FAULL & NIKPAY
THE EC LAW OF COMPETITION

FAULL & NIKPAY

THE EC LAW OF COMPETITION

SECOND EDITION

Edited by

JONATHAN FAULL

Director General, European Commission
Professor of Law, Vrije Universiteit Brussel

ALI NIKPAY

Senior Director, Office of Fair Trading
Visiting Fellow, London School of Economics

OXFORD
UNIVERSITY PRESS

OXFORD
UNIVERSITY PRESS

Great Clarendon Street, Oxford OX2 6DP

Oxford University Press is a department of the University of Oxford.
It furthers the University's objective of excellence in research, scholarship,
and education by publishing worldwide in

Oxford New York

Auckland Cape Town Dar es Salaam Hong Kong Karachi
Kuala Lumpur Madrid Melbourne Mexico City Nairobi
New Delhi Shanghai Taipei Toronto

With offices in

Argentina Austria Brazil Chile Czech Republic France Greece
Guatemala Hungary Italy Japan Poland Portugal Singapore
South Korea Switzerland Thailand Turkey Ukraine Vietnam

Oxford is a registered trade mark of Oxford University Press
in the UK and in certain other countries

Published in the United States
by Oxford University Press Inc., New York

British Library Cataloguing in Publication Data
Data available

Library of Congress Cataloging in Publication Data
Faull & Nikpay, the EC law of competition / edited by Jonathan Faull, Ali Nikpay.—2nd ed.
    p. cm.
  Includes bibliographical references and index.
  ISBN 978-0-19-926929-7 (alk. paper)
  1. Restraint of trade—European Union countries. 2. Antitrust law—European Union countries.
3. Competition, Unfair—European Union countries. I. Faull, Jonathan. II. Nikpay, Ali.
III. Title: EC law of competition. IV. Title: Faull and Nikpay.
    KJE6456.F38 2007
    343.24'0721—dc22   2007007599

Typeset by Cepha Imaging Private Ltd, Bangalore, India
Printed in Great Britain
on acid-free paper by
CPI Bath Press

ISBN 978-0-19-926929-7

1 3 5 7 9 10 8 6 4 2

EDITORS

Jonathan Faull

Ali Nikpay

CONTRIBUTORS

Svend Albaek

François Arbault

José Luis Buendia Sierra

Sarah Cardell

Peder Christensen

Kevin Coates

Eddy De Smijter

Carles Esteva Mosso

Jonathan Faull

Mario Filipponi

Kyriakos Fountoukakos

Hubert Gambs

Francisco Enrique González Díaz

Maria Jaspers

Lars Kjølbye

Andreas Knaul

Eduardo Martinez Rivero

Renato Nazzini

Monique Negenman

Albert Nijenhuis

Ali Nikpay

Harold Nyssens

Luc Peeperkorn

Tony Penny

Francisco Pérez Flores

Stephen Ryan

Stephen A. Ryan

Ewoud Sakkers

Wolf Sauter

Dominik Schnichels

Konrad Schumm

Dan Sjöblom

Joos Stragier

María Luisa Tierno Centella

Vincent Verouden

Rita Wezenbeek

Donncadh Woods

FOREWORD

It is not a vice, it is a virtue for this book to be so hard to define that the authors themselves find it difficult to do it. In the Preface to the first edition they write that it is not a textbook, but is intended to be a 'practical guide'. But, they add, it is a practical guide which also explains, quite extensively the rationale underpinning the law. The definition is more than humble and after reading the new edition it definitely appears to be an understatement. Undeniably the book provides clear guidance for practitioners and others interested in the subject to the substantive and procedural intricacies of competition law. To give an example, it is reassuring for the non-specialist to find a preliminary listing of sectors to which competition law does not apply, as well as the limits of such immunity. However, there is much more to the book than this, revealed and reflected by the architecture of the work, in which principles play a primary and pervasive role.

Firstly 'the economics of competition', and therefore the conceptual framework of law and economics, essential to competition law, is set out; secondly the basic principles and the rationale of each of the main antitrust provisions of the Treaty are discussed and clarified and thirdly the principles thus expounded are applied to types of conduct (agreements, practices, abuses, mergers etc.) and to sectors. The architecture reflects the activities of the editors and contributors and the nature of the institution to which most of them have devoted their working lives, the Competition Directorate of the European Commission: on the one hand enforcers of the law and thus practitioners themselves, on the other hand members of the wider community of scholars who analyse the context and meaning of the provisions to be enforced. In other fields it is not so frequent for practitioners and scholars to belong to the same community and therefore to share background, language, readings and writings. It happily happens in competition law and it explains the particular nature of 'practical' guides such as this one.

The authors explicitly underline that the opinions and views they express are theirs, not the Commission's. And we can believe it. However, their institutional role might be one of the reasons behind a visible thread that runs through their work: despite profound changes in analysis and interpretation, consistency has nevertheless remained a feature of European competition policy and a (relatively) unambiguous and clear use of the existing normative instruments can be relied upon for the sake of certainty and of the parties to whom the law is applied. Several purely academic scholars would put it differently, stressing underlying ambiguities and inconsistencies. Yet, Savigny is more on the side of our authors than of others.

All of us are well aware that the use of economic analysis has brought about an almost complete reversal of the mission itself of our competition law, from the protection of individual freedom against abusive powers (the heritage of the Freiburg School) to the promotion of efficiency and the protection of consumer welfare (the teaching of Chicago). We are equally aware that these changes have profoundly affected the interpretation of Article 81, and in particular its paragraph 1, in ways which make the new divide between paragraphs 1 and paragraph 3 highly problematic.

Sometimes I ask myself why our European institutions have not found the courage of the American Courts, which openly overruled precedents (and therefore arguments) clearly incompatible with the new doctrines they were adopting (for example in *Sylvania*). Are agreements still declared illegal in Europe for their object alone? Have not we reached the point of assessing every agreement in relation to its effects before prohibiting it? Some of our scholars give a clear-cut answer. Our institutions do not and clearly prefer building up the coherence of our system on the basis of a reassuring continuity between its past and its present. The authors of this volume describe the development of the law and look ahead to its possible future.

To say the least, they have good arguments in stressing continuity. We Europeans have made remarkable progress by using economic analysis and in a certain sense we have become adult. Nowadays we know that perfectly undistorted competition is not attainable. Eventually we have learnt that reducing market power is a more realistic goal (as did the authors and enforcers of the Clayton Act, long before Chicago). But we are still convinced that competition is not only instrumental to efficiency, but also a goal in its own right. Furthermore we find it hard to abandon the idea that freedom—freedom of choice for the consumer and freedom of entrance for the producer—has to play a role in giving meaning to the type of welfare protected by competition law. Making the original and the supervening notions and cultures compatible with each other is not at all easy, and yet we keep both of them alive for both of them are alive within the set of European values and principles. Reading this volume demonstrates that it may not always be an unproblematic endeavour, but that it is one with real substance and merit.

Giuliano Amato*

*Professor, European University Institute, Florence.

PREFACE

Much has changed since the first edition of this book was published in 1999. Competition law and the way it is applied in the European Union has undergone a process that can be described without exaggeration as revolutionary: new rules have been enacted, policies announced and enforcement systems radically altered. The system in force at the end of the twentieth century is no more. To mention just two major changes: Regulation 17/62 has given way to Regulation 1/2003 and the key substantive test for the assessment of mergers has been changed.

These developments have resulted in important changes to the book: for example, the treatment of cartels has expanded significantly. Where previously it was dealt with in the chapter on horizontal agreements, it now has its own chapter. We have also added new chapters on state aid, motor vehicle distribution and the new enforcement system under Regulation 1/2003. Existing chapters have either been rewritten entirely or heavily revised and expanded. As a result the book has now doubled in length.

That being said, the aim of the second edition is the same as the first; that is to provide a concise description of the law and to identify and, where possible, explain the rationale which underpins it. Where the law is not fully consistent with announced policy, we have attempted to describe and explain both. In so doing, we hope to have provided our readers with some insight into where the law and policy are likely to go next. However, we must repeat what we wrote in 1999: readers will search in vain for insiders' secrets or indiscretions. The opinions expressed in this book are ours and those of the contributors alone: they cannot be taken as representing the views of the institutions for which we work.

As well as the book's size, the number of people we would like to thank has also grown significantly. Like its predecessor, this book is the result of a collective effort by many people. The contributors deserve our heartfelt thanks for accomplishing the mammoth task of describing and explaining EC competition law in a period of major change, some aspects of which are still on the journey from policy intent to possibly settled law. The fact that many contributors are now in more senior positions within the Commission, while some have taken up senior positions in private practice—Kyriakos Fountoukakos is partner at Herbert Smith in London, José Luis Buendia Sierra is partner at Garrigues in Brussels, Francisco Enrique González Díaz is partner at Cleary Gottlieb Steen & Hamilton in Brussels, Mario Filipponi is Assistant General Counsel for Verizon Business in Brussels and Andreas Knaul is partner at CMS Reich-Rohrwig Heinz TOV in Kiev—as well as the fact that some have become parents in the intervening years(!) adds to their extraordinary achievement.

The editors and contributors are very grateful to Lars Albath, Michael Albers, Eric Barbier de la Serre, Marc Barennes, Matthew Benson, Hubert Beuve-Méry, Simon Bishop, André Bouquet, Philip Brentford, Jason Cawley, Frances Dethmers, Jonathan Dykes, Eliana Garcés Tolón, José Garrido Otaola, Paul Hofer, Giles Holman, Jenine Hulsmann, Sir Robin Jacob, Barbara Jankovec, Manuel Kellerbauer, Nicholas Khan, Jindrich Kloub, Gabrielle Knoll, Antón Leis Garcia, Victoria Louri, Bryan McGuire, Adrian Majumdar,

Wessel Marquering, Philip Marsden, Kirti Mehta, Elliot Milton, Sam Momtaz, Giorgio Monti, Jayne Morris, Michael C. Naughton, Alex Nourry, Fay Poosti, Maria Rehbinder, Nino Schober, Tom Sharpe, Elizabeth Simpson, Katerina Soteri, Rostom Stepanian, John Temple Lang, Fabienne Timmermans, Sir John Vickers, Greg Werden, Justin Woodward and Lawrence Wu.

In addition we are extremely grateful to Philip Collins, Amelia Fletcher, Mark Griffiths, John Kallaugher, Dorothy Livingston, Henrike Mueller, Thomas Mueller, Sarah Northam, Robert O'Donoghue, John Osborne, Michail Papadakis, Mark Powell, Steven Preece, Simon Priddis, Martin Smith, Vincent Smith and Mark Williams. This distinguished group helped us to ensure that the second edition remained focused on practitioners' needs, without losing the particular features which in our view make the work different from other books on the subject. Of course, any errors or omissions remain the responsibility of the editors and contributors.

Eagle-eyed readers will also notice that the names of Renato Nazzini, Sarah Cardell and Tony Penny appear on the list of contributors but not in the table of contents. Their names have been added to the list to reflect the important contribution each made on different chapters or to the process as a whole.

We would also like to thank Chris Rycroft, our commissioning editor at Oxford University Press. His understanding of the subject-matter, his patience, and the skill with which he managed the process at OUP have been invaluable. Thanks too to his colleagues at OUP, especially Annette Lord.

Producing this book has been a demanding but ultimately hugely rewarding experience for the contributors and editors. Its impact on our partners and families, however, has been far less benign—for the last three years they have had to live with the constant tapping of computer keys during holidays, weekends and the early hours of the morning as we wrote and rewrote our chapters. Without their support the book would not have been written. We would therefore like to dedicate it to them with our heartfelt thanks.

Jonathan Faull and Ali Nikpay
Brussels and London
February 2007

CONTENTS—SUMMARY

CONTENTS

I GENERAL PRINCIPLES

3. Article 81

II SPECIFIC PRACTICES

III SPECIAL SECTORS

11. Financial Services

IV STATE AID

16. State Aid

TABLES OF CASES

1. TABLES OF EUROPEAN COURT OF JUSTICE (ECJ) AND COURT OF FIRST INSTANCE (CFI) CASES

A. ALPHABETICAL (ECJ AND CFI COMBINED)

ABB Asea Brown Boveri v Commission (Case T-31/99) [2002]
ECR II-1881 .... 8.121, 8.227, 8.228, 8.233, 8.267, 8.454, 8.691, 8.694, 8.737, 8.750
AKZO Chemie BV and AKZO Chemie UK Ltd v Commission (Case 53/85) [1986]
ECR 1965; [1987] 1 CMLR 231 .... 2.188, 2.194, 2.199, 8.459, 8.462
AKZO Chemie BV v Commission (Case 5/85) [1986] ECR 2585 .... 8.399
AKZO Chemie BV v Commission (Case C-62/86) [1991] ECR I-3359;
[1993] 5 CMLR 215 .... 4.49, 4.89, 4.271, 4.287, 4.444, 8.453, 14.69
AOIP v Beryrard (76/29) [1976] OJ L6/8; [1976] 1 CMLR D14 .... 8.553
AOK Bundesverband (Cases C-264, 206, 254 and 355/01) [2004] ECR I-2493;
[2004] 4 CMLR 22 .... 6.22, 11.142, 11.145, 11.147, 11.152
ARBED v Commission (Case C-176/99) [2003] ECR I-10687 .... 8.571
ARD v Commission (Case T-158/00) [2003] ECR II-3825 .... 5.652, 5.655, 13.286
AEG v Commission (Case 107/82) [1983] ECR 3151; [1984] 3 CMLR 325 .... 3.67, 3.72,
3.362, 3.363, 3.367, 8.463, 8.560, 8.568, 8.837, 9.36, 9.332
A Brünsteiner GmbH and Autohaus Hilgert GmbH v Bayerische Motorenwerke AG
(BMW) (Joined Cases C-276/05 and C-377/05),
not yet reported 15.17, 15.77, 15.83, 15.107
Aalborg Portland (Case C-204/00) [2004] ECR I-124; [2004] 4 CMLR 13 .... 2.25, 3.52,
3.95, 3.111, 3.149, 3.399, 8.268, 8.308, 8.452, 8.453, 8.457,
8.458, 8.463, 8.469, 8.491, 8.497, 8.501, 8.509, 8.515,
8.532, 8.534, 8.546, 8.547, 8.574, 8.576, 8.714

B. NUMERICAL TABLE OF ECJ CASES

C. NUMERICAL TABLE OF CFI CASES

2. TABLES OF EUROPEAN COMMISSION DECISIONS

A. ALPHABETICAL (ALL TYPES OF DECISION COMBINED)

B. NUMERICAL TABLE OF NON-MERGER DECISIONS

C. NUMERICAL TABLE OF MERGER DECISIONS

D. NUMERICAL TABLE OF JOINT VENTURE DECISIONS

Note: For Commission Decisions of a legislative nature and Commission State Aid Decisions, see the Tables of EU/EC Legislation, Part C, below.

3. TABLE OF NATIONAL AND OTHER CASES

TABLES OF TREATIES AND LEGISLATION

1. TABLE OF EU/EC TREATIES

Paragraph numbers in bold relate to parts of the book dealing specifically with the article named

Treaty establishing the European Coal
and Steel Community (ECSC Treaty)
(1951). 3.04, 8.650, 12.09
Art 60 . . . . 8.776
Art 65 . . . . 8.23, 8.70, 8.715, 8.776
    (1) 8.03, 8.20, 8.50, 8.51
    (2) 12.342
    (5). 8.10, 8.70, 8.420, 8.471,
              8.501, 8.587, 8.611
Art 66 . . . . 5.1
    (7) 4.38
Treaty establishing the European Atomic
Energy Community 1957, as
amended (Euratom Treaty). 3.04,
                  12.12, 12.60
Art 40 . . . . 12.16
Arts 67–76 . . . . 12.15
Treaty establishing the European Economic
Community—Rome 1957, as
amended (**EC Treaty**) 2.164,
      2.197, 2.244, 2.245, 3.04,
      4.364, 8.459, 8.476,
      10.17, 12.06, 12.09, 12.12,
      12.15, 14.05, 16.01, 16.56,
      16.265, 16.386
Art 2 . . . . . 4.411, 5.653, 6.04, 9.38, 16.113

Art 3 . . . . 3.02, 3.13, 6.04, 12.91
    (1)(g) 2.57, 2.142, 3.341, 14.88
    (c). 9.38
    (g) 4.01, 4.350, 4.411, 6.04,
           6.05, 6.06, 6.92, 9.38
Art 5 (ex Art 10) 4.102
    (2) 16.255
Art 6 (ex Art 3c) 3.13, 16.113
    (3) 14.14
Art 8
    (1) 4.417
    (2) 4.343, 4.344, 4.350,
              4.416, 4.417
Art 10 (ex Art 5) 2.155, 2.164,
      2.195, 2.270, 6.04–6.06, 6.92,
      8.244, 8.407, 12.91, 13.32,
      13.33, 14.87, 16.334
    (2) 14.88
Art 12 (ex Art 6) 4.398, 6.08, 6.09,
      6.50, 6.98, 12.389
Art 16 (ex Art 7d). 6.213,
      6.214, 16.217
Art 28 (ex Art 30) 6.49, 6.51,
      6.97, 6.100–6.105, 6.120, 6.121,
      6.130, 6.158, 6.245, 7.386,
      10.10, 10.49, 10.173

2. TABLES OF EU/EC LEGISLATION

A. REGULATIONS

B. DIRECTIVES

C. DECISIONS

State Aid Decisions

3. TABLE OF EU/EC NOTICES, GUIDELINES AND OTHER INFORMAL TEXTS

4. TABLE OF NATIONAL LEGISLATION

5. TABLE OF NON-EU/EC TREATIES AND AGREEMENTS

Part I

GENERAL PRINCIPLES

1

THE ECONOMICS OF COMPETITION

Luc Peeperkorn and Vincent Verouden

A. Introduction

1.01 Nowadays, there is a clear awareness among competition policy makers, competition lawyers and judges of the importance of economics for their daily work. In the EU and in the US it is normal practice to discuss competition cases in terms of economic concepts such as market power, entry barriers, and sunk costs, and to evaluate cases according to their effects on the market. Competition policy is economic policy concerned with economic structures, economic conduct, and economic effects. It is for this reason that in a book on competition law an introduction to the economics of competition is of importance.

1.02 The growing acceptance and importance of economics in competition policy raises questions regarding the usefulness of economics, both for devising competition rules and for deciding on competition cases. A word of caution is appropriate in this respect. Economic thinking and economic models have proved not to be perfect guides.

1.03 Economic theories and models are built on and around assumptions. This approach has the benefit of making explicit the various elements relied upon in arriving at a particular conclusion or insight. At the same time, these assumptions by definition do not cover (all) real world situations. In addition, when the assumptions are changed the outcomes of the models may look very different. It is for these reasons that the application of economic theories may not always be able to give a clear and definite answer, for example as to what will happen in a market when companies merge, or when companies try to collude or engage in specific types of conduct.

1.04 The best that the application of economic principles can do in general is to provide a coherent framework of analysis, to provide relevant lines of reasoning, to identify the main issues to be checked in the context of certain theories of competitive harm, and possibly to exclude certain outcomes. In other words, it helps to tell the most plausible story. In individual cases it will be necessary first to find the concepts and the model that best fit the actual market conditions of the case and then to proceed with the analysis of the actual or possible competition consequences. Economic insights can also be useful in the formulation of policy rules, indicating under what conditions anti-competitive outcomes are very unlikely, very likely, or rather likely, and helping to devise safe harbours.

1.05 The competition policy practitioner is advised to follow the mainstream of economics in order to avoid too much contradiction and too many untested assumptions. This chapter gives a short introduction to the main insights of industrial economics.[1] It has the following structure:

- Section B briefly describes the main historical trends in the field of industrial economics;
- Section C describes the static welfare aspects of market power;
- Section D describes the dynamic welfare aspects of market power;
- Section E describes market definition as a method for identifying the extent to which products exert a competitive constraint on each other;
- Section F looks into the concepts of market power and market dominance in further detail and discusses the ways in which market power may be maintained or enhanced through anti-competitive means; and
- Section G presents a number of empirical methods to verify the existence of competitive constraints and market power.

B. Structure, Conduct, Performance

(1) Early Developments

Interest in the issues of market power and cartels arose well before the twentieth century. **1.06** Descriptions of the dangers of monopoly can be found in ancient Greek written sources as well as in the Bible. Adam Smith in his *Wealth of Nations* (1776) made the famous remark that people of the same trade seldom meet, even for merriment and diversion, without it ending in a conspiracy to raise prices. In general, Smith warned against the negative effects of monopoly, both private monopoly and monopoly sponsored by a government.

In the nineteenth century, neoclassical authors such as Augustin Cournot and Alfred Marshall **1.07** laid the basis for modern microeconomics with the development of simple models of perfect competition, monopoly, and duopoly. The hallmark of neoclassical economics is the paradigm of rational economic agents maximising their utility. The model of perfect competition was especially useful for developing theory on general equilibrium for the whole of the economy. However, these models were ill-equipped to explain market developments at the end of the nineteenth/beginning of the twentieth century, in particular market concentration, the emergence of trusts, product differentiation, non-price competition, and advertising.

Research in the first half of the twentieth century also seemed to indicate that companies were **1.08** not always producing, as the model of perfect competition would predict, at minimum/ lowest average costs.[2] Instead, they were producing on a decreasing cost curve, ie where

---

[1] Industrial economics or industrial organisation can be described as applied microeconomics: it uses the models and concepts of microeconomics in an effort to understand the development of real world markets and company behaviour. For an excellent introduction see FM Scherer and D Ross, *Industrial Market Structure and Economic Performance* (3rd edn, Boston: Houghton Mifflin Company, 1990). More recent: J Church and R Ware, *Industrial Organization – A Strategic Approach* (Boston: McGraw-Hill, 2000); and DW Carlton and JM Perloff, *Modern Industrial Organization* (3rd edn, Reading: Addison Wesley Longman, Inc, 2000). More technical and elaborate is the *Handbook of Industrial Organization* edited by R Schmalensee and R Willig (Amsterdam: North Holland, 1989); and J Tirole, *The Theory of Industrial Organization* (MIT Press, 1988).

[2] For the concepts used see Section C, in particular paras 1.28–1.32 and 1.54–1.74.

there are increasing returns to scale, without, however, becoming much bigger. This phenomenon, known as the Great Cost Controversy, led several authors like Piero Sraffa, Edwin Chamberlin, and Joan Robinson to write about imperfect and monopolistic competition, that is, those situations in between the two extremes of perfect competition and monopoly which perhaps more accurately describe how markets function. In order to provide a rationale for imperfect and monopolistic competition, they explored the role of product differentiation and advertising in their models.

(2) The Harvard School

1.09 Not satisfied with the limited, rather simple models mentioned above, at around the time of World War II a number of economists such as John Clark, Edward Mason, and Joe Bain started to look for more empirically supported explanations of market phenomena.[3] They tried to develop a kind of applied microeconomics. Instead of deduction based on assumptions they wanted to take account of the richness of the real world. Data were gathered and by induction they tried to develop general insights concerning likely company behaviour, effects on the market, and possibilities for government intervention.

1.10 The main result of this so-called Harvard School, that dominated the industrial economics scene for many years, is the Structure-Conduct-Performance (S-C-P) paradigm. In its simplest form it states that market structure determines companies' market behaviour which in turn determines market performance. Market structure, being the basis of the explanation, is seen as of paramount importance. In its most mechanistic form the study of conduct becomes quite irrelevant. It is the structure that is responsible for the final market outcome. Studies were done for several sectors collecting market structure data such as concentration ratios and the height of entry barriers. These data were linked to performance indicators such as profit levels. The general conclusion of these studies was that concentrated markets with entry barriers showed above average profitability. This approach fitted well with the general trend for structuralist theories and explanations developed in the social sciences in the 1940s, 1950s, and 1960s.

Figure 1 The simple S-C-P scheme

1.11 The main policy conclusion flowing from the simple S-C-P scheme has been that competition policy should concentrate on the structure of markets and on structural remedies, ensuring that markets do not become (overly) concentrated or entry barriers be erected. This was reflected, for example, in the use of market concentration measures in assessing merger cases in the 1968 Horizontal Merger Guidelines issued by the US Department of Justice. Behavioural remedies to a competition problem were seen as ineffective without the necessary structural changes.

---

[3] See, eg, JM Clark, 'Toward a Concept of Workable Competition' (1940) 30 Am. Econ. Rev. 241.

(3) The Chicago School

A number of economists like George Stigler, Harold Demsetz, and Yale Brozen questioned **1.12**
the S-C-P framework and its conclusion that market concentration in general leads to
monopoly profits. This group of scholars, also known as the Chicago School, argued that
competition policy should be less concerned with market structure and should focus more
directly on the concept of economic efficiency (welfare) in evaluating business conduct or
mergers.[4]

The Chicago School criticised the empirical studies underlying the S-C-P paradigm. By **1.13**
applying different techniques to the same data and by using improved or new data they
showed that the relationship between concentration, entry barriers and monopoly profits
was not so stable or strong and, at times, was even non-existent. More important, however,
was their theoretical questioning of the S-C-P paradigm.

The Chicago School argued that the causal link is not between high concentration on the one **1.14**
hand and high profits on the other. Instead, they argued that the causality runs as follows:
increased firm size leads to increased firm efficiency, which in turn leads to market concentration and ultimately to possibly higher profits. Central to this reasoning is the role of
economies of scale and scope and a general belief that competition forces companies to
become superior in terms of efficiency. The companies that succeed in this way will grow
faster than others who may even go out of business. This may at times lead to higher concentration levels in the industry but, if this is the product of the market process which seeks
and obtains efficiency, this is therefore desirable from a competition policy point of view.
It leads to more efficient firms, even when it would also result in profits in excess of the competitive norm. Monopoly profits would not be very likely to arise and certainly would not
be durable, as it was argued that entry barriers are rarely very high and can be overcome in
time. The more extreme statement of the Chicago School is that the only high and durable
entry barriers are those created by the State, thereby telling governments to clean up their
own act instead of pursuing vigorous competition policy.

These attacks of the Chicago School, that started in the 1960s but culminated in the 1970s **1.15**
and 1980s, brought back a greater reliance on the [self-correcting] forces of competition.
High concentration is not necessarily bad and only in very particular circumstances is competition policy action called for. This fitted well with the general trend in the 1970s and
especially the 1980s of seeing limits to the effectiveness of and scope for government interference.[5]

---

[4] The term 'efficiency' (or 'economic efficiency') generally refers to the extent to which welfare is optimised
in a particular market or in the economy at large. Welfare can be conceived as the (weighted) sum of consumer
surplus (the difference between consumers' willingness to pay for consumption and the price paid) and producer surplus (profits): see Section C. The weights accorded to consumer surplus and producer surplus imply
a certain value judgment. The Chicago School proposed to use equal weights, arguing that not antitrust, but
other laws should address the ways prosperity is used or distributed. See R Bork, *The Antitrust Paradox:
A Policy at War with Itself 90* (1978). For a detailed account of the Chicago school, see Herbert Hovenkamp,
Federal Antitrust Policy: The Law of Competition and Its Practice (2nd edn, 1999), p 60; MW Reder, 'Chicago
Economics: Permanence and Change' (1982) 20 J. Econ. Lit. 1.
[5] cf Eleanor Fox, 'What is harm to competition? Exclusionary practices and anticompetitive effect' (2002)
70 Antitrust Law Journal 371–411 at 377.

(4) More Recent Developments

1.16 The Chicago School returned in part to the deductive approach of the microeconomic models, focusing more on the theoretical underpinnings than on empirical testing. It highlighted the main theoretical weaknesses in the arguments of the Harvard School and it forced a reconsideration of the S-C-P framework that, as a consequence, has been extended and refined over the years. It has been recognised that a wide array of other basic conditions such as consumer preferences and technological developments influence the market structure and that these basic conditions may themselves change. Just as important, it has been accepted that conduct is not a negligible factor when it comes to explaining performance. In addition it is recognised that conduct and also performance may help shape the market structure. In other words, although the main causal link may still run from market structure to market conduct to market performance, feedback mechanisms complicate the picture. In schematic terms, the resulting extended S-C-P framework can be illustrated as in Figure 2.[6]

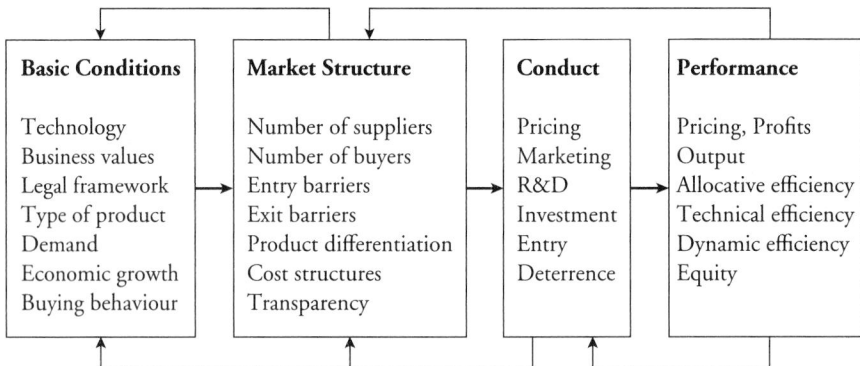

Figure 2 The extended S-C-P framework

1.17 This extended S-C-P framework is still important today in industrial economics and in competition policy, not as the perfect explanatory framework but as a good way to organise one's thoughts. Market structure is still the starting point for competition policy arguments and it is generally accepted that certain market structure conditions are a prerequisite for anti-competitive conduct and performance. However, these necessary conditions may not be sufficient. Conduct such as limit pricing or excess capacity creation may play their own role. Structural conditions can be used to describe safe harbours: that is, situations in which anti-competitive behaviour or effects are highly unlikely. However, to find anti-competitive situations, usually structural, behavioural and performance aspects will have to be taken account of. Under Articles 81 and 82 of the EC Treaty it is in general not enough to show that the market structure enables anti-competitive conduct; also the conduct itself and/or the likely negative effects that may result from this conduct must be shown. The same holds true under the EC Merger Regulation where, to assess the impact of a merger on competition, a purely structural analysis may not suffice.

---

[6] Adapted from Scherer and Ross, figure 1.1, p 5 (see n 1).

The renewed attention to the behaviour of companies is also reflected in the latest develop- **1.18** ment in industrial economics, sometimes called New Industrial Economics. The centre of attention is the possible strategic behaviour of companies in oligopolistic situations. It tries to deduce, within the framework of more sophisticated microeconomic models and with the help of game theory, what the most likely company strategies are and whether collusive strategies are likely or not. It fits in well with the more moderate, less ideological, and more technical approach to problems of the 1990s and the turn of the century. It has cast more light on the (efficiency) rationale behind certain types of company behaviour, such as the use of vertical restraints, without however always leading to particularly robust outcomes useful for competition policy.

C. Static Welfare Analysis of Market Power

(1) Introduction

In a nutshell, one could say that the economics of competition is about market power: what **1.19** it is, how it is created or sustained, and what its effects are. The answer given by economists on the first question—what is market power?—concentrates on the power to raise price above the competitive level. In the short run this means the power to raise price above marginal cost and in the long run above average total cost.[7] In other words a company has market power if it has a perceptible influence on the price against which it can sell and if by charging a price above the competitive level it is able, at least for a significant period, to obtain 'supra-normal' profits.

This makes it very clear that market power is not a black and white concept and that com- **1.20** panies can have different degrees of market power. In principle the appropriate measuring rod would be the net present value of the monopoly profits a company can make. The net present value is today's value of the profit of this period and all future periods. It depends therefore on the monopoly profit per period, on the number of periods a monopoly profit can be sustained before entry or expansion by competitors takes the profit away, and on the discount rate against which future profits are evaluated.[8]

A firm with market power may raise its price by reducing its own output or by making com- **1.21** petitors reduce theirs. As stated above, this price increase should increase the firm's profits and do so for a significant period of time. Under the merger rules, the test is, in practice, whether the merging companies involved will, with high likelihood, be able to obtain supra-normal profits for a period longer than two years. Under Articles 81 and 82 shorter periods are also normally taken into account.

The second question about how market power is created or sustained brings us back to the **1.22** question of the relevant elements of market structure and conduct. And so does the third

---

[7] The terminology used comes back and is explained in later parts in this Section.

[8] The present value of a stream of profits is given by: $NPV = \sum_{i=1}^{n} \frac{1}{(1+r)^i} \pi_i$, where n is the number of periods a monopoly profit is made, π_i is the profit in period i, r is the discount rate, and Σ the summation sign for the different periods. As discount rate, usually the competitive rate of return on capital or the rate at which the company can lend money is taken, since this measures the opportunity cost of using the company's own funds.

question about its effects. This section is devoted to a static welfare analysis of these questions. By static it is meant that the state of technology is assumed to be constant and effects of market power on innovation and vice versa are ignored. The latter effects are dealt with in Section D, not surprisingly titled 'Dynamic Welfare Analysis of Market Power'.

1.23 Welfare economics is the branch of microeconomics concerned with the efficiency of the company/the market/the economy.[9] A welfare economic analysis of the effects of market power concentrates on the effects on efficiency, both allocative and technical efficiency,[10] and therewith the effect on total welfare. This is measured in terms of consumer surplus and company profits. The following subsections provide an explanation of these and other microeconomic concepts and analyse the market structures of perfect competition, monopoly, and oligopoly.

(2) Basic Microeconomic Concepts

1.24 In this subsection, the following basic microeconomic concepts are discussed: consumer surplus, (short and long run) production costs, profit maximisation, economies of scale, minimum efficient scale, entry barriers, and contestable markets.

(a) Consumer Surplus

1.25 Consumer surplus is the net benefit consumers obtain by buying a certain good or service. It is the difference between their willingness to pay, sometimes called their reservation price, and the price actually paid. As consumers have different preferences and incomes some are normally willing to pay more than others for a certain good. Also, the higher the quantity of the good a particular consumer obtains the lower in general his willingness to pay for an additional unit. These characteristics mean that a demand curve, which shows for an individual or a whole market the relationship between the willingness to pay and the quantity bought, is normally downward sloping. This is shown in Figure 3, where the individual and collective consumer surplus at a market price of five are presented by the shaded areas.

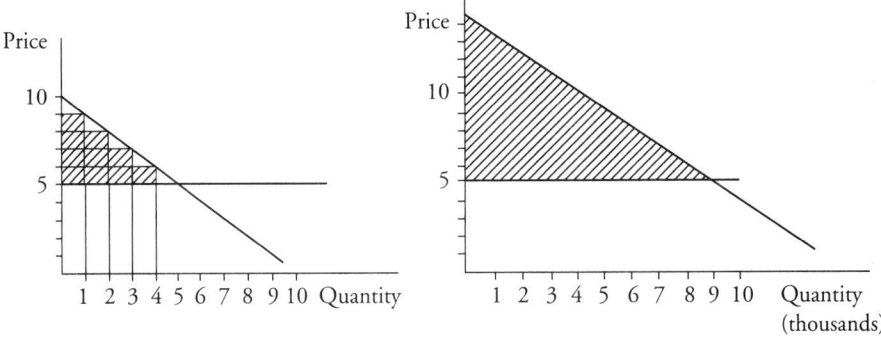

Figure 3 Individual demand curve   **Market demand curve**

---

[9] T Scitovsky, *Welfare and Competition* (London: Unwin University Books, 1952). For the term efficiency, see also n 4.

[10] For an explanation of these terms, see paras 1.32 and 1.59–1.60.

(b) Production Costs

Production costs of a company can be represented as curves. These cost curves are of course **1.26** not the same for different companies and different industries. Some firms are capital inten- sive while others are labour intensive, some have high fixed costs while others have high variable costs, some experience economies of scale while others have flat cost curves or even experience diseconomies of scale. However, there are some general characteristics to cost curves.

These general characteristics depend very much on whether one looks at the short or long **1.27** run. In the short run many production factors may be fixed, that is the producer is not able to vary the quantity used of these factors in response to demand changes. This is usually true for the buildings and other main capital goods and the production process adopted. But it may also be true for labour, at least in a downward sense when rules on firing make adaptation difficult and slow, and sometimes in an upward sense when, for example, train- ing for specific capabilities takes a long time. Other inputs like raw materials, intermediate goods, and energy are often variable. In the long run all factors become variable as plants, production processes, and personnel (including management) can be totally replaced.

(c) Short Run Production Costs

The general characteristics of the short run cost curves are best explained by what econo- **1.28** mists call the law of increasing and decreasing returns. Let us assume for the moment that we have only two factors of production, capital and labour. The former is fixed while the latter is variable.[11]

To produce, a company must employ labour to work with the available fixed capital. At first, **1.29** employing more labour will lead to a more efficient use of labour, eg through specialisation. By adding an employee the productivity of every employee will rise: the returns are increasing. In other words, the marginal productivity, that is the change in total output resulting from the use of one more employee, is increasing. This means that the costs of producing a unit of output are decreasing. This is so for the average total cost (ATC), that is all fixed and vari- able costs divided by total output, as well as for the average variable cost (AVC), that is all variable cost divided by total output. It is also true for marginal cost (MC), that is the cost of producing the last unit of output.

With the fixed capital as a constraint there comes a point where adding another employee **1.30** will lead to less extra output when compared to adding the penultimate employee. The marginal productivity is declining and the returns start to decrease. The moment the mar- ginal productivity starts to decline the marginal cost starts to increase: producing one more unit of output becomes more expensive than the previous unit of output in terms of employee time used.[12] By adding more employees the marginal cost will rise further and

---

[11] The law of increasing and decreasing returns is related to the concept of economies of scale. The latter concept concerns increasing returns in a long run context, where all production factors are variable and where thus increasing capacity by adding more capital is possible; see Section C(2)(f) below.

[12] It is assumed that the price of the production factor, in this example the wage rate, is constant and not influenced by the quantity demanded by the company.

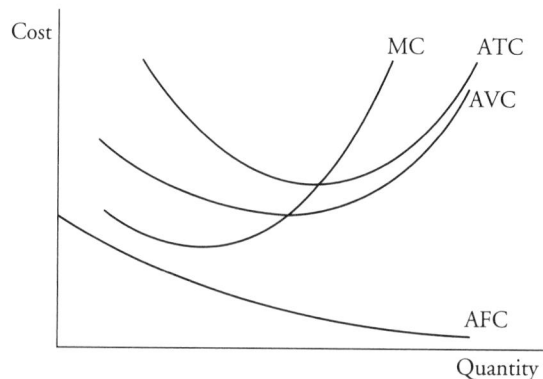

Figure 4 A company's short run cost curves ATC, AVC, AFC, and MC

will cut the average variable and average total cost curves at their lowest point, as depicted in Figure 4.

1.31   That the MC curve cuts the other two curves at their minimum is easily explained: when the extra costs incurred by producing one more unit of output are still lower, respectively, than the average variable or average total costs, producing this extra output will further sink these averages. However, the moment that producing this extra unit has marginal costs that are higher as the respective average, the average will start to rise.

1.32   In Figure 4, also, the average fixed cost (AFC) curve is depicted. This average will decline as long as output grows, as the fixed costs are spread over more units of output. In Figure 4 the cost curves are only drawn in so far as it is economically interesting. That means not too far left or right from the minimum of ATC. The further away from this minimum the less efficient the company produces. At its minimum the company reaches productive or technical efficiency.[13]

(d) Profit Maximisation

1.33   What range of the cost curves is economically interesting is linked to the goal of the company. Usually it is assumed that this goal is profit maximisation. Certainly in a competitive environment where profits are under pressure a company is best advised to try to maximise its profits in order to survive in the long run. In a situation of fierce competition, profits will be rather low, just high enough to attract the required production effort, and a deviation from profit maximisation will quickly lead to losses. It is only when a company has a certain degree of market power that it can afford to pursue other goals such as sales maximisation with a minimum profit constraint.[14]

---

[13] It is not relevant to see what happens if more and more employees are added to the fixed capital, making the average costs rise further and further and eventually leading to a decline in output. Nor is it interesting to see what happens when the company produces far below its optimal scale.

[14] Whether a company with market power actually will deviate from the goal of profit maximisation will depend on the incentives of management, the control of ownership over management, and in general the restraining influence of the capital markets.

To maximise its profits or when times are bad to minimise its losses a company should **1.34** ensure that the additional costs of producing one extra unit of output are still covered by the additional revenue earned by this extra unit of output: the marginal cost should equal the marginal revenue (MC=MR). This rule holds good for companies with or without market power.

The MR curve will depend on the demand curve the company is facing. When the company **1.35** operates in a perfectly competitive market it is a price taker: its output has no influence on the price in the market. If it raises its price above the market price demand for its product will drop to zero. Its marginal revenue equals the market price. Graphically this means the MR curve is a horizontal line at the level of the market price. In that situation the MC curve represents the supply curve of the profit-maximising firm: at each price level, the MC curve indicates the supply of a given firm (MC=MR=p).

If, on the other hand, the company faces a downward sloping demand curve, meaning that **1.36** by varying its output it can change the price at which it can sell, the MR curve will lie beneath the demand curve. Given that the demand curve is downward sloping, the company has to lower its price if it wants to sell more units of output. This price decrease applies not only to the additional sales but to all its sales.[15] As a result, the additional revenue following the expansion of output is lower than the price at which the expansion takes place.

Let us assume for the moment that the company is a price taker. In Figure 5 this means that **1.37** as long as the market price is below p1 the company is better advised not to produce at all: the price does not even cover the average variable costs. With a price above p1 the profit maximising company will produce the amount where its marginal cost (MC) equals the price. Producing less would mean that marginal cost is smaller than marginal revenue (MC is below MR), indicating that producing an extra unit of output will make it earn more. Producing more than the amount for which marginal cost equals marginal revenue would mean that marginal cost is higher than marginal revenue, indicating that reducing output

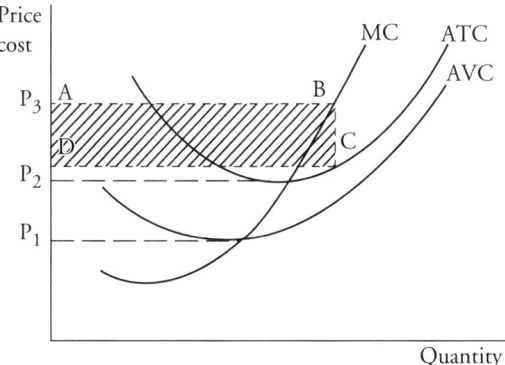

Figure 5 A company's cost curves and profit

---

[15] If there is no price discrimination.

will make it earn more. With a market price between p1 and p2 the company is in fact minimising its losses, as the price does not yet cover all average total costs. When the price rises above p2 the company will make a profit, as the price exceeds the average total costs. With a price of p3 the profit will be the shaded area ABCD.

(e) Long Run Production Costs

1.38 It was stated above that the cost curves depend very much on whether the short or long run is analysed. In the short run the law of increasing and decreasing returns indicates that the ATC, AVC, and MC curves will first decline and then increase. An area where average costs are constant over a certain range of output is possible, but inevitably the cost curves will rise as more variable production factors are added to the fixed factors. The optimal capacity utilisation will not vary much in the short run.

1.39 In the long run, when the fixed production factors are also variable, the picture looks different. If a company producing at its minimum short run average total cost would like to double its output, it could do so by duplicating the existing plant. This means that the long run ATC curve will have a flat section. The long run average total cost is therefore in general depicted as in Figure 6. In the same picture different short run ATC curves are drawn belonging to different output levels. The long run ATC curve represents the lowest short run average total cost achievable for every output.[16]

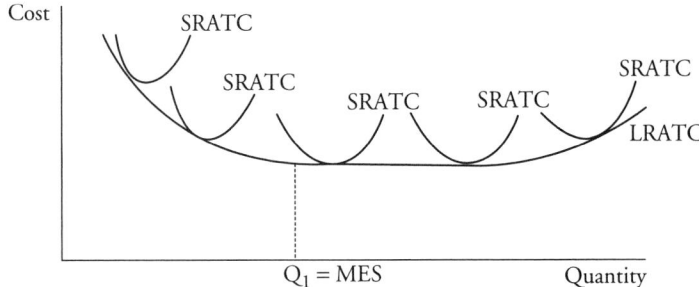

Figure 6 Long and short run ATC

(f) Economies of Scale and Minimum Efficient Scale

1.40 The long run ATC curve drawn in Figure 6 makes two other important concepts clear: that of economies of scale and the minimum efficient scale (MES). In Figure 6 an output below Q1 will be produced at higher average total cost than is attainable when more than Q1 is produced. Up to Q1 increasing capacity will lead to economies of scale: a higher capacity reduces the average costs. These economies of scale result often from the indivisibility of certain production factors: the bigger truck that transports more while still requiring only one driver, the bigger company that can afford to have a full-time specialist employed for every relevant area, the bigger plant that does not need to keep more spare parts in stock than the

---

16 The short run costs are the real costs of a company, used for instance when it has to calculate its profit or loss. In a static world, the long run costs indicate the possibility frontier where the state of technology is assumed to be constant (see Sections C(1) and D(1)).

smaller plant. Economies of scale may also result from technical-physical relationships, like the bigger oil tanker that requires relatively less steel to be built, or from economies of increased dimensions, like the larger company that may obtain discounts when buying larger amounts of input or borrowing larger sums.[17] More generally, increased output brings a different, more efficient production process within reach.

Beyond Q1 no more economies of scale can be reaped. This point is called the minimum efficient scale. Although in practice not always easy to establish, it is an important concept helping to explain concentration in a market. The MES determines the maximum number of companies that can operate efficiently in a market, at least when producing below MES level results in significantly higher costs per unit of output. The extent to which producing below MES level results in higher costs is measured by the cost gradient; that is the steepness of the slope of the cost curve. For example, when the cost gradient is significant and the MES equals 10 per cent of total demand there is room for at most ten efficient companies. **1.41**

In the example of a MES of 10 per cent of market demand it can also be expected that a company having capacity to produce 20 per cent of the market will be able to produce at the same low ATC. In theory a company can have any size above MES and produce at the same low ATC. In order to produce more its management could simply copy MES size units. In practice, however, it can be expected that above a certain size diseconomies of scale will also appear. Management may become too complex, the number of management layers will increase, and motivation may reduce. The long run ATC may creep up when size continues to increase. **1.42**

Economies of scale, especially when they are substantial, are an important explanation for concentration tendencies in a market. By indicating the maximum number of firms that can operate efficiently in the market the MES determines the minimum concentration degree. As some companies will be above MES scale the overall concentration in the market will usually be higher. This makes it quite clear that more companies in a market does not necessarily lead to a better market outcome as production may take place at sub-optimal levels and that protecting competitors is not the same as protecting competition or consumers' interests. **1.43**

The economies of scale described above are sometimes referred to as static internal economies of scale; internal because they are related to the plant or firm, static because they are not related to past production. Estimates of the importance of these static internal economies of scale depend to a degree on the method of measurement.[18] Econometric studies based on cross-section or time-series data on costs and profits tend to find only limited economies of scale. For example, Lyons found that in the UK for most of the studied 118 trades, MES **1.44**

---

[17] In the latter case a distinction is made between real economies, based on actual cost savings on the side of the input producer/bank, and pecuniary economies that (merely) reflect a benefit at the expense of the input producer/bank resulting from a different balance of power.

[18] Karsten Junius, *Economies of Scale: A Survey of the Empirical Literature*, Kiel Working Paper No 813 (Kiel Institute of World Economics, 1997). See also European Commission, *The Single Market Review*, Subseries V: Volume 4: Economies of Scale (1997); and J Stennek and F Verboven, *Merger Control and Enterprise Competitiveness: Empirical Analysis and Policy Recommendations*, in *The Efficiency Defence and the European System of Merger Control, European Economy*, Reports and Studies No 5/2001, European Commission, 2001.

was below 250 employees.[19] However, engineering estimates, that is cost estimates by managers, engineers, etc, tend to give more weight to economies of scale. In his study for the Commission, Pratten found very important economies of scale in a number of sectors like motor vehicles, other means of transport, chemicals, machinery and instrument manufacturing, and paper and printing, that is in particular in the production of industrial goods. Pratten estimated that 27 per cent of EU output is produced in industries whose MES is above 5 per cent of the whole EU market.[20]

1.45 In addition to static internal economies of scale, dynamic internal economies of scale are distinguished.[21] The latter refer to a lowering of the costs of production over time as a result of experience obtained on past cumulative output. They are also referred to as learning effects. In terms of Figure 6, these economies of scale lead to a downward shift of the long run ATC curve. These economies of scale are not so much an explanation for concentration tendencies but may be part of a first mover advantage. The company or companies that entered the market first were possibly able to recoup the higher original costs while latecomers may have to sell immediately at lower prices dictated by the first entrants having gained some experience in the market. Such learning effects are more likely in new industries, especially when operating with much skilled labour, and less likely in mature industries with known technologies, especially when operating with much fixed capital.

(g) Entry Barriers

1.46 As already indicated in the previous paragraph economies of scale are also an important element when describing another main concept of industrial economics, the concept of entry barriers. It was Bain who stressed the importance of entry barriers as a condition for companies with a significant market share to have market power and turn this into high (monopoly) profits. Without entry barriers easy entry would quickly eliminate such profits. Entry barriers, according to Bain, are 'the advantages of established sellers in an industry over potential entrant sellers, these advantages being reflected in the extent to which established sellers can persistently raise their prices above a competitive level without attracting new firms to enter the industry'.[22] In other words, the incumbent companies have certain advantages that allow them to increase their price above minimum ATC without attracting entry.

1.47 This definition of entry barriers is often used in competition policy as it indicates situations in which a competition concern is likely to arise. In a market with entry barriers further concentration through mergers may have to be stopped, especially when the incumbent firms already experience reduced competition. A competition authority will also have to be more alert to abuse of a dominant position in a case where a company with a high market share operates on a market shielded off by entry barriers.

---

[19] B Lyons, *A New Measure of Minimum Efficient Plant Size in the UK Manufacturing Industry* (Economica, 1980).

[20] C Pratten, *A Survey of the Economies of Scale*, Economic Papers of the European Commission, No 67 (1988).

[21] In the literature (static and dynamic) external economies of scale are also distinguished (see Karsten Junius, 1997). These refer to positive external effects resulting from firms being situated near each other. These economies are, however, less relevant for industrial economics and competition policy and play a role in regional economics and trade theory.

[22] See J Bain, *Barriers to New Competition* (Cambridge: Harvard University Press, 1965) p 3.

The above definition of entry barriers, however, does not always give the right policy insights. **1.48**
When the question comes up as to whether a competition authority should stimulate or force
entry in a particular market another definition, first proposed by Stigler, is superior. He
defined entry barriers as costs that new entrants have to bear, but which are not incurred by
the incumbents.[23]

The difference with Bain's definition is most easily explained with the example of economies **1.49**
of scale. Economies of scale qualify as an entry barrier under the definition of Bain. As new
companies in general enter at a small scale they will experience a cost disadvantage compared
to the incumbents. This will allow the latter, when competition between them is already
reduced, to keep their price above their own minimum average total cost and earn high
(monopoly) profits.[24] However, the incumbents were also faced with scale economies when
they entered. In addition, new entrants may be able to enter at minimum efficient scale.
Scale economies therefore do not qualify as an entry barrier under the definition of Stigler.
Forcing entry by the competition authority will be inefficient when it increases the number
of companies above the number of companies that can efficiently operate in the market,
that is when the incumbents are not much bigger than minimum efficient scale.

In addition to economies of scale a number of other factors are sometimes mentioned in **1.50**
competition policy analysis as entry barriers, although these may not always qualify as such
under the definition of Stigler. Government regulations, especially when establishing exclusive
rights, may work as an entry barrier, for example when only a limited number of licences
are provided. State aid, when only available to incumbents, will work as an entry barrier.
Import tariffs have the same effect on foreign suppliers. Intellectual property rights or ownership of absolutely scarce resources (for example, platinum mines) may also inhibit access by
those that cannot avail themselves of these patents or scarce resources. An essential facility,
defined as a facility that is required to be able to produce another good or service (eg the
railway track and the railway service), may work as an entry barrier if access to the facility
is not open to competitors. Vertical links or vertical integration may make access more difficult and foreclose potential competitors. Economies of scope, that is lower average total
cost as a result of producing a larger product range, may also make entry more difficult. The
same can be said of brand loyalty of customers, for example stimulated by high advertising
outlays, as it makes customers less willing to switch to comparable or better offers. More
generally, when a customer will have to bear a high cost in order to switch to a new supplier,
such switching costs may hinder entry of new suppliers. It may be added that many of these
factors may not work only as an entry barrier but may also work as a barrier to expansion,
preventing companies already in the market from expanding their output.

The question of whether certain of the above-mentioned factors should be described as **1.51**
entry barriers partly depends on whether the necessary outlays are sunk costs. Sunk costs
are those costs that have to be made to enter or be active on a market but that are lost when

---

[23] George J Stigler, 'Barriers to entry, economies of scale and firm size' in Irwin RD, *The Organization of Industry* (Homewood, 1968). For a review of the various definitions of entry barrier, see R Preston McAfee, HM Mialon and MA Williams, 'What is a barrier to entry?' (2004) 94(2) American Economic Review 461.

[24] Where the entrant considers entry at large scale it will seriously have to estimate the influence of its additional output on the market price. If it expects the price to drop to competitive levels entry may not be attractive.

the market is exited. Advertising costs to build consumer loyalty will work as an entry barrier if an exiting firm can not sell its brand name nor use it somewhere else without a loss. The more costs are sunk, the more potential entrants will have to weigh the risks of entering the market and the more credibly incumbents can threaten that they will match new competition as they will not leave the market.[25] High sunk costs invested in excess capacity may be an especially credible threat that the incumbent(s) cannot leave the market and will increase output and lower prices upon entry.

(h) Contestability

1.52 It was Baumol, Panzar, and Willig who stressed the importance of sunk costs with their theory of contestable markets in the early 1980s.[26] A market is said to be contestable if there are no sunk costs or other entry barriers and consumers are willing to switch quickly, before incumbents can react, to the better offer of new entrants. Under these conditions so-called hit-and-run entry is possible. When the incumbents charge a price above minimum average total cost it becomes profitable to enter, if not to stay in the market for at least the time it takes before the incumbents lower their price. The threat of such hit-and-run entry, in other words the existence of potential competition, will discipline the incumbents, even when they have very high market shares.

1.53 At a conceptual level the theory of contestable markets helped to underline and delineate the possible role of potential competition. In practice not many markets are truly contestable. The important question is the degree to which markets are contestable. In general, entry requires sunk costs, sometimes minor and sometimes major, and incumbents are often in the position to react quickly, that is before consumer loyalty wears down. Even in transport markets, where it is possible in theory to redirect assets, like ships or planes, at short notice from one route to another, other entry barriers like the non-availability of necessary slots may delay or impede entry. Actual competition is therefore still to be preferred above potential competition.

(3) Perfect Competition

(a) The Model

1.54 When market models are put on a market power scale, perfect competition is the extreme at the low end. There is no company that holds market power and competition policy enforcers can quietly write books during office hours. Unfortunately, markets rarely fulfil the conditions of this model. However, the model is useful for two reasons. First, it highlights the two very important welfare economic concepts, of allocative and technical efficiency. Secondly, in certain respects, it is useful as a benchmark against which to measure the competitiveness of actual markets.

1.55 In order to be called perfectly competitive a market must have a number of characteristics, of which the following are the main ones: there must be many suppliers and many buyers,

---

[25] This commitment element also applies to the entrant after market entry. The difference is the incumbent is already in the market whereas the entrant still has to decide whether to enter.

[26] WJ Baumol, JC Panzar and RD Willig, *Contestable Markets and the Theory of Industry Structure* (New York: Harcourt Brace Jovanovich, 1982).

there are no entry barriers, the product is homogeneous, and there is full transparency. This means that the MES must be small compared to total market demand, so that many companies are able to operate in the market and produce at minimal costs. The condition of transparency means that suppliers and potential suppliers are aware of every change in demand and price and, as there are no entry barriers, swiftly react by expanding or reducing supply. The condition also implies that companies are aware of the most efficient production techniques and that no company is more efficient than the others.

A company operating under such conditions will be a price taker, as briefly indicated in the   **1.56** previous section. The price is determined by the market and a company's own output is so small compared to total output that a change in the company's output has no perceptible influence on the market price. As entry and exit are swift and without costs, the market will always quickly return to its equilibrium where the price exactly matches market demand and market supply, as shown on the right-hand side of Figure 7. If demand rises, graphically this means the demand curve shifting to the right, the price will rise as the current output is not able to satisfy all demand. Entry of new firms or expansion of existing firms will immediately increase output until the equilibrium price is restored. A fall in demand, graphically the demand curve shifting to the left, leads to firms leaving the market until output is sufficiently reduced and equilibrium restored.

At the equilibrium market price every company in the market will produce at the same   **1.57** minimum average total cost and will make no profits. This is shown on the left-hand side of Figure 7. By 'no profits' it is meant that the company's income is just enough to cover the rewards that all factors of production, including capital, need to make them stay in this company. In economic terminology they receive their opportunity cost (the money they would make elsewhere, that is on other markets), but not more. In other words, the situation of no profits allows for normal accounting profits that are necessary to make capital stay in the company. These normal profits are part of the ATC cost curve. However, no excess profits are made.

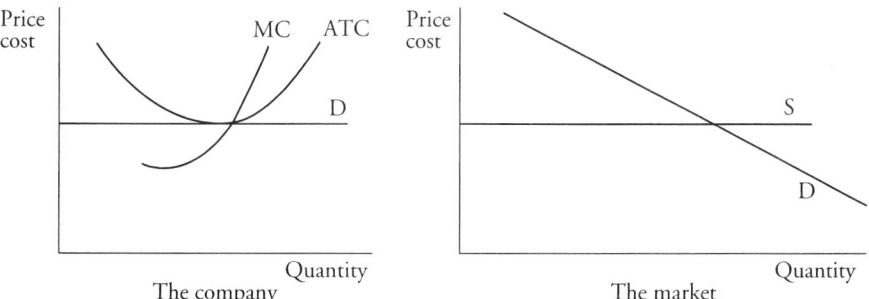

Figure 7 Perfect competition

(b) The Effects

Figure 7 deserves some further explanation as it shows a number of important issues. First,   **1.58** there is the difference between the market demand curve and the company's demand curve, ie the demand the company faces for its own output. The market demand curve is downward sloping, as explained in paragraph 1.25 (see Figure 3). The company's demand curve is (practically) horizontal at the level of the market price. At that price the company, given its small capacity, can sell as much as it wants. It does not need to lower its price to sell more. It is also not in a position to lower its price since that would lead to immediate losses as the price would go below marginal cost as well as average total cost. Increasing its price above the market price would lead to an immediate loss of all sales and imply the company's exit from the market.

1.59   Secondly, Figure 7 highlights that in perfect competition there is *technical/productive efficiency*: with given resources the maximum output is produced. This results from every company producing at the minimum average total cost. If a company is less efficient it will make a loss and exit the market, in which a new efficient entrant will take its place. If a firm introduces a new cost saving technique this will be copied immediately by all the others, graphically represented by a downward shift of the supply curve, after which a new equilibrium will be realised at a lower price.

1.60   Thirdly, Figure 7 indicates that in the equilibrium situation there is *allocative efficiency*: welfare is maximised.[27] Welfare is maximised as consumer surplus is at its largest. If less output than the equilibrium quantity is produced welfare will be lower, because there will be buyers willing to pay more than the equilibrium price but who are not served. That means these buyers would be willing to pay more than it costs to produce more units and welfare could thus be increased by expanding output. Expanding output beyond the equilibrium would also lower welfare as the extra costs exceed the price level, in other words the extra costs exceed the willingness to pay of the marginal consumer. Productive resources are used at the wrong place: elsewhere, that is on other markets, they could be used to produce goods for which there is a higher willingness to pay. The allocative efficiency is reflected at company level by every company obtaining a price equal to its marginal costs (P=MC).

(4) Monopoly

(a) The Model

1.61   Monopoly is at the other extreme of the market power scale. In the fully-fledged monopoly model the monopolist has the maximum achievable market power. One might expect that competition policy enforcers when such a situation occurs have to give up the possibility of writing books during office hours. However, this may not be the case as the analysis of pure monopoly situations is rather straightforward and markets rarely fulfil the conditions of this model. The model of monopoly is, however, very useful as it helps to highlight a number of important concepts and it provides the clearest example of what competition policy tries to prevent or remedy.[28]

1.62   In order to be called purely monopolistic a market must have a number of characteristics, the main ones being that there is only one supplier while there are many buyers and that there are entry barriers that practically prevent entry.

---

[27] See also n 4.
[28] This is not to say that competition policy is only concerned with static monopoly or market power. The dynamic point of view is important as well. See in particular Sections D and F.

A company operating under such conditions will be a price setter. As it is the only company **1.63** in the market, market demand is the demand for the company's product. By varying its output the monopolist can determine the market price along the demand curve. As entry is impossible it can quietly try to maximise its profits or pursue other goals.

(b) The Effects

Assuming that profit maximisation is the monopolist's goal it will produce that output **1.64** where its marginal revenues equal its marginal costs (see paragraph 1.34). In Figure 8 this is at quantity Qm. With a demand curve that is downward sloping its marginal revenue curve will also slope downwards and lie beneath the demand curve. The reason is simple. When the monopolist wants to sell an extra unit of output it has to lower the price somewhat. When price discrimination is assumed impossible the monopolist has to lower the price not only for this last unit but for all units it wants to sell. This means that the marginal revenue at a particular output is the new price minus the cumulative price loss it has to take on all other units.[29] In Figure 8 it is further assumed that average total cost and marginal cost are constant (the ATC and MC curves of the monopolist are horizontal), that is there are no fixed costs and no economies of scale. This assumption simplifies the drawings without changing the principal outcome of the model.

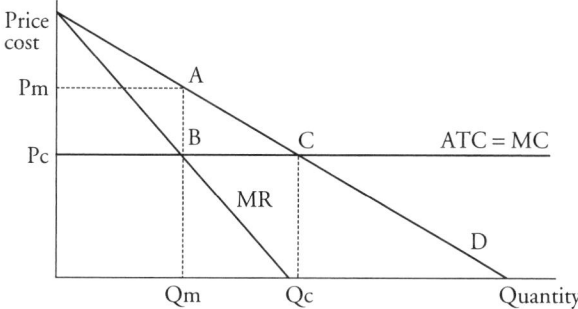

Figure 8 Pure monopoly

Figure 8 clearly shows the main disadvantages of monopoly. The monopolist sells Qm, **1.65** which is less than the output Qc under competition. As a result the price the consumers have to pay is higher: Pm compared to Pc. This has two main welfare effects. First, there is a loss of welfare as consumers acquire fewer products than before. The area ABC is what is generally called the dead-weight welfare loss of monopoly. It is 'dead-weight' in the sense that the consumer surplus is really lost: it is not acquired by anyone in the economy. Secondly, there is a transfer of income from consumers to monopolist. The monopolist makes a profit of PmABPc. This amount used to be consumer surplus, but with the higher price the consumers have to pay it is turned into profits for the monopolist.

It can be debated whether the monopolist's profit should be counted as a welfare loss or not. **1.66** One could argue that the transfer of income from consumers to monopolist does not

---

29 See also para 1.36.

change society's welfare as a whole, as some gain what many lose.[30] However, for a competition authority the case may be quite straightforward. As the goal of competition policy is in general stated in terms of protection of competition to further the interests of the consumer, there can usually be no doubt that monopoly profits—in particular where they persist—must be seen as something negative which competition policy should try to avoid.

1.67 The allocative inefficiency, ie the dead-weight welfare loss, is evidenced by the difference between P and MC. As the monopoly price Pm is higher than the marginal costs, welfare could be increased by producing extra units. The consumers are willing to pay more for these units than it would actually cost to produce them.

1.68 Another question is whether the monopolist is technically efficient. In the example of Figure 8 the answer is 'yes'. The monopolist is producing at minimum ATC. But there are good reasons to believe a monopolist may not always be so efficient. Not feeling the heat of competition the company may become slow and inefficient. Slack eats away part of the possible monopoly profits. Taking life easy instead of profit maximisation may have become important, especially when the owners (shareholders) do not exercise effective control. It was Leibenstein who coined the phrase 'X-inefficiency', meaning internal inefficiency in the form of too high salaries, excessive corporate jets, a surplus of employees, etc. That this leads to an additional welfare loss is shown in Figure 9.

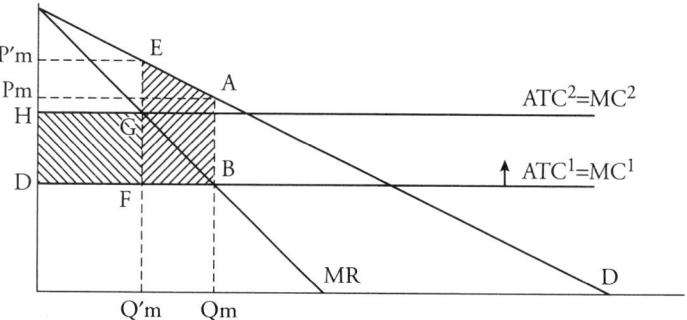

Figure 9 A monopolist with X-inefficiency

1.69 The X-inefficiency is reflected in higher ATC and higher MC cost curves. This results in a new equilibrium with the lower quantity Q'm and the higher price P'm. The consumer is paying for the higher costs with a higher price. There is an extra dead-weight welfare loss of EABF. In addition, productive factors of the area HGFD are lost to society, as what was previously monopoly profit has now been used to produce inefficiently.

1.70 A last loss of welfare caused by monopoly could be named 'the price of success'. A monopoly position is very attractive and many resources may be wasted both by those that defend it and those that attack it. Those who defend it may try to erect and maintain entry barriers

---

[30] According to the neo-Paretian principle often used in welfare economics, the income transfer does not change total welfare because the monopolist could (not should) compensate the consumers for their loss of income. Only the dead-weight welfare loss is a clear loss of total welfare under this principle.

by keeping excess capacity, by excessive product differentiation, by political lobbying, by starting entry-delaying lawsuits, etc. Those who attack the monopoly position have to spend resources to overcome these barriers. In theory all monopoly profits could be wasted in the struggle for a share of the pie.

Not everyone will recognise these costs as a welfare loss. When competition is seen as rivalry— a fight for temporary advantages, a struggle to gain market power before being overtaken by the next wave of competition—at least part of these costs may be seen as the necessary price to be paid for vigorous competition. However, most competition authorities will, for example, be rather suspicious when finding dominant companies running up costs to maintain excess capacity, which could be used to predate. **1.71**

Monopoly may not only have negative effects but may also lead to certain advantages for consumers. First, it may be the case that economies of scale require such a size that only one company in the market can produce at minimal cost. This is what is called a natural monopoly.[31] Producing with more companies would necessarily lead to inefficient production. The deadweight loss and the price asked by the monopolist may compare favourably with the welfare loss due to higher costs and the price level asked under competition. If protecting consumer welfare is the aim, then the only relevant question in such a static analysis is whether the price asked under monopoly is higher or lower than the price asked under competition. If the protection of total welfare is the aim, it would be preferable to have a monopoly not only when it would lead to a lower price, but also if it would lead to a higher price but the resulting production efficiency gains outweigh the dead-weight welfare loss created by the higher price. **1.72**

A second possible positive effect of monopoly, which may be relevant in the context of innovation and patents, is that the prospect of monopoly profits may spark more effort on the part of companies to invest in innovation. The trade-offs in this area are considered in more detail in Section D. **1.73**

A third possible positive effect has less relevance for competition policy. Some authors argue that the lower output and higher price of monopoly may counterbalance certain negative externalities in production or consumption. Less consumption of environmentally unfriendly products and less use of limited natural resources might actually increase welfare. **1.74**

(5) Oligopoly

(a) Introduction

The models of monopoly and perfect competition may be on opposite sides of the market power scale, but they are remarkably similar in their emphasis on market structure and neglect of company behaviour. The only behavioural assumption that is introduced is that **1.75**

---

[31] In case not even a monopolist has sufficient scale to produce at MES level, this has consequences for technical and allocative efficiency. Technical inefficiency will persist until demand grows and allows attainment of MES size. Similarly, as long as ATC is falling over the relevant output range, pricing at marginal cost, ie allocative efficiency, would result in a price below ATC and would thus result in overall losses, which would need to be recovered with the help of, for instance, general taxation or dual pricing.

companies are profit maximisers. The C of the S-C-P paradigm can be ignored as the models are quite straightforward; the market structure leads *linea recta* to a specific market performance.

1.76   This is not the case for oligopoly, the most important intermediate market form on the market power scale. Oligopoly is the market structure in which there are a few suppliers, at least two while the maximum number of companies is not clearly determined. The main characteristic is that the companies in such a market realise or believe that their individual behaviour concerning output, price, etc has a perceptible influence on the market outcome and therefore may provoke reactions from the side of competitors. In the fisheries sector a fisherman rightly ignores the influence of his catch on the market price of fish. In the oligopolistic car market a large manufacturer cannot and will not ignore the impact its decisions have on the market and on its competitors and vice versa. This means that the C of the S-C-P scheme becomes more important in oligopolistic markets. It also means that competition issues in such markets are rather complicated. Competition policy enforcers faced with such markets are forced to write their books in the evening hours.

1.77   Oligopolistic markets are difficult to analyse. The outcome of oligopolistic behaviour can vary to such an extent that one of the more popular statements is that 'with oligopoly anything goes'. The market price may be as low as under perfect competition or as high as under pure monopoly or anywhere between these two. The economic models of oligopoly reflect well this complexity. The outcome of oligopoly models is often highly specific to the exact assumptions used in the model. It is therefore important to identify and analyse the model specifications that best fit the actual market conditions. But even then the economic models of oligopoly may leave a wide range of possible outcomes.

1.78   This does not mean that competition policy has no function in oligopolistic markets. Experience shows that anti-competitive outcomes can often arise in such markets; they should probably therefore be the focus of competition policy. However, given the complexity of these markets and the limited guidance offered by economic models, the ambitions of the competition enforcer should be modest. Oligopoly cases are the clearest example of what was said in the introduction: that competition cases are concerned with identifying the most plausible story or explanation of the market outcome. A good part of this story will consist of analysing the factors that either enhance or decrease the possibilities of collusion and anti-competitive effects and choosing the model and specifications that best fit the actual market conditions. Empirical verification is in this context of great importance.

1.79   In the limited space of this chapter no more than a brief introduction to oligopoly theory can be provided.[32] The literature on oligopoly is vast and sometimes very technical. For a layman it may be disappointing to see that the various models are often not very helpful for answering concrete policy questions. The models do not answer the question of which market conditions will lead companies in an oligopolistic market to compete fiercely on all the important parameters (price, quality, and innovation) and of when competition will be

---

[32] For more extensive introductions, see, for example, Scherer and Ross or Church and Ware (n 1 above); or, more technical, A Koutsoyiannis, *Modern Microeconomics* (London: Macmillan, 1979); and J Tirole (n 1 above).

replaced, on one or all parameters, by collusive behaviour. There is no super model that includes all possible relevant factors. Most models concentrate on the effects and interaction of a limited number of factors, abstracted away from more realistic settings.

(b) Game Theory

Most advances in oligopoly theory have been made since the World War II by using game theory, especially non-co-operative game theory.[33] Game theory studies situations of strategic interaction using mathematical models. A game theory model specifies the players in a game (for example, firms in a market or individuals in an organisation), the information they have (or do not have), the actions they can choose, the timing of these actions, and the pay-offs for each player that result from these actions. In such a model, each player is assumed to choose a strategy (a plan of action) that maximises his pay-offs based on the information available to him and his expectations about rivals' actions.

1.80

The main idea behind non-co-operative games, as opposed to co-operative games, is that the parties cannot make binding agreements. A non-co-operative game setting seems to be the appropriate framework to apply as competition rules make anti-competitive agreements unenforceable in court. Cartel members may make agreements, but these are not binding.

1.81

In non-co-operative game theory, fully rational oligopolistic behaviour requires an assessment of the potential actions of competitors. That is, the oligopolists take account of the interdependence of strategies. An equilibrium will therefore only exist when the decisions of companies lead to a 'self-reinforcing set of strategies in which each strategy is a best response to the other strategies'.[34] Such an equilibrium is called a Nash equilibrium, that is 'a set of actions is in Nash equilibrium if, given the actions of its rivals, a firm cannot increase its own profit by choosing an action other than its equilibrium action'.[35] In other words, the game finds a stable outcome once every oligopolist sticks to its current strategy, for example concerning the price it sets for its own product, in the light of the strategies chosen by the other oligopolists.

1.82

Game theory has been applied extensively to study the strategic behaviour of companies in oligopolistic markets. Game models with multiple stages are particularly appropriate to study situations in which a company, for example the incumbent, has a first-mover advantage over other market players. Such analysis has been applied to examine the scope for entry deterrence strategies such as creating excess capacity or product proliferation (introducing products in the market to deter entry, not because it is in itself profitable), as well as limit pricing (pricing low to signal that market conditions are not favourable for entry).[36] Also vertical restraints have been studied extensively for their impact on competition, by focusing

1.83

---

[33] Game theory as a formal theoretical analysis started with the book of the mathematician John von Neumann and the economist Oskar Morgenstern, *Theory of Games and Economic Behaviour* (Princeton: Princeton University Press, 1944).

[34] D Yao and S DeSanti, 'Game theory and the legal analysis of tacit collusion' (1993) The Antitrust Bulletin, 113–141.

[35] J Tirole (n 1 above) at 206.

[36] For an overview and discussion of such strategies, see Scherer and Ross, above n 1, Ch 10; and Tirole, above n 1, Ch 8.

on the strategic value that such restraints may provide.[37] For example, economic models have shown that single branding/exclusive dealing contracts may be tools for foreclosing markets, in particular when they render the anti-competitive strategy (foreclosure) more credible and time-consistent.[38] Similarly, delegating pricing decisions to exclusive distributors may allow producers to credibly commit to less competitive behaviour towards each other (to 'soften' competition), because exclusive distributors have different pricing incentives than distributors facing intra-brand competition.[39]

1.84 As noted above, the outcomes of the models of strategic interaction tend to rely heavily upon the precise modelling assumptions. One of the important assumptions in this respect concerns the way in which companies are thought to compete. Two stylised modes of competition are often considered: Bertrand competition (price competition) and Cournot competition (quantity competition).[40]

1.85 Under Cournot competition it is assumed that each company in the market decides on its profit-maximising output assuming the other's output will remain unchanged. In the [Nash] equilibrium, each company chooses a level of output that is optimal (profit-maximising) in view of what the other market players produce. The equilibrium of this model features a market price below the monopoly level but (well) above marginal cost (the benchmark of perfect competition).

1.86 Competition in output is often identified with situations where output or capacity decisions are the main drivers of the price level in the market. Conceptually, firms choose output or capacity and then, given the level of demand, adjust prices to sell this output. This might apply, for instance, to certain basic commodity industries, where price levels are primarily determined by the overall level of output in the market, but also to a variety of other markets, such as those for package holidays, hotel accommodation, and office space. In markets where output or capacity decisions are the most important strategic decisions of the firms, the important concern for firms is how their output decision influences market prices.

1.87 Under Bertrand competition it is assumed that each company in the market decides on its price assuming that other prices in the market will remain unchanged. In the corresponding Nash equilibrium, each company chooses a price level that maximises profit in view of what the other market players charge. The equilibrium of this model features a market price equal to marginal cost in the case of homogeneous products[41] and a price that is higher in the case of differentiated products.

---

[37] For an overview see, eg, M Waterson 'Vertical integration and vertical restraints' in Jenkinson T (ed), *Readings in microeconomics* (Oxford Univeristy Press, 1996); or V Verouden, 'Vertical Agreements: Motivation and Impact', forthcoming in Collins W (ed) *Directions in Competition Law and Policy*.

[38] cf P Aghion and P Bolton, 'Contracts as a barrier to entry', (1987) 77 Journal of Economic Theory 388–401.

[39] cf P Rey and J Stiglitz, 'The Role of Exclusive Territories in Producers' Competition' (1995) 26 Rand Journal of Economics 431. With exclusive distribution, producers face sales volumes that react less strongly to rises in their own producer prices and as a result final demand will drop by less than otherwise might have been the case. This may make producers inclined to carry through price increases, amounting to a 'softening of competition'.

[40] The two modes of competition are identified with the nineteeth century economists Bertrand and Cournot, respectively.

[41] In case there are cost differences between the companies, the price will be equal to the marginal cost of the second-most efficient firm.

Competition in prices often refers to situations where firms set prices and adjust their pro- **1.88**
duction levels according to demand. Competition in markets for consumer products and
for capital goods can often be characterised in this way. In many such markets, capacity and
output levels are less determinative of the eventual market outcome. Rather, factors like
product differentiation (the products offered differ in the eyes of buyers with respect to one
or more important parameters) provide each firm a certain margin of manoeuvre in its
price setting behaviour.[42]

The above distinction in types of competition is of course a stylised one: there will be many **1.89**
cases where the type of competition cannot be characterised as being one or the other. Even
in markets where 'output drives price' or where competition is 'mostly on price', it is not to
be taken for granted that competition is Bertrand or Cournot. Most markets feature business decisions that go well beyond a choice of price or a choice of quantity at a given point
in time. For instance, markets in practice may turn largely on innovation (both product
and process innovation) or on building consumer loyalty. Nonetheless, it may be useful to
consider the generic market types and to distil some key factors to be examined in each of
these. It is the purpose of the economic models to clarify what factors are the more relevant
in precise market settings. The role of the investigator is to see to what extent any given
model is useful in light of the facts of the case.

(c) The Scope for Collusion Illustrated with the Prisoner's Dilemma

Another important area in which game theory has played a role in clarifying the main issues **1.90**
is that of collusion in oligopolistic markets. Collusion and collusive behaviour are used in
this chapter as in the economic literature, ie as any situation in which market players do not
compete 'to the fullest' as a more competitive attitude would trigger a rational reaction or
retaliation from its rivals in later periods.[43] It therefore includes not only explicit collusion
in the form of agreements or concerted action but also tacit collusion. The latter is what
lawyers define as (conscious) parallel behaviour. Collusion in the economic sense is possible
without communication between the companies involved. Economists thus define collusion
in terms of effects. This stands in contrast to legal definitions of collusion, which are usually
limited to agreements and concerted practices, stressing the possibility for competition
rules to provide a remedy for the situation.

Within the non-co-operative game setting, the game that provides most insight into the **1.91**
difficulties and possibilities of collusion is the prisoner's dilemma game.[44] The original example used to explain the game went along the following lines. A murder is committed, and two

---

[42] Products may be differentiated in terms of, for instance, technical specifications, quality, brand image,
level of service, or geographic location. The presence of switching costs can also induce buyers to consider products to be differentiated, since they would have to incur costs in order to switch to a competitor's product.

[43] cf Tirole, n 1 at 207.

[44] Games with this structure were devised and discussed by Merrill Flood and Melvin Dresher in 1950 as part
of their work for the Rand Corporation. The title 'prisoner's dilemma' and the version with prison sentences as
pay-offs are due to Albert Tucker (Stanford Encyclopedia of Philosophy at <http://plato.stanford.edu/entries/
prisoner-dilemma/>). Much of the theory of tacit coordination derives from the work of G Stigler, 'A Theory
of Oligopoly' (1964) 72(4) Journal of Political Economy 44–61. The economic literature on tacit coordination
is relevant to all forms of coordination not based on legally enforceable contracts.

suspects are arrested. Not having enough evidence, the police need them to confess in order to have a conviction for murder. If one of the prisoners testifies against the other, the first goes free if the other has not testified against him, and the second goes to jail for ten years. If neither testifies, both get a sentence of one year only for illegal possession of firearms. Lastly, if both testify, both go to prison for seven years.

1.92 The structure of the game can be presented in the diagram shown in Figure 10, commonly referred to as the 'pay-off matrix'. In this case the pay-off matrix illustrates all the possible outcomes or pay-offs for the two suspects (the first number provides A's jail sentence in years, the second B's sentence).

		Player B		
		N	T	
	N	1,1	10,0	N = not testify
Player A				
	T	0,10	7,7	T = testify

Figure 10 The prisoner's dilemma game

1.93 It is clear upon close examination that the best strategy for both suspects in this case is to testify. If A does not testify it is better for B to testify and vice versa. If A testifies it is also better for B to testify and vice versa. In the jargon of game theory, to testify is the dominant strategy. The result is that both go to jail for seven years as they testify against each other. The collectively optimal outcome of each serving only the light sentence is not attained because the suspects cannot make a binding agreement.

1.94 This analysis can easily be extended to the study of oligopolistic behaviour of companies. Although oligopolists are normally not confined to choosing between two prices, two quantities, etc, it can be assumed that the basic choice is between competing and colluding. Instead of the decisions being 'not testify' and 'testify' they could be labelled 'co-operate' or 'defect' in relation to collusive behaviour in the market. The pay-off matrix would then have the structure represented in Figure 11. The first figure provides company A's profit, the second company B's profit.

1.95 In the situation of Figure 11 the dominant strategy for both companies is to defect, in other words to compete. When the other company in the market will restrict output and thereby ensure a high market price it is advantageous not to restrict output. Similarly, when the other company will not restrict output it is against one's own interest to restrict output.

		Company B		
		C	D	
	C	3,3	1,4	C = co-operate
Company A				
	D	4,1	2,2	D = defect

Figure 11 The prisoner's dilemma applied to a duopoly

As a result, the two companies will not co-operate and will forgo the collective optimal outcome and end up with the equilibrium with the lower collective profit. The latter is the Nash equilibrium of the prisoner's dilemma game.

If all oligopolistic markets would follow the simple rules of the prisoner's dilemma game just **1.96** described there would not be many competition problems. Even duopolists would compete with each other down to the competitive price level. The prisoner's dilemma shows the basic instability present in many situations of collusion. The collusive outcome creates the possibility to free ride or cheat on the co-operative behaviour of the others, as witnessed in practice by the breaking down and erosion of many cartel agreements.

However, competition policy practice and simulation experiments show that a collusive **1.97** outcome is attainable. In practice, to co-operate does seem to be the dominant or chosen strategy in a not insignificant number of cases. This is explained by a number of factors.

The first factor that makes a collusive outcome more likely is that oligopolists usually do **1.98** meet each other many times in the market-place; the game is not played once but more than once. Intuitively this means that although the prisoner's dilemma pay-off structure may indicate it is rational to compete if one only looks at one round, such competitive behaviour may spoil future profits that could possibly be attained by collusion. Past behaviour and possible future profits become important when formulating a strategy. In game theory one usually distinguishes in this context between games that are infinite versus games that are played a finite number of times.

In a prisoner's dilemma setting that is played an infinite number of rounds the players **1.99** might come to a collusive outcome. Such an infinitely repeated single-period game is called a supergame. Whether a collusive outcome results depends on the balance for each player of the gains from competing in the first period against the loss of a part of the collusive (monopoly) profit for every period or at least a number of periods thereafter. The incentive to compete will be weighed by each player against the possible punishment the other players may inflict on him in the future in case he does not co-operate. Such punishment will in turn depend on the possibilities and rationality of punishing possible competitors. The punishment may consist in returning to the competitive outcome on the market because all firms expand their output. The players may also try to reduce for all players the attractiveness of competing by limiting the time or scope of possible competition and/or increasing the possibilities of punishment.[45] The exchange of sensitive market information may be used by the players to help to detect competition.

Also when the game is played a limited and not an infinite number of times a collusive out- **1.100** come may result in a non-co-operative setting with a prisoner's dilemma pay-off matrix. Theoretically collusion becomes, however, more difficult. This is explained by backward induction. In a one-period prisoner's dilemma type game the best strategy for each player is, as explained before, not to co-operate. This means that in a multi-period game it is rational

---

[45] The punishment strategy that is chosen by the players influences the pay-off that results after the competing behaviour has been detected. As the question of the best punishment strategy seems still unresolved this is not discussed further here.

for both players not to co-operate in the last period. Given the certainty that both will not co-operate in the last period it is also not rational to co-operate in the penultimate period, as there can be no reward in terms of co-operation in the last period etc. Thus collusion will not be achieved in any period.

1.101 However, as soon as the players do not have full information but instead have imperfect information and have to make up their minds about their best strategy under uncertainty—the common situation in real markets—collusion again becomes a possible outcome. Players may not know the number of times the game will be played, may have to guess about the costs and possibilities of the others to punish, may assign probabilities to the possible strategies of the others, etc. This may make it rational to co-operate, at least until someone starts to compete.

1.102 Different strategies can be imagined in repeated games. A most successful strategy in simulation that is also very simple is the so-called tit-for-tat strategy: co-operate on the first round and thereafter do whatever the other player did in the previous round. It has the advantage of starting with a co-operative strategy in the first round to try to reap the gains of collusion. In addition, it provides a quick reaction by hitting back when competitive behaviour is detected. After such punishment it offers the other the possibility to restore the collusive equilibrium.

1.103 A second factor that makes a collusive outcome more likely is that companies, also in a setting of a non-co-operative game like the prisoner's dilemma, may behave more as if they are in a co-operative game setting. Companies in general do not behave as nakedly rational as non-co-operative game theory usually assumes. Social constraints, moral codes of conduct, etc do influence behaviour. Business ethics may 'command' that oral non-binding agreements are kept; 'a man a man, a word a word'.[46]

1.104 This also means that communication on future prices and output, sometimes described as 'cheap talk' as it does not involve binding commitments and does not change the pay-off matrix, may not be all 'cheap talk'. To discuss and hammer out agreements detailing how much each will produce and what price will be charged may be quite vital as companies may become rather nervous about their co-operative attitude when there is not enough communication. Communication may be essential to 'prevent' companies from starting to behave as rationally as the underlying non-co-operative game assumes.

1.105 From experiments with the prisoner's dilemma it is known that the narrow 'self-regarding' perspective is in general not realistic. The experiments of Flood and Dresher[47] in the early 1950s already show this. In a 100-round prisoner's dilemma experiment they find that even

---

[46] This does not necessarily mean that players act irrationally, it may mean that their perspective becomes less 'self-regarding' and more 'other regarding'. One could be 'other regarding' and have as moral principle that one does not want to be the first who cheats. When applied rationally this leads to collusion. Also, sometimes certain deliberations do not enter the pay-off matrix; from a manager's point of view it may be very rational when he does not want to isolate himself on the green on Saturday by being the one who 'ruins' the market. See, for further details, H Pellikaan, *Anarchie, Staat en het Prisoner's Dilemma* (Delft: Eburon, 1996) Ch 8.

[47] See n 44.

highly qualified players let their choice, while non-collusion is the dominant strategy, be influenced by emotional considerations and feelings of revenge and that the players act in a surprisingly co-operative manner; in sixty rounds both co-operated at the same time while only in fourteen rounds both defected.[48]

(d) Some Results

Real oligopoly situations are more complicated than the stylised games described above. **1.106** In an oligopoly there are usually more than two players, and each company has the choice not simply between competing or colluding but has to decide on a number of parameters that are important for competition; not just price or output, but also promotional activity, product differentiation, product and process innovation. On each of these parameters there are not just two options and two pay-offs but usually a range of options and pay-offs. It is therefore not surprising that there is no super oligopoly model that by incorporating all the parameters and strategies provides clear-cut solutions to the oligopoly game. However, game theory helps to understand the inherent tension between competition and collusion within oligopolistic markets.

Game theory has helped to identify a number of factors which influence the scope for col- **1.107** lusion between market players. Some of the more important are the following:[49]

- *The number of sellers*: The fewer the sellers, the easier it is to agree on the terms of collu-sion (eg to arrive at a 'focal price') and to monitor adherence. Furthermore, the greater the number of sellers, the greater is the incentive to deviate given that each company has more market share to gain while its lower price will have less effect on the revenues from the output it already sells.
- *Market transparency*: The more transparent the market is in terms of, for instance, the avail-ability of pricing data or market share data, the easier it becomes for the colluding firms to detect competitive behaviour.
- *Product differentiation*: The main reason why product differentiation makes tacit collusion more difficult is that it may exacerbate informational problems in non-transparent mar-kets. When product differentiation is also related to quality differences, companies produc-ing high quality products may have a greater incentive to deviate than low quality firms: they may have more to gain from deviating and less to fear from retaliation by others.
- *Cost asymmetries*: The higher the disparities in terms of cost structure, the less likely it is that tacit collusion will result in a market. First, companies may find it difficult to agree on a 'common price': low-cost companies typically prefer a lower collusive level than high-cost companies. Secondly, low-cost companies are more difficult to discipline. This reasoning also underlies the idea that 'maverick' firms make collusion more difficult.
- *Symmetry of market shares*: Lack of symmetry in market shares is not by itself an indication that collusion is difficult to achieve in a market. However, when market shares are asym-metric in a given industry, this may be the result of different cost levels and/or differences

---

[48] See W Poundstone, *Prisoner's Dilemma* (New York: Doubleday, 1992) 106–116.
[49] The list of factors is based on M Ivaldi, B Jullien, P Rey, P Seabright and J Tirole, *The Economics of Tacit Collusion*, Report to DG Competition (available at <http://europa.eu.int/comm/competition/index_en.html>), with the exception of the item 'ringmaster'.

in product characteristics. These more profound differences are factors that may affect the scope for collusion (see above).

- *Frequency of interaction*: Companies will find it easier to sustain coordination when they interact more frequently. This is because companies can react more quickly to a deviation by any of the other firms. Bidding markets featuring large and infrequent contracts are therefore less prone to collusion.

- *Entry barriers*: Tacit collusion is more difficult to sustain when entry barriers are low. In deciding whether or not to adhere to the terms of coordination, companies make a trade-off between the short-term gains of deviating and the loss in future profits associated with collusion. The prospect of future entry tends to reduce the scope for future collusion, making the latter aspect less relevant in the trade-off.

- *Excess capacity*: The impact of capacity constraints (or the absence thereof) on the scope for tacit collusion is not so clear-cut. When companies are capacity constrained, they lack both the incentive to deviate (there is little scope for increasing market share), and the ability to react against another company that deviates from the collusion. It appears that the situation where some companies are capacity constrained and others are not hampers collusion.

- *Demand growth*: In principle, demand growth increases the value of future gains from collusion and thereby the incentive to adhere to the terms of coordination. However, given that demand growth increases the prospect of future entry it may also reduce the incentive to collude (see above).

- *Innovation*: Innovation makes tacit collusion more difficult. The prospect of innovation reduces both the (expected) value of future coordination and the degree to which other firms can retaliate against a company deviating from the collusion.

- *The presence of a 'ringmaster'*[50]: The existence of a dominant firm acting as a price leader and as a swing producer, should changes in demand conditions require it, can be materially important in maintaining price discipline. Rival companies in such a market may choose not to contest the leadership position of the dominant firm, but instead prefer to live under the shelter of the price level maintained by this firm.

1.108 Game theory also puts in a clearer perspective the role played by so-called facilitating devices. A number of such practices that facilitate co-operation are described in the literature. Rees, for example, mentions the following facilitating devices: information exchange, trade associations, price leadership, collaborative research and cross-licensing of patents, most-favoured-customer (mfc) and meeting-competition (mc) clauses in sales contracts, resale price maintenance, basing point pricing, common costing books.[51] What all these devices have in common is the exchange of information as central element. This is obvious for the direct exchange of information between competitors or the exchange through an intermediary like a trade organisation (collection and dissemination of data, forecasting

---

[50] The term 'ringmaster' appears in T Krattenmaker and S Salop, 'Anticompetitive Exclusion: Raising Rivals' Costs to Achieve Power over Price' (1986) 96(2) Yale Law Journal 211. For similar notions, see S Salop, *Assessment of Dominance: Unilateral and Co-ordinated Effects*, speech delivered at the IBA Conference, Brussels, 8 November 2002. Salop describes a scenario of an asymmetric Stigler-type detection/punishment oligopoly (see Stigler, n 44 above), in which a dominant firm acts as the leader and enforcer of coordinated interaction. The 'ringmaster' concept does not feature explicitly in the report by Ivaldi et al, n 49 above, and it must be acknowledged that there is, as yet, little formal analysis of the 'ringmaster' in the context of collusion.

[51] R Rees, 'Tacit Collusion' (1993) Oxford Review of Economic Policy 27, 35–37.

studies, common costing books, etc). But it is also the case when the exchange runs via the customers (price leadership, mfc and mc clauses, resale price maintenance, basing point pricing). These devices may all be used to limit the influence of factors that destabilise co-operative outcomes or strengthen the factors that support co-operative outcomes. This is done by limiting the gains of competing, by monitoring each other's behaviour thus making detection of competing easier, by better targeting the infliction of punishment, or by making it easier for firms to reach a view on the appropriate collusive strategy by reducing the effects of factors such as product heterogeneity, uncertainty about future cost, demand, or capacity, and technological change.

In terms of the prisoner's dilemma game described above, such facilitating practices may **1.109** reduce the gains of defecting/competing. They reduce the pay-off/profits that can be obtained from competing while the others act in a collusive manner. In the extreme case the pay-off matrix may change so much that it is no longer a prisoner's dilemma type of game. An example of this extreme case is given by the pay-off matrix represented in Figure 12.

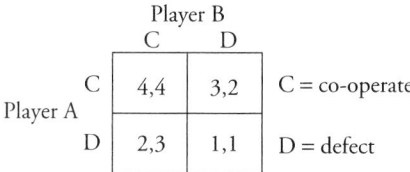

Figure 12 **A non-co-operative game with co-operation as the dominant strategy**

In such a case, by reducing its price each player loses more in profits on its current sales than **1.110** it could gain in profits from newly attracted sales. To restrict output has become the dominant strategy for both players and the high price outcome ensues without collusion. Competing is not anymore an attractive option. Such a matrix is unlikely under most market conditions, but the oligopolists may take steps to worsen their possible gain from competing, to make the pay-off structure change from a prisoner's dilemma to a setting where restricting output is the dominant strategy. For instance, the adoption by the oligopolists of a most favoured customer plan, guaranteeing to pay customers retro-actively any possible discount the company will give within, for example, the next one year. Such a plan may significantly undermine an oligopolist's gain from competing, as the lower price offered to lure new customers away from its competitors will have to be awarded to all its customers of the past year. If applied simultaneously by all it will reduce each firm's gain from competing. However, to start colluding and to implement such facilitating practices that worsen the possible gain from competing, will itself require overcoming a prisoner's dilemma.

Although an accurate, predictive and encompassing oligopoly model does not yet exist, **1.111** what can one conclude as to the scope for collusion? The factor that is often taken as a starting point for competition policy analysis is the number of firms and their market shares and the resulting market concentration.

With a limited number of firms in the market, prices and profits may be significantly higher **1.112** than these would be in a market with many firms. The economic literature does not provide a specific number of firms below which or a particular level of market concentration above which supra-normal prices and profits will be likely to arise.[52] As explained, the likelihood of such effects lowers as the number of firms increases. The likelihood and effects are likely to become rather small above a certain number of firms, possibly when there are more than ten or twelve main firms in the market.[53]

1.113 In the context of merger control, which is by its nature forward looking, one can only confidently predict collusion to result from a merger in (highly) concentrated markets. This is reflected in the indications given in the 1992 Horizontal Merger Guidelines issued by the US Department of Justice and Federal Trade Commission as well as those of the European Commission. The US Guidelines state that a merger is 'likely to create or enhance market power or facilitate its exercise' when the Herfindahl-Hirschman Index (HHI) is above 1800 and the HHI increase resulting from the merger exceeds 100.[54] The HHI threshold of 1800 implies there are roughly five or six equally large firms in a market. However, this does not mean that, in the US, mergers in such situations are systematically forbidden. It is a rebuttable presumption and other factors such as entry barriers, countervailing power, efficiencies, etc also play a role in the assessment. In the EU Merger Guidelines, the Commission only formulates negative presumptions using the HHI. It is stated that the Commission is unlikely to identify horizontal competition concerns in a market with a post-merger HHI below 1000, in a market with a post-merger HHI between 1000 and 2000 where the HHI increase resulting from the merger remains below 250 and in a market with a post-merger HHI above 2000 where the HHI increase resulting from the merger remains below 150. Above these thresholds there is no negative or positive presumption of competition concerns. Other factors that may make collusion easier, more stable or more effective, such as the possibility to monitor, deter, and raise entry barriers will have to be evaluated. EC competition policy practice has been rather cautious and has attacked mergers on the basis of collective dominance mainly in cases where there are two or three main companies in the market.[55]

---

[52] A specific number is mentioned by Selten in an article of 1973 and Phlips in later work which builds upon the ideas of Selten. See: R Selten, 'A simple model of imperfect competition where four are few and six are many' (1973) 2 International Journal of Game Theory 141–201; L Phlips, *Competition Policy: a Game-Theoretic Perspective* (Cambridge: Cambridge University Press, 1995); and L Phlips, 'On the detection of collusion and predation' (1996) 40 European Economic Review 495–510. Their conclusion is that '4 are few and 6 are many', that is when there are four firms or less in a market the likelihood of collusion will be one while this likelihood drops to close to nil when the number of firms becomes six or more. However, their conclusion is only valid with the restrictive assumptions underlying their model. The model of Selten, which is also the basis of Phlips's work, excludes the possibility of cheating. Each company decides beforehand whether it will co-operate or not. Once it has decided to co-operate it sticks to its promise. This therefore resembles the situation of a co-operative game with enforceable agreements. The model shows that such binding agreements will be formed with a likelihood of one as long as the number of firms does not exceed four.

[53] Scherer and Ross (n 1 above) 277 state: 'As a very crude general rule, if evenly matched firms supply homogeneous products in a well-defined market, they are likely to begin ignoring their influence on price when their number exceeds ten or twelve.' This number of ten or twelve companies does not necessarily include fringe companies and companies supplying niche markets, which can also be active on the market while not exerting an important competitive pressure.

[54] The HHI is a measure of concentration defined as the sum of the squared market shares of all the firms in the market.

[55] See, eg, the following merger cases: Case IV/M190 *Nestlé/Perrier* [1992] OJ L356/1; Case IV/M308 *Kali & Salz* [1994] OJ L186/38, and [1998] OJ C275/3; Case IV/M619 *Gencor/Lonhro* [1997] OJ L11/30; Case COMP/M3099 *Areva/Urenco/ETCJV* (2004, not yet reported).

In the context of antitrust enforcement under Articles 81 and 82, competition authorities **1.114** may want to concentrate on the detection of explicit collusion and in addition on the detection and analysis of facilitating practices. Investigation of facilitating devices offers the possibility to scrutinise conscious parallelism as closely as possible and take remedial action by, if necessary, disallowing the facilitating device. In terms of the US antitrust practice it means defining the 'plus' in 'conscious parallelism plus something else' that together restrict competition.

Many of the negative decisions on cartels taken under Article 81 seem to corroborate the **1.115** above analysis. Although it is not always easy to establish the number of competitors in the relevant market(s) in past decisions as it was not always considered necessary to carefully define the market(s) in cases of clear-cut price fixing and market sharing cartels, the number of main competitors seems in general to have been below twelve. In most cases the cartel consists of between three and eight members and covers all or most of the market.[56] Exceptions to this rule are mainly found in decisions involving trade associations,[57] liner conferences,[58] or previously regulated industries such as the steel industry,[59] where for different reasons effective cartels were able to operate with a higher number of main players.

There was also a limited number of firms in the market in the *Fatty Acids* case and in the **1.116** *UK Tractors* case, two cases where exchange of information as a facilitating device for parallel behaviour was the sole competition infringement.[60] In these cases important elements of a game-theoretical analysis can be found. In the *Fatty Acids* case the description of the parties' motivation contains many elements of a non-co-operative game with a prisoner's dilemma; companies are afraid of being misunderstood by their competitors, afraid to provoke price-cutting which again would make retaliation necessary, when business is stolen

---

[56] See the following cases: *Polypropylene* [1986] OJ L230/1; *Meldoc* [1986] OJ L348/50; *Belasco* [1986] OJ L232; *Fatty Acids* [1987] OJ L3/17; *Italian flat glass* [1989] OJ L33; *Soda ash/Solvay* [1991] OJ L152/21; *UK Tractors* [1992] OJ L68/19; *Cement* [1994] OJ L343/1; *Carton Board* [1994] OJ L243/1; *Ferry Operators* [1996] OJ L26/23; *Alloy Surcharge* [1998] OJ L100/55; *British Sugar; Tate & Lyle; Napier Brown; James Budgett* [1999] OJ L76/1; *Greek Ferries* [1998] OJ L109/24; *Pre-insulated Pipe Cartel* [1999] OJ L24/1; *Seamless Steel Tubes* [2003] OJ L140/1; *Amino Acids* [2001] OJ L152/24; *SAS/Maersk Air* [2001] OJ L265/15; *Graphite Electrodes* [2002] OJ L100/1; *Sodium Gluconate* (not yet published); *Vitamins* [2003] OJ L6/1; *Citric Acid* [2002] OJ L239/18; *Belgium Breweries* [2003] OJ L200/1; *Luxembourg Breweries* [2002] OJ L253/21; *Zinc Phosphate* [2003] OJ L153/1; *German Banks* [2003] OJ L15/1; *Carbonless Paper* [2004] OJ L115/88; *Specialty Graphite* (not yet published); *Plasterboard* [2005] OJ L166/8; *Methylglucamine* [2004] OJ 38/18; *Fine Art Auction Houses* [2005] OJ L200/92; *Methionine* [2003] OJ L255/1; *Austrian Banks – 'Lombard Club'* [2004] OJ L56/1; *Industrial and Medical Gases* [2003] OJ L84/1; *Food Flavour Enhancers* [2004] OJ L75/1; *Sorbates* [2005] OJ L182/20; *Electrical and Mechanical Carbon and Graphite Products* [2004] OJ L125/45; *Organic Peroxides* [2005] OJ L110/44; *Industrial Copper Tubes* [2004] OJ L125/50; *Copper Plumbing Tubes* (not yet published); *Sodium Gluconate* (not yet published); *French Beer* (not yet published); *Raw Tobacco in Spain* (not yet published); *Hard Haberdashery/Needles* (not yet published); and *Choline Chloride* (not yet published).
[57] See the following cases: *SPO* [1992] OJ L92; *CNSD* [1993] OJ L203/27; *SCK/FNK* [1995] OJ L312/79; *COAPI* [1995] OJ L122/37; *FENEX* [1996] OJ L181/28; *FEG; TU* [2003] OJ L39/1; *Concrete Reinforcing Bars* (not yet published); *French Beef* [2003] OJ L209/12; *Raw Tobacco in Spain* (not yet published).
[58] See the following cases: *TAA* [1994] OJ L376; *Far Eastern Freight Conference* [1994] OJ L378/17; *TACA* [1999] OJ L95/1; *FETTCSA* [2000] OJ L268/1.
[59] See the following cases: *Welded Steel Mesh* [1989] OJ L260/1; *Steel Beams* [1994] OJ L116/1; *Wirtschaftsvereinigung Stahl* [1998] OJ L1/10.
[60] *Fatty Acids* [1987] OJ L3/17; *UK Tractors* [1992] OJ L68/19.

recouping it elsewhere would be detrimental to the current equilibrium, output needs to be controlled and monitoring of respective market positions is essential to allow 'orderly marketing'. In the *UK Tractors* decision the Commission emphasised the context of a concentrated market, the creation of market transparency which is likely to destroy what hidden competition there remains in that market, the elimination of uncertainty about competitors' actions, the shortened reaction lag to price competition which greatly reduces the advantage of a company that tries to undercut, the situation that targeted punishment is made possible and the possible effect that a reduction of intra-brand competition may have on inter-brand competition, which all fit very well in a game theoretical explanation.

D. Dynamic Welfare Analysis of Market Power[61]

(1) Innovation and Welfare

1.117 The static welfare analysis described in Section C above does not take dynamic aspects of competition, most notably innovation, into account. Technological developments are abstracted away, by assuming the level of technology as constant. This of course is at best reflective of reality in the short term and certainly not in the longer term. In the real world product markets develop and change over time because of innovation; improved or new products and production processes are introduced. New or improved products will in general lead to greater consumer satisfaction and improved or new production processes will lead to lower production costs. In other words, these dynamic efficiencies lead to welfare gains. A proper welfare analysis of market power should thus not only take the static but also the dynamic efficiencies into account and in case the rate of innovation is affected by the market structure or the level of competition it may be necessary to assess any trade-off between static and dynamic efficiencies.

1.118 There is agreement that competition is the driving force for static allocative efficiency. Competition forces companies in a market with a given technology to offer the best quality products at the lowest prices. However, it is also a generally accepted and well-substantiated point of view that innovation is the main source of increases in economic welfare. The literature shows that technological innovation together with an increased ability on the part of the labour force are the main driving forces behind productivity gains and welfare growth.[62] This explains why societies in general try to spur the creation and dissemination of innovation. In case of a choice between dynamic and static efficiencies, the former will quickly outweigh the latter.

(2) Different Views

1.119 This has led to the question whether innovation instead of price competition should be the focal point of competition policy and if so whether this should lead to a drastic revision of

---

[61] This section is based on L Peeperkorn, 'IP Licenses and Competition Rules: Striking the Right Balance' (2003) 26 World Competition 527–539.

[62] See Scherer and Ross, Ch 17; RM Solow, 'Technical Change and the Aggregate Production Function' (1957) Review of Economics and Statistics, 312–320; WK Tom, Background Note, pp 21–22, *Roundtable on Competition Policy and Intellectual Property Rights*, Committee on Competition Law and Policy, OECD, October 1997.

competition policy. This question goes to the heart of competition policy and questions its general validity when applied to markets for new and existing products. The assumption is that there may be a contradiction between innovation and (price) competition, or at least that by focusing on the preservation of (price) competition the rate of innovation may be harmed. Underlying this assumption is the view that (high) concentration may have a positive influence on the rate of technological progress.

There is no clear agreement in the economic literature concerning the benefit of competition for innovation and hence dynamic efficiency. There are economists who, in the footsteps of Schumpeter, claim that innovation is spurred by monopoly.[63] Monopoly profits may fund research and development (R&D) and a high market share may help to appropriate the value of the resulting innovations. They argue that there is therefore a conceptual flaw in competition policy. Competition policy, by attacking monopoly and preventing market power from arising, may have a positive effect on static allocative efficiency but at the same time undermines dynamic efficiency. As the latter is much more important for welfare growth it is argued that competition policy easily leads to unwanted policy results, ie less growth and less welfare. **1.120**

The Schumpeterian view has been contradicted by Arrow[64] and also by other economists, who have put forward a number of reasons why competition may provide more incentives than monopoly for innovation. A firm under competitive pressure will be less complacent and will have more market share to gain through innovation. In addition, in the case of a product invention the new product will not cannibalise the firm's own market as it would under monopoly. It is also argued that innovation incentives depend not so much on the post-innovation profits *per se*, but on the difference between post-innovation and pre-innovation profits. The direct effect on welfare is also supposed to be better under competition, especially in the case of a process invention, as the innovation will be applied to a higher output than under monopoly.[65] Greater product market competition and a strict competition policy both work as an effective stick to foster innovative effort.[66] **1.121**

(3) Some Empirical Results

Empirical research on the relationship between market structure and innovation, usually the litmus test in case of theoretical controversy, does not give unequivocal results but tends to support the view of Arrow. In general, competition and open markets provide the better incentives for innovation while monopoly and high concentration retard innovation.[67] There are some indications of an inverted U relationship between concentration and the ratio of industry R&D to industry sales, with the highest R&D/sales ratios occurring **1.122**

---

[63] J A Schumpeter, *Capitalism, Socialism and Democracy* (1942).

[64] K J Arrow, 'Economic Welfare and the Allocation of Resources for Invention'[1962] The rate and Direction of Inventive Activity: Economic and Social Factors 609–625.

[65] Static welfare analyis indicates that industry output is higher under competition than under monopoly. See Section C.

[66] P Aghion, N Bloom, R Blundell, R Griffith and P Howitt, 'Competition and Innovation: An Inverted-U Relationship' (2005) 120 Quarterly Journal of Economics 701; S Martin, 'Competition Policy for High Technology Industries' [2001] Journal of Industry, Competition and Trade 441–465.

[67] See Scherer and Ross, Ch 17 (n 1); Tom, p 22 (n 62); and 'Patents, Competition and Innovation', Background note by the Secretariat, pp 27–38, Competition Committee, OECD, September 2006.

where the four biggest companies in the industry sell 50–60 per cent of total industry sales.[68] However, it is also clear that other factors such as the technological opportunity of the sector are more important to explain R&D intensity. Using data for the UK and controlling for technological opportunity Geroski found higher seller concentration and increases in other monopoly related variables to have a significant negative impact on the emergence of innovations.[69] In a study analysing reports in specialised technical literature covering the entire manufacturing sector, Acs and Andretsch found that the average small-firm innovation rate is higher than the large-firm innovation rate.[70] Other research points to the very important role of newcomers, especially where the invention of radically new products and concepts is concerned, and to the related interest in keeping entry barriers at modest levels. Lastly, it should be noted that research into the relationship between market structure and innovation is complicated by the fact that to a certain extent both are endogenous: both depend on more basic factors such as technological opportunities for innovation and demand conditions.

(4) The 'New Economy'

1.123 Recently there has been a more refined debate, as to whether the supposed different dynamics of competition in sectors undergoing rapid technological change requires a more or less fundamental revision of competition policy for those sectors.[71] For instance Evans and Schmalensee argue that competition in important new industries centres on investment in IP. Firms engage in competition for the market through sequential winner-takes-all races to produce drastic innovations, rather than through price/output competition in the market and through incremental innovation.[72] They argue that firms will obtain considerable short-term market power, but ignoring their dynamic vulnerability may lead to misleading antitrust conclusions.

1.124 For competition policy it would therefore be important to distinguish between industries where markets are (continuously) destroyed and replaced through drastic innovations on the one hand and, on the other hand, industries where within markets innovation develops incrementally. Evans and Schmalensee identified the following industries as having Schumpeterian dimensions: computer software, computer hardware, internet based businesses (portals,

---

[68] P Aghion, N Bloom, R Blundell, R Griffith, P Howitt, *Competition and Innovation: An Inverted U Relationship*, The Institute for Fiscal Studies, WP02/04, February 2002.

[69] P Geroski, 'Innovation, Technological Opportunity, and Market Structure' [1990] Oxford Economic Papers 42. See also Scherer and Ross, Ch 17 (n1).

[70] ZJ Acs and DB Andretsch, 'Innovation, Market Structure and Firm Size' (1987) LXIX Review of Economics and Statistics 567–574.

[71] It is sometimes argued, often in a rather loose way, that the pace of technological change is increasing or has increased in recent times. There seems little evidence of this trend. Traditional indicators such as productivity growth rates have not shown a clear upward trend in the pace of innovation. Some claim that the rate of innovation is poorly measured by such indicators as many qualitative improvements are not captured: however the same applies for the productivity figures of the past and to show a clear upward trend in the pace of innovation one should in that case show that qualitative improvements have become more important over time. It seems more likely that the impression that innovation is increasing in pace is only a matter of perception: changes in ones own time always seem more rapid and upsetting, just like the perception of speed will be stronger if one is near to a passing train than when one is looking at the train from a distance.

[72] DS Evans and R Schmalensee, *Some Economic aspects of Antitrust Analysis in Dynamically Competitive Industries*, NBER Working Paper 8268, May 2001.

BtoB exchanges), communications networks, mobile telephony, biotechnology and, to a lesser extent, pharmaceuticals.

This is again in the first place an empirical question. Evans and Schmalensee acknowledge that an initial phase with bursts of innovation may only characterise the infant stage of a new industry and may very well be followed by a long period of comparative stability and incremental innovation. They for instance refer to the car industry having had Schumpeterian aspects around 1910 and decades of stability afterwards. Other examples are the chemical and electronics industries that were described in the 1950s as 'new-economy'.[73] It seems most likely that also today's 'new economy' industries will turn into more 'normal and traditional' industries if they have not done so in good part already.

1.125

In addition, Evans and Schmalensee recognise that many of the sectors they assess as having Schumpeterian characteristics also have network effects and that these effects tend to reinforce the market leaders' position. Network effects can make markets tip and become highly concentrated and can impose significant barriers to entry. Similarly, switching costs and lock-in may prevent displacement of market leaders.

1.126

In line with the general conclusion in the literature, Evans and Schmalensee do not contend that dynamically competitive industries should be immune from careful antitrust scrutiny, nor do they contend that the basic principles of antitrust should be modified.[74] Price fixing, foreclosure, market partitioning, etc can and will still harm consumers, also in the 'new economy'. However, as is the case for every sector, also for the new-economy industries competition policy needs to take account of industry or technology specific characteristics. According to Evans and Schmalensee in particular market definition and market power analysis have to be modified when applied to highly innovative sectors.

1.127

In their view traditional market definition and market share analysis does not acknowledge that in Schumpeterian industries companies are constrained from doing harm to consumers by dynamic competition. An essential element of market power analysis should be an examination of actual and potential innovative threats, also from alternative technologies. Where the market leader's position may not be based on durable assets like production capacity but based on the quality of its current products and IP it may therefore be fragile. They argue that in these sectors a market share at best measures static market power. Static market power does not provide a useful measure of the real competitive constraints on the leading firms in these sectors. They may not be constrained by the behaviour of existing competitors as the latter are often few or absent and scale economies and network effects may form effective barriers to the entry of similar products. The real and dynamic constraints come from firms actually or potentially making significant R&D investments to replace the current products. The question whether these are around and how credible the threat might be, they argue, cannot be measured by market share. Dynamic competition

1.128

---

[73] See DE Lilienthal, *Big Business: A New Era* (1952).

[74] See also, for instance, *E-Commerce and its Implications for Competition Policy*, Discussion Paper 1, OFT, August 2000, p 1: '. . . e-commerce will not give rise to any entirely new forms of anti-competitive behaviour, nor will it raise any new issues that cannot be dealt with under the existing competition law framework. However, . . . there are . . . areas where detailed application of the rules may require some adjustment.'

may not be effective when the leading company owns all IP necessary for radical innovation or when it forecloses important distribution channels. It may be, though, that several companies are or could make significant R&D investments and that experts consider the outcome of the rivalry in doubt, in which case dynamic competition may be effective.

(5) Some Concluding Remarks

1.129 In conclusion, there seems to be no important conflict between innovation and competition policy aimed at product market competition and there seems to be no fundamental flaw in competition policy. Competition policy, by defending competition and open markets, will in general have a positive impact on both static and dynamic efficiency. Companies under competitive pressure will be less complacent and will have more incentive to innovate and gain market share. Product market competition and a strict competition policy generally work as an effective stick to promote innovative effort. With the possible exception of those industries where during an initial phase markets are continuously destroyed and replaced through drastic innovations, a company's position on the market is in general well reflected by its market share and that share is generally the best available indicator of its market power.

E. Market Definition[75]

1.130 Antitrust analysis focuses on the question of whether companies are, or will be, in a position to exercise market power. It is difficult to think of this question without reference to a proper context, without reference to a 'market'. For example, the analysis of an agreement between two companies might indicate that certain clauses in the agreement restrict the competitive conduct of one or both of the parties. However, the effects of the clauses at issue can only be expected to have a significant impact, on any relevant market and hence on market variables such as price or output, if the agents concerned possess some market power. In order to identify the existence or creation of market power, one typically needs to proceed to an analysis of the market.[76]

1.131 What is the right context for antitrust analysis? What is the 'relevant market'? Though obviously related, the relevant market for antitrust purposes does not always coincide with the market as it is described in marketing reports or other business reports. Companies, when thinking of what constitutes the relevant market, naturally consider this question from a business perspective. For example, many European companies nowadays operate in several parts of Europe and the world, with a view to expanding their business. For them, the relevant geographic market is European, if not global. Similarly, many well-known

---

[75] This section and the next build on a text written by Kirti Mehta for the previous edition of this book. The authors wish to thank Greg Werden for his comments. All errors, if any, are the responsibility of the present authors.

[76] As a general rule, market definition is more relevant where the analysis is prospective than in situations where the anti-competitive nature or effect can be analysed more directly, *ex post*. In the context of horizontal cartels, for example, the anti-competitive object of the behaviour is clear and does not require any market definition. In the latter case, it may still be useful to proceed to a definition of the market in order to evaluate the impact of the situation.

companies would broadly describe their relevant area of activity as 'consumer electronics', 'healthcare', or 'automotive'. Market definition for antitrust purposes starts, however, from a different perspective: what options are open for the customers to acquire the product they wish to acquire? What alternatives do they have? Are they good alternatives? It is this perspective that determines, in large part, whether a company has the ability to exercise market power (eg raise price) vis-à-vis its customers, or not.

Whether or not a company can exert market power depends on a number of factors. The **1.132** availability of substitute products for the products offered by the company under consideration is only one of them. The strength of competitors, the presence of entry barriers, the presence of buyer power are other relevant factors. Nonetheless, it is useful to proceed in steps. The objective of defining a market, the first step, is to identify, both in the product and geographic dimension, those products that are capable of constraining the commercial behaviour of the company concerned in that they form sufficiently good substitutes for the product in question.[77] It thereby provides a context within which to assess the competition issue, be it the competitive impact of a given agreement, a certain type of company conduct, or a merger.

Beyond providing context, it is clear that market definition also serves an important practi- **1.133** cal purpose. Once the market is defined it is possible to assign market shares to the various companies active in the relevant market, so as to obtain a first impression of their relative importance in the competitive process. Market definition thereby allows for a first screening of cases, to see whether there may be competitive issues or not.[78]

The subsections below discuss the main principles of market definition, first in the context **1.134** of product market definition and then in the context of geographic market definition. The section concludes with a number of further considerations on market definition.

(1) Product Market Definition

The key concept in the definition of a relevant product market for antitrust purposes is **1.135** *substitutability*, ie the extent to which customers are able and willing to switch to other products.

Two main avenues of substitution are often considered in the context of market definition: **1.136** demand-side substitution and supply-side substitution.[79] Demand-side substitution relates to the possibility of customers switching to alternative products that are already on offer. Supply-side substitution relates to the possibility of turning to products that are not yet offered by particular competitors, but that would readily be offered by them in the event of a higher price of the product in question.

---

[77] cf Commission's Notice on the Definition of the Relevant Market for the Purposes of Community Competition Law [1997] OJ C372/5 (hereinafter Commission Notice on market definition).

[78] While there can be some debate as to whether high market shares are good indicators of market power, there is less doubt on low market shares being good indicators of the absence of market power. See also Section F.

[79] As will be discussed below, the US approach to supply-side substitution differs somewhat from that of the EU.

(a) Demand-side Substitution

1.137 The most immediate constraint upon the terms on which a firm supplies a product is the competitive pressure represented by adequate substitute products available (in the relevant geographic area). In the case of a price increase of the product in question, the customer would readily shift to such substitute products. In practice, the market definition problem thus reduces itself to determining the range of products that constitute good substitutes for the customer or, rather, for a sufficiently important number of customers.

1.138 The importance of demand-side substitution is underlined in the traditional description given in the EU to the concept of relevant product market: 'A relevant product market comprises all those products and/or services which are regarded as interchangeable or substitutable by the consumer, by reason of the products' characteristics, their prices and their intended use.'[80]

1.139 While the underlying idea is clear, in practice it is often rather difficult to determine whether products are good substitutes for each other by focusing on factors such as product characteristics, prices, or intended use alone. For some products it may be readily possible to identify a number of good substitutes on this basis, but more often than not the above factors are unlikely to provide a clear basis for deciding which products should be considered part of the relevant market and which should not be considered part of the market. To take an example, different types of malt whisky may well be considered part of the same market. But can malt whisky be considered in the same relevant market as blended whisky? And what about vodka or gin? On the one hand, one would be tempted to say that malt whisky is different from blended whisky and very different from vodka or gin. On the other hand, there are a number of similarities as well: all the products are spirits, their (quality adjusted) prices are comparable, and the products are consumed in rather similar circumstances.

1.140 Furthermore, it must be realised that not all customers are alike. Basing market definition on the 'average customer', where there are significant differences among customers, may lead to erroneous results. In determining whether or not other products constitute a competitive threat to the product in question, one needs to focus on the so-called *marginal customers*, ie those who generally value the product at the price paid and not much more. It is those consumers who would be likely to shift their demand, in whole or in part, to substitutes if the relative price of the product increases. If the proportion of marginal customers is sufficiently large relative to the other customers (called the infra-marginal consumers[81]), a relative price increase might well result in a substantial loss of sales.

1.141 Finally, even when one has reliable information about the actual degree of substitutability between products for the group of customers under consideration, on what basis does one conclude that the substitutability is high enough for products to form part of the same relevant market? Where should one draw a line between the products? What is the benchmark?

---

80 See, eg, the Commission Notice on market definition, above n 77, para 2.
81 Infra-marginal consumers have, by way of definition, a willingness to pay for the product that is higher than the price they have to pay for it and so they would substitute less, or not at all, if the relative price increases.

As it turns out, it is useful to apply a 'unifying principle' to market definition and to think of **1.142** a relevant market as 'something worth monopolising'[82] (if a company had a monopoly for this particular type of product, would it want to raise the price of it?). This idea is embodied in the SSNIP methodology for analysing economic substitutability, which we discuss next.

(b) The SSNIP Test

The need for a framework to assess economic substitutability has led to the development of **1.143** the SSNIP test, also known as the 'hypothetical monopolist test' or '5-10 per cent price test'.[83] SSNIP stands for 'Small but Significant Non-transitory Increase in Price'. The SSNIP test links up with the purpose of market definition itself; that is, to identify the products that are capable of constraining the commercial behaviour of the company supplying the product under consideration. It proposes to make—in an iterative way—a distinction between products that would prevent a company, even if it were a monopolist, from raising the price for the product in question and those products that do not. Thus, the *benchmark* is whether it would be profitable for such a supplier (the 'hypothetical monopolist') to raise the price for the product concerned or not. The *methodology* is iterative.

Specifically, the SSNIP approach suggests the following line of enquiry: start with the prod- **1.144** uct in question, postulate a hypothetical small but significant increase (eg in the range of 5–10 per cent) in the price at which that product is made available (the prices of the alternative products are held constant), and assess the likely reactions of customers to that increase.[84] If substitution away from the product by customers would be enough to make the price increase unprofitable because of the resulting loss of sales, then the product is not a relevant market by itself: there are other products that exercise a sufficient competitive constraint in that they prevent a company, even if it had a 'monopoly' on the product, from raising the price.[85]

If the price increase of the product is unprofitable, the next step of the SSNIP test is to **1.145** consider the situation where a company would be the sole supplier of the product under

---

[82] Term used in B Owen and S Wildman *Video Economics* (Harvard University Press, 1992) (quoted in S Bishop and M Walker, *The Economics of EC Competition Law* (2002), p 84).

[83] For a more elaborate discussion of the SSNIP test, see GJ Werden, 'The 1982 Merger Guidelines and the Ascent of the Hypothetical Monopolist Paradigm' (2003) 71 Antitrust Law Journal 253–276.

[84] What price increase is significant or insignificant depends on the industry. In some markets, eg the market for crude oil, smaller price increases could be considered significant. However, taking a price increase that is too small would not capture the reactions of all the marginal customers, and might understate the extent of likely customer switching. Using a very large price increase would be likely to capture the reactions of significant portions of the infra-marginal customers. If used as a basis for defining the market, this would lead to very wide markets, hiding otherwise significant competition concerns. Further, it must be noted that the '5–10%' does not constitute a 'tolerance level' below which price increases would be acceptable (see also US Horizontal Merger Guidelines, Section 1.0).

[85] This might raise the question of how any firm producing this product can ever be found dominant on this product or on a wider market given that not even a 'hypothetical monopolist' could profitably raise price by more than 5–10% on the product concerned. The answer is simple. At each iteration the SSNIP test assumes that prices of the products outside the postulated (narrow) market remain constant. This assumption may well be incorrect in light of the nature of competition in the market. Especially in oligopolistic markets, producers of competing products may adjust their prices upwards in response to the price increase of the product concerned (see Sections C(5) and F(3) for more details). The SSNIP test abstracts away from these competition aspects so as to purely focus on the question of the degree to which products are substitutes.

consideration and also its next best substitute (the product to which the greatest proportion of customers switches when the price of the reference product goes up). Would such a company want to raise prices? If it would not, then these two products still do not constitute a relevant market, and it is appropriate to include additional substitutes. If raising prices were profitable, then the two products can be considered a relevant market, given that there are no other products that exert sufficient competitive pressure on the two products. More generally, the steps would be repeated until the set of products is such that small, lasting increases in relative prices would be profitable (the resulting set of products is 'something worth monopolising').[86]

1.146 In our spirits example, if, in the event of a price increase for malt whisky, customers would switch to blended whisky to such an extent that the price increase for malt whisky would not be profitable due to the resulting loss of sales, then the market would comprise at least all whiskies. The process would have to be extended to other available drinks (eg vodka, gin, jenever, etc) until a set of products is identified for which a price rise would not induce a significant enough substitution in demand. This would then be the relevant antitrust market from the perspective of malt whisky customers.

1.147 One might be left with the impression, from reading the above, that the SSNIP approach is a very 'quantitative' tool, and relies on the availability of detailed demand and cost data.[87] In our view, the complexity of the SSNIP test should, however, not be overemphasised. The most important aspect of SSNIP is its conceptual side, not its quantitative side.[88] Even when no detailed data are available, it is useful to think of the market definition question in terms of SSNIP. By asking a question which is directly linked to the purpose of antitrust analysis (is the exercise of market power an issue for this collection of products or not?), it brings a certain structure and consistency to the market definition exercise. The SSNIP concept provides for a framework within which to consider the question of economic substitution.

1.148 In applying the SSNIP test, and in particular for the analysis of merger cases, the reference price to use will normally be the prevailing market price. Special care, however, needs to be taken in the context where the prevailing price has been determined in the absence of sufficient competition. In particular for investigation of abuses of dominant positions, the fact that the prevailing price might already have been substantially increased by a given practice or conduct should be taken into account. If not, this would lead to overly wide markets being defined, and to an understatement of the firm's true market power.[89] In the context

---

[86] If for a given collection of products a price increase is profitable, this is because the next best substitute does not exercise a sufficient constraining influence; hence a wider market including the next best substitute could also be deemed to be the relevant market as on this wider market too a price rise will be profitable. It is for this reason that for competitive analysis the antitrust authorities normally seek to define the narrowest market.

[87] Cost levels matter in view of the profitability question ('would it be profitable to raise the price?').

[88] For similar views, see JB Baker, '*Market Definition*', in Collins WD (ed) *Directions in Competition Law and Policy* (forthcoming).

[89] It is often the case that customers become more willing to switch to other products as the price of a given product increases. Assessing the degree of subsitutability at this high price might wrongly suggest that more products are part of the relevant market. This is the so-called *Cellophane fallacy* (named after a case in 1956 where a US court overlooked this issue).

of mergers, the proper reference price depends on the reason why there is insufficient competition.[90] When it is due to collective dominance (tacit or explicit coordination) pre-merger, it would be appropriate to start from the 'competitive' level (the price level in the absence of coordination), to identify the products relevant for maintaining collective dominance. When the high price is related to a single dominant position, the concern is that the merger may take away a next best substitute at current (high) prices.[91]

(c) Elasticity Concepts and the Diversion Ratio

An important concept in the assessment of demand substitution is the price elasticity of **1.149** demand. The price elasticity of a product measures how demand for that product changes with the price of the product, keeping other prices constant (this elasticity is also called the *own-price elasticity*). In particular, it measures the %-change in demand following a 1 per cent increase in its price. If the price elasticity is, for example, 2.0, this means that, following a 1 per cent price increase, demand for the product goes down by 2.0 per cent. The own price elasticity is, normally speaking, negative: demand for a product falls when its price increases. However, it is common to leave the 'minus' sign away and speak of a high elasticity when the elasticity is high in absolute terms.

The price elasticity is in fact a summary indicator of the extent to which a product is sub- **1.150** ject to demand-side constraints. When the price of a product is raised, customers may, to various extents, switch away from it: they either switch to competing products, or they stop purchasing the product altogether. The (own-) price elasticity of a good captures both these movements. The higher the own-price elasticity, the more the product is subject to demand-side constraints.

A related elasticity concept is the *aggregate price elasticity*, which measures how total market **1.151** demand (combined demand for all products in a particular market) changes with a price increase of 1 per cent (keeping other prices constant).

The own-price elasticity of demand (or, more generally, the aggregate price elasticity for a **1.152** group of products) provides direct input into the SSNIP test for market definition. For example, if the elasticity of the set of products one posits to be in the same relevant product market is equal to 1.5, the unit sales for the products will go down by approximately 7.5 per cent if prices for the products go up by 5 per cent (the usual SSNIP). Depending on the initial gross profit margins of the products involved, this may be profitable or not profitable. If initial margins are low, the price increase is more likely to be profitable.[92]

---

[90] See also the US Horizontal Merger Guidelines, Section 1.11, and the UK Competition Commission Merger Guidelines, paras 2.09–2.10.

[91] After all, the objective of market definition is to identify the products that are capable of exerting some competitive pressure on the merging entities' products, so as to see whether a merger involving these products is problematic from the competition point of view. When the high price is related to coordination among the existing market players, the main concern is that the merger reinforces this coordination by making it less likely to break down in the future. See also Baker, above n 88. When the high price is related to a single dominant position, there are no products exerting significant competitive pressure at the 'competitive' level (if there were, prices would not be that high). Instead, the focus should lie on identifying the products that exert competitive pressure at the higher price level, to see whether a merger involving these products allows the dominant company to further raise price.

[92] An example is developed in Section G(2).

1.153   Another elasticity concept, the *cross-price elasticity*, is also relevant for analysing demand-side substitution, but from a different perspective. The cross-price elasticity measures how demand for a product changes when the price of some other product changes. For example, if the cross-price elasticity of product A vis-à-vis the price of B is 0.8, this means that, when the price of B goes up by 1 per cent, demand for product A goes up by 0.8 per cent. Similarly, there is a cross-price elasticity for product B with respect to the price of A. Cross-price elasticities provide useful information on substitution patterns, but provide less direct input to the SSNIP test than the own-price elasticity. The SSNIP test is primarily concerned with the question of whether a market is 'worth monopolising', so with the question of how much demand for product A changes with the price of A. This is measured by the own-price elasticity. The SSNIP test is only in the second instance also concerned with the question to which products demand switches away. Generally, however, the higher the cross-price elasticity of product B with respect to the price of A, the more product B forms a competitive constraint for product A, and the less likely it is that product A is 'worth monopolising'.[93] If the cross-price elasticity is zero, then the products concerned are not competing. Accordingly, when, on the basis of the own-price elasticity, one concludes that a given product (or set of products) does not constitute a market on its own, an analysis of cross-price elasticities can point to the products that should be included in the relevant market.

1.154   A concept which is closely related to the cross-price elasticity is the *diversion ratio*.[94] The diversion ratio from product A to product B measures the proportion of the sales of product A lost due to a price increase of A that are captured by product B. The diversion ratio and the cross-price elasticity are alternative ways to measure product substitution, with the former being viewed as somewhat more insightful.[95] It has become customary to define the 'next best substitute' of a product as that product for which the diversion ratio is highest.

(d) Supply-side Substitution

1.155   Supply-side substitution relates to the possibility for customers to turn to products that are not yet offered, but that would readily be offered by companies (either new or existing) in the event of a higher price of the product in question.

1.156   Under the Commission's Notice on market definition, supply-side substitution may be taken into account for market definition purposes in those situations in which its effects are 'equivalent to those of demand substitution in terms of effectiveness and immediacy'.[96]

---

[93] Some caution is necessary in interpreting cross-price elasticities, especially when the sales levels of products A and B are very different. For example, if the cross-price elasticity of product B vis-à-vis the price of A is 10.0, this means that when the price of A goes up by 1%, demand for product B goes up by 10%. If, however, the initial sales level of product A is 100 units and that of product B is only 10 units, then the 10% increase in product B only represents one unit of B and, correspondingly, a decrease of only one unit of A (on a total of 100, ie a 1% decrease). Furthermore, it is possible that the cross-price elasticity is high simply because the price of the product under consideration is itself already high (cf the *Cellophane fallacy* problem discussed in the previous subsection). This consideration is, however, not specific to the cross-price elasticity, it is also relevant to the own-price elasticity.

[94] For a presentation, see C Shapiro, 'Mergers with Differentiated Products' Antitrust Magazine, Spring 1996, pp 23–30.

[95] Also in view of the issues described in n 93 above.

[96] Commission Notice on market definition, above n 77, para 20.

This requires that such alternative suppliers be able and willing to switch production to the relevant products and market them in the short term[97] without incurring significant additional costs or risks in response to small and permanent changes in relative prices (the SSNIP). When these conditions are met, the additional production that is put on the market may have a disciplinary effect on the competitive behaviour of the companies involved that is equivalent to that of demand substitution.[98] The products are then in general considered to be in the same relevant market, irrespective of whether there is substitutability from a demand perspective.

A classical example of the role of supply-side substitution is the case of paper.[99] Paper is usu- **1.157** ally supplied in a range of different qualities, from standard writing paper to high quality papers to be used for instance to publish art books. From a demand point of view, different qualities of paper cannot be used for a specific use. For example, office paper of format A4 is typically not substitutable with office paper format A3. Similarly, an art book or a high quality publication often cannot be produced on lower quality papers. However, it is possible that paper plants are prepared to manufacture the different qualities, and that production can be adjusted with negligible costs and in a short time frame. In the absence of particular difficulties in distribution, paper manufacturers are able therefore to compete for orders of the various qualities. Under such circumstances, it makes sense not to define a separate market for each quality of paper and respective usage, but to view the various qualities of paper as part of one relevant market.

A practical question that arises in this context is how far one must take the argument that **1.158** supply-side substitution warrants the grouping of various products into a broader market. Suppose, for example, that there is a product A that is produced by various companies, and a product B that is supplied by a number of other companies. Suppose further that only one of the B-companies uses a production technology that allows it to swiftly switch production from product B to product A (the other B-companies use a technology that only allows them to produce B). Would this be sufficient to conclude that product markets A and B constitute one relevant product market on the basis of supply-side substitution? Grouping the whole A and B market into one would mean that all the single-purpose B-companies are somehow viewed as constraining the A-companies from raising price, whereas in fact this is not the case. The same would apply when all B-companies can switch production to product A, but in reality only a few will do so, given that the margins obtained on producing the B product are higher. In such circumstances, it is more appropriate to only take the B-companies into account *to the extent* they are able and willing to swiftly participate in the A market.

---

[97] A relevant time frame in this respect is often thought of as one year.

[98] When switching production is possible, but would require significant additional investments or time delays (eg due to the need to adjust existing tangible and intangible production assets), this possibility is not considered at the stage of market definition, but rather at the stage of considering potential competition. This is logical given that market definition is a step in the analysis identifying products that already constitute some form of competitive constraint on the product(s) in question. It makes sense therefore to limit attention to those companies that have the ability to provide a *swift* supply response, and to leave the more involved assessment of other entry to the stage of the detailed competition assessment. Proceeding in this way also avoids the practical difficulty of having to assign hypothetical market shares to potential producers, of whom only an undefined proportion may become actual producers.

[99] Example featuring in the Commission Notice on market definition, above n 77, para 22.

1.159 The response formulated to the above-described issue in the Commission's Notice is to note that it is appropriate to group products into one product market on the basis of supply substitutability, provided that *most* of the suppliers are able to offer and sell the various qualities under the conditions of immediacy and absence of significant increase in costs.[100]

1.160 Arguably, the principle that supply-side substitution may be taken into account for market definition in those situations in which its effects are 'equivalent to those of demand substitution in terms of effectiveness and immediacy' mandates that a cautious approach is also applied where margin differences (eg as in the case of branded versus private label products) limit supply substitution. Indeed, a useful line of enquiry for analysing supply substitution is suggested by the examination of the margins or gross returns in the production of supply substitutes as compared to the product in question. These margins should tend to equality if the supply substitutes are correctly identified, either because the prices and costs are the same or because quality-adjusted prices and costs tend to converge. Put differently, in the absence of switching barriers, the gross returns to the producers of supply substitutes cannot get too much out of line with those earned by producers of the product in question.

1.161 It is worth noting that the US approach to supply-side substitution is different from the one applied in the EU. In principle, supply-side factors are not, as such, taken into account in the US in defining the scope of the relevant product market.[101] They are instead considered in identifying firms *participating* in the relevant market (these firms are called 'firms that participate through supply response' or 'uncommitted entrants').[102] Correspondingly, in measuring a firm's market share, the US agencies include its sales or capacity only to the extent that the firm's capacity is not 'committed or so profitably employed outside the relevant market that it would not be available to respond to an increase in price in the market'.[103]

1.162 In the example given above, the relevant market in the US would be the 'market for A'. The multi-purpose B-company would be considered a *player* in this A-market, but only to the extent it would be likely to switch production from B to A in the event of a price increase of A; the single-purpose B-companies would not be viewed as players in the A-market.

1.163 Having established the principle, the US Guidelines indicate however that 'if production substitution among a group of products is nearly universal among firms selling one or more of those products . . . the Agency may use an aggregate description of those markets as a matter of convenience'.[104] This *aggregation* of markets bears resemblance to the approach taken in the Commission Notice to grouping markets on the basis of supply-side substitution when most of the suppliers are able to swiftly offer and sell the various products.[105]

---

[100] Commission Notice on market definition, above n 77, at para 21 (emphasis added).

[101] See also Baker, above n 88.

[102] US Horizontal Merger Guidelines, Section 1.32.

[103] US Horizontal Merger Guidelines, Section 1.41.

[104] US Horizontal Merger Guidelines, Section 1.321, fn 14. See also GJ Werden, *Market Delineation Algorithms Based on the Hypothetical Monopolist Paradigm* (US DOJ Antitrust Division Economic Analysis Group Discussion Paper No 02–8; 27 July 2002), Section 7.

[105] This requirement is also captured by another characterisation of the relevant market sometimes used, and according to which a relevant market is a product space in which the 'conditions of competition are sufficiently homogeneous'.

(2) The Relevant Geographic Market

The relevant geographic market is traditionally defined as comprising 'the area in which the **1.164** undertakings concerned are involved in the supply and demand of products or services, in which the conditions of competition are sufficiently homogeneous and which can be distinguished from neighbouring areas because the conditions of competition are appreciably different in those areas'.[106] Despite this somewhat general wording, the main objective of defining a market, also in its geographic dimension, is to identify those competitors that are capable of constraining the commercial behaviour of the company under consideration, in that they supply products (or are able to do so in a short time frame) that are sufficiently good substitutes for the product in question. Also in the geographic dimension, it is possible to distinguish between demand-side substitution and supply-side substitution (although the latter term is less often used in this context).

(a) Demand-side Substitution

The analysis of demand-side substitution in the context of geographic market definition **1.165** focuses on the extent to which customers in a given geographic area are able and willing to switch to suppliers located in other areas. The conceptual approach to geographic market definition can again be based on the SSNIP test. One has to assess to what extent the customers of a given product or group of products would switch to suppliers located elsewhere in response to a hypothetical small but significant (in the range of 5–10 per cent), non-transitory increase in the price of the products in the area being considered (prices in other areas held constant). If substitution would be enough to make the postulated price increase unprofitable because of the resulting loss of sales, additional geographic areas are included in the relevant market. This would be done until the set of geographic areas is such that the postulated price increase would be profitable[107] (until the area would be 'something worth monopolising').

In order to establish whether companies in different areas constitute an actual alternative **1.166** source of supply for consumers a number of relevant factors can be taken into account, such as transportation costs for the products involved, the need for (locally provided) sales support or maintenance services, the importance of national or local preferences, purchasing habits of customers, and product differentiation. All these factors have an impact on the attractiveness of products offered outside the geographic market under consideration for customers located within the relevant market.

(b) Supply-side Substitution

Supply-side substitution relates to the possibility for customers to turn to products that are **1.167** not yet offered by particular competitors, but that would readily be offered in the event of a higher price of the product in question. In the context of geographic market definition this relates to the possibility of suppliers located outside a certain geographic area to (swiftly) start supplying into that area. Thus, whereas demand-side substitution relates to the prospect

---

[106] Commission Notice on market definition, above n 77, para 8. See also Case 27/76 *United Brands* [1978] ECR 207, para 11.
[107] Commission Notice on market definition, above n 77, para 29.

of customers (or their agents) turning to other areas to obtain the product demanded, supply-side substitution relates to the prospect of outside suppliers turning to the area under consideration to start offering their products.

1.168 In this context, it is important to investigate the various supply factors to see whether those companies located in distinct areas face significant impediments to developing their sales on competitive terms throughout the geographic market. Possible impediments may result from requirements for a local presence in order to sell in that area, the conditions of access to distribution channels, costs associated with setting up a distribution network, and the existence or absence of regulatory barriers such as administrative authorisations and packaging regulations.

1.169 Whereas demand-side substitutability is often seen as being the main form of substitution in the context of product market definition, the relative importance of demand-side and supply-side substitution is probably more in balance in the context of geographic market definition. In the product dimension, supply-side substitution relates to the ability of companies to swiftly change production from one product to another. The product areas which lend themselves to such substitution are probably limited in number, and may well fall short of the number of cases where companies are able to swiftly offer, in a different area, products they already produce.

(3) Specific Issues in the Context of Market Definition

1.170 It is worth addressing three specific situations, where care has to be taken in the context of market definition.

(a) *Chains of Substitution*

1.171 In certain cases, the existence of *chains of substitution* may warrant a definition of a single relevant market, even where products or areas at either end of the market do not directly compete with one another. Consider, for example, a product with significant transport costs such as construction materials. In such a case, deliveries from a given plant are limited to a certain area around the plant because of transport costs. Such an area could, in principle, constitute the relevant geographic market. However, if the distribution of plants is such that there are considerable overlaps between the areas around the different plants, it is possible that the pricing of those products will be constrained by a chain substitution effect: prices in one area constrain prices in an adjacent area, which in turn constrain prices in another area (not adjacent to the first). If the 'chain' that links the three areas is strong enough, it would be proper to define the relevant market as including these three areas. Note that application of the SSNIP methodology would indeed identify the relevant market as such, whereas an overly strong emphasis on factors such as transport costs would not.

1.172 Chains of substitution may also be relevant in the context of product market definition.[108] Suppose that products A and C are single-purpose software programs each suitable for doing a different computing task and that product B is a dual-purpose software product

---

[108] It should be noted that chains of substitution are probably less prevalent in the context of product market definition than in the context of geographic market definition.

that can be used for both tasks. Even if products A and C are not direct demand substitutes, it is proper to view them as belonging to the same relevant product market when their respective pricing is sufficiently constrained by substitution to product B (in the sense of the SSNIP concept) and vice versa. Product B can then be seen as forming the 'link' between products A and C.

(b) Price Discrimination

In certain markets, it is possible for suppliers to engage in price discrimination, ie to charge different prices to different customers depending on their buyer characteristics.[109] Price discrimination is possible when suppliers can identify to which group an individual customer belongs at the moment of selling the relevant product, and trade among customers (or arbitrage by third parties) is not feasible. In such cases, demand substitution (the ability of customers to obtain substitute products, or to obtain them elsewhere at better terms) may be impaired. If also supply substitution is difficult or impossible, it is appropriate to define a market by reference to the group of customers that may be the subject of such price discrimination. In terms of the SSNIP principle: the possibility of targeting a price increase raises the likelihood of such a price increase being profitable. **1.173**

Importantly, the chain of substitution effect described in the previous subsection no longer holds as a factor linking together distinct products or geographic areas when price discrimination is possible. For example, in the context of the software products example described above, if a hypothetical sole supplier of products A and B could identify customers by their specific software needs, it could increase price on the A product and, to those customers that are in need of the software function performed by A, also on the dual-purpose B product. It cannot even be excluded that, for a hypothetical sole supplier of products A and B, raising price on A alone might be profitable (some customers may switch to product B, but, given that B also belongs to the hypothetical monopolist, this need not be problematic). In market definition, the operational response to the possibility of price discrimination is to define markets by reference to the group of customers that may be the subject of such price differentiation (in the example, the customers in need of the software function performed by A). **1.174**

In the context of geographic markets, it is often the case that customers located close to the border are familiar with trading conditions across the border and ready to obtain the products needed there. Similarly, outside suppliers located near the border may be relatively quick at supplying across the border when the opportunity arises. When there is great demand and supply-side substitutability at the borders, this would point towards a geographic market that is wider than the area delineated by the border if the SSNIP test is applied with a uniform price increase of 5 per cent in mind. An issue to be checked in such cases is whether a sole owner of the production or supply locations in the area could practice geographic price discrimination (in other words, whether a uniform price increase over the area is the appropriate benchmark). If the location of the production or supply locations **1.175**

---

[109] Bidding markets may be examples of markets where price discrimination is possible. In essence, these are markets where companies compete for specific contracts and where each customer gets, or may get, a personalised offer.

is such that prices further inland could be different from (ie higher than) those near the border, then the area under consideration might be 'worth monopolising' after all.[110] In such a case, it might be appropriate to define the relevant geographic market as the original area under consideration, not wider.

(c) Captive Production

1.176 The definition of the relevant market involving intermediate products is often fairly complex. Intermediate product markets may feature both specialised producers and integrated producers captively producing all or a sizeable proportion of their output for internal use. The competitive constraints on a non-integrated supplier in such a market situation are not just the demand substitution possibilities of its customers (whether integrated or non-integrated), but also the supply possibilities of integrated producers who are currently only participating in the merchant supply a little, if at all.

1.177 In defining product markets for intermediate goods it is customary to first focus on what is called the 'merchant market', ie that part of the product market for which transactions take place between entities not belonging to one and the same group. This is because of the idea that, in response to a reduction in supply by any given company active on the merchant market, other non-integrated suppliers can normally be assumed to exert a competitive constraint by increasing their supply, whereas an integrated company may be more reluctant to increase supplies on the merchant market (if it is already active on it) or to become active on it (if it is not yet active).[111] Even when one decides that the integrated firm is likely to increase supplies or to become active, the question remains how much of its sales or capacity to take into account.[112] These factors make it appropriate to pay attention to the merchant market as such, especially at the early stages of the investigation.

1.178 At the same time, it is important not to lose sight of the relationship between captive sales and merchant sales in the overall market. It has to be realised (in application of the SSNIP test) that the incentive to raise the price on the merchant market becomes less, the more the customers of such suppliers (the non-integrated downstream companies) would lose sales and market share to the integrated companies who would not be confronted with an increase in the price at which they can obtain input supplies. If it is the case that raising the price for merchant supplies would be unprofitable in view of the strong presence of integrated suppliers,

---

[110] While it is true that customers located further inland could turn to the (lower priced) areas near the border, when these border areas are also under the control of the hypothetical monopolist, the incentive on the part of the hypothetical monopolist to raise prices inland is higher than when the border areas are not under his control.

[111] The integrated firm's decision whether to (increase) supply on the merchant market is a function of the impact this has on the profitability of its business activities further downstream (the stage that uses the intermediate product as an input). Such an impact may exist not only where increasing supplies into the merchant market implies cutting back on the internal use of the intermediate product (and, hence, reducing output of the downstream subsidiary), but also where supplying more of the intermediate product means more competition for the downstream subsidiary from non-integrated downstream rivals using the intermediate product.

[112] As with supply substitution in general, it would make sense to take the integrated firm's sales or capacity into account in measuring market shares only to the extent that the firm would be available to respond to an increase in price in the merchant market (part of the firm's capacity may be committed or more profitably employed internally).

this would plead in favour of looking at the captive sales and merchant sales as a whole. All in all, the best response to the complexity of market definition in the context of intermediate goods would seem to be to consider both possible market definitions (merchant market and combined market) and, when the companies involved have important market positions on either market, to proceed to a full analysis of competition.

(4) Further Considerations

(a) *Market Definition in Practice*

At the start of this section, it was mentioned that market definition serves the purpose of **1.179** putting the assessment of market power in a proper context. The more alternatives are available to customers, the less market power the companies supplying a given product are likely to have. Even when companies have a 'monopoly' on a given product, they may not have market power over that product when sufficient alternatives are present. By contrast, when there are few alternatives, it is opportune to see whether any particular company, or group of companies, has market power.

In many cases, the starting point of market definition is to describe clearly the product or **1.180** service in question and to think of various conceivable markets. This then permits one to decide, from a summary examination of market shares on the various conceivable markets, whether in relation to the operation under analysis there are any competition issues, even on the narrowest conceivable market.[113] This allows for a first screening of cases, to see whether there may be competitive issues or not.

Having determined that an accurate market definition is needed, the SSNIP methodology **1.181** suggests the following line of enquiry: start with the product under consideration and assess what proportion of the customers would switch away, in whole or in part, from the product if its price were to be raised by a small but significant proportion, and to which substitutes would they switch. To obtain a first indication, an enquiry into the opinions, primarily of customers but also of competitors, can be undertaken concerning the extent to which the products under consideration are adequate substitutes. The accuracy of the enquiry can, in subsequent stages, be improved by addressing more customers and competitors (a wider base of respondents) and asking for more specific information. In this context, evidence of customer switching in the past would be particularly informative. Data on price-cost margins can shed further light on the question whether a 'hypothetical monopolist' would find it profitable to raise the price or not.

Various additional quantitative and empirical methods are available that can provide infor- **1.182** mation on the degree to which products face demand-side constraints. These methods include the analysis of prices and price movements of the products under consideration to see to what extent they move together over time, the estimation of price elasticities, critical loss analysis, event analysis (to see whether particular events in the past shed light on the

---

[113] This is not to say that the narrowest market necessarily is the one where the parties' market shares are the highest. After all, when product markets are defined very narrowly, there may be no competitive overlap in the first place. It remains important also to look at wider possible market definitions.

question of which products compete with one another), and the analysis of bidding data. These methods are presented in further detail in Section G.

(b) Defining the Market: Not an End in Itself

1.183 While one may debate the various alternative approaches to market definition, the essential point is that the market defined must seek to include the products (and the firms producing them) that represent a competitive constraint on the product(s) in question. Often the difficult issue in market definition is that, whatever the operational formulation or the test employed, the appropriate boundaries of the market cannot be decided precisely. Market definition will indicate which products provide an immediate constraint on the product under investigation, but not that all these products are of equal constraining influence. In the context of differentiated product markets in particular, the issue of differing degrees of competitive pressure between products, even within one and the same relevant market, may be of great importance.[114]

1.184 The boundaries within which competition is at work cannot be fully captured by the classification of products into different 'markets'. This merely recalls the fact that market definition is not a goal in itself but an intermediate step for structuring the analysis. The aim of market definition is to analyse the economic substitutability of products in a structured way, not to represent a full analysis of competition among the companies supplying the products.[115]

F. Market Power and Dominance[116]

1.185 Market power is often broadly referred to as the power to raise price above the competitive level. While the general idea behind this characterisation of market power is fairly clear, a number of comments can be made. This section starts by addressing some of the questions the concept raises. It focuses in particular on the question of how to identify market power in a given market context. The next part then addresses the relationship between market power and the concept of 'dominance', as it is known in Article 82 EC and the EC Merger Regulation. The section ends with a discussion of ways in which market power may be maintained or enhanced through anti-competitive means, which is the main focus of competition policy.[117]

(1) Market Power

(a) Concept

1.186 Market power can manifest itself in a number of dimensions, such as high prices, reduced output, reduced choice and quality, or diminished technological innovation. The former

---

[114] See also Section F(1).

[115] See also n 85 on the difference between iteratively assessing the SSNIP question (involving a 'hypothetical monopolist') and assessing competition in actual markets.

[116] This section builds on a text written by Kirti Mehta for the previous edition of this book and, for the discussion of unilateral effects and tacit coordination, on V Verouden, C Bengtsson and S Albæk, 'The EU Notice on Horizontal Mergers: A Further Step Towards Convergence' [2004] The Antitrust Bulletin 243–285. All errors, if any, are the responsibility of the current authors.

[117] Market power is not a negative thing *per se*. Often companies obtain market power in entirely legitimate ways, eg by producing more efficiently than other players, by making better quality products, or by being more innovative. Consequently, competition policy is not concerned with market power as such. Rather, it is concerned with the ways in which market power may be maintained or enhanced through anti-competitive means. See Section F(3).

dimensions—price and output—are normally the focus for analysis of the static welfare impact of a given merger, agreement, or conduct. The latter dimensions—choice, quality, and innovation—are of particular importance when it comes to assessing the dynamic welfare impact.

While the dynamic perspective of market power is arguably of great importance, antitrust **1.187** analyses typically start by considering whether a company has (or will obtain) static market power. After all, without market power in a static sense, it is unlikely that a company has market power in the dynamic sense.

The static notion of market power concentrates on the power to raise price above the com- **1.188** petitive level. From a short-term perspective, the competitive price level is often taken to mean the marginal cost level. Market power then refers to the ability to sell a product at a higher price than it actually costs to produce at the margin. If a company has static market power, this implies that there is a certain welfare loss (also called *inefficiency*) stemming from the fact that some customers do not obtain the product although they have a willingness to pay for the product that is higher than it actually costs the company to make the product. From a longer-term perspective, the competitive price level is often taken to mean the average cost level, where the cost benchmark includes a reasonable rate of return on investment.[118] Market power then refers to the ability to make supra-normal profits, ie profits that are higher than customary in similar market settings, over a sustained period.

Obviously, any company can raise the price at which it sells. What is meant by the ability **1.189** to raise price above the competitive level is the ability to do so *profitably*. This is only possible for a firm that does not face such pressure from its competitors that any reduction in its own output is easily made up for by the competitors. In such a case, the sales loss facing the company when it raises price above the competitive level is limited,[119] and increasing price above the competitive level may be profitable. The less competitors pose a competitive constraint on the firm in question, the more that firm is said to have market power. It follows that a situation of market power cannot arise in a market where expanding output (or indeed entry) is easy, since in such conditions the pressure on prices charged by the incumbent firm(s) is rather persistent.

There are, in essence, three principal reasons why competitors may not easily make up for **1.190** a reduction in output of the firm with market power. The first is product differentiation. Product differentiation means that the products that are being offered are imperfect substitutes for each other.[120] When rival producers offer alternative products, but these products

---

[118] The cost benchmark is sometimes taken to be forward-looking (ie what would it cost to start production with current technology).

[119] Technically speaking, the firm-specific demand curve is downward sloping and not flat, as would be the case with perfect competition.

[120] Products may be differentiated in various ways. Differentiation may be based on brand image, technical specifications, product quality, or level of service. It may also find its origin in buyers having to incur switching costs to use a competitor's product. There may also be differentiation in terms of geographic location, based on branch or stores location. For example, location matters for retail distribution, banks, travel agencies, or petrol stations. Note that products can be imperfect substitutes even where they are part of the same relevant market. Substitutability is a matter of degree.

are not as attractive as the ones offered by the firm raising the price (at least from the viewpoint of the customers of the firm raising the price), customers may prefer to stay with that company even when it raises the price. As a result, the firm in question has a certain leeway, or margin of manoeuvre, in its pricing behaviour. The more the products offered by competitors are close substitutes (or the more easily competitors can reposition their products), the less market power a company is likely to have.

1.191 The second reason why a company may have market power is that rival suppliers, though offering equivalent or similar products to those of the company with market power, are not capable of supplying more in response to a price increase of the firm in question.[121] A prime example is the situation where rivals have capacity constraints or face other barriers to expansion. Rivals may, for example, have insufficient access to input supplies, relevant infrastructure, or distribution networks to provide a supply response. Also in these situations, the firm in question has a certain leeway to set prices.

1.192 A third important source of market power is differences in productive efficiency. Where economies of scale or scope are important, a company with high production levels is able to produce more cheaply at the margin than companies operating at sub-optimal levels.[122] This source of market power translates into the inability of rivals to compete at low prices and allows the company with the cost advantage a possibly considerable margin to set prices.

1.193 An extreme case of market power is the situation where a firm has a monopoly on the relevant market, so that there are no rival companies to constrain the firm. A monopoly may be seen as entailing all or some of the sources of market power mentioned above: strong product differentiation (the product in question basically forms a relevant product market by itself), inability of rivals to provide a supply response (entry barriers[123]), or substantial efficiency differences (no rival is able to supply at competitive prices).

1.194 The fact that setting price above competitive levels is only possible for a firm that does not face such pressure from its competitors so that any reduction in its own output is easily made up for by the competitors suggests an alternative (but equivalent) way of thinking of market power. In this perspective, market power relates to the ability of a firm to significantly influence, through its own output level, the aggregate output of the market.[124] The characterisation captures quite well the three sources of market power identified above. Where products are differentiated, the reduction of output by one firm is likely to lead to a reduction of aggregate output, since other rivals' products are not able to make up for the difference. Similarly, where competitors have capacity constraints or face other barriers to expand output,

---

121 More generally, rivals face increasing marginal cost levels when production levels go up.

122 See Section C(2). As already indicated, market power is not in itself a bad thing. This holds in particular where the market power stems from superior efficiency.

123 Monopoly positions are normally linked to barriers to entry, such as legal barriers to entry (patents on technology, brand names, statutory monopolies), technological barriers (extreme economies of scale or scope), or strategic entry barriers (related to the incumbent firm's behaviour or reputation). See Section C(2).

124 cf B Klein, 'Market Power in Antitrust: Economic Analysis after Kodak' (1993) 3 *Supreme Court Economic Review* 43–92 at 76. See also J Azevedo and M Walker, 'Dominance: Meaning and Measurement' (2002) 23 *European Competition Law Review* 363–367.

the reduction of output by one firm is likely to have an impact on total output. Finally, where a company has a significant cost advantage it can, at least within certain boundaries, determine the output level in the market.[125]

(b) Identification of (Static) Market Power

The usual starting point for determining whether a company has market power is to con- **1.195** sider the relative position of the company vis-à-vis its competitors on the market. Market shares, the main indicators used in this respect, often give at least some indication of the degree to which companies have, or do not have, market power.

Market shares are used extensively for the purpose of identifying market power, not only **1.196** because they are relatively simple measures, but also because the more direct methods to measure market power are difficult to use. The definition of static market power—the ability to raise price over cost—suggests that one looks at the profit margin of a firm to find out whether this firm has market power. For example, the gross margin is a measure of the degree by which a firm's price exceeds marginal cost. This margin, while in principle ascertainable, is often difficult to assess in practice. Accounting costs, ie the costs as they appear in the company's accounts, need not be accurate measures of the costs involved in producing additional units of output, which is the relevant economic benchmark.[126] Accounting costs are often based on aggregate costs calculated over the entire production, rather than cost levels at the margin. In addition, those costs that cannot be directly attributed to the production of a specific product or service (where common production factors are involved) are normally attributed according to standard accounting rules that have little connection with what it costs to increase production.

If instead the elasticity of demand facing the firm is known with some precision, then that **1.197** information could give some indication about the firm's margin. This idea underlies the so-called Lerner index, which is defined as the firm's gross margin in relation to the current price set by the firm. Economic theory predicts that, at its profit-maximising point, a firm's margin will be the reciprocal of the elasticity of demand facing it: where the demand elasticity is low, the firm's margin is high, and vice versa. However, the elasticity of demand facing a firm is also usually not known, at least not with sufficient precision.

Even when one has (directly or indirectly) established the relevant margin, the question **1.198** remains as to what is a high margin. Industries may feature different gross and net margins depending on the level of fixed investment, the stage of the industry (growing or stagnant), or the degree of risk involved (the fact that margins turn out to be high *ex post* may be a proper compensation for the risk incurred *ex ante*). Pharmaceutical companies, for example, often feature high gross and net margins on a limited number of products because R&D expenditure is both significant and risky, and marginal costs of production are low or negligible.

---

[125] It is only after the price has risen above a certain level that the other companies become competitive and may start to produce or increase output.

[126] From an economic perspective, the marginal cost of production and, on a longer perspective, the incremental cost of production are the relevant benchmarks when assessing how much it actually costs to produce more at the margin. They identify whether customers are left unserved, whose willingness to pay for the product exceeds the cost of production but is below the price charged.

One would need therefore to make comparisons with appropriate benchmarks, preferably from the same sector but in a different geographic area. It is clear, however, that finding appropriate benchmarks is one of the more difficult issues in the identification of market power through margin analysis.

1.199 Market shares are, by contrast, comparatively simple indicators of market power. The main question is, of course, how good market shares are as an indicator for market power. On the one hand, they are likely to contain some information on the competitive strength of each of the market players. In a competitive market with many players each firm tends to be a price taker, ie acts as if facing an infinitely elastic demand curve, irrespective of whether the total market demand is price elastic or inelastic. Similar technology, absence of scale or scope economies, and the commodity nature of products all tend to ensure that many companies are active in the market and that there is no great variation of market shares. Where, however, certain firms have relatively high market shares this may be an indication that such firms are either cost leaders or have product advantages in a differentiated product market. Alternatively, it may reflect a difference in production capacities. In such cases, the practical approach based on market shares can be considered a useful, if approximate, way of identifying firms with market power.

1.200 On the other hand, the observation that one or more companies in a market have significant market shares is compatible with a whole range of market settings, both competitive and less competitive ones. To take one example: a company may have a high market share for merely historical reasons and lack the ability to raise prices above any competitive level because other market participants face no problems in expanding output in response to a price increase by the former company.

1.201 Whether it is appropriate to use market shares as a proxy for market power also strongly depends on the quality of the definition of the 'relevant market'. In differentiated product markets, in particular, the degree of competition between the respective products may vary in ways not represented by market shares. It may well be that the company with the highest market share faces more competition than niche players with lower market shares. Market shares do not tell how close a substitute one product is vis-à-vis another product.

1.202 Another example of a market where market shares may be less informative is bidding markets. The fact that other firms did not make a sale in a particular bidding contest does not mean that these firms did not pose a significant competitive constraint on the winning firm.[127] In addition, the link between market share and market power is probably less direct in bidding markets than in most other markets.[128] In bidding markets each customer gets, or may get, a personalised offer. Where this is the case, companies can decide to compete more aggressively on the margin, without this necessarily having a direct impact on the margins obtained on their existing customer base. When individual contracts are large and

---

[127] This may be the case in particular where the number of bids in a given year is small. When the number of bids gets larger, one can expect market shares to better reflect competitive strength.

[128] For a critical analysis of this argument, see P Klemperer, *Bidding Markets*, forthcoming in Buccirossi P (ed) *Advances in the Economics of Competition Law* (MIT Press).

infrequent, the incentive to compete for each of them may be especially strong. Similar arguments can be raised in contexts where competition is 'for the market' instead of in the market.

It is clear that both the approach based on relative market positions and the more direct **1.203** measurements of market power have certain drawbacks. In identifying whether a company has market power, it remains therefore indispensable to focus on the causes of market power, to focus on those factors that enable the company to raise price: the degree of product differentiation in the market, the presence of barriers to entry and expansion on the part of rivals, and differences in productive efficiency. It is only when such factors are present that one can persuasively say that a company has market power.

(2) Dominance

As the name suggests, the term 'dominance' refers to a strong form of market power. A distinc- **1.204** tion is commonly made between two forms of dominance, single dominance and collective dominance. The first refers to a situation where a single company has substantial market power, the second to a situation where a group of companies jointly hold such market power giving rise to collusion.

(a) Single Dominance

The traditional characterisation of the term 'dominant position' in EC competition law is **1.205** that it relates to a 'position of economic strength enjoyed by an undertaking which enables it to prevent effective competition being maintained on the relevant market by giving it the power to behave to an appreciable extent independently of its competitors, customers and ultimately of its consumers'.[129]

The latter part of the above definition, relating to 'the power to behave to an appreciable **1.206** extent independently of its competitors, customers and ultimately of its consumers' is closely related to the three factors giving rise to market power discussed in the previous subsection. Product differentiation in the market, the presence of barriers to entry and expansion on the part of rivals, and differences in productive efficiency all may provide a given company with substantial leeway in determining prices. It is of course true that no company can act entirely independently of competitors, customers, and consumers. It is only natural that a company, even when it is dominant, takes account of the fact that competitors may produce a bit more if it raises its price. Similarly, it will realise that customers are likely to consume less when the price goes up (the 'discipline of the demand curve'). Whether or not a company has market power and has the ability to set the price above the competitive level is a matter of degree. Whereas, legally speaking, a company either is or is not dominant, it is important to realise that, from an economic standpoint, the underlying variables determining the degree of market power rather form a continuum.

For a firm to be considered dominant in practice, it must normally have a large market **1.207** share, in the range of 40 per cent of recent sales or more, with the other market participants

---

[129] Case 27/76 *United Brands v Commission* [1978] ECR 207.

holding (substantially) lower market shares. The importance of market shares is qualified by the extent to which they convey information on the ability of rivals to provide a competitive constraint on the dominant firm. The Court has held in this respect that, although the importance of market shares may vary from one market to another:

> the view may legitimately be taken that very large shares are in themselves, and save in exceptional circumstances, evidence of the existence of a dominant position. An undertaking which has a very large market share and holds it for some time, by means of the volume of production and the scale of the supply which it stands for - *without those having much smaller market shares being able to meet rapidly the demand from those who would like to break away from the undertaking which has the largest market share* - is by virtue of that share in a position of strength which makes it an unavoidable trading partner and which, already because of this secures for it, at the very least during relatively long periods, that freedom of action which is the special feature of a dominant position.[130]

1.208   Thus, dominance is said to exist only when the situation of substantial market share is expected to be sustained over a period of time during which incumbents and entrants cannot be expected to bid away the dominant firm's market share through lower pricing and superior quality products.

1.209   In general terms, the factors that are taken into account in determining dominance all relate to the ability and incentive of the smaller competitors to increase their production or otherwise provide a constraining force. Economies of scale and scope, control over input supplies, patents, or distribution networks, and other strategic advantages for the dominant firm (eg branding and reputation) are the more important ones in this respect. Such factors may make expansion of smaller firms or entry of new competitors difficult, either in the short term (eg when the new entity controls input supplies) or in the long run (eg when the possession of patent portfolios reduces the ability of competitors to innovate). Similarly, the above factors may dissuade smaller rivals from expanding and thereby affect their incentive to provide a competitive constraint. Here one can think, for instance, of cases where the company in question has control over the main distribution networks in an industry, leading to a significant reduction in competing rivals' incentive to invest in marketing effort or R&D. In such circumstances, an asymmetric market structure may prevail in which one firm dominates production and is the principal decision maker with market power.

1.210   It is worth noting that in economics there also exists a concept called the 'dominant firm', but that it has a meaning that is often more specific than the one commonly used in the EC competition context. It refers to a market situation where a single large actor faces a number of fringe competitors (often called the model of the 'dominant firm and the fringe').[131] In this model, the fringe competitors are price takers, so that they supply up to the point where their marginal costs equal the market price.[132] By contrast, the single large firm dominates production of the final good because of a cost advantage and acts strategically with

---

130   Case 85/76 *Hoffmann-La Roche & Co AG v Commission* [1979] ECR 461, para 41. Emphasis added.
131   The model is due to K Forchheimer, 'Theoretisches zum unvollständigen Monopole' (1908) 32 Schmollers Jahrbuch für Gesetzgebung, Verwaltung und Volkswirtschaft 1-12. See also M Riordan, 'Anticompetitive Vertical Integration by a Dominant Firm' (1988) 88 American Economic Review 1232–1248.
132   The fringe players do not assume that their individual actions have an influence on the price level in the market, so that the marginal revenue of supplying more equals the price level.

respect to the fringe. The situation of a dominant firm in the total market can be depicted as in Figure13.[133] The dominant firm faces a firm-specific demand curve (ED, in the right hand picture) which is obtained by deducting from market demand (DD, in the left hand picture), at each price, the supply responses of all the other firms (SS) in the market. The dominant firm would maximise profits by producing where its marginal costs equal its marginal revenue; this is at the output Q_1, which implies the price P_1, leaving the balance of the output being produced by smaller firms. The small firms accept the price set since their supply response is limited (their marginal costs are increasing and exceed, at some point, the price charged by the dominant firm).

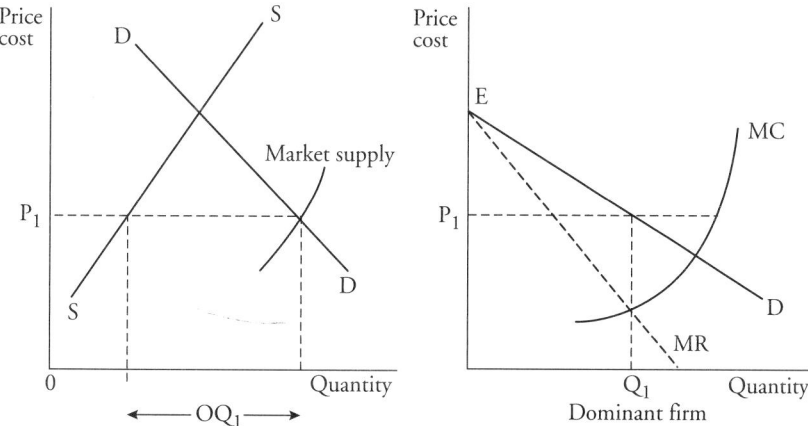

Figure 13 A dominant firm

(b) Collective Dominance

Collective dominance refers to a situation where a group of companies jointly hold market power giving rise to explicit coordination (eg by way of a collusive agreement) or tacit coordination. As explained in Section C(5), the theory of coordination[134] is anchored in economic models that explain how competitors can cancel the mutual competitive pressure by a coherent system of implicit threats. In a non-collusive setting, each competitor constantly has an incentive to compete. This incentive is ultimately what keeps prices low, and what prevents firms from *jointly* maximising their profits. Coordination emerges when this short-run incentive is overruled by a stronger long-term incentive: each firm in the market exercises a self-imposed competitive restraint in the short run only because it knows that this restraint will be 'rewarded' in the long run by the other firms exhibiting similar restraint.   **1.211**

Coordination is more likely to emerge in markets where it is fairly easy to establish the terms of coordination and where such coordination is sustainable.[135] Sustainability requires that   **1.212**

---

[133] P Hardwick, B Khan and J Langmead, *An Introduction to Modern Economics* (Longman, 1992).
[134] The economic literature on tacit coordination is relevant to all forms of coordination not based on legally enforceable contracts.
[135] EU Horizontal Merger Guidelines, para 41.

there is: (i) sufficient market transparency, so that the coordinating firms are able to monitor to a sufficient degree whether the terms of coordination are being adhered to; (ii) the existence of a disciplining mechanism to ensure adherence to the coordination; and (iii) the absence of possible actions of outsiders, such as current and future competitors, as well as customers, that can jeopardize the results expected from the coordination.

1.213   The degree to which the above conditions are fulfilled all vary with the characteristics of the firms, markets, and products concerned. The reader is referred to Section C(5) for an overview of the most relevant factors.

(3) Enhancing Market Power

1.214   The existence of market power, in particular static market power, on the part of a single firm is not a negative thing *per se*. Often companies obtain market power in entirely legitimate ways, eg by producing more efficiently than other players, by making better quality products, or by being more innovative. Indeed, the prospect of obtaining (some) market power is a major determinant for companies to invest in product and process innovation. Consequently, competition policy is normally not concerned with market power as such. Rather, it is concerned with the ways in which market power may be maintained or enhanced through anti-competitive means.

1.215   Apart from collusion with other market players,[136] one commonly distinguishes between two main ways in which companies may enhance their market power: (i) through merger with a competitor; and (ii) through exclusion.

(a) Merger with a Competitor: Unilateral versus Coordinated Effects

1.216   While the existence and extent of any negative impact of a merger on competition will depend on many factors (such as the market position of the companies concerned, the strength of the competitors, the nature of the products, efficiencies, etc), the immediate reason why a merger can have a negative impact is often the same: a merger may diminish the degree of competition in a market by removing important competitive constraints on one or more sellers, who consequently find it profitable to increase prices (or to reduce output, or to take other action to the detriment of consumers).

1.217   The first competitive constraint being removed is that which previously existed between the merging firms. Whereas, before the merger, the merging parties exercised a competitive constraint on each other, in the sense that, if one party were to raise price, it would lose customers to the other party and vice versa, the merger lifts this particular constraint: part of the sales lost due to a price rise on one product will now flow to the product of the merger partner and, as a result, such a price increase may be profitable, while it would not have been profitable before the merger.

---

136 See Section C(5). One could debate whether (tacit and explicit) coordination can itself be viewed as a way to achieve market power (as is argued by P Hofer, M Williams and L Wu, 'Principles of Competition Policy Economics' [2004] The Asia-Pacific Antitrust Review 4) or that it rather should be viewed as the expression of the *exercise* of market power. Although ability and effect are difficult to disentangle in the context of collusion, it is true that, in principle, the ability to overcome the prisoner's dilemma, and thereby being able to collude, is not the same as actually colluding.

To illustrate, let us consider the example of high-quality cars and let us imagine that German **1.218**
purchasers of cars essentially make a choice between brands A (say, an Audi), B (a BMW),
M (a Mercedes), and S (a Saab).[137] A reasonable starting point for any market analysis is to
assume that pre-merger all producers are marketing their cars in an optimal way. Car manufacturers may pursue varying strategic objectives,[138] but let us assume that each producer
tends to choose a selling price that is optimal in view of what the other producers are charging
for their product. Accordingly, a reason why, for example, Audi is not charging more for its
cars is that it realises that it would probably lose too many sales to the other three producers.
The reason that it does not decrease its price is that it would lose margin and not sufficiently
increase volumes. Each producer makes a trade-off between volume and margin.

How would a merger between, for instance, Audi and BMW change the picture? Suppose **1.219**
that Audi and BMW were competitively interdependent in the following way: if Audi were
to increase prices by 10 per cent, half of the customers who would stop purchasing Audi
would instead purchase a BMW.[139] Similarly, if BMW were to increase prices by 10 per cent,
one-third of the customers who would stop purchasing BMW would instead purchase an
Audi. The merger would change the marketing strategy of the new company fundamentally. After all, in deciding on the price of the Audi model, the fact that half of the Audi customers that would be lost following a price increase on Audi would turn up to buy a BMW
would be a rather comforting thought for the new company's management. In the absence
of other factors (such as new entry or the realisation of efficiencies through the merger), the
likely result of the merger would be an increase in the price of Audi and, by analogy, also of
BMW.[140]

Such effects are not conditional on competitors changing their way of interacting in a given **1.220**
market (for instance, by starting to coordinate) but are instead the consequence of the
merged firm's optimal response to the new market configuration where the merging firms
no longer compete. The merged firm's behaviour is profitable *even if* rivals continue to compete in the same way as they would have done in the absence of the merger. Accordingly,
such merger effects are often called 'unilateral' or 'non-coordinated'.[141]

---

[137] This is a highly stylised example, which ignores, for instance, the presence of other car manufacturers in the
high-quality segment and the fact that each car manufacturer typically has several models within this segment.

[138] Such as a market penetration or a product positioning objective.

[139] In other words, suppose that the *diversion ratio* from Audi to BMW (following a price increase of the
Audi model of 10%) equals 50%.

[140] Strictly speaking, one must also take into account the loss of sales on the Audi model following the 10%
price increase. If this loss were very large, the capturing of half of the sales by the BMW model might not be
enough to make a 10% price increase profitable for the new entity. At the margin, however (ie at lower levels of
price increase), price rises would be likely to be profitable. The point to remember is that an extra factor—the
sales captured by the other model—enters into the pricing equation of the new entity, changing its pricing
incentives for each model.

[141] The term 'unilateral' might leave the impression that the effects only relate to actions of a single firm, ie
the merged entity. As will be developed further in the paragraphs below, competitors may also change their price
or output levels in response to a merger. For this reason, some have suggested that 'unilateral effects' are better
referred to as 'multilateral effects'. See, eg J Vickers, Competition Economics and Policy, speech delivered at
Oxford University, 3 October 2002 (*available at* <http://www.oft.gov.uk/news/speeches/2002/index.htm>).
A decisive factor for effects to be 'unilateral' (or 'multilateral') is that they do not depend on companies in the
market starting to coordinate. For this reason, the EU Horizontal Merger Guidelines and the Merger Guidelines
of the UK Office of Fair Trading use the term 'non-coordinated effects'.

1.221 This is not to say that competitors cannot also benefit from reductions in competitive pressure as a result of a unilateral price increase by the merging companies. In a way, a merger takes out a source of competition in a market. Other firms' likely responses to this may be to also increase prices, albeit perhaps to a lesser extent. Therefore, the incentive to raise prices on the side of the merging firms may lead to price increases for all firms that are present in the same market.

1.222 To come back to our car example: the moment that, as a result of the merger, both Audi and BMW have become more expensive, more customers will show up at the doorsteps of the Mercedes and Saab dealers. The management of those two companies, confronted with more demand for their products, would make the usual trade-off between volumes and margins. They would be likely to increase their prices and margins a little, so as to benefit optimally from the increase in demand they face.

1.223 While competitors may react by raising their prices, it is important to note that it is not these reactions that make the unilateral price rise profitable in the first instance. In the case of unilateral effects, the incentive of the new entity to raise its price stems entirely from the elimination of the competitive constraints that the two merger companies exercised on each other pre-merger, not from the new firm anticipating that its competitors will raise prices. While the magnitude of the price increase may depend on how the other remaining companies respond and vice versa, this is not the underlying reason for the price increase. This is different from the so-called 'coordinated effects' which may result from a merger. These refer to price effects (or other effects) which are profitable to the merging firms *only because* other companies in the market choose to refrain from competing in a strong manner, eg choose to coordinate.[142]

1.224 The precise nature of the competitive constraints between the parties that a merger eliminates can vary from merger to merger. In some mergers, it may be the fact that the merging entities produce relatively close substitutes that is the important aspect of the merger (our car example). In other mergers, the focus may be on the elimination of direct competition by the combination of important production capacities of the two firms.[143] In yet other mergers it may be the combination of two market participants that previously provided important innovations and thereby influenced the nature of competition significantly. Unilateral effects analysis is therefore not confined to the context of differentiated products.

1.225 It is also worth noting that the above-described effects have by themselves little to do with the question of whether or not the merging firms will become the largest player in a market. What matters is that the merger involves companies that, pre-merger, formed a significant

---

[142] See the previous section for more details on the scope for tacit coordination in a given market.

[143] In markets where output or capacity decisions are the most important strategic decisions of the firms, the important concern for firms is how their output decision influences market prices. In such circumstances, the merged firm may have an incentive to reduce output relative to the pre-merger levels, thereby raising the market price. This incentive is likely to be larger, the larger the sales volume of the merged firm, since the corresponding price increase will benefit a larger base of sales. The combination of market shares from two previously independent firms will in some cases thus produce an incentive to reduce output or capacity. For more details, see Ivaldi et al, above n 49.

competitive constraint on each other and that the market context is one where the remaining competitors do not form a fully effective competitive constraint.

In the car example, what drove the result was the fact that a merger between Audi and BMW **1.226** would eliminate competition between the two and that the two remaining companies would exert only a partial constraint on Audi and BMW. For example, in case of a price increase of 10 per cent on Audi, half of the former Audi customers would go to BMW and not to Mercedes or Saab. In this sense, Mercedes or Saab exert only a partial constraint on Audi; the remaining part comes from BMW.[144]

Consequently, a fundamental aspect in determining whether a merger should be consid- **1.227** ered anti-competitive is the degree to which the remaining companies exert a competitive constraint on the merging parties.

In practice, therefore, there is a high degree of overlap between those cases where the merg- **1.228** ing parties end up being the dominant player in the market and the cases in which *significant* unilateral effects are likely to arise. This does not mean to say that market dominance (in the usual sense of the word of being the largest company in the market) is either a necessary or a sufficient condition for negative consequences to occur, but there is a strong correlation.[145]

(b) Exclusionary Strategies

A firm with market power may raise prices by reducing its own output or by making competi- **1.229** tors reduce theirs. Strategies that seek to achieve the latter are commonly referred to as 'exclusionary'.[146] A company with market power may seek to exclude rivals in a variety of ways.

In the context of agreements between companies at different levels in the production or dis- **1.230** tribution chain (vertical agreements), antitrust concerns may arise when an agreement results in market foreclosure.[147] For example, it may be possible for a company to conclude exclusive agreements with the most important suppliers of raw materials or relevant infrastructure in the industry and thereby prevent competitors' access to these inputs or make such access more expensive for them (input foreclosure). When such foreclosure has the effect of significantly increasing the cost levels at which rivals can operate, it may increase the

---

[144] This example can also serve to illustrate that it is not strictly necessary that the merging parties' products are 'closest' for the merger to produce a (noticeable) price effect. What matters is the degree to which the remaining products exert a competitive constraint on those of the merging parties. However, it is true that the more the merging products are considered to be 'closest' by customers, the more likely it is that a noticeable effect will result (all else being equal).

[145] See also the EU Merger Guidelines, para 25, where it is stated that 'Generally, a merger giving rise to such non-coordinated effects would significantly impede effective competition by creating or strengthening the dominant position of a single firm, one which, typically, would have an appreciably larger market share than the next competitor post-merger'.

[146] The term 'exclusion' is broadly used for any (anti-competitive) practice which leads competitors to produce less; it is not limited to situations where competitors are forced to exit the market altogether. The same holds for the term 'foreclosure'.

[147] cf S Salop and D Scheffman, 'Raising Rivals' Costs' (1983) 73 American Economic Review 267; Krattenmaker and Salop, above n 50. For an elaborate analysis of foreclosure, see P Rey and J Tirole, 'A Primer on Foreclosure' in Armstrong M and Porter R (eds), *Handbook of Industrial Organization*; M Riordan and S Salop, 'Evaluating Vertical Mergers: a Post-Chicago Approach' (1995) 63 Antitrust Law Journal 513–568; and J Church, *The Impact of Vertical and Conglomerate Mergers on Competition*, Report for DG Competition, September 2004.

market power of the company having concluded the agreement and lead to higher prices downstream. This scenario is known as enhancing market power through *raising rivals' costs*.

1.231 Rivals' costs may also be increased through agreements that lead to the foreclosure of access to important sales channels (customer foreclosure). Such concerns typically arise in the context of exclusive dealing arrangements in the retailing or distribution sector. Indirectly, and to the extent that foreclosure impacts upon the revenue streams of rivals and their ability to invest in R&D and cost reduction, it may also affect their ability to compete in the longer run.

1.232 Although vertical mergers differ from exclusive vertical agreements in that the divisions of the integrated firm can remain active as players in the intermediate goods markets, a vertical merger can modify the incentives of the integrated firm in its dealings with competitors upstream or downstream. For instance, a vertically integrated firm, when deciding to supply its competitors downstream with inputs, will take into account how these supplies affect the profits of its own downstream division. If the merged entity has substantial market power in the upstream market, it may have an incentive to raise the price level in that market as that will raise the costs of all non-integrated downstream firms, whereas the integrated firm has access to the input at the true production cost. The change in prices in one market may thus reduce competitive pressure on the integrated firm in the downstream market, leading to overall increases in prices for downstream customers.

1.233 Assessing whether or not vertical integration or a vertical agreement has the effect of raising rivals' costs is in practice a fairly difficult matter. For input foreclosure to be a concern, it must generally be the case that the merging or contracting party involved in the input market has substantial market power: without such market power, it is difficult to see how price can be raised in the input market as a means to raise rivals' costs. One further needs to see to what extent rival companies lack sufficient alternative sources of supply and, where relevant, the ability to adopt counter-strategies (eg in the form of concluding their own contracts with players upstream, or to vertically integrate by way of merger). Furthermore, it is well recognised that vertical relationships may provide considerable scope for efficiency gains.[148] They may reduce transaction costs between the two companies[149] and better align the incentives of the companies in bringing a product to market.[150] As a result of such efficiency gains competition in the market may intensify, rather than diminish.

---

[148] cf Riordan and Salop, above n 147, at 523.

[149] Transaction costs can be understood as the usual costs of searching for a trading partner and of drawing up and enforcing contracts, but also as inefficiencies that result from not being able to write contracts as comprehensive as one might wish (incomplete contracts), which may reduce the willingness to invest in assets which are specific to the vertical relationship. Mergers, but also exclusive contracts, can have the effect of restoring such incentives. See, eg O Williamson, 'Transaction Cost Economics' in Schmalensee R and Willig R (eds), *Handbook Of Industrial Organization* (1989).

[150] The incentives of the upstream and downstream companies are not necessarily well aligned. One classic example is the problem of double mark-ups. When the upstream and downstream markets are imperfectly competitive, both the downstream and the upstream company set a mark-up, as a result of which the joint mark-up may be too high from the point of view of the vertical structure. Depending on the market conditions, reducing the combined mark-up (ie the price) may allow the vertical structure to significantly expand output on the downstream market and increase profits.

Apart from creating market power in a given market, vertical contracts or mergers can also **1.234** serve to protect market power, by increasing entry barriers into a market. Vertical linkages can raise the costs at which potential competitors can operate on a market (input foreclosure), or reduce the revenue streams that can be expected after entry (customer foreclosure). Because of foreclosure, potential competitors may have to enter two markets instead of one: entrants would also have to set up their own input production facilities or distribution system. When this is the result, a company with market power in either of the two relevant markets has become less exposed to potential competition.

In settings where two or more products are often bought or used in combination, exclusion- **1.235** ary conduct can also take the form of tying or bundling. 'Tying' occurs when customers that purchase one good (the tying good) are required also to purchase another good from the producer (the tied good). 'Bundling' refers to selling the goods as a single package.[151] Tying and bundling can be used to 'leverage' a strong market position from one market to another market.[152] The main antitrust concern in this context is again foreclosure, more particularly customer foreclosure. Such foreclosure may be inspired by the desire to gain market power in the tied goods market, to protect market power in the tying goods market, or a combina- tion of the two.[153] As with vertical foreclosure concerns, it is fairly difficult to predict when bundling and tying are detrimental to competition, not least because bundling and tying also have a potential to lead to efficiency gains.

A final way in which rivals may be excluded in an anti-competitive way is through predatory **1.236** pricing. Predation refers to the strategy of a (dominant) company to charge very low prices for its products so as to prompt the exit or marginalisation of its rivals unable to sustain the losses incurred for a prolonged period. Following the exit or marginalisation of rivals, the company would be in a situation of enhanced market power and be able to raise prices. While the idea of predation is rather straightforward, it is clear that there are quite substan- tial hurdles for such a strategy to work. Not only must rivals be marginalised or forced to exit, it must also be the case that, following their exit, there is no entry by new companies or re-entry by the old ones.

A complication with pursuing cases of exclusion, especially when they are of the customer **1.237** foreclosure type, is that the type of behaviour pursued may so closely resemble acts of normal competition. The concept of 'exclusion' is inherent in any process of competition. When companies seek to supply customers and are very successful in doing so, some rivals are 'excluded' in passing and may even have to exit the market. Such exclusion should, in prin- ciple, be of no concern to competition policy. Indeed, competition policy should ensure that the normal competitive process is able to perform its task in benefiting the companies that are the more efficient in producing goods and services and the more effective in catering for the customers' needs. This ground principle, however, also mandates that competition

---

[151] More generally: the price paid for the two goods is the same, whether one buys one product or both.
[152] There is no received definition of 'leveraging' but, in its most neutral sense, it is being able to increase sales in one market (the tied market), by virtue of the strong market position of the product to which it is tied or bundled (the tying market).
[153] See, eg M Whinston, 'Tying, Foreclosure and Exclusion' (1990) 80 American Economic Review 837 2859.

policy should keep an eye on companies that—though 'successful' in selling to customers— seek to exclude rivals in ways that are not compatible with the competitive process in the long run. At the same time, the fact that real competition ('competition on the merits') and exclusionary practices are so difficult to disentangle only highlights the need to be cautious in intervening in free market processes out of a concern that a given company is seeking to exclude rivals. Companies may restrict competition, but so may antitrust authorities— when their policies are too interventionist.

G. Empirical Methods for Market Definition and the Assessment of Market Power[154]

1.238 Both market definition (an intermediary step in the analysis of market power) and the assessment of market power itself address the following central question: to what extent do companies compete with one another?

1.239 This question, in the majority of cases, is an empirical question. One needs to consider the specific facts of the case. In certain cases, where sufficient data are available, it is possible to apply quantitative, empirical methods to study this question.

1.240 In this section, we will discuss the main methods that are available. These methods are: the analysis of prices and price movements in the market, the estimation of price elasticities, critical loss analysis, price concentration analysis, event analysis, the analysis of bidding data, and, finally, techniques involving merger simulation.

1.241 As this review will show, empirical analysis does not need to be sophisticated, nor does it need to rely on having access to numerous data. Some methods are relatively simple. What matters most is that a method is chosen that is sound for the case under investigation. Help from econometricians is valuable in this respect, but using one's own common sense is also an important ingredient.

(1) Analysis of Prices and Price Movements

1.242 Prices are probably among the main competitive variables in any market. Analysis of prices, and of price movements, is therefore likely to provide useful first information on the degree to which products compete.

1.243 **Price Correlation Analysis**   One intuitive tool for analysing prices is price correlation.[155] The main idea behind price correlation analysis is that, when two products are in the same relevant product market, over time their prices are likely to move together relatively closely. After all, when products are substitutes in the eyes of customers, the prices of these products are likely to constrain each other. Note that this does not mean that the prices themselves

---

154   The authors wish to thank Lawrence Wu, Wessel Marquering, and Eliana Garces Tolon for their comments on earlier versions of this section. All errors, if any, remain the responsibility of the authors.
155   Price correlation analysis has been applied or discussed in various Commission cases, eg *Nestlé/Perrier* [1992] OJ L356/1; *Procter&Gamble/Schickedanz* [1994] OJ L354/33; *Gencor/Lonrho* [1997] OJ L11/30; *CVC/Lenzing* [2004] OJ L082/20; and *Blackstone/Acetex* [2005] L312/60.

have to be at the same level; low-priced products of a lower quality may well constrain high-priced goods of a higher quality, and vice versa.

To illustrate, suppose we have the following monthly price levels for two products A and B, **1.244**
for the years 2002–2004:

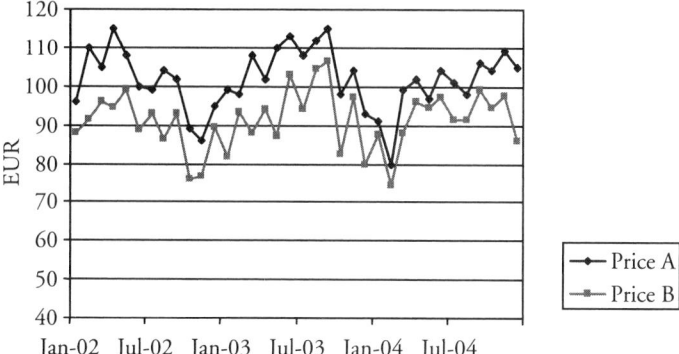

Figure 14 Price development of products A and B over time

From Figure 14, there appears to be some correlation between the two price series, but it is not perfect. In most months, the prices move in parallel (for instance, both prices make substantial drops in the second half of 2002, and again in early 2004), but in some months, they move in opposite directions.

The degree to which two prices move together is measured by the *correlation coefficient*, **1.245**
a measure that can take a value between −1 and 1. The coefficient is calculated on the basis of the deviations of the prices from their average values at each point in time.[156] When the correlation coefficient is equal to one, the correlation is perfect. It is zero when the prices move independently of each other; it is −1 when the prices persistently move in opposite directions.

The fact that in the Figure 14 above there appears to be some positive correlation between **1.246**
the two price series is also conveyed by the correlation coefficient, which equals 0.77 in this case (positive value but less than one).

When two products are in the same relevant product market, one would expect the corre- **1.247**
lation coefficient to be fairly high as this would be consistent with prices closely moving together over time. A first, practical question that arises is: how high does the correlation

---

[156] The correlation coefficient between two price series is equal to the covariance (joint variance) of the price series divided by the product of the standard deviations of the two individual price series. Specifically, if P_t^A denotes the price of product A at time t, and P_t^B the price of product B at time t, the covariance of the two price series is $(1/n) \Sigma (P_t^A - P^A) (P_t^B - P^B)$, where P^A and P^B are the average values of the price of A and B, respectively; n is the number of observations; and Σ the summation sign. The standard deviation of the price series is a measure of the variability of the price over time. For product A, it is the square root of $(1/n) \Sigma (P_t^A - P^A)^2$, for product B it is the square root of $(1/n) \Sigma (P_t^B - P^B)^2$. Thus, the correlation coefficient (r) is given by the following formula: $r = (1/n) \Sigma (P_t^A - P^A) (P_t^B - P^B) / \sqrt{(1/n) \Sigma (P_t^A - P^A)^2} \sqrt{(1/n) \Sigma (P_t^B - P^B)^2}$. The correlation coefficient is always pair-wise (eg between two series of prices).

coefficient need to be, for the products to be considered in the same relevant market? One must have some idea of what is the relevant benchmark for comparison. One suggested way is to take two products that are known to be in the same relevant market (because of their identical product characteristics, for example), and to see how much their prices are correlated. This approach is known as benchmarking. In our example above, the idea would be to compare the correlation of 0.77 with the correlation between product B and another product C known to be in the same market as B.

1.248 A problem with benchmarking is, however, that, if one takes two close substitutes with a price correlation of say, 0.90, a third product may be perhaps not so correlated (not so close), but still be close enough to be in the same relevant market. The 'benchmark' obtained from two products in the same relevant market should not be used too strictly, therefore, but rather as a rough indication.

1.249 Another important point to be aware of is that prices may be correlated for reasons that have nothing to do with competition between these products. For example, if prices follow the same trend (eg upwards, due to general inflation), this would show up in the correlation coefficient. The problem becomes particularly relevant when two products are made with the same major input. The classic example is prices at the petrol station. It may very well be that prices at the petrol station in Sweden and Portugal are highly correlated but this probably says very little about the relevant geographic market for petrol distribution. Rather, the correlation is likely to be the result of developments in the price of crude oil. Correlation driven by this sort of factor is called 'spurious' (spurious in the sense that there is correlation due to reasons unrelated to substitutability).

1.250 One must also think of the proper time dimension. The degree of correspondence between two prices depends on the speed with which prices can react to each other. Prices may constrain each other, but only with a certain delay. This would be the case, for example, for a commodity that is traded both at the merchant market and on a supply contract basis, with monthly revisions of the supply price. Prices in the contracted market may well react to spot market prices, but can do so only at the revision dates or after the contracts have expired. In this case, the correlation between daily or weekly prices may turn out to be relatively low, while the correlation between monthly prices is probably higher. In such an instance, the appropriate correlation coefficient to look at would be the one based on monthly prices.

1.251 While it is certainly useful to have a look at price correlation (in particular by looking at the graphs), one must realise that it does not provide the full answer to the question whether products belong to the same relevant market. If there is a high correlation between the prices of two products, this simply means that, on average, when the price of one product went up, the price of the other product went up as well, and vice versa. It does not address the question of *how many* customers would switch in the event of a price increase on a product (or group of products), which is the central question for market definition purposes (the SSNIP test). It is true that a high correlation coefficient suggests a strong competitive relationship in this sense, but it can only be taken as indicative evidence. A high correlation coefficient is a necessary, but not a sufficient condition for two products to be in the same market.

Extension: Stationarity/Co-integration   As noted above, measuring price correlation **1.252** may give rise to misleading ('spurious') results if, for example, the prices of two products follow the same general (upward or downward) trend. A price series following a certain trend is in fact a special instance of a price series that is *non-stationary*: the series cannot be said to move around a stable mean over time.[157] When working with price series that are non-stationary, there is a high risk that the correlation coefficient is unreliable.

Co-integration analysis is a rather technical way of analysing price series that are non- **1.253** stationary.[158] It starts from the idea that two price series that are non-stationary may still be 'connected' to each other, ie co-integrated (eg price A usually 40 per cent higher than price B). The intuition underlying co-integration analysis is in fact the same as that of price correlation analysis: when two products are in the same relevant product market, their prices are likely to move together over time. This can be translated into analysing the difference between two price series (in absolute or relative terms), and to see whether that difference follows a stable pattern, ie is stationary. The statistical test used to analyse whether a series is stationary is rather involved, and typically requires expert input.[159]

(2) Analysis of Price Elasticities of Demand

The price elasticity of a product measures how demand for that product changes with the **1.254** price of the product (this elasticity is also called the *own-price elasticity*). In particular, it measures the %-change in demand following a 1 per cent increase in the price. If the price elasticity is for example –2, this means that, following a 1 per cent price increase, demand goes down by 2 per cent.

As indicated in Section E(1), the price elasticity is a summary indicator of the extent to **1.255** which a product is subject to competitive constraints (due to customer reactions and the presence of competitors). When the price of a product is raised, customers switch away from it: they either switch to competing suppliers, or they stop purchasing the product altogether. The (own-) price elasticity of a good captures both these movements. The higher the own-price elasticity, the more the product is subject to competitive constraints. Alternatively, the lower the own-price elasticity, the higher the degree of market power for the supplier concerned.[160]

Price elasticity analysis provides direct input into the SSNIP test for market definition. For **1.256** example, if the aggregate elasticity[161] of the set of products one posits to be in the same relevant product market is equal to 1.5, the unit sales for the products will go down by approximately 7.5 per cent if prices for the products go up by 5 per cent (the usual SSNIP). Depending on the initial gross profit margins of the products involved, this may be profitable or not profitable.

---

[157] Another example of a price series that is non-stationary is one where a random price movement at one point in time appears to have effects that persist (eg 'random walk').

[158] Co-integration tests have been applied or discussed in a small number of Commission cases, eg *Gencor/Lonrho* [1995] OJ 314; *CVC/Lenzing* [2004] L082/20; and *Blackstone/Acetex* [2005] L312/60.

[159] See the next subsection for more information on the subject of statistical testing.

[160] Note that the own-price elasticity of a product is normally higher than 1. If it were lower, eg 0.5, the supplier of the good could make more money by raising its price (a price increase of 1% would result in only 0.5% less demand, and hence lead to a net increase in profit).

[161] See Section E(1)(c). The aggregate elasticity measures how total market demand (combined demand for all products in a particular market) changes with a price increase of 1%.

If these margins are around 40 per cent, the 5 per cent price increase represents a $5/40 = 12.5\%$ increase in the profits made on the $(100 - 7.5 =)$ 92.5% of sales retained. Comparing the profit gain on retained sales $(0.925 \times 12.5\% = 11.6\%)$ with the margin loss on sales lost $(0.075 \times 100\% = 7.5\%$[162]$)$, the price increase would be profitable.

1.257 The *cross-price elasticity* measures how demand for a product changes with the price of some other product. For a set of products, there is an array of cross-price elasticities, each corresponding to an individual pair of products. The cross-price elasticity between competing products is normally positive (if the cross-price elasticity is zero, then the products concerned are not competing). Generally, the higher the cross-price elasticity of B with respect to the price of A, the more product B forms a competitive constraint for product A. Cross-price elasticities are thus particularly helpful in evaluating the 'closeness' of substitute products (relevant both for market definition and for evaluating possible unilateral effects arising from mergers).

1.258 Information on elasticities can be obtained in various ways.[163] Some rudimentary information can result from customer surveys that ask the question: 'in the face of a 1 per cent price increase for product X, and assuming that the price of alternative products did not change, would you switch? If so, by how much?' If, out of 100 respondents, five indicate that they would switch away half of their demand to other suppliers, this could indicate that the own-price elasticity of the product in question is about –2.5 per cent (assuming the respondents are more or less of equal size). The same question can also be asked for a group of products to see what the elasticity is for the group as a whole.[164]

1.259 An issue with surveys is that the results should be representative for the larger group of customers. This is not always easy to achieve, if only for practical reasons (one may need a substantial group of respondents to have representative results). Further, the questions asked should be accurate enough, so that they leave relatively little room for misinterpretation. Finally, the question is—by definition—a hypothetical one: 'what would you do if'. The answers from respondents to a survey are unlikely to be as well thought through as business decisions in the case of real price increases. With these caveats, however, surveys remain a useful tool, and certainly a good starting point.

1.260 Further (and more affirmative) information on switching behaviour can be obtained from looking at actual decisions to switch in the past. If there are quite a few respondents that indicate they have switched in the past to take advantage of price differences between products, this signals that the elasticity for a particular product (or set of products) is likely to be substantial.

1.261 To avoid the problem of representativeness of limited groups of respondents, information on switching behaviour can also be obtained from looking at historic market sales and

---

162 The full margin (100%) is lost on the units no longer sold.

163 The Commission considers price elasticities mostly on the basis of surveys. The more sophisticated regression techniques have been applied or discussed in, for instance, *Procter&Gamble/Schickedanz* [1994] OJ L354/33; *Guinness/Grand Metropolitan* [1998] OJ L288/24; and *TetraLaval/Sidel* [2004] OJ L43/13.

164 A small but significant minority of switching customers may already be enough for the own-price elasticity of a product to be substantial. See Section D.

price data. These data may reveal a certain pattern, namely that, on average, falls (or increases) in the sale price are followed by a certain increase (or fall) in sales. From this it may be possible to distil the price elasticity of demand.

To illustrate, suppose that in addition to information on monthly prices in the period **1.262** 2002–2004 (depicted in Figure 14), we also have data on the monthly quantities of product A bought. The observed quantities and prices of product A may look as follows:[165]

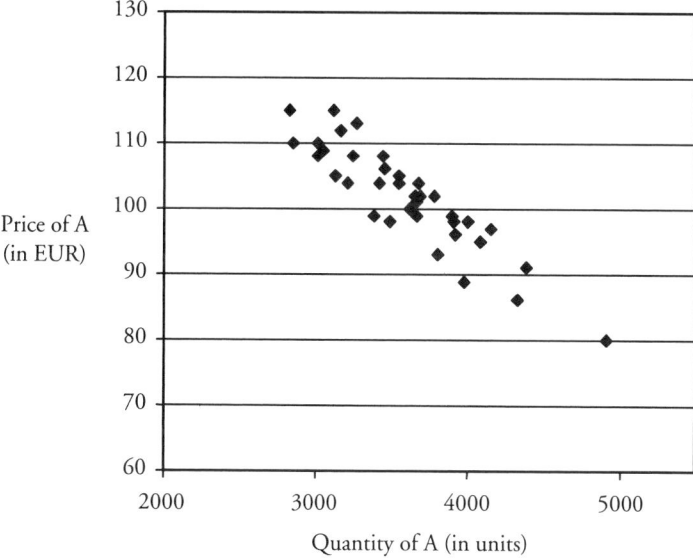

Figure 15 Observed prices vs quantities

Each 'dot' represents a combination of the observed price and quantity of product A in a particular month (there are 36 dots). The dots indicate a negative relationship between prices and quantities. We can even recognise something like a 'demand curve' in the picture, by drawing a line that 'best fits' the points in the graph. An example of such a curve is depicted in Figure 16. It is downward sloping, and seems to have a slight curvature. Note however that, strictly speaking, one cannot call the curve a 'demand curve' (a curve expressing demand as a function of price), unless one knows that there are no other (important) factors that have changed in the period under investigation that influence the demand for product A at a certain price of A.[166]

The slope of the demand curve gives information on the demand elasticity. The greater the **1.263** slope of the demand curve (the steeper the demand curve) at a given price level, the lower

---

[165] In economics, it is customary to display prices on the vertical axis and quantities on the horizontal axis, even when quantities are thought to be a function of prices, rather than the opposite.

[166] As will be discussed further below, the price of substitute products may substantially influence demand for a given product. This will have to be taken into account. Another equally fundamental issue is that in each given period the observed prices and quantities are a reflection of the *equilibrium* in the market (ie the situation where supply equals demand), not of the demand curve as such. It is only possible to interpret the dots in Figure 15 as a demand curve if this relationship is stable and does not 'move' from one period to the other. When the demand curve is not stable, one is faced with the problem of *identification*: how to identify the true relationship between demand and price. For this, more advanced econometric analysis is needed.

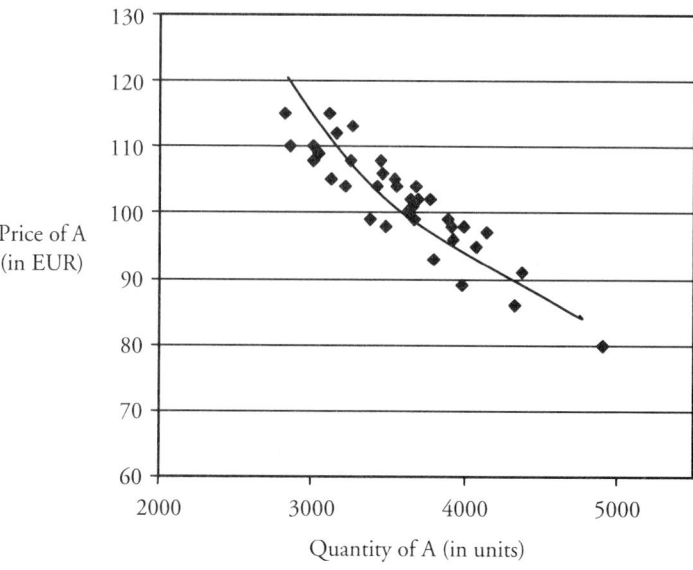

Figure 16 A line of best fit

the price elasticity at that price: a change in price has little impact on the quantity bought. Note that the price elasticity and the slope cannot be 'equated', however. The slope relates quantity changes (in units) with price changes (in euros). An elasticity is about relating %-changes, which is different. For instance, for a given price increase of 1 per cent, a drop in sales of 100 units starting from a level of, say, 5000 units is not the same as a drop of 100 units at a level of 3000 units. The former drop is lower in percentage terms than the latter (2 per cent vs 3.33 per cent).[167] In order to identify (and estimate) elasticities more easily, the data is therefore usually transformed by taking the *logarithms* of prices and quantities (essentially expressing prices and quantities in terms of growth rates starting from a certain base level, eg the lowest level observed in the sample). The slope of a curve in the resulting plot does indicate an elasticity: the slope relates a %-change in the price with a %-change in the quantity.

1.264 If there are no other factors to take account of ('all else being equal'), an estimate of the price elasticity for product A is obtained from the demand curve that best fits the data points observed. It is common to start with the assumption that the elasticity is constant across (the relevant range of) the demand curve, so that there is only one value to be estimated. This assumption determines the shape of the curve.[168] The assumption is not entirely innocuous, as the price elasticity of a product tends to increase when the price increases (demand often

---

[167] In general terms, the relation between elasticity and the slope of the demand curve is as follows. For a certain unit change in price (Δp) and corresponding unit change in demand (Δq), the elasticity is approximately $(\Delta q/q)/(\Delta p/p) = (\Delta q/\Delta p) \times (p/q)$, ie the (inverse) slope of the demand curve multiplied by price level p divided by quantity q.

[168] Assuming that the elasticity is constant across the demand curve amounts to assuming that the relationship between the *logarithms* of quantities and prices is linear.

becomes more elastic at higher prices). However, it is a good assumption to start with and its appropriateness can be checked later.[169]

The standard statistical tool used by economists to find and evaluate a relationship between observed data points is *regression analysis*. Broadly speaking, regression analysis aims at identifying a line through data points that provides the best fit, ie which minimises the differences between the actual observations and the plotted line.[170] It then evaluates whether the differences between the actual observations and the plotted line are substantial or not, in view of the number of data points available. The better the 'fit', the more 'precise' the estimated relationship can be deemed to be.

1.265

How confident can we be that the resulting elasticity estimate is precise and reliable? In general, the more data points one has, and the better the fit, the more one can be confident of having found a reliable estimate. The extent to which elasticity estimates obtained from regression are 'precise' in a statistical sense is answered in the following way. There is a 'true' price elasticity of demand, and there is the elasticity estimate found by drawing the line through the available data. In econometrics, when establishing a relationship between variables, it is recognised that there may still be other (small) factors, and measurement errors on the variables, that may produce an observed relationship that is not exactly identical to the 'true' relationship. Taken together, these other factors and the measurement errors form a certain 'chance' component in the observations (this produces the 'scatter' in the graph).

1.266

Technically, econometricians say that they estimate the following 'model':

1.267

$$Q_t^A = \alpha - \beta \cdot P_t^A + \varepsilon_t,$$

where Q_t^A stands for the quantity (in logarithms) of product A bought in month t (t = January 2002, ..., December 2004), P_t^A the price (in logarithms) of product A in that month, β represents the 'true' relationship between the quantity of A and the price of A (when quantities and prices are expressed in terms of logarithms, coefficient β is an elasticity[171]), and where ε_t is the error term, ie the 'chance' component in the observations at time t. Parameter α is a constant term to improve the fit. Under conditions of normality,[172] and as long as the error

---

[169] Other simplifications are used as well, especially when simultaneously evaluating the price elasticities (both cross- and own-price elasticity) of various products. For example, the cross-price elasticity of a product A with respect to the price of B and that of product B with respect to the price of A are sometimes assumed to satisfy a symmetry condition (such as 'Slutsky symmetry') or the stronger 'Independence of Irrelevant Alternatives' condition. The purpose of these initial—and testable—assumptions is to reduce the number of parameters to be estimated. This method is often needed when the number of data points available is itself relatively low.

[170] To measure difference, one can use the absolute differences between the observations and the plotted line, or other measures of difference. The most practical method has proved to be to take the squared differences, and to draw a line such that the sum of the squared differences is minimised. This method is called Ordinary Least Squares (OLS). Statistical tests have been developed for the OLS method, and its variants.

[171] See para 1.263 above.

[172] Normality conditions in this context means that the error term follows a 'normal distribution' with a mean equal to zero (ie the error is on average zero). The 'normal distribution' is a distribution of values with a certain shape. The term 'normal' is not taken by chance, in fact. It appears that many things, especially in nature (eg the height of oak trees), follow some normal distribution. A normal distribution is thought to result when the variable itself (height) is the result of many small and independent events influencing the variable (the amount of rain fall during each month; the amount of sunlight; branches breaking off during storms; young couples carving their names into the tree; etc). The—more prosaic—events in economics relate to measurement error, small random events determining demand, etc.

is not 'systematic' (as would be the case if there were still some other relevant, but omitted variable in the model), it can be shown statistically that, 95 per cent of the time, the 'true' elasticity lies within about *two standard deviations* of the elasticity estimate obtained from the data sample.[173] The standard deviation of the estimated elasticity is an estimate of the variability of the elasticity estimate.[174]

1.268   If we conducted a regression analysis on the data shown in Figure 15, we would find that the own-price elasticity of product A would be estimated to be 1.40.[175] Allowing for the 'chance' component that may have produced this result, it can be said with 95 per cent confidence that on the basis of this regression the 'true' elasticity lies between 1.17 and 1.65.[176] This interval is called the *95 per cent confidence interval*. In principle, the narrower the confidence interval (the more closely it surrounds the estimate of 1.40), the more precise the estimate can be considered to be.

1.269   'Preciseness' and 'reliability' are, however, relative concepts. As indicated above, a problematic issue in the interpretation of the curve in Figure 15 arises from the fact that it relates the observed quantities of product A only to the observed prices of A. There may be other factors that influence the quantities of A bought, not just the price of A. When this is the case, then the relationship found by mechanically comparing observed quantities and prices of A (as done above) is unlikely to be the correct one: the found elasticity estimate is then called 'biased'. And when the elasticity estimate is itself 'biased', the confidence intervals surrounding the estimate do not mean much either.

1.270   For instance, when a product B is a good substitute for product A, an obvious factor influencing the demand for A is the price of product B. The way to obtain correct (unbiased) elasticity estimates is to add the price of product B into the analysis as a possible explanatory variable for the demand for A. By explicitly adding the 'price of B' in the analysis, the real effect of the 'price of A' on 'quantities of A bought' gets identified. In graphical terms, the picture becomes three-dimensional, with on the vertical axis 'quantities of A bought' and on the two ground axes 'price of A' and 'price of B'.[177] Econometric estimation (regression) finds the line that best fits all the data points in the three-dimensional plot.[178] The slope of

---

173   The factor 'two' (in '*two* standard deviations') is in fact closer to 1.96, and is linked to the assumption of normality (see footnote above). With a distribution different from the normal distribution, one would need a different factor. The same holds if one were to take a different confidence level (eg with 90% instead of 95%, the factor becomes 1.64).

174   Remember that there is a 'chance' component in the whole exercise, so that the estimate obtained is itself also influenced by chance. Hence, one can speak of a certain (intrinsic or underlying) variability of the estimate, even though we end up having only one estimate of the coefficient.

175   Estimate obtained using a software package.

176   Note that this does not mean that the true elasticity lies in the interval with 95% probability. Either the true elasticity lies within the interval (in which case the probability of the true elasticity lying in the interval is 100%) or it does not (in which case the probability of the true elasticity lying in the interval is zero).

177   These axes are chosen for ease of presentation.

178   Technically, econometricians now estimate the following 'model': $Q_t^A = \alpha - \beta . P_t^A + \gamma . P_t^B + \varepsilon_t$, where Q_t^A stands for the quantity (in logarithms) of product A bought in month t (t = January 2002, ..., December 2004), P_t^A the price (in logarithms) of product A in that month, P_t^B the price (in logarithms) of product B in that month, β and γ represent the 'true' relationships between on the one hand the quantity of A and on the other hand the price A and B respectively, and where ε_t is the error term, ie the 'chance' component in the observations at time t. Parameter α is a constant term to improve the fit.

the (new) line with respect to the price of A provides an estimate of the own-price elasticity of product A. The slope of the line with respect to the price of product B gives an estimate of the cross-price elasticity of product A with respect to the price of B.

Suppose the prices of product B over the period 2002–2004 are those depicted in Figure 14. Using this information with the data on the prices and quantities of product A shown in Figure 15, the own-price elasticity of product A would be estimated to be 2.23. Allowing for the 'chance' component that may have produced this result, the 'true' elasticity is between 2.09 and 2.37, with about 95 per cent confidence. Note that demand for product A thus turns out to be more elastic than that suggested by the previous regression (2.23 is greater than 1.40). This is consistent with the fact that the prices of product A and B were quite correlated (see Section G(1)), suggesting they might be in the same relevant market. On average, increases in the price of A were accompanied by increases in the price of B, limiting the actual sales loss of product A from an increase in its price. However, when prices of B are held constant (the 'all else being equal' aspect inherent in the notion of 'elasticity'), the sales loss of A is higher. **1.271**

Regression analysis also can be used to help us test hypotheses. For example, a regression analysis could be used to test whether or not two products are, in fact, substitute products. One hypothesis that can be tested is this: products A and B are not substitutes, which means that the cross-price elasticity is (close to) zero. A regression analysis can help us test this hypothesis by providing an estimate of the cross-price elasticity between products A and B along with the standard deviations of the estimate. In our example, the regression produces an estimate of the cross-price elasticity with respect to the price of B equal to +0.98, with a 95 per cent confidence interval between 0.86 and 1.11. Given that the confidence interval is such that it does not include zero, it can be concluded with 95 per cent confidence that the true coefficient is not zero (in other words, one can be rather confident that the two products indeed are substitutes). In this case, econometricians say that the found coefficient is in statistical terms *significantly different from zero*, or in short 'statistically significant'.[179] **1.272**

In a case where the confidence interval is such that it includes zero, it cannot be excluded with 95 per cent confidence that the true coefficient is in fact different from zero. Suppose, for example, that we had found a cross-price elasticity of +0.21 and a confidence interval between –0.05 and 0.47. In that case, econometricians would say that the found elasticity estimate of 0.21 is statistically not significantly different from zero. In other words, although the found estimate of the cross-price elasticity is positive (+0.21), one would not be able to confidently say that the two products are in a competitive relationship. **1.273**

---

[179] Closely related to confidence intervals are the concepts of *t-statistic* and *p-value*. Whereas confidence intervals depict the range of values around the obtained estimate for which we can be 95% certain that it will contain the 'true' coefficient, the *t-statistic* is the transformation of the obtained estimate into a test variable (think of *t-statistic* as meaning 'test statistic'), which is known to follow a certain standard probability distribution. Hence, we can test its significance and, accordingly, that of the corresponding elasticity estimate. When the *t-statistic* is larger than the critical value 'two', it is said to be significantly different from zero at the 95% confidence level (on the number 'two', see n 173 above). The *p-value* is the probability that an estimate as large as or larger than the one obtained from the sample is obtained, when the true elasticity is in fact zero. When the *p-value* is low (eg below 5%), it is unlikely that the true elasticity is indeed zero. At this point, one can conclude that the elasticity is significantly different from zero.

1.274   There are three broad reasons why estimates may not be significantly different from zero. The first, obvious possibility is that the coefficient being estimated is indeed zero or close to zero. Secondly, the data set may be too small to be confident that the result is different from zero: small data sets usually lead to wide confidence intervals, and this shows up in the estimate being 'statistically insignificant'. Thirdly, the differences between the actual observations and the plotted line are substantial (ie the 'fit' is not good enough), so that the confidence interval around the estimate includes 'zero'. The statistical significance test alerts us that one of these situations applies.

1.275   As noted, estimates obtained from regression analysis are likely to be biased whenever variables that have a significant impact on the dependent variable are omitted from the analysis. In order to have fully reliable results, it would be necessary to check whether there are no omitted variables left. The added value of regression analysis is that it allows account to be taken of many factors that may potentially have an influence on the variable to be explained. Sometimes it is possible to think of potentially omitted variables. For instance, one could see if there have been promotion campaigns for either product A or B, and include such information into the analysis. In this way one can check whether the influence of promotion campaigns is statistically significant or not. Alternatively, one can do some (econometric) checks to see whether the differences between the observed data points and the plotted line do not follow some systematic (yet unexplained) pattern, which would suggest that there may still be other factors at play.

1.276   A final remark relates to the relation between statistical significance and economic significance. The two concepts are obviously related, but not identical. For example, the estimate of a cross-price elasticity may, through the wealth of data available, be statistically distinguishable from zero, but it may still be very low in economic terms (eg 0.15). Similarly, while an own-price elasticity estimate may, due to a lack of data, not be statistically different from zero, it may still be quite high and important (eg 3.0). It is important to ask oneself why an estimate may be statistically significant or insignificant, and to keep an eye on the value of the estimates, to see whether they are important.

(3) Critical Loss Analysis

1.277   Critical loss analysis is another method addressing the market definition question: would a hypothetical monopolist want to raise price on a set of products or not? It addresses the SSNIP test from the other angle: rather than evaluating actual or likely demand-side responses to a price increase (eg through estimation of price elasticities), it looks at the supply-side and asks: given a price increase of X per cent, what would the percentage loss in unit sales have to be to make the price increase unprofitable? If the actual loss of sales is larger then this amount, then a price increase is unlikely to be profitable. If it is less, it is profitable.

1.278   For example, if the price-cost margin is 40 per cent, a 5 per cent price increase represents a $5/40 = 12.5\%$ increase in the profits made on the sales that continue to be made.[180] At the same

---

[180] This assumes that the price-cost margin is constant over the sales base. The price-cost margin, also called gross profit margin, is the difference between price (p) and the incremental cost (c) of supplying one more unit of output, expressed as a percentage of price: $(p-c)/p$.

time, the full margin (100%) is lost on the units no longer sold. Let the percentage of sales lost be denoted by L. Then the gain of the price increase is equal to 12.5% · (100 – L); the loss is 100% · L. The critical loss is given by that L for which there is no net gain: 12.5% · (100 – L) = 100% · L. The critical loss is therefore equal to 11.1%.[181]

Critical loss analysis provides a benchmark with which the estimate of the actual sales loss in the case of a price increase can be compared. In the context of market definition, when an estimate of the price elasticity for a group of products in the candidate relevant market is available, one can compare the estimated sales loss (based on the price elasticity) following a 5–10 per cent price increase with the critical loss benchmark or threshold. If the former is higher than the latter, this indicates that the price increase would be unprofitable and that the relevant market should be wider. If not, the candidate market is an antitrust market (and maybe it is even taken too large).

1.279

If no estimate of the price elasticity is available, one can still see whether the critical loss analysis suggests that the elasticity would have to be unrealistically low (or high) for the products to be in the same (or a different) relevant antitrust market. Note that a critical loss easily translates into a 'critical elasticity': if the critical loss in the context of a 5 per cent price increase is 11.1 per cent (as in the example above), this means that the critical elasticity is 11.1% / 5% = 2.2.

1.280

The critical loss benchmark for a given product (or group of products) depends on the price-cost margin on the product(s) and on the hypothesised price increase. The larger the margin, the smaller the critical loss will be. This is not surprising given that it is much more costly to lose sales when margins are high than when they are low.

1.281

One common misunderstanding is that, because high margins mean that the critical loss benchmark for a given group of products is low, it follows that the relevant market is probably wider than that group of products. This may indeed be the case, but one must keep an eye on what causes the high margins in the first place. Notably, high margins may be the result of a degree of product differentiation. In such a case, the critical loss may be low, but so is—in all likelihood—the actual loss in case of a price increase. A comparison of critical loss and (likely levels of) actual loss remains therefore preferable in many cases.

1.282

(4) Price Concentration Analysis

A promising avenue for investigating whether products or companies are the subject of significant competitive constraints opens up where it is possible to compare markets with one another, either a comparison between different markets (eg different geographic markets) or a comparison of markets over time (eg before or after some important event in the industry).

1.283

An example of comparing markets with one another is price concentration analysis.[182] The object of study of price concentration analysis is to see whether prices are systematically

1.284

---

[181]   A general formula for critical loss is given by: *Critical Loss* $= \Delta p / (\Delta p + m)$, where Δp denotes the % price change, and m the price-cost margin (in %). The formula only holds good when the price-cost margin m is constant over the sales base (in other cases, it is an approximation). In the example, it gives 5% / (5%+40%) = 11.1%.

[182]   This technique has so far been considered by the Commission in relatively few cases. Examples are *Nordic Capital/Mölnlycke Clinical/Kolmi* [1998] OJ C39/19 and a number of cases involving airlines (to investigate

higher in markets where there are a few players (high market concentration), than in markets where there are many players (low market concentration). If so, this is an indication that an increase in market concentration (eg through a merger) may lead to price increases. Alternatively, in a case where market concentration is high due to the presence of a firm with a very large market share, it is an indication that this firm is exerting market power and can be deemed dominant in this market.

1.285 Figure 17 provides an example of a positive relationship between concentration and price for a sample of distinct geographic areas.

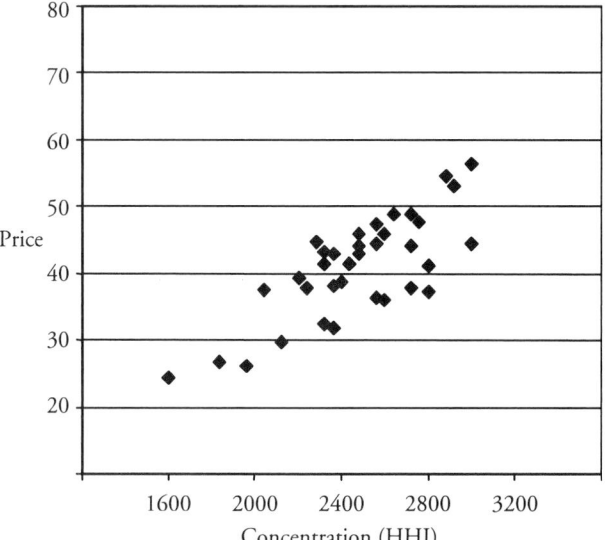

Figure 17 Price vs concentration

When there is no clear relationship between concentration and price, this signals that in the more concentrated markets there is not more market power than in less concentrated markets. It can also signal that the 'markets' (on the basis of which concentration is measured) are themselves not really relevant product or geographic markets, but rather part of a broader relevant product or geographic market. For instance, one would expect to find little relation between the number of malt whisky producers and the price of malt whisky, if the relevant market in reality includes both malt whisky and blended whisky.

1.286 The relationship between price and concentration can also be investigated using econometric methods. The relationship can be estimated by drawing a line that best fits all the data points in the plot (regression analysis). The greater the slope of this line, the stronger is the relationship (all else being equal). Econometric tests can then be performed to see how precise the found relationship can be considered to be, on the basis of the 95 per cent

whether certain city-to-city routes constitute separate relevant markets). The somewhat related technique of comparing the level of discounts and the number of bidders participating in tenders for contracts is discussed in Section G(6) below.

confidence interval around the price concentration relationship found, and to test whether the relationship is indeed significant from a statistical point of view.

Importantly in this context, the regression analysis allows for taking account of factors **1.287** other than concentration that also affect price. For example, if it is the case that in certain countries the costs of running a business are high, so that: (i) prices are relatively high; and (ii) fewer firms are active; then this by itself shows a certain relationship between price and concentration. It is necessary to take such other factors into account, because the relation found between price and concentration by mechanically comparing those two variables alone is likely to be the incorrect one for the purpose of antitrust analysis.

To make meaningful comparisons, it is necessary to compare 'like with like'. When the prod- **1.288** ucts whose prices are being compared are not identical across the regions, price disparities might be the result of differences in the product characteristics and costs, rather than of differences in the degree of competition present in the market. Incorporating product characteristics and costs directly into the analysis may be difficult when data on these variables are difficult to obtain. In such cases, it is preferable to work with margin data, given that margins typically better control for differences in product characteristics and costs than prices.

(5) Event Analysis

Relevant information for the purpose of market definition and impact assess-ment can also **1.289** be derived from the analysis of past 'events' or 'shocks' occurring in the industry.[183] The idea is to consider the event, and to see how customers and/or companies reacted to it. Typically, but not necessarily, this analysis would involve some type of econometric analysis.

The 'events' can be of various sorts. An important type of event is past market entry. For **1.290** instance, if, following the market entry by a company A, company B lost many sales, but company C's sales remained constant, then it may be concluded that A and B's products are in the same relevant market, and C's products are probably not. This analysis may also be applied on a more general basis, to see which products rather than others are closer substitutes for each other. If B's sales reacted a lot, but C's sales much less, then one could conclude that products A and B are closer substitutes than products A and C.

Other examples of 'events' include supply shortages, shocks in input prices, regulatory **1.291** intervention, technological change, and promotional and advertising activity. For example, if a promotional activity on one branded good (eg a strong advertisement campaign, or heavy discounting) resulted in a capture of market share of one other brand in particular, this may be taken as evidence that those two goods are in close competition with each other.

Exchange rate developments, given that they relate to trade between countries, may provide **1.292** insight into the question of geographic market definition. For example, if in the past, following a strong depreciation of the US dollar persisting over a lengthy period, US exports of the product under consideration did not increase, this could be taken as an indication that the

---

[183] This type of analysis has been applied in some Commission cases, eg *Procter&Gamble/Schickedanz* [1994] OJ L354/33; *Kimberley-Clark/Scott* [1996] OJ L183/1; *Blackstone/Acetex* [2005] L312/60; and COMP/37.507 *Generics/Astra Zeneca* (2005, not yet reported). Obviously, the industry under investigation must have witnessed an 'event' in order to apply this technique.

US and the EU formed separate geographic markets for this product. Obviously, with the arrival of the euro, the 'exchange rate event' is likely to become less often applicable in EU investigations, but, in cases involving both euro and non-euro countries, it remains a potential source of information.

(6) Analysis of Bidding Data

1.293   Certain markets can be characterised as bidding markets. In essence, these are markets where companies compete for specific contracts. The term 'bidding market' covers both situations where customers use formal bidding rules (as is the case in public procurement) and situations where customers simply elicit bids from sellers during negotiations.

1.294   Analyses of bidding data are often helpful in evaluating the nature of competitive interaction among firms in the market place. They can be used to assess market definition by helping to identify the firms that participate or compete in a bid. They can also be used to assess market power by identifying the firms whose presence is most important in determining the outcomes of bidding situations.

1.295   A particular issue in the context of bidding markets is the question of what role market shares play in the competition assessment. In each particular bidding contest, there is normally only one winner. The fact that another firm did not make a sale in a particular bidding contest does not mean that this firm did not pose a significant competitive constraint on the winning firm. In such a case, market shares (which give an indication of the firms' success in bids) may not be a good reflection of the competitive significance of firms, especially when the number of bids in a given year is small (when the number of bids gets larger, one can expect market shares to better reflect competitive strength).

1.296   In addition, the link between market share and market power is probably less direct in bidding markets than in most other markets.[184] In bidding markets each customer gets, or may get, a personalised offer. Where this is the case, companies can decide to compete more aggressively on the margin, without this necessarily having a direct impact on the margins obtained on their existing customer base. Especially when individual contracts are large and infrequent, the incentive to compete for each of them may be strong.

1.297   Accordingly, in bidding markets it is useful to seek direct information on the importance of the respective market players in the bidding process, and to see whether market shares overstate or understate market power. Three forms of bidding analysis are often applied, mostly with a view to establishing which firms have been competing strongly against each other for certain types of contracts.[185]

1.298   *Frequency of encounter analysis* consists in counting how often specific firms meet. For example, if firm A meets firm B more than 80 per cent of the time in those bids in which it participates, but meets firms C and D only 30 per cent and 20 per cent of the time, respectively,

---

[184] But see Klemperer, above n 128, for a critical discussion.

[185] Bidding data have been analysed by the Commission in a number of cases, for example *Boeing/McDonnell Douglas* [1997] OJ L336/16; *PriceWaterhouse/Coopers & Lybrand* [1999] OJ L50/27; *Philips/Agilent* [2001] OJ C92/10; *Buhrmann/Samas Office Supplies* [2003] OJ C117/5; *GE/Instrumentarium* [2004] OJ L109/1; and *Oracle/Peoplesoft* (2004, not yet reported).

this can be an indication that firms A and B are 'close' competitors for the customers they supply.[186]

Runner-up analysis seeks to provide more accurate information on the 'closeness' of competitors by looking at the number of times a company A has come second when company B has won a bid, and vice versa. The more often two companies have put in the two most competitive bids, the more they represent the main competitive threat to each other.   **1.299**

Price impact analysis (discount analysis) investigates whether the number (and possibly the identity) of bidders present in a bid has a significant impact on the prices (or discounts) being offered. When prices are, on average, higher when the number of bidders is low, this indicates that the number of bidders in the market matters, and that a merger may lead to price increases. One can also investigate whether the prices offered by a company A tend to be lower when company B is bidding as well (and vice versa). This would give an indication of the likely price impact of a merger between companies A and B.   **1.300**

Also in this context one should compare 'like with like'. When the contracts are very diverse in nature or size, it is probably better to compare discounts than actual prices (discounts normally vary less with differences in the actual contract to be performed). Even then, however, one still needs to be aware of factors influencing the level of discounts, such as the value of the deal (large values usually attract large discounts).   **1.301**

A systematic way to investigate the relationship between discounts and the number (or identity) of bidders, and to properly control for other factors influencing the level of discounts, is to do a regression analysis. Econometric tests can then be performed to see how precise the found relationship between the number (identity) of bidders and discounts can be deemed to be, on the basis of the 95 per cent confidence interval, and to test whether the relationship is indeed significant from a statistical point of view.   **1.302**

In certain industries the number of bidders taking part in any particular bid is determined by the customer itself. If so, and when the number of potential bidders exceeds the number of bidders usually invited, the impact of the observed relationship between the number of bidders and the discount is likely to be small. This is likely to show up in an estimate for this relationship that is insignificant.   **1.303**

(7) Merger Simulation

Merger simulation is a recent technique to simulate the impact of mergers in specific markets.[187] Two ingredients go into this technique: information on demand ('demand elasticities') and an assumption about the nature of competition in the market ('a model').   **1.304**

---

[186] Note that such a pattern may be perfectly compatible with a market context where all four firms have equal market share (25%). For instance, companies C and D may meet each other more often (and secure more wins) in bidding contests for other customers.

[187] Merger simulation was first used by the Commission in the case of *Volvo/Scania* [2001] OJ L143/74. In this case, the Commission decided that, in view of the novel character of the approach and some not fully resolved issues on the reliability of the results and the data, it would not rely on the simulation results for deciding the case. In the case *Lagardere/Natexis/VUP* [2004] OJ L125/54, the Commission did rely on the results, but only as part of the wider body of evidence. Merger simulation studies were also considered in the cases of *Philip Morris/Papastratos* (2003); *Sydkraft/Graninge* (2003); and *Oracle/Peoplesoft* (2004).

1.305   The idea behind merger simulation is that if one knows the demand elasticities, and knows the model according to which companies compete, it is possible to predict how prices will change once two firms in the model have merged.

1.306   Also when data on certain model parameters are not available (eg the precise cost levels of the firms, or possibly even the price elasticities of some of the products), it may be possible to 'retrieve' these parameters by fitting the market outcome as is predicted by the model for the situation pre-merger (eg in terms of market shares or prices) to the market outcome actually observed pre-merger. This step is called 'calibrating the model'. With all the model parameters available, it is then possible to 'recalculate' the model, but with two firms in the model having merged.

1.307   Merger simulation has so far been developed for three main industry settings: differentiated product markets (where companies are assumed to compete on prices à la Bertrand), commodity markets (where companies are assumed to compete on output à la Cournot), and bidding markets (where competition between firms can be modelled as an auction).

1.308   Provided it is done properly, the main advantage of merger simulation is that it casts some light on the magnitude of effects that can be expected following the merger, and on the question of whether they will be substantial or minimal. In that sense, the technique is a useful companion to merger analysis that mainly relies on the (qualitative) analysis of the change in market structure. Especially in industry settings where market shares are not necessarily informative (in particular, in differentiated product markets, where market definition itself is a difficult exercise, and in bidding markets), merger simulation can provide added value.[188]

1.309   In addition, merger simulation can allow for the explicit consideration of merger efficiencies. When one expects the merger to produce significant cost savings (notably, in the form of marginal cost savings), the model can be recalculated on the basis of the new, lower cost level for the merged entity. Merger simulation is thereby a means to directly assess the *net* impact of a merger on the market. Potentially, this is a major advantage of merger simulation in comparison with more traditional, market structure-based analyses of competition.

1.310   The main weaknesses of merger simulation are also well known. The 'model' content in the exercise is very high, possibly to the detriment of the empirics. In its purest form, empirical analysis is about observing things, and drawing inferences that are consistent with what is observed. Merger simulation also considers data, but draws inferences partly on the basis of a model, which is not the same. For example, when merger simulation involves calibration to obtain information on the value of parameters pre-merger, it obtains such estimates on the basis of a model (the model imposes a 'structure' on the data). Also, for its predictions, merger simulation clearly relies on the correctness of the specific model being used.

1.311   It is therefore important that one follows a strict approach in the application of merger simulation techniques in the assessment of mergers. Leading experts in this field commonly emphasise that it is essential that the model used and the estimates obtained provide a good

---

[188]   Merger simulation may better incorporate the fact that demand substitutability is a matter of degree. The products do not have to be regarded as either 'in' or 'outside' the market.

'fit' for the industry at hand, in that they 'explain' the past history of the industry at a fairly high level of generality,[189] and that sensitivity analysis is performed. When the model does fit the industry, merger simulation has a number of potential advantages. As a general rule, however, it appears best not to rely on merger simulation alone, but to use it as part of a wider body of evidence.

---

[189] G Werden, L Froeb and D Scheffman, 'A Daubert Discipline for Merger Simulation', (2004) 18 Antitrust Magazine 89-95 (the name 'Daubert' refers to the doctrine of the same name of the US Courts with respect to the admissibility of expert economic evidence).

2

THE ENFORCEMENT SYSTEM UNDER REGULATION 1/2003

Eddy De Smijter and Lars Kjølbye

A. The Legal Exception System

(1) Introduction

2.01 Regulation 1/2003 on the implementation of the rules on competition laid down in Articles 81 and 82 of the Treaty[1] has replaced Regulation 17/62[2] with effect from 1 May 2004. The new Regulation introduces a fundamental change in the procedural framework for applying the Community competition rules.

2.02 Regulation 17/62 created a notification and authorisation system whereby undertakings had to notify agreements to the Commission in order to benefit from the exception contained in Article 81(3) of the Treaty. The Commission had exclusive competence to apply this Treaty provision. National competition authorities and courts had no power to apply Article 81(3). Moreover, in the case of horizontal agreements, Article 81(3) could be applied only with effect from the date of notification. Thus agreements which had already been implemented could not benefit from Article 81(3) for the period prior to notification. In the case of vertical agreements, Article 4(2) of Regulation 17/62 allowed for retroactive application of Article 81(3). Commission exemption decisions applying Article 81(3) had the effect of binding national competition authorities and courts until the expiry date of the particular decision.

2.03 Regulation 1/2003 replaces the centralised notification and authorisation system by an enforcement system based on direct application of Articles 81 and 82 as a whole. Now, the Commission, the competition authorities, and courts of the Member States all have the power to apply Articles 81 and 82 in full. Moreover, agreements caught by Article 81(1)

---

[1] [2003] OJ L1/1. Regulation 1/2003 took effect on 1 May 2004. The adoption of the Regulation on 16 December 2002 was preceded by a Commission proposal of 27 September 2000 (COM(2000) 582 final) and a Commission White Paper on modernisation of the rules implementing Arts 81 and 82 of the EC Treaty adopted on 28 April 1999. The present chapter deals only to a limited extent with the history of what eventually became Regulation 1/2003. On the procedural framework under Regulation 1/2003 and its implementation, see R Nazzini *Concurrent Proceedings in Competition Law: Procedure, Evidence and Remedies* (Oxford University Press, 2004), and in particular ch 2, 6, 7 and 8.

[2] First Regulation implementing Arts 81 and 82 of the Treaty [1962] OJ 13/204.

but which satisfy the conditions of Article 81(3) are valid and enforceable, no prior decision to that effect being required.[3] Notification is no longer a condition for Article 81(3) to apply. Indeed, agreements can no longer be notified to the Commission or the national competition authorities as far as the application of Community competition law is concerned. Undertakings themselves must assess whether their agreements and practices comply with Articles 81 and 82. In the new system cases are either initiated *ex officio* or upon complaint.

(2) The Aims of the System Change

The aim of the modernisation reform is to create an enforcement system that ensures more effective enforcement of the Community competition rules throughout the internal market. This overall aim can be broken down into a number of objectives that contribute to achieving this goal. **2.04**

(a) Increased Application of Articles 81 and 82 at Member State Level

Articles 5 and 6, in combination with Article 3(1) of the Regulation, give to national competition authorities and courts the power and obligation to apply Articles 81 and 82 in cases where trade between Member States is capable of being affected. As a result national competition authorities and courts will be involved to a much greater extent in the application of Community competition law. This greater involvement of Member State bodies is often referred to as 'decentralisation'. The reform does indeed imply—and intentionally so—a measure of decentralisation since the Commission's exclusive competence to apply Article 81(3) is abolished. However, the system created by Regulation 1/2003 does not amount to devolution and should not be seen as an exercise in subsidiarity. The Commission retains full parallel competence in all cases and plays a particular role in ensuring consistent application and in defining the orientation of Community competition policy. '*Communitarisation*' of enforcement of competition law, therefore, may be a more fitting term.[4] **2.05**

The greater involvement of national competition authorities has a number of advantages. It paves the way for greater co-operation and coordination of enforcement activities within the Union. The Commission and the national competition authorities have created a network (the European Competition Network) which provides a framework for work sharing and exchanging information. This is intended to ensure that cases are dealt with by the most appropriate authorities. Close co-operation in the application of a common set of rules also promotes consistency and legal certainty by creating a common competition culture. In addition the Regulation contains a number of instruments aimed specifically at ensuring consistency in the application of the law. **2.06**

The elimination of the notification system and the Commission's exclusive power to apply Article 81(3) removes an important obstacle to private enforcement of the Community competition rules. In the system created by Regulation 17/62 private enforcement of **2.07**

---

[3] See Art 1(2) of Regulation 1/2003.

[4] The Regulation is largely limited to regulating issues of procedure at Community level. It only regulates to a very limited extent national procedures. Articles 81 and 82 are applied at Member State level on the basis of Member State rules on procedures and sanctions.

Article 81 could often be effectively blocked by a notification of the agreement to the Commission. If it were not abundantly clear that Article 81(3) was not applicable, the national court would have to suspend proceedings.[5] Being aware of this, complainants generally went direct to the Commission.

2.08   Action by private individuals is an important complement to public enforcement. One does not need to look beyond the borders of the European Union to realise this. In other areas of Community law such as free movement of goods, persons, services, and capital, the development of the law has been driven to a substantial extent by private action; not by Commission action.[6] The Court of Justice has also explicitly recognised the importance of private enforcement in the field of competition.[7] However, it is unlikely that Regulation 1/2003 in itself is sufficient to substantially increase the level of private enforcement in the Community.[8]

(b) Commission Focus on Enforcement

2.09   The Commission, like any other enforcement agency, has limited resources, and from the explanatory memorandum to the Commission's proposal[9] it is clear that the Commission did not consider that the enforcement system of Regulation 17/62 allowed it to make the best use of resources: 'the notification regime no longer constitutes an efficient tool for the protection of competition. It only rarely reveals cases that pose a real threat to competition. In fact, the notification system prevents the Commission's resources from being used for the detection and punishment of serious infringements.'

2.10   One of the objectives of the reform is to allow the Commission to focus its resources in areas where they make a significant contribution to the enforcement of the Community competition rules. Under Regulation 1/2003 the Commission will have three main tasks: (a) to enforce the rules; (b) to develop the orientation of the Community competition rules; and (c) to contribute to the enforcement activities of other enforcers in particular with a view to ensuring consistent application.

2.11   Effective enforcement presupposes both the power to set priorities and the availability of effective tools for that task. The Community Courts recognise the power to set priorities.

---

5   See Case C-234/89 *Stergios Delimitis v Henninger Bräu* [1991] ECR I-935, para 50.

6   One example is the principle confirmed in a preliminary reference case that a Member State may be liable to pay damages caused by a violation of Community law; see in this respect Joined Cases C-46/93 and C-46/93 *Brasserie du Pêcheur and Factortame* [1996] ECR I-1029; and Case C-224/01 *Gerhard Köbler* [2003] ECR I-10239.

7   See Case C-453/99 *Courage v Crehan* [2001] ECR I-6297, paras 26 and 27 where the Court held that the full effectiveness of Art 81 and, in particular, the practical effect of the prohibition laid down in Art 81(1) would be put at risk if it were not open to any individual to claim damages for loss caused to him by a contract or by conduct liable to restrict or distort competition. The Court also held that the existence of such a right strengthens the working of the Community competition rules and discourages agreements or practices, often covert, which are liable to restrict or distort competition and that from that point of view, actions for damages before the national courts can make a significant contribution to the maintenance of effective competition in the Community.

8   See also the Commission Green Paper on damages actions for breach of the EC antitrust rules (COM(2005) 672), available at <http://europa.eu.int/comm/competition/antitrust/others/actions_for_damages/gp_en.pdf>.

9   See COM(2000) 582 final, p 2.

The case law allows the Commission to assign differing degrees of priority to complaints brought before it and to reject complaints for lack of sufficient Community interest.[10] The Commission applies internal principles to set priorities that aim to identify at an early stage the cases that merit further investigation. No single criterion can be decisive in setting priorities. However, given the increasing focus on protecting competition for the benefit of consumers,[11] it can be expected that the likely impact of the alleged infringement on consumers will be an increasingly important element. Given the role of the Commission in defining the orientation of Community competition policy it can also be expected that the Commission will have particular regard to the value of precedents in deciding individual cases.[12]

(3) Self-assessment and Legal Certainty

The abolition of the notification system implies that undertakings cannot require the Commission (or the national competition authorities) to assess the compatibility of their agreements with the Community competition rules and make findings of conformity. Undertakings themselves must assess whether their agreements are compatible with Articles 81 and 82. In making this assessment they can find guidance in the case law and in Commission guidelines.   **2.12**

The Commission has acknowledged that in certain circumstances it may be useful for it to give informal guidance on novel questions concerning the application of Articles 81 and 82. The Commission's policy in this regard is developed in its Notice on guidance letters.[13] Guidance letters are not intended to be a substitute for the notification system that was abolished by Regulation 1/2003. There is no legal right to obtain guidance letters. Such letters are issued at the Commission's discretion taking account of its enforcement priorities. Since the main aim of Regulation 1/2003 is to strengthen enforcement of the Community competition rules, enforcement action will be given priority.[14]   **2.13**

---

[10] See eg Case T-24/90 *Automec v Commission* [1992] ECR II-2223, paras 77 and 85. This case law is reflected in recital 18 of Regulation 1/2003.

[11] See in this respect para 13 of the Commission Guidelines on the application of Art 81(3) of the Treaty [2004] OJ C101/97, and para 5 of the Commission Guidelines on the application of Art 81 of the EC Treaty to technology transfer agreements [2004] OJ C101/2.

[12] The Notice on co-operation within the Network of Competition Authorities, [2004] OJ C101/43, may also have an impact on priority setting at Commission level. It follows from this notice that the Commission is particularly well placed to deal with cases involving agreements and practices that produce effects in more than three Member States; cases that are linked to other provisions of Community law which are exclusively or more efficiently applied by the Commission; and cases where the Community interest requires the adoption of a Commission decision in order to ensure effective enforcement or the development of Community competition policy. It is important to note, however, that the notice only sets out categories of cases where the Commission is *particularly* well placed to act. The Commission's powers of investigation extend to the whole of the Union and the Commission is well placed to deal with cases that are not captured by the criteria set out in the Notice. Moreover, in Case C-344/98 *Masterfoods* [2000] ECR I-11369, para 48, the Court of Justice held that the Commission was entitled to adopt at any time individual decisions under Arts 81 and 82 of the Treaty, even where an agreement or practice has already been the subject of a decision by a national court and the decision contemplated by the Commission conflicts with that national court's decision. It is submitted that the same principle applies in the case of Member State competition authorities.

[13] See Commission Notice on informal guidance relating to novel questions concerning Arts 81 and 82 of the Treaty that arise in individual cases (guidance letters) [2004] OJ C101/78.

[14] So far, no guidance letter has been issued.

2.14 Guidance letters are not formally binding on the Commission. However, according to the notice the Commission will take a previous guidance letter into account, subject in particular to changes in the underlying facts, to any new aspects raised by a complainant, to developments in the case law of the European courts or wider changes in the Commission's policy. It follows that a guidance letter does give rise to a certain legitimate expectation on the part of the recipient. Departure from a previous guidance letter must be justified by the Commission, *inter alia*, in light of the factors cited in the Notice.

2.15 To guide it in the exercise of its discretion the Commission has established a number of criteria against which it will assess whether to respond positively to a request and issue a guidance letter. These criteria operate at three levels: (a) the absence of clarity of the law; (b) the public and private interest in the issue of a guidance letter; and (c) the level of available information and other circumstances pertaining to the request for guidance.

2.16 It is an overriding condition that the issues that are raised with the Commission concern application of the law not previously clarified. If there is existing case law or Commission practice and guidance clarifying the issues raised, then the request for guidance will be denied. The Notice makes clear that the Commission will only issue guidance letters in respect of clearly defined, unresolved issues. The Commission will not consider requests that ask it to take a position on an agreement as a whole.[15]

2.17 At the next level the Commission takes into account public and private interests in determining whether it would be useful to issue a guidance letter. The Notice lists the following elements:

(a) the economic importance from the point of view of the consumer of the goods and services concerned by the agreement or practice; and/or

(b) the extent to which the agreement or practice corresponds to or is liable to correspond to more widely spread economic usage in the marketplace; and/or

(c) the extent of the investment linked to the transaction in relation to the size of the companies concerned and the extent to which the transaction relates to a structural operation such as the creation of a non-full function joint venture.

It follows from the use of the words 'and/or' that each element may lead the Commission to conclude that a guidance letter should be issued. For instance, the combination of a high degree of uncertainty as to the application of the law (level 1) with a high degree of financial risk (level 2) may be sufficient to warrant a guidance letter.

2.18 Finally, there is a requirement that a guidance letter can be issued on the basis of the information provided and that, as a consequence, no further fact-finding is required. It is made clear in the notice that no guidance letter will be issued in cases which are pending before the European Courts, national courts, the Commission or a national competition authority. Moreover, the Commission will not consider hypothetical questions or issue guidance letters in the case of agreements or practices that are no longer being implemented.

---

15 The approach under the notice is somewhat similar to the Art 234 preliminary reference procedure according to which the requesting Member State court is required to specify the issues of interpretation on which it seeks a preliminary ruling.

(4) The Direct Effect of Articles 81 and 82

Articles 81(1) and 82 are directly applicable provisions of Community law, creating rights for **2.19** individuals that can be invoked before national courts.[16] Article 81(3) on the other hand does not have direct effect. This follows from Article 83(2)(b), which requires the Community legislator to lay down detailed rules for the application of Article 81(3). In spite of the content of this provision, which does lend itself to direct application, the power accorded to the Community legislator under Article 83 implies that Article 81(3) is not sufficiently unconditional to produce direct effect. Article 83(2)(b) expressly provides for the adoption of detailed implementing measures as a necessary condition for applying Article 81(3).

When adopting Regulation 17/62 the Community legislator exercised this power to lay **2.20** down detailed rules creating a notification system and granting the Commission the exclusive power to apply Article 81(3). Only the Commission could authorise agreements caught by Article 81(1). Neither national courts nor national competition authorities had the power to apply the exception rule of Article 81(3). If a national court considered a notified agreement to be caught by Article 81(1) it would have to suspend its proceedings and await the outcome of the Commission's proceedings unless it was abundantly clear that the Commission would find the conditions of Article 81(3) had not been satisfied.[17] In cases where the agreement had not been notified and where retroactive notification was not possible[18] the national court would have to strike down the agreement even if it considered that the conditions of Article 81(3) were satisfied. Needless to say, this system led to very limited application of Article 81 at Member State level and it was left almost entirely to the Commission to enforce this important Treaty provision.

Regulation 1/2003 removes the obstacles to effective application of Articles 81 and 82 at **2.21** Member State level by abolishing the exclusive competence of the Commission to apply Article 81(3). This is achieved by rendering Article 81(3) directly applicable. Article 1(2) of Regulation 1/2003 provides that agreements, decisions, and concerted practices caught by Article 81(1) which satisfy the conditions of Article 81(3) shall not be prohibited, no prior decision to that effect being required. Conversely, agreements, decisions, and concerted practices caught by Article 81(1) which do not satisfy the conditions of Article 81(3) are prohibited, no prior decision to that effect being required; see Article 1(1) of the Regulation.[19] It follows that whereas under Regulation 17/62 a formal Commission act was required for the exception to apply, Article 81(3) now applies whenever the four conditions are satisfied. The prohibition rule of Article 81(1) applies as long as the conditions for its application are satisfied and the conditions for the application of the exception rule of Article 81(3) are not satisfied.

National competition authorities are empowered by Article 5 of the Regulation to apply **2.22** Articles 81 and 82. However, it is for the Member States to designate the specific authority

---

[16] See eg Case C-453/99 *Courage v Crehan* [2001] ECR I-6297, para 23.
[17] See in this respect Case C-234/89 *Stergios Delimitis v Henninger Bräu* [1991] ECR I-935, paras 50–54.
[18] See Art 4(2) of Regulation 17/62.
[19] So far as Art 82 is concerned, Art 1(3) provides that the abuse of a dominant position referred to in Art 82 shall be prohibited, no prior decision to that effect being required.

or authorities responsible for the application of Articles 81 and 82. In so doing they must ensure that the Regulation is effectively complied with.[20] Article 6 of the Regulation provides that national courts shall have the power to apply Articles 81 and 82 of the Treaty. However, this provision is in principle superfluous. It follows from Article 1 of the Regulation combined with the principle of direct effect that national courts have the right and the obligation to apply Articles 81 and 82 in full in cases pending before them.

2.23   Various articles of the Regulation make clear that neither at Community nor at national level, is it possible to maintain a notification system for the application of Articles 81 and 82. This is achieved by stipulating exhaustively the manner in which proceedings may be initiated. As far as the Member State competition authorities are concerned Article 5 provides that with a view to adopting specified types of decisions they may act on their own initiative or alternatively on a complaint. They may not act upon a request from parties seeking a positive decision. As is clear from Articles 7–10 the same limitation applies to the Commission. In no case is the Commission empowered to adopt a positive decision upon request.

(5) Burden and Standard of Proof

2.24   Regulation 1/2003 does not affect the substance of Article 81. It merely regulates the procedure for applying this Treaty provision. In particular the Regulation does not change the fact that Article 81 comprises a prohibition rule, requiring an analysis of likely anti-competitive effects, and a defence,[21] requiring an analysis of likely pro-competitive effects and the weighing up of these pro-competitive and anti-competitive effects.[22] Regulation 1/2003 does not lead to an integration of Article 81(1) and (3) and the creation of a unified rule limiting the enquiry to whether, on balance, the agreement is anti-competitive. While the overall analysis provides an answer to this question, the fact remains that the analysis is composed of two separate assessments each subject to distinct rules on the burden of proof.

2.25   Article 2 of Regulation 1/2003 provides that the burden of proving an infringement of Article 81(1) rests on the party or authority alleging the infringement, whereas the undertaking claiming the benefit of Article 81(3) bears the burden of proving that the conditions of that paragraph are satisfied.[23] Article 81(3) is a defence that can be invoked against a finding of an infringement.[24] In accordance with general principles of law it is for the party claiming a defence to prove that the conditions applicable to the defence are satisfied. Moreover, the information required to prove that the conditions of Article 81(3) are satisfied is generally in the hands of the undertaking that seeks to rely on the defence. For instance, the parties to the agreement control the cost data and other information required to substantiate claims that the agreement gives rise to objective economic benefits.

---

[20] See Art 35(1) of Regulation 1/2003.
[21] See recital 5 of Regulation 1/2003.
[22] See recital 5 of Regulation 1/2003.
[23] The allocation in Art 2 of the burden of proof was confirmed by the Court of Justice in Joined Cases C-204/00 and others *Aalborg Portland* [2004] ECR I-124, para 78.
[24] See recital 5 of Regulation 1/2003.

They are also in a better position to explain why the agreement is indispensable for producing efficiencies and to demonstrate the benefits passed on to consumers. If the burden of proof under Article 81(3) were to be placed on the party seeking to establish an infringement the prohibition could be undermined, thereby affecting the very substance of Article 81. Recital 5 also refers to Article 82, stipulating that it is for the party claiming an infringement to prove its existence. This does not mean, however, that the party seeking to establish an infringement must prove the lack of a defence. When stating that it is for the party relying on a defence to prove the existence of conditions for that defence, recital 5 not only refers to Article 81(3), but to all cases in which a defence can be claimed.

Article 2 of the Regulation does not determine the standard of proof. This is reflected in recital 5 according to which the Regulation affects neither national rules on the standard of proof nor obligations on competition authorities and courts of the Member States to ascertain the relevant facts of the case. However, in each case it is a condition that such rules and obligations are compatible with general principles of Community law, in particular with the principle of effectiveness (*effet utile*). This implies in particular that the standard of proof cannot be set at such a high level that the application of Article 81(1) becomes impossible or unduly difficult. In determining the appropriate standard of proof the economic nature of the rule must be taken into account. Moreover, there is nothing to prevent a graduated approach where the standard of proof depends on the nature of the alleged infringement. It is submitted that this is the approach of the European courts. The term 'requisite legal standard' consistently used by the European courts covers a graduated approach with the highest standard being applied in the area of cartels and other cases leading to high fines. **2.26**

The second proviso in recital 5, concerning obligations on national competition authorities and courts to ascertain the relevant facts of the case, was introduced to accommodate concerns in Member States where public authorities are obliged to investigate the case actively, including elements of the case that favour the defendant. The actual wording of recital 5 is inspired by *Consten and Grundig*[25] where the Court held that the Commission 'may not confine itself to requiring from undertakings proof of the fulfilment of the requirements for the grant of exemption but must, as a matter of good administration, play its part, using the means available to it, in ascertaining the relevant facts and circumstances'. This statement does not affect the allocation of the burden of proof. It merely implies that a public authority is obliged to consider of its own motion obvious arguments and facts that may speak in favour of the defendant. The role of the Commission is not to enforce the rules *per se* but to apply the rules pursuant to their underlying aim. The aim of Articles 81 and 82 is to protect competition in the market for the benefit of consumers.[26] Striking down a pro-competitive agreement simply because the defendant did not raise certain obvious facts and arguments would not contribute to the furtherance of this goal. **2.27**

---

[25] See Joined Cases 56/64 and 58/66 *Consten and Grundig* [1966] ECR 429.
[26] See para 13 of the Commission Guidelines on the application of Art 81(3) of the Treaty [2004] OJ C101/97.

B. The Relationship between Community Competition Law and National Competition Law

(1) Introduction

2.28 In the European Union, Community competition law and national competition laws have coexisted. The Treaty does not expressly exclude the application of national competition laws to agreements and practices capable of affecting trade between Member States. However, dual application raises the question of which law prevails in case of conflict. Two theories have been put forward.[27] Under the so-called double barrier theory conflicts are solved in favour of the strictest rule. Prohibitions always win. Under the so-called single barrier theory Community law trumps national law in case of conflict, whether or not Community law is stricter. Until the adoption of Regulation 1/2003, the relationship between Community competition law and national competition law was regulated exclusively by the principle of primacy of Community law laid down by the Court of Justice in *Walt Wilhelm*.[28] Regulation 17/62 did not regulate the relationship between Community competition law and national competition law. In *Walt Wilhelm* the Court held that parallel application of national competition law is only permissible in so far as it does not prejudice the uniform application throughout the common market of the Community competition rules.

2.29 Regulation 1/2003, on the other hand, makes use of the power laid down in Article 83(2)(e) of the Treaty for the Community legislator to regulate the relationship between national competition law and the Community competition rules. These regulatory rules are contained in Article 3, which constitutes one of the pillars of the enforcement system created by Regulation 1/2003.

2.30 Article 3 follows the line of *Walt Wilhelm* to the extent that it does not exclude the application of national competition law to agreements and practices capable of affecting trade between Member States.[29] Parallel application of Community competition law and national competition law remains possible. However, the application of national competition law is subject to two important conditions. First, whenever the national competition authorities and courts apply national competition law to agreements and abusive practices, which may affect trade between Member States, they must also apply Articles 81 and 82 (see Article 3(1)). Secondly, agreements which may affect trade between Member States and which are not prohibited under Community competition law cannot be prohibited under national competition law (see Article 3(2)).[30] This latter obligation is referred to as the '*convergence rule*'. The convergence rule only applies to agreements; it does not apply in the field of unilateral conduct, ie *part* of the scope of application of Article 82.

---

[27] For a discussion see Waelbroeck & Frignani, *Commentaire Megret, Concurrence* (1997) Ch 3.

[28] Case 14/68 *Walt Wilhelm* [1969] ECR 1. The primacy principle is dealt with in section C.5 below.

[29] The Commission's original proposal (COM(2000) 582 final of 27 September 2000) provided for exclusive application of Arts 81 and 82 to agreements and abusive practices capable of affecting trade between Member States.

[30] These two obligations ensure that Art 3 achieves essentially the same aims as the Commission's original proposal.

(2) Article 3(1): The Obligation to Apply Articles 81 and 82

Article 3(1) provides that where the competition authorities and courts of the Member **2.31**
States apply national competition law to agreements, decisions of associations of undertakings, or concerted practices within the meaning of Article 81(1) which may affect trade
between Member States, or to any abuse prohibited by Article 82, they must also apply
Articles 81 and 82 to such agreements, decisions or concerted practices.

(a) *Scope of Article 3(1)*

National competition authorities and courts have the power to apply national competition **2.32**
laws to agreements and abusive practices of dominant undertakings, which may affect
trade between Member States. However, when they do so, they are obliged to also apply
Articles 81 and 82.

Article 3(1) only imposes obligations as to the application of national competition law. **2.33**
Nothing prevents national competition authorities and courts from applying only Articles
81 and 82 to agreements and practices capable of affecting trade between Member States.

Under Article 3(1) there are only two situations in which the Community competition **2.34**
rules need not be applied:

(a) the agreement or practice is not capable of affecting trade between Member States; or
(b) the case involves the application of *stricter* national competition laws to unilateral con-
    duct which does not constitute an abuse prohibited by Article 82.

The latter situation may arise where national law is applied to unilateral conduct below the
level of dominance or to unilateral conduct which is not considered abusive within the
meaning of Article 82. In those circumstances Article 82 is not applicable and as a consequence
the obligation contained in Article 3(1) does not apply. It is not sufficient to escape the obligation of Article 3(1) that national law has a wider scope of application than Article 82. There
must be stricter application in the individual case. Moreover, to the extent that Article 82
is applied to certain parts of the case, Article 3(1) applies to those parts.

The facility for national competition authorities and courts to apply stricter national com- **2.35**
petition laws to unilateral conduct follows from the scope of application of Article 3(2).
The convergence rule does not apply to unilateral conduct leaving open the application of
stricter national competition laws to such conduct.

However, given the obligation to apply Article 82 when this Treaty provision is applicable **2.36**
and the fact that a decision adopted in breach of Article 3(1) is challengeable[31] Member
State competition authorities and courts are as a practical matter obliged to give reasons
why Community law is not being applied. Article 3(1) thereby increases transparency.
Moreover, in cases where the national law provision applying to unilateral conduct is a copy
of Article 82, it may be difficult to justify why that national law prohibition should be given
a wider interpretation than that contained in Article 82. This is particularly true of
Member States like the United Kingdom where there is an obligation under national law to

---

[31] See section 4 below.

interpret provisions of national competition law in accordance with Community law precedents.[32] It is likely, therefore, that the main scope for applying stricter national competition law to unilateral conduct will be found where a national law prohibition covers conduct engaged in by firms that are not dominant.

2.37 All agreements capable of affecting trade between Member States are covered by the convergence rule in Article 3(2), which precludes the application of stricter national competition laws. The combination of Article 3(1) and (2) thus excludes all stand-alone application of national competition laws to agreements capable of affecting trade between Member States. In the field of agreements parallel application of national competition law serves only one purpose, namely to protect national proceedings against legal challenges based on the effect on trade criterion. If Member State enforcers were obliged to make a choice between national law and Community law in each and every case, depending on whether trade between Member States was capable of being affected, there would be a risk that the choice made would be challenged systematically. While the effect on trade concept has been substantially clarified in the case law of the European courts, the Community legislator considered it desirable to enable national competition authorities and courts to avoid such challenges by applying a double legal base. Even if one legal base falls, the decision still stands.

(b) Primary Functions of Article 3(1)

2.38 Recital 8 of Regulation 1/2003 explains that Article 3(1) serves the purpose of ensuring effective enforcement of the Community competition rules and the proper functioning of the co-operation mechanisms contained in the Regulation.

2.39 The obligation to apply Articles 81 and 82 to agreements and abusive practices affecting trade between Member States increases the number of cases in which the Community competition rules are being applied. It thereby ensures that they are enforced more effectively. Article 3(1) changes fundamentally the situation prevailing under Regulation 17/62 where there was very little application of Articles 81 and 82 at Member State level. In particular, the national competition authorities applied national competition law almost exclusively. In an enlarged European Union, national competition authorities and courts need to participate actively in the enforcement of Articles 81 and 82. As is clear from other areas of Community law the Commission alone cannot ensure effective enforcement of the law. The principle of direct effect on which Regulation 1/2003 is based has contributed greatly to the effective enforcement of Community law.[33]

2.40 The second objective referred to in recital 8 relates to the co-operation mechanism contained in Regulation 1/2003. These co-operation mechanisms concern the relationship between the competition authorities, including the Commission, and between national courts and the Commission. It is a precondition for applying these co-operation mechanisms that

---

[32] See s 60 of the UK Competition Act. It is not necessary for individual rights to be conferred by a Community measure for that measure to be held to have direct effect, see in this respect Case C-194/94 *CIA International* [1996] ECR I-2201; and Case C-72/95 *Kraaijeveld* [1996] ECR I-5403. The principle of direct effect was developed first and foremost to ensure the effective application of Community law.
[33] For a recent example see Case C-198/01 *Consorzio Industrie Fiammiferi (CIF)* [2003] ECR I-8055.

Articles 81 and 82 are applied.[34] By creating an obligation to do so, Article 3(1) ensures the effectiveness of the co-operation mechanisms. In the absence of Article 3(1) the co-operation mechanisms could have been avoided simply by applying national competition law.

The co-operation mechanisms contained in the Regulation are aimed particularly at ensuring effective enforcement and at maintaining consistent application within the internal market. The main co-operation mechanisms are contained in Article 11, which constitutes the legal backbone of the European Competition Network (ECN).[35] The main function of the ECN is to promote effective enforcement by ensuring an efficient use of resources as well as consistent application of the Community competition rules. These two aims are reflected in Article 11 of Regulation 1/2003. According to Article 11(3) the competition authorities of the Member States must inform the Commission of new cases at an early stage. Similarly, under Article 11(2), the Commission must inform the Member State competition authorities of new cases. This information provides a basis for reallocating individual cases to other authorities that are well placed to deal with them. Moreover, Article 11(4) provides that the national competition authorities must inform the Commission no later than thirty days before they adopt a negative decision and provide a copy of the draft decision or any other document setting out the envisaged course of action. This obligation ensures that policy questions and other issues requiring consistent application are discussed within the ECN before a decision is adopted. In the case of disagreement, the Commission has the power to resolve the conflict and protect consistency by withdrawing the case from the Member State competition authority in question. According to Article 11(6) the competition authorities of the Member States are relieved of their competence to apply Articles 81 and 82 when the Commission opens proceedings in the same case. **2.41**

It is important to appreciate the relationship between Article 3 and 11(6). The opening of proceedings by the Commission under Article 11(6) only relieves the Member State competition authorities of their competence to apply Articles 81 and 82. However, when combined with Article 3, the opening of proceedings will in a great many cases also prevent the Member State competition authorities from acting under national competition law. In combination, Article 3(1) and 3(2) limit the scope for stand-alone application of national competition law. Such application only remains possible in respect of aspects of cases that involve the application of stricter national law to unilateral conduct. In all other cases stand-alone application of national competition law is excluded. In the case of agreements capable of affecting trade between Member States national competition law can only be applied in parallel with the Community competition rules. The same is true of unilateral conduct prohibited by Article 82. In the case of such conduct national competition law can only be applied in parallel with Community law. In all these cases the application of Community law is thus a *sine qua non* for applying national competition law. When the Commission opens proceedings under Article 11(6) this condition can no longer be satisfied since the national competition authorities are no longer competent to **2.42**

---

[34] With the limited exception of Art 12(2) the Regulation does not lay down rules on co-operation in the application of national competition law.
[35] See section E.2 below.

apply Articles 81 and 82 in the case at hand. National competition law therefore cannot be applied.

(3) The Convergence Rule of Article 3(2)

2.43 Recital 8 explains that, in order to create a level playing field for agreements,[36] it is necessary to provide that the application of national competition laws to agreements within the meaning of Article 81(1) may not lead to the prohibition of such agreements if they are not also prohibited under Community competition law. This is reflected in Article 3(2) according to which the application of national competition laws must not lead to the prohibition of agreements, decisions of associations of undertakings, or concerted practices[37] which may affect trade between Member States but which do not restrict competition within the meaning of Article 81(1), or which fulfil the conditions of Article 81(3), or which are covered by a block exemption Regulation for the application of Article 81(3). Recital 8 also explains that Member States should not be precluded under the Regulation from adopting and applying on their territory stricter national competition laws which prohibit or impose sanctions on unilateral conduct engaged in by undertakings. These stricter national laws may include provisions which prohibit or impose sanctions on behaviour towards economically dependent undertakings. In this respect Article 3(2) does not prevent the application of stricter national competition laws to unilateral conduct engaged in by undertakings. It follows that the relevant distinction within Article 3(2) is between agreements and unilateral conduct. It is not between Article 81 and 82 or between dominant firms and non-dominant firms. Dominant undertakings also benefit from the convergence rule of Article 3(2). This interpretation is confirmed by recital 8 according to which agreements within the meaning of Article 81(1) cannot be prohibited if they are not also prohibited by 'Community competition law', ie Articles 81 and 82. This also follows from the fact that Article 81 applies to any agreement capable of affecting trade between Member States irrespective of the market position of the parties. Article 81 covers the complete range from zero market share to monopoly. In the field of agreements Articles 81 and 82 overlap. Articles 81 and 82 may apply simultaneously to the same practice.[38]

2.44 The aim of Article 3(2) is to create a level playing field within the internal market for agreements capable of affecting trade between Member States. Such agreements are subject to a

---

[36] The notions of agreements, decisions, and concerted practices are autonomous concepts of Community competition law covering the coordination of undertakings on the market as interpreted by the Community Courts, see recital 8 of the Regulation.

[37] In the following the term 'agreement' covers 'agreements', 'decisions', and 'concerted practices'.

[38] See Joined Cases C-395/96 P and C-396/96 P *Compagnie maritime belge* [2000] ECR I-1365, para 33. Articles 81 and 82 pursue the same aim: see Case 6/72 *Continental Can* [1973] ECR 215, para 25. The analysis of the same set of facts under either Article should therefore lead to the same result. In particular, as both provisions aim at protecting competition in the market (see recital 9 to Regulation 1/2003) it is difficult to imagine an agreement which would not be restrictive of competition within the meaning of Art 81(1) but would nevertheless constitute an abuse under Art 82. It may happen that a block-exempted agreement is abusive. In that case, national competition authorities and courts have the power to apply Art 82, since a block exemption does not prevent the application of Art 82. However, as a consequence of Art 3(2), national competition authorities and courts are precluded from applying national competition law to block exempted agreements.

single competition law standard, namely that of Articles 81 and 82. They cannot be prohibited by national competition law. Article 3(2) thereby relieves undertakings of the burden of having to check their agreements against up to twenty-six different sets of competition rules.[39] The obligation in Article 3(2) prevents the adoption of decisions that prohibit agreements capable of affecting trade between Member States which are not prohibited by Community competition law.

Article 3(2) does not prevent the application of instruments of national competition law **2.45** in the investigatory phase. For instance, Article 3(2) does not prevent the application of market investigation instruments and the drawing up of reports on the functioning of particular markets. It follows that Article 3(2) does not interfere with the exercise of powers such as those conferred on the Commission under Article 17 of Regulation 1/2003. Under this Article the Commission may conduct an inquiry into particular sectors of the economy or into a particular type of agreement across various sectors and publish a report on the results of its inquiry. However, when it comes to acting upon any recommendation contained in such reports the obligation contained in Article 3(2) must be complied with.[40] This means that agreements identified in a report resulting from an inquiry can only be prohibited in so far as they are also prohibited under Community competition law. For instance, if in an inquiry it is found that the functioning of a market could be improved by reducing the duration of contracts imposing exclusive purchasing obligations on retailers, such a finding can only be implemented if the agreements in question infringe the Community competition rules. This would require that the agreements in question affect actual or potential competition to such an extent that on the relevant market negative effects on prices, output, innovation, or the variety or quality of good and services can be expected with a reasonable degree of probability and that the agreements do not satisfy the conditions of Article 81(3), for instance because the restrictions are reasonably necessary to recoup a pro-competitive investment.[41]

The prohibition on applying stricter national competition laws to agreements capable of **2.46** affecting trade between Member States applies in all cases where an agreement is not prohibited by Community competition law. The reason for non-prohibition under Community competition law may be that the agreement in question does not restrict competition in the first place or that it is covered by the exception in Article 81(3) either following individual assessment or by virtue of a block exemption. In the case of non-restrictive agreements it is immaterial whether the agreement falls outside Article 81(1) either because the agreement does not give rise to any restriction of competition or because it does not appreciably restrict competition. Agreements that are de minimis under Community law cannot be prohibited under national competition law.

---

[39] Ideally, the same principle should apply in the case of unilateral conduct. See in this respect the Commission's original proposal (COM(2000) 582 final of 27 September 2000). However, this proposal did not find sufficient support in the Council.

[40] Similarly the obligation contained in Art 3(1) must be complied with. The case for imposing remedies must therefore also be argued on the basis of Community law.

[41] See the Commission's Guidelines on the application of Art 81(3) of the Treaty [2004] OJ C101/97, paras 24 and 44.

2.47 Before the adoption of Regulation 1/2003 it was argued by some that what may not be appreciable from a Community perspective may be appreciable from a Member State perspective and that in such cases Member States should not be subject to Article 3. This argument was rejected, rightly. It is based on the erroneous assumption that the perspective necessarily differs under Community competition law and national competition law in terms of the effects that are taken into account.[42] The Community competition rules constitute a fully-fledged system in its own right and are not intended as a supplement to the national systems. Articles 81 and 82 not only pursue the objective of market integration. Their primary and fundamental objective is to preserve undistorted competition and open competitive markets.[43] Moreover, Articles 81 and 82 cover not only restrictions that interfere directly with cross-border trade, but also all other restrictions of competition that are common to fully fledged competition laws. When, for example, foreclosure effects are analysed under Articles 81 and 82, not only are the effects on undertakings from other Member States taken into account but the Community competition rules, when applicable, also require that a full analysis be made of the possibilities available to all competitors to enter the market or expand their market positions.

2.48 The application of Article 3(2) does not create an enforcement lacuna at Member State level. Agreements are analysed within the confines of a relevant antitrust market, which is defined on the basis of the possibilities for substitution. When markets are held to be Community-wide it is not because Articles 81 and 82 apply to the whole of the European Union but because it is found that suppliers in the Community place an effective competitive constraint on each other due to the absence of barriers to entry.[44] When significant barriers to entry exist the geographic market will be defined more narrowly. Agreements which are capable of affecting trade between Member States and which do not appreciably restrict competition within the relevant market are compatible with Article 81(1). This is because such agreements produce only insignificant anti-competitive effects, if any, within the relevant market and, as a consequence, are either neutral or pro-competitive. There is no good reason why the outcome should differ under national competition law. In particular, there is no reason why, within the same relevant antitrust market, the notion of appreciability should differ depending on which law applies.

---

[42] In Case 14/68 *Walt Wilhelm* [1969] ECR 1 the Court of Justice held that Member State law and Community law view practices from a different perspective. However, the Court made this finding in the context of rejecting the argument that the principle of *ne bis in idem* prevents the fining of a restrictive agreement under both Member State law and Community law. The Court thus ensured that the application of Community law would not be barred because of the prior application of national law, which from a Community law perspective would have been undesirable. The judgment does not imply that the substantive analytical approach under Community law and Member State law is inherently different.

[43] See in this respect Case C-198/01 *Consorzio Industrie Fiammiferi (CIF)* [2003] ECR I-8055, para 47.

[44] According to the so-called SSNIP test, the relevant geographic market must be expanded to include neighbouring areas, if a hypothetical monopolist in the area tested would not be able to raise prices 5–10% without attracting entry from neighbouring areas to such an extent that the price increase would be unprofitable. In that case the products offered by suppliers in these other areas are substitutable and thus place an effective competitive constraint on the hypothetical monopolist in the test area.

(4) The Legal Consequences of Infringing Article 3(1) and 3(2)

Articles 3(1) and 3(2) have direct effect. Both provisions impose unconditional and precise **2.49**
obligations on national competition authorities and courts, which undertakings can rely
on directly. Moreover, it is submitted that decisions adopted in breach of the obligations
contained in Article 3 are invalid and unenforceable.

The obligation contained in Article 3(1) constitutes a fundamental procedural safeguard. **2.50**
The importance of Article 3(1) derives from the fact that national competition authorities
and courts are also obliged to argue their cases on the basis of Articles 81 and 82, rendering
transparent any deviation on the basis of national competition law.[45] Thus it strengthens
the effectiveness of Article 3(2) and the fundamental principle of primacy of Community
law. Moreover, Article 3(1) is of fundamental importance due to its intrinsic link to the network mechanisms and in particular Article 11(4) and (6). The act of applying Community
law triggers further obligations aimed at ensuring consistent application and protecting the
integrity of the internal market. Article 3(1) is thus not a mere formality.[46] It is the glue that
makes the rest of the Regulation stick. As an essential procedural requirement, the failure
to respect Article 3(1) affects the very substance of the decision and thereby its validity.[47]
If the competition authorities and courts of the Member States fail to observe the obligation
imposed by Article 3(1), they expose their decisions to legal challenges and invalidity.

Article 3(2), like Article 3(1), is a directly applicable rule that can be relied on before national **2.51**
courts. Moreover, it is a rule of substance the effect of which is to relieve undertakings of the
burden of having to comply with more than one set of rules. By prescribing a common competition law standard, Article 3(2) creates a level playing field within the internal market.
Against this background it would appear beyond doubt that a decision adopted in breach of
Article 3(2) is invalid and unenforceable. In this respect the provision has the same effect as
any other directly effective rule of Community law, rendering inapplicable any conflicting
Member State measures.

(5) Article 3 and the Primacy Rule

According to the primacy rule the application of national law must not prejudice the full **2.52**
and uniform application of the Community competition rules within the internal market.
In *Walt Wilhelm*[48] the Court of Justice held, *inter alia*, that agreements benefiting from an
exemption under Article 81(3) cannot be prohibited by national competition law.
However, the Court has not had occasion to rule on the applicability of the primacy rule to
agreements and practices which are not caught by Article 81(1), because they do not
restrict competition within the meaning of that provision.[49] The number of such cases has

---

[45] It is submitted that the term 'apply' contained in Art 3(1) implies that Arts 81 and 82 must find expression in the operative part of the decision.
[46] Compare in this respect the information mechanism considered by the Court of Justice in Case 380/89
Enichem Base [1989] ECR 2491.
[47] See in this respect Case C-194/94 *CIA International* [1996] ECR I-2201 and section E.2.b.iii below.
[48] See Case 14/68 *Walt Wilhelm* [1969] ECR 1.
[49] It has been forcefully argued by Tesauro AG in Case C-266/93 *Volkswagen* [1995] ECR I-3479 (see paras
58 and 59 of the opinion) that when the Court of Justice or the Commission have found that an agreement

increased considerably in recent years as a consequence of the application of a more effects-based approach to Article 81(1).

2.53 Article 3(2) removes uncertainty as to the scope of the primacy rule by establishing in addition a clear convergence rule for the non-prohibition aspect of Article 81(1). Agreements that fall outside the prohibition of Article 81(1), because from the point of view of Community competition law they do not restrict competition at all or do not restrict it appreciably, cannot be prohibited by stricter national competition laws. Article 3 also creates a stronger rule by requiring that Member State authorities must also argue the case on the basis of Community law. Under the primacy rule, undertakings must prove to the requisite legal standard that there is a conflict between a Community law measure and a national law measure. By virtue of Article 3 national competition authorities and courts are obliged to apply Articles 81 and 82 and are precluded from deviating from the Community law outcome when considering agreements.

2.54 Importantly, however, Regulation 1/2003 leaves the primacy rule untouched. This clear and necessary intention finds expression in the second sentence of Article 3(2) according to which 'Member States shall not *under this Regulation* be precluded from adopting and applying on their national territory stricter national laws which prohibit or sanction unilateral conduct engaged in by undertakings' (emphasis added). It is also expressed in Article 3(3) according to which the exceptions contained in that provision are 'without prejudice to general principles and other provisions of Community law'. It follows in particular that Article 3 does not in any way interfere with the fundamental principle according to which Community law prohibitions trump more lenient treatment under Member State law.[50] It also leaves open the possibility for further developments of the non-prohibition aspect of the primacy rule, which remains relevant to unilateral conduct. On the basis of the *Walt Wilhelm*, it can be argued that in cases where the Commission adopts a non-infringement decision under Article 10 of Regulation 1/2003, and finds that certain unilateral conduct does not constitute an abuse of a dominant position, that conduct cannot be prohibited under national competition law. Article 10 decisions relating to the application of Articles 81 and 82 are to be adopted only in the Community public interest and it is submitted that such decisions constitute positive action in the same way as the exemption decisions adopted under Regulation 17/62.[51] Indeed, it follows from Article 16 of Regulation 1/2003

---

affecting trade between Member States does not constitute a threat to competition for the purposes of Art 81(1), such an agreement cannot be prohibited under national law, the requirements for asserting the primacy of Community law being satisfied. Even if the Court of Justice were to concur with this interpretation, Article 3 would retain its importance since its application does not depend on the existence of a prior Community act. Article 3 obliges Member State courts and competition authorities to apply Arts 81 and 82 to all agreements and abusive practices capable of affecting trade between Member States and precludes any application of stricter national competition laws to agreements.

  50 For a recent expression of this principle see Case T-203/01 *Michelin (II)* [2003] ECR II, para 112 where the Court of First Instance held that the fact that the practice in question was compatible with national law was immaterial given the primacy of Community law and the direct effect of Art 82.

  51 In para 5 of the judgment in *Walt Wilhelm* the Court of Justice acknowledged that the Treaty permits the Community authorities to carry out certain positive, though indirect, action with a view to promoting a harmonious development of economic activities within the Community. Article 10 of Regulation 1/2003 is a reflection of this principle.

that the national competition authorities and courts cannot adopt decisions that run counter to, *inter alia*, non-infringement decisions adopted by the Commission.[52] While Article 16 only applies to Member State decisions adopted on the basis of Articles 81 and 82, it can be argued that the purpose of Article 10 read in conjunction with Article 16, namely to enable the Commission to develop Community competition policy and to promote its consistent application throughout the internal market, must be taken into account in the application of the primacy rule.

(6) Exceptions to Article 3

Article 3(1) and (2) cover national competition laws. They do not apply to other national **2.55** laws. Moreover, the last paragraph of Article 3 contains two express exceptions, the second being a reflection of the general limitation of the scope of application of Article 3 to national competition laws. According to Article 3(3), Article 3(1) and (2) do not apply when national competition authorities and courts apply national merger control laws. They also do not preclude the application of provisions of national laws that predominantly pursue an objective different from that pursued by Articles 81 and 82. Finally, the last sentence of recital 8 provides that Regulation 1/2003 does not apply to national laws that impose criminal sanctions on natural persons except to the extent that such sanctions are the means by which competition rules applying to undertakings are enforced.

(a) National Competition Laws

As stated above, Article 3, including the convergence rule of Article 3(2), applies only to **2.56** national competition laws.[53] It does not apply to other types of national laws. It is submitted that it could not be otherwise. Indeed, it is not because an agreement is compatible with the Community competition rules that it is immune to intervention on the basis of any other type of law. The purpose of Article 3 is to ensure effective enforcement of Articles 81 and 82 and to create a level playing field for agreements in the area of competition law, not to prevent Member States from interfering with agreements in the pursuit of legitimate objectives other than the protection of competition. Such measures enacted by Member States must, however, comply with the Treaty rules and secondary legislation in the field of free movement of goods, services, persons, and capital.

According to Article 3(3) the point of departure is each individual provision of national law **2.57** and not the overall statute in which it is contained. For each relevant provision it must be determined whether or not it is a provision of national competition law. Both Article 3(3) and recital 9 include guidance as to what constitutes a provision of national competition law, in particular as regards the distinction between national competition laws and national laws on unfair trading practices. Under Article 3(3) a provision does not to lie within the sphere of national competition law if it predominantly[54] pursues an objective different

---

[52] Article 16 codifies the judgment of the Court of Justice in Case C-344/98 *Masterfoods* [2000] ECR I-11369.

[53] This was also the case with the Commission's original proposal.

[54] In the case of provisions with multiple objectives, the predominant objective must be ascertained. This assessment must be made provision by provision.

from that pursued by Articles 81 and 82. Recital 9 explains that Articles 81 and 82 have as their objective the protection of competition on the market. The meaning of the term 'protection of competition on the market' becomes clearer when read in conjunction with Article 3(1)(g) of the Treaty, according to which distortion of competition in the internal market must be avoided.[55] Competition is distorted when agreements and practices interfere with the competitive process. When viewed as process competition implies that economic operators seek to attract demand by offering products that consumers want.[56] The competitive process is an interplay between existing and new players on the market. Articles 81 and 82 apply[57] to agreements and practices that harm existing competition and prevent new competition from developing.[58]

2.58 Provisions of national law covered by Article 3 are those that predominantly pursue the objective of protecting competition on the market and which therefore prohibit acts that have actual or presumed effects on competition on the market. The reference to '*actual or presumed effects*' is very important. It reflects the distinction between restrictions of competition by object and restrictions of competition by effect, which is recognised in most competition law systems and which implies that no analysis of anti-competitive effects is required in respect of certain types of restraints. It is thus not decisive whether the application of the national law provision in question requires market analysis. National *per se* rules are covered by Article 3 to the extent that they predominantly pursue the objective of protecting competition on the market. This is the case where the prohibition is imposed because it is presumed that the agreement or conduct in question produces adverse effects on the market. The only difference between 'by object' rules and 'by effect' rules is the fact that in the former case the assessment of the impact on the market is made *ex ante* at the time of adoption of the rule, obviating the need to analyse the effect on competition in individual cases.

2.59 The distinction between national competition laws and other laws may be particularly difficult to draw in repect of national unfair trading laws. Recital 9 explains that the exception of Article 3(3) covers:

> . . . national legislation that prohibits or imposes sanctions on acts of unfair trading practice, be they unilateral or contractual. Such legislation pursues a specific objective, irrespective of the actual or presumed effects of such acts on competition on the market. This is particularly the case of legislation which prohibits undertakings from imposing on their trading partners obtaining or attempting to obtain from them terms and conditions that are unjustified, disproportionate or without consideration.

---

[55] As to the relationship between Art 3(1)(g) and Arts 81 and 82, see eg Case 6/72 *Continental Can* [1973] ECR 215, para 23.

[56] In the context of Art 82 this process is referred to as competition on the merits, see eg Case T-203/01 *Michelin (II)* [2003] ECR II, paras 54 and 97.

[57] This is not meant to imply that an agreement or practice is prohibited merely because it impacts on the competitive process. At the end of the day what matters is the overall impact on consumers' welfare.

[58] In Joined Cases C-241/91 P and C-242/91 P *RTE* (*Magill*) [1995] ECR I-743, a refusal to license was prohibited because it prevented the introduction of a new product. In Case C-234/89 *Delimitis* [1991] ECR I-935, the Court held that the impact of networks of agreements on the possibility for new entry must be examined.

It is submitted that the main distinguishing feature between the examples of provisions of unfair trading laws referred to in the last sentence of recital 9 and provisions of national competition law is whether the aim of the provision is confined to regulating a contractual relationship with a view to protecting a weaker party against a stronger party or whether (in addition) the market context is taken into account either in the elaboration of the rule or its application. The reference to competition on the market implies that the objective of the national law provision must go beyond the mere regulation of a (contractual) relationship between two undertakings. As soon as it is, for instance, a condition for the application of the national law provision that one of the parties possesses market power, the provision should be qualified as one of national competition law. Similarly, provisions of national law that aim at protecting smaller undertakings in a market against their larger competitors should be qualified as competition law provisions. Even if for lack of appreciable restrictive effects no violation were to be found under Articles 81 and 82, the fact remains that such provisions aim at protecting competition on the market, which is the decisive element.

2.60 Provisions of national law that regulate contractual relationships by stipulating what are the terms and conditions that must be offered—for instance, by a supplier to distributors—should frequently be classified as provisions of unfair trading law. For example, Directive 86/653 on commercial agents[59] regulates, *inter alia*, termination notices and the compensation that must be provided by the principal to the agent in a case of termination of the agreement. Such measures are wholly unrelated to the actual or presumed impact of the agreement on competition on the market and therefore fall outside the scope of application of Article 3. Similarly, provisions in unfair trading laws applying to non-contractual relationships such as provisions prohibiting passing-off apply irrespective of the market context and any actual or presumed effects on competition. For instance, the assessment of whether a firm has applied a layout which is unduly close to that of another firm is a question which can and should be answered without taking into account market factors such as the market position of the defendant.

2.61 In some cases it may be relevant to consider the extent to which the national law provision aims at protecting consumer welfare.[60] It is submitted that such provisions should qualify as provisions of national competition law where they regulate the conduct of undertakings in relation to other undertakings. For instance, if a provision of national law prohibits exclusive dealing in a particular sector because such dealing is considered to reduce choice for consumers the provision in question should be considered to belong to the sphere of national competition law. In the case of provisions that directly regulate the conduct of undertakings in respect of final consumers, relying on the consumer welfare criterion is more difficult. Consumer protection legislation, which is not covered by Article 3, can also be said to promote consumer welfare, although in a different way. It is submitted that contrary to competition laws, consumer protection laws are first and foremost based on

---

[59] Directive 86/653 on the coordination of the laws of the Member States relating to self-employed commercial agents [1986] OJ L382/17.

[60] The Commission Guidelines on the application of Art 81(3) [2004] OJ L101/97, para 13, provide that the objective of Art 81 is to protect competition on the market as a means of enhancing consumers' welfare and of ensuring an efficient allocation of resources.

principles of fairness. While Article 82 admittedly also contains elements of fairness[61] it is submitted that its core aim is to prevent agreements and unilateral conduct that interfere with the competitive process and thereby produce inferior market outcomes in terms of prices, quality, output, variety, innovation, etc. Provisions of national consumer protection law that prohibit certain kinds of advertising[62] or certain commercial practices such as 'cold calling'[63] are not concerned with market outcomes but rather with protecting consumers against undue influences caused by certain commercial practices.

(b) National Laws Implementing Community Law Directives

2.62 Over time the Community has adopted a number of directives aimed at liberalising various sectors of the economy such as telecommunications, gas, and electricity. Such measures are intended to introduce competition into and protect such competition on the market. They thus pursue the same primary objective as Articles 81 and 82, which are not limited to protecting existing competition. They also apply to agreements and conduct that prevent new competition from developing.[64]

2.63 The question remains, however, whether national measures implementing such directives can be considered to constitute provisions of 'national law'. Given their Community law origin, it can be argued that such measures do not constitute national competition laws for the purposes of Article 3. While such measures are incorporated into national law, the implementation of a Community directive into national law is often a fairly mechanical process, which does not deprive the measure of its Community law origins. However, to the extent that a measure implementing a Community directive contains provisions that are not derived from the directive, such provisions clearly constitute provisions of national competition law for the purposes of Article 3, provided that they pursue predominantly the same objective as Articles 81 and 82. Since the assessment is made provision by provision it is immaterial that the overall measure implements a Community directive.

2.64 In interpreting the notion of 'national law', it is necessary to consider the impact on the effectiveness of Regulation 1/2003, of excluding from the scope of Article 3 provisions of national law that implement Community directives. It is clear that including such measures under Article 3 enhances the effectiveness of the network and the mechanisms for maintaining consistency. The exclusion from Article 3 of Member States implementing provisions implies that the various co-operation mechanisms contained in Regulation 1/2003 may not come into play because they only apply in cases where Articles 81 and 82 are being applied. However, while it may be desirable to enhance co-operation in all areas of competition law enforcement, it is not clear that Article 3 was intended to impose networking in areas covered by special Community law regimes. Indeed, these measures may set out special co-operation mechanisms that are tailored to the specific instrument.[65] Moreover, given the common origin of the provisions in question, the risk of inconsistency is less pronounced than in the case

---

[61] See eg Case T-203/01 *Michelin (II)* [2003] ECR II, para 150.
[62] See eg Joined Cases 34-36/95 *De Agostini* [1997] ECR I-3843.
[63] See eg Case C-384/93 *Alpine Investments* [1995] ECR I-1141.
[64] See section 6.a. above.
[65] See eg Art 7 of Directive (EC) 2002/21 on a common regulatory framework for electronic communications networks and services [2002] OJ L108/33.

of measures adopted and applied purely within each national legal order. Community liberalisation measures contain common rules that are specifically tailored to opening up the sectors in question. In contrast to purely national measures, it may reasonably be assumed that, in devising these rules, the Community interest has been taken into account and that consequently there is less need to insist on systematic parallel application of Articles 81 and 82. It remains to be seen how the European courts will interpret the concept of national competition law contained in Article 3.

(c) Member State Measures Covered by Article 86 of the Treaty

According to Article 86 of the Treaty, Member State measures that grant special or exclusive **2.65** rights to undertakings are subject to the rules of the Treaty including Articles 81 and 82. Member State measures granting special or exclusive rights do not constitute national competition laws for the purposes of Article 3. Indeed, they restrict competition rather than protecting it. The very purpose of Article 86 is to ensure that such measures do not unduly restrict competition in violation of the Community competition rules.

The question remains as to how to classify provisions contained in national measures **2.66** intended to regulate the exercise of special or exclusive rights granted by such measures. For instance, is a provision of national law that imposes on the holder of the special or exclusive right an obligation to supply third parties on fair and non-discriminatory terms a provision of national competition law? Viewed in isolation the purpose of such a provision is to protect competition on the market, namely the downstream market for the goods and services produced by the holder of the special or exclusive right. The fact that the object of the assessment under Article 3(3) is the individual provision of a national measure and not the measure as such supports to a certain extent the inclusion of such provisions within the scope of application of Article 3. Individual provisions may constitute national competition law for the purposes of Article 3 even if the main thrust of the measure under examination pursues a distinct objective. However, where the conditions imposed form an integral part of the overall measure granting special and exclusive rights, it can be argued that it would be artificial to consider each individual condition in isolation. Even if individual provisions aim at protecting competition on the market, the predominant objective of such provisions, considered in the overall context in which they occur, is not to protect competition on the market. Their aim is merely to regulate the use of the special or exclusive rights granted by the measure. On this interpretation the individual condition forms an integral part of the grant of the special and exclusive right and thus falls outside the scope of Article 3. It remains to be seen how the European courts will interpret such provisions.

(d) National Merger Control Laws

According to Article 3(3) the first two paragraphs of this Article do not apply in the case of **2.67** national merger control laws. Transactions that qualify as mergers under national law are thus not subject to the obligations contained in Article 3(1) and (2). This exception has its origin in the Commission's original proposal for Article 3, which provided for exclusive application of Articles 81 and 82 to all agreements and abusive practices capable of affecting trade between Member States. Exclusive application of the Community competition rules on the basis of the Regulation would have meant that no system of *ex ante* control of agreements and abusive practices within the meaning of Articles 81 and 82 would have been possible at national level. The Regulation precludes any notification system for the application of Articles 81 and 82.[66] Indeed, it follows from Article 5 of Regulation 1/2003 that the competition authorities of the Member States are only competent to apply Articles 81 and 82 on their own initiative or on a complaint. Since a number of transactions falling under Articles 81 and 82 are subject to the system of *ex ante* control of the Merger Regulation,[67] mergers were excluded from the scope of application of Article 3 at an early stage in the negotiations concerning the Commission's original proposal.[68] Subsequently, when Article 3 acquired its current shape and form, it would have been sufficient to limit this exclusion to the application of Article 3(1). It is the obligation to apply Articles 81 and 82 that precludes a system of *ex ante* control. However, it did not prove possible to limit the exclusion of mergers to Article 3(1). As the merger tests of dominance or substantial impediment to effective competition are normally more difficult to meet than the test of appreciable restriction of competition under Article 81(1), it is unlikely that this exclusion has a detrimental impact on the level playing field inside the internal market, taking into account the general principle of primacy of Community law.

2.68　Moreover, general principles of Community law impose some limitations on the scope of the exception. It follows expressly from Article 3(3) that the exception is without prejudice to such general principles. It is a general principle of Community law that exceptions are to be interpreted restrictively. Moreover, the principle of effectiveness (*effet utile*) implies that the useful effect of Article 3 and the rest of Regulation 1/2003 must be preserved. Accordingly, there are limits as to how far Member States are able to expand the scope of national merger control to escape the obligations of Article 3. While it is in principle for the Member States to determine the scope of their merger control laws, the exercise of this power is subject to the control of the Court of Justice, which has the power to review the limits within which recourse can be had to the exception.[69] Member States cannot go beyond what can reasonably be defined as mergers. Some form of structural operation must thus be present.

(e) Criminal Sanctions on Natural Persons

2.69　A final exception, concerning Member State laws imposing criminal sanctions on natural persons, is reflected in recital 8 to Regulation 1/2003. The last sentence of recital 8 provides that 'Regulation 1/2003 does not apply to national laws, which impose criminal sanctions on natural persons except to the extent that such sanctions are the means whereby competition rules applying to undertakings are enforced'. When the last sentence of recital 8 applies it is not only Article 3 that does not apply. It is the entire Regulation that does not apply.[70]

---

[66] The Regulation, on the other hand, does not interfere with national notification systems for the application of national competition law. However, as a consequence of the primacy of Community law prohibitions, national exemptions cannot protect agreements against intervention on the basis of Arts 81 and 82.

[67] See Art 3(4) of Regulation 139/2004 on the control of concentrations between undertakings [2004] OJ L24/1; and Case 6/72 *Continental Can* [1973] ECR 215.

[68] See Commission Staff Paper on Art 3 submitted to the Council working group.

[69] See in this respect eg Case C-7/98 *Krombach* [2000] ECR I-1935.

[70] This implies for instance that Art 12, which provides for the exchange and use in evidence of confidential information, is not applicable. Information exchanged under the Regulation cannot be used for the purposes of imposing criminal sanctions on natural persons in the context of enforcing a separate and distinct offence as set out in recital 9.

The exception contained in recital 8 has not found expression in Article 3 or any other **2.70** operative part of the Regulation. Since recitals do not create new law but rather serve to interpret the operative parts of the legislation, it would appear that the basis for the exception lies in the distinction made in Article 3(3) between national competition laws and other types of national laws. A criminal offence that applies irrespective of any finding of an infringement on the part of undertakings is thus deemed not to belong to the sphere of national competition law in the sense of Article 3. This reading is consistent with the fact that according to the recital it is the entire Regulation that does not apply.

The last sentence of recital 8 was introduced primarily in order to avoid the application of **2.71** Article 3(1) to certain types of criminal proceedings against individuals. It was feared that the obligation to apply Community law including the exception in Article 81(3) would make it unduly difficult to impose sanctions on individuals. However, it is submitted that this concern is unwarranted. The exception in Article 81(3) only applies when the four cumulative conditions for exception are satisfied, including the conditions that the restrictions must be indispensable and that consumers must receive a fair share of the benefits. In the case of hardcore cartels that have as their object raising prices to the detriment of consumers these conditions are not satisfied.

The exception contained in recital 8 envisages national laws that define a violation on the **2.72** part of natural persons, which is distinct and separate from any violation of competition rules by undertakings. For the exception to apply the criminal offence must apply irrespective of any finding of an infringement on the part of undertakings. In that case the criminal sanctions are not the means by which competition rules applying to undertakings are enforced. The exception is not considered to apply where the sanction on natural persons is imposed as a result of their participation in an infringement found on the part of undertakings or where a sanction imposed on natural persons is a condition for imposing sanctions on undertakings. It is submitted that in such cases there is no violation on the part of the natural person separate and distinct from the infringement on the part of the undertaking. It is merely the means by which competition rules applying to undertakings are enforced. In practice, however, this distinction may be difficult to draw. In particular, in instances where the factual basis for the case is a price fixing cartel, it would appear somewhat artificial to distinguish the violation on the part of the undertaking and a violation on the part of an individual based on his participation in the operation of the cartel.

Recital 8 and Article 3(3) only exclude the application of Regulation 1/2003 to certain **2.73** criminal offences that do not belong to the sphere of national competition law. They do not prevent Member States from empowering their competition authorities or courts, as the case may be, to impose sanctions on individuals for their participation in infringements of Articles 81 and 82. It is for the Member States to determine the types of sanction that can be applied in case of violation of Articles 81 and 82. The fact that the prohibitions contained in Articles 81 and 82 are addressed to undertakings does not imply that sanctions cannot be imposed on individuals for their participation in infringements. In Regulation 1/2003 the Community legislator has chosen not to empower the Commission to impose sanctions on individuals. However, it is submitted that there is no obstacle to making a different choice in the future. Article 83 of the Treaty does not limit the Community legislator to the provision of sanctions on undertakings.

C. Powers and Decisions of National Competition Authorities

(1) Introduction

2.74 According to Article 5 of Regulation 1/2003 the competition authorities of the Member States (hereafter 'national competition authority' or 'NCA') shall have the power to apply Articles 81 and 82 EC in individual cases. This provision gives a clear and directly applicable legal basis for NCAs to apply these EC competition law provisions in their entirety. Article 5 marks a radical change in the enforcement of EC competition rules, in particular by granting to NCAs the power to apply Article 81(3), a power which they lacked until 1 May 2004. By empowering NCAs to apply Article 81 as a whole, as well as Article 82, Article 5 of the Regulation indeed completes, together with Articles 1 (the legal exception system) and 3 (the compulsory and convergent application of EC competition law) of Regulation 1/2003, the *communitisation* of the enforcement of EC competition law.

(2) The National Competition Authority

2.75 Since Article 5 is directly applicable, no national legislation is necessary to give the national competition authority the power to apply Articles 81 and 82 EC. That being said, most if not all of the EU Member States have confirmed in national legislation that their national competition authority can apply the EC competition law provisions.[71] In so doing, the legislator has at the same time (implicitly) designated the NCAs as responsible for the application of Articles 81 and 82 EC within the meaning of Article 35(1) of Regulation 1/2003. Indeed, the designation referred to in Article 35(1) of Regulation 1/2003 does not require a specific legislative act further to the adoption of Regulation 1/2003. The designation may as well result from acts prior to the date of adoption of Regulation 1/2003 (16 December 2002), as long as it is unambiguously clear which national authority acts as NCA within the meaning of Regulation 1/2003. One could even argue that as soon as a national authority has been empowered to apply national competition law (meaning provisions which predominantly pursue the objective of protecting competition on the market),[72] that authority has implicitly been designated as a competition authority within the meaning of Article 35(1) of Regulation 1/2003 and is thus also empowered to apply Articles 81 and 82 EC.

2.76 When requiring the Member States to designate an NCA, Regulation 1/2003 does not impose a specific national enforcement model. The only requirement laid down in Article 35(1) is that the designation should guarantee that the provisions of the Regulation are complied with effectively. Subject to the condition of effectiveness, Member States are free to designate their competition authority or authorities. The result is a variety of national enforcement models: some Member States have designated one single NCA, responsible for the application of EC competition rules in their territory, others have designated several NCAs,

---

[71] By the time Regulation 1/2003 was adopted, 12 of the then 15 EU Member States already had legislation empowering their national competition authority to apply Arts 81(1) and 82 EC. See the table in the European Commission's XXXIInd Report on Competition Policy—2002, pp 336 and 337.

[72] One can deduce from Art 3(3) of Regulation 1/2003 that provisions of national law that predominantly pursue an objective different from that pursued by Arts 81 and 82 EC are not considered to be provisions of national competition law. Recital 9 indirectly clarifies what the objectives pursued by Arts 81 and 82 EC are.

whose competences are divided according to the sector of the economy[73] or according to the provisions of the Regulation.[74] The latter model is explicitly referred to in Article 35(2), according to which 'Member States may allocate different powers and functions [referred to in Regulation 1/2003] to (. . .) different national authorities, whether administrative or judicial'.

The Regulation does not contain any criteria to determine whether or not a given designa-   **2.77**
tion of a national competition authority guarantees effective compliance with the provisions of the Regulation. One can assume, however, that it implies, among other criteria, that NCAs should be able to find and fine infringements of EC competition rules, that they can actively assist Commission officials during their inspections and that they should be organised in such a way that they can fully participate in the ECN. On this latter requirement, the European Parliament Committee on Economic and Monetary Affairs, in its report on the Commission's proposal for the new Council regulation, contended that NCAs should be 'equipped to organise an effective network with the Commission and with other member states. The human and technical resources available to national competition authorities may therefore have to be reinforced'.[75]

(3) The Decisions of a National Competition Authority

Article 5 of Regulation 1/2003 lists the decisions a national competition authority can take   **2.78**
when applying Articles 81 or 82 EC. According to that provision, the NCA may require that an infringement be brought to an end; order interim measures; accept commitments; impose fines, periodic penalty payments or any other penalty provided for in its national law; or it may decide that there are no grounds for action on its part. The list of decisions contained in Article 5 is an exhaustive list, without it being necessary for NCAs to be able to take all decisions listed.

(a) Article 5: Nothing More, Maybe Less

Article 5 contains an exhaustive list because when applying Articles 81 or 82 EC, NCAs   **2.79**
cannot take any decision other than those listed in Article 5. This is particularly relevant in respect of the second paragraph of Article 5, which addresses the situation in which the NCA, on the basis of the information in its possession, comes to the conclusion that the conditions for prohibition are not met. In those circumstances, the NCA cannot find that Articles 81 or 82 are not applicable,[76] but it may decide that there are no grounds for action on its part. When applying Articles 81 or 82, NCAs are thus prevented from adopting positive decisions.

---

[73] See eg the designation in the UK in s 54 of and Sch 10 to the Competition Act 1998 and the Competition Act 1998 (Concurrency) Regulations 2004.

[74] See eg the designation in Ireland, Statutory Instruments (SI) 2004/195—European Communities (Implementation of the Rules on Competition laid down in Articles 81 and 82 of the Treaty) Regulations 2004 of 30 April 2004.

[75] The report of the EP Committee on Economic and Monetary Affairs of 21 June 2001 on the Commission's proposal for a Council regulation on the implementation of the rules on competition laid down in Arts 81 and 82 of the Treaty and amending Regulations (EEC) 1017/68, (EEC) 2988/74, (EEC) 4056/86 and (EEC) 3975/87 (A5-0229/2001), p 24.

[76] Only the Commission can make findings of inapplicability, pursuant to Art 10 of Regulation 1/2003.

2.80 Conversely, Article 5 does not require NCAs to have all powers listed. The designated national competition authority should thus not necessarily be able to take all decisions listed in Article 5 when applying Articles 81 or 82. There are, however, two limitations to this autonomous determination of the kind of decisions NCAs may take, which both flow from Article 10 EC.

2.81 The first limitation is linked to the fact that Article 10 EC requires Member States to take all appropriate measures to guarantee the full scope and effect of Community law, a requirement that is also echoed in Article 35(1) of Regulation 1/2003. NCAs therefore need to have the necessary powers to contribute to the effective enforcement of the EC competition rules. It is submitted that this requirement entails, first of all, that an NCA should be able to require that an infringement be brought to an end: when it finds an infringement of the EC competition rules, an NCA should at least be able to remedy that situation for the future. That in itself is, however, not sufficient to guarantee the full scope and effect of Community law. Indeed, when the only risk run by an infringer of EC competition rules is that he must stop his infringing behaviour, there is no real incentive for undertakings to respect those rules. Article 10 EC therefore requires NCAs to be able to deter potential infringers of EC competition rules effectively. In order to achieve that objective, an NCA should be able to impose effective, proportionate, and dissuasive penalties when it finds that Articles 81 or 82 are infringed.[77]

2.82 The second limitation is known as the principle of equivalence. According to that principle, the procedural rules applicable to the enforcement of Community law may not be less favourable than the rules applicable to the enforcement of equivalent national law.[78] The idea is that it may not be more difficult to enforce EC law than it is to enforce equivalent national law. That principle, although mainly applied by the Court of Justice in cases where a national court has been asked to ensure the protection of the rights which citizens have through the direct effect of Community law, implies that the means by which national authorities enforce EC competition rules must not be less favourable than the means used to enforce national competition rules. Read together with the obligation under Article 3 of Regulation 1/2003 to apply national and EC competition law simultaneously to agreements that may affect trade between Member States, it is submitted that a Member State, when determining which decisions its NCA may take when applying EC competition law, should allow the NCA to take the same decisions as it may take when it is applying national competition law, provided of course that those decisions are included in Article 5 of Regulation 1/2003.

(b) The Decisions Listed in Article 5

2.83 The decisions listed in Article 5 largely correspond to the decisions the Commission can take when enforcing Articles 81 and 82; with the significant exception that only the Commission

---

[77] Case 68/88 *Commission v Greece* [1989] ECR 2965, para 23. On the necessity of deterrence, compare with the reasoning of the Court in Case 14/83 *Von Colson and Kamann* [1984] ECR 1891, paras 22 and 23 on equal treatment for men and women in labour conditions.

[78] See, eg, Case 33/76 *Rewe* [1976] ECR 1989, para 5.

may find those provisions to be inapplicable.[79] This correspondence does not mean, however, that the scope of the NCA decisions is identical or even similar to that of the 'corresponding' Commission decision. For instance, although the ability of a national competition authority to require that an infringement be brought to an end may also include the power of the NCA to impose remedies to bring the infringement to an end, that does not necessarily imply that the NCA can also impose structural remedies. Similarly, the procedural requirements of a national decision-making process may be different from those of the Commission when taking a 'corresponding' decision. There is for instance no reason why an NCA that wants to accept commitments should be required to publish the main content of those commitments allowing interested third parties to submit observations (see Article 27(4) of Regulation 1/2003). Finally, although an NCA should be able to impose effective, proportionate, and dissuasive penalties when it finds that Articles 81 or 82 have been infringed, Regulation 1/2003 does not harmonise the national sanctions applicable to EC competition law infringements. Nothing in the Regulation requires the EU Member States to allow their NCAs to impose (only) those sanctions which the Commission can impose when it finds an infringement of Articles 81 or 82, nor should the fines and periodic penalty payments necessarily be the same as those provided in Articles 23 and 24 of the Regulation, nor should the fining policy of NCAs necessarily be similar to that of the Commission.[80]

2.84 The main limitations on the EU Member States' freedom to determine both the scope of the decisions (including the sanctions) NCAs can take and the procedural requirements that must be respected when taking those decisions are the limitations mentioned above: the principle of effectiveness (the national rules may not make the enforcement of EC competition law excessively difficult or practically impossible) and the principle of equivalence (the national rules for the enforcement of EC competition law may not be less favourable than the rules applicable to the enforcement of national competition law). In addition, when enforcing EC (competition) rules, national authorities must also respect the general principles of Community law, in particular the fundamental rights of all those involved in the enforcement of Community law. As a consequence, the national procedures for taking the decisions listed in Article 5 of Regulation 1/2003 should also respect the general principles of Community law.

(4) Triggering a Decision of a National Competition Authority

(a) The National Competition Authority Acts on its Own Initiative or on a Complaint

2.85 Article 5 states that a national competition authority may only apply Articles 81 and 82 when it acts on its own initiative or on a complaint. This constraint on the activities of an NCA applies to all decisions listed in Article 5, including the decision that there are no grounds for action on the part of the NCA. The latter might be subject to discussion because the last sentence of Article 5 does not explicitly repeat the said constraint. Yet, it follows from

---

[79] Compare with Arts 7–10, 23 and 24.
[80] See the Guidelines on the method of setting fines imposed pursuant to Art 23(2)(a) of Regulation No 1/2003 [2006] OJ C210/2.

the text of Article 5, second paragraph, and from the context in which this provision should be read that an NCA cannot upon request from an undertaking decide that there are no grounds for action on its part.[81]

2.86　Indeed, the text of Article 5, second paragraph, indicates that the information which is in the possession of the NCA is aimed at proving an infringement. However, when that information is not sufficient to prove that the conditions for prohibition are met, the NCA may decide that there are no grounds for action on its part. The fact that the NCA is not obliged to take such a decision is yet another textual argument to show that NCAs are not taking such decisions on request from an undertaking. Finally, recitals 3 and 4 of Regulation 1/2003 indicate that the notification system was replaced by a directly applicable exception system in order to allow authorities to concentrate resources on curbing the most serious infringements. Replacing the system of notification to the Commission by a system of notification to the NCAs therefore runs counter to the aims of the Regulation. Article 5, second paragraph, therefore, cannot be interpreted as establishing a system of EC competition law notification to NCAs. Thus, NCAs can only decide that there are no grounds for action on their part when acting on their own initiative or on a complaint.

(b) National Notification Systems

2.87　The fact that Regulation 1/2003 replaced the system of notification with a directly applicable exception, however, does not exclude Member States maintaining—or even introducing—a system of notification in order to obtain an exemption under national law. The possibility of national notification, which at the time of writing still exists in eight of the twenty-five Member States,[82] leads to a peculiar situation when the notified agreement is capable of affecting trade between Member States. When that is the case, Article 3(1) of the Regulation requires the acting NCA also to apply Article 81, although what is meant by 'apply' remains unclear. Surely, the NCA cannot exempt under national law an agreement that restricts competition within the meaning of Article 81(1) but does not fulfil the conditions of Article 81(3). Indeed according to Article 1(1) of the Regulation '[a]greements (. . .) caught by Article 81(1) of the Treaty which do not satisfy the conditions of Article 81(3) of the Treaty shall be prohibited'. The primacy of that rule implies that NCAs may only apply exemptions under national law when the agreement fulfils the conditions of Article 81(3) EC. Conversely, it is theoretically possible that, in order to obtain an exemption decision from an NCA, national law could impose conditions over and above those of Article 81(3). However, under Article 3(2) of the Regulation, agreements could not be prohibited even if such additional conditions have not been fulfilled. Adding conditions to Article 81(3) in order to obtain an exemption under national law would create a grey area between

---

[81] This also appears from the explanatory memorandum on Art 5 in the proposal of the Commission: '[i]f the competition authority of a Member State finds that behaviour, acting on a complaint or on its own initiative does not infringe Article 81 as a whole or Article 82, it can close the proceedings or reject the complaint by decision, finding that there are no grounds for action', [2000] OJ C365E/284.

[82] The notification system still exists in Bulgaria, Cyprus, Denmark, Estonia, Greece, Italy, Latvia, Romania, and Spain and to some extent also in Portugal. Cyprus, Romania, and Spain are considering abolishing the notification system.

prohibition and exemption and, to ensure legal certainty, is therefore to be avoided. Thus it appears that the requirement of Article 3(1) for an NCA to 'apply Article 81' to notified agreements which may affect trade between Member States at least refers to the convergence obligation in the application of national competition law to these agreements, for example an NCA exemption decision under national law.

But the requirement of Article 3(1) to 'apply Article 81' may go further than this convergence obligation. One could argue that Article 3(1) requires the NCA to which an agreement capable of affecting trade between Member States has been notified, to take a decision. If after analysing the agreement, the NCA were to come to the conclusion that the agreement can be exempted under national law, the requirement 'to apply Article 81' would then imply that the NCA, on its own initiative, should add the decision that under Community law, there is no ground for action on its part, as is provided by Article 5, second paragraph, of the Regulation. Whatever the precise scope of the requirement for the NCA 'to apply Article 81', it is clear that exemptions under EC law are excluded even if an NCA is allowed to take exemption decisions under national law. **2.88**

Without delving further into the politics of discussing the soundness of maintaining or introducing a national notification system when Regulation 1/2003 has abolished the option of notification at European level, one needs to keep in mind the limited value of a national exemption decision. Although it is undoubtedly true that in some economic systems a national notification system can offer legal certainty to companies whose business affairs keep within the boundaries of the Member States, genuine legal certainty disappears when business is conducted at an inter-state level. Indeed, since the jurisdiction and thus the authority of an NCA decision is generally limited by the boundaries of its own Member State, the NCA's exemption decisions will only create legitimate expectations in respect of itself. No other member of the ECN is bound in European law by the decision of an NCA. A company that has received an exemption decision from an NCA is therefore not protected against an action by any other ECN member in respect of that exempted behaviour. **2.89**

D. Commission Powers and Decisions

(1) Introduction

Article 4 of Regulation 1/2003 provides that, for the purpose of applying Articles 81 and 82 of the Treaty, the Commission shall have the powers provided for by the Regulation. Articles 7–10 go on to stipulate the types of decisions that the Commission is empowered to adopt. It is these provisions and the powers of investigation vested in the Commission by Articles 18–21 of the Regulation that enable the Commission to enforce the Community competition rules effectively. **2.90**

The Treaty itself, however, assigns the Commission a special role in the enforcement of the Community competition rules. Case law confirms that the Commission, entrusted by Article 85(1) of the Treaty with the task of ensuring application of the principles laid down in Articles 81 and 82 of the Treaty, is responsible for defining and implementing the orientation of Community competition policy. It is for the Commission, subject to review by the Court of First Instance and the Court of Justice, to adopt individual decisions in accordance **2.91** with the procedural rules in force and to adopt exemption regulations.[83] In order to fulfil the role assigned to it by the Treaty, the Commission is not bound by decisions given by national courts and competition authorities applying Articles 81 and 82 of the Treaty. The Commission is entitled to adopt individual decisions under Articles 81 and 82 of the Treaty at any time, even when an agreement or practice has already been the subject of a decision by a Member State competition authority or court and the decision contemplated by the Commission conflicts with that prior decision.[84]

2.92   The special responsibility of the Commission in enforcing Articles 81 and 82 and in defining and implementing Community competition policy is reflected in Regulation 1/2003, in particular in the various provisions intended to ensure consistent application of Articles 81 and 82. It is also reflected in Article 16 of the Regulation under which Member State competition authorities and courts cannot take decisions contradicting those adopted or contemplated by the Commission. Article 16 strengthens the effect of Commission decisions in the new enforcement system.

(2) Article 7: Finding and Termination of Infringements

2.93   Article 7 of Regulation 1/2003 empowers the Commission to find an infringement and order the undertakings concerned to bring it to an end. This provision raises three main issues, namely the scope of the Commission's power to find infringements, the scope for the Commission to impose remedies and finally the rights of complainants.

(a) *The Power to Find Infringements*

2.94   Article 7(1) provides that where the Commission, acting either on a complaint or on its own initiative, finds that there is an infringement of Article 81 or Article 82 of the Treaty, it may by decision require the undertakings and associations of undertakings concerned to bring the infringement to an end. Article 7(1) thus empowers the Commission to find an infringement and impose a cease and desist order in cases where the infringement is ongoing. Article 7(1) further provides that if the Commission has a legitimate interest in doing so, it may also find that an infringement has been committed in the past. The Commission must substantiate in light of the facts of the individual case the reasons why it considers that the legitimate interest condition is satisfied.[85]

2.95   A legitimate interest may exist in particular in the following three situations:

(a) Deterrence. The Commission has a legitimate interest in finding a past infringement with a view to imposing a fine. An example would be a cartel that has been brought to an end before the Commission has adopted a decision. In order to ensure effective enforcement through punishment of the perpetrators it is essential that past infringements can be found and adequately fined. However, deterrence does not only stem from fines. It may also stem from the very fact of finding and making public a very serious infringement on the part of an undertaking. The interest in enabling the injured

---

[83] See in particular Case C-344/98 *Masterfoods* [2000] ECR I-11369, para 46.
[84] ibid para 48.
[85] See Joined Cases T-22/02 and T-23/02 *Sumitomo* [2005] ECR II-4065, para 138.

parties to bring matters before the national civil courts may also contribute to deterrence and give the Commission legitimate reasons to find a past infringement.[86]

(b) Clarification so as to avoid the infringement being repeated. In *GVL*[87] the Court of Justice held that the Commission had a legitimate interest in finding a past infringement in a case where there was a real danger of a resumption of the practice.

(c) Policy development.[88] If a case involving a past infringement raises new policy issues or issues of consistent application, for instance because Member States competition authorities and courts have arrived at different outcomes in similar situations, there may be a need for the Commission to find that an infringement has been committed in the past.

The fact that the possibility to find a past infringement exists does mean that the Commission should always act on it. In the exercise of its power the Commission must balance the benefits of making such a finding against the resources that must be committed in order to do so. Since Regulation 1/2003 is intended to allow the Commission to focus on the prosecution of the most serious infringements, the Commission can be expected to exercise its powers sparingly in cases where fines are not likely to be imposed. **2.96**

(b) The Power to Impose Remedies

Article 7(1) of Regulation 2003 provides that the Commission may impose any behavioural or structural remedies which are proportionate to the infringement committed and necessary to bring the infringement effectively to an end. Structural remedies can only be imposed either where there is no equally effective behavioural remedy or where any equally effective behavioural remedy would be more burdensome for the undertaking concerned than the structural remedy. **2.97**

(i) General Principles   Remedies serve to bring an identified infringement of the Community competition rules to an end. Remedies cannot serve as a penalty. The only penalties foreseen in Regulation 1/2003 are fines and periodic penalty payments.[89] While in many cases a cease and desist order is sufficient to bring the infringement to an end, there are circumstances in which it is neccesary to impose further obligations. Such obligations may for instance be required when negative effects remain after an agreement or practice has been prohibited or when the prohibited conduct takes the form of a refusal to engage in certain conduct.[90] **2.98**

Since the purpose of any obligation imposed must be designed to bring the infringement to an end, there must be a link between the infringement and the obligations imposed. Moreover, the principle of proportionality requires that the burden imposed on the undertaking in order to end the infringement must not exceed what is appropriate and necessary to attain the objective sought, namely re-establishment of compliance with the rules infringed.[91] **2.99**

---

[86] ibid, para 137.

[87] Case 7/82 *GVL* [1983] ECR 483, para 27.

[88] See p 17 of the Explanatory Memorandum to the Commission's proposal of 27 September 2000 (COM (2000) 582 final).

[89] See Arts 23 and 24 of Regulation 1/2003.

[90] See eg Joined Cases 6/73 and 7/73 *Commercial Solvents* [1974] ECR 223.

[91] See Joined Cases C-241/91 P and C-242/91 P *RTE and ITP (Magill)* [1995] ECR I-743, para 93.

If several effective and proportionate remedies are available the undertaking is entitled to choose which remedy to comply with.[92] If one proportionate remedy is more effective than other available remedies, the Commission can impose the most effective one. The assessment of the effectiveness and necessity of any remedy must be based on the facts and circumstances of the individual case. A remedy is only effective if in the specific circumstances of the case it cures the competition problem that has been identified.

2.100 The effectiveness of a remedy depends not only on the capacity of the remedy to address a competition problem which has been identified but also its enforceability. For a remedy to be effective it must be possible to monitor compliance. Complex behavioural remedies are often ineffective. As the complexity of a remedy increases, the less likely it is that it will address the competition problem effectively. Behavioural remedies often suffer from a high degree of complexity compared to structural remedies. However, in the field of Articles 81 and 82, behavioural remedies cannot be avoided because the competition problem often arises from the behaviour of the undertaking.

2.101 **(ii) Structural and Behavioural Remedies**   Article 7(1) of Regulation 1/2003 empowers the Commission to impose any remedy whether behavioural or structural. The term '*structural remedy*' covers a wide range of remedies but all must affect the assets of the undertaking. Examples of structural remedies include obligations to dispose of a shareholding in a competitor or to partly or wholly dissolve a joint venture.[93] The most far-reaching structural remedy is a break-up of a pre-existing entity, ie an entity as it existed before the infringement was committed.

2.102 Article 7(1) establishes a presumptive hierarchy between the two categories of remedy: where an equally effective behavioural remedy exists it must be chosen unless it is more burdensome for the undertaking concerned. The stated preference for behavioural remedies is based on the assumption that such remedies are less burdensome for the undertaking concerned. It would be disproportionate to impose a structural remedy where an equally effective behavioural remedy is available. However, as is clear from Article 7(1) itself, the presumption may be rebutted in individual cases. Therefore, an assessment of several equally effective remedies must be made, to determine which is the least burdensome.

2.103 The benchmark established by Article 7(1) is whether an alternative less burdensome remedy is '*equally effective*'. The Commission is not obliged to choose a less effective behavioural remedy if a structural remedy is more effective in terms of bringing the infringement to an end. The intention is merely to ensure in accordance with the principle of proportionality, that, when faced with two equally effective remedies, the Commission imposes the least burdensome one. It follows that Article 7(1) does not impose restrictions on the choice of remedies beyond those that already flow from general principles.[94]

2.104 **(iii) Break-ups**   Recital 12 of Regulation 1/2003 provides that changes to the structure of an undertaking as it existed before the infringement was committed would only be

---

[92] See Case T-24/90 *Automec* [1992] ECR II-2223, paras 51 and 52.
[93] See eg Commission Decision in *Gillette* [1993] OJ L116/21.
[94] See Case T-24/90 *Automec* [1992] ECR II-2223, paras 51 and 52.

proportionate where there is a substantial risk of a lasting or repeated infringement that derives from the very structure of the undertaking. This recital deals with the most far-reaching structural remedy, namely the break-up of a pre-existing undertaking. The recital reflects the principle of proportionality. Given the far-reaching nature of a break-up, this type of remedy is disproportionate save in exceptional cases.

According to recital 12, a break-up may be warranted in cases where the infringement **2.105** derives from the very structure of the undertaking. This is because, in such cases, it may be very difficult to devise an effective behavioural remedy and to ensure that it continues to be respected. Such situations may in particular arise in cases where an undertaking operates in two or more related markets and where the undertaking controls essential infrastructure or input in an upstream market.[95] This situation can be illustrated by a case that fell within the ambit of Article 86. In *Raso*,[96] an undertaking had been granted the exclusive right to provide temporary labour services to undertakings providing dock work services to the users of the Port of La Spezia. The undertaking holding the exclusive right was also a service provider in the downstream market in which the monopoly service was an input. The monopolist was thus itself active on the downstream market. The Court of Justice held that the exclusive right violated Article 86 in conjunction with Article 82 because it enabled the undertaking to distort in its favour the equal conditions of competition between the various operators on the downstream market for dock work services. The undertaking was enabled, in particular, to impose unduly high costs on its competitors or to supply them with labour that was less suited to the work to be done. To bring the infringement to an end the Member State in question either had to eliminate the exclusive right or ensure that the holder ceased to be active on the downstream service market.

Given the very far-reaching nature of break-ups as a remedy, it is submitted that the fol- **2.106** lowing minimum conditions should be met before considering the imposition of such a remedy:

(i) the infringement has a substantial impact on competition and consumers;
(ii) the undertaking has engaged in repeated infringements or the structure of the undertaking causes it to infringe the Community competition rules, for instance, by creating an inherent conflict of interest;
(iii) other available remedies are ineffective; and
(iv) break-up does not lead to a significant loss of efficiency at the level of the undertaking, which would undermine the pro-competitive effects of the remedy.

The last condition reflects the fact that the ultimate aim of Articles 81 and 82 is to protect competition in the market for the benefit of consumers. If the integration of the assets in question leads to significant efficiencies, a break-up should only be imposed where on balance it would lead to greater benefits for consumers when compared to an alternative remedy.

---

[95] Often such markets are regulated and thus subject to a special framework. It can be expected that in devising remedies deference will be given to the special framework. For a break-up to be imposed there should therefore be particularly clear evidence that the framework in question is inadequate in terms of ensuring compliance with the Community competition rules.

[96] See Case C-163/96 *Raso* [1998] ECR I-533. See also Case C-18/88 *RTT v GB-Inno-BM* [1991] ECR I-5941, where the Court of Justice applied the same reasoning.

(c) Complaints

2.107   Article 7 decisions can be adopted either at the Commission's own initiative or in response to a complaint. According to Article 7(2) natural or legal persons who can show a legitimate interest and Member States are entitled to lodge complaints. Formal complaints are subject to a particular procedure. Complainants are entitled to have their complaint rejected by a formal and challengeable decision in the event that the Commission decides not act upon the complaint.

2.108   The complaint procedure is set out in Commission Regulation 773/2004 relating to the conduct of proceedings by the Commission pursuant to Articles 81 and 82 of the Treaty[97] and is further described in the Commission Notice on the handling of complaints by the Commission under Articles 81 and 82 of the Treaty.[98] The Notice requires compliance with a special form, Form C, in order for a complaint to be treated as a formal complaint. The purpose of Form C is to ensure that complainants provide as useful information as possible, as early as possible. As a *quid pro quo*, the Commission undertakes to inform the complainant within four months whether it intends to investigate the complaint further. Even if it does not intend to investigate, the Commission must still reject the complaint to the extent that the complainant pursues it. Early communication to the complainant of the Commission's intentions has two main advantages. It allows the complainant to pursue without undue delay alternative solutions to the alleged competition problem such as litigation before Member State courts. It also means the Commission must declare early on whether it will give priority to the complaint and commit the necessary resources to further investigate it.

2.109   Case law confirms that the Commission is entitled to give different priority to cases brought before it and to reject cases for lack of Community interest.[99] National courts are obliged to decide on all cases brought before them, but by contrast, the Commission, as a competition authority, is entitled to concentrate its resources on the most important cases. However, because of the rights granted to complainants under the Regulation, the Commission is nevertheless obliged to explain in a challengeable act why it considers that it is not in the Community interest to investigate the complaint further. Complaints may also be rejected on substantive grounds, ie that there is no infringement of Articles 81 and 82. However, following the logic of Regulation 1/2003, complaints will increasingly be rejected for lack of Community interest on the ground that the case is not a priority. Since Regulation 1/2003 is intended to enable the Commission to focus on prosecuting the most serious infringements, the Commission is placing renewed emphasis on priority setting. Relevant factors include the strategic importance of the case, the impact of the infringement on competition and consumers and the importance of the case from the point of view of developing Community competition policy. Cases that are not given priority are likely to be closed or rejected.

(3) Article 8: Interim Measures

2.110   Article 8(1) of Regulation 1/2003 provides that in cases of urgency due to the risk of serious and irreparable harm to competition, the Commission, acting on its own initiative,

---

[97] [2004] OJ L123/18, hereafter also 'Commission implementing Regulation'.
[98] [2004] OJ C101/65.
[99] See eg Case C-344/98 *Masterfoods* [2000] ECR I-11369, para 47.

may order interim measures by decision, on the basis of a *prima facie* finding of infringement. Article 8(2) further provides that an interim measures decision shall apply for a specified period of time and may be renewed as necessary. Article 8 largely codifies the case law that developed under Regulation 17/62. In *Camera Care*[100] the Court of Justice held that the Commission has the power to adopt interim measures in cases proved to be urgent, in order to avoid a situation likely to cause serious and irreparable damage to the party seeking their adoption, or because the situation is against the public interest. It was further held that such measures must be of a temporary and conservatory nature and restricted to what is required in the circumstances.

However, Article 8 qualifies the pre-existing state of the law in two important respects. **2.111** First, interim measures decisions can only be adopted on the Commission's own initiative. The wording of Article 8 differs from that of Article 7 by not mentioning complaints. Complainants are not granted specific rights in the context of Article 8. It follows that complainants have no legal entitlement to request that interim measures be adopted and that the Commission has no obligation to formally reject requests that it considers ill-founded. However, in the same way that complainants may submit informal complaints, they may also draw to the Commission's attention cases in which they consider interim measures to be warranted. Secondly, interim measures can only be adopted in case of urgency due to serious and irreparable harm to competition. It is not sufficient that serious and irreparable harm be caused to an individual undertaking. There must also be indications that competition will be harmed. This qualification reflects the fact that the purpose of Articles 81 and 82 is to protect competition in the market and that the Commission, in its capacity as a competition authority, acts in the public interest to protect competition. National courts are better placed to protect the interests of individual companies.

(4) Article 9: Commitments

(a) Introduction

Article 9 of Regulation 1/2003 empowers the Commission to adopt an entirely new type **2.112** of decision, namely a decision whereby commitments offered by undertakings are made binding and enforceable on the undertakings concerned. Commitments serve the same purpose as a cease and desist order and remedies imposed by an Article 7 decision: to bring an effective end to an identified competition problem.

Article 9(1) provides that where the Commission intends to adopt a decision requiring that **2.113** an infringement be brought to an end and the undertakings concerned offer commitments to meet the concerns expressed to them by the Commission in its preliminary assessment, the Commission may by decision make those commitments binding on the undertakings. Such a decision may be adopted for a specific period and shall conclude that there are no longer grounds for action by the Commission.

According to Article 27(4) of Regulation 1/2003, the adoption of an Article 9 decision **2.114** must be preceded by publication of a document inviting third parties to submit comments

---

[100] See eg Case T-24/90 *Automec* [1992] ECR II-2223, para 76.

on the commitments offered. In order to enable them to do so, the document must contain a summary of the Commission's concerns and the main content of the commitments.

(b) The Nature of Article 9 Decisions

2.115 An Article 9 decision is an enforcement instrument. It is not an instrument for providing legal certainty to companies, nor is it a substitute for exemption decisions. Undertakings are not entitled to a commitments decision. Commitments decisions are adopted in circumstances where the Commission intends to adopt a prohibition decision but the commitments offered address effectively the competition concerns identified by the Commission. The decision thus has its origin in an enforcement action.

2.116 According to Article 9(1) and recital 13 the operative part of an Article 9 decision must find that there are no longer grounds for action by the Commission without concluding whether or not there has been or still is an infringement. The operative part of Article 9 decisions has implications for their effect in law. As explained in recital 13, commitments decisions are without prejudice to the powers of national competition authorities and courts to find an infringement and decide upon the case. National competition authorities and courts can both make a finding of a past infringement and a continuing future infringement. Article 16 of Regulation 1/2003, which stipulates that national competition authorities and courts must not adopt decisions that run counter to those adopted by the Commission, does not preclude such a finding. The finding of an infringement is not in conflict with a Commission decision that limits itself to finding that there are no longer grounds for action in its part. Defendants will no doubt cite commitments decisions as de facto evidence against any claim that an infringement continues, since commitments serve the same purpose as an Article 7 decision. Article 9 decisions are adopted by the Commission where it would otherwise have proceeded with the adoption of a prohibition decision. The fact that the Commission accepts the commitments is at least an indication that the commitments remedy the competition problem for the future, provided that the underlying facts remain materially the same.

2.117 The operative part of an Article 9 decision not only finds that there are no longer grounds for action by the Commission. It also renders the commitments binding on the undertakings. This part of the decision is binding on national competition authorities and courts in the sense that they are precluded from adopting decisions that render ineffective the commitments contained in the operative part of the Commission's decision, nor can they release the undertakings from those commitments.

2.118 Commitments contained in an Article 9 decision can be enforced by the Commission against the addressees by means of fines and periodic penalty payments. According to Article 23 of Regulation 1/2003 fines of up to 10 per cent of the total turnover of the undertaking concerned in the preceding business year may be imposed where, whether intentionally or negligently, the undertaking fails to comply with commitments that have been made binding. Moreover, periodic penalty payments of up to 5 per cent of the undertaking's average daily turnover in the preceding business year may be imposed in order to compel undertakings to respect their commitments.

2.119 The Regulation is silent on the question as to whether or not third parties can rely on commitments before Member State courts. In other words, it is an open question whether third parties can enforce the commitments and invoke them as a basis for claiming damages. For instance, if an undertaking has made a binding commitment to supply third parties on certain terms and conditions and fails to do so, can the third party in question bring a claim directly on the basis of the commitments decision? Regulation 1/2003 deliberately leaves open this question.[101] It is submitted, however, that this question should be answered in the affirmative. According to Article 249 of the Treaty, Community decisions are binding in their entirety on those to whom they are addressed. Moreover, it is a fundamental principle of Community law that clear and unconditional provisions contained in Community acts have direct effect and can be invoked before national courts. There is no reason why this general principle of Community law should not also apply to commitments rendered binding by a Community act.

(c) The Purpose of Article 9 Decisions

In the past the Commission from time to time would close a case informally on condition **2.120** that the undertakings concerned undertook to abstain from or adopt certain conduct in the future. When a satisfactory solution had been found it was often considered an unnecessary use of resources to proceed with the case and adopt a prohibition decision, although such action was necessary in order to render the obligations accepted by the undertakings concerned binding and enforceable. In the case of an informal settlement the only response to a breach of the settlement was the reopening of proceedings with a view to adopting a prohibition decision. By offering the Commission the option of making commitments binding and enforceable, Article 9 remedies the weakness inherent in informal settlements. This is the main attraction of Article 9 decisions from the point of view of the Commission. It allows for effective enforcement of the Community competition rules by remedying an identified competition problem and at the same time enables the Commission to save scarce enforcement resources. From the point of view of undertakings Article 9 decisions may be attractive in that they avoid the adoption of a formal finding of an infringement. Article 16 of the Regulation allows such a finding to serve as a basis for claiming damages. As Article 9 decisions make no such finding they merely constitute an element of fact to be taken into account by national competition authorities and courts.

Article 9 decisions are designed for cases where the objective of the enforcement action is **2.121** to remedy an identified competition problem for the future. As stated in recital 13 to Regulation 1/2003, commitments decisions are not appropriate where the Commission intends to impose a fine. It is not possible in an Article 9 decision for the Commission to accept a commitment to pay a sum of money.[102] If the Commission intends to impose a fine, it must proceed with an Article 7 decision.

The statement in Article 13 to the effect that commitments decisions are not appropriate **2.122** where the Commission intends to impose a fine does not imply that the adoption of an Article 9

---

[101] Recital 12 of the Commission's proposal of 27 September 2000 (COM (2000) 582 final) provided that the commitments could be relied upon by third parties. However, certain Member States considered it more appropriate to leave this question to be decided by the Community Courts. The statement was therefore deleted.

[102] This limitation follows from the Regulation and not from the Treaty itself.

decision is excluded in all cases where in a statement of objections the Commission has indicated that it may impose a fine. The intention was not to prevent the Commission from bringing an end to an identified competition problem merely because of a prior statement to the effect that fines may be imposed. Any such statement in the statement of objections is required from the point of view of rights of defence[103] and should not prejudice the final outcome in the case. The assessment of whether the Commission has a legitimate interest in adopting an Article 9 decision as opposed to an Article 7 decision imposing fines should be made at the time the decision is adopted.[104] The Commission should be entitled to balance the interest in deterring anti-competitive behaviour through fines against the interest in improving the functioning of a market by eliminating a competition problem for the future. In the individual case it may be more important to bring an end to a competition problem more speedily by imposing binding, effective, and enforceable remedies than to impose a fine. Moreover, the fact that in the past the Commission has imposed fines in a similar case should not in itself bar it from adopting an Article 9 decision in a future case. The intention behind recital 13 is two-fold. First, the aim is to avoid a situation where, in the same case or group of cases, commitments decisions are adopted in respect of some undertakings but fines are imposed on others. In such circumstances the Commission has, through its conduct in relation to certain undertakings, expressed a clear intention to impose a fine and should not therefore treat other undertakings differently. Secondly, the aim is to exclude the adoption of Article 9 decisions in cartel cases where due to the serious nature of the infringement the Commission has a consistent policy of imposing fines. In such cases there is no appropriate commitment. The proper response from the Commission is the imposition of a cease and desist order and deterrent fines.

(d) The Procedure for Adopting Article 9 Decisions

2.123 Procedures that are terminated with an Article 9 decision start like any other prohibition proceeding, with a complaint or an *ex officio* investigation. Investigations are conducted in the same way, the objective being to identify possible competition problems. Moreover, nothing prevents the Commission from pursuing its investigation of a case while assessing the commitments offered. If the commitments are considered insufficient to meet its concerns the Commission may at any point in time opt for the adoption of an Article 7 decision.

2.124 Procedurally, however, Article 9 decisions do have certain distinctive features. The first element is the requirement that the Commission must have expressed its concerns in '*its preliminary assessment*'.[105] In cases where a statement of objections has been issued this document and the preliminary assessment will be one and the same. However, this need not be the case. The preliminary assessment may be a separate document. This interpretation is confirmed by Article 2(1) of Commission Regulation 773/2004 according to which the Commission must initiate proceedings no later than the date on which it issues a preliminary assessment or a statement of objections whichever is earlier. It follows that the

---

[103] See eg Case T-15/02 *BASF* [2006] ECR II-000, para 48.

[104] This is also the point in time at which the Commission has to decide whether the commitments offered address its concerns.

[105] The preliminary assessment is a Commission document. It must therefore be adopted in accordance with the Commission's internal decision-making procedure.

preliminary assessment may be issued earlier than the statement of objections. In that case the analysis may be (substantially) less detailed than that found in a statement of objections. Even so, a preliminary assessment will generally be preceded by a detailed investigation since, without it, the Commission is not in a position to assess whether the commitments are sufficient to meet its concerns.

The preliminary assessment summarises the main facts of the case and identifies the competition concerns that in the Commission's view would warrant the adoption of a prohibition decision. In other words, the preliminary assessment sets out the nature of the infringement alleged by the Commission. The purpose of the preliminary assessment is two-fold. First, it serves as a basis for the undertakings concerned to assess what are the Commission's allegations. On that basis they can decide whether it is appropriate to offer commitments, and if so, what they should cover.[106] Secondly, the preliminary assessment is intended to avoid the Commission negotiating and accepting commitments without having sufficiently investigated the case and identified the competition problems which it creates. As an enforcement authority, the Commission must ensure that the commitments that it accepts do address the competition problem effectively. In most cases a detailed investigation is required before it is possible to identify the true nature of the competition problem and the appropriate remedy. **2.125**

According to Article 9(1), commitments are offered after the Commission has issued the preliminary assessment. However, in practice it is likely that discussions on the issue of commitments will commence before the preliminary assessment is issued. If there is no statement of objections, the preliminary assessment is issued only when the adoption of an Article 9 decision is envisaged. The parties will therefore often have indicated a willingness to offer commitments. However, the undertakings concerned are not required to set out their commitments in any detail before the preliminary assessment has been issued. **2.126**

Before adopting the decision the Commission is required to market test the commitments. This market testing is formalised in Article 27(4), according to which an Article 9 decision must be preceded by the publication in the Official Journal of a concise summary of the case and the main content of the commitments. Interested third parties may submit their observations within a time limit which is fixed by the Commission (and included in the summary published in the Official Journal) and which may not be less than one month. An Article 27(4) publication is in some respects equivalent to the Article 19(3) publications that preceded the adoption of an exemption decision under Regulation 17/62. It is submitted, however, that the context in which the decisions are adopted makes a difference. In the case of exemption decisions adopted under Article 8 of Regulation 17/62, the parties would request the Commission to review a notified agreement and adopt a favourable decision protecting the agreement against third party challenges. Such agreements rarely gave rise to competition concerns. Once the Commission had come to the conclusion that the agreement as amended by the parties was unproblematic, the Article 19(3) publication was more or less a formality. The statement in an Article 19(3) publication, containing the Commission's favourable opinion of the agreement, was **2.127**

---

[106] The Regulation does not prevent undertakings from withdrawing their commitments up until the time when the Commission renders them binding.

indeed favourable. Third party comments had to be quite substantial for the final outcome to be significantly different.[107] By contrast, according to Article 27(4), the publication must indicate that the Commission intends to adopt an Article 9 decision. This statement is merely an indication that the Commission considers the commitments sufficiently sound to warrant market testing and does not in any way prejudice the final assessment of the sufficiency of the commitments post-market test. An Article 9 decision is an enforcement instrument and the decision is a substitute for a prohibition decision. The Commission is dealing with the case on its own initiative or on a complaint, not at the request of the parties. Moreover, the case has been considered of sufficient importance to merit continued investigation. The Commission is therefore likely to be more critical of the commitments and their effectiveness. Early experience confirms that third party comments constitute an indispensable check on whether the commitments are effective. If not, the Commission should seek additional commitments or proceed to an Article 7 decision.[108] If the input from third parties leads the Commission to identify new concerns, it must issue a supplementary preliminary assessment. Conversely, third party comments may lead the Commission to conclude that certain concerns expressed in the preliminary assessment should not be retained. The Article 27(4) publication and third party input is therefore an important part of the procedure.

2.128 The requirement that an Article 27(4) publication be made does not prevent the Commission from proactively complementing the market test by directly contacting third parties that are thought to possess relevant information. The Commission systematically employs this approach in the field of mergers and it is also likely to make frequent use of it in the antitrust field.[109]

(e) Adoption of the Decision and Reopening of the Proceedings

2.129 At the end of the procedure and provided that the commitments are deemed sufficient to address the Commission's concerns[110] the Commission adopts a decision incorporating the commitments and rendering them binding. Without making a determination as to whether there has been or still is an infringement, the decision also briefly describes the conduct engaged in by the undertakings concerned, otherwise it would not be possible to understand the activity addressed by the commitments. The decision may be unlimited in time or adopted for a specific period.[111]

---

[107] In practice the Commission rarely received comments on a significant scale. It is clearly intended that the Art 27(4) publication should constitute a real market test and it can only be hoped that interested third parties will make full use of the opportunity to make comments.

[108] The Commission has in several cases obtained additional commitments after the market test.

[109] The Commission's proposal of 27 September 2000 (COM(2000) 582 final) did not provide for the Art 27(4) procedure, the reason being that it was considered more efficient to rely on proactive and targeted market testing. Article 27(4) was introduced at the insistence of the Member States which considered that third parties should be made aware of the main content of the commitments in their own language and have the possibility to make comments on their own initiative.

[110] A literal reading of Art 9(1) suggests that the commitments must meet the Commission's concerns as they stand at the time of the preliminary assessment. It is submitted, however, that the relevant moment in time to assess whether the commitments meet the Commission's concerns is at the time when the decision is adopted. It is at this moment in time that the Commission has the fullest basis for assessing the case. In particular, certain concerns expressed in the preliminary assessment may need to be modified after the market test, as it may lead the Commission to conclude that certain concerns were unwarranted. If the Commission identifies new concerns, it must issue a supplementary preliminary assessment.

[111] Current Commission practice suggests that decisions will be limited in time.

In order to comply with the obligation under Article 253 of the Treaty to state reasons, the **2.130** decision must set out at least briefly why the Commission considers that the commitments are sufficient to meet its concerns. The Commission must find a fine balance between the Treaty obligation to give reasons and the obligation under Regulation 1/2003 not to conclude whether there has been or still is an infringement.[112]

According to Article 9(2) of Regulation 1/2003 the Commission may, subject to certain **2.131** conditions, reopen the proceedings on its own initiative or upon request. Proceedings can be reopened where any of the following three conditions are satisfied:

(a) there has been a material change in any of the facts on which the decision was based;
(b) the undertakings concerned act contrary to their commitments;
(c) the decision was based on incomplete, incorrect or misleading information provided by the parties.

The term 'reopening of proceedings' covers the situation where the Commission considers that the commitments are insufficient and therefore acts with a view to prohibiting certain practices. Article 9(2) takes account of the legitimate expectation of the addressees by limiting the circumstances in which the Commission can act to their detriment by reopening its proceedings. Article 9(2) also envisages the situation where the Commission considers that the addressees should be released wholly or partly from their commitments. The Commission has not agreed to introduce review clauses going beyond the scope of Article 9(2).[113]

Article 9(2)(a) provides that proceedings may be reopened when there has been a material **2.132** change in any of the facts on which the decision was based. A commitments decision addresses competition concerns identified by the Commission in light of the facts pertaining at the time of the decision. If the facts change materially it may be necessary to reopen proceedings with a view to adjusting the commitments to the new factual situation. For instance, it may be that over time the market position of the addressees has increased to such an extent that the commitments are no longer sufficient. It may even be that the changes are such that the appropriate course of action is the adoption of a prohibition decision. If at the time of adoption of the decision it is likely that market conditions will change in the foreseeable future, it may be appropriate to limit the duration of the decision to a specified period.[114] Such limitation allows the situation to be assessed afresh after a certain period of time. It may also be appropriate to limit the decision in time where the impact of the commitments is uncertain. In such circumstances the Commission may have an interest in limiting the duration of the decision so that it can reassess the effectiveness of the commitments

---

[112] Compare in this respect the Commission Decision in *DFB* (Decision of 19 January 2005 in Case 37.214) and the subsequent decision in *Coca-Cola* (Decision of 22 June 2005 in Case 39.116), both published on the DG Competition website. It is submitted that the approach of the latter decision, which was made later, is more satisfactory. The language used in para 41 of the decision in *DFB* could be read to suggest that the Commission had only carried out a cursory investigation and assessment, which was not the case.

[113] The *Coca-Cola* case (Decision of 22 June 2005 in Case 39.116) provides an interesting illustration of this. The Art 27(4) publication contained a more extensive review clause, but this clause was not retained in the final decision and the Commission has not accepted the introduction of more extensive review clauses since then. Such clauses would introduce an unwarranted asymmetry between the rights and obligation of the parties to the settlement.

[114] Early experience suggests that the Commission will generally limit Art 9 decisions in time.

in light of experience. The undertaking concerned may have a similar interest if there is a risk that the commitments may be unnecessarily intrusive. If the decision is of unlimited duration proceedings cannot be reopened merely because experience shows that the commitments are ineffective or unnecessarily intrusive. There must be a material change in the relevant facts.

2.133 Article 9(2)(b) provides that proceedings may be reopened when the undertakings concerned act contrary to their commitments. When the addressees of an Article 9 decision act contrary to their commitments the normal response of the Commission will be to reopen proceedings with a view to adopting a decision imposing fines and/or periodic penalty payments as provided for in Articles 23 and 24 of the Regulation. In such a decision the Commission is required to demonstrate that the commitments have been breached. It is not required to show that the conduct in question constitutes an infringement of Articles 81 and 82. The Commission may also reopen proceedings with a view to adopting a prohibition decision under Article 7 of the Regulation.

2.134 Finally, proceedings may be reopened where the parties have provided incomplete, incorrect, or misleading information, in which case the commitments accepted by the Commission are likely to be insufficient, and proceedings are likely to be reopened with a view to adopting a prohibition decision imposing remedies.

(f) The Scope for Legal Challenges

2.135 Case law shows that Commission decisions can be challenged in so far as the measure in question produces legal effects that are binding on, and capable of affecting the interests of the applicant by having a significant effect on his legal position.[115] Commitments decisions produce legal effects on the addressee. The addressee is obliged to act in accordance with the commitments and adapt his market conduct accordingly. However, the question remains on what grounds a commitments decision can be challenged by the addressee. As the commitments are offered by the addressee, it is submitted that he would not be able to argue that the commitments go further than is necessary to eliminate the competition problem, especially since the decision does not find that, prior to the commitments, the agreement or practice infringed Article 81 or 82. On the other hand the addressee would be able to argue that the Commission has abused its powers by forcing it to offer the commitments, that the commitments offered are not correctly reproduced in the decision, or that procedural guarantees have not been respected, for example that the Commission failed to issue a preliminary assessment in accordance with Article 9(1).

2.136 As regards third parties, it is useful to distinguish complainants and other third parties. The Commission must follow the normal complaints procedure set out in Commission Regulation 773/2004. If the complaint is pursued in spite of the Commission having accepted the commitments, the complaint must be rejected by decision. The decision rejecting the complaint may be challenged before the Community Courts. The complainant must also be able to challenge the commitments decision in which the Commission closes the case in respect of those parts of the complaint not covered by the commitments. Although the complaint is rejected by separate decision, the two decisions are intrinsically linked.

---

[115] See eg Joined Cases C-68/94 and C-30/95 *France and Others v Commission* [1998] ECR I-1375, para 62.

Indeed, the complainant's right to challenge the rejection decisions can only be maintained by also allowing him to challenge the commitments decision which precludes the Commission from reopening the proceedings to the detriment of the addressee save in the special circumstances set out in Article 9(2).

It might be argued that Article 9 decisions do not significantly affect the legal position of **2.137** third parties. Case law shows that an action for annulment brought by a natural or legal person is admissible only in so far as that person has an interest in the annulment of the contested measure. This means that, the annulment of the measure must of itself be capable of having legal consequences.[116] Unlike exemption decisions adopted under Article 8 of Regulation 17/62, commitments decisions do not make a formal finding of non-infringement and do not legally prevent subsequent challenges before national courts or complaints to national competition authorities.[117] Moreover, third parties are also free to complain to the Commission provided that they submit material new information. While it is true that as long as the facts are the same the Commission is precluded from reopening the proceedings, this fact may well be insufficient for a finding that annulment is capable of having legal consequences for the party bringing the action.

Alternatively, it might be argued that a distinction should be drawn between third parties **2.138** that have responded to the Article 27(4) publication and third parties that have not. In *Kruitvat*,[118] the Court of Justice held that a third party that had not participated in the administrative procedure leading to the adoption of the decision could not be regarded as being individually concerned within the meaning of Article 230 of the Treaty, as it was in a situation which could not be distinguished from that of numerous other economic operators. In the case of Article 9 decisions the way in which third parties can participate in the procedure is by responding to the Article 27(4) publication.

(5) Article 10: Finding of Inapplicability

(a) Introduction

Article 10 empowers the Commission to adopt an entirely new type of decision, namely **2.139** a decision finding that an agreement or practice does not infringe Article 81 or 82. Article 10 provides that where the Community public interest relating to the application of Articles 81 and 82 of the Treaty so requires, the Commission, acting on its own initiative, may by decision find that Article 81 is not applicable to an agreement, a decision by an association of undertakings, or a concerted practice, either because the conditions of Article 81(1) are not fulfilled, or because the conditions of Article 81(3) are satisfied. The Commission may likewise make such a finding with reference to Article 82 of the Treaty. According to Article 27(4) of the Regulation the adoption of an Article 10 decision must be preceded by a publication in the Official Journal of a concise summary of the case and the proposed course of action, ie the adoption of a non-infringement decision.

---

[116] See eg Case T-310/00 *MCI v Commission* [2004] ECR II, para 44.

[117] It is not sufficient that a commitments decision may de facto be taken into account by national competition authorities and courts, see in this respect Joined Cases T-125/97 and T-127/97 *Coca-Cola* [2000] ECR I-1733, para 92.

[118] Case C-70/97 P *Kruitvat* [1998] ECR I-7183.

As in the case of Article 9 decisions interested third parties must thus be invited to submit observations for the same purpose, namely to market test the Commission's preliminary findings.

(b) The Nature and Purpose of Article 10 Decisions

2.140 The Commission has exclusive competence to adopt decisions that make a formal finding of non-infringement. The competition authorities of the Member States have no such power.[119] Recital 14 provides some insight into the reasons why the Commission was granted this special power and into the nature of the scope of this power.

2.141 Recital 14 provides that, in exceptional cases where the public interest of the Community so requires, it may be expedient for the Commission to adopt a decision of a declaratory nature finding that the prohibition in Article 81 or 82 of the Treaty does not apply, with a view to clarifying the law and ensuring its consistent application throughout the Community, in particular with regard to new types of agreements and practices that have not been settled in the existing case law and administrative practice. It follows from Article 10 and recital 14 that non-infringement decisions may only be adopted on the Commission's own initiative and in exceptional circumstances. These limitations are introduced in order to ensure that Article 10 decisions do not become a substitute for exemption decisions previously adopted under Regulation 17/62.

2.142 The reference to the Community public interest, relating to the application of Articles 81 and 82, serves the same purpose. Article 10 decisions cannot be adopted in the private interest of individual undertakings. The specific reference to Articles 81 and 82 makes clear that Article 10 decisions are a competition instrument. They cannot be used to promote interests other than those which can be subsumed under Articles 81 and 82. Other public interest considerations, such as industrial policy objectives cannot be used to establish a Community public interest within the meaning of Article 10 of the Regulation. The concept of Community public interest is thus intrinsically linked to the fundamental aim in Article 3(1)(g) of the Treaty of establishing a system of undistorted competition.[120]

2.143 The purpose behind Article 10 decisions is to provide the Commission with an instrument allowing it, where necessary, to clarify the law and ensure its consistent application throughout the Community. Article 10 thereby links in with the special responsibility of the Commission to define and implement the orientation of Community competition policy and to maintain its consistent application. Indeed, one of the main concerns voiced during the elaboration of Regulation 1/2003 was that the empowerment of Member State competition authorities and courts to apply Articles 81 and 82 in full would endanger the consistent application of Community competition. Article 10 provides the Commission with the means to intervene *ex ante* and orientate Community competition policy by adopting non-infringement decisions in respect of new types of agreements and practices. It also allows the Commission to intervene *ex post* and address an inconsistency in the application of the law.

---

[119] See section C.3.a above.

[120] This notion must be clearly distinguished from the (lack of) 'Community interest' concept developed in the case law and which governs the rejection of complaints.

For instance, if at Member State level the same type of agreement or practice has given rise to diverging decisions, the Commission may intervene and determine the correct approach by adopting an Article 10 decision. However, as is clear from Article 10 and recital 14, the adoption of non-infringement decisions is the exception rather than the rule. The Commission should use the instrument sparingly, reserving it for cases where there is a real need to intervene in favour of an agreement or a practice. Article 10 decisions may be appropriate in particular where an agreement as a whole is considered pro-competitive and has effect in large parts of the Community. In order to ensure that such pro-competitive agreements are allowed to develop, it may be appropriate that the Commission adopts a decision explaining in detail why the agreement is viewed positively.[121]

(c) The Legal Effects of Article 10 Decisions

In their operative part Article 10 decisions make a formal finding that the agreement or practice in question is compatible with Article 81 or 82. It follows from Article 16 that national competition authorities and courts cannot take decisions that run counter to *inter alia* Article 10 decisions adopted by the Commission. Article 10 decisions therefore have strong legal effects. Once adopted, national competition authorities and courts cannot contradict such decisions. Only the European courts have the power to do so, either in the context of a direct action or a preliminary reference under Article 234 of the Treaty.[122]   **2.144**

The statement in recital 14 to the effect that Article 10 decisions are declaratory in nature does not detract from the fact that they have strong legal effects. This statement is meant to distinguish Article 10 decisions from exemption decisions previously adopted under Regulation 17/62 by making it clear that the effects of Article 10 decisions are linked to the underlying facts and not to a pre-defined period of time. Non-infringement decisions state the law as it stands in light of the facts on which they are based. As long as the facts remain substantially the same the binding effect of the decision remains intact. However, if the facts change materially, the assessment may also change affecting the basis for the decision. In other words, Article 10 decisions are binding *rebus sic stantibus*. If it is clear that on the basis of new facts, the Commission would no longer consider the agreement compatible with Articles 81 and 82, national competition authorities and courts can intervene against the agreement or practice without violating their obligations under Article 16. However, in order to avoid being proved wrong at a later point in time, national competition authorities and courts would be well-advised in such circumstances either to contact the Commission[123] or, in the case of the national courts, to make a preliminary reference to the   **2.145**

---

121 Article 10 decisions differ from guidance letters (see section A.5 above) in two ways. First, they have a much broader scope. Guidance letters are confined to addressing specific pre-defined issues whereas Art 10 decisions address the agreement or practice as a whole. Secondly, the legal effects of Art 10 decisions are considerably stronger.

122 A decision which has not been challenged by the addressee within the time limit laid down by Art 230 of the Treaty becomes definitive as against him; see Case C-188/92 *TWD Textilwerke Deggendorf* [1994] ECR I-833, para 13. The addressee cannot subsequently challenge the decision before national courts and rely on the Art 234 reference procedure to have it annulled by the Court of Justice. National courts are not competent to annul Community acts, see Case 314/85 *Foto Frost* [1987] ECR 4199, para 17.

123 Under Art 15(1) of Regulation 1/2003 Member State courts have the right to request opinions from the Commission.

Court of Justice under Article 234 of the Treaty with a view to ascertaining whether the new facts provide a sufficient basis for deviating from the Article 10 decision.

2.146 **The Relationship between Articles 9 and 10**   As a condition for adopting an Article 10 decision the Commission may request that the agreement or practice be modified in certain ways so as to render the agreement or practice compatible with Articles 81 and 82. Article 10, however, does not provide an explicit basis for rendering commitments binding and enforceable. For instance, it may be that for a practice to be compatible with Article 82, the undertaking in question must undertake to grant certain access rights to third parties. Such conditions may be incorporated into the decision, making clear that the undertaking concerned must respect the conditions in order to benefit from the favourable decision. If not, it exposes itself to third party actions and complaints. The fact remains, however, that from the point of view of effective enforcement it would be desirable if commitments could be rendered binding and enforceable, as is the case under Article 9. The question is whether Article 9 and 10 decisions can be combined.

2.147 Regulation 1/2003 is silent on the matter and ultimately it will be for the European courts to decide. However, there would appear to be no fundamental obstacles to an affirmative answer. The fact that, according to recital 13, commitments decisions do not incorporate a conclusion as to whether an infringement still exists and the fact that Article 10 decisions make a formal finding of non-infringement would not appear to speak decisively against a combination of the two instruments. Article 9 decisions leave open the question as to whether an infringement still exists, in order to avoid binding NCAs and national courts with a decision which does not contain detailed legal reasoning showing why the commitments effectively cure the competition problem. By reason of Article 16, this would have been the consequence of making a finding that, following the commitments, there was no longer any infringement. This does not, however, preclude combining an Article 9 decision with an Article 10 decision, which does contain detailed reasoning why the agreement or practice is compatible with Articles 81 and 82 and therefore addresses the concern that underlies the statement in recital 13.

E. Co-operation Between Enforcers

(1) Introduction

2.148 The enforcement system established by Regulation 17/62 implied that the Commission was de facto the foremost, if not the only enforcer of the EC competition rules. Moreover, it meant the Commission spending much of its resources on dealing with notifications rather than on finding and sanctioning infringements of the rules.[124] One of the objectives of Regulation 1/2003 was therefore to enhance the enforcement of the EC competition

---

[124] According to recital 3 of Regulation 1/2003, '[t]he centralised scheme set up by Regulation No 17 (. . .) hampers application of the Community competition rules by the courts and competition authorities of the Member States, and the system of notification it involves prevents the Commission from concentrating its resources on curbing the most serious infringements'.

rules via an increased involvement of the NCAs and the national courts.[125] This increase in enforcers raises questions concerning co-operation and the sharing of work between them and the appropriate instruments to guarantee a consistent application of the rules. The co-operation mechanisms between the competition authorities (the Commission and the national competition authorities) are laid down in Articles 11–14, 16(2) and 22 of Regulation 1/2003 and are further elaborated in the Commission notice on the European Competition Network (also referred to as the 'Network Notice'),[126] whereas the co-operation mechanisms between the Commission and the national courts are the subject of Articles 15 and 16(1) of Regulation 1/2003, which are also further elaborated in a Commission notice (also referred to as the 'notice on co-operation with national courts').[127]

(2) Co-operation within ECN

Regulation 17/62 provided for few co-operation mechanisms between the Commission **2.149** and the national competition authorities. The main forms of co-operation were related to the investigatory powers of the Commission and to the consultation of the NCAs via the Advisory Committee on Restrictive Practices and Monopolies prior to the Commission taking any enforcement decision.[128] Those co-operation mechanisms were clearly insufficient to support the new enforcement model which called for a greater involvement of the NCAs in the enforcement of Articles 81 and 82 EC. The major changes brought about by Regulation 1/2003 relate to: (a) the work sharing amongst the competition authorities; (b) the possibility for NCAs to ask other NCAs to carry out investigations or other fact-finding measures; and (c) the possibility of exchanging information between the competition authorities and of using the exchanged information in evidence for the purpose of applying EC competition law.

(a) The Sharing of Work Amongst the Competition Authorities

Articles 4 and 5 of Regulation 1/2003 give the Commission and the NCAs full parallel **2.150** competence to apply Articles 81 and 82 of the EC Treaty.[129] In the absence of any further provision concerning the division of competence between the ECN members, the question as to which ECN member is dealing with a particular case is not a matter of jurisdiction, but merely of work sharing among the competition authorities. In that context, terms like 'allocation' or 're-allocation' of a case are often used, although both might give the wrong impression of the ECN as a clearing house, where cases are being allocated to one or more

---

125 See recitals 6 and 7 of Regulation 1/2003. For an assessment nearly one year after the date of application of Regulation 1/2003, see the many contributions in 'Title 1: Enhanced Enforcement of EC Competition Rules since 1 May 2004 by the Commission and the National Competition Authorities' in Lowe P and Reynolds M (eds) *Antitrust Reform in Europe: A Year In Practice* (London: International Bar Association, 2005), pp 11–87.

126 The Commission notice on co-operation within the Network of Competition Authorities [2004] OJ C101/43. See also recital 15 of Regulation 1/2003.

127 The Commission notice on the co-operation between the Commission and the courts of the EU Member States in the application of Articles 81 and 82 EC [2004] OJ C 101/54.

128 See respectively Arts 11(1) and 14(5) and Art 10(3) of Regulation 17/62.

129 Point 11 of the Joint Statement of the Council and the Commission on the functioning of the network, available from the Council register at <http://register.consilium.eu.int> (document 15435/02 ADD 1), and point 5 of the Network Notice.

ECN members or transferred from one competition authority to another. Practice so far has shown, however, that very few cases have been transferred from one competition authority to another: cases stay with the competition authority that started proceedings following a complaint, a leniency application or any other indication of a competition law infringement.[130] It is only when the involvement of another competition authority is necessary to ensure the effective enforcement of the EC competition rules in a particular case that the case may change hands.

2.151 In order to ensure that cases are dealt with by the ECN member(s) that can effectively enforce the EC competition rules—the so-called 'well placed competition authority'[131]—ECN members inform one another as soon as they start investigating a case.[132] This early information system permits the network to detect multiple procedures and it allows for a quick and efficient sharing of work within the ECN.[133] Indeed, following the early information, any other competition authority may decide to open proceedings in the same case.[134] When that latter authority is the Commission, Article 11(6) of Regulation 1/2003 states that the NCA that initially dealt with the case is relieved of its competence to apply Articles 81 and 82 EC for that part of the case for which the Commission has initiated proceedings. Conversely, when that latter authority is an NCA, the competition authority

---

[130] See K Dekeyser and D Dalheimer, 'Co-operation within the European Competition Network—taking stock after 10 months of case practice' in Lowe P and Reynolds M (eds) *Antitrust Reform in Europe: A Year In Practice* (London: International Bar Association, 2005) pp 105–123. See also point 6 of the Network Notice.

[131] The Joint Statement referred to in n 129 introduced the notion of 'well placed competition authority' to deal with a case. The Network Notice lists three cumulative conditions to be met for an authority to be considered well placed to deal with a case: '(1) the agreement or practice has substantial direct actual or foreseeable effects on competition within its territory, is implemented within or originates from its territory; (2) the authority is able to effectively bring to an end the entire infringement, ie it can adopt a cease-and-desist order the effect of which will be sufficient to bring an end to the infringement and it can, where appropriate, sanction the infringement adequately; (3) it can gather, possibly with the assistance of other authorities, the evidence required to prove the infringement' (point 8 of the Network Notice). Apart from these criteria, the Commission is said to be particularly well placed to deal with a case 'if more than three Member States are substantially affected by an agreement or practice, if it is closely linked to other Community provisions which may be exclusively or more effectively applied by the Commission, if Community interest requires the adoption of a Commission decision to develop Community competition policy particularly when a new competition issue arises or to ensure effective enforcement' (point 19 of the Joint Statement, see also points 14 and 15 of the Network Notice). These criteria must make the work sharing in the ECN more transparent; they cannot be qualified as jurisdictional criteria: 'each network member retains full discretion in deciding whether or not to investigate a case' (point 5 of the Network Notice).

[132] Pursuant to Art 11(3) of Regulation 1/2003, NCAs inform the Commission when they are acting under Arts 81 or 82 EC, before or without delay after commencing the first formal investigative measure. It has been agreed amongst the members of the ECN that the NCAs will also get that information (point 17 of the Network Notice). Similarly, the Commission will inform the other ECN members when it starts investigating a case (see Art 11(2) of Regulation 1/2003). In accordance with point 17 of the Network Notice, the ECN members give each other only limited details of the pending case, such as the product, territories and parties concerned, the alleged infringement, the suspected duration of the infringement, and the origin of the case.

[133] Practice so far shows, however, that work sharing in the network is often being organised informally in the earliest stages of the procedures, even before the other ECN members are formally informed about a new case. See K Dekeyser and D Dalheimer, 'Co-operation within the European Competition Network—taking stock after 10 months of case practice', referred to above in n 130, p 112.

[134] See, however, n 159 and the accompanying text on the limitations on using information voluntarily submitted by a leniency applicant.

that initially dealt with the case can continue dealing with the case in parallel or, preferably,[135] it may abstain from acting, suspend or close its file either on the basis of its discretion (not) to act or on the basis of Article 13 of Regulation 1/2003.

Article 13 of Regulation 1/2003 offers the ECN members a stand-alone legal basis to sus- **2.152** pend or to close proceedings because another ECN member is dealing or already has dealt with the case.[136] The direct effect and the primacy of this rule implies that no further national (implementing) act is needed for an NCA to use Article 13, nor can a (conflicting) national provision prevent, limit, or condition such use. At the same time, it should be recalled that Article 13 confers a discretionary power upon the ECN members. That means that although there can be no generic limitation to the use of Article 13, an ECN member can in an individual case decide not to suspend or close its proceedings in order to ensure an effective enforcement of the EC competition rules.[137]

There follow some further reflections on the fact that an ECN member is able to suspend **2.153** or close its own proceedings on the basis 'that a case is (being) dealt with' by another ECN member:

- Although Article 13 is not explicit on this point, one can deduce from the fact that it is meant to contribute to the work sharing within the ECN that Article 13 can only be used as a legal basis to suspend or to close proceedings if the competition authority that is already acting or that has already acted on a case, is doing/has done so on the basis of Article 81 or 82 EC, with or without a parallel application of national competition law.[138] Indeed, when a case is being dealt with or has been dealt with solely on the basis of national competition law, an ECN member cannot invoke a satisfactory enforcement of EC competition law as a justification to suspend or to close its own proceedings under Article 81 or 82. It is, however, submitted that the suspension of proceedings or the rejection of a complaint can be legitimately based on Article 13 if at the time of the suspension or rejection another ECN member was dealing with the case under EC competition law, regardless of the outcome of the latter proceedings; this is so even if the proceedings did not finally lead to the application of Articles 81 or 82 because, for example, on the basis of the investigation, it was finally concluded that trade between Member States was not affected.
- For an ECN member to be able to suspend or to close proceedings on a case, another competition authority has to be dealing or to have dealt with the same case. According to Article 13 a case can be considered to be the same when it concerns 'the same agreement, decision of an association or practice'. In the Network Notice, this precondition has been

---

135 According to recital 18 of Regulation 1/2003, 'the objective [is] that each case [is] handled by a single authority'. However, '[p]arallel action by two or three NCAs may be appropriate where an agreement or practice has substantial effects on competition mainly in their respective territories and the action of only one NCA would not be sufficient to bring the entire infringement to an end and/or to sanction it adequately' (point 12 of the Network Notice).

136 Although Art 13(1) only mentions the rejection of a complaint, it can be argued that those NCAs which formally need to close an *ex officio* proceeding can base such closure on Art 13(1) of Regulation 1/2003. See also, implicitly, points 24 and 25 of the Network Notice.

137 See point 22 of the Network Notice.

138 See the first sentence of recital 18 of Regulation 1/2003.

tightened by requiring that 'the [same] competition issue' is/has been dealt with, which implies that the agreement, decision, or practice involves 'the same infringement(s) on the same relevant geographic and product markets'.[139]

- In order to clarify what is meant by 'dealing with a case', the Network Notice states that another competition authority is required to be investigating or to have investigated the case.[140] It is thus not necessary for that latter competition authority to have opened proceedings in the case. Since ECN members inform one another as soon as they start investigating a case, that information can be referred to as proof of the fact that the case is being dealt with.

(b) The NCA's Request to another NCA to Carry Out an Investigation

2.154 Regulation 1/2003 also introduced, in Article 22(1), the possibility of NCAs carrying out inspections or other fact-finding measures in their territory at the request and for the benefit of another NCA. Previously, only the Commission could request such assistance from an NCA.[141] Together with the possibility of exchanging information and using it in evidence pursuant to Article 12 of Regulation 1/2003, this new facility was necessary to bring about efficient work sharing within the ECN and thus effective enforcement of the EC competition rules.[142] Without it, it would indeed have been impossible for the particular NCA dealing with a case to obtain all necessary evidence to effectively apply Articles 81 and 82 EC. The result would have been that all cases where the evidence is spread over more than one Member State would have had to be dealt with by the Commission or by several NCAs in parallel. Article 22(1) now permits enforcement by the single national competition authority considered well placed to deal with the case.

2.155 Similar to other provisions of Regulation 1/2003, Article 22(1) offers NCAs a stand-alone legal basis with which to carry out inspections or other fact-finding measures on the request of another NCA.[143] The direct effect and the primacy of this rule implies that no further national (implementing) act is needed for an NCA to make use of Article 22(1), nor can a (conflicting) national provision prevent, limit, or condition such use. At the same time, it should be recalled that Article 22(1) confers a discretionary power upon the NCAs. That means that although there can be no generic limitation to the use of Article 22(1), an NCA can in an individual case decide not to carry out the requested inspection or fact-finding measure. It is submitted, however, that, because of the obligation of 'close co-operation' within the network, which is 'dedicated to the effective enforcement of EC competition rules', an NCA can only refuse such assistance in exceptional circumstances.[144]

2.156 When an NCA carries out an inspection or another fact-finding measure on behalf of another NCA, it does so 'under its national law' and 'pursuant to its own rules of procedure,

---

[139] Point 21 of the Network Notice.
[140] Point 20 of the Network Notice.
[141] Article 13 of Regulation 17/62, now Art 22(2) of Regulation 1/2003.
[142] See recital 28 of Regulation 1/2003.
[143] See eg paras 2.161–2.168 below on Art 12 and para 2.152 above on Art 13.
[144] Article 11(1) of Regulation 1/2003 and point 5 of the Joint Statement referred to in n 129. It could even be argued that the duty of loyal co-operation as laid down in Art 10 EC would oblige an NCA to provide the necessary assistance for the purpose of applying the EC competition rules.

and under its own powers of investigation'.[145] That implies, for example, that companies' rights relating to the inspection are determined by the national law of the assisting NCA. Thus, the question whether information was collected legally or not is determined by the national law of the assisting NCA that has collected the information. However, Article 12 of Regulation 1/2003 governs the subsequent exchange and use of the information collected in an investigation pursuant to Article 22(1).[146]

(c) The Exchange of Information and its use in Evidence

Regulation 17/62 contained little provision for exchange of information between the Commission and the national competition authorities and none at all for exchange of information between the NCAs. Apart from the provisions on the basis of which the Commission informed an NCA about its investigation initiatives in that particular Member State,[147] Regulation 17 dealt with the exchange of information between competition authorities in its Articles 10 and 11(1). Article 11(1) allowed the Commission to 'obtain all necessary information from the Governments and competent authorities of the Member States', whereas Article 10(1) obliged the Commission to send the competent authorities of the Member States copies of the most important documents lodged with the Commission for the purpose of enforcing the EC competition rules. Whereas the former 'exchange' aimed at providing the recipient, *in casu* the Commission, with the evidence it could use in its proceedings, the latter 'exchange' of information did not have that objective at all. **2.157**

Article 11 listed some of the tools available to the Commission for gathering the information necessary to apply Articles 81 and 82 EC. The information Member States sent to the Commission could thus be used in evidence by the latter. By contrast, the information sent to the NCAs on the basis of Article 10(1) was meant 'to inform Member States of Community proceedings relating to undertakings situated within their territories and (. . .) to enhance the provision of information to the Commission by enabling it to compare the particulars given by the undertakings with such indications and observations as may be made to it by the Member State concerned'.[148] Since the information which the Commission sent to the NCAs by virtue of Article 10(1) was intended to allow the Commission to apply Articles 81 and 82 EC in accordance with the provisions of Regulation 17 and not to furnish evidence to be used by NCAs in proceedings governed by national law, any use in evidence of that information by an NCA would violate the fundamental rights of undertakings and the professional secrecy rules as laid down in Article 20 of Regulation 17. Indeed, the Court of Justice found that: **2.158**

> . . . professional secrecy [makes] it impossible for the authorities legally in possession of such information to use it, in the absence of an express provision allowing them to do so, for a reason other than that for which it was obtained. Those safeguards would be violated if

---

[145] Article 22(1) of Regulation 1/2003 and point 29 of the Network Notice.

[146] Conversely, it is submitted that the information obtained during the inspections referred to in Art 22(2) must be sent to the Commission in accordance with Art 18(6) of Regulation 1/2003.

[147] See Arts 11(2) and (6), 14(2) and (4) of Regulation 17/62.

[148] Case C-67/91 *Dirección General de Defensa de la Competencia v Asociación Española de Banca Privada and others* [1992] ECR I-4785, para 34.

an authority other than the Commission were able to use, as evidence in procedures not governed by Regulation 17, information obtained [by the Commission for the purpose of applying Articles 81 and 82 EC].[149]

2.159 In order to enhance co-operation between the European competition authorities in the enforcement of the European competition rules, Article 12 of Regulation 1/2003 removes the restrictions that flow from the *Spanish Banks* case law. In contrast with the regime that existed before 1 May 2004, Regulation 1/2003 contains an explicit provision concerning the exchange of information between the European competition authorities and the use of such exchanged information for the purpose of applying the EC competition rules. These powers constitute a cornerstone of the efficient and effective work sharing and handling of cases within the ECN. As it is now possible to exchange information within the ECN, it no longer matters which competition authority discovered the evidence necessary to find the infringement: the authority that can stop and sanction the infringement will be able to obtain the evidence from other competition authorities and use it to prove the infringement.

2.160 This section discusses first in (i), the main features of the exchange of information regime within the ECN as it has been established by Regulation 1/2003, focusing in paragraphs 2.161–2.168 on the power of ECN members to exchange information between themselves, in particular the exchange of information voluntarily submitted by a leniency applicant, and, in paragraphs 2.169–2.172 on the safeguards linked to the exchange of confidential information; and in (ii), the use of the exchanged information in evidence.

(i) The Exchange of Information within the ECN

'[T]he Commission and the [National] Competition Authorities (. . .) shall have the Power to provide one another with and use in Evidence'

2.161 *Empowering ECN members to exchange information*   Article 12 of Regulation 1/2003 *empowers* the ECN members to exchange information between themselves and to use that information as evidence in their cases. The right of NCAs to exchange and to use information flows directly from the Council Regulation and because of the primacy of European law, it can neither be jeopardised nor conditioned by a national provision. Since the Council Regulation constitutes a sufficient legal basis for the ECN members to exchange information within the ECN, the legality of such exchange cannot be challenged.

2.162 The same goes for the use of exchanged information in evidence: as long as the information has been legally collected by the transmitting ECN member, its use by the receiving ECN member cannot be challenged. The limitations on the use in evidence of exchanged information that would exist under the domestic rules of the receiving ECN member are irrelevant because of the primacy of European law. This implies that an ECN member can

---

[149] ibid, paras 37 and 38. The Court accepted, however, that 'Member States are not required to ignore the information disclosed to them and thereby undergo (. . .) "acute amnesia". That information provides circumstantial evidence which may, if necessary, be taken into account to justify initiation of a national procedure' (para 39).

lawfully use in evidence information that was legally collected by another ECN member, even if the former could not itself have obtained that information.[150]

Allowing ECN members to exchange information   Article 12, however, *does not oblige* ECN **2.163** members to exchange information; it only allows them to do so. Again, that does not mean that a national provision could deprive NCAs of the benefit of the Council Regulation nor could its use be limited in a *general* way.[151] The option laid down in Article 12 just implies that in a *specific* case, an ECN member itself has the discretion not to exchange information or not to use the information exchanged in evidence.

How the *option* of Article 12 of Regulation 1/2003 relates to the *duty* of loyal co-operation **2.164** as laid down in Article 10 EC nevertheless remains an open question. In its interpretation of that Treaty provision, which obliges the EU Member States to facilitate the achievement of the Community's tasks, the Community courts found that Article 10 EC imposes on the European institutions and the EU Member States mutual duties of sincere co-operation with a view to attaining the objectives of the EC Treaty.[152] In the context of co-operation between the Commission and the national courts, this provision was referred to by the Court of Justice in order to oblige the Commission to transmit information it held to national courts that were dealing with an infringement of Community rules.[153] One may wonder whether such an obligation on the part of the Commission also exists in relation to the national competition authorities and, whether or not an NCA is under a duty to provide other NCAs with the information it holds.[154] The main argument in favour of such reading of Article 10 EC is its rationale, namely the need for Community institutions and national authorities to assist one another in the application of European rules. The consequence would thus be that the option laid down in Article 12 of Regulation 1/2003 should be interpreted as an obligation to exchange the information requested by another ECN member for the purpose of applying the EC competition rules.[155] One could argue, however, that the Council clearly did not intend to impose such an obligation on the ECN members when it expressly provided for the *option* to exchange evidence. So specific a provision would then prevail over the more general obligation of mutual assistance laid down in Article 10 EC, which is only applicable to the extent that Community legislation

---

[150] See also Margaret Bloom, 'Benefits and challenges of leniency programmes in the context of EC modernisation' in *Antitrust between EC law and national law*, UAE Symposium, VI Conference at Treviso, Italy, 13/14 May, Enrico Adriano Raffaelli (ed), (Bruylant: Brussels, 2005). When using the evidence exchanged under Art 12 of Regulation 1/2003, the Commission and the national competition authorities obviously must respect the general principles of Community law, such as the rights of defence of the parties involved. This issue is further elaborated under paras 2.174–2.175 below.

[151] eg a national provision that would prohibit an NCA from using in evidence documents from in-house lawyers, even if those documents were lawfully obtained from another ECN member that had legally collected the documents, would violate Art 12.

[152] See eg Case C-2/88 *Imm Zwartveld* [1990] ECR I-3365, para 17.

[153] Case T-353/94 *Postbank* [1996] ECR II-921, para 64. Further under paras 2.264–2.267 below.

[154] Pursuant to Art 18(6) of Regulation 1/2003, NCAs already have a duty to provide the Commission with the information it asks for in order to apply Arts 81 and 82 EC.

[155] The question is particularly relevant to the exchange of information between NCAs, since an NCA is already pursuant to Art 18(6) of Regulation 1/2003 obliged to 'provide the Commission with all necessary information to carry out the duties assigned to it by th[e] Regulation'.

remains silent as to the co-operation between the European institutions and the Member States.[156]

2.165 In instances where the combined reading of Article 10 EC and Article 12 of Regulation 1/2003 would lead to an obligation on the ECN members to exchange information between themselves, such an obligation obviously cannot be unlimited. Indeed, the Court's case law concerning the limitations applicable to the obligation on the Commission to transmit information it holds to national courts would also have to apply *mutatis mutandis* to the exchange of information within the ECN. That would imply, for example, that the Commission may refuse to transmit information for overriding reasons relating to the need to safeguard the interests of the Community or to avoid any interference with its functioning and independence, in particular by jeopardizing the accomplishment of the tasks entrusted to it.[157] The Commission relies on this exception, for instance, to avoid transmission to national courts of information voluntarily submitted by a leniency applicant without the consent of that applicant.[158] This concern to protect the information voluntarily submitted by a leniency applicant, and thus to protect the leniency programme of the competition authority, lies at the heart of some detailed provisions in the Network Notice regarding the exchange of such information.

2.166 *Exchanging information voluntarily submitted by a leniency applicant*   The Network Notice affirms as a main principle that an ECN member will only transmit information voluntarily submitted by a leniency applicant to another ECN member when the leniency applicant consents to that exchange.[159] The reasoning behind this rule is obvious: potential leniency applicants will no longer apply for leniency if the information they voluntarily submit to one ECN member (which in return grants immunity or reduction of fine to the applicant) can be used against them by another ECN member, in particular when the latter does not run a leniency programme and the leniency applicant was thus not even able to apply for leniency to the would-be receiving ECN member.[160] The same applies, of course, to the information that has been gathered as a result of the leniency application (eg incriminating documents

---

[156] On the complementary nature of Art 10 EC, see Case 2/73 *Riseria Luigi Geddo v Ente Nazionale Risi* [1973] ECR 865, para 4: 'In providing that Member States shall take all appropriate measures to ensure that their obligations are carried out and shall abstain from any measure liable to jeopardize the attainment of the objectives of the Treaty, Article 5 [now Article 10 EC] imposes a general obligation on Member States, the actual significance of which depends, in each particular case, on the provisions of the Treaty or on the rules laid down within its general framework.'

[157] Compare with Case C-2/88 *Zwartveld* [1990] ECR I-4405, paras 10 and 11; Case T-353/94 *Postbank* [1996] ECR II-921, para 93; and Case C-275/00 *First and Franex* [2002] ECR I-10943, para 49.

[158] See point 26 *in fine* of the Commission Notice on co-operation with national courts.

[159] See in particular points 40 and 41. For the sake of completeness, it should be recalled that the Network Notice also provides for protective measures in the case of other exchanges within the ECN of information voluntarily submitted by a leniency applicant (see point 39 of the Network Notice), eg information submitted to the network pursuant to Art 11 of Regulation 1/2003 (for work sharing purposes or coherence check) cannot be used by other ECN members as the basis for starting an investigation on their own behalf. Similarly, information transmitted with a view to obtaining assistance from the receiving ECN member under Arts 20, 21 or 22 of Regulation 1/2003 may only be used for the purpose of the application of the said Articles.

[160] At present, five EU Member States do not run a leniency programme: Denmark, Italy, Malta, Slovenia and Spain. By law of 4 August 2006, the Italian competition authority has also been formally entitled to adopt a leniency programme. For a regular update, see <http://europa.eu.int/comm/competition/antitrust/legislation/authorities_with_leniency_programme.pdf>.

found during an inspection). If there were a free exchange of the latter information, the leniency applicant could still suffer from a sanction imposed by another ECN member, if the latter were able to prove an infringement of the competition rules on basis of information that was found as an indirect consequence of the leniency application. Information obtained as a result of the leniency application therefore cannot be transmitted to another ECN member without the consent of the leniency applicant.

Although these principles guarantee the required adequate protection of the leniency **2.167** applicant, they might have the adverse effect that not only the leniency applicant but also other participants in the agreement or conduct that infringes the competition rules will escape from effective sanctioning. Indeed, the exchange of information between ECN members will most likely take place because the ECN member wishing to transmit information cannot or can only partially effectively sanction the infringement of the competition rules. The ECN member wishing to receive the information is therefore the authority most likely to be involved in the sanctioning of the infringement. If the exchange between ECN members of information obtained through a leniency application solely depends on the consent of the leniency applicant, the latter will only give its consent when it does not risk any sanction being imposed by the intended recipient ECN member. Under the current rules, that implies that the leniency applicant also applied for leniency to the intended recipient ECN member. It goes without saying that in such a scenario the exchange of information is of little use since the intended recipient ECN member would have obtained the information directly from the leniency applicant. The chances are therefore high that the limitations to the exchange of information as explained in the previous paragraph lead to no information being exchanged at all, which implies an unwanted scenario of structural under-punishment because not only the leniency applicant but also the other participants in the behaviour infringing the competition rules will escape effective punishment.

In order to guarantee effective punishment for infringements of the European competition **2.168** rules, the Network Notice therefore provides for the possibility of an exchange of information between ECN members in the absence of the consent of the leniency applicant, while maintaining the effectiveness of the leniency programme of the transmitting ECN member.[161] In order to reconcile these two objectives, the ECN members guarantee to the leniency applicant that he will not be punished by the receiving ECN member on the basis of the information transmitted, nor will he be punished on the basis of any other information subsequently obtained.[162] To that end, the recipient ECN member will give a commitment

---

[161] Apart from the scenario described in this paragraph, there are two further situations where consent is not required for an exchange between ECN members of information obtained through or as a result of a leniency application between ECN members: (1) information may be sent to an ECN member that received a leniency application relating to the same infringement from the same applicant; and (2) if the ECN member that received the leniency application asks an NCA to conduct inspections on its territory, the latter NCA may send the information obtained to the ECN member that initially asked for this assistance.

[162] The guarantee is laid down in the Network Notice. The Commission is bound by the notices it issues and, for this particular notice, all NCAs have signed a statement declaring that they will also abide by the principles set out in the notice, in particular the principles 'relating to the protection of applicants claiming the benefit of a leniency programme, in any case in which [they are] acting or may act and to which those principles apply'. For the list of NCAs that have signed the said statement, see <http://europa.eu.int/comm/competition/antitrust/legislation/list_of_authorities_joint_statement.pdf>.

in writing not to use such information to impose sanctions on the leniency applicant or on any other natural or legal person the applicant wishes to protect. The leniency applicant will receive a copy of this written commitment.[163]

2.169 **'[A]ny Matter of Fact or of Law, including Confidential Information'** Article 12 of Regulation 1/2003 allows the ECN members to exchange all information between them, explicitly emphasising that this also includes confidential information. It is only by allowing ECN members to exchange confidential information that the ECN member dealing with a case can obtain all evidence necessary to prove the alleged infringement. It may be that some ECN members may be reluctant to divulge confidential information, because they were previously precluded from disclosing business secrets or any other confidential information they obtained in the exercise of their function.[164] However, confidential information can be safely exchanged within the ECN, because in that context the Regulation has replaced the national guarantees for protection of confidential information with a Community-wide one.

2.170 *The relation between Article 12 and the national law provisions prohibiting NCAs from divulging confidential information* Most, if not all, EU Member States have rules preventing NCAs from disclosing confidential information they obtain in the exercise of their duties. It is, however, difficult to reconcile those rules with an efficient allocation of cases within the ECN. Indeed, one can easily imagine a situation in which one ECN member is dealing with a case for which another ECN member holds part of the evidence. If in those circumstances, the latter ECN member was prevented from sending the confidential parts of the said evidence, the former ECN member could encounter difficulties in the enforcement of the EC competition rules. Article 12 therefore explicitly allows for the exchange of confidential information and, due to the primacy of EU law, NCAs cannot rely on national law provisions in order to avoid sending the confidential information to other ECN members.[165]

2.171 The exchange of confidential information not only contributes to the efficient sharing of work within the ECN. Moreover, it releases ECN members from a duty that might exist under own national provisions, to verify, assess, and pronounce themselves on the confidential nature of (parts of) the information they have obtained and intend to send to another ECN member. Since the nature of the information cannot determine whether it is to be exchanged or not, the ECN member intending to transmit the information does not need

---

[163] According to point 41(2) of the Network Notice '[n]o consent is required where the receiving authority has provided a written commitment that neither the information transmitted to it nor any other information it may obtain following the date and time of transmission as noted by the transmitting authority, will be used by it or by any other authority to which the information is subsequently transmitted to impose sanctions (a) on the leniency applicant, (b) on any other legal or natural person covered by the favourable treatment offered by the transmitting authority as a result of the application made by the applicant under its leniency programme or (c) on any employee or former employee of any of the persons covered by (a) or (b). A copy of the receiving authority's written commitment will be provided to the applicant'.

[164] For the Commission, this rule is an emanation of the general duty not to disclose information of the kind covered by the obligation of professional secrecy (Art 287 EC), whereas for NCAs the obligation follows from provisions in their national law.

[165] See para 2.161.

to classify the information. Furthermore, to the extent that the original information is being sent, the transmitting ECN member can no longer respond to a demand for access to that information, so the ECN member intending to transmit the information does not need to classify the information that is to be exchanged for that purpose either. Even if the ECN member transmitting the information decides to send copies to the requesting ECN member, the decision whether or not to exchange information should not be influenced by the fact that such information has been classified or may at a later stage be classified as confidential.[166] Indeed, because of the common ECN minimum standard for the protection of confidential information, the intended recipient ECN member will also be required to guarantee the confidentiality of the exchanged information.

A wider umbrella for the protection of confidential information   The exchange of confiden-   **2.172**
tial information within the ECN must not mean that once such information is within the ECN, it can 'escape' via the ECN member whose own national rules, if any, provide the lowest degree of protection for confidential information. Regulation 1/2003 therefore contains a common European minimum standard for the protection of confidential information throughout the European Union. According to Article 28(2) of Regulation 1/2003, the ECN members 'shall not disclose information acquired or exchanged by them pursuant to this Regulation and of the kind covered by the obligation of professional secrecy'. This implies that all European competition authorities must have an effective procedure to ensure that information which circulates within the ECN and which is covered by professional secrecy, remains within the ECN. The common European concept of professional secrecy, which encompasses the protection of business secrets and other confidential information, thus constitutes an appropriate protection of such information within the ECN.[167]

(ii)   The Use in Evidence of the Information Exchanged within the ECN

Article 12 of Regulation 1/2003 not only regulates the exchange of information within the   **2.173**
ECN, but also constitutes an important legal basis for the use in evidence of information exchanged. In contrast with the regime that existed before 1 May 2004, Article 12 allows the ECN members to use in their proceedings all information received from another ECN member, notwithstanding any national provision to the contrary.[168] The only limitations to this power are those contained in Article 12:

- the information should be used for the application of EC competition rules;
- the information should be used in respect to the subject matter for which it was collected by the transmitting ECN member; and

---

[166] In those exceptional cases where the transmitting ECN member—before or after the transmission—has classified information as confidential on the basis of national legislation, such qualification can obviously not bind the receiving ECN member. The latter will, however, most likely take into account the views indicated by the transmitting ECN member as much as possible. Because of the primacy of European law, a Commission decision regarding the confidentiality of information binds the other ECN members.

[167] See further on the implication of Art 28 in paras 2.185–2.202 below.

[168] National law provisions can thus not limit this facility. Further on this argument, see paras 2.161–2.162.

- application of the restrictions in Article 12(3) with regard to the use of information in evidence when imposing sanctions on natural persons.

Before examining these restrictions further, however, it may be useful also to recall the restrictions on the use of information that flow from the respect for the general principles of Community law and in particular the fundamental rights as guaranteed by the European Convention for the Protection of Human Rights and Fundamental Freedoms ('ECHR').

2.174 **The general principles of Community law** All EU Member States have signed and ratified the ECHR and the European Union itself is bound to respect the fundamental rights as guaranteed by that Convention.[169] It did not come as a surprise, therefore, that the Court of Justice identified these fundamental rights as integral to the general principles of Community law, which should be respected by both the European institutions and the EU Member States, when the latter apply Community law.[170] It is precisely this common minimum standard of fundamental rights which is at the heart of the regime of Article 12, where it states that the ECN member receiving information from another ECN member can use that information in evidence against an undertaking without any restriction other than those listed in Article 12. Without this common minimum standard, the implicit mutual recognition of each other's standard of protection of the rights of defence enjoyed by undertakings would have been impossible.[171] In the same way, this mutual recognition of each other's standard of protection of fundamental rights is necessary to bring about an effective exchange of information within the ECN and thus to an efficient work sharing within the ECN. Indeed, without this mutual recognition of standards of fundamental rights, the use in evidence—and thus the preceding exchange—of information would be seriously limited. That would mainly be so because the exchange would depend on whether or not in the state of the ECN member intending to transmit the information the standard of fundamental rights for the collection of the information is such that the information exchanged can be used in evidence under the standards of the intended recipient ECN member. It could further be assumed that such exercise of comparative law would give rise to perpetual and even vexatious challenges by the undertakings involved.

2.175 The fact that Article 12 of Regulation 1/2003 provides for an implicit mutual recognition of standards of fundamental rights implies that such challenges are meaningless. It may indeed happen that the national rules of the recipient ECN member offer greater protection of the rights of defence than is guaranteed under the ECHR standard or under the national standard of the transmitting ECN member. However, because of the implicit mutual recognition such a difference in standards cannot prevent the recipient ECN member from using in evidence information exchanged to the extent that the information was collected legally by the transmitting ECN member in accordance with

---

[169] Article 6(2) EU.

[170] Case 5/88 *Hubert Wachauf v Germany* [1989] ECR 2609, para 19.

[171] According to recital 16 of Regulation 1/2003, '[t]he rights of defence enjoyed by undertakings in the various systems can be considered as sufficiently equivalent'.

its domestic rules.[172] For instance, even if the national law of the receiving NCA grants legal privilege to documents emanating from in-house lawyers, that NCA can without any problem lawfully use in evidence such documents where they are received from an NCA whose law does not extend the legal privilege to such documents and who thus has collected them legally. It is therefore possible that the primacy of European law results in an NCA using in evidence information that has been collected by another (transmitting) ECN member by a means unavailable to the recipient ECN member.[173]

Information exchanged can only be used in evidence for the application of EC Competition rules   Article 12(2) states that '[i]nformation exchanged shall only be used in evidence for the purpose of applying Article 81 or Article 82 of the Treaty', thereby excluding the use of information in evidence for any other purpose, such as the application of other Community law provisions or of national competition law. This limitation reflects the respect for professional secrecy rules and the rights of the defence, according to which, in the absence of an explicit derogation, information can only be used for the purpose for which it was obtained.[174] Since the information is being exchanged for the purpose of applying Articles 81 and/or 82 (see Article 12(1) of the Regulation), the recipient competition authority cannot use the exchanged information in evidence for a different purpose. Moreover, that restriction is directly related to the legal basis of Regulation 1/2003, namely Article 83, which allows the European institutions to adopt regulations 'to give effect to the principles set out in Articles 81 and 82' EC only. It was thus legally impossible for the Council to empower the competition authorities to exchange and to use in evidence information for the purpose of applying only national competition law. **2.176**

However, since the final version of Article 3 of Regulation 1/2003 allows NCAs and national courts to apply national competition rules to cases which fall within the realm of Articles 81 or 82 EC and obliges NCAs and national courts to apply the EC competition rules in those cases as well, it was not feasible to limit the use in evidence of exchanged information to the application of Articles 81 and 82 EC alone.[175] Indeed, allowing the use in evidence of exchanged information for the application of EC competition law, while excluding such use for the parallel application of national competition law to the same case would have a chilling effect on the application of national rules as that application is **2.177**

---

172 It cannot be excluded that the legality of the collection of the information by the transmitting ECN member is challenged. It has been agreed within the ECN that the transmitting ECN member may inform the receiving ECN member whether the gathering of the information was contested or could still be contested (point 27 of the Network Notice).

173 This finding is particularly important when read in combination with Art 22 of Regulation 1/2003, which allows (or when requested by the Commission 'obliges') an NCA to carry out any inspection or other fact-finding measure on its territory under its national law in response to a demand from another NCA. The collected evidence is subsequently exchanged and used in accordance with Art 12.

174 See Case C-67/91 *Dirección General de Defensa de la Competencia v Asociación Española de Banca Privada and others* [1992] ECR I-4785, para 37; and Case 85/87 *Dow Benelux* [1989] ECR 3137, para 18. Although in the latter case, the court addressed the scenario of the use of information that was obtained beyond the scope (subject matter and purpose) of an investigation, the finding of the court probably also holds for the use of information beyond the scope of the investigation.

175 Compare Arts 3 and 12(2) of the Commission proposal ([2000] OJ C365E/284) with the ultimate version of those provisions.

allowed by Article 3. Article 12(2) therefore, by way of explicit derogation from the absolute parallelism between the purpose of the exchange of information and the use of that information, does allow the use of exchanged information for the application of national competition law where the latter is applied both in the same case and in parallel to EC competition law.

2.178 In addition to the requirement of parallel application, Article 12(2) limits the use of exchanged information for the application of national competition law to situations in which the latter does not lead to a different outcome than would the application of EC competition law. Read together with the last sentence of Article 3(2) which contains an exception to the convergence rule, this further limitation implies that NCAs cannot use information exchanged under Article 12(1) to apply stricter national competition law which prohibits or sanctions unilateral conduct that would be permitted under EC competition law. It could also be argued that Article 12(2) excludes the use of exchanged information to grant an exemption under national law, even if applied in parallel with EC competition law, since that outcome is excluded when the NCA is applying the latter rules.[176]

2.179 **Information exchanged can only be used in evidence in respect of the subject matter for which it was collected**   Article 12(2) further limits the use of the exchanged information in evidence by the recipient competition authority to 'the subject-matter for which it was collected by the transmitting authority'. Again, this limitation reflects the respect for professional secrecy rules and the rights of the defence enjoyed by the undertaking against which the information is being used.[177] In order to define the scope of 'the subject-matter for which [the information] was collected', inspiration may be drawn from the European courts' case law regarding the limitations imposed by the subject matter of an investigation on the subsequent use by the Commission of the information obtained during that investigation. In *Hoechst*, the Court linked the requirement for the Commission to specify the subject matter of an inspection to its obligation to 'clearly indicate the presumed facts which it intends to investigate'.[178] That would imply that the receiving competition authority could only use the information exchanged in evidence to prove an infringement relating to the same factual context as that which underlay the information gathering measure of the transmitting authority.

2.180 The Court's case law seems to suggest that this factual context is composed of the product and the conduct under scrutiny.[179] Clearly, the identity of the undertaking under scrutiny is not part of that factual context: thus the information obtained from one undertaking by the transmitting authority can be used against another undertaking by the recipient authority.[180] Similarly, it is submitted that the legal classification of the

---

[176] On the national notification systems and how they relate to Arts 3 and 5 of Regulation 1/2003, see paras 2.87–2.89 above.

[177] See n 174 and point 28(b) of the Network Notice.

[178] Joined Cases 46/87 and 227/88 *Hoechst* [1989] ECR 2859, para 41.

[179] ibid, para 42.

[180] Joined Cases T-305/94 to T-307/94, T-313/94 to T-316/94, T-318/94, T-325/94, T-328/94, T-329/94 and T-335/94 *Limburgse Vinyl Maatschappij and others ('PVC II')* [1999] ECR II-931, paras 509 and 512; and

investigated conduct as a particular infringement is not part of the subject matter of the information gathering measure because it goes beyond the pure factual setting of the investigative measure. As a result, the fact that the transmitting authority has classified some specific behaviour as a possible infringement of national competition rules and collected information for the purpose of applying those rules cannot prevent the receiving authority from using the collected and subsequently exchanged information for the purpose of applying EC competition rules, provided the factual context remains the same.

The limitations with regard to the use of information in evidence to impose sanctions on natural persons   Whereas the Commission cannot impose sanctions on natural persons, NCAs can impose whatever penalty is provided for in their national law, including sanctions on natural persons.[181] If an NCA that has received information from another ECN member would like to use that information in evidence against a natural person, Article 12(3) of Council Regulation 1/2003 sets further limitations on that use. According to that provision: **2.181**

> [i]nformation exchanged pursuant to [Article 12(1)] can only be used in evidence to impose sanctions on natural persons where (-) the law of the transmitting authority foresees sanctions of a similar kind in relation to an infringement of Article 81 or Article 82 of the Treaty or, in the absence thereof, (-) the information has been collected in a way which respects the same level of protection of the rights of defence of natural persons as provided for under the national rules of the receiving authority. However, in this [latter] case, the information exchanged cannot be used by the receiving authority to impose custodial sanctions.

It is not surprising that these limitations are formulated as a conditional mutual recognition of standards of fundamental rights. Indeed, the very reason for these limitations is the difference in fundamental rights protection for natural and legal persons. To treat proceedings against natural persons and those against legal persons in the same way—which would have been the consequence of an absolute mutual recognition of fundamental rights standards—was considered to be an inappropriate circumvention of the higher level of protection accorded to the fundamental rights of natural persons. As a consequence, the unconditional use in proceedings against natural persons of evidence that was collected in proceedings against an undertaking is replaced by a conditional use.   **2.182**

In much the same fashion as the implicit mutual recognition of standards of fundamental rights for the use of exchanged information in evidence against legal persons as outlined in paragraphs 2.174–2.175 above, the first indent of Article 12(3) reveals that the ECN members recognise each other's standards on condition that the law of both the transmitting and the receiving ECN member foresees 'sanctions of a similar kind'. Whether a sanction is of a similar kind does not depend on the classification of the sanctions under   **2.183**

Joined Cases T-67/00, T-68/00, T-71/00 and T-78/00 *JFE Engineering and others ('seamless steel tubes and pipes')* [2004] ECR II-2501, para 192: 'no provision or any general principle of Community law prohibits the Commission from relying, as against an undertaking, on statements made by other incriminated undertakings.'

[181] Compare Arts 23 and 24 of Regulation 1/2003 with Art 5 of the Regulation.

national law (eg 'administrative' or 'criminal'). The Regulation refers rather to the underlying difference in fundamental rights depending on whether the proceedings may result in custodial sanctions or in other types of sanctions, such as fines.[182] If in that regard the legal systems of both the transmitting and the receiving ECN members provide for sanctions of a similar kind (eg fines), the procedural safeguards in both systems are deemed to be equivalent. The result of this irrefutable presumption is that there can be no further limitation on the recipient ECN member using the information exchanged in evidence.

2.184 If, however, the laws of the transmitting and the receiving ECN member do not provide sanctions of a similar kind, there can no longer be any presumption of equivalence of procedural safeguards. That does not mean that the use in evidence of information exchanged is completely excluded. Article 12(3) still allows an ad hoc equivalence check. If the result of such a check is that the information has indeed been collected by the transmitting ECN member in a manner which respects the same level of protection of the rights of defence enjoyed by natural persons as provided for under the national rules of the receiving ECN member, the latter can use the information exchanged in evidence. There is, nevertheless, one further limitation to the latter use, which results from a negative presumption raised by a number of Member States during the negotiations in Council. According to that irrefutable negative presumption it is impossible to equate the procedural safeguards in proceedings that may result in custodial sanctions and procedural safeguards with other proceedings. Consequently, the recipient ECN member can only use the information exchanged in evidence to impose custodial sanctions where the first indent of Article 12(3) applies, namely where the laws of both the transmitting and the receiving ECN member provide for a custodial sanction.

(d) The Obligation of Professional Secrecy and the Need to Disclose Information

2.185 The obligation of professional secrecy refers to the duty imposed by law on officials and other servants in respect of confidentiality. One reason for this obligation is to ensure that undertakings cannot plead commercial sensitivity as an excuse for withholding relevant documents from investigators, thus enabling the Commission and the competition authorities of the Member States to collect the information they need on the widest possible scale.[183] At Community level, the concept of professional secrecy is laid down in Article 287 EC, which states that: 'the members of the institutions of the Community, the members of committees, and the officials and other servants of the Community shall be required, even after their duties have ceased, not to disclose information of the kind covered by the obligation of professional secrecy, in particular information about undertakings, their business relations or their cost components.' This Treaty provision is repeated and extended in Article 28(2) of Regulation 1/2003.

2.186 Article 28(2) of Regulation 1/2003 requires officials and civil servants from national authorities and from the Commission, as well as other persons working under the supervision of these authorities, not to disclose information acquired or exchanged by them pursuant to the

---

[182] See point 28(c) of the Network Notice.
[183] Case C-85/76 *Hoffman-La Roche v Commission* [1979] ECR 46, para 14.

Regulation and of the kind covered by the obligation of professional secrecy. The Community law concept of professional secrecy used in Article 28 thus creates a common minimum level of protection throughout the Community. It is submitted that this common minimum level implies that all ECN members need to have an effective procedure for the protection of information that is covered by professional secrecy. It is therefore necessary to identify the scope and the limitations of the Community law concept of professional secrecy.

(i) Which Information is Covered by Professional Secrecy?

The wide coverage of professional secrecy The case law of the Court of Justice does not **2.187** contain a general definition of what is covered by professional secrecy. There are only a few cases in which the Court has observed that particular information falls within the realm of the obligation of professional secrecy.

In *Adams*, the Court of Justice pointed out that, although Article 287 EC primarily refers **2.188** to information gathered from undertakings, the expression 'in particular' shows that the principle in question is a general one which applies also to information supplied by natural persons, if that information is of the kind that is confidential.[184] In his opinion in *AKZO*, Advocate General Lenz considered that Article 20(2) of Council Regulation 17/62—which contains similar obligations to those in Article 28(2) of Regulation 1/2003—does not only cover business secrets but also information internal to the administration in charge of the application of competition law.[185]

In an attempt to grasp what is covered by the concept of professional secrecy, one could say **2.189** that it probably extends to all information that comes to the knowledge of the ECN members in the exercise of their functions, except for information that is already in the public domain. The concept of professional secrecy thus does not focus on the nature of the information itself but on the circumstances in which it is communicated or obtained.

Specific sub-category within the wider concept of professional secrecy: business secrets **2.190** **and other confidential information** Although the obligation of professional secrecy extends beyond the protection of business secrets or other confidential information, these types of information are the most disputed. It is therefore useful to explore their scope under Community law.

Business secrets In *Postbank*, the Court of Justice defined business secrets as 'information **2.191** of which not only disclosure to the public but also mere transmission to a person other than the one that provided the information might seriously harm the latter's interests'.[186]

---

[184] Case 145/83 *Adams* [1985] ECR 3539, para 34.
[185] Opinion of Lenz AG in Case 53/85 *AKZO Chemie BV and AKZO Chemie UK Ltd v Commission* [1986] ECR 1965, paras 5.2 and 5.3.
[186] Case T-353/94 *Postbank* [1996] ECR II-921, para 87. According to point 18 of the revised Commission notice on the rules for access to the Commission file, information about an undertaking's business activity constitutes business secrets in so far as disclosure of such information could result in a serious harm to that undertaking (Commission Notice of 13 December 2005 on the rules for access to the Commission file in cases pursuant to Articles 81 and 82 of the EC Treaty, Articles 53, 54 and 57 of the EEA Agreement and Council Regulation (EC) No 139/2004, available at <http://europa.eu.int/comm/competition/antitrust/legislation/notice_en.pdf>).

The revised Commission notice on the rules for access to the Commission file mentions the following examples of information that may qualify as business secrets: technical and/or financial information relating to an undertaking's know-how; methods of assessing costs; production secrets and processes; supply sources; quantities produced and sold; market shares; customer and distributor lists; marketing plans; cost and price structure; and sales strategy.[187]

2.192   It is clear that information covered by the notion of business secrets may evolve over time: what is commercially important today is not necessarily commercially important at a later stage (eg production secrets and processes for products which are no longer on the market). Moreover, business secrets need no longer be protected when they are in the public domain. This would be the case, for example, when a third party is able to obtain that information without great effort. Therefore, documents containing information which could be obtained from other sources or which is commercially available on the market (eg comparative data, including market share figures, collected by a third party for commercial purposes) can never be regarded as containing business secrets.

2.193   Although it is for each competition authority to assess whether or not a particular document contains business secrets, inspiration may be drawn from the following non-exhaustive list of criteria which the Commission applies to determine whether information can be deemed to constitute business secrets: to what extent is the information known outside the company; to what extent measures have been taken to protect the information within the company; the value of the information for the company and its competitors; the effort or investment which the undertaking had to make to acquire the information; the effort which others would need to go to in order to acquire or copy the information; and the degree of protection offered to such information under the legislation of the Member State concerned.[188]

2.194   *Other confidential information*   The Commission has established that 'other confidential information' means information other than business secrets, which may be considered as confidential in so far as its disclosure would significantly harm an undertaking or a person.[189] This would cover, for instance, voluntarily supplied information for which confidentiality was requested in order to protect the informant's anonymity. Indeed, the Court of First Instance and the Court of Justice have acknowledged the legitimacy of the reluctance displayed by the Commission in revealing certain letters received from customers of the undertaking which is being investigated, since their disclosure might easily expose the authors to the risk of retaliatory measures. Such retaliation might be feared where undertakings are able to place very considerable economic or commercial pressure on their competitors or on their trading partners, customers, or suppliers.[190] Therefore the concept of

---

187   Point 18 of the notice referred to in n 175. See also point 10 of the Commission communication COM(2003) 4582 of 1 December 2003 on professional secrecy in state aid decisions [2003] OJ C297/6.

188   Point 13 of the Commission communication referred to in n 176.

189   Recital 13 of the Commission implementing Regulation. The Eighteenth Report on Competition Policy (1988), para 43 specified that the harm would be caused to the supplier of the information.

190   Case T-65/89 *BPB Industries and British Gypsum* [1993] ECR II-389; Case C-310/93P *BPB Industries and British Gypsum* [1995] ECR I865; and Case T-5/02 *Tetra Laval* [2002] ECR II-4381, paras 98ff.

other confidential information may extend to information that would enable the parties to identify complainants or other third parties where those parties wish to remain anonymous.[191] The category of other confidential information also includes military secrets.[192]

(ii) The Disclosure of Information Acquired or Exchanged Pursuant to Regulation 1/2003

According to Article 28(2) of Regulation 1/2003, the ECN members, and also the staff of **2.195** other Member States' authorities that receive such information, are prevented from disclosing information that is covered by the professional secrecy obligation and which has been acquired or exchanged pursuant to the Regulation.[193] The prohibition not only covers the information the Commission acquires pursuant to its powers of investigation (Articles 17–21 of the Regulation) and the information an NCA acquires during an inspection or other fact-finding measure pursuant to Article 22 of the Regulation, but it extends to all other information that an ECN member or another national authority acquires or exchanges in the context of the co-operation mechanisms provided for in Chapter IV of Regulation 1/2003.[194]

The obligation of professional secrecy, however, cannot prevent the ECN members from **2.196** using the co-operation mechanisms as foreseen within Regulation 1/2003 itself. Article 28(2) of Regulation 1/2003 therefore confirms that the exchange and use of information which takes place in the context of Articles 11 (co-operation between the Commission and the NCAs), 12 (exchange of information and use of exchanged information), 14 (Advisory Committee), and 15 (co-operation with national courts) of the Regulation cannot be regarded as a violation of the obligation of professional secrecy. Article 28(2) further excludes the use of information under Article 27 from the realm of professional secrecy. That provision allows the Commission to disclose and use information acquired or exchanged pursuant to Regulation 1/2003 in order to prove an infringement of the EC competition rules (paragraphs 2.198–2.199 below) and to grant access to the file (paragraphs 2.200–2.202 below).

Beyond the exceptions explicitly mentioned in Article 28(2), one may ask whether there **2.197** are further circumstances in which the ECN members are entitled to disregard the professional secrecy obligation imposed by that provision. As the obligation is laid down in an EC Regulation, the exceptions, if any, would have to flow from the EC Treaty,[195] the general principles of Community law, an international agreement concluded by the EC[196] or

---

[191] When information is confidential from an objective point of view, that information is covered by the obligation of professional secrecy. The subjective wish of the supplier of information to keep that information confidential is therefore irrelevant (Opinion of Lenz AG in Case 53/85 *AKZO Chemie BV and AKZO Chemie UK Ltd v Commission* [1986] ECR 1965, para 5.4).

[192] Points 19 and 20 of the Commission notice on access to the file, referred to in n 186.

[193] In addition to the professional secrecy obligation laid down in Art 28(2), Arts 14(6), 27(2) and (4) and 30(2) of Regulation 1/2003 provide further particular protection for business secrets.

[194] It is submitted that this implies that also the comments of DG Competition to the information sent pursuant to Art 11(4) of Regulation 1/2003 are covered by the prohibition laid down in Art 28(2).

[195] eg the duty of loyal co-operation resulting from Art 10 EC requires the Commission to disclose documents to national courts. See points 21–26 of the Commission notice on co-operation between the Commission and national courts and paras 2.265–2.272.

[196] See eg Protocol 23 to the EEA Agreement, as recently amended, [2005] OJ L64/57 and L133/35.

from the requirement to guarantee the useful effect of the exceptions explicitly stated in Article 28(2). Exceptions could surely not be based on national provisions, because that would jeopardize the common minimum level of protection created by Article 28(2) of Regulation 1/2003.[197] However, it is submitted that to the extent that a national provision emanates from a general principle of Community law (eg access to the file in the context of the rights of defence) or is necessary to guarantee the useful effect of the exceptions explicitly stated in Article 28(2) (eg disclosure of information exchanged pursuant to Article 12 in order to prove an infringement of EC competition law), that national provision can be upheld against the obligation of professional secrecy. These further exceptions, however, should be applied strictly and can thus not go beyond what is required according to the general principles of Community law or what is necessary to guarantee the useful effect of the exception explicitly stated in Article 28(2).

2.198 **Disclosure necessary to prove an infringement of Articles 81 or 82** According to the last sentence of Article 27(2) of Regulation 1/2003 and to Article 15(3) of the Commission Implementing Regulation, nothing in Article 27(2) or in the Implementing Regulation, respectively, prevents the Commission from disclosing information necessary to prove an infringement of Articles 81 or 82 EC. This means, for example, that information received from other network members may be disclosed by the Commission to the other parties to the proceedings if that is necessary to prove an infringement.

2.199 Where disclosure of business secrets or other confidential information is necessary to prove an infringement, recital 14 of the Implementing Regulation requires the Commission to assess in the case of each individual document whether the need to disclose is greater than the harm that might result from disclosure. If the Commission intends to disclose information provided by an undertaking, which is claimed to be a business secret or other confidential information, the *AKZO* procedure is followed: the Commission informs the undertaking in question in writing of its intention and of its reason for disclosing the information. It also sets a time limit for the undertaking to respond. If the undertaking continues to object to the disclosure, the Commission adopts a reasoned decision on the disclosure of the given piece of information.[198]

Disclosure in granting access to the file

2.200 *Access to the file for the addressee of a statement of objections* The obligation of professional secrecy laid down in Article 28(2) does not prevent the Commission from granting the addressee of a statement of objections access to the file on the basis of which the

---

[197] This implies, eg, that the receiving NCA cannot transmit the information exchanged to other national or foreign authorities, even if national law provisions or an international agreement would allow or oblige it to do so (Case C-67/91 *Dirección General de Defensa de la Competencia v Asociación Española de Banca Privada and others* [1992] ECR I-4785, paras 41 and 42). It is, however, submitted that disclosure to other national authorities of information exchanged or acquired pursuant to Regulation 1/2003 is possible, when the NCA is obliged to do so for the purpose of applying Art 81 or 82 EC. However, that other national authority is also covered by Art 28(2) and therefore cannot use this information for any other purpose, nor can it disclose it further.

[198] The procedure is named after Case 53/85 *AKZO Chemie BV and AKZO Chemie UK Ltd v Commission* [1986] ECR 1965.

Commission formulated its objections.[199] This access to all documents, including those exchanged or acquired pursuant to Regulation 1/2003, relied upon by the Commission in making its findings is intended to allow the effective exercise of the rights of defence against the objections.[200] This access to the file, however, does not extend to business secrets or other confidential information, nor does it extend to internal documents of the Commission or NCAs, in particular correspondence between the Commission and the NCAs or between NCAs.[201]

With respect to the category of internal documents, it is clear from case law that the rea- **2.201** son why they are not accessible is that Commission departments must be able to express themselves freely within their institution concerning all aspects of ongoing cases.[202] The idea behind this is that internal documents are, at most, evaluative in nature and cannot be incriminating nor exculpatory. They cannot be used in evidence and thus access to them is not necessary in order to respect the rights of defence.[203] The enforcement system established by Regulation 1/2003 requires this reasoning to be extended to the internal documents and correspondence that circulate within the network. If, however, the Commission or another ECN member finds some of that information necessary to prove an infringement of Articles 81 or 82 EC, the principles described in paragraphs 2.198–2.199 above apply.

Access to information by other parties with legitimate interest, in particular complainants **2.202** The last sentence of Article 27(1) states that '[c]omplainants shall be associated closely with the proceedings'. That means that, unlike addressees of a statement of objections, complainants only have the right to participate in the administrative procedure. Therefore they cannot claim a right of access to the Commission's file on the same basis as the undertakings under investigation.[204] Article 8 of the implementing Regulation establishes this right for a complainant to participate in the procedure by giving him access 'to the documents on which the Commission bases its provisional assessment. For this purpose, the complainant may however not have access to business secrets and other confidential information belonging

---

[199] Article 27(2), first sentence, of Regulation 1/2003 and Art 15(1) of the Commission Implementing Regulation.

[200] Point 7 of the Commission notice on access to the file, referred to in n 186.

[201] Article 27(2) of Regulation 1/2003 and Arts 15(2) and 16(1) of the Commission Implementing Regulation.

[202] Joined Cases T-25/95 et al *Cimenteries CBR SA et al* [2000] ECR II-491, para 420.

[203] Case T-7/89 *Hercules Chemicals* [1991] ECR II-1711, paras 51, 52 and 54: 'regard for the rights of the defence requires that an applicant must have been put in a position to express, as it sees fit, its views on all the objections raised against it by the Commission in the statement of objections addressed to it and on the evidence which is to be used to support those objections and is mentioned by the Commission in the statement of objections or annexed to it (. . .). However, regard for the rights of the defence does not require that an undertaking involved in a procedure pursuant to Article [81(1) EC] must be able to comment on all the documents forming part of the Commission's file since there are no provisions requiring the Commission to divulge the contents of its files to the parties concerned (. . .). It follows that the Commission has an obligation to make available to the undertakings involved in Article [81(1) EC] proceedings all documents, whether in their favour or otherwise, which it has obtained during the course of the investigation, save where the business secrets of other undertakings, the internal documents of the Commission or other confidential information are involved.'

[204] Case T-17/93 *Matra-Hachette* [1994] ECR II-595, para 34.

to other parties involved in the proceedings'. Although Article 8 does not refer to the (exclusion of) access to the internal documents of the ECN members, in particular to the correspondence between them, it seems obvious that since the addressees of a statement of objections have no access to these documents, third parties, which includes complainants, *a fortiori* cannot have access to them either.

(3) Consistent Application within ECN

(a) Introduction

2.203 The need to ensure consistent application of Articles 81 and 82 throughout the internal market was one of the main drivers behind the creation of ECN and a number of the supporting co-operation mechanisms contained in Regulation 1/2003. Prior to the adoption of Regulation 1/2003 there was widespread fear that the empowerment of national courts and competition authorities to apply Articles 81 and 82 in full would lead to inconsistent application of Community competition law. The European Parliament expressed the concern that the reform would lead to a re-nationalisation of Community competition law.[205]

2.204 Regulation 1/2003 takes these concerns very seriously and creates a number of mechanisms that aim at promoting consistent application. These mechanisms constitute the backbone of ECN's framework for ensuring consistency. The network itself, however, is not regulated by the Regulation in any detail. The only reference in the operative part of the Regulation is in Article 11(1), which merely requires the Commission and the competition authorities of the Member States to apply the Community competition rules in close co-operation. Recital 15 further provides that the Commission and the competition authorities of the Member States should form together a network of public authorities applying the Community competition rules in close co-operation, and that for that purpose it is necessary to establish arrangements for information exchange and consultation. Recital 15 also states that further modalities for the co-operation within the network will be laid down and revised by the Commission in close co-operation with the Member States. These further means of co-operation are contained in the Network Notice.

(b) The Consultation Procedure in Article 11(4)

2.205 One of the key instruments for maintaining consistent application of the Community competition rules at the level of the national competiton authorities is contained in Article 11(4) of Regulation 1/2003, which provides that:

> No later than 30 days before the adoption of a decision requiring that an infringement be brought to an end, accepting commitments or withdrawing the benefit of a block exemption Regulation, the competition authorities of the Member States shall inform the Commission. To that effect, they shall provide the Commission with a summary of the case, the envisaged decision, or in the absence thereof, any other document indicating the proposed course of action. This information may also be made available to the competition authorities of the other Member States. At the request of the Commission, the acting competition authority shall make available to the Commission other documents it holds which are necessary for the assessment of the case. The information supplied to the Commission may be made available

---

[205] See Report of Mr Jonathan Evans of 21 June 2001 (A-0229/2001 Final).

to the competition authorities of other Member States. National competition authorities may also exchange between themselves information necessary for the assessment of cases that they are dealing with under Article 81 or Article 82 of the Treaty.

In order to appreciate the full impact of Article 11(4) this provision should be read in conjunction with Article 11(6) according to which the initiation by the Commission of proceedings for the adoption of a decision under Chapter III of the Regulation relieves the national competiton authorities of their competence to apply Articles 81 and 82 of the Treaty. The Commission may exercise this power in the context of a consultation pursuant to Article 11(4).

(i) The Scope of the Article 11(4) Procedure

National competiton authorities are obliged to inform the Commission no later than thirty **2.206** days before adopting certain types of decisions. Consultation may occur earlier. However, in order for the consultation to achieve its intended aim the case must have developed to such an extent that it is possible to define the proposed course of action. Moreover, if the course of action is significantly modified subsequently, Article 11(4) requires that the Commission be consulted again, in which event the Commission has another thirty days to respond. This is the case where, for instance, the competition authority in question, after the first consultation, adds new objections or where the competition authority in question re-orients the case from a prohibition to a commitments decision.

Nothing prevents the Commission from replying to the consultation prior to the expiry of **2.207** the thirty-day period, in which case, the national competiton authorities may adopt the decisions without further delay. A national competition authority may ask the Commission for a response before the end of the thirty-day period, on the basis of special circumstances, in which case the Commission will endeavour to respond as quickly as possible.[206]

The obligation to consult covers decisions requiring that an infringement be brought **2.208** to an end, accepting commitments or withdrawing the benefit of a block exemption Regulation.[207] The wording of Article 11(4) does not expressly mention decisions limited to imposing fines and could therefore be read as not including such decisions. However, this would not be a correct interpretation of Article 11(4). It clearly follows from the explanatory memorandum to the Commission's proposal, which contained the same wording, that decisions imposing fines are covered.[208] The inclusion of decisions imposing fines is also necessary in order to preserve the effectiveness of Article 11(4), which is intended to ensure that Articles 81 and 82 are applied in a consistent manner in the case of negative decisions adopted by Member State competition authorities. The types of decision covered by Article 11(4) are the national equivalents of the decisions adopted by the

---

[206] See para 47 of the Network Notice.

[207] Article 11(4) does not mention interim measures decisions. As a consequence, the obligations of Art 11(4) do not apply to interim measures decisions. Article 114 applies to negative decisions except decisions prescribing interim measures.

[208] See Commission proposal of 27 September 2000 (COM(2000) 582 final) pp 9 and 21, which refers to prohibition decisions in general and all decisions by Member States' authorities aimed at terminating or penalising an infringement of Arts 81 or 82.

Commission under Articles 7 and 9 of Regulation 1/2003, which cover the finding and termination of infringements, the imposition of fines for such infringements, and the acceptance of commitments. Decisions withdrawing the benefit of a block exemption Regulation do not constitute a separate category in practice. In the case of withdrawal, the competition authorities concerned must demonstrate that the agreement infringes Article 81(1) and that it does not fulfil the conditions of Article 81(3).[209] A withdrawal must therefore be accompanied by a negative decision addressing the competition problem for the future.

2.209 There is no obligation to consult the Commission on rejections of complaints and other types of decisions whereby national competition authorities decide that there are no grounds for action on their part. While national competition authorities are free to use the provision in Article 11(5) and consult the Commission also on such cases, there is no obligation to do so.[210] Given the number of rejections of complaints and other decisions whereby files are closed, substantial resources would have been occupied if such decisions had been made subject to mandatory consultation. Moreover, the aim of ensuring consistent application does not require such consultation. Positive decisions adopted by NCAs within the limits provided for in Article 5 of the Regulation do not as a matter of law prevent other players in the system from acting. The fact that a particular authority has found that there are no grounds for action on its part, does not prevent other competition authorities or national courts from finding otherwise and prohibit the agreement or practice in question. The fact that Article 11(4) only covers negative decisions is therefore not an indication that over-enforcement is perceived as a greater problem than under-enforcement. It is a mere recognition of the fact that in the enforcement system created by Regulation 1/2003 negative decisions always win.[211] The only exceptions are Article 10 decisions adopted by the Commission, so that all that is required is a system that prevents the adoption by national competition authorities of unwarranted negative decisions. Once adopted and implemented negative decisions are difficult to undo.

2.210 When consulting the Commission the national competition authorities must provide it with a summary of the case, the envisaged decision, or in its absence, any other document indicating the proposed course of action. Although the language could have been clearer in this respect, the intention is that the national competition authorities must in all cases provide a summary of the case. In addition they must provide either a draft decision or, in its absence, any other document indicating the proposed course of action. This latter option is particularly relevant where the national competition authority does not itself draft the final decision but rather submits a statement of objections or a writ or indictment to another authority including a court that adopts the final decision. The language used allows Member States to organise procedures such that Member State courts do not have to consult the Commission on draft decisions. Instead, consultation may take place on the writ or indictment submitted to the court.[212]

---

[209] See in this respect para 36 of the Commission Guidelines on the application of Art 81(3) of the Treaty [2004] OJ C101/97.

[210] National competition authorities have occasionally made use of this facility following the entry into force of Regulation 1/2003.

[211] It would have been otherwise if national competition authorities had been empowered to adopt constitutive exemption decisions, see in this respect the White Paper on modernisation, paras 58ff.

[212] This measure of flexibility is reflected in Art 35(1) and (2) of Regulation 1/2003.

Under Article 11(4) the Commission is the main interlocutor. National competition **2.211** authorities are obliged to provide the Commission with the specified information and allow the Commission thirty days to scrutinise the documents submitted. There is no equivalent obligation in respect of the other national competition authorities. There is a right but no obligation to inform them. This choice was made in order to avoid situations where failure in an individual case to inform one or more of the national competition authorities would expose the subsequent decision to legal challenge.

(ii) The Consultation Process and its Objective

The purpose of the consultation procedure established by Article 11(4) is to enable the **2.212** Commission (and the national competition authorities) to detect potential problems of inconsistent application and cure them prophylactically. In general, consistency is maintained through dialogue. However, if the issue is sufficiently serious and no common ground is found, the Commission may open proceedings with the effect of relieving the national competition authority concerned of its competence to apply Articles 81 and 82.[213]

In the context of Article 11(4) consultation the Commission can make comments in any **2.213** appropriate form. The Network Notice expressly acknowledges that the Commission may make written observations.[214] The intervention of the Commission is thus not limited to deciding whether or not to exercise its power under Article 11(6). Indeed, by making reasoned comments on the drafts submitted by the national competition authorities the Commission can play an important role in terms of ensuring consistency and promoting the development of a common competition culture.[215]

Comments made by the Commission and discussions between the Commission and the **2.214** national competition authorities are internal to the network. The parties to the proceedings in question have no right to be heard or otherwise comment on the view expressed by the Commission. The exclusion of the parties from the consultation procedure is considered unproblematic from the point of view of rights of defence. To the extent that the consultation process leads to certain objections being dropped, it is for the benefit of the parties.[216] If the consultation process leads to new objections being raised, the undertakings concerned must be given the opportunity to comment. Rights of defence are therefore protected in the proceedings of the consulting national competition authority.

(iii) The Legal Consequences of Failure to Comply with Article 11(4)

It is submitted that there can be little doubt that decisions adopted in breach of Article 11(4) **2.215** are invalid and unenforceable. Article 11(4) imposes a clear and unconditional obligation on the national competition authorities. Before adopting certain types of decision they must

---

[213] See Art 11(6).
[214] See para 46.
[215] A unit has been created within DG Competition to handle, *inter alia*, Art 11(4) consultation.
[216] In the case of complaints, the national competition authority may under the applicable national law on procedure have to reject specific complaints that are not being pursued. Depending on the applicable law such rejections may be challengeable. In such an event, it makes no difference whether a national competition authority decides not to pursue a complaint on its own initiative or following comments in the context of the consultation process.

inform the Commission and submit to it certain specified information that allows the Commission to assess the case. Moreover, additional documents must be supplied where necessary for the assessment of the case. The Commission is entitled to comment on the draft with a view to ensuring consistent application and may also exercise its power under Article 11(4) and withdraw the case from the national competition authority in question. Article 11(4) constitutes an essential procedural requirement that is closely linked to the substantive decision adopted by the national competition authority in question.

2.216 The argument that a decision adopted in violation of Article 11(4) is invalid finds support in the judgment of the Court of Justice in *CIA International*.[217] This case concerned Directive 83/189 laying down a procedure for the provision of information in the field of technical standards and regulations.[218] Under Article 8 of this Directive Member States must immediately communicate to the Commission any draft technical regulation. The Commission notifies the other Member States of any draft it has received and the Commission and the Member States may make comments to the Member State which has forwarded the draft technical regulation and that Member State must take such comments into account as far as possible in the subsequent preparation of the technical regulation. Moreover, Article 9 provides that Member States shall postpone the adoption of a draft technical regulation for six months from the date of notification referred to in Article 8(1) if the Commission or another Member State delivers a detailed opinion, within three months of that date, to the effect that the measure envisaged must be amended in order to eliminate or reduce any barriers which it might create to the free movement of goods. It is also provided that, if the Commission ascertains that a communication pursuant to Article 8(1) relates to a subject covered by a proposal for a directive or regulation submitted to the Council, it must inform the Member State concerned of this fact within three months of receiving the communication. Member States are obliged to refrain from adopting technical regulations on a subject covered by a proposal for a directive or regulation submitted by the Commission to the Council before the communication provided for in Article 8(1) for a period of twelve months from the date of its submission.

2.217 In *CIA International*, the Court of Justice held[219] that Directive 83/189 is to be interpreted as meaning that breach of the obligation to notify renders the technical regulations concerned inapplicable and unenforceable against individuals. In reaching this conclusion, the Court referred to the fact that the aim of the procedure was to eliminate obstacles to trade by giving the Commission and the other Member States time to react and to propose amendments for lessening restrictions to the free movement of goods arising from the envisaged measure and to afford the Commission time to propose a harmonising directive. The Court also stated that the wording of Articles 8 and 9 of Directive 83/189 was clear in that those articles laid down a procedure for Community control of draft national regulations and the date of their entry into force was made subject to the Commission's agreement or lack of opposition.

---

[217] Case C-194/94 *CIA International* [1996] ECR I-2201.
[218] [1983] OJ L109/8 as amended by Council Directive (EEC) 88/182 [1988] OJ L81/75.
[219] See paras 50 and 54.

The Article 11(4) procedure serves an equivalent objective, namely that of ensuring consistent **2.218**
application of Articles 81 and 82. Moreover, the powers of the Commission are, if anything, more
extensive under Regulation 1/2003 than under Directive 83/189, since the Commission has the
power under Article 11(6) to prevent the adoption of the decision at Member State level and not
merely have it suspended. Undertakings that engaged in proceedings before Member State competition authorities are therefore well-advised to require proof that the obligations under Article
11(4) have been complied with, otherwise any subsequent decision is invalid and unenforceable.

(c) Article 11(6): The Commission's Power to Withdraw a Case

Article 11(6) provides that the initiation by the Commission of proceedings for the adop- **2.219**
tion of a decision under Chapter III shall relieve the national competition authorities of
their competence to apply Articles 81 and 82 of the Treaty. If a national competition
authority is already acting in a case, the Commission shall only initiate proceedings after
consulting with that authority.

Article 11(6) forms an essential part of the mechanisms in the Regulation intended to ensure **2.220**
consistent application. This fact is explained in recital 17, which provides that, if the competition rules are to be applied consistently, and at the same time, the network is to be managed in the best possible way, it is essential to retain the rule that the competition authorities
of the Member States are automatically relieved of their competence if the Commission initiates its own proceedings. As is clear from the word 'retained', the rule of Article 11(6) is not
new. An equivalent rule was contained in Article 9(3) of Regulation 17/62. However, the
combination of Article 11(6) and Article 3 with its obligation to apply Articles 81 and 82
and the consultation procedure of Article 11(4) has greatly enhanced its importance.

(i) The Legal Nature of Article 11(6)

Article 11(6) is a rule of competence. When the Commission opens proceedings in a case, **2.221**
the competence of the national competition authorities to deal with that same case is eliminated. The opening of proceedings by the Commission is a formal act by which the
Commission indicates its intention to adopt a formal decision under Chapter III of the
Regulation.[220] It can occur at any stage of the investigation of a case.[221]

In instances where the Commission is the first to open proceedings in a case, the effect of **2.222**
Article 11(6) is to ensure that the Commission remains the only authority to deal with it.
This is a rational solution since the Commission has the power to enforce the Community
competition rules throughout the European Union. The Commission can provide one-
stop enforcement anywhere in the EU. Once the Commission acts there is no need for
national competition authorities to act as well. Indeed, if they were to do so, it would lead
to duplication of work and create a risk of inconsistent outcomes. In cases where a national
competition authority is already dealing with a case the effect of the Commission opening
proceedings is to withdraw the case from the competition authority in question.[222]

---

[220] See, concerning Art 9(3) of Regulation 17/62, Case 48/72 *Brasserie de Haecht* [1973] ECR 77, para 16.
[221] See para 52 of the Network Notice. Traditionally, proceedings have been opened at the stage of the
statement of objections. However, it appears that the Commision will increasingly open proceedings at an earlier stage when it has decided to give priority to a case.
[222] This aspect of Art 11(6) is dealt with in more detail in section (iii) below.

2.223   When the Commission closes its proceedings the national competition authorities regain their competence. In order to prevent the national competition authorities from adopting a conflicting decision in the case the Commission must itself adopt a decision. Once adopted, a Commission decision will have the effect provided for in Article 16, preventing the national competition authorities from adopting conflicting decisions.[223]

(ii)   The Authorities Covered by Article 11(6)

2.224   According to Article 11(6) the national competition authorities are relieved of their competence when the Commission opens proceedings. Article 35(3) and (4) of Regulation 1/2003 provide further insight into which national competition authorities are relieved of their competence. According to Article 35(3) the effects of Article 11(6) apply to the authorities designated by the Member States including national courts, which exercise functions relating to the preparation and the adoption of the types of decisions under Article 5 of Regulation 1/2003. On the other hand, the effects of Article 11(6) do not extend to courts in so far as they act as review courts in respect of such decisions.

2.225   Article 35(4) contains a further proviso, that, notwithstanding Article 35(3), in the Member States where, in order to adopt certain types of decision provided for in Article 5 of the Regulation, an authority brings an action before a judicial authority that is separate and different from the prosecuting authority and provided that the terms of Article 35(3) are complied with, the effects of Article 11(6) shall be limited to the authority prosecuting the case which shall withdraw its claim before the judicial authority when the Commission opens proceedings and this withdrawal shall bring the national proceedings effectively to an end. The only purpose of Article 35(4) is to allow Member States to arrange their procedures so as formally to avoid the Commission withdrawing a case from a national court in circumstances where cases are brought before the court by a prosecutor.[224] In such cases the application of Article 11(6) can be arranged in such a way that the prosecutor withdraws its claim before the court. It is a condition however that such withdrawal effectively brings the national proceedings to an end. If not, the court in question is automatically relieved of its competence. Moreover, Article 35(4) is carefully drafted to ensure that it does not apply to individual authorities that comprise both prosecutorial and judicial arms. The exception does not apply where one part of the authority prepares the statement of objections or equivalent and another part of the same authority takes the decision. In such cases the decision-making body is automatically relieved of its competence.

2.226   Article 11(6) in conjunction with Article 35(3) and (4) ensure that the Commission has effective means at its disposal to prevent the adoption of a conflicting decision. The opening of proceedings by the Commission prevents the adoption of a decision at Member State level. It follows from the combined rule of Article 35(3) and (4) that the effects of

---

[223] The Commission's decision can be challenged before the European Courts. According to Art 230 of the Treaty Member States always have standing to challenge acts adopted, *inter alia*, by the Commission.

[224] Article 35(4) was introduced to accommodate the sensitivities of certain Member States where the first decision-maker is a court.

Article 11(6) apply until the adoption of the first decision on the merits of the case at national level.[225]

It is submitted that it would have given rise to considerable difficulties if Article 11(6) had **2.227** been extended to review courts or appeal courts that decide on the legality of already adopted decisions. In order to achieve the aim of Article 11(6) it would not be sufficient to relieve such courts of their competence. It would in addition be necessary to undo a decision which had already been adopted. Once a decision is adopted at national level recourse to other means to resolve a conflict is required. One option is for the Commission to make an *amicus curiae* submission to the appeals court in accordance with Article 15(3) of the Regulation. Another option for the Commission is to adopt a contrary decision with the effect of Article 16 and thus bind the appeal court, subject to the power of the court to make a preliminary reference to the Court of Justice under Article 234 of the Treaty.[226]

(iii) Circumstances in which Withdrawal may be Envisaged

The Network Notice distinguishes two situations in which the Commission opens pro- **2.228** ceedings with the effect of withdrawing the case from a national competition authority. In both situations the Commission is obliged to consult the authority in question before opening proceedings.[227] However, national competition authorities cannot prevent the Commission from opening proceedings which have the effect of Article 11(6). This is in line with the fact that, according to precedent, the Commission is entitled, at any time, to adopt individual decisions under Articles 81 and 82 of the Treaty, even where an agreement or practice has already been the subject of a decision at Member State level and the decision contemplated by the Commission conflicts with that decision.[228]

The first situation dealt with in the Notice is where the Commission opens proceedings **2.229** after a national competition authority has informed the network of a new case pursuant to Article 11(3) of the Regulation but before the end of the initial indicative allocation period of two months. In this situation the opening of proceedings is a mere reflection of the fact that the Commission is well placed to deal with the case as an enforcer and that as a consequence the case is allocated to the Commission for further investigation.[229]

The second situation concerns cases where proceedings are opened after the initial alloca- **2.230** tion period and where the case is already therefore being investigated by a national competition authorities. The withdrawal of a case in such circumstances is a far-reaching measure, which is likely to be used in only a limited number of circumstances. The Network Notice provides guidance as to the circumstances in which this may be envisaged.[230] However, Article 11(6) itself does not impose any limitations of a substantive nature on the Commission.

---

[225] This represents a limitation compared to Art 9(3) of Regulation 17/62 which in Case 127/73 *BRT v SABAM* [1974] ECR 51, paras 18–20 were held to extend to courts reviewing the legality of decisions as well.

[226] See in this regard section 3.b. (*ii*) below.

[227] See Art 11(6) of the Regulation.

[228] See Case C-344/98 *Masterfoods* [2000] ECR I-11369, para 48.

[229] The Network Notice develops some broad criteria for determining when network members are well placed to deal with cases and when a re-allocation of a case may be warranted, see section 1.a. above.

[230] See para 54.

The Commission has full discretion and the examples contained in the Network Notice are merely illustrative in nature. This fact is confirmed in the Notice itself, which employs the words 'in principle' when listing the circumstances in which the Commission would consider intervening. The situations expressly mentioned in the Network Notice are the following:

(a) network members envisage conflicting decisions in the same case;
(b) network members envisage a decision which is obviously in conflict with consolidated case law; the standards defined in the judgments of the Community courts and in previous decisions and regulations of the Commission should serve as a yardstick; concerning facts, only a significant divergence will trigger an intervention of the Commission;
(c) network member(s) is (are) unduly drawing out proceedings;
(d) there is a need to adopt a Commission decision to develop Community competition policy in particular when a similar competition issue arises in several Member States;
(e) the national competition authority does not object.

Although this list is not exhaustive, it is considered that the categories listed do in fact allow the Commission to intervene in all cases where it would have a legitimate interest in doing so. The main effect of the list is to make clear that the Commission cannot make use of Article 11(6) merely because it finds a particular case interesting. Article 11(6) is not a cherry-picking instrument. However, this goes without saying. Given the co-operative nature of the network and the need for continuing close co-operation in order for the network to function as intended, it would not be in the Commission's interest to use Article 11(6) for such purposes.

2.231 When network members envisage conflicting decisions in the same case there may be, according to letter (a) above, a need for the Commission to intervene in order to prevent the conflict from arising. However, there is no obligation for the Commission to do so. Given that, in the enforcement system created by Regulation 1/2003, prohibition decisions trump non-action decisions adopted by national competition authorities under Article 5 of the Regulation, there is only a need to intervene where the Commission takes the view that a certain agreement or practice should not be prohibited.

2.232 According to letter (b) above, there may also be a need to intervene when a decision envisaged by a national competition authority is in obvious conflict with existing case law. Intervention in such cases goes beyond the avoidance of conflicting decisions in the same case. The aim is to preserve the integrity and consistency of the established body of case law. In this regard the Commission's role may complement that of the European courts. Given the absence of an integrated system of community courts in the EU and the limits of the Article 234 preliminary reference procedure only a Commission decision can trigger a full review by the European courts.

2.233 Alternatively (b) provides that, as regards facts, only a significant divergence will trigger an intervention by the Commission. This distinction between law and facts is considered justified. From the point of view of maintaining consistency it is essential to ensure that there are no major divergences in terms of the analytical approach. For instance, it would be problematic if in one Member State parallel trade restrictions were assessed under the effects standard but at Community level such restrictions were considered restrictions by object. Such differences would strike at the heart of the Community competition rules. The same may not be so when it comes to assessing the facts of individual cases. It may not be unreasonable for two national competition authorities to reach different conclusions when assessing the facts of a case. For instance, the fact that in one case the relevant market has been considered national does not necessarily mean that it is problematic if in a subsequent case it is found that the relevant market is (now) Community-wide. As stated in the Network Notice there is only a need to intervene as regards the assessment of the facts when there is a significant divergence.[231]

According to (c) above, the Commission may intervene when a network member is pro- **2.234**
longing proceedings unduly. The Commission may thus act in order to ensure effective enforcement of the Community competition rules when national competition authorities for whatever reason fail to do so. This follows from the last part of (d), which provides that the Commission may open proceedings when there is a need to adopt a Commission decision to ensure effective enforcement. This may be the case, for instance, where experience has shown that national competition authorities do not intervene effectively against certain types of infringement.

The policy-developing role of the Commission is expressly recognised in (d) above, accord- **2.235**
ing to which there may be a need to adopt a Commission decision to develop Community competition policy. It is particularly relevant for the Commission to do so when new types of agreements and practices are being implemented in the Community. By adopting a leading decision, the Commission can send a strong signal to the market as to how such agreements and practices will be assessed under the Community competition rules. The Network Notice gives the example of similar competition issues arising in several Member States. However, this is only one example of circumstances in which intervention may be warranted. Moreover, (d) is not limited to developing new policy orientations. The opening of proceedings with the effect of Article 11(6) may also be warranted in order to maintain the coherence of existing policy instruments such as guidelines. According to case law[232] the Commission is responsible for defining and implementing the orientation of Community competition policy. Guidelines play an important role in terms of defining policy. It is for the European courts as opposed to national competition authorities and courts to determine whether the policy orientations developed by the Commission are in accordance with the legal rules laid down in Articles 81 and 82.

Finally, it follows from (e) above that there is no need for the Commission to justify its interven- **2.236**
tion in light of the situations described under the previous headings where the affected competition authority does not object. This heading is added for the sake of avoiding any doubt.

(iv) The Procedure for Applying Article 11(6)

Article 11(6) provides that if a national competition authority is already acting in a case, **2.237**
the Commission shall only initiate proceedings after consulting with the competition

---

[231] See para 54(b).
[232] See eg Case C-344/98 *Masterfoods* [2000] ECR I-11369, para 46.

authority in question. It follows from the Notice[233] that a national competition authority is deemed to be acting in a case when it has informed the network pursuant to Article 11(3). The obligation of consultation imposed on the Commission under Article 11(6) implies that it must explain to the authority in question the reasons why it intends to open proceedings. The national competition authority has the right to make comments.

2.238 Recital 17 provides that in circumstances where a national competition authority is already dealing with a case and the Commission intends to open proceedings, it should endeavour to do so as soon as possible. The aim is to ensure that the Commission intervenes as soon as possible so as to limit duplication of work and unnecessary use of resources at Member State level.

2.239 According to Article 14(7) the competition authority concerned also has the right to call a meeting of the Advisory Committee to discuss the matter. However, according to the same provision the Committee does not issue an opinion in such cases and neither the Committee nor the competition authority concerned has the power to prevent the Commission from opening proceedings.

(4) Consistent Application by National Courts

(a) *The Competence of National Courts to Apply EC Competition Rules*

2.240 As early as the 1970s, the Court of Justice stated that Articles 81(1) and 82 EC 'tend by their very nature to produce direct effects in relations between individuals. [T]hese Articles create direct rights in respect of the individuals concerned which the national courts must safeguard'.[234] Nevertheless, in the following thirty years, national courts rarely applied the EC competition rules. One may wonder why that is so. Part of the explanation is that national courts were not allowed to apply Article 81(3) EC, which meant that a party could de facto block national procedures by making a notification to the Commission. Another reason may be the fact that complainants often choose the 'easy' alternative of coming to the Commission, even if the latter cannot award damages. Yet another reason might be that parties' lawyers simply did not invoke the EC competition rules, which they were not acquainted with. And finally one should not exclude the reticence of some national judges to apply rules other than their domestic provisions. This general observation becomes even more apparent when one looks at the application of EC competition rules in particular. A review of the Commission's Annual Reports on Competition Policy indicates that the application of EC competition rules by national judges has not been an unmitigated success. For example, the 2003 Annual Report only had reports from five of the (then) fifteen EU Member States on the application of Articles 81 and 82 EC by national courts.[235]

---

[233] See para 54.

[234] Case 127/73 *BRT v SABAM (BRT I)* [1974] ECR 51, para 16.

[235] In 2003, the competition authorities of Austria, Denmark, Finland, France, Greece, Spain, Ireland, Luxembourg, Portugal, and Sweden have not reported any decisions by their courts applying the EC competition rules or referring a question to the European Court of Justice for a preliminary ruling. That may of course be due to the fact that the NCAs were not aware of the application by their national courts, but the possibility that there was nothing to report on should not be excluded.

In one of his last public speeches as Commissioner for Competition, Mario Monti **2.241** emphasised the importance of private enforcement of the EC competition rules through national courts as 'a powerful additional incentive for companies to comply with [those competition rules]'.[236] According to him, Regulation 1/2003 constituted a first step in the direction of stimulating private enforcement. Because that was not the prime intention of Regulation 1/2003, that objective was not realised directly by harmonising national procedural rules,[237] but rather by modifying the way in which EC competition rules are enforced.

A first modification concerned the abolition of the Commission's monopoly on exemp- **2.242** tion. This change in the system should lead to an increased flow of cases before national courts, because it has removed the opportunity for defendants to prolong proceedings before a national court unduly by notifying an agreement to the Commission.[238] It may be assumed that as a result, complainants will now be more inclined to start proceedings before national courts, for instance in order to obtain damages.[239] Once a national court is dealing with a case, Article 3(1) of Regulation 1/2003 imposes on national courts the obligation to apply Articles 81 and 82 as soon as they apply national competition law to agreements, decisions, or abuses within the meaning of Articles 81 or 82. The mere possibility of national courts applying EC competition rules has thus been turned into an obligation to apply EC competition rules. This obligation does not only exist for procedures that were launched after 1 May 2004, but for all procedures that were pending before a national court on that day, regardless of when the facts underlying the procedure took place or the capacity in which the court is looking at the case.[240] This temporal effect of Article 3(1) is the result of the fact that it is a procedural provision[241] and according to the case law of the

---

[236] Mario Monti, 'Competition for consumers' benefit', The Netherlands European Competition Day, Amsterdam, 22 October 2004. The speech can be found on the website of DG Competition: <http://europa.eu.int/comm/competition/speeches/text/sp2004_016_en.pdf>.

[237] Only Arts 2 and 15 of Regulation 1/2003 contain elements of harmonisation of procedural rules for national courts.

[238] For national courts, the elimination of the Commission's exemption monopoly has been confirmed by Art 6 of Regulation 1/2003.

[239] On the right of natural and legal persons to seek compensation for loss caused by an infringement of Arts 81 or 82, see Case C-453/99 *Courage v Crehan* [2001] ECRI-6297, para 26 and the judgment of 13 July 2006 in Joined Cases C-295/04 to C-298/04 *Manfredi* not yet reported, para 60. On 19 December 2005, the Commission adopted a Green Paper on damages actions for breach of the EC antitrust rules (COM(2005) 672, available at <http://europa.eu.int/comm/competition/antitrust/others/actions_for_damages/gp_en.pdf>). The Green Paper sets out a number of possible options to remedy the obstacles in current national procedural law for bringing antitrust damages actions. It is said that by facilitating damages claims for breaches of the EC antitrust rules the enforcement of those rules will be strengthened and it will also make it easier for consumers and companies who have suffered damage from an infringement of EC antitrust rules to recover their losses from the infringer.

[240] eg a court reviewing a decision of an NCA that was taken prior to 1 May 2004, a court reviewing an appeal or as last instance court a judgment of a first instance court that was given prior to 1 May 2004, a court that, in conformity with national procedural rules, is responding to a preliminary request of another national court that has asked the question prior to 1 May 2004, etc.

[241] Leaving aside the temporal application in respect of the EU Member States which acceded in May 2004—an issue which is dealt with generally in the accession treaties—it is clear that the obligation on NCAs and national courts to apply Arts 81 and 82 in cases falling within the substantive scope of application of those provisions is of a procedural nature. Indeed, Art 3(1) of Regulation 1/2003 does not impose a new substantive rule upon undertakings (they were already bound by Arts 81 and 82 before the Regulation entered into force), it only regulates the way in which the substantive rules are being enforced.

Court of Justice, procedural rules are generally held to apply to all proceedings pending at the time when they enter into force.[242]

2.243 This immediate application of Article 3(1) of Regulation 1/2003 becomes particularly relevant when read in combination with the reminder that has been put in the Commission's notice concerning the co-operation between the Commission and the national courts, that the EC competition law provisions are a matter of public policy.[243] The consequence of such classification is that even if none of the parties in a (pending) national procedure rely on Articles 81 or 82 EC, the national judge is obliged to apply those provisions of his own motion, as soon as his domestic law also obliges or allows him to apply domestic public policy rules.[244]

(b) The Coherent Application of EC Competition Rules by National Courts

2.244 The enhanced role of national courts in the enforcement of EC competition rules may have led to some uncertainty as to the coherent application of those rules by the courts.[245] One should not overestimate the possibility of uncertainty, however, as the question of how to secure coherent application of EC rules by national courts is neither new nor unique to the field of competition law. Both the EC Treaty and the case law of the Court of Justice provide for a number of mechanisms aimed at ensuring coherent application of EC rules and in particular, the EC competition rules.

2.245 The main mechanism provided for by the EC Treaty is the preliminary rulings procedure under Article 234 EC. Although this mechanism remains the most conclusive guarantee of a coherent application of the EC competition rules and is compulsory for last instance courts,[246] it appears to be rarely used by national courts.[247] The most obvious reason for this

---

242 Case C-61/98 *De Haan Beheer v Inspecteur der Invoerrechten en Accijnzen te Rotterdam* [1999] ECR 5003, para 13.

243 Point 3 of the notice on co-operation with national courts. See Case C-126/97 *Eco Swiss* [1999] ECR I-3055, para 36; Case T-34/92 *Fiatagri UK and New Holland Ford* [1994] ECR II-905, para 39; and Case T-128/98 *Aéroports de Paris* [2000] ECR II-3929, para 241; and the judgment of 13 July 2006 in Joined Cases C-295/04 to C-298/04 *Manfredi* not yet reported, para 31.

244 There is only one proviso, namely that national courts cannot be required to raise of their own motion an issue concerning the breach of an EC competition law provision where the examination of that issue would oblige them to abandon the passive role assigned to them by going beyond the ambit of the dispute as it has been defined by the parties (Joined Cases C-430/93 and C-431/93 *van Schijndel* [1995] ECR I-4705, paras 13–15 and 22).

245 One of the recurrent observations made during the process that led to Regulation 1/2003 was that national judges were not ready to apply EC competition rules, in particular Art 81(3) EC, because 'they cannot deal with substantive economic assessments of both the anti- and pro-competitive impacts of agreements' (Report of the EP Committee on Economic and Monetary Affairs of 21 June 2001 on the proposal for a Council regulation on the implementation of the rules on competition laid down in Articles 81 and 82 of the Treaty (A5-0229/2001), p 25).

246 National courts against whose decisions there is no judicial remedy under national law are obliged to ask the Court of Justice a preliminary question (Art 234, third paragraph, EC) whenever they are confronted with a novel and not-straightforward issue (Case 283/81 *CILFIT v Ministry of Health* [1982] ECR 3415, paras 13 and 14).

247 Between 1997 and 2005, the Court of Justice received 78 preliminary questions regarding EC competition rules (varying between one request in 2002 and 15 requests in 2001), which as a total constitutes less than 4% of all preliminary questions it received over that period (see the annual reports of the Court of Justice on <http://curia.eu.int/en/instit/presentationfr/index_cje.htm>).

reluctance is probably the fact that it takes the Court of Justice almost two years to reply to the preliminary request,[248] which constitutes a great disincentive, particularly in private antitrust actions, where parties frequently ask for interim measures and for injunctions as speedy remedies for alleged infringements.

Recently, the Court itself limited the opportunity for a national court operating as an NCA **2.246** to ask preliminary questions when the Court found that it had no jurisdiction to answer the questions of the Greek Competition Commission.[249] The Court came to this conclusion because it found the Greek Competition Commission not to be sufficiently independent from the Government and from the prosecuting authority and—more surprisingly— because it can be relieved of its competence to apply Articles 81 and 82 EC pursuant to Article 11(6) of Regulation 1/2003.[250] Since a national court may refer a question to the Court only if it is called upon to give judgment in proceedings intended to lead to a decision of a judicial nature and the opening of proceedings by the Commission relieves the Greek Competition Commission from its competence, the Court found that whenever the latter happens, 'the proceedings initiated before that authority will not lead to a decision of a judicial nature'.[251] The latter argument comes as a surprise, not only because it seems to be based on a misreading of earlier case law of the Court,[252] but mainly because the Article 11(6) effect—which 'essentially maintains the rule in Article 9(3) of Council Regulation 17'[253]— did not prevent the Court from answering the question posed by the Spanish *Tribunal de Defensa de la Competencia*, also a national competition authority.[254] One may therefore assume that the Court will not use Article 11(6) as a basis simply to refuse jurisdiction to answer a question referred by any of the national courts that act as an NCA. The fact that the Court concludes that the Greek Competition Commission is not a court or tribunal within the meaning of Article 234 EC on basis of 'the factors examined, *considered as a whole*' (emphasis added)[255] seems to support that view. NCAs such as the *Tribunal de Defensa de la Competencia* will thus probably still be able to ask the Court of Justice for a preliminary ruling.[256]

---

[248] See the 2004 annual report of the Court of Justice on <http://www.curia.eu.int/en/instit/presentationfr/rapport/stat/st04cr.pdf>.

[249] Judgment of the Court of Justice of 31 May 2005 in Case C-53/03 *Syfait* [2005] ECR I-4609. In his opinion of 28 October 2004, Jacobs AG came to the opposite conclusion.

[250] Case C-53/03 *Syfait* paras 29–38.

[251] ibid, para 36.

[252] Both in Case C-134/97 *Victoria Film* [1998] ECR I-7023, paras 14–18 and in Case C-195/98 *Österreichischer Gewerkschaftsbund* [2000] ECR I-10497, paras 25–29 the criterion that a national court may refer a question to the Court only 'if it is called upon to give judgment in proceedings intended to lead to a decision of a judicial nature' has been introduced to exclude bodies which act in a more administrative capacity. In *Syfait*, the Court shifts the focus from the nature of the outcome, a judicial decision, to the outcome itself and thus seems to add the condition that the proceedings not only should be *intended* to lead to a decision of a judicial nature, but should effectively *result* in such a decision.

[253] Case C-53/03 *Syfait*, para 34.

[254] Case C-67/91 *Dirección General de Defensa de la Competencia v Asociación Española de Banca Privada and others* [1992] ECR I-4785.

[255] Case C-53/03 *Syfait*, para 37.

[256] Point 1 of the notice on co-operation with national courts defines national courts within the meaning of the notice as 'those courts and tribunals within an EU Member State that can apply Articles 81 and 82 EC and that are authorised to ask a preliminary question to the Court of Justice of the European Communities pursuant to Article 234 EC'. The consequence of the *Syfait* case would thus be that, until the Court of Justice

2.247　The limited use of the preliminary rulings procedure has a huge impact as it essentially neutralises what is intended to be the main mechanism for coherence provided for by the EC Treaty. In order to offer some comfort for judges who would like their judgments to be coherent with the *acquis communautaire*, but who choose not to refer a preliminary request to the Court of Justice, the Commission has taken a number of initiatives, which, although not leading to binding guidance, may contribute to coherent application of EC competition rules by national courts. In addition, Article 15 of Regulation 1/2003 sets a framework for close co-operation between national courts and the Commission.[257]

(i) Commission Initiatives towards Coherent Application of EC Competition Rules

2.248　In order to give the national judges some guidance in their application of Articles 81 and 82 EC, the Commission has taken the following initiatives: it issues policy notices and guidelines; it co-finances the training of national judges; and it makes publicly available the judgments of national courts applying EC competition rules.

2.249　**The Commission's policy notices and guidelines**　When a national court is dealing with a case in which European competition rules are to be applied, it will most likely look for guidance in the case law of the Court of Justice and/or in the decisions and publications of the Commission. Those texts do not all have the same status for guidance purposes. Leaving aside the implications of individual Commission decisions (dealt with in paragraphs 2.254–2.259), it is important to be aware of the fact that the Court's case law, like the Commission's block exemption Regulations, gives *binding* guidance to the national judge.[258] By contrast, in the Commission's notices, guidelines and even in its annual report on competition policy, the national judge can find *non-binding* guidance for his judicial work.[259]

2.250　Although non-binding, the Commission's notices and guidelines offer an excellent tool for enhancing the coherent application of EC competition rules. To the extent that national courts from all over the EU take account of the notices and guidelines when applying EC competition law, the outcome of their reasoning becomes more predictable and thereby contributes to the legal certainty for business. In particular notices which clarify the Commission's view of key concepts in the enforcement of competition rules, such as the Notice on the definition of the relevant market for the purposes of EC competition law[260]

---

rules differently, the Commission will treat bodies such as the Greek Competition Commission as not being covered by Art 15 of Regulation 1/2003. The practical consequences of this finding should not be overestimated, though, since those bodies can still enjoy the co-operation mechanisms provided within the ECN.

[257]　The co-operation between the national courts and the Commission as established by Art 15 is dealt with in paras 2.260–2.278.

[258]　Case 63/75 *Fonderies Roubaix* [1976] ECR 111, paras 9–11; and Case C-234/89 *Delimitis* [1991] ECR I-935, para 46.

[259]　Case 66/86 *Ahmed Saeed Flugreisen* [1989] ECR 803, para 27; Case C-234/89 *Delimitis* [1991] ECR I-935, para 50; and Joined Cases C-319/93, C-40/94 and C-224/94 *Dijkstra* [1995] ECR I-4471, para 32. The annex to the notice on co-operation with national courts contains a list of Commission guidelines, notices and regulations in the field of competition policy, in particular the block exemption Regulations. The list is also available and regularly updated on the website of DG Competition: <http://europa.eu.int/comm/competition/antitrust/legislation/>.

[260]　[1997] OJ C372/5.

or the Notice on the effect on trade concept contained in Articles 81 and 82 EC,[261] or guidelines which give further details on the application of the binding Commission block exemption Regulations have a high potential for building coherence. The interpretation by national judges of these non-binding notices and guidelines is likely to be rather coherent. The reason for this optimism lies in the fact that national judges, to the extent that they are at all inclined to ask the Commission for assistance, will most likely consider it to be appropriate to address themselves to the author of the notices and guidelines in cases where these texts raise some doubts. It may therefore be expected that most questions the Commission will receive pursuant to Article 15(1) of Regulation 1/2003 will have a bearing on its notices and guidelines, either regarding their content or perhaps even more regarding their perceived 'lacunae'.

Co-financing the training of national judges in EC competition rules When the **2.251** European Parliament (EP) was considering its position on the Commission's proposal to replace Regulation 17/62 by a regulation establishing a new enforcement system, the Committee on Economic and Monetary Affairs seemed to share the general concerns regarding the application of EC competition rules by national judges. In order to ensure both the effective and the coherent application of those rules, the EP Committee suggested that 'the practicalities of further training or the creation of specialised courts would need extensive further consideration and discussion if the regime is to operate effectively'.[262] The Committee did not elaborate further the idea of creating specialised courts as an undoubtedly stimulating factor of coherence; most likely because it considered that, as a matter of sovereignty, the EU Member States should decide upon that themselves. However, with regard to the aspect of training, it called 'on the Commission to propose (. . .) a programme for the continuing training and education in Community competition law of national judges (. . .) in pursuit of the principle of the uniform application of Community law'.[263]

The Commission immediately took up this suggestion and, as early as 2002, launched its **2.252** programme to finance the training of national judges in EC competition law. Indeed, the Commission opted not to organise the training itself, because that could have been seen as an undue interference with the independence of the judiciary, but rather to prompt European non-profit organisations to organise the training for national judges. So far, the Commission has co-financed thirty training projects all over the EU and envisages continuing its training efforts.[264] With these projects, the Commission not only wants to encourage the training of national judges in the application of EC competition rules, but also to strengthen judicial co-operation and networking between national competition judges in order to contribute to a coherent application of the rules.

---

[261] [2004] OJ C101/81.

[262] Report of the EP Committee on Economic and Monetary Affairs of 21 June 2001, referred to in n 245, p 26.

[263] ibid, p 63.

[264] Neelie Kroes, 'Taking Competition Seriously—Anti-Trust Reform in Europe', International Bar Association/European Commission Conference 'Anti-trust reform in Europe: a year in practice', Brussels, 10 March 2005. The speech can be found on the website of DG Competition: <http://europa.eu.int/comm/competition/speeches/index_2005.html>.

2.253 **A database on national judgments** While fully conscious of the principle of independence of judges, the authors of Regulation 1/2003 were also aware of the risk to coherent application of the law that might result if judges did not talk to other enforcers or communicate their rulings applying Articles 81 and 82 other than to the parties to the national proceedings. Consequently, under Article 15(2) of Regulation 1/2003, the Commission must receive a copy of any written judgment relating to the application of Articles 81 or 82. DG Competition now makes available on its website non-confidential versions of these received national judgments in their original language. This also allows potential publishers to analyse and comment on these judgments so that they also become known outside the Member State where they were issued.[265]

(ii) Consistency in the Case of Parallel or Consecutive Application of EC Competition Rules

2.254 The thorniest issue regarding coherent application of the EC competition rules and the related co-operation between the national courts and the Commission, is the situation in which a national court is applying EC competition law to an agreement, decision, concerted practice, or unilateral behaviour affecting trade between Member States at the same time as, or after, the Commission.[266] In the *Delimits* and *Masterfoods* cases,[267] the Court of Justice had occasion to clarify how consistency could be guaranteed in those circumstances and the Council codified this case law in Article 16(1) of Regulation 1/2003. Depending on who decides first, the national court or the Commission, the obligations for national courts are slightly different.

2.255 The most likely situation is the one in which the Commission reaches a decision before the national court. In those circumstances, the national court cannot make a decision running counter to that of the Commission. If, however, the national court doubts the legality of the Commission's decision and it would therefore prefer not to follow it, it can only do so once the Court of Justice has pronounced itself on the illegality of the Commission's decision. A national court seeking to deviate from a Commission decision in the same case must therefore suspend the national proceedings and ask the Court of Justice for a preliminary ruling.[268]

2.256 It may also be that while the case is pending before the national court, the Court of First Instance is reviewing the Commission's decision at the request of the party to whose detriment the Commission has decided. In such circumstances, the national judge should suspend the national proceedings until the final judgment in the annulment action is taken by the Community courts. There seem to be two exceptions to this latter obligation, where: (1) the national court considers the validity of the Commission's decision to be irrelevant

---

[265] See <http://europa.eu.int/comm/competition/antitrust/national_courts/index_en.html>.

[266] Article 11(6), *juncto* Art 35(3) and (4) of Regulation 1/2003 prevents a parallel application of Arts 81 or 82 EC by the Commission and a national court only when the latter has been designated as a national competition authority.

[267] Case C-234/89 *Delimitis* [1991] ECR I-935; and Case C-344/98 *Masterfoods* [2000] ECR I-11369. For a comment on *Masterfoods*, see L Kjølbye, [2002] CML Rev 175–184 and R Nazzini *Concurrent Proceedings in Competition Law*, refered to above in n 1, pp 182–200. On the scope of *Masterfoods*, see the speeches of the Lords of Appeal for judgment in the case *Inntrepreneur Pub Company and others v Crehan* [2006] UKHL 38.

[268] Case 314/85 *Foto-Frost* [1987] ECR 4199, paras 12–20.

172

to the case it is dealing with; or (2) the national court considers it more appropriate to ask the Court of Justice to pronounce on the validity of the Commission's decision.[269] The latter option may be chosen for instance in a case where the national court fears an appeal against the judgment of the Court of First Instance and seeks to speed up the process by directly asking the Court of Justice for a preliminary ruling.

The alternative scenario is the one in which the national court comes to a decision before **2.257** the Commission does, since there is—by definition—no Commission decision which the national court would have to take into account. Article 16(1) of Regulation 1/2003, echoing the case law of the Court of Justice, states that in those circumstances, the national court must avoid adopting a decision that would conflict with a decision contemplated by the Commission. In contrast to the previous scenario, where Article 16(1) imposes an obligation as to the result that is to be achieved (namely no deviation), this sounds more like an obligation of best efforts on the part of the national court. As a consequence, this is probably the 'ideal' scenario in which the co-operation mechanisms between the national courts and the Commission could contribute to guaranteeing a coherent outcome.

Indeed, apart from the most obvious solution which would imply that the national court **2.258** will suspend its proceedings until the Commission has made a decision, one can also imagine that the obligation to avoid a judgment that would conflict with a future decision of the Commission implies that the national court will use the co-operation mechanisms provided for by Article 15 of Regulation 1/2003 to try to ensure coherence. For instance, the national court could ask the Commission whether it has initiated proceedings relating to the same agreements, decisions or practices that the national court is dealing with.[270] If so, the court could also enquire of the Commission as to the progress of its investigation and proceedings and the likelihood of a decision in that case.[271] Furthermore, when a national court considers staying proceedings pending the outcome of the Commission's proceedings in order to safeguard the legal certainty and thus coherence, it may also be useful for the national court to ask the Commission when a decision is likely to be taken. Whenever the Commission is informed of the fact that the case in which it has opened proceedings is also pending in parallel before a national court and that the national court considers its own proceedings to depend on the outcome of the Commission's proceedings, the latter will endeavour to give priority to such cases, 'in particular when the outcome of a civil dispute depends on them'.[272]

Finally, whenever the national court cannot reasonably have doubts as to the nature of the **2.259** Commission's contemplated decision or where the Commission has already decided on a

---

[269] Case C-344/98 *Masterfoods* [2000] ECR I-11369, paras 52–59.

[270] According to the Court of Justice, the initiation of proceedings implies an authoritative act of the Commission, evidencing its intention of taking a decision (Case 48/72 *Brasserie de Haecht* [1973] ECR 77, para 16). The Commission may make public the initiation of proceedings with a view to the adoption of a decision pursuant to Arts 7–10 of Regulation 1/2003 (see Art 2(2) of Commission Implementing Regulation). When proceedings are opened in parallel with the publication of the notice pursuant to Art 27(4) of Regulation 1/2003, the national court will obviously know that the Commission intends to adopt a decision pursuant to Art 9 or 10.

[271] Case C-234/89 *Delimitis* [1991] ECR I-935, para 53; and Joined Cases C-319/93, C-40/94 and C-224/94 *Dijkstra* [1995] ECR I-4471, para 34.

[272] Point 12 of the notice on co-operation with national courts.

similar case, the national court should be able to decide on the case pending before it in accordance with that contemplated or earlier decision without needing to ask the Commission for the information referred to above or awaiting the Commission's decision.

(c) The Co-operation between the Commission and the National Courts

2.260 The co-operation between the national courts and the Commission in the application of EC competition rules is a delicate exercise, in which one has to reconcile the independence of the judiciary with the need for consistent application of Articles 81 and 82. The independence of the judiciary means that co-operation between the national courts and the Commission, as distinct from the co-operation within the ECN, is mainly *demand-driven*, ie originating from the national courts.[273] In order for a demand-driven co-operation to lead to coherence, national courts must both be able to identify any difficulty related to the application of competition rules and subsequently be willing to seek support from a 'coherence fostering' European authority to contribute to resolving that difficulty.

2.261 In order to help the national courts apply the EC competition rules, the Commission as early as in 1993 issued a Notice on co-operation with national courts.[274] When drafting Regulation 1/2003, the Commission undertook also to revise the old notice on co-operation with national courts. The new Notice is intended to serve as a practical tool for national judges who apply Articles 81 and 82 EC in conformity with Regulation 1/2003. It assembles the relevant case law of the Court of Justice, thus clarifying the procedural context in which national judges are operating.

2.262 Before turning to the detail of those co-operation mechanisms between the Commission and the national courts, the notice emphasises the fact that the co-operation mechanisms are intended to assist the national courts. The qualification 'assistance' reflects the non-binding character of the co-operation. The assistance is non-binding in that a national judge is not obliged to seek the Commission's assistance, nor is (s)he bound by the assistance given.[275] The assistance provided by the Commission under Article 15 of Regulation 1/2003 is also intended exclusively to help the judge. Although that assistance might favour the position of one of the parties over that of the other, the parties' interest is not relevant as regards the Commission's assistance. Indeed, the co-operation mechanisms have as their sole objective the guarantee of consistent application of EC competition rules throughout the European Union. The Commission is thus endeavouring to protect the general interest and not the private interest of any one of the parties. This is why the notice on co-operation with national courts states that 'the Commission will not hear any of the parties about its

---

[273] It goes without saying that a network such as the ECN could not be established with national courts. Not only would that not have been practically feasible, but it is mainly a matter of independence of the judiciary. Many national judges, however, seek contacts with their peers in order to exchange experience and to establish some 'best practices' for the swift and coherent application of the EC competition rules. The Association of European Competition Law Judges is probably the best known network in that respect.

[274] [1993] OJ C39/6.

[275] Note the difference from the preliminary rulings procedure: national courts against whose decisions there is no judicial remedy under national law are obliged to ask the Court of Justice a preliminary question (Art 234, third paragraph, EC). The rulings given by the Court bind all national courts (Case 68/74 *Alaimo v Préfet du Rhône* [1975] ECR 109).

assistance to the national court' and it will even inform the court of any contacts it has had with the parties.[276]

Turning now to the precise co-operation mechanisms between the Commission and the **2.263** national courts as they are laid down in Article 15, one may distinguish two basic categories: (i) the possibility for national judges to ask the Commission for information or for its opinion; and (ii) the possibility for the Commission and for national competition authorities to submit written and oral observations to national courts.

(i) The Opportunity for the National Courts to ask the Commission for Information or for its Opinion

Article 15(1) of Regulation 1/2003 provides a clear and sufficient legal basis for national **2.264** judges to ask the Commission for any information it has in its possession or for its opinion on questions concerning the application of EC competition rules. This provision is complementary to the obligation of the Commission under Article 10 EC to assist the Member States in the application of EC competition law.

The opportunity to ask the Commission for information   On the basis of Article 10 EC, **2.265** the Commission is obliged to provide the national judge with such information in its possession as the latter may request. That information may be very general, for example reports the Commission has drawn up, or it may be case-specific, where the judge wants to know whether there are any precedents to the case, whether the Commission has or intends to open its own proceedings in the case, or where the court is asking for specific documents that could help it in the factual, legal, or economic assessment of the case pending before it. The information requested may be publicly available, but it may also be confidential, for example, business secrets or other confidential information.

As a matter of principle, information requested by a national judge will be sent to that **2.266** judge. There are, however, two exceptions to this general principle. First, the Commission may refuse to transmit information to national courts for overriding reasons relating to the need to safeguard the interests of the Community or to avoid any interference with its functioning and independence, in particular by jeopardizing the accomplishment of the tasks entrusted to it.[277] In its notice on co-operation with national courts, the Commission interpreted this exception as covering, amongst others, the refusal to transmit to national courts information voluntarily submitted by a leniency applicant without the consent of that applicant.[278] This position echoes the agreement within the ECN not to exchange information voluntarily submitted by a leniency applicant.[279]

Secondly, as the Court of First Instance has explained in the *Postbank* case, the co-operation **2.267** with national courts may not lead the Commission to undermine the guarantees given to

---

[276] Point 19 *in fine* of the notice on co-operation with national courts.

[277] Case C-2/88 *Zwartveld* [1990] ECR I-4405, paras 10 and 11; Case C-275/00 *First and Franex* [2002] ECR I-10943, para 49; and Case T-353/94 *Postbank* [1996] ECR II-921, para 93.

[278] Point 26 of the Notice on co-operation with national courts.

[279] See point 40 of the Network Notice. The exceptions laid down in point 41, such as the written commitment by the receiving authority not to sanction, cannot be fulfilled by a national court. Point 26 of the Notice on co-operation with national courts therefore does not contain any exception.

natural and legal persons by the Community provisions concerning professional secrecy.[280] The Commission shall therefore inform the national court of the confidential nature of the documents it transmits. It is then the responsibility of the national court to guarantee protection of the confidentiality of such information. Where the national court cannot provide a sufficient guarantee of confidentiality, the Commission is entitled to refuse to send the confidential documents. To the extent that the requirement to guarantee confidentiality prevents the national court from disclosing the information it has received from the Commission to the parties in the pending case or to their legal representatives, this form of co-operation between the Commission and national courts risks becoming meaningless. Indeed, the fundamental right to be heard implies that the court cannot base its decision on information which is not also available to the parties. Since it cannot be assumed that the Court of First Instance intended to render meaningless the duty of sincere co-operation between the Commission and national courts, the question remains to what extent the Commission can send confidential information to the national courts and to what extent the latter can use such information in its ongoing proceedings.

2.268 This brings us to the more general question: to what extent do the limitations which flow from Article 12(2) and (3) of Regulation 1/2003 to the use by a competition authority of information exchanged within the ECN, also apply *mutatis mutandis* to the information the Commission has sent to a national court following a request pursuant to Article 15(1)? It can be argued that, although Regulation 1/2003 only regulates very marginally the use by national courts of information received from the Commission, the restrictions laid down in Article 12(2) and (3) also restrict the use by national courts of information received from the Commission.

2.269 The constraints of Article 12(2) are relevant for national courts because of the general principles of Community law and the framework within which the Commission transmits information to national courts. It has indeed been argued that the limitation on use of the exchanged information in evidence only in respect of the subject matter, for which it was collected, reflects the basic rights of defence of the undertakings against which the information is being used.[281] Since the rights of defence, as with all fundamental rights, fall under the general principles of Community law, which all national authorities must respect when applying Community law, national courts should also respect this limitation and thus only use the information received from the Commission in evidence in respect of the subject matter for which it was collected.

2.270 Article 12(2) clarifies further that '[i]nformation exchanged shall only be used for the purpose of applying Article 81 or 82' EC. That limitation is repeated in Article 15(1) ('In proceedings for the application of Article 81 or Article 82 of the Treaty') as a limitation to the request. That same limitation returns in the next phase of the co-operation, namely the transmission of information by the Commission. That phase is not dealt with in Regulation 1/2003, nor is it referred to explicitly in the EC Treaty. The Notice on co-operation with national courts recalls, however, that the Community courts inferred from Article 10 EC an obligation on the part of the Commission to assist national courts when they apply

---

[280] Case T-353/94 *Postbank* [1996] II-921, para 90.
[281] See paras 2.179–2.180 above.

Community law.[282] Such a general obligation would probably not exist when the latter only apply national law.[283] Since the purpose both of the request and of the transmission of the information by the Commission is to assist the national court in the application of the EC competition rules, it is submitted that any other use by a national court would constitute an abuse of Article 15(1) and of Article 10 EC. One should not exclude the possibility that such an abuse could be invoked as a ground for the annulment of (that part of) the judgment made on the basis of the transmitted information.

However, there seems to be one exception to the general limitation on the co-operation **2.271** between the Commission and national courts relating to the latter's application of EC law. When a national court, pursuant to Article 3 of Regulation 1/2003, applies EC and national competition law in parallel in the same case, it would be absurd to prevent that court from basing its judgment on the information received from the Commission when applying national competition law, while allowing it for the application of EC competition law. Logic thus suggests that the opening provision in Article 12(2) of Regulation 1/2003 in respect of the use of information exchanged within the ECN for the parallel application of national competition law also applies *mutatis mutandis* to the use by a national court of information transmitted by the Commission.[284] It is debatable, however, whether the additional condition of Article 12(2), namely that the parallel application of national competition law should not lead to a different outcome than that of the application of EC competition law, would also apply to the use by a national court of the information transmitted by the Commission. Indeed, to the extent that this condition goes beyond the convergence requirement of Article 3(2) of Regulation 1/2003 and in the absence of any explicit provision like Article 12(2), there seems to be no imperative reason why such additional condition would limit the use by a national court of the information transmitted by the Commission to apply EC and national competition law in parallel in the same case.

Finally, it is also contended that the restrictions contained in Article 12(3) of Regulation **2.272** 1/2003 apply to national courts. Article 12(3) concerns the limitations on the use in evidence of information exchanged within the ECN in order to impose sanctions on natural persons. It is clear from the context and the wording of that provision[285] and from its interpretation in the Network Notice[286] that the sanctions referred to are those included in Article 5, first paragraph, last indent, of Regulation 1/2003. Those sanctions could be administrative or criminal fines, custody or other personal sanctions, such as a professional disqualification. A national court that can impose the sanctions included in Article 5

---

[282] Point 15 of the Notice on co-operation with national courts, Case C-2/88 *Imm Zwartveld* [1990] ECR I-3365, paras 16–22; and Case C-234/89 *Delimitis* [1991] I-935, para 53.

[283] See, however, Case C-275/00 *First and Franex* [2002] ECR I-10943, para 49, in which the Court seems to extend the duty of loyal co-operation to those situations in which a national court needs information that *only* the Commission can provide, irrespective of whether that national court applies EC law or national law.

[284] See paras 2.176–2.178 above.

[285] Article 12(3) deals with the use of information exchanged within the ECN pursuant to Art 12(1). Since the Commission can only impose sanctions on undertakings, Art 12(3) regulates the use in evidence of exchanged information by NCAs in their application of EC competition rules. The application of EC competition rules by an NCA cannot lead to any decision other than those enumerated in Article 5 of Regulation 1/2003 (see also paras 2.79–2.82 above).

[286] See point 28(c) of the Network Notice.

would thus be designated (implicitly) as a national competition authority within the meaning of Article 35(1) of Regulation 1/2003. Consequently, the transmission of information by the Commission to such a national court would be covered by Article 12 of Regulation 1/2003 and the limitations of Article 12(3) to the use of such information by the recipient NCA, *in casu* a national court, would thus apply automatically. As a result, the use by a national court of information received from the Commission following a request pursuant to Article 15(1) of Regulation 1/2003 is necessarily conditioned by the limitations of Article 12(3).

2.273 **The opportunity of asking the Commission for its opinion** National judges can ask the Commission any question relating to a competition issue raised by the facts of a case and request its interpretation of the EC competition rules. The opinion sought can be legal and/or economic, sectoral or general, procedural or factual. As mentioned in paragraph 2.250 above, one can anticipate that national courts will mainly question the Commission about the interpretation and the concrete application of the texts it has authored, such as notices, guidelines or block exemption Regulations. Although the Commission's opinion is only indicative, without taking any final position on the merits of a pending case,[287] it can be assumed that the Commission's opinions, particularly on the texts it has authored, will have the effect of fostering consistency. That also explains why the Commission announced that it may make its opinions available on its web site. In any case, the Commission gives an overview of its co-operation with national courts in its annual Report on Competition Policy.[288] That channel permits the Commission to give a wider publicity to those (parts of) opinions that may be relevant beyond the specific factual settings of the national court case in which it was asked for its opinion.

(ii) The Submission of Observations

2.274 Apart from the option available to a national court to ask the Commission for assistance in a case it is dealing with, Article 15 of Regulation 1/2003 provides an opportunity for the Commission and for the national competition authorities to submit observations to national courts. For most Member States, this possibility constitutes a novelty. According to Article 15(3), all ECN members have the right to submit written observations on their own initiative. The Commission can submit observations where the consistent application of Articles 81 or 82 so requires. With the permission of the national court, the Commission and/or the national competition authority may also come to the courtroom and present oral observations. Although these observations do not bind the national court, they will constitute an important tool enabling the Commission to draw the attention of a national court to an issue relating to consistent application of EC competition rules. So far, the Commission has not considered it necessary to submit observations pursuant to Article 15(3).

---

[287] National courts can always turn themselves directly to the Court of Justice for a binding interpretation of the rules under the preliminary ruling procedure, which is provided for in Art 234 EC. See, however, the judgment of the Court of Justice of 31 May 2005 in Case C-53/03 *Syfait* [2005] ECR I-4609. The judgment has been commented in para 2.246 above.

[288] Point 20 of the notice on co-operation with national courts. For an initial overview, see points 112 and 113 of the 2004 Report on Competition Policy, SEC(2005) 805 of 17 June 2005, available at <http://europa.eu.int/comm/competition/annual_reports/2004/en.pdf>.

For the Commission or an NCA to intervene in a pending national proceeding, they of course must be aware of the cases pending before a national court in which it could be appropriate for them to submit observations. In a number of Member States, courts are obliged by law to inform the NCA—and in some also the Commission—about any case brought before them which concerns the application of Articles 81 or 82.[289] There is also an obligation under Article 15(2) of Regulation 1/2003 to inform the Commission—and in some Member States also the NCA, pursuant to national law—about all judgments in which a national court applies EC competition law.[290] Whenever a judgment brought to their attention raises particular concerns, the Commission and NCAs may proactively explore whether that judgment has been appealed and if so, they may consider submitting observations. **2.275**

Compared to the *ex ante* line of information (about a pending case), the *ex post* line (about a closed case) has the obvious drawback of depending on whether or not the parties appeal the judgment which gives rise to concern. Moreover, it also excludes the intervention by the competition authorities before the judge of first instance. That in itself should not necessarily be regarded as a negative feature, however. One could argue that it is more appropriate for a competition authority to intervene at a later stage, when the facts have been established and when the domestic judicial protection system has the opportunity to correct itself. However, one should also have regard to the scope and the frequency of (the last instance) review in competition matters in the Member State concerned in order not to miss an occasion to usefully submit observations. **2.276**

A final method by which information can be provided will of course be when one of the parties themselves direct the competition authorities' attention to a pending case in which an intervention is considered expedient. Although the competition authorities should not act upon a request from a party seeking to defend its private interest, the information provided may nevertheless trigger an autonomous decision by the authority to submit observations. When the Commission decides to submit observations following a request from one of the parties, it will obviously not contact that party on the content of its submission and will inform the court about the request it received.[291] **2.277**

Finally, it should be emphasised that Regulation 1/2003 merely provides an opportunity to submit observations to national courts, without elaborating the procedural context within which this new coherence instrument will be exercised. The Regulation only states that in order to allow them to adequately prepare their observations, the Commission and the national competition authorities may ask the court for documents which they feel are necessary for assessing the case. Naturally this information cannot be used by the authority for any other purpose. All other procedural issues, such as when the observations should be submitted or when and how the parties in the case can respond to the observations, are to **2.278**

---

[289] See eg Art 90(1) of the German competition law, Art 91/H of the Hungarian competition law, Art 35 of the Latvian competition law, Art 50(2) of the Lithuanian competition law, and Art 82a of the Slovak Civil Procedure Code.

[290] See para 2.253 above.

[291] Point 19 of the Notice on co-operation with national courts.

be dealt with under national law. Member States' procedural rules and practices determine the relevant procedural framework, duly taking into account the rights of defence of the parties to the proceedings.[292] This presumably implies that the court should forward the observations from the competition authority to the parties in order for them to reply. In the absence of a procedural framework, the national court, in compliance with the principle of effectiveness and, where applicable, of equivalence, will have to ensure in any event that the Commission or the NCA can use its right.[293] This is most likely to mean that the national court will apply *mutatis mutandis* the domestic rules on intervention by an expert.

---

[292] Recital 21 of Regulation 1/2003 and point 35 of the Notice on co-operation with national courts. See eg Art 90a of the German competition law and for Ireland, r 22 of the Rules of the Superior Courts (Competition Proceedings) 2005 (SI 2005/130).

[293] Where a Member State has not established the relevant procedural framework, the national court has to determine which national procedural rules are appropriate for the submission of observations in the case pending before it. According to the principle of effectiveness, those national procedural rules may not make the submission of observations by the Commission or by an NCA excessively difficult or practically impossible. According to the principle of equivalence, the national procedural rules for submitting observations in a case regarding the enforcement of EC competition law may not be less favourable than the rules applicable to the submission of observations in a case regarding the enforcement of national competition law.

3

ARTICLE 81

*Ali Nikpay, Lars Kjølbye and Jonathan Faull**

* Sections A–C are by Ali Nikpay and Jonathan Faull. Sections D–F are by Lars Kjølbye, Ali Nikpay and Jonathan Faull.

A. Introduction

3.01   The purpose of the following overview of Article 81 of the EC Treaty (formerly Article 85) is to consider certain general features of that provision as it is interpreted and applied. The aim is to highlight some of the key legal and policy issues and debates arising from its application, in order to introduce and underpin the substantive chapters.

B. Scope of Article 81

(1) Scope

3.02   Pursuant to Article 3 of the EC Treaty, 'the activities of the Community shall include, as provided in this Treaty and in accordance with the timetable set out therein: . . . (g) a system ensuring that competition in the internal market is not distorted'. Article 81 is interpreted and applied, together with other Treaty provisions, in order to create and sustain that system.

In general Article 81 applies to all sectors of the economy except those where the Treaty **3.03** itself grants exceptions. In accordance with Article 36 the competition rules apply to the production of, and trade in, agricultural products only to the extent determined by the Council within the framework of Article 37(2) and (3) and in accordance with the procedure laid down therein, account being taken of the objectives set out in Article 33. These products are listed in Annex II of the Treaty. Regulation 26 of 4 April 1962,[1] which was adopted on the basis of Articles 36 and 37, provides that Articles 81 to 86 of the Treaty and all the provisions adopted to implement them are also applicable to agriculture, although it gives three exceptions. Under Article 2(1) of the Regulation, Article 81(1) of the Treaty does not apply to agreements, decisions, and practices which form an integral part of a national market organisation or are necessary for the attainment of the objectives set out in Article 33 of the Treaty. In particular it does not apply to agreements, decisions, and practices of farmers, farmers' associations, or associations of such associations belonging to a single Member State which concern the production or sale of agricultural goods or the use of joint facilities for the storage, treatment, or processing of agricultural products, and under which there is no obligation to charge identical prices. This is so unless the Commission finds that competition is thereby excluded or that the objectives of Article 33 of the Treaty are jeopardized.[2]

(2) Coal and Steel

The EC Treaty has applied to the coal and steel sectors since the expiry of ECSC Treaty in 2002.[3] **3.04** The nuclear sector is still governed by the Euratom Treaty.

(3) Defence

Particular attention must be paid to the application of the competition rules to the defence **3.05** sector.

Article 296 provides that: **3.06**

1. The provisions of this Treaty shall not preclude the application of the following rules:
   (a) no Member State shall be obliged to supply information the disclosure of which it considers contrary to the essential interests of its security;
   (b) any Member State may take such measures as it considers necessary for the protection of the essential interests of its security which are connected with the production of or trade in arms, munitions and war material; such measures shall not adversely affect the conditions of competition in the common market regarding products which are not intended for specifically military purposes.
2. The Council may, acting unanimously on a proposal from the Commission, make changes to the list, which it drew up on 15 April 1958, of the products to which the provisions of paragraph 1(b) apply.

---

[1] Council Regulation 26/62/EEC applying certain rules of competition to production of and trade in agricultural products [1962] OJ 30 as amended by Council Regulation 49 of 29 June 1962 [1962] OJ 53.

[2] See also Council Regulation (EEC) 2077/92 of 30 June 1992 concerning inter-branch organisations and agreements in the tobacco sector [1992] OJ L215/80.

[3] Communication from the Commission concerning certain aspects of the treatment of competition cases resulting from the expiry of the ECSC Treaty, OJ L222/1.

3.07   Pursuant to Article 298:

> If measures taken in the circumstances referred to in Articles 223 and 224 [now Articles 296 and 297] have the effect of distorting the conditions of competition in the common market, the Commission shall, together with the State concerned, examine how these measures can be adjusted to the rules laid down in the Treaty. By way of derogation from the procedure laid down in Articles 226 and 227, the Commission or any Member State may bring the matter directly before the ECJ if it considers that another Member State is making improper use of the powers provided for in Articles 223 and 224.

3.08   In a number of merger cases,[4] the Commission has noted that Governments of Member States have instructed the undertakings notifying a concentration not to notify information relating to their military activities. The Commission considered information supplied by the governments concerned and noted that:

- the un-notified part of the concentration related only to the production of or trade in arms, munitions and war material mentioned in the list referred to in Article 296(2);
- the measures taken by the Member States were necessary for the protection of essential security interests;
- there were no spill-over effects from military to non-military applications of dual use products;
- the merger would have no significant impact on suppliers and sub-contractors of the undertakings concerned or defence Ministries in other Member States;
- intermediate consumers would be little affected.

3.09   In these circumstances, the Commission declared itself satisfied with the measures taken by the governments concerned and saw no need to invoke Article 298. It limited its decisions to non-military applications of dual use products.

3.10   It seems from the above analysis that the Commission will defer to Member States' refusal to allow undertakings to notify concentrations relating to solely military products. However, the Commission reserves the right to invoke Article 298 if these conditions are not met. The same principles apply, *mutatis mutandis*, to the other competition rules.

3.11   In other cases[5] in which no Member State invoked Article 296, the Commission has applied the Merger Regulation in the normal way to defence or military markets. The Commission has pointed out that 'markets for defence equipment have shown a move towards a more international approach to procurement over recent years'.[6] This suggests that competition in defence markets is ceasing to be a purely national concern. This of course reflects general trends in defence policy in Europe in recent years. Again these principles apply, *mutatis mutandis*, to the other competition rules.

---

[4] See eg *British Aerospace/VSEL* (Case IV/M528) (1994) (United Kingdom); *GEC/VSEL* (Case IV/M529) (1994) (United Kingdom); *British Aerospace/Lagardèe SCA* (Case IV/M820) (1996) (United Kingdom/France).

[5] *Matra Marconi Space/British Aerospace Space Systems* (Case IV/M437) (1994); *CGI/Dassault* (Case IV/M571) (1995); *Thomson CSF/Teneo/Indra* (Case IV/M620) (1995); *Thomson/CSF/Finmeccanica/Elettronica* (Case IV/M767) (1996); *Matra BAe Dynamics/DASA/LFK* (Case IV/M945) (1998); *Snecma/Messier Dowty* (Case IV/M1159) (1998).

[6] *Matra BAe Dynamics/DASA/LFK* (Case IV/M945) (1998), para 23.

(4) Environment and Culture

In addition to these provisions there are also a number of other rules which are relevant to **3.12** a discussion of the scope of the Article 81. In particular, environmental and cultural issues may be taken into account in applying the competition rules. However, they will only be relevant to policy considerations arising under Article 81(3), as they do not have any impact on the notion of the restriction of competition for the purposes of Article 81(1).

Article 6 provides: 'Environmental protection requirements must be integrated into the **3.13** definition and implementation of the Community policies and activities referred to in Article 3, in particular with a view to promoting sustainable development.' This integration requires the Commission and other bodies applying Article 81 to take account of the impact of the agreements, decisions or concerted practices under consideration on the promotion of sustainable development, and of their impact on that goal. This will be particularly important in applying Article 81(3). It does not mean that, in the event of a clash between policies, an agreement which should be prohibited on competition grounds but which promotes sustainable development must be allowed to proceed. The Treaty does not prescribe any such hierarchy and an anti-competitive agreement should not be allowed on environmental grounds alone. There may be other ways of protecting the environment and promoting sustainable development.[7]

That said, two recent decisions show an increased willingness to give greater weight to envi- **3.14** ronmental arguments. In *DSD*[8] the Commission exempted an agreement, at least in part, because it provided 'direct practical effect to environmental objectives' set out in the Directive on Packaging Waste. Similarly in *CECED*[9] the Commission exempted an agreement between many European producers of washing machines to stop manufacturing the least energy-efficient machines identified in Commission Directive 95/12 (EC). Although a clear restriction of competition, the Commission decided to exempt the agreement, *inter alia*, because it was likely to lead to more efficient and technologically advanced products replacing machines which consumed high quantities of electricity. On announcing the decision, the then Commissioner, Mario Monti declared that '. . . environmental concerns are in no way contradictory with competition policy. This decision clearly illustrates this principle, enshrined in the Treaty, provided that restrictions of competition are proportionate and necessary to achieving the environmental objectives aimed at, to the benefit of current and future generations'.[10]

In addition, Article 151 provides: 'The Community shall contribute to the flowering of the **3.15** cultures of the Member States, while respecting their national and regional diversity and at the same time bringing the common cultural heritage to the fore . . . 4. The Community shall take cultural aspects into account in its action under other provisions of this Treaty, in particular in order to respect and to promote the diversity of its cultures.' The interface between culture and

---

[7] Similarly, an agreement which is innocent in competition terms, but favours unsustainable development, should be dealt with by other means than the prohibition of Art 81(1).

[8] OJ 2001 L 319/1.

[9] OJ 2000 L 187/47.

[10] Commission press release IP/00/148 of 11 February 2000.

competition has proved controversial and difficult to resolve in recent years as the Commission has grappled with resale price maintenance for books and the activities of public television companies. In such cases, insofar as agreements have an appreciable effect on competition and trade,[11] cultural benefits are likely to be relevant[12] but only under Article 81(3).[13]

(5) Sport

3.16 There is no general exclusion for sport from the application of the competition rules. However, matters which are of a 'purely sporting interest and, as such, have nothing to do with economic activity'[14] fall outside the scope of the law. This is because (as in any other case) the law applies only to the extent that the agreement/concerted practice/conduct in question constitutes an economic activity.[15]

3.17 There has been much debate about the scope of application of the concept of a 'purely sporting interest'. In a recent landmark judgment, *Meca-Medina and Majcen v Commission*[16] the ECJ clarified, albeit in a highly elliptic manner, that European law applies in a far wider range of circumstances than many, including the CFI and the Commission, had assumed; in many ways it can be argued that the ECJ's judgment in this case has all but removed the safe harbour provided by this concept in cases involving restrictions on the freedom of professional and semi-professional sportsmen and women to provide their services. This does not of course mean that such restrictions automatically fall within Article 81(1); rather that such sporting cases will be assessed according to the normal rules.

3.18 *Meca-Medina and Majcen v Commission* concerned the anti-doping rules of the International Olympic Committee. The ECJ confirmed that European law did not apply to rules 'concerning questions which are of purely sporting interest'. However the Court found that it was often difficult to sever the sporting aspects from the economic ones in cases involving professional and semi-professional sports.[17]

3.19 In such cases the approach set out in the ECJ's judgment in *JCJ Wouters, JW Savelbergh and Price Waterhouse Belastingadviseurs BV v Algemene Raad van de Nederlandse Orde van Advocaten*[18] applied. More specifically the following factors were relevant:[19]

---

11 In Commission press release IP/02/461 of 22 March 2002 the Commissioner, Mario Monti stated that 'the Commission has no problem with national book price fixing agreements which do not appreciably affect trade between Member States'. This conclusion raises a number of difficult issues. See Monti 'Article 81 EC and Public Policy' [2002] 5 CML Rev 39 1084–1086.

12 It has been argued that the Commission is unable, as a matter of law, to take national interests, including cultural ones, into account in applying Art 81; see Monti, n 11 above.

13 See Commissioner Van Miert's answer to MEP's written question on 28 April 1998; [1999] 4 CMLR 394–395.

14 Case C-519/04 *Meca-Medina and Majcen v Commission*, judgment of 18 July 2006, not yet published, para 25.

15 See section C.(1) below for a general discussion of the concept of 'economic activity'.

16 Case C-519/04 *Meca-Medina and Majcen v Commission*, judgment of 18 July 2006, not yet published.

17 ibid, para 26.

18 Case C-309/99 [2002] ECR I-1577. In *Wouters* the ECJ held, in essence, that restraints which are necessary for the implementation of a public interest objective fall outside the scope of Art 81(1); see 3.189. The Commission has relied on *Wouters* in reaching a number of decisions, both formal and informal, in sporting cases. For example in 2002 it rejected a complaint that rules which restricted the ownership of shares in more than one football club competing in the Champions League tournament did 'not go beyond what is necessary to ensure its legitimate aim: ie to protect the uncertainty of the results in the interest of the public': IP/02/942 (27/06/2002).

19 Case C-519/04 *Meca-Medina and Majcen v Commission*, para 42.

- first 'the overall context in which the decision of the association of undertakings was taken or produces its effects and, more specifically, [. . .] its objectives';
- second 'whether the consequential effects restrictive of competition are inherent in the pursuit of those objectives'; and
- third whether these 'consequential effects' are 'proportionate'.

As regards the 'overall context', the Court found that the Commission had been entitled to take the view that the general objectives of the IOC anti-doping rules (to safeguard athletes' health, the integrity of the sport and its ethical values) were legitimate: 'even if the rules at issue were to be regarded as limiting the appellants' freedom of action, they did not necessarily constitute a restriction of competition since they were justified by a legitimate objective'. **3.20**

On the second issue, the Court found that the limitations placed on athletics by the rules were 'inherent in the organisation and proper conduct of competitive sport' because their 'very purpose is to ensure healthy rivalry between athletes'. **3.21**

On the third issue, that of proportionality, the ECJ acknowledged that the penal nature of the rules and the magnitude of the penalties applicable were capable of producing adverse effects on competition because they could result in an athlete's exclusion from sporting events 'and thus in impairment of the conditions under which the activity at issue is engaged in'. To fall outside Article 81(1) they therefore 'had to be limited to what was necessary to ensure the proper conduct of competitive sport'; on the facts they were. **3.22**

C. Article 81(1)

Article 81 provides: **3.23**

1. The following shall be prohibited as incompatible with the common market: all agreements between undertakings, decisions by associations of undertakings and concerted practices which may affect trade between Member States and which have as their object or effect the prevention, restriction or distortion of competition within the common market, and in particular those which:
   - (a) directly or indirectly fix purchase or selling prices or any other trading conditions;
   - (b) limit or control production, markets, technical development, or investment;
   - (c) share markets or sources of supply;
   - (d) apply dissimilar conditions to equivalent transactions with other trading parties, thereby placing them at a competitive disadvantage;
   - (e) make the conclusion of contracts subject to acceptance by the other parties of supplementary obligations which, by their nature or according to commercial usage, have no connection with the subject of such contracts.
2. Any agreements or decisions prohibited pursuant to this Article shall be automatically void.
3. The provisions of paragraph 1 may, however, be declared inapplicable in the case of:
   - — any agreement or category of agreements between undertakings;
   - — any decision or category of decisions by associations of undertakings;
   - — any concerted practice or category of concerted practices, which contributes to improving the production or distribution of goods or to promoting technical or economic progress, while allowing consumers a fair share of the resulting benefit, and which does not:

    (a) impose on the undertakings concerned restrictions which are not indispensable to the attainment of these objectives;

    (b) afford such undertakings the possibility of eliminating competition in respect of a substantial part of the products in question.

3.24 Article 81 deals with the impact on competition of contractual (and other consensual arrangements) between undertakings. Where the undertakings concerned are actual or potential competitors, what they decide to do together may be of interest to competition authorities. Even if they are not competitors, those authorities may legitimately take an interest in the impact of their commercial arrangements on third parties and the competitive process.

3.25 The competitive relations with which Article 81 deals are thus traditionally divided into two categories: horizontal (between undertakings competing in respect of research, development, production, purchase, or sale of different goods or services) and vertical (between undertakings engaged in the research, development, production, purchase or sale of one and the same set of goods or services, but operating at different economic levels). This useful simplification is followed in Community policy and will be used in this chapter where necessary.

3.26 The following sections will consider the constituent elements of Article 81. Before doing so it should be recalled that Community law has its own definitions for a number of the terms found in Article 81. Thus, for example, the meaning of '*undertaking*' or '*agreement*' in Article 81(1) is different from both the ordinary meaning of those words in English and any special meaning which may have been ascribed to them in legal systems in Member States of the Community (or elsewhere) which use the English language. The terms of Article 81 have the same meaning in all the Community's official languages. Article 81(1) contains a number of conditions, all of which have to be fulfilled if its prohibition is to apply.

(1) Undertakings

(a) Definition

3.27 Article 81(1) only applies to *undertakings*. In order to be an undertaking an entity must be 'engaged in an economic activity'.[20] This is defined as '*any* activity consisting in offering goods and services on a given market'[21] in order to ensure that the rules apply widely, thereby limiting the circumstances in which anti-competitive agreements (or behaviour in relation to Article 82) can escape from the prohibitions by virtue of their legal form rather than their object or effect. As such, entities do not have to be incorporated under company law or take any other legally recognised form in order to be deemed an undertaking. Similarly, pursuit of profit is not essential.[22] In *Fédération Française des Sociétés d'Assurances and Others v Ministère de l'Agriculture et de la Pêche*,[23] the ECJ held that a non-profit-making organisation which managed a voluntary supplementary pension scheme under rules laid

---

[20] Case C-41/90 *Klaus Höfner and Fritz Elser v Macrotron GmbH* [1991] ECR I-1979, para 21; Case C-35/96 *Commission v Italian Republic* [1998] ECR I-3851, para 49; Case C-244/94 *Fédération Française des Sociétés d'Assurances and Others v Ministère de l'Agriculture et de la Pêche* [1995] ECR I-4013, para 14; and Case C-55/96 *Job Centre coop arl* [1997] ECR I-7119, para 21.

[21] Case C-118/85 *Commission v Italy* [1987] ECR 2599, para 7 (emphasis added).

[22] Case 7/82 *GVL v Commission* [1983] ECR 483.

[23] Case C-244/94 *Fédération Française des Sociétés d'Assurances and Others v Ministère de l'Agriculture et de la Pêche* [1995] ECR I-4013, para 17.

down by public authorities was an undertaking because it carried on an activity in competition with life assurance companies. The position is perhaps best summarised in *Film Purchases by German Television Stations*,[24] where the Commission stated that the term 'covers any activity directed at trade in goods or services irrespective of the legal form of the undertaking and regardless of whether or not it is intended to earn profits'.

The wide definition given to this term means that the competition rules apply not only to companies but also to partnerships, the self-employed[25] (including performing artists),[26] agricultural co-operatives,[27] protection and indemnity (P and I) clubs,[28] and sports associations. For example, in *Distribution of Package Tours during the 1990 World Cup*,[29] the Commission held that FIFA, football's world governing body, and the Italian Football Association carried out activities of an economic nature and were therefore undertakings. **3.28**

It is worth noting however that an entity may be an undertaking in certain circumstances but not in others.[30] Practically speaking, this is most likely to be relevant in cases involving state or state-related bodies. Thus a state school is unlikely to be found to be engaging in an economic activity when providing educational services free at the point of use; however it is likely to be an undertaking when renting out its facilities.[31] **3.29**

In theory this line of argument could also apply to businesses. However advisors should take great care in relying on it as competition authorities and the courts are likely to be highly sceptical of arguments that a business is not engaged in an economic activity—for example, the mere provision of a product or service free to customers would not, in and of itself, be sufficient. In practice this argument is only likely to succeed where the business in question can show that it is acting either as an agent or as a sub-contractor for another entity as prescribed in the relevant Commission Guidelines and Notices.[32] **3.30**

---

[24] [1989] OJ L284/36.

[25] *Coapi* [1995] OJ L122/37, para 32. On the other hand individuals acting solely in their capacity as employees are not considered to be undertakings. See, for example, Joined Cases 40–48, 50, 54–56, 111, 113 and 114-173 *Coöperative Vereniging "Suiker Unie" UA and others v Commission* [1975] ECR 1663. Similarly agents may, in certain circumstances, not be undertakings. See section D.3 of Chapter 9.

[26] *RAI/UNITEL* [1978] OJ L157/39.

[27] Case 61/80 *Coöperatieve Stremsel-en Kleurselfabriek v Commission* [1981] ECR 851.

[28] *P&I Clubs* [1985] OJ L376/2, [1999] OJ L126/12. In its decision of 19 May 1999, the Commission stated at para 50: "The pooling Agreement and the IGA are agreements between the P&I Clubs. These must be considered non-profit-making undertakings performing an economic activity. In fact, they compete between themselves as well as other mutuals and profit-making insurers in some segments of the P&I insurance business.'

[29] *Distribution of Package Tours during the 1990 World Cup* 1992] OJ L326/31.

[30] See A-G Jacobs' Opinion in Case C-67/96 *Albany International BV v Stichting Bedrijfspensioenfonds Textielindustrie* [1999] ECR I-5751, para 207.

[31] See discussion of Public Bodies below at section C.1(c); see also *Spanish Courier Services* [1990] OJ L233/19; Case C-41/90 *Höfner and Elser* [1991] ECR I-1979; Case C-179/90 *Merci Convenzionali Porto di Genova SpA v Siderurgica Gabrielli SpA* [1991] ECR I-5889; Case C-475/99 *Firma Ambulanz Glöckner v Landkreis Südwestpfalz* [2001] ECR I-8089; see also *Eco-Emballages* OJ [2001] L 233/37, para 70 in which local authorities were found to be undertakings when entering into contracts for the collection of waste.

[32] The competition rules relating to both agency and sub-contracting agreements are complex. See Chapter 9, at D.3 and section D generally. See also the Commission's Guidelines on Vertical Restraints OJ [2000] C291/1 paras 12-20 (for agency) and the Commission's Notice of 18 December 1978 concerning its assessment of certain subcontracting agreements in relation to Art 81(1) of the EEC Treaty [1979] C 1/2 (3.1.1979) (for sub-contracting).

3.31 An individual acting as a final consumer will, however, never constitute an undertaking.[33] In theory the logic behind the rule could again apply to businesses, particularly partnerships and the self-employed. However, it seems likely that almost all purchases made by such entities would be inputs into the products or services that they market or would, in some other way, be closely linked to the economic activity in which they engage. For example in *Pavel Pavlov v Stichting Pensioenfonds Medische Specialisten*[34] the ECJ found that the self-employed entities in question had acted as undertakings, rather than as consumers, when making contributions to a particular pension scheme which was closely linked to the economic activity in which they engaged.

3.32 However, in certain circumstances intermediate purchases may not constitute an economic activity. In *FENIN v Commission*,[35] the CFI held that an organisation which purchased products—even in great quantity—not for the purpose of supplying goods and services as part of an economic activity, but in order to use them in the context of a different activity, 'such as one of a purely social nature, does not act as an undertaking simply because it is a purchaser in a given market. Whilst an entity may wield very considerable economic power, even giving rise to a monopsony, it nevertheless remains the case that, *if the activity for which that entity purchases goods is not an economic activity*, it is not acting as an undertaking for the purposes of Community competition law [emphasis added]'.[36]

(b) Professions

3.33 Although in most Member States, members of the liberal professions ('professionals' hereinafter) are regulated by law and are considered, to some extent, to exercise public interest functions, the European Courts and the Commission have been careful to ensure that the normal rules apply: professionals are undertakings within the meaning of Article 81 if their activities are economic in nature; the fact that their endeavours are intellectual and may require authorisation from a state sanctioned regulatory body and/or compliance with conditions imposed by that body is insufficient to take them outside the scope of Article 81.[37] For example, in *Pavel Pavlov v Stichting Pensioenfonds Medische Specialisten*, the ECJ held that medical specialists in the Netherlands were undertakings because they 'provide, in their capacity as self-employed economic operators, services on a market, namely the

---

[33] See Joined Cases C-180/98 to C-184/98 *Pavel Pavlov v Stichting Pensioenfonds Medische Specialisten* [2000] ECR I-6451, paras 79–81. The main exception to this is Case T-319/99 *Federación Nacional de Empresas de Instrumentación Científica, Médica, Técnica y Dental (FENIN) v Commission* [2003] ECR II-357, paras 35–37.

[34] Joined Cases C-180/98 to C-184/98 *Pavel Pavlov v Stichting Pensioenfonds Medische Specialisten* [2000] ECR I-6451, paras 79–81.

[35] Case T-319/99 *Federación Nacional de Empresas de Instrumentación Científica, Médica, Técnica y Dental (FENIN) v Commission* [2003] ECR II-357, para 37. The judgment was upheld by the ECJ in Case C-205/03 P (11 July 2006), para 25.

[36] The judgment does not deal with the thorny issues of whether such an organisation would be an undertaking if it *also* uses the products/services purchased to supply goods/services as part of an economic activity (eg where a national health service charges non-EU patients for services). It is submitted that in such cases the European Courts are more likely than not to find the organisation to be an undertaking for the purposes of Art 81. See n 30 above. How they would do so however is unclear given the fact that it will usually be difficult to distinguish between purchases made for the provision of economic and non-economic activities downstream. The issue was raised both before the CFI and the ECJ but declared inadmissible as it had been raised for the first time at the appeal stage.

[37] Case C-35/96 *Commission v Italy* [1998] ECR I-3851, para 38.

market in specialist medical services. They are paid by their patients for the services they provide and assume the financial risks attached to the pursuit of their activity'. The ECJ also reiterated that the complexity and technical nature of the services in question and the fact that the medical profession is regulated are immaterial to the question of whether the members of the profession were undertaking for the purpose of Article 81.[38] In *JCJ Wouters, JW Savelbergh and Price Waterhouse Belastingadviseurs BV v Algemene Raad van de Nederlandse Orde van Advocaten*[39] the ECJ found that 'members of the Bar offer, for a fee, services in the form of legal assistance consisting in the drafting of opinions, contracts and other documents and representation of clients in legal proceedings' and as such are undertakings.[40]

Similarly the bodies which regulate the professions are likely to be found to be association of undertakings and therefore subject to the law—the European Courts and the Commission have been extremely reluctant to expand the scope of the exclusion from the rules enjoyed by certain public bodies[41] to such regulatory entities. For example, in *Commission v Italy*[42] the ECJ found that customs agents were undertaking and that their regulatory body, the National Council of Customs Agents ('NCCA'), was an association of undertakings. Relying on *Bureau National Interprofessionnel du Cognac v Guy Clair*,[43] the Court went on to hold that the public law nature of the body under review did not take it outside the scope of the rules. However, it may be worth noting that in making this judgment the Court relied on the fact that the Italian State had no power to intervene, directly or indirectly, in the appointment of the members of the NCCA and there was nothing in law to prevent the NCCA from acting in the exclusive interest of the profession. **3.34**

The Court relied on similar findings in *Wouters*.[44] In that case it was common ground that the Bar of the Netherlands ('the Bar') was a statutory body governed by public law and had been entrusted with making regulations in the public interest binding on the members of the profession as well as on third parties. The ECJ was asked whether in these circumstances a regulation prohibiting lawyers from entering into partnership with accountants fell within the scope of Article 81(1). It found that when adopting the regulation in question the Bar was neither fulfilling a social function based on the principle of solidarity nor was it exercising powers which were typically those of a public authority. By adopting the regulation in question, the Bar was merely regulating the exercise of an economic activity (the provision of legal services). **3.35**

---

[38] Joined Cases C-180/98 to C-184/98 *Pavel Pavlov v Stichting Pensioenfonds Medische Specialisten* [2000] ECR I-6451, paras 74–77.

[39] Case C-309/99 *JCJ Wouters, JW Savelbergh and Price Waterhouse Belastingadviseurs BV v Algemene Raad van de Nederlandse Orde van Advocaten, intervener: Raad van de Balies van de Europese Gemeenschap* [2002] ECR I-1577.

[40] The same issues in relation to the members of the Italian Bar are discussed in the Opinion of Advocate General Léger in Case C-35/99 *Criminal proceedings against Manuele Arduino, third parties: Diego Dessi, Giovanni Bertolotto and Compagnia Assicuratrice RAS SpA* [2002] ECR I-1529.

[41] See section C.1(c) below.

[42] Case C-35/96 *Commission v Italy* [1998] ECR I-3851.

[43] Case 123/83 [1985] ECR 391, para 17.

[44] Case C-309/99 *JCJ Wouters, JW Savelbergh and Price Waterhouse Belastingadviseurs BV v Algemene Raad van de Nederlandse Orde van Advocaten, intervener: Raad van de Balies van de Europese Gemeenschap* [2002] ECR I-1577.

3.36   In making this judgment, the ECJ highlighted four elements. First was the fact that the governing bodies of the Bar had all been elected by members of the profession. Second the State had no power to intervene in these appointments. Third, when exercising its regulatory powers, the Bar was 'not required to do so by reference to specified public-interest criteria'—the relevant legislation merely required the Bar to act 'in the interest of the proper practice of the profession'. Fourth, by prohibiting multi-disciplinary partnerships, the regulation in question influenced the conduct of member of the Bar on the market for legal services, ie it regulated an economic activity. Taken together these factors meant that the regulation was merely an expression of the intention of the delegates of the members of this profession to act in a particular manner in carrying out their economic activity.

3.37   This judgment suggests that the scope for argument that regulatory bodies are not undertakings/association of undertakings is extremely narrow—following *Wouters*, the argument is only likely to carry any force where legislation has laid down clearly defined criteria according to which the body in question *must* exercise its function and/or where the state appoints the members of that body's ruling committee. However, in our view, even in this situation the likelihood of success for such arguments is uncertain given the clear reluctance of the European Courts and the Commission to limit the *scope* of the competition rules. *Wouters* itself provides perhaps the strongest indication of this—it is clear from the judgment that the ECJ did not want the regulation in question to fall within the scope of Article 81(1). Instead of finding that the Bar was not an association of undertakings, which would have been a relatively easy thing to do on the facts, the ECJ choose to deal with the matter by finding that the particular regulation in question did not have as its object or effect the restriction of competition (a far more complex matter).[45] This enabled it to find that the competition rules did apply to entities such as the Dutch Bar but did not to the particular activity under review.

(c) Public Bodies Exception

3.38   The European Courts and the Commission have followed a similar expansive approach to the jurisdictional reach of Article 81 in cases involving public bodies, or other entities operating under State aegis. In essence, a distinction is drawn 'between a situation where the State acts in the exercise of official authority and that where it carries on economic activities of an industrial or commercial nature by offering goods or services on the market'.[46] It is only in the former that the competition rules do not apply (referred to as 'public sector exception' in the remainder of this chapter). This meant, for example, that a Soviet trading organisation forming part of a Ministry[47] has been found to be an undertaking for the purposes of Article 81.

3.39   A critical factor in determining whether the public sector exception applies is the nature of the *activity* carried out by the relevant entity (as distinct from the nature of the *body* performing a particular activity). Does the activity in question form part of the essential functions of the State? Put another way, is the activity connected with the exercise of powers which are

---

[45]   See para 3.188 *et seq* below.
[46]   Case C-343/95 *Diego Cali & Figli Srl Servizi ecologici porto di Genova SpA (SEPG)* [1997] ECR I-547; [1997] 5 CHLR 484, para 16. See also Case 118/85 *Commission v Italy* [1987] ECR 2599, para 7.
[47]   *Aluminium imports from Eastern Europe* [1985] OJ L92/1.

typically those of a public authority? In *Klaus Höfner and Fritz Elser v Macrotron*,[48] the ECJ held that the Federal German Employment Agency was an undertaking since the service it provided, employment procurement, *was* an economic activity and one which did not necessarily have to be provided by the State.

Conversely in *Corinne Bodson v SA Pompes Funèbres des Régions Libérées*,[49] where the per-   **3.40** formance of funeral function was, as a matter of law, entrusted to local communes, the ECJ held that Article 81 did 'not apply to contracts . . . concluded between communes acting in their capacity as public authorities and undertakings entrusted with the operation of a public service'. Similarly, in *Diego Calì & Figli Srl v Servizi ecologici porto di Genova SpA (SEPG)*, the ECJ held that the activities of a limited company which had been granted the exclusive right to carry out anti-pollution services on the Genoa Port Authority's behalf were *not* of an economic nature, notwithstanding the fact that the company charged vessels a fee, albeit one set unilaterally by the Port Authority, for its services. The ECJ found that:

> The anti-pollution surveillance for which SEPG was responsible . . . *forms part of the essential functions* of the State as regards protection of the environment in maritime areas. Such surveillance is connected by its nature, its aim and the rules to which it is subject with the exercise of powers relating to the protection of the environment which *are typically those of a public authority*. It is not of an economic nature justifying the application of the Treaty rules on competition. The levying of a charge by SEPG for preventive anti-pollution surveillance is an integral part of its surveillance activity in the maritime area of the port and cannot affect the legal status of that activity.[50]

Similarly, in *Eurocontrol*,[51] the ECJ held that Eurocontrol's activities were connected with   **3.41** the exercise of powers relating to the control and supervision of air space 'which are typically those of a public authority'. They were therefore 'not of an economic nature justifying the application of the Treaty rules of competition'.[52]

However, it is important to stress that the mere fact that an activity has a public interest   **3.42** dimension, and/or that the bodies carrying on the activity may be the subject of public service obligations, does not mean that the competition rules will not apply. In *Firma Ambulanz Glöckner v Landkreis Südwestpfalz*, the ECJ found that medical aid organisations entrusted under the relevant legislation with the task of providing ambulance services were undertakings within the meaning of EC competition law; this was the case even though the organisations were specifically named in the legislation and were subject to public service obligations not imposed on private sector competitors. The Court relied on the fact that the services in question were subject to payment from users and that they did not necessarily have to be provided by the named medical organisations or by public authorities; indeed they were at the time also supplied by private firms. The provision of such services, therefore, constituted an economic activity for the purposes of the application of EC competition law.[53]

---

[48] Case C-41/90 *Höfner and Elser* [1991] ECR I-1979.

[49] Case 30/87 [1988] ECR 2479, at para 35.

[50] Case C-343/95 *Diego Cali & Figli Srl Servizi ecologici porto di Genova SpA (SEPG)* [1997] ECR I-547; paras 22–24; emphasis added.

[51] Case C-364/92 [1994] ECR I-43.

[52] ibid, para 30.

[53] Case C-475/99 *Firma Ambulanz Glöckner v Landkreis Südwestpfalz* [2001] I-8089, paras 19–22.

3.43 A key factor in determining whether the public body exception applies is the way an entity is financed. In *Christian Poucet v Assurances Générales de France and Caisse Mutuelle Régionale du Languedoc-Roussillon*,[54] ('*Poucet*') the ECJ was asked whether an organisation charged with managing a special social security scheme is to be regarded as an undertaking for the purposes of Articles 81 and 82 of the Treaty. In response the ECJ stated that '[s]ickness funds, and the organisations involved in the management of the public social security system, fulfil an exclusively social function. That activity is based on the *principle of national solidarity* and is entirely non-profit-making . . . The benefits paid are statutory benefits *bearing no relation to the amount of the contributions*. Accordingly, that activity is not an economic activity and, therefore, the organisations to which it is entrusted are not undertakings [emphasis added]'.

3.44 The crucial fact was that the scheme was run on the basis of 'solidarity'. Solidarity was 'embodied in the fact that the contributions paid by active workers serve to finance the pensions of retired workers. It is also reflected by the grant of pension rights where no contributions have been made and of pension rights that are not proportional to the contributions paid'. It follows, the ECJ said, 'that the social security schemes, as described, are based on a system of compulsory contribution, which is indispensable for application of the principle of solidarity and the financial equilibrium of those schemes.' Put another way, the very essence of the system was to perform a social function which was inherently non-economic (benefits did not depend on the contribution made nor the success of a particular investment) and was based on the reallocation of resources for social policy reasons. The CFI applied a similar approach in *FENIN v Commission*, where it found that the Spanish national health system was not an undertaking, in part, because 'it operates according to the principle of solidarity-it was funded from social security contributions and other State funding and provided services free of charge to its members on the basis of universal cover'.[55] This approach was upheld by the ECJ on appeal.[56]

3.45 It is important to stress that the principles in *Poucet* have usually been applied narrowly. For example, in *Fédération Française des Sociétés d'Assurances and Others v Ministère de l'Agriculture et de la Pêche*,[57] the ECJ found that a non-profit-making organisation managing a supplementary pension scheme under rules laid down by public authorities could be an undertaking. It rejected the French Government's argument that the scheme was based on the principle of 'solidarity', drawing attention in particular to the fact that the pension scheme under review was one that beneficiaries entered into on a voluntary, rather than a compulsory, basis. Furthermore, the benefits payable depended on the amount of the contributions and the financial results of the investments made. Thus the scheme effectively operated like other pension schemes offered by the private sector; the fact that the body managing the pension scheme pursued a social policy objective under national law, was non-profit-making

---

[54] Joined Cases C-159/91 and C-160/91 *Christian Poucet v Assurances Générales de France and Caisse Mutuelle Régionale du Languedoc-Roussillon* [1993] ECR I-637, paras 4, 18, 19, 11, and 13.

[55] Case T-319/99 *Federación Nacional de Empresas de Instrumentación Científica, Médica, Técnica y Dental (FENIN) v Commission* [2003] ECR II-357, para 39, upheld on appeal in Case C-205/03 P (11 July 2006).

[56] Case C-205/03 P (11 July 2006).

[57] Case C-244/94 *Fédération Française des Sociétés d'Assurances and Others v Ministère de l'Agriculture et de la Pêche* [1995] ECR I-4013.

and was restricted in the type of investments it could make was not sufficient to bring the scheme within the public sector exemption.

The ECJ has made similar findings in a number of other cases. For example in *Albany* **3.46** *International BV v Stichting Bedrijfspensioenfonds Textielindustrie*,[58] it found Article 81 to apply even though the pension scheme was compulsory, non-profit-making and operated under criteria which had a social dimension (the benefits to be paid were calculated with reference to the average salary and did not depend on contributions made by a particular beneficiary; also, the pension rights continued to accrue even if the beneficiary ceased to contribute because of ill health or because the employer had become insolvent). In rejecting the argument that the scheme was based on the principle of solidarity, the ECJ highlighted that the pension fund itself determined the amount of the contributions and benefits and that the fund operated in accordance with the principle of capitalisation: accordingly, the amount of benefits provided by the fund depended on the financial results of the investments made by it.[59] The position is however perhaps best by Advocate General Fennelly's opinion in *Sodemare v Regione Lombardia* where he stated that solidarity is 'the inherently uncommercial act of involuntary subsidisation of one social group by another'.[60]

(2) Agreements

(a) General Definition

The term 'agreement' is defined widely for the purposes of Article 81(1). For an agreement **3.47** to exist it 'is sufficient if the undertakings in question should have expressed their joint intention to conduct themselves on the market in a specific way'.[61] The concept 'centres around the existence of a concurrence of wills between at least two parties the form in which it is manifested being unimportant so long as it constitutes the faithful expression of the parties' intention'.[62]

(b) Requires At Least Two Undertakings

In order for an agreement to exist the concurrence of wills must, as common sense dictates, **3.48** be between at least two parties. This means that unilateral conduct does not fall within the scope of Article 81.[63]

(c) Form Irrelevant

A 'concurrence of wills' does not have to take the form of a legally binding contract for an **3.49** agreement to exist under Article 81(1)—in fact its form is almost entirely irrelevant. It can be written or oral,[64] signed or unsigned.[65] The concept is wide enough to catch arrangements

---

[58] Case C-67/96 *Albany International BV v Stichting Bedrijfspensioenfonds Textielindustrie* [1999] ECR I-5751, paras 71–87.

[59] Paras 81–82. See also Joined Cases C-180/98 to C-184/98 *Pavel Pavlov v Stichting Pensioenfonds Medische Specialisten* [2000] ECR I-6451, paras 108–119.

[60] Case C-70/95 [1997] ECR I-3395, para 29.

[61] Case T-7/89 *SA Hercules Chemicals NV v Commission* [1991] ECR II-1711, para 2.

[62] Case T-41/96 *Bayer AG v Commission* [2000] ECR II-3383, para 69.

[63] See section C.2(e) below.

[64] Case 28/77 *Tepea BV v Commission* [1978] ECR 1391.

[65] *BP Kemi—DDSF* [1979] OJ L286/32.

such as gentlemen's agreements',[66] simple 'understandings',[67] the constitution of a trade association[68] or non-binding marketing guidelines. For example, in *Anheuser-Busch Incorporated—Scottish & Newcastle*,[69] the Commission decided that guidelines on the positioning and marketing of Budweiser beer in the UK produced by Anheuser, the receipt of which was acknowledged by S&N with the 'pledge to use its reasonable efforts to ensure compliance . . . with such . . . guidelines'[70] by its staff and customers was an agreement for the purposes of Article 81(1). This was even though the document may not have constituted a legally binding agreement under the relevant national law, could have been unilaterally altered by Anheuser, and was posited on its face as 'non-binding recommendations as to steps which S&N *could* take to promote the beer's image as a premium lager'.

3.50 The existence of an 'expression of a joint intention' or the 'concurrence of wills' is particularly easy to show in horizontal cases. An arrangement between competitors is an agreement even if it does not prescribe in detail the conduct to be undertaken; in order to qualify it is sufficient for it to set the broad framework under which the parties will cease to operate independently. Thus 'inchoate understandings', 'conditional agreements' and 'loose' arrangements have all been considered to fall within the scope of term 'agreement'.[71] In *Polypropylene*, the Commission held that an agreement exists merely 'if the parties reach a consensus on a plan which limits or is likely to limit their commercial freedom by determining the lines of their mutual action or abstention from action in the market'.[72]

3.51 Thus an undertaking can be party to an agreement even if it attends a meeting with its competitors at which it is passive and in which only one participant reveals its intentions.[73] In *Thyssen Stahl AG v Commission of the European Communities*[74] the CFI held that mere attendance by an undertaking at meetings involving anti-competitive activities can suffice.[75] In *Commission v Anic Partecipazioni*[76] the ECJ found that since 'the Commission had been able to establish that Anic had participated in the meetings at which price initiatives had been decided on, planned and monitored, it was for Anic to adduce evidence that it had not subscribed to those initiatives'.

3.52 In order to avoid such a finding, the undertaking in question must either prove that it did not allow the information it had received in any way to influence it actions[77] (which would seem almost impossible to do in practice) or have publicly distanced itself from what was discussed so as not to give the impression to the other participants that it subscribed

---

[66] Case 41/69 *ACF Chemiefarma NV v Commission* [1970] ECR 661.
[67] *SSI* [1982] OJ L31/1.
[68] *Re Nuovo CEGEAM* OJ [1984] L 99/29.
[69] Case No IV/34.237/F3 OJ [2000] L49/37.
[70] ibid, para 53.
[71] See generally Case T-9/99 *HFB Holding für Fernwarmetechnik Beteiligungsgesellschaft mbH & Co. KG and Others v Commission (Pre-Insulated Pipe Cartel)* [2002] ECR II-1487.
[72] [1986] OJ L230/1, para 81.
[73] Cases T-202/98 *Tate & Lyle v Commission* [2001] ECR II-2035, para 54.
[74] Case T-141/94 *Thyssen Stahl AG v Commission* [1999] ECR II-347, para 177.
[75] See also discussion of presumption in concerted practice at para 3.110 below.
[76] Case C-49/92 P *Commission v Anic Partecipazioni* [1999] ECR I-4125, para 96.
[77] C-199/92 P *Hüls AG v Commission* [1999] ECR I-4287, para 162.

to the aim of the meeting and would act in conformity with it.[78] In practical terms this is likely to require the undertaking to end its participation in the meeting as soon as the anticompetitive nature of the gathering becomes apparent, stating why it is doing so to the attendees. It must also not engage in any activities linked in any way to the meeting.

In vertical cases this means that where the Commission has adduced evidence of the existence of an agreement, it is for the dealer wishing to escape from the scope of Article 81(1) to 'adduce evidence that it distanced itself from that agreement, [the] evidence . . . must demonstrate a clear intention, brought to the notice of the other participating undertakings, to withdraw from that agreement'.[79]   **3.53**

An agreement is reached even if one or more of the undertakings involved intends to ignore its provisions.[80] In *Roofing Felt Cartel*,[81] the Commission found that seven members and two non-members of a trade association had fixed prices. The non-members argued that they had joined the cartel for fear of retaliation. They had given the impression of going along with the cartel's plans, while having no real intention of abiding by its disciplines. They also argued that there was no evidence of their having observed the agreements in practice. However, the Commission held that 'neither the state of mind of the non-members when they entered into such agreements as to their intention of abiding by them, nor the fact that the non-members did not in fact observe the agreements (as some evidence suggests) would affect the Commission's finding that the agreements were made and that the non-members were parties to them'.   **3.54**

Similarly an agreement may be found even if undertakings were forced into it.[82] Even cheating or occasional outbreaks of fierce competition do not prevent an arrangement from constituting an agreement for the purposes of Article 81(1) where there is a common and continuing objective to co-operate.[35] In *Cimenteries CBR SA v Commission* the CFI held that 'it is settled law that the fact that an undertaking does not abide by the outcome of meetings which have a manifestly anti-competitive purpose is not such as to relieve it of full responsibility for the fact that it participated in the agreement or concerted practice'.[83]   **3.55**

In *Commission v Anic Partecipazioni*[84] the ECJ confirmed that 'there is no need to take account of the concrete effects of an agreement once it appears that it has as its object the prevention, restriction or distortion of competition'. Thus 'Anic's arguments that its conduct on the market had been independent of the price initiatives referred to in the Polypropylene   **3.56**

---

[78] Case T-9/99 *HFB Holding für Fernwärmetechnik Beteiligungsgesellschaft mbH & Co KG and others v Commission (Pre-Insulated Pipe Cartel)* [2002] ECR II-1487, para 223; Case T141/89 *Tréfileurope Sales SARL v Commission* [1995] ECR II-791, para 85. *Aalborg Portland and others v Commission*, para 55, paras 81–84; and Case T-61/99 *Adriatica di Navigazione v Commission* [2003] ECR II 5349, paras 135–138).

[79] See Joined Cases C-2/01 P and C-3/01 *Bundesverband der Arzneimittel-Importeure and Commission v Bayer* [2004] ECR I-23, para 82.

[80] Joined Cases 209–215 and 218/78 *Heintz Van Landewyck SARL and others v Commission* [1980] ECR 3125.

[81] [1986] OJ L232/15, para 86, upheld on appeal: Case 246/86 *SC Belasco and others v Commission* [1989] ECR 2117.

[82] Cases T-25/95 *Cimenteries CBR SA v Commission* [2000] ECR II-491, para 2557.

[83] ibid, para 1389.

[84] Case C-49/92 P *Commission v Anic Partecipazioni* [1999] ECR I-4125, paras 96–99.

Decision are irrelevant, since agreements within the meaning of Article 85 [now 81] of the Treaty were involved here'.

(d) Single Continuous Infringement Doctrine

3.57 As a matter both of evidence and of substantive law[85] it is not necessary for an undertaking to have actively participated in, give its express consent to, or even to have been aware of each and every individual aspect or manifestation of an agreement for it to be party to that agreement. In *Polypropylene*,[86] the Commission decided that the 15 firms involved had reached an agreement even though some had not been to every meeting or been involved in every decision that had been made '[i]n the present case the producers, by subscribing to a common plan to regulate prices and supply in the polypropylene market, participated in an overall framework agreement which was manifested in a series of more detailed sub-agreements worked out from time to time.' Similarly in *Pre-Insulated Pipes*[87] the CFI found that although it was clear that during the cartel negotiations one of the participants, Tarco, had 'refused to participate in any agreement on prices without a parallel agreement on market-share quotas' it could not be 'inferred from the fact that Tarco adopted such a position that it was opposed to the principle of sharing the German market'.

3.58 In *Citric Acid*,[88] a cartel involving five producers in which some 20 multilateral and ten bilateral meetings had been held over a four-year period, the Commission stated that '... the term 'agreement' can properly be applied not only to any overall plan or to the terms expressly agreed but also to the implementation of what has been agreed on the basis of the same mechanisms and in pursuance of the same common purpose ... where the various concerted practices followed and agreements concluded form part of a series of efforts made by the undertakings in pursuit of a common objective of preventing or distorting competition, the Commission is entitled to find that they constitute a single continuous infringement'. This means, amongst other things, that an agreement will exists even if the terms of, or the parties to, it change over time. In *Pre-Insulated Pipes*, which was largely upheld on appeal, the Commission decided that each such change did not imply that a new 'agreement' had come into force for the purposes of Article 81(1).[89]

3.59 It is also worth noting that an undertaking participating in a single complex infringement may be held responsible for the conduct of other undertakings throughout the period of its participation. This could be the case where it is proved 'that the undertaking in question was aware of the unlawful conduct of the other participants, or could reasonably foresee such conduct, and was prepared to accept the risk'.[90] Relying on paragraph 203 of

---

85 See, for example, Case C-49/92P *European Commission v Anic Partecipazioni* [1999] ECR I-4125; Case T-1/89 *Rhône Poulenc v Commission* [1991] ECR II-867, para 126; Case T-141/89 *Tréfileurope Sales SARL v Commission* [1995] ECR II-791, para 85; Cases T-305/94 etc *Limburgse Vinyl Maatschappij NV and other v Commission* [1999] ECR II-931.
86 [1986] OJ L230/1.
87 Case T-9/99 *HFB Holding fur Fernwarmetechnik Beteiligungsgesellschaft mbH & Co. KG and others v Commission (Pre-Insulated Pipe Cartel)* [2002] ECR II-1487, para 205.
88 [2002] OJ L239/18 (6.9.2002), paras 145–147.
89 *Pre-Insulated Pipes* [1999] OJ L24/1, paras 129–138.
90 Case T-9/99 *HFB Holding fur Fernwarmetechnik Beteiligungsgesellschaft mbH & Co. KG and others v Commission (Pre-Insulated Pipes)* [2002] ECR II-1487, para 231.

Commission v Anic,[91] the CFI held that such a conclusion was 'not at odds with the principle that responsibility for such infringements is personal in nature, nor does it neglect individual analysis of the evidence adduced, in disregard of the applicable rules of evidence, or infringe the rights of defence of the undertakings involved'.

The rationale for the concept that parties may be held responsible for a 'single continuous infringement' even though they are shown to have participated only directly in one or some of its constituent elements (sometimes referred to as the 'single overall agreement concept') is perhaps most clearly set out in (then) Advocate General Vesterdorf's joined opinions in *Rhône Poulenc*:[92] **3.60**

> If one considers how the alleged cartel probably worked in practice, it is plain to see that it can be extraordinarily difficult to determine in detail the degree of involvement of each party. Who had the idea of taking this or that initiative? Who sought to persuade those others who were perhaps less enthusiastic? Who came to the meetings best prepared? And so on. It is self-evident that where there are no admissions on the part of the participating undertakings, it is often not possible to unravel all those threads in an administrative procedure in which most of the evidence is based on written documents . . . . [therefore] some relaxation of the requirements of proof must be regarded as unobjectionable. Otherwise, in many cases the Commission would in all likelihood have to abandon prosecution from the outset in cases where there is unquestionably an unlawful cartel but where it is not possible to adduce detailed proof of each party's involvement in the cartel's activities. Such a result would in practice rob Article [81] of much of its effectiveness.

Though the 'single continuous infringement' doctrine gives the courts and competition authorities a powerful tool in handling cartel, the *scope* of its application is, however, subject to two caveats. First, as the CFI held in *Limburgse Vinyl Maatschappij NV and other v Commission*, an undertaking can be found liable in this way 'only if it is shown that it knew, or must have known, that the collusion in which it participated . . . was part of an overall plan intended to distort competition'.[93] The CFI applied this test in *Cimenteries*, but replaced the words 'must have known' with the term 'ought to have known'.[94] This follows the ECJ judgment in *Commission v Anic Partecipazioni* where the Court confirmed the objective nature of the test by holding that the Commission had to establish 'that the undertaking in question was aware of the offending conduct of the other participants or that it could *reasonably have foreseen it* and that it was prepared to take the risk'[95] (emphasis added). **3.61**

Second the particular infringement must be part of, or fall within, the broad framework under which the parties cease to operate independently; in other words it must be demonstrated that 'the overall plan included all the constituent elements of the cartel'[96] as found by the Commission. This means that different arrangements can only be regarded as constituent elements of a single agreement if they form part of an overall plan pursuing a **3.62**

---

[91] Case C-49/92 P *Commission v Anic Partecipazioni* [1999] ECR I-4125.

[92] Case T-1/89 *Rhône Poulenc v Commission* [1991] ECR II-867.

[93] Joined cases T-305/94 etc *Limburgse Vinyl Maatschappij NV and other v Commission* [1999] ECR II-931, para 773.

[94] Cases T-25/95 *Cimenteries CBR SA v Commission* [2000] ECR II-491, para 4109.

[95] Case C-49/92 P *Commission v Anic Partecipazioni* [1999] ECR I-4125, para 83.

[96] Joined cases T-305/94 etc *Limburgse Vinyl Maatschappij NV and other v Commission* [1999] ECR II-931, para 773.

common objective;[97] this would be the case where, for example, they were 'intrinsically linked'. In *Buchmann GmbH v Commission*[98] the Commission had decided that Buchmann had been party to an overall agreement covering price fixing, output limitation and market sharing. This was the case even though Buchmann had not participated in any of the discussions on market sharing. According to the Commission, Buchmann and other suppliers were 'well aware of the general understanding between the major producers to maintain "constant levels of supply" [ie market sharing] and, no doubt, of the need to adapt their own conduct to it'.[99] On appeal, the CFI rejected the Commission's view that Buchmann 'must have been aware of the market sharing'[100] on two principal grounds. First, the Commission had not provided any evidence to show that despite Buchmann's absence from the meetings on market sharing, it had 'subscribed to a general agreement providing, in particular, for the freezing of the market shares of the main producers'.[101] Second it found that 'the mere fact that those undertakings participated in collusion on prices and collusion on downtime [output limitation] does not demonstrate that they also participated in collusion on market shares. Contrary to the Commission's apparent claim, the collusion on market shares was *not intrinsically linked* to collusion on prices and/or collusion on downtime' (emphasis added).[102] The Commission had therefore not proved that 'the applicant knew, or must have known, that its own unlawful conduct was part of an overall plan which included, over and above the collusion on prices and the collusion on downtime in which it actually participated, also collusion on the market shares of the major producers'.[103]

3.63 The CFI made a similar finding in *Cimenteries* where it rejected the Commission's argument that a particular infringement (exchange of prices between Français Ciments and Buzzi) had been part of the overall agreement (between numerous producers across Europe to stay out of each other's home markets). The CFI reached this conclusion because the only evidence upon which the Commission had relied in respect of this particular infringement was a fax which did 'not express any intention on the part of those undertakings to observe any principle of non-transhipment to home markets'.[104] In addition the Commission had not stated 'anywhere in the contested decision that by the exchange of prices .... Ciments Français and Buzzi sought to observe such a principle'[105] or indeed how the exchange of this information 'pursued the same anti-competitive object'[106] as the main agreement.[107]

3.64 It has been suggested to the authors that a third caveat or limitation exists: that the concept applies only in the context of a *complex* cartel of *long* duration. Proponents of this view rely on two arguments. First, the concept has been applied only in such situations. Second, they point

---

[97] Case T-1/89 *Rhône Poulenc v Commission* [1991] ECR II-867, para 126.
[98] Case T-295/94 *Buchmann GmbH v Commission* [1998] ECR II-813.
[99] ibid, para 115.
[100] ibid, para 118.
[101] ibid.
[102] ibid, para 119.
[103] ibid, para 123.
[104] Cases T-25/95 *Cimenteries CBR SA v Commission* [2000] ECR II-491, para 4041.
[105] ibid, para 4041.
[106] ibid, para 4057.
[107] It is worth noting that the fact that an agreement or concerted practice is not part of a particular cartel does not mean that it is legitimate by virtue of that fact alone.

to cases such as *Citric Acid* where the Commission stated that 'a complex cartel may properly be viewed as a single continuing cartel for the time frame in which it existed . . . . Indeed, in a complex cartel of *long duration*, where the various concerted practices followed and agreements concluded form part of a series of efforts made by the undertakings in pursuit of a common objective of preventing or distorting competition, the Commission is entitled to find that they constitute a single continuous infringement.' (emphasis added).[108]

The authors do not share this view for two main reasons. First, the mere fact that the concept has, thus far, only been applied in particular types of cases does not, in and of itself, mean that it cannot be used in other situations. Second, the very rationale underpinning the concept, best captured by Advocate General Vesterdorf's opinion in *Rhône Poulenc*,[109] mitigates against such a view. **3.65**

Whilst the situation described by Vesterdorf is most likely to feature in cartels of a long duration, it can also arise in relation to less complex, shorter agreements: there is therefore no reason as a matter of principle to limit its application in the way suggested—as the CFI observed in *Hercules v Commission*,[110] it would be artificial to split up continuous conduct, characterised by a single purpose, by treating it as consisting of a number of separate infringements. **3.66**

(e) Tacit Acquiescence in Relation to the Particular Anti-Competitive Measure in Question is the Minimum Requirement in Vertical Cases

Unlike cartels, in which agreements or concerted practices are readily found, the European Courts have, at least in more recent judgments,[111] been more circumspect in applying a wide definition to the terms 'expression of a joint intention' or 'concurrence of wills' in vertical cases. Whilst acknowledging that in certain instances[112] 'measures adopted or imposed in an apparently unilateral manner by a manufacturer . . . have been regarded as constituting an agreement [with its distributor] within the meaning of Article 81(1) EC',[113] the European Courts have in recent cases gone on to underline that an agreement requires *at least* the 'implied participation'[114] or 'tacit acquiescence' of dealers.[115] **3.67**

This is the case even in the context of an ongoing business relationship where, until very recently, it had been thought by many commentators that, at least as far as selective distribution **3.68**

---

108 [2002] OJ L239/18 (6.9.2002), paras 146–147.
109 Case T-1/89 *Rhône Poulenc v Commission* [1991] ECR II-867. See quotation at para 3.60 above.
110 Case T-7/89 *SA Hercules Chemicals NV v Commission* [1991] ECR II-1711, paras 262–263.
111 Given the way in which the CFI and the ECJ distinguished *Bayer* and *Volkswagen II* from previous judgments, great care must be taken in drawing any conclusions from older cases. See Christopher Brown, '*Bayer v Commission*: the ECJ Agrees' [2004] ECLR 388.
112 The Court explicitly refers to the following judgments in this regard: Joined Cases 32/78, 36/78–82/78 *BMW Belgium v Commission* [1979] ECR 2435, paras 28–30; Case 107/82 *AEG v Commission* [1983] ECR 3151, para 38; Joined Cases 25/84 and 26/84 *Ford v Commission* [1985] ECR 2725, para 21; Case C-277/87 *Sandoz prodotti farmaceutici v Commission* [1990] ECR-I 45, paras 7–12; Case C-70/93 *Bayerische Motorwerke v ALD* [1995] ECR-I 3439 (*BMW*), paras 16 and 17, and Case T-41/96 *Bayer v Commission* [2000] ECR-II 3383, para 70.
113 Case T-208/01 *Volkswagen AG v Commission* [2003] ECR II-5141, para 34.
114 Case T-41/96 *Bayer v Commission* [2000] ECR II-3383, para 71.
115 ibid.

systems were concerned, dealers could be found to have agreed to whatever sales policies the manufacturer had chosen to adopt by *the very fact* of agreeing to becoming part of a network.

3.69   This position is no longer tenable following recent judgments. In *Bayer* the ECJ clearly stated that '[t]he mere concomitant existence of an agreement which is in itself neutral and a measure restricting competition that has been imposed unilaterally does not amount to an agreement prohibited by that provision. Thus, the mere fact that a measure adopted by a manufacturer, which has the object or effect of restricting competition, falls within the context of continuous business relations between the manufacturer and its wholesalers is not sufficient for a finding that such an agreement exists'.[116] This, together with the European Courts' findings in *Bayer* and *Volkswagen II* in the previous case law, suggests that, unlike cartels, where the 'single overall agreement' concept can apply, for vertical agreements, Article 81(1) requires that the express or tacit acquiescence must be in relation to the particular measure in question.[117]

3.70   *Volkswagen II*[118]   The CFI's judgment in *Volkswagen II* (which was upheld in almost all respects on appeal)[119] perhaps summarises best many aspects of the law.

3.71   The dealership agreement under review required dealers to comply with all instructions issued regarding the distribution of new Volkswagen cars, the stocking of replacement parts, customer service, sales promotion, advertising, training, and the ensuring of quality in each area of Volkswagen's business. It also permitted Volkswagen to issue non-binding price recommendations concerning retail prices and discounts. On 6 July 2001 the Commission issued a decision[120] in which it found that Volkswagen had infringed Article 81 by sending circulars/letters (referred to hereinafter as 'calls') instructing its German dealers to grant limited discounts, or no discounts at all, on the new Passat model. Volkswagen appealed, arguing that the Commission had failed to show that the issuing of the 'calls' constituted an agreement under Article 81(1).

---

[116] Joined Cases C-2/01 P and C-3/01 *Bundesverband der Arzneimittel-Importeure and Commission v Bayer* [2004] ECR I-23, para 141.

[117] This conclusion is not invalidated, it is submitted, by the CFI's statement in para 77 of Case T-168/01 *GlaxoSmithKline Services v Commission* that the Commission is 'not required to establish the existence of a joint intention to pursue an *anti-competitive aim*' [emphasis added]. This statement was made in response the parties' argument that they had not manifested a concurrent will *to restrict competition*, but merely a concurrent will to *sell and purchase medicines* according to the terms set out in the General Sales Conditions (these were contractually binding sales conditions relating to the sale of medicines to Spanish wholesalers. The arrangements incorporated a dual pricing system which resulted in Spanish wholesalers being charged a higher price for drugs resold in other Member States than for those resold in Spain). The CFI found, in paras 78–81, that Glaxo and its wholesalers had infact conducted themselves on the market in the manner specified in General Sales Conditions (in terms used in para 3.69 of this chapter, the General Sales Conditions were the 'the particular measure in question'). As such there was an agreement—the fact that the Commission had not adduced evidence of a joint intention to restrict competition through a formal prohibition on exports did not change that finding.

[118] Case T-208/01 *Volkswagen AG v Commission* [2003] ECR II-5141.

[119] Case C-74/04 P *Commission v Volkswagen AG* (13 July 2006). The only material issue on which the ECJ did not uphold the CFI was the latter's finding that where the parties had entered into a lawful contract, 'an unlawful . . . variation could not be regarded as having been accepted in advance'. The ECJ held that no such assumption could be made: an assessment of the clauses in dispute had to be made 'individually, taking account, where applicable, of all other relevant factors, such as the aims pursued by that agreement in the light of the economic and legal context in which it was signed' (para 45).

[120] *Volkswagen* [2001] OJ L262/14 (2.10.2001).

On appeal, the Commission asserted that 'according to the *AEG*,[121] *Ford*[122] *BMW*,[123] and **3.72** *Volkswagen I*[124] judgments it is not necessary, at least in the case of selective distribution systems ... to look for acquiescence to a call by the manufacturer in the behaviour which the dealer adopts in the context of that call ... Such acquiescence must be regarded as established as a matter of principle, from the mere fact that the dealer has entered the distribution network. It is therefore deemed to have been given by the dealer ...'.[125] It went on to add that it 'is presumed that by joining a distribution system, the dealer approves the manufacturer's distribution policy in advance, a policy which is naturally not foreseeable in all its details when the dealer joins. Those principles apply also to the manufacturer's policy in relation to resale prices'.[126]

The CFI held that the Commission had misinterpreted the case law in deciding that acqui- **3.73** escence could be regarded as having been established 'as a matter of principle by the mere fact that the dealer has entered the distribution network'. The Court went on to say for example that, contrary to the Commission's claim, in *AEG* the Court of Justice had found that the distributors in question had acquiesced in AEG's anti-competitive actions. This was because AEG operated a distribution system under which it could refuse to appoint any dealer it chose, including those qualified to enter. Therefore by entering the system, distributors were, by definition, agreeing to and benefiting from AEG's appointment policy.

As for *Ford* and *BMW*, the CFI essentially held that those cases were not about whether an **3.74** agreement had been entered into at all but whether the circulars sent by these manufacturers to their dealers could be said to have been incorporated into *existing* agreements. Thus the CFI distinguished *Ford* from *Volkswagen II* by holding that in the former case it was common ground that the circular had been implemented in practice by Ford and that, despite protests from certain quarters, dealers had complied with it. The *Ford* judgment was therefore about whether the circular in question could be said to have been incorporated into the Ford dealership agreement and should therefore have been assessed together with the main agreement under Article 81(3); the case was therefore not about whether the sending of a circular constituted an agreement in itself. Similarly the CFI did not think that the *BMW* judgment was directly relevant. This was because in *BMW* the question was not so much whether an agreement had actually been reached by BMW and its dealers as a result of the circular sent by former but rather whether such a request, assuming that it was accepted and therefore constituted an agreement within the meaning of Article 81(1) EC, came within the relevant exempting regulation.

(i) What Does Tacit Acquiescence Require?

In *Bayer*[127] the ECJ confirmed that an agreement could not be regarded as having been **3.75** concluded 'by tacit acceptance' if all that existed was a unilateral decision by the supplier to

---

[121] Case 107/82 *AEG v Commission* [1983] ECR 3151.
[122] Joined Cases 25/84 and 26/84 *Ford v Commission* [1985] ECR 2725.
[123] Case C-70/93 *Bayerische Motorenwerke v ALD* [1995] ECR I-3439
[124] Case T-62/98 *Volkswagen v Commission* [2000] ECR II-2707.
[125] Case T-208/01 *Volkswagen AG v Commission* [2003] ECR II-5141, para 25.
[126] ibid, para 26.
[127] All Bayer quotes in the following paragraphs are, unless otherwise stated, taken from Joined Cases C-2/01 P and C-3/01 *Bundesverband der Arzneimittel-Importeure and Commission v Bayer* [2004] ECR I-23, paras 100–101.

follow a particular course of action. On the facts, the Court found that Bayer's had decided to limit the amount it supplied to certain distributors unilaterally: it had neither told these suppliers where they should sell the product nor made supply conditional on the final destination of the product. Consistent with this, Bayer had not checked to see where sales had been made following the reduction in supply. There was therefore no agreement for the purposes of Article 81.

3.76 Tacit acquiescence requires an express or implied 'invitation' from one party to the other party to fulfil an anti-competitive goal 'jointly'. This can 'be deduced from the conduct of the parties concerned'.

3.77 In deciding whether an invitation has been made the Commission and the European Courts are likely to consider whether the supplier is able to achieve its aims without the dealers' assistance. For example, in rejecting the Commission's finding of an agreement, the ECJ noted that Bayer was able to reduce parallel imports simply by unilaterally cutting the amount it supplied its dealers.[128] The Court distinguished this situation from that in *Sandoz* where the supplier needed the assistance of its distributors to eliminate or reduce parallel imports. This also distinguishes *Bayer* from *Volkswagen II*—in the latter, the practice in question, resale price maintenance, required the co-operation of dealers to succeed. In such circumstances it is likely to be relatively easy to show tacit acceptance.[129]

3.78 In the absence of an 'invitation', tacit acquiescence can still be found *if* the dealer shares the same intention as the supplier—thus in *Bayer* the question was whether wholesalers 'shared the intention of Bayer to prevent parallel imports'.[130] In this regard, the ECJ's judgment could be read as implying that it may be sufficient for the dealer merely 'to give [the supplier] the impression' of going along with the latter's strategy.[131] However, the Court's reference in the judgment to the need to consider the 'genuine wishes'[132] of the wholesalers and its focus on assessing the behaviour of the wholesalers following the adoption of the policy by Bayer suggests that this may not be enough. Instead the European Courts and the Commission are likely, in order to determine whether dealers share the intention of the supplier, to consider a number of factors. In particular the Courts are likely to consider whether it is in the interest of dealers to observe the supplier's policy. Conversely in *Bayer* the supplier's policy was to prevent parallel imports from Spain to the UK being made. This was clearly not in the interest of dealers in Spain who lost profitable export opportunities as a result.

3.79 As part of its assessment, the European Courts may consider the 'actual conduct'[133] of the dealers to determine whether there has been acquiescence. In *GSK*[134] the CFI held that

---

[128] Although the ECJ did not explain the relevance of this factor, it might have resulted from the Court asking itself the following question: 'would an invitation have been made if assistance had not been needed?' Common sense would suggest an answer in the negative.

[129] For instance, the fact that some dealers may have offered discounts on the resale price of a supplier is unlikely to be sufficient, on its own, to prevent the European Courts from finding an agreement—it may very well be that the discounting would have been deeper in the absence of the supplier's invitation to coordinate.

[130] *Bayer*, para 121.

[131] ibid, para 122.

[132] ibid, para 121.

[133] ibid, para 129.

[134] Case T-168/01 *GlaxoSmithKline Services v Commission* (judgment of 27 September 2006, para 83). In making this finding the CFI relied expressly on paras 82 and 100 of the ECJ's judgment in *Bayer*.

'evidence may consist of direct evidence, taking the form, for example, of a written document or, failing that, indirect evidence, for example in the form of conduct'. In *Volkswagen I* the ECJ relied on the fact that the dealers had complied with the manufacturer's initiatives and had refused to sell to their foreign customers to find the existance of an agreement.[135] In *Bayer* the CFI relied on dealers' conduct to find that no agreement existed:[136] the Court found that the dealers could not have shared Bayer's intention; in fact, their action demonstrated their firm intention to continue with parallel exporting.[137] The fact that they had kept their intention secrets and indeed may have deliberately attempted to give Bayer the impression they were acting in accordance with the manufacturer's policy did not vitiate the Court's finding (as the Commission had suggested) as they had done this in order to secure supplies for export.[138]

(ii) Care Should be Taken in Applying the Bayer/Volkswagen II Approach

The *Bayer/Volkswagen II* judgments have reignited debate about the concept of an agreement and the scope of application of Article 81(1).[139] Some commentators have suggested that the European Courts have, through these cases, increased the hurdle for the European Commission and NCAs in vertical cases where there is no direct evidence of agreements existing.   **3.80**

The authors do not share these views, other than to a limited extent. Although these judgments are important, and may require the Commission to analyse the facts more closely, they do not mean that agreements which would have been caught in the past are now significantly more likely to fall outside Article 81(1).   **3.81**

Great care therefore needs to be taken by undertakings seeking to rely on these judgments to escape Article 81(1). It is worth noting, for example, that the way in which the ECJ distinguished *Bayer* from its judgment in *Sandoz* suggests that the European Courts may not require much more than passive acquiescence in cases where the supplier has sought the co-operation of dealers. The ECJ noted that the fact that the dealers in that case had continued to purchase from Sandoz after it had inserted the words 'export prohibited' on invoices was sufficient for an agreement to exist. In *Bayer* the emphasis the CFI placed on evidence such as the fact that some wholesalers had continued to seek additional supplies for export[140] suggests that, had they merely reduced or eliminated exports *with no more*, the CFI may have found tacit acquiescence.   **3.82**

---

[135] Case T-208/01 *Volkswagen AG v Commission* [2003] ECR II-5141, para 53.
[136] Joined Cases C-2/01 P and C-3/01 [2004] ECR I-23, para 21 quoting para 154 of the CFI's judgment in the same case.
[137] For instance the Court noted that dealers had responded to Bayer's policy by, *inter alia*, trying to persuade Bayer that domestic demand had grown (for example, by establishing new wholesalers).
[138] Case T-41/96 *Bayer v Commission* [2000] ECR II-3383, paras 152–157.
[139] For example, F Wijckmans, F Tuytschaever and A Vanderelst *Vertical Agreements in EC Competition Law* (OUP, 2006), 65–71; C Brown, '*Bayer v Commission*: the ECJ Agrees' [2004] ECLR 386; D Bailey, 'Reaching Agreement' Comp LI 2005 4(20) 3; SB Völcker, 'Developments in EC Competition Law in 2003: An Overview' [2004] CML Rev 1031–3; A Jones and B Sufrin, *EC Competition Law, Text, Cases and Materials* (2nd edn, OUP, 2004), 138–146.
[140] Case T-41/96, para 126.

3.83 Particular care needs to be taken where the dealers' co-operation is necessary for the achievement of the supplier's policy or where it is in their interest to observe the supplier's policy.[141]

(f) Formal Termination May Not be Sufficient

3.84 The formal termination of an agreement does not necessarily mean that there is no longer a violation of Article 81. In *EMI Records Limited v CBS United Kingdom Limited*,[142] the ECJ held that for Article 81 to apply 'it is sufficient that such agreements continue to produce their effects after they have formally ceased to be in force'. However, the ECJ added that '[a]n agreement is only to be regarded as continuing to produce its effects if from the behaviour of the parties concerned there may be inferred the existence of elements of concerted practice and of coordination peculiar to the agreement and producing the same result as that envisaged by the agreement'.[143] Thus, the agreement must continue to influence the conduct of the parties on the market.[144]

3.85 The fact that the terms of, or the parties to, an arrangement change over time does not mean that as a result it ceases to be an agreement under Article 81(1). In *Pre-Insulated Pipes*, the Commission decided that each such change did not imply that a new 'agreement' had come into force for the purposes of Article 81(1).[145]

3.86 Agreements made before accession of a Member State will be deemed to be agreements for the purposes of Article 81(1) if they continue to produce their effects within the European Community after the date of accession.[146] In any event, the fact that an agreement was concluded outside the EC does not prevent Article 81(1) applying to it if the general rules on Community jurisdiction apply.[147]

(g) The Single Economic Unit Doctrine (No Intra-Enterprise Conspiracy in EC Law)

3.87 As already noted above, for the purposes of Article 81(1) at least two undertakings must be party to an agreement. However, two or more legally separate entities may be treated as a single undertaking under the competition rules if their relationship justifies regarding them as a single economic unit. In this case, agreements between them, even legally enforceable ones, will usually be regarded as an internal allocation of functions within a corporate group rather than an agreement between independent undertakings capable of falling within the prohibition of Article 81(1). This means that Article 81 will not apply to arrangements between them, however anti-competitive they may seem to be.[148] However, it also means that parent companies, including those based outside the Community, can be held liable under Article 81 for the behaviour of their subsidiaries operating within the EU, since the undertaking *as a whole* is active there.[149]

---

141 Case T-41/96, para 129. See above at paras 3.77–3.79.
142 Case 51/75 [1976] ECR 811, para 30.
143 ibid, para 31.
144 *Soda-ash/Solvay, ICI* [1991] OJ L152/1, para 54.
145 *Pre-Insulated Pipes* [1999] OJ L24/1, paras 129–138.
146 Case 40/70 *Sirena Srl v Eda Srl and others* [1971] ECR 69.
147 On jurisdiction, see section D below.
148 Art 82 may, however, apply.
149 Case 48/69 *ICI v Commission* [1972] ECR 619.

In *Centrafarm v Sterling Drug*,[150] the ECJ held that an agreement between undertakings **3.88** belonging to the same group and having the status of parent and subsidiary was not caught by Article 81(1) 'if the undertakings form an economic unit within which the subsidiary has no real freedom to determine its course of action on the market, and if the agreements or practices are concerned merely with the internal allocation of tasks as between the undertakings'. In *Viho Europe BV v Commission*,[151] the ECJ held that Article 81(1) could not apply where a subsidiary did not freely determine its conduct on the market, but instead carried out the instructions given to it directly or indirectly by the parent company.

Determining whether related firms are independent in their decision making can, in prac- **3.89** tice, be difficult. The Commission's decisions under the EC Merger Regulation, and its Notice on the concept of concentration,[152] provide perhaps the best guidance on this issue. In general, where a subsidiary is wholly owned, or where a parent company has a majority shareholding in a subsidiary, there is a presumption that the subsidiary is controlled by its parent.[153] Minority holdings may also give the parent company control[154] where specific rights are attached to the minority shareholding which enable the minority shareholder to determine the strategic commercial behaviour of the other company (such as the power to appoint more than half of the members of the supervisory board or the administrative board). A minority shareholder may also be deemed to have control if it is likely to achieve a majority at the shareholders' meeting, given that the remaining shares are widely dispersed.

The situation is more complex where a subsidiary is jointly controlled by two companies or **3.90** persons. In *Gosme/Martell*,[155] DMP was a joint subsidiary of Martell and Piper-Heidsieck. The Commission found that Martell was not in a position to control DMP's commercial activities because the parent companies each held 50 per cent of DMP's capital and voting rights; half the supervisory board members represented Martell shareholders and half Piper-Heidsieck shareholders; DMP also distributed brands not belonging to its parent companies; Martell and Piper-Heidsieck products were invoiced to wholesalers on the same document; and DMP had its own sales force and alone concluded the conditions of sale with the buying syndicates. The Commission therefore concluded that DMP, the subsidiary, and Martell, a parent company, were independent undertakings.

Similarly, in *Ijsselcentrale*,[156] four electricity generation companies had established a joint **3.91** subsidiary to act as a vehicle for co-operation between them. The parties had argued that the subsidiary and the electricity generators formed an economic unit because they were components of one indivisible public electricity supply system. The Commission rejected this argument. It held that the four participants did not belong to a single group of companies.

---

[150] Case 15/74 *Centrafarm v Sterling Drug* [1974] ECR 619, para 1147.
[151] Case C-73/95 *Viho Europe BV v Commission* [1996] ECR I-5457.
[152] [1998] OJ C66/5.
[153] See para 13 of the Commission Notice On The Concept Of Concentration under Council Regulation (EEC) No 4064/89 on the control of concentrations between undertakings. See also *Zurich/MMI* (Case IV/M286) (1993) OJ C112/0; *Crédit Lyonnais/BFG Bank* (Case IV/M296) (1993) OJ C45/0.
[154] See para 14 of the Commission Notice on the Concept of Concentration under Council Regulation (EEC) No 4064/89 on the control of concentrations between undertakings.
[155] *Gosme/Martell–DMP* [1991] OJ L185/23.
[156] *Ijsselcentrale and others* [1991] OJ L28/32.

They were separate legal persons, and were not controlled by a single person, natural or legal. Each generating company determined its own conduct independently. The fact that the generators formed an indivisible part of the public electricity supply system did not mean that they were part of the same economic unit. The Commission also held that the subsidiary was not part of the same economic unit as its parents but rather a joint venture controlled by them together.

3.92 While property rights and shareholders' agreements are the most important factors in determining whether undertakings belong to the same economic unit, they are not the only ones. The fact that a company does not legally belong to a group is not decisive. Account must also be taken of the nature of the relationship between the undertakings belonging to that group.[157] Purely economic relationships may also play a role. In certain circumstances, a situation of economic dependence may lead to control on a de facto basis where, for example, important long-term supply agreements or credits provided by suppliers or customers, coupled with structural links, confer decisive influence on one party over another.[158]

(h) Successor Undertakings

3.93 Two legally separate entities may also be treated as one for the purposes of competition law where one is the economic successor of the other. The ECJ has held that 'a change in the legal form and name of an undertaking does not create a new undertaking free of liability for the anti-competitive behaviour of its predecessor, when, from an economic point of view, the two are identical.'[159] At issue is 'whether there is a functional and economic continuity between the original infringer and the undertaking into which it was merged'.[160]

3.94 Where an undertaking subsequently acquires the entity that has infringed the law, the ECJ has held that it 'falls in principle, to the legal or natural person managing the undertaking in question when the infringement was committed to answer for that infringement, even if, when the Decision finding the infringement was adopted, another person had assumed responsibility for operating the undertaking.'[161] Thus in *Zinc Phosphate*, the Commission decided that, 'when an undertaking committed an infringement of Article 81(1) . . . and when this undertaking later disposed of the assets that were the vehicle of the infringement and withdrew from the market concerned, the undertaking in question will still be held responsible for the infringement *if it is still in existence*'[162] (emphasis added).

3.95 Recently however, in *Aalborg v Commission*,[163] the ECJ examined whether the Commission can treat an undertaking as accountable for the anti-competitive conduct of another, when

---

[157] Case 30/87 *Corinne Bodson v SA Pompes Funèbres des Régions Libérées* [1988] ECR 2479.

[158] See, eg para 9 of Notice on the Concept of Concentration; see also *CCIE/GTE* (Case IV/M258) [1992] OJ C265; *Lockhead Martin/Loral Corporation* (Case IV/M697) [1996] OJ C314/9.

[159] Joined Cases 29/83 & 30/83 *Compagnie Royale Asturienne des Mines SA and Rheinzink GmbH v Commission* [1984] ECR 1679, para 9.

[160] *PVC* OJ [1989] L74/1, para 42.

[161] Case C-279/98 P *Cascades v Commission* [2000] ECR I-9693, para 78.

[162] OJ [2003] L153/1, para 238, referring to Case T-80/89 *BASF and others v Commission* (polypropylene) [1995] ECR II-729, which judgment was upheld by the ECJ in Case C-49/92 P *Commission v Anic Partecipazioni SpA* [1999] ECR I-4125.

[163] Joined Cases C-204/00 P, C- 205/00 P, C-211/00 P, C-213/00 P, C-217/00 P and C-219/00 P *Aalborg Portland A/S and others v Commission* [2004] ECR I-123.

the conduct occurred prior to its formation. More specifically, the ECJ considered whether the fact that the (original) infringing entity still exists wholly and necessarily precludes the Commission from proceeding against the successor.

Aalborg Portland A/S ('Aalborg') was formed on 26 June 1990 and acquired, with retroactive effect to 1 January 1990, the cement plant of Aktieselskabet Aalborg Portland-Cement Fabrik ('Aktieselskabet'). For its part, Aktieselskabet became a holding company, with it and another company, Blue Circle, each owning 50 per cent of the shares in Aalborg. **3.96**

The CFI upheld the Commission's decision to hold Aalborg accountable for Aktieselskabet's participation in the cement cartel during the 1980s, considering that the events in 1990 described above (and by which time the infringements had ceased) constituted a reorganisation of the group and that Aalborg and Aktieselskabet were one and the same economic entity. On appeal, Aalborg pointed to the Court's case law (eg in *Anic*) stating that 'the economic continuity test can only apply where the legal person responsible for running the undertaking [in this case, Aktieselskabet] has ceased to exist in law after the infringement has been committed.'[164] **3.97**

In its decision, the ECJ rejected Aalborg's appeal. It considered that the CFI's finding should be taken to mean that the undertaking run by Aalborg from 1990 was the same as that previously run by Aktieselskabet and the fact that Aktieselskabet still existed as a legal entity did not invalidate that finding. While the Court acknowledged its previous decision in *Anic*, it distinguished that case as being one concerning two existing and functioning undertakings one of which had simply transferred part of its activities to the other and where there was no structural link between them.[165] In the present case, Aktieselskabet remained as one of Aalborg's holding companies. **3.98**

(i) Judicial Settlement

It is not certain whether a settlement reached before a national court which constitutes a judicial act is an agreement capable of falling within the prohibition of Article 81(1). In *Bayer AG and Maschinenfabrik Hennecke GmbH v Heinz Süllhöfer*, the ECJ held that '[i]n its prohibition of certain 'agreements' between undertakings, Article 85(1) [now Article 81(1)] makes no distinction between agreements whose purpose is to put an end to litigation and those concluded with other aims in mind'. However, it went on to note that 'this assessment of such a settlement is without prejudice to the question whether, and to what extent, a judicial settlement reached before a national court which constitutes a judicial act may be invalid for breach of Community competition rules.'[166] There is no doubt that agreements between undertakings to settle actual or potential litigation, for example on matters of intellectual property, may fall under Article 81(1).[167] **3.99**

---

[164] ibid, para 347.
[165] ibid, para 359.
[166] Case 65/86 *Bayer AG and Maschinenfabrik Hennecke GmbH v Heinz Süllhöfer* [1988] ECR 5249, paras 1 and 15.
[167] See eg *Toltecs-Dorcet* [1982] OJ L379/19.

(3) Decisions by Associations of Undertakings

3.100 Article 81(1) explicitly recognises that collusion can take place through the medium of an association. As with the other terms of Article 81(1), the word 'association' is defined widely and is not restricted to trade associations. Thus such bodies as agricultural co-operatives,[168] associations entrusted with statutory functions,[169] and associations of trade associations[170] have been held to be 'associations of undertakings' under Article 81(1).

3.101 Similarly the word 'decision' has a wider meaning under Article 81(1) than might appear at first glance. Thus where an association of undertakings is found to exist, its 'decisions' do not need to be binding on its members to bring them within the scope of Article 81(1). All that is required is that the 'decision' be made with the object or effect of influencing the commercial behaviour of the association's members. In *Verband der Sachversicherer eV v Commission*,[171] an association of German insurers issued a recommendation to its members to raise premiums. The association had argued that this recommendation had been made by a committee which was not competent to adopt decisions binding on the association or its members. The recommendation therefore fell outside the scope of the prohibition. The ECJ held that the recommendation was a decision as it reflected the association's resolve to co-ordinate the conduct of its members on the German insurance market in accordance with the terms of the recommendation.

3.102 It should be noted that if a recommendation is carried out or, indeed, if it merely influences the behaviour of the members of the association, this can also amount to an agreement or a concerted practice as between the members themselves.[172] The importance of the concept of 'decisions by associations of undertakings' therefore lies in the fact that it enables those applying Article 81(1) to hold associations liable for the anti-competitive behaviour of their members.

(4) Concerted Practices

(a) Definition

3.103 A concerted practice is a form of co-ordination where undertakings,[173] without concluding any sort of agreement or establishing a plan of action, 'knowingly substitute practical co-operation between them for the risks of competition'.[174] The aim of the Treaty, in establishing the concept of concerted practice, is to prevent undertakings from evading the application of Article 81(1) by colluding in an anti-competitive manner which falls short of an agreement.

3.104 In *Imperial Chemical Industries Ltd (ICI) v Commission*, the ECJ held that, although undertakings were free to alter their behaviour to take into account the present or foreseeable

---

168 *MELDOC* [1986] OJ L348/50.
169 *Pabst & Richarz/BNIA* [1976] OJ L231/24; *Coapi* [1995] OJ L122/37.
170 *Milchförderungsfonds* [1985] OJ L35/35.
171 Case 45/85 [1987] ECR 405.
172 *Roofing Felt Cartel* [1986] OJ L232/15, upheld on appeal: Case 246/86 *SC Belasco and others v Commission* [1989] ECR 2117.
173 It has been suggested that concerted practices can also cover vertical arrangements. This is discussed in section C.4(c) below.
174 Case 48/69 *ICI v Commission* [1972] ECR 619, para 64.

conduct of their competitors, it was nevertheless 'contrary to the rules on competition contained in the treaty for a producer to cooperate with his competitors, in any way whatsoever, in order to determine a co-ordinated course of action . . . and to ensure its success by prior elimination of all uncertainty as to each other' s conduct regarding the essential elements of that action'.[175]

The ECJ confirmed and developed this definition in *Coöperatieve Vereniging 'Suiker Unie'* **3.105** *and others v Commission*.[176] The Commission had decided that sugar producers in Belgium, Germany, and Holland had engaged in a concerted practice to control the supply of sugar into The Netherlands. The producers had argued that for a concerted practice to exist it would have been necessary for them to have established a plan which removed in advance any doubt as to their future conduct; otherwise, they asserted, every attempt by an undertaking to react intelligently to the acts of its competitors could be portrayed as an offence. In their case no plan had been worked out, so no concerted practice had taken place.

The ECJ again acknowledged that the law did not deprive economic operators of the right **3.106** to adapt themselves intelligently to the conduct of their competitors. However, the underlying notion of competition in the EC Treaty was that each economic operator had to 'determine independently the policy which he intends to adopt on the common market including the choice of the persons and undertakings to which he makes offers or sells'. The law therefore strictly precluded 'any direct or indirect contact between such operators, the object or effect whereof is either to influence the conduct on the market of an actual or potential competitor or to disclose to such a competitor the course of conduct which they themselves have decided to adopt or contemplate adopting on the market'. Thus the law 'in no way requires the working out of an actual plan'[177] for a concerted practice to exist; nor does it require the consensus necessary to be reached orally or to come about from direct contact.

In *SA Hercules Chemicals NV v Commission*,[178] the CFI applied the tests laid down in *ICI* **3.107** and *Suiker Unie*. The Commission had found that the applicant had participated in meetings during which it discussed with its competitors matters such as the prices they wished to see charged on the market, the prices they intended to charge, their profitability thresholds, they judged to be necessary, their sales figures and the identity of customers. The CFI confirmed that the applicant, through its participation in those meetings, had taken part, together with its competitors:

> in concerted action the purpose of which was to influence their conduct on the market and to disclose to each other the course of conduct which each of the producers itself contemplated adopting on the market. Accordingly, not only did the applicant pursue the aim of eliminating in advance uncertainty about the future conduct of its competitors but also, in determining the policy which it intended to follow on the market, it could not fail to take account, directly or indirectly, of the information obtained during the course of those meetings. Similarly, in determining the policy which they intended to follow, its competitors were bound to take into account, directly or indirectly, the information disclosed to them by the

---

[175] ibid, para 118.
[176] Joined Cases 40 to 48, 50, 54–56, 111, 113 and 114/73 [1975] ECR 1663.
[177] Case T-202/98 *Tate & Lyle v Commission* [2001] ECR II- 2035, para 55.
[178] Case T-7/89 [1991] ECR II-1711.

applicant about the course of conduct which the applicant itself had decided upon or which it contemplated adopting on the market.[179]

3.108 Thus it would seem that to prove a concerted practice a number of elements will usually have to be identified. First, some form of contact between undertakings is necessary; however this 'contact' can be indirect and 'weak'. For example if A makes a public announcement of its intention to behave in a particular manner, 'contact' may be held to have taken place if A did so in the knowledge that its competitors would follow its lead.

3.109 Secondly, there must some meeting of minds or consensus between the parties to co-operate rather than compete. However, as with 'contact', this 'meeting of minds' can be found easily. In *Cimenteries CBR SA v Commission* the CFI found that Lafarge was party to a concerted practice merely because it had received information about the commercial activities of its competitors. In this regard the CFI found that the existence of a concerted did not require a formal understanding to be given as to future conduct.[180] It went on to recall that 'it is settled law that the fact that an undertaking does not abide by the outcome of meetings which have a manifestly anti-competitive purpose is not such as to relieve it of full responsibility for the fact that it participated in the agreement or concerted practice'.[181]

3.110 Third, 'the concept of a concerted practice . . . implies, besides undertakings' concerting with each other, subsequent conduct on the market, and a relationship of cause and effect between the two'.[182] However, again the threshold for proving this is low: for example, in *Hüls* the ECJ held that since the Commission had established that the applicant had participated in meetings between undertakings of a manifestly anti-competitive nature, it 'did not have to adduce evidence that their concerting together had manifested itself in conduct on the market or that it had had effects restrictive of competition'[183] ie in hardcore horizontal cases, once there is 'contact' and a 'meeting of minds', there is a 'presumption'[184] that conduct will follow.

3.111 The European Courts have however made clear that this presumption can be rebutted if the undertaking in question is able to adduce 'proof'[185] that the concertation did not have 'any influence whatsoever on its own conduct on the market'.[186] The practical implications of this are however likely to be limited. For example, in the case of a meeting between competitors at which commercially sensitive matters are discussed, the undertaking wishing to rebut the presumption must show that it did not engage in any activities linked to the concertation and that it did not, in anyway, take into account the commercial information it had learned at the meeting in determining its conduct on that market.[187] This is because it

---

179 Case T-7/89, paras 259–260. See also *Pre-Insulated Pipes* [1999] OJ L24/1, paras 129–138.
180 Cases T-25/95 *Cimenteries CBR SA v Commission* [2000] ECR II-491, para 1852.
181 ibid, para 1389.
182 Case C-199/92 P *Hüls AG v Commission* [1999] ECR I-4287, para 161.
183 ibid, para 167.
184 ibid, para 162; see also Cases T-25/95 *Cimenteries CBR SA v Commission* [2000] ECR II-491, para 1865.
185 Joined Cases T-25/95 etc *Cimenteries CBR SA v Commission* [2000] ECR II-491, para 1865. The case was largely upheld on appeal in Joined Cases C-204/00 P, C-205/00 P, C-211/00 P, C-213/00 P, C-217/00 P and C-219/00 P *Aalborg Portland A/S v Commission* [2004] ECR I-123.
186 Case C-199/92 P *Hüls AG v Commission* [1999] ECR I-4287, para 167.
187 Case C-199/92 P *Hüls AG v Commission* [1999] ECR I-4287, para 162.

is assumed that 'the recipient of the information in question cannot normally fail to take that information into account when formulating its policy on the market'.[188]

Thus, whilst theoretically possible, this hurdle would seem too high for undertakings to overcome in most cases—it is worth recalling in particular that evidence showing a lack of effect on the market (for example on price) is unlikely, in an of itself, to be sufficient. Case law suggests that to rebut the presumption the undertaking in question must at least have ended its participation in the meeting as soon as the anti-competitive nature of the gathering became apparent[189] and to have 'publicly distance[d] itself from what was discussed' so as not to give the impression to the other participants that it subscribed to the aim of the meeting and would act in conformity with it.[190] Thus in *Huls* the ECJ implied that Huls could have escaped the scope of Article 81(1) if it had put 'forward evidence to establish that its participation in those [manifestly anti-competitive] meetings was without any anti-competitive intention by demonstrating that it had indicated to its competitors that it was participating in those meetings in a spirit that was different from theirs'.[191] **3.112**

(b) Can a Concerted Practice be Inferred from Circumstantial Evidence Alone?

Although in most cases involving concerted practices there will be evidence of contact and a common intent to co-operate rather than compete, in certain circumstances a concerted practice may be inferred from circumstantial evidence alone. The test, however, is strict and hard to meet. In *ICI*,[192] the Commission found that the major producers of aniline dyes in the Community, who had all raised their prices by similar amounts on three separate occasions between 1964 and 1967, had engaged in a concerted practice. The parties appealed arguing that the increases could be explained by the oligopolistic nature of the markets concerned. Dismissing the appeal, the ECJ held that while parallel behaviour by itself did not constitute a concerted practice 'it may however amount to strong evidence of such a practice if it leads to conditions of competition which do not correspond to the normal conditions of the market having regard to the nature of the products, the size and number of undertakings, and the volume of the said market'.[193] The ECJ found that the market for aniline dyes was not oligopolistic. It was national in scope with clear differences in characteristics between the different geographic markets. It was therefore 'hardly conceivable that the same action could be taken spontaneously at the same time, on the same national markets and for the same range of products'[194] as a result of independent decision making. **3.113**

In *Ahlström Osakeyhtiö et al v Commission (Wood Pulp II)*,[195] the ECJ clarified further the standard of proof required. It noted that Article 81 did not deprive economic operators of **3.114**

---

[188] *Argos Limited and Littlewoods Limited v Office of Fair Trading* [2004] CAT 24, para 663.
[189] Case T-9/99 *HFB Holding für Fernwärmetechnik Beteiligungsgesellschaft mbH & Co KG and Others v Commission (Pre-Insulated Pipes)* [2002] II-1487, para 223.
[190] Case T141/89, para 85.
[191] Case C-199/92 P *Hüls AG v Commission* [1999] ECR I-4287, para 155.
[192] Case 48/69 *ICI v Commission* [1972] ECR 619.
[193] ibid, para 66.
[194] ibid, para 109.
[195] Joined Cases C-89/95, C-104/85, C-114/85, C-116/85, C-117/85 and C-125/85–C-129/85 [1993] ECR I-1307.

the right to adapt themselves intelligently to the existing and anticipated conduct of their competitors. Thus parallel conduct in itself 'cannot be regarded as furnishing proof of concertation unless concertation constitutes the only plausible explanations for such conduct. Accordingly, it is necessary in this case to ascertain whether the parallel conduct alleged by the Commission cannot, taking account of the nature of the products, the size and the number of the undertakings and the volume of the market in question, be explained otherwise than by concertation.'[196]

3.115 In *Compagnie Royale Asturienne des Mines SA and Rheinzink GmbH v Commission*,[197] the Commission had held that two zinc producers had engaged in a concerted practice to prevent parallel imports from Belgium to Germany by terminating deliveries to their Belgian distributor within a week of each other. To refute this argument the ECJ held that it would be sufficient for the applicants to prove circumstances which cast the facts established by the Commission in a different light and which thus allow another explanation of their parallel behaviour. In this case the termination of deliveries could be explained by non-payment of invoices by the distributor over the preceding few months.

(c) Vertical Concerted Practices

3.116 It has been suggested to the authors that the concept of a concerted practice has no application in the context of a vertical relationship between suppliers and their distributors. Those who advocate this view draw on the classic, often-repeated definitions of concerted practice given in two of the leading cases, *ICI v Commission*[198] and *Suiker Unie*[199] which seems to limit the scope of the concept to competitor interaction only. Thus in the former the ECJ defined concerted practice as a form of co-ordination where undertakings 'knowingly substitute practical co-operation between them for the *risks of competition*' whilst in the latter it referred to '. . . any direct or indirect contact between such operators, the object or effect whereof is either to influence the conduct on the market of an *actual or potential competitor* or to disclose to such a *competitor* the course of conduct which they themselves have decided to adopt or contemplate adopting on the market'.[200] In addition proponents of this view argue that the jurisprudence and principles summarised above only make sense in the context of competitor co-ordination since vertical relationships are generally pro-competitive.

3.117 The view summarised above is, as a matter of law, erroneous—there is nothing either in the wording of Article 81(1) itself or any of the jurisprudence which definitively takes vertical cases outside the scope of the concept of concert practice. Indeed the opposite is true. Thus, for example, in *SA Musique Diffusion française and others v Commission*[201] the ECJ found that Pioneer, a supplier of camera equipment, had engaged in a concerted practice with three of its distributors to prevent parallel imports. The ECJ made the same finding on similar facts in *Hasselblad (GB) Limited v Commission*.[202]

---

[196] *Ablström*, paras 61–72.
[197] Joined Cases 29/83 and 30/83 [1984] ECR 1679.
[198] Case 48/69 *ICI v Commission* [1972] ECR 619, para 64.
[199] Joined Cases 40/73 etc [1975] ECR 1663.
[200] ibid, para 174.
[201] Joined Cases 100 to 103/80 [1983] ECR 1825, paras 72–80.
[202] Case 86/82 [1984] ECR 883, paras 24–29.

However, as a matter of practice, there is some merit to the ideas set out in paragraph 3.116 **3.118** above. Two points are worth stressing in this regard. First, whilst it is easy, for example, to understand why a meeting between competitors at which commercially sensitive matters are discussed creates a presumption of anti-competitive conduct, the same is not true for contact between a supplier and a distributor. By definition, they have a commercial relationship which often requires contact and possibly some co-ordination of commercial activities (most obviously in the case of selective distribution). This is not to suggest that the concept of concerted practice does not apply in vertical cases but rather that the principles set out thus far by the Commission and the European Courts have a limited application because they were developed in the context of catching competitor collusion.

Secondly, and perhaps more importantly, though formally about the concept of an agreement, **3.119** it seems clear that *Bayer v Commission* has, for now, set the upper limit for scope of application of Article 81(1) in vertical cases (ie that there must be, at a minimum, tacit acquiescence for Article 81(1) to apply).[203] It seems inconceivable, given the clear statements by both the CFI and the ECJ that the European Commission, Member State competition authorities or national courts would try to bypass the test set therein. The only exception to this is likely to be in a case where the facts are similar to those in *Musique Diffusion Française* and *Hasselblad*, ie where the supplier plays a co-ordinating role of some sort in a concerted practice *between* its distributors.[204]

(5) Distinction Between Agreements and Concerted Practices

It can be difficult to identify exactly where an agreement ends and a concerted practice starts. **3.120** The concepts are fluid and may overlap. An infringement may begin in one form and, as it evolves over time, progressively assume some or all the characteristics of another. In fact it often makes little sense to try to draw a distinction between the two concepts as an infringement may present simultaneously the characteristics of an agreement and a concerted practice.[205] Indeed, in cartel cases, the Commission often alleges that an agreement and/or concerted practice has taken place without distinguishing between the two. Nothing turns on the precise distinction for the purposes of the substantive analysis under Article 81(1).[206] This is clear from the Commission's *Pre-Insulated Pipes* decision, in which it held that:

> where the various concerted practices followed and agreements concluded form part of a series of efforts made by the undertakings in pursuit of a common objective of preventing or distorting competition, the Commission is entitled to find that they constitute a single continuous infringement. As the Court of First Instance observed on this point in Case T-1/89: it would be artificial to split up such continuous conduct, characterised by a single purpose, by treating it as a number of separate infringements: 'The fact is that the (undertakings) took part—over a period of years—in an integrated set of schemes constituting a single infringement, which progressively manifested itself in both unlawful agreements and unlawful concerted practices'.[207]

---

[203] See section C.2(e) above.
[204] See, for example, the judgment of the UK's Competition Appeal Tribunal in *JJB Sport v Office of Fair Trading* [2004] CAT 17.
[205] *Pre-Insulated Pipes* [1999] OJ L24/1, paras 129–138.
[206] *Polypropylene* [1986] OJ L230/1, para 85.
[207] [1999] OJ L24/1, para 131.

3.121 The validity of the Commission's practice of classifying infringements as 'agreements and/or concerted practices' has been upheld on numerous occasions. In *Commission v Anic*, the ECJ held that a 'comparison between that definition of agreement and the definition of a concerted practice . . . shows that, from the subjective point of view, they are intended to catch forms of collusion having the same nature and are only distinguishable from each other by their intensity and the forms in which they manifest themselves'.[208]

3.122 In the *Limburgse Vinyl Maatschappij NV v Commission*[209] the CFI rejected the argument made that the concept was cumulative ('and') rather than alternative ('or') ie that '[o]nly if proof of both classifications were established'[210] could the concept apply. It held that 'the dual classification must be understood not as requiring simultaneous and cumulative proof that every one of those factual elements reveals the factors constituting an agreement and a concerted practice, but rather as designating a complex whole that includes factual elements of which some have been classified as an agreement and others as a concerted practice within the meaning on Article 85(1) of the Treaty, which does not provide for any specific classification in respect of that type of complex infringement.'[211]

3.123 The CFI further explained that in the context of a 'complex infringement involves many producers seeking over a number of years to regulate the market between them' the Commission could not 'be expected to classify the infringement precisely, for each undertaking and for any given moment'. In fact the Commission was 'entitled to classify that type of complex infringement as an agreement "and/or" concerted practice, inasmuch as the infringement includes elements which are to be classified as an "agreement" and elements which are to be classified as a "concerted practice"'.[212]

3.124 This leaves one obvious question unanswered: does the concept only apply to complex cartels of a long duration as the quote above suggests? It is certainly true that the European Courts have used the formulation above, or a version of it, on more than one occasion.[213] However, as a practical matter, this is fact alone is likely to be of limited use to parties seeking to challenge a Commission decision. There are two main reasons for this. First the 'jurisdictional' concepts inherent in Article 81(1) such as 'undertaking',[214] 'agreement',[215] 'concerted practice'[216] and 'effect on trade'[217] have evolved in such a way as to ensure that undertakings engaging in anti-competitive practices do not escape the scope of Article 81(1) through use of clever legal arguments. Given this it seems likely that, if called to define either of the terms 'complex' or 'long duration' in a future case, the European Courts would do so in such a manner as to ensure that enforcement is not undermined. Second, and perhaps

---

[208] Case C-49/92 P *Commission v Anic Partecipazioni* [1999] ECR I-4125, para 131.

[209] Joined Case T-305/94 etc *Limburgse Vinyl Maatschappij NV and other v Commission* [1999] ECR II-931.

[210] ibid, para 692.

[211] ibid, para 698.

[212] ibid, paras 696–697.

[213] See for example Case T-1/89 *Rhône-Poulenc SA v Commission*, para 127 or Case T-9/89 *Hüls AG v Commission*, para 299

[214] See section C.1 above.

[215] See section C.2 above.

[216] See section C.4 above.

[217] See section D below.

more importantly from a practical viewpoint, given that the European Courts have acknowledged that the concept is not 'cumulative' but rather is 'alternative', it would matter little if the Commission fell on the first, higher leg of the concept (ie proving an 'agreement'). As long as there was sufficient evidence to support a finding of a concerted practice Article 81(1) could apply. The one proviso to this may be in vertical cases where scope of application of 'concerted practice' may have narrowed following *Bayer v Commission*.[218]

(6) State Compulsion

Article 81 does not apply if 'anti-competitive conduct is *required* of undertakings by national legislation or if the latter creates a legal framework which itself *eliminates any possibility* of competitive activity on their part'[219] (emphasis added). **3.125**

As the quote above suggests, the scope of application of this 'exclusion' is extremely narrow. Thus in *Aluminium Imports From Eastern Europe* the Commission rejected the cartel members' argument that their conduct fell outside the scope of Article 81 because it had the backing of the UK authorities. The Commission, whilst acknowledging that the UK Government had 'supported and encouraged' the anti-competitive arrangements, found that the parties had not been placed under any legal obligation to behave in an anti-competitive way. As such Article 81(1) applied.[220] In *SSI* the Commission decided that whilst competition in the cigarette industry in the Netherlands was limited because of the heavy taxes imposed there was still 'a sufficient margin within which manufacturers/importers and dealers could compete with one another'. Article 81 applied since it could not be argued that there was 'no scope at all for competition or that the scope is so limited that there would no longer be any scope for active competition'. In fact, in such a situation, 'it is even more important . . . that firms should not make agreements or engage in practices that eliminate the scope for competition that remains'.[221] This suggests that the test set out in paragraph 3.125 is cumulative: state compulsion itself is not enough; it must also eliminate 'any margin of autonomy on the part of those undertakings'.[222] **3.126**

More recently, the European Courts appear to have loosened marginally the criteria by holding that Article 81 would not apply if there was 'objective, relevant and consistent evidence' that undertakings had been obliged to engage in conduct 'through the exercise of irresistible pressures, such as, for example, the threat to adopt State measures likely to cause them to sustain substantial losses'[223] ie the 'exclusion' does not appear to require the existence of binding regulatory provisions; threats may suffice. **3.127**

In *CIF*, a reference under Article 234 from the *Tribunale Amministrativo per il Lazio*, the ECJ confirmed that 'the duty to disapply national legislation which contravenes Community **3.128**

---

[218] Joined Cases C-2/01 P and C-3/01 *Bundesverband der Arzneimittel-Importeure and Commission v Bayer* [2004] ECR I-23. See section C.2(e).

[219] Case T-228/97 *Irish Sugar v Commission* [1999] ECR II-2969, para 130; Case T-513/93 *Consiglio Nazionale degli Spedizionieri Doganali v Commission* [2000] ECR II-1807, para 58.

[220] OJ [1985] L 92/1 paras 6–10.

[221] OJ [1982] L 232/1 para 100.

[222] Case T-387/94 *Asia Motor France and others v Commission* [1996] ECR II-961, para 63.

[223] See for example Case T-66/99 *Minoan Lines SA v Commission (Greek Ferries)* [2003] ECR II-5515, para 179.

law applies not only to national courts but also to all organs of the State, including administrative authorities'.[224] The Court also highlighted the distinction between conduct by an undertaking that is *required* by national legislation and conduct that is '*merely facilitated or encouraged*' by it. For the former, an NCA may not impose penalties on the undertaking in respect of past conduct, as the offending national law constitutes a 'justification which shields the undertaking concerned from all the consequences of an infringement'.[225] (The NCA may, however, impose penalties for conduct *subsequent* to the decision to disapply the national legislation). On the other hand, if a national law 'merely encourages, or makes it easier for an undertaking to engage in autonomous anti-competitive conduct', the undertaking remains subject to Articles 81 and 82 and may incur penalties. However, when setting the level of the penalty, the undertaking's conduct may be assessed in the light of the national legal framework, as a mitigating factor.[226]

(7) 'which have as their object or effect the prevention, restriction or distortion of competition within the common market' [227]

3.129   The central debate within Article 81(1) has always revolved around the following question: 'what is a restriction of competition and how is it to be measured?' Put another way, what is the provision supposed to protect? Many different answers have been given: some see the EC's competition rules as about the maximisation of consumer welfare; others look to concept such as fairness and the ordo-liberal view that the aim of competition law is to control private economic power; alternatively it is argued that the purpose of Article 81 (and 82) is to protect the process of rivalry itself; yet others point to the role of competition as a tool to help the Community to fulfil overarching objectives such as market integration,[228] etc. Whilst this debate may at first seem of academic interest only, it is of crucial importance to an understanding of how and why the Commission and the European Courts have applied the rules in the past and how they are likely to do so going forward.

3.130   It is worth noting at the outset that the EC's competition rules were incorporated into the EEC Treaty at the insistence of the German delegation and were based on the laws in force in Germany. In addition it should be recalled that until the appointment of Philip Lowe in 2002, every Director General of DG Competition but one had been German. The German approach to competition law, which itself was based on the ordo-liberal philosophy[229] of the 'Freiburg School', was therefore of paramount importance to the development of competition law in the Community.

3.131   At its core the Freiburg School sought to limit and control private economic power by prohibiting agreements that placed unjustified limits on the competitive autonomy of firms.

---

224   Case C-198/01 *Consorzio Industrie Faimmiferi (CIF)* [2003] ECR I-8055, para 49.
225   ibid, para 54.
226   ibid, para 57.
227   Unless specified to the contrary, reference hereinafter to 'agreement' should be taken as encompassing concerted practices and decisions of associations.
228   For a brief account, see F Souty, *Le droit de la concurrence de l'Union Européenne* (2nd edn, Paris: Montchrestien, 1999) 23 *et seq.*
229   For a detailed discussion of the ordo-liberal approach and its impact see D Gerber, '*Law and Competition in 20th Century: Protecting Promotheus*', (Oxford, Clarendon Press: 1998).

Its goal was not to maximise efficiency (although consumer benefits were recognised and valued) but rather 'the protection of individual economic freedom of action'[230] in the interest of a free and fair political/social order. Freedom and fairness meant that markets should be kept as open as possible—clauses which limited sources of supply or the access of third parties from markets were therefore viewed with suspicion.

The Commission added an economic element to these ideas by arguing that the *process* of **3.132** competition itself, or, to be more precise, the process of rivalry between undertakings, produced the best *economic* results. For example, in its *Report on Competition Policy 1971* (Vol I), the Commission described competition as 'the best stimulant of economic activity'. It went on to argue that competition, '[t]hrough the interplay of decentralised decision-making machinery', enabled enterprises 'continuously to improve their efficiency which is the sine qua non for a steady improvement in living standards and employment prospects. From this point of view, competition policy is an essential means for satisfying to a great extent the individual and collective needs of our society.' Over a decade later, in its Fifteenth Report, the Commission described the role of competition, and thus of Article 81(1), as preserving 'the freedom and right of initiative of the individual economic operators' and fostering 'the spirit of enterprise'. Thus for the Commission the protection of rivalry and the freedom of action of the parties to the agreement (as well as those third parties affected by it) has been, until very recently, an end in itself.

In practice this philosophy often led to a legalistic examination of the clauses in agreements **3.133** to identify whether restraints had been placed on the commercial conduct of the parties or third parties;[231] analysis of economic effects was almost exclusively done under Article 81(3).

Given the nature of most contracts, the impact of this policy was felt most powerfully by those **3.134** entering into vertical agreements which often contained restraints of one sort or another (eg the granting of exclusivity). In this way, the Commission's approach to the concept of a 'restriction of competition' drew thousands of agreements, the vast majority of which were harmless or efficiency-enhancing, into the scope of Article 81(1).

This effect was strengthened by the determination of the Community institutions to create **3.135** and sustain the Single Market. The competition rules were seen as an important way of preventing firms from establishing barriers to trade and allowing consumers to purchase freely from anywhere within the EC.[232] As a result agreements which potentially harmed the Single Market were found to fall foul of Article 81 even if, in certain cases, their prohibition hurt consumers directly.[233] However, the Single Market objective also reinforced the scepticism of the Commission towards all vertical agreements containing territorial restrictions.

---

[230] Möschel, 'Competition Policy from an Ordo Point of View' in Peacock and Willgerodt (eds), *German Neo-liberals and the Social Market Economy* (Macmillan, 1989).

[231] See, for example, Barry E Hawk, 'System Failures: Vertical Restraints and EC Competition Law' 32 CML Rev 973, 977 (1995).

[232] See for example, D Deacon, 'Vertical Restraints Under EU Competition Law: New Directions 1995' in Fordham Corp. L. Inst. 1996 (Barry Hawk, ed), pp 307, 309.

[233] See for example the *Distillers Company Limited, Conditions of Sale and Price Terms* [1978] OJ L50/16.

3.136 These attitudes began to change with the adoption of the Green Paper on Vertical Agreements in EC Competition Policy in 1996 [234] as economic analysis increasingly came to be at the forefront of the Commission's activities. This culminated in 2004 with the Commission stating explicitly in its *Guidelines on the application of Article 81(3) of the Treaty* ('Article 81(3) Guidelines' hereinafter) that the 'objective of Article 81 is to protect competition on the market as a means of enhancing consumer welfare and of ensuring an efficient allocation of resources'.[235] Although much of the policy had already been developed in preceding documents such as the Commission's *Guidelines on Vertical Restraints*[236] and its *Guidelines on the applicability of Article 81 of the EC Treaty to horizontal cooperation agreements*,[237] this bold statement confirmed that nothing less than a seismic shift had taken place in the enforcement of Article 81. Today, for example, for the Commission to find an agreement to be restrictive by effect 'it must affect actual or potential competition to such an extent that on the relevant market negative effects on prices, output, innovation or the variety or quality of goods and services can be expected with a reasonable degree of probability . . . it is not sufficient in itself that the agreement restricts the freedom of action of one or more of the parties'.[238]

3.137 More recently, in *GSK*,[239] the CFI placed consumer welfare at the centre of its analysis. It held that 'the objective assigned to Article 81(1) EC . . . is to prevent undertakings, by restricting competition between themselves or with third parties, *from reducing the welfare of the final consumer for the products in question*' (emphasis added). Echoing to some extent the Article 81(3) Guidelines, the Court went on to hold that a key issue for the application of Article 81(1) was the 'repercussions' which an agreement 'has or may have on one or other of the parameters of competition, such as the quantity in which a product is supplied or the price at which it is sold, that provides evidence of such a restriction'.[240]

3.138 These developments are of course welcome and, arguably, long overdue. However, for a number of reasons, practitioners will need to treat them with at least a degree of caution. First whilst an increasing number of commentaries[241] have reinterpreted some of the existing case law in line with the approach set out in recent Commission policy statements, many[242]

---

[234] COM(96) 721, January 1997.

[235] Communication from the Commission, 'Guidelines on the application of Article 81(3) of the Treaty' [2004] OJ C101/97 (27.4.2004), para 13.

[236] Commission Notice, 'Guidelines on Vertical Restraints' [2000] OJ C291/1 (13.10.2000).

[237] Commission Notice, 'Guidelines on the applicability of Article 81 of the EC Treaty to horizontal cooperation agreements' [2001] OJ C3/2 (6.1.2001).

[238] See Commission's 'Guidelines on the application of Article 81(3) of the Treaty' [2004] OJ C101/97, para 24 and n 31.

[239] Case T-168/01 *GlaxoSmithKline Services v Commission*, judgment of 27 September 2006, para 118.

[240] ibid, para 167.

[241] See for example Chapter 2 of the first edition of this book; see also Nazzini, 'Article 81 EC between time present and time past: a normative critique of "restriction of competition" in EU law' [2006] CML Rev 43: 497–53; Odudu, 'Interpreting Article 81(1): Demonstrating Restrictive effect' 26 EL Rev (2001) 261, 271–272.

[242] See, for example, Giorgio Monti, *European Competition Policy* (Cambridge: Cambridge University Press, 2007, forthcoming); Bellamy and Child, *European Community Law of Competition* (6th edn, Oxford: Oxford University Press, 2007, forthcoming); Butterworths *Competition Law* (December 2005); Whish, *Competition Law* (5th edn, LexisNexis Butterworths, 2003); Pietro Manzini, 'The European Rule of Reason-Crossing the Sea of Doubt' (2002) 8 ECLR 392.

(arguably the majority) continue to provide a more traditional interpretation of the case law.[243] Second, and perhaps more importantly from a practitioner's perspective, the policy reforms initiated by the 1996 Green Paper on Vertical Agreements have not, as yet, been endorsed by the ECJ. Nor have they resulted in a slew of Commission decisions or CFI judgments which have plainly adopted the new approach—*GSK* is, in fact, one of only a small number of cases in which a European Court has *explicitly* applied a consumer welfare test under Article 81.[244] Indeed it can be argued with some force that in at least one recent case [245] the CFI relied on an ordo-liberal type approach to reach its conclusions.

Given all this, practitioners would be well-advised to consider the factors highlighted above **3.139** and below when counselling clients until the new approach has been confirmed by the ECJ. Four points in particular are worth highlighting in this regard.

First, whilst the European Courts have, in recent years, shown much greater willingness to **3.140** overturn parallel import decisions[246] (and the Commission has sought to rationalise its Single Market objective on economic, rather than political, grounds[247] thereby allowing itself greater flexibility in such cases)[248] it is still very likely that absolute territorial protection will, in most circumstances, fall foul of Article 81 even if strong countervailing efficiencies exist.[249]

Second, the Commission and the European Courts continue to look unfavourably on cer- **3.141** tain kinds of agreements if their duration is considered to be excessive. Thus, for example, an obligation or incentive scheme exceeding five years under which a buyer agrees to purchase all (or nearly all) its requirements on a particular market from a particular supplier will, in most cases, fall foul of Article 81 without requiring the effects analysis set out in paragraph 3.136 above to be carried out.[250]

---

[243] This may of course be more a reflection of the date of publication of a number of these books and articles—many were written prior to the adoption of the Art 81(3) Guidelines. That said, as noted above, the Art 81(3) Guidelines were merely the culmination of a policy decision which was clear from the time of the adoption of the Guidelines on the applicability of Art 81 of the EC Treaty to horizontal cooperation agreements in 2001 and also, arguably though less explicitly, from the Guidelines on Vertical Restraints in 1999.

[244] See Case 28/77 *Tepea v Commission* [1978] ECR 1391, para 56; Joined Cases T-213/01 and T-214/01 *Osterreichische Postsparkasse and Bank für Arbeit und Wirtschaft v Commission* (judgment of 7 June 2006, para 115); and Joined Cases 56/64 and 58/64 *Consten and Grundig v Commission* [1966] ECR 299, which also refer to consumer welfare in a less forthright manner.

[245] Case T-112/99 *Métropole Télévision v Commission* [2001] ECR II-2459; see Pietro Manzini, 'The European Rule of Reason—crossing the sea of doubt' [2002] ECLR 392; see also Monti (2007, forthcoming).

[246] See for example Case T-41/96 *Bayer v Commission* [2000] ECR II-3383; Case T-168/01 *GlaxoSmithKline Services v Commission* (judgment of 27 September 2006)

[247] In para 13 of its Guidelines on the application of Art 81(3) of the Treaty [2004] OJ C101/97, the Commission states that 'preservation of an open single market promotes an efficient allocation of resources throughout the Community for the benefit of consumers'.

[248] The most obvious example of a slight relaxation in the Commission's approach to absolute territorial protection is rule 10 in para 119 of the Guidelines on Vertical Restraints. This states that '... vertical restraints linked to opening up new product or geographic markets in general do not restrict competition. This rule holds, irrespective of the market share of the company, for two years after the first putting on the market of the product. It applies to all non-hardcore vertical restraints and, in the case of a new geographic market, to restrictions on active and *passive sales* ...' (emphasis added).

[249] See para 46 of the Art 81(3) Guidelines and Case 258/78 *Nungesser* [1982] ECR 2015, para 77. See also F.3(a) and section B(3) of Chapter 9.

[250] See Commission's 'Guidelines on Vertical Restraints' OJ [2000] C 291/1, para 141.

3.142 Third, the Commission and the European Courts share the view that agreements which restrict intra-brand competition do not fall outside the scope of Article 81(1) merely because they increase inter-brand competition.[251] Though this is only likely to be of practical relevance when market shares are above 30 per cent,[252] it underlines the view that the Community institutions continue to see merit in protecting, albeit to a significantly lesser degree than in the past, the process (or as one Commission official has put it the 'conditions')[253] of competition rather than focusing exclusively on the direct or probable economic effects of agreements. This means that in certain circumstances agreements which have a neutral or even *net positive* effect on consumer welfare and allocative efficiency can fall within the scope of Article 81(1).

3.143 Fourth, and perhaps most importantly from a private enforcement perspective, it will take time for the new policy to be reflected in the case law of the European Courts and the decisional practice of the European Commission. As such the impact of existing jurisprudence which, to varying degrees, was influenced by the Commission's former emphasis on 'free' competition, will continue to be felt before national courts. It is to be hoped however that whilst acknowledging the old case law, national judges will feel sufficient confident to apply the consumer welfare standard adopted in *GSK*[254] and the approach enunciated by the Commission in the various notices and guidelines that have been issued since 1999 (when the new Vertical Block Exemption Regulation[255] and Guidelines on Vertical Restraints were adopted). Failure to do so would create a significant and damaging divergence with the approach that will be taken by the Commission/national competition authorities to cases under Article 81.[256]

3.144 The remainder of this section will consider the concept of a restriction of competition in more detail. Five preliminary points are worth noting at the outset. First, for an agreement or concerted practice to be caught by Article 81(1) it must have the *object or effect* of preventing, restricting, or distorting competition. Object and effect are alternative and not cumulative requirements.[257] Thus if an agreement restricts competition by object, it is not necessary to show that it is also restrictive by effect or vice versa.[258] Second, nothing turns on the terms

---

[251] See the Commission's 'Guidelines on the Application of Article 81(3) of the Treaty' [2004] OJ C101/97, para 17 where the Commission states that 'Article 81(1) prohibits restrictions of both inter-brand competition and intra-brand competition.' See also Case T-112/99 *Métropole Télévision (M6), Suez-Lyonnaise des Eaux, France Télécom and Télévision française 1 SA (TF1) v Commission* [2001] ECR II-2459 and the discussion of this at para 3.248 et seq below.

[252] See Commission's 'Guidelines on Vertical Restraints' OJ [2000] C 291/1, para 21. Below 30%, most restrictions are covered by the safe harbour created by the Vertical Block Exemption Regulation.

[253] For an excellent discussion of the evolving role of economic analysis under Art 81(1), see Vincent Verouden, 'Vertical Agreements and Article 81(1) EC' Antitrust Law Journal [2003] Vol 71 No 2, 525–575.

[254] Case T-168/01 *GlaxoSmithKline Services v Commission*, judgment of 27 September 2006, para 118.

[255] Commission Regulation 2790/99/EC on the application of Art 81(3) of the Treaty to categories of vertical agreements and concerted practices [1999] OJ L336/21 (29.12.1999).

[256] In a recent judgment (Case No 1041/2/1/04 *The British Horseracing Board v OFT*, para189) the UK's Competition Appeals Tribunal (CAT) considered whether the Office of Fair Trading had shown that the price in question 'was' above the competitive level. Though part of the OFT's case, it can be argued with some force that, in requiring the OFT to demonstrate an actual, rather than a likely effect on price the CAT went too far.

[257] Case 56/65 *Société Technique Minière v Maschinenbau Ulm GmbH* [1996] ECR 235, at 249.

[258] Case 56/65 *Société Technique Minière v Maschinenbau Ulm GmbH* [1996] ECR 235; Case 45/85 *Verband der Sachversicherer v Commission* [1987] ECR 405.

prevention, restriction and distortion. Third, whilst Article 81(1) does not contain the word 'appreciable', it is clear from the case law of the European Courts and the administrative practice of the Commission that a restriction of competition will not fall within the scope of Article 81(1) unless it has an *appreciable* impact on competition in the relevant market.[259] Fourth, Article 81 is applicable both to horizontal and vertical agreements.[260] Fifth, Article 81(1) applies not only to restrictions of actual but also potential competition.[261]

(a) Restriction by Object

Agreements[262] which are restriction by object fall within the scope of Article 81(1). The ECJ has stated clearly on several occasions that, once an anti-competitive object has been shown, 'there is no need to take account of the concrete effect of an agreement'.[263] Thus if the object of an agreement is to fix prices it will not be necessary to show that actual prices were in fact affected. Similarly, arguments which purport to show that such agreements may also have pro-competitive effects will not be considered under Article 81(1).[264]   **3.145**

However, no agreement is automatically restrictive by object: agreements must be assessed in their legal and economic context.[265] In the types of cases listed in paragraphs 3.149 and 3.150 this can usually be done on a relatively cursory basis. However, a more detailed examination of the facts underlying an agreement and the specific circumstances in which it operates may sometimes be required.[266] In *GSK*[267] the CFI held that whilst an agreement to limit parallel trade 'must in principle' be considered to have as its object the restriction of competition, that would be the case only in so far as the agreement may be presumed to deprive consumers of the advantages of effective competition in terms of supply or price.[268] In *GSK* the Commission had failed to examine the specific and essential characteristics of the sector, in particular the fact that the prices of the products in question were fixed by Member States. It could not therefore 'be taken for granted at the outset that parallel trade tends to reduce [. . .] prices and thus to increase the welfare of final consumers'. Consequently, the Commission's conclusion that the agreement 'must be considered to be prohibited by Article 81(1) EC in so far it has as its object the restriction of parallel trade, cannot be upheld'.[269]   **3.146**

Similarly in *SPRL Louis Erauw-Jacquery v La Hesbignonne SC*, the ECJ held, relying on *Nungesser v Commission*,[270] that an agreement prohibiting a licensee from exporting, directly   **3.147**

---

[259] Case 56/65 *Société Technique Minière v Maschinenbau Ulm GmbH* [1996] ECR 235.
[260] Joined Cases 56 and 58/64 *Consten and Grundig v Commission* [1966] ECR 299.
[261] Case T-504/93 *Tiércé-Ladbroke v Commission* [1997] ECR II-923.
[262] As noted in n 227, the term 'agreement' should be read as covering concerted practices and decisions of associations.
[263] Joined Cases 56 and 58/64 *Consten and Grundig v Commission* [1966] ECR 299.
[264] Cases T-374/94 etc *European Night Services v Commission* [1998] ECR II-3141, para 136; see also Case 19/77 *Miller International Schallplatten v Commission* [1978] ECR 131.
[265] See Joined Cases 56 and 58/64 *Consten and Grundig v Commission* [1966] ECR 299. See also, for example, Joined Cases 29/83 and 30/83, *CRAM and Rheinzink* [1984] ECR 1679, para 26, and Joined Cases 96/82 and others, *ANSEAUNAVEWA* [1983] ECR 3369, paras 23–25.
[266] Para 22 of the Commission's 'Guidelines on the application of Article 81(3) of the Treaty' [2004] OJ C101/97.
[267] Case T-168/01 *GlaxoSmithKline Services v Commission*, judgment of 27 September 2006.
[268] ibid, para 121.
[269] ibid, para 147; see also paras 33–134.
[270] Case 258/78 [1982] ECR 2515.

or indirectly, certain varieties of cereal seeds protected by plant breeders' rights did not infringe Article 81(1) given the costs and risks involved in developing seed varieties.[271] Likewise in *Javico v Yves Saint Laurent Parfums*, the export ban imposed on distributors in Russia and Ukraine did not have as its object the restriction of competition within the Community though it could be restrictive by effect.[272]

3.148   It is important to note however that these cases are not authority for the proposition that an extensive analysis of actual or likely effects of an agreement is necessary for it to be restrictive by object. In fact, in the vast majority of cases, the types of agreements listed in paragraphs 3.149–3.150 below will easily be found to fall within Article 81(1)—cases such as *GSK* are distinguishable on their facts and do not undermine the basic position set out by the ECJ in *Consten and Grundig*. Indeed in *GSK* itself, the CFI noted that the factual matrix of the case was 'largely unprecedented': 'the prices of the products in question . . . *unlike the prices of other consumer goods* . . . such as sports items or motor cycles, are . . . to a significant extent shielded from the free play of supply and demand' (emphasis added).[273] This meant that it could not 'be presumed that parallel trade has an impact on the prices charged to the final consumers', a point the Commission itself had implicitly noted.[274]

(i) Types of Agreement Typically Restrictive by Object

3.149   Other chapters in this book will identify and cover in detail the types of clauses or activities which have been deemed to be restrictive by object.[275] For present purposes it is sufficient to note that agreements between competitors[276] which have the obvious consequence of price fixing, market sharing or collective exclusive dealing[277] (more commonly known as 'group boycotts') will, almost certainly, fall into this category. In the context of a cartel, the exchange of commercially sensitive information is also highly likely to be caught by object;[278] in fact in *Aalborg Portland A/S v Commission*,[279] the ECJ confirmed the CFI's finding that though the information in that case had been 'in the public domain or related to historical and purely statistical prices' its exchange had infringed because it 'underpinne[d] another anti-competitive arrangement. That interpretation is based on the consideration that the circulation of price information limited to the members of an anti-competitive cartel has the effect of increasing transparency on a market where competition is already much reduced and of facilitating control of compliance with the cartel by its members'.

---

[271] Case 27/87 *SPRL Louis Erauw-Jacquery v La Hesbignonne SC* [1988] ECR 1919, paras 10–11.

[272] Case C-306/96 *Javico International and Javico AG v Yves Saint Laurent Parfums SA (YSLP)* [1998] ECR I-1983, para 19.

[273] Case T-168/01 *GlaxoSmithKline v Commission*, judgment of 27 September 2006, para 133.

[274] ibid, para 135.

[275] See, for example, B.3 in Chapter 9 (hardcore restrictions in vertical agreements), 7.260 (joint selling agreements), 8.50 (exchange of confidential information).

[276] See Chapter 7 on horizontal agreements.

[277] See, for instance, *Nederlandse Federative Vereniging voor de Groothandel op Elektrotechnisch Gebied and Technische Unie (FEG and TU)* [2000] L39/1.

[278] See for example Cases T-25/95 etc *Cimentaries v Commission* [2000] ECR II-491.

[279] Joined Cases C-204/00 P, C-205/00 P, C-211/00 P, C-213/00 P, C-217/00 P and C-219/00 P *Aalborg Portland A/S v Commission* [2004] ECR-I 123, para 281.

For vertical agreements,[280] only those which impede parallel trade within the Community[281] **3.150** or enforce resale price maintenance[282] are likely to be considered restrictive by object.[283] In addition the Commission's Guidelines on Vertical Restraints[284] state that an obligation or incentive scheme exceeding five years under which a buyer agrees to purchases all (or nearly all) its requirements on a particular market from a particular supplier will, in most cases, fall foul of Article 81 without requiring an effects analysis.[285]

It is important to stress that few types of agreement have as their object the restriction of **3.151** competition; conversely agreements other than those listed above may be restrictive by object: paragraphs 3.149 and 3.150 merely list those which the Community institutions have thus far deemed to fall into this category.

Object restrictions are those which have by 'their very nature the potential for restricting **3.152** competition'[286]—the subjective intent of the parties 'is a relevant factor'[287] but is not, in any way, determinative. Thus agreements can be restrictive by object even if the parties to it are able to show that restricting competition was not their aim, or that they had other laudable motives.[288] Conversely the Commission and the European Courts cannot find that a particular agreement has as its object a restriction of competition merely because the aim of the parties is to restrict competition.

Typically object restrictions are those which, *prima facie*, do not have any significant beneficial **3.153** effects but 'have such a high potential of negative effects on competition that it is unnecessary for the purposes of applying Article 81(1) to demonstrate any actual effects on the market.'[289]

In the Article 81(3) Guidelines the Commission has identified the following factors as **3.154** being relevant 'in particular' to its assessment of whether an agreement has as its object the restriction of competition:[290]

- 'the content of the agreement and the objective aims pursued by it';
- 'the actual conduct and behaviour of the parties on the market'. According to the Guidelines '[t]he way in which an agreement is actually implemented may reveal a restriction by

---

[280] See section C.7(b) below.

[281] See, eg, Joined Cases 56 and 58/64 *Consten and Grundig v Commission* [1966] ECR 299; Case 19/77 *Miller International Schallplatten v Commission* [1978] ECR 131.

[282] Case 234/83 *SA Binon & Cie v SA Agence et Messageries de la Presse* [1985] ECR 2015, para 44.

[283] This policy is reflected in para 276 of the Green Paper on Vertical Restraints, where it is stated that: 'The policy of treating *resale price maintenance* and *impediments to parallel trade* as serious violations of the competition rules would continue. It is proposed that they be treated as per se contrary to Article 85(1) [now Article 81(1)], as long as the agreement, concerted practice or decision concerned may affect trade between Member States. They are also unlikely to benefit from an exemption under Article 85(3).' See section B(3) of Chapter 9.

[284] See OJ [2000] C 291/1, para 141.

[285] See also section C.7(b) below.

[286] See para 21 of the Commission's 'Guidelines on the application of Article 81(3) of the Treaty' [2004] OJ C101/97; Case 19/77 *Miller International Schallplatten v Commission* [1978] ECR 131.

[287] See para 22 of the Commission's 'Guidelines on the application of Article 81(3) of the Treaty' [2004] OJ C101/97.

[288] See, for example, Joined Cases 96–102, 104, 105, 108 and 110/82 *NV IAZ International Belgium and others v Commission* [1983] ECR 3369.

[289] Para 21 of the Commission's 'Guidelines on the application of Article 81(3) of the Treaty' [2004] OJ C101/97.

[290] See para 22 of the Commission's 'Guidelines on the application of Article 81(3) of the Treaty' [2004] OJ C101/97.

object even where the formal agreement does not contain an express provision to that effect';

- 'the context in which it [the agreement/concerted practice] is (to be) applied' ('the specific circumstances in which it operates').

3.155 No further guidance is however provided in the Article 81(3) Guidelines as to how these factors are to be applied in practice. This is largely because the determination as to whether an agreement or concerted practice is an object restriction is, predominantly, a question of *policy* for the Community institutions.[291] Thus in its Article 81(3) Guidelines the Commission states that in determining its stance it bases itself 'on *experience* showing that restrictions of competition by object are likely to produce negative effects on the market and to jeopardise the objectives pursued by the Community competition rules' (emphasis added). Amongst other things, this 'policy' element means that there is very little room for NCAs or national courts to expand the scope of restrictions caught by object beyond those explicitly identified as such by the European Courts in case law and by the Commission in its Notices and Guidelines (or 'the black clauses'[292] in its block exemptions).

3.156 In practical terms, the importance of the criteria set out above is likely to lie in the flexibility they give the Commission and NCAs to find that a particular agreement (or types of agreements)[293] which, *prima facie*, falls into the categories listed in paragraphs 3.149 and 3.150 above (eg price fixing, market sharing, etc) is not restrictive by object. For example, in *Visa International—Multilateral Exchange Fee*,[294] the fee paid by the acquiring bank to the issuing bank[295] for transactions was set by Visa in the EU and the EEA. The Commission found that the scheme under which this fee was established was an agreement between competitor banks which restricted their freedom to decide their pricing policy.[296] In the vast majority of cases this would be an object restriction as horizontal pricing fixing is usually considered the most heinous of antitrust infringement. However, in the instant case, the Commission expressly stated that the agreement did not have as its object the restriction of competition. This was because the 'objectives' of the scheme were to increase the efficiency and stability of the Visa four-party system and to enable it to compete vigorously with other systems such as the three-party system operated by American Express.[297] Put another way, the Commission decided that agreement was not restrictive by competition given (in the language of the Article 81(3) Guidelines) its 'objective aims'[298] and the nature of the product and the market concerned.

---

[291] See in this respect Whish, '*Competition Law*' (5th edn, LexisNexis Butterworths, 2003), p 112.

[292] See in particular para 11 of Commission Notice on agreements of minor importance [2001] OJ C 368/12; Arts 4(a) and 4(b) of Regulation 2790/99; Art 5 of both Regulations 2658/00 and 2790/00.

[293] See for example Art 3 of Regulation (EEC) No 4056/86 in the transport sector, providing for an exemption for price agreements between liner conferences under certain conditions and obligations and Art 4 of Regulation (EEC) No 1617/93, providing for a group exemption for price agreements between airlines with regard to IATA interlineable fares: OJ L 155/18 [1993].

[294] *Visa International—Multilateral Exchange Fee* [2002] OJ L318/17.

[295] The issuing bank is the bank issuing the Visa card to the consumer while the acquiring bank is the bank which agrees the terms for acceptance of the Visa card and handles the transaction with the merchant.

[296] *Visa International—Multilateral Exchange Fee* [2002] OJ L318/17, para 66.

[297] ibid, para 69.

[298] See para 22 of the Commission's 'Guidelines on the application of Article 81(3) of the Treaty' [2004] OJ C101/97.

However care should be taken by practitioners in applying the criteria set out above—in most cases claims from the parties as to the legitimate 'objective aims' of the agreement are unlikely to be successful. For example in *IAZ International Belgium v Commission*[299] the parties challenged a decision in which the Commission had held that the object of an agreement between them was to restrict competition. The parties were manufacturers and exclusive importers of washing machines affiliated to certain trade organisations in Belgium. They had agreed that one of them would carry out checks on appliances and grant a conformity label to machines fulfilling the relevant criteria. According to the parties the purpose of the agreement was to monitor the conformity of washing machines in order to preserve the quality of drinking water. However, whilst acknowledging this, the Commission had, in its decision, concluded that the agreements also hindered parallel trade as it 'enable[d] sole importers to check parallel imports and to take any other restrictive measures to prevent them'.[300] The ECJ held that, notwithstanding the fact that the agreement pursued the objective of protecting public health and reducing the cost of conformity checks, its object was to restrict competition within the common market. The ECJ further held that it did not matter for this purpose that it had not been established that the intention of all the parties was to restrict competition.

3.157

(b) Restriction by Object and Appreciability

An agreement which, *prima facie*, has as its object the restriction of competition can nevertheless escape the prohibition of Article 81(1) if it has only an 'insignificant effect'[301] on the market or on trade.[302] Thus in *Società Italiana Vetro, Fabbrica Pisana and PPG Vernante Pennitalia v Commission*[303] the CFI rejected the Commission's submission that the evidence of the agreements between the parties was so unambiguous and explicit that any investigation whatsoever into the structure of the market had been entirely superfluous. While acknowledging that the Commission was not required to discuss in its decisions all the arguments raised by undertakings, the CFI held that the Commission ought to have examined more fully the structure and the functioning of the market in order to show why the conclusions drawn by the applicants were groundless.[304] The ECJ affirmed this position in *Javico* where it held that: '. . . even an agreement imposing absolute territorial protection may escape the prohibition laid down in Article 85 [now Article 81] if it affects the market only insignificantly, regard being had to the weak position of the persons concerned on the market in the products in question.'[305]

3.158

What is an '*insignificant effect*'? As a preliminary point it is worth noting that the Commission is not required to prove that an object restriction has or even could have the effect of raising

3.159

---

[299] Joined Cases 96–102, 104, 105, 108 and 110/82 *NV IAZ International Belgium and others v Commission* [1983] ECR 3369; see also, eg, *AROW/BNIC* [1982] OJ L379/1.

[300] *NAVEWA-ANSEAU* [1982] OJ L167/39, para 56.

[301] Case 5/69 *Völk v Vervaecke* [1969] ECR 295, paras 5/7.

[302] Not all commentators accept this view. Note, in respect of vertical restrictions, that in many cases the appreciability of the restriction appears to be assumed, with the analysis of appreciability concentrating upon effect on trade between Member States: see section B.4 of Chapter 9.

[303] Joined Cases T-68/89, T-77/89 and T-78/89 [1992] ECR II-1403.

[304] ibid, para 159.

[305] Case C-306/96 *Javico International v Yves Saint Laurent Parfums* [1998] ECR I-1983, paras 15–17.

prices or restricting output. European competition law assumes that object restrictions will potentially have this effect.[306] Rather the issue is whether the effect is likely to be of sufficient magnitude to affect competition appreciably. For object restrictions this is largely assessed with reference to the market position of the parties.[307] In its submission in *Völk v Vervaecke*,[308] a case concerning absolute territorial protection, the Commission stated that the production of washing machines by Mr Völk's company represented 0.08 per cent of the total production of the common market and 0.2 per cent of production in the Federal Republic of Germany. Its market share of sales in Belgium and Luxembourg, the territory of its exclusive distributor Vervaecke, was approximately 0.6 per cent. On the basis of these small market shares the Commission accepted that the agreement did not appreciably restrict competition. On the other hand in *Miller*,[309] which concerned a territorial restriction by object, the ECJ found that the company concerned, which had a market share of the German market in sound recordings which varied between 5 per cent and 6 per cent, could not be compared with the undertakings in the *Völk* case and that Article 81(1) was infringed.

3.160 These cases suggest that for *vertical* restrictions, shares below 1 per cent are likely to be 'insignificant' while above 5 per cent, the effect is likely to be appreciable and Article 81(1) is likely to apply. Between 1 per cent and 5 per cent is best described as a grey area.

3.161 As for *horizontal* cases, it seems highly unlikely that, even if applicable, market shares in this region would ever be relevant from a practical perspective: it is difficult to conceive of price fixing or market sharing agreements between entities with combined market shares in single digits on a properly defined market. In any event, given the general tenor of the case law on cartels,[310] it would seem implausible that the European Courts would permit cartels to escape the Article 81 prohibition on the basis of low market shares alone.

(c) The Commission's Approach to Appreciability in Object Cases

3.162 It is worth noting that through its Notices, Guidelines and Block Exemptions, the Commission has, arguably, conveyed its desire for a stricter approach than that set out in the

---

[306] See para 21 of the Commission's 'Guidelines on the application of Article 81(3) of the Treaty' [2004] OJ C101/97.

[307] It is worth noting that whilst the appreciability doctrine is usually thought of in market share terms, it can also not apply if the restriction itself is insignificant. For example in joined cases C-180/98–C-184/98 *Pavel Pavlov v Stichting Pensioenfonds Medische Specialisten* ECR 2000 I-06451, the ECJ found that a decision to set up a pension fund entrusted with the management of a supplementary pension scheme was not an appreciable restriction. This was because the pension fund produced 'restrictive effects only in relation to one cost factor of the services offered by self-employed medical specialists . . . which is insignificant in comparison with other factors, such as medical fees or the cost of medical equipment. The cost of the supplementary pension scheme has only a marginal and indirect influence on the final cost of the services offered by self-employed medical specialists'. In *UEFA's broadcasting regulations* the Commission decided that regulations which prevented the live transmission of matches at certain times, in order to protect amateur participation in sport and to encourage live attendance at football matches, was not an appreciable restriction. See also *Irish Banks' Standing Committee* [1986] OJ L295/28; *Visa International* [2001] OJ L293/24, on appeal Case T-28/02 *First Data Corp v Commission* (judgment pending); *Identrus* [2001] OJ L249/12.

[308] Case 5/69 [1969] ECR 295.

[309] Case 19/77 *Miller International Schallplatten GmbH v Commission* [1978] ECR 131.

[310] See para 3.149 above.

case law discussed above.[311] Unlike the ECJ's case law, these documents and legislative instruments provide no[312] 'safe harbours' for object restrictions. For example, the Commission expressly states that its *Notice on agreements of minor importance* (which establishes market share thresholds below which, in the Commission's view, there is no appreciable restriction of competition)[313] does not apply to agreements containing the following 'hardcore' restrictions:[314]

1. as regards agreements between competitors as defined in point 7,[315] restrictions which directly or indirectly, in isolation or in combination with other factors under the control of the parties, have as their object or effect;[316]
    (a) the fixing of prices when selling the products to third parties;
    (b) the limitation of output or sales;
    (c) the allocation or markets or customers;
2. as regards agreements between non-competitors as defined in point 7,[317] restrictions which, directly or indirectly, in isolation or in combination with other factors under the control of the parties, have as their object:
    (a) the restriction of the buyer's ability to determine its sales price, without prejudice to the possibility of the supplier imposing a maximum sale price or recommending a sale price, provided that they do not amount to a fixed or minimum sale price as a result of pressure from or incentives offered by, any of the parties;
    (b) the restriction of the territory into which, or of the customers to whom, the buyer may sell the contract goods or services, except the following restrictions which are not hardcore—

---

[311] But see Case 30/78 *Distillers Co v Commission* [1980] 3 CML R 121, where the ECJ concluded that an agreement affecting the distribution of Pimms was of importance, notwithstanding its small market share, because its producer Distillers occupied an important position on the market for drinks generally. Similarly in Cases 100–103/80 *Musique Diffusion Française v Commission* [1983] ECR 1825, the ECJ held that a concerted practice was not within the de minimis doctrine where the parties' market shares were small but the market was a fragmented one, their market shares exceeded those of most competitors and their turnover figures were high.

[312] Save for agreements between small and medium-sized undertakings, as identified in the Annex to Commission Recommendation 96/280/EC (OJ L107/4, 30.4.96), which it has been acknowledged are rarely capable of appreciably affecting trade between Member States. Small and medium undertakings are currently identified in that recommendation as undertakings which have fewer than 250 employees and have either an annual turnover not exceeding EUR 40 million or an annual balance-sheet total not exceeding EUR 27 million. It should be noted that, according to the Commission's Notice on agreements of minor importance (footnote 3), the recommendation will be revised and that 'it is envisaged to increase the annual turnover threshold from EUR 40 million to EUR 50 million and the annual balance-sheet total threshold from EUR 27 million to EUR 43 million.'

[313] OJ C368/13 (22.12.2001). See para 3.237 *et seq* below.

[314] Point 11 of the Notice on agreements of minor importance. These restrictions essentially equate to the 'object' restrictions noted in paragraph 3.149 above. See also section B.3 in Chapter 9 (hardcore restrictions in vertical agreements), 7.260 (joint selling agreements), 8.50 (exchange of confidential information).

[315] Competitors are defined as undertakings which are actual or potential competitors on any relevant market affected by the agreement (see point 7(a) of the Notice on agreements of minor importance).

[316] The Notice on agreements of minor importance will apply, however, to situations of joint production with or without joint distribution: see Art 5, para 2 of Commission Regulation (EC) No 2658/2000 (on specialisation agreements) and Art 5, para 2 of Commission Regulation (EC) No 2659/2000 on (research and development agreements), OJ L304/5.12.2000, pp 3 and 7 respectively.

[317] Non-competitors are defined as undertakings which are not actual or potential competitors on any relevant market affected by the agreement (see point 7(b) of the Notice on agreements of minor importance).

— the restriction of active sales into the exclusive territory or to an exclusive customer group reserved to the supplier or allocated by the supplier to another
buyer, where such a restriction does not limit sales by the customers of the buyer,

— the restriction of sales to end users by a buyer operating at the wholesale level of
trade,

— the restriction of sales to unauthorised distributors by the members of a selective distribution system, and

— the restriction of the buyer's ability to sell components, supplied for the purposes of incorporation, to customers who would use them to manufacture the
same type of goods as those produced by the supplier;

(c) the restriction of active or passive sales to end users by members of a selective distribution system operating at the retail level of trade, without prejudice to the possibility of
prohibiting a member of the system from operating out of an unauthorised place of
establishment;

(d) the restriction of cross-supplies between distributors within a selective distribution
system, including between distributors operating at different levels of trade;

(e) the restriction agreed between a supplier of components and a buyer who incorporates those components, which limits the supplier's ability to sell the components as
spare parts to end users or to repairers or other service providers not entrusted by the
buyer with the repair or servicing of its goods;

3. as regards agreements between competitors, where the competitors operate, for the purposes of the agreement, at a different level of the production or distribution chain, any
of the hardcore restrictions listed in 1. and 2. above.

3.163 The approach taken by the Commission in the *Notice on agreements of minor importance*
means, for instance, that the Notice would not apply to a case where market shares were akin
to those in *Völk*.[318] Similarly the vertical and horizontal block exemptions do not apply to
agreements which contain even one black listed clause[319]—although Block Exemptions
are only relevant in the context of Article 81(3), they indicate the Commission's overall
view, and the message it wishes to convey, as to the seriousness of particular restrictions.

3.164 On the other hand, as a matter of prosecutorial discretion it is unlikely that the Commission
(or indeed NCAs applying Article 81) would allocate resources to cases in which market
shares were in single digits. Such considerations are of course not of direct relevance to cases
brought before national courts by private litigants.[320] Given the general tenor of the case law
and the implicit policy stance taken by the Commission in its guidelines/block exemptions,

---

[318] Case 5/69 [1969] ECR 295.

[319] For example, when a technology transfer agreement contains a hardcore restriction of competition as
listed in Art 4 of Regulation 772/2004/EC, the agreement as a whole falls outside the scope of the block exemption: Commission's Guidelines on the application of Art 81 of the EC Treaty to technology transfer agreements
[2004] OJ C101/2 (27.4.2004) para 75. For further details, see section C(5) in Chapter 10 (Intellectual
Property). Similarly, Art 5(1) of Commission Regulation 2659/2000/EC on the application of Art 81(3) of
the Treaty to categories of research and development agreements [2000] OJ L304/7 (5.12.2000) (see section
7.125 of Chapter 7 (Horizontal Agreements)) and Art 4(1) of Commission Regulation 1400/2002/EC on the
application of Art 81(3) of the Treaty to categories of vertical agreements and concerted practices in the motor
vehicle sector [2002] OJ L203/30 (1.8.2002) (see section 15.23 of Chapter 15 (Motor Vehicles)).

[320] They may, however, be one of the considerations taken into account by national courts when assessing
the likelihood of anti-competitive harm, perhaps on applications for summary judgment.

it is highly likely that the rules would be applied strictly. Thus, in summary, it would seem fair to conclude that, even for companies with little market power, agreements containing restrictions by object run a very serious risk of infringing Article 81(1).

(d) Restriction by Effect [321]

3.165 If an agreement does not have the object of restricting competition 'the consequences of the agreement should then be considered and for it to be caught by the prohibition it is then necessary to find that those factors are present which show that competition has in fact been prevented or restricted or distorted to an appreciable extent. The competition in question must be understood within the *actual context* in which it would occur *in the absence of the agreement in dispute*'[322] (emphasis added).

3.166 In other words, if there is appreciably less competition as a result of the agreement, Article 81(1) will apply. This apparently simple formulation, however, masks a heated debate. What does 'appreciably less competition' mean and how is it to be measured? This is such a key point of analysis that it merits a separate section its own, as follows immediately below.

(8) Restriction by Effect

3.167 As noted in section C.7 above, the Commission centred its assessment,[323] until fairly recently,[324] on the impact of the agreement on the:

- process of rivalry between the parties and/or from third parties through either foreclosure of potential new entrants or hindrance of existing players in the market; and
- Single Market.

3.168 In doing so it focused, to varying degrees, on the extent to which agreements limited the commercial freedom of action of the parties or third parties. For example, in its Twenty-Third Report on Competition Policy the Commission explained that an exclusive distribution agreement 'is viewed as restricting competition since it *limits the parties' freedom of action in the territory covered*' (emphasis added).[325]

(a) European Courts Broadly Endorsed the Commission's Traditional Approach

3.169 The impact of agreements on the process of rivalry, whether between the parties to the agreement and/or from third parties, has also been an important feature of the case law of

---

[321] This chapter focuses on the broad analytical framework established by the Commission in its policy statements and relevant decisional practice. It will also examine the case law of the European Courts from this perspective. Chapters 7 and 9 will consider the detailed framework set out in the guidelines on horizontal co-operation agreements and on vertical restraints respectively for analysis of the competitive impact of various types of agreements.

[322] Case 56/65 *Société Technique Minière v Maschinenbau Ulm GmbH* [1996] ECR 235, at 249 and 250; this formulation was repeated most recently in Case T-328/03 O2 (Germany) *GmbH & Co. v Commission*, judgment of 2 May 2006, at para 68.

[323] See for example: *Bayer/Gist Brocades* [1975] OJ L30/13; *Vacuum Interrupters Ltd* [1977] OJ 48/32 (section II, para 17); *Rennet* [1980] OJ L51/19; *Carlsberg* [1984] OJ L207/26 (para II(A)(3)(i) and (ii); *VIFKA* [1986] OJ L291/46 (para 12); *Dutch Banks* [1989] OJ L253/1 (para 55); *Twenty-Third Report on Competition Policy* (1993) para 212; *Van den Bergh Foods Limited* [1998] OJ L246/1 (paras 143 and 184); *Eurovision (Métropole)* [2000] L151/18 (para 107).

[324] See section C.9 below.

[325] *Twenty-Third Report on Competition Policy* (1993), para 212.

the European Courts. For example in its 1967 preliminary ruling, *SA Brasserie de Haecht v Consorts Wilkin-Janssen*,[326] the ECJ was asked to consider whether, on the facts of the case, it was necessary to take into account under Article 81(1) 'the simultaneous existence of a large number of contracts of the same type . . .' or whether 'consideration must be limited to an examination of the effects on the market of the said agreements considered in isolation'. The ECJ replied that 'the existence of similar contracts may be taken into consideration for this objective to the extent to which the general body of contracts of this type *is capable of restricting the freedom of trade*' (emphasis added).

3.170 This focus on rivalry is clear even from cases which have traditionally been relied upon by those who see a 'rule of reason'[327] in the jurisprudence of the European Courts. For example, in *Delimitis v Henninger AG*,[328] a preliminary reference case relating to a beer supply agreement, the Court required a detailed economic assessment to be made. However, this was done in order to analyse the impact of the agreement (together with other contracts of the same type) '*on the opportunities of national competitors*, or those from other Member States, *to gain access to the market* . . . or to increase their market share'. The Court held that 'a beer supply agreement is prohibited by Article 85(1) [now Article 81(1)]. . . if two cumulative conditions are met. The first is that . . . it is *difficult for competitors* who could enter the market or increase their market share to gain access to the national market for the distribution of beer in premises for the sale and consumption of drinks. . . The second condition is that the agreement in question must make a significant contribution to the *sealing-off effect* brought about by the totality of those agreements in their economic and legal context' (emphasis added).[329] As in *Brasserie de Haecht*, no assessment as to the likely effect of this foreclosure on market parameters (such as price or output) or weighing up of the pro- and anti-competitive effects was required. The key issue was whether, as a matter of economic reality, the agreements hindered entry of potential competitors or the expansion of existing players.

3.171 A similar conclusion can be drawn from the *European Night Services v Commission* judgment in which the CFI held, referring specifically to *Delimitis*, 'that the examination of conditions of competition is based not only on existing competition between undertakings already present on the relevant market but also on potential competition, *in order to ascertain whether . . . there are real concrete possibilities for the undertakings concerned to compete among themselves or for a new competitor to penetrate the relevant market and compete with the undertakings already established* (Delimitis, cited above, paragraph 21)' (emphasis added).[330] Again the focus was on the impact of the agreement on entry and expansion.

---

[326] Case 23/67 *SA Brasserie de Haecht v Consorts Wilkin-Janssen* [1967] ECR 407.

[327] Whereby the competitive benefits and harms of a practice will be balanced before its legality is determined. For arguments in favour of the use of the rule of reason, see eg Joliet, '*The Rule of Reason in Antitrust Law; American, German and Common Market Laws in Comparative Perspective*' (The Hague: Martinus Nijhoff, 1967); Forrester and Norall, 'The Laicization of Community Law: Self-Help and the Rule of Reason: How competition law is and could be applied' (1984) CML Rev 21; Schechter, 'The Rule of Reason in European Competition Law' Legal Issues of European Integration Vol 2 (1983) at 1.

[328] Case C-234/89 [1991] ECR I-935.

[329] Para 27.

[330] Joined Cases T-374/94, T-375/94, T 384/94 and T-388/94 [1998] ECR II-3141, para 137.

Yet more recently in *Van den Burgh Foods*, the CFI's attention was, once again, on the impact **3.172** of the agreement on the ability of actual or potential competitors to enter or expand. Thus it stated that 'in order to determine whether HB's exclusive distribution agreements fall within the prohibition contained in Article 85(1) it is appropriate . . . to consider whether . . . those agreements cumulatively have the effect of *denying access to that market to new competitors*. If . . . such examination reveals that it is *difficult to gain access to the market*, it is then necessary to assess the extent to which the agreements at issue contribute to the cumulative effect produced, on the basis that only those agreements which make a significant contribution to any partitioning of the market are prohibited' (emphasis added).[331]

The CFI took a similar approach in *Métropole Télévision v Commission*,[332] a case concern- **3.173** ing the pay-TV market in France. The Court upheld the Commission's finding that a clause obliging the parents of a joint venture to supply certain channels exclusively to their subsidiary fell foul of Article 81(1). The Commission had found that whilst these channels did not constitute a type of content that was 'essential for pay-TV', the exclusivity clause denied 'competitors access to attractive programmes'[333] and, as such, had a foreclosure effect sufficient to bring it within the scope of Article 81(1).

However in a more recent judgment,[334] the CFI adopted an approach which appeared to **3.174** focus on the impact of the agreement on the intensity of competition in the market: '[i]n the present case, it cannot therefore be ruled out that a roaming agreement of the type concluded between T-Mobile and O2, instead of restricting competition between network operators, is, on the contrary, capable of enabling, in certain circumstances, the smallest operator to compete with the major players, such as in this case T-Mobile but also D2 Vodafone on the retail market, or even dominant operators, as T-Mobile is on the wholesale market.'[335]

O2 is a potentially significant development in the CFI's case law, particularly when **3.175** combined with the CFI's focus in GSK[336] on consumer welfare. However, as noted below,[337] it is possible to distinguish O2, at least to some extent, on its facts and in light of some of the language used by the CFI.

(b) European Courts have Modified the Traditional Approach in a Number of Important Ways

As noted above, the European Courts have broadly endorsed the Commission's traditional **3.176** interpretation of the concept of a 'restriction of competition'. However, in several important judgments they modified the approach in a number of significant respects. Most importantly, they held that restrictions of rivalry were not, in and of themselves, restrictions of competition for the purposes of Article 81(1)—rather, restrictions had to be

---

[331] Case T-65/98 [2003] ECR II-4653, para 83.
[332] Case T-112/99 [2001] ECR II-2459.
[333] *TPS* [1999] OJ L90/6, para 107. See also discussion below at para 3.202.
[334] Case T-328/03 *O2 (Germany) GmbH & Co. v Commission,* judgment of 2 May 2006.
[335] ibid, para 109.
[336] Case T-168/01 *GlaxoSmithKline Services v Commission* (judgment of 27 September 2006). See also paras 3.137–3.148.
[337] See para 3.269 below.

assessed in their specific market context. This introduced a stronger economic element to Article 81(1) and ultimately led to the adoption of the Article 81(3) Guidelines which explicitly relies on an assessment of market power and/or the likely impact of agreements on price[338] to determine the application of Article 81(1).

(c) Restrictions of Rivalry Must be Assessed in Their Market Context

3.177 A restriction of rivalry is not, in and of itself, sufficient for the application of Article 81(1): agreements must be assessed in their specific market context. This is clear from the ECJ's first competition law judgment, *Société Technique Minière v Maschinenbau Ulm GmbH*. The Court held that 'in order to decide whether an agreement containing a clause "granting an exclusive right of sale" is to be considered as prohibited by reason of its object or of its effect, it is appropriate to take into account in particular the nature and quantity, limited or otherwise, of the products covered by the agreement, the position and importance of the grantor and the concessionaire on the market for the products concerned, the isolated nature of the disputed agreement or, alternatively, its position in a series of agreements, the severity of the clauses intended to protect the exclusive dealership or, alternatively, the opportunities allowed for other commercial competitors in the same products by way of parallel re-exportation and importation'.[339]

3.178 In the following year, the ECJ made the need for market analysis even more clear: in *Brasserie de Haecht v Wilkin* it held that 'it would be *pointless* to consider an agreement, decision or practice by reason of its effect if those effects were to be taken distinct from the markets in which they are seen to operate . . . [t]hus in order to examine whether it is caught by Article 85 [now Article 81] an agreement cannot be examined in isolation from . . . the factual or legal circumstances causing it to prevent, restrict or distort competition'[340] (emphasis added).

3.179 In fact, over the years, there have been numerous examples of the European Courts finding clauses which restrict rivalry between the parties and/or from third parties and which fall outside Article 81(1) because of the market context in which they were applied. Such cases fall into four, to some extent, overlapping categories.

3.180 First are cases in which the restrictive clause under review is objectively necessary for the implementation of a legitimate purpose. These types of clauses are known as 'ancillary restraints'. Second are exclusivity clauses without which the relevant goods/services would not be supplied because of the commercial risks involved (these are referred to below as clauses where exclusivity is necessary for supply). Third are those cases that do not affect competition[341] 'to an appreciable extent'.[342] This category covers restrictions that have an insignificant effect on the market either because of the weak position of the parties or because they have a de minimis impact on rivalry given their 'nature'.[343] Fourth are vertical

---

[338] The term 'price' is used as short-hand for the various market parameters which the Commission may consider. These include output, innovation, and the variety or quality of goods and services.

[339] Case 56/65 *Société Technique Minière v Maschinenbau Ulm GmbH* [1996] ECR 235, para 250.

[340] Case 23/67 *SA Brasserie de Haecht v Consorts Wilkin-Janssen* [1967] ECR 407.

[341] There will also have to be an effect on trade. This is dealt with in section D below.

[342] See Case 22/71 *Beguelin* [1971] ECR 949, para 16.

[343] The 'nature' of an agreement relates to factors such as 'the area and objective' of the arrangement, 'the competitive relationship between the parties' and the 'extent to which they combine their activities; Commission,

restraints which do not have a foreclosure effect either because there are 'real concrete'[344] ways for competitors to enter or expand or, where such opportunities do not exist, because they do not make a significant contribution to the sealing-off effect.[345] This is often referred to as the 'cumulative effect doctrine'.

(d) Ancillary Restraint Doctrine

Clauses which restrict rivalry between the parties and/or third parties fall outside Article 81(1)   **3.181** if they are directly related and necessary to the implementation of a legitimate purpose; this purpose may be commercial or relate to a public interest.

(i) Commercial Ancillarity

In a number of important and oft-cited judgments, the European Courts held that restric-   **3.182** tions which are necessary for the implementation of a legitimate commercial purpose fall outside Article 81(1). For example, in *Metro I* the Court found that, given the characteristics of the market in question, 'selective distribution systems constituted . . . an aspect of competition which accords with Article 85(1), provided that resellers are chosen on the basis of objective criteria . . . and that such conditions are laid down uniformly for all potential resellers and are not applied in a discriminatory fashion'.[346] Having found the selective distribution to be legitimate, the Court went on to hold that clauses which limited the freedom of the parties or third parties but which were necessary for the system to function, and proportionate, fell outside Article 81(1). The clearest example of this is at paragraph 27 where the Court held that to 'be effective, any marketing system based on the selection of outlets necessarily entails the obligation upon wholesalers forming part of the network to supply only appointed resellers . . .' The Court went on to find that 'provided that the obligations undertaken in connection with such safeguards do not exceed the objective in view they do not in themselves represent a restitution on competition but are the corollary of the principle obligation and contribute to it fulfilment'.[347]

The ECJ took a similar approach to distribution through franchising. In *Pronuptia*,[348] the   **3.183** ECJ found that a system under which 'an undertaking, which has established itself as a distributor on a given market and thus developed certain business methods, grants independent traders, for a fee, the right to establish themselves in other markets using its business name and the business methods which have made it successful . . . does not in itself interfere with competition'.[349] It went on to find that for the system to work the franchisor must be able to communicate his know-how to the franchisees and provide them with the necessary

---

'Guidelines on the applicability of Article 81 of the EC Treaty to horizontal cooperation agreements' [2001] OJ C3/2 (6.1.2001), paras 21–23.

[344] Case C-234/89 *Delimitis v Henninger AG* [1991] ECR I-935, para 21.

[345] ibid, para 27, Case T-65/98 *Van den Bergh Foods* [2003] ECR II-4653, paras 109–118. See also Chapter 9 on Vertical Agreements.

[346] Case 26/76 *Metro SB-Grossmärkte GmbH* [1977] ECR 1875, para 20. The question of whether this constitutes a rule of reason approach is dealt in paras 3.248–3.255 below.

[347] ibid, para 27.

[348] Case 161/84 *Pronuptia de Paris v Pronuptia de Paris Irmgard Schillgalis* [1986] ECR 353.

[349] ibid, paras 14–15. The question of whether this constitutes a rule of reason approach is dealt with in paras 3.248–3.255 below.

assistance in order to enable them to apply his methods, without running the risk that that know-how and assistance might benefit competitors, even indirectly. It followed from this that provisions which were essential 'to avoid that risk, do not constitute restrictions on competition for the purposes of Article 85(1)'. Similarly the franchisor had to be able to take the measures which were necessary to maintain the identity and reputation of the network bearing his business name or symbol. This meant that obligations on the franchisee to apply the business methods developed by the franchisor and to use the know-how provided or clauses which allowed the franchisor to select the products offered by the franchisee or a provision requiring the franchisee to sell only products supplied by the franchisor (or other franchisees) did not fall within Article 81(1)—this was the case despite the fact that such clauses clearly limited the commercial freedom of the franchisee and potentially third parties.

3.184 Whilst the ancillary restraints doctrine has been seen as particularly important in vertical cases, it can apply to any type of agreement which might fall within the scope of Article 81(1). Thus in *Erauw-Jacquery*,[350] the Court held that a clause preventing a licensee from exporting seeds protected by plant breeders' rights could fall outside Article 81(1) where it was necessary to enable the licensor to select its licenses. Similarly in *Coditel 2*,[351] the ECJ held that an exclusive licence to exhibit a film in a particular territory would not restrict competition if it was necessary to protect the investment of the licensee.

3.185 In *Gøttrup-Klim*,[352] the ECJ was asked to consider whether a joint buying co-operative which prevented its members from buying through other similar arrangements (referred to in the judgments as the '[p]rohibition of dual membership')[353] fell within Article 81(1). It held that such a restriction could be lawful if it was necessary for the effective operation of the co-operative: '[w]here some members of two competing cooperative purchasing associations belong to both at the same time, the result is to make *each association less capable of pursuing its objectives for the benefit of the rest of its members*, especially where the members concerned, as in the case in point, are themselves cooperative associations with a large number of individual members. It follows that such dual membership *would jeopardize both the proper functioning of the cooperative and its contractual power in relation to producers*. Prohibition of dual membership does not, therefore, necessarily constitute a restriction of competition within the meaning of Article 85(1) of the Treaty and may even have beneficial effects on competition' (emphasis added).

3.186 However, the ECJ underlined that 'in order to escape the prohibition laid down in Article 85(1) of the Treaty, the restrictions imposed on members by the statutes of co-operative purchasing associations must be *limited to what is necessary* to ensure that the cooperative functions properly and maintains its contractual power in relation to producers' (emphasis added); ie the restrictions must be proportionate.[354]

3.187 The Commission has, albeit to a lesser extent, also applied the doctrine. The best example of this is *Elopak/Metal Box—Odin*, in which the Commission considered the overall effect

---

[350] Case 27/87 [1988] ECR 1919.
[351] Case 262/81 [1982] ECR 3381.
[352] Case C-250/92 [1994] ECR I-5641.
[353] ibid, para 34.
[354] See para 3.256 below.

of the creation of a joint venture called Odin and came to the conclusion that it did not fall within Article 81(1). It went on to say however that the 'specific provisions of the agreement must . . . be examined to ascertain whether such provisions restrict competition within the meaning of Article 85(1), or whether they are no more than is necessary to ensure the starting up and the proper functioning of the joint venture'.[355] Analysing the clauses, the Commission found that they were either 'provisions not restricting competition in the sense of Article 85(1), or provisions which in other contexts might restrict competition but which in the context of the present case do not. Since such provisions cannot be disassociated from the creation of Odin without undermining its existence and purpose and since the creation of Odin does not fall within the scope of Article 85(1), these specific provisions also fall outside the scope of Article 85(1)'.[356]

(ii) Public Interest Ancillarity

The cases outlined above cover what one leading commentator has described as 'commercial ancillarity',[357] that is, restrictions which are necessary for the implementation of a legitimate commercial purpose. However, in its *EPI Code of Conduct*[358] decision the Commission appeared to extend the concept to cover restraints which are necessary on public interest grounds.[359] The case concerned the code of conduct of the Institute of Professional Representatives before the European Patent Office (EPO). The Commission found that a number of these rules fell outside Article 81(1) because: '[t]hey are necessary, in view of the specific context of this profession, in order to ensure impartiality, competence, integrity and responsibility on the part of representatives, to prevent conflicts of interest and misleading advertising, to protect professional secrecy or to guarantee the proper functioning of the EPO'.[360]   **3.188**

The legitimacy of this approach was challenged by Advocate General Léger in *JCJ Wouters, JW Savelbergh and Price Waterhouse Belastingadviseurs BV v Algemene Raad van de Nederlandse Orde van Advocaten*.[361] In essence he argued that the ancillary restraint doctrine was 'strictly confined to a purely *competitive* balance-sheet of the effects of the agreement. Where, taken as a whole, the agreement is capable of encouraging competition on the market, the clauses essential to its performance may escape the prohibition laid down in Article 85(1) of the Treaty. The only legitimate goal which may be pursued in accordance with that provision is therefore exclusively *competitive* in nature' (emphasis added).[362] The Commission's approach   **3.189**

---

[355] [1990] OJ L209/15, paras 28–29.
[356] ibid, para 36.
[357] Whish, *Competition Law* (5th edn, LexisNexis Butterworths, 2003), p 119.
[358] [1999] OJ L106/14.
[359] It has been argued that the main reason the Commission adopted this approach, rather than issuing an exemption or comfort letter, was that it wanted to avoid a flood of notifications of the rules of bodies which regulate professions; it should be recalled that under Regulation 17/62 agreements falling within the scope of Art 81(1) had to be notified to the Commission if they were to be exempted under Art 81(3). See, for example, H Nyssens, 'Concurrence et ordres professionnels: les trompettes de Jéricho sonnent-elles?' Revue de Droit Commercial Belge (1999) 475.
[360] [1999] OJ L106/14, para 38.
[361] Case C-309/99 [2002] ECR I-1577.
[362] Para 104 of the Advocate General's opinion.

in the *EPI Code of Conduct* decision[363] on the other hand effectively introduced into Article 81(1) considerations which were linked to the pursuit of a public interest objective. It also implied that the Commission and European Courts should not only consider the question of whether a restriction of competition exists, but also whether or not it might be justified under Article 81(1). Such an interpretation, warned the Advocate General, was 'liable to negate a great part of the effectiveness'[364] of Articles 81(3).

3.190   Without explicitly referring to it, the ECJ's judgment clarified that the ancillary restraints doctrine does not apply exclusively to restrictions which are necessary for the attainment of a legitimate *commercial* objective. The Court held that 'a national regulation such as the 1993 Regulation adopted by a body such as the Bar of the Netherlands does not infringe Article 85(1) of the Treaty, since that body could reasonably have considered that that regulation, despite the effects restrictive of competition that are inherent in it, is *necessary for the proper practice* of the legal profession, as organised in the Member State concerned' (emphasis added).[365]

3.191   Naturally, since *Wouters* was an Article 234 reference, the Court limited itself to answering the specific question put to it. However, other than the allusion in the paragraph quoted above to 'a national regulation . . . adopted by a body such as the Bar', there is nothing in the judgment which limits its application to the rules of regulatory bodies. Indeed most[366] commentators have, correctly, concluded that the judgment applies to any[367] public interest objective. The Commission has taken a similar position: in a recent complaint rejection decision, it applied *Wouters* to rules which restricted the ownership of shares in more than one football club competing in the Champions League tournament. It decided that 'the limitation of the freedom of action of clubs and investors which the rule entails does not go beyond what is necessary to ensure its legitimate aim: ie to protect the uncertainty of the results in the interest of the public'.[368]

3.192   More recently in *Meca-Medina and Majcen v Commission*,[369] the ECJ held that the anti-doping rules of the International Olympic Committee fell outside the scope of Article 81(1) since

---

[363] [1999] OJ L106/14.

[364] Para 107 of the Advocate General's opinion.

[365] Case C-309/99 [2002] ECR I-1577, para 110.

[366] See, for example, Monti, 'Article 81 EC and Public Policy' [2002] 5 CML Rev 39 1057–1099. A similar, though not identical, interpretation is given in Komninos, 'Non-competition Concerns: Resolution of Conflicts in the Integrated Article 81 EC' Working Paper (L) 08/05 Oxford Centre for Competition Law & Policy. Komninos argues that the *Wouters* approach is based on 'the theory of mandatory requirements that was developed in the Court's four freedoms case law.' However, Whish, *Competition Law* (5th edn, LexisNexis Butterworths, 2003), at p 122, states that the judgment is limited to 'regulatory rule[s] adopted for the protection of consumers'. However closer examination of Whish suggests that this is not the case: the author specifically refers to the press release in *UEFA/ENIC*, a case relating to rules which restricted the ownership of shares in more than one football club competing in the Champions League tournament. The press release (IP/02/942 dated 27/06/2002) clearly states that 'the limitation of the freedom of action of clubs and investors which the rule entails does not go beyond what is necessary to ensure its legitimate aim: ie to protect the uncertainty of the results in *the interest of the public*' (emphasis added).

[367] It should be noted, however, that where the public interest relates to a Community policy, the judgment in *Brentjens' Handelsonderneming BV* (Joined Cases C-115/97, C-116/97 and C-117/97 [1999] ECR I-6025) is more likely to be considered the leading authority.

[368] IP/02/942 (27/06/2002).

[369] Case C-519/04 *Meca-Medina and Majcen v Commission*, judgment of 18 July 2006.

they were 'justified by a legitimate objective', were 'inherent in the organisation and proper conduct of competitive sport'[370] were 'not . . . disproportionate'.[371] In doing so, the ECJ explicitly applied the approach set out in *Wouters*.[372]

(iii) The Narrow Scope of the Ancillary Restraint Doctrine

Although it is now clear that the scope of application of the ancillary restraint doctrine is broader than some had assumed (in the sense that it can be used on non-commercial grounds),[373] its usefulness is, in fact, limited in practice. **3.193**

The *Pronuptia* case itself provides a good example of this—the ECJ held that since a franchise agreement typically resulted in a sharing of markets between the franchisor and the franchisees or between franchisees, its restrictive clauses could, in certain circumstances,[374] fall within Article 81(1) even if 'a prospective franchisee would not take the risk of becoming part of the chain, investing his own money, paying a relatively high entry fee and undertaking to pay a substantial annual royalty, unless he could hope, thanks to a degree of protection against competition on the part of the franchisor and other franchisees, that his business would be profitable. That consideration, however, is relevant only to an examination of the agreement in the light of the conditions laid down in Article 85(3).'[375] **3.194**

This narrowness of application was confirmed by the CFI's judgment in *Métropole*.[376] The Court explained that the concept only covered clauses which are 'directly related and necessary to the implementation of a main agreement'.[377] **3.195**

Directly Related and Subordinate A restriction is said to be 'directly related to [the] implementation of a main operation' if it is 'subordinate to the implementation of that operation and . . . has an evident link with it'.[378] **3.196**

This element of the doctrine is relatively straightforward to understand and apply: the activity covered by the clause must be part of, or at least be closely linked to, the main agreement; however it must not be the main purpose for which the parties come together. Thus, for example, in *Métropole* the main operation was the establishment of a joint venture in the pay-TV market, whilst a clause through which the parties granted certain exclusive rights to the joint venture was found to be subordinate and linked. The justification for this is obvious: there is a clear connection between a pay-TV platform and the supply of content; however supplying the channels to the joint venture was, in this case, not the main reason the parties entered into the business relationship. Another example would be a clause in a franchise agreement which allows a franchisor to select the products offered by the franchisee. **3.197**

---

[370] ibid, para 45.
[371] ibid, para 55.
[372] Case C-309/99 [2002] ECR I-1577; see also paras 3.33–3.37.
[373] See para 3.188 *et seq* above.
[374] See section E(5) of Chapter 9 (Vertical Agreements).
[375] Case 161/84 *Pronuptia de Paris v Pronuptia de Paris Irmgard Schillgalis* [1986] ECR 353, para 24.
[376] Case T-112/99 *Métropole Télévision (M6), Suez-Lyonnaise des Eaux, France Télécom and Télévision Française 1 SA (TF1)* [2001] ECR II-2459; see also subsequently Case T-65/98 *Van den Bergh Foods* [2003] ECR II-4653.
[377] *Métropole*, para 104.
[378] ibid, para 104.

This restraint clearly covers an activity which is subordinate but nevertheless closely linked to the implementation of a franchise system (which is the main operation).[379]

3.198 **Necessary**   Relying on the ECJ's judgment in *Remia*,[380] the CFI held in *Métropole* that for the necessity element of the doctrine to apply two conditions had to be satisfied:

- first, the restriction had to be objectively necessary for the implementation of the main operation; and
- second, it had to be proportionate.

3.199 **Objective necessity for the implementation of the main operation**   *Objective necessity* means that in the absence of the clause in question, the main operation would be 'difficult[381] or even impossible to *implement*' (emphasis added).[382] In *Métropole* and subsequently in *Van den Bergh Foods*[383] the CFI held that determination of this did not require a weighing-up of the pro- and anti-competitive effects of the clause in question;[384] rather a 'relatively abstract'[385] examination needed to be conducted.

3.200 Thus the key question is not whether the restriction is indispensable to the *commercial* success of the main operation but rather its importance for the implementation of the main agreement.

3.201 In many ways this distinction is difficult to understand: undertakings enter into commercial agreements to make or save money. Commercial considerations are therefore at the very core of these agreements. From an economic perspective, there would therefore appear to be little difference between clauses which are necessary from a commercial perspective and those which are required for the 'implementation' of agreements.

3.202 The need for the distinction becomes clearer, however, when viewed through a legal or policy lens. Although it is not immediately evident from *Métropole*, the Court appears to have drawn a distinction between clauses which are required for the main agreement to *function at all* and clauses which may or may not be necessary depending on the *economic circumstances* of each particular case: the applicants had submitted that a clause granting a new joint venture exclusive rights to certain general-interest channels was indispensable to its penetration of the pay-TV market in France. Therefore it was ancillary. In response the CFI found that 'the fact that the exclusivity clause would be necessary to allow [the joint venture] to establish itself on a long-term basis on that market it is not relevant to the classification of that clause as an ancillary restriction . . . such considerations, relating to the indispensable nature of the restriction in the light of the *competitive situation on the relevant market* . . . can be taken into account only in the framework of Article 85(3) of the Treaty'.[386] The CFI

---

[379] Case 161/84 *Pronuptia de Paris v Pronuptia de Paris Irmgard Schillgalis* [1986] ECR 353.
[380] Case 42/84 [1985] ECR 2545, para 20.
[381] Para 111 of *Métropole* appears to give some guidance on what the Court meant by 'difficult' by referring, without dissent, to various Decisions in which the Commission had found clauses to be ancillary where 'the operation in question . . . could only be implemented under more uncertain conditions, at substantially higher cost, over an appreciably longer period or with considerably less probability of success'.
[382] *Métropole*, para 109.
[383] Case T-65/98 [2003] ECR II-4653.
[384] *Métropole*, para 107.
[385] ibid, para 109.
[386] ibid, paras 120–121.

went on to observe that although the applicants had been able to establish to the requisite legal standard that the exclusivity clause was directly related to the establishment of TPS, they had not shown that the exclusive broadcasting of the general-interest channels was 'objectively necessary' for that operation: 'as the Commission has rightly stated, a company in the pay-TV sector can be launched in France without having exclusive rights to the general-interest channels'.[387]

In explaining this distinction the CFI referred to the *Remia* judgment[388] in which the ECJ **3.203** held that a non-compete clause was 'objectively necessary for a successful transfer of undertakings, in as much as, without such a clause . . . . It is clear that the agreement for the transfer of the undertaking *could not be given effect*. The vendor . . . would still be in a position to win back his former customers immediately after the transfer and thereby drive the . . . [transferee] out of business' (emphasis added).[389] The ECJ's concern here was that the contract would not be entered into at all, but for the non-compete clause.

The CFI also sought to explain its logic by drawing on previous Commission decisions, in **3.204** particular those which related to P&I Clubs.[390] These are mutual non-profit association of ship-owners, charters and operators who share the risk of providing their members with protection and indemnity insurance. The Commission found that such 'claim-sharing arrangement *cannot function* properly without at least one level of cover to be offered being agreed by all its members. The reason is that *no member* would be willing to share claims brought to the pool by other clubs of a higher amount than the ones it can bring to the pool.' According to the Commission since mutuals do not charge premiums in claim-sharing agreements, there is '*no workable* method available to force the members which would bring larger claims to compensate the others'[391] ie the system could not function without claim-sharing.

The distinction drawn by the CFI in *Métropole* is also found in previous ancillary restraint **3.205** judgments, in particular *Pronuptia*. In that judgment the ECJ drew, in broad terms, a distinction between two types of clauses. The first were those which were necessary 'for the system to work',[392] such as obligations requiring the franchisee to use the business methods and know-how developed by the franchisor, or to sell the contract goods only in premises laid out and decorated according to the franchisor' s instructions.[393] Without these there could be no franchise system. The second were clauses which dampened price competition between franchisees. Whilst recognising that it was 'of course possible that a prospective franchisee would not take the risk of becoming part of the chain, investing his own money, paying a relatively high entry fee and undertaking to pay a substantial annual royalty, unless he could hope, thanks to a degree of protection against competition on the part of the franchisor and other franchisees, that his business would be profitable',[394] the Court held that

---

[387] ibid, para 122.
[388] Case 42/84 [1985] ECR 2545.
[389] *Métropole*, para 110.
[390] [1999] OJ L125/12.
[391] ibid, para 77.
[392] Case 161/84 [1986] ECR 353, para 15.
[393] ibid, see generally paras 16–22.
[394] ibid, para 24.

this was not an assessment that should be made under Article 81(1): such consideration were relevant only to an examination under Article 81(3).

3.206 There are two main policy reasons for drawing this distinction. First, as the Commission argued in its *White Paper on Modernisation of the Rules Implementing Articles 85 and 86*,[395] 'if more systematic use were made under Article 85(1) of an analysis of the pro and anti-competitive aspects of a restrictive agreement, Article 85(3) would be cast aside, whereas any such change could be made only through revision of the Treaty'.[396] The Court explicitly echoed this by holding that 'it would be wrong, when classifying ancillary restrictions, to interpret the requirement for objective necessity as implying a need to weigh the pro and anti-competitive effects of an agreement [under Article 81(1)]. Such an analysis can take place only in the specific framework of Article 85(3) [now Article 81(1)] of the Treaty'.[397]

3.207 Second, the very fact that only an 'abstract'[398] analysis should be done and, indeed, that ancillary restraints are cleared, irrespective of their effect, means that clauses which could be harmful may be taken outside Article 81(1). Prudence would seem to dictate that the scope of application of the doctrine should not be too wide.

3.208 It is worth noting that the objective necessity test also applies in 'public interest' ancillarity cases. In *Wouters*[399] the ECJ found that a regulation prohibiting multi-disciplinary partnerships imposed by the Bar of the Netherlands fell outside the scope of Article 81(1), despite its restrictive effects, since it could 'reasonably be considered to be necessary in order to ensure the proper practice of the legal profession, as it is organised in the Member State concerned'.[400]

3.209 Although this language is not identical to that used in *Métropole*, the underlying approach is, it is submitted, the same: was the restraint in question (here a regulation) objectively necessary, or in the language of the judgment 'could . . . reasonably be considered to be necessary', for the implementation of a legitimate purpose? The Court found that the regulation was necessary to ensure that the professional conduct rules for members of the Bar were complied with, having regard to the way the profession was organised in that State. The Court based this on its finding that members of the Bar might no longer be in a position to advise and represent their clients independently and in the observance of strict professional secrecy if they belonged to an organisation such as an accountancy firm—clearly a legitimate public policy concern.

3.210 **Proportionality**   Where a restriction is objectively necessary, it is still necessary to verify whether its duration and its material and geographic scope exceed what is necessary to implement the main operation. If the duration or the scope of the restriction is excessive, the clause must be assessed separately under Article 81(3) of the Treaty.[401]

---

[395] European Commission: *White Paper on Modernisation of the Rules Implementing Arts 85 and 86 of the EC Treaty—Commission programme No 99/027* COM(1999) 101, April 1999.

[396] ibid, para 57.

[397] *Métropole*, para 107.

[398] ibid, para 109.

[399] Case C-309/99 [2002] ECR I-1577.

[400] ibid, para 107; see also Case C-519/04 *Meca-Medina and Majcen v Commission*, judgment of 18 July 2006.

[401] See to that effect, Case T-61/89 *Dansk Pelsdyravlerforening v Commission* [1992] ECR II-1931, para 78.

This apparently clear formulation masks an important evidentiary point: careful examina- **3.211**
tion of the relevant cases in this area shows that very little is required to take a clause outside
the scope of the doctrine. For example, in *Métropole* the CFI found that a clause granting a
new joint venture exclusive rights to certain general-interest channels for a period of ten
years was disproportionate. The reasons given for this finding amounted to no more than
mere assertion:[402] the Court found, without any real evidence to support its position, that
it was 'quite probable' that the competitive disadvantage from which the joint venture suffered at its creation (principally its lack of access to exclusive film and sports rights) would
diminish over time. Similarly, it argued that the clause deprived the joint venture's actual
and potential competitors of access to the programmes that were considered 'attractive by
a large number' of French television viewers—no real attempt was however made by the
Commission, nor deemed necessary by the CFI, to assess the nature or extent of the foreclosure or indeed to establish, in any concrete way, the importance of this content to competition in this market. Finally, the Court pointed to the existence of so-called 'shadow
zones' in France—ie areas with poor reception of free-to-air television. It found that those
viewers in these areas who wanted to subscribe to a pay-TV company which also broad-
casted general-interest channels could only turn to the joint venture. Again, there is very
little in either the Commission's decision or the Court's judgment on the likely impact of
this on competition; even basic questions such as whether this group was of sufficient size
to prevent entry of other players into the market were not considered necessary.[403]

Once again, it is worth noting that, as with objective necessity, the proportionality test also **3.212**
applies in 'public interest' ancillarity cases. In *Wouters*[404] the ECJ found that a rule prohibiting multi-disciplinary partnerships imposed by the Bar of the Netherlands had restrictive effects; however these effects did not 'go beyond what is necessary in order to ensure the
proper practice of the legal profession'.[405]

(iv) Concluding Remark: Ancillary Restraint Doctrine of Limited Practical Use

Notwithstanding the clarification of certain elements of the ancillarity test by the CFI in **3.213**
Métropole, it is clear that the concept still raises more questions than it answers. It is very
difficult, if not impossible, to identify in the abstract whether a particular restraint will be
treated as ancillary to a particular type of agreement. Of course, similar problems exist
when applying the concept of indispensability under Article 81(3).[406] However, in such
cases, advisers can often turn to the 'black lists' in the various block exemption regulations
or the existing case law. Unfortunately, there is little case law under Article 81(1) to guide

---

[402] *Métropole*, paras 123–126.

[403] Although mere speculation, given the European Courts' approach in previous cases, the CFI's failure
to conduct a more detailed assessment may simply have reflected the nature of the submissions made by the
applicants in *Métropole*—careful reading of the *Van den Burgh Foods* judgment, for example, suggests that the
submissions made by the applicants in that case were far more detailed and sophisticated than in *Métropole*.

[404] Case C-309/99 [2002] ECR I-1577.

[405] See also Case C-519/04 *Meca-Medina and Majcen v Commission*, judgment of 18 July 2006.

[406] Is this different from the indispensability test under Art 81(3)? Under Art 81(3), the test is whether the
clause is necessary for the attainment of the benefits identified. Under Art 81(1), the question is whether
the clause is necessary for the existence and implementation of the agreement.

companies and their advisers.[407] The doctrine cannot therefore be applied with certainty by those who wish to argue that a particular restrictive clause in an agreement falls outside Article 81(1). Perhaps, more importantly, whilst the distinction drawn by the CFI between 'implementation' and 'commercial needs' makes a degree of sense from a policy viewpoint, it is very difficult to apply from a practical perspective.

(e) Exclusivity Necessary for Supply

3.214 The preceding sections considered one category of cases in which the European Courts have found restrictive clauses to fall outside Article 81(1) because of the market context in which they were applied. Another category covers the situation whereby goods/services would not be supplied by an undertaking without at least a degree of exclusivity because of the commercial risks involved. Thus in *Société Technique Minière*,[408] the Court held that 'it may be doubted whether there is an interference with competition if the said agreement seems really necessary for the penetration of a new area by an undertaking'.[409] Similarly in *Nungesser v Commission*,[410] the Court found the exclusivity under review to be compatible with Article 81(1):[411] having regard to the specific nature of the products in question the ECJ concluded that an undertaking 'which was not certain that it would not encounter competition from other licensees for the territory granted to it, or from the owner of the right himself, might be deterred from accepting the risk of cultivating and marketing that product; such a result would be damaging to the dissemination of a new technology and would prejudice competition in the community between the new product and similar existing products'.[412]

3.215 The logic underlying these cases (and those discussed below) is the same: Article 81(1) does not apply if, from an objective perspective, it is clear that undertakings could not, or would not, supply or enter the market in the absence of the restraint in question given the risks involved. Put differently, Article 81(1) does not apply in such cases because in the absence of the 'necessary' restraint the undertakings in question (or at least 'objective' undertakings in a similar setting) would not participate in the market and compete.

(i) Exclusivity Must be Objectively Necessary

3.216 As with ancillary restraints doctrine, this line of case law only applies to restrictions which are objectively necessary—the subjective views of the parties may of course, in certain circumstances, be relevant but they will in no way be determinative. Thus in assessing whether 'the said agreement seems really necessary' the ECJ did not consider the subjective intention or needs of the parties in *Société Technique Minière*. Instead it focused on objective market characteristics 'in particular the nature and quantity, limited or otherwise, of the products covered

---

[407] Nor can the decisions under the Merger Regulation be relied on under Art 81 except, perhaps, for structural operations.

[408] Case 56/65 *Société Technique Minière v Maschinenbau Ulm GmbH* [1966] ECR 235.

[409] ibid at 250; see more recently Case T-328/03 *O2 (Germany) GmbH & Co. v Commission*, judgment of 2 May 2006, at para 68.

[410] Case 258/78 [1982] ECR 2515.

[411] Insofar as it did not prevent parallel imports. See para 3.231 dealing with this below.

[412] Case 258/78 [1982] ECR 2515, para 57.

by the agreement, the position and importance of the grantor and the concessionaire on the market for the products concerned, the isolated nature of the disputed agreement or, alternatively, its position in a series of agreements, the severity of the clauses intended to protect the exclusive dealership or, alternatively, the opportunities allowed for other commercial competitors in the same products by way of parallel re-exportation and importation'.[413] Similarly in *Nungesser v Commission*, the ECJ did not consider or refer to the particular applicant's needs or its appetite for risk; instead it focussed on an objective assessment and made a generic finding that 'an undertaking established in another Member State . . . might be deterred from accepting the risk . . . [h]aving regard to the specific nature of the product in question'.[414]

(ii) It is Unclear Whether this Doctrine Applies to Agreements Between Competitors

It has been suggested by some commentators[415] that this line of case law is relevant only to distribution and licensing agreements and does not apply to agreements between competitors. Paragraphs 18(2) and 29 of the Article 81(3) Guidelines, when read together, seem to make, or at least imply, a similar point.[416]   **3.217**

However it is worth noting that the logic underlying these cases is close, if not identical to that used in potential competition cases: it is settled law that Article 81 only applies to agreements between actual or potential competitors;[417] it does not apply to agreements between undertakings which do not compete with each other (nor are likely to do so within a reasonable timescale).[418] Amongst other things this means that Article 81 does not apply to agreements which are necessary for entry to take place. For example, in *European Night Services*,[419] a case concerning agreements establishing a joint venture (the 'ENS JV') between several of European rail companies to provide train services through the Channel Tunnel, the parties appealed the Commission's decision to grant a conditional exemption. They argued that their agreements did not restrict competition because, *inter alia*, the evidence showed that none of the railway undertakings alone would have accepted the risks of supplying the service. Moreover, the procurement of rolling stock involved various fixed costs such that an undertaking could only make a profit by increasing output to a minimum efficient size—individually, none of the railway undertakings would have been in a position to increase the level of services to that minimum.   **3.218**

In response, the Commission argued that the fact that the parties had assumed significant commercial risks and incurred high costs did not mean that appreciable competition was   **3.219**

---

[413] Case 56/65 *Société Technique Minière v Maschinenbau Ulm GmbH* [1966] ECR 235 at 250.

[414] Case 258/78 [1982] ECR 2515 paras 57–58.

[415] See, for example, Butterworths *Competition Law* (December 2005), I/126, para 203 (Issue 54).

[416] See section C.9(a) below for a fuller discussion of the treatment of this issue in the Art 81(3) Guidelines.

[417] For a detailed discussion and definition of potential competition and competitors, see 7.126–7.138. See also *Convention Chaufourniers* OJ [1969] L122/8; *Clima Chappée—Buderus* OJ [1969] L195/1; *Wild—Leitz* OJ [1972] L61/27; *Vacuum Interrupters Ltd* OJ [1977] L48/32; *Sopelem/Vickers* OJ [1978] L70/47; *The Distillers Co. Ltd—Victuallers* OJ [1980] L233/43; *Re UK Agricultural Tractor Registration Exchange* OJ [1992] L68/19; *HOV SVZ/MCN* OJ [1994] L104/34; *BNP/Dresdner Bank—Austrian JV* (Case IV/M1340) (1998); *Iridium* OJ [1997] L16/87; *Air France/Alitalia* OJ [2003] C297/10; Case T-374/94 *European Night Services* [1998] ECR II-3141. Also, Case T-504/93 *Tiércé-Ladbroke v Commission* [1997] ECR II-923, where the CFI annulled a Commission decision which failed to take into account a possible restriction of potential competition.

[418] Insofar as they do not restrict competition from or between third parties.

[419] Case T-374/94 ECR II-3141, para 137.

improbable: a railway undertaking established in one Member State could, for example, form an international grouping with another railway undertaking established in another Member State and obtain from Eurotunnel, the infrastructure manager, the paths necessary to pass through the Channel Tunnel and thus operate international transport services.

3.220   The CFI rejected the Commission's arguments finding, *inter alia*, that it was unrealistic, given the novelty and the specific features of the night rail services in question, to enter in the way envisaged by the Commission. The prohibitive cost of the investment required for such services through the Channel Tunnel and the fact that there were no economies of scale in the operation of a single route, as opposed to the four routes to be operated together by ENS JV, made entry of the type envisaged by the Commission unrealistic. In making this finding, the Court drew attention to the fact that no rail company had ever entered the market of another Member States in the manner implied by the Commission's arguments. The CFI held that 'the examination of conditions of competition is based not only on existing competition between undertakings already present on the relevant market but also on potential competition in order to ascertain whether, in the light of the structure of the market and the economic and legal context within which it functions, there are *real concrete possibilities for the undertakings concerned to compete among themselves or for a new competitor to penetrate the relevant market* and compete with the undertakings already established'. The Court went on to note that the 'assumption of potential competitive circumstances presupposes *that each parent alone is in a position to fulfil the tasks assigned to the [joint venture]* and that it does not forfeit its capabilities to do so' by the creation of the joint venture (emphasis added).

3.221   More recently in *O2 v Commission*[420] a case concerning infrastructure sharing and national roaming in Germany between two mobile operators (O2 and T-Mobile), the CFI relied explicitly on the formulation set out in *Société Technique Minière*, that 'interference with competition may in particular be doubted if the agreement seems really necessary for the penetration of a new area'.[421]

(iii) Doctrine Only Likely to Apply in Clear-cut Cases

3.222   At one level the logic of this approach (that is, exclusivity being necessary for supply) suggests that a thorough examination of the market is required in order to assess the level of risk and extent of exclusivity needed. Indeed in *Société Technique Minière* the ECJ held that 'in order to decide whether an agreement containing a clause 'granting an exclusive right of sale' is to be considered as prohibited . . . it is appropriate to take into account in particular the nature and quantity, limited or otherwise, of the products covered by the agreement, the position and importance of the grantor and the concessionaire on the market for the products concerned, the isolated nature of the disputed agreement or, alternatively, its position in a series of agreements, the severity of the clauses intended to protect the exclusive dealership or, alternatively, the opportunities allowed for other commercial competitors in the same products by way of parallel re-exportation and importation'.

3.223   However, in practice, this level of analysis may not be necessary or required—for example the ECJ's assessment in *Nungesser* was relatively superficial and impressionistic. In fact it

---

[420]   Case T-328/03 *O2 (Germany) GmbH & Co. v Commission*, judgment of 2 May 2006, para 68.
[421]   ibid, para 77.

can be argued with some force that the European Courts are likely to adopt an approach similar to that used in ancillary restraint cases—in *Métropole* the CFI held that it would be inappropriate to conduct a full market analysis when determining whether a clause was ancillary; instead a 'relatively abstract'[422] examination was required. This was, at least in part, because it felt that Article 81(3) 'would lose much of its effectiveness if [a detailed] examination had already to be carried out under Article 85(1) of the Treaty'.[423] A priori, it is difficult to identify reasons why this logic would not apply in *Société Technique Minière/Nungesser* type cases.

In practice this is likely to mean that the *Société Technique Minière/Nungesser* approach will only apply in clear-cut cases; in situations where the facts are more complex (or where a more thorough analysis is required for some other reason) it is likely that the Court will, assuming all other conditions are met, bring the case within the scope of Article 81(1) in order to assess, under Article 81(3), the claims made by the parties.[424]   **3.224**

Exception to General Rule   The main exception to this general rule is likely to be in potential competition cases, ie where an assessment has to be made of the likelihood of entry by undertakings which are not actual but may be potential competitors. According to both the Commission and the CFI the analysis in such cases has 'to be based on realistic grounds, the mere theoretical possibility to enter a market is not sufficient'.[425] In *European Night Services*[426] the CFI held that this involved an examination of 'the structure of the market and the economic and legal context within which it functions' in order to determine whether there are '*real* concrete possibilities'[427] (emphasis added) for the undertakings concerned to compete among themselves or for a new competitor to penetrate the relevant market and compete with the undertakings already established.   **3.225**

Similarly in *O2*,[428] the CFI criticised the Commission for undertaking an insufficiently detailed assessment of this issue under Article 81(1). In particular the Court found that the Commission had been wrong to assume that it was unnecessary to consider in 'more detail' under Article 81(1) 'whether, in the absence of the agreement, O2 would have been present on the [new] 3G market work'.[429]   **3.226**

Perhaps more significantly, the Court found, at least in respect of this issue, that the Commission should not have limited its detailed economic analysis to Article 81(3)—its findings under Article 81(3) implied 'some uncertainty concerning the competitive situation and, in particular, as regard O2's position in the absence of the agreement'. This showed, the CFI concluded, that the presence of O2 on the 3G communications market could not be   **3.227**

---

[422] Case T-112/99 *Métropole Télévision (M6), Suez-Lyonnaise des Eaux, France Télécom and Télévision Française 1 SA (TF1)* [2001] ECR II-2459, para 109.

[423] ibid, para 74; see also *Van den Burgh*, para 107.

[424] See discussion at para 3.232 below.

[425] Commission Notice, 'Guidelines on the Applicability of Article 81 of the EC Treaty to Horizontal Cooperation Agreements' OJ [2001] C 3/02 n 9; see also the Commission's Thirteenth Report on Competition Policy, point 55. Commission Decisions include 90/410/EEC *Elopak/Metal Box-Odin* OJ L 209 [1990] and *Iridium* OJ [1997] L16/87. For the CFI see in particular Case T-374/94 *European Night Services* ECR II-3141, para 137 and the discussion in this chapter at paras 3.218–3.220.

[426] Case T-374/94 ECR II-3141.

[427] Case T-374/94 [1998] *European Night Services* ECR II-3141, para 137.

[428] Case T-328/03 *O2 (Germany) GmbH & Co. v Commission*, judgment of 2 May 2006.

[429] ibid, para 77.

taken for granted, as the Commission had assumed, and that 'an examination in this respect was *necessary not only for the purposes of granting an exemption but, prior to that, for the purposes of the economic analysis of the effects of the agreement on the competitive situation determining the applicability of Article 81 EC'* (emphasis added).[430]

3.228 The fact that a more through analysis is required in such cases is not surprising given the greater risks associated with horizontal agreements. However, a degree of care should be taken in relying too heavily on the statements in *European Night Services* and *O2*. In the former case the CFI appears to have been heavily influenced by the fact that the contested decision and the documents before it contained little if any evidence as to the existence of undertakings in other Member States which had entered or intended to enter this or similar markets; indeed the converse was true: there was evidence from third parties on the Commission's file which indicated that other operators shared the parties' views as to the viability of entry.[431] Thus for example part of the Commission's case was that each of the parent undertakings could set up subsidiaries in the Member States of the other parent undertakings and form, either with its own subsidiaries or with other railway undertakings established in the other Member States concerned, international groupings in direct competition with ENS. The Court considered this to be 'a hypothesis unsupported by any evidence or any analysis of the structures of the relevant market from which it might be concluded that it represented a real, concrete possibility'. Indeed there was 'no indication either in the contested decision or in the documents before the Court that there are any railway undertakings with sub-sidiaries in other Member States having themselves the status of railway undertakings, such as to demonstrate any actual exercise of the right to freedom of establishment on the market for rail transport in the Community'. In essence the CFI found that the Commission's case was, at least on this point, based on no more than a theoretical possibility of entry. In the circumstances the CFI approach is not surprising.

3.229 Similarly in *O2* the CFI was, as is clear from the citations given in paragraphs 3.226 and 3.227 above, highly critical of the Commission's factual analysis and approach under Article 81(1), in particular its assumption as to the ability of O2 to enter the new 3G market and compete, given its findings under Article 81(3) on O2's likely competitive position.

3.230 It is also worth comparing the approach taken in *European Night Services*, and to a lesser extent *O2*, with that in *Tiércé-Ladbroke v Commission*,[432] a judgment handed down only 15 months before *ENS*. In the latter case the CFI annulled the decision because Commission had failed to take into account a possible restriction of potential competition. The level of analysis it conducted on this issue however was little short of cursory and may not, it is submitted, have withstood the type of scrutiny undertaken in its own *European Night Service/O2* judgments: although the parties could have entered the market with ease (entry in this case meant granting a licence) there was no evidence that they either intended, or had a particular incentive, to do so, ie it could be argued with at least a degree of force that their entry was no more than a theoretical possibility (albeit one that could have occurred very easily had they chosen to do so).

---

[430] *O2 (Germany)*, para 79.
[431] See, in this regard, *European Night Services*, para 145.
[432] Case T-504/93 [1997] ECR II-923.

(iv) *Approach Does Not Apply to 'Object' Cases*

It is worth noting that the Court has explicitly limited the application of this doctrine to agree- **3.231** ments which did not entail absolute territorial protection: '[t]he Court has consistently held . . . that absolute territorial protection granted to a licensee in order to enable parallel imports to be controlled and prevented results in the artificial maintenance of separate national markets, [is] contrary to the Treaty'.[433]

(v) *Difference Between Exclusivity Necessary for Supply and Ancillary Restraint Doctrines*

At first glance there appears to be a degree of tension between the *Société Technique Minière/* **3.232** *Nungesser* approach and the ancillary restraints doctrines. In *Métropole* and subsequently *Van den Bergh Foods*[434] the CFI held that a clause would be ancillary if in its absence, the main operation would be 'difficult or even impossible to *implement*';[435] the question of whether the restriction was necessary for the *commercial success* of the main operation was, for the reasons outlined in preceding section, a matter largely for Article 81(3). However, under the *Société Technique Minière/Nungesser* case law, the commercial aspects of the case are central to the analysis.

These judgments are not inconsistent with one another. The *Société Technique Minière/* **3.233** *Nungesser* line of cases applies to agreements in which *market entry would not occur at all* but for the restrictive clause. Conversely, in *Métropole* the Court found that a company *could be launched* in the relevant market without the exclusivity granted in the agreement under review.[436] As such the restrictive clause under review went to the *commercial success* of the joint venture rather than whether entry could take place *at all*.[437]

This distinction has arguably been muddied slightly by the CFI's recent reliance under Article **3.234** 81(1) in *O2* (a case concerning 3G mobile telephony) on factors normally considered under Article 81(3) (speed of roll-out, better coverage, quality and transmission rates, etc).

Two points are worth noting in this regard however. First, the CFI considered these factors as **3.235** part of its assessment of whether O2 could enter the market and be an 'effective competitor'[438] in the absence of the agreement. It found that 'O2's competitive position . . . would probably not have been secure without the agreement, and it might even have been jeopardised.'[439] It is submitted that this approach is not significantly different to that taken in the *STM/ Nungesser/ENS* line of cases.

Second, the CFI explicitly recognised that it had not, in this judgment, ruled on the cor- **3.236** rect test in this regard. It held that '[t]he argument relied on by the defendant at the hearing that there is a significant difference between not being able to penetrate a market and being able to do so with difficulty cannot, in any event, invalidate the above considerations

---

[433] Case 258/78 [1982] ECR 2515, para 61.

[434] Case T-65/98 [2003] ECR II-4653.

[435] *Métropole*, para 109. There is also a proportionality leg to the test; see para 3.198 above.

[436] *Métropole*, paras 120–122.

[437] It is worth noting that the test is likely to be an objective one: *Métropole*, para 109; see also Case C-234/89 *Delimitis* [1991] ECR I-935, para 21 where the ECJ referred to 'real concrete possibilities . . . for a new competitor to penetrate the relevant market and compete with the undertakings already established'.

[438] Case T-328/03 *O2 (Germany) GmbH & Co. v Commission* (judgment of 2 May 2006), para 78.

[439] ibid, para 114.

since, in the Decision, the Commission specifically failed to analyse objectively the competition situation in the absence of the agreement under Article 81(1)'.[440]

(f) Appreciability

3.237   Agreements which restrict competition will nevertheless fall outside Article 81(1) if they do not have an appreciable impact on competition (or on inter-state trade).[441] In *Volk v Vervaecke*,[442] one of its earliest competition cases, the ECJ held that:

> An agreement falls outside the prohibition in Article 85(1) where it has only an insignificant effect on the market, taking into account the weak position which the persons concerned have on the market of the product in question.

3.238   The Commission has given guidance on this concept (also known as the de minimis doctrine) in its Notice on Agreements of Minor Importance.[443] This Notice provides market share[444] thresholds below which, in Commission's view [445] an agreement [446] can not have an appreciable effect on competition. The thresholds [447] are as follows:

(a)   the aggregate market share held by the parties to the agreement does not exceed 10 per cent on any of the relevant markets affected by the agreement, where the agreement is made between undertakings which are actual or potential competitors ('horizontal' agreements); or

(b)   if the market share held by each of the parties to the agreement does not exceed 15 per cent on any of the relevant markets affected by the agreement, where the agreement is made between undertakings which are not actual or potential competitors ('vertical' agreements or 'agreements between non-competitors').

3.239   In the case of a mixed horizontal/vertical agreement or where it is difficult to classify the agreement as either horizontal or vertical, the 10 per cent threshold is applicable. The threshold is reduced further to 5 per cent, for both horizontal and vertical agreements, where there is a parallel network of agreements having similar foreclosure effects on the relevant market, ie only those suppliers or distributors with a market share of less than 5 per cent can rely on the provisions of this Notice to escape the scope of Article 81(1). As for cumulative foreclosure itself,[448] the Notice states that such effects are unlikely to occur if

---

[440]   *O2 Germany*, para 115.

[441]   See also section D.5 below.

[442]   Case 5/69 [1969] ECR 295, paras 5/7.

[443]   OJ C 368, 22.12.2001, 13–15. See also discussion above at section C.7(b) and C.9, in particular at para 3.310 et seq, below. See also para 7.264 and section D(2) in Chapter 9.

[444]   Market shares are to be calculated on the basis of sales value data or, where appropriate, purchase value data. If value data are not available, estimates based on other reliable market information, including volume data, may be used.

[445]   Though binding only on itself, the Commission expressly states that the aim of the Notice is 'to give guidance to the courts and authorities of the Member States in their application of Article 81'; see para I.4 of the Notice.

[446]   The Notice does not apply to 'hardcore restrictions'—see para II.11 of the Notice. See also C.7(b) above as well as paras 7.391 and section D(2) of Chapter 9.

[447]   The thresholds are, to some extent, flexible: para 9 states that agreements will benefit from the safe harbours provided by the Notice as long as market shares do not exceed the thresholds, in two successive calendar years, by more than two percentage points.

[448]   For an explanation of cumulative effects doctrine see section C.8(9) below, as well as section C of Chapter 9.

less than 30 per cent of the relevant market is covered by parallel networks of agreements having similar effects.

It is important to stress, however, that agreements which breach the thresholds of the **3.240** Notice do not necessarily fall within the scope of Article 81(1). In *European Night Services v Commission*, the CFI held that the 'mere fact that [the] threshold may be reached and even exceeded does not make it possible to conclude with certainty that an agreement is caught by Article 85(1) [now Article 81(1)] of the Treaty'.[449] Thus, even where agreements exceed the thresholds set out in the Notice 'the Commission must provide an adequate statement of its reasons for considering such agreements to be caught by the prohibition' of Article 81(1).[450] This is reflected in the Notice itself which expressly states that '[i]n this notice the Commission quantifies, with the help of market share thresholds, what is *not* an appreciable restriction of competition under Article 81 of the EC Treaty. This *negative* definition of appreciability does not imply that agreements between undertakings which exceed the thresholds set out in this notice appreciably restrict competition'.[451] As such the Notice effectively sets 'safe harbours' below which agreements can not be said to have an appreciable effect on competition.

It is also important to note that 'appreciability' and 'market power' are not, at this stage in **3.241** the development of EC competition law, synonymous.[452] The former is an economic idea which has yet to be defined by the European Courts but which the Commission has recently adopted[453] as the threshold beyond which restrictive agreements are likely *to be caught* by Article 81(1), ie it helps define what *is* a restriction of competition.

The latter is a legal concept which the ECJ introduced to ensure that the Freedom of Action doc- **3.242** trine, which as noted above was at the centre of competition enforcement in the Community until very recently, did not ensnare agreements with had an 'insignificant', or in the Commission's words 'negligible' effect on the market.[454] Without such an instrument the Freedom of Action theory would have brought within the scope of Article 81(1) a far larger number of agreements since, almost by definition, most contracts limit, to some extent, the commercial freedom of the parties.

---

[449] Case T-374/94 [1998] ECR II-3141, para 102; see also Case T-7/93 *Langnese-Iglo GmbH v Commission* [1995] ECR II-1533, para 98.

[450] Case T-374/94 [1988] *European Night Services v Commission* [1998] ECR II-3141, para 102.

[451] Para I.2 of the Notice.

[452] However, whilst in line with the jurisprudence, the relevance of the distinction drawn between appreciability and market power is less easy to explain from a practical perspective. See paras 3.332–3.336 below.

[453] See paras 3.332–3.336 below.

[454] It is worth noting that whilst the appreciability doctrine is usually thought of in market share terms, it can also not apply if the restriction itself is insignificant. For example in Joined Cases C-180/98 to C-184/98 *Pavel Pavlov v Stichting Pensioenfonds Medische Specialisten* ECR 2000 I-06451, the ECJ found that a decision to set up a pension fund entrusted with the management of a supplementary pension scheme was not an appreciable restriction. This was because the pension fund produced 'restrictive effects only in relation to one cost factor of the services offered by self-employed medical specialists . . . which is insignificant in comparison with other factors, such as medical fees or the cost of medical equipment. The cost of the supplementary pension scheme has only a marginal and indirect influence on the final cost of the services offered by self-employed medical specialists.' In *UEFA's Broadcasting Regulations* the Commission decided that regulations which prevented the live transmission of matches at certain times, in order to protect amateur participation in sport and to encourage live attendance at football matches, was not an appreciable restriction. See also *Irish Banks' Standing Committee* OJ [1986] L295/28; *Visa International* OJ [2001] L293/24, on appeal Case T-28/02 *First Data Corp v Commission* (judgment pending); *Identrus* OJ [2001] L249/12.

(g) Cumulative Effects Doctrine

3.243 The cumulative effects doctrine covers the fourth category of cases in which the European Courts have found restrictive clauses to fall outside Article 81(1) because of the market context in which they operate.

3.244 Under the doctrine, vertical agreements containing restrictions do not fall within the scope of Article 81(1) if there are 'real concrete possibilities'[455] for new players to enter the market or for existing participants to expand. Where this is not the case (ie where the market is foreclosed), exclusive agreements can still escape the application of Article 81(1) if they do not significantly contribute to the foreclosure effect.

3.245 The doctrine is set out most clearly in *Van den Burgh Foods* where the CFI held[456] that '[w]hen examining the correctness of the Commission's assessment of the existence and degree of market foreclosure, the Court cannot confine itself to looking at the effects of the exclusivity clause, considered in isolation, referring only to the contractual restrictions imposed by [the supplier's] distribution agreements on individual retailers'. In order to determine whether such agreements falls within Article 81(1) it is necessary to consider whether 'all the similar agreements entered into in the relevant market and the other features of the economic and legal context of the agreements at issue, show that those agreements cumulatively have the effect of denying access to that market to new competitors. If, on examination, that is found not to be the case, the individual agreements making up the bundle of agreements cannot impair competition within the meaning of Article 85(1) of the Treaty.' If, on the other hand, such examination shows that it is 'difficult to gain access to the market, it is then necessary to assess the extent to which the agreements at issue contribute to the cumulative effect produced, on the basis that only those agreements which make a significant contribution to any partitioning of the market are prohibited'.

3.246 It is worth noting that the scope of application of the doctrine is not as wide as it might, at first, seem: if a bundle of contracts from a particular producer makes a sufficient contribution to the foreclosure effect to fall within Article 81(1) then every agreement within the bundle, however small, will be caught.

3.247 The cumulative effects doctrine raises a number of complex practical and theoretical issues. These are discussed in Chapter 9 at section C.[457]

(h) The Purpose of the Market Analysis

(i) No Rule of Reason under Article 81(1)

3.248 As discussed in section C.8(c), a restriction of rivalry is not, in and of itself, sufficient for the application of Article 81(1): agreements must be assessed in their specific market context. In a series of appeals including, most recently, *Métropole*[458] and *Van den*

---

[455] Case C-234/89 *Delimitis* [1991] ECR I-935, para 21.

[456] Case T-65/98 [2003] ECR II-4653, paras 82–83.

[457] See also Case C-234/89 *Delimitis* [1991] ECR I-935, paras 14–27; Case T-7/93 *Langnese-Iglo GmbH v Commission* [1995] ECR II-1533, especially paras 94–95 and 101.

[458] Case T-112/99 *Métropole Télévision (M6), Suez-Lyonnaise des Eaux, France Télécom and Télévision Française 1 SA (TF1)* [2001] ECR II-2459.

Bergh Foods,[459] it was argued by the applicants that this meant that agreements fell within Article 81(1) only where a weighing up of the pro- and anti-competitive effects showed that there was a net negative impact on competition. This approach, sometimes known as the 'rule of reason' was challenged by the Commission and rejected by the CFI.

The question of whether Article 81(1) requires (or at least should require) a balancing exer- **3.249**
cise of this nature to be conducted has long been debated[460] and has not, in the view of some commentators, been settled by the CFI's judgments in *Métropole* and *Van den Bergh Foods*. Those who believe that Article 81(1) requires such approach rely on the line of (mostly ECJ) cases discussed in sections C.8(d) and (e) above in particular *Metro I and II*,[461] *Nungesser*,[462] *Coditel*,[463] *Pronuptia*,[464] *Gøttrup-Klim*,[465] *European Night Services*,[466] *Wouters*[467] and *O2*.[468] In summary the argument is as follows:[469] in these cases the European Courts found restrictive clauses to fall outside Article 81(1) either because they were necessary for the implementation of a legitimate commercial or public policy purpose ('ancillary restraints doctrine') or for goods/services to be supplied at all because of the commercial risks involved ('necessity for supply doctrine'). A balancing of pro- and anti-competitive effects is inherent in such approaches. Thus, the very finding that a particular activity is legitimate implies a value judgment; in a commercial ancillarity case this will inevitably involve an assessment of whether the main agreement 'taken as a whole . . . is capable of encouraging competition on the market'[470] or is, at least neutral in competitive terms; in a vertical 'necessity for supply' doctrine case it could involve a balancing of increased inter-brand competition against a reduction in intra-brand competition.

---

[459] Case T-65/98 [2003] ECR II-4653.

[460] See for example Joliet, '*The Rule of Reason in Antitrust Law: American, German and Common Market Laws in Comparative Perspective*' (The Hague, 1967); Korah, 'The rise and fall of provisional validity: The need for a Rule of Reason in EEC Antitrust' (1981) Northwestern J of Intl L and Business 320; Steindorff, 'Article 85 and the Rule of Reason' 21 CML Rev (1984) 639; Gyselen, 'Vertical restraints in the distribution process: Strength and weakness of the free rider rationale under EEC Competition Law', 21 CML Rev (1984) 647; Forrester and Norall, 'The laicization of Community law: Self-help and the Rule of Reason: how competition law is and could be applied', 21 CML Rev (1984) 11; Whish and Sufrin, 'Article 85 and the Rule of Reason' 7 YEL (1987) 1; G Wils, ' "Rule of Reason": Une Regle Raisonnable en Droit Communautaire?' (1990) CDE 19; Manzini, 'The European Rule of Reason: Crossing the sea of doubt' (2002) ECLR 392; Butterworths *Competition Law*, issue 54 [2003], Division I, para 188–205; Nicolaides, 'The Balancing Myth: The Economics of Article 81(1) & (3)' (2005) LIEI 1236.

[461] Case 26/76 [1977] ECR 1875; Case 75/84 [1986] ECR 3021.

[462] Case 258/78 [1982] ECR 2515.

[463] Case 262/81 [1982] ECR 3381.

[464] Case 161/84 *Pronuptia de Paris v Pronuptia de Paris Irmgard Schillgalis* [1986] ECR 353.

[465] Case C-250/92 [1994] ECR I-5641, paras 32–34.

[466] Case T-374/94 [1998] ECR II-3141.

[467] Case C-309/99 [2002] ECR I-1577.

[468] Case T-328/03 *O2 (Germany) GmbH & Co. v Commission*, judgment of 2 May 2006.

[469] This is a very simplified version of the argument based on Chapter 2 of the first edition of this book and sections C.8(d) and C.8(e) above. For a different elegant exposition of this view see Nazzini, 'Article 81 EC between time present and time past: a normative critique of "restriction of competition" in EU law' [2006] CML Rev 43: 497–53.; and Odudu, 'Interpreting Article 81(1): Demonstrating Restrictive effect' 26 EL Rev (2001) 261, 271–272.

[470] Case C-309/99 *JCJ Wouters, JW Savelbergh and Price Waterhouse Belastingadviseurs BV v Algemene Raad van de Nederlandse Orde van Advocaten, intervener: Raad van de Balies van de Europese Gemeenschap* [2002] ECR I-1577, opinion of Advocate General Léger, para 104.

3.250 The need for a balancing of the kind envisaged by the parties in *Métropole* and *Van den Bergh Foods* has however been rejected by the majority of commentators. There are a number of reasons for this. First, as noted in paragraphs 3.165–3.175 above the Commission's and the European Courts' focus had, until very recently, been on whether the agreement under review hindered the entry of potential competitors or the expansion of existing players. A rule of reason approach however requires a weighing up of the pro- and anti-competitive effects to determine an agreement's net effect on competition—the impact of the agreement on existing or potential players would be but one element within this.

3.251 Second, whilst a degree of balancing is clearly inherent in the 'ancillary restraints' and 'necessity for supply' doctrines, with the exception of the *Metro cases*,[471] *Gøttrup-Klim*,[472] *Wouters*[473] and *O2*[474] there is little in the language of the judgments referred to in paragraph 3.249 to suggest that a fuller market assessment was conducted by the European Courts in order to ascertain the overall, or net, impact on competition.

3.252 Rather in the cases categorised in paragraph 3.249 above as falling within the ancillary restraints doctrine, the European Courts appear to have taken the 'common-sense' view that certain forms of activity such as franchising (*Pronuptia*) and the sale of a business (*Remia*) were legitimate activities which would have been harmed by an overly expansive application of Article 81(1). By taking this approach the European Courts prevented Article 81(1) from 'extending wholly abstractly and without distinction to all agreements whose effect is to restrict the freedom of action of one or more of the parties'.[475]

3.253 In the case of the 'necessity for supply' doctrine the level of economic analysis conducted by the ECJ in its leading judgments was, it is submitted, too superficial and impressionistic to suggest that a balancing of the kind necessary under the rule of reason approach was conducted.

3.254 As for the judgments referred to in paragraph 3.249, it will be argued below that they are either distinguishable (*Metro I/II* and, with greater difficulty, *O2*) or are best interpreted as ancillary restraints cases (*Gøttrup-Klim* and *Wouters*).

3.255 Third is the clear, unambiguous rejection of the approach by the CFI in *Métropole* and *Van den Bergh Foods*.

(ii) Gøttrup-Klim[476]

3.256 In this case the ECJ was asked to consider whether a joint buying co-operative which prevented its members from buying through other similar arrangements (referred to in the judgments as the '[p]rohibition of dual membership')[477] fell within Article 81(1). In setting out its view the Court used language which could be read as implying a consideration of the overall effect on competition: it held that 'the activities of cooperative purchasing associations may . . . *make way for more effective competition* . . . [the p]rohibition of dual

---

[471] Case 26/76 [1977] ECR 1875; Case 75/84 [1986] ECR 3021.
[472] Case C-250/92 [1994] ECR I-5641, paras 32–34.
[473] Case C-309/99 [2002] ECR I-1577.
[474] Case T-328/03 *O2 (Germany) GmbH & Co. v Commission,* judgment of 2 May 2006.
[475] *Métropole,* para 77.
[476] Case C-250/92 [1994] ECR I-5641, paras 32–34.
[477] ibid, para 34.

membership does not, therefore, necessarily constitute a restriction of competition . . . *and may even have beneficial effects on competition*' (emphasis added).

However, the Court's conclusion was, it is submitted, primarily driven by the imbalance in the bargaining position of the sellers and buyers in this market: the Court found that the joint buying co-operative 'constitute[d] a significant counterweight to the contractual power of large producers' and that the prohibition of dual membership was necessary for its effective operation. The Court found that where some members of two competing cooperative purchasing associations belong to both at the same time, 'the result is to make each association less capable of pursuing its objectives for the benefit of the rest of its members', especially where the members concerned, as in the case in point, are themselves cooperative associations with a large number of individual members. It followed from this that such 'dual membership would jeopardize both the proper functioning of the cooperative and its contractual power in relation to producers'. The ECJ went on to hold that 'in order to escape the prohibition laid down in Article 85(1) [now Article 81(1)] of the Treaty, the restrictions imposed on members by the statutes of cooperative purchasing associations must be limited to what is necessary to ensure that the cooperative functions properly and maintains its contractual power in relation to producers'.[478]

3.257

Therefore, whilst not impossible to argue the contrary, the case is better understood as one in which the ancillary restraints doctrine was applied in a market context in which the relevant undertakings had little economic power. Put differently, whilst the case may be consistent with a rule of reason approach, it would be dangerous for advisors to rely overly on it as precedent for the proposition that a real balancing of pro- and anti-competitive effects[479] is necessary under Article 81(1) given (i) the fact that the case was about a joint purchasing arrangement in which the purchasers were evidently in a much weaker position that the suppliers and (ii) the fact that the ECJ's approach is consistent with the ancillary restraints doctrine—a doctrine which, unlike the rule of reason, has explicitly been confirmed by both the Commission and the CFI as being a legitimate creature of European competition law.

3.258

(iii) Wouters[480]

A similar conclusion can be drawn from *Wouters*—a reference under Article 234 of the Treaty in which the ECJ found a national regulation ('Regulation') prohibiting multi-disciplinary partnerships between member of the Dutch bar and accountants to fall outside the scope of Article 81(1). As with *Gøttrup-Klim*, it is possible to argue that *Wouters* is an example of the balancing of pro- and anti-competitive effects under Article 81(1): the Court found that the Regulation was liable to limit production and technical development within the meaning of Article 81(1)(b) of the Treaty. It gave three reasons for this: first, since legal services more and more frequently required recourse to an accountant, a multi-disciplinary partnership of members of the Bar and accountants would make it possible to offer a wider range of services. Clients would thus be able to turn to a single entity for a large part of the services necessary for the organisation, management and operation of their business (ie 'the

3.259

---

478 ibid, para 35.
479 See Verouden, 'Vertical Agreements and Article 81(1) EC' Antitrust Law Journal [2003] Vol 71 p 528.
480 Case C-309/99 [2002] ECR I-1577.

one stop shop advantage').[481] Second, a multi-disciplinary partnership would be capable of satisfying the needs of what the Court referred to as 'the increasing interpenetration of national markets and the consequent necessity for continuous adaptation to national and international legislation'. Third, the Court found that it was not inconceivable that the economies of scale resulting from such multi-disciplinary partnerships might have positive effects on the cost of services.

3.260 On the other side, the Court went on to identify benefits which flowed from the Regulation. First it found that the conflict of interest requirement on law firms could, if they were permitted to enter into partnership with accountancy firms, lead to a reduction in the number of undertakings offering legal services. This was because the accountancy market was already highly concentrated.[482] Second it found that members of the Bar 'might no longer be in a position to advise and represent their clients independently and in the observance of strict professional secrecy if they belonged to an organisation which was also responsible for producing an account of the financial results of the transactions in respect of which their services were called upon and for certifying those accounts'.[483]

3.261 Although these findings were based on assertion rather than detailed argument backed by facts or any real analysis, the ECJ would appear to have engaged in at least a degree of balancing between pro- and anti-competitive effects under Article 81(1). This has led some[484] to argue that in doing so the ECJ adopted a rule of real approach (albeit a highly superficial one).

3.262 This interpretation is not however easy to reconcile with the main thrust of the judgment, which focussed on whether the prohibition was necessary for the proper practice of the legal profession (rather than whether its pro-competitive benefits outweigh its anti-competitive harm).

3.263 The Court held that in applying Article 81(1) 'account must be taken of [the Regulation's] objectives . . . [i]t has then to be considered whether the consequential effects restrictive of competition are inherent in the pursuit of those objectives'.[485] The Court found that the aim of the Regulation was to ensure that the rules of professional conduct for members of the Bar were complied with, having regard to the prevailing perceptions of the profession in that country. The Bar of the Netherlands was entitled to consider that its members might no longer be in a position to act independently and in the observance of strict professional secrecy if they belonged to an organisation which 'was also responsible for producing an account of the financial results of the transactions in respect of which their services were called upon and for certifying those accounts'. In addition accountants in the Netherlands were not bound by a rule of professional secrecy which was comparable to those of the Bar. In light of these considerations, the ECJ concluded that it 'does not appear that the effects restrictive of competition such as those resulting for members of the Bar practising in the Netherlands from a Regulation such as the 1993 Regulation *go beyond what is necessary* in order to ensure the proper practice of the legal profession' in the Netherlands.

---

481 Para 87.
482 Paras 91–93.
483 Para 105.
484 See for example Nazzini [2006] cited above.
485 Case C-309/99 [2002] ECR I-1577, para 97.

Thus (as with *Gøttrup-Klim*) whilst not impossible to argue the contrary, the most prudent **3.264** course for advisors would be to consider this case as one in which the ancillary restraints doctrine was applied (but on public interest grounds).[486] From a rule of reason type perspective, *Wouters* is, at most, authority for the proposition that public policy considerations can, in certain circumstances, outweigh harm to competition. This is however some way from the proposition that *Wouters* is authority for the view that Article 81(1) applies only where the pro-competitive effects of an agreement outweigh its anti-competitive harm (such that the overall, or net, effect *on competition* is neutral or positive).[487]

(iv) Metro I and II [488]

In these cases the ECJ held that selective distribution systems based only on qualitative and **3.265** non-discriminatory criteria ('simple selective distribution') did not fall within the scope of Article 81(1), notwithstanding the fact that they might have a dampening effect on price competition. It stated that the price effect was counterbalanced by competition on the quality of the services supplied to customers, which was not normally possible in the absence of an adequate profit margin covering the higher costs entailed by such services.[489]

The language and approach adopted by the ECJ indicate that a degree of balancing was **3.266** conducted. However, even those who see these cases as authority for a rule of reason approach acknowledge that the judgments do not allow for a clear conclusion to be reached as to where the Court drew the line between Article 81(1) and 81(3).[490] For example, in *Metro II* the Court considered the increase in the degree of concentration on the market as 'a factor to be taken into consideration in examining an application for the renewal of an exemption under Article 85(3) of the Treaty'[491]—however most commentators would agree that under a rule of reason approach the degree of concentration would, first and foremost, be a matter for Article 81(1). Furthermore, any conclusions which may be drawn from these cases on this issue is clouded by the fact that the Court also relied on tests such as the reasonableness of the requirement (paragraph 33) and the necessity of the clause for the attainment of a (legitimate) objective (paragraph 27) to reach it conclusion.

It can also be argued that the agreements fell outside Article 81(1) because there was no **3.267** foreclosure effect. First, in a simple selective distribution system there is generally no restriction of rivalry since there is no limit on the number of undertakings that can join. In such circumstances, there is only likely to be a foreclosure effect of the type relevant to

---

[486] See also para 3.258 above.

[487] But see Nazzini 'Article 81 EC between time present and time past: a normative critique of "restriction of competition" in EU law' [2006] CML Rev 43: 497–53. One of Nazzini's arguments is that the proper practice of the legal profession benefits consumers. This allows him to interpret any weighing up that may have taken place as being economic (rather than public interest) in nature and therefore within the rule of reason; see also Monti, 'Article 81 EC and Public Policy' [2002] 5 CML Rev 39 pp 1084-1086; cf Komninos 'Non-competition Concerns: Resolution of Conflicts in the Integrated Article 81 EC', Working Paper (L) 08/05 Oxford Centre for Competition Law & Policy.

[488] Case 26/76 [1977] ECR 1875; Case 75/84 [1986] ECR 3021.

[489] See paras 20-22 of *Metro I* and para 45 of *Metro II* (Case 75/84 ECR 1986 3021) where the ECJ summarised it own findings in its previous judgment.

[490] See n 53, Nazzini 'Article 81 EC between time present and time past: a normative critique of "restriction of competition" in EU law' [2006] CML Rev 43: 497–536.

[491] Case 75/84 [1986] ECR 3021, para 88.

Article 81(1) where the existence of a number of similar systems leaves no room for other methods of distribution.[492] Second and perhaps more importantly, are the particular facts of the *Metro* cases themselves: for example in *Metro II* the Commission had submitted evidence which showed that Metro had been excluded from only 'three 'simple' distribution systems and four systems entailing other obligations. By contrast, some leading manufacturers distribute their products without resorting to any selection'. The Court found that it was 'possible for Metro [the would be distributor] or other self-service wholesalers to market consumer electronics equipment, and colour television sets in particular, obtained from other producers . . . Metro has not, however, proved that other methods of distribution of a different kind, such as the self-service wholesale trade, no longer exist on the relevant market'.[493] It is possible to see this as a finding that the market was not foreclosed—an undertaking wishing to enter could do so in other ways.

3.268   Given all this, even if a balancing exercise of some sort was conducted by the Court, it would be prudent for advisors to regard this area of law as sui generis. It is interesting to note in this regard that these cases do not appear to have been relied upon by the applicants in any of the recent appeals based on the rule of reason.[494]

(v) O2 v Commission [495]

3.269   This case concerned an infrastructure sharing and national roaming arrangement in Germany between two mobile operators, O2 and T-Mobile. The CFI explicitly relied on the test set out by the ECJ in *Société Technique Minière (STM)*[496] in reaching its conclusions: the Court held that for an agreement to be restrictive by effect 'it is necessary to find that those factors are present which show that competition has in fact been prevented or restricted or distorted to an appreciable extent. The competition in question must be understood within the actual context in which it would occur in the absence of the agreement in dispute; the interference with competition may in particular be doubted if the agreement seems really necessary for the penetration of a new area.' On the facts, the CFI found that the Commission had failed to assess properly 'the extent to which the agreement was necessary for O2 to penetrate the 3G mobile communications market'.[497] The Court went on to find that O2's position on the 3G market would 'probably not have been secure without the agreement, and it might even have been jeopardised'.[498]

---

[492] ibid, paras 41–42. But see Case T-19/92 *Groupement d'Achat Edouard Leclerc v Commission* [1996] ECR II-1851, paras 178–192 and Case T-88/92 *Groupement d'Achat Edouard Leclerc v Commission* [1996] ECR II-1961, paras 170–184 where these types of arguments were rejected.

[493] Case 75/84 *Metro II* [1986] ECR 3021, paras 64–66.

[494] See Case T-112/99 *Métropole Télévision (M6), Suez-Lyonnaise des Eaux, France Télécom and Télévision Française 1 SA (TF1)* [2001] ECR II-2459, para 68; Joined Cases T-374/94, T-375/94, T 384/94 and T-388/94 *European Night Services* [1998] ECR II-3141, para 119; Case T-65/98 *Van den Bergh Foods* [2003] ECR II-4653, para 53.

[495] Case T-328/03, para 68.

[496] Case 56/65 [1966] ECR 235, at 249–250. See also para 3.177.

[497] Case T-328/03 *O2 (Germany) GmbH & Co v Commission* (judgment of 2 May 2006), para 77.

[498] ibid, para 114.

In reaching this conclusion however the Court appeared to rely on factors such as the efficiency, efficacy and speed of entry.[499] In particular the Court found that the 'roaming agreement of the type concluded . . . is capable of enabling, in certain circumstances, the smallest operator [O2] to compete with the major players'. In essence the Court appeared to find that in the absence of these arrangements O2 would have been a less effective competitor to the major incumbents. **3.270**

Under the more traditional approach the Court would have limited itself to considering whether the 'the agreement seems really necessary for the penetration of a new area'.[500] The 'pro-competitive' assessment of whether the agreement enabled a weaker competitor to compete more effectively with strong incumbents would have been considered under Article 81(3). **3.271**

Does O2 Signal a Change in Direction?   The case can be interpreted in two different ways. On the one hand, the Court itself argued that such an approach did 'not amount to carrying out an assessment of the pro- and anti-competitive effects of the agreement and thus to applying a rule of reason, which the Community judicature has not deemed to have its place under Article 81(1)'.[501] **3.272**

It is also worth noting that *O2* contains a number of elements which suggest that the CFI's findings were case-specific. First the Court is very careful to stress the 'specific characteristics'[502] of (what it refers to on a number of occasions in the judgment as) this 'emerging market'.[503] **3.273**

Second, when noting the pro-competitive elements of the arrangements, the Court often uses language which is highly qualified. For instance the quote set out in paragraph 3.270 above contains a significant number of caveats—for the sake of clarity it is repeated here with added emphasis: '*[i]n the present case, it cannot be ruled out* that a roaming agreement *of the type concluded* . . . is . . . capable of enabling, *in certain circumstances*, the smallest operator to compete with major players . . .'(emphasis added).[504] **3.274**

Third it is evident from the language used that the CFI was unimpressed by the Commission's case—the judgment could thus be seen as a 'common-sense' one in which **3.275**

---

[499] The Court implied that the factors the Commission had relied upon to grant an exemption were relevant to the assessment under Art 81(1). In particular the Court noted the following from the Decision:
    • O2 'would not have been able to gain access to the market efficiently' and would likely have been unable, at least in certain geographic areas, unable to fulfil its obligations under its operating licence (paras 111–112);
    • O2 was unlikely to be in a position to quickly build out a high-quality network covering a sufficient area to enable the company to compete effectively from the outset against other established licensed operators (para 112);
    • '[w]ithout access to national roaming for 3G services on T-Mobile's network, O2 . . . would be a less effective competitor during its roll-out phase and would be unlikely to enter 3G wholesale and retail markets as a nationwide competitor (or in any event as a competitor offering the broadest geographical scope that is likely to be available at that time)' (recital 135) (para 113).
[500] Para 68. It is worth noting this in regard that the Court did not find that without rapid, efficient entry O2 would not have been unable to enter the market.
[501] Para 69.
[502] Para 110.
[503] Para 114.
[504] Para 109.

the Court refused to find anti-competitive an agreement which helped a very weak competitor to enter and compete more effectively with a much stronger incumbents.

3.276 Fourth, unlike cases such as *Métropole*[505] and *Van den Bergh Foods*,[506] the agreements in *O2* raised no foreclosure issues. They also did not appear to harm the process of rivalry between the parties. The Court found 'that the general assessment in recital 107 of the Decision that national roaming restricts competition because it enables a roaming operator to slow down the roll-out of its network and places it in a situation of technical and commercial dependence on the network of the visited operator is not based on any concrete evidence specific to the agreement and contained in the Decision'.[507]

3.277 Finally, and perhaps most significantly, the judgment is not clear as to the importance of the agreement for O2's participation in the market: whilst some paragraphs, such as 109, suggest that agreements merely permitted O2 to compete more vigorously with bigger players, others, in particular paragraph 114, suggest that O2 position was far more precarious: '[i]t is therefore apparent,' the Court concluded, 'that, in the light of the specific characteristics of the relevant emerging market, O2's competitive situation on the 3G market would probably not have been secure without the agreement, and it might even have been jeopardised'. This finding arguably brings this case in line with the 'necessity for supply' doctrine.

3.278 That all said, in light of the nature of the assessment made, and the focus of the CFI on consumer welfare in other recent cases,[508] it is however possible to argue, at least with a degree of force, that *O2* is a turning point in the approach taken by the CFI to Article 81(1).

3.279 First, unlike *Métropole* and *Van den Bergh Foods* the judgment in *O2* was handed down *after* the adoption of the Article 81(3) Guidelines.[509] Although the European Courts have increasingly shown less deference to the Commission, the position taken by the CFI in this case is broadly in line with the general approach set out in the Guidelines.

3.280 Second, and more importantly, it is clear from the judgment that the Court could easily have overturned the Decision on the basis of the Commission's failure to take into account properly relevant facts such as changes to the duration of the agreements made by the parties after notification. For instance the Court found that 'the general assessment of the restrictive nature of roaming is not substantiated in the light of the key parameter consisting in the duration of the agreement, that is to say taking account of the timetable for phasing out roaming envisaged for each area'.[510] Had the Commission 'actually taken into account the amendments to the agreement concerning roaming in urban areas in the examination of whether the agreement is compatible with the common market, it is possible that it would have made findings which differ from those which it reached in the Decision, in particular as regards the need for those new elements for O2 to gain access to the 3G market in

---

[505] Case T-112/99 [2001] ECR II-2459.
[506] Case T-65/98 [2003] ECR II-4653.
[507] Case T-328/03 *O2 (Germany) GmbH & Co. v Commission* (judgment of 2 May 2006), para 102.
[508] Case T-168/01 *GlaxoSmithKline Services v Commission* (judgment of 27 September 2006); see discussion above at paras 3.136–3.138. See also Joined Cases T-213/01 and T-214/01 *Österreichische Postsparkasse and Bank für Arbeit und Wirtschaft v Commission* judgment of 7 June 2006.
[509] See section C.9 at para 3.292 *et seq* below.
[510] Case T-328/03 *O2 (Germany) GmbH & Co. v Commission* judgment of 2 May 2006, para 93.

urban areas'.[511] Similarly, the Court found that the Commission was wrong to work on the assumption that since O2 was present on the 2G market, it would, in the absence of the agreement, necessarily also be present on the 3G market: '[i]t must be held that that assumption is not supported in the Decision by any analysis or justification showing that it is correct, a finding that, moreover, the defendant could only confirm at the hearing. Given that there was no such objective examination of the competition situation in the absence of the agreement, the Commission could not have properly assessed the extent to which the agreement was necessary for O2 to penetrate the 3G mobile communications market. The Commission therefore failed to fulfil its obligation to carry out an objective analysis of the impact of the agreement on the competitive situation.'[512] In summary the CFI found that the Decision 'suffers from insufficient analysis' and complained that the Decision was confined, in respect of roaming at least, 'to a petitio principii and to broad and general statements'.[513]

Instead of overturning the Decision on the basis of these flaws the Court however chose to undertake a detailed analysis of the market under Article 81(1) which encompassed 'pro-competitive' factors traditionally reserved for consideration under Article 81(3). It is worth noting in this regard that the Court appeared, at least implicitly, to acknowledge the difference between its approach and the more traditional view advocated by the Commission at the hearing: '[t]he argument relied on by the defendant at the hearing that there is a significant difference between not being able to penetrate a market and being able to do so with difficulty cannot, in any event, invalidate the above considerations since, in the Decision, the Commission specifically failed to analyse objectively the competition situation in the absence of the agreement under Article 81(1) EC and Article 53(1) of the EEA Agreement'.[514] **3.281**

(vi) Explicit Rejection of the Rule of Reason under Article 81(1) by the CFI

In *Métropole*[515] and subsequently in *Van den Bergh Foods*[516] (and more recently, though more indirectly in *O2*)[517] the CFI explicitly rejected the rule of reason approach under Article 81(1). The Court held that the requirement to assess agreements in their market context did not mean that 'it is necessary to weigh the pro and anti-competitive effects of an agreement in order to determine whether it is caught by the prohibition laid down in [Article 81(1)]'.[518] This is because such an approach would be 'difficult to reconcile with the rules prescribed by [Article 81].'[519] Article 81 'expressly provides, in its third paragraph, for the exemption of agreements that restrict competition where they satisfy a number of conditions. . . It is only within the specific framework of that provision that the pro and anti-competitive aspects of a restriction may be weighed.' The Court explained that Article 81(3) 'would lose much of its effectiveness if such an examination had already to be carried out under Article 85(1) [now Article 81(1)] of the Treaty'.[520] **3.282**

---

[511] Para 95.
[512] Para 77.
[513] Para 116.
[514] Para 115.
[515] Case T-112/99 [2001] ECR II-2459.
[516] Case T-65/98 [2003] ECR II-4653.
[517] Case T-328/03 *O2 (Germany) GmbH & Co. v Commission*, judgment of 2 May 2006.
[518] *Métropole*, para 72.
[519] ibid, para 73.
[520] *Métropole*, para 74; *Van den Burgh*, para 107.

(i) Extent of Market Analysis

3.283 Having rejected the rule of reason, the CFI went on to hold that the purpose of the market analysis is to prevent Article 81(1) from 'extending wholly abstractly and without distinction to all agreements whose effect is to restrict the freedom of action of one or more of the parties'.[521]

3.284 However, given its objective, the extent of the analysis may vary from case to case. In *Delimitis v Henniger Bräu* the ECJ conducted a detailed analysis of the market to determine whether access was appreciably impeded by the vertical agreements under review. This involved not only the definition of the relevant antitrust market but also identification and consideration of the options available to undertakings wishing to enter the market in light of the number and duration of other restrictive agreements already in place. In a similar case, *Van den Burgh Foods*, the CFI arguably undertook an even more exhaustive factual analysis to ascertain the degree to which the market was foreclosed to potential new entrants, and/or existing players wishing to expand, and whether Van den Burgh's agreement appreciably contributed to this foreclosure.[522] It is worth noting however that the analysis conducted by the Court in this case, whilst relatively detailed in comparison to many of its other judgments, was not especially precise on the question of whether there were, *in fact*, sufficient opportunities for new competitors to penetrate that market. For example, it did not consider what the minimum number of sales outlets necessary for the profitable entry were in this market.[523]

3.285 In *O2*,[524] the CFI was critical of the Commission for its failure to undertake a thorough assessment. For example it held that the Commission had been wrong to work on the assumption that, in the absence of the agreement, O2 would be present on the 3G mobile market agreement merely because it was present on the 2G one: '[i]t must be held that that assumption is not supported in the Decision by any analysis or justification showing that it is correct, a finding that, moreover, the defendant could only confirm at the hearing. Given that there was no such objective examination of the competition situation in the absence of the agreement, the Commission could not have properly assessed the extent to which the agreement was necessary for O2 to penetrate the 3G mobile communications market. The Commission therefore failed to fulfil its obligation to carry out an objective analysis of the impact of the agreement on the competitive situation.'[525] Similarly, as regards the impact of agreement on wholesale prices, the CFI found that the Commission's case had 'not been demonstrated'. Indeed the Commission's findings were, according to the CFI, 'belied by the statement in the Decision that the parties to the agreement have different pricing principles (recital 140). Moreover, in response to the questions put by the Court of First Instance, referred to in paragraph 36 above, concerning O2's price structure, the applicant has supplied information from which it is apparent that, by means of different types of products and services, a variety of subscription packages and pricing formulae combining many variables, it attempts to differentiate itself from T-Mobile.'[526]

---

[521] *Métropole*, para 77.
[522] Case T-65/98 [2003] ECR II-4653, see in particular paras 108–118.
[523] See Chapter 9 (Vertical agreements), sections C(2) and (3).
[524] Case T-328/03 *O2 (Germany) GmbH & Co. v Commission*, judgment of 2 May 2006.
[525] ibid, para 77.
[526] ibid, para 100.

Conversely in *Métropole*,[527] a case concerning the pay-TV market in France, the CFI's lim-　**3.286**
ited itself merely to upholding, with little further, the Commission's cursory analysis of the
impact of a clause obliging the parents of a joint venture to supply certain channel exclusively to their subsidiary. The Commission had found that although these channels did not
constitute a type of content that was 'essential for pay-TV', and that two other digital bouquets had been launched (one of which, according to the Commission itself, had been a
'great success') without offering this content, the exclusivity clause nevertheless had a foreclosure effect sufficient to bring it within the scope of Article 81(1) because:

(a) the channels supplied by the JV's parents 'traditionally attract the largest audience
    shares in France, namely 90% of viewers, if all methods of transmission are aggregated,
    and 75.1 % of cable viewers';
(b) 'There is also potential demand for the general-interest channels broadcast in digital
    mode, which could largely be accounted for by a peculiarity concerning the reception
    of terrestrial broadcasts in France. Although broadcasting via terrestrial frequencies is
    by far the most common method of transmission, reception of the programmes is occa-
    sionally poor or even impossible in some areas of France. According to a survey con-
    ducted by Médiamétrie over the period November to December 1997(25), 9,254,000
    of the 22,330,000 homes with a television set were located in areas where reception of
    the general-interest channels is poor . . .'
(c) the attractiveness of the general-interest channels as part of TPS's bouquet was esti-
    mated in surveys carried out on behalf of the company: [. . .] of interviewees stated that
    they had decided to subscribe because of the presence of the general-interest channels.

In comparison to the approach taken by the European Courts in *Delimitis, Van den Burgh*　**3.287**
Foods, and O2, the analysis in *Métropole* was fleeting—no real attempt was made by the
Commission, nor deemed necessary by the CFI, to assess the nature or extent of the foreclosure or indeed to establish, in any concrete way, the importance of this content to competition in this market.[528] In essence the Commission had found, and the CFI had
confirmed, that the exclusivity clause was restrictive of competition because it denied
'competitors access to attractive programmes'.[529]

The discrepancy between the European Courts' approaches in these cases creates a degree　**3.288**
of uncertainty as to the extent of analysis and evidence that is required for Article 81(1) to
apply. Although tempting for the Commission, NCAs and plaintiffs to follow *Métropole*, it
is submitted that the cursory analysis and level of detail relied upon by the CFI in that case
is something of an aberration.

(j) Restrictive Clauses are Not a Necessary Condition for the Application of Article 81(1)

Both the Commission and the European Courts have recognised that agreements which do not　**3.289**
contain clauses restricting the commercial freedom of the parties can restrict rivalry between

---

[527] Case T-112/99 *Métropole Télévision (M6), Suez-Lyonnaise des Eaux, France Télécom and Télévision Française 1 SA (TF1)* [2001] ECR II-2459.
[528] Although mere speculation, given the European Courts' approach in previous cases, the CFI's failure to conduct a more detailed assessment may simply have reflected the nature of the submissions made by the applicants in *Métropole*—careful reading of the *Van den Burgh Foods* judgment, for example, suggests that the submissions made by the applicants in that case were far more detailed and sophisticated than in *Métropole*.
[529] *TPS* [1999] OJ L90/6, para 107.

them or adversely affect the position of third parties, and therefore fall within Article 81(1). For example, in *UK Agricultural Tractor Registration Exchange*,[530] an information sharing system had been set up which had the effect of revealing to all competitors the market positions and strategies of individual undertakings. The system did not contractually limit the participants' freedom to take independent commercial decisions. The Commission and subsequently the ECJ found that, on a highly oligopolistic market, uncertainty about the future conduct of competitors was one of the only remaining spurs to competition. The exchange of information which reduced this uncertainty was therefore likely to impair substantially competition between them. Thus the agreement fell within Article 81(1) even though it did not explicitly limit the parties' commercial freedom. Similarly, in *British-American Tobacco Company and RJ Reynolds Industries v Commission*,[531] the ECJ held that an acquisition of a minority shareholding in a competitor could fall within Article 81(1) if, *inter alia*, it served as an instrument for influencing the commercial conduct of the companies in question or created a structure likely to be used for such co-operation between them.

3.290 A comparable logic has been used by the Commission in some of its decisions. In *GEC Weir Sodium Circulators*, the Commission held that: '[e]ven in the absence of express provisions, the creation of a joint venture generally has a notable effect on the conduct of parent parties who have a significant holding in the joint venture. Within the field of the joint venture and in related fields such parties are likely to co-ordinate their conduct and be influenced in what would otherwise have been their independent decisions and activities. Where the parent parties are actual or potential competitors, their participation in a joint venture is accordingly likely to impair free competition between them, regardless of the existence of explicit restrictive provisions to that effect.'[532]

3.291 More recently in its Guidelines on the Applicability of Article 81 to Horizontal Cooperation Agreements[533] the Commission stated that the application of Article 81(1) depends on the 'economic context taking into account both the nature of the agreement and the parties' combined market power which determines—together with other structural factors—the capability of the cooperation to affect overall competition'.[534] Contractual terms in the agreement which limit the participants' freedom to take independent commercial decisions are just one of the factors taken into account when this analysis is made.

(9) Commission's new policy

3.292 The Commission's traditional approach, which was heavily criticised by many commentators,[535] gradually changed from the mid-1990s onwards to encompass greater economic

---

[530] [1992] OJ L68/19, paras 36–37; Case C-7/95 *John Deere Ltd v Commission* [1998] ECR I-3111; Case C-8/95 *New Holland Ford Ltd v Commission* [1998] ECR I-3175.
[531] Joined Cases 142 and 156/84 [1987] ECR 4487, paras 37–39.
[532] [1977] OJ L327/26, section II, para 2.
[533] Commission Notice, 'Guidelines on the applicability of Article 81 of the EC Treaty to horizontal cooperation agreements' [2001] OJ C3/2 (6.1.2001).
[534] ibid, para 20.
[535] See for example Barry E Hawk, 'System Failure: Vertical Restraints and EC Competition Law' (1995) 32 CML Rev 973; Ian Forrester and Christopher Norall, 'The Laicization Of Community Law: Self-Help And The Rule Of Reason: How Competition Law Is And Could Be Applied' (1984) CML Rev 21.

analysis.[536] It culminated in 2004 with the adoption of the Article 81(3) Guidelines which explicitly state that 'Article 81(1) only applies where on the basis of a proper market analysis it can be concluded that the agreement has likely anti-competitive effects on the market'.[537] Underpinning this is an assessment of market power and/or the likely impact of agreements on price, output, innovation, the variety or quality of goods and services.[538]

How is this 'economic' approach applied in practice? The Article 81(3) Guidelines set out a two-step test for the assessment of cases under Article 81(1). The first step consists of counterfactuals, one for agreements affecting inter-brand competition and the other for restrictions on intra-brand competition, which are applied to determine whether the agreement is *capable* of restricting competition. **3.293**

The second step involves an assessment of the likely impact of the agreement on the parameters of competition: for an agreement to fall within Article 81(1) 'it must affect actual or potential competition to such an extent that on the relevant market negative effects on prices, output, innovation or the variety or quality of goods and services can be expected with a reasonable degree of probability'.[539] **3.294**

(a) Step 1—The Counterfactuals

Paragraph 18 of the Article 81(3) Guidelines sets out two counterfactuals which the Commission now uses to assess cases under Article 81(1). The first is applied to agreements which allegedly affect inter-brand competition between the parties or from third parties. It seeks to determine whether 'the agreement restrict[s] actual or potential competition that would have existed without the agreement'. If the answer is yes, the 'agreement may be caught by Article 81(1)'.[540] **3.295**

The guidelines provide examples of how the counterfactual might be applied in practice. The first is where two undertakings established in different Member States undertake not to sell products in each other's home markets. In this case, potential competition that existed prior to the agreement is restricted. The second example given is that of a supplier imposing obligations on its distributors not to sell competing products. These obligations foreclose third party access to the market. As such, actual or potential competition that would have existed in the absence of the agreement is restricted. **3.296**

The Article 81(3) Guidelines make clear that the economic and legal context will be taken into account in assessing whether the parties to an agreement are actual or potential **3.297**

---

[536] See, for example, para 19 of the Commission's 'Guidelines on the applicability of Article 81 of the EC Treaty to horizontal cooperation agreements' [2001] OJ C3/2.

[537] See para 24 the Commission's 'Guidelines on the application of Article 81(3) of the Treaty' [2004] OJ C101/97.

[538] This policy shift however is not, as yet, reflected in the Commission's decisional practice or, with the important exception of the *GSK* judgment (Case T-168/01, judgment of 27 September 2006), in the case law of the European Courts. Existing case law is therefore still of relevance; indeed it has been argued that the CFI's 2001 judgment in Case T-112/99 *Métropole Télévision v Commission* [2001] ECR II-2459 reaffirmed the ordo-liberal underpinnings of Art 81(1). See, in particular, the seminal article by Giorgio Monti, 'Article 81 EC and Public Policy' [2002] 5 CML Rev 39, pp 1057–1099; Pietro Manzini, 'The European Rule of Reason—crossing the sea of doubt' [2002] ECLR 392.

[539] See para 24 of the Art 81(3) Guidelines.

[540] ibid, para 18(1).

competitors. For instance, 'if due to the financial risks involved and the technical capabilities of the parties it is unlikely on the basis of objective factors that each party would be able to carry out on its own the activities covered by the agreement the parties are deemed to be non-competitors in respect of that activity'. However, 'it is for the parties to bring forward evidence to that effect'.[541]

3.298 The second counterfactual seeks to determine whether 'the agreement restrict[s] actual or potential competition that would have existed in the absence of the contractual restraint(s)'.[542] Although the literal interpretation of this phrase suggests otherwise, paragraph 18(2) of the Guidelines makes it clear that the counterfactual relates to intra-brand competition only. The example given in the Guidelines is of a supplier restricting its distributors from competing with one another through the use of resale price maintenance and territorial or customer sales restrictions—in this situation '(potential) competition that could have existed between the distributors absent the restraints is restricted'.

3.299 The distinction drawn between inter- and intra-brand competition at this level of the analysis appears to have been made for two reasons. First, to underline the implications of the ECJ's judgment in *Consten and Grundig* where the Court held that: 'although competition between producers is generally more noticeable than between distributors of products of the same make, it does not thereby follow that an agreement tending to restrict the latter kind of competition should escape the prohibition of Article 85(1) [now Article 81(1)] merely because it might increase the former'.[543] By setting out two separate counterfactuals, the Guidelines underline the view that agreements that restrict intra-brand competition are caught by Article 81(1) even if they also promote inter-brand competition.[544]

3.300 The second, and in practical terms the more important, reason for two counterfactuals is to allow the Commission to take into account, at this stage in the analysis, the approach outlined by the ECJ in *Société Technique Minière*[545] and the cases where exclusivity is necessary

---

541 Guidelines, para 18(1).

542 ibid, para 18(2).

543 Joined Cases 56/64 and 58/66 *Consten and Grundig* [1966] ECR 429.

544 Case T-112/99 *Métropole Télévision (M6), Suez-Lyonnaise des Eaux, France Télécom and Télévision Française 1 SA (TF1)* [2001] ECR II-2459. The CFI's explicit refusal in *Métropole* to take into account either the degree of inter-brand competition existing in the market at the time of entry—the incumbent operator, Canal+ was almost certainly dominant—or its likely development had led some authors to call into question the effect based approach set out in the Commission Guidelines on Art 81(3); see, eg, Nazzini, 'Article 81 EC between time present and time past: a normative critique of "restriction of competition" in EU law' [2006] CML Rev 43: 497–536; see also Verouden, 'Vertical Agreements and Article 81(1) EC' Antitrust Law Journal [2003] Vol 71 No 2, pp 525–575 (this paper was published before the Art 81(3) Guidelines were adopted. As such it does not explicitly challenge the position set out therein). In essence these commentators argued that a focus on the effects of agreements on price and output requires a holistic (or what Verouden calls a 'net effect'—see p 528) assessment of competition to be made. In the case of *Métropole* this would have required an analysis of the restraints in light of the degree of inter-brand competition in the market; it would also have required an assessment to be made of the impact of the restraint on the development of inter-brand competition. In simple terms, it is argued that if the likely effect of the restraints in *Métropole* was to promote inter-brand competition (by enabling the new entrant to compete more vigorously with the dominant incumbent) then the likely effect of the clause, had it not been challenged, would have been more vigorous price/service/quality competition. As such, Art 81(1) could not be said to apply.

545 Case 56/65 *Société Technique Minière v Maschinenbau Ulm GmbH* [1996] ECR 235.

for supply.[546] These judgments made clear that restraints which restrict intra-competition but are 'objectively necessary for the *existence* [*note not implementation or commercial success*][547] of an agreement of that type or that nature' [emphasis added] are excluded from the application of Article 81(1).[548] The rationale for the '18(2) exclusion' is subtle but convoluted: the starting point is the fact that there can be no intra-brand competition without vertical agreements. Therefore, as a matter of logic, if a restraint is necessary for the conclusion of a vertical agreement then it can be said to be necessary for the very existence of the intra-brand competition that the agreement creates. Put differently, without the 'necessary' restraint, there would be no agreement and therefore no intra-brand competition for Article 81(1) to protect (at least not the intra-brand competition which would have been created by the agreement). As such intra-brand restraints that are 'objectively necessary' for the existence of a vertical agreement fall outside Article 81(1).

What does 'objectively necessary' mean? The Guidelines make clear that this 'exclusion of the **3.301** application of Article 81(1) can only be made on the basis of objective factors external to the parties themselves and not the subjective views and characteristics of the parties. The question is not whether the parties in their particular situation would not have accepted to conclude a less restrictive agreement, but whether given the nature of the agreement and the characteristics of the market a less restrictive agreement would not have been concluded by undertakings in a similar setting.'[549] In other words the '18(2) exclusion' does not apply merely because, in the absence of the restraint, the parties to the agreement would not have concluded it. The '18(2) exclusion' only applies if, in the absence of the restraint, undertakings in a similar setting would likely not have concluded an agreement of the same type or nature.

The description given in the Guidelines of the '18(2) exclusion' is, at least linguistically, **3.302** almost identical to that used for ancillary restraints.[550] However, the Article 81(3) Guidelines assert that whilst the two concepts are 'similar', they are not the same. As explained elsewhere in this chapter,[551] the ancillary restraints doctrine is relevant only to the practical implementation, as opposed to commercial success of an agreement. Its scope of application is therefore narrower than that of the '18(2) exclusion'.[552] From a practical perspective, the important implication of this is that the assessment of commercial risk under Article 81(1) is generally only relevant to intra-brand restraints—arguments based on the commercial need for restraints on inter-brand competition are unlikely to be successful in taking agreements outside Article 81(1). This is reflected in the examples given in the Article 81(3) Guidelines of situations covered by the '18(2) exclusion'. The first is where a potential licensee would not take a licence for a new technology which requires large up-front investment without initial

---

[546] This conclusion is derived from para 29 of the Guidelines which states that '[i]t follows that the ancillary restraints test is similar to the test set out in paragraph 18(2) above. However, the ancillary restraints test applies in *all cases* where the main transaction is not restrictive of competition. It is *not limited to determining the impact of the agreement on intra-brand competition*' (emphasis added). See also para 3.181 *et seq* above.

[547] See discussion on ancillarity above at 3.232 *et seq* and para 3.295 below.

[548] Para 18(2) of the Art 81(3) Guidelines.

[549] ibid, para 18(2).

[550] ibid, para 29.

[551] See para 3.177 above.

[552] See paras 30–31 of the Art 81(3) Guidelines.

protection from licensees in other territories.[553] The second is where a licensor would be unlikely to license widely if he faced direct competition from his own licensees.[554]

3.303   As an aside it is also worth noting that whilst the '18(2) exclusion' is built on the logic of the ECJ's judgments in *Société Technique Minière* and the cases where exclusivity is necessary for supply, it also introduced a new aspect by including within its scope elements which are akin to those found under the 'objective justification' defence to Article 82—the example given in the Article 81(3) Guidelines is of 'a prohibition imposed on all distributors not to sell to certain categories of end users . . . for reasons of safety or health related to the dangerous nature of the product in question'.[555]

(b) Step 2—Assessment of the Likely Effect of the Agreement Restraint on Prices, Output, Innovation or the Variety or Quality of Goods or Services

3.304   The second step in the analysis is to consider whether the agreement affects actual or potential competition[556] to such an extent that on the relevant market appreciable negative effects on prices, output, innovation or the variety or quality of goods and services can be expected with a reasonable degree of probability.

3.305   For the avoidance of doubt, this step is only relevant if application of the counterfactuals shows that an agreement is capable of restricting competition.

3.306   In certain cases, it may be possible to show anti-competitive effects, such as price increases, directly by analysing the conduct of the parties to the agreement on the market and/or the available data. However, in most instances, this will not be possible either because the data does not exist or because the agreement has yet to be put into effect.

3.307   According to the Article 81(3) Guidelines in such cases analysis of the restrictive effects of the agreement requires consideration 'inter alia [of] the nature of the products, the market position of the parties, the market position of competitors, the market position of buyers, the existence of potential competitors and the level of entry barriers'.[557] The aim of this analysis is to ascertain if 'the parties individually or jointly have or obtain some degree of market power and [whether] the agreement contributes to the creation, maintenance or strengthening of that market power or allows the parties to exploit such market power'.[558] Where this is the case the Article 81(3) Guidelines assume that 'negative effects on competition within the relevant market are likely to occur'.[559]

3.308   Market power is defined as 'the ability to maintain prices above competitive levels for a significant period of time or to maintain output in terms of product quantities, product quality and variety or innovation below competitive levels for a significant period of time . . . [i]t is when competitive constraints are insufficient to maintain prices and output at competitive

---

[553] See para 101 of the Commission's 'Guidelines on the application of Article 81 of the EC Treaty to technology transfer agreements' [2004] OJ C101/2.

[554] ibid, para 172.

[555] Para 18(2) of the Art 81(3) Guidelines.

[556] See paras 7.126–7.138.

[557] Para 27 of the Art 81(3) Guidelines.

[558] ibid, para 25.

[559] ibid.

levels that undertakings have market power within the meaning of Article 81(1)'.[560] The Article 81(3) Guidelines go on to confirm that the degree of market power normally required for the finding of an infringement under Article 81(1) is less than that required for a finding of dominance under Article 82. However, crucially, no further guidance is provided in this document as to how market power is to be identified.

Some guidance can however been gleamed, to varying degrees, from Block Exemptions and Commission policy statements in particular the *Notice on Agreements of Minor Importance* (alternatively known as the *de minimis Notice*), the Guidelines on Vertical Restraints and the Guidelines on the applicability of Article 81 to horizontal co-operation agreements (see the next section). **3.309**

(c) Community Guidance on Market Power under Article 81(1)

(i) Notice on Agreements of Minor Importance [561]

This Notice provides market share thresholds below which, in Commission's view,[562] an agreement *can not have an appreciable effect*[563] on competition. **3.310**

The thresholds are as follows: **3.311**

(a) the aggregate market share held by the parties to the agreement does not exceed 10 per cent on any of the relevant markets affected by the agreement, where the agreement is made between undertakings which are actual or potential competitors ('horizontal' agreements); or

(b) if the market share held by each of the parties to the agreement does not exceed 15 per cent on any of the relevant markets affected by the agreement, where the agreement is made between undertakings which are not actual or potential competitors ('vertical' agreements or 'agreements between non-competitors').

In the case of a mixed horizontal/vertical agreement or where it is difficult to classify the agreement as either horizontal or vertical, the 10 per cent threshold is applicable. The threshold is reduced further to 5 per cent, for both horizontal and vertical agreements, where there is a parallel network of agreements having similar foreclosure effects on the relevant market, ie only those suppliers or distributors with a market share of less than 5 per cent can rely on the provisions of this Notice to escape the scope of Article 81(1). As for cumulative foreclosure itself, the Notice states that such effects are unlikely to occur if less than 30 per cent of the relevant market is covered by parallel networks of agreements having similar effects. **3.312**

It is important to stress, however, that agreements which breach the thresholds of the Notice do not necessarily fall within the scope of Article 81(1). In *European Night Services v* **3.313**

---

[560] ibid.

[561] 'Commission Notice on agreements of minor importance which do not appreciably restrict competition under Article 81(1) of the Treaty establishing the European Community *(de minimis)'* [2001] OJ C368/13.

[562] Though binding only on itself, the Commission expressly states that the aim of the Notice is 'to give guidance to the courts and authorities of the Member States in their application of Article 81'; see para I.4 of the Notice.

[563] The Notice does not apply to horizontal agreements which are caught by object or to vertical agreements between competitors—see para II.11 of the Notice. See also para 3.146 above as well as para 7.391 in Chapter 7 and section B(5)(b) of Chapter 9.

Commission, the CFI held that the 'mere fact that [the] threshold may be reached and even exceeded does not make it possible to conclude with certainty that an agreement is caught by Article 85(1) [now Article 81(1)] of the Treaty'.[564] Thus, even where agreements exceed the thresholds set out in the Notice 'the Commission must provide an adequate statement of its reasons for considering such agreements to be caught by the prohibition' of Article 81(1).[565] This is reflected in the Notice itself which expressly states that '[i]n this notice the Commission quantifies, with the help of market share thresholds, what is *not* an appreciable restriction of competition under Article 81 of the EC Treaty. This *negative* definition of appreciability does not imply that agreements between undertakings which exceed the thresholds set out in this notice appreciably restrict competition'.[566] As such the Notice effectively sets 'safe harbours' below which the parties can not be said to have market power; *it does not however provide a starting point for the existence of market power.*

(ii) Vertical Block Exemption Regulation ('VBER')[567]

3.314   The VBER exempts all vertical agreements:[568]

(a) where the market share of the supplier, or in the case of exclusive supply obligations[569] the buyer, does not exceed 30 per cent; and

(b) which do not contain the hardcore restrictions set out in Articles 4 and 5.

3.315   From a practical perspective the existence of a high market share threshold, combined with a short hardcore list, means that for the vast majority of vertical agreements the test set out in the Article 81(3) Guidelines, indeed the very question of whether Article 81(1) is engaged, is largely irrelevant[570]—the Commission's enforcement activities (in particular under the ECMR) suggest that few undertakings have shares in excess of 30 per cent.

3.316   For cases falling outside the scope of the VBER, the 30 per cent threshold is important only insofar as it establishes a market share level beyond which agreements *may* be at risk; however, it is important to note that the VBER does not establish a starting point for the existence of market power[571] and thus the application of Article 81(1): neither the recitals nor the terms

---

[564] Case T-374/94 [1998] ECR II-3141, para 102; see also Case T-7/93 *Langnese-Iglo GmbH v Commission* [1995] ECR II-1533, para 98.

[565] Case T-374/94 [1988] *European Night Services v Commission* [1998] ECR II-3141, para 102.

[566] Para I.2 of the Notice.

[567] Commission Regulation 2790/99/EC on the application of Art 81(3) of the Treaty to categories of vertical agreements and concerted practices [1999] OJ L336/1 (29.12.1999).

[568] The rationale behind this approach is set out in recital 8 of the VBER: 'where the share of the relevant market accounted for by the supplier does not exceed 30%, vertical agreements which do not contain certain types of severely anti-competitive restraints generally lead to an improvement in production or distribution and allow consumers a fair share of the resulting benefits'. See also section D(1) of Chapter 9.

[569] As defined in Art 1(c) of the VBER.

[570] It can be argued that where such agreements do not affect trade between Member States, they may be at risk from national competition laws. However, in most cases, this risk is more theoretical than practical. This is because the competition laws of the majority of Member States mirror the wording of Art 81. It is also worth recalling that European law is always likely to be stricter than national law in this area since one of the objects of Art 81 is protection of the Single Market. Taken together, it would therefore seem highly unlikely that that an agreement fulfilling the two main criteria of the VBER (market share below 30% and no hardcore restrictions) would be found to breach most national competition laws.

[571] Recital 9 which states that above 30% 'there can be no presumption that vertical agreements . . . will usually give rise to objective advantages of such a character and size as to compensate for the disadvantages which

of the block exemption create any kind of presumption that agreements in which market shares are above 30 per cent automatically fall within Article 81(1).

(iii) Vertical Guidelines[572]

The Vertical Guidelines are important for the application of Article 81(1) in three main respects. **3.317**

First, they identify the factors which the Commission considers are 'the most important' in establishing 'whether a vertical agreement brings about an appreciable restriction of competition under Article 81(1)'.[573] These include the market position of the supplier; the market position of competitors; the market position of the buyer; entry barriers; the maturity of the market; the level of trade; the nature of the product; whether there is a cumulative effect; whether the agreement is 'imposed' or 'agreed'; the regulatory environment; and any behaviour that may indicate or facilitate collusion. It is worth noting these factors are ones typically used to determine the existence and degree of market power (although the term itself is not used in the Guidelines in relation to Article 81(1): unlike subsequent policy documents such the Article 81(3) Guidelines, the vertical one does not draw a clear distinction between Article 81 as a whole and its constituent parts in this respect). **3.318**

Second the Guidelines provide some indication as to the relative weight to be placed on each factor. Thus, for example, the Guidelines explain that in relation to *non-compete obligations*:[574] **3.319**

- the 'market position of the supplier is of *main importance* to assess possible anti-competitive effects';
- 'entry barriers are *important* to establish whether there is real foreclosure';
- '[c]ountervailing power is *relevant*, as powerful buyers will not easily allow themselves to be cut off from supply of competing goods or services';
- '[l]astly, 'the level of trade' is *relevant* for foreclosure. Foreclosure is less likely in case of an intermediate product' (emphasis added).

Thus, whilst of central importance to any assessment made, market share is just one factor, amongst a number of others, which is taken into account. As such the Guidelines effectively confirm (albeit implicitly) that Article 81(1) is not engaged merely because the share threshold in the Guidelines is breached. **3.320**

Third, the Vertical Guidelines identify the types of negative effect that may flow from each category of vertical agreement. For example the possible competition risks of exclusive distribution agreements are listed as 'mainly reduced intra-brand and market partitioning, which may in particular facilitate price discrimination. When most or all of the suppliers apply exclusive distribution this may facilitate collusion, both at the suppliers' and distributors' level'.[575] **3.321**

---

they create for competition' should be read in this light. Indeed as the Commission itself has stressed, there is no 'presumption of illegality' for agreements falling outside the scope of the VBER. See para 62 of the Commission Guidelines on Vertical Restraints [2000] OJ C291/1. See also the discussion at para 3.316 below and Chapter 9.

[572] Commission Guidelines on Vertical Restraints [2000] OJ C291/1.
[573] See section D(5) of Chapter 9.
[574] Paras 140–146 of the Vertical Guidelines.
[575] ibid, para 161.

3.322   Taken together these elements establish, for the first time, a coherent explanation of why vertical agreements may fall within Article 81(1) and the factors which the Commission, NCAs and national courts should consider in assessing cases. However, they do not explain in any detail how this framework (and therefore by extension the market power test set out in the Article 81(3) Guidelines) should be applied in practice.

(iv) Research and Development and Specialisation Block Exemptions[576]

3.323   These block exemptions are, in many ways, similar in form to the VBER: they have market share thresholds and a short hardcore list. Given this, they also have a similar impact:[577] they reduce the number of cases requiring actual analysis under Article 81(1) (and of course Article 81(3)).

3.324   The similarity to the VBER also extends to the impact of their market share thresholds on cases falling outside of their scope of application: as with the VBER, the thresholds are important only in so far as they establish a market share level beyond which agreements *may* be at risk; they do not determine a starting point for the existence of market power[578] in such case.

(v) Guidelines on the Applicability of Article 81 to Horizontal Co-operation Agreements (the 'Horizontal Guidelines')[579]

3.325   The Horizontal Guidelines perform a similar function to the Vertical Guidelines: they establish an analytical framework for the assessment of particular types of agreements—in this case co-operation between competitors which fall outside the scope of the R&D[580] and Specialisation[581] Block Exemptions.

3.326   The framework in the Horizontal Guidelines is an embryonic version of the one found in the Article 81(3) Guidelines. Using language that is very similar to that found in the Article 81(3) Guidelines, paragraphs 19–20 outline, for the first time in a policy document, the guiding philosophy behind the Commission's new economic approach to Article 81(1): '. . . it is not sufficient that the agreement limits competition between the parties. It must also be likely to affect competition in the market to such an extent that negative market effects as to prices, output, innovation or the variety or quality of goods and services can be expected . . . . [this] depends on the economic context taking into account both the nature of the agreement and

---

[576]   Commission Regulation 2659/2000/EC on the application of Art 81(3) of the Treaty to categories of research and development agreements [2000] OJ L304/7; Commission Regulation 2658/2000/EC on the application of Art 81(3) of the Treaty to categories of specialisation agreements [2000] OJ L304/3.

[577]   However, given that they cover co-operation between competitors, they have, to some extent, a more limited scope of application than the VBER—their market share thresholds are lower and they require that a number of other conditions are fulfilled before they apply.

[578]   Recital 9 of the VBER which states that above 30% 'there can be no presumption that vertical agreements . . . will usually give rise to objective advantages of such a character and size as to compensate for the disadvantages which they create for competition' should be read in this light. Indeed as the Commission itself has stressed, there is no 'presumption of illegality' for agreements falling outside the scope of the VBER. See para 62 of the Vertical Guidelines. See also the discussion at para 3.316 above and Chapter 9.

[579]   Commission Guidelines on the applicability of Art 81 of the EC Treaty to horizontal cooperation agreements [2001] OJ C3/2.

[580]   Commission Regulation 2659/2000/EC on the application of Art 81(3) of the Treaty to categories of research and development agreements [2000] OJ L304/7.

[581]   Commission Regulation 2658/2000/EC on the application of Art 81(3) of the Treaty to categories of specialisation agreements [2000] OJ L304/3.

the parties' combined market power which determines—together with other structural factors—the capability of the cooperation to affect overall competition to such a significant extent.'

Under the Guidelines the starting point for an Article 81(1) analysis is the position of **3.327** the parties in the markets affected by the cooperation (since this 'determines whether or not the parties are likely to maintain, gain or increase market power through the cooperation, ie have the ability to cause negative market effects as to prices, output, innovation or the variety or quality of goods and services').[582] If the parties together have a low combined market share, a restrictive effect of the co-operation is considered to be unlikely and no further analysis is generally required.

The reverse is not, however, true: high market shares are not, in and of themselves, suffi- **3.328** cient for Article 81(1) to bite: paragraph 28 expressly states that it is 'impossible to give a general market share threshold above which sufficient market power for causing restrictive effects can be assumed'.

The Guidelines go on to explain that market concentration, ie the position and number of **3.329** competitors, may also have to be taken into account in assessing the impact of the cooperation. Some guidance is provided through reference to the Herfindahl-Hirshman Index (HHI): the Guidelines state that below 1,000 the market concentration can be characterised as low, between 1,000 and 1,800 as moderate and above 1,800 as high.

Depending on the market position of the parties and the concentration in the market, other **3.330** factors such as the stability of market shares over time, entry barriers and the likelihood of market entry, the countervailing power of buyers/suppliers or the nature of the products (eg homogeneity, maturity) may, under the Guidelines, also have to be considered.

Unlike its counterpart for Verticals, the Horizontal Guidelines also provide useful worked **3.331** examples of how the framework should be applied in practice. That said, few broadly appli- cable conclusions can be drawn from the examples—whilst in many of the problematic examples market shares are in excess of 40 per cent, in others combined shares are as low as 25 per cent[583] (although in general, where market shares are below 40 per cent the markets tend to be highly concentrated with HHIs in excess of 1,800);[584] examples are also given of agreements which may not raise competition problems despite shares that are well over 40 per cent.[585]

(vi) Link Between Appreciability and Market Power

The Article 81(3) Guidelines go on to state that where these effects are appreciable Article **3.332** 81(1) will apply. At the theoretical level this makes eminent sense—although some com- mentators have attempted to equate market power and appreciability, the two concepts are

---

[582] Para 27 of the Commission Guidelines on the applicability of Art 81 of the EC Treaty to horizontal cooperation agreements [2001] OJ C3/2.
[583] ibid, see para 138.
[584] See, eg, para 108.
[585] See, eg, para 110.

not, at this stage in the development of EC competition law, synonymous. The former is an economic idea which has yet to be defined by the European Courts but which the Commission has adopted as the threshold beyond which restrictive agreements *are likely* to be caught by Article 81(1), ie it helps define what *is* a restriction of competition.

3.333 The latter is a legal concept which the ECJ introduced to ensure that the Freedom of Action doctrine, which as noted above was at the centre of competition enforcement in the Community until very recently, did not ensnare agreements with had an 'insignificant', or in the Commission's words 'negligible' effect on the market. Without such an instrument the Freedom of Action theory would have brought within the scope of Article 81(1) a far larger number of agreements since, almost by definition, most contracts limit, to some extent, the commercial freedom of the parties.

3.334 However, whilst in line with the jurisprudence, the relevance of the distinction drawn between appreciability and market power in the Article 81(3) Guidelines is less easy to explain from a practical perspective. There are two distinct but inter-related reasons for this. First the Guidelines' analytical framework is, in practice, relevant only in the small number of cases where market shares exceed the thresholds set in the relevant block exemptions (why worry about Article 81(1) when you know that your agreement would, in any event, be cleared automatically by the Block Exemption?). Put another way, the distinction suggests that the Commission could find an agreement not to be appreciable *even though* the market share thresholds in the block exemptions were breached. This is possible but would seem unlikely in the majority of cases given the fact that dominance was, under the old EC Merger Regulation, found with market shares as small as 35 per cent.[586]

3.335 Second, more importantly, it is difficult to conceive of too many cases where the parties have sufficient market power for negative effects to arise but where it could be plausibly argued that the appreciability criteria had not been met. This is particularly so where the Commission assumes, rather than quantifies, the negative effect.

3.336 However, it may be that under the new test appreciability will develop into a tool which the parties under investigation could use to rebut the presumption of negative effects based on market power. An example of this might be where a distributor agrees to purchase all its requirements from a supplier with market power (ie he enters into a non-compete obligation). If the distributor is small, and there are no network effects, it could be argued that the agreement is not appreciable.[587] Another example might be where competitors establish a joint production venture to produce a particular input. If the cost of the input is a small fraction of the overall costs of the parties then the agreement is unlikely to affect competition appreciably even where their combined downstream market position is strong.[588]

---

[586] See para 17 of Commission Guidelines on assessment of horizontal mergers [2004] OJ C31/5, in particular n 22; eg *Nestlé/Ralston Purina* (Case COMP/M.2337) (2001) points 44–47, where the Commission regarded 35% as a level above which dominant concerns might arise.

[587] Case C-234/89 *Stergios Delimitis v Henninger Bräu AG* [1991] ECR I-935.

[588] Para 27 of the Commission Guidelines on the applicability of Art 81 of the EC Treaty to horizontal cooperation agreements [2001] OJ C3/2.

D. Jurisdiction

(1) General

It is a condition for applying Articles 81 and 82 that the agreement or practice in question **3.337** 'may affect trade between Member States'. In the absence of such effect the Community competition rules do not apply, with the result that the agreement or practice is subject only to Member State or third country competition law, as the case may be. The effect on trade criterion thus determines the jurisdictional reach of Articles 81 and 82.

The effect on trade concept also determines the scope of the obligation under Article 3(1) **3.338** of Regulation 1/2003 of the NCAs and national courts to apply Articles 81 and 82 and the obligation under Article 3(2) not to prohibit agreements that are compatible with the Community competition rules. In the enforcement system created by Regulation 1/2003, the effect on trade concept is thus of particular significance.

The Commission has adopted Guidelines on the effect on trade concept contained in **3.339** Articles 81 and 82 (the 'Effect on Trade Guidelines').[589] In the Effect on Trade Guidelines the Commission largely limits itself to restating principles derived from the existing case law of the European Courts. It is an interpretative text in which few attempts are made to develop the law. In particular, there is deliberately no attempt to limit the scope of the effect on trade concept. This is hardly surprising given the fact that any such attempt would expose more agreements to stand-alone application of national competition law. Indeed, the spirit of Article 3 of Regulation 1/2003 points in the opposite direction: the Community competition rules should constitute the common competition law standard for the internal market.

(2) The Concept of Trade between Member States

The function of the concept of 'trade' is to establish a nexus between the case at hand and **3.340** Articles 81 and 82 so as to justify Community law jurisdiction. According to the case law of the ECJ the concept of 'trade' is a wide one covering all cross-border economic activity including establishment.[590] This interpretation reflects the fundamental objective of the Union to create an internal market with free movement of goods, services, persons and capital. Limiting the jurisdictional reach of Articles 81 and 82 to agreements and practices influencing cross-border exchanges of goods and services would ignore the wider objective of the Community and would therefore be unduly narrow.

In interpreting the concept of trade it is also necessary to take into account the fact that **3.341** according to Article 3(1)(g) of the Treaty one of the objectives of the Community is the creation of a system ensuring that competition in the internal market is not distorted. As competition inside the internal market is necessarily distorted when the competitive structure within the Community is impaired, Articles 81 and 82 also apply to agreements and

---

[589] Commission Notice [2004] OJ C101/81 (27.4.2004).
[590] See Case 172/80 *Züchner* [1981] ECR 2021, para 18. See also Case C-309/99 *Wouters* [2002] ECR I-1577, para 95, Case C-475/99 *Ambulanz Glöckner* [2001] ECR I-8089, para 49, Joined Cases C-215/96 and 216/96 *Bagnasco* [1999] ECR I-135, para 51, Case C-55/96 *Job Centre* [1997] ECR I-7119, para 37, and Case C-41/90 *Höfner and Elser* [1991] ECR I-1979, para 33.

practices that affect the competitive structure within the internal market by eliminating or threatening to eliminate a competitor.[591] It is not a condition for Community law jurisdiction to exist in such cases that the output of the undertaking in question be sold on the Community market. In *Commercial Solvents*[592] the ECJ held that Article 82 was applicable even though the output of the targeted undertaking was sold mainly to third countries.

3.342 The requirement that there must be an effect on trade 'between Member States' implies that there must be an impact[593] on cross-border economic activity involving at least two Member States. It is not required that the agreement or practice affect trade between the whole of one Member State and the whole of another Member State. Articles 81 and 82 may be applicable also in cases involving part of a Member State, provided that the effect on trade is appreciable.[594]

3.343 The application of the effect on trade criterion is independent of the definition of relevant geographic markets. Trade between Member States may be affected also in cases where the relevant market is national or sub-national.[595] This is important from the point of view of Article 3 of Regulation 1/2003. The obligations contained in this article will apply to a number of cases where the relevant market does not extend beyond the territory of a single Member State.

(3) The Link Between Trade and the Agreement or Practice

3.344 In the case of Article 81, it is the agreement that must be capable of affecting trade between Member States. It is not required that each individual part of the agreement, including any restriction of competition which may flow from the agreement, be capable of doing so.[596] If the agreement as a whole is capable of affecting trade between Member States, there is Community law jurisdiction in respect of the entire agreement, including any parts of the agreement that individually do not affect trade between Member States.[597]

3.345 In cases where the contractual relations between the same parties cover several activities, these activities must, in order to form part of the same agreement, be directly linked to and form an integral part of the same overall business arrangement.[598] If not, each activity constitutes a separate agreement. On the other hand, it is immaterial whether or not the participation of a particular undertaking in the agreement has an appreciable effect on trade between Member States.[599] An undertaking cannot escape Community law jurisdiction merely because its own contribution to an agreement, which itself is capable of affecting trade between Member States, is insignificant.

---

[591] See, eg, Joined Cases T-24/93 and others *Compagnie Maritime Belge* [1996] ECR II-1201, para 203, and Joined Cases 6/73 and 7/73 *Commercial Solvents* [1974] ECR 223, paras 32 and 33.

[592] idem.

[593] Which may be direct or indirect, actual or potential; see para 3.358 *et seq* below.

[594] See, eg, Joined Cases T-213/95 and T-18/96 *SCK and FNK* [1997] ECR II-1739.

[595] See Effect on Trade Guidelines, para 22.

[596] See Case 193/83, *Windsurfing* [1986] ECR 611, para 96, and Case T-77/94, *Vereniging van Groothandelaren in Bloemkwekerijprodukten* [1997] ECR II-759, para 126.

[597] See Effect on Trade Guidelines, para 14.

[598] See Case T-77/94, *Vereniging van Groothandelaren in Bloemkwekerijprodukten* [1997] ECR II-759, paras 142–144.

[599] See, eg, Case T-2/89 *Petrofina* [1991] ECR II-1087, para 226.

In the case of Article 82 it is the abuse that must affect trade between Member States. This **3.346** does not imply, however, that each element of the behaviour engaged in by the dominant undertaking must be assessed in isolation. Conduct that forms part of an overall strategy pursued by the dominant undertaking must be assessed in terms of its overall impact. Where a dominant undertaking adopts various practices in pursuit of the same aim, for instance practices that aim at eliminating or foreclosing competitors, it is sufficient in order for Article 82 to be applicable to all the practices forming part of this overall strategy, that at least one of these practices be capable of affecting trade between Member States.[600]

(4) The Notion of 'May Affect'

(a) Introduction

The notion 'may affect' determines the nature and intensity of the influence on trade **3.347** between Member States that must be established for Articles 81 and 82 to be applicable. According to the standard test developed by the ECJ, 'it must be possible to foresee with a sufficient degree of probability on the basis of a set of objective factors of law or fact that the agreement or practice may have an influence, direct or indirect, actual or potential, on the pattern of trade between Member States'.[601] In addition, according to settled case law the influence on trade must be 'appreciable'.[602] As we shall see, appreciability is assessed on the basis of the position and importance on the market of the undertakings concerned.

The test developed by the ECJ is relatively abstract in nature. It is submitted that it could **3.348** not be otherwise. The establishment of jurisdiction cannot depend on detailed factual analysis. If that were the case it would be difficult to assess *ex ante* what is the applicable law. There would also be a risk that jurisdiction would be unstable, frequently disappearing and re-emerging over time. The principles developed by the ECJ make it possible to assess the issue of Community law jurisdiction on the basis of a limited number of core elements which are often available *ex ante* or after relatively limited enquiry.

(b) A Sufficient Degree of Probability

The words 'may affect' and the reference by the ECJ to 'a sufficient degree of probability' **3.349** imply that, in order for Community law jurisdiction to be established, it is not required that the agreement or practice actually has had, has or will have an effect on trade between Member States. It is sufficient that the agreement or practice be 'capable' of having such an effect.[603] It is not possible to point to a single decisive factor for the assessment. The ability

---

[600] See in this respect Case 85/76 *Hoffmann-La Roche* [1979] ECR 461, para 126, and the Effect on Trade Guidelines, para 17.

[601] See eg Case 172/80 *Züchner* [1981] ECR 2021, Case 319/82 *Kerpen & Kerpen* [1983] ECR 4173, Joined Cases 240/82 and others *Stichting Sigarettenindustrie* [1985] ECR 3831, para 48, and Joined Cases T-25/95 and others *Cimenteries CBR* [2000] ECR II-491, para 3930. In some judgments, mainly relating to vertical agreements, the European Courts have added wording to the effect that the agreement was capable of hindering the attainment of the objectives of a single market between Member States, see eg Case T-62/98 *Volkswagen* [2000] ECR II-2707, para 179, Joined Cases C-215/96 and 216/96 *Bagnasco* [1999] ECR I-135 para 47, and Case 56/65 *Société Technique Minière* [1966] ECR 337. The impact of an agreement on the single market objective is thus a factor which can be taken into account.

[602] See in this respect Case 22/71 *Béguelin* [1971] ECR 949, para 16.

[603] See eg Case T-228/97 *Irish Sugar* [1999] ECR II-2969, para 170, and Case 19/77 *Miller* [1978] ECR 131, para 15.

of an agreement to affect trade between Member States is based on several factors that individually may not be decisive.[604]

3.350   The analysis is based on three main elements:[605]

   (i)   The nature of the agreement and practice;
   (ii) The nature of the products covered by the agreement or practice;
   (iii) The position and importance of the undertakings concerned.[606]

3.351   The nature of the agreement and practice provides important insight into its ability to affect trade between Member States. Some agreements and practices are, by their very nature, capable of affecting trade between Member States. For example, cross-border cartels and agreements concerning imports and exports are necessarily capable of affecting trade between Member States as they have a direct impact on cross-border economic activity. Moreover, such agreements are directly linked to the very essence of the internal market and the objective of the Community competition rules of ensuring that competition in the internal market is not distorted. It would deprive the Community competition rules of their raison d'être if they were not applicable to agreements such as cross-border cartels. On the other hand, certain other types of agreements are not, by their very nature, capable of affecting trade between Member States and require more detailed analysis. This is, for example, the case with joint ventures confined to a single Member State: such agreements do not have an inherent link with cross-border economic activity.

3.352   The nature of the products covered by the agreements or practices also provides an indication of whether or not trade between Member States is capable of being affected. When, by their nature, products are easily traded across borders or are important for undertakings that want to enter or expand their activities in other Member States, Community jurisdiction is more readily established than in cases where, due to their nature, there is limited demand for products offered by suppliers from other Member States or where the products are of limited interest from the point of view of cross-border establishment or the expansion of the economic activity carried out from such place of establishment.[607]

3.353   The domicile of the undertakings concerned is also taken into account. The ECJ has thus held that the mere fact that the participants in a national arrangement also include undertakings from other Member States is an important, but not decisive, element.[608]

3.354   The market position of the undertakings concerned and their sales volumes are indicative, from a quantitative point of view, of the ability of the agreement or practice concerned to affect trade between Member States.

---

[604]   See eg Joined Cases C-295/04 to C-298/04 *Manfredi* (judgment of 13 July 2006) para 43, and Case C-250/92 *Gøttrup-Klim* [1994] ECR II-5641, para 54.

[605]   See the Effect on Trade Guidelines, para 28.

[606]   See eg Case C-306/96 *Javico* [1998] ECR I-1983, para 17, and Case 22/71 *Béguelin* [1971] ECR 949, para 18.

[607]   Compare in this respect Joined Cases C-295/04 to C-298/04 *Manfredi* (judgment of 13 July 2006), para 49, Case C-309/99 *Wouters* [2002] ECR I-1577, para 95, and Joined Cases C-215/96 and 216/96 *Bagnasco* [1999] ECR I-135, para 51.

[608]   See Joined Cases C-295/04 to C-298/04 *Manfredi* (judgment of 13 July 2006), para 44.

In addition to the factors already mentioned, it is necessary to take account of the legal and **3.355** factual environment in which the agreement or practice operates. The relevant economic and legal context provides insight into the potential for trade between Member States to be affected. If there are absolute barriers to cross-border trade between Member States, which are external to the agreement or practice, trade is only capable of being affected if those barriers are likely to disappear in the foreseeable future. In cases where the barriers are not absolute but merely render cross-border activity more difficult, it is of the utmost importance to ensure that agreements and practices do not further hinder such activities. Agreements and practices that do so are capable of affecting trade between Member States.[609]

(c) An Influence on the Pattern of Trade

The term 'pattern of trade' is neutral. It is not a condition that trade be restricted or reduced.[610] **3.356** Patterns of trade can also be affected when an agreement or practice causes an increase in trade. Indeed, Community law jurisdiction is established if trade between Member States is likely to develop differently with the agreement or practice as compared to the way in which it would probably have developed in the absence of the agreement or practice.[611]

Moreover and importantly, it is not necessary, for the purposes of establishing Community **3.357** law jurisdiction, to establish a link between the alleged restriction of competition and the ability of the agreement to affect trade between Member States. Non-restrictive agreements may also affect trade between Member States. This is reflected in Article 3(2) of Regulation 1/2003 which, *inter alia*, provides that agreements which may affect trade between Member States but which do not restrict competition within the meaning of Article 81(1) cannot be prohibited by national competition law. The Community legislator has thus assumed that non-restrictive agreements may affect trade between Member States. That being said, however, the alleged restrictions arising from an agreement may provide a clear indication as to the ability of the agreement to affect trade between Member States. For instance, a distribution agreement prohibiting exports is by its very nature capable of affecting trade between Member States, although not necessarily to an appreciable extent.

Direct or Indirect, Actual or Potential   The required influence of agreements and prac- **3.358** tices on patterns of trade between Member States can be 'direct or indirect, actual or potential'. When attempting to establish the true meaning of these terms, it is important to keep in mind that it is only required to show that the agreement is capable of affecting trade between Member States. The assessment remains fairly abstract as regards direct and actual effects. The main focus is on the link between the agreement and practice and the cross-border economic activity which is allegedly capable of being affected. There is no obligation or need to calculate the actual volume of trade between Member States affected by the agreement or practice.

---

[609] See Effect on Trade Guidelines, para 32.

[610] See eg Case T-141/89 *Tréfileurope* [1995] ECR II-791, Case T-29/92 *Vereniging van Samenwerkende Prijsregelende Organisaties in de Bouwnijverheid (SPO)* [1995] ECR II-289, as far as exports were concerned, and Commission Decision in *Volkswagen (II)* OJ 2001 L 262/14.

[611] See in this respect Case 71/74 *Frubo* [1975] ECR 563, para 38, Joined Cases 209/78 and others *Van Landewyck* [1980] ECR 3125, para172, Case T-61/89 *Dansk Pelsdyravler Forening* [1992] ECR II-1931, para 143, and Case T-65/89, *BPB Industries and British Gypsum* [1993] ECR II-389, para 135.

3.359 Direct effects normally occur in relation to the products covered by the agreement or practice.[612] An agreement whereby the parties agree not to sell into certain territories produces direct effects on trade between Member states. Actual effects are produced when an agreement that is capable of affecting trade between Member States has been implemented.[613]

3.360 Indirect effects often occur in relation to products that are related to those covered by an agreement or practice. For instance, in *BNIC v Clair*[614] the ECJ held that trade between Member States was capable of being affected in the case of an agreement involving the fixing of the price of spirits used in the production of cognac. The spirits in question were not exported and only spirits made from grapes grown in the Cognac region could be used in the production of cognac. The agreement therefore did not produce direct effects on trade between Member States. However, given that the product covered by the agreement was used in the production of a product that was traded between Member States, the agreement was capable of producing indirect effects on trade between Member States.

3.361 Indirect effects on trade between Member States may also occur in relation to the products covered by the agreement or practice. For instance, agreements whereby a manufacturer limits warranties to products sold by distributors within their Member State of establishment create disincentives for consumers from other Member States to buy the products because they would not be able to invoke the warranty.[615] Export by official distributors and parallel traders would be more difficult because, in the eyes of consumers, the products are less attractive without the manufacturer's warranty.[616]

3.362 Potential effects are those that may occur in the future with a sufficient degree of probability. It follows that market developments must be taken into account.[617] Even if trade is not capable of being affected at the time the agreement is concluded or the practice is implemented, Articles 81 and 82 remain applicable if the factors which led to that conclusion are likely to change in the foreseeable future. If cross-border economic activity is not possible due to barriers to entry, it must be considered whether those barriers are going to be eliminated or sufficiently reduced within a reasonable period of time. If so, Community jurisdiction is established *ex ante*. Intervention does not have to wait for the point in time when cross-border economic activity becomes possible.

3.363 Even if, at a given point in time, cross-border economic activity does not occur, the Community competition rules are applicable if, due to the nature of the products concerned, cross-border economic activity is possible and the agreement is capable of affecting such activity. For instance, it may be that at a given point in time market conditions are unfavourable to cross-border trade, for example because prices are similar in the Member States in question.[618]

---

[612] See Effect on Trade Guidelines, para 39.

[613] idem, para 40.

[614] See Case 123/83 *BNIC v Clair* [1985] ECR 391, para 29.

[615] See Commission Decision in *Zanussi* [1978] OL L322/36, para 11.

[616] See in this respect Case 31/85 *ETA Fabrique d'Ebauches* [1985] ECR 3933, paras 12 and 13.

[617] See Joined Cases C-241/91 P and C-242/91 P *RTE (Magill)* [1995] ECR I-743, para 70, and Case 107/82 *AEG* [1983] ECR 3151, para 60.

[618] In *Austrian banks* [2004] OJ L56/1 market conditions were such that it was not attractive for Austrian customers to borrow from banks established in Germany. However, the continuous monitoring of rates offered by German banks indicated that the services in question were tradeable and that the cartel agreement

Trade is nevertheless capable of being affected if the situation may change as a result of changing market conditions.[619] What matters is the ability of the agreement or practice to affect trade between Member States and not whether at any given point in time it actually does so.

The inclusion of indirect or potential effects in the analysis of effect on trade between Member States does not mean that the analysis can be based on remote or hypothetical effects. The likelihood of a particular agreement to produce indirect or potential effects must be explained by the competition authority or party claiming that trade between Member States is capable of being appreciably affected. Hypothetical or speculative effects are not sufficient for establishing Community law jurisdiction.[620]   **3.364**

(5) Appreciability

(a) General Principles

Agreements and practices fall outside the scope of application of Articles 81 and 82 when they affect the market only insignificantly.[621] For Community law jurisdiction to be established, the agreement or practice must be capable of *appreciably* affecting trade between Member States.[622]   **3.365**

Appreciability is assessed, in particular, by reference to the position and the importance of the relevant undertakings on the market for the products concerned.[623] The stronger the market position of such undertakings, the more likely it is that an agreement or practice capable of affecting trade between Member States can be held to do so appreciably.[624] However, it is important also to take account of other factors such as the nature of the agreement and practice and the nature of the products that they cover. When, by its very nature, an agreement or practice is capable of affecting trade between Member States, the appreciability threshold is lower than in the case of agreements and practices that are not, by their very nature, capable of affecting trade between Member States.[625]   **3.366**

In a number of cases concerning imports and exports, the ECJ has considered that the appreciability requirement was fulfilled when the sales of the undertakings concerned accounted for about 5 per cent of the market.[626] Market share alone, however, has not always been considered the decisive factor. In particular, it is necessary also to take account of the turnover   **3.367**

---

was capable of producing potential effects on trade between Member States. Similarly, in Case C-359/01 P *British Sugar* [2004] ECR I, para 81, the fact that the parties has continuously monitored import levels and engaged in limit pricing to control imports was held by the ECJ to confirm the Commission's finding that trade between Member States was capable of being affected.

[619] See Case 107/82 *AEG* [1983] ECR 3151, para 60.

[620] See Effect on Trade Guidelines, para 43. This is in line with the case law of the ECJ in the field of free movement of goods: see, eg Case C-379/92 *Peralta* [1994] ECR I-3453, para 24, where the ECJ held that the restrictive effect that the measure in question might have on the free movement of goods was too uncertain and indirect for it to be regarded as being of a nature to hinder trade between Member States.

[621] See Case 5/69 *Völk* [1969] ECR 295, para 7.

[622] See Case 22/71 *Béguelin* [1971] ECR 949, para 16.

[623] See eg Case C-305/96 *Javico* [1998] ECR I-1983, para 17, and Case T-65/89 *BPB Industries and British Gypsum* [1993] ECR II-389, para 138.

[624] See *BPB Industries and British Gypsum* (cited above), para 138.

[625] See *Effect on Trade Guidelines*, para 45.

[626] See eg Case 19/77 *Miller* [1978] ECR 131, paragraphs 9 and 10 and Case 107/82 *AEG* [1983] ECR 3151, para 58.

of the undertakings in the products concerned. In *Musique Diffusion Française*, where the products in question accounted for just above 3 per cent of sales on the national markets concerned, the ECJ held that the agreements, which hindered parallel trade, were capable of appreciably affecting trade between Member States due to the high turnover of the parties and the relative market position of the products, compared to those of products produced by competing suppliers.[627] It follows that the application of the appreciability test does not necessarily require that relevant markets be defined and market shares calculated.[628] The sales of an undertaking in absolute terms may be sufficient to support a finding that the impact on trade is appreciable.

(b) Quantification

3.368 The Effect on Trade Guidelines do not contain elaborate criteria for determining when the effect on trade of an agreement or practice on trade between Member States *is* appreciable. With one exception the Commission has limited itself to setting out a presumption indicating when trade between Member States *is not* capable of being appreciably affected. This presumption must be distinguished from the *de minimis* rule contained in the Commission Notice on agreements of minor importance (the *'de minimis* Notice').[629] The latter rule concerns only the question of what constitutes an appreciable restriction of competition within the meaning of Article 81(1), which is a distinct issue. The *de minimis* Notice has no bearing on whether or not an agreement is capable of appreciably affecting trade between Member States. The Effect on Trade Guidelines contain in paragraph 52 a distinct negative rebuttable presumption[630] according to which

> 'the Commission holds the view that in principle agreements are not capable of appreciably affecting trade between Member States when the following cumulative conditions are met:
>
> (a) The aggregate market share of the parties on any relevant market within the Community affected by the agreement does not exceed 5%, and
> (b) In the case of horizontal agreements, the aggregate annual Community turnover of the undertakings concerned[631] in the products covered by the agreement does not exceed 40 million Euro. In the case of agreements concerning the joint buying of products the relevant turnover shall be the parties' combined purchases of the products covered by the agreement.
>
> In the case of vertical agreements, the aggregate annual Community turnover of the supplier in the products covered by the agreement does not exceed 40 million Euro. In the case of licence agreements the relevant turnover shall be the aggregate turnover of the licensees in the products incorporating the licensed technology and the licensor's own turnover in such products. In cases involving agreements concluded between a buyer and several suppliers the relevant turnover shall be the buyer's combined purchases of the products covered by the agreements.'

---

[627] See Joined Cases 100/80 and others *Musique Diffusion Française* [1983] ECR 1825, para 86.

[628] See in this respect Case T-62/98 *Volkswagen* v *Commission* [2000] ECR II-2707, paras 179 and 231 and Case T-213/00, *CMA CGM and others* [2003] ECR II-913, paras 219 and 220.

[629] Commission Notice on agreements of minor importance which do not appreciably restrict competition under Art 81(1) of the Treaty [2001] OJ C368/13.

[630] The Guidelines refer to this presumption as the NAAT-rule (no appreciable affectation of trade). From a linguistic point of view the word 'affectation', which appears to have been borrowed from the French, is somewhat unfortunate. In the present context, the NAAT-rule is referred to as the negative presumption.

[631] The term 'undertakings concerned' includes connected undertakings as defined in para 12.2 of the *de minimis* Notice.

According to paragraph 52 of the Effect on Trade Guidelines the negative presumption **3.369** remains applicable where during two successive calendar years the turnover threshold is not exceeded by more than 10 per cent and the market threshold is not exceeded by more than two percentage points. In cases where the agreement concerns an emerging not yet existing market and where as a consequence the parties neither generate relevant turnover nor accumulate any relevant market share, the negative presumption does not apply. The Effect on Trade Guidelines provide that in such cases appreciability may have to be assessed on the basis of the position of the parties on related product markets or their strength in technologies relating to the agreement.

It is also worth mentioning that according to paragraph 56 of the Effect on Trade Guidelines, **3.370** in the case of networks of agreements entered into by the same supplier with different distributors, sales made through the entire network are taken into account. Moreover, according to paragraph 57, contracts that form part of the same overall business arrangement constitute a single agreement for the purposes of the negative presumption. Undertakings cannot bring themselves below the thresholds by dividing up an agreement that from an economic perspective forms a whole.

The two cumulative conditions of the negative presumption can be traced back to case law. **3.371** The 5 per cent market share threshold follows from *Miller*[632] according to which a market share of 5 per cent is sufficient to be appreciable, at least in the case of agreements that by their very nature are capable of affecting trade between Member States. The turnover threshold as such is derived from *Musique Diffusion Française*[633] where the ECJ held that trade was capable of being appreciably affected due to the large turnover of the undertakings concerned in spite of the fact that their market share was around 3 per cent.

The turnover threshold of 40 million euro is calculated on the basis of the Community **3.372** turnover in the products covered by the agreement.[634] This calculation method differs from that contained in Commission Recommendation 96/280/EC concerning the definition of micro, small and medium-sized enterprises,[635] which uses total turnover. There is no link between the *Effect on Trade Guidelines* and Commission Recommendation 96/280/EC.[636] A threshold based on agreement-specific turnover is clearly more difficult to apply than a threshold based on total turnover. However, it is submitted that it is a better proxy for appreciable effects on trade. In the case of multi-product firms, the total turnover of an undertaking may say very little about the ability of an agreement to affect trade between Member States, which is the relevant issue.

The wording of the two cumulative thresholds of the negative presumption suffers from a **3.373** certain lack of clarity. The reference to 'aggregate market share' in paragraph 52(a) makes

---

[632] Case 19/77 *Miller* [1978] ECR 131.
[633] See Joined Cases 100/80 and others *Musique Diffusion Française*, [1983] ECR 1825, para 86.
[634] In the 1986 *de minimis* Notice ([1986] OJ C231/2) which also covered appreciability in relation to effect on trade, the turnover threshold was calculated on the basis of total turnover, which explains the higher threshold of 300 million Euro.
[635] [1996] OJ L107/4. With effect from 1 January 2005 this Recommendation was replaced by Commission Recommendation 2003/361/EC concerning the definition of micro, small and medium-sized enterprises [2003] OJ L124/36.
[636] See Effect on Trade Guidelines, para 50.

sense in the case of agreements between undertakings operating at the same level of trade. However, in the case of agreements between undertakings operating at different levels of trade, such as agreements between a supplier and its distributor where the supplier itself does not also distribute, there is nothing to aggregate. There is only one market share on each relevant market, namely that of the supplier or the distributor as the case may be. Paragraph 52(a) should therefore be read as providing that market shares must be calculated for each relevant market affected by the agreement and that, where applicable, the market shares of the parties must be aggregated.

3.374   The purpose of paragraph 52(b) is to identify the relevant turnover. However, the relationship between the two parts is not entirely clear. In particular, it is unfortunate that in the second part, which deals with vertical agreements, reference is made to the licensor's turnover on the product market.[637] The text would have been clearer if all horizontal agreement in respect of which aggregation is relevant had been dealt with in the first part and the second part had been confined to purely vertical agreements in respect of which the parties do not generate turnover on the same relevant market.

3.375   In the case of horizontal agreements the relevant turnover is that which the parties generate on the relevant markets where they act as sellers. The only explicit exception is purchasing agreements where the relevant turnover is the turnover generated on the purchasing market. However, as regards licence agreements it is necessary to read the part of paragraph 52(b) dealing with horizontal agreements in light of the second part dealing with vertical agreements. It follows from a combined reading of these two parts that, in the case of licence agreements, the relevant turnover of the licensor is the combined turnover of the licensees and the licensor in the products incorporating the licensed technology and the relevant turnover of the licensee is its turnover in products that compete with the products covered by the agreement.

3.376   In the case of vertical supply agreements the relevant turnover is that of the supplier[638] and in the case of vertical purchasing agreements, ie agreements whereby a buyer sources from several suppliers, the relevant turnover is that of the buyer. A particular rule applies to licence agreements: the turnover of the licensor in its capacity as licensor is limited to royalties. Royalties are generally calculated as a percentage of the price of the product or a fixed amount per product sold by the licensee. Royalty income of 40 million euro thus represents a much larger turnover on the market for products incorporating the licensed technology, which generally is the market on which the effects of the agreement are analysed.[639] This must be taken into account when assessing whether the agreement is capable of appreciably affecting cross-border economic activity. The Effect on Trade Guidelines reflect this fact

---

[637] As opposed to the technology market; as to this distinction see the Commission Guidelines on the application of Art 81(3) of the Treaty to categories of technology transfer agreements [2004] OJ C101/2, paras 20 and 22.

[638] In the case of networks of agreements entered into by the same supplier with different distributors, sales made through the entire network are taken into account, see para 56 of the Effect on Trade Guidelines. This means that the relevant turnover is that of the supplier vis-à-vis all its distributors.

[639] See in this respect para 23 of the Commission Guidelines on the application of Art 81 of the Treaty to technology transfer agreements [2004] OJ C101/2.

when providing that in respect of licence agreements the relevant turnover is that of the licensees on the market where they sell the products incorporating the licensed technology.

In addition to the negative presumption, the Effect on Trade Guidelines also set out a pos- **3.377**
itive rebuttable presumption of appreciable effects on trade. In this respect paragraph 53 provides that:

> the Commission will also hold the view that where an agreement by its very nature is capable of affecting trade between Member States, for example, because it concerns imports and exports or covers several Member States, there is a rebuttable positive presumption that such effects on trade are appreciable when the turnover of the parties in the products covered by the agreement . . . exceeds 40 million euro. In the case of agreements that by their very nature are capable of affecting trade between Member States it can also often be presumed that such effects are appreciable when the market share of the parties exceeds the 5 per cent threshold . . . . However, this presumption does not apply where the agreement covers only part of a Member State.

This positive presumption reflects case law according to which the definition of relevant **3.378**
markets and thus the calculation of market shares is not a precondition of assessing appreciability.[640] When by its very nature an agreement is capable of affecting trade between Member States, turnover may be sufficient. However, the positive presumption based on turnover may be rebutted where the turnover in question is insignificant in comparison to the overall size of the market. The Effect on Trade Guidelines also recognise that market share is not always a good indicator of the ability of an agreement to appreciably affect trade between Member States. The relevant market may for instance be local, in which case market share provides no useful information on the question of appreciability. For this reason the positive presumption based on market shares does not apply in the case of sub-national markets.

(6) Assessment of Various Types of Agreement and Practices

(a) Introduction

With a view to illustrating the general principles developed in previous sections, the Effect **3.379**
on Trade Guidelines deal with various types of agreements and abusive practices in three separate sections. These sections cover (a) agreements and practices covering or implemented in several Member States;[641] (b) agreements and practices covering a single, or only part of a, Member State;[642] and (c) agreements and practices involving imports and exports with undertakings located in third countries, and agreements and practices involving undertakings located in third countries.[643]

(b) Agreements and Practices Concerning Imports and Exports and Agreements and Practices Implemented in Several Member States

The first category covers agreements concerning imports and exports and agreements and **3.380**
practices such as cross-border cartels, joint ventures and abusive practices that by their very nature are capable of affecting trade between Member States. In these cases the main issue to

---

[640] See Case T-62/98 *Volkswagen* [2000] ECR II-2707, paras 179 and 231, and Case T-213/00 *CMA CGM and others* [2003] ECR II-913, paras 219 and 220.
[641] See para 3.1 of the Effect on Trade Guidelines.
[642] ibid, para 3.2.
[643] ibid, para3.3.

be considered is that of appreciability. If this condition is satisfied it is uncontroversial that there should be Community law jurisdiction in the case of cross-border agreements and practices and agreements concerning imports and exports such as agreements that hinder parallel trade. Such agreements and practices go to the heart of Articles 81 and 82, namely the protection of undistorted competition within the internal market. If the Community competition rules were not applicable, for instance to cross-border cartels, the only alternative would be to apply national competition law, which fails to take into account the Community dimension.

(c) Agreements and Practices Confined to the Whole or Part of a Member State

3.381 The issue becomes more complex in the case of agreements and practices that do not extend beyond the territory of a single Member State. In such cases it may be necessary to proceed with a more detailed inquiry into the ability of the agreements or abusive practices to affect trade between Member States. This is particularly warranted in the case of agreements that are not by their very nature capable of affecting trade between Member States. This is, for instance, likely to be the case with horizontal cooperation agreements and in particular non-full function joint ventures, which are confined to a single Member State and which do not directly relate to imports and exports. Such agreements may, in particular, be capable of affecting trade between Member States where they have foreclosure effects.[644] Similarly, vertical agreements covering the whole of a Member State may, in particular, be capable of affecting patterns of trade between Member States when they concern imports and exports and when they make it more difficult for undertakings from other Member States to penetrate the national market in question, either by means of exports or by means of establishment.[645]

3.382 In a number of cases that have mainly involved cartels, sector-wide horizontal agreements, agreements hindering parallel trade and abuse of dominance[646] the ECJ has held that agreements and practices extending over the whole territory of a Member State have by their very nature the effect of reinforcing the partitioning of markets on a national basis by hindering the economic penetration which the Treaty is designed to bring about. Agreements and abusive practices that cover the whole of a Member State often make it more difficult for undertakings from other Member States to engage in economic activity in the Member State in question. These difficulties may stem from the fact that the agreement or practice creates barriers to entry, as is the case where a dominant firm concludes exclusive dealing agreements with a number of customers,[647] or from the fact that in order to sustain the agreement the parties need to take action against outsiders. For example, in the case of a cartel the participating undertakings normally need to take action to exclude competitors from other Member States or alternatively include them in the cartel.[648] If they do not, the cartel risks being undermined by competition from such undertakings.

---

[644] See Effect on Trade Guidelines, para 84.

[645] ibid, para 86.

[646] See eg Case C-309/99 *Wouters* [2002] ECR I-1577, para 95; Case T-62/98 *Volkswagen* [2000] ECR II-2707, para 179; Case C-70/93 *Bayerische Motorenwerke* [1995] ECR I-3439, para 20; and Case T-29/92 *SPO* [1995] ECR II-289, para 229.

[647] See Case 61/80 *Coöperative Stremsel- en Kleurselfabriek* [1981] ECR 851, para 15.

[648] See eg Case 246/86 *Belasco* [1989] ECR 2117, paras 32-38, Case 45/85 *Verband der Sachversicherer* [1987] ECR 405, para 50, and Case C-7/95 P *John Deere* [1998] ECR I-3111, and Joined Cases C-295/04 to C-298/04 *Manfredi* (judgment of 13 July 2006), para 49.

In assessing whether agreements covering the whole of a Member State may affect trade   **3.383**
between Member States it is, in addition to the nature of the agreement, particularly relevant
to take into account whether or not the products covered by the agreement are 'tradeable'.
A product is tradeable if there is cross-border demand for it or if the product constitutes a
significant factor in the choice made by undertakings from other Member States whether or
not to establish themselves in the Member State in question. The importance of tradeability
is illustrated by the judgments in *Bagnasco*[649] and *Wouters*.[650] The *Bagnasco* case concerned
an agreement in the Italian banking sector establishing standard terms and conditions for
current account credit facilities. The ECJ held that trade between Member States was not
capable of being appreciably affected. In so holding, the ECJ referred to the fact that the
Commission had found that the banking service in question involved economic activities
that had a very limited impact on trade between Member States and that the participation
of the subsidiaries or branches of non-Italian financial establishments was limited. The
Commission had also made clear, in reply to a question put to it by the Court, that potential recourse to contracts for credit facilities and contracts for the provision of general guarantees by the main customers of foreign banks, that is to say large undertakings and foreign
economic operators, was not great and, in any event, was not a factor of decisive importance in the decision made by foreign banks whether or not to establish themselves in Italy.
The ECJ concluded that the Commission's findings had not been called into question in
the proceedings. Conversely, in *Wouters*, where the ECJ considered a rule laid down by the
Dutch Bar Association prohibiting joint partnerships between lawyers and accountants,
the ECJ applied the standard formula on cases covering the whole of a Member State to
find that trade between Member States was capable of being affected. It added that the
effect was all the more appreciable because the agreement applied equally to visiting lawyers
who were registered members of the Bar of another Member State, because economic and
commercial law more and more frequently regulates transnational transactions and, lastly,
because the firms of accountants looking for lawyers as partners were generally international groups present in several Member States. In other words, the services in question
were clearly tradeable.

(d) *Agreements and Practices Covering Part of a Member State*

In assessing agreements and practices that only cover part of a Member State, it is necessary   **3.384**
to consider what proportion of the Member State in question is covered by the agreement
and what proportion of its territory is open to trade.[651] If, for example, transport costs render it economically unviable for undertakings from other Member States to serve the entire
territory of another Member State, trade is capable of being affected if the agreement forecloses access to the part of the territory of a Member State that is open to trade, provided
that this part is not insignificant.[652]

---

[649] Joined Cases C-215/96 and 216/96 *Bagnasco* [1999] ECR I-135, para 51.
[650] Case C-309/99 *Wouters* [2002] ECR I-1577, para 95. This full Court judgment makes clear that there
is no basis for interpreting *Bagnasco* (see previous footnote) as contracting the scope of application of
Community law. In *Wouters* the ECJ expressly upholds prior case law including the judgment in Case 8/72
Vereeniging van Cementhandelaren [1972] ECR 977, para 29.
[651] See Effect on Trade Guidelines, para 89.
[652] See in this respect Joined Cases T-213/95 and T-18/96 SCK and FNK [1997] ECR II-1739, paras 177–181.

3.385 When an agreement forecloses access to a regional market, the volume of sales affected must be significant in proportion to the overall volume of sales of the products concerned inside the Member State in question.[653] This assessment cannot be based merely on geographic coverage. The market share of the parties to the agreement must also be given fairly limited weight. Even if the parties have a high market share in a properly defined regional market, the size of that market in terms of volume may still be insignificant when compared to total sales of the products concerned within the Member State in question. In general, the best indicator of the capacity of the agreement to (appreciably) affect trade between Member States is the share of the national market in terms of volume that is being foreclosed. Agreements covering areas with a high concentration of demand will thus more readily affect trade between Member States than those covering areas where demand is less concentrated. For Community jurisdiction to be established, the share of the national market that is being foreclosed must be significant. Agreements that are local in nature are in themselves not capable of appreciably affecting trade between Member States.[654] This is the case even if the local market is located in a border region. Conversely, if the foreclosed share of the national market is significant, trade is capable of being affected even where the market in question is not located in a border region. The same is true for abusive practices.[655] Trade may not be capable of being appreciably affected if the abuse is purely local in nature or involves only an insignificant share of the sales of the dominant undertaking.[656]

3.386 According to paragraphs 92 and 97 of the Effect on Trade Guidelines, some guidance may be derived from the condition in Article 82 that the dominant position must cover a substantial part of the common market. Agreements and abusive practices that, for example, have the effect of hindering competitors from other Member States in their efforts to gain access to part of a Member State, which constitutes a substantial part of the common market, should be considered as having an appreciable effect on trade between Member States. In the application of this criterion regard must be had in particular to the size of the market in question in terms of volume. Regions and even a port or an airport situated in a Member State may, depending on their importance, constitute a substantial part of the common market.[657] In these cases, it must be considered whether the infrastructure in question is used to provide cross-border services and, if so, to what extent. Where infrastructures such as airports and ports are important in providing cross-border services, trade between Member States is capable of being affected. The Guidelines do not suggest that trade is not capable of affecting trade between Member States when the agreement or practice does not cover a substantial part of the Common market. It is only a positive presumption.

(e) Agreements and Practices Involving Third Countries

3.387 Articles 81 and 82 apply irrespective of where the undertakings are located or where the agreement was concluded. Articles 81 and 82 may also apply to agreements and practices

---

[653] See Effect on Trade Guidelines, para 90.

[654] ibid, para 91.

[655] ibid, para 96.

[656] ibid.

[657] See eg Case C-475/99 *Ambulanz Glöckner* [2001] ECR I-8089, para 49, Case C-179/90 *Merci convenzionali porto di Genova* [1991] ECR I-5889, and Case C-242/95 *GT-Link* [1997] ECR I-4449.

that cover third countries and are entered into or conducted by undertakings established in those countries, provided that the agreements and practices are capable of affecting trade between Member States. According to paragraph 100 of the Effect on Trade Guidelines Community law is applicable if the agreement or practice is either implemented or produces effects inside the Community. As such the application of Community law is compatible with the requirements of public international law.

The leading case on the implementation doctrine is *Woodpulp*[658] where the ECJ held that: **3.388**

> It should be observed that an infringement of Article [81], such as the conclusion of an agreement which has had the effect of restricting competition within the common market, consists of conduct made up of two elements, the formation of the agreement, decision or concerted practice and the implementation thereof. If the applicability of prohibitions laid down under competition law were made to depend on the place where the agreement, decision or concerted practice was formed, the result would obviously be to give undertakings an easy means of evading those prohibitions. The decisive factor is therefore the place where it is implemented.

> The producers in this case implemented their pricing agreement within the common market. It is immaterial in that respect whether or not they had recourse to subsidiaries, agents, sub-agents, or branches within the Community in order to make their contacts with purchasers within the Community.

> Accordingly the Community's jurisdiction to apply its competition rules to such conduct is covered by the territoriality principle as universally recognized in public international law.

It follows that as soon as undertakings established outside the Community take steps to implement agreements and abusive practices within the Community, Articles 81 and 82 may be applied provided the requisite effect on trade between Member States can be established.

Under the effects doctrine, jurisdiction can be established simply on the basis of economic **3.389**
effects produced within a given territory: implementation within that territory is not required. Following the judgment in *Woodpulp*, it was an open question as to whether the effects doctrine was recognised in Community law. However, this has now been accepted by the CFI in *Gencor*[659] where it held that the application of the Merger Regulation was justified under public international law when it is foreseeable that a proposed concentration will have an immediate and substantial effect in the Community. It follows therefore that the effects doctrine is, as a matter of law, compatible with the Community legal order. Although this conclusion was reached in the context of a merger case, there is no reason to believe that the European Courts would not also apply the effects doctrine within the field of Articles 81 and 82. The fact that under the Merger Regulation jurisdiction is based on turnover threshold rather than the effect on trade concept should not considered decisive. When agreements and practices produce effects within the Community, they may well affect patterns of trade within the Community, thereby satisfying the requirements for finding an effect on trade.

Where the object of the agreement is to restrict competition inside the Community, the **3.390**
required effect on trade between Member States is more readily established than where the object is predominantly to regulate competition outside the Community. In the former case,

---

[658] See Joined Cases C-89/85 and others *Ahlström Osakeyhtiö (Woodpulp)* [1988] ECR 651, paras 16–18.
[659] See Case T-102/96 *Gencor* [1999] ECR II-753.

the agreement or practice has a direct impact on competition inside the Community and trade between Member States. Such agreements and practices, which may concern both imports and exports, are normally by their very nature capable of affecting trade between Member States. In the case of imports, this category includes agreements that bring about an isolation of the internal market.[660] In the case of exports, this category includes cases where undertakings that compete in two or more Member States agree to export certain (surplus) quantities to third countries with a view to co-ordinating their market conduct inside the Community.[661]

3.391 In the case of agreements and practices the object of which is not to restrict competition inside the Community, it is relevant to examine the effects of the agreement or practice on customers and other operators inside the Community who rely on the products of the undertakings that are parties to the agreement or practice.[662]

3.392 Trade may also be capable of being affected when the agreement prevents re-imports into the Community. This may, for example, be the case with vertical agreements between Community suppliers and third country distributors, imposing restrictions on resale outside an allocated territory, including the Community. If, in the absence of the agreement, resale to the Community would be possible and likely, such imports may be capable of affecting patterns of trade inside the Community.[663] However, for such effects to be likely, there must be an appreciable difference between the prices of the products charged in the Community and those charged outside the Community, and this price difference must not be eroded by customs duties and transport costs. In addition, the product volumes exported compared to the total market for those products in the territory of the common market must not be insignificant.[664] If these product volumes are insignificant compared to those sold inside the Community the impact of any re-importation on trade between Member States will not be appreciable. In making this assessment, regard must be had not only to the individual agreement concluded between the parties, but also to any cumulative effect of similar agreements concluded by the same and competing suppliers.[665] It may be, for example, that the product volumes covered by a single agreement are quite small, but that the product volumes covered by several such agreements are significant. In that case the agreements taken as a whole may be capable of appreciably affecting trade between Member States.

---

660 See in this respect Case 51/75 *EMI v CBS* [1976] ECR 811, paras 28 and 29 and Commission Decision in *Siemens/Fanuc* [1985] OJ L376/29.

661 See in this respect Joined Cases 29/83 and 30/83 *CRAM and Rheinzink* [1984] ECR 1679, and Joined Cases 40/73 and others *Suiker Unie* [1975] ECR 1663, paras 564 and 580.

662 See Joined Cases T-24/93 and others *Compagnie Maritime Belge* [1996] ECR II-1201, para 203.

663 See in this respect Case C-306/96 *Javico* [1998] ECR I-1983. It is submitted that it ought to suffice that such price differences may arise. As it stands it is difficult to reconcile this part of the Effect on Trade Guidelines with the principles developed in earlier parts according to which it is sufficient to show a potential effect on trade. The language used by the ECJ in *Javico* to which the Guidelines refer may be explained by the fact that the Court dealt with the issues of effect on trade and restriction of competition at the same time. The analysis of restrictive effects under Art 81(1) is a continuous process. It can therefore be argued that in a case such as *Javico* a finding of restrictive effects requires the presence of material price differences. However, this distinction between effect on trade and restriction is not clearly drawn in this part of the Effect on Trade Guidelines.

664 ibid, paras 24–26.

665 See Effect on Trade Guidelines, para109. It is submitted that it should suffice that the quantities in question are large compared to the quantities sold in the Member State of importation. Such imports can affect prices in the importing Member State and thereby parallel trade between this Member State and other Member States. For Art 81 to be applicable it is not required that the agreement affects trade throughout the Community.

E. Article 81(2)

Pursuant to Article 81(2), 'any agreements or decisions prohibited pursuant to this Article **3.393** shall be automatically void'. The agreements and decisions as a whole are unenforceable, unless the restrictive elements (ie that which is prohibited by Article 81(1) and not saved by Article 81(3)) can be separated from the remainder. If so, only those restrictive elements are void and unenforceable. Severability is a matter for the national court applying its own contract law, as long as the Community law requirement that no effect be given to the restrictive elements is respected. The ECJ has held[666] that 'the automatic nullity decreed by Article 85(2) [now Article 81(2)] of the Treaty applies only to those contractual provisions which are incompatible with Article 85(1). The consequences of such nullity for other parts of the agreement, and for any orders and deliveries made on the basis of the agreement, and the resulting financial obligations are not a matter for Community law. Those consequences are to be determined by the national court according to its own law.'

It is beyond the scope of this chapter to delve into the many interesting questions which **3.394** arise in respect of Article 81(2). Similarly, we have decided not to examine the issue of provisional validity and the impact of accession to the Community, which are dealt with extensively in other works.

F. The Article 81(3) Exception

(1) Introduction

Article 81(3) of the Treaty contains an exception[667] to the prohibition of restrictive agree- **3.395** ments contained in Article 81(1). Agreements, concerted practices and decisions of associations of undertakings caught by Article 81(1) that satisfy the conditions of Article 81(3) are valid and enforceable, no prior decision to that effect being required.[668]

On 30 March 2004 the Commission adopted new guidelines on the application of Article **3.396** 81(3)[669] (the Guidelines). The Guidelines develop a methodology for the application of Article 81 based on the economic approach which the Commission has applied in recent years. The methodology in the Guidelines is intended to apply in all areas of application of Article 81, including those covered by existing Commission guidelines. The analytical framework of the Guidelines is more elaborate than that of the existing guidelines and includes some new policy orientations. The Guidelines provide a useful indication for firms and their advisers when dealing with cases involving the application of Article 81.

---

[666] Case 319/82 *Société de Vente de Ciments et Bétons de l'Est SA v Kerpen & Kerpen GmbH und Co KG* [1983] 4173, paras 11 and 12.

[667] With the entry into force of Council Regulation 1/2003 on the implementation of the rules on competition laid down in Arts 81 and 82 of the Treaty [2003] OJ L 1/1 Art 81(3) of the Treaty has become a directly applicable exception. The term 'exemption', which was closely related to the previous enforcement system based on notifications, is no longer used.

[668] See Art 1(2) of Regulation 1/2003.

[669] See [2004] OJ C 101/97.

3.397 The application of Article 81(3) is subject to four cumulative conditions, two of which are positive and two of which are negative:

(a) The agreement must contribute to improving the production or distribution of goods or contribute to promoting technical or economic progress,

(b) Consumers must receive a fair share of the resulting benefits,

(c) The restrictions must be indispensable to the attainment of these objectives, and

(d) The agreement must not afford the parties the possibility of eliminating competition in respect of a substantial part of the products in question.

3.398 When these four conditions are satisfied, the agreement enhances competition within the relevant market, since it leads the undertakings concerned to offer cheaper or better products to consumers, compensating the latter for the adverse effects of the restrictions of competition.[669A] The very essence of competition is the effort to win customers by offering cheaper, better and more innovative products on the market. Agreements that, on balance, improve supply to the market are pro-competitive.

3.399 Article 81(3) can be applied either to individual agreements or to categories of agreements by way of a 'block exemption regulation'. In individual cases, Article 81(3) provides a defence against a finding of an infringement of Article 81(1). The burden of proof under Article 81(3) rests on the party seeking to rely on it.[670] The extent of the burden depends on the strength of the case made by the party claiming a breach of Article 81(1). In *GlaxoSmithKline*[670A] the CFI found that the likely negative effects of the agreements concluded by the defendant were limited. Only limited benefits were therefore required to outweigh the negative effects. When an agreement is covered by a block exemption, the parties to the restrictive agreement are relieved of the requirement to show that their individual agreement satisfies each of the conditions of Article 81(3). They need only prove that the restrictive agreement benefits from the block exemption.

3.399A The person who relies on Article 81(3) must demonstrate that the four conditions are satisfied by means of convincing arguments and evidence .[670B] When this threshold is reached the person claiming an infringement of Article 81(1) must adduce additional convincing arguments and evidence in order to undermine the defence.

3.399B Before making a finding of infringement, the Commission is obliged to adequately examine all relevant evidence brought forward by the defendant under Article 81(3) and, so far as necessary, refute it by means of arguments and evidence capable of substantiating its conclusion. Failing such explanation or justification, it may be concluded that the burden of proof borne by the person who relies on Article 81(3) has been discharged.[670C]

[669A] In Case T-168/01 *GlaxoSmithKline* (judgment of 27 September 2006) at paras 118 and 171, the CFI confirmed that the objective of the Community competition rules is to prevent undertakings from reducing consumer welfare.

[670] See Art 2 of Regulation 1/2003. This rule was confirmed by the Court of Justice in Joined Cases C-204/00 and others *Aalborg Portland* [2004] ECR I, para 78.

[670A] See Case T-168/01 *GlaxoSmithKline* (judgment of 27 September 2006).

[670B] idem, para 235.

[670C] idem.

(2) The Relationship Between Article 81(1) and Article 81(3)

The aim of Article 81 is to identify and prohibit agreements that harm competition on the **3.400** market and thereby harm consumers. It is only after analyzing both Article 81(1) and Article 81(3) that one can conclude whether or not an agreement is anti-competitive.

The bifurcation of Article 81 does not affect the nature and content of the analysis. **3.401** Article 81(1) and (3) contain all the necessary elements of a rule of reason approach, with the anti-competitive aspects of agreements analysed under Article 81(1) and the pro-competitive elements analyzed and balanced against the anti-competitive elements under Article 81(3). There is no balancing of overall effects under Article 81(1).[671] The prohibition applies where the agreement and its restraints appreciably affect competition in the market.[672]

When applying Article 81(1) and Article 81(3) it is important to maintain a balance **3.402** between the two paragraphs so as to ensure that the prohibition effectively catches agreements that harm competition while leaving untouched innocuous and pro-competitive agreements. The Guidelines seek to achieve this balance by combining the fairly narrow scope of Article 81(1) with a similarly narrow interpretation of Article 81(3). According to paragraph 24 of the Guidelines 'the prohibition of Article 81(1) only applies where on the basis of proper market analysis it can be concluded that the agreement has likely anti-competitive effects on the market.'[673] Likely negative effects occur when 'on the relevant market negative effects on prices, output, innovation or the variety or quality of goods and services can be expected with a reasonable degree of probability.'[674] As a consequence of this economic approach to Article 81(1), which gives Article 81(1) a fairly narrow scope of application, the Guidelines are also fairly demanding in terms of the evidence required before the conclusion can be drawn that the pro-competitive benefits flowing from the agreement outweigh the anti-competitive effects.

(3) General Principles for the Application of Article 81(3)

(a) Introduction

Article 81(3) provides a structured framework for assessing the economic benefits gener- **3.403** ated by restrictive agreements and balancing them against the anti-competitive effects. This analysis of economic benefits forms an inherent part of any competition law system that has as its ultimate aim the protection of economic welfare in general and consumer welfare in particular.

---

[671] See Case T-65/98 *Van den Bergh Foods* [2003] ECR II, para 107, and Case T-112/99 *Métropole Télévision (M6) and others* [2001] ECR II-2459, para 74. In these cases the Court of First Instance held that it is only in the precise framework of Art 81(3) that the pro- and anti-competitive aspects of a restriction may be weighed.

[672] See Joined Cases 56/64 and 58/66 *Consten and Grundig* [1966] ECR 429. The fact that there is no rule of reason under Art 81(1) does not imply that efficiencies are entirely irrelevant in the context of Art 81(1). Efficiencies may affect the incentives of the parties and make collusion in the market less likely. This may for instance be the case where the agreement creates a maverick. In such cases the agreement may fall outside Art 81(1) for lack of likely anti-competitive effects.

[673] See in this respect Joined Cases T-374/94 and others *European Night Services* [1998] ECR II-3141.

[674] See Guidelines, para 24.

3.404   According to settled case law the four conditions of Article 81(3) are cumulative:[675] they must all be satisfied in order for the exception rule to be applicable. If they are not, Article 81(3) will not apply.[676] The four conditions of Article 81(3) are also exhaustive: when they are met the exception applies and is not dependent on any other condition.[677]

3.405   Article 81(3) does not exclude *a priori* certain types of agreement from its scope. All restrictive agreements that fulfil the four conditions of Article 81(3) are covered by the exception rule.[678] Article 81 does not contain a *per se* rule. However, this fact is not as significant as it might seem: restrictions of competition that can be qualified as 'hardcore' are very unlikely to fulfil the conditions of Article 81(3).[679] Such agreements generally fail (at least) the first two conditions of Article 81(3): they neither create objective economic benefits nor do they benefit consumers.[680] For example, a horizontal agreement to fix prices limits output and leads to the misallocation of resources. It also transfers value from consumers to producers since it leads to higher prices without producing any countervailing value to consumers within the relevant market. Hardcore restrictions generally also fail the indispensability test under the third condition.[681] However, the absence of a *per se* rule introduces a useful check on hardcore lists: if in a significant number of cases hardcore restrictions do satisfy the conditions of Article 81(3), the restriction in question should be re-classified. A restriction should only be classified as hardcore if upon individual assessment such agreements would almost always be prohibited. Naked cartels, for instance, clearly satisfy this test.

(b) The Nature of the Benefits that Can be Taken into Account

3.406   The Treaty pursues a number of objectives, some of which must explicitly be taken into account in the pursuit of other policies.[682] Such objectives may be taken into account in the application of Article 81(3) on condition that they can be subsumed under the four conditions of Article 81(3).[683] In order for Article 81(3) to apply, the objective in question must translate into economic benefits that satisfy the four conditions of that provision, including the requirement that consumers must receive a fair share of the resulting benefits.[684]

3.407   This interpretation is confirmed by the case law. In *Metro (I)*[685] the Court referred to the provision of employment in the following way: 'Furthermore, the establishment of supply

---

675   See eg Case T-185/00 and others *Métropole Télévision SA (M6)* [2002] ECR II-3805, para 86; Case T-17/93 *Matra* ECR [1994] II-595, para 85; and Joined Cases 43/82 and 63/82 *VBVB and VBBB* [1984] ECR 19, para 61.

676   See Case T-213/00 *CMA CGM and others* [2003] ECR II-913 para 226.

677   See Case T-168/01 *GlaxoSmithKline* (judgment of 27 September 2006), para 234 and Guidelines, para 42.

678   See Case T-168/01 *GlaxoSmithKline* (judgment of 27 September 2006), para 233 and Case T-17/93 *Matra Hachette* [1994] ECR 595, para 139.

679   See Guidelines, para 46.

680   See eg Case T-29/92 *Vereniging van Samenwerkende Prijsregelende Organisaties in de Bouwnijverheid (SPO)* [1995] ECR II-289.

681   See eg Case 258/78 *Nungesser* [1982] ECR 2015, para 77, concerning absolute territorial protection.

682   See Art 153(2) of the Treaty concerning consumer protection.

683   See Guidelines, para 42.

684   In the enforcement system created by Regulation 1/2003 this is very important. It is not the task of the enforcement agencies and courts to permit anti-competitive agreements in order to promote other policy objectives. If that were possible, the scope for inconsistent application and divergence would be significant.

685   Case 26/76 *Metro (I)* [1977] ECR 1875.

forecasts for a reasonable period constitutes a stabilising factor with regard to the provision of employment which, since it improves the general conditions of production, especially when market conditions are unfavourable, comes within the framework of the objectives to which reference may be had pursuant to article 81(3).' The Court did not consider employment as such to be an objective economic benefit falling under Article 81(3). However, the stabilising effect on employment was relevant because it improved production. Fluctuating demand forces an undertaking at one point in time to reduce personnel and at another point in time to increase it. This imposes costs in the form of transaction costs, training costs and loss of valuable skills. The stabilising effect of an agreement on employment may thus translate into cost savings and other efficiency gains. The benefit referred to by the Court could thus without difficulty be subsumed under the first condition of Article 81(3). Similarly in *Matra*[686] the CFI emphasised the fact that the Commission's reference in *Ford/Volkswagen*[687]—the decision under review—to the project's impact on public infrastructure and on employment in a region in Portugal had no bearing on the assessment under Article 81(3), thereby confirming the fact that the benefits in question, as such, did not constitute objective economic benefits within the meaning of Article 81(3).

In *CECED*[688] the Commission went some distance towards accepting restrictive agreements on environmental protection grounds. While this is a fairly recent decision, it does not appear to reflect current Commission thinking as laid down in the Guidelines. The case concerned an agreement between producers and importers of washing machines, who accounted for 90 per cent of the market, to cease producing and importing machines in energy classes E to D. The Commission found that the agreement was caught by Article 81(1)[689] but that it satisfied the conditions of Article 81(3). The benefits under Article 81(3) were considered to be twofold. First, the Commission argued convincingly that the agreement would reduce energy consumption leading to direct savings for users which would compensate them relatively quickly for the higher price that they would probably have to pay for washing machines. Secondly, the Commission considered that the agreement would reduce pollution to the benefit of society and consumers at large. There are several problems with this argument. It leads to a situation where one group of consumers, namely users of washing machines, through the higher price for washing machines, bear the cost of a benefit bestowed, at least principally, on other consumers. The decision thereby departs from the principle, which is now clearly stated in the Guidelines, that the group of consumers that is harmed by the anti-competitive effects of the agreement must also derive countervailing benefits from the agreement.[690] Given the wider scope of the analysis, this issue was not sufficiently addressed. Moreover, even the benefits to consumers at large depended on the

3.408

---

[686] Case T-17/93 *Matra Hachette* [1994] ECR 595, para 139.

[687] [1993] OJ L 20/14.

[688] [2000] OJ L 187/47.

[689] The Commission considered *inter alia* that the agreement reduced the demand for electricity, which it equated with an output restriction. By qualifying a clear-cut efficiency as an output restriction the decision runs counter to the normal interpretation of Art 81 where efficiencies are taken into account as pro-competitive effects in the application of Art 81(3).

[690] See the following section.

method employed for generating electricity. In regions relying on, for instance, hydro-electric power the benefits derived from the agreement would be non-existent.[691]

(c) The Relevant Market as the Proper Framework for Applying Article 81(3)

3.409   Under the Guidelines, benefits flowing from restrictive agreements are in principle analysed within the confines of each relevant market to which the agreement relates.[692] The Guidelines thereby adhere to the traditional antitrust approach of using the relevant market as the basis for analysing anti-competitive and pro-competitive effects. Moreover, the fact that under Article 81(3) consumers must receive a fair share of the benefits resulting from the agreement implies that negative effects on consumers in one product or geographic market cannot normally be balanced against and compensated for by positive effects for consumers in another unrelated product or geographic market. The only exception[693] is where two markets are related, in which case benefits achieved on separate markets can be taken into account 'provided that the group of consumers affected by the restriction and benefiting from the efficiency gains are substantially the same'. Taken as a whole the principles contained in the Guidelines thus require that the consumers who pay and the consumers that benefit must be substantially the same. A departure from this approach would require complex inter-personal comparisons to be carried out in each and every case where competition concerns and efficiencies occur in distinct markets.[694]

3.410   The approach set out in the Guidelines is considered to be in line with recent case law of the European Courts. In *Shaw*[695] the CFI held that the assessment under Article 81(3) had to be

---

[691]   The decision attempts to address under Art 81(3) a perceived externality, namely pollution of the environment. However, it was not argued that the washing machines themselves caused pollution. The source of pollution was certain forms of electricity generation required for the machine to run. In such cases the externality should be addressed at source, *in casu* electricity generation, and not by accepting restrictive agreements that at best have an indirect effect on the problem. Moreover, it is submitted that it would be more appropriate to take externalities into account under Art 81(1). The environment is a resource which is used by polluters but which, in the absence of a tax or other instrument, is not factored into the price of the product. It can be argued that agreements which internalise genuine externalities in a proportionate manner are not restrictive of competition in the first place.

[692]   See Guidelines, para 43. This is also the approach set out in para 79 of the Commission's horizontal merger guidelines [2004] OJ C 31/5), and n 36 of the US merger guidelines.

[693]   See Guidelines, para 43.

[694]   Having to engage in inter-personal comparisons is fraught with difficulty, as can be illustrated by the following examples taken from *Lars Kjølbye*, 'The new guidelines on the application of Art 81(3): an economic approach' [2004] ECLR 566:

A and B produce heart drugs for which there are no substitutes. They also produce a diabetes drug for which three other substitutes exist. A and B agree to pool their respective R&D activities in both fields of activity. In the context of Art 81(1) it is found that the agreement is likely to lead to higher prices and reduced R&D on the market for heart decease drugs whereas consumers of diabetes drugs obtain an improved product. How should one balance these two effects?

A and B manufacture heavy trucks. They establish a joint venture combining their distribution and service organisations in several Member States. Relevant markets are national. In one Member State where the parties have a relatively weak market position, the agreement does not appreciably restrict competition. In fact, the agreement is pro-competitive because it allows the parties to compete more effectively with larger incumbents. In another Member State where the parties have a strong position, the agreement is caught by Art 81(1) because it allows the parties to increase their market power, making price increases likely. Again, how should one balance a likely higher price for consumers in one Member State against a likely lower price for consumers in the other Member State?

[695]   See Case T-131/99 *Shaw* [2002] ECR II-2023, para 163.

made within the same analytical framework as that relevant to analysing the restrictive effects of the agreement, which can reasonably be interpreted as being the relevant market.

In *Compagnie Générale Maritime and others*[696] the CFI held that 'regard should naturally **3.411** be had to the advantages arising from the agreement in question, not only for the relevant market, namely that for inland transport services provided as part of intermodal transport, but also, in appropriate cases, for every other market on which the agreement in question might have beneficial effects, and even, in a more general sense, for any service the quality or efficiency of which might be improved by the existence of that agreement.' On its face, this statement could be interpreted as requiring a balancing of anti-competitive and pro-competitive effects across markets. It is submitted, however, that the statement should be read in light of the judgment in *Shaw* and the facts of the case. When due regard is given to the facts, it becomes clear why the CFI considered that it was an 'appropriate case' for taking account of benefits produced in a distinct market. The case concerned intermodal transport services. These services encompassed, *inter alia*, inland and maritime transport services provided to shippers across the Community. The restrictions related to inland transport services, which were held to constitute a distinct relevant market, whereas the benefits were claimed to occur in the separate market for maritime transport services. Both services were demanded by shippers requiring intermodal transport services between northern Europe and Southeast and East Asia. The affected group of consumers was therefore the same. When an agreement covering services affects the same group of consumers, the overall impact of the agreement on this group of consumers must be analysed. It was therefore entirely appropriate and consistent with the approach of the Guidelines in the specific case to analyse pro-competitive effects and anti-competitive effects across the relevant markets involved. This reading appears to be confirmed by the CFI in *GlaxoSmithKline*[696A] where it emphasised that the final consumers likely to benefit from the efficiencies were the same as those that suffered from the likely negative effects.

(d) The Temporal Application of Article 81(3)

Article 81 applies to agreements according to the actual legal and economic context in which **3.412** they occur.[697] The application of Article 81(1) and Article 81(3) thus depends crucially on the facts pertaining at the point in time when the assessment is made. It follows that the assessment cannot be made exclusively on the basis of the facts pertaining at the time when the agreement was concluded. If the circumstances subsequently change, the assessment may also change. It would be neither legally possible nor economically justified to base the assessment exclusively on the situation *ex ante*. The mere fact that at the time of conclusion

---

[696]   Case T-86/95 *Compagnie Générale Maritime and others* [2002] ECR II-1011, paras 343–345. See also Case T-213/00 *CMA CGM and others* [2003] ECR II-913, para 226. This case concerned a situation where the agreement, while covering several distinct services, affected the same group of consumers, namely shippers of containerised cargo between northern Europe and the Far East. Under the agreement the parties fixed charges and surcharges relating to inland transport services, port services and maritime transport services. The Court of First Instance held (cf paras 226–228) that in the circumstances of the case there was no need to define relevant markets for the purpose of applying Art 81(3). The agreement was restrictive of competition by its very object and there were no benefits for consumers.

[696A]   See Case T-168/01 *GlaxoSmithKline* (judgment of 27 September 2006), para 251.

[697]   See eg Joined Cases 25/84 and 26/84 *Ford* [1985] ECR 2725, para 33.

an agreement is not caught by Article 81(1) or satisfies the conditions of Article 81(3), does not imply that the agreement is immune to subsequent intervention. Undertakings are obliged to re-assess their agreements when circumstances change materially.

3.413 This principle does not mean that the *ex ante* situation is irrelevant. It merely implies that all relevant facts have to be taken into account, whether or not they pre-date or post-date the agreement. In order not to discourage pro-competitive agreements it is particularly important to take account of *ex ante* investments committed by the parties. The Guidelines[698] expressly recognise that it is necessary to take into account the initial sunk investments made by any of the parties and the time needed and the restraints required to commit and recoup an efficiency-enhancing investment. The risk facing the parties and the sunken investment that must be committed to implement the agreement may thus lead to the agreement falling outside Article 81(1) or fulfilling the conditions of Article 81(3), as the case may be, for the period of time required to recoup the investment.[699]

3.414 The Guidelines[700] make one exception to the principle that agreements are assessed on the basis of the facts pertaining at the time the assessment is made. In certain cases the agreement is an irreversible event, in the sense that once the restrictive agreement has been implemented the *ex ante* situation cannot be re-established. In such cases the assessment must be made exclusively on the basis of the facts pertaining at the time of implementation. The Guidelines give the example of a research and development agreement whereby the parties agree to abandon their respective research projects and pool their capabilities. In such a case, from an objective point of view, it may be technically and economically impossible to revive a project once it has been abandoned. The assessment of the anti-competitive and pro-competitive effects of the agreement to abandon the individual research projects must therefore be made as at the time of the completion of its implementation. If at that point in time the agreement is compatible with Article 81, for instance because a sufficient number of third parties have competing research and development projects, the parties' agreement to abandon their individual projects remains compatible with Article 81, even if at a later point in time the third party projects fail. The Guidelines caution, however, that the prohibition of Article 81 may apply to other parts of the agreement in respect of which the issue of irreversibility does not arise. If, for example, in addition to joint research and development, the agreement provides for joint exploitation, Article 81 may apply to this part of the agreement if, due to subsequent market developments, the agreement becomes restrictive of competition and does not (any longer) satisfy the conditions of Article 81(3).

---

[698] See para 44.

[699] The Guidelines on technology transfer agreements, [2004] OJ C 101/2 give examples of both situations. Para 101 provides that in the case of agreements between non-competitors it is likely—given the investment required by licensees penetrating a new territory—that licensees would not enter into a licence agreement without an initial period of protection against passive sales from licensees in other territories, ie protection against intra-brand competition, in which case the agreement falls outside Art 81(1). Para 170 provides that restrictions on active sales in non-reciprocal agreements between competitors may satisfy the conditions of Art 81(3), in particular, where the licensee has a relatively weak market position in the territory allocated to him and has to make a significant investment in order to exploit the licensed technology efficiently.

[700] See para 45.

(e) Block Exemptions

Block exemption regulations are Community acts that produce effects *erga omnes*.[701] **3.415**
Agreements that benefit from a block exemption are presumed to satisfy the conditions of
Article 81(3) and thus to be legally valid and enforceable.

In the enforcement system created by Regulation 1/2003 only the Commission (and the **3.416**
Council)[702] has the power to adopt block exemption regulations concerning the application of Article 81(3). The national competition authorities of Member States (NCAs) may
apply Articles 81 and 82 in individual cases.[703] The Commission's powers are laid down in
enabling regulations adopted by the Council.[704] So far these cover vertical agreements,
agreements concerning the acquisition and use of industrial property rights, research and
development and specialisation agreements, insurance, liner shipping consortia, interlining and slot allocation.[705]

The application of Article 81(3) to categories of agreements by way of block exemption **3.417**
regulation is based on the presumption that restrictive agreements that fall within their
scope[706] fulfil each of the four conditions laid down in Article 81(3). A block exemption is
therefore appropriate only when it can reasonably be assumed that upon individual assessment the vast majority of agreements falling within its scope would satisfy the conditions
of Article 81(3). This is the reason why recent block exemptions have incorporated market
share thresholds to limit their scope. These block exemptions have a wide scope of application in terms of the restrictions covered. Every provision which is not identified as a hardcore or excluded restriction benefits from the block exemption. In the absence of market
share thresholds it is not possible to assume that agreements falling within the scope of the
block exemption will satisfy the conditions of Article 81(3).

The mere fact that an agreement is covered by a block exemption does not imply that it is **3.418**
necessarily caught by Article 81(1). Block exemptions formally cover a number of agreements that may not restrictive of competition in the first place. The fact that an agreement

---

[701] See in this respect Art 249 of the Treaty.
[702] In the past certain block exemptions have been adopted by the Council. Block exemptions are enforcement instruments applying Art 81(3) of the Treaty. They are therefore different from other types of legislative
acts adopted by the Community legislator. It is therefore a welcome development that in recent years the
Council has confined itself to granting legislative powers to the Commission, refraining from adopting block
exemptions itself.
[703] See Art 5 of Regulation 1/2003.
[704] The Council did not in Regulation 1/2003—as proposed by the Commission—grant the latter a
general power to adopt block exemptions.
[705] See Council Regulation 19/65 on the application of Art 81(3(to certain categories of agreements and
concerted practices OJ [1965] 36 as amended by Council Regulation 1215/1999 OJ [1999] L148/1, Council
Regulation 2821/71 on the application of Art 81(3) to categories of agreements and concerted practices
[1971] OJ L 285/46, Council Regulation 1534/91 on the application of Art 81(3) to certain categories of
agreements, decisions and concerted practices in the insurance sector [1991] OJ L143/1, Council Regulation
479/92 on the application of Art 81(3) to certain categories of agreements, decisions and concerted practices
between liner shipping companies (consortia) [1992] L 55/3, and Council Regulation 3976/87 on the application of Art 81(3) to certain categories of agreements and concerted practices in the air transport sector
[1987] OJ L374/9.
[706] The fact that an agreement is block exempted does not in itself indicate that the individual agreement
is caught by Art 81(1).

is not block exempted does not give rise to any presumption that the agreement in question is caught by Article 81(1) or that it fails to satisfy the conditions of Article 81(3).[707] Individual assessment is required. The only exception is where the agreement contains hardcore restrictions in which case there is a presumption that the agreement is incompatible with Article 81.[708]

3.419 If, in an individual case, the agreement is caught by Article 81(1) and the conditions of Article 81(3) are not fulfilled, the block exemption may be withdrawn. According to Article 29(1) of Regulation 1/2003 the Commission has the power to withdraw the benefit of a block exemption when it finds in a particular case that an agreement covered by a block exemption regulation has certain effects that are incompatible with Article 81(3). Pursuant to Article 29(2) of Regulation 1/2003 an NCA may also withdraw the benefit of a Commission block exemption regulation in respect of its territory (or part of its territory), if this territory has all the characteristics of a distinct geographic market. In the case of withdrawal it is for the NCA concerned to demonstrate that the agreement infringes Article 81(1) and that it does not fulfil the conditions of Article 81(3). Since withdrawal implies that the agreement is incompatible with Article 81 as a whole, withdrawal necessarily implies the adoption of a decision under either Article 7 or Article 9 of Regulation 1/2003 or equivalent national provisions.

(4) The Four Conditions of Article 81(3)

(a) Introduction

3.420 Article 81(3) contains four cumulative tests the purpose of which is to identify the economic benefits produced by agreements and their overall impact on consumers. In its past practice the Commission focussed mainly on the two last conditions of Article 81(3) concerning indispensability and no elimination of competition. It focused less on the quantification and verification of efficiency claims and on verifying that consumers received a fair share of the efficiencies.[709] The Guidelines aim at putting more emphasis on the first two conditions of Article 81(3) and bringing the application of all four conditions into line with the regime created by Regulation 1/2003, where undertakings have to rely on self-assessment and where the Commission is focussing on pro-active enforcement against agreements and practices that give rise to real competition concerns. As a result of the more economic approach under Article 81(1), fewer cases will be caught by the prohibition rules. However, when Article 81(1) does apply, careful analysis of all four conditions of Article 81(3) is required.

(b) The First Test of Article 81(3): Efficiency Gains

3.421 According to the first condition of Article 81(3), the restrictive agreement must contribute to improving the production or distribution of goods or to promoting technical or economic progress. This provision refers expressly only to goods, but applies by analogy to services.[710]

---

707 See eg para 37 of the Guidelines on the application of Art 81 to technology transfer agreements.
708 See para 46 of the Guidelines.
709 The system of prior notification and authorisation created by Regulation 17/62 led to a reactive enforcement culture where the Commission spent a considerable amount of time checking individual clauses in notified agreements. The condition of indispensability was well suited for that purpose.
710 See para 48 of the Guidelines.

Under the Guidelines, no enquiry is conducted into whether the restraints are indispens- **3.422** able or what the benefits are for consumers. The purpose of the first condition is to identify all economic benefits flowing from the restrictive agreement. In *Van den Bergh Foods* and *GlaxoSmithKline*[711] the CFI held that 'the improvement must in particular display appreciable objective advantages of such a character as to compensate for the disadvantages which they cause in the field of competition'. Although it is not entirely clear what is meant by 'in the field of competition', this passage would appear to imply that an analysis of the impact of the agreement on total economic welfare is required. However, such an interpretation leads to a double welfare test, since the condition that consumers must receive a fair share of the benefits already requires that for Article 81(3) to apply the agreement must not lead to a loss of consumer welfare. As the consumer welfare standard is more strict than the total welfare standard, it makes little sense to apply both in the same case. It is therefore submitted that the better approach is that no balancing of positive and negative effects is required under the first condition.

The benefits that are taken into account under the first condition need not flow from the **3.423** restrictions contained in the agreement. The link between the benefits and the restrictions is analysed under the condition of indispensability. In general, relevant economic benefits stem from the economic activity which is regulated by the agreement and more specifically from an integration of economic activity whereby undertakings combine assets to achieve what they could not achieve as efficiently on their own or whereby they entrust another undertaking with tasks that can be performed more efficiently by that other undertaking.[712] The research and development, production and distribution process may be viewed as a chain[713] that can be divided into a number of stages. Co-operation between undertakings at each stage of this chain may give rise to economic benefits within the meaning of Article 81(3).[714] To the extent, however, that an agreement has wider efficiency-enhancing effects within the relevant market, for example because it leads to a reduction in industry-wide costs, these additional benefits are also taken into account.[715]

Only objective benefits can be taken into account.[716] Benefits are not assessed from the sub- **3.424** jective point of view of the parties.[717] Cost savings that arise from the mere exercise of market power by the parties cannot be taken into account. For example, when companies agree to fix prices or share markets they reduce output and production costs. Reduced competition may also lead to lower sales and marketing expenditure. Such cost reductions are a direct consequence of a reduction in output and value. They do not produce any pro-competitive effects on the market and cannot be taken into account.[718]

---

[711] See Case T-65/98 *Van den Bergh Foods* [2003] ECR II-4653, para 139 and Case T-168/01 *GlaxoSmithKline* (judgment of 27 September 2006), paras 247 and 304 to 307.
[712] See Guidelines, para 60.
[713] This term has been developed by Porter, *Competitive Advantage* (The Free Press, 1985).
[714] See Guidelines, para 61.
[715] ibid, para 53.
[716] See eg Joined Cases 56/64 and 58/66 *Consten and Grundig* [1966] ECR 429.
[717] See in this respect Commission Decision in *Van den Bergh Foods* [1998] OJ L 246/1.
[718] See Guidelines, para 49.

3.425   In its Guidelines the Commission uses the term 'efficiencies' to capture all the various economic benefits covered by Article 81(3). The scope of this term is wider than that flowing from the traditional definition of efficiencies in economics, where it generally covers the production of a certain product using fewer resources. In the Guidelines the notion of 'efficiencies' covers static and dynamic efficiencies in the shape of cost savings, new or improved products, enhanced product variety and innovation.[719]

3.426   The Guidelines do not expressly refer to the market integration goal of the Community competition rules. However, this should not be taken as an indication that the market integration goal is being de-emphasised or abandoned. It merely reflects the fact that in the context of Article 81(3) market integration and the benefits flowing from the internal market must and normally will translate into the types of efficiencies that are covered by Article 81(3). Only benefits that can be subsumed under the four conditions of Article 81(3) can be taken into account.[720] This can be illustrated by the Commission's decision in *Uniform Eurocheques*[721] where the efficiencies took the form of an improved cross-border payment system. This agreement clearly promoted market integration. Importantly, however, it did so by making available an improved service to consumers; a type of efficiency that falls squarely within the scope of Article 81(3).

(i) Examples of Relevant Types of Efficiencies

3.427   The Guidelines distinguish two basic categories of efficiencies, namely 'cost efficiencies' and what, for lack of a better term, are called 'qualitative efficiencies', encompassing *inter alia* new and improved products. These are broad categories of efficiencies and the Guidelines do not express any preference for any particular category. Cost savings are not given more weight than other types of efficiencies.

3.428   Cost efficiencies can stem from agreements resulting in the development of new production technologies and methods. As stated in the Guidelines, it is generally when technological advances are made that the greatest potential for cost savings is achieved.[722] Synergies resulting from the integration of existing assets are another source of efficiency. When the parties to an agreement combine their respective assets they may be able to attain a cost/output configuration that would not otherwise be possible. The combination of two existing technologies that have complementary strengths may reduce production costs or lead to the production of a higher quality product.[723] Undertakings concluding agreements may also be able to achieve lower costs as a result of economies of scale, ie declining cost per unit of output as output increases, and economies of scope, which arise when firms achieve cost savings by producing different products on the basis of the same input. Cost reductions may also result from agreements that allow for better planning of production, reducing the need to hold expensive inventory and allowing for better capacity utilisation.

---

[719] See also the Guidelines on technology transfer agreements which emphasise the fact that innovation constitutes an essential and dynamic component of an open and competitive market economy.

[720] See Guidelines, para 42 and section F.3(b) above.

[721] See [1985] OJ L 35/43.

[722] See Guidelines, para 64.

[723] ibid, para 65.

Agreements between undertakings may also generate efficiencies of a qualitative nature. **3.429**
Depending on the individual case, such efficiencies may be of equal or greater importance
than cost efficiencies.[724] Technical and technological advances form an essential and dynamic
part of the economy, generating significant benefits in the form of new or improved goods
and services. By co-operating, undertakings may be able to create efficiencies that would not
otherwise have been possible or would have been possible only with substantial delay or at
higher cost. In the same way that the combination of complementary assets can give rise to
cost savings, combinations of assets may also create synergies that create efficiencies of a
qualitative nature. The combination of research and development and production assets in
the context of a joint venture or a licence agreement may for instance lead to the production of new products, products with novel features or higher quality products.

(ii) The Substantiation of Efficiency Claims

In order to maintain a proper balance between Article 81(1) and Article 81(3) and as a con- **3.430**
sequence of the greater weight attributed to economic analysis and the consumer welfare
objective, the Guidelines impose more rigour in the assessment of efficiency claims.
Efficiency claims must be backed up by evidence before they can be given weight by the
Commission. The Guidelines[725] provide that all efficiency claims must be substantiated so
that the following can be verified:

(a) The *nature* of the claimed efficiencies;
(b) The *link* between the agreement and the efficiencies;
(c) The *likelihood* and *magnitude* of each claimed efficiency; and
(d) *How* and *when* each claimed efficiency would be achieved.

Point (a) is intended to enable the Commission to verify that the claimed efficiencies are **3.431**
objective in nature and therefore capable of being taken into account. Clarifying the nature
of the claimed efficiencies is also important to the subsequent analysis of whether consumers
receive a fair share of the benefits. Certain types of efficiencies are more likely to be passed
on to consumers than others.[726]

Point (b) allows the Commission to verify whether there is a sufficient causal link between **3.432**
the agreement and the claimed efficiencies. At this stage of the analysis the inquiry is limited to examining whether the claimed efficiencies flow from the agreement. The analysis
of the link between the efficiencies and the restrictions of competition caused by the agreement is conducted within the framework of the condition of indispensability. Generally
the claimed efficiencies will result from the economic activity covered by the agreement
itself, but sometimes agreements have wider efficiency-enhancing effects, for example
because they lead to a reduction in industry-wide costs, in which case such additional
benefits are also taken into account.[727]

---

[724] ibid, para 69.
[725] See paras 98 and 102.
[726] See further section F.4(c) below.
[727] See Guidelines, para 53.

3.433   According to the Guidelines, the causal link between the agreement and the claimed efficiencies must normally be direct.[728] A direct causal link exists for instance where a technology transfer agreement allows the licensees to produce new or improved products or a
distribution agreement allows products to be distributed at lower cost or valuable services
to be produced. As regards indirect effects the Guidelines provide that as a general rule such
effects are too uncertain and too remote to be taken into account.[729] The use of the term
'as a general rule' implies that indirect effects can be taken into account. However, their
existence must be proved convincingly.[730]

3.434   The purpose of points (c) and (d) is to enable the Commission to verify the value of the
claimed efficiencies, which in the context of the third condition of Article 81(3) must be
balanced against the negative effects identified under Article 81(1).[731] Efficiency claims
must be substantiated. Unsubstantiated claims are rejected. The parties must describe the
method(s) by which the efficiencies have been or will be achieved. If the agreement has yet to
be fully implemented the parties must substantiate any projections concerning the date from
which the efficiencies will become operational so as to have a significant positive impact in the
market.[732] The data submitted must be verifiable so that there can be a sufficient degree of
certainty that the efficiencies have materialised or are likely to materialise. The Guidelines also
require that, in the case of claimed cost efficiencies, the undertakings concerned calculate or
estimate as accurately as reasonably possible the value of the efficiencies and describe in detail
how the amount has been computed.[733] In the case of claimed efficiencies in the form of new
or improved products and other non-cost based efficiencies, the undertakings claiming the
benefit of Article 81(3) must describe and explain in detail the nature and value of the
efficiencies and how and why they constitute an objective economic benefit.[734]

3.435   While the Guidelines clearly establish a rigorous framework for assessing efficiency claims,
they explicitly acknowledge that efficiencies are not an exact science. Words such as 'as accurately as reasonably possible' suggest that that the obligation imposed is one of best efforts.
Moreover, the Guidelines as a whole are based on a sliding scale approach:[735] the greater the
competition concerns identified under Article 81(1), the greater must be the efficiencies and
the more they must be substantiated. The analysis of pro-competitive and anti-competitive
effects under Article 81 is often a question of probabilities.[735A] What the undertaking
invoking Article 81(3) is required to do is to make a convincing case in its favour.

(c) The Second Test of Article 81(3): Indispensability

3.436   The Guidelines deal with the third condition of Article 81(3) before the second condition.
It is submitted that in general there are good reasons for doing so. The second condition,

---

[728]   ibid, para 54.
[729]   ibid, para 54.
[730]   See Case T-168/01 *GlaxoSmithKline* (judgment of 27 September 2006), para 280.
[731]   See Guidelines, para 55.
[732]   ibid, para 58.
[733]   ibid, para 56.
[734]   See Guidelines, para 57.
[735]   See eg para 90.
[735A]   See Case T-168/01 *GlaxoSmithKline* (judgment of 27 September 2006), para 302.

according to which consumers must receive a fair share of the benefits, implies a balancing of pro-competitive and anti-competitive effects. This balancing exercise should not include restrictions that in any event are unnecessary to achieve the efficiencies. If it were otherwise an agreement might be denied the benefit of Article 81(3) in its entirety even though the second condition could be satisfied if certain unnecessary restrictions were eliminated. This is particularly relevant in cases where a restriction can be eliminated or modified without undermining the commercial arrangement covered by the agreement. Automatic nullification under Article 81(2) only extends to those parts of the agreement that are incompatible with Article 81, provided that such parts are severable from the agreement as a whole.[736] If only part of the agreement is null and void, the consequences thereof for the remaining part of the agreement must be determined according to the applicable national law.[737]

When applying the indispensability test, the decisive factor is whether or not the restrictive **3.437** agreement and individual restrictions make it possible to perform the underlying economic activity more efficiently than would probably have been the case in the absence of the agreement or the restriction concerned.[738] The question is not whether, in the absence of the restriction, the agreement would have been concluded or not, but whether more efficiencies are produced with the agreement or restriction than would have been the case in the absence of the agreement or restriction.[739]

The indispensability test contained in Article 81(3) requires an assessment of whether the **3.438** efficiencies are specific to the agreement and its individual restrictions. There must be a causal link between the efficiencies and the restrictions showing that the restrictions are necessary in order to obtain the efficiencies that flow from the agreement. The test applied in the Guidelines is one of 'reasonable necessity'.[740] The Commission does not interpret the concept of indispensability as implying a test of 'strict necessity'. In a world where business decisions must be made on the basis of imperfect information and where enforcement agencies are not often well-placed to second guess such decisions, a certain margin of error is considered justified.

The assessment of indispensability is made by reference to the actual context in which the **3.439** agreement operates and must take account in particular of the structure of the market, the economic risks related to the agreement, and the incentives for the parties.[741] The more uncertain the success of the product covered by the agreement, the more a restriction may be required to ensure that the efficiencies will materialise. In some cases a restriction may be indispensable only for a certain period of time, in which case the exception of Article 81(3) applies only during that period. In making this assessment it is necessary to take due account of the period of time required for the parties to achieve the efficiencies justifying the application of the exception rule.[742] In cases where the benefits cannot be achieved

---

[736] See Case 56/65 *Société Technique Minière* [1966] ECR 337.
[737] See in this respect Case 319/82 Kerpen & Kerpen [1983] ECR 4173, paras 11 and 12.
[738] See Guidelines, para 74.
[739] In the case of intra-brand restrictions, Art 81(1) does not apply if in the absence of the restraint such an agreement would not have been concluded: see Guidelines, para 18(1).
[740] See Guidelines, para 73.
[741] See Guidelines, para 80.
[742] See Joined Cases T-374/94 and others European Night Services [1998] ECR II-3141, para 230.

without considerable investment, account must be taken in particular of the period of time required to recoup that investment.

3.440 In some cases the agreement as such is restrictive of competition. This may be the case for instance where the very creation of a production joint venture restricts competition between the parties in a downstream market. In such cases it is necessary to assess whether the efficiencies could have been achieved by means of a less restrictive alternative, whether by a different type of agreement or by the parties acting individually. The parties must explain and demonstrate why seemingly realistic and significantly less restrictive alternatives to the agreement would be significantly less efficient.[743] The Guidelines stress that the Commission will not second guess the business judgment of the parties.[744] The Commission will intervene only when it is reasonably clear that there are realistic and attainable less restrictive alternatives to the agreement entered into by the parties. It is submitted that, under the policy orientations contained in the Guidelines, the Commission will only rarely find that the agreement as a whole is not indispensable. In most cases it will therefore only be necessary to assess whether the individual restrictions contained in the agreement are necessary to produce the efficiencies identified in the application of the first condition of Article 81(3).

3.441 Once it is found that the agreement in question is necessary in order to produce the efficiencies, the indispensability of each restriction of competition flowing from the agreement must be assessed. A restriction is indispensable if its absence would eliminate or significantly reduce the efficiencies achieved by the agreement or make it significantly less likely that they will materialise.[745] The assessment of alternative solutions must take into account the actual and potential improvement in competition by the elimination of a particular restriction or the application of a less restrictive alternative. The third condition of Article 81(3) thus incorporates a sliding scale. The more restrictive the restraint, the stricter the test under the third condition.[746] Restrictions that are black-listed in block exemption regulations or identified as hardcore restrictions in Commission guidelines and notices are unlikely to be considered indispensable.

(d) The Third Test of Article 81(3): A Fair Share for Consumers

3.442 According to Article 81(3) consumers must receive a fair share of the benefits that have been identified in the context of the first condition. Consumers within the meaning of the second condition of Article 81(3) are the users of the product covered by the agreement. The term 'consumers' is thus not synonymous with 'final consumers'.[747] The Guidelines refer to 'direct or indirect' users.[748] The reference to indirect users is particularly intended to cover situations where the direct buyer does not pay for the product and as a consequence is not the one who benefits from a passing on of cost efficiencies. For instance, prescription

---

[743] In this regard the Guidelines reflect the fact that in the new enforcement system the Commission will focus on cases that give rise to real competition concerns and will not engage in micromanagement of agreements.

[744] See Guidelines, para 75.

[745] ibid, para 79.

[746] Case T-86/95 *Compagnie Générale Maritime and others* [2002] ECR II-1011, paras 392–395.

[747] The French version of the Treaty uses the term 'utilisateurs'. Certain other language versions use a similar term, which is wider than that of final consumer.

[748] See para 84.

drugs are generally paid wholly or partly by social security bodies. In such cases, the (main) beneficiary of any cost efficiencies will be the social security scheme which pays the bill rather than the patient who consumes the product. In this example the social security body is an indirect user.

The reference in the Guidelines[749] to 'direct and indirect users' and 'customers of the parties and subsequent buyers' is not intended to impose on the parties a requirement to show that the benefits are passed to final consumers. As stated above, the concept of consumer is not synonymous with final consumer. If the buyers of the products receive a fair share of the efficiencies generated by the agreement, the third condition of Article 81(3) is satisfied even if for some reason these benefits are not passed on to final consumers. For instance, it may be that due to the presence of market power at the level of the immediate buyers, cost savings stemming from the agreement are not passed on to subsequent buyers. However, this does not lead to Article 81(3) being inapplicable. Pro-competitive agreements should not be struck down because of a competition problem at the next level. This interpretation is in line with the general principle of the Guidelines according to which the group of consumers that is adversely affected by the agreement must also benefit from the efficiencies.[750] Once this condition is satisfied it is not necessary for subsequent buyers to benefit as well. **3.443**

The concept of 'fair share' establishes the benchmark for assessing whether a sufficient portion of the efficiencies is passed on to consumers for the second condition of Article 81(3) to be satisfied. According to the Guidelines[751] this test is met when pass-on is such that it at least compensates consumers for any actual or likely negative impact caused to them by the restriction of competition found under Article 81(1). If on balance an agreement has no likely negative effect on consumer welfare it should not be prohibited. Article 81 prohibits anti-competitive agreements, ie agreements that have likely adverse effects on competition and consumers. While on equity grounds it might be considered desirable that consumers obtain a certain proportion of the efficiency gains, it is submitted that the Guidelines rightly reject such an approach, which can only lead to arbitrary outcomes and introduction of elements into the analysis that are foreign to Article 81. **3.444**

For consumers to obtain a fair share of the benefits it is not necessary for them to receive a share of each and every efficiency gain identified under the first condition. It suffices that sufficient benefits are passed on so as to compensate for the negative effects of the restrictive agreement. In that case consumers obtain a fair share of the overall benefits.[752] The essence of this analysis is captured in the following two questions: (i) are prices in the market likely to increase and (ii) if so, are such price increases likely to be offset by product improvements or other efficiencies? In general, it can reasonably be assumed that if prices are unlikely to rise either in absolute terms or relative to the value of the products, then consumers of the products in question are not adversely affected and the agreement is not anti-competitive as regards that group of consumers. However, as these questions do not deal with, in particular, positive and adverse effects on innovation, they should not be applied mechanically. **3.445**

---

[749] idem.
[750] See section F.3(c).
[751] See para 85.
[752] See in this respect Case 26/76 *Metro (I)* [1977] ECR 1875, para 48.

3.446   In previous guidelines[753] the Commission assumed that sufficient pass-on will normally occur if sufficient competition that effectively constrains the parties to keep to the agreement is maintained on the market. The Guidelines have abandoned this presumption. In the absence of restrictions by object, Article 81(1) applies only when the parties have or obtain a significant degree[754] of market power and the agreement contributes to the creation, maintenance or strengthening of market power. In other words, Article 81(1) applies only where the undertakings concerned are not subject to an effective competitive constraint.[755] In such cases it cannot be assumed that residual competition on its own is sufficient to ensure that adequate pass-on occurs. This is not to say that residual competition is irrelevant. However, if residual competition is insufficient to prevent the parties from exercising market power, it is difficult to see why residual competition in itself would be sufficient to force the parties to pass on efficiencies to consumers. It is necessary to consider a number of factors.

3.447   The factors that according to the Guidelines are particularly relevant are (a) the characteristics and structure of the market, (b) the nature and magnitude of the efficiency gains, (c) the elasticity of demand, and (d) the magnitude of the restriction of competition.[756] The reference to market structure and characteristics captures the degree of residual competition in the relevant market.

3.448   The second factor reflects the fact that some types of efficiency are more likely to be passed on than others. Indeed, efficiencies of a qualitative nature that manifest themselves in the goods and services sold to consumers are necessarily passed on. If a production joint venture leads to the production of an improved product or a distribution agreement leads to the provision of improved services, these benefits are necessarily passed on to users of the goods and services in question. In such cases, the main task is to assess whether these benefits are sufficient to compensate for any price increase or other likely anti-competitive effects resulting from the agreement such as foreclosure of competitors and a resulting loss of product variety.

3.449   In the case of cost efficiencies the situation is more complex. Cost savings will generally only benefit consumers if they lead the undertakings concerned to lower prices. Economic theory suggests that this is more likely to occur in the case of reductions in variable costs than in the case of fixed cost reductions. Undertakings maximise their profits by selling units of output until marginal revenue equals marginal cost. Marginal revenue is the change in total revenue resulting from selling an additional unit of output. Marginal cost is the change in total cost resulting from producing that additional unit of output. If marginal costs fall, even undertakings with market power may have an incentive to reduce prices. This can be illustrated by the following example.[757] Undertaking X produces under licence and pays a royalty

---

[753] See para 34 of the Guidelines on horizontal co-operation agreements and para 136 of the Guidelines on Vertical Restraints.

[754] This term is used in several places in the Guidelines on technology transfer agreements to signify the degree of market power required for Art 81(1) to apply. This degree of market power is not the same as that required for a finding of dominance, which in the said guidelines is referred to as 'substantial' market power.

[755] The reference in the Guidelines on horizontal co-operation agreements and Vertical Restraints to effective competitive constraints raises the question why the agreement is caught by Art 81(1) in the first place.

[756] See para 96.

[757] The example is taken from *Lars Kjølbye*, 'The new Commission Guidelines on the application of Article 81(3)' [2004] ECLR 575.

of 10 euro per unit. Assuming that there are no other costs, X will produce and sell units until the extra sales generates less than 10 euro in additional revenue per unit. X now terminates the agreement and takes out another licence for a lump sum payment of EUR 1 million. X will now produce and sell units until the extra sales make no addition to total revenues. The investment of 1 million euro in the licence does not necessarily affect X's pricing. Feeding fixed costs into pricing decisions does not increase revenues and profits. Clearly, the difference between total revenues and total costs determines whether X is profitable. However, that is a different issue from the one that is relevant in this context, namely whether cost efficiencies are likely to be passed on to consumers in the form of price reductions.

These considerations are reflected in the Guidelines,[758] according to which 'undertakings   **3.450** may have a direct incentive to pass on to consumers in the form of higher output and lower prices efficiencies that reduce marginal costs, whereas they have no such direct incentive with regard to efficiencies that reduce fixed costs. Consumers are therefore more likely to receive a fair share of the cost efficiencies in the case of reductions in variable costs than they are in the case of reductions in fixed costs.' This passage does not rule out the taking into account of fixed costs savings. However, given that economic theory predicts that undertakings have no direct incentive to pass on fixed cost reductions, the burden of proof is higher in the case of such efficiencies. It may be that in reality reductions in fixed costs do have an impact on pricing decisions, and if undertakings can make a robust case in their favour, the Guidelines leave the door open for taking such efficiencies into account.

The extent to which cost savings will lead to an increase in output and a reduction in price   **3.451** also depends on the elasticity of demand. The actual pass-on rate depends on the extent to which consumers respond to changes in price. The greater the increase in demand caused by a decrease in price, the greater the pass-on rate. This follows from the fact that the greater the additional sales caused by a price reduction due to an increase in output, the more likely it is that these sales will offset the loss of revenue caused by the lower price resulting from the increase in output.[759] In the absence of price discrimination, the lowering of prices affects all units sold by the undertaking, in which case marginal revenue is less than the price obtained for the marginal product.[760]

Finally, the second condition of Article 81(3) implies that the pro-competitive effects and   **3.452** the anti-competitive effects created by the agreement must be balanced against each other and the pro-competitive effects must outweigh the anti-competitive effects. The efficiency effect must dominate the market power effect of the agreement. While this exercise forms an inherent part of any rule of reason analysis embedded in Article 81 as a whole, it can in practice be a difficult one. It is therefore important that the Guidelines[761] provide that if the restrictive effects of an agreement are relatively limited and the efficiencies are substantial, it is likely that a fair share of the cost savings will be passed on to consumers. In such cases it is therefore normally not necessary to engage in a detailed analysis of the second condition

---

[758] See para 98.
[759] See Guidelines, para 99.
[760] idem. If the undertakings concerned are able to charge different prices to different customers, ie price discriminate, pass-on will normally only benefit price sensitive consumers.
[761] See paras 90 and 91.

of Article 81(3), provided that the three other conditions for the application of this provision are fulfilled. Conversely, if the restrictive effects of the agreement are substantial and the cost savings are relatively insignificant, it is very unlikely that the second condition of Article 81(3) will be fulfilled. Full-blown balancing is thus confined to 'grey zone' cases, where it is unavoidable, unless the agreement has already failed one of the other cumulative conditions of Article 81(3).

(e) The Fourth Test of Article 81(3): No Elimination of Competition in Respect of a Substantial Part of the Products in Question

3.453 According to the fourth condition of Article 81(3) the agreement must not afford the undertakings concerned the possibility of eliminating competition in respect of a substantial part of the products in question. When competition is eliminated, the competitive process is brought to an end and short-term efficiency gains are outweighed by longer-term losses stemming *inter alia* from expenditures incurred by the incumbent to maintain its position (rent seeking), misallocation of resources, reduced innovation and higher prices.[762]

3.454 In the past the Commission took the view that elimination of competition could be equated with dominance. This view is reflected in the guidelines on vertical restraints and horizontal cooperation agreements which state that where an undertaking is dominant or becoming dominant as a consequence of an agreement, restrictions which produce anti-competitive effects can in principle not be exempted.[763]

3.455 However, in recent case law, the CFI has held that 'the prohibition on eliminating competition is a narrower concept than that of the existence or acquisition of a dominant position, so that an agreement could be regarded as not eliminating competition within the meaning of Article 81(3)(b) of the Treaty, and therefore qualify for exemption, even if it established a dominant position for the benefit of its members.'[764] It follows that the concept of dominance is not synonymous with the concept of elimination of competition. Given that dominance is a question of degree,[765] dominance may be sufficient for a finding of elimination of competition. However the mere finding of dominance is not sufficient. Further enquiry into the degree of market power and the relationship between the agreement and such market power is required.[766]

3.456 In light of this case law the Guidelines do not rule out the application of Article 81(3) to dominant undertakings. Instead, they provide[767] that not all restrictive agreements concluded by a dominant undertaking constitute an abuse of a dominant position in which case Article 81(3) remains applicable until competition is being eliminated. It is explained

---

[762] See Guidelines, para 105.

[763] See paras 135 and 35 respectively of these Guidelines.

[764] See judgment of 30.9.2003, Joined Cases T-191/98, T-212/98 and T-214/98 *Atlantic Container Line (TACA)*, para 939, not yet reported, and Case T-395/94 *Atlantic Container Line* [2002] ECR II-875, para 330.

[765] Compare eg Case T-65/89 *BPB Industries and British Gypsum* [1993] ECR II-389 and Case T-219/99 *British Airways* [2003] ECR II.

[766] Once remedies that reduce the impact on competition below the threshold of elimination of competition are found, the last condition of Art 81(3) cannot serve as a basis for removing further restrictions of competition. This can be required only if the other three conditions of Art 81(3) are not satisfied.

[767] See para 106.

in a footnote[768] that this is how the Guidelines on Vertical Restraints and the Guidelines on horizontal cooperation agreements should be understood when they state that, in principle, restrictive agreements concluded by dominant undertakings cannot be exempted. The Guidelines thereby effectively amend the pre-existing guidelines. This new line is also reflected in the DG Competition discussion paper on the application of Article 82 of the Treaty.[769] In this, DG Competition proposes to apply the analytical framework of Article 81(3) in the analysis of Article 82 cases.

In referring to the concept of abuse, the Guidelines reflect the case law according to which **3.457** the application of Article 81(3) cannot prevent the application of Article 82 of the Treaty.[770] Agreements that constitute an abuse of a dominant position cannot benefit from Article 81(3). Since Articles 81 and 82 are both aimed at maintaining effective competition on the market, consistency requires that Article 81(3) be interpreted as precluding any application of the exception rule to restrictive agreements that constitute an abuse of a dominant position.[771] It is thus important to determine what constitutes abuse of dominance. This issue is dealt with the in the context of the Commission's on-going review of its policy in the field of Article 82.

Whether or not competition is eliminated within the meaning of the last condition of **3.458** Article 81(3) depends on the degree of competition existing prior to the agreement and on the impact of the restrictive agreement on such competition, ie the reduction in competition brought about by the agreement. The more competition is already weakened in the market concerned, the slighter the further reduction required for competition to be eliminated within the meaning of Article 81(3).[772]

The Guidelines refrain from establishing threshold values for finding elimination of com- **3.459** petition. However, in its Article 82 discussion paper,[773] DG Competition has suggested an indicative threshold of 75 per cent market share for this. However, it is clear that the analysis cannot be based on market share alone. The last condition of Article 81(3) requires a careful analysis of the various sources of competitive constraint. This analysis is based on the same factors that are relevant in the context of Article 81(1), namely the market position of the parties to the agreement, the market position of competitors and their ability to compete, the market position of buyers and barriers to entry. As regards the market position of buyers, what matters is not whether certain strong buyers may be able to extract more favourable conditions from the parties to the agreement than their weaker competitors.[774] The presence of strong buyers can only serve to counter a *prima facie* finding of elimination of competition if it is likely that the buyers in question will pave the way for effective new entry.

---

[768] See n 92.
[769] Published in December 2005 on the DG Competition web site.
[770] See Joined Cases C-395/96 P and C-396/96 P *Compagnie Maritime Belge* [2000] ECR I-1365, para 130.
[771] See in this respect Case T-51/89 *Tetra Pak (I)* [1990] ECR II-309, and Joined Cases T-191/98, T-212/98 and para 1456 of the judgment in *TACA*, cited in n 99.
[772] See Guidelines, para 107.
[773] See para 3.456 above.
[774] See in this respect Case T-228/97 *Irish Sugar* [1999] ECR II-2969, para 101 and the Guidelines, para 115(v).

3.460   The last condition of Article 81(3) refers to 'a substantial part of the products concerned' which appears to be distinct from the concept of 'relevant market' which is the traditional framework for competition law analysis. While it is clear that the issue of elimination of competition will generally be assessed with regard to a relevant market, the more open-ended language leaves room for taking account of the impact of the agreement on competition within a differentiated product market. This is reflected in the Guidelines[775] which acknowledge that, when undertakings offer differentiated products, the competitive constraint that individual products impose on each other differs according to the degree of substitutability between them. The Guidelines therefore require consideration of the degree of substitutability between the products offered by the parties, ie the competitive constraint that they impose on each other. The more closely substitutable the products of the parties to the agreement, the greater the likely restrictive effect of the agreement. The more substitutable the products the greater the likely change brought about by the agreement in terms of restriction of competition in the market and the more likely it is that competition in respect of a substantial part of the products concerned risks being eliminated.

---

[775] See para 113.

4

ARTICLE 82

Carles Esteva Mosso, Stephen A. Ryan, Svend Albaek
and María Luisa Tierno Centella

A. Introduction

(1) General

4.01 Article 82 of the EC Treaty provides as follows:

> Any abuse by one or more undertakings of a dominant position within the common market or in a substantial part of it shall be prohibited as incompatible with the common market insofar as it may affect trade between Member States.
>
> Such abuse may, in particular, consist in:
> (a) directly or indirectly imposing unfair purchase or selling prices or other unfair trading conditions;
> (b) limiting production, markets or technical development to the prejudice of consumers;
> (c) applying dissimilar conditions to equivalent transactions with other trading parties, thereby placing them at a competitive disadvantage;
> (d) making the conclusion of contracts subject to acceptance by the other parties of supplementary obligations which, by their nature or according to commercial usage, have no connection with the subject of such contracts.

Together with Article 81, which has been analysed in the previous chapter, Article 82 constitutes a basic provision of EC competition law. Both articles promote one of the main objectives of the EC Treaty which, according to Article 3(g), consists in establishing: 'a system ensuring that competition in the internal market is not distorted'.[1]

4.02 It is clear from the wording of Article 82 that it regulates the unilateral behaviour of one or, in certain specific cases, more undertakings. This is a basic difference from Article 81, which deals with situations involving collusive behaviour between several undertakings, ie agreements, decisions of an association of undertakings, or concerted practices.

4.03 Article 82 also differs from Article 81 in that it cannot be applied to any undertaking. It only applies to those undertakings which have a 'dominant position'. As will be explained below (see 4.37 and following sections), undertakings in a dominant position are basically undertakings holding a substantial amount of market power in one or more of the markets in which they operate.

4.04 Article 82, therefore, makes a distinction between two types of undertakings, those which hold a dominant position and those which do not. It places particular obligations upon the former. As the Court of Justice said in *Michelin I*:[2]

> A finding that an undertaking has a dominant position . . . simply means that, irrespective of the reasons for which it has such a dominant position, the undertaking concerned has a *special responsibility* not to allow its conduct to impair genuine undistorted competition on the common market.

4.05 In other words, undertakings which do not hold a dominant position will need only to comply with the general competition rules contained in Article 81, while the firms which

---

[1] See R. Nazzini, 'Article 81 EC between time present and time past: a normative critique of "restriction of competition" in EU law' [2006] CMLR 43: 502–505.

[2] Case 322/81 *NV Nederlandsche Baden-Industrie Michelin v Commission* [1983] ECR 3461, para 57 (emphasis by the authors).

are dominant will have to comply with the provisions of Article 82, in addition to those of Article 81. The relationship between the two Articles will be further analysed below (see Section E of this chapter).

Article 82 does not prevent the mere creation or possession of a dominant position. As its **4.06** wording clearly states, it prohibits 'abuses' of such a dominant position. These abuses may consist in one of the four different actions listed in the second paragraph of Article 82. The list included in that paragraph, however, is not exhaustive. As the Court of Justice clarified in *Continental Can*,[3] its first decision concerning Article 82, the list is merely indicative. Abuses may also consist, as it will be explained below (see Section C of this chapter), in any kind of behaviour by a dominant undertaking that appreciably distorts competition or exploits customers in the market in question.

Finally, abuses of a dominant position are prohibited only insofar as they may affect trade **4.07** between Member States. This condition, also included in Article 81, limits the sphere of application of EC competition law. Its precise meaning will be detailed below (see Section D of this chapter).

The wording of Article 82 does not make any reference to the consequences of the violation **4.08** of the prohibition that it establishes. As will be explained in more detail below (see 4.434), an abuse of a dominant position may have the consequence that the agreements concluded in exercise of such abuse are void. In addition, competition authorities applying the EC Competition rules can order that the infringement be terminated and may impose fines on undertakings found to have breached Article 82. Damages arising from infringements of this article can be sought in national courts.

(2) Rationale for Article 82

Article 82, as explained, is one of the provisions of the EU Treaty that ensures that compe- **4.09** tition in the internal market is not distorted. In particular, it attempts to achieve this goal in those markets where firms enjoy a substantial amount of market power. It does so by prohibiting certain types of unilateral conduct by such dominant firms.

Debate about Article 82 has generally centred on the purpose of the prohibition of abusive **4.10** behaviour.[4] Put another way, what is the provision supposed to protect? Many different explanations have been given: some see the EC's competition rules as concerned with the maximisation of consumer welfare; others look to concepts such as fairness and the ordo-liberal view that the aim of competition law is to control private economic power; elsewhere, it is argued that the purpose of Article 82 is to protect the process of rivalry itself; others point to the role of competition as a tool to help the Community to fulfil overarching objectives such as market integration.[5]

---

[3] Case 6-72 *Europemballage Corporation and Continental Can v Commission* [1971] ECR 215, para 26.
[4] This debate relates to competition policy in general rather than to Art 81 or Art 82 in particular. For a fuller discussion of the development of Community competition policy, see Ch 2.
[5] For a brief account, see F. Souty, *Le Droit de la concurrence de l'Union Européenne* (2nd edn, Paris: Montchrestien, 1999), 23 *et seq.*

4.11   As discussed more fully in Chapter 3 the German approach to competition law, which itself was based on the ordo-liberal philosophy[6] of the 'Freiburg School', has played an important role in influencing the development of competition law in the Community. At its core the Freiburg School sought to limit and control private economic power by prohibiting behaviour that placed unjustified limits on the competitive autonomy of firms. Its goal is not to maximise efficiency (although consumer benefits were recognised and valued) but rather 'the protection of individual economic freedom of action'[7] in the interest of a free and fair political/social order. Freedom and fairness mean that markets should be kept as open as possible—behaviour which limited sources of supply or the access of third parties from markets was therefore viewed with suspicion. As far as unilateral exercise of market power is concerned, some members of the Freiburg School advocated for a sort of 'as if' test whereby firms having market power should be required to behave 'as if' they were acting in a competitive environment.

4.12   Some have added to these ideas by arguing that the *process* of competition itself, or, to be more precise, the process of rivalry between undertakings, produces the best *economic* results. For example, in its *Report on Competition Policy 1971* (Vol. I), the Commission described competition as 'the best stimulant of economic activity'. It went on to argue that competition, '[t]hrough the interplay of decentralised decision-making machinery', enables enterprises 'continuously to improve their efficiency which is the *sine qua non* for a steady improvement in living standards and employment prospects. From this point of view, competition policy is an essential means for satisfying to a great extent the individual and collective needs of our society.' Over a decade later, in its Fifteenth Report, the Commission described the role of competition, and thus of Article 81(1), as preserving 'the freedom and right of initiative of the individual economic operators' and fostering 'the spirit of enterprise'. These Commission statements appear therefore to regard the protection of rivalry and the freedom of action of the parties to the agreement (as well as those third parties affected by it) as an end in itself.

4.13   Some critics consider that this philosophy has led to an overly rigid or legalistic application of Article 82 to certain types of behaviour and to the approach which seeks to identify whether the commercial conduct and freedom of action of third parties had been interfered with by the dominant undertaking. The same critics point to the fact that, in some Commission decisions applying Article 82, analysis of the economic effects of the abuse played a limited role.

4.14   The Commissioner's approach to the application of Article 82 cannot fully be understood without reference to the determination of the Community institutions to create and sustain the Single Market. The competition rules have often been seen as an important way of preventing firms from establishing barriers to trade and perpetuating differences in national markets. As a result, behaviour which potentially harmed the Single Market has been found to fall foul of Article 82.

---

[6] For a detailed discussion of the ordo-liberal approach and its impact see D. Gerber, *Law and Competition in 20th Century Europe: Protecting Promotheus* (Oxford: Clarendon Press, 1998).

[7] Möschel, 'Competition policy from an ordo point of View', in A. Peacock and H. Willgerodt (eds), *German Neo-liberals and the Social Market Economy* (London: Macmillan, 1989).

The emphasis of Community competition policy has shifted somewhat in recent years, **4.15** with the adoption of a more robust economic approach to the application of Article 81[8] and of the Merger Regulation.[9] However, the case law and Commission practice on Article 82 still reflects an approach to the abuse of a dominant position which, in the view of some commentators, gives too little weight to the effects of the behaviour on the market and, ultimately, on consumer welfare. Following the policy shifts in the application of Article 81 and the Merger Regulation, the Commission has come under increasing pressure to adopt a more economics-based approach to abuse of dominance. Open discussion has already commenced on the shape of a possible new policy, with the publication by the Commission's DGF competition of a Staff Discussion Paper in December 2005. However, it is at the time of publication, still unclear to what extent the Commission's policy will be re-cast. This chapter discusses the current case law and practice and endeavours to highlight tensions and problems that may lead to future developments in the policy.

(a) Alternative Approaches to Unilateral Conduct by Firms Holding Substantial Market Power

The problem of the purpose of the prohibition is linked to, but distinct from, the question **4.16** of how best Article 82 should be enforced to ensure that competition is not distorted and customers are not harmed. There are two alternative approaches. Competition rules can attempt to prevent direct harm by prohibiting exploitative behaviour and, therefore, by regulating market outcomes, or they can try to achieve the same result indirectly, by prohibiting exclusionary behaviour, thereby ensuring that competition on the merits takes place between the firms holding substantial market power and their competitors, thus ultimately benefiting customers.

Prohibition of customer exploitation   By prohibiting customer exploitation, competition **4.17** rules focus on the effects of the exercise of market power. The exercise of market power leads to market outcomes that can be less beneficial for consumers than those of competitive markets, in terms of higher prices, reduction of output or various types of customer discrimination. By limiting those effects, for instance by prohibiting excessive prices, competition rules can prevent a certain degree of exploitation of customers in those markets where firms enjoy substantial market power.

This approach, however, presents several problems.[10] First, it is difficult to distinguish the exer- **4.18** cise of market power from its possession. Indeed, firms with market power will, by behaving in a 'commercially sensible' manner (ie trying to maximise their profits), inevitably charge higher prices and produce less output than firms in a competitive market structure. Therefore, the prohibition of customer exploitation may lead, if broadly interpreted, to the prohibition of the mere existence of firms holding market power.

---

8 See Ch 3.
9 See Ch 5.
10 See V. Korah, *EC Competition Law and Practice* (5th edn, London: Hart, 1994), 97; L. Gyselen, *Abuse of Monopoly Power within the Meaning of Art 86 of the EEC Treaty: Recent Developments* (Fordham Corporate Law Institute, 1989); and T. E. Kauper, *Whither Art 86? Observations on Excessive Prices and Refusals to Deal* (Fordham Corporate Law Institute, 1989).

4.19   Second, the exercise of market power by incumbents will normally attract new entrants into the market (at least, in industries with limited barriers to entry). Incumbents, by charging higher prices than in a competitive market, obtain supra-competitive profits that other firms will want to share. The entry of such firms will normally increase competition, reduce prices, and automatically improve consumer welfare. It can legitimately be asked whether a competition authority should intervene in such situations.

4.20   Finally, any intervention by authorities to curb exploitative behaviour will require them to determine the parameters of output to be provided and the price that should be charged by the dominant undertaking. This task amounts, in some cases, to direct regulation of prices and output for the industry in question: neither competition authorities nor courts are particularly well suited to this task.

4.21   **Prohibition of exclusionary practices**   A second possible approach for dealing with firms holding substantial market power consists in prohibiting conduct which is not based on normal business performance but excludes or seeks to exclude competitors from the market. This approach does not seek to prohibit the mere possession of market power or the effects of such possession, but the increase or maintenance of such power by anti-competitive means.

4.22   This approach avoids direct regulation of the prices and output of dominant firms. It relies on the self-regulating mechanism of the market for preventing dominant undertakings from harming consumer welfare. That is why its main aim is to ensure that the market functions properly and that competition is not distorted by anti-competitive conduct.

4.23   This is the approach adopted by US Courts in interpreting Section 2 of the Sherman Act, which prohibits monopolisation. As Judge Hand said in *Alcoa*,[11] this provision does not prevent undertakings from excluding competitors by 'superior skill, foresight and industry'. It does not prevent, as also stated by the US Supreme Court,[12] 'growth or development as a consequence of superior product, business acumen or historic accident'.

4.24   The difficulty inherent in this approach is how to distinguish situations where competitors are harmed or excluded from the market due to competition on the merits, which is permitted, from harm or exclusion by anti-competitive means, which is not. If the notion of anti-competitive conduct is too widely defined, there is a risk of creating disincentives for innovation and investment by efficient leading firms and artificially enabling inefficient competitors to stay in the markets. If, on the contrary, it is too narrowly defined, rivals may be discouraged from competing on the merits, and less efficient leading firms may ultimately prevail in the market.

4.25   In order to find the proper balance, several tests to define the boundaries between competition on the merits and anti-competitive conduct could be developed.[13] One option is to

---

[11] *US v Aluminium Co.*, 148 F2d, 416 (2d Cir. 1945).

[12] *US v Grinnell Corp.*, 348 US 563 (1966).

[13] T. Muris, 'The FTC and the law of monopolization', Antitrust Law Journal (2000); E. Fox, 'What is harm to competition? Exclusionary practices and anti-competitive effect', Antitrust Law Journal (2000); E. Elhauge, 'Defining better monopolization standards', Stanford Law Review, 56 (2003); J. Vickers, 'Abuse of market power', Economic Journal (2005).

determine that a dominant firm only engages in exclusionary conduct when its behaviour does not make economic sense but its goal is to reduce or eliminate competition. Under a similar formulation of the same principle, it can be considered that a dominant firm commits an abuse only when it harms or excludes competitors on a basis other than behaviour that enhances its own efficiency.

A different approach for formulating a similar test is to focus on the type of competitors to **4.26** be excluded. A practice would only be considered exclusionary if it led to the foreclosure of competitors at least as efficient as the dominant firm. The exclusion of less efficient competitors is part of the normal competitive process and, therefore, legal under Article 82. Some argue that this test must be applied dynamically, and must take into account the fact that a competitor may not be just as efficient as a dominant company when the latter engages in the exclusionary practice, but the former does have the potential to become as efficient (eg because it has not yet reached the most efficient production scale).

Finally, one could simply focus on the final effects of the practice to determine whether it **4.27** is anti-competitive. In this case the test would be whether the dominant company behaviour is likely to harm competitors, by increasing prices or reducing output. Proof of actual effects, however, should not normally be required if one expects enforcement to be capable of intervention in a time frame sufficient to avoid or limit the harm.

(b) Approach Used in Article 82 of the EC Treaty

The wording of Article 82 is not clear enough to determine which of the prohibition meth- **4.28** ods described above is prescribed by the provision. Indeed, although Article 82 prohibits abuses of a dominant position, no definition of what amounts to an abuse is to be found in that or any other article of the EC Treaty.

The first commentators on Article 82 were divided on this issue. Some[14] tended to believe **4.29** that the provision was a clear prohibition of exploitative behaviour. They supported this view by reference to the list of prohibited conducts detailed in Article 82 (ie unfair prices and terms of trade, limitation of output, discrimination, and tying practices) which relates to instances where market power is exercised to the detriment of customers or suppliers, independently of the effects on competition. Others,[15] by contrast, supported an interpretation of Article 82 as extending to exclusionary practices as well.

Both the practice of the Commission as well as the decisions of the Court of Justice have **4.30** followed the latter school of thought and interpreted Article 82 as also embodying a prohibition of exclusionary practices. In *Continental Can*[16] the Court took the earliest opportunity

---

[14] R. Joliet, *Monopolization and Abuse of Dominant Position: A Comparative Study of the American and European Approaches to the Control of Economic Power* (Liège: Faculté de Droit, 1970).

[15] EEC Commission, *Concentration of Enterprises in the Common Market, Memorandum to the Governments of the Member States* (1965). It largely reproduced the conclusions of a group of professors appointed by the Commission two years earlier to study the problems raised by the interpretation of Art 82. See also M. Siragusa, *Application of Art 86: Tying Arrangements, Refusals to Deal, Discrimination and Other Cases of Abuse* (Bruges, 1974). In 1974 he had already considered that Art 82 should mainly apply to exclusionary behaviour and be interpreted so as to limit cases of exploitative abuse to those listed in the second paragraph of the article.

[16] Case 6-72 *Europemballage Corporation and Continental Can v Commission* [1971] ECR 215, para 26.

to say that Article 82 'is not only aimed at practices which may cause damage to consumers directly, but also at those which are detrimental to them through their impact on an effective competition structure'. Most of the cases in which Article 82 has been applied (eg exclusive dealing, refusals to deal, tying, pricing practices) fall into this second category.

4.31 As to the concept of exclusionary conduct adopted, the Court has accepted that only the 'recourse to methods different from those which condition normal competition in products or services on the basis of the transactions of commercial operators'[17] can be deemed abusive. A more specific test, however, has not been defined in general terms and the specific conditions to determine what is abusive have differed depending on the type of abuse in question. This issue will be analysed in more detail below (see 4.142).

4.32 The exploitative practices explicitly mentioned in the wording of Article 82 are still prosecuted in certain circumstances but less frequently than would be expected given the wording of the provision. This is probably explained by the self-policing character of these abuses (see 4.19 above) as well as by the fact that authorities applying it may well baulk at making a subjective decision that a particular course of conduct is either unfair or unreasonable.

4.33 There are circumstances, however, in which exploitative abuses are continued. First, there is some economic sense in engaging in these abuses in markets with high barriers to entry, where extra competitive profits will not attract new entrants, and which are not regulated at a national level. Second, they have been used in markets in the process of liberalisation, sometimes in conjunction with Article 86 in relation to undertakings benefiting from exclusive rights.[18] Thirdly, in some cases, this type of abuse has been engaged in because the practice in question helped the dominant undertakings in question to infringe other principles of the EC Treaty, in particular when they created obstacles to the establishment of the Single European market.[19]

B. Dominant Position

(1) Market Power in the Sense of Article 82—What is 'Dominance'?

4.34 The debate about the purpose of, and the economic approach to, Article 82 is not only relevant to the analysis of the abuse but also to the assessment of dominance. While dominance has been linked to the economic concept of market power relatively early and there appears to be little doubt today that substantial market power is at least a necessary condition for a finding of dominance, in the enforcement of Article 82 often an excessive weight has been placed on market shares rather than on the competitive pressure faced by the allegedly dominant undertaking.

---

[17] Case 85/76 *Hoffmann-La Roche v Commission* [1979] ECR 46, para 91.

[18] For instance, in C-41/90 *Hofner and Elser v Macrotron* [1991] ECR I-1979 the Court considered that the Bundesanstalt für Arbeit, a German agency with the monopoly on the provision of placement services, had failed to meet the demand for its services and that it had, therefore, abused its dominant position. This was considered an infringement of both Arts 86 and 82.

[19] For instance, Case 26-75 *General Motors Continental NV v Commission* [1975] ECR 1367, where a surcharge applied by General Motors in Belgium to certifications of imported cars which prevented imports from other Member States was considered to be an excessive price caught by Art 82.

Dominance is a position of substantial economic power, held for a period of time by a firm **4.34A**
over its competitors, customers, and/or suppliers in a market, which enables the firm to
impede effective competition. Ultimately, such market power gives a firm the ability to
restrict output and/or raise prices above the level that would prevail in a competitive market,
without existing rivals or new entrants taking its customers away over time (a detailed
economic discussion of market power is contained in Chapter 1).

Dominance is not synonymous with monopoly. Nor is it an absolute concept, with a fixed **4.35**
threshold of some kind above which it can be inferred. To be considered dominant, an
undertaking should hold a substantial amount of market power and be able to behave independently from its competitors but it is not necessary that all competitors be eliminated
from the relevant market. Although market power may be found to exist to a greater or
lesser extent, or for longer or shorter periods of time, the following paragraphs analyse whether
the concept of dominance as such can be modulated accordingly. Monopolies (whether *de
jure* or de facto) are invariably dominant undertakings within the meaning of Article 82.

The temporal element is crucial to the existence of dominance. In the absence of insur- **4.36**
mountable barriers to entry, market forces should normally ensure that dominance is not
sustainable over the long term. Indeed, new companies should normally attempt to enter
the market, attracted by the supra-competitive profits obtained by the incumbent, and
would erode the latter's market power and position. During the period of time needed for
new entrants to establish a presence in the market, however, the dominant undertaking
may engage in exclusionary practices aimed at securing its position. Competition policy is
concerned with impeding such behaviour during this period, even if market forces alone
might over the longer term restore consumer welfare. A company will therefore normally
be considered dominant if it holds market power for a period of time long enough to enable
it to behave independently from competitors and customers, and to allow it to obtain an
economic benefit from such a position.

The Court of Justice's definition   The classic definition of the nature of a dominant posi- **4.37**
tion within the meaning of Article 82 is contained in the ECJ's judgment in the *United
Brands* case, where it was described as follows:

> a position of economic strength enjoyed by an undertaking which enables it to prevent effec-
> tive competition being maintained on the relevant market by giving it the power to behave
> to an appreciable extent independently of its competitors, customers and ultimately of con-
> sumers. In general it derives from a combination of factors which taken separately are not
> determinative.[20]

The Court has in successive judgments essentially retained this definition.[21] The Court **4.38**
emphasises the concept of a dominant firm's independence from the competitive forces normally constraining a supplier in the market. This does not mean that a firm, in order to be dominant, must be able to ignore competition entirely and do as it wishes by, for example, raising
prices without any constraint. Indeed, a firm can be dominant even in circumstances where

---

[20] Case 27/76 *United Brands v Commission* [1978] ECR 207.
[21] Cases 85/76 *Hoffmann-La Roche v Commission* [1979] ECR 461, Case 322/81 *NV Nederlandsche
Baden-Industrie Michelin v Commission* [1983] ECR 3461.

it must sometimes take competitive factors into account in determining its commercial behaviour.[22] In *Hoffmann-La Roche*, the Court noted that a dominant position 'does not preclude some competition . . . but enables the undertaking which profits by it, if not to determine, at least to have an appreciable influence on the conditions under which competition will develop, and in any case to act largely in disregard of it so long as such conduct does not operate to its detriment'. If a firm can substantially disregard, and keep safely at bay, its competitors over a long period of time, this is a clear indication of dominance.

4.38A   The idea of independence of behaviour was also found in Article 66(7) of the ECSC Treaty,[23] which enabled the Commission to address recommendations to dominant undertakings in the coal and steel sectors. Indeed, this provision defines dominant undertakings as: 'public or private undertakings which, in law or in fact, hold or acquire in the market for one of the products within its jurisdiction a dominant position shielding them against effective competition in a substantial part of the common market'. The Court of Justice in *Hoffmann-La Roche* has also characterised a dominant firm in terms of its being 'an unavoidable trading partner' for its customers. This notion of economic dependence has been a characteristic of numerous cases involving the application of Article 82. In *Virgin/British Airways*,[24] for example, the CFI upheld the Commission's finding that British Airways constituted an 'obligatory business partner' for UK travel agencies, in the sense that these agencies needed to be able to sell BA tickets to their customers.

4.39   **The Merger Regulation concept of dominant position**   The concept of dominance is also central to the substantive standard of review in the Merger Regulation.[25] Article 2 of the Regulation states that 'a concentration which would significantly impede effective competition in the common market or in a substantial part of it, in particular as a result of the creation or strengthening of a dominant position, shall be declared incompatible with the common market.' Article 2 of the old Merger Regulation[26] (in force until 1 May 2004) had framed the substantive standard more directly in terms of dominance by stating that 'a concentration which creates or strengthens a dominant position as a result of which effective competition would be significantly impeded in the common market or in a substantial part of it shall be declared incompatible with the common market'.

4.40   There is no reason to believe that the concept of dominant position included in the Merger Regulation has—in essence—a meaning different from the concept contained in Article 82 of the EC Treaty.[27] However, both provisions have substantially different purposes and scope, which necessarily means that this same concept is applied from two different perspectives. First, while Article 82 applies to existing dominant positions, and requires a fundamentally

---

[22]   See J. Temple-Lang, 'Some aspects of abuse of dominant positions in European Community anti-trust law' (1979) 3 Fordham International Law Forum.

[23]   The Treaty expired in 2002.

[24]   OJ [2000] L30/1; Case T-219/99 of 17 December 2003 *British Airways v Commission*. This decision is under appeal to the ECJ.

[25]   Council Regulation 139/2004 of 20 January 2004 on the control of concentrations between undertakings (OJ L24, 29.01.2004).

[26]   Council Regulation 4064/89 of 21 December 1989 on the control of concentrations between undertakings (OJ L395, 30.12.1989).

[27]   See C-395/96 P and C-396/96 P *Compagnie Maritime Belge and Dafra-Lines v Commission*, opinion of AG Fennelly; 29.10.1998; paras 26 and 27.

retrospective analysis, the Merger Regulation assesses the possibility of a dominant position being created or strengthened, thus requiring a prospective analysis. Second, Article 82 is ultimately not concerned with the possession of market power as such, stemming from the existence of a company with a dominant position, but with the abuses that such market power may permit a company to engage in. The Merger Regulation, on the other hand, is concerned with the effects on competition resulting from the enhancement of market power through concentration, and in particular by the creation or strengthening of a dominant position.

In the course of the review of the Merger Regulation leading up to the adoption of Regulation 139/2004, one of the most controversial discussions centred on the question of whether the concept of dominance in the Regulation extends also to post-merger situations where the market power of multiple firms would be enhanced, but without the firms being able to adopt a common policy on the market in the manner normally associated with joint dominance in the sense of Article 82.[28] Due largely to uncertainty as to whether the concept of dominance could be used in this way, the substantive test in the Regulation was changed so that dominance was one, but not necessarily the only, post-merger scenario that could justify intervention. (For a detailed analysis of the concept of collective dominance, see below. For a detailed analysis of the Merger Regulation, see Chapter 5.) **4.41**

(2) Determining Dominance

The existence of a dominant position in a particular market is normally inferred from a variety of quantitative and qualitative factors, some of which may carry more weight than others. These factors relate to the nature and structure of the market—in particular the barriers to entry thereto, to the firm's position on the market as well as to its own characteristics and competitive conduct.[29] It should be stressed that determining whether or not there is dominance should not be seen as a mechanical process but rather as an assessment which takes all of the dynamics of the relevant market, and the particularities of the allegedly dominant firm, into account. **4.42**

(a) The Relevant Market

In determining the existence of a dominant position, it is first necessary to identify the relevant product and geographic markets. Dominance can only be appraised by reference to a defined category of products within a specified geographical area; it is thereby possible to establish whether or not an allegedly dominant firm is facing competitive pressures that enable it to behave in relative disregard of its competitors.[30] It should be stressed, however, **4.43**

---

[28] During the review, it was widely objected that such an interpretation would stretch the dominance concept in the ECMR far beyond its plain language meaning, something which was undesirable not only in terms of legislative clarity more generally, but also in terms of the consequences this sometimes 'tortured' interpretation was having on the interpretation of the identically worded concept in Art 82. Particular concern was expressed about the confusion that might result from an 'extension' of the concept of dominance to 'non-collusive oligopolies', and what this would mean in terms of the possible imposition of the special responsibilities of Art 82 on the members of such an oligopoly.

[29] In analysing these factors, this chapter will focus on analysis conducted by the Commission and the Court of Justice when applying Art 82 of the EC Treaty. In some cases, however, decisions adopted under the Merger Regulation assessing the existence of a dominant position will also be referred to.

[30] See Commission Notice on the definition of the relevant market for the purposes of Community competition law OJ C372/03, 09.12.1997.

that defining a market and establishing a firm's share thereof constitutes no more than a starting point in the assessment of whether or not the firm in question enjoys genuine market power. Market definition is dealt with in detail in Chapter 1.[31]

(b) Measuring Market Power: Market Shares

4.44 As also explained in Chapter 1, there are various methods of assessing market power. The primary albeit imperfect indicator of dominance is usually to be found by examining the allegedly dominant company's share of the relevant market (ie the percentage that the sales of the undertaking represent in relation to the whole market turnover). If a company is dominant on that market, it is logical that it will have succeeded in gaining a large share of it. The Court of Justice in *Hoffmann-La Roche*[32] stated that:

> the existence of a dominant position may derive from several factors which taken separately are not necessarily determinative but among these factors a highly important one is the existence of very large market shares.

4.45 It should be stressed at the outset, however, that market shares provide no more than a starting point for assessing the existence of market power. As will be explained in detail below, market share may not be an indication of market power in markets where there are relatively few or insignificant barriers to entry and expansion by rival firms. Moreover, market shares recorded at a particular point in time may not be sufficient to illustrate the true dynamics of a market, particularly where that market is subject to volatility or experiences rapid growth or sharp decline. In order to obtain an accurate picture of a particular market, it may therefore be necessary, on the one hand, to examine historical market shares observed over a period of time and, on the other, to forecast future market shares adjusted to take account of reasonably foreseeable market developments.

4.46 **Very high or very low market share levels**   It is not possible to point to a specific share of the market above which a firm is conclusively dominant, and below which it is not. Neither have the Commission or Court of Justice taken such a simplistic line. Certain levels will however give rise to strong indications one way or the other.

4.47 Very high market shares provide in themselves virtually conclusive proof that a firm is dominant. The Court of Justice in *Hoffmann-La Roche* stated that:

> although the importance of the market shares may vary from one market to another the view may legitimately be taken that very large market shares are *in themselves, and save in exceptional circumstances*, evidence of the existence of a dominant position [emphasis added].

4.48 In that case, Hoffmann-La Roche held very high shares of a number of markets. These very high shares ranged from approximately 75 per cent to approximately 87 per cent of a series of specific Community vitamin markets, and the Court considered that they were so high

---

[31] Particular care should be attached to the application of the so-called SSNIP test, which is based on the assumption that prevailing market prices are the appropriate benchmark for measuring the likelihood of a 5–10 per cent price increase being successful, in cases involving the application of Art 82. In markets characterised by dominance, the prevailing price may already be well above competitive levels, a phenomenon sometimes referred to as 'the cellophane fallacy'. See para 19 of the Commission Notice on the definition of the relevant market for the purposes of Community competition law, OJ C372/03, 09.12.1997.

[32] Case 85/76 *Hoffmann-La Roche v Commission* [1979] ECR 461.

as to require no further examination of other factors before concluding that dominance existed. In *Hilti*[33] the Court of Justice upheld the Commission's view that market shares of between 70 and 80 per cent were so high as not to require further corroboration. The same situation arose in *Tetra-Pak*,[34] where the undertaking concerned held a market share of around 90 per cent.

High market shares (of over about 50 per cent), held over a period of time, are considered to be strong prima facie evidence of dominance and effectively create a presumption that a firm is dominant. In *Michelin I*,[35] market shares of 57 and 65 per cent were considered, in the absence of any countervailing indications, sufficient evidence of dominance. In *AKZO*,[36] a market share of 50 per cent over at least three years was considered strong evidence of the existence of a dominant position. If, however, high market shares are only held—or are only likely to be held?for relatively short periods of time, or where the firm's market power is kept in check by countervailing constraints, such high shares may not be sufficient in themselves to establish the existence of dominance.[37]   **4.49**

Low market shares on the other hand (less than 40 per cent or so) are generally considered to be indicative of a firm not occupying a dominant position. In the case of market shares of between about 25 and 40 per cent, it must be considered unlikely that a single company could be held to occupy a dominant position, unless the shares of the firm's competitors are very fragmented. In *Grundig*,[38] the Commission did not find dominance with market shares of 23 and 33 per cent by the two leaders in the German colour TV market. In *Virgin/British Airways*,[39] however, British Airways was held by the Commission to be in a dominant position in the air travel agency services market with a share of slightly less than 40 per cent (39.7 per cent). In a number of instances, the Commission has intervened against mergers resulting in market shares below the levels normally associated with dominance.[40]   **4.50**

Market shares of less than 25 per cent are very unlikely to be associated with dominance by a company. Whilst the Courts have never explicitly articulated a presumption of the absence of dominance below a given market share threshold, it should be noted that recital 32 to the Merger Regulation indicates that concentrations 'where the market share of the undertakings concerned does not exceed 25 per cent either in the common market or in a substantial part of it' are presumed to be compatible with the common market.   **4.51**

Finally, very low shares of the relevant market are considered definitive indicators of the absence of dominance. In the *Metro* and *SABA II* cases,[41] for example, market shares   **4.52**

---

[33] T-30/89 *Hilti v Commission* [1992] ECR 1439 and C-53/92 P.

[34] T-83/91 *Tetra Pak International v Commission* [1994] ECR II-755.

[35] Case 322/81 *NV Nederlandsche Baden-Industrie Michelin v Commission* [1983] ECR 3461.

[36] C-62/86 *AKZO Chemie BV v Commission* [1991] ECR I-3359.

[37] See M.42 *Alcatel/Telletra* [OJ L122/48 of 17 May 1991] where the Commission authorised the creation of a firm with a combined post-merger market share of 83 per cent, essentially because of countervailing buyer power in the markets concerned. See also M.2876 *Newscorp/Telepiù* [OJ C255 of 23.10.2002], where the Commission authorised the merger although the merged entity would have no real competitors.

[38] *Grundig* [1985] OJ L233/1.

[39] OJ [2000] L30/1; Case T-219/99 of 17 December 2003 *British Airways v Commission*. This decision is under appeal to the ECJ.

[40] See, for example, M.1684 *Carrefour/Promodes*, and M.2337 *Nestle/Ralston Purina*.

[41] *Metro* and *SABA II*.

of 7 per cent and 10 per cent were considered by the Court to be conclusive of an absence of dominance.

4.53 **Market share levels over time**   Market shares should be held over a certain period of time to constitute evidence of a dominant position. The Court, in *Hoffmann-La Roche*,[42] has stressed the importance of this temporal element:

> an undertaking which has a very large market share *and holds it for some time* . . . is by virtue of that share in a position of strength which makes it an unavoidable trading partner and which, already because of this secures for it, *at the very least during relatively long periods*, that freedom of action which is the special feature of a dominant position [emphasis added].

4.54 The length of the period of time over which large market shares should be maintained in order to prove dominance is a question that must be answered by considering the specifics of each individual case, principally as a function of the barriers to entry in the relevant market. In *Hoffmann-La Roche* the Court of Justice considered that the company's fluctuating share of the vitamin B3 market (ranging from 29 to 51 per cent over a three-year period) could not be considered sufficient evidence of dominance. Large market shares in a market which is in an early stage of its development and which is characterised by low barriers to entry may also not be considered evidence of a dominant position.[43]

4.55 **Market share levels relative to competitors**   In the case of large market shares which are nevertheless not so great that they provide more or less conclusive proof of dominance it is usually necessary also to assess the shares of the company's closest rivals. The Court of Justice in *Hoffmann-La Roche* accepted the Commission's finding of dominance in relation to the company in the Vitamin A market (where its share was 47 per cent), in particular because of the smaller relative size of the company's competitors' shares (27, 18, 7, and 1 per cent) in what the Court described as a 'narrow oligopolistic market'. A share of between 40 and 45 per cent in another vitamin market was also found to amount to a dominant position. The Court pointed out that this share was 'several times greater' than that of its nearest rival, and that its other rivals were considerably further behind again in terms of market share. In *Michelin I*,[44] none of the dominant firm's rivals had individual market shares exceeding 8 per cent. In *Virgin/British Airways*,[45] while upholding the Commission's finding that British Airways occupied a dominant position in the air travel agency services market with a share of less than 40 per cent, the Court of First Instance placed particular emphasis on the substantial gap between BA's market share and that of its main competitors.

4.56 **Market share levels and differentiated products**   The value of market shares as reliable indicators of market power may be somewhat diminished, however, in markets where products tend to be differentiated to a significant degree. Products may, for example, be differentiated by virtue of differing characteristics, quality, or brand image, and competing products may be more or less substitutable as a result. In such markets, where competition is more intense between some products than between others, shares of the overall market

---

[42] Case 85/76 *Hoffmann-La Roche v Commission* [1979] ECR 461.

[43] MSG Media Services; 9/11/1994, para 55.

[44] Case 322/81 *Michelin v Commission* [1983] ECR 3461.

[45] OJ [2000] L30/1; Case T-219/99 of 17 December 2003 *British Airways v Commission*. This decision is under appeal to the ECJ.

will not necessarily provide an altogether accurate picture of a particular firm's market power. In order to obtain a better understanding of the market power enjoyed by a specific firm in those circumstances, it is necessary to examine the extent to which its pricing can be constrained by firms which are producing products which are closely substitutable. Generally speaking, therefore, the greater the extent of product differentiation in a particular market, the less reliable will be market share data taken alone.

(c) *Measuring Market Power: Price Elasticity of Demand*

The market power held by a particular undertaking can also be directly measured by esti- **4.57** mating the price elasticity of demand of the enterprise in question. Price elasticity of demand is the percentage by which the output sold by the undertaking decreases in relation to an increase in its price. In general, the lower its price elasticity of demand, the greater is the market power held by the firm in question.

Estimating price elasticity of demand, however, requires a substantial amount of detailed **4.58** data on levels of prices and output sold that is rarely available and often not easily obtainable. In view of this difficulty, authorities enforcing competition rules, as explained above, normally define a market and assess the position of the undertakings in question on that market as a surrogate means of assessing market power, or at least as a starting point in such an assessment.

(d) *Measuring Market Power: Profitability Measurement*

Measuring the levels of profits of an undertaking has sometimes been considered an alter- **4.59** native means of inferring market power, or of providing corroborating evidence of the existence of such power. Inferences may, for example, be drawn from the extent to which a firm's prices relate to its marginal costs. This can, however, be a misleading tool and so is best treated with caution.[46] It is true that supra-competitive profits can be associated with a dominant position, but this correlation is easily broken. Indeed, non-dominant firms can be particularly profitable, due to superior performance in terms, for example, of greater innovation, risk taking, or efficiency than the firm's rivals. Conversely, low profits or even losses can sometimes be explained by poor performance in the market, and are necessarily not inconsistent with dominance.[47]

(e) *Other Factors to be Taken into Account in Determining Dominance: Barriers to Entry and Expansion*

In addition to establishing the market share that a company enjoys on the relevant market, **4.60** it is of particular importance in determining whether such a company holds a dominant position to take account of any barriers to entry or expansion in that market. Indeed, a company will only be able to exert market power if potential or existing competitors are prevented from easily and profitably entering the market, or expanding their share in it.

---

[46] The UK authorities have on a number of occasions relied on such profitability assessments in measuring market power.

[47] In Case 27/76 *United Brands v Commission* [1978] ECR 207, the Court did not consider relevant the fact that the company had suffered losses for a number of years; those losses had been due to extraneous factors (climactic conditions, accidents etc); see also *Irish Sugar* [1997] OJ L258/1.

If entry is easy and sufficiently profitable, companies which increase prices will not be able to retain their share of the market, no matter how large that share, and will inevitably lose market share to new entrants or to incumbents.

4.61 Case law does not provide a clear definition of the concept of barrier to entry. The concept does, however, comprise a multiplicity of elements and these have been taken into account in case law concerned with determining the existence of dominance. These elements are classified into three different categories and discussed in detail below. The notion of barriers to expansion is then dealt with. For a discussion of the economic importance of barriers to entry and potential competition, see Chapter 1.

(f) Structural Factors: Characteristics Inherent in the Relevant Market

4.62 **Legal or administrative barriers to entry**   Any exclusive right to operate in a certain market, granted by a legal or administrative provision, constitutes a barrier to entry. Case law has dealt with several of those barriers: national monopolies in certain sectors,[48] restrictions on the number of licences available for operating in a market,[49] or the need to obtain an administrative authorisation.

4.63 A particular type of legal barrier to entry is *intellectual property rights* (patents, trademarks, designs, or copyrights). These confer on their holders the exclusive ownership for a period of time of certain intellectual creations. These rights may allow their holders, therefore, to exclude competitors from certain activities that cannot be performed without the use of the intellectual property rights in question.

4.64 Some types of intellectual property rights will be more likely than others to confer a dominant position. Patents covering a new production method, for instance, have been considered several times by the jurisprudence as conferring dominance in the market in question.[50] The same reasoning could apply to copyrights for certain information needed in order to provide a product or service.[51] Trademarks, in themselves, are less likely to confer dominance. They may, however, be an important factor contributing to a conclusion that dominance exists, particularly if they concern well-established brands enjoying strong consumer loyalty.[52]

4.65 **Sunk costs of entry**   Sunk costs are those costs of entry that cannot be recovered if entry fails. The Court has recognised that they constitute barriers to entry. In *United Brands*[53] for instance, it stated that:

> The barriers to competitors entering the market are the exceptionally large capital investments required . . ., the economies of scale from which newcomers to the market cannot

---

[48] Merger Decision *Elf/Ertoil* (M.063; 29.4.1991).

[49] See Commission decisions in merger cases M.1430 *Vodafone/Airtouch*, at point 27 and M.2016 *France Telecom/Orange*, at point 33.

[50] T-83/91 *Tetra Pak International v Commission* [1994] ECR II-755. See also Merger Decisions *ATT/NCR* (M.050; 18.1.1991) and *Boeing/McDonnell Douglas* (M.877; 30.7.1997).

[51] T-69/89 *Radio Telefis Eireann v Commission* [1991] ECR II-485; T-70/88 *BBC Enterprises Ltd. v Commission* [1991] ECR II-535 and T-76/89 *Independent Television Publications v Commission* [1991] ECR II-575.

[52] See the Commission decision in *Van den Bergh Foods* [1998] OJ L246/1, and the judgment of the CFI in Case T-65/98 *Van den Bergh Foods v The Commission* [2003] ECR II-4653, at para 156. See also, in the merger control context, the Commission decision in case M.833 *The Coca-Cola Company/Carlsberg A/S*.

[53] Case 27/76 *United Brands v Commission* [1978] ECR 207, para 122.

derive any immediate benefit and the actual cost of entry made up *inter alia* of all the general expenses incurred in penetrating the market such as the setting up of an adequate commercial network, the mounting of very large-scale advertising campaigns, all those financial risks, the costs of which are irrecoverable if the attempt fails.

Sunk costs which are fixed (ie they do not depend on the amount of output to be produced) **4.66** lead to the existence of *economies of scale*. Indeed, the larger the output produced, the larger the spread of the fixed sunk costs between those units produced and the lower the average costs obtained, ie the larger the economies of scale. The existence of such economies of scale, therefore, also constitutes a barrier to entry.[54] In its Horizontal Merger Guidelines,[55] the Commission notes that 'entry is . . . less likely if it would only be economically viable on a large scale, thereby resulting in significantly depressed price levels'.

In the same Guidelines, the Commission also indicates that possible entry should be 'suffi- **4.67** ciently swift and sustained' and 'of sufficient scope and magnitude' to deter or defeat the exercise of market power. The Guidelines note that 'what constitutes an appropriate time period depends on the characteristics and dynamics of the market, as well as the specific capabilities of the potential entrants'. The same is true in the context of Article 82. If an undertaking enjoys a very high market share, and the barriers to entry are such that significant and timely entry is unlikely, the firm is likely to be found to be in a dominant position.[56]

Different types of sunk costs have normally to be incurred in order to enter a new market. **4.68** They may differ according to a company's field of activity (production, research and development (R&D), distribution, and marketing costs).

As far as production costs are concerned, sunk costs include investments in plant and other **4.69** production facilities that could not be recovered if entry fails constitute barriers to entry.

With regard to R&D, in markets where innovation plays an important role, a lead in R&D **4.70** or technological level constitutes a factor contributing particularly to dominance. Indeed, in order to replicate such a lead, new entrants may have to incur substantial R&D costs that are often difficult to quantify in advance because it can be difficult to forecast the extent to which such investment will lead to effective results.

The Court of Justice has cited technical lead as a barrier in *United Brands*, where it indicated **4.71** that UBC's rivals could not 'develop research at a comparable level and are in this respect at a disadvantage'. It has also been relied on as a relevant factor by the Commission and Court in some other cases.[57] Merger decisions have also often referred to technological advantage in order to determine whether a dominant position is being created.[58]

---

[54] Merger Decisions *Procter & Gamble/Schickedanz* (M.430; 21.6.1994) or *Nestlé/Perrier* (M.190; 22.7.1993).

[55] Guidelines on the assessment of horizontal mergers under the Council Regulation on the control of concentrations between undertakings; OJ C31/5, 5.2.2004.

[56] ibid, paras 74–5.

[57] Case 85/76 *Hoffmann-La Roche v Commission* [1979] ECR 461, para 48, Case 322/81 *NV Nederlandsche Baden-Industrie Michelin v Commission* [1983] ECR 3461 (para 58), T-30/89 *Hilti v Commission* [1992] ECR II-1439 and C-53/92 P.

[58] *Saint Gobain/Wacker-Chemie/Nom* (M.774; 4.12.96).

4.72   In low-technology markets or markets where the relevant patents have expired (as was the case in *Hoffmann-La Roche*) this factor should not play an important role. It is certainly arguable that technology which can easily be replicated by competitors should not be treated as a barrier. The dominant firm may have had to make considerable investments in order to develop such a technology but this level of investment might not need to be replicated by newcomers to the same extent.

4.73   Sunk costs in distribution facilities also constitute barriers to entry. The Court of Justice, for instance, in *Hoffmann-La Roche* considered the fact that the company had an extensive sales network to be a factor leading to dominance. In *Van den Bergh Foods*, the Commission placed reliance on the company's nationwide distribution network.

4.74   Finally, as far as marketing is concerned, investments in building a reputation and in particular in promoting a trademark are also normally sunk. A brand signals the quality and origin of a product and, in markets of non-homogeneous products, and particularly luxury products, amounts to one of the basic parameters of competition. A leading trademark, therefore, is an additional factor to be taken into account when evaluating dominance.

4.75   In *United Brands* the strength of UBC's brands was taken into account in the Commission and Court's assessment of the existence of dominance. In *Van den Bergh Foods*, the strength of Unilever's ice cream brands in Ireland was relied on by the Commission and by the CFI as being one of the considerations relevant to the finding of dominance.[59] Several decisions assessing the compatibility of concentration within the common market have also referred to this factor.[60]

4.76   **Switching costs for customers**   Barriers to entry will not only derive from the costs that the entrant will have to support, but also from costs that new entry would create for the customers. Indeed, a barrier to entry will exist when a customer will have to bear a high cost in order to switch to a competitor. This will be the case when, for instance, it has to invest in new facilities in order to be supplied by the competitor or when it has to train its workforce to use the new entrant's product. In all these cases, the new entrant will have to support part of these switching costs in order to make its way into the market, while the incumbent company will not.

4.77   The Commission acknowledged that switching costs can constitute a barrier to entry in the *Tetra Pak I*[61] case. In order to determine whether Tetra Pak, a producer of milk packaging systems, held a dominant position the Commission examined whether customers of Tetra Pak could easily switch to its competitors. It considered that the choice for a dairy of the type of packaging system it will use is an important investment decision because, not only must packaging machinery specific to the package employed be purchased, but milk treating and storing equipment also needs to be adapted.

4.78   **Taking account of market dynamics**   Proper account should be taken of the dynamic aspects of the relevant market. Dominance will normally be more difficult to establish in

---

[59] See Case T-65/98 *Van den Bergh Foods v The Commission* [2003] ECR II-4653, at para 156.

[60] *Coca-Cola/Amalgamated Beverages* (M.794; 22.1.1997); *Guinness/Grand Metropolitan* (IV/M.938; 15.10.97).

[61] *Tetra Pak I* [1988] OJ L272/37, para 37.

markets which historically have seen frequent and successful market entry. Moreover, if a market is characterised by rapid growth, and/or by frequent technological 'leap-frogging', dominance will generally be less readily established. Conversely, mature or declining markets may be more readily dominated by an incumbent firm.

High-technology ('new economy') markets, where the parameters of competition are often **4.79** determined by the pace of innovation, are a case in point. The incumbent in a new market of this kind may have a very high market share, even a quasi-monopoly, but the position may be a transient one, and easily challenged by a rival's competing technology.[62] In time, however, high-technology markets may more easily and sustainably be dominated by a single incumbent than many other industries because of the phenomenon of so-called 'network externalities'. Put simply, this refers to the phenomenon whereby customers will be attracted to the network with the most users, which in turn can become the industry standard, the most obvious example being Microsoft's Windows operating system for personal computers.[63]

Countervailing buyer power   If a market is characterised by the presence of significant **4.80** buyer power in the form of a single buyer or a small number of large buyers, this may constitute evidence offsetting an initial conclusion as to the existence of dominance in that market. Buyer power in this context means the bargaining strength which a buyer enjoys in relation to its suppliers by virtue of its size and commercial significance to the seller.[64] The countervailing impact of the buyers must be such that they are credibly, and within a reasonably short period of time, able to turn to an alternative source/s of supply, if a prima facie finding of dominance is to be set aside.[65] It will not normally be sufficient, however, if the buyers are only likely to offset price increases for themselves, and not in the market more generally.

(g) Structural Factors: Characteristics Specific to the Allegedly Dominant Firm

Size of operations   Sheer size, established on the basis of turnover or any other similar **4.81** measure (eg volume of assets), should not normally be considered a factor relevant to a finding of dominance. Large size can result from the fact that a company is operating in several different relevant markets which does not have any particular relevance for the appreciation of whether the undertaking concerned has market power in just one of these markets. The Court of Justice in *Hoffmann-La Roche*[66] dismissed this as a valid criterion, even for the purpose of corroborating apparent dominance based on high market shares. However, a company's size relative to other competitors in a market may be a factor relevant to establishing dominance. Moreover, as discussed above, an incumbent's size, insofar as it gives rise to economies of scale in markets requiring significant sunk costs, may be considered to constitute a barrier to entry, particularly if only large-scale entry could be profitable.

---

[62] See C. Ahlborn and D. Evans, 'Competition policy in the new economy: is competition law up to the challenge?' [2001] ECLR 156.

[63] See Commission decision in *Microsoft*, 24 March 2004. This decision is under appeal to the CFI.

[64] The concept of countervailing buying power is dealt with in some detail in the Commission's Guidelines on the assessment of horizontal mergers under the Council Regulation on the control of concentrations between undertakings; OJ C31/5, 5.2.2004, at paras 64–67.

[65] See Case T-228/97 *Irish Sugar* [1999] ECR II-2969, para 101.

[66] Case 85/76 *Hoffmann-La Roche v Commission* [1979] ECR 461.

4.82 Conversely, small firms may sometimes be dominant. In *Boosey & Hawkes*,[67] the Commission found that a musical instrument maker occupied a dominant position in the supply of instruments for British-style brass bands. The company's annual worldwide turnover amounted only to some £38 million sterling.

4.83 **Wide geographical presence**   Wide geographical presence is a factor that could be relevant for dominance when large multinational conglomerates benefit from group synergies at different levels (purchasing, technological development, distribution channels, etc.), which can give them the opportunity to behave, to some extent, independently from competitors. If these synergies are not apparent, the mere presence in different geographic markets is not particularly helpful to determine whether the company in question holds market power precisely in one of such markets.

4.84 In *Michelin I*[68] the Court accepted as relevant to the issue of dominance that the company appeared to gain advantages from the fact that it had subsidiaries operating throughout Europe and the world. The Commission has sometimes also mentioned this factor[69] both in Article 82 as in merger decisions to establish the existence of a dominant position.[70] Conversely, competitors with large market shares have sometimes not been found dominant when they face competitors belonging to large multinational groups.[71]

4.85 **Financial resources**   Ready access to considerable finance (ie deep pockets) has been used by the Commission[72] and the Court of Justice[73] as an additional factor to establish dominance under Article 82. The Merger Regulation, in its Article 2, also refers to financial power as one of the elements to be taken into account to assess whether a concentration creates or strengthens a dominant position and several Merger Decisions have mentioned it.[74] It should be noted, however, as some economists have pointed out,[75] that if financial markets are efficient in allocating capital resources, then this should not be a relevant factor for assessing dominance.

---

[67] *Boosey & Hawkes* [1987] OJ L286/36.

[68] Case 322/81 *NV Nederlandsche Baden-Industrie Michelin v Commission* [1983] ECR 3461. However, the Court of Justice, in Case 85/76 *Hoffmann-La Roche v Commission* [1979] ECR 461, did not consider relevant to the issue of dominance the fact that Roche was the biggest producer of vitamins in the world, noting that several of its competitors were also companies with a wide geographical presence.

[69] *United Brands*, T-83/91 *Tetra Pak International v Commission* [1994] ECR II-755, *Van den Bergh Foods* [1998] OJ L246/1. See also Case T-65/98 *Van den Bergh Foods v Commission* at para 156, where the CFI, in confirming the Commission's finding of dominance, explicitly referred to the fact 'that HB has the most extensive and most popular range of products on the relevant market, that it is the sole supplier of impulse ice-cream in approximately 40 per cent of outlets in the relevant market, that it is part of the multinational Unilever group which has been producing and marketing ice creams for many years in all Member States and many other countries, in which undertakings in the group are often the major supplier in their respective market, and that the HB brand is very well known.'

[70] *BT/MCI* (M.856; 14.5.1997); *Nestlé/Perrier* (M.190; 22.7.1992); *Boeing/McDonnell Douglas* (M.877; 30.7.1997).

[71] *Unilever France/Ortiz Miko* (M.422; 15.3.1994).

[72] See, for instance, C-310/93 P *BPB Industries pcl & Anor v EC Commission*, para 115.

[73] Case 27/76 *United Brands v Commission* [1978] ECR 207.

[74] *Lyonnaise des Eaux/Suez* (M.916 ; 5.6.1997).

[75] C. Baden Fuller, 'Article 86 EEC: economic analysis of the existence of a dominant position' (1979) 4 ELR 423.

Vertical integration. If vertical integration allows a firm to have exclusive access, or better access **4.86** than its rivals, to raw materials or other inputs, particularly scarce ones, or easier access than its rivals to distribution outlets, this could no doubt constitute a relevant factor to a finding dominance.

In *United Brands*, for instance, the Commission pointed to the vertical integration in UBC **4.87** of the various stages in bringing bananas to market—a characteristic not shared with its rivals— as a further supporting factor (in addition to its high market shares) indicating the company's dominance. In *Hoffmann-La Roche*, the company's wide distribution network was considered by the ECJ to confer a significant advantage on it over its competitors.[76] Vertical integration has also been mentioned in several merger decisions[77] as a factor contributing to dominance.

Product range or differentiation   A wide range of products is not always an indicator of **4.88** dominance. It should only be so when it allows the firm in question to obtain significant costs savings by exploiting economies of scope or when there are consumers interested in purchasing the whole range of products. In this case, a company offering the full range will reduce the transaction and supply costs for the customers and will also be able to maximise its promotion campaigns (by, for instance, offering discounts across the range). This advantage enjoyed by a firm offering a full range of products is sometimes referred to as 'portfolio effect'. In cases where such effects do not exist, the fact that a company is present in different product markets does not say anything about its dominance in one of them.

The Commission has referred several times to a large range of products as a contributing fac- **4.89** tor to dominance. In *Tetra Pak II*,[78] for instance, it pointed out that 'the diversity of its products' increased market power. In *Van den Bergh Foods*, the breadth of the dominant company's range of products compared to those of its rivals is also mentioned by the Commission as a factor influencing the finding of dominance. The Court of Justice has also accepted this position in several cases.[79] Several merger control decisions point also to this factor.[80]

Subjective factors   It is questionable whether it is appropriate to place much reliance on **4.90** subjective factors in reaching a conclusion as to whether a particular firm/s is or are dominant. An example of such a factor might be evidence that the firm's senior management considers that the firm is dominant on a particular market, and has perhaps expressly stated as much in internal memoranda or even in published materials. It is submitted that, while

---

[76] See also *Van den Bergh Foods* [1998] OJ L246/1 and *Napier Brown/British Sugar* [1988] L 284/41.

[77] *Mannesman/Hoesch* (M.222; 12.11.92); *Nestlé/Perrier* (M.190; 22.7.92); *Nordic Satellite Distribution* (M.490; 19.7.1995).

[78] *Tetra Pak II* [1992] OJ L72/1.

[79] Case 322/81 *NV Nederlandsche Baden-Industrie Michelin v Commission* [1983] ECR 3461, para 55; C-62/86 *AKZO Chemie BV v Commission* [1991] ECR I-3359, para 58; in case 85/76 *Hoffmann-La Roche v Commission* [1979] ECR 461, however, considered that Roche's wide range of vitamins was not relevant to any of its findings of dominance, but this seems to have been because the company's rivals also supplied a range of vitamins, and any advantage that might otherwise have accrued to Hoffmann-La Roche was thereby neutralised.

[80] *Guiness/Grand Metropolitan* (IV/M.938; 15.10.1997); *Nestlé/Perrier* (M.790; 22.7.1992); *Kimberly-Clark/Scott* (M.623; 16.1.1996), among others.

such evidence may be useful as corroboration or illustration of an objective finding, no particular weight should be attached to it as evidence in its own right.

(h) Behavioural Factors: Conduct of the Allegedly Dominant Firm

4.91 **Can dominance be inferred from 'abusive' conduct?** It should finally be discussed whether a dominant position could also be inferred from the conduct of the alleged dominant firm. It has been explained that a dominant position is a position that allows a company to behave independently from its competitors and customers. It could be argued, therefore, that the very evidence of such independent behaviour could also be used to prove the existence of a dominant position.

4.92 Both the Court of Justice and the Commission have sometimes used behavioural elements to demonstrate the existence of a dominant position. For instance, in *Hoffmann-La Roche*,[81] the Court analysed whether the company could behave to a large extent independently of competitors. It considered that, should the company have been forced to reduce its prices in reaction to competitors' discounts, it would not have been possible to conclude that it behaved independently and, therefore, that it held a dominant position.[82]

4.93 There is clearly a danger of circular reasoning if strategic behaviour, without reference to other factors, is taken as sufficient and conclusive evidence of dominance. In none of the cases involving the application of Article 82 to date, however, has the assessment of behavioural factors alone sufficed, or provided a substitute for an analysis of the structure of the market and of the position of the allegedly dominant company in that market. To the extent that behavioural factors are considered, they are therefore complementary to such a structural analysis.[83]

4.94 **Strategic behaviour** A barrier to entry can derive from the behaviour of the firm holding a dominant position. The threat to engage in a price war, or to expand output, in response to a new entry can amount to a barrier sufficient to deter new entrants. Major investments in publicity or product range, for instance, may also raise the cost of entry of the rivals and constitute barriers. In its Horizontal Merger Guidelines,[84] the Commission notes that 'entry is likely to be more difficult if the incumbents are able to protect their market shares by offering long-term contracts or giving targeted pre-emptive price reductions to those customers that the entrant is trying to acquire'.

4.95 The existence of excess capacity,[85] in particular, could constitute a barrier because it may allow the dominant company to prevent entry through strategic behaviour. The fact that a

---

[81] Case 85/76 *Hoffmann-La Roche v Commission* [1979] ECR 461, para 71.

[82] See also, Case 27/76 *United Brands v Commission* [1978] ECR 207, paras 67 and 68 or case 85/76 *Hoffmann-La Roche v Commission* [1979] ECR 461, para 71.

[83] M. Waelbroeck and A. Frignani, *Commentaire J. Megret*, iv: *Concurrence* (Brussels: Éditions ULB, 1997), 244.

[84] Guidelines on the assessment of horizontal mergers under the Council Regulation on the control of concentrations between undertakings; OJ C31/5, 5.2.2004.

[85] It is important to distinguish 'excess' capacity from 'idle' capacity. The former allows a firm to increase its level of production at short notice and without substantial capacity maintenance costs. The latter, often the result of the advent of new technology, is capacity whose usage is expensive and usually not economically viable. It should not therefore be taken into account as a factor supporting a finding of dominance.

company is able to increase its output at short notice because it is not using all its production capacity, allows it to respond to any potential entry or expansion by its competitors or potential competitors, and hence may contribute to the company's dominance.[86] Conversely, the existence of competitors with substantial excess capacity may lead to the conclusion that a company with large market shares is not dominant, because any attempt to exploit its position would be met by an increase in production by its competitors.[87]

It is not necessary to determine whether strategic behaviour in itself constitutes an abuse in order to consider it as a barrier to entry and thereby to draw a conclusion as to the existence of a dominant position. It is clear that an exclusionary abuse may in turn create a barrier to entering the market in question. That is not to say, however, that any strategic behaviour intended to raise the cost of entry for rivals may be deemed to constitute an abuse in the sense of Article 82 of the EC Treaty. **4.96**

(i) Barriers to Expansion

A final concept to take into consideration in this context is that of barriers to expansion. Instead of preventing companies not present in the market from entering it, barriers to expansion prevent firms already present in the market from increasing their market share. This type of barrier is also relevant for the determination of a dominant position because, in the absence thereof, a dominant firm will not be able to exert market power: if it raises prices, output will be easily lost to its competitors. **4.97**

The term 'barriers to expansion' has not yet been used as such in case law, but the concept has been taken into account by the Courts in order to determine dominance. For instance, the Court of Justice has considered that dominance could be established when competitors having smaller market shares than the leading undertaking were not 'able to meet rapidly the demand from those who would like to break away from the undertaking which has the largest market share'.[88] **4.98**

Most of the elements listed above as barriers to entry (sunk costs, switching costs, strategic behaviour, etc.) could also be considered to constitute barriers to expansion. In general, barriers to expansion tend to be high in sectors where increase in capacity requires large investments (eg building production plants, finding new sources of supply, expanding distribution networks), but are low in those sectors where, once a large entry investment has been made, the marginal cost of supplying a new product unit is very low. **4.99**

(3) Particular Situations of Dominance

Some specific examples of dominance are described below. First, those situations will be dealt with in which undertakings, due to a particular characteristic, will always be considered to be in a dominant position. This will be the case for statutory monopolies. Secondly, consideration is given as to whether it is appropriate to adopt a 'sliding scale' approach to **4.100**

---

[86] The Court of Justice, in Case 85/76 *Hoffmann-La Roche v Commission* [1979] ECR 461, accepted that the company's overcapacity was a factor relevant to the issue of dominance.

[87] See Merger Decisions *Mannesmann/Vallourec/Ilva* (31.1.1994) or *Aérospatiale/MBB* (25.2.1991).

[88] Case 85/76 *Hoffmann-La Roche v Commission* [1979] ECR 461.

the concept of dominance, with greater responsibilities being placed on firms approaching monopoly. Thirdly, the question of whether a company is always dominant in its aftermarkets (eg markets for the supply parts of a certain brand) and markets for which it holds intellectual property rights is discussed. Fourthly, an explanation is provided of the extent to which Article 82 can also be applied to oligopolies or, in other words, whether dominant positions can be held by several undertakings. The concept of a so-called collective dominant position is described in this context. Fifthly, there is an assessment of whether Article 82 can apply to the behaviour of firms in a certain market where they do not have a dominant position, notably in markets neighbouring those in which the firm holds a dominant position. Finally, the extent to which a dominant buyer can also be considered to have a dominant position and, therefore, be subject to Article 82, is discussed.

(a) Statutory Monopolies or Companies with Exclusive Rights

4.101   Public monopolies or undertakings that have been granted an exclusive right to operate in a particular market will always be considered to be in a dominant position if the market in question constitutes the relevant market for competition purposes. Multiple examples of these kinds of monopolies are to be found in the case law. Statutory monopolies have been found, *inter alia*, in the markets for certificates for conformity for imported cars;[89] the operation of railway infrastructure;[90] telecommunications services;[91] provision, maintenance, and repair of telecommunications equipment;[92] recruitment services;[93] postal delivery;[94] harbour pilot and other services;[95] as well as broadcasting.[96]

4.102   Such statutory monopolies, for so long as they do not operate as public authorities, are subject to Article 82 of the EC Treaty in the same way as any other undertaking holding a dominant position. In fact, Article 5 of the EC Treaty imposes an obligation on Member States not to adopt any measure that can deprive this or other Treaty articles of its effectiveness. Furthermore, if the state measure granting the exclusive right leads the monopoly to abuse its dominant position, it might also infringe Article 86 of the EC Treaty (ex Article 90) (see a detailed analysis of this article in Chapter 6). Even if the statutory monopoly has been entrusted with the operation of services of general economic interest, Article 82 will apply, according to Article 86(2), insofar as its does not obstruct the performance, in law or in fact, of the particular tasks assigned to the undertaking in question.

(b) Super-dominance?

4.103   Recent pronouncements by the ECJ and by Advocate General Fennelly in *Compagnie Maritime Belge*[97] appear to indicate that a graduated approach to the determination of dominance

---

[89] Case 26/75 *General Motors Continental v Commission* [1975] ECR 1367.
[90] See Commission decision of 28 August 2003 in Case COMP/D-1.37.685 *GVG/FS*, at paras 82–85.
[91] Case 41/83 *Italian Republic v Commission* [1985] ECR 880.
[92] Case C-202/88 *French Republic v Commission* [1991] ECR I-1223 and C-18/88 *RTT v GB-Inno-BM* [1991].
[93] Case C-41/90 *Klaus Hofner and Fritz Elser v Macrotron Gmbh* [1991] ECR I-1979.
[94] Case C-320/91 *Corbeau v Belgian Post Office* [1993] ECR I-2533.
[95] C-179/90 *Porto di Genova* [1991] ECR I-5889; C-18/93 *Corsica Ferries Italia Srl v Corpo dei Piloti del Porto di Genova* [1994] ECR I-1812.
[96] Case 311/84 *Télémarketing* [1985] ECR 3261.
[97] Case C-395/96 *Compagnie Maritime Belge Transports SA v Commission* [2000] 4 CMLR 1076, at para 114 et seq. In his opinion (at para 136), Fennelly AG appears to suggest that the responsibility of a

may sometimes be appropriate, and that certain categories of behaviour may be considered abusive when engaged in by firms occupying a position of particular strength on a market, but not when engaged in by other dominant firms. In the case in question the ECJ left open the possibility that the same behaviour impugned in that case (price discrimination) might not be abusive if engaged in by a firm not enjoying a position comparable to the 90 per cent market share held by the shipping conference. In his opinion, Fennelly AG appears explicitly to endorse a 'sliding scale' approach to the assessment of dominance, in the following terms: 'Article 82 cannot be interpreted as permitting monopolists or quasi-monopolists to exploit the very significant power which their *super dominance* confers so as to preclude the emergence of a new or additional competitor' (emphasis added).

It is submitted that this graduated approach, which appears to imply that special rules may **4.104** be applicable to some firms (which could be characterised as 'super-dominant') has certain drawbacks in terms of legal certainty. That said, the reference to the concept of super-dominance may be no more than acknowledgement of an obvious fact, namely that a firm with overwhelming market power will have enormous capacity and incentive to exploit that position to its advantage.

(c) Dominance in Aftermarkets

In some instances, the Commission and the Court of Justice have considered that a com- **4.105** pany held a dominant position in the aftermarkets (or secondary markets) of the products it provides. By aftermarket (or secondary market) is normally meant the markets for products or services complementary to the main product that the undertaking provides (primary market), such as spare parts or reparation and maintenance services.

Two examples follow. In *General Motors*[98] it was considered that the firm, which was not **4.106** dominant on the car manufacturers' market (primary market), held a dominant position in the market for delivery of certificates for conformity for imported cars into Belgium (secondary market). This certificate was necessary for cars which were the subject of parallel imports (ie not imported by the manufacturer itself but by other car dealers) to be allowed to be driven in the country, and only car manufacturers were authorised by law to deliver such certifications to cars of their own brand. The second example, the *Hugin*[99] case, involved a producer of cash registers (primary market), which did not hold a dominant position on this market, but was found to be in such a position in the market for spare parts to be used for the repair or maintenance of Hugin cash registers.

It cannot be inferred from these cases, however, that a manufacturer will always be considered **4.107** to hold a dominant position in its aftermarkets. Indeed, if the manufacturer is not dominant in the primary market it will not normally be considered as such in the secondary one.

---

dominant firm may be greater than usual in circumstances where the firm 'enjoys a position of dominance approaching a monopoly'. In Case C-334/94 *Tetra-Pak v Commission* [1996] ECR I-5951, at para 24, the ECJ indicated that the extent of the special responsibility imposed on a firm under Art 82 must be considered in the light of the particular circumstances of each case.

[98] Case 26/75 *General Motors Continental v Commission* [1975] ECR 1367. See also C226/84 *British Leyland v Commission* [1986] ECR 3263.

[99] 22/78 *Hugin v Commission* [1979] ECR 1869. See also T-30/89 *Hilti v Commission* [1992] ECR II-1439 and C-53/92 P.

Rational consumers and producers should take into account the conditions in the aftermarkets at the moment of purchasing or selling the primary product and, therefore, a producer will avoid abusing its position in the aftermarkets in order not to damage its competitive position on the primary market.

4.108 In some cases, however, consumers might not take into account the behaviour of the producers in the aftermarkets when purchasing the primary product, in particular if information concerning the aftermarkets is not available or not disclosed to the customer at that time. This may, for example, be the case when the customer is unaware when purchasing the primary product of difficulties in finding compatible secondary products as well as cases where the lifetime of the primary product is relatively long.[100] This may be the case when the cost of the secondary product is a small fraction of the cost of the primary product and, therefore, is not taken into account when the primary product is purchased.[101] However, even in such situations the competitors in the primary market typically will be fully aware of the link between the primary and the secondary market, and the competitive pressure in the primary market may be sufficient that there is no dominance in the aftermarket. Often high aftermarket prices will be compensated by low primary market prices, bringing the price of the 'system' down. Only in the limited circumstances when such mechanisms are not at work, non-dominant manufacturers of the main product might be considered to hold a dominant position in the aftermarkets.[102]

(d) Collective Dominance

4.109 Article 82 refers to abuses by 'one or more undertakings'. This wording implies that Article 82 is addressed, not only to single dominant firms, but also to more than one undertaking which together have a dominant position. The Article does not spell out in what circumstances several firms can be considered as holding together a dominant position. Over time, however, case law has clarified what is meant by the concept of collective dominance to the point where it is now clear that it encompasses any situation of oligopoly where explicit or even tacit collusion are likely. Early cases seemed to limit the concept to circumstances in which several firms were jointly dominant on a market by virtue of the existence of structural or contractual links of some kind which enabled them to behave as a single entity. More recent cases confirm, however, that the notion of collective dominance also applies to oligopolies where only the likelihood of tacit collusion can be demonstrated.

4.110 **Concept of a collective dominant position** The concept of a collective dominant position was first recognised by the European courts in *Flat Glass*,[103] where the Court of First

---

[100] Commission Notice on the definition of the relevant market for the purposes of Community competition law [1997] OJ C372/5, para 56.

[101] Digital; XXVII Report on Competition Policy, point 69, where Digital was considered dominant on the maintenance of computers it had sold. See also Philip Andrews, 'Aftermarket power in the computer services market: the Digital undertaking' (1998) ECLR. By contrast, in *Pelycan v Kyocera*, XXV Report on Competition Policy, p 140. Kyocera was not considered dominant in the market for toner cartridges for its printers because it was not dominant in the printer market.

[102] See also *Eastman Kodak Co. v Image Technical Services Inc.* 112 S. Ct. 2072 (1992), a landmark case where the US Supreme Court rejected Kodak's contention that lack of market power in service and replacement parts for copying equipment must be assumed when such power is absent in the primary equipment market.

[103] Cases T-68/89, T-77/89, and T-78/89 *Societa Italiano Vetro SPA, Fabrica Pisana SPA and PPG Vernante Pennitalia SPA v Commission* [1992] ECR II-1403. The CFI considered that the Commission had not proved the existence of a collective dominant position and, therefore, partially annulled its Decision.

Instance, while finding that collective dominance had not been established in that specific case, stated that:

> There is nothing, in principle, to prevent two or more independent economic entities from being, on a specific market, united by such economic links that, by virtue of that fact, together they hold a dominant position vis-à-vis the other operators in the same market.

This conceptual approach appeared to be endorsed, and its economic meaning further elucidated, several years later by the Court of Justice in the *Almelo*[104] case, where it stated that: 'In order for such a collective dominant position to exist, the undertakings must be linked in such a way that they adopt the same conduct on the market'. Both the Court of Justice and the CFI have elaborated upon this definition in subsequent judgments where the concept of a collective dominant position has been discussed.[105] However, it was not until the ECJ's judgment in *Compagnie Maritime Belge*[106] that the nature of the 'economic links' required for a finding of collective dominance was comprehensively set out. In that judgment, upholding a Commission decision finding an abuse of collective dominance by a maritime conference, the Court of Justice stated that two independent undertakings may be collectively dominant if 'they present themselves or act together on a particular market as a collective entity'. As to the nature of the economic links that must be shown to exist between the companies, the Court makes it clear that there is no requirement for formal, contractual links, but only for 'factors which give rise to a connection between the undertakings' such that they behave as a collective entity on the market. Indeed, the Court goes on to stress that 'the existence of an agreement or of other links in law is not indispensable to a finding of a collective dominant position; such a finding may be based on other connecting factors and would depend on an economic assessment and, in particular, on an assessment of the structure of the market in question'.[107] It is interesting to note that, some years previous to the ECJ judgment in *Compagnie Maritime Belge*, the Commission had already indicated that this less formalistic interpretation of the concept of collective dominance under Article 82 is the one that it considered appropriate.[108]

From this body of case law, two central conclusions can be drawn regarding the notion of a collective dominant position. First, the companies occupying the collective dominant position will normally be independent economic entities.[109] A collective dominant position is

4.111

---

[104] Case C-393/92 *Almelo* [1994] ECR I-1477.

[105] Case C-96/94 *Centro Servizi Spediporto* [1995] ECR I-2883; C-140/94, C-141/94, C-142/94 *DIP v Comune di Bassano del Grappa* [1995] ECR I-3257; T-24/93, T-25/93, T-28/93 *Compagnie Maritime Belge Transports SA, Dafra-Lines A/S, Deutsche Afrika-Linien GmbH & Co and Nedlloyd Lijnen BV v Commission* [1996] ECR II-1201.

[106] Cases C-395/96 and C-396/96 *Compagnie Maritime Belge NV v Commission* [2000] 4 CMLR 1076.

[107] The Court of First Instance has followed the ECJ's approach, using very similar language, in upholding the Commission's decision in the *TACA* case, in which the Commission had found an abuse of collective dominance by a liner shipping consortium: see joined Cases T-191/98, T-212/98, T-213/98, T-214/98 of 30.09.2003.

[108] Notice on the application of the Competition Rules to access agreements in the telecommunications sector [1998] OJ C265/02, para 79: 'for two or more companies to be jointly dominant it is necessary, though not sufficient, for there to be no effective competition between the companies on the relevant market. This lack of competition may be due to the fact that the companies have links such as agreements for cooperation, or interconnection agreements. The Commission does not however consider that either economic theory or Community law implies that such links are legally necessary for a joint dominant position to exist.'

[109] In Case CT-228/97 *Irish Sugar v Commission* of 7.10.1999, the CFI upheld a Commission decision in which Irish Sugar and its distribution subsidiary SDL were found to be in a 'vertical collective dominant position'.

not a concept limited to firms belonging to the same group, and therefore constituting a single economic unit,[110] but also applies to undertakings independent one from the other. Second, such undertakings must be connected or interrelated in such a way as to enable them to behave as a single collective entity on the market, irrespective of whether or not that relationship is characterised by formal links of one kind or another.

4.112   **The notion of economic links**   The crucial element needed to infer the existence of a collective dominant position is, therefore, the existence of links between the undertakings in question. The case law does not prescribe the form those links should take, but only specifies that the links should unite the undertakings in such a way that they adopt the same conduct on the market. In its Notice on the application of the Competition Rules to access agreements in the telecommunications sector, the Commission has gone some way in explaining its understanding of the interrelationship by indicating that, for two or more companies to be in a joint dominant position, they must first together have the same position in relation to their customers and competitors as a single company would have if it were in a dominant position.[111]

4.113   **Contractual or structural links**   The most obvious example of a collective dominant position is that in which the link between the undertakings is of a contractual nature. In *Flat Glass*,[112] the CFI cited as an example of undertakings with economic links those which jointly have licences which give them a technological lead in relation to the remaining competitors. It has also been suggested that football clubs involved in the organisation of a professional league,[113] or two air carriers sharing an air route constituting a distinct market,[114] together hold a dominant position. The Commission has also applied this concept to two companies jointly managing a port and jointly operating ferry services from it,[115] and to insurance undertakings participating in a re-insurance pool which covers a substantial share of the relevant market.[116]

4.114   Collective dominant positions could also exist when the undertakings in question are not linked by contractual relationships but have a structural link that leads them to behave as a single undertaking. Cross shareholdings or common directorships could constitute such links.[117]

4.115   There are some cases where the contractual link between undertakings holding a collective dominant position consists in an agreement or concerted practice which falls under Article 81(1) of the EC Treaty.[118] The clearest example of this situation is found in the Commission

---

[110] Until the decision in *Flat Glass*, it was widely felt that the 'or more undertakings' in Art 82 should be interpreted narrowly as only applying to companies within the same group. This was the position adopted by the UK government in its intervention in the *Flat Glass* case.

[111] Notice on the application of the Competition Rules to access agreements in the telecommunications sector [1998] OJ C265/02, paras 78–79.

[112] Cases T-68/89, T-77/89, and T-78/89 *Societa Italiano Vetro SPA, Fabrica Pisana SPA and PPG Vernante Pennitalia SPA v Commission* [1992] ECR II-1403.

[113] Case C-415/93 *Bosman* [1997], opinion of Advocate General Lenz.

[114] Case 66/86 *Ahmed Saeed Flugreisen v Zentrale zur Bekampfung Unlauteren Wettbewerbs* [1989] ECR 803, opinion of Advocate General Lenz.

[115] *Port of Rødby* [1994] OJ L55/52.

[116] *P&I Clubs* [1999] OJ L125/12.

[117] Joined Cases C-395/96 P and C-396/96 P. *Compagnie Maritime Belge NV and Dafra-Lines v Commission* [1998] Opinion of Advocate General Fennelly.

[118] For a detailed analysis of the relationship between Arts 81 and 82 in situations of collective dominance, see T Soames, 'An analysis of the principles of concerted practice and collective dominance: a distinction without a difference?' [1996] 1 ECLR, 24-39.

decisions concerning maritime conferences.[119] These are agreements between shipowners to share a particular route and agree on uniform rates and transport conditions for that route. These agreements are caught by Article 81(1) but benefit from a block exemption regulation.[120] This has not, however, prevented the Commission from considering that the members of such conferences, by virtue of the agreements concluded between them, hold a collective dominant position in the maritime route in question, and that they abuse it by engaging in exclusionary practices. This approach has now been confirmed by both the CFI and the ECJ.[121]

Oligopolies without contractual or structural links   It now seems clear that the concept   **4.116**
of collective dominance in Article 82 can also be applied to an oligopoly characterised by a parallelism of behaviour between the oligopolists, even in the absence of any contractual or structural links. In this regard, it is important to recall that the notion of collective dominance has also evolved in the context of the application of the Merger Regulation, and that the concept of collective dominance has been applied to precisely this kind of scenario, namely to oligopolies not necessarily involving contractual or structural links between the oligopolists, but nonetheless characterised by a likelihood of tacit collusion between them (see below).

It is submitted that the definition of collective dominance used by the ECJ in *Compagnie*   **4.117**
Maritime Belge is fully consistent with the case law on collective dominance under the ECMR. Indeed, the Court explicitly cites its judgment in *Kali und Salz*,[122] in addition to other precedents under Article 82, as authority for its conclusions. In *Gencor*, the CFI likewise confirmed that its findings on collective dominant positions also apply to Article 82.[123] A more recent judgment of the Court of First Instance in *Laurent Piau*[124] cites 'three cumulative conditions' which 'must be present for a finding of collective dominance', namely the so-called '*Airtours* criteria' which are set out below. This would appear to mean that the notion of collective dominance is for all intents and purposes identical under Article 82 and the Merger Regulation.

In oligopolistic markets, a limited number of undertakings exert significant market power.   **4.118**
Depending on the characteristics of the industry in question, the interdependence between the members of the oligopoly may result in consumer harm, in the form of excessive prices,

---

[119] *French-West African Shipowners' Committees* [1992] OJ L134/1 and *Cewal* [1992] OJ 1993 L34/20. See also *P&O/Nedlloyd* (IV/M.831) [1996], para 53.

[120] Council Regulation (EEC) 4056/86 on the determination of application modalities of Arts 85 and 86 of the EC Treaty to maritime transports [1986] OJ L378.

[121] T-24/93, T-25/93, T-28/93 *Compagnie Maritime Belge Transports SA, Dafra-Lines A/S, Deutsche Afrika-Linien GmbH & Co. and Nedlloyd Lijnen BV v Commission* [1996] ECR. See also C-395/96 P and C-396/96 P *Compagnie Maritime Belge and Dafra-Lines v Commission*, opinion of AG Fennelly, 29.10.1998; Cases C-395/96 and C-396/96 *Compagnie Maritime Belge NV v Commission* [2000] 4 CMLR 1076.

[122] Cases C-68/94 and C-30/95 *French Republic, Société Commerciale des Potasses et de l'Azote and Entreprise Minière et Chimique v Commission* [1998] ECR I-1375.

[123] See T-102/96 *Gencor Ltd. v Commission* [1999] ECR II-753, at paras 273–7. See also C-395/96 P and C-396/96 P *Compagnie Maritime Belge and Dafra-Lines v Commission*, opinion of AG Fennelly, 29.10.1998, para 27, where it considers that there is no fundamental difference in the requirement of 'economic links' under Art 82 case law and of 'factors giving rise to a connection' under Merger Regulation case law.

[124] Case T-193/02 *Laurent Piau v Commission*; judgment of 26 January 2005. It should be noted that this was a case in which the collectively dominant undertakings (football clubs) were in any event contractually linked via the FIFA organisation.

output restrictions, or a stifling of innovation.[125] From an economic point of view, and to the extent that the oligopolists behave on the market in a collective fashion, there does not seem to be any policy reason to treat these situations any differently from those resulting from the existence of a single dominant firm.

4.119 The European Courts, in applying the Merger Regulation (see Chapter 5), concluded in 1995 that the concept of a collective dominant position extends to oligopolistic situations, even in the absence of structural or contractual links between the oligopolists. In *Kali und Salz*,[126] the courts confirmed the Commission's view[127] that mergers creating an oligopolistic market structure (duopolistic in the case in question) could be covered by Article 2(3) of the Merger Regulation, which prohibited concentrations that create or strengthen a dominant position as a result of which effective competition would be impeded. The ECJ has defined a collective dominant position under the Merger Regulation as follows:

> a situation in which effective competition in the relevant market is significantly impeded by the undertakings involved in the concentration and one or more other undertakings which together, in particular because of factors giving rise to a connection between them, are able to adopt a common policy on the market and act to a considerable extent independently of their competitors, their customers, and also of consumers.[128]

4.120 The ECJ considered that such a situation could be found when several characteristics are met. In particular, it referred to the factors mentioned by the Commission in its decision, such as the homogeneity of the product; the maturity and transparency of the market; the high degree of concentration; the similar market share of the members of the oligopoly. It also referred to structural links between the companies in question, such as participation in the same export cartel and use in one Member State, by one of the companies, of the distribution network of the other.

4.121 A year later the CFI further clarified the notion in *Gencor*,[129] a case again involving a duopoly, when it stated that:

> there is no reason whatsoever in legal or economic terms to exclude from the notion of economic links the relationship of interdependence existing between the parties to a tight oligopoly within which, in a market with the appropriate characteristics, in particular in terms of market concentration, transparency and product homogeneity, those parties are in a position to anticipate one another's behaviour and are therefore strongly encouraged to align their conduct in the market, in particular in such a way as to maximise their joint profits by restricting production with a view to increasing prices.

4.122 Structural links, therefore, do not need to be proved in order to determine collective dominance. In *Gencor* the Commission relied on several other elements to prove such dominance,

---

[125] See a seminal article from J. Stigler, 'A theory of oligopoly' (1964) 72 *J. Pol. Econ.* 44.

[126] Cases C-68/94 and C-30/95 *French Republic, Société Commerciale des Potasses et de l'Azote and Entreprise Minière et Chimique v Commission* [1998] ECR I-1375.

[127] *Kali und Salz/MdK/Treuhand* (IV/M.308) (1994) OJ L186/38, but also previous decisions such as *Alcatel/ AEG/Kabel* (IV/M.165); *Nestlé/Perrier* (IV/M.190) (1992); *Dalmine/Mannesmann/Vallourec* (IV/M.315) (1994) among many others.

[128] Cases C-68/94 and C-30/95 *French Republic, Société Commerciale des Potasses et de l'Azote and Entreprise Minière et Chimique v Commission* [1998], para 221.

[129] T-102/96 *Gencor Ltd. v Commission* [1999], para 276.

including the following: a high degree of market concentration; the similarity of cost structures of the undertakings holding the collective dominant position; market transparency; product homogeneity; moderate growth in demand; price inelastic demand; mature production technology; high entry barriers; and a lack of negotiating power on the part of purchasers.[130]

In *Airtours/First Choice*,[131] in striking down a Commission decision prohibiting a merger in the UK tour operators market on the grounds that it would create a tight oligopoly involving three firms, the CFI went still further in spelling out clearly the conditions necessary for a finding of collective dominance under the Merger Regulation: the oligopolists must be able to reach terms of (tacit) collusion with relative ease; it must be possible for the oligopolists to monitor deviations from these terms, and to deter such deviation or retaliate effectively, if necessary; and it must not be impossible for the reactions of other competitors or potential competitors to jeopardise the effectiveness of the tacit collusion. **4.123**

Given the fact that the concept of dominant position under Article 82 and the Merger Regulation are essentially equivalent (see 4.39 above), this case law under the Merger Regulation is of direct relevance for the application of Article 82.[132] Although there has been no case law to date involving the application of Article 82 in scenarios not involving contractual or structural links of some kind, it is not difficult to conceive of circumstances in which the members of a tight oligopoly might engage in exclusionary behaviour aimed at 'fringe' competitors or potential entrants, with a view to safeguarding their market position. It is also conceivable, however difficult this might prove in practice, to envisage that oligopolists might be found to have exploited their dominance by charging excessive prices. **4.124**

It should, however, be stressed that it is very unlikely that a case could be taken under Article 82 against oligopolists for engaging in tacit collusion *per se*. It is submitted that, if the collusion is not such that it is capable of being addressed under Article 81, it would not be appropriate to do so 'through the back door' under Article 82. It is only when that tacit collusion results in the commission of an abuse that Article 82 can be applied. **4.125**

An interesting question which can be posed in this context is whether it is possible to prosecute one oligopolist for abuse of collective dominance or whether such cases will always involve a finding of abuse committed by all of the members of the oligopoly. While the logic underlying the notion of collective dominance implies that an oligopolist engaging in exclusionary behaviour is in a sense doing so on behalf of the collective entity (the collectively dominant firms may, for example, be 'taking turns' to take measures against potential entrants or fringe players), it seems now to be clearly established that it is nonetheless possible to prosecute oligopolists individually.[133] Indeed, the notion of applying Article 82 to a firm which is not directly engaging in any exclusionary conduct seems to stretch the legal **4.126**

---

[130] ibid, para 159.

[131] Case T-342/99 *Airtours plc v The Commission*, 6 June 2002; [2002] ECR II-2585.

[132] See also the Commission's Guidelines on the assessment of horizontal mergers under the Council Regulation on the control of concentrations between undertakings; OJ C31/5, 5.2.2004, at paras 39–57.

[133] The CFI acknowledged this in *Irish Sugar*, when it stated that 'undertakings occupying a joint dominant position may engage in joint or individual abusive conduct'; see Case T-228/97 [1999] ECR II-2969, at para 66, and in the *TACA* case, when the CFI stated that: 'Although the existence of a collective dominant position may be deduced from the position which the economic entities concerned together hold on the market in

fiction of abuse of collective dominance beyond reasonable limits. The same seems all the more true in the case of an oligopolist engaging in exploitative behaviour.

(e) Dominance and Neighbouring Markets

4.127 Normally, abuses within the meaning of Article 82 can only be committed in the market where the dominant position is established. However, in special circumstances, it would seem that a dominant undertaking may commit an abuse in a market neighbouring that where it holds a dominant position, at least insofar as the markets are closely associated with each other and the impugned conduct seems likely to reinforce the firm's position in the market where it is dominant.

4.128 In *Tetra Pak II*, the CFI[134] and the Court of Justice[135] confirmed the Commission's finding that Tetra Pak had committed abuses in the markets for non-aseptic packaging machines and non-aseptic cartons, while Tetra Pak's dominant position had only been established in the markets for aseptic packaging machines and aseptic cartons (where it had a market share of nearly 90 per cent). The Court[136] acknowledged that:

> the application of Article 86[82] to conduct found on the associated, non-dominated market and having effects on that associated market can only be justified by special circumstances.

In this case, the decision was justified by the leading position that Tetra Pak held in these neighbouring markets (even if it did not amount to a dominant position), and because of the strong links existing between the aseptic and non-aseptic packaging machines and cartons markets. In particular, the Court referred to the fact that both aseptic and non-aseptic products were used for packaging the same products (ie fruit juices and dairy products); that a substantial proportion of Tetra Pak's customers operated in both sectors; and that several important competitors also operated in both sectors.

4.129 In *Interbrew*[137] the Commission indicated that Article 82 would be applicable to an abuse in the same product market, but outside the geographic market where dominance was held. In that case, Interbrew subsidiaries outside Belgium (where the company is dominant) pursued a policy of not supplying beer to customers likely to export outside their territory, including Belgium. The fact that the abuses had the effect of protecting the Belgian market would appear to have provided the necessary link between the latter market, where dominance was held, and those where the abuses were allegedly committed.

4.130 It has been asked whether it is reasonable to sanction under Article 82 an undertaking's exclusionary behaviour in a market in which it is not dominant.[138] In fact, no exclusionary

---

question, the abuse does not necessarily have to be the action of all the undertakings in question. It need only be capable of being identified as one of the manifestations of such a joint dominant position'; see Case T-191/98, T-212/98, T-213/98, T-214/98 of 30 September 2003, at para 633.

[134] Case T-83/91 *Tetra Pak International v Commission* [1994] ECR II-755.
[135] Case C-333/94 P *Tetra Pak International v Commission* [1996] ECR I 5951.
[136] Case T-83/91 *Tetra Pak International v Commission* [1994] ECR II-0755, para 27.
[137] 1996 Annual Competition Report, para 53.
[138] R. Subiotto, 'The special responsibility of dominant undertakings not to impair genuine undistorted competition' [1995] World Competition 18/3.

practice will normally be successful if the undertaking engaging in it cannot rely on a certain amount of market power in the market where the alleged abuse occurs. Nevertheless, it may be true that in some exceptional cases the mere possession of market power in neighbouring markets will suffice to make such a practice succeed or, as the Court has stated, to enjoy a freedom of conduct compared with the other economic operators in those markets. This may in particular be the case where an alleged abuse is carried out by a firm in a market where it is not dominant but where the apparent motive for the behaviour is the protection of that firm's dominance in a neighbouring market. In such circumstances, the application of Article 82 may be justified.[139]

(f) Buyer's Dominance

An undertaking may hold a dominant position in relation either to its customers or to its suppliers. In the latter case, it is referred to as buyer's dominance.[140] The Commission has acknowledged the possibility of applying Article 82 to abuses of a buyer's dominant position but there is little case law actually applying this concept. | **4.131**

Most cases of buyer's dominance will arise in relation to companies that hold a monopolistic position in their own markets and, therefore, are also the single buyer for certain components of the products or services they supply. In the guidelines for the application of competition rules to the telecommunications sector,[141] the Commission has indicated that monopolist telecom operators might abuse their dominant purchasing position by imposing on suppliers excessively favourable prices or other trading conditions.[142] The *Tabacalera/Filtrona*[143] case constitutes an example of an investigation in which the issue of buyer's dominance was encountered: Tabacalera was the dominant producer of cigarettes in Spain and it decided to stop buying filters from Filtrona, because it had started to produce them on its own. The Commission considered that Tabacalera had a dominant position on the filters buying market and that a refusal to buy from a certain competitor could constitute an abuse covered by Article 82. Nevertheless, in that instance it was considered that the refusal was objectively justified by the economies of scale and reduction of costs that Tabacalera would achieve by producing filters on its own. | **4.132**

In *Virgin/British Airways*,[144] the CFI confirmed a Commission decision finding that the commissions paid by BA to travel agents in the UK pursuant to a performance award scheme | **4.133**

---

[139] Notice on the application of the Competition Rules to access agreements in the telecommunications sector [1998] OJ C265/02, paras 65–67. The Commission applies this analysis to the telecommunications sector. Another example of this is found in a merger case, *Guinness-Grand Metropolitan*, where the Commission applied the portfolio effects theory, which suggests that companies might exert market power in several linked markets even if they only hold a traditional position in one of them because of the combined effects of its position in all these markets.

[140] A single buyer, in economic terms is referred to as a monopsony.

[141] Guidelines for the application of competition rules to the telecommunications sector [1991] OJ C233, paras 116–120.

[142] See also the Commission's Guidelines on the assessment of horizontal mergers under the Council Regulation on the control of concentrations between undertakings; OJ C31/5, 5.2.2004, at paras 61–62.

[143] European Commission's XIXth Annual Report on competition policy, para 61.

[144] [2000] OJ L30/1; Case T-219/99 *British Airways v Commission* [2003] ECR II-5917. This judgment is under appeal to the ECJ: Case C-95/04 *British Airways v Commission* (Kolkott AG's opinion delivered on 23 February 2006).

were equivalent to loyalty discounts and hence abusive within the meaning of Article 82.[145] In so doing, it confirmed that Article 82 applies both to undertakings with a dominant position in relation to their suppliers and to those whose dominance is established in relation to its customers.

4.134 This issue is also of particular relevance in relation to the retailing industry. The increasing concentration of this sector in most European markets may lead to situations of buyer's dominance and to a more frequent application of Article 82 in these situations. Merger control has already on a number of occasions taken buyers' market power into account in the assessment of concentrations between retailers.[146]

(4) Dominant Position in a Substantial Part of the Common Market

4.135 There is an additional criterion specified in Article 82 in relation to the geographic scope of a finding of dominance, namely that the relevant geographic market must constitute the whole of the common market or at least 'a substantial part' thereof. In practice, this further requirement has essentially been applied as a de minimis criterion, and the Court of Justice has had a number of opportunities to interpret its meaning. In *Suiker Unie*, the Court said that:

> for the purpose of determining whether a specific territory is large enough to amount to 'a substantial part of the common market' within the meaning of Article 86 of the Treaty, the pattern and volume of the production and consumption of the said product as well as the habits and economic opportunities of vendors and purchasers must be considered.

4.136 This means that an analysis is required, not just of the geographic extent of the market, but also a quantitative assessment of the economic importance of the market relative to the total Community market. The Court found in the instant case that the sugar market in Belgium and Luxembourg constituted such a substantial part of the common market. In reaching that conclusion, it took account of the volumes of production and consumption of sugar in the area, and of the proportion of the Community market that these represented: production levels amounted to some 9 per cent of the total Community's production and consumption accounted for about 5 per cent of total consumption in the Community.

4.137 Determining what is substantial and what is not can be approached from a number of different angles. It seems that the entire territory of a Member State, even the smallest,[147] will usually be considered a substantial part of the common market. The Court has also held that

---

[145] The performance award scheme formed part of a series of agreements between BA and travel agents established in the UK for the purposes of providing air transport agency services, including the issuing of tickets to travellers and the provision of ancillary promotional services. At the time, 85 per cent of air tickets sales in the UK were made through travel agents.

[146] *Kesko/Tuko* (M.784; 20.11.1996); *Rewe/Meindl* (M.1221; 23.10.1999); *Carrefour/Promodes* (M.1684, 25.1.2000). See also, in other sectors, *Crown Cork/Carnaud Metalbox* (M.603, 14.11.1995).

[147] In the *Magill* case, the Commission found that the market for TV licences in Ireland was substantial (*c*.1 per cent of total Community licences); in *BP v Commission*, AG Warner indicated that Luxembourg would be likely to be considered a substantial part of the common market. See also the CFI judgment in *Irish Sugar*, Case T-228/97 [1999] ECR II-2969, at para 99.

large areas falling short of the entire territory of a Member State can also be substantial.[148] In *Ambulanz Glöckner*,[149] the Court of Justice held that the German region of Rheinland-Pfalz constitutes a substantial part of the common market on the sole ground that it 'covers a territory of almost 20 000 km² and has a high number of inhabitants, around four million, which is higher than the population of some Member States'. By contrast, the English and Irish courts have found respectively that the North of England[150] and County Kerry[151] in Ireland do not constitute substantial parts of the common market.

In a number of cases, the Commission has considered that geographically small areas with a specific economic significance may in themselves constitute substantial parts of the common market. Several major transport terminals such as the ports of Genoa[152] in Italy, Rodby[153] in Denmark, Holyhead[154] in the UK, Roscoff in France, as well as Brussels airport,[155] have been placed into this category. The traffic in terms of freight or passengers using these facilities will be of particular importance in deciding whether they constitute a substantial part of the common market. **4.138**

When a transaction raises concerns on several local markets for the same product/service, such markets may be aggregated so as collectively to cover an area which may be considered a substantial part of the common market, at least if there is some geographical continuity between these local markets. In *La Crespelle*, it was held that a French law created a dominant position in a substantial part of the common market because it was 'establishing, in favour of those undertakings, a contiguous series of monopolies territorially limited but together covering the entire territory of a Member State'.[156] If considered independently, most of the local areas in question would not have constituted a substantial part of the common market. **4.139**

Likewise, it seems that local markets within the same Member State can sometimes also be aggregated, even if they are not contiguous, for the purposes of determining whether they together constitute a substantial part of the common market. In *Bodson*,[157] the Court of Justice ruled that 'Article [82 EC] applies in a case in which a number of communal monopolies are granted to a single group of undertakings whose market strategy is determined by the parent company, in a situation in which those monopolies cover a certain part of the national territory'. In this case, the group of undertakings controlled by 'Pompes Funèbres Générales' held an exclusive concession in less than 10 per cent of communes in France, the population of which, however, accounted for more than one-third of the total **4.140**

---

148 In *Suiker Unie*, and in *BP v Commission*, the Court found that southern Germany was a substantial part of the common market; in *Hugin*, the City of London was held to be such a substantial part.
149 Case C-475/99, at para 38.
150 *Cutsforth v Mansfield Inns* [1986] 1 WLR 558 (QBD).
151 *Cadbury Ltd v Kerry Co-op* [1982] ILRM 77.
152 *Porto di Genova* [1997] OJ L301.
153 Commission Annual Report (1994), point 226.
154 ibid (1993), point 234.
155 ibid (1995), point 120.
156 Case C-323/93, *Société Civile Agricole du Centre d'Insémination de la Crespelle Contre Coopérative d'Élevage et d'Insémination Artificielle du Département de la Mayenne* [1994]ECR I-5077.
157 Case 30/87 *Bodson* [1988] ECR 2479.

population since most concessions were granted in big cities. Although there was therefore no geographic continuity between these local markets, there was nevertheless *an economic link* between them, because the strategy was determined by the parent company at the national level.

C. Abuse

(1) General

4.141 The holding of a dominant position is not in itself objectionable under Article 82. It is the abuse of that position which contravenes the provision.

4.142 Article 82 itself does not provide any definition of what constitutes an abuse of a dominant position. It is still debated what conduct is, or should be, prohibited under Article 82. Some take the view that only behaviour that reduces consumer welfare (or total welfare) should be caught by the prohibition. Others believe that Article 82 protects the 'process of competition' in itself, from which economic benefits are assumed to flow. The early approach has often been to protect the economic freedom of other players in the market, particularly competitors. This debate is not settled. This section follows the distinction between exclusionary and exploitative abuses. It identifies certain elements that are common to both categories of abuse before analysing the different types of abuse as identified by the case law and the Commission practice.

4.143 As explained in detail in the introduction to this chapter, a controversy on the types of behaviour prohibited by Article 82 arose in the early years of application of EC competition law. It is now established that this is not an unequivocal concept but that it covers both exclusionary and exploitative practices by dominant undertakings.

4.144 Exclusionary abuses are those practices not based on normal business performance which seek to harm the competitive position of the dominant company's competitors, or to exclude them from the market altogether, ultimately causing harm to the customer. Exclusionary abuses may not have a directly harmful effect on the customers of the dominant firm, and may indeed result in at least short-term benefits for them (eg predatory pricing). However, by foreclosing the market to actual or potential competitors, exclusionary abuses result in long-term harm to the dominant firm's customers or trading partners.

4.145 Exploitative abuses, on the other hand, involve the attempt by a dominant company to exploit the opportunities provided by its market strength in order to harm customers directly, for instance by imposing excessive prices.

4.146 Exploitative abuses can also include discriminatory practices, by which the dominant company applies different treatment, for instance different prices or trading conditions, to similar customers. Discrimination on the basis of nationality or geographic location is one example of such an abuse.

4.147 Any definition that encompasses all these concepts of abuse would be too wide to become a useful analytical tool. Some elements of the concept of abuse, however, are common to exclusionary and exploitative conducts. These are analysed below (see 4.148 to 4.151). The main characteristics and types of exclusionary and exploitative abuses are then described.

(a) Abuse as an Objective Concept: Intent not Required

The concept of abuse is an objective one, not requiring any subjective dimension as to the **4.148** mindset of the dominant firm.[158] It is simply a question of fact to be determined, and it is therefore not necessary to prove that an abuse was intentionally committed.

Notwithstanding the fact that lack of intent cannot be put forward as a defence, it can prove **4.149** to be one of the factors taken into account in assessing the effects of alleged abuse, since the intent explains the motive of an undertaking and, if it is assumed that undertakings act rationally, it could be treated as evidence against the dominant undertaking.

Furthermore, the mental element is relevant to the level of fine which may be imposed by **4.150** the Commission. Negligent or unconscious behaviour will attract a less severe fine than will intentional conduct. Indeed, the Commission guidelines on the method of setting fines consider as an attenuating circumstance the fact that the infringements were committed as a result of negligence or unintentionally.[159]

(b) Abuse by an Undertaking in a Dominant Position

A particular practice may only be considered to constitute an abuse when it has been per- **4.151** formed by an undertaking in a dominant position. Exactly the same practice would not constitute an abuse, and would therefore be perfectly legal, when performed by any other undertaking. The concept of abuse, therefore, even if it is an objective one, only applies to particular entities: those undertakings that have a dominant position. As explained in the introduction to this chapter, this is because these companies have a 'special responsibility not to allow its conduct to impair genuine undistorted competition on the common market'.[160] The economic rationale for the 'special responsibility' of dominant firms is that, in order for unilateral behaviour to reduce consumer welfare or allocative efficiency, the firm is normally required to have a certain degree of market power.

(2) Exclusionary Abuses

(a) General Characteristics

The Court of Justice has, on several occasions, defined exclusionary abuses using the **4.152** following words:

> The concept of an abuse is an objective concept relating to the behaviour of an undertaking in a dominant position which is such as to influence the structure of a market where, as a result of the very presence of the undertaking in question, the degree of competition is weakened and which, through recourse to methods different from those which condition normal competition in products or services on the basis of the transactions of commercial operators, has the effect of hindering the maintenance of the degree of competition still existing in the market or the growth of that competition.[161]

This definition starts by describing the characteristics common to all abuses, in particular **4.153** the fact that an abuse is an objective concept and that it can only be committed by

---

[158] Case 85/76 *Hoffmann-La Roche v Commission* [1979] ECR 461, para 91.
[159] Guidelines on the method of setting fines imposed pursuant to Art 15(2)(a) of Regulation n° 1/2003, OJ C210, 1.09.2006.
[160] Case 322/81 *NV Nederlandsche Baden-Industrie Michelin v Commission* [1983] ECR 3461, para 57.
[161] Case 85/76 *Hoffmann-La Roche v Commission* [1979] ECR 46, para 91.

a dominant undertaking. It then spells out the two particular elements of exclusionary abuses. First it refers to the fact that an abuse only takes place when 'methods different from those which condition normal competition' are used. Second, such methods should have the effect of 'hindering the maintenance of the degree of competition still existing in the market or the growth of that competition'.

(b) Competition on the Merits Distinguished

4.154 The key element in defining exclusionary abuses by firms in a dominant position is the need to distinguish anti-competitive behaviour from the pro-competitive behaviour which the competition rules are intended to foster. The primary question to be considered in determining whether a practice that excludes competitors from the market is abusive or not is whether the practice has been the result of competition on the merits. Any firm will try to exclude its competitors from the market by performing more effectively than them. A firm only abuses its position when the exclusion of competitors is not the consequence of better performance.

4.155 In order to distinguish competition on the merits from exclusionary abuses, it is essential to analyse whether the practice in question may be justified by any reason other than the mere aim to exclude competitors. If the practice reduces the costs of the dominant undertaking or otherwise increases its efficiency it will normally be considered as an example of normal competition, even if it contributes to the elimination of competitors not able to match this increase in performance. If, on the other hand, a practice leads to the exclusion of competitors without increasing the efficiency of the dominant undertaking at all, it is much more likely that such a practice would be considered as an abuse within the meaning of Article 82.

4.156 An example can be used to clarify this issue. The granting of volume rebates (ie rebates granted when customers reach a certain volume of purchases from the dominant undertaking) can in some cases be an abuse and in others a straightforward instance of competition on the merits. If the market concerned enables the achievement of important economies of scale, a dominant undertaking might be interested in offering volume rebates in order to attract new business, increase its output, and therefore profit from the economies of scale and obtain lower average costs. If no such economies of scale are attainable, however, volume rebates could not contribute to an increase in the dominant undertaking's efficiency. In both cases the rebates may have as an effect the exclusion of competitors from the market, but only in the latter circumstances should their granting be considered an abuse.

4.157 In light of the Commission guidelines on the application of Article 81(3) and the horizontal merger guidelines, which make clear that efficiency considerations can be taken into account, it is relevant to ask whether the concept of objective justification under Article 82 could be clarified and perhaps extended to include efficiency considerations similar to those relevant to Article 81(3) and merger control.

4.158 For reasons of consistency, this would probably entail a clear consumer focus, that is, it would have to be decided whether consumers ultimately would be better off if the prima facie abusive behaviour were allowed. Similarly, as under Article 81(3), it would also seem reasonable to require indispensability and no elimination of competition. The Commission's *Microsoft* *decision*[162] gave an example of how such a balancing could be performed. Microsoft argued that efficiencies arising from tying the Windows Media Player with the Windows operating system would outweigh any possible anti-competitive effects from the tying. The Commission, however, considered that what Microsoft presented as benefits of tying could be achieved in the absence of Microsoft tying Windows Media Player with Windows (ie the indispensability test was not met) or that they primarily related to Microsoft's own profitability and hence could not outweigh the distortion to competition created by the tying.

An otherwise abusive practice can be justified by reasons other than proving that the practice **4.159** enhances efficiency. Such reasons can relate to the need to protect subjective rights or other general interests. For example, a dominant undertaking that refuses to supply an existing customer who, as a consequence, is excluded from the market, normally contravenes Article 82. The refusal can be justified if it is adopted in reaction to a breach of contract by the customer. Indeed, in such a case, the general interest in ensuring that contractual obligations can be enforced (and, therefore, that a breach can be sanctioned) may prevail over competition rules objectives. Other objective justifications for each of the most common abuses are described below.

(c) Exclusionary Effect

The second specific element included in the definition of exclusionary abuse reproduced **4.160** above is that the behaviour of the dominant undertaking 'has the effect of hindering the maintenance of the degree of competition still existing in the market or the growth of that competition'.

In order to analyse this element of the definition, it must first be said that the effect required **4.161** by the definition of the Court of Justice can be either actual or potential. Indeed, in order to consider conduct by a dominant undertaking as abusive, there is no need to prove that it has actually hindered competition. It is enough to demonstrate that the conduct is likely to produce such an effect or, as the Court said in *Commercial Solvents*,[163] that it 'risks' producing it. This is the same interpretation that the Court has adopted for the equivalent provision of Article 81.

Second, the definition of the Court of Justice requires that the behaviour from the domi- **4.162** nant undertaking 'hinders the degree of competition' in the relevant market. It appears that this should be understood as requesting that the behaviour in question is able to alter the structure of the market, by weakening or eliminating competitors. There is no need, however, to prove that such an effect is substantial. Indeed, in markets where an undertaking holds a dominant position, competition is already weakened and any further modification of the market structure could strengthen the market power of the undertaking. In this respect, therefore, the interpretation of Article 82 differs from the interpretation of Article 81, which requires the existence of an appreciable anti-competitive effect.

In practice, and depending on the characteristics of the market analysed, the Court of **4.163** Justice has applied Article 82 to practices affecting market structure in different ways.

---

162 *Microsoft* [2004]. This decision is under appeal to the CFI.
163 See, for instance, *Commercial Solvents*, para 25.

In some cases, the weakening of one competitor has been sufficient for the Court to consider that the conduct producing such effect was abusive. In other cases, the Court has required, at least, the exclusion of a competitor,[164] even if other competitors could remain in the market. Finally, more recently, the Court has required proof that the conduct would completely eliminate any competition from the market in question.[165] In all these cases, however, the likely result of the behaviour pursued would have been the maintenance or strengthening of the market power of the dominant undertaking.

4.164 In some cases, however, the Court of Justice has applied Article 82 to behaviour not at all likely to affect market structure and, therefore, the degree of competition in the market.[166] In these isolated cases, Article 82 appears to be used in order to pursue different objectives and, in particular, to ensure fairness between the different companies operating in a certain market.

(d) Types of Exclusionary Abuses

4.165 Exclusionary behaviour may take many diverse forms. Any type of behaviour by a dominant undertaking that can, directly or indirectly, affect the competitive position of a competitor might be caught by Article 82. Many different denominations and classifications of types of abusive behaviour have been suggested by the doctrine.[167]

4.166 The different possible types of exclusionary abuses are classified below in a few broad categories according to the methods used to commit the abuse. Abuses committed by means of a refusal to deal are analysed first. This category includes different types of pure refusals to deal, unilaterally adopted by the dominant undertaking (eg refusals to supply, refusals to grant a licence, refusals to access to an essential facility). It also covers refusals to deal found in contracts between the dominant undertaking and its customers or suppliers (ie exclusive dealing). Finally, it also includes refusals to deal by a dominant undertaking towards customers which do not accept the imposition of supplementary obligations not having any connection with the supply of the product or service for which the undertaking in question is dominant (ie tying).

4.167 The second broad category analysed below concerns abuses committed by means of pricing practices. All undertakings active in the internal market are expected to engage in price competition for the benefit of consumers and for the sake of a good allocation of resources. Undertakings enjoying a dominant position should be encouraged to charge competitive prices, since their market power generally enables them to set prices above competitive levels. However, price cutting undertaken by a dominant company to implement its exclusionary strategies is not legitimate. This includes predatory practices (ie pricing below costs), as well as practices aimed at squeezing competitors (ie pricing intermediate components to inhibit competition in the final product market) or at discriminating between customers. As discounts and rebates may constitute exclusionary abuses and constitute one of the main

---

[164] See, for instance, ibid.

[165] Case C-7/97 *Oscar Bronner GmbH & Co. v Mediaprint Zeitungs* [1998], para 41.

[166] See, for instance, Case 27/76 *United Brands v Commission* [1978] ECR 207.

[167] See, for instance, M. Waelbroeck et A. Frignani. *Comentaire J. Megret*, iv: *Concurrence* (Brussels: Éditions ULB, 1997), 244.

methods used to price discriminate between customers; abuses committed through these practices (eg fidelity rebates, target discounts) are also covered under this section. Finally, a pricing policy could be also used by a dominant undertaking to induce customers to accept tying. In this case we will refer to bundling.

Third, different possible types of abuse aimed at raising competitors' costs will be described. **4.168** In particular, this section will deal with legal harassment, a practice intended to increase the legal costs incurred by competitors. Fourth, the abuses committed by means of allocating costs from the activity where the undertaking is dominant to activities where it faces competition (ie cross-subsidisation) will be dealt with.

Finally, some types of structural abuses will be analysed. Structural abuses consist in those **4.169** types of commercial actions by dominant firms, or transactions involving them, which produce an immediate change in the structure of the market to the detriment of competition. These include, for instance, acquisitions by the dominant undertaking of control in another undertaking (or of minority shareholdings).

(e) Refusal to Deal

(i) Unilateral Refusals to Deal

General principles In most EC Member States, the legal order embodies the principles **4.170** of a market economy and the freedom to engage in business activities. A corollary of these principles is the freedom granted to undertakings to deal with whomsoever they like. These principles are also enshrined in EU competition rules. As the CFI has stated 'The case law of the ECJ indirectly recognizes the importance of safeguarding free enterprise when applying the competition rules of the Treaty where it expressly acknowledges that even an undertaking in dominant position may, in certain cases, refuse to sell . . . without failing under the prohibition laid down in Article 82.'[168]

Freedom to deal is a principle which, in addition to its legal and political nature, is also jus- **4.171** tified by economic considerations. Indeed, ensuring that companies will be able freely to use their assets and output fosters investment, innovation, and competition in the long term. If companies knew in advance that they would normally be obliged to give competitors access to their assets or output, for instance a facility that they have built or a new production process that they have developed and patented, the incentive to engage in such activities might be reduced.[169]

In view of the above, the legal order would normally oblige a firm to deal against its will only **4.172** in those rare situations when it is necessary in order to protect a public interest. It is clear from case law concerning the application of Article 82 that the refusal to deal or the exercise of an exclusive right by the owner may involve abusive conduct only in situations where there is particular harm to competition.

Elements of the abuse The general conditions that are necessary to establish an abusive **4.173** refusal to deal—the conduct, the effects, and the absence of objective justification—are

---

[168] Case T-41/96 *Bayer AG v Commission* [2000] ECR II-3383, para 180.
[169] See para 57 of Opinion of Advocate General Jacobs in Case C-7/97 *Oscar Bronner GmbH & Co. v Mediaprint Zeitungs.*

described in the following paragraphs. Afterwards, each of these conditions is examined in greater detail for specific types of refusals to deal.

4.174 *Conduct: refusal to deal* There is a wide array of conduct that can be classified as refusal to deal. The following is a non-exhaustive list of types of refusal that might be caught by Article 82: refusal to supply products and services; refusal to provide information; refusal to license intellectual property rights; refusal to grant access to an essential facility; or refusal to become part of a network. A refusal to deal can, obviously, take the form both of a refusal to start dealing, as well as of the unilateral termination of an ongoing deal (eg a withdrawal of supply).

4.175 The concept of a refusal to deal covers not only the pure refusal, but also agreement by the dominant company to deal but under unreasonable conditions. In this regard, price and non-price conditions can be distinguished. As to the latter, the Commission has acknowledged that non-refusal conditional upon acceptance of other unrelated products or services could be considered an abuse.[170] An obligation imposed by a dominant supplier to indicate the geographical destination of the goods supplied and the identity of the final customers may also considered an abuse of a dominant position.[171]

4.176 Excessive prices, as well as being abusive in themselves, may also amount to an effective refusal[172] (see below a detailed analysis of the concept of excessive prices). Finally, the Commission has acknowledged that undue and inexplicable or unjustified delays in responding to a request for access may also constitute an abuse.[173]

4.177 *Effects: harm to competition* A refusal to deal should only be covered by Article 82 when it harms competition in a particular market. The market in question may be either the market where the dominant undertaking is present (referred to as a primary line abuse) or any other market (referred to as a secondary line abuse).

4.178 In the first case, the refusal can directly harm competitors. The most obvious example is that of a dominant undertaking in an upstream market (eg managing harbour facilities), which also operates in a market downstream (eg operating ferries) from the market where it is dominant. The dominant undertaking might be abusing its position if it refuses to deal in the upstream market with undertakings competing in the downstream market, in order to strengthen its position in this second market.

4.179 In the second case (secondary line abuse) the refusal to deal with particular customers operating in a market where the dominant undertaking is not present can discriminate between them, which might harm competition in this market. The refusal, however, may also be addressed to customers (eg distributors) who favour competitors to the dominant undertaking. In this case the refusal would also indirectly harm competition in the market where the dominant undertaking is present.

---

[170] Notice on the application of the EC competition rules to cross-border credit transfers [1995] OJ para 26.

[171] *Polaroid/SSI Europe*, 13th Report on Competition Policy, paras 155–157.

[172] Notice on the application of the Competition Rules to access agreements in the telecommunications sector (1998) OJ C265/02, para 97.

[173] ibid, para 95.

In order to determine whether competition will be harmed by a refusal to deal, the first **4.180** question to examine is the extent of the handicap imposed on an actual or potential competitor by such a refusal. If the competitor remains able to operate in the market by other means (eg to obtain the inputs required to operate in such a market from another supplier or to replicate the essential facility by itself) without its efficiency being seriously impaired (to the point when it becomes no longer a competitive constraint) it is clear that the refusal should not be considered an abuse.

In order ultimately to harm consumers, however, it is not enough that a refusal to deal **4.181** weakens a competitor or excludes it from the market. The elimination or weakening of such a competitor should be likely to have an impact in market prices or outputs. This can be the case if the refusal to deal blocks the emergence of a new service or product, or if, by eliminating competitors as efficient (or likely to become as efficient) as the dominant firm, it weakens the competitive pressures exerted over the dominant firm. The case law in relation to this issue, ie to what degree competition in the market in question should be harmed to establish that a refusal to deal violates Article 82, also differs, depending on the type of refusal concerned.

Absence of an objective justification   A refusal to deal by a dominant undertaking that prima **4.182** facie harms competition as described above will not be considered an abuse under Article 82 of the EC Treaty if it is objectively justified. This will be the case if the refusal can be justified on business grounds other than the intention to eliminate a competitor from the market.

The justifications may relate, first, to the characteristics of the dominant undertaking. For **4.183** instance, such an undertaking cannot be required to supply a customer or a competitor if it does not have enough capacity to satisfy its own needs[174] or if the costs of dealing render the deal unprofitable. It should also be possible to refuse to supply a competitor if, for efficiency reasons, the dominant undertaking decides to stop providing the product or service independently. It must be noted, however, that such efficiency considerations have played a limited role in case law. For instance, in *Commercial Solvents*,[175] the Court condemned a refusal to supply an intermediate product to a competitor, even where the dominant undertaking had decided to integrate vertically and itself produce the final product.

Secondly, the justifications may refer to the behaviour of the undertaking requesting the trans- **4.184** action. For instance, a dominant undertaking cannot be required to deal with a company which is at risk of bankruptcy, which does not respect the agreed conditions of the deal, or which might put in danger the quality and reputation of the supplier.

Neither can a dominant undertaking be obliged to treat its clients equally in all circum- **4.185** stances. In times of shortages, for instance, a dominant firm is allowed to favour its more regular customers over occasional ones.[176] It is not permitted, however, to favour those exclusively dealing with it over those also dealing with competitors.[177]

---

[174] *Filtrona/Tabacalera*. XVIVth Report on Competition Policy (1989), point 61.
[175] Case 6-7/73 *Commercial Solvents v EC Commission* [1974] ECR 223.
[176] Case 77/77 *BP v Commission* [1978] ECR 1513, para 34.
[177] Case C-310/93 P *BPB Industries pcl & Anor v EC Commission*.

4.186 **Types of unilateral refusals to deal**   Different types of refusal to deal can be distinguished, according to the relationship prevailing between the dominant company and the company subject to the refusal. First of all, refusals to deal with competitors will be examined. A distinction will be made between interruption to supply (ie refusal to continue dealing with a current customer who is also a competitor downstream) and refusal to deal for the first time with a rival. In this second category, some specific refusals will be examined, in particular refusal of access to an essential facility and refusal to license intellectual property. Finally, refusals to supply distributors or retailers (secondary line abuse) will be examined briefly.

4.187 *Ceasing to supply a competitor*   The most obvious instance of a refusal to deal is the interruption of supply to a competitor of a raw material needed in order to be present in the market. The classic case in EC case law in this field is *Commercial Solvents*.[178] This US company had a dominant position on the market for aminobutamol, a chemical used in the production of ethambutol and drugs based on this component. Through its Italian subsidiary it sold aminobutamol to an Italian company, Zoja, for more than three years. After this period, Commercial Solvents' Italian subsidiary modified its strategy and started to produce drugs based on ethambutol and decided no longer to supply aminobutamol, the intermediate product. Zoja complained and both the Commission and the Court considered the refusal to deal to be an abuse within the meaning of Article 82 of the EC Treaty. The Court rejected the argument that the Italian subsidiary of Commercial Solvents had started to produce the final product as a justification for the termination of supply, which had resulted in the exclusion from the market of one of its main competitors.

4.188 An interruption in supply to competitors may also involve final products. The Commission prohibited the refusal by British Sugar to supply industrial sugar to Napier Brown, an established customer, after the latter had attempted to compete with British Sugar in the retail sugar market.[179] The refusal could also relate to secondary products, such as spare parts. In *Hugin*,[180] for instance, the Court considered that a Swedish manufacturer of cash registers abused its dominant position for terminating its supply of spare parts to Lipton, a UK company operating in the market for repair and maintenance of cash registers, where Hugin was also present. A similar abuse was found in Hilti.[181]

4.189 The termination of other types of contract with competitors, substantially harming competition as a consequence, might also be covered by Article 82. The Commission Decision in *British Midland/Aer Lingus*[182] is an example of this. The case concerned the refusal to interline, which is an airline practice consisting in issuing tickets on behalf of other airlines, allowing passengers to use a single ticket for a journey made on two different airlines. In the case in question, Aer Lingus, the dominant operator on the Dublin–London route, terminated its agreement to interline with British Midland when the latter started to compete on the Dublin–London route. It must be noted that the absence of interlining would not have

---

[178] Case 6-7/73 *Commercial Solvents v EC Commission* [1974] ECR 223.
[179] *Napier Brown/British Sugar* [1988] OJ L284/41.
[180] Case 22/78 *Hugin v Commission* [1979] ECR 1869.
[181] Case T-30/89 *Hilti v Commission* [1992] ECR 1439 and C-53/92 P.
[182] *British Midland/Aer Lingus* [1992] OJ L96/34. See also *Lufthansa/Air Europe*. 20th report on Competition Policy 1991, p 83.

prevented British Midland from operating on the route, but would have probably forced it to offer more flights and incur additional costs. The Commission considered that the significant handicap imposed on British Midland was enough to consider the refusal to interline an abuse of a dominant position.

As to the required harm to competition, case law appears less strict in cases where the refusal **4.190** concerns an existing customer than in refusals to deal for the first time. While in some cases where the ECJ has found an abuse, such as *Commercial Solvents*,[183] the existing customer was clearly forced out of the market due to the refusal to supply by the only provider of an indispensable raw material, completely eliminating competition in the downstream market, in other cases where a refusal was considered abusive there were alternative sources of supply available to existing customers. From an economic point of view, the effects are likely to be the same if the refusal affects a new or an existing customer and, therefore, there should be no reason to treat refusals to existing customers more leniently.[184]

It is only when objective justifications are examined that the two situations may be dealt with **4.191** differently. Indeed, the existence of an ongoing commercial relationship can contribute to prove that dealing with that specific customer is a profitable activity for the dominant firm and, therefore, makes it more difficult for the dominant firm to justify the refusal on pure commercial grounds.

Refusal to deal with a competitor   The refusal by a dominant company in an upstream **4.192** market to deal for the first time with a company that would become its competitor in a downstream market may, in certain circumstances, become an abuse. Two situations will be examined in particular: refusal of access to an essential facility and refusal to license intellectual property.

Refusal to grant access to an essential facility   The Commission defines an essential facil- **4.193** ity as a 'facility or infrastructure which is essential for reaching customers and/or enabling competitors to carry on their business, and which cannot be replicated by any reasonable means'.[185] In accordance with application of the general principles applying to other types of refusals to deal, the refusal to grant access to such an essential facility, which eliminates competition in a downstream market and which is not objectively justified is prohibited by Article 82.[186]

As its name indicates, the basic characteristic of the concept of essential facility is that access **4.194** to it is essential in order to operate in a particular market. In other words, it is not sufficient

---

[183] Case 6-7/73 *Commercial Solvents v EC Commission* [1974] ECR 223.

[184] See, for instance, R. Subiotto and R. O'Donoghue, 'Defining the scope of the duty of dominant firms to deal with existing customers under Article 82 EC' [2003] ECLR.

[185] Notice on the application of the Competition Rules to access agreements in the telecommunications sector [1998] OJ C265/02, para 68.

[186] See, on essential facilities in general: J. Temple Lang, 'Defining legitimate competition: companies' duties to supply competitors and access to essential facilities' [1994] Fordham International Law Journal 2; D. Glasl, 'Essential facilities doctrine in EC anti-trust law: a contribution to the current debate' [1994] 6 ECLR; J. S. Venit and J. J. Kallaugher, *Essential Facilities: A Comparative Law approach* (Fordham Corporate Law Institute, 1994); R. Derek, 'Essential facilities and the obligations to supply competitors under UK and EC competition law' [1996] ECLR 8.

that the dominant undertaking's control over the facility gives it a competitive advantage; it should give it a genuine stranglehold on the market in question. The duplication of the facility must be impossible or extremely difficult owing to physical, geographical, or legal constraints.[187] As to the latter, it should be proved that it is totally uneconomical to duplicate the facility, in other words that the total income generated in the market in question would not generate profits from two facilities. It is not enough to prove that it is not economical for a given competitor to duplicate the facility, because the competitor has a limited turnover.[188]

4.195 The concept of essential facility was first used by the Commission in relation to transport infrastructures and, in particular, in relation to harbour facilities. In *Sea Containers v Stena Sealink*,[189] an interim measures decision concerning the port of Holyhead in Wales, the Commission concluded that Stena Sealink, the port operator, had abused its dominant position in the market for port services by refusing access to its harbour to a potential competitor in the market for ferry services. Through this refusal, Stena Sealink, which was also a ferry operator, was protecting its position in this market.[190]

4.196 Access to harbour facilities has become a common subject of cases concerning essential facilities. The Commission has also adopted a decision concerning the access to the Port of Rødby[191] (Denmark), and has intervened in relation to the access to the Ports of Elsinore (Denmark), and Roscoff[192] (France). It has also applied Article 82 to the imposition of non-equitable conditions in relation to access to the Port of Genoa (Italy).[193] In some of these cases, where ports are operated by public companies or companies entrusted with special rights, the Commission considered that Article 86 had been infringed together with Article 82 of the EC Treaty.

4.197 Several cases of access to essential facilities have also arisen in the air transport field. In *London European-Sabena*[194] the Commission declared the refusal by Sabena to give a competing airline access to its computer reservation system (CRS) to be an abuse of the dominant position that the former held in the Belgian market for computer reservation services. Sabena had engaged in this conduct in order to force the competing airline to raise its fares for the London–Brussels line, for which there was limited competition. In the same aviation sector, landing and take-off slots,[195] landing lanes,[196] and underground pipes used for

---

[187] See opinion of the Advocate General Jacobs in C-7/97 *Oscar Bronner Gmbh & Co. v Mediaprint Zeitungs* [1998].

[188] Case C-7/97 *Oscar Bronner GmbH & Co v Mediaprint Zeitungs* [1998], para 45. See also the opinion of the Advocate General in the same case.

[189] *Sea Containers v Stena Sealink (Interim Measures)* [1993] OJ 1994 L15/8.

[190] The evolution of this particular market may have proved the Commission wrong in defining such a harbour as an essential facility. Indeed, competition to the same route seems to have been developed from the Liverpool harbour, which had been excluded by the Commission decision from the relevant market. See National Economic Research Associates (NERA), Competition Brief No. 4, January 1999.

[191] *Port of Rødby* [1994] OJ L55/52.

[192] Commission Annual Report (1996), point 131.

[193] *Porto di Genova* [1997] OJ L301.

[194] *London European-Sabena* [1988] OJ L317/47.

[195] See Council Regulation 95/93 on common rules for the allocation of slots at Community airports [1994] OJ L14/1.

[196] *Flughafen Frankfurt/Main AG* [1998] OJ L72/30.

refuelling aircrafts[197] have also been considered essential facilities. On the other hand, loco- motives or train crews were considered not to be such essential facilities by the Court in *European Night Services*.[198]

Essential facilities cases may also arise in recently liberalised markets, where former monop- **4.198** olists still hold the ownership of infrastructure needed by new entrants in the market. This is the case for the telecommunications market, where the dominant telecommunications operators own the main networks, as well as energy markets, where former monopolists control electricity lines, pipelines, and other facilities to which access is required in order to compete in the energy distribution market. The Commission has adopted a Notice on the application of the Competition Rules to access agreements in the telecommunications sector,[199] which clarifies how it intends to apply Article 82 to these issues.

In addition to transport and liberalised markets, essential facilities can be found in other **4.199** sectors. In the financial services sectors, payment systems (ie systems established between financial entities in order to allow their customers to use non-cash payment instruments such as credit transfers, cheques, or cards) can also sometimes be considered essential facil- ities. In the Notice on the application of competition rules to cross-border credit transfers the Commission considers that such a system will be an essential facility when participa- tion in it is necessary for banks to compete on the relevant market, which would be the case if a new competitor could not feasibly gain access to another system or create its own system in order to compete on the relevant market.[200]

The Commission has actually considered that certain cross-border transfers systems notified **4.200** to it were essential facilities,[201] but that access was granted on a non-discriminatory basis and that, therefore, the competition rules were not infringed. In a single case, concerning the refusal to allow La Poste to have access to SWIFT, a network for processing and transmitting cross-border bank operations, the Commission appeared ready to apply Article 82 to a refusal to deal in this sector. However, Swift adopted non-discriminatory access conditions and the case was closed without a final decision.[202]

The leading case concerning 'essential facilities' is the preliminary ruling in *Oscar Bronner*,[203] **4.201** where the Court analysed whether a national newspaper home delivery service could be considered an essential facility. It concluded that it was not, because first, another nation- wide distribution system could be established. The Court did not consider material that a newspaper with limited circulation would not find it economic to establish a nationwide distribution system. Rather, to consider the system as an essential facility, it was necessary

---

[197] *Disma*, 23th Report on Competition Policy (1994), p 80.

[198] Joined cases T-374-75/94, T-384/94, and T-388/94 [1998] *European Night Services v Commission*.

[199] Notice on the application of the Competition Rules to access agreements in the telecommunications sector (1998) OJ C265/02.

[200] Notice on the application of the EC competition rules to cross-border credit transfers [1995] OJ C251/3.

[201] See Luc Gyselen, *EU Antitrust Law in the Area of Financial Services: Capita Selecta for the Cautious Shaping of a Policy* (Fordham Corporate Law Institute, 1986), 359–61.

[202] Publication of an undertaking. *La Poste v Swift + GUF* [1997] OJ C335/3.

[203] Case C-7/97 *Oscar Bronner GmbH & Co. v Mediaprint Zeitungs* [1998], para 41. See also, opinion of Advocate General in the same case.

to prove that the market could not sustain a competing system at all. Second, the Court also pointed out that there were alternative, even if less convenient, means to distribute newspapers, such as mail deliveries or conventional newspaper retail outlets.

4.202   As far as harm to competition is concerned, the Commission considers that the refusal of access to an essential facility must lead to the competitor's activities being made either impossible or seriously and unavoidably uneconomic.[204] In *Oscar Bronner*[205] the Court took a similar position on this point. It held that the refusal to grant access to a distribution facility would constitute an abuse only if there was no real or potential substitute for it. In the same judgment the ECJ established that the effect of the refusal should be the elimination of competition in the downstream market.[206]

4.203   *Refusal to license intellectual property rights*   As explained above, the existence of a patent, trademark, or copyright is not sufficient to establish a dominant position. Nevertheless, when it is established that the existence of such rights confers a dominant position, in exceptional circumstances, the refusal to license them may constitute an abuse of that dominant position.

4.204   Intellectual property rights are established in order to reward the creativity, quality, or innovation of their holders. They grant to their holders the exclusive use of an intellectual creation, a trademark or a patent for a certain period of time. This may lead to the elimination of competition in the market for which the right was granted, but this is a consequence of the existence of such a right and a refusal to license it cannot be considered as an abuse of the dominant position of the holder of the right. If this were the case, those rights would no longer fulfil their main purpose, and creativity or innovation would no longer be rewarded. Nevertheless, in some cases the refusal to license such rights may go beyond what is necessary to fulfil their essential function and may harm competition in a market related to the one for which the right was granted.[207] In such exceptional cases, Article 82 may oblige the holder of the right to license it.

4.205   One example of a case where the refusal to grant a license of an IP right was not considered an abuse is *Volvo v Veng*.[208] Independent producers of spare parts for cars were prevented from competing with car manufacturers because they held design rights and refused to license them. The Court established the principle that it is lawful for a dominant company to obtain exclusive rights under intellectual property legislation and that a refusal to license them does not itself constitute an abuse within the meaning of Article 82.

4.206   In a more recent case, however, the Court confirmed the Commission's view that in certain circumstances a refusal to grant an intellectual property right could amount to an abuse of

---

[204]   Notice on the application of the Competition Rules to access agreements in the telecommunications sector [1998] OJ C265/02, para 91.

[205]   Case C-7/97 *Oscar Bronner GmbH & Co. v Mediaprint Zeitungs* [1998], para 41. See also, opinion of Advocate General in the same case.

[206]   Case C-7/97 *Oscar Bronner GmbH & Co. v Mediaprint Zeitungs* [1998].

[207]   See interpretation of previous case law by Advocate General Jacobs in its opinion on Case C-7/97 *Oscar Bronner GmbH & Co. v Mediaprint Zeitungs* [1998], para 43.

[208]   238/87 *Volvo AB v Erik Veng* [1988] ECR 6211. See also 53/87 *Consorzio Italiano della Componentistica di Ricambio per Autoveicoli v Régie Nationale des Usines Renault* [1988] ECR 6039.

a dominant position. Indeed, in *Magill*[209] the Commission considered that RTE and BBC, the main broadcasters in Ireland, held dominant positions on the markets for the supply of their programme lists (protected by a copyright) and that they had abused this dominant position by refusing to give details of their programmes to other magazines more than a day in advance. This made it impossible for anyone to publish a single independent weekly magazine covering all broadcasters' programmes. Both the CFI[210] and the Court of Justice[211] confirmed this view. They relied on the fact that the refusal to license had prevented the appearance of a new product for which there was a potential consumer demand; that there was no justification for such refusal either in the activity of television broadcasting or in that of publishing television magazines, and that the broadcasters, by their refusal, had reserved to themselves the secondary market of weekly television guides by excluding all competition on that market.

The position of the CFI and the Court of Justice in *Magill* was subject to considerable criticism for eroding the content of intellectual property rights.[212] In a subsequent case, *Tiercé Ladbroke*,[213] the CFI confronted this criticism by specifying the exceptional circumstances in which a refusal to license an IP right may infringe Article 82. The case concerned the Commission's rejection of a complaint by the leading operator in the Belgian horse betting market against the refusal by undertakings holding the video and audio rights on French horse races to license such rights for use in the complainant's betting shops in Belgium. The CFI considered that, whereas in *Magill* the refusal to grant IP rights had impeded the complainant from entering a market, in the instant case the complainant was not only present, but was the leading operator in the market for which the use of the right was requested. In addition to this, the refusal to grant a licence applied to all Belgian betting operators and, therefore, did not entail any discrimination. It concluded by saying: 'The refusal to supply the applicant could not fall within the prohibition laid down by Article 8[2] unless it concerned a product or service which was either essential for the exercise of the activity in question, in that there was no real or potential substitute, or was a new product whose introduction might be prevented, despite specific, constant and regular potential demand on the part of consumers'. **4.207**

The conditions necessary to establish whether a refusal to license IP rights could be considered abusive have recently been clarified by the ECJ's preliminary ruling in the *IMS* case.[214] The ruling related to the refusal by IMS, the leading provider of pharmaceutical sales data **4.208**

---

[209] T-69/89 *Radio Telefis Eireann v Commission* [1991] ECR II-485; T-70/88 *BBC Enterprises Ltd. v Commission* [1991] ECR II-535 and T-76/89 *Independent Television Publications v Commission* [1991] ECR II-575.

[210] T-69/89 *Radio Telefis Eireann v Commission* [1991] ECR II-485; T-70/88 *BBC Enterprises Ltd. v Commission* [1991] ECR II-535 and T-76/89 *Independent Television Publications v Commission* [1991] ECR II-575.

[211] C-241 and 242/91 *RTE and ITP v Commission* [1995] ECR I-743.

[212] See Opinion of the Advocate General Gulman on cases C-241 and 242/91 *RTE and ITP v Commission* [1994] and also I. Forrester, 'Software licensing in the light of current EC competition law considerations' [1992] *ECLR* 5, 5–20 and R. Subiotto, 'The right to deal with whom one pleases under EEC Competition Law: small contribution to a necessary debate' [1992] *ECLR* 13, 234–244.

[213] T-504/93 *Tiercé Ladbroke v Commission* [1997] ECR II-923; appeal pending (C-300/97 P).

[214] Case C-418/01, *IMS Health* (2004). The Commission had previously adopted an interim measures decision in relation to the same practice, which was suspended by order of the President of the CFI (order upheld by the President of the ECJ) and finally withdrawn by the Commission.

in Germany, to license its IP rights concerning the structure used to divide Germany into geographic areas ('brick structure') in order to present sales data to customers. The structure appeared to have been developed with participation by the pharmaceutical laboratories, which could have created a particular dependency by users with respect to that structure.

4.209   The ECJ started by summarising existing case law as imposing three conditions for determining a refusal to license an IP right as abusive: preventing the emergence of a new product for which there is a potential consumer demand; being unjustified; and excluding any competition on a related market. It then transposed these conditions to the facts of the case, and left it to the national court to decide, first, whether the 'undertaking which requested the licence intends to offer, on the market for the supply of the data in question, new products or services not offered by the copyright owner and for which there is potential consumer demand'; second whether the 'brick structure constitutes, upstream, an indispensable factor in the downstream supply of German regional sales data for pharmaceutical products'; and finally 'whether the refusal by IMS to grant a licence to use the structure is capable of excluding competition on the market for the supply of German regional sales data on pharmaceutical products'.

4.210   With regard to the condition of the abuse concerning harm to competition, in *Magill*[215] and *IMS*[216] the ECJ followed an approach, in relation to the refusal to provide IP rights, similar to that established in *Oscar Bronner* in relation to access to essential facilities. The ECJ established that the effect of the refusal should be the elimination of competition in the downstream market.[217] It clearly indicated that the dominant company is normally allowed to reserve for itself the market for which the IP right was granted (to create such a monopoly is, indeed, the basic function of IP rights) and that a refusal would be abusive only when it would prevent the emergence of a new product in a downstream market.

4.211   The concept of new product was clarified by the ECJ in *IMS*, by indicating that 'the refusal . . . may be regarded as abusive only where the undertaking which requested the licence does not intend to limit itself essentially to duplicating the goods or services already offered on the secondary market by the owner of the copyright, but intends to produce new goods or services not offered by the owner of the right and for which there is a potential consumer demand'.[218] While *Magill* could have been read as requesting the exclusion of a totally new category of product (a television guide), this paragraph from *IMS* can be read as simply requesting the exclusion of a product within the same category but with different characteristics (different presentations of data on sales of pharmaceutical products).

4.212   *Refusal to provide information*   In some cases, companies cannot have access to certain markets if they do not obtain proprietary information from their competitors. In such cases, the refusal to provide this information can also constitute an abuse under Article 82 of the EC Treaty.

---

215   T-69/89 *Radio Telefis Eireann v Commission* [1991] ECR II-485.
216   Case C-418/01 *IMS Health* [2004].
217   Case C-7/97 *Oscar Bronner GmbH & Co. v Mediaprint Zeitungs* [1998].
218   Case C-418/01 *IMS Health* [2004], para 49.

The Commission, for instance, obliged *IBM*[219] to provide technical information to man- **4.213** ufacturers of peripheral computer products (eg printers) in sufficient time to allow them to compete with IBM in the market for such products. In other cases, the modification of technical standards without informing competitors has also been considered an abuse. For instance, in *Decca Navigator System*,[220] the dominant manufacturer of electronic equipment for maritime navigation modified the electronic signals produced by its equipment, without informing manufacturers of competing equipment, with the consequence that all competing equipment produced unreliable results. The Commission considered that this practice constituted an abuse within the meaning of Article 82 of the EC Treaty.

Not only technical information has been the subject of this type of abuse. In *ITT Promedia/* **4.214** *Belgacom*[221] the Commission considered that the refusal by the dominant telecom operator in Belgium to provide, on reasonable terms, data about customers of telephone services to a new entrant in the telephone directories market also constituted an abuse of dominant position.

The most recent Commission decision[222] in this area concerns the practices of *Microsoft* in **4.215** the market for operating systems for work group servers. The Commission found that Microsoft had committed an abuse by refusing to disclose certain information to its competitors which prevented their operating systems for work group servers from enjoying full interoperability with the Microsoft PC operating system and servers.

In order to conclude that such a refusal was abusive, the Commission established, first, that **4.216** interoperability with the Windows PC operating system, in view of the position enjoyed by Microsoft in this market, was necessary for a work group server operating system vendor viably to stay in the market and that there are no actual or potential substitutes to disclosures by Microsoft of such information.[223]

Second, it established that, while competitors are still active in the market for work group **4.217** server operating systems, the refusal to provide interoperability allowed Microsoft to increase its market share to the level of dominance and risked eventual elimination of competition in the market. Indeed, the refusal was already reducing the level of innovation in the market and diminishing customers' choices. It must be noted that Microsoft's refusal to provide interoperability had not prevented its competitors from offering operating systems for work group servers, but it prevented them from offering certain innovative features in their own operative systems for work group servers. According to the Commission, the impossibility of competitors being able to offer such innovations risked eliminating competition in this market.[224]

---

[219] Undertakings offered by IBM [1984], 14th report on Competition Policy, paras 94–95.

[220] *Decca Navigator System* [1988] OJ L43/27, paras 108–110.

[221] IP/97/292.

[222] Commission Decision COMP/37.792—*Microsoft* (24.03.06). This decision is under appeal to the CFI. Case T-201/04 *Microsoft v Commission*.

[223] It must be noted that the Commission also established that Microsoft had discontinued previous levels of supply by progressively reducing the information available to competitors, as stated in the Decision, 'it has been highlighted that the European Courts have given weight to circumstances where a refusal to supply constituted a disruption of previous levels of supply'(para 578).

[224] Commission Decision COMP/37.792—*Microsoft* (24.03.06), paras 693–701. This decision is under appeal to the CFI: Case T-201/04 *Microsoft v Commission*.

4.218   The Commission also examined whether some justifications advanced by Microsoft could be taken into account. First, it dismissed the claim that, by imposing interoperability, the Commission was obliging Microsoft to reveal IP rights and allowing customers to clone its products. Second, it also refused to accept that Microsoft's practices could be justified in order to protect its incentives to innovate. The Commission considered not only that, despite the obligation to facilitate interoperability, Microsoft would have an interest in improving the interoperability between its own Windows PC and work group server operating systems, but also that, in any event, the incentives to innovate that Microsoft could derive from such a refusal would be compensated by the positive impact that interoperability would have on the degree of innovation by the whole industry.

4.219   ***Refusals to deal with retailers or customers***   This category of refusals to supply concerns customers which are not competitors of the dominant undertaking. Normally such a refusal will not affect competition in the markets where the dominant company operates. In certain instances, however, the refusal may be addressed to retailers or other specific customers in order to prevent them from favouring competitors of the dominant undertaking. In this case the refusal would also indirectly harm competition in the market where the dominant undertaking is present.

4.220   In *United Brands*, for instance, the Court condemned a producer of bananas for refusing to supply to Olesen, a Danish distributor which had taken part in an advertising campaign by one of United Brands' competitors. The Commission also adopted interim measures against the refusal by Boosey & Hawkes, the leading UK manufacturer of brass instruments, to supply to two of its customers, resellers of brass instruments, when it discovered that they had created BBI, a competing manufacturer of brass instruments.[225]

4.221   As for harm to competition, it must be noted that in these cases the refusal would not have changed substantially the level of competition existing in the downstream market. Nevertheless, the conduct was found to be abusive because it threatened to eliminate competition in the upstream market where the dominant firm operated.

4.222   With regard to objective justifications, it should also be clear that a dominant undertaking is entitled to refuse to supply a customer who is damaging its legitimate distribution policy. The opposite position would impede dominant undertakings from enforcing efficient methods of improving distribution. Nevertheless, case law is contradictory on this issue. In *United Brands*[226] the Court accepted that a dominant undertaking is entitled to defend its commercial interests provided that the measures taken are proportionate. Nevertheless, the ECJ went as far as stating as a general principle that 'a firm cannot stop supplying a long standing customer who abides by regular commercial practice',[227] independent of the availability of alternatives for the customer in question.

4.223   Also, in *BBI/Boosey & Hawkes*,[228] the Commission stated in general terms that when the customer transfers its principal activity to the promotion of a competing brand, the dominant

---

225   *BBI/Boosey & Hawkes* [1987] OJ L286/36.
226   Case 27/76 *United Brands v Commission* [1978] ECR 207.
227   ibid.
228   *BBI/Boosey & Hawkes* [1987] OJ L286/36, para 19.

undertaking may even be entitled to protect its commercial interests by terminating, in a timely manner, a special supply relationship with a customer. Nevertheless, it considered that in the case in question the dominant undertaking's refusal to supply was not proportionate and was deemed to be an infringement of Article 82 of the EC.

(ii) Refusal to Deal: Exclusive Dealing

The imposition of exclusivity obligations by a dominant firm on its trading partners (ie **4.224** customers, suppliers) obliges them to refuse to deal with any other party than the dominant undertaking. Such exclusivity imposed by a dominant firm will attract the sanction of Article 82 where the consequence is that the market is substantially foreclosed to the dominant company's competitors.

In *Hoffmann-La Roche*, the Court of Justice made a comprehensive statement explaining **4.225** when exclusivity obligations of this kind imposed on, or agreed with, customers, would infringe Article 82, saying that 'an undertaking which is in a dominant position on a market and ties purchasers—even if it does so at their own request—by an obligation or promise on their part to obtain all or most of their requirements exclusively from the said undertaking abuses its dominant position within the meaning of Article 8[2]'.

Elements of the abuse

Conduct: legal or de facto exclusivity   Article 82 applies to exclusivity obligations imposed **4.226** either legally or de facto. The Irish ice cream cases provide a good example of both situations. Originally, *Van den Bergh Foods*, a dominant producer of impulse ice cream, supplied freezer cabinets to small outlets, provided they purchased exclusively its own brands. This legal exclusivity provision was eliminated after the Commission addressed a formal Statement of Objections to the dominant undertaking.[229] It was replaced by a prohibition on outlets against stocking other ice cream brands in Van den Bergh Food's freezers. The Commission considered that such a prohibition led to de facto exclusivity because most outlets do not have space or means to have a second freezer and it prohibited this in a formal decision.[230]

The Court of First Instance confirmed the finding in 2003[231] that the dominant company **4.227** was abusing its position 'by inducing retailers who, for the purpose of stocking impulse ice-cream, did not have their own freezer cabinet, or a cabinet made available by an ice-cream supplier other than HB, to accept agreements for the provision of cabinets subject to a condition of exclusivity'. The CFI clearly stated that it was appropriate to analyse 'not only the provisions of Van den Bergh Food's distribution agreements, which do not formally preclude retailers from stocking other suppliers' ice creams in their sales outlets, but also the application of those agreements in the relevant market and the commercial options actually open to retailers pursuant to those agreements'.[232] Offering to supply freezer cabinets to the retailers and to maintain the cabinets free of any direct charge to the retailers constituted an abuse in the specific circumstances of the case.

---

[229]   Case 98/531 *Van den Bergh Foods* [1998] OJ L246, p 1.
[230]   ibid.
[231]   Case T-65/98 *Van den Bergh Foods Ltd. v Commission of the European Communities* (23 October 2003), paras 160 and 161.
[232]   Case T-65/98 *Van den Bergh Foods v Commission*, 23 October 2003.

4.228 The Court of First Instance reached this conclusion despite the fact that the provision of freezer cabinets on a condition of exclusivity constituted a standard practice on the relevant market. It argued that in a competitive market, those agreements are concluded in the interests of the two parties, whereas in a market characterised by a dominant position held by one of the parties, the assessment might be different.

4.229 *Effects: substantial foreclosure*   The imposition of an exclusivity obligation would constitute an abuse if it forecloses or is likely to foreclose a substantial share of the market to actual and potential competitors and, therefore, harms competition in it. In the above mentioned Irish ice cream cases, the Court of First Instance concluded: 'The fact that an undertaking in a dominant position on a market ties de facto—even at their own request—40 per cent of outlets in the relevant market by an exclusivity clause which in reality creates outlet exclusivity constitutes an abuse of a dominant position.' In order to estimate the market share foreclosed to competitors, it is necessary to consider further to the coverage and the duration of the exclusivity obligation, the degree to which buyers are dependent on the dominant company, whether it supplies 'must-carry' products without a formal exclusivity obligation attached to them or whether and to what extent other suppliers are in the position to supply the same quantities in equivalent conditions.

4.230 The fact that a company holds a dominant position normally implies that its products benefit from the preference of a significant part of the demand. Therefore, the Guidelines on vertical restraints[233] conclude that 'for a dominant company, even a modest tied market share may already lead to significant anticompetitive effects. The stronger its dominance, the higher the risk of foreclosure of other competitors.'

4.231 *Absence of objective justification*   The imposition of exclusivity arrangements may in certain circumstances be considered objectively justifiable. This will normally only be the case where the anti-competitive effects are kept to the minimum necessary for the attainment of some economic advantage. Exclusive supply contracts of a limited duration, for example, have been accepted by the Commission on the grounds that they provide the customer with the benefit of security of supply. In an earlier case concerning the European soda-ash market,[234] for example, the Commission objected (in a proceeding terminated informally) to contracts between ICI and Solvay on the one hand, and their customers on the other, which provided for exclusive supply. The Commission, however, accepted amendments to those contracts which provided for supply of fixed tonnage for periods not exceeding two years, pointing out that this amendment amounted to a balance between the customer's need for security of supply and the freedom to turn elsewhere for supplies.

4.232 In *Van den Bergh Foods*, however, the CFI refused to consider as an objective justification the fact that the provision of freezer cabinets on a condition of exclusivity would constitute standard business practice, that would satisfy the interest of both the ice cream supplier and the retailer. The CFI indicated that it could not accept the argument that this practice should be criticised only if there were no objective commercial justification for it. It stated that such standard business practices, which would not be objectionable in a competitive

---

[233] OJ 2000 C 291/1, para 147.
[234] 11th Annual Competition Report, paras 73–76.

market, 'cannot be accepted without reservation in the case of a market on which, precisely because of the dominant position held by one of the traders, competition is already restricted'.[235] These clear statements appear to limit considerably the possibility of invoking legitimate business reasons as a justification for this type of abuse.

Types of exclusive dealing abuses

Requirements contracts (imposition of exclusive obligations to customers)   Dominant   **4.233**
companies will infringe Article 82 if they oblige their customers to purchase from them all or most of their requirements, if this can be demonstrated to have a substantially foreclosing effect on competing suppliers. In *Hoffmann-La Roche*, exclusivity obligations of this kind were contained in some of the company's agreements with customers. The same cases also concerned agreements imposing on customers the obligation to obtain quantities which were close to their total requirements, thereby producing a level of foreclosure similar to that produced by total requirements contracts. In the *Soda Ash* cases, Solvay and ICI used similar mechanisms, including the use of 'tonnage contracts' (where the tonnage corresponded more or less to a customer's total requirements) ensuring virtual de facto exclusivity. It remains to be seen whether a parallel will be established between the concept of exclusive dealing under Article 82 ('all or almost all of the requirements') and a loose definition of non-compete obligations (80 per cent or more of the requirements). Article 1(b) of the Block Exemption Regulation for vertical restraints[236] and the Guidelines on vertical restraints[237] define 'non-compete obligations as 'obligations that require the buyer to purchase from the supplier or from another undertaking designated by the supplier more than 80 per cent of the buyer's total purchases during the previous year of the contract goods and services and their substitutes . . . thereby preventing the buyer from purchasing competing goods or services or limiting such purchases to less than 20 per cent of total purchases'.

Imposition of exclusive obligations on distributors   In *Hachette*,[238] a case which did not   **4.234**
result in a formal decision, the Commission objected to the imposition, by the two dominant newspaper distributors in France, of exclusive distribution arrangements on French publishers seeking to export newspapers/periodicals to other Member States, as well as on foreign publishers wishing to import such publications into France from other Member States. The Commission was of the view that the exclusive obligations rendered access to these import and export markets very difficult. In another case resolved without a formal decision, Visa International abandoned a plan to introduce exclusivity obligations in its arrangements with banks. Those arrangements, which would have prohibited the banks from issuing competing cards, had been objected to by the Commission on account of their probable anti-competitive consequences.[239]

Imposition of exclusive obligations on suppliers   In the *IRI/Nielsen*[240] case, the Commission   **4.235**
provisionally concluded (this case was resolved informally) that Nielsen had abused its

---

[235] Case T-65/98 *Van den Bergh Foods v Commission*, 23 October 2003, para 159.
[236] OJ L336, 29.12.1999, pp 21–25.
[237] OJ 2000 C 291/1, para 58.
[238] 8th Annual Competition Report, paras 114–115.
[239] 1996 Annual Competition Report, para 63.
[240] ibid, para 64.

dominant position on the European market for retail tracking services by concluding exclusivity contracts with retailers. These contracts were patently exclusionary, in that they prevented those retailers from providing certain kinds of market data, a type of raw information crucial to produce retail tracking reports, to competitors of Nielsen. In *BPB Industries and British Gypsum*,[241] a case concerning exclusive supply obligations imposed by a dominant buyer to its providers, the Court of First Instance reiterated the principle stated in *Hoffmann-LaRoche* and added that the conclusion of exclusive supply contracts in respect of a substantial proportion of purchases constitutes an unacceptable obstacle to entry. This finding was later upheld by the Court of Justice.[242]

4.236 *'English clauses'*   So-called 'English clauses' or 'most favoured customer clauses' included in supply contracts allow the purchaser to switch from one supplier to another if that other supplier is able to offer more favourable terms which the dominant supplier is not willing to match. These clauses impede other suppliers from attracting a customer through a lower offer unless the actual dominant supplier allows it. In *Hoffmann-La Roche*, the Court of Justice was very critical of English clauses, stressing that 'even in the most favourable circumstances, the English clause does not in fact remedy to a great extent the distortion of competition [caused by the exclusivity clauses]. By virtue of the machinery of the English clause it is for Roche itself to decide whether, by adjusting its prices or not, it will permit competition.' The Guidelines on vertical restraints[243] define an English clause as a clause 'requiring the buyer to report any better offer and allowing him only to accept such an offer when the supplier does not match it'. It 'can be expected to have the same effect as a non-compete obligation, especially when the buyer has to reveal who makes the better offer'; it 'may also work as quantity-forcing'. The same Guidelines conclude that English clauses are contrary to Article 82.

4.237 English clauses enhance transparency in the market and increase the likelihood that a competitor lowering prices will not gain market share but will prompt the incumbent supplier to match the lower price. The generalisation of these clauses in highly concentrated markets, therefore, could lead to a parallelism of conduct between different players and would avoid price competition between them. Should it be possible to prove that a collective dominant position exists in such a market, challenging such clauses as an abuse would be one of the means available to competition authorities to reduce anti-competitive effects of oligopolies.

(iii) Refusal to Deal: Tying

4.238 **Concept of tying**   According to Article 82(d) of the EC Treaty an abuse may, in particular, consist in:

> making the conclusion of contracts subject to acceptance by the other parties of supplementary obligations which, by their nature or according to commercial usage, have no connection with the subject of such contracts.

4.239 This provision covers those cases where a company that holds a dominant position forces its customers to purchase the goods or services for which it is dominant together with other goods or services for which it is not (the former products or services are commonly referred

---

[241] Case T-65/89 *BPB Industries Plc and British gypsum Ltd. v Commission* [1993] ECR II-389, para 68.
[242] Case C-310/93P *BPB Industries plc & Anor v Commission* [1995] ECR I-865, para 68.
[243] OJ 2000 C 291/1, para 152.

to as the tying market and the latter as the tied market). Such a practice might distort competition in the tied market by driving out of the market or marginalising those providers who only sell the tied products. Indeed, if most of the tied product consumers are also in need of the tying product, they would inevitably obtain the tied product together with the tying one and would not need, therefore, to obtain it from other suppliers.

The classic example of tying in EC competition law is found in the *Hilti* case. This case concerned a company trading in nail guns and their accessories (cartridge strips and nails) which attempted to eliminate independent producers of nails compatible with its guns, first, by selling its cartridge strips only to those customers who accepted to buy its own nails and, second, by reducing discounts to the customers who only ordered its cartridge strips and bought compatible nails from independent manufacturers. The Commission[244] considered that these practices constituted abuses within the meaning of Article 82 of the EC Treaty and imposed a 6 million ECU fine upon Hilti. Both the CFI[245] and the ECJ[246] upheld the Commission's decision. **4.240**

Elements of the abuse

Dominance in the tying market   In general, only a company which holds a dominant position in a given market can successfully impose tying on its customers. Indeed, a company would only be able to force its customers to purchase two distinct products or services together if the customers were dependent on the company for the supply of one of those products. Otherwise, customers would buy these products from other suppliers other than the dominant company in order to avoid the tying practice. **4.241**

Tying of two distinct products or services   Tying exists, by definition, when a dominant company forces its customers to buy two distinct products or services together. In order to prove that tying has occurred it is therefore necessary to show that the two products or services are distinct from each other. One would consider a car and its tyres as a single product, or that an air flight and the meal served in it are a single service but it might be more debatable, for instance, whether a computer operating unit and its screen are also the same product. **4.242**

According to Article 82, this should be determined either by analysing the nature of the products or services in question or by assessing whether they are normally sold together ('according to commercial usage'). These two criteria will allow a determination in most cases of whether two or more products or services sold together are indeed a single unit. These criteria have been sufficient for the ECJ and the CFI to conclude on the main tying cases brought before them. In *Tetra Pak II*,[247] for instance, it was concluded that the packaging machines and the packaging materials used by these machines were two distinct products, not linked by their nature, and which could perfectly well be manufactured and sold separately.[248] **4.243**

---

[244] *Eurofix-Bauco/Hilti* [1988] OJ L65/19.
[245] Case T-30/89 *Hilti AG v Commission* [1991] ECR II-1439.
[246] Case C-53/92 P *Hilti AG v Commission* [1994] ECR I-667.
[247] Case T-83/91 *Tetra Pak International v Commission* [1994] ECR II-755.
[248] It should, however, also be noted that the ECJ in *Tetra Pak II* 'stressed that the list of abusive practices set out . . . in Article 8[2] is not exhaustive. Consequently, even when tied sales of two products are in accordance with commercial usage or there is a natural link between the two products in question, such sales may still constitute abuse within the meaning of Article 8[2] unless they are objectively justified'; Case C-333/94 P *Tetra Pak International v Commission* [1996] ECR I-5951, para 37.

4.244   Nevertheless, in some cases and, in particular, in relation to new products brought to the market, nature and commercial usage will not be criteria of much help. Indeed, deciding whether a new product is by nature a single unit or whether each of its components should be considered as a distinct product becomes a rhetorical question and, as the product is new, there is no commercial usage to look at. In these cases, the weight of the analysis may shift from the question of whether the products sold together are distinct, to the question of whether it is objectively justifiable to sell them together (see 4.254 below). Alternatively, a forward-looking analysis could be conducted, in which the question is asked whether it is likely that the two products in the future will be sold together by effectively all companies operating in competitive markets.

4.245   Indeed, it must be noted that the consideration of two products as distinct products evolves with time. What in a certain stage of technological development could be considered as two separate products might, at a later stage, become a single integrated product. A good example of this is the *IBM System 370* case,[249] where the Commission considered that selling computer central units together with memory devices and basic software applications amounted to illegal tying. Shortly thereafter, integrating and selling these components as a single product became common in the computer industry. Article 82 should be applied carefully in these cases in order to avoid hampering technological development by preventing such integration.

4.246   The issue of technological integration arose again in the Commission's Microsoft decision.[250] Microsoft argued that its World Media Player was an integral part of the Windows operating system and not a product distinct from Windows. The Commission, however, dismissed this argument since the market provided media players separately some four years after Microsoft started tying World Media Player with Windows.

4.247   *Coercion to purchase two products or services together*   This has been considered a crucial element of the abuse. Any company, even a dominant one, is free to sell two or more products together. The abuse will only occur when the customers of a dominant company are pressured into purchasing two products together against their will.

4.248   There are varying degrees of coercion. The most extreme coercion would consist in making the purchase of the tied products or services an absolute condition for the selling of the tying ones. This condition may be embodied in the contract concluded between the dominant company and its customers[251] or in the contract concluded between the dominant company and its distributors.[252] The condition can also be applied de facto by the dominant company: it does not sell the tying products unless customers buy also the tied ones.[253]

4.249   Pressure could also be applied by withdrawing some benefits from customers who purchase the two products or services separately. The most obvious example of this is the withdrawal

[249] Bull CE 10/84, para 3.4.1. See also the US *Microsoft* case, concerning whether integrating the internet navigator software with the operating system software constituted an instance of unlawful tying (*United States v Microsoft Corp.*, 253 F.3d 34 (D.C. Cir.), cert. denied, 534 US 952 (2001)).

[250] *Microsoft* [2004]. This decision is under appeal to the CFI.

[251] Case T-83/91 *Tetra Pak International v Commission* [1994] ECR II-755.

[252] *Windsurfing* [1983] OJ L229/1.

[253] Case T-30/89 *Hilti AG v Commission* [1991] ECR II-1439.

of the guarantee for a product if the customers do not use spare parts or accessories from the same manufacturer. A recent example of this type of tying is *Novo Nordisk*,[254] a case where a manufacturer of an insulin-injecting pen disclaimed liability for the malfunction of its pen products or refused to guarantee such products when they were used in conjunction with compatible components (eg disposable needles) manufactured by its competitors.

A degree of coercion could also be expressed through pricing incentives. A dominant com- **4.250** pany could reduce rebates to customers purchasing both products separately[255] or could increase these rebates to customers purchasing both the tying and the tied product[256] (see also below the analysis of exclusionary pricing abuses). If these pricing incentives are so powerful that no rational customer would choose to buy the products separately, their effect can be similar to tying. Some commentators refer to this less stringent type of tying as bundling.

Distortion of competition in the tied market In order to be considered an abuse, tying **4.251** should affect or be capable of affecting competition in the tied market. This will be the case if the tying practice forecloses the tied market to suppliers of the tied product or service alone, which will only happen when the majority of customers of the tied product are also customers of the tying one. If this is not the case, the suppliers of the tied product or service will be able to remain in the market selling to those customers who are not in need of the tying product.

In *Hilti*, for instance, the tying practice intended to prevent independent nail manufactur- **4.252** ers from entering the market for Hilti-compatible nails by tying these nails to Hilti cartridge strips. As most consumers of Hilti-compatible nails were the purchasers of Hilti cartridge strips, the tying practice could have had success and might have foreclosed independent nail manufacturers completely from the market for nails.

In *Microsoft*, the Commission argued that Microsoft's tying of Windows Media Player **4.253** (WMP) foreclosed competition in the market for media players as alternative distribution channels (for instance, downloading) did not enable media players competing with WMP to match the ubiquitous and guaranteed presence of the pre-installed WMP. The Commission considered that this provided WMP with a significant competitive advantage which was liable to have a harmful effect on the structure of competition, raise entry barriers and, ultimately, stifle innovation to the detriment of consumers.

Absence of an objective justification A tying practice will not constitute an abuse if it can **4.254** be justified by objective reasons. The most obvious reason is likely to be that the tying prac- tice enhances efficiency, in other words, that it would be more costly to produce or distribute the tied products or services independently. As to productive efficiency, one example is inte- grating the different components of a computer in a single unit. As to distributive efficiency, it results from selling together products that most people would buy together (eg right and left shoes), which would save the extra costs (ie packaging, storage) that would result from selling each unit independently.

---

[254] European Commission, XXVIth Report on Competition Policy [1996] p 35.
[255] Case T-30/89 *Hilti AG v Commission* [1991] ECR II-1439.
[256] Case 85/76 *Hoffmann-La Roche v Commission* [1979] ECR 461, para 71 and *IRI/Nielsen*, XXVIth Report on Competition Policy [1996] pp 144–148.

4.255 Other possible justifications may relate to a guarantee of the quality, safety, and good usage of the products provided. A tying practice may help the provider to ensure the quality of all the elements of the system it provides and to be able to guarantee the good functioning of the whole system. Nevertheless, in the actual cases where this justification has been advanced,[257] the Commission concluded that the use of elements manufactured by third parties would not damage the systems in question and that tying would, therefore, not be justified. In any case, tying would be justified only if it was the least restrictive means of ensuring the quality of the products sold.

4.256 In *Hilti*, for instance, the Commission remarked that a selective distribution system (that Hilti had already notified) would have been a less restrictive means of ensuring that its products were sold together with the appropriate components. The CFI added that it was 'clearly not the task of an undertaking in a dominant position to take steps on its own initiative to eliminate products which, rightly or wrongly, it regards as dangerous or at least as inferior in quality to its own products', when there are laws 'attaching penalties to the sale of dangerous products and to the use of misleading claims as to the characteristics of any product'.[258] The CFI reiterated this line in *Tetra Pak II*, stating that 'even if using another brand of cartons on Tetra Pak machines involved a risk it was for [Tetra Pak] to use the possibilities afforded it by the relevant national legislation in the various Member States'.[259]

4.257 **Types of tying**   As explained, a tying practice may involve any combination of separate product or services. The most common types of tying are described below.

4.258 *Tying of products with their accessories*   Several examples of tying already mentioned, such as *Hilti*, *Tetra Pak*, and *Novo Nordisk*, involve a product and the accessories needed for its functioning. In these cases, one of the main issues is whether the market for the accessories is a relevant product market on its own (see above a discussion about dominance in aftermarkets).

4.259 *Tying of complementary products*   A tying may involve two complementary products, that is two products intended to be used together. In *Windsurfing*[260] (a case involving the application of Article 81), for instance, the Commission and the ECJ considered that selling windsurf boards and sails together constituted tying. It is in particular in such cases that the tying might be justified by efficiencies in distribution.

4.260 *Tying of products in the same range*   In *Hoffmann-La Roche* the Commission condemned a practice consisting in granting particular rebates to customers purchasing the whole range of vitamins supplied by this dominant company. If such rebates are not justified by economies of scope (ie reduction of the average cost of producing the whole range of products), they may constitute tying contrary to Article 82 of the EC Treaty.

---

[257] Case T-30/89 *Hilti AG v Commission* [1991] ECR II-1439, Case T-83/91 *Tetra Pak International v Commission* [1994] ECR II-755, *Novo Nordisk*, European Commission, XXVIth Report on Competition Policy [1996] p 35.
[258] Case T-30/89 *Hilti AG v Commission* [1991] ECR II-1439, para 118.
[259] Case T-83/91 *Tetra Pak International v Commission* [1994] ECR II-755, para 139.
[260] Case 193/83 *Windsurfing International v Commission* [1986] ECR 611.

Tying of a product and related services   This is the type of tying that arises when a domi-   **4.261**
nant company only sells a product if the customer also purchases some related services from
it. For instance, such a tying would exist in cases where a dominant company would only
sell spare parts if it is also allowed to perform the repairing service. A similar situation arose
in *British Sugar*,[261] where in certain instances the dominant company only agreed to sell
sugar if it could also transport it to the final destination.

Tying of the same product in different geographic markets   A tying practice does not only   **4.262**
involve different product markets but it could also concern different geographic markets
for the same product. In *IRI/Nielsen*[262] the Commission considered that Nielsen had abused
its dominant position in the market for retail tracking services by applying discounts in
exchange for commitments from customers to call upon its services in a wide range of
countries. This involved the bundling of countries where Nielsen was the sole provider of
these services with countries that IRI was entering, and prevented the latter company from
establishing a presence in Europe.

(f) Pricing Practices

(i) Predatory Pricing

Predatory pricing is a commercial strategy by which a dominant firm first lowers its price   **4.263**
to a level which will ultimately force its rivals out of the market. When the latter have been
successfully expelled, the company can raise the price again and reap the rewards. The logic
is that the company chooses to incur short-term losses in an attempt to obtain long-term
profit gains through the future exercise of market power. Predatory pricing is an exclusionary pricing strategy. It is forbidden under Article 82 EC not only when it has actually produced the pursued exclusionary effects, such as the elimination of competition or entry
deterrence, but also whenever it is likely to attain them. The Court of Justice has held that:
'It must be possible to penalize predatory pricing whenever there is a risk that competitors
will be eliminated' since the 'aim pursued, which is to maintain undistorted competition,
rules out waiting until such a strategy leads to the actual elimination of competitors.'[263]
The Court of Justice has further ruled that predatory pricing strategies may be penalized
without requiring evidence that the dominant company has '*a realistic chance of recouping
losses*' once its competitor has been eliminated (this issue is discussed below under the heading 'Need to recoup losses').

Therefore, it seems that a dominant firm engages in predatory pricing falling under Article 82   **4.264**
EC when it deliberately incurs and sustains short-run losses by temporarily charging unreasonably low prices with the intention of eliminating competitors, disciplining them, or deterring their entry in order to protect or further increase its market power in the longer run.

Predator pricing strategies are normally targeted at actual or potential competitors.   **4.265**
Dominant firms usually charge below cost only the minimum amount of products and customers necessary to achieve the exclusionary aim, thereby reducing the amount of losses

---

[261] *Napier Brown/British Sugar* [1988] OJ L284/41.
[262] European Commission, XXVIth Report on Competition Policy, p 36.
[263] Case C-333/94P *Tetra Pak International SA v Commission of the European Communities* (*Tetra Pak II*)
[1996] ECR I-5951, para 44.

incurred and facilitating a recovery strategy. Therefore, predatory pricing strategies often involve price discrimination.

Elements of the abuse

4.266 *Level of prices*   Prices set at unreasonably low levels having regard to the dominant firm's structure of costs and the price opportunities and constraints featuring in the relevant market result in short-run losses which the dominant company could have avoided or reduced. Not every price below cost will be considered predatory.

4.267 The US Courts have developed a relatively simple, objective cost-based rule for dealing with cases of predatory pricing. The so-called Areeda & Turner rule [264] states that a price at or above average variable cost (cost which varies according to the quantity produced) benefits from a presumption of legality, while a price below that level may be unlawful. Areeda & Turner had originally proposed marginal costs as a benchmark to establish predatory prices because a company not covering marginal costs incurs an immediate loss with the production and sale of each output unit. The company could generally have been better off simply by not producing each unit. However, companies do not normally run their business on the basis of calculations of marginal costs and in most case there are no data available to calculate them. Therefore, the two professors introduced average variable costs as a proxy for marginal costs.[265] This does not exclude the possibility that other proxies could also reflect whether a company is deliberately incurring avoidable losses, thereby justifying the finding of predatory pricing.[266] In particular, average avoidable costs have been proposed as a standard benchmark for the finding of predatory pricing. Average variable costs are often the equal to average avoidable costs for the production of a given part of output, except in cases where the production of that given part of output requires incurring not only variable investments, but also fixed or sunk costs. In such cases, since average avoidable costs take into account all relevant costs, they stand for a higher figure than average variable costs.

4.268 As described below, the Commission and Court of Justice have, in contrast, evolved an approach based, not solely on a cost analysis but partly on the proven intent of the dominant firm.

4.269 The Commission made its first finding of predatory pricing in 1985, in the *AKZO* case.[267] The case involved a complaint to the Commission by ECS, a competitor of AKZO's in the supply of organic peroxides to millers in the UK and Ireland. Initially, ECS did not supply these products outside the flour industry, but in 1979 it decided to expand its activities and approached a German plastics' manufacturer (BASF) with a view to supplying it. When AKZO learned of this, it met with ECS and threatened to eliminate it from the market, unless ECS would agree to cease supplying the plastics industry. When ECS failed to do so,

---

[264] P. Areeda and D. F. Turner, 'Predatory pricing and related practices under Section 2 of the Sherman Act' (1975) Harvard Law Review.

[265] The costs incurred in producing one additional unit of output.

[266] More recently, a judgment of the US Court of Appeals for the Third Circuit, *LePage's Inc. v 3M* (2002 WL 46961 (3rd Cir. 2002)) held that the general proposition that a company's pricing practices are lawful so long as its prices are above cost, does not apply to a monopolist: '*a monopolist is not free to take certain actions that a company in a competitive (or even oligopolistic) market may take, because there is no market constraint on a monopolist's behaviour*'.

[267] *AKZO* [1985] OJ L374/1.

AKZO proceeded to offer organic peroxides to ECS's regular customers at prices well below those which it offered its normal customers. ECS alleged to the Commission that the prices were below average variable cost and that their only rationale could be the elimination of ECS from the market. As a consequence, ECS suffered considerable loss of market share, and only managed to sustain a foothold in the market by reducing prices to below cost for those customers which it retained. A surprise Commission inspection uncovered internal documents at AKZO premises which appeared to confirm ECS's allegations of below-cost selling and of a deliberate attempt to oust it from the market.

In finding that AKZO's behaviour in offering below-cost prices to ECS's customers was abusive, the Commission expressly rejected the need to adopt a purely cost based rule for establishing the existence of predatory pricing.[268] Instead, the Commission emphasised that a deliberate attempt to impair competition in the market, by seeking to eliminate or harm the competitive position of a competitor/s, must be demonstrated. **4.270**

Although the Court of Justice upheld the Commission's finding[269] of predatory pricing by AKZO, it rejected the test which the Commission had employed. The Court emphasised that the concept of an abuse is an objective one, although the test which it devised retains an element of subjectivity. The test is a two-pronged one: **4.271**

(i) prices set at *below* average *variable* cost[270] 'by means of which a dominant undertaking seeks to eliminate a competitor'[271] are presumed to be predatory and thus abusive, as such a price necessarily implies a loss of all the fixed costs and at least some of the variable costs. This sacrifice can hardly respond to any other conceivable economic purpose than the elimination of a competitor. In principle, a dominant company would be better off not producing or procuring the items at all than by selling them at a price implying the loss of all fixed costs and the loss of part or all variable costs incurred in the production or acquisition of each item. The Court of Justice has held that 'a dominant undertaking has no interest in applying such prices except that of eliminating competitors so as to enable it subsequently to raise its prices by taking advantage of its monopolistic position, since each sale generates a loss, namely the total amount of the fixed costs (that is to say, those which remain constant regardless of the quantities produced) and, at least, part of the variable costs relating to the unit produced.'

(ii) prices set at *below* average *total* cost,[272] *but above* average *variable* cost, are not considered predatory, except when there is evidence that they are part of a plan to exclude competition; the Court made it clear that for such prices to be abusive they must have been set within the framework of a specific plan aimed at eliminating the competitor/s.

In the instant case, the Court found, applying the test just described, that all but one of the prices offered to AKZO's customers were between average variable and average total cost; the other price was below even average variable cost. It held that 'such prices can drive from **4.272**

---

[268] The Commission's rejection of the need for a thorough cost-based analysis could be explained by the fact that the case appeared to be so clear-cut on the facts.
[269] It reduced the level of the fine by 25 per cent, however, in view of the novelty of predatory pricing as an abuse.
[270] ie costs which vary according to the quantity produced or procured.
[271] Case C-62/86 *AKZO Chemie BV v Commission* [1991] ECR I-3359, para 71.
[272] ie variable costs plus fixed costs.

the market undertakings which are perhaps as efficient as the dominant undertaking but which, because of their smaller financial resources, are incapable of withstanding the competition waged against them'.

4.273 Principally because the prices had not also been offered to AKZO's normal customers, the Court found that AKZO must have intended to exclude ECS from the market, or at least severely harm its competitive position. The file also contained documentary evidence of direct threats, as well as a note by a manager of AKZO including a detailed plan, with figures, describing the measures that would be put into effect if ECS did not refrain from supplying its products, as well as statements by other employees, records of meetings, and affidavit of the High Court in London.

4.274 A few years later, the Court of Justice applied the same test and reasoning in its judgment of 14 November 1996 in *Tetra Pak II*.[273] Tetra Pak was condemned for having sold at a loss its non-aseptic cartons in seven Member States. It had been able to subsidise this practice from its profits in the market for aseptic cartons where it was a quasi-monopolist, holding 90 per cent market share. The Commission had based its decision on the AKZO presumption that prices below average variable costs are predatory, and gathered further evidence to conclude that sales at a loss were the result of a deliberate policy aimed at eliminating competition.[274] The Commission Decision also considered whether exceptional circumstances independent of Tetra Pak's will had forced it to make losses, but it found none. Both the CFI and the ECJ upheld the decision.

4.275 Prices set at levels above average variable costs do not entail losses by the mere production or procurement for sale of each output unit. According to the Court of Justice, in those cases, the finding that a price is unreasonably low cannot rest only on the level of the price and the cost structure of the alleged predator, since sales which do not cover total costs may still allow some return on capital. There may be a variety of constraints or considerations that could objectively explain why a dominant company would temporarily endure certain levels of losses, irrespective of whether the prices it charges would eliminate other competitors or deter their entry. Furthermore, although those prices may be capable of threatening the viability of efficient competitors, they are not, as such, so incontrovertibly likely to exclude them. Therefore, those price levels will only be regarded as predatory if it can be established that those price levels have been devised by the dominant company for an exclusionary purpose. Predatory pricing strategies are subject to scrutiny from the beginning of their implementation, although mere plans do not constitute an abuse until they are not put into effect.

4.276 Some commentators consider that the Court's approach is open to criticism because the intention to exclude rivals is not in itself anti-competitive; indeed, it is often inherent in the competitive process that firms will seek to eliminate each other. A further disadvantage of this approach is that it provides less legal certainty than a completely objective cost-based rule. Professor Baumol, for instance, has often said that there is no good way to determine what the management of a firm really had in mind and economists have no particular professional qualifications for delving into anyone's mental state.

---

[273] Case C-333/94P *Tetra Pak II*, paras 41 and 42.
[274] OJ 1992 L72/1, para 147.

On the other hand, there is no doubt that predatory pricing is an exclusionary pricing strategy. **4.277**
Below average variable costs or another appropriate proxy to marginal costs, such as average
avoidable costs, the conclusion that those prices respond to a predatory strategy is the most
plausible explanation. This presumption is not valid for other price levels.

In the absence of any evidence of a predatory strategy, prices set above average variable costs **4.278**
(or an equivalent proxy for marginal costs) will not be caught by Article 82 EC. If it can be
objectively established with documentary or behavioural evidence that the dominant firm's
intention in setting unreasonably low prices was to exclude competition at the expense of
incurring and sustaining losses, this would exclude any legitimate intent such as defeating
competitors by outperforming the rivals. Furthermore, it is implausible that a dominant
company would embark on this loss-making strategy if it does not anticipate exclusionary
effects, ie if it is not persuaded that its pricing policy is likely to effectively eliminate viable
and efficient competitors or discipline or deter their entry and that it can finance a sufficient
scale of losses during the requisite time. Objective factors such as the scale of the losses, their
continuity and the foreseen or actual duration of the practice, as well as the fact that the predatory efforts would be targeted at some competitors are mentioned in case law as elements
showing the existence of predatory intent. It could be added that the precedents where
predatory pricing has been found were also cases involving other exclusionary abuses

Since *AKZO* and *Tetra Pak II* there have been other Commission decisions[275] involving **4.279**
predatory pricing: *Napier Brown/British Sugar*,[276] *Wanadoo Interactive*,[277] and *Deutsche
Post AG*.[278] In *Napier Brown* the Commission found that British Sugar had abused its dominant position by charging predatory prices to sugar packers for raw sugar (see further in
footnote 286 below). In *Wanadoo Interactive*, the Commission scrutinised a pricing strategy
for Wanadoo's ADSL high-speed Internet access services. During the period covered by the
decision nearly all ADSL lines in France were operated by the incumbent operator France
Télécom holding almost 100 per cent of the market for wholesale ADSL services for Internet
services providers (including Wanadoo). Alternative networks such as cable networks had
limited coverage in France and were not in a position to be considered competitors at
national level. Wanadoo, which was a (72 per cent) subsidiary of France Télécom from
March 2001 to October 2002 was setting prices at loss-making levels, while its parent company, France Télécom, was anticipating considerable profits in the near future on its own
wholesale ADSL products. From January 2001 to September 2002, Wanadoo's market
share rose from 46 per cent to 72 per cent on a market which saw more than a fivefold
increase in its size over the same period. The Commission concluded that Wanadoo was
charging predatory prices for its high-speed Internet access services, not covering variable
costs until August 2001 or total costs from then onwards, as part of a plan to pre-empt the

---

[275] In the 1987 Annual Competition Report (paras 334–336), the Commission detailed its policy (on the
basis of a study which it had commissioned) in relation to predatory pricing, largely reaffirming its rejection
of a purely cost-based rule and in particular of a rule providing for *per se* legality for prices above marginal cost.
The Commission emphasised that 'predatory pricing practices must be regarded as part of an abusive global
strategy aimed at eliminating other producers in an anti-competitive manner'.
[276] *British Sugar* [1988] OJ L284/41.
[277] Decision COMP/38.233 of 16 July 2003.
[278] OJ [2001] L125, p 27.

market in high-speed Internet access during a key phase in its development. In this case, the AKZO-test was applied to the specific features of the product, which was not a one-off shopping product, but a service to which the end user subscribed for a period of time.

4.280 New developments in EU decision making show that the Commission is willing to use in each case the cost benchmark that best justifies the finding of predation.[279] *Deutsche Post AG I* was the first case in which a test based on incremental costs was applied in a formal decision, and it was the first decision adopted under Article 82 EC leading to a *structural remedy*, namely the structural separation of two branches of a formerly integrated undertaking. The Commission found that DPAG had abused its statutory monopoly in the German market for the delivery of mail-order parcels by engaging in predatory pricing and granting fidelity rebates. No fine was imposed for the first infringement because the economic cost concepts used to identify the predatory pricing behaviour were not sufficiently developed at the time the abuse occurred. The complainant, United Parcel Service (UPS), a private operator in the business parcel sector active in Germany and other European States, alleged that DPAG was using revenues from its profitable letter-mail monopoly to finance a strategy of below-cost selling in business parcel services, which are open to competition. DPAG did not cover the costs incremental to providing the mail-order delivery service for five years. The Decision establishes that any service provided by the beneficiary of a monopoly in open competition has to cover at least the additional or incremental cost incurred in branching out into the competitive sector.

4.281 The Commission Notice on the Application of the Competition Rules to Access Agreements[280] in the field of telecommunications suggests that a standard based on long-run incremental costs might be more suitable for network industries, where fixed costs for infrastructure are very high and variable costs are low.

4.282 *Limit pricing* Limit pricing, whereby a firm sets prices (and output) at a level which ensures that there is not enough demand left for another firm to profitably enter the market, is not regarded as abusive, unless it is predatory, even if it might have the effect of keeping out potential market entrants.

4.283 Need to recoup losses. As explained before, a firm engaging in predatory pricing, to be successful, must keep the price at the level at which its rivals are forced to withdraw from the market, give up vigorous competition, or refrain from entry. It must therefore be able to survive the low price levels for longer than its competitors can. The firm would then be able to raise its price to a level sufficiently high, and for a sufficiently long period of time, to enable it not only to recoup the losses incurred by the predation, but also to secure higher profits than it would have obtained had it not engaged in the predatory behaviour. The lower the barriers to entering the market, the more difficult it will be for the predator to recoup his losses and then reap the monopoly profits.

---

[279] Out of respect for the principle of legal certainty, the Commission ultimately refrains from imposing fines whenever a new cost benchmark is used for the first time, in the absence of any policy paper or guideline warning companies of this possibility.

[280] OJ 1998 C 265/2, paras 113–115.

Nevertheless, it seems that to establish this abuse there is no need to demonstrate that the **4.284** exclusionary strategy in question is specifically designed for the additional and implicit purpose of recouping the losses incurred or that the dominant company will be able to raise prices following the expulsion of its competitors sufficiently to enable it to recoup its losses and then enjoy supra-competive profits.[281] In *Tetra Pak II* the Court stated that it was not necessary 'in the circumstances of the present case, to require in addition proof that Tetra Pak had a realistic chance of recouping its losses'.[282] It will suffice for the Commission to simply demonstrate that the predatory price is likely to eliminate the dominant firm's rivals.

This is probably explained by the fact that the authorities' intervention is likely to occur **4.285** before the victims of predation have been excluded altogether from the market, and probably before the dominant firm will have succeeded in fully recouping its losses. For this reason, proving the abuse will generally involve a degree of conjecture as to the behaviour's likely ultimate consequences. Moreover, it is implausible that a dominant company would engage itself in this sacrifice strategy if it does not anticipate recovery in the long run of the losses incurred in the short run, through the future exercise of market power, without thereby attracting new entry. Nevertheless, it is not a condition for the finding of an exclusionary abuse under Article 82 EC that there could also be established the existence or the likelihood of a subsequent exploitative abuse by the dominant company, such as excessive or discriminatory prices to recoup the losses incurred. The dominant company would already have breached its duty not to impair genuine competition conditions on the market by denying other operators their right to access markets competing on the merits, whether it finally manages to recoup the losses or not.

It may be argued, in this regard, that establishing dominance already implies that entry bar **4.286** riers are sufficiently high to presume the possibility of recovery. Therefore it is not necessary to provide further separate proof of recovery in order to find an abuse.

Objective justification   A real difficulty from the point of view of applying Article 82 to **4.287** allegations of predatory pricing is to distinguish legitimate, competitive conduct from predatory, anti-competitive behaviour.[283] A price below cost may be consistent with a number of other competitively legitimate explanations such as, for example, the need to clear stocks, for instance of perishable goods, or to meet a competitor's offer. It is likely that the presumptions of abuse contained in the Court's test are rebuttable in the light of evidence that the prices charged were objectively justified by these or similar legitimate commercial considerations. Examples of circumstances that might justify loss-making prices could include the obligation of a dominant company to honour long-term contracts with fixed prices which have become loss making due to unforeseeable increases in input prices. Likewise, a dominant company may be minimizing its losses in the short run or by temporarily maintaining

---

[281] This is in contrast with US case law which requires that the alleged predator be shown to have a reasonable likelihood of recouping the losses it suffered by predation—see *Brooke Group v Brown and Williamson Tobacco* (1993).

[282] The Court of Justice said that 'it must be possible to penalise predatory pricing whenever there is *a risk* that competitors will be eliminated' (emphasis added, para 44).

[283] AG Lenz noted that the Commission seemed to have ignored the defence of 'meeting competition' in C-62/86 *AKZO Chemie BV v Commission* [1991] ECR I-3359.

a certain scale of production when this would be less costly than closing a plant and restarting production after a while.

Other predatory strategies

4.288 *'Fighting Ships'* This is a strategy, sometimes adopted by the members of a shipping 'conference', designed to harm non-member shipping companies. The abuse consists of the predatory shipping conference sailing a ship (a so-called 'fighting ship') in competition with the non-member (ie on the same route and on approximately the same date), and charging rates which are below those which the conference normally charges, with the aim of eliminating the non-member. The members then share the loss of revenue between them. The Commission found in *CEWAL*,[284] that the conference in question used the strategy over an 18-month period and that it formed part of a deliberate plan aimed at eliminating its principal competitor on routes between the North Sea and Zaire. The special characteristic of the abuse is that it presupposes a finding of joint dominance on the part of the members of the shipping conference, which the Commission did in this case. The decision was upheld by the Court of First Instance. Neither the Commission, nor the Court of First Instance or the Court of Justice expressly qualified this conduct as 'predatory pricing', probably on account of the fact that the tariffs were set at levels covering total costs. They nevertheless concluded that this practice was exclusionary.

(ii) Pricing Practices: Price Squeezing

4.289 A price squeeze (or 'vertical margin squeeze') is a form of pricing behaviour by a company that, being dominant in both an upstream and a downstream market, charges a price in the upstream market that does not enable its competitors to operate profitably in the downstream one. Even if neither the upstream nor downstream price is in itself abusive (ie excessive or predatory) the combination of the two (the squeeze) is contrary to Article 82.

4.290 In *Industrie des Poudres Sphériques*,[285] the Court of First Instance described the abuse in the following terms:

> Price squeezing may be said to take place when an undertaking which is in a dominant position on the market for an unprocessed product and itself uses part of its production for the manufacture of a more processed product, while at the same time selling off surplus unprocessed product on the market, sets the price at which it sells the unprocessed product at such a level that those who purchase it do not have a sufficient profit margin on the processing to remain competitive on the market for the processed product.[286]

4.291 Therefore, engaging in an abuse of this kind requires the imposition of a margin between the two prices that must be insufficient to allow an as efficient competitor to achieve an

---

[284] *CEWAL* [1993] OJ L34/20.

[285] Case T-5/97 *Industrie des Poudres Sphériques SA v Commission* [2000], para 178.

[286] Likewise, in *Napier Brown*, British Sugar was dominant in both the upstream (industrial sugar) and downstream (retail sugar) markets. Napier Brown was dependent on supplies of industrial sugar from British Sugar in order to be able to operate in the retail sugar market. The margin between the price British Sugar charged Napier Brown for the industrial sugar, on the one hand, and the price British Sugar charged for its own consumer sales, on the other, was below British Sugar's own repackaging and selling costs, and thus did not allow Napier Brown to remain viable as a packer and seller of retail sugar. The Commission also relied on evidence that the behaviour formed part of a deliberate price-cutting campaign by British Sugar aimed at excluding Napier Brown from the retail market.

acceptable rate of return and thus remain competitive on the market. It is important to note that the cost structures that are relevant for this assessment should be those of the dominant company,[287] but not necessarily those of the squeezed company. There should only be an infringement of Article 82 EC to the extent that competition is impacted by the elimination of an as efficient competitor. In some circumstances, a rival may feel it is being 'price squeezed', where in reality the 'squeeze' results from its own processing costs which may be higher than those of the dominant firm.[288] In any event, a dominant company cannot be required to make its commercial decisions on the basis of data that it does not know and that it cannot be expected to know, as would normally be the case with regard to the cost structure of its competitors.

Such abuses may be particularly relevant in network industries, where access to infrastructure is granted by a dominant firm. In *Deutsche Telekom*,[289] for example, the Commission found that DT had imposed a vertical margin squeeze, in breach of Article 82, on new entrants to the German fixed-line telephony market by means of the prices it charged for wholesale local access to its fixed telephony network ('the local loop', ie the final section of cable connecting a customer with the local switching point). The access fees which it charged were either higher than those which DT charged its own retail customers, or so close to the latter price that the margin would not even have covered DT's own costs in providing the retail services. This made it impossible for the new entrants to compete with DT in the retail market. **4.292**

(iii) Pricing Practices: Exclusionary Discounts and Rebates

General   Discounts are generally offered on individual transactions, while rebates are normally deductions or cash payments made retrospectively to a customer in accordance with the latter's purchases over a period of time. These terms will often be used interchangeably in this section.[290] **4.293**

Discounts and rebates are often used as instruments of healthy and legitimate price competition. Since dominant firms are not subject to effective competitive constraints, they should in principle be allowed and encouraged to share their profits by offering discounts and rebates, provided that this does not ultimately lead to depriving customers of the benefits of residual competition. The difficulty for the competition authority or other enforcer of the competition rules is, as with so many alleged abuses of market power, to distinguish such genuinely pro-competitive behaviour from anti-competitive or exploitative conduct. At one end of the spectrum, where the discount/rebate is a direct reflection of the dominant company's efficiency, it will be unobjectionable. At the other end, where the only commercially **4.294**

---

[287] As the Court of First Instance recalled in para 179 *in fine*, '*a producer, even in a dominant position, is not obliged to sell its products below its manufacturing costs*'.

[288] In *Industrie des Poudres Sphériques*, para 180, the CFI argued against the finding of an abuse because the applicant had not shown that the price for the unprocessed product was such as to eliminate an efficient competitor from the market for the processed product.

[289] Case COMP/C-1/37451, 37.578, 37.579; OJ L263 of 14.10.2003.

[290] Sometimes, however, the words are used interchangeably, because commercial relationships between undertakings normally have a regular basis and both discounts and rebates are included in an accounting system, rather than being actually discounted or paid back in cash for each transaction. In fact, except in the case of prospective target discounts, all other discounts and rebates (standard or individualised volume discounts, fidelity and retroactive target discounts, etc.) show a retroactive nature, because the price is reduced across all purchases once a threshold is reached.

rational explanation for the discount/rebate is in terms of an attempt to exclude competitors or exploit customers, it will fall foul of Article 82.

4.295 In deciding whether a firm is objectively justified in granting the discount or rebate, it is normally necessary to have regard to whether the discount/rebate reflects gains in efficiency or economic savings made by the dominant firm, arising from its supply to the recipient of the discount[291] or from the business brought by supplier receiving a reward,[292] or from early payment or payment in cash or in a certain currency, etc. The assessment further requires consideration of whether the rules governing the discount scheme are objective. It is also necessary to examine the extent to which the discount/rebate has the effect of restricting the customer's commercial likelihood of deciding whether to purchase from another supplier, and whether the efficiency gains or economic savings are passed on to consumers. Finally, the likely harm to the dominant firm's rivals needs to be assessed, as well as the extent to which the discounts/rebates will be likely to shore up its dominant position.

4.296 Many commentators tend to criticise the Commission and the Courts for basing their assessment of rebate schemes on the schemes themselves and the dominant company's cost structure, but not on the actual cost structures of the rivals at risk of being eliminated or deterred from entry. This might be consistent with economic models and fully transparent markets. However, the mere elimination of a particular rival does not necessarily involve direct harm to competition or indirect harm to consumers, since that elimination may be the consequence of genuine competition and a specific rival may not be an efficient competitor. It is more relevant to assess whether the practice is capable of impairing competition conditions and likely to hamper, eliminate, or deter efficient competitors, and whether the practice can be objectively justified by the dominant company.[293] It is the rules and working of a given scheme or the conditions attached to the rebates that may actually handicap competitors, and not merely the lower price. Furthermore, the enforcement of Article 82 EC is subject to some constraints stemming from market reality and legal safeguards: a dominant company cannot be required to make its commercial decisions on the basis of data unknown to it or which it cannot be expected to know legally. Most of the time this is the case with regard to its competitors' cost structures.

4.297 **Non-exclusionary discounts or rebates** Most common types of discounts and rebates do not fall foul of Article 82. First, discounts or rebates based on the quantity, value, or volume purchased per single transaction are normally not exclusionary. According to precedent, such discounts/rebates 'are deemed to reflect gains in efficiency and economies of scale made by the undertaking in a dominant position'.[294] This, however, needs to be qualified.

---

[291] Case T-203/01 *Michelin v Commission* [Michelin II], 30/11/2003, para 58.

[292] Case T-219/99 *British Airways v Commission*, 17/12/2003, para 284.

[293] This approach broadly recalls a classical definition of 'exclusionary conduct': '*Exclusionary comprehends at the most behaviour that not only (1) tends to impair the opportunities of rivals, but also (2) either does not further competition on the merits or does so in an unnecessarily restrictive way*'; Areeda & Turner (1978) Antitrust Law 78.

[294] Quantity discounts, rebates, and rewards grow in relation to the absolute size of the order. Other discounts, rebates, and rewards grow in proportion to the share of the each buyer's increased purchases from the dominant supplier over a certain reference period or in proportion to the share of the supplier's business provided to the dominant reseller. In Hoffmann-La Roche, the Court described the latter 'as those designed through the grant of a financial advantage to prevent customers from obtaining their supplies from competing producers'.

When the volume required to obtain the discount or rebate represents a large share of the customer's needs, the discount may be objectionable (see below under target rebates).

The Commission has rarely required the direct correlation with efficiencies to be quanti- **4.298** fied, since those are presumed when the standardised rebate schemes are objectively established on the basis of quantities, value, or volume purchased, and are open to all customers. Nevertheless, the Court of First Instance in *Michelin II* has confirmed that even these rebate schemes can be found to infringe Article 82 EC if they do not actually respond to real efficiencies or cost savings obtained by the dominant company.

Some commentators argue that both the Commission and the European Courts have failed to **4.299** consider the efficiencies on the demand side. Although the debate is far from closed, it seems that the Commission and the Courts do concentrate on the exclusionary effects for efficient rivals of the dominant firm rather than on the better prices for the dominant firms' customers because it is taken for granted that the demand side always benefits from obtaining rebates (except in cases where the rebates are applied discriminatorily). The debatable issue would be rather whether those efficiencies on the demand side could ever outweigh a loss of competition at the supply level and whether different rebate, discount, and reward schemes could offer different degrees of relevant efficiencies depending on their context, which seems to be the case.

Discounts or rebates not permissible under Article 82   Some other types of discounts or **4.300** rebates would normally fall foul of Article 82. They are discussed below.

In *Michelin I*[295] the Court considered that in order to establish that a dominant company **4.301** had abused its position by applying a discount system, it was

> necessary to consider all the circumstances, particularly the criteria and rules for the grant of the discount, and to investigate whether, in providing an advantage not based on any economic service justifying it, the discount tends to remove or restrict the buyer's freedom to choose his sources of supply, to bar competitors from access to the market, to apply dissimilar conditions to equivalent transactions with other trading parties or to strengthen the dominant position by distorting competition.

Discounts conditional upon the acceptance of exclusive dealing or of requirement clauses **4.302** **(referred to in the case law as 'fidelity or loyalty rebates')**   Such rebates seek to reward customers for their pattern of purchases from a dominant firm. Customers are normally rewarded for de facto exclusive purchasing. Although it is arguable that fidelity rebates amount to no more than vigorous price competition, the Commission and Court have come close to establishing a presumption of illegality for such schemes, without developing any systematic analysis of the ability of efficient competitors to profitably match the strategy of the dominant company. US law tends to take a more robust view of the merits of rebates and discounts of this kind.

Fidelity rebates are often used by a dominant company to make it difficult, or commercially **4.303** irrational, for the customer to switch to another supplier. This can have the effect, on the one hand, of foreclosing a substantial part of the market in question to the competitors of the dominant firm. Indeed, the dominant firm's competitors would have to match the level of rebates granted by their more powerful competitor in order to be able to sell to

---

[295] Case 322/81 *NV Nederlandse Banden—Industrie Michelin v Commission* [1983] ECR 3461, para 73.

the customer in question. On the other hand, where the dominant supplier's customers are competitors of each other, those not receiving the rebate are thereby placed at a competitive disadvantage in relation to those who do.

4.304   The Commission first objected to fidelity rebates in *Suiker Unie*, where the dominant sugar supplier granted rebates to loyal customers, namely those who met the totality of their requirements from the dominant supplier. The Commission found that, even though the dominant supplier's competitors were offering lower prices, these were not sufficient to match the rebate and attract customers receiving the rebate. The Commission's findings were upheld by the Court of Justice.

4.305   In *Hoffmann-La Roche*, the Court gave its most comprehensive indication that fidelity rebates would infringe Article 82. It said that, not only will a firm in a dominant position on a market infringe Article 82 when it ties purchasers *de jure* through exclusivity obligations (as described above at 4.224), but that

> the same applies if the said undertaking [the dominant firm], without tying the purchasers by a formal obligation, applies, either under the terms of agreements concluded with these purchasers or unilaterally, a system of fidelity rebates, that is to say discounts conditional on the customer's obtaining all or most of its requirements, whether the quantity of its purchases be large or small, from the undertaking in a dominant position.

4.306   In the instant case, the fidelity rebates were progressive with regard to the proportion of the customer's purchases taken from Hoffmann-La Roche; that is to say that the greater the proportion of requirements accounted for by such purchases, the greater the rate of rebate accorded to the customer. This had a clear tying effect on the dominant supplier's customers, making it more difficult for them to turn elsewhere with every additional unit which they purchased. As with *de jure* exclusivity obligations, the Court also made it clear that such rebates were caught by Article 82 even if they had been expressly requested by the customer.

4.307   This critical approach to exclusivity rebates is common in both sides of the Atlantic and it largely extends to rebates rewarding partial exclusivity such as market-share discounts.[296] Exclusive dealing and bundled rebates may qualify as exclusionary conduct under §1 of the Sherman Act, §3 of the Clayton Act, and §5 of the FTC Act. In a recent judgment of the US Court of Appeals for the Third Circuit, *LePage's Inc. v 3M*,[297] it is clearly stated that 'Exclusionary conduct, such as the exclusive dealing and bundled rebates proven here, can sustain a verdict under §2 against a monopolist.'[298]

---

[296]   eg in 'Anticompetitive aspects of market-share discounts and other incentives to exclusive dealing' (2000) 67 Antitrust Law 615, William K. Tom, David A. Balto, and Neil W. Averritt (FTC officials) argue that market-share discounts structured to produce total or partial exclusivity should be judged according to the same economic principles as exclusive dealing and that the case law makes it possible to condemn them under the Sherman Act or FTC Act.

[297]   2002 WL 46961 (3rd Cir. 2002).

[298]   See also the OECD study 'Loyalty and fidelity discounts and rebates' published on 4 February 2003 including the answers to a questionnaire by all OECD countries and the European Commission. That study does not only relate to 'loyalty and fidelity discounts and rebates' in the EC law sense (those rewarding exclusivity or quasi-exclusivity), but also to what the EC case law would consider as quantity rebates, fidelity-inducing rebates, predatory rebates, and others. According to the OECD, 'the probability that a fidelity discount will have anticompetitive effects essentially depends on whether, and to what degree, the discount reduces price transparency, excludes or restricts actual or potential competitors, and/or raises the probability of anticompetitive co-ordination'.

Target and long-term rebate schemes   Article 82 can also be infringed where dominant companies grant rebates on the basis of the customer having reached a specified sales target, if this has the effect of inducing the latter to purchase larger quantities from the former. For target rebates to produce loyalty enhancing effects, the threshold triggering the attainment of a rebate must be set at a higher level than the volume, value, or quantity of requirements normally demanded by its customers, in the absence of any obligation or rebate, ie it should be capable of inducing incremental purchases from the dominant provider by leveraging between the 'contestable' and the 'non-contestable' part of the demand. Such rebates are often fixed bilaterally between the dominant supplier and its customer and do not blatantly depend on any customer's obligation to achieve all or most of his requirements from the supplier. According to case law and Commission practice, the compatibility of such schemes with the Treaty will depend *inter alia* on the length of the reference period upon which the rebate is calculated, and on the degree to which the criteria for granting the rebate are objective and transparent. In our view, the assessment of this kind of rebate should also take into account whether an as efficient competitor could successfully compete for the incremental purchases. Such an assessment requires the exercise of some judgment: using the 'as efficient competitor test' has the practical advantage for dominant companies' management and for competition agencies of being a clear and predictable test, because it relies mainly on the dominant company's costs and performance. However, if in order to qualify as 'efficient competitor', a company must be 'as efficient' as the dominant company, new entrants and currently small incumbents will hardly ever have the chance to become 'as efficient' as the dominant company, even if they have the potential to do so. Since Article 82 EC is not meant to protect (individual) competitors for their own sake, but only to protect and foster competition for the benefit of consumers, the benefit of consumers and the need to maintain the existing competition are relevant factors when searching for the right criterion to balance the 'right' of a potentially as efficient player to compete for potentially available portions of the demand and the 'right' of the dominant company to offer better prices for the benefit of consumers.

The precedents allow us to distinguish between rebates linked to the attainment of individualised targets over a relatively long reference period and rebates linked to the attainment of generally applicable volume targets over a relatively long reference period. **4.308**

Rebates linked to the attainment of individualised targets over a relatively long reference **4.309**
period   These so-called 'target rebates' were discussed at length by the Court of Justice in *Michelin I*.[299] In that case, specific targets were fixed between Michelin and its customers at the beginning of each year, based on the latter's purchases in the previous year. If the target was reached or exceeded, an individually negotiated discount would be granted. In finding the rebate system abusive, the Court placed particular emphasis on the length of the reference period (one year), pointing out that the supplier would be unlikely to switch suppliers at any point during the year (but particularly as the year progressed) for fear of not qualifying for the rebate. The Court also relied, though to a lesser extent, on the secret manner in which the rebates were agreed, and the general lack of uniformity and transparency characterising the system.

---

[299] Case 322/81 *Michelin* [1983] ECR 3461.

4.310 Target rebates will, however, only be objectionable if they have an appreciable tying effect on customers (ie if they inhibit customers from switching to a competitor). In the first *Coca-Cola*[300] case, which was resolved without the need for a formal decision, the Commission objected to Coca-Cola's target rebate scheme for its customers in Italy, which used a reference period of one year for the calculation of the rebate. As in *Michelin I*, the Commission felt that such a scheme had a tying effect on purchasers, thereby substantially foreclosing the market to Coca-Cola's competitors. When the company volunteered to reduce the reference period to three months, however, the Commission accepted that the scheme no longer substantially impeded the company's customers from switching suppliers.

4.311 The Commission revisited Coca-Cola's rebate system in a second *Coca-Cola* case in 2005 where Coca-Cola offered commitments based on a so-called 'preliminary assessment' by the Commission that several of Coca-Cola's marketing practices raised competition concerns.[301] With respect to the target rebates the preliminary assessment found that, notwithstanding the quarterly reference period adopted after the first *Coca-Cola* case, there were still competition concerns as the rebates were calculated on the overall purchases of the customer. The rebates were therefore likely to offer strong financial incentives for the customer's additional purchases once he approached the threshold, thereby increasing the customer's switching costs and binding him to Coca-Cola. The commitments specify that Coca-Cola will refrain from offering individually set target rebates.[302]

4.312 Target rebates were also the subject of the *Irish Sugar* judgment by the Court of First Instance on 7 October 1999.[303] A number of small companies had entered the Irish retail sugar market as sugar packers, and sourced most of their requirements from Irish Sugar. The dominant company was at that time the only domestic sugar packer operating on the Irish market. Irish Sugar was abusing its position of dominance by offering selective target rebates to certain wholesalers and retailers, based on target increases in their total sugar purchases from Irish Sugar. The scheme was not governed by objective award criteria and it had the effect of discouraging the recipient wholesalers and retailers from purchasing sugar from Irish Sugar's sugar-packaging competitors.

4.313 Several of these packers also complained to the Commission that they were the only bulk sugar customers of Irish Sugar who did not receive any non-volume-related discounts.[304] The Commission found that this too amounted to an abuse of Irish Sugar's dominance, in that it placed those sugar packers (the ones sourcing from Irish Sugar) at a competitive disadvantage in relation both to Irish Sugar itself as a sugar packer, and to other sugar packers sourcing from elsewhere.

---

[300] IP/88/615 (13/10/88).

[301] Case COMP/39.116 *Coca-Cola*, decision of 22.06.2005. See also P. Gasparon and B. Višnar, *Coca-Cola: Europe-wide Remedies in Fizzy Drinks*, Competition Policy Newsletter Number 3, Autumn 2005.

[302] In addition to target and growth rebates, the commitment decision covers a variety of other practices, such as exclusivity and exclusivity related practices, and tying, assortment, and space-to-sales arrangements.

[303] Case T-228/97 *Irish Sugar plc v Commission of the European Communities*.

[304] These were primarily so-called 'promotional' discounts.

In *British Airways*,[305] the CFI scrutinised a reward scheme for the travel agents established   **4.314**
in the United Kingdom and who were marketing British Airways' plane tickets. According
to the Court, it was necessary to determine whether the marketing agreements and the
reward scheme had a fidelity building effect in relation to those travel agents and, if they did,
whether they were based on an economically justified consideration. The schemes were
found to have fidelity building character 'by reason of their progressive nature with a very
noticeable effect at the margin'. The increased commission rates could rise exponentially from
one reference period to another, as the successive reference periods progressed. Furthermore,
the higher the revenues obtained by the travel agents, the stronger the penalty they would
face even in the case of a slight decrease in sales of BA tickets compared with the previous reference period. Therefore, transport agents were deterred from offering tickets from BA's competitors. The CFI did not accept the argument that the agents could hardly influence the
travellers' choice of airlines, since they filter information on air transport availability and fare
structures. The CFI further considered that BA's five main competitors on the UK market[306]
were not in the position to match the advantages offered by BA, in order to counteract the
exclusionary effect of the reward scheme. The reward scheme was also considered to be
discriminatory.

Rebates linked to the attainment of generally applicable volume targets over a relatively   **4.315**
long reference period   In *Michelin II*, the CFI condemned uniformly set annual targets
by distinguishing them from straightforward quantity rebates. A system of quantity rebates
linked exclusively to the volume of purchases and based on efficiency gains and economies
of scale does not generally foreclose competition. A discount applicable to the whole of the
turnover achieved in a reference period has a loyalty enhancing effect. The longer the period
(one year) the more loyalty enhancing it becomes. That effect is limited when the additional
rebate applies only to quantities exceeding a certain threshold. According to the CFI, a dominant company which operates loyalty inducing discounts and bonuses inhibits normal price-
based competition and infringes Community law.

Top slice rebates   A so-called 'top-slice rebate' is a specific form of rebate resulting from the fact   **4.316**
that purchasers sometimes obtain the bulk of their requirements (or their 'core requirements')
from a single supplier and the rest from elsewhere. In such circumstances, dominant firms
may seek to induce the purchaser to purchase in addition that remnant (the so-called 'top
slice') from it by offering a special discount on the top slice tonnage. In the *Soda Ash* cases,
the Commission penalised the chemical company ICI for pursuing such pricing policies,
relying also on the fact that the rebates were not granted at a uniform rate to all recipients.

Tying or aggregated rebates   If a discount is granted only on condition that the customer   **4.317**
agrees to buy several different types of products and/or services, this will not normally be
permitted under Article 82. Such rebates can have exclusionary effects in a number of markets simultaneously. In *Hoffmann-La Roche*, for example, the Court held that the dominant
company's system of fidelity rebates, calculated on a customer's purchases of a variety of

---

[305] Case T-219/99 *British Airways* 17/12/2003. This decision is under appeal to the ECJ.
[306] BA sold a multiple of the sales achieved by the cumulative sales of those five competitors.

products in different product markets, also constituted an infringement of Article 82(d)[307] (see also an analysis of tying in 4.237 et seq. above).

(iv) Pricing Practices: Discriminatory Pricing

4.318 **Price discrimination generally** Price discrimination occurs when a firm charges different prices to different customers for identical goods or services. Firms often discriminate between customers for legitimate commercial reasons. In some cases they charge different prices for a same product to different customers (ie medical or legal services are sometimes priced according to the wealth of the patient). Price discrimination does not consist in direct pricing abuses alone, but can also (and in fact more usually does) occur as a result of indirect pricing practices, principally by means of the granting of discounts or rebates.

4.319 Discrimination can only occur if three conditions are fulfilled. First, the firm engaging in it should have some market power. Firms are not able to discriminate in a competitive market. Second, there should be different groups of customers with different elasticities of demand (ie ready to buy the products at different prices) and, finally, arbitration between these groups of customers should not be possible.

4.320 Discrimination is not always economically harmful. To the extent that discrimination enhances output, by enabling a firm to sell more than it would have in the absence of the discrimination, it increases consumer welfare. In some cases, however, price discrimination produces anti-competitive effects. In analysing the exclusionary effects produced by price discrimination, it is useful to distinguish between what is termed 'primary-line price discrimination', which harms the direct competitors of the dominant company by foreclosing access to the market were the dominant firm is present, and 'secondary-line price discrimination', which harms customers of the dominant company who are competing with each other. As an exclusionary abuse, price discrimination is used by a dominant firm to protect or increase market power. In addition to these two forms of discrimination, Article 82 is arguably also concerned with price discrimination which simply exploits the dominant firm's customers, and possibly consumers, by extracting higher surplus from them (see exploitative abuses below).

4.321 **Elements of the abuse** Article 82(c) states that an abuse may consist in 'applying dissimilar conditions to equivalent transactions with other trading parties, thereby placing them at a competitive disadvantage'. It is established that this provision also implies a ban on the equal treatment of non-equivalent transactions.[308]

4.322 *Equivalent transactions* In order to fulfil the first criterion of Article 82(c), it is necessary to decide in what circumstances transactions are 'equivalent'. This involves an evaluation of the nature of the products and/or services concerned, and may necessitate consideration *inter alia* of their composition, quality, variety, of the speed or time of delivery, of marketing costs, or of any other relevant factors. The most obvious method to conclude that two

---

[307] Similar abuses were the subject of the *Digital* case, which was resolved with undertakings—see 1997 Annual Competition Report, para 69.
[308] See the bundled pricing cases discussed at 4.329 et seq. below: *Napier Brown* and *Van den Bergh Foods*.

transactions are not equivalent is to show that the dominant company's costs in providing the product and/or service were not the same.

Both the Commission and the Court, in order to avoid geographic price discrimination, **4.323** which undermines the single market, have been particularly careful in considering as equivalent transactions those which could be differentiated on the basis of nationality. More controversially, in some cases they have also regarded transactions involving identical goods, but where the goods are sold in different geographic markets, as equivalent (see the *United Brands* and *Tetra Pak* cases, discussed below under geographical price discrimination). Nevertheless this seems to have changed and at present a detailed analysis of transport costs is made before considering two transactions as equivalent. In the Commission's decision in *HOV SVZ/MCN* (1994),[309] for example, the Commission did not accept the German rail operator's assertion that its freight carriage costs to Dutch and Belgian ports were higher than to North German ports. This is also the case for quantity discounts based on cost savings, as will be seen below.

Placing trading parties at a competitive disadvantage The second condition of Article **4.324** 82(c) requires that the dominant firm's trading parties be placed at a competitive disadvantage as a result of the discrimination. This condition is somewhat ambiguous. The customer of the dominant firm may be placed at a competitive disadvantage in relation to the dominant firm itself (primary line discrimination), or in relation to other customers of the dominant firm (secondary line discrimination). Beyond the wording of Article 82(c), price discrimination may also be found when a dominant company uses selective pricing targeting potential customers of a competitor to deter its entry as in *Irish Sugar*.

Perhaps on account of this ambiguity, the requirement to demonstrate that trading parties **4.325** have been placed at a competitive disadvantage has been substantially neglected by the Commission and by the Courts in cases where price discrimination is used for exclusionary purposes rather than exploitative ones. In most of the principal cases dealing with price discrimination as an exclusionary abuse (*United Brands* and *Hoffmann-La Roche*, for example), this aspect, or at least the precise wording, was entirely neglected, while in others (*Suiker Unie* and *Irish Sugar*, for example) only brief reference was made to it.

Objective justification As a general rule, it will be a legitimate defence to the application **4.326** of Article 82 to discrimination by dominant firms to demonstrate that the behaviour can be objectively justified. The most obvious instance of objective justification in this context is to show that the dominant company is forced to discriminate in order to meet a competitor's offer. The extent to which the Commission and Court will be prepared to admit the defence of meeting competition is unclear, though there are some indications that a dominant firm will be given greater leeway in more competitive markets. In *BPB Industries*,[310] for example, the Commission considered that specific prices discounts, accorded to customers in a geographic market where competition was particularly vigorous, were justifiable.

---

[309] *HOV SVZ/MCN* [1994] OJ L104/34.
[310] C-310/93 P *BPB Industries pcl & Anor v EC Commission.*

4.327 **Discriminatory rebates and discounts** Customers obtaining a rebate for buying a large quantity of a given good will pay a lower unitary price of the goods purchased than customers buying the same product but in less quantity. Precedent determines that the rules for calculating discounts and rebates must not result in the application of dissimilar conditions to equivalent transactions with other trading parties within the meaning of Article 82(c). Although this principle concerns even purely quantitative rebates, its application requires judgment:

> the mere fact that the result of quantity discounts is that some customers enjoy in respect of specific quantities a proportionally higher average reduction than others in relation to the difference in their respective volumes of purchase is inherent in this type of system, but it cannot be inferred from that alone that the system is discriminatory.[311]

In economic terms, quantity discounts or rebates are more accurately described as an instance of non-uniform pricing rather than pricing which is discriminatory between customers. The Commission has rarely condemned quantity rebate schemes where all customers are treated equally, ie where the scheme is entirely objective in terms of its qualification criteria.

4.328 Where the differences of treatment are not justified by the volume of business they bring or by economies of scale, there might be scope for a finding of an infringement of Article 82 on the basis of discrimination.

4.329 A volume discount specifically targeted to favour a particular customer might also have exclusionary effects for the favoured customer's competitors. This was the case in the *Brussels Airport*[312] case, where the Commission found such a scheme to be contrary to Article 82, because it seems to have been tailored so that only the airport's largest customer, Sabena, would benefit. Other rebates which are likely to be accepted, because they normally confer an economic benefit on the dominant supplier, include: discounts corresponding to services rendered by the customers, for example 'functional discounts' sometimes granted to wholesalers;[313] discounts given for cash payment; discounts given for prompt payment; and rebates given because of quality defects.

(v) Pricing Practices: Bundled Pricing

4.330 Another form of exclusionary pricing practice, similar to a tying practice and to discriminatory pricing, is bundling through the pricing of a product or service (see also below). This is an instance of applying equivalent conditions to non-equivalent transactions. In *Napier Brown*, the Commission found British Sugar's policy of 'delivered pricing' to be discriminatory. This policy involved charging all purchasers of sugar a bundled price (a 'delivered price') which included the cost of delivery, even when buyers did not wish to have the sugar delivered by British Sugar. The Commission's intervention ensured that British Sugar introduced an alternative 'ex factory' price for customers not taking delivery from the company.

---

[311] eg Case C-163/99 *Portugal v Commission* (Portuguese Airports) [2001], paras 50–52.
[312] See Commission's XXVth Annual Competition Report (1986), point 120.
[313] In the *Coca-Cola* case, for example, the Commission indicated that rebates granted in return for distributors' use of Coca-Cola's advertising material would be objectively justified.

In *Van den Bergh Foods*,[314] the Commission indicated[315] that Unilever's previous policy of **4.331** so-called 'inclusive pricing', whereby the costs of freezer cabinet provision and of the ice cream products themselves were bundled together in a single price charged to all retailers, would amount to an abuse within the meaning of Article 82. The pricing policy had the effect of discriminating against retailers who bought Unilever's ice cream but didn't take its cabinets. No formal finding was made, however, because the alleged abuse had been terminated following the Commission's statement of objections.

Legal harassment   An undertaking may abuse its dominant position by an excessive use **4.332** against competitors of the instruments that the legal order puts at its disposal to defend its rights. Two different types of this abuse can be distinguished:

• Abuse of legal proceedings, and
• Abuse of claims for performance of a contract

Abuse of legal proceedings   The fact that an undertaking with a dominant position on a **4.333** particular market brings legal proceedings against a competitor on that market may constitute an abuse within the meaning of Article 82 of the EC Treaty. Nevertheless, as the CFI pointed out in *ITT Promedia*:[316]

> As access to the Court is a fundamental right and a general principle ensuring the rule of law, it is only in wholly exceptional circumstances that the fact that legal proceedings are brought is capable of constituting an abuse of a dominant position within the meaning of Article 82 of the EC Treaty.

The Commission[317] has laid down two cumulative criteria for determining in which cases **4.334** bringing such legal proceedings would constitute an abuse: first, the legal action cannot reasonably be considered as an attempt to establish the rights of the undertaking concerned, and can therefore only serve to harass the competitor; and, second, the legal action must be conceived in the framework of a plan whose goal is to eliminate competition. Since the two criteria constitute an exception to the general principle of access to the Courts they must be construed and applied strictly.

As to the first criterion, the CFI specified[318] that it should not be interpreted as a question **4.335** of determining whether the rights that the dominant undertaking was asserting actually existed or whether the action was well founded. It is a question of simply assessing whether the legal action is intended to assert what the dominant undertaking could reasonably consider to be its rights. In view of this interpretation, the first criterion will probably only be satisfied when it can be proved that the only aim of the action is to harass a competitor. As to the interpretation of the second criterion, there is no particular guidance provided by

---

[314] Case 98/531 *Van den Bergh Foods* [1998] OJ L246, p 1.

[315] ibid, p 76.

[316] T-111/96 *ITT Promedia NV v Commission* [1998] para 60. On this judgment, see R. Nazzini, *Concurrent Proceedings in Competition Law: Evidence, Remedies and Procedure* (Oxford: Oxford University Press, 2004) 398–399.

[317] *ITT Promedia/Belgacom* (IV/35.258) [1996] not published. Mentioned in *ITT Promedia* (see previous note), para 55. The CFI did not explicitly confirm that the two criteria were well founded because the claimant did not challenge them, but gave some indications as to how they should be interpreted.

[318] T-111/96 *ITT Promedia NV v Commission* [1998], paras 72–73 and 93.

case law, but it can be assumed that it will only be satisfied if there is evidence of intention to eliminate competition through the legal action.

4.336 A different modality of this type of abuse involves the misuse by a dominant company of regulatory procedures in order to raise rivals' costs or to keep competitors out of the market. The only example to date of this type of abuse being prosecuted under EC law is the decision adopted against AstraZeneca for misusing the patent system and other regulatory procedures for the marketing of pharmaceutical products.[319] In its findings, the Commission considered that two different practices could be considered abusive. The first involved misrepresentations by AstraZeneca before a certain number of national patent offices with a view to extend in certain countries the patent protection for Losec, the leading anti-ulcer drug. The second practice related to a misuse of rules and procedures applied by the national medicines agencies which issue market authorisations for medicinal products. The effect of both practices was to block or delay entry to the market for generic versions of Losec.

4.337 *Abuse of claims for performance of a contract*   In the same *ITT Promedia case*[320] the CFI ruled that a claim for performance of a contractual obligation may also constitute an abuse for the purposes of Article 82 of the EC Treaty if, in particular, that claim exceeds what the parties could reasonably expect under the contract or if the circumstances applicable at the time of the conclusion of the contract have changed in the meantime. In any other case, if the conclusion of the contract in itself was not deemed to be abusive, it would not be possible to rule that a claim for performance of that contract is contrary to Article 82 of the EC Treaty.

(g) Cross-subsidisation

4.338 Cross-subsidisation occurs when one undertaking allocates all or part of the costs of its activity in one or more product or geographic market to its activity in another product or geographic market.

4.339 If an undertaking in a dominant position engages in cross-subsidisation from the market where it is dominant to a market where it is not, it could benefit from its position in the first market in order to artificially offset its costs in the second market internally. It would not, therefore, compete purely on the basis of efficiency in this second market, which could distort competition there. It is conceivable, therefore, that cross-subsidisation might constitute an abuse within the meaning of Article 82 of the EC Treaty.

4.340 Cross-subsidisation will normally allow the dominant company to charge lower prices than those it would have charged in the absence of cross-subsidisation. If a cross-subsidisation abuse exists at all, however, it would be independent of the level at which these prices are set. There would be no need to prove that the prices are predatory in order for cross-subsidisation to be considered abusive. Indeed, evidence that the lower prices can be explained by the existence of cross-subsidies would be enough to conclude that the dominant company is not competing on the merits. In the absence of such evidence, Article 82 would only be applicable if the price levels could be shown to be predatory (ie it would have to be demonstrated that the prices were set below variable average cost).

---

[319] IP/05/737 of 15 June 2005.
[320] T-111/96 *ITT Promedia NV v Commission* [1998], para 140.

Types of cross-subsidisation   To date, the possibility of finding a cross-subsidisation abuse   **4.341**
has only been considered in relation to companies enjoying monopolies and, in particular, when
the activities in these reserved markets subsidise activities in markets open to competition.

The case law to date casts some doubt, however, on the existence of an independent abuse of   **4.342**
cross-subsidisation, and it may be that cross-subsidisation does no more than facilitate the
commission of an abuse. In *Deutsche Post AG I*,[321] the Commission found that Deutsche
Post had engaged in predatory pricing in the market for business parcel services. Deutsche
Post's below-cost selling in the latter market (which was open to competition) had been
partly financed by its revenues in its reserved letter mail delivery market. For five years,
Deutsche Post had not covered the additional or incremental cost involved in moving into the
new market. The Commission decided that any beneficiary of a monopoly branching out
into a new competitive market must ensure that the activities in the new market must 'pay for
themselves' by bearing at least these incremental costs. No fine was imposed on Deutsche Post
for this abuse, because of the novelty of applying an incremental cost standard for predatory
pricing. (This case is also discussed in the section on predatory pricing— see 4.262.)

It should be noted, however, that the Guidelines on the application to EC competition   **4.343**
rules in the telecommunications sector[322] the Commission stated that 'subsidising activities under competition, by allocating their costs to monopoly activities, is likely to distort
competition in violation of Article 8[2]'.

Likewise, in the Notice on the application of the Competition rules to the Postal Sector and   **4.344**
on the assessment of certain state measures relating to postal services, the Commission
claims that 'cross-subsidisation in the postal sector, where nearly all operators provide
reserved and non-reserved services, can distort competition and lead to competitors being
beaten by offers which are made possible not by efficiency and performance but by cross-
subsidies'. The Commission concludes by saying that 'subsidising activities open to competition by allocating their costs to reserved services is likely to distort competition in
breach of Article 8[2]'.

According to the Commission,[323] this type of cross-subsidisation can take different forms.   **4.345**
It can be carried out either by funding the activities in question with capital remunerated
substantially below the market rate, or by providing premises, equipment, experts, and/or
services for those activities at a remuneration substantially lower than the market price.
It is submitted, however, that the Commission did not necessarily mean that such cross-
subsidisation would constitute an abuse *per se*, but that it might facilitate the commission
of an abuse (such as predatory pricing, for example).

Such cross-subsidisation is considerably easier to detect if monopolies are obliged to   **4.346**
keep separate financial records, identifying separately costs and revenues associated with
the provision of services supplied under their exclusive rights and those provided under

---

[321] Case COMP/35.141 (OJ L125, 5.5.2001).
[322] OJ C233/02 [1991], paras 102–110.
[323] Guidelines on the application to EC Competition rules in the telecommunications sector, OJ C233/02
[1991], para 104.

competitive conditions. EC law imposes such an obligation on telecommunications operators and the Commission considers that Members States should also require it from postal operators.[324] In certain other cases,[325] such as where a condition was required for the grant of an exemption pursuant to Article 81(3), the Commission has imposed separated cost accounting and transparency requirements.

4.347 Other types of cross-subsidisation also involving telecommunications or postal monopolies would not be considered restrictive of competition. Cross-subsidies within or between reserved activities are allowed, not only because they cannot restrict competition, but also because they might be necessary in order to enable the monopolists to perform their obligation to provide a universal service (eg profitable mail delivery in urban areas may subsidise unprofitable delivery in rural ones). The need for these cross-subsidies to ensure the financial viability of monopolies entrusted with a service of general interest may even justify maintaining an exclusive right in relation to activities that should otherwise be opened up to competition.[326]

4.348 As for cross-subsidies from non-reserved activities to reserved ones, they are rarely likely to occur. Such cross-subsidies would not normally make commercial sense as, unless it is more efficient than its competitors, the cross-subsidies would impede the monopolist from offering a competitive price for its non-reserved activities. Even if they did occur, they would not be restrictive of competition because they would only affect the market already reserved to the monopolist.

(h) Structural Abuses

4.349 **General principles** The concept of structural abuse consists in a commercial action by, or transaction involving, a dominant firm which produces an immediate change in the structure of the market to the detriment of competition. Structural abuses are distinct from the other exclusionary abuses detailed above, in that the latter are essentially behavioural in nature, and generally result from a course of conduct over a period of time. Structural abuses, by contrast, are usually one-off occurrences. Such an abuse might consist in, for example, the acquisition by a dominant company of a minority shareholding or of a technology licence. The creation by a dominant firm of a co-operative joint venture or other long-term co-operation agreement might also be considered to constitute an abuse of a structural kind.

4.350 The concept of structural abuse was first recognised by the Court of Justice in its seminal 1973 ruling in *Continental Can*. The Court established the principle that *any commercial practices* which are damaging to the maintenance of an effective competitive structure are prohibited by Article 82. The Court said that the Article

> is not only aimed at practices which may cause damage to consumers directly, but also at those which are detrimental to them through their impact on an effective competition structure, such as is mentioned in Article 3(f) [now 3(g)] of the Treaty. Abuse may therefore occur if an undertaking in a dominant position strengthens such position in such a way that the degree of dominance

---

[324] Notice on the application of the Competition rules to the Postal Sector and on the assessment of certain state measures relating to postal services, para 8(b).
[325] *Atlas and Phoenix* [1996] OJ L239 and *Unisource* [1997] OJ L318.
[326] See case C-320/91 *Procureur du Roi v Corbeau* [1993] ECR I-2533.

reached substantially fetters competition, ie that only undertakings remain in the market whose behaviour depends on the dominant one . . .

The Court goes on to stress that 'the strengthening of the position of an undertaking may be an abuse and prohibited by Article 8[2] of the EC Treaty, regardless of the means and procedure by which it is achieved, if it has the effects mentioned above.'

Acquisition of control of another undertaking   As explained above, in Continental Can   **4.351**
it was established that Article 82 is applicable to concentrations which *strengthen an already existing dominant position*. It is not clear, however, whether it could also be applicable to concentrations which *create a dominant position*.[327] At present this discussion becomes largely academic because the Commission can no longer take action on the basis of Regulation 17 against such operations.[328] Since the adoption of the Merger Regulation in 1989, concentrations (as defined in the Regulation) with a 'Community dimension' (as defined in the Regulation) are assessed by the Commission on the basis of the Regulation (see Chapter 5).

Acquisition of minority shareholdings   It has been established that Article 82 may be appli-   **4.352**
cable to acquisitions of shareholdings which do not confer on the acquirer sole or joint control of the enterprise of which the acquired shareholding represents a stake. In *BAT and Reynolds*,[329] the Court stated that, where a company in a dominant position acquires a minority shareholding in another company, 'an abuse of such a position can only arise where the shareholding in question results in *effective control* of the other company *or at least in some influence on its commercial policy* [emphasis added]'.[330]

The Commission appears to have gone further than that by finding Article 82 applicable to   **4.353**
the acquisition by a dominant firm of minority shareholdings which confer little if any determinative control over the company in which the stake was acquired. In *Warner-Lambert/Gillette*,[331] the Commission held that the acquisition by Gillette, which was dominant in the wet-shaving market in Europe, of a minority shareholding in its principal competitor, was contrary to Article 82. The Commission reached this conclusion notwithstanding the fact that the 22 per cent stake in question conferred on Gillette very few formal powers, it obtained no voting rights or board representation. The Commission pointed out that 'the structure of the wet-shaving market in the Community has been changed by the creation of a link between Gillette and its leading competitor' and that the change would have an adverse effect on competition. Referring to *BAT and Reynolds*, the Commission concluded

---

[327] Although the Court of Justice has never addressed this question, it is highly debatable whether Art 82 could be extended to include the prohibition of such operations; note that in its decision in *Metaleurop* (1990), a decision taken before the Merger Regulation came into force, the Commission seemed to imply (see para 18) that Art 82 could be applicable to concentrative operations which created a dominant position.

[328] It could, however, act on the basis of Art 85 (formerly Art 89), either on its own initiative or at the request of a Member State/s. Nor is that to say that national courts cannot apply Art 82: the Treaty provision, being directly applicable, is not affected by secondary legislation such as the Merger Regulation. It should also be noted that Member State authorities can apply Art 82 to concentrations without a Community dimension—see recital 29 to the Merger Regulation, and Art 84 (formerly Art 88) of the Treaty; the latter provision provides that Member State authorities can apply the competition rules in the absence of implementing legislation pursuant to Art 83 (formerly 87); since neither Regulation 17, nor the Merger Regulation, apply to concentrations without a Community dimension, there is no such implementing legislation for these operations.

[329] Cases 142 and 156/84 *BAT and Reynolds* [1986] ECR 1899.

[330] ibid, para 65.

[331] Case 93/252 *Warner-Lambert/Gillette* L116, 12.5.1993, p 21.

that the management of Gillette's competitor would be 'obliged to take into account' the position of Gillette, and that the minority stake would thereby influence its commercial conduct. The Commission ordered Gillette to dispose of the minority shareholding.

4.354 **Acquisition of a licence**   In *Tetra Pak I*,[332] the firm, which was dominant in the markets for aseptic milk cartons and filling machinery, acquired a competitor, thereby also acquiring an exclusive licence to a new technology for filling packages. The Court of First Instance held that, in doing so, Tetra Pak had abused its dominant position. The abuse, according to the Court, did not consist in the concentrative aspect of the operation but in the fact that the transaction gave Tetra Pak access to a technology which would strengthen its dominance, and have a substantial foreclosure effect on the company's rivals for a long period of time.

4.355 In *Carlsberg/Interbrew*,[333] a case which did not result in a formal decision, the Commission objected to an exclusive licence from Carlsberg to the Belgian brewer Interbrew for the distribution of the former company's beer products in Belgium. The Commission was of the view that the licence would result in a strengthening of Interbrew's dominance in the Belgian beer market by increasing the portfolio of beers it could offer to consumers, as well as by making it more difficult for its competitiors to make a comparable offer. In response to the Commission's objections, Carlsberg rendered the licence non-exclusive, and created a second distributor for its products in partnership with a local wholesaler.

4.356 The Commission has even acted against licensing arrangements which have been in operation for a long time. In *Svenska Tobaks*,[334] also a case resolved informally, the Commission expressed doubts as to the compatibility with Article 82[335] of a long-standing[336] exclusive licensing arrangement between the dominant cigarette company in Sweden (the licensee) and a Danish cigarette company (the licensor). The licence concerned the manufacture, distribution, and sale of one of the major cigarette brands in Sweden. The Commission was of the view that such a long-term licensing arrangement produced anti-competitive effects, thereby strengthening the licensee's dominance in the Swedish cigarette market. Following the Commission's intervention, the licence was essentially reduced to a subcontracting arrangement.

4.357 **Co-operative joint ventures/co-operation agreements**   In line with the approach taken towards the applicability of Article 82 to licensing arrangements, it would seem that the same principles would apply in relation to co-operative joint ventures or long-term co-operation agreements between competitors. There appears to be no case law relating specifically to this question, which may be explained by the fact that Article 81 is almost invariably sufficient to deal with such cases.

(3) Exploitative Abuses

4.358 By exploitative abuses is normally meant those practices by dominant undertakings which, while not directly harming competitors in the market, reduce the welfare of consumers.

---

[332] Case T-51/89 *Tetra Pak I* [1991].
[333] See 1994 Annual Competition Report, paras 209, 213.
[334] See 1997 Annual Competition Report, para 66.
[335] The Commission also considered that the arrangements infringed Art 81.
[336] The original licence was granted in 1961.

This reduction of welfare or exploitative effect can take several forms, such as excessive prices, insufficient quality or diversity of products, reduction of innovation, or discriminatory treatment of customers.

(a) Exploitative Effects

As explained in the introduction to this chapter, the assessment of exploitative effects presents some important conceptual and practical difficulties. The main conceptual problem is that, theoretically, an exploitative abuse could be committed every time that a company with market power operates in the market. Indeed, by definition, companies with market power charge a higher price or produce lower output than companies operating in a pure competitive situation and, therefore, reduce the welfare of customers. **4.359**

This conceptual problem is closely linked to a practical difficulty in assessing exploitative effects: in order to determine whether a particular firm is exploiting its customers it must be determined at what level of prices and/or output it would not be doing so. The level of prices and output that would prevail in a competitive situation would be the appropriate reference, but in most cases it will be impossible for competition authorities and courts to determine this. Other references, therefore, have been used, such as a comparison to the situation in similar markets or an assessment of the level of satisfaction of demand in the market in question. **4.360**

The determination of an exploitative effect necessarily involves, therefore, the need to make an assessment of the appropriate level of prices and output in a particular market. It can be observed that, probably in order to limit the risks inherent to any such judgment, competition authorities and Courts tend to restrain themselves and only pursue exploitative behaviour in cases where the reduction of consumer welfare is particularly clear. **4.361**

(b) Unfair or Excessive Prices

Article 82(a) of the EC Treaty expressly states that an abuse may, in particular, consist in indirectly imposing unfair purchase or selling prices or other unfair trading conditions. Generally speaking, such abuses will consist in the charging of unfairly high prices by dominant suppliers, but could also include the extraction of unfairly low prices by dominant buyers. **4.362**

(i) Excessive prices

General   In economic terms, excessive prices are those which are set at above the competitive level as a result of the exercise of market power. It is often pointed out that excessive prices are not anti-competitive, that is to say that in a functioning market economy they should have the effect of attracting new entrants who will force the price down, and that they consequently should not be the concern of antitrust authorities. It is often argued that to prohibit a dominant company from charging high prices amounts to unfairly penalising the company's competitive success in achieving dominance by depriving it of its just reward for that endeavour. This, broadly speaking, is the approach adopted by the US courts,[337] which have repeatedly refused to countenance a 'reasonable price' test, principally on account of the inherent uncertainty of such a test. **4.363**

---

[337] See, for instance, the judgment by the US Supreme Court in *Verizon Communications INC v Law Offices of Curtis V Trinko LLP*, 540 US 398 (2004). The approach is also favoured by some commentators on EC law: see V. Korah's *EC Competition Law and Practice* (London: Hart, 2000).

4.364 The EC Treaty, however, is expressly concerned with a dominant firm's ability to exploit consumers by charging them unfairly high prices. Intervention against excessive pricing can moreover be supported by a number of economic and policy justifications.[338] While economic theory may predict that new firms should enter a market, the reality may prove otherwise, particularly where a market is characterised by structural problems, hence the need for intervention. Protecting consumers is moreover a legitimate policy objective of antitrust law. Where, for example, the barriers to entering a market are particularly high, such a policy interest may be particularly compelling. Furthermore, while competition rules should not deprive a firm of the fruits of its genuine success in the market-place, it is legitimate to prevent the undue exploitation of its market power. It should also be added that, in some instances, a firm's dominance arises as a result of forces other than competition.

4.365 Excessive pricing has, however, proved to be a notoriously difficult abuse to prosecute, principally on account of the complexity involved in calculating what amounts to an unreasonably high price. Taking such cases is also unsatisfactory in the sense that the intervening authority is expected to take on the role of a quasi-price regulator, with the task of second-guessing the market as to what is the correct price level. Conversely, from a dominant company's point of view, the control of excessive pricing poses a problem of legal certainty: how high can its prices lawfully be set? It is perhaps not surprising therefore that the Commission has only rarely taken decisions making a finding of excessive pricing, notably in the *General Motors* and in the *United Brands* cases and, even then, the findings were in both instances subsequently struck down by the Court of Justice.

4.366 *General Motors* In this case, the Commission held that General Motors had abused its dominant position on the market for granting Opel car conformity certificates in Belgium by charging excessively high fees for the service. The Court of Justice struck down the finding, however, because of the relative triviality of the allegations, and because General Motors had terminated the alleged abuse even before the Commission's intervention. Nevertheless, the Court made it clear that excessive pricing could in principle constitute an abuse [339] if the price was excessive in relation to the economic value of the service provided, and if it had the effect of either curbing parallel trade (thereby eliminating the possibility of competition from lower prices charged elsewhere) or of unfairly exploiting customers.

4.367 *United Brands* The prices charged by UBC in the various Member States where it operated varied considerably: the greatest price difference was between Ireland and Denmark, the level being 138 per cent higher in the latter than in the former. Using the Irish prices as a base, the Commission concluded that the prices charged by UBC were 'excessive in relation to the economic value of the product supplied',[340] that the differences could not be accounted for by transport costs, and that the prices were excessive by comparison with those charged

---

[338] See more generally Conor Hanly, 'Pricing: A Behavioural Approach to Abuses of Market Power' (Ph.D. thesis, UCD, unpublished, 1994).

[339] The Court had given earlier signals that it was prepared to entertain findings of excessive pricing; see the *Sirena* and *Deutsche Grammophon* cases.

[340] They were 30–40 per cent higher than the prices charged for unbranded bananas, which were only of slightly inferior quality.

by UBC's competitors. No detailed cost/price analysis was, however, carried out. The Commission proceeded to require UBC to reduce its prices by a fixed percentage in certain Member States.

The Court of Justice's test   The Court of Justice, while reiterating that excessive prices   **4.368** would fall foul of Article 82 where they bore no reasonable relation to the economic value of the product supplied and resulted in harm being caused to consumers, nevertheless held that the Commission's economic analysis in the instant case had been flawed. The Court made it clear that it was necessary for a detailed cost analysis to be made, stating that the question to be determined is 'whether the difference between the costs actually incurred and the price actually charged is excessive and, if the answer to this question is in the affirmative, to consider whether a price has been imposed which is either unfair in itself or when compared to competing products'.

This is a twofold test: the first part requires a cost/price analysis, followed by a determination   **4.369** as to whether the difference is excessive; the second part necessitates determining whether a price is either excessive in itself or by comparison to competitors' products. Applying the test in the instant case, the Court found that UBC's prices were only 7 per cent greater than those of its main competitors, and so annulled the Commission's finding of excessive pricing.

It is submitted that the Court's failure to articulate a more objective, and perhaps a more   **4.370** workable, test is to be regretted. In applying both parts of the test, the question of what is meant by 'excessive' arises, and the Court provides no real guidance which might relieve this uncertainty. The Court does not describe exactly what costs should be taken into account in making the cost/price analysis. Nor does it shed light on when a price should be considered 'in itself' excessive. The requirement to make a comparison with the prices of competing products is moreover potentially unreliable in that the prices compared to may themselves be unfair.

The *United Brands* case highlights the major difficulties of proof associated with finding an   **4.371** abuse of excessive pricing, and probably explains the relative dearth of instances in which the Commission has intervened.

The ECJ has also dealt with alleged excessive prices in two cases referred to it by French   **4.372** courts. In *Bodson*[341] the issue was whether the prices for certain 'external services' relating to funerals were excessive. The prices in question were charged by a private undertaking which had been given a concession to provide these services in 2,800 French communes. The Court held that a basis for deciding whether the prices of the private undertaking were excessive would be a comparison with the prices in the 30,000 communes that either had left the provision of 'external services' unregulated or operated the services themselves.

In *Lucazeau v SACEM*[342] the Court held that a dominant national copyright-management   **4.373** society imposes unfair trading conditions where it on a consistent basis charges appreciably

---

[341] Case 30/87 *Corinne Bodson v SA Pompes Funèbres des Regions Libérées* [1988] ECR 2479.
[342] Joined Cases 110/88, 241/88, and 242/88 *François Lucazeau and others v Societé des Auteurs, Compositeurs et Editeurs de Musique (SACEM) and others* [1989] ECR 2811.

higher royalties to discothèques than those charged in other Member States. The Court's judgments in these two cases hinted at some possible comparisons but gave no indications of how large differences need to be before a finding of excessive prices is appropriate. To date, there is, therefore, still no clear guidance on this issue from the European courts.

4.374   In 2004 the Commission applied the *United Brands* twofold test in rejecting two parallel complaints alleging that the Port of Helsingborg charged excessive port fees for services provided to ferry operators active on the Helsingborg–Elsinore route between Sweden and Denmark.[343] The Commission found that the revenues derived from the ferry operations 'would seem to exceed the costs actually incurred by the port to provide services and facilities to these users'. However, the Commission did not determine whether the difference was sufficiently large for the prices to be considered excessive, on the basis that in any event it had to address the second limb of the *United Brands* test. After detailed analysis the Commission found that there was 'insufficient evidence' to conclude that the port fees were unfair either compared to prices charged to other users or by other ports or in themselves.

4.375   These cases illustrate the difficulties of showing that prices are excessive if there are no obvious comparators. The Commission sought to compare the prices charged by the Port of Helsingborg with prices charged by other ports and between the fees charged by the Port to ferry operators and those charged to cargo vessels. However, it argued that differences in charging systems and the services provided made it very difficult to compare prices in a meaningful way and that in the end there was 'insufficient evidence' to conclude on the basis of such comparisons that the prices were unfair.

4.376   As to the issue of whether prices were unfair in themselves, the Commission argued that non-cost factors also had to be taken into account in order to assess the 'economic value' of the services provided. One such factor was the good location of the Port of Helsingborg which allowed its customers an attractive short distance service. On the basis of these considerations the Commission again found that there was 'insufficient evidence' to conclude that prices were unfair in themselves.

4.377   **The United Kingdom *Napp* case**   This case provided the Office of Fair Trading (OFT)[344] and the Competition Appeals Tribunal (CAT)[345] with the opportunity to address the issue of how to establish that prices are excessive. Napp had sold certain strengths of its brand of sustained release morphine to the hospital segment at prices below direct cost while prices charged to the 'community segment' (medicine prescribed by general practitioners) were much higher. The CAT confirmed the findings by the OFT that Napp had supplied hospitals at 'excessively low' (ie predatory) prices and charged excessively high prices to the community segment.

---

[343]   Cases COMP/36.568 *Scandlines Sverige AB v Port of Helsingborg* and COMP/36.570 *Sundbusserne v Port of Helsingborg*, decisions of 23.07.2004. See also M. Lamalle, L. Lindström-Rossi, and A. C. Teixeira, 'Two important rejection decisions on excessive pricing in the port sector', *Competition Policy Newsletter* No. 3, Autumn 2004.

[344]   Case No. CA98/2/2001 *Napp Pharmaceutical Holdings Limited and Subsidiaries* [2001].

[345]   Case No. 1001/1/1/01 *Napp Pharmaceutical Holdings Limited and Subsidiaries v Director General of Fair Trading* [2002].

The OFT argued that to show that prices are excessive, it must be demonstrated that **4.378** (i) prices are higher than what would be expected in a competitive market, and (ii) there is no effective competitive pressure to bring them down to competitive levels, nor is there likely to be.

The OFT relied on following facts: Napp's prices in the community segment were typically **4.379** 30–50 per cent higher than its competitors; Napp's prices in the community segment had basically remained the same for more than twenty years, even after the expiry of its formulation patent; for the tablet strengths on which it faced competition, Napp's list price (less wholesale discount) in the community segment was on average 1,400 per cent higher than its prices in the hospital segment and at its highest level 2,000 per cent higher; Napp's prices in the community segment were over 500 per cent higher than its prices for export on a contract manufacture basis; Napp's gross profits margin on sales to the community segment was more than 80 per cent, compared with a margin in the 30–50 per cent range in the hospital segment; Napp's gross profit margin on sales to the community segment was in excess of 80 per cent compared with a gross profit margin on less than 70 per cent for Napp's next most profitable competitor; if Napp's manufacturing margin was recalculated on the basis of the costs of its next most profitable competitor, Napp's gross margin was less than 90 per cent compared with that competitor's margin of less than 70 per cent.

The CAT concluded that the comparisons listed above amply supported the conclusion of **4.380** the OFT that Napp's prices were well above what would have been expected in competitive conditions. The fact that Napp at the same time had retained a market share of the community segment of some 96 per cent also supported the proposition that Napp's community prices had not been subject to competitive pressure.

Although this was not entirely clear from the decision, the OFT at the appeal stated that it **4.381** would not wish to maintain the abuse of excessive pricing in the community segment if the CAT found that there had been no exclusionary conduct in the hospital segment. The OFT took the view that since pricing in the pharmaceutical industry is, to a certain extent, regulated, a case of alleged excessive pricing by a pharmaceutical company, in which there was no suggestion of any exclusionary conduct, would be a different case, and would require a more detailed and complex analysis than the OFT thought it necessary to undertake in the Napp case. The CAT took the opportunity to clarify that, as a matter of law, nothing in *United Brands* suggests that the existence of exclusionary conduct is a prerequisite to a finding that prices are excessive.

(ii) Unfairly low prices extracted by dominant buyers

Although instances appear to be rare, it has been established that Article 82 can also be **4.382** applied in relation to the behaviour of a company (or companies in the case of joint dominance) which is a dominant purchaser in the relevant market, and which exercises its buying power to extract unfairly low prices from its suppliers. In particular, concern is increasingly being expressed by suppliers and consumers about the power of the major retail groups in certain Member States.[346]

---

[346] See 16th Annual Competition Report, at paras 345–348, re the increasing buying power of large retail chains and the increasing incidence of purchasing associations.

4.383 In the *CICCE*[347] case, the Commission rejected a complaint from a film distributors' association against the three French TV stations, in which the complainants alleged that the stations charged unfairly low broadcasting fees for the airing of their films. While accepting that the TV stations did possess the requisite buying power to enable them to commit an abuse by charging excessively low fees, the Commission's rejection of the complaint was upheld by the Court on the grounds that the allegation was unsupported by sufficiently detailed evidence demonstrating that the fees bore no reasonable relation to the economic value of the films: a value which would vary according to each individual film. Once again, the difficulty of proving these unfair pricing abuses is evident.

(c) Imposing Other Unfair Terms

4.384 In addition to condemning excessive prices, Article 82(a) also considers that the imposition of other unfair trading conditions may constitute an abuse. Determining whether a trading condition imposed by a dominant undertaking is unfair presents the same problems as determining whether a price is fair or excessive.

4.385 As explained above, determining whether a price or trading condition is unfair requires the authorities to apply Article 82 to assess what would be the prices or conditions that would prevail in a competitive environment.

4.386 In exceptional cases, however, the Commission and the Court have considered that conditions imposed by dominant undertakings were unfair and, therefore, contrary to Article 82. In *BRT v SABAM*,[348] a case concerning a performing rights society, it was considered that restrictions imposed on the authors who were members of the society were unfair insofar as they were not necessary to allow the performing rights society to conduct its business properly (ie to negotiate with radio and TV stations over copyright licences).

4.387 In other cases, the criteria for determining whether a trading condition was fair or not have focused on the burden that the condition places on customers. In *Alsatel*,[349] a case concerning the rental of telecommunication equipment, the Court considered that a clause allowing the dominant company to increase unilaterally the rent and automatically extend for fifteen years the rental contract was excessive. Similarly, in *Tetra Pak II*,[350] a clause obliging the payment of a rent at the beginning of the contract of almost the same amount as the value of the machine was considered unfair. Indeed, it would force the customer to pay as much as if it had purchased the machine, but would deprive it of the legal benefits of being the owner.

4.388 In *AAMS*, the Court of First Instance[351] confirmed a Commission decision[352] finding that the Italian state tobacco monopoly had abused its de facto monopoly on the market for wholesale distribution of cigarettes in two ways. First, AAMS inserted into distribution contracts clauses which gave it as the distributor of foreign cigarettes the right to intervene in certain choices of the foreign firms and, therefore, limit the competitive initiatives of

---

347 Case 298/83 *CICCE* [1985] ECR 1105.
348 Case 127/73 *BRT v SABAM* [1974] ECR 51.
349 Case 247/86 *Alsatel* [1988] ECR 5987, para 10.
350 Case 92/163 *Tetra Pak II* [1991] OJ L72, 18.3.1992, p 1, paras 135–138.
351 Case T-139/98 *Amministrazione Autonoma dei Monopoli di Stato (AAMS)* [2001] ECR II-3413.
352 *Amministrazione Autonoma dei Monopoli di Stato* [1998] OJ L252/47.

these firms on the Italian market. For instance, the contracts only allowed foreign firms to introduce new brands twice a year and limited in various ways the quantities of cigarettes that the foreign firms could bring into the market. Secondly, AAMS unilaterally took certain decisions with regard to imported cigarettes which amounted to abusive behaviour. These included AAMS refusing to authorise increases in cigarette imports within the limits of the distribution contracts and taking actions aimed at ensuring that independent parts of the Italian distribution system downstream from AAMS would favour domestic cigarettes over foreign cigarettes

4.389 Finally, excessive conditions have also been considered abusive when imposed by dominant buyers. In *Eurofima*[353] (a company created by the main European rail operators in order to develop new rail passenger carriages), the Commission considered that a dominant buyer of railway stock was abusing its dominant position by inviting tenders for development contracts on condition that unlimited patent licenses should be granted to it without further remuneration.

(d) Limiting Production, Markets, or Technical Development

4.390 Another example of exploitative abuse is contained in Article 82(b) of the EC Treaty, which states that an abuse may, in particular, consist in limiting production, markets, or technical development to the prejudice of consumers.

4.391 As in relation to other exploitative abuses, there are no simple criteria for determining what should be the amount and quality of output produced by an undertaking in a dominant position (or the level of technical development that it should attain) in order not to prejudice consumers and, therefore, not to engage in an abuse within the meaning of Article 82.

4.392 Theoretically, it could be said that an undertaking holding a dominant position abuses this position when it produces a lower level of output or innovation than what a competitive environment would produce. However, authorities applying competition rules do not have the means to perform such an analysis and, therefore, are obliged to find other, less perfect, criteria for determining when Article 82(b) of the EC Treaty is infringed.

4.393 The simplest situation to assess is that in which a company holding a dominant position ceases to provide a product or service that it was providing previously. In such a case, if the interruption prejudices customers and is not justified by any reasonable business objective (eg to eliminate the losses that such a product generated) it may be deemed to constitute an abuse of a dominant position. In *British Leyland*,[354] for instance, the refusal by a British car manufacturer to renew the certifications for left hand drive cars that it had been granting in the past was considered to be an abusive limitation of output. In this particular case, British Leyland could not advance any business justification for its decision because it was obvious that the main motivation behind it was to foreclose the British market from parallel imports.

4.394 A criterion to be used more generally is to assess whether the output produced by the dominant undertaking, both in qualitative and quantitative terms, leaves a substantial amount

---

[353] *Eurofima*, IIIrd Report on Competition Policy [1973], para 68.
[354] Case 226/84 *British Leyland* [1986] ECR 3263, paras 12–21.

of the demand unsatisfied. If this is the case, the undertaking may be found to have infringed Article 82 of the EC Treaty.

4.395 The Court has applied this criterion to undertakings entrusted by Member States with an exclusive right to perform certain activities. In *Hoffner and Elser v Macrotron*,[355] it considered that the Bundesanstalt für Arbeit, a German agency with the monopoly on the provision of placement services, had failed to meet the demand for its services and that it had, therefore, abused its dominant position. Similarly, in *Port of Genoa*,[356] the Court considered that the undertaking with the exclusive right to organise dock work had abused its dominant position by failing to use modern technology, which resulted in increased costs and longer service delays. In both cases the Court found that granting exclusive rights under such conditions constituted an infringement of Article 82 together with Article 86 of the EC Treaty.

4.396 This criterion has been used not only in the case of legal monopolies, but also in relation to private undertakings holding a dominant position. The Commission considered, for instance, that the *International Group of P&I Clubs*,[357] which covers around 90 per cent of the market for maritime third party liability insurance, had abused its dominant position by only providing a single level of insurance cover, thereby leaving a substantial proportion of the demand unsatisfied.

(e) Discriminatory Practices

4.397 Article 82(c) prohibits discriminatory practices and, in particular, discriminatory pricing. The elements of this abuse have been discussed above (see 4.317 et seq.) insofar as the abuse may amount to an exclusionary practice. Discrimination can however also be exploitative. Some particular types of exploitative discriminatory pricing are discussed below.

4.398 **Discrimination based on nationality**   Nationality can never constitute an admissible ground for discrimination. To do so would fly in the face of a fundamental tenet of Community law, enshrined in Article 12 of the Treaty, namely that discrimination on the basis of nationality is absolutely prohibited. Discrimination on the basis of nationality has the effect of impeding the development of the single market. The European competition rules serve the purpose, not only of protecting competition, but also of ensuring the integration and proper functioning of that market. For that reason, this form of discrimination can legitimately be prohibited by Article 82.

4.399 The prohibition covers both direct and indirect discrimination, and so extends to discrimination on the basis, for example, of domicile or place of establishment. In *Corsica Ferries*,[358] the Court of Justice found that pilot tariffs had been set in such a way as to discriminate indirectly against certain ships on the basis of nationality. In *GVL*,[359] the Court held that a refusal by a dominant company to supply a category of customers, defined according to those customers' nationality or domicile, was contrary to Article 82.

---

[355] C-41/90 *Hofner and Elser v Macrotron* [1991] ECR I-1979.
[356] C-179/90 *Port of Genoa v Gabrielli* [1991] ECR I-5889.
[357] *International Group of P&I Clubs* [1999] OJ L125.
[358] Case C-18/93 *Corsica Ferries Italia Srl v Corpo dei Piloti del Porto di Genova* [1994] ECR I-1783.
[359] Case 7/82 *GVL* [1983] ECR 2327.

Geographical price discrimination   The *United Brands* and *Tetra Pak* cases demonstrate   **4.400**
that, if a dominant firm charges different prices in different Member States, it can also
attract the sanction of Article 82. It seems clear that, in these cases, the Commission and
Court have been motivated by the desire to prevent the segmentation of the market along
national lines. These cases are less straightforward, however, than the cases involving discrimination on the basis of nationality, because it is not clear whether it is the discrimination as such which has been condemned, or the discrimination combined with other
market partitioning factors specific to those cases.

In *United Brands*, UBC had a long-standing policy of supplying bananas to ripener-   **4.401**
distributors in the various Member States where it operated, at considerably varying price
levels. The bananas were of identical quality, were sold in an identical condition, and in the
same place (usually Bremerhaven or Rotterdam). The Commission, in a decision upheld
by the Court of Justice, found this to be an infringement of Article 82(c).

It seems rather far-reaching, on the face of it, that Article 82 should be extended to apply to   **4.402**
a company which pursues a different pricing policy in different national markets. It should
be noted however that the Commission and Court appear to have been particularly influenced by what they saw as UBC's deliberate attempt to partition the Community along
national market lines, in particular by imposing obligations on its customers not to resell
green bananas. This additional restriction had the effect of rendering more difficult the
possibilities for arbitrage through the development of a cross-border wholesale trade in
bananas. The resale restrictions and discriminatory pricing were separately condemned by
the Commission and Court.

UBC argued that its pricing policy was objectively justified in that it was charging what the   **4.403**
market would bear, and that this differed significantly from one geographic market to the
other. The reasons for these differences depended, according to UBC, on a variety of locally
specific factors such as seasonal demand variations and so on.

The Commission and Court refused to accept that different market conditions pertaining in   **4.404**
the various Member States could amount to an objective justification for the price differences.
In reaching this conclusion, the Commission placed particular emphasis on the fact that identical bananas were usually sold in the same place at widely varying prices. The Court appeared
also to rely on the fact that UBC was not itself directly selling in the markets concerned, but
only to resellers who were selling there; only the latter were bearing the risks inherent in the
local markets, and so only they would need to take into account local market specificities in
setting price levels. This may indicate that the closer is a dominant company's direct involvement in the market, the more it will be permitted to price discriminate.

In *Tetra Pak II*, however, the Commission and Court condemned geographical price   **4.405**
discrimination by a vertically integrated dominant firm selling directly to customers in a
variety of national markets. In that case also, the differences between the prices charged in
the various Member States were very considerable. The Commission and Court did not
accept that the price differences could have any legitimate explanation other than as an
attempt to partition the common market along national lines. Again, as in *United Brands*,
the Commission and Court placed reliance on the fact that resale restrictions were imposed

on Tetra Pak's customers and, again, the resale restrictions and discriminatory pricing were separately condemned.

4.406 This approach has, with a degree of justification, been sharply condemned by some commentators. It can be argued that, in cases such as those just described, it is the resale restrictions alone which should be condemned. The possibility of arbitrage should ensure that markets become more integrated notwithstanding the price discrimination (though in the case of integrated firms selling directly to consumers, this would be more difficult).

4.407 It is certainly unjust, however, to prohibit geographical price discrimination, at least by integrated firms, where selling costs (advertising, promotional, or fiscal costs, for example) in the various national markets differ to any great extent. It is even arguable that the approach adopted by the Commission and Court in *United Brands* and *Tetra Pak II* amounts to giving dominant companies the responsibility for the implementation of public policy. The approach might be seen as requiring such firms to charge more or less uniform prices across all Member States, thereby depriving them of the possibility of pricing optimally (availing of the differing price levels in the different Member States) in the same way as non-dominant companies can.

4.408 In *Irish Sugar*, the Commission impugned a series of abuses aimed at protecting the Irish sugar market from imports. These included an ad hoc rebate scheme operated periodically by the dominant supplier of sugar in Ireland, whose purpose was patently protectionist. The scheme sought to restrict imports from Northern Ireland (where sugar prices were usually lower than in the Republic), including re-imports of Irish Sugar's own products, by offering so-called 'border rebates' to customers on the Irish side of the border area, the clear aim being to discourage them from importing sugar from Northern Ireland. The company also indulged in 'selective pricing' of Irish Sugar's own retail brand, offering it to some customers at lower prices than others—particularly where those customers had started to stock, or had expressed an interest in stocking, imported sugar brands.[360]

4.409 Finally, a peculiar form of geographical price discrimination was also sanctioned by the Commission in *Irish Sugar*. The dominant supplier had been operating a system of so-called 'sugar export rebates', whereby rebates were granted on sales of industrial sugar to companies exporting the final processed products from Ireland to other Member States. The Commission found that this scheme of rebates was a clear example of discrimination with trade distorting consequences. Irish Sugar claimed that domestic processors were not placed at a competitive disadvantage in relation to the exporters, as the two were competing on different markets. However, the Commission pointed out that the rebate scheme also discriminated against the local processors by placing them at a competitive disadvantage in relation to third parties, such as importers into Ireland of processed sugar products from other Member States.[361] It remains to be seen whether the Courts will uphold the

---

[360] Similar rebates were also impugned by the Commission and Courts in *BPB Industries plc* [1989] OJ L10/50, rectified in [1989] OJ L52/42; *Case T-65/89 BPB Industries Plc and British Gypsum v Commission* [1993] ECR II-389; *Case C-310/93P BPB Industries Plc and British Gypsum v Commission* [1995] ECR I-865.

[361] See Decision at para 140.

Commission's interpretation of what is meant by the notion of 'competitive disadvantage' in this context.

D. Effect on Trade between Member States

The same principle outlined in relation to Article 81 applies to Article 82. The effect on **4.410** trade criterion is a jurisdictional standard, confining the scope of application of Article 82 to abuses of a dominant position appreciably influencing, either directly or indirectly, actually or potentially the patterns of trade of goods or services or other cross-border economic activity between Member States, (see Chapter 3 for a more detailed analysis of these notions.) Furthermore, the concept of 'effect on trade' determines the ambit of the convergence rules established in Article 3 of Regulation 1/2003,[362] which governs the parallel application of Articles 81 and 82 EC and of national law (see below under the heading 'Parallel application of Article 82 and national law to unilateral and concerted conduct').

E. Relationship between Article 81 and Article 82

A common purpose Both Articles 81 and 82 serve the principles set out in Articles 2 and **4.411** 3(g) of the Treaty. That is to say, they are both instrumental in facilitating the establishment and maintenance of a common market, and they together comprise 'a system ensuring that competition . . . is not distorted'[363] in that market. The two provisions are aimed at policing the market behaviour of commercial undertakings. Article 86 and Articles 88–91 (formerly Articles 92–4), by contrast, are concerned with public measures which have the effect of distorting competition in the common market.

The Court of Justice clearly sees Articles 81 and 82 as the two branches of a single bifurcated **4.412** antitrust system. In *Continental Can*,[364] the Court stressed that, because the two Articles ultimately pursue the same basic objective, they 'cannot be interpreted in such a way that they contradict each other'. This means that care must be taken to ensure that Articles 81 and 82 are applied in a coherent fashion.

Articles 83–5 (formerly Articles 87–89) of the EC Treaty, as well as the relevant implement- **4.413** ing legislation, in particular Council Regulation 1/2003, apply to both Articles 81 and 82. Article 83 provides the legal basis for such implementing rules, while Article 85 specifically prescribes an enforcement function for the Commission in respect of Articles 81 and 82. Article 84 (formerly Article 88) is concerned with transitional arrangements.

Differences While Articles 81 and 82 serve the same basic purpose, they are nevertheless **4.414** independent instruments, designed to remedy broadly different commercial situations. The principal differences between them can be summarised as follows.

---

[362] Regulation 1/2003 on the implementation of the rules on competition laid down in Arts 81 and 82 of the Treaty (OJ L1, 4.1.2003, p 1).
[363] Art 3(g) EC Treaty.
[364] [1973] ECR 215, para 25.

4.415 Article 81 addresses concerted behaviour or agreements between companies, and does not address undertakings' unilateral conduct, whereas Article 82 is mainly concerned with unilateral responsibility of dominant firms,[365] whether the conduct is implemented unilaterally or by means of concerted behaviour or agreements. A finding that Article 81 has been infringed must involve establishing that the agreement has an anti-competitive object or effect. Exploitative conduct falling foul of Article 82 need only to have been engaged in by a dominant company. As regards exclusionary abuses, it is necessary to show that the conduct of the dominant firm is likely to eliminate or deter competition because it resorts to strategies other than competition on the merits. In contrast to Article 81, the relevant market for the application of Article 82 must constitute the whole or at least a substantial part of the common market. Finally, Article 82 contains neither a provision for automatic nullity equivalent to Article 81(2), nor a provision equivalent to Article 81(3).

4.416 **Parallel application of the two Articles** The Court of Justice made it clear in *Hoffmann-La Roche*[366] that, where an agreement appears to infringe both Articles 81 and 82, *either* Article may be applied. It also now seems clear that *both* Articles 81 and 82 can be applied simultaneously to the same agreement or conduct. The Commission sought to apply both Articles in *Italian Flat Glass*, a case involving the notion of collective dominance (discussed in detail at 4.110 *et seq* above). The Court of First Instance recognised that the same conduct could be incompatible with both Article 81(1) and 82, but it went on to say that 'for the purposes of establishing an infringement of Article 8[2], it is not sufficient . . . to "recycle" the facts constituting an infringement of Article 8[1]'.

4.417 There had initially been some doubt as to the Court of Justice's attitude towards the simultaneous application of both Articles to the same subject matter. In *Ahmed Saeed*,[367] the Court seemed to consider that it would only be possible to apply Article 82 to an agreement falling foul of Article 81 where the agreement 'simply constitutes the formal measure setting the seal on an economic reality characterized by the fact that an undertaking in a dominant position has succeeded in having the . . . [agreements] in question applied by other undertakings'. This seemed to imply that, in order for there to be simultaneous application of the two Articles it would be necessary to demonstrate that the abuse in reality consisted in a unilateral imposition by the dominant company of the agreements in question. In *Almelo*,[368] however, the Court of Justice clearly held that the application by a group of companies holding a collective dominant position of an exclusive purchasing obligation could be at the same time contrary to both Articles 81 and 82. This position was confirmed in *Compagnie Maritime Belge*[369] by explicitly stating: 'It is clear from the very wording of Articles 8[1](1)(a), (b), (d) and (e) and 86(a) to (d) of the Treaty that the same practice may give rise to an infringement of both provisions. Simultaneous application of Articles 8[1] and 8[2] of the Treaty cannot therefore be ruled out a priori. However, the objectives pursued by each of those two provisions must be distinguished.'

---

[365] Or, in the case of collective dominance, by more than one dominant company.
[366] Case 85/76 *Hoffmann-La Roche v Commission* [1979] ECR 461, para 116.
[367] Case 66/86 [1989] ECR 803.
[368] Case C-393/92, [1994] I ECR 1477.
[369] Joined Cases C-395/96 P, C-396/96 P, [2000] ECR I-1365, para 33.

Relationship between Articles 81(3) and 82   It is in principle possible for a dominant   **4.418**
company to benefit from the application of Article 81(3), since that provision does not
exclude any kind of undertaking from its scope of application. However, if the company at
stake is not simply dominant, but the behaviour (agreement or concerted practice) falling
under Article 81 also qualifies as abusive, Article 82 may be applied as well. The fact that Article
81(3) may be applicable to an agreement falling under Article 81(1) does not preclude the
application of Article 82 to the same agreement. Furthermore, the economic approach
characterising the application of Article 81 EC under the new rules concerning vertical
restraints and horizontal co-operation, as well as the principles set out in the Commission
Notice on the Guidelines on the application of Article 81(3) of the Treaty[370] makes it essential to consider whether the firms taking part in an agreement enjoy a sufficient degree of
market power enabling them to distort competition. Therefore, it is extremely unlikely that
Article 81(3) may be applicable to an agreement constituting an abuse of a dominant position, which is a very high and durable degree of market power. In particular, exploitative
abuses implemented through agreements are by nature unlikely to satisfy any requirement
to pass on to consumers a fair share of the advantages obtained by the dominant firm.

A possible conflict between Article 81(3) and Article 82 in the context of an agreement   **4.419**
which benefits from a block exemption is also unlikely, in practice, since the new generation of block exemptions also hinges on the concept of market power and does not normally cover agreements or concerted conduct undertaken by dominant companies. If this
were to be exceptionally the case, those block exemption regulations expressly reiterate the
principle that the applicability of a block exemption does not imply that Article 82 is not
infringed, and it therefore provides no protection against this prohibition. Apart from the
fact that no individual assessment will have been made of the agreement in question,
a block exemption is a piece of secondary legislation and cannot therefore override a Treaty
provision. Furthermore, Article 29 of Regulation 1/2003 allows the Commission and
the National competition authorities (within the limits set in paragraph 2) to withdraw
the benefits of a block exemption regulation for the future in an individual case.

In *Tetra Pak I*, the Court of First Instance confirmed the Commission's finding that the   **4.420**
acquisition by Tetra Pak of an exclusive patent licence was contrary to Article 82. The fact
that the licence containing the exclusivity provision benefited from an exemption by virtue
of the patent licensing block exemption (Reg. 2349/84) did not affect the possibility of
finding such an infringement. The Commission in any event made it clear that, had Tetra
Pak not renounced all claims to the exclusivity before the Commission Decision was taken,
it would have withdrawn the benefit of the block exemption and found an infringement
of Article 81. Indeed, in a block exemption concerning shipping conferences,[371] the
Regulation explicitly provided that where the Commission finds that the conduct of
the conferences benefiting from the exemption has effects which are incompatible with
Article 82, it may withdraw the benefit of the block exemption and take measures to
terminate the infringements.

---

[370] OJ 2004/C 101/08.
[371] Commission Regulation 4056/86, Art 8.

4.421 **Parallel application of Article 82 and national law to unilateral and concerted conduct** Article 83(2)(e) of the Treaty gives to the Council the power to regulate the relationship between Articles 81 and 82 EC and national competition laws. This was exercised for the first time in Article 3 of Council Regulation 1/2003. The most relevant parts of this provision as regards Article 82 are the following:

1. . . . Where the competition authorities of the Member States or national courts apply national competition law to any abuse prohibited by Article 82 of the Treaty, they shall also apply Article 82 of the Treaty.
2. The application of national competition law may not lead to the prohibition of agreements, decisions by associations of undertakings or concerted practices which may affect trade between Member States but which do not restrict competition within the meaning of Article 81(1) of the Treaty, or which fulfil the conditions of Article 81(3) of the Treaty or which are covered by a Regulation for the application of Article 81(3) of the Treaty. Member States shall not under this Regulation be precluded from adopting and applying on their territory stricter national laws which prohibit or sanction unilateral conduct engaged in by undertakings.

4.422 According to Article 3(1), it is no longer possible to apply only national law to prohibit a violation of Article 82 EC. Therefore, national competition authorities and national courts must enforce Article 82 EC whenever they apply national law to deal with an abuse of a dominant position in the common market or a substantial part thereof, which appreciably affects trade between Member States. The application of Article 82 EC as a common standard triggers the co-operation mechanisms within the European Competition Network as well as those with national judges.

4.423 The eventual application of national competition law is subject to the conditions spelled out in Article 3(2), which was drafted to distinguish purely unilateral conduct from agreements, decisions by associations of undertakings, or concerted practices within the meaning of Article 81 EC. Unilateral conduct by dominant companies is only subject to scrutiny under Article 82 EC, and Member States are not precluded from adopting national laws stricter than Article 82 EC and applying them to it. This includes, for instance, many pricing practices, de facto tying, and refusals to supply when they do not qualify as 'agreements' or 'concerted practices' between undertakings. On the other hand, abuses of a dominant position falling under Article 82 may constitute the implementation of agreements, decisions of an association of undertakings or concerted practices in the sense of Article 81 EC, such as contractual tying, agreed target or loyalty rebates, English clauses, or exclusivity obligations. In this case, Article 81 EC will normally also be applicable and Member States are precluded from enforcing stricter national competition law.

4.424 **The burden of proof** Article 2 of Regulation 1/2003 establishes that the burden of proving an infringement of Article 82 shall rest on the party or the authority alleging the infringement. This provision only codifies the current Commission practice [372] and a general principle of law

---

[372] See Case C-185/95 P *Baustahlgewebe v Commission* [1998] ECR I-8417, para 58. See, on the subject of the burden of proof, R. Nazzini 'The wood began to move: an essay on consumer welfare, evidence and burden of proof in Article 82 EC cases' [2006] ELR (forthcoming).

(*secundum allegata, probata*), extending it to all other enforcers. Article 2 does not regulate the kind of evidence or standard of proof required or how the evidence should be brought in order to be admissible. Furthermore, it does not establish whether or to what extent an authority must investigate both incriminating and exculpating evidence. For national proceedings, those issues remain subject to national law, which in any event should not jeopardise the effectiveness of Article 82 EC; whereas Commission proceedings follow Community law, in particular the principles set out by the Court of Justice.

F. Remedies

Article 82 prohibits the abuse of a dominant position but it does not make any reference to the remedies to be applied once such abuse has taken place. Regulation 1/2003, however, does include some general rules on this issue. These rules, as well as remedies that have been imposed by the Commission and the Courts, are described below. **4.425**

Termination of the infringement   Article 7 of Regulation 1/2003 provides for the Commission to adopt a decision requiring undertakings to terminate their infringements of the competition rules of the EC Treaty. This decision is binding on the undertakings to which it is addressed and normally takes effect immediately, although in some cases the Commission grants a delay for the termination of such infringements.[373] **4.426**

A decision to terminate an abuse within the meaning of Article 82 will normally consist of an order to cease an action. The order can also extend to any future behaviour which has an effect similar to the conduct deemed to be abusive.[374] **4.427**

Behavioural remedies   In order to secure the termination of the infringement, the decision may also require the undertaking which has abused its dominant position to adopt a certain course of action. As the Court of Justice held in *Commercial Solvents*,[375] the decision can include: **4.428**

> an order to do certain acts or provide certain advantages which have been wrongfully withheld, as prohibiting the continuation of certain actions, practices or situations which are contrary to the EC Treaty.

An order to adopt a certain course of action will be more likely in cases of refusal to deal. It may require a resumption of supply when this has been interrupted by the dominant undertaking,[376] or the provision of access to any facility or information for which this access has been denied. In both cases, the Commission can order that the access terms be reasonable,[377] but should not interfere in the principle of freedom of contract if it is not strictly necessary.[378] **4.429**

---

[373] For instance, in *Magill TV Guide* [1989] OJ L78/43, the parties were given two months to bring the infringements to an end.

[374] *Hilti*, [1988] OJ L65/19.

[375] Case 6 and 7/73 *Commercial Solvents v Commission* [1974] ECR 223.

[376] ibid.

[377] As it did in *Magill TV Guide* [1989] OJ L78/43.

[378] See Case T-24/90 *Automec v Commission* [1992].

4.430   The Commission decision in the *Microsoft*[379] case provides a recent example of behavioural remedies. Indeed, to terminate a refusal to provide information to competitors in the server operating system markets (see 4.214 above), the Commission imposed on Microsoft the obligation to make interoperability information available and allow its use on reasonable and non-discriminatory terms to any undertaking with an interest in developing and distributing work group server operating system products. In addition, in order to terminate the tying abuse identified, Microsoft was obliged to offer a full-functioning version of its Operating System, the tying product, which did not incorporate Windows Media Player, the tied product. However, Microsoft retained the right also to offer a bundle of both products.

4.431   **Structural remedies**   Article 7 of Regulation 1/2003 enables the Commission to:

> impose any behavioural or structural remedies which are proportionate to the infringement committed and necessary to bring the infringement effectively to an end. Structural remedies can only be imposed either where there is no equally effective behavioural remedy or where an equally effective behavioural remedy would be more burdensome for the undertaking concerned than the structural remedy.

4.432   This provision grants an explicit power to the Commission to impose structural remedies to terminate an infringement of Articles 81 and 82. However, this is not an unqualified power. Structural remedies are considered as a last resort solution; they can only be imposed when there is no equivalent behavioural remedy or when the equivalent behavioural remedy would be a more burdensome one. In the remaining cases, the Commission must impose a behavioural remedy leading to the termination of the infringement, as described above.

4.433   Structural remedies would normally be appropriate in cases where the abuse produces a change in the market structure (see above under structural abuses). For instance, in *Continental Can*,[380] the Commission considered that a purchase of a competitor by a dominant undertaking was an abuse of Article 82 and required the dominant company to make a disposal of the acquired company. The order was not applied, however, because the ECJ annulled the decision on substantive grounds. In *Gillete*,[381] the Commission considered that the acquisition of a 22 per cent share of the company that had acquired Wilkinson Sword, a competitor, constituted an abuse and expressly imposed an obligation on Gillette to dispose of that equity stake.

4.434   Structural remedies will also be appropriate in other cases where there is a risk of a lasting or repeated infringement that derives from the very structure of the undertaking.[382] This could be the case, for instance, in a situation in which an undertaking holding an exclusive right or a clearly dominant position in an upstream market and competing in a downstream one repeatedly abused its dominant position upstream.

4.435   **Nullity of agreements concluded in breach of Article 82**   Article 82 does not include a provision equivalent to Article 81(2), which prescribes that any agreements or decisions prohibited

---

379   Commission Decision COMP/37.792—Microsoft; 24 March 2004.
380   Case 6/72 *Europemballage and Continental Can v Commission* [1973] ECR 215.
381   Commission Decision in *Warner-Lambert/Gillette and BIC/Gilette*, OJ 1993 L116, p 21.
382   See Recital 12 of Regulation 1/2003.

by Article 81(1) shall be automatically void. Nevertheless, the ECJ has stated that a similar consequence applies to any breach of Article 82.[383] Nullification of contracts concluded in breach of Article 82 can be enforced by national Courts due to the direct effect of Article 82.

Commitment decisions   Article 9 of Regulation 1/2003 establishes that: **4.436**

> Where the Commission intends to adopt a decision requiring that an infringement be brought to an end and the undertakings concerned offer commitments to meet the concerns expressed to them by the Commission in its preliminary assessment, the Commission may by decision make those commitments binding on the undertakings.

In June 2005 the Commission adopted the first Article 9 decision relating to a potential   **4.437** Article 82 infringement. The decision was addressed to Coca-Cola and referred to three types of concern: exclusivity related practices, growth and target rebates, and bundling practices.[384] According to the preliminary analysis of the Commission, these practices could have led to less downwards pressure on prices and loss of product variety.

The Commitments offered by the parties, however, were considered sufficient to remove   **4.438** these concerns. First, the parties undertook to refrain from concluding exclusivity agreements save in specific circumstances and from granting growth and target rebates. Second, by providing that requirements concerning assortment and shelf-space must be defined separately for certain categories of brands, the commitments addressed the concern that strong brands would be leveraged in favour of weaker ones. Finally, in regard to financing agreements and technical equipment arrangements, the commitments would reduce contract duration, give customers the option of repayment and termination without penalties and free up a certain share of cooler space, thus addressing the concerns that the pre-existing arrangements would unduly bind customers and lead to outlet exclusivity.

It is difficult to draw general conclusions on the basis of this single precedent as to the future   **4.439** use of Article 9 decisions. The Commission, however, appears ready to contemplate concluding complex proceedings with commitment decisions, rather than continuing the procedure until the adoption of an infringement decision. Ensuring an immediate impact of the commitments on the market and avoiding litigation may justify this policy. In fact, several Article 82 proceedings had already been brought to an end by virtue of commitments proposed by the parties, even when the Commission did not have powers under Regulation 17 to make them binding. The binding character of Article 9 and the powers to impose substantial fines for possible violations of the commitments (see Article 23.2 of Regulation 1/2003) should provide sufficient reassurance to the Commission to use this instrument further in the future.

G. Fines

Article 23 of Regulation 1/2003 allows the Commission to impose fines on undertakings   **4.440** that infringe Article 82. Fines can be applied for infringements made both intentionally

---

[383] Case 172/73 *BRT v SABAM* [1974] ECR 51.
[384] Commission decision of 22 June 2005 relating to a proceeding pursuant to Art 82 of the EC Treaty and Art 54 of the EEA Agreement (Case COMP/A.39116/B2/*Coca-Cola*).

or negligently. They may range from 1,000 to 1,000,000 euros, or a sum in excess thereof but not exceeding 10 per cent of the turnover in the preceding business year of each of the undertakings participating in the infringement.

4.441 According to the Guidelines on the method of setting fines adopted by the Commission[385] an abuse of a dominant position will normally constitute a serious infringement, with starting amounts between EUR1 million and EUR20 million. Clear-cut abuses of a dominant position by undertakings holding a virtual monopoly, however, might be considered very serious infringements, which will attract fines above EUR20 million.

4.442 Within each of these categories the fine will be set according to the nature of the infringement committed, the effective economic capacity of offenders to cause significant damage to other operators, the deterrent effect, and the size of the undertaking committing the infringement. In addition, for infringements of medium duration (one to five years) the fine could be increased by up to 50 per cent, and for infringements of long duration (more than five years) by up to 10 per cent per year. Aggravating and attenuating circumstances will also be taken into account.

4.443 Since the adoption of the Guidelines on the method of setting fines the Commission has imposed fines in eleven Article 82 cases. In eight cases it considered the infringement serious.[386] In two cases, *TACA* and *Microsoft*, the infringement was considered very serious. In *TACA*,[387] a case that concerned an abuse of a collective dominant position, a starting amount of EUR20 million was imposed on the worst infringers. The total fines imposed amounted to EUR273 million, but were annulled by the CFI on substantive and procedural grounds. In *Microsoft*,[388] the Commission considered the different abuses jointly as a very serious infringement and imposed a preliminary fine of EUR165.7 million, which took into account the fact that the abuses were particularly anti-competitive in their nature, had a significant impact in markets of strategic importance in the IT sector, and affected the whole EEA. The final fine amounted to EUR497 million, which represented the largest fine ever imposed by the Commission on an individual company. Finally, in one case,[389] the Commission imposed a symbolic fine because it was the first time it had considered the practice in question as abusive.

4.444 Before the adoption of the Guidelines on the method of setting fines, the largest fines in a case involving an abuse of a single dominant position were imposed in *Tetra Pak II*[390] and

---

[385] Guidelines on the method of setting fines imposed pursuant to Art 15(2) of Regulation No. 17 and Art 65(5) of the ECSC Treaty (1988) OJ C9.

[386] The eight Art 82 decisions where the infringement was considered as serious are: AAMS (starting amount EUR3 million; final amount EUR6 million); Virgin-BA (starting amount EUR4 million; final amount EUR6.8 million); Deutsche Post (starting amount EUR12 million; final amount EUR24 million); Michelin (starting amount EUR8 million; final amount EUR19.76 million); La Poste (starting amount EUR2 million; final amount EUR2.5 million); Deutsche Telekom (starting amount EUR10 million; final amount EUR12.6 million); Wanadoo (starting amount EUR9 million; final amount EUR10.35 million) and AstraZeneca (final amount EUR60 million; the Commission took into account the fact that some features of the abuses could be considered as novel; see IP/05/737 of 15 June 2005).

[387] *TACA* [1998] OJ L95/1 (9.4.1999).

[388] See, in particular, paras 1059 to 1080.

[389] *Deutsche Post AG—Interception of cross-border mail* [2001] OJ L331/40.

[390] Case T-83/91 *Tetra Pak International v Commission* [1994] ECR II-755.

they amounted to 75 million ECU. Other substantial fines in Article 82 cases had been imposed in *AKZO*,[391] where they amounted to 7.5 million ECU, in *British Sugar*[392] and *BPB Industries/British Gypsum*,[393] in each of which a fine of 3 million ECU was imposed.

H. The Commission's December 2005 Discussion Paper

In December 2005 the Commission published a document entitled 'DG Competition **4.445** discussion paper on the application of Article 82 of the Treaty to exclusionary abuses'. The accompanying press release[394] stated that '[t]he Discussion Paper is designed to promote a debate as to how EU markets are best protected from dominant companies' exclusionary conduct, conduct which risks weakening competition on a market. The paper suggests a framework for the continued rigorous enforcement of Article 82, building on the economic analysis carried out in recent cases, and setting out one possible methodology for the assessment of some of the most common abusive practices, such as tying, and rebates and discounts.' The press release indicates that other forms of abuse, such as discriminatory and exploitative conduct, will be the subject of further work by the Commission in 2006.

The Commission invited comments on the Paper by 31 March 2006. As to the future of **4.446** the Paper, the Commission stated that it was not yet decided whether the Paper would be turned into Commission Guidelines on Article 82. The decision would await the results of the public consultation. Although '[i]t is clear that the Commission would like to give guidance on the application of Article 82', the Commission would 'reflect on the precise form this guidance will take following the consultation'.[395]

The Paper covers market definition in Article 82 cases as well as the analysis of dominance, **4.447** but the major part of the Paper is devoted to the analysis of abuses. The sections on market definition and dominance closely follow recent case law and decision-making practice of the Commission. The main new development is that the so-called 'AKZO presumption' of dominance relating to a company with a market share above 50 per cent[396] is referred to as an 'indication' of dominance and not as a 'presumption': '[i]t is very likely that very high market shares, which have been held for some time, indicate a dominant position. This would be the case where an undertaking holds 50 per cent or more of the market, provided that rivals hold a much smaller share of the market.'[397]

In a 2005 speech, Competition Commissioner Neelie Kroes explained the reasoning **4.448** behind the decision not to choose the term 'presumption': 'I consider that high market shares are not—on their own—sufficient to conclude that a dominant position exists. Market share presumptions can result in an excessive focus on establishing the exact market shares of the various market participants. A pure market share focus risks failing to take proper account

---

391 Case C-62/86 *AKZO v Commission* [1991] ECR I-3359.
392 *British Sugar* [1988] OJ L284/41.
393 Case T-65/89 *BPB Industries/British Gypsum* [1993].
394 IP/05/1626.
395 MEMO/05/486.
396 See 4.49 above.
397 Art 82 Discussion Paper, para 31 (footnotes omitted).

of the degree to which competitors can constrain the behaviour of the allegedly dominant company. That is not to say that market shares have no significance. They may provide an indication of dominance—and sometimes a very strong indication—but in the end a full economic analysis of the overall situation is necessary.'[398]

4.449 The main body of the Paper dealing with abuses is introduced by a section called 'Framework for analysis of exclusionary abuses', followed by sections on individual abuses such as 'Predatory pricing', 'Single branding and rebates', 'Tying and bundling', and 'Refusal to supply'. A final section deals with the analysis of aftermarkets.

4.450 The framework section attempts to 'describe in general terms the framework that could be used by the Commission in its analysis of exclusionary abuses'.[399] It describes the 'essential' objective of Article 82 with respect to exclusionary abuses as 'the protection of competition on the market as a means of enhancing consumer welfare and of ensuring an efficient allocation of resources'.[400] In line with its policy for Article 81[401] and mergers,[402] the Commission thus explicitly confirms consumer welfare as the yardstick for the enforcement of Article 82.

4.451 The Paper argues that the 'concern' of Article 82 enforcement is 'to prevent exclusionary conduct of the dominant firm which is likely to limit the remaining competitive constraints on the dominant company, including entry of newcomers, so as to avoid that consumers are harmed'.[403] The Paper continues that 'the purpose of Article 82 is not to protect competitors from dominant firms' genuine competition based on factors such as higher quality, novel products, opportune innovation or otherwise better performance, but to ensure that these competitors are also able to expand in or enter the market and compete therein on the merits, without facing competition conditions which are distorted or impaired by the dominant firm'.[404] This could be read as a kind of 'safe haven' for certain categories of conduct ('higher quality, novel products, opportune innovation or otherwise better performance') but the Paper is not explicit on this.

4.452 The Paper argues that not only actual but also likely anti-competitive effects in the market are prohibited. Also, conduct which can harm consumers directly or indirectly is prohibited. As to the time frame, short-, medium-, and long-term harm arising from foreclosure are all taken into account.[405]

---

[398] Neelie Kroes, 'Preliminary Thoughts on Article 82 Review', speech at the Fordham Corporate Law Institute, 23 September 2005.

[399] Art 82 Discussion Paper, para 51.

[400] Ibid, para 54.

[401] Commission Guidelines on the application of Art 81(3) of the Treaty, OJ C101, 27.04.2004, 97–118.

[402] Commission Guidelines on the assessment of horizontal mergers under the Council Regulation on the control of concentrations between undertakings, OJ C31, 05.02.2004, 5–18.

[403] Art 82 Discussion Paper, para 54. This is repeated in a slightly different formulation in para 56: 'The central concern of Article 82 with regard to exclusionary abuses is thus foreclosure that hinders competition and thereby harms consumers.'

[404] ibid.

[405] ibid, para 55.

The Paper suggests that the definition of exclusionary abuse given by the European Court **4.453** of Justice in *Hoffmann-La Roche*[406] implies a three-limb test: first, the conduct must 'have the capability, by its nature, to foreclose competitors from the market. To establish such capability it is in general sufficient to investigate the form and nature of the conduct in question'.[407] The second limb is that 'in the specific market context, a likely market distorting foreclosure effect must be established'.[408] The third limb is that the exclusionary conduct should not be objectively justified or produce efficiencies which 'outweigh the negative effect on competition'.[409]

The term 'capability' seems to be used mainly as a screen to distinguish between price-based **4.454** behaviour that normally cannot be considered abusive and that which might be abusive. While single branding obligations 'by their nature' have the capacity to foreclose,[410] in the case of priced-based conduct the Commission only considers that the conduct has the capability to foreclose competitors if an equally efficient competitor cannot compete with the dominant company.[411]

The Paper divides the term 'market distorting foreclosure effect' in two parts. It first defines **4.455** foreclosure as meaning that 'actual or potential competitors are completely or partially denied profitable access to a market'.[412] Foreclosure is then said to be 'market distorting' if it 'likely hinders the maintenance of the degree of competition still existing in the market or the growth of that competition and thus have as a likely effect that prices will increase or remain at a supra-competitive level'.[413] The term 'foreclosure' therefore relates to the effect on competitors while 'market distorting' relates to consumers (through higher prices).

The Paper then turns to what is needed in order to establish a market distorting foreclosure **4.456** effect and mentions that market coverage, selective foreclosure of customers, network effects, economies of scale and scope and the degree of dominance may all be relevant factors.[414] The thinking seems to be that if it can be established to a sufficient degree that the market is foreclosed to competitors, it can normally be assumed that consumers are harmed by such foreclosure. Consumer harm is thus not analysed directly, but rather indirectly through the foreclosure of the market.

The Paper appears to opt for a rather broad 'test' focusing directly on harm to consumers, **4.457** whose protection is seen as the 'essential objective' of Article 82. However, when it comes to price-based exclusionary conduct (predation, rebates, margin squeeze), the Paper abandons the broad test and opts for the so-called 'as efficient competitor' test, stating that the 'more detailed principles described in this paper for assessing allegedly price based exclusionary

---

[406] See 4.152 above.
[407] Art 82 Discussion Paper, para 58.
[408] ibid.
[409] ibid, para 77.
[410] ibid, para 148.
[411] ibid, para 66.
[412] ibid, para 58. The Paper also argues that rivals do not need to exit the market to be foreclosed; it suffices that they are 'disadvantaged and consequently led to compete less aggressively'.
[413] ibid.
[414] ibid, para 59.

conduct are based on the premise that in general only conduct which would exclude a hypothetical "as efficient" competitor is abusive'.[415] The reason for this choice may be that it would be rather difficult to apply the broad consumer harm test when it comes to price-based abuses, and that the resulting uncertainty could limit the willingness of dominant firms to compete hard on prices.

4.458 The Paper does, however, retain the option not to adhere strictly to the 'as efficient competitor' test. In particular, it is said that 'it may sometimes be necessary in the consumers' interest to also protect competitors that are not (yet) as efficient as the dominant company'. This could be done by, for instance, 'taking account of economies of scale and scope, learning curve effects or first mover advantages that later entrants can not be expected to match even if they were able to achieve the same production volumes as the dominant company'.[416]

4.459 A major new development is the discussion of possible defences. Besides objective justifications and the 'meeting competition defence', which are known from the case law, the Paper also has a section on efficiencies. The approach taken in the Paper is that an efficiency defence under Article 82 should be applied basically in the same way as Article 81(3). The underlying argument is presumably that Articles 81 and 82 can often be applied to the same behaviour and the treatment should therefore be consistent.[417]

4.460 The Paper therefore proposes criteria similar to the criteria for applying Article 81(3)[418] and states that the following conditions must be fulfilled:

(i) that efficiencies are realised or likely to be realised as a result of the conduct concerned;
(ii) that the conduct concerned is indispensable to realise these efficiencies;
(iii) that the efficiencies benefit consumers;
(iv) that competition in respect of a substantial part of the products concerned is not eliminated.[419]

4.461 The four conditions are described in terms very similar to those used in the Article 81(3) notice. The fourth condition, however, receives special attention in the Paper, because of the considerable debate that there has been over the issue. The Paper interprets the condition as meaning that it is 'highly unlikely that abusive conduct of a dominant company with a market position approaching that of a monopoly, or with a similar level of market power, could be justified on the ground that efficiency gains would be sufficient to counteract its actual or likely anti-competitive effects'.[420]

4.462 The Paper gives this statement more precise content by continuing that '[a] dominant company is in general considered to have a market position approaching that of a monopoly if its market share exceeds 75 per cent and there is almost no competition left from other actual competitors in the market, for instance because they are producing at considerably

---

[415] Art 82 Discussion Paper, para 63.
[416] ibid, para 67.
[417] See discussion above 4.155–4.158.
[418] See Ch 3.
[419] Art 82 Discussion Paper, para 84.
[420] ibid, para 91.

higher costs and/or are severely capacity constrained for a longer period of time, and entry barriers are so substantial that relevant entry can not be expected in the foreseeable future'.[421]

As mentioned above, the Paper also applies these principles to various individual abuses. **4.463**
Some of the sections dealing with these abuses (predation, tying and bundling, refusal to supply) do not necessarily add much to recent case law. The main new development is to be found in the rebates section, where the basic message is that an assessment of the effects of so-called 'retroactive' or 'roll-back' rebates has to be made over a 'relevant volume' and not at the 'margin' (or over the entire volume purchased). The Paper proposes to apply the 'as efficient competitor' test in such a situation and describes a methodology that could be used for performing à price-cost test over such a 'relevant volume'. The relevant volume is determined by what are commercially viable amounts for the competitors of the dominant supplier to supply. The Paper suggests calculating an effective price over such a volume by spreading the savings achieved by receiving a retroactive rebate over this volume. The next question asked is whether the effective price covers the average total costs of production.

The Paper is an important step towards an effects-based approach to Article 82. It anchors the **4.464**
Commission's analysis within a consistent framework clarifying the Commission's position and confirms recent moves towards a more effects-based analysis in some major Article 82 cases such as *Microsoft*. Whether the Paper in the end will be transformed into formal Commission Guidelines remains to be seen. However, its publication and the debate that has followed have already made a significant contribution towards modernising the application of Article 82 in line with what has happened for Article 81 and merger control.

---

[421] ibid, para 92.

5

MERGERS

Peder Christensen, Kyriakos Fountoukakos and Dan Sjöblom

A. Introduction to the Merger Regulation

(1) A Merger Control System for the European Union—From the Original Merger Regulation to Regulation 139/2004

(a) The Original Merger Regulation

Council Regulation (EEC) 4064/89 on the control of concentrations between undertak-ings [1989][1] ('the original Merger Regulation') provided the Community, for the first time, with a specific instrument for the control of cross-border concentrations. While Article 66 of the European Coal and Steel Treaty of 1951 provided for *ex ante* control of concentra-tions, the original Merger Regulation introduced for the first time a fully developed frame-work for merger control at the European level with general applicability across all industry sectors.   **5.01**

From the outset the original Merger Regulation has had two functions. First, it has pro-vided a means to assess, remedy or even prevent concentrations with anti-competitive effects in the common market or a substantial part of it. Secondly, the Regulation has pro-vided a single procedural and substantive framework within which such transactions can be assessed.   **5.02**

Whereas the first function is a *sine qua non* for any serious merger control policy, and, indeed, for complementing the Community rules on antitrust and state aid, the second function is equally important from an industry perspective. For cases which have a Community dimension, the 'one stop shop' assessment by the Commission replaces the need to apply for clearance under multiple national merger control regimes.   **5.03**

The original Merger Regulation is justly considered to be a particularly successful piece of EU legislation. It served to facilitate corporate restructuring in Europe, by ensuring cen-tralised, transparent regulatory scrutiny within a timetable reflecting the needs of business. Far from standing in the way of industrial restructuring in Europe, the original Merger Regulation facilitated it, while ensuring that it did not result in damage to competition. It provided a 'one stop shop' for the scrutiny of large cross-border mergers, dispensing with the need for companies to file in a multiplicity of national jurisdictions in the EU. It guaranteed that merger investigations were completed within tight, pre-determinable deadlines; a remarkable degree of transparency was maintained in the rendering of decisions with each and every merger notified to the Commission resulting in the communication and publication of a reasoned decision.   **5.04**

As can be seen from the statistical table in para 5.20 below, only a very limited proportion of these notified transactions under the original Merger Regulation required intervention by the Commission. Outright prohibitions have indeed been very rare: the total of 18 such prohibitions since 1990 represents just under 1 per cent of all notified transactions.   **5.05**

---

[1] OJ [1989] L395/1 (amended OJ [1990] L257/13).

During the same period, a further 6 per cent or so of notifications resulted in clearances conditional on the acceptance of remedies. All the remaining cases were cleared, mostly in a period of one month after notification, resulting in legal certainty for the companies concerned.

(b) The 2002–2003 Review Leading to the Adoption of the New Merger Regulation

5.06 Subsequent reviews of the original Merger Regulation have been mindful to build on its strengths. The first such review, which led to the adoption of Council Regulation (EC) 1310/97,[2] amended the Regulation in several respects, the most notable of which related to jurisdictional issues, with the intention of further strengthening the 'one stop shop'.[3]

5.07 The most recent review, which concluded with the adoption of the current Merger Regulation, Council Regulation (EC) 139/2004[4] ('the Merger Regulation' or 'the new Merger Regulation') was also triggered by a need to review the jurisdictional mechanisms of the original Merger Regulation, following a report from the Commission to the Council on the functioning of the relevant turnover thresholds.[5,6] In this report, the Commission announced its intention to embark on a wide-ranging review of the procedural and substantive aspects of the Regulation. The review was therefore to be much more ambitious in its ambit than the previous review of the original Merger Regulation. The report on the functioning of the turnover thresholds was followed by a comprehensive Green Paper,[7] which launched a wide-ranging public consultation[8] culminating in a Commission proposal for a new Merger Regulation.[9]

5.08 The context of the review merits some further discussion, particularly since the review, which took place during 2002–2003, appears to have been very timely in several senses.

5.09 First, the impending (and now completed) enlargement of the European Union necessitated some rethinking of the system of allocation of cases between the Commission and national authorities. Allocation of cases in a Union of 25 Member States may not necessarily work in the same way as in a Union of 15.

---

[2] Council Regulation (EC) 1310/97 amending Regulation (EEC) 4064/89 on the control of concentrations between undertakings, OJ [1997] L180/1.

[3] Notable amendments included the introduction of a lower set of thresholds for notification in Art 1(3) and simplification of the treatment of joint ventures under Art 3(2).

[4] Council Regulation (EC) No 139/2004 of 20 January 2004 on the control of concentrations between undertakings, OJ [2004] L24/1.

[5] COM(2000) 399 final—28.06.2000.

[6] As required by Art 1(4) of the original Merger Regulation.

[7] Green Paper on the Review of Council Regulation (EEC) No 4064/89, COM(2001) 745/6—11.12.2001.

[8] The Green Paper launched a wide public consultation exercise. The consultation focused on issues of jurisdiction, substantive review, and merger control procedures, on the effectiveness of the administrative system generally, including the due process guarantees and 'checks and balances' built into the system.

There was very considerable feedback on the Green Paper, with the submission of over 120 replies. Nearly half the submissions were from industry (industry associations and individual companies), and more than a quarter from law firms. In addition, submissions were received from trade unions, consumer organisations and academics. Several Member States also submitted written comments, as well as several of the, then, accession candidate countries. The European Parliament and ECOSOC also submitted comments. For a comprehensive summary of responses received, see DG Competition's web site at <http://ec.europa.eu/comm/competition/index_en.html>.

[9] Proposal for a Council Regulation on the control of concentrations between undertakings OJ C20, 28.01.2003, pp 4–57.

Second, notwithstanding what was generally regarded as a positive track-record, there was **5.10** undoubtedly some scope for improving the original Merger Regulation's effectiveness, and for better adapting it to the economic realities of the 21st century. The system had exhibited some signs of strain, notably on account of increasing pressures resulting from the growth in the number of merger cases and higher expectations of the quality of the Commission's analysis of merger cases.

Indeed, as can be seen from the table in para 5.20 below, merger activity had increased **5.11** beyond most expectations since the introduction of the original Merger Regulation. The number of concentrations notified to the Commission increased spectacularly during the 1990s, to the point where, by 2003, the Commission was annually reviewing more than three to four times as many cases as in the early years, notwithstanding the slowdown in merger activity in 2003. Not only the number but also the complexity of cases had increased exponentially. In particular, higher levels of industrial concentration necessitated greater sophistication in the economic analysis contained in the Commission's reasoned decisions and the emergence of a specialised competition bar heightened expectations of economic analysis in Commission merger decisions.

Importantly, litigation and scrutiny by the Community courts was also on the increase in **5.12** the relevant review period. In the period intervening between the report to the Council and the Commission's proposal, the Court of First Instance ('CFI') overturned the Commission's prohibition decisions in three important merger cases, *Airtours*,[10] *Schneider/Legrand*,[11] and *Tetra Laval/Sidel*.[12]

Whilst the CFI's annulments were not at the heart of the then ongoing review, the com- **5.13** bined critique that came through in these CFI judgments of the Commission's analysis and procedures in the field of mergers demonstrated that the Commission's investigation of merger cases would be subject to close and intense scrutiny by the Community courts. The CFI's criticisms also fuelled a debate started by the Green Paper regarding the relative merits of administrative merger control systems versus prosecutorial ones. In this discussion, some held the view that a clear separation between investigative and decisional powers (as, for example, in the US) provided better checks and balances on the investigating agency's powers, and was therefore the preferred model, whereas others felt that due process could be equally well provided by administrative systems, and favoured the benefits of such systems in terms of speed and transparency. In the end the Council decided to retain the administrative model, which is more in line with the systems applied in most Member States. However, in response to the debate, several measures (legislative and others) were adopted by the Commission in order to ensure a better functioning of its internal checks and balances. These measures are discussed in detail in Section D on 'Procedure' below.

Finally, it is worth noting that many of these discussions were taking place at an unprece- **5.14** dented international level, reflecting perhaps the ever more international aspect of mergers and merger control. Thus, the period when the Commission was reviewing its rules and

---

[10] Case T-342/99 *Airtours plc v The Commission*, 6 June 2002.
[11] Case T-301/01 *Schneider Electric v The Commission*, 22 October 2002.
[12] Case T-5/02 *Tetra Laval v The Commission*, 25 October 2002.

procedures also saw the birth of the International Competition Network (ICN),[13] and thus the review incorporated some amendments with the specific purpose of ensuring compatibility with ICN merger notification and review process recommendations.

5.15 The reform therefore sought to redress shortcomings that had emerged over the years. As a result, the review touched upon almost all aspects of merger control. The reform package that was put in place at the end of the review, and which is analysed in greater detail in the remainder of this chapter, aimed to improve the EC merger control regime and to enable the Commission to grapple with the evolving challenges ahead, whilst preserving the very real merits inherent in the original system.

(c) Overview of the New EC Merger Control Regime[14]

5.16 The 2002–2003 review culminated in the adoption of a substantially revised Merger Regulation in the form of Council Regulation (EC) 139/2004.[15] The new Merger Regulation introduced not only important further jurisdictional changes to optimise the allocation of merger cases between the Commission and National Competition Authorities in the light of the principle of subsidiarity and with the aim of alleviating the 'multiple filings' problem in Europe. It also included several major improvements to the procedural setting of the EC merger control regime, and, moreover, introduced the first changes to the substantive assessment criteria since the introduction of merger control at the Community level, see section C1 below.

5.17 The adoption of the new Merger Regulation was followed by the adoption of a new Commission Implementing Regulation[16] and guidance Notices[17] (these will be commented on in detail below in the appropriate sections dealing with jurisdiction (Section B), substantive assessment (Section C), and procedure (Section D)).

5.18 In addition to those legislative changes, the review also included the introduction of comprehensive Commission guidelines on the assessment of horizontal mergers and a set of best practice guidelines on the conduct of merger investigations.[18] The former set out, for the first time, the analytical framework that the Commission intends to apply in assessing mergers between competing firms, and provide a framework for the treatment of efficiencies in merger analysis. The latter are intended to further increase transparency on the day-to-day

---

[13] See <http://www.internationalcompetitionnetwork.org/index.html>.

[14] For a more detailed exposition of the changes made through the 2004 reform see DG Competition Newsletter, Special edition—The EU gets new competition powers for the 21st century, 2004 available at <http://www.ec.europa.eu/comm/competition/publications/cpn/special_edition.pdf>.

[15] Council Regulation (EC) No 139/2004 of 20 January 2004 on the control of concentrations between undertakings, OJ [2004] L24/1.

[16] Commission Regulation (EC) 802/2004 of 7 April 2004 implementing Council Regulation (EC) No 139/2004 on the control of concentrations between undertakings, [2004] OJ L133/1.

[17] Guidelines on the assessment of horizontal mergers under the Council Regulation on the control of concentrations between undertakings, OJ C31/5, 5 February 2001, Commission Notice on a simplified procedure for treatment of certain concentrations under Council Regulation (EC) No 139/2004, OJ C56, 05.03.2005 and Commission Notice on restrictions directly related and necessary to concentrations, Official Journal C56, 05.03.2005.

[18] DG Competition Best Practices on the Conduct of Merger Proceedings, published at <http://www.ec.europa.eu/ comm/competition/mergers/legislation/regulation/best_practices.pdf>.

handling of merger cases by DG Competition and the Commission's relationship with the merging parties and interested third parties on issues such as the timing of state-of-play meetings and due process in merger proceedings.

Finally, a number of measures relating to the staffing and resources of DG Competition **5.19** have also been introduced, including a new position of Chief Competition Economist, with a staff of ten or so PhD economists, the systematisation of internal panels to scrutinise proposals by case-teams, the appointment of a Consumer Liaison Officer, and a re-organisation of the Competition DG. (These internal reform measures are outlined in greater detail in section D 'Procedure' below).

(2) Statistics 1990–2005

The growth in the number of cases notified under the Merger Regulation is illustrated in **5.20** the table below.

Beyond the statistics showing the number of notified cases, it is interesting to note the rel- **5.21** ative stability in terms of proportion of cases notified that require in-depth investigation, remedial action or even prohibition. Over the whole period, somewhere between 90–95 per cent of all cases are cleared without the need to open second phase proceedings. Thus, for the great majority of cases, the Merger Regulation's 'one stop shop' provides a definitive clearance throughout the EU within a time frame of, normally, one month.

Looking at the more complex cases, one finds that with the exception of the years 1992 and **5.22** 1999/2000,[19] the proportion of cases with phase one remedies is at 5 per cent (or below). The Commission is positive towards solving limited and clear-cut competition concerns without resorting to a more protracted investigation period than is necessary. Apart from demonstrating a pragmatic attitude, also benefiting the notifying parties, the policy of accepting remedies, rather than seeking prohibitions, has allowed for the creation of a considerable amount of case law and experience in terms of crafting proportionate, but effective remedies to address various types of competition concerns.[20]

Finally, it is interesting to note that the proportion of prohibitions, although so low as to **5.23** make statistical analysis difficult, normally remains at about 1 per cent of all cases, only exceeding 2 per cent in 1996.

B. Jurisdiction

(1) Concept of a Concentration

(a) Introduction

The Merger Regulation applies exclusively to *concentrations with a Community dimension*. **5.24** On the one hand, this means that, pursuant to Article 21(1), the Merger Regulation is the

---

[19] The increased number of Phase I remedies in those years is probably attributable partly to the merger boom, but also to the fact that the amendments introduced though Regulation 1310/97 made explicit reference to the possibility of such decision, something which previously had been assumed by analogy from the provision in Art 8.2 relating to Phase II proceedings.
[20] See for details section C(6) on remedies and the remedy study in particular.

Notifications	90	91	92	93	94	95	96	97	98	99	00	01	02	03	04	05	Total
Notified cases	11	64	59	59	95	110	131	168	224	276	330	335	277	211	247	313	2910
Withdrawn — Phase 1			3	1	6	4	5	9	5	7	8	8	3	0	3	6	68
Withdrawn — Phase 2				1			1		4	5	5	4	1	0	2	3	26
Final decisions	**90**	**91**	**92**	**93**	**94**	**95**	**96**	**97**	**98**	**99**	**00**	**01**	**02**	**03**	**04**	**05**	**Total**
6.1(a)	2	5	9	4	5	9	6	4	4	1	1	1	1	0	0	0	52
6.1(b)	5	47	43	49	78	90	109	118	196	225	278	299	238	203	220	276	2474
6(2)		3	4		2	3		2	12	16	26	11	10	11	12	15	127
6.1 (b) + 6.2	5	50	47	49	80	93	109	120	208	241	304	310	248	214	232	291	2601
9.3 referral			1	1	1		3	7	4	5	5	7	11	9	3	6	63
Phase I	7	55	57	54	86	102	118	131	216	247	310	318	260	223	235	297	2716
9.3 referral										1		0	0	0	0	0	1
8.1/8.2		1	1	1	2	2	1	1	3	0	3	5	2	2	2	2	28
8.2 with remedies		3	3	2	2	3	3	7	4	7	12	9	5	6	4	3	73
8.3 prohibition		1			1	2	3	1	2	1	2	5	0	0	1	0	19
8.4 restore competition								2					2				4
Total Art 8		5	4	3	5	7	7	11	9	8	17	19	9	8	7	5	124
Phase II		5	4	3	5	7	7	11	9	9	17	19	9	8	7	5	125

	90	91	92	93	94	95	96	97	98	99	00	01	02	03	04	05	Total
Total final decisions	7	60	61	57	91	109	125	142	225	256	327	337	269	231	242	302	2841
Decisions other Articles																	
6(1) (c) opening proceedings	6	4	4	6	7	6	11	11	20	18	21	7	9	8	10	10	148
6.3 (a) Revoked										1						0	1
8.5 (a) Revoked																0	0
Art 14 Fines									1	4	1		1		1	0	8
Art 22 referral to COM				1		1	1	1					2	1	1	4	12
Art 22 referral rejected by COM																1	1
Art 9 rejected by decision	1									1				1		0	3
Art 7 derogation suspension	1	2	2	3	3	2	4	5	13	7	4	7	14	8	10	6	90

Source: E.C., COMP Merger Registry

only piece of legislation that applies to concentrations,[21] and that the competition legislation in the Member States cannot be applied to such concentrations.[22] On the other hand, it means that the Merger Regulation cannot be applied to transactions which do not meet its definition of a concentration in Article 3.

5.25   The new Merger Regulation did not make any major changes to the concept of a concentration of the original Merger Regulation. Although the Commission plans to revise and update the four interpretative Notices adopted in 1998[23] under the original Merger Regulation, probably in the course of 2006/2007, the guidance set out in those Notices also remains largely applicable under the new Regulation. This section will therefore summarise the general approach set out in those Notices, while commenting on developments brought about either by the new Merger Regulation or by intervening decision-making practice or case law.

5.26   The logic of the four Notices is as follows: the Notices on the concept of 'concentration' and on the concept of a 'full-function joint venture' provide the basis for deciding whether a given operation meets the definition of a concentration. If it does, the other two Notices, on the concept of 'undertakings concerned' and 'calculation of turnover', help determine whether it has Community dimension.

(b) Concept of a Concentration: Article 3 of the Merger Regulation

5.27   Under Article 3(1) a concentration is defined as a change of control that takes one of two main forms, ie whereby two previously independent parties merge or whereby control is acquired over the whole or parts of another undertaking. Article 3(4) adds to this by stating that the creation of a full-function joint venture is also considered a concentration.[24]

5.28   Internal restructuring does not fall within the scope of the Merger Regulation, and is therefore in general of little or no relevance for the application of the Regulation. However, where, as in *Astra-Zeneca/Novartis* (Case M.1806 [2000]) internal restructuring is carried out in connection with a concentration, it may be of relevance in determining the scope of the concentration.

---

[21] Theoretically, the Commission could apply Arts 81 and 82 of the EC Treaty by means of Art 85 of the EC Treaty. However, the Commission has stated that it normally does not intend to use this possibility (see Commission Notes on Council Regulation (EEC) 4064/89, published together with the original Merger Regulation). In practice, the Commission has not intervened against any concentration on this basis.

[22] The Merger Regulation's approach to exclusive jurisdiction differs fundamentally from that which applies in relation to Arts 81/82 following the introduction of Regulation 1/2003, where the latter is based on a system of parallel competence between the Commission and Member States which will be co-ordinated in a network approach.

[23] Commission Notice on the concept of a concentration under Council Regulation (EEC) No 4064/89, OJ C66/5, 2.3.1998, Commission Notice on the concept of full-function joint ventures under Council Regulation (EEC) No 4064/89, OJ C66/1, 2.3.1998, Commission Notice on the concept of undertakings concerned under Council Regulation (EEC) No 4064/89, OJ C66/14, 2.3.1998 and Commission Notice on calculation of turnover under Council Regulation (EEC) No 4064/89, OJ C66/25, 2.3.1998.

[24] Joint ventures that do not meet the requirements for being considered as 'full-function' fall outside the scope of the Merger Regulation and are instead subject to the rules of Art 81 of the EC Treaty. For further detail on full-functionality, see paras 5.57ff below.

Article 3(1), first sentence, of the new Merger Regulation introduced some clarifications in **5.29** order to state explicitly that a concentration arises only where a 'change of control' occurs on 'a lasting basis'. This was previously said only in the recitals of the original Merger Regulation, but the express acknowledgement of that rule in the new Regulation implies no change in the scope of the Merger Regulation.

The main principles for deciding whether a given operation meets the definition of a con- **5.30** centration in Article 3 are set out in the Notice on the concept of concentration under the original Merger Regulation on the control of concentrations between undertakings.[25] This Notice is of general applicability to all mergers and acquisitions of sole or joint control. Additional guidance on the application of Article 3, sub-paragraph 4, in the specific cases of joint ventures is provided in the Notice on the concept of full-function joint ventures under Council Regulation (EEC) No 4064/89 on the control of concentrations between undertakings.[26]

(i) Mergers—Article 3(1)(a) of the Merger Regulation   Under Article 3(1)(a) of the **5.31** Merger Regulation, the term 'merger' has a specific meaning, which may not be identical to the colloquial use of the term in other situations. For the purposes of the Merger Regulation, a merger occurs when two or more independent undertakings amalgamate to form a new undertaking, thereby ceasing to exist as separate legal entities. A merger may also occur when one undertaking is absorbed by another, in which case the latter retains its legal identity while the former ceases to exist as a legal entity ie in essence for the purposes of the Merger Regulation a 'merger' is where A merges with B to form a new entity C.

It is worth noting however that even in the absence of a legal merger, an operation result- **5.32** ing in the legal or de facto creation of a single economic unit into which the activities or interests of previously independent undertakings are transferred may be considered to be a merger (see, for example *RTZ/CRA* (Case IV/M.660 [1995]), *KLM/Alitalia* (Case IV/JV.19 [1999]), *Exxon/Mobil* (Case IV/M.1383 [1999]), *AOL/Time Warner* (Case COMP/M.1845 [2000]) or *Carnival Corporation/P&O Princess(II)* (Case COMP/M.3071 [2003])). A pre-requisite for a finding of a single economic unit is the existence of a permanent, single economic management. The other factors mentioned in point 7 of the Commission Notice on the concept of a concentration (ie internal profit and loss compensation, joint liability and cross-shareholdings may be of relevance, as in *Price Waterhouse/ Coopers&Lybrand* (Case IV/M.1016 [1998]), but they normally play a lesser role in deciding whether to consider merged entities forming an economic unit.

From a jurisdictional viewpoint, 'mergers' tend to be relatively uncomplicated. First, these **5.33** cases clearly constitute concentrations within the meaning of the Merger Regulation. An issue that arises occasionally is that the parties to a concentration, for reasons unrelated to competition issues, wish to characterise their concentration as a 'merger between equals', whereas,

---

[25] Commission Notice on the concept of a concentration under Council Regulation (EEC) No 4064/89, OJ C66/5, 2.3.1998.
[26] Commission Notice on the concept of full-function joint ventures under Council Regulation (EEC) No 4064/89, OJ C66/1, 2.3.1998.

legally speaking, the transaction takes the form of one party acquiring control over the other. In such circumstances, it is not uncommon that the Commission is asked to describe the transaction as a merger under Article 3(1)(a), rather than an acquisition pursuant to Article 3(1)(b). However, acceding to such a request would not only mean that the Commission was not applying the Merger Regulation correctly, but would also have an impact on the rights and obligations of the participants.[27]

5.34 **(ii) The Acquisition of Control (Article 3(3) of the Merger Regulation)**   The vast majority of all concentrations notified under the Merger Regulation are acquisitions of control in the sense of Article 3(1)(b). Control in the sense of the Merger Regulation is therefore a central concept and is explained in Article 3(3), which states that control is linked to *the possibility of exercising decisive influence* over one or more other undertakings. Control can be exercised on a legal or de facto basis, and it can be direct or indirect.

5.35 The most common means of acquiring control is through share purchases and/or shareholders' agreements. Control may also be conferred by other agreements relating to intellectual property rights, long-term supply arrangements or credits or any other means, see eg *Blokker/Toys R Us* (Case IV/M.890 [1997]) and *KLM/Air UK* (Case IV/M.967 [1997]). What ultimately matters is not the form,[28] but whether the acquiring party or parties, based on a qualitative assessment of all facts, will have the ability to determine strategic decisions, such as budgets, business plans and the appointment of senior managers of the target firm(s). Mere ability in this content is sufficient so there is no need to demonstrate whether such ability will be exercised in practice. It is also not relevant whether the acquisition of control was the intended result of the transaction. Control could even be acquired by one party as a result of action by a third party, see eg *RTL/M6* (Case COMP/M.3330 [2004]).

5.36 Such acquisitions can be made by one company ('sole control'), or by two or more companies ('joint control'). Sole control confers the positive ability to impose strategic decisions on the controlled entity, and is dealt with in greater detail below in paras 5.40ff. By contrast, joint control distinguishes itself primarily by providing the holders of such control with a negative form of control, eg to veto strategic decisions proposed by other jointly controlling partners. Joint control issues are dealt with in paras 5.48ff below.[29]

---

[27] See Art 11 of the Implementing Regulation, according to which all parties to a merger under Art 3(1)(a) are referred to as 'notifying parties', whereas the target company in acquisitions falling under Art 3(1)(b) are referred to as 'other involved parties'. Consequently, the responsibility for making the notification, and the associated responsibility for the veracity of the information it contains does not rest on companies that are the target of an acquisition. On the other hand, the Commission will only address its ultimate decision to notifying companies.

[28] Art 3(5) of the Merger Regulation contains three limited exceptions to the principle that an acquisition of control constitutes a concentration. These exceptions relate to temporary (one-year) holdings by financial institutions, liquidation and similar proceedings and acquisitions by financial holding companies within the meaning of Council Directive (EEC) 78/660 based on Art 54 (3) of the Treaty on the annual accounts of certain types of companies [OJ L222, 14.8.1978 p11, last amended through EP/Council Directive (EC) 2003/51, OJ L178, 17.7.2003, p16]. As exceptions, these provisions have in practice been narrowly interpreted, see eg *Lagardère/Natexis/VUP* (Case COMP/M.2978 [2004]).

[29] The question whether an operation gives rise to the acquisition of sole or joint control has important consequences for the definition of the 'undertakings concerned', and therefore for the question whether an operation has Community dimension, as well as to the rights and obligations of the various parties.

(iii) The Acquirer   In most cases the legal persona of the acquirer is of no consequence   **5.37**
for the Merger Regulation. This is the case in all circumstances when control is acquired
by a private undertaking. The Merger Regulation is also applicable if one or more natural
persons acquire control over an undertaking, provided that they already control at least one
undertaking (see Article 3(1)(b)).[30]

Whilst internal re-organisation within a group of companies does not constitute a concen-   **5.38**
tration, a specific situation occurs when transactions involve state-owned or other public
entities. An acquisition by one state-owned company of another public entity falls under
the Merger Regulation if the two undertakings have been part of different economic units
with independent powers of decision, irrespective of the way in which their capital is held
(see recital 22 of the Merger Regulation).[31]

(iv) The Object of Control   The target of a notified concentration is normally one or   **5.39**
several legal entities, including subsidiaries and other participations. However, the object
of an acquisition of control can also be specific parts of the assets of a company, eg brands
or licences, provided that the assets in question constitute a business to which [a market
turnover exceeding the thresholds in Article 1 can be attributed] (see eg *Saint-Gobain/
Wacker Chimie/NOM* (Case IV/M.774 [1996]) or *Fortune Brands/Allied Domecq* (Case
COMP/M.3813 [2005])).[32] Acquisitions of certain assets in relation to an outsourcing
agreement may be caught by this provision where the transferred business is or has the
means to supply the relevant products or services also to third parties (see eg *Celestica/IBM*
(Case COMP/M.1841 [2000]) or *Flextronics/Nortel* (Case COMP/M.3583 [2004])).
Franchise agreements, on the other hand, normally do not confer control over the franchisee's business (see *UBS/Mister Minute* (Case IV/M.940 [1998])).

(v) The Concept of Sole Control   An operation involving the acquisition of sole control   **5.40**
can take two forms. The acquirer may, prior to the operation, be in a position of having no
decisive influence over the target company (change from no control to sole control).
Alternatively, the acquirer may already prior to the operation have joint control over the
target company (change from joint to sole control).[33] The latter scenario normally does not

---

[30] In *EDF/Graninge* (Case IV/M.1169 [1998]) joint control over Graninge was acquired by the Electricité
de France group (EDF) and a number of individuals, who were all descendants of the founder of the company.
None of these individuals held economic interests outside Graninge. The question of whether these individuals could be considered as undertakings concerned was however left open, since EDF would in any case
acquire (joint) control over Graninge, which meant that the operation, regardless of the position of the
family members, constituted a concentration with a Community dimension (see also *Asko/Jakobs/Adia* (Case
IV/M.082 [1991]) and *Spohn Cement/Heidelberg Cement* (Case COMP/M.3926 [2005])).

[31] An example of this was the merger between the two Finnish state controlled companies Neste and IVO.
Although the companies previously had been controlled by the same Member State, the operation was
considered to constitute a concentration in the meaning of the Merger Regulation since the companies had
had separate and independent management (*Neste/IVO* (Case IV/M.931 [1998])). See also *Pechiney/Usinor*
(Case IV/M.097 [1991]).

[32] OJ [1997] L247/1.

[33] The latter situation, which was first considered in *ICI/Tioxide* (Case IV/M.023 [1990]), is considered to
create a concentration in the meaning of the Merger Regulation because decisive influence exercised alone is
substantially different from decisive influence exercised jointly.

raise any substantive doubts and is therefore, unless special circumstances apply, subject to a short-form notification.[34]

5.41 Sole control is normally based on the ownership of an amount of shares in the target company, which is sufficient to control the company. Sole control can be found on the basis of ownership rights coupled with contractual arrangements between two or more shareholders, as was the case in *Ford/Hertz* (Case IV/M.397 [1994]). Finally, more exceptionally, other contractual arrangements, such as those concerning the management of another undertaking may lead to a finding of sole control.[35] Similarly, very important supply contracts, options or financing arrangements may lead to a finding of sole control.[36]

5.42 *Considerations based on ownership of shares*   As indicated earlier, sole control confers the positive ability to impose strategic decisions on the controlled entity. In the normal case of acquisitions of shares, the important test is therefore the proportion of voting rights the acquirer will control after the operation. If the Memorandum or Articles of Association of the target company do not contain any specific requirements regarding qualified majorities for strategic decisions, an acquisition of shares that will give the acquirer more than 50 per cent of the votes will be seen as an acquisition of sole control.

5.43 In publicly quoted companies in particular, an acquisition of a qualified minority holding of less than 50 per cent of the voting rights will normally be sufficient to confer de facto sole control. This is because, in such companies, it is unlikely that all smaller shareholders will be present or represented at a shareholders' meeting. Based on evidence of the presence of shareholders at such meetings in previous years (normally the last three years), an assessment must be made to determine whether the holder of a particular share will be likely to achieve a majority at future meetings. Where that is the case, sole control is deemed to exist. Such findings have in practice been found where the shareholding of the acquirer was as low as 25–30 per cent in the target company.[37]

5.44 *Considerations based on contractual arrangements*   The most common type of contractual arrangement conferring control over another company is the shareholders' agreement. The most common function of such agreements is to provide the contracting parties with joint control over the target company. However, a shareholders' agreement is sometimes concluded in a manner that provides a single shareholder with the ability to manage or

---

[34] Regarding special circumstances, that would justify not treating the case as a simplified procedures case, the Commission Notice refers to cases where the hitherto existing joint venture has enjoyed a degree of independence from the parent that proposes to acquire sole control, as in *KLM/Martinair* (Case IV/M.1328 [1999]). See also Section D.3 'Notification-Short Form CO and Simplified Procedure' below.

[35] See, eg, *Lehman Brothers/SCG/Starwood/Le Meredien* (Case COMP/M.3858 [2005]).

[36] See, eg, *Coca-Cola/Amalgamated Beverages* (Case IV/M.794 [1997]), *Scottish & Newcastle/Groupe Danone* (Case COMP/M.1925 [2000]) or *Shell/DEA* (Case COMP/M.2389 [2001]).

[37] For example, see *Société Genérale de Belgique/Genérale de Banque* (Case IV/M.343 [1993]), where a shareholding just below 26% would have been sufficient to provide a majority at previous shareholder meetings, *Crown Cork & Seal/Carnauld Metalbox* (Case IV/M.603 [1995]), concerning a 32% shareholding, *Anglo American Corporation/Lonrho* (Case IV/M.754 [1997]), where a holding of 27.5% was considered to give Anglo American sole control over Lonrho or *Aker Maritime/Kvaerner* (Case COMP/M.2117 [2000]) where a 26.7% shareholding was held to confer sole control.

determine the strategic behaviour of the target company, or to appoint the majority of its managing body. For example, in *Ford/Hertz* (Case IV/M.397 [1994]), a shareholders' agreement enabled Ford unilaterally to take control over the board of Hertz by converting some of its C-shares. Equally, in cases where a shareholders' agreement provides only one company with veto rights over the appointment of senior management and/or the adoption of budgets or business plans, that shareholder can be considered to have sole control over the company, see *Nabisco/United Biscuits* (Case COMP/M.1920 [2000]).

Options and other financial arrangements Put and call options are contractual arrange- **5.45**
ments whereby two or more parties agree the terms of a future transaction. Although such agreements may, at the time of their exercise, be relevant to control of the target company, they do not normally, prior to their exercise, lead to a change in the control structure. Option agreements in isolation are therefore not considered to trigger a concentration in the sense of the Merger Regulation.[38]

However, in situations where it is clear that the option will be exercised in the near future, **5.46**
in accordance with legally binding arrangements, the option agreements are taken into consideration along with other elements, such as contractual arrangements or minority acquisitions. Thus, if, based on an overall assessment, it is concluded that de facto a change of control will occur prior to the exercise of the option, a notifiable concentration will be deemed to arise at that earlier date. In some transactions option agreements are included in a manner to allow divestitures to take place in two or more stages. In *Scottish & Newcastle/ Groupe Danone* (Case COMP/M.1925 [2000]), stage one would have lasted for a maximum of three years during which S&N would have managed the relevant businesses, and during which time Danone had a put option to require S&N to buy Danone's interests. If the put option were not exercised, the agreement provided, in a second stage, for the relevant businesses to come under sole control by S&N. The whole operation was found to result immediately in the acquisition of sole control by S&N. Also in *Shell/DEA* (Case COMP/M.2389 [2001]), the parties had agreed a transaction structure whereby Shell and RWE would each hold 50 per cent in DEA for an initial period, during which RWE had a put option to sell its 50 per cent stake to Shell, and if the put option were not exercised, a mechanism was in place to ensure that Shell would increase its stake in DEA to a level of sole control within a three-year period. Again, the transaction was regarded as immediately giving rise to sole control. In *KLM/Air UK* (Case IV/M.967 [1997]) the Commission found that KLM had acquired de facto joint control of Air UK through a minority holding (14.9 per cent) and option agreements coupled with a complex package of financial arrangements. KLM was able to demonstrate that, partly due to the option agreements, in practice it had the power to exercise a joint decisive influence over the target company.

In *BBVA/BNL* (Case COMP/M.3768 [2005]) the Commission found that a change in the **5.47**
quality of control constituted a notifiable concentration when a pre-existing shareholder, who alone had previously held negative control over the target company, ie had been the

---

[38] Case T-2/93 *Air France v Commission* [1994] ECR II-323.

only shareholder able to block the adoption of strategic decisions, acquired the ability positively to impose its views with regard to such strategic decisions.

5.48 **(vi) The Concept of Joint Control**[39]   Under the Merger Regulation a company that is jointly controlled by two or more parents, and is established on a lasting basis (in practice, usually at least three years)[40] is referred to as a joint venture. As indicated above, joint control is distinguished by the fact that the jointly controlling companies (the parent companies) must all agree on the major decisions concerning the joint venture. The decisive influence exercised by the parents of a joint venture means the power to veto decisions which are decisive for the strategic commercial behaviour of the joint venture. The power to veto such actions will result in deadlock, unless an agreement between all controlling parent companies is reached. Since the joint venture would not be able to function properly in that deadlock situation, the parent companies will be forced to reach an agreement, or simply to terminate the joint venture. Therefore, each parent company has decisive influence over the joint venture.

5.49 *Equal voting rights*   The most clear-cut form of joint control exists when two companies each hold 50 per cent of the shares in another company. Neither parent will then be able to determine the strategy of the joint venture, so they will effectively have to agree about all matters relating to the joint venture. Situations where two or more shareholders are in the same position through other means are treated in the same way. Such other means may include situations where they otherwise hold equal voting rights (as opposed to share in the joint venture's capital), or where in accordance with the statutes of the joint venture they all have to agree to strategic decisions.[41] In line with paragraph 37 of the Notice on the concept of a concentration the Commission has in certain situations found joint control to exist despite procedures for mediation by an independent third party (*Leisureplan* (Case IV/M.662 [1995])) or after an arbitration procedure (*Wacker/Air Products* (Case IV/M.1097 [1998])). In both these cases the time required for the relevant procedure would be in the region of at least three months.

5.50 *Veto rights*   In the absence of equal voting rights, joint control may arise out of veto rights granted in a shareholders' agreement or through special quorum requirements in the company's statutes to one or more minority shareholders. Depending on the organisational set-up, veto rights may confer decisive influence over the joint venture by enabling the holder of such rights to block strategic decisions of the shareholders' meeting, the board of directors, the supervisory board or other relevant body. Veto rights regarding normal minority protection issues, however, do not confer joint control (see *Eridania/ISI* (Case IV/M.062 [1991])).

5.51 Generally speaking, veto rights that enable their holder to block the adoption of appointment of senior management, the company's budget or business plans will be deemed to

---

[39] Commission Notice on the concept of a concentration, points 18–38.

[40] In *BS/BT* (Case IV/M.425 [1994]) the Commission concluded that a situation of joint control that would last only for a start-up period of, at most, three years gave rise to an acquisition of sole control for the parent that would retain its decisive influence after the start-up period. See also *Albacom* (Case IV/M.604 [1995]) and *Mannesmann/Olivetti/Infostrada* (Case IV/M.1025 [1998]).

[41] See eg *Matra/CAP Gemeni Sogeti* (Case IV/M.272 [1993]), *Pasteur-Mérieux/Merck* (Case IV/M.285 [1993]) or *Philips/LG Electronics/JV* (Case COMP/M.2263 [2001]).

confer joint control. If the joint venture's budgets and/or business plans are detailed and thus provide little scope for the company to vary its commercial behaviour, a veto right relating to such a document may suffice in itself to confer joint control, see *Preussag/ Nouvelle Frontières* (Case COMP/M.2186 [2000]). Whilst a veto right regarding the appointment of senior management will always be a candidate for concluding that joint control exists, it is submitted that such veto rights increase in importance where the budget and business plan are of a relatively general nature, thus leaving the management of the company with more freedom in determining the strategic decisions.

Other veto rights, including those that relate to investment decisions, have been found suf-**5.52** ficient to confer joint control. Such veto rights will, however, not be seen to confer joint control if the value of investments that need approval by minority shareholders is set at a very high level. The likelihood of a veto right on investments being considered to confer joint control will increase if the joint venture's activities are likely to frequently involve new investments and if the value where the veto comes into play is set at a low level.[42]

De facto joint control or shifting alliances?   Minority shareholders could, even in the **5.53** absence of any agreement, on a de facto basis, jointly control another company if they were united by a sufficiently strong common interest, leading to the assumption that they would act together in exercising their voting rights. The Commission has found such common interests to give rise to de facto joint control in relatively few cases. Illustrative examples can be found in *Philips/Grundig* (Case IV/M.382 [1993]), where three minority financial owners could only block action by the industrial owner if they acted together, and in *Hutchinson/RCPM/ECT* (Case COMP/JV.55 [2001]), where the two largest shareholders, with a combined share of 70 per cent, on the basis of, *inter alia*, past links and a high degree of mutual dependency would have a strong common interest not to vote against each other on strategic issues regarding the joint venture.[43]

Other situations where no stable voting majority can be attributed to two or more minor-**5.54** ity shareholders will not constitute a concentration. For example where two shareholders each hold 40 per cent in the target company, but no quorum rules are laid down in its statute and no pooling agreement exists, each party will, in future voting situations, have to rally support from other smaller shareholders, with the result that the control over the company is subject to shifting alliances and that neither of the 40 per cent shareholders has a lasting majority.[44]

Changes in the structure or quality of control   It should be noted that the Merger **5.55** Regulation does apply to transactions leading to a change from sole to joint control

---

[42] For an example of a case where a veto right over investments in an emerging, technology-driven market was considered to confer joint control, see *Bell Cablemedia/Cable & Wireless/Videotron* (Case IV/M.853 [1996]) or *TUI Group/ GTT Holding* (Case COMP/M.1898 [2000]).

[43] For cases where this has been unsuccessfully argued by the notifying parties, see *Channel Five* (Case IV/M.673 [1995]), *Nokia Oy/SP Tyres* (Case IV/M.548 [1995]), *Ericsson/Nokia/Psion/Motorola* (Case IV/JV.12 [1998]).

[44] However, since an operation that creates such a structure would not constitute a concentration, within the meaning of the Merger Regulation, no obstacles would exist against applying Art 81 of the EC Treaty and/or national competition rules to the operation (see Art 21(1) and (3) of the Merger Regulation).

(or addition of further controlling companies),[45] as well as to a change from joint to sole control. While the former scenario always requires a full investigation into the substance, the latter does not usually give rise to any competition concerns.[46]

5.56 Transactions whereby the number of controlling shareholders in a joint venture is increased, or where one controlling shareholder is replaced by a new parent company will constitute notifiable concentrations under the Merger Regulation. Similarly, cases where new assets are contributed to an existing joint venture will generally constitute notifiable concentrations, as the other controlling parent companies through such transactions gain joint control over the contributed assets (see *Bertelsmann/Kirch/Premiere* (Case IV/M.993 [1998]). In *Coca-Cola/Nestlé/JV* (Case COMP/M.2276 [2001]) the Commission found that a transaction whereby a pre-existing joint venture was transformed into a full function entity was notifiable under the Merger Regulation.

5.57 **(vii) Full function joint ventures (Article 3(4))** Not all joint ventures are caught by the Merger Regulation. According to Article 3(4), joint ventures that perform on a lasting basis all the functions of an autonomous economic entity are considered concentrations for the purposes of the Merger Regulation. Joint ventures that do not satisfy these criteria fall instead to be assessed under Article 81 of the EC Treaty. The concept of a full function joint venture was clarified in the amendments to the original Merger Regulation in 1997 which included an abandonment of the concept of 'concentrative JVs' in favour of 'full-function JVs'. This concept corresponded better to all transactions with a (structural effect) on the market. This structural effect can create a new player on a market where neither party has previously been active or combine their existing activities on a market, or lie anywhere between these two extremes. What is important as regards the full function criteria is that the concept focuses on transactions that result in the joint venture being an active market participant. No changes were made to this concept in the new Merger Regulation.[47]

5.58 Full function joint ventures under the Merger Regulation are defined in Article 3(4) as 'the creation of a joint venture performing on a lasting basis all the functions of an autonomous economic entity'. In practice, this excludes certain operations where the joint venture is created for a short, finite duration. It also excludes operations where a joint venture is not equipped to function on the market in its own right. The latter assessment will focus mainly on whether the joint venture has been given sufficient assets to carry out a business activity, so that it, rather than its parent companies, will de facto act on the market.

5.59 Under the Merger Regulation therefore, a joint venture must perform, on a lasting basis, all the functions of an autonomous economic entity in the relevant market. The concept of

---

[45] The opposite situation, a reduction in the number of controlling companies would be considered a concentration if the changing structure were to affect the quality of control enjoyed by the remaining parent companies.

[46] Exceptionally, however, a change to sole control can lead to competition concerns, see *KLM/Martin Air* (Case IV/M.1328), XXIXth Report on Competition Policy 1999—SEC(2000) 720 final, points 165–166.

[47] The concept of a full function joint venture was clarified in the amendments to the original Merger Regulation in 1997 which included an abandonment of the concept of 'concentrative JVs' in favour of 'full-function JVs'. This concept corresponded better to all transactions with a structural effect on the market which ought to be reviewed under the Merger Regulation.

'lasting basis' has only rarely raised difficulties. The Commission's Notice of full function joint ventures states in paragraph 15 that, 'The fact that the parent companies commit to the joint venture the resources [needed for it to be an autonomous economic entity] normally demonstrates that [the joint venture is intended to operate on a lasting basis]'. In other words, where the parent companies create a joint venture that is equipped to become an autonomous market participant, there is a sort of presumption that the 'lasting basis' criterion will be fulfilled. In *John Deere Capital Corp/Lombard North Central plc* (Case IV/M.823), the Commission concluded that the joint venture could be considered to have been set up on a lasting basis, even though the agreement, which set it up for an indefinite duration, could be terminated by either parent by giving one year's notice after a minimum of three years.

5.60 *Full functionality*   Questions on the full function character of a joint venture are often very factual and depend on the circumstances of the case in question. As a basic principle, a joint venture will normally be considered equipped to operate on a market if, in comparison with other companies active on that market, the joint venture has all the resources necessary to do so.

5.61 The Commission has consistently held that joint ventures that merely fulfil functions that are auxiliary to one or more of its parent companies (eg limited to R&D, production or sales) are not regarded as performing all the functions of an autonomous economic entity (see *Baxter/Nestlé/Salvia* (Case IV/M.058 [1991]) or *Electrabel/Energia Italiana/Interpower* (Case COMP/M.3003 [2003])).

5.62 The joint venture agreement between the parent companies will normally set out the joint venture's business objectives, and is therefore the first source of information, describing the parent companies' intentions when setting up the joint venture. The joint venture agreement will normally indicate the economic field of activity of the joint venture, the resources allocated for the attainment of its objectives, its management structure and the extent to which the joint venture will continue to rely on its parent companies, for example in terms of supply and purchase relationships.[48]

5.63 It is common and acceptable that full function joint ventures can be relatively dependent on one or more parent companies for administrative services and/or for commercial relationships (up- or downstream) during a start-up period, normally not exceeding three years.[49]

5.64 Where the dependency on the parent companies is not limited to a start-up period, a distinction must be made between situations where the joint venture will be active on markets upstream or downstream of the parent companies.

---

[48] In *Thomson /Deutsche Aerospace AG* (Case IV/M.527 [1994]), the licensing of certain intellectual property rights was considered equivalent to the transfer of those rights. Similarly, in *British Gas Trading/Group 4 Utility Services* (Case IV/M.791 [1996]) one of the parent companies sold certain assets to a financial institution, which subsequently leased the assets to the joint venture.

[49] See, eg, *EDS/Lufthansa* (Case IV/M.560 [1995]), *Nokia/Autoliv* (Case IV/M.686 [1996]), *RSB/ Tenex/Fuel Logistic* (Case IV/M.904 [1997]) or *Schneider/Thomson Multimedia/JV* (Case COMP/M.2403 [2001]). If special circumstances so require, a longer period of dependency may be accepted, see, eg, *Siemens/Italtel* (Case IV/M.468 [1995]).

5.65 *Joint venture active upstream of parent companies*   Where the joint venture will be active on upstream markets, the relative proportion of its sales to the parent companies will be an important factor. Where such sales, on a continuous basis, will make up a significant proportion of the joint venture's total production, the operation comes closer to a production joint venture and will fall outside of the Merger Regulation, unless it can be demonstrated that the joint venture is, owing to specific market circumstances, nonetheless geared to play an active role on the market. This will normally not be the case with regard to joint ventures created as a form of outsourcing, which typically will be strongly focused on carrying on the outsourced activity. In other such cases, factors that may be of importance in deciding whether the joint venture can be considered full function will include the question as to whether the sales to parent companies are made on normal commercial terms (see, for example, *Zeneca/Vanderhave* (Case IV/M.556 [1996]), *Bayer/Hüls—Newco* (Case IV/M.751 [1996]) or *Philips/LG Electronics/JV* (Case COMP/M.2263 [2001])). In some cases, one or more parent companies may act as sales agencies for the joint venture. The role of an agent does not include assuming the commercial risk. The joint venture will, therefore, in such situations, be seen as the real market player. Consequently, a joint venture may, in such circumstances, be considered as full function, even though a large part of its sales are made through the parent companies. See, for example, *TNT/Canada Post, DBP Postdienst, La Poste, PTT Post and Sweden Post* (Case IV/M.102 [1991]), where an exclusive agency agreement was accepted for an initial start-up period of two years. A similar case is *Smith & Nephew+Breiersdorf/JV* (Case COMP/JV.54 [2001]).

5.66 *The joint venture will be active downstream of the parent companies*   In situations where the joint venture will be active on a market which is downstream of the parent companies, the question whether or not it can be characterised as full function will not depend only on the relative proportion of its sales that will be made up by products supplied by its parent companies. Equally important is the question whether the joint venture will add significant value to the parents' products.[50] This may be the case where the parent companies supply semi-manufactured materials to the joint venture, which will then further process these materials and provide additional service elements, such as installation. On the other hand, if the activities of the joint venture are limited to mere assembly of the materials supplied by the parent companies, it may in reality be closer to a common sales agency, which will normally not be considered as an autonomous economic entity and thus fall outside the scope of the Merger Regulation.

5.67 The only exception where a joint venture may be regarded as a full-function entity, despite essentially only selling the parent companies' products is where the joint venture will be active on a trade market. Such a trade market was first discussed in *Texaco/Norsk Hydro* (Case IV/M.511 [1995]). A trade market is characterised by the presence of companies specialising in sales and distribution, without being active at the upstream production level. Moreover, a trading company can normally be distinguished from a sales agency by its

---

[50] In *Cargill/Vandemoortele—JV* (Case IV/M.1227 [1998]) an estimated value-added between 25% and 40% was considered sufficient. In *BP/NOVA* (Case COMP/M.3578 [2005]), 30% value-added was considered sufficient.

ability to obtain deliveries from a large number of suppliers. Any quasi-exclusivity provision between the parent companies and the joint venture is therefore prima facie incompatible with the finding that the joint venture will act as a trading company. A joint venture active on a trade market will be considered as full-function, if it has all the functions of companies active on that market.

(c) Multiple Transaction Concentrations

The need for specific treatment of multiple concentrations The above sections identify **5.68** the types of 'concentrations' to which the Merger Regulation applies. The definitions in Article 3(1) are result-oriented and do not specify any requirements relating to the format that such concentrations can take. Specifically, the Merger Regulation does not contain any general rule to indicate the number of transactions that can constitute 'one' concentration for the purposes of the Merger Regulation. Article 5(2)(2) provides a legal definition covering a specific situation in which the legislator has ensured that a certain form of staggered transaction would always be treated as a single concentration. The idea behind Article 5(2)(2) was to avoid circumvention of the Merger Regulation's notification thresholds by slicing up a transaction into multiple pieces, each of which could then fail to meet the turnover thresholds (sometimes referred to as 'salami tactics'). As such, this provision applies automatically once the legal conditions are met, regardless of whether, for example, the two transactions relate to entirely different businesses.[51] On the other hand, the provision provides no guidance as to *other* situations where two or more parties conclude multiple agreements that may lead to one or several concentrations.

Recital 20 to the new Merger Regulation In order to provide further clarity as regards the **5.69** legal situation for transactions that take place in stages or are otherwise linked in one way or another, additional guidance has been introduced in recital 20 to the Merger Regulation which describes the concept of a concentration and adds that:

> It is moreover appropriate to treat as a single concentration transactions that are [i] closely connected in that they are linked by condition or [ii] take the form of a series of transactions in securities taking place within a reasonably short period of time.

Treatment of two or more linked transactions The recital clarifies that transactions that **5.70** are 'linked by condition' should be treated as a single concentration. This would cover situations where two or more transactions are legally linked because one would not take place without the other. The choice of wording is not insignificant, as it allows for situations beyond reciprocal inter-conditionality (A does not take place without B and vice versa) to be covered, for example, situations where there are three transactions, A, B and C, and where both transaction A and C are conditional upon transaction B, but not upon each other.[52]

One specific situation is the joint acquisition of a target with a view to splitting the assets. This **5.71** involves multiple transactions, which, if linked by condition (so that all transactions must proceed for any of them to go ahead), are to be regarded as one concentration, unless the assets are

---

[51] See, eg *Volkswagen/RollsRoyce/Cosworth* (Case IV/M.1383 [1998]).
[52] See *Kingfisher/Wegert/ProMarkt* (Case IV/M.1188 [1999]).

to be split up completely and immediately.[53] This was the situation in case *Ratos/3i Group/Atle* (COMP/M.2384), where the various agreements concluded between Ratos, 3i and the sellers of Atle provided for Ratos and 3i each to acquire certain parts of Atle, and joint ownership of the remaining parts. As all the acquisitions were linked by condition and the assets were not to be completely split up, all of the transactions were considered as a single concentration. It should be noted that stock exchange rules may exclude such conditionality for joint bids relating to listed companies, as the acquirers may not be allowed to condition their bid for the target company on subsequently receiving regulatory approvals for a certain division of the assets. Thus, if the public bid as such will be able to proceed, regardless of the subsequent split of the assets of the target, the bid will be considered as a separate concentration.[54]

5.72   Another such situation is the acquisition of joint control of one part and sole control of another part of an undertaking, which, if linked by condition, can also constitute one concentration.[55]

5.73   These and other points of possible consistency between the new Merger Regulation and the existing guidance notices on jurisdictional matters will be the subject of review by the Commission in 2006. The implications of recital 20 and the treatment of multiple transactions will therefore be clarified further in the context of the revision of the existing Notices or in a separate Commission Notice.

5.74   In addition to recital 20, there is considerable guidance to be found in the numerous cases where the Commission has had to decide on the very question of whether or not multiple transactions should be seen as a single concentration.[56] This has indeed come up on many occasions over the years, and the Commission has examined from different viewpoints linkages of various kinds and degrees. Generally speaking, the starting point for such considerations is that the treatment of a number of transactions as one concentration is justified if the transactions are linked together in such a way that the end result is equivalent to a concentration arising out of a single transaction. A test question for this assessment is normally whether the parties would abandon all the transactions or renegotiate the whole package of transactions if one or more of them could not go ahead for any reason. If the reply to the question is positive, treatment as a single concentration is warranted,[57] otherwise it is not.[58]

---

[53] See para 24 of Commission Notice on the concept of undertakings concerned under Council Regulation (EEC) No 4064/89 on the control of concentrations between undertakings (OJ C 66, 02.03.1998, p 14) and *Ratos/3i Group/Atle* (Case COMP/M.2384).

[54] See, eg the related cases *Pernod Ricard/Allied Domecq* (Case COMP/M. 3779 [2005]) and *Fortune Brands/Allied Domecq* (Case COMP/M.3813 [2005]).

[55] See *Flaga/Progas* (Case COMP/M.4028 [2006]).

[56] On the issue of multiple concentrations and the Commission's past practice under the original Merger Regulation, see also the recent judgment of the Court of First Instance in Case T-282/02 *Cementbouw Handel & Industrie v Commission*, judgment of 23.2.2006, not yet published in the ECR.

[57] IV/M.102—*TNT/Canada Post/DBP Postdienst/La Poste/PTT Post/Sweden Post*, which is also given as an example in the Commission notice on undertakings concerned. Par. 29; IV/M.222—*Mannesmann/Hoesch*; IV/M.450—*AGF/Assubel*; IV/M. 853—*Cable Media/ Cable&Wirless/ Videotron*; IV/M.1006—*UPM-Kymmene*; IV/M.1188—*Kingfisher/Wegert/ProMarkt*; IV/M.1696—*Onex/Air Canada/Canadian Airlines*; COMP/M.2389—*Shell/DEA*; COMP/M.2404—*Elkem/Sapa*; COMP/M.2420—*Mitsui/CVRD/Caemi*; COMP/M.2854—*RAG/Degussa*: COMP/M.2897—*SITA Sverige AB and Sydkraft Ecoplus AB*; COMP/M.2926—*EQT/H&R/Dragoco*.

[58] IV/M. 853—*Cable Media/Cable&Wirless/Videotron*; IV/M.1188—*Kingfisher/Wegert/ProMarkt*; Cases COMP/M.1663—*Alcan/Alusuisse* and COMP/M.1715—*Alcan/Pechiney*; Cases COMP/M.1817—*BellSouth/*

It should be noted that de-mergers and exchanges of assets or 'swaps' are not treated as a **5.75** single concentration, even if, strictly speaking, such transactions are normally interdependent in the sense that one side of the swap cannot go ahead in isolation.[59] For such cases, emphasis is thus put on the final situation envisaged by the parties. In other words, where there will be no remaining link between the two (or more) sides of the transaction, each part of it will be treated separately as a concentration.

Determining whether transactions should be regarded as being linked in this respect is impor- **5.76** tant for identifying the undertakings concerned, and therefore for purposes of calculating turnover to establish whether the Commission has jurisdiction over the concentration.

Beyond this, the issue of multiple transaction concentrations also has a determinative **5.77** impact on other important issues, namely the transaction(s) to which a Commission decision extends, or, indeed, whether numerous decisions are necessary. This can be decisive, since, for example, a second phase may be necessary for some transactions, but not for others.[60] The assessment must therefore be made in every case where it is possible that more than one transaction may be involved. The issue of multiple transaction concentrations is also important in relation to enforcement issues, including the extent of the 'stand still' obligation under Article 7(1).[61] The issue of multiple transaction concentrations is furthermore relevant in determining the extent to which the transaction(s) can be restored to the status quo ante under Article 8(4) if the concentration has already been implemented and prohibited. More generally, determining which transactions are covered by a prohibition or a conditional clearance depends on the definition of concentration.

Creeping take-overs　With the clarification inserted into recital 20, the legislator has **5.78** removed any existing uncertainty that the Merger Regulation will treat as a single concentration so-called 'creeping take-overs' or any other take-overs where control is acquired by purchasing numerous shares from several independent sellers on the stock market in order

---

Vodafone (E-plus), COMP/M.1821—*BellSouth/VRT (E-plus)* and COMP/JV.38—*KPN/BellSouth/E-plus*; Cases COMP/M.2097—*SCA/Metsa Tissue*; COMP/M.2032—*SCA Packaging/Metsa Corrugated* and COMP/ M.2020—*Metsä-Serla/Modo*; COMP/M.2404—*Elkem/Sapa*; Cases COMP/M.2498—*UPM-Kymmene/Haindl* and COMP/M.2499—*Norske Skog/Parenco/Walsum*; Cases COMP/M.2533—*BP/E.ON* and COMP/M2761— *BP/ Veba Öl*.

[59] In para 49 of the Commission Notice on the concept of undertakings concerned (Commission Notice on the concept of undertakings concerned under Council Regulation (EEC) No 4064/89 on the control of concentrations between undertakings (OJ C66, 02.03.1998, p 14)) the exchange of assets is always considered to be two concentrations.

[60] Cases COMP/M.1922—*Siemens/Bosch/Atecs*, COMP/M.2059—*Siemens/Dematic/VDO/Sachs*, COMP/ M.2060—*Bosch/Rexroth*: three simultaneous and related, but ultimately not inter-conditional, transactions in which the engineering and automotive activities of Mannesmann were split between Siemens and Bosch. Ultimately Bosch acquired Rexroth, Siemens acquired Dematec, VDO and Sachs, but both jointly acquired control over Demag. These transactions were considered as different concentrations, COMP/M.1922 was cleared unconditionally in first phase, COMP/M.2059 was cleared in first phase with commitments and COMP/M.2060 was cleared in second phase with commitments. Cases COMP/ M.2097—*SCA/Metsa Tissue*, COMP/M.2032—*SCA Packaging/Metsa Corrugated* and COMP/M.2020—*Metsä-Serla/Modo*: Three transactions forming part of an extensive exchange of assets, but not being conditional upon each other thus constituting three concentrations with different outcomes out of which two (COMP/M.2032 and COMP/ M.2020) were approved in phase I, one of which (COMP/M.2020) with remedies, COMP/M.2097—was prohibited after a phase II investigation.

[61] See Section D.3 Procedure, Suspensory Effect, Article 7, below.

to acquire control over a company.[62] The requirement for such transactions to take place within a 'reasonably short period of time', rather than over a fixed number of months or years should be regarded in the context of the general purpose of the Regulation, which is to assess concentrations from an economic viewpoint, rather than a formalistic one. While this provision makes it clear that creeping take-overs will be treated as a single concentration for the purposes of assessing their compatibility with the Common Market, at the same time it has been clarified that such operations, for the purposes of the suspensive obligation in Article 7, will be treated in the same way as public bids and should therefore be exempt from the bar on closing provided that the conditions in Article 7(2) are met.[63] Arguably, a creeping take-over, by analogy with public bids in Article 4(1)(2), can be notified once the acquirer has made it public that it intends to acquire control over another company through such means. In any case, once control has been achieved, Articles 4(1) and 7(2) impose the need to notify without delay and restrict the ability to use the attached voting rights.

5.79 Given the complexity of the issues that can arise in cases involving multiple transactions, parties may wish to consult with DG Competition informally at the pre-notification stage (see Section D.2. Procedure, Pre-Notification, below).

(2) Concept of Community Dimension

5.80 The Merger Regulation is intended to apply to concentrations of a significant size, the basic assumption being that such operations have a cross border impact across more than one Member State and therefore can be more effectively assessed at a European level.

5.81 After having established that a particular transaction constitutes a concentration within the meaning of Article 3 of the Merger Regulation, the second part of the jurisdictional test assesses whether the concentration has a 'Community dimension'. This analysis requires, first, the identification of the 'undertakings concerned' and secondly, establishment of the fact that the turnover attributable to these undertakings meets the thresholds laid down in Article 1 of the Merger Regulation.

(a) Identifying the Undertakings Concerned (Article 1)

5.82 As an introductory remark it should be noted that the purpose of this Article is to measure the total amount of turnover[64] being combined through a concentration. It follows from this that the seller of a business will not be considered as an undertaking concerned, unless it retains a jointly controlling interest in the divested business. Consequently, the turnover of the seller (and its group) is only of interest if it retains such joint control.

5.83 (i) **Mergers** In the most straightforward scenario, the undertakings concerned will be each of the merging entities.

5.84 (ii) **Acquisition of Sole Control** Here, the undertakings concerned will be the company acquiring control and the target of the acquisition. In cases of sole control there can only be

---

[62] See, eg, IV/M.754—*Anglo American Corporation/Lonrho*; IV/M.1157—*Skanska/Scancem*; COMP/M.2117—*Aker/Kvaerner*; COMP/M.2404—*Elkem/Sapa*.

[63] See Section D.3 Procedure, Suspensory Effect, Article 7, below.

[64] The aggregate level of turnover is calculated on the basis of the group to which each undertaking concerned belongs. See below, section on 'The turnover of groups—the application of Article 5(4)'.

one undertaking concerned on the acquiring side, the entity that is the actual acquirer. However, Article 3(3)(b) allows one to 'see through' the formal acquirer of control, if an acquisition vehicle is used by another person or undertaking that will in fact exercise the control. If a joint venture is used as a vehicle, the parent companies will be regarded as undertakings directly concerned;[65] *since* the joint venture *is* a mere vehicle for the acquisition it is *not* an undertaking concerned.[66]

The other undertaking concerned, the target of the acquisition, can be one or more whole **5.85** companies, or parts thereof, including business assets that may not make up a legal entity, for example a division, unit or only certain assets (eg brands or licences). According to Article 5(2)(1), in such cases, the assets must constitute a business to which a market turnover can be attributed.[67]

(iii) Acquisition of Joint Control When a new joint venture is created, the undertakings **5.86** concerned will be each of its controlling parent companies. The joint venture, which at the time of the transaction does not exist, will not be considered as an undertaking concerned.[68] If the parent companies contribute various businesses to the new joint venture, the turnover attributable to each such business will already be included in that of the respective parent company.

In cases where a pre-existing company or business comes under the joint control of two **5.87** or more parents, each of the controlling parents will be considered as undertakings concerned, regardless of whether or not they also, prior to the transaction, were solely or jointly controlling the target company.

The pre-existing target company will be considered an undertaking concerned in all situa- **5.88** tions except one, namely where, prior to the transaction, it was solely controlled by one parent company, and this parent will retain joint control. In this situation the target company has so far been part of the initial parent's group, as defined by Article 5(4) (see below). To avoid double counting or making an artificial separation of the initial group solely for the purpose of defining the undertakings concerned, the target company will not, in this situation, be considered an undertaking concerned.

(iv) Change in the Shareholding in Cases of an Existing Joint Venture If one existing **5.89** parent acquires sole control over a company that has hitherto been a joint venture, the undertakings concerned are the acquiring company and the target company (which ceases to be a joint venture). Any other change in the structure of control over a joint venture, by

---

[65] In the *TNT/Canada Post, DBP Postdienst, La Poste, PTT Post and Sweden Post* (Case IV/M.102 [1991]), five national postal administrations had set up a company (GD Net), specifically for the purpose of participating in the notified transaction. The Commission found that each of the five postal administrations had joint control over GD Net and therefore looked through the veil of GD Net and considered each of the postal administrations as undertakings concerned. Another example can be found in *Danish Crown/HK Ruokatalo/Sokolów* (Case COMP/M.3522 [2004]).

[66] In such cases, or otherwise when an acquisition is made through a subsidiary, the Commission will normally assume that the concentration is notified by the parent company.

[67] For an example regarding the acquisition of trade marks, see *Fortune Brands/Allied Domecq* (Case COMP/M.3813 [2005]).

[68] See, eg, *The Post Office/TPG/SPPL* (Case COMP/M.1915 [2001]).

which one or more undertakings acquire joint control (whether by the entry of a new controlling parent, or the replacement for an exiting parent) will be deemed to constitute a concentration. In such cases the undertakings concerned will be each controlling parent company and the target company.[69] If, on the other hand, the joint venture has three or more controlling parents and one of them exits with no impact on the relative power of the remaining parent companies, this will not constitute a concentration.

5.90 (v) **Multiple Transaction Concentrations**   As indicated at para 5.69 above, recital 20 to the new Merger Regulation clarifies that transactions that are linked by condition are to be regarded as constituting a single concentration. Where this is the case, it will have an impact on the identification of the undertakings concerned in the concentration and possibly on the jurisdictional division between the Commission and the Member States. However, as already stated, a demerger, ie an operation reversing a previous merger or joint venture, is still considered to constitute two or more separate concentrations.[70] The undertakings concerned will be, on the one hand, each party that acquires control of certain assets, and on the other hand, the assets that are acquired by each party.

5.91 For swap agreements, ie where two or more undertakings agree to exchange certain assets with one another, the undertakings concerned are each of the acquiring parties and each of the acquired assets.

5.92 (vi) **Other Situations**   According to Article 3(1)(b) of the Merger Regulation an individual will be regarded as an undertaking concerned if he/she, prior to the transaction under consideration, already controls at least one other undertaking.[71]

5.93 Similarly the fact that two companies ultimately are controlled by the same state (or regional or local public entity) does not automatically mean that they will not be separate undertakings under the Merger Regulation. The decisive criterion is whether the two companies form part of different economic units with independent powers of decision. If that is indeed the case the Merger Regulation will be applicable, and each of the companies involved in the concentration will be regarded as undertakings concerned.[72]

(b) Calculation of Turnover (Article 5)

5.94 After the undertakings concerned have been identified, the question of whether a concentration has a Community dimension will depend on a purely quantitative test of whether or not the turnover attributable to those undertakings is sufficient to reach the thresholds set out in Article 1(2) or 1(3).[73]

---

[69] See, eg, *Synthomer/Yule Catto* (Case IV/M.376 [1993]).

[70] In *Solvay/Laporte* (Case IV/M.197 [1992]) the Commission concluded that the break-up of a previous joint venture constituted two separate operations, and issued a combined Art 6(1)(a) and 6(1)(b) decision for both operations. See also *Shell/BEB* (Case COMP/M.3293 [2003]) and *ExxonMobil/BEB* (Case COMP/M.3294 [2003]).

[71] See *Asko/Jacobs/Adia* (Case IV/M.082) [1991]) and *EDFI/Graninge* (Case IV/M.1169 [1998]).

[72] See, eg, *CEA Industries/France Telecom/SGS-Thomson* (Case IV/M.216 [1993]) and *Neste/IVO* (Case IV/M.931 [1998]).

[73] For more details, see Commission Notice on calculation of turnover under Council Regulation (EEC) No 4064/89 on the control of concentrations between undertakings [1998] OJ C66/25 ('the turnover Notice').

These two sets of thresholds are alternative, so that the Article 1(3) threshold only becomes **5.95** applicable in situations where the Article 1(2) threshold is not met.

Article 1(2) contains the threshold test which was also included in the original Merger **5.96** Regulation. This is a threefold test requiring (i) a combined world-wide turnover of all parties concerned greater than EUR 5 billion; (ii) a Community-wide turnover greater than EUR 250 million for each of at least two parties; and (iii) that each of the undertakings concerned does not achieve more than two thirds of its Community-wide turnover in one and the same Member State (the so called 'two-thirds rule').

Only in cases where these thresholds are *not* met, do the parties need to consider the set of **5.97** thresholds in Article 1(3). This establishes five conditions: (i) a combined world-wide turnover of all parties concerned greater than EUR 2.5 billion; (ii) a Community-wide turnover greater than EUR 100 million for each of at least two parties; (iii) a combined turnover of all parties concerned of more than 100 million EUR in each of at least three EU Member States; (iv) that in each of at least three EU Member States included in condition (iii), each of at least two parties has a turnover of more than EUR 25 million; (v) that the two-thirds rule is not met.

In relation to the EEA agreement it should be noted that the turnover thresholds relate to **5.98** the Community as such. Only EU Member States count for the purposes of the turnover thresholds of Article 1. This means, *inter alia*, that it is not possible to apply Article 1(3) by fulfilling the requirement of EUR 25 and EUR 100 million in one EFTA State and two Member States. Such a case would not have a Community dimension.

The 2004 revision of the Merger Regulation has not affected Articles 1(2) and 1(3), despite **5.99** the fact that the Commission's report[74] on these provisions in June 2000 provided strong indications that the thresholds did not capture effectively all cases with a Community interest. Upon reflection, it was felt that the introduction of more complex thresholds would not be the optimal solution for improving the system of allocation of competencies for merger control between the Commission and the Member States. Leaving the turnover thresholds unchanged,[75] the 2004 revision instead introduced a more streamlined system for reallocating jurisdiction through referral of cases and made such referrals possible even before the notification of a case.[76]

(i) Turnover: an Accounting and 'Net' Concept   In order to provide the intended reflec- **5.100** tion of the economic strength of the undertakings concerned, the Merger Regulation's turnover concept is based on 'net sales'. The main rule is therefore that, regardless of whether the undertaking's activities consist of the sale of products or the provision of services, the financial resources combined through the concentration—as indicated by the net sales—will determine the jurisdictional issue. In this context it should be noted that the

---

[74] COM(2000) 399 final—28.06.2000.

[75] In November 2005, Commissioner Kroes announced an initiative that will reflect on the functioning of the 2/3-rule contained in both Arts 1(2) and 1(3). Following this, the Commission may, if appropriate make a proposal to amend or even abandon this rule, possibly in the course of 2006.

[76] See Section B.3 below.

entire turnover of the merging groups is considered, not merely the proportion thereof which is achieved on markets that are affected by the transaction.

5.101 The Commission will normally base its decision on audited accounts for the last financial year. However, if more recent figures are available in a final form, and if the result of using these figures would be decisive for the jurisdictional question, the Commission may in exceptional circumstances agree to take the unaudited figures into account. The undertakings concerned however, in order to achieve this, would have to provide clear-cut evidence that the unaudited figures should replace the audited ones. The hostile takeover in *Gas Natural/Endesa* (Case COMP/M.3986 [2005]), involved two Spanish companies active in the field of energy. The latter proposed that the Commission should accept a large number of adjustments to its legally audited accounts and thereby conclude that the transaction would be of Community dimension. After detailed examination, the Commission, however, concluded that the reasons put forward provided an insufficient basis to disregard the legally audited accounts.[77]

5.102 The turnover thresholds should reflect the economic strength of the undertakings concerned at the time of the event that triggered the notification (ie the conclusion of the agreement, the announcement of the public bid or the acquisition of a controlling interest).[78] The turnover attributable to the acquirer(s) as well as to the target company should therefore always be adjusted to take account of any acquisitions or disposals that have taken place between the last audited accounts and the date of the event triggering the concentration or, at the latest, the date of the notification. Moreover, if a divestiture or closure of existing divisions, subsidiaries, etc is a pre-condition for the notified transaction, it is appropriate to deduct the turnover attributable thereto.[79]

5.103 In other service sectors, the normal principle of calculating the total amount of sales is no different from that for the sale of products. The fact that certain categories of service providers act as intermediaries is not necessarily different from the situation regarding the sale of products, which may equally include intermediaries, such as agents whose role is limited to provide a meeting place for sellers and buyers, but who do not resell the goods or services in question and whose liability is limited to the service provided. Such undertakings can include for example various kinds of agencies (travel, ticketing, advertising, employment) as well as various kinds of exchanges (stock market, electricity, etc). The relevant turnover to be considered for such companies will be the amount of commission received. To the extent undertakings act at the same time as intermediaries and for their own account, the relevant turnover will consist of a combination of commission received and sales made.

---

[77] The Commission decision rejecting jurisdiction is published at <http://www.ec.europa.eu/comm/competition/mergers/cases/additional_data.html>. See also IP/05/1425 of 15/11/2005.

[78] The Commission considers these triggering events to remain the decisive date for calculation of turnover even though the 2004 revisions have abandoned the previously existing obligation to notify within one week of any such event. However, if, as is now possible under Art 4(1), the parties chose to notify on the basis of a good faith intention to proceed to a concentration, the decisive date for turnover calculation would be at the latest the date of the notification.

[79] See judgment of the Court of First Instance in Case T-3/93, *Air France v Commission* [1994] ECR II-12, paras 102–105.

(ii) Group Turnover—the Application of Article 5(4) In order to reflect accurately the **5.104** financial strength of an undertaking concerned, its turnover will be combined with that of all other companies in the same group. The turnover to be taken into account will thus include all parent and sister companies as well as subsidiaries within the meaning of Article 5(4) of the Merger Regulation. This provision essentially focuses on quantitative, rather than qualitative criteria for this assessment and includes (i) ownership of more than half the capital or business assets, (ii) power to exercise more than half the voting rights, (iii) power to appoint more than half the members of the board or other bodies legally representing the undertaking, or (iv) the right to manage the undertakings' affairs.

In the specific case of pre-existing joint ventures between a company in the group and one **5.105** or more third parties, the Commission has consistently allocated the turnover of that joint venture in proportion to the *number* of controlling parents (see *Ameritech/Tele Denmark* (Case M.1046 [1997])). Consequently, for example, even if there are three controlling parents of a joint venture with shareholdings of 40 per cent, 30 per cent and 20 per cent (and a fourth with 10 per cent but no veto rights), the turnover of the joint venture has been allocated equally between the three controlling parents.

(iii) Geographical Allocation of Turnover The audited accounts of an undertaking will **5.106** not necessarily contain a precise break-down of turnover for each Member State or even the EU as a whole. This does not normally cause any problem, since, in most cases, it can be clearly shown that the Community-wide threshold is exceeded and that less than 2/3 of this turnover is achieved in a single Member State. In such cases it is normally not necessary to provide exact figures for each Member State. If a detailed break-down is necessary in order to settle the jurisdictional test, the general principle is to attribute turnover to the location of the customer, which provides the best indication of where competition to achieve the sales actually took place. If the Community-wide turnover thresholds are satisfied on this basis, no further investigation is normally required.

A particular question concerns companies with central purchasing strategies, ie where, for **5.107** example, the company headquarters engages in purchasing for the entire group. In such cases it may be necessary to consider on a case-by-case basis where the competition to win such contracts took place. Turnover should be allocated geographically to the place where the head office is located if goods are both purchased and delivered there even if further deliveries are made within the company to various other areas. However, in other situations where it is the local subsidiaries that are in contact with potential suppliers and where subsequent deliveries are made at that level, this should be reflected in the turnover calculation, even if the formal purchases are placed centrally through the company headquarters, on the basis of, for example, framework agreements.

In the field of services, and air transport and telecommunication services in particular, the **5.108** nature of the services in question has caused certain questions to arise as to the most proper method of geographical allocation of turnover. In *Delta Airlines/Pan Am* (Case M.130 [1991]) and subsequent cases in the airline sector, the Commission considered, in addition to the above-mentioned method of allocating the turnover to the area where the sales actually took place, the effect of allocating the turnover to the place of the destination or of allocating the turnover on a 50/50 basis between the place of departure and the place of arrival. As the relevant turnover thresholds were met irrespective of the method employed, this question was left open.[80]

5.109   **(iv)   Credit and Other Financial Institutions and Insurance Undertakings**   Article 5(3)(a) specifies that the calculation of turnover for financial institutions will follow Council Directive (EEC) 86/635 on the annual accounts and consolidated accounts of banks and other financial institutions [1986].[81] The turnover Notice sets out these rules in detail.

(3)   Re-allocation of Jurisdiction ('Referrals')

5.110   The Merger Regulation contains four distinct rules allowing a case to be referred, fully or partially, from the Commission to one or more Member States (Articles 4(4) and 9) or vice versa (Article 4(5) and 22). Referrals under Article 4 can only occur prior to notification to the Commission or Member States, referrals under Articles 9 and 22 can only occur after notification. Each type of referral is explained below.

(a)   Introduction—The Concept and Rationale behind the System for Referral of Cases

5.111   As explained above, Community jurisdiction in the field of merger control is defined by the application of a matrix of turnover-related criteria contained in Articles 1(2) and 1(3)[82] of the Merger Regulation. For practical purposes, this means that the division of jurisdiction between the Community and national levels is based on objective and quantitative criteria, thereby providing legal certainty about where a concentration should be notified.

5.112   This bright-line test, however, does not come without some drawbacks in a minority of cases. Fixed turnover-related criteria cannot serve as more than proxies for the category of transactions which the Commission is best placed to deal with in order to assess their impact on competition. This is why from the outset the Merger Regulation envisaged the possibility of cases being referred by the Commission to Member States (Article 9) and vice versa (Article 22). Such referrals could be made only after notification of a case upon request of the Member State(s) concerned and provided certain criteria are fulfilled.

5.113   When the Merger Regulation was first adopted in 1989, it was envisaged by the Council and Commission that referrals (notably referrals from the Commission to Member States pursuant to Article 9) would only be resorted to in 'exceptional circumstances' and where 'the interests in respect of competition of the Member State concerned could not be adequately protected in any other way'.[83] Over time referrals tended, however, to become less controversial and were resorted to in less restrictive circumstances. Factors contributing to this development certainly included the introduction of merger control laws in all

---

[80] Similar alternatives for the geographic allocation of turnover have been considered in the telecommunication sector, see *British Telecom/MCI (II)* (Case IV/M.856 [1997]).

[81] OJ [1986] L372/1, last amended by European Parliament and Council Directive (EC) 2003/51.

[82] The jurisdictional criteria set out in Art 1(2) were supplemented in 1997 by a more complex set of criteria designed to catch transactions not caught by Art 1(2) but nonetheless having a significant cross-border impact.

[83] See the Notes on Council Regulation (EEC) 4064/89 ('Merger Control in the European union', European Commission, Brussels-Luxembourg, 1998, at p 54).

Member States, and, more importantly, the benefit of experience gained by competition authorities as well as notifying companies and their advisors. Through these developments it became more routine for the Commission to agree, in appropriate circumstances, to refer cases to Member States pursuant to Article 9 where it was felt that the Member State in question was better placed to carry out the investigation. Since 1990, there have been 69 requests under Article 9,[84] of which 62 resulted in a full or partial referral. More than half of these Article 9 requests were submitted between 2001 and 2005. Likewise, referral requests pursuant to Article 22 have recently become more common in cases where several Member States have considered the Commission to be the authority best placed to carry out the investigation.[85] Overall, there have been 12 such requests since 1990, eight of which were submitted between 2002 and 2005.

The revised rules retain the possibility of post-notification referrals upon Member State request pursuant to Articles 9 and 22 and provide for significant procedural improvements, in particular as regards joint referrals under Article 22. However, the main intention of the new rules is to provide the merging companies with a greater involvement in the process at the pre-notification stage. Thus, two new provisions in the Merger Regulation, Articles 4(4) (for pre-notification referrals from the Commission to Member States) and 4(5) (for pre-notification referrals from the Member States to the Commission) allow the parties the option of triggering, at as early a stage as possible, a decision as to where jurisdiction for scrutiny of their operation will ultimately lie. This should minimise any delay and expense involved in referral cases. **5.114**

The Commission's Notice on referrals[86] describes for each of the relevant provisions (Articles 4(4), 4(5), 9 and 22), not only the legal criteria that must be fulfilled in order for referrals to be possible, but also the factors which the Commission and Member States will take into consideration when deciding upon referral requests. It also provides practical guidance regarding the mechanics of the referral system, in particular regarding the pre-notification referral mechanism provided for in Article 4(4) and (5) of the Regulation. **5.115**

(b) General Substantive Considerations in Deciding Whether a Referral is Warranted

(i) **Identifying the 'More Appropriate Authority'**   In principle, jurisdiction should only be re-assigned to another competition agency in circumstances where the latter is better placed to deal with a merger, having regard to the specific characteristics of the case as well as the investigative and enforcement tools and expertise available to the agency. **5.116**

---

[84] Reflects the situation as of 30 November 2005, see <http://www.ec.europa.eu/comm/competition/mergers/cases/stats.html>.

[85] In a parallel development, the Member States' competition authorities have formed a European Competition Authorities' association ('ECA'), which has issued a recommendation to provide guidance as to the principles which national competition authorities should apply when dealing with cases eligible for joint referrals under Article 22 ECMR (*Principles on the application, by National Competition Authorities within the ECA network, of Article 22 of the EC Merger Regulation*). This document is available at the home pages of most of the Member State Competition Authorities (available for example at: <http://www.oft.gov.uk/NR/rdonlyres/DDCC8138-88EB-413B-8CD5-724511D36DFE/0/ecaprin.pdf>).

[86] Commission Notice on Case Referral in respect of concentrations, OJ C56, 05.03.2005.

5.117   From an agency viewpoint, the likely locus of any impact on competition resulting from the merger will normally be the most important consideration, and tends to go hand in hand with other agency interests, such as increasing administrative efficiency by avoiding duplication and fragmentation of enforcement efforts. This does not exclude having due regard to the administrative effort involved for the parties. However, particularly as regards pre-notification referral requests, the parties should be aware that Member States may be less likely to refer competition-neutral cases with effects on, at most, national markets, even if this may be more convenient for the merging parties. From the perspective of the agencies, the case for re-assigning jurisdiction is likely to be more compelling where it appears that a particular transaction may have a sufficiently significant impact on competition and thus may deserve careful scrutiny.

5.118   **(ii) Avoiding Fragmentation of Cases**   In an *obiter dictum* to its decision in *Philips v Commission*, the CFI took the view that 'fragmentation' of cases, ie simultaneous treatment by several competition agencies in the EU, although possible as a result of the application of Article 9, was 'undesirable in view of the "one-stop-shop" principle on which Regulation 4064/89 was based'.[87] Fragmentation of cases through referral should therefore be avoided where possible unless it appears that multiple authorities would be in a better position to ensure that competition in all markets affected by the transaction is effectively protected. Accordingly, while partial referrals are possible under Articles 4(4), 9 and 22 (but not under Article 4(5)), it would normally be appropriate for the whole of a case to be dealt with by a single authority.[88] At the pre-notification stage, the parties' request will determine the possible scope of the referral. Thus, only upon request may such a case end up as a partial referral. In the post-notification situation, there may still be situations where a partial referral is deemed appropriate despite potentially leading to fragmentation. It may, for example be appropriate that a Member State deals with the effects of a transaction on market X, which remains a national market and where there are only significant effects in that Member State, while the Commission deals with market Z, which is EU-wide in scope. Proceeding in this way will ensure that all connected parts of a transaction are assessed by a single authority.

5.119   **(iii) Ensuring Legal Certainty**   Due account should also be taken of the importance of legal certainty regarding jurisdiction over a particular concentration, from the perspective of all concerned.[89] Accordingly, a referral should normally only be made where there is a compelling reason for departure from the 'original jurisdiction', as expressed by the turnover thresholds in Article 1. This applies particularly at the post-notification stage.

---

[87] Case T-119/02 *Royal Philips Electronics NV v Commission*, OJ C213/33 of 6.9.2003 (see paras 350 and 380).

[88] This is consistent with the Commission's decision in Cases M.2389 *Shell/DEA* and M.2533 *BP/E.ON* to refer to Germany all of the markets for downstream oil products. The Commission retained the parts of the cases involving upstream markets. Likewise, in M.2706 *P&O Princess/Carnival*, the Commission exercised its discretion not to refer a part of the case to the UK, because it wished to avoid a fragmentation of the case (see Commission press release of 11/04/2002, IP/02/552).

[89] See recital 11 of the Merger Regulation.

Similarly, if a referral has been made prior to notification, a post-notification referral in the same case should be avoided as far as possible.[90]

(c) Pre-notification Referrals

Pre-notification referrals are governed by Articles 4(4) and 4(5) of the Merger Regulation **5.120** depending on whether the referral is from the Commission to the Member States or vice versa.

Pre-notification referrals are intended to enhance efficiency by re-allocating jurisdiction to **5.121** an appropriate authority before any notification has been made. Pre-notification referrals are entirely voluntary in the sense that they can only be requested by the notifying parties. In line with the aim of allowing a more active role in referral discussions to the parties, who in particular at this early stage have much greater in-depth knowledge of the case and the relevant markets, pre-notification referrals can only be triggered by a reasoned submission lodged by the parties to the concentration.

(i) Article 4(4)

Legal requirements for referrals from the Commission to Member States under Article 4(4) **5.122** Article 4(4) specifies that the undertakings concerned may make a referral request by means of reasoned submission (Form RS), 'prior to the notification of a concentration within the meaning of paragraph 1'. This means that the request can only be made where no Form CO has formally been submitted pursuant to Article 4(1). In addition, Article 4(4) sets out the two legal requirements necessary for a referral. There must exist indications *that the concentration may significantly affect competition* in one or more markets, and such market or markets must *present all the characteristics of a distinct market* within the Member State to which referral is sought.

As to the degree of impact on competition, it would normally be sufficient for the parties **5.123** to show the existence of 'affected markets' within the meaning of Form RS[91] in order to meet the requirements of Article 4(4). However, the parties can point to any factors which may be relevant for the competitive analysis of the case (market overlap, vertical integration, etc), and they do not need to provide more than preliminary indications without prejudice to the outcome of the investigation.[92]

The requesting party or parties must also show that the geographic market in which com- **5.124** petition is affected by the transaction is national, or narrower than national in scope, in view of the product characteristics (eg low value of the product as compared to costs

---

[90] See recital 14 of the Merger Regulation. This is of course subject to the parties having made a full and honest disclosure of all relevant facts in their request for a pre-filing referral.

[91] An affected market exists in horizontal relationships if the joint market share is 15% or more, or in vertical relationships, if the market share is 25% or more on either market.

[92] It was considered important to ensure that parties would not be in a position where they would be asked to 'self-incriminate', in order to obtain a desired result on the jurisdiction of their case. For this reason, whilst the legal criteria of Art 4(4) and the guidance on Art 4(5) ask the parties to provide indications *that the concentration may significantly affect competition*, recital 16 of the Merger Regulation provides that such effects need not be detrimental to competition.

of transport), specific characteristics of demand (eg end consumers sourcing in their own locality) and supply, significant variation of prices and market shares across countries or regions, national consumer habits, different regulatory frameworks, taxation or other legislation.[93]

5.125 The Commission will address its decisions under Article 4(4) to both the Member State to which the referral is made and the party or parties that lodged the request.

5.126 *The EEA context* By its decisions of 8 June 2004,[94] the EEA joint Committee extended the applicability of the Merger Regulation to the three EFTA States that are parties to the EEA agreement, namely Iceland, Liechtenstein and Norway. Under the old EEA rules, the Commission had the power to refer a case with a Community dimension to one of these countries, but none of those countries had any right to initiate a referral. Under the new rules, merging parties can, using the same legal requirements as for an Article 4(4) referral request to a Member State, also request referral to one of these EFTA states.[95]

5.127 *Other factors to be considered for referrals from the Commission to Member States under Article 4(4)* Other than verification of the legal requirements, anyone who is contemplating making a reasoned submission under Article 4(4) should also consider whether the agencies involved are likely to consider the request appropriate. The intention of the Commission's Guidance Notice is to assist in this process, even if, ultimately, the national agencies are not formally bound by the contents of a Commission Notice. In any case, early informal discussions with the Commission and the Member State(s) concerned is certainly recommended.

5.128 *Impact limited to national or sub-national markets in a single Member State* Concentrations with a Community dimension which are likely to affect competition in markets that have a national or narrower than national scope, *and* whose effects are likely to be confined to, or have their main economic impact in, a single Member State,[96] are the most appropriate candidate cases for referral to that Member State. This applies in particular to cases where the impact would occur on a distinct market which does not constitute a substantial part of the common market. To the extent that referral is confined to a single Member State, the benefit of a 'one stop shop' is also preserved.

5.129 *Impact not excluded from extending into other Member States* Referral to a single Member State is not excluded even if a concentration has potentially significant effects on competition in a nation-wide market as well as potentially substantial cross-border effects. Such cross-border effects may result from spill-over into neighbouring geographic markets in

---

[93] Further guidance can be found in the Commission notice on the definition of the relevant market for the purposes of Community competition law (OJ C372, 9.12.1997, p 5).

[94] Decisions 78 and 79/2004 of the EEA Joint Committee.

[95] See Annex XIV to the EEA Agreement (Joint Committee Decision—No 1037163, Annex I, letter (j)) and Art 6 (4) of the Protocol 24 to the EEA Agreement.

[96] See, eg, the Commission's referral of certain distinct oil storage markets for assessment by the French authorities in Cases M.1021 *Compagnie Nationale de Navigation-SOGELF*, M.1464 *Total/Petrofina*, and Case M.1628 *Totalfina/Elf Aquitaine*, Case M.1030 *Lafarge/Redland*, Case M.1220 *Alliance Unichem/Unifarma*, Case M.2760 *Nehlsen/Rethmann/SWB/Bremerhavener Energiewirtschaft*, and Case M.2154 *C3D/Rhône/Go-ahead*; Case M.2845 *Sogecable/Canal Satelite Digital/Vias Digital*.

other Member States, or from foreclosure effects and consequent fragmentation of the common market. As more experience is gained, it will be possible to tell whether any general rule can be established regarding such cases. Until then, in such situations parties should discuss these issues informally with both the Commission and the Member State/s concerned, not least because both agencies retain a considerable margin of discretion in deciding whether or not to refer such cases.[97]

Impact on the same market in a series of Member States   Where a concentration with a   **5.130**
Community dimension potentially affects competition in a series of national or narrower than national markets in more than one Member State, a case by case assessment will also be needed. Such cases may still be appropriate candidates for referral to several Member States, should the parties so request. This will depend on factors specific to each individual case, such as the number of national markets likely to be significantly affected, the prospect of addressing any possible concerns by way of proportionate, non-conflicting remedies, and the investigative efforts that the case may require. Where a case may engender competition concerns in several Member States, the parties are not likely to seek partial referral to each of them.[98] However, if they do, and if the case clearly requires coordinated investigations and remedial action, this will militate in favour of the Commission retaining jurisdiction over the whole of the case in question.[99] On the other hand, to the extent that the case gives rise to competition concerns which, despite involving national markets in more than one Member State, do not appear to require coordinated investigation and/or remedial action, a referral may be appropriate. In a limited number of past cases,[100] the Commission has found it appropriate to refer a concentration to more than one Member State, because of the significant differences in competitive conditions that characterised the affected markets in the Member States concerned. While fragmentation of the treatment of a case deprives the merging parties of the benefit of a one stop shop in such cases, this consideration would be less pertinent at the pre-notification stage, since the referral is triggered by a voluntary request from the merging parties.

As far as possible, consideration should also be given to whether the national competition   **5.131**
authority or authorities to which referral of the case is contemplated may possess specific

---

[97] See Case M.580 *ABB/Daimler Benz*, where the Commission did not accede to Germany's request for referral of a case under Art 9 in circumstances where, while the competition concerns were confined to German markets, the operation (which would create the largest supplier of railway equipment in the world) would have significant repercussions throughout Europe. See also Case M.2434 *Hidroelectrica del Cantabrico/EnBW/Grupo Vilar Mir*, where, despite a request by Spain to have the case referred under Art 9, the Commission pursued the investigation and adopted an Art 8(2) decision.

[98] By year end 2005, no request for referral to more than one Member State had been received by the Commission.

[99] For some examples, see M.1383 *Exxon/Mobil*, where the Commission, despite the UK request to have the part of the concentration relating to the market for motor fuel retailing in the north west of Scotland referred to it, pursued the investigation because the case required a single and coherent remedy package designed to address all the problematic issues in the sector concerned; see also M.2706 *P&O Princess/ Carnival*, where, despite the fact that the UK authorities were assessing a rival bid by Royal Caribbean, the Commission did not accede to a request for a partial referral, so as to avoid a fragmentation of the case and secure a single investigation of the various national markets affected by the operation.

[100] See M.2898, *Le Roy Merlin/Brico*, M.1030, *Redland/Lafarge*, M. 1684, *Carrefour/Promodes*.

expertise concerning local markets,[101] or is examining, or about to examine, another transaction in the sector concerned.[102]

(ii) Article 4(5)

5.132 *Legal Requirements for referrals from the Member States to the Commission under Article 4(5)* Article 4(5) specifies that a request must be made 'prior to any notification to the competent [national] authorities'. This means that the concentration in question must not have been formally notified in any EU jurisdiction for this provision to apply. Even one notification anywhere in the EU will preclude the undertakings concerned from triggering the mechanism of Article 4(5).

5.133 By contrast with Article 4(4), the legal requirement for requesting a referral to the Commission under Article 4(5) does not contain a competition test. Parties are simply required to show that their transaction is a concentration within the meaning of Article 3 of the Merger Regulation, and that the concentration is outside the scope of the Merger Regulation, but is *capable of being reviewed under the national competition laws of three or more Member States*.

5.134 'Capable of being reviewed' or reviewable should be interpreted as meaning a concentration which falls within the jurisdiction of a Member State under its national competition law for the control of mergers. There is no need for a mandatory notification requirement in national law, only a requirement that the national authority in question is empowered under national law to review the concentration in question. This covers, where appropriate, voluntary merger control regimes, such as that of the UK.

5.135 These legal requirements that are relatively easy to meet are counterbalanced by the establishment of an 'all or nothing' system whereby each and every Member State that had original jurisdiction over the case can veto the entire referral process by refusing to refer

---

[101] In Case M.330 *MacCormick/CPC/Rabobank/Ostmann*, the Commission referred a case to Germany, because it was better placed to investigate local conditions in 85,000 sales points in Germany; a referral to the Netherlands was made in Case M.1060 *Vendex/KBB*, because it was better placed to assess local consumer tastes and habits; see also Case M.1555 *Heineken/Cruzcampo*, Case M.2621 *SEB/Moulinex* (where consumer preferences and commercial and marketing practices were specific to the French market); Case M.2639 *Compass/Restorama/Rail Gourmet/Gourmet*, and Case M.2662 *Danish-Crown/Steff-Houlberg*.

[102] In Case M.716 *Gehe/Lloyds Chemists*, for example, the Commission referred a case because Lloyds was also subject to another bid not falling under ECMR thresholds but being scrutinised by the UK authorities: the referral allowed both bids to be scrutinised by the same authority; In M.1001/M.1019 *Preussag/Hapag-Lloyd/TUI*, a referral was made to Germany of two transactions, which together with a third one notified in Germany, would present competition concerns: the referral ensured that all three operations were dealt with in like manner; In Case M.2044 *Interbrew/Bass*, the Commission referred the case to the UK authorities, because they were at the same time assessing Interbrew's acquisition of another brewer, Whitbread, and because of their experience in recent investigations in the same markets; Similarly, see also Cases M.2760 *Nehlsen/Rethmann/SWB/Bremerhavener Energiewirtschaft*, M.2234 *Metsalilitto Osuuskunta/Vapo Oy/JV*, M.2495 *Haniel/Fels*, M.2881 *Koninklijke BAM NBM/HBG*, and M.2857/M.3075-3080 *ECS/IEH* and six other acquisitions by Electrabel of local distributors. In M.2706 *P&O Princess/Carnival*, however, despite the fact that the UK authorities were already assessing a rival bid by Royal Caribbean, the Commission did not accede to a request for a partial referral. The Commission had identified preliminary competition concerns in other national markets affected by the merger and thus wished to avoid a fragmentation of the case (see Commission press release of 11/04/2002, IP/02/552).

the case. The veto stops the entire process not just the referral from the vetoing Member State. In light of this rule, the system, although potentially applicable to many cases, in particular following the enlargement of the EU, is one which requires consensus among the requesting parties and *all* Member States concerned. The Commission, on the other hand, has no discretion, and the reason for this is that it seems hardly conceivable that the Commission would have any reason to oppose such a consensus, and that removing any Commission discretion allows for a shortening of the procedure.

The EEA context By its decisions of 8 June 2004,[103] the EEA Joint Committee has also **5.136** extended the applicability of Article 4(5) to Iceland, Liechtenstein and Norway with certain adaptations. Under the new rules, merging parties, using the same legal requirements as for a request for referral from Member States, may also request referral to the Commission from any number of these EFTA States competent to assess the case under their national rules.[104] Where parties make such a request for referral to the Commission from both EU and EFTA States, the veto mechanism has been adapted so as to allow the EFTA States only to block the referral as it relates to those three countries. If, on the other hand, no veto is raised by any competent state, the Commission acquires full jurisdiction over the entire EEA, which is consistent with the one stop shop principle.

The issue of the relationship between Article 4(5) and 7(3), which allows parties to seek a **5.137** derogation from the 'stand-still' obligation, has arisen. Although Article 7(3) is in principle also applicable before notification, it was concluded that this provision would not be applicable prior to the event establishing that the case will have a Community dimension. Thus, the Commission will not be able to grant such derogations prior to the expiry of the period during which the Member States concerned may veto a referral request.

Other factors to be considered for referrals from Member States to the Commission under **5.138** *Article 4(5)* Given this combination of relatively easily satisfied legal requirements and discretion on the part of the competent Member States, the Commission's guidance Notice endeavours to explain in what circumstances a referral of the case is likely to be considered appropriate. Whilst Member States are not formally bound by its content, it is likely that parties who submit well-reasoned requests that are in line with the guidance in the Notice will find it easier to convince Member States of their view that the Commission is the more appropriate authority for dealing with their case and thus avoid a veto of their referral request. By the end of 2005, there had only been two vetoes submitted in relation to requests under Article 4(5). In one of these cases, one Member State was of the opinion that the request failed to provide sufficient information about market conditions that it considered to be specific to its territory. In the other case, the referral request, in the view of one Member State, failed to consider the impact of the proposed transaction on parallel cases dealt with by that Member State. A common feature of both vetoes was that the focus of the respective transactions lay within the objecting Member State. In both cases, the affected

---

[103] Decisions 78 and 79/2004 of the EEA Joint Committee.
[104] See Annex XIV to the EEA Agreement (Joint Committee Decision—No 1037163, Annex I, letter (j)) and Art 6 (4) of the Protocol 24 to the EEA Agreement.

markets were also more likely than not to be at most national in scope. Proper contacts with all competent Member States, and in particular Member States where the transaction has its centre of gravity, will reduce the risk of a veto and provide the parties with a better view as to what information will be needed for the purposes of the request.

5.139   Recital 16 of the Merger Regulation makes it clear that requests for pre-notification referral to the Commission would be particularly pertinent in situations where the concentration would affect competition beyond the territory of one Member State. Particular consideration should therefore be given to the likely locus of any competitive effects resulting from the transaction, and to how appropriate it would be for the Commission to scrutinise the operation.

5.140   Referrals of cases that are genuinely cross-border in nature, having regard to elements such as its likely effects on competition and the investigative and enforcement powers likely to be required to address any such effects should normally not be controversial. As in the case of Article 4(4), the existence of 'affected markets' beyond a single Member State should generally be considered sufficient. In addition, the parties can point to any factors they consider relevant for the competitive analysis of the case (market overlap, vertical integration, etc), and there is no need to demonstrate that the effect on competition is likely to be an adverse one.

5.141   *Impact on markets that reach beyond a single Member State*   Cases where the market/s in which there may be a potential impact on competition is/are wider than national in geographic scope,[105] or where some of the potentially affected markets are wider than national and the main economic impact of the concentration is connected to such markets, are the most appropriate candidate cases for referral to the Commission. Such cases require investigative efforts in several countries, and should concerns be confirmed, also appropriate remedial and enforcement powers. The Commission is likely to be in the best position to handle such cases.[106]

5.142   *Impact in a series of national markets*   The Commission may also be more appropriately placed to deal with cases affecting a series of national or narrower than national markets located in a number of different countries in the EU.[107] The Commission is likely to be in the best position to carry out the investigation in such cases, given the desirability of ensuring consistent and efficient scrutiny across the different countries, of available investigative powers, and of addressing any competition concerns by way of coherent remedies.[108]

---

[105]   See the joint referral by seven Member States to the Commission of a transaction affecting worldwide markets in M.2738 *GE/Unison*, and the joint referral by seven Member States to the Commission of a transaction affecting a Western European market in M.2698 *Promatech/Sulzer*; see also *Principles on the application, by National Competition Authorities within the ECA network, of Article 22 of the EC Merger Regulation*, a paper published by the European Competition Authorities (ECA), at para 11.

[106]   An example of such a case dealt with on the basis of Art 4(5) is M.3692 *Reuters/Teletrade* [2005].

[107]   This may, for example, be the case in relation to operations where the affected markets, while national (or even narrower than national in scope for the purposes of a competition assessment), are nonetheless characterised by common Europe-wide or world-wide brands, by common Europe-wide or world-wide intellectual property rights, or by centralised manufacture or distribution—at least to the extent that such centralised manufacture or distribution would be likely to impact upon any remedial measures.

[108]   Examples of such cases dealt with on the basis of Art 4(5) are M.3465 *Syngenta/Advanta* and M.3570 *Piaggio/Aprilia*, both 2005.

Other factors to consider   It may also be that the Commission is better equipped than the   **5.143**
competent Member States properly to scrutinise the case, in particular with regard to factors
such as specific expertise, or past experience in the sector concerned. There may also be specific
circumstances relating to the case at hand that may mitigate in favour of a referral to the
Commission, for example where two cases are connected, albeit not in a form sufficient to treat
them as one concentration under Article 3, and where one case has a Community dimension,
whereas the other falls to be assessed by several Member States.[109] Parties who wish their case
to undergo a referral are advised to bring up any such specific reasons in their request.

Competition-neutral cases   The legal requirements in Article 4(5) do not in any way   **5.144**
inhibit the parties from seeking referral in cases where there is an apparent absence of effects
on competition. They may simply want to make use of this provision to avoid being subject to multiple filing requirements within the EEA. They may then argue, with reference
to recitals 12 and 16 of the Merger Regulation, that there is a compelling case for having
the operation treated by the Commission due to factors such as the cost and time delay
involved in submitting multiple Member State filings. The Commission's experience by the
end of 2005 was that about 35 per cent of all cases notified after a referral under Article 4(5)
could be treated under the Simplified Procedure, and, thus, that Member States when
requested are also able to agree to referrals of competition-neutral cases. Nonetheless, it is
advisable for parties that are considering such requests to make informal contact with the
Commission and each of the competent Member States.

(iii) Mechanics of the Pre-notification Referral System   Articles 4(4) and 4(5) of the   **5.145**
Merger Regulation together with the Implementing Regulation set out a self-contained
mechanism for referrals from and to the Commission. The Commission's Notice provides
additional guidance as to the mechanics of the referral system.

As noted above, pre-notification referrals can only be requested by the undertakings con-   **5.146**
cerned,[110] and for this purpose they must submit a reasoned request on Form RS. The
request is transmitted without delay by the Commission to all Member States.[111] The fact
that a Form RS has been lodged will not be published, and, consequently, non-public
transactions can be the subject of a pre-notification referral request.

The remainder of the process differs under Articles 4(4) and 4(5).   **5.147**

Article 4(4)
   (i) Under Article 4(4), the Member State/s concerned[112] have 15 working days from the   **5.148**
        date they receive the submission within which to express agreement or disagreement

---

   [109] See M.3465 *Syngenta/Advanta* [2005].
   [110] The term 'undertakings concerned' includes 'persons' within the meaning of Art 3(1)(b).
   [111] Both the Commission and all NCAs, their officials and other servants, and other persons working under
the supervision of these authorities as well as officials and civil servants of other authorities of the Member
States, will be bound by the professional secrecy obligations set out in Art 17 of the Merger Regulation. They
shall not disclose non-public information they have acquired through the application of the Merger
Regulation, unless the natural or legal person who provided that information has consented to its disclosure.
   [112] The Member State/s concerned are those identified in Form RS to which the case will be referred if the
request is granted.

with the request. The fact that this period is calculated from the date of receipt means that, where the Form RS, as is strongly encouraged by the Commission, is submitted in an electronic format suitable for electronic transmission to the Member States, this will have the potential to reduce the total length of this period.

   (ii) Silence on the part of a Member State is deemed to constitute agreement. This mechanism is an essential feature of all referral procedures set out in the Merger Regulation. The mechanism is often referred to as 'positive silence' or non-opposition, and means that failure to make a negative decision on the part of the Commission or a Member State will be deemed to constitute the making of a positive decision.

  (iii) If the Member State or States concerned agrees to the referral, the Commission has an additional period of approximately 10 working days (25 working days from the date the Commission received Form RS) in which it may decide to refer the case. Silence on the part of the Commission is deemed to constitute assent.

  (iv) If the Commission assents, the case (or the requested part/s thereof) is referred to one or more Member States as requested by the undertakings concerned.

   (v) If the referral is made, the Member State(s) concerned applies its national law to the referred part of the case.[113] Articles 9(6)–9(9) apply.

Article 4(5)

5.149   (i) Under Article 4(5), the Member States concerned have 15 working days from the date they receive the submission within which they can express agreement or disagreement with the request. A 'concerned' Member State is one where the concentration is reviewable and which therefore has the power to examine the concentration under its national competition law.

5.150 Experience shows that during this period there may be some limited scope for the parties to supplement the information provided in Form RS, so as to satisfy information needs of concerned Member States. Requesting parties should, however, be warned that the Member States are in no way required to seek such additional information, but can instead resort directly to a veto if the form is insufficient for their needs. Moreover, there are clearly limits as to how much extra information can be gathered and digested by the Member States during this short period, which, contrary to the position following notification of a concentration, cannot be interrupted owing to incompleteness of the information contained in the Form. For these reasons it is very important that requesting parties consider very carefully the information needs of each Member State concerned prior to filing their request. Informal contact with all competent Member States is therefore recommended.

---

[113] Art 4(4) allows merging parties to request partial or full referrals. The Commission and Member States must either accede to or refuse the request, and may not vary its scope by, for example, referring only a part of case when a referral of the whole of the case had been requested. In the case of a partial referral, the Member State concerned will apply its national competition law to the referred part of the case. For the remainder of the case, the Merger Regulation will continue to apply in the normal way, so that the undertakings concerned will be obliged to make a notification of the non-referred part of the concentration on Form CO pursuant to Art 4(1) of the Merger Regulation. By contrast, if the whole of the case is referred to a Member State, Art 4(4) final sub-para specifies that there will be no obligation to notify the case also to the Commission. The case will thus not be examined by the Commission. The Member State concerned will apply its national law to the whole of the case; no other Member State can apply national competition law to the concentration in question.

(ii) The Commission checks whether, at the end of the 15 working days, any Member **5.151**
State competent to examine the concentration under its national competition law has
expressed disagreement. If there is no such expression of disagreement, the case is
deemed to acquire a Community dimension and is thus referred to the Commission
which has exclusive jurisdiction over it. It is then for the parties to notify the case to
the Commission, using Form CO.

(iii) On the other hand, if one or more competent Member States has/have expressed **5.152**
its/their disagreement, the Commission informs all Member States and the undertakings concerned without delay of any such expression of disagreement and the referral
process ends. It is then for the parties to comply with any applicable national notification rules.

Important procedural issues regarding pre-notification referrals correct and complete information **5.153**
The fact that the deadlines applicable to pre-notification referrals cannot be interrupted
by a declaration of incompleteness does not mean that there is no sanction against such
behaviour.

If parties submit incorrect or incomplete information, the Commission has the power: **5.154**

(i) to adopt a decision pursuant to Article 6(1)(a) of the Merger Regulation (where failure to fulfil the conditions of Article 4(5) comes to its attention during the course of
the investigation), or

(ii) to revoke any Article 6 or 8 decision it adopts following an Article 4(5) referral, pursuant to Article 6(3)(a) or 8(6)(a) of the Merger Regulation.

Following the adoption of a decision pursuant to Article 6(1)(a) or following revocation, **5.155**
national competition laws would once again be applicable to the transaction.

In the case of referrals under Article 4(4) made on the basis of incorrect or incomplete **5.156**
information, the Commission may require a notification pursuant to Article 4(1).

In addition, the Commission has the power to impose fines under Article 14(1)(a) of the **5.157**
Merger Regulation.

Finally, if a referral is made on the basis of incorrect or incomplete information included in **5.158**
Form RS, the Commission and/or the Member States have the power to correct this by
making a post-notification referral reversing a pre-notification referral based on such incorrect or incomplete information.

Concentrations eligible for referral   Only concentrations within the meaning of Article 3 of **5.159**
the Merger Regulation are eligible for referral pursuant to Articles 4(5) and 22. Only concentrations falling within the ambit of the relevant national competition laws for the control of mergers are eligible for referral pursuant to Articles 4(4) and 9.[114]

Pre-filing referral requests pursuant to Articles 4(4) and 4(5) of the Merger Regulation **5.160**
must concern concentrations for which the plans are sufficiently concrete. In that regard,

---

[114] By contrast, the reference to 'national legislation on competition' in Arts 21(3) and 22(3) should be
understood as referring to all aspects of national competition law.

there must at least exist a good faith intention to merge on the part of the undertakings concerned, or, in the case of a public bid, at least a public announcement of an intention to make such a bid.[115] In other words, the standard for initiating an Article 4(4) or 4(5) procedure is the same as the requirement for notification under the Merger Regulation.[116]

(d) Post-notification Referrals

5.161 Many of the principles described above for pre-notification referrals were replicated from the procedures and experiences of the post-notification systems included in Articles 9 and 22 which have existed since the inception of the original Merger Regulation. These provisions, contrary to the pre-notification rules, can be triggered exclusively through a request by a Member State and not by the parties.

(i) Article 9

5.162 *Legal Requirements for Referrals from the Commission to Member States pursuant to Article 9*
Under Article 9 there are two options for a Member State wishing to request referral of a case following its notification to the Commission: Articles 9(2)(a) and 9(2)(b) respectively.

5.163 *Article 9(2)(a)*   In order for a referral to be made to a Member State or States pursuant to Article 9(2)(a), the concentration must:

    (i) threaten to affect competition in a market significantly, and
    (ii) the market in question must be *within the requesting Member State, and present all the characteristics of a distinct market.*

5.164 Member States are thus, in essence, requested to demonstrate that there is a real risk that the transaction may have a significant adverse impact on competition, and thus that it deserves close scrutiny. Such preliminary indications may be in the nature of prima facie evidence of such a possible significant adverse impact, but would be without prejudice to the outcome of a full investigation. Given that the Member State will have had only 15 working days to review the concentration, it would not be feasible to impose more onerous requirements. At the same time, the fact that Member States have this time to consider the relevant issues involved also makes it reasonable to put the requirements at a slightly higher level, compared to those in Article 4(4). This is the intention behind the use of the term 'threaten to' in this provision, rather than the 'may' included in Article 4(4). The presence of 'affected markets' would, for example, normally not be sufficient in isolation to meet the Article 9 threshold.

5.165 The Member State is also required to provide at least sufficiently strong prima facie evidence that a geographic market in which competition is affected by the transaction is national, or narrower than national, in scope.

5.166 The Commission has discretion whether or not to agree to Article 9 requests. For this purpose, apart from these legal requirements, an assessment will be made of the appropriateness of a referral. This will involve an examination of the same guiding principles referred

---

[115] See recital 34 and Art 4(1) of the Merger Regulation.
[116] See Section D, Procedure, Notification, below.

to in the section on Article 4(4) above, and in particular whether the competition authority or authorities requesting the referral of the case is/are in a better position than the Commission to deal with the case. The likely locus of the competitive effects of the transaction will be of key importance in this assessment.

Article 9(2)(b)   Article 9(2)(b) was introduced in recognition of the fact that there are   **5.167** certain types of cases where the discretion that the Commission enjoys under Article 9 could be limited, so as to reduce, in those situations, the legal uncertainty inherent in any discretionary assessment. In order for a referral to be made to a Member State or States pursuant to Article 9(2)b a concentration must:

(i) *affect competition in a market*, and
(ii) the market in question must be *within the requesting Member State, present all the characteristics of a distinct market, and not constitute a substantial part of the common market.*

As regards the *first criterion*, a requesting Member State is required to show, based on a pre-   **5.168** liminary analysis, that the concentration is (liable) to have an impact on competition in a market. Such preliminary indications may be in the nature of prima facie evidence of a possible adverse impact, but would be without prejudice to the outcome of a full investigation. The Member State is then required to show not only that the market in which competition is affected by the operation constitutes a distinct market within a Member State, but also that the market in question does not constitute a substantial part of the common market. Experience so far, based on the past practice and case law,[117] indicates that such situations are generally limited to markets with a narrow geographic scope, within a Member State. Where these conditions are met, the Commission has an obligation to refer the case.

The EEA context   By its decisions of 8 June 2004, the EEA Joint Committee has extended   **5.169** the applicability of Article 9 to Iceland, Liechtenstein and Norway. These countries will now

---

[117] See Commission referrals granted under Art 9(2)(b) in: M.2446, *Govia/Connex South Central*, where the operation affected competition on specific railway routes in the London/Gatwick-Brighton area in the UK; in M.2730, *Connex/DNVBVG*, where the transaction affected competition in local public transport services in the Riesa area (Saxony, Germany); and in M. 3130, *Arla Foods/Express Dairies*, where the transaction affected competition in the market for the supply of bottled milk to doorstep deliverers in the London, Yorkshire and Lancashire regions of the UK. For the purpose of defining the notion of a non-substantial part of the Common Market, some guidance can also be found in the case law relating to the application of Art 82 EC Treaty. In that context, the Court of Justice has articulated quite a broad notion of what may constitute a substantial part of the common market, resorting *inter alia* to empirical evidence. In the case law there can be found, for instance, indications essentially based on practical criteria such as 'the pattern and volume of the production and consumption of the said product as well as the habits and economic opportunities of vendors and purchasers', see Case 40/73, *Suiker Unie/Commission*, 1975, ECR 1663. See also Case C-179/90, *Porto di Genova*, 1991, ECR 5889, where the Port of Genova was considered to constitute a substantial part of the common market. In its case law the Court has also stated that a series of separate markets may be regarded as together constituting a substantial part of the common market. See, eg, Case C-323/93, *Centre d'Insémination de la Crespelle*, para 17, where the Court stated 'In this case, by making the operation of the insemination centres subject to authorization and providing that each centre should have the exclusive right to serve a defined area, the national legislation granted those centres exclusive rights. By thus establishing, in favour of those undertakings, a contiguous series of monopolies territorially limited but together covering the entire territory of a Member State, those national provisions create a dominant position, within the meaning of Article 86 of the Treaty, in a substantial part of the common market'.

be able to request a referral from the Commission under the same legal requirements and circumstances that are applicable to EU Member States.

(ii) Article 22

5.170 *Legal Requirements for Referrals from Member States to the Commission—Article 22* A case (but not parts of a case) can be referred to the Commission by one or more Member States pursuant to Article 22 if the concentration:

(i) affects trade between Member States, and

(ii) threatens to significantly affect competition within the territory of the Member State or States making the request.

5.171 According to past experience, the *first criterion* is not a significant problem for Member States to establish. A concentration fulfils this requirement to the extent that it is liable to have some discernible influence on the pattern of trade between Member States.[118]

5.172 A referring Member State is then required to demonstrate that, based on a preliminary analysis, there is a real risk that the transaction may have a significant adverse impact on competition, and thus that it deserves close scrutiny. Such preliminary indications may be in the nature of prima facie evidence of such a possible significant adverse impact, but would be without prejudice to the outcome of a full investigation.

5.173 The text of Article 22 suggests that a Member State can refer a concentration that meets the two above-mentioned criteria even where it is not competent to review the case under its own national law (eg the national thresholds are not met) or even where it has no national merger control legislation.[119]

5.174 *Other factors to be considered* As post-notification referrals to the Commission may entail additional cost and time delay for the merging parties, they should normally be limited to those cases which appear to present a real risk of negative effects on competition and trade between Member States, and where it appears that these would be best addressed at the Community level.[120] The Commission views the categories of cases normally most appropriate for referral to the Commission pursuant to Article 22 to be the following:

(i) Cases which give rise to serious competition concerns in a market/s which is/are wider than national in geographic scope, or where some of the potentially affected markets

---

[118] See eg *Kesko/Tuko* (Case IV/M.784 [1996]). See also, by analogy, the Commission Notice on the notion of effect on trade concept contained in Arts 81 and 82 of the Treaty (OJ [2004] C101, 27.04.2004, pp 81–96).

[119] Originally, the main purpose of Art 22 was precisely to permit Member States without the relevant powers to review a potentially harmful concentration to request the Commission to examine it on their behalf. The provision was therefore known as the 'Dutch clause' because, at the time of the adoption of the original Merger Regulation, the Netherlands did not have national merger control laws.

[120] See the joint referral by seven Member States to the Commission of a transaction affecting world-wide markets in M.2738 *GE/Unison*, and the joint referral by seven Member States to the Commission of a transaction affecting a Western European market in M.2698 *Promatech/Sulzer*; see also *Principles on the application, by National Competition Authorities within the ECA network, of Article 22 of the EC Merger Regulation*, a paper published by the European Competition Authorities (ECA), at para 11.

are wider than national, and where the main economic impact of the concentration is connected to such markets.

(ii) Cases which give rise to serious competition concerns in a series of national or narrower than national markets located in a number of countries of the EU, in circumstances where coherent treatment of the case (regarding possible remedies, but also, in appropriate cases, the investigative efforts as such) is considered desirable, and where the main economic impact of the concentration is connected to such markets.

The EEA context   By its decisions of 8 June 2004,[121] the EEA Joint Committee has also **5.175** extended the applicability of Article 22 to Iceland, Liechtenstein and Norway. In order to respect the two-pillar system of the EEA agreement some adaptations have been agreed to the rules applicable between the Commission and the Member States.[122] Following these adaptations, the rules provide that, where a concentration may affect trade between one or more EU Member States and one or more EFTA States, the Commission shall inform the ESA of any request received from an EU Member State pursuant to Article 22 of Regulation No 139/2004 without delay. One or more EFTA States may join such a request where the concentration affects trade between one or more EU Member States and one or more EFTA States and threatens to significantly affect competition within the territory of the EFTA State or States joining the request. This means that the EFTA States, in such cases, are granted a right to join a request already made by an EU Member State. The EFTA States do not have a right to initiate a request under Article 22 in other circumstances.

In procedural terms, upon receipt of a copy of request, all national time limits relating **5.176** to the concentration shall be suspended in the EFTA States until it has been decided where the concentration shall be examined. As soon as the EFTA State has informed the Commission and the undertakings concerned that it does not wish to join the request, suspension of its national time limits shall end. Where the Commission decides to examine the concentration, the EFTA State or States having joined the request shall no longer apply their national legislation on competition to the concentration.

(iii) Mechanics of the Post-notification Referral System   Pursuant to Articles 9(2) and **5.177** 22(1), post-notification referrals are triggered by Member States either on their own initiative or following an invitation by the Commission pursuant to Articles 9(2) and 22(5). The procedures differ according to whether the referral is from or to the Commission.

Article 9

(i) A Member State may request that the Commission refer to it a concentration with **5.178** Community dimension, or a part thereof, which has been notified to the Commission and which threatens to significantly affect competition within a distinct market within that Member State (Article 9(2)(a)), or which affects such a distinct market not constituting a substantial part of the common market (Article 9(2)(b)).

---

[121] As regards Art 22, the Joint committee decision requires certain constitutional procedures in the EFTA States prior to its entry into force. This has now occurred.

[122] See Art 3 (1) of the Joint Committee Decision—No 1042011 (by which Art 6 of the Protocol 24 to the EEA Agreement is amended).

(ii) The request must be made within 15 working days from the date the Member State received a copy of Form CO.

(iii) The Commission must first verify whether those legal criteria are met. It may then decide to refer the case, or a part thereof, exercising its administrative discretion. In the case of a referral request made pursuant to Article 9(2)(b), the Commission has no discretion and must make the referral if the legal criteria are met. The decision must be taken within 35 working days from notification or, where the Commission has initiated proceedings, within 65 working days.[123]

(iv) If the referral is made, the Member State concerned applies its own national competition law, subject only to Article 9(6) and 9(8).

5.179 Regulation 139/2004 has clarified Article 9(6), which previously included a less precise provision[124] which risked being interpreted differently by the Member States, depending, *inter alia*, on their domestic merger control rules. This provision was therefore clarified and it now provides that, when the Commission refers a notified concentration to a Member State in accordance with Article 4(4) or 9(3), the national authority must deal with the case 'without undue delay'. Accordingly, the competent authority concerned should deal as expeditiously as possible with the case under national law. In addition, Article 9(6) provides that the competent national authority shall inform the undertakings concerned of the result of the 'preliminary competition assessment' and what 'further action', if any, it proposes to take within 45 working days after the Commission's referral or, if required, following a notification being submitted at the national level.[125] Accordingly, within 45 working days after the referral or following notification, the merging parties should be provided with sufficient information to enable them to understand the nature of any preliminary competition concerns the authority may have and be informed of the likely extent and duration of the investigation. The Member State concerned may only exceptionally suspend this time limit, where necessary information has not been provided to it by the undertakings concerned as required under its national competition law.

5.180 *Article 22*   Prior to the amendments brought about by the new Merger Regulation, the procedure surrounding the use of Article 22 left much to be desired, which may well be one of the reasons why it has been used very infrequently over the past years. Following these amendments, the procedures have been streamlined in order to increase legal certainty and to make this provision a more operational tool. It now works as follows:

(i) A Member State may request that the Commission examine a concentration which has no Community dimension but which affects trade between Member States and threatens to significantly affect competition within its territory.

---

[123] As regards cases where the Commission takes preparatory steps within 65 working days, see Art 9(4)(b) and 9(5).

[124] 'The publication of any report or the announcement of the findings of the examination of the concentration by the competent authority of the Member state concerned shall be effected not more than four months after the Commission's referral.'

[125] 45 working days represents a compromise period which is not significantly longer than that when the parties would, at the latest, have received an Art 6(1)(c) decision, had the case remained with the Commission.

(ii) The request must be made within 15 working days from the date of national notification or, where no notification is required, the date when the concentration was 'made known' to the Member State concerned. The Commission interprets the notion of 'made known' as implying sufficient information to make a preliminary assessment as to the existence of the criteria for the making of a referral request pursuant to Article 22.

(iii) The Commission transmits the request to all Member States.

(iv) Any other Member State can decide to join the request within a period of 15 working days from the date it received a copy of the initial request. It should be noted that any national time limits relating to the concentration running at that time are suspended until a decision on where the request will be examined has been reached. A Member State can, however, re-start its national time limits before the expiry of the 15 working day period by informing the Commission and the merging parties that it does not wish to join the request.

(v) Within 10 working days following this 15 working day period, the Commission must decide whether to accept the case from the requesting Member State/s.

(vi) If the Commission accepts jurisdiction, national proceedings in the referring Member State/s are terminated and the Commission examines the case pursuant to Article 22(4) of the Merger Regulation on behalf of the requesting State/s. Although this Article provides the Commission with discretion as to whether to require a notification, experience suggests that the merging parties will be asked to provide a full notification, because the various documents exchanged during the Article 22 request will not normally cover all aspects of the Form CO and exchanges up to that point may well have been in several community languages. Where the Commission examines a concentration on behalf of one or more Member States pursuant to Article 22, it can adopt all the substantive decisions provided for in Articles 6 and 8 of the ECMR. This is established in Article 22(4) of the Merger Regulation. It is to be noted that the Commission examines the concentration upon the request of and on behalf of the requesting Member States. The Commission therefore examines the impact of the concentration within the territory of only those Member States. The Commission will only examine the effects of the concentration in the territory of Member States which have not joined the request where such examination is necessary in order to assess the effects of the concentration and remedies within the territory of the requesting Member States (normally where the geographic market extends beyond the territory/ies of the requesting Member State/s).

(vii) By contrast with Article 4(5) cases, cases that come to the Commission via Article 22 do not achieve a 'Community dimension'. Non-requesting Member States can therefore continue to apply national law.

C. Substantive Assessment of Mergers

(1) The Substantive Test in the Merger Regulation

(a) *The Purpose of Merger Control*

The purpose of merger control is to prevent increases in market power which significantly impede effective competition. By its very nature and in contrast with cases of abuse under **5.181**

Article 82 of the EC Treaty, the assessment of merger cases is forward-looking. The focus is on the impact of the merger on future competition rather than on how competition has evolved in the past (although the latter is clearly relevant to an assessment of the former). Consequently the analysis must also take account of likely future industry changes in order to assess properly the impact of a particular transaction. Industry dynamics may, for example, lead to a change in supplier structure in the near future, which could lead to a higher level of potential competition, or market delineations may be about to change due to changes in regulatory regimes on a market or technological innovation (see section on potential competition below).[126] Therefore, merger control involves a market forecast of how competition will develop in the future. On the basis of such a market forecast the Commission assesses whether a merger will lead to a critical increase in market power that, for example, would allow the merged entity to raise prices or reduce quality. The assessment is made in accordance with the substantive test of the Merger Regulation as explained below.

(b) Article 2—The Test for Assessing Mergers under the Merger Regulation

5.182 Article 2 is the provision that contains the main criteria and test for assessing merger cases. According to Article 2(1)(a) the Commission shall take into account the need to develop and maintain effective competition within the common market, and according to Article 2(1)(b) the Commission shall take into account:

> The market position of the undertakings concerned and their economic and financial power, the alternatives available to suppliers and users, their access to supplies or markets, any legal or other barriers to entry, supply and demand trends for the relevant goods and services, the interest of the intermediate and ultimate consumers, and the development of technical and economic progress provided that it is to the consumers' advantage and does not form an obstacle to competition.

5.183 Articles 2(2) and 2(3) set out the substantive test for the assessment of the compatibility of mergers with the common market. According to Article 2(3), 'A concentration which would significantly impede effective competition in the common market or in a substantial part of it, in particular as a result of the creation or strengthening of a dominant position, shall be declared incompatible with the common market'.

5.184 This so-called 'SIEC' test ('Significantly Impede Effective Competition') was introduced for the first time in the new Merger Regulation. The background to the SIEC test merits some further explanation.

5.185 (i) **The Original 'Dominance' Test** Under the original Merger Regulation the test for whether the threshold for intervention by the Commission had been reached was solely a test for dominance. The test for dominance continues to be important and therefore warrants discussion.

---

[126] Dynamics on the demand side are considered in the market definition. For example, as regards the geographic scope of the relevant market, competition may at present occur mostly within national boundaries, but may be expected for various reasons to develop across the EU within a relatively short time period, and the relevant geographic market may, therefore, be considered an EU market.

The original Merger Regulation set out in Article 2(3) the creation or strengthening of **5.186** 'a dominant position as a result of which effective competition would be impeded in the common market or a substantial part of it' as the substantive test for whether a concentration is or is not compatible with the common market. For the purpose of the Merger Regulation the Commission has used the definition of dominance as defined by the European Court of Justice in past cases under Article 82 EC:

> The dominant position referred to (in Article 86 [now Article 82]) relates to a position of economic strength enjoyed by an undertaking which enables it to prevent effective competition being maintained on the relevant market by giving it the power to behave to an appreciable extent independently of its competitors, customers and ultimately of its consumers.[127]

And:

> such a position does not preclude some competition, which it does where there is a monopoly or quasi-monopoly, but enables the undertaking which profits by it, if not to determine, at least to have an appreciable influence on the conditions under which that competition will develop, and in any case to act largely in disregard of it so long as such conduct does not operate to its detriment.[128]

Consequently, according to the Court of Justice, a company is dominant if it has the power **5.187** to act to an appreciable extent independently of its competitors, customers and ultimately consumers. However, a dominant position need not amount to a true monopoly or quasi-monopoly. For example, in an industry consisting of one large and a number of smaller firms, the large firm could under certain circumstances be dominant within the meaning of the old Merger Regulation (see sections C2 and C3 below).

The concept of dominance as defined by the Court of Justice is a legal rather than an eco- **5.188** nomic concept (ie it is not a term of art in economic theory). However, it must necessarily be given an economic interpretation, since the assessment of the impact on competition of a merger requires an economic analysis focusing on the potential increase in market power resulting from a merger. Applying the dominance test, the relevant question is whether a merger increases the market power of the merging parties to such an extent that it creates or strengthens the ability 'to act to an appreciable extent independently of [their] competitors, customers and ultimately of consumers'.

In terms of standard economic theory, the focus of the analysis of market power is whether **5.189** the merging parties would be able to increase prices (either directly or indirectly as a consequence of reducing output) after having implemented a merger. However, while the potential for price increases is often one of the main concerns in the assessment of the negative effects of dominance, the Commission's assessment may go further. For example, the potential for a company to establish a 'gatekeeper' function, whereby it would be in a position to control entry to a market has played an important role in a number of cases.[129]

---

[127] Case 27/76 *United Brands Company and United Brands Continental BV v Commission* [1978] ECR 207.
[128] Case 85/76 *Hoffmann-La Roche & Co AG v Commission* [1979] ECR 461.
[129] For example, *The Coca-Cola Company/Carlsberg A/S* (Case IV/M.833 (1997)) [1998] OJ L145/41; *MSG Media Service* (Case IV/M.469[1994]) OJ L364/1; and *Nordic Satellite Distribution* (Case IV/M.490 (1995)[1996]) OJ l53/20.

The concern is not only the potential to earn monopoly profits, but also the negative impact on consumer choice over time. Further concerns could include, for example, increased scope for predatory pricing or the negative effects of a refusal to supply third parties. These are all examples of negative market behaviour, which may become possible as a consequence of a merger resulting in the creation or strengthening of a dominant position, and will be further elaborated below in the sections on the anti-competitive effects of mergers.

(ii) The Change to the SIEC Test

5.190 *Background—treatment of coordinated and unilateral effects under the original Merger Regulation* The reasons for the change to the SIEC test stem from the development of the treatment of collective (or oligopolistic) dominance under the original Merger Regulation. When the original Merger Regulation entered into force in 1990, the question was raised whether it could be used to prevent the creation or strengthening of collectively dominant positions. The Commission believed this was the case and considered collective dominance in a string of cases, such as *Nestlé/Perrier*, *DMV*, *Kali & Salz*, *Pilkington/SIV* and *Gencor/ Lonrho*.[130] However, the question was not finally settled until the judgment in *Kali & Salz* in 1999, when the ECJ confirmed that collective dominance was covered by the original Merger Regulation.[131]

5.191 After the ECJ judgment in *Kali & Salz* and the CFI judgment in *Gencor/Lonrho*[132] in 1999, the Commission dealt with oligopolies in a number of decisions such as *Veba/Viag*, *Exxon-Mobile*, *ABB/Daimler-Benz*,[133] *Price Waterhouse/Coopers & Lybrand*,[134] and *Airtours/First Choice*.

5.192 In *Airtours/First Choice*, the Commission for the first time prohibited a merger which it considered would have created a collective dominant position on the part of three firms. Airtours subsequently appealed the decision to the CFI, arguing among other things that the Commission's decision should be annulled because it was based on 'unilateral effects' (or 'non-coordinated' effects, for a further discussion see section C.3 below). According to Airtours the Commission had sought to develop a case based on unilateral effects and had therefore applied an incorrect definition of collective dominance (ie Airtours argued that the Commission had misapplied the test for dominance as set out in Article 2 of the original Merger Regulation since this test extended to collective dominance in the form of coordinated effects but not non-coordinated effects). Airtours further argued that the Commission had failed to established collective dominance in the form of coordinated effects on the facts of the case.

---

130 Case IV/M.190 *Nestlé/Perrier* [1992] OJ L356/01, Case IV/M.315 *Dalmine/Mannesmann/Valourec* (DMV), [1994] OJ L102/15, Case IV/M.308 *Kali & Salz/MDK/Treuhand* [1994] OJ L1186/38, Case IV/M.358 *Pilkington-Techint/SIV* [1994] OJ L158/24, Case IV/M.619 *Gencor/Lonrho* [1997] OJ L11/30.

131 Joined Cases C-68/94 and C-30/95 *France v Commission*.

132 Case T-102/96 *Gencor v Commission*.

133 Case IV/M.580 *ABB/Daimler-Benz* [1997] OJ L11/01.

134 Case IV/M.1016 *Price Waterhouse/Coopers & Lybrand* [1999] OJ L050/27.

The essence of the argument as regards unilateral effects is that oligopolists behaving in a **5.193** non-coordinated manner cannot be considered to be 'collectively' dominant. This argument is not entirely unreasonable, since the ECJ has laid down as key criteria for a finding of collective dominance that the undertakings 'act together' and present themselves as a 'single entity' to the market (see for example the judgment in *Compagnie Maritime Belge*).[135] In the *Airtours* judgment the CFI stated that companies must 'adopt a common policy' and present themselves to the market as a 'single economic entity'. On the other hand, according to the judgment in *Kali & Salz* it is clear that the ECJ has accepted that the intention of the legislator was to cover all anti-competitive effects of mergers. In the *Airtours* judgment the CFI did not accept Airtours' argument that the decision was based on unilateral effects, concentrating instead on whether the Commission had established collective dominance in the form of coordinated effects (see further section C3 below). Ultimately the CFI was not convinced by the Commission's finding of collective dominance and annulled the decision, without explicitly pronouncing on whether collective dominance could also be interpreted as covering non-coordinated effects in oligopolies.

The *Airtours* decision and the subsequent court proceedings led to a debate about whether **5.194** there was a 'gap' in the Merger Regulation in the sense that anti-competitive effects resulting from the non-coordinated behaviour of undertakings in an oligopolistic market (which was not therefore characterised by single firm dominance) were not caught by the regulation.[136] The question surfaced again to some extent in the *Volvo/Scania*[137] merger. That merger was prohibited due to the creation of traditional single dominant positions in a number of European markets for busses and trucks. However, in an econometric study produced for the Commission, it was found that there could have been significant non-coordinated effects in a number of other countries, where the combined market shares of Volvo and Scania were only in the 30–40 per cent range and where there were other strong competitors present. The reason for this finding seemed to be that Volvo and Scania were each other's closest competitor on these markets. However, the question was never fully examined in these other markets.

Commission Consultation and Green Paper   Given the uncertainty surrounding the appli- **5.195** cation of the original dominance test to non-coordinated oligopoly scenarios, the Commission decided to launch a debate on the merits of that test and, in its 2001 Green Paper launching the reform that led to the adoption of the new Merger Regulation, it invited comments on whether the dominance test functioned properly or whether a move to a new test, most notably a 'substantial lessening of competition' test ('SLC') would be preferable.

The debate following the Green Paper spawned numerous comments by Member State **5.196** authorities, academics, law firms and the business community. The position of the Commission and some Member States during the merger review was that such effects

---

[135] Joined Cases C-395/96 and C-396/96 *Compagnie Maritime Belge Transport SA and others v Commission*.
[136] For further discussion see Massimo Motta, 'EC Merger Policy and the Airtours case', European Competition Law Review, April 2000, 21(4); Ali Nikpay and A Houwen, 'Tour de force or a little local turbulence? A heretical view on the Airtours judgment', European Competition Law Review, May 2003, 24(5).
[137] Case M.1672—*Volvo/Scania* (2000), OJ L143 [2001].

were covered by the original Merger Regulation but that a new test was necessary as a clarification. Following this debate, the Commission proposed to amend the original Regulation by adding a paragraph clarifying that dominance would cover non-coordinated oligopolies. The Commission's proposal was criticised as being too prescriptive (in essence it redefined the meaning of dominant position) and not effectively dealing with the issue at hand. The matter was also debated in the Council and the debate ultimately led to the adoption of the SIEC test which is enshrined in Article 2 of the new Merger Regulation.[138]

5.197   During the period between the *Airtours* judgment in June 2002 and the entering into force of the SIEC test under the new Merger Regulation in May 2004, the Commission's case-load included a significant in-depth investigation into an oligopolistic market in the *Oracle/PeopleSoft*[139] case. The case was notified on 14 October 2003 before the new Merger Regulation entered into force and, therefore, had to be assessed exclusively under the dominance test. The case is of interest in highlighting the impact of the debate regarding the change to the SIEC test.

5.198   *Oracle/PeopleSoft* involved a proposed merger of the second and third largest players in the relevant markets for enterprise application software. The presence of SAP as the number one supplier meant that single firm dominance was not a real issue. However, consistent with its position during the merger review, the Commission explicitly assessed both potential coordinated and non-coordinated effects to determine whether the merger would result in the creation of a dominant position. Nevertheless, the question of non-coordinated effects was not addressed expressly in the decision since further evidence which had been submitted in respect of the relevant market (essentially broadening the relevant market and thus increasing the number of players in that market) led the Commission to conclude that the merger was unlikely to result in anti-competitive non-coordinated effects. Turning to the possibility of coordinated effects, the Commission conducted its assessment using the analytical framework for establishing collective dominance which the CFI had set out in the *Airtours* judgment. However, in view of its conclusions regarding the relevant market definition, the Commission considered that it was not possible to conclude that the merger would lead to a collective dominant position based on coordinated effects. The merger was consequently cleared. For a more detailed discussion of how the Commission is likely to assess potential coordinated and non-coordinated effects in future merger cases, see section C3 below.

(iii) Impact of the SIEC Test

5.199   *Closure of perceived 'gap' and likely future approach*   With the change in the substantive test to a SIEC test, it has now been clarified that anti-competitive effects resulting from non-coordinated behaviour in oligopolistic markets are effectively covered by EU merger control law. The main effect of the change is therefore to close any 'gap' that may have been

---

[138] For a more detailed discussion of the debate leading to the adoption of the SIEC test see Kyriakos Fountoukakos and Stephen Ryan, 'A New Substantive Test for EU Merger Control', European Competition Law Review (ECLR) 2005, issue 26(5).

[139] COMP/M.3216—*Oracle/PeopleSoft* [2005] OJ L218/6.

perceived to exist under the original Merger Regulation. However, the change should not be exaggerated.[140] The SIEC test is not intended to change fundamentally the process and scope of EU merger control. On the contrary, it is apparent from the wording of Articles 2(2) and 2(3) as well as recital 26 of the new Merger Regulation that an assessment of dominance is intended to remain as the main criterion for deciding whether mergers are incompatible with the common market. This is also clear from recital 25 of the new Merger Regulation where it is stated that 'the notion of significant impediment to effective competition in Article 2(2) and 2(3) should be interpreted as extending beyond the concept of dominance, *only to the anti-competitive effects of a concentration resulting from the non-coordinated behaviour of undertakings which would not have a dominant position on the market concerned*' (emphasis added). Consequently, even though the substantive test has been changed, the large body of established case law remains valid for the assessment of dominance.[141]

The first two years of the new Merger Regulation show that the practical impact of the change to the SIEC test is likely to be limited and that changes will come only gradually. In line with its promise to ensure continuity the Commission has continued to apply the original dominance standard as the main test, which has been used successfully under the original Merger Regulation since 1990. Furthermore, if judged on the basis of the few cases in the past where single dominance has not been found but where non-coordinated effects have nonetheless been raised as an issue, it seems likely that there will be few pure non-coordinated effects cases.[142] However, it would also be natural if the application of the SIEC test were to evolve over the coming years in particular in the area of oligopolies, and it would also be natural if this were to result in some evolvement of application of the test for single dominance (see section C3 below).[143]   **5.200**

However, even if there are relatively few pure non-coordinated effects cases, it is quite possible that the SIEC test will lead to a more subtle treatment of certain cases. In a case such as *Volvo/Scania*, for example, it would have been natural to include an assessment of non-coordinated effects in the markets where the parties had relatively low market shares. At the time the Commission was criticised, in the context of the *Volvo/Scania* merger, for putting big companies from small countries at a disadvantage by preventing them from merging in their home markets. If the non-coordinated effects on these other markets had been proven, that would have given the decision a broader base and would to some extent have countered this criticism.   **5.201**

---

[140] Commissioner Monti stressed in a speech that the change in the substantive test should not be seen as a 'shift in enforcement policy or a revolution'. See Monti, 'Private litigation as a key complement to public enforcement of competition rules and the first conclusions on the implementation of the new Merger Regulation', IBA 8th Annual Competition Conference, Fiesole, 17 September 2004, available at <http://www.ec.europa.eu/comm/competition/speeches/index_2004.html>.

[141] See also paras 1–4 of the Commission's Guidelines on the assessment of horizontal mergers under the Council Regulation on the control of concentrations between undertakings, OJ C31/5, 5.2.2004 ('Horizontal Guidelines').

[142] See para 4 of the Horizontal Guidelines.

[143] For further discussion see Lars-Hendrik Röller and Miguel de la Mano, 'The Impact of the New Substantive Test in European Merger Control', European Competition Journal, April 2006.

5.202   It has sometimes been argued that the threshold for prohibiting mergers was lowered with introduction of the SIEC test in the sense that mergers will in the future be considered problematic at lower levels of market power. It is clear from the recitals in the new Merger Regulation that this is not the intention. From the Commission's perspective, the SIEC test does not represent a lowering of the market power thresholds for intervention, but only a clarification that all types of mergers including mergers with non-coordinated effects are covered. However, if one were of the view that anti-competitive effects resulting from the non-coordinated behaviour of undertakings in a market were not caught by the original Merger Regulation, then it could be considered that the SIEC has led to a 'widening' of the substantive test to cover that scenario.

5.203   Consequently, the basic approach to the Commission's assessment of merger cases is not expected to change dramatically with the introduction of the SIEC test even though the SIEC test focuses the analysis more directly on an economics-based, effects-based approach. As in the past, the Commission will, when assessing merger cases, continue to weigh a number of factors such as market position, countervailing buyer power and potential competition simultaneously against each other in reaching a conclusion on whether a merger leads to an increase in market power. Although the change to the SIEC test is not expected to result in a fundamental shift in the Commission's approach to assessing merger cases, greater insight into the principles which will guide the Commission's assessment, in particular as far as horizontal mergers are concerned, has been provided with the publication of the Horizontal Guidelines[144] which are analysed in greater detail below.

5.204   *International convergence*   As regards international convergence of merger laws, it should be noted that, whilst US and EU assessment of notified mergers had in practice already converged to a large extent under the dominance test of the original Merger Regulation, the new SIEC test together with the inclusion of an explicit assessment of efficiencies (see below), is expected to increase consistency at the level of applicable rules to the benefit of even more pronounced convergence.[145]

5.205   *Use of quantitative evidence*   It is notable that the economic analysis of mergers has become increasingly sophisticated, sometimes including the use of econometric models, in recent years. In addition to (and in part in conjunction with) the need to address the specific issue of coordinated and non-coordinated effects discussed above, the new Merger Regulation and the Horizontal Guidelines to some extent reflect this general trend towards increased use of more sophisticated economic analysis. Wilst the Commission is keen to ensure that its use of economic analysis is both appropriate and rigorous, it is again not expected that this will lead to a fundamental reorientation or change in the way it assesses mergers. In academic economics literature a number of quantitative methods have existed

---

[144] See n 141.
[145] See speech by Commissioner Monti on 'Competition Policy Convergence in EU-US antitrust policy regarding mergers and acquisitions: an EU perspective' at the UCLA Law First Annual Institute on US and EU Antitrust Aspects of Mergers and Acquisitions, Los Angeles, 28 February 2004, available at: <http://www.europa.eu.int/rapid/pressReleasesAction.do?reference=SPEECH/04/107&format=HTML&aged=0&language=EN&guiLanguage=en>.

for some time, for example for assessing market power by estimating the residual demand elasticity of an undertaking following a concentration. However these types of analyses normally require a large amount of data, and yet in most cases can only be expected to give a limited indication of whether a merger significantly increases market power. Consequently, while the Commission is expected to use quantitative evidence whenever it is useful and sufficiently sound, in the large majority of cases the assessment of mergers will continue to involve, as in the past, a qualitative analysis based on a mix of quantitative and qualitative evidence.

5.206 In this regard, it is worth noting that merging parties are now contracting with external economic experts to a greater extent than in the first years of EU merger control in order to support their cases. While it is always useful to have as solid an economic assessment of a case as possible, it is also clear that studies produced for the purpose of a particular merger proceeding have been prepared with a particular aim in mind. The Commission will naturally take this into consideration when reviewing such studies and will rely on them in its assessment only to the extent that their basis is sufficiently sound. This implies among other things that the Commission should be able to assess whether the methodology proposed is the most appropriate one, for example because it corresponds to the way businesses usually analyse their market. Furthermore, the assumptions used should be clear, and the data should be unbiased and provided in a form that allows the Commission to calculate the results itself.

5.207 Having identified and understood in principle the substantive test to be applied by the Commission when assessing mergers under Article 2 of the Merger Regulation, the remainder of this section considers how the Commission will typically apply that test in practice.

(2) The Assessment of Market Concentration

5.208 The assessment of the change in market concentration (and consequently in most cases market power) caused by a merger is at the core of merger control. In order to be able to assess the impact of a merger on market concentration, the Commission will typically begin by identifying the possible relevant product and geographic markets before proceeding to the assessment of market concentration.[146] It is notable that the Commission may in certain cases refrain from reaching a definitive view as to the precise boundaries of the relevant market, because there is no SIEC regardless of the precise market definition.

5.209 Having examined the scope of the relevant market, the Commission's assessment of the impact of the merger on competition will often commence with an initial consideration of market share and concentration levels.

(a) Market Shares

5.210 An examination of market shares is a useful first step in the assessment of whether a concentration will significantly impede effective competition. As noted above, the Commission

---

[146] For a more detailed discussion of how the Commission performs a market definition analysis see Chapter 1, Section E on market definition above as well as the Notice on market definition, 'Notice on the definition of the relevant market for the purpose of Community competition law', OJ C372/5, 9 December 1997.

will often examine several different possible market definitions and, where appropriate, will also consider different possible ways of calculating market shares. If such examination leads to the conclusion, in view of the low levels of post-merger market concentration, that a merger would not significantly impede effective competition, then the case is usually cleared unless there are special circumstances requiring further investigation such as those outlined in the section on the Herfindahl-Hirschman Index (HHI) below. This initial assessment of a merger on the basis of market shares does not reflect any particular line of economic thinking, but is simply a way of ensuring that the resources of the Commission are used in the most efficient way.

5.211 The Commission has in the past relied on current market shares in its initial assessment of the market power of the parties and their competitors. Post-merger market shares are typically calculated based on the combined pre-merger market shares of the parties. However, in certain cases adjustments may be made to the calculation of the post-merger market shares. For example, in highly dynamic markets characterised by significant innovation or growth, or where there is a strong likelihood of future entry (or exit), it may be appropriate to adjust post-merger market share forecasts accordingly. Equally, in markets characterised by volatility of market shares (for example in bidding markets or other markets characterised by large and infrequent 'lumpy' orders), it may be appropriate to modify forecasts of future market shares by reference to historical patterns and volatility. In *Gencor/Lonrho*, for example, it was clear that the assessment of current market shares underestimated the future actual market power of the South African producers. Conversely, in a recent case in the automotive sector, it was clear that the high and leading market share of the parties did not reflect actual market power. In particular, in that bidding market it was not unlikely that parties could easily and rapidly lose their leading market position.[147]

5.212 In applying the dominance test in the past, the Commission normally considered that market shares below 25 per cent did not give rise to concerns under the old Merger Regulation, and that market shares usually had to be above 40 per cent in order for single dominance to be a concern. However, the Commission's conclusion would ultimately depend on the facts of the individual case.

5.213 The Horizontal Guidelines reflect this approach, which is consistent with the Community courts' case law. According to the guidelines '. . . very large market shares—50 per cent or more—may in themselves be evidence of the existence of a dominant market position. However, smaller competitors may act as a sufficient constraining influence if, for example, they have the ability and incentive to increase their supplies.'[148] The guidelines further note that 'The Commission has in several cases considered mergers resulting in firms holding market shares between 40 per cent and 50 per cent and in some cases below 40 per cent[149] to lead to the creation or the strengthening of a dominant position.' The guidelines then go on to state that 'Concentrations which, by reason of the limited market share of the undertakings

---

147 COMP/M.3486—*Magna/New Venture Gear.*
148 The Horizontal Guidelines, para 17.
149 Case IV/M.1221—*Rewe/Meinl* and Case COMP/M.2337 *Nestlé/Ralston Purina.*

concerned, are not liable to impede effective competition may be presumed to be compatible with the common market . . . an indication to this effect exists, in particular, where the market share of the undertakings concerned does not exceed 25 per cent'[150] (although this is stated to be subject to market definition and does not apply to collective dominance cases).

It is not possible to be more exact as to what precise level of market share would lead to a **5.214** finding of dominance in a particular market and the 40 per cent marker should be taken as a potential indicator rather than a presumption of dominance. As is clear from the Horizontal Guidelines, the significance of a particular market share level will depend on the structural and dynamic features of the market in question, such as the size of other competitors in the market, their access to technology or inputs, the presence of capacity constraints and the extent of barriers to entry etc. For example, in a particular case the Commission may be more concerned about, say, a 40 per cent market share in a market where the rest of the suppliers are highly fragmented and therefore more likely to follow the actions of the market leader. Conversely, the presence of a more limited number of sizeable suppliers who are able to challenge the market leader could mean that even a 40 per cent market share will not significantly impede effective competition. Equally, as noted above, the Commission's assessment is always forward looking and based on the particular context of the case. Consequently, the question of whether the increase in market share indicates that the merger will significantly impede effective competition must take into account likely future changes in market dynamics due, for example, to new entry or innovation.

(b) The Herfindahl-Hirschman Index (HHI)

In the past the Commission has in some cases, in addition to market shares, also used the **5.215** HHI to measure the level of market concentration.[151] The advantages of the HHI compared to simple market shares are in particular that it measures the overall level of concentration level of a market pre- and post-merger, and that it attaches proportionally more weight to large firms. With the introduction of the Horizontal Guidelines the Commission now relies more systematically on the HHI in addition to considering market share levels.

(c) Indicative Thresholds

The Horizontal Guidelines set out certain thresholds in terms of the HHI indicating the **5.216** levels of concentration where it is unlikely that a merger would cause horizontal competition concerns. The thresholds do not constitute a set of presumptions but rather helpful indicators. In particular, the Guidelines state that the Commission is unlikely to find horizontal competition concerns in cases where the post-merger HHI is less than 1000. The same is also true if the post-merger HHI is between 1000 and 2000 with a delta[152]

---

150 The Horizontal Guidelines, para 18 referring to recital 32 of the Merger Regulation.

151 The HHI is the sum of the squared market shares of all suppliers in a market. In a market with three market participants with 40%, 30% and 30% market share respectively, eg, the HHI is $40^2 + 30^2 + 30^2 = 3400$. The HHI can range from close to zero in markets having many small suppliers to 10,000 in pure monopoly markets.

152 'Delta' is the change in the HHI resulting from a concentration. The Delta of a concentration can be calculated only on the basis of information about the market shares of the merging parties. If, for example, two companies each with a market share of 30% merge, then the Delta is $60^2 - (30^2 + 30^2) = 1800$.

below 250, or if the HHI is higher than 2000 with a delta below 150, except in special circumstances as discussed further below. Table 1 provides a summary of the 'safe harbour' ranges.

5.217   Special circumstances may result in the Commission identifying competition concerns even if a merger falls within one of the 'safe harbour' range of HHI levels and deltas identified above. Such special circumstances could arise if the current competitive force of one of the merging parties is not adequately reflected in the market share and/or concentration levels such that the HHI do not fully capture the potential impact of the merger on competition. This could be the case, for example, if one or more of the following factors applies: the merger involves a potential or recent entrant; one of the merging parties is an important innovator; one of the parties has a pre-merger market share of more than 50 per cent and may be dominant; there are significant cross-share holdings between market participants;[153] or there are indications of coordination between market participants (particularly if one of the parties is a 'maverick' firm which would otherwise be likely to disrupt coordinated conduct).

5.218   Some commentators have suggested that the inclusion of the HHI thresholds in the horizontal merger guidelines is an indication that the thresholds for intervention have been reduced on the basis that there would be no reason to include them otherwise[154] and that different permutations of market shares could now give rise to intervention at lower levels than was previously the case. However, the thresholds were identified on the basis of an examination of market shares showing which market shares did or did not give rise to intervention in past cases. Moreover, exceeding the thresholds will not automatically lead to a finding of anti-competitive effects but will instead simply act as an initial indicator of whether further investigation may be required. Equally, there may in the future also be

Table 1   'Safe harbours'—ranges of the HHI and delta

HHI	Delta
HHI < 1000	Size not important
1000 < HHI < 2000	Delta < 250 *
2000 < HHI	Delta < 150 *

* Except in special circumstances

---

153   In the assessment of current competition in a market, it is sometimes the case that a company has joint control or some other degree of influence over another supplier. The Court of First Instance recognised in *Gencor v Commission* that in such a situation there can be competition between such entities even though one company has some degree of control over the other. Therefore, in such cases the Commission must assess the extent to which there is competition between such entities. However, no firm rules can be made in this respect: the analysis must be conducted on a case by case basis. As for market share calculations, the Commission may also adjust the HHI to take into account joint venture or cross shareholdings, as appropriate.

154   Mike Walker, 'Le nouveau règlement sur les concentrations et les lignes directrice sur les concentrations horizontales apporteront-ils un changement?' CRA articles sur la politique de la concurrence, Charles River Associates Limited, June 2004.

some cases falling below these indicative thresholds which nonetheless give rise to competition concerns meriting further investigation. However, by focusing on the market share and concentration levels which have typically given rise to intervention in past cases, the Commission has tried to ensure that the thresholds reflect past practice in the best possible way. Therefore, the thresholds cannot be assumed to indicate, as seems to be implied, that there will, in the future, be a higher number of cases with competition concerns. Moreover, the continued emphasis on the dominance criterion and the wish to continue to be able to rely on existing case law are clear indications that the intention was not to lower the intervention threshold in this way.

(3) Types of Cases and their Anti-competitive Effects

The central question in merger control is the change in the future conditions of competition **5.219** that the merger creates. If there is no change, then there can be no significant impediment to effective competition resulting from the merger and it should therefore be approved. This is the case no matter whether the merger is horizontal, vertical or conglomerate, and regardless of whether one or more of the parties was already dominant in one or more markets before the merger.

(a) *Horizontal Mergers*

(i) Non-coordinated and Coordinated Effects   Horizontal mergers can have two main **5.220** types of anti-competitive effects: non-coordinated and coordinated effects. The Horizontal Guidelines explicitly refer to the distinction between non-coordinated and coordinated effects by specifying that harm to competition can arise in two principal ways:

(a) By eliminating important competitive constraints on one or more firms, which consequently would have increased market power, without resorting to coordinated behaviour (non-coordinated effects);

(b) By changing the nature of competition in such a way that firms that previously were not coordinating their behaviour, are now significantly more likely to coordinate and raise prices or otherwise harm effective competition. A merger may also make coordination easier, more stable or more effective for firms which were coordinating prior to the merger (coordinated effects).[155]

Non-coordinated or unilateral[156] effects arise where the merger results in the removal of **5.221** direct competitive constraints such that the merged entity (and possibly one or more other firms) enjoys increased market power which, for example, enables it unilaterally without any coordinated action, to raise prices above the pre-merger level. Critically, the fundamental character of competition in the market will remain the same pre- and post-merger: firms will continue to compete against one another to maximise their profitability on an independent, non-coordinated basis. However, to the extent that the merger removes significant competitive constraints on one or more suppliers who consequently enjoy increased

---

[155] The Horizontal Guidelines, para 22.
[156] In the US Horizontal Merger Guidelines the term 'unilateral effects' is used. From the point of view of economic theory 'unilateral effects' and 'non-coordinated effects' are the same.

market power, the merger may result in a reduction in the *intensity* of competition without fundamentally changing the way in which firms interact. The Commission recognises that this alteration in the intensity of competition as a consequence of non-coordinated effects may in practice occur in two forms: either through the creation or strengthening of a dominant position of a single firm (likely to account for the majority of cases involving non-coordinated effects) or, in oligopolistic markets, through a reduced intensity of competition even in the absence of coordination. Both are discussed further below.

5.222 By contrast, and as discussed in greater detail below, a merger resulting in coordinated effects in a market not previously characterised by coordination brings about a fundamental change in the *nature* of competition in the relevant market. This occurs where, as a consequence of the merger, the market participants are able to recognise and act on a mutual understanding that a certain level of prices and/or quantities achieved through coordination of their competitive interaction is in the best interest of all players. A merger may make the market more transparent or predictable, for example, by removing a 'maverick' firm. As a result, the remaining firms may collectively find it attractive and possible to adopt coordinated market behaviour rather than to compete. No explicit agreement as found in cartels is necessary for such coordination to occur. Market participants will still take their decisions independently. However, there is a realisation amongst the market participants that a coordinated outcome is in their mutual interest. In addition, a merger may also result in coordinated effects in a market already characterised by coordination but where the merger facilitates more effective coordination as discussed further below.

5.223 The assessment of non-coordinated and coordinated effects in merger analysis grounds the analysis firmly in economic theory. While these effects have been analysed in the past, their explicit inclusion in the Horizontal Guidelines clarifies how the Commission assesses horizontal mergers and will serve to better focus the Commission's analysis on the economic aspects of a case. However, the change in approach is not expected to be dramatic. Retaining the dominance analysis used in the past as the main criterion of assessing mergers means that the Commission will continue to rely on its past approach and the existing case law for the large majority of cases (ie both non-coordinated effects cases which are characterised by single firm dominance as well as coordinated effects (collective dominance) cases). However, it is expected that the analysis of certain types of mergers will be clearer in the future. This is notably the case for the assessment of mergers in oligopolistic markets where it will be appropriate to consider the possibility of both non-coordinated and coordinated effects. For the purpose of the subsequent discussion a distinction will be made between the following three types of anti-competitive horizontal mergers:

— Non-coordinated effects in single dominance cases
— Non-coordinated effects in oligopoly cases
— Coordinated effects in oligopoly cases

5.224 **(ii) General Approach to Assessing Non-coordinated Effects**   As explained above, a merger may significantly impede effective competition by removing important competitive constraints on one or more sellers who consequently have increased market power. The most direct effect of the merger will be the loss of competition between the merging firms A and B (for example where A was previously constrained from increasing prices due to the risk of lost sales to B). However, non-merging firms in the relevant market may also benefit from a reduced competitive constraint. For example, if as a result of the elimination of direct competition between the merging firms the merged entity is able to raise prices, some customers may switch to rival firms who may in turn find it profitable to increase their prices.

A number of factors are relevant to an assessment of whether a merger is likely to result **5.225** in significant anti-competitive non-coordinated effects (both as regards single firm dominance and oligopoly cases). These factors will typically need to be considered in combination although it will not be necessary for all such factors to be present in a particular case for such effects to be likely.

Consistent with past practice, the starting point will typically be an assessment of market **5.226** shares. As noted above, this assessment must be conducted with regard to the specific characteristics of the market in question. However, in general, the higher the market shares the more likely it is that the merged firm will have market power, and the greater the increase in market shares the more likely it is that the merger will lead to an increase in market power. This in turn makes it more likely that the merged entity would find a post-merger price increase profitable, notwithstanding the accompanying reduction in sales that would entail.

In a differentiated product market, the risk of non-coordinated effects is also likely to be **5.227** higher if the merging firms are close competitors. In this case, the competitive constraint eliminated as a consequence of a merger between producers of close substitutes will be greater while the remaining competitive constraint from more distant competitors will be weaker. Consequently the opportunity for a profitable price increase by the merged entity will be enhanced.[157] However, in markets where the remaining competitors produce more distant substitutes, the Commission will also consider the ease with which such producers could reposition or extend their product offering to compete more directly with the merged entity.

The Commission will also examine other factors such as whether customers of the merging **5.228** parties have limited opportunities to switch suppliers, either because there are few alternative suppliers or because they face substantial switching costs. Such customers are particularly vulnerable to post-merger price increases by the merged entity. In this context it may also be necessary to consider the scope for price discrimination where only certain customers are constrained in their ability to switch supplier.

In addition, where competitors of the merging parties are capacity constrained, it is more **5.229** likely that the merger will lead to significant non-coordinated effects because, in such situations, competitors cannot respond to a price increase by increasing supply. In some cases the merged entity may also be able to hinder the expansion of competitors and thus undermine

---

[157] In *Volvo/Scania*, eg, Volvo and Scania were found to be each other's closest substitutes. It is likely that this type of analysis will be included more and more, as appropriate, in the analysis of differentiated product markets. See, eg, the analysis of the market for endovascular stents in COMP/M.3687—*Johnson&Johnson/Guidant* [2005], paras 265–272.

their ability to act as an effective competitive constraint on the merged entity. This could be due, for example, to the merged entity's control of inputs, distribution channels or intellectual property rights such as patents.

5.230 On the other hand, if competitors are not capacity constrained, that could be an indication that the merger will not significantly impede effective competition. This may be the case under certain circumstances even if the merging parties have relatively high market shares. In a bidding market with few large bids every year, for example, it may not be a problem that one firm has a much higher market share than its competitors, as long as the bidding process is effective and competitors are not capacity constrained.

5.231 A merger may also eliminate an important competitive force where it involves a firm with more influence on the competitive process than its current market share would suggest. Effective competition may, for example, be significantly impeded by a merger between two important innovators. A firm with a relatively small market share may also be an important competitive force if it possesses new technology or pipeline products or if it is a recent entrant with potential to exert significant pressure on more established competitors in the future.

5.232 **(iii) Non-coordinated Effects in Single Dominance Cases**   The vast majority of cases under the old Merger Regulation involved assessing whether the merger would lead to the creation or strengthening of a single dominant firm. This is not expected to change under the new Merger Regulation since, as noted above, the majority of cases where a merger is considered likely significantly to impede effective competition as a result of non-coordinated effects will involve the creation or strengthening of a single dominant position. This is also the experience of the first year with the new SIEC test, where the Commission continued to follow the existing case law applicable to single dominance cases. In such cases the merged entity would typically have an appreciably larger market share than the next competitor post-merger, and as outlined above, the anti-competitive non-coordinated effect may occur as a result of the elimination of the competitive constraint the merging firms previously imposed on one another and the resulting increase in market power enjoyed by the merged entity. This anti-competitive effect may be magnified if the fringe players are also able to increase their prices post-merger. The intensity of competition in the market will consequently be reduced. However, the fundamental character of that competition (as between the merged entity and the remaining firms) will not alter.

5.233 Consequently, in single dominance cases the Commission will, as in the past, assess whether a merger will lead to very high market shares and whether this and other pertinent factors (including those identified above in the general discussion on non-coordinated effects) can lead to the conclusion that the merged entity will acquire or strengthen a dominant position as a result of the merger. As noted above, the existing case law on single firm dominance will continue to apply in these cases.

5.234 **(iv) Non-coordinated Effects in Oligopoly Cases**   In some oligopolistic markets a merger may give rise to significant anti-competitive non-coordinated effects even if the market shares of the merging parties do not reach a level normally considered to constitute single dominance (and sizeable competitors remain on the market). These are the so-called 'gap' cases which the change to the SIEC test was intended to clarify as discussed above.

This situation could arise, for example, in differentiated product markets if two close com-   **5.235**
petitors were to merge. In the *Volvo/Scania* case there were indications that this was the situation in some European markets where the combined market share of Volvo and Scania
was only in the range of 30–40 per cent. This would not necessarily have been indicative of
a single dominant position in this case, but an econometric study carried out for the
Commission showed substantial non-coordinated effects on some of these markets.[158]
However, the merger was ultimately prohibited due to the creation of single dominant
positions on a number of markets, and the case for non-coordinated effects in these other
European markets was not pursued since the Commission would have had to investigate
these effects in greater detail in order to be able to conclude whether the merger would have
produced appreciable non-coordinated effects.

The Commission has so far only investigated non-coordinated effects in oligopolies in rel-   **5.236**
atively few cases and in varying degrees of detail. Even though the Horizontal Guidelines
set out an economic framework for assessing such situations, at this stage the Commission
still needs to develop an approach in practice. It is likely that a first focus will be on how
to assess mergers in differentiated product markets between firms which are close
competitors. Such an analysis could start with an assessment of the strategic positioning of
the merging parties in the market as well as an assessment of product characteristics,
customer groups, switching costs for customers when changing supplier and so on. If,
for example, customers were to incur substantial switching costs when changing suppliers,
and if customers therefore used a dual sourcing strategy as a means of obtaining
competitive prices, then a merger in such a market could have substantial non-coordinated
effects if it eliminated an independent second source of supply. This was, for example,
one of the Commission's concerns in *Oracle/PeopleSoft* although the non-coordinated
effects argument in that case was ultimately not pursued for the reasons explained above.

Econometric estimates of non-coordinated effects can be useful as a way of quantifying   **5.237**
such effects. However, econometric calculations are not usually sufficiently robust to
be relied on as the sole piece of evidence in merger cases (the potential problems associated with such an analysis were, for example, highlighted in the *Oracle/PeopleSoft*[159] case)
and earlier in *Volvo/Scania*.[160] On the other hand, a finding of non-coordinated effects
in an oligopolistic market made solely on the basis of qualitative information may also
be insufficient.

---

[158] For further details on the econometric estimations in the *Volvo/Scania* case see Marc Ivaldi, Frank
Verboven, 'Quantifying the effects from horizontal mergers in European competition policy' [December
2005] International Journal of Industrial Organisation, Volume 23.

[159] COMP/M.3216—*Oracle/PeopleSoft*, paras 197–204.

[160] For a complete overview of the econometric arguments for and against in *Volvo/Scania* see M Ivaldi and
F Verboven, 'Quantifying the effects from horizontal mergers in European Competition policy'; JA Hausman
and GK Leonard, 'Using merger simulation models: testing the underlying assumptions'; M Ivaldi and
F Verboven, 'Quantifying the effects from horizontal mergers: Comments on the underlying assumptions', all
in [December 2005] International Journal of Industrial Organisation, Volume 23.

5.238 Another area where practice will need to be developed, and may be of particular importance to non-coordinated effects cases in oligopolistic markets, is the assessment of efficiencies. Substantial efficiencies may render a merger pro-competitive in such a context and a careful assessment of the potential pro- and anti-competitive effects will therefore be required (see further the section on efficiencies below).

5.239 In conclusion, it is likely that the Commission will have to use a mix of qualitative and quantitative evidence, including econometric calculations, to inform its analysis in these types of cases.

(v) Assessment of Coordinated Effects in Oligopoly Cases

5.240 *Form of coordination in collective dominance cases*   In some concentrated markets, a merger may make it possible and economically rational for competitors to pursue coordinated market behaviour which would lead to the creation or strengthening of a collective dominant position and therefore significantly impede effective competition, for example by facilitating coordination of higher prices on a sustainable basis.

5.241 Coordination leading to a finding of collective dominance under the Merger Regulation is not based on explicit collusion. In the words of the Horizontal Guidelines, a merger in a concentrated market may significantly impede effective competition, because it increases '. . . the likelihood that firms are able to coordinate their behaviour in this way and raise prices, even without entering into an agreement or resorting to a concerted practice within the meaning of Article 81 of the Treaty.' This type of coordination leading to the creation or strengthening of a collective dominant position under the Merger Regulation is often called 'tacit collusion' by economists. However, coordination seems a better term for legal purposes, since no 'collusion' in the sense of Article 81 is necessary in order for coordinated effects to occur.

5.242 Coordination of market behaviour may take various forms. It could be coordination on prices, on quantities supplied or both. It may also take the form of dividing the market by geographic areas, customer groups or allocation of bidding contracts. In past merger cases coordination has mainly been in terms of price or quantities supplied. In *Nestlé/Perrier*, for example, the concern was on coordination on price, whereas in *Gencor/Lonrho* and *Airtours/First Choice* the concern was coordination on quantities supplied. However, this is not an indication that in merger cases the Commission will not also consider other forms of coordination.

5.243 Typically, coordinated effects may occur in certain concentrated industries where two or more firms not only recognise that it is in their mutual interest to align their conduct and thus act collectively to increase their market power but are also able, in view of the market characteristics and the competitive interaction between the major players, to coordinate their market behaviour accordingly without entering into any explicit agreement to that effect. One may debate the exact meaning of terms such as 'recognise their mutual interest' or 'implicit agreement' and 'be able to coordinate'. However, in principle coordinated effects in the economic sense of the term could arise without any particular intention of collusion, but simply due to the fact that it is rational for the oligopolists to take commercial decisions in such a way that the resulting market outcome is coordinated. As a result they act collectively with greater market power and thus, for example, achieve increased profits through higher prices compared to the most competitive market outcome.[161]

The necessary conditions for coordination to be sustainable   Earlier case law dealing   **5.244**
with collective dominance under Article 82 had suggested that some form of structural or economic link between the oligopolists might be a necessary condition for a finding of collective dominance.[162] However, the precise nature or extent of the requisite link was unclear. In *France v Commission* (*Kali & Salz*) the ECJ for the first time had to address collective dominance in a merger case. The Court stated that the Commission was in such cases obliged to assess, using a prospective analysis of the reference market, whether the undertakings involved in the concentration and one or more other undertakings together 'in particular because of correlative factors which exist between them, are able to adopt a common policy on the market and to act to a considerable extent independently of their competitors, their customers, and also of consumers'.[163] This was reiterated by the CFI in *Gencor v Commission* where it stated that the objective of the Merger Regulation was to prevent the creation or strengthening of anti-competitive market structures including 'market structures of an oligopolistic kind where each undertaking may become aware of common interests and, in particular, cause prices to increase without having to enter into an agreement or resort to a concerted practice'.[164] The CFI further referred to 'the relationship of interdependence existing between the parties to a tight oligopoly within which, in a market with the appropriate characteristics . . . those parties are in a position to anticipate one another's behaviour and are therefore strongly encouraged to align their conduct in the market, in particular in such a way as to maximise their joint profits by restricting production with a view to increasing prices'.[165] The Court's judgments in *France v Commission* and *Gencor v Commission* (as well as those in *Airtours* and *Compagnie Maritime Belge* discussed below) made it clear that structural links were not essential, the key factor instead being a (potentially looser) connection or relationship of interdependence between the oligopolists that allow parties to anticipate each other's behaviour and lead to an alignment of their conduct.

In *Compagnie Maritime Belge*, an Article 82 case, the ECJ sets out the decisive criteria   **5.245**
for collective dominance as being that, from an economic point of view, firms 'present themselves or act together on a particular market as a collective entity'.[166] Subsequently the CFI in the *Airtours* judgment expanded on the criteria for establishing collective dominance. It is clear from the Horizontal Merger Guidelines that, in order to establish that a merger will result in the creation or strengthening of a collective dominant position

---

161   In this context the most competitive market outcome is not necessarily the market outcome of a perfectly competitive market as described in basic microeconomics. Technically the most competitive market outcome is a 'Nash equilibrium', where the price level may be higher than the theoretical perfectly competitive market outcome.

162   See, eg, Case T-68/89 [1992] ECR II-1403 (*Italian Flat Glass*), para 358.

163   Joined Cases C-68/94 and C-30/95 *France v Commission*, para 221.

164   Case T-102/96 *Gencor v Commission*, para 277.

165   Case T-102/96 *Gencor v Commission*, para 276.

166   Joined Cases C-395/96 and C-396/96 *Compagnie Maritime Belge Transports v Commission*, para 36.

in future cases, the Commission will follow the principles set out by the CFI in the *Airtours* judgment. The Horizontal Guidelines identify three necessary conditions for coordination to be sustainable:[167]

> First, the coordinating firms must be able to monitor to a sufficient degree whether the terms of coordination are being adhered to. Second, discipline requires that there is some form of credible deterrent mechanism that can be activated, if deviation is detected. Third, the reactions from outsiders such as current and future competitors not participating in the coordination, as well as customers, should not be able to jeopardise the results expected from the coordination.

These three conditions were laid down by the CFI in the *Airtours* judgment and are sometimes referred to as 'the *Airtours* criteria'. As a fourth point, also stressed by the CFI, one may add the need for the merger to bring about a sufficient change in the competitive dynamics of a market as discussed further below. In *Impala v Commission*[168] the CFI provided further guidance as to how these conditions should be applied in a case where the Commission is assessing the existence rather than the creation of a collective dominant position, see further below.

5.246 *Condition 1: 'Ability to monitor to a sufficient degree whether the terms of coordination are being adhered to'*   The Commission must first establish that it is possible for the market participants to reach a common understanding (without any express agreement) on the terms of coordination and to monitor whether the terms of coordination are being adhered to. Coordination is more likely to occur in markets where it is relatively simple to reach a common understanding on the terms of coordination because competing firms can more easily arrive at similar views on how coordinated market behaviour would function. This is generally easier in less complex and relatively stable environments with few players. It is, for example, easier to coordinate on one price for a homogeneous good rather than on hundreds of price points for numerous differentiated products. Similarly, it is easier to coordinate on price or quantity if market conditions are relatively stable. Consequently it may, for example, be more difficult to reach and monitor a coordinated outcome in markets characterised by significant growth, highly volatile demand or frequent new entry since all of these characteristics may disrupt efforts to reach a common understanding on the terms of coordination. This may also be problematic in markets with high rates of innovation resulting in more frequent changes in products or processes and where competition on innovation drives the market, because no firm can afford not to innovate.

5.247 The degree of market transparency is likely to be critical in assessing the ability of the market participants to reach a mutual understanding on the terms of coordination and to monitor adherence to those terms. Transparency is often higher the lower the number of market participants. Moreover, market transparency depends on how transactions take place. In some markets transactions are, for example, negotiated confidentially and the degree of market transparency may accordingly be lower than, for example, in markets

---

[167] The Horizontal Guidelines, para 41.
[168] Case T-464/04 *Impala v Commission*, judgment of 13 July 2006, not yet reported in the ECR.

where transactions take place on a public exchange or in an open auction. It may also be easier to reach a common understanding on the terms of coordination where firms are relatively symmetric in terms of factors such as market shares, cost structures, capacity levels and vertical integration, and thus have more closely aligned commercial incentives. The existence of structural links may also align the incentives of firms and facilitate the adoption of a common policy.

Firms may also find ways to overcome the problems of complexity of the market to estab-   **5.248**
lish points of coordination. This could, for example, be achieved through common pricing rules. In *DMV*, the existence of common pricing rules was thought to make the market for stainless seamless steel tubes more conducive to coordination, and in *Sony/BMG* use of a Published Price to Dealers (PPDs) pricing system by the major record companies was thought to make it more likely that the major record companies would be able to coordinate their prices for recorded music CDs.

The Commission will assess whether the market is sufficiently transparent on the key   **5.249**
parameters where coordination is expected to take place such that firms can monitor whether competitors are deviating from or adhering to the common policy. It is rarely the case that competitors will have full information on all aspects of each other's business. In *Airtours/First Choice*, for example, the Commission did not argue that it was necessary for the market actors to be able to monitor each other's prices, but rather that there was sufficient transparency on capacity decisions (although the CFI held that there was not sufficient transparency on the facts of the case). Similarly in *Gencor/Lonrho*, the Commission did not argue that the market participants had full knowledge of the properties of each other's mines, but rather that the capacity decisions were sufficiently transparent for monitoring. The Commission has also not always accepted that bilaterally negotiated transactions were not transparent. In *Nestlé/Perrier*, for example, despite the fact that prices were negotiated bilaterally between supermarket chains and producers of source water, the market transactions were considered to be sufficiently transparent to allow the market actors to detect deviations.

It is therefore necessary to consider whether the relevant market characteristics are likely to   **5.250**
facilitate or hinder monitoring of potential deviations. Equally the Commission will consider whether, even where general market conditions would appear to make monitoring of deviations difficult, certain market practices may in fact enhance transparency. These might include meeting competition or most favoured customer clauses (which encourage customers to report back on prices or other terms offered by competitors and thus enhance visibility in this regard) as well as publication or announcements of relevant information, even where the primary purpose of such practices is not to facilitate monitoring of competitors' conduct.

However, it is not sufficient to be able to reach a common understanding on the terms of   **5.251**
coordination in order for a collective dominant position to be created or strengthened. Coordination must also be sustainable over time.

Condition 2: 'Requires that there is some form of credible deterrent mechanism, that can be acti-   **5.252**
vated, if deviation is detected'   As noted above, it is not sufficient that any deviation from

the coordinated outcome can be easily detected. In addition, and critically, a credible, timely and sufficient threat of future retaliation is necessary to deter market actors from deviating from the terms of coordination in the first place. The most obvious form of retaliation would be to cut prices or increase the quantities supplied to the market. However, retaliation may take many forms (for example cancelling joint ventures or other forms of co-operation) and may not necessarily have to take place in the same market as that in which coordination takes place.

5.253   Assessing the scope for a credible threat of future retaliation is not an easy matter and it depends critically on the incentives facing the deviating and non-deviating (retaliating) firms. Put simply, the threat of retaliation will only be an effective deterrent if the benefit to an individual firm from sticking to the coordinated outcome exceeds the gain to be derived from deviation less the pain of any subsequent retaliation. It is normally considered that delayed retaliation is less likely to be an effective deterrent since the impact will be less immediate (in contrast to the gain from deviation) and may also be less certain (particularly if the incentives for the non-deviating firms to carry out such retaliation are lower than in the case of more immediate retaliation). Furthermore, it is also normally considered that if targeted retaliation, hurting only the deviating firm, is possible, then this is likely to be more effective and credible than retaliation hurting the whole market. However, it should be noted that in principle, depending on the market, a sufficient deterrent making coordination sustainable does not need to be more complicated than the simple threat that a firm starts to compete. Consequently the nature and extent of retaliation necessary to establish an effective and credible deterrent in a particular case will depend on the specific market in question.

5.254   In past collective dominance cases, until *Airtours/First Choice*, the Commission did not outline a specific retaliation mechanism. In *Gencor/Lonrho*, for example, it described the characteristics of the demand and supply structure which it found to be conducive to collective dominance, as well as how the merger would change the incentives of the two duopolists and make coordination more likely.[169] However, the decision did not explain how the Commission saw the specific retaliation mechanism functioning in that market. In *Airtours/First Choice*, the Commission used the same approach as in *Gencor/Lonrho*, but in addition attempted to describe the specific deterrent mechanism which in its view would lead to sustainable coordinated effects.[170] The CFI found that the Commission had not sufficiently proven its case in this regard and annulled the decision. However, the CFI also found, consistent with the judgment in *Gencor/Lonrho*, '. . . that the Commission must not necessarily prove that there is a "specific" retaliation mechanism involving a degree of severity, but it must none the less establish that deterrents exist, which are such that it is not worth

---

[169] This has sometimes somewhat unfairly been referred to as the 'checklist' approach, because the Commission examined a set of factors such as points of coordination, transparency, cost structures, rate of market growth, rate of innovation, structural links, etc as part of its analysis of whether a merger would be likely to lead to collective dominance.

[170] Peder Christensen and Valérie Rabassa, 'The Airtours Decision: Is There a New Commission Approach to Collective Dominance', European Competition Law Review, June 2001.

the while of any member of the dominant oligopoly to depart from the common course of conduct to the detriment of the other oligopolists.'[171]

It might therefore be considered that the question still remains rather open as to what pre-   **5.255**
cisely the Commission has to prove in terms of the retaliation mechanism in collective dominance cases. However, it is clear from the CFI's judgment in *Airtours* (as reflected in the Horizontal Guidelines) that assessment of the structural features of the market is not sufficient. Comparing *Gencor/Lonrho* and *Airtours/First Choice* it is possible that a more complex analysis of deterrents will be required in coordinated effects cases involving more than two firms than the Commission had conducted prior to *Airtours*.

In *Sony/BMG* (Case M.3333), for example, the Commission examined whether there was   **5.256**
coordination amongst the major record companies[172] in respect of the pricing for CDs at wholesale level. The Commission found that some indications of past coordinated behav-iour were present in the market but that there was a lack of actual evidence as regards past retaliatory action. It further considered that there was insufficient evidence to demonstrate that the reduction from five to four major market participants would facilitate trans-parency and retaliation to such an extent that the transaction would result in the creation of a collective dominant position (see further discussion below regarding the CFI's judg-ment in this case).

In conclusion, it seem likely that the Commission will develop its analysis of the scope for   **5.257**
retaliation even further, in particular in coordinated effects cases involving coordination between more than two firms. The challenge for the Commission will be to put evidence of retaliatory actions into a relevant market context in such a way that it demonstrates convincingly that this is sufficient to sustain a coordinated market outcome. In some cases this may even require a degree of economic modelling, which despite the possibility of limited extension of the investigation under the new Merger Regulation, is likely to be constrained by the tight deadlines for merger procedures. In the past the Commission may have refrained from economic modelling and from investigating the specific retalia-tion mechanism in a given market in greater detail, because this would have increased significantly the burden of investigation. However, in order to examine fully the possibility of coordinated effects in more complex oligopolies than duopolies, this approach may be necessary.

Condition 3: 'the reactions from outsiders such as current and future competitors not participat-   **5.258**
ing in the coordination, as well as customers, should not be able to jeopardise the results expected from coordination'   In its assessment of collective dominance the Commission has always had to assess the behaviour of the collectively dominant firms against that of the outsiders (the 'fringe' players as well as potential competitors and customers). If outsiders are capable of reacting sufficiently to coordinated behaviour to jeopardise the coordinated outcome, then it is unlikely that coordination is sustainable.[173] The analysis in past cases such as

---

[171] The *Airtours* judgment, para 195.
[172] Sony, BMG, EMI, Universal, and Warner.
[173] See eg the cases of *Nestlé/Perrier*, *DMV*, *Gencor/Lonrho*, *Airtours/First Choice*.

Gencor/Lonrho and *Airtours/First Choice* focused on the ability of the fringe players to increase supply in the face of a reduction of supply by the collectively dominant firms. In *Gencor/Lonrho* this was not found to be the case due to a lack of access to mining rights or an inability to increase ore extraction. In *Airtours/First Choice*, lack of access to low cost seats was considered by the Commission to be a barrier (although the CFI considered that the Commission's conclusion was wrong in this regard).

5.259   It is also necessary to consider whether potential new entrants could destabilise a coordinated outcome. This involves an assessment of the costs of, and barriers to, new entry. As a general principle, for entry to be considered a sufficient competitive constraint, it must be shown to be likely, timely and sufficient to deter or defeat any potential anti-competitive effects of the merger (see further the discussion of barriers to entry below). Finally, the Commission must consider whether the market is characterised by the presence of countervailing buyer power sufficient to destabilise a coordinated outcome. This issue is discussed in greater depth below. By way of example, it may be possible for a large buyer to undermine an attempt to coordinate by offering substantial and/or long-term contracts which may tempt one of the market participants to deviate from the terms offered under the coordinated outcome.

5.260   *Need to identify the alterations to competition resulting from a merger*   In order to reach a finding that a merger will lead to the creation or strengthening of a collective dominant position, the Commission must also prove that, as a consequence of the merger, there would be a change in the competitive dynamics of the market such as either to facilitate coordination in a previously competitive market or to make coordination easier, more stable or more effective in a market previously characterised by coordination. In the *Airtours* judgment, the CFI highlighted the need for the Commission to identify the change in the competitive dynamics resulting from the merger, stating that 'if there is no substantial alteration to competition as it stands, the merger must be approved'.[174] Since the Commission had accepted that the pre-merger market was not characterised by collective dominance, it had to prove that, in view of the relevant market characteristics, approval of the merger would have resulted in the creation of a collective dominant position 'inasmuch as Airtours/First Choice, Thomson and Thomas Cook would have had the ability, which they did not previously have, to adopt a common policy on the market by setting capacity lower than would normally be the case in a competitive market'.[175]

5.261   In assessing the change in the competitive dynamics of a market, the reduction in the number of firms may in itself be a factor that facilitates coordination (particularly if the merger involves the elimination of a 'maverick' firm that has a history of disrupting attempts at coordination). However, this is usually not sufficient. The Commission has in past cases, therefore, looked as well at other factors that could result in an alteration in market dynamics and which would make coordination easier to achieve and sustain. In *Gencor/Lonrho*, for example, the Commission found that the merger would have resulted in an

---

174   Case T-342/99 *Airtours v Commission*, para 58.
175   Case T-342/99 *Airtours v Commission*, para 77.

alignment of the cost structures (and therefore incentives) of the two duopolists. In *Airtours/First Choice*, the Commission found, among other things, that the merger would have resulted in more transparency and a much tighter oligopoly with increased entry barriers (although the CFI did not agree that these factors were sufficient to 'tip' the market into coordination). In this connection one may argue that where the relevant market characteristics would not change appreciably as a consequence of the merger, it will be more important for the Commission to be able to provide evidence of past coordination to support a finding of collective dominance. However, evidence of past coordination is not always that relevant for the assessment of future behaviour. The fact that there has been a cartel in a market cannot, for example, necessarily be taken as an indication of a higher likelihood of a coordinated market outcome.

The requirement to show an alteration to the competitive dynamics of a market poses **5.262** the interesting question of what would be the most appropriate point of intervention in oligopolistic markets for a competition authority. If one imagines a market which consolidates gradually through successive mergers from ten to three suppliers, then it may not be possible to demonstrate a substantial change to the competitive dynamics at any specific point in the process of consolidation, but cumulatively the change may be very important, and the market may have become much less competitive, possibly through coordinated effects. If the Commission is not able to intervene at the most appropriate point in time in such a case, then it may hamper the development of an effective policy against consumer harm in such cases.[176]

(vi) Assessment of an Existing Collective Dominant Position   In *Impala v Commission* **5.263** the CFI drew a distinction between the assessment of an *existing* collective dominant position as opposed to the *creation* of a collective dominant position (which was the situation addressed by the Court in *France v Commission*, *Gencor* and *Airtours*). The Court appeared to suggest that, when assessing an existing collective dominant position, a less theoretical approach might be warranted with relatively more weight being attached to factual evidence regarding past or existing market conditions and characteristics. The CFI indicated that, whilst the three conditions set out in *Airtours* remained necessary, 'they may, however, in the appropriate circumstances, be established indirectly on the basis of what may be a very mixed series of indicia and items of evidence relating to the signs, manifestations and phenomena inherent in the presence of a collective dominant position'.[177] Indeed the CFI

---

[176] Massimo Motta and Helder Vasconcelos in an interesting article, 'Efficiency gains and myopic antitrust authority in a dynamic merger game' ([December 2005] International Journal of Industrial Organisation, Volume 23) seeks to address this question from the point of view of economic theory. Their proposal is basically that competition authorities should seek to take into account possible future mergers, when assessing a particular merger, because a merger may 'trigger' other mergers. This is an interesting idea. However, it would seem difficult to implement in practice for legal reasons. If one takes as a purely hypothetical example the market for recorded music, then putting into practice this idea would have meant that when assessing the Polygram/Seagram merger (that led to the combination of Universal Music and Polygram), the Commission should at the same time have tried to anticipate and include the future merger of Sony/BMG seven year later in its assessment. This would not seem practical and there would have been major legal issues with such an approach.

[177] Case T-464/04 *Impala v Commission*, para 251.

indicated that certain evidence, in particular the close alignment of prices above the competitive level over a long period together with the presence of certain other factors characteristic of a collective dominant position, could in the absence of an alternative reasonable explanation give rise to a presumption, or at least a strong indication, of an existing collective dominant position. Hence it might be presumed from such alignment that the market was sufficiently transparent to allow price coordination without the need for direct evidence of strong market transparency (contrary to the CFI's requirement in *Airtours*). However, since the Applicant had not formulated its case on this basis, the CFI went on to consider whether the Commission had properly applied the three conditions set out in *Airtours*.

5.264 The CFI also indicated in *Impala* that a different approach might be taken to the examination of deterrents in relation to an existing collective dominant position. The Court reiterated the requirement to show 'adequate deterrents' as part of the test to establish collective dominance as set out in *Airtours* and confirmed that the 'mere existence of effective deterrent mechanisms is sufficient, in principle, since if the members of the oligopoly conform with the common policy, there is no need to resort to the exercise of a sanction . . . the most effective deterrent is that which has not been used'. Nonetheless, the Court went on to observe that, when looking at the existence rather than the creation of a collective dominant position 'it might be considered that the condition relating to retaliation may consist, not, as was the case in *Airtours* . . . in ascertaining the mere existence of retaliatory measures, but in examining whether there have been any breaches of the common course of conduct which have not been followed by retaliatory measures'. This requires two cumulative conditions to be satisfied, namely proof of (i) deviation from the common conduct and (ii) absence of retaliatory measures. Although the Commission had not argued (either in the decision or before the Court) that the test for adequate deterrents should be different when examining *existing* collective dominance, the CFI nonetheless examined whether the findings in the decision satisfied this formulation of the test.[178]

5.265 **(vii) Concluding Comments on Non-coordinated and Coordinated Effects in Oligopoly Cases** Conceptually, the distinction between non-coordinated and coordinated effects is clear. However, as is evident from the preceding discussion, in practice it may be very difficult to determine empirically whether a merger in an oligopolistic market leads to non-coordinated or coordinated effects. It is also possible that firms may only coordinate certain aspects of their market behaviour and may therefore not achieve complete coordination (which would enable them to behave as a monopolist). Consequently, it is entirely possible that the Commission may wish to investigate both non-coordinated and coordinated effects in a particular market. As a result of its investigation the Commission may base any objections to a merger purely on non-coordinated effects, purely on coordinated effects or on both non-coordinated and coordinated effects.

5.266 In the latter situation it is clear that a market cannot be characterised as both a non-coordinated and a coordinated market outcome at a given point in time. However, for

---

[178] Case T-464/04 *Impala v Commission*, in particular paragraphs 466, 468 and 469.

mergers in oligopolistic industries, it could still be relevant to assess non-coordinated and coordinated effects in a two step procedure starting with the former and then going on to consider the latter.

If both the non-coordinated and coordinated effects analysis are retained, then the result-   **5.267**
ing market outcome is one of coordination, and the analysis of non-coordinated effects can be used as an intermediate step in the assessment of the coordinated effects. The assessment in *Oracle/PeopleSoft*[179] was essentially carried out in just such a two step procedure, but ulti-mately neither the objections based on non-coordinated nor on coordinated effects were retained and the merger was approved.

(viii) Merger with a Potential Competitor   A merger between a company already active   **5.268**
in a particular relevant market and a potential competitor to the company on that market can have horizontal anti-competitive effects similar to those of a merger between firms already active in the same relevant market (whether non-coordinated or coordinated). For this to be the case, the potential competitor would usually possess the relevant assets needed to enter the market without incurring significant sunk costs or, alternatively, would be very likely to incur the sunk costs necessary to enter in a relatively short time frame after which that competitor would constrain the behaviour of current market participants.[180] In addi-tion, two conditions usually need to be fulfilled for significant anti-competitive horizontal effects to arise in a merger with a potential competitor. First, the potential competitor is already, or is forecast within the near future to become, a significant competitive force able to exert a material constraining influence on the market. Second, there must be an insuffi-cient number of other potential competitors able to act as a sufficient competitive con-straint after the merger.[181]

In Case M.3440—*EDP/GDP/ENI*,[182] the Portuguese national electricity company EDP   **5.269**
and ENI of Italy proposed to acquire joint control over the national Portuguese gas com-pany GDP. The Portuguese gas and electricity markets were in the process of being liber-alised. A number of distinct relevant gas and electricity markets were identified in Portugal. The Commission also found that there were important links between some of the markets which facilitated cross-market entry. It was noted, for example, that natural gas will in the future play a crucial role for electricity generation in Portugal, that EDP was the most likely new entrant to the liberalised Portuguese gas market and that GDP was the most likely potential new entrant to the liberalised Portuguese electricity market. Sufficient entry by other potential competitors was not considered likely, and the merger was subsequently prohibited. The decision was appealed.[183]

The Court of First Instance found that the Commission had erred in law due to the dero-   **5.270**
gation granted to Portugal under the Second Gas Directive, which meant that the merger could not lead to a strengthening of dominant positions which would impede competition

---

[179] COMP/M.3216—*Oracle/PeopleSoft* [2005] OJ L218/6, para 189.
[180] See, eg, Case IV/M.1630 *Air Liquide/BOC*, paras 196–222.
[181] See the Horizontal Guidelines, para 60.
[182] Case COMP/M.3440—*EDP/GDP/ENI* (2004), OJ L302, 19.11.2005.
[183] See Case T-87/05 *EDP v Commission*.

on the gas markets.[184] However, for the electricity markets, the Court of First Instance accepted the principles and fully upheld the Commission's analysis of impact of the merger on potential competition.

5.271 A similar assessment to the one in *EDP/GDP/ENI* was carried out in the case of *DONG/Elsam/Energi E2*,[185] which concerned a merger in the Danish energy sector. The case has similarities with the *EDP/GDP/ENI* case, but the market context was somewhat different from the situation in Portugal. In *DONG/Elsam/Energi E2* the competition concerns were *inter alia* identified on the wholesale market for gas, where it was found that DONG's dominant position would be strengthened by the removal of E2 as an important source of potential and actual competition. The merger was subsequently cleared with remedies.

5.272 In the *Guidant Corporation/Johnson & Johnson* case[186] on the other hand, the Commission had to assess whether eliminating Guidant Corporation as a potential competitor to Johnson & Johnson in the market for coronary drug eluting stents (expandable wire tubes that are placed in occluded coronary arteries in order to remove plaque and support the walls of the blood vessel) would significantly impede effective competition. This is a fast growing market, where only Johnson & Johnson and Boston Scientific compete at the moment. The Commission found that Guidant Corporation was likely to have been one of the future key players in this market, but other significant players were also likely to exercise a significant competitive constraint in the future, compensating for the loss of competition resulting from the merger. The Commission therefore concluded that there was no significant impediment to effective competition on this market as a result of the loss of potential competition from Guidant Corporation.

5.273 **(ix) Mergers Creating or Strengthening Buyer Power in Upstream Markets**   Mergers may also result in an increase in the buying power of the merging parties, which could have detrimental effects in markets upstream from the affected relevant market as well as in downstream markets.[187] If, for example, a merger were to create a dominant buying position, then this could in itself lead to welfare losses due to a negative impact on competition in the relevant market concerned. However, an increase in buying power may also lead to negative effects in downstream markets. This could be the case if the increase in buyer

---

184   GDP had been granted a monopoly position, which would be in place for a number of years under a derogation granted in accordance with the Second Gas Directive. In the view of the CFI, since GDP had a monopoly position, it was not possible that the merger could lead to a strengthening of that position and since there was no competition on the gas markets, the merger could not further impede competition on those markets. The Court of First Instance also rejected the Commission's argument that it had to apply the Merger Regulation to the period after the derogation had expired, because this could influence the opportunities for the Portuguese state to organise the gas market in the derogation period. Consequently, the decision would have prohibited the parties from benefiting from the merger in the derogation period, which was not acceptable to the Court. Because of the derogations under the Second Gas Directive, the circumstances that caused the CFI to annul that part of the Commission's decision were quite particular. It is not clear whether general principles can be drawn from the court's analysis of this point.

185   Case COMP/M.3868—*DONG/Elsam/Energi E2* [2006], forthcoming.

186   Case COMP/M.3687 *Johnson & Johnson/Guidant* [2005].

187   See the Horizontal Guidelines, para 61.

power were to enable the merging parties to foreclose access to or increase the costs of an input for their competitors in downstream markets.[188] On the other hand, increased buyer power may in certain circumstances be beneficial where, for example, it lowers input costs without restricting downstream competition such that those reduced costs are to some extent passed on to consumers. The Commission's assessment will therefore require consideration of both potential positive and negative effects in this scenario.

(b) Vertical Mergers

5.274 Vertical mergers involve companies active at different stages of a production or distribution process. A producer of a certain product may, for example, decide to buy one of its distributors or a distributor of a competing producer. In purely vertical mergers, no addition of market shares within a given market takes place, so any increases in market power within a particular market come about through the vertical links between the markets where the merging entities are present.

5.275 A vertical merger will usually only give rise to competition concerns where the merged entity will be dominant in at least one market in the relevant supply chain and where the merger is expected to result in market foreclosure, for example if the vertical integration resulting from the merger will increase entry barriers or make it more difficult or costly for rivals to gain access to key inputs or distribution channels (or, in an extreme case, refuse such access altogether).[189] Vertical mergers may in certain circumstances also facilitate coordination in one or more markets as discussed further below.

5.276 (i) **Commission Assessment of Vertical Mergers and Market Foreclosure Prior to *GE/ Honeywell***   The cases discussed below provide an overview of the Commission's approach to assessing the vertical effects of mergers prior to the *GE/Honeywell* case. For example, *MSG Media Service* involved a proposed joint venture, MSG, between Bertelsmann AG, Deutsche Bundespost Telekom and Kirch to provide technical, administrative and related services for pay TV providers. The Commission considered that MSG could be expected to hold a lasting monopoly position as an operator of digital infrastructure for pay TV and that Bertelsmann/Kirch already had a very strong position on the German pay TV market. The Commission went on to identify a number of anti-competitive vertical effects expected to arise from the creation of the joint venture including the fact that, through their controlling influence in MSG, Bertelsmann/Kirch could directly influence the prices and other terms offered to other future pay TV suppliers and could influence the marketing of competing programmes in terms of the placing of such programmes on the smart cards issued by MSG. The Commission therefore concluded, *inter alia*, that the proposed

---

[188] See Cases M.1221—*Rewe/Meinl*, OJ L274, 23.10.1999, T-22/97—*Kesko v Commission*, [1999] ECR II-3775; M.877—*Boeing/McDonnell Douglas*, OJ L336, 8.12.1997.

[189] See, eg, *MSG Media Service* (Case IV/M.469 [1994]) OJ L364/1, *Nordic Satellite Distribution* (Case IV/M.490 [1996]) OJ L53/20, *RTL/Veronica/Endemol* (Case IV/M.553 [1996]) L134/32, *The Coca-Cola Company/Carlsberg A/S* (Case IV/M.833), *Skanska/Scancem* (Case IV/M.1157 [1999]) OJ L183/1, *Vivendi/ Canal+/Seagram* (Case COMP/M.2050), *AOL/Time Warner* (Case COMP/M.1845 (2000), OJ L268/28 [2001]), *General Electric/Honeywell* (Case COMP/M.2220 (2001)) OJ L048/1 [2004]), and subsequent CFI judgment in Case T-210/01 *GE v Commission*, not yet published but available on the ECJ web site.

joint venture would create a durable dominant position for Bertelsmann/ Kirch on the pay TV market in Germany and prohibited the concentration.

5.277 In *Skanska/Scancem*, the merged entity's combined activities would have covered the whole supply chain in the construction sector from raw materials such as cement and intermediate construction materials such as concrete through to the end construction market. The case involved both horizontal and vertical effects. As regards the latter, the anti-competitive effects identified by the Commission included the fact that Scancem, which already had a dominant position on the Swedish cement market, would as a consequence of the merger be able to foreclose access to that market by competing cement importers. This market foreclosure was expected to occur through a number of channels including the fact that Skanska, which was by far the largest downstream purchaser of cement for concrete production, would have no incentive post-merger to buy cement from Scancem's competitors. The Commission further noted that Skanska, as a major construction company, was a principal downstream customer of many of Scancem's other customers active in the concrete production market and considered that the merged entity would be able to exploit this dependency on Skanska as a downstream customer to induce greater loyalty in terms of upstream cement purchases by these companies from Scancem. The Commission therefore considered that these effects would strengthen the already dominant position of the merged entity in the cement market. In addition, the merged entity would be in a position both to raise the input costs of rival concrete producers and/or to affect their level of sales by reducing its purchases from them, thus enhancing its market position in the intermediate market for ready-mix concrete (which, in combination with the horizontal effects, would lead to the creation of a dominant position in that market). Skanska was therefore required to divest its entire shareholding in Scancem.

5.278 In *AOL/Time Warner*, the Commission had to assess vertical effects in the emerging market for online music delivery and, related to this market, in the market for music player software. At the time, measured on market capitalisation, this was the biggest merger operation ever notified under the Merger Regulation. AOL was the leading provider of internet online services. Time Warner was the largest media and entertainment company in the world. Among other things Time Warner, through it its subsidiary Warner Music Group, was one of the 'five major' suppliers of recorded music.[190] In this connection, it was significant that AOL also had two joint ventures in Europe with Bertelsmann, another of the major suppliers of recorded music, which the Commission considered gave it preferential access to Bertelsmann Music Group's music catalogue. In addition, in parallel to the AOL/Time Warner merger, the parties had also notified a proposal to merge the music business of Time Warner with the music business of EMI. Consequently, the parties would have had preferential access to the combined music catalogues of Warner Music Group, EMI and Bertelsmann for online music delivery.

5.279 The Commission was therefore concerned that the AOL/Time Warner merger would enable the parties to foreclose and dominate the emerging market for online delivery of music.

---

190 The five major players were: Warner Music, Universal Music, EMI, BMG (Bertelsmann), and Sony.

This concern remained even after the proposed merger with EMI was abandoned by the parties at a late stage of the procedure. For example, the Commission considered that one entity controlling such a sizeable music catalogue could exercise substantial market power by refusing to license its rights, or by doing so on discriminatory terms (eg to third party Internet distribution companies). Equally, the Commission considered that AOL could use its strong position in online distribution to favour Time Warner and Bertelsmann, either by charging supra-competitive prices for the delivery of third party music content or by restricting access for competing content providers.

The Commission further considered that the merged entity would be in a position to **5.280** dictate the technical standards for online music delivery and in effect establish its own technology as an industry standard, for example by leveraging the breadth of its music catalogue and threatening not to license its own proprietary technology to developers of music players unless they agreed to refrain from supporting competing technologies. Through its control over the relevant technology the merged entity could, it was argued, then raise the costs incurred by competing record companies since they would be required to format their music for online distribution using the merged entity's technology and could therefore be charged excessive technology licensing fees. The Commission addition-ally contended that the merged entity could alternatively format Time Warner and Bertelsmann music to make it compatible only with Winamp (the AOL music player) and, by refusing to license its technology, could thus create a dominant position in the market for music player software since Winamp would be the only player able to decode the proprietary format of the extensive Time Warner and Bertelsmann music catalogue.

In order to resolve the competition concerns identified by the Commission, the parties **5.281** submitted a set of undertakings which effectively severed all structural links between AOL and Bertelsmann, thus materially reducing the market power which would have been enjoyed by the merged entity in terms of preferential access to music publishing rights necessary for online music distribution. Consequently the Commission considered that the proposed remedies would *inter alia* prevent the creation of a dominant position in the emerging markets for online music delivery and music player software such that it was possible for the Commission to clear the merger.

(ii) Impact of *GE/Honeywell* for the Future Assessment of Vertical Mergers In *General* **5.282** *Electric/Honeywell*, the Commission's grounds for prohibiting the merger included the con-tention that it would have led to foreclosure effects due to vertical relationships between General Electric and Honeywell. Specifically, the Commission concluded that the merger would have resulted in the strengthening of the dominant position of General Electric in the market for engines for large commercial aircrafts, because of the foreclosure of compet-ing engine manufacturers arising from the vertical relationship between GE as an engine manufacturer and Honeywell as a supplier of engine starters to engine manufacturers. The Commission found that Honeywell was the leading, if not only, independent supplier of engine starters and considered that the merged entity would have an incentive to delay or disrupt its supply of engine starters to competing engine manufacturers, and/or to increase the price of engine starters supplied to such manufacturers, thus undermining the ability of other engine suppliers to compete with the parties after the merger.

5.283   The Commission's vertical analysis (as well as conglomerate analysis for which see below) was reviewed by the CFI on appeal. The CFI's judgment provides relevant guidance for the assessment of vertical mergers.

5.284   *Burden of proof and evidence required*   First, as regards the burden of proof and evidence required in such cases, the CFI emphasised that since the Commission's case concerning the anti-competitive vertical effects of the merger hinged on the merged entity's future conduct, the onus was on the Commission to produce convincing evidence as to the likelihood of that behaviour (as is also the case for the prospective analysis required to establish collective dominance and anti-competitive conglomerate effects—see the discussion above and below respectively). The CFI observed that such evidence might, for example, consist of economic studies establishing the likely development of the market situation and demonstrating an incentive for the merged entity to behave in a particular way. However, where it was obvious that the commercial interests of an undertaking militate predominantly in favour of a given course of conduct, 'the simple economic and commercial realities of the particular case' may constitute such convincing evidence.[191]

5.284A   *Potential deterrent effect of legal constraints*   On the facts of the case, the CFI considered that, in view of the post-merger market structure and in particular the dependence of Rolls Royce (a competing engine manufacturer) on the supply of engine starters by Honeywell, the Commission's case that the merged entity would face an incentive to limit or disrupt supplies of engine starters to competing engine manufacturers was prima facie persuasive. Thus the Commission's analysis of potential vertical foreclosure effects was in principle upheld. In particular the CFI noted that (in view of the relative value of engine starters), any profits foregone from lost sales of engine starters to competing engine manufacturers would be minimal in comparison with the increased profits to be derived from a higher market share in the market for large commercial aircraft engines. However, and critically, the CFI considered that the Commission had failed to take proper account of the legal constraints which might have precluded the behaviour foreseen by the Commission. In particular, applying the principles that the CFI had first used in its review of the *Tetra Laval/Sidel* decision and in the light of the ECJ's judgment in the same case (see section on conglomerate mergers below), the CFI found that the Commission had failed to assess whether the anticipated conduct would constitute an infringement of Article 82 and thus made an error of law in failing to take into account the deterrent effect which that might have had on the merged entity. While the CFI upheld the decision as such, it therefore found that this part of the decision relating to the strengthening of GE's pre-merger dominant position on the market for large commercial aircraft engines as a consequence of the vertical overlap with Honeywell's manufacture of starter engines was not sufficiently established.[192] The interplay between Article 82 and merger control in vertical and conglomerate mergers is discussed in further detail below in the section on Conglomerate Mergers which contains an analysis of the CFI's and ECJ's approach on this issue.

---

[191]   Case T-210/01, *General Electric Company v Commission*, paras 295–297.
[192]   Case T-210/01, paras 301–312.

(iii) Possible Developments in Policy in Vertical Cases   The Commission's assessment **5.285** of vertical links in mergers hitherto has therefore typically focused on potential foreclosure effects of the sort discussed above. In cases where no foreclosure effects have been found, the Commission has not normally been concerned about the vertical aspects of the merger. It is expected that this will continue to be a principal focus for the Commission's analysis in such cases in the future. However, it is possible that the Commission's approach to assessing vertical mergers will be further developed in the future for two reasons. First, as noted above, vertical mergers may also facilitate coordination in one or more markets. This could be the case, for example, if vertical integration results in increased transparency (either in terms of upstream input costs or downstream retail prices), leads to a greater degree of alignment of commercial interests amongst rival undertakings, and/or increases the number of commercial links between competing firms. In appropriate future cases, the Commission may therefore consider whether vertical integration resulting from a merger may facilitate coordination and significantly impede competition.

Second, it is to be expected that the Commission's assessment of vertical mergers will in the **5.286** future include a fuller assessment of potential efficiency gains. Vertical mergers are often efficiency-enhancing, for example as a consequence of greater commercial alignment of upstream and downstream operations. The assessment of vertical mergers, like horizontal mergers, may therefore warrant a trade-off between any negative effects such as foreclosure effects and the efficiencies created by the merger. However, just as is the case for horizontal mergers, efficiencies resulting from a vertical merger would appear insufficient to justify the creation of a monopoly (see further the discussion on efficiencies below).

(c) Conglomerate Mergers

(i) Overview of Anti-competitive Conglomerate Effects   Conglomerate mergers are **5.287** mergers where several different relevant product markets are affected but (in their conventional form) where no horizontal or vertical issues arise. Such mergers will only occasionally give rise to significant competition concerns. In particular it is highly unlikely that cases where the affected markets are completely unrelated in terms of physical product characteristics, customer groups, production facilities, distribution channels, etc should give rise to conglomerate concerns. The impact of the merger on competition in each of the various affected markets would normally be assessed separately and no consideration would be given to links between the markets. However, occasionally the situation may be different where the various affected markets are related. In neighbouring markets, for example, the products concerned may be complementary (one is always used with the other, eg engines and avionics) or be part of a range of products sold to the same customers (eg different beverages or different packaging machinery for beverages). In such cases, the Commission will include the relationships between the affected markets in its assessment of the impact of the merger on competition.

Anti-competitive conglomerate effects, whilst relatively rare, might in certain cases signif- **5.288** icantly impede effective competition, for example, either by leading to the reinforcement of an existing dominant position and/or enabling a company which is already dominant in one market to leverage its position and create a dominant position in a second, related market. In either case, the key consideration is whether any competitive advantage which the merged entity may derive from the conglomerate nature of the transaction (in terms of the relationship between the affected markets) can be used to foreclose rivals from one or more of those markets. The Commission has yet to publish guidelines providing a definitive view of its theory of competitive harm in respect of conglomerate mergers. However its approach in this area has developed over recent years, including in light of Court intervention in the *Tetral Laval/Sidel* and *GE/Honeywell* cases, and may be further refined in the future.

5.289 **(ii) Historic Approach to Conglomerate Mergers**   The factors historically considered by the Commission in assessing potential anti-competitive conglomerate effects have included the creation of 'portfolio power' (or 'range effects') on the part of the merged entity. In *Tetra Pak/Alfa-Laval*,[193] the Commission considered whether there were potential anti-competitive effects resulting from the complementarity between the parties' product ranges in the sense that Alfa-Laval produced all equipment used for processing milk and juice until it was packaged and Tetra Pak produced the machines used to package the milk and juice. The Commission concluded that the creation of a full-line processing and packaging capability on the part of the merged entity would not in fact confer a significant competitive advantage to the detriment of actual or potential competitors on the market for aseptic carton packaging machines and that the existing dominant position of Tetra Pak in that market would not therefore be strengthened as a consequence of the merger. In conducting its assessment, the Commission effectively focused on the scope for leveraging existing market power. Relevant considerations for the Commission's analysis included the fact that, in practice, the demand for simultaneous purchases of processing and packaging machines was extremely limited and that the technical interface between processing and packaging machines was not complex and thus facilitated substitution between different manufacturers. For broadly the same reasons, the Commission concluded that the merger would not create or strengthen a dominant position in the non-aseptic carton packaging market nor in the markets for processing machines.

5.290 Similarly, in certain previous cases involving consumer products markets such as beer, soft drinks or spirits, the Commission considered whether the ability to offer a portfolio of products within a particular category (such as a range of spirits) would give the merged entity an advantage which could lead to anti-competitive effects.[194] The Commission's analysis of portfolio effects has usually focused on the scope for leveraging existing market power and this has also been the focus of the Commission's analysis in more recent conglomerate effects cases, including both *General Electric/Honeywell*,[195] and *Tetra Laval/Sidel*,[196] each of which is discussed in more detail below.

(iii) Assessment of Leveraging in Recent Cases

5.291 *Approach taken by the Commission in* **Tetral Laval/Sidel** *and* **GE/Honeywell**   In *Tetra Laval/Sidel* the Commission concluded that the merger would have united the dominant company in carton packaging, Tetra Pak, with the leading company in PET (plastic)

---

[193] Case IV/M68 [1991] OJ L290/35.
[194] *The Coca-Cola Company/Carlsberg A/S and Guinness/Grand Metropolitan* (Case IV/M938)(1997) OJ L288/24.
[195] Case COMP/M.2220 (2001) OJ L048 [2004].
[196] Case COMP/M.2416 (2001) OJ L043 [2004].

packaging equipment, Sidel. In addition to finding horizontal and vertical effects, the Commission found that the merger would have enabled the merging parties to turn the leading position in PET packaging equipment into a dominant position by leveraging Tetra Pak's existing dominant position in cartons into the neighbouring PET packaging equipment market. The argument was based particularly on an analysis of market characteristics such as Tetra's dominance in the first market, Sidel's 'leading position' in the second market, high barriers to entry and the close relationship between the two markets.

According to the Commission, carton and PET represented distinct but closely related **5.292** product markets with a common pool of customers, namely producers of beverages such as milk, juice, iced tea and flavoured drinks, where carton and PET are technical substitutes in that they can both be used to package such products. Moreover the Commission considered that PET would in the future be expected to become an increasingly attractive substitute for carton in certain end-use segments and was therefore expected to win market share from carton. In the Commission's view, the merged entity's existing dominant position in carton, and its close and well established customer relationships in that market, meant that it would be particularly well placed to win additional share in the PET market as demand increased (including via switching from carton). The Commission therefore considered that the merged entity would have both the ability and incentive to leverage the existing dominant position of Tetra Pak in carton in order to increase Sidel's already leading share (of approximately 60 per cent) in the PET market to the level of dominance. Specific leveraging practices identified by the Commission, which it considered could be targeted at certain categories of customers, included the possibility of tying carton packing equipment with PET equipment and using pressure or incentives (such as predatory pricing, price wars or loyalty rebates) to induce Tetra Pak's carton customers to buy PET equipment from Tetra Pak/Sidel, to the detriment of the merged entity's competitors.

The Commission also dealt with conglomerate effects in *GE/Honeywell*. In that case, the **5.293** Commission considered that the merged entity would be uniquely placed to sell packages of complementary products including engines (where GE was already dominant), avionics and non-avionics (where Honeywell already enjoyed a leading position). The Commission argued that this could be achieved through one or more of mixed bundling (where the price of the package was set at a discount to the price of the individual products), pure bundling (where the products were only offered for sale as a package) and technical bundling (where the individual products would only function effectively as part of the bundled system and could not be integrated with other suppliers' products). Each was expected to lead to a reduction in competitors' market shares and, ultimately, market exit and foreclosure. The Commission considered that this would have contributed to the creation of a dominant position on the markets for SFE (Supplier-Furnished-Equipment) and BFE (Buyer-Furnished-Equipment) avionics as well as the creation of a dominant position on the market for non-avionics (auxiliary power units, electric power, wheels and brakes, etc). The Commission also argued that it would have had the effect of strengthening GE's existing dominant position in the engines market.

The Commission set out a further objection to the merger arguing that the merged entity **5.294** would be able to leverage its financial strength and existing vertical integration into aircraft leasing and financing to establish a dominant position in respect of Honeywell's avionics and non-avionics products.[197] In assessing GE's pre-merger dominance in large commercial engines, the Commission had identified its vertical integration into aircraft leasing and financing as a factor which reinforced GE's dominance. The Commission considered that this occurred, for example, where GE Capital provided financial support to airframe manufacturers in return for engine exclusivity and because GECAS, as a significant aircraft purchaser, could influence airframe manufacturers' choice of engine and in many cases adopted a policy of only selecting GE engines when purchasing new aircraft. The Commission argued that this relationship could be extended to Honeywell's avionics and non-avionics products following the merger, leading to an additional foreclosure effect in those markets.

Impact of recent European court judgments on the assessment of conglomerate mergers

5.295 *General observations relevant to the assessment of a conglomerate merger* The Commission's decision in *Tetra Laval/Sidel* was subsequently annulled by the Court of First Instance on appeal in *Tetra Laval v Commission*.[198] The Court's judgment provides some important guidance as to the key factors to be taken into consideration by the Commission when reviewing conglomerate mergers. First, the CFI observed that conglomerate mergers are generally considered to be neutral or even beneficial in terms of their impact on competition but confirmed that, in certain cases, conglomerate effects may result in the creation or strengthening of a dominant position. The CFI therefore agreed with the Commission that, in principle, the Merger Regulation gave it the power to control such mergers. However, the Court emphasised the high evidential burden facing the Commission, stating that:

> the Commission's analysis of a merger transaction which is expected to have an anti-competitive conglomerate effect calls for a particularly close examination of the circumstances which are relevant for an assessment of that effect . . . where the Commission takes the view that a merger should be prohibited because it will create or strengthen a dominant position within a foreseeable period, it is incumbent upon it to produce convincing evidence thereof . . . the proof of anti-competitive conglomerate effects of such a merger calls for a precise examination, supported by convincing evidence, of the circumstances which allegedly produce those effects.[199]

5.296 The CFI then gave detailed consideration to the specific nature of potential conglomerate effects and, in this context, distinguished between what in its view are structural effects occurring directly as a consequence of the merger and behavioural effects resulting from the post-merger conduct of the merged entity such as leveraging of an existing dominant position. As regards the latter, the CFI further emphasised that where the Commission's assessment relies on foreseeable conduct which is likely to constitute an abuse of an existing

---

[197] The financial strength of the merged entity was also considered by the Commission to be a relevant factor in a number of other conglomerate merger cases such as *Magneti Marelli/CEAC* (Case IV/M43 [1991] OJ L222/38), *Accor/Wagon-Lits* (Case IV/M126 [1992] OJ L204/1), *ABB/Daimler-Benz* (Case IV/M580 (1995) [1997] OJ L11/1), and *Boeing/McDonnell-Douglas* (Case IV/M877 [1997] OJ L336/16). However, the Commission has never considered financial strength to be the only decisive element in the concluding whether or not a merger was compatible with the Common Market.

[198] Case T-5/02 *Tetral Laval v Commission*, ECR [2002] II-4381.

[199] Case T-5/02 *Tetra Laval v Commission*, paras 150–155.

dominant position under Article 82, it must take into account whether the illegal nature of that conduct and/or the risk of detection and the imposition of penalties would reduce or eliminate the incentive to engage in such conduct.[200] (The relationship between the Merger Regulation and Article 82 in such cases is discussed further below.) The CFI further held that the Commission ought to have taken into account any behavioural commitments not to engage in such conduct when assessing the likelihood of leveraging.

The Commission appealed the CFI's judgment to the ECJ on important points of law. The **5.297** ECJ upheld the CFI's judgment in a case that contains important principles for the assessment of conglomerate cases under the Merger Regulation.[201] Notably, the ECJ confirmed the CFI's position regarding the standard of proof and evidential burden to be met by the Commission when seeking to prohibit a conglomerate merger as outlined above. In doing so, the ECJ emphasised the prospective and uncertain nature of the assessment required in such cases to establish anti-competitive effects and highlighted the fact that the quality of evidence to be produced by the Commission was therefore particularly important.[202] However, the ECJ did critically review the extent of the obligation imposed on the Commission by the CFI in terms of the requirement to take into consideration whether the leveraging methods it had identified would constitute an abuse under Article 82 as discussed further below.

In *GE v Commission* the CFI reiterated the framework for assessing conglomerate effects **5.298** which was set out by the CFI and ECJ in the *Tetra Laval* case. In particular, the CFI emphasised that the onus was on the Commission to provide convincing evidence that the merged entity was likely to adopt the particular anticipated course of conduct following the merger, including an evaluation of the possible deterrent effect of Article 82.[203]

The requirement for the Commission to base its conclusions on sufficiently convincing **5.299** evidence underpinned the CFI's assessment of the specific conglomerate effects identified by the Commission in *GE/Honeywell*. The CFI first examined the argument that the merged entity would be able to leverage its financial strength and vertical integration through GE Capital and GECAS. Although the CFI had accepted that the financial strength and vertical integration derived from GE Capital and GECAS was a factor in establishing GE's pre-existing dominant position in large commercial engines, it found that the Commission had not provided sufficient evidence to show that the merged entity would have leveraged this relationship to create a dominant position for Honeywell's products following the merger. The CFI emphasised that, in line with the court judgments in *Tetra Laval*, it was necessary for the Commission not only to show that the merged entity was able to transfer the practices in question to the relevant avionics and non-avionics markets but also to establish, based on convincing evidence, that it was likely the merged entity would engage in such conduct and furthermore that those practices would create

---

[200] Case T-5/02 *Tetra Laval v Commission*, para 159.
[201] Case C-12/03 *Commission v Tetra Laval*, ECR [2005] I-987.
[202] Case C-12/03, paras 39 and 44. For a further discussion on the standard of proof, see below section on Judicial Review.
[203] *GE v Commission*, paras 65–76.

a dominant position in the relevant markets in the relatively near future. The CFI considered that the requisite 'convincing evidence' as to the likelihood of the predicted conduct might, for example, have consisted of actual evidence of intent to exploit the strength of GE Capital and GECAS on the avionics and non-avionics markets after the merger. However, given the absence of such factual evidence, the Commission was required to conduct an economic assessment of the merged entity's incentives to do so and could not simply rely on GE's past practice in the distinct market for large commercial engines. The CFI concluded that the Commission's assessment of the incentives to engage in, and hence the likelihood of, the anticipated conduct was inadequate and, moreover, that the Commission did not sufficiently establish that such practices would have led to the creation of a dominant position.[204]

5.300   Regarding the assessment of bundling, the CFI applied the same analytical framework emphasising that it was not sufficient for the Commission to establish that the merged entity would be capable of bundling, but that it must also demonstrate that it would have been likely (ie that it would have faced sufficient incentives) to engage in such practices. The Court first identified some general problems with the Commission's arguments on bundling in this case. It then reviewed the Commission's separate arguments in relation to pure, mixed and technical bundling, identifying a number of flaws in each case.[205]

5.301   *Relationship between the Merger Regulation and Article 82*   The emphasis both the CFI and ECJ put on the relationship between the Merger Regulation and Article 82 in *Tetra Laval* is of particular interest and has significant implications for future cases. As noted above, the CFI stressed that for a merger to create a dominant position it must be clear that the merger would create conditions 'allowing the merged entity to leverage its way so as to acquire, in the near future, a dominant position on the other market'.[206] However, if the effects are not likely to take place in the near future, then they cannot be considered as causal to the merger and (by implication) would have to be dealt with under Article 82. Furthermore, the CFI stressed that, when assessing the opportunities for leveraging, the Commission was required to take into account the disincentives that flow from the illegality of the alleged conduct and to consider whether, in the light of those disincentives, it was likely that the merged entity would engage in anti-competitive conduct.

5.302   The ECJ clarified the extent of this obligation, stating that the CFI was right to hold that an assessment of the likelihood of adoption of particular leveraging methods must take account 'both of the incentives to adopt such conduct and the factors liable to reduce or even eliminate those incentives, including the possibility that the conduct is unlawful'. However, the ECJ criticised the CFI's analysis on this point and agreed with the Commission that a requirement to undertake an exhaustive and detailed examination of the extent to which those incentives would be reduced or eliminated as a result of the

---

[204]   *GE v Commission*, paras 315–365.
[205]   ibid, paras 399–473.
[206]   Case T-5/02, para 151.

unlawfulness of the conduct in question, the likelihood of its detection and the financial penalties which could ensue would run counter to the preventative purpose of the Merger Regulation.[207]

The precise scope of the obligation imposed on the Commission in this regard was also addressed in *GE v Commission*. In that case the CFI again criticised the Commission for not having taken into account the possible impact, on the markets in question, of the potential deterrent effect of Article 82. However, in *GE* the CFI had to take into account the ECJ's criticism, in *Tetra Laval*, of the CFI's analysis on this point. The CFI therefore attempted to reconcile its own view of the interplay of Article 82 and merger control with that of the ECJ as established in *Tetra Laval*. The CFI confirmed that the Commission, in examining the potential anti-competitive effects resulting from a merger, is required to assess whether the deterrent effect of Article 82 is sufficient to eliminate the anticipated negative effects of a merger. However, at the same time the CFI (in the light of the ECJ's judgment) only asked for a summary analysis based on available evidence, and did not require the Commission to conduct an investigation similar to a full Article 82 type of investigation in merger cases:[208] **5.303**

> It follows that the Commission must, as a rule, take into account the potentially unlawful, and thus sanctionable, nature of certain conduct as a factor, which might diminish, or even eliminate, incentives for an undertaking to engage in particular conduct . . . However, it is not required to establish that the conduct foreseen in the future will actually constitute an infringement of Article 82 EC or that, if that were to be the case, that infringement would be detected and punished, the Commission being able to limit itself in that regard to a summary analysis based on the evidence available to it.[209]

This is the CFI's interpretation of the ECJ's judgment in *Commission v Tetra Laval* (paragraphs 74–78), where the ECJ points out that such a requirement would run counter to the Merger Regulation's preventative purpose. It remains to be seen how these requirements will be applied in practice by the Commission and the courts in future cases. **5.304**

In *Tetra*, the ECJ moreover held that the CFI was right to have found that the Commission ought, in its assessment of the likelihood that such leveraging would occur, to have taken into account the commitments submitted by Tetra with regard to its future conduct[210] (see further section C6 below on remedies). **5.305**

Commission's recent approach following Court Judgments An example of the Commission's approach to assessing potential anti-competitive conglomerate effects in the wake of the CFI's judgment in *Tetra Laval* is provided by the decision in *GE/Amersham*.[211] That merger involved a combination of GE's diagnostic imaging equipment and Amersham's diagnostic pharmaceuticals and thus did not give rise to any horizontal overlaps. The **5.306**

---

[207] Case C-12/03, *Commission v Tetra Laval*, paras 74–78.
[208] From a practical point of view this would also be difficult, since merger cases involve an assessment of the future market development, whereas Art 82 cases examines past market behaviour.
[209] Case T-210/01, para 304.
[210] Case C-12/03, *Commission v Tetra Laval*, para 89.
[211] Case COMP/M.3304.

Commission considered that the products could, however, be viewed as complements since both were required by hospitals to provide an imaging medical service to patients. The Commission therefore investigated whether the merged entity might acquire 'the ability and economic incentive to foreclose competition, by leveraging its pre-merger market power from one market to another through exclusionary practices, such as bundling and/or tying'.[212] In framing its investigation in these terms, the influence of the CFI's judgment in *Tetra Laval* was clear. It was equally evident in the Commission's structured approach to its more detailed analysis which covered commercial (mixed) bundling, forced (pure) bundling and technical tying. For example, in assessing the scope for commercial bundling, the Commission noted that for such a practice to result in foreclosure it was necessary for the merged entity to be able to leverage its pre-merger dominance in one product to another product and, for such a strategy to be profitable, there must be a reasonable expectation that rivals will be forced to exit the market as a result and that the merged entity would then subsequently be able to implement sustainable unilateral price increases (which was not found to be the case on the facts). The Commission concluded that the merger would not result in anti-competitive conglomerate effects and it was therefore cleared.

(d) Other Factors Affecting the Competitive Assessment of the Merger

5.307 The competitive pressure on the merging parties is not only exercised by their direct competitors, but may also come from their customers or potential entrants. Such constraints on the merged entity's behaviour are therefore important factors to be taken into account when assessing the impact of the merger on competition. Furthermore, the overall assessment of a merger may also need to take into consideration factors such as the potential efficiencies created by the merger as well as whether the failing firm defence applies.

5.308 **(i) Countervailing Buyer Power** The Horizontal Guidelines define countervailing buyer power as 'bargaining strength that the buyer has vis-à-vis the seller in commercial negotiations due to its size, its commercial significance to the seller and its ability to switch to alternative suppliers'. Usually individual consumers in consumer product markets are not considered to have countervailing buyer power. However, in the *Airtours* judgment the Court of First Instance seems to say that the simple fact that individual consumers in consumer product markets can shop around could be a countervailing influence on the potential anti-competitive effects of the merger. The Court appeared to consider that it was not necessary for customers individually to have significant countervailing power if their ability to switch to fringe suppliers in sufficient numbers meant that, collectively, they could destabilise the coordinated outcome. While this analysis may be valid, the conclusion seems to hinge on the Court's rejection of the Commission's finding of collective dominance on other grounds as discussed above. Certainly the Court provided no guidance as to how this approach should be applied in practice and where any boundaries should be set to avoid a finding of buyer power in almost any case involving a multitude of small consumers.

---

212 Para 31.

More typically, countervailing buyer power tends to be found in situations where a business **5.309** customer could credibly threaten to switch to other sources of supply, vertically integrate upstream, or sponsor upstream entry by a potential entrant, for example, by placing a big order. In *Enso/Stora*, for example, the merging parties were estimated to have a market share of 60 per cent of the market for liquid packaging board used for packing products such as milk and juice. Enso/Stora was faced with a very concentrated buyer structure with essentially three big buyers, including notably Tetra Pak, accounting for more than 60 per cent of the purchases of liquid packaging board. Tetra Pak had been instrumental in growing the market and had developed several of the suppliers of liquid packaging board. It was concluded that the purchasers had sufficient countervailing buyer power, for example through an ability to develop alternative suppliers, and the merger was authorised.

It is more likely that large sophisticated buyers may possess this kind of countervailing **5.310** buyer power than a larger number of smaller firms in a fragmented market. However, the Commission has in the past been wary of accepting that the buyer power of large firms is sufficient, in and of itself, to overcome a prima facie case that the merger will lead to the creation or strengthening of a dominant position. In order to possess countervailing buying power, it has normally not been considered sufficient that a firm is large, if it is not a large purchaser of a particular product. Moreover, even large purchasers may not have countervailing buyer power if they do not have sufficient alternative sources of supply.

In some cases buyer power may be an insufficient constraint on the merged entity's ability **5.311** to exercise market power even where a group of customers in a market have considerable bargaining power, if other customer groups do not. Large supermarket chains may for example possess more bargaining power than smaller stores. However, even if one or more large buyers have countervailing buyer power, but the merging parties are able to price discriminate between customers and therefore exploit their position towards smaller customers with no countervailing buyer power, then the Commission would normally not accept that countervailing buyer power eliminates the competition concerns created by the merger.[213] Furthermore, such bargaining power may not necessarily be sufficient to neutralise the negative effects of a merger on overall market prices.

It is also not sufficient that buyer power may exist before the merger, because one effect of **5.312** the merger may be to reduce pre-existing buyer power. In the past the Commission has only accepted the argument of countervailing buyer power if specific reasons for the buyer power could be identified and if it could be shown that it would neutralise the negative effects of the merger, such as was the case in *Enso/Stora*.

(ii) Entry

Importance of scope for new entry as part of the merger review   Potential new entrants can **5.313** exercise a constraining force on companies in a given market, if entry barriers are low and consequently entry is easy and rapid. In such cases an otherwise problematic merger may not pose any significant anti-competitive risk. On the other hand if entry barriers are high, and consequently entering the market is difficult and slow, competition from potential

---

[213] See, eg, Case COMP.M/3486—*Magna/New Venture Gear*.

new entrants may not be sufficient to remove or reduce any anti-competitive effects of a merger. Incumbent firms may, for example, be able to increase prices following a merger, without any risk of new entry being prompted by the higher prices. For entry to be a sufficient constraining force, it must be shown to be likely, timely, and sufficient to defeat or deter any anti-competitive effects. Relevant evidence could, for example, consist of examples of successful past entry or take the form of an objective analysis of what would be required in terms of effort and time for a new entrant to enter a market. Furthermore, it would be useful for the Commission to be made aware, if it is known, of plans of potential entrants to enter a market.

5.314 *Types of entry barriers* Entry barriers are specific features of the market which give incumbent competitors an advantage over new entrants. Entry barriers can take various forms. There are legal barriers such as tariffs or trade barriers. The incumbents may also have technical advantages such as preferential access to natural resources,[214] essential facilities or intellectual property rights,[215] various scale or scope advantages, possession of powerful distribution networks,[216] access to important technologies and so on. Incumbent firms may also have advantages due to their established position in markets, where experience or reputation is necessary to compete effectively. A typical example is a case where it is necessary to build a brand in order to compete in a market. Such brand building may require heavy advertising expenditure, which would be sunk costs and would therefore increase the risk of entering the market. Close relationships between buyers and sellers in industrial markets, for example, joint development of technology, may also represent a barrier for new entrants to overcome. The expected development of a market is also essential in the assessment of the likelihood of entry. A growing market is for example normally easier and more attractive to enter than a stagnant or declining market.

5.315 *Relevant considerations for an assessment of potential entry* The Commission relied in part on likely entry from potential competitors in its decision to clear the merger of *Mercedes-Benz/Kässbohrer*.[217] In this case the question was how quickly potential competitors could enter the German bus market. Competitors such as Volvo and Renault were already in the process of entering the German market for buses, and it was found that entry was likely to have an impact on the market within a relatively short time period. In *Saint Gobain/Wacker Chemie/NUM*[218] on the other hand, the question was whether potential Chinese and Eastern European producers would be able to enter the EEA market for silicon carbide. It was found that entry was likely only to take place after several years. Potential competition was not considered a sufficiently strong constraining force on the merging parties in that case. Similar arguments were considered in two aerospace mergers.[219]

---

[214] See eg, Case IV/M.754—*Anglo American Corporation/Lonrho* (1997), OJ L149, 20.5.1998, p 21 points 118–119.

[215] See eg Case IV/M.269—*Shell/Montecatini* (1994), OJ L332, 22.12.1994, p 48 point 32.

[216] See eg Case IV/M.833—*The Coca-Cola Company/Carlsberg* (1997), OJ L145, 15.5.1998, p 41 point 74.

[217] Case IV/M.477 [1995] OJ L211/1.

[218] Case IV/M.774 [1996] OJ L247/1.

[219] *Aerospatiale-Alenia/de Havilland* (Case IV/M.53 [1991] OJ L334/42) and *Boeing/McDonnell-Douglas* (Case IV/M.877 [1997] OJ L336/16).

In *Boeing/McDonnell-Douglas*, for example, it was important that research and development costs for a large new jet aeroplane were substantial and production involved large scale advantages in terms of learning curve effects.

Mergers may also change entry barriers. In *Kesko/Tuko*,[220] it was concluded that the merger **5.316** would have led to an increase in entry barriers, for example because it eliminated an independent company which could have served as an acquisition target providing a springboard for new entry, or as a wholesale trading partner providing access to competitively priced goods.

Entry is more likely to be considered as a relevant competitive constraint in the assessment **5.317** of a concentration if potential entrants already possess appropriate production facilities that could easily be switched to production for the market in question. The Commission will normally not consider entry sufficiently timely, if it cannot be shown to be likely to occur within two years. It must also be sufficient to act as a threat or deterrent. Therefore, prediction of small scale entry, for example targeting a market niche, is not likely to be considered sufficient to remove any anti-competitive effects of a merger.

(iii) Efficiencies

Assessment under the original Merger Regulation   In some cases under the original **5.318** Merger Regulation the Commission included an assessment of the technical and economic progress resulting from a particular merger, usually prompted by the merging parties bringing forward such arguments. However, while the original Merger Regulation allowed for efficiencies to be considered in the overall assessment of dominance 'provided that it is to the consumer's advantage and does not form an obstacle to competition' (Article 2(1)(b)), there was no developed framework for how such an assessment would be made, and efficiency arguments were rarely made with any conviction.

Assessment under the new Merger Regulation   The new Merger Regulation contains the **5.319** same provisions for taking into account efficiencies as the original Merger Regulation. However, in recital 29 of the new Merger Regulation the Commission is required to take into account any substantiated and likely efficiencies put forward by the merging parties. It is also stated that it is possible that efficiencies brought about by a concentration might counteract the effects on competition and the potential harm to consumers, and as a consequence, the concentration may not significantly impede effective competition. In conclusion, the Commission is now required to assess efficiencies in the overall appraisals of concentrations more systematically. On this basis in some cases it may find that a merger should be allowed, because the efficiencies it generates will be pro-competitive to the benefit of consumers and thereby outweigh any negative impact of the merger. This approach has been used in the past including in some collective dominance cases,[221] where the Commission has assessed efficiencies in order to determine whether efficiencies were likely to reduce or remove the risk of coordinated effects. However, this will require further development in the future.

---

[220] Case IV/M784 (1996) [1997] OJ L110/53.
[221] For example *Danish Crown/Vestjyske Slagterier* and *Airtours/First Choice*.

5.320 The Commission was also required by the new Merger Regulation to publish guidance on the conditions under which it may take efficiencies into account in the assessment of a concentration. Therefore, the Horizontal Guidelines set out how efficiencies will be assessed under the new Merger Regulation and explain that, in order for the Commission to take efficiencies into account, they must benefit consumers, be merger-specific and verifiable. Efficiencies should also in principle benefit consumers in those markets where the competition concerns may occur. In other words the Commission will not trade-off efficiency gains in one market with increases in market power in another market. It would not be acceptable, for example, for the consumers in country A to pay higher prices in order for consumers in country B to benefit from efficiencies. Furthermore, efficiencies will also have to be timely and substantial in order to be taken into account. The Commission will put less weight on efficiencies which are more distant and therefore uncertain.

5.321 Mergers may bring about various types of efficiencies, such as cost savings relating to production or distribution, which may enable the merged firm to lower prices to consumers. Cost efficiencies relating to variable costs or marginal costs are more likely to be recognised by the Commission, because such costs are more likely to lead to lower prices than reductions in fixed costs. Consumers may also benefit from efficiencies in research and development allowing the merging parties to bring out new products.

5.322 According to the Horizontal Guidelines, efficiencies will only be included in the assessment to the extent that they are merger-specific, ie they cannot be achieved through other means such as licensing agreements, co-operative joint ventures or a differently structured merger. In this regard the Commission will only consider alternatives that are reasonably practical from a business perspective.

5.323 Efficiencies must be verifiable so that the Commission can be reasonably certain that they will materialise. The burden of proof in this regard lies with the merging parties, because only they have access to the type of information necessary to demonstrate the extent of the efficiencies. Documents relied on by the merging firms in deciding on whether to merge are particularly useful evidence in this regard.

5.324 The new Merger Regulation and the Horizontal Guidelines are expected to result in a more explicit and elaborate assessment of efficiencies than in the past. However, it is unlikely that this will radically alter the decision-making practice of the Commission and lead to any general increase in the threshold for intervention. This is indicated in the Horizontal Guidelines where it is stated that the greater the potential negative effects of a concentration, the greater the claimed efficiencies will have to be in order for the Commission to clear the merger. Furthermore, it is considered highly unlikely that a merger leading to a near monopoly or a similar level of market power could be declared compatible with the common market on efficiency grounds. This is consistent with the provisions in Article 2(1)(b), since a position of near monopoly would constitute an obstacle to competition which is unlikely to be outweighed by any benefits resulting from efficiencies.

5.325 While the decision-making practice may not change significantly, the assessment of efficiencies is expected to result in a more complete economic analysis of concentrations. This will clarify how efficiencies are taken into account in individual cases. The Commission has in the past occasionally been accused of applying an 'efficiency offence' by which is meant a situation where a merger creates substantial efficiencies, which will increase the competitive advantage of the merging parties and therefore enable them to increase their (high) market share further. Prohibiting such a merger would in reality denote to objecting to the efficiencies. It is to be welcomed, if the new approach can reduce the number of such complaints by clarifying the treatment of efficiencies.

(iv) Failing Company The failing company defence concerns a situation where an otherwise anti-competitive merger can be approved because the deterioration of the competitive structure that follows a merger would in any event have occurred without the merger, due to the failing firm exiting the market. In such a situation, it cannot be concluded that *the merger* itself will significantly impede effective competition. **5.326**

The Horizontal Guidelines spell out three criteria which need to be fulfilled in order for this condition to be fulfilled: **5.327**

- First, the allegedly failing firm would in the near future be forced out of the market because of financial difficulties, if not taken over by another undertaking.
- Second, there is no less anti-competitive alternative purchase than the notified merger.
- Third, in the absence of a merger the assets of the failing firm would inevitably exit the market.

Furthermore, the Horizontal Guidelines stress that it is for the merging parties to demonstrate that the deterioration of the competitive structure following a merger is not caused by the merger. **5.328**

So far the failing company defence has only been accepted in the case of *Kali-Salz/MDK/Treuhand*, where a dominant position was found to have been created in the German market for potash. However, the case was cleared because it was found that a prohibition would have led to the same market outcome as a clearance. The three criteria set out in the Horizontal Guidelines were basically laid down in that decision and the subsequent Court judgment. The Horizontal Guidelines only contain one minor variation compared to the decision in *Kali-Salz/MDK/Treuhand*. The Guidelines require that, in the absence of the merger, the assets of the failing firm would inevitably exit the market, meaning that the assets would no longer be used to supply the market in question, whereas the decision emphasises that the market shares of the failing company would in any event go to the merging party. **5.329**

The wording of the Horizontal Guidelines should not be interpreted as a major relaxation of the failing firm defence. It should be noted that the criteria as set out in *Kali-Salz/MDK/Treuhand* in fact basically imply that a failing firm defence could only be used in mergers to monopoly. The Horizontal Guidelines in principle raise the possibility of also using the failing company defence in mergers which do not lead to monopoly. However, the criteria for using the failing firm defence are otherwise the same and still quite strict. It is also notable that in the past the Commission has not accepted an extension of the failing company defence to failing divisions or to companies having entered a so-called 'death spiral', by which is meant that it is predicted that a company or division will fail at some point in the future. In conclusion, the guidelines do not signal a major change as regards the future **5.330** application of the failing company defence. In particular, for the failing company defence even to be considered, it must be evident that the company has failed or is about to fail.

(4) The Assessment of Spill-over Effects in Co-operative Joint Ventures

(a) Meaning of 'Spill-over' Effects

5.331   Article 2 of the Merger Regulation provides that all full function joint ventures satisfying the turnover thresholds will be assessed under the regulation. Any co-operative aspects, or 'spill-over' effects, will be assessed within the same procedure as the merger analysis. 'Spill-over' effects can analytically be distinguished from ancillary restrictions. Whereas the latter are based on contractual provisions related to a concentration (see section C5 below), the former are more likely to flow more or less automatically from the structure that is created by the concentration. Spill-over effects are unlikely to be based on contractual arrangements.

(b) Framework for Assessment of Spill-over Effects under the Merger Regulation

5.332   In particular Article 2(4) provides the following:

> To the extent that the creation of a joint venture constituting a concentration pursuant to Article 3 has as its object or effect the coordination of the competitive behaviour of undertakings that remain independent, such coordination shall be appraised in accordance with the criteria of Article 81(1) and (3) of the Treaty, with a view to establishing whether or not the operation is compatible with the common market.

5.333   And Article 2(5) provides:

> In making this appraisal, the Commission shall take into account in particular:
>
> — Whether two or more parent companies retain to a significant extent activities in the same market as the joint venture or in a market which is downstream or upstream from that of the joint venture or in a neighbouring market closely related to this market,
>
> — Whether the coordination which is the direct consequence of the creation of the joint venture affords the undertakings concerned the possibility of eliminating competition in respect of a substantial part of the products or services in question.

5.334   The principles contained in Articles 2(4) and 2(5) are further expanded in recital 27 of the new Merger Regulation, where it is said that the criteria of Article 81(1) and 81(3) of the Treaty should be applied to full function joint ventures, 'to the extent that their creation has as its consequence an appreciable restriction of competition between undertakings that remain independent.' It follows that the joint venture will be subject to the SIEC test of Article 2(1)–(3) and, to the extent that, as a direct consequence of the merger, it will bring about co-operative 'spill-over' effects, these will be assessed according to the criteria of Article 81(1) and (3) of the EC Treaty.

5.335   Normally spill-over effects would be found between two or more parent companies, when they retain significant activities either in the market of the joint venture or in a closely related market such as upstream, downstream or neighbouring markets. However, nothing excludes a finding of spill-over effects outside these areas. Significant effects on potential competition between the parent companies, for example, are also conceivable. In any event, the Commission is not precluded from applying Article 81(1) outside the scope of the Merger Regulation, if for example the required causality link between the joint venture and the effect on competition between the parent companies on markets other than the market(s) of the joint venture cannot be established. In this regard, and in line with general principles, a company could only invoke Articles 2(4) and 2(5) as a defence against possible future measures under Regulation 1/2003 to the extent that it has made full and honest disclosure of all relevant facts at the time of the merger proceedings.

The second indent of Article 2(5) would seem to indicate a strong requirement for causality **5.336** ('direct consequence'), and that the appraisal of the competitive impact may require a substantial impact to be shown ('possibility of eliminating competition'), which leads in the direction of the significantly impeding competition test. Again, it may, however, be useful to note that these are the factors that the Commission must take into account '*in particular*'. Consequently, other factors (such as the other three criteria in Article 81(3) of the EC Treaty) may be considered in specific cases.

(c) Considerations Relevant to an Assessment of Spill-over Effects

The investigation of spill-over effects under Articles 2(4) and 2(5) would normally include **5.337** the following issues: the spill-over markets, the parent companies' incentives to coordinate, and the causality between the creation of the joint venture and the spill-over effects.

The first case where the issue of spill-over effects were significantly discussed was *Telia/* **5.338** *Telenor/Schibsted*.[222] In this case, the joint venture was to be active in the provision of various services linked to the use of the Internet. The creation of the joint venture was to be assessed under the dominance test of Article 2, and raised no serious doubts. The Commission also made an Article 2(4) assessment of the impact on the 'candidate markets' for spill-over effects. These markets were the market for web site production, where the joint venture and two of the parent companies were active, and in addition, the market for the provision of 'dial-up' access to the Internet, a market upstream to that of the joint venture, where at least two of the parent companies would remain active.

In relation to the web site production market, the Commission concluded that the com- **5.339** bined market share of the parent companies and the joint venture would be so low that, even if the parent companies were to coordinate their activities, such coordination could not lead to an appreciable restriction of competition. Therefore, it was not necessary to consider whether there was a causal link between the creation of the joint venture and the behaviour of the parent companies outside the joint venture. The 'dial-up' Internet access market was competitive and growing, and therefore not likely to be conducive to coordination of competitive behaviour. The fact that this market was substantially larger than the markets of the joint venture was considered to reduce the likelihood of coordination further. In conclusion, there was no likelihood that the parent companies would coordinate on the 'dial-up' Internet access market. Consequently, it was not necessary to examine any causal link between the creation of the joint venture and the behaviour of the parent companies outside the joint venture on that market.

---

[222] Case IV/JV1 (1998).

5.340 Recently, spill-over effects were assessed in COMP/M.3333 *Sony/BMG*[223] and COMP/ M.3099 *Areva/Urenco/ETC JV*.[224] *Sony/BMG* concerned the merger of the recorded music businesses of Sony and BMG. Both Sony and BMG also had significant activities in the neighbouring market of music publishing, which is a much smaller market than recorded music. The music publishing businesses were not included in the merger. Therefore, the question arose whether the merger of the recorded music businesses could lead to a spill-over effect, which would result in coordination of the market behaviour of the parties in the music publishing market. Neither Sony nor BMG appeared to have very high market shares in the music publishing market. More importantly the Commission could exclude the risk of coordination due to the fact that in the music publishing market coordination could only materialise to a rather limited extent since the administration of the publishing rights is mainly carried out by the collecting societies, which collect the revenues from the exploitation of rights and distribute the revenue on to the holders of the rights.

5.341 The *Areva/Urenco/ETC JV* case concerned the upstream market for uranium enrichment technology. Areva and Urenco are two competing companies active in the enrichment of uranium fuel. Pre-merger, Urenco solely controlled the company Enrichment Technology Limited (ETC), which was active in the development, design and manufacturing of centrifuges for uranium enrichment. The merger operation consisted in Urenco and Areva taking joint control over ETC. Areva was at the time operating a uranium enrichment plant based on gas diffusion technology. This technology was more expensive than using centrifuges and needed to be phased out. The merger was a means of allowing Areva to acquire access to the centrifuge technology and equipment for uranium enrichment.

5.342 The Commission found that the merger did not lead to serious doubts on the upstream market for uranium enrichment technology. However, there were serious doubts about whether the ETC joint venture would have as its effect the coordination of the parties' decisions on capacity and output on the downstream market for enriched uranium. Notably, the Commission was concerned that each of the parties might be able to veto any increase in capacity of the other. The parties subsequently offered sufficient commitments to change their agreements so that these concerns were eliminated. The Commission consequently cleared the operation.

5.343 The application of the Articles 81(1) and 81(3) criteria will not always be easy within the framework of a merger proceeding. It seems clear that the Commission will consider the criteria for Article 81(1) to have been met if the substantive analysis of a spill-over market indicates that the merger would significantly impede effective competition in that market, as was the case in *Areva/Urenco*. This, of course, is also the test to be applied to the joint venture as such under the new Merger Regulation.

5.344 Since the introduction of Article 2(4) a considerable number of joint ventures have required assessment against the criteria of Article 81(1) and (3). The analysis in these cases has followed broadly the same lines as above. The experience shows that it is nonetheless rare

---

[223] COMP/M.3333—*Sony/BMG* (2004).
[224] COMP/M.3099—*Areva/Urenco/ETC JV* (2004).

that this examination leads to concerns as regards the compatibility of the transaction with the common market. However, a merger may still be prohibited on the basis of Article 2(4) under exceptional circumstances, for example, if a cartel has been falsely presented as a joint venture. The greatest benefit of Article 2(4), however, is probably the removal of the rather theoretical distinction between concentrative and co-operative joint ventures included in the Merger Regulation until the 1997 amendments.

(5) Ancillary Restrictions

(a) Introduction

The term 'ancillary restrictions' refers to contractual arrangements agreed between the parties to a concentration, which would ordinarily be regarded as restrictive of competition, but which are deemed to be directly related and necessary to the implementation of a concentration. The Merger Regulation provides in Article 6(1)(b), second subparagraph, in Article 8(1), second subparagraph and Article 8(2), third subparagraph that a decision declaring a concentration compatible with the common market 'shall be deemed to cover restrictions directly related and necessary to the implementation of the concentration'. Article 21(1) of the Merger Regulation provides that this regulation alone applies to ancillary restrictions to the exclusion of Council Regulation 1/2003.

5.345

Furthermore, recital 21 explains that the Commission does not have to assess the ancillary restrictions in individual cases: 'Commission decisions declaring concentrations compatible with the common market in application of this Regulation should automatically cover such restrictions, without the Commission having to assess such restrictions in individual cases'.

5.346

Accordingly, the parties to a transaction must assess such restrictions themselves. This approach is consistent with the regime for the enforcement of Articles 81 and 82 set out in Regulation (EC) No 1/2003.

5.347

However, in specific circumstances, the Commission retains a residual function. According to recital 21, the Commission should, at the request of the undertakings concerned, expressly assess whether such restrictions are ancillary, if a case presents 'novel and unresolved questions giving rise to genuine uncertainty'. The recital then defines a 'novel or unresolved question giving rise to genuine uncertainty' as a question that is 'not covered by the relevant Commission notice in force or a published Commission decision'.[225]

5.348

The main purpose of the new Notice[226] on ancillary restrictions is to provide better guidance for the interpretation of the notion of 'ancillary restrictions' in order to facilitate the parties' self-assessment and to improve legal certainty. The Notice covers the large majority of agreements that in the Commission's experience are normally claimed to be ancillary to concentrations. The Notice also uses more clear-cut provisions, for example by simplifying

5.349

---

[225] A decision is considered to have been published when it has been published in the Official Journal of the European Union or when it has been made available on the Commission's web site.
[226] Commission Notice on restrictions directly related and necessary to concentrations, OJ C56, 05.03.2005, pp 24–31.

the maximum periods for which restrictions can be accepted. However, clauses that depart from the principles set out in the Notice may well be regarded as ancillary restrictions in exceptional circumstances. In line with recital 21 of the Merger Regulation, for further guidance the Notice refers the parties to the Commission's published decisions.[227] When the specific circumstances of a case are covered neither by the Notice nor by previous decisions of the Commission, the Commission will assess the case individually if the parties so request.

5.350 Restrictions that are not directly related to and necessary for the implementation of a merger are not implicitly authorised and therefore may fall within Articles 81 and 82. Disputes as to whether restrictions are directly related and necessary to the implementation of a concentration and, if not, whether they are anti-competitive under Articles 81 or 82 may be resolved by national courts. This approach is consistent with the enforcement of Articles 81 and 82 as provided for in Council Regulation 1/2003.

5.351 As the term ancillary 'restriction' indicates, the measures in question must constitute a restriction of competition in the sense of Article 81(1). It follows that not all contractual arrangements concluded in relation to a merger bring about restrictions of competition. Any provisions which do not infringe Article 81(1) will obviously not need to be covered by the decision in any event. One example is a clause in an agreement to sell a certain business, specifying that the seller will not take any measures adversely affecting the business between the date of the agreement and the closing date.[228] Another type of measure that cannot in itself be considered restrictive is one that is integral to the concentration.[229] Examples of the latter are contractual arrangements that organise the control structure of the target company following the concentration.

5.352 Agreements must be necessary for the implementation of a concentration in order to be ancillary. This means that without the agreements the concentration could not be implemented or could only be implemented under considerably more uncertain conditions, at substantially higher costs, over an appreciably longer period or with considerable difficulty.[230] Ancillary restrictions are typically related to agreements which aim at protecting the value of the assets transferred,[231] maintaining continuity of supply[232] or facilitating the start-up of a new entity.[233] In determining whether a restriction is necessary it also necessary to assess the duration, subject matter and geographical field of application. If equally effective alternatives are available, the parties must choose the least restrictive one.

---

[227] See eg the decisions in Cases COMP/M.1980—*Volvo/Renault* [2000], para 56—*high degree of customer loyalty*; IV/M.1298—*Kodak/Imation* [1998, para 73—*long product life cycle*; IV/M.550—*Union Carbide/Unichem* [1995], para 99—*limited number of alternative producers*; IV/M.197—*Solvay-Laporte/Interox* [1992], para 50—*longer protection of know-how required.*

[228] See eg *Textron/Valois* (Case IV/M.721(1996)).

[229] See eg Cases IV/M.206—*Rhône-Poulenc/SNIA* [1992], para 8.3; IV/M.113—*Courtaulds/SNIA* [1991], para 35; IV/M.102—*TNT/Canada Post/DBP Postdienst/La Poste/PTT Poste & Sweden Post* [1991], para 46.

[230] See eg Case COMP/M.1886—*Vodafone/Airtel JV* [2000], para 20.

[231] See eg Case COMP/M.2227—*Goldman Sachs/Messer Griesheim* [2001], para 11.

[232] See eg Case COMP/M.1841—*Celestica/IBM* [2000].

[233] See eg Case COMP/M.2243—*Stora Enso Assidomän/JV* [2000], paras 49, 56, 57.

(b) Ancillary Restrictions in Acquisitions

(i) Non-compete Clauses   The most common type of restrictive agreement in relation   **5.353**
to acquisitions of undertakings is the non-compete clause, by which the seller undertakes
not to compete with the divested business or otherwise solicit its clients (or employees).
Such clauses are in principle accepted as ancillary to the concentration, as they allow for the
transfer of the full value of the acquired business. However, for a clause to be considered
ancillary, the legitimate protection of the buyer may not exceed what is necessary.
Therefore, the product and geographic scope[234] of the non-compete clause should be limited to correspond to the areas of the divested business. Non-compete clauses cannot be
considered necessary when the transfer is limited to physical assets such as land, buildings
or machinery, or to exclusive industrial and commercial property rights where the rights-
holders could take immediate action against infringements by the seller of such rights.

In terms of the acceptable duration, the Commission considers non-compete clauses justi-   **5.354**
fied for periods of up to three years,[235] when the transfer of the undertaking includes the
transfer of customer loyalty in the form of both goodwill and know-how.[236] When only
goodwill is included, they are justified for periods of up to two years.[237]

(ii) Licence Agreements   The second broad category of arrangements that are often   **5.355**
included in the transfer of businesses are those related to intellectual property rights
(patents, trademarks, know-how, etc). If the divested business has been using such rights,
owned by the selling company, which will continue to use those rights in other fields,
a licence will normally serve as a substitute for an outright transfer. Such licences (which
need not be limited in time and may be limited to certain fields of use, to the extent that
these correspond to the activities of the undertakings concerned) can be considered necessary to the implementation of the concentration and may even be seen as an integral part
of the concentration, and consequently would not need to be considered as ancillary
restrictions. However, territorial limitations in terms of product or geographic scope, on
the field of use allowed for the licensee (reflecting the territory of the transferred activities),
may effectively amount to a market sharing arrangement, and may not be justified as ancillary restrictions.

(iii) Purchase and Supply Obligations   The third most common form of ancillary   **5.356**
restriction is the purchase, supply, service or distribution agreement. These can be in favour
of either the seller or the acquirer and are normally acceptable as they allow for a smooth
transition from established intra-group relationships to the new situation where the seller

---

[234] See eg Cases COMP/M.2355—*Dow/Enichem Polyurethane* [2001], para 28; COMP/M.2305—
Vodafone GROUP PLC/EIRCELL [2001], para 22; COMP/M.1979—*CDC/BancoUrquijo/JV* [2000] para 18;
IV/M.884—*KNP BT/Bunzl/Wilhelm Seiler* [1997] para 17; IV/M.1482—*KingFisher/Grosslabor* [1999], para 27.
[235] There may be exceptional circumstances justifying a longer period in some cases. See eg Cases COMP/
M.1980—*Volvo/Renault* [2000], para 56; IV/M.1298—*Kodak/Imation* [1998], para 74; IV/M.612—*RWE-DEA/
Enichem Augusta* [1995], para 37.
[236] See eg Cases COMP/M.2305—*Vodafone Group plc/Eircell* [2001], paras 21 and 22; COMP/
M.2077—*Clayton Dubilier / Rice/Iteltel* [2000] para 15; IV/M.1127—*Nestlé/Dalgety* [1998], para 33.
[237] See eg Cases IV/M.1482—*Kingfisher/Grosslabor* [1999], para 26; IV/M.884—*KNP BT/Bunzl/Wilhelm
Seiler* [1997], para 17.

and the divested business will form separate economic entities. The underlying reasons justifying such clauses cannot, however, legitimately be extended to a period going beyond a transitional period required to establish new purchase, supply, service or distribution relationships for each of the two groups. A five year transition period is normally considered acceptable.[238] Supply and purchase obligations providing for fixed quantities, possibly with a variation clause, are recognised as ancillary. However, obligations amounting to exclusive supply and purchasing arrangements are not considered necessary to the implementation of a concentration.[239]

(c) Ancillary Restrictions in Joint Ventures

5.357 (i) **Non-compete Obligations** In cases where the parent companies have been active on the same markets of the joint venture non-compete obligations between the parent companies and the joint venture may be considered ancillary to the concentration, where such obligations correspond to the products, services and territories covered by the joint venture. Such non-competitive arrangements can, for example, be necessary to protect the joint venture from competitive acts by one of the parents facilitated through privileged access of the parent company to know-how and goodwill transferred to the joint venture.[240] However, the geographical scope must, as a rule, be limited to the territory where the parent offered products and services before the joint venture whilst the product scope should be limited to the products and services of the joint venture.[241] In any event such non-compete obligations can only be considered ancillary to the implementation of the concentration for the lifetime of the joint venture.

5.358 (ii) **Licence Agreements** A licence granted by the parents to the joint venture may be considered ancillary. This is the case whether or not it is exclusive and whether or not it is limited in time or restricted to a particular use. Licences granted by the joint venture to one of its parents or cross-licence agreements can also be regarded as directly related and necessary to the implementation of the concentration. However, licence agreements between the parents are not considered ancillary.

5.359 (iii) **Purchase and Supply Obligations** The creation of a joint venture will often involve questions concerning contractual arrangements between the parent companies and their joint venture relating to purchase, supply, or distribution obligations. Such arrangements may or may not be seen as restrictive, and to the extent they are restrictive they may or may not be regarded as ancillary to the concentration. The assessment of such purchase, supply,

---

[238] See eg Cases IV/M.651—*AT&T/Philips* [1996], VII; IV/JV.15 *BT/AT&T* [1999], para 209. In exceptional cases longer periods may be acceptable. See eg Cases IV/M.550—*Union Carbide/Enichem* [1995], para 99; *RWE-DEA/Enichem Augusta* [1995], para 45.

[239] Exclusive arrangements have only been accepted in exceptional cases such as when there is de facto no market. See eg Cases IV/M.612—*RWE-DEA/Enichem Augusta* [1995], para 45; IV/M.550 *Union Carbide/Enichem* [1995] paras 92–96. See also para 34 of the Notice.

[240] See Cases COMP/M.1832—*Ahold/ICA Förbundet/Canica* [2000], para 26; IV/M.1042—*Eastman Kodak/Sun Chemical* [1998] para 40; IV/M.727—*BP/Mobil* [1996], para 51; IV/M.751—*Bayer/Hüls* [1996], para 31.

[241] See eg COMP/M.2243—*Stora Enso/Assidomän/JV* [2000], para 49; COMP/M.1913—*Lufthansa Menzies/LGS/JV* [2000], para 18.

or distribution obligations should follow the same principles as described above in relation to the acquisition of businesses.

(6) Remedies

(a) *General Considerations*

(i) **The Purpose of Remedies**   If in a particular case the Commission has established that **5.360** a merger will lead to a significant impediment of effective competition, it may often still be possible to proceed with the merger, if a satisfactory remedy to the competition problem created by the merger can be found. Remedies are considered satisfactory if they eliminate the identified competition problems and restore effective competition, and if they are proportionate to the competition concerns identified.

In the past, the Commission has always been willing to consider remedies and has worked **5.361** constructively with the merging parties to solve the competition problems otherwise created by a merger. A prohibition decision has been taken only if no satisfactory remedy could be found. Consequently, most cases which were likely to lead to a creation or strengthening of a dominant position have in the past been cleared with one or more remedies. The change in the substantive test from a dominance test to a SIEC test should not result in any change to this constructive approach nor should it result in any material change to the nature or assessment of remedies.

(ii) **Types of Remedies**   In order for the Commission to take proposed remedies into **5.362** account, they normally have to be of a structural nature. 'Structural' refers to the need for the remedies to re-establish the market structure in such a way that effective competition is restored to its pre-merger level. The focus of the remedy is, therefore, the maintenance of competitive market structures. An example of a structural remedy could be a divestiture of a business or sale of assets such as brands or production capacity. In contrast, so-called 'behavioural' remedies are not normally accepted under the Merger Regulation. By behavioural remedies are meant remedies which amount to statements of intent or promises not to abuse the increased market power resulting from a merger. They could, for example, require undertakings not to increase prices or to continue to supply competitors on a non-discriminatory basis following a merger. While recognising that such behavioural undertakings may not be without value in a particular market context, the Commission has not normally based its decisions on them. This is a logical approach, since the purpose of the Merger Regulation is to maintain competitive market structures.

In this regard it is important to note the position taken by the CFI in the *Gencor* judgment, **5.363** where the CFI specifically stated that the decisive point is not whether a remedy is behavioural or structural in nature, but whether it prevents the creation or strengthening of a dominant position. Similarly, in *Tetra Laval v Commission*[242] the CFI held that behavioural remedies should be taken into account when assessing whether the merged entity would be likely to engage in a particular type of anti-competitive conduct. This view was subsequently confirmed by the European Court of Justice.[243] In particular both the CFI and the

---

[242] Case T-5/02.
[243] Case C-12/03.

ECJ held that the Commission ought to have taken account of the behavioural commitments offered by Tetra which were intended to offset the Commission's concerns that the merged entity would be able to leverage its dominant position in carton packaging to gain a dominant position in PET packaging, in particular through bundling. The proposed behavioural commitment included the separation of Sidel from Tetra Pak and a commitment not to bundle the products in question. The Commission considered that, since the proposed commitments were purely behavioural, they were not suitable to restore the conditions of effective competition on a permanent basis since they did not address the permanent change in market structure created by the merger. However, the court judgments make it clear that the Commission must consider whether a behavioural commitment constitutes an effective remedy at least in certain circumstances. The ECJ emphasised that, whilst in the *Gencor* case the structure of the market on which competition would be impeded as a consequence of the merger was directly altered by the merger, in *Tetra Laval* the relevant market structure would only be altered (and competition therefore impeded) as a consequence of leveraging. The Court therefore considered that it was in this case appropriate for the Commission to take account of behavioural commitments offered which were intended to prevent the merged entity from engaging in that future conduct.

5.364 While the CFI and the ECJ disagreed with the Commission's assessment and dismissal of the behavioural remedies in the *Tetra Laval* case, the case cannot be interpreted as calling for a fundamental change in the consideration of behavioural remedies. In particular there is no principal contradiction between the stance of the CFI and the ECJ and the past policy of the Commission. However, the Commission has rightly been cautious in accepting behavioural remedies, since one of the main reasons for the existence of the Merger Regulation is the wish to maintain competitive market structures rather than to undertake market regulation. Consequently, it would not seem logical for the Commission to base merger decisions to a greater extent on behavioural undertakings such as, for example, promises of the parties not to wield their new market power and increase prices. Ultimately, there would be little need for the Merger Regulation if this became the prevailing policy towards mergers. Furthermore, structural remedies such as divestitures may also be more clear-cut, and it may, therefore, be easier for the parties to convince the Commission that a remedy solves the problem. Finally, a more practical consideration favouring structural remedies is that it can be demanding in terms of resources for the Commission to monitor, and the parties to ensure, ongoing compliance with a non-structural commitment over a prolonged period of time.

5.365 **(iii) Timing of Remedies Proposal** The Commission may accept remedies in both phase I and phase II (for the procedural aspects in submitting remedies see Section D below). In phase II, remedies are normally given after an in-depth investigation, and the competition concerns are clear. Remedies given after an in-depth investigation aim at removing the significant impediment to effective competition created by the merger. On the other hand, remedies given in phase I must remove the 'serious doubts' identified. In some cases removing 'serious doubts' may require more wide-ranging remedies from the merging parties, because 'serious doubts' is usually a lower threshold of intervention than a 'significant impediment to competition'. Furthermore, in phase I without the benefit of a full investigation and in order to be certain that 'serious doubts' are removed, the

Commission has normally had to insist on quite clear-cut remedies. It should also be noted that according to Article 6(2), the Merger Regulation imposes on the Commission the obligation to clear a case immediately, when it has become clear that 'serious doubts' have been removed. Consequently, if the merging parties produce remedies to that effect at the beginning of phase II, then the Commission will have to immediately clear the case.[244]

(b) Divestiture Remedies

The most common type of remedy is divestiture. However, as discussed below, other types of remedy are also possible, depending on the specific case.[245] **5.366**

(i) **Identifying the Business to be Divested** If, for example, a merger involves a horizon- **5.367** tal overlap in a market as a result of which the merger would create a significant impediment to effective competition in that market, then the most obvious and clear-cut remedy is for the parties to divest one of the businesses creating the overlap.

Such a divestiture must normally constitute a viable business which already exists, and **5.368** which can operate on a stand alone basis, at least after a transitory period. Normally, the merging parties would have to divest the most appropriate business from a competition policy point of view. The most appropriate business may be the business of the acquiring or the acquired company. In the case of a hostile bid, the most appropriate business may belong to the acquiring company, since the bidder may have difficulties knowing in sufficient detail whether the target's business, if divested, will be a viable competitor.

The Commission has in the past in some cases allowed the parties to choose between alter- **5.369** native divestiture commitments. In *Akzo Nobel/Courtaulds*,[246] for example, the merger threatened to create a dominant position in aerospace coatings. Akzo Nobel and Courtaulds each had a market share of some 40 per cent. However, in addition to the aerospace coatings business, Courtaulds was also active in aerospace sealants, which was an attractive business for Akzo Nobel. Consequently Akzo Nobel, as the acquiring firm, proposed to sell its own aerospace coatings business and keep Courtaulds' business. The Commission accepted this remedy in this particular case, but insisted that if Akzo Nobel's business could not be sold, then the parties would have to divest Courtaulds' business. Ultimately, Akzo Nobel struggled to sell its own business and did in the end have to sell Courtaulds' business. The implementation of the remedy was made more complicated by its structure, which allowed for choice, and in the end it was more difficult to implement and took longer to implement than would otherwise have been the case. A remedy allowing for a 'swap' may also in other cases raise the question whether the incentives to compete are changed as a result of the 'swap'.

---

[244] For a discussion of the Commission's role in reviewing remedies, see also the recent judgments of the CFI in Case T-87/05 *EDP v Commission*, judgment of 21.9.2005, not yet published in the ECR; and in Case T-282/02 *Cementbouw Handel & Industrie v Commission*, judgment of 23.2.2006, not yet published in the ECR.

[245] See also the Commission Notice on remedies acceptable under Council Regulation (EEC) No 4064/89 and under Commission Regulation (EC) No 447/98.

[246] Case IV.M.1182—*Akzo Nobel/Courtaulds* (1998).

5.370 In certain cases, for example in *Crown Cork & Seal/CarnaudMetalbox*,[247] the Commission has accepted a divestiture combining certain assets from the target and the purchaser. In *Kimberley-Clark/Scott Paper*, the Commission even accepted a divestiture package including only brands and related production assets as sufficient to recreate the conditions for effective competition. The purpose is usually to allow the parties to enjoy the benefits of the merger, while at the same time ensuring that the merger does not significantly impede competition. The result may be that competition will be less intense after the merger, but not so far as significantly to impede competition. However, in this type of situation there are often additional risks of viability and efficiency, which render such divestiture remedies unconvincing.

5.371 Furthermore, in cases where the merger significantly impedes effective competition as a result of coordinated or non-coordinated effects in oligopolistic markets, satisfactory divestiture remedies may be particularly difficult to achieve. Frequently, in such cases the parties would have to dispose of assets with the purpose of 'recreating' the competitor lost through the merger. Such a disposal will often contradict the logic of the merger, and may not be feasible for the merging parties. The outcome, therefore, could well be a prohibition or a collapse of the merger. In *Nestlé/Perrier* a disposal of certain assets was deemed to be feasible and sufficient, whereas in *Gencor/Lonrho*, despite serious attempts to put together a satisfactory divestiture package, it was ultimately not possible for the parties to put forward a package which was acceptable to the Commission.

5.372 Divestitures to remove a horizontal overlap created by a merger are the most common types of divestures. However, in some cases divestitures may also be used to remedy other competition problems. A divestiture may also, for example, be a means of removing a structural link through a joint venture or minority share holding creating concerns for coordinated effects in an oligopolistic market.

5.373 **(ii) Identifying a Suitable Purchaser**   In addition to the need for the business to be a viable business capable of restoring effective competition, it is also a condition that the business is sold to a suitable purchaser. The potential of the business to attract a suitable purchaser is an important element in the assessment of the appropriateness of the proposed remedy. There are cases where the viability of a remedy depends on the purchaser. In such cases, the Commission will not clear the merger unless the parties undertake not to implement the merger until they have entered into a binding agreement with the purchaser for the divested business which is subject to prior approval by the Commission (a so-called 'upfront buyer' remedy).

5.374 **(iii) Typical Requirements for Divestiture Remedies**   When submitting a divestiture commitment the parties need to define carefully and describe all the assets included in the commitment. The commitment must also include a mechanism regulating how the acquirer can select and retain the relevant personnel in order to run the business. This may be particularly relevant if there are personnel who have not worked directly for the business but in supporting functions such as R&D in the parent company.

---

[247] OJ L75, 23.3.1996, p 38.

The commitments must set out the timing for their implementation. The timing of the **5.375** various stages of the commitments, including the various agreements such as binding letters of intent, final agreement, and the transfer of legal title, must be specified and agreed with the Commission. The commitments should also set out the 'purchaser standard'. Normally it is required that the acquirer of a divested business is a viable existing or potential competitor independent of and unconnected to the parties, and who possesses the financial resources and financial expertise, and has the incentive to develop the business as a viable competitor of the merging parties.[248]

The parties are required to maintain the competitive potential of the business to be divested **5.376** in the interim period until the divestiture can be implemented. The Commission will require the parties to make commitments to 'ring fence' the business to be divested in order to maintain its economic viability and saleability during the interim period. In addition, as the Commission does not have the ability continuously to oversee the 'hold separate' provisions in detail, the Commission will usually require the appointment of a 'hold separate trustee', who will oversee the hold separate arrangements and periodically report to the Commission. The trustee's mandate must be approved by the Commission as part of the appointment process. The mandate will usually include provisions on the trustee's supervision responsibilities and possibly the right to propose and impose certain measures as necessary to ensure compliance with the commitments.

The Commission usually also lacks the expertise and the resources to oversee all aspects of **5.377** the divestiture itself. It is, therefore, common to ask the parties to appoint a 'divestiture trustee', who will oversee the divestiture itself and report regularly to the Commission. Often, depending on the structure of the remedy, the divestiture trustee will have to oversee the parties' efforts to sell the business in a first phase, and if the parties are not successful at selling the business, then the trustee will be given an irrevocable mandate to sell the business at any price within a specific deadline, but with the approval of the Commission (this is known as a 'fire sale').

The 'hold separate trustee' and the 'divestiture trustee' may or may not be the same person or **5.378** organisation. However, the function of hold separate and divestiture can be quite different. The hold separate trustee may require more management and accounting expertise than the divestiture trustee, who on the other hand may need expertise as an investment banker. In the past the two trustee functions have, therefore, often been separated.

It is for the parties to remunerate the trustees. The fee structure should be such that it does **5.379** not endanger the independence and effectiveness of the trustees. After the passage of legal title of the divestiture package, the trustee's mandate will normally provide that the trustee should ask that the Commission be discharged from its responsibilities.

When the parties or the trustee have identified a suitable purchaser, they must, before pro- **5.380** ceeding with the divestiture, ask the Commission to approve the purchaser on the basis of evidence that the purchaser meets the requirements as set out in the commitments. If the

---

[248] Commission Notice on remedies acceptable under Council Regulation (EEC) No 4064/89 and under Commission Regulation (EC) No 447/98, para 49.

Commission finds that the purchaser does not fulfil the requirements, then it will communicate this formally to the parties.[249] If the purchaser fulfils the criteria, then the divestiture can go ahead. The divestiture constitutes a new concentration and as such it is subject to merger control. If the divestiture fulfils the criteria for the Merger Regulation, then it will have to be notified to the Commission. Since the Commission will have approved the purchaser already, the divestiture will normally just be cleared under the usual procedure. If the divestiture does not need to be notified under the Merger Regulation, then the operation may need to be notified to national competition authorities.

5.381   Finally, when a merger has been implemented, it is not normally possible to restore competition to the pre-merger level, despite the potential for certain interim provisions such as 'hold separate' provisions in divestitures. Therefore, the length of time within which undertakings must be implemented is normally quite short.

(c) Non-divestiture Remedies

5.382   Normally, divestiture remedies are the preferred type of remedy, because they provide a clear-cut solution to the competition problem. However, other types of remedy are possible in specific circumstances. The foreclosure effect of existing exclusive long term supply agreements, for example, may contribute to a merger significantly impeding effective competition.[250] It is also possible that barriers to entry may arise due to control over infrastructure or key technology in the form of patents, know-how or intellectual property rights. In such circumstances, remedies may consist of a commitment to ensure access to the necessary infrastructure or key technology. In relation to key technology in particular, the preferred remedy is a divestiture of the patents or intellectual property rights. However, if that is not possible the Commission may accept a licence agreement, which is preferably exclusive and without restrictions as to the use of the licence.

5.383   In some cases the most appropriate remedy is to open the market for new entrants. This has been the approach used in a certain number of airline cases. In these cases each individual route is usually considered to constitute a relevant market. In *Air France/KLM*,[251] for example, the parties would have achieved very high market shares on the routes between Paris and Amsterdam. The parties gave a commitment to make a sufficient number of slots available to allow a new entrant on the Paris–Amsterdam city pair to enter that market.

5.384   As noted above, the Commission is normally sceptical about so-called behavioural commitments. Behavioural remedies amounting to mere statements of intent or promises of the merging parties not to abuse their post-merger market power are not normally considered sufficient to remove the significant impediment to effective competition created by a merger.

---

[249] Usually a remedy specifies a procedure for its implementation and decisions are taken in accordance with this procedure. Some decisions relating to remedies may be taken by a non-opposition procedure, where it is specified that unless the Commission reacts within x days, the proposal of the parties is accepted. In other cases a formal decision by the Commission may be required. If a formal decision is required, the Commissioner for Competition has normally been empowered to implement remedies, and he or she can then take the decision without consulting the full Commission.

[250] See for example IV/M.1571 *New Holland/Case*, OJ C130, 11.5.2000.

[251] Case COMP/M.3280—*Air France/KLM* (2004).

On the other hand, behavioural remedies may in some cases have a real market impact. In *Enso/Stora*, for example, the parties committed to giving the competitors to Tetra Pak conditions in line with the conditions of Tetra Pak in their purchases of liquid packaging board. The purpose of the undertaking was to ensure that the countervailing buyer power of Tetra Pak spilled over to the whole market, thereby preventing any price discrimination by the merging parties against the smaller competitors of Tetra Pak. However, the *Enso/Stora* case was in this regard a rather exceptional case, and in normal circumstances such remedies are not attractive. First of all, they normally require some continuous monitoring on the part of the Commission, and DG COMP is not well equipped and does not in general have the resources to carry out the type of price monitoring necessary in such cases. Second, it is clear that this type of remedy can be quite interventionist, effectively resulting in the Commission regulating the pricing on a market. It is far from obvious that this will in all cases produce the best market outcome for competition and ultimately consumers. However, it is to be noted that the CFI and the ECJ in their judgments in the *Tetra Laval* case, held that the Commission cannot dismiss behavioural remedies outright without explaining why they are not sufficient to solve the competition problems identified, in that case to prevent the merged entity from engaging in the future conduct which would have led, according to the Commission, to the creation of a dominant position. [252]

D. Merger Regulation Procedure

(1) Overview—The Basic Features of the Merger Regulation Procedure

The Merger Regulation and accompanying legal instruments establish a detailed and self-contained procedural framework for the administrative processing of merger cases governing all aspects of examination of a case, from pre-notification to final decision. Before proceeding with a detailed analysis of the procedure to be followed under the Merger Regulation, it is useful to set out briefly a summary of the legal instruments applicable to merger proceedings, the main actors involved in merger proceedings and a synoptic timetable. **5.385**

(a) Legal and Soft-law Instruments Governing Merger Proceedings

(i) **The Merger Regulation**[253] The Merger Regulation contains a number of provisions governing procedure. The most important ones are: Article 4 on notifications, Article 7 on suspension of concentrations and derogations, Articles 6 and 8 on decision-making powers, Article 10 on time limits, Articles 11–13 on investigation powers, Articles 14–15 **5.386**

---

[252] See also Case T-177/04 *easyJet v Commission*, judgment of 4.7.2006, not yet reported in the ECR, where the CFI summarised the previous case law on behavioural remedies as follows (para 182): '. . . it must be borne in mind that behavioural commitments are not by their nature insufficient to prevent the creation or strengthening of a dominant position, and that they must be assessed on a case-by-case basis in the same way as structural commitments.' (*EDP v Commission*, para 44 above, para 100; see also, to that effect, *Gencor v Commission*, para 40 above, para 319; Case T-5/02 *Tetra Laval v Commission* [2002] ECR II-4381, para 161, confirmed in Case C-12/03 *P Commission v Tetra* Laval [2005] ECR I-987, para 85.)

[253] Council Regulation (EC) 139/2004 of 20 January 2004 on the control of concentrations between undertakings, [2004] OJ L24/1.

on fining powers, Article 17 on confidentiality, Article 18 on rights of defence, Article 19 on the role of the Advisory Committee and Article 20 on publication of decisions. Article 16 governs judicial review with respect to fines.

5.387 (ii) **The Implementing Regulation**[254]   The Implementing Regulation is a Commission Regulation adopted on the basis of Article 23 of the Merger Regulation. It governs details of the Merger Regulation's procedural system by laying down rules on notifications, time limits, hearings and rights of defence. The Implementing Regulation prescribes specific forms for the notification of merger cases (Form CO and Short Form CO) as well as for referral requests (Form RS).

5.388 (iii) **The Notice on Simplified Procedure**[255]   This Notice sets out a simplified procedure for certain cases which are considered not to pose competition concerns.

5.389 (iv) **The Best Practices on the Conduct of Merger Proceedings**[256]   The Best Practices is a soft-law instrument created by DG Competition. It sets out, in a comprehensive manner, practical rules for the day to day handling of merger cases dealing in particular with pre-notification contacts, meetings with the parties and third parties, investigation, and review of documents in the Commission's file.

5.390 (v) **The Notice on Access to the File**[257]   This Commission Notice deals with the rights of parties to have access to the Commission's file and the procedure for obtaining such access.

5.391 (vi) **The Hearing Officer's Mandate**[258]   This Commission instrument establishes the position of an independent hearing officer with the task of overseeing procedural rights during merger proceedings. It also governs confidentiality issues, access to the file, the conduct of oral hearings and procedural aspects of market testing of remedies.

5.392 (vii) **The Notice on Remedies**[259]   and accompanying documents (the Best Practice Guidelines for Divestiture Commitments and the Commission's model texts for divestiture

---

[254] Commission Regulation (EC) 802/2004 of 7 April 2004 implementing Council Regulation (EC) No 139/2004 on the control of concentrations between undertakings, [2004] OJ L133/1.

[255] Commission Notice on a simplified procedure for treatment of certain concentrations under Council Regulation (EC) 139/2004 [2005] OJ C56/04. The Notice can be found at <http://www.ec.europa.eu/comm/ competition/mergers/legislation/regulation/>.

[256] DG Competition Best Practices on the Conduct of Merger Proceedings, published at <http://www.ec.europa.eu/comm/competition/mergers/legislation/regulation/best_practices.pdf>.

[257] Commission Notice on the rules for access to the Commission file in cases pursuant to Arts 81 and 82 of the EC Treaty, Arts 53, 54 and 57 of the EEA Agreement and Council Regulation (EC) 139/2004, hereinafter referred to as the 'Notice on Access to the File' [2005] OJ C325/7. The Notice on Access to the File replaced the previous notice which had been in force since 1997 (for the 1997 Notice, see: Notice on the internal rules of procedure for processing requests for access to the file in cases under Arts 85 and 86 of the EC Treaty, Arts 65 and 66 of the ECSC Treaty and Council Regulation (EEC) 4064/89 [1997] OJ C23/3).

[258] Commission Decision of 23 May 2001 on the terms of reference of hearing officers in certain competition proceedings, hereinafter referred to as the Hearing Officer Mandate [2001] OJ L162/21.

[259] Commission Notice on remedies acceptable under Council Regulation (EEC) 4064/89 and under Commission Regulation (EC) 447/98 [2001] OJ C68/3. The Notice remains relevant under the new Merger Regulation.

commitments and trustee mandates) set out sample texts for the submission of remedies and explain the Commission's substantive practice with respect to remedies.

All the above texts can be found at DG Competition's web site.[260]   **5.393**

(b) The Basic Procedural Features of EU Merger Control

The basic procedural features of the EU merger control regime, which are set out below,   **5.394** have remained relatively constant since the inception of the original Merger Regulation in 1989.[261]

- **administrative system**: the Commission, which is an administrative body, has the power to assess merger cases and authorise or prohibit mergers. The Commission's decisions are subject to external judicial review by the Community Courts.
- *ex ante* **system**: mandatory notification of all concentrations with Community dimension and a bar on closing ('suspensive effect' or 'stand-still obligation') prior to authorisation by the Commission;
- **predictable timetable**: processing of cases by the Commission within pre-determined, short and legally binding deadlines;
- **legal certainty and transparency**: at the end of the process, the Commission takes a legally binding and reasoned decision which is communicated to the parties and, subject to confidentiality, made public;
- **involvement of Member States**: the Commission must liaise closely with national competition authorities (NCAs) and representatives of NCAs advise the Commission formally in complex (Phase II) cases;
- **rights of defence**: before taking adverse decisions, the Commission must communicate all its objections to the merging parties, allow them to respond in writing and at a formal oral hearing and give them access to its file.

The Merger Regulation and accompanying instruments retain and improve all the above   **5.395** procedural features of EC merger control. It is to be noted, in particular, that the transparency of EC merger control procedures has been increased significantly following the adoption of DG Competition's Best Practices which seek to increase understanding of the investigation process and thereby to further enhance the efficiency of investigations and to ensure a high degree of transparency and predictability of the review process.[262]

(c) The Principal Actors in EU Merger Proceedings

During the assessment of a merger case from pre-notification to final decision, a multitude   **5.396** of parties, Commission services and national authorities are involved. Their roles are explained briefly below.

(i) **The Merging Parties**   The merging parties (or undertakings concerned) are the compa-   **5.397** nies directly involved in the merger, the acquirer and the target company. Parties acquiring

---

[260] See <http://www.ec.europa.eu/comm/competition/mergers/legislation/>.

[261] Council Regulation (EEC) 4064/89 of 21 December 1989 on the control of concentrations between undertakings [1989] OJ L395/1; corrigendum in [1990] OJ L257/13. Regulation No 4064/89 was amended by Council Regulation (EC) 1310/97 of 30 June 1997 [1997] OJ L180/1.

[262] See para 1 of the Best Practices.

control (normally the acquiring company only but including all companies acquiring joint control) are under an obligation to notify the case and are also known as the 'notifying parties'. The target company and the seller are known as 'involved parties'.

5.398 **(ii) Third Parties** Third parties involved in a merger proceeding include normally customers, suppliers and competitors of the merging parties, employees and their representatives, shareholders and other interested third parties such as consumer associations.

5.399 **(iii) The Commission** The Commission is the body responsible for adopting decisions under the Merger Regulation. The Commission takes decisions as a collegiate body but decision making can be delegated to the Competition Commissioner. The most important decisions (under Article 8 of the Merger Regulation) are taken by the College whereas decisions in the first phase of proceedings have been delegated to the Competition Commissioner (at the time of writing, Ms Neelie Kroes) who can in turn delegate certain tasks to the Director General of DG Competition (at the time of writing, Mr Philip Lowe). The Competition Commissioner is assisted by a Cabinet consisting of seven members.[263] A specific Cabinet member is entrusted with the portfolio of merger control issues, essentially reviewing draft merger decisions and advising the Commissioner.

5.400 **(iv) DG Competition and the Merger Control Network** DG Competition is the Commission Directorate-General responsible for dealing with merger cases under the Merger Regulation.[264]

5.401 Until May 2004, a specific directorate within DG Competition, Directorate B, also known as the Merger Task Force, was solely responsible for examining notifications and preparing decisions under the Merger Regulation. DG Competition has been re-organised as part of the merger review exercise which took place in 2003 and culminated with the adoption and entry into force of the Merger Regulation in 2004.[265]

5.402 Following this re-organisation and further changes made during 2005, the Merger Task Force has been dispersed in a number of merger units contained within sectoral directorates. DG Competition now contains four sectoral directorates (B-E) dealing respectively with the following economic sectors: B-Energy, basic industries, chemicals and pharmaceuticals; C-Information, communication and media; D-Services; and E-Industry, consumer goods and manufacturing. Each of these directorates contains a specific unit dealing with merger cases within that sector.[266] In addition, a merger policy and coordination unit has been created within directorate A of DG Competition. A Deputy Director General for Mergers has been entrusted with the task of overseeing merger work within DG Competition. A central registry dedicated to merger notifications has been retained.

---

[263] For more information on the Cabinet's composition see <http://www.ec.europa.eu/comm/ commission_barroso/kroes/index_en.html>.

[264] For details of posts within DG Competition and persons holding those posts see <http:// www.ec. europa.eu/comm/dgs/competition/index_en.htm>.

[265] For a summary of the merger reform package see DG Competition Newsletter, 2004 Special Edition, available at http://www.ec.europa.eu/comm/competition/publications/cpn/special_edition.pdf.

[266] See DG Competition's web site at http://www.ec.europa.eu/comm/dgs/competition/ index_en.htm.

The merger units and merger registry form a Merger Control Network (MCN) under the authority of the sectoral Directors, the DDG for Mergers, the Director General of DG Competition and ultimately the Competition Commissioner.

A position of Chief Economist has also been established within DG Competition. This is **5.403** a specific position created within DG Competition headed by an eminent economist with significant expertise in industrial economics. The Chief Economist is supported by officials with expertise in industrial economics.

DG Competition has also created a position of Consumer Liaison Officer. This position is **5.404** held by a senior official within DG Competition who is entrusted with the task of liaising with and assisting consumer organisations to be effectively involved in merger proceedings.

The MCN is responsible for the examination of merger notifications and for preparing **5.405** draft decisions. In exercising its duties, the MCN liaises with other areas of DG Competition such as Directorate A and the office of the Chief Economist. It also consults other relevant Commission services, which always includes the Legal Service, which must give its prior clearance before decisions can be taken, as well as other services with interest in merger control including notably DG Enterprise, DG Ecfin (Economic and Financial Affairs), DG Sanco (Consumer Protection), DG Tren (Transport and Energy) or DG Infso (Information society). The MCN is constituted by approximately 70 officials, including staff on temporary contracts and national experts seconded by national competition authorities. This body of staff is mainly composed of lawyers and economists with expertise in antitrust and merger control.

(v) **The Hearing Officer**   The Commission has created the position of 'Hearing Officer'[267] **5.406** whose role is to ensure that the effective exercise of the right to be heard is respected in competition proceedings before the Commission including in merger proceedings. The hearing officer's role is set out in the Hearing Officer Mandate. He or she is attached, for administrative purposes, to the Competition Commissioner and is thus independent from DG Competition.

(vi) **The Member States and the Advisory Committee**   The Commission is under a **5.407** duty to liaise closely with Member State authorities (Article 19 of the Merger Regulation). In complex, phase II, cases the Commission is obliged to consult an Advisory Committee on concentrations composed of representatives of the competent authorities of the Member States.

(vii) **International Competition Authorities (ESA and Third Country Authorities)** **5.408** Third country competition authorities will normally also be involved to a lesser or greater extent during an EC merger proceeding. This is because a case falling within the Commission's jurisdiction under the Merger Regulation may also fall to be assessed by third country authorities under their national law and the Commission may be under a bilateral or multilateral obligation to co-operate with such authorities.

---

[267] At the time of writing there were two officials holding the position of Hearing Officer: Mr Serge Durande and Ms Karen Williams.

5.409 In the case of the EFTA countries, formal agreements divide competence between the Commission and the EFTA Surveillance Authority and a co-operation procedure has been established. The relevant rules are contained in Articles 57–58 of the EEA Agreement, in Protocol 24 to the EEA Agreement and in Decisions No 78/2004 and 79/2004. These decisions set out the applicability of the EC Merger Regulation to the entire EEA-area.[268] In practice, since the establishment of the EEA agreement, all cases have fallen under the competence of the Commission.

5.410 The Commission has also signed bilateral agreements with a number of third countries,[269] notably with the United States authorities,[270] Canada[271] and Japan[272] with which close co-operation has been established.

(d) Synopsis of Timetable of a Merger Proceeding

5.411 Before analysing in further detail the procedural aspects of the EC merger control regime, it is worth setting out a brief synopsis of the main stages through which a merger case may pass. These are:

Pre-notification: informal and confidential discussions with the Commission services before notification of a case either to establish whether notification is necessary or to discuss preparation of notification and jurisdictional issues.

Notification: submission of a merger case to the Commission on the prescribed forms in accordance with the rules set out in the Merger Regulation and Implementing Regulation.

Phase I procedure: investigation of the case to determine whether it should be cleared, with or without modifications, within the first phase deadline set out in the Merger Regulation or whether a second phase in-depth investigation ought to be launched on the basis that the concentration raises serious doubts as to its compatibility with the common market.

Phase II procedure: in-depth investigation of complex cases which raise serious doubts as to their compatibility with the common market. During this phase of the procedure, the Commission investigates the case in depth. If its serious doubts as to the compatibility of the merger with the common market are not dispelled, the Commission sends the parties a Statement of Objections ('SO'), allows the parties access to the file and the opportunity to present their views formally in writing and at an oral hearing, consults representatives of the Member States in the Advisory Committee and finally adopts and publishes a decision either authorising the merger, with or without conditions, or prohibiting the merger.

---

268 See <http://www.ec.europa.eu/comm/competition/mergers/legislation/regulation/regulation 139/>.

269 See <http://www.ec.europa.eu/comm/competition/international/bilateral/bilateral.html>.

270 Agreement between the Government of the United States of America and the Commission of the European Communities regarding the application of their competition laws, 23.9.1991, [1995] OJ L95/47, and Agreement between the European Communities and the Government of the United States of America on the application of positive comity principles in the enforcement of their competition laws, 4.6.1998, [1998] OJL173/28. See also the EU-US Best Practices on cooperation in merger cases, available at <http://www.ec. europa.eu/comm/competition/mergers/others/eu_us.pdf>.

271 Council and Commission Decision of 29 April 1999 concerning the conclusion of the Agreement between the European Communities and the Government of Canada regarding the application of their competition laws [1999] OJ L175/49.

272 http://www.ec.europa.eu/comm/competition/international/bilateral/extracts/jp2a_en.pdf.

Judicial review: Commission decisions can be appealed to the Court of First Instance (CFI) and a judgment of the CFI concerning a Commission merger decision can then be appealed to the European Court of Justice (ECJ).

A synoptic table setting out the full timetable of a merger case from pre-notification to final decision is set out below.

5.412

SYNOPTIC TIMETABLE[273]

Pre-notification	
Initiation of contacts	at least 2 weeks before notification[274]
Submission of Memorandum	at least 2 weeks before notification and at least 3 days before any meeting
Allocation of case team	within 1 week of submission
Discussions with case team	normally one or more meetings
Submission of draft Form CO	allow at least 5 days for comments
Green light given for submission of Form CO	within 5 days of submission

Phase I	
Notification	**Day N**
COM sends copies to Member States	Day N+1-3
Publication in the OJ	Day N+3 (normally)
Usual deadline for submission of 3rd party comments	Day N+13
Phase I State of Play Meeting	Day N+15
Deadline for MS Art 9 request	Day N+16–18
Deadline for Remedies	Day N+20
Deadline for Art 6 decision	**Day N+25**
Extended deadline for Art 6 decision	**Day N+35**

Phase II	
Initiation of Proceedings (Art 6(1)(c) decision)	**Day P**
Post 6.1.c State of Play Meeting	Day P+10
Deadline for unilateral Art 10(3) extension request	Day P+15
Investigation	Day P to ~Day P+30[275]
(also review of key documents and triangular meetings)	
Scrutiny Panel	~[276]Day P+30
Pre-SO State of Play Meeting	~Day P+30
Statement of Objections	~Day P+35

---

[273] This timetable takes the reader through the main steps of a merger proceeding. All days are expressed in 'working days' ('WD'). The Implementing Regulation specifies that deadlines indicated in the Merger Regulation start on the working day following that of the triggering event.

It should be noted that precise calculation of deadlines requires careful consideration of the relevant provisions of the Merger Regulation and Implementing Regulation. A precise calculation following the provisions of the Merger Regulation and Implementing Regulation must be undertaken for each merger case.

See 'Deadlines' below for more information on the calculation of relevant deadlines under the Merger Regulation.

[274] Normally a much longer pre-notification period is required in order to allow sufficient time for any necessary amendments to the draft Form CO.

[275] All following steps may be held up to 20WD later where an Art 10(3) extension has been granted.

[276] The sign is used to denote 'approximately'.

SYNOPTIC TIMETABLE (*cont.*)

Phase II (*cont.*)

Access to the File	~Day P+35–36
Reply to SO	~Day P+45
Oral Hearing	~Day P+50
Post-SO State of Play Meeting	~Day P+50–55
Deadline for Remedies	**Day P+65**
Market Test of Remedies	~Day P+65 to P+70
Pre-AdCom State of Play Meeting	~Day P+70
Advisory Committee Meeting	~Day P+75
Deadline for Art 8 decision	**Day P+90**
Extended (remedies) deadline for Art 8 decision	**Day P+105**
Maximum extended deadline for Art 8 decision (including Art 10(3) extension)	**Day P+125**

---

(2) The Pre-Notification Stage

(a) *Role and Purpose*

5.413 The Best Practices contain useful information as to the role, purpose, and format of pre-notification contacts.[277] The Commission actively encourages parties to engage in pre-notification contacts even in seemingly simple cases.[278]

5.414 In brief, the role and purpose of the pre-notification meeting is:

- for the Commission to provide informal guidance to the parties on technical, jurisdictional and other aspects of the Merger Regulation, eg whether a given case is notifiable or not under the Merger Regulation;
- for the parties to inform the Commission about the background to an intended concentration;
- for the parties and the Commission to discuss the timing of the notification and of the subsequent procedure;
- for the parties and the Commission to discuss the type and quantity of data that will be necessary in the notification; and,
- for the parties to gain some idea as to the likely attitude of the Commission on substantive issues arising from the operation.

(b) *Confidentiality*

5.415 The first thing to be noted in the context of pre-notification discussions and discussions with the Commission in general is that all such discussions take place under strict and legally binding conditions of confidentiality.

5.416 The relevant provision of the EC Treaty, Article 214, requires that officials do not reveal business secrets. Similarly, Article 17(2) of the Merger Regulation forbids officials (and other servants) from disclosing information acquired through the application of the

---

[277] See para 5 of the Best Practices.
[278] ibid.

Merger Regulation. The same applies to officials of national competition authorities who receive information under the Merger Regulation.[279]

As regards pre-notification contacts in particular, the Commission understands that parties **5.417** do not wish news of their operation to become public prior to formal notification to the Commission. The Commission therefore agrees to maintain a high degree of confidentiality until notification takes place.[280] For example in all written correspondence between the parties and the Commission code names may be employed to conceal the identities of the parties. Similarly, code names are used even for internal purposes. However, it is obvious that the case team will have to be aware of the identities of the parties in order to appreciate the nature, scope and potential problems that the operation involves. It must be appreciated that the less the case team knows of the parties to the operation, the less able it will be to provide constructive advice leading to a satisfactory outcome for both the parties and the Commission.

DG Competition takes confidentiality very seriously. It has adopted internal security measures **5.418** and imposes strict obligations on all its officials who have to sign appropriate confidentiality documents. DG Competition has a solid record of maintaining confidential pre-notification contacts. Parties should therefore approach the Commission in full confidence that the information they submit in pre-notification will be treated as strictly confidential.

Following notification, the Commission is bound by strict confidentiality obligations in **5.419** accordance with Article 287 of the EC Treaty, Article 17 of the Merger Regulation and Article 18 of the Implementing Regulation. The Commission will, therefore, throughout its investigation, protect confidential information and business secrets contained in submissions provided by all parties involved in EC merger proceedings. Given the short legal deadlines of EC merger procedures, parties supplying information to the Commission must clearly identify any material which they consider to be confidential, giving reasons, and must provide a separate non-confidential version by the date set by the Commission.[281] The Commission may expressly require a party providing information to identify business secrets in any submission it makes.[282]

The Best Practices encourage parties to clarify as soon as possible any queries related to confidentiality claims with members of the case team.[283] Guidance on what is considered to constitute business secrets or other confidential information is provided in the Commission's Notice on Access to the File. In case of dispute, the Hearing Officer can be involved pursuant to Article 9 of the Hearing Officer Mandate.

(c) *Informal Consultations on Jurisdiction ('Notifiability')*

The complex jurisdictional questions of the Merger Regulation (discussed in Section B: **5.421** Jurisdiction above) may result in uncertainty on the part of the merging parties and their

---

[279] See Art 17(2) of the Merger Regulation.
[280] See para 8 of the Best Practices.
[281] See Art 18(3) of the Implementing Regulation.
[282] ibid.
[283] See paras 37 and 47 of the Best Practices.

advisers as to whether their operation is notifiable under the Merger Regulation. In such cases, where there is genuine uncertainty on the part of the merging parties, the merging parties can approach the Commission and seek informal guidance on technical aspects of the Merger Regulation including in particular the notifiability of a given transaction.[284]

5.422   The parties should approach the Commission by writing to a person responsible within the Merger Control Network, either the DDG for Mergers, the Merger Registry or the Head of the relevant Merger Unit. Sufficient information must be disclosed including the identity of the parties as the MCN is reluctant to give advice on the basis of abstract information.[285] The MCN will be ready to issue an informal 'comfort' letter confirming whether in its view the operation is or is not notifiable under the Merger Regulation. Such letters normally contain disclaimers specifying that the letter expresses the view of the MCN and does not bind the Commission. The CFI has accepted that such a disclaimer is sufficient in order to avoid the Commission being formally bound by the MCN's views.[286]

(d) Informal Consultations on Referrals

5.423   Pre-notification contacts are also the appropriate forum for discussions concerning the possibility of pre-notification referrals under Articles 4(4) and 4(5) of the Merger Regulation. The Best Practices expressly invite parties to contact the Commission services on an informal basis and highlight DG Competition's readiness to discuss with notifying parties informally the possibility of such pre-notification referrals and to guide them through the pre-notification referral process.[287]

(e) International Dimension

5.424   Many merger cases falling within the scope of the Merger Regulation will also fall to be notified in jurisdictions outside the EU, notably the United States. In such cases, pre-notification contacts will be useful to discuss the timing of the case with a view to enhancing the efficiency of the respective investigations, reducing burdens on the merging parties and third parties, and increasing the overall transparency of the merger review process.

5.425   In cases where co-operation with the United States authorities takes place, the parties should have regard to the bilateral agreements regulating co-operation between the United States authorities and the Commission in the field of competition as well as to the EU-US Best Practices on co-operation in merger proceedings.[288] DG Competition normally asks the parties to produce waivers, even at pre-notification, so that it can begin exchanging information

---

[284] See para 24 of the Best Practices.

[285] ibid, para 25.

[286] See Case C-170/02 P *Schlusselverlag JS Moser and others v Commission* [2003] ECR I-9889 and Case T-3/02 *Schlusselverlag JS Moser and others v Commission* [2002] ECR II-1473.

[287] See Best Practices, n 10.

[288] Agreement between the Government of the United States of America and the Commission of the European Communities regarding the application of their competition laws, 23.9.1991, [1995] OJ L95/47, and Agreement between the European Communities and the Government of the United States of America on the application of positive comity principles in the enforcement of their competition laws, 4.6.1998, [1998] OJ L173/28. See also the EU-US Best Practices on cooperation in merger cases, available at <http://www.ec. europa.eu/comm/competition/mergers/others/eu_us.pdf>.

and discussing immediately the prospective merger case with its US counterparts.[289] While there is no obligation on the parties to produce such waivers, it may be in their interests to do so. Careful consideration of the international aspects of a transaction at this stage is therefore necessary.

DG Competition is an active participant in the International Competition Network (ICN), **5.426** which has produced a model form or forms for use by merging parties and competition agencies governing waivers of confidentiality protection for materials submitted in connection with merger review.[290]

(f) Discussions on the Content and Timing of a Notification of a Case and Substantive Issues

The most important aspect of pre-notification discussions will concern the content and tim- **5.427** ing of a notification of a merger case as well as preliminary discussions on the substantive merits of the case.

The pre-notification contacts will be initiated by the merging parties by submitting a mem- **5.428** orandum informing the Commission of the merger and providing sufficient information so that DG Competition can allocate a suitable case team taking into account the sector concerned and linguistic requirements.[291]

Once the case team has been allocated, discussions and meetings with DG Competition **5.429** will follow on the content of the notification, timing issues and a preliminary indication of substantive issues that may be raised by the case. The Best Practices set out in detail when and how the parties should contact DG Competition to discuss such issues.[292]

It is important to bear in mind that, given the time constrains, once formal notification has **5.430** taken place, the pre-notification phase is of particular importance. It provides a valuable opportunity to clarify issues from the very beginning of the process, to familiarise the case team with the case and to set the stage for an efficient and productive procedure following formal notification. All issues should be discussed in a co-operative manner with full disclosure of all relevant facts. Parties are encouraged to submit as much information and documentation as possible even at the pre-notification stage and to raise issues such as efficiencies if relevant.[293]

The investigation with third parties will normally not commence at the pre-notification **5.431** stage. However, in cases where the parties, for example because of special timing constraints, wish the Commission to launch its investigation before the formal notification, this can also be discussed with the case team. If the parties provide valid reasons for wanting to proceed in such a manner and provided there are no reasons to assume that this would hinder an effective investigation, the Commission may agree to such a procedure.

---

[289] See para 25 of the Best Practices. For a model waiver form see <http://www.ec.europa.eu/ comm/ competition/mergers/others/npwaivers.pdf>.

[290] <http://www.internationalcompetitionnetwork.org/notification.html>.

[291] For this purpose, the initial memorandum should specify the language in which the parties intend to notify their merger case.

[292] See paras 10–23 of the Best Practices.

[293] See paras 16–18 of the Best Practices.

(g) Draft Form CO and Completeness of Notification—Waivers

5.432 The pre-notification stage helps the parties to prepare their notification adequately so as to ensure that the Commission will accept their notification as being complete in all material respects. This is extremely important because only a complete notification can trigger the formal start of the procedure (see Section (3) Notification below).

5.433 The Best Practices specify that parties ought to submit a complete draft of the notification for discussion with DG Competition before filing formally.[294] Experience shows that notifications that have not been preceded by any pre-notification contacts should be avoided to the greatest extent possible as pre-notification contacts are invaluable in ensuring that any final notification will contain the requisite information and thus avoid declarations of incompleteness.[295] DG Competition will endeavour to review draft notifications within five working days and will confirm whether it considers a draft notification adequate and will provide comments where necessary.

5.434 Article 4(2) of the Implementing Regulation permits the Commission to dispense with the obligation on the parties to provide any information or documents required by the notification form where the Commission considers that such information or documents are not necessary for the examination of the case. The Implementing Regulation does not require that the parties formally request a waiver from submitting data; nor does it require the Commission to respond formally to such a request.

5.435 A waiver may also be sought from any requirement contained in Form RS, where the parties feel that certain information is not relevant to assess their request for a pre-notification referral. The Commission will generally adopt a particularly cautious attitude towards such requests, given that this form provides the basis for the assessment to be made, not only by the Commission, but more importantly by the Member States concerned. Consequently careful note should be taken at pre-notification meetings to ensure that both the parties and the Commission agree as to the exact extent and nature of any requested waiver. In the context of a Form RS, it may well be appropriate for the parties to discuss issues of sought waivers with the Member States concerned as well.

5.436 The pre-notification stage should also be used to discuss with DG Competition whether the case should benefit from the simplified procedure and whether a short-form notification in accordance with Article 3(1) of the Implementing Regulation could be used (see Section (3) (c) (ii) Notification below).

(3) Notification

(a) The Obligation to Notify—Who Must Notify—Article 4(1)

5.437 The Merger Regulation sets out a preventive, *ex ante* system of merger control with mandatory notifications. Article 4(1) of the Merger Regulation provides that all concentrations with Community dimension, including those referred to the Commission under Article 4(5), must be notified to the Commission before their implementation.

---

[294] ibid, para 15.
[295] ibid, para 7.

Article 4(2) specifies that the obligation to notify rests with the parties acquiring control **5.438** over the target company.[296] In cases of a legal merger, both merging parties will be obliged to notify jointly. The same is also true for joint ventures (acquisitions of joint control): all parties acquiring joint control must notify jointly.[297] In cases of straightforward acquisitions, only the acquirer is obliged to notify. The seller or target company has no obligation to notify even though its assistance will be required in order to provide information necessary for the examination of the case.

(b) *When to Notify—Triggering Event and Deadline*

The Merger Regulation allows the notifying parties significant flexibility as to the timing **5.439** of their notification. While notification is mandatory, there is no deadline by which the parties must notify their operation as long as they do not implement it. According to Article 4(1) notification can be made at any time prior to implementation of the merger and following the conclusion of the agreement giving rise to the concentration, or the announcement of a public bid or the acquisition of a controlling interest.

Article 4(1), second sub-paragraph, also permits 'early notifications'. Thus, the parties may **5.440** decide to notify an intended concentration even before the conclusion of a legally binding agreement, announcement of a public bid or acquisition of a controlling interest. The Commission will accept such early notifications where the parties can demonstrate a good faith intention to proceed with the intended concentration. Recital 34 of the Merger Regulation explains that the parties ought to satisfy the Commission that they intend to enter into an agreement which will give rise to a concentration with Community dimension and that their plan for the proposed concentration is sufficiently concrete. A signed memorandum of understanding, heads of terms or letter of intent signed by the undertakings concerned could suffice to satisfy the Commission of the parties' good faith intent. In cases of public bids, an announcement of the intention to make the bid could also suffice. The parties should have sufficiently concrete plans so that their concentration can be identified precisely (who will buy what) and Form CO can be filled in correctly and accurately.

(c) *Notification Forms—Form CO, Short Form CO (Simplified Procedure)*

Notification must be made on specified forms which are annexed to the Implementing **5.441** Regulation. There are two such forms: Form CO and Short Form CO.

(i) **Form CO**   Form CO is the standard form for notifications of merger cases under the **5.442** Merger Regulation. It constitutes Annex I to the Implementing Regulation. Form CO

---

[296] See also Art 2 of the Implementing Regulation and section 2 of Form CO.

[297] Art 2(3) of the Implementing Regulation specifies that joint notifications should be submitted by a joint representative who is authorised to transmit and to receive documents on behalf of all notifying parties. Whilst the provision and section 2.3 of Form CO appear to imply that the jointly notifying parties should appoint a single representative, it is submitted that it would be unreasonable if this provision were taken to mean that the parties acquiring joint control and thus notifying jointly are obliged to instruct one and the same legal representative. It is therefore submitted that each party acquiring joint control could instruct its own legal representative and fill in the details of such representative in sections 2.3 Form CO. Nonetheless, the MCN may insist that one single representative be appointed for the purposes of correspondence with the Registry. The details of this joint representative should be filled in section 2.3.4 of Form CO.

specifies the information that the notifying parties need to complete when notifying a merger case to the Commission. Form CO requires a large amount of up-front information in order to enable the Commission to examine the case within the short deadlines imposed by the Merger Regulation, providing the Commission with the information required to carry out the necessary investigation, to assess the impact of the concentration on the markets concerned and to produce a duly motivated decision at the end of phase I. It is a document which requires significant input by the parties, and their legal and economic advisers.

5.443   Form CO requires *inter alia* the following key information:

- Section 1: description of the concentration including an executive summary.
- Section 2: background information as to the parties and their legal representatives.
- Section 3: details of the concentration (legal agreements, structure of the deal, value of the deal) and information on the parties' turnover.
- Section 4: details on the ownership and control of the undertakings involved in the concentration including personal and financial links and previous acquisitions of the parties.
- Section 5: supporting documentation including copies of the documents creating the concentration (agreements, bid documents), annual accounts, and the so-called section 5.4 documents, ie copies of all relevant analyses, reports, studies, surveys etc. assessing or analysing the concentration and market conditions.
- Section 6: market definition of all markets affected by the concentration. This is an important section where the parties must identify which product and geographic markets are affected by the concentration.
- Section 7 and section 8: detailed information on the identified affected markets including market shares of the parties and their competitors, HHI calculation, information (including contact details) on competitors, customers and suppliers, barriers to entry, structure of demand and supply, research and development and relevant IP rights.
- Section 9: overall context of the concentration and efficiency claims.

5.444   **(ii) Short Form CO and Simplified Procedure**   Article 3(1) of the Implementing Regulation permits the submission of a short form notification where cases meet the conditions specified in the Short Form CO which is annexed to the Implementing Regulation. These are cases which are unlikely to raise competition concerns. The following three main categories are identified in Short Form CO:

(a) Joint ventures with no, or negligible, actual or foreseen activities within the territory of the EEA, ie where (a) the turnover of the joint venture and/or the turnover of the contributed activities is less than EUR 100 million in the EEA territory; and (b) the total value of the assets transferred to the joint venture is less than EUR 100 million in the EEA territory.

(b) Cases with no affected markets: either the parties are not engaged in business activities in the same product or geographic markets or related upstream or downstream markets (no horizontal or vertical relationships at all) or where the parties engage in such activities but have a combined market share of less than 15 per cent in horizontal relationships or less than 25 per cent in vertical relationships.

(c) Cases where a party is to acquire sole control of an undertaking over which it already has joint control.

The Commission retains discretion to request a full form notification where it appears **5.445** either that the conditions for using the Short Form are not met, or, exceptionally, where they are met, the Commission determines, nonetheless, that a notification under Form CO is necessary for an adequate investigation of possible competition concerns. Short Form CO sets out exhaustively the situations where this might occur.[298]

Information to be provided on Short Form CO is significantly less than that required by **5.446** the full form notification. In particular, the information required on the relevant reportable markets is substantially less burdensome. There is also no requirement to produce the so-called section 5.4 documents.

Cases notified on Short Form CO will normally also benefit from a simplified procedure. **5.447** The simplified procedure was first introduced in July 2000 through the issuing of a Commission Notice.[299] The Notice was revised in 2004.[300] The conditions under which a case may benefit from the simplified procedure are identical to those specified in the Short Form CO. However, even where the parties have submitted a full notification they can still benefit from the simplified procedure if the relevant conditions are met.

The Commission reserves the right to use the full procedure in circumstances where this is **5.448** deemed appropriate. These circumstances are set out in points 6–12 of the Simplified Procedure Notice. The Commission can revert to a normal procedure where, for example, it is difficult to define the relevant product and geographic markets or to determine the parties' market shares, where the parties are active in closely related neighbouring markets, where there are high barriers to entry or the market is highly concentrated or the markets are new, where there are issues of coordination within the meaning of Article 2(4) of the Merger Regulation or in certain circumstances where changes from joint to sole control may give rise to competition concerns.[301]

Where the simplified procedure is used, the Commission will not launch an investigation. **5.449** It will publish the fact of the notification in the Official Journal with an indication that the case is a candidate for the simplified procedure and will invite comments. If no comments are submitted, the Commission will adopt a short form decision authorising the merger as soon as possible after the 15 working day deadline for Member States to request a referral of the case pursuant to Article 9. On the other hand, should the publication in the Official Journal lead to substantial comments being addressed to the Commission, it would normally revert to a normal procedure. If the simplified procedure is followed through to the end, the short-form decision will contain the information about the notified concentration

---

[298] See Short Form CO, point 1.2.

[299] [2000] OJ C217/32.

[300] Commission Notice on a simplified procedure for treatment of certain concentrations under Council Regulation (EC) 139/2004 [2005] OJ C56/04. The Notice can be found at <http://www.ec.europa.eu/comm/competition/mergers/legislation/regulation/>.

[301] For instance, where a former joint venture is integrated into the group or network of its remaining single controlling shareholder, whereby the disciplining constraints exercised by the potentially diverging incentives of the different controlling shareholders are removed and as a result its strategic market position is significantly strengthened. See eg *KLM/Martinair* (Case COMP/M.1328 [1999]) Art 6(1)(C) decision of 01.02.1999.

published in the Official Journal at the time of notification (names of the parties, their country of origin, nature of the concentration and economic sectors concerned) and a statement in the decision that the concentration is declared compatible with the common market because it falls within one or more of the categories described in the Notice on simplified procedure, with the applicable category(ies) being explicitly identified.[302]

(d) Submitting the Notification—Formalities—The Merger Registry

5.450 The Implementing Regulation, Form CO, and Short Form CO set out the formal requirements which must be met by notifications.

5.451 Notifications must be in one of the official languages of the EU or in the language of an EFTA State; in this case, a translation into an official EU language is also required. Supporting documents are to be submitted in their original language; where this is not an official language of the Community, they must be translated into the language of the proceedings (Article 3(4) of the Implementing Regulation).[303]

5.452 It is important to follow closely the format of Form CO or Short Form CO and to fill in all the relevant sections. Annexes can be provided but the information required by the Form must be found in its main body. In order to facilitate and expedite the process, contact details for competitors, customers and suppliers must be provided in a format specified by DG Competition. The parties should contact the case team or the case team secretary for details of the appropriate electronic format.

5.453 One original and 35 copies of the forms and all supporting documents must be provided.[304] This requirement is to ensure distribution of the form to national authorities and relevant internal Commission departments.

5.454 Notifications must be signed by those submitting them; where they are signed by representatives of persons or of undertakings, such representatives must produce written proof that they are authorised to act.[305]

5.455 The notification and copies must be delivered to the Merger Registry at the time and address specified from time to time on DG Competition's web site in accordance with Articles 3(2) and 23(1) of the Implementing Regulation and according to the security procedure specified on DG Competition's web site.[306]

(e) Effective Date of Notification—Completeness of Notification

5.456 Submission of notification is an extremely important step in the Merger Regulation procedure. It is this event that triggers the relevant binding deadlines under the Merger Regulation.[307]

---

[302] For an example, see *Allianz/Four Seasons* (Case COMP/M.3523 [2004]) OJ C184/3.

[303] The overwhelming majority of merger notifications are submitted in English. A much smaller percentage is submitted in French and German followed by very limited percentages in other official languages.

[304] Art 3(2) of the Implementing Regulation. See also a recent Communication in [2006] OJ C251/2 on the format for delivery of notifications.

[305] ibid, Art 2(2).

[306] See Communication pursuant to Art 23(1) of Commission Regulation (EC) 802/2004 implementing Council Regulation (EC) 139/2004 on the control of concentrations between undertakings [2004] OJ C139/2. See also <http://www.ec.europa.eu/comm/competition/mergers/others/>.

[307] See Art 10 of the Merger Regulation.

In view of the legal consequences of submission, the Implementing Regulation (Article 5) specifies precisely when a notification becomes effective for the purposes of the Merger Regulation. The effective date is the date on which the Commission receives a notification which is complete in all material respects.

What is meant by 'material completeness' is not clarified. Article 5(4) of the Implementing **5.457** Regulation specifies that incorrect information will be considered incomplete information. The definition of 'material incompleteness' is naturally subjective but the concept is unlikely to be invoked if the notifying parties have made their best efforts to answer fully all questions contained in the notification form or have agreed any sought waivers with the case-team. DG Competition has emphasised that the notifying parties should take special care to provide the appropriate contact details for customers, suppliers and competitors. If such information is not correct or not provided in full it will significantly delay the investigation and therefore may lead to a declaration of incompleteness.[308]

Article 5(2) of the Implementing Regulation gives the Commission the power to declare a **5.458** submitted notification incomplete. The Commission must inform the parties in writing without delay and fix an appropriate time limit for submission of the complete information. Only where that information has been submitted can the notification be considered complete thus triggering the relevant deadlines of the Merger Regulation (Article 10(1) of the Merger Regulation and 5(2) of the Implementing Regulation). In addition, pursuant to Article 5(3) of the Implementing Regulation, if after the submission of a complete notification, there are material changes in the facts, the parties must communicate them to the Commission without delay. Where such facts significantly affect the assessment of the case, the Commission may declare the notification complete as from the date when the full facts have been disclosed. The Commission must always inform the parties in writing. The Commission must also publish the effective date of notification (and any changes thereto) in the Official Journal pursuant to Article 5(5) of the Implementing Regulation.

In practice, the procedure upon submission of notification to the Merger Registry is as fol- **5.459** lows. Upon receiving the notification the Merger Registry will issue a receipt. In the event that DG Competition discovers omissions in the Form CO after formal notification, the notifying parties may be given an opportunity to rectify such omissions urgently before a declaration of incompleteness is adopted; due to the time constraints in merger procedures, the time allowed for such rectification is normally limited to one or two days but this opportunity will not be granted in cases where DG Competition finds that the omissions immediately hinder the proper investigation of the proposed transaction.[309] However, should the notification then be found to be incomplete in a material respect by the Merger Registry or the case team, the Commission will inform the notifying parties, in writing, without delay and will set a deadline for the submission of the missing information. This declaration prevents the relevant deadlines from being triggered. Upon receipt of the

---

[308] See para 20 of the Best Practices.
[309] See para 23 of the Best Practices.

missing information, a further letter will be issued acknowledging receipt of the missing information, stating that the notification is complete and giving the effective date on which the data has been received and the deadlines start running.

5.460 In order to be as sure as possible that a declaration of incompleteness is avoided, the notifying parties should discuss notification requirements with the Commission services at a pre-notification meeting and obtain appropriate waivers for the submission of specific data (see Section (2) The Pre-Notification Stage above).

(f) Incorrect Information in the Notification—Fines

5.461 Notification forms are legally binding documents and there are significant penalties and consequences for the provision of incorrect information.

5.462 Under Article 14(1)(a) of the Merger Regulation, notifying parties who, either intentionally or negligently, supply incorrect or misleading information, may be liable to fines of up to 1 per cent of the aggregate turnover of the undertaking concerned. In addition, pursuant to Article 6(3)(a) and Article 8(6)(a) of the Merger Regulation, the Commission may revoke its decision on the compatibility of a notified concentration where it is based on incorrect information for which one of the undertakings is responsible.

(g) Withdrawal of Notification

5.463 The submission of a notification is a formal act with significant legal consequences. It puts in motion the administrative system for the assessment of a merger case under the Merger Regulation. Consequently, notifying parties may not withdraw notifications at will without *any* consequences. If this were permitted, notifying parties could trigger the relevant deadlines again and again by submitting, withdrawing and re-submitting notifications. As a result, provided that the agreement is still in place, withdrawal of a notification does not deprive the Commission of jurisdiction over a concentration with Community dimension.[310]

5.464 However, in the absence of a notification, the Commission is not bound by the deadlines specified in Article 10(1) of the Merger Regulation which speaks only of 'notified' concentrations.

5.465 In the *MCI v Commission* judgment,[311] the CFI confirmed that, under the old Merger Regulation, a withdrawal did not as such suffice to deprive the Commission of its competence. However, in that case, according to the CFI, the parties had shown that their concentration, 'in the form presented in the notification', had actually been abandoned. In such circumstances, the Commission could not adopt a decision, since the concentration no longer existed in the form dealt with by the Commission. That withdrawal together with the abandonment therefore deprived the Commission of its competence, and the CFI

---

[310] The power of the Commission to adopt decisions even in the absence of a notification was expressly confirmed in the judgment of the CFI in T-310/00 *MCI v Commission*, judgment of 28.9.2004, [2004] ECR-II 3253 (paras 93–96).

[311] Case T-310/00 *MCI v Commission* judgment of 28.9.2004, [2004] ECR II-3253.

therefore annulled the Commission's decision.[312] In addition, the CFI held that the Commission had infringed the legitimate expectation of the parties by departing from previous administrative practice which, according to the CFI, consisted in accepting withdrawals even in the absence of a real abandonment.[313]

The new Merger Regulation, which did not apply in the *MCI* case but was adopted before **5.466** the CFI delivered its judgment in *MCI*, clarifies matters to a certain extent. Article 6(1)(c) of the Merger Regulation makes clear that, where the Commission has initiated proceedings, the proceedings must close with a final decision unless the parties demonstrate 'to the satisfaction of the Commission that they have abandoned the concentration'. In such a case, the Commission can therefore simply close the file without adopting any decision. This provision does not apply prior to the initiation of proceedings, ie in Phase I.

DG Competition has issued an Information Note on abandonment of concentrations pursuant to Article 6(1)(c) of the Merger Regulation.[314] According to the Information Note, in order for the parties to demonstrate to the satisfaction of the Commission that a concentration has indeed been abandoned, a mere withdrawal of the notification does not suffice. On the contrary, the requirements for the proof of the abandonment must correspond in terms of legal form, format, intensity, etc to the initial act that was considered sufficient to make the concentration notifiable. Thus, a binding agreement bringing about the concentration must be cancelled, a good faith intention to conclude an agreement must be reversed through adequate documentation to this effect, an announcement of a public bid or intention to launch a public bid must be reversed and the bidding process stop and, in cases of implemented concentrations, the situation prevailing before implementation must be re-established.

As a practical matter of administrative practice, it is to be noted that the Commission has **5.468** no interest in pursuing investigations unnecessarily. As a result, in Phase I, where the above considerations imposed by Article 6(1)(c) do not apply, the Commission is therefore normally unlikely to want to continue its investigation of a merger case where the parties withdraw their notification, demonstrate their intention to re-notify and do not take any steps to implement the operation in the meantime.[315]

In any case, it is generally prudent for parties wishing to withdraw their notification to seek **5.469** and receive specific confirmation by the Commission as to the consequences of such action.

---

[312] It should be noted that the CFI's ruling in *MCI v Commission* that an abandonment of plans to implement the merger 'in the form presented in the notification' equated to an abandonment of the merger agreement itself may be criticised for not allowing the Commission a reasonable margin of discretion insofar as it was not clear whether the agreement in question had indeed been rescinded by the parties (see points 84–87 of the judgment; point 20 of the judgment reveals that the actual abandonment of merger plans followed only on 13 July 2004, after the Commission's decision, in view of opposition by the US authorities).

[313] See paras 108–113 of the judgment in case T-310/00 *MCI v Commission*.

[314] DG Competition Information Note on Art.6(1)(c) 2nd sentence of Regulation 139/2004 (abandonment of concentrations), available at: <http://www.ec.europa.eu/comm/competition/mergers/legislation/abandonment_of_concentrations_en.pdf>.

[315] The Commission normally announces the fact that a notification has been withdrawn in the Official Journal. See eg *ONO/Hidrocantábrico/Retecal* (Case COMP/M.3364 [2004]) OJ C46/26.

(h) Suspensory Effect—Article 7

5.470 The requirement of Article 4(1) for mandatory notification of all concentrations with Community dimension goes hand in hand with the requirement of Article 7(1) that such concentrations should not be implemented without being notified and prior to an express or deemed authorisation by the Commission (either an authorisation decision under Articles 6 or 8 or a deemed authorisation pursuant to Article 10(6) for inaction during the relevant deadlines).

5.471 Thus, Article 7(1) establishes a 'suspensory effect' or 'bar on closing' until express or deemed authorisation. The parties are not permitted to close the deal or take any steps that can be deemed to be implementation of the operation without notifying and before authorisation by the Commission unless they benefit from a derogation pursuant to Article 7(2) or 7(3).

5.472 What can be considered as 'implementing' the concentration is not clarified in the provision and there is no case law specifically on this point. The main reason for this is that most discussions about whether specific actions would fall under the suspensory effect tend to take place informally between the parties and the Commission. The following guidance can be given. First, it should be noted that the suspensory effect covers both full and partial implementation. While it may be difficult to establish a rule that is easily applicable to all possible scenarios, the limit is generally that each party can take legitimate commercial steps to prepare its own businesses for the change of control. Joint planning between the merging parties for actions to be taken upon closing may be permissible. However, steps that involve coordination of the businesses to be merged or the new entity anticipating amendments to existing contracts with third parties would go too far.[316]

5.473 It follows that closing the deal by transferring legal title of the target undertaking to the acquirer is clearly implementation of the concentration. The same goes for any exercise of control over the target undertaking. Other practices may fall into a grey zone.

5.474 Consultation with the Commission is advisable as well as the seeking of express authorisation, if necessary, in order to avoid the serious consequences that unauthorised implementation entails.

5.475 **(i) Consequences of Unauthorised Implementation**   The consequences of unauthorised implementation of a merger are serious. First, Article 7(5) specifies that transactions in breach of Article 7(1) are dependent on a subsequent authorisation decision. If no authorisation is granted the transactions are invalid.[317] Second, the Commission can impose substantial fines of up to 10 per cent of the aggregate annual turnover of the undertakings concerned (Article 14(2)(a) and (b) of the Merger Regulation). Third, the Commission can take interim measures to safeguard effective competition under Article 8(5)(a) of the Merger Regulation and can take measures to dissolve the concentration following the procedure of

---

[316] These issues are also known, in the United States, as 'gun jumping'.

[317] Art 7(5), second sub-para, however, specifies that Art 7(5) has no effect on the validity of transactions in securities including those convertible into other securities admitted to trading on a market such as a stock exchange, unless the buyer and seller knew or ought to have known that the transaction was carried out in contravention of Art 7(1).

Article 8(4) of the Merger Regulation. Articles 8(4) and 8(5) are discussed in greater detail in Section 6(b)'Dissolution Orders and Interim Orders-Articles 8(4)–8(5)' below.

(ii) Derogation for Public Bids and Stock Exchange Transactions—Article 7(2)   Article 7(2) **5.476** permits the implementation of public bids and other stock exchange transactions even before an authorisation decision is granted or even before notification provided that certain conditions are met. First, the transaction must be a public bid or a transaction in securities trading on a stock exchange. Second, the merger must be notified without delay to the Commission pursuant to Article 4. Third, the acquirer must not exercise the voting rights attached to the securities in question or, if it does, it does so only to maintain the full value of its investments based on an ad hoc derogation granted by the Commission under Article 7(3).[318]

(iii) Ad hoc Derogations—Article 7(3)   Article 7(3) allows the Commission to grant ad **5.477** hoc derogations from the suspensory obligation of Article 7(1) upon a reasoned request by the parties. The parties can apply for a derogation at any time even prior to notification. In deciding on the request, the Commission takes into account *inter alia* the effects of the suspension on one or more undertakings concerned in the concentration or on a third party and the threat to competition posed by the concentration. Such derogation may be made subject to conditions and obligations in order to ensure conditions of effective competition. Provided the parties can show that there is a real commercial interest in closing the deal early in order to avoid negative effects on them or third parties and that the transaction poses no effects on competition, the Commission would normally not be reluctant to grant an ad hoc derogation. This will be the case especially in concentrations benefiting from the simplified procedure where no competition concerns are raised.[319] Nonetheless, derogations remain exceptional and the Commission does not appear willing to grant them as a matter of course.

The procedure for the granting of derogations under Article 7(3) is not entirely straightfor- **5.478** ward. No specific form is required for the parties to make their request. There are also no deadlines. The Commission will examine the request and will then adopt a decision which takes the form of a reasoned letter addressed to the parties. In cases of favourable unconditional acceptance of the request the matter can be resolved quickly and the decision can be short form. In cases of rejection of the request or acceptance with conditions, the decision is longer and the requesting parties and, possibly, third parties have the right to be heard (Article 18(1) of the Merger Regulation). The Commission must inform them of its objections and fix a time limit within which they can make known their views (Article 18(1) of the Merger Regulation and Article 12(1) of the Implementing Regulation). It can also adopt a provisional decision pursuant to Article 18(2) of the Merger Regulation and allow the parties to be heard afterwards. In this situation, the decision will become final only after the parties have been heard (Article 12(2) of the Implementing Regulation).

---

[318] For a case implemented under the equivalent provision of Regulation 4064/89 where such ad hoc derogations to permit exercise of voting rights attached to shares purchased pursuant to Art 7(2), see *Tetra Laval/Sidel* (Case COMP/M.2416 [2003]).

[319] The Commission has indicated its willingness to grant derogations in such cases in the Explanatory Memorandum accompanying its legislative proposal for the Merger Regulation COM(2002) 711 final [2003] OJ C20/4, points 67–68.

(4) Phase I

5.479   The overwhelming majority of notified merger cases will only need to go through a short examination period leading to a decision pursuant to Article 6 of the Merger Regulation.[320] This is the so-called Phase I of the merger procedure. Apart from cases benefiting from the much simpler simplified procedure (which has been analysed in Section (3) Notification above), Phase I cases will invariably follow the procedure outlined in this section.

(a) Publication in the Official Journal

5.480   Once the Commission has received a complete notification it will first of all announce in the Official Journal the fact that the notification has been received. Pursuant to Article 4(3) of the Merger Regulation, the Commission will indicate the names of the undertakings concerned, their country of origin, the nature of the concentration and the economic sectors involved, taking account of the legitimate interest of undertakings in the protection of their business secrets.

(b) Deadlines and Timetable

5.481   All deadlines under the Merger Regulation are calculated in 'working days'.[321] Article 24 of the Implementing Regulation specifies that a working day for the purposes of the Merger Regulation is any day other than Saturdays, Sundays, and Commission holidays as published in the Official Journal of the European Union before the beginning of each year.[322] Articles 7 and 8 of the Implementing Regulation explain that all relevant time periods start on the working day following a specified event and end on the last working day of the relevant period.

5.482   According to Article 10(1), the Commission has 25 working days to complete its investigation and adopt a decision pursuant to Article 6 of the Merger Regulation either putting an end to the procedure or opening an in-depth investigation (the so-called Phase II proceedings). The clock for the 25 working day deadline starts ticking on the first working day following that on which the Commission receives a complete notification.[323]

5.483   The deadline for the adoption of an Article 6 decision is strict and legally binding. Pursuant to Article 10(6), if the Commission fails to adopt a decision within this deadline, the concentration is deemed to be authorised.

5.484   The Phase I deadline is automatically extended to 35 working days where the parties submit commitments or where a Member State makes a referral request pursuant to Article 9.[324] The deadline for the parties to submit commitments is within not more than 20 working days from the date of the notification in accordance with Article 19(1) of the

---

[320]   In 2003, of a total of 222 decisions adopted under the Merger Regulation, 214 were adopted at the end of Phase I.

[321]   This is a procedural improvement compared to the regime of Regulation 4064/89 which involved more complex calculations on the basis of a system of calendar months, weeks and recovery of holidays.

[322]   For example, for 2004, see [2003] OJ C284/10. A link should normally be available on DG Competition's web site's at http://www.ec.europa.eu/comm/competition/mergers/legislation/holidays.htm>.

[323]   Art 10(1) of the Merger Regulation.

[324]   ibid, Art 10(1), second sub-para.

Implementing Regulation. The deadline for a Member State to make an Article 9 referral request is 15 working days from the date of receipt of a copy of the notification in accordance with Article 9(2) of the Merger Regulation.

It is also to be noted that in appropriate cases, ie those requiring careful scrutiny of their **5.485** impact on competition, a State of Play meeting is normally held no later than 15 working days into Phase I.[325] These issues are discussed in greater detail below.

Example:

Notification (Day N)	18.6.2004 (Friday)
(assume notification complete)	
Start of 25WD period	21.6.2004 (Monday)
(WD following complete notification)	
State of Play Meeting	before 9.7.2004
(Before Day N+15WD)	
Deadline for Submission of Remedies	16.7.2004
(Day N+20WD)	
Normal Deadline for Article 6 Decision	26.7.2004
(Day N+25 WD)	
(NB: 21.7.2004 is an official holiday and should	
not be counted)	
Extended Deadline for Article 6 Decision	9.8.2004
(Day N+35WD)	

(c) *The Phase I Investigation*

During Phase I, the Commission will investigate the case by examining the notification, ver- **5.486** ifying facts and performing a market investigation by contacting competitors, customers and suppliers of the merging parties as weil as other interested parties. The Commission also has the power to inspect business premises. These powers are analysed here.

It is to be noted that any information gathered by the Commission under the Merger **5.487** Regulation is subject to strict confidentiality provisions. The information can only be used for the purposes of the merger investigation in question and the Commission, its officials and national authorities cannot disclose information which is covered by the obligation on professional secrecy.[326]

(i) Information Gathering—Article 11 Written Requests The powers of the Commission **5.488** to request information are contained in Article 11 of the Merger Regulation. The Commission has the power to request written information from undertakings and associations of undertakings, persons controlling undertakings within the meaning of Article 3(1)(b)[327] and Member State authorities.[328] The main addressees of such requests during an investigation are the merging parties, their customers, suppliers and competitors.[329]

---

[325] See para 33(a) of the Best Practices.
[326] Subject to the possibility of limited disclosures for the purposes of publications and hearings under Arts 4(3), 18 and 20 of the Merger Regulation. See also Art 17(2) of the Merger Regulation.
[327] ibid, Art 11(1).
[328] ibid, Art 11(6).
[329] See paras 26–28 of the Best Practices.

5.489 The Commission has two ways whereby it can request information in writing. It can either send a so-called simple request (also known as an Article 11 letter) or request information by decision.[330] Normally the Commission will follow a two-stage process by sending first a simple request followed by a request by decision only where the recipient fails to respond or to supply certain requested information. However, Article 11(3) permits the Commission to proceed by way of decision straight away. This may be the case where the information is essential for the investigation and the two-stage approach would waste precious time for the Commission's investigation.

5.490 The request for information must set out the legal basis for and purpose of the request; identify the information required; set out the penalties that may levied if the information provided is incorrect or misleading and specify the date for a response. Should the requested information not be provided within the stated time period or if only an incomplete response is given, the Commission may, by way of a decision, require that the information be provided pursuant to Article 11(3). Should this decision be ignored the Commission may impose fines on the non-compliant undertaking by virtue of Articles 14 and 15 of the Merger Regulation (see Section (v) on 'Penalties' below).

5.491 In practice, requests for information take the form of a letter signed by senior DG Competition management (at the level of at least a Head of Unit). They contain the legal requirements set out above as well as contact details of members of the case team responsible for assessing the case. The questions are normally attached in an annex. If a question is unclear or should a company require more time in which to respond, the case team should be contacted as soon as possible. Explanations can then be given and, more than likely, the deadline for a response extended by a short period of time.[331] The language regime of requests for information is also of importance. The detailed questionnaires attached to an Article 11 request are normally drafted in the language of the case and not necessarily the language of the recipient as, despite best efforts, it is not always possible for DG competition to have the questionnaires translated into the recipient's language in good time for the investigation. Recipients may approach the case team to seek clarifications if the language used is not one with which they are familiar and request translations should they be unable to understand the language in question.

5.492 It is to be noted that Member States where the recipient is located or whose territory is affected receive copies of Article 11 decisions (Article 11(5)). They can also receive copies of all simple Article 11 requests upon express request (Article 11(5) of the Merger Regulation).

5.493 **(ii) Non-submission of Information or Incomplete Information—Article 10(5) Suspension of Deadline**   Fines are not the only consequence for refusing to submit complete information to the Commission. Since it is important for the Commission to receive accurate and timely information in order to assess the case within the deadlines imposed by

---

[330] Art 11(1) of the Merger Regulation.
[331] As will be appreciated, the deadline given for a response may often appear short. However it must be understood that the case team only has approximately one month in which to reach a conclusion on a notified operation: two-thirds of this time will comprise the actual investigation.

the Merger Regulation, Article 10(5) provides for the suspension of the relevant Phase I or Phase II deadlines where, owing to circumstances for which one of the undertakings involved in the concentration is responsible, the Commission has had to request information by decision pursuant to Article 11 or to order an inspection by decision pursuant to Article 13. Article 9 of the Implementing Regulation specifies that, in such cases, the time limits are suspended from the working day following the expiry of the time limit fixed for response in the original Article 11 request (or in the Article 11 decision where only a decision was issued) until the submission of the full and complete information requested.[332]

The CFI has acknowledged the importance of the receipt of complete information by the Commission for the purposes of its investigation and has accepted that the Commission has wide discretion to request information it deems necessary, imposing very short deadlines, and to stop the clock where this information is not submitted within the imposed deadline.[333] **5.494**

Example:

Article 11 request sent	1.9.2004
Article 11 request deadline	8.9.2004
Parties fail to respond by deadline	
Commission adopts Article 11 decision on	10.9.2004
Decision sets deadline for	17.9.2004
Decision triggers suspension of Article 10(5) deadline	
Parties provide complete information on	15.9.2004
Deadline is suspended from 10.9.04 to 15.9.04	
(from the working day following original deadline of Art. 11 request until complete information was submitted)	

NB: It is important to note that, for the purposes of the deadline calculation in situations of a simple request followed by an Article 11 decision, like in this example, it is immaterial that the parties responded within the Article 11 Decision deadline. This is important only in the context of imposition of fines (in this example, no fines will be imposed since the parties responded within the deadline) but not for the suspension of the Article 10 deadline. In such situations, the deadline is suspended automatically, the triggering event being the adoption of the Article 11 decision, from the working day following the date of the original Article 11 request deadline until the provision of complete information.

(iii) Oral Interviews—Article 11(7) of the Merger Regulation Article 11(7) of the Merger Regulation empowers the Commission to interview any natural or legal person who consents to be interviewed for the purpose of collecting information relating to the subject matter of an investigation. **5.495**

At the beginning of the interview, which may be conducted by telephone or other electronic means, the Commission must state the legal basis and the purpose of the interview. Where the interview takes place in person and outside the Commission's premises, the **5.496**

---

[332] The suspension ends, in accordance with Art 9(4) of the Implementing Regulation, with the end of the day on which complete information is submitted; where such date is not a working day, the suspension ends with the end of the following working day.

[333] See Case T-310/01 *Schneider Electric v Commission* [2002] ECR II-4071, paras 21–23 and 74–113. The CFI held that 'given the circumstances of the present case . . . and the requirement for speed which characterises the overall scheme of Regulation No 4064/89, the Court regards the time-limit for responding . . . by the letter of 6 April 2001, which expired on 18 April 2001, as reasonable', para 100 of the judgment.

Commission is obliged to inform in advance the competent national authorities and national officials may assist the Commission officials in the interview.[334]

5.497 Oral interviews may be a useful method of gathering information in a speedy way, in particular in Phase I, given the tight deadlines imposed by the Merger Regulation. In practice, the Commission will take short minutes of the interviews and can subsequently require the undertakings concerned to confirm what was said orally by sending an Article 11 request in order to receive a written response where the interviewed person confirms or amends the minutes.

5.498 The Commission cannot fine interviewees for refusing to be interviewed or for giving incorrect information in an oral interview.

5.499 **(iv) Inspections** Article 13 of the Merger Regulation empowers the Commission to carry out inspections ('dawn-raids') of undertakings' business premises (those of the parties and of third parties). The Commission does not have the power to search private residences under the Merger Regulation.

5.500 The Commission officials conducting the inspection will require either an authorisation pursuant to Article 13(3) or a Commission decision pursuant to Article 13(4) of the Merger Regulation. They can be assisted by national officials pursuant to Article 13(5). Should the company resist the inspection order, measures to enforce the order will be taken by the national authorities, including involvement of the police.[335] Judicial authorisation may be required and the Merger Regulation sets out a procedure for such authorisation.[336]

5.501 In the course of an inspection the authorised officials are empowered to enter the premises of the company, to examine all business records and take copies thereof, to ask for oral explanations on facts or documents relating to the inspection on the spot and to record the answers.[337] They can also seal premises if the inspection is to last for more than one day.[338]

5.502 Under the Merger Regulation the Commission will not normally have to resort to using these powers as most companies involved in notifiable mergers provide the requested information voluntarily, in order to obtain, as speedily as possible the legal certainty that is provided by a decision under the Merger Regulation. However, if there are indications that the companies involved are not providing the required information in full, the Commission may use its powers under these provisions in appropriate cases.[339]

---

334 Art 11(7), second sub-para.

335 Art 13(6) of the Merger Regulation.

336 ibid, Art 11(7) and (8).

337 ibid, Art 13(2).

338 ibid, Art 13(2)(d). Recital 39 of the Merger Regulation clarifies that the power to seal premises will only be used exceptionally and only for the period of time strictly necessary for the inspection, normally not for more than 48 hours. Seals can be used particularly in circumstances where there are reasonable grounds to suspect that a concentration has been implemented without being notified; that incorrect, incomplete or misleading information has been supplied to the Commission; or that the undertakings or persons concerned have failed to comply with a condition or obligation imposed by decision of the Commission.

339 This happened for example in *Skanska/Scancem* (Case IV/M.1157 [1998]) where the Commission conducted an investigation at the premises of the parties in order to clarify in part the transactions, agreements and other arrangements relating to the establishment of Scancem, in part other events and circumstances relevant to Scancem's operations in order to assess the notifiability of the operation.

Under Article 12, national authorities, at the request of the Commission, can undertake **5.503** inspections. In such cases, national officials will operate in accordance with national law and may be assisted by Commission officials.[340]

(v) Penalties There are significant penalties regarding both Article 11 requests for **5.504** information and Article 13 inspections. These are set out in Articles 14 and 15 of the Merger Regulation. As noted above, there are no penalties concerning oral interviews under Article 11(7).

Under Article 14, the Commission can inflict penalties of up to 1 per cent of the aggregate **5.505** annual turnover of undertakings concerned where they supply incorrect or misleading information in a response pursuant to an Article 11(2) simple request (Article 14(1)(b)) or where they supply incorrect, misleading or incomplete information or fail to provide information within the specified time limit pursuant to an Article 11(3) decision (Article 14(1)(c)); where they refuse to submit to an inspection following a decision under Article 13(4) (Article 14(1)(d)); where, during an inspection, they produce the required book or records in incomplete form (Article 14(1)(d)); they give incorrect or misleading answers (Article 14(2)(e)), or fail to mmission (Article 14(2)(e)); fail to provide a complete answer on facts relating to an inspection (Article 14(2)(e)); or break seals (Article 14(f)).

Article 15 empowers the Commission to inflict periodic penalties. The Commission can **5.506** impose a penalty of up to 5 per cent of the daily aggregate turnover of the undertakings concerned in order to compel them to provide information requested by an Article 11(3) decision (Article 15(1)(a)) or to submit to an inspection ordered under Article 13(4) (Article 15(1)(b)).

(d) The Phase I State of Play Meeting and Remedies

Where, following its market investigation and internal analysis, the Commission believes **5.507** that there are serious doubts as to the compatibility of the merger with the common market which could lead to the opening of in-depth proceedings, the case team will communicate its concerns to the parties informally as soon as possible and will hold a State of Play discussion not later than 15 working days into Phase I.[341]

This Phase I State of Play meeting, like all State of Play meetings, takes place at the **5.508** Commission's premises, or alternatively, if appropriate, by telephone or video conference and is normally chaired by senior DG Competition management. In addition to informing the notifying parties of the preliminary result of the initial investigation, this meeting provides an opportunity for the notifying parties to prepare the formulation of a possible remedy proposal in Phase I before expiry of the 20 working day deadline for the submission of remedies set out in Article 19(1) of the Implementing Regulation. The procedure for the submission of remedies which is the same under Phase I and Phase II is discussed in more detail under Section (5) Phase II below.

---

[340] Art 12(1) and 12(2) of the Merger Regulation.
[341] See para 33 of the Best Practices.

(e) The Article 6 Decision

5.509 The first phase procedure is ended by the adoption of a decision in accordance with Article 6 of the Merger Regulation.

5.510 **(i) Possible Decisions**   There are four possible categories of Commission decision putting an end to Phase I:

* the concentration does not fall within the scope of the Merger Regulation (Article 6(1)(a));
* the concentration is declared compatible with the common market (Article 6(1)(b));
* the concentration, following the receipt of appropriate modifications, is declared compatible with the common market subject to conditions and obligations (Article 6(1)(b) in conjunction with Article 6(2));
* the concentration raises serious doubts as to its compatibility with the common market and proceedings (a Phase II investigation) are initiated (Article 6(1)(c)).

5.511 **(ii) Adoption of the Article 6 Decision**   The Article 6 decision is prepared by the relevant MCN case team. Other Commission services provide comments in writing or orally at so-called inter-service meetings. Inter-service meetings are normally held at key stages of the procedure, in order to consider draft documents such as a draft Phase I decision and, in Phase II, a draft Statement of Objections, and a draft decision before it is submitted to the advisory committee and the final draft decision before this is submitted to the College of Commissioners. The Legal Service also scrutinises draft decisions and Statements of Objections and provides its input. Its authorisation is important before these documents are adopted.

5.512 Article 6 decisions are adopted in the name of the Commission by the Competition Commissioner who is so empowered by the College of Commissioners. The Article 6 decision takes the form of a letter addressed to the notifying party(ies) and is signed by a Commissioner or through sub-delegation by the Director General.

5.513 **(iii) Notification and Publication of Decision**   The Article 6 decision is notified to the notifying parties without delay,[342] normally on the same day as its adoption. Notification is made by the Secretariat General of the Commission, normally by fax (only the operative part of the decision) and by courier (original of the full decision). Member States receive copies soon thereafter.[343] While there is no obligation to send the decision to other involved parties such as the target company or the seller, the Commission services are prepared to provide copies upon request but only once all business secrets have been removed.[344]

5.514 In the vast majority of cases, the removal of any business secrets contained in a decision, which is necessary for dissemination of the decision to third parties and to the public, is

---

[342] Art 6(5) of the Merger Regulation.

[343] ibid, Art 6(5).

[344] For the removal of business secrets, the Commission's obligation not to disclose confidential information and the role of the Hearing Officer in solving disputes concerning such issues, see Section 5(j)(v) 'Access to the File—Involvement of the Hearing Officer' below.

readily achieved by way of dialogue between the Commission services and the notifying parties. However, in some cases even extended dialogue cannot resolve all the differences of opinion. The Hearing Officer can be involved pursuant to Article 9 of the Hearing Officer Mandate to mediate between the Commission and the parties in cases of dispute.[345] The final decision as to the public version rests with the Commission which will have to take care in removing all business secrets.

Following the removal of business secrets the public version of the decision becomes available. Even though there is no legal obligation to publish Article 6 decisions in the Official Journal,[346] the Commission has adopted a practice of informing the general public of the fact that a decision has been adopted by way of the publication of a summary notice in the Official Journal of the European Communities entitled 'non-opposition to a notified concentration';[347] moreover the full text of the decision, normally only in the original language of procedure, becomes available on DG Competition's web site.[348] **5.515**

(f) *Revocation of Article 6 Decision*

It is important to note that Article 6(3) of the Merger Regulation allows the Commission to formally revoke an Article 6 decision it has previously adopted where (a) the decision is based on incorrect information for which one of the undertakings is responsible or where it has been obtained by deceit, or (b) the undertakings concerned commit a breach of an obligation attached to the decision.[349] **5.516**

It is important moreover to note that, if an Article 6 decision is subject to conditions such as, for example, a divestiture and these conditions are not fulfilled, the authorisation for the merger falls apart as the situation authorised by the decision fails to materialise. **5.517**

(5) Phase II

If at the end of the Phase I period, the Commission finds that the concentration raises serious doubts as to its compatibility with the common market, it will adopt a decision initiating proceedings pursuant to Article 6(1)(c) of the Merger Regulation. The procedure which starts with the initiation of proceedings and ends with the adoption of a final decision under Article 8 of the Merger Regulation is known as an in-depth investigation or Phase II procedure. **5.518**

---

[345] Art 9 of the Hearing Officer Mandate requires that the undertaking be informed of the fact that a business secret will be disclosed together with the reasons therefore. A time limit is also fixed for the undertaking's response. Following the receipt of the undertaking's comments, and assuming that the Commission considers that disclosure is still required, a reasoned decision would be drafted and notified to the undertaking concerned. This decision would specify the date on which the information would be disclosed. The decision must allow at least a week between the dates of notification and future disclosure. This is to allow the undertaking leave to appeal the Hearing Officer's decision.

[346] It is to be noted that recital 42 of the Merger Regulation invites the Commission to publicise its decisions as much as possible. It states: 'For the sake of transparency, all decisions of the Commission which are not of a merely procedural nature should be widely publicised.'

[347] For examples of such publications in the Official Journal see <http://www.ec.europa.eu/comm/competition/mergers/oj/>.

[348] <http://www.ec.europa.eu/comm/competition/mergers/cases/>.

[349] See *Sanofi/Synthélabo* (Case IV/M.1397 [1999]).

(a) Overview of Phase II Timetable

5.519 A Phase II investigation triggers an extensive and extremely demanding procedure for everybody involved: the Commission services, the merging parties and their legal and economic advisers, and third parties. It is a procedure which involves significant amounts of information gathering, meetings (including at least four State of Play meeting), the sending of a Statement of Objections, access to the Commission's file, a formal hearing where the parties and third parties can present their views orally, a meeting of the Advisory Committee on concentrations and, finally, the adoption of a final decision by the full College of Commissioners which either authorises or prohibits the merger under examination.

5.520 In Phase II, the Commission has a total of 90 working days (approximately four and half months) in which to adopt a decision pursuant to Article 8 (subject to extensions of the deadline as outlined below in Section (5) 'Phase II, The Article 8 Decision').

5.521 While this 90 working day period may appear to grant the Commission services a great deal of time in which to assess a case, it is interesting to understand how this time period of some 18 weeks breaks down in practice.

5.522 Broadly speaking, the Commission services have six to eight weeks in which to raise further questions with the parties, their suppliers, customers and competitors and to analyse their responses. If appropriate, two weeks are then given over to the preparation of the Statement of Objections and discussion with other Commission services involved in the investigation. Upon the dispatch of the Statement of Objections the parties are permitted to have access to the Commission's file and are given approximately two weeks for preparation of their response to the Statement of Objections and to allow time to prepare for the Oral Hearing.

5.523 After the Oral Hearing, the Commission services have a further week to prepare a draft of the final decision. This must be sent to the Member States at least 10 working days prior to the meeting of the Advisory Committee (Article 19(5) of the Merger Regulation).

5.524 Before the Advisory Committee meeting, the Commission will have held at least four State of Play meetings with the parties at key stages of the procedure: within 10 working days of the Article 6(1)(c) decision, before the issuing of a Statement of Objections, following the Oral Hearing, and before the meeting of the Advisory Committee.[350]

5.525 Following the Advisory Committee meeting, the Commission services must make the appropriate changes to the draft final decision; consult associated services and submit the draft decision to the Secretariat General of the Commission. This requires some two weeks. Finally a gap of around a further 10 days is necessary between the submission of the draft decision to the Secretariat General and its adoption by the College of Commissioners. Decisions tend to be adopted at least one week prior to the legal deadline, as a safety margin in case the College needs to discuss the matter more than once.

---

[350] See para 33 of the Best Practices.

(b) Deadlines and Extensions

(i) **Legal Deadline**   According to Article 10(3), a final decision pursuant to Article 8 must **5.526** be taken at the latest within not more than 90 working days of the date of the Article 6(1)(c) decision which initiated the proceedings.[351]

If the Commission fails to adopt a final Article 8 decision with regard to a notified con- **5.527** centration[352] within the specified deadline of Article 10(3), the merger is deemed to be authorised pursuant to Article 10(6) of the Merger Regulation. This deadline can, however, be extended in various ways as outlined here.

The fact that Article 10(3) specifies an ultimate deadline for the adoption of an Article 8 **5.528** decision does not mean that the Commission must exhaust the timetable in every Phase II case. On the contrary, Article 10(2) of the Merger Regulation obliges the Commission to adopt decisions authorising a notified concentration (under Article 8(1) or 8(2) of the Merger Regulation) as soon as the serious doubts identified in its Article 6(1)(c) decision have been removed, in particular as a result of commitments offered by the parties. It may be the case that adequate commitments dispelling the serious doubts are offered at the very beginning of Phase II, or in any case prior to the sending of a Statement of Objections. In such a situation, the case may come to an end without the need to follow through the rest of the procedure and even without having to send a Statement of Objections.[353]

(ii) **Automatic (Remedies) Deadline Extension**   By virtue of Article 10(3), first sub- **5.529** paragraph, the submission of commitments by the parties triggers an automatic extension of the deadline by 15 working days to a total of 105 working days from the initiation of proceedings *unless* the commitments are offered less than 55 working days after the initiation of proceedings; in such cases, the early submission of commitments allows sufficient time for further investigation and negotiation without the need to extend the timetable.

(iii) **Voluntary Extension ('Stop-the-Clock')**   Article 10(3), second sub-paragraph **5.530** allows for ad hoc extensions of the timetable which cannot total more than 20 working days. There are two ways for such an extension to take place. First, the notifying parties can make a request for an extension in the first 15 working days of Phase II. The notifying parties can make only one such request and they can request any period of extension up to 20 working days. The Commission must accept this request. Second, the Commission may extend the deadline at any time during Phase II provided that the notifying parties expressly agree and provided that the total duration of any extensions effected under Article 10(3), second sub-paragraph, does not exceed 20 working days.[354]

---

[351] Deadlines are calculated in working days and according to Arts 7 and 8 of the Implementing Regulation (see Phase I deadlines above).

[352] Art 10 deadlines and Art 10(6) consequences for missing a deadline only apply with respect to 'notified' concentrations. Where the Commission exercises its powers ex officio with respect to an un-notified concentration or following the revocation of a previous decision, it is not bound by deadlines (Arts 6(4) and 8(7) of the Merger Regulation).

[353] For example, see *Allied Signal/Honeywell* (Case COMP/M.1601 [1999]) and *Siemens/ Draegerwerk/JV* (Case COMP/M.2861 [2003]).

[354] Art 10(3), second sub-para, was applied for the first time in *E.ON/MOL* (Case COMP/M. 3696 [2005]).

5.531 The following table provides an example of the relevant deadlines and their calculation.

Example:	
Article 6(1)(c) decision (Day P)	9.8.2004
Start of Phase II proceedings (working day following 6(1)(c) decision)	10.8.2004
Normal deadline (Day P + 90) (NB: 1 and 2.11.2004 are official holidays and should not be counted)	15.12.2004
Parties request for a 12 WD extension (must be submitted before Day P+15)	
Extended Deadline following parties' request (NB: 24-31 December and 1-2 January are holidays and should not be counted) Parties offer commitments not before Day P+55	10.1.2004
New Extended Deadline (Extended Remedies Deadline of 13.1.2005—Day P + 105 + 12 WD of stop-the-clock)	31.1.2005
Commission requests 8 WD extension and parties agree (NB: COM can only request up to 8 days given that 12 days have already been requested by the parties)	
Final Extended Deadline (Day P + 125: this is the maximum extension possible under Article 10(3))	10.2.2005

5.532 **(iv) Article 10(5) Suspension**   As under Phase I, the Phase II deadlines can be suspended pursuant to Article 10(5) of the Merger Regulation and in accordance with Article 9 of the Implementing Regulation where the Commission has to request information by decision pursuant to Article 11(3) of the Merger Regulation or must order an inspection pursuant to Article 13 of the Merger Regulation in circumstances where the parties involved in the concentration are responsible (see Section (4) (c) Phase I above).

(c) The Post-Article 6(1)(c) State of Play Meeting

5.533 The post-Article 6(1)(c) meeting is held within the first 10 working days of Phase II.[355] The main purpose of the meeting is to facilitate the notifying parties' understanding of the Commission's concerns at an early stage of the Phase II proceedings, to discuss the framework of the Phase II investigation, and to discuss the envisaged timetable of the Phase II procedure, in particular the need for any Article 10(3) stop-the-clock extensions. Normally, the parties will also provide the Commission with a written memorandum containing their comments on the Article 6(1)(c) decision.[356]

(d) The Phase II Investigation—Information Gathering—Triangular Meetings—Early Review of Key Documents

5.534 **(i) What a Phase II Investigation Involves**   The Commission's powers to gather information, conduct interviews and make inspections are the same as those in Phase I (see Section (4)

---

[355] See para 33(b) of the Best Practices.
[356] ibid, para 33(b).

Phase I above). During Phase II, however, the Commission will use its information-gathering powers extensively. Hundreds, even thousands, of Article 11 requests may be sent to the parties, their customers, suppliers and competitors. The MCN case team may also find it useful to conduct site visits, for example, of a factory plant, to get a better idea of the functioning of the relevant product market.

In addition, in complex Phase II cases, the Commission may commission specialist studies **5.535** consisting of market analyses and economic, in particular, econometric analysis, reports. The merging parties will in all likelihood need to use specialist economic advisers and must be ready to respond to the Commission's highly technical questionnaires within a short time frame.

During the Phase II investigation, the Commission services will have to undertake a thor- **5.536** ough analysis of the significant amount of data gathered, to cross-verify facts and to come to preliminary conclusions as to whether the serious doubts identified in the Article 6(1)(c) decision have been dispelled or, on the contrary, confirmed, in which case the Commission will issue a Statement of Objections. It goes without saying that during this phase of the procedure, the merging parties will often try hard to convince the Commission that the serious doubts are dispelled and that the case does not merit the issuance of a Statement of Objections.

Given the complexity of the matters at stake, the Chief Economist's office will normally **5.537** also be involved. One or more members of the Chief Economist's team will be entrusted with the case. They can be appointed at any stage of the procedure, but are usually appointed immediately after the initiation of proceedings. The Chief Economist and his team can provide valuable input in the case team's investigation and analysis but their role also consists of scrutinising the case team's conclusions. The Chief Economist's findings are reported directly to the Director General of DG Competition and the Competition Commissioner.

(ii) Triangular Meetings and Early Review of Key Documents   The Best Practices provide **5.538** the Commission with two tools for the better verification of facts and understanding of the case before it decides to send a Statement of Objection: triangular meetings and early review of key documents.

During the Phase II investigation, in situations where two or more opposing views have **5.539** been put forward as to key market data and characteristics and the effects of the concentration on competition in the markets concerned, the Commission may hold so-called triangular meetings between the Commission services, the merging parties and third party complainants.[357] These will enable the Commission services to hear the views of those parties in a single forum. Experience with this kind of procedure is still relatively limited. Among the possible aims of such a meeting may be to enable DG Competition to reach a more informed conclusion as to the relevant market characteristics and to clarify issues of substance before deciding on the issuing of a Statement of Objections. The meeting may,

---

[357] See para 38 of the Best Practices.

however take place at any time in the procedure, and there have been examples of such meetings usefully taking place regarding disputes relating to the implementation of remedies.

5.540 Triangular meetings are voluntary and would normally be chaired by senior DG Competition management. To the extent possible, taking into account confidentiality issues, preparation of a triangular meeting will normally include a mutual exchange of non-confidential submissions between the notifying parties and the third party in question sufficiently in advance of the meeting.[358]

5.541 From DG Competition's perspective, triangular meetings may provide an extremely useful tool for the better understanding of the case by the Commission services at an early, pre-Statement of Objections, stage of the procedure. However, due to their voluntary nature, it will not always be possible for DG Competition to organise such meetings as both the merging parties and complainants would need to agree to attend them. Notifying parties and their advisers as well as third parties should think carefully whether the issues at stake merit the investment needed for such meetings. In most situations, this will be the case, as such meetings will provide a good opportunity to clarify contentious points, convince the Commission services of the correctness of a point of view and lead to a more focused debate on the relevant issues.

5.542 As with triangular meetings, the possibility for early review of documents laid out in the Best Practices[359] can be a useful tool for all concerned. In the Best Practices, DG Competition has highlighted its wish to provide the notifying parties with the opportunity of reviewing and commenting on 'key documents' obtained by the Commission, such as substantiated submissions of third parties running counter to the notifying parties' own contentions, shortly after the initiation of proceedings.[360] The main aim is to allow for better verification of facts and better understanding of the issues involved at an early stage, before a Statement of Objections is issued and formal access to the file is granted. As with triangular meetings, however, the voluntary nature (absence of a legal obligation) of such early review of key documents may mean that it will not be possible for DG Competition, despite its best endeavours, to provide this opportunity in all cases. DG Competition has stressed that it must respect justified requests by third parties for non-disclosure of their submissions prior to the issuing of the Statement of Objections, when such requests relate to genuine concerns regarding confidentiality, including fears of retaliation and the protection of business secrets.[361]

(e) The Pre-Statement of Objections ('Pre-SO') State of Play Meeting

5.543 The Commission will offer the parties the opportunity to attend a pre-SO State of Play meeting. This pre-SO meeting gives the notifying parties an opportunity to understand DG Competition's preliminary view on the outcome of the Phase II investigation and to be informed of the type of objections DG Competition may set out in the Statement

---

[358] See para 39 of the Best Practices.
[359] ibid, section 7.
[360] See para 46 of the Best Practices.
[361] ibid, para 46.

of Objections. The meeting may also be used by DG Competition to clarify certain issues and facts before it finalises its proposal on the issuing of a Statement of Objections.[362] The parties may use this meeting as a last attempt to avoid the issuance of a Statement of Objections or limit a Statement of Objections' scope by convincing the Commission of some of their views or by offering suitable remedies.[363]

(f) The Scrutiny Panel

Before the Commission issues a Statement of Objections or, at a later stage, before it sends a draft decision to the Advisory Committee, DG Competition may decide to make use of an internal Scrutiny Panel (also knows as 'Devil's Advocate Panel').   **5.544**

Even though this is a procedure that the Commission had been using informally under Regulation 4064/89, it has been formalised in the context of the recent reforms of the Commission's merger control process.[364] DG Competition has created a scrutiny unit within Directorate A with the task of examining the draft decisions prepared by the relevant MCN case team.[365]   **5.545**

The way the scrutiny panel procedure works is as follows: In Phase II merger cases, a panel composed of a number of experienced DG Competition officials is created. Members of associated services, including the Legal Service, may also participate. The panel is normally headed by the Head of Unit of the Directorate A unit responsible for decision scrutiny. The members of the panel have access to all relevant documents and are instructed to examine the draft decision thoroughly. They have access to the case team for clarifications and document requests. Before the issuance of the Statement of Objections or a draft decision, the panel meets formally within DG Competition and debates the draft document prepared by the case team. During the meeting, the Panel can ask any questions it sees fit to members of the case team. Following the meeting, the Panel can report its findings to the Director General of DG Competition and to the Competition Commissioner either supporting the case team, opposing the conclusions reached by the case team or proposing modifications. The ultimate decision as to how the Commission should proceed naturally rests with the Competition Commissioner.   **5.546**

The Scrutiny Panel is an entirely internal procedure and the parties have no access to the Panel or to any reports produced. It is a procedure designed to enhance the quality of decision making within the Commission. It can be argued that the internal nature of the Panel actually enhances its effectiveness as its members feel free to express their opinions without   **5.547**

---

[362] ibid, para 33(c).

[363] A good example is *GE/Instrumentarium* (Case COMP/M.3083 [2003]) where the parties managed to resolve a major issue relating to vertical concerns prior to the issuance of a Statement of Objections thus avoiding the raising of objections with regard to this particular aspect of the case. This enabled the parties to focus on the main horizontal issues in the post-SO period. See point 351 of the Commission's decision in that case.

[364] The formalisation of the use of scrutiny panels was first announced by Commissioner Monti at his speech before the IBA Conference on EU Merger Control held in Brussels on 7 November 2002. The speech is available at: http://www.ec.europa.eu/comm/competition/speeches/index_speeches_by_the_commissioner.html.

[365] Currently Unit A3 'Enforcement priorities and decision scrutiny'. See <http://www.ec.europa.eu/comm/dgs/competition/index_en.htm>.

fearing that they will be made public. The panel members can thus be as harsh or as complimentary as they see fit when discussing the case team's draft decision.

(g) The Statement of Objections

5.548 In cases where, following the initiation of the second phase procedure and further investigation and analysis, the Commission's doubts on the compatibility of a concentration with the common market persist, a statement pursuant to Article 18 of the Merger Regulation (the 'Statement of Objections') is prepared and dispatched to the notifying parties.

5.549 (i) **Purpose of the Statement of Objections**   The purpose of the Statement of Objections is to fulfil the Commission's obligation, contained in Article 18(1) of the Merger Regulation, to allow the undertakings concerned to make known their views on the objections levelled against them. Article 18(1) of the Merger Regulation obliges the Commission to send a Statement of Objections before it can adopt a final decision under Article 8 of the Merger Regulation. This requirement is reiterated in Article 13 of the Implementing Regulation. Thus, the Statement of Objections is a crucial stage of the procedure without which the Commission cannot proceed to the adoption of a final negative decision.

5.550 (ii) **Form and Content of the Statement of Objections**   The Statement of Objections takes the form of a reasoned letter, which addresses all the points that could be expected to be found in the final decision.[366] Therefore the SO discusses the operation/nature of the concentration, the product and geographic markets and details of the creation or strengthening of a dominant position. In addition, should the parties have already submitted a remedy which has been found to be insufficient, this would also be included.

5.551 The Statement of Objections must contain all the objections against the parties which the Commission intends to include in its final decision (Article 18(3)). This is because Article 18(3) of the Merger Regulation specifies that the Commission can base its decision only on objections on which the parties have been able to submit their observations. The introduction of further objections, subsequent to the sending of the Statement would therefore require a second Statement of Objections. The Commission generally avoids the sending of such supplementary Statements mainly in order not to disrupt the tight Phase II timetable. However, it has engaged in this practice in the past and there is nothing unusual about it.[367]

5.552 (iii) **Timing of the Statement of Objections**   As regards the timing of the sending of a Statement of Objections, neither the Merger Regulation nor the Implementing Regulation contains any legal deadline within which the Commission must act. However, the steps that must be taken after a Statement of Objections has been issued (Reply to the SO,

---

[366] It should, however, be noted that, according to well-established case-law, the final decision need not necessarily replicate the statement of objections. Thus, it is permissible to supplement the statement of objections in the light of the parties' response, whose arguments show that they have actually been able to exercise their rights of defence. The Commission may also, in the light of the administrative procedure, revise or supplement its arguments of fact or law in support of its objections in the final decision (see, to that effect, Case T-310/01 *Schneider Electric v Commission* [2002] ECR II-4071, para 438).

[367] See *Tetra Laval/Sidel* (Case COMP/M.2416 [2003]), n 125.

formal hearing, Advisory Committee, preparation and adoption of final decision) dictate that the Statement of Objections must be sent to the notifying parties at least seven to eight weeks before the legal deadline for adoption of a final Article 8 decision.

(iv) Who Receives the Statement of Objections—Non-confidential Version The **5.553** Commission is required to communicate its objections to the undertakings concerned pursuant to Article 18(1) of the Merger Regulation. A copy of the Statement of Objections is therefore addressed to each party against whom objections are raised. More specifically, Article 13(2) of the Implementing Regulation requires the Commission to send the Statement of Objections to the notifying parties and to inform other involved parties in writing of the objections. As regards third parties, Article 16(1) of the Implementing Regulation specifies that where third parties with a sufficient interest in the procedure have applied in writing to be heard pursuant to Article 18(4), second sentence, of the Merger Regulation, the Commission must inform them in writing of the nature and subject matter of the procedure.

Normally the Commission will therefore send a copy of the Statement of Objections to **5.554** other involved parties (namely, the target company) and third parties having a sufficient interest which have applied in writing to be heard.[368]

The Commission will only send a non-confidential version of the Statement of Objections **5.555** to such parties after removal of business secrets. For this purpose, on the dispatch of the Statement of Objections to the notifying parties, the Commission will require them to identify any business secrets contained in the Statement of Objections in order that they may be removed.[369] The non-confidential version of the Statement of Objections is provided under strict confidentiality obligations and restrictions of use, which the third parties must accept prior to receipt.[370]

(h) Procedural Rights Following the Statement of Objections—Rights of Defence

Following the issuance of a Statement of Objections, the merger procedure becomes more **5.556** adversarial in nature. It is only after a Statement of Objections has been issued that the Commission has a 'case' against the parties by having raised objections to their planned merger. This post-Statement of Objections stage is therefore characterised by a more formalised procedure, ensuring respect of the rights of defence of the merging parties.[371] Other parties also acquire more formal rights under the Merger Regulation during this stage of the procedure.[372]

Three main categories of parties need to be distinguished as each category enjoys different **5.557** procedural rights under the Merger Regulation and the Implementing Regulation: notifying

---

[368] For the procedure and criteria for showing 'sufficient interest' in order to demand participation at the oral hearing see Section (5) Phase II, 'The Oral Hearing' below.

[369] For the removal of business secrets, the Commission's obligation not to disclose confidential information and the role of the Hearing Officer in solving disputes concerning such issues, see below Section (5) Phase II 'Access to the File—Involvement of the Hearing Officer'.

[370] See para 36 of the Best Practices.

[371] Art 18(3) of the Merger Regulation specifies that '[t]he rights of the defence shall be fully respected in the proceedings'.

[372] ibid, Art 18(4).

parties, involved parties and third parties. Notifying parties are those who submit a notification pursuant to Article 4 of the Merger Regulation. Involved parties mainly consist of the target company in the merger and the seller. Third parties having a sufficient interest include customers, suppliers and competitors, members of the administration or management organs of the undertakings concerned or recognised workers' representatives of those undertakings.

5.558   **(i) What Rights Exist—Who Enjoys Them**   First, the notifying parties, other involved parties and third parties with a sufficient interest which have applied in writing to be heard, are entitled to receive a copy of the SO, if necessary after elimination of business secrets.[373]

5.559   Second, the notifying parties, other involved parties and third parties with a sufficient interest which have applied in writing to be heard, are entitled to put their comments on the SO in writing to the Commission within a time limit set by the Commission.[374]

5.560   Third, notifying parties and other involved parties which have made a request to this effect in their written comments, are entitled to present their views orally including at a formal oral hearing.[375] The Commission may also, where appropriate, allow third parties which have shown sufficient interest, to participate in the oral hearing (Article 16(2) of the Implementing Regulation).

5.561   Fourth, notifying parties and other involved parties have a right to access the Commission's file subject to confidentiality restrictions. There is a distinction to be made between notifying parties which receive access to the file upon request in order to exercise their rights of defence[376] and involved parties which can only be granted access to the extent that they can demonstrate that this is necessary for the purposes of preparing their comments on the SO.[377] Under the Merger Regulation, third parties do not enjoy a right to access the Commission's file.[378]

5.562   Fifth, all parties concerned benefit from the involvement of and access to an independent Hearing Officer whose role is to oversee the respect of rights of defence during this stage of the procedure, to chair the formal oral hearing and to intervene in disputes concerning access to documents or as regards confidentiality.

5.563   Parties other than notifying parties, involved parties and third parties having a sufficient interest do not acquire formal rights. However, the Commission may invite any other

---

[373] Arts 13(2) and 16(1) of the Implementing Regulation.
[374] ibid, Art 13(2) with respect to notifying and involved parties and Art 16(2) of the Implementing Regulation with respect to third parties.
[375] Art 14(1) and 14(2) of the Implementing Regulation.
[376] Art 17(1) of the Implementing Regulation.
[377] ibid, Art 17(2).
[378] However, it should be noted that third parties, like any member of the public, may seek to have access to documents in the Commission's possession under the provisions of Regulation (EC) 1049/2001 of the European Parliament and of the Council of 30 May 2001 regarding public access to European Parliament, Council and Commission documents ('Regulation 1049/2001') [2001] OJ L145/43. Normally, however, while a case is still pending, the Commission will be able to refuse access to documents using the exceptions set out in Art 4 of Regulation 1049/2001. This is discussed in greater detail in 'Access to the File' below.

natural or legal person to express their views, in writing as well as orally, including at the formal oral hearing.[379]

A summary of the rights enjoyed by the various categories of parties can be seen in the following table.   **5.564**

	Receipt of Statement of Objections	Right of response to Statement	Access to the file	Attendance at Oral Hearing	Right to speak at Oral Hearing
Notifying parties	Yes	Yes	Yes	Yes	Yes
Involved parties	After deletion of business secrets	Yes	Insofar as is necessary in order to prepare their comments	Yes	Yes
Third Parties with sufficient interest	Limited to 'nature and subject matter of procedure'	Yes	No	Yes	Yes

(i) The Reply to the SO (Timing and Content)

Following receipt of the SO, notifying parties have the right to provide their comments to the Commission in writing.[380] A response to the SO is a right of the notifying parties and not an obligation, but, in the overwhelming majority of cases, notifying parties submit a written response.   **5.565**

The Reply to the SO and comments by involved parties and third parties to the SO must be provided within the time limit fixed by the Commission.[381] This is normally a period of two weeks but can be extended by the Hearing Officer in agreement with the case team or in case of dispute with the case team where, for example, the relevant party believes that the time limit imposed for its reply is too short.[382] In this case, the party may, within the original time limit, seek an extension of that time limit by means of a reasoned request to the Hearing Officer. The applicant is informed in writing whether the request has been granted.[383] The time limit for reply is important, as the Commission is not obliged to take into account comments received after its expiry.[384]   **5.566**

---

[379] Art 16(3) of the Implementing Regulation.
[380] Art 13(2) of the Implementing Regulation, second sub-para.
[381] ibid, Arts 12(2) and 16(1).
[382] The CFI has acknowledged that, given the necessity for speed in proceedings under the Merger Regulation, the parties may only invoke the shortness of the periods allowed to them inasmuch as those periods are disproportionate to the duration of the proceedings as a whole. A period of 11 working days plus one additional working day extension was held to be not disproportionate in the context of the proceedings of the case in question in Case T-210/01 *General Electric v Commission*, judgment of 14.12.2005, not yet published in the ECR, paras 703–706.
[383] Art 10 of the Hearing Officer Mandate.
[384] Art 13(2)(5) of the Implementing Regulation.

5.567 Article 13(3) of the Implementing Regulation sets out the formalities regarding the submission of the Reply to the SO. According to this provision, the parties may set out all facts and matters known to them which are relevant to their defence, and must attach any relevant documents as proof of the facts set out; they may also propose that the Commission hear persons who may corroborate those facts. One original and 10 copies of the Reply must be submitted at the same address used for the submission of notifications, ie at DG Competition's Merger Registry. An electronic copy must also be submitted at the same address and in the format specified by the Commission.

5.568 The Commission forwards copies of the Reply without delay to the competent authorities of the Member States.[385] In addition the Commission services have adopted a policy of making such parties' responses available to the other parties, after removal of business secrets.

(j) Access to the File

5.569 Access to the Commission's file is a fundamental right of defence[386] and an obligatory step in the Phase II procedure by virtue of Article 18(3) of the Merger Regulation and Article 17 of the Implementing Regulation. The Commission's policy on access to the file has been codified in the recently adopted Notice on Access to the File.[387]

5.570 (i) **Who has Access to the File?** The Merger Regulation and the Implementing Regulation are clear on who has access to the file: only notifying and involved parties.[388] Third parties do not enjoy such rights to access the Commission's file under the Merger Regulation.

5.571 It should, nevertheless, be noted here that access to documents in the Commission's possession is also governed by Regulation 1049/2001 on access to documents by the general public.[389] Regulation 1049/2001 gives a general right of access to any document held by the Commission or Council subject to specific exceptions stipulated in Article 4 of that Regulation. As a result, third parties, who do not enjoy access to the file rights under the Merger Regulation, may seek to use Regulation 1049/2001 to obtain access to documents in the Commission's file. In such situations, while a case is pending, the Commission will normally be entitled to refuse access on the basis of the exception set out in Article 4, in particular Article 4(2) and 4(3) of Regulation 1049/2001, which permits the Commission to refuse access to a document under that Regulation where disclosure of the document would undermine the protection of commercial interests of a natural or legal

---

[385] ibid, Art 13(3).

[386] See Case T-210/01 *General Electric v Commission*, judgment of 14.12.2005, not yet published in the ECR, para 629 *et seq*.

[387] Notice on Access to the File [2005] OJ C325/7 (also available at <http://www.ec.europa.eu/comm/competition/mergers/legislation/access.htm>). The Notice replaced the 1997 Notice on the internal rules of procedure for processing requests for access to the file in cases under Arts 85 and 86 of the EC Treaty, Arts 65 and 66 of the ECSC Treaty and Council Regulation (EEC) 4064/89 [1997] OJ C23/3.

[388] See Art 18(3) of the Merger Regulation and Art 17(1) of the Implementing Regulation with respect to notifying parties and Art 17(2) with respect to involved parties. See also Notice on Access to the File, paras 7, 33 and 34.

[389] Regulation (EC) 1049/2001 of the European Parliament and of the Council of 30 May 2001 regarding public access to European Parliament, Council and Commission documents ('Regulation 1049/2001') [2001] OJ L145/43.

person, including intellectual property, court proceedings and legal advice, the purpose of inspections, investigations and audits, or where the document relates to a matter where the decision has not been taken by the institution and disclosure of the document would seriously undermine the institution's decision-making process.[390]

(ii) When is Access Granted?   In accordance with Article 18(1) and (3) of the Merger   **5.572** Regulation and Article 17(1) of the Merger Implementing Regulation, the notifying parties will be given access to the Commission's file upon request at every stage of the procedure following the notification of the Commission's objections up to the consultation of the Advisory Committee.[391]

The notifying parties may have access as soon as they have received the Statement of   **5.573** Objections, although a slight delay, to allow a digestion of its contents may be appropriate thus permitting a more thorough understanding of the contents of the file. DG Competition normally endeavours to allow the notifying parties to have access to the file the same day they receive the SO or the following day.

Involved parties would normally have access to the file at a later date, if at all. This is due to   **5.574** the fact that involved parties normally should receive the SO at a later date after elimination of business secrets from that document. Involved parties would first need to receive the SO in order to motivate their request for access to the file: Article 17(2) of the Implementing Regulation allows them access only insofar as is necessary for the purposes of preparing their comments. In addition, a separate version of the file would normally need to be prepared, removing the business secrets of the notifying parties.

Following the initial access to the file after the issuance of an SO, the parties will continue   **5.575** to receive access to any accessible documents received after the SO is issued up to the stage of consultation of the Advisory Committee (Article 18(1) and (3) of the Merger Regulation and Article 17(1) of the Implementing Regulation).[392]

It should be stressed that, under the Merger Regulation, the parties have no right of access   **5.576** to the file prior to the issuance of the Statement of Objections.[393] Any provision of documents prior to that stage is on a voluntary basis and mainly aims to assist DG Competition in better verification of facts at an early stage.[394]

(iii) Which Documents?   The Commission's 'file' consists of all documents which have   **5.577** been obtained, produced and/or assembled by DG Competition during the investigation.[395]

---

[390] For the application of Regulation 1049/2001 in the context of competition proceedings which had already come to an end when access was requested, see Case T-2/03, *Verein für Konsumenteninformation v Commission*, judgment of 13.4.2005, [2005] ECR II-1121.

[391] See Notice on Access to the File, para 28.

[392] See also para 43 of the Best Practices.

[393] See Notice on Access to the File, para 28. This was confirmed by the CFI in the recent judgment in Case T-210/01 *General Electric Company v Commission*, judgment of 14.12.2005, not yet published in the ECR, paras 694–696, where the CFI held the view that no formal right to access the file exists prior to the issuance of a Statement of Objections and rejected the applicant's argument that the Commission is obliged to grant access on a continuous basis throughout the proceedings.

[394] See paras 45 and 46 of the Best Practices.

[395] Notice on Access to the File, para 8.

5.578 All documents in the Commission's file are, in principle, accessible with the exception of internal documents and documents containing business secrets or other confidential information.[396]

5.579 Article 17(3) of the Implementing Regulation expressly specifies that right of access to the file shall not extend to confidential information, or to internal documents of the Commission or of the competent authorities of the Member States or to correspondence between the Commission and the competent authorities of the Member States or between the latter.

5.580 The Commission's Notice on Access to the File contains more information on the rules relating to internal documents and business secrets/confidential information.

5.581 In essence, documents produced by the Commission's services (including drafts, opinions, memos or notes from Commission departments, correspondence between the Commission and Member State authorities[397] and notes of meetings that have not been agreed)[398] will be considered as internal documents and hence non-accessible. The same goes for correspondence between the Commission and a contractor who has been commissioned to produce a study.[399] The final study and the methodology for it are, however, accessible.[400]

5.582 Business secrets include information about an undertaking's business activity the disclosure of which could harm its legitimate interests such as business plans, sales figures, market share figures, etc.[401] Other confidential information includes information the disclosure of which could significantly harm a person or undertaking.[402] In such cases, information may be produced in anonymous form to protect the provider of information from possible retaliatory measures.[403]

5.583 **(iv) How does Access to the File Take Place?**   The mystery of access to the file has been largely reduced by the Commission's Notice on Access to the File. However it is useful to set out what may take place when a company's representatives arrive at the Commission to review the contents of the file.

---

[396] ibid, para 10. See also Case T-210/01 *General Electric v Commission*, judgment of 14.12.2005, not yet published in the ECR, para 630.

[397] See, however, para 16 of the Notice on Access to the File which specifies that, in certain exceptional circumstances, the Commission will grant access to documents originating from Member States, the EFTA Surveillance Authority or EFTA States, after deletion of any business secrets or other confidential information. The Commission will consult the entity submitting the document prior secrets or other confidential information.

[398] According to para 13 of the Notice on Access to the File, however, where the person or undertaking in question has agreed the minutes, such minutes will be made accessible after deletion of any business secrets or other confidential information. Such agreed minutes constitute part of the evidence on which the Commission can rely in its assessment of a case.

[399] ibid, para 14.

[400] ibid, para 11.

[401] ibid, para 18.

[402] ibid, para 19. Para 20 also specifies that military secrets constitute confidential information.

[403] This practice has been accepted as legitimate by the Court of First Instance in case T-05/02 *Tetra Laval v Commission* [2002] ECR II-4381, para 98 *et seq.* See also Case T-210/01 *General Electric v Commission*, judgment of 14.12.2005, not yet published in the ECR, para 649 *et seq.*

At this point the contents of the file will have been divided into those to which the parties **5.584** can have access (or partial access) and those which are inaccessible. The Commission services will have spent considerable time going through the contents of the file to arrange documents in this way and, in particular, to contact third parties in order to confirm whether their submissions contain confidential information and, if so, to receive non-confidential versions of the information submitted.[404]

Wholly accessible papers will comprise the data submitted by the parties themselves **5.585** together with Commission questionnaires sent to third parties, information in the public domain (press articles, independent statistical data, Commission reports on the industry/ sector in question, etc) and information submitted by third parties which is non-confidential in its entirety. Partially accessible data will generally comprise those parts of third party responses submitted to the Commission which do not contain business secrets or those from which any business secrets have been deleted. Non-accessible papers include internal Commission documents, correspondence with the Member States and business secrets data and other confidential information submitted by third parties.

The Notice on Access to the File (para 44) specifies that the Commission may determine **5.586** that access to the file shall be granted in one of the following ways, taking due account of the technical capabilities of the parties: by means of a CD-ROM(s) or any other electronic data storage device as may become available in future; through copies of the accessible file in paper form sent to them by mail; by inviting them to examine the accessible file on the Commission's premises. The Commission may choose any combination of these methods.

In practice, the notifying parties' representatives receive a list of all documents in the **5.587** Commission's file which are numbered consecutively according to the chronological order in they were received or sent out by the Commission. The list specifies whether a document is accessible, non-accessible or partially accessible. The notifying parties are then permitted to photocopy the accessible and partially accessible papers or receive copies of those papers directly. DG Competition has established a practice whereby the accessible and partially accessible papers are provided to the notifying parties in electronic format (on DVD-ROMs). This speeds up access to the file considerably and is a significant practical improvement in the procedure.

(v) Involvement of the Hearing Officer It is possible that a dispute may arise over access **5.588** to certain documents insofar as a party enjoying a right to access the Commission's file believes that the Commission has documents in its possession which have not been disclosed and should be disclosed to it. In such a situation, the Notice on Access to the File specifies that the said party should submit a reasoned request to that end to the Commission. If the services of DG Comp are not in a position to accept the request and if

---

[404] It should be recalled here that all parties submitting information to the Commission are obliged to provide a non-confidential version of the information pursuant to Art 18(2) and (3) of the Implementing Regulation. See also paras 21–25 and 35–43 of the Notice on Access to the File.

the party disagrees with that view, the party in question may turn to the procedure contained in the Hearing Officer's Mandate.[405]

5.589   Article 8(1) of the Hearing Officer Mandate permits the recipient of the Statement of Objections to issue a reasoned request to the Hearing Officer indicating which documents it believes are in the Commission's possession, which have not been disclosed and which are necessary for a proper exercise of the right to be heard. Article 8(2) of the Hearing Officer Mandate requires that a reasoned decision be adopted by the Hearing Officer in respect of any such request.[406]

5.590   Conversely, where the Commission wishes to disclose information and a person, be it the parties, involved parties or third parties, objects to such disclosure on the basis that the document contains confidential information, the procedure set out in Article 9 of the Hearing Officer mandate can be used. Such issues can arise at any time during the procedure where the Commission wishes to disclose information, either for the purposes of the investigation, or in the context of access to the file or when providing non-confidential versions of an Article 6(1)(c) decision or SO or finally, at the stage of publication of the non-confidential version of a final decision.

5.591   In such cases, point 42 of the Access to the File Notice and Article 9 of the Hearing Officer Mandate obliges the Commission to inform an undertaking in writing of its intention to disclose the sensitive information and the reasons for the disclosure. A time limit is fixed within which the undertaking concerned may submit any written comments. Where the undertaking concerned objects to the disclosure of the information the Hearing Officer considers the matter. If he or she finds that the information is not protected and therefore may be disclosed, that finding is stated in a reasoned decision which is notified to the undertaking concerned. The decision specifies the date after which the information will be disclosed. This date cannot be less than one week from the date of notification.

5.592   It should be noted that, while Article 9 speaks of 'business secrets', its scope may cover any kind of confidential information, that is information covered by the obligation of professional secrecy which, if disclosed, could harm the interests of the undertaking or person concerned.[407]

(k)   The Oral Hearing

5.593   (i) **Purpose and Timing**   The purpose of the oral hearing is to give the notifying parties, against whom a Statement of Objections has been issued, the right to respond and formally set out their counter arguments to the Commission's objections. In addition, the oral hearing provides the forum for other involved parties and for interested third parties to comment on the positions of both the Commission and the notifying parties.

---

[405] Commission Decision of 23 May 2001 on the terms of reference of hearing officers in certain competition proceedings [2001] OJ L162/21 (also available at: <http://www.ec.europa.eu/ comm/competition/ mergers/legislation/access.htm>).

[406] Such a decision could of course be challenged before the Court of First Instance (see Section (7) Due Process and Judicial Review below).

[407] See Case T-198/03 *Bank Austria Creditanstalt AG v Commission of the European Communities*, judgment of 30th May 2006, not yet published in the ECR, for issues of disclosure of information and Art 9 of the Hearing Officer Mandate.

The oral hearing takes place some two weeks after the dispatch of the Statement of **5.594** Objections and some three weeks before the meeting of the Advisory Committee. The Hearing Officer, in consultation with the DG Competition director responsible for the case, determines the precise date, the duration and the place of the hearing and decides on any possible postponement of the hearing.[408]

(ii) Who Can Attend?   The oral hearing is mainly held for the exercise of the notifying **5.595** parties' rights of defence. The hearing can, however, be held whether the notifying parties request it or not as third parties may wish to attend it even in the absence of the notifying parties.[409] A hearing is not always held, however, as no party may have expressed a wish to attend.[410]

The oral hearing is not open to the public. A party wishing to attend must receive an express **5.596** invitation. Parts of the hearing may be held separately so as to protect business secrets of the parties concerned.[411]

The Commission invites recipients of the SO (notifying parties, involved parties and third **5.597** parties having shown sufficient interest) to express whether they wish to attend an oral hearing at a date already specified by the Commission in the SO cover letter. Notifying parties will be permitted to attend upon request in their written Reply that they be afforded the opportunity to present their views orally at a formal hearing.[412] Involved parties[413] and third parties[414] having a sufficient interest can also apply in writing to attend the oral hearing. As regards third parties, which must show that they have a sufficient interest before they can be admitted, Article 6 of the Hearing Officer Mandate contains a specific procedure for their applications. Applications must be submitted in writing, together with a written statement explaining the applicant's interest in the outcome of the procedure. Decisions as to whether third parties are to be heard are taken by the Hearing Officer after consulting the DG Competition director responsible for the case. Where it is found that an applicant has not shown a sufficient interest to be heard, he is informed in writing of the reasons for the finding and a time limit is fixed within which he may submit any further written comments.[415]

From the administration side, the oral hearing is attended by the Commission case team **5.598** and management, other associated services of the Commission including the Legal Service, and representatives of the Member States.[416] Notifying parties, involved parties and third parties permitted to attend, in addition to their lawyers, may also bring along economic or other advisers and experts that have been admitted by the Hearing Officer.[417]

---

[408] Art 12(1) of the Hearing Officer Mandate.
[409] Art 16(3) of the Implementing Regulation.
[410] See eg *CVC/Lenzing* (Case COMP/M.2187 [2001]), para 11.
[411] Art 15(6) of the Implementing Regulation.
[412] Art 18(1) of the Merger Regulation and Art 14(1) of the Implementing Regulation.
[413] Art 18(1) of the Merger Regulation and Art 14(2) of the Implementing Regulation.
[414] Art 18(4) of the Merger Regulation and Art 16(2) of the Implementing Regulation.
[415] Art 6 of the Hearing Officer Mandate.
[416] Art 15(2) of the Implementing Regulation.
[417] ibid, Art 15(5).

5.599 **(iii) Preparation of the Oral Hearing—The Role of the Hearing Officer** The Hearing Officer is responsible for the smooth operation of the oral hearing from its preparation to its conduct on the day. Article 11 of the Hearing Officer Mandate specifies that, where appropriate, in view of the need to ensure that the hearing is properly prepared and in particular that questions of fact are clarified as far as possible, the Hearing Officer, after consulting the director responsible, may supply in advance to the parties invited to the hearing a list of the questions on which he or she wishes them to make known their views. He or she may also hold a meeting with the parties invited to the hearing and, where appropriate, the Commission staff, in order to prepare for the hearing itself.[418] Article 11 of the Hearing Officer Mandate also allows the Hearing Officer to ask for prior written notification of the essential contents of the intended statement of persons whom the parties invited to the hearing have proposed for attendance, such as experts.

5.600 **(iv) What Takes Place at the Oral Hearing?** The procedure for the Oral Hearing is as follows: first, the Commission services present the case, summarising the objections to the concentration. Subsequently, the notifying parties present their view of the concentration and answer the Commission's objections. Once the notifying parties' presentation has been made, the Member States' representatives, third parties and the Commission services are invited to pose questions. Obviously, the notifying parties are expected to respond. A novelty introduced in the Implementing Regulation is that, in contrast to the regime under Regulation 4064/89, the parties may be allowed to pose questions to the Commission's case team.[419]

5.601 The next rounds of presentations are made by the involved parties followed by the third parties: questions are raised on their presentations by the Member States, other parties and Commission services in turn. The final stage of the Oral Hearing is left for the notifying parties to make concluding remarks.

5.602 Statements made at the oral hearing are recorded and the recordings are made available to attendees, if necessary after removal of business secrets.[420]

5.603 **(v) Role of Hearing Officer following the Oral Hearing** Following the oral hearing, the Hearing Officer reports to the Competition Commissioner on the hearing and the conclusions he/she draws from it, with regard to the respect of the right to be heard. Article 13 of the Hearing Officer Mandate sets out the procedure with respect to this report. The observations in this report concern procedural issues, including disclosure of documents and access to the file, time limits for replying to the Statement of Objections and the proper conduct of the oral hearing. A copy of the report is given to the Director-General for Competition and to the director responsible for the case. In addition to this report, the Hearing Officer may make observations on the further progress of the proceedings.

---

[418] Art 15(7) of the Implementing Regulation and Art 11 of the Hearing Officer Mandate.

[419] Art 15(7) of the Implementing Regulation. This introduction was intended to make the oral hearing more interactive following criticism by many notifying parties that the oral hearing did not allow for a properly adversarial exchange of views and appeared to be a stale exercise in consecutive monologues.

[420] Art 15(8) of the Implementing Regulation.

Such observations may relate among other things to the need for further information, the withdrawal of certain objections, or the formulation of further objections.

Finally, the Hearing Officer prepares a final report in which he/she opines on the exercise **5.604** of the right to be heard and generally on whether the procedure has been respected, in particular whether any final draft decision prepared by the Commission services is based only on objections to which the parties have had the right to comment.[421] This final report is sent to the Competition Commissioner, Director General of DG Competition, director responsible for the case, and is also attached to the draft decision sent to the College of Commissioners for adoption.[422] It is communicated to the addressees of the Decision and published in the Official Journal.[423]

(l) The Post-SO and Pre-Advisory Committee State of Play Meetings

Following the oral hearing, the Commission will offer the parties two State of Play meetings: **5.605** one shortly following the oral hearing (or if no oral hearing was held, following the reply to the SO); and a further State of Play meeting before the meeting of the Advisory Committee.

The Best Practices clarify that the post-SO State of Play meeting provides the notifying par- **5.606** ties with an opportunity to understand DG Competition's position after it has considered their reply and heard them at an Oral Hearing. If DG Competition indicates that it is minded to maintain some or all of its objections, the meeting may also serve as an opportunity to discuss the scope and timing of possible remedy proposals.[424]

The primary purpose of the pre-Advisory Committee State of Play meeting is to enable the **5.607** notifying parties to discuss with DG Competition its views on any proposed remedies and where relevant, the results of the market testing of such remedies. It also provides the notifying parties, where necessary, with the opportunity to formulate improvements to their remedies proposal.[425] The meeting is also colloquially known as the 'last cigarette' meeting as it essentially consists of the last formal stage for the parties to secure an authorisation decision for their merger.

(m) Submission of Remedies[426]

If the undertakings concerned decide to offer commitments in order to avoid a prohibition **5.608** decision, they must follow the procedure set out in the Implementing Regulation and must take into account the Commission's Notice on Remedies,[427] the Best Practice Guidelines

---

[421] Art 16 of the Hearing Officer Mandate.

[422] ibid, Art 16(1).

[423] ibid, Art 16(3). For a list of published Hearing Officer reports see http://www.ec.europa.eu/comm/ competition/mergers/cases/index/by_dec_type_art_18_hearing_officer.html.

[424] See para 33(d) of the Best Practices.

[425] ibid, para 33(e).

[426] For substantive issues concerning remedies, including suitability and content of various types of remedies see Section C: Substantive Assessment of Mergers, subsection (6) Remedies above.

[427] Commission Notice on remedies acceptable under Council Regulation (EEC) 4064/89 and under Commission Regulation (EC) 447/98 [2001] OJ C68/3 (also available at <http://www.ec.europa.eu/comm/ competition/mergers/legislation/remedies.htm>). The Notice remains relevant under the new Merger Regulation.

for Divestiture Commitments and the Commission's model texts for divestiture commitments and trustee mandates.[428] The Remedies Notice sets out the general principles applicable to remedies, the main types of commitments that have previously been accepted by the Commission, the specific requirements which proposals of remedies need to fulfil in both phases of the procedure, and guidance on the implementation of remedies.

5.609 The Best Practices invite parties to seek the Commission's guidance in formulating their remedies proposals.[429] The Best Practices specify that although it is for the notifying parties to formulate suitable remedies proposals, DG Competition will provide guidance to the parties as to the general appropriateness of their draft proposal in advance of submission. In order to allow for such discussions, a notifying party should contact DG Competition in good time before the relevant deadline for submission, in order to be able to address comments DG Competition may have on the draft proposal.

5.610 Phase II commitments must be submitted within not more than 65 working days from the date on which proceedings were initiated.[430] However, where extensions of the legal deadline for a final decision have occurred pursuant to Article 10(3), second sub-paragraph, of the Merger Regulation, this 65 working day period is also extended by the same number of working days.[431]

5.611 Article 19(2), third sub-paragraph, of the Implementing Regulation allows the Commission, in exceptional circumstances, to accept commitments offered after the expiry of the time limit provided that there is sufficient time to comply with the relevant time limits and procedure set out in Article 19(5) of the Merger Regulation for consultation of the Advisory Committee.[432] Point 43 of the Commission Notice on Remedies specifies that, where the parties modify their commitments after the relevant deadline of Article 19(2) of the Implementing Regulation, the Commission may only accept these modified commitments where it can clearly determine—on the basis of its assessment of information already received in the course of the investigation, including the results of prior market testing, and without the need for any other market test—that such commitments, once implemented, resolve the competition concerns identified and allow sufficient time for proper consultation of Member States.[433]

---

[428] All documents can be found at DG Competition's web site at: http://www.ec.europa.eu/comm/competition/mergers/legislation/.

[429] See para 41 of the Best Practices.

[430] Art 19(2) of the Implementing Regulation.

[431] ibid, Art 19(2), second sub-para.

[432] The CFI has held that, whilst the parties to a concentration cannot oblige the Commission to take account of commitments and modifications to them submitted after the time-limit of three weeks, the Commission must nevertheless be able, where it considers that it has the time necessary to examine them, to authorise the concentration in light of those commitments even if modifications are made after expiry of the three-week time limit (Case T-114/02 *Babyliss v Commission* [2003] ECR II-1279, para 140).

[433] In Case T-87/05 *EDP v Commission*, judgment of 21.9.2005, not yet published in the ECR, the CFI held (at paras 67 and 69) that the parties are indeed entitled to submit modification of commitments after the deadline specified in the Implementing Regulation provided they respect the conditions set out in para 43 of the Notice on Remedies.

Commitments must be submitted to the Merger Registry of DG Competition in one original and 10 copies; a copy must also be provided in electronic format.[434] Submitting parties must also provide, at the same time, a non-confidential version which the Commission will use in any market testing of the remedies.[435] Member States also receive copies of commitment proposals.[436]   **5.612**

Remedies proposals in Phase II are habitually market tested through the sending of questionnaires to competitors, customers and suppliers of the parties. The same procedure is followed as for an Article 11 request. Deadlines for responses are naturally particularly short given the time constraints at this stage of the procedure. The parties receive access to the responses to the market test,[437] if necessary after removal of business secrets or in summary form.[438] The parties may also seek the intervention of the Hearing Officer who can report on the objectivity of the market test by reviewing the selection of respondents and the methodology used.[439]   **5.613**

Where commitments are accepted by the Commission in order to declare a concentration compatible with the common market, the Commission can attach conditions and obligations to its authorisation decision to ensure that the undertakings concerned comply with the commitments they have entered into.   **5.614**

A distinction must be made between conditions and obligations. The Remedies Notice explains that the requirement for achievement of each measure that gives rise to the structural change of the market is a condition, for example, a condition that a business is to be divested. The implementing steps which are necessary to achieve this result are generally obligations on the parties, eg such as the appointment of a trustee with an irrevocable mandate to sell the business. Where the undertakings concerned commit a breach of an obligation, the Commission may revoke clearance decisions issued either under Article 6(2) or Article 8(2) of the Merger Regulation, acting pursuant to Article 6(3) or Article 8(7), respectively. The parties may also be subject to fines and periodic penalty payments as provided in Article 14(2)(a) and 15(2)(a) respectively of the Merger Regulation. Where, however, the situation rendering the concentration compatible with the common market does not materialise, that is, where a condition is not fulfilled, the compatibility decision no longer stands at all. In such circumstances, where in the absence of the condition, the merger would have been found to be incompatible with the common market, the Commission   **5.615**

---

[434] Art 20(1) of the Implementing Regulation.

[435] ibid, Art 20(2).

[436] ibid, Art 20(1).

[437] The Best Practices specify that the notifying parties will be given the opportunity to have access to documents received after the issuing of the SO up until the consultation of the Advisory Committee (Best Practices, para 43). Such documents will mainly comprise responses to the market testing of remedies proposals.

[438] This practice, which DG Competition has followed in certain cases in order to protect the anonymity of respondents, has been accepted by the Court of First Instance in Case T-5/02 *Tetra Laval v Commission* [2002] ECR II-4381. See paras 98–101 of the judgment.

[439] Art 14 of the Hearing Officer Mandate. For an example of a case where this procedure was used, see *Tetra Laval/Sidel* (Case COMP/M.2416 [2001]). The Commission's decision was upheld on procedural grounds (but annulled on substantive grounds) by the CFI in Case T-5/02 *Tetra Laval v Commission* [2002] ECR II-4381. See paras 110–117 of the judgment on the Hearing Officer's report concerning the objectivity of the market test.

may, pursuant to Article 8(4) of the Merger Regulation, order the full dissolution of the concentration.[440]

(n) The Advisory Committee

The Advisory Committee consists of representatives of the competent authorities of the Member States (one or two representatives per Member State) who are normally required to be experts in antitrust matters (Article 19(4) of the Merger Regulation).

5.616 Article 19(3) specifically requires the Commission to consult the Advisory Committee prior to adopting a decision on the basis of Article 8 (termination of the second phase procedure), or a decision imposing a fine on an undertaking (Articles 14 and 15).[441]

5.617 The meeting of the Advisory Committee is convened by the Commission. The Advisory Committee is provided with a copy of the Commission's proposed decision, a summary of the case and an 'indication of the most important documents' relevant for an appreciation of the case.[442]

5.618 The meeting of the Advisory Committee should take place not less than 10 working days following the invitation but this period can be shortened if necessary for the purposes of the case.[443] In the past, the Commission had to shorten this period in many cases due to the time constraints in Phase II and in particular due to late submission of remedies by the notifying parties necessitating last minute drafting of decisions before they could be sent to the Advisory Committee. Recourse to this option should in the future be reserved to exceptional circumstances under the Merger Regulation since more time is available when remedies are offered thanks to the automatic extension of the deadline by 15 working days. Indeed, it is important for the Advisory Committee to receive the relevant documents in good time in order to provide meaningful input during the meeting.

5.619 The meeting of the Advisory Committee is chaired by a representative of DG Competition (normally from Directorate A). In addition, a representative from one of the Member States' delegations acts as a 'rapporteur' and is responsible for drawing up an agenda for the meeting, presenting the case, and drawing up the Advisory Committee's conclusions. The Commission services associated with the case are represented at the meeting and members of the Advisory Committee may pose questions to the case-team. The parties or any other external persons are not permitted to attend this meeting. It is an internal affair where the Commission and representatives of the Member State authorities can debate the case with complete openness.

5.620 Normally the meeting will consider whether the concentration is of Community dimension, whether the relevant product and geographic markets have been properly defined,

---

[440] See Section (6) Enforcement Powers below.

[441] The Commission has a general obligation, pursuant to Art 19(2) of the Merger Regulation, to maintain a close and constant liaison with the competent authorities of the Member States.

[442] Art 19(5) of the Merger Regulation.

[443] Art 19(5) of the Merger Regulation. The CFI has upheld the Commission's practice of shortening this period where necessary and has held that a failure to respect this provision cannot lead to an automatic annulment of a Commission decision. See Case T-290/04, *Kaysersberg SA v Commission* [1997] ECR II-2137.

whether the concentration significantly impedes effective competition, in particular as a result of the creation or strengthening of a dominant position, and whether any remedies proposed by the parties to counter the negative competitive effects are appropriate.

At the end of the meeting, the Advisory Committee delivers an opinion on the Commission's draft decision, if necessary by taking a vote.[444] The Advisory Committee may deliver an opinion even if some members are absent and unrepresented. The opinion is delivered in writing and is appended to the draft decision.[445] **5.621**

While the opinion of the Advisory Committee is not binding, Article 19(6) obliges the Commission to take the utmost account of it and to inform the Committee of the manner in which it does this. In practice, the Advisory Committee meeting has an important place in the Phase II procedure. It has the role of an external scrutiny of the draft decision produced by the Commission services. An opinion against the draft Commission decision has major repercussions within the Commission and would in all likelihood lead to heavy debates within DG Competition, before the Legal Service, the Competition Commissioner and the College of Commissioners. Ultimately, the Commission can override the Advisory Committee's opinion if there are good reasons to do so. **5.622**

The opinion's importance is reflected in the fact that it is communicated to the addressees of the final decision and published together with the decision in the Official Journal.[446] It is to be hoped that opinions of the Advisory Committee, which in the past have been rather laconic, will in the future provide more extensive reasoning shedding further light on the Commission's assessment of the case. **5.623**

(o) The Article 8 Decision

(i) **Possible Decisions** Phase II ends with the adoption of a final decision under Article 8 of the Merger Regulation.[447] **5.624**

There are three main categories of decisions that may put an end to Phase II proceedings: **5.625**

- The concentration is declared compatible with the common market (Article 8(1) of the Merger Regulation).
- The concentration is declared compatible with the common market subject to conditions and obligations following modifications by the parties (Article 8(2) of the Merger Regulation).
- The concentration is declared incompatible with the common market (Article 8(3) of the Merger Regulation).[448]

---

[444] For an example of an Advisory Committee Opinion containing majority and minority opinions see *Siemens/Draegerwerk/JV* (Case COMP/M.2861 [2003]).

[445] Art 19(6) of the Merger Regulation.

[446] Art 19(7) of the Merger Regulation.

[447] That proceedings must be closed by means of an Art 8 decision is specified in Art 6(1)(c) of the Merger Regulation. However, where the parties have abandoned their concentration, there is no such obligation to close proceedings by means of decision.

[448] In this case, further measures for the dissolution of the merger may also be taken under Art 8(4) of the Merger Regulation. See Section (6) Enforcement Powers below.

5.626 **(ii) Adoption of the Decision** By contrast to Phase I decisions which are adopted by the Competition Commissioner acting under empowerment (*'habilitation'*), Phase II decisions are adopted by the full College of Commissioners.

5.627 The process up to adoption is as follows. Normally there are three to four weeks between the meeting of the Advisory Committee and the legal deadline for the case. During this period the Commission services must adjust the decision for comments made by the Advisory Committee; consult associated services in respect of such amendments; discuss the draft decision at a meeting of the competition experts of the Commissioners' private offices and finally submit the proposed decision for adoption by the College of Commissioners. The last two steps take a minimum of seven working days.

5.628 **(iii) Notification and Publication of the Decision** The Decision is adopted in the language of the case and is communicated to the notifying parties without delay.[449] The operative part of the decision is communicated to the parties or their specified legal advisers immediately by telefax. The full decision is then sent to the notifying parties by courier through the Commission's Secretariat General.[450] A non-confidential version may also be sent to other involved parties. Copies of the decision are sent to the Member State authorities.[451] Together with the decision, notifying parties receive the Hearing Officer's final report[452] and the Advisory Committee's opinion.[453]

5.629 Article 8 decisions must be published in the Official Journal in all official languages of the European Union. The publication must state the names of the parties and the main content of the decision, having regard to legitimate interests of undertakings in the protection of their business secrets.[454] The parties are requested to identify any business secrets contained in the decision. Ultimately, it is up to the Commission to decide on the version to be published and to remove all business secrets or, in the case of figures, replace them with indicative ranges. If there is a dispute between the Commission and the parties with respect to business secrets, the matter can be resolved by the Hearing Officer.[455]

5.630 As for any publication in the Official Journal, translations into all Community languages are needed. This is a task which may take a considerable amount of time, and publication in the Official Journal has in the past taken up to 12 months in certain cases. DG Competition will therefore normally make available a public non-confidential version of the decision, in the language of the case, on its web site prior to publication in the Official Journal. DG Competition may also in the future decide to limit the publication in the

---

[449] Art 8(8) of the Merger Regulation.
[450] As this may take a few days for administrative purposes, the parties may ask DG Competition to provide them informally with a full copy of the decision. It is up to the case team to decide whether it wishes to proceed this way taking into account that official notification must always be done by the Secretariat General.
[451] Art 8(8) of the Merger Regulation.
[452] Art 16(3) of the Hearing Officer Mandate.
[453] Art 19(7) of the Merger Regulation.
[454] Art 20(1) and (2) of the Merger Regulation.
[455] Art 9 of the Hearing Officer Mandate. (See above Section (5)(j)(v) Phase II Access to the File—Involvement of the Hearing Officer.)

Official Journal to the 'main content of the decision' as required by Article 20(2) of the Merger Regulation in order to ensure speedier publication.

(p) Revocation of Article 8 Decision

Article 8(6) of the Merger Regulation allows the Commission to formally revoke an Article 8 **5.631** decision it has previously adopted where (a) the decision is based on incorrect information for which one of the undertakings is responsible or where it has been obtained by deceit, or (b) the undertakings concerned commit a breach of an obligation attached to the decision.

It is moreover important to note that, as with the case of Article 6 decisions, where an **5.632** Article 8 decision is subject to a condition (as opposed to obligations), for example a divestiture, and this condition is not fulfilled, the authorisation for the merger falls apart as the situation authorised by the decision fails to materialise.

(6) Enforcement Powers

(a) Fines and Periodic Penalties

The Commission's powers to fine undertakings and persons for infringements under the **5.633** Merger Regulation have been discussed throughout this section in the appropriate sub-sections.[456] It is useful, however, to summarise briefly here in a comprehensive manner the Commission's fining powers. These are to be found in Articles 14 and 15 of the Merger Regulation and relate to procedural and substantive infringements. It should be noted that in setting the amount of the fine the Commission must have regard to the nature, gravity and duration of the infringement.[457] Pursuant to the Merger Regulation, fines under the Merger Regulation are not of a criminal law nature.[458]

(i) Substantive Infringements   Under Article 14(2), the Commission can impose fines **5.634** not exceeding 10 per cent of the aggregate turnover of the undertaking concerned where, either intentionally or negligently, it:

(a) fails to notify a concentration prior to its implementation without authorisation;
(b) implements a concentration in breach of Article 7;
(c) implements a concentration declared incompatible with the common market by decision pursuant to Article 8(3) or does not comply with any measure ordered by decision pursuant to Article 8(4) or (5);
(d) fails to comply with a condition or an obligation imposed by decision pursuant to Articles 6(1)(b), Article 7(3) or Article 8(2), second sub-paragraph.

In the first case in which a fine was imposed under Article 14(2) of the Merger Regulation, **5.635** the South Korean company Samsung was fined ECU 33,000 for its failure to notify the acquisition of AST Research Inc. and for implementing the transaction without Commission approval.[459] The Commission will not hesitate to impose significantly larger fines if it learns of a failure to notify a case with more significant effects on competition, if the failure

---

[456] See Section (4)(c)(v) Phase I, Phase I Investigation Penalties above.
[457] Art 14(3) of the Merger Regulation.
[458] ibid, Art 14(4).
[459] See Commission press release IP/98/166 of 18 February 1998.

to notify was intentional or if the company concerned does not co-operate with the Commission when its failure to notify has been discovered.

5.636 **(ii) Procedural Infringements**   Under Article 14(1) of the Merger Regulation, the Commission can impose fines not exceeding 1 per cent of the aggregate turnover of the undertakings concerned where, intentionally or negligently:

(a) they supply incorrect or misleading information in a submission, certification, notification or supplement to a notification;

(b) they supply incorrect or misleading information in response to an Article 11(2) request;

(c) they supply incorrect, incomplete or misleading information or do not supply information within the required time limit in response to a request made by an Article 11(3) decision;

(d) they produce the required books or other records related to the business in incomplete form during inspections under Article 13, or refuse to submit to an inspection ordered by decision taken pursuant to Article 13(4);

(e) in response to a question asked during an inspection in accordance with Article 13(2)(e), they give an incorrect or misleading answer, they fail to rectify within a time limit set by the Commission an incorrect, incomplete or misleading answer given by a member of staff, or they fail or refuse to provide a complete answer on facts relating to the subject matter and purpose of an inspection ordered by a decision adopted pursuant to Article 13(4);

(f) they have broken seals affixed by officials or other accompanying persons authorised by the Commission in accordance with Article 13(2)(d).

5.637 Even though the infringements set out in Article 14(1) are procedural in nature, the strict time limits imposed on the Commission for the assessment of merger cases make it extremely important that undertakings respond to the Commission's questions accurately, truthfully and in a timely manner. In past decisions adopted under Article 14, the Commission has stated in very clear terms that the intentional or negligent provision of incorrect or misleading information is an infringement of considerable gravity because it creates the risk that important aspects relevant for the competitive assessment of the transaction may never be investigated or analysed by the Commission, thus leading to a final decision based on incorrect information.[460] The Commission will therefore not hesitate to impose fines whenever it finds that the conditions of Article 14(1) are met.[461]

5.638 **(iii) Periodic Penalty Payments**   Under Article 15 of the Merger Regulation, the Commission can impose periodic penalty payments not exceeding 5 per cent of the average

---

[460] See *BP/Erdoelchemie* (Case COMP/M.2624 [2004]) OJ L91/40, para 48. There have been five cases imposing fines for the submission of incorrect or incomplete information: *Sanofi/Synthelabo* (Case M.1543 [1999]); *KLM/Martinair II* (Case M.1608 [1999]); *Deutsche Post/TransoFlex* (Case M.1610 [1999]); *BP/Erdoelchemie* (Case M.2624 [2002]); and *Tetra Laval/Sidel* (Case M.2416 [2003]). A list of Art 14 decisions can be found at http://www.ec.europa.eu/ comm/competition/mergers/cases/index/by_dec_type_art_14.html.

[461] See, most recently, *Tetra Laval/Sidel* (Case M.2416 [2003]) where the Commission imposed a fine of EUR 90,000 and issued a press release IP/04/863 of 7 July 2004 outlining the importance of Art 14(1).

daily aggregate turnover of the undertaking concerned for each working day of delay, calculated from the date set in the decision, in order to compel the undertaking:

(a) to supply complete and correct information which it has requested by decision taken pursuant to Article 11(3);

(b) to submit to an inspection which it has ordered by decision taken pursuant to Article 13(4);

(c) to comply with an obligation imposed by decision pursuant to Article 6(1)(b), Article 7(3) or Article 8(2), second sub-paragraph; or

(d) to comply with any measures ordered by decision pursuant to Article 8(4) or (5).

In case M.1431, a fine totalling EUR 900,000 was imposed on Mitsubishi, a third party in the case, for failure to provide information requested pursuant to an Article 11 decision.[462] **5.639**

(b) Dissolution Orders and Interim Orders—Articles 8(4)–8(5)[463]

The Merger Regulation provides the Commission with effective powers enabling it to control concentrations which, despite the *ex ante* system of merger control put in place by the Merger Regulation, are implemented in breach of the Merger Regulation: these include concentrations which are implemented without authorisation or are implemented and then found to be incompatible with the common market or are implemented in breach of conditions attached to an authorisation decision. These powers are contained in Articles 8(4) and 8(5) of the Merger Regulation.[464] **5.640**

Article 8(4) of the Merger Regulation empowers the Commission to order the dissolution of an implemented merger which is incompatible with the common market.[465] Two categories of implemented incompatible mergers may fall within this provision: implemented mergers which have been expressly prohibited under Article 8(3) of the Merger Regulation; and mergers implemented in contravention of a condition attached to an Article 8(2) decision which found that, in the absence of the condition, the concentration would be incompatible with the common market.[466] **5.641**

---

[462] See press release IP/00/764 of 12 July 2000.

[463] For a more detailed analysis of Arts 8(4) and 8(5) see DG Competition Newsletter, Spring 2004 issue, K Fountoukakos, 'Unscrambling the Eggs: Dissolution orders under Article 8(4) of the Merger Regulation', available at http://www.ec.europa.eu/comm/competition/publications/ cpn/cpn2004_1.pdf.

[464] See also recital 31 of the Merger Regulation.

[465] The text of Art 8(4) was amended in the recent reform of the Merger Regulation to improve the clarity of the original text of the same provision in Regulation 4064/89. There have been four cases adopted under Art 8(4) of Regulation 4064/89: *Kesko/Tuko* (Case M.784 [1996]) OJ L110/53; *Blokker/Toys R Us* (Case M890 [1997]); *Schneider/Legrand* (Case M.2283 [2001]); *Tetra Laval/Sidel* (Case M.2416 [2001]). The two latter decisions were annulled by the CFI on appeal in, respectively, Case T-77/02 *Schneider Electric v Commission* [2002] ECR II-4201 and Case T-80/02 *Tetra Laval v Commission* [2002] ECR II-4519.

[466] Reading Art 8(4)(b) in conjunction with Art 8(7)(a)(ii), two distinct forms of breach of Art 8(2) conditions can be distinguished: (i) conditions attached to Art 8(2) decisions which had found that, in the absence of the conditions, the merger would be incompatible with the common market; and (ii) conditions attached to Art 8(2) decisions which had only found that, in the absence of the conditions, the concentration would raise serious doubts. Normally, an Art 8(2) decision will fall within the former category. However, the latter situation may arise where, eg, the parties offer commitments early in Phase II and a Statement of Objections is not sent to the parties or if sent does not include certain objections in relation to which the serious doubts were dispelled early (see, eg, *GE/Instrumentarium* (Case M.3083) and *Siemens/Draegerwerk/JV*

5.642 In such situations, the Commission may order the complete dissolution of the prohibited concentration, so as to restore the situation prevailing prior to the implementation of the concentration. Normally this will take place through the dissolution of the merger or the disposal of all the shares or assets acquired.[467] The Commission may also impose other flanking measures to ensure compliance with its dissolution order. These measures will normally entail the appointment of an independent trustee.

5.643 Orders under Article 8(4) can be taken by separate decision or together with an Article 8(3) decision. The procedure followed is the same as in a Phase II proceeding but the Commission is not bound by deadlines.

5.644 Article 8(5) of the Merger Regulation empowers the Commission to take interim measures to maintain or restore conditions of effective competition where a concentration has been implemented without authorisation,[468] or in breach of a conditional decision[469] or in spite of a prohibition decision.[470] Interim measures will include hold-separate orders, appointment of a trustee and other measures ensuring that pending final resolution of the matter, conditions of effective competition are not compromised. The Commission can adopt such decisions quickly by adopting a provisional decision, ie without the need to resort to Statements of Objection, hearings, etc, under the procedure established in Article 18(2) of the Merger Regulation.

(7) Due Process and Judicial Review

(a) Introduction

5.645 The Merger Regulation and its accompanying measures put in place an administrative system of merger control which must respect due process and the parties' rights of defence. Respect for the rights of defence is explicitly enshrined in Article 18(3) of the Merger Regulation.

5.646 A number of features of the Merger Regulation and its accompanying measures are primarily concerned with safeguarding due process. These include the requirement to adopt reasoned decisions whenever proceedings are initiated, the requirement to inform the parties of all objections against them in a formal statement, to allow them access to the Commission's file and to grant them the opportunity to respond to the Commission's

---

(Case M.2861 [2003])). In such cases, the Art 8(2) decision only finds that the serious doubts have been dispelled but does not make an express finding of incompatibility in the absence of the condition. Such decisions therefore become akin to Phase I conditional decisions. In the absence of a finding of incompatibility, the Commission does not have the power, under Art 8(4), to order directly the dissolution of a merger but must first proceed to examine the case pursuant to Art 8(7).

[467] See, eg, *Tetra/Sidel* (Case M.2416 [2003]), adopted under the old version of Art 8(4) in Regulation 4064/89, where the Commission ordered Tetra to dispose of all the shares it held in Sidel. The decision was annulled by the Court of First Instance on appeal (Case T-5/02) but the CFI essentially agreed with the Commission's analysis that the complete separation of the undertakings concerned is the logical consequence of prohibition. Art 8(4) of the Merger Regulation now makes it clear that this is the primary consequence of a prohibition.

[468] Art 8(5)(a) of the Merger Regulation.

[469] ibid, Art 8(5)(b).

[470] ibid, Art 8(5)(c).

objections in writing as well as at a formal hearing chaired by an independent Hearing Officer, the Commission's commitment to keep the parties fully apprised of all developments through formalised State of Play meetings at key stages of the procedure and to allow them to have early review of key documents and to confront third parties' views at triangular meetings.

Checks and balances on the work of the case team in the procedure include supervision by **5.647** and involvement of senior DG Competition management at key stages of the procedure including State of Play meetings, the use of Scrutiny Panels, the involvement of associated Commission services, scrutiny of the legal content of a decision by the Legal Service, scrutiny of the economic analysis by the Chief Economist, scrutiny of all procedural aspects by the Hearing Officer, scrutiny of the whole draft decision by the Advisory Committee and finally adoption of Phase II decisions by the full College of Commissioners.

Most importantly, in addition to such due process features of the EC system of merger con- **5.648** trol, the Commission's merger decisions are subject to judicial review by the Court of First Instance ('CFI') and, on appeal on points of law, by the European Court of Justice ('ECJ'). Judicial review is the ultimate guarantor of the parties' rights of defence and the ultimate external, independent check and balance on the Commission's powers under the Merger Regulation.[471]

(b) Jurisdiction of the CFI to Review Merger Decisions

The CFI's jurisdiction is enshrined directly in the EC Treaty and there is no need for addi- **5.649** tional provisions in the Merger Regulation granting the court such jurisdiction. Nonetheless, the Merger Regulation makes specific references to the court's jurisdiction in Article 21(2) which provides that '*subject to review by the Court of Justice*, the Commission shall have sole jurisdiction to take the decisions provided for in this Regulation.'[472] Article 10(5) of the Merger Regulation expressly envisages a specific procedure to be followed in case of annulment of the Commission's decisions by the CFI. Finally, Article 16 of the Merger Regulation confers on the CFI unlimited jurisdiction (as opposed to judicial review juris-diction) with respect to fines. The CFI can therefore 'cancel, reduce or increase the fine or periodic penalty payment imposed'.[473]

(c) Grounds of Appeal

Pursuant to Article 230 of the EC Treaty, the CFI has the power to review the legality **5.650** of acts, such as Commission decisions, on the following grounds: (i) lack of competence, (ii) infringement of an essential procedural requirement, (iii) infringement of the Treaty or any rule of law relating to its application, and (iv) misuse of power. The Court has adopted a flexible approach to Article 230 and to a large extent those grounds have lost their indi-vidual importance. Infringement of procedural requirements and infringement of rules of

---

[471] For a more detailed analysis on the role of judicial review see Bo Vesterdorf, *Judicial Review in EC Competition Law: Reflections on the Role of the Community Courts in the EC System of Competition Law Enforcement*, Competition Policy International, Vol 1, No 2, Autumn 2005.
[472] Emphasis added.
[473] Art 16 of the Merger Regulation.

law will normally be the grounds capable of challenging most aspects of a Commission merger decision.

5.651 Infringement of procedural requirements can lead to annulment of a decision where the procedural breach affected the outcome of the case.[474] Lesser infringements or minor procedural irregularities might lead only to partial annulment or be disregarded by the Court. The test is whether, but for the breach of the procedure, the decision might have been different.[475] This plea can involve in particular questions relating to access to the file and whether the Statement of Objections included all the objections on which the final decision was based.

5.652 Infringement of the Treaty or any rule of law relating to its application is the widest ground of appeal. Parties can plead this to argue that the Commission has breached any provision of the Merger Regulation, most often Article 2 of the Merger Regulation itself. In essence, the plea is that the Commission's analysis that the merger is or is not compatible with the common market is manifestly wrong and thus breaches the Merger Regulation.[476] The plea can also be used to challenge the Commission's findings on jurisdiction (calculation of turnover, questions of joint control, etc)[477] or to argue that the Commission's acceptance or non acceptance of remedies is erroneous.[478] The parties can also plead breach of fundamental principles of Community law under this heading including in particular proportionality, protection of fundamental rights, and legitimate expectations.

---

[474] As was the case in Case T-310/01 *Schneider Electric v Commission* [2002] ECR II-4071; see in particular, paras 421–465 (especially para 437 *et seq*) of the judgment where the CFI held that the fact that the Commission did not include with sufficient clarity in the Statement of Objections all the competition problems it subsequently relied on in the final decision prohibiting the merger in question infringed the applicant's rights of defence insofar as the omission did not permit the applicant to assess the full extent of the competition problems to which the Commission claimed the concentration would give rise. According to the CFI, had the applicant been given such an opportunity, the Commission could have reconsidered its position or, alternatively, have provided further evidence in support of its proposition, so that the Decision might have been different. This resulted in the decision being vitiated by an infringement of the rights of defence which led the CFI to annul it.

See Case T-210/01 *General Electric v Commission*, judgment of 14.12.2005, not yet published in the ECR, para 632 *et seq* for an explanation of the circumstances where a procedural infringement may lead to annulment of a Commission decision.

[475] In the recent merger judgment in Case T-5/02 *Tetra Laval v Commission* [2002] ECR II-4381, the CFI summarised its jurisprudence on this point. It stated, at point 90 of the judgment: 'It must also be recalled that, in order to hold that the rights of the defence have been infringed, it is sufficient for it to be established that the non-disclosure of the documents in question might have influenced the course of the procedure and the content of the decision to the applicant's detriment (Case T-36/91 *ICI v Commission* [1995] ECR II-1847, para 78; Joined Cases T-305/94, T-306/94, T-307/94, T-313/94, T-314/94, T-315/94, T-316/94, T-318/94, T-325/94, T-328/94, T-329/94 and T-335/94 *Limburgse Vinyl Maatschappij and Others v Commission* [1999] ECR II-931, para 1021; and Case T-221/95 *Endemol Entertainment Holding BV v Commission* [1999] ECR II-1299, para 87)'.

[476] See, eg, Case T-342/99 *Airtours plc v Commission* [2002] ECR II-2585; Case T-310/01 *Schneider Electric v Commission* [2002] ECR II-4071; and Case T-5/02 *Tetra Laval v Commission* [2002] ECR II-4381.

[477] See, eg, Case T-3/93 *Air France v Commission* [1994] ECR II-121. See also case T-417/05 *Endesa v Commission*, judgment of 14.7.2006, not yet published in the ECR.

[478] See, eg, Case T-158/00 *ARD v Commission*, judgment of 30.9.2003. For an appeal against a Commission decision on the implementation of commitments see Case T-342/00 *Petrolessence v Commission*, [2003] ECR II-1161. See also Case T-282/02 *Cementbouw Handel & Industrie v Commission*, judgment of 23.2.2006, not yet published in the ECR, where the parties appealed against the conditional authorisation decision of 26.6.2004 in case M2650 *Haniel/Cementbouw/JV (CVK)* (2002).

Finally, it should be noted here, that an applicant can also bring an action for damages **5.653** suffered because of an illegal Commission decision pursuant to Article 2 of the EC Treaty. No judgments have been rendered in this respect with regard to concentrations but two cases are currently pending before the CFI.[479]

(d) Which Decisions can be Appealed

Any decision producing binding legal effects which can affect the interests of the party **5.654** bringing the action can be challenged before the CFI under Article 230 EC. [480]

It is well established that Commission final decisions in merger proceedings fall within the **5.655** term 'act' which may be subjected to judicial review. Thus, the main decisions adopted by the Commission under Articles 6(1)(b)/6(2), 8(2), 8(3), and 8(4) of the Merger Regulation are all 'challengeable' acts.[481] Other decisions that, in principle, can be appealed are those under Articles 6(1)(a),[482] 7(3), 14 and 15 and referral decisions under Articles 9 and 22(3).[483]

Certain specific situations merit further discussion. First, it is to be noted that where a final **5.656** act is challenged on grounds that do not affect the applicant's legal rights, the CFI will hold the action inadmissible. This will be the case where a party challenges an authorisation decision favourable to it for findings contained in it that it deems prejudicial but which do not affect its legal rights.[484] Second, the courts' case law makes clear that the parties to a merger 'retain their legal interest' and are thus entitled to challenge a merger decision even though, because of the disappearance of the contractual basis underlying it, the transaction can no longer be carried out, even if the court finds in favour of the parties.[485] An Article 6(1)(c) decision is a preparatory step and does not put a final end to proceedings. As such, it should

---

[479] Case T-351/03 *Schneider Electric v Commission*, pending; for details of the appeal see [2004] OJ C7/37; and Case T-212/03 *My Travel v Commission*, pending; for details of the appeal see [2003] OJ C200/28.

[480] See Case C-60/81, *IBM v Commission* [1981] ECR 2639, para 9.

[481] Commission decisions under those provisions have been challenged before the CFI without any problems as to the admissibility of the action. See, eg: Art 6(1)(b)/6(2): Case T-114/02 *Babyliss v Commission* [2003] ECR II-1279; Case T-158/00 *Arbeitsgemeinschaft der öffentlichrechtlichen Rundfunkanstalten der Bundesrepublik Deutschland (ARD) v Commission* [2003] ECR II-3825; Art 8(2): Case T-282/02 *Cementbouw Handel & Industrie v Commission*, judgment of 23.2.2006, not yet published in the ECR; Art 8(3): Case T-5/02 *Tetra Laval v Commission* [2002] ECR II-4381; Art 8(4): Case T-80/02 *Tetra Laval v Commission* [2002] ECR II-4519.

[482] In the *Generali/Unicredito* case (Case T-87/96 *Assicurazioni Generali SpA and Unicredito SpA* [1999] ECR II-203), the CFI held that a decision under Art 6 (1) (a) of Regulation 4064/89 affected the legal position of the parties concerned in the case to the extent that it put an end to the procedure set out in the Merger Regulation.

[483] For the 'challengeability' of referral decisions under Article 9 of the Merger Regulation, see Case T-119/02 *Royal Philips Electronics v Commission* [2003] ECR II-1433, paras 267-308 and Joined Cases T-346/02 and T-347/02 *Cableuropa SA and Others v Commission* [2003] ECR II-4251.

[484] See eg, Joined Cases T-125/97 and 127/97 *The Coca Cola Company and Coca Cola Enterprises v Commission* [2000] ECR II-1733, where Coca Cola challenged an authorisation decision favourable to it on the grounds that it disagreed with the Commission on the market shares and market definitions made by the Commission in the decision. The CFI considered that there was no legitimate interest in appealing the decision due to the lack of legal effects on the legal position of the addressee.

[485] See Case T-310/00 *MCI v Commission*, judgment of 28.9.2004 [2004] ECR II-3253, paras 44–64 for an exposition of the relevant case law. In this case, the CFI held that, even though MCI had abandoned its merger with Sprint following a Commission decision declaring the merger incompatible with the common market, it was still entitled to bring proceedings for the annulment of the Commission's decision. Indeed, the CFI annulled the decision on the basis that the withdrawal of the notification and abandonment of the merger before the adoption of the decision deprived the Commission of its competence to adopt the decision.

normally not be subject to appeal. This has recently been confirmed by the CFI in an Order declaring an action against a Commission Article 6(1)(c) decision inadmissible.[486]

5.657 Decisions by the Hearing Officer refusing a request for access to the file (under Article 8 of the Hearing Officer Mandate) or, conversely, confirming that the Commission will disclose information contrary to a party's claim that such information is confidential (under Article 9 of the Hearing Officer Mandate), may also be considered, in principle, as challengeable acts as they affect the legal situation of their addressee.[487]

5.658 In addition to the above formal acts, there are a number of other acts adopted by the Commission which do not expressly take the form of a decision but which may affect the legal position of the addressee. The courts have held such acts to be 'appealable'. For example, the CFI ruled that the statement of the spokesman for the Commissioner for Competition considering a merger without community dimension, constituted a definitive decision under the terms of Article 230 EC.[488] A letter from the Director of the Merger Task Force with an express disclaimer to the effect that it is not binding on the Commission will not be considered a challengeable act whereas the same letter but without a suitable disclaimer may be considered such an act.[489]

5.659 Finally, it should be noted that an action can be brought for failure to act under Article 232 EC or, under Article 230 EC, against decisions of the Commission closing a file following a complaint. For instance, a party which believes that the Commission, and not national authorities, ought to take jurisdiction over a given merger due to the jurisdictional turnover test being met, can bring an action against the Commission for failure to act or against a Commission decision which decides not to act on its complaint.[490]

(e) *Who can Bring an Appeal*

5.660 Pursuant to Article 230 EC, addressees of a Commission decision under the Merger Regulation will have a right to bring an action against the decision addressed to them.

5.661 On the other hand, other applicants who are not addressees of the decision, such as the target company, competitors, customers, suppliers, employees or shareholders of the merging companies, must meet the requirements of Article 230 EC by showing that they are *directly* and *individually* concerned by the decision they are challenging. There is significant case law on the concept of direct and individual concern[491] including in the merger field.

---

[486] See Order of the CFI of 31.1.2006 in Case T-48/03 *Schneider Electric v Commission*, not yet published in the ECR. It is not entirely clear whether the CFI ruled that the action was inadmissible in the particular circumstances of the case or that any such action against a Commission Art 6(1)(c) decision would be inadmissible. Para 79 *et seq* of the Order suggest this but the CFI's statements were made in subsidiary order ('*à titre surabondant*'). An appeal against the Order has been lodged before the ECJ. See Case C-188/06P.

[487] See Case T-198/03 *Bank Austria Creditanstalt AG v Commission of the European Communities*, judgment of 30 May 2006, not yet published in the ECR.

[488] Case T-03/93 *Air France v Commission* [1994] ECR II-121.

[489] Case C-170/02 P *Schlusselverlag JS Moser and others v Commission* [2003] ECR I-9889 and Case T-3/02 *Schlusselverlag JS Moser and others v Commission* [2002] ECR II-1473.

[490] See Case C-170/02 P *Schlusselverlag JS Moser and others v Commission* [2003] ECR I-9889 and Case T-3/02 *Schlusselverlag JS Moser and others v Commission* [2002] ECR II-1473.

[491] See judgment of the ECJ in Case C-263/02 P *Commission v Jego Quéré* [2004] ECR I-3425. See in particular Advocate General Jacobs' opinion in that case for an analysis of those requirements under Art 230 EC. See also Case T-119/02 cited in n 483 above.

It will be easy for the merging parties, regardless of whether they are addressees of the deci- **5.662**
sion or not, to show that they are directly and individually concerned by a merger decision.

The principal competitors of the merging parties will also normally be able to show that **5.663**
they have *locus standi* if they can prove that their market position is significantly affected by
the merger in a way which distinguishes them from other market operators.[492] Specific
involvement in the administrative procedure will also help to show that the applicant is
individually concerned.[493] Similar considerations apply to customers and suppliers of the
merging parties. Shareholders will normally not be able to prove that they are directly and
individually concerned[494] but may be able to do so under particular circumstances; the case
law is not clear on this point. Finally, the case law shows that workers' representatives only
have *locus standi* to the extent that the object of the action is to ensure that the procedural
rights recognised in the Merger Regulation have been respected.[495]

(f) Timing and Procedure for Appeal

Appeals against merger decisions must follow the same procedure as all other appeals **5.664**
respecting the relevant rules of procedure of the CFI and ECJ.[496] A detailed exposition of
the procedure is beyond the scope of the present chapter.

Briefly, appeals under Article 230 EC must be lodged within two months of the notifica- **5.665**
tion to the addressee or, in the absence thereof, the day on which it came to the knowledge
of the addressee or where the measure is published, from the 15th day after publication.[497]
This two-month period is automatically extended by ten calendar days due to presumed
distance of the applicant from Luxembourg.[498] Vacations or public holidays do not interrupt the periods but if the deadline ends on a Sunday or a public holiday it is extended to
the following working day. The CFI and ECJ may accept late submission of appeals only
where there are special circumstances of *force majeure*.

All applications initiating proceedings must contain the statements prescribed by **5.666**
Article 44(1) and (2) of the Rules of Procedure of the CFI.[499]

---

[492] For a recent CFI order discussing admissibility of third parties in merger cases, see order in Case
T-350/03, not yet published in the ECR.

[493] See Case T-03/93 *Air France v Commission* [1994] ECR II-121.

[494] See Case T-83/92 *Zunis Holding v Commission* [1993] ECR II-1169 where the Court held that, in principle, a merger decision is not of such a nature as by itself to affect the substance or extent of the rights of those
shareholders, either as regards their proprietary rights or the ability to participate in the company management conferred on them by such rights (para 35).

[495] Case T-96/92 *Comité d'Entreprise v Commission* [1996] ECR I-1213.

[496] The Community courts' rules of procedure can be found at http://www.curia.europa.eu.

[497] Art 230 EC.

[498] Art 102(2) of the Rules of Procedure of the CFI; Art 81(2) of the Rules of Procedure of the Court of
Justice.

[499] Art 44 (1): 'An application of the kind referred to in Article 21 of the Statute of the Court of Justice shall
state: (a) the name and address of the applicant; (b) the designation of the party against whom the application
is made; (c) the subject-matter of the proceedings and a summary of the pleas in law on which the application
is based; (d) the form of order sought by the applicant; (e) where appropriate, the nature of any evidence
offered in support. (2). For the purposes of the proceedings, the application shall state an address for service
in the place where the Court of First Instance has its seat and the name of the person who is authorised and
has expressed willingness to accept service.'

5.667 The rules of procedure of the CFI set out the procedure to be followed. The normal procedure consists of two exchanges of written pleadings followed by an oral hearing and the judgment of the court.[500] The court may adopt measures of instruction or organisation of procedure including in particular requests of documents and the posing of written questions.[501]

5.668 In view of the timing considerations affecting merger decisions (in a prohibition decision situation, commercially, the companies may not wish to wait until the outcome of litigation and may prefer to withdraw from the contract and equally in a clearance situation, it is important to know whether the Commission's authorisation would stand or not), speed in the judicial review of merger decisions is particularly important. The CFI has introduced an expedited procedure which can be applied to merger appeals.[502] An applicant wishing to benefit from this procedure must lodge a separate document at the same time as the application initiating the proceeding or the defence.[503] The CFI decides whether to adjudicate the case under the expedited procedure having regard to its particular urgency and circumstances of the case. The Court therefore exercises its discretion on whether to grant the 'fast track' procedure on a case-by-case basis. When agreeing to adjudicate under the expedited procedure, the CFI may prescribe conditions as to the volume and presentation of the pleadings, the subsequent conduct of proceedings or as to the pleas in law and arguments on which the CFI will be called upon to decide. Non-compliance by the parties may lead to revocation of the expedited procedure, following which the ordinary procedure applies.[504]

5.669 When an applicant has requested the expedited procedure, the time limit for lodging the defence is one month (rather than the usual two months).[505]

5.670 Once the request for the expedited procedure has been approved by the CFI, the written and oral procedures follow modified rules: (i) the case is given priority in the court;[506] (ii) the written procedure is simplified and limited to a single exchange of pleadings

---

[500] See Arts 43–63 of the Rules of Procedure of the CFI; 37–44 and 55–62 of the Rules of Procedure of the ECJ.

[501] Arts 64 and 65 of the Rules of Procedure of the CFI; Arts 45 and 54a of the Rules of Procedure of the ECJ.

[502] Art 76(a) of the Rules of Procedure of the CFI and Art 62(a) of the Rules of Procedure of the ECJ. A similar procedure is established in Art 62(a) of the Rules of Procedure of the ECJ. For a more detailed analysis of the functioning of the expedited procedure see DG Competition Newsletter, 3rd issue, October 2002, K Fountoukakos, 'Judicial Review and Merger Control: the CFI's expedited procedure', available at http://www.ec.europa.eu/comm/competition/publications/cpn/ and Eric Barbier de la Serre, 'Accelerated and Expedited Procedures before the EC Courts: a review of the practice', Common Market Law Review, Vol 43, No 3, June 2006.

[503] Pursuant to Art 76a(1): 'The application may state that certain pleas in law or arguments or certain passages of the application initiating the proceedings or the defence are raised only in the event that the case is not decided under an expedited procedure, in particular, by enclosing with the application an abbreviated version of the application initiating the proceedings and a list of the annexes which are to be taken into consideration only if the case is decided under an expedited procedure.' This provision, which was introduced in the recent amendment of Art 76a (see OJ L298 of 15.11.2005, p 1), in essence invites the parties to agree to limit their pleadings if the expedited procedure is granted.

[504] See Art 76a(4).

[505] However, if the CFI decides not to adjudicate under the expedited procedure, the defendant will be given an additional month in order to lodge, or as the case may be, supplement its defence (Art 76a(2)).

[506] Derogation from Art 55 of the Rules of Procedure of CFI. See Art 76a(1), last sentence.

(application and defence);[507] (iii) the CFI will make greater use of pre-hearing measures of organisation of procedure;[508] (iv) the Court will in principle devote more time to the oral procedure allowing all aspects of the case to be argued comprehensively and in depth;[509] and (v) the expedited procedure will, normally, lead to a judgment being rendered within a maximum period of less than 12 months.[510]

The expedited procedure has been used successfully in recent merger cases[511] and it should continue to provide a means for timely and effective judicial review to applicants challenging Commission decisions in the field of mergers. It should be noted, however, that this procedure places enormous strain on the CFI's limited resources and, as a result, the court may be reluctant to grant the benefit of the expedited procedure in a large number of cases.[512]   **5.671**

Another means of obtaining speedy judicial intervention is for applicants to seek interim measures by lodging a separate action for the suspension of a contested Commission decision or other interim measures pursuant to Articles 242 and 243 EC and Articles 104–110 of the Rules of Procedure of the CFI. Applicants need to show that they have a prima facie case, that there is urgency which makes interim measures necessary and that the balance of interests leans in their favour. The precedents from the Court make it extremely difficult to obtain interim measures in general[513] and in merger cases in particular.[514]   **5.672**

---

[507] A written reply and rejoinder as well as interventions and replies to interventions will only be allowed exceptionally by way of measures of organisation of procedure in accordance with Art 64 of the Rules of Procedure of CFI (see Art 76a(2), second sub-para).

[508] Such measures can include the clarification of orders sought or of the pleas in law and arguments between the parties, amicable settlements of proceedings, taking of evidence, submission of written questions by the Court to the parties, etc.

[509] To facilitate the oral hearing, the parties should submit to the CFI and to the other parties an outline of the arguments which they intend to present at the oral hearing approximately two weeks in advance of the hearing. At the oral hearing, the parties may supplement their arguments and offer further evidence. They must, however, give reasons for the delay in offering such further evidence.

[510] It should be stressed that there is no guarantee as to timing as this is not specified in the Rules of Procedure. Indeed, the recent judgment in *Impala v Commission*, judgment of 13.7.2006, not yet published in the ECR, was delivered approximately 19 months after the appeal was lodged even though the case was adjudicated under the expedited procedure.

[511] See in particular Case T-87/05 *EDP v Commission*, judgment of 21.9.2005, not yet published in the ECR, Case T-5/02 *Tetra Laval v Commission* [2002] ECR II-4381 and Case T-310/01 *Schneider Electric v Commission* [2002] ECR II-4071. The *EDP* judgment was delivered in a record time of just under seven months from the lodging of the application.

[512] See Bo Vesterdorf, *Judicial Review in EC Competition Law: Reflections on the Role of the Community Courts in the EC System of Competition Law Enforcement*, Competition Policy International, Vol. 1, No. 2, Autumn 2005. In this paper (see footnote 50), Bo Vesterdorf highlights that the CFI has been able to grant the benefit of the expedited procedure in the overwhelming majority of merger cases in which it was requested and that over 70% of all expedited procedure cases before the CFI are merger cases.

[513] For the difficulties in meeting the condition on urgency, see case T-201/04 R, *Microsoft v Commission* [2004] ECR II-2977.

[514] The President of the CFI has granted interim measures to a third party challenging a Commission merger decision in only one case: Case T-88/94R *Société Commerciale des Potasses v Commission* [1994] ECR II-401. It should be noted here that it would be difficult for merging parties to seek suspension of a prohibition decision. This is because such a decision is a 'negative' act and its suspension does not in principle have the effect of changing the legal situation of the applicant (see for negative acts in general—not in a merger context— Case T-369/03 R *Arizona Chemicals and others v Commission*, Order of 16.1.2004 [2004] ECR II-205, at paras 61–62. In the field of mergers, a suspension of a prohibition decision would not therefore automatically

(g) Standard and Role of Judicial Review[515]

5.673 When scrutinising the Commission's merger decisions, the CFI applies the so-called judicial review standard or 'manifest error' standard of review.[516] This standard of review is normally inherent in an administrative system in which the court is entrusted with the task of reviewing the legality of the administration's decisions and does not have jurisdiction to re-try cases *de novo*.

5.674 According to the manifest error standard, the CFI will scrutinise the Commission's decisions closely for correct application of the law and correctness of the underlying primary facts but when it comes to matters of complex economic appreciation of facts (such as the overall economic assessment under Article 2 of the Merger Regulation), the CFI will allow the Commission a considerable margin of appreciation and will only annul a Commission decision where it finds that the Commission has committed *manifest* errors of appreciation.[517] Since it only has a judicial review role and not the role of a court trying a case on its merits, the CFI is not permitted to substitute its own view for that of the Commission.[518]

---

result in a positive permission to consummate the merger. For a recent interim measures merger case, see Case T-417/05 R *Endesa v Commission*, Order of the President of the CFI of 1.2.2006, not yet published in the ECR.

[515] For a detailed discussion of the standard of review and standard of proof in merger cases see the following article by the President of the CFI, Bo Vesterdorf, 'Standard of proof in merger cases: reflections in the light of recent case law of the Community Courts', European Competition Law Journal (March 2005), p 3.

[516] See Joined Cases C-68/94 and C-30/95 *Kali & Salz* [1998] ECR I-1375; and Case T-102/96 *Gencor v Commission* [1999] ECR II-753. See also Case T-210/01 *General Electric v Commission*, judgment of 14.12.2005, not yet published in the ECR, paras 60–76, for a discussion of the appropriate standard of review in merger cases.

[517] See paras 223-224 of the *Kali & Salz* judgment (Case C-68/94), where the Court held that the Merger Regulation's provisions 'confer on the Commission a certain discretion, especially with respect to assessments of an economic nature' and that consequently 'review by the Community judicature of the exercise of that discretion, which is essential for defining the rules on concentrations, must take account of the discretionary margin implicit in the provisions of an economic nature which form part of the rules on concentrations'. This test was reaffirmed by the ECJ in Case C-12/03 P *Tetra Laval v Commission* [2005] ECR I-987, para 38. The ECJ's language suggests, however, a tightening of this standard. See para 39 of the judgment and para 5.676 *et seq* below.
The distinction of the intensity of review as regards review of facts or review of assessment of facts has been highlighted by Advocate General Tizzano in his Opinion in Case C-12/03P *Commission v Tetra Laval*, para 86. The AG stressed that, 'With regard to the findings of fact, the review is clearly more intense, in that the issue is to verify objectively and materially the accuracy of certain facts and the correctness of the conclusions drawn in order to establish whether certain known facts make it possible to prove the existence of other facts to be ascertained. By contrast, with regard to the complex economic assessments made by the Commission, review by the Community judicature is necessarily more limited, since the latter has to respect the broad discretion inherent in that kind of assessment and may not substitute its own point of view for that of the body which is institutionally responsible for making those assessments'.

[518] See Case T-342/00 *Petrolessence v Commission* [2003] ECR II-1161, where the Court held that the applicants' arguments could be accepted 'only if they show that the Commission's appraisal . . . is *manifestly* erroneous. However, it must be observed that the applicants have not established that the Commission's appraisal of those points is clearly mistaken and it must be concluded that the applicants' present arguments consist in inviting the Court of First Instance *to substitute a different appraisal of their candidacy for that of the Commission*' something which the CFI refused to do (point 103 of the judgment, emphasis added). In his Opinion in Case C-12/03P *Commission v Tetra Laval*, para 89, Advocate General Tizzano stressed this point by stating that '[t]he rules on the division of powers between the Commission and the Community judicature, which are fundamental to the Community institutional system, do not however allow the judicature to go further, and particularly . . . to enter into the merits of the Commission's complex economic assessments or to substitute its own point of view for that of the institution'.

The judicial review standard does not mean that scrutiny by the CFI is lax. Quite the **5.675** contrary.[519] The CFI will not hesitate to annul Commission decisions where the underlying facts on which the Commission relies to support its case are erroneous, where the Commission has committed procedural breaches which have a significant impact on the outcome of the case or where the Commission's assessment of facts or economic reasoning reveals manifest errors of appreciation. The CFI's demanding level of review was clearly demonstrated in a 2002 series of merger prohibition decisions which were annulled by the CFI for procedural breaches, errors of fact, lack of evidence and manifest errors of appreciation.[520]

It should be noted that the issue of the appropriate standard of review was expressly **5.676** addressed by the ECJ in the *Tetra Laval* judgment. The ECJ confirmed that the standard of review remains the manifest error standard which has been consistently applied by the Community courts. However, the ECJ did not agree with the Commission that the CFI had exceeded this standard by reviewing particularly closely the Commission's assessment of the Tetra Laval/Sidel merger.[521] Suggesting a possible tightening of the traditional manifest error standard, the ECJ held that '[w]hilst the Court recognises that the Commission has a margin of discretion with regard to economic matters, that does not mean that the Community Courts must refrain from reviewing the Commission's interpretation of information of an economic nature. Not only must the Community Courts, inter alia, establish whether the evidence relied on is factually accurate, reliable and consistent but also whether that evidence contains all the information which must be taken into account in order to assess a complex situation and whether it is capable of substantiating the conclusions drawn from it. Such a review is all the more necessary in the case of a prospective analysis required when examining a planned merger with conglomerate effect.'[522]

Following *Tetra Laval*, the CFI had the opportunity to adjudicate on a number of merger cases **5.677** reviewing both prohibition[523] and authorisation decisions.[524] In a number of those cases, the CFI appeared to be applying the traditional standard of judicial review. For example,

---

[519] See Advocate General Tizzano's Opinion in Case C-12/03P *Commission v Tetra Laval*, para 88 where the learned AG stated that the duties imposed on the Commission under the Merger Regulation 'make it possible for the Community judicature to exercise an adequate review'.

[520] Case T-342/99 *Airtours plc v Commission* [2002] ECR II-2585; Case T-310/01 *Schneider Electric v Commission* [2002] ECR II-4071; and Case T-5/02 *Tetra Laval v Commission* [2002] ECR II-4381.

[521] However, the complexity and subjective nature of this issue is perhaps reflected in the fact that the Commission's arguments on the standard of review were largely upheld by Advocate General Tizzano in his opinion which, on this point, was not followed by the ECJ. See Opinion in Case C-12/03P *Commission v Tetra Laval*. On the standard of proof issue, Advocate General Tizzano stressed that the Commission's objections on this point 'hit the mark' and that 'the Court of First Instance incorrectly substituted its own point of view for the Commission's, formulating its own autonomous prediction of future developments in the market' and thus 'that court therefore plainly overstepped the bounds of its judicial review' (points 93 and 94 of the Opinion).

[522] Case C-12/03 P, *Commission v Tetra Laval* [2005] ECR I-987.

[523] Case T-210/01 *General Electric v Commission*, judgment of 14.12.2005, not yet reported in the ECR; and Case T-87/05 *EDP v Commission*, judgment of 21.9.2005, not yet reported in the ECR.

[524] Case T-177/04 *easyJet v Commission*, judgment of 4.7.2006, not yet reported in the ECR; Case T-464/04 *Impala v Commission*, judgment of 13.7.2006, not yet published in the ECR; and Case T-282/02, *Cementbouw v Commission*, judgment of 23.2.2006, not yet published in the ECR (on appeal Case C-202/06 P).

in *easyJet v Commission* (review of an authorisation decision) the CFI referred to the traditional standard of review whereby 'review by the Community judicature of complex economic assessments made by the Commission in the exercise of the power of assessment conferred on it by [the Merger Regulation] is limited to ensuring compliance with the rules governing procedure and the statement of reasons, as well as the substantive accuracy of the facts and the absence of manifest errors of assessment or misuse of powers'. [525] This standard of review was also clearly referred to by the CFI in *EDP v Commission* (review of a prohibition decision) where the CFI also stated clearly that '*it is still the case that the errors invoked by the applicant must be manifest if the contested decision is to be annulled*'[526] and in *Cementbouw v Commission* where the CFI also added that, given this standard, 'it is not for the Court of First Instance to substitute its own economic assessment for that of the Commission'.[527]

5.678 By contrast, in cases such as *General Electric v Commission*[528] (review of a prohibition decision), and *Impala* v *Commission*[529] (review of an authorisation decision), the CFI appeared to follow the arguably stricter post-*Tetra Laval* standard of review and made specific reference to the ECJ's dicta in *Tetra Laval* indicating a heightened standard of review (see para 5.676 above).

5.679 For example, in *General Electric v Commission* the CFI went through an analysis of the appropriate standard of review (at para 57 *et seq*), referred to the ECJ's judgment in *Tetra Laval* and stated that 'effective judicial review is all the more necessary when the Commission carries out a prospective analysis of developments which might occur on a market as a result of a proposed concentration'.[530] In a conglomerate merger situation where the Commission argues that dominance would be created due to a particular conduct adopted by the parties following the merger, 'the Commission had the onus to provide convincing evidence to support its conclusion that the merged entity would probably behave in the way foreseen'.[531]

5.680 The CFI's judgment in *Impala v Commission* merits further discussion as to the standard of review applied by the CFI. The CFI's demanding level of review was clearly demonstrated in this judgment where the CFI, clearly referring to the standard of review set out by the ECJ in *Tetra Laval*, held that the Commission's assessment of whether a collective dominant position existed prior to the merger was inadequately reasoned and characterised by manifest errors of assessment. What distinguishes this judgment from the 2002 annulments (and from *General Electric v Commission*) is that it concerned a Commission *authorisation* decision and not a prohibition decision. The CFI showed clearly that, even when reviewing

---

[525] Case T-177/04 *easyJet v Commission*, judgment of 4.7.2006, not yet reported in the ECR, at para 44.

[526] Case T-87/05 *EDP v Commission*, judgment of 21.9.2005, not yet reported in the ECR, at para 152 (emphasis added).

[527] Case T-282/02,*Cementbouw v Commission*, judgment of 23.2.2006, not yet published in the ECR (on appeal Case C-202/06 P), at para 197.

[528] Case T-210/01 *General Electric v Commission*, judgment of 14.12.2005, not yet reported in the ECR.

[529] Case T-464/04 *Impala v Commission*, judgment of 13.7.2006, not yet published in the ECR. The judgment has been appealed. See Case C-413/06 P.

[530] Case T-210/01 *General Electric v Commission*, para 64.

[531] ibid, para 69.

the legality of an authorisation decision, it may scrutinise the Commission's evidence, reasoning and assessment closely. The CFI was highly critical of the Commission's (lack of) reasoning and assessment of the evidence. In the CFI's view the evidence and the Commission's assessment and reasoning were manifestly erroneous and clearly inadequate to support a finding of absence of collective dominance before the merger and the absence of creation of dominance after the merger. On the contrary, the CFI thought that the extensive evidence to which the Commission itself referred in the decision (for example as regards market transparency) appeared to support the opposite conclusion. The CFI was also highly critical of the Commission's inability to explain material inconsistencies in the facts and its position with regard to the facts between the SO and the final decision.[532]

While the 2002 annulments, the ECJ's judgment in *Tetra Laval*, and the subsequent CFI judgments in *General Electric v Commission* and *Impala v Commission* appear to indicate a marked shift towards closer scrutiny of Commission decisions, in other post-*Tetra Laval* judgments, the CFI appears to have applied a more traditional standard of review. Each case is clearly affected by its own circumstances and facts and it remains to be seen how the CFI will exercise its judicial review function and what standard of review it will apply in future merger cases.[533] **5.681**

(h) Procedure Following Annulment

Where the CFI annuls a Commission decision undertaken under the Merger Regulation, it has a judicial review role and cannot authorise or prohibit the merger itself. The case reverts to the Commission for re-examination. Article 10(5) of the Merger Regulation governs the procedure to be followed. **5.682**

The case must be re-examined starting from the beginning of the procedure in Phase I with a view to adopting an Article 6 (Phase I) decision either authorising the case or proceeding to an in-depth (Phase II) investigation and ultimately an Article 8 final decision.[534] **5.683**

---

[532] The CFI's judgment in *Impala* also provides interesting commentary regarding the extent of any requirement for consistency between the SO and the decision in merger proceedings. The CFI confirmed that the Commission was 'not obliged to explain any differences by comparison with the statement of objections, since that is a preparatory document containing assessments which have purely provisional in nature' and noted the Commission's obligation 'to drop any objections which may have proved unfounded'. Consequently the mere fact that the Commission did not explain in the body of the decision the change in its position by comparison with that set out in the statement of objections cannot as such constitute a lack of, or an insufficient, statement of reasons'. On the other hand, the CFI observed that although the SO is only a provisional document and 'the Commission is perfectly entitled, and indeed obliged, to modify its position in light of the information which it has obtained in the course of its investigation, it cannot suppress certain relevant elements on the sole ground that they might not be consistent with its new assessment'. Critically, the Court held that 'the Commission must be in a position to explain, not in the decision admittedly, but at least in the context of proceedings before the Court, its reasons for considering that its provisional findings were incorrect' and 'above all, the findings set out in the decision must be compatible with the findings of fact made in the statement of objections, in so far as it is not established that the latter findings were incorrect'. (Case T-464/04 *Impala v Commission*, in particular paras 284, 285, 300 and 335).

[533] As noted above, the classic manifest error standard appears to have been applied by the CFI in the (later than *Tetra Laval*) *EDP* judgment of 21 September 2005, Case T-87/05 *EDP v Commission*, not yet published in the ECR, at para 151.

See also Case T-210/01 *General Electric v Commission*, judgment of 14.12.2005, not yet published in the ECR, in particular para 57 *et seq*, for a discussion of standard of review and standard of proof issues.

[534] Article 10(5), first sub-para, of the Merger Regulation.

5.684 The case must be examined in the light of current market conditions.[535] This is a reasonable requirement since a lengthy period of time may have passed between the original examination and the annulment of the Commission's decision.

5.685 As the re-examination goes back to the beginning of Phase I and is done in the light of current market conditions, Article 10(5) of the Merger Regulation requires the parties to submit a new notification or supplement the original notification, without delay, where the original notification has become incomplete by reason of intervening changes in market conditions or in the information provided. If there are no such changes, the parties must provide a certification to this effect. The Phase I deadlines of Article 10(1) start on the working day following that of the receipt of complete information in a new notification, a supplemented notification, or a certification. The provisions relating to Form CO are also applicable to supplements and certifications.[536]

5.686 The normal Phase I procedure is then followed. The Commission re-examines the case not only in the light of the new notification and new market conditions but also taking into account the findings in the CFI's judgment.[537,538]

---

[535] ibid, Art 10(5), second sub-para.

[536] Art 6(2), second sub-para of the Implementing Regulation.

[537] For a case examined pursuant to Art 10(5) of Regulation 4064/89 see case M.2416 *Tetra Laval/Sidel* [2003]. The Commission re-examined the case following annulment of its first prohibition decision by the CFI in Case T-5/02 *Tetra Laval v Commission* [2002] ECR II-4381. Following the second examination and taking into account the CFI's judgment, the Commission authorised the merger subject to conditions and obligations pursuant to Art 6(2) of Regulation 4064/89. See Commission press release IP/03/36 of 14/01/2003.

[538] Art 233 of the EC Treaty requires institutions to draw the consequences of a judgment of the Community courts annulling one of their decisions. The CFI cannot, on the contrary, instruct the Commission to act in a particular way. Its judgment should be limited to confirming or annulling, partially or wholly, the Commission's decision.

6

ARTICLE 86—EXCLUSIVE RIGHTS AND OTHER ANTI-COMPETITIVE STATE MEASURES

José Luis Buendia Sierra

A. Introduction

Competition law normally deals only with the behaviour of undertakings   Competition **6.01** law has traditionally dealt with anti-competitive behaviour of undertakings. The private or public nature of ownership is irrelevant in that respect. In principle both public (ie State controlled) and private undertakings are subject to competition rules.

6.02 **State defence doctrine** The normal competition rules (ie Articles 81 and 82 (former Articles 85 and 86) of the EC Treaty) only apply to the autonomous behaviour of undertakings. Such rules can only be infringed (and the undertaking held responsible) when the behaviour is the result of an autonomous decision of the undertaking. The autonomous character of the behaviour is not excluded by mere persuasion or encouragement from the State. However, binding State measures imposing particular behaviour on an undertaking do exclude such autonomy of decision. In principle, a State-imposed behaviour cannot constitute an infringement of normal competition rules by the undertaking. The undertaking may invoke this 'State defence doctrine' to avoid antitrust liability when the behaviour is imposed by law. This lack of liability on the part of the undertaking is to some extent compensated for by State liability under Article 86(1) (former Article 90(1)) of the EC Treaty.[1]

6.03 **State liability under competition law** Although competition law has traditionally been regarded as dealing only with the behaviour of undertakings, it is obvious that State measures imposing anti-competitive behaviours may easily undermine the effectiveness of EC competition rules. This has led the European Court of Justice (following the example of the US Supreme Court) to establish a doctrine that allows for a limited application of antitrust rules to State measures which force or induce undertakings to behave anti-competitively.

Application of Articles 3(g), 10 and 81/82 of the EC Treaty to anti-competitive state measures

6.04 *Initial position (broad interpretation)* This doctrine was based on the combined application of Article 3(g),[2] Article 10,[3] and Articles 81 and/or 82 (former Articles 3(g), 5 and 85/86) of the EC Treaty and was established in the *Inno/ATAB* case.[4] The basic reasoning was as follows: Article 10 prevents Member States from adopting measures depriving EC rules of their *effet utile*. Article 3(g) establishes undistorted competition as one of the main Community goals and Articles 81 and 82 prohibit anti-competitive behaviour by undertakings. Taken together, all these provisions were interpreted by the Court of Justice as prohibiting Member States from depriving competition rules of their *effet utile* by adopting measures that would allow the undertakings to ignore the limits imposed by Articles 81 and 82 of the Treaty.[5] At one point this case law seemed to imply that every State measure producing

---

[1] See para 6.59 below.

[2] Art 3 of the EC Treaty reads as follows: 'For the purposes set out in Article 2, the activities of the Community shall include, as provided in this Treaty and in accordance with the timetable set out therein:... (g) a system ensuring that competition in the internal market is not distorted ...'.

[3] Art 10 (former Art 5) of the EC Treaty reads as follows: 'Member States shall take all appropriate measures, whether general or particular, to ensure fulfilment of the obligations arising out of this Treaty or resulting from action taken by the institutions of the Community. They shall facilitate the achievement of the Community's tasks. They shall abstain from any measure which could jeopardise the attainment of the objectives of this Treaty.'

[4] Case 13/77 *Inno v ATAB* [1977] ECR 2144, paras 31–33.

[5] The leading cases of the Court of Justice were: Case 229/83 *Leclerc v Au Blé Vert* [1985] ECR 1; Case 231/83 *Cullet* [1985] ECR 305; Case 123/83 *BNIC v Clair* [1985] ECR 391; Joined Cases 209–213/84 *Nouvelles Frontières* [1986] ECR 1425; Case 311/85 *Vlaamse Reisbureaus* [1987] ECR 3801; Case 267/86 *Van Eycke* [1988] ECR 4769. For some of the literature on the subject see F Castillo de la Torre, 'State Action defence in EC Antitrust Law' [2005] 28 World Competition 407–431; Y Galmont and J Biancarelli, 'Les réglementations nationales en matière de prix au regard du droit communautaire' [1985] RTDE 299; G Marenco, 'Le Traité CEE interdit-il aux Etats membres de restreindre la concurrence?' [1986] CDE 294–295; G Marenco, 'Effets des règles communautaires de concurrence (art 85 et 86) sur l'activité des Etats membres'

restrictive effects on competition would have *effects* similar to those of a cartel (or to those of an abuse of a dominant position). As a consequence every State measure producing restrictive *effects* on competition would be contrary to Articles 3(g), 10 and 81 (or 82) of the EC Treaty, even in the absence of any behaviour by the undertaking. This would mean that every measure taken by the State having an impact on the price or the quantity of goods or services would be prohibited. Such an approach would have greatly reduced the ability of Member States to intervene in the economy.

Court narrows interpretation   Although the theoretical implications of this doctrine were far-reaching, its practical impact has been much more limited. The reasons are twofold. First of all, the Court of Justice has subsequently interpreted this *effet utile* in a restrictive way. According to this more restrictive case law, which originated in 1993 with the *Meng*, *Reiff* and *Ohra* cases, a mere anti-competitive effect cannot in the absence of *behaviour* of undertakings mean that the State measure is contrary to Articles 3(g), 10 and 81 or 82 of the EC Treaty.[6] Only those State measures that impose or induce anti-competitive behaviour by undertakings, reinforce the effects of anti-competitive behaviour or delegate regulatory powers to private operators can be considered as violating these provisions. This very strict test dramatically reduces the scope of application of Articles 3(g), 10 and 81/82 as regards anti-competitive State measures.[7]   **6.05**

Moreover, this case law on Articles 3(g), 10 and 81/82 of the EC Treaty has not provided significant added value to EC law. The reason is that EC competition law, contrary to many other competition systems (such as US antitrust), has always had specific provisions dealing with the most significant anti-competitive State measures, such as State aids or exclusive rights. The need for 'creative' jurisprudence was therefore much less marked and its re-definition in a restrictive way has meant that it has had, in practice, a very limited impact.   **6.06**

Application of Articles 86, 87 and 88 to anti-competitive state measures   EC competition law therefore includes not only Articles 81 and 82, the rules addressed to undertakings, but also Articles 86, 87 and 88 (former Articles 90, 92 and 93), the rules addressed to the   **6.07**

---

in J Schwarze (ed), *Les pouvoirs discrétionnaires des EE.MM. de la CE dans le domaine de la pol. économique et leurs limites en vertu du TCEE*, Contributions to an International Colloquium of the European University Institute, Florence 14–15 May 1987 (Baden-Baden: Nomos Verlagsgesellschaft, 1988) 53–67; P Pescatore, 'Public and Private Aspects of Community Competition Law' [1986] FCLI 381–430; M Waelbroeck, 'Les rapports entre les règles sur la libre circulation des marchandises et les règles de concurrence applicables aux entreprises dans la CEE' in Various, *Du droit international au droit de l'intégration—Liber Amicorum Pierre Pescatore* (Baden-Baden: Nomos Verlagsgesellschaft, 1987) 781–803; R Joliet, 'Réglementation étatiques anticoncurrentielles et Droit communautaire' [1988] CDE 363–382; L Gyselen, 'Anticompetitive State measures under the EC Treaty: towards a substantive legality standard' [1994] ELR Competition checklist 55 *et seq*; JF Verstrynge, 'The Obligations of Member States as Regards Competition in the EEC Treaty' [1988] FCLI 17.1–17.43; U Bøegh Henriksen, *Anti-Competitive State Measures in the European Community* (Copenhagen: Handelshøjskolens Forlag, 1994) 21–29.

  6 Case C-2/91 *Meng* [1993] ECR I-5797, para 14; Case C-185/91 *Reiff* [1993] ECR I-5847, para 14; and Case C-245/91 *Ohra* [1993] ECR I-5851, para 10. This case law has been largely confirmed in many subsequent judgments, such as: Case C-35/99 *Arduino* [2002] ECR I-1529; Case C-309/99 *Wouters* [2002] ECR I-1577; and Case C-198/01 *CIF* [2003] ECR I-8055.

  7 N Reich, 'The "November Revolution" of the European Court of Justice: Keck, Meng and Audi revisited' [1994] 21 CML Rev 459–492; B Van Der Esch, 'Loyauté fédérale et subsidiarité: à propos des arrêts du 17 novembre 1993 dans les affaires C-2/91 (Meng), C-245/91 (Ohra) et C-185/91 (Reiff)' [1994] CDE 536; A Bach, 'Judgments of the Court, Cases C-185/91 Reiff, C-2/91 Meng and C-245/91 Ohra' [1994] CML Rev 1357–1374.

Member States. Articles 87 and 88 deal with one of the more characteristic instruments for State intervention in the market: State aids. Due to their specific character, State aids fall outside the scope of this chapter.[8] The other provision, Article 86, refers to exclusive rights granted by the State in favour of certain undertakings and also to other kinds of restrictive State measures related to public or privileged undertakings. This provision also contains a limited exception from competition and other EC rules in favour of services of general economic interest. Finally, Article 86 also provides for a special procedure. These three dimensions of Article 86 are examined in this chapter.

B. Article 86(1): State Measures in Respect of Public or Privileged Undertakings

(1) Addressees and Regulatory Content

6.08   Article 86(1) (former Article 90(1)) provides:

> In the case of public undertakings and undertakings to which Member States grant special or exclusive rights, Member States shall neither enact nor maintain in force any measure contrary to the rules contained in this Treaty, in particular those rules provided for in Articles 12 and 81 to 89.

Article 86(1) of the EC Treaty is only addressed to Member States.[9] As interpreted by the Court of Justice this provision prohibits Member States from adopting or maintaining in force any measures contrary to the Treaty:

- when such measures benefit Public undertakings or undertakings to which Member States grant exclusive or special rights; or
- when these undertakings are the instrument used by the Member State for the implementation of the measures.[10]

---

[8] See J-P Keppene, *Guide des aides d'Etat en droit communautaire* (Bruxelles: Bruylant, 1999) for a general overview of State aid rules.

[9] Case C-41/90 *Höfner* [1991] ECR I-2015, para 16; Case C-320/91 *Corbeau* [1993] ECR I-2533, paras 10–12.

[10] See JL Buendia Sierra, *Exclusive Rights and State Monopolies in EC Law* (Oxford University Press, 1999) Chapters 4–6; and F Blum and A Logue, *State Monopolies under EC Law* (Chichester: Wiley, 1998). Different collective works have dealt with Art 86: Various, *Concorrenza tra settore pubblico e privato nella CEE*, Colloquio di Bruxelles della 'Ligue Internationale contre la concurrence déloyale' 5–6 March [1963] RDI anno XII 1–256; Various, *L'entreprise publique et la concurrence. Les articles 90 et 37 du Traité CEE et leurs relations avec la concurrence*, Semaine de Bruges 1968 (De Temple, Bruges, 1969); Various, *Equal treatment of public and private enterprises*, 1978 FIDE Congress in Copenhagen [1978] FIDE Copenhagen volume 2; Various, *Le processus de libéralisation d'activités économiques et de privatisation d'entreprises face au Droit de la concurrence*, XVI Congrès de la FIDE [1994] FIDE Rome iii. Among the individual contributions see: R Joliet, 'Contribution à l'étude du régime des entreprises publiques dans la CEE' [1965] AFDL i 23–92; G Marenco, 'Public Sector and Community Law' [1983] 20 CML Rev 495–527; J Temple Lang, 'Community Antitrust Law and Government Measures relating to Public and Privileged Entreprises: Article 90 EEC Treaty' [1984] FCLI 543–581; H Papaconstantinou, *Free Trade and Competition in the EEC. Law, Policy and Practice* (London/New York: Routledge, 1988); LM Pais Antunes, 'L'Article 90 du Traité CEE—Obligations des Etats Membres et pouvoirs de la Commission' [1991] RTDE ii 187–209; D Edward and M Hoskins, 'Article 90: deregulation and EC Law. Reflections arising from the XVI FIDE Conference' [1995] 32 CM LRev 157–186; R Kovar, 'Droit communautaire et service public: esprit d'orthodoxie ou pensée laïcisée' [1996] RTDE xxxii (ii) 215–242, xxxii (iii) 493–533.

Article 86(1) is also interpreted as applying to the *granting* of exclusive rights to any undertaking when such a grant is contrary to another Article of the EC Treaty.[11]

State measures which are related to public or privileged undertakings only fall under **6.09** Article 86(1) if they are 'contrary to the rules contained in this Treaty, in particular those rules provided for in Articles 12 and 81 to 89'. This means that Article 86(1) is not entirely self-contained, and cannot be applied alone. In order to establish a specific obligation for Member States the provision must always be applied 'in combination with' another rule of the EC Treaty. This implies that Article 86(1) has a multiplicity of legal content with different spheres of application.

(2) State Measures

Whilst Articles 81 and 82 refer to the behaviour of undertakings, Article 86(1) refers to **6.10** State measures. A State measure is an act undertaken by a public entity in its role as a public authority. However, the distinction between State measures and behaviour of undertakings cannot be based solely on the private or public nature of the entity. Even if private entities cannot, as a general rule, adopt State measures, public entities may undertake economic activities. In this case, the commercial activities of the public entities are clearly subject to Articles 81 and 82, even if fulfilled directly by a public body.[12] It is therefore necessary to differentiate between the different acts of public entities, ie between 'State measures', to which Article 86(1) may apply, and the 'behaviour of public undertakings', to which Articles 81 and 82 may apply.

Formal criteria are not decisive in defining 'state measures'   It is very tempting to rely **6.11** solely on formal criteria to make the distinction referred to above. According to this approach, public law instruments would be examined under Article 86(1) and private law instruments under Articles 81 and 82.[13] This has the advantage of being a rather simple and easy-to-use criterion. It is also a reasonably realistic one. After all, State measures are normally adopted through laws, acts, regulations, administrative rules, or other instruments of public law. Private law contracts are normally used by public entities when exercising a commercial activity.

The function of the Act is the decisive factor in defining 'state measures'   However, **6.12** although the form of the relevant instrument is an important factor, it cannot be the sole factor. EC law has always been reluctant to rely on formal criteria in order to define the scope of its different provisions. The reason for this reluctance is that, very often, the different Member States use different legal instruments to achieve the same results. In order to be credible, EC law must be able to apply similar rules to situations that are similar from a substantive point of view. This means that the criterion of the private or public law form of the relevant act must be complemented with another criterion: that of its functional nature. An act whose function is to regulate the market-place from the perspective of the

---

[11] Paras 6.46–6.47 below.
[12] Case C-393/92 *Almelo* [1994] ECR I-1517, para 31.
[13] In Case C-18/93 *Corsica Ferries* [1994] ECR I-1825, para 43, the Court of Justice applied Art 86 to an act as commercial in nature as a tariff. The criterion used was obviously a formal one.

public interest would be a 'State measure'.[14] This would be the case even if adopted under the form of a private law contract.[15] An act of a purely commercial nature would fall under Articles 81 and 82 even if adopted under a public law form.[16]

6.13 **The form of the Act creates a presumption, but its function is the decisive criterion in defining it as a 'state measure'** It follows from this that the functional nature of the act—rather than its form—should, at least in theory, be the decisive criterion in determining the borderline between Article 86(1) on the one hand and Articles 81 and 82 on the other hand. In practice, however, a private law form will create a strong presumption that one is dealing not with a State measure but with the 'behaviour' of a public undertaking. It would nevertheless still be possible—but not easy—to destroy this presumption by relying on the regulatory nature of the act.

6.14 **State measures may be adopted by any type of public authority** State measures can be adopted by any public entity of a Member State provided that the entity is invested with some kind of public authority role. Local or regional authorities, for instance, can adopt State measures like national authorities.[17]

(3) Related to Public or Privileged Undertakings

6.15 In order to fall under Article 86(1), a State measure must have a link with one or more 'undertakings' (ie, entities exercising an 'economic activity'). In principle, this undertaking must be either a 'public undertaking' or an 'undertaking to which the Member State grants exclusive or special rights'. These different concepts, and the precise nature of this link between the measure and the undertaking, are examined below.

(i) 'Economic activity'

6.16 *Article 86(1) applies to State regulation of economic activities* Article 86(1) only applies if the State measure relates to one or more entities that engage in an 'economic activity'. The State *measure* itself must of course have a regulatory nature, but the *activity*, which is being regulated by that measure, must be of an economic nature. In other words, Article 86(1) applies to State regulation of economic activities. Regulatory measures relating to non-economic activities (such as 'exclusive rights' in respect of national defence, public security, etc) are not covered by Article 86(1).

6.17 *Definition of 'economic activity'* The existence of an 'economic activity' is a prerequisite for the application, not only of Article 86(1), but of any competition rule. This notion embraces all activities of a commercial or industrial nature. Unfortunately, the borderline between economic and non-economic activities is particularly difficult to draw in the public sector. Indeed, the State provides its citizens with many 'services' in areas such as utilities, health, social security, education, or defence and it is not always easy to determine which ones are 'economic' (and whose regulation is therefore subject to Article 86(1)) and

---

[14] Case 30/87 *Bodson* [1988] ECR 2479.

[15] For instance, local authorities in Germany usually grant public service concessions to electricity distributors by means of private law contracts. It is submitted that these concessions should be treated as State measures to the extent that their aims are to regulate the market place from a perspective of public interest.

[16] Case 41/83 *British Telecommunications* [1985] ECR 873, paras 19–20.

[17] Case 30/87 *Bodson* [1988] ECR 2479; Case C-323/93 *La Crespelle* [1994] ECR I-5077.

which ones are not. Utilities, such as telecommunications, energy, transport, or postal services, are clearly economic activities. However, other public sector activities, such as health, social security or education, have a less clear status. This makes it necessary to find rational criteria by which to differentiate between the two groups.

Criteria used by the European Court of Justice In its *Höfner* judgment, the Court of Justice **6.18** seemed to imply that any activity that may conceivably be exercised by a private undertaking should be considered as an economic activity, irrespective of its actual mode of financing.[18] This seems a rather objective and simple criteria: it is in principle enough to show that the activity has been or is being fulfilled by private undertakings in another geographical area. [19]

The problem with such interpretation is that it perhaps construes the concept of economic **6.19** activity too widely. Indeed, it implies that activities such as health or social security are 'economic' and should, therefore, in principle, be subject to the competition rules.

However, the Court of Justice did not want to go that far. It therefore excluded certain **6.20** sectors from the scope of 'economic activities'. Such exclusions are based on a rationale not entirely consistent with the logic used in *Höfner*, even though the judgments may pay lip service to this logic.

For instance, the *Poucet* judgment made clear that 'compulsory social security systems' **6.21** cannot be considered as economic activities.[20] The reason for this seemed to be the mode of financing, based on 'solidarity' amongst contributors. Subsequent judgments explained that the exclusion of the 'economic' character of a given system of social security requires a detailed analysis of the 'solidarity' elements that are present in its financing mechanisms.[21] Social security systems based on a capitalisation model, of voluntary membership and whose perceptions are proportional to the contributions of each member are considered 'economic'.

Case law has sometimes relied on other, less apposite, criteria such as the exercise of public **6.22** prerogatives,[22] the pursuit of objectives of general interest,[23] or the fact that the activity is subject to the control of the State.[24] These criteria have introduced a certain degree of confusion into the definition of economic activity. Indeed, it seems obvious that certain entities may fulfil what is materially an economic activity while at the same time exercising public prerogatives. This latter fact cannot deprive the activity of its 'economic' character nor the entity of its 'entrepreneurial' nature.[25] It is also clear that there cannot be a contradiction between the 'economic' nature of an activity and the fact that it pursues 'objectives of general interest'. Otherwise Article 86(2) EC would serve no purpose. Finally, the mere fact that an activity is subject to

---

[18] Case C-41/90 *Höfner* [1991] ECR I-2015, paras 20–22.
[19] Case C-475/99 *Ambulanz Glöckner* [2001] ECR I-8089, para 20; Case T-1278/98 *Aéroports de Paris* [2000] ECR II-3929, para 124.
[20] Cases C-159 and 160/91 *Poucet* [1993] ECR I-637, paras 17–19.
[21] Case C-67/96 *Albany* [1999] ECR I-5751, paras 77–87; Cases C-115 to 117/97 *Brentjens* [1999] ECR I-6025, paras 77–87; Case C-219/97 *Drijvende* [1999] ECR I-6121, paras 67–77; Cases C-180 to 184/98 *Pavlov* [2000] ECR I-6451, paras 108–119; Case C-218/00 *Cisal di Battistello Venanzio* [2002] ECR I-691, paras 31–42; Cases C-264, 206, 254 y 355/01 *AOK Bundesverband* [2004] ECR I-2493, paras 45–66.
[22] Case C-364/92 *Eurocontrol* [1994] ECR I-43, paras 24–30.
[23] Case C-343/95 *Calì* [1997] ECR I-1547, paras 22–23.
[24] Case C-218/00 *Cisal di Battistello Venanzio* [2002] ECR I-691, paras 43–45.
[25] Case T-1278/98 *Aéroports de Paris* [2000] ECR II-3929, para 108.

State control cannot be relevant in its qualification as 'economic', since—by definition—all 'public undertakings' are fulfilling economic activities while subject to the control of the State.

6.23 Apart from these few debatable judgments, recent case law appears to have finally arrived at definitions of 'economic activity' and 'undertaking' that are reasonably clear and practical. According to this case law, the concept of 'undertaking' covers any entity engaged in economic activity, regardless of the legal status of the entity or way in which it is financed. An 'economic activity' is an activity consisting of offering goods and services on a given market.[26] The underlying logic is pure *Höfner* logic: any activity that may be fulfilled by a private undertaking must be considered 'economic' in nature. This can be established, for instance, by showing that the activity is actually being or has been fulfilled by private undertakings in another geographical area.

6.24 As an exception to this general concept, case law has excluded from the scope of 'economic activities' compulsory social security systems to the extent that they are based on the principle of 'solidarity'. Such exclusion is rather a deliberate choice by the Court than a logical extension of the general concept. Similarly, the case law has also excluded workers from the notion of 'undertakings'.[27] The Court might perhaps in the future use this same approach to exclude other sensitive sectors, such as national systems of compulsory education.

6.25 One should not forget that merely classifying an activity as 'economic' does not automatically imply an obligation to open up that activity to competition. Issues such as 'solidarity' in the financing or the character of 'general interest', even if they do not exclude the 'economic' nature of the activity, may justify the application of the exception set out in Article 86(2).[28]

6.26 **(ii) 'Public' undertaking** Article 86(1) applies, first of all, to State measures having a link with one or more 'public undertakings'. The concept of a public undertaking embraces all undertakings that are subject to the dominant influence of the public administrations of a Member State (at national, regional, or local level).

6.27 *Definition of public undertaking* The Commission has defined 'public undertaking' as any undertaking in which the public administrations may exercise, directly or indirectly, a dominant influence.[29] This dominant influence may be the result of ownership, financial participation, or the rules governing the undertaking. Dominant influence is presumed when the public administrations, whether directly or indirectly, control either the majority of the capital of the undertaking, or the majority of the places on the governing or controlling bodies of the undertaking. This concept of 'dominant influence' is closely connected with the concept of 'control' under the Merger Regulation.[30]

---

[26] Case C-218/00 *Cisal di Battistello Venanzio* [2002] ECR I-691, paras 22–23; Case C-475/99 *Ambulanz Glöckner* [2001] ECR I-8089, para 19; Cases C-180 to 184/98 *Pavlov* [2000] ECR I-6451, paras 74, 75 and 108–119.

[27] Case C-22/98 *Becu* [1999] ECR I-5665, paras 21–30.

[28] See paras 6.131 ff below. See *Buendia Sierra* (n 10 above) paras 1.141–1.201, for a detailed study of the concept of 'economic activity'.

[29] Art 2 of Commission Directive (EEC) 80/723 concerning the transparency of financial relations between Member States and their public undertakings [1980] OJ L195/35.

[30] Art 3(2) of Council Regulation (EC) 139/2004 on the control of concentrations between undertakings [2004] OJ L24/1.

A separate legal entity is not necessary   Public undertakings are often organised as   **6.28**
autonomous entities with distinct legal personalities. However, this is not always the case.
A public administration can also be considered as a public undertaking to the extent that it
is directly involved in the operation of an economic activity.[31]

Public undertakings after privatisation   The 'public' character of undertakings has rarely   **6.29**
been controversial in the past, but privatisation may have changed this. Even if privatisation
normally implies that a 'public undertaking' becomes a 'private undertaking', this is not always
the case. In some cases, the Government loses ownership but retains a 'golden share' in the privatised company. Recent judgments make clear that such mechanisms are likely to conflict
with EC rules on establishment.[32] Moreover, the powers connected with this 'golden share'
may in some cases be so important as to lead to 'dominant influence' by the public authorities.
In such a scenario a privatised undertaking may well remain a 'public undertaking' at least
from the point of view of Article 86(1).

(iii) 'privileged' undertakings   Article 86(1) also applies to State measures concerning   **6.30**
'undertakings to which Member States grant exclusive or special rights'. These 'privileged'
undertakings may be public or private.[33] This means that Article 86(1) may well apply to
State measures concerning a particular kind of private undertaking. What characterises
these undertakings is the granting by the Member State of 'special or exclusive rights'. It is
therefore necessary to examine these concepts.

Exclusive rights
Notion of 'exclusive right'   An 'exclusive right' is the right granted by a State measure to one   **6.31**
undertaking to engage in an economic activity on an exclusive basis. The legal notion of
'exclusive right' roughly corresponds to the popular notion of 'monopoly'.

The definition of exclusive rights means that, for each economic activity and in a given territory,   **6.32**
there is a single beneficiary: a monopolist.[34] It is also possible for exclusive rights to be granted in
parallel to different undertakings provided that they operate in different territories.[35] In this
case, each of the operators is a monopolist within its reserved territory. However, when the
activity is reserved to more than one competing undertaking, the State has not granted an
exclusive right, but 'special' rights.[36]

---

[31] Case 118/85 *Commission v Italy* (transparency) [1987] ECR 2599, para 11.
[32] Case C-98/01 *Commission v UK* [2003] ECR I-4641; Case C-463/00 *Commission v Spain* [2003] ECR
I-4581; Case C-503/99 *Commission v Belgium* [2002] ECR I-4809; Case C-367/98 *Commission v Portugal*
[2002] ECR I-4731; Case C-483/99 *Commission v France* [2002] ECR I-4781.
[33] The expression 'privileged enterprises' was used by J Temple Lang, 'Community Antitrust Law and
Government Measures relating to Public and Privileged Enterprises: Article 90 EEC Treaty' [1984] FCLI 543–581.
[34] Case C-203/96 *Dusseldorp* [1998] ECR I-4075, para 58; Case T-260/94 *Air Inter* [1997] ECR II-997,
paras 120–121. See *Buendia Sierra* (n 10 above) Ch 1, for a detailed study of the concept of 'exclusive right'.
[35] Case 30/87 *Bodson* [1988] ECR 2479; Case C-323/93 *La Crespelle* [1997] ECR I-5077, para 17.
[36] However, Case C-209/98 *Sydhavnens* [2000] ECR I-3743, paras 53–54, used the expression 'exclusive
rights' to refer to the rights granted to tree undertakings for the fulfilment of the same activity in the same territory. It is submitted that the correct qualification in such case should have been 'special rights'.

6.33   *Exclusive right and dominant position are different things*   Some judgments of the Court of Justice[37] and some Decisions of the Commission[38] suggest that the mere existence of an exclusive right automatically puts its holder in a dominant position. However, it is submitted that no such automatic link exists. The concept of an exclusive right is closely connected to but independent from the concept of 'dominant position' under Article 82 of the EC Treaty. The existence of an exclusive right depends entirely on legal factors. The existence of a dominant position depends on a number of economic factors. It is true that in most cases the protection from competition granted by the exclusive right puts the undertaking in a dominant position, as the Court stated in *Télémarketing*,[39] but this is not always the case. The key question, as the Court explained in *Bodson*,[40] is whether the scope of the exclusive right embraces a substantial part of a market which is 'relevant' from an economic point of view.[41] If so, the exclusive right will lead to a dominant position on that market (and Article 82 may apply). If this is not the case, the holder of the exclusive right may not have attained a dominant position within the meaning of Article 82. In any event, contrary to some interpretations, it is clear that the mere existence of an exclusive right does not automatically imply the existence of a dominant position.

6.34   *Exclusive rights are created by State measures*   In order to fall under Article 86(1), the exclusive right must be created by a State measure.[42] This means that it must be granted by a public administration acting in its role as a public authority. Exclusive rights granted by a public undertaking acting as an economic operator do not fall under Article 86(1) but under Article 81. For instance, in the *Almelo* case, an exclusive purchase contract between a local council (acting in its capacity as undertaking in charge of distribution of electricity) and a regional distributor was examined within the framework of Article 81.[43] The Commission seems to consider that Article 86(1) only applies if the exclusive right is granted through law, administrative regulation, or other act with a public law form.[44] However, although State measures normally have a public law form, this is not essential. An exclusive right granted by a public authority through a private law contract may fall under Article 86(1) if its regulatory rather than commercial function can be proved.[45]

6.35   *Need for a discretionary decision by the State*   The granting of the exclusive right must be the result of a *discretionary* decision by the public authority. This may consist in an artificial

---

[37] Case C-41/90 *Höfner* [1991] ECR I-2015, para 28; Case 260/89 *ERT* [1991] ECR I-2925, para 31; Case C-179/90 *Port of Genoa* [1991] ECR I-5889, para 14; Case C-18/93 *Corsica Ferries* [1994] ECR I-1783, paras 39–41; Case C-323/93 *La Crespelle* [1997] ECR I-5077, paras 17 and 24; Cases C-180 to 184/98 *Pavlov* [2000] ECR I-6451, paras 124–126.

[38] *British Telecommunications* [1982] OJ L360/36, para 26.

[39] Case 311/84 *Télémarketing* [1985] ECR 3261, para 16.

[40] Case 30/87 *Bodson* [1988] ECR 2479, paras 26–29.

[41] This was the approach followed by the Court of First Instance in Case T-1278/98 *Aéroports de Paris* [2000] ECR II-3929, paras 147–151.

[42] The notion of 'State measure' has been examined at paras 6.10 ff above.

[43] Case C-393/92 *Almelo* [1994] ECR I-1517, paras 30–31.

[44] See the definition of 'exclusive rights' contained in Art 2(1) of Commission Directive (EC) 94/46 on satellite communications [1994] OJ L268/15; and in Art 2(1)f of Commission Directive (EEC) 80/723 concerning the transparency of financial relations between Member States and their public undertakings [1980] OJ L195/35, as modified by Commission Directive (EC) 2000/52 [2000] OJ L193/75.

[45] For instance, it is submitted that electricity concessions in Germany could be treated as State measures, despite their private law form, to the extent that the aim of the granting authorities is to regulate the market place from a perspective of public interest.

limitation of the number of players to a single one and/or in the discretionary choice of the single operator when a natural monopoly exists. In both cases the undertaking may feel an obligation towards the public authority whose discretionary decision is at the origin of its monopoly position. This may give the public authority some influence over the behaviour of the undertaking. This is not the case in respect of patents and other intellectual property rights, which are granted automatically once the various legal conditions are fulfilled. The Court of Justice considers that intellectual property rights are not 'exclusive rights' within the meaning of Article 86.[46]

As explained below[47] exclusive rights have a dual role within Article 86(1). On the one hand, **6.36** the provision refers to State measures concerning undertakings to which Member States *have previously granted* exclusive rights. On the other hand, Article 86(1), as interpreted by the Court of Justice, also applies to the *original* granting of an exclusive right to an undertaking.

Special Rights   The concept of 'special rights' and its relationship with that of 'exclusive rights' **6.37** has been and still remains controversial. The controversy arose in 1991 when the Court of Justice condemned the Commission for its failure to differentiate between these categories.[48]

Following that judgment the Commission provided, in its 'Satellites' Directive (1994), a **6.38** definition of 'special rights'.[49] The Commission included in this definition two different kinds of rights. 'Special rights' are, first of all, rights to engage in an economic activity in a given territory granted by a State measure *only to a limited number of undertakings*. If the legal notion of 'exclusive right' finds a parallel in the popular notion of 'monopoly', these 'special rights' roughly correspond with the popular notion of 'oligopoly'. Special rights of this kind only exist if there is a *discretionary* decision by the public authority. This may consist in an artificial limitation of the number of players and/or in the discretionary choice of the operators. No special rights exist when the access to an activity (such as a profession) is restricted to those fulfilling certain predetermined conditions, provided there is no limitation on the number of operators.[50]

Secondly, the Commission also considers as 'special rights' the legal advantages granted by **6.39** State measures to only some of the undertakings that are active in a market which is, in principle, open to competition. In this second scenario, public authorities do not restrict the number of operators but give some of them other legal privileges implying a competitive advantage. An example of this kind of special right is the right granted to some telecommunication operators to manage the numbering system in a Member State. The qualification of these rights as 'special rights' means that Article 86(1) EC would continue to apply as regards these undertakings, even if they no longer enjoy either exclusive rights or special rights of the

---

[46] Case 13/77 *Inno v ATAB* [1977] ECR 2115, para 41.
[47] See paras 6.46–6.48 below.
[48] Case C-202/88 *Terminal equipment for telecommunications* [1991] ECR I-1223, paras 45–47; Cases C-271, 281 and 289/90 *Telecommunications services* [1992] ECR I-5883, paras 28–32.
[49] This definition of 'special rights' is currently contained in Art 1(6) of Commission Directive (EC) 2002/77 on competition in the markets for electronic communications networks and services [2002] OJ L249/21, but it originally appeared in Directive (EC) 94/46 on satellite communications [1994] OJ L268/15 (no longer in force). A similar definition appears in Art 2(1)(e) of Commission Directive (EEC) 80/723 concerning the transparency of financial relations between Member States and their public undertakings [1980] OJ L195/35, as modified by Commission Directive (EC) 2000/52 [2000] OJ L193/75.
[50] Case 13/77 *Inno v ATAB* [1977] ECR 2115, para 41.

first category. In other words, Article 86(1) EC will continue to be applicable in sectors that have been liberalised but that are still subject to an intense degree of regulatory intervention.

6.40 The same logic probably lies behind the *Ambulanz Glöckner* judgment, which has substantially modified the landscape as regards the concepts of exclusive and special rights. Indeed, in this judgment the Court establishes a common definition embracing both exclusive and special rights. In so doing, the Court goes back to the initial situation where both concepts were considered synonyms. The (new) concept of 'special or exclusive right' refers to situations where:

   (i) a legislative measure;
   (ii) confers protection on a limited number of undertakings;
   (iii) which may substantially affect the ability of other undertakings to engage in the economic activity in question in the same geographical area under substantially equivalent conditions.[51]

6.41 From a substantive point of view this new definition merely combines within a single concept the cases previously caught by the notions of exclusive rights and special rights. The only new element is the requirement of a 'legislative measure'. This is a surprising new feature. Previous case law merely required a 'State measure' without specifying that it had to be necessarily of a 'legislative' nature. Also Advocate General Jacobs in his opinion in *Ambulanz Glöckner* had merely required a grant by the Member State authorities. It is submitted that this line is more consistent with the functional logic behind Article 86 EC.

(iv) The connection between the measure and the undertaking

6.42 *Kinds of connection required by Article 86(1)*   Article 86(1) only applies to State measures that have some kind of connection with public or privileged undertakings. General measures affecting all undertakings (public and private—privileged or not) in the same manner do not fall within Article 86(1).

6.43 However, the precise nature of the connection required by Article 86(1) is not explained. Article 86(1) merely says that 'in the case of' these undertakings, Member States shall neither adopt nor maintain in force measures contrary to the rules of the Treaty. As interpreted by the Court of Justice and the Commission, this means that a State measure falls under Article 86(1):

   (a) when such *measures benefit* public undertakings or undertakings to which Member States grant exclusive or special rights; and/or
   (b) when these public or privileged *undertakings are the instrument* used by the Member State for the implementation of the measures; and/or
   (c) when the measure consists of the granting or maintenance in force of an *exclusive right*.

6.44 *State measures which benefit the undertaking*   Most State measures fall under Article 86(1) because they benefit a public undertaking or an undertaking to which a Member State grants exclusive or special rights. The granting of an exclusive right to an undertaking, for instance, obviously benefits that undertaking.

6.45 *State measures which use the undertaking as an instrument*   This kind of beneficial effect is not essential in order for Article 86(1) to apply, however. The provision also applies to measures that use public or privileged undertakings as instruments by imposing on them certain kinds

---

[51] Case C-475/99 *Ambulanz Glöckner* [2001] ECR I-8089, para 24.

of behaviour, even when the measures do not benefit the undertakings in question. For instance, in the *Corsica Ferries* case, the Court of Justice found that Article 86(1) applied to a measure imposing on an undertaking having an exclusive right for 'pilotage' services in the Port of Genoa a system of tariffs, which discriminated according to the national or foreign origin of each transport service.[52] This discrimination was not beneficial for the undertaking which had the exclusive right but was nevertheless found to be an Article 86(1) State measure.

State measures granting an exclusive right   As has been shown above, the general rule is that State measures fall under Article 86(1) when such measures benefit public undertakings or undertakings to which Member States grant exclusive or special rights and/or when these undertakings are the instrument used by the Member State for the implementation of the measures. However, State measures consisting of the granting or maintenance in force of *exclusive rights* fall under a particular regime.   **6.46**

It was thought by some commentators that exclusive rights would only be considered State measures falling under Article 86(1) when they were granted to either a *public* undertaking or to a private undertaking to which a Member State *had previously granted* an exclusive or special right. However, the Court of Justice has interpreted Article 86(1) as applying to the *original* granting of an exclusive right to an undertaking as well, even if the undertaking in question is neither a public undertaking nor a private undertaking to which Member States had previously granted an exclusive right.[53] In the *Port of Genoa* case, for instance, the Court found that the only exclusive right granted to a private undertaking, the company of dockers, fell under Article 86(1).[54] In *La Crespelle* the exclusive rights granted to various private undertakings were also examined under Article 86(1).[55]   **6.47**

The dual role of exclusive rights within Article 86(1)   This approach means that the exclusive right may be, in respect of Article 86(1), both the *State measure* and/or the element that makes the *undertaking* fall under that provision. Indeed, exclusive rights play a dual role within Article 86(1). On the one hand, the provision refers to State measures concerning undertakings to which Member States *have previously granted* exclusive rights. On the other hand, Article 86(1), as interpreted by the Court of Justice, also applies to the *original* granting of an exclusive right to an undertaking. The original granting of an exclusive right is a 'State measure' under Article 86(1) even if the undertaking in question is neither a public undertaking nor a private undertaking to which Member States have previously granted an exclusive right.   **6.48**

General measures do not fall under Article 86(1)   Article 86(1) only applies to State measures to the extent that these measures are connected—in one of the above-mentioned ways—with public or privileged undertakings. When such a link or connection does not exist (because the measure applies in the same way and with similar effects to all of the undertakings in a particular sector), the measures are 'general' measures to which Article 86(1) does not apply.[56] This does not exclude the possible application of other provisions of the EC Treaty, such as Articles 28 or 49 (former Articles 30 and 59).   **6.49**

---

[52] Case C-18/93 *Corsica Ferries* [1994] ECR I-1783.
[53] Case C-203/96 *Dusseldorp* [1998] ECR I-4075, paras 53–63.
[54] Case C-179/90 *Port of Genoa* [1991] ECR I-5889, para 2.
[55] Case C-323/93 *La Crespelle* [1997] ECR I-5077, paras 15–22.
[56] *Temple Lang* (n 10 above) 552; *Pais Antunes* (n 10 above) 200.

(4) Contrary to Another Provision of the EC Treaty

6.50 State measures which are related to public or privileged undertakings only fall under Article 86(1) if they are 'contrary to the rules contained in this Treaty, in particular those rules provided for in Articles 12 and 81 to 89'. This means that Article 86(1) cannot be applied alone—in order to establish a specific obligation for Member States—but must always be applied 'in combination with' another rule of the EC Treaty. Article 86(1) is therefore a 'règle de renvoi' whose legal content depends on that of the rule which is applied in combination with it.

6.51 This means that Article 86(1) has a multiplicity of legal content with different spheres of application. As a result, a State measure may in some cases violate both Article 86(1) in combination with Article 82, and Article 86(1) in combination with Article 28[57] or with Article 49.[58] In other cases, a State measure may be compatible with Article 86(1) in combination with Article 82 while being incompatible with Article 86(1) in combination with Articles 28 or 49,[59] or vice versa.[60]

6.52 It is therefore necessary, in order to analyse the legal content of Article 86(1), to distinguish between its application in combination with the antitrust rules and its application in combination with the free movement rules.

(5) Article 86(1) in Combination with the Competition Rules Addressed to Undertakings

6.53 Article 86(1) not only reminds Member States of their obligation to respect the rules of the EC Treaty that are addressed to them, but also prohibits Member States from adopting measures contrary to Articles 81 and 82 of the EC Treaty, rules that in principle are addressed not to the Member States but to undertakings. As Articles 81 and 82 have as their object the behaviour of undertakings and not State measures,[61] their application to Member States through Article 86(1) in some cases requires an adaptation of their logic.[62] In other words, when applied in combination with Article 86(1) as regards State measures, the contents and scope of Articles 81 and 82 are not necessarily the same as when these Articles are directly applied to the behaviour of undertakings.

(a) *Article 86(1) in Combination with Article 82*

6.54 The precedents from the Court of Justice and the doctrine of the European Commission indicate that a State measure concerning a public or privileged undertaking will infringe Article 86(1) in combination with Article 82 when the following conditions are met:

(1) the undertaking is in a dominant position on a market which is relevant from an economic point of view and which embraces a substantial part of the common market;

---

[57] Case C-179/90 *Port of Genoa* [1991] ECR I-5889, paras 21 and 24; Case C-18/88 *RTT* [1991] ECR I-5941, paras 28 and 36.

[58] Case 260/89 *ERT* [1991] ECR I-2925, paras 26 and 38.

[59] Case C-323/93 *La Crespelle* [1997] ECR I-5077, paras 22 and 29.

[60] Case C-41/90 *Höfner* [1991] ECR I-2015, paras 34 and 40.

[61] See Section A of this chapter.

[62] *Buendia Sierra* (n 10 above) Chs 4 and 5; A Pappalardo, 'Régime de l'Article 90 du Traité CEE: les aspects juridiques', in Various, *L'entreprise publique et la concurrence. Les articles 90 et 37 du Traité CEE et leurs relations avec la concurrence*, Semaine de Bruges 1968 (De Temple, Bruges, 1969), 94; *Papaconstantinou* (n 10 above) 76.

(2) the measure:
   — either actually leads the undertaking to behave in such a way as to abuse its domi-
      nant position,
   — or has the potential to lead the undertaking to behave in such a way as to abuse its
      dominant position,
   — or produces effects similar to those of an abusive behaviour;
and
(3) the effects of the abuse or the effects of the State measure are capable of affecting intra-
    Community trade.

(i) Dominant position   For Article 86(1) to apply in combination with Article 82, the **6.55**
public or privileged undertaking must be in a dominant position in a market which is relevant from an economic point of view and which embraces a substantial part of the common market. This dominant position may well be the result of State measures, such as an
exclusive right, but the mere existence of an exclusive right does not automatically imply
the existence of a dominant position.[63] The notion of 'dominant position' is an economic
one. In principle, this concept does not vary when Article 82 is applied in combination
with Article 86(1). It is true that in most cases the protection from competition granted by
the exclusive right puts the undertaking in a dominant position, as the Court said in
Télémarketing,[64] but this is not always the case. The key question, as the Court explained in
Bodson, [65] is whether the scope of the exclusive right embraces a substantial part of a market which is 'relevant' from an economic point of view. If so, the exclusive right will imply
a dominant position on that market. If that were not the case, Article 86(1) might not be
applied in combination with Article 82. In practice, however, both the Court of Justice and
the Commission often presume the existence of a dominant position from the existence of
an exclusive right.[66] It is submitted that it should be possible to reverse that presumption
with economic analysis showing that, despite enjoying the exclusive right, the undertaking
is not in a dominant position.

(ii) State measures leading to actual abusive behaviour of the undertakings   Article 86(1) **6.56**
in combination with Article 82 applies first of all to State measures that lead, or may lead, a
public or privileged undertaking to behave in such a way as to abuse its dominant position.
Any behaviour which would normally be considered as an abuse contrary to Article 82 if
spontaneously adopted by a dominant undertaking, will fall under Articles 86(1) and 82
when it is imposed or induced by a State measure.

Different kinds of abuses   Among the more typical abuses under Articles 86(1) and 82 are **6.57**
those related to prices. Price regulation is a common instrument for State intervention in the
utilities sector, where the presence of public undertakings or undertakings with exclusive or

---

⁶³ See para 6.33 above.
⁶⁴ Case 311/84 *Télémarketing* [1985] ECR 3261, para 16.
⁶⁵ Case 30/87 *Bodson* [1988] ECR 2479, paras 26–29.
⁶⁶ Case C-41/90 *Höfner* [1991] ECR I-2015, para 28; Case 260/89 *ERT* [1991] ECR I-2925, para 31;
Case C-179/90 *Port of Genoa* [1991] ECR I-5889, para 14; Case C-18/93 *Corsica Ferries* [1994] ECR I-1783,
paras 39–41; Case C-323/93 *La Crespelle* [1997] ECR I-5077, paras 17 and 24; *British Telecommunications*
[1982] OJ L360/36, para 26; Case C-163/96 *Raso* [1998] ECR I-533, para 25; Case C-203/96 *Dusseldorp*
[1998] ECR I-4075, para 60.

special rights is also normal. The tariffs applied by these undertakings are often established and/or approved by the public authorities. In some cases these State-approved tariffs may lead the undertaking to engage in discriminatory,[67] excessive,[68] and/or predatory pricing which, if adopted spontaneously, would infringe Article 82. If this is the case, the State-approved tariff would infringe Article 86(1) in combination with Article 82. The substantive criteria for determining the discriminatory, excessive, or predatory character of a price are the same, irrespective of whether Article 82 is applied alone or in combination with Article 86(1).

6.58   Other typical abuses under Articles 86(1) and 82 are those implying a 'refusal to deal' resulting, not from an autonomous behaviour of the monopolist, but from a State measure. A typical example is the refusal to grant access to an 'essential facility' such as the refusal to grant a ferry operator access to a port.[69] The conditions qualifying this kind of abuse were clarified in the *Bronner* judgment.[70]

6.59   *Only the State is responsible for State-imposed abuses*   It has always been accepted that Article 86(1) in combination with Article 82 prohibits Member States from *obliging* their public or privileged undertakings to abuse their dominant position.[71] One should keep in mind that Article 82 taken in isolation can only be infringed (and the undertaking held liable) when the behaviour is the result of an autonomous decision of the undertaking. In principle, a State-imposed behaviour cannot constitute an infringement of normal competition rules by the undertaking.[72] Thus, by interpreting Articles 86(1) and 82 as an obligation upon Member States to refrain from imposing abusive behaviour on their public or privileged undertakings, the lack of liability of the undertaking under Article 82 is compensated for by the liability of the State under Articles 86(1) and 82.

6.60   *Both the State and the undertaking are liable for State-induced abuses*   In general, Article 86(1) in combination with Article 82 prohibits Member States from legally obliging public or privileged undertakings to abuse their dominant position. However, in the absence of a binding obligation to abuse, it is generally agreed that Article 86(1) in combination with Article 82 also prohibits Member States from merely *inducing* their public or privileged undertakings to abuse their dominant position. Of course, the mere presence of State inducement does not exclude either the autonomous character of the behaviour of the undertaking or its potential liability under Article 82.[73] This might at most be considered as a mitigating factor in the establishment of fines.[74] These non-binding inducements may, however, have a very severe anti-competitive impact on the market. It is therefore logical to establish in these cases two parallel potential liabilities: one for the State under Articles 86(1)

---

[67] Case C-18/93 *Corsica Ferries* [1994] ECR I-1781, para 43; Case C-242/95 *GT Link* [1997] ECR I-4449; *Zaventem* [1995] OJ L216/8.

[68] Case C-179/90 *Port of Genoa* [1991] ECR I-5889, para 19; Case C-242/95 *GT Link* [1997] ECR I-4449.

[69] *Rødby* [1994] OJ L55/52.

[70] Case C-7/97 *Bronner* [1998] ECR I-7791.

[71] Case 30/87 *Bodson* [1988] ECR 2479, para 33.

[72] Case T-65/99 *Strintzis Lines* [2003] ECR II-5433, paras 119–122.

[73] Case T-65/99 *Strintzis Lines* [2003] ECR II-5433, paras 119–122. *Temple Lang* (n 10 above) 558.

[74] Case T-65/99 *Strintzis Lines* [2003] ECR II-5433, para 171.

and 82 for having induced the undertaking to abuse; and one for the undertaking under Article 82 for having responded when it was not bound to do so.[75]

State inactivity   Some authors even suggest that the simple *inactivity* of the Member State   **6.61**
when faced with abusive behaviour by a public or privileged undertaking should be enough for Article 86(1) in combination with Article 82 to apply.[76] However, nothing in the case law of the Court of Justice or in the practice of the Commission suggests that a mere failure to prevent an abuse triggers the responsibility of the Member State.[77]

(iii) State measures affecting the structure of competition and leading to potential abusive behaviour of undertakings

No need for actual abuses   Even if some kind of positive action by the Member State is   **6.62**
always required for Article 86(1) to apply, such positive action need not be related to one specific abuse. Article 86(1) also applies as regards State measures affecting the structure of the market if the resulting structure leads an undertaking to abuse. This means that, for Articles 86(1) and 82 to apply, there is no obligation to establish first that an actual abuse has been committed. What is required is establishment of the fact that the State measure is such as could lead an undertaking to abuse. Of course, being able to prove that actual abuses have been committed will help in establishing that a measure leads an undertaking to abuse, but it is not an absolute requirement. In the *RTT* judgment, the Court of Justice stated clearly that Articles 86(1) and 82 may apply even in the absence of actual abuses.[78]

The granting of regulatory powers to an undertaking   There is broad consensus that   **6.63**
Article 86(1) in combination with Article 82 is violated when a Member State entrusts a public undertaking active in a competitive market with regulatory tasks. Such a measure creates for the undertaking a conflict of interest between its regulatory mission and its commercial objectives. As a regulator of the market-place, the undertaking can easily use its regulatory powers to inflict competitive disadvantages on its competitors. The combination of the granting of a substantive regulatory power with the objective situation of a conflict of interest will inevitably lead the public undertaking to abuse its dominant position. The accumulation of commercial and regulatory functions in the same entity is therefore incompatible with Articles 86(1) and 82 of the EC Treaty.[79] This incompatibility does not occur if the regulatory functions in question only consist in a role of formal verification. [80]

---

[75] A Pappalardo, 'Measures of the States and Rules of Competition of the EEC Treaty' [1984] FCLI 527–528.

[76] I Hochbaum, 'Commentaire de l'Article 90 du Traité CEE' in Thiesing, Schröter and Hochbaum, *Les ententes et les positions dominantes dans le Droit de la CEE*, updated translation of the 2nd German edn 1974 (Paris: Editions Jupiter, Editions de Navarre, 1977) 284; P Mathijsen, 'Egalité de traitement des entreprises dans le Droit des Communautés européennes', in Various, *Equal treatment of public and private enterprises*, vol 2 (Copenhagen: FIDE, 1978), 11.4; A Deringer, 'Equal treatment of public and private enterprises. General report' in Various, *Equal treatment of public and private enterprises*, vol 2 (Copenhagen: FIDE, 1978), Ch 1, 1.19; AC Page, 'Member States, Public Undertakings and Article 90' [1982] ELR 24; CD Ehlermann, 'Managing Monopolies: The Role of the State in Controlling Market Dominance in the European Community' [1993] 2 ECLR 65–66.

[77] *Temple Lang* (n 10 above) 559.

[78] Case C-18/88 *RTT* [1991] ECR I-5941, paras 23–24; Case C-163/96 *Raso* [1998] ECR I-533, para 31.

[79] Case C-202/88 *Terminal equipment for telecommunications* [1991] ECR I-1223, paras 48–52; Case C-18/88 *RTT* [1991] ECR I-5941, paras 25–28; Cases C-46/90 and C-93/91 *Lagauche* [1993] ECR I-5267; Case C-69/91 *Decoster* [1993] ECR I-5335; Case C-92/91 *Taillandier* [1993] ECR I-5383.

[80] Case C-67/96 *Albany* ECR [1999] I-5751, paras 112–117.

6.64 ***The 'bundling' of regulatory and commercial activities***   Thus Article 86(1) in combination with Article 82 prohibits the 'bundling' of, on the one hand, the regulatory functions of the State and, on the other hand, the entrepreneurial activities of the State. In other words, public undertakings must be 'independent' from the bodies that regulate their markets and vice versa. The key question is the degree of separation necessary to achieve such 'independence'. The Court of Justice has already made clear that two directorates within the same administration cannot be considered as being independent.[81] This implies at least that a mere functional unbundling within a single entity (public undertaking or administration) is not enough to fulfil the obligation of independence. The Commission considers that the independence requirement is fulfilled, first of all, where a former public undertaking belongs to private shareholders and not to the State. It is obvious that, in such a situation, the exercise of regulatory functions by the public administration does not raise any concern about conflict of interest. The requirement is also fulfilled where the State keeps its financial interest in the commercial undertakings but transfers the regulatory functions to a body 'independent from the relevant Ministry'.[82]

6.65 ***The granting of an exclusive right***   The granting of an exclusive right is a positive State measure that may, in some circumstances, 'lead' the undertaking to abuse its dominant position. In a way, this might be seen as a wide interpretation of the notion of inducement: by assuring a dominant position through the granting of an exclusive right, the State would 'induce' the undertaking to abuse of this dominant position. However, not every exclusive right necessarily leads the beneficiary to abuse. The Court of Justice has restricted this reasoning by requiring some additional circumstances also to be present.

6.66 ***The demand limitation doctrine***   First of all, an exclusive right is found to 'inevitably lead' the undertaking to abuse when the undertaking is not in a position to satisfy properly existing demand for that type of service. This demand limitation doctrine was established in the *Höfner* case.[83] The issue was that the exclusive rights enjoyed by the German federal office for employment placed that entity in a dominant position in the executive recruitment market. However, the entity was clearly not capable of satisfying the existing demand in the market for this type of activity. Article 82(b) defines as abusive the behaviour of undertakings which consists in 'limiting production, markets or technical development to the prejudice of consumers'. The fact that an activity is reserved to an entity which is not in a position to carry it out will necessarily lead to abuses of this type being committed. In such circumstances, the grant of exclusive rights would be contrary to Articles 86(1) and 82. This 'demand limitation doctrine' can also be found in other judgments[84] and Decisions.[85]

6.67 ***The conflict of interest doctrine***   The *RTT* case made clear that Article 86(1) in combination with Article 82 is violated when a State measure creates a situation of conflict of interest

---

[81] Case C-69/91 *Decoster* [1993] ECR I-5335, para 21.

[82] Commission Communication on the status and implementation of Directive (EEC) 90/388 on competition in the markets for telecommunications services [1995] OJ C275/2, see p 10.

[83] Case C-41/90 *Höfner* [1991] ECR I-2019.

[84] Cases C-180 to 184/98 *Pavlov* [2000] ECR I-6451, para 127; Case C-67/96 *Albany* ECR [1999] I-5751, para 95.

[85] *Dutch Courier Services* [1990] OJ L10/50, paras 14–15; *Spanish Courier Services* [1990] OJ L233/22, para 11.

between the regulatory mission entrusted to an undertaking and its commercial objectives. This is not, however, the only kind of conflict of interest that may occur. A conflict of interest may also be created between two different commercial activities of a single undertaking. This approach was established in the *ERT* case,[86] which concerned the Greek television monopoly. The Greek authorities had granted ERT the exclusive right both to broadcast programmes produced by itself and programmes produced abroad. It was obvious that in such a situation the monopoly would logically tend to prefer the programmes which it had produced itself over programmes from other Member States. This would constitute an abuse of a dominant position contrary to Article 82. As the judgment said, Article 86(1) of the Treaty prohibits the granting of an exclusive right to retransmit television broadcasts to an undertaking which has an exclusive right to transmit broadcasts, where those rights are liable to lead that undertaking to infringe Article 82 of the Treaty by virtue of a discriminatory broadcasting policy which favours its own programmes.

In *ERT* the circumstance which led the beneficiary of the exclusive rights to act in an abusive **6.68** manner was the existence of a conflict of interest. Although the grant of the exclusive rights did not legally oblige the undertaking benefiting from them to discriminate in favour of its own programmes, it is obvious that the temptation would be very difficult to resist in practice. The grant of exclusive rights to an undertaking with such a conflict of interest creates a structure favouring abusive behaviour. This 'conflict of interest doctrine' has been relied upon in the *Raso* judgment.[87]

No smoke without fire In very rare cases, the Court of Justice has concluded, on the basis **6.69** of the gravity and repetition of particular abuses, that they were an inevitable consequence of the existence of an exclusive right. The judgment in *Port of Genoa* is the clearest example.[88] The facts were as follows: the undertaking Sidelurgica had applied to Merci, holder of exclusive rights for the organisation of dock works, for a ship to be unloaded in the port of Genoa. Various problems arose, including a strike in the dock work company, Compagnia. As a result, delays occurred and Sidelurgica suffered losses. In the subsequent litigation, the question arose as to the compatibility of the exclusive rights enjoyed by Merci and Compagnia with Articles 86(1) and 82. The Court listed no fewer than four different types of abuse which had occurred (demanding payment for unrequested services, charging excessive prices, engaging in discriminatory pricing, and not using technologically advanced unloading equipment). The surprising point was that the Court moved from the existence of these abuses of a dominant position to the conclusion that the abuses were the result of the exclusive rights without examining the causal relationship.[89] It seems that the variety, seriousness, and repeated nature of the abuses committed led the Court to the presumption that the very structure of the market (the operation of exclusive rights) favoured the commission of abuses and for that reason was incompatible with Articles 86(1) and 82 of the Treaty.

---

[86] Case 260/89 *ERT* [1991] ECR I-2925.
[87] Case C-163/96 *Raso* [1998] ECR I-533, paras 28–31.
[88] Case C-179/90 *Port of Genoa* [1991] ECR I-5889.
[89] The Court limited itself to stating that: 'it appears from the circumstances described by the national court and discussed before the Court of Justice that the undertakings enjoying exclusive rights in accordance with the procedures laid down by the national rules in question are, as a result, induced either to demand payment for services or to commit the rest of the abuses mentioned above'. Case C-179/90 *Port of Genoa* [1991] ECR I-5889.

6.70 **(iv) Effects similar to those of abusive behaviour**   Article 86(1) in combination with Article 82 also applies to some State measures having effects similar to those of abusive behaviour, even in the absence of any actual or potentially abusive behaviour by the undertaking.

6.71 *The doctrine of the extension of a dominant position*   This doctrine holds that the grant to an undertaking, which is already dominant in one market, of exclusive rights in another adjacent but distinct market is contrary to Articles 86(1) and 82, unless such a grant can be objectively justified.

6.72 The doctrine of the extension of a dominant position was used for the first time in the framework of Articles 86(1) and 82 in the *RTT* case.[90] In this judgment the Court considered that an exclusive right was contrary to Articles 86(1) and 82 not because it resulted in real or potential abuse of a dominant position, but rather because it produced a similar effect to such abuse.

6.73 The undertaking GB-Inno-BM had imported and sold telephones in Belgium without having them approved by RTT, the public telecommunications operator. The Court appears to have assumed that RTT had not decided independently to exclude competitors but rather that such exclusion was a direct consequence of the legislation. The Court also appears to have identified RTT's power to approve its competitors' telephones with a true exclusive right for the sale of terminals. RTT, which already enjoyed a monopoly in the operation of the network, thus received a second exclusive right from the State, for the sale of telephones. On this basis, it was considered that there was an extension of RTT's dominant position from one market to another. The extension was not the result of abuses committed by RTT but instead was due to the State granting RTT the exclusive power to approve competitors' telephones. Such extension by law of a dominant position is illegal not because it induces or favours abuse, but rather because it produces effects identical to those which would be produced by abusive behaviour contrary to Article 82.

6.74 In this way, on the basis of effects rather than behaviour, the Court established its doctrine of the extension of a dominant position. This doctrine, which was used again by the Court of Justice in its 1992 judgment concerning the telecommunications services Directive[91] and in the 2001 judgment *Ambulanz Glöckner*[92] has come to play a key role in the liberalisation process.

6.75 Of course, apart from exclusive rights, other State measures may extend the dominant position of a public or privileged undertaking, thus falling under Article 86(1) in combination with Article 82. This may be the case, for instance, of national regulatory measures imposing, all other things being equal, higher licence fees on newcomers than on incumbent operators. [93]

6.76 *The automatic abuse doctrine*   The abovementioned precedents clearly show a tendency restricting the ability of Member States to grant or maintain exclusive or special rights. The initial presumption of compatibility of exclusive rights had suffered so many exceptions

---

[90] Case C-18/88 *RTT* [1991] ECR I-5941. This theory had previously been used by the Commission in its two decisions based on Art 86 concerning courier postal services in The Netherlands and Spain.

[91] Cases C-271, 281 and 289/90 *Telecommunications Services Directive* [1992] ECR I-5868, paras 35–36.

[92] Case C-475/99 *Ambulanz Glöckner* [2001] ECR I-8089, paras 40–43.

[93] Case C-426/99 *Connect Austria* [2003] ECR I-5197, paras 80–95; Commission decisions *GSM Italy* [1995] OJ L280/49; *GSM Spain* [1997] OJ L76/19.

that it seemed about to be reversed. The Court has subsequently retreated from this position: in the *Corbeau* case the Court of Justice seemed to consider that, even in the absence of these circumstances, an exclusive right would automatically lead the beneficiary to abuse, therefore falling under Articles 86(1) and 82.[94]

The facts of the case were as follows. Paul Corbeau provided services consisting in the collection and delivery of mail in the city of Liège, Belgium. Despite the services offered being superior to those of the State postal service, the charges were slightly lower. Belgian legislation imposed on the Régie des Postes a universal obligation to ensure basic postal services throughout Belgian territory at a uniform tariff. In exchange, the Régie des Postes was granted an exclusive right over postal services without distinguishing between basic postal services and more profitable services such as courier services. The Régie des Postes started criminal proceedings against Paul Corbeau for breach of the exclusive rights and the matter was referred to the Court of Justice. **6.77**

In the judgment, the Court did not regard it as necessary to look for even the slightest hint of abusive behaviour. It limited itself to stating the obligation of Member States not to compromise the *effect utile* of Article 82. It is submitted that this expression has to be understood as a general reference to the effects theory. Without ever reaching any specific conclusions as to what the obligations of Member States are under Article 86(1), the Court surprisingly went on to examine the scope of the exception contained in Article 86(2).[95] While the reasoning may be scant, the conclusion the Court reached was clear: if the grant of exclusive rights was only permitted under Article 86 to the extent that it came within the exception contained in Article 86(2), that meant that in principle all grants of exclusive rights were contrary to Article 86(1) unless they were objectively justified.[96] **6.78**

Corbeau was simply the final consequence of the effects theory. If the role of Article 82 was to prevent the distortion, restriction or elimination of competition caused by the behaviour of undertakings, a State measure which totally eliminated competition would have the same effect, if not worse, as such behaviour. Since the behaviour of undertakings would have been contrary to Article 82, such State measures were contrary to Article 86(1) in conjunction with Article 82. **6.79**

The overall effect of *Corbeau* was simply to reverse the burden of proof. Until *Corbeau*, the starting point had been that exclusive rights were prima facie legal (*Sacchi*). They would only be contrary to Articles 86(1) and 82 if it was shown that they led undertakings to engage in abusive behaviour (*Höfner*, *ERT* and *Port of Genoa*) or if they constituted an extension of a dominant position (*RTT*, *Telecommunications Services*). Following *Corbeau*, exclusive **6.80**

---

[94] Case C-320/91 *Corbeau* [1993] ECR I-2533.

[95] Art 86(2) reads as follows: 'Undertakings entrusted with the operation of services of general economic interest or having the character of a revenue-producing monopoly shall be subject to the rules contained in this Treaty, in particular to the rules on competition, in so far as the application of such rules does not obstruct the performance, in law or in fact, of the particular tasks assigned to them. The development of trade must not be affected to such an extent as would be contrary to the interest of the Community.'

[96] It is therefore no coincidence that this new approach coincided with a new emphasis on the exception under Art 86(2), which would permit, *inter alia*, those exclusive rights which were indispensable to ensure objectives of general economic interest being allowed.

rights were presumed to be illegal, unless they could be objectively justified or unless they were necessary to guarantee the effective carrying out of a project of general economic interest. The effect of *Corbeau* was simply to bring the approach in relation to Articles 86(1) and 82 into line with that concerning the free movement of goods. That is, restrictions on trade and free competition were in principle prohibited unless they existed because of mandatory requirements of general interest and they respected the principle of proportionality.

6.81   *The* La Crespelle *case*   The automatic abuse doctrine established in *Corbeau* has subsequently been abandoned by the Court of Justice. In October 1994 the judgment in *La Crespelle* heralded a change of approach.[97] A local monopolist brought proceedings against the La Crespelle centre for breach of its exclusive right to artificially inseminate cattle. According to this judgment, while the legislation in question authorised the insemination centres to freely establish their charges, it did not encourage them to demand exorbitant prices. Therefore it could not be concluded that such legislation led undertakings to abuse their dominant positions. This last statement involved a radical change of direction in the interpretation of the expression 'led to abuse'. Until that moment, the case law had suggested that if a monopoly 'facilitated' the possibility of abuse, that was sufficient to constitute 'leading' the undertaking to abuse. Given that all monopolies, by definition, facilitated the charging of abusive prices, the logical conclusion was that all monopolies were prima facie contrary to Articles 86(1) and 82. This was the position taken in *Corbeau*. However, faced with a similar situation in *La Crespelle* the Court reacted in a different way and held that the presence of possible abuses derived from the exercise of the exclusive right could not automatically be imputed to the mere existence of the exclusive right. The fact that the monopolist had abused its dominant position by demanding excessive prices could justify the application of Article 82 to such behaviour, but could not on its own lead to an action against the Member State under Articles 86(1) and 82. Such action would only be justified if a causal relation between the State measure and the abuse were demonstrated.[98]

6.82   *Recent cases*   However, *La Crespelle* was apparently not the last word of the Court on this issue. Indeed the *Dusseldorp* (1998) and *Deutsche Post* (2000) judgments relied again on the 'automatic abuse' doctrine.[99] These judgments used an approach very similar to the one used on Corbeau: the exclusive right is implicitly presumed incompatible unless justified as necessary for an objective of general interest.

6.83   The more recent *Sydhavnens* judgment (2000) aims to strike a delicate balance between both approaches.[100] The Court starts with the presumption of legality of the exclusive rights and with the 'behaviour theory' in line with the approach used in *La Crespelle*. The conclusion is that the exclusive right at stake does not infringe Articles 86(1) and 82 EC. Despite this finding, the Court went on examining whether the exclusive right was acceptable under the exception foreseen in Article 86(2) EC for services of general economic interest. This second analysis corresponds with the approach used in *Corbeau, Dusseldorp*

---

[97]   Case C-323/93 *La Crespelle* [1997] ECR I-5077.

[98]   Case C-387/93 *Banchero* [1995] ECR I-4663.

[99]   C-203/96 *Dusseldorp* [1998] ECR I-4075, paras 53–68; Cases C-147 and 148/97 *Deutsche Post* [2000] ECR I-825, paras 39–41.

[100]   Case C-209/98 *Sydhavnens* [2000] ECR I-3743.

and *Deutsche Post*. However, such approach comes as a surprise: if the exclusive right does not infringe Articles 86(1) and 82 EC it is hard to understand why it is necessary to examine its justification under Article 86(2) EC.

The current status quo   It follows from the above description that the European Courts have **6.84** not yet made a clear choice between the 'effects theory' and the 'behaviour theory'. On the one hand the language used in most of the recent judgments rather relies on the 'behaviour theory' as shown in the following example:

> It must be borne in mind that the mere creation of a dominant position through the grant of special or exclusive rights within the meaning of Article 90(1) of the Treaty is not in itself incompatible with Article 86 of the Treaty. A Member State will be in breach of the prohibitions laid down by those two provisions only if the undertaking in question, merely by exercising the special or exclusive rights conferred upon it, is led to abuse its dominant position or where such rights are liable to create a situation in which that undertaking is led to commit such abuses (. . .).[101]

Similarly, different recent judgments rely on constructions based on the behaviour of the operator, like the 'demand-limitation' or 'conflict of interests' doctrines.[102]

On the other hand, even some of these judgments rely on the extension of dominant posi- **6.85** tion which, as explained above, is nothing but an application of the 'effects theory'.[103] Other judgments seem to rely directly on the 'effects theory'.[104]

One may conclude that (with the possible exception of the 'automatic abuse theory') all the **6.86** approaches developed by the case law for the joint application of Articles 86(1) and 82 EC, as described in the present chapter, are still accepted by the European Courts. Thus, the granting of regulatory powers to one of the players in the market or the granting of exclusive rights to an undertaking unable to satisfy demand, are likely to infringe Articles 86(1) and 82 EC. The same may be said about the granting of exclusive rights to an undertaking in a situation of conflict of interest or its granting to an undertaking previously dominant in a neighbouring market.

This situation may not be entirely satisfactory from a theoretical point of view but seems to **6.87** work reasonably well in practice. The scope of the prohibition resulting from the accumulation of the abovementioned approaches is indeed rather wide. In practical terms the current situation is not very different in its effects from the hypothetical effects of the application of the 'automatic abuse' theory. Perhaps this explains why the consolidation of the case law on Articles 86(1) and 82 EC has coincided in time with a development in the case law on the exception contained in Article 86(2) EC (examined later in this chapter).

(v) **Effect upon intra-Community trade**   For Article 86(1) to apply in combination **6.88** with Article 82 the effects of the abuse or the effects of the State measure should be capable

---

[101] Case C-475/99 *Ambulanz Glöckner* [2001] ECR I-8089, para 39. Similar statements appear in Case C-209/98 *Sydhavnens* [2000] ECR I-3743, para 66; Cases C-180 to 184/98 *Pavlov* [2000] ECR I-6451, para 127; and Case C-340/99 *TNT Traco* [2001] ECR I-4109, para 44.

[102] Case C-163/96 *Raso* [1998] ECR I-533, paras 28–31; Case C-67/96 *Albany* [1999] ECR I-5751, para 95; Cases C-180 to 184/98 *Pavlov* [2000] ECR I-6451, para 127.

[103] Case C-475/99 *Ambulanz Glöckner* [2001] ECR I-8089, para 40.

[104] Case C-147 and 148/97 *Deutsche Post* [2000] ECR I-825, paras 39–41; Case C-203/96 *Dusseldorp* [1998] ECR I-4075, paras 53–68.

of affecting intra-Community trade.[105] It is not necessary to prove that trade is actually been affected, a mere potential effect being enough for the condition to be fulfilled.[106] It is enough to have a certain degree of probability of such effects and to show that such effects would not be insignificant.[107] The condition is an objective one: it does not prevent an undertaking from invoking Articles 86(1) and 82 in respect of a measure of its own Member State.[108]

(b) Article 86(1) in Combination with Article 81

6.89 In theory, Article 86(1) may apply in combination with the prohibition of anti-competitive agreements between undertakings contained in Article 81 (former Article 85). In practice, however, there are few examples so far of such application in the case law of the Court of Justice and in the practice of the Commission.

6.90 The most obvious situation in which Article 86(1) could in theory apply in combination with Article 81 would be a State measure inducing one or more public or privileged undertakings to agree between themselves and/or with other undertakings in order to restrict competition. However, there are no examples of such a 'compulsory cartel' in the case law or in the practice of the Commission.

6.91 In the *Ahmed Saeed* case, the Court of Justice found that Article 86(1) in combination with Article 81 applied to the approval by a Member State of tariffs agreed by the two air carriers operating on a given route as a result of a bilateral Treaty.[109] This suggests that Articles 86(1) and 81 combine to prohibit Member States from adopting measures reinforcing the effects of anti-competitive agreements in which at least one public or privileged undertaking takes part.

6.92 An analogy with the case law of the Court of Justice in respect of Articles 3(g), 10 and 81 suggests that Article 86(1) in combination with Article 81 would also prohibit State measures that either impose or induce anti-competitive agreements in which at least one public or privileged undertaking takes part.[110]

6.93 It goes without saying that, for Articles 86(1) and 81 EC to be applicable, the agreement at stake must be an agreement between two or more undertakings. An agreement between a public authority and an undertaking does not fall within the scope of Article 81 EC and cannot therefore trigger the combined application of Articles 86(1) and 81 EC.[111]

(6) Article 86(1) in Combination with the Treaty Rules Addressed to the Member States

(a) The Double Function of Article 86(1)

6.94 Article 86(1) can also be applied in combination with the rules of the Treaty that are addressed to the Member States, such as the rules on free movement of goods, the rules on

---

[105] Case 30/87 *Bodson* [1988] ECR 2479, paras 24–25.
[106] Case C-41/90 *Höfner* [1991] ECR I-2015, paras 32–33; Case C-179/90 *Port of Genoa* [1991] ECR I-5889, para 20.
[107] C-475/99 *Ambulanz Glöckner* [2001] ECR I-8089, paras 47–49.
[108] Case C-320/91 *Corbeau* [1993] ECR I-2533; L Hancher, 'Case C-320/91, Corbeau' [1994] 21 CML Rev 114.
[109] Case 66/86 *Ahmed Saeed* [1989] ECR 803, paras 47–58.
[110] Opinion of Van Gerven AG, point 23, Case C-179/90 *Port of Genoa* [1991] ECR I-5889.
[111] C-475/99 *Ambulanz Glöckner* [2001] ECR I-8089, para 27.

freedom to provide services, and the rules on freedom of establishment. When applied in combination with these rules, Article 86(1) may play two different roles. First of all, it serves as a reminder to Member States that these rules must also be respected when adopting measures concerning public or privileged undertakings. Secondly, Article 86(1) prevents Member States from using their public or privileged undertakings as instruments in order to circumvent the application of these rules.

Article 86(1) as a 'reminder' of prohibitions As stated above, when applied in combina- **6.95** tion with the rules of the Treaty addressed to the Member States, Article 86(1) reminds them that these rules must also be respected when adopting measures concerning public or privileged undertakings.[112] From a substantive point of view this reminder is totally redundant. Whether applied in combination with Article 86(1) or not, the measures in question would in any event infringe the rules of the Treaty. The value-added provided by Article 86(1) is of a procedural nature. When the State measures are contrary to one of the rules of the Treaty addressed to the Member States but also have a link with a public or privileged undertaking so as to fall under Article 86(1), this opens up the possibility of using the special procedures established in Article 86(3).

The 'lifting of the veil' Although Article 86(1) is in principle addressed to the Member **6.96** States, it also has some impact on public and privileged undertakings. Thus, Article 86(1) in combination with the rules of the Treaty addressed to the Member States prohibits behaviour of public or privileged undertakings that, if engaged in directly by the State, would infringe the rules of the Treaty addressed to the Member States. This simply means that Member States cannot do *indirectly* (through their influence over these undertakings) what they cannot do *directly* (through behaviours of public authorities). Article 86(1) allows one to 'lift the veil' of apparent autonomy of the undertaking so as to attribute to the Member State responsibility for the acts of the undertaking that do not fit into an entrepreneurial logic.

It is well known that if a *public* undertaking transfers funds to another undertaking, these **6.97** funds may well be State aids within the meaning of Article 92, even if they come from a public undertaking and not directly from the Member State itself.[113] This same logic may apply, by virtue of Article 86(1), as regards other rules addressed to Member States. For instance, if a public or privileged undertaking follows a 'buy national' procurement policy which is irrational from a purely entrepreneurial point of view, the Member State may be found responsible for this behaviour under Articles 86(1) and 28.[114]

A good example of the attribution to a Member State of responsibility for the behaviour of **6.98** a public undertaking can be found in the *Transmediterranea* case. In 1987 the Commission adopted a Decision, based on Articles 90(1) and 7 of the EEC Treaty (now Articles 86(1) and 12 of the EC Treaty), against a Spanish law obliging transport operators to give discounts only to Spanish nationals on trips to the Canary and Balearic islands.[115] After the

---

[112] *Buendia Sierra* (n 10 above) paras 6.06–6.13; *Temple Lang* (n 10 above) 550.
[113] See, however, Case C-482/99 *Stardust* [2002] ECR I-4397, which requires additional elements showing the 'imputability' of the conduct to the State.
[114] *Buendia Sierra* (n 10 above) paras 6.02–6.05; Commission, *Report on Competition Policy 1972* (Vol II) para 129; *Report on Competition Policy 1976* (Vol VI) para 275.
[115] *Spanish Transport Tariffs* [1987] OJ L194/28.

repeal of these legal provisions, a public undertaking called Transmediterranea started offering similar discounts in favour of nationals. The undertaking claimed that these were the result of an autonomous commercial decision and therefore immune from the former Article 7, which was a rule addressed solely to the Member State. The Commission found, however, that this behaviour could not be explained on a commercial basis, but only on a governmental one. It therefore concluded that the behaviour of Transmediterranea constituted a new State measure contrary to the former Articles 90(1) and 7.[116]

6.99 Having examined in general terms how Article 86(1) functions in combination with the rules of the Treaty addressed to the Member States, it is now necessary to examine how the provision works in combination with each particular category of rules.

(b) Article 86(1) in Combination with the Rules on Free Movement of Goods— Articles 28 and 31

6.100 Measures taken by a Member State that restrict access to its markets for goods imported from other Member States will often conflict with the rules of the Treaty on free movement of goods.[117] When this type of restrictive State measure is linked with a public or privileged undertaking, then the rules of the Treaty on free movement of goods will apply in combination with Article 86(1), and the special procedures of Article 86(3) may be used.

6.101 When considering the Treaty rules on free movement of goods, a distinction must be drawn between the general regime based on Article 28 (former Article 30) and the special regime under Article 31 (former Article 37) applying to State monopolies of a commercial character.

6.102 **(i) The general regime: measures of equivalent effect and Article 28** Article 28 prohibits so-called 'measures of equivalent effect to quantitative restrictions on imports'. This notion was traditionally interpreted by the Court of Justice, notably in its *Dassonville* judgment, in a very broad manner, including all State measures restricting imports irrespective of their discriminatory or non-discriminatory character.[118] According to the *Cassis de Dijon* doctrine, only measures that are equally applicable to both national and foreign products and that are necessary to guarantee certain 'mandatory requirements' may avoid failing under the prohibition contained in Article 28.[119]

6.103 However, the interpretation of Article 28 has subsequently been restricted by the Court of Justice in its *Keck* judgment.[120] The Court distinguishes between two groups of measures. As regards measures concerning the characteristics of products (composition, packaging, labelling, etc), nothing has changed: measures that restrict imports, even if they are non-discriminatory, can only avoid prohibition under Article 28 if they are necessary to guarantee 'mandatory requirements'.[121] The change comes when considering measures related to the circumstances

---

[116] Commission, *Report on Competition Policy 1991* (Vol XXI) para 334.

[117] See P Oliver, *Free Movement of Goods in the European Community under Articles 28 to 30 of the EC Treaty* (4th edn, London: Sweet & Maxwell, 2003); *Buendia Sierra* (n 10 above) paras 6.14–6.115 for a general overview.

[118] Case 8/74 *Dassonville* [1974] ECR 87, para 5.

[119] Case 120/78 *Cassis de Dijon* [1979] ECR 649, para 8.

[120] Cases C-267 and 268/91 *Keck* [1993] ECR I-6097.

[121] Cases C-267 and 268/91 *Keck* [1993] ECR I-6097, para 15.

in which the products are traded (the so-called 'modalités de vente'): irrespective of their restrictive effect these measures would only fall under Article 28 if they discriminate, in law or in fact, against imported products.[122] Of course, the borderline between measures concerning the characteristics of products and measures related to the circumstances in which the products are traded is not at all easy to draw.[123]

Although a more detailed analysis of Article 28 is beyond the scope of this book, it is in any **6.104** event clear that State measures related to public or privileged undertakings dealing in goods would in many cases fall under the prohibition of Article 28. It also follows from the case law that State measures related to public or privileged undertakings and restricting exports may enter into conflict with Article 34 EC.[124] Such State measures may assume various forms: obligations to purchase, special rights, etc.

In principle, exclusive rights relating to goods can also be considered as 'measures of equivalent **6.105** effect' contrary to Article 28[125] and there are plenty of examples of this in the case law of the Court of Justice and in the practice of the Commission, both before[126] and after[127] the *Keck* judgment. However, the application of this rule must take into account the existence of a specific provision, Article 31, which applies to State measures concerning the functioning of State monopolies of a commercial character. Although the precise borderline between Articles 28 and 31 is difficult to determine (because of the hesitations of the Court of Justice on this issue),[128] it seems clear that exclusive rights would in many cases have to be examined under Article 31.[129]

(ii) The special regime: State monopolies and Article 31   Article 31 provides: **6.106**

(1) Member States shall adjust any State monopolies of a commercial character so as to ensure that no discrimination regarding the conditions under which goods are procured and marketed exists between nationals of Member States. The provisions of this

---

[122] Cases C-267 and 268/91 *Keck* [1993] ECR I-6097, paras 16–17.

[123] N Reich, 'The "November Revolution" of the European Court of Justice: Keck, Meng and Audi revisited' (1994) 21 CML Rev 470; A Mattera, 'De l'arrêt Dassonville à l'arrêt Keck: l'obscure clarté d'une jurisprudence riche en principes novateurs et en contradictions' [1994] RMUE i 153.

[124] Case C-209/98 *Sydhavnens* [2000] ECR I-3743, paras 31–43.

[125] M Van Der Woude, 'Article 86: "Competing for Competence",' (1991) ELR Competition Law Checklist 72.

[126] Commission Directive (EEC) 88/301 on competition in the markets for telecommunication terminal equipment [1988] OJ L131/73, para 3, confirmed by the Court of Justice in the judgment of Case C-202/88 *Terminal equipment for telecommunications* [1991] ECR I-1223, paras 33–39; Case C-179/90 *Port of Genoa* [1991] ECR I-5889, para 21.

[127] Cases C-277, 318 and 319/91 *Ligur Carni* [1993] ECR I-6621, paras 35–38, Case C-323/93 *La Crespelle* [1997] ECR I-5077, paras 28–29.

[128] This question is analysed later in this section.

[129] See JL Buendia Sierra, *Exclusive Rights and State Monopolies in EC Law* (Oxford University Press, 1999) Ch 3. On the doctrine see: Pierre-Alex Franck, 'Les entreprises visées aux articles 90 et 37 du Traité CEE' in Various, *Les articles 90 et 37 du Traité CEE et leurs relations avec la concurrence*, Semaine de Bruges 1968 (De Temple, Bruges, 1969), 44; CA Colliard, 'Régime de l'Article 37 du Traité CEE: les aspects juridiques' in Various, *L'entreprise publique et la concurrence. Les articles 90 et 37 du Traité CEE et leurs relations avec la concurrence*, Semaine de Bruges 1968 (De Temple, Bruges, 1969), 143; R Franceschelli, 'Rapport sur l'Article 37 du Traité CEE (présenté le 26 octobre 1967 à la Ligue Internationale contre la concurrence déloyale)' in Various, *L'entreprise publique et la concurrence. Les articles 90 et 37 du Traité CEE et leurs relations avec la concurrence*, Semaine de Bruges 1968 (De Temple, Bruges, 1969), 481; GC Rodriguez Iglesias, *El régimen jurídico de los monopolios de Estado en la Comunidad Económica Europea* (Madrid: Instituto de Estudios Administrativos, 1976); F Burrows, 'State Monopolies' [1983] YEL 25–47.

Article shall apply to any body through which a Member State, in law or in fact, either directly or indirectly supervises, determines or appreciably influences imports or exports between Member States. These provisions shall likewise apply to monopolies delegated by the State to others.

(2) Member States shall refrain from introducing any new measure which is contrary to the principles laid down in paragraph 1 or which restricts the scope of the Articles dealing with the prohibition of customs duties and quantitative restrictions between Member States.

(3) If a State monopoly of a commercial character has rules which are designed to make it easier to dispose of agricultural products or obtain for them the best return, steps should be taken in applying the rules contained in this Article to ensure equivalent safeguards for the employment and standard of living of the producers concerned.

6.107 Article 31 EC corresponds with former Article 37 of the Treaty with a few minor changes.[130]

'State monopolies of a commercial character'   This concept of 'State monopolies of a commercial character' has traditionally been interpreted in a very restrictive and formalistic way, as referring only to public undertakings that have been conferred, by law, with exclusive rights for the production, commercialisation, importing and/or exporting of goods. A careful reading of the two paragraphs of Article 31(1) shows, however, that the concept embraces all situations in which a Member State can influence imports or exports through an undertaking. What is essential is, on the one hand, the existence of an undertaking (the 'monopoly')[131] which can appreciably[132] influence the import or export of goods[133] between Member States.[134] This ability to influence may result from exclusive rights for import[135] or export, from exclusive rights over other activities (commercialisation, production, etc), from special rights,[136] or simply from the existence of a dominant position.[137] The other essential element for a State monopoly

---

130   The Treaty of Amsterdam repealed paras 3, 5 and 6 of former Art 37 because these paragraphs had become redundant once the transitional period ended. Paras 1, 2 and 4 of former Art 37 are now paras 1, 2 and 3 of Art 31. The only substantive change was the elimination of the word 'progressively' and of the reference to the transitional period, which had become redundant.

131   Art 31 also applies to situations where the State influences imports through a greater number of undertakings: Case 30/87 *Bodson* [1988] ECR 2479, paras 12–14.

132   Complete control over imports or exports is not necessary for Art 31 to apply. In Case C-347/88 *Greek oil monopoly* [1990] ECR I-4747, para 41, the Court of Justice found that control over 65% of imports implied an appreciable influence.

133   In principle, Art 31 only applies to goods, not to services: Case 155/73 *Sacchi* [1974] ECR 409, para 10; Case 271/81 *Mialocq* [1983] ECR 2057, para 8; Case 30/87 *Bodson* [1988] ECR 2479, para 10; Case C-17/94 *Gervais* [1995] ECR I-4353, para 35; Case C-6/01 *Anomar* [2003] ECR I-8621, paras 57–61. However, Art 31 may apply to cases where an undertaking can appreciably influence the trade in certain goods because it has a monopoly over certain services: Case 271/81 *Mialocq* [1983] ECR 2057, para 10; Case C-17/94 *Gervais* [1995] ECR I-4353, paras 36–37. A monopoly over funeral services, for instance, might in some cases allow the undertaking to influence the trade in coffins: Case 30/87 *Bodson* [1988] ECR 2479, para 10. Electricity is considered a good, not a service, and therefore electricity monopolies are subject to Article 31, as confirmed by the Court in Case C-393/92 *Almelo* [1994] ECR I-1517, para 28; and Case C-158/94 *Italian electricity monopoly* [1997] ECR I-5789, para 17.

134   Imports coming directly from third countries are not covered by Art 31: Case 91/78 *Hansen* [1979] ECR 935, para 19.

135   Case C-157/94 *Dutch electricity monopoly* [1997] ECR I-5699, para 20.

136   Case C-157/94 *Dutch electricity monopoly* [1997] ECR I-5699, paras 17–18.

137   This clearly results from the text of Art 31(1), second para. However, the Court of Justice seems reluctant to admit it: Case 271/81 *French artificial insemination monopoly* [1983] ECR 2079, paras 14–18; Case C-393/92

to exist is that the Member State[138] should either control the undertaking (in this case it would be a public undertaking) or have an appreciable influence over its behaviour. This influence can be presumed when the undertaking is a private undertaking that has been granted exclusive or special rights by the State.[139] This concept of 'monopolies delegated by the State to others' under Article 31(1), paragraph 2, corresponds to the notion of privileged undertakings under Article 86(1).

Obligations contained in Article 31   Once the concept of 'State monopolies of a commer- **6.108**
cial character' is defined, it is necessary to determine what the obligations are that Article 31 imposes on Member States. A distinction must be made, in that respect, between the obligations that apply during the transitional period and those that apply thereafter.[140] Former Article 37 contained some provisions that were applicable only during the transitional period. As the transitional period has ended these provisions have become redundant and the new Article 31 does not include them.

Obligations during the transitional period   During the transitional period, former Article 37 **6.109**
contained (a) an obligation for Member States to *progressively* adjust their State monopolies of a commercial character; (b) a provisional exemption from other Treaty provisions; and (c) an obligation to maintain a position of standstill as regards new restrictive measures.

The progressive adjustment of State monopolies is the main obligation arising out of former **6.110**
Article 37(1) during the transitional period. This provision obliged Member States to 'progressively adjust' their State monopolies 'so as to ensure that when the transitional period has ended no discrimination regarding the conditions under which goods are procured and marketed exists between nationals of the Member States'. The 'adjustment' was presented in this provision as a *process* that had to take place during the transitional period, in order to achieve a *result* by the end of that period. This result was 'to ensure that . . . no discrimination regarding the conditions under which goods are procured and marketed exists between nationals of the Member States'. The precise meaning of this obligation of non-discrimination will be discussed later. One must focus first upon how this process of adjustment had to be managed. Ideally, the adjustment should have been effected by the Member State in a progressive way. However, former Article 37 left Member States with a wide margin of discretion in determining the rhythm and the manner in which the adjustment had to take place.[141] The Commission could only formulate non-binding recommendations in relation to these questions. What was essential was that the result of non-discrimination was

---

Almelo [1994] ECR I-1517, paras 29–32. Most commentators also restrict the application of Art 31 to *de jure* monopolies: *Franck* (n 104 above) 47; *Rodriguez Iglesias* (n 104 above) 32; *De Cocborne* (n 104 above) 313.

[138]   The concept of Member State is not restricted to the national government but includes all the public authorities of the country (regional governments, local councils, etc): Case 30/87 *Bodson* [1988] ECR 2479, para 13.

[139]   Case C-157/94 *Dutch electricity monopoly* [1997] ECR I-5699, para 20. Opinion of Roemer AG, point 63, Case 82/71 *SAIL* [1972] ECR 119.

[140]   The transitional period ended on 31 December 1969 for the original Member States, on 31 December 1977 for the United Kingdom, Ireland and Denmark, on 31 December 1985 for Greece, on 31 December 1991 for Spain, and on 31 December 1992 for Portugal. No transitional period was foreseen for Finland, Sweden and Austria (except for a three-year transitional period for the Austrian tobacco monopoly).

[141]   Case C-361/90 *Portuguese alcohol monopoly* [1993] ECR I-95, paras 12–18.

achieved by the end of the transitional period. Before that moment the obligation to progressively adjust the monopolies did not have direct effect.[142]

6.111 Former Article 37 provided a transitory exception during the transitional period. The definitive regime applying to monopolies only applies at the end of the transitional period.[143]

6.112 Article 31(2) (and former Article 37(2)) contain a standstill clause which prohibits Member States from adopting new discriminatory or restrictive measures during the transitional period. This standstill obligation has direct effect.[144]

6.113 *Obligations after the transitional period* Once the transitional period has ended, Article 31 obliges Member States 'to ensure that no discrimination regarding the conditions under which goods are procured and marketed exists between nationals of the Member States'. This obligation has direct effect.[145] The precise content of this obligation is to some extent still controversial, as it depends on how the notion of 'discrimination' is interpreted[146] and also on the interpretation given to the expression 'to ensure that no discrimination exists'.

6.114 State measures that directly discriminate against imported goods are clearly prohibited by Article 31(1). This is the case in respect of measures imposing quantitative limits on imports, by the monopoly, discriminatory fiscal measures,[147] or measures fixing the price of products in such a way as to discriminate against imports.[148]

6.115 Discriminatory behaviours of the monopoly as regards imported goods, even in the absence of any explicit State measure, also seem to fall under Article 31(1),[149] although this interpretation is controversial.[150]

6.116 Exclusive rights granted to a State monopoly are clearly affected by Article 31. However, the precise impact of the provision is still to some extent controversial. Some commentators have argued in the past that, since Article 31 did not require the *abolition* of State monopolies but only *adjustment*, this meant that any exclusive rights that they held were legal. It is clear that even if the provision does not impose the elimination of all exclusive rights, it does require the elimination of exclusive rights having a discriminatory character.[151] The question is how to determine which exclusive rights are discriminatory and which are not.

---

[142] Case C-76/91 *Caves Neto Costa* [1993] ECR I-117, para 8.

[143] Case 45/75 *Rewe* [1976] ECR 196, para 24; Case 86/78 *Peureux I* [1979] ECR 897, para 31.

[144] Case 6/64 *Costa v ENEL* [1964] ECR 1141.

[145] Case 45/75 *Rewe* [1976] ECR 196, para 4.

[146] MG Ross, 'Article 37—Redundancy or Reinstatement' [1982] 7(4) ELR 281–299.

[147] Case 13/70 *Cinzano* [1970] ECR 1089; Case 91/75 *Miritz* [1976] ECR 217; Case 45/75 *Rewe* [1976] ECR 196.

[148] Case 91/78 *Hansen* [1979] ECR 935; Case 78/82 *Italian tobacco monopoly* [1983] ECR 1955.

[149] Case C-438/02 *Hanner* [2005] ECR I-4551, para 38; Case 91/78 *Hansen* [1979] ECR 935, para 14; *Report on Competition Policy 1971* (Vol I) para 196; *De Cockborne* (n 104 above) 322 and 342. See JL Buendia Sierra, *Exclusive Rights and State Monopolies in EC Law* (Oxford University Press, 1999) paras 3.117–3.126.

[150] The Court of Justice seemed to reject this interpretation in other cases: Case 30/87 *Bodson* [1988] ECR 2479, para 14; Case C-393/92 *Almelo* [1994]1 ECR I-1517, paras 29–32.

[151] *Rodriguez Iglesias* (n 104 above) 87–88.

Since the *Manghera* case[152] the Court of Justice has held that exclusive rights over the activities of importing,[153] exporting,[154] and/or the wholesale distribution[155] of goods are *per se* discriminatory and therefore contrary to Article 31.

6.117

Much less clear is the status of exclusive rights over sales at the retail level. The recent *Franzén* judgment suggests that such exclusive rights do not fall under Article 31 if the monopoly is organised in such a way as to avoid discrimination between national and foreign goods.[156] However, this approach seems incompatible with the traditional interpretation of Article 31 and also with three other judgments adopted by the Court of Justice that same day.[157] Indeed, the *Franzén* judgment ignores the fact that Article 31 not only bans discrimination between national and foreign *goods* but also discrimination between national and foreign *operators and customers*. A retail monopoly, by preventing foreign producers from reaching the customers of that Member State directly and by preventing national consumers from reaching foreign operators directly, clearly discriminates between national and foreign *operators and customers*. It is therefore submitted that exclusive rights for sales at the retail level should also be considered as contrary to Article 31.[158]

6.118

It has traditionally been thought that exclusive rights in respect of the production of certain types of goods do not fall under Article 31 due to their 'industrial' (as opposed to 'commercial') character.[159] This highly questionable interpretation has never been either confirmed or denied by the Court of Justice. It seems clear, however, that, even if these exclusive rights of production were not caught by Article 31, they may fall under other provisions (such as Article 43 (former Article 52)).

6.119

(iii) The borderline between the general and special regimes In principle, Article 31 only applies as regards State measures (such as exclusive rights) that are closely 'linked' with the existence and the functioning of a monopoly. Measures that do not have such a close link are considered as 'detachable' or general measures that are subject to Article 28.[160]

6.120

---

152 Case 59/75 *Manghera* [1976] ECR 91.

153 Case 59/75 *Manghera* [1976] ECR 91, paras 9–13; Case C-347/88 *Greek oil monopoly* [1990] ECR I-4747, paras 42–44; Case C-157/94 *Dutch electricity monopoly* [1997] ECR I-5699, paras 15 and 17; Case C-158/94 *Italian electricity monopoly* [1997] ECR I-5789, paras 23 and 32; Case C-159/94 *French electricity and gas monopolies* [1997] ECR I-5815, paras 33, 39 and 40.

154 Case C-158/94 *Italian electricity monopoly* [1997] ECR I-5789, paras 24 and 25; Case C-159/94 *French electricity and gas monopolies* [1997] ECR I-5815, paras 34 and 35.

155 Case C-347/88 *Greek oil monopoly* [1990] ECR I-4747, paras 43, 44 and 56.

156 Case C-189/95 *Franzén* [1997] ECR I-5909, paras 37–66.

157 Case C-157/94 *Dutch electricity monopoly* [1997] ECR I-5699, paras 21–23; Case C-158/94 *Italian electricity monopoly* [1997] ECR I-5789, paras 23 and 32; Case C-159/94 *French electricity and gas monopolies* [1997] ECR I-5815, paras 33 and 38–40.

158 See JL Buendia Sierra, *Exclusive Rights and State Monopolies in EC Law* (Oxford University Press, 1999) paras 3.162–3.172. Léger AG followed this same line in his Opinion Case C-438/02 *Hanner*, paras 62 and 115. However, the Court maintanted the Franzén approach in its judgment in Case C-438/02 *Hanner* [2005] ECR I-4551, para 35.

159 This is the dominant opinion: RC Beraud, 'L'aménagement des monopoles nationaux prévu à l'Article 37 du Traité CEE à la lumière des récents développements jurisprudentiels' [1979] RTDE iv 586; F Wooldridge, 'Some recent decisions concerning the ambit of Article 37 of the EEC Treaty' [1979] LIEI i 120; *Oliver* (n 93 above) 320; *Mattera* (n 93 above) 36; M Bazex, 'L'entreprise publique et le Droit européen—Public Enterprise and European Law' [1991] RDAI—IBLJ iv 471.

160 Case 91/78 *Hansen* [1979] ECR 935, para 9; Case 86/78 *Peureux I* [1979] ECR 897, paras 35–37; Case C-387/93 *Banchero* [1995] ECR I-4661, para 29; Case C-189/95 *Franzén* [1997] ECR I-5909, paras 35–36.

6.121   This dual regime is not always applied in a coherent way. First of all, the distinction between 'linked' and 'detachable' measures is not a clear one. In addition, the Court of Justice has in the past often applied Article 28 as regards exclusive rights, which are the measures most closely 'linked' with the existence and the functioning of a monopoly.[161] Happily, these ambiguities have a rather limited practical impact. The reason is that the prevailing interpretation of Article 31 as prohibiting discrimination between national and foreign operators and customers makes this provision very similar in substance to the prohibition contained in Article 28.

(c) Article 86(1) in Combination with the Rules on Freedom to Provide Services and on Establishment—Articles 43 and 49

6.122   State measures that restrict the provision of services by undertakings established in other Member States will often conflict with Article 49 (former Article 59), the Treaty rule on freedom to provide services. State measures that restrict the establishment of undertakings coming from other Member States will often conflict with Article 43 (former Article 52), the Treaty provision on freedom of establishment.[162] When restrictive State measures of this type are linked with a public or privileged undertaking, then the Treaty rules on freedom to provide services and establishment will apply in combination with Article 86(1), and the special procedures of Article 86(3) may be used.

6.123   **Article 86(1) in combination with Article 49**   Article 49 of the EC Treaty, as interpreted by the Court of Justice, prohibits Member States from adopting measures that unduly restrict the provision of cross-border services by undertakings established in other Member States. Of course, this provision clearly prohibits restrictions having a discriminatory character, either in law or in fact, against foreign service providers and in favour of national ones. However, Article 49 also prohibits certain non-discriminatory but clearly restrictive State measures. Indeed, the *Mediawet* judgment has made it clear that State measures restricting the provision of services that on the face of it apply equally to both foreigners and nationals still fall under Article 49 unless they can be justified as being necessary to guarantee certain 'mandatory requirements'.[163]

6.124   Exclusive rights in the field of services would normally impede the access of foreign service providers to the relevant national market for services.[164] Special rights may also restrict market access for foreign undertakings. Such exclusive or special rights would only be compatible with Article 49 if they could be proven to be proportional.[165]

---

[161] Case C-347/88 *Greek oil monopoly* [1990] ECR I-4747; Case C-202/88 *Terminal equipment for telecommunications* [1991] ECR I-1223, paras 33–43; Case C-323/93 *La Crespelle* [1994] ECR I-5077, paras 28–39.

[162] See G Marenco, 'The Notion of Restriction on the Freedom of Establishment and Provision of Services in the Case-law of the Court' [1991] 11 YEL 111–150, for an interesting study of both Articles. See also *Buendia Sierra* (n 10 above) paras 6.116–6.275.

[163] Case C-353/89 *Mediawet* [1991] ECR I-4069, paras 14–19; Case C-288/89 *Stichting Collectieve Antenne Gouda* [1991] ECR I-4007, paras 10–15; Case C-124/97 *Läärä* [1999] ECR I-6067, paras 29–30; Case C-6/01 *Anomar* [2003] ECR I-8621, para 65. However, the recent case law seems to exclude non-discriminatory measures from Art 49: Cases C-544 & 545/03 *Mobistar* [2005] ECR I-7723, para 31.

[164] Case 352/85 *Bond van Adverteerders* [1988] ECR 2085, paras 24–26; Case C-3/88 *Commission v Italy* (*data services*) [1989] ECR 4035, paras 8–9; Case C-353/89 *Mediawet* [1991] ECR I-4069, para 25; Case 260/89 *ERT* [1991] ECR I-2925, paras 19–26.

[165] Case C-3/88 *Commission v Italy* (*data services*) [1989] ECR 4035, paras 10–11; Case C-353/89 *Mediawet* [1991] ECR I-4069, para 42; Case C-288/89 *Stichting Collectieve Antenne Gouda* [1991] ECR I-4007, para 24;

Article 86(1) in combination with Article 43 Article 43 obliges Member States to autho- **6.125** rise the establishment within their territories of undertakings from other Member States on the same terms as apply to their own nationals. This means that, unlike Article 49, Article 43 in principle only prohibits restrictive State measures that discriminate against foreigners.[166]

However, the Court of Justice interprets the concept of discrimination in this context in a very **6.126** broad manner. It embraces not only formal but also material discrimination. Even measures that on their face apply equally to both nationals and foreigners are considered discriminatory if in fact they make establishment more difficult for foreigners than for nationals.[167]

Exclusive rights were at first considered to be non-discriminatory measures, as (apart from **6.127** the monopolist) all national and foreign undertakings were treated on an equal footing.[168] The Court of Justice has subsequently made clear that a measure that discriminates in favour of a single national undertaking (and therefore against all the other undertakings, national and foreign) is also considered to be a discriminatory restriction of establishment contrary to Article 43.[169]

Thus, the granting of an exclusive right to a national undertaking may in principle fall **6.128** under Article 43. The application of this provision should be excluded, however, when the Member State can prove that the selection of the undertaking that benefits from the exclusive right has been made in an objective and transparent way.[170]

Need for a cross-border element Article 86(1) in combination with Articles 43 and 49 **6.129** only applies to situations where a cross-border element exists. This is the case where an undertaking wants to establish in another Member State, or wants to provide services to customers residing in that Member State, and is prevented from doing so by the existence of an exclusive right. However, in contrast to the way that Article 86(1) operates in combination with Article 82, Article 86(1) in combination with Articles 43 and 49 cannot be invoked by a national against an exclusive right granted by the authorities of his own Member State.[171]

(7) Direct Effect

Article 86(1), when applied in combination with Articles 82, 28, 31, 43 or 49 has direct **6.130** effect.[172] It can therefore be applied not only by the European Commission, but also by national courts.

Case C-124/97 *Läärä* [1999] ECR I-6067, para 33; Case C-451/03 *Calafiori* [2006] not yet published, para 33–37. In the sector of gambling the margin of discretion of Member States is wider (Case C-67/98 *Zenatti* [1999] ECR I-7289; Case C-6/01 *Anomar* [2003] ECR I-8621, paras 73–87) but still subject to certain limits (see Case C-243/01 *Gambetti* [2003] ECR I-13031, paras 65–76).

[166] *Marenco* (n 136 above) 111–128. There are, however, some judgments about non-discriminatory restrictions: Case 107/83 *Klopp* [1984] ECR 2971; Case 96/85 *Commission v France* [1986] ECR 1475; Case 143/87 *INASTI* [1988] ECR 3877. See also *Greek Insurances* [1985] OJ L152/25.

[167] Case C-3/88 *Commission v Italy* (*data services*) [1989] ECR 4035, paras 8–9.

[168] Case 6/64 *Costa v ENEL* [1964] ECR 1141; Case 90/76 *Van Ameyde* [1977] ECR 1091, paras 26–30.

[169] Case C-3/88 *Commission v Italy* (*data services*) [1989] ECR 4035, paras 8–9; Case C-243/01 *Gambetti* [2003] ECR I-13031, para 48; Case C-451/03 *Calafiori* [2006] not yet published, paras 34–35.

[170] See Case C-458/03 *Parking Brixen* [2005] not yet published, according to which Arts 43 EC and 49 EC, and the principles of equal treatment, non-discrimination and transparency, preclude a public authority from awarding, without putting it out to tender, a public service concession.

[171] Case C-41/90 *Höfner* [1991] ECR I-2015, paras 35–41; Case C-17/94 *Gervais* [1995] ECR I-4353, paras 23–28. However, these Community provisions may have an indirect impact whenever national law protects its nationals from 'reverse discrimination'; Case C-451/03 *Calafiori* [2006] not yet published, paras 28–29.

[172] *Temple Lang* (n 10 above) 544; Case C-179/90 *Port of Genoa* [1991] ECR I-5889, para 23.

C. Article 86(2): Services of General Economic Interest and Other Public Interest Objectives

6.131   The strict regime contained in Article 86(1) as regards anti-competitive State measures must be balanced by the exceptions foreseen in the Treaty for those restrictions that may be justified by public interest objectives. Article 86(2) (former Article 90(2)), in particular, may allow derogation from the prohibitions contained in Article 86(1) when this is necessary for the achievement of a purpose of general economic interest (public service) that has been entrusted by the State to one undertaking.[173]

6.132   Article 86(2) provides that:

> Undertakings entrusted with the operation of services of general economic interest or having the character of a revenue-producing monopoly shall be subject to the rules contained in this Treaty, in particular to the rules on competition, in so far as the application of such rules does not obstruct the performance, in law or in fact, of the particular tasks assigned to them. The development of trade must not be affected to such an extent as would be contrary to the interest of the Community.

This provision aims to find a balance between the Community objective of market integration on the one hand and national public service objectives on the other hand. These sets of objectives are not necessarily in conflict: the opening of certain activities to competition has often led to lower prices and increased choice for consumers. However, such conflict may indeed arise in certain cases. This possibility of conflict increases with the progress of market integration. This explains the increased importance of Article 86(2) EC in recent years from an obscure provision rarely applied to the object of hot legal and political debates.

(1)   The Undertakings to which Article 86(2) Relates

6.133   Article 86(2) refers to certain 'undertakings'. This means that to be able to rely on the exception the entities in question must carry out 'economic activities'. Two different types of undertaking are capable of coming within the scope of Article 86(2): first those undertakings entrusted with the management of services of general economic interest and secondly those undertakings which are revenue-producing monopolies.

6.134   **Undertakings**   As previously explained, the Community competition rules only apply to 'undertakings', that is to entities which carry out 'economic activities'. In the same way,

---

[173] See JL Buendia Sierra, *Exclusive rights and State Monopolies in EC Law* (Oxford University Press, 1999) Ch 8. For discussion of the underlying theory see: Various, *Concorrenza tra settore pubblico e privato nella CEE*, Colloquio di Bruxelles della 'Ligue Internationale contre la concurrence déloyale' 5–6 March [1963] RDI anno XII 1–256; L Hancher, 'Case C-320/91, Corbeau' [1994] 21 CML Rev 105–122; A Wachsmann and F Berrod, 'Les critères de justification des monopoles: un premier bilan après l'affaire Corbeau' [1994] RTDE xxx (i) 39–61; R Kovar, 'Droit communautaire et service public: esprit d'orthodoxie ou pensée laïcisée' [1996] RTDE xxxii (ii) 215–242, xxxii (iii) 493–533; D Simon, 'Les mutations des services publics du fait des contraintes du Droit communautaire', in R Kovar and D Simon, (eds) *Service public et Communauté européenne: entre l'intérêt général et le marché, Actes du colloque de Strasbourg, 17–19 octobre 1996* (Paris: La Documentation Française, 1998) 65; JL Buendia Sierra, 'La Communication sur les services d'intérêt général en Europe et la politique communautaire de concurrence' in R Kovar and D Simon (eds) *Service public et Communauté européenne: entre l'intérêt général et le marché, Actes du colloque de Strasbourg, 17–19 octobre 1996* (Paris: La Documentation Française, 1998) 461–473. K Lenaerts, 'Les services d'intérêt général et le Droit Communautaire', in Conseil d' Etat, *Rapport public 2002—Collectivités locales et concurrence* (Paris, 2002) 425–437.

only those exclusive rights concerning the exercise of economic activities come within the scope of Articles 31 and 86(1) of the Treaty. Accordingly, it is only in respect of these exclusive rights and as regards the carrying out of economic activities that the exception contained in Article 86(2) can possibly apply.

The case law of the Court of Justice has always distinguished between non-economic activities (not subject to the competition rules) and activities of general economic interest (subject to the competition rules but capable of falling within Article 86(2)). In this context, it is necessary to point out that the criteria employed to distinguish between economic and non-economic activities do not coincide with those used to decide what *economic* activities must be considered to be of general economic interest. The analysis of the possible application of Article 86(2) presupposes that it is beyond doubt that the activity in question is 'economic' in nature. If an activity is non-economic, Member States are free to grant or maintain exclusive rights without the need to justify them in the context of Articles 31 and 86 EC. [174]   **6.135**

Undertakings entrusted with the operation of services of general economic interest   **6.136**
Article 86(2) refers first to those undertakings to which a public authority has entrusted the operation of a service of general economic interest. The scope of Article 86(2) is defined by the role of the undertakings in question and not by their public or private nature. Both public and private undertakings come within this provision.[175]

The types of undertakings referred to in Article 86(2) do not coincide exactly with the concept of undertaking set out in Section (1) above. However, it is clear that exclusive rights and/or the public ownership of many of the undertakings included in Article 86(1) are explained by the fact that they are undertakings to which tasks of general economic interest have been entrusted under Article 86(2).   **6.137**

There are two parts of this definition which cause problems: the meanings of 'entrusted' and the content of public service. Each will now be examined in turn.   **6.138**

Services of general economic interest   The concept of 'services of general economic interest' contained in Article 86(2) is a Community law concept. A service of general economic interest is a service of an economic nature the provision of which to the general public is considered essential, which justifies a degree of intervention of the public authorities in order to the show that a given service is actually provided and to control the conditions under which it is provided.   **6.139**

Article 86(2) specifies that the general interest must be of an economic nature. This requirement is frequently omitted by the Court of Justice in its judgments which appears to indicate that the Court considers the adjective 'economic' to be redundant, adding nothing in the context of Article 86(2). 'General interest' and 'general economic interest' thus appear to be the same thing.[176] The economic nature of the general interest protected must be broadly defined to include, for example, cultural activities.[177]   **6.140**

---

[174] Commission Communication concerning services of general interest in Europe [1996] OJ C281/3–12 para 18.
[175] Case 127/73 *BRT II* [1974] ECR 318, para 20; Case 172/80 *Züchner* [1981] ECR 2030, paras 6–7. Commission Communication concerning services of general interest in Europe [1996] OJ C281/3–12 para 10.
[176] Case C-393/92 *Almelo* [1994] ECR I-1520–1521, paras 46, 47, 49.
[177] Case 155/73 *Sacchi* [1974] ECR 430, para 14.

6.141 The Commission has distinguished between 'services of general interest' and 'services of general *economic* interest'. The former category includes the provision of any service considered of general interest by the public authorities, regardless of whether it is of an economic nature or not. The latter category forms part of the former and only includes the provision of services of an economic nature.[178] The competition rules, and in particular Article 86(2), would only apply to this latter category.

6.142 A service or benefit offered only to certain undertakings or economic sectors cannot in principle be considered to be of 'general' interest. To come within this definition, the service must concern general economic activity.[179] The Court suggested that this was the case in *BRT II*, when affirming that a copyright management undertaking 'to which the State has not assigned any task and which manages private interest, including intellectual property rights protected by law' is not an undertaking entrusted with a task of general economic interest.[180] The same theory has been supported by the Commission in the *GEMA*[181] and *GVL*[182] decisions, which both concerned copyright management companies.

6.143 Regional policy and in particular the correction of regional imbalances can be considered to be tasks of *general* interest, although limited to certain geographical areas.[183] The same applies to actions directed at certain disadvantaged groups of people. The essential point is that the considerations upon which such actions are based are of a general nature, although their application in practice is logically directed at certain groups.

6.144 It follows that the concept of 'services of general economic interest' roughly corresponds to the concept of 'public service' used by certain Member States.[184] The Court of Justice has also sometimes used both terms as if they were synonymous.[185] The fact that Article 86(2) does not actually refer to 'public service' is probably due to the desire to emphasise the fact that it is a Community law concept, and as such it need not correspond exactly to the concepts of public service employed in some Member States.[186]

---

178 Commission Communication concerning services of general interest [1996] OJ C281/4, para 10.

179 This was the view of Dutheillet de Lamothe AG in his Opinion in Case 10/71 *Puerto de Mertert* [1971] ECR 739. See also H Papaconstantinou, *Free Trade and Competition in the EEC: Law, Policy and Practice* (Routledge: London-New York, 1988) 88. Against this see the Opinion of Roemer AG in Case 82/71 *SAIL (milk wholesale markets)* [1972] ECR 147 and the Opinion of Reischl AG in Case 52/76 *Benedetti* [1976] ECR 192.

180 Case 127/73 *BRT II* [1974] ECR 318, para 23.

181 Commission Decision (EEC) 71/244 *GEMA* [1971] OJ L134/27, para III.2.

182 Commission Decision (EEC) 81/1030 *GVL* [1981] OJ L370/58, paras 67–68.

183 Case 66/86 *Ahmed Saeed Flugreisen and Silver Line Reisebüro GmbH v Zentrale zur Bekämpfung Unlauteren Wettbewerbs e V* [1989] ECR 853, para 55; Case T-260/94 *Air Inter* [1997] ECRII-997, para 140. See also *Papaconstantinou, op cit*, 88.

184 This was the position of the majority of participants in the Brussels Coloquium 1963 *Concorrenza tra settore . . ., cit.* Joliet, R, pointed out that this Community concept was French inspired in 'Contribution à l'étude du régime des entreprises publiques dans la CEE' [1965] AFDL i 86. Among recent academic contributions see Kovar, *op cit*, 241.

185 Case C-18/88 *RTT* [1991] ECR I-5980, para 22; Case C-393/92 *Almelo* [1994] ECR I-1520–1521, paras 47, 49.

186 This was the position of the majority of participants in the Brussels Coloquium 1963: Hartmann (70 ff), Franceschelli (85 and 240), Delvaux y Faber (156 ff) Snoy Et D'oppuers (247 ff), *Concorrenza tra settore . . ., cit.* Others also agreeing with this position are L Ferrari-Bravo, 'Les articles 90 et 37 dans leurs rélations avec un régime de concurrence non falsifiée. Les incidences des règles de concurrence et de l'article 222 sur les possibilités de nouvelles nationalisations ou socilisations de secteurs économiques' in Various *L'entreprise publique . . ., cit.* 424; A Deringer, *op cit* 1.25.

Stating that the concept of 'services of general economic interest' is a Community concept in no **6.145** way implies that deciding which general economic interest services a given Member State can offer to its citizens is a matter for the Community authorities. This would be the case in areas in which a Community harmonisation of the public service objectives has taken place, such as telecommunications or postal services. However, in the absence of a Community harmonisation, this is a task for the public authorities of the Member State in question. In this scenario the public authorities of each Member State are in principle free to decide which public services they wish to guarantee for their citizens, without those services necessarily having to coincide with others offered in different countries. However, this discretion is limited rather than absolute.

Indeed, the Community concept of 'services of general economic interest' should be under- **6.146** stood as a *maximum standard* beyond which Member States cannot go. If this were not the case, a Member State might artificially set too wide a concept of public service with the sole objective of giving excessive protection to a certain operator. This concept therefore acts as the final barrier preventing the exception of Article 86(2) EC being abused by Member States.[187] This is clear from judgments of the Court of Justice such as *Port of Genoa* (port activities which were the object of a legal monopoly)[188] and *BRT II* (the management of copyrights).[189] A more or less similar line has been followed by the Court of First Instance.[190]

The following activities have been considered by the Court or by the Commission to be **6.147** 'services of general economic interest', even without discussion:

- the operation of a river port which handles the majority of river traffic in goods in a Member State;[191]
- the establishment and operation of a public telecommunications network;[192]
- water distribution;[193]
- the operation of television services;[194]
- electricity distribution;[195]
- the operation of certain transport lines;[196]
- employment recruitment;[197]
- basic postal services;[198]

---

[187] Page, *op cit* 29–30; Kovar, *op cit* 233; Simon, *op cit* 19.
[188] Case C-179/90 *Port of Genoa* [1991] ECR I-5931, para 27.
[189] Case 127/73 *BRT II* [1974] ECR 318, para 23.
[190] Case T-106/95 *FFSA* [1997] ECR II-229, paras 108 and 192, have sometimes been understood as supporting a purely 'national' definition of services of general economic interest. However, a careful reading shows that the limits to Community control in paras 108 and 192 do not refer to the definition of the activity as 'service of general economic interest' but to the efficiency of the operator and the level of its costs.
[191] Case 10/71 *Port of Mertert* [1971] ECR 730, para 11. See also the Opinion of Dutheillet De Lamothe AG in the same case [1971] ECR 739.
[192] Case 41/83 *Italy v The Commission (British Telecom Decision)* [1985] ECR 888, paras 29–33; Case C-18/88 *RTT* [1991] ECR I-5979, para 16.
[193] Commission Decision (CEE) 82/371 *Navewa-Anseau* [1982] OJ L167/48, para 66.
[194] Impliedly in Case 155/73 *Sacchi* [1974] ECR 430–431, paras 14–15, in Commission Decision (EEC) 91/310 *Screensport* [1991] OJ L63/43, para 69 and less obviously in Commission Decision (EEC) 89/536 *German Televisions* [1989] OJ L284/41, para 40.
[195] Commission Decision (EEC) 91/50 *IJsselcentrale* [1991] OJ L28/43, para 40; and Case C-393/92 *Almelo* [1994] ECR I-1520–1521, para 47.
[196] Case 66/86 *Ahmed Saeed* [1989] ECR 853, para 55.
[197] Case C-41/90 *Höfner* [1991] ECR I-2017, para 24.
[198] Case C-320/91 *Corbeau* [1993] ECR I-2568, para 15.

- the maintenance of a postal service network in rural communities;[199]
- regional policy within a Member State;[200]
- port services;
- waste management;
- ambulance services.

In general the Court of Justice and the Commission have, as far as possible, avoided stating clearly that a given activity is or is not a service 'of general economic interest'. Frequently, it is assumed, for the sake of argument, that an activity has such a nature in order for it then to be shown that in any event the application of the Treaty provisions would not endanger the fulfilment of its task.

6.148 Moreover, the concept of 'services of general economic interest' is a dynamic one, capable of changing with time, according to factors such as technological advances, the state of Community integration, or variations in society's perception of the needs which must be covered by the State. In other words, what is considered today to be a service of general economic interest may be considered differently in the future and vice versa.[201]

6.149 **Entrustment**   In order for Article 86(2) to apply to an undertaking it is necessary for the management of a service of general economic interest to have been entrusted to it by a public authority.[202] In this context, public authorities can be of a national, regional or local nature.[203]

6.150 The public entity that grants the task in question to an undertaking must do so in the exercise of its functions as a public authority.[204] The assignment of the task in question may be carried out by an act of State in the exercise of its prerogative power.[205] It can be operated without doubt through a legal provision[206] and/or through another public law instrument (regulation, public law contract, grant, etc).[207]

6.151 Whether a service of general economic interest under Article 86(2) can be entrusted to an undertaking by means of a simple private law contract is debatable.[208] Without doubt, in such cases the State does not exercise its *prerogative* powers, but this does not necessarily mean that it does not act in the exercise of public authority *functions*. It is perfectly possible and even normal for a public authority, in the exercise of its everyday administrative functions, to make use of private law instruments.

6.152 On the contrary, if a public entity enters into a contract governed by private law with an undertaking for the purpose of carrying out of an economic activity it is not, by definition, acting in the exercise of public authority *functions*. Such a contract could not come within the meaning of Article 86(2).[209]

---

[199]   Case T-106/95 *FFSA* [1997] ECR II-229, paras 108, 192.
[200]   Case T-260/94 *Air Inter* [1997] ECRII-997, para 140.
[201]   Case C-18/88 *RTT* [1991] ECR I-5979, para 16. See also the Commission Communication concerning services of general interest, *op cit* 7, para 29.
[202]   Cases T-204 and 270/97 *EPAC* [2000] ECR II-2267, paras 125–128.
[203]   Commission Decision (CEE) 82/371 *Navewa-Anseau* [1982] OJ L167/48, para 65.
[204]   Franck, *op cit* 39; Papaconstantinou, *op cit* 83.
[205]   Case 127/73 *BRT II* [1974] ECR 318, para 20; Case 172/80 *Züchner* [1981] ECR 2030, para 7.
[206]   Case 10/71 *Port of Mertert* [1971] ECR 730, para 11.
[207]   Case C-159/94 *Electricity and Gas Monopolies—France* [1997] ECR I-5815, para 66.
[208]   This was the position of Joliet, *op cit* 82–83 and Papaconstantinou, *op cit* 83.
[209]   Case C-393/92 *Almelo* [1994] ECR I-1517, para 31.

In principle, if a public authority merely *authorises* the exercise of certain activities this does **6.153** not in itself mean that the activity has been 'entrusted' within the meaning of Article 86(2).[210] Equally, the fact that certain activities undertaken by private initiative obtain the express approval of the public authorities does not automatically mean that they have been 'entrusted' either.[211] The 'entrustment' under Article 86(2) may however occur following a suggestion by an operator. The important element is the underlying positive decision by public authorities to consider an activity 'of general interest'.

The assignment of the task must be to one or more specific undertakings in an individu- **6.154** alised manner.[212]

The assignment by the public authority of a task of general interest to an undertaking is a **6.155** different act from the possible grant of an exclusive right to that undertaking.[213] Of course, in many cases both acts will be carried out in a parallel manner and the function of the exclusive right will be to allow the task to be properly fulfilled. Nevertheless it is necessary to distinguish clearly between them.[214]

Revenue-producing monopolies   Apart from undertakings entrusted with services of **6.156** general economic interest, Article 86(2) also refers to another category of undertakings: revenue-producing monopolies. There is a general consensus, however, that exclusive rights whose only objective is the generation of revenues would never be justified under Article 86(2).[215] This is because revenue-producing monopolies would normally fail to sat- isfy the proportionality test, as there are less restrictive means available for obtaining such revenues, such as fiscal measures.[216]

(2) Article 86(2) as an Exception Applicable to the Behaviour of Undertakings and to State Measures

Articles 81 and 82 are provisions addressed to undertakings. As such, they apply directly **6.157** not only to private but also to public undertakings. The point of departure is therefore that these provisions apply to all undertakings. Article 86(2), however, expressly provides for a limited exemption: Articles 81 and 82 will only apply to the behaviour of an undertaking that has been entrusted with a service of general economic interest to the extent that their application does not endanger the fulfilment of the undertaking's specific role. It follows from this that Article 86(2) can be invoked by these undertakings in the context of proce- dures based on Articles 81 and/or 82 of the EC Treaty.[217]

---

[210] Commission Decision (EEC) 81/1031 *GVL* [1981] OJ L370/58, para 66; Kovar, *op cit* 234.

[211] Commission Decision (EEC) 85/77 *Uniform Eurocheques* [1985] OJ L35/48, para 29.

[212] Case C-159/94 *French electricity and gas monopolies* [1997] ECR I-5815, paras 69–70.

[213] Kovar, *op cit* 234.

[214] Kovar, *op cit* 239 clearly distinguishes between both questions and suggests that the confusion is, in many cases, deliberate, since 'defending public service often includes defending monopolies'. See also Simon, *op cit* 9.

[215] *Franck* (n 104 above) 39; *Papaconstantinou* (n 10 above) 90; R Wainwright, 'Public Undertakings under Article 90' [1989] FCLI 249.

[216] This position was adopted by the Commission in Recommendation 62/1500 *French tobacco monopoly* [1962] OJ 48; and Recommendation 62/1502 *French matches monopoly* [1962] OJ 48.

[217] Case C-393/92 *Almelo* [1994] ECR I-1517, paras 33–50; Case 41/83 *British Telecommunications* [1985] ECR 873, paras 28–35.

6.158   Despite some early doubts,[218] it is now clear that the exception provided for in Article 86(2) can also apply to State measures (such as exclusive or special rights) that are contrary to a rule of the Treaty addressed to the Member States,[219] such as Article 86(1) in combination with Articles 28, 31, 43, 49 or 82.

6.159   The relationship of Article 86(2) with the rules on State aids (Articles 87 and 88) has traditionally been controversial. According to certain case law, subsidies granted in consideration of additional costs incurred as a result of public service obligations were State aids whose compatibility had to be examined under Article 86(2). [220] Other judgments indicated that such subsidies are not to be considered as State aids within the meaning of Article 87(1), so that the exemption of Article 86(2) would have no role to play as regards State aids.[221] The recent *Altmark* judgment has taken an intermediate approach: this judgment considers that the non-aid character can only be accepted for public service compensations granted in accordance with certain strict conditions.[222] This judgment appears to suggest that many public service compensation schemes imply State aids. Therefore it is now clear that the exception provided for in Article 86(2) can also apply to State aids. The detailed conditions of application have been clarified recently with the adoption in July 2005 of a Commission Decision addressed to all Member States under Article 86(3) dealing with public service compensation (ie aids granted by Member States to compensate undertakings in charge of services of general economic interest for the additional costs resulting from these duties). This instrument specifies that certain types of compensation (those below a certain threshold and fulfilling certain conditions) are considered compatible with Article 86(2) and are exempted from the notification obligation of Article 88. The Commission also adopted a communication explaining its future approach as regards those cases that fall outside the scope of the decision and must therefore be examined on an individual basis.[223]

(3) Conditions for the Application of Article 86(2)

6.160   One must keep in mind that Article 86(2), as with any exception, will be interpreted strictly.[224] It goes without saying that the mere invocation of Article 86(2) by a Member State or by an undertaking does not automatically mean that the exception will be applied. This would only happen if all the conditions set out in the provision are fulfilled. The first condition, that a service of general economic interest must have been entrusted by the State to one undertaking,

---

[218] Case 72/83 *Campus Oil* [1984] ECR 2727, para 19.

[219] Case C-157/94 *Dutch electricity monopoly* [1997] ECR I-5699, paras 27–31; Case C-158/94 *Italian electricity monopoly* [1997] ECR I-5789, paras 38–44; Case C-159/94 *French electricity and gas monopolies* [1997] ECR I-5815, paras 44–50.

[220] Case T-106/95 *La Poste* [1997] ECR II-233, para 172; Case T-46/97 *SIC* [2000] ECR II-2125; Case C-332/98 *CEFL* [2000] ECR I-4833, paras 27–32.

[221] Case C-53/00 *Ferring* [2001] ECR I-9067, paras 27–33.

[222] Case C-280/00 *Altmark* [2003] ECR I-7747, paras 87–94.

[223] Commission Decision (EC) 2005/842 on the application of Article 86(2) of the EC Treaty to State aid in the form of public service compensation granted to certain undertakings entrusted with the operation of services of general economic interest [2005] OJ L312/67; and Community framework for State aid in the form of public service compensation [2005] OJ C297/4. For a detailed analysis of the application of Art 86(2) to State aids see JL Buendia Sierra, 'An Analysis of Article 86(2) EC' in Sanchez Rydelski (ed) *The EU State aid regime* (London: Cameron May, 2006) 541–574.

[224] Case 127/73 *BRT II* [1974] ECR 313, paras 20–21; Case T-260/94 *Air Inter* [1997] ECR II-997, para 135; Case T-128/98 *Aéroports de Paris* [2000] ECR II-3929, para 227.

has already been examined. The other two conditions are that the restriction must be proportionate (or necessary) and the interest of the Community must be respected.

(i) The necessity of the measure   Article 86(2) only applies to the extent that the restriction is *necessary* for the fulfilment of the relevant purpose of general economic interest. In other words, the exception will only apply if the *proportionate* character of the restriction can be proved. Thus, the legality of many State measures or behaviour of undertakings will depend on the interpretation given to this condition. It goes without saying that this fact makes its interpretation highly controversial.

6.161

The proportionality principle   The proportionality test contained in Article 86(2) is no different from those existing in other areas of EC law. The proportionality test is considered to be fulfilled when the following three elements are proved:[225]

6.162

(1) that a causal link exists between the measure and the objective of general interest;
(2) that the restrictions introduced by the measure are balanced by the benefits to the general interest; and
(3) that the objective of general interest cannot be achieved through other less restrictive means.

The question of causation is relatively simple and objective. In order to be protected by Article 86(2) an exclusive right must contribute in some way to the carrying out of a task of general economic interest. The second element is confused in practice with the last requirement of Article 86(2) concerning the interest of the Community, which will be analysed later. The main problems arise in connection with the question of necessity (the objectives cannot be achieved by less restrictive methods).

6.163

The functioning of the proportionality test in the field of Article 86(2) which has just been described is identical to that employed in the field of free movement of goods. However, there is at first sight an important difference *in content* between mandatory requirements and Article 30 (former Article 36) on the one hand and the exception contained in Article 86(2) on the other.

6.164

Indeed the Court has always maintained that the exceptions contained in Article 30 cannot be used to safeguard interests of an economic nature. The same is probably true of mandatory requirements, the exception first laid down in *Cassis de Dijon*.[226] In order to be covered by these exceptions the requirements or interests protected by the State measure in question must be of a non-economic nature. The Court has held that a Member State cannot evade its obligations under the Treaty on the pretext of economic problems caused by the elimination of barriers to intra-Community trade.[227] However, restrictive national regulations can sometimes be justified to protect the health of consumers or the protection of the environment, these being non-economic interests.

6.165

Putting to one side the terminology employed, in reality the objective of guaranteeing certain public services to citizens is not, in this sense, an objective of an economic nature. Such an objective is perfectly comparable to that of other interests contemplated in Article 30 or in

6.166

---

[225] J Schwarze, *European Administrative Law* (Office for Official Publications of the European Communities, Sweet and Maxwell, 1992), 854; G De Burca, 'The Principle of Proportionality and its Application in EC Law' [1993] YEL xiii 113.
[226] Case 120/78 *Cassis de Dijon* [1978] ECR 649.
[227] Case 72/83 *Campus Oil* [1984] ECR 2752, para 35.

the (open) list of mandatory requirements recognised by the Court: the protection of health, the protection of the environment, and so on. If the case law relating to both types of exception is carefully examined it can be seen that the differences which exist are not based on the objectives but on the *means* employed in order to justify such objectives. In other words, the difference stems from the criteria employed to evaluate *proportionality* in the two different fields.

6.167 Traditionally, in the field of Article 30 and of mandatory requirements, the Court has only tended to admit State measures which have been *indispensable* to achieve the aim (of a non-economic nature) pursued by the Member State in question. A monopoly is always the most restrictive possible measure and therefore it will only be allowed if another less restrictive type of measure is insufficient to guarantee the desired objective. However, in the field of Article 86(2) the Court has in recent times left open the possibility of a more flexible interpretation.

6.168 *The old approach: A strict interpretation of the proportionality test* The traditional approach to Article 86(2) came within the strict interpretation of the proportionality principle, similar to that employed in the field of Article 30 and of mandatory requirements. Thus only those restrictions which are *indispensable* in order to achieve an objective of general interest will be allowed. Accordingly, faced with a particular measure the question which must be asked is whether or not other less restrictive measures exist by which this end could be achieved. If such measures exist Article 86(2) cannot be relied on.[228] Not surprisingly, the exception contained in this Article has rarely been found to apply.

6.169 *The need for a more flexible interpretation* This strict interpretation of the principle of proportionality is no longer valid, at least as regards the legality of *exclusive rights*. Indeed, if the majority of exclusive rights breach, in principle, Articles 31 and/or 86(1) the question of whether they can find support in Article 86(2) becomes crucial. This question in turn forms part of the larger question of the proportionality of the exclusive right in relation to the objectives of general interest which are adduced. The legality or illegality of the majority of exclusive rights will depend on how this principle of proportionality is interpreted. This explains the hesitancy and the ambiguity of the two European courts as well as the seesaw nature of the case law. It also explains the Commission's approach, the sudden academic attention and the intense political interest caused by an apparently simple legal question.

6.170 In order to be protected by Article 86(2) exclusive rights can refer to different types of tasks of general economic interest. The need to ensure supplies can be invoked to justify exclusive rights to import gas or electricity, the protection of public health can be invoked to justify exclusive rights for the retail sale of alcoholic products, and so on. Different legitimate objectives of general interest are capable of being invoked to justify exclusive rights. However, without doubt the most typical objective, and also the one which creates the most problems, is the obligation to provide a universal service.

6.171 *Universal service as a justification for exclusive rights* The aim of the obligation to provide a universal service is to guarantee the access of all citizens, wherever their place of residence, to certain essential services at a reasonable price.[229] In many cases, the State requires the establishment of a uniform tariff throughout the whole of its territory. In these cases, the

---

[228] *Navewa-Anseau* [1982] OJ L167/39, para 66; *British Telecommunications* [1982] OJ L360/36, para 41; Case C-18/88 *RTT* [1991] ECR I-5941, para 22.

[229] Commission Communication concerning services of general interest in Europe [1996] OJ C281/3.

undertaking enjoys an exclusive right in exchange for taking on a series of obligations of universal service which are imposed on it by the State. For example, it is normal for the electricity distribution companies to receive a monopoly in exchange for agreeing to offer electricity to all consumers, wherever they are, at uniform rates. The same occurs with postal services.

In such a situation those consumers located in densely populated urban areas are paying a **6.172** much higher price for the supply of the product or service in question than the actual cost to the company. On the other hand, the price paid by consumers in rural areas does not cover the costs incurred by the company in guaranteeing them the product or service in question.

If the monopoly did not exist, other undertakings would offer their services to the consumers **6.173** located in the areas where prices are greater than costs. These competitors would thus take the best clients away from the monopoly and make the continued supply of rural areas at the prices previously offered more difficult. Accordingly, the monopoly is necessary to ensure the economic stability of the undertaking which guarantees the fulfilment of the public service objective. This approach is commonly known by its French sobriquet *écremage*: the newly arrived competitors cream off the best clients in the urban areas leaving the somewhat ordinary milk to the old monopoly. In English, this practice is known as 'cherry picking': the best cherries are picked off by the competition leaving the less appetising specimens to the old monopoly.

This argument starkly illustrates the choice between a strict interpretation and a more flexi- **6.174** ble interpretation of the principle of proportionality. The supporters of a strict interpretation argue that the grant of exclusive rights is not *indispensable* to ensure the existence of a universal service. If a Member State wishes to guarantee a universal service it can always grant to the operator subsidies which compensate it for the losses it makes from operating the service. This mechanism would permit the existence of competition in profitable sectors with the maintenance of a universal service. The supporters of a more flexible interpretation argue that the elimination of an exclusive right would make the maintenance of a universal service *much more difficult*, by ruling out the possibility of the undertaking financing these requirements itself and by obliging the undertaking to have recourse to external financing from the State.

In order for the exception contained in Article 86(2) to apply, the question is therefore **6.175** whether there is no realistic alternative to the exclusive right or whether it would be sufficient for the alternatives which exist to be much more difficult to organise. It is clear that this is not a black and white choice; instead, there is a certain degree of flexibility which the Commission and the European courts have exploited.

In the field of the free circulation of goods, the Court had previously firmly rejected the **6.176** *écremage* argument (according to which a monopoly is necessary to ensure the economic stability of the undertaking which guarantees the objective of general interest being pursued). Thus, in *Campus Oil* the Court stated that a less restrictive alternative than a monopoly was available: the grant of State aid.[230] In a similar context the Court could have been expected to interpret restrictively the exception contained in Article 86(2).[231]

---

[230] Case 72/83 *Campus Oil* [1984] ECR 2754, paras 45–46 (especially end of para 46); in fact the measure in question in that case was even less restrictive than a monopoly (the oil product distributors were obliged to buy some of their supply from the national refinery).
[231] Case 172/82 *Used Oils* [1983] ECR 567, para 15; and the Opinion of Rozes AG in the same case [1983] ECR 581, para 3.

6.177 *The* Corbeau *case* When faced with the same dilemma in later cases concerning the application of Article 86(2), the Court appears to have taken a different approach. In *Corbeau* the Court of Justice openly accepted the *écremage* argument for the first time. The Court held that the exception contained in Article 86(2) can justify a State measure which consists in the grant of an exclusive right to an undertaking if this is necessary for the undertaking to be able to offer a universal service in acceptable economic conditions.[232]

6.178 The facts of the case were as follows. Mr Corbeau, a Belgian citizen, offered a service which consisted of the collection and delivery of post within the city of Liège, Belgium. He charged slightly less than the Régie des Postes (the State postal service) but offered a superior service (collection from sender's address, quicker delivery, and so on). The Belgian legislation imposed on the Régie des Postes a universal obligation to ensure the provision of basic postal services at a fixed rate throughout Belgian territory. In return, the Régie des Postes was granted a monopoly over postal services, without distinguishing between basic services and additional services such as courier services. The Régie des Postes took the view that Corbeau was skimming off a considerable part of its 'cream' and as a result brought criminal proceedings against him for infringement of the exclusive rights contained in the Belgian legislation. The Belgian Court referred the question of whether the Belgian legislation was compatible with Articles 86 and 82 to the Court of Justice for a preliminary ruling.

6.179 Faced with these facts the Court of Justice accepted for the first time the *écremage* argument:

> The starting point of such an examination must be the premise that the obligation on the part of the undertaking entrusted with that task to perform its services in conditions of economic equilibrium presupposes that it will be possible to offset less profitable sectors against the profitable sectors and hence justifies a restriction of competition from individual undertakings where the economically profitable sectors are concerned.

> Indeed, to authorize individual undertakings to compete with the holder of the exclusive rights in the sectors of their choice corresponding to those rights would make it possible for them to concentrate on the economically profitable operations and to offer more advantageous tariffs than those adopted by the holders of the exclusive rights since, unlike the latter, they are not bound for economic reasons to offset losses in the unprofitable sectors against profits in the more profitable sectors.[233]

6.180 In the following paragraph the Court of Justice clarified that financial resources needed to compensate non-profitable sectors of activity did not necessarily have to come from general economic interest activities. An activity which was objectively distinct from the service of general economic interest which is to be guaranteed could be monopolised if that were necessary for the economic stability of the latter service:

> However, the exclusion of competition is not justified *as regards specific services dissociable from the service of general interest* which meet special needs of economic operators and which call for certain additional services not offered by the traditional postal service, such as collection from the senders' address, greater speed or reliability of distribution or the possibility of changing the destination in the course of transit, in so far as such specific services, by their nature and the conditions in which they are offered, such as the geographical area in which

---

[232] Case C-320/91 *Corbeau* [1993] ECR I-2568-2569, paras 15–18.
[233] Case C-320/91 *Corbeau* [1993] ECR I-2533, paras 17–18.

they are provided, *do not compromise the economic equilibrium of the service of general economic interest* performed by the holder of the exclusive right. [Author's emphasis added] [234]

So, faced with the *écremage* problem, the Court accepted the principle that it was possible to create monopolies in activities which were not of general economic interest if such monopolies are necessary, at a given moment, to guarantee the economic stability of other activities which *are* of general economic interest.

The Almelo *case*   In *Almelo*,[235] the Court of Justice again accepted the *écremage* argument   **6.181**
as justifying certain restrictions on competition. However, unlike *Corbeau* the restrictions in question were not of a legal origin but were the result of the independent behaviour of undertakings entrusted with the management of a public service.

In the context of litigation in the Netherlands between various local electricity distribution   **6.182**
companies and a regional distribution company, the former companies queried whether the exclusive purchasing and sale clauses contained in the supply contracts entered into by each one of them with the regional distributor were compatible with Community competition law. Although the legislation in force in the Netherlands at the time did not establish any monopoly or any type of restriction on the import of electricity, the effect of these clauses was to make the direct import of electricity from other Member States by the local companies impossible. The national court referred the matter to the Court of Justice for a preliminary ruling on the compatibility of these contractual restrictions with Community competition rules.

Having found the clauses in question infringed Articles 81(1) and 82, the Court of Justice   **6.183**
went on to examine whether the undertaking responsible for the infringement could invoke the exception contained in Article 86(2). The Court of Justice, after reiterating the application of the proportionality principle, went on to suggest that this principle had to be interpreted with a certain degree of flexibility:

> The Restrictions on competition from other economic operators must be allowed in so far as they are necessary in order to enable the undertaking entrusted with such a task of general interest to perform it. In that regard, *it is necessary to take into consideration the economic conditions in which the undertaking operates*, in particular the costs which it has to bear and the legislation, particularly concerning the environment, to which it is subject. [Author's emphasis added] [236]

Thus the Court appears to accept that the universal distribution of electricity needs to be   **6.184**
organised as a monopoly, since otherwise the profitable sectors would be creamed off by the competition and the operator entrusted with providing the universal service would not be able to maintain its economic stability. The question of whether or not less restrictive alternatives exist is hardly discussed. The reason for this is that in *Almelo* the problem is examined not from the perspective of the Member State but rather from that of the operator, and certain solutions which are open to Member States are not available to the operators. Thus, in organising the universal service a Member State can contemplate alternatives such as

---

[234] Case C-320/91 *Corbeau* [1993] ECR I-2533, para 19.
[235] Case C-393/92 *Almelo* [1994] ECR I-1520-1521 paras 46 ff.
[236] Case C-393/92 *Almelo* [1994] ECR I-1521, para 49.

external financing through subsidies, the financing of sectors through a universal service fund or internal financing supported by exclusive rights. However, in the absence of State intervention the operator has far less room to manoeuvre.

6.185 *More recent cases* In the *Monopolies of Electricity and Gas* judgments the Court of Justice reiterated that it is incumbent on the Member State which wishes to rely on Article 86(2) to prove that all the conditions for that provision to apply exist. The Court nevertheless marked certain limits to this burden of proof, pointing out that the Member State does not have to show positively that there is no other imaginable (by definition hypothetical) measure which would permit the fulfilment of the tasks in question. In the above cases the Court held that the Member States had sufficiently explained the problems that would result if the exclusive rights to import were eliminated. On the other hand, the Commission had limited itself merely to submitting legal arguments without having attempted to answer the economic arguments put forward by the Member States.[237]

6.186 In *Ambulanz Glöckner* the Court has introduced some interesting nuances.[238] This case examined the compatibility of a State measure granting the exclusivity for non-urgent patient transport to an entity previously entrusted with the exclusivity for emergency ambulance services. The Court considered that this measure was an extension of dominant position contrary to Articles 86(1) and 82 EC. The Court also examined whether it could be justified under Article 86(2). In this respect the Court noted on the one hand that both activities—urgent and non-urgent ambulance services—were different but closely related. On the other hand, the extension of the exclusivity to cover also non-urgent services made it possible to assume both activities in conditions of economic equilibrium. Both elements pointed towards accepting the application of Article 86(2). However the Court introduced a new limit to the application of this provision:

> However, as the Advocate General explains in point 188 of his Opinion, it is only if it were established that the medical aid organisations entrusted with the operation of the public ambulance service were manifestly unable to satisfy demand for emergency ambulance services and for patient transport at all times that the justification for extending their exclusive rights, based on the task of general interest, could not be accepted.[239]

6.187 This judgment seems to transfer to the application of Article 86(2) the demand limitation doctrine initially set out by the *Höfner* judgment in the framework of Article 86(1) in combination with Article 82 EC. Indeed *Ambulanz Glöckner* seems to imply that the inability of a monopolist to meet demand not only produces a prima facie infringement of Articles 86(1) and 82 but excludes the possibility of justifying the exclusivity under Article 86(2) EC. In other words, the judgment suggests that, in order to be covered by the exception of Article 86(2), undertakings entrusted with services of general economic interest must operate with a minimum level of efficiency.

---

[237] Case C-159/94 *Gas and Electricity Monopolies—France* [1997] ECR I-5815, paras 90–107; Case C-158/94 *Electricity Monopoly—Italy* [1997] ECR I-5789, paras 46–60; Case C-157/94 *Electricty Monopoly—Netherlands* [1997] ECR-I 5699, paras 48–64.

[238] Case C-475/99 *Ambulanz Glöckner* [2001] ECR I-8089, paras 55–65.

[239] Case C-475/99 *Ambulanz Glöckner* [2001] ECR I-8089, para 62.

So, the precedents from the Court of Justice cannot be interpreted as a blanket statement **6.188** that where a universal service exists this automatically implies that the exclusive rights which are granted in order to finance such a service are legal. In *Corbeau* and *Ambulanz Glöckner* the Court clearly marked out the limits of the possibility of allowing exclusive rights over activities other than the basic service. In neither judgment did the Court of Justice *actually decide* the legality of the exclusive rights in question.

The question of the legality of an exclusive right justified by a universal service can only be **6.189** answered in the light of the different circumstances of each sector and of each specific case. This is also shown by the case law of the Court of First Instance.

Case law of the Court of First Instance   In *FFSA*,[240] the Court of First Instance rejected an **6.190** appeal against a Commission Decision. In this decision, the Commission declared, on the basis of Articles 87 and 86(2) of the Treaty, that tax exemptions granted to the French public undertaking La Poste were compatible with the Treaty, since they amounted to compensation for this undertaking taking on public interest obligations.[241] These obligations consisted in the maintenance of non-profitable offices and postal services in rural areas. Proceedings had been started as a result of the complaint of various insurance undertakings, which considered that the tax exemptions in question favoured La Poste, which was an undertaking active in the insurance services market as well as enjoying a monopoly in postal services.

In this case the Commission had undertaken an analysis of the economic cost which such **6.191** tasks entailed and had quantified the impact of the advantages received. Having done this, the Commission reached the conclusion that the advantages were outweighed by the costs involved and accordingly the tax exemptions were compatible with the Treaty. The Court agreed with the overall analysis carried out by the Commission and emphasised the fact that the Commission enjoyed a great deal of discretion under Article 86.

In the judgment in *Air Inter*[242] the Court of First Instance had the opportunity to analyse **6.192** fully the interpretation of the principle of proportionality of Article 86(2) when this provision is invoked in order to justify exclusive rights.

Once again the case involved an appeal against a Commission Decision. The decision in **6.193** question was made under powers granted to the Commission by one of the regulations concerning the liberalisation of air transport, Regulation (EEC) 2408/92, which concerned the access of Community airline companies to intra-Community air routes.[243] The origin of the proceedings was a complaint presented to the Commission by the private airline company TAT against the French Government, who had refused TAT the right to operate between Orly airport in Paris and Toulouse and Marseille airports. The reason given by the French Government for its refusal was the existence of exclusive rights over

---

[240] Case T-106/95 *FFSA* [1997] ECR II-229, paras 117–199.
[241] Commission Decision [1995] OJ C262/11 concerning proceedings applying Art 93 of the EC Treaty—State Aid n NN135/92, competition activities of French La Poste.
[242] Case T-260/94 *Air Inter* [1997] ECR II-997, paras 129–141.
[243] Council Regulation (EEC) 2498/92 concerning the access of Community airline companies to intra-Community routes [1992] OJ L240/8.

such routes, which had been granted to the public undertaking Air Inter. In its decision, the Commission declared that such exclusive rights were incompatible with the Community rules relating to the liberalisation of air transport and obliged France to grant the rights sought by TAT.[244]

6.194 The French public undertaking Air Inter claimed it was prejudiced by the loss of its exclusive rights over the routes in question and appealed against this decision. One of the arguments relied on by Air Inter was that the exclusive rights in question were justified by Article 86(2) of the Treaty. Thus, Air Inter carried out a general interest task, which consisted in its contribution to the opening up of a large number of French cities and regions in the context of regional development, based on a cross-subsidy of tariffs, which enables it to finance about twenty unprofitable domestic air routes thanks, essentially, to the profitability of the Paris–Marseille and Paris–Toulouse routes. Citing *Corbeau* and *Almelo*, Air Inter defended the legality of these exclusive rights as measures which were proportionate to the general interest objective pursued.[245] In other words, the Court of First Instance was faced with a variant of the *écremage* argument.

6.195 In its judgment, the Court of First Instance reiterated that as an exception, Article 86(2) 'it must be strictly interpreted (. . .) and its application is not left to the discretion of the Member State which has entrusted an undertaking with the operation of a service of general economic interest' (paragraph 135). Thereafter, the Court of First Instance reaffirmed, with surprising strength, the strict interpretation of the principle of proportionality underlying Article 86(2):

> The application of those articles could, however, be excluded only in as much as they 'obstructed' performance of the tasks entrusted to the applicant. Since that condition must be interpreted strictly, it was not sufficient for such performance to be simply hindered or made more difficult (. . .)(paragraph 138).

6.196 In addition, the Court of First Instance reiterated very clearly the principle that the burden of proving the proportionality of the exclusive right was on the party invoking the exception contained in Article 86(2). The Court of First Instance considered that in this particular case the burden of proof had not been discharged. Air Inter had limited itself to merely stating that the loss of the exclusive right would make it impossible to fulfil its task, without quantifying either the cost of the task or the additional income which allegedly resulted from the operation of the exclusive right. The Court of First Instance emphasised once again the need for an economic analysis to be carried out when evaluating the possibility of applying the exception. Further, the Court of First Instance highlighted the difference between *means* and *ends*, a distinction which was essential for the correct application of the principle of proportionality within the field of Article 86(2):[246]

> In any event, the domestic air network system combined with the internal cross-subsidy system to which the applicant refers in support of its case did not constitute an aim in themselves,

---

[244] Commission Decision (EC) 94/291 concerning proceedings applying Council Regulation (EEC) 2498/92 [1994] OJ L127/32.

[245] Case T-260/94 *Air Inter* [1997] ECR II-997, paras 129–130.

[246] Case T-260/94 *Air Inter* [1997] ECR II-997, paras 138–139.

but were the means chosen by the French public authorities for developing the French regions. The applicant has not argued and still less established that, following the entry into force of Regulation No 2408/92, there was no appropriate alternative system capable of ensuring regional development and in particular of ensuring that loss-making routes continue to be financed (. . .) (paragraph 140)

Article 86(2) recognises in principle the legitimacy of the *ends* of public service but subjects the *means* to these ends to an examination of proportionality. The legal consequences of this can be very significant. For example, in *Air Inter* if the maintenance of the compensation system of tariffs between different airline routes had been accepted as an end in itself, perhaps it would have been possible to demonstrate (obviously backed up by the appropriate figures) the necessity of the exclusive rights. **6.197**

Nevertheless, the most important question is in fact a different one: whether other means of achieving regional policy goals and the maintenance of non-profitable routes exist. The answer is 'yes'. The Community rules concerning the air transport sector (Regulation (EEC) 2408/92) provide that the loss-making routes which are declared to be of general interest cannot be financed through the grant of exclusive rights over other profitable routes. Instead, they would have to be directly subsidised by the State in accordance with the Regulation. With those arguments in mind the Court of First Instance declared that Article 82(2) could not be applied to justify the exclusive rights enjoyed by Air Inter. **6.198**

Need for an economic analysis It follows from the case law that even if the proportionality test is applied in a flexible way, an economic analysis will be necessary in order to apply the exception in Article 86(2). This analysis should be conducted as follows:[247] **6.199**

• the net cost of providing a universal service must be evaluated in an objective manner;[248]
• the economic advantages inherent to the State measure in question must also be evaluated;
• the two figures should then be compared;
• due account must be taken of State aids and other advantages also received by the undertaking as compensation for the universal service cost.

The dynamic character of proportionality The proportionality of the means used to perform a role of general economic interest must be evaluated according to the circumstances at the relevant time. An exclusive right may have been fully justified in the past, but following developments of a technological, economic, legal, social, or other nature, may cease to be justified in the future.[249] For example, starting in the mid-nineties, the Commission began to change its approach to the telecommunications sector. Once the universal coverage of the telecommunication networks was assured, the justification for the voice telephony monopolies disappeared. For that reason, following a review of the situation in the sector, **6.200**

---

[247] Case C-334/03 *Commission v Portugal* [2005] not yet published, para 33; Case T-260/94 *Air Inter* [1997] ECR II-997, paras 138–140.

[248] In principle the only relevant cost in the application of Art 86(2) is the *actual* cost incurred by the undertaking, irrespective of its level of efficiency. The compensation of the costs of a highly efficient operator may under certain conditions not even be considered State aid; see Case C-280/00 *Altmark* [2003] ECR I-7747, para 93. Moreover, Case C-475/99 *Ambulanz Glöckner* [2001] ECR I-8089, para 62, could be interpreted as suggesting that Art 86(2) could not be used to justify the compensation of costs of highly inefficient operators.

[249] Case C-18/88 *RTT* [1991] ECR I-5941, para 16.

the Commission decided to modify its Directives in order to liberalise the services.[250] In the future, universal telecommunications services will have to be assured without exclusive rights. Cross-subsidisation (ie from long-distance to metropolitan calls) will no longer be sustainable (thus leading to the rebalancing of tariffs by incumbents). Universal telecommunication services will have to be financed by other mechanisms, more neutral from a competitive point of view. The net cost of providing a universal service will have to be calculated in an objective way. The provider of the universal service could for instance be compensated for these net costs with money coming from a 'universal service fund'. Such a fund could be established with contributions from all the operators that are active in the market and the contributions calculated following an objective and non-discriminatory method. This example illustrates the dynamic character of the exemption contained in Article 86(2).

6.201 *Different approaches depending on the sector* The Court of First Instance, in the *Air Inter* case, rejected the application of Article 86(2) to justify exclusive rights in the air transport sector. The undertaking invoked the 'cherry-picking' argument to defend its exclusive rights over some profitable air routes which were allegedly used to cross-subsidise other non profitable routes (it was a universal service type of argument). The Court, however, relying on a strict interpretation of the proportionality test, suggested that there were means less restrictive than exclusive rights to achieve the objective of integrating the territory.[251]

6.202 *The strict approach and the flexible approach* The previous examples show that, when evaluating the legality of exclusive rights for the provision of universal services, Article 86(2) has sometimes been applied in a traditional, strict way and sometimes in a more flexible way. It is submitted[252] that this apparent inconsistency can be explained by taking into account two factors: the traditional or newly created character of the universal service in question, and the presence or lack of Community intervention in the sector.

6.203 A more flexible approach is followed as regards existing exclusive rights that have traditionally served to finance a classical universal service.[253] This 'acquired rights' approach no longer applies once the Commission uses its discretionary powers under Article 86(3) to opt for the stricter approach,[254] or when other Community legislation liberalises the sector.[255] Of course, the greater flexibility implicit in the 'acquired rights' approach should never benefit newly created (or extended) exclusive rights or newly designed universal service obligations.

6.204 *Universal services and other services of general economic interest* Universal service is the most typical justification of exclusive rights, but exclusive rights may be justified for reasons other than universal service.[256] It is only one among the various kinds of services of general economic interest to which Article 86(2) refers. In principle, there is nothing to prevent a

---

[250] Directive (EC) 96/19 on full competition in telecommunications [1996] OJ L74/13, paras 13–24.

[251] Case T-260/94 *Air Inter* [1997] ECR II-997, paras 138–140.

[252] See JL Buendia Sierra, *Exclusive Rights and State Monopolies in EC Law* (Oxford University Press, 1999) paras 8.238–8.243 for more details.

[253] This was the case of the postal and electricity monopolies at the time of the *Corbeau* and *Almelo* cases.

[254] This is the case in the telecommunication sector.

[255] This is the case in the air transport sector.

[256] Commission communication on 'Services of General Interest in Europe' [1996] OJ C281/3; *Kovar* (n 146 above) 242 and 515.

Member State from establishing exclusive rights for the provision of other kinds of (non-universal) public services. It is submitted that in all these cases the proportionality test under Article 86(2) must be applied strictly.[257]

(ii) The interest of the Community The second sentence of Article 86(2) makes clear that, **6.205** for the exemption to apply, the development of trade must not be affected in a manner contrary to the Community interest. The majority view is that this is not an additional condition, but merely a clarification concerning the proportionality requirement contained in the previous sentence.[258] According to this view, Article 86(2) as a whole has direct effect and national courts can directly apply the exemption without a previous decision by the Commission.

It is submitted that there is also another plausible interpretation: that direct effect is restricted **6.206** only to the first sentence of Article 86(2).[259] This would mean that national courts are competent to apply the exemption as regards national measures that they consider to be proportionate. However, the Commission would retain the exclusive competence to declare, subject to the review of the Court of Justice, that the 'interest of the Community' is being infringed. The second sentence of Article 86(2) would therefore be 'an exception to the exception'.

(4) Invocation of Article 86(2) and Burden of Proof

Article 86(2) is an exception. This means that it can only be applied to a case if it is invoked by the **6.207** Member State or by the undertaking which is in charge of the service of general economic interest.[260] Neither the Commission nor the Courts can be obliged to apply this provision *ex officio*.

In principle, those invoking the exception have the burden of proving that all the conditions of Article 86(2) are fulfilled.[261] The Member State and/or the undertaking would have to prove that a role of general economic interest had been entrusted to the undertaking and that the measure or behaviour concerned was proportionate. This is logical, as these elements fall within their sphere of knowledge. It would be absurd to require the Commission to prove the lack of proportionality of a measure whenever anyone invoked Article 86(2). Such an approach would transform the provision into a quasi-automatic scapegoat. However, the Court of Justice has to an extent slightly altered the issue of the burden of proof, by making clear that the Commission is obliged to respond to the legal and economic arguments put forward by the State or undertaking.[262]

---

[257] See JL Buendia Sierra, *Exclusive Rights and State Monopolies in EC Law* (Oxford University Press, 1999) para 8.244; V Hatzopoulos, 'L'Open Network Provision (ONP) moyen de la dérégulation' [1994] RTDE xxx (i) 87 and 96.

[258] *Wainwright* (n 153 above) 251; *Wachsman and Berrod* (n 146 above) 53; Case C-202/88 *Terminal equipment for telecommunications* [1991] ECR I-1223, paras 11–12.

[259] This position was defended by Van Gerven AG in Case C-179/90 *Port of Genoa* [1991] ECR I-5889, paras 26–28; and by the CFI in Case T-16/91 *Rendo* [1992] ECR II-2417. The Court of Justice, however, refused to endorse this position in its appeal judgment, Case C-19/93P *Rendo* (appeal) [1995] ECR I-3319, paras 18–19.

[260] *Zaventem* [1995] OJ L216/8, para 20; *GSM Italy* [1995] OJ L280/49, paras 26–27; *GSM Spain* [1997] OJ L76/19, para 30.

[261] Case 155/73 *Sacchi* [1974] ECR 409, para 15; Case 41/83 *British Telecommunications* [1985] ECR 873, para 33; Case T-260/94 *Air Inter* [1997] ECR II-997, para 138.

[262] Case C-157/94 *Dutch electricity monopoly* [1997] ECR I-5699, paras 48–64; Case C-158/94 *Italian electricity monopoly* [1997] ECR I-5789, paras 46–60; Case C-159/94 *French electricity and gas monopolies* [1997] ECR I-5815, paras 90–107.

(5) Relationship between Article 86(2) and Other Exceptions

6.209 **'Mandatory requirements' in the framework of Article 86(2)**   Under the 'Cassis de Dijon' doctrine, general measures falling within the rules on free movement could only be justified on the basis of 'non-economic' objectives such as the protection of human health, culture, etc.[263] Economic objectives, such as the promotion of national industry, were clearly not admissible. The only Treaty exception allowing 'economic' objectives to be taken into account was Article 86(2) (objectives of general 'economic' interest).

6.210 Furthermore, Article 86(2) has traditionally been interpreted as referring *only* to objectives of an 'economic' nature.[264] According to this view, the notion of objectives of 'general economic interest' did not include 'non-economic' objectives.

6.211 Today it is obvious that many restrictions concerning public or privileged undertakings (and therefore falling within Article 86(1)) may be justified for non-economic reasons, such as the protection of public health (this may be the case of alcohol monopolies) or the promotion of culture (television monopolies). The Court of Justice has made clear that these restrictions can also in some cases benefit from the exception in Article 86(2).[265] This means that these non-economic objectives (or 'mandatory requirements') may also be objectives of general interest under Article 86(2). Strictly speaking, therefore, the adjective 'economic' used in this provision refers to the means (a commercial activity) and not necessarily to the objectives.

6.212 **Article 81(3)**   It follows from the *Eurovision* case that the exception provided by Article 86(2) may overlap from a substantive point of view with the exemption that the Commission may grant on the basis of Article 81(3) (former Article 85(3)).[266] A notifying party may therefore invoke Article 86(2) within the framework of a notification to the Commission under Article 81(3).

(6) Relationship between Article 86(2) and Article 16

6.213 The 1997 Treaty of Amsterdam introduced into the Treaty a new Article 16 (former Article 7D) which reads as follows:

> Without prejudice to Articles 73, 86 and 87, and given the place occupied by services of general economic interest in the shared values of the Union as well as their role in promoting social and territorial cohesion, the Community and the Member States, each within their respective powers and within the scope of application of this Treaty, shall take care that such services operate on the basis of principles and conditions which enable them to fulfil their missions.[267]

The Treaty of Amsterdam also included the following declaration in the Final Act:

> The provisions of Article 7d of the Treaty establishing the European Community on public services shall be implemented with full respect for the jurisprudence of the Court of Justice,

---

[263] Case 120/78 *Cassis de Dijon* [1979] ECR 649, para 8.
[264] Opinion of Tesauro AG, Case C-320/91 *Corbeau* [1993] ECR I-2531, para 14.
[265] Case C-18/88 *RTT* [1991] ECR I-5941, para 22.
[266] Cases T-528, 542, 543 and 546/93 *Eurovision* [1996] ECR II-649, paras 114–126.
[267] Art III-6 of the Draft Treaty establishing a Constitution for Europe retains this same provision with a new phrase at the end: 'European Laws shall define these principles and conditions' (<http://european-convention.eu.int/docs/Treaty/cv00850.en03.pdf>). This draft provision would add another legal basis to those already provided for in the EC Treaty, like Art 86(3) EC.

inter alia as regards the principles of equality of treatment, quality and continuity of such services.

In 2000 the Charter of Fundamental Rights of the European Union included a provision, **6.214** Article 36, on 'Access to services of general economic interest' which reads as follows:

> The Union recognises and respects access to services of general economic interest as provided for in national laws and practices, in accordance with the Treaty establishing the European Community, in order to promote the social and territorial cohesion of the Union.[268]

It is submitted that these new provisions do not modify Article 86(2) but rather reaffirm the logic behind the provision while underlining its importance. Indeed, the formula used in Article 16 ['(. . .) the Community (. . .) shall take care that such services (of general economic interest) operate on the basis of principles and conditions which enable them to fulfil their missions'] does not seem different in content from the formula used in Article 86(2) ['(. . .) services of general economic interest (. . .) shall be subject to the rules contained in this Treaty (. . .) in so far as the application of such rules does not obstruct the performance, in law or in fact, of the particular tasks assigned to them (. . .)']. The declaration to the Final Act of the Treaty of Amsterdam underlines the need to interpret the new provision in the light of the previous case law of the Court of Justice. Obviously the previous case law is based on Article 86(2). Moreover, the text of Article 16 makes clear that this provision is without prejudice to Article 86.

Despite these changes, the relationship between services of general economic interest and **6.215** Community law remains a matter of debate. The European Council invited the Commission to consider the option of a 'framework Directive' on services of general economic interest and on 'guidelines' on State aids in this field. The Commission published a Green Paper in 2003 and launched a public consultation on these issues. The Commission concluded in 2004 that the case for a 'framework Directive' was not made out but that some action was needed in the area of State aids. In this respect the Commission adopted a horizontal Decision in 2005 under Article 86(3) to deal with aids to compensate undertakings in charge of services of general economic interest for the additional costs resulting from these obligations. This instrument specifies that certain types of compensation (those below a certain threshold and fulfilling certain conditions) are considered compatible with Article 86(2) and are exempted from the notification obligation of Article 88 EC.[269] The Commission also adopted a framework explaining the criteria that would be applicable to the cases that would remain subject to notification.[270]

The experience of recent Intergovernmental Conferences suggests that the relationship between **6.216** services of general economic interest and Community Competition Law will remain controversial. The reason is that Article 86(2) is the result of a difficult balancing exercise between very different ideas of the role that the State should play in the markets (interventionist vs liberal). This provision is thus the point of contact between two 'tectonic plates' moving in opposite

---

[268] [2000] OJ C364/1.

[269] Commission Decision (EC) 2005/842 on the application of Article 86(2) of the EC Treaty to State aid in the form of public service compensation granted to certain undertakings entrusted with the operation of services of general economic interest [2005] OJ L312/67.

[270] Community framework for State aid in the form of public service compensation [2005] OJ C297/4.

directions, so that regular seismic movement is to be expected. Since these underlying differences remain, the likelihood of the Member States agreeing on a substantial modification of Article 86(2) appears rather limited. This explains why the new Treaty provisions adopted so far in this area are mere reformulations of the same basic principles.

D. Article 86(3): Procedural Rules Applying to Anti-Competitive State Measures

6.217 Article 86(3) (former Article 90(3)) provides:

> The Commission shall ensure the application of the provisions of this Article and shall, where necessary, address appropriate directives or decisions to Member States.

Thus Article 86 contains in its third paragraph procedural rules for the application of the substantive provisions contained in the first two paragraphs. Article 86(3) gives the Commission, on the one hand, the power to adopt *decisions* declaring that a Member State has infringed Article 86(1) and obliging this Member State to put an end to the infringement. On the other hand, it also gives the Commission the power to adopt *Directives* with binding effects on all Member States, in order to specify the obligations contained in Article 86(1) and/or to prevent future infringements of the obligations.[271]

(1) Article 86(3) Decisions

6.218 **(i) General issues** Article 86(3) gives to the Commission the power to adopt *decisions* declaring that Article 86(1) has been infringed and obliging the Member State to put an end to the infringement. This procedure constitutes an exception to the general procedure of Article 226 (former Article 169), in which it is up to the Court of Justice to declare that the Treaty has been infringed, but is not a revolutionary idea. Indeed, the Commission has similar powers as regards anti-competitive behaviour of undertakings (Articles 81 and 82)[272] and as regards State aids (Articles 87 and 88). This suggests a design giving the Commission similar powers to react quickly against all restrictions of competition, irrespective of their public or private origin.[273]

6.219 *Analogy with other procedures* There is no supplementary text that specifies Article 86(3) procedure in greater detail. The obvious temptation is to turn to the analogy with other procedures, such as the antitrust procedure,[274] the State aids procedure,[275] or the Article

---

271 On the doctrine see: JL Buendia Sierra, 'Public Undertakings and Exclusive or Special Rights—Article 86(3) EC' in L Ortiz Blanco (ed) *EC Competition Procedure* (2nd edn, Oxford University Press, 2006) 725–781; C Hocepied, 'Les directives Article 90, paragraphe 3. Une espèce juridique en voie de disparition?' [1994] RAE ii 49–63; A Pappalardo, 'State Measures and Public Undertakings: Article 90 of the EEC Treaty Revisited' [1991] 1 ECLR 29–39; M Kerf, 'The Policy of the Commission of the EEC Toward National Monopolies. An Analysis of the Measures Adopted on the Basis of Article 90(3) of the EEC Treaty' (September 1993) 17(1) World Competition 73–111; LM Pais Antunes, 'L'Article 86 du Traité CEE—Obligations des Etats Membres et pouvoirs de la Commission' [1991] RTDE ii 187 ff; H Papaconstantinou (n 10 above); F Melin-Soucramanien, 'Les pouvoirs spéciaux conférés à la Commission en matière de concurrence par l'Article 86.3 du Traité de Rome' [1994] 382 RMCUE 601–610.

272 L Ortiz Blanco (ed) *EC Competition Procedure* (2nd edn, Oxford University Press, 2006).

273 *Papaconstantinou* (n 10 above) 102–104.

274 Rejected by the CFI in Case T-32/93 *Ladbroke I* [1994] ECR II-1015, para 38.

275 Case C-18/88 *RTT* [1991] ECR I-5941, para 31; Opinion of La Pergola AG, Case C-107/95P *Expert Accountants* [1996] ECR I-957, paras 14–21.

226 procedure.[276] However, these analogies must be used with care, taking due account also of the differences between these rules and Article 86.

Discretionary character of the procedure under Article 86(3) Even if the Commission **6.220** always has the ability to act (*ex officio* or following a complaint) on the basis of Article 86(3), the provision does not oblige the Commission to commence infringement proceedings whenever a violation of Article 86(1) comes to light. In principle, case law suggests that the Commission has a wide margin of discretion in this respect.[277]

A 2002 judgment of the Court of First Instance in the *max.mobil* case put into jeopardy **6.221** this well-established line of jurisprudence.[278] This judgment restricted the margin of discretion of the Commission by stating that the Commission was obliged to examine complaints based on Article 86 EC in a diligent and objective way. This implied on the one hand that, after an analysis of the complaint, the Commission must at least indicate why it considered that there was (or there was not) an infringement and whether it considered it necessary to intervene. On the other hand judicial review on these two points (and in particular on the opportunity to intervene) would in any case be minimal and limited to manifest errors.[279]

However on appeal in 2005 in the *max.mobil* case,[280] the ECJ overruled the finding of the **6.222** CFI on the basis that, contrary to what happens in the field of Articles 81 and 82 EC, the Commission's refusal to act under Article 86 is not susceptible to judicial review under Article 230 EC, especially because that particular act could not be regarded as producing a legal effect. This confirms that the Commission enjoys a wide margin of discretion when deciding whether to initiate proceedings against a Member State for breach of Article 86(1) of the Treaty. This discretion greatly limits the chances for individuals who are complaining about such infringements to appeal successfully against the Commission's Decision.

This margin of discretion also exists as regards the choice between the different proce- **6.223** dures.[281] The Commission is not obliged to use Article 86(3) to act against infringements of Article 86(1). The option to use the Article 226 procedure still remains, although Article 86(3) would normally be preferred due to its nature.

---

[276] Opinion of Van Gerven AG, Case C-18/88 *RTT* [1991] ECR I-5941, para 8.

[277] Case C-163/99 *Portuguese Airports* [2001] ECR I-2613, para 20; Case T-266/97 *VTM* [1999] ECR II-2329, para 75; Case T-111/96 *ITT Promedia* [1998] ECR II-2937, para 97; Case T-575/93 *Koelman* [1996] ECR II-1, paras 70–73; confirmed by Case C-59/96P *Koelman* (appeal) [1997] ECR I-4809, paras 57–58; Case T-32/93 *Ladbroke I* [1994] ECR II-1015, paras 37–38; Case T-548/93 *Ladbroke II* [1995] ECR II-2565, para 45; Case T-84/94 *Expert Accountants* [1995] ECR II-101, para 31; confirmed by Case C-107/95P *Expert Accountants* (appeal) [1996] ECR I-957, para 27.

[278] Case T-54/99 *max.mobil* [2002] ECR II-313, paras 54–55. See also Case T-17/96 *TF 1* [1999] ECR II-1757, paras 49–57.

[279] Case C-141/02 P *max.mobil* (appeal) [2005] ECR I-1283.

[280] Case C-141/02 P *max.mobil* (appeal) [2005] ECR I-1283, paras 68–73. Poiares Maduro AG had issued a considered opinion recommending the repeal of the CFI judgment although without endorsing the line suggested by the Commission, but he has not been followed by the Court of Justice. Even before that judgment the Court of First Instance had already gone back to the traditional approach in Case T-52/00 *Coe Clerici* [2003] ECR II-2123, paras 82–106.

[281] Case T-266/97 *VTM* [1999] ECR II-2329, para 75; *Papaconstantinou* (n 10 above) 113; J Flynn and E Turnbull, 'Joined Cases C-48/90 and C–66/90, (the "Dutch Couriers" Case)' [1993] CML Rev 402; *Hocepied* (n 271 above) 55.

6.224   **(ii) Lodging of complaints and *ex officio* cases**   The Commission may act *ex officio* or following a complaint. Complaints and *ex officio* cases based on Article 86 are registered and examined during a preliminary phase. During this phase, the Commission may request additional information from the complainant or from the Member State. At the end of the preliminary phase, the Commission decides whether an infringement procedure should be opened and informs the complainant of its decision.

6.225   *Dismissal of complaints*   The Commission has in principle a wide margin of discretion in deciding whether to open an infringement procedure under Article 86(3). The Commission may therefore reject a complaint not only on substantive grounds, but also on opportunity grounds (because the case is considered as non-priority). The Court of First Instance considered in *max.mobil* that the Commission may react to a complaint based on Article 86 EC by adopting a Decision refusing to take action.[282] However the Court of Justice rejected this approach in its 2005 judgment on the appeal. According to this judgment, such letters cannot be regarded as having legal effect and cannot be the subject of an action for annulment.[283]

6.226   Of course, persons and undertakings wishing to complain about an alleged infringement of Article 86(1) always have the right to invoke the direct effect of this provision before national courts. This right is totally independent from the possibility of filing a complaint with the Commission and—legally speaking—it is not affected by the outcome of such complaint.

6.227   The opportunities for complainants to react to an implicit or explicit refusal by the Commission are much less clear. Traditionally it was considered that complainants did not have *locus standi* to either bring an Article 230 (former Article 173) annulment action against the Commission's refusal to open a procedure[284] or bring an Article 232 (former Article 175) action against the Commission's failure to act following a complaint based on Article 86.[285] According to the Court of Justice such actions could only be introduced in 'exceptional situations'.[286]

6.228   The *max.mobil* judgment of the CFI seemed to interpret these 'exceptional situations' very widely. According to this approach, a complainant could attack the Commission's refusal to act or its lack of action if the complaint refers not to measures of general application but to specific measures favouring a competitor.[287] This distinction seems hardly operational, however, in the area of Article 86(1). Indeed, one of the necessary conditions for this provision to apply is precisely that the measure at stake is not general but specific to public or privileged undertakings. So the 'specificity' criteria will—by definition—be automatically fulfilled in *all* Article 86(1) cases.

---

[282]   Case C-141/02 P *max.mobil* (appeal) [2005] ECR I-1283.

[283]   Case C-141/02 P *max.mobil* (appeal) [2005] ECR I-1283, para 70.

[284]   Case T-84/94 *Expert Accountants* [1995] ECR II-101, para 31; confirmed by Case C-107/95P *Expert Accountants* (appeal) [1996] ECR I-957, para 27.

[285]   Case T-32/93 *Ladbroke I* [1994] ECR II-1015, paras 34–36.

[286]   Case C-107/95P *Expert Accountants* (appeal) [1996] ECR I-957, para 25.

[287]   Case T-17/96 *TF 1* [1999] ECR II-1757, paras 52–57; Case C-141/02 P *max.mobil* (appeal) [2005] ECR I-1283.

On appeal in the *max.mobil* case,[288] the ECJ overruled the CFI judgment on the basis that **6.229** the Commission's refusal to act under Article 86 is not susceptible to judicial review under Article 230. This confirms that the Commission enjoys a wide margin of discretion when deciding whether or not to initiate proceedings against a Member State for breach of Article 86(1) of the Treaty.

(iii) The infringement procedure

Interim measures   The infringement procedure is normally opened by a letter of formal **6.230** notice. However, an analogy with the procedure of Regulation 17/62 suggests that it should be possible for the Commission to adopt interim measures in cases where there is a clear urgency and a serious and irreparable risk for the complainant or for the general interest.[289]

Letter of formal notice   The Court of Justice in its *Dutch PTT* case made clear that, before the **6.231** adoption of an Article 86(3) Decision, the Commission must inform the Member State of its intention and the supporting legal reasoning and give the Member State the opportunity to make observations.[290] These requirements arise as a result of the rights of defence of the Member State. This communication normally takes the form of a letter of formal notice addressed by the Commission to the Member State. The letter must clearly identify the State measures that are the subject of controversy and warn explicitly of the possibility of a future Article 86(3) Decision.

The rights of the Member State and of the undertaking that benefits from the measure **6.232** According to the *Dutch PTT* case, as the Member State is the sole addressee of an Article 86(3) Decision, it is also the only party that has rights of defence within the framework of the procedure.[291] The undertaking that benefits from the State measure at stake does not have such a right of defence, but merely a right to be heard.[292] This right implies a right to be informed of the position of the Commission and a right to make comments to the Commission. However, the undertaking does not have a right to know the comments made by the Member State nor a right to receive a copy of the complaint.[293]

End of the procedure without a formal decision   The infringement procedure may con- **6.233** clude without a formal decision. This happens when the Member State decides to put an end to the infringement before the adoption of a decision, and also when the Commission changes its mind as a result of the comments made by the Member State. The Commission is not bound within the framework of Article 86 EC to adopt a formal decision stating that this provision has not been infringed. So, contrary to what happens in State aid control, there is normally no 'positive' Article 86 EC Decision.

(iv) The formal decision and its effects
If the dispute remains after the answer to **6.234** the letter of formal notice, then the Commission may adopt a formal Decision based on

---

[288] Case C-141/02 P *max.mobil (appeal)* [2005] ECR I-1283, paras 68–73.
[289] Case 792/79R *Camera care* [1980] ECR 119.
[290] Cases C-48 and 66/90 *Dutch PTT* [1992] ECR I-565, para 45.
[291] Case T-266/97 *VTM* [1999] ECR II-2329, paras 32–37.
[292] Cases C-48 and 66/90 *Dutch PTT* [1992] ECR I-565, paras 50–51.
[293] Case T-266/97 *VTM* [1999] ECR II-2329, para 37.

Article 86(3). The Commission retains a wide margin of discretion to decide whether or not to adopt such a Decision. The Commission has so far adopted 16 Decisions of this kind.[294]

6.235 An Article 86(3) Decision is a decision within the meaning of Article 249. As such, it must contain a statement of its legal basis and of the steps requested to be taken by the Member State. When a choice exists as regards the means to put an end to an infringement, the Commission has the power to ask for one specific means rather than another.[295] An Article 86(3) Decision is notified by the Commission to the recipient Member State, and takes effect from the date of notification. The Decision must also establish a deadline for the notification by the Member State of the implementing measures.

6.236 *Binding effects*   Article 86(3) Decisions are, as with any other Decision, binding on the Member States to which they are addressed.[296] This means that their direct effect can probably be invoked before a national court once the deadline has expired without the measures being implemented.[297]

---

[294] The decisions are as follows:
- Commission Decision (EEC) 85/276 regarding the insurance in Greece of public goods and of loans granted by Greek public banks [1985] OJ L152/25;
- Commission Decision (EEC) 87/359 regarding the tariff reductions on air and shipping transport reserved exclusively to Spanish residents in the Canary and Balearic islands [1987] OJ L194/28;
- Commission Decision (EEC) 90/16 regarding the provision in the Netherlands of courier postal services [1990] OJ L10/47;
- Commission Decision (EEC) 90/456 regarding the provision in Spain of international courier postal services [1990] OJ L233/19;
- Commission Decision (CE) 94/119 regarding the refusal of access to the installations of the port of Rødby (Denmark) [1994] OJ L55/52;
- Commission Decision (EC) 95/364 regarding the discount system in the landing tariffs in the national airport of Brussels [1995] OJ L216/8;
- Commission Decision (EC) 95/489 regarding the conditions imposed upon the second operator of radio-telephonic GSM services in Italy [1995] OJ L280/49;
- Commission Decision (EC) 97/181 regarding the conditions imposed upon the second operator of radio-telephonic services GSM in Spain [1997] OJ L76/19;
- Commission Decision (EC) 97/606 on the exclusive right to broadcast television advertising in Flanders [1997] OJ L244/18;
- Commission Decision (EC) 97/744 on the provisions of Italian ports legislation relating to employment [1997] OJ L301/17;
- Commission Decision (EC) 97/745 regarding the tariffs for piloting in the Port of Genoa [1997] OJ L301/27;
- Commission Decision (EC) 99/199 Portuguese airports [1999] OJ L69/31;
- Commission Decision (EC) 2000/521 Spanish airports [2000] OJ L208/36;
- Commission Decision (EC) 2001/176 in relation to the provision of certain new postal services with a guaranteed day- or time-certain delivery in Italy [2001] OJ L63/59;
- Commission Decision (EC) 2002/344 on the lack of exhaustive and independent scrutiny of the scales of charges and technical conditions applied by La Poste to mail preparation firms for access to its reserved services [2002] OJ L120/19;
- An Art 86(3) Decision was adopted on 20 October 2004 but is not yet published in the OJ (Press release IP/04/1254 of 'The Commission acts against the discrimination of mail preparation service providers in Germany').

[295] Cases C-48 and 66/90 *Dutch PTT* [1992] ECR I-565, para 28; Case C-107/95P *Expert Accountants* (appeal) [1996] ECR I-947, para 23.

[296] Case C-163/99 *Portuguese Airports* [2001] ECR I-2613, paras 19–20; Case 226/87 *Greek Insurances* [1988] ECR 3611, para 12.

[297] *Pais Antunes* (n 271 above) 205–206; *Hocepied* (n 271 above) 55.

Action for annulment against an Article 86(3) decision If the Member State disagrees with **6.237**
the Decision, it has to bring an action for annulment under Article 230 before the Court of
Justice within two months of its notification. An Article 230 action may also be introduced
before the Court of First Instance by third parties that are directly and individually affected
by the Decision (such as the undertaking that benefits from the State measure in question)
within two months of their becoming aware of the Decision (ie two months from notification
or of publication, depending on the case).[298] In principle, an action for annulment does not
suspend the binding nature of the Decision, although the Member State may ask the Court
to adopt an interim suspension.[299] The suspension would only be granted if the usual conditions for interim measures (*fumus boni iuris*, urgency and balance of public and private interests) are fulfilled. If no action is brought within the two months or if the action is rejected by
the Court the Decision becomes final and its legality cannot be further challenged, unless
there are devices available such as to declare it non-existent.[300]

Action for failure to implement an Article 86(3) decision Once the deadline given to the **6.238**
Member State expires without the Decision having been correctly implemented (and unless
the Court has adopted an interim suspension), the Commission may open an Article 226
action against the Member State for failure to respect the Decision. The Commission is
obliged to send a letter of formal notice first and then a reasoned opinion to the Member State
before bringing the case to the Court of Justice. It must be stressed that the substance of the
case (the legality of the Decision) cannot be further argued at this stage (unless as referred to
above, there are devices available such as to seek a declaration of non-existence).[301]

As well as facing the intervention of the Commission and the Courts, a Member State that **6.239**
has been found to be in breach of its Community obligations under Article 86 may face
actions from particular bodies asking for indemnities under the *Francovitch* doctrine.[302]

(2) Article 86(3) Directives

(i) Preventive functions of Article 86(3) directives The Commission is entrusted with **6.240**
a duty of vigilance as regards the respecting by Member States of the Treaty rules and of
Article 86 in particular. In view of this duty, Article 86(3) grants the Commission not only
powers to act against concrete infringements but also *preventive* powers as regards future
infringements. Indeed, apart from the power to adopt individual Decisions addressed to a
Member State, Article 86(3) also gives to the Commission the power to adopt *Directives*
with binding effect on all Member States.

Article 86(3) EC does not refer to 'regulations'. However, in theory the Commission may **6.241**
also adopt under Article 86(3) Decisions addressed not to one individual Member State
but to all Member States. The nature of such 'horizontal' Decisions would be very similar
to that of Directives, both having binding effect on Member States. The main difference

---

[298] Case C-107/95P *Expert Accountants* (appeal) [1996] ECR I-957, para 24; Cases C-48 and 66/90
Dutch PTT [1992] ECR I-565, para 50; and Opinion of Van Gerven AG in that case, para 5.
[299] See, for instance, Case T-53/01 R *Poste Italiane* [2001] ECR II-1479.
[300] Case 226/87 *Greek Insurances* [1988] ECR 3611, paras 12–16.
[301] ibid.
[302] Cases C-6 and 9/90 *Francovich* [1991] ECR I-5357, paras 36–37.

would be that Decisions automatically have a 'direct effect' while Directives only have such effect in certain circumstances. The references made in this chapter to 'Directives' may be understood to be also applicable to such kind of 'horizontal Decisions'.

6.242   The aim of Directives is to prevent future infringements of the obligations contained in Article 86(1). Unlike individual Article 86(3) Decisions, the Directives based on this provision do not have a repressive function: they do not constitute a declaration that actual infringements have been committed.[303]

6.243   The prevention of future infringements is achieved in two ways. First of all, the Commission may use an Article 86(3) Directive to create instrumental obligations aimed at making possible the detection of future infringements. Secondly, the Commission may also use an Article 86(3) Directive to specify the meaning and extent of the obligations that already exist under Article 86(1) and/or of the exception under Article 86(2) of the Treaty. This means that under Article 86(3) the Commission has certain quasi-legislative powers, even if it is subject to strict limits and under the legal control of the Court of Justice. This raises delicate legal and political issues.

6.244   *Article 86(3) Directives as instruments for detecting future infringements*   The most obvious example of the use of Article 86(3) Directives as an instrument for detecting future infringements is the 'transparency' Directive, originally adopted in 1980 and subsequently modified in 1985 and 1993.[304] This Directive creates an obligation on Member States to set up transparent accounting systems reflecting on the one hand the financial relationships between the public administrations and public undertakings and on the other hand the costs and revenues that can be ascribed to the different activities performed by the undertakings.[305] The idea was to make possible the detection of State aids to public undertakings. The obligation to set up transparent accounts did not exist prior to the adoption of the Directive. It was created as a new obligation ancillary to the State aid rules. Thus, this new obligation was a means of guaranteeing that existing rules were respected. The Court of Justice confirmed in 1982 that Article 86(3) gave the Commission the power to adopt such preventive measures.[306]

6.245   *Article 86(3) Directives as instruments for 'specifying' the provisions of the Treaty* Article 86(3) Directives may also be used to 'specify' the meaning and extent of the obligations that already exist under Article 86(1) of the Treaty.[307] The first example of this approach was the 'telecom terminals' Directive, in which the Commission 'specified' that

---

303 Case C-202/88 *Terminal equipment for telecommunications* [1991] ECR I-1223, para 17.

304 Commission Directive (EEC) 80/723 concerning the transparency of financial relations between Member States and their public undertakings [1980] OJ L195/35. This Directive has been modified by the following directives:
   • Commission Directive (EEC) 85/413 [1985] OJ L229/20;
   • Commission Directive (EEC) 93/84 [1993] OJ L254/16;
   • Commission Directive (EC) 2000/52 [2000] OJ L193/75;
   • Commission Directive (EC) 2005/81 [2005] OJ L312/47.

305 According to Art 1(2) this latter obligation also applies to *private* undertakings to which Member States have granted exclusive or special rights.

306 Cases 188, 189 and 190/80 *Transparency directive* [1982] ECR 2545.

307 Case C-163/99 *Portuguese Airports* [2001] ECR I-2613, paras 26 and 28.

the exclusive rights granted to the telecommunications operators for the import and commercialisation of terminal equipment were incompatible with Article 86(1) in combination with Articles 28, 31, 49 or 82.[308] On the basis of this 'specification', the Directive obliged Member States to abolish these exclusive rights. A similar approach has been used in many other Article 86(3) Directives.[309] The Court of Justice fully confirmed the legality of this approach in 1991 and 1992.[310]

The 'specification' function of Article 86(3) is not restricted to 'obligations' imposed on Member States. It may also be used to 'specify' the meaning and extent of the exception provided by Article 86(2) for services of general economic interest. In this respect the Commission adopted in 2005 a horizontal Decision under Article 86(3) to deal with public service compensation (ie: aids granted by Member States to compensate undertakings in charge of services of general economic interest for the additional costs resulting from these obligations). This instrument specifies that certain types of compensation (those below a certain threshold and fulfilling certain conditions) would be considered compatible with Article 86(2) and would be exempted from the notification obligation of Article 88 EC.[311] **6.246**

In situations where a Treaty obligation can be implemented in different ways, the power to 'specify' these obligations implies a power to impose on Member States one specific means of implementation.[312] **6.247**

(ii) Legal regime of Article 86(3) directives
The exclusive competence of the Commission   The Commission has exclusive competence to adopt Article 86(3) Directives and a total discretion as to when to use this power. **6.248**

---

[308] Commission Directive (EEC) 88/301 on competition in the markets for telecommunications terminal equipment [1988] OJ L131/73, para 3.

[309] The Directives adopted under Art 86(3) are the following:
- Commission Directive (EEC) 88/301 on competition in the markets in telecommunications terminal equipment [1988] OJ L131/73–77;
- Commission Directive (EEC) 90/388 on competition in the markets for telecommunications services [1990] OJ L192/10–16;
- Commission Directive (EEC) 94/46 amending Directive (EEC) 88/301 and Directive (EEC) 90/388 in particular with regard to satellite communications [1994] OJ L268/15–21;
- Commission Directive (EC) 95/51 amending Directive (EEC) 90/388 with regard to the abolition of the restrictions on the use of cable television networks for the provision of already liberalized telecommunications services [1995] OJ L256/49–54;
- Commission Directive (EC) 96/2 amending Directive (EEC) 90/388 with regard to mobile and personal communications [1996] OJ L20/59–66;
- Commission Directive (EC) 96/19 amending Directive (EEC) 90/388 with regard to the implementation of full competition in telecommunications markets [1996] OJ L74/13–24;
- Commission Directive (EC) 99/64 amending Directive 90/388/EEC in order to ensure that telecommunications networks and cable TV networks owned by a single operator are separate legal entities [1999] OJ L175/39;
- Commission Directive (EC) 2002/77 on competition in the markets for electronic communications networks and services [2002] OJ L249/21.

[310] Case C-202/88 *Terminal equipment for telecommunications* [1991] ECR I-1223, para 17; Cases C-271, 281 and 289/90 *Telecommunications services* [1992] ECR I-5883, para 12.

[311] Commission Decision (EC) 2005/842 on the application of Article 86(2) of the EC Treaty to State aid in the form of public service compensation granted to certain undertakings entrusted with the operation of services of general economic interest [2005] OJ L312/67.

[312] Cases C-271, 281 and 289/90 *Telecommunications services* [1992] ECR I-5883, paras 17 and 22; L Hancher, 'Judgments of the Court Lagauche, Decoster & Taillandier' [1994] 21 CML Rev 857–873.

Although the Treaty does not require the intervention of any other institution, in practice the Commission normally consults the European Parliament, the Member States and the interested parties. Often, a draft Article 86(3) Directive is published first in the C series of the Official Journal to invite comments from institutions and bodies who may wish to intercede. The Directive is only adopted by the Commission after taking into account the results of this consultation.[313]

6.249 *Limits to the Commission's competence*   Irrespective of this policy of searching for consensus, from a legal point of view the Commission has sole responsibility for the adoption of Article 86(3) Directives. However, this power to adopt Directives under Article 86(3) is not a general legislative competence but a precisely defined competence which is exercised under the legal control of the Court of Justice. Some of the limits on the regulatory power of the Commission are examined in the following paragraphs.

6.250 *Article 86(3) Directives cannot deal with the autonomous behavior of undertakings*   In principle, the target of Article 86(3) Directives must be State measures, not the behaviour of undertakings.[314] Moreover, these State measures must be connected in one way or another with public or privileged undertakings or with public services (ie falling within Article 86(1) or 86(2)).

6.251 *Formal limits to the Commission's power under Article 86(3)*   The power that Article 86(3) grants to the Commission of creating obligations (either preventive or mandatory) must be exercised using a binding legal form, ie: a Directive or a Decision. The use of non-binding instruments, such as a communication, would undermine legal certainty and would be illegal.[315]

6.252 An Article 86(3) Directive has all the characteristics of a normal Directive within the meaning of Article 249 (former Article 189) of the EC Treaty. It must contain a clear legal basis.[316] In accordance with Article 254(2) (former Article 191(2)) the Directive will be published in the L series of the Official Journal and will enter into force 20 days after its publication, unless otherwise specified.

6.253 *Binding effects*   Article 86(3) Directives are obligatory for the Member States to which they are addressed. This obligatory effect is independent of the obligatory effect of the Treaty rules on which the Directive is based.[317]

6.254 *Lack of direct effect*   In principle, Directives are not directly applicable but require the adoption of implementing measures at national level. However, provisions having an unconditional and precise enough content may be recognised as having a direct effect once the deadline has expired without their being implemented.[318]

---

[313] *Report on Competition Policy 1995* (Vol XXV) para 100.

[314] Case C-202/88 *Terminal Equipment for Telecommunications* [1991] ECR I-1223, paras 55–57; Cases C-271, 281 and 289/90 *Telecommunications Services* [1992] ECR I-5883, paras 24–26.

[315] Case C-325/ 91 *Transparency Communication* [1993] ECR I-3283.

[316] Case C-202/88 *Terminal Equipment for Telecommunications* [1991] ECR I-1223, paras 45–47; Cases C-271, 281 and 289/90 *Telecommunications Services* [1992] ECR I-5883, paras 28–31.

[317] *Edward and Hoskins* (n 10 above) 184; *Pais Antunes* (n 271 above) 203.

[318] Cases C-46/90 and C93/91 *Lagauche* [1993] ECR I-5267, and Opinion of Lenz AG on this case at paras 13–19; Case C-69/91 *Decoster* [1993] ECR I-5335, and Opinion of Tesauro AG on this case; Case C-92/91 *Taillandler* [1993] ECR I-5383.

(iii) Relationship between directives under article 86(3) and harmonising **6.255**
directives   Even though the Court of Justice has repeatedly confirmed its legal validity,
the quasi-legislative competence that Article 86(3) gives to the Commission has been the
subject of political controversy. Those powers, however, fit well into the logic of the EC
Treaty where the provisions addressed to the Member States, such as Article 86, are not of
a programmatic nature but are rather directly obligatory rules. This makes it difficult to
distinguish between 'creating law' and 'applying existing law'. Article 86 Directives simply
testify to this ambiguity.

Article 86(3) overlaps with other Treaty provisions   The competence of the Commission   **6.256**
under Article 86(3) coexists with the legislative competences of the Council of Ministers
and the European Parliament under Article 95 (former Article 100A) and many other provisions. The Court of Justice has confirmed that certain matters may be regulated either by
a Directive of the Council and the Parliament or by a Directive of the Commission.[319] This
happens in particular in the case of liberalisation of the utilities sectors.

The dissuasive role of Article 86(3)   The political implications of this overlapping of com-   **6.257**
petences are delicate. The participation of the European Parliament in the legislative procedure under Article 95 gives to the relevant Directives a democratic legitimacy that does
not exist in the case of Article 86(3) Directives. This clearly reduces, from a political point
of view, the margin of discretion of the Commission in choosing the appropriate legal basis
for its liberalisation Directives. This may explain the restraint shown by the Commission
in the use of Article 86(3) Directives: so far this instrument has only been used in the area
of financial transparency between Member States and public undertakings and in the
telecommunications sector. The Commission has not used this legal basis in the liberalisation of the electricity, gas, air transport, railways or postal sectors. It would be a mistake,
however, to think that Article 86(3) has not played any part in these liberalisation
processes. It is clear that the mere possibility of the Commission adopting an Article 86(3)
Directive has had an influence upon the attitudes of the actors in the legislative process.
It is submitted that this 'dissuasive' role of Article 86(3) is an essential factor in achieving a
balanced Community approach to liberalisation.

---

[319] Cases 188, 189 and 190/80 *Transparency directive* [1982] ECR 2545, paras 11–14; Case C-202/88
Terminal equipment for telecommunications [1991] ECR I-1223, paras 23–26; Cases C-271, 281 and 289/90
Telecommunications services [1992] ECR I-5883, para 14.

PART II

SPECIFIC PRACTICES

7

HORIZONTAL CO-OPERATION AGREEMENTS

Francisco Enrique González Díaz

A. Introduction

(1) Definition of Horizontal Agreements and Practices

7.01   In this context, horizontal agreements refer to agreements between companies operating at the same level in the production/distribution chain, for example in research or production. In the majority of cases the focus of the antitrust rules will be on horizontal agreements between actual and/or potential competitors. However, agreements between companies that have complementary skills or technology may also be of concern to the antitrust authorities to the extent that such agreements harm the competitive position of third parties, for example by foreclosing market entry.

(2) Classification of Horizontal Agreements and Practices

7.02   Depending on their effects on competition, horizontal agreements can be classified into two broad categories, '*per se*' and 'non-*per se*'.

7.03   Agreements falling into the so-called '*per se*' category, such as price-fixing cartels etc, are considered as being illegal in themselves, without regard to any anti-competitive effects that they might produce, and are unlikely to have any redeeming virtues. The underlying idea being that *per se* offences are invariably harmful to competition. These inherently unlawful agreements have been analysed in a previous chapter.

7.04   The assessment of 'non-*per se*' co-operation agreements is quite different. The principle involved here is that these arrangements are not necessarily harmful to competition. Their effect on competition depends, *inter alia*, on the nature of the agreement and on market conditions. Therefore their assessment is primarily carried out on a case-by-case basis.

(3) Use of Commission Decisions

7.05   The Commission generally publishes decisions when it wishes to establish points of principle and to give greater clarity as to how it assesses individual cases. However, it is important also to realise that the Commission policy has developed over time. This is in part a reaction to changing markets as well as a refining of the analytical approach and techniques open to it, and in part due to experience. This chapter does not attempt to provide a detailed review of Commission decisions; rather it discusses general points of principle and illustrates these points, where possible, with recent Commission decisions.

B. Co-operation Agreements

(1) Introduction

7.06   It is increasingly common in today's economic environment for companies to choose to co-operate with each other. This is usually for pro-competitive reasons. It allows companies to spread the costs and risks associated with investment in R&D or new production facilities. It also allows them to pool the expertise or market information that is necessary to launch new products or to enter new geographic markets. Such co-operation is often a response to the increasing competitive pressure of modern global and high technology markets. It can lead to significant advantages for consumers if the efficiencies achieved through co-operation are passed on through lower prices, or if new products are brought to market more quickly.

If the *per se* or 'hardcore' restrictions that were mentioned earlier are avoided, then experience has shown that such agreements are less likely to raise competition concerns. However, the Commission's policy has for many years been to apply Article 81(1) very widely to co-operation agreements, even if ultimately they have been frequently exempted unchanged. This has led many firms to notify their agreements to the Commission for the sake of legal security and to avoid the potential problem of litigation under Article 81(2). **7.07**

Several statements by the Commission did, however, refer to the need for a greater economic analysis in assessing competition cases.[1] In recent times, enforcement practice and experience have also tended to focus on a more economic-oriented analysis of the application of Article 81(1). This trend has led the Commission to adopt a set of Guidelines on horizontal co-operation agreements, published in January 2001.[2] The Guidelines were designed to provide an analytical framework for the assessment of most types of co-operation agreements under Article 81(1), with greater emphasis on economic criteria, in light of the Commission's decisional practice and the European Courts' case law. Following this policy driver, the Commission recognises the various potential efficiencies brought about by horizontal co-operation, which will be weighed against the possible negative effects on competition, instead of following a formalistic approach. Further, the Community courts appear to be pushing the Commission in the direction of a more effects-based approach to Article 81 in general, and co-operation agreements in particular.[3] **7.08**

There is no precise definition of what constitutes a co-operation agreement. Agreements are sometimes structured as joint ventures, sometimes as looser co-operation arrangements. Generally it is only agreements between actual or potential competitors that will cause competition problems, although agreements between non-competitors which significantly affect the position of third parties, by perhaps foreclosing a market, can also fall within Article 81(1). In the following sections most types of co-operation will be covered. Vertical agreements and technology licensing agreements are covered elsewhere.[4] **7.09**

The 2001 Guidelines generally distinguish three types of agreements. At one end of the spectrum, agreements between non-competitors, agreements between competing companies that cannot conduct the project or activity covered by the agreement independently from one another and agreements concerning an activity which does not influence the relevant **7.10**

---

[1] Report on Competition Policy 1983 (Vol XIII).

[2] Commission's Notice on the applicability of Article 81 to horizontal co-operation agreements [2001] OJ C3/2 ('2001 Guidelines').

[3] As a recent example, the CFI annulled a Commission decision, concluding that national roaming agreements between competing network operators 'by definition' restrict competition and thus had an anti-competitive 'effect' under Article 81(1). The CFI noted that in order to assess the effects of one of these agreements in a particular case, the Commission should have analysed what the competition situation would have been in the absence of the agreement and demonstrated in concrete terms that the roaming agreement had restrictive effects on competition. Case T-328/03 *O2 (Germany) v Commission*, judgment of 2 May 2006 (not yet published).

[4] Art 5 of Commission Regulation (EC) 772/2004 of 27 April 2004 on the application of Article 81(3) of the Treaty to certain categories of technology transfer agreements, discussed under technology licensing agreements in the context of joint ventures.

parameters of competition are not *normally* deemed to fall under Article 81(1). Such agreements may, however, fall under Article 81(1) if they involve firms with significant market power[5] and raise foreclosure concerns. At the other end of the spectrum certain categories of agreements are deemed to *almost always* fall under Article 81(1). These are arrangements which specifically aim at restricting competition such as price fixing, output limitation or market/customer sharing agreements. Agreements not falling into either category are deemed to require further analysis concerning various market-related criteria such as the market position of the parties involved and other structural factors.[6]

7.11 The legal form of an agreement should not fundamentally alter the assessment under the competition rules. However, there are certain elements of the assessment that are peculiar to certain forms of agreements. *Joint ventures* are discussed in the next section. The subsequent sections consider other 'types' of co-operation agreements that occur commonly. These can be broadly identified as co-operation at the various stages of industrial activity, ie *R&D*, *production* (including *specialisation*), *buying/purchasing*, or *commercialisation* (encompassing *joint selling, distribution* and *promotion*), all of which are specifically addressed in the 2001 Guidelines. In addition, the Commission's Guidelines include an analysis of agreements on standards and environmental agreements.

7.12 An agreement concerning each of these activities can raise different issues and will require an adaptation of the basic analytical approach. Therefore for each type of agreement we consider the general Commission policy towards such agreements, the likelihood of an agreement falling under Article 81(1), and the criteria for exemption. Other factors such as particular problems relating to market definition and the attitude of the Commission to certain common restrictions are also discussed.

7.13 However, agreements rarely fall squarely into any of these categories. Often they involve elements of co-operation at more than one level. As a general rule an agreement that is primarily concerned with one area of co-operation, such as joint R&D, will be assessed as such. The provisions related to co-operation in other areas, such as joint exploitation of this R&D, will be looked at in the light of their importance to the main co-operation. Paragraph 12 of the Commission's Guidelines attempts to clarify the kind of assessment that must be pursued for each of these complex agreements by focusing on the so-called 'centre of gravity of the co-operation'. For this centre of gravity to be determined, two factors must be considered, namely the starting point of the co-operation and the degree of integration of the different functions combined in the context of the collaboration.[7] Once the centre of gravity of the agreement has been identified, the analysis of the entire agreement will be undertaken under the relevant legal standards.

---

[5] The concept of 'market power' in the present context must be distinguished from dominance and generally refers to a lower threshold of market power.

[6] 2001 Guidelines, para 26.

[7] The Guidelines illustrate this scheme by pointing out that a co-operation involving both R&D and joint production of the results of the innovation would 'normally' be evaluated under the criteria laid down for joint R&D efforts, as the joint production would only be implemented if the R&D programme is successful. 2001 Guidelines, para 12.

There are also several Notices and Regulations in the field of horizontal co-operation. These, together with the relevant decisions, will be referred to and discussed in the context of the individual agreements. **7.14**

C. Joint Ventures

(1) Definition and Constitution of a Joint Venture

Definition Joint ventures ('JVs') have been defined in several different ways. In fact, virtually any commercial arrangement involving two or more firms could be called a 'joint venture'. As it has been pointed out,[8] in defining JVs one must focus on those factors that make these kinds of business transactions a distinctive subject of antitrust concern. For the purposes of this chapter JVs will be defined as agreements by which two or more independent undertakings proceed to the partial integration of their business operations which are put under joint control in order to achieve some commercial goal.[9] In practice, JVs encompass a broad range of operations, from merger-like operations to co-operation for particular functions such as R&D, production or distribution. **7.15**

Constitution of a joint venture A JV can be the result of the pooling of two companies' potential capacity to produce, distribute, etc,[10] a specific product or service through the setting up of a new business entity (whether or not endowed with the corporate form). This type of joint venture may bring about not only the potential benefits derived from integration of commercial activities or technological expertise but also the addition, at least in principle, of a new competitive force to the market (*ex novo* creation) and in this respect it differs from the categories that follow. **7.16**

A second possibility consists of the pooling of two companies' existing capacity to produce, distribute, etc, a specific product or service falling short of a complete merger between them but entailing the total and irreversible withdrawal of their independent activities at least in a particular product and geographic market. **7.17**

And finally, although not significantly different from the last option, the pooling of existing assets might affect either one (for example through the acquisition of shares of an existing enterprise) or all the undertakings party to the agreement *without* giving rise to their total withdrawal, actual or potential, from the markets concerned. **7.18**

All these varied forms of constitution share the same common denominator: a limited integration of operations coupled with the preservation of the economic independence of the companies party to the joint venture agreement (the parent companies). Because of these two common features these sorts of arrangement can give rise to both a positive and a negative presumptive attitude of the antitrust laws. **7.19**

---

[8] Brodley, 'Joint Ventures and Antitrust Policy' (1982) 95 Harv. L. Rev. at 1525.

[9] The Commission's Notice on co-operative and concentrative JVs describes them as 'undertakings controlled by two or more other undertakings'. Commission Notice on the distinction between concentrative and co-operative joint ventures [1994] OJ C385/1 (para 2).

[10] Carry out R&D, buy, sell, etc.

7.20 Indeed, it could be argued that, as mergers, JVs have a potential for the generation of efficiencies and other economic benefits and therefore should deserve the more favourable treatment dispensed to mergers. If, in addition, it is considered that, as opposed to mergers, some JV agreements do not entail the total elimination of the parent companies as actual or potential competitors in the market of the JV, preserving thus their independence as economic agents, and that in a majority of cases they also give rise to the creation of a new competitive force in the market, it could be concluded that they even deserve a more permissive approach than that granted to mergers.[11]

7.21 However, as seen below, the very fact that the undertakings party to the JV agreement remain independent after its setting up can give rise to competition concerns as to the extent to which the existence of the JV may unite the economic interests of the parent companies thus facilitating the conclusion of restrictive arrangements or the creation of anti-competitive spillover effects.[12]

7.22 These are some of the reasons why JVs have caused so much legal debate on both sides of the Atlantic.

(2) Distinction Between Co-operative and Concentrative Joint Ventures

7.23 There is an important distinction between the so-called concentrative JVs, ie JVs falling under the Merger Regulation[13] and subject exclusively to the test set out in its Article 2(3),[14] and co-operative JVs, ie JVs to which Article 81 applies. Within this latter category a further distinction must be made between those JVs falling under the Merger Regulation, the so-called co-operative full-function JVs, which are subject both to the Merger test and Article 81, and those falling under Regulation 1/2003 and other implementing regulations, the so-called co-operative non-full-function JVs, to which only Articles 81 and 82 apply.

7.24 Indeed, under Article 3 of the Merger Regulation a JV falls outside the provisions of Regulation 1/2003[15] if it can be regarded as a concentration, that is to say if it performs on a lasting basis all the functions of an autonomous economic entity.[16] However, whenever

---

[11] In relation to this see Brodley, above, at 1523 ff.

[12] F E González Díaz, 'Joint Ventures under EC Competition Law: the New Boundaries', in Bruylant, *Mélanges en Homenage á Michel Waelbroeck* Vol II, (1999), pp 1024–1028.

[13] Council Regulation (EC) 139/2004 of 20 January 2004 on the control of concentrations between undertakings [2004] OJ L24/1.

[14] The actual test laid down in the new Merger Regulation of 2004 goes beyond the old dominance criterion stating that '[a] concentration which would significantly impede effective competition, in the common market or in a substantial part of it, in particular as a result of the creation or strengthening of a dominant position, shall be declared incompatible with the common market.' Basically, the new test is liberated from the potentially legal 'corset' of dominance and becomes the one and only substantive test applicable to all concentrations, with the only exception of full-function JVs. For a detail comment on this issue, see F E González Díaz, 'The Reform of European Merger Control: *Quod Novi Sub Sole?*' (2004) 27 (2) World Competition 177-199; and this book's chapter on Mergers.

[15] Council Regulation (EC) 1/2003 of 16 December 2002 on the implementation of the rules on competition laid down in Articles 81 and 82 of the Treaty [2003] OJ L1/1.

[16] Art 3(4) of Council Regulation (EC) 139/2004 of 20 January 2004 on the control of concentrations between undertakings. See also Commission Notice on the Concept of full-function joint ventures under Council Regulation (EEC) 4064/89 on the control of concentrations between undertakings [1998] OJ C66/1.

the creation of full-function JVs leads to the coordination of the competitive behaviour of companies that remain independent the Commission must apply Article 81 to this aspect of the transaction.[17]

(3) The Rationale Behind the Difference in Treatment Between Concentrative and Co-operative Joint Ventures

Concentrative JVs are subject to a more benign regulatory framework in terms of substance than co-operative full-function JVs since the former are only subject to the Merger Regulation test while the latter are subject to both the Merger Regulation test and to Article 81. **7.25**

This difference in treatment has given rise to a considerable number of criticisms from the legal community.[18] The main criticism levelled at the distinction between co-operative and concentrative JVs, in particular with regard to co-operative full-function JVs, is that the Commission would treat differently economically similar transactions, thus deterring the formation of desirable JVs, and that this ultimately leads to less competitive markets in European industries.[19] It has thus been argued that the principal rationale for the distinction between co-operative and concentrative JVs, ie that co-operative JVs create greater risks of competitive harm and fewer opportunities for competitive benefits than full mergers and acquisitions and that these competitively 'worse' transactions can only be adequately regulated under the stricter enforcement regime of Article 81, does not survive close analysis.[20] This is so, the argument goes, because most JVs, especially those with a limited duration or only partial contribution from their parents' operations: (a) typically create lower (and certainly no greater) risks of competitive harm than full mergers and acquisitions involving the **7.26**

---

[17] Art 2(4) of the Merger Regulation reads:

'To the extent that the creation of a joint venture constituting a concentration pursuant to Article 3 has as its object or effect the coordination of the competitive behaviour of undertakings that remain independent, such coordination shall be appraised in accordance with the criteria of Article 81(1) and (3) of the Treaty, with a view to establishing whether or not the operation is compatible with the common market.'

In making this appraisal, the Commission shall take into account in particular, and according to Art 2(5) of the Merger Regulation:

— 'whether two or more parent companies retain, to a significant extent, activities in the same market as the joint venture or in a market which is downstream or upstream from that of the joint venture or in a neighbouring market closely related to this market,

— whether the coordination which is the direct consequence of the creation of the joint venture affords the undertakings concerned the possibility of eliminating competition in respect of a substantial part of the products or services in question.'

[18] F E González Díaz, 'Joint Ventures under EC Competition Law: the New Boundaries', at 1024.

[19] Hawk, 'A Bright Line Shareholding Test to End the Nightmare Under the EEC Merger Regulation' [1993] 30 CMLR 1155. Firms are encouraged to merge their competing operations fully and permanently rather than engage in limited duration/partial function joint ventures that create fewer long-term risks of competitive harm. Other criticisms levelled at the co-operative/concentrative distinction are the following: the cost, unpredictability and time-consuming nature of applying the distinction to individual cases, the risk of forum shopping and of alteration of private transactions to fit the definition of concentrative JV, and the corruption of substantive antitrust principles when used for jurisdictional purposes. Hawk, 'A Bright Line', 1162–1167.

[20] Hawk, 'A Bright Line,' relying on the seminal work of Joseph Brodley, above, at 1521.

same parties;[21] and (b) are often equally likely to involve functional integration of economic resources (and thus result in economic efficiencies and other competitive benefits).[22]

7.27 However, in order to fully understand the rationale for this difference in treatment between concentrative and co-operative JVs, one needs to bear in mind why mergers and acquisitions of single control are given a more favourable treatment under EC competition law. The reasons appear to be twofold. First of all, this type of transaction is considered to be more likely to produce efficiency gains through the integration of resources of previously independent companies than other kinds of transactions such as co-operative JVs, licensing agreements, cartels, etc where the level of economic integration is either less important or practically non-existent. Secondly, one would expect the risk of such efficiencies not being fully exploited to the benefit of consumers to arise only in cases where the concentration in question would create or strengthen a dominant position or otherwise significantly impede effective competition.

7.28 Under EC law, the 'concentration privilege' is thus only reserved for those transactions which could be presumed to give rise to significant levels of efficiency in terms of economic integration between undertakings.

7.29 As far as JVs are concerned, the need to bring about a considerable degree of economic integration in order to qualify as a concentration has been essentially embodied in the legal requirement that the JV under scrutiny be full-function, ie it must perform on a lasting basis all the functions of an autonomous economic entity.[23]

7.30 However, this rationale does not explain the reason why some co-operative JVs—and in particular those bringing about the creation of a full-function JV—were excluded from the scope of application of the first Merger Regulation[24] prior to the entry into force of Regulation 1310/97,[25] which amended it.

7.31 The answer lies not in the inability of a co-operative full-function JV to bring about a significant degree of economic integration in such cases but, rather, in its ability to give rise to the coordination of the competitive behaviour of undertakings which remain independent in areas which have not been 'merged' within the JV.

7.32 Thus the Council's rationale for not applying the Merger Regulation appears to have been based on the Commission's belief that JVs which could lead to the coordination of the competitive

---

[21] This would be so because a JV can never eliminate competition more than a full merger between the same parties since full mergers totally and permanently eliminate all actual and potential competition between the parties. In comparison, JVs (especially limited duration and/or partial function ventures) often create lower risks of competitive harm than full mergers because JVs may preserve some degree of competition between the parents in the JV's market and may be more likely to break up at some later date, which could either maintain or reintroduce both parents as independent competitors in the JV's market. Even if the JV creates a very high spillover risk, the total harm to competition can never be greater than that which would occur if the same parties entered into a full merger.

[22] The types and magnitude of economic integration created by a (non-sham) JV would often equal those created by a full merger between the same parties in terms of scale or scope economies, risk allocation, facilitation of new product development or geographic entry, and synergies resulting from combining complementary operations.

[23] F E González Díaz, 'Joint Ventures under EC Competition Law: the New Boundaries,' at 1020.

[24] Council Regulation (EEC) 4064/89 of 21 December 1989 on the control of concentrations between undertakings [1989] OJ L385 (no longer in force).

[25] Council Regulation (EEC) 1310/97 of 30 June 1997 [1997] OJ L180/1 (no longer in force).

behaviour of undertakings with regard to business activities which are not pooled within the JV, and which consequently are not integrated within a single economic entity, do not deserve the benefit of the 'concentration privilege'. In other words, so the argument goes, there is no reason to give the benefit of the Merger Regulation test to a restriction of competition in areas of business activity of the parent companies which do not give rise to an increase in the level of economic integration and which consequently cannot compensate its anti-competitive effects with the creation of significant efficiencies.

In addition, and in particular in cases where the parent companies operate in the same market as the JV, the coordination of the competitive behaviour of the parent companies and the JV could also potentially lead to a decrease in the level of efficiency generated by the integration of economic activities within the JV. This is because the JV might not act as a profit maximising company, given the need to take into account the interests of the parent companies in deciding its pricing and output strategies. **7.33**

In sum, a considerable number of full-function JVs were subject to the strictures of Article 81, Regulation 17 (today Regulation 1/2003), and other implementing regulations, since they had the potential to give rise to the coordination of the competitive behaviour of parent companies that remained independent in areas of business activity where they had not pooled their activities and, consequently, had not created any significant efficiency gains. **7.34**

In this regard, the comparison made by some commentators[26] between a full-function JV leading to the coordination of the competitive behaviour of the parent companies with regard to business activities which are not the subject of any integration other than that resulting from collusion and a merger of the same parent companies in respect of the same activities, does not seem appropriate. Indeed, the first scenario may bring about coordination without any redeeming virtue. In the second scenario, however, although there is an elimination of competition, this is accompanied by an integration of economic activity likely to give rise to significant efficiencies. Against this background, it is difficult to accept the contention that the Commission incorrectly applied a different treatment to fully equivalent business transactions. **7.35**

However, these commentators are right to point out that, by applying Article 81(1) not only to the coordination of the competitive behaviour of the parent companies, but also to the actual pooling of activities within the JV, the Commission was likely to treat the potential for efficiencies created by a co-operative full function JV more harshly than the equivalent potential for efficiencies stemming from the setting up of a concentrative JV.[27] **7.36**

(4) The Application of Article 81(1) by the Commission to Co-operative Joint Ventures prior to the Entry into Force of the 1997 Amendment to the First Merger Regulation

This section will describe the way in which the Commission has assessed under Article 81 those JVs which, in spite of involving a significant degree of integration (R&D, production and/or distribution of goods or services), did not qualify, under its approach, as concentrative JVs. **7.37**

---

[26] Hawk, 'A Bright Line', 1162–1167.
[27] This potential for discrimination has been acknowledged by the Commission in its Green Paper on the Review of the Merger Regulation and, as noted below, was the basis of the Commission's proposal to the Council to modify the Merger Regulation with regard to JVs.

7.38 One of the most complete descriptions of the competitive risks associated with the formation of a JV under Article 81 can be found in the *GEC-Weir Sodium Circulators* decision of 21 November 1977.[28] This decision concerned a joint venture agreement entered into between General Electric Company Ltd of London (UK) and Weir Group Ltd of Glasgow (UK), for the purposes of joint development, production and sale by the parties of sodium circulators and for the allocation between the parties of work for the development and production of such circulators. In finding that the JV had as its object or effect the prevention, restriction, or distortion of competition within the meaning of Article 81(1) the Commission stated that:

7.39 First—from a structural point of view, the mere setting up of a JV between two undertakings which were, prior to the occurrence of this event, at least potential competitors in the field of activity of the JV is to be considered a restriction of competition due to the replacement of two undertakings by one, the joint venture.[29]

7.40 Secondly—the collusive effect, either in the JV's market or in related ones where the parents are in competition, arising out of the joint management of their offspring, is also a restriction of competition as such: the joint fixing of prices, production targets, etc, of the joint venture normally leads, in the absence of an express agreement, to the alignment of the commercial policies of the parties involved thereto and in any case the joint management of the JV generates a kind of co-operative atmosphere giving rise to a decrease of the competitive zeal between the parent companies in other related areas.

7.41 Thirdly—even in the absence of an express agreement not to compete, the parent companies of a JV will normally not compete with it.

7.42 Fourthly—in the case of JVs vertically related to the parent companies the position of third parties will be affected to the extent that the joint venture will be preferred as a source of supply or as an outlet, producing a foreclosure effect restrictive of competition.

7.43 These three last restrictions represent what has been characterised above as the so-called spillover effect.

7.44 In more recent cases,[30] Article 81(1) has also been applied to the network effect resulting from the setting up of the so-called interlocking JVs, ie JVs with at least one common parent company.

7.45 The Commission's analysis of spillover effects under Article 81(1) to date[31] can be thus summarised as follows: once a JV has been characterised as a co-operative JV the Commission

---

[28] [1977] OJ L327/26.

[29] The Commission thus carries out a merger-like assessment of the transaction under Art 81 with regard to the loss of competition resulting from the integration of activities of the parent companies.

[30] See for example *Optical Fibres* [1986] OJ L236/30; and *Night Services* [1994] OJ L259/20.

[31] For more recent cases following the same basic approach see: *Unisource* [2001] L52/30 (appeal to Decision 97/780 [1997] L318/1); *Lufthansa/SA* [1996] OJ L54/28; *Atlas* [1996] OJ L239/23; *Exxon/Shell* [1994] OJ L144/20; *Philips/Osram* [1994] OJ L378/34; *IPSP* [1994] OJ L354/75; *Pasteur Merieux/Merck* [1994] OJ L309/1; *Asahi/Saint-Gobain* [1994] OJ L354/87; *Night Services* [1994] OJ L259/20; *ACI* [1994] OJ L224/28; *BT/MCI* [1994] OJ L223/36; *Astra* [1993] OJ L2/23; *Ford/VW* [1993] OJ L20/14; *Gosme/Martell* [1991] OJ L185/23.

assesses the anti-competitive effects arising out of its creation not only with regard to spillover effects as defined above but also with regard to the pooling of activities within the JV.

For example, if company A and company B, both active in the manufacture and sale of say **7.46** widgets and gadgets, decided to pool their widget operations within a JV, the Commission would examine under Article 81(1) not only the possible spillover effects stemming from the setting up of the JV on the gadget market (where both parent companies would remain competitors) but also the anti-competitive effects resulting from the addition of market share (or the loss of potential competition) arising out of the combination of their activities on the widget market. In other words, once the JV was characterised as a co-operative JV the Commission would proceed not only to the assessment of the anti-competitive effects of the JV on the market where collusion was likely to occur but also on the market where the parties had merged their activities thus carrying out a limited form of merger control under Article 81(1).

In addition to that, and despite the fact that the coordination of the competitive behaviour **7.47** of the parent companies and the JV was abandoned in the 1994 Notice as a jurisdictional criterion to determine whether or not a JV had to be characterised as concentrative or co-operative, if the Commission came to the conclusion that the JV fell into the latter category, then the coordination of the competitive behaviour of the parent companies and the JV was also assessed under Article 81. For instance, if in our example only company A had transferred its widget activities to the JV, then the Commission would have examined separately under Article 81 the possible coordination of the competitive behaviour between company B and the JV on the widget market.[32]

Finally, the Commission also assesses under Article 81 the possible foreclosure effect stem- **7.48** ming from the creation of the JV wherever the parent companies and the JV are in a vertical relationship. For instance, if in our example company A was also a manufacturer of an input for the production of widgets, the Commission would examine the possible foreclosure effects in terms of the de facto exclusivity granted to the JV,[33] resulting from the setting up of the JV.

The most striking feature of the Commission's analysis of co-operative JVs (both full-function **7.49** and not full-function) under Article 81 was, despite its stated policy in point 26 of the 1993 Notice on co-operative JVs[34] and some isolated cases,[35] the almost automatic conclusion that once the parent companies of the JV and the JV itself were in any of the situations described above the JV would lead to an appreciable restriction of competition provided the thresholds of the Notice on agreements of minor importance[36] were exceeded.

---

[32] See for example *Mitchell Cotts/Sofiltra* [1987] OJ L41/31; and *Gosme/Martell—DMP* [1991] OJ L185/23.

[33] See for example *Night Services* [1994] OJ L259/20.

[34] Commission Notice concerning the assessment of co-operative joint ventures pursuant to Article 85 [now Article 81] of the EEC Treaty [1993] OJ C43/2.

[35] See cases cited by Pathak, 'The EC Commission's Approach to Joint Ventures: A Policy of Contradictions' [1991] 5 ECLR 171.

[36] Today, Commission's Notice on agreements of minor importance which do not appreciably restrict competition under Article 81(1) of the Treaty establishing the European Community (de minimis) [2001] OJ C368/13.

7.50 There was some tension, it is submitted, between this policy and the analysis developed by the Court of Justice in dealing with (a) the appreciability of alleged anti-competitive effects of agreements likely to produce significant efficiency gains;[37] and (b) the need to show a sufficient degree of causality between the creation of a structure which might be presumed likely to lead to anti-competitive effects and actual anti-competitive effects,[38] and by the Commission itself in some areas of its decisional practice including some JV cases[39] and, in particular, in the context of exchange of information agreements,[40] in dealing both with the issue of appreciability and with the conditions likely to lead to the coordination of competitive behaviour among competitors in the absence of an express agreement to collude.

7.51 The following section will develop in more detail the notion and role of potential competition in assessing the validity of JVs under Article 81.

(5) The Notion and Role of Potential Competition in Assessing the Validity of Joint Ventures under Article 81

7.52 In its early decisions considering joint ventures under Article 81,[41] the Commission seemed to be quite willing to embrace a rather broad notion of the conditions required to assert that one or more companies were in a situation of potential competition (defined in this setting as the ability to enter the JV market). In effect, the Commission adopted this approach not only where the partners would have been able independently to engage in the activities exercised by the JV, but also where the JV enabled the parties to develop a new product or to enter a new market which neither of them would have been able to develop or enter into independently. Such competitive benefit was taken into consideration by the Commission only when assessing whether the conditions of Article 81(3) were fulfilled.[42] The Commission in these decisions based its determination of the existence of potential competition as between the parent companies on presumptions related to the previous activities and expertise of the parent companies, their theoretical access to the necessary technology, and their financial resources.[43]

---

[37] See for example, Case C-234/89 *Stergios Delimitis v Henninger Bräu AG* [1991] ECR I–935; and Case C-306/96 *Javico AG v Yves Saint Laurent Parfums SA (YSLP)* [1998] ECR I–1983; Case C-250/92 *Gøttrup—Klim ea Grouvareforeninger* [1994] ECR I–5641; and Case C-399/93 *HG Oude Luttikhuis ea* [1995] ECR I–4515.

[38] Joined Cases C-68/94 and C-30/95 *French Republic and Société commerciale des potasser et de l'azote (SCPA) and Entreprise minière et chimique (EMC) v Commission* [1998] ECR I–1375.

[39] See cases cited by Pathak above.

[40] Commission decision of 17 February 1992, *UK Agricultural Tractor Registration Exchange* [1993] OJ L68/19. The Commission's approach towards the coordination of the competitive behaviour resulting from the setting up of an exchange of information system among competitors has been recently endorsed both by the Court of First Instance (Case T–34/92 *Fiatagri and New Holland Ford v Commission* [1994] ECR II–905; and Case T-35/92 *John Deere Ltd v Commission* [1994] ECR II–957); and by the Court of Justice (Case C-7/95P *John Deere Ltd v Commission* [1998] ECR I–1311; and Case C-8/95P *New Holland Ford Ltd v Commission* [1998] ECR I–3175).

[41] *KEWA* [1976] OJ L51/15; *Vacuum Interrupters* [1976] OJ L48/32; *GEC-Weir Sodium Circulators* [1977] OJ L327/26; *Beecham/Parke Davis* [1979] OJ L70/11; *Langenscheidt-Hachette* [1982] OJ L39/25; *Amersham-Buchler* [1982] OJ L314/34, 35; *Rockwell-Iveco* [1983] OJ L224/19; *VW-MAN* [1983] OJ L376/11; *Carlsberg* [1984] OJ L207/26.

[42] See Waelbroeck, 'Antitrust Analysis under Article 85(1) and (3)' [1987] Annual Proceedings of the Fordham Corporate Law Institute 716.

[43] For a commentary on this issue see FL Fine, *Mergers and Joint Ventures in Europe* (Graham & Trotman, 1989) at 60.

This approach gave rise to an easy and sometimes cursory consideration of many joint ventures **7.53** as restrictive of competition and to the consequent increase of the Commission's powers of supervision under Article 81 of the Treaty. This led the Commission to reconsider its gauging of the potential competition issue. In this connection, the Commission stated in the *Thirteenth Report on Competition Policy* that in order to evaluate, in an individual case, whether the formation of a JV in the production field restricts potential competition, it may use the following checklist of questions with respect to each of the partners. The basic point is that the degree of potential competition depends largely on the nature of the product manufactured or the services offered by the JV.

In addition, the following individual questions may be relevant: **7.54**

(a) *Input of the Joint Venture.* Does the investment expenditure involved substantially exceed the financing capacity of each partner? Does each partner have the necessary technical know-how and sources of input products?

(b) *Production of the Joint Venture.* Is each partner familiar with the process technology? Does each partner itself produce inputs for or products derived from the JV's product and does it have access to the necessary production facilities?

(c) *Sales by the Joint Venture.* Is the actual or potential demand such that it would be feasible for each of the partners to manufacture the product on its own? Does each of them have access to the necessary distribution channels for the joint venture's product?

(d) *Risk Factor.* Could each partner bear the technical and financial risks associated with the production operations of the JV alone?[44]

This relaxation in the Commission's approach has manifested itself in certain decisions (*Optical* **7.55** *Fibres*,[45] *Mitchell Cotts/Sofiltra*,[46] *Olivetti/Canon*[47]) where, for example, it has not deemed the considerable technological and financial resources of the parties sufficient to establish that the parent companies were in a position to enter the joint venture market independently.[48]

This apparently more lenient stance towards the potential competition issue could dimin- **7.56** ish the relevance of one of the more thorny legal problems, at least from the point of view of a coherent antitrust analysis and enforcement, posed by the Commission implementation of Article 81(1) and (3) to JVs.

Indeed, in the event that it is established that the formation of the JV restricts competition **7.57** because of the substitution of one competitor, the JV, for two, it has to be shown that such agreement does not impose on the undertakings concerned restrictions which are not indispensable to the attainment of objectives such as the improvement of the production

---

[44] It is interesting the way in which the Commission avoids any reference to the so called 'perceived' potential competition as a decisive element in order to decide whether or not the formation of the joint venture leads to a lessening of competition on the relevant market.

[45] [1986] OJ L236/30. See also Korah, 'Critical Comments on the Commission's Recent Decisions Exempting Joint Ventures to Exploit Research that Needs Further Development' [1987] European Law Review 18, 37.

[46] [1987] OJ L41/31.

[47] [1988] OJ L52/51.

[48] However, the Commission has also developed additional means of establishing potential competition. In several decisions, the Commission considered: (i) whether the JV partner is a potential competitor of the joint venture itself (*Iveco/Ford* [1988] OJ L230/39; and *Mitchell Cotts/Sofiltra*); and (ii) whether there are JVs in competition with each other (*Optical Fibres*).

or distribution of goods, the promotion of technical or economic progress, etc for the agreement to benefit from Article 81(3).

7.58   If the parents were able to enter the market independently, then, how could the Commission justify the indispensability of the JV under Article 81(3)?

7.59   In essence, the Commission examines whether the parent companies could with their own resources and capabilities alone develop the JV products and whether other forms of co-operation such as a licence agreement, a specialisation agreement, etc[49] could be expected to lead to the same type of benefits.

7.60   In the *Engine Alliance* decision,[50] however, the Commission exempted a JV despite its finding that the two partners, GE and Pratt & Witney, were potential competitors. The partners joined efforts to manufacture and market a new jet engine, destined to fit a new Airbus aircraft. The Commission acknowledged that developing the engine in co-operation may have been more efficient, but nevertheless considered it economically and technically feasible for both parties to develop the new engine independently. The parties were therefore deemed potential competitors in a very tight oligopolistic market since the co-operation reduced the number of market players from three to two.

7.61   The Commission nevertheless considered that the JV met the conditions for an exemption under Article 81(3). In particular, the JV was deemed indispensable to develop the new engine within the time frame and costs requirements imposed on the JV. In light of the efforts of the only competitor to adapt its existing engine to the new aircraft, the co-operation was deemed necessary to market a competing engine. The exemption, however, contained obligations designed to ensure that the co-operation was strictly limited to that specific engine.

(6) Conditions Leading to the Incentive to Coordinate (Spillover Effects)

7.62   **(i) Introduction**   Although not discussed in the 1990, 1993 and 1994 Commission Notices, economic theory appears to support the view that the setting up of a JV can lead either to anticompetitive parallel behaviour (tacit collusion) by the parent companies[51] (or by the parent companies and third companies[52]) or to independent behaviour having equivalent effects.[53]

7.63   Generally, the parent companies of a JV can be presumed to have an incentive to coordinate their competitive behaviour where this coordination is likely to be profitable,

---

[49]   For a more recent example see *Atlas* [1996] OJ L239/23.

[50]   Case IV/36.213/F2 *GEAE/P & W* [2000] OJ L58/16.

[51]   Or in the case of a joint venture where the parent companies operate on the same market as the joint venture. F E González Díaz, 'Joint Ventures under EC Competition Law: the New Boundaries', at 1029.

[52]   The likelihood of coordination between the new JV and the other duopolist on the market was analysed in *P&O Stena Line* [1999] OJ L163/61, where the Commission concluded that despite the combination of the ferry operations of P&O and Stena in the proposed JV and Eurotunnel, they were expected to compete with each other, rather than act in parallel to raise prices on the short Channel crossing tourist market. The joint venture was thus exempted under Art 81(3) for a period of three years. The exemption was renewed in 2001 for an additional period of six years (See Press Release in IP/01/806 of 7 June 2001). See also F E González Díaz, 'Recent Developments in EC Merger Control with Regard to Remedies and Joint Ventures' [April 1999] SEW 144-165.

[53]   Stephen Martin, 'Joint Ventures and Market Performance in Oligopoly', EUI Working Papers No 88/368, Florence, 1988, at 1.

ie economically rational. Such a situation may arise, in particular, when the parent companies in question, either on their own or in combination with third parties, acquire and/or increase their ability to raise prices above the competitive level and/or to exclude competitors, ie whenever they acquire or increase their market power beyond some significant level.

In the context of homogeneous products, this can be the case, in particular, whenever the establishment of a JV leads to the creation of a market setting in which anti-competitive parallel behaviour becomes a rational option for the parent companies or for the parent companies and third parties.[54]   **7.64**

For heterogeneous products, be they in the same or in neighbouring relevant markets, coordination may become a rational option, in particular, where the parent companies, as a result of the creation of the JV, can acquire or increase their market power by taking advantage of the product range effect deriving from the coordination of their competing brands,[55] for instance by favouring their JV to the detriment of third parties.   **7.65**

One of the key issues in deciding whether the setting up of a JV would lead to the coordination of the competitive behaviour of the parent companies or of the parent companies and their JV is the causal link between the creation of the JV and this putative coordination. In other terms, in what way does the creation of a JV modify the incentive of the parent companies to compete?[56]   **7.66**

There are a number of factors, other than the ability to exercise market power, that can have a bearing on the incentive of the parent companies to compete after the creation of a joint venture. Such factors include the ownership and control structure operating within the new entity,[57] the size of the joint venture compared to that of the parents' independent operations,[58] the duration of the agreement,[59] the degree and the extent of the exchange of   **7.67**

---

[54] The need for tacit coordination with third parties would be required in those situations where the parent companies (and the JV where the parents operate in the same product and geographic market as the JV) do not jointly have market power.

[55] For an application of the product range effect theory in the context of merger control see Case IV/M.938 *Guinness/Grand Metropolitan* [1998] OJ L288/24.

[56] For a review of the economic literature on the non-coordinated effects of the setting up of JVs see generally F E González Díaz, 'Joint Ventures under EC Competition Law: the New Boundaries'.

[57] Variations in the ownership and control of the JV may significantly affect the incentives of the parent companies to continue competing with each other or with the JV. The greater the parent's stake in the JV, the less likely the parent will continue to compete against the venture in the relevant market. See Robert Pitofsky, 'Joint Ventures Under the Antitrust Laws: Some Reflections on the Significance of Penn-Olin' (1969) 82 Harv. L. Rev. at 1007, 1012. Similarly, the parent's ability to coordinate its independent business decisions with those of the JV increases as its control over the venture increases. A controlling parent may attempt to ensure that the joint venture does not cannibalise the parent's independent sales in the JV market. See TF Bresnahan and SC Salop, 'Quantifying the Competitive Effects of Production Joint Ventures' (1986) 4 Intl. J. Ind. Org. 155, 156. However, this approach is probably more relevant to the analysis of the non-co-operative effects of the operation of the JV than to the analysis of collusion.

[58] For example, a 50% stake in a venture that is five times larger than the parent's independent operations in the relevant market will reduce the incentive of the parent to compete against the JV. See E Kitch, 'The Antitrust Economics of Joint Ventures' (1987) 54 Antitrust L. J. at 957, 962.

[59] The shorter the duration, the more likely the parties will continue to compete against each other in markets affected by the JV. Indeed, when the duration of the JV is limited, the parents will continue to compete in the relevant market knowing that their collaboration's end is on the near horizon. See A Piriano, 'Beyond Per Se, Rule of Reason or Merger Analysis: A New Antitrust Standard for Joint Ventures' (1991) 76 Minn. L. Rev. 1, 65.

commercially sensitive information,[60] etc. All these factors may be examined at a number of levels.

7.68 **(ii) Spillovers on the same market as a joint venture**   If the parents are present on the same market as the JV the first question to address is whether the JV will reduce the incentive of the parent companies to compete on that market.

7.69 The likelihood of anti-competitive effects will depend, other than on the structural characteristics of the relevant market, upon the economic importance of the JV to the parents. Thus if the JV produces a significant proportion of the parents' output it can lead to a coordination of all their interests on that market. The 1993 Notice on co-operative JVs includes, in paragraph 26, a reference to the criteria to be applied in assessing whether a JV leads to an appreciable restriction of competition, and in particular to the coordination of the parents' behaviour. However, these are only qualitative indications. The Commission's practice to date has been to apply Article 81(1) almost automatically to a JV between competitors and to aggregate their market share in the assessment.

7.70 The *Exxon/Shell* decision of 1994 is a rare example where the coordination effect is discussed in more detail. Exxon and Shell agreed to create a JV, Cipen, to produce certain grades of polyethylene (PE) in Europe. This PE would be supplied back exclusively to the parents who would then sell on to final consumers. Shell and Exxon had a combined share of 20 per cent of the EU production capacity for these grades of PE and the JV represented 17 per cent of this combined capacity. The Commission argued that:

> the flow of information between Exxon and Shell allowed by the JV structure is the basis on which each partner can plan its polyethylene production and adapt it to the choices of the other partner [. . .]. In fact any increased reduction or halt in production decided by one partner in order to adjust its behaviour to one other partner's choices in the joint venture entails a general reconsideration of the production plans of all (polyethylene) sites belonging to that partner's group.[61]

7.71 As a result, the Commission concluded that the parents would be likely to coordinate their behaviour on the EU market for these grades of PE through the JV. Therefore the agreement fell under Article 81(1).

7.72 It is not just the relative importance of a JV to the parents' activities on the market that will determine whether they will coordinate their behaviour. The greater the parents' combined market share on the market the stronger the incentive there is for them to coordinate and hence even a smaller JV can be the source of anti-competitive coordination.

7.73 The Commission has stated on several occasions that it is necessary to undertake an economic analysis of the incentives on the parents to coordinate their behaviour, as well as the effects of doing so in order to assess whether a JV will lead to an 'appreciable' restriction of competition.

---

[60] JVs may serve as conduits for coordinating the participants' market behaviour or for exchanging competitively sensitive information. See J Kattan, 'Antitrust Analysis of Technology Joint Ventures: Allocative Efficiency and the Rewards of Innovation' (1993) 61 Antitrust L. J. at 937, 949.

[61] *Exxon/Shell* [1994] OJ L144/20, para 63.

This was reconfirmed by the Court in the more recent judgment on the *European Night* **7.74** *Services* decision.[62] In the original 1994 decision,[63] the Commission exempted, with certain conditions, a JV, European Night Services, between several European rail companies to provide train services through the Channel Tunnel to cities beyond London, Paris and Brussels. However the parties appealed against this decision arguing that the JV in fact did not fall under Article 81(1) at all and that the Commission had not provided sufficient reasoning for its decision. The Court upheld the appeal on a variety of grounds including the fact that the Commission had not demonstrated sufficient economic reasoning that the agreements fell under Article 81(1).[64]

(iii) Spillovers on to other markets   The second question to answer is whether the JV **7.75** may provide a means for coordination of the parties' behaviour on an adjacent product or geographic market. Typically these markets will be upstream or downstream of the co-operation.

Spillovers on to downstream markets   Joint production of an input that represents a sig- **7.76** nificant proportion of the costs of the final product may significantly reduce the scope for competition on the downstream product market.

The *Philips/Osram* decision of 1994[65] illustrates this concept. The case concerned a JV to **7.77** manufacture lead glass tubing for incandescent and fluorescent lamps. The parties had approximately 65 per cent of the EEA capacity for the production of lead glass. The parties also produced, separately, the final lamps and produced over two-thirds of the European market for lamps. They were also competitors in most segments of this downstream lamp market. However, the lead glass tubing represented only 0.67 per cent of the final costs of the lamp, and therefore, even though there were other small elements of common cost structure, the Commission concluded that: 'given the very small importance of lead glass on the manufacturing costs of lamps, such standardisation is not considered relevant enough to constitute a restriction of competition'.

Spillovers on to adjacent product markets   If the parties are competitors on markets other **7.78** than that of the JV the mere fact of having made significant investment in a JV on one market may reduce the incentive to compete as actively in these markets. However, this would only be likely if these markets are closely related. The Commission Notice on co-operative joint ventures[66] noted in paragraph 41 that:

> Where the JV operates on a market adjacent to that of its parents, competition can only be restricted when there is a high degree of interdependence between the two markets. This is especially the case when the JV manufactures products that are complementary to those of its parents.

---

[62] [1998] ECJ II-3141.
[63] *European Night Services* [1994] OJ L259/20.
[64] See in particular paras 135–160 of the judgment.
[65] *Philips/Osram* [1994] OJ L378/37.
[66] Notice Concerning the Assessment of co-operative joint ventures pursuant to Article 85 [now Article 81] of the EEC treaty [1993] OJ C43/2.

7.79 The Commission has never taken a formal decision based on these potential spillover effects. In the *Ford/Volkswagen* decision of 1992,[67] concerning a JV to develop a range of multi-purpose vehicles, so-called 'people carriers', the Commission noted that:

> the co-operation between Ford and VW will furthermore lead to an extensive exchange and sharing of, *inter alia*, technical know-how which could affect the competitive behaviour of the two partners in neighbouring market segments like those of estate cars or light vans.

7.80 However, the main reason why the Commission argued that this JV fell within Article 81(1) remained the fact that two major competitors on the EU car market were jointly developing a major new product.

7.81 *Spillovers on to adjacent geographic markets*   The argument that a JV can limit competition on adjacent markets applies equally to adjacent geographic markets. In the *Atlas* decision of 1996,[68] the Commission exempted a JV, Atlas, between France Telecom (FT), and Deutsche Telekom (DT), to provide international telecom services to corporate customers. However, several conditions were imposed upon the parents. In particular, there was concern that neither parent would enter each other's domestic market after the full liberalisation of the telecommunications market in 1998. Under the JV agreement each parent would distribute Atlas services within its own national market and refrain from active selling of such services into each other's home market. The Commission required the divestiture of a FT subsidiary in Germany.

7.82 **(iv) Network effects**   Finally, a JV may also be one of several JVs between the parents in the same or related markets. Individually these JVs may not be regarded as sufficient to lead to a restriction of competition but the combined effect of several such JVs may be. These are commonly referred to as *network effects*.

7.83 The situations in which networks of JVs may give rise to concern were well described in the Notice on co-operative joint ventures (paragraphs 27–31). In essence a JV should not be assessed without taking account of all other relevant interests of the parents on that market or on related markets.

7.84 The *Optical Fibres* decision of July 1986[69] usefully illustrates this concern. In this case the Commission ultimately granted an exemption to a series of JV agreements between Corning, a US producer of glass fibre for fibre optic cable, and a number of EU cable manufacturers. The agreements were designed to develop and produce fibre optic cable for EU markets. While the Commission noted that neither Corning nor its individual European partners were actual or potential competitors for the manufacture of fibre optic cables, the individual JVs were. The Commission argued that Corning's presence as a common party to each JV would restrict competition between them, hence Article 81(1) applied. Therefore, as a condition for exemption, Corning's individual influence on each JV was reduced and they were required to meet unsolicited orders into each other's territory.

7.85 In the *European Night Services* judgment of 1998, overturning the earlier Commission Decision of 1994, the Court rejected the Commission's argument that the fact that the parents had interests in a series of other JVs to transport goods and passengers through the

---

[67] *Ford/Volkswagen* [1993] OJ L20/14.
[68] *Atlas* [1996] OJ L239/23.
[69] [1986] OJ L236/30.

Channel Tunnel would lead to a restriction of competition. In particular the Commission was concerned about the ACI JV between BR and SNCF to transport goods through the tunnel and the Autocare Europe JV between BR and SNCB to transport motor vehicles. In rejecting the Commission's arguments the Court noted that these JVs were not in the same market as ENS, passenger services, but in related markets. The 1993 Notice stated that when parent undertakings set up JVs for 'non-complementary' services competition may be restricted when these 'non-complementary' services are marketed by the parent undertakings themselves. However in this case none of the parents sold the services of these JVs themselves and the Commission in its decision did not explain how the participation of the parents in such a network of JVs would lead to a restriction of competition. Therefore the Court rejected this element of the Commission decision.

(7) Direct Contractual Restrictions between Parents

There can be express restrictions of competition between the parents of a JV resulting from direct contractual agreements between them. Agreements to fix prices or share markets would fall automatically within Article 81(1). Other restrictions would have to be assessed on an individual basis taking into account the presence of the parties on all affected markets. These restrictions would be assessed under the procedures laid down in Regulation 1/2003 as for all other co-operation agreements. However, those restrictions that are directly related to the setting up and functioning of a JV and are regarded as necessary for the operation of the JV may be ancillary to the JV and as such assessed together with the JV.[70] For instance, in its *Cégétel + 4* decision,[71] the Commission cleared the creation of a joint venture between Vivendi and various telecom operators containing a non-compete clause. Such a restriction of competition was considered to be the product of a commitment by all the parent companies to guarantee that each of them would channel its activities in France through the new company. Further, the Commission also cleared an exclusive distribution agreement whereby Cégétel would be the only distributor of the services supplied by the parents on the ground that it would contribute to ensure competition with France Telecom, then dominant on the market. The argument of creating or improving competition on the market through the market entry of the JV was also put forward in *Télévision Par Satellite (TPS)*, where many restrictive agreements ancillary to the creation of a new operator on the pay-TV market were exempted on the ground that they were essential for the new company successfully to enter the market and compete with the incumbent monopoly, Canal+/Canal Satellite.[72]

7.86

(8) Spillovers under the Merger Regulation

As outlined above the Merger Regulation allows for the coordination effects arising from a full function co-operative JV to be assessed under Article 81.[73] This results from the 1997

7.87

---

[70] 1993 Notice on co-operative JVs, part V; see also Commission Notice on restrictions directly related and necessary to concentrations [2001] OJ C188/5.

[71] [1999] OJ L218/14. The Commission also authorised the creation of a JV between Cégétel and the SNCF, the French national railway company which would provide telecommunications services along the railway network (*Télécom Développement* [1999] OJ L218/24).

[72] [1999] OJ L90/6.

[73] See Art 2(4) of the Regulation.

amendment to the first Merger Regulation (which entered into force in March 1998), which was kept intact in the current Merger Regulation of 2004. Since 1997, the Commission has examined a significant number of full function JVs where there were possible coordination effects.[74] The majority of these JVs have been set up in the telecoms, Internet, or related industries. Due to the number of closely related markets in these sectors JVs are perhaps more likely to lead to spillover effects.

7.88 It should be stressed from the outset that the Commission has chosen not to issue guidelines on the application of Article 2(4) to the spillover effects stemming from the setting up of a joint venture. Indeed, at footnote 3 of its Notice on the concept of full function JVs it stated that it intended, in due course, to provide guidance on the application of Article 2(4). Pending the adoption of such guidance, interested parties are referred to the principles set out in paragraphs 17 to 20 of its 1994 Notice on the distinction between concentrative and co-operative joint ventures.[75]

7.89 However, early decisions applying Article 2(4) have proved to be extremely helpful in providing guidance as to the way in which the Commission intends to apply this provision of the Merger Regulation. In that respect, the adoption of Regulation 1310/97 might constitute a significant departure from the Commission's traditional approach to the notion of restriction of competition, at least with regard to the spillover effect generated by structural operations, and the consolidation of a more economic driven analysis of this type of economic phenomenon.

7.90 The first case in which the Commission had the opportunity to develop its new approach towards the spillover effects stemming from the creation of a full function joint venture under Article 2(4) was *Telia/Telenor/Schibsted* (Case IV/JV.1) (1998).

7.91 This case concerned the setting up of a JV (Scandinavia OnLine) between Schibsted Multimedia AS,[76] Telenor Nextel AS[77] and Telia AB[78] for the provision of certain Internet services to consumers and business customers mainly in Sweden. The JV company was to take over the assets and activities of Telia InfoMedia and Scandinavia On-Line AB (SOL) and to operate on the market for web site production for third parties, including design of web sites and related programming (services were to be provided in the Swedish language).

7.92 After finding that the operation constituted a concentrative joint venture within the meaning of Article 3 of the Merger Regulation, the Commission proceeded to the definition of

---

[74] (October 1998) 3 Competition Policy Newsletter, 30.

[75] [1994] OJ C385/1.

[76] Telia AB, wholly owned by the Swedish State, was the main telecommunications operator in Sweden, providing a broad range of telecommunications services both in Sweden and abroad, including enhanced services through its shareholding in Unisource. Telia was also an Internet Service Provider (ISP). Internet services in the Swedish language were provided by Telia InfoMedia Interactive AB.

[77] Telenor AS was the main Norwegian telecommunications operator. Its subsidiary, Telenor Nextel AS, offered a number of Internet related services. It was a shareholder in Telenordia (33%, the other parent companies are BT and TeleDanmark), which provided telecommunications services in the Swedish market. Telenordia's subsidiary Algonet was an ISP on the Swedish market.

[78] The Norwegian Schibsted group was involved in a range of media related activities such as newspapers, television, films and multimedia. Its subsidiary Schibsted Multimedia AS had a number of Internet related activities, including the provision of content, in Sweden via Scandinavia On-Line AB, which was jointly owned by Telenor AS. Schibsted also had a stake in Aftonbladet, a newspaper in Sweden, which also had an Internet edition.

the relevant product and geographic markets for the purposes of its assessment under the dominance test (Article 2(3) of the First Merger Regulation). The Commission defined three relevant markets, all of them having a national dimension or possibly a linguistic dimension: the markets for Internet advertising, paid-for content provision, and web site production. It found that the operation did not create a dominant position in any of these markets.

7.93 With regard to Article 2(4), the Commission defined, at point 28 of the decision, what appears to be a new, more economic-driven, approach to the treatment of spillover effects under Article 81(1). Indeed, according to the Commission, '[i]n order to establish a restriction of competition in the sense of Article 85(1) [now Article 81(1)] EC-Treaty, it is necessary that the coordination of the parent companies' competitive behaviour is likely and appreciable and that it results from the creation of the joint venture, be it as its object or its effect'.

7.94 In this regard, it should be noted that, although the requirement of appreciability was already part of the Commission's normal practice in dealing with spillover effects, the need to show likelihood on more than a purely theoretical basis and, above all, the requirement to prove causality constitute two significant and welcome developments in the Commission's approach to the applicability of Article 81(1) to JVs.

7.95 Having defined the framework for analysis under Article 81(1), the Commission proceeded to the identification of the so-called candidate markets for coordination, ie those on which the JV and at least two parent companies are active, or closely related neighbouring markets where at least two parent companies remain active. The Commission identified two candidate markets for coordination: (i) web site production and related services; and (ii) dial-up Internet access.[79]

7.96 Dial-up Internet access was considered a candidate market for coordination because Telia and Telenordia (Algonet) provided dial-up Internet access to users and because access to the Internet is a necessary prerequisite for any use of the Internet. This market was thus considered as a market upstream to the JV's markets and thus as closely related to the JV's markets.[80]

7.97 As far as the assessment under Article 2(4) is concerned, the Commission reached the following conclusions:

(a) In the absence of clear indications to prove that the object of the creation of the JV is the coordination of the competitive behaviour of the parent companies, an intended coordination of the parent companies' behaviour could not be established (decision at point 38). However, the effect of the operation might be to give way to the coordination of competitive behaviour.

---

[79] See points 29 to 37 of the decision. With regard to geographic market definition, the Commission found that for web site production the relevant geographic market was at least as wide as Sweden or Sweden plus the Swedish language communities in other Nordic countries. However, the Commission indicated there were no technical barrier to these services being provided outside Sweden and the Nordic countries. The Internet services of the JV would be offered in the Swedish language for private and business users in Sweden. Although access to Internet content in Sweden was available from outside Sweden, this did not widen the market definition as the content offered was aimed specifically at consumers in Sweden. Therefore, the relevant geographic market for dial-up Internet access was defined as Sweden.

[80] It is to be noted that the impact of the JV on the web site and related services market was already assessed and cleared under the old dominance test.

(b) On the web site production market, the Commission indicated that the combined market share of the parent companies did not exceed [. . .][81] per cent and the JV would have a market share of [. . .][82] per cent. The Commission considered that this total market share of [. . .][83] per cent on the Swedish market, which was the narrowest and most unfavourable to the parties, in any event, would not allow the conclusion that any restriction of competition was appreciable.

Therefore, the Commission concluded that even if the parent companies were to coordinate their activities on the web site production market this coordination could not lead to an appreciable restriction of competition and that, as a result, it was not necessary to establish a causal link between the creation of the JV and the behaviour of the parent companies outside the JV on this closely related market.

(c) With regard to the dial-up Internet access market, the Commission found that it was characterised by high growth[84] and relatively low barriers to entry. The costs of starting a small ISP providing a dial-up service were low and small companies can and do provide dial-up Internet access. According to the information supplied by the parties, there were around 100 such ISPs in Sweden. Entry was also possible from both local start-up ISPs and global ISPs. In addition, as the market was very price-sensitive, in particular given low switching costs, this would prevent higher prices through coordination from being sustained. Any increase in prices would result in the parties quickly losing market share to rival companies as new subscribers opted for lower price offerings.

7.98 Telia was present on this market. Telenor, through Telenordia (the other parent companies being BT and TeleDanmark), was also present. Telia and Telenordia held substantial market shares.[85] However, the Commission considered that market shares were of limited significance in this growing market. In any case, the combined market share of Telia and Telenordia had fallen by between 15 and 20 per cent of the total market over the last nine months.

7.99 Against this background, the Commission concluded that the market structure was not conducive to coordination of competitive behaviour. The Commission also stated that the relative size of the markets for Internet advertising, content and web site production (the markets of the JV), compared with that of dial-up Internet access, was relevant to the likelihood of coordination. The dial-up Internet access market was substantially larger than the other markets[86]

---

81 Business secret: less than 5%.

82 Business secret: less than 5%.

83 Business secret: less than 10%.

84 According to information obtained during the Commission's investigation, the growth rate in Sweden in the three years following the decision would be around 30%.

85 Telia had a 30–40% market share and Telenordia had 15–20% of the market. The largest service provider offering dial-up Internet access in Sweden was Tele2 (a telecommunications company which is a member of the Kinnevik Group, a leading Nordic media company), which had at the time of the investigation a 40–50% market share. However, on the basis of other information received, it appeared that if the market share of Telenordia were to be attributed to Telenor, their total market share would be 45–60%. This data was based on information obtained from the notifying parties and other third parties during the investigation.

86 According to information obtained by the Commission during its investigation, the proportion of revenues derived from access was 93% in Sweden compared with 7% from all other Internet revenue sources.

and, therefore, given the relative sizes of the markets concerned, the likelihood of coordination was reduced further.[87]

The Commission thus found that, even on the basis of the narrowest market definition, there was no likelihood that the parent companies would coordinate their competitive behaviour on the dial-up Internet access market and it was therefore not necessary to establish a causal link between the creation of the JV and the behaviour of the parent companies outside the JV on this related market. **7.100**

The approach developed in these early cases has been confirmed in more recent merger decisions adopted by the Commission. A good example may be the clearance decision in *Sony/BMG* (Case COMP/M.3333) (2004). **7.101**

In January 2004, Sony and BMG notified their agreement to create a new JV, SonyBMG, that aimed to combine their recorded music businesses worldwide, except for Japan. The scope of the JV only covered the so-called 'Artist and Repertoire' (A&R) activities, which comprise the discovery and development of performing artists as well as the marketing and sale of the records. A number of related activities (eg manufacturing and physical distribution, music publishing, etc) were thus kept outside the JV and remained in the hands of the parents. **7.102**

The structure of the record industry was characterised by the presence of five 'majors', including both Sony and BMG. Following the creation of the JV, Universal and SonyBMG would both hold about 25 per cent of the market, ahead of EMI and Warner. The Commission noted that market demand had been declining since 2000 although some signs of a market recovery were detected in certain countries. **7.103**

The Commission analysed the case under the substantial test of Regulation 4089/89 (as the case was notified before the entry into force of Regulation 139/2004). The Commission decided to open an in-depth investigation in connection with the three relevant markets where the JV would be active: recorded music, licences for online music and online music distribution. In addition, it also assessed whether the JV would lead to coordination between its partners on a closely related market: the music publishing market. **7.104**

---

[87] In Case IV/JV.5 *Cegetel/Canal+/AOL/Bertelsmann* (1998) the Commission took into account, in excluding the likelihood of coordination in a vertically related market, the provision of network distribution services, the fact that, according to the parties, the JV would not be the main customer for the network distribution services provided by the parent companies. Their infrastructures were to be used primarily for telecommunications and TV distribution and not for dial-up Internet access services respectively, so the JV would not create economically meaningful incentives for coordination in network distribution service offerings to ISPs. In Case IV/JV.12 *Ericsson/Nokia/Psion* (1998) the Commission found that the creation of a JV would not lead to the coordination of the competitive behaviour of the parent companies on the downstream markets for wireless information devices and mobile phones. With regard to wireless information devices, the Commission based its analysis on the lack of commonality of costs, the fact that the cost of the operating system produced by the JV was likely to be relatively low as an overall proportion of the costs of the wireless information devices, the presence of actual or potential competition, the need to establish the new operating system on the market, the ongoing development of this kind of device (decision, points 31, 32 and 33) and the wide scope for product differentiation (decision, points 34 and 35). With regard to mobile phones, the Commission's analysis rested on the fact that the operating system to be developed by the JV would not be included in mobile phones, on the lack of direct connection between the JV and the technology used in mobile phones, on the existence of sufficient actual competition (despite the fact that Nokia and Ericsson account together for around 50% of the market), on market performance (prices have decreased steadily over the past five years) and on the relative sizes of the markets (the revenue from the JV would be extremely small in proportion to the overall revenue generated by their mobile telephony activities) (decision, points 37 and 38).

7.105   Whereas the Commission's analysis of collective dominance attracted most of the attention by commentators, the decision also contains an interesting assessment of the possible spillover effects of the transaction on the upstream markets for music publishing.[88] Music publishers manage the rights of authors and composers as opposed to record companies which sign singers and other performing artists. The Commission concluded that coordination was unlikely as the management of mechanical rights (due by the record companies for the reproduction of musical creations) and performance rights (payable by radio and TV broadcasters, concert organisers and the like for the public performance of music) is mainly carried out by collecting societies such as GEMA in Germany and SACEM in France. Licences are normally granted by those entities on a non-discriminatory basis and royalties are determined by them in agreement with publishers, authors and composers. The Commission therefore concluded that coordination was unlikely.

7.106   To sum up the Commission's approach can be described as follows:

(a) The Commission determines first whether the JV performs on a lasting basis all the functions of an autonomous economic entity. If it does the Merger Regulation applies. In reaching this conclusion account must be taken of the Notice on the notion of full function joint ventures of 2 March 1998.

(b) Once the JV has been characterised as a concentration the Commission will examine whether it significantly impedes effective competition, in the common market or in a substantial part of it, in particular as a result of the creation or strengthening of a dominant position.

(c) The Commission will proceed then to examine whether the creation of the JV will lead to the coordination[89] of the competitive behaviour of the parent companies on the JV market or on related markets (upstream, downstream or neighbouring).

---

[88] Paras 176 ff of the decision.

[89] In assessing the likelihood of coordination the Commission will take into account both actual and potential competition. See in this sense Case IV/JV2 *ENEL/FT/DT* (1998). This case concerned the creation of a JV, WIND Telecomunicazioni SpA (Wind) between ENEL SpA (ENEL), France Telecom SA (FT) and Deutsche Telekom (DT) for the provision of a full range of domestic and international telecommunications services combining mobile and fixed line telecommunications activities to business and residential customers located in Italy, in competition with the incumbent telecommunications operator, Telecom Italia, and other new market entrants. Following the methodology laid down in its *Telia* decision, the Commission identified the following candidate markets for coordination of the competitive behaviour of FT and DT: fixed line telephony, ie domestic and international voice and data telecommunications services in Italy, France and Germany, advance international services, and mobile telephony in Italy and in Western Europe. As to the domestic and international voice and data telecommunications services in Italy, the Commission considered that in view of the substantial investments in Wind which both FT and DT had already made or would need to make, it was unlikely that they would enter these markets on their own in the future. The markets for domestic and international voice and data telecommunications services in France and Germany were considered as closely related markets within the meaning of Art 2(4) in view of their geographic proximity and their importance to Italy. (Germany and France are the two most important countries for Italy in terms of bilateral traffic. In 1997, for example, bilateral traffic between Italy and Germany alone amounted to around 700 million minutes.) Both DT and FT hold a strong (if not dominant) position in these markets in their respective countries. FT has not so far expanded its operations to Germany to any important degree since it sold its shares in Info AG in the context of the Atlas/GlobalOne transaction. Neither had DT entered the French markets to any noticeable extent. FT and DT could however be considered as at least potential competitors on the French and German markets. A recent analysis of potential competition (with a negative conclusion) can be found in Case COMP/M.3817 *Wegener/PCM/JV* (2005).

(d) In doing so, the Commission will identify first the candidate markets for coordination, ie those markets in which the parent companies either compete or are in a vertical or conglomerate relationship.[90] Secondly it will determine whether the coordination of the parent's competitive behaviour is likely, appreciable, and results from the creation of the JV be it as its object or its effect. If any of these tests are not met Article 2(4) does not apply and the Commission does not examine the other ones.

(e) With regard to the likelihood of coordination test, the Commission seems to focus on the question whether the market characteristics, including the market position of the JV

---

[90] In Case IV/M.1327 *NC/Canal+/CDPQ/BankAmerica* (1998), the Commission had the opportunity to examine the effects of the setting up of a JV in the French pay TV market on a neighbouring market (the Spanish pay TV market) under Art 2(4) of the amended Merger Regulation. This case concerned the acquisition of joint control by Canal+, Caisse de dépôt et placement du Québec, and BankAmerica Corporation over Numéricable (NC), a French cable television network operator previously controlled by Canal+. After concluding that the notified operation did not give rise either to the creation or strengthening of a dominant position or to the coordination of the competitive behaviour of the parent companies in the French pay TV market, the Commission assessed the impact of the notified transaction on the Spanish pay TV market including the wholesale supply of films and sports channels for retail pay TV under Art 2(4). This assessment was based on the fact that: (a) the BankAmerica and CDPQ's groups have controlling interests (joint control) in Cableuropa, a significant network cable operator in the Spanish pay TV market and a buyer of pay TV rights; and (b) Sogecable (a significant supplier of pay TV rights in Spain) is under joint control of Prisa and Canal+. Therefore, all the undertakings concerned were active both in the same product/service market as NC (pay television) and in the vertically related market (the wholesale supply of films and sports channels for retail pay TV) in a neighbouring geographical market (Spain). The Commission had thus to examine the potential anti-competitive spillover effects arising out of the newly created link between Canal+/Sogecable and BankAmerica-CDPQ/Cableuropa in the Spanish pay TV market. In making this assessment the Commission took into account the significant position of Sogecable in the Spanish TV market and the highly concentrated nature of this market. As to the possibility of vertical coordination between Canal+/Sogecable and BankAmerica-CDPQ/ Cableuropa (a buyer of pay TV rights in Spain), the Commission concluded that, as a result of the NC deal, there were strong indications (amounting to serious doubts within the meaning of Art 6(1)(c) of the Merger Regulation) that both companies had a significant incentive to coordinate their competitive behaviour at least with regard to access to Sogecable's content. In particular, the Commission deemed that Canal+ had a strong incentive to favour Cableuropa in its supply arrangements to the detriment of other players in the cable segment of the pay TV market in Spain. The Commission based its conclusion on Cableuropa's significant and real power to retaliate against Canal+ in France if it was not given favourable conditions in the access to the audio-visual rights that it needs to develop its pay TV activities in Spain and on the fact that some days after the NC deal was signed, Sogecable and Cableuropa reached a content distribution agreement on a non-exclusive basis.

Although the notifying parties contested this analysis they submitted undertakings to the Commission in order to remove the competitive concerns raised by the Commission with regard to the Spanish pay TV market. These undertakings essentially consisted of an obligation not to discriminate in the granting of access to pay TV rights for as long as the conditions in the Spanish market and the shareholdings of Canal+, BankAmerica and CDPQ in Sogecable, Cableuropa and NC remained substantially the same. The Commission concluded that the undertakings were sufficient to remove its serious doubts within the meaning of Art 6(1)(c) of the Merger Regulation and to render the concentration compatible with the common market.

This case illustrates how the Commission will not limit its assessment under Art 2(4) of the amended Merger Regulation to potential spillover effects on the same product and geographic markets as those of the JV or to horizontal coordination between the parent companies. Indeed, as shown in the *NC/Canal+/CDPQ/ BankAmerica* decision, the Commission will also examine the effects resulting from the creation of a JV in neighbouring markets both at the horizontal and vertical/conglomerate levels. Obviously, the Commission's findings in this case were strongly conditioned by the very strong position held by Sogecable in the Spanish pay TV market and by the need to limit the creation of further links, or of their effects, in an already highly concentrated market. See also, Case COMP/M.3099 *AREVA/Urenco/ETC* (2004), where the parties had to offer a number of commitments in order to mitigate the risk of coordination in a downstream market, in particular concerning capacity expansions.

and its size, are conducive to coordination of the competitive behaviour. As to the appreciability test, the Commission seems to go beyond the strict limits imposed by the Notice on agreements of minor importance. Finally, as regards the causality test, the Commission examines whether or not the creation of the JV, and not any other factor such as the existence of previous links between the parent companies, is the real cause of the putative coordination of the competitive behaviour between the parent companies.[91] The Commission has followed this basic approach in various cases to date.[92]

---

[91] In Case IV/JV.2 *ENEL/FT/DT* (1998) the Commission found that the creation of Wind would not lead to the coordination of the competitive behaviour of FT and DT in each other's markets (ie the restriction of potential competition) on grounds of lack of causality. Indeed, according to the Commission: 'As mentioned above, DT and FT have already so far (at least since the Atlas/GlobalOne transaction) not competed strongly with each other in their respective home countries despite the possibilities to do so which the liberalisation of the telecommunications sector has created. The two companies have, through their joint venture Atlas, entered into a joint venture with Sprint Corporation (GlobalOne) for the purpose of providing advanced telecommunications services. The lack of competition on their respective home markets in the past therefore appears to stem from a deliberate choice on the part of these companies. It is not possible to claim with the requisite degree of certainty that such lack of competition (if it were to continue in the future) would be the result of the creation of Wind.'
The lack of causality argument has also been used by the Commission to conclude that the creation of a JV will not lead to the coordination of the competitive behaviour of two parent companies active on the same market as the JV in Case IV/JV.3 *BT/AirTouch/Grupo Acciona/Airtel* (1998) at point 25 and in Case IV/JV.4 *Viag/Orange* (1998) at point 32.
In Case IV/JV.5 *Cegetel/Canal+/AOL/Bertelsmann* (1998) the Commission concluded that although only Vivendi, one of the parent companies (via its Info On-Line site), had declared its intent to offer paid-for content in France, and had suspended its product line earlier that year, it could be stated that after the creation of the JV all four parties and the JV were also potential competitors on the paid-for content market, either because they developed content or because they were active in the traditional media market, and were therefore likely to use proprietary content to provide paid-for content. Therefore the Commission considered this market as a candidate market for coordination. With regard to network distribution services, the Commission equally considered the issue of potential competition in the following terms: 'Cegetel is the second long distance carrier on the French telecommunications market, as well as the second French mobile GSM operator. The notifying parties submitted that no other party to the concentration is active in France in the market for network distribution services for ISPs. However, Canal+ is active in the broadcasting (both analogue and digital), and the distribution of television services by cable and satellite. CanalSatellite, a general partnership managed by Canal+, has started testing a dial-up Internet access service via DTH satellite transmission. NC Numéricâble, a subsidiary of Canal+, operates cable networks for the provision of CA-TV in various locations in France. In particular, Télériviera, a company jointly owned by NC Numéricâble and TDS, a subsidiary of Cegetel, has experimented a dial-up Internet access service via its cable in the Nice area. In any case, cable modems allowing cable networks to be used as local loops have been developed, and although Numéricâble's cable network has not been used for this purpose yet, it is likely to be in the future.' However, the Commission cleared the transaction on grounds of lack of appreciable effect given the low market shares of the parties (below 10%).
[92] See, eg Case COMP/M.3333 *Sony/BMG* (2004); Case JV.55 *M. Hutchinson/RCP/ECT* (2001); Case JV.56 *Hutchinson/ECT* (2001); Case JV.37 *BSkyB/KirchPayTV* (2000); Case JV.17 *Mannesman/ Bell Atlantic/Omnitel* (2000); Case JV.19 *Alitalia/KLM* (2000); Case JV.18 *Chronopost/Correos* (1999); Case JV.25 *Sony/Time Warner/ CD Now* (1999); Case IV/JV.1 *Telia/Telenor/Schibsted* (1998); Case IV/JV.2 *ENEL/FT/DT* (1998); Case IV/JV.3 *BT/AirTouch/Grupo Acciona/AirTel* (1998); Case IV/JV.5 *Cegetel/Canal+/AOL/Bertelsmann* (1998); Case IV/JV.6 *Ericsson/Nokia/Psion* (1998); Case IV/JV.4 *Viag/Orange UK* (1998); Case IV/JV.7 *Telia/Sonera/ Lithuanian Telecommunications* (1998); Case IV/JV.9 *Telia/Sonera/ Motorola/Omnitel* (1998); Case IV/JV.11 *@ Home Benelux BV* (1998); Case IV/JV.8 *Deutsche Telekom/Springer/Holtzbrink/Infose* (1998); Case IV/JV.14 *Panagora/DG Bank* (1998); Case IV/M.1327 *NC/Canal+/CDPQ/BankAmerica* (1998); Case IV/JV.13 *Wintershall/ EnBW/MVV/ WV/DED* (1998); and Case IV/JV.15 *BT/AT&T* (1998). The Commission decided to open a detailed inquiry into a proposed JV between British Telecommunications and AT&T, two of the world's largest telecommunications operators. The joint venture would provide a broad range of telecommunications services to multinational corporate customers as well as international carrier services to other carriers. The Commission enquired into the effects

D. Research and Development Agreements

(1) Introduction

In many industries a company's level of innovation may become a key competitive factor. **7.107**
From pharmaceuticals to computing and electronics it is not just price and quality that give
firms a competitive edge but their technical know-how and ability to develop new products.

Co-operation at the level of research and development is therefore increasingly important to **7.108**
many companies. The costs and risks associated with R&D can be very high. Many companies choose therefore to co-operate to spread these risks. There are also potentially enormous
benefits in avoiding expensive duplication of effort and in the cross-fertilisation of ideas and
experience that come from R&D co-operation.[93] It is for these reasons that the Commission
has taken a generally positive view of R&D co-operation.

Co-operation in R&D can take place at many levels. In some cases the co-operation is in **7.109**
fundamental research projects far from the market often in collaboration with universities
or publicly funded research programmes. In other cases R&D constitutes basically no more
than incremental improvements to existing products and may be an adjunct to a joint production arrangement.

R&D agreements are equally structured in many different forms. These may range from JVs **7.110**
to subcontracting arrangements. However, the assessment of R&D arrangements should
not depend upon the legal form of the agreement.

The Commission has identified three types of competition problems in R&D agreements. **7.111**
The first is that the contractual terms affecting the exploitation of the results of the R&D
may limit competition. The second is that the agreement may not leave sufficient competition at the level of the R&D itself. The third is that as a result of the co-operation third
parties may be foreclosed from access to a given technology or R&D capability.

In most of the Commission's published Notices, including its Guidelines on horizontal **7.112**
co-operation agreements, and decisions it is the first problem that has most concerned the
Commission.

(2) Application of Article 81(1) to R&D Agreements

The Commission has often stated that it sees little problem with co-operation in R&D[94] **7.113**
and indeed, over the recent years it has actively encouraged, through the various Community

---

of the JV on several global telecommunications markets. The Commission expressed concerns in the following
areas: the parties' combined market position on the markets for the provision of global telecommunications services to large multinational companies and for international carrier services; the effect of the creation of the JV
leading to the possible creation or strengthening of a dominant position for certain telecommunications services
in the UK; and the possible coordination effects of the proposed JV in the UK between ACC, a wholly owned
subsidiary of AT&T, and between BT and Telewest, in which AT&T through TCI will have a jointly controlling
stake. The Commission did ultimately clear the transaction.

[93] See 2001 Horizontal Guidelines, para 40. Additionally, the Guidelines mention the necessity for SMEs
to co-operate with each other to undertake joint R&D efforts. A positive attitude towards this type of collab-
orations would lead to a more vigorous competition with stronger market players.

[94] Report on Competition Policy 1984 (Vol XIV); Report on Competition Policy 1985 (Vol XV).

research programmes, co-operation in R&D and in the dissemination of its results. R&D agreements are also one of the few types of horizontal agreements to benefit from a block exemption.[95] This Regulation has been supplemented with the Commission's Guidelines on horizontal co-operation agreements. However, despite all these legislative efforts, there remains some confusion as to when co-operation in R&D will fall under Article 81. Many companies find it difficult to assess the potential effect of such agreements on markets where there may not yet be an actual product and there is no guarantee as to whether the R&D will be successful.

7.114 The following subsections examine the different legal issues raised by R&D agreements under Article 81, preceded by a brief description of the R&D block exemption.

7.115 **(i) Basic framework in the R&D block exemption** The R&D block exemption, in common with most block exemptions, does not explicitly define when a R&D agreement falls within Article 81(1). Instead it states that to the extent that agreements covered by the block exemption do fall within Article 81(1) they would be exempted. The 2001 Horizontal Guidelines are more helpful in this respect, as they make clear that some agreements 'do not fall under Article 81(1)', ie generally 'most R&D agreements', and in particular, 'R&D co-operation between non-competitors' and 'pure' research agreements;[96] and that certain others are 'almost always' caught by this provision, ie disguised hardcore cartels.[97] All the cases falling between these two extremes of the spectrum will deserve a more detailed analysis, a description of which can be found in the block exemption and the Horizontal Guidelines.

7.116 The block exemption Regulation excludes the application of Article 81(1) to agreements between two or more undertakings concerning the following matters, as well as all the ancillary provisions that may be 'directly related to and necessary for their implementation':[98]

(a) joint research and development of products or processes and joint exploitation of the results of that research and development;

(b) joint exploitation of the results of research and development of products or processes jointly carried out pursuant to a prior agreement between the same parties; or

(c) joint research and development of products or processes excluding joint exploitation of the results.[99]

7.117 The block exemption recognises the importance of market power to an assessment of R&D agreements and it therefore gives some useful guidance as to which markets should be considered when assessing R&D co-operation.

7.118 The block exemption states in recital 15 that:

It is necessary to exclude from the block exemption agreements between competitors whose combined share of the market for products capable of being improved or replaced by the results of the research and development exceeds a certain level at the time agreement is entered into.

---

[95] Commission Regulation (EC) 2659/2000 of 29 November 2000 [2000] OJ L304/7 (replacing Regulation (EEC) 418/85 of 19 December 1984 [1985] OJ L53/5).

[96] 'Pure' R&D agreements refer to those which do not include the joint exploitation of results by means of licensing, production and/or marketing (2001 Horizontal Guidelines, para 58).

[97] 2001 Horizontal Guidelines, paras 55–58 and 59.

[98] Block exemption Regulation, Art 1(2).

[99] Block exemption Regulation, Art 1(1).

As a result, Article 4 of the block exemption sets out limits to its application depending **7.119** upon the market share of the parties on possibly affected markets.

Article 4(1) of the block exemption states: **7.120**

> Where the participating undertakings are *not competing undertakings*, the exemption pro-
> vided for in Article 1 shall apply for the duration of the research and development. Where the
> results are jointly exploited, the exemption shall continue to apply for seven years from the
> time the contract products are first put on the market within the common market.

This article grants the benefit of the block exemption to those R&D agreements where the **7.121** parents are not already present on the product markets likely to be affected by the results of the R&D. Thus a R&D agreement covering a completely new product in a new market would be covered by the Regulation. Similarly a new product that might compete in an existing market on which the parents were not present would also be covered by the exemp- tion. There is *no* market share limit for the duration of the R&D programme and for the first seven years after the product is first put on the market.

Article 4(3) sets out the conditions of application of the block exemption after the end of **7.122** seven years:

> the exemption shall continue to apply as long as the combined market share of the participat-
> ing undertakings does not exceed 25% of the relevant market for the contract products.

However, if the R&D relates to improvements to existing products or to new products that **7.123** are capable of replacing the parties' existing products on a market, then the Commission imposes a market share threshold in Article 4(2) *ab initio*:

> the exemption [. . .] shall apply [. . .] only if, at the time the agreement is entered into, the
> combined market share of the participating undertakings does not exceed 25% of the rele-
> vant market for the contract products.

The Commission presumes that if the parties have some degree of market power on the **7.124** 'existing' product market they may be able to reduce or delay innovation on this market.

It must be noted as well that the block exemption contains a 'blacklist' with a set of agree- **7.125** ments excluded from the scope of the exemption (Article 5). This list includes, *inter alia*, the restriction of the parties' ability to carry on R&D efforts in a field unconnected to that to which the relevant R&D relates and even in the same or connected fields when restrictions apply after the completion of the R&D programme; and all possible hardcore restraints, eg price fixing, market allocation, etc.[100]

(ii) Potential competition As noted above, Article 81(1) applies, in particular, to agree- **7.126** ments where the parties are actual or potential competitors.[101] The notion of a potential

---

[100] Art 5(2) clarifies that the black list does not include 'the setting of production targets where the exploitation of the results includes the joint production of the contract products' and 'the setting of sales tar- gets and the fixing of prices charged to immediate customers where the exploitation of the results includes the joint distribution of the contract products.'

[101] The 2001 Horizontal Guidelines point out that 'R&D co-operation between non-competitors does gen- erally not restrict competition' (para 56). The criterion laid down to analyse the competitive relationship between the parties is the feasibility of individual and independent R&D, in accordance with the previous case law.

competitor has been discussed earlier in the context of JVs. The Commission's decisional practice confirms the importance of this notion in the context of R&D co-operation.

7.127 The Commission policy towards potential competition in R&D is usefully set out in the 1990 *Elopak/Metal Box—Odin* decision.[102] Elopak and Metal Box agreed to set up a JV, Odin, to research, develop and ultimately manufacture and distribute a new type of packaging involving a carton base and a separate closure that could be filled with UHT and processed food. The technology was new and involved contributions of existing know-how from both parents. In the Commission's view 'neither party could in the short term enter the market alone as such entry would require a knowledge of the other party's technology which could not be developed without significant time and investment'.

7.128 Therefore it did not regard the parties as potential competitors and the JV did not fall within Article 81(1).

7.129 Similarly, in the 1990 *Konsortium ECR 900* decision[103] the Commission issued a negative clearance to a development agreement between AEG, Alcatel and Nokia, to respond to calls for tender to develop systems and equipment related to the GSM mobile telephone system in Europe. The Commission concluded that the parties were effectively not credible potential competitors. None of the parties individually would have been able to comply with the timetable set in the tender documents if they were to proceed individually nor would they have been able to bear the considerable financial risk involved.

7.130 It is therefore clear that as far as R&D co-operation is concerned there must be some reasonable likelihood that the parties could undertake the R&D effort independently and that they already have the essential background know-how to do so.

7.131 The *KSB/Goulds/Lowara/ITT* decision[104] of 1990 set out some of the limits to this approach. The parties, who were all existing manufacturers of pumps with significant presence in European and US markets, had argued that without co-operation they would not have invested in the necessary development work for a new generation of chrome nickel steel pumps, and therefore negative clearance was appropriate. The Commission, however, decided that due to the size of each of the parties they would have been capable of bearing the necessary financial cost of the development work. The parties also argued that they needed the technical know-how belonging to one of the parties, Lowara. However, the Commission also argued that such basic technology was available under licence from other manufacturers. The Commission went on to argue that there were other ways to recover the development costs such as licensing to third parties rather than producing jointly.

7.132 The agreement fulfilled all the criteria of the 1984 version of the block exemption except for the market share threshold of 20 per cent, and therefore the Commission granted an individual exemption. Interestingly in the Commission's analysis under Article 81(3) it argued that the restrictions inherent in the agreement were indispensable to the project

---

[102] *Elopak/Metal Box—Odin* [1990] OJ L209/15.
[103] *Konsortium ECR 900* [1990] OJ L228/31.
[104] *KSB/Goulds/Lowara/ITT* [1991] OJ L19/25.

since the development costs could be justified economically only if a minimum level of production units was attained.

In the 1994 *Asahi/Saint Gobain* decision,[105] the Commission also rejected the parties' arguments that they were not potential competitors. The companies had set up a R&D JV to develop a new type of safety glass for use in the automotive industry. They argued that as they carried out R&D efforts in different regions, Asahi in Japan, St Gobain in Europe, and there were certain key patents in Europe that blocked entry into that market, they were not potential competitors. However, both companies had already developed pilot plants and submitted samples to potential customers, thus the Commission argued that they could continue with their R&D programmes independently. **7.133**

In the 1994 *Pasteur Mérieux/Merck* decision,[106] exempting a JV in the field of child vaccines, the Commission made some attempt to analyse potential competition in R&D. The JV was established to develop, produce and distribute the parties' existing and future vaccines in Europe. The Commission identified several restrictions of competition related to the development of future products resulting from the JV. **7.134**

In particular it argued that: **7.135**

> as regards future products in an advanced stage of clinical trials ('pipeline products'), it is realistic to assume that the parties, in view of their past performance, financial strength and existing vaccine knowledge, can be considered as potential competitors for those new [products] for which their actual R&D portfolio shows an overlap.

However, for R&D programmes more distant from the market the Commission recognised the difficulty of assessing whether the parties were potential competitors: **7.136**

> An assessment of the restriction of competition between the parties for other new [products] in earlier stages of R&D ('future pipeline products') is far more difficult, in view of the extremely broad range of such future research and the lack of precise indications as to the chances of bringing successful products to the markets.

More specifically the Commission argued that: **7.137**

> It is, furthermore, not accepted that the parties could be considered as potential competitors for the development of these [new products] simply because of their ability to obtain access to the missing (antigens) via licences to proprietary know-how and/or patents, and possibly bulk supplies from other manufacturers.

While the assessment of potential competition clearly varies with the specific details of each case, the inherent uncertainty in any R&D project makes the assessment of whether companies are potential competitors for that R&D project extremely difficult. It is notably difficult to be conclusive as to whether a company could have successfully completed a R&D project without the co-operation. However, as the decisions referred to above have illustrated, it is essentially when the R&D effort has led to some successful outcome, such as a prototype or perhaps a drug entering the later stages of clinical trials, that the Commission has found that the companies involved can be considered potential competitors. **7.138**

---

[105] *Asahi/Saint Gobain* [1994] OJ L354/87.
[106] *Pasteur Mérieux/Merck* [1994] OJ L309/1.

7.139 (iii) **Market position on R&D and related markets**   In common with most agreements, the assessment of the parties' market position is a key element in the assessment of R&D arrangements under Article 81(1).

7.140 Market definition in R&D cases can be extremely difficult. The R&D co-operation may relate to improvements in existing products, to the development of new products that will compete on an existing market, or to new products that will create a completely new market. In some cases the application of the Commission's Notice on market definition to such agreements is therefore not entirely straight forward.

7.141 The 2001 Horizontal Guidelines pay attention to competition in both existing markets (both the market for existing products related to the innovation and the technology markets involved) and innovative efforts.

7.142 The examination of existing markets will be relevant when the R&D project is aimed at the improvement or replacement of existing products. If this is the case, incumbent and new or upgraded products may not belong to the same relevant market, as substitution between them may be imperfect or long-term. However, the market for existing products may still be relevant if the pooling of R&D is 'likely to result in the coordination of the parties' behaviour as suppliers of the existing products'. For this scenario to take place, it is essential that the parties have a strong market position with respect to both the existing product market and the R&D efforts. Markets for existing products must also be subject to analysis when the R&D concerns an important (a 'key element', as termed by the Guidelines) component of the final product, eg a car market may be affected by a joint R&D programme related to a new type of engine.[107]

7.143 Existing markets relevant to the assessment of R&D agreements do not only include those where the final products are commercialised, but also the technology markets where the rights to intellectual property are marketed separately from the products to which they relate. Technology markets consist of the intellectual property licensed and its close substitutes. Actual market shares and potential entry in the relevant technology market should be weighed in order to determine the effects of the R&D agreement.[108]

7.144 Finally, the analysis of both the markets for existing products and for technology should be coupled with a careful examination of the effects brought about by the R&D co-operation on the competition in innovation. This question will be specifically addressed below.

7.145 But the identification of the relevant markets is not the only obstacle to be overcome. It can also be difficult to identify at what level of market power R&D co-operation is likely to lead to an appreciable restriction of competition. Markets where R&D and technological development are important are often characterised by both high and large fluctuations in market shares as a new product may arrive on the market and temporarily have very high market shares. If the R&D leads to a completely new product market the parties may, initially, have a temporary monopoly.

---

[107] 2001 Horizontal Guidelines, paras 44–46.
[108] 2001 Horizontal Guidelines, paras 47–49.

The following sections will address first the basic framework provided by the exemption **7.146**
Regulation and the 2001 Horizontal Guidelines and, subsequently, the problems that can
be raised in connection with the different markets that may be relevant for the assessment
of a R&D agreement.

(iv) R&D and innovation markets, 'poles of research' The Commission has referred on **7.147**
several occasions to the need to ensure sufficient competing 'poles of research', both in the
recitals to the block exemption and in the 1993 Notice on co-operative JVs.

More specifically, the Guidelines on horizontal co-operation agreements are concerned with **7.148**
the possibility that R&D co-operation may affect not only competition in existing markets,
but also competition in innovation. Therefore, it is essential to examine the effects of the
agreement on the possible poles of research existing in the relevant economic sector.[109] This
requires an assessment of what is sometimes referred to as a 'R&D' market or a 'potential'
market. In essence this requires an assessment of the numbers of alternative research efforts
directed at a particular market that are likely to be successful within a short period of time
and therefore provide a credible constraint on the co-operation of the parties. The
Guidelines go on to distinguish two possible scenarios. The first relates to markets where
the process of innovation is structured in such a way that it is possible to identify R&D
poles at an early stage, eg the pharmaceutical industry, credible competing poles must be
identified. Hence, the coordination must not lead to a situation where no other research
efforts can be feasibly pursued. For a competing R&D pole to be considered 'credible', several factors should be analysed (eg nature, scope, financial and human resources, timing,
capability for exploitation and so on). The second scenario is where there is not a clear
R&D market structure. In this case, the Commission would, absent extraordinary circumstances, limit its assessment to product and/or technology markets related to the R&D
co-operation, ie actual, existing markets.

The Commission has not published any decisions under Article 81 explaining this concept **7.149**
in detail. However, the *Pasteur Mérieux/Merck* decision[110] did discuss the effects of the JV
on the development of vaccines in the future. In this case the Commission noted that the
JV might lead to a reduction in the incentives of the parties to improve existing products,
and to a coordination of their R&D programmes.

Some merger decisions have also provided useful insights into the Commission's assess- **7.150**
ment of R&D markets.

In the *Glaxo/Wellcome* decision,[111] the Commission included R&D projects in its competitive **7.151**
assessment of the concentration. In the pharmaceutical sector the Anatomical Therapeutic
Classification ('ATC') system is used to group medicines according to their composition
and therapeutic properties. This system applies to both medicines in clinical trials as well as
those already on the market. It therefore provides a method for assessing whether given

---

[109] Commission's Notice on the applicability of Art 81 to horizontal co-operation agreements [2001] OJ
C3/2, para 50.
[110] *Pasteur Mérieux/Merck* [1994] OJ L309/1.
[111] Case IV/M555 *Glaxo/Wellcome* [1995] OJ C65/3.

R&D efforts are 'competing poles of research' as well as whether they are likely to compete with existing medicines.

7.152 The decision argues, in paragraph 9, that:

> In the pharmaceutical sector, in order to be complete a competition assessment will require scrutiny of products which are not yet on the market but which are at an advanced stage of development (normally after a very considerable investment of resources of time and money). The potential of such products to compete with other products either in development or already on the market can only be assessed by reference to their characteristics and intended use.[112]

7.153 The Commission found when it applied the ATC classification to Glaxo and Wellcome's existing range of drugs and to those at research stage and in clinical trials that there were some overlaps, in particular in the market for anti-migraine products. Both Glaxo and Wellcome had strong existing products in these markets and R&D programmes in the latter stages of clinical trials. Several other major pharmaceutical firms had anti-migraine research programmes and at least two of these had drugs in Phase III clinical trials. Therefore in assessing the market position of the parties the Commission took into account both the market shares of any existing products and the number of research programmes aimed at the same market.

7.154 The Commission did not argue that Glaxo/Wellcome had a dominant position for migraine products but, to remedy any possible concern, the parties agreed to grant an exclusive licence to one of their drugs in clinical trials to a third party.

7.155 It seems reasonable to assume that the same approach could be taken in Article 81 cases. Thus market definition may involve looking not just at existing market shares but also at R&D programmes.

7.156 The Commission has not stated explicitly how many 'competing poles of research' would be necessary to maintain effective competition in the R&D market. It is clear that research is inherently uncertain and it is difficult to judge whether one pole is more likely to succeed than another. While a co-operation between companies undertaking similar or competing R&D may conceivably fall within Article 81(1) if as a result of it there remain too few independent R&D programmes, the Commission has never yet explicitly indicated how many competing R&D programmes are appropriate.

7.157 **(v) Technology licensing markets** The other market definition issue relevant for the analysis of R&D arrangements is that relating to the licensing of technology. In the *Shell/Montecatini* decision,[113] the Commission considered the worldwide market for the necessary technology to produce polypropylene (PP) from propylene. As the decision noted:

> it appears that the licensing of advanced PP technology and other associated services [. . .] constitutes a distinct product market upon which the effects of the proposed joint venture should be assessed. [. . .] Dominance in the PP technology market would enable a PP technology provider to exercise market power with regard to an essential element of PP production.

The decision went on to conclude that the resulting JV would lead to a dominant position **7.158**
on the PP technology market and to require Montecatini's subsidiaries to transfer their
PP technology business, including related R&D facilities and staff, out of the JV into a
separate company.

This decision illustrates that the licensing of technology can constitute a distinct antitrust **7.159**
market.

(vi) Restriction of competition   In its policy statements on co-operation in R&D the **7.160**
Commission has usually taken the line that R&D agreements that do not impose restrictions on the parties' use of the results of that R&D or on their activities in other areas do
not constitute a restriction of competition.

Thus the 1968 Notice on co-operation agreements[114] stated that: **7.161**

> Agreements having as their sole object:
> (a) the joint implementation of research and development projects,
> (b) the joint placing of research and development contracts,
> (c) the sharing out of research and development projects among participating enterprises.

do *not* fall under Article 81(1). It went on to note that the mere exchange of information **7.162**
on experience in or results of R&D will not lead to a competition problem and nor will
agreements on the joint execution of research work up to the stage of industrial application.
Paragraph 55 of the Commission's Guidelines on horizontal agreements echoes this
favourable attitude towards R&D co-operation, plainly stating that '[m]ost R&D agreements do not fall under Article 81(1)'.

This is repeated in recital 3 of the R&D block exemption, which notes that: **7.163**

> agreements on the joint execution of research work or the joint development of the results of
> the research, up to but not including the stage of industrial application, *generally* do not fall
> within the scope of Article 81(1) of the Treaty. In certain circumstances, however, such as where
> the parties agree not to carry out other research and development in the same field thereby fore-
> going the opportunity of gaining competitive advantage over other parties, such agreements may
> fall within Article 81(1) [. . .].

Therefore those agreements that do impose restrictions on the parties' freedom to carry out **7.164**
competing R&D projects or on the exploitation of the results of the R&D such as how the
parties may grant licences to each other or to third parties, *may* fall within the scope of
Article 81(1).

Clearly, in practical terms, most agreements involving R&D co-operation include contrac- **7.165**
tual terms on the exploitation of the results of that R&D. They may also include other
restrictions relating to the use of any know-how contributed, etc. It is these contractual
terms that have often been the basis of much of the Commission's analysis of co-operation
in R&D. This is discussed further under the section on Article 81(3).

---

[114] Notice concerning agreements, decisions and concerted practices in the field of co-operation between
enterprises [1968] OJ C75/3–6.

7.166 However, it is important to note that if the parties are not actual or potential competitors and the co-operation does not have an appreciable effect on competition then the agreements bringing about this co-operation do not fall under Article 81(1).

7.167 **(vii) Foreclosure effects** Agreements may fall under Article 81(1) if they have significant foreclosure effects on the market. Thus if a company with a key, or dominant, technology enters into an exclusive co-operation in R&D with another company, third parties may be restricted in their access to the necessary technology to compete on the relevant R&D and downstream markets.

7.168 The Guidelines on horizontal co-operation agreements, referring to R&D co-operation between non-competitors, make clear that this modality of collaboration 'does generally not restrict competition'.[115] Further, the 1993 Notice on co-operative JVs between non-competitors states that '[t]his group rarely causes problems for competition [. . .] one must simply examine whether market access of third parties is significantly affected by the co-operation'.

7.169 The 1994 *Pasteur Mérieux/Merck* decision discusses in some detail the effect of the JV on third parties. In this case, the Commission considered that the exclusivity granted to the JV with regard to existing technology and 'pipeline products', together with the parties' strong position in the relevant markets, could affect the position of third parties, and hence a restriction of competition was found:

> Other producers will, in view of these arrangements, be limited in their possibilities to collaborate either with the parent companies or with the JV as a source for them to get access to 'missing' [elements for new products] or vaccine technologies. This outside sourcing could become important for the development of [new products].[116]

7.170 However, when the Commission considered the market for future vaccines, it did not find a restriction of competition. Although R&D efforts in vaccine technology were carried out in Europe by only four firms, two of which were the parties, spending more than ECU 25 million a year on vaccine-related R&D, many other bodies carried out research in this area:

> There are, therefore, in view of the number of potential competitors for the wide range of future vaccines and vaccine technology, no indications that the creation of the JV will lead to appreciable restrictions of competition by reducing the sourcing-out possibilities of third producers for future vaccines and vaccine technology.

7.171 Thus the Commission appears only to be concerned with foreclosure effects when the degree of remaining actual and/or potential competition is considered to be insufficient.

(3) Grounds for Exemption

7.172 **(i) The R&D block exemption** In the year 2000, the Commission published a block exemption covering certain categories of R&D agreements,[117] to replace a previous block

---

[115] Commission's Notice on the applicability of Art 81 to horizontal co-operation agreements [2001] OJ C3/2, para 56.
[116] *Pasteur Mérieux/Merck* [1994] OJ L309/1, para 69.
[117] Commission Regulation (EC) 2659/2000 of 29 November 2000 [2000] OJ L304/7.

exemption Regulation, dating back to 1984.[118] At the time, and in contrast to other block exemptions, such as those for distribution agreements, the 1984 R&D Regulation was not drafted as a response to a problem of mass notifications but rather as an attempt to encourage more R&D co-operation at a time when Europe was felt to be falling behind Japan and the US in key technological areas. The substance of the Regulation, however, was deemed too narrowly drawn, focusing too much on regulating in detail what contractual clauses could and could not benefit from the exception. The new Regulation adopts a different, more economic-based approach based on the parties' level of market power. In short, the new block exemption moves away from the previous list-based approach to embrace a new scheme consisting of broad definitions of the exempted agreements up to a certain level of market power coupled with the specification of all the restrictions or clauses that are not to be included in such agreements.[119]

There are several key elements of an R&D agreement that are necessary for it to fall within **7.173** the terms of the block exemption, these are set out in Article 3 of the Regulation.

R&D is defined very broadly as:								**7.174**

> the acquisition of know-how relating to products or processes and the carrying out of theoretical analysis, systematic study or experimentation, including experimental production, technical testing of products or processes, the establishment of the necessary facilities and the obtaining of intellectual property rights for the results.

Any joint exploitation must relate only to results which are protected by intellectual prop- **7.175** erty, or constitute know-how, which substantially contribute to technical or economic progress and which are decisive for the manufacture of any contract products (Article 3(4)).

The undertakings in charge of the manufacture by way of specialisation in production **7.176** must be required to fulfil orders for supplies from all the parties, except when the R&D agreement also provides for joint distribution (Article 3(5)).

Finally, the new block exemption relaxes the market share requirement by raising the **7.177** threshold for the aggregate market share of the participating undertakings to 25 per cent, instead of the 20 per cent applied under the old Regulation.

The Commission would appear to require some evidence to support the application of **7.178** these criteria. In the *KSB/Goulds/Lowara/ITT* decision of 1990, the Commission accepted that the combined R&D programme of the four parties involved did meet these criteria. It referred in this respect to the various patents granted, awards for innovative research, and the clear description in the JV agreement of the R&D work that was to be jointly exploited.

The block exemption appears to contemplate a model of R&D co-operation between equal **7.179** partners. There are certain key elements required in any R&D agreement that reflect this. Thus under Article 3(2) and (3) all parties must have access to the results of the R&D and if there is no joint exploitation each party must be allowed to exploit them separately.

---

[118] Commission Regulation (EEC) 418/85 of 19 December 1984 ([1985] OJ L53/5) as amended by Commission Regulation (EEC) 151/93 of 23 December 1992 (no longer in force).
[119] Commission Regulation (EC) 2659/2000 of 29 November 2000 [2000] OJ L304/7, recital 7.

7.180   However, many agreements are more one-sided. It is not completely clear how these would be treated under the block exemption. The definition of 'joint exploitation' in Article 2(11) is deliberately wide, covering both the exploitation of the results by a JV, by a jointly-entrusted third party or by 'allocation between the parties by way of specialisation in research, development, production or distribution'.

7.181   Nevertheless, while subcontracting or original equipment manufacturing (OEM) agreements may not always fall under the block exemption it is rather likely that they would benefit from an individual exemption, provided the other elements of the block exemption such as the market share thresholds are met.

7.182   Despite these limitations the Commission has tried to emphasise that it generally takes a liberal policy towards R&D co-operation and that in many cases individual exemption for agreements falling outside the block exemption is still possible.

7.183   **(ii) Individual exemption**   Even if a particular agreement does not meet all the requirements laid down in the block exemption Regulation, there is always room for the agreement to be individually exempted from the application of Article 81(1). To qualify for such individual exemption an agreement must fulfil the four criteria of Article 81(3). Namely it must contribute to technical or economic progress; allow consumers a fair share of the resulting benefit; not impose restrictions which are not indispensable; nor allow the parties the possibility of eliminating competition in respect of a substantial part of the products in question.

7.184   In practice for R&D agreements the first condition is usually fulfilled in the form of 'cost savings and cross fertilisation of ideas and experience, thus resulting in improved or new products and technologies being developed more rapidly than would otherwise be.'[120] 'Indispensability' essentially refers to the exclusion of the hardcore restraints listed in Article 5 of the block exemption from the scope of the Regulation itself. The Commission's analysis generally focuses on the question of elimination of competition and on the nature and effect of any restrictions imposed, which are analysed separately below.

7.185   *Elimination of competition*   The issue of market definition for agreements related to R&D has been discussed earlier. In many cases, the parties' position in existing markets is assessed on the basis of the principles set out in the R&D block exemption. In the *Asahi/St Gobain* decision and the *KSB/Goulds/Lowara/ITT* decision, the parties all had strong existing market shares; in both cases above the 20 per cent threshold provided for in the 1984 block exemption.

7.186   In these cases, the result of the R&D was likely to be a product that would compete directly with the parties' existing products, in one case autoglass, and in the other liquid pumps. However, more recently the Commission has recognised that this measure of market power may not be appropriate in R&D leading to new products and possibly new markets. In cases such as *Elopak*, reference has been made to the fact that a significant number of firms with the relevant or competing technologies remain outside the co-operation. This concept of a 'pole' of research has been used in the US for some years and in some recent Commission merger decisions.

---

[120] 2001 Horizontal Guidelines, para 68.

However, an analogy with the 25 per cent threshold might suggest that if at least four other **7.187** 'poles' of research were identifiable an R&D co-operation might well be exemptable even if it did not benefit explicitly from the R&D block exemption. It is hard to imagine the Commission finding that such a collaboration violated Article 81(1) at all. In fact, the Guidelines on horizontal co-operation agreements cautiously refer to the combination of the only two existing poles of research by the R&D agreement as an example of elimination of competition.

Contractual restrictions   The type and scope of the contractual restrictions that can be **7.188** accepted as part of an R&D agreement is a key issue to industry and to its advisers. As discussed in earlier sections, if an agreement falls within Article 81(1) the restrictions in question must, *inter alia*, be indispensable to the achievement of the objectives of the agreement, ie they must go no further than is necessary to achieve these objectives.

This section deals with the most common contractual restrictions and the Commission's **7.189** likely response to their presence in a R&D contract. As with earlier discussions, the Commission's move towards a more economic-based approach is perhaps likely to limit its concerns with individual restrictions in the future.

Joint R&D together with joint exploitation   The extension of an R&D collaboration into **7.190** joint production, and sometimes joint distribution and sales, is increasingly common. It is also increasingly common that the parties wish to set out the terms of these arrangements at the beginning of the R&D collaboration.

The block exemption specifically allows for the joint exploitation of the results of a R&D **7.191** programme, whether in the form of joint manufacture or joint licensing of the results (Articles 1(1)(b) and 2(8)). However, this is constrained by a market share limit of 25 per cent (Article 4(2)).

The market share threshold refers to the market for 'products which are considered by users **7.192** to be equivalent in view of their characteristics, price and intended use'. Individual exemptions are clearly possible above this market share limit and many of the Commission's published decisions in this area relate to R&D together with joint production. For example, in the *Olivetti/Canon* decision of 1987,[121] the Commission argued that a JV to develop, design and produce copying machine products, laser beam printer products and facsimile products, fell under Article 81(1) as the parents were existing competitors for some products and potential competitors for others. The parties' combined market share in some of the product categories was as high as 30 per cent. However, an exemption under Article 81(3) was appropriate, among other reasons because, as stated in paragraph 54 of the Decision:

> The expansion of production in the EEC which is the effect of the joint venture enables the parties to spread the costs of these investments [in R&D] over a larger number of products: otherwise the costs of these products would be too high for producers to be able to sell them at a competitive price.

Similarly, in the *Fujitsu/AMD Semiconductor* decision,[122] the Commission stated that an **7.193** R&D and production JV was exemptable, *inter alia*, because 'new product lines require

---

[121] *Olivetti/Canon* [1988] OJ L52/51.
[122] *Fujitsu/AMD Semiconductor* [1994] OJ L341/66.

considerable investment. This investment is risky [...] The JV will allow each parent substantially to reduce these costs and risks.'

7.194 In these cases the market to be assessed seemed to be that for the final product rather than that for the R&D itself. However, as discussed earlier, the Commission is more and more likely to examine R&D markets and therefore the parties to an agreement may need to consider their position on both the R&D and downstream product markets.

7.195 *Joint exploitation of joint R&D between non-competitors*   The Commission's approach to this question is not completely clear. However, the *Mitchell Cotts/Sofiltra* decision of 1986[123] appears to say that although the parties to the agreement were not potential competitors for the production of the product in question, high quality air filters, they were potential competitors for its distribution. The implication of this decision is that although the parties were not competitors initially, once they had collaborated and had therefore had access to the results of the R&D they became potential competitors and Article 81(1) could apply.

7.196 *Joint marketing*   The new block exemption defines 'joint exploitation of the results of research and development' (Article 1(1)) as meaning, *inter alia*, 'the production or distribution of the contract products' thus including joint marketing in the very definition of exempted agreements.

7.197 Two decisions had previously illustrated the generally favourable approach taken towards joint marketing in those industries where complex tendering procedures are required. In the 1990 *Alcatel Espace/ANT Nachtrichtentechnik* decision,[124] the Commission accepted that a joint R&D, production and marketing agreement was exemptable as competition in the procurement industry for satellites generally required the setting up of consortia. The decision noted that: 'in this particular case the benefits of joint R&D and joint manufacture can only be achieved if they are combined with a degree of joint marketing'.

7.198 In the 1990 *Konsortium ECR 900* decision,[125] the Commission actually decided that the agreements to set up a consortia to bid for tendered contracts for mobile phone technology did not in fact fall under Article 81(1) at all as the parties would not have been able to tender independently.

7.199 *Territorial restrictions on manufacturing or sales*   It is also extremely common for the parties to an R&D agreement to allocate exclusive territories to each other, whether within Europe or worldwide. The block exemption appears to reflect a certain relaxation of the Commission's policy towards territorial restrictions.[126] Furthermore, the new block exemption lengthens the period during which the parties are allowed to ban active sales within a specified territory from five to seven years (Article 5 (g)).

---

[123] *Mitchell Cotts/Sofiltra* [1987] OJ L41/31.
[124] *Alcatel Espace/ANT Nachtrichtentechnik* [1990] OJ L32/19.
[125] *Konsortium ECR 900* [1990] OJ L228/31.
[126] *Beecham/Parke Davis* [1979] OJ L70/11: 'To qualify for an exemption in these circumstances joint research co-operation can only be admitted if the results of such joint research can be used by both parties freely and independently without any territorial or other restrictions on production or marketing within the common market.'

On the other hand, however, absolute territorial protection banning passive sales is considered **7.200** a *per se* prohibited restriction (Article 5(f)). In addition, the exemption does not apply to territorial restrictions on active sales after seven years from the time the contract products were first marketed. The Commission's practice also indicates which territorial restrictions are clearly not allowed. The *Siemens Fanuc* decision of 1985[127] concerned an R&D agreement between Siemens and Fanuc, a subsidiary of Fujitsu, for the development and sale of numerical controls for machine tools. The parties entered into an exclusive distribution agreement whereby Siemens sold Fanuc's products in Europe and Fanuc sold Siemens's products in Asia. The agreement was never notified. Following an investigation the Commission found that prices for Fanuc's products were higher in Europe than in Asia and that it was almost impossible for third parties to purchase direct from Fanuc. The Commission found that the R&D elements of the agreement were secondary to the exclusivity arrangements and in no way justified them.

This principle was reaffirmed in the *Quantel International-Continuum/Quantel SA* deci- **7.201** sion of 1992.[128] This decision concerned an import restriction in the context of the sale of a business whereby the seller agreed not to sell the products in question, lasers, into the European market. The Commission reaffirmed that such absolute territorial restrictions were not permissible. It also confirmed that the territorial exclusivity permitted by the block exemption must be limited to five years (under the old block exemption) after the products come onto the market and must refer to the results of a specific R&D programme.

Prohibitions on engaging in competing R&D　These are common contractual restrictions and **7.202** are usually regarded as ancillary to the main agreement. They generally cover both individual efforts outside the co-operation and co-operation with third parties. Such restrictions are allowed by the R&D block exemption (Article 1(1)). However, these non-compete restrictions must be limited to the given field of co-operation. The *Fujitsu/AMD Semiconductor* decision[129] illustrates these principles. A basic non-compete clause for the life of the JV is:

> a restriction of competition which is ancillary to the JV in so far as it has to be considered necessary to the setting up and proper operation of the JV. In view of the difficulty, risks and costs involved in successfully developing NVMs, [microchips], this non-competition clause is necessary to allow each party to obtain the benefit of its investment.

In addition, short periods of post-term non-compete obligations may also be allowed. For **7.203** example, if a JV is created, the parties may be required not to compete for a period of typically three years after they sell their interest. This would ensure that a buyer can be found as any purchaser would wish to be protected for a limited period of time to prevent free riding from the seller.

Prohibition from engaging in unconnected R&D　These covenants would not be regarded **7.204** as acceptable restrictions and are specifically included as a black clause in Article 5(a) of the block exemption.

It is clear that these restrictions can be similar in object and scope to the 'field of use' restric- **7.205** tions discussed below. While the Commission has generally taken a more positive approach

---

[127] *Siemens/Fanuc* [1985] OJ L376/29.
[128] *Quantel International-Continuum/Quantel SA* [1992] OJ L235/9.
[129] *Fujitsu/AMD Semiconductor* [1994] OJ L341/66.

to the latter, specific prohibitions on unrelated activity are too close to blatant 'market sharing' restrictions and are thus regarded with greater suspicion.

7.206 *Field of use restrictions* It is common for companies entering a R&D co-operation agreement to wish to limit the co-operation to a fairly specific field of operation. They may see advantages in a collaboration in one area but do not want the technology they contribute to the co-operation to be used by their partner in another unrelated field. To a certain extent such restrictions are covered by normal intellectual property rules. Thus if a company grants a licence for its know-how, it can impose certain restrictions on the use of that technology.

7.207 The block exemption allows field of use restrictions in areas where the parties are not competing at the time the agreement is entered into (Article 3(3)). However, in the context of a R&D co-operation or JV the parties cannot impose restrictions on product markets or other R&D co-operations that its partners can enter into in other areas (Article 5(a)).

7.208 *Granting of licences to partners, JVs; Grant backs of technical improvements; and Cross-licensing after termination of a co-operation* It is frequently the case that the parties to an agreement, or a JV, wish to grant licences for all necessary technology to the JV on an exclusive basis. This may often include provisions on further technical developments from either of the parents. These provisions do not come under Article 81(1) if the co-operation does not. The exclusivity is merely a guarantee that the parties will commit all efforts and investment to the success of the JV.

7.209 Conditions imposed on a JV that it will grant back any improvements made to its parents during its life are also not restrictions of competition. Nor are agreements to cross license any necessary technology after the termination of a co-operation to ensure that each parent has the necessary technology to use the results satisfactorily. However, any post-term links or exchanges of information would need to be considered in the light of the prevailing market structure as they may limit subsequent competition as between the parties.

7.210 *Allocation of royalties* In general, contractual agreements on the allocation of royalties between the parties to an agreement will not lead to a restriction of competition unless they significantly distort the incentive on the parties to compete with each other in the exploitation of the R&D co-operation. That assessment will depend upon the nature of the market and the structure of the royalty payments. In particular any uneven royalty payments may distort the incentives on the parties to compete.

(4) Duration of Exemption

7.211 For a long time there was no standard Commission policy towards the duration of an exemption granted under Article 81(3). Article 4 of the R&D block exemption grants an initial seven years' exemption from the point at which the products arising from an R&D collaboration arrive on the market. This will continue to apply after the seven-year period provided the market share of the parties concerned does not exceed 25 per cent.

7.212 In several decisions, notably *Asahi/St Gobain* in 1994 and *KSB/Goulds/Lowara/ITT* in 1990, the Commission had accepted a duration similar to that of the 1984 R&D Exemption Regulation (five years). However, the Court of First Instance decision in the *European*

Night Services case[130] held that the Commission, in granting exemptions for limited periods, should take account of the period necessary for the parties to recoup their investment. In paragraph 230 of this decision the court states that: 'the length of time required to ensure a proper return on that investment is necessarily an essential factor to be taken into account when determining the duration of an exemption'.

E. Joint Production Agreements

(1) Legislation

The Commission has published three useful pieces of legislation relevant to the treatment of production arrangements. These are the Guidelines on Horizontal co-operation agreements,[131] the block exemption on specialisation agreements,[132] and the Notice on co-operative joint ventures.[133] The Commission's Guidelines set out the general principles for the assessment of horizontal agreements under Article 81 and complement the specialisation block exemption Regulation. The specialisation Regulation is restricted to a fairly limited form of co-operation, and while it has been amended on several occasions, it is of limited use. The Notice on co-operative JVs while providing less legal certainty than a Regulation, gives some useful guidance as to how production JVs should be analysed under Article 81. It has, however, been superseded to a certain extent by the last amendment to the old Merger Regulation[134] and the new Merger Regulation of 2004. Each of these pieces of legislation is analysed separately below.   **7.213**

Guidelines on horizontal co-operation agreements   Chapter 3 of the Guidelines distinguishes between three categories of production agreements: those which *do not fall* within Article 81(1), those which *almost always fall* within Article 81(1) and, more generally, those which *may fall* within Article 81(1).   **7.214**

The first category covers, in essence, situations where it is unlikely that the parties to the joint production agreement will coordinate their competitive behaviour. Two types of agreements are distinguished. On the one hand, production agreements between non-competitors normally fall outside of Article 81(1), unless they raise foreclosure concerns. On the other hand, certain agreements between competitors also normally fall outside Article 81(1). This is the case if both undertakings compete on markets closely related to the one concerned with the agreement if such co-operation is their only commercially justifiable way to enter the new market. This is also the case where the parties share a small proportion of their respective total costs (low commonality of costs), eg the joint production of an intermediate product accounting for a small part of total costs incurred in (separately) producing the final product.   **7.215**

---

[130] Judgment of the Court of First Instance 15 September 1998 in Joined Cases T–373/94, T–375/94, T–384/94 and T–388/94 *European Night Services v Commission* [1998] ECR II–3141, para 230.

[131] Commission Notice, Guidelines on the applicability of Article 81 of the EC Treaty to horizontal co-operation agreements [2001] OJ C3/2.

[132] Commission Regulation (EC) 2658/2000 of 29 November 2000 on the application of Article 81(3) of the Treaty to categories of specialization agreements [2000] OJ L304/3.

[133] Notice concerning the assessment of co-operative joint ventures pursuant to Article 85 [now Article 81] of the EEC Treaty [1993] OJ C43/2.

[134] Council Regulation (EC) 1310/97 of 30 June 1997 [1997] OJ L180/1 (no longer in force).

7.216 The second category covers joint production agreements fixing prices for the parties' output, limiting the parties' output, sharing markets or customer groups. Joint producers are however allowed to agree on the level of output or price for the production directly concerned by the agreement.

7.217 Finally, other agreements may fall under Article 81(1) and require to be analysed in their economic context.

7.218 **Specialisation block exemption**   The rationale for this block exemption is set out in its recital 8:

> Agreements on specialisation in production generally contribute to improving the production or distribution of goods, because undertakings concerned can concentrate on the manufacture of certain products and thus operate more efficiently and supply the products more cheaply.

7.219 The Regulation is primarily aimed at small and medium-sized enterprises. The assumption is that this type of co-operation will allow them to compete more effectively with larger companies by using their assets more efficiently. The basic concept is set out in Article 1(b) and (c) of the Regulation, which exempts the following agreements from application of Article 81(1):

> (a) unilateral specialization agreements, by virtue of which one party agrees to cease production of certain products or to refrain from producing those products and to purchase them from a competing undertaking, while the competing undertaking agrees to produce and supply those products; or
> (b) reciprocal specialization agreements, by virtue of which two or more parties on a reciprocal basis agree to cease or refrain from producing certain but different products and to purchase these products from the other parties, who agree to supply them; or
> (c) joint production agreements, by virtue of which two or more parties agree to produce certain products jointly.

7.220 The scope of the Regulation is clearly not limited to reciprocal obligations and includes both unilateral agreements and joint ventures.

7.221 There are no explicit cross-supply obligations imposed under the block exemption but if the parties wish to impose an exclusive supply/purchase obligation on each other then these are covered by Article 3(a).

7.222 The block exemption is however restricted to agreements between undertakings whose combined share in the relevant product market is less than 20 per cent (Article 4).

7.223 **Notice on co-operative joint ventures**   This Notice provides a general overview of the Commission's policy towards JVs. However, it has particular relevance to production agreements as these are frequently organised through JVs and many JVs also include an element of joint production. Despite the fact that the Notice was complemented by the more extensive Guidelines on horizontal co-operation agreements, it remains highly illustrative of the Commission's approach to co-operative JVs.

7.224 This Notice was drafted at the time when the Commission's policy debate focused on the distinction between co-operative and concentrative JVs, and hence on whether or not the provisions of the Merger Regulation[135] applied. Since then the Merger Regulation has been revised. The main policy distinction now rests on the question whether the JV is full function and autonomous from its parents. This is discussed in more detail in Section C above.

The Notice on co-operative JVs, however, provides some guidance as to the Commission's **7.225** policy towards production JVs under Article 81. Clearly, for Article 81(1) to apply, the creation of the JV must restrict actual or potential competition between the parents or the creation of the JV must have a significant detrimental effect on third parties' ability to compete on the market. The restriction of competition must, of course, be appreciable.

Not only must the effect of the JV itself be assessed, but also the competitive relationship **7.226** between the JV and its parents and between the parents themselves. This assessment will depend, *inter alia*, on whether they are present on the same markets as the JV and/or adjacent markets (upstream or downstream), and on the economic importance of the JV to the parents.

(2) Application of Article 81(1)

The Commission has generally applied Article 81(1) to the creation of JVs among actual or **7.227** potential competitors despite policy claims to the contrary, one of the most significant exceptions being the *Elopak* decision.[136]

Whilst many early decisions of the Commission focused more on the question whether the **7.228** JV agreements restricted the freedom of action of the parties to the JV agreement, the Commission has emphasised the importance of a more economic approach on several occasions. This trend has led to the adoption of the 2001 Guidelines. Although the Guidelines themselves do not provide a definitive market share threshold indicating market power, they do acknowledge that when the parties combined market share is above 20 per cent, the market impact of the joint production agreement must be assessed in more detail.[137] In this event, the degree of market concentration is to be assessed with reference to the HHI index. Other factors may also come into play, such as network effects, that may render collusion likely. Joint production of an upstream input may also raise foreclosure concerns if the parties are strong on the upstream market, or spillover effects concerns if the input in question is an important element of cost and the parties have a strong position in the downstream market.

The following sub-sections analyse: (i) the peculiarities of market definition in connection **7.229** with joint production arrangements; and (ii) the substantive assessment of production JVs under Article 81.

Market definition   The basic principles are set out in the Commission's Notice on market **7.230** definition. However, there are certain aspects of the analysis that are peculiar to production agreements.

---

[135] Then Council Regulation 4064/89 of 21 December 1989 on the control of concentrations between undertakings [1989] OJ C395/1 (no longer in force).

[136] *Elopak/Metal Box—Odin* [1990] OJ L209/15.

[137] The guidelines initially refer to the 20% market share threshold in the specialisation agreements block exemption (at para 93). However, reference is later made to a more general 20% market share threshold applied to production agreements (at para 96).

7.231 One of the most important difficulties in assessing production JVs relates to the distinction between captive and free production. In many sectors, such as the chemical industry, a proportion of the output of a plant is used internally by a company and a proportion is sold on the free market. Therefore when considering the market position of the parties to an agreement it is not always clear whether it is the share of the free market or that of total production that is relevant. This can be further complicated by swap arrangements between companies and by the difference between the theoretical capacity of a manufacturing facility and what it actually produces.

7.232 In assessing market power the Commission focuses on those products, or production facilities, that act as a competitive constraint on the behaviour of an undertaking. Thus captive production that could easily be switched to the free market if prices rose would be included in the market share calculations. Similarly if there is overcapacity in the market this may be considered a competitive constraint provided that the marginal costs of increasing production are not too high.

7.233 **Production joint ventures**   The Notice on co-operative JVs discusses, in paragraph 40, two possible types of non-full-function production JV. In the first scenario 'the JV manufactures primary or intermediate products for competing parent companies, which are further processed by the parents into the final product'. A restriction of competition may arise depending, *inter alia*, upon the importance of the initial product to the price of the finished product. Thus the higher the price of the input product the more significant the commonality of cost between the competing parents and the less scope they have for effective competition.

7.234 In the second scenario:

> the JV undertakes the processing of basic materials supplied by the parents, or the processing of half-finished into fully-finished products, with the aim of resupplying the parents, then competition between the participating undertakings, taking into consideration the market proximity of their co-operation and the inherent tendency to align prices, will usually exist only in a weaker form. This is particularly so when the entire production activities of the parents are concentrated in the JV and the parents withdraw to the role of pure distributors. This leads to the standardisation of manufacturing costs and the quality of the products so that essentially the only competition between the parents is on trade margins. This is a considerable restriction of competition, which cannot be remedied by the parents marketing the products under different brand names.

7.235 These scenarios may be usefully illustrated by three Commission decisions. In the *Philips/ Osram* decision of 1994,[138] the parents created a JV to manufacture lead glass tubing for incandescent and fluorescent lamps. This tubing was an intermediate product, which was to be sold back to the parents for incorporation in the lamps and also onto the free market for those manufacturers without their own production facilities. The JV involved the combination of the parties' existing production facilities in the EEA together with investment in new plant. However, outside the EEA the parties continued to produce independently.

7.236 The Commission argued that there was likely to be no effect on the market for lamps as the lead glass represented typically only 2 per cent of the cost of the final product. The Commission

---

[138] *Philips/Osram* [1994] OJ L378/37.

therefore concluded that there was no restriction of competition on the market for lamps: 'given the very small importance of lead glass on the manufacturing costs of lamps, such standardisation is not considered relevant enough as to constitute a restriction of competition'. However, Article 81(1) did apply to the JV given the likely effect on the market for lead glass, as prior to the setting up of the JV the parties accounted for approximately 66 per cent of production capacity on the EEA market for lead glass.

In the *Ford/Volkswagen* decision of 1992,[139] Ford and Volkswagen agreed to set up a JV to **7.237** design, develop, and manufacture a 'People Carrier' or Multi Purpose Vehicle (MPV). These vehicles would be supplied exclusively to the parents for distribution and sale. The parents agreed to make some attempt to differentiate the products through the use of different engines in most models and through different exterior design and appearance.

The Commission was clearly concerned about the very limited possibility for competition **7.238** between the two companies' final products given the virtual identity of the final product. However, the analysis under Article 81(1) was limited to the fact that both firms were potential entrants onto the MPV market and that by investing in this project they effectively precluded separate entry. The Commission also examined the possible spillover effects on the adjacent markets for 'estate cars and light vans'. The substantive analysis of whether there was in practice any scope for competition between the parents was discussed under Article 81(3).

The *Exxon/Shell* decision of 1994[140] provides a more detailed analysis of why Article 81(1) **7.239** applies to a production JV. The two companies agreed to set up a JV to construct and operate a new plant to manufacture Linear Low Density Polyethylene (LLDPE) on the EU market.

The EC market for LLDPE and its substitutes, various other forms of PE and polypropylene, **7.240** was deemed to be oligopolistic. Together Exxon and Shell had approximately 20 per cent of the EC LLDPE capacity. The JV represented 17 per cent of the parents' EC capacity.

As the JV would effectively source all its raw materials exclusively from the parents and then **7.241** supply all its output to the parents, the JV was not full function. It was also under the joint control of the parents who, through the management structure, had an active role in the JV's commercial decisions.

Exxon and Shell remained competitors on the LLDPE market and were capable of build- **7.242** ing plants separately. Therefore in assessing whether Article 81(1) applied the Commission argued that 'account must be taken of the legal and economic context, in particular in the light of the situation on the relevant market and the position of the parties thereon.' It also stated that in line with the Notice on co-operative JVs:

> As the joint venture processes feedstock provided by the parent companies into polyethylene (which continues also to be individually produced and marketed by Exxon and Shell) to be supplied back to them, competition between undertakings—taking into account the market proximity of their co-operation and the inherent tendency to align prices—will exist in a weaker form only.

More specifically the decision argues that decisions on investment, either within the JV or **7.243** separately, will inevitably take into account the interests of the other party. Similarly, it

---

[139] *Ford/Volkswagen* [1993] OJ L20/14.
[140] *Exxon/Shell* [1994] OJ L144/20.

states that the parents will be led to coordinate their production with the other party and the JV. The fact that the parents continue to market the LLDPE products independently was not deemed to reduce the anti-competitive effect: 'As sales prices are largely similar, the major competition parameter is the overall strategy on investment and production which is precisely the concern of the coordination within the joint venture'.

(3) Application of Article 81(3)

7.244   In common with Commission decisions in many other areas the analysis of production agreements under Article 81(3) is not always consistent and rigorous. However, an attempt is made here to emphasise the more recent and hopefully more relevant points in various exemption decisions. A recent application of Article 81(3) to a co-operative JV can be found in the Commission decision on *O2 UK Limited/T-Mobile UK Limited*.[141] This decision relates to a collaboration scheme concerning infrastructure sharing and national roaming on the UK market for the third generation of mobile telecommunications networks. The rationale for the exemption was that the two operators will be able to improve the coverage, quality and transmission rates for both wholesale and retail levels. Consumers will notably benefit through cheaper prices and more innovation as a result of the creation of more incentives for competitors to introduce new products on the market. The Commission took note of the fact that the agreement leaves scope for competition between the parties thereof, and that each one will control its core network and thus be able to offer a differentiated product.

7.245   The approach of the Commission concerning each of the requirements laid down in Article 81(3) can be summarised as follows.

7.246   **Improvement of production and promotion of technical progress**   This condition is rarely given much weight and is usually fulfilled by the parties investing in new production facilities or reorganising existing plants or capacities.

7.247   **Benefits to consumers**   This condition is not usually discussed extensively. In those cases where it is, reference is made to the benefits of improved products, greater energy efficiency, or other environmental advantages. In *Austrian Airlines/Deutsche Lufthansa*, the Commission imposed several conditions on the parties for their co-operation agreement to be cleared, as it was not convinced that consumers would receive a share of the benefits arising from the expected cost savings via lower prices.[142]

7.248   **Indispensable restrictions of competition**   The Commission's assessment of this condition focuses on two main elements. The first one, as developed in part in the *Ford/ Volkswagen* and *Exxon/Shell* decisions, relates to the assessment of whether the overall arrangement is the least restrictive way to achieve the objectives of the collaboration.

7.249   Thus in the *Ford/Volkswagen* decision the Commission accepted the parties' argument that 'the partners each acting on its own could not develop and produce the MPV in the same conditions so rapidly and so efficiently as their co-operation will enable them to do'.

---

[141] [2003] OJ L200/59.
[142] [2002] OJ L242/25. Among these conditions, the Commission required both airlines to admit competitors to their frequent flier programme and to make up to 40% of their slots on a route available to a new entrant that wishes to operate in that route.

Similarly in *Exxon/Shell* the Commission considered the possibility of alternative arrangements such as a toll manufacturing agreement and accepted that for technical reasons and reasons of investment they would not have achieved the same advantages as the JV.

The second relates to the assessment of individual restrictions such as exchanges of informa- **7.250** tion, length of supply agreements, or non-compete obligations. The Commission's position is that none of these restrictions should go any further or last longer than is appropriate.

Elimination of competition As in the assessment of other types of agreements the upper **7.251** limit of market share or market concentration at which the Commission has indicated it would prohibit a production agreement would be that of dominance. The Commission frequently takes into account the restraining effect of potential competition from imports outside the EU, and of countervailing buying power from customers.

F. Joint Selling Agreements

(1) Introduction

Definition The agreements covered in this section involve co-operation in the selling of **7.252** products or services between companies operating at the same level of the supply chain. Joint selling covers a range of different forms of coordination of sales policy: market prospecting; reciprocal assistance at the distribution stage (reciprocal supply arrangements); and joint selling as such. In the latter situation, producers grant to a common agent or a joint sales organisation, whether or not on an exclusive basis, the right to sell their products or services on either all markets or a number of them. In this section joint selling will be used in this sense, but will also include reciprocal supply arrangements.

A distinction can be drawn between those agreements where the selling of a product or service **7.253** is an adjunct to another co-operation, for example the joint selling of the output resulting from joint production which has already been or can be challenged under Article 81(1), and those agreements where joint selling is the main joint activity of the partners involved. Where joint selling is the adjunct of an anti-competitive practice, its assessment under Article 81(1) must be carried out in combination with that practice. This section thus analyses agreements having joint selling as their sole or principal object. Full function joint ventures performing the functions of an autonomous economic entity engaged in joint selling will not be considered here as they fall either under the EC Merger Regulation or, in a case where they fall below the thresholds thereof, under the jurisdiction of Member States' competition rules.

Potential or actual competitors In the 1968 Notice concerning agreements, decisions, **7.254** and concerted practices in the field of co-operation between enterprises,[143] it was pointed out under heading II (6) that Article 81(1) does not apply to:

Agreements having as their sole object:

(a) joint selling arrangements,
(b) joint after-sales and repairs service, provided the participating enterprises are not competitors with regard to the products or services covered by the agreement.

---

[143] [1968] OJ C75/3, rectified in [1968] OJ C84/14.

7.255   Thus, competition problems are only likely to arise when the parties to the joint selling agreement are actual or potential competitors. This very principle is also present in the 2001 Guidelines, which confirm that commercialisation agreements are only likely to fall under the competition rules 'if the parties to [such] agreements are competitors' (paragraph 143).

7.256   In addition, a distinction can be made between the horizontal and vertical nature of a selling agreement between what appear to be potential competitors. An undertaking may choose a competing undertaking to sell its products in a particular market. Provided the selling undertaking controls prices and other distribution aspects, he acts as a reseller and the relationship is of a vertical nature. However, if the supplying undertaking keeps control over the price of the product the other undertaking sells, the relationship is of a horizontal nature between competitors and must be assessed as such.

7.257   **Consortia**   If a consortium is being set up for the joint supply of goods or services, and the parties are not competitors as regards these goods or services, the whole operation falls outside the scope of Article 81. For example, in a case where a consortium allows the undertakings involved to introduce a tender for a project that they would not be able to fulfil, or would not have bid for, individually, the parties are not considered to be potential competitors.[144] This circumstance has been expressly recognised in the 2001 Guidelines on horizontal co-operation agreements.[145] However, the Commission has also indicated in its 1968 Notice that 'if the absence of competition between the enterprises and the maintenance of this situation are based on agreements or concerted practices, there may be a restraint of competition'.[146]

7.258   **No joint sales**   There is no restraint of competition, even if they are competitors, in a case where 'several manufacturers, without acting in concert with each other, arrange for an after-sales and repair service for their products to be provided by an enterprise which is independent of them'.[147] The reason is that such an activity is not considered to fall within the category of joint selling activities, as the parties do not act together.

7.259   **Main competition issues**   Joint sales agreements normally lead to the coordination of prices and sales conditions, and sometimes even to output restrictions and market sharing. These issues can therefore be considered as the main competition problems in respect of these agreements. As a result such agreements will normally be prohibited, in particular if they involve price-fixing and market sharing, both regarded as hardcore restrictions.

(2) **Application of Article 81(1) to Joint Selling Agreements**

7.260   (i) **Introduction**   The Commission's attitude towards joint selling among competing undertakings has changed since the late sixties and early seventies, as clearly shown in its Notice concerning the assessment of co-operative joint ventures pursuant to Article 81 of

---

144   *Eurotunnel* [1988] OJ L311/86.
145   Commission Guidelines on horizontal co-operation agreements, para 143.
146   Heading II(5) of the 1968 Notice.
147   Heading II(6), last para, of the 1968 Notice.

the EC Treaty[148] and the section of the 2001 Guidelines dealing with 'commercialisation agreements'. The Notice states that:

> Sales JVs belong to the category of classic horizontal cartels. They have as a rule the object and effect of coordinating the sales policy of competing manufacturers. In this way they not only close off price competition between the parents but also restrict the volume of goods to be delivered by the participants within the framework of the system of allocating orders. The Commission will therefore in principle assess sales JVs negatively.[149]

In principle all joint selling arrangements between competitors are caught by Article 81(1) as they normally lead to the coordination of prices and sales conditions, and sometimes even to output restrictions or market sharing.

7.261

Joint selling agreements are covered by chapter 5 of the Horizontal Guidelines[150] on commercialisation agreements. The Guidelines exclude agreements between non-competitors from the scope of Article 81(1). As noted above, the Commission is primarily concerned with agreements tending to price-fixing and is therefore particularly wary of joint selling agreements since they are deemed to 'have as a rule the object and effect of coordinating the pricing policy of competing manufacturers'. The exclusive nature of the agreement bears no consequence on the Commission's approach, as long as it can be presumed that the agreement will lead to an overall coordination on price.

7.262

The following subsections examine the main factors that are normally taken into account in the assessment of a joint selling arrangement under Article 81. Those factors generally relate to: (i) the characteristics of the selling market and the undertakings concerned; and (ii) the behaviour of the seller(s).

7.263

(ii) Characteristics of the selling market and the undertakings concerned

Size of the undertakings concerned   This question is particularly relevant in connection with small or medium-sized enterprises (SMEs). The 1968 Notice indicates that very often there is no appreciable restriction of competition if joint selling is undertaken by SMEs, even if they are competing with each other. However, no definition of SMEs was given in the Notice. It is only since 1996 that a Community definition of SMEs exists.[151] Nonetheless, even in the presence of such a definition, it should be borne in mind that the Notice does not exclude the application of Article 81(1) in a case where joint selling is agreed upon between a number of SMEs. Indeed, the Notice says that *very often* no appreciable restriction of competition will occur in a case of joint selling by SMEs, but this cannot be totally excluded. In this context, the subsequent 2001 Commission Notice on agreements of minor importance which do not fall under Article 81(1)[152] (known as the 'De Minimis Notice') also defines the field of application of Article 81(1) with regard to

7.264

---

[148] [1993] OJ C43/2.

[149] Points 38 and 60 of the 1993 Notice.

[150] Commission Guidelines on the applicability of Article 81 of the EC Treaty to horizontal co-operation agreements [2001] OJ C3/2.

[151] [1996] OJ L107/4.

[152] [2001] OJ C368/13, replacing Commission Notice of 3 September 1986 ([1986] OJ C231/2–4).

co-operation between SMEs and between other undertakings. The De Minimis Notice[153] builds on the 1968 Co-operation Notice and refers essentially to the appreciable effect on competition. Agreements concluded between undertakings having a market share of not more than 10 per cent (agreements between competitors) or 15 per cent (agreements between non-competitors) of the relevant product and geographical markets do generally not have an appreciable effect on competition within the meaning of Article 81(1). In view of the 10 per cent market share threshold, SMEs are likely to benefit from this Notice. However, the applicability of Article 81(1) cannot be ruled out in the case of agreements representing serious restrictions of competition, including the sharing of sources of supply. Yet, the Commission will only act upon such agreements if the Community interest so requires and in particular if they affect the proper functioning of the single market.[154]

7.265 The Commission's policy towards joint selling carried out by competing SMEs is illustrated in the *SAFCO (Société Anonyme des Fabricants des Conserves Alimentaires)* decision.[155] SAFCO was the first decision where a joint selling agency, responsible for sales to other Member States, was granted a negative clearance because of the small size of the undertakings concerned.

7.266 *Market structure; Oligopolistic markets*   In general, joint sales organisations set up by the biggest undertakings in a concentrated market are likely to infringe Article 81(1) and are very unlikely to be exempted, because they may exclude competition to a very large extent. Furthermore, co-operation through joint selling will not be exempted if it injures competition by reducing the level of potential competition, especially if competition in the relevant market is already weak and the potential competitors are the only credible entrants, as for example in the *Floral* case.

7.267 The Commission's *Floral* decision[156] relates to the sales of compound fertilisers produced by the three leading French manufacturers of fertilisers. Their production accounted for more than two-thirds of total French production. Moreover, at that time France was second only to the United Kingdom in the production of compound fertilisers in the Community. French exports to Germany in the mid-seventies accounted for two-thirds of intra-Community exports. Large quantities of compound fertilisers were imported both into France and Germany, which were also major exporters. The customers were around thirty co-operatives and fertiliser wholesalers.[157] All the parties' products for export to Germany passed through Floral. Although they had not explicitly undertaken to channel all their exports to Germany exclusively through Floral, they nevertheless did so for a period of more than five years. Later on the bulk of such exports was channelled through Floral. Exports to other Member States took place on an individual basis. The three French manufacturers sold their products to Floral at varying prices. However, the products were

---

153 First issued in 1970, [1970] OJ C64/1 (5% market share and aggregate annual turnover of ECU 15 million) and amended for the first time in 1977, [1977] OJ C313/3 (5% market share and ECU 50 million). The 1986 Notice contained a turnover threshold of ECU 200 million, last amended in 1994 (ECU 300 million), [1994] OJ C368. In 1997 the turnover threshold was abandoned. The latest Notice dates from 2001 (10% market share for agreements between competitors, 15% for agreements between non-competitors), as noted above.

154 Report on Competition Policy 1996 (Vol XXVI) point 38.

155 *SAFCO* [1972] OJ L13/44.

156 *Floral* [1980] OJ L39/51.

157 Point 5 of the decision, 53.

resold at uniform prices (including identical rebates) and on uniform terms.[158] The prices were aligned on those of German manufacturers which were on average 5 per cent to 10 per cent, and sometimes as much as 15 per cent, higher than in France. German buyers were thus faced with identical prices and identical sales conditions for products of the same type.

The Commission concluded that the organisation of export sales in this manner, ie chan- **7.268** nelled and standardised through Floral, amounted to an export sales agency. By refraining from exporting to Germany otherwise than through Floral, the parties excluded competition between them on the German market.

In order to measure the impact of Floral on the relevant market, the Commission took into **7.269** account the following factors: (i) the three manufacturers were France's largest manufacturers; (ii) they also were large manufacturers in relation to total Community production, ie representing together more than 10 per cent; (iii) they had a substantial exportable output and their plants were capable of exporting on their own to Germany; (iv) freight costs for Germany were to a large extent not higher than those for destinations in France; and (v) the structure of the German market, where the number of competitors was very small, ie dominated by three companies. The Commission thus concluded that the market concerned had an oligopolistic structure. The Commission also concluded that, if on such a market three of the few suppliers channel and standardise their supply through a joint sales organisation, the oligopoly becomes even tighter. Individual sales, even in relatively small quantities, can, in such a market, have an appreciable impact on market conditions.

The Commission adopted a similar approach in *Ansac*.[159] Ansac (American Natural Soda **7.270** Ash Corporation) was the export cartel of the United States natural soda ash industry. Between 1982 and 1990, imports of US natural soda ash into the Community were restricted by anti-dumping measures. In 1983 the US producers concluded a membership agreement under which they agreed to make all their export sales through Ansac. Ansac would decide on the products to be sold, the choice of customers, and the prices to be charged. This agreement would allow for only one new entrant on the European market. However, the Commission considered that Ansac's members were all large undertakings, capable of selling regularly on an individual basis within the Community. If Ansac were allowed to enter the Community market, this would not lead to the improvement of the market structure nor improve competition in the Community's soda ash market in general, as there would be no possibility between Ansac's members to compete between themselves and between them and Community producers. The Community soda ash market at the time could be characterised as having a rigid and oligopolistic structure. The Commission took the view that the anti-competitive agreements between Community producers did not as such keep out competition from third parties. If their collusive prices were set above the market level, competitors outside these agreements could still enter the European market by applying a lower price. In such a market it was not necessary for the US producers to combine their sales in the Community in order to be able to enter into this rigid market. The principal obstacles to the entry of US natural soda ash were the Community anti-dumping

---

158 Point 6 of the decision, 53 and 54.
159 *Ansac* [1991] OJ L152/54.

measures and the exclusionary rebates systems operated by a couple of Community producers, both of which were removed.

7.271 *Market entry*   In *SAFCO*,[160] it was shown that a joint sales agency of SMEs can facilitate and increase new export activities to markets outside the normal spheres of activity of the undertakings involved, and be thus desirable from a competition point of view. The economic rationale behind this decision was to encourage market entry by facilitating this kind of co-operation between SMEs, thus making them become more competitive and able to strengthen the competitive structure of the market.

7.272 Encouragement of market entry by facilitating joint sales was also the underlying rationale in *Cekacan*,[161] which concerned a co-operation agreement concluded between two packaging companies in Sweden and in Germany. The object of the agreement was to extend throughout Europe the use of a new packaging, known as Cekacan. In this respect the parties envisaged setting up a new company, Ceka Europe, allowing the parties to introduce and market the new process in other Member States. The agreement appeared to be aimed solely at co-operation in an initial phase for the introduction of the new product, taking advantage of the experience obtained by the German partner in using the processes in question. The introduction of the processes concerned in other Member States' markets, including Germany where the German partner had been using the processes in question, would thus be undertaken only through the joint venture Ceka Europe. The JV would also be the sole supplier of materials and services required in the production of Cekacan. The Commission considered that the establishment of Ceka Europe would prevent the German partner from developing its practice as regards the use of the relevant processes, thereby removing an independent competitor from the market. Secondly, the joint sales of materials and services related to the production of Cekacan by the JV would affect the position of the German partner. Indeed, the exclusive supply clauses contained in the agreement would remove any incentive for the German party to manufacture the necessary materials, since it would not be able to sell them for Cekacan products. This would also restrict its competitive position towards third parties manufacturing such materials which were free to market them to Cekacan customers.

7.273 In its assessment of the agreement under Article 81(3), the Commission took into account that the agreement allowed for the extension of the use of the Cekacan product, which represented a substantial technological innovation. The agreement was also necessary to enable the participants to establish an efficient distribution system in a new market. Thus, the agreement would help to improve production and in particular the distribution of this product within the single market, using the experience of the German partner. This would result in a more rapid increase in the number of customers using Cekacan packaging.

(iii) **Types of seller behaviour**

7.274 *Price restrictions*   Price competition is expressly covered in Article 81(1)(a) in the sense that agreements or concerted practices that directly or indirectly fix selling prices are prohibited.

---

[160] *SAFCO* [1972] OJ L13/44.
[161] *Cekacan* [1990] OJ L299/64.

Price is directly linked to supply, and thus is of special importance in cases involving joint selling agreements.

Belgian-German fertilisers[162] concerned a reciprocal supply arrangement, operated by a **7.275** Belgian and two German manufacturers of fertilisers. The Belgian manufacturer sold each of the German parties every month an agreed quantity of fertilisers. The fertiliser was then delivered, not in Germany, but to the Belgian clients of the German manufacturers. The German manufacturers sold equivalent quantities to their Belgian partner, but supplied them directly to the latter's customers in Germany. Manufacturers of fertilisers sell their products at prices including transport costs, ie the cost of carriage to the station or port of destination. At the time German prices were around 12 per cent higher than Belgian prices. The price for the reciprocal sales between the Belgian and the two German producers was the same. Although the parties did not sell directly to their foreign customers, they nonetheless compared actual freight costs with the higher transport costs that would have been incurred if they had sold directly to those customers. The companies then shared the difference. The price for sales to local customers was the same as the price offered in the country of destination to their foreign customers. However, the arrangement left the parties free to determine this price. Although there was no formal agreement to align prices, the Commission considered that this system in practice led to price coordination between the three parties.

Output restrictions   Joint selling agreements may influence the parties' output. Any lim-   **7.276** itation thereof, for example through sales quotas, necessarily has an impact on the volume of goods to be delivered and hence limits the choice of purchasers. These output restrictions may also be a means of controlling prices through controlling supply. Output restrictions intended to reduce overcapacity are not dealt with in this chapter.

Ansac[163] can also serve as a good example of the effect joint selling can have on output.   **7.277** Ansac's overall goal was to market the natural soda ash produced by its members in Europe and to this end to enter the European market, but only as a second supplier to glass manufacturers. To do this, it decided to limit its sales in the Community to 5 per cent of total demand. At the time of the Ansac membership agreement, the few Community producers of soda ash were involved in collusive pricing and marketing agreements.[164]

In general terms the Ansac membership agreement restricted competition with respect to   **7.278** output and prices in an oligopolistic market. It was Ansac's intention to limit its sales in the Community to 5 per cent of total demand, thereby accepting the role of a secondary supplier and leaving the soda ash market in the hands of the European producers. This would minimise the competitive effect Ansac's supplies might have on the sales of Community producers and clearly restricted output. This meant that the customers of the Community soda ash producers were not offered a real alternative in terms of supply.

[162] Report on Competition Policy 1976 (Vol VI) points 126–128.
[163] *Ansac* [1991] OJ L152/54.
[164] *Solvay/ICI* [1991] OJ L152/1; *Solvay/CFK* [1991] OJ L152/16; *Solvay* [1991] OJ L152/21; *ICI* [1991] OJ L152/40.

7.279 *Exclusivity clauses*   It should be noted from the outset that, in the Commission's view, it is not important whether or not the agreement commits the parties to sell exclusively through the joint sales agency. What counts is whether, as was shown in both the *Floral* and *Soda Ash* decisions, in practice they do so, irrespective of whether this is done in order to obtain the rationalisation benefits of a single organisation. The 2001 Guidelines confirm this view (paragraph 145).

7.280 In two recent decisions concerning football broadcasting rights, the Commission has elaborated on the implications of exclusivity in connection with joint selling agreements.

7.281 In *UEFA—Champions League*,[165] the Commission cleared the joint selling agreement implemented by UEFA to manage the TV broadcasting rights relating to the Champions League tournament, after some concessions were made to allow individual clubs to exploit such rights for both the Internet and the UMTS mobile phone technology. UEFA, as the private organisation that runs and regulates European football, manages and sells media rights to the Champions League on behalf of the clubs participating in the contest. The Commission maintained that the central selling scheme ran afoul of Article 81 EC, since it raised problems at both the horizontal (curbing competition between individual clubs for the sale of TV rights) and the vertical level (foreclosing access to the rights by broadcasters). The final settlement included the separation of matches between different packages, the most attractive to be sold by UEFA on an exclusive basis. However, room was left for the clubs to manage individually the TV rights of some matches and the rights on other platforms such as the Internet and the third generation of mobile telephony. Further, exclusivity agreements with national broadcasters were limited to a maximum period of three years. In view of these conditions, an exemption under Article 81(3) was granted.

7.282 Similarly, in *German Bundesliga*,[166] the Commission accepted a series of commitments offered by the German football league providing for the liberalisation of the central marketing of Bundesliga rights. These remedies were essentially similar to those imposed in the context of the *UEFA* case, ie the creation of several packages available to broadcasters and the limitation of the exclusivity to three seasons.

(3) Application of Article 81(3) to Joint Selling Agreements

7.283 **Efficiencies**   As expressly indicated in the 1968 Notice,[167] the Commission gives favourable consideration to agreements leading to the achievement of economies of scale, such as joint storage and transport facilities. However, it is considered that, in general, joint selling arrangements largely exceed what might be necessary to achieve economies of scale by the parties concerned. It is therefore unlikely that they can be exempted under Article 81(3). In particular, joint sales organisations established among the biggest producers in a market are highly unlikely to be exempted.

7.284 In both the *Soda Ash* and the *Floral* cases, the Commission prohibited joint sales because of, *inter alia*, the size of each of the parties to the agreements. If the parties to a joint selling

---

165 *UEFA—Champions League* [2003] OJ L291/25.
166 A summary of the commitment decision was published in [2005] OJ L134/46.
167 [1968] OJ C75/3, point II (4).

agreement are capable of selling on an individual basis, they will have to provide strong justifications in order to demonstrate the need for their co-operation, especially in terms of efficiencies.

Also, when joint selling arrangements like the Ansac membership agreement largely exceed **7.285** what might be necessary to achieve the economies of scale that result from joint storage and transport facilities, these efficiencies cannot outweigh the anti-competitive effects resulting from the joint selling agreement. In any event, no efficiencies can justify a joint selling agreement that leads to price fixing.

Specific circumstances allowing for an exemption Although joint selling arrangements **7.286** are rarely exemptable, specific circumstances may allow for an exemption to be granted.

The 2001 Guidelines state that '[p]rice fixing can generally not be justified, unless it is **7.287** indispensable for the integration of other marketing functions, and this integration will generate substantial efficiencies'. In addition, the 1993 Notice indicated that:

> The Commission takes a positive view however of those cases where joint distribution of the contract products is part of a global co-operation project which merits favourable treatment pursuant to Article 85(3) [now Article 81(3)] and for the success of which it is indispensable. [. . .] In other cases, an exemption can be envisaged only in certain specific circumstances.[168]

In this respect attention should be drawn to *UIP*,[169] which is the most obvious example of **7.288** such 'specific circumstances'.

The decision concerns the distribution and licensing by United International Pictures **7.289** (UIP) on an exclusive basis of feature motion pictures, short subjects, and trailers produced and/or distributed by three production companies (Paramount, MCA and MGM), all engaged in the production and distribution of feature films and other entertainment programmes for exhibition in cinemas, on television and through other media. The parent companies originally distributed their own films within the Community through their own separate distribution organisations.

A first important feature of the market for the exhibition of films is that there are a number **7.290** of means to measure its size. The decision mentions the following ones: (a) the number of films; (b) the number of tickets sold or admissions; (c) box office receipts, ie the amount paid by the public to see a film; and (d) rentals, ie the part of box office receipts paid by the cinemas to the distributor for the right to show a film.[170] The Commission chose box office receipts as the most meaningful way of measuring the size of the relevant market. On this basis the three parent companies accounted for some 22 per cent of gross Community box office receipts. However, their market share sometimes varied considerably from one Member State to the other (from 13 per cent in Greece up to 35 per cent in the UK). A second important characteristic of this market is the wide variation in market share from year to year depending on the success of the films shown. In this respect the Commission notes

---

[168] Point 60 of the 1993 Notice.
[169] *UIP* [1989] OJ L226/25, exemption renewed for five years in 1999.
[170] Point 12 of the decision, 26.

that the cinema industry has suffered from 'a remarkable decline both in admissions and in box-office receipts in the years prior to the agreements'.

7.291 UIP was granted a right of first refusal to distribute its parents' films. However, UIP must distribute a film if a parent, holding the distribution rights in any territory, so directs.

7.292 The parties to the agreements indicated that the purpose in forming UIP was to enhance efficiencies by reducing fixed overhead costs while maximising for each parent the gross receipts from the films distributed.[171]

7.293 The specific characteristics of the cinema industry played an important, even decisive role in the Commission's considerations to grant an exemption. Indeed, the Commission attached particular importance to the important changes that affected the cinema industry over a period of more than fifteen years prior to the conclusion of the agreements concerned. During that period (1970–1986) cinema admissions fell by an average of 40 per cent. Box office revenue fell by around 26 per cent. This decline resulted from structural changes in the market. The introduction of new technologies associated with television, such as cable, satellite television and video cassettes, allowed for a growth of film presentation through these media to the detriment of cinemas. In addition costs related to production and distribution had risen sharply. Within this economic environment, the Commission found the JV indispensable for the continuation of the international distribution of the parents' films.

7.294 These characteristics also strongly influenced the economic power UIP could exercise on the relevant market, normally measured in terms of market share. Although it had an average market share of 22 per cent in the Community, the Commission considered that competition in this market tends to be localised due to language barriers, national regulations and different patterns of distribution. However, more important were the observed wide variations in market share from year to year depending on the success of the films shown in a given Member State. Thus, the market share UIP held in various Member States did not necessarily reflect its economic power in these countries.

7.295 This analysis was confirmed in 1999, when the Commission renewed the exemption for an additional five year period.[172] The Commission found that, despite the strength of the film distribution market, UIP's performance had been moderate during the period covered by the exemption, its market share decreasing to 17 per cent in 1998. UIP also faced competition from a number of distributors and exhibitors with countervailing power. In these conditions, and given the amendments and undertakings attached to the original agreement, the Commission concluded that there was no indication that UIP held market power.

(4) Practices Restricted to a National Market

7.296 **The Cobelaz doctrine** The initial position taken by the Commission with regard to joint sales agencies set up by competing undertakings restricted to a national market, was reflected in its *Report on Competition Policy 1971* (Volume I). Two decisions taken at the end of the sixties and early seventies articulated this position in what is known as the

---

171 Point 15 of the decision, 27.
172 See press release IP/99/681 of 14 September 1999.

Cobelaz[173] doctrine. In these cases, the Commission granted a negative clearance[174] after joint selling systems were altered by the parties so that they were restricted to national markets and to markets outside the then EEC. It was considered that purely national sales organisations did not affect trade between Member States and therefore were not caught by Article 81(1). However, at the same time the Commission indicated that it would undertake investigations in order to find out whether or not the maintenance of national joint sales agencies would lead to a protection of national markets which would be incompatible with the competition rules.[175]

The CSV doctrine   In contrast with the *Report on Competition Policy 1971* (Volume I), **7.297** neither the 1993 Notice concerning the assessment of co-operative joint ventures pursuant to Article 81 of the EC Treaty[176] nor the 2001 Guidelines makes a distinction between national joint sales agencies and those which coordinate sales from and to the markets of Member States. Following the Commission decision in the *CSV* case, it is established case law that nationwide joint sales agreements may affect trade between Member States.

CSV[177] marks the second stage in the case law relating to joint selling agreements applied **7.298** on the territory of a single Member State. As in the *Cobelaz* case, which concerned a Belgian joint sales agency of fertilisers, the CSV sales agency was granted an exclusive right to sell for the territory of a single Member State, this time the Netherlands. In both cases each of the parties retained its individual right to sell in other Member States. In the *Cobelaz* case this led the Commission to grant a negative clearance, as it considered such an agreement, confined to a national market, not to affect trade between Member States. However, in the *CSV* case, the Commission shifted its position considerably.

CSV (Centraal Stikstof Verkoopkantoor) was a joint sales agency of two Dutch manufac- **7.299** turers of straight nitrogenous fertilisers. Between them they accounted for 80 per cent of Dutch production and 16 per cent of Community production of this type of fertiliser. Moreover, their major competitors in the Community each accounted for between 7 and 8 per cent of total Community production. Under the CSV agreement the sales agency was responsible for marketing all straight nitrogenous fertilisers manufactured by the two parties in the Netherlands and on export markets outside the Community. To this extent, the parties notified to CSV their production and sales forecasts before the beginning of each marketing year. On the basis of the information collected by CSV, the parties adjusted their figures on volumes produced and sold on the various markets in the previous month on a monthly basis and corrected the forecasts for the remaining months of the year. Every month a planning committee discussed stocks, production and sales in order to verify whether the parties were in line with the forecasts. This system also included exports within the Community. Due to the monthly planning, the export levels for exports within the Community set by the parties at the beginning of the year were not exceeded. Additional quantities were made available to the joint sales agency, in order to avoid the risk of these

---

[173] *Cobelaz/Febelaz* [1986] OJ L276/13; *Cobelaz Cokeries* [1986] OJ L276/19.
[174] *SEIFA* [1969] OJ L173/8; *Supexie* [1970] OJ L10/10.
[175] Report on Competition Policy 1971 (Vol I), point 13.
[176] [1993] OJ C43/2.
[177] *CSV* [1978] OJ L242/15.

quantities being sold twice. A steering group discussed, every two months, questions relating to sales in the Netherlands, prices, rebates, deliveries to competitors, imports, exports, etc. As regards prices, uniform prices were applied, since the other sellers aligned their prices with those of CSV.

7.300 Despite the fact that exports to other Member States were not handled by CSV, the co-operation between the two parties affected their entire production and distribution policy. Although at the beginning of each marketing year the parties were free to decide on the quantities they would sell through CSV and the quantities they would sell themselves, in practice the planning system led to the coordination of their plans. Corrections to these plans were also harmonised in the course of the year. In such a situation the effect of the agreement on trade between Member States could be considered as appreciable, because the parties accounted for some 16 per cent of Community production of the product concerned.

G. Joint Buying Agreements

(1) Introduction

7.301 **Definition**   Joint buying covers a wide range of different forms of coordination of the parties' purchase policy. Joint buying can take place through central buying organisations, by means of a JV, or on the basis of looser forms of co-operation. Experience shows that joint buying is most likely to happen in the retail sector, especially the food retail sector.

7.302 **Associations of retailers**   Joint buying by so-called associations of retailers such as co-operatives, whereby the central buying organisation is owned by the members of the co-operative, can contain both horizontal and vertical elements. Depending on the specific features of the case, such agreements will be considered either as vertical arrangements or horizontal agreements.

7.303 **Co-operatives**   A co-operative may have an effect on competition in two ways. First, a co-operative, by reason of the very principles that govern it, may affect the free play of competition as regards the activity constituting its object as a co-operative. Secondly, the obligations imposed on the members of a co-operative, and in particular the obligations associated with the principle of 'fidelity to the co-operative', by virtue of which the co-operative generally imposes on its members obligations to supply to it or to take supplies from it in return for the particular advantages which it grants them, are liable to influence both the economic activity of the co-operative and the free play of competition between its members and vis-à-vis third parties. Thus, it cannot be considered that the exercise of an economic activity by a co-operative society is, as a matter of principle, not subject to the provisions of Article 81(1) of the Treaty or that the conditions for the applicability of the Community competition rules, as such, to the co-operative sector are of a different nature from those applying to the other forms of organising economic activity. In assessing the effects on a given market of the presence of a co-operative, account will be taken of the particular features of that form of association of undertakings, but that exercise must be carried out *inter alia* in the light of Article 81(3) of the Treaty.[178]

---

[178] Case T–61/89 *Dansk Pelsdyravlerforening v Commission* [1992] ECR II–1931 (exclusive supply obligations).

Potential or actual competitors   For joint buying to constitute a real competition problem **7.304** the parties to the joint buying agreement must be either potential or actual competitors. In *Screensport/EBU*,[179] the Commission considered that the Eurosport Consortium members and Sky could be qualified as potential competitors in the market for transnational television sports channels. In deciding so, it attached much importance to the fact that the Eurosport Consortium members (an association of broadcasting organisations which are also members of the European Broadcasting Union (EBU), as well as Sky Television and News International) decided to establish a new satellite television sports channel, while at the same time Sky actively tried to acquire rights to sports events and was also contemplating the establishment of a satellite sports channel. Sky thus had the potential to become a direct competitor to the satellite sports channel the interested EBU members wanted to establish.

Two views of buyer power   Two contrasting views can be identified when it comes to the **7.305** possible consequences of buyer power. Both have been recognised by the Commission in paragraph 127 of the 2001 Guidelines. The first one is a positive or benign view of buyer power. It takes as a starting point the fact that retailers' buyer power can be used to counter the market power of suppliers, thus preventing the latter from fully exploiting their market position. Buyer power could then lead to lower prices which, as a result of effective competition on the downstream market, would be passed on to consumers. The contrary or deleterious view is that buyer power may have damaging effects in the longer run for two reasons. First, because of the effects it may have on the profitability of suppliers, which may result in lower investments in branded products and in the development of new products. Secondly, it might lead to a weakening of smaller retailers, as wholesale prices for them may rise as a response of suppliers to the lower wholesale prices the bigger retailers are able to obtain. The fear is that brands might disappear and that a small number of retailers would mainly supply their own brands. This would finally mean reduced choice and possibly in some cases higher consumer prices.

The economic welfare trade-offs   It seems useful to keep these two views in mind when **7.306** examining buyer power, as they allow for the consideration of a number of trade-offs. The first of them is a short run trade-off between increased buyer power of a retailer (as a result of a merger) or a group of retailers (as a result of a joint buying agreement) on the upstream market and increased retailer power on the downstream market where it operates as a seller. If a retailer increases its market share, it may use its increased buyer power to put downward pressure on wholesale prices. At the same time, its stronger position on the downstream market could be used to raise rather than lower final prices. The second trade-off is a trade-off between the short run benefits of lower final prices and the longer term damage to manufacturer competition from weakened brands and greater own-label penetration and the distortion of retail competition on the downstream market in favour of large retailers. Given these trade-offs, it cannot be anticipated what will be the net economic welfare effect of buyer power.

Main competition issues   Competition problems may arise on the purchasing market **7.307** when the parties to the agreement pool their buyer power and coordinate their purchase

---

[179] *Screensport/EBU* [1991] OJ L63/32.

prices and other purchase conditions. Joint buying might also lead to coordination between the parties on the downstream market. Furthermore, account has to be taken of efficiencies realised through joint buying.

7.308 The 1968 Notice does not deal with joint buying as such. Reference is made to 'agreements, which have as their sole object the joint use of [. . .] storing and transport equipment'.[180] However, joint buying agreements cannot benefit from that Notice, as they normally do not have as their sole object joint storing and transport of the goods bought. Joint buying agreements go well beyond these organisational and technical aspects.[181] It is not uncommon for parties to a joint buying agreement to engage also in developing products under a common label. In this respect the 1968 Notice indicates that 'agreements having as their sole object the use of a common label to designate a certain quality, where the label is available to all competitors on the same conditions' do not restrict competition.[182] Again, the parties to a joint buying agreement normally do not limit themselves to this joint activity.

7.309 In contrast, the 2001 Guidelines deal with joint buying agreements more extensively, taking the view that joint buying agreements between SMEs are normally deemed pro-competitive, because the concentration of buying power enables the partners to achieve volumes and discounts similar to their bigger competitors.

7.310 The main competition issues arising out of joint buying agreements are also briefly set out in the 1993 Notice concerning the assessment of co-operative joint ventures pursuant to Article 81.[183] Compared to the position taken by the Commission towards joint selling, the position reflected in its 1993 Notice is less negative towards joint purchasing co-operative JVs:

> Purchasing JVs contribute to the rationalisation of ordering and to the better use of transport and store facilities but are at the same time an instrument for the setting of uniform purchase prices and conditions and often of purchase quotas. By combining their demand power in a JV, the parents can obtain a position of excessive influence vis-à-vis the other side of the market and distort competition between suppliers. Consequently, the disadvantages often outweigh the possible benefits, which can accompany purchasing JVs, particularly those between competing producers.
>
> The Commission is correspondingly prepared to grant exemptions only in exceptional cases and then only if the parents retain the possibility of purchasing individually.[184]

(2) Buyer Power—Definition

7.311 Buyer power enables an undertaking to influence the price and other terms at which it obtains its products from suppliers. The concept of buyer power in this very broad definition is analogous to the concept of market power.

7.312 In 1981 the OECD defined buyer power as 'a situation which exists when a firm or a group of firms, either because it has a dominant position as a purchaser of a product or service or because it has strategic or leverage advantages as a result of its size or other characteristics,

---

180 Heading II (4) of the 1968 Notice.
181 See, for example, the case mentioned in the *Report on Competition Policy 1983* (Vol XIII), point 130.
182 Heading II(8) of the 1968 Notice.
183 [1993] OJ C43/2.
184 Point 61 of the 1993 Notice.

is able to obtain from a supplier more favourable terms than those available to other buyers'.[185] This definition relies mainly on whether a buyer or a group of buyers can obtain favourable terms compared to other buyers. It has the disadvantage that it ignores an obvious source of price differences, namely those that arise from cost-related discounts. If, for example, a retail chain, by setting up its own central depot, absorbs a part of the distribution costs that was borne before by suppliers, one would expect the retailer to obtain a lower purchasing price as a result thereof.

7.313 The OECD definition also does not catch the situation where the members of a purchasing group are competitors at the downstream level. In such a situation, joint buying may also affect their behaviour as suppliers on the retail market. For the analysis of buyer power it makes a difference whether there is a situation of power on both the upstream (procurement) and downstream (retail) markets, or whether there only exists a situation of power on the procurement market but not on the retail market.

7.314 The research paper on the welfare consequences of the exercise of buyer power, prepared for the OFT in 1998,[186] also refers to the more favourable terms an undertaking or a group of firms can obtain from suppliers when describing buyer power. However, compared to the OECD definition, it is a broader one. It distinguishes between more favourable terms in general, namely more favourable terms than those available to other buyers, and those terms that are more favourable than 'would otherwise be expected under normal competitive conditions'. The latter part of the definition is interesting in the sense that it seems to suggest that in some cases the exercise of buyer power might be the result of lack of sufficient competition in the market concerned. However, this definition also shows the same deficiencies as that of the OECD in so far as it is also based on the more favourable terms approach without singling out cost-related discounts.

7.315 In 1998 another attempt within the OECD was made to define buyer power.[187] This time, the definition says that:

> a retailer is defined to have buyer power if, in relation to at least one supplier, it can credibly threaten to impose a long term opportunity cost which, were the threat carried out, would be significantly disproportionate to any resulting long term opportunity cost to itself. By disproportionate, we intend a difference in relative rather than absolute opportunity cost, eg Retailer A has buyer power over Supplier B if a decision to de-list B's product could cause A's profit to decline by 0.1 per cent and B's to decline by 10 per cent.

7.316 Again, the 1998 OECD definition does not catch the situation where members of a purchasing group are downstream competitors. The situation described in its paper also seems to point towards a dependency relation, where a retailer is exploiting the state of economic dependence of a supplier, which has no real alternative. In terms of competition the relationship

---

[185] OECD, *Buying Power: The Exercise of Market Power by Dominant Buyers*, Report of the Committee of Experts on Restrictive Business Practices (Paris, 1981).
[186] PW Dobson, M Waterson and A Chu, *The Welfare Consequences of the Exercise of Buyer Power*, Research Paper 16 (London, Office of Fair Trading, 1998).
[187] OECD, *Buyer Power of Large Scale Multiproduct Retailers*, Background Paper by the Secretariat, Round Table on Buying Power (Paris, 1998).

between a retailer and a supplier can be described as asymmetric. Indeed, a retailer, by the sheer fact that he/she sells a broad range and a great diversity of products (on average a supermarket may offer 18,000 different products), often represents a significant proportion of the overall sales of a supplier, whereas the products of the supplier may represent a much smaller percentage of the retailers' turnover. The example given by the OECD would also indicate that concerns about buying power relate to the distribution of economic rents, namely the division of profits and not to the impact of the retailers' behaviour on economic welfare. However, when buyer power is mainly a matter of distribution of economic rents, it may be better dealt with as an issue of unfair competition. Under traditional antitrust law, economic dependence may be of concern if it results in adverse welfare effects in terms of under-investment by suppliers or higher consumer prices.

7.317 The foregoing shows that the concept of buyer power is not easy to define. This seems at least partly related to the confusion that may arise out of the concept of most favourable terms in relation to buyer power. Indeed, although buyer power inevitably translates itself into more favourable supply contracts, the fact that some buyers are successful in obtaining more favourable purchasing terms than others does not automatically mean that there might be a case of buyer power, especially in cases of cost-related discounts. More favourable terms as such are therefore not sufficient evidence of buyer power. Thus, it seems more appropriate to distinguish at least between cost-related discounts and more favourable purchasing terms not related to cost savings. This distinction can also serve as an indicator of competition problems, especially with regard to the question whether buyer power generates efficiencies or not. It seems also appropriate to identify those cost-related discounts that are the result of the acquisition of a high volume of products. In such a case, depending on the volume bought, more favourable discount can be the result of buyer power. Thus, some cost-related discounts can serve as evidence of buyer power and some cannot.

7.318 Another problem in relation to the concept of buyer power is the issue of a supplier's economic dependence on a retailer. It is not clear under which circumstances the exploitation of a supplier's economic dependence can be considered as an expression of buyer power. It is particularly difficult to determine whether there is a case of unfair competition or loss of economic welfare. For this reason, examples of economic dependence are often used in order to describe buyer power, but they might well fail to show any real detrimental impact on competition in terms of damage to economic welfare.

(3) The Existence of Buyer Power

7.319 The existence of buyer power in a given market depends on a number of factors. Some of these factors have already been mentioned briefly in relation to the concept of buyer power. They relate to the structure of the markets, the degree of commonality of costs among the members to a joint buying agreement and the parties' conduct in terms of pricing and strategic buyer behaviour.

7.320 Competition concerns may arise if a joint buying agreement allows the buying group to gain or increase market power over suppliers and if the agreement facilitates the coordination of the parties' competitive behaviour on the downstream selling market where they are active as suppliers.

There is no absolute threshold to measure buyer power. It is a matter of degree. Buyer **7.321** power depends on a number of factors, such as the market position of the parties and their competitors on the relevant market(s), the concentration of the market(s), barriers to entry, the countervailing power of suppliers, the nature of the products and the degree of elasticity of supply. Due to the potential asymmetric relation between suppliers and retailers (see the concept of buyer power), the market share threshold at which joint buying might have a negative effect on competition might be lower than the threshold indicating a supplier's seller power.

The 2001 Guidelines nevertheless take the view that below a 15 per cent combined market **7.322** share, it is unlikely that the parties have sufficient market power for the joint buying agreement to raise concerns.

The different methods to measure market power are discussed below. **7.323**

Direct measurement of buyer power: elasticity of supply   The Buying Power Index **7.324** (BPI) of Blair and Harrison[188] is based on the elasticity of supply. The underlying idea is that if the supply of a good is perfectly elastic, a monopsonist, ie a monopoly buyer, cannot exert buyer power through a restriction of supply. The less elastic the supply, the greater the possibility for a monopsonist to exert buyer power. This index thus examines the scope for a single buyer to use buyer power. However, it can only be used in a monopsony type of situation. Within monopsony situations, the index can be especially relevant if the supply side is perfectly competitive. In other situations, demand interferes as a factor and supply can no longer serve as the overall factor determining the measurement of buyer power. Furthermore, elasticities of supply are difficult to measure and this index seems therefore of limited use in practice in order to draw conclusions with regard to buyer power. It requires a substantial amount of detailed data on levels of prices and output sold which is rarely available. In view of this difficulty, other methods are used for assessing buyer power.

Indirect measurement of buyer power: market shares   As in the case for market power **7.325** in general, buyer power is most likely to occur when one or a few undertakings dominate as buyers on the procurement market. Although buyer concentration is no definitive proof of the existence of buyer power and other factors need to be taken into consideration, it can serve as a useful indicator of the existence of buyer power. In this respect, buyer concentration relates both to the number of undertakings and to the difference in size between them. For example, buyer concentration may arise when in a given market only three dominant buyers operate, each of them having 30 per cent of the market. In another situation, buyer concentration may arise when one player holds 40 per cent of the market and its competitors each only around 5 per cent. Especially in the latter situation, it seems desirable to pay attention to the leading undertakings' market share, as well as to the direction in which it has developed over a number of years. Changes in market share can serve as an indicator for the dynamics of the market concerned and point at an increase, stabilisation, or decrease of buyer concentration. The use of market shares as a proxy for the existence of buying power has been endorsed by the 2001 Guidelines, establishing a presumption of an

---

[188] OFT Research Paper, 50, endnote 7.

absence of negative impact in all cases where the parties to the agreement have a combined market share below 15 per cent. Above this threshold, other factors will take part in what the Guidelines name 'a more detailed assessment of the impact of a joint buying agreement on the market', such as market concentration and the possible existence of countervailing power on the part of suppliers.[189]

7.326 There are several ways to measure buyer concentration using market share. The most common are the buyer concentration ratio and the so-called HHI.

7.327 The buyer concentration ratio focuses on the market share of the largest buyers in the market. The ratio depends on the number of undertakings one wants to take into account. Thus, if the ratio is four, this means that the market share of the four largest buyers serves as an indicator of buyer power on the market. The advantage of this method is that it is easy to apply. The disadvantage is that it does not take account of all the market players and therefore may not always present a complete picture of the situation.

7.328 The Herfindahl-Hirschman Index (HHI) measures the sum of the squared market shares of undertakings buying a particular product. The advantage of this index is that it takes account of the market share of each of the competitors in the market. However, a problem might arise if not all market shares are known, but the extent of this problem depends on which undertakings' market share data are missing.

7.329 **Performance measures** A third method to measure buyer power is to measure output or performance variables such as profitability or the price–cost margin. Taking a competitive price and competitive purchasing conditions as a basis, buyer power would then be measured in terms of the size of the discount compared to the competitive price and the value of special purchasing conditions obtained from suppliers compared to competitive purchasing terms. As with the Buying Power Index, this system has the disadvantage that it would be difficult to put in practice, as it requires a lot of data that are not readily available.

7.330 Price–cost margins of undertakings may be more readily accessible. However, it is not an indicator of buyer power alone. Price–cost margins may reflect cost savings obtained as a result of the efficient operation of an undertaking or cost savings handed over by the supplier to the buyer as a result of cost savings related to the handling of the goods bought. For these reasons price–cost margins as such are not a very useful indicator of buyer power.

7.331 **Other variables** Additional methods to measure buyer power, used in combination with the above-mentioned measures, can be the weighted annual average purchases per undertaking (this captures the impact of large buyers having strong bargaining power), and a measure of the dispersion of sales across industries (this reflects the relation between the dependency and the bargaining power of suppliers).[190]

(4) Relevant Markets and Substantive Assessment

7.332 The effects on competition of buying power must be assessed on two categories of markets. First, on the relevant upstream (procurement) market. Secondly, on the relevant downstream

---

189 Commission's Guidelines on horizontal co-operation agreements, para 131.
190 OFT Research Paper, 53, endnote 27.

(selling) market, ie the market where the parties to the joint buying agreement are active as suppliers. Indeed, co-operation in the field of buying can lead to competition problems on the selling market, although the initial co-operation is undertaken on the procurement market. The existence of this complex group of relevant markets has been recognised by the Commission in the 2001 Guidelines (paragraph 119).

The definition of the relevant product and geographic markets is carried out on the basis of the methodology laid down in the Commission's Notice on Market Definition.[191] However, it has to be noted that the definition of substitutability on a procurement market is different. While substitutability in a selling market is defined from the viewpoint of consumers, in a procurement market it is defined from the viewpoint of suppliers. Thus, the alternatives suppliers have in the case of a small but lasting price *decrease* are decisive to identify the competitive restraints on purchasers. **7.333**

In order to examine a joint buying arrangement under Article 81, two elements should be taken into account: the situation in the two categories of markets mentioned above, and the behaviour of the undertakings concerned, including the terms and conditions of the agreement. **7.334**

(i) Procurement market   Buyer power on the procurement market can be assumed if a buying agreement accounts for a sufficiently large proportion of the total volume of a procurement market, so that the buyer, by restricting demand, can drive prices down below the competitive level or access to the market can be foreclosed to competing buyers.[192] *Socemas*[193] is a good example of a lack of buyer power in relation to joint purchasing. The members of Socemas used their organisation in order to import products from other Community countries for sale on the French market. Socemas operated primarily as an intermediary. The parties to the agreements together had a market share of 9 per cent of the French food market. The products imported through Socemas represented no more than 0.1 per cent of their aggregated turnover. This percentage had not changed over the years. In view of these facts the Commission concluded that the agreements had no appreciable effect on competition. **7.335**

A similar position was taken in *Intergroup*.[194] Intergroup is a co-operation between SPAR chains established in a number of Community countries. The chains are composed of food retailers and wholesalers entitled to use the SPAR symbol. In 1973, these chains comprised about 35,000 retailers and 180 wholesalers. In the same year, the total volume of imports carried out by each SPAR chain via Intergroup accounted for between 0.06 and 0.89 per cent of the total turnover of all the SPAR wholesalers. Their 1973 turnover was less than 4 per cent of the total EC food retail turnover. Although Intergroup concluded in most cases the contracts in the name of the SPAR members, the latter remained free to determine the resale prices of the product purchased through or after negotiation by Intergroup. Since imports effected by the members through or after negotiation by Intergroup represented only a **7.336**

---

[191] [1997] OJ C372/5–13.
[192] Commission's Guidelines on horizontal co-operation agreements, para 126.
[193] *Socemas* [1968] OJ L201/4.
[194] *Intergroup* [1975] OJ L212/23.

small part of their total turnover, and because purchases effected or negotiated by Intergroup accounted for a relatively small proportion of the total turnover in the retail food trade in each of the Member States of the then EEC, the agreements fell outside Article 81(1).

7.337 At first sight lower prices resulting from buyer power might be seen as pro-competitive, as long as they are passed on to final consumers due to competition in the selling market. However, this does not automatically mean that in such a situation there is effective competition on these markets. In particular, buyer power exercised by a group of undertakings may lead to raising rivals' costs because suppliers will try to recover price reductions or other advantages for one group of buyers by increasing prices or reducing favourable purchasing conditions for other buyers. Furthermore, in a case where prices are forced below a competitive level by buyer power, inefficiencies on the supply side, such as quality reductions or less innovation, may be generated.

7.338 On the procurement market it is essential to evaluate the balance of power between sellers and buyers. A clear distinction should be made between situations where buyer power is being exercised against suppliers that have no seller power (unilateral power situation) as opposed to situations where suppliers have countervailing power (bilateral power situation).

Unilateral power situation

7.339 *Upward sloping supply function*   In this situation, the competition analysis is similar to the one applied in the case of a monopsony, ie a single buyer, or an oligopsony, where a number of sellers are confronted with a few buyers. Some conditions have to be fulfilled if such a situation is to appear. First, the buying agreement should account for a substantial proportion of the total volume of a procurement market. In case of oligopsony, the higher the concentration level in terms of buyers, the greater the impact will be. Secondly, there are barriers to entry into the buyer's market. Thirdly, and this is very important, the supply curve of the product or service has to be upward sloping, indicating an increase in the unit cost of production in the case of an increase of production due to increased demand. Thus, each marginal unit costs more than the average cost. This leads to diminishing returns as output increases. Under these circumstances buyer power means that the buyers are able to depress the price paid for a product or a service to a level that is below the competitive level, thereby depressing output. The social welfare consequence is that too few production resources are being employed. Moreover, the lower the elasticity of supply, the steeper the supply curve will be.

7.340 *Dynamic effects*   Joint buying may offer the participants an opportunity to obtain more favourable purchasing conditions from suppliers. The parties to the agreement may be better off, but some of the suppliers concerned might be worse off. Thus, attention needs to be paid to the consequences of buyer power on the position of suppliers, especially in a case where the prices at which they sell are forced below competitive level by buyer power. Possible detrimental welfare effects may relate to a reduction in the ability of suppliers to invest, for example in innovation or rationalisation, and an increased concentration on the supply level as some suppliers might be driven out of the market. These considerations relate to the possible dynamic effects of buyer power and are more difficult to assess, as they are likely to occur only in the medium or long term, if they occur at all.

Efficiencies   Attention should also be drawn to the fact that joint buying can contribute **7.341** to efficiencies, for example in terms of lower prices, product variety or availability, better use of transport and store facilities, and possible other economies of large-scale purchases. The economic benefits resulting from joint buying may outbalance the above-mentioned competition problem, but this depends on the circumstances of each case. However, these benefits have to be scrutinised carefully in the case of buyer power. Special attention will be paid to situations where joint buying agreements mainly have the objective of gaining or increasing buyer power while generating only limited efficiencies. It is unlikely that these agreements will be exempted under Article 81. On the basis of the above competition analysis joint buying cannot be considered as representing the simple 'mirror' situation of joint selling.

Bilateral power situation   In a situation of bilateral power, the undertakings exercising **7.342** buyer power are confronted with seller power on the supply side. Bilateral power can range from a bilateral monopoly (ie a monopoly exists on both the upstream and downstream markets) or bilateral oligopoly to a lesser but still sufficiently concentrated number of undertakings on both the buying and selling sides. A bilateral power situation is even less clear cut in competition terms than a unilateral power situation, because the detrimental social welfare effects are much less obvious due to the more complicated situation as a result of the mutual interdependence between the two sides. Neither of them can dominate in terms of price, as is the case in a unilateral power situation. It is therefore not unlikely that both buyer(s) and seller(s) will try to set a price that maximises their profits. However, if the buyer is a monopolist on the downstream market, the buyer can use this position in order to restrict quantity below the competitive level.

Original versus opposing power[195]   Sometimes it is claimed that buyer power is a response **7.343** to the selling power of suppliers. In this view, selling power is the original power, whereas buyer power is the opposing power, countervailing the selling power of suppliers. It is also claimed that in such a situation the opposing power may be beneficial to competition, as it weakens the original power. Two observations can be made in this respect. First, it seems too general a statement to say that buyer power has developed as a response to suppliers' selling power. Concentration on the suppliers' side may have occurred in certain product segments, but not in others. Secondly, even if buyer power in some cases can be considered as opposing selling power, competition concerns cannot be excluded, especially if the buyer, as already indicated above, has seller power in the downstream market.

SMEs   Joint buying is often carried out by SMEs to achieve similar volumes and discounts **7.344** to their bigger competitors. If large suppliers dominate the procurement market, joint buying by SMEs normally does not constitute a case of bilateral power. *EEIG Orphe*[196] shows that if joint buying is undertaken by SMEs, this is very likely to fall outside the scope of Article 81(1). The European Economic Interest Group (EEIG) Orphe was set up by seven SMEs, most of them co-operatives, specialising in the wholesale distribution of pharmaceuticals. Because of the fact that very large wholesalers dominated the market concerned,

---

[195]   OFT Research Paper, 19.
[196]   EEIG Orphe, Report on Competition Policy 1990 (Vol XX) 80, point 102.

the Commission considered that joint buying enabled the SMEs concerned to obtain a better place in the market. This can be considered as desirable from a competition point of view. It is important to note that the parties remained free to determine the prices and conditions of sale of their products, including those bought through their central purchasing organisation. Moreover, market entry may thus be encouraged by facilitating this kind of co-operation between SMEs.

7.345 *Efficiencies* In *National Sulphuric Acid Association*,[197] the members of the joint buying pool were allowed jointly to purchase 25 per cent of sulphur for sulphuric acid production. The members of the pool accounted for more than 80 per cent of the UK and 100 per cent of the Irish output of sulphuric acid. The 25 per cent was considered necessary to enable the pool to maintain sufficient buyer power towards the major suppliers, only eight worldwide. Since sulphur accounts for up to 80 per cent of sulphuric acid production cost, the cost and distribution benefits resulting from the pool were taken into account, especially for those requiring only small amounts of sulphur.

7.346 *Retailers' gatekeeper role* As a result of the considerable concentration on retail markets in Europe and technological changes such as scanning, retailers have obtained a considerable advantage over suppliers in terms of controlling access to consumers, both in terms of access to sales outlets and access to information on consumers' buying behaviour. This has led to a shift in the balance of power away from suppliers to retailers. In this respect mention should also be made of the rise and success of retailers' brands or own-label products as opposed to suppliers' brands. They represent a key factor in the relation between retailers and suppliers. First, own-label products will not suffer from practices such as de-listing, as suppliers' brands sometimes might. Secondly, in setting the final price for his own-label products, a retailer can more easily take into account the consumer price of a competing product set by a supplier.

7.347 (ii) **Selling market** In cases where the parties to a joint buying agreement are also downstream competitors on their selling market, joint buying may also affect their behaviour as suppliers on this market. This effect is explained by the commonality of costs and its influence on the total output of the parties in the seller market. As to the effect on the market, the following principle applies: the higher the proportion the parties buy together, the higher the degree of commonality of costs and the more competition between them is restricted. If a high proportion (for example 40 per cent) of goods is bought jointly, coordination of the parties' behaviour as market suppliers may be inevitable and competition will be substantially reduced. On the other hand, if the parties only buy a small proportion (for example 5 per cent) of their needs jointly, and the remaining 95 per cent are still bought independently, a restrictive effect on their competitive behaviour as suppliers is unlikely. Thus, joint buying may lead to a significant degree of commonality of costs among the participants of the buying group, provided that joint buying amounts to a sufficient proportion of their total costs. Commonality of costs facilitates the coordination of the parties' competitive behaviour as suppliers in their selling markets. However, this is only a profitable strategy if the parties would gain or increase market power by coordinating their behaviour.

---

[197] *National Sulphuric Acid Association* [1980] OJ L260/24 and [1989] OJ L190/22.

The restrictive effect between the parties should therefore not be seen in isolation from the issue of market power. The possibility to achieve a higher degree of market power provides an incentive to coordinate competitive behaviour, even if the effects caused by commonality of costs are moderate. Consequently, the higher the degree of market power held in the market, the lower the degree of commonality of costs which is regarded as sufficient for a restrictive effect to be assumed. The effects of joint buying can be therefore rather similar to joint production.

In *M6 and others v Commission*,[198] the Court of First Instance annulled a Commission decision exempting the European Broadcasting Union (EBU)'s system of joint acquisition and sharing of TV rights for sporting events. EBU members are TV broadcasters, coming together *inter alia* to purchase broadcasting rights associated with major sporting events. Despite its decline in the last ten years, the Commission found that the parties still held a strong market position in the acquisition of international sports events due to the fact that its members are mostly broadcasters of free-TV and provide a one-shop-stop to events organisers, thus guaranteeing them a large audience. The exemption was annulled based on the Court's finding that the sub-licensing scheme organised under the system did not, contrary to the Commission's view, allow for sufficient access to rights to transmit sporting events to EBU competitors. **7.348**

(iii) **Types of buyer behaviour**   Through joint purchasing, buyers may employ a number of practices,[199] other than pricing behaviour, to exploit their joint forces. The OFT research paper mentions the following examples of strategic buyer behaviour: (a) slotting allowances;[200] (b) exclusive distribution; (c) conditional purchase behaviour;[201] (d) exclusivity contracts; (e) cloning behaviour;[202] (f) joint marketing by seller and buyer; (g) predatory buying of inputs;[203] (h) strategic purchasing of facilities;[204] (i) reciprocal dealing; and finally (j) terms of business. These practices may serve a number of different purposes. Some can enhance efficiencies, some can distort competition, while others allow buyers to obtain a greater share of profits, so-called rent shifting. **7.349**

A number of these practices concern vertical restraints, such as exclusive distribution, exclusivity contracts, and reciprocal dealing which are dealt with elsewhere in this book. However, in dealing with the possible anti-competitive effects resulting from vertical restraints, it might be argued that, due to the asymmetric relation between suppliers and retailers, the market share threshold at which joint buying might have a negative effect on **7.350**

---

[198] Joined Cases T-185/00, T-216/00, T-299/00 and T-300/00 *M6 and others v Commission,* [2002] ECR II-3805.

[199] OFT Research Paper 16, 22.

[200] Payments of a supplier to a buyer in order to obtain the right to have one's goods displayed at all or in a particular place on the shelves in the latter's shops.

[201] The purchase of goods only on the condition that significant concessions are made by the supplier of such goods.

[202] Close copy or 'look-alike' of trade marks and similar devices.

[203] Cost raising strategy in order to induce exit and eventually to deter market entry.

[204] Retail outlets, in particular large store formats such as super- and hypermarkets, have become the dominant form of access for suppliers to reach consumers, thus control of such facilities provides retailers with bargaining power over suppliers.

competition might be lower than the threshold applied in case of a supplier's selling power. Other practices come close to unfair competition, like cloning behaviour and slotting allowances, often observed in the context of the economic dependency of a supplier. In all these examples, it has to be examined whether there is any detrimental impact on economic welfare. Experiences drawn from Member States' competition authorities show that this proves to be a difficult exercise in practice.

7.351 The main concern in this type of agreement is the existence of *exclusive purchasing obligations*. The Commission has challenged joint buying agreements covering a significant part of the market when they include exclusive purchasing obligations.[205] In *Rennet*[206] the Cooperatieve Stremsel- en Kleurselfabriek accounted for 90 per cent of the Dutch market for the production of rennet. Its members were under the obligation to buy all their rennet from the co-operative. The purchasing obligation was further strengthened by a penalty provision in case this obligation was not met. The Commission considered that the efficiencies resulting from the joint production, such as improvement of the quality of rennet and cost saving, could still be obtained if the members were allowed greater freedom of choice in terms of buying.

7.352 In *National Sulphuric Acid Association*,[207] the exclusive purchase clause obliging all pool members to buy their total requirements of imported sulphur for sulphuric acid production through the pool had to be abolished before an exemption could be granted. The members of the pool accounted for over 80 per cent of the UK and 100 per cent of the Irish sulphuric acid output. The purchasing obligation was brought down to 25 per cent, allowing the pool to maintain a strong negotiation position with the major suppliers, of which only eight existed worldwide. In *ARD/MGM*,[208] the joint buying of exclusive television broadcasting rights for films was exempted after so-called 'windows' allowing broadcasting by third parties during certain periods had been accepted by the parties.

7.353 In *National Sulphuric Acid Association* and *ARD/MGM*, joint buying was associated with a restriction of the freedom to buy independently. In *Socemas* and *Intergroup*, the parties' freedom to buy was not restricted. Although the existence of such an express restriction is important, what may ultimately matter is whether or not the parties in practice buy exclusively or partly through the joint buying organisation.

7.354 In contrast, the creation of a common trademark may give rise to more limited concern under Article 81. In *Orphe*,[209] its members engaged in joint buying of pharmaceutical and parapharmaceutical products and created a common trademark, which would appear beside the trademark of each member on the products distributed by the members. Since the members were SMEs and very large wholesalers dominated the procurement market, the agreement was considered beneficial, among other things because it would allow for wider product choice.

---

[205] *GISA* [1972] OJ L303/45.
[206] *Rennet* [1979] OJ L51/19.
[207] *National Sulphuric Acid Association* [1980] OJ L260/24 and [1989] OJ L190/22.
[208] *ARD/MGM* [1989] OJ L284/36.
[209] EEIG Orphe, Report on Competition Policy 1990 (Vol XX) 80, point 102.

H. Information Exchange Agreements

(1) Introduction

Definition   An information exchange agreement is an arrangement whereby undertak-   **7.355**
ings organise themselves in such a way that they can gather and exchange certain information between them or supply such information to a common agency responsible for
centralising, compiling and processing this information before returning it to the participants
in the form and at the frequency agreed. The information exchanged can contain different
kinds of data. Information exchange agreements can relate to the collection of individual data
and/or aggregate data. Individual data are data relating to a designated or directly or indirectly
identifiable undertaking. Aggregate data are data relating to at least three undertakings. Data
relating to only two undertakings cannot be regarded as aggregate, since it enables each of the
two undertakings concerned to know precisely, by subtraction, the data relating to the other.

A distinction should be drawn between those cases where the exchange of information is   **7.356**
the adjunct of an anti-competitive practice which has already been or can be challenged
under Article 81(1) and those cases where the system as such constitutes a threat to competition. Where an exchange of information is the adjunct of an anti-competitive practice, its
assessment will be carried out in combination with that practice.[210] The Commission classified this issue in *VVVF* and *IFTRA*.[211]

This kind of information exchange agreement will not be dealt with in this section. This section   **7.357**
analyses information exchange which might constitute a threat to competition in its own right.
This comprises cases where, without there being evidence of other collusive practice that is caught
by Article 81(1), the information exchange agreement causes undertakings to change their conduct in a way which damages competition. *Fatty Acids*[212] is the first example of a prohibition
of an information exchange agreement that is not the adjunct of an otherwise demonstrated,
illegal practice but which in itself already infringes EC competition law. It therefore marks the
first important stage in the case law concerning information exchange and EC competition law.

Internal and external effects   Information exchanges have two main effects. First, there is an   **7.358**
internal effect, namely information sharing increases the information available within the
group of undertakings participating in the exchange. This, in turn, is likely to reduce the uncertainty among its members. Secondly, there are external effects, which will depend on the nature
of the market in which they operate. These effects can vary but are likely to include price and
output setting. Of course, the consequences for economic welfare will depend on the extent to
which prices or quantities are the main strategic variables used by the undertakings concerned.

Public versus private market transparency   It is important to distinguish between public   **7.359**
and private market transparency.[213] Public market transparency is transparency for consumers,

---

[210] Case T–1/89 *Rhône-Poulenc* [1991] ECR II–867.
[211] *VVVF* [1969] OJ L168/22; *IFTRA-Glass containers* [1974] OJ L160/1; and *IFTRA-Aluminium* [1975]
OJ L228/3; *Ciment* [1994] OJ L343/1, in particular Art 2 thereof.
[212] *Fatty Acids* [1987] OJ L3/17.
[213] European Commission, Information exchanges among firms and their impact on competition (1995), 92.

while private market transparency is transparency for undertakings. It has been argued that public market transparency is essential for competition, since it allows consumers effectively to compare products and services. This kind of exchange of information is therefore likely to intensify competition. Therefore, the publication of prices, for example, via advertisements will increase both public and private market transparency. On the other hand, private market transparency only increases market transparency for the undertakings involved and may, through collusive behaviour on prices and output, have an adverse effect on competition. Indeed, in terms of effect on competition, public market transparency can be seen as the opposite of private market transparency. As a consequence thereof, private market transparency will be the main concern of competition authorities.

7.360 **Price announcements** In view of the foregoing, it has been considered that price announcements made by producers to users do not constitute a concerted practice within the meaning of Article 81(1), since the producers who made them have no guarantee regarding the conduct that will be adopted by their competitors, as was shown in *Wood Pulp*.[214]

7.361 **Main competition issues** The main reason for competition authorities to be concerned with information exchange agreements lies in the potential of these agreements to facilitate collusive behaviour among competing undertakings, since they are likely to improve the monitoring of activities of competitors.

7.362 In the 1968 Co-operation Notice, the Commission takes the view that the following agreements do not restrict competition:

> Agreements having as their sole object:
> (a) an exchange of opinion or experience,
> (b) joint market research,
> (c) the joint carrying-out of comparative studies of enterprises or industries,
> (d) the joint preparation of statistics and calculation models.[215]

7.363 The Commission thus considered information exchange agreements as a form of co-operation that can be assessed under the EC competition rules. The Notice was a first attempt to develop criteria for such an assessment. As regards agreements not falling under Article 81(1), it indicated that:

> Agreements whose sole purpose is the joint procurement of information which the various enterprises need to determine their future market behaviour freely and independently, or the use by each of the enterprises of a joint advisory body, do not have as their object or effect the restriction of competition.

7.364 The 2001 Guidelines on horizontal co-operation agreements are silent about the matter.

(2) Information Exchange—Criteria for Assessment

7.365 The assessment of an information exchange agreement depends mainly on three factors: (i) market structure; (ii) the type of information exchanged; and (iii) the frequency of information exchange.

---

[214] Case C-89/85 *Wood Pulp* [1993] ECR I–1307.
[215] [1968] OJ C75/3, heading II(1).

In its *Report on Competition Policy 1977* (Volume VII), the Commission established guide- **7.366**
lines for the assessment of exchanges of information along the lines indicated by the Court
of Justice in the *Sugar* case.[216] The Commission stated that it had no fundamental objection to the exchange of statistical information either direct or through trade associations or
reporting agencies, even when they provide a breakdown of the figures, as long as the information exchanged does not enable the identification of individual undertakings.[217] The
Commission went on to say that it would generally regard the organised exchange of individual data from individual undertakings, such as figures or quantities produced and sold, prices
and terms for discounts, higher and lower rates, credit notes, and general terms of sale, delivery and payment, as practices which have as their object or effect the restriction or distortion
of competition and which are therefore prohibited. The Commission also explained that the
distinction between good and bad information exchange systems can be made only on a case-
by-case basis in the light of all features of each agreement, having regard in particular to the
structure of the market and the nature of the information exchanged.

As the Commission stated very clearly in its *Report on Competition Policy 1977* (Volume VII): **7.367**

> the area between permissible and prohibited exchange of information is defined by the dis-
> tinction between a purely statistical arrangement with a breakdown of data by product,
> country and period of time which is not conducive to collusion, and the kind of arrangement
> which clearly relates to individual firms.[218]

(i) Market structure   The exchange of sensitive individual data on an atomistic market **7.368**
does not enable undertakings to predict or anticipate the conduct of all of their competitors because of the fragmented nature of the market. The concentration ratio of the market
concerned is of particular importance for the assessment of information exchange agreements, as this element greatly influences the competitive structure of the market. The market can be more or less concentrated in itself, or alternatively the number of participants to
the agreements may be such as to cover a substantial part of the market. In this respect the
Court in *New Holland Ford* observed that:

> on a truly competitive market transparency between traders is in principle likely to lead to the
> intensification of competition between suppliers, since in such a situation the fact that a trader
> takes into account information made available to him in order to adjust his conduct on the mar-
> ket is not likely, having regard to the atomised nature of the supply, to reduce or remove for the
> other traders any uncertainty about the foreseeable nature of its competitors' conduct.[219]

The Court further stated that: **7.369**

> general use, as between main suppliers, of exchanges of precise information at short intervals,
> identifying registered vehicles and the place of their registration is, on a highly concentrated
> oligopolistic market such as the market in question and on which competition is as a result
> already greatly reduced and exchange of information facilitated, likely to impair considerably
> the competition which exists between traders. In such circumstances, the sharing, on a regu-
> lar and frequent basis, of information concerning the operation of the market has the effect

---

[216] Joined Cases 40–48/73 *Suiker Unie and others v Commission* [1975] ECR 1663.
[217] Report on Competition Policy 1977 (Vol VII), point 7.
[218] ibid.
[219] Case C-8/95 *New Holland Ford* [1998] ECR I-3175.

of periodically revealing to all the competitors the market positions and strategies of the various individual competitors.

7.370 **(ii) Type of information exchanged**   Two main elements must be examined in connection with the information exchanged: (i) its level of detail; and (ii) whether it constitutes historical information or recent data.

Level of detail

7.371 *The level of aggregation of data*   To analyse the effects of an information exchange agreement from a competition point of view, it is important to determine the level of aggregation of data. Indeed, the harmfulness in terms of competition depends on the possibility of identifying sensitive data. Identification of such data is possible where the data exchanged are individual data. Identification is also possible sometimes in the case of aggregate data. When confronted with an apparently general data system, one has to ensure for oneself that the degree of aggregation of data is sufficient to prevent any identification.

7.372 *Statistics*   A first group of data which is very often the subject of exchange of information comprises statistics. Statistical material which sets out production and other figures for the industry or trade in question without identifying individual undertakings, as is the practice in official statistics, is a fine example of aggregate data which do not allow for the identification of individual undertakings. The exchange of these data is perfectly legitimate.

7.373 A second group of data which can be identified in information exchange agreements comprises statistical data, broken down by product, country or period of time. Depending on whether the breakdown of figures enables a party to the information exchange to identify or not the competitive behaviour of the other parties, the data will or will not be regarded by the Commission as restricting or distorting competition.

7.374 *Individual data*   A third group of data concerns individual data from individual undertakings, such as figures on prices, production, sales, customers, delivery and payment. Under this heading we can distinguish a number of elements which undertakings are interested in for the purpose of information exchange: (i) prices, production, sales, market share and customers; (ii) costs and demand structure; (iii) capacity; and (iv) R&D. Some of these elements can be refined. Prices, for example, include not only prices as such, but also price changes and price factors such as discounts, rebates and reductions. As far as customers are concerned, lists of customers, as well as information on the order book, are relevant elements in this respect. In relation to capacity, one can identify information on investments as well as on capacities and production-capacity utilisation rates. With regard to R&D, not only R&D programmes but also the results thereof can be of interest to undertakings. The Commission will generally regard the organised exchange of this kind of data as likely to restrict or distort competition. It should be noted that individual data not only enable the parties to identify the nature of each other's commercial strategies, but also facilitate the enforcement of a cartel as it will be easier to identify an undertaking deviating from the cartel strategy.

7.375 The organised exchange of individual data from individual companies will generally be regarded by the Commission as likely to restrict or distort competition, as shown by *UK Tractor* and related Court cases.[220] More recent developments also confirm this negative stance of the Commission on the exchange of individual data.[221]

The Commission's *UK Agricultural Tractor Registration Exchange*[222] decision marks the sec- **7.376** ond stage in the case law relating to information exchange agreements. It is a concrete example of the application of the Commission's competition policy towards the exchange of aggregate data which nonetheless allow for identification of the conduct of competitors. Furthermore, the case is the first one in which the information exchange system did not directly concern prices.

The agreement concerned an exchange of information identifying the volume of retail sales **7.377** and market shares of eight, later seven, manufacturers and importers of agricultural tractors on the UK market. The exchange was managed by the Agricultural Engineers Association Ltd (the AEA), the UK trade association of manufacturers and importers of agricultural machinery.

The members could obtain three sets of data. First, they were offered information on aggregate **7.378** industry sales. This information could be broken down by geographic areas, land use, counties, dealer territories and postcode sectors. It could be made available for yearly, quarterly, monthly and weekly time periods. In addition to these data, each member could obtain information identifying the volume of retail sales and market shares of each individual member to the agreement, with detailed breakdowns by model, product groups, geographic areas, and by yearly, quarterly, monthly and daily time periods. Finally, a third group of data was provided for and concerned information on sales by dealers belonging to the dealer network of each member, in particular the imports and exports in their respective territories. In the Commission's view this permitted each party to monitor every other party's sales.

With regard to the first group of data, the aggregate industry sales data, the Commission **7.379** observed in its decision that it did not in principle object to the availability of these data because they do not identify the retail sales of the individual members. However, in this particular case the Commission did object to the exchange of these data. Since there were a small number of producers by category or product or geographic area, or the number of units sold in a given period was low, or the frequency of exchanges was high, the information exchange allowed for the identification of undertakings.

Age of the information exchanged   The age of data can be grouped in three categories: **7.380** (i) historical information, being more than one year old; (ii) recent information, being less than one year old; and (iii) future information. Depending on the age of the information, the exchange thereof will be more or less harmful for competition. As a rule, it can be said that the exchange of historical information is usually not caught by Article 81(1), unless it is the adjunct of another anti-competitive arrangement.

---

[220] Joined Cases T–34 and 35/92 *Fiatagri and John Deere* [1994] ECR II–905 and 957; Joined Cases C-7 and 8/95 *New Holland Ford (formally Fiatagri) and John Deere* [1998] ECR I-3111.
[221] See eg *Amino Acids* [2001] OJ L152/24, where a worldwide network of lysine producers exchanged firm-specific information concerning sales volumes between at least 1990 and 1995.
[222] *UK Agricultural Tractor Registration Exchange* [1992] OJ L68/19.

7.381 It is sometimes argued that the exchange of information about past conduct cannot be anti-competitive and that only the exchange of information about future conduct may be anti-competitive. This argument must be viewed with care, as it would be impossible to sustain collusion in the absence of information about past behaviour.[223]

7.382 Following the Court of Justice's 1998 judgments[224] upholding its *UK Agricultural Tractor Registration Exchange* decision, the Commission undertook to bring all similar exchanges in the EU into line. To this effect, the Commission established a number of principles that may serve as guidelines for information exchanges in other sectors that are as concentrated as the tractor and agricultural machinery market.[225]

7.383 In essence, the exchange of individual data should be withheld until a 12-month period has elapsed between the event constituting the subject of the data and the date of exchange. With respect to aggregate market data, it may be exchanged even if it is less than 12 months old if it is being supplied by at least three dealers belonging to different individual industrial or financial groups. If not, data may be exchanged only if the figure in question concerns more than ten units.

7.384 **(iii) Frequency of information exchange**   The frequency of information exchange plays an important role in affecting the scope of collusion. The effect will certainly grow with the frequency at which data are being exchanged. This also strongly influences the age of the information, as a frequent exchange of data normally implies that the most recent information is being exchanged. This may further strengthen collusion.

I. Standardisation Agreements

(1) Introduction

7.385 Standardisation agreements are covenants that have as their main purpose 'the definition of technical or quality requirements with which current or future products, production processes or methods may comply', as the 2001 Horizontal Guidelines put it.[226] There exist a myriad of contexts in which these agreements may appear. The setting of some sort of standard or technical specification may be present in sectors where interoperability among all products or systems put into the market is essential, or simply where the production covers a variety of sizes and models that may be harmonised all across the market. Also, standards are often used as conditions that must be complied with in order to have access to a particular quality mark or plainly to observe the rules laid down by a regulatory body, either public or of a mixed nature.

7.386 Agreements on standards have traditionally been regarded with a favourable stance by the competition authorities in general and the European Commission in particular, despite the

---

[223] European Commission, Information exchanges among firms and their impact on competition (1995), 99.

[224] Cases C-7/95 *John Deere v Commission* [1998] ECR I-3111; and C-8/95 *New Holland Ford v Commission* [1998] ECR I-3175.

[225] *See Report on Competition Policy 1999* (Vol XXIX), pp 156–58 and Commission press release of 20 September 1999 (IP/99/690).

[226] 2001 Horizontal Guidelines, para 159.

existence of some acknowledged potential sources of concern. This positive view is grounded on two different lines of reasoning.[227] First, standardisation is regarded as a fundamental force supporting market integration all across the Union. By harmonising the quality level or the technical characteristics of products and services supplied within the Community, free movement of goods pursuant to Article 28 of the EC Treaty is enhanced. Moreover, setting EC-wide standards, either by regulators or by the regulated themselves, can be useful to dispose of national specifications that may act in practice as barriers to free exchange of goods and services within the Community. Secondly, some potential economic benefits may be linked to standard setting. Product interoperability, rationalisation of production, economies of scale and the creation of unified platforms for both R&D efforts and the development of new products can be cited here as examples of such beneficial effects.[228]

However, standards may also pose some threats for competition. It is more than clear that agreements imposing certain conditions on market operators concerning their goods or the production thereof have an impact on the market. First, standardisation agreements can be in reality pacts among companies to exclude actual or potential rivals as part of a more general restrictive scheme (eg when non-compliers are subject to boycotting by the members of the agreement).[229] Also, standards may be applied in a manner that grants the parties joint control over production or innovation efforts, thereby limiting competition among themselves on product characteristics, and at the same time affecting suppliers, purchasers or other third parties.[230] Finally, and even if not explicitly mentioned in the Horizontal Guidelines, standardisation platforms could be also used for exchanges of sensitive information, thereby facilitating collusion.

7.387

According to the 2001 Guidelines, three different markets may be affected by the implementation of any standard.[231] First and more obviously, the product market to which the standard applies is subject basically to the same kind of concerns raised by the R&D agreements reviewed above. But in the event that different standardisation bodies or agreements exist, the agreement would be problematic only on the service market for standard setting (eg a situation where different quality marks compete among themselves to grandfather prospective products). Finally, there could also be a distinct market for testing and certification upon which the standardisation agreement may have some prejudicial effects.

7.388

(2) Agreements on Standards under the 2001 Horizontal Guidelines

Application of Article 81   The 2001 Guidelines deal with the specifics of the standardisation agreement in a manner that evidences the positive approach that the Commission takes in this field. The Guidelines apply to all agreements whereby standards are set, either

7.389

---

[227] Dolmans, 'Standards for Standards' (2002) 26 Fordham Int. L. J. at 165-166.
[228] Dolmans, 'Standards for Standards' (2002) 26 Fordham Int. L. J. at 166. Dolmans also mentions the fact that standardization may give rise to opportunities for SMEs.
[229] 2001 Horizontal Guidelines, para 165, concerning 'agreements that almost always fall under Article 81(1).'
[230] 2001 Horizontal Guidelines, para 166, on 'agreements that may fall under Article 81(1).'
[231] 2001 Horizontal Guidelines, para 161.

concluded between private parties or implemented 'under the aegis of public bodies or bodies entrusted with the operation of services of general economic interest'.[232]

7.390   Under the Commission perspective, standardisation agreements do not fall under the scope of Article 81(1) of the EC Treaty, and therefore, do not raise antitrust concerns, so long as 'participation in standard setting is unrestricted and transparent' and the agreements themselves either provide for 'no obligation to comply with the standard' or 'are parts of a wider agreement to ensure compatibility of products'. Therefore, the basic rule is that standard setting is acceptable under a competition law perspective when there is open and non-discriminatory access for the generality of competitors on the market and the procedures for their implementation are transparent. Access to the initial agreement and later entrance must not be burdensome for interested parties.

7.391   It must also be noted that agreements with a negligible or 'de minimis' effect benefit from a safe harbour provided that they do not involve hardcore violations (eg price fixing etc).[233] Further, Article 81(1) will not apply to all cases where the participants in the agreement are SMEs willing to standardise access forms or conditions to collective tenders or harmonise certain minor product characteristics.[234]

7.392   When the standardisation agreement disguises or complements a general collective strategy aimed at excluding actual or potential competitors, Article 81(1) applies 'almost always' as the Guidelines state (eg standards coupled with boycotting schemes targeted at outsiders).[235]

7.393   Application of Article 81(1) also takes place when the agreement affords the parties 'joint control over production and/or innovation' thereby restricting competition among themselves.[236] However in the latter case, a detailed, case-by-case assessment of the transaction must be undertaken. Such an analysis must focus on the nature of the standard and its likely effect on the market, as well as the scope of possible restrictive purposes beyond the mere standardisation. The key element is that the agreement in order to escape the application of Article 81(1) must leave room for the parties involved to develop alternative standards or to commercialise non-complying products. Hence, agreements that either confer single bodies the exclusive right to test compliance with the standard or impose restrictions on marking of conformity with standards, unless imposed by regulatory provisions, may also restrict competition within the meaning of Article 81(1).[237] The evil of standardisation is basically the reduction of technological diversity on the market, which can lead in turn to innovation paralysis. So long as the parties to the agreement remain free to carry out their

---

[232] 2001 Horizontal Guidelines, para 162. Note, however, that the Guidelines expressly exclude from their scope all '[s]tandards related to the provision of professional services, such as rules of admission to a liberal profession' (para 160).

[233] For an agreement to be labelled as 'de minimis' the general rule of thumb laid down in the de minimis Notice ([2001] OJ C368/13) applies. If the parties entering the agreement do not enjoy a market share above 10%, the covenant falls outside Art 81(1). It must be kept in mind that agreements exceeding this threshold may still qualify for individual exemption under Art81(3).

[234] 2001 Horizontal Guidelines, para 164.

[235] 2001 Horizontal Guidelines, para 165.

[236] 2001 Horizontal Guidelines, para 166.

[237] 2001 Horizontal Guidelines, para 167.

activity beyond the standards, technological variety is not severely compromised and the application of Article 81(1) is likely to be ruled out.

Even if Article 81(1) applies to a particular agreement, it may qualify for individual exemp- **7.394** tion under Article 81(3). For this possibility to be available, a number of conditions must be fulfilled.

Economic benefits   All agreements that attempt to be exempted on an individual basis **7.395** must be coupled with the public availability of the information needed to implement the standard. In other words, access to the agreement must remain open to all companies will-ing to join it, and for this purpose, they must be able to know how to comply with the stan-dards laid down thereby. In addition, an 'appreciable proportion of the industry' must be involved in the setting of the standard. The rationale for such a requirement is twofold: first, a significant degree of participation is necessary for the agreement to produce worthy economic efficiencies; secondly, the Commission is willing to assure a certain level of equal-ity of opportunities among the different competitors.[238] In accordance with this scheme, the Guidelines only allow for restrictions on admission to the agreement if they are objec-tive and adequately explained. It must be recalled that for interested firms to be able to enter the agreement, information concerning the standards themselves and the results thereof must remain publicly available. Finally, the parties must make sure that the agreement does not hinder or curb innovation in any possible way.[239]

Indispensability   The setting of the standard may not be based on capricious assessments. **7.396** On the contrary, non-discrimination must be the rule. As the Guidelines point out, '[i]deally, standards should be technologically neutral'. When different standards are feasi-ble, the parties must provide a reasoned explanation of their final choice after having afforded all competitors in the markets involved an opportunity to engage in the discus-sions. This openness can only be excepted if the parties demonstrate that important ineffi-ciencies would arise from it, or if some form of collective representation of interests (eg as in formal standards bodies) is available.[240] In sum, selection of the technology must be per-formed in an open and objective manner.

Additionally, the Commission is also concerned with the depth of the standard set by the **7.397** parties.[241] Hence, standardisation agreements must not fall beyond what is necessary to ensure their purposes (ie technical compatibility, certain level of quality). Practices that clearly exceed these ends, such as collective boycotts against non-complying products, are deemed to be restrictive. The same conclusion must be drawn for all standards concerning design or other features of the product that go beyond technical requirements or quality specifications. It must be noted, however, that the line dividing technical or functional specifications and rules concerning other characteristics of the product can be blurred.

Non-elimination of competition   For the covenants to be exempted under Article 81(3), **7.398** the Guidelines oblige the parties to set the standards in the most transparent, non-discriminatory

---

[238] M Dolmans, 'Standards for Standards' (2002) 26 Fordham Int. L. J. at 171.
[239] 2001 Horizontal Guidelines, para 170.
[240] 2001 Horizontal Guidelines, para 172.
[241] M Dolmans, 'Standards for Standards' (2002) 26 Fordham Int. L. J. at 174-175.

and open way. Access to the standard must be afforded on equal terms and in a reasonable manner to any party willing to participate. Limitations on admission would only be acceptable, ie exemptable under Article 81(3), if they are necessary, objective and relevant, and so long as decisions can be appealed to a neutral arbitrator or court.[242] Justifications based on logistics and workability are deemed to be sufficiently objective.[243]

7.399 An example that may be illustrative of the Commission's approach described in the precedent paragraphs is its positive attitude towards Stack International, a non-profit company created by several international companies in the information technology sector.[244] The basic activities of this firm consist in setting different standards for components such as integrated circuits, memory circuits, memory modules and similar products, as well as in certifying compliance with these standards. This agreement was notified for the first time to the Commission in 1976 and again in 1997, including updated versions of the agreements and a wider membership list. The conclusion of the Commission was positive, and the case was closed by a comfort letter providing for negative clearance. A number of factors were used in support of the Commission's view.

7.400 First, the agreement neither imposed on the members any sort of restriction concerning their freedom to choose different components from those certified by Stack nor gave special consideration to complying suppliers.

7.401 Secondly, there was no significant exchange of sensitive information capable of facilitating collusion.

7.402 Thirdly and finally, membership was open to companies showing an interest in joining the agreement.

J. Environmental Agreements

(1) Introduction

7.403 For many years, the European Community has witnessed many examples of industry-led initiatives that attempt to achieve various environmental programmes, in parallel to the efforts made by the public enforcers at both the national and the Community levels.[245] Environmental agreements or commitments by companies are generally welcomed by the Commission, and its approach, reflected in the 2001 Horizontal Guidelines, strongly encourages co-operation in this field. Moreover, in many cases voluntary agreements are

---

[242] M Dolmans, 'Standards for Standards' (2002) 26 Fordham Int. L. J. at 172.

[243] *X/Open Group* [1987] OJ L35/36, cited by Dolmans, above at 172.

[244] See Report on Competition Policy 1998 (Vol XXVIII), pp 153–154. Note that the assessment by the Commission took place before the Horizontal Guidelines were drafted, but nevertheless the same basic principles were applied.

[245] The present EC policy on the environment is embodied in the VI Community Environment Community Programme (Decision (EC) 1600/2002 of the European Parliament and of the Council of 22 July 2002 [2002] OJ L242/1). One of the themes of this programme is the willingness of the European authorities to '[work] with business and consumers to achieve more environmentally friendly forms of production and consumption' (see Press Release, IP/01/102). It is in this context, therefore, where environmental agreements between undertakings on the markets have a role to play.

much more efficient and effective for accomplishing environmental objectives than the implementation of compulsory rules by public regulators.

The concept of environmental agreement is limited by the Horizontal Guidelines to all **7.404** covenants whereby 'the parties undertake to achieve pollution abatement, as defined in environmental law, or environmental objectives, in particular, those set out in Article 174 of the [EC] Treaty'.[246] In any event, the target of the measures agreed upon must be 'directly linked to the reduction of a pollutant or a type of waste identified as such in relevant regulations', eg pertinent Community directives. This requirement attempts to avoid the use of environmental pretexts to cover broader restrictive purposes. The Guidelines themselves mention various examples where possible restrictive effects on competition may be ruled out: standards on the environmental performance of products, covenants providing for the common attainment of environmental targets (eg recycling, emission reduction, etc), and industry-wide schemes implemented in order to fulfil environmental obligations of its members, such as recycling or energy saving, which are very common in many Member States.[247]

The markets affected are those to which the environmental measure relates. When the pollut- **7.405** ant at which the agreement is targeted is not a product in itself (eg an input used in the production chain), the relevant market will be that of the product in which the pollutant is incorporated.[248] It must be noted that in most cases environmental agreements simply encompass standards with an environment-enhancing aim, but standards at last. Thus, the same problematic described above for standardisation agreements may apply *mutatis mutandis* here.

(2) Environmental Agreements under the 2001 Horizontal Guidelines

The Guidelines make a distinction between situations in which the environmental **7.406** compromise at stake '[does] not fall under Article 81(1)', 'almost always' comes under this provision and 'may fall' within the range of cases to which it applies.

First, the Commission devises a 'safe harbour' for agreements that it considers to be free **7.407** from any restrictive effect within the meaning of Article 81(1), regardless of the aggregated market share of the companies involved. Three examples are cited by the Commission.

Where the environmental agreement does not impose a 'precise obligation' upon the par- **7.408** ties or if they are just 'loosely committed to contributing to the attainment of a sector-wide environmental target', restrictive effects on competition are in principle nonexistent, at least for antitrust purposes.[249] As for the second situation, the relevant benchmark is the

---

[246] 2001 Horizontal Guidelines, para 179. The objectives laid down in Art 174 are the following: 'preserving, protecting and improving the quality of the environment'; 'protecting human health'; 'prudent and rational utilisation of natural resources'; and 'promoting measures at international level to deal with regional or worldwide environmental problems'.

[247] The positive stance of the Commission on agreements implementing joint recycling or waste packaging schemes is reflected on a variety of cases (See eg Report on Competition Policy 2000 (Vol XXX), p 148, for joint recycling systems; and Decisions on *Eco-Embalages* ([2001] OJ L233/37) and *Duales System Deutschland* ([2001] OJ L319/1), for waste packaging programmes.

[248] 2001 Horizontal Guidelines, para 182. Concerning the specific case of collection or recycling agreements, the Guidelines point to the 'market(s) on which the parties are active as producers or distributors' and the 'market of collection services' as the focal points for analysis.

[249] 2001 Horizontal Guidelines, para 185.

degree of discretion left to the parties regarding the means to attain the agreed objective. A good case in point is that of the commitment made by ACEA (Association of European Automobile Manufacturers) to reduce carbon dioxide emissions from passenger cars marketed by its members. The agreement, which was to be jointly monitored by the Member States and the Commission, was notified to the Commission in September 1998 and received a favourable comfort letter a month latter.[250] This positive assessment was essentially justified by the fact that the agreement consisted of an overall average target for all ACEA members, rather than individual objectives for each participant. Therefore, manufacturers remained free to apply more or less stringent levels of pollutant, so long as the average goal was met.[251]

7.409 The second category of 'safe' environmental agreements involves environmental standards which 'do not appreciably affect product and production diversity in the relevant market or whose importance is marginal for influencing purchase decisions'.[252] What the Commission sets out here is a sort of 'de minimis' exception for all agreements having a negligible effect on competition.

7.410 Finally, the third class of agreements falling outside Article 81(1) is that of covenants 'which give rise to genuine market creation', eg recycling agreements. The sole condition laid down for this exclusion to apply is that the parties must not be capable of conducting such activities in isolation, 'whilst other alternatives and/or competitors do not exist'.[253]

7.411 A second basic group of agreements is composed by all compromises between competitors with an environmental nature that 'may', some conditions fulfilled, hinder or curb competition, and therefore fall under Article 81(1). The Guidelines use here a rule based on an 'appreciability standard' whereby if the restriction imposed by the agreement on the ability of the parties to devise the characteristics of their products or the methods to produce them is 'appreciably restricted', then Article 81(1) comes into play.[254] The evil to be avoided is twofold: first, restrictive agreements may grant the parties some degree of influence over each other's production of sales; secondly, spillover effects affecting third parties (eg suppliers, purchases) may appear. The basic criterion for assessment is based on the market shares of the parties involved.[255] In the *CEDED* case,[256] the Commission took the position that a European association of manufacturers of electrical domestic equipment restricted competition

---

[250] Report on Competition Policy 1998 (Vol XXVIII), p 151; and Press Release (IP/98/865).

[251] The Association of Japanese Automobile Manufacturers (JAMA) and its Korean peer (KAMA) subsequently notified similar agreements responding to that by ACEA. These schemes, identical to ACEA's, were equally deemed not to restrict competition within the meaning of Art 81(1). (Report on Competition Policy 1999 (Vol XXIX), p 160, and Press Release IP/99/922).

[252] 2001 Horizontal Guidelines, para 186.

[253] 2001 Horizontal Guidelines, para 187.

[254] 2001 Horizontal Guidelines, para 189.

[255] The Guidelines mention different examples where a large market share may raise antitrust concerns: allocation of individual pollution quotas, agreements on products or processes affecting an important proportion of the parties' sales and exclusivity concerning the provision of collection and/or recycling services for the parties' products. In the latter case, for the agreement to fall under Art 81(1), other actual or realistic potential providers must exist. 2001 Horizontal Guidelines, paras 190 and 191.

[256] [2000] OJ L187/47.

under Article 81(1) when it implemented an agreement to reduce the electricity consumption of washing machines. The Commission relied, *inter alia*, on the fact that the members of the association exceeded 95 per cent of the relevant market. Nevertheless, an individual exemption under Article 81(3) was finally awarded.

Finally, the Guidelines distinguish a set of situations where the environmental agreement **7.412** in reality disguises an unlawful cartel involving hardcore restrictions, ie price fixing, output limitation or market allocation. If this is the case, the agreement will 'almost always' fall under Article 81(1).

To conclude the analysis of the 2001 Horizontal Guidelines, it must be kept in mind that **7.413** even if the agreement at stake is deemed to restrict competition, it may nevertheless benefit from an individual exemption under Article 81(3) of the Treaty, provided that all the conditions laid down in this provision are met.[257] In short, environmental agreements must: have a positive effect on consumers, thereby outweighing their negative effect on competition; be indispensable for the intended goal (or supported at least by a cost-benefit analysis showing that alternative means would be economically or financially costly); and must not eliminate competition in terms of product or process differentiation, technological innovation or market entry.[258] If these requirements are fulfilled, then the agreement can be exempted on an individual basis.

---

[257] For an example of an individual exemption under Art 81(3), see the *CEDED* decision ([2000] OJ L187/47). In that case, the Commission acknowledged that the agreement would boost the introduction of technologically advanced washing machines, that consumers would benefit in form of savings on electricity bills and that competition on prices, performance, etc would continue despite the agreement.
[258] 2001 Horizontal Guidelines, paras 192–197.

8

CARTELS

François Arbault and Ewoud Sakkers

A. Introduction

8.01 **Definition**[1]   In its simplest form, a cartel is an agreement between competitors aimed at raising the price of a product or service to a level higher than the one that would have prevailed under normal competitive conditions. Cartels may take the form of formal agreements between their members to adopt a given (anti-competitive) conduct in the market but may also consist of looser forms of coordination of each party's commercial behaviour. Such arrangements are commonly reached by informal means, often merely orally, because of their blatantly illegal nature and obviously adverse effect on customers. Intense efforts are

---

[1] The history of cartels and the origins of the term 'cartel' itself are not discussed in this chapter. There is an abundant literature on the subject, including: DJ Gerber, *Law and Competition in Twentieth Century Europe: Protecting Prometheus* (1998); C Harding and J Joshua, *Regulating Cartels in Europe: A Study of Legal Control of Corporate Delinquency* (2003); PZ Grossman (ed), *How Cartels Endure and How they Fail—Studies of Industrial Collusion* (2004).

usually made to keep them secret. Apart from outright agreements on the prices to be charged to customers, cartels also typically involve collusion in respect of the commercial terms to be applied to transactions, as well as output levels, the allocation of market shares, specific customers or geographic areas, or other arrangements such as which competitor should win a given contract ('bid rigging'). Each of these elements will ultimately influence the price level of the products or services concerned.

In view of their complex and informal nature, as well as the large variety of collusive arrange- **8.02** ments that they may comprise, it is difficult to formulate a clear and exhaustive definition of cartels. In its 1998 Recommendation Concerning Effective Action against Hard Core Cartels,[2] the OECD Council attempted to define a 'hard core' cartel as 'an anticompetitive agreement, anticompetitive concerted practice or anticompetitive arrangement by competitors to fix prices, make rigged bids (collusive tenders), establish output restrictions or quotas, or share or divide markets by allocating customers, suppliers, territories, or lines of commerce'. By referring to 'hard core' cartels, the OECD made it clear that this category 'does not include agreements, concerted practices or arrangements that i) are reasonably related to the lawful realisation of cost-reducing or output-enhancing efficiencies, ii) are excluded directly or indirectly from the coverage of a Member country's own laws, or iii) are authorised in accordance with those laws'. 'Hard core cartels' are therefore those agreements or practices which are so intrinsically detrimental to the competitive process that they would never produce countervailing benefits and, thus, will never be held as lawful under competition law.[3]

The *per se* prohibition of cartels by EC competition law   As the most restrictive forms of **8.03** horizontal arrangements, hard core cartels have as their *object* the restriction of competition with a view to extracting supra competitive profits. As such, provided that they (at least potentially) affect trade between Member States, they fall under the prohibition of Article 81(1) EC[4] and amount to appreciable restrictions of competition *per se* irrespective of their effects in the market.[5]

---

[2] Recommendation of the OECD Council concerning Effective Action Against Hard Core Cartels, adopted by the Council at its 921st Session on 25 March 1998.

[3] Cartel behaviour has been described as 'a practice without defenders in the economic profession' (I Stelzer, quoted by JR Kinghorn and R Nielsen, 'A Practice without Defenders: The Price Effects of Cartelization', in PZ Grossman (ed), *How Cartels endure and How they Fail—Studies of Industrial Collusion* (2004).

[4] A similar prohibition was included in Art 65(1) ECSC (the ECSC Treaty expired in July 2002 and cartel conduct in the coal and steel sectors now falls under the general prohibition of Art 81(1) EC). It is also worth mentioning that special rules apply to certain agricultural products by virtue of Reg No 26 applying certain rules of competition to production of, and trade in, agricultural products [1962] OJ L30/993 (English special edition: Series I Chapter 1959–1962, 129). Thus, by way of exception, Art 81 EC is not applicable to certain restrictive practices pertaining to the Common Agricultural Policy (CAP).

[5] The CFI has held that a clear infringement of Art 81 EC such as price fixing, output limitation or market sharing 'precludes the application of a rule of reason, assuming such a rule to be applicable in Community competition law' and 'must be regarded as an infringement per se of the competition rules': see Case T-14/89 *Montedipe SpA v Commission* [1992] ECR II-1155, para 265. Also the CFI stated in Joined Cases T-374/94, T-375/94, T-384/94 and T-388/94 *European Night Services v Commission* [1998] ECR II-3141, at para 136, that 'it must be borne in mind that in assessing an agreement under Article [81(1)] of the Treaty, account should be taken of the actual conditions in which it functions, in particular the economic context in which the undertakings operate, the products or services covered by the agreement and the actual structure of the market concerned [. . .], unless it is an agreement containing obvious restrictions of competition such as price-fixing, market-sharing or the control of outlets [. . .]. In the latter case, such restrictions may be weighed against their claimed pro-competitive effects only in the context of Article [81(3)] of the Treaty [. . .]".

8.04   One may wonder, however, whether a cartel could, in spite of its restrictive object, be held as lawful under Article 81(3) EC. If one follows to the OECD definition of hard core cartels, this should never be the case, as the notion explicitly excludes agreements, concerted practices or arrangements which could be deemed lawful under competition law. This does not mean, however, that agreements tantamount to cartels could never be held to be compatible with EC competition law.[6] In the past, the Commission has occasionally allowed so-called 'crisis cartels', by exempting restructuring agreements between competitors that aimed to secure a concerted reduction of capacity in sectors hit by severe structural overcapacity.[7] Those exemptions were, however, subject to drastic conditions and dependent upon due notification to the Commission.[8] Today, such schemes would probably no longer be considered to fulfil the conditions of Article 81(3) EC, as illustrated by the Commission Guidelines on the application of Article 81(3) EC.[9] In this context, and for the purpose of this chapter, the term 'hard core cartels' is used in the sense of agreements or concerted practices which do not pursue any legitimate goal and thus cannot be considered lawful under Article 81(3) EC. In what follows, references to 'cartels' should be taken to mean 'hard core' cartels in this sense, unless the context clearly implies otherwise.[10]

8.05   **Harm caused by cartels**   Cartels cause considerable economic damage and have been publicly described by regulators in terms as severe as 'cancers on the open market economy',[11] 'fraud upon consumers [. . .] equivalent of theft by well-dressed thieves',[12] or as the

---

   6   The CFI has ruled that 'in principle, no anti-competitive practice can exist which, whatever the extent of its effects on a given market, cannot be exempted, provided that all the conditions laid down in Article [81(3)] of the Treaty are satisfied and the practice in question has been properly notified to the Commission' (Case T-17/93 *Matra Hachette SA v Commission* [1994] ECR II-595, para 85).

   7   In principle, the Commission considers that it is for each undertaking to decide when overcapacity is no longer economically sustainable and to take the required restructuring measures. Nevertheless, the Commission has acknowledged that in cases of severe structural overcapacity, market forces may fail to bring about a restructuring process capable of ensuring, in the long run, a return to competitive structures. Whilst consumers would at first sight seem to benefit from an excess supply situation, they may ultimately have to bear the costs of the inefficiencies caused by structural overcapacity.

   8   See eg *Synthetic Fibres* [1984] OJ L212/1 and *Stichting Baksteen* [1994] OJ L131/15.

   9   [2004] OJ C101/97. The Commission states in the Guidelines that 'Article 81(3) does not exclude a priori certain types of agreements from its scope' and that 'as a matter of principle all restrictive agreements that fulfil the four conditions of Article 81(3) are covered by the exception rule'. However, it goes on to state that 'hard core' restrictions 'generally fail (at least) the two first conditions of Article 81(3). They neither create objective economic benefits nor do they benefit consumers. For example, a horizontal agreement to fix prices limits output leading to misallocation of resources. It also transfers value from consumers to producers, since it leads to higher prices without producing any countervailing value to consumers within the relevant market. Moreover, these types of agreements generally also fail the indispensability test under the third condition'. The Commission adds that '[a]ny claim that restrictive agreements are justified because they aim at ensuring fair conditions of competition on the market is by nature unfounded and must be discarded [. . .] The protection of fair conditions of competition is a task for the legislator in compliance with Community law obligations and not for undertakings to regulate themselves' (paras 46 and 47).

   10   In the maritime sector, restrictive agreements entered into by liner shipping conferences in the context of the related block exemption under Reg No 4056/86 [1986] OJ L378/4 long raised complex issues as to the compatibility of certain price-fixing practices with Art 81 EC. This is not dealt with in this chapter. Reg No 4056/86 has now been repealed by Reg 1419/06 [2006] OJ L269/1, which has simultaneously amended Regulation (EC) No 1/2003, in that the scope of the latter has been extended to include cabotage and international tramp services.

   11   M Monti (then European Commissioner in charge of competition), opening speech at the 3rd Nordic Competition Policy Conference, Stockholm, September 2000.

   12   JM Griffin (then Deputy Assistant Attorney General, Antitrust Division, US Department of Justice ('DOJ')), 3rd Nordic Competition Policy Conference, Stockholm, September 2000.

'most intolerable form of abusive practice' whose 'long term eradication' is 'essential'.[13] Cartels go against the most fundamental principles of free market economics, according to which the levels of prices and output should be determined by competition, providing consumers with the highest quality goods at the lowest possible price, as well as resulting in a high level of innovation. By artificially reducing output and/or fixing prices, cartels mimic a monopoly situation, in which supra competitive profits are shared out between their members. They create an unjustified transfer of wealth to the exclusive benefit of their members and divert resources from their optimal use elsewhere in the economy. Cartels tend to align prices and commercial strategy with those of the least competitive of their members. This results in higher costs for customers, a slowdown in innovation and the artificial survival of 'lame ducks'. By eliminating the pressure that encourages companies to invent new products or services, to improve distribution and to reduce production costs, collusion results in both productive and allocative inefficiency. Cartels reduce both social welfare and the consumer surplus.[14]

8.06 From an EC perspective, cartels are all the more damaging since they frustrate the attainment of the Community's policies. Not only do they tend to reduce the benefits expected from the proper functioning of an open market economy but, through the artificial partitioning of their market, they also obstruct the development of a true single European market, intended to facilitate the attainment of the economic and political goals of European integration.[15] It is therefore essential to ensure that regulatory barriers to trade, which have been dismantled over past decades, are not replaced by invisible barriers set up by private operators. Success in fighting cartels is also particularly important in the context of the liberalisation of certain markets, as the intensification of competition may create further incentives to collude.

8.07 **Quantifying the harm** It is not easy to assess in economic terms the precise harm that cartels cause.[16] In its 2003 Report on cartels,[17] the OECD highlighted this difficulty, noting

---

[13] Neelie Kroes (European Commissioner in charge of competition) in her speech, 'The first hundred days', 7 April 2005. Ms Kroes added: 'I am an economist by training. My analytical experience tells me that it is rare in life that issues are either entirely one thing or another—or, if you like, purely black or white. But with cartels my judgement is clear-cut. Cartel behaviour is illegal, unjustified and unjustifiable—whatever the size, nature or scope of the business affected'. See on Commission's website: SPEECH/05/205.

[14] See Chapter 1 of this book.

[15] In Case T-241/01 *Scandinavian Airline System v Commission* [2005] ECR II-95, at para 85, the CFI stated that '[a]part from the serious distortion of competition that they entail, such agreements, by obliging the parties to respect distinct markets, often delimited by national frontiers, cause the isolation of those markets, thereby counteracting the EC Treaty's main objective of integrating the Community market'. The European Courts have also consistently held that it is relevant when setting the amount of the fines in a cartel case to 'ensure that its action has the necessary deterrent effect, especially as regards those types of infringement which are particularly harmful to the attainment of the objectives of the Community' (eg Joined Cases 100/80, 101/80, 102/80 and 103/80 *Musique diffusion française and others v Commission* [1983] ECR 1825, para 106).

[16] First, cartels have both price and non-price effects and the indirect loss of welfare (lower quality and choice, reduced innovation and marketing efforts) caused by the sheltering of the cartel from a truly competitive process is virtually impossible to estimate. Second, a reliable calculation of the excess price imposed by cartels would require comparison of the situation in the cartelised market to the one that would normally prevail. Such a comparison would be of dubious reliability in view of the complex interplay of factors that characterises the functioning of a market.

[17] OECD, *Hard Core Cartels, Recent progress and challenges ahead* (2003). See also the 2002 Report of the OECD Competition Committee on the nature and impact of hard core cartels and sanctions against cartels under national competition laws.

that competition regulators generally do not attempt to quantify the damage caused by cartels, since that is not usually a legal requirement. Although it had conducted a wide-ranging survey, the OECD acknowledged that estimating the harm resulting from cartels remained an elusive goal and that 'one can only conclude that the total harm from cartels is significant indeed, surely amounting to many billions dollars each year'.[18] There are nevertheless examples of attempts to quantify the damage caused by cartels. These indicate the considerable extent of the harm caused, which may correspond to between 15 and 20 per cent of the value of the affected trade[19] and to a median overcharge of 25 per cent.[20]

8.08 In spite of the difficulty of computing their negative effects with any precision, Commission decisions provide revealing examples of the great harm that cartels cause. In *Welded Steel Mesh*, the Commission noted that the agreement concerning the French market, which involved price fixing and limitation of imports, had enabled prices to rise spectacularly. In less than one year, prices had increased by 58 per cent, a rate much higher than in other Community producing countries.[21] In *Cartonboard*, according to the producers' own figures, the series of price initiatives between 1988 and 1991 boosted West European basic list prices by an average of 42 per cent in absolute terms.[22] In *Graphite Electrodes*, the Commission found that the relevant prices had increased by 50 per cent during the period of operation of the cartel.[23] The effects of a cartel are not restricted to prices alone. In other cases, cartels may for instance aim to slow down an anticipated price fall or to delay the introduction of a more efficient, but perhaps less lucrative process.[24] The result, however, is a net harm to customers.

8.09 **The intensification of the Commission's fight against hard core cartels**   In view of the threat posed to the economy, it is essential for Community 'anti-cartel' policy to have a deterrent effect. With the adoption of Regulation 17 in 1962, the Commission was granted important powers enabling it to investigate cartels, to order them to cease and desist and, most importantly, to impose on each of the cartel members financial penalties representing up to 10 per cent of their annual turnover. The first fines were imposed as early as 1969,

---

[18] 2003 OECD Report on hard core cartels, p 9.

[19] ibid. The OECD stated that in 14 large cartel cases prosecuted during the survey period (1996–2000), estimates of harm expressed as a percentage of affected commerce could be calculated. These estimates ranged from a low of 3% to a high of 65% and the median was between 15 and 20%.

[20] JM Connor, *Price-Fixing Overcharges: Legal and Economic Evidence*, available at SSRN: <http://www.ssrn.com/abstract=787924>. In this paper, based on an extensive study of several hundred hard core cartels, Connor found that the median cartel overcharge for all types of cartels over all time periods is 25%. This median overcharge would be 32% for international cartels, making international cartels about 75% more effective in raising prices than domestic cartels. Connor states that his findings are generally consistent with the few previously published works that survey cartel overcharges.

[21] [1989] OJ L260/1, para 25.

[22] [1994] OJ L243/1, para 21. In real terms, the increase in announced prices during this period averaged 26% in Western Europe while actual prices went up 19% before dropping somewhat in the second half of 1991.

[23] [2002] OJ L100/1, para 70. This is confirmed in *Specialty Graphite* (Decision of 17 December 2002, full text of the decision available on DG COMP's web site), where the Commission reported at para 129 that during a top level cartel meeting in 1993, the chairman of a member of the cartel indicated that, thanks to the collaboration achieved in the market for graphite electrodes, the parties had succeeded in increasing prices by 50%. He encouraged members to cooperate in the business of specialty graphite as well, with a view to halting the price decline in that market.

[24] In *Graphite Electrodes* [2002] OJ L100/1, a cartel participant produced a type of electrode which, although smaller and cheaper than those produced by the other participants, could successfully compete with them. The cartel forced the undertaking concerned to cease manufacture of the cheaper product (see para 56).

in the *Quinine*[25] and *Dyestuff*[26] cases. In the 1970s, several cartels were prohibited by the Commission, but the imposition of fines remained sporadic, as some of these agreements had been notified, thus benefiting by law from a provisional immunity from fines.[27] As cartel participants became more aware of the illicit nature of their practices, as well as of the legal consequences of such behaviour, cartels went underground and the Commission had to focus on detection and punishment. From the early 1980s, fines were imposed systematically and their level increased progressively.

The intensity of the Commission's fight against cartels dramatically increased from the mid-1990s, when it became apparent, through the unearthing of very large and sophisticated international collusive schemes, such as the *Cartonboard*, *PVC* or *Cement* cartels, that such practices were widespread. The process of globalisation also increased awareness of the threat to consumer welfare posed by (worldwide) cartels. During the second half of the 1990s, the Commission took important steps to render its enforcement policy more effective. Its strategy consisted largely of a 'carrot and stick' policy. On the one hand, in 1996 the Commission adopted its first leniency programme,[28] aimed at encouraging cartel members voluntarily to disclose illegal practices in exchange for reductions in fines up to 100 per cent in certain cases. On the other hand, it adopted a tougher policy on fines with the publication in 1998 of guidelines on a new method for setting fines (the '1998 Guidelines'),[29] which resulted in levels of punishment with a greater deterrent value. The Commission's new strategy yielded tangible results, with the adoption, in 2001, of an unprecedented number of cartel decisions (10), resulting in the imposition of a total of over EUR 1,000 million in fines. The Commission has since confirmed its determination: over the period 2001–2006, the Commission adopted 39 cartel decisions and imposed over EUR 6,000 million in fines. In 2002, it adopted a renewed leniency programme aimed at providing greater incentives for companies to come forward. This programme was again modified in 2006, with a view to further improving its effectiveness.[30] In 2003, the Council granted the Commission increased investigatory powers to fight cartels with the adoption of Regulation 1/2003, and in 2006 the Commission adopted new guidelines for setting fines (the '2006 Guidelines')[31] which, it is expected, will again increase the level of the fines imposed on cartels.[32]

8.10

---

[25] [1969] OJ L192/5.

[26] [1969] OJ L195/11.

[27] The notification of outright violations of Art 81 EC was not uncommon in the early years of competition law enforcement. See eg *Cardboard Tubes Producers* [1970] L242/18; *Vereeniging van Cementhandelaren* [1972] OJ L13/34; *IFTRA rules for producers of virgin aluminium* [1975] OJ L228/3.

[28] Commission notice on the non-imposition or reduction of fines in cartel cases, [1996] OJ C207/4.

[29] Guidelines on the method of setting fines imposed pursuant to Art 15(2) of Reg No 17 and Art 65(5) of the ECSC Treaty, [1998] OJ C9/3.

[30] Commission notice on immunity from fines and reduction of fines in cartel cases, [2006] OJ C298/17. See also IP/06/1705 and MEMO/06/469.

[31] IP/06/857.

[32] From an organisational point of view, the intensification of the Commission's fight against cartels was embodied by the setting-up of a dedicated 'Cartel' unit within the Commission's Directorate General for Competition on 1 December 1998. A further step was taken in 2005, with the creation within the same Directorate General of an entire 'Cartel' directorate, employing in 2006 approximately 50 dedicated case-handlers. Competition Commissioner, Neelie Kroes described this decision 'as a very concrete expression of the zero tolerance policy the European Commission is committed to implement in the face of this most damaging type of anti-competitive practice' ('Taking Competition Seriously—Anti-Trust Reform in Europe', speech at the IBA/European Commission Conference 'Anti-trust reform in Europe: a year in practice', Brussels, 10 March 2005).

8.11 **Incentives for firms to form cartels**   According to the perfect competition model,[33] open market economies should produce an optimal outcome as long as there is more than one seller in the market. However, this model does not take into account the fact that the interaction between firms affects the result of the competitive process between market players. Indeed, undertakings are well aware that the profitability of their market strategies is often dependent on those pursued by competing firms, and take this into account in their business decisions. Non-cooperative game theory has shown however, through the so-called 'Nash equilibrium', as illustrated by the 'prisoners' dilemma', that despite firms having a shared interest in charging a price above the competitive level, they will normally end up charging the competitive price.[34]

8.12   In response to these factors, firms may be tempted to enter into agreements or less formal arrangements which, although not formally binding, may help them to suppress the uncertainty characterising the 'prisoner's dilemma', thus enabling them to reduce the effectiveness of the competitive process and to increase price above the competitive level. Through explicit collusion, that is voluntary coordination of their behaviour, cartel participants may eliminate competition between themselves and extract supra competitive profits.[35] Nevertheless, as game theory also shows, whilst there is an incentive for firms to engage in explicit collusion, there is also a temptation for them to cheat on the arrangements: once a high price has been agreed by the cartel, it may be extremely profitable for one of its members—provided that the others stick to the agreement—to 'free-ride' by undercutting the collusive price. However, if all cartel participants cheat, collusion fails to produce its expected results. Sustaining effective collusion will therefore be difficult: instability is inherent in cartels and the likelihood of obtaining 'positive' results will largely depend on the cartel's capacity to monitor compliance with the cartel agreement and to punish cheats effectively.

8.13 **Factors conducive to the setting up of cartels**   Cartels can develop in almost any industry. Their occurrence may result from 'human' factors (collusive 'culture', bad habits of certain managers), but will also critically depend on 'objective' factors such as specific incentives to cooperate or to cheat or opportunities to monitor and enforce collusive arrangements. In this respect, some sectors may be more prone to collusion than others. Explicit collusion is easier in oligopolistic market structures, as the small number of players makes it easier to agree, monitor and enforce restrictive arrangements. Significant barriers to entry are also conducive to collusion, in that price increases will not immediately provoke entry into the market by potential competitors, which would in turn destabilise the cartel. Homogeneity of products also favours collusion, as it is easier to agree on the

---

[33] See Chapter 1 of this book, paras 1.54ff. Under the (theoretical) perfect competition model, companies hold no market power and are therefore price takers. The functioning of the market is characterised by a permanent equilibrium where the price exactly matches demand and market supply. At this point of equilibrium, the price charged by the seller equals its marginal cost and its total average cost, and no excess profit can be made. Sellers cannot charge above the competitive price, as the response of competitors would be immediate and result in losses. At this point of equilibrium, productive efficiency is attained, as all goods are being produced at the lowest possible cost, because an undertaking that did not produce at this lowest possible cost would immediately be forced out of the market. In such a situation, technical progress and innovation will always be sought and will spread immediately throughout the market, leading to a new equilibrium at a lower price.

[34] See Chapter 1 of this book, paras 1.80ff.

[35] See Chapter 1 of this book, paras 1.90ff.

prices of products with common features.[36] It is therefore not surprising that cartels have traditionally flourished in commodity markets, basic industry and intermediary goods sectors. Cartels have, however, also been found in less 'traditional' sectors such as services or consumer goods. In recent years, cartels have been unearthed in sectors as varied as banking (*Austrian Banks*),[37] transport services (*Greek Ferries*,[38] *FETTCSA*,[39] *SAS/Maersk Air*),[40] agriculture (*French Beef*,[41] *Raw Tobacco Spain*[42] and *Raw Tobacco Italy*)[43] textiles and harberdashery (*Needles*,[44] *Thread*)[45] food and beverages (*Belgian Beer*,[46] *Luxembourg Brewers*)[47] or even the fine arts business (*Fine Arts Auction Houses*).[48]

B. Typology of Cartel Arrangements and Common Features of Collusion

(1) Typology of Cartel Arrangements

Cartels are usually complex schemes combining distinct restrictive practices in the pursuance **8.14** of their overall goal, the achievement of supra competitive profits. Although cartel practices are generally closely intermingled, it is possible to classify them according to their nature.

(a) *Direct or Indirect Fixing of Purchase or Selling Prices or any other Trading Conditions*

Price-fixing arrangements can take many different forms. Although it is not easy to present **8.15** a clear typology, it is nevertheless possible to distinguish a number of basic features pertaining to cartels, as described below, where they relate to the fixing of prices. In addition to fixing the *level* of prices, cartel members also frequently agree on the *timing* of their price increases, thereby depriving customers of bargaining power through coordinated price 'campaigns', as shown below. Cartels will often mix price-fixing techniques in a global, multi-faceted effort to eliminate competition. Most full-blown cartel cases will thus be characterised by a more or less sophisticated combination of price-fixing techniques, as illustrated by many Commission decisions.

Uniform prices and price formulae   The joint fixing of prices can first take the form of **8.16** common selling prices. In *Greek Ferries*,[49] the Commission found that seven ferry operators

---

[36] Similarly, where branding and marketing have a low impact, or where there is a low rate of product innovation, there will exist a more stable environment for competing firms to reach an understanding. In this respect, similar cost structures and the use of mature technologies are also relevant to collusive tendencies. Other factors may also be relevant, such as specific business values, and established communication channels between competitors, transparency of prices, the existence of a dominant firm acting as price leader, recession, or excess capacity.

[37] [2004] OJ L56/1.

[38] [1999] OJ L109/24.

[39] [2000] OJ L268/1.

[40] [2001] OJ L265/15.

[41] [2003] OJ L209/12.

[42] Decision of 20 October 2004, IP/04/1256 (full text of the decision available on DG COMP's web site).

[43] Decision of 20 October 2005, IP/05/1315 (full text of the decision available on DG COMP's web site).

[44] Decision of 26 October 2004, IP/04/1313 (full text of the decision available on DG COMP's web site).

[45] Decision of 4 September 2005, IP/05/1140 (full text of the decision available on DG COMP's web site).

[46] [2003] OJ L200/1.

[47] [2002] OJ L253/21.

[48] [2005] OJ L200/92 (full text of the decision available on DG COMP's web site).

[49] [1999] OJ L109/24.

had fixed prices for roll-on and roll-off services on all Greece–Italy routes over several years. Common prices were fixed for each line and for each type of vehicle. Similar practices can be found in many other cartel decisions.[50] Collusion on prices can also take the form of a common price calculation scheme. In *Roofing Felt*, the members of the trade association 'Belasco' had agreed on a common price system for their product (bituminous roofing felt).[51] In *Agreements between manufacturers of glass containers*,[52] European producers of glass containers had agreed, through so-called 'IFTRA[53] rules', upon a harmonisation of prices at common market level by applying a standard calculation scheme.[54] This method enabled its users to reach similar if not identical cost curves.[55] The Commission found that '[t]he implementation [. . .] of a common system of calculating costs in order to determine sales prices ha[d] [. . .] a direct effect on the process of determining price of each undertaking in question, since it enable[d] the latter to more easily compare their respective prices and thus to coordinate their action on the market'.[56] The rules also provided that export prices had to be fixed on the basis of the parties' domestic prices in the destination country.[57] In addition, the rules provided for a common delivered-price system and for the use of a common price calculation formula.[58] Another example of such practices can be found in *Electrical and Mechanical Carbon and Graphite Products*, where cartel participants also relied on a commonly agreed price formula to impose general price increases throughout Europe.[59]

8.17 **Minimum prices**   Price-fixing can also take the form of minimum prices to be applied by all cartel participants, leaving upward deviations to the individual decisions of the cartel members. In *BNIC*,[60] the Commission condemned industry agreements by which producers, cooperatives, distillers and shippers of Cognac, represented through their professional and trade organisations within the 'BNIC',[61] fixed minimum selling prices. In *Raw Tobacco Spain*, the three Spanish unions of tobacco producers agreed on the average minimum price

---

[50] See eg *Quinine* [1969] OJ L192/5, para 22; *Flat Glass Benelux* [1984] OJ L212/13, paras 7–8 and 40–43) and *Methylglucamine* [2004] OJ L38/18, paras 83–87.

[51] [1986] OJ L232/15.

[52] [1974] OJ L160/1.

[53] International Fair Trade Practice Rules Administration.

[54] As differences in selling prices between producers and between national markets were caused by differences between methods of calculating costs, a single calculation method was established 'so that the progressive dismantling of customs barriers would not lead customers and wholesalers to take advantage of differences between national calculation methods to the detriment of producers'.

[55] It was 'to be used for sales pricing and not for purposes of internal management'. Companies could work out their costs according to the traditional method, but they had to compare them with costs established under the IFTRA method subsequently, in order to avoid 'serious mistakes' (paras 19–20).

[56] Para 46.

[57] This meant that all glass container producers agreed to align their prices with the domestic producers' prices, thereby eliminating price competition in each Member State.

[58] Paras 11–12.

[59] [2004] OJ L125/45 (full text of the decision available on DG COMP's web site), paras 91–97. Such increases covered all products and countries covered by the cartel agreement (paras 102ff). The participants had devised a highly sophisticated method for the calculation of the price of the products with reference to a number of objective factors such as the price of raw materials, the size of the product or the number of components it included. This formula, called the 'barème', was intended to enable each cartel participant to calculate the price of its products in a way that guaranteed a perfect uniformity of the prices notwithstanding the differences in the specifications of the product.

[60] [1982] OJ L379/1.

[61] Bureau National Interprofessionnel du Cognac.

per producer and producer group that they would subsequently negotiate with the tobacco processors.[62] Collusion on minimum prices was also found in *Scottish Salmon Board*,[63] *French Beef*[64] and many other cartel decisions.[65] This often implies close coordination: in *Cast Iron and Steel Rolls*,[66] a large number of producers of industrial rolls had set up a sophisticated system of mutual prior consultations regarding quotations in respect of specific enquiries from customers.[67] In *Organic Peroxides*, the cartel, which lasted over 37 years, was initially based on a written contract, signed in 1971, stating *inter alia* that '[n]o party will give prices lower than any agreed minimum prices for any product to any new customer, or reduce prices for any product to existing customers without prior discussions with the other two parties'.[68]

'Target' prices are also a common feature of cartels. Participants agree on a common price **8.18** objective to be achieved over a given period of time. Target prices may be set by category of product, or grade of product (as in *Polypropylene*),[69] but may also be set out in detail in respect of specific customers (as in *Food Flavour Enhancers*[70] or *Industrial Tubes*).[71] In *Vereeniging van Cementhandelaren*,[72] the ECJ ruled on appeal that the fixing of a target price 'affects competition because it enables all the participants to predict with a reasonable degree of certainty what the pricing policy pursued by their competitors would be'.[73] In *Polypropylene*, the Commission stated that '[t]he setting of a particular price level which has been presented to the market as "the list price" or "the official price" meant that the opportunities for customers to negotiate with producers were already circumscribed and that they were deprived of many of the benefits which would otherwise be available from the free play of competition forces'.[74] On appeal, the CFI found that 'for the purposes of the application of Article [81(1) EC] the fixing of target prices constitutes direct or indirect fixing of selling prices as mentioned, by way of example, in point (a) of that provision. [. . .] The purpose of Article [81(1) EC], and in particular of point (a) thereof, is to prohibit undertakings

---

[62] Decision of 20 October 2004 (full text of the decision available on DG COMP's web site), para 68.

[63] [1992] OJ L246/37. Norwegian and Scottish producers of salmon had agreed on minimum prices applicable to their product, in order to impose discipline in the market and, ultimately, to raise prices.

[64] [2003] OJ L209/12. The Commission condemned an agreement between farmers' and slaughterers' federations fixing minimum sales (and purchase) prices regarding cows. The prices set were 10% to 15% above the prices existing before the entry into force of the agreement (paras 39–40).

[65] See eg *Sodium Gluconate* (para 88), *Industrial and Medical Gases* (paras 101, 343), *Thread* (para 282), and *Industrial Bags* (para 279).

[66] [1983] OJ L317/1.

[67] A trade association had been created for this purpose, and a neutral office located in Switzerland was responsible for notifying to all interested parties the price enquiry received by the respective producers. The competitors would contact each other to establish suitable prices, which could not be lower than those of the last similar transaction and had to respect the minimum price levels agreed.

[68] [2005] OJ L110/44 (full text of the decision available on DG COMP's web site), para 85.

[69] [1986] OJ L230/1.

[70] [2004] OJ L75/1, para 94. The target prices for production in 1990 were discussed on the basis of 'guidelines for pricing in the European market in 1990', which indicated different target prices based on the volume ordered by a customer (large, medium-sized, or small customer).

[71] [2004] OJ L125/50 (full text of the decision available on DG COMP's web site), para 100. Price increase targets were broken down by customer and by country.

[72] [1971] OJ L13/34.

[73] Case 8/72 *Vereeniging van Cementhandelaren v Commission* [1972] ECR 977, para 21.

[74] [1986] OJ L230/1, para 90.

from distorting the normal formation of prices on the markets'.[75] This was confirmed by the CFI in its *PVC* judgment.[76]

8.19 **Recommended prices** agreed upon by competitors will also be considered restrictive. In *Welded Steel Mesh*, the price agreements entered into by the producers during cartel meetings were not 'binding', but the Commission found that they were no less contrary to Article 81(1) EC, as they replaced competition with a form of price cooperation.[77] In *SCK/FNK* (*'Dutch Cranes'*), members of FNK, the association of Dutch crane-hire companies, were obliged to charge 'reasonable' rates for the hiring of cranes. To this end, FNK published cost calculations and recommended rates based on them. The Commission established that 'jointly recommended prices, which may or may not have been observed in practice, make it possible to predict with reasonable certainty what the pricing policy of competitors would be'.[78] This was upheld by the CFI.[79] Likewise in *Fenex*, where an association of Dutch forwarding companies circulated recommended tariffs, the Commission stated that '[t]he circulation of recommended tariffs [. . .] is liable to prompt the relevant undertakings to align their tariffs, irrespective of their cost prices. Such a method dissuades undertakings whose cost prices are lower from lowering their prices and thus creates an artificial advantage for undertakings which have the least control over their production costs'.[80]

8.20 **Agreement on part of the price or on price supplements**   Price-fixing may concern only an element of the final selling price. In *Building and Construction Industry in the Netherlands*, the Commission concluded that the mere fixing of a part of the price (through the systematic addition of uniform price increases to the price tenders of contractors) amounted to an infringement of Article 81(1) EC.[81] This was confirmed by the CFI on appeal.[82] Other types of agreement on part of the price can be found in *Eurocheque/Helsinki Agreement*[83] and in *Industrial Tubes*.[84] 'Price supplements', 'charges' or 'surcharges' may also be just another

---

[75] Case T-13/89 *ICI v Commission* [1992] ECR II-1021, paras 310–311.

[76] Joined cases T-305/94, T-306/94, T-307/94, T-313/94 to T-316/94, T-318/94, T-325/94, T-328/94, T-329/94 and T-335/94 *LVM and others v Commission* [1999] ECR II-931 paras 739 and 745.

[77] [1989] OJ L260/1.

[78] [1995] OJ L312/79, para 20.

[79] Joined cases T-213/95 and T-18/96 *SCK and FNK v Commission* [1997] ECR II-1739.

[80] [1996] OJ L181/28, para 61.

[81] [1992] OJ L92/1. The Commission objected to a system of complex rules set up by the SPO, an association of contractors established in the Dutch building market, whose object was to 'promote and administer orderly competition, to prevent improper conduct in price tendering and to promote the formation of economically justified prices'. Among the rules objected to was one that provided for two types of price increase to be added uniformly to the price tenders of the various contractors, to be borne by the party awarding the contract, consisting first in the reimbursement of the costs of calculating the work estimates and secondly in contributions to the operating costs of the trade organisations (see para 31).

[82] Case T-29/92 *SPO and others v Commission* [1995] ECR II-289, para 146.

[83] [1992] OJ L95/50, paras 46–49. All French banks constituting the Groupement des Cartes Bancaires CB entered into an agreement on the principle of charging a commission to their customers and on the amount charged.

[84] [2004] OJ L125/50 (full text of the decision available on DG COMP's web site). In this market, the total price of the product resulted from the metal price element, based on the London Metal Exchange (LME) index, and a 'conversion price' corresponding to the value added by the manufacturing company. Within the cartel, price cooperation related to the 'conversion price', ie to the added value representing a percentage of the final product value. The Commission concluded that the agreement on part of the tubes price amounted to an agreement on the price of tubes.

form of price-fixing. In *Ferry operators—Currency surcharges*, the Commission condemned an agreement between several ferry operators concerning the amount (and the date of introduction) of a surcharge on freight shipments following the devaluation of the pound Sterling.[85] Similar agreements can be found in *Steel Beams*,[86] *Alloy surcharge*[87] and *Electrical and Mechanical Carbon and Graphite Products*.[88] On appeal in *Alloy Surcharge*, the CFI again confirmed that the prohibition of Article 81(1) EC extends to agreements relating to the fixing of a part of the final price.[89]

Maximum rebates   Arrangements concerning rebates or discounts have also been con-   **8.21** demned by the Commission. They may consist of rules imposed by associations of undertakings, or of specific agreements between cartel members. In *Agreements between manufacturers of glass containers*, the Commission found that the clauses relating to price discounts and terms of trade all had the similar object of suppressing normal competitive behaviour.[90] Similar conclusions about rebates were reached in *Fedetab*,[91] *Roofing Felt*[92] and *FETTSCA*.[93] The prohibition of rebates may target or exclude specific customers or categories of customers. In *Quinine*, the cartel members agreed on the rebates to be granted to each customer.[94] In *Citric acid*, the cartel participants agreed that no customer would be granted discounts. An exception was made for the five major purchasers since it was unrealistic to expect them to pay the published list price. Those customers could be offered a discount of up to 3 per cent off the list price.[95] In *Fine Art Auction Houses*, Christie's and

---

[85] [1997] OJ L26/23.

[86] [1994] OJ L116/1, paras 244–249. The Commission found that the cartel had agreed on the amount of so-called 'extras', ie price supplements charged in regard of specific quality or dimension criteria. It stated that such harmonisation agreements were agreements to fix prices contrary to Art 65(1) ECSC, since extras formed part of the ultimate price to be paid for the products in question.

[87] [1998] OJ L100/55. The Commission condemned an agreement between stainless steel producers on a formula calculating the price supplement ('alloy surcharge') applicable to the price of stainless steel products. The price supplement, which was based on the evolution of the price of the alloys used to obtain stainless steel, represented an important part of the price of the final product. The formula was considered to be a price recommendation restrictive of competition.

[88] Paras 111–114. Price supplements were agreed upon by the cartel members when price increases were too difficult to justify to customers. These price supplements were justified as packaging, transport or recycling costs.

[89] Joined cases T-45/98 and T-47/98 *Krupp Thyssen Stainless and Acciai speciali Terni v Commission* [2001] ECR II-3757, para 15.

[90] This included a clause prohibiting special prices, discounts and other conditions, a clause prohibiting any secret departure from published offers or price lists and a clause which deemed it an unfair practice to depart, whether secretly or not, from price lists. See [1974] OJ L160/1, para 36.

[91] [1978] OJ L224/29, para 98(b). The Commission found that a recommendation by a trade association regarding the end-of-year rebates system effectively stifled all competition in this field. Indeed, the recommendation meant that the total rebate granted by each manufacturer was calculated by applying the appropriate rate to the customer's total turnover, regardless of the quantity of goods actually purchased each year from an individual manufacturer. There was no incentive for intermediaries to make greater competitive efforts with a view to obtaining improved benefits from manufacturers, or to take their custom exclusively to one manufacturer with a view to being rewarded with a larger rebate.

[92] [1986] OJ L232/15. The Commission found that an agreement between manufacturers of bituminous felt to set maximum discounts was intended to facilitate the imposition of minimum prices for the product.

[93] [2000] OJ L268/1. An agreement not to discount from published charges and surcharges applicable to basic ocean rates constituted an infringement of Art 81(1) as it restricted competition between liner shipping companies as regards the final price charge to shippers (para 134).

[94] [1969] OJ L192/5, para 22.

[95] [2002] OJ L239/18, para 83.

Sotheby's agreed to make their vendor's commissions non-negotiable, that is to exclude any rebates save permitted exceptions identified in so-called 'grandfather lists'.[96] In *Electrical and Mechanical Carbon and Graphite Products*, the cartel reached an agreement on the discounts to be granted to customers depending on the method of delivery.[97] The finding that agreements on maximum rebates amount to price-fixing has been upheld by the European Courts.[98]

8.22 Agreements on other trade conditions   Cartels may involve arrangements on trading conditions other than price. Such restrictions will generally be considered as *per se* infringements, as they have a direct or indirect influence on the selling price.[99] In *Vereeniging van Cementhandelaren*,[100] the Commission condemned a series of agreements and decisions taken by the Dutch cement dealers' association concerning the sale of cement in the Netherlands which, *inter alia*, strictly limited the commercial benefits which might be granted to purchasers and prevented any services being provided for customers which fell outside the framework of what was regarded as 'normal'. In *Agreements between manufacturers of glass containers*,[101] the Commission found that the system of 'free delivered' price agreed upon[102] had the object of nullifying any competitive advantage which a producer of glass containers could gain from having greater proximity to its customers, and consequently distorted competition between these undertakings and between the users of glass containers.[103] In *Vimpoltu*,[104] the Commission condemned a decision by a Dutch association of importers of agricultural machinery laying down, *inter alia*, standard delivery and payment terms and rules on sales promotions. In *Fine Arts Auction Houses*, the two cartel members agreed on a wide array of trade terms.[105] Similar attempts to harmonise trading

---

[96] [2005] OJ L200/92 (full text of the decision available on DG COMP's web site), paras 116–118. As they agreed to introduce new sliding scales, Christie's and Sotheby's had made it clear in their press releases that goods already consigned for future sales would not be affected by the new scale. These exceptions opened the door to cheating, as the two auction houses could not trust each other not to offer attractive terms in getting a particularly high profile sale on the basis that this followed from past obligations. In order to ensure that neither took on new business at the old rate or at no commission, the two CEOs exchanged lists of 'grandfathered' clients. These lists identified the customers with whom conditions had been agreed, prior to the announcement of the new scale.

[97] [2004] OJ L125/45 (full text of the decision available on DG COMP's web site), paras 115–117.

[98] Joined cases 209 to 215 and 218/78 *van Landewyck and others v Commission* [1980] ECR 3125, paras 142–146; Joined Cases T-39/92 and T-40/92 *CB and Europay v Commission* [1994] ECR II-49, paras 84–86, and Case T-213/00 *CMA CGM and others v Commission* [2003] ECR II-913, para 175.

[99] See eg Joined cases 209 to 215 and 218/78 *van Landewyck and others v Commission* [1980] ECR 3125, paras 147–156.

[100] [1971] OJ L13/34.

[101] [1974] OJ L160/1.

[102] The price corresponded to the price of the goods plus average transport costs. Since users and retailers compare not only prices but also sales terms, this made it easier for manufacturers to sell products at a long distance since it precluded unfavourable comparisons of the low prices of nearby plants with the higher prices of distant plants.

[103] Para 48.

[104] [1983] OL L200/44.

[105] [2005] OJ L200/9 (full text of the decision available on DG COMP's web site), para 76. The agreement included refusal to give vendors at auction guarantees as to the minimum price, refusal to make advances to vendors on single lots, the setting of minimum interest rates for loans, and the limitation of credit terms to trade buyers at 90 days.

conditions can be found in *Specialty graphites*,[106] *Electrical and Mechanical Carbon and Graphite Products*[107] and *Industrial Tubes*.[108]

Agreement on the purchase price of raw materials   Cartel participants may also agree on **8.23** the price of purchase of raw materials from their suppliers. In *German Scrap Iron*, the Commission found that agreements and concerted practices fell under the prohibition of Article 65 ECSC as they instituted a system of buying quotas which brought about a limitation of demand intended to reduce prices.[109] In *Belgian Agreement on Industrial Timber*, the Commission intervened against an agreement under which Belgian customers of industrial timber had agreed not to purchase the product above a given price.[110] In *Zinc Producer Group*, an agreement by an association of undertakings regarding the fixing of the price of purchase ('producer price') for their zinc metal requirements was condemned. The Commission stated that the agreement had the object and effect of restricting price competition within the European Community, by restricting the parties' freedom to negotiate their purchase prices with zinc mining companies and to set their selling prices for zinc metal to zinc metal purchasers to their own best commercial advantage.[111] In *Raw Tobacco Spain*[112] and *Raw Tobacco Italy*,[113] processors of raw tobacco agreed between themselves the maximum purchase price that they would pay to their suppliers, the tobacco producers. The objective was to ensure that prices paid to the suppliers would not rise above certain maximum levels.

Co-ordinated price increase 'campaigns'   Apart from deciding on a price levels, cartel **8.24** participants often endeavour to eliminate any uncertainty about their future commercial behaviour by agreeing on the rate, date and place of price increases. Such practices may be made systematic through the conduct of wide-ranging price increase 'campaigns' aimed at secretly depriving customers of their bargaining power. Such arrangements have been condemned by the Commission from its very first cartel decisions, in *Quinine*[114] and *Dyestuff*.[115]

---

[106] Decision of 17 December 2002 (full text of the decision available on DG COMP's web site), para 100. There were agreements on premiums for non standard products, agreements on billing conditions, on discounts, as well as on 'standard' exchange rates.

[107] [2004] OJ L125/45 (full text of the decision available on DG COMP's web site). The cartel agreed on payment terms and conditions. See paras 118–119.

[108] [2004] OJ L125/50 (full text of the decision available on DG COMP's web site). The cartel participants agreed on commercial terms such as payment terms, delivery and consignment stock. See paras 102 and 195.

[109] [1970] OJ L29/30. See also First Commission Report on Competition Policy (1971), para 10.

[110] See Fifth Commission Report on Competition Policy (1975), para 37. The agreements were terminated without a formal decision having to be issued.

[111] [1984] OJ L220/27, para 66. See also *Bitumen Netherlands*, Decision of 20 September 2006, IP/06/1179.

[112] Decision of 20 October 2004 (full text of the decision available on DG COMP's web site), paras 67 and 74–76.

[113] Decision of 20 October 2005 (full text of the decision available on DG COMP's web site), paras 115, 126–127 and 238.

[114] [1969] OJ L192/5. The Commission found that the producers of quinine (a substance used for the production of medicines) had agreed on simultaneous and identical price increases, as well as on the level of the commissions and rebates granted to purchasers.

[115] [1969] L195/11. In this case concerning colouring agents, the Commission found, following complaints by customers, that the implementation by the dyestuff industry of identical and simultaneous price increases in several Member States was the result of a concerted action. The Commission established that price increases for the same products were characterised by the same rates and had been instituted on the same dates. It also found that the memos sent out to the sales offices had been drafted in an almost identical way, following contacts between the producers.

In the latter case, the ECJ stated on appeal that the function of price competition is 'to keep prices down to the lowest possible level and to encourage the movement of goods between the member states, thereby permitting the most efficient possible distribution of activities in the matter of productivity and the capacity of undertakings to adapt themselves to change'.[116] It added that 'the fact that the increases were uniform and simultaneous has in particular served to maintain the status quo, ensuring that the undertakings would not lose custom, and has thus helped to keep the traditional national markets in those goods "cemented" to the detriment of any real form of movement of the products in question in the common market'.[117]

8.25 Price campaigns can take different forms: increases may be simultaneous, as in *Quinine*[118] or *Dyestuff*,[119] or carefully staggered, as in *Polypropylene*,[120] or in *Graphite Electrodes*.[121] They may be prepared down to the most specific detail in order to ensure success, and to avoid detection. In *PVC II*, customers were psychologically prepared through reports in the specialist trade press alluding to particular target levels.[122] The initiative in altering the price lists was not always taken by the same producer, and to avoid the risk of not being followed by its competitors, each producer took the precaution of checking, prior to an actual price increase, whether the others were prepared to follow suit.[123] In *Polypropylene*, price 'initiatives' were signalled by a press announcement that one producer was planning a price increase which the others were 'supporting' or 'following'.[124]

8.26 Price increase campaigns may not be aimed at imposing identical prices, but rather at maintaining the status quo between suppliers. In *Pre-insulated Pipes*, a cartel participant stated that the purpose of the agreement 'was to increase prices by approximately 30 to 35 per cent within a period of two years. It was expected that there would be gradual increases every quarter. The companies were not supposed to increase their prices by the same percentage at the same time. The usual practice was to have a 6 to 8 per cent increase per quarter [. . .]'.[125]

---

[116] Case 48-69 *ICI v Commission* [1972] ECR 619, para 115.

[117] ibid, para 123.

[118] [1969] OJ L192/5.

[119] [1969] OJ L195/11.

[120] [1986] OJ L230/1. Cartel participants agreed on concerted price 'initiatives' sometimes lasting for a period of several months and consisting of several separate 'step' increases. Tables or lists of target prices for each principal product grade were drawn up for each local market, in the relevant currency (para 21).

[121] [2002] OJ L100/1. Tables were circulated, indicating price increases in each country and currency, with the date on which they were supposed to take place (para 62). Increases came into effect on different dates in different countries. The cartel decided which undertaking would make the first move and the others agreed not to undercut the quoted price (para 66). There was a market leader in charge of taking the initiative of setting the price increase in each relevant region. As soon as the price increase announced by the market leaders was accepted by customers, the smaller producers would follow the major producers and apply the new prices (para 69(2)).

[122] [1994] OJ L239/14. An internal memo from a cartel member stated that the target prices in Europe were fairly well known through the industry and as such were 'posted levels'. The memorandum went on to state that '[. . .] these posted levels will not be achieved in a slack market [. . .] but the announcement does have a psychological effect upon the buyer. An analogy would be in car sales where the "List price" is set at such a level that the purchaser is satisfied, when he obtains his 10–15% discount, that he has struck a "good deal"' (para 19).

[123] ibid, paras 18–19.

[124] [1986] OJ L230/1, para 67.

[125] [1999] OJ L24/1, para 58.

In addition to the general objective of pushing prices upwards, concerted price increases may also respond to specific needs. In *Franco-Japanese Ball-Bearings Agreement*,[126] French and Japanese manufacturers of ball-bearings aimed to increase the prices of Japanese products imported into France and bring those prices in line with the domestic ones. In *Vegetable Parchment*, producers agreed on several general price increases applicable for 'export markets' where no cartel member was established.[127] In *Citric Acid*, the cartel paid great attention to the fluctuations in exchange rates in order to maintain prices at the same level in Europe and in the US, and its members made an explicit commitment not to allow prices to diverge substantially so as to prevent trans-shipments between the two areas.[128]

(b) Limitation or Control of Production, Markets, Technical Development or Investment

Since the price of a product is a function of output and demand, a restriction in output by **8.27** producers will affect prices. It should come as no surprise, therefore, that parties to an agreement on prices sometimes also enter into an agreement to limit production in order to support their price objectives, or that on occasions an agreement solely aims to restrict output, in consideration of the (anticipated) effect on price.

Production or sales quotas Output restrictions are commonly achieved through produc- **8.28** tion or sales quotas which, in most cases, consist of the cartel participants allocating between themselves a maximum permissible volume of production or deliveries. Quotas are often fixed according to the respective (agreed) market shares of the cartel members, as in *Italian Cast Glass*[129] and *Welded Steel Mesh*[130] and are seen as ancillary to the cartel's attempts to raise prices. In *Polypropylene*[131] and *Cartonboard*,[132] some permanent system of volume control was deemed necessary to the success of 'price initiatives'. In *Vitamins (A and E)*, the fundamental idea underlying the cartel was to freeze the quantities put on the market at the level of the year preceding the beginning of the cartel. The control of the volumes was ensured through so-called annual 'budgets'.[133] Further examples of sales quotas can be found, inter alia, in *Amino Acids*[134] or *Sodium Gluconate*.[135]

Other types of joint limitation or control of production may be resorted to with a view to **8.29** restricting competition. In *Cimbel*[136] the Commission condemned an agreement which

---

[126] [1974] L343/19.
[127] [1978] OJ L70/54, paras 40–52.
[128] [2002] OJ L239/18, paras 93, 95.
[129] [1980] OJ L383/19. The three Italian producers of cast glass agreed on quotas for sales on the Italian market.
[130] [1989] OJ L260/1. The participants established delivery quotas for welded steel mesh for the French, German and Benelux markets.
[131] [1986] OJ L230/1. Volume targets in tonnes were set for each producer, and the quota system had as its ultimate objective the creation of artificial conditions of 'stability' favourable to price rises. Another measure taken by the cartel was the diversion of supplies as far as possible to deep sea markets so as to create a shortage in Western Europe conducive to a price increase (para 27).
[132] [1994] OJ L243/1. The 'price before tonnage' policy led to the strict control of volumes put on the market (see eg paras 51–60).
[133] [2003] OJ L6/1, paras 189–196.
[134] [2001] OJ L152/24, paras 211–223.
[135] Paras 83–87.
[136] [1972] OJ L303/24.

provided, among other things, that the building of new cement plants had to be subject to prior approval by all contracting parties. In *Zinc Producer Group*,[137] in order to support the common agreed price, the cartel members had agreed to curtail production and to notify investment projects to all the members of the group. In *French-West African shipowners' committees*, the agreement had as its object the control of the supply of transport services available to shippers wishing to import or export goods between France and the African States concerned.[138] In *Polypropylene*, an exchange of information took place regarding planned temporary plant closures which might be helpful in reducing overall supply.[139] In *Cartonboard*[140] several producers coordinated their downtime in order to restrict supply and keep prices up. This constituted an element of the so-called 'price before tonnage policy' strategy. On appeal, the CFI confirmed that the Commission had adequately established the existence of collusion on downtime and that this formed part of an anticompetitive strategy.[141] In *Graphite Electrodes*, one of the governing principles of the cartel was the freezing of production capacities. Moreover, a limitation on the transfer of technology outside the cartel was agreed, in order to prevent market entry by any third party.[142]

8.30   **The control or limitation of commercial investment** may also constitute methods of restricting competition. In *Belgian Beer*,[143] the cartel arrangements included agreements to limit advertising and other marketing activities (promotion campaigns and services to retailers) as well as investment in distribution. In *Electrical and Mechanical Carbon and Graphite Products*, cartel members agreed not to conduct publicity campaigns and to abstain from taking part in trade fairs.[144] In addition to explicit restrictions on investment, joint investment strategies in the context of a collusive scheme may also be considered restrictive. In *Roofing Felt*,[145] the cartel had agreed to defend the members' collective interests, by jointly agreeing to refrain from individual advertising. The Commission found that this was an objectionable part of an agreement which also provided for restrictions on prices and products and for quotas. As the products were largely standardised, individual advertising could (and should) have been a means whereby suppliers still competed with one another.[146] On appeal, the ECJ upheld the Commission's analysis, stating that '[. . .] joint advertising measures, such as use of [a common mark], restricted competition in so far as they presented a uniform image of products in a sector in which individual advertising may facilitate differentiation and therefore competition'.[147]

---

137   [1984] OJ L220/27.

138   [1992] OJ L134/1. Due to the freezing of market shares induced by cargo-sharing, members of the committees could not increase their supply of transport services over and above the quotas set by the committees. Any third country lines wishing to supply such services had no choice but to be co-opted by the members of the committees and limit their supply to the cargo quotas imposed by the committees, or otherwise to give up all activity in these trades, unless they were willing to run the risk of incurring penalties (see para 41).

139   [1986] OJ L230/1, para 27.

140   [1994] OJ L243/1.

141   See eg Case T-352/94 *Mo och Domsjö AB v Commission* [1998] ECR II-1989, paras 133 and 139.

142   [1999] OJ L24/1, paras 2, 110.

143   [2003] OJ L200/1.

144   [2004] OJ L125/45 (full text of the decision available on DG COMP's web site), paras 152–153.

145   [1986] OL L232/15.

146   The Commission stated that there were reasons to believe that the joint advertising was intended to support the other restrictive features of the cartel agreement by fostering users' impression of a homogeneous product and so limiting the scope members ought to have had to compete by differentiating their products (para 73).

147   Case 246/86 *Belasco and others v Commission* [1989] ECR 2117, para 30.

Collusive product specialisation   Arrangements whereby one party refrains from produc-   **8.31**
ing certain products in favour of the other party are also common in cartels and equally prohibited under Article 81(1) EC. In *Quinine*, the gentleman's agreements prohibited the
production of a certain type of product by certain cartel participants, so that others could
keep the (joint) monopoly on the product. The trade-off was that those undertakings
refraining from production benefited from the protection of their domestic market for the
products that they did continue to sell.[148] The Commission found that such agreements
prevented the undertakings concerned from competing against each other. A similar practice was found in *Welded Steel Mesh*, where a gentleman's agreement between certain producers to mutually refrain from manufacturing the type of product manufactured by other
party was regarded as a restriction of competition, in so far as each party had relinquished its
right to manufacture and sell the product yielded to the other party through its own sales network.[149] The CFI upheld the Commission's finding.[150] In *SAS/Maersk Air*, the Commission
found that similar arrangements had been put into practice in air transport: the two cartel
members had agreed that each of them would cease to operate certain routes and so eliminated competition between them.[151]

Channelling output   Elimination of competition may also be sought by channelling the   **8.32**
cartel's output only through certain of its members. In *European Sugar Industry*,[152] the principle of mutual respect of domestic markets was implemented through the practice of
limiting the sales of sugar to be sold outside the domestic sales zone to the direct or indirect
channels of the competitors established in the destination market. Similar arrangements
were condemned in *Vegetable Parchment*,[153] *Aluminium Imports from Easter Europe*[154] and
Seamless Steel Tubes.[155] In *Food Flavour Enhancers*, part of the cartel arrangement consisted
of so-called 'counterpurchasing agreements' according to which the Japanese producers
were committed to purchasing product from the Koreans in exchange for which those producers agreed to limit their sales to certain markets as well as to certain customers.[156]

Grant of reciprocal selling rights and joint sales arrangements   Agreements granting   **8.33**
reciprocal selling rights between competitors or providing for joint sales constitute another
means of eliminating competition at sales level by channelling output through a single route.

---

[148] [1969] OJ L192/5, para 30.
[149] [1989] OJ L260/1, para 172.
[150] Case T-141/89 *Tréfileurope Sales v Commission* [1995] ECR II-797, para 97.
[151] [2001] OJ L265/15, paras 24, 69.
[152] [1973] OJ L140/17.
[153] [1978] OJ L70/54. The Commission found that the European producers had engaged in a concerted practice whereby the French and German undertakings agreed, after a British competitor shut down its pro-duction plant, to supply the British undertaking with vegetable parchment for the British market on an exclu-sive basis. Continental European producers supplied this undertaking with the quantities which it required in order to meet British demand in full and refrained from supplying users directly.
[154] [1992] OJ L92/1. The Commission condemned an agreement whereby all the primary producers of alu-minium in the EC had agreed to purchase the entire supplies of aluminium offered by the State Trading agencies of the Eastern bloc countries, which in turn agreed to sell exclusively to the EC primary aluminium producers.
[155] [2003] OJ L140/1. It was agreed as a cartel sub-agreement that British Steel, which ceased to produce tubes, would continue to supply the UK market through the purchase of these tubes from three other European cartel participants. The aim was the protection of the UK market as a 'national' market, and the exclusion of Japanese competitors from entry (paras 78–82).
[156] [2004] OJ L75/1, para 64.

In *Siemens/Fanuc*,[157] the Commission condemned an agreement by which the two competitors had granted each other exclusive selling rights for numerical controls in Europe and Asia respectively. Thus, Siemens neutralised the direct impact of an important competitor in Europe and prevented all other undertakings in the common market from buying directly from Fanuc. In *Dutch Nitrogenous Fertilizers (CSV)*, the Commission condemned an agreement by which the two major Dutch producers had set up an organisation (CSV) aimed at handling joint sales of their products in the Netherlands and for export.[158] The Commission found that competition had been eliminated between the two producers and that parallel sales were also discouraged by their joint operation. In *Floral*,[159] the Commission prohibited an agreement by which French producers of fertiliser had set up a joint-sales organisation for the purpose of exporting to Germany and shared the profits through their equity holding.

8.34 Standard setting   The setting of industry standards may also be used in various ways to eliminate competition or exclude potential competitors. In *Roofing Felt*[160] the Commission found that the agreement to promote the standardisation of the products was, in view of the restrictive nature of the overall cartel arrangement and of the way it was applied, at least partly intended to restrict members' freedom to differentiate their products. On appeal, the Court upheld the Commission's analysis, stating that '[t]he standardization measures were intended to prevent the members from differentiating their products and to obviate competition between members [. . .]'.[161] In *Pre-insulated Pipes*, the cartel brought pressure to bear on a member which had introduced a new industrial process allowing savings of 15 to 20 per cent of production costs and which tended to charge lower prices. Other producers arranged to limit the expansion of this new technology and to maintain the old standards.[162] In *Copper Plumbing Tubes*, the cartel's anti-competitive strategy included the joint use of a single trademark, and the participants agreed that copper plumbing tubes should not be put in the market under other trademarks.[163]

8.35 Other practices limiting production or technological development have also been condemned. In *Roofing Felt*, the cartel members took coordinated action with regard to an undertaking that went bankrupt in order to ensure that its production facilities would continue to be controlled by the cartel.[164] The Court upheld the Commission's finding and stated that

---

157 [1985] OJ L376/29.

158 [1978] OJ L242/15. CSV also provided for the exchange and joint discussion of detailed information concerning production, storage and sales forecasts and figures for each product and destination, including deliveries to other Member States.

159 [1980] OJ L39/51.

160 [1986] OJ L232/15.

161 Case 246/86 *Belasco and others v Commission*, [1989] ECR 2117, para 30.

162 [1999] OJ L24/1. The creation of a trade association officially aimed at promoting the exchange of technology within the industry was instrumental to this effort to discriminate against a technically superior product. The ringleader had stated in this respect that the new standard should not be accepted as resulting cost savings would mean a reduction of 10 to 15% in market volume and 'none of [the cartel participants] would become richer' (see paras 113–116).

163 Decision of 3 September 2004 (full text of the decision available on DG COMP's web site), para 119.

164 [1986] OJ L232/15. At a meeting with the regional economic authorities, the representatives of Belasco, the trade association under cover of which the cartel operated, urged against the undertaking being taken over by foreign interests lest this 'upset the already very precarious balance on the market'. They also expressed an interest in taking over the firm themselves (see para 64).

'the applicants endeavoured to avoid the possibility of a takeover of [the insolvent undertaking], by one or more foreign undertakings because they were not members of the cartel. It must be acknowledged that that concerted action, which formed part of a campaign against other producers and importers, was intended to restrict competition or to strengthen the applicants' position on the market'.[165] In *Graphite Electrodes*, pressure was brought to bear on a cartel participant whose US subsidiary produced 28¾-inch electrodes. This product was competing with their 30-inch electrodes but its price was that of 28-inch electrodes. The cartel members asked the undertaking concerned to cease to produce this product, or to raise its price. In the end, the manufacture of the product was abandoned.[166]

(c) Sharing of Markets, Customers or Sources of Supply

Market sharing arrangements are often the corollary of price-fixing and output restrictions. However, they may also exist separately, as a means of influencing the overall price level, particularly where an agreement on price may be difficult to reach or control. In addition to the mere allocation of a given share of the market subject to collusion, such arrangements may involve the allocation of specific territories within those markets, or of customer groups or individual customers. Sources of supply may also be shared between cartel members, as a form of market sharing at the purchase level. Typically, the adherence of each party to its specified share will be monitored in order to detect possible cheats, in which case penalties may be imposed.

8.36

Allocation of market shares   Market-sharing practices can take many different forms, as illustrated, *inter alia*, by *Quinine*,[167] *French-West African shipowners' committees*,[168] or *Flat Glass Benelux*.[169] Compliance with the allocated market shares is often closely monitored, as in *Cartonboard*[170] or *Graphite Electrodes*.[171] Market shares may be defined at a global (world) level, as in *Citric Acid*,[172] at a broad regional level, as in *Sodium Gluconate*,[173] at a

8.37

---

[165] Case 246/86 *Belasco and others v Commission* [1989] ECR 2117, para 28.

[166] [1999] OJ L24/1, para 56.

[167] [1969] OJ L192/5. In the first cartel condemned by the Commission, quotas were fixed on the basis of the total sales of all cartel participants. The sharing out of the sales thus compromised all markets.

[168] [1992] OJ L134/1. The committees had shared among their members the markets constituted by the cargoes carried by liner vessel between France and 11 African States.

[169] [1984] OJ L212/13. The Commission found that the two cartel members and their subsidiaries, and associated companies in the Benelux countries had shared out the market by predetermining the two groups' relative positions within a narrow band (between 60/40 and 62/38). The 60/40 ratio related to the two groups' installed capacity in the Benelux countries. The Commission stated that this 'meant that their respective capacities were operated at similar levels at any given time' and that this was 'an extremely serious restriction of competition which was designed to keep the parties' market shares stable and so largely insulate them from customer pressures'.

[170] [1994] OJ L243/1. The so-called 'price before tonnage' scheme was implemented through a 'freezing' of the market shares of the major producers on the basis of their respective positions in 1987 and through the constant monitoring and analysis in meetings of 'market share development' and fluctuations in the market shares of the major producers (see para 130).

[171] [2002] OJ L100/1. Specific market shares were attributed to each cartel member in 1992 and were meant to remain stable. At their subsequent 'Working Level' meetings, the participants reviewed their sales in the different markets and exchanged information in order to monitor observance of the allocated quotas.

[172] [2002] OJ L239/18. Each producer was assigned a worldwide market share expressed as a percentage of total sales by the trade association members in a given year. Quotas were initially set in terms of total tonnage but it was subsequently decided to express the quotas in terms of market share figures instead. Market share quotas for each company were set out in great detail and the figures included decimals (see para 97).

[173] Overall sales quotas were set at world level, but the world was divided into five 'regional' areas (US, Europe, Canada, Japan, rest of the world) in which each party was allocated a specific market share.

European level, as in *Zinc Phosphate*[174] or even at a national level.[175] The sharing-out of the market and subsequent freezing of market shares may be applied with particular rigour. In *Pre-insulated Pipes*, the principle underlying the quota system was that in future market share could only be 'bought'.[176] In many cases, the strict implementation of the sharing-out of the market implies that undertakings which have sold more than their respective quotas are obliged to compensate other cartel members, for instance by buying up quantities from their competitors, as in *Quinine*,[177] *Citric Acid*,[178] *Vitamins*[179] or *Organic Peroxides*.[180] 'Swap deals', that is *ad hoc* arrangements regarding the exchange of previously allocated quantities for reasons of convenience, are also a common feature in market sharing arrangements. In *Pre-insulated Pipes*,[181] producers whose market shares in specific countries were considered too low were encouraged or required to withdraw from those markets because their marginal commercial presence tended to push down price levels. In return for giving up this business, they received compensation in the form of an increase of their quota allocation in other markets in which they were already present.

8.38 **Allocation of territories or distribution channels** among cartel members is a frequent feature of cartels. The 'home market' rule, that is an arrangement whereby the stronghold of an undertaking in its domestic market is respected by the other competitors who agree not to enter or to refrain from increasing sales in that market, constitutes the most obvious means of territorial allocation. Since it runs directly counter to the establishment of a common market, one of the fundamental objectives of the Treaty, it has always been severely condemned by the Commission. In *Quinine*, the gentleman's agreement had as its object the protection of the German, French and Dutch markets to the benefit of the local producers, and exports to those markets by other members were prohibited.[182] In *European Sugar Industry*,

---

174 [2003] L153/1. Sales quotas were in principle allocated at the European level (para 66).

175 See eg *Carbonless Paper* [2004] OJ L115/1, paras 241–251, and *Industrial Bags*, decision of 3 May 2006, para 318.

176 [1999] OJ L24/1. The ringleader insisted on a 'deadlock' in the market, which meant that market shares were to be frozen. If a producer wanted to increase its overall market share, it could only do so through acquisition of a competitor.

177 [1969] OJ L192/5. The cartel agreement provided for such compensation in case of deviation from the agreed quotas.

178 [2002] OJ L239/18. It had been decided that if a company exceeded its assigned quota in any one year, it would be obliged to purchase product from the company or companies with sales below their quota during the following year (para 88). This led to several important transactions between companies, especially as one company tended to fall short of its quota, whilst another one tended to remain ahead of it (paras 102–111).

179 [2003] OJ L6/1. When a party exceeded its sales quota, it was obliged to 'slow down' its sales in order to allow other cartel participants to catch up. If at the end of the year a producer was substantially above its sales quota, it had to buy the product from others in order to compensate for the deficit they had suffered (see para 196).

180 [2005] OJ L110/44 (full text of the decision available on DG COMP's web site). The initial cartel agreement signed in 1971 read as follows: 'All future sales of initiators in the geographical area will be shared between the parties in accordance with a quota system. [. . .] The quota will be maintained by exchanging every quarter the uncertified sales figures of the past three months. [. . .] If the exchange of figures shows that the sales of a party in any country have exceeded the quota for any category then that party will modify its sales policy in succeeding months with the object of arriving eventually at a tonnage for the whole of the calendar year which does not exceed his percentage quota' (see para 85).

181 [1999] OJ L24/1.

182 [1969] OJ L192/5. Cartel members agreed not to make offers in the 'reserved markets', but measures were taken to conceal market partitioning. Sales in reserved markets could exceptionally be made, subject to quota compensations, in order to avoid suspicion.

a large market partitioning scheme had been set up by the Community sugar producers.[183] Whilst cross-border sales became necessary because of shortages in certain Member States, the cartel members ensured that this would not disrupt prices by devising a 'stay-at-home' policy and setting-up a complex scheme that guaranteed that imported sugar would be sold at the same price as domestic production.[184] The Commission's finding that this scheme was a blatant infringement of Article 81(1) EC was largely endorsed by the ECJ.[185] Similar schemes were condemned in *Vegetable Parchment*,[186] *Peroxygen Products*[187] and *Graphite Electrodes*[188] and *Cement*.[189] Examples of market partitioning in the transport sector include *CEWAL*[190] (maritime shipping lines) and *SAS/Maersk Air* (airline connections).[191] *Seamless Steel Tubes*[192] provides an example of how market-sharing can be organised at an inter-continental level. In that case, the cartel agreement included an arrangement concerning mutual self-restraint between European and Japanese producers.[193] Cartel members may also agree on the mutual allocation of distribution channels. In *Belgian Beer*, the cartel agreement between Interbrew and Danone included a general non-aggression pact and a sharing out of the 'on-trade' distribution channels in Belgium, notably through an agreement

---

[183] [1973] OJ L140/17. As the Common Market replaced national market organisations, the producers endeavoured to restrict competition on their respective domestic markets.

[184] Deliveries were subject to the consent of competitors established in the sales zone and the sales price was aligned to the domestic prices. Cross-border sales were also channelled through local producers, in order to ensure uniformity in price and sales conditions.

[185] The Decision was however partly annulled on other grounds. See Joined cases 40 to 48, 50, 54 to 56, 111, 113 and 114–73 *Suiker Unie and others v Commision*, [1975] ECR 1663.

[186] [1978] OJ L70/54. The producers agreed to share out markets where no producer was established, but there was an agreement to respect each other's domestic markets by refraining from exporting to those markets.

[187] [1985] OJ L35/1. The cartel members conducted their commercial operations in the Community on the basis of an agreement or understanding that each national market was to be reserved for those producers who manufactured inside the territory in question (the 'home market rule'). Each producer limited its sales to end-users in those Member States where it possessed production facilities (see paras 9–10).

[188] [2002] OJ L100/1. Non-domestic producers were supposed to refrain from competing aggressively with home producers. Ultimately, non-domestic producers were meant to withdraw from home markets (see para 50).

[189] [1994] OJ L343/1. The *Cement* case is a good example of how markets may be shared out pursuant to complex and detailed rules: the European producers of cement agreed to ensure non-transhipment to home markets and to regulate cement transfers from one country to another. They had to refrain from selling outside their home market, or to comply with the price and sales conditions applied by local producers. Cartel members could claim priority in respect of certain markets if they had long term contracts. However, in case of failure to supply, they were obliged to share the supplies equitably with their competitors.

[190] [1993] OJ L34/20. The members of three maritime conferences had agreed that the members of one conference would refrain from operating as an independent shipping company ('outsider') in the area of activity of the other two conferences. The Commission found that such trade-sharing agreements amounted to agreements between the members of these conferences not to compete with each other as outsiders in their respective areas of operation. They had the effect of partitioning off each group of shipping routes (paras 33, 37).

[191] [2001] OJ L265/15. The two Nordic airline companies had entered into an overall market sharing agreement by which SAS undertook not to compete with Maersk Air as regards connections to and from Jutland, whilst Maersk Air undertook to refrain from competing with SAS on all international routes to or from Copenhagen. The parties had also colluded to share out 'inland connections' (see para 69).

[192] [2003] OJ L140/1.

[193] The Commission found that that European and Japanese producers of steel tubes used in the oil industry had entered into a market sharing agreement called the 'Europe-Japan Club'. According to the so-called 'fundamentals', ie the basic rules to be observed by the parties to the agreement, the producers had to respect each other's home market. Japanese producers could not deliver their products in Europe and vice versa. Within Europe, producers agreed to respect each other's domestic market and to submit price offers in tenders that would be between 8 and 10% above the price of the local producer (paras 62 to 68).

that the two companies would not 'steal' each other's traditional outlets.[194] In *French Beer*, Danone and Heineken agreed upon a temporary freeze on the acquisition of wholesalers, and the establishment of equilibrium between their respective distribution networks in the French sector for 'on-trade' consumption of beer.[195]

8.39 **Allocation of customers and other customer-specific practices** Market sharing can also take the form of customer specific measures. This may consist of respecting each cartel member's 'traditional' customers. In *Roofing Felt*, several Belgian producers had agreed to supply only their own customers. Under the expression 'stability of clientèle', the members made it a principle that every producer should keep its own customers. One object of the agreement was to avoid a member's customers being approached by other members.[196] The 'established customer' principle was also applied, for example, in *Pre-insulated Pipes*,[197] *Luxembourg brewers*,[198] *Methylglucamine*[199] and *Food Flavour Enhancers*.[200]

8.40 The sharing out of non-'traditional', important customers is also a feature of many cartels. In *Polypropylene*, a system known as 'account management' (or in a later, more refined form, 'account leadership') had been set up to ensure the effective implementation of an agreed price increase by nominating one supplier (secretly) to coordinate their dealings with a particular customer.[201] In *Vitamins*, the producers of Vitamin C had set up a highly sophisticated system for the treatment of 'key' customers for which a detailed sales plan was determined. Each cartel participant was in charge of controlling a specific customer. The cartel participants agreed to share out the supplies to the largest global customers.[202] In *Electrical and*

---

194 [2003] OJ L200/1 see eg paras 60, 73, 239, 243.

195 *Kronenbourg/Heineken* ('*French Beer*'), [2005] OJ L184/57 (full text of the decision available on DG COMP's website).

196 [1986] OJ L232/15, para 51.

197 [1999] OJ L24/1. For most projects, the traditional supplier was designated the 'favourite' and the other producers had either to decline to bid or to give a higher 'protect' quote so as to ensure that the former received the contract. In the case of major projects, where several suppliers could be envisaged, the producers who traditionally supplied the customer were expected to bid and to share the contract between them (see para 68).

198 [2002] L253/21. The brewers had entered into a market-sharing agreement having as its object the protection of each party's clientéle. By a written agreement signed in 1985, the parties agreed not to supply beer to any customer in the hospitality sector who was tied to another party by an exclusive purchasing agreement ('beer tie'). This beer tie guarantee extended to beer ties which were invalid or unenforceable in law, as well as to supply arrangements where a brewer simply invested in a drinks outlet but did not sign an exclusive purchasing contract. The beer tie guarantee was reinforced by a consultation mechanism obliging the parties to check with each other about the presence of a beer tie before supplying new customers, as well as by financial penalties for non-compliance.

199 [2004] OJ L38/18. The cartel agreement was based on the mutual respect of each party's customers. Each party undertook to quote higher prices than its competitor to ensure that the customer would stay with its traditional supplier (see paras 98ff).

200 [2004] OJ L75/1. An agreement existed between the cartel members not to sell to each other's respective 'traditional' European customers. In order to protect this agreement, cartel members also entered into a 'counter-purchasing' agreement whereby Japanese producers agreed to purchase product from their Korean competitors in exchange for which the respective competitors would limit their sales to the European customers.

201 [1986] OJ L230/1. Later on, a more general adoption of the system was proposed, with an account leader named for each major customer who would 'guide, discuss and organize price moves'. Other producers who had regular dealings with the customer were known as 'contenders' and would cooperate with the account leader in quoting prices to the customer in question. To 'protect' the account leader and contenders, any other producers approached by the customer were to quote prices higher than the desired target. These producers were called 'non-contenders' (para 27).

202 [2003] OJ L6/1, paras 402–414.

Mechanical Carbon and Graphite Products, a system of 'account leadership' was meant to overcome the difficulty of ensuring a uniformity of prices with regard to large customers enjoying buying power.[203] Other examples of the sharing out of customers can be found in *Seamless Steel Tubes*,[204] *Sodium Gluconate*[205] or *Industrial Tubes*.[206] Customer allocation may be organised using very sophisticated mechanisms. In *Industrial Tubes*, major customers were identified by number-codes.[207]

Agreement may also be reached on collusive practices specific to a certain category of customer. In *Flat Glass Benelux*,[208] the cartel members had classified their customers in several classes, each class qualifying for different rates in the confidential price-lists. In *Electrical and Mechanical Carbon and Graphite Products*, the cartel participants devised a pricing strategy specific to car equipment manufacturers. Since these customers were multinational companies, the cartel was afraid that they could benefit from the price differences between countries to source their éntire needs from the cheapest country. To counteract this risk, cartel members set up a pricing policy that was specific to these customers and aimed at ensuring the uniformity of the prices quoted throughout Europe.[209] **8.41**

Bid rigging is a specific form of customer allocation between suppliers and constitutes, as **8.42**
such, a blatant violation of Article 81(1) EC. Collusive behaviour in tendering procedures is all the more serious since the Community has endeavoured, through the adoption of successive Directives, to harmonise procedures for the award of public contracts and to ensure transparency so as to promote competition with regard to public tenders. The Commission's position on bid rigging was made clear as early as 1973 in its *European Sugar Industry* decision,

---

[203] [2004] OJ L125/45 (full text of the decision available on DG COMP's web site), paras 128ff. For each of the main customers, the cartel member who was the most important supplier was appointed as the 'leader' of the account and meant to lead the price negotiation and to obtain the highest possible price, whilst competitors had to follow its instructions when quoting prices to the same customer.

[204] [2003] OJ L140/1. British Steel, a cartel participant which had ceased to produce steel tubes, agreed with the other European producers of the cartel that the supply of its needs would be shared out between them and that the Japanese producers would be excluded (see paras 78–82).

[205] A detailed sharing out of major customers was implemented. For instance, each cartel member was allocated a specific subsidiary of a large multinational customer (para 90). The allocation of specific customers was also used to enable cartel participants to adjust their sales to the agreed quotas.

[206] The cartel did not resort to general price increases as purchasers were big companies with which prices were individually negotiated once a year. Instead, cartel participants devised tables containing detailed indications as to volumes per producer and per customer and future prices to be achieved, as well as the sequence in which the producers were expected to submit price quotations to each customer (para 99).

[207] Each customer's identification number was first known only to its respective suppliers and the exchange of information took place on the basis of spreadsheets and handwritten statistics. Cartel participants attending to a certain customer knew each others' prices and volumes. The allocation of key customers and volumes was also monitored though so-called 'customer leadership rules'. One of the cartel members described the mechanism as follows: '[during the cartel meetings] a customer's identification number would be called. The manufacturers supplying that customer would answer the call and withdraw from the meeting in order to discuss how to proceed vis-à-vis the customer in terms of pricing, supply quantities and terms and conditions. If another manufacturer also wanted to supply the customer concerned, he would contact M. It was then up to the current supplier(s) whether to grant the manufacturer a supply share with respect to the said customer. In the event that several members simultaneously submitted an offer at the same price, the suppliers agreed that each manufacturer would tell the (usually major) customer that it was only able to deliver a limited quantity of tubes. The remaining quantities could then be supplied by the other manufacturers' (para 106).

[208] [1984] OJ L212/13.

[209] [2004] OJ L125/45 (full text of the decision available on DG COMP's web site), paras 124–127.

where it stated that '[i]n a system of tendering, competition is of the essence. If the tenders submitted by those taking part are not the result of individual economic calculation, but of knowledge of the tenders by other participants or of concertation with them, competition is prevented, or at least distorted or restricted'.[210] In *Building and construction in the Netherlands*,[211] the Commission condemned the rules and regulations of the umbrella association of the federations of Dutch builders and contractors (SPO) which provided, among other things, for exchanges of information prior to tendering and for collusion on price tenders for building and construction contracts. Moreover, it shared the demand side of the market between members through the prior designation of successful tendering undertakings and the protection of entitled undertakings. The CFI, which rejected the appeal by the undertakings, stated that 'concertation by contractors regarding the manner in which they intend responding to an invitation for tender is incompatible with article 81(1) of the Treaty, even if the invitation sets unreasonable conditions. It is for each contractor to determine independently what it regards as reasonable or unreasonable and to conduct himself accordingly'.[212] In *Pre-insulated pipes*, the members of the cartel had set up a system through which they could allocate individual projects between themselves by manipulating bidding procedures so that they could decide in advance which producer would be awarded the contract.[213] In *Raw Tobacco Italy*, the processors of tobacco coordinated their conduct in respect of the bids placed at public auctions organised for the purchase of tobacco by the Italian monopoly ATI.[214]

8.43 **Sharing sources of supply** Cartel participants may also agree to share out their sources of supply. In *Raw Tobacco Spain*, the four Spanish processors of raw tobacco agreed each year on the quantities of each variety of raw tobacco that each of them would undertake to purchase from the group of producers.[215] In *Raw Tobacco Italy*, the tobacco processors also allocated to themselves suppliers and quantities to be purchased.[216]

(d) Co-ordinated Boycotts, Bans on Imports, Concerted Refusal to Deal

8.44 Cartellists may also agree upon concerted action to prevent the entry of new competitors to the market or upon retaliatory measures against undertakings refusing to comply with their restrictive arrangements.

8.45 **Keeping competitors away from the cartel's market** In several cases, the Commission has condemned coordinated measures designed to keep competitors away from the market. In *Meldoc*, a particularly serious dimension of the cartel was that it was aimed at protecting

---

[210] [1973] OJ L140/17, 28.
[211] [1992] OJ L92/1.
[212] Case T-29/92 *SPO and others v Commission* [1995] ECR II-289, para 119.
[213] [1999] OJ L24/1. The cartel members had agreed that the other producers would submit higher offers in the tendering procedure. In return, unsuccessful bidders would be granted the opportunity to participate in the project as subcontractors. There was also another 'compensation system' which corrected departures from the quota if the selected producer failed to win the bid. Likewise, a monitoring system was set up for the cases where a producer undercut the allocated 'favourite', and would be called to account and pressurised to withdraw its bid or to increase its price to allow the favourite win.
[214] Decision of 20 October 2005 (full text of the decision available on DG COMP's web site), paras 126, 150, 240.
[215] Decision of 20 October 2004 (full text of the decision available on DG COMP's web site), para 67.
[216] Decision of 20 October 2005 (full text of the decision available on DG COMP's web site), paras 240 and 246–249.

the Dutch market by blocking imports of cheaper milk from Belgium and Germany, thereby having a clearly adverse effect on consumer interests and obstructing the achievement of one of the most fundamental objectives of the Treaty, the integration of the economies of the Member States.[217] A focus on import restrictions was also an important aspect of the cartel agreements in *Welded Steel Mesh*. Here, a series of agreements between French producers and producers from Italy, Germany and Belgium who traditionally exported to France included terms setting quotas for imports into France. These restrictions on the volume of foreign deliveries to the French market made it possible to enter into a price agreement; the prices charged on the French market were set at a level far higher than the average in other Community countries, without this producing an increase in imports as would normally be expected.[218] In *Luxembourg Brewers*, the cartel agreement was intended to keep foreign brewers out of Luxembourg.[219] In *French Beef*, the Commission condemned an agreement entered into by farmers' and slaughterers' federations, which had as its object a temporary commitment to suspend all imports of beef.[220]

Placing certain competitors at a competitive disadvantage Agreements may also be **8.46** reached in order to oblige other parties to adopt a given behaviour, or to place downstream operators at a competitive disadvantage. In *Fedetab*,[221] the Commission condemned the agreement between Belgian and Luxembourg producers of manufactured tobacco not to supply several large distribution firms which did not stock a minimum range of brands. In *Electrical and Mechanical Carbon and Graphite Products*, cartel participants sold 'rough' carbon blocks in addition to their finished products and found themselves in competition on the downstream market with 'cutters', who bought the rough carbon blocks from them and transformed them into finished products. In order to limit competition from these cutters, the cartel had agreed to keep the cutters in a position of competitive disadvantage by selling the carbon blocks to them at an artificially high price.[222]

Boycott of reluctant undertakings Action may also be taken to boycott undertakings **8.47** showing reluctance to comply with the collusive arrangements. In *Cement*, cartel members agreed upon a collective response to what was perceived as the problem posed by the Greek producers, whose conduct was destabilising the cement industry. A 'stick and carrot' approach was devised in order to 'persuade' them to cooperate. The short term punitive actions considered, called 'stick actions', were aimed at defending European domestic markets.[223]

---

[217] [1986] OJ L348/50, para 82.

[218] [1989] OJ L260/1, para 159.

[219] [2002] OJ L253/21. In this case, a common defensive mechanism was instituted whereby the parties agreed to consult each other first if a foreign brewer attempted to negotiate a supply contract with one of their tied outlets. Priority would then be allocated to one of the cartel participants, in an attempt to keep the outlet as a customer. If that party succeeded in negotiating a new contract with the outlet, it was obliged to compensate the party which had lost the outlet by transferring an equivalent outlet to him. Other clauses allowed for the exclusion from the cartel of any party which cooperated with a foreign brewer or distributed its beer.

[220] [2003] OJ L209/12, para 38.

[221] [1978] OJ L224/29.

[222] [2004] OJ L125/45 (full text of the decision available on DG COMP's web site), paras 154–156.

[223] [1994] OJ L343/1, para 25(4). The 'stick' actions consisted of resorting, *inter alia*, to: administrative obstacles; quality standards; action by associations; penalising of customers purchasing imported cement; attacks on the export markets of the producers who were destabilising the market by taking the place of those producers in various countries or by making Greek exports unprofitable; boycotts of shipping lines controlled by the producers who were destabilising the market; adoption of 'guerilla' tactics in the Greek market; and seeking the assistance of international banks to 'convince' the recalcitrant producers to cooperate.

In *Pre-insulated Pipes*, the Commission found that the cartel participants had devised and enforced a sophisticated strategy to eliminate a competitor who had refused to participate in their bid-rigging scheme. The award to this undertaking of the largest contract in Germany for ten years sparked off a particularly violent reaction, and a collective boycott of this undertaking was instigated. The cartel decided to cease any supply to this undertaking and its subcontractors.[224]

(e) Exchange of Commercially Sensitive Information

8.48 Under normal competitive conditions, information regarding, for example, capacity, use of capacity, production levels, customers, prices charged and conditions applied to customers, would not be exchanged between competitors. However, the exchange of such commercially sensitive information usually does take place within cartels, as a means to prepare, implement or monitor the restrictive agreement(s) or arrangements. The question is whether such exchanges of information, where they are connected to an identified infringement, are also separately caught by the prohibition of Article 81 EC, and therefore whether such exchanges are also caught when they take place in complete isolation, ie in the absence of any additional restrictive arrangements.

8.49 **A constituent of the 'cartel offence'**   The exchange of commercially sensitive information is often ancillary to other *per se* violations of Article 81 EC, such as price fixing, or market-sharing. It is thus not generally considered separately by the Commission, in that evidence of the exchange of confidential information is used to provide additional proof of the overall cartel arrangements, and the Commission finds a single cartel infringement (implicitly) including the exchange of confidential business information. In such instances, the exchange of information is found to have taken place either by way of preparation and implementation or for the monitoring of the cartel arrangements, and with the same object as was identified for the main (*per se*) infringement. It is worth noting, however, that the Commission has in many cases singled out exchanges of information as a distinct part of the *per se* infringement, thereby considering them not merely as a 'facilitating' device but as a separate constitutive element of the 'cartel offence'.[225]

8.50 **A 'cartel offence' in its own right?**   An important issue, however, is whether the exchange of business sensitive information may constitute an infringement of Article 81 EC on a stand-alone basis. On appeal in *Steel Beams*, the CFI concluded that, contrary to the Commission's contention during the Court proceedings, the 'information exchange systems' referred to in the decision had been considered by the Commission as separate infringements of Article 65(1) ECSC.[226] The CFI subsequently considered that such systems

---

[224] [1999] OJ L24/1, paras 98–107.

[225] This was the case, for instance, in *Cartonboard* [1994] OJ L243/1, paras 61–64, 105–106 and 134; *Seamless Steel Tubes* [2003] OJ L140/1, para 153, third indent; *Belgian Beer* [2003] OJ L200/1, para 265; *Zinc Phosphate* [2003] OJ L153/1, para 215; *Methionine* [2003] OJ L255/1, para 214; *Methylglucamine* [2004] OJ L38/18, para 184; *Food Flavour Enhancers* [2004] OJ L75/1, para 172; *Thread*, (para 282) and *Industrial Bags* (paras 521–523).

[226] Case T-141/94 *Thyssen Stahl v Commission* [1999] ECR II-347, paras 379–392. In *Steel Beams*, the Commission had described at length systems of exchange of confidential information, but claimed on appeal before the CFI that it had considered that the disputed information systems did not constitute a separate infringement of Art 65(1) ECSC but formed part of wider infringements consisting, in particular, of price-fixing and market-sharing agreements. The Commission argued that the exchange of information infringed Art 65(1) ECSC insofar as the exchange made it easier for those other infringements to be committed.

for the exchange of (confidential) information could indeed be regarded having the restriction of competition as their object.[227] This was confirmed on appeal by the ECJ.[228] It seems that the Commission has now fully embraced the idea that information exchanges can be considered *per se* infringements. In *Plasterboard*, the Commission regarded the exchange of confidential information as the essential element of the 'cartel offence'. Its finding of a *per se* infringement of Article 81 EC was based mostly on the existence of several exchanges of confidential business information. The Commission concluded that there had existed 'between 1992 and 1998 at least in the four major European plasterboard markets a complex, continuous agreement having as its object the restriction of competition'.[229] Interestingly, the Commission pointed out that the parties had at certain times knowingly exchanged incorrect information, which confirmed that the exchange of information had had a restrictive object as it was actually used as a monitoring mechanism.[230]

Conclusion   In answering the question of whether the concerted practice of information exchange can be illegal in itself, the first issue is therefore to see whether the exchange of information can be demonstrated to have as its *object* the restriction of competition.[231] If such an object cannot be demonstrated, then other relevant factors may need to be considered.   **8.51**

---

[227]   The CFI stated in particular that 'the information which the undertakings received under the arrangements in question was capable of appreciably influencing their conduct, by reason of the fact that each undertaking knew that it was being kept under close surveillance by its competitors and that it could, if necessary, react to the conduct of its competitors, on the basis of considerably more recent and accurate data than those available by other means' and that 'data, indicating the very recent market shares of participants and not publicly available, are by their very nature confidential data, as confirmed by the fact that interested undertakings could receive the data distributed by the secretariat only on a reciprocal basis' (para 403). The CFI concluded that 'the information exchange systems in question appreciably reduced the decision-making independence of the participating producers by substituting practical cooperation between them for the normal risks of competition' (para 406).

[228]   Case C-194/1999 P *Thyssen Stahl AG v Commission* [2003] ECR I-10821, paras 59–90.

[229]   [2005] OJ L166/8 (full text of the decision available on DG COMP's web site), para 434. The Commission stated in particular at paras 449 and 450 that 'an information exchange constitutes *per se* an infringement of Article 81(1) EC if the requirement of independence according to which each trader must determine independently his conduct on the market is undermined as a result. This requirement of independence will without a doubt be affected if the exchange takes place in a highly concentrated market and if it reduces the risk of uncertainty for the trader. These two conditions are manifestly met in the present case inasmuch as the market is an oligopolistic one and the uncertainty has disappeared since the parties agreed [. . .] to put an end to the aggression reigning on the market, this wish being manifested, moreover, on a number of occasions on the relevant markets. The Commission considers therefore that the system constitutes an infringement of Article 81(1) EC'.

[230]   The Commission stated at para 452 that '[t]his body of evidence permits the Commission to assert that the [. . .] agreement concerning the exchange of information [. . .] was intended to enable participants therein to monitor the conduct of their competitors at least on the relevant markets and constitutes a manifestation of the common wish of the parties to restrict competition on the plasterboard market in the four major European markets. In so doing, the Commission characterises the agreement as restrictive of competition within the meaning of Article 81(1) EC, being a particular manifestation of the complex, continuous agreement having as its object the restriction of competition on the plasterboard market at least in the four major European markets'.

[231]   In *Steel Beams* [1994] OJ L116/1, the Commission had described at length, in its decision, systems of exchange of confidential information, but claimed on appeal before the CFI that it had considered that the disputed information systems did not constitute a separate infringement of Art 65(1) ECSC but formed part of wider infringements consisting, in particular, in price-fixing and market-sharing agreements. The Commission argued that the exchange of information thus infringed Art 65(1) ECSC insofar as the exchange made it easier for those other infringements to be committed. See C-194/1999 P *Thyssen Stahl AG v Commission* [2003] ECR I-10821 para 384.

These are, *inter alia*: the nature of the information exchanged, the level of aggregation and the age of the data, and the concentration of the industry. The Commission has accepted that, depending on an examination of the individual case, exchange of information schemes can be held to be lawful.[232] It may indeed be legitimate for companies to pool information about the market in which they operate, as a certain degree of transparency may lead to a more efficient functioning of the market. The CFI confirmed the validity of this approach in *John Deere v Commission*.[233] That said, and as mentioned above, exchanges of information that create an artificial level of transparency and thus a reduction in the uncertainty about competitors' behaviour in the market are generally considered anti-competitive. For a detailed analysis of the compatibility of exchange of information schemes with EC competition law, see Chapter 7 of this book, at paras 7.355 and following.

(f) The Problem of 'Tacit Collusion'

8.52 Can economic evidence of the parallel conduct of certain undertakings in the market, in the absence of any proof of collusion, enable the Commission to determine the existence of a 'cartel' prohibited under Article 81?[234]

8.53 **The theory of tacit collusion** According to economic theory, it is possible for firms in an oligopolistic market to tend towards a monopoly-type price equilibrium in the absence of any kind of explicit collusion. Owing to the interdependence that characterises firms in an oligopolistic context, where each market operator takes into account the anticipated reaction of its competitors for the purpose of determining its own market strategy, firms may de facto find that they are coordinating their market behaviour without engaging in any form of consultation. What is thus described by economic literature as 'tacit collusion' consists of each undertaking aligning its commercial behaviour with the conduct of the price leader (or of the first mover) by imposing prices increases as soon as the latter does so.

8.54 **Does tacit collusion amount to cartel behaviour?** The question of whether tacit collusion amounts to cartel behaviour, ie whether it constitutes a *per se* infringement of Article 81 EC, raises complex issues that still remain somewhat unresolved today. The notion of 'concerted

---

[232] *Steel Beams* [1994] OJ L116/1. The Commission has however chosen not to address these within the context of the Guidelines on horizontal cooperation agreements (see Commission Guidelines on the applicability of Art 81 of the EC Treaty to horizontal cooperation agreements, [2001] OJ C3/2, para 10). Interestingly, the Commission stated that the Guidelines are 'only concerned with those types of cooperation which potentially generate efficiency gains', implying that this is not the case for exchange of information schemes.

[233] Case T-35/92 *John Deere v Commission* [1994] ECR II-957. The CFI found at para 51 that 'on a truly competitive market transparency between traders is in principle likely to lead to the intensification of competition between suppliers, since in such a situation, the fact that a trader takes into account information made available to him in order to adjust his conduct on the market is not likely, having regard to the atomized nature of the supply, to reduce or remove for the other traders any uncertainty about the foreseeable nature of its competitors' conduct'.

[234] This question is of a different nature from the question whether, in the absence of material evidence of an agreement that is restrictive in object or of a concerted practice, evidence of an anticompetitive intention can be deduced from economic evidence of parallel conduct in the market. The latter question relates to the burden of proof that the Commission must discharge to establish the existence of a common will to restrict competition. As to the former question, it raises the issue whether, in certain market conditions, it is possible for the Commission to conclude that undertakings have engaged in illegal behaviour in respect of their ability to jointly restrict competition, by tacitly colluding, ie by aligning their behaviour with their competitors by anticipating and/or following their behaviour.

practice' as defined by case law does indeed seem very close to the notion of 'tacit collusion', in that the fulfilment of the corresponding test ('conscious substitution of practical cooperation between undertakings for the risks of competition') does not seem to require much evidence of explicit coordination. However, it seems that a finding of concerted practices nevertheless requires an effective breach of the obligation for a firm to determine its market behaviour independently that must go beyond mere tacit collusion.

Indeed, the Court in *Suiker Unie*, having reiterated that each economic operator must **8.55** independently determine the policy which it intends to adopt in the market, stated that 'this requirement of independence does not deprive economic operators of the right to adapt themselves intelligently to the existing and anticipated conduct of their competitors'. The Court went on to confirm that 'it does however strictly preclude any direct or indirect contact between such operators, the object or effect whereof is either to influence the conduct on the market of an actual or potential competitor or to disclose to such a competitor the course of conduct which they themselves have decided to adopt or contemplate adopting in the market'.[235] The reference to the term 'contact' (whether indirect or not) seems to rule out the possibility that the notion of concerted practice includes 'tacit collusion'.

In its *Wood Pulp II* judgment, the ECJ gave additional useful indications as to the value of **8.56** economic evidence for the purpose of establishing cartel behaviour. In *Wood Pulp*,[236] the Commission had found that several producers had engaged in unlawful behaviour which, the Commission submitted, was essentially established by the fact that the firms' quarterly price announcements were near-simultaneous and identical. On appeal, the Court annulled the Commission decision on the grounds that the latter had not established an infringement of Article 81 EC to the required legal standard.[237] The Court stated on this occasion that parallel conduct could not be regarded as furnishing proof of concertation unless that collusion constituted the only plausible explanation for such conduct, recalling the right of economic operators to adapt themselves intelligently to the existing and anticipated conduct of their competitors.[238]

Conclusion   In the light of the case law discussed above, it seems that tacit collusion can- **8.57** not, as such, be regarded as cartel behaviour. The Community judicature seems ready to accept, albeit under extremely strict conditions (which, it is submitted, are extremely difficult for the Commission to satisfy), that economic evidence may be resorted to in order to establish that prior concertation took place between competitors, in cases where that cannot

---

[235] Joined Cases 40–48, 50, 54–56, 111 and 113–114/73 *Suiker Unie and Others v Commission* [1975] ECR 1663, paras 173–174.

[236] [1985] OJ L85/1.

[237] Since the Commission had no documents which directly established the existence of collusion between the producers concerned, the Court stated that it was 'necessary to ascertain whether the system of quarterly price announcements, the simultaneity or near-simultaneity of the price announcements and the parallelism of price announcements [. . .] constitute[d] a firm, precise and consistent body of evidence of prior concertation' (Joined cases C-89/85, C-104/85, C-114/85, C-116/85, C-117/85 and C-125/85 to C-129/85 *A. Ahlström Osakeyhtiö and others v Commission* [1993] ECR I-1307, para 70).

[238] To discharge the burden of proof of cartel conduct, the Commission was required to establish, 'taking account of the nature of the products, the size and the number of the undertakings and the volume of the market in question' that the alleged parallel conduct of the undertakings could 'not be explained otherwise than by concertation'. The Court found that the Commission had failed to do this (paras 71 and 72).

be established through material evidence of actual contacts. But one should remain careful not to interpret the case law as implying that 'tacit collusion' can be legally qualified as a cartel behaviour. The *Wood Pulp II* judgment addresses the question of the standard of proof applicable to the demonstration of classical cartel behaviour, rather than the possibility of tacit collusion *per se* being caught under Article 81 EC. If the Commission is not able to establish to the required standard that contacts between competitors have taken place, it seems that parallel conduct in the market will not be deemed unlawful, as uncertainty about the future conduct of each undertaking in the market is preserved. This is so, even if economic theory might suggest that the conditions for tacit coordination do exist.

(2) Common Features of Collusion

8.58 Analysis of Commission decisions regarding cartels reveals that collusive schemes have many common operational features. Classic patterns of cartels concern their establishment, organisational aspects and the manner in which collusion is conducted on a day-to-day basis.

(a) Factors Conducive to the Establishment of Cartels

8.59 Cartels will often develop in markets which have a number of characteristics that are favourable to collusion. A specific event affecting the market will generally convince cartel instigators that concerted reaction is needed. In turn they will often convince others to engage in collusion, thereby acting as a catalyst.

8.60 **Oligopolistic markets**   Collusion is made easier in oligopolistic markets. In *Italian Flat Glass II*, the Commission noted that the flat-glass market was dominated by a tight oligopoly.[239] Similar features can be found in *Alloy Surcharge*,[240] *Belgian Beer*[241] and *Zinc Phosphate*, where the five cartel members controlled, in spite of their small size, 90 per cent of the EEA market.[242] In *French Beer*, a non-aggression pact was made between the two main market players who agreed that neither of them should become dominant.[243] Cartels have sometimes been formed after a process of intense concentration has taken place, as in *Carbonless Paper*[244] or *Plasterboard*.[245] They may nevertheless involve a relatively high number of players. This is workable in homogeneous product markets, in particular when strongly established trade associations are able to ensure adequate coordination, as in *Cartonboard*[246] or *Cement*.[247]

8.61 **Collusive business values and established communication channels**   Sector-specific values may result in operators looking upon the control of competition between them in a

---

[239] [1989] OJ L33/44, para 12.
[240] [1998] OJ L100/55. The stainless steel market was described as a highly concentrated market.
[241] [2003] OJ L140/1. The cartel was set up by the two main actors in the market, who together controlled over 70% of the entire market.
[242] [2003] OJ L153/1.
[243] [2005] OJ L184/57 (full text of the decision available on DG COMP's web site).
[244] [2004] OJ L115/1. The Commission observed that the production of carbonless papers in Europe had become increasingly dominated by a relatively small number of major producers as smaller suppliers had withdrawn from the market. At the time of the infringement, the cartel members controlled between 85 and 90% of the EEA market for carbonless paper, with the four biggest players controlling around 60% of the market (paras 14–16).
[245] [2005] OJ L166/8 (full text of the decision available on DG COMP's web site), paras 48–51.
[246] [1994] OJ L243/1.
[247] [1994] OJ L343/1.

positive way. Such values may be diffuse, but have been clearly exposed in certain cartel cases, such as *Agreements between manufacturers of glass containers*[248] or *Building and Construction Industry in the Netherlands*.[249] The *Austrian Banks* cartel is probably one of the best illustrations of the influence of specific business values on cartel conduct. In a sector long characterised by a very high level of public ownership and considerable oversupply, market players saw cartel agreements (the 'Lombard club') as a welcome means to combat 'destructive, cut-throat competition', or free competition, as it might simply be termed.[250] Established communication channels between competitors may also be conducive to cartel behaviour. This may result from the existence of long established and carefully structured trade associations (*Cartonboard*,[251] *Cement*),[252] from a (legitimate) regulatory framework providing opportunities for discussions between competitors (*Belgian Beer*),[253] or simply from privileged personal contacts between individuals (*Fine Art Auction Houses*).[254]

Exogenous triggering events   Cartels may simply arise from a desire to extract supra competitive profits but they are often triggered by an exogenous event resulting in concerted response from the industry. The *Quinine* cartel was formed when the suppliers of this substance (used for producing medicines against Malaria) were faced with a situation of considerable oversupply following the end of the Second World War.[255] In *European Sugar Industry*,[256] the cartel was set up as a concerted attempt to neutralise the effects of the creation of a European common market for sugar. In *BNIC*, the cartel of cognac producers was triggered by the severe imbalance of supply and demand resulting from the breaking out of the oil crisis in 1973, as 80 per cent of the sales of this luxury good were

8.62

---

[248] [1974] OJ L160/1. The 'International Fair Trade Practice Rules Administration' (IFTRA) had established a considerable number of rules to be applied by European manufacturers of glass containers which qualified and prohibited as 'unfair practices' conduct that was really just competitive behaviour.

[249] [1992] OJ L92/1. The trade association, SPO, which gathered 28 associations of undertakings representing over 4,000 members of the building sector in the Netherlands, had adopted a 'Code of Honour' and its object was 'to promote and administer orderly competition, to prevent improper conduct in price tendering and to promote the formation of economically-justified prices' (paras 3, 12, 47–48).

[250] [2004] OJ L56/1. Episodes of more or less unrestricted competition used to be described by the banks as 'hyperactivity' and bank charges were seen in this context, not so much as a factor of competition, but more as 'a joint earnings opportunity', to the detriment of customers. Despite repeated warnings, before the accession of Austria to the EC, that the system would be deemed illegal, banks did not terminate their agreements and the Lombard Club remained in existence, as the banks considered that cartels 'had always been part' of banking and they therefore did not in the least intend to change this now simply because of the applicability of European antitrust law (paras 6, 37).

[251] [1994] OJ L243/1.

[252] [1994] OJ L343/1.

[253] [2003] OJ L140/1.

[254] [2005] OJ L200/92 (full text of the decision available on DG COMP's web site). Such factors explain why recidivism is not rare. Several undertakings have been condemned repeatedly on the basis of the same type of facts. This may also explain the phenomenon of 'contamination' from one product market to a neighbouring one. Thus, links can be established between the *Graphite Electrodes*, *Specialty Graphite* and *Electrical and Mechanical Carbon and Graphite Products* cartels, between the *Amino Acid* and *Food Flavour Enhancers* cartels, and between the *Citric Acid* [2002] OJ L239/18 and *Sodium Gluconate* cartels.

[255] [1969] OJ L192/5. New plantations of cinchoma had been established in Africa and Asia, resulting in a strong rise in the supply of bark and the situation became even more critical when the US government decided to dispose, at auction, of very large stocks accumulated over the previous years. The producers reacted by agreeing on the price of bark, allocating between themselves purchases of the US stocks, protecting their respective domestic markets and sharing out others.

[256] [1973] OJ L140/17.

destined for export.[257] In *Steel Beams*, the cartel resulted partly from a desire to follow up on the anti-crisis measures initiated and operated by the Commission in the 1980s, which came to an end in 1988.[258] In *Ferry Operators—Currency surcharges*,[259] Channel ferry companies colluded in response to the devaluation of the pound in September 1992. Similar examples can be found in *Alloy Surcharge*,[260] *French Beef* [261] and *Raw Tobacco Spain*.[262]

8.63   **The determining role of instigators**   Particular instigators often play a determining role in the formation of cartels. In *Zinc Producer Group*, the Commission noted that 'the initiative [. . .] came from the Canadian and Anglo-Australian zinc companies, whilst the Continental European companies joined only after some hesitation'.[263] In *PVC II*, the cartel originated in a collusive plan formulated at ICI's, and the discussions and consultations which followed.[264] In *Pre-insulated Pipes*, the Commission found that ABB, viewing the price-cutting policies of its competitors as 'irresponsible' in view of the weak state of the market, initiated a series of meetings with competitors in order to find a 'solution'.[265] *Amino Acids* [266] is also illustrative of typical instigator behaviour. In 1989, ADM decided to start producing lysine when it became aware that two other undertakings were about to set up production facilities in North America. ADM's production facilities for lysine doubled the world's capacity and it was known that the company had strong financial means and access to cheap raw materials. ADM sent signals to the incumbent producers that, though it intended to be a big player in the lysine market, it would prefer coordination to price war. In order to convince the incumbent producers of the seriousness of its intentions and the penalties of not agreeing, ADM granted its competitors the opportunity to inspect its production plant, and commenced significant sales at low prices. This caused the incumbent producers to drastically lower their prices in an attempt to keep market shares. They finally agreed to cooperate with ADM.

---

[257] [1982] OJ L379/1. The same phenomenon can be observed in *Fine Arts Auction Houses*, where the cartel was formed at a time when the international art market was undergoing a period of recession, in the context of the economic downturn of the early 1990s (see para 78).

[258] [1994] OJ L116/1, para 308.

[259] [1997] OJ L26/23.

[260] [1998] OJ L100/55. The cartel was triggered by a surge in the price of nickel, an important component of stainless steel, at a time when the price for alloys and stainless had fallen sharply (see para 20).

[261] [2003] OJ L209/12. The defensive cartel was triggered by a sharp fall in the slaughterhouse entry prices that farmers were receiving for cattle, reaching levels that were even lower than during the second outbreak of the 'mad cow' crisis, despite the Community adjustment measures (see para 184).

[262] Decision of 20 October 2002 (full text of the decision available on DG COMP's web site). The agreement between the tobacco processors on maximum prices for the purchase of tobacco leaves resulted from the opening of this activity to competition. Until 1990, one public company had held a legal monopoly over the processing of raw tobacco in Spain and had negotiated the purchase price. In the mid-90s, three new players entered the market, triggering a rise in the average buying price and placing Spanish tobacco at a competitive disadvantage on export markets. The processors began discussions on the setting of a maximum purchase price 'to avoid price escalation' (see para 84).

[263] [1984] OJ L220/27, para 15.

[264] [1994] OJ L239/14. Two planning documents amounting to a blueprint for the cartel were found at ICI, the first proposing a new framework of meetings to administer a revised quota system and price fixing scheme, and the second recording the generally favourable reaction of other producers to the ICI proposals.

[265] [1999] OJ L24/1, para 30.

[266] [2001] OJ L152/24.

(b) Organisational Aspects of Cartels

As complex, often multinational, multilateral and secretive schemes, cartels are difficult to **8.64** operate and considerable effort is frequently devoted to ensuring their success. Their intrinsic instability adds to the difficulty of maintaining their functionality. Cartel participants often have to make significant efforts to design the 'modus operandi' of their collusion. Cartels generally involve frequent meetings and delegation of specific coordinating roles to their members. In some cases these tasks are carried out by trade associations or fiduciary companies, which may in in certain circumstances be set up exclusively for the purpose. Great efforts are also made to ensure the concealment of the collusive practices, as the participants are aware of the illegality of their behaviour.

(i) Regular Meetings

A key feature of most cartels is the need for regular contact and meetings to administer the col- **8.65** lusive behaviour. Whilst the development of electronic communication tools might be expected to render physical gatherings less necessary, it nevertheless appears that the complexity of the objectives pursued, the multilateral dimension of collusion and the need for confidence building all mean that physical meetings are still indispensable. Such gatherings are often convened in international hotels, where anonymity can be respected, or in other convenient places such as airports, where company representatives gather for this sole purpose before taking their plane home. Cartel meetings are often scheduled, for opportunistic reasons, before or after official gatherings of industry representatives, such as meetings of trade associations or international fairs. Of course, such meetings can later provide an apparently innocent explanation for having been present at a particular location at the same time as competitors.

From informal contacts to highly institutionalised schemes Certain cartels may only **8.66** need sporadic, informal meetings between top executives or sales managers (*Belgian Beer*,[267] *Zinc Phosphate*).[268] However, in view of the technical complexity of implementing restrictive schemes, cartels may require the organisation of a large number of meetings at different levels, from the highest executive circles down to the level of sales managers in local areas. International cartels are often organised along sophisticated lines. The Commission's cartel decisions are full of vivid descriptions of sophisticated cartel structures.[269] Although it

---

[267] [2003] OJ L140/1.
[268] [2003] OJ L153/1.
[269] In *Cartonboard* [1994] L243/1, the cartel was headed by a 'President Working Group' (PWG) of managing or commercial directors, which met five or six times a year. The PWG reported to a 'President conference' consisting of all producers. Below the PWG, a 'Joint Marketing Committee' (JMC) at marketing manager level also included nearly all producers. The JMC prepared and briefed the PWG and executed its directives. It met once a month. Besides the JMC, an Economic Committee also included most producers and reported to the 'President Conference' and the 'JMC' on the state of the market in various countries. In *Pre-insulated Pipes* [1999] OJ L24/1, the supervisory body was known as the 'directors' club', or the 'Elephant group' and consisted of the chairman and managing directors. As for the 'marketing' or 'contact' groups, they consisted of sales managers and administered the cartel arrangement under the supervision of the directors' club. They were set up in each country and their task was to assign individual projects and coordinate the collusive bidding procedure. In *Specialty graphite*, decision of 17 December 2002 (full text of the decision available on DG COMP's web site), there were four different levels of meeting: 'Top level meetings', attended by the top executives of the companies; 'International Working Level meetings' (or 'International' meetings), consisting of experts in the senior management; 'Regional (European) meetings and Local (national) meetings which were meant to implement the principles agreed at the International meetings and were attended by local managers.

operated within a single Member State, the *Austrian Banks* cartel provides one of the most striking examples of the degree of institutionalisation reached by certain cartels. The Commission stated that 'the agreements were comprehensive as regards their contents, highly institutionalised and closely interconnected, and covered the entire country, "down to the smallest village" [...]. For every banking product there was a separate committee on which the competent employee at the second or third level of management sat'.[270]

8.67   **Multiple working levels**   Cartels are generally characterised by a ladder of several working levels. *Top level* meetings are usually convened once or twice a year. They act as the cartel 'board' and provide the highest, 'political level' input.[271] *High level technical meetings* normally include top ranking sales executives. They are aimed at administering the cartel arrangements, under the supervision of the top level (*Pre-insulated Pipes*),[272] by translating the broad objectives defined in operational goals and agreeing on the techniques to attain them.[273] *Regional or local meetings* constitute the lowest end of the cartel and ensure their smooth day-to-day running.[274]

8.68   'Pre-meetings' and 'ad hoc meetings' are also a frequent feature of cartels. They are generally used to agree in advance upon common positions between undertakings sharing the same kind of interests, or as follow-up to 'plenary' meetings. In *Polypropylene*, the so-called

---

270 [2004] OJ L56/1. The cartel structure included the Lombard Club, specialist committees, special committees and regional committees. The top-level body (Lombard Club) met every month and was composed of senior representatives of the largest Austrian banks. In addition to matters of general interest that were clearly neutral from a competition point of view, [they] discussed changes in interest rates, advertising measures, etc. One level down consisted of product-based specialist committees. The most important of these were the 'Lending Rates Committees' and the 'Deposit Rates Committees', which, as their names suggest, dealt with lending and deposit interest rates and were convened either separately or jointly. There was a constant flow of information between these committees, in particular with the Lombard Club at the top. Both the Lombard Club and the Vienna Lending and Deposit Rates Committees sent out signals to the diverse and numerous 'regional committees', which held regular meetings in every province of Austria. In some provinces even the hierarchical structure of 'Lombard' and specialist committees was replicated. The views expressed in the provinces flowed in the opposite direction back to meetings of the 'Federal Lending and/or Deposit Rates Committees', in which bank representatives from Vienna met with their opposite numbers from the provinces and whose decisions were in principle valid for the whole of Austria.

271 They ensure adherence to the collusive scheme (*Vitamins*) and take major strategic decisions as regards the cartel (*Cartonboard*). Top meetings are also aimed at ensuring the stability of the cartel by resolving internal conflicts (*Electrical and Mechanical Carbon and Graphite Products*). They define the main principles of collaboration for subsequent implementation at lower managerial level (*Specialty Graphite*) and agree on quotas at a global level. They may sometimes go as far as allocating individual market shares in the national markets or agreeing overall price increases (*Pre-insulated Pipes*). Conversely, 'Summit' meetings may also serve to take notice of agreed price levels and other decisions taken in technical meetings (*Electrical and Mechanical Carbon and graphite products*).

272 [1999] OJ L24/1.

273 In *Specialty Graphite*, 'International Working Level meetings' consisted of experts in the senior management, who discussed at this level the classification of the products in different categories or groups and established European minimum prices for each group. In *Vitamins*, 'Marketing directors' meetings took place at three different levels, from the worldwide level to the regional level. Their role was to take operational decisions regarding implementation of the agreement, to monitor sales, to ensure respect of the quotas and to implement price increases.

274 In *Specialty Graphite* 'Local meetings' were meant to implement the principles agreed at international technical meetings and were attended by local managers. In *Electrical and Mechanical Carbon and Graphite Products* [2004] OJ L125/45 (full text of the decision available on DG COMP's web site), local meetings were organised on an 'ad hoc' basis in each country and dealt with the implementation of the cartel decisions in each country and discussed local customers' accounts (see paras 74–77).

'big four' met in restricted session the day before each 'bosses' meeting'. These so-called 'pre-meetings' provided a forum in which the four major producers could agree a position between themselves prior to the full meeting. The idea was that the four major producers, with some 50 per cent of the market in their hands, could, by adopting a united approach, encourage moves towards price stability.[275] Similar practices have been identified in *Seamless Steel Tubes*,[276] *Graphite Electrodes*[277] and *Citric Acid*.[278] Commission decisions also highlight numerous examples of bilateral meetings aimed at sorting out specific problems regarding, for instance, compliance with agreed quotas or the mutual allocation of specific customers. Bilateral meetings are also often used to prepare for negotiations in multilateral meetings and to secure the support of 'allied' undertakings.[279]

(ii) The Role of Trade Associations and Fiduciary Companies

Many Commission decisions show that trade associations or fiduciary companies play a **8.69** central role in the establishment and, in certain cases, the management of cartels. In nearly all cases, the activities of a trade association or of a fiduciary organisation processing market data on behalf of competitors in a given market are part of the general context in which the collusive trade associations or fiduciary companies operate.

Liability of trade associations   Cartel decisions adopted in the early years of enforcement **8.70** reveal that, at that time, trade associations were often directly involved in anticompetitive activities, if not created exclusively for anticompetitive purposes. However, the Commission did not always work on the basis that the associations themselves should be held personally responsible for the infringements found, as illustrated in *Vegetable Parchment*,[280] *Cast Iron and Steel Rolls*[281] or *Zinc Producer Group*.[282] It soon became the

---

[275] [1986] OJ L230/1, para 68.
[276] [2003] OJ L140/1. European producers used to coordinate their positions during preparatory meetings, before taking part in the general meetings (see para 59).
[277] [2002] OJ L100/1. 'European meetings' were convened in the absence of the Japanese cartel members.
[278] [2002] OJ L239/18. Representatives from the two US undertakings met on at least on 10 separate occasions to prepare positions prior to multilateral meetings (para 86).
[279] In *Food Flavour Enhancers* [2004] OJ L95/1, the Commission noted that 'bilateral' meetings were also used to influence the outcome of the 'general' competitors meetings. For example, two undertakings met the day before the multilateral meeting because one of them wanted to secure the support of the other in relation to a price increase to be applied to a customer (para 135).
[280] [1978] OJ L70/54. Nearly all cartel participants were members of a trade association named the 'Genuine Vegetable Parchment Association' (GVPA), which played a central role in the cartel. The GVPA secretariat collected all invoices for export sales issued by its members and established statistical tables setting out the tonnages exported by each producer. It also received the price schedules established by manufacturers during the general assembly, such as the rates of increase and the dates on which the new prices were to become applicable and sent them to the other members. However, the Commission addressed the prohibition decision only to the GVPA members (paras 36–40).
[281] [1983] OJ L317/1. The creation of the 'International Rolls Manufacturers Association' (IRMA) was purely instrumental in the implementation of the cartel agreements. Cartel members agreed to set up a more elaborate organisation for the purpose of coordinating the notification of individual enquiries and the fixing of quotation prices. IRMA was at the core of the cartel and all strategic decisions were taken within the framework of the association's meetings. However, the Commission did not include IRMA among the addressees of the prohibition decisions, only its members.
[282] [1984] OJ L220/27. The establishment of the cartel could not be dissociated from the creation of the 'Zinc Producer Group' (ZPG), an institutionalised organisation which ran the cartel in practice for 13 years. It is worth noting that the Commission did not address the prohibition decision to ZPG, but only to undertakings which were members of the ZPG and active in the Community. The Commission stated that '[t]he

Commission's practice, however, to hold trade associations directly responsible for cartel infringements alongside its members. In *Belgian Wallpaper*, the trade association, whose 'internal regulation' was held to be a factor in the infringement, was an addressee of the decision although no fine was imposed on it.[283] The same approach was followed in *Fedetab*[284] and in *Italian Flat Glass I*.[285] In *Steel Beams*, trade association Eurofer had facilitated the implementation of infringements of Article 65 ECSC by its members by organising an exchange of some of the necessary information. The Commission stated that although Article 65(5) provided only for fines against undertakings, an infringement committed by an association would expose the undertakings which belonged to it to the risk of a fine.[286] With *BNIC*,[287] the Commission started to impose fines on trade associations themselves. Trade association BNIC,[288] which played a central role in the cartel, was deemed to be an association of undertakings and was held directly responsible for the infringement. It was the addressee of the prohibition decision and the fine was imposed on it (and not directly on its members). In *Roofing Felt*, the Commission found that trade association 'Belasco' was not involved in all aspects of the cartel's operation, but in one of its most serious aspects, namely the system of quotas. The Commission found that although Belasco's members were also members of the cartel, the association itself had to be held responsible, independently of its members, for its involvement in operating the cartel.[289] A fine was imposed on Belasco and the Commission decision was upheld on appeal.[290] As a further example, the *Cement* case provides a particularly clear illustration of how directly trade associations can be involved in cartels.[291]

ZPG must be seen as a worldwide cartel whose centre of gravity was always outside the European Community. As well as the firms with which this Decision is concerned, a large number of other firms were involved in it which did not, and do not, have any registered office or subsidiary in the Community and did not operate to any significant extent or only sporadically in the Community. For the ZPG, which controlled about 80% of the world zinc market, the European Community was only one of several regional markets [. . .]. The initiative to form the ZPG and the driving force which carried it along came from non-Community firms. A report [. . .] written [. . .] on the foundation of the ZPG [. . .] speaks of a "diktat" by the British, Australian and Canadian companies. However, the situation of the zinc market was such that, even in the absence of the restrictive agreements, these third-country companies would not have made any significant contribution to improving competitive conditions in the Community, so that their participation in the ZPG had only indirect effects on the Community'. It was therefore appropriate to consider Art 81 EC as applying only to the undertakings which were indirectly involved in the manipulation of competition within the Community.

[283] [1974] OJ L237/3.

[284] [1978] OJ L224/29.

[285] [1981] OJ L326/32. The Commission found that three associations of Italian glass producers had been directly involved in the cartel as their internal regulations, which were binding on their members, were at the heart of the restrictive arrangements. These associations were addressees of the Commission's prohibition decisions, together with their members, but no fine was imposed in recognition of the short duration of the infringement.

[286] [1994] OJ L116/1 para 317. No additional fines were imposed however, since individual undertakings were already being fined.

[287] [1982] OJ L379/1.

[288] 'Bureau National Interprofessionnel du Cognac'.

[289] [1986] OJ L232/15, paras 114, 115.

[290] Case 246/86 *Belasco and others v Commission* [1989] ECR 2117.

[291] [1994] OJ L343/1. In addition to fining individual undertakings, the prohibition decisions imposed heavy fines on the European Cement Association (Cembureau) and eight national cement associations. Although officially entrusted with fully legitimate goals, Cembureau was at the core of the cartel agreements. Through the collection and dispatch of information and the organisation of regular meetings between 'head

Over time, cartels have drawn lessons from the Commission's practice and trade associa- **8.71** tions are today less overtly involved in anti-competitive activities. However, recent decisions show that cartels continue to originate in the contacts developed within the context of trade associations and that trade associations continue to be used as legitimate covers for illegal activities, as shown in *Amino acids*,[292] *Citric Acid*[293] or *Carbonless paper*.[294] In *Industrial Tubes*, the Commission noted that towards the late 1980s, the producers, organised within the trade association Cuproclima, extended the scope of their cooperation to competition issues. Cuproclima meetings were held twice a year, and provided a regular opportunity to discuss and fix prices and other commercial conditions for industrial tubes once the official agenda of the meetings had been concluded.[295]

The role played by certain fiduciary companies in facilitating collusion The collection and **8.72** processing of (individual) market data to obtain a reliable picture of the size and evolution of the market is an entirely legitimate activity provided that it does not lead to the disclosure of individualised figures to competitors (see Chapter 7 of this book, paras 7.355 and following). However, undertakings may be tempted to go beyond what is allowed, exchanging individual figures in order to set up and monitor collusion. In certain cases, cartel members organise the collection and exchange of data themselves.[296] However, the Commission's decisions over the years show that in other cases the cartel delegates this activity to a fiduciary company or a notary's office. In such cases, the fiduciary often carries out an entirely legitimate activity, whereas the cartel participants exchange individual figures between themselves.[297]

---

delegates' (the representatives of the member undertakings), Cembureau organised the collusion on prices and established what was known as the 'Cembureau agreement or principle of non transhipping to internal European markets', in the implementation of which it actively participated. In addition to the heavy fines imposed on its members, Cembureau itself incurred a fine of EUR 100,000. This fine was however subsequently annulled by the CFI.

[292] [2001] OJ L152/24. In order to avoid arousing suspicion over the meetings they attended, the cartel members created an 'amino acid working group' of the wholly legitimate European Feed Additives Association, whose sole purpose was to provide a 'perfect cover' for their price-fixing meetings. See JM Griffin, 'An inside look at a cartel at work: Common characteristics of international cartels', in Konkurrensverket/ Swedish Competition Authority (ed), *Fighting Cartels—why and how?* (2001) p 43.

[293] [2002] OJ L239/18. Cartel members used the cover of the legitimate meetings of the Brussels-based trade association ECAMA to hold their meetings, which would typically take place the evening prior to the official ECAMA meeting (see para 87).

[294] [2004] OJ L115/1. General cartel meetings were convened under cover of the official meeting of the trade association AEMCP. Cartel discussions first took place during the trade association meetings, but it was subsequently decided that official and collusive activities should be separate. Cartel meetings were then held before or after official meetings (see paras 83–86).

[295] The Commission noted that '[d]iscussions concerning price, customers, individual sales volumes and market shares mostly took place on the second day of the Cuproclima meeting session after the official agenda had been discussed' (paras 78 and 82).

[296] See eg *Methylglucamine* [2004] OJ L38/18, paras 76–82), *Choline Chloride* [2005] OJ L190/22 (full text of the decision available on DG COM's web site), para 92.

[297] In *Peroxygen Products* [1985] OJ L35/1, the three cartel participants which supplied the French market exchanged detailed information on their respective production and sales. This was effected every month through a body known as the 'Chambre Syndicale de l'Eau Oxygénée et des Persels'. This body collected statistics from each of the producers and issued them with composite figures for the whole French market. In addition to the monthly statistics issued by the 'Chambre Syndicale', the producers exchanged further and more detailed information on matters not covered by the 'official' exchange. The data available through the 'Chambre Syndicale' did not include details of sales to individual customers. However, the individual producers exchanged the data with each other (see para 30). See also, eg *Sodium Gluconate* and *Zinc Phosphate* [2003] OJ L153/1.

However, there are a number of examples where the fiduciary companies actively take part in the illegal exchange of detailed competitor data. In *Italian Cast Glass*, a fiduciary company was entrusted by the cartel members with the task of supervising the proper implementation of the cartel agreement at issue.[298] In *Cast Iron and Steel Rolls*, the cartel agreement contained an obligation to pass on all customer enquiries immediately to a neutral office in Zurich (Switzerland). It was that office's responsibility to notify all interested parties of the other producers who had received the enquiry. The competitors would then contact each other to establish suitable prices.[299] In *Cartonboard*, the cartel also used the services of a fiduciary company located in Zurich. This company provided the secretariat for the Paperboard product board and was present at all cartel meetings.[300]

8.73 **Towards a systematic sanctioning of fiduciary companies' direct involvement** For a long time, the Commission had tended not to hold fiduciary companies responsible for the cartel infringement to which they contributed. However, in *Italian Cast Glass*, evidence of the fiduciary involvement was so strong that the Commission considered that the fiduciary company had been a party to the anti-competitive agreement and addressed the decision to it.[301] No fines were imposed, however. Nevertheless, it appears that the Commission's attitude towards cartel facilitators is no longer so lenient. In *Organic Peroxides*, the Commission imposed a symbolic fine on a Zurich-based fiduciary for its blatant involvement in the implementation of cartel activity, thus signalling that such behaviour is at risk of being severely punished in the future.[302]

---

298 [1980] OJ L383/19. The fiduciary company had to draw up monthly summaries of shipments, containing information on average prices for each product and each undertaking, and to carry out on their premises verifications of the information provided, including verification of the quantities dispatched and of their consistency with the store accounts and with the general accounts. If it deemed it appropriate, the fiduciary could request additional information and even carry out random checks on the physical quantities compared with the accounting quantities indicated or appearing in the store accounts.

299 [1983] OJ L317/1. The Commission decision contains considerable evidence of the office's direct involvement in the cartel, which took detailed minutes of the cartel arrangements made at the cartel meetings and implemented concealment measures (see paras 10, 31).

300 [1994] OJ L243/1. The Commission noted with scepticism, however, that the fiduciary's claims that it had not kept any record of the cartel working groups, contrary to what its practice had been for the other committees. In that case, the fiduciary was entrusted with the task of running a very sophisticated statistical system which was used to assist in the determination and monitoring of individual market shares and in the analysis of capacity utilisation.

301 [1980] OJ L383/19. The Commission stated that '[i]n assessing whether the agreements concluded between [the cartel members] on the one hand and Fides on the other were liable to restrict competition on the market in cast glass, despite the fact that the first three companies are manufacturing undertakings and Fides a service undertaking, it must be borne in mind that Fides enabled and consciously assisted the implementation of the restrictions of competition which were the very purpose of the agreements, and consequently it is jointly responsible for the resulting restrictive effects' (see point II.A.4 of the decision).

302 [2003] OJ L6/1 (full text of the decision available on DG COMP's web site). See also IP/03/1700. In this case, the Commission found, *inter alia*, that the fiduciary had stored the initial cartel agreement in a safe; organised the meetings of the cartel members; taken charge of reimbursing the travel expenses of the participants in order to avoid traces of the cartel meetings in the undertaking's accounts; produced, distributed and collected the so-called 'pink' and 'red' papers with the agreed market shares which were, because of their colours, easily distinguishable from other meeting documents and which were not allowed to be taken outside the fiduciary's premises; acted as a moderator in case of tensions within the cartel; and even instructed all participants on the legal dangers of the meetings and of measures to take to avoid detection (see paras 91–105).

(iii) Concealment Measures

In view of the blatant illegality of their behaviour and the severe penalties incurred if they are **8.74** discovered, cartels generally deploy considerable efforts to avoid detection. Concealment measures of all types can be found in cartel decisions.

Covering the cartel's tracks A basic security measure is to ensure that cartel meetings, and the **8.75** matters discussed at them, remain secret. To that end, many cartel meetings have been convened in hotels in large international cities, and reservations for meeting rooms and accommodation made under false names. In *Amino Acids*,[303] the cartel members took care to stagger their arrival and departure times for the cartel meetings so as not to arouse suspicion by having the entire group enter and leave the room at the same time. In *Food Flavour Enhancers*, cartel meetings were sometimes limited to just a few undertakings who acted on behalf of the other competitors in order to limit the risk of detection.[304] In many cases, cartel meetings have been organised just before or after official meetings of a legitimate trade association meeting, or during a trade fair.

Paperless policy Cartel members also often endeavour to refrain from taking written **8.76** notes during cartel meetings or from taking such notes away from the meeting room, or they ensure subsequent destruction of any minutes or notes. In *Cartonboard*, the Commission noted that there were, surprisingly, no notes of certain working groups whilst other, more innocent meetings were documented in great detail.[305] There are many examples of instructions to destroy all notes after the end of the meeting.[306] In *SAS/Maersk*, several measures were taken to avoid keeping a full written record of the points on which the cartel members had agreed.[307] In *Industrial Tubes*, the unofficial meetings were conducted without documentary support, implying that normally no minutes or agenda were drafted. The Commission found evidence of a cartel document specifying the security rules as 'no paper, no document, only with diskette'. In *Organic Peroxides*, a fiduciary company produced and distributed data on agreed market shares in the form of 'pink' and 'red' papers which were easily distinguishable from other papers and were collected up at the end of the meetings.[308]

Storing cartel documents in private homes The use of private homes as places of storage **8.77** of cartel documents, or as 'safe' mailboxes for the exchange of sensitive information, is also

---

[303] [2001] OJ L152/24.

[304] [2004] OJ L75/1. The Commission reports that in one high level meeting, a Japanese company represented all other Japanese members. This company stated that 'it would look suspicious if the Japanese producers all went to a Korean resort together'. In *Organic Peroxides* [2005] OJ L110/44 (full text of the decision available on DG COMP's web site), a Swiss-based fiduciary company reimbursed travel expenses to avoid leaving traces in the cartel members accounts and in *Graphite Electrodes* [2002] OJ L100/1, expenses for meetings were paid in cash with no explicit reference to those meetings.

[305] [1994] OJ L243/1.

[306] See, for example, *Graphite Electrodes* [2002] OJ L100/1. In *Copper Plumbing Tubes* (decision of 3 September 2004, full text of the decision available on DG COMP's web site), the Commission noted that if anyone sent notes to one of the cartel participants, this person was reminded by phone to destroy the paper (see para 129).

[307] Thus, in *SAS/Maersk* [2001] OJ L265/15, the Commission uncovered a cartel document reading: '[t]he parts of the documents that infringe Article [81(1)], although they cannot be agreed upon and cannot be put on paper, we presume that because some people will not be present (in the future), these parts will have to be written anyway and be put in escrow in the offices of lawyers from both sides' (see para 89). All material on price agreements, market-sharing agreements and the like had to be destroyed after the meetings and any controversial material on PCs had to be deleted.

[308] [2003] OJ L6/1 (full text of the decision available on DG COMP's web site).

a classic feature of hard core cartels. In *SAS/Maersk*, the Commission found the minutes of an internal meeting of Maersk reporting a statement from a company's representative that 'all material on price agreements, market-sharing agreements and the like had to be destroyed before going home today. Anything that might be needed had to be taken home'.[309] In *Graphite Electrodes*, for the specific purpose of keeping these contacts secret, a sales manager had a special dedicated telephone installed at his home with a fax machine.[310] In *Vitamins*, the cartel members made great efforts to keep track of incriminating documents and destroy them, including the conduct of international audits to verify that such documents no longer existed.[311]

8.78 **Using code names**   The use of code names to designate cartel members is also a frequent feature of cartel documents. For example, in *Cast Iron and Steel Rolls*, the Commission notes that the cartel decided, as a precaution in case of cartel investigations, to use a code in place of the abbreviations of members' names previously used by the fiduciary company. In *Graphite Electrodes*, a sophisticated system of code names was used to conceal the real identity of both undertakings and individuals.[312] In *Belgian Beer*, the cartel agreements were referred to by cryptic names such as 'project Green' or 'Université de Lille'.[313] In *Industrial Tubes*, a coding system was used to hide the identity of the producers in the cartel documents and in spreadsheets concerning target prices.

8.79 *Other measures* may also be taken to hide specific cartel implementation measures. In *Food Flavour Enhancers*, the so-called 'counter-purchases' between competitors, which were part of the collusive scheme, were made under sophisticated covers: a cartel member purchased the product of another cartel member through the distributor of a third one.[314] Emergency measures may also be taken in view of a growing danger of discovery. In *Graphite Electrodes*, one of the cartel leaders warned all other cartel participants that on-the-spot investigations from the Commission could be expected. With that in mind, all relevant files were reviewed and incriminating documents were destroyed or kept in safe places, such as private homes.[315] In *Vitamins*, as the result of a recent criminal investigation in the US involving ADM, the cartel members agreed on a principle of 'complete security'. Direct contact with the subsidiaries in the US would be suspended and contact would be made with the headquarters.[316]

---

309 [2001] OJ L265/15, para 89. In *Electrical and Mechanical Carbon and Graphite Products* [2004] OJ L125/45 (full text of the decision available on DG COMP's web site), there were instructions not to keep any cartel document in the undertakings' premises or even at home but to destroy them after use. In the first years of the cartel, communication was conducted through 'mailboxes' and there were instructions to use the telephone rather than faxes.

310 [2002] OJ L100/1. In the same cartel decision, the Commission notes that telephone conversations regarding prices were made from a mobile phone registered in Switzerland (see para 59).

311 [2003] OJ L6/1. Certain documents that had to be kept were copied onto computer disks and hidden in the eaves of one employee's grandmother's house. See 2003 OECD Report on Hard Core Cartels.

312 [2002] OJ L100/1. SGL was named 'BMW', UCAR got the name of 'Pinot' and the group of Japanese companies were dubbed 'Cold', a derivation from the first letters of their individual code names 'Chivas', 'Ocean', 'Lawn' and 'Dry'. VAW Carbon was known as 'Wave'. Individuals were also given code names, such as 'Artemis', 'Moustache' and 'Taurus' (see para 59).

313 [2003] OJ L140/1.

314 [2004] OJ L75/1, para 83.

315 [2002] OJ L100/1, para 33.

316 [2003] OJ L6/1, see para 452.

In *Electrical and Mechanical Carbon and Graphite Products* a 'security committee' was even created in 1998, after the opening in Europe of an investigation into other activities of the cartel members.[317]

(c) Running the Business of Collusion

Besides purely organisational aspects, it is worth describing the common features of the management of collusive activities. The elimination or reduction of competition can be a complex task requiring a particular form of management. In spite of their joint intention to collaborate, a degree of rivalry and distrust will always remain between cartel members. The undercurrent of distrust in cartels means that they require a certain degree of leadership and coordination. Devising sophisticated cartel management tools is often necessary. In spite of such measures, cartels nevertheless appear to be characterised by an inherent instability. **8.80**

(i) Managing the Elimination of Competition

Getting other market operators on board   Efforts are often made by large cartel members to convince unruly players to join the cartel. In *Vitamins*, the Commission noted several examples of efforts used by the ringleaders to convince other participants to enter into the restrictive agreements. In the Vitamin B5 cartel, a representative of Roche travelled to Tokyo to convince Daiichi to limit its exports to other markets as this was pushing down the price. Since Daiichi doubted that the cartel would succeed without BASF, Roche promised to invite BASF to a trilateral meeting convened to promote a collusive scheme regarding vitamin B5.[318] *In Industrial Tubes*, the Commission quoted a cartel participant as stating that small participants were invited to join cartel meetings 'to have better control, because with a fairly small market share these companies still had a big impact on prices'.[319] **8.81**

Achieving comparability of the products   An acceptable degree of comparability of the products sold by each member appears to be relevant to most cartels. Significant efforts may be dedicated to this. In *Sodium Gluconate*, discussions concerned the proper way to define the product and the opportunity to include in the calculation of market shares a partial substitute, as certain producers of that product were suspected of free riding on the other cartel members.[320] In *Specialty Graphite*, in order to be able to fix prices according to equivalent categories of products, the parties established a complex 'Product Grouping Standard'. This classification of grades was devised in accordance with the product applications.[321] In *Electrical and Mechanical Carbon and Graphite Products*, cartel participants had devised a highly sophisticated method for the calculation of the price of the products with reference to a number of objective factors such as the price of raw materials, the size of the product or the number of components it included.[322] **8.82**

---

[317] [2004] OJ L125/45 (full text of the decision available on DG COMP's web site), paras 81–86.
[318] [2003] OJ L6/1, para 297.
[319] [2004] OJ L125/50, para 89.
[320] Paras 111, 135.
[321] Decision of 17 December 2002 (full text of the decision available on DG COMP's web site), para 99.
[322] [2004] OJ L125/45 (full text of the decision available on DG COMP's web site). This formula, called the 'barème', was meant to enable each cartel participant to calculate the price of its products in a way that guaranteed a perfect uniformity of the prices notwithstanding the differences in the specifications of the product. This effort towards a total harmonisation of the prices was the subject of many technical meetings of the cartel (see paras 91–97).

8.83 **Collection of data and circulation of detailed implementation documents**   The day-to-day management of cartels often involves a sophisticated exchange of important quantities of data such as sales volumes, price lists, tables of market shares or annual 'budgets', either for planning fresh agreements or monitoring existing ones. Cartels often rely on the legitimate statistical activities of a trade association to obtain the basic data on which they rely to exchange further information and to make their decisions (*Sodium Gluconate*, *Zinc Phosphate*).[323] However, the collection and processing of data may be done by the cartel members themselves, with a view to saving costs and/or minimising the risks of detection.[324] Such cartel documents may be very sophisticated, as illustrated by numerous cartel decisions.[325] In *Vitamins*, extremely detailed documents were maintained and circulated. All three major European producers supplied to the Commission tables and spreadsheets created and used for the purposes of calculating, reviewing and agreeing the sales quotas of vitamins A and E for each regional and national market.[326]

8.84 **'Coordinators' and 'market leaders'**   Cartels often show a high degree of coordination and contact within the network. Specific coordination measures may also be taken. In *Pre-insulated Pipes*, a retired business executive with close personal connections to the ringleader of the cartel was engaged as a consultant to act as the 'coordinator' of the cartel.[327] A 'contact group' also played a fundamental role in the coordination of the cartel. The Commission noted that this 'complex mechanism enabled the German contact group to monitor some 1,400 to 1,500 projects per year which were over a DEM 50,000 threshold'.[328]

8.85 The appointment of 'market leaders' of particular regional or national markets often serves to ensure the coordination of cartel measures, such as collective price initiatives. The market leaders are supposed to take a 'first mover' role in any price movement in the markets for which they have been designated. In *Vegetable Parchment*,[329] the cartel members fixed prices for 'free export markets', that is countries in which no member manufacturer was established. Once the cartel members had fixed the date and rate of the price increase 'price-leaders' in each market sent to the trade association secretariat, for circulation to the other members, the applicable price schedules.[330] In *Graphite Electrodes*, the 'home producer' was

---

323 [2003] OJ L153/1.

324 In *Sodium Gluconate*, the cartel participants had ceased to resort to a Swiss fiduciary but resumed discussions on this point as mutual suspicion of cheating was growing (paras 119, 195, 196). In *Citric Acid* [2002] OJ L239/18, each participant reported the tonnage sold in each region to the secretariat of the (rotating) president of the trade association, which assembled the data and reported them back to the members by telephone, broken down by firm and by region (para 100).

325 See eg, in *Citric Acid* [2002] OJ L239/18, the description of certain cartel documents at para 101. Very detailed market share and price increase tables were circulated in *Graphite Electrodes* [2002] OJ L100/1, and *Carbonless Paper* [2004] OJ L115/1.

326 [2003] OJ L6/1. The Commission described these documents as consisting of worksheets or support documents used to fix the annual 'budget' for each producer on a country-by-country basis and charts comparing the actual sales of each producer with their respective 'budgeted volumes', ie their quota for each regional and national market both on an annual basis and for interim periods (see paras 190–191).

327 [1999] OJ L24/1, para 33.

328 Para 72.

329 [1978] OJ L70/54.

330 Para 40.

made responsible for fixing the price on its domestic territory, and the other cartel members were expected to follow its price initiatives.[331] Similar practices are described in *Sodium Gluconate*[332] and *Industrial Tubes*.[333]

(ii) Enforcing Cartel Arrangements between the Participants

As regards the risk of 'free riding' inherent in any collusive schemes, the enforcement of the   **8.86** restrictive arrangements by the members is generally a major source of concern for companies involved in cartels. Monitoring schemes aimed at ensuring compliance are therefore frequently set up, and deviations from the agreements are often subject to peer pressure or even penalties.

Monitoring schemes   The monitoring of compliance with the cartel agreements may simply   **8.87** take the form of an informal agreement between cartel members to provide each other with evidence of the implementation of the measures taken.[334] However, in many cases, the monitoring takes a more structured form. Compliance is often verified by cross-checking the individual data supplied by cartel members with global market data processed by a coordinator.[335] The monitoring of compliance may even take the form of more intrusive methods and may lead to coercive measures. In *Preserved Mushrooms*, cartel members had agreed that on request, each party would allow the other to check sales, production and dispatch documents; a joint accounting organisation would also be appointed to collect such data for the common information of the parties.[336] In *Italian Cast Glass*,[337] a fiduciary company

---

[331] [2002] OJ L100/1. One undertaking was appointed as the market leader for the US and certain parts of Europe, whilst another was responsible for the rest of Europe. Japanese producers were market leaders in the Far East (see para 50).

[332] A market leader was appointed in each country and was in charge of setting the target price. The market leader was chosen on the basis of its thorough knowledge of the country and of its influence in the said country (see para 89).

[333] [2004] OJ L125/50. 'Market leaders' were appointed, who were responsible for certain Member States. The market leader was the member of the cartel with the highest sales in a given country. Market leaders were in charge of monitoring customer visits, of gathering information in their respective territory and deciding upon target price changes. A cartel participant stated that 'the mission of the cartel leader [was] to protect the interests of each member as agreed'. He had to be informed of all visits to customers and to be immediately informed of the negotiations. 'Only the market leader [could] change the targets if necessary and [had to] inform immediately all the companies involved. [. . .] In case of disagreement between a member and a market leader, the market leader would take the final decision' (see para 108).

[334] In *Carbonless Paper*, the monitoring of compliance with the price-fixing agreements was conducted through the exchange of the standard letters announcing price increases to customers. The Commission found in the premises of one undertaking a bundle of standard letters from a competitor to its customers, together with a card sent 'with the compliments of' another competitor (paras 102–103). In *Industrial Tubes*, compliance was monitored through exchanges of detailed information between members on deliveries, market shares, customers and prices, primarily within the framework of the cartel meetings, as well as by fax, e-mail and telephone.

[335] In *Specialty Graphite* (decision of 17 December 2002, full text of the decision available on DG COMP's web site), the frequent exchanges of shipment records among competitors allowed a detailed monitoring of sales and the detection of possible deviations from the cartel instructions. A trade association or a fiduciary company may be entrusted with the task of collecting and aggregating individual sales data. Monitoring may also be carried out by a cartel member. In *Sodium Gluconate*, sales monitoring was initially conducted on the basis of the statistics supplied by a Swiss fiduciary, but to save costs, one undertaking was put in charge of collecting sales data a few days before the multilateral cartel meetings instead (paras 92–93). Similar schemes were identified in *Citric Acid* [2002] OJ L239/18 (paras 100–101) and *Amino Acids* [2001] OJ L152/24 (paras 224–227).

[336] [1975] OJ L29/26, para 4(d).

[337] [1980] OJ L383/19.

was entrusted by the cartel members with the task of drawing up monthly summaries of shipments and carrying out, in the premises of the undertaking, verification of the information provided. The fiduciary could even carry out random checks on the physical quantities compared with the accounting quantities indicated or appearing in the store accounts. In *Roofing Felt*, an accountant was appointed and was in charge of monitoring compliance with quotas and prices.[338] In *French Beef*, the Commission found that three farmers' federations had used physical force to set up mechanisms to verify that the agreement was being applied, such as illegal 'inspections' to establish the place of origin of meat.[339]

8.88 **Penalties and compensation measures** Cartels frequently agree on compensation measures or even penalties to be applied to members who have not complied with the restrictive agreements. In *Roofing Felt*, a member in breach of its obligations could be ordered to pay a standard penalty into a common fund, failing which the sum could be deducted from the security the member had lodged in the guarantee fund.[340] In *Pre-insulated Pipes*, the performance of each producer against quota was ascertained and discrepancies would be regularised either in the allocation of the following year's quotas or by payment of compensation.[341] In *Citric acid*,[342] a compensation scheme was agreed as a corollary to the quota agreements, in order to penalise those companies selling above their assigned sales quotas and at the same time compensate those that did not reach theirs.

8.89 **Threats, boycotts and coordinated attacks on competitors** In addition to the enforcement of compliance schemes 'voluntarily' agreed upon by the members, it is not uncommon for cartels to take steps aimed at forcing reluctant market players to align their commercial behaviour, so that the anticipated results of the cartel are not undermined. In *Roofing Felt*, the cartel members took or planned concerted action against other manufacturers and importers to discourage them from pursuing a price-cutting policy, and to take customers away from them.[343] In *Electrical and Mechanical Carbon and Graphite Products*, cartel members exchanged information on their competitors and engaged in concerted actions in order to persuade or force them to cooperate.[344] In *Carbonless Paper*, threats were

---

[338] [1986] OJ L232/15. To facilitate monitoring of quotas, members were required to make monthly returns to the accountant stating their purchases and movements of stocks of raw materials and finished products and their exports. They also had to keep numbered invoices on both sales and purchases and to keep full accounts, with supporting documents, for regular or extraordinary inspection. The accountant also administered the arrangements for penalising those who exceeded their quotas and acted as secretary to the general meetings (see para 20).

[339] [2003] OJ L209/12, paras 30, 38, 80, 126, 133, 173.

[340] [1986] OJ L232/15, para 21.

[341] [1999] OJ L24/1, para 65.

[342] [2002] OJ L239/18. It had been decided that if a company exceeded its assigned quota in any one year, it would be obliged to purchase product from the company or companies with sales below their quota during the following year. According to the Commission, this led to several important transactions between companies, especially as one company tended to fall short of its quota, whilst another one tended to remain ahead of it (see paras 88 and 102–111).

[343] [1986] OJ L232/15, para 59.

[344] [2004] OJ L125/45 (full text of the decision available on DG COMP's web site). On several occasions small local producers were persuaded to take part in local cartel meetings. In other instances, competitors were forced to withdraw from the market, or were even taken over by the cartel members, who subsequently ensured that their subsidiary complied with the cartel rules (see para 167).

made against recalcitrant competitors. A representative of the ringleader stated that he would 'personally take care' of those who would not play by the rules. The company in question, which enjoyed market power, threatened to destroy any competitor that adopted a competitive attitude. It was reported to have executed this threat with regard to an Italian competitor.[345] Measures to 'convince' companies to cooperate may even take the form of (threats to take) initiatives aimed at having their behaviour sanctioned by public authorities. In *French-West African Shipowners' Committees*, the committees deployed efforts to ensure that the African public authorities adopted rules protecting their activities and providing for penalties on members exceeding their quotas and on independent lines operating without the approval of the committees.[346] In *Amino Acids*,[347] and *Citric Acid*, recalcitrant third-country producers were threatened with anti-dumping actions.[348] Targeted concerted actions against competitors may also be taken. In *Pre-insulated Pipes*,[349] considerable efforts were devoted to taking a small but active competitor out of the market. In *Citric Acid*, the increasing availability of Chinese production in the European market and the need for a more forceful stance by the cartel members to maintain their level of sales were the subject of discussion at the cartel meetings. A price war against the Chinese competition was decided upon, at whatever price was necessary.[350]

(iii) The Instability of Collusive Schemes

Cartels are unstable by nature. They are subject to the economic cycles of the markets in which they operate, all the more so because they often occur in sectors with a high degree of cyclicality, such as commodity markets, where surges in demand result in massive expansion in capacity which ineluctably trigger crises of overcapacity. Instability is also inherent in collusive schemes, where supra competitive profits may only be attained through collective discipline, but where the temptation to poach customers by undercutting collusive prices is high, as this may result in even higher benefits for the individual firm. Despite the efforts deployed to ensure mutual control, tensions within cartels are therefore frequent, and mutual grievances often result from the eagerness or the lack of discipline of certain members.[351]   **8.90**

Claims for higher quotas   Cartel participants may threaten the other participants by adopting competitive behaviour in order to obtain more favourable treatment within the cartel. In *Sodium Gluconate*, a previous cartel had collapsed because a participant had decided to   **8.91**

---

[345] [2004] OJ L115/1, paras 104–106.

[346] [1992] OJ L134/1, para 25.

[347] [2001] OJ L152/24. The two ringleaders envisaged economic sanctions against a Korean producer who did not comply with the cartel agreement. In particular they threatened it with an anti-dumping action in Europe if it did not limit sales quantities in this area. The Korean producer subsequently agreed to comply with the cartel agreement (see paras 88, 330).

[348] [2002] OJ L239/18. With regard to the growing competition from Chinese producers, the cartel members decided that on forthcoming trips by representatives of the cartel members to China, the local producers were to be threatened with an anti-dumping complaint (see para 122).

[349] [1999] OJ L24/1.

[350] [2002] OJ L239/18. Target customers were allocated to each cartel member. This catalogue of target customers came to be known as the 'Serbia List' and was the subject of regular monitoring and discussion.

[351] On the inherent instability of cartels and the determining factors of their stability, see PZ Grossman (ed), *How Cartels Endure and How they Fail—Studies of Industrial Collusion* (2004). See also MC Levenstein and VY. Suslow 'What determines Cartel Success?' (2002), available at SSRN: <http://ssrn.com/abstract=299415>.

expand its production capacity by constructing new plant. After a period of intense price war, the cartel was reformed after the undertaking which had led to the collapse managed to obtain a higher quota which took into account its expanded capacity. In *Vitamins*, Takeda's entry into the cartel arrangements for vitamin B2 provoked intense negotiations regarding annual quotas, with Takeda alleging that Roche had made a mistake in the calculation of market shares and demanding a higher allocation. The Commission noted that 'Takeda's volume aspirations were clearly a cause of irritation for Roche'.[352] In *Citric Acid*, disputes also arose because certain undertakings were unhappy with the quotas that had been allocated to them.[353]

8.92 **Mutual suspicion of cheating** Grievances frequently result from suspicions that certain cartel members are not complying with their obligations. In *Sodium Gluconate*[354] and *Citric Acid*,[355] for instance, tensions arose regarding the monitoring of sales data, as certain cartel participants were accused of cheating. *Food Flavour Enhancers* provides numerous examples of tensions between cartel participants. For instance, one participant would no longer agree to cooperate on pricing unless another participant agreed to buy certain quantities of the product from it.[356] Grievances regarding alleged non compliance were also numerous.[357] Similar episodes can be found in *Carbonless Paper*[358] and *Austrian Banks*.[359]

8.93 **Leniency programmes as an additional factor of instability** On top of the natural instability of cartels, the adoption of leniency programmes by a large number of competition enforcement authorities has added an additional and significant source of distrust between cartel members. In the EU, the chance of obtaining full immunity in exchange for reporting an unknown cartel to the Commission has considerably increased the incentive for cartel members to denounce their peers before another participant does so. It is likely that the facts that will be set out in future cartel decisions will illustrate this new and important source of tension within collusive schemes.

---

[352] [2003] OJ L6/1, para 280.

[353] [2002] OJ L239/18, para 97.

[354] Para 93.

[355] Jungbunzlauer was seen to be 'causing problems' in the group because it did not strictly adhere to the agreement at all times and was perceived to be 'ill-disciplined' by the other cartel participants (para 117).

[356] [2004] OJ L75/1, para 102.

[357] Paras 114, 116.

[358] [2004] OJ L115/1. The Commission reports that a cartel participant who doubted the accuracy of the figures submitted by another asked for, and obtained, the right to directly verify the figures in question at the premises of that undertaking (see para 106).

[359] [2004] OJ L56/1. The case of one bank cutting interest 'without prior notice' prompted strong and immediate reactions from the other cartel members, who immediately convened the relevant cartel committee. The Commission reports that '[f]eelings ran high at the meeting and the undertaking in question, which had already not complied with other cartel measures and which had not provided appropriate information to competitors on the measures taken, was fiercely attacked by the other banks. It was "the unanimous opinion" that there was "no justification" for the measure taken and that it "contradicted the stated objective of all the relevant committee meetings" ie "not to go along with" any cuts in interest rates on loans. Any "such senseless competition" was downright dangerous' (see para 172).

C. Investigating Hardcore Cartels

(1) The Initiation of a Case: Information Sources

The information that may prompt the Commission to start an investigation can come from **8.94**
a variety of sources. It is widely known that a prime case-generator is the Commission's
Leniency Notice.[360] Under the Leniency Notice, undertakings that self-report a cartel
infringement and provide sufficient evidence to the Commission can receive immunity
from fines.[361] The Commission also has other means of tracing cartels: an investigation
may result from the Commission's own monitoring of markets, from information transmitted to the Commission by Member State authorities or by third country agencies; it
may also originate from submissions by complainants (private customers or industrial
clients), or from whistleblowers (for instance (ex-)employees who wish to report wrongdoing). Each of these possibilities is discussed in greater detail below. Given the important
place of the Commission's Leniency Notice as an investigative tool in cartel proceedings, a
full in-depth section is dedicated to a discussion of all aspects of its functioning.[362]

(a) Market Monitoring and Information from Other Investigations

The Commission may put itself on the track of collusive behaviour through so-called 'mar- **8.95**
ket monitoring'. The term relates to the informal gathering of information and finding of
possible illegal behaviour in a given market, based on indications, first and foremost of an
economic nature, through an analysis of structural, behavioural and performance indicators. The Commission may search for particular occurrences or trends that go against the
expected economic development of those markets, such as a sudden (upward) swing in the
movement of prices or strong price differentials between geographic markets. Furthermore,
the Commission can examine the mechanisms by which particular markets operate and as
a result of which (price) transparency is achieved.

Unless a market monitoring exercise leads to the actual acquisition of evidence of a hard- **8.96**
core cartel (which is relatively unlikely), the results may still provide the Commission with
a sufficient basis for issuing requests for information. The question, however, is whether the
Commission will be able to obtain sufficient information through market monitoring to
enable it actually to carry out (surprise) inspections.[363] In any case, it is difficult to see how
the Commission can obtain sufficient leads without actually requesting information from

---

[360] The Commission stated in 2004: 'In recent years, most cartels have been detected by the European
Commission after one cartel member confessed and asked for leniency, [. . .]'. See the brochure *EU competition
policy and the consumer*, European Commission, 2004, available at <http://www.publications.eu.int/>. (It should
be noted that the Leniency Notice does not require a specific *confession* (as the brochure states) by the undertaking
requesting immunity or a reduction of fines. On the specifics of the Leniency Notice, see further para 8.104.)

[361] If the Commission issues a final prohibition Decision with fines after the conclusion of its investigation, the undertakings whose (conditional) immunity is confirmed in that Decision will nevertheless be
named in it, with all relevant facts about their participation. Also, a fine will be calculated for it, from which
it is then granted immunity.

[362] See paras 8.105–8.257, below.

[363] It should be noted that the mere fact that an industry appears not to be performing in a competitive manner, cannot, by itself, constitute proof of an infringement, unless—according to *Woodpulp*—there exists no other
explanation for the malfunctioning of the market than an agreement or a concerted practice between competitors.

the market (so that the companies concerned would become aware of the Commission's interest, thereby reducing the surprise effect of inspections).

8.97 Apart from more general market monitoring, the Commission may also obtain leads from other investigations. In cases where the Commission has discovered materials, for instance during an inspection in one investigation, about a different infringement, it cannot use the information in evidence in that second case, but it could not be prevented from using the information to commence a new and separate investigation.[364]

8.98 **Sector inquiries** The Commission has a specific power to carry out sector inquiries, under Article 17 of Regulation 1/2003.[365] (Article 17 in fact speaks of 'investigations into sectors of the economy and into types of agreement', but the general term 'sector inquiries' is commonly used.) Rather than serving as a specific tool for detecting evidence of (secret) cartels (although that may of course occur), their purpose is to study the functioning of certain markets or industry sectors.[366] Within the framework of sector inquiries, Article 17 does allow for the possibility of carrying out unannounced inspections.

(b) *Information Received from Other Authorities*

8.99 **Pre-investigation exchanges of information within the European Competition Network (ECN)** With the entry into force of Regulation 1/2003, and the lifting of previous impediments to the exchange of confidential information between Member States and the Commission (see Article 12 of the Regulation), the Commission can benefit from information available from the NCAs (National Competition Authorities), which can be used not only as a lead for an investigation of its own, but also as evidence of an infringement.[367]

(Joined cases C-89/85, C-104/85, C-114/85, C-116/85 and C-125/85 to C-129/85 *A Ahlström Osakeyhtiö and others v Commission* [1993] ECR I-1307 (*Woodpulp II*), para 71: 'In determining the probative value of those different factors, it must be noted that parallel conduct cannot be regarded as furnishing proof of concertation unless concertation constitutes the only plausible explanation for such conduct. It is necessary to bear in mind that, although Article 85 of the Treaty prohibits any form of collusion which distorts competition, it does not deprive economic operators of the right to adapt themselves intelligently to the existing and anticipated conduct of their competitors (see the judgment in Suiker Unie, cited above [in the judgment], para 174).' Having said that, the same standard of evidence for proving an infringement may not be applicable at the stage of deciding on inspections (where a well-founded suspicion may suffice to start an investigation).

[364] See Case 85/87 *Dow Benelux v Commission* [1989] ECR 3137, para 9.

[365] Such sector enquiries were for many years rarely used, but Commissioner Kroes announced that the Commission would increasingly resort to them (see SPEECH/05/157, 10 March 2005, Taking Competition Seriously—Anti-Trust Reform in Europe; Preliminary Report of 16 February 2006, available at the DG COMP's web site; For recent examples of sector inquiries: see Press release IP/06/174 of 16/02/2006: Competition: energy sector inquiry confirms serious problems and sets out way forward; MEMO/06/78 of 16/02/2006: MEMO/05/425 of 15/11/2005: Competition: Commission sector inquiry reveals serious problems in energy markets; MEMO/05/203 of 13/06/2005: Energy sector competition inquiry—frequently asked questions; IP/05/716 of 13/06/2005; Commission opens sector inquiry into gas and electricity. For a discussion of this instrument: D Wood and N Baverez, 'Sector Inquiries under EU Competition Law', Competition Law Insight, February 2005.

[366] Art 17(1) of Regulation 1/2003 refers to the '. . . the trend of trade between Member States, the rigidity of prices or other circumstances that suggest that competition maybe restricted or distorted within the common market'.

[367] This is an important innovation compared to the situation before Regulation 1/2003 when information exchanged could not be used directly in evidence but only as a lead, so that the receiving authority first had to use

More detailed rules on the exchange of information between the NCAs and the Commission have been laid down in the so-called 'Network Notice' that was part of the 2004 Modernisation package.[368] The Network Notice establishes the principle that in relation to infringements that cover more than three Member States the Commission is the authority that is 'well placed to act'.[369] Just as the Commission can benefit from information submitted to it, so the NCAs can benefit from information in the possession of the Commission or their NCA-counterparts, relating to infringements on which they themselves are active.[370]

Exchange of information with third country authorities   Information leading to an   **8.100** investigation may also originate from third country authorities. There exists no general framework for the exchange of information in antitrust matters between the Commission and third countries. There are, however, antitrust agreements with certain individual jurisdictions: with the States of the European Free Trade Association (EFTA), through the EEA Agreement;[371] with the United States;[372] with Canada;[373] and with Japan.[374] The EEA Agreement is the most far-reaching and allows the Commission to work closely together with the EFTA Surveillance Authority (ESA), including through investigative assistance.[375] The other

---

its own investigative procedures to obtain the information (Case C-67/91 *Dirección General de la Competencia v Asociación Española de Banca Privada and others v Commission* [1992] ECR I-4785, paras 33 and 39).

> In that general context, the purpose of a request for information addressed to an undertaking on the basis of Article 11 of Regulation No 17 is to provide the Commission with the factual or legal information needed to enable it to exercise its powers. The probative value of the information thus communicated and the conditions under which such information may be relied on against undertakings are, consequently, defined by Community law and confined exclusively to proceedings governed by Regulation No 17. The purpose of the request for information is not to furnish evidence to be used by the Member States in proceedings governed by national law.

Such an interpretation does not in any way run counter to the requirements of the principle of cooperation between the Community institutions and the Member States. The Member States are not required to ignore the information disclosed to them and thereby undergo—to echo the expression used by the Commission and the national court—'acute amnesia'. That information provides circumstantial evidence which may, if necessary, be taken into account to justify initiation of a national procedure (see, to that effect, the judgment in Case 85/87 *Dow Benelux v Commission* [1989] ECR 3137, paras 18 and 19).

[368] Commission Notice on Co-operation within the Network of Competition Authorities, [2004] OJ C101/03, hereinafter referred to as the 'Network Notice'.

[369] Point 14 of the Network Notice.

[370] Points 16 *et seq.* of the Network Notice. On the exchange of information between the Commission and the Member States, see also chapter 2 of this book. As regards the aspects of information exchange relevant to leniency applications, see section C(3) of this chapter.

[371] Agreement on the European Economic Area. (Decision of the Council and the Commission of 13 December 1993 on the conclusion of the Agreement on the European Economic Area between the European Communities, their Member States and the Republic of Austria, the Republic of Finland, the Republic of Iceland, the Principality of Liechtenstein, the Kingdom of Norway, the Kingdom of Sweden and the Swiss Confederation (94/1/ECSC, EC), [1994] OJ L1/1).

[372] Agreement between the European Communities and the Government of the United States of America regarding the application of their competition laws. Decision of the Council and the Commission of 10 April 1995 (95/145/EC, ECSC). ([1995] OJ L95/47; [1995] OJ L131/38.)

[373] Council and Commission Decision of 29 April 1999 concerning the conclusion of the Agreement between the European Communities and the Government of Canada regarding the application of their competition laws ([1999] OJ L175/49).

[374] Council Decision of 16 June 2003 concluding the Agreement between the European Community and the Government of Japan concerning co-operation on anti-competitive activities. ([2003] OJ L183/12.)

[375] See Protocol 23, Art 8 of the EEA Agreement.

official antitrust agreements (with the US, Canada and Japan) are oriented more towards co-operation and co-ordination as well as the exchange of information, although in limited cases they also provide for forms of investigative assistance.[376] Apart from its close links with the ESA, in the area of cartel investigations the relationship of the Commission with the United States (the US Department of Justice) is the closest.[377]

8.101 Although the rules of professional secrecy prevent the Commission from sharing with third country agencies any evidence that has been obtained through its investigations,[378] this does not mean that no relevant information at all can be shared. Especially at the pre-investigation stage (ie before the Commission makes use of its formal powers of investigation as a result of which the rules of professional secrecy come into full play), information can be shared that will be important in enabling the recipient authority to consider taking appropriate (investigative) action. Such an exchange can take place even in the absence of any particular bilateral agreement, although the existence of an actual treaty provides a stronger impulse for doing so.[379] Since at the pre-investigation stage the supply of information to the authorities usually takes place on a voluntary basis (usually in applications for immunity), the exchange of the information between jurisdictions is less problematic in terms of legal obstacles. Authorisation by the provider of the information—a confidentiality waiver—is of course required, including in the case of applicants for immunity.[380] (For more on international co-operation in cartel investigations, see paras 8.433–8.448 below.)

---

[376] See for instance Art V(2) of the EC/U.S. Agreement of 10 April 1995 (see n 371 above).

[377] R Hewitt Pate, the then Assistant Attorney General for Antitrust at the US Department of Justice: 'Now, we [the European Commission and the US DoJ] routinely share information and coordinate investigative strategies in our international cartel investigations with the end result being coordinated, simultaneous raids on targets located in the United States and Europe.' (R Hewitt Pate, *Antitrust In A Translantic Context—From The Cicada's Perspective*, presented at the 'Antitrust In A Translantic Context' Conference, Brussels, 7 June 2004).

[378] See section C(3) of this chapter and in particular para 8.448 below on international aspects of Commission investigations. See also Kyryazis, *Jurisdiction and co-operation issues in the investigation of international cartels*, paper for the ABA Advanced International Cartel Workshop, February 2001, and Parisi, *Enforcement co-operation among Antitrust Authorities*, November 1999, available at <http://www.ftc.gov/speeches/other/ ibc99059911update. htm>. Ortiz Blanco notes that the obligation not to disclose information is also incumbent on the national competition authorities of the Member Sates where they apply Art 81 or 82 EC. However, Art 28 concerns information that comes into the possession of the Member States 'pursuant to Regulation 1/2003'. It therefore does not seem that Member States, at least not from the wording in Art 28 of Regulation 1/2003, are, *through Regulation 1/2003* prevented from sharing information that they have obtained via an investigation that is based on their respective national procedures. The prohibition that Ortiz signals may perhaps be argued based on the spirit of Regulation 1/2003 and by analogy to Art 12 of Regulaton 1/2003, and may of course follow from the application of national law. (L Ortiz Blanco (ed), *EC Competition Procedure* (2nd edn, 2005, para 7.16).

[379] For instance, the EU/US Agreement, n 371 above, in Art III(3), states that 'Each party will provide the other party with any significant information that comes to the attention of its competition authorities about anticompetitive activities that its competition authorities believe is relevant to, or may warrant, enforcement activity by the other Party's competition authority.' It is submitted that this provides a clear foundation for passing on information about a cartel that also affects the jurisdiction of the other party (unless that would be prohibited by Art 28 of Regulation 1/2003 or would not have the agreement of the source of the information, ie a whistleblower or immunity applicant).

[380] Where information has been submitted by complainants or informants on a voluntary basis, or where information came into the possession of the authorities other than by means of using (compulsory) investigative powers, the sharing of such information, it is submitted, would generally be permissible under Art 28 of Regulation 1/2003. (Art 28 refers only to information acquired 'pursuant to this Regulation'.) Nevertheless, the general rules on professional secrecy, under Art 287 of the EC Treaty, should be respected. For the notion of professional secrecy and its application in competition procedures see Case T-198/03 *Bank Austria Creditanstalt AG v Commission*, judgment of 30 May 2006, not yet reported. (For the obligation on the

(c) Complaints (Formal and Informal)

Complaints about possible cartel infringements can originate from customers, who may **8.102** claim to be subject to practices such as a synchronised increase in prices and/or a reduction in sources of supply, which they suspect to be the result of collusion between the suppliers.[381] Competitors may also sometimes manifest themselves as complainants: for example, those that are outside the cartel and find themselves confronted with co-ordinated measures from alleged cartel members to expel them from the market, in reaction to their competitive ('disturbing') behaviour.[382] Regulation 1/2003 and Commission Regulation 773/2004, together with the 2004 Commission's Notice on the handling of complaints,[383] provide two options for submitting complaints: the submission of a formal complaint through a dedicated form,[384] or the submission of information in a less formal manner.[385] The Commission requests that

---

Commission to protect the identity of an informant, see the judgment in *Stanley Adams*. The Court held that Art 214 of the EEC Treaty (now Art 287 EC), which lays down the secrecy obligations of the members and civil servants of Community institutions, contains a general principle that applies not only to confidential information gathered from companies, but also to information supplied by natural persons (para 34 of the judgment). The Court found that the Commission was bound by a duty of confidentiality toward Mr Adams, a previous employee of the firm Hoffman-LaRoche & Co ('Roche'). What made this case remarkable was that in the course of the antitrust proceedings the Commission disclosed information to Roche that assisted Roche in identifying Mr Adams as an informant. This eventually led to his arrest, detention, and conviction in Switzerland on economic espionage charges. The Commission was held liable by the Court for having transmitted information to Roche that, together with other information, permitted the identification of Mr Adams as the source, and was ordered to pay compensation for non-contractual liability (Case 145/83, *Stanley George Adams v Commission* [1985] ECR 3539). Regarding information submitted under the Commission's Leniency programme, particular care needs to be taken about any onward transmission, because as a policy matter, the sharing of information without the agreement of the supplier could have a significant chilling effect on the functioning of the Commission's Leniency programme. Information received from applicants for immunity or a reduction in fines will therefore be transmitted only with the approval of the source, in the form of a waiver. (Remarks of Commission officials G De Bronett and EC Sakkers at the *International Cartel Workshop* of the American Bar Association, New York, February 2004.)

[381] See for instance the Commission's investigation in *Greek Ferries* which had been initiated as a result of a complaint by a single customer (Commission Decision of 9 December 1999, in case IV/34.466—*Greek Ferries*, OJ [1999] L109/24). For another example of an investigation that was—reportedly—started on the basis of customer complaints, see the Commission's investigation in *Cross Channel Ferries* (see 'Euro inspectors sift ferry evidence', <http://www.news.bbc.co.uk/1/hi/business/3079574.stm>, and Commission MEMO/03/167 of 03/09/2003, available at <http://www.europa.eu.int/rapid/pressReleasesAction.do?reference=MEMO/03/167&format=HTML&aged=1&language=EN&guiLanguage=en>).

[382] An example of such a complainant was the company, Powerpipe in the *Pre-insulated Pipes* case. Powerpipe complained to the Commission that its competitors had taken concerted steps to confine Powerpipe's activities to Sweden by, *inter alia*, unlawfully interfering with its contractual relations with customers and suppliers (Commission Decision of 21.10.1998, [1999] OJ L24). For another example of a collective boycott, see *Luxemburg Brewers*, Commission Decision of 5.12.2001, [2002] OJ L253. In this case the incumbent brewers in Luxemburg endeavoured to keep foreign competitors out of the market by collectively disallowing them access to their established distribution networks. On collective boycotts see further the discussion in paras 8.44ff of this chapter.

[383] *Commission Notice on the handling of complaints by the Commission under Articles 81 and 82 of the EC Treaty*, OJ [2004] C101/05, accessible at: <http://www.europa.eu.int/dgcomp/info-on-anti-competitive-practices>, hereinafter also referred to as the 'Complaints Notice'.

[384] Art 5 of Regulation 773/2004.

[385] See paras 3 and 4 of the Complaints Notice (n 383 above). Formal complainants have a number of procedural rights and participate in the Commission's procedure. Their position is further explained in Regulation 773/2004 (Chapter IV, Arts 5–9), and the Complaints Notice. Citizens and undertakings that may wish to provide information to the Commission about suspected infringements can do so at a special mailbox: COMP-MARKET-INFORMATION@ec.europa.eu. Contact may also be made with DG Competition's 'Consumer Liaison Officer'.

complaints be submitted through a dedicated web site, although paper submissions are also possible. It is important to emphasise that the Commission will treat a complainant's information and/or its identity as confidential, including from the undertakings whose behaviour has been complained of, if the divulging of the information could have repercussions for the provider of the information.[386]

(d) Informants/Whistleblowers

8.103 Another possible avenue through which the Commission may receive leads or evidence is through 'informants'. The term informant, or 'whistleblower', is applied, for example, to (ex-) employees of a company who (without its authorisation) provide information about the company's activities to the Commission.[387] It is not to be confused with those providing (corporate) confessions made under the Leniency Notice. Submissions by informants may be formally registered by the Commission under Article 19 of Regulation 1/2003 ('the power to take statements'), but the Commission will certainly also be ready to allow other informal means of communication.[388] The Commission will of course treat the information received by an informant confidentially, and will protect the identity of the provider of the information under its duty of care.[389]

(e) Applications under the Leniency Notice

8.104 It is well known that many of the cases that the Commission deals with result from information submitted under its Leniency Notice. The Commission's Leniency programme has proved to be a very useful instrument in generating information about cartels, both as regards previously undetected infringements and in relation to ongoing investigations (in applications for a reduction in fines). The Leniency Notice can therefore be regarded as an 'investigation tool' in its own right. Given the specificity of the Leniency Notice and its procedural intricacies, it is dealt with below in a distinct section that precedes the section on the other investigative tools of the Commission.

(2) Leniency: Inducing Insiders to Break Rank

(a) Rationale and Origins of the EC Leniency Policy

8.105 **The problem of deterring cartel behaviour** Hardcore cartels are *per se* infringements and their perpetrators are generally fully aware of the blatant illegality of their behaviour. In this context, the ultimate goal of any enforcement policy should be to deter companies from entering into such agreements. Deterrence will be effective if a company abstains from taking part in a cartel because the prospect of loss, in terms of sanctions, is higher than the

---

[386] See point 81 of the Complaints Notice.

[387] The most famous (or perhaps one should say infamous) example of an informant is that of Stanley Adams, referred to in n 379 above. Mr. Adams was an employee of the Swiss company, Hoffmann-La Roche & Co. AG ('Roche') in the 1970s. In 1973 Mr Adams contacted the European Commission to inform it of anti-competitive practices that he believed were being engaged in by Roche. The information provided by Mr Adams led the Commission to start an investigation into Roche's activities and, in 1976, to adopt Decision 76/642/EEC ([1976] OJ L223/27), in which the Commission found that Roche had abused its dominant position in the market for bulk vitamins. (See Case 145/83 *Stanley George Adams v Commission* [1985] ECR 3539.)

[388] Citizens and undertakings wishing to provide information to the Commission about suspected infringements can do so at a special mailbox: COMP-MARKET-INFORMATION@ec.europa.eu.

[389] On the duty to protect the source of information, see n 380 above.

prospect of gain.[390] To influence companies in this way the Commission can only rely on its power to 'name and shame' companies in formal decisions and to impose heavy fines on them. The general deterrent effect of fines depends not only on their absolute level, but also on the likelihood that the cartel will be detected and actually punished. What is relevant to the decision making process of a potential cartel member is the level of the 'expected' fine, which, mathematically, is the nominal amount of the fine multiplied by the probability that the fine will in fact be imposed. Enforcers must therefore not only focus their attention on the general level of fines but also on increasing detection rates.[391]

Difficulties in detecting and proving cartels   Owing to their secret nature, cartels are dif-   **8.106** ficult to detect and investigate. Enforcers must not only become aware of the existence of a cartel but must also prove the infringement to the requisite legal standard. Over time, cartel members, aware of the risks involved, have made ever greater efforts to conceal their illegal activities. During the first decades of enforcement the Commission relied almost exclusively on the investigative powers granted by Regulation 17. In terms of detection this meant that the Commission essentially had to rely on complainants, on the observation of abnormal market behaviour, or on information submitted by whistleblowers such as disgruntled employees. As these sources of evidence are rare in the case of cartels, evidence of an infringement was particularly difficult to collect. Although the Commission could rely to a certain extent on the effectiveness of its on-the-spot investigations, it generally found itself faced with the difficulty of establishing the infringement as a whole. Hence, the interests of the companies under investigation was often to adopt a confrontational stance in the course of the administrative procedure, both with a view to restricting the Commission's ability to establish the infringement, and in the hope that the final decision would either be quashed by the Courts, or the fines at least reduced.[392]

The rationale for a leniency policy: the prisoner's dilemma   Faced with such difficulties,   **8.107** the Commission considered it to be in the public interest to induce cartel members to come forward by granting them lenient treatment in exchange for their co-operation.[393] The basic rationale for such a leniency policy is threefold. First, it is expected to increase the probability of both detection and effective punishment, and thus the overall level of deterrence.[394] Secondly, the leniency policy has a 'preventive' dimension. The existence of an attractive leniency programme creates a 'prisoner's dilemma' and implants a permanent fear within cartels

---

[390] The deterrence problem is particularly acute because certain considerations that would normally induce companies to comply with competition rules can appear to have insufficient preventive effects in respect of cartels. For instance, cartel members have no need to fear the civil consequences of a declaration of nullity under Art 81(2) EC, which would be the case in respect of a legally binding contract.

[391] See para 8.856 below.

[392] C Harding and J Joshua, *Regulating Cartels in Europe: A Study of Legal Control of Corporate Delinquency* (2003), see especially chapters 5 and 6.

[393] The underlying assumption is that the interest of consumers and citizens in ensuring that secret cartels are detected and punished outweighs the interest in fining the individual undertakings that have enabled the authority to detect and punish such practices (see point 4 of both the 1996 and the 2002 Leniency Notices).

[394] In order to entice undertakings to self-report, reductions in fines should, first, be proportional to the added value brought by the co-operating company to the investigation and, secondly (and consequently), be restricted, at least as regards large reductions, to the first company to come forward.

that a member will report it to the enforcement authorities, thus getting 'off the hook' itself at the expense of the other members of the cartel. This increases the risk associated with cartel behaviour and creates a climate of permanent suspicion between the cartel members which not only maximises the inherent instability of cartels but may also simply discourage companies from engaging in such behaviour in the first place. Thirdly, leniency is a cost-effective enforcement tool which enables enforcement authorities to detect and punish cartels without having to resort to other costly and time-consuming methods of investigation.

8.108 **Practice of leniency before the adoption of the 1996 Leniency Notice** It was already a practice of the Commission, prior to the adoption of a formal leniency policy, to reward the co-operative attitude of parties to competition cases when setting their fines.[395] The investigation of the *Cartonboard* cartel[396] marked a turning point in the understanding that leniency could play a more major role in cartel investigations. For the first time an undertaking, in this case the Swedish company, Stora, decided to co-operate with the Commission to an unprecedented extent, thus considerably facilitating the Commission's investigation of the case and the finding of the infringement. Another company (Rena) also voluntarily supplied incriminating cartel documents. The Commission consequently granted Stora and Rena very substantial reductions in the fines that would otherwise have been imposed upon them.[397]

8.109 **Experience from US corporate leniency policy** The US Department of Justice (DoJ) was the first enforcement authority to formally adopt a leniency programme, in October 1978. Under the 'Corporate Leniency Policy', companies coming forward to the Antitrust Division of the DoJ before any investigation was initiated could ask for complete amnesty from fines. The grant of amnesty, however, was not automatic, but subject to the prosecutorial discretion of the Attorney General. Despite its aims, the 1978 leniency policy was not a success. The legal uncertainty and lack of transparency in the process were considered to be a disincentive to companies reporting their activities. In almost 15 years following the introduction of the leniency policy only 17 companies applied for amnesty and a mere ten of them qualified successfully.[398] In view of these limited results the US authorities decided

---

[395] In *Wood Pulp* ([1985] OJ L85/1, para 149) and *Polypropylene* ([1986] OJ L230/1, para 109), the Commission stated that it had taken account, in mitigating the fine imposed, of the fact that some addressees had co-operated with the Commission during the proceedings. In *French-West African Shipowners' Committees* [1992] OJ L134/1, it stated further that there were 'grounds for exempting from fines the four shipping companies which, although members of the committees, contributed in drawing the attention of the Commission to the practices dealt with in this Decision' ([1992] OJ L134/1, para 74(e)). Conversely, the Commission had also treated lack of co-operation or obstruction of the investigation as aggravating factors when calculating the fine.

[396] [1994] OJ L243/1.

[397] [1994] OJ L243/1, para 171. The Commission stated in its final decision that '[a]lthough there was already strong documentary evidence to prove the existence of a cartel, Stora's spontaneous admission of the infringement and the detailed evidence which it provided to the Commission [. . .] contributed materially to the establishment of the truth, reduced the need to rely upon circumstantial evidence and no doubt influenced other producers who might otherwise have continued to deny all wrongdoing. Rena for its part provided important documentary evidence to the Commission on a voluntary basis'.

[398] GR Spratling, DJ Arp and AJ Shepard, 'The Increasing Globalization of International Cartel Enforcement', Antitrust Report, Spring 2004.

to modify certain features of the programme. The new leniency policy adopted in 1993 contained three significant changes.[399] As a consequence there was a considerable increase in the number of amnesty applications. The average rose from one application per year under the old policy to three applications per month under the new policy.[400] This led in particular to the rapid unearthing of many large international cartels[401] and contributed greatly to the introduction of leniency policies around the world.

Adoption of the Commission's 1996 Leniency Notice   Drawing lessons from **8.110** *Cartonboard*[402] and from the success of the new US corporate leniency programme, the Commission adopted its first leniency policy in 1996. Little publicity was given to it,[403] probably as a result of certain reservations that existed at the time regarding the perceived thinking behind the new policy.[404] The Commission made it clear in the introductory part of the 1996 Leniency Notice that leniency would only be applicable to 'secret cartels between enterprises aimed at fixing prices, production or sales quotas, sharing markets or banning imports or exports'. The rationale behind this was that other serious restrictions of competition such as abuses of dominant position or vertical restrictions are not usually conspiratorial and/or the behaviour is not generally kept secret. The Commission stated that it considered that it was in the Community interest to grant favourable treatment to enterprises which cooperate. It pointed out that consumers and citizens are better served by ensuring that cartels are detected and prohibited rather than fining enterprises which cooperate with the Commission.

Rapid change of attitude towards leniency policies and adoption of the 2002 Leniency **8.111** **Notice**   In view of the undeniable success of the Commission leniency policy, which resulted in a significant increase in anti-cartel enforcement and a highlighting of the extent

---

[399] First, amnesty became automatic in cases where no prior investigation had been initiated, thus providing more (and earlier) legal certainty. Secondly, an 'alternative' amnesty could be granted, on certain conditions, even if the company came forward after an investigation had started. Thirdly, it was decided that amnesty would be granted automatically to all employees of the successful applicants.

[400] GR Spratling, DJ Arp and AJ Shepard, 'The Increasing Globalization of International Cartel Enforcement', Antitrust Report, Spring 2004.

[401] Whilst from the passage of the Sherman Act in 1890 to August 1998, when the new leniency policy was adopted, only eight non-US companies had been prosecuted for cartel activity in the United States, 72 non-US companies had been prosecuted on similar grounds by August 2003. See ibid.

[402] [1994] OJ L243/1.

[403] In a very succinct press release, the Commission stated '[i]n its uneasy fight against cartels which becomes more sophisticated every day, the Commission has [. . .] decided, under these circumstances, to either reduce or drop fines for companies which inform the Commission of certain types of secret cartels'. See IP/96/629.

[404] The European Parliament ('EP') criticised the very concept of leniency and expressed doubts as to its compatibility with the fundamental principles of EC law. In its Resolution on the XXVIth Competition Policy report, the EP stated in particular that 'it [could] neither accept the contents nor the form of the [1996 Leniency Notice]' and called upon 'a legally binding instrument duly tak[ing] account of the legal traditions of the majority of the Member States' (see XXVIIth Competition Policy Report, p 351). In the European context, where cartel behaviour had long been considered benign if not simply morally justifiable, certain policy makers were reluctant to recognise the legitimacy of a 'trade-off' policy which they considered morally unacceptable. As for certain members of the business community, they considered that 'breaking rank' amounted to a kind of betrayal running counter to an unwritten 'code of honour'.

of the phenomenon, initial reservations faded. The business community also seemed to undergo a complete change of attitude, possibly as a result of the rapid evolution of corporate culture due to globalisation, but no doubt equally from a greater awareness of the considerable risks incurred due to the increasingly high fines imposed. Such a change of mind also facilitated the revision of the Commission's leniency policy after six years of application, which led to the adoption in 2002 of a new Notice intended to provide even greater incentives to companies to co-operate. The 2002 Leniency Notice has in turn been amended, with the publication of a revised Notice on 8 December 2006, incorporating small but significant changes aimed at further reinforcing its effectiveness ('the 2006 Leniency Notice').[405]

8.112 Detailed descriptions of the 2002 Leniency Notice as amended in 2006 and the 1996 Leniency Notice are given below. As at 31 December 2005 the Commission had received 167 applications under the 2002 Leniency Notice. Eighty-seven applications had been dealt with as applications for immunity and 80 as applications for a reduction of fine. Fifty-one conditional immunity decisions had been granted.[406] By 31 December 2006, only six cartel decisions based on the 2002 Leniency Notice had been adopted, not all of which had been made publicly available.[407] In view of the fact that the Commission is, at the time of writing, still issuing certain cartel decisions based on the 1996 Leniency Notice,[408] the provisions of the 1996 Leniency Notice are considered in detail below.

(b) The 1996 Leniency Notice

(i) Content of the 1996 Leniency Notice

8.113 **Basic principles**   The 1996 Leniency Notice distinguished three degrees of co-operation. These were described in Sections B, C and D, and provided for decreasing, non-overlapping ranges of reductions in the level of the fines to be imposed. Each Section listed a number of cumulative requirements to be fulfilled by applicants. Section E clarified certain procedural aspects. The underlying rationale of the scheme was that a company could expect a reduction in the fine which would otherwise have been imposed in proportion to the value of its co-operation. Thus, the first company to submit decisive evidence of a cartel could qualify

---

[405] Commission Notice on Immunity from fines and reduction of fines in cartel cases, [2006] OJ C298/17. The 2006 Leniency Notice replaced the 2002 Leniency Notice from the date of its publication on 8 December 2006 for all cartel cases in which no undertaking has contacted the Commision in order to take advantage of the favourable treatment set out in that notice (see point 37 of the 2006 Leniency Notice).

[406] In cases where several applications were received in relation to the same infringement, the first application was considered as an application for immunity and the others as applications for a reduction of fine, unless the first application was rejected, in which case the second application was considered as an application for immunity. See P Lowe, 'La lutte contre les cartels et la politique de clémence', speech at the European Competition Forum, Brussels, 28 April 2006, published in Concurrences, issue 3 (2006).

[407] *Rubber Chemicals* (IP/05/1656), *Raw Tobacco Italy* (IP/05/1315, decision of 20 October 2005, full text of the decision available on DG COMP's web site), *Hydrogen Peroxide and Perborate* (IP/06/560), *Methacrylates* (IP/05/1315), *Bitumen Netherlands* (IP/06/1179), *Synthetic Rubber* (IP/06/1647).

[408] See eg the Commission decision of 20 September 2006 imposing a global fine of EUR 314.7 million to the *Copper Fittings* cartel, where the 1996 Leniency Notice was applied. The 1996 Leniency Notice is applicable when at least one undertaking involved in the cartel had contacted the Commission in order to take advantage of the leniency policy prior to the date of adoption of the 2002 Leniency Notice, ie prior to 14 February 2002. See point 28 of the 2002 Leniency Notice.

for a 'substantial' reduction in the fine (a least 50 per cent) provided the Commission was not already in the possession of such evidence. This reduction could rise to a 'very substantial' reduction, or even complete immunity from fines (100 per cent reduction) provided that no inspection had already been carried out at the time of the submission. As for subsequent applicants, they could still hope to benefit from 'significant' reductions of their fines depending on the importance of their contribution to the investigation.

Section B: from 75–100 per cent reduction (total exemption) from the fine   In order to qualify for a reduction in its fine from 75–100 per cent the applicant was expected to fulfil five cumulative conditions, namely: (a) to be *the first to report* a cartel to the Commission *before* it had carried out inspections (ordered by decision) at the premises of suspected participants; (b) to be the first to *adduce decisive evidence* of the cartel's existence;[409] (c) to have *terminated involvement* in the cartel at the time of disclosure; (d) to *provide all the relevant information and evidence* available to it regarding the cartel and maintain *continuous and complete co-operation* throughout the investigation; and (e) *not to have acted as an instigator of, or played a determining role in the cartel or compelled* another company to take part in it.   **8.114**

Section C: from 50–75 per cent reduction in the fine   Companies which satisfied the conditions set out in Section B, points (b) to (e), but which disclosed the secret cartel only *after* the Commission had carried out an inspection (ordered by decision) at the premises of (at least one of) the cartel participants could benefit from a reduction of 50–75 per cent of the fine. This was on the condition that the inspections in question had failed to provide sufficient grounds for initiating a procedure leading to a decision.   **8.115**

Section D: reductions from 10–50 per cent of the fine   Companies which co-operated with the Commission without fulfilling all the conditions set out in Sections B or C could still benefit from a significant reduction in their fine under section D. Two specific situations were distinguished. First, where a company had provided the Commission, *before a Statement of Objections was sent*, with information, documents or other evidence which materially contributed to establishing the existence of the infringement. Secondly, where a company, *after receiving a Statement of Objections*, informed the Commission that it 'd[id] not substantially contest the facts on which the Commission bas[ed] its allegations'.[410] However, the Commission did not specify the differential in the reductions of fines to be expected under each type of co-operation.   **8.116**

Procedural aspects (Section E)   The Commission made the following procedural rules: only persons authorised to represent the company for that purpose could apply for leniency; the Commission would only determine which section of the notice the applicant would benefit from in the final decision;[411] although the notice would create legitimate   **8.117**

---

[409] Implying that the Commission did not already have sufficient information to establish the existence of the alleged cartel.

[410] This established, in practice, a distinction between 'active' co-operation (before the sending of the Statement of Objections), and 'passive' co-operation (merely consisting of the company refraining from contesting the facts as set out in the Statement of Objections).

[411] The Commission indicated in the notice that this was justified by the fact that the conditions of eligibility applied throughout the entire administrative procedure. Another reason was that during the administrative procedure the Commission's services could not take a decision binding the College of Commissioners.

expectations on which companies could rely, failure to meet any of the requirements of Sections B and C would result in the loss of the favourable treatment set out therein;[412] benefit from leniency could not protect a company from the civil law consequences of its participation in an illegal agreement, and each company should be aware that the role played by it in the cartel would be described in full in the final decision; and finally, the Commission indicated that if a company subsequently contested facts in proceedings before the CFI which were formerly uncontested in front of the Commission, the Commission would 'normally ask that court to increase the fine imposed on that enterprise' if the company had benefited from a previous reduction under Section D.

(ii) Application of the 1996 Leniency Notice

8.118   **Tangible results**   Whilst a number of other factors may explain the intensification of the Commission's anti-cartel activity since the late 1990s (see para 8.10 above), the adoption of a leniency policy has undoubtedly been a major contributor. As at 31 December 2006, the Commission had applied the 1996 Leniency Notice in no less than 37 formal decisions with fines, out of a total of 47 cartel decisions adopted since 1 January 1998.[413] As compared to the overall amount of fines imposed, the 'value' of the overall reductions in fines granted corresponds to an average reduction per case of approximately 40 per cent, showing that the leniency policy provides tangible benefits for companies that choose to co-operate with the Commission.[414]

8.119   **Section B: a trend towards the granting of 100 per cent reductions**   The 1996 Leniency Notice was applied to cartel cases where a first leniency application was made within a time period of some six years (July 1996–February 2002). As at 1 October 2006, 18 undertakings had qualified for a reduction in their fine under Section B.[415] These 18 cases corresponded

---

[412]   In such circumstances, however, a company could still benefit from a reduction in the fine under Section D.

[413]   Excluding cases where the 2002 Leniency Notice has been applied.

[414]   See eg F Arbault and F Peiro 'The Commission's new notice on immunity and reduction of fines in cartel cases: building on success', Competition, Policy Newsletter, Number 2 (2002) and C Veljanovski 'Cartel Fines in Europe—Law, Practice and Deterrence', World Competition (2007), available at SSRN: http://ssrn.com/abstract=920786. Nevertheless, statistics should not be misinterpreted. Individual reductions granted ranged from total immunity from fines (100% reduction) to only small reductions (10%). Whilst a small number of companies received very favourable treatment because of the decisive importance of the evidence provided and their early co-operation, many other applicants received only a 10% reduction of their fine because their co-operation was limited to not substantially contesting the facts as set out in the Statement of Objections, rather than actively co-operating with the Commission.

[415]   The undertakings were Fujisawa (*Sodium Gluconate*, IP/01/1355), Aventis (*Vitamins* [2003] OJ L6/1), Cerestar (*Citric Acid* [2002] OJ L239/18), Brasserie de Luxembourg (*Luxembourg Brewers* [2002] OJ L253/21), Sappi (*Carbonless Paper* [2004] OJ L115/1), Aventis (*Methionine* [2003] OJ L255/1), Christie's (*Fine Arts Auction Houses* [2005] OJ L200/92, full text of the decision available on DG COMP's website), Merck (*Methylglucamine* [2004] OJ L38/18), Takeda (*Food Flavour Enhancers* [2004] OJ L75/1), UCAR (*Specialty Graphite*, IP/02/1906, full text of the decision available on DG COMP's web site), Chisso (*Sorbates* [2005] OJ L182/20, full text of the decision available on DG COMP's web site), Morgan (*Electrical and Mechanical Carbon and Graphite Products* [2004] OJ L125/45, full text of the decision available on DG COMP's web site), Akzo (*Organic Peroxides* [2005] OJ L110/44, full text of the decision available on DG COMP's web site), Müller (*Copper Plumbing Tubes*, IP/04/1065, full text of the decision available on DG COMP's web site), Entaco (*Raw Tobacco Spain*, IP/04/1256, full text of the decision available on DG COMP's web site), Clariant (*MCAA*, IP/05/61), BPI (*Industrial Bags*, IP/05/1508), and Müller (*Copper Fittings*, IP/06/1222).

to roughly half of the 38 formal prohibition decisions in which the 1996 Leniency Notice had been applied by that date. It seems possible to identify an evolution in the Commission's and/or the undertakings' practice(s). Until 1 August 2002 (the date by which half of the 38 decisions where the 1996 Leniency Notice was applied had been adopted), the benefit from Section B had been granted in only six out of the 19 cartel decisions under the 1996 Leniency Notice (out of 21 cartel decisions where the 1996 Leniency Notice could have been applied).[416] Only three companies had benefited from a 100 per cent reduction in their fine, whilst two others benefited respectively from only 80 per cent and 90 per cent reductions because their co-operation had not been entirely of their own initiative (they had approached the Commission only after having received specific requests for information).[417] Over the following four years (August 2002–1 October 2006),[418] the 1996 Leniency Notice was applied in nearly all 18 cartel decisions[419] and the Commission granted the benefit of Section B in 12 out of the 17 decisions where the Notice was applied. All 11 companies which qualified under Section B received complete immunity from fines (100 per cent reduction). This suggests that after an initial period of reluctance to come forward voluntarily, cartel participants began to realise the possibilities offered by the 1996 Leniency Notice and decided to take advantage by coming forward *before* the Commission was made aware of the cartel. For its part, the Commission proved its determination to meet the expectations of applicants and did not hesitate to grant *complete* immunity from fines where all relevant conditions were met.

Section C: almost unused   Out of 38 cases in which the 1996 Leniency Notice had been **8.120** applied by 1 October 2006, only one company had benefited from section C (50–75 per cent reduction for an application filed after inspections).[420] Although surprising at first sight, this may be considered positively from the Commission's point of view because it seems to highlight the effectiveness of the Commission's investigative powers. Indeed, it would appear that even in cases where the Commission had not received evidence from a 'Section B' applicant prior to the conduct of its inspections, dawn raids did generally result in the collection of 'decisive evidence', thereby depriving potential applicants of the possibility of benefiting from Section C. Companies deciding to co-operate after on-the-spot investigations were often only left with the possibility of benefiting from a 'significant' reduction in their fine under Section D.

Section D: reductions for 'active' co-operation   It is difficult to draw general conclusions **8.121** from the Commission's broad practice of granting reductions for 'active' co-operation

---

[416]   The 1996 Leniency Notice was not applied in *FEG/TU* [2000] OJ L39/1, *German Banks* [2003] OJ L15/1.

[417]   The three undertakings which received a 100% reduction were Rhône-Poulenc (now Aventis), with regard to two of the three infringements in which it was found to have participated in *Vitamins* [2003] OJ L6/1; Brasserie de Luxembourg (a subsidiary of Interbrew) in *Luxembourg Brewers* [2002] OJ L253/21, and Sappi, in *Carbonless Paper* [2004] OJ L115/1. Two undertakings benefited from a very substantial reduction in their fines for their decisive co-operation under Section B, namely Fujisawa in *Sodium Gluconate* (80% reduction) and Cerestar Bioproducts in *Citric Acid* [2002] OJ L239/18 (90% reduction).

[418]   The 1996 Leniency Notice was replaced by a new Notice on 14 February 2002, but continued to be applied in all cases where at least one undertaking contacted the Commission for the purpose of benefiting from the leniency policy prior to 14 February 2002.

[419]   With the noticeable exception of *French Beef* [2003] OJ L209/12.

[420]   Showa Denko received a 70% reduction of its fine in *Graphite Electrodes* [2002] OJ L100/1.

under Section D. The evaluation of each applicant's contribution to the investigation of the case has been done on a 'case by case' basis,[421] and the reductions of fine imposed, resulting from an evaluation of the value of each applicant's cooperation in both 'absolute' and 'relative' terms, have varied from 10 per cent to 50 per cent.[422] The reductions varied according to the timing of the co-operation, as well as to the nature and degree of detail of the information supplied. Timing has clearly played a significant role in the percentage of reduction obtained, on the basis that the information initially supplied was substantial enough to be taken into consideration. Continuity of co-operation has also played an important role. However, when applicants have been able to supply the Commission with evidence of great value this has generally been taken into account even if the applicant concerned was not the first to come forward.

8.122 **Section D: reductions for 'passive' co-operation**   In several decisions, the Commission seems to have implicitly taken into account the fact that applicants had not substantially contested the facts by granting them a 50 per cent reduction under Section D despite the Commission refering solely to their 'active' co-operation.[423] When applicants were found to have limited their co-operation to not contesting the facts the Commission has generally granted a reduction of 10 per cent, although in two early decisions, *Seamless Steel Tubes*[424] and *Greek Ferries*, it granted a 20 per cent reduction on the same grounds. The Commission has refused to grant a reduction for non-contestation when the company has contested an important factual aspect of the infringement as described in the Statement of Objections, such as duration of the cartel, or when the Commission has considered that the company has limited its non-contestation to those facts which it had itself brought to the attention of the Commission (*Belgian Beer*).[425]

---

[421]   The CFI has determined that the mere fact that the Commission had granted a certain rate of reduction in previous decisions for specific conduct did not imply that it was required to grant the same proportionate reduction when assessing similar conduct in a subsequent administrative procedure, as each case must be assessed on its own merits (Case T-31/99 *ABB Asea Brown Boveri v Commission* [2002] ECR II-1881). See para 8.233 below.

[422]   Section D did not establish a distinction between the percentages of reduction to be granted for 'active' and 'passive' co-operation. It seemed however that one could deduce from the wording of the Notice, in which the Commission mentioned both the maximum and the minimum percentages of reduction that could be expected under Section D (50% and 10%), that 'active' co-operation could be rewarded by a maximum 40% reduction, which together with the 10% reduction associated with the non-contestation of the facts would reflect the maximum reduction available under Section D (50%). Initially, however, the Commission's practice was not entirely clear. In certain early decisions the Commission granted a 50% reduction in consideration of what seemed to solely correspond to 'active' co-operation, without bothering to specify whether it had also taken into consideration the fact that the applicant had not substantially contested the facts (see, *inter alia*, *Amino Acids* [2001] OJ L152/24, *Graphite Electrodes* [2002] OJ L100/1, *Citric Acid* [2002] OJ L239/18). This lack of precision could be seen as problematic since it appeared that 'active' co-operation did not necessarily imply 'passive' co-operation. For instance, in *Belgian Beer* [2003] OJ L200/1, the Commission granted a 10% reduction to Danone in consideration of its (limited) 'active' co-operation, whilst refusing to grant the latter a reduction for 'passive' co-operation, because it considered that Danone had contested the facts as set out in the Statement of Objections. However, in later decisions, the Commission expressly stated that the overall percentage of reduction reflected both the 'active' and 'passive' co-operation of the applicant (see, *inter alia*, *Methionine*, *Industrial and Medical Gases*, *Plasterboard*, *Food Flavour Enhancers*, *Sorbates*, *Organic Peroxides*, and *Industrial Tubes*). This would suggest that 'active' co-operation can indeed be rewarded by a maximum reduction of 40%.

[423]   See n 422, above.

[424]   [2003] OJ L140/1.

[425]   [2003] OJ L 200/1.

(iii) Issues Regarding the Effectiveness of the 1996 Leniency Notice

The Commission's 1996 Leniency Notice proved to be effective when combined with the **8.123** Commission's other investigative tools. Nevertheless, experience of its day to day implementation revealed that a number of factors prevented the policy from fully developing its potential, both in the reporting of undetected cartels and the establishment of the evidence required for the adoption of final decisions.

Difficulty of obtaining early information on undetected cartels The mere knowledge of **8.124** the existence of a cartel has an intrinsic value since the Commission has effective investigative tools at its disposal. It should also be in the interest of potential leniency applicants to cooperate as early as possible in order to maximise their chances for qualifying for a 100 per cent reduction. In spite of this, it appears that under the 1996 Leniency Notice cartels have rarely reported to the Commission prior to the start of an investigation. A seemingly widespread concern among companies was a perceived uncertainty with regard to their final treatment under the 1996 Leniency Notice which resulted in a reluctance to come forward spontaneously.[426]

Sub-optimal contribution to the collection of valuable evidence The 1996 Leniency **8.125** Notice did not contribute in a fully satisfactory manner to the uncovering and collection of decisive evidence of an infringement. An application was generally filed only once the company felt that it had little choice because an investigation had already been opened against it.[427] When applications were filed rather late in the course of the proceedings, the 'surprise effect' of confronting other cartel members with incriminating evidence was often lost, and some applicants limited themselves to confirming what the Commission was already aware of, without bringing any significant added value to the Commission's investigation. This reflected a defensive attitude consisting of attempting to limit the damage of what appeared to be an unavoidable outcome. As the imposition of a fine became increasingly likely, filing an application at a late stage in the proceedings, whilst maintaining an ambiguous stance

---

[426] Three causal factors were identified. First, neither DG COMP nor the Commissioner in charge of competition could make a formal prior commitment to the leniency applicant, since the final prohibition decision is taken by the College of Commissioners. Undertakings therefore considered that they did not have sufficient guarantees that the Commission would, at the end of the process, grant the total immunity provided in Section B of the notice. Secondly, there was an apparent 'double' requirement in Section B of the 1996 Leniency Notice—an applicant not only had to be (i) the *first* to apply, but also needed to (ii) produce *decisive evidence* of the infringement. Thus, supplying evidence which was not decisive disqualified the applicant, and providing this 'decisive evidence' after the Commission was in possession of this type of material also prevented the applicant from qualifying. This was seen as placing potential applicants in an 'untenable' position, especially in view of the lack of clarity as to the 'decisive evidence requirement'. The fact that under Section B the Commission retained a certain amount of discretion to determine the applicable reduction within a band (75–100% reduction) reinforced this level of uncertainty and may have fuelled some scepticism on the part of industry. A third factor was the fact that the 1996 Leniency Notice excluded from Section B any undertaking which had played 'a determining role in the illegal activity', so that undertakings that had been major cartel players were unsure whether they could actually qualify. This provision, aimed at excluding ringleaders from full immunity, was perceived to be too wide-ranging, discouraging spontaneous and early applications by companies which had had a significant role in the cartel and which feared that they would ultimately be excluded from the benefit of this section of the Notice.

[427] Experience showed that many companies filed an application once they discovered that the Commission was already aware of the main aspects of a case (generally upon receipt of a very detailed request for information).

and providing the Commission with a minimum amount of 'usable' evidence seemed to be a conscious strategy in certain cases.

(c) The 2002 Leniency Notice and its 2006 revision

8.126   In the 1996 Leniency Notice the Commission had stated that, as soon as it had acquired sufficient experience of its application, it would consider modifying its policy if necessary. Almost six years after its adoption, and on the basis of the lessons drawn from its application in 16 cases, the Commission adopted a new Notice, introducing significant changes in its policy. Nearly five years later, small but significant changes were made to the 2002 Leniency Notice, resulting in the publication of a revised notice, the 2006 Leniency Notice.

(i) Principles Governing the Revision of the 1996 Leniency Notice

8.127   The revision of the 1996 Leniency Notice was intended to tackle the issues identified from experience of the application of the 1996 Notice. First, it was thought necessary to grant a very significant reward, upfront, to the first company enabling the Commission to take a decisive step in the prosecution of a cartel. Secondly, the level of the reduction in fines granted to subsequent applicants was to be related to the real added value of their co-operation. Thirdly, the Commission sought to introduce more legal certainty in the system and to render it more transparent.[428]

8.128   **Full immunity: a major incentive to report or contribute to prove a cartel**   In order to maximise the incentive to co-operate fully and to do so at the earliest possible stage of an investigation, the Commission decided to provide conditional immunity, immediately and in writing, to the first company to come forward with enough evidence to enable the Commission to start an investigation by adopting a decision ordering a surprise inspection. The minimum threshold to qualify for immunity when the cartel was undetected was therefore significantly lower than in the 1996 Leniency Notice where the test was the supply of 'decisive evidence'.

8.129   However, in situations where the Commission had already started an investigation but had not gathered sufficient evidence to find an infringement of Article 81 EC, the provision of such information would still be of crucial interest to the Commission, in spite of its prior knowledge of the cartel. Hence, the first company to provide evidence 'enabling the Commission to find an infringement of Article 81 EC' could also qualify for a full immunity from fines, even if an investigation had already started. The Commission was also aware that granting immunity is a very significant derogation from the imposition of fines in the case of the most serious violations of competition law. It was therefore decided that only one undertaking, the first one to meet either of the two criteria, would be granted immunity from fines in any given cartel case.

8.130   **Alignment of the reductions of fines to the real value of the co-operation**   Once the Commission has granted immunity to an applicant, or has itself obtained sufficient evidence to find an infringement under Article 81 EC, there may still be justification for

---

[428] See press release on the adoption of the 2002 Leniency Notice: IP/02/247 and the associated 'Questions and Answers' memo: MEMO/02/223.

reducing the fines imposed on subsequent applicants that provide information within the framework of the investigation. It was nevertheless thought that the magnitude of the reduction granted should reflect the effective contribution to the investigation. Therefore, in order to qualify for a reduction, applicants should provide the Commission with evidence representing 'significant added value' when compared with the evidence already in the Commission's possession at the time of the submission. As the relative added value of any evidence submitted diminishes as more undertakings apply for reduction, it was decided that when the Commission approached the conclusion of the investigation, the band within which the reduction in fines should be determined ought also to depend on whether the applicant was the first, second, third or subsequent undertaking to meet the criterion of 'significant added value'.

The Commission also took steps to deal with the concern that potential leniency applicants **8.131** would be discouraged from coming forward, fearing that the same information which led to a reward would at the same time increase the potential level of the fine to which they would be exposed.[429] In order to tackle this issue, the Commission adopted the principle that where an applicant provides evidence of facts previously unknown to the Commission, which have a direct bearing on the gravity or duration of the suspected cartel, the Commission will not take those elements into account when setting the level of the fine to be imposed on that applicant.

Greater certainty and transparency An important concern for the Commission was to **8.132** increase certainty and transparency for potential applicants. Not only did the Commission decide that it would grant at a very early stage, and in writing, conditional immunity from fines to the successful applicant, but it also took other measures to promote legal certainty. The Commission also decided to adopt a more restrictive definition of the criteria leading to the exclusion of an applicant from any immunity by narrowing the scope of the notion of 'ringleader' of the cartel. Another means of increasing legal certainty was to provide immunity applicants with the opportunity to check with the Commission on an anonymous basis and in hypothetical terms whether the kind of information in their possession would indeed qualify.

Not surprisingly, the Commission decided not to grant subsequent applicants as much **8.133** upfront certainty as the first (immunity) applicant. In order to qualify for a reduction, the subsequent applicant must provide the Commission with evidence representing 'significant added value'. This notion is not straightforward because of the 'relative' nature of its content, and, consequently, the Commission can only assess whether this test is passed by reference to the information already in its possession. Nevertheless, it was decided that applicants for a reduction in fine would also benefit from increased transparency as compared with the previous practice: they would be informed of the band within which the Commission would determine the applicable reduction no later than on the date on which the Statement of Objections is sent (rather than in the final decision as was formerly the case).

---

[429] For example, a leniency applicant could be deterred from supplying evidence of a cartel of longer duration or wider geographical scope than the Commission was aware of because of the automatic increase in the fine this might trigger.

(ii) Changes introduced in the 2006 Leniency Notice

8.134 **Small but significant amendments** After nearly five years of implementation of the 2002 Leniency Notice and following a public consultation, the Commission adopted a new Leniency Notice in December 2006. Rather than introducing a radical change in the Commision's approach to leniency, the 2006 Leniency Notice consists of a limited revision of the 2002 Leniency Notice, incorporating small but nonetheless significant changes, drawing lessons from the experience gained, and aimed at further reinforcing the effectiveness of the programme.

8.135 **Five main changes** Have been introduced in the 2006 Leniency Notice. First, the two immunity thresholds have been clarified to set out more clearly what type of information and evidence the applicants must submit to qualify for immunity. Secondly, as regards application for reductions in fines, the Commission has clarified that only evidence that requires little or no corroboration has a particularly great value which may be rewarded outside of the normal bands provided that the applicable conditions are met. Thirdly, the general conditions to be complied with by leniency applicants have been made more explicit. Fourthly, a discretionary marker system has been introduced with respect to immunity applications. Finally, the Commision has developed a procedure to protect corporate statements given under the 2006 Leniency Notice from discovery in civil damages procedures.[430]

(iii) Content and Implementation of the 2002 and 2006 Leniency Notices

8.136 The 2002 and 2006 Leniency Notices are still almost identical in substance. However, certain important changes have been introduced in the 2006 Leniency Notice. As a significant number of cartel cases are still to be decided by the Commission under the rules set out in the 2002 Leniency Notice, it remains appropriate to highlight the specificities of each Notice.

8.137 Both the 2002 and 2006 Leniency Notices comprise two distinct sections. Sections A of the 2002 Leniency Notice and II of the 2006 Leniency Notice deal with *immunity* from fines, and sections B of the 2002 Leniency Notice and III of the 2006 Leniency Notice with *reductions* in fines. Both sections explain in detail the applicable substantive test and the corresponding procedure.

(iv) Immunity under the 2002 and 2006 Leniency Notices

8.138 1. **Substantive tests** One of two alternative tests must be satisfied in order to qualify for conditional immunity from fines. Both are set out in point 8 of each Notice and are generally known as '8(a)' or '8(b)' tests.

8.139 *'8(a)' test* Pursuant to point 8(a) of the 2002 Leniency Notice, an applicant could qualify for immunity if it was the first to 'submit evidence which in the Commission's view may enable it to adopt a decision to carry out an investigation in the sense of Article 14(3) of Regulation 17' (the reference to Article 14(3) of Regulation 17 is now understood as a reference

---

[430] See IP/06/1705, as well as MEMO/06/469 and MEMO 06/470.

to Article 20(4) of Regulation 1/2003). In the 2006 Leniency Notice, the Commission has slightly changed the formulation of the '8(a)' test, in that it now reads that the applicant must be the first to submit '*information* and evidence which in the Commission's view enable it to carry out a *targeted* inspection in connection with the alleged cartel' (emphasis added).

This reflects a desire on the part of the Commission to ensure that the information submit-   **8.140** ted as a counterpart to conditional immunity will in effect enable the Commission to carry out inspections with a sufficient likelihood of success. The applicant should be in a position to provide the Commission with such 'insider' information on the cartel that would allow the Commission to better target its inspection with more precise information as to, for instance, what to look for and where in terms of evidence.

The Commission has listed in point 9 of the 2006 Leniency Notice what the applicant   **8.141** should provide in order to enable it to carry out a targeted inspection, 'to the extent that this, in the Commision's view, would not jeopardize the inspections'. This includes: (a) a corporate statement and (b) other evidence relating to the alleged cartel in possession of the applicant or available to it at the time of the submission, including in particular any evidence contemporaneous to the infringement.

Pursuant to point 9(a) of the 2006 Leniency Notice, the corporate statement to be submit-   **8.142** ted should include, insofar as it is known to the applicant at the time of the submission: (i) a detailed description of the alleged cartel arrangement, including, for instance, its aims, activities and functioning; the product or service concerned, the geographic scope, the duration of and the estimated market volumes affected by the alleged cartel; the specific dates, locations, content of and participants in alleged cartel contacts, and all relevant explanations in connection with the pieces of evidence provided in support of the application; (ii) the name and address of the legal entity submitting the immunity application as well as the names and addresses of all the other undertakings that participate(d) in the alleged cartel; (iii) the names, positions, office locations and, where necessary, home addresses of all individuals who, to the applicant's knowledge, are or have been involved in the alleged cartel, including those individuals who have been involved on the applicant's behalf; and (iv) information on which other competition authorities, inside or outside the EU, have been approached or are intended to be approached in relation to the alleged cartel.

'8(b)' test Alternatively, pursuant to point 8(b), an applicant may qualify for immunity   **8.143** if it is the first to 'submit evidence which in the Commission's view may enable it to find an infringement of Article 81 EC in connection with the alleged cartel'. That evidence may be submitted either before or after the start of an investigation. If evidence is submitted after the launch of an inquiry, the fact that the Commission has already conducted an investigation, or is in a position to do so without there being an '8(a)' type applicant, does not necessarily disqualify the applicant. However, in order for the applicant to be able to obtain immunity at a later stage of the Commission's investigation it must supply information enabling the Commission to find an infringement under Article 81 EC which the Commission had not been able to establish until then. This requirement is therefore more demanding than that of '8(a)': applicants are expected to give very concrete and direct evidence of the infringement in question. In the 2006 Leniency Notice, the Commission has

clarified that in order to qualify, the applicant 'must be the first to provide contemporaneous, incriminating evidence of the alleged cartel as well as a corporate statement containing the kind of information specified in point (9)(a), which would enable the Commission to find an infringement of Article 81 EC'.[431]

8.144   *Only one immunity per cartel*   There can only be one successful immunity applicant per infringement. If the Commission has already granted conditional immunity from fines under 8(a), no further applicant is eligible for immunity under 8(b), even if the Commission is still not in possession of evidence enabling it to find an infringement under Article 81 EC.[432] However, should an undertaking be willing to come forward and supply such evidence, it may receive a significant reduction in its fine (to the maximum of 50 per cent) under the leniency procedure (Section B, discussed further below) and, where appropriate, the information will not be used against it.

8.145   **2. Other conditions which must be satisfied in order to qualify for immunity**   In accordance with point 11(a) of the 2002 Leniency Notice, immunity applicants were under a general obligation to co-operate 'fully, on a continuous basis and expeditiously with the Commission throughout the Commission's administrative procedure'. An applicant had therefore the obligation to provide the Commission with 'all evidence that [came] into its possession or [was] available to it relating to the suspected infringement'. This implied, in particular, that an immunity applicant had to supply the *entirety* of the evidence available to it at the time of its initial submission, that is, not only to the extent necessary to satisfy '8(a)' test.[433] The content of the requirements under point 11(a) of the 2002 Leniency Notice has been further clarified in what is now point 12 of the 2006 Leniency Notice.

8.146   Under points 12 and 13 of the 2006 Leniency Notice, and in addition to the specific requirements set out in points 8(a), 9 and 10 or 8(b) and 11, an applicant must meet five

---

[431] Point 11 of the 2006 Leniency Notice. The content of the 'corporate statement specified in point 9(a)' is set out in fn 469 below, at para 8.172.

[432] Point 11 of the 2006 Leniency Notice provides that '[i]mmunity pursuant to (8)(b) will only be granted on the cumulative conditions that the Commission did not have, at the time of the submission, sufficient evidence to find an infringement of Article 81 EC in connection with the alleged cartel and that no undertaking had been granted conditional immunity from fines under point (8)(a) in connection with the alleged cartel.

[433] Already before the publication of the 2006 Leniency Notice, the duty to fully co-operate seemed to be construed widely by DG Competition officials. It was publicly stated that there was an obligation for the immunity applicant to search actively for any piece of evidence relating to the infringement and to communicate it to the Commission. The applicant should look for, and supply, any element and fact relating to the infringement, concerning both its own participation and that of the other members of the cartel. The applicant was also required to be able to testify, upon requirement, to all the initiatives taken to that effect, to all sources that were used to collect relevant information, and to all measures taken to prevent the destruction or concealment of any relevant piece of evidence. The applicant was also expected to ensure that any person informed, directly or indirectly, of the relevant facts was interviewed and that the outcome of these interviews was reported to the Commission. In case of contradictory statements, the Commission expected to be informed of the various accounts given. The immunity applicant also had to be prepared to be subjected to an inspection should it be deemed necessary by the Commission. See F Laina, 'L'intensification de la lutte contre les cartels: Quelques observations sur les amendes et le fonctionnement du programme de clémence', Speech at the European Competition Forum, Brussels, 28 April 2006, published in Concurrences, issue 3 (2006).

cumulative conditions. The applicant must first, genuinely, fully, continuously and expeditiously co-operate with the Commission throughout the administrative procedure; secondly, end its involvement in the alleged cartel; thirdly, not have, when contemplating its application, destroyed, falsified or concealed evidence; fourthly, not have disclosed its intention to file a leniency application, and, finally, not have taken steps to coerce other undertakings to remain in it.

Duty to co-operate genuinely, fully, on a continuous basis and expeditiously   The duty to   **8.147**
co-operate genuinely, fully, on a continuous basis and expeditiously throughout the administrative procedure includes the following obligations:

- providing the Commission promptly with all relevant information and evidence relating to the alleged cartel that comes into its possession or is available to it;
- remaining at the Commission's disposal to answer promptly any request that may contribute to the establishment of the facts;
- making current (and, if possible, former) employees and directors available for interviews with the Commission;
- not destroying, falsifying or concealing relevant information or evidence relating to the alleged cartel; and
- not disclosing the fact or any of the content of its application before the Commission has issued a Statement of Objections in the case, unless otherwise agreed.

Obligation not to reveal immunity application without the Commission's approval   It is   **8.148**
worth emphasising that the duty to co-operate fully includes the obligation not to reveal to third parties the existence of the immunity application, without prior approval from the Commission. A violation of this obligation would disqualify the applicant from immunity as this would severely undermine the effectiveness of the Commission's investigative powers. The Commission has stated in particular that it is aware that publicly listed companies may be subject to legal obligations regarding information to be given to financial stakeholders, but that it will nevertheless not permit any disclosure by the applicant before the Commission has taken the relevant investigative steps (whenever possible, the Commission carries out surprise inspections within a few weeks of an application).[434] However the Commission is more open to allowing disclosure once inspections have taken place.

The Commission first revoked a decision of conditional immunity from fines in *Raw*   **8.149**
Tobacco Italy. In that case, Deltafina was originally granted conditional immunity from fines, but the Commission later found that it had failed to comply with its duty of full co-operation under point 11(a). During the hearing it became clear that before the Commission carried out its on-the-spot inspections Deltafina had disclosed to the other cartel members the fact that it had applied for immunity.[435] Whilst observing that Deltafina had drawn attention to the potential difficulty of keeping the information secret before the investigation could take place, the Commission noted that Deltafina had chosen not to inform the Commission that it had revealed its immunity application to the

---

[434] B Van Barlingen and M Barennes, 'The European Commission's Leniency Notice in Practice', Competition Policy Newsletter, issue No 3, Autumn 2005, pp 12–13.
[435] Decision of 20 October 2005 (full text of the decision available on DG COMP's web site), paras 408–460.

other cartel members. The Commission revoked Deltafina's conditional immunity from fines and refused to consider its application as an application for a reduction in its fine under Section B of the 2002 Leniency Notice instead, although Deltafina did benefit from a reduction of 50 per cent of the basic amount of its fine in recognition of the attenuating circumstance that it had co-operated with the Commission beyond the scope of the 2002 Leniency Notice (see para 8.758).[436]

8.150 *Obligation to end involvement in the cartel* Under point 12(b) of the 2006 Leniency Notice, there is an obligation that the immunity applicant 'ended its involvement in the alleged cartel immediately following its application'. The same obligation existed under point 11(b) of the 2002 Leniency Notice. However, the Commision has specified in the 2006 Leniency Notice that this obligation applies 'except for what would, in the Commision's view, be reasonably necessary to preserve the integrity of the inspections'. This shows that the Commission had to strike a delicate balance between the logical requirement to cease the infringing conduct and the need to ensure the efficacy of its investigations. It is obviously extremely important to ensure that the other members of the cartel do not realise too soon that one of them has blown the whistle. In the case of an infringement that is ongoing at the time of the application, such awareness might be the result of one cartel member abruptly ending its participation without there being a valid alternative explanation. On the other hand, active continued participation in the cartel could not be allowed, if not from a moral perspective, at any rate because the Commission might expose itself to accusations of condoning continued harm to customers. In cases where there is a risk of creating suspicion among other cartel members, the Commission may discuss with the applicant appropriate solutions that would still fall within the obligation to end the infringement. Therefore the Commission might not oppose the suggestion that an undertaking, for instance, will simply abstain from any active form of participation until after an investigation has commenced, at which point its withdrawal from any illicit contacts has to be complete.[437] Where an undertaking does not break off all cartel contacts, and does so with the consent of the Commission in order to ensure the integrity of the investigation, the fact that it has not distanced itself from the cartel more clearly should in any event not be regarded as continued *participation* in the infringement, but rather as taking precautions to ensure compliance with the 2006 Leniency Notice.

8.151 *Obligation not to destroy, falsify or conceal evidence* The Commission has introduced under point 12(c) in the 2006 Leniency Notice, a specific obligation for a company contemplating making an application not to destroy, falsify or conceal evidence of the alleged cartel. This is to prevent companies being tempted to get rid of the incriminating information in their possession before filing their application, or to falsify the information

---

[436] Whilst it is clear that the revocation of conditional immunity granted to one applicant may not result in granting *ex post* immunity to the undertaking that subsequently came forward, it remains debatable whether the revocation of an applicant's conditional immunity should result in the latter being barred from then claiming a reduction of fine under Section B of the 2002 Leniency Notice.

[437] This may imply that the applicant undertaking should in any event not use the information received for the determination of its commercial conduct.

submitted to the Commission with a view to exculpating themselves or to artificially put the responsibility on other parties.

Obligation not to disclose the fact or any of the content of a contemplated application, except to other competition authorities   Under point 12(c) of the 2006 Leniency Notice, the Commission has also expressly prohibited a company considering the filing of an application from disclosing the fact or any of the content of the contemplated application. This is also to prevent any possible attempt by cartel members to co-ordinate their conduct in the context of their respective applications under the Leniency Notice.   **8.152**

Coercion of other companies as a cause for exclusion from immunity   Under point 11(c) of the 2002 Leniency Notice, an undertaking could benefit from immunity from fines only if it 'did not take steps to coerce other undertakings to participate in the infringement'.[438] The Commission considered that it would not be acceptable for companies that have taken steps to coerce other companies to enter into the cartel to be in a position to then report them, thus getting 'off the hook' themselves. In the revised Notice, the scope of this cause for exclusion has been enlarged. Under point 12(c) of the 2006 Leniency Notice, undertakings which 'took steps to coerce other undertakings to join the cartel *or to remain in it*' are not eligible for immunity from fines (emphasis added). As at 31 December 2006, there had been no known instances where the Commission had refused (conditional) immunity or where conditional immunity had been withdrawn on that basis. The standard of proof required from the Commission to establish 'coercion' by one undertaking can now be expected to be quite high.   **8.153**

3. Procedural aspects

First contact   A company wishing to apply for immunity must contact DG Competition.[439] To facilitate this, dedicated secure phone and fax numbers have been put in place.[440] At the request of an applicant, a meeting will be organised as quickly as possible, at the date and time proposed by the applicant provided it falls within the normal working hours of the Commission.[441] Pursuant to point 12 of the 2002 Leniency Notice, if it became apparent that the applicant did not qualify for immunity under point 8(a) or 8(b), either because the substantive tests are not met or because another applicant has already been granted conditional immunity, the applicant was to be 'immediately' informed of that fact. Under point 20 of the 2006 Leniency Notice, the Commission indicates that it will do so in writing. Under both 2002 and 2006 Leniency Notices, the unsuccessful applicant may withdraw the evidence disclosed for the purpose of its immunity application or request that the Commission consider its application for a reduction in fines under Section B (2002 Leniency Notice) or Section III (2006 Leniency Notice).[442] This does   **8.154**

---

[438] This possibility of exclusion has been significantly limited as compared to that set out in the 1996 Leniency Notice which excluded from Section B or C any company found to have instigated the cartel or played a determining role in it. The purpose of this change was to encourage immunity applicants to come forward even if they have played a significant or even central role in the cartel.

[439] Point 12 of the 2002 Leniency Notice and point 14 of the 2006 Leniency Notice.

[440] The dedicated phone numbers are +32-2-298-41-90 or 298-41-91. The dedicated fax number is +32-2-299-45-85.

[441] These are Monday to Friday from 08.30 to 13.00 and from 14.15 to 17.30.

[442] Point 17 of the 2002 Leniency Notice and point 20 of the 2006 Leniency Notice.

not prevent the Commission from using its normal powers of investigation in order to obtain the information.[443]

8.155 Notwithstanding that 'hypothetical' applications for immunity are possible, the Commission refuses to allow 'testing of the water', that is (anonymous) enquiries into the availability of immunity, with no clear intention to apply. This would make it too easy for a cartel member to abuse the system so as to obtain confirmation that none of the other members has blown the whistle, thus establishing that the cartel is safe before simply walking away. However, when dealing with a hypothetical application genuinely made for the purpose of testing the sufficiency of the evidence provided, the Commission does not require the applicant to identify itself at the stage of the first enquiry. Nevertheless, it must necessarily identify at least the broad product sector covering the relevant product, before the Commission can determine whether immunity is available.[444] Then, if the Commission already has information of its own or has received a prior immunity application, the applicant will have to become more specific until the Commission can state with certainty whether immunity is available. It is also assumed by the Commission that if the initial enquiry leads to the conclusion that immunity is indeed available, the applicant should immediately lodge an application.[445]

8.156 *No 'marker' system under the 2002 Leniency Notice*   The 2002 Leniency Notice clearly worked on a 'first come, first served' basis. The point in time at which an application was made, that is at which the evidence was submitted, was therefore of crucial importance, as it determined the place in line of the applicant and thus the possibility of obtaining immunity.[446] The Commission did not operate any 'marker' system, whereby a company preparing an application could provisionally secure its place simply by informing the authority of the existence of an infringement and its intention to submit further information, thereby provisionally preventing other applications from being taken into consideration. For the submission to be deemed a valid application and considered for conditional immunity it had to be immediate and substantial, and to provide all the evidence and information that the applicant had at its disposal at that point in time.[447]

---

[443] Point 17 of the 2002 Leniency Notice and point 20 of the 2006 Leniency Notice.

[444] Depending on the case, the Commission may require the applicant to identify more precisely the category of product concerned.

[445] In this respect, one may reasonably assume that the building of a relationship of mutual trust between competition lawyers and Commission officials is sought by both parties.

[446] In other words, it is not the one with the *best* information who obtains immunity, but rather the *first* one through the door with *enough relevant* information.

[447] The Commission had drawn the attention of potential applicants to the fact that they had to take this into account when scheduling their immunity application. Thus, if an immunity application was not finalised over a single, uninterrupted period (even if for instance the meeting had to be temporarily interrupted because it extended beyond normal working hours), any second immunity application lodged in the meantime (that is during the interruption) made it impossible for the first applicant to complete its application. The first application would then be evaluated on the basis of the evidence supplied until the moment the second application was made. See B Van Barlingen and M Barennes, 'The European Commission's Leniency Notice in Practice', Competition Policy Newsletter, issue No 3, Autumn 2005, p 10). The absence of a marker system could be seen as lacuna in the Commission's leniency system. Its absence was a disadvantage both to undertakings and to the Commission. Undertakings, when discovering an infringement, had no opportunity to report at a very early stage, when they may have had every intention to follow up on an initial application. The Commission, in turn, often had to consider incomplete applications and/or allow staggered applications rather than allowing firms to apply once with a perfected submission.

Introduction of a 'marker' system in the 2006 Leniency Notice   The Commission has **8.157** introduced a discretionary 'marker' system in its revision of the 2002 Leniency Notice. Under point 14 of the 2006 Leniency Notice, an undertaking that intends to self-report a cartel 'may either initially apply for a market or immediately proceed to make a formal application'. During this period it has the opportunity to complete the evidence it expects to submit in its application.[448]

According to point 15 of the 2006 Leniency Notice, 'the Commission services may grant a **8.158** marker protecting an immunity applicant's place in the queue for a period to be specified on a case-by-case basis in order to allow for the gathering of the necessary information and evidence'. To be eligible to secure a marker the applicant must provide the Commission with information concerning its name and address, the parties to the alleged cartel, the affected product(s) and territory(/ies), the estimated duration of the alleged cartel and the nature of the alleged cartel conduct. The applicant must also inform the Commission of other past or possible future leniency applications to other authorities in relation to the alleged cartel, and justify its request for a marker. Where a marker is granted, the Commission services will determine the period within which the applicant has to perfect the marker by submitting the information required to meet the relevant threshold for immunity. Undertakings which have been granted a marker will not be allowed to perfect it by means of a formal application in hypothetical terms. If the applicant perfects the marker within the period set by the Commission services, the information and evidence provided will be deemed to have been submitted on the date when the marker was granted. It is important to note that the granting of a marker is made 'by the Commission services', as referred to at the beginning of point 15 of the 2006 Notice. It may be expected that the granting of a marker will not be automatic on fulfilling the above conditions. That also follows from the frequently asked questions/explanatory note which accompanied the adoption of the 2006 Notice (Memo/06/469) in which it is stated that the marker will be discretionary. It appears therefore that a marker will only be granted when, apart from fulfilling the requirements of point 15, an undertaking can provide particular circumstances as a result of which it has not yet been in a position to acquire the evidence needed. Furthermore, it should be noted that marker periods will be short, ie undertakings should count on days or weeks, but not months. This is clear from the text of Point 15 and the explanatory note: the Commission's philosophy as regards a marker appears to be that the usual race to the door by applicants providing sufficient evidence to qualify for immunity should prevail, but that in certain situations a marker can be a justifiable means of providing a (temporary) guaranteed spot at the front of the queue for a particular applicant.

---

[448] When adopting the 2002 Leniency Notice, the Commission decided against a marker system, although this constituted an established feature of US practice, which generally was a source of inspiration for the Commission. Presumably the Commission considered that companies should not come forward with under-prepared applications and that the 'race to the door' should be between companies that would be providing full evidence, rather than between those merely providing indications of a cartel. Undoubtedly, the Commission's stance also related to the fact that the '8(a)' standard for obtaining immunity was rather low, so that a marker was perceived to be unnecessary and unjustified, since a company would receive upfront immunity under the new system. Practitioners have nevertheless often stated that the absence of a marker is a considerable practical lacuna in the current system. See eg JM Joshua, 'That Uncertain Feeling: the Commission's Leniency Notice', paper given at the 11th EU Competition Law and Policy workshop, European University Institute, Florence, 2–3 June 2006.

8.159 *Hypothetical application*   To provide greater reassurance to potential applicants the Commission has set up a mechanism allowing for so-called 'hypothetical applications'.[449] This procedure allows the company to know whether or not it will satisfy conditions 8(a) or 8(b) before disclosing to the Commission its identity together with the relevant facts and evidence. The applicant must present a descriptive list of the evidence it proposes to disclose at an agreed later date. The decision to grant immunity is then taken solely on the basis of the descriptive list. The content of the list is therefore crucial and applicants should pay great attention to it. This list must describe in detail the nature of the content of the evidence it proposes to disclose (type of document, date, information contained in it, origin, etc). Expurgated copies of the relevant documentation should be annexed.[450] In order to obtain a reliable answer from the Commission as to whether it will qualify, the applicant's list should enable the Commission to form a very clear opinion on whether it will pass the test of 8(a) or 8(b). The descriptive list alone should suffice to establish whether the applicable test is passed. The subsequent comparison with the actual evidence when disclosed amounts merely to verification. The Commission also insists that the evidence described in the list must already be in the possession of the applicant when the list is handed over, as the evidence must be available for immediate submission.

8.160 *Oral application*   Under the 2002 Leniency Notice, the Commission indicated that a written corporate statement produced for the sole purpose of applying for immunity under the Commission's leniency programme should not be discoverable for purposes other than Article 81 EC enforcement by the Commission, for example in civil litigation in third country jurisdictions.[451] There was, however, a risk that immunity applicants may be obliged to produce their written statements under discovery procedures used in the context of civil actions, notably in the US.[452] In order not to deter applicants, the Commission indicated that as long as there was a risk that immunity applications may be subject to discovery procedures, it was prepared to accept oral applications.[453] The guiding principle for the Commission

---

[449] Points 13(b) and 16 of the 2002 Leniency Notice, and 16(b) and 19 of the 2006 Leniency Notice.

[450] In practice, therefore, the applicant should ensure that the entire application is ready when presenting it in its hypothetical form.

[451] Point 33 of the 2002 Leniency Notice. See also Art 15(4) of Regulation 773/2004 and point 48 of the Commission Notice on the rules for access to the Commission file in cases pursuant to Arts 81 and 82 of the EC Treaty, Arts 53, 54 and 57 of the EEA Agreement and Council Regulation (EC) No 139/2004, [2005] OJ C325/7.

[452] To further protect leniency application corporate statements, the Commission has intervened in several cases before US courts as *amicus curiae* in civil litigation, or has in various instances submitted letters to a party involved in such litigation, for submission by that party to the competent court. The Commission submitted in this respect that the granting of discovery in relation to self-incriminating statements would put at risk the effectiveness of the (worldwide) fight against cartels, including in the US, if the EU leniency policy was undermined by the disclosure of EU immunity applications before US civil courts. The results of these interventions have been varied. However, it may be hoped that, from the point of view of promoting its leniency policy, the Commission will succeed in convincing US (district) court judges that plaintiffs' requests for the discovery of corporate statements made under the 2002 Leniency Notice should be denied in order to protect the effectiveness of this enforcement tool.

[453] The Commission made it clear that it is not its intention to hinder civil litigation in any civil jurisdiction, but also indicated that it did not believe that 'plaintiffs in civil litigation should gratuitously benefit from the entirely unrelated and autonomous procedure of the Commission's leniency program, thereby undermining the latter programme in the process'. See B van Barlingen, 'The European Commission's 2002 Leniency Notice After One Year of Adoption', Antitrust, Spring 2002, p. 87.

is that applicants under the Leniency Notice should not be put in a worse position in civil litigation than companies that do not co-operate.[454]

In the 2006 Leniency Notice, the Commission has expressly stated its intention to protect voluntary statements submitted under its leniency programme. It indicated in the introductory statement that such statements 'have proved to be useful for the effective investigation and termination of cartel infringements' and that they 'should not be discouraged by discovery orders issued in civil litigation'.[455] An entire section of the 2006 Leniency Notice concerns 'Corporate statements made to qualify under this Notice',[456] which expressly provides that the Commission may accept that corporate statements be provided orally.

8.161

The opportunity to make oral immunity applications has not, so far, been conditional upon the applicant establishing that it would actually face a serious risk of discovery. In point 32 of the 2006 Leniency Notice, the Commission has however made clear that it is upon the applicant's request and provided that the applicant has not 'already disclosed the content of the corporate statement to third parties' that it will accept that such a statement be provided orally. To avoid possible misunderstandings and omissions, oral corporate statements are recorded and transcribed at the Commission's premises.[457] The evidence provided is contained in the oral statement itself and any transcript has the status of an internal Commission document. All corporate statements are therefore considered as internal Commission documents, whether formally signed or not. If the undertaking refuses to sign its statement, a record ('procès-verbal') is signed by Commission officials. It can be agreed between the Commission and the applicant that all documents produced by the Commission (including the decision granting conditional immunity) will be served (and will remain) at the premises of the Commission to a representative of the applicant.[458] The transcript of the oral statement will serve as evidence, but if necessary it can be supplemented before the European Courts with the original recordings.

8.162

No subsequent application will be considered before a position is taken on a prior one Pursuant to point 18 of the 2002 Leniency Notice and to point 21 of the 2006 Leniency

8.163

---

[454] It should be clear however that the Commission considers that documents that were already in the possession of the applicant before it asked for immunity and that were thus not prepared especially for this purpose (eg minutes of meetings) were discoverable before the lodging of the application. They must be submitted to the Commission as part of the application. The Commission does not accept that such pre-existing documents become non-discoverable by reason of their inclusion in an application under the Commissions Leniency Notice.

[455] Point 6 of the 2006 Leniency Notice. The Commission added that '[p]otential leniency applicants might be dissuaded from cooperating with the Commission under this Notice if this could impair their position in civil proceedings, as compared to companies who do not cooperate. Such undesirable effect would significantly harm the public interest in ensuring effective public enforcement of Article 81 EC in cartel cases and thus its subsequent or paralle effective privarte enforcement'.

[456] Section IV of the 2006 Leniency Notice.

[457] Pursuant to point 32 of the 2006 Leniency Notice, undertakings making oral corporate statements will be granted the opportunity to check the technical accuracy of the recording to to correct the substance of their oral statement within a certain time limit.

[458] See also the draft procedure for corporate statements made for the purpose of obtaining immunity from fines or reduction of fine in cartel cases, available on DG COMP's web site at the following address: <http://ec.europa.eu/comm/competition/antitrust/legislation/l3_en.pdf>. That procedure (as amended from the draft) has now been incorporated in the 2006 Leniency Notice. It applies to all applications that were pending at the time of the adoption of the 2006 Leniency Notice, according to point 37 of the 2006 Leniency Notice.

Notice, the Commission will not consider other applications for immunity from fines before it has taken a position on an existing application in relation to the same alleged infringement.[459] Such a principle is logical, as immunity from fines may only be granted to one applicant. Application of this principle might, however, turn out to be difficult for the Commission to implement because delay in the handling of the first immunity application may place the second applicant in a position of uncertainty. However, one would expect the second applicant still to apply for a reduction in fines as the second best option, and its application can then be considered retroactively as an application for immunity should the first applicant fail to qualify for immunity.

8.164 *Acknowledgement of receipt and verification of evidence submitted*   Pursuant to the 2002 Leniency Notice, after the applicant had handed over the evidence (or the descriptive list under the procedure for 'hypothetical' applications), the Commission provided the applicant with an acknowledgement of receipt, indicating the date and the content of the submission. Under the 2006 Leniency Notice, this acknowledgement of receipt is only delivered upon the applicant's request (point 17 of the 2006 Leniency Notice). If the evidence has been submitted directly, the Commission then checks whether the evidence disclosed meets the applicable criteria as set out in points 8(a) or 8(b) of the Notice. If so, the Commission grants the applicant conditional immunity from fines by way of decision. Alternatively it rejects the application, also by decison.

8.165 In the case of hypothetical applications, the decision-making process takes place in two stages. The Commission first assesses whether the evidence in the list will meet the applicable criteria. If so, the Commission will adopt a first decision informing the applicant that conditional immunity from fines *will* be granted. The applicant must then disclose the actual evidence referred to in the descriptive list. Once the Commission has verified that the evidence submitted corresponds to the description made in the list, it then grants the applicant conditional immunity from fines by way of a second decision. If the application has been made in good faith, the second decision should follow automatically.[460] If that is not the case, the Commission must revoke the first decision.

8.166 *'Non eligibility letter'*   Although both the 2002 and 2006 Leniency Notices make it clear that they concern only secret cartels,[461] there may be cases where undertakings file an immunity application relating to business practices other than cartel conduct.[462] In such cases, the Commission services may send the applicant a short and standard administrative letter stating that the reported practice does not fall within the scope of the Leniency Notice and

---

459   In the 2006 Leniency Notice, the Commission has indicated that this is 'irrespective of whether the immunity application is presented formally or by requesting a marker'.

460   This means that it is on the basis of the hypothetical list that the actual evaluation of the evidence is conducted.

461   Point 1 of both the 2002 and 2006 Leniency Notices.

462   B van Barlingen and M Barennes point to an 'unwelcome' development in that undertakings have asked for immunity with regard to general clauses in business contracts or to vertical agreements. They interpret this as a possible attempt to 're-create something similar to the previous notification system that was abolished with the entry into force of Regulation 1/2003'. See B Van Barlingen and M Barennes, 'The European Commission's Leniency Notice in Practice', Competition Policy Newsletter, issue No 3, Autumn 2005, p 11.

that this letter is without prejudice to the question of the compatibility of the practice in issue with EC competition rules.[463]

'Rejection decision'   If the Commission concludes that the application does not qualify   **8.167**
for immunity, it adopts a so-called 'rejection decision' informing the applicant that the Commission services consider that the evidence does not meet the requirements set out in points 8(a) or 8(b).[464] This letter, although it doubtlessly constitutes a legal act, is construed by the Commission as not being challengeable in its own right. This is because the effect of the rejection of immunity will only appear if and when the Commission takes a final prohibition decision with fines. The unsuccessful applicant may subsequently challenge a Commission decision imposing a fine on it. If immunity is rejected, the applicant may lodge a new application for immunity seeking to meet the criteria laid down in points 8(a) of 8(b) of the Notice. Alternatively, the applicant may apply for a reduction in the fine under the relevant section of the Notice.

'No action letter'   There may be situations where the Commission considers that the con-   **8.168**
ditions of the Leniency Notice are not met with certainty (for instance, if there is doubt as regards the possible effect on trade between Member States or whether a practice is one that actually qualifies as a hardcore (secret) cartel) as well as the fact that the practices in any case may not be considered a priority for the Commission. In such cases the Commission may not want to take a position as to whether conditional immunity can be granted. In these circumstances the Commission services have sometimes sent a so-called 'no action' letter to the applicant stating that, on the basis of a preliminary assessment showing that the conditions of application of the Notice would not be met, it is not the Commission services' intention to investigate the case further. However, the letter states that, should the Commission change its position, it will take a formal position on the application for immunity. Thus, whilst the case is put on hold, the applicant's place in the queue is 'safeguarded' should the Commission subsequently restart its investigation, for instance on the basis of a second application.

'Conditional immunity decision'   The Commission grants conditional immunity from   **8.169**
fines by a formal decision taken by the Commissioner in charge of competition matters. This authority is delegated to the Commissioner by the College of Commissioners.[465] The decision is therefore binding upon the latter which will confirm the decision if all conditions remain fulfilled at the time of the adoption of the final prohibition decision imposing fines. The decision is addressed to the legal entity (one entity only, which is why it is preferable that the parent entity of a group applies rather than a subsidiary; see para 8.176 below) which filed the application and is not published. The Commission specifies the infringement which is covered by the conditional immunity by describing the product(s) concerned

---

[463] The Commission also indicates that the evidence disclosed may be withdrawn without prejudice to the ability of the Commission to use its investigative powers subsequently to obtain the information.

[464] Rejection decisions are taken by the Commissioner in charge of competition by authority delegated by the College of Commissioners ('empowerment').

[465] The issuance of a conditional immunity decision may take several weeks from the date of the submission of the relevant evidence. In the case of hypothetical applications, the procedure is longer. In general, the speed with which an application can be processed depends to a large extent on its quality.

and its presumed geographical coverage and duration. The decision typically reads that 'at the end of the administrative procedure, the Commission will grant the applicant immunity from fines with regard to any infringement(s) that the Commission has found as a result of its investigation in connection with the evidence the applicant submitted in relation to the alleged cartel, provided that the applicant has met the conditions set out in point 11 of the [2002] Leniency Notice'.[466]

8.170 *Withdrawal of conditional immunity* If an applicant benefiting from conditional immunity fails to comply with the duty of full co-operation as set out in point 11 of the 2002 Notice or in point 12 of the 2006 Leniency Notice, the Commission may withdraw the immunity. This was the case in *Raw Tobacco Italy* under the 2002 Leniency Notice. The conditional immunity granted to Deltafina in that case was withdrawn because although Deltafina was aware of the Commission's intention to carry out inspections, it had disclosed its application under the 2002 Leniency Notice to the other cartel members before the Commission had the opportunity to carry out inspections.[467] The Commission sent to all the addressees of the Statement of Objections an 'Addendum to the Statement of Objections' where it stated its intention to withdraw Deltafina's conditional immunity. An oral Hearing also took place on this matter. It is submitted however that the right to be heard on this matter concerns primarily the immunity applicant and that the Commission may well limit itself to sending a Statement of Objections announcing an intention to withdraw the immunity solely to the undertaking concerned.

8.171 *2006 Leniency Notice: no position is taken on applications concerning infringements in respect of which the imposition of fines is time-barred* Under point 36 of the 2006 Leniency Notice, the Commission will not take a position under the Leniency Notice 'if it becomes apparent that the application concerns infringements covered by the five years limitation period for the imposition of penalties stipulated in Article 25(1)(b) of Regulation 1/2003, as such applications would be devoid of purpose'. The Commission has indicated in this respect that '[t]reating leniency requests in such situations would create unnecessary administrative workload detracting resources from action against other cartels', given that in those cases no fine could be imposed.[468]

4. The Commission's practice in dealing with immunity applications

8.172 *Content requirement for a successful immunity application* Irrespective of whether the application is made under point 8(a) or 8(b), the applicant is required to provide the Commission with at least the following: (i) *a corporate statement* prepared for the purpose

---

[466] The obligation to fully co-operate is stressed in the decision. Thus, immunity decisions routinely reiterate that the applicant shall not reveal the existence of the application to third parties without prior approval from the Commission (something which is equally included in the 'acknowledgement of receipt' letters). In exceptional cases, the immunity decision may also contain certain clarifications as to the exact content of the duty to fully cooperate set out in point 11 of the Notice.

[467] See *Raw Tobacco Italy*, Decision of 20 October 2005 (full text of the decision available on DG COMP's web site), paras 408–460.

[468] See MEMO/06/357: 'Competition: Commission proposes changes to the Leniency Notice—frequently asked questions'.

of the application containing a detailed account of its participation in the cartel;[469] (ii) *copies of original cartel documents or pieces of evidence* when available; (iii) *precise information as to the names, functions and office location(s) of other participants* in the cartel;[470] and (iv) a *power of attorney* if the applicant is represented by outside counsel. In any event, the undertaking is well advised to provide the Commission with all relevant information in order to maximise its chance of qualifying for conditional immunity.[471]

Specificity of '8(a)' applications   Applications under point 8(a) raise the delicate issue of   **8.173** the nature and scope of the 'evidence' that the Commission may require from an immunity applicant in exchange of conditional immunity. Under point 8(a) of the 2002 Leniency Notice the applicant was required to submit 'evidence' which 'in the Commission's view' enabled it to adopt a decision to carry out an investigation in the sense of [now Article 20(4) of Regulation 1/2003] in connection with an alleged cartel affecting the Community'. In the 2006 Leniency Notice, the applicable test has been slightly modified. The applicant is now required to 'submit *information* and evidence which in the Commission's view will enable it to carry out a *targeted* inspection in connection with the targeted cartel' (emphasis added).

There is a link between the test to be met by the applicant and the requirement placed   **8.174** on the Commission for the purpose of adopting a decision ordering inspections under Article 20(4) of Regulation 1/2003. Under Article 20(4) of Regulation 1/2003, 'the decision shall specify the subject matter and purpose of the inspection'. This, however, does not help much to benchmark the requirements placed on the immunity applicant. Indeed, the exact legal standard applying to the reasoning of inspection decisions has not been defined in great detail by case law. However, the obligation to state reasons seems to be confined to a minimum.[472] In this context, it should be emphasised that under the 2002 Leniency Notice the Commission already seemed to retain discretion, as point 8(a) provided that (provisional) immunity was conditional upon the submission of evidence which '*in the Commission's view*' may enable it to adopt a decision to carry out an investigation' (emphasis added). With the new test contained in the 2006 Leniency Notice, the margin of discretion retained by the Commission has been underlined. It is indeed for the Commission to determine not only whether the information contained in the submission is sufficient to form the basis of a decision ordering an inspection, but also whether the information

---

[469] The statement should be based on all available information in the possession of the applicant at that point in time and describe the product or service concerned, the production process, the market, the customers and, in particular, the precise functioning of the cartel including its membership, period of functioning, geographic area, activities, internal rules, and the particulars of meetings and other contacts.

[470] This will be considered of particular importance in the case of '8(a)' applications where it is crucial that the Commission be in a position to carry out 'targeted' dawn raids.

[471] It should be noted that the Commission will routinely ask for a waiver in the case of simultaneous leniency applications in other (non-EU) countries. The Commission will also ask to be informed about Member States where applications have been made.

[472] Whilst the Commission decision must comply with the duty to state reasons under Art 253 EC, the requirement on the Commission appears to be limited. The Commission must specify the 'subject-matter and purpose of the investigation' (Joined Cases 46/87 and 227/88 *Hoechst v Commission* [1989] ECR 2859, para 41. This formula is now referred to in Art 20 of Regulation 1/2003). The Commission must also clearly indicate the presumed facts which it intends to investigate, but is not required to communicate to the addressee of the decision all the information at its disposal concerning the presumed infringements (Case 85/87 *Dow Benelux v Commission* [1989] ECR 31338, para 9).

submitted will in fact enable the Commission to carry out 'targeted' inspections, ie inspections that are more likely to be successful. In this regard, the requirement on the applicant to provide not only 'evidence' of the cartel, but also 'information' manifests the Commission's concern to maximise the chances of success of 'dawn raids'.

8.175 *'One infringement, one immunity decision'* Each infringement reported is evaluated separately by the Commission as to whether the relevant information supplied qualifies for the granting of immunity. Whether separate infringements exist can only be decided on a case-by-case basis. This will depend on factors such as the products or services affected, whether geographical coverage is the same, or whether the cartel participants are the same. However, this analysis may prove difficult at such an early stage of the investigation. Indeed the existence of a 'complex scheme' and its exact scope is often difficult to determine based solely on the information supplied by the immunity applicant. In any case, the scope of the immunity is a very sensitive question because the line taken by the Commission may have an impact on the opportunities for other undertakings to lodge other applications. However, this issue should not be blown out of proportion. It is clearly in the applicant's interest to be as exhaustive as possible in terms of disclosure. If an undertaking has been granted immunity for more than it can prove, the Commission may be expected to correct that by a separate decision in order to clear the way for other applications.

8.176 *Immunity only for one legal entity* An immunity decision must be addressed to a legal entity that made the application. Immunity covers the liability of all subsidiaries under the effective control of the applicant with regard to the product(s) mentioned in the immunity decision. If immunity has not been requested by the highest entity of the group, the parent company may still be held liable for the payment of the fine. This would not be the case if, as was established by the Commission in *MCAA*[473] and *Rubber Chemicals*[474], the liability of the parent company is not based on evidence of its direct involvement in the cartel, but rather on the exercise of effective control on the conduct of its subsidiary.[475] If, however, the parent company is found to have participated in the cartel directly, or where it is shown not to have co-operated with the investigation, it will not be covered by the immunity granted to its subsidiary and will have to pay a fine. As a consequence undertakings wishing to apply for leniency are best advised to apply at the highest level at which their liability may be established.

8.177 *Joint ventures* If a joint venture has been involved in a cartel and has applied for immunity, the question of the liability/immunity of the parent companies arises. If none of the parent companies have ever been involved in the cartel the Commission appears willing to envisage that the parents may benefit from the immunity obtained by the joint venture.[476]

---

[473] Decision of 19 January 2005 (full text of the decision available on DG COMP's web site).

[474] Decision of 21 December 2005 (full text of the decision available on DG COMP's web site).

[475] The Commission considers that if a parent company is found to (have) exercise(d) effective control on the conduct of its subsidiary, both entities can be considered to form part of the same 'undertaking' for the purpose of EC competition law. In that respect, the application of the subsidiary is deemed to cover the entire 'undertaking', ie the parent company as well, provided that the latter has not itself been directly involved in the collusive practices.

[476] The underlying assumption would be that the joint venture and its parent companies constitute one and the same 'undertaking' for the purpose of the case (and for the purpose of leniency).

However, the Commission has stated that if one or more of the parent companies have been actively involved in the collusive practices the application filed by the joint venture cannot cover the behaviour of the parent company (or companies).[477] The Commission's view that several parents of a joint venture may benefit from the protection of the joint venture's application is, it is submitted, debatable. Either the parent company has not been directly involved in the cartel *and* has not exercised any effective control over the joint venture, in which case it should not be found liable for the infringement, or the parent company is found to have exercised effective control over the joint venture, in which case it could be held liable for its conduct. Thus if, for example, two parent companies were found to have jointly exercised effective control over the joint venture even though they were not directly involved in the cartel, they should each be held liable of a separate fine. In such a case, if the Commission permitted the two parent undertakings to benefit from the immunity obtained by their subordinate joint venture, that would amount to granting immunity to two separate undertakings.

(v) Reduction in the fine under the 2002 and 2006 Leniency Notices

Undertakings that do not meet the conditions for conditional immunity under Section A of the 2002 Leniency Notice or Section II of the 2006 Leniency Notice may be eligible to benefit from a reduction in any fine that would otherwise have been imposed on them under Section B of the 2002 Leniency Notice or Section III of the 2006 Leniency Notice. **8.178**

1. Substantive tests   The relevant substantive test in order to qualify for a reduction in fine is the so-called 'significant added value' (SAV) test. Another important substantive test—applicable only after passing the SAV test—is set out in the last paragraph of point 23 of the 2002 Leniency Notice and of point 26 of the 2006 Leniency Notice. In effect this provides for partial immunity from fines where the information not only qualifies for SAV (and, pursuant to the 2006 Leniency Notice, constitutes 'compelling evidence') but also adds to the gravity or duration of the infringement. **8.179**

'Significant added value' (SAV) test   To qualify for a reduction in the fine under section B of the 2002 Leniency Notice or Section III of the 2006 Leniency Notice, the applicant must, apart from terminating its involvement in the suspected infringement, provide the Commission with evidence representing 'significant added value' with respect to the evidence already in the Commission's possession in relation to the same case. Evidence amounts to 'added value' if it 'strengthens, by its very nature and/or its level of detail, the Commission's ability to prove the alleged cartel'.[478] In assessing this, the Commission will generally attribute greater value to written and contemporaneous evidence (eg handwritten notes of cartel meetings) than to evidence subsequently created (statements of facts, or testimonies). **8.180**

---

[477] Both the 2002 and 2006 Leniency Notice clearly provide that a leniency application can only be made by a single undertaking. The Commission may also want to ensure that there is no possibility of abusing the Notice through artificial legal arguments aimed at avoiding liability.

[478] Point 25 of the 2006 Leniency Notice. The wording of point 22 of the 2002 Leniency Notice is almost identical.

Similarly, greater value will be attached to direct evidence (eg a list of agreed 'target' prices) than to circumstantial evidence (eg records of travel expenses pertaining to cartel meetings).[479] There is no definition of 'significant' (added value) in the Notice. It was considered that providing such a definition would have been meaningless as such significance can only be determined in the context of each particular case.

8.181   *Greater value of 'compelling evidence'*   In the 2006 Leniency Notice, the Commission has further clarified the relative value it attributes to the evidence provided by the applicant. Hence, it indicates in point 25 that '[i]ncriminating evidence directly relevant to the facts in question will generally be considered to have a greater value than that with only indirect relevance'. The Commission also indicates that 'the degree of corroboration from other sources required for the evidence submitted to be relied upon against other undertakings involved in the case will have an impact on the value of that evidence, so that compelling evidence will be attributed a greater value than evidence such as statements which require corroboration if contested'. This new notion of 'compelling evidence' is of direct relevance for the assessment of whether the applicant may benefit from partial immunity under point 26 (last paragraph) of the 2006 Leniency Notice, as is explained below.

8.182   *'Partial immunity within the context of an application for a reduction of a fine*   According to point 23 (last paragraph) of the 2002 Leniency Notice, 'if an undertaking provides evidence relating to facts previously unknown to the Commission which have a direct bearing on the gravity or duration of the suspected cartel, the Commission will not take these elements into account when setting any fine to be imposed on the undertaking which provided this evidence'. In other words, the Commission does not take into account the increased gravity or duration of the infringement resulting from the consideration of these facts when setting the fine for the undertaking that supplied that information.[480] This means that the actual reduction in the applicant's fine may, in effect, be greater than the respective 50 per cent, 30 per cent and 20 per cent ceilings set out in section 23(b) of the Notice. This provides another incentive for an applicant to provide as much information as possible and to also apply as early as possible, in order to maximise the overall reduction in fines resulting from the application.

8.183   In the 2006 Leniency Notice, the Commission has made the benefit of 'partial immunity' within the context of an application for a reduction in fines conditional upon the provision of 'compelling evidence' within the meaning of point 25 of the Notice, that is to say evidence that does not require corroboration. This clearer (and apparently tighter) requirement implies that in order to benefit from immunity in respect of additional facts that increase the gravity or the duration of the infringement under the 2006 Leniency Notice, the applicant for a reduction in fines has to submit direct and self-standing incriminating evidence.

---

[479] For a comparative analysis of different types of evidence, see section D(2)(e) below.

[480] Facts 'previously unknown' should not be confused with facts 'not yet proven' (to the requisite standard). They are facts which had neither been brought to the Commission's attention nor discovered by the latter as a result of the investigation at the time they are submitted by the applicant.

2. Available bands of reduction and relevant criteria In its final decision, the Commission **8.184**
determines whether the evidence provided by a an applicant for a reduction in fines represents significant added value with respect to the evidence in the Commission's possession
at the time. If the Commission comes to the preliminary conclusion that the evidence submitted by the applicant constitutes added value within the meaning of the relevant points
of the applicable notice,[481] it will inform the undertaking in writing, no later than the date
on which a Statement of Objections is notified, of its intention to apply a reduction in a fine
within a specified band, as provided in point 23(b) of the 2002 Leniency Notice and in
point 26 of the 2006 Leniency Notice.[482] Under the 2006 Leniency Notice, this is however
also subject to the applicant fulfilling the conditions set out in points 12 and 27 of the
Notice. This means, first, that the applicant must have made clear, at the time of any voluntary submission, that it formed part of an application for a reduction in fines (point 27 of
the Notice). Second, the applicant must have complied with the duty of full co-operation as
set out in point 12 of the 2006 Leniency Notice.

Available bands of reduction For each undertaking found to have provided evidence repre **8.185**
senting significant added value, the Commission will grant a reduction in the fine within a
given band. The first company to qualify will benefit from a reduction in the fine of between
30 and 50 per cent and the second a reduction of between 20 and 30 per cent. Subsequent
undertakings that have passed the SAV test will receive a reduction of up to 20 per cent.[483]

Relevant criteria for the determination of the reduction within each band Two factors **8.186**
determine the level of reduction within each band: the time at which the submission of the
evidence satisfying the SAV test was made (in relation to the stage of the Commission's proceedings), and the extent to which it provided added value.[484] Under the reduction in fines
section of the 2002 Leniency Notice, there was no explicit *obligation* on the applicant to co-
operate fully and continuously with the Commission, so the granting of a reduction in fines
depended on whether the applicant provided significant added value to the Commission's
investigation at the time of the submission.[485] However in the light of case law developments[486] the Commission introduced in the 2006 Leniency Notice a general obligation to
fully co-operate throughout the administrative procedure which applies also to applicants
for a reduction in fines. In order to benefit from a reduction in fines, any applicant under
Section III of the 2006 Leniency Notice must therefore comply with the conditions as set
out in point 12(a) to 12(c) of the 2006 Leniency Notice (see para 8.196 below).

---

[481] ie point 22 of the 2002 Leniency Notice, point 24 and 25 of the 2006 Leniency Notice.
[482] Indeed, the Commission usually provides such an indication only at a rather late stage in the investigation, because its assessment can only become final after a complete evaluation of all the evidence on file: see
para 8.191 below.
[483] Point 23(b), first para of the 2002 Leniency Notice and point 26 of the 2006 Leniency Notice.
[484] Point 23(b), second para of the 2002 Leniency Notice and point 26, second para of the 2006 Leniency
Notice.
[485] The extent and continuity of the co-operation provided could be taken into account, however, in the
determination of the final percentage of reduction granted within a given band.
[486] The ECJ has emphasised the requirement of a spirit of 'genuine cooperation' on the part of any leniency
applicant. See para 8.227 below.

3. Procedural aspects

8.187 *Requirement to make a formal application for a reduction in fines under the 2006 Leniency Notice* 'Under the 2002 Leniency Notice the Commission did not require formal applications for the reduction in fines.[487] This could lead to 'hidden' applications, that is, information contained in a response to a request for information from which the Commission was effectively required to 'detect' any voluntary submission of evidence. It was therefore deemed preferable for all parties involved[488] that applications for reduction in fines must be made in an explicit form. Thus, pursuant to point 27 of the 2006 Leniency Notice, 'an undertaking wishing to benefit from a reduction in a fine must make a formal application to the Commission' and 'any voluntary submission of evidence to the Commission which the undertaking that submits it wishes to be considered for the beneficial treatment [under the 'reduction of fines' section] must be clearly identified at the time of its submission as being part of a formal application for a reduction of a fine'.

8.188 *Acknowledgement of receipt upon request* Pursuant to point 25 of the 2002 Leniency Notice, the Commission delivered an acknowledgement of receipt recording the date on which the relevant evidence was submitted (when a formal application was made, (see para 8.164 above). Under point 28 of the 2006 Leniency Notice, only 'if requested' will DG COMP provide such an acknowledgement. The Commission will not consider any application for a reduction in fine before it has taken a position in respect of any existing application for conditional immunity from fines in relation to the same alleged cartel.

8.189 *A reduction in fines under the Leniency Notice is not an alternative in case of revocation of conditional immunity* The Commission considers that the withdrawal of a conditional immunity from fines does not enable the undertaking concerned to have the evidence it supplied in the context of its immunity application considered alternatively under Section B. In *Raw Tobacco Italy* the Commission found that, as regards an immunity applicant, 'subsidiary applications for reductions can only be accepted in cases where the request for immunity does not comply with the requirements of points 8(a) and 8(b) of the Notice. [. . .] In fact, once immunity is granted to a company, any subsidiary application for reduction in the fine which may have been included in its original application loses all purpose and legal effect'.[489] However, in *Raw Tobacco Italy* the Commission considered that in view of the exceptional circumstances of the case, the added value of the co-operation provided by the applicant whose immunity was revoked justified a reduction in the fine as an attenuating circumstance.[490]

8.190 *Applications are considered until the issuance of the Statement of Objections* The 2002 Leniency Notice did not set out any time limit as regards the opportunity to file an

---

[487] Applications for immunity under the 2006 Leniency Notice, by contrast, need to be made formally.

[488] This is especially true because the place in line, and band of reduction of fines, that one company obtains, depends on the submissions and evaluation of what another company has provided. Hence, companies involved in cartel proceedings should be able to identify clearly, during the administrative proceedings, what information the Commission should take into account when awarding reductions in fines.

[489] Decision of 20 October 2005 (full text of the decision available on DG COMP's web site), paras 464 and 466.

[490] A reduction of 50% of its fine was therefore granted to Deltafina.

application for a reduction in a fine. However, it was understood that applications for reductions of fines would normally not be considered once a Statement of Objections had been sent.[491] It may indeed be assumed that the issuance of the Statement of Objections in a given case implies that the Commission has gathered all the information needed to form its objections and, subject to the exercise of the right to be heard, to adopt a final decision. Under such an assumption, there is no room for the provision of evidence of 'significant added value' to the investigation after the sending of a Statement of Objections.[492] This has been clarified by the Commission in the 2006 Leniency notice, which provides in point 29 that 'the Commission may disregard any application for a reduction of fines on the grounds that it has been submitted after the statement of objections has been issued'.

Informing the undertaking that SAV has been provided and of the band of reduction within   **8.191**
which the application falls   Pursuant to both the 2002 and the 2006 Leniency Notices, if the Commission comes to the preliminary conclusion that the evidence submitted by the undertaking constitutes added value within the meaning of the relevant provisions,[493] it will inform the undertaking in writing, no later than the date on which a Statement of Objections is notified, of its intention to apply a reduction in a fine within a specified band.[494] Under the 2006 Leniency Notice, the Commission must also consider that the applicant has so far complied with its duty of full and continuous co-operation as set out in point 12. In effect, the Commission informs those applicants which, in the Commission's preliminary view, have qualified for a reduction in fine, by means of an individual decision before the Statement of Objections is sent. The Commission also indicates the band of reduction within which the applicant is placed.[495]

Notification of failure to meet the SAV test   Unlike immunity applications, if an applicant   **8.192**
for a reduction in fine submits evidence which does not represent significant added value, the Commission does not issue a 'letter of rejection'. Indeed, applications for a reduction in fines can be supplemented with further evidence throughout the administrative procedure until the Statement of Ojections is sent (see para 8.194 below). Under the 2002 Leniency Notice, the Commission progressively developed a practice, once it had reached a final conclusion with regard to the value of the evidence submitted by each applicant for a reduction in fine, of informing, by means of an individual decision, those applicants who had not provided significant added value and therefore did not qualify for a reduction in

---

[491] This logically stems from point 26 of the 2002 Leniency Notice, according to which 'if the Commission comes to the preliminary conclusion that the evidence submitted by the undertaking constitutes added value [. . .] it will inform the undertaking in writing, *no later than the date on which a statement of objections is notified* [. . .]' (emphasis added).

[492] It is still possible, however, that upon receipt of a Statement of Objections, an addressee that may have not been in contact with the Commission previously could cast substantially new light on certain aspects of an infringement. Such a scenario should result in the issue of a new Statement of Objections, which would allow the submission to be taken into account. However, it is unlikely that this would actually happen in practice.

[493] ie point 22 of the 2002 Leniency Notice and points 24 and 25 of the 2006 Leniency Notice.

[494] As set out in point 23(b) of the 2002 Leniency Notice and point 26 of the 2006 Leniency Notice.

[495] In principle, the Commission should notify its decision as soon as possible after receiving the application and assessing the evidence, so as to increase legal certainty. However, notification of the decision can also be made shortly before the Statement of Objections is notified.

their fine.[496] This has been incorporated in the 2006 Leniency Notice, according to which the Commission will systematically, no later than the date on which a Statement of Objections is notified, 'inform the undertaking in writing if it comes to the preliminary conclusion that [it] does not qualify for a reduction of a fine'.

8.193 *Provisional decisions on SAV test are not deemed challengeable*   Indeed, it is only in the final prohibition decision that the final reduction in the fine is determined. Such decisions allow applicants for a reduction in fines to exercise their right to be heard before a final decision is taken. However, they are deemed to constitute only a preparatory act, and the applicant has an opportunity to challenge the Commission's finding in the final decision.

8.194 *Successive submissions and their assessment by the Commission*   Applications for a reduction in fine need not necessarily take the form of a single, one off, submission and there is no such requirement in the Notice. Applicants may find that they can only supply evidence to the Commission in stages as the relevant material becomes available to them in the course of an internal investigation. On the other hand, contrary to the rule set out with regard to immunity applications, the Commission is under no obligation to take a position on a first application for reductions of fines prior to the examination of a second application. This creates a strong incentive for applicants to supply as much evidence as possible as quickly as possible, as undertakings must compete with each other for the purpose of passing the SAV test that will secure their place along the decreasing scale of the available bands of reductions. This raises the question of the way in which the Commission handles successive applications by the same applicant.

8.195 How successive applications for a reduction in fines may be assessed, was revealed in the Commission's Competition Policy Newsletter.[497] Successive applications are examined in chronological order. For each application, the Commission verifies whether the SAV test is met on the basis of all the information submitted by the applicant, even if another applicant for a reduction in fine has also submitted relevant information in the meantime. In other words, the SAV test is applied to the cumulative amount of relevant information that has been submitted by a given applicant at the time of the assessment of the latest submission.[498] For the avoidance of doubt, it must be emphasised that any previous

---

[496] However, it is understood that the Commission did not consider the provision of such information as an obligation under the 2002 Leniency Notice. For cases that are being dealt with under that Notice it is therefore not certain that the Commission will indeed send 'negative' reduction of fines letters to applicants.

[497] B Van Barlingen and M Barennes, 'The European Commission's Leniency Notice in Practice', Competition Policy Newsletter, issue No 3, Autumn 2005.

[498] B van Barlingen and M Barennes (ibid) provide a hypothetical example of one possible approach to achieving the SAV threshold: 'Let us assume that 100 points are needed to reach the threshold of significant added value. Undertaking A makes a first submission. It is worth 70 points, taking into account the evidence the Commission already had at that moment. At this point in time, undertaking A has not yet qualified for significant added value. One week later, undertaking B makes a voluntary submission of evidence. Based on the evidence the Commission already had, including the submission of undertaking A, the value of this submission is considered to be 80 points. Undertaking B also does not qualify yet. Again one week later, undertaking B comes back with a second submission, worth 20 points, taking into account as always all the evidence the Commission had gathered until then. Undertaking B has now accumulated 100 points in total and is the first undertaking to qualify for significant added value, even if undertaking A was the first applicant for a reduction of fines. Undertaking B will thus benefit from a reduction between 30% and 50%. If undertaking A then comes back again a week later with a second submission worth 80 points, it will have accumulated 150 points and will be the second undertaking to qualify. It will thus receive a reduction between 20% and 30%'.

submissions of an applicant ('Applicant A') who failed to qualify for a reduction in fine initially may ultimately be taken into consideration in the context of a subsequent application from the same applicant, even if another applicant ('Applicant B') has supplied relevant information in the meantime. The assessment of the added value provided by B is made on the basis of the information already collected by the Commission *including* the submission(s) of A.[499]

Duty of full and continuous cooperation for applicants for a reduction in a fine under the **8.196**
2006 Leniency Notice   Under the 2002 Leniency Notice, a requirement of full and continuous co-operation only existed in respect of applicants for immunity from fines. Applicants for *reductions* in fines were not subject to any obligation in this respect, although the Notice provided that the Commission could take into account the degree of co-operation provided when determining the fine within a given band.[500] The Community courts however recently clarified that a 'spirit of co-operation' may be expected from applicants under the Leniency Notice (see para 8.227 below). Consequently, the Commission has indicated in the 2006 Leniency Notice that a duty to co-operate fully and continuously also applies to applicants for a reduction in fines.[501] The Commission had indeed stated that 'the requirement of full and continuous co-operation with the Commission investigation is an essential feature of the Leniency Notice', and that 'the co-operation ha[d] to be sincere and [that] there [was] no reason to distinguish between applicants for immunity and those for reduction of fines'.[502] The detailed content of the duty for the applicant for a reduction in fine to co-operate 'genuinely, fully, on a continuous basis and expeditiously' from the time it submits its application is set out in point 12 of the 2006 Leniency Notice (see para 8.147 above).

It is submitted, however, that the introduction of such a requirement profoundly modifies   **8.197**
the economy of the Leniency Notice. In the absence of a duty to fully and continuously co-operate, applicants for a reduction in fine were rewarded solely with regard to the objective, actual value of their contribution to the current investigation of the cartel. This had the advantage of leaving it to the applicant to decide the extent to which it was willing to take advantage of the possibility offered by the leniency programme. The Commission, in fact, relied on the clearly established principle that an applicant may receive lenient treatment only in proportion to the degree to which it facilitated the Commission's investigation.

---

[499] This means that the information supplied by B which may already have been supplied by A cannot be considered for the purpose of overall assessment of the added value provided by B. Thus, there is no risk that information be rewarded twice in the context of section B of the Notice. Although the information initially supplied by A becomes part of the evidence in the possession of the Commission, it is 'rewarded' exclusively on the condition that ultimately, A manages to pass the SAV test on the basis of the entirety of the information supplied to the Commission.

[500] Point 23, penultimate para of the 2002 Leniency Notice provides that '[i]n order to determine the level of reduction within each [. . .] band the Commission [. . .] may [. . .] also take into account the extent and continuity of any cooperation provided by the undertaking following the date of its submission'.

[501] It is indicated in point 24 of the 2006 Leniency Notice that applicants for a reduction of fines must meet the same obligation of full and continuous co-operation as that applicable to applicants for immunity from fines, as set out in point 12(a) to (c) of the Notice.

[502] See MEMO/06/357: 'Competition: Commission proposes changes to the Leniency Notice—frequently asked questions'.

Against this background, the introduction of a duty of full and continuous co-operation may well not put the Commission in a more favourable position. First, failure to co-operate fully and continuously will not be easy for the Commission to establish and might result in a burdensome dispute, and possibly related litigation. Secondly, the threat represented by the potential finding of a breach of the duty to co-operate might well reinstate within the 2006 Leniency Notice a degree of uncertainty, the limitation of which was one the main reasons justifying revision of the Commission's leniency policy in 2002. It will, however, act as a safety valve aimed at ensuring maximum input from those who wish to benefit from the possible rewards the leniency programme offers.

4. 'Significant Added Value' Test: Commission Practice

8.198 *Requirements established by the SAV test*   Under points 21 of the 2002 Leniency Notice and 24 of the 2006 Leniency Notice, the Commission indicates that in order to qualify for a reduction in a fine 'an undertaking must provide the Commission with evidence of the suspected infringement which represents significant added value with respect to the evidence already in the Commission's possession'. This means that an applicant for a reduction in fines must meet four distinct, cumulative criteria. In its application the undertaking must submit (i) 'evidence' or (ii) 'compelling evidence' (2006 Leniency Notice), (iii) 'of the alleged cartel'[503], which provides (iv) 'added value' which is found to be (v) 'significant'. However, no further guidance is provided. This seems justified by the fact that such an assessment must be done on a case by case basis.[504] Each of the above criteria will be examined in turn.

8.199 *'Evidence'*   The Notice is silent as to what constitutes 'evidence'. Points 22 of the 2002 Leniency Notice and 25 of the 2006 Leniency Notice merely indicate that contemporaneous evidence will generally be considered of a greater value than evidence subsequently established and that evidence 'directly relevant to the facts in question' will generally be considered to have a greater value than 'that with only indirect relevance'. On the notion of evidence in the investigation of cartel cases, reference is made to section D(2) of this chapter where this question is discussed in detail. It is nonetheless worth recalling here that the following conclusions can be drawn from case law.

8.200 First, a single piece of evidence may suffice to establish an infringement provided that its evidential value is not in doubt. However, this does not apply to a statement if the statement is contested by another undertaking incriminated by the statement in question,

---

[503] This is the wording of the 2006 Leniency Notice. The 2002 Leniency Notice read 'of the suspected infringement'.

[504] In this regard, reference to the Commission's decision-making practice is not very helpful, as the Commission does not explain in great detail the way it applies the SAV test. (At 31 December 2006, the Commission had applied the SAV test to applicants for a reduction of fines pursuant Section B of the 2002 Leniency Notice in 6 cartel decisions: *Raw Tobacco Italy*, *Industrial Bags*, *Rubber Chemicals*, *Hydrogen Peroxides and Perborate*, *Methacrylates*, and *Synthetic Rubber*.) However, apart from this and the guidance given in the wording of Notice itself, the Commission officials have provided certain useful indications in this respect. See B Van Barlingen and M Barennes, 'The European Commission's Leniency Notice in Practice', Competition Policy Newsletter, issue No 3, Autumn 2005, p. 6.

unless the Commission can rely on other evidence corroborating it. Secondly, oral information can be used as evidence to establish an infringement. Thirdly, it is not necessary for every piece of evidence relied upon by the Commission to be sufficiently precise and consistent to prove every element of the infringement. It suffices for the body of evidence viewed as a whole to be sufficiently precise and consistent to prove that the infringement took place. In this respect, in the case of secret infringement such as cartels where evidence may be expected to be fragmentary and sparse, evidence of an infringement may result from coincidences and indications taken together in the absence of any other plausible explanation.

'Compelling evidence'   The notion of 'compelling evidence' was introduced in the 2006   **8.201**
Leniency Notice, where the Commission states in point 25 that 'the degree of corroboration from other sources required for the evidence submitted to be relied upon against other undertakings involved in the case will have an impact on the value of that evidence, so that compelling evidence will be attributed a greater value than evidence such as statements which require corroboration if contested'. The Commission will therefore better reward 'conclusive, stand-alone evidence as compared with, for instance, a corporate statement uncorroborated by other pieces of evidence which would not be used as evidence against other parties to the cartel if they all contradicted it in similar statements'.[505] It should also be noted that the benefit from 'partial immunity' within the context of an application for a reduction in fines will be conditional upon the provision of 'compelling evidence' (see paras 8.181 to 8.183 above).

Contemporaneous vs 'subsequently' established evidence   Contemporaneous evidence as   **8.202**
understood in the 2006 Leniency Notice (see also section D(2) of this chapter for a description of the notion of evidence in cartel cases) can be documentary (eg minutes of meetings, hand-written or computer-based tables setting out agreed market shares or price increases, e-mails, internal memos) or take an audio or audiovisual form (eg a tape or video-tape recording a cartel meeting). Evidence may however be 'subsequently established' for the purpose of the application for a reduction in fines. It will then take the form of a written or oral, corporate or individual statement.

'Direct' vs 'indirect' evidence   The notion of direct evidence as used in the 2006 Leniency   **8.203**
Notice, refers to contemporaneous or subsequently established evidence that is directly relevant to the facts considered to constitute the infringement (eg a table setting out agreed market shares, an e-mail summarising an agreement on a price increase, or a statement reporting the setting out of quotas between cartel members). Indirect evidence will provide circumstantial elements relevant to the finding of an infringement. It may, for example, consist of a planned meeting entry in a diary, a hotel bill or a travel record.

Evidence 'of the alleged cartel'   Pursuant to points 22 of the 2002 Leniency Notice and 25 of   **8.204**
the 2006 Leniency Notice, added value refers to the extent to which the evidence provided strengthens the Commission's ability 'to prove the facts in question' (2002 Leniency Notice)

---

[505] In 'Revised Leniency Notice—frequently asked questions', MEMO/06/469. The Commission adds that '[t]his does not mean that corporate statements can never provide significant added value, but it signals that they are more likely to provide it when they corroborate other statements or pieces of evidence'.

or 'to prove the alleged cartel' (2006 Leniency Notice). Evidence of the suspected infringement must therefore effectively contribute to the Commission discharging the burden of proof of the infringement and must therefore constitute incriminating evidence. Any other evidence submitted which does not contribute to establish the infringement (such as information on the market, barriers to entry, supply and demand, etc) will not be deemed to provide added value and will therefore not be rewarded under the 2002 Leniency Notice.

8.205 *Requirement to supply 'added value'*　Cartel infringements constitute a restriction by object. It is therefore settled case law that the Commission's ability to find the infringements is not conditional on the finding of actual effects in the market. Regard must be had to the conduct of the parties. This implies that evidence submitted under Section B of the 2002 Leniency Notice (Section III of the 2006 Leniency Notice) will represent added value only if it pertains to *conduct* falling under the prohibition of Article 81 EC. Points 22 of the 2002 Leniency Notice and 25 of the 2006 Leniency Notice clarify that the evidence submitted must ease the Commission's burden of proof by its 'very nature and/or its level of detail'. This implies that the submission of facts which do not pertain to the behaviour of the cartel members such as, for example, evidence of the effects or impact of the anticompetitive conduct, may well not be rewarded by the Commission under the Notice. Indeed, such evidence, albeit useful to the Commission, does not fall within the ambit of what must be proved by the Commission in order to establish the infringement.

8.206 *Requirement to supply 'significant' added value*　It can be expected that the mere strengthening or confirmation of evidence already in the Commission's possession does not constitute *significant* added value. SAV will be provided only by evidence enabling the Commission to prove certain facts. The evidence submitted should therefore either enable the Commission to prove *all or part of the facts* already known to it (eg by generally corroborating prior statements which in all likelihood would not suffice to prove the infringement on a stand-alone basis), or enable the Commission to prove *facts not yet known* to it.[506] Whether the submission of evidence by an applicant provides significant added value enabling the Commission to prove facts certainly requires the exercise of judgement that must take into account all the specific circumstances of a case.

8.207 *Consequences of failure to meet the 'SAV' test*　An applicant under Section B of the 2002 Leniency Notice or Section III of the 2006 Leniency Notice cannot be assured that the evidence submitted will satisfy the SAV test. This uncertainty might be perceived as a disincentive to co-operate. It may fuel concern that the Commission might refuse to reward the provision of useful information whilst nevertheless using it as evidence in the prohibition decision. However, it is submitted that such wariness would not be well founded. Evidence that is necessary for the Commission to establish (a part of) the infringement should normally be rewarded simply on the basis that the Commission relies on such evidence to prove the infringement. That being said, there may be a risk that an undertaking's evidence is used—even extensively—as further information showing the infringement, but that no

---

[506] This could be the case, eg, where, prior to the submission, the only evidence available to the Commission was a statement (most likely to be contested by the incriminated party(ies)), or where the submission elucidates evidence already in the Commission's possession, or where the applicant submits evidence which by its level of detail enables the Commission to prove all or part of the facts.

reward is given. This could happen when other information establishing (those elements of) the infringement was already available to the Commission. Hence the frequency of use of evidence is not a guarantee that an undertaking qualifies for SAV. Although this can be interpreted as a disincentive to an undertaking to apply, account must be taken of the fact that the undertaking cannot weigh up that incentive when applying, and that, from the Commission's point of view, the overall message of the leniency programme is clear: make sure not only that the evidence is good, but also that you bring it in as early as possible. At any rate, any denial of a reward by the Commission for the information supplied by applicants can easily be subjected to effective judicial control on the basis of the content of the prohibition decision and the access to the file that has taken place during the administrative procedure.

Criteria for the determination of appropriate reduction in fines within each band   The   **8.208** fulfilment of the SAV test entitles the applicant to benefit from a reduction in fine within a given band. To that end, the Commission takes into account 'the time at which the evidence fulfilling the [SAV test] was submitted and the extent to which it represents added value.[507] Under the 2002 Leniency Notice, the Commission may also take into account the extent and continuity of any cooperation provided by the undertaking following the date of its submission'.[508] This criterion has disappeared from the 2006 Leniency Notice, as applicants for a reduction in fines are now subject to a duty of full co-operation as set out in point 30(b).

By referring to the time at which the evidence was supplied, the Commission does not refer   **8.209** to the ranking of the applicant, as under the section regarding immunity applications, but to the stage reached in the investigation when the evidence was supplied. Logic suggests that evidence submitted at a very early stage of the investigation, for example shortly after inspections are carried out, will be considered of a higher value than evidence supplied after months of investigation, in recognition of the saving to the Commission in enforcement costs.

The Commission reserves the right, notwithstanding the fact that the evidence was in any   **8.210** case considered of significant added value, to make the level of reduction granted conditional upon the intrinsic value of the evidence submitted. Thus it is to be expected that submission of contemporaneous, directly incriminating documents should attract greater reward than the production of mere statements. This has been confirmed by the 2006 Leniency Notice, where the Commission states explicitly that it attributes greater value, for the purpose of its assessment, to 'compelling' self-standing evidence. Very detailed and substantiated statements can also be expected to warrant a higher reduction than less substantive statements.

As regards the criterion of the quality of the applicant's co-operation throughout the   **8.211** administrative procedure, which now applies only in relation to the 2002 Leniency Notice, it is submitted here that 'the *extent* and *continuity*' of the applicant's co-operation should be construed as a single general criterion of the usefulness of an applicant's co-operation rather

---

[507] Point 23(b), second para of the 2002 Leniency Notice and point 26, second para of the 2006 Leniency Notice.

[508] Point 23(b), second para of the 2002 Leniency Notice.

than being analysed as two distinct criteria. Indeed, it would seem legitimate to consider that co-operation in terms of extent should not be compromised if that co-operation has not developed into a form of continuous exchange with the Commission. Conversely, an applicant's repeated contact or correspondence with the Commission should not be considered as particularly valuable if they did not result in the provision of a significant amount of evidence. It is also considered that the co-operation provided is in fact encapsulated in the value and timing of the evidence rather than in the overall attitude of the applicant. A further evaluation of co-operation, or rather a demonstrated lack thereof, it is suggested, will hence only have a downward influence on the level of reduction granted, it being quite impossible for the Commission to (separately) evaluate and reward what may constitute 'good co-operation'.

(vi) Treatment of the Information Obtained under the 2002 and 2006 Leniency Notices

8.212 **A sensitive aspect of the Commission's leniency policy** By voluntarily providing the Commission with information about a cartel in which they took part, leniency applicants not only help to incriminate other cartel members, but also themselves. This is attractive when it results in full immunity or in a reduction in fine. However, self-incrimination may indirectly result in a greater exposure of the applicant in the context of subsequent judicial proceedings, thereby deterring potential applicants from coming forward.

8.213 One outstanding issue is that voluntary submissions made by immunity or leniency applicants may become available to potential or actual plaintiffs, in particular in respect of certain features of the US (civil) legal system.[509] First, by virtue of the US Federal Rules of Civil Procedures, a party to a civil action can request a US district court to order the discovery of documents held by the other party. Plaintiffs seeking treble damages in regard of cartel conduct have thus started to introduce requests for discovery of EC leniency statements in order to benefit from the self-incriminating nature of such documents. US courts, which have traditionally taken a liberal approach in this regard, may consider such requests favourably in spite of the Commission's declared opposition to such a practice.[510] Secondly, by virtue of Section 1782 of the US Code, a separate discovery rule allows judges to order the production of documents at the request of a party to a proceeding before a foreign or international Tribunal. This may also result in leniency applicants being obliged to produce leniency statements in the context of civil proceedings virtually anywhere in the world. Such a situation may have a considerable chilling effect on the readiness of undertakings to apply for leniency in regard of the risks involved in civil proceedings.[511]

---

[509] Other legal systems may have similar implications for the EC leniency policy. However, a detailed discussion of this issue would go far beyond the scope of the present chapter.

[510] The Commission has in the recent past intervened as *amicus curiae* in US proceedings, but has also written to parties in the framework of such litigation, stating that discovery of leniency statements should not be made discoverable. A request for discovery was finally turned down in the context of antitrust litigation in *Methionine*. However, the production of EC leniency submissions was ordered in the context of the antitrust litigation in *Vitamins*. See eg K Nordlander, 'Discovering Discovey—US Discovery of EC Leniency Statements', ECLR, issue 10 (2004).

[511] For a detailed discussion of the issue, see eg K Nordlander, 'Discovering Discovey—US Discovery of EC Leniency Statements', ECLR, issue 10 (2004).

A second outstanding issue is that self-incriminating information submitted in the context **8.214** of a leniency application may possibly be subsequently used for initiating criminal proceedings at national level against the individuals who, as the leniency applicant's employees, personally took part in the cartel. The Commission must therefore consider the issue of the treatment of the information obtained under its leniency programme with great care.

Identity of immunity applicants   The Commission will not disclose the identity of an **8.215** immunity applicant to any third party[512] without permission, until the Statement of Objection has been issued.[513] At that time the applicant's identity will become known because the Commission must describe in detail the cartel and its investigation, including the fact that the immunity applicant came forward.[514] It is worth noting, however, that the issuing of the Statement of Objections takes some time. In practice, it generally takes at least a year from the date of the inspection(s). It should also be noted that the Statement of Objections is sent only to the parties involved in the proceedings and should not serve any purpose other than the exercise of the right of defence by its addressees.[515] Nevertheless, the Commission will also indicate in the final decision that immunity was granted and who benefited from the immunity, as well as the role played by each cartel member in the infringement.

Access for third parties to statements made under the Notice   Access to the documents **8.216** submitted by the immunity applicant in the context of its co-operation with the Commission will be granted to other parties in accordance with the Commission Notice on rules for access to the Commission file.[516] In point 33 of the 2002 Leniency Notice, the Commission stated that 'any written statement made vis-à-vis the Commission in relation to the Leniency Notice forms part of the Commission's file and may not, as such, be disclosed or used for any other purpose than the enforcement of Article 81 EC'.[517] Point 34 of the 2006 Leniency Notice, makes this even clearer and provides that 'access to the file is only granted to the addressees of a statement of objections on the condition that the information thereby obtained may only be used for the purposes of judicial or administrative proceedings for the application of the Community competition rules at issue in the related administrative proceedings'. This means in particular that access to statements submitted

---

[512] For the avoidance of doubt, the notion of 'third party' excludes National Competition Authorities (see section C(2)(e) below).

[513] If a second company has applied for immunity in a case where conditional immunity has already been granted, the Commission must inform the second applicant that immunity is no longer available or that it is not the first to apply. The Commission does not, however, disclose the identity of the first applicant.

[514] The Commission indicates in point 39 of the 2006 Leniency Notice that '[i]n line with the Commission's practice, the fact that an undertaking cooperated with the Commission during its administrative procedure will be indicated in any decision, so as to explain the reason for the immunity or reduction of the fine. The fact that immunity or reduction in respect of fines is granted cannot protect an undertaking from the civil law consequences of its participation in an infringement of Article 81 EC'.

[515] See point 33 of the 2002 Leniency Notice; points 6, 7 and 34 of the 2006 Leniency Notice; Art 15(4) of Regulation 773/2004, and point 48 of the Commission Notice on the rules for access to the Commission file in cases pursuant to Arts 81 and 82 of the EC Treaty, Arts 53, 54 and 57 of the EEA Agreement and Council Regulation (EC) No 139/2004, [2005] OJ C325/7.

[516] [2005] OJ C325/7.

[517] It is understood that the notion of 'enforcement of Article 81 EC' is narrowly construed here, in that it refers to the enforcement of Art 81 EC by competition authorities and does not cover private enforcement.

by an applicant in the context of the 2002 Leniency Notice will be confined strictly to the purpose of the exercise of the rights of defence. Parties may not use the documents to which they were granted access for other purposes, for example, private litigation.[518]

8.217 **Limitations in the conditions of access to corporate statements** Pursuant to point 33 of the 2006 Leniency Notice, access to corporate statements is only granted to the addressees of a Statement of Objections 'provided that they commit, together with the legal counsel getting access on their behalf, not to make any copy by mechanical or electronic means of any information in the corporate statement to which access is being granted and to ensure that the information to be obtained from the corporate statement will solely be used for the purposes of judicial or administrative proceedings for the application of the Community competition rules at issue in the related administrative proceedings'. Point 33 also provides that 'other parties such as complainants will not be granted access to corporate statements'.

8.218 Parties seeking access to corporate statements are required to sign a document whereby they agree to abide by the provision of Article 15(4) of Regulation No 773/2004 stating that documents obtained through access to the file may only be used for the purposes of judicial or administrative proceedings for the application of Article 81 EC.

8.219 **Sanctions for violation of the limitation imposed in respect of access to file** The 2006 Leniency Notice provides for a set of possible sanctions in the case of violation of the limitations applicable to the use of the information obtained through access to the file. First, the use of such information for a different purpose during the proceedings may be regarded as lack of co-operation within the meaning of points 12 and 27 of the 2006 Leniency Notice. Secondly, if any such use is made after the Commission has already adopted a prohibition decision in the proceedings, the Commission may, in any legal proceedings before the Community Courts, ask the Court to increase the fine in respect of the responsible undertaking. Thirdly, should the information be used for a different purpose, at any point in time, with the involvement of an outside counsel, the Commission may report the incident to the bar of that counsel, with a view to disciplinary action.

8.220 **Leniency and public access to documents** As regards public access to documents (outside of the scope of access to file), the Commission has taken the position that the disclosure, at any time, of documents received under the Leniency Notice would undermine 'the purpose of inspections and investigations' within the meaning of Article 4(2) of Regulation No 1049/2001 regarding public access to the documents of the EC institutions.[519] This is spelled

---

[518] In this regard, legal representatives are given access to documents only after signing a formal commitment that the information to which they will be given access will not be used for any purpose other than defence of their client's rights in the Commission proceedings.

[519] Regulation (EC) No 1049/2001 of the European Parliament and of the Council of 30 May 2001 regarding public access to European Parliament, Council and Commission documents [2001] OJ L145/43. Limited exceptions to the right of access are listed in Art 4(1) and 4(2). Pursuant to Art 4(2), 'the institutions shall refuse access to a document where disclosure would undermine the protection of commercial interests of a natural or legal person, including intellectual property, court proceedings and legal advice [and] *the purpose of inspections, investigations and audits*, unless there is an overriding public interest in the disclosure' (emphasis added).

out in both point 32 of the 2002 Leniency Notice and point 40 of the 2006 Leniency Notice. The disclosure of such documents would therefore be subject to the applicable restrictions. The underlying rationale is that undertakings which are being investigated have a legitimate expectation that information they supply to the Commission on an obligatory or a voluntary basis within the framework of an investigation under Article 81 EC will not be disclosed and that it will be used only for the purposes of the Commission proceedings. Also, the disclosure of such information could place the provider in a worse position in terms of any claims for civil damages than companies not co-operating with the Commission.[520]

Communication of leniency documents to other enforcement authorities   As regards the   **8.221** communication of leniency documents to other enforcement authorities, two situations should be distinguished. On the one hand, leniency applications are treated on a confidential basis with regard to enforcement authorities outside the ECN. In the context of international cartels, however, the Commission may ask—and this is always the case in practice—the undertaking to waive the confidentiality in respect of third country jurisdictions where the applicant has also applied for leniency.[521] On the other hand, as regards communication with National Competition Authorities (NCAs) within the EU the situation is governed by Regulation No 1/2003 which provides that the Commission and the NCAs are, under specific conditions, entitled to exchange information in the context of a leniency application without the prior authorisation of the applicant. However, this power is subject to strict conditions. Guarantees exist in particular as regards the exchange of information relating to the conduct of individuals. This aspect is dealt with in more detail in paras 8.240 to 8.242 below.

(d) *Judicial Review of the Commission's Leniency Policy*

The Community courts have had several opportunities to take a position on the principle   **8.222** of leniency and on the application of the 1996 Leniency Notice by the Commission. However, as at 31 December 2006, the Community courts had not rendered any judgment concerning cartel decisions where the 2002 Leniency Notice was applied.[522] This section therefore only describes the judicial review of the application of the 1996 Leniency Notice. However, apart from a few aspects which have lost their relevance under the new Notices, most of the findings of the courts can be considered relevant under the 2002 or 2006

---

[520] In spite of the rather unclear drafting of the exception in Regulation No 1049/2001, there would appear to be sound reasons for considering that the purpose of investigations and inspections would be undermined if the release of leniency statements was possible, even after an investigation is closed. It would jeopardise the willingness of parties to co-operate fully with the Commission's investigation and thus prejudice the Commission's ability to conduct its present and future investigations in an effective manner. It would put into question the openness of the exchange of information with the Commission on which the Commission relies in conducting successful investigations. Parties would be reluctant to co-operate fully and would retain information essential to the Commission's fair and objective handling of the case. In general, the Commission's ability to carry out investigations and fulfil its duty under the Treaty to apply the competition rules as provided by Art 4(2) of Regulation 1049/2001 would therefore be jeopardised.

[521] In such cases, the Commission will ask the applicant to provide a waiver so that the Commission can discuss the case with these authorities and share information without restriction. Such a waiver allows, in particular, coordination of simultaneous enforcement actions by the authorities concerned.

[522] The first time the Commission applied the 2002 Leniency Notice was in *Raw Tobacco Italy*. The decision was adopted on 17 October 2005 (full text of the decision available on DG COMP's web site).

Leniency Notices. Overall, the courts have largely upheld the Commission's practice. They have nevertheless clarified a number of important points as to how the Commission must assess co-operation under its leniency policy.

8.223 **Recognition of the rationale of leniency**   Prior to the adoption of the 1996 Leniency Notice, the European Courts had already stated that a reduction in the fine imposed on an undertaking was justified when the latter had facilitated the finding of an infringement. In the context of *Polypropylene*,[523] one of the first cases where the Commission had taken into consideration the co-operation of certain undertakings in setting fines, the CFI reduced the fine imposed on ICI on account of its co-operation with the Commission during the administrative procedure. The CFI stated that without ICI's very detailed reply to a request for information, 'it would have been much more difficult for the Commission to establish and bring to an end the infringement [. . .]. Even though the applicant's cooperation was not forthcoming until after the Commission had found compromising documents on its premises, it would have been more difficult for the Commission to understand the significance of those documents and of those which it had taken from other producers' premises and to draw the necessary inferences from those documents so as to establish the existence of the infringement and bring it to an end if it had not had the benefit of the applicant's reply to the request for information'.[524]

8.224 **Co-operation must facilitate the finding of the infringement**   The CFI specified the rationale of leniency in the *Cartonboard* case, where it explicitly spelled out that '[a] reduction on grounds of cooperation during the administrative procedure is justified only if the conduct enabled the Commission to establish an infringement more easily and, where relevant, to bring it to an end'.[525] This implies that a reduction in the fine is justified only if, by co-operating, the applicant went beyond its legal obligations, in particular its duty to reply to requests for information.[526] Thus in *Cascades v Commission*, where the applicant claimed that the reductions of fines granted to other undertakings showed that the mere reply to requests for information justified a reduction, the CFI rejected the argument by stating that one of the undertakings concerned had provided information 'well in excess of that which the Commission may require under Article 11 of Regulation 17 (now Article 18 of Regulation 1/2003)'.[527] The CFI and the ECJ subsequently confirmed that only co-operation going beyond the legal obligations of an undertaking can justify reducing the fine under the Leniency Notice.[528]

---

[523] [1986] OJ L230/1.

[524] Case T-13/89 *ICI v Commission* [1992] ECR II-1021, paras 393–394.

[525] Case T-338/94 *Finnboard v Commission* [1998] ECR II-1617, para 363, upheld by the ECJ in Case C-298/98 P *Finnboard v Commission* [2000] ECR I-10157. See also Joined Cases T-45/98, and T-47/98 *Krupp Thyssen Stainless and Acciai speciali Terni v Commission* [2001] ECR II-3757, para 270, and Case T-279/02 *Degussa v Commision*, not yet reported, para 380.

[526] Case T-12/89 *Solvay v Commision* [1992] ECR II-907, paras 341 and 342.

[527] See Case T-308/94 *Cascades v Commission* [1998] ECR II-925, para 262.

[528] See Case T-230/00 *Daesang v Commission* [2003] ECR II-2733, para 137, Case T-38/02 *Groupe Danone v Commission*, [2005] ECR II-4407, para 451, and Case T-48/02 *Brouwerij Haacht v Commision*, not yet reported, para 106. See also Case C-301/04 P *SGL Carbon v Commission*, not yet reported, paras 39–50, where the Court rejected the finding of the CFI in Joined Cases T-236/01, T-239/01, T-244/01 to T-246/01, T-251/01 and T-252/01 *Tokai Carbon and others v Commission* [2004] ECR II-1181, paras 408–409 and confirmed that the submission, in response to a request for information, of information falling within the scope of this request does not constitute cooperation justifying a reduction of the fine under the leniency policy.

Co-operation must relate to the infringement for which the applicant is liable   Under   **8.225**
the same principle, the co-operation provided must consist of supplying the Commission
with information facilitating the finding of the infringement for which the undertaking
can be held liable.[529] Where an undertaking provides the Commission with information
that does not, as such, assist the Commission in establishing the existence of an infringement, but which does enable it to evaluate more precisely the degree of co-operation offered
by another undertaking during the administrative procedure, the provision of that information cannot be regarded as co-operation falling within the scope of the Leniency Notice.
However, it may in exceptional circumstances amount to 'effective cooperation outside the
scope of the [Leniency] Notice', that is to an attenuating circumstance pursuant to the
Guidelines on fines justifying, on that ground, a reduction in the amount of the fine.[530]
This does not imply, however, that the provision of information or evidence that failed to
justify a reduction in fine under the Commission leniency programme should nevertheless
be rewarded as constituting some kind of co-operation outside of the scope of the Leniency
Notice. When the information provided could have been be rewarded under the Leniency
Notice had the applicable test been met, failure to pass the test should normally exclude any
other kind of reward.

Co-operation must be truly useful to the Commission   In order to be considered as   **8.226**
facilitating the finding of the infringement, the applicant's co-operation must be truly
useful to the Commission. In the *Cascades* judgment the CFI had stated that a reduction in fine was justified because the undertaking concerned had supplied information
that went 'well in excess of that which the Commission may require' under its investigation powers. This raised the question as to whether the resulting requirement was
for the applicant to provide information 'well in excess' (as had actually been the case in
Cascades) or simply 'in excess' of that which the Commission may require. Subsequent
case law appears to have established that the factual finding in *Cascades* has become the
applicable test. Indeed, the CFI found in its judgments regarding *Amino Acids* and
Belgian Beer that 'a reduction in the fine is justified where an undertaking provides the
Commission with information *well in excess* of that which the Commission may require
under [its investigative powers]'.[531] The CFI has also found that where the declaration
of an applicant merely confirms, albeit less precisely and less explicitly, some of the
information already provided by another undertaking, and when its usefulness lies
exclusively in the fact that it corroborates to a certain extent information which the
Commission already had at its disposal, such a declaration does not facilitate the
Commission's task significantly and therefore does not justify a reduction in the fine on

---

[529]   Where, in the course of the Commission's investigation of a cartel, an undertaking makes available
to it information concerning actions for which it could not in any event have been required to pay a fine,
that does not amount to co-operation falling within the scope of the Leniency Notice (see Case T-224/00
ADM v Commission [2003] ECR II-2957, para 297, and Case T-38/02 *Groupe Danone v Commission* [2005]
ECR II-4407, para 452).

[530]   Case T-224/00 *ADM v Commission* [2003] ECR II-2957, paras 304–307.

[531]   See Case T-230/00 *Daesang v Commission* [2003] ECR II-2733, para 137, Case T-38/02 *Groupe
Danone v Commission* [2005] ECR II-4407, para 451, and Case T-48/02 *Brouwerij Haacht v Commision*, not
yet reported, para 106.

grounds of co-operation.[532] Thus an 'efficiency threshold' applies with respect to leniency and a reduction can only be justified if the undertaking's cooperation has indeed been of significant added value to the Commission.

8.227 **Duty to demonstrate a genuine spirit of co-operation** The Court found on appeal in *Pre-insulated Pipes* that a reduction under the leniency programme can be justified only where the information provided and, more generally, the conduct of the undertaking concerned might be considered to demonstrate 'genuine cooperation' on its part. It follows that even if an applicant provided information capable, in principle, of meeting the conditions that permit a reduction in the fine under the Leniency Notice, this does not oblige the Commission to grant the applicant a reduction under that notice.[533] Thus, the Commission is entitled to refuse to grant a reduction in the fines when the applicant provides incomplete or partly inaccurate information. This has been confirmed on appeal in *Graphite Electrodes* where the Court found that by giving incomplete and misleading answers to questions it was not obliged to answer, the behaviour of SGL Carbon had not reflected 'a spirit of cooperation within the meaning of the judgment in *Dansk Rørindustri and others v Commission*'.[534]

8.228 **Lack of spontaneity in co-operation may be taken into account** The Court also confirmed that the Commission, when deciding the level of any reduction, is entitled to take into account the fact that the cooperation was not entirely on the initiative of the party. In *ABB v Commission*, the Court stated that 'it was perfectly admissible for the Commission not to grant the maximum reduction envisaged by section D of the 1996 Leniency Notice to the applicant, which did not declare its willingness to cooperate until after receiving a first request for information.[535] Also, even if there has been a certain degree of helpful cooperation, the Commission is justified in refusing to grant a reduction if the undertaking has provided it with incomplete or inexact information'.[536]

8.229 **Non-contestation of facts must be express (1996 Leniency Notice only)** In order to receive a reduction in the fine on the ground of not contesting the facts, as was provided for in point D.2 of the 1996 Leniency Notice, the undertaking was required to have informed

---

[532] Case T-44/00 *Mannesmann Röhrenwerke v Commission* [2004] ECR II-2223, para 301, and Case T-38/02 *Groupe Danone v Commission* [2005] ECR II-4407, para 455. This is, however, debatable. Indeed, in many cases, the corroborative value of the evidence brought by an applicant may be of great importance in relation to the Commission's ability to find the infringement (see section D(2) of this chapter). It is therefore submitted that the conclusion drawn by the CFI should be valid mainly in situations where the evidence supplied only corroborates facts which the Commission is already capable of establishing to the requisite legal standard.

[533] Joined Cases C-189/02 P, C-202/02 P, C-205/02 P to C-208/02 P and C-213/02 P *Dansk Rørindustri and others v Commission*, not yet reported, paras 392–403. The ECJ upheld the finding of the CFI that the conduct of the undertaking Henss/Isoplus had not demonstrated genuine co-operation by providing incomplete and, in part, inaccurate information. The Court also confirmed that there had been no breach of what the appellant alleged to be the criminal law principle that an admission, even where it is only a partial admission, must necessarily lead to a reduction in the fine. No breach of the rights of the defence or of the principle *non bis in idem* was found either.

[534] Case C-301/04 P *SGL Carbon and others v Commission*, not yet reported, paras 66–70.

[535] Case T-31/99 Case T-31/99 *ABB Asea Brown Boveri v Commission* [2002] ECR II-1881, para 238 and T-17/99 *Ke Kelit v Commission*, para 181–182.

[536] Case T-9/99 *HFB Holding für Fernwärmetechnik and others v Commission* [2002] ECR II-1487, paras 616–619.

the Commission expressly that it had no intention of substantially contesting the facts, after reviewing the Statement of Objections.[537] In the absence of such an express declaration, mere silence on the part of an undertaking could not be considered to facilitate the Commission's task because the Commission is then required to establish the existence of all the facts in the final decision without being able to rely on a declaration by the undertaking.[538] In the same vein, it was found insufficient for an undertaking to state in general terms that it does not contest the facts alleged (in accordance with the 1996 Leniency Notice) if, in the circumstances of the case, that statement is not of any help to the Commission.[539] Nor can a statement that the undertaking does not substantially contest the facts be considered as facilitating the Commission's task where the statement is accompanied by a series of observations by which the applicant allegedly seeks to clarify the significance of certain facts but which, in reality, amounts to contesting those facts.[540]

Retraction of non-contestation (1996 Leniency Notice only)   However, the Court has   **8.230**
found that a subsequent submission by an undertaking seeking legal qualification of the facts, and which differed from the initial submission, would not be considered a retraction as long as the facts themselves were not contested.[541] Also, the Commission would not consider it a failure to co-operate if an undertaking contested an element of the infringement which the Commission had ultimately not been able to prove in the decision even if, allegedly, the Commission's failure to prove this element of the infringement resulted directly from the undertaking's retraction.[542] However the CFI has found that in the case of an agreement which has an anticompetitive object, such as a cartel, 'an admission of the truth of the facts is sufficient, in principle, to establish two of the essential elements of an infringement of Article 81(1) EC, namely the existence of an agreement and its anti-competitive object'.[543] It follows that an undertaking cannot, in its response to the Statement of Objections, contest the 'infringing nature' of the facts which the Commission has validly established and which themselves constitute the infringement in question, without substantially contesting the facts within the meaning of the second indent of Section D.2 of the Leniency Notice.[544]

Lenient treatment and admissibility of pleas contesting facts before the CFI   Where an   **8.231**
undertaking expressly acknowledges the facts, thereby explicitly admitting during the

---

[537] Case T-347/94 *Mayr-Melnhof v Commission* [1998] ECR II-1751, para 309.
[538] Case T-44/00 *Mannesmann Röhrenwerke v Commission* [2004] ECR II-2223, para 303.
[539] Case T-48/00 *Corus UK v Commission* [2004] ECR II-2325, para 193, and Case T-38/02 *Groupe Danone v Commission* [2005] ECR II-4407, para 505.
[540] Case T-38/02 *Groupe Danone v Commission* [2005] ECR II-4407, para 515.
[541] In *British Sugar* [1999] OJ L76/1, the Commission had granted only a 50% reduction to the first applicant, under Section D and not Section B, in the light of what was alleged to be the retraction of its admission of certain facts or legal qualifications in the course of the proceedings. The CFI found that the Commission has erred in law on this point in Joined cases T-202/98, T-204/98 and T-207/98 *Tate & Lyle, British Sugar and Napier Brown v Commission* [2001] ECR II-2035, para 161. See also Case T-15/02 *BASF v Commision*, not yet reported, para 93.
[542] Joined cases T-202/98, T-204/98 and T-207/98 *Tate & Lyle, British Sugar and Napier Brown v Commission* [2001] ECR II-2035, para 161.
[543] Case T-48/00 *Corus UK v Commission* [2004] ECR II-2325, para 195 and T-38/02 *Groupe Danone v Commission* [2005] ECR II-4407, para 514.
[544] Case T-38/02 *Groupe Danone v Commission* [2005] ECR II-4407, para 514.

administrative procedure the substantive truth of the facts which the Commission alleges against it in the Statement of Objections, those facts must thereafter be regarded as established and the undertaking is estopped in principle from disputing them during the procedure before the Court.[545] However, if an undertaking has not expressly acknowledged the facts during the administrative procedure, but has merely stated that it was not expressing any view on the Commission's factual allegations, thereby failing to acknowledge the correctness of those allegations, it is not barred from putting forward before the Court any plea in its defence which it deems appropriate.[546]

8.232 When the participation of the undertaking in the cartel has been inferred by the Commission, not from a clear and precise statement made by the undertaking, but from a range of evidence such as its conduct towards the Commission during the administrative procedure and its rather general 'no contest' statements, the undertaking in question cannot be prevented from pleading before the Court that that range of evidence was misinterpreted as proving its participation during the relevant period.[547] However, in such a case, the Commission, facing a belated challenge of certain facts, is entitled, for the purpose of establishing before the Court the participation of the undertaking in the infringement, to rely on the attitude taken by the undertaking during the course of the administrative procedure, namely that the undertaking did not dispute that it had taken part in the infringement during the relevant period.[548] It follows, from the option left to the Commission to rely on the undertaking's attitude during the administrative procedure as evidence of its participation in the infringement, that the Commission's task of establishing the facts constituting the infringement may, in effect, have been made easier during the administrative procedure by the undertaking's conduct and statements. Furthermore, if the undertaking's attitude ultimately suffices for the Commission to establish to the requisite legal standard before the Court that the undertaking took part in the infringement without having to adduce fresh evidence, the result is that the Commission's task was not in itself rendered objectively more difficult due the fact that the Commission's findings were subsequently challenged by the undertaking before the Court. Therefore, this is not a justification for the Court, at the request of the Commission, to annul the reduction granted to the undertaking in the final decision. However, with regard to the additional effort that the belated and unexpected challenge of certain facts requires from the Commission before the Court, the latter may, in the exercise of its unlimited jurisdiction, and in view of the fact that the infringement has been established, decide to increase the fine imposed on the undertaking.[549]

---

[545] Case T-224/00 *ADM v Commission*, para 227; Joined cases T-236/01, T-239/01, T-244/01 to T-246/01, T-251/01 and T-252/01 *Tokai Carbon and others v Commission* [2004] ECR II-1181, para 109. However, the applicant is permitted to argue the legal basis for the facts before the CFI. See Case T-15/02 *BASF v Commission*, not yet reported, para 293.

[546] Case C-297/98 P *SCA Holding v Commission* [2000] ECR I-10101, para 37; Cases T-224/00 *ADM v Commission*, para 227; Joined cases T-236/01, T-239/01, T-244/01 to T-246/01, T-251/01, and T-252/01 *Tokai Carbon and others v Commission* [2004] ECR II-1181, para 108.

[547] Joined cases T-236/01, T-239/01, T-244/01 to T-246/01, T-251/01 and T-252/01 *Tokai Carbon v Commission* [2004] ECR II-1181, para 109.

[548] ibid, para 110.

[549] ibid, paras 111–112.

Leniency and equal treatment   The CFI has confirmed that the granting of different levels **8.233** of reduction in the fines by the Commission by virtue of its leniency policy does not constitute a breach of the principle of equal treatment. Indeed, a reduction in the fine is justified only if the conduct of the undertaking concerned enabled the Commission to establish the infringement more easily. The Commission is thus perfectly entitled to grant leniency applicants different reductions in fines corresponding to the differences in the value and timing of their co-operation.[550] In cases where the Commission has itself solicited information, such a differentiation cannot however depend on purely random factors, such as the order in which companies are questioned by, or answer to, the Commission.[551] Any differential treatment must therefore be clearly justified. Equal treatment does not imply, however, that the Commission must apply the same reduction in fine for the same co-operative conduct or in each case. The mere fact that the Commission has in previous decisions granted a certain rate of reduction for a specific co-operative conduct does not imply that it is required to grant the same proportionate reduction when assessing similar conduct in a subsequent administrative procedure.[552] Each case must be assessed on its own merits.

Co-operation under the leniency notice must be differentiated from co-operation as an **8.234** **'attenuating circumstance'**   In *HFB v Commission*, the Court found that the Commission was right not to take account of the applicant's co-operation as a mitigating factor in the case of cartels, since such co-operation clearly falls to be assessed under the Leniency Notice in such cases.[553] However, as the 1998 Guidelines also did before them, the 2006 Guidelines on fines clearly set out that the effective co-operation of an undertaking outside of the scope of the Leniency Notice may nevertheless be taken into account as an attenuating circumstance. It is submitted, however, in line with the Court's finding, that such an attenuating circumstance should apply only in regard of effective co-operation which, despite facilitating the Commission's investigation, could because of its nature not be considered for a reduction under the applicable leniency programme. It should not be used to reward the provision of information failing to pass the relevant thresholds of the applicable Leniency Notice, such as the 'SAV' test, as this would result in a circumvention of the leniency programme (on this topic, see also para 8.225 above).

(e) Leniency within the European Competition Network

The entry into force of Regulation No 1/2003 has introduced very significant changes **8.235** as regards the enforcement of European competition law. It has established a European

---

[550] Cases T-21/99 *Dansk Rørindustri v Commission* [2002] ECR II-1681, para 245.

[551] Such a situation could arise under the 1996 Leniency Notice. On appeal in *Alloy Surcharge* [1998] OJ L100/55, the CFI found that the Commission had erred in law by granting lower reductions to certain companies because the content of their submission disclosed nothing more than had previously been disclosed by other applicants: as the same questions had been put at the same time to the companies, the Court concluded that the extent of their co-operation had to be 'regarded as comparable in so far as those undertakings provided the Commission, at the same stage of the administrative procedure and in similar circumstances, with similar information concerning the conduct imputed to them' (Case T-48/98 *Acerinox* [2001] ECR II-3859, para 140, and Joined case T-45/98 and T-47/98 *Krupp Thyssen Stainless and Acciai speciali Terni v Commission* [2001] ECR II-3757, para 246).

[552] Case T-31/99 *ABB Asea Brown Boveri v Commission* [2002] ECR II-1881, para 239.

[553] Case T-9/99 *HFB Holding für Fernwärmetechnik and others v Commission* [2002] ECR II-1487, paras 608–610.

network of competition authorities (ECN) including the Commission and the NCAs, capable of referring cases to each other and exchanging information, as well as a system of close co-operation between the ECN and national courts (see Chapter 2 of this book, in particular Section E). Although the changes are not directly linked to the operation of leniency programmes, they entail significant consequences for companies applying for leniency.[554] This has been considered in the design of the new system, which includes measures to preserve the effectiveness of leniency programmes in the EU in an environment where not all NCAs conduct a leniency policy.[555]

8.236 **Advantages of the new system and measures taken to tackle potential risks** From the perspective of an applicant for immunity or for a reduction in fine, one of the advantages of the new system is that, in contrast to the previous regime, the opening of proceedings by the Commission under Article 11(6) of the Regulation automatically deprives NCAs of their competence to investigate the case not only under Article 81 EC, but also under their national competition law.[556] Thus, if the Commission grants immunity to an applicant and subsequently opens proceedings, the undertaking concerned does not run the risk of further proceedings in a Member State. Also, the Commission Notice on Cooperation with the Network of Competition Authorities ('the Network Notice)[557] means that the information provided to an NCA under an application for leniency will not be transferred to an authority that has no leniency programme unless the receiving authority guarantees the applicant the same beneficial treatment as the transmitting authority.[558]

8.237 However, the new system raises some potential issues of serious concern. First, in the absence of any harmonisation by Regulation No 1/2003 of the sanctioning regimes, there is no obligation for NCAs to adopt a leniency policy. Although many NCAs have now adopted leniency programmes,[559] and in spite of their similarities, their terms are country-specific and there is, notwithstanding the existence of an ECN 'model programme' adopted in September 2006, no programme common to all ECN members under which a cartel participant may apply. Thus, an applicant who has supplied information under one particular leniency programme might fear that it will subsequently find itself exposed to sanctions in another jurisdiction where it could not apply, or has not applied, for immunity or leniency. Secondly, the criminalisation of cartel behaviour in some Member States could become a deterrent factor if the transfer to other NCAs, under Regulation No 1/2003, of the names of individuals having taken part in the cartel were to lead to their criminal prosecution in the Member States where penal sanctions apply. Thirdly, undertakings contemplating co-operation under a leniency programme could fear that in national court

---

[554] C Swaak and MR Mollica, 'Leniency Applicants Face to Modernisation of EC Competition Law' (2005) ECLR.

[555] See eg S Blake and D Schnichels, 'Leniency Following Modernisation: safeguarding Europe's leniency programmes', Competition Policy Newsletter, No 2, Summer 2004; C Gauer, 'Les programmes de clémence au regard du droit communautaire', Concurrences, issue No 3 (2005); C Gauer and M Jaspers, 'The European Competition Network Achievements and Challenges—a case in point: leniency', Competition Policy Newsletter No 1, Spring 2006.

[556] See Art 3 of Regulation No 1/2003.

[557] [2004] OJ C101/43.

[558] See paras 8.240 to 8.243 below.

[559] 19 Member States on 1 July 2006. A list is available at: <http://europa.eu.int/comm./competition/antitrust/legislation/authorities_with_leniency_programme.pdf>.

proceedings regarding claims for losses suffered by a party as a result of cartel behaviour, the Commission might transmit to that court information voluntarily submitted as part of the leniency application.[560] Such uncertainties could seriously undermine the effectiveness of the leniency programmes of the Commission and the Member States.

The Commission and NCAs have sought to address these concerns through specific rules **8.238** provided not only in Regulation No 1/2003, but also in two of the Commission Notices that followed as part of the so-called 'modernisation package', namely the Network Notice and the Commission Notice on the Cooperation between the Commission and Courts of the EU Member States in the application of Articles 81 and 82 EC (the 'Notice on the Cooperation with the Courts').[561] The Network Notice addresses two of the above mentioned concerns. First, that due to co-operation under Article 11 of Regulation 1/2003, a leniency application to one ECN member might trigger an investigation by another ECN member to which the applicant has not also applied for leniency and, secondly, that the information volunteered to one ECN member, together with any information consequently obtained by the latter, might be transmitted to another ECN member under Article 12 of Regulation 1/2003 and used as evidence to impose sanctions on the applicant.

Leniency applications and Article 11 of Regulation No 1/2003 Pursuant to Article 11(3) of **8.239** Regulation No 1/2003, an NCA taking action under Article 81 EC—including as a result of a leniency application—must inform the Commission before, or without delay, after commencing the first formal investigative measure.[562] The Network Notice provides that the information contained in a leniency application submitted to an ECN member may not be used by another ECN member as a basis for starting an investigation on its own behalf, whether under Article 81 EC or—as regards NCAs—under their national competition or other laws.[563] Whilst another ECN member is not precluded from investigating the case, nevertheless,[564] it may not solicit such information unless it provides guarantees that the applicant who applied to the transmitting authority will be granted the same favourable treatment. It is worth emphasising that the risk to the leniency applicant of another authority independently receiving information and initiating an investigation on its own behalf is not due to Regulation No 1/2003. The same risk actually existed before 1 May 2004 and therefore does not result from the co-operation which is encouraged under Regulation No 1/2003 and the Network Notice.[565]

---

[560] Pursuant to Art 15(1) of Regulation 1/2003, national courts may in proceedings for the application of Arts 81 EC and 82 EC ask the Commission to transmit to them information in its possession or its opinion on questions concerning the application of the Community competition rules.

[561] OJ [2004] C101/54.

[562] Regulation 1/2003 also provides that the information may be made available to other NCAs. The Commission has accepted a similar obligation to inform NCAs under Art 11(2) of the Regulation. The information transmitted includes the name of the authority dealing with the case, the product, territories and parties concerned, the nature and suspected duration of the alleged infringement, and the origin of the case.

[563] Para 39 of the Network Notice. It is understood by the ECN members that this commitment covers all forms of communications about such cases, and not only the specific information which is submitted to the common case-management system (see C Gauer and M Jaspers, 'The European Competition Network Achievements and Challenges—a case in point: leniency', Competition Policy Newsletter No 1, Spring 2006).

[564] Another NCA can nevertheless open an investigation on the basis of information received from other sources, such as a complainant, an informant, or another leniency applicant.

[565] S Blake and D Schnichels, 'Leniency Following Modernisation: safeguarding Europe's leniency programmes', Competition Policy Newsletter, No 2, Summer 2004.

8.240 **Leniency applications and Article 12 of Regulation No 1/2003**   Under Article 12 of Regulation No 1/2003, ECN members have the power, for the purpose of applying Articles 81 or 82 EC, and only upon request, to provide one another with, and to use in evidence, any matter of fact or law, including confidential information. The Network Notice indicates how the ECN exercises this power in cases where leniency applications have been filed.[566] Two categories of information are considered, namely, information voluntarily submitted by a leniency applicant and information obtained as the result of investigatory powers such as inspections or any other fact-finding measures which could not have been carried out in the absence of a leniency application. Under the Network Notice, such information may be transmitted from one ECN Member to another only in one of the three following alternative circumstances: (i) the leniency applicant has consented to the transmission of the information submitted as part of its leniency application;[567] (ii) the ECN member requesting the information has also received from the same undertaking a leniency application relating to the same infringement;[568] or (iii) the authority to which the information is transmitted has given guarantees concerning the use that will be made of that information and of any additional information obtained as a result of the information transmitted.[569]

8.241 **Guarantees to be provided by the receiving authority**   Where the leniency applicant has neither consented to the transmission of information to another NCA nor made a (parallel) application under the leniency programme of that NCA, the receiving authority must first guarantee that not only the information transmitted to it, but also that any information it may subsequently obtain on this basis, will not be used either by it or by any other authority to which the information is subsequently transmitted to impose sanctions on: (i) the leniency applicant; (ii) any other person covered by a favourable treatment offered by the transmitting authority as a result of its leniency programme; or (iii) any employee or former employee of any of the persons covered by (i) or (ii). Thus the guarantee given confers on the applicant immunity from any fine which the receiving authority might otherwise have imposed on it, unless the latter already possessed sufficient evidence to impose a sanction on the undertaking concerned. A copy of such a guarantee, when it is issued, is to be provided to the leniency applicant.[570]

---

[566] Paras 40 and 41 of the Network Notice.

[567] Under Art 12 of the Regulation, the transmission of information does not normally require the prior consent of the party that provided the information.

[568] Thus, once a leniency applicant has made the decision to apply to more than one authority within the ECN, it must accept that the authorities to which it applied will no longer require its consent in order to exchange information amongst themselves. It should be noted in this respect that at the time the information is transmitted, it must not be open to the applicant to withdraw its leniency application from the authority to which the information is to be transmitted. This proviso is necessary so as not to nullify provisions such as that in the Commission's leniency programme allowing an applicant for immunity to withdraw its evidence if it fails to meet the requirements for conditional immunity.

[569] Of course, if the Commission investigates the case itself, it may be necessary to pass information to certain Member States for the purpose of preparing inspections and subsequently in the context of the administrative procedure preceding the adoption of a formal decision prohibiting the cartel. In such circumstances however, Member States are subject to an obligation of professional secrecy under Art 28 of Regulation No 1/2003 and cannot use the information received as evidence in their national law enforcement.

[570] This provision applies not only to applicants who have been awarded immunity by the transmitting authority, but in general also to those that have voluntarily supplied information: the receiving authority cannot use that information for any sanction to be imposed on the applicant.

Guarantees regarding the information relating to individuals   In order to deal with the   **8.242**
issue of the exchange of (voluntarily supplied) information in a context where such information may trigger prosecution against individuals, Article 12(3) of Regulation No 1/2003
provides that information within the ECN can only be used as evidence for the imposition
of sanctions on natural persons where the information has been collected in a way that
respects the same level of protection of the rights of defence of natural persons as is provided under the rules of the receiving authority. This condition, it is submitted, is not met
in relation to immunity applications filed with the Commission that would be transferred
to an NCA which applies criminal sanctions, as their voluntary nature is entirely different
from the nature of criminal proceedings. Therefore any information originating from
immunity applications filed with the Commission could be used to impose sanctions on
individuals for cartel behaviour in the case of national criminal proceedings.[571]

Binding nature of the policy set out in the Network Notice   The Network Notice is a   **8.243**
Commission Notice. As such, its provisions, as described above, can be deemed to create
legitimate expectations on which leniency applicants may rely in so far as the Commission's
conduct is concerned. Nevertheless, even though the Network Notice alone does not bind
NCAs, the latter have committed themselves to respecting the principles set out in the
Network Notice.[572] All NCAs have signed a declaration acknowledging those principles
and have declared that they will abide by them.[573] The declaration is annexed to the
Network Notice. Thus, irrespective of the NCA to which the application is made, protected leniency information will only be transmitted to another ECN member under the
three conditions described above.

Leniency applications and transmission of information to national courts   Regulation   **8.244**
No 1/2003 establishes mechanisms ensuring co-operation between the ECN members
and national courts. The Regulation provides in particular that the national courts may ask
the Commission, in the context of proceedings under Article 81 or 82 EC, to provide
them with information in its possession.[574] As proceedings before national courts may consist of actions for damages relating to the harm caused by a cartel, leniency applicants may

---

[571] Theoretically, however, this does not preclude a Member State from acting against individuals on the
basis of national laws that are not competition laws, provided that the proceedings are not based on evidence
received through the ECN under Art 12. It is feasible that criminal proceedings could be brought against
employees of a company which has received immunity from the Commission on the basis of information
resulting from the final Decision. Such initiatives would, however, go directly against the purpose of the EC
leniency policy. It can therefore be assumed that the Commission and the Member States will work in close
co-operation to avoid such contradictions, in order to continue the battle against cartels effectively. Worth
noting in this respect is that the UK Office of Fair Trading has publicly stated that the employees of an undertaking that benefits from immunity before the Commission will receive a 'no action letter' which protects
them from prosecution under national law (see brochure of the Office of Fair Trading 'The Cartel offence.
Guidance on the issue of no action letters for individuals', points 3.5 and 3.6, available at: <http://www.oft.gov.uk/
entrepriseact.htm>).
[572] The same applies where a case has been initiated by the Commission as a result of a leniency application under the Commission's leniency policy (para 42 of the Network Notice).
[573] Available at: <http://europa.eu.int/comm/competition/antitrust/legislation/list-of-authorities-joint-
statement.pdf>.
[574] Art 15(1) of Reg No 1/2003. National courts may also request the Commission's opinion on questions
concerning the application of the Community competition rules. This provision is essentially a reflection of
the duty of loyal co-operation that already exists under Art 10 EC.

understandably be concerned if the information that they have voluntarily submitted to the Commission were subsequently to be transmitted to a national court. This concern has been addressed in the Notice on the Cooperation with the Courts. Under this Notice the Commission may refuse to transmit information to courts for overriding reasons relating to the need to safeguard the interest of the Community or to avoid any interference with its functioning and independence, in particular by jeopardising the accomplishment of the tasks entrusted to it. In this regard the Commission made it clear in the Notice that it would not make available to a national court information voluntarily submitted by a leniency applicant without the consent of the applicant.[575]

8.245 **Where best to file leniency applications within the ECN?**   Pursuant to Article 11(6) the initiation of proceedings by the Commission relieves the NCAs of their competence to apply EC and national competition law. In such cases, applicants who have applied to the Commission for leniency are placed in a more secure position under Regulation No 1/2003 than they were previously.[576] This does not mean, however, that by applying for leniency to the Commission an applicant can avoid the risk of being investigated and sanctioned by an NCA, as there is no guarantee that the Commission will necessarily initiate proceedings in the case, and, if it does so, this may take place only at the time a Statement of Objections is issued.[577] Given the very serious nature of cartel infringements, the Commission is clearly likely to start an investigation (note: this does not imply the (later) opening of proceedings) where the cartel is worldwide, Europe-wide, or where more than three Member States are involved.[578] In the case of more local cartels, however, the Commission may indeed choose not to investigate. If so, an undertaking applying for leniency exclusively to the Commission and relying on the use of Article 11(6) of Regulation 1/2003—especially in the case of a purely national or regional cartel—exposes itself to the risk that another cartel member may in the meantime apply for leniency to the relevant NCA(s) that is (are) also well placed to act. Should the Commission choose not to take up the case the applicant which applied only to the Commission would clearly be exposed relative to another cartel member that applied to the NCA(s) that finally deal(s) with the case and impose(s) the relevant sanctions.

8.246 In this context it is crucial for a cartel participant wishing to come forward to consider carefully the authority(/-ies) to which a leniency application should be made.[579] It would appear that the most prudent course of action for the prospective applicant is first to identify those authorities which have jurisdiction in relation to the territory affected by the infringement and

---

575 Para 26 of the Notice on the Cooperation with the Courts.

576 See Case 14/68 *Walt Wilhelm* [1969] ECR 1, where the ECJ had held that under Regulation No 17, national authorities could take action against an agreement in accordance with their competition laws even when an examination of the agreement under EC law was pending before the Commission (subject to the condition that the application of national law did not prejudice the full and uniform application of Community law or the effects of measures taken to implement it (see para 9).

577 Only the initiation of the proceedings under Art 11(6) would relieve the Member States from the possibility of acting under Art 81 (or Art 82) on the matter, as well as, de facto, to act under national law (through the application of Art 3 of Regulation No 1/2003).

578 See para 14 of the Network Notice.

579 A similar type of analysis is conducted by leniency applicants in the context of global cases, where applications may have to be filed (simultaneously) with competition agencies in Europe, in the US, Canada, Japan, and possibly with other authorities.

to verify whether a leniency programme is available with those authorities.[580] Having excluded the authorities that do not have a leniency programme, it will then need to decide which of the authorities that have jurisdiction over the case is (are) most likely to deal with it. Finally, it will need to decide in respect of each authority whether it actually wants to make an application in view of the limited likelihood of an investigation being started by a particular authority.[581] This is a delicate exercise which requires taking into account many different factors, including the risk of being sanctioned by the authority in question (eg, if another cartel member were to apply to that authority for leniency), the nature and size of potential sanctions that the authority may impose, the particular terms of the authority's leniency programme, and the costs of making a leniency application to it. The outcome in each case will depend on its particular facts.

An undertaking seeking to exclude any risk should apply to all authorities potentially able **8.247** to investigate the case, thus securing its position under the leniency programme of each authority that might (theoretically) exercise its jurisdiction to impose sanctions. Preferably, this should be done simultaneously. Some commentators have pointed out that this may be difficult and too costly[582] and have called for a 'one stop shop' harmonised system of immunity programmes within the ECN (see paras 8.249 to 8.253 below). It is submitted, however, that in most cases an applicant would not need to consider applying for leniency to more than four ECN members, including the Commission. Indeed, the principles of case allocation set out in the Network Notice envisage the possibility of parallel action by a maximum of three NCAs, each of them acting for its respective territory.[583] This implies that where the effects of the infringement are felt in more than three Member States, the Commission will normally be considered well placed to act (although it is not obliged to do so). In the case of Europe-wide or global cartels, the Commission is likely to investigate the case and it would clearly make sense for leniency applicants in such cases to prioritise applying to the Commission only.[584] Conversely, in the case of purely national or regional cartels affecting a maximum of up to three Member States, leniency applicants would be well advised to file a leniency application to the NCA of each of the Member States concerned, and possibly the Commission.[585]

---

[580] Assuming that trade between Member States is affected and that Art 81 EC therefore applies, these will always include the Commission.

[581] Of course, a 'best protective' approach would mean submitting applications in all Member States where the cartel has effect, ie in the case of an EU-wide cartel in the 18 jurisdictions that operate a leniency programme: see below.

[582] JM Joshua and PD Camesasca, 'Where angels fear to tread: the Commission's 'new' leniency policy revisited' European Antitrust Review (2005), the European Antitrust Review; V Turner, 'International Cartel Enforcement: Multijurisdictional Defence Strategies' paper submitted at ABA Section of International Law Annual Conference, Brussels, 26–29 October 2005; JM Joshua, 'That Uncertain Feeling: the Commission's 2002 Leniency Notice', paper submitted at the 11th EU Competition Law and Policy Workshop, European University Institute, Florence, 2–3 June 2006.

[583] Network Notice, point 14.

[584] In certain Member States, the NCA may allow, if it is not likely to take an investigative action, a summary application and/or a 'marker', and may only decide on a course of action once the other authority(ies) have decided on the immunity application. See para 8.253 below.

[585] At any rate, it should be recalled that the principles of allocation set out in the Network Notice are not binding rules of jurisdiction on which undertakings may rely, but rather general principles aimed at ensuring an optimal enforcement of competition law within the EC.

(f) *Leniency in the EU: Prospects for Evolution*

8.248 In view of the various issues that the application of the Commission's 2002 Leniency Notice had raised and the developments surrounding the application of leniency programmes within the ECN, the Commission undertook to revise its leniency programme and published on 8 December 2006 a new Leniency Notice. Although the 2006 Leniency Notice contains certain significant changes when compared to the 2002 Leniency Notice, the Commission's policy has remained substantially the same. Whilst this may simply point at a high degree of confidence in the efficiency of the current model, it nevertheless seems worthwhile to examine what the future directions of a further evolution of the Commission's leniency programme could be. Two issues can be mentioned in particular: a possible evolution towards an EU-wide leniency programme, and the possibility of a so-called 'amnesty plus' system. Other possible features will also be reviewed briefly.[586]

(i) *The Call for an EU-wide Approach to Leniency*

8.249 In view of the complexity deriving from the coexistence of differing leniency programmes with parallel competence, and indeed from the lack of such programmes in certain Member States, it has been suggested that an EU-wide leniency programme be adopted which would be binding on all NCAs, thereby creating a single, EU-wide leniency system.[587]

8.250 **An EU-wide leniency programme: mission impossible?** It seems that such a system was not genuinely considered during the drafting of Regulation No 1/2003. A number of reasons for this may be put forward. First, some Member States had so far refused to adopt a leniency policy. Thus it may have been considered unlikely that a sufficient number of Member States would agree to an overarching programme.[588] Secondly, and more importantly, it may have been considered virtually impossible to make such a system function to the requisite standards of reliability and certainty. Indeed a Community-wide leniency programme would imply that leniency applications could be filed once within the European Competition Network and take effect throughout the whole Network. Multiple leniency 'entry points' would in all likelihood be necessary, as the Commission would be unable to handle all incoming cases. Moreover, the existence of multiple entry points would necessarily imply that any of them would be capable of making a decision binding the Network in its entirety. This would pose two main problems. First, a uniform system would imply that the standards of examination of a leniency application should be identical in any point of the network in order to guarantee a level playing field and to avoid forum shopping.[589] Secondly, because of the critical importance of the timing of leniency applications, a uniform system would require a perfect and instantaneous transmission of information between all contact points.[590]

---

[586] The issue of 'direct settlements', although associated with leniency, is considered in section D(1)(g) on fines.

[587] See eg D Henry, 'Leniency Programmes: An Anaemic Carrot for Cartels in France, Germany and the UK?' (2005) ECLR 13.

[588] Pursuant to Art 83 EC, Regulations or Directives to give effect to the principles set out in Arts 81 and 82 EC shall be laid down by the Council acting by a qualified majority.

[589] In view of the complexity associated with the examination of an immunity application, of the requirement of secrecy that it implies, and of the stakes involved, the ability of the system to ensure a perfect uniformity in both the substantive and procedural aspects of the test applied would be far from certain.

[590] On receipt of an immunity application from an undertaking concerning a Community-wide cartel, an NCA would need to be able to check, before granting conditional immunity from fines, that no other undertaking in the same cartel had already applied for immunity at any other entry point in the ECN.

Such an approach probably appeared to be impracticable, likely to become overly bureaucratic, and—in view of the likelihood of its failure to be watertight—liable to create damaging uncertainty for leniency applicants.[591]

Favouring convergence: the ECN Model leniency programme   In the absence of an EU-   **8.251**
wide leniency programme in the foreseeable future, ECN members have focused their efforts on the reduction of any discrepancy or contradiction between their respective leniency programmes that may discourage potential applicants from coming forward. Co-operation within the ECN has resulted in a collective screening of the possible conflicting requirements and in a common understanding as to how to overcome certain potential issues.[592] On 29 September 2006, the ECN adopted and published of a 'Model leniency programme' (MLP) intended to serve as a reference point and foster convergence between the various leniency programmes in the EU.[593] The ECN MLP, which has been drafted as a coherent programme setting out the essential procedural and substantial requirements that the ECN believe every leniency programme should contain, provides a basis for soft harmonisation of the European leniency programmes.[594] It also introduces a model for a uniform summary application system for immunity applications (see para 8.253 below). The heads of the European competition authorities have agreed to use their best efforts to align their current and future European leniency programmes with the provisions of the ECN MLP. The state of convergence of the leniency programmes is due to be assessed in 2008.[595]

Towards a one stop shop system?   In the absence of the likelihood of a full harmonisation   **8.252**
of European leniency programmes in the near future, it is desirable that practical solutions be found that minimise the unfavourable consequences of the existence of possibly divergent leniency programmes. In 2005, Commissioner Neelie Kroes had already hinted at what she referred to as a 'one-stop-shop' system.[596] It is difficult, at the time of writing to postulate what practical options are open to the Commission and the other ECN members.

---

[591] The only alternative that might overcome the obstacles described above would lie in the centralisation of all immunity or leniency applications with the Commission. It is nevertheless submitted that this would not only be undesirable for the Commission from an organisational point of view, but that it would also be overtly contrary to the philosophy underlying the modernisation reform. Thus, the approach followed in the Network Notice, which consists of placing the responsibility on companies by obliging them to simultaneously file an application in any jurisdiction where they consider the case may ultimately investigated, appears to be a reasonable one; all the more so since it may be assumed that it should not lead to more than three or four separate applications, as explained above.

[592] See C Gauer and M Jaspers, 'The European Competition Network Achievements and Challenges—a case in point: leniency', Competition Policy Newsletter No 1, Spring 2006.

[593] Mentioned by P Lowe, Director General of DG COMP, at the International Cartel Workshop of the ABA conference, London, February 2006.

[594] The ECN Model Programme is accompanied by Explanatory Notes providing further explanations and practical guidance. It is available in all official languages.

[595] For more detailed information, see IP/06/1288 and MEMO/06/356: 'Competition: the European Competition Network launches a Model Leniency Programme—frequently asked questions'. The ECN Model programme is available on the ECN Website at: <http://ec.europa.eu/comm/competition/antitrust/ecn/ecn_home.html>.

[596] Neelie Kroes, Commissioner in charge of competition matters, 'The First Hundred Days' speech at the 40th Anniversary of the Studienvereinigung Kartellrecht 1965–2005, International Forum on European Competition Law, Brussels, 7 April 2005. In spite of the term used, the Commissioner made it clear that a fully centralised system was not the solution that would be foreseen and that '[t]he design of any future system [would have] to take full account of the specific needs of those who will eventually have to operate it. This means that rather than limiting ourselves to centralising solutions, we have to look at the options for one-stop leniency which fully exploit the dimension of the network.'

In the meantime however, the Commission has stated that a possible way to provide legal certainty in the case of multiple filings may consist of organising some form of EU-wide 'marker' system in combination with short form pro forma applications. This would enable leniency applicants to protect their position within the ECN without having to provide full and complete information to each network member capable of pursuing the case.[597]

8.253 **The model 'summary application system': a concrete step forward**   It should be noted that the ECN MLP (see para 8.251 above) includes a model 'summary application system', which is intended to help applicants make a plurality of (near) simultaneous immunity applications and to help competition authorities process them in cases where it is likely that the Commission will deal with the case. If the summary application system—which already exists in certain Member States—is put into practice, immunity applicants, rather than having to file full and complete applications with authorities that could be considered 'well placed' to act on the case, may limit themselves to supplying a short description of the cartel that has been reported to the Commission. Such a summary application would act as a permanent 'marker' enabling the applicant to keep its 'place in the queue' in order to lodge a full application should the case ultimately be transferred to the NCA concerned.

(ii)   Other possible features of the EC leniency programme

8.254 **'Immunity plus' and 'penalty plus'**   A recurring question about the leniency policy of the Commission is whether the Commission should grant to a company co-operating in a cartel case an additional reduction in its fine in an ongoing investigation where that company discloses the existence of another cartel in which it is involved. This system has been adopted by the US where it is known as 'Amnesty Plus'.[598] It has also recently been adopted by the UK.[599] Under the US leniency programme, 'amnesty plus' is complemented by the so-called 'penalty plus' principle. This means that a company under investigation in a cartel X which fails to reveal its involvement in another cartel Y under the 'amnesty plus' provision may ultimately receive a greater punishment in respect of cartel X than would initially have been the case if its involvement in the cartel is subsequently discovered.[600]

8.255 **'Leniency plus': pros and cons**   'Amnesty plus' has often been described by US DOJ officials as a very efficient lever of enforcement.[601] Against this background, the Commission

---

[597] C Gauer and M Jaspers, 'The European Competition Network Achievements and Challenges—a case in point: leniency', Competition Policy Newsletter No 1, Spring 2006.

[598] The so-called 'amnesty plus' system consists of providing a company which failed to qualify for immunity in cartel case X but who reports another cartel Y, for which they get immunity, with an increased reduction of fine in cartel case X. See eg US DoJ, Antitrust division, 'Status Report: An Overview Of Recent Developments In The Antitrust Division's Criminal Enforcement Program' (February 2004), available on the US DoJ website at: <http://www.usdoj.gov/atr/public/guidelines/202531.htm>.

[599] See eg 'Leniency Plus' section in OFT, 'Leniency and No-action', OFT803, July 2005 and sections 3.16 and 3.17 of the OFT's Penalty Guidance.

[600] On 'amnesty plus' in the US, see eg G Spratling 'Making Companies an Offer They Shouldn't Refuse', speech before Bar Association of the District of Columbia's 35th Annual Symposium on Associations and Antitrust, 16 February 1999.

[601] US DoJ, Antitrust division, 'Status report: An Overview of Recent Developments In the Antitrust Division's Criminal Enforcement Program' (February 2004). <http://www.usdoj.gov/atr/public/guidelines/202531.pdf>. According to the US DoJ, of 50 grand jury investigations relating to cartels, almost half were initiated as a result of investigations in separate product markets. See also Scott D Hammond, 'Measuring the Value of Second-In Cooperation in Corporate Plea Negotiations'—speech before the 54th Annual American Bar Association Section of Antitrust Law, 29 March 2006.

has been criticised by certain commentators for not having seized the opportunity when revising its 1996 Leniency Notice to include an 'amnesty plus' (and possibly a 'penalty plus') system in the 2002 Leniency Notice.[602] Overall, the gist of the argument is that amnesty plus provides stronger incentives to report the second cartel and critically increases the natural instability of cartels by encouraging a 'spill over' effect from ongoing investigations. Indeed, its benefit would lie in a stronger incentive for a cartel member to report a so far undisclosed cartel and thereby minimise the damage caused by the prosecution of the first one.[603] However, the Commission has so far chosen not to adopt it. One reason for this may lie in the conviction that once a cartel participant has been caught by the Commission, there is a strong motivation for it to decide to 'come clean' more generally and apply for immunity with regard to any involvement it has in other cartels the severe additional punishments meted out to recidivist offenders may play a role in such assessment. The suggestion that an undertaking may choose not to disclose its participation in other cartels on the assumption that it will not be discovered cannot, it is submitted, be sustained.[604] Against that background the Commission may have considered that the additional reduction in fines entailed by the 'amnesty plus' approach was not needed.[605] Another reason may be found in the legal constraints imposed on the Commission in finding and sanctioning infringements. 'Immunity plus' means that the fine imposed on an undertaking for a given infringement is reduced because of co-operation offered in relation to another infringement. This may raise various legal and practical issues that would add to the (already) complex nature of Commission proceedings, and the complexities arising from parallel competences within the ECN.[606] 'Immunity plus' may well trigger many unsubstantiated

---

[602] See eg M Jephcott, 'The European Commision's New Leniency Notice—Whistling the right tune?' (2002) ECLR, 378; D McElwee, 'Should the European Commission Adopt 'Amnesty Plus' in its Fight Against Hard-core cartels?', (2004) ECLR, 558; and D Henry, 'Leniency Programmes: An Anaemic Carrot for Cartels in France, Germany and the UK?' (2005) ECLR, 13.

[603] Such an approach is based on two underlying assumptions: first, that the undertakings involved in cartels have a natural tendency to replicate their collusive conduct in the various markets in which they are active; and secondly, in the absence of an additional reward relating to the initial cartel case in the context of which they have been caught, such companies have no incentive to disclose their involvement in another cartel if they are sufficiently confident that the other cartel members will not come forward and that the Commission will not, *ex officio*, detect their involvement in the latter cartel if, for instance, it relates to a completely unrelated market.

[604] Indeed, cartels tend to spread from one market to a neighbouring one and it can be assumed that is extremely rare for a company to be involved in separate cartels characterised by completely different 'competitors'. In most cases, at least some of the cartel participants in cartel A will also be involved in cartel B. Thus, as soon as there is a suspicion that one cartel has been detected, the incentive for participants in 'collateral' cartels to come forward before the others do can be assumed to be extremely strong even in the absence of an 'amnesty plus' programme.

[605] The experience of the first years of implementation of the 2002 Leniency Notice would seem to confirm the 'domino' effect that has triggered new applications and investigations.

[606] Legal issues may result, eg, from the fact that the Commission would find itself under an obligation to determine the fines in one prohibition decision on the basis of factual elements pertaining to another case, itself subject to a subsequent prohibition decision, with the consequent implications for the legality of the decision (notably in relation to the principle of equal treatment). The Commission could find itself facing practical issues such as the necessity to grant a reduction in fine on the basis of 'leniency plus' in the formal decision relating to cartel X before having finalised its investigation of cartel Y in respect of which amnesty plus was claimed. This would mean that a reduction in fines would formally be granted in cartel X at a point in time where the applicant would only have received conditional immunity from fines in cartel Y, the actual grant of immunity being subject to a duty of continuous co-operation throughout the entire proceedings.

requests for immunity for different (alleged) infringements with the mere purpose (for the applicants) of getting a higher reduction in cartel X.[607] Such applications may well also include all kinds of local or national cartels falling under Article 81 EC but that would normally be expected to be dealt with at the level of NCAs. 'Immunity plus' may also create intricate problems in relation to the connection it would imply between the cases, both in terms of access to file and judicial review.[608] Whilst such problems may not be insuperable, they might explain why the Commission did not adopt 'amnesty plus'. It will be interesting to see whether any future revision produces a different outcome, but in a European context, the disadvantages seem to outweigh the benefits.

8.256 **'Penalty plus': pros and cons** It would appear for similar reasons to be difficult to put in place an EC 'penalty plus' system. Such a system implies that immunity is revoked and a fine is imposed in a cartel X on the basis of the applicant's failure to report the existence of a cartel Y when it applied for leniency in cartel X. A 'penalty plus' system would have the advantage of creating a strong 'spill over effect' in that any immunity applicant would have to engage into a 'spring cleaning' process and report any possible form of cartel involvement to the Commission. However, it is submitted that such a system would probably be too complex to implement in practice, as well as being excessively detrimental to the legal certainty required from an efficient leniency programme. In addition, this would in all likelihood be incompatible with the constraints of the Community's legal order, in so far as it implies that the position of the applicant in cartel X may be negatively affected in respect of its alleged failure to report its participation in a cartel not yet proven against it.

8.257 **Compulsory restitution by leniency applicants** Another possible change in the Commission's leniency programme might consist of imposing on applicants an obligation to pay compensation to customers who have suffered harm.[609] Such an obligation is already a feature of the US leniency programme and does not seem to be a major disincentive to leniency applications. However, one may wonder whether such a system could or should be imported into the EC leniency programme. First, in the absence of criminal sanctions for cartel behaviour in Europe, immunity from which would be a strong incentive to apply regardless of other possible consequences, the prospect of having to negotiate restitution for customers might well significantly undermine the efficiency of the leniency programme. Secondly, it may be more appropriate for the award of damages to be left to national courts rather than being partially determined by the Commission.

Whilst a possible revocation of immunity with regard to cartel Y would not necessarily mean that the additional reduction of fine obtained in cartel X should be annulled, one may wonder whether it should not affect the level of that reduction.

[607] On this phenomenon in the context of the US leniency programme, see DC Klawiter, 'U.S. Corporate Leniency after the Blockbuster Cartels: Are we entering a new Era?', paper given at the 11th EU Competition Law and Policy workshop, European University Institute, Florence, 2–3 June 2006.

[608] This is because a reduction in cartel X would be made dependent on an application in cartel Y being well-founded.

[609] The Commission has already taken account, when calculating the fine to be imposed on an undertaking, of restitutions already made to the customers who have suffered harm. See para 8.763 of the section on fines below.

(3) The Commission's Powers of Investigation: Information Requests, Interviews, Inspections

(a) Preliminary Observations

The Commission's fact-finding powers, which have been referred to as 'sweeping' by the **8.258** Commission itself,[610] play a crucial role in its cartel investigations.[611] Where a case may be opened on the basis of information volunteered in an immunity application or may be derived from a complainant or whistleblower,[612] the investigation that the Commisssion will subsequently need to carry out is meant to 'acquire the additional information it will need if it is to give a ruling on the legality of the practices in question'.[613] Indeed, in enquiries which may lead to hefty fines, undertakings cannot be expected to voluntarily submit information which will be used against them.

The Commission possesses the following investigative powers, contained in Articles 18 to 21 **8.259** of Regulation 1/2003:

  (i) Requests for Information—Article 18;
  (ii) Interviews—Article 19;
 (iii) Inspections into business premises—Article 20; and
 (iv) Inspections into other premises (private homes)—Article 21.

The rules relating to the Commission's investigative powers and procedures are laid down in **8.260** Council Regulation 1/2003, complementary provisions being contained in Commission Regulation 773/2004. Other notices and communications also contain relevant rules, in particular the Commission's Leniency Notice[614] and the Notice on Access to the File.[615] Furthermore, the case law of the European Courts and the decisions of the Commission constitute important sources for the interpretation of the Commission's investigation powers. It is noted that where Member States apply Article 81 and/or 82 EC to cases they investigate,

---

[610] *Dealing with the Commission*, Publication of the European Commission, 1997, available at <http://europa.eu.int/comm/competition/publications/dealen1_en.pdf>, section 5.5 at p 38. The principles evoked in this brochure, although it was written well before the adoption of Regulation 1/2003, remain applicable as regards the various principles laid down therein for the conduct of Commission investigations, notably as regards on-site investigations.

[611] The investigative powers used in cartel cases also apply to investigations into other violations of the EC competition rules under Arts 81 and 82 of the EC Treaty, for instance relating to vertical agreements or abuse of a dominant position. However, the discussion in this chapter concentrates on their use in investigations into hardcore cartels. For other literature about the Commission's powers of inspection, see, for instance CS Kerse and N Khan, *EC Antitrust Procedure* (5th edn, 2005); L Ortiz Blanco, *EC Competition Procedure* (2nd edn, 2006); D Dalheimer, C Feddersen and G Miersch, *EU Kartellverfahrensverordnung* (Verlag CH Beck, 2005); G De Bronett, *Kommentar zum europäischen Kartellverfahrensrecht*, Luchterhand Kommentar, 2005; L Ritter and WD Braun, *European Competition Law: A Practitioners Guide* (3rd edn, 2004); and R Whish, *Competition Law* (5th edn, 2003).

[612] See paras 8.94–8.103 above for a discussion about the various information sources for starting an investigation.

[613] *Dealing with the Commission*, n 610 above, section 3.1 at p 21.

[614] See for instance point 22 of the 2002 Leniency Notice, which gives indications as to the merit of information in relation to the notion of 'significant added value'. (Commission Notice on Immunity From Fines and Reduction of Fines in Cartel Cases [2002] OJ C45/03).

[615] Commission Notice on the rules for access to the Commission file in cases pursuant to Arts 81 and 82 of the EC Treaty, Arts 53, 54 and 57 of the EEA Agreement and Council Regulation (EC) No 139/2004, [2005] OJ C325/07.

their procedures and powers of investigation are those available under national law. Also noteworthy is that the Commission's investigative powers can also be applied against undertakings in EFTA countries.[616]

8.261   **Documented evidence as the principal basis for Commission cartel decisions**   In coming to decisions in which it prohibits and fines cartels, the Commission seeks to rely principally on contemporaneous, documentary evidence of illegal behaviour. This does not mean, however, that the Commission bases itself solely on (pre-existing) documents. It also relies on *ex post facto* descriptions. In recent years the importance of such statements has grown because it is less and less the case that the Commission can obtain written (contemporaneous) cartel evidence: often cartel participants are well aware of the illegal nature of their activities, and endeavour not to create, or to conceal, any traceable evidence. As a result, the Commission increasingly has to base its conclusions on written or oral accounts by natural or legal persons, notably those received in the context of applications for reduction in fines under the Leniency Notice. Such statements, if provided orally, are recorded by the Commission services (DG Competition), and may be set out in a transcript. They are added to the Commission's investigation file and can be used in evidence.[617]

8.262   **Investigations under the Merger Regulation**   The discussion below focuses on the application of the Commission's investigative instruments under Regulation 1/2003. Under the Merger Regulation the Commission has investigative powers that are similar.[618] The carrying out of inspections in merger cases, however, is a rare phenomenon.[619] Although on-site inspections are theoretically possible in State aid cases in certain circumstances, the investigative powers in the field of State aid are also not considered in this chapter.[620]

8.263   **Applicability to the transport sector** [621]   Air, maritime and rail transport services were, until 1 May 2004, subject to special procedural rules contained in three sector-specific

---

[616] See para 8.438.

[617] For the relevance of information provided orally see for instance the Commission Decision in *Vitamins* and the judgment of the CFI in *BASF*, where the CFI, on the question of whether the Commission could rely in its decision on evidence supplied orally, noted that not only 'documents' but also 'information' may constitute evidence. The CFI also noted that, 'Furthermore, the oral disclosure of information has no major disadvantage from the point of view of legal certainty, since information provided orally to a public administration in a meeting is normally likely to be preserved by sound recording and/or in written minutes'. (Case T-15/02 *BASF v Commission*, judgment of 15 March 2006, not yet reported, paras 496 and 498, and the case law cited therein). It is noted that although the Commission does take oral statements in its investigations, any 'direct testimony' before the College of Commissioners is not provided for in the decision-making process. For a further explanation about the *Schriftlichkeitsprinzip* of Commission competition procedures see: G De Bronett, *Kommentar zum europäischen Kartellverfahrensrecht* (Luchterhand Kommentar, 2005), at p 25.

[618] Council Regulation (EC) No 139/2004 of 20 January 2004 on the control of concentrations between undertakings (the 'Merger Regulation'). See Art 11 of the Merger Regulation as regards requests for information, Art 11(7) as regards interviews, and Art 13 as regards inspections. Inspections into 'other premises' are not provided for under the Merger Regulation.

[619] See, for example, *Skanska/Scancem* (Case IV/M.1157), Commission Decision of 11 November 1998 [1999] OJ L183.

[620] See Art 22 of Council Regulation (EC) No 659/99 of 22 March 1999 laying down detailed rules for the application of Art 93 of the EC Treaty, [1999] OJ L83/1. Inspections are restricted to '*ex-post*' verifications at publicly held companies. A secondary set of (procedural) legislation for the execution of such investigations is lacking, however, and the powers have not been used in practice.

[621] On the particular rules applying to the transport sector, see also Chapter 14.

implementing Regulations.[622] Regulation 1/2003 revoked the procedural provisions of these Regulations and brought transport services under the same enforcement rules that are applicable to all other areas of activity.[623] As a result, the Commission's investigative powers became applicable to investigations in the transport sector. At that time, two exceptions remained, however, in Regulation 1/2003, namely the exclusions contained in the air and maritime implementing regulations (for air services between the Community and third countries, maritime cabotage and tramp vessel services).[624] Since then, through the adoption of Regulation 411/2004, the exception for air transport has been removed.[625] As regards the exceptions for maritime transport, a proposal for a Council Regulation was launched in December 2005 to include cabotage and tramp vessel services within the framework of Regulation 1/2003. This proposal was adopted in September 2006 by Regulation 1419/06.[626]

Relevance of interpretation under Regulation 17/62   In providing an overview of the   **8.264**
Commission's fact-finding powers under Regulation 1/2003, it is necessary to have reference to the broadly similar powers that existed under its predecessor, Regulation 17/62. Indeed, the powers incorporated in Regulation 1/2003 can only be analysed and understood by having regard to the issues of interpretation that have arisen over the many years of application of Regulation 17/62. The Commission's decision-making practice, as well as the jurisprudence of the European Courts (the Court of Justice and the Court of First Instance) remain valid sources when considering the scope of the Commission's powers under Regulation 1/2003, especially since the core powers (requests for information/inspections into business premises) have stayed broadly the same. Even as regards the new competences of the Commission, such as the power to seal offices during inspections, to put oral questions to designated members of staff during inspections, and to take oral statements, prior case law will help to provide guidance for the interpretation of these (new) powers.[627]

Outline for discussion   The investigation powers of the Commission will be discussed   **8.265**
below in the order in which they are found in Regulation 1/2003: requests for information, interviews, inspections at business premises, and inspections at other premises. Before discussing the powers individually, a number of general aspects will be dealt with that govern

---

[622] Although for instance Art 18 of Regulation No 4056/86 provided for the same inspection powers as those contained in Art 14 of Regulation 17/62 (now Art 20 of Regulation 1/2003). (Council Regulation (EEC) No 4056/86 of 22 December 1986, [1986] OJ L 378/4.)

[623] See recital 36, as well as Arts 36–43 of Council Regulation (EC) No 1/2003 of 16 December 2002. See also the White Paper on modernisation of the rules implementing Arts 85 and 86 of the EC Treaty, Commission Programme No 99/027, [1999] OJ C132/1, and the Proposal for a Council Regulation on the implementation of the rules on competition laid down in Arts 81 and 82 of the EC Treaty and amending Regulations (EEC) No 1017/68, (EEC) No 2988/74, (EEC) No 4056/86 and (EEC) No 3975/87, [2000] OJ C365/284.

[624] Art 32 of Regulation 1/2003.

[625] Council Regulation (EC) No 411/2004 of 26 February 2004 repealing Regulation (EEC) No 3975/87 and amending Regulations (EEC) No 3976/87 and (EC) No 1/2003, in connection with air transport between the Community and third countries [2004] OJ L68/1.

[626] Council Regulation (EC) No 1419/2006 of 25 September 2006 repealing Regulation (EEC) No 4056/86 laying down detailed rules for the application of Articles 85 and 86 of the Treaty to maritime transport, and amending Regulation (EC) No 1/2003 as regards the extension of its scope to include cabotage and international tramp services ([2006] OJ L269/1).

[627] Where existing case law does not provide for conclusive answers we have endeavoured to provide an informed opinion intended to be of use to the practitioner when being confronted with particular questions about the Commission's investigative powers.

the Commission's investigation powers as a whole. These common features include the application of general principles of law and fundamental rights, and within those the rights of defence, as well as other (practical) features. A section dedicated to 'international co-operation in cartel investigations', which is becoming an increasingly important issue in the fight against cartels, is included at the end of this chapter.

(b) General Aspects of the Commission's Fact-finding Powers

(i) Principles of law and fundamental rights applicable to Commission investigations

8.266 **The applicability of general principles of law and fundamental rights** Fundamental rights, which are part of the general principles of Community law as recognised by the European Courts, permeate the various provisions of law that govern cartel proceedings.[628] In situations where specific legal provisions are lacking or where these leave room for interpretation, principles of law are usually relied on.[629] Recital 37 of the Preamble to Regulation 1/2003 demonstrates the relevance of principles of law and fundamental rights for interpretation purposes. It states: 'This regulation respects the fundamental rights and observes the principles recognised in particular by the Charter of Fundamental Rights of the European Union. Accordingly, this Regulation should be interpreted and applied with respect to those rights and principles.'[630] In defining the principles of law that are applicable to competition proceedings, the European Courts have generally drawn inspiration from the European Convention of Human Rights (ECHR), recognising particular rights that are included in the ECHR as part of the legal tradition common to the Member States.[631] The ECHR is, however, not legally binding within the Community legal order[632] and the same holds true for the

---

[628] Case T-112/98 *Mannesmannröhren-Werke AG v Commission* [2001] ECR II-729, para 60.

[629] Reference to the respect of the principles of law is often made in the case law of the CFI and ECJ. There is an example of the applicability to the general principles of law in the CFI's judgment in *Industrial Gases*: 'First of all, it should be recalled that according to settled case-law, when determining the amount of each fine, the Commission has a discretion and is not required to apply any particular arithmetical formula. [. . .] Its assessment must, however, be carried out in compliance with Community law, which includes not only the provisions of the Treaty *but also the general principles of law* (Case C-50/00 P *Unión de Pequeños Agricultores* v *Council* [2002] ECR I-6677, para 38).' (Case T-304/02 *Hoek Loos NV v Commission*, judgment of 4 July 2006, not yet reported, at para 68, emphasis added.)

[630] Charter of Fundamental Rights of the European Union [2000] OJ C346/1. The Charter is not legally binding, although the Council, by referring to the Charter in Regulation 1/2003 has raised its importance as regards competition proceedings. The European Courts also appear to have accepted its relevance as a point of orientation in their jurisprudence. (See for a discussion, CS Kerse and N Khan, *EC Antitrust Procedure* (5th edn, 2005), at paras 3-002 and 3-003 and the jurisprudence referred to there). The draft European Constitution, which would have become binding had it been ratified, incorporates a section on fundamental rights. (*Treaty Establishing a Constitution for Europe* [2004] OJ C310/41, Part II—The Charter of Fundamental Rights.) The European Constitution was intended to enter into force on 1 November 2006, but at the time of writing the Constitution had received a no-vote in France and the Netherlands, as a result of which the ratification process was halted.

[631] See the ECJ in *PVC II*: '[. . .] Article F.2 of the Treaty on European Union (now, after amendment, Article 6(2) EU) provides that [t]he Union shall respect fundamental rights, as guaranteed by the [ECHR] and as they result from the constitutional traditions common to the Member States, as general principles of Community law.' (Joined Cases C-238/99 P, C-244/99 P, C-245/99 P, C-247/99 P, C-250/99 P to C-252/99 P and C-254/99 P *Limburgse Vinyl Maatschappij (LVM) and others v Commission* [2002] ECR I-08375, para 167 confirming on this point the judgment of the CFI in the same matter, in Joined Cases T-305/94 to T-307/94, T-313/94 to T-316/94, T-318/94, T-325/94, T-328/94, T-329/94 and T-335/94 *Limburgse Vinyl Maatschappij (LVM) and others v Commission* [1999] ECR II-931, para 120.

[632] Case T-347/94 *Mayr-Melnhof Kartongesellschaft v Commission* [1998] ECR II-1751, para 31 and case T-112/98 *Mannesmannröhren-Werke AG v Commisson* [2001] ECR II-729, para 59. For a further discussion on this topic and references to relevant literature see L Ortiz Blanco, *EC Competition Procedure* (2nd edn, 2006) at paras 4.36 *et seq.*

jurisprudence of the European Court of Human Rights (ECtHR).[633] That being said, the European Courts do attach 'great value to the case-law of the European Court of Human Rights', to use the words of Advocate-General Geelhoed in *SGL*.[634]

General principles and fundamental rights particularly relevant to cartel investigations **8.267**
Of chief importance to cartel proceedings is the category of fundamental rights which can be listed under the heading 'rights of defence'. Other general principles and fundamental rights that help establish procedural safeguards and ensure due process include the principle of proportionality,[635] the principle of the presumption of innocence,[636] the principle of equal treatment,[637] the right to the protection of confidential information,[638] the right to privacy,[639] and the recognition of legitimate expectations.[640] These fundamental rights and principles of law are not considered separately in this chapter, but are identified where a reference is required in the light of the particular topic that is being discussed.[641] Because of their particular importance in cartel proceedings, an exception is made for certain of the rights of defence, notably the right against providing self-incriminating statements and the right to the protection of lawyer-client communications.

(ii) The Rights of Defence

In all Community proceedings in which sanctions may be imposed, observance of the **8.268** rights of defence is a fundamental right of Community law which must be complied with, even if the proceedings in question are administrative in nature.[642] In the words of AG Ruiz-Jarabo: '[t]he Commission has wide powers of investigation and inquiry but, precisely

---

[633] See also case C-94/00 *Roquette Frères* [2002] ECR I-9011, paras 22–29, where the ECJ considered the extent to which consideration should be given to the ECHR and the case law of the ECtHR.

[634] AG Geelhoed in *Graphite Electrodes*, Case C-301/04 *Commission v SGL Carbon*, Opinion of 19 January 2006, not yet reported, para 62. In *Greek Ferries*, for instance, the Court referred directly to the principles laid down in Art 8 ECHR. (Case C-121/04 P, *Minoikes Grammes ANE (Minoan Lines SA) v Commission*, Order of 17 November 2005, not yet reported, para 47.) For a more detailed discussion on this subject see Riley, 'The ECHR Implications of the Investigation Provisions of the Draft Competition Regulation' 51 International Competition Law Quarterly 2002, 55. See also para 8.273 on the relevance of the ECHR and the case law of the ECtHR, particularly as regards the issue of self-incrimination.

[635] See, for instance, Case T-304/02 *Hoek Loos NV v Commission*, judgment of 4 July 2006, not yet reported, para 96 and the case law cited there.

[636] See, for instance, Case C-235/92 P *Montecatini v Commission* [1999] ECR I-4539, para 175. Also Case T-67/00 *JFE Engineering v Commission* [2004] ECR II-2501, para 178, and Case T-279/02 *Degussa AG v Commission*, judgment of 5 April 2006, not yet reported, para 115.

[637] See, for instance, Case T-252/01 *Tokai Carbon Co. and others v Commission (Tokai I)* [2004] OJ C251, para 394.

[638] See, for instance, the ECJ judgment in *PVC II*, n 645 above, paras 294 *et seq*.

[639] See, for instance, Case 136/79 *National Panasonic (UK) Ltd v Commission* [1980] ECR 2033, paras 17–19.

[640] See, for instance, Case T-31/99 *ABB Asea Brown Boveri v Commission* ('*Pre-insulated Pipes*') [2002] ECR II-1881, para 126.

[641] For a more in-depth discussion, reference is made to the great quantity of literature that exists on the subject. See, for instance, CS Kerse and N Khan, *EC Antitrust Procedure* (5th edn, 2005), chapters 3 and 4. See also L Ortiz Blanco, *EC Competition Procedure* (2nd edn, 2006), para 1.20 *et seq*.; W Wils, *Principles of European Antitrust Enforcement* (Hart Publishing, 2005), notably chapter 2. For a listing of different rights see L Ritter and WD Braun, *European Competition Law: A Practitioners Guide* (3rd edn, 2004), at p 1031 *et seq*.

[642] Case 85/76 *Hoffmann-La Roche v Commission* [1979] ECR 461, para 9. Cartel proceedings have even been been characterised as 'having a criminal law character' in *Rhone Poulenc* (by Judge Vesterdorf, acting as Advocate-General in Case T-1/89 *Rhône Poulenc v Commission* [1991] ECR II-00867 at section I.A.3, where he stated that such a qualification supposes a high level of protection of the rights of the defence within the proceedings).

because of that nature and because one and the same body is invested with the power to conduct investigations and the power to take decision, the rights of defence of those subject to the procedure must be recognised without reservation and respected.'[643] The rights of defence are indeed pervasive throughout the Commission's investigation, although they may apply differently depending on the stage of the Commission proceedings (ie whether they are in the preliminary/investigative stage) or at the adversarial stage (ie after the issuance of a Statement of Objections). Notably, the right to be heard only comes fully into play once the Commission has formulated its preliminary findings in a Statement of Objections.[644] Other rights, such as the right against self-incrimination, are applied throughout the administrative process in order to protect those rights from being irredeemably impaired during the fact-finding phase.[645] Two rights of defence are particularly relevant in the investigative stage, the right against self-incrimination and the privilege of lawyer-client communications, each of which merits separate discussion (see below). Another right of defence, the right to legal assistance, is briefly touched upon, as well as an explanation of why, during the stage of the investigation, the right to be heard plays a lesser role.

1. The privilege against supplying self-incriminating information

8.269 *An EU competition law version of 'the right to remain silent'*   One of the most important principles in the administration of cartel cases, applicable both to requests for information and in on-site inspections, is the right of an undertaking not to make statements that are self-incriminating.[646] This right to remain silent within EU competition proceedings is only relevant as regards undertakings,[647] because Commission investigations do not address private persons.[648]

---

[643] Opinion in Joined Cases C-204-5, 211, 213, 217, and 219/00 P *Aalborg A/S and others v Commission* [2004] ECR I-123, para 26.

[644] See paras 8.450ff, for a further discussion on the procedure for adopting a final prohibition decision and the right to be heard.

[645] Case 374/87 *Orkem v Commission* [1989] ECR 3283, para 27.

[646] For a discussion of the scope of the protection from self-incrimination, including its compatibility with the ECHR and the jurisprudence of the ECtHR see amongst others: K Dekeyser and C Gauer, 'The New Enforcement System for Articles 81 and 82 and the Rights of Defence', in BE Hawk (ed), Annual proceedings of the Fordham Institute [2005]; WPJ Wils, 'Self-incrimination in EC Antitrust Enforcement: A Legal and Economic Analysis' [2003] World Competition, Volume 26, Issue 4; PR Willis, '"You have the right to remain silent", or do you? The privilege against self-incrimination following Mannesmannröhren-Werke and other recent decisions', ECLR, August 2001; and B Vesterdorf, 'Legal Professional Privilege and the Privilege against Self-incrimination in EC Law: Recent Developments and Current Issues' [2005] Fordham International Law Journal, 1197–1215.

[647] Interestingly, under US law no right to silence exists for undertakings. The 5th amendment can only be invoked by private persons. *Hale v Henkel*, 201 US 43 (1906); *Braswell v United Sates*, 487 US 99 (1988); and *White v United States*, 322 US 649 (1944).

[648] Given the fact that certain Member States have (criminal) legislation applying to individuals involved in cartel conduct, an issue arises as to the extent to which the personnel of an undertaking, when asked questions by the Commission in the framework of an inspection, may refuse to provide an answer on the basis that the information would become available to the Member States and may ultimately be used against them in national criminal proceedings. Given the safeguards included in Regulation 1/2003 (Art 12) and the Commission's 'Network Notice' to which the Member States adhere (points 26–28) as regards the exchange and use of information between the competition agencies of the European Competition Network (ECN), such a claim would appear unfounded, however, the Commisson has no power to compel replies from individual employees. This issue is further discussed in para 8.367ff, dealing with the Commission's power to

The Commission has explicitly recognised the privilege against self-incrimination in the preamble to Regulation 1/2003.[649] In so doing, it has followed the jurisprudence of the European Courts, notably the 1989 judgment in *Orkem*, where the Court of Justice stated that the Commission 'may not compel an undertaking to provide it with answers which might involve an admission on its part of the existence of an infringement which it is incumbent on the Commission to prove'.[650]

8.270

There is no absolute right for an undertaking to remain silent. According to the European Courts, a complete right to silence for undertakings would constitute an undue hindrance to the Commission in the accomplishment of its task under the Treaty and go beyond what would be necessary to preserve the rights of defence.[651] For the Commission, the fact that no absolute right of silence exists is crucial, as such a right would be likely to render its investigatory tools ineffective. In the words of Joshua, to import any right for a firm to withhold the very evidence that would prove an infringement 'would stultify the whole purpose of the Regulation'.[652]

8.271

According to the ECJ, the Commission 'is entitled to compel an undertaking to provide all necessary information concerning such facts as may be known to it and if necessary such documents relating thereto as are in its possession, even if the latter may be used to establish, against it or against another undertaking, the existence of anti-competitive conduct'.[653] The right to silence for undertakings is therefore restricted. As explained below, it

8.272

---

request clarifications on the spot. It is noted that the privilege against self-incrimination cannot be invoked with regard to national civil proceedings in which Arts 81 or 82 EC are invoked, as such proceedings before a national court cannot lead to the imposition of penalties by a public authority (Case C-60/92 *Otto v Postbank* [1993] ECR I-5683).

[649] Recital 23 of the preamble of Regulation 1/2003 reads: 'The Commission should be empowered throughout the Community to require such information to be supplied as is necessary to detect any agreement, decision or concerted practice prohibited by Article 81 of the Treaty or any abuse of a dominant position prohibited by Article 82 of the Treaty. When complying *with a decision* of the Commission, undertakings *cannot be forced to admit* that they have committed an infringement, but they are in any event *obliged to answer factual questions and to provide documents*, even if this information may be used to establish against them or against another undertaking the existence of an infringement.' [emphasis added].

[650] Case 374/87 *Orkem v Commission* [1989] ECR 3283, paras 34 and 35. See also cases T-112/98 *Mannesmannröhren-Werke AG v Commission* ('*Mannesmann*') [2001] ECR II-729, paras 66 and 67; Case T-34/93 *Société Générale v Commission* [1995] ECR II-545, para 74; Joined Cases C-238/99P, C-244/99P, C-245/99P, C-247/99P, C-250/99P, C-252/99P and C-254/99P *Limburgse Vinyl Maatschappij and others v Commission* (*PVC II*) [2002] ECR I-8357, paras 258–293. Case T-48/02 *Brouwerij Haacht v Commission* [2006] OJ C36, not yet reported, para 107. Case C-301/04 *Commission v SGL Carbon* AG, judgment of 29 June 2006, not yet reported, para 42. It is important to note that the privilege against self-incrimination cannot be invoked in the context of national civil proceedings based on Arts 81 and/or 82 EC because civil proceedings cannot lead, directly or indirectly, to the imposition of a sanction by a public authority: (Case C-60/92 *Otto v Postbank* [1993] ECR I-5683, paras 15–17, referred to in L Ortiz Blanco, *EC Competition Procedure* (2nd edn. 2006), para 7.43.

[651] See the judgment of the Court of First Instance in *PVC II*, Joined Cases T-305/94, T-307/94, T-313/94, T-316/94, T-318/94, T-325/94, T-328/94, T-329/94 *Limburgse Vinyl Maatschappij and Others v Commission* [1999] ECR II-931, para 448.

[652] JM Joshua, 'The element of surprise: EEC competition investigations under Article 14(3) of Regulation 17', European Law Review [1983] Vol 8, pp 3–23.

[653] As stated in Case 374/87 *Orkem v Commission* [1989] ECR 3283, para 34. See also Case T-112/98 *Mannesmannröhren-Werke AG v Commission* [2001] ECR II-729, para 65.

does not cover pre-existing documentation or any other factual information about past occurrences, even if incriminating.[654]

8.273 *Compatibility of the right against self-incrimination as established in* Orkem *with the European Convention of Human Rights and its case law*   The European Courts have held that the (restricted) privilege against self-incrimination under Community law is compatible with the principles of the ECHR and the case law of the European Court of Human Rights (ECtHR) in Strasbourg.[655] In relation to this, it has considered it relevant that the Commission's procedures are administrative in nature rather than of a criminal law character, as well as the fact that the Commission proceedings are addressed to undertakings and not to private persons.[656]

8.274 *Precise scope of the privilege against self-incrimination: the elements of 'compulsion' and 'admission'*   In *PVC II* it was made clear that undertakings can only invoke the right against self-incrimination where the Commission *compels* information from them.[657]

---

[654] Case 374/87 *Orkem v Commission* [1989] ECR 3283, paras 34 and 35. See also Case T-112/98 *Mannesmannröhren-Werke AG v Commission* [2001] ECR II-729, paras 66 and 67; Case T-34/93 *Société Générale v Commission* [1995] ECR II-545; Joined Cases T-305/94, T-307/94, T-313/94, T-316/94, T-318/94, T-325/94, T-328/94, T-329/94 *Limburgse Vinyl Maatschappij and Others v Commission (PVC II)* [1999] ECR II-931, para 444 *et seq*; Joined Cases C-238/99P, C-244/99P, C-245/99P, C-247/99P, C-250/99P, C-252/99P and C-254/99P *Limburgse Vinyl Maatschappij and Others v Commission (PVC II)* [2002] ECR I-8357, para 272. Case C-301/04, *Commission v SGL Carbon* AG, judgment of 29 June 2006, not yet reported, para 44 *et seq*.

[655] In *PVC II*, the ECJ dealt with the issue whether developments in the case law of the European Court of Human Rights should lead to a widening of the privilege against self-incrimination. The Court denied such an extension stating that even taking into account the ECtHR case law, the scope of the privilege should not be widened. The CFI, in para 120 of its judgment in *PVC II* (confirmed by the ECJ in para 274) phrased it as follows:

> 'The Community judicature has consistently held that fundamental rights form an integral part of the general principles of Community law whose observance it ensures (see, in particular, Opinion 2/94 [1996] ECR I-1759, paragraph 33; Case C-299/95 *Kremzow* v *Austria* [1997] ECR I-2629, paragraph 14). For that purpose, the Court of Justice and the Court of First Instance rely on the constitutional traditions common to the Member States and the guidelines supplied by international treaties and conventions on the protection of human rights on which the Member States have collaborated or to which they are signatories. The ECHR has special significance in that respect (Case 222/84 *Johnston* v *Royal Ulster Constabulary* [1986] ECR 1651, paragraph 18; *Kremzow*, paragraph 14). Moreover, Article F.2 of the Treaty on European Union states that "[t]he Union shall respect fundamental rights, as guaranteed by the [ECHR] and as they result from the constitutional traditions common to the Member States, as general principles of Community law".'

The ECJ added in para 274 *et seq*. that even subsequent jurisprudence of the ECtHR did not alter the position expressed by the CFI. See also Case C-301/04 *Commission v SGL Carbon* AG, judgment of 29 June 2006, not yet reported, at para 44, where the ECJ confirms *PVC II* on this point.

[656] Given the level of the sanctions that the Commission can apply as well as their purpose (punishment as well as deterrence), some scholars have argued that Commission procedures should be seen as criminal in nature, and should therefore be accompanied by a higher level of protection of the rights of defence, including an absolute right to silence. See for instance P Meyer and S Kuhn, 'Befugnisse und Grenzen kartell-rechtlicher Durchsuchungen nach VO Nr. 1/2003 und nationalem Recht', Wirtschaft und Wettbewerb, 9/2004, pp 880–892. See also WP Wils, *Principles of European Antitrust Enforcement* (Hart Publishing, 2005), at pp 76–77. Judge Vesterdorf, acting as Advocate-General in Case T-1/89 *Rhône Poulenc v Commission* [1991] ECR II-00867 at section I.A.3, characterises competition law proceedings as criminal in character.

[657] See the judgment of the CFI in *PVC II*, n 41 above, at paras 439 *et seq*. on the question of whether the Commission may use information that was obtained from (self-incriminating) questions in a simple request for information. That judgment leaves unanswered the question whether an undertaking other than the one questioned can challenge the use of information obtained by the Commission in violation of a rule of law or principle that could have been applicable or used by the undertaking to which the questions were put. In *Greek Ferries* a much similar question was answered positively; The CFI was dealing with the question of whether evidence which was claimed to have been illegally obtained from one party from an inspection could be used against another. (Case T-59/99 *Ventouris Group Enterprises SA v Commission* [2003] ECR II-5257, at para 107 *et seq*.)

Therefore it is relevant in two instances, namely where: (a) the Commission requires information from undertakings by information request under a binding decision based on Article 18(3) of Regulation 1/2003 (not under Article 18(2)[658]), and/or (b) the Commission uses its power to put questions to the undertaking during inspections carried out pursuant to Article 20(4).[659]

Furthermore, according to the ECJ in *Orkem*, the right against self-incrimination only **8.275** applies where an undertaking is, in effect, requested to *admit* its participation in an infringement. To provide an admission can be interpreted as giving a qualifying, testimonial statement to that effect in reply to a question by the Commission.[660] The *Mannesmann* case provides an example of this. The Commission had requested Mannesmann to describe the 'purpose' of certain identified meetings (this question—one of many in the request for information—was put to the undertaking in case it had no documentary information available to it about the meetings, such as agendas or minutes). When the company refused to answer to the entirety of the request, the Commission issued a decision with procedural fines against Mannesmann, which the company subsequently challenged. Mannesmann's appeal was (partly) successful: the CFI considered that certain of the questions, those about the 'purpose' of certain meetings, placed an obligation on the undertaking to provide an *ex post* qualification of events that might imply admission of an infringement of the competition rules on its part.[661] (This judgment can be contrasted, however, with a more recent judgment of the CFI in *Brouwerij Haacht*, where a question about the 'subject-matter' of meetings appears to have been acceptable in relation to its self-incriminating nature.[662])

Pre-existing documents and factual information must be supplied Based on the limita- **8.276** tions described above, recourse to the privilege against self-incrimination is not available when

---

[658] An undertaking may refuse to respond to a request under Art 18(2), so if it does answer it cannot claim to have been compelled. (See *PVC II*, n 654 above, at para 279.)

[659] It is arguable whether in a case where the Commission addresses a question to a member of staff of an undertaking, rather than to a 'representative' of the undertaking under Art 20(2)(e), whether that individual could invoke a right not to self-incriminate. This issue is relevant because the Commission cannot 'compel' the individual to reply, so if the *PVC II* principle were applied, a right of silence could not be invoked. It is submitted, as Vesterdorf suggests, that in such a circumstance the member of staff could not avoid a question by relying on that principle, as he or she cannot be forced to answer under pain of sanction. A possible solution could lie in the approach of attributing the answer of the employee to the undertaking, as a result of which compulsion would apply, and consequently the privilege could be invoked (B Vesterdorf, n 646, above at p 1214, discussed in L Ortiz Blanco (ed.), *EC Competition Procedure* (2nd edn, 2006), para 7.47.

[660] In other words, the respondent's answer could not have existed outside the will of the respondent. In this sense, see PR Willis, '"You have the right to remain silent", or do you? The privilege against self-incrimination following Mannesmannröhren-Werke and other recent decisions', ECLR, August 2001.

[661] The question at issue was: 'In the case of meetings for which you are unable to find the relevant documents, please describe the purpose of the meeting, the decisions adopted and the type of documents received before and after the meeting'. (Case T-112/98 *Mannesmannröhren-Werke AG v Commission* [2001] ECR II-729, para 6). The undertaking had decided not to respond to the *entirety* of the request for information, ie including those questions that were clearly factual or asked for the production of pre-existing documents, and to which it was obliged to answer. Therefore, its appeal was only partly successful (paras 69–79 of the judgment). (Incidentally, from the German version of the question, which asked for a reply as regards the '*Themen*', it is less clear that this would have the same, self-incriminating, meaning as that attributed to the word 'purpose'.)

[662] Case T-48/02 *Brouwerij Haacht v Commission*, judgment of 6 December 2005, not yet reported, at para 113 *et seq*. An explanation may be that a question about the subject matter is considered as 'factual' whereas asking about the 'purpose' requires a qualification by the provider of the information.

pre-existing (contemporaneous) documentation or any other factual information about past occurrences is requested.[663] *Orkem* made clear that an undertaking could not avoid investigation on the grounds that its answers to such questions might provide evidence of an infringement by the undertaking. It was also clarified in *Orkem* that an undertaking must co-operate actively, which implies that it must make available to the Commission all information relating to the subject matter of the investigation. Consequently, the Commission can compel an undertaking to provide all necessary information and documents in its possession, even if the latter may be used to establish the existence of anti-competitive conduct.[664] The company can always clarify for the Commission, when exercising its rights of defence, that the facts or documents have a different meaning than that ascribed to them by the Commission.[665]

8.277 Regarding documents, the above principles leave little or no room for interpretation. However, answering the question of what constitutes 'factual information' is less straightforward and thus providing guidance on this point is more difficult. The CFI provided some clarification in *PVC II*, stating that the self-incriminating nature of any 'facts' that the Commission may request should be judged solely by the nature of the question and not in relation to the evidence which the Commission previously held.[666] However, this still leaves unanswered the question of what the notion of 'facts' encompasses.

8.278 It is difficult to provide a conclusive answer on this issue. In line with the above principles it would appear that a question on any matter which requires an opinion or qualification from an undertaking as to what has occurred is not 'factual', and therefore does not have to be answered.[667] Also 'leading questions', through which an undertaking would be asked for confirmatory statements and would be pushed in a particular direction, would not

---

[663] AG Geelhoed in *SGL* made a clarifying distinction between 'documents' and 'answers'. He emphasised that as regards documents there is no distinction to be made between 'admissible' and 'inadmissible' documents. (AG Geelhoed, Opinion in Case C-301/04 *Commission v SGL Carbon*, not yet reported, at para 56 *et seq.*)

[664] *Orkem*, n 654 above, para 34; Case T-112/98 *Mannesmannröhren-Werke AG v Commission* [2001] ECR II-729 para 65, *Société Générale*, n 654 above, para 74; CFI in *PVC II*, n 654 above, para 447, Joined Cases T-236/01, T-239/01, T-244/01 to T-246/01, T-251/01 and T-252/01 *Tokai Carbon Co and others v Commission (Tokai I)*, at para 403. The CFI, in *Tokai I*, fully endorsed the above principles and stated unequivocally that the mere fact of being obliged to answer purely factual questions and to comply with requests for the production of documents already in existence cannot constitute a breach of the principle of respect for the rights of defence or impair the right to a fair legal process. In the same judgment, and referring to *Mannesmann*, the CFI stated that questions relating to the 'object of meetings' did not need to be complied with. Then, a few paragraphs later in the same judgment, the CFI stated, quite surprisingly, that a number of pre-existing documents did *not* have to be produced in view of their incriminating nature (para 407). That contradiction was challenged by the Commission, relying on established case law. In his Opinion on the case, AG Geelhoed advised the ECJ to overturn the judgment, referring to the principles set out in *Orkem*. (Opinion in case C-301/04 *Commission v SGL Carbon*, not yet reported, at para 32 *et seq.*). The ECJ followed the AG on this point. (*Commission v SGL Carbon AG*, judgment of 29 June 2006, not yet reported, at para 48.)

[665] *Mannesmann*, n 664 above, paras 77 and 78.

[666] The CFI in its judgment in *PVC II*, n 654 above, para 458. Hence an undertaking cannot refuse to answer a question about, for instance, the presence of an executive at a meeting with competitors, even if it is clear that the Commission is aware (as the undertaking would most likely be) that the meeting concerned was of an illegal nature and therefore the confirmation of their presence would consistitute evidence of infringing behaviour.

[667] By way of comparison, in *Saunders*, a case before the ECtHR, it was concluded that the material which 'has an existence independent of the will of the suspect' did not qualify under the privilege. (See *Saunders v UK* (1997) 23 EHRR 313, paras 68, 69.)

require response.[668] AG Geelhoed in *SGL* suggested that asking for 'facts of an objective kind' would be permissible.[669] Lenaerts and Maselis conclude that factual information would include items such as: the dates of meetings, the persons attending the meetings, the capacity in which they attended, and—notably—the subjects discussed during the meetings.[670] Indeed for certain questions (*purpose/object/subject-matter*) there may be a fine line between the ones that are '*Orkem*-proof' and those that are not.[671]

In conclusion, the Commission should be careful about the manner in which it puts questions, and companies should be clear that they are indeed under an obligation to respond to the Commission's queries, even if the facts requested and the documents that are asked for could be used against them. The procedural options for an undertaking that considers it is not under an obligation to reply (because it would be submitting self-incriminating statements covered by *Orkem*) are briefly touched upon in the sections dealing with Article 18 requests, and with oral questions during inspections under Article 20.[672]   **8.279**

2. Legal professional privilege

The right to the protection of lawyer-client correspondence   Another component of the   **8.280**
rights of the defence in relation to cartel investigations is that of an undertaking to refuse to provide to the Commission its communications with its legal advisors. This right is referred to as 'legal professional privilege' or 'legal privilege'.[673]

---

[668] In that sense see M Guerrin and G Kyriazis, 'Cartels: Proof and Procedural Issues', Fordham International Law Journal Vol 16:266, 1992–1993.

[669] A-G Geelhoed in Case C-301/94 *Commission v SGL*, Opinion of 19 January 2006, not yet reported, at para 77 appears to have put a rather large frame around the category of information that may be considered factual in referring to 'facts of an objective kind' (although the meaning of this concept is not entirely clear either).

[670] K Lenaerts and I Maselis, 'Procedural Rights and Issues in the enforcement of Articles 81 and 82 of the EC Treaty', Annual Proceedings of the Fordham Corporate Law Institute, [2000] v.27, at p 284.

[671] A question such as providing information of 'subjects discussed' in relation to a possible meeting seems to stand squarely on that dividing line. Is the answer to that question 'factual' or will it lead to an 'admission'? Whether or not the summoning of the production of certain information leads to answers that go beyond what *Orkem* allows, would appear to depend a lot on the way the Commission puts a question: if it were it to ask, for instance, whether the subjects discussed during a meeting included 'an exchange of customer prices', thus putting words into the respondent's mouth, that question, though it may indeed relate to a fact, could well be considered as 'leading', and the answer could be construed as requiring a direct admission of illegal activity. If, however, the Commission simply asks for the items on the agenda of the meeting, that may be considered a purely factual question, and the undertaking would be obliged to list the items truthfully, including the item on 'customer pricing', even if that fact could be used as incriminating information against the undertaking.

[672] See paras 8.309ff and 8.367ff. For a further discussion as regards the aspects of leniency see paras 8.224ff.

[673] For an impressive and comprehensive overview of the rationale for legal professional privilege and its application under EC law, see E Gippini-Fournier, 'Legal Professional Privilege in Competition Proceedings before the European Commission: Beyond a Cursory Glance' Annual proceedings of the Fordham Institute, (BE Hawk, ed.) [2005] p 575. For another (more) general source, notably about the theory of legal privilege under common law, see J Auburn, *Legal Professional Privilege—Law and Theory* (Hart Publishing, 2000). See furthermore K Dekeyser and C Gauer, 'The New Enforcement System for Articles 81 and 82 and the Rights of Defence', (BE Hawk, ed), Annual proceedings of the Fordham Institute [2005]. See also the discussion in CS Kerse and N Khan, *EC Antitrust Procedure* (5th edn, 2005), Chapter 3 and L Ortiz Blanco, *EC Competition Procedure* (2nd edn, 2006), para 7.41 *et seq*. The underlying rationale for the principle of legal privilege is that 'to encourage candour between the lawyers and client encourages the client to consult with counsel more readily as to how the client should proceed so as to remain within the bounds of the law.'

8.281   Neither Regulation 1/2003 nor the Commission's implementing regulation (Regulation 773/2004) deal with the question of legal privilege. The principle of the protection of lawyer-client communications was established by the Court of Justice in the *A.M.&S.* case[674], which concerned a Commission investigation into the zinc sector. [675] In *A.M.&S.* the Court of Justice recognised the existence of a general principle of Community law, common to the legal orders of the Member States, which confers on an undertaking a right to the protection of the confidentiality of its communications with its lawyers. That principle applied, according to the Court, not only to proceedings before the European Court of Justice itself, but also to administrative proceedings before the Commission.

8.282   *Scope of legal professional privilege under Community law*   In the context of EC law, the issue of legal professional privilege may arise when the Commission *compels* the production of information, either during inspections or under requests for information. However, as with the privilege against self-incrimination, legal privilege is not an unqualified or absolute right and are restricted as set out below.

8.283   First, as the Court of Justice made clear in *A.M.&S.*, *legal privilege is confined to communications between the undertaking and external lawyers,* ie qualified lawyers who are not bound by an employment relationship with the undertaking.[676] The privilege does not, therefore, extend to correspondence with in-house counsel, even where in-house lawyers are admitted to the bar (and hence may be subject to the same professional-ethical rules as independent lawyers). This is because the EC doctrine relies on the assumption that in-house counsel is not considered sufficiently independent from the undertaking, regardless of such bar membership. In the words of Gippini-Fournier, '. . . the Court did not consider that bar membership alone guaranteed the appropriate level of independence to trigger a privilege against compelled production of evidence'.[677] The legal department within an undertaking is therefore not a 'safe haven', protected from the scrutiny of Commission inspectors.[678]

In more general terms it concerns the right of any natural or legal person to freely consult its lawyer, without the possibility of any records of such consultations being obtained by a public authority. (See *Upjohn Co. v United States*, 449 US 383 (1981) at 389, referred to in Gippini-Fournier, in fn 29, as well as the jurisprudence mentioned there.)

[674]   Case 155/79 *Australian Mining and Smelting Europe (A.M.&S.) v Commission* [1982] ECR 1575.

[675]   The Commission first recognised that it would not use as evidence 'legal papers' in 1978. (Written Question No. 63/78 of MEP Cousté, [1987] OJ C188/30.)

[676]   *A.M.&S.*, n 674 above, at paras 21 and 24. It is important to note that the principle in fact only applies to external lawyers who have been admitted to a bar organisation of one of the Member States, and not to lawyers who have qualified in third countries. Nevertheless, the Commission is known in practice also to have accepted the principle as extending to correspondence with outside counsel admitted to a non-EU bar organisation.

[677]   Gippini-Fournier, n 673 above, at section II, B. Indeed, in order to judge independence, the court in *A.M.&S.* considered first and foremost the question of the employment relationship. Where independence exists, the Court of Justice stated that a distinct criterion needed to be fulfilled, that of being a qualified member of the regulated legal profession in a Member State, ie a bar-admitted lawyer. See *A.M.&S.*, n 674 above, paras 21 and 24.

[678]   The question whether (bar-admitted/*admis au barreau*) in-house counsel should also benefit from legal privilege has been the subject of much academic debate since *A.M.&S.* and was raised again before the European Courts in 2003, some 20 years after the *A.M.&S* judgment, in an application made by Akzo Chemicals Ltd and its subsidiary Ackros Chemicals within the framework of an investigation into the product heat stabilisers. Akzo/Ackros brought an appeal and an application for interim measures against a decision of the Commission to retain copies of documents—allegedly covered by legal privilege—uncovered during an

A second limitation introduced by the Court of Justice in *A.M.&S.* is that only correspon- **8.284**
dence with a lawyer that is admitted to a bar *of a Member State* can benefit from legal privilege. In spite of what was stated in *A.M.&S.*, the Commission reportedly does not apply
that rule rigorously and has in practice accorded legal privilege—on occasion—to advice
from non-EU registered counsel where it was clear that such external counsel was admitted
to a national bar which applies similar deontological rules as those applicable in the
Member States.[679]

A third limitation on the protection afforded by legal privilege is that the documents for **8.285**
which privilege is claimed must have been *prepared for the purposes and in the interests of the
client's rights of defence and in the framework of obtaining legal advice in relation to the subject-
matter of the procedure*.[680] It is noted that undertakings cannot claim legal privilege protection
for documents that are annexed to a request for advice from (outside) counsel. In other words,
there exists no 'privilege by paperclip'.[681] It is quite clear from the above qualification by the
ECJ that the Commission is entitled to take copies of such annexed documents because, at
the time of their creation, they were not prepared for the purpose of obtaining legal advice.

As regards the criterion that the documents must have been drafted 'for the purposes of **8.286**
seeking legal advice in relation to the subject-matter of the procedure', the Court has provided
two clarifications. In *A.M.&S.*[682] the Court indicated that the protection extends to written
communications from a date earlier than the start of the Commission's investigation, as long
as these communications relate to the subject-matter of the proceedings (ie even if those proceedings only commenced at a later stage). Furthermore, in *Hilti*, the Court of Justice clarified that '. . . internal notes which are confined to reporting the text or the content of those

---

inspection at Ackros Chemicals. In its decision, the Commission denied Akzo's request to return documents.
The documentation in question included a set of documents which emanated from the company's in-house
counsel (or on which the latter had allegedly provided advice). The undertaking claimed that such communications deserved the same protection as that of external counsel. At the time of writing, the outcome of the
case before the CFI in the main proceeding was not yet known. In the case on interim measures, the president
of the CFI had stated that the possibility that an in-house counsel's correspondence could not benefit from
legal professional privilege merited careful (re)consideration. In the appeal on interim measures lodged by the
Commission, the President of the Court of Justice did not examine this issue in depth as he overturned the
President's Order in the interim measures on the basis of the requirement of urgency, which was stated not to
have been correctly considered by the CFI. The President of the ECJ concluded that as no serious and
irreparable harm could be foreseen from the Commission having had access to the documents, the application for interim measures had to be dismissed. At the time of writing, no judgment had been reached in the
main proceedings before the CFI on the issue of the possible extension of legal privilege to cover in-house
counsel. (Case T-125/03, and Joined Cases T-125/03 R and T-253/03 R *Akzo Nobel Chemicals Ltd and Ackros
Chemicals Ltd v Commission* and, on appeal, Case C-7/04 P(R) *Commission v Akzo Nobel Chemicals Ltd and
Ackros Chemicals Ltd,* order of 27 September 2004 [2004] ECR I-8739.) For a description of the proceedings
in *Akzo Ackross* and the issues at stake see B Vesterdorf, 'Legal Professional Privilege and the Privilege against
Self-incrimination in EC Law: Recent Developments and Current Issues' [2005] Fordham International Law
Journal, 1197–1215.

[679] However, this would be a matter for the undertaking to demonstrate. See D Dalheimer, C Feddersen
and G Miersch, *EU Kartellverfahrensverordnung*, Verlag CH Beck, 2005), at p 133.

[680] *A.M.&S.*, n 674 above, at para 23 and Case T-30-89 *Hilti Aktiengesellschaft v Commission* [1990]
ECR II-00163, at para 13.

[681] See Joshua, 'Proof in contested EEC Competition cases, a comparison with the rules of evidence in
common law', Eur Law Rev, 1987, p 343.

[682] *A.M.&S.*, n 674 above, para 23.

communications [with outside counsel]. . .' are also protected.[683] In the *Akzo/Ackros* case, the question arose to what extent internal working documents (allegedly) made in preparation of (future) communications with outside counsel could also be covered by the privilege.[684] At the time of writing, this question was still before the CFI in the main proceedings.

8.287   ***Is the Commission permitted to 'inspect' a document for which legal privilege is claimed?*** *A.M.&S.* and *Akzo/Ackross* have highlighted a fundamental question regarding the right that legal privilege is supposed to protect: is it supposed to protect lawyer-client correspondence from *use in the investigation*, or does the privilege serve to protect against possible *use in evidence*? According to the first interpretation—possible use in directing the investigation—inspecting the information before deciding whether legal privilege applies, even cursorily, may influence the Commission's attitude during the inquiry and help orientate its subsequent steps in the investigation.[685] For instance, a legal opinion from outside counsel may conclude that a violation of the competition rules has indeed occurred and may discuss certain facts of which the Commission was previously unaware and which might affect the Commission's mindset in the the investigation.

8.288   According to the second interpretation—protection against use in evidence—there should be no controversy about the Commission reviewing such documents on the spot. When it has assessed whether the document is covered by legal privilege or not, the Commission can decide to take a copy if it considers that legal privilege does not apply. Use of such a document in evidence and any conclusion based upon it can be contested later, if and when the Commission ultimately issues a prohibition decision with fines against the undertaking.[686]

8.289   The question of which right the recognition of legal privilege is aimed to protect has never been fully elucidated in case law, but the *Akzo/Ackross* case may produce some clarification. Gippini-Fournier considers that the right at stake is the use of the information in evidence and that view appears to be supported by the President of the Court of Justice in his Order in *Akzo/Ackross*.[687] In *A.M.& S.*, however, the Court clearly appears to have

---

[683]   *Hilti*, n 680 above, para 18.

[684]   *Akzo/Ackros*, Case C-7/04 P (R) *Commission v Akzo Nobel Chemicals Ltd and Ackros Chemicals Ltd*, order of 27 September 2004, [2004] ECR I-8739, para 97. The Order of the President of the CFI suggested that 'working or summary documents' might also be covered by legal privilege, whereas in the case of *Hilti* the Court only referred to summaries of '. . . internal notes which are confined to reporting the text or the content of those communications [with outside counsel]. . .'. (See *Hilti*, n 680, at para 18.) The CFI President's Order also considered whether an exchange of documents relating to a compliance programme 'set up by external lawyers' would qualify as such a working or summary document. The answer to that question was negative, due to the wide scope that such compliance programmes may have.

[685]   It may be presumed that the Commission will not suffer from 'acute amnesia' once it has seen certain information (Case C 67/91 *Dirección General de la Competencia v Asociación Española de Banca Privada and other* [1992] ECR I-4785, at para 39). The argument is that investigation may be directed in such a manner that the Commission would be able to obtain information, the evidentiary value of which could not be challenged on the ground of a violation of legal privilege.

[686]   At the same time, as regards use in evidence, it is debatable what evidentiary value the opinion of outside counsel can have, if a document solely contains that opinion and no other relevant information: the Commission will then have to make its *own* assessment, based on the facts, rather than rely on the opinion of any outside party.

[687]   *Akzo/Ackross*, Order of the President of the Court of Justice, n 684 above.

moved in the opposite direction: the judgment states that the undertaking cannot be requested to divulge the content of the communications. The outcome of the main proceedings in *Akzo/Ackross* will have greatest importance for future practice in relation to defining the nature of the right that legal privilege is supposed to protect, together with the issue of the possible extension of legal privilege to in-house counsel.

Procedure for claiming legal privilege   Whatever the exact scope of legal privilege in EC   **8.290**
law, the Commission has accepted that documents which are legally privileged have a special status, even at the stage of their collection (ie not only at the stage of their use in evidence). The Commission accepts, in recognition of *A.M.&S.*, that an undertaking which is the subject of an inspection under Article 20 of Regulation 1/2003, and which claims legal privilege in respect of a document, is not obliged to allow the Commission to actually study the contents of the document. The undertaking must, however, provide the Commission inspectors with 'relevant material' of such a nature as to demonstrate that the communication fulfils the conditions for classification under legal privilege.[688] Providing relevant material to satisfy the Commission would mean, for instance, showing the originator or addressee of the document (is it from/to outside counsel?), the subject mentioned, the (sub)headings contained in it, and that no annexes exist that consist of pre-existing documents (to which the privilege does not apply). Therefore, a mere claim of legal privilege by an undertaking is not sufficient. In any case, if the Commission considers the claim unjustified, it can either take a copy of the document using its powers under Article 20(2) and 20(6) of Regulation 1/2003 or impose periodic penalty payments under that Regulation as a penalty for the undertaking's refusal to supply the additional evidence as to the nature of the document.[689] In that case the undertaking, in order to attempt to have the document struck from the file, will have to ask formally for the return of the documents, and may appeal the decision if it is refused.[690]

Envelope procedure   Where genuine doubt exists on the part of the Commission and it   **8.291**
cannot make an appropriate on-the-spot assessment as to whether or not legal privilege applies, it has occasionally allowed undertakings more time to substantiate their claim, after the inspection, by way of the so-called 'envelope procedure'. This procedure involves putting the document(s) for which a claim is made in a sealed envelope, which is to be kept unopened until the undertaking, within a set time, has provided further arguments for its claim. If the undertaking's arguments are accepted, the documents will be returned. If, on the other hand, the Commission considers the arguments insufficient, it will inform the undertaking by way of formal decision of its intention to open the envelope.

---

[688] It is submitted that this also applies to requests for information under Art 18 of Regulation 1/2003, in that undertakings that are requested to produce particular documents are bound to refer the Commission to any documents falling within the ambit of the request and to which they consider legal professional privilege to attach, together with relevant material that allows the Commission to assess whether the claim is justified.

[689] See Case 155/79 *Australian Mining and Smelting Europe (A.M.&S.) v Commission* [1982] ECR 1575, at para 31. The taking of copies, absent a satisfactory explanation for the Commission's case team, occurred, for instance, in the *Akzo/Ackross* case: Case T-125/03, and Joined Cases T-125/03 R and T-253/03 R *Akzo Nobel Chemicals Ltd, and Ackros Chemicals Ltd v Commission* and, on appeal, Case C-7/04 P (R) *Commission v Akzo Nobel Chemicals Ltd and Ackros Chemicals Ltd* [2004] ECR I-8739.

[690] As did *Akzo/Ackross*, ibid.

That decision constitutes an act that is challengeable before the CFI, so that the undertaking can request an independent court review of the issue. This whole process was followed in *Akzo/Ackros*.[691] The Commission cannot be expected to apply the envelope procedure often. Doing so might lead to a considerable disruption of a Commission investigation, ie if several documents were to become the subject of (lengthy) court proceedings before they could be used in the investigation.

8.292 **3. The right to legal assistance** The right to legal assistance was referred to by the Court of Justice in *Hoechst* as one of the rights that the Commission must respect as early as at the investigative stage.[692] It is firmly enshrined in the Commission's practice, both as regards information requests and inspections, although there is no general reference to this right in Regulation 1/2003. Regarding requests for information, Regulation 1/2003 does clarify that lawyers are allowed to answer questions on behalf of their clients.[693] As regards inspections at business premises, an undertaking is entitled to have legal assistance present on the spot, although the Court clarified that this is not a prerequisite for the validity of the inspection.[694] It is considered that, by way of analogy at least, a right to legal assistance also exists in the case of inspections into other premises (private homes) under Article 21. As regards interviews under Article 19, as these are conducted on a voluntary basis, it appears evident that the interviewee can have a lawyer present if so desired.

8.293 **4. No right to be heard prior to investigative measures** Even though the rights of the defence are to be protected throughout the entirety of the administrative process, as was made clear in *Orkem*,[695] their application is of a different nature depending on the stage of the Commission investigation. The Court of Justice emphasised this fundamental difference in *National Panasonic*.[696] Regulation 1/2003 provides undertakings with no right to be heard prior to the Commission exercising its investigative powers.[697] This is because measures taken under Articles 18, 20 and 21 of Regulation 1/2003 are aimed merely at information gathering and therefore have lesser consequences for the undertakings concerned than a final cartel decision by which particular conduct is prohibited (and penalties are imposed).

---

[691] If the Commission were to insist on the spot on making a contested document part of the investigation file and therefore copy it, the better option for the undertaking would be to formally request the return of the document, the formal response to which would constitute a challengeable decision. That procedure was followed in *Akzo/Ackross* for the so-called 'Set A' documents (described more elaborately in the Order of the President of the CFI in *Akzo/Ackros*, Joined Cases T-125/03 R and T-253/03 R *Akzo Nobel Chemicals Ltd and Ackros Chemicals Ltd v Commission* [2004] ECR II-4771, at paras 6–10).

[692] The Court stated that the right to legal assistance is to be respected, like the respect for legal professional privilege, during both the investigation stage and the stage of the contentious procedure. See Joined Cases 46/87 and 277/88 *Hoechst AG v Commission* [1989] ECR 2859, para 16. See also *Dealing with the Commission* [1997], p 38.

[693] Art 18(4) of Regulation 1/2003.

[694] See also Case 136/79 *National Panasonic (UK) Ltd v Commission* [1980] ECR 2033. On the right to legal assistance during inspections see para 8.383.

[695] Case 374/87 *Orkem v Commission* [1989] ECR 3283, para 27.

[696] See case 136/79 *National Panasonic (UK) Ltd v Commission*, n 694 above, at para 21.

[697] Art 27 of Regulation 1/2003, which lays down the right to be heard but does not make reference to decisions taken under Arts 18, 20 and 21.

Regarding investigative measures, especially inspections, granting a right to be heard to undertakings before such steps are taken would frustrate the very purpose of investigations.

(iii) Other General Features of the Commission's Investigative Powers

1. Application of the principle of proportionality—practical implications

The investigative action must be proportionate to the goal pursued   The Commission's   **8.294**
investigative actions are measured in accordance with the principle of proportionality. This influences not only *what* the Commission can obtain in its investigations but also *how much* it can ask for. The fact that the Commission can ask only for 'necessary information'[698] that remains within the subject matter of the inquiry, as well as the fact that it can conduct inspections that are 'necessary'[699] may be seen as expressions of that overall principle.[700] As the principle of proportionality permeates what the Commission undertakes in terms of investigations, its practical consequences are dealt with in more depth in the paragraphs below, but will also be touched upon in the sections that deal with information requests and inspections.

'Necessity'   The Commission has wide powers to obtain information. Article 18(1) of   **8.295**
Regulation 1/2003 states, in relation to requests for information, that: 'In order to carry out the duties assigned to it the Commission may require undertakings . . . to supply all necessary information'. The Commission has confirmed its adherence to the principle of proportionality in exercising its investigative powers.[701] In principle it is for the Commission to determine what is 'necessary information' in a given case and, as regards requests for information, the Commission has a wide power of discretion, as the Court has confirmed.[702] Provided its requests are necessary, the Commission is entitled to ask for any piece of (factual) information

---

[698]   Art 18(1) of Regulation 1/2003.

[699]   Art 20(1) of Regulation 1/2003.

[700]   The question of the necessity of information may also be seen as an issue distinct from that of proportionality and rather as a 'limitation of purpose' (CS Kerse and N Khan, *EC Antitrust Procedure* (5th edn, 2005), at para 3-006). The ECJ, in *SEP*, framed the issue of necessity within the principle of proportionality. ('As regards the third plea in law, alleging a breach of the principle of proportionality, it should first of all be observed that the implementation of Article 11 of Regulation No 17 is subject to compliance with that principle. A mere relationship between a document and the alleged infringement is not sufficient to justify a request for disclosure; the relationship must be such that the Commission could reasonably suppose, at the time of the request, that the document would help it to determine whether the infringement had taken place.' Case T-39/90 *SEP v Commission* [1991] ECRII-1947, at para 25.)

[701]   *Dealing with the Commission*, Publication of the European Commission, 1997, available at <http://europa.eu.int/comm/competition/publications/dealen1_en.pdf>, p 28.

[702]   See Case 374/87 *Orkem v Commission* [1989] ECR 3283, paras 15 and 16. That same discretion would apply to Commission inspections. The Court of Justice decided that although the Commission has considerable discretion as to what is necessary for its investigation, it must be considered whether the information may exceed what is necessary in the light of the investigation. (In this conection see Kerse and Khan, n 700 above, at para 3-006. See also, *Société Générale*, where the CFI stated, in relation to Société Générale contesting the scope of particular questions in a request for information: 'The Commission's obligation to specify the subject matter [. . .] is a fundamental requirement both in order to show that the information requested of the undertaking concerned is justified and also to enable those undertakings to assess their duty to co-operate whilst at the same time safeguarding their rights of defence. It follows that the Commission is entitled to require the disclosure only of information which may enable it to investigate putative infringements which

within the compass of the subject matter of the investigation.[703] The principle of proportionality is also relevant to the decision to carry out on-the-spot enquiries. For instance, the Commission must have regard to that principle in selecting the method of investigation, which should be the least intrusive means possible (ie requests for information should be considered in place of invading the privacy of a legal person by way of a dawn raid)[704] even though no hierarchical order exists between the different means of investigation.[705]

8.296 *The principle of proportionality and the quantity of information requested/burden on the undertaking* The rule of proportionality also comes into play where the information requested is very difficult for an undertaking to obtain because of its volume or because of the research needed to obtain the data.[706] As the Court of Justice put it in *SEP*: '. . . the implementation of Article 11 of Regulation No 17 [currently Article 18 of Regulation 1/2003] is subject to compliance with the principle of proportionality. It is not enough for the information requested to be connected with the subject-matter of the inquiry. What is also necessary is that an obligation imposed on an undertaking to supply an item of information should not constitute a burden on that undertaking which is disproportionate to the requirements of the inquiry.' Where the need for an extension can be justified, the Commission is unlikely to take an unreasonable position and will in practice limit its request or allow an extension to answer a questionnaire.[707] Ultimately, if the undertaking cannot agree on a solution with the Commission in terms of reducing the request or allowing more time for its answer, it may ask the Court of First Instance to review the matter.[708]

---

justify the conduct of the inquiry.' (Case T-34/93 *Société Générale v Commission* [1995] ECR 545, at para 40.) Similarly, Case T-39/90 *SEP v Commission* [1991] ECR II-1947, at para 25. In *SEP*, the Court of First Instance clarified that: 'As regards the third plea in law, alleging a breach of the principle of proportionality, it should first of all be observed that the implementation of Article 11 of Regulation No 17 is subject to compliance with that principle. A mere relationship between a document and the alleged infringement is not sufficient to justify a request for disclosure; the relationship must be such that the Commission could reasonably suppose, at the time of the request, that the document would help it to determine whether the infringement had taken place.'

[703] Information sought must at least have the potential to help to determine whether the alleged infringement has taken place. For the notion of 'factual information' see paras 8.276ff.

[704] That being said it may be hard to determine how/where the boundary would lie for the Commission. (See CS Kerse and N Khan, *EC Antritrust Procedure* (5th edn, 2005), p 158, n 45, referring to A.G. Roemer in Case 31/59 *Acciaieria e Tubeficio di Brescia v High Authority* [1960] ECR 71 at 88–89.) It is noted that if an undertaking considers an inspection to constitute a disproportionate mode of investigation, this is unlikely to provide sufficient basis for an undertaking to prevent an inspection from actually proceeding (see paras 8.404ff on the possible ways to challenge an inspection decision or the materials obtained therein).

[705] Case 136/79 *National Panasonic v Commission*, n 694 above, at paras 12 and 30.

[706] *Dealing with the Commission*, n 701 above, section 4.3. The Commission recognises that an excessively short time limit would constitute an infringement of the rights of the defence.

[707] Similarly, during inspections, the Commission will be open to discussing a mitigation of its request for the production of documents if the original question would have led to the production of an excessive amount of information.

[708] See, for instance, the judgment of the Court of First Instance in *SEP*, Case T-39/90 *SEP v Commission* [1991] ECR II-1947, paras 51 and 52 (as well as the case law referred to therein), where the CFI stated:

'As regards the third plea in law, alleging a breach of the principle of proportionality, it should first of all be observed that the implementation of Article 11 of Regulation No 17 is subject to compliance with that principle. It is not enough for the information requested to be connected with the subject-matter of the inquiry. What is also necessary is that an obligation imposed on an undertaking to supply an item of information should not constitute a burden on that undertaking which is disproportionate to the requirements of the inquiry.'

2. The content and form of information/business records that may be requested **8.297**
In considering what information an undertaking may be required to produce in reply to a
request for information or during an inspection, a distinction must be made between *content*
and *form*. In other words, the question is, on the one hand, what substantive information
can be requested and, on the other, what form the information can take.

Content The Commission may obtain any information that falls within the subject mat- **8.298**
ter of the investigation,[709] as long as its requests are necessary and proportionate, as has
been explained above. The fact that a document contains business secrets cannot be relied
upon to prevent its disclosure to the Commission. (The protection of any business secrets
or other confidential information against access by third parties is safeguarded through
Article 28 of Regulation 1/2003 and the procedures relating to access to the file, described
in paras 8.459 and following.) The fact that particular business records may not be direct
proof of the infringement cannot be used by an undertaking to refuse their submission, as
long as the Commission stays within the limits of 'information which may enable it to
investigate putative infringements'.[710] That said, part of the purpose of an inspection is to
allow the Commission to assess information in order to make a decision about whether or
not it is relevant to the inquiry.

Form As regards the *types of business records* that the Commission can ask for, no restric- **8.299**
tions are placed on the Commission: no matter how the information has been recorded
(official or unofficial, in draft form or as definitive, signed or unsigned, typed or handwritten, stored electronically or 'physically', non-confidential or confidential) the Commission
can request the submission of those records and take copies. The Commission may even
ask to see documents that are claimed to be of a personal nature in order to ascertain that
those documents are indeed private. The categories of documents sought by the
Commission typically include minutes of meetings, fax communications, e-mail messages,
extracts from diaries, information from electronic equipment such as mobile telephones
and PDAs, notepads with hand-written information in them, expense records, etc.
Although the Commission may always request the production of existing business records,

---

That view is confirmed by settled case law. In its judgment in Case 136/79 *National Panasonic*, cited above,
para 30, the Court of Justice considered whether, in implementing Art 11 of Regulation No 17, 'the Commission's
action . . . was disproportionate to the objective pursued and therefore violated the principle of proportionality'. Similarly, it expressly recognised in its judgment in Joined Cases 46/87 and 227/88 *Hoechst*, cited above,
para 19, relating to a proceeding applying Art 14 of Regulation No 17, that the need for protection against
arbitrary or disproportionate intervention by public authorities in the sphere of the activities of any person,
whether natural or legal, constitutes a general principle of Community law. (See also Case C-94/00 *Roquette
Frères*, ECR I-9011, para 27, referring to *Hoechst*.)

[709] In the terminology of Art 20(2) of Regulation 1/2003, these would be 'business records', defined by the
Court of Justice as 'documents concerning the market activities of the undertaking'. (See *A.M.&S.*, n 689
above, para 16; Case C-94/00 *Roquette Frères SA*, ECR I-9011, para 45.)

[710] See Case T-34/93 *Société Générale v Commission* [1995] ECR II-545, para 40 and Case T-39/90 *SEP v
Commission* [1991] ECR II-1947, para 25. In *A.M.&S.* the Court clarified that: 'It is in principle for the
Commission itself, and not the undertaking concerned or a third party, whether an expert or an arbitrator, to
decide whether or not a document must be produced to it'. (*A.M.&S.*, n 689 above, at para 17.)

it may also request the production of other (factual) information,[711] either by request for information or during an inspection, including information not previously documented.[712]

8.300   **3. The undertakings from which information may be sought: suspected cartel participants as well as other parties**   The undertakings (including associations of undertakings) which may be subjected to the Commission's investigatory powers may include not only the undertakings that are suspected of having been involved in an infringement, but also third parties, for instance suppliers or customers. However, surprise inspections are in general reserved for undertakings believed to have been (directly) involved in an infringement. Similarly, it is rather exceptional in a cartel case for the Commission to address a request for information to any party other than a suspected cartel member, although it may do so if information relevant to establishment of the infringement or other more general information needed for the inquiry may be obtained from that source. For instance, the Commission may seek further information from customers regarding their knowledge about price increases or more generally about the functioning of the industry.

8.301   **4. The territorial scope of the Commission's investigation powers**   In the context of increased internationalisation of business activities, many undertakings operate in several countries and continents. Correspondingly, evidence of cartels that affect the common market is increasingly located in other jurisdictions. The ability to obtain such evidence is crucial to the successful prosecution of (international) cartels. Jurisdictional constraints, however, affect the Commission's capacity to obtain evidence from undertakings located outside the EEA.

8.302   The competence of the Commission to proceed against anti-competitive conduct of an undertaking is not linked to where the undertaking is based, but relates to whether the anti-competitive behaviour is implemented in or has effects in the Community.[713] Consequently, the Commission imposes prohibition decisions against EU and non-EU based firms alike where they have participated in a cartel that affects trade between EU Member States. However, the Commission's powers of investigation are much less obviously applicable against non-EU-based entities.

---

[711] On the issue of 'factual information', see paras 8.276–8.279.

[712] Information may be supplied in writing or in oral form, as appropriate. As regards inspections, see Art 4 of Regulation 773/2004.

[713] The territorial scope of the Commission's powers in the field of competition law can be defined either by the 'economic entity', 'implementation' or 'effects' doctrine. On the *implementation doctrine*, see Case 48/69 *ICI v Commission* ('*Dyestuffs*') [1972] ECR 619, paras 125–142; Cases 89/85, 104/85, 114/85, 116/85, 117/85, 125 to 129/85. See also discussions in Whish, *Competition Law* (5th edn, 2003), p 436; Jones/Sufrin, *EC Competition Law* (2nd edn, 2004), p 1254. On the *effects doctrine*, see AG Darmon in *Woodpulp* ([1988] ECR 5193, para 50); in relation to merger control, see Case T-102/96 *Gencor v Commission* [1999] ECR II-753, paras 76–110. For the *effects doctrine* see also L Ritter and WD Braun, *European Competition Law: A Practitioners Guide* (3rd edn, 2004), p 71. The European Court has never explicitly recognised the effects doctrine although in *Gencor* it did allude to the applicability of the effects doctrine for establishing jurisdiction, but based the existence of the Commission's jurisdiction on the implementation of the merger agreement in the EU.

The jurisdictional scope of the Commission's investigative powers: subject matter jurisdiction **8.303**
versus *enforcement jurisdiction*   In considering the scope of the Community's jurisdiction
in antitrust matters, a distinction may be drawn between 'subject matter jurisdiction' and
'enforcement jurisdiction'. Subject matter jurisdiction (also referred to as the 'jurisdiction to
prescribe') is the power to lay down general or individual rules or decisions through legislative, executive or judicial bodies.[714] Subject matter jurisdiction of the Community over non-
EU based entities, eg the authority to adopt prohibition decisions with fines against cartels
that affect the EEA, has been upheld by the European Courts.[715] Enforcement jurisdiction
can be described as the power to give effect to a general rule or an individual decision by means
of issuing implementing measures.[716] Such decisions compel undertakings to act in a certain
way. Inspection decisions would fall within this category because they order companies to
subject themselves to an on-site investigation. The distinction between subject matter jurisdiction and enforcement jurisdiction, however, can be quite unclear.[717] By way of example,
the Commission targets EU and foreign-based entities alike in its cartel decisions, in which it
combines the imposition of fines (an exercise of its subject matter jurisdiction) with a 'cease
and desist' obligation on those undertakings (a form of enforcement jurisdiction).[718] The
Commission has also asserted jurisdiction to enforce on an extraterritorial basis by issuing
decisions which included (behavioural) orders against non-EU undertakings, such as a
supply obligation, and the ECJ has upheld the Commission's authority to do so.[719]

State sovereignty   A crucial principle to consider in relation to the Commission's inves- **8.304**
tigative jurisdiction is that of state sovereignty, which constitutes an established principle
under public international law.[720] In application of that principle, the Commission cannot
conduct inspections outside the borders of the EU,[721] even if the undertakings that are
located outside the EU are active on EU markets. Should the Commission wish to seek,
on the spot, information held by companies outside the EU, it would have to rely on international agreements. At present, only the EEA Agreement can be used for that purpose.

---

[714] For example, the prohibition on restrictions of competition contained in Art 81, as well as the individual prohibition decisions of the Commission addressed to undertakings.

[715] Case *ICI v Commission* (*Dyestuffs*), n 713 above; *A Ahlström Oy v Commission* (*Woodpulp*), n 713 above;
see also H Sauter in Langen/Bunte, *Kommentar zum deutschen und europäischen Kartellrecht* (8th edn, 1998),
VO 17/62, para 27 *et seq.*

[716] For example, a decision requiring the execution of remedies or a decision imposing interim measures
may be seen as such an enforcement decision.

[717] Cf. AG Darmon in *Woodpulp*, n 713 above, para 28 *et seq.*

[718] The making of a cease and desist order may be considered as an exercise of enforcement jurisdiction.
(cf Whish, *Competition Law* (5th edn, 2003), p 438; CS Kerse and N Khan, *EC Antitrust Procedure* (5th edn,
2005), para 6-020.

[719] Cases 6/73 & 7/73 *Commercial Solvents v Commission* [1974] ECR, para 223. In that case the
Commission imposed a re-supply obligation on a US based company, which was upheld by the Court; see also
Commission Decision in *Warner-Lambert/Gillette* (OJ [1993] L116/21), in which the Commission obliged
a US-based company to dispose of its equity interest and its interest as a creditor. The imposition of such
behavioural measures are now provided under Regulation 1/2003, under Art 8 (interim measures) and Art 9
(commitments).

[720] Friedel-Souchu, *Extraterritorialité du droit de la concurrence aux États-Unis et dans la Communauté
européenne*, 1994, p 36; R Whish, *Competition Law* (5th edn, 2003), p 435 *et seq.*; CS Kerse and N Khan,
EC Antitrust Procedure (5th edn, 2005), para 3-030; De Bronett in Schröter/Jakob/Mederer, *Kommentar zum
europäischen Wettbewerbsrecht*, 2003, VO 17, Vorbemerkung, para 5.

[721] R Whish, *Competition Law* (5th edn, 2003), pp 437–438.

The Commission cannot rely on other treaties, such as mutual legal assistance treaties (MLATs) or equivalent agreements.[722]

8.305   As regards requests for information, the legal situation is less clear, however. As far as is known, the Community Courts have never answered the question of whether information can be compelled from entities located outside the EU. The Commission considers, however, that it ought not to apply the power to impose sanctions on undertakings located outside the EU that fail to provide a complete response to a request for information or that supply incorrect or misleading information.[723] Certain authors have suggested that requesting information concerning a possible infringement of a substantive rule of law is merely an extension of subject-matter jurisdiction, so that the Commission could very well issue requests for information to third country undertakings, even by decision.[724] It seems, therefore, that rather than being based on any legal impossibility,[725] the choice not to issue Article 18 requests with reference to procedural fines has been a policy choice by the Commission, against the background of sovereignty arguments and a desire to preserve harmonious international relations for the EC.[726] It is submitted, however, that on the basis

---

[722]   The EEA agreement stipulates that, on request, investigations can take place on the request of a contracting party, in accordance with the internal rules of the requested party. EEA Agreement, Protocol 23, Art 8(3). For an example see the investigation in *Zinc Phosphate*, where inspections under Art 14(2) were carried out in Norway. (See Commission Decision in *Zinc Phosphate* [2001] L153/1.)

[723]   The Commission therefore only issues (simple) requests for information, in which it even refrains from indicating the possibility of imposing fines for incomplete, misleading or incorrect answers, as provided in Arts 23 and 24 of Regulation 1/2003. See also *Dealing with the Commission*, European Commission, 1997, p 22.

[724]   Gleiss/Hirsch and Whish argue that the request for information represents the enforcement of EC competition law through compulsory measures. The Commission therefore cannot compel the production of information outside its territory. (Gleiss/Hirsch, *Kommentar zum EG-Kartellrecht* (4th edn, 1993) Einleitung B, paras 45, 46); R Whish, *Competition Law* (5th edn, 2003), pp 437–438. Other authors (Rehbinder/Sauter) argue that the subject matter jurisdiction of the Commission actually includes procedural competence (*Gleichlaufprinzip*) and therefore includes the right to request information by decision from non EU-based undertakings (Rehbinder/Sauter, in Immenga/Mestmäcker Gesetz gegen Wettbewerbsbeschränkungen (GWB), Kommentar (3rd edn, 2001). See also Meng, in Von der Groeben/Thiesing/Ehlermann, *Extraterritoriale Anwendung des EU-Rechts* (5th edn, 1997), p 1244, para 98. By contrast, other authors hold a view that is somewhere in between these two positions: the mere *imposing of fines* on entities located in third countries without being able to *enforce* these fines, does not represent the enforcement of the request for information and is thus not part of the jurisdiction to enforce. According to these authors, the power to order is not limited to the borders of a country, only the power to compel by pecuniary sanction is limited (eg Friedel-Souchu, *Extraterritorialité du droit de la concurrence aux États-Unis et dans la Communauté européenne*, 1994, pp 41, 193; B Goldman, *Observations sur les arrêts 'Matières colorantes'*, JDI (Clunet, 1973), p 935. Also compare A-G Darmon in *Woodpulp*, n 713 above, para 30 ('Accordingly, it is specific measures of enforcement and coercion that are excluded. However, as others have written before, "to order is not to compel".').

[725]   JM Joshua, 'Requests for information in EEC fact finding procedures', ECLR 1982, vol 3 no 1, at pp 175, 176. Joshua explains that perceived difficulties with enforcement (execution) and 'national sensitivities' have played a role in the Commission's decision to merely send requests for information on an informal basis to entities located outside the Community.

[726]   Indeed, should the Commission endeavour to pursue decisions requesting information against foreign located entities, it may provoke a reaction of other jurisdictions of either creating or applying so-called 'blocking statutes' or of applying the same assertion of jurisdiction towards EU located entities, which may be considered to be an unwelcome consequence. (Hence, the most appropriate way forward would be to conclude bilateral or multilateral treaties in this respect.) At the same time, it is submitted, in the current geopolitical climate of strong enforcement against cartels, the Commission should feel less restrained from considering the option of issuing requests under Art 18 to foreign entities. Another reason for considering issuing the same types of requests for information to EU and non-EU based undertakings alike is that treating them differently as regards the information that they would be obliged to submit is no longer appropriate in an environment of internationalisation of business activity.

of the above arguments it would be legally defensible if the Commission were to issue requests for information in the same way for undertakings located inside and outside the EEA. In practice, the Commission has tried to overcome the above restraint by addressing requests for information to subsidiaries in the EU intended for (parent) entities outside the EU.[727] The logic applied is that 'the undertaking', to which both parent and subsidiary belong, has a presence in the EU. Valid notification of a request for information destined for the parent entity can be effected by service on the subsidiary.[728]

Information stored electronically may be treated differently, in spite of the above princi- **8.306** ples. The principle that the Commission applies is that, since its powers of inspection permit access to information that is available on the premises of the undertaking inspected, it will also be permitted to access information that is electronically accessible from the premises, even if the information is 'physically stored'—if one can apply such a term to electronically stored information—on a server that is located outside the Commission's jurisdiction.[729]

5. The timing of any investigative steps/application of limitation periods The Commission **8.307** is not restricted on the timing for initiating its investigations and it can send information requests or launch inspections at any time during an investigation. The Commission is not required to apply one investigative measure before it can apply another, ie to launch on-the-spot investigations only after it has sent requests for information.[730] Certain temporal limits are placed on the Commission regarding the imposition of penalties, though these rules do not affect the Commission's ability to investigate. The limitation rules, which are set out in Chapter VII of Regulation 1/2003,[731] provide that the Commission cannot impose fines if the infringing behaviour of the undertaking had ceased five years before the Commission took any

---

[727] Case 48/69 *ICI v Commission (Dyestuffs)* [1972] ECR 619, paras 34–44; Case 6/72 *Continental Can v Commission*, [1973] ECR 215, paras 9–10; See also L Ritter and WD Braun, *European Competition Law: A Practitioners Guide* (3rd edn, 2004) at p 72.

[728] *Dyestuffs*, n 715 above, at paras 42–43. See also CS Kerse and N Khan, *EC Antitrust Procedure* (5th edn, 2005), para 3-030. That solution may not be a perfect substitute for the (perceived) lack of ability to issue requests for information to entities located outside the EU. First, this option may not be available where the parent entity has no subsidiary in the EU. Secondly, where there is a subsidiary in the EU, but it is involved in a different business altogether and has no connection with the subject-matter of the investigation, it is submitted that one may view a request made *to that subsidiary* to be a measure of investigation that is disproportionate against that legal entity. An analogy may be drawn with the question of liability for the infringement itself: if a legal entity cannot be held liable for the infringement because it was neither involved in the cartel behaviour nor exercised decisive influence over another entity that was, it is difficult to see how such an entity could be forced to answer an Art 18 request that would in fact be destined for its parent or another (sister) entity in the group (see para 8.553 on the issue of liability). On this point see also: Burrichter/Hauschild in Immenga/Mestmäcker, *EG Wettbewerbsrecht*, 1997, VO 17, Art 11, para 19; H Sauter in Langen/Bunte, *Kommentar zum deutschen und europäischen Kartellrecht* (8th edn, 1998), VO 17/62, Art 11, para 13 *et seq.*; G De Bronett in Schröter/Jakob/Mederer, *Kommentar zum europäischen Wettbewerbsrecht*, 2003, VO 17 Art 11, para 2. See also paras 8.294ff on the issue of the proportionality requirements for requests for infromation.

[729] The Commission's powers of investigation should not be frustrated by the mere fact that an undertaking has decided to store certain information that is under its control outside the Community. (For a short discussion, see CS Kerse and N Khan, *EC Antritrust Procedure* (5th edn, 2005), para 3-031.) As regards the Commission's powers of inspection see section D(3)(e).

[730] Case 136/79 *National Panasonic (UK) Ltd v Commission* [1980] ECR 2033, at para 11, also discussed in para 8.295.

[731] See Art 25, paras (1)–(5) of Regulation 1/2003.

investigative action. To 'take action' means to take steps by whatever means of investigation, whether formal or informal.[732] Any such action will make the five-year period start afresh.[733] Where the Commission has started an investigation within five years of the termination of the infringement, there is a second, absolute time bar on its ability to impose any fines: where the participation in the infringement ceased more than 10 years before.[734] In these circumstances a decision imposing fines may no longer be taken.[735] That said, the Commission may still issue a prohibition decision against a cartel member, in spite of the fact that imposing a fine for participation in the cartel would be time-barred, as long as it provides its reasons for doing so in the decision.[736] It should be noted that the limitation period for the imposition of fines or periodic penalty payments is suspended for as long as the decision of the Commission is the subject of proceedings pending before the Court of Justice.[737]

8.308   **6. The duty of active co-operation and its implication for requests for information and inspections**   One reason why the Commission's investigative powers are effective is that 'an obligation to co-operate actively' is imposed upon the undertakings, as described by the Court of Justice in *Orkem*.[738] That obligation implies that undertakings, as long as their fundamental rights are not violated, '. . . must make available to the Commission all information relating to the subject matter of the investigation'.[739] The principle is applicable to both information requests and inspections.[740] The duty to make information available applies even if the data may serve to establish the infringement by the undertaking. The only exception is that, as explained in paras 8.296 and following, an answer that may lead to the admission of an infringement need not be supplied, as that would violate the fundamental right against self-incrimination.[741] The duty of active co-operation means, as

---

[732] Art 25(3) speaks of 'any action' in this respect. It lists (non-exhaustively) the procedural steps that are to be considered as 'actions'.

[733] However, the Commission may not, for instance, use requests for information that are without relevance to the investigation as an artificial means of avoiding the prescription rules. In *FETTSCA*, the Court applied a narrow interpretation of the rule applying to the interruption of the five-year limitation period, in holding that a request for information on turnover figures, made purely to provoke a prolongation of prescription periods, could not have that effect. (Case T-213/00 *CMA CGM v Commission* [2003] ECR II-913, para 448).

[734] 'Twice the limitation period'—see Art 25(5) of Regulation 1/2003.

[735] As regards the imposition of fines for procedural infringements, eg for a refusal during an inspection or a refusal to reply to an Art 18 request by decision, the time periods are respectively three and six years. (See Art 25(1)(a) and (5) of Regulation 1/2003.) It is noted that whereas Art 25 of Regulation 1/2003 governs restrictions on *imposing* penalties for substantive or procedural infringements, Art 26 covers the limitation periods for the *collection* of any fines imposed. The basic rule is that the Commission has five years from the date of the decision to enforce it.

[736] In such a case the Commission must provide grounds for doing so. Joined Cases T-22/02 and T-23/02 *Sumitomo Chemical and Sumika Fine Chemicals v Commission*, judgment of the CFI of 6 October 2005 (not yet reported), at paras 136 *et seq*.

[737] Art 25(6) of Regulation 1/2003.

[738] See for instance Case 374/87 *Orkem v Commission* [1989] ECR 3283, para 27; Joined Cases C-204–5, 211, 213, 217, and 219/00 P *Aalborg A/S and others v Commission* [2004] ECR I-123, at para 61 *et seq*.

[739] See Commission decisions (in relation to the production of documents during inspections) in *Fabrica Pisana* and *Fabrica Sciara*, [1980] OJ L75/30 and 35.

[740] Whereas *Orkem* (Case 374/87 *Orkem v Commission* [1989] ECR 3283) was a matter that related to an inspection having been carried out under Art 14 of Regulation 17/62, the principle was also established in litigation concerning requests for information under Art 11 of Regulation 17/62. (See notably Case T-34/93 *Société Générale v Commission* ECR II-545, at para 72, in which the Court refers more generally to a duty of active co-operation under Regulation 17/62).

[741] Case *Orkem*, ibid, at paras 34 and 35, and *Société Générale*, ibid, at para 74.

regards requests for information, that the undertaking must consider the spirit and purpose of the request and provide answers which may go beyond the particulars of the questions posed.[742] In relation to inspections it implies, for instance, that an undertaking cannot adopt a passive attitude and that it will have to indicate the whereabouts of documents when so requested.[743] Indeed, an answer along the lines of 'we are happy to come and meet you to explain our views' would not be sufficient answer to a request for information.[744] The obligation to co-operate actively should be seen separately from the duty to allow an inspection to proceed and the duty to provide access to business records. These obligations flow directly from Article 20 of Regulation 1/2003. The duty of active co-operation can be seen as a distinct, supplementary requirement upon undertakings.

(c) Requests for Information—Article 18

(i) The Use of Requests for Information in Cartel Cases

Various aspects in relation to the issuing and answering of questionnaires are described below. This overview does not pretend to be exhaustive. It does not, for example, enter into the particular procedural issues surrounding the issue and receipt of Article 18 letters. It does aim, however, to discuss the most relevant aspects for practitioners involved in cartel investigations. Reference is made to other literature dealing in greater detail with the issue of requests for information.[745] **8.309**

The power of the Commission to issue requests for information is enshrined in Article 18 of Regulation 1/2003. That power already existed under Regulation 17.[746] Requests for information are used very commonly in cartel cases[747] and throughout the course of a cartel investigation an undertaking may receive multiple requests.[748] 'Information' in relation to Commission procedures is a notion that is wide-ranging and undefined.[749] It refers to (pre-existing) documents and other factual data. **8.310**

---

[742] See also *Dealing with the Commission*, at sections 4.1 and 4.5.

[743] It is also noted that the duty of co-operation applies fully in the case of (voluntary) inspections under Art 20(3): once the undertaking has allowed the inspection to take place, it cannot reverse that position later in the process [see also para 8.337, fn 812].

[744] See Case T-46/92 *The Scottish Football Association v Commission* [1994] ECR II-1039.

[745] For a more complete overview of the Commission's powers in relation to requests for information, and more generally the procedural aspects of the fact-finding process, see for instance L Ortiz Blanco, *EC Competition Procedure* (2nd edn, 2006), ch 7; CS Kerse and N Khan, *EC Antitrust Procedure* (5th edn, 2005), ch 3; Korah, 'Narrow or misleading replies to Requests for Information', 1982 3 Bus L Rev 69; JM Joshua, 'Requests for information in EEC fact finding procedures' [1982] ECLR, vol 3 no 1, pp 173–184. C. Lavoie, 'The Investigative Powers of the Commission with respect to Business Secrets under Community Competition Rules' [1992] Eur L Rev, Vol 17, no 1, pp 20–40.

[746] Art 11 of Regulation 17/62.

[747] This is usually different for companies that benefit from conditional immunity under the Leniency Notice because they have a duty of full co-operation and therefore may receive questions on an informal basis. A need for the Commission to rely on its formal powers is considered to be at odds with this duty of co-operation. Nevertheless, applicants for immunity from fines are not excluded from receiving requests for information based on Art 18.

[748] It is also possible, however, that an undertaking, or a legal entity within that undertaking, is not asked questions during the administrative phase and that the first communication from the Commission it receives is a Statement of Objections.

[749] For the notion of 'information', see CS Kerse and N Khan, *EC Antitrust Procedure* (5th edn, 2005), at para 3-009.

8.311 In a typical cartel investigation, a first request for information will follow on-site inspections. Where the inspection was not the initial step in the investigation, or where the undertaking was not amongst the companies visited, the sending of a request for information will be the first formal investigative measure.[750] In a request for information the Commission may seek information that is directly relevant to the establishment of the infringement (eg about participants to cartel meetings), but may also request information that is relevant to other issues (eg information about volume of commerce of the products or services in question, which may be used later in the administrative procedure in determining the level of the fines). The Commission's power under Article 18 is far-reaching and, as explained in paras 8.296 and following, in requests for information it may compel disclosure of incriminating evidence (facts or documents), with the exception of statements that form an admission of the infringement.

(ii) Two Types of Request for Information: 'Simple Requests' and 'Requests by Decision'

8.312 Under Article 18 of Regulation 1/2003, the Commission has two means of obtaining information in writing: either through a 'simple request' under Article 18(2) of Regulation 1/2003, under which no sanction can be applied if an answer is not provided, or through a 'request by decision' under Article 18(3), where the answer is compelled under threat of pecuniary sanctions. Under Regulation 1/2003, the Commission has discretion to decide whether or not to resort to issuing a request by decision.[751] The fact that under a simple request no sanction applies for not answering does not mean, however, that responding to such a request is to be seen as voluntary co-operation.[752]

8.313 **1. Procedural requirements: the duty to state the legal basis and purpose of the request and to set a time-limit** Article 18 requests must fulfil certain procedural requirements. Both Articles 18(2) and 18(3) require the Commission to state the legal basis and the purpose of the request.[753] In stating the purpose the Commission can be relatively succinct: it must

---

[750] This can happen, eg, in cases where an application for immunity exists, but the need for, or usefulness of, a search for evidence in the companies is limited. This can happen for instance in a case where the reported infringement is relatively old and few documents of probative value, if any, are likely to surface during an on the spot investigation.

[751] Under Art 11 of Regulation 17/62, the Commission first had to ask its questions by simple request—to which an undertaking was not obliged to answer—before resorting to an information request by decision. Even though undertakings did usually comply with the simple request, in a considerable number of cases, the Commission had to seek compliance by issuing a decision. This has often created a substantial delay in the investigation as a result of the two-stage process. Under Regulation 1/2003 the obligatory two-stage process has been abolished, as compared to Regulation 17/62. It is therefore likely that in cartel cases the Commission will increasingly make use of the option of requesting information by decision immediately. This is principally because the evidence sought in a cartel investigation is often litigious, as it is used in one way or another to formulate objections against the undertakings concerned. Full (voluntary) compliance cannot always be expected under those circumstances. (Decisions ordering companies to produce information are not always published by the Commission. In certain cases, however, the Commission has decided to publish the decision. See for instance the Commission Decision compelling information in *Fides* [1979] OJ 157/33.) For a list of decisions in which procedural fines were imposed see M Van Der Woude and C Jones, *EC Competition Law Handbook* (2004/2005 edn), p 197.

[752] Only providing information that goes 'far beyond' that which an entity is obliged to supply can be seen as voluntary co-operation and is therefore capable of leading to a reduction in fines under the Leniency Notice. (Case T-48/02 *Brouwerij Haacht v Commission*, judgment of 6 December 2005, not yet reported, at para 106 and the jurisprudence cited there.)

[753] As regards the requirements for the statement of purpose, see also the judgment in Case C-94/00 *Roquette Frères* [2002] ECR I-9011, at paras 82–84.

indicate the main features of the conduct it is investigating.[754] The statement of purpose is relevant for the undertakings to assess the scope of their duty to co-operate. Of course, the request must specify the information requested, which the Commission often does in an annex to an otherwise standardised letter. Also, for simple requests and those by decision under Article 18(3) the Commission must fix a time limit.[755] Furthermore, the Commission is required to state what procedural penalties may apply pursuant to Article 23 (see the section below), but not necessarily the level of the fine for failing to provide the requested information within the set time limit.

2. Sanctions for late, incomplete, incorrect or misleading replies   The Commission can **8.314** punish an undertaking by way of procedural (financial) penalties for providing information *late* or in *incomplete* form, or for supplying *incorrect* or *misleading* information.[756] Procedural sanctions for late and incomplete replies can only apply to requests for information by decision, the logic of which is that undertakings have no obligation to answer 'simple' requests for information. It is to be noted, however, that if the Commission considers that false replies to requests for information constitute a means of obstructing the investigation, it may, as an alternative to punishing such behaviour through a procedural sanction, treat the conduct as an aggravating circumstance when determining the ultimate cartel fine.[757] This may also affect the potential of undertakings that have made an application under the Leniency Notice to obtain any reward.[758]

Procedural sanctions for late and incomplete replies to requests by decision   The **8.315** Commission, when sending a request for information, will set a time for the reply. The deadline given is usually three weeks for any substantial questionnaire, but can vary, depending on the volume of the information requested.[759] A late or partial reply to simple requests under Article 18(2) (ie not replying at all or replying in incomplete form) cannot lead to penalties because answering such requests is not compulsory. In the case of failure to (fully) answer a simple request, the Commission has to resort to requesting the information by decision based on Article 18(3), in which it fixes a compulsory time-limit for the reply. When a request has been made by a Commission Decision under Article 18(3) of Regulation 1/2003, an undertaking is compelled to answer. A late or incomplete decision may attract fines which, under Article 23(2), may be up to 1 per cent of annual (group) turnover.

[754] Case C-36/92 P *SEP v Commission* [1994] ECR I-1911, para 21.
[755] The fixing of a time limit in a simple request was not a requirement specified in Art 11(3) of Regulation 1/2003.
[756] It is important to note the distinction between an answer being *late* or *incomplete*, or being *incorrect* or *misleading*. The latter kind of defective answers are subject to sanctions even in the case of simple requests for information (for a discussion of the sanctions, see below).
[757] See para 8.317 and paras 8.719ff.
[758] Case C-310/04 *Commission v SGL Carbon AG*, judgment of 26 June 2006, not yet reported, at para 68 and the case law cited there. The Court confirms that that an undertaking wishing to benefit from a reduction under the Leniency Notice must demonstrate a 'genuine spirit of cooperation', which SGL Carbon had failed to do in providing incomplete information to the Commission.
[759] What matters is that the amount of time given is proportionate. In cartel cases the Commission may even issue requests with a deadline for reply of one or two days, for instance when asking for details of a contact person to whom a decision addressed to the undertaking is to be sent.

Furthermore, the Commission has the power to levy periodic (daily) penalties, based on Article 24(1)(d) of Regulation 1/2003, in order to force the undertaking to comply with an information request by decision.[760] The periodic penalty can amount to a maximum of 5 per cent of the daily turnover of the undertaking, calculated on the basis of the preceding business year.[761] The amount of the periodic penalty itself can be set in the decision requesting information, but can also be fixed subsequently in a separate decision. The aggregate periodic penalty is then issued in a second (or third) decision against which an appeal to the CFI can be made.

8.316 *Procedural sanctions for incorrect or misleading replies*   Regulation 1/2003 provides that an undertaking can be punished, both as regards answers to simple requests and requests by decision, for having provided 'incorrect' or 'misleading' answers.[762] The Commission has defined incorrect or misleading information as 'Any statement [. . .] which gives a distorted picture of the true facts asked for and which departs significantly on major points. Where a statement is thus false or so incomplete that the reply in its entirety is likely to mislead the Commission about the true facts, it constitutes incorrect information within the meaning of Article 15(1)(b) [of Regulation 17]'.[763] Given that sanctions also apply in the case of an incorrect or misleading answer to a (simple) request for information under Article 18(2), a company that chooses to answer a simple request (even though it cannot be compelled to do so) should be careful to provide information that is accurate. The maximum fine for incorrect or misleading replies is 1 per cent of daily (group) turnover.[764] The amount due is fixed in a separate decision in respect of which the undertaking has a right to be heard and which, as mentioned above, may be challenged before the CFI.

8.317 **3. Incomplete or untruthful replies are considered to obstruct the investigation**   As noted above, although the Commission has procedural means to target companies that supply it with wrong or incomplete information, the Commission is not limited to using the procedural sanctions under Articles 23 and 24 of Regulation 1/2003. Depending on the circumstances, it can also treat answers that are considered obstructive to the investigation as an 'aggravating circumstance' and apply a percentage increase to the basic amount of the fine as calculated in the ultimate cartel decision.[765] Such a possibility is provided for under

---

[760]   Art 24(1)(d) of Regulation 1/2003 and Art 23(1) (a) and (b). For any fine to be levied under Arts 23 and 24(2), the fines ultimately imposed can only be established after the undertaking has been heard by the Commission (see Art 27 of Regulation 1/2003). The undertaking has a right to appeal the decision in which fines are imposed before the CFI, under Art 230 EC.

[761]   By comparison with Art 16(1)(c) of Regulation 17/62, where the maximum daily penalty was €1,000 per day, the current rules provide much stronger incentives for undertakings to comply fully with decisions requesting information in a timely fashion.

[762]   Art 23(1)(a) and (b) of Regulation 1/2003.

[763]   See Commission Decision in *Telos* [1982] OJ L58/19.

[764]   Here too, when compared Regulation 17, under which a fine of €5,000 was the maximum, the current penalties under Art 23 provide significantly stronger incentives for undertakings to submit appropriate replies.

[765]   In *Graphite Electrodes*, the CFI stated that if the act of the undertaking is intended to 'frustrate the Commission's inquiry', and hence does not constitute a specific and autonomous infringement, the Commission can apply an aggravating circumstance when determining the overall fine. (Case T-308/04 *SGL Carbon AG v Commission*, judgment of 29 June 2006, not yet reported, at para 64 *et seq.*)

Section 2, second indent of the Commission's Guidelines on Fines. The increase in fines can be significant. In *Greek Ferries*, the Commission applied a 10 per cent increase to the cartel fine, corresponding to €340,000, for having tried to mislead the Commission through answers to a request for information. Similarly in *Pre-insulated Pipes* the Commission treated the deliberate obstruction of its investigation as an aggravating circumstance for the purpose of calculating the level of fine imposed.[766]

4. Article 18 requests, the duty of co-operation and reductions of fines for voluntary submissions In answering a request for information, an undertaking has a duty to consider the spirit and purpose of the request and must provide answers which may go beyond the particulars of the questions posed.[767] It may refuse to answer questions that are not *Orkem*-proof, ie questions that lead to self-incriminating answers (except when the information concerns pre-existing documents or other factual information).[768] Should an undertaking nevertheless— voluntarily—supply such self-incriminating information, it cannot later claim the illegality of the decision requesting the information.[769] However, supplying such self-incriminating information may entitle an undertaking to a reduction in its fine. In *Brouwerij Haacht* the CFI confirmed that in order to be eligible for a reduction in fines on that basis, an answer needs to go 'far beyond' that which an undertaking could be expected to provide and that a reduction in the fine '. . . is justified only if the conduct of the relevant undertaking concerned enabled the Commission to establish the infringement more easily . . .'.[770] (As regards the interplay of the Leniency Notice and requests for information, see paras 8.126–8.257 dealing with the Leniency Notice.)

8.318

5. Various other aspects of requests for information
No right to be heard Article 27 of Regulation 1/2003, governing the right to be heard, makes no reference to Articles 18 or 20, but only to those decisions in which final sanctions are

8.319

---

[766] In *Greek Ferries*, the Commission increased the fine because one undertaking, after receiving a request for information, suggested to the other cartel members that they differentiate prices by 1% for four cabin categories. In the response to the request for information, the price differentiation was presented as being the result of actual competition. The Commission decision was fully upheld by the CFI on this point (Case IV/34.466—*Greek Ferries*, Commission Decision of 9 December 1998 ([1999] OJ L109/24), recitals 160, 161; on appeal, Case T-66/99 *Minoan Lines v Commission* [2003] ECR II-5515 and on appeal before the ECJ Case C-121/04, order of 17 November 2005, not yet reported). In *Pre-insulated Pipes*, a company provided misleading information about the group structure. (Case IV/35.691—*Pre-Insulated Pipes* OJ [1999] L24/1; upheld on appeal by the CFI in Case T/9/99 *HFB Holding v Commission* [1999] ECR II-2429 and by the ECJ in Joined Cases C-189/02P, 202/02P, 205-208/02P and 213/02P *Dansk Rørindustri and others v Commission* [2005] ECR I-5425.) Another example concerns misleading information supplied about contract provisions, referred to in the Commission's Decision in *Nintendo* (Cases COMP/35.587 *PO Video Games*, COMP/35.706 *PO Nintendo Distribution* and COMP/36.321 *Omega—Nintendo*, OJ [2003] L255/33).
[767] On the duty to co-operate in relation to requests for information see for instance Case T-46/92 *The Scottish Football Association v Commission* [1994] ECR II-1039.
[768] See paras 8.269ff as regards the issue of self-incrimination.
[769] Where an undertaking supplies an answer to self-incriminating questions, it must be prepared to accept the consequence that the decision requesting the information itself cannot be challenged later on that ground. (See *PVC II*, Case C-238/99 etc P *Limburgse Vinyl Maatschappij and others v Commission* [2002] ECR I-8375, para 441).
[770] Case T-48/02 *Brouwerij Haacht v Commission*, judgment of 6 December 2005, not yet reported, para 104 and the case law cited therein.

imposed (ie the prohibition decision with fines in the case of cartels).[771] Hence the only time when a company will be heard concerning a request for information is when the Commission considers the imposition of fines in relation to the answer provided (or the absence of an answer).[772]

8.320 *Formal requirements as regards the justification for issuing an information request* The requirement on the Commission is relatively light in this respect. The Commission needs only to indicate what the suspected (cartel) infringement is, so that undertakings can assess the proportionality of the request and hence the scope of their duty to co-operate.[773] A generic description of the types of business practices concerned will suffice with an indication that the behaviour, if established, may constitute an infringement of Article 81 or 82 EC. Also, the request must state the applicable penalties provided for in Regulation 1/2003, the actual warning being dependent on whether the Commission relies on Article 18(2) or 18(3).[774]

8.321 *No duty on the Commission to issue requests for information or to issue them simultaneously to all undertakings concerned by an investigation* The Commission is under no obligation to issue requests for information to the parties involved in a cartel investigation. Indeed, there is no right to receive such questions or to be made aware of the existence of an investigation and Article 18 cannot be considered to be a vehicle for the rights of defence.[775] Nor is there a requirement on the Commission, if it sends information requests to various undertakings, to do so simultaneously or to include the same questions to all of them.[776] The purpose of the Commission's investigation is to clarify, for each undertaking individually, its role in the infringement.

---

[771] Final decisions to terminate and declare cartel behaviour incompatible are granted a higher level of protection under rights of defence than decisions that attract less definitive consequences, ie those taken in exercise of investigative powers (see above para 8.268). It is only when the Commission, by separate decision, takes final decisions as regards infringements of a procedural nature, based on Arts 23 and/or 24, that an undertaking may be heard, so that it can express its views as regards the Commission's reasoning for fixing a procedural fine.

[772] On the absence of the right to be heard during the investigative stage see also para 8.268.

[773] Case C-36/92 P *SEP v Commission* [1994] ECR I-1911, at para 21.

[774] The mention of the provisions on sanctions in Art 18 requests may be omitted when the seat of the legal entity to which the request is addressed is based outside the EU. On the issue of extraterritoriality of the Commission's investigative powers, see paras 8.301ff.

[775] See L Ortiz Blanco, *EC Competition Procedure* (2nd edn, 2006) at para 7.21, and Case 27/88 *Solvay v Commission* [1989] ECR 3355, paras 12, 13; Case 374/87 *Orkem v Commission* [1989] ECR 3283, paras 15–16; Joined Cases 46/87 and 227/88 *Hoechst AG v Commission* [1989] ECR 2859, para 25.

[776] There would be one instance in which the Commission would have to be careful about the timing of its requests. That is where the request includes self-incriminating questions to which more than one undertaking may be able to supply an answer. In *Krupp-Thyssen* the Commission issued a request for information to one undertaking, and the same request only later to other undertakings involved in the same infringement. The first undertaking received a reduction in fines for having been the first company to have submitted particular information. Other undertakings received the same questions and provided similar answers within a similar time-frame, but did not receive a reward (as by that time the Commission was already aware of the information). The CFI corrected the Commission and stated that the manner in which the undertakings were rewarded could not depend on purely random factors (such as when they were asked by the Commission) and it ought to give the same rewards to all of the companies who provided an identical response (in this case: an actual acknowledgement of the infringement), even if they did so at somewhat different points in time (Joined Cases T-45/98 and T-47/98 *Krupp Thyssen Stainless GmbH and Acciai speciali terni SpA v Commission* [2001] ECR II-03757, paras 237–247. In view of *Krupp-Thyssen*, it is submitted that if the Commission were to consider issuing any self-incriminating questions the answer to which would lead to a reduction in fines for co-operation, it should do so simultaneously to all undertakings that are in a position to answer such questions, or take the risk that it must provide rewards for the same information to more than one undertaking.

Answers may be provided by the undertakings or their lawyer   Article 18(3) provides that   **8.322**
questionnaires are sent to the undertakings themselves, rather than to their legal representatives (external lawyers). Nevertheless, according to Article 18(4), in line with the right to
legal representation, a lawyer may supply the answer if duly authorised by its client, but the
undertaking still remains responsible for the information supplied. Where the undertaking
itself replies, the answer must be given by its owners, or the persons who are authorised to
represent it by law or by constitution.[777] This is to prevent any scope for undertakings to
claim that an answer should be disregarded on the basis that it was provided by an unauthorised individual[778] and thus to challenge reliance by the Commission on the answer.

(d) Interviews (The Power to Take Statements)—Article 19

(i) Rationale

The rationale for seeking this power is mentioned in the Preamble to Regulation 1/2003,   **8.323**
where the Commission states that the 'detection of infringements of the competition rules is
growing ever more difficult' and that the purpose of the power is to enable the Commmission
to obtain 'useful information' in the possession of (legal or natural) persons.[779] In drawing up
its proposals for Regulation 1/2003 in its 1999 White Paper, the Commission intended to
obtain a true 'power' to take statements, including a capacity to summon individuals to
provide statements.[780] However, in the face of criticism of its White Paper, notably regarding the proposal that the Commission be provided with a power to impose sanctions on
natural persons for failure to comply, the power to take statements was watered down as
regards the element of compulsion. What remained was a voluntary interview process and
to label this new instrument as a 'power' is somewhat inaccurate. Unlike other Commission
investigative powers, ie inspections and requests for information decisions, the use of this
tool is entirely subject to the consent of the interviewee and no procedural sanctions are
foreseen for providing incorrect or misleading statements.[781]

Prior to the entry into force of Regulation 1/2003,[782] there does not appear to have been   **8.324**
anything to prevent oral statements being recorded and used by the Commission.

---

[777] Art 18(4) of Regulation 1/2003.

[778] For an example of such a claim see Commission Decision *Viho/Parker Pen* [1992] OJ L233/27.

[779] Recital 25 of the Preamble of Regulation 1/2003.

[780] See para 114 of the White Paper on 'Modernisation of the rules implementing Articles 85 and 86 [now Arts 81 and 82] of the EC Treaty': '. . . in order to increase the effectiveness of its enquiries the Commission should also be empowered to summon to its own premises any person likely to be able to provide information that might be helpful to its enquiries, and to take minuted statements.' (Commission programme No 99/027, 28 April 1999).

[781] Nevertheless, if the statements are aimed at frustrating the Commission's investigation or otherwise mislead the Commission, this may lead to the Commission applying a percentage increase to the fine for aggravating circumstances. If false statements are provided by an applicant under the Leniency Notice, the undertaking may lose its beneficial treatment, as undertakings wishing to benefit from the Leniency Notice should show a 'spirit of co-operation' (Case T-301/04 P *Commission v SGL Carbon AG*, judgment of 29 June 2006, not yet reported, para 68 and the case law cited there.)

[782] The ability to interview on a voluntary basis and use the information in evidence already existed before Regulation 1/2003. See for instance the use of the interview of MrVerluca referred to in, Joined Cases T-67/00, T-68/00, T-71/00 and T-78/00 *JFE Engineering and other v Commission (Seamless Steel Tubes)* [2004] ECR II-2501.) See also the Commission Decision in *Pre-insulated Pipes* ([1999] OJ L24/1) and *Zinc Phosphate* ([2003] OJ L153/1). See also the use of evidence presented orally by the undertaking BASF in *Vitamins* (Commission Decision of 21 November 2001, [2003] OJ 16/1) and the evaluation of such evidence by the CFI in Case T-15/02 *BASF v Commission*, judgment of 15 March 2006, not yet reported, at para 495 *et seq*.

However, the creation in Community law of a new, general tool that formalises the incorporation of oral information as evidence in EC competition proceedings, notwithstanding its non-compulsory nature, is an important development. Indeed, the flexibility of oral interviews and the information that may follow from question-and-answer sessions would appear to make oral interviews an attractive means of investigation for the Commission. It is likely, however, that information gathered by the Commission under Article 19 will be subject to challenge by third parties as regards its admissibility and use as evidence.[783] Due to the non-compulsory nature of the instrument, it may be expected that third parties affected by statements under Article 19 will raise issues in their defence, such as that the statements are not compelled, they are not taken under oath, the statements may be self-serving, untruthfulness remains unsanctioned by procedural penalties, and third parties have no opportunity to test (cross-examine) the individual on the information that was submitted. Certainly these are factors that the Commission and the Court will have to take account of when deciding on the credibility of the information provided.[784] Given these potential arguments, and given that the Commission can solicit answers from any undertaking—in writing and under pain of sanction—based on Article 18 of Regulation 1/2003, it may generally be expected that the Commission will not use the (voluntary) Article 19 instrument to any great extent in order to record (oral) evidence of an infringement.[785]

(ii) Legal Basis

8.325 Article 19 provides the Commission with the 'power to take statements', whereby it 'may interview any natural or legal person who consents to be interviewed for the purpose of collecting information relating to the subject-matter of an investigation'. The power of the Commission to take statements must be distinguished from the power of the Commission to request explanations during inspections (of facts or documents) from any representative or member of staff, on pain of sanction for the undertaking.[786] A second, relevant legislative provision concerning the power to take statements is Article 3 of Regulation 773/2004, which presents further procedural rules for the way in which interviews are conducted and recorded. These rules are discussed below.

(iii) Possible Interviewees: Natural and Legal Persons

8.326 According to Article 19 of Regulation 1/2003, the Commission may conduct interviews with 'any legal or natural person'. It is important to highlight the possibility of interviewing *legal persons*—though the person providing the answers will of course be an individual—as greater evidentiary value may be ascribed to statements where they are made on behalf of an undertaking than to statements that are made (only) on behalf of a private person.[787]

---

[783] On the use of oral statements in evidence, see generally JM Joshua, 'Oral Statements in EC Competition Proceedings: a Due Process Short-Cut?', Competition Law Insight, 7 December 2004.

[784] See also para 8.519 on the use in evidence of such statements.

[785] Of course, such questions would have to stay outside the boundaries of what can be considered self-incriminating under EC law.

[786] Pursuant to Article 20(2)(e) of Regulation 1/2003.

[787] Mr Verluca's statements in *Seamless Steel Tubes* were considered to have been provided *on behalf of* the undertaking, Vallourec, rather then on a personal basis, which, according to the CFI, added to their evidential value. (Case *JFE Engineering*, n 782 above, at para 205.) On the notion of evidence, see also section D(2).

Potential categories of interviewees under Article 19 would include, for instance, ex-employees **8.327** of an undertaking, victims of a cartel (complainants), competitors, or (personnel of) applicants for immunity or reduction in fines.[788] The undertakings which are the target of the Commission's investigation (and their employees), are, however, unlikely to volunteer to be interviewed, unless they have decided that to do so would be in their best interest. The (un)willingness of a cartel participant to be interviewed will almost certainly be dependent on whether the interviewee is (an employee of) a legal person that is an applicant for (conditional) immunity under the Leniency Notice, or whether the interviewee aims to obtain a reduction in fines. The undertaking that has applied for immunity, as part of its duty of co-operation, may be expected to provide to the Commission all requisite information. That obligation includes facilitating access to its employees for interviews.[789] As regards applicants for reduction in fines under Section B of the 2002 Leniency Notice, no explicit co-operation obligation exists, and hence there is no obligation to make personnel available. However, it may well happen that the Commission asks to receive a first-hand account about certain information previously submitted by the applicant for reduction in fine. The applicant has no obligation to respond to a request to be interviewed, although doing so would generally appear in its best interest, since the level of co-operation provided may play a role in the level of the reduction it receives under the (2002) Leniency Notice and it would be required to do so following the obligation of genuine co-operation under the 2006 Leniency Notice.[790] In any case, in view of the principle of non-discrimination, the Commission will have to move carefully and in a well-considered manner when using interviews actively to seek new information.[791]

(iv) Procedural Aspects and Rights of the Interviewee

The Commission may conduct interviews on or off its premises.[792] It can conduct inter-   **8.328** views by any means, including by telephone. A record of the interview may be made 'in

---

[788] As regards applicants for reduction of fines under the 2002 Leniency Notice, the Commission, when (actively) involved in taking statements (interviewing), must be attentive to the issue of discrimination against other undertakings involved in the investigation. Allowing only one undertaking the benefit of being asked certain questions, the answers to which may result in a benefit of a reduced fine, may potentially be considered as a form of discrimination, if other parties had been able to respond to those questions as well, by analogy to the *Krupp Thyssen* judgment. (Joined Cases T-45/98 and T-47/98 *Krupp Thyssen Stainless GmbH and Acciai speciali terni SpA v Commission* [2001] ECR II-03757, paras 237–247.) At the same time, it is submitted, parties that do not endeavour to collaborate by making their employees available for interview are objectively not in the same position as parties who do, so that there would be no ground for a claim based on discriminatory treatment. Furthermore, the Commission should be granted a certain level of discretion in order to structure its investigations, so as not to become paralysed by potential claims from the undertakings involved.

[789] Or at least, for the undertaking, applying its best efforts to do so. (Depending on the circumstances, employees may feel uncomfortable about the risk of a transfer of the information to Member State authorities in combination with the risk of prosecution leading to personal (criminal) sanctions, including imprisonment, under national law. However, Regulation 1/2003 (Art 12) and the Network Notice (points 26–28) provide important safeguards in this respect (see section C(2)(e)).)

[790] Under point 23, last para of the 2002 Leniency Notice, and points 12 and 24 of the 2006 Leniency Notice (for a discussion see paras 8.196ff).

[791] The argument would be that the Commission had intervened in the leniency process by granting one undertaking an opportunity to qualify within a band of reduction, whilst withholding that opportunity from others. (See n 788 above, referring to *Krupp Thyssen*.)

[792] Pursuant to Art 19(2), in cases where the Commission takes a statement in the territory of a Member State, the competition officials of that Member state may assist the Commission officials.

any form', ie including in electronic form.[793] The Commission has a duty, at the beginning of the interview, to state the purpose and legal basis of the interview and, if applicable, to inform the interviewee of the intention to record the conversation.[794] The recording, if any,[795] must be made available to the interviewee, who has a right to communicate to the Commission any corrections to be made to the statement.[796] As has been emphasised, under Article 19 there is no obligation to submit to an interview and the Commission cannot impose any procedural sanctions (similar to those for replies to Article 18 requests by decision) if the individual or legal person chooses to refuse a request to appear for an interview. Nor can an interviewee who provides incorrect or misleading answers—whether a natural or legal person—be penalised by any procedural penalty.[797] That said, negative consequences for providing false or incomplete information may follow where the position of the undertaking/interviewee under the Leniency Notice is assessed. If the undertaking is an immunity applicant, submitting false information may lead to a withdrawal of the conditional immunity decision (the immunity status being conditional on the requirement of full co-operation). The position of applicants that have applied for a reduction in fines may also be affected if they have provided wrong information. First, under the 2002 Leniency Notice, if the information is of such a nature that the provider is considered not to be acting in a 'spirit of co-operation',[798] the applicant's status under the Leniency Notice may be prejudiced. Under the points 24 and 12 of the 2006 Leniency Notice,[799] an express obligation of genuine co-operation exists, for applicants for reductions in fines, so that there is now a clearer requirement in the Notice itself for providing complete and truthful information. Secondly, if the untruthful nature of the information was not of such an importance as to exclude all benefit of the Leniency Notice, the level of the reduction (within the fixed bands) might still be affected, since the ultimate reduction may depend on the level of co-operation shown. Providing false information is likely to play a role in that regard.[800] Last but not least, if the information is considered to be obstructive to the investigation, the Commission, it is submitted, can not only withhold a benefit, but also take the provision of false information into account as an aggravating circumstance when determining the ultimate fine for the cartel infringement.[801]

---

[793] See Art 3(2) of Regulation No 773/2004. It is submitted that there is no obligation on the Commission to record and transcribe complete interviews, but it is bound by the principle of good administration in this regard. (See Case T-15/02 *BASF AG v Commission*, judgment of 15 March 2006, paras 501–502.) Depending on the circumstances, minutes of such interviews can be made by the Commission in which the essential elements of the interview can be set out (and which can be recorded by the interviewee).

[794] Art 3(1) of Regulation 773/2004.

[795] There is no general obligation on the Commission to produce minutes of meetings. (Case T-38/02 *Groupe Danone v Commission* [2005] ECR II-4407, para 66 and the case law cited there.)

[796] Art 3(3) of Regulation 773/2004. If no corrections are provided, the Commission could enhance and safeguard the evidential value of the information by obtaining a written confirmation of the correctness of the minutes of the interview.

[797] Unlike answers to a simple request for information under Art 18(2), which are also not provided under compulsion, but where incorrect or misleading answers from a legal person can indeed be penalised.

[798] As to the required 'sprit of co-operation', see Case T-301/04 P *Commission v SGL Carbon AG*, judgment of 29 June 2006, not yet reported, para 68 and the case law cited there.)

[799] Commission Notice on Immunity from Fines and Reduction of Fines in Cartel Cases [2006] OJ C298/17.

[800] See above paras 8.196ff regarding the 2002 and 2006 Leniency Notices.

[801] Case T-308/04 *SGL Carbon AG v Commission*, not yet reported, at para 64 *et seq.* and the case law cited there.

(e) Inspections of Business Premises—Article 20

The most high profile and widely reported power of the Commission is the ability to carry out on-the-spot investigations. The Commission is allowed to '[. . .] undertake such inspections as are necessary to detect any agreement, decision or concerted practice prohibited by Article 81 of the Treaty or any abuse of a dominant position prohibited by Article 82 of the Treaty.'[802] **8.329**

Inspections are frequently used as a means of investigation in cartel cases, and the record shows that in most of the cases that lead to prohibition decisions the Commission has indeed used its power to inspect in order to gather evidence on the spot.[803] If the Commission has decided to use inspections in a given investigation against the various undertakings that are suspected cartel participants, these usually take place simultaneously.[804] In cartel cases of international scope, such investigative measures are often co-ordinated, and as far as possible, synchronised with those foreign antitrust agencies that are also carrying out enquiries.[805] **8.330**

Three types of on-the-spot investigation by the Commission are provided for in Regulation 1/2003: **8.331**

(a) inspections based on an authorisation from the Director-General of DG Competition, under Article 20(3) (hereinafter referred to as 'announced inspections');

(b) inspections by formal decision of the Commission, under Article 20(4) (hereinafter referred to as 'unannounced inspections'); and

(c) inspections of 'other premises', by formal Commission decision combined with a national judicial authorisation, under Article 21 (also referred to as 'private home inspections').

Furthermore, Regulation 1/2003 provides, in Article 22(2), that Member States can carry out investigations at the request of the Commission. Such inspections are conducted by the national competition authorities (NCAs) under their respective domestic laws, and the powers of the NCAs may be different from those of the Commission. A separate sub-section **8.332**

---

[802] See para 24 of the preamble of Regulation 1/2003.

[803] For instance, the Commission's 2005 decision in *MCAA*, shows that crucial contemporaneous evidence was found during the on-site inspections at the premises of the cartel participants. (Commission decision of 19 January 2005, available at <http://ec.europa.eu/comm/antitrust/cases/decisions/37773/en.pdf>). The Commission need not use inspections in all cases to gather proof of the infringement. For instance, in *Fine Art Auction Houses*, the evidence that the Commission relied on consisted foremost of the information submitted voluntarily by Christie's and Sotheby's as well as that gathered through requests for information. No inspections were carried out. (*Fine Art Auction Houses* [2005] OJ L200/92. The full text of the decision is available on the DG COMP web site at: <http:// ec.europa.eu/comm/competition/index_en.htm>.

[804] In a typical investigation, the Commission will visit five to ten sites at the same time, but it can be more or less, depending on the case. In one instance, the Commission reportedly carried out concurrent investigations at more than 20 company sites in the European Union (Case COMP 38.456—*Bitumen*, press memo of 10 October 2002, MEMO/02/211).

[805] Such simultaneous action usually follows from the fact that the same applicant will have informed the Commission and other agencies of the existence of a cartel more or less at the same time (under their respective leniency programmes), as a result of which investigations can be organised within a similar timeframe. Examples of such co-ordination include: *Heat Stabilisers and Impact Modifiers* (press release of 14 February 2003, MEMO/03/33), *Copper Concentrate* (press release of 14 May 2003, MEMO/03/107), and *Deep Sea Chemical Shipping* (press release of 19 March 2003, MEMO/03/38). See further paras 8.433–8.448 on international co-operation.

is devoted to such inspections and their place in Commission proceedings,[806] but a detailed discussion of such national procedures would go beyond the scope of this chapter.

8.333 **Outline of discussion**   In the paras below (8.334–8.410) the Commission's powers of inspection regarding business premises are dealt with. The difference between announced and unannounced inspections is explained, and their features are discussed (notably the on-the-spot powers, which are the same for announced and unannounced inspections). The separate (procedural) aspects for each of the two types of inspection are dealt with next, followed by a review of various aspects of inspections by Member States under Article 22. As for inspections on other premises (private home inspections), they are discussed in a separate section (section (f) at para 8.416) in view of the special characteristics of this power.

(i) The Difference Between 'Announced' and 'Unannounced' Inspections

8.334 When considering gathering information on the spot at undertakings, the Commission can choose between announced and unannounced inspections.[807] In cartel investigations, the Commission will usually want to take advantage of the element of surprise in order to maximise the chances of obtaining information that may serve as incriminating evidence of a 'hardcore' infringement. Such surprise inspections, given the perception that they commence at the break of day, are often referred to as 'dawn raids'.[808]

8.335 Announced inspections, under Article 20(3) of Regulation 1/2003, take place on a non-compulsory basis. The undertaking to be investigated is normally forewarned by the Commission of the planned visit, although there is no rule that prescribes an advance warning. Announced inspections are used much less frequently by the Commission in cartel investigations than unannounced inspections. Clearly the element of suprise is normally important. Also, undertakings are not likely to co-operate of their own will and volunteer evidence that may attract severe financial penalties, so the Commission prefers to resort to inspections by binding decision.[809] Nevertheless, announced inspections do take place occasionally, for instance in situations where a second, follow-up inspection takes place at an undertaking that is already aware of an investigation, or where co-operation by the undertaking has been previously established (eg an applicant for immunity that is under a duty to co-operate). Announced inspections are based on a written authorisation that can be signed by the Director-General for Competition.[810]

8.336 Unannounced inspections are based on a Commission decision, as provided for in Article 20(4) of Regulation 1/2003, and undertakings must allow these surprise inspections to take place.

---

[806] See paras 8.411ff.

[807] Arts 20(3) and 20(4) are independent provisions. The Court of Justice has clarified, in *National Panasonic*, that the Commission need not first try to establish whether an undertaking will (voluntarily) submit to an inspection by authorisation, before subjecting it to an inspection by decision. (Case 136/79 *National Panasonic (UK) Ltd v Commission* [1980] ECR 2033 at para 15, where it is stated that the two procedures '[. . .] constitute two alternative checks the choice of which depends on the special features of each case.')

[808] In reality, however, inspections usually commence at the start of business hours.

[809] Information would indeed be at risk of disappearing if an undertaking were forewarned and had the opportunity to refuse the inspection, which it could do without any legal consequences if the inspection were based on an authorisation. The Commission confirmed this in answer to Written Question No 677/79 [1979] OJ C310/30.

[810] Note that the authorisation is not a formal Commission Decision.

The power to issue decisions based on Article 20(4) of Regulation 1/2003 is a (collegiate) power of the Commission that has been delegated to the Commissioner for Competition, and in turn has been sub-delegated to the Director-General for Competition.[811] Although nothing prevents the Commission from announcing inspections by decision, the Commission will not usually do so because of the risk of concealment or disappearance of evidence in the kind of cases where inspection decisions are being used.

(ii) General Aspects Common to Inspections by Authorisation and Inspections by Decision

As indicated above, the main difference between inspections under Article 20(3) and **8.337** Article 20(4) is that undertakings are not obliged to submit to an inspection by authorisation, whereas undertakings have a duty to submit to an inspection by decision.[812] Other than that, the on-the-spot powers of the Commission and most other features are no different between the two alternative inspection methods. These elements, common to both types of inspection, are discussed below.

1. Commission inspections and the principle of the 'inviolability of the home'

Intrusion into the private sphere of undertakings must not be arbitrary or excessive   In its **8.338** judgment in *Hoechst*,[813] the Court of Justice stated that no right to the protection of the 'private sphere' existed for undertakings. In that case it was argued that, based on Article 8 of the European Convention of Human Rights (ECHR)—which confers a right to the protection of the private sphere to 'everyone'[814]—the right should also apply to legal persons. The Court of Justice, whilst affirming its earlier case law on the particular significance of the ECHR (when considering the scope of the fundamental rights that form part of the general principles of Community law), made clear in *Hoechst* that the protective aegis of Article 8 of the ECHR involved a *man's* personal freedom and ought not to be extended to business premises.[815] Subsequently, in *Roquette*, the ECJ took a different position (based on

---

[811] In accordance with Arts 13(1) and 13(3) of the Commission Rules of Procedure (amended) and Commission Decision of 15 November 2005 [2005] OJ L347/83. On 28 April 2004 the Commission adopted a decision with a comprehensive set of empowerments (PV(2004) 1655, SEC(2004) 520/2) for the Competition Commissioner for the application of the Modernisation Regulation No 1/2003 and implementing Commission Regulation No 773/2004. The decision to order inspections under Art 20(4), although in substance approved by the Commissioner for Competition, is amongst those that can be signed by the Director-General, following the decision of 27 May 2004 of the Commissioner for Competition (PH/2004/769). Signature can be further delegated to a Deputy Director-General in cases where the Director-General is prevented from carrying out his duties, and in accordance with Art 27 of the Commission Rules of Procedure. Inspection decisions that include procedural fines (periodic penalties) under Art 24(1)(e) have not been sub-delegated to the Director-General.

[812] Once an undertaking has decided to (voluntarily) submit to an inspection under Art 20(3) it is held to an equal duty of co-operation. See for instance Commission Decision *FNICF* [1982] OJ L319/12, where the French Shoemakers' Federation claimed, when confronted with a Statement of Objections following a refusal to produce certain documents during an inspection, that it was unaware that it could have refused the inspection (which had been based on Art 14(2) of Regulation 17/62, now Art 20(3) of Regulation 1/2003).

[813] Joined Cases 46/87 and 227/88 *Hoechst AG v Commission* [1989] ECR 2859, para 13.

[814] See Art 8(1) of the Convention, which reads: 'Everyone has the right to respect for his private and family life, his home and his correspondence.' For the place of the ECHR and the case law of the European Court of Human Rights (ECtHR) in the Community's legal order, see para 8.266.

[815] Joined Cases 46/87 and 227/88 *Hoechst AG and others v Commission* [1989] ECR 2859, para 13.

developments in the jurisprudence of the ECtHR, notably in *Colas Est*),[816] namely that a right to the protection of the private sphere, as foreseen in Article 8 of the ECHR, also exists for business premises in certain circumstances. Although it is not clear from the judgment in *Roquette* whether the ECJ has fully embraced the idea that the principle of the protection of private sphere exists in the same way for business as it does for individuals,[817] it is safe to say that the Court considers that inspections of business premises under compulsion should satisfy the requirements of Article 8(2) of the ECHR and the case law of the ECtHR.[818] That implies that that interference with the right to the protection of the private sphere should be surrounded by the following safeguards: it must be based on the law, it must have a lawful purpose, and there must be protection against abuse.[819] Whereas in the case of inspections by the Commission satisfaction of the first two conditions appears quite clear (a legislative basis exists, together with a formal inspection decision, and the aim pursued is legal), fulfilment of the third condition depends upon applying the principles of non-arbitrariness and proportionality that follow from *Hoechst*.[820] In applying these principles to its inspection decisions, the Commission must provide reasons (although succinctly) for its intended action.[821] A second

---

[816] Case C-94/00 *Roquette Frères SA v Directeur-Général de la Concurrence, de la Consommation et de la Répression des Fraudes* [2002] ECR I-9011, paras 27–29, which refer to the ECtHR judgment in *Colas Est*. In the latter case, the Paris Court of Appeal had condemned the practice of the French DGCCRF (*Direction-Générale de la Concurrence, de la Consommation et de la Répression des Fraudes*) of conducting inspections, including the use of force, without sufficient justification or court approval. The ECtHR indicated that Art 8 of the ECHR, which enshrines the principle of the inviolability of the home, applies to businesses (legal persons) as well to private persons. The statute under which the inspection was carried out, which did not require court approval even for the use of coercive measures, was changed in 1986, soon after the inspections that became subject of the court proceedings took place. (*Société Colas Est and Others v France* (2004) 39 EHRR 17.)

[817] Indeed, as regards the privilege against self-incrimination, a distinction has been made by the Courts between the privilege as it may apply to private individuals and the more limited right applicable to undertakings (see paras 8.269ff). See also G Miersch, in D Dalheimer, C Feddersen, and G Miersch, *EU Kartellverfahrensverordnung* (Verlag C.H. Beck, 2005), at p 156.

[818] It is noted that any claim related to a *breach* of the privacy of an undertaking can in any event only apply to inspections ordered by decision. In *PVC II* the CFI (Joined Cases T-305/94 to T-307/94, T-313/94 to T-316/94, T-318/94, T-325/94, T-328/94, T-329/94 and T-335/94 *Limburgse Vinyl Maatschappij and others v Commission* [1999] ECR II-931, paras 417–427) and later the Court of Justice (Joined Cases C-238/99, etc *Limburgse Vinyl Maatschappij NV and others v Commission* [2002] ECR I-8375, paras 236–257) rejected the claims by DSM about the unlawfulness of the inspection, on the grounds that since the inspection had been based on an *authorisation*, DSM had voluntarily allowed it to take place, so that any arguments relating to a 'violation' of its right to privacy could not be upheld. DSM had put forward the argument that the judgment of the European Court of Human Rights of 1992 in *Niemitz* should be taken account of and alter the position the ECJ had adopted at the time in *Hoechst* (in 1989, which it had taken with regard to inspection decisions adopted around the same time as the inspection authorisations and decisions in the PVC case, namely 1987). DSM claimed that the CFI had erred in failing to take into account the developments in the case law of the ECtHR since then, notably the *Niemitz* case (*Niemitz v Germany* Series A No 251-B (1993) 16 ECRR 97, para 31). That precedent, DSM claimed, should have led the Courts to reconsider its position regarding the protection of undertakings. The CFI (in para 120 of its judgment) and the ECJ (para 274), disagreed with that proposition.

[819] For a discussion of these principles, see CS Kerse and N Khan, *EC Antitrust Procedure* (5th edn, 2005), paras 3-047, 3-048 and 3-049.

[820] For a reference to the fact an intervention under EC law may not be arbitrary or excessive see also Case C-121/04 P *Minoan Lines v Commission*, Order of 17 November 2005, not yet published, at para 30.

[821] The Commission must indicate the subject matter and purpose in its investigative decisions. (*Hoechst*, para 29.) Other cases in which this point was dealt with are Case 85/87 *Dow Benelux v Commission* [1989] ECR 3137, para 8, and joined cases 97/87, 98/87 and 99/87 *Dow Chemical Ibérica and others v Commission* [1989] ECR 3165, para 26. Furthermore, the Court of Justice confirmed the *Hoechst* jurisprudence in its judgment in *PVC II*. (Joined Cases C-238/99 *Limburgse Vinyl Maatschappij NV and others v Commission* [2002] ECR I-8375, para 254.)

safeguard follows from the control by the national judicial authority, which will verify that the envisaged coercive measures under national law in the framework of Commission inspections are not disproportionate.[822] Since in the case of Commission inspections there will be a reasoned decision before an inspection can be carried out, and recourse to coercive measures requires prior court approval, it is submitted that such procedures would indeed stand scrutiny against the ECtHR case law.

Role of the national courts Depending on the provisions of national law, the relevant **8.339** Member State authority providing assistance to the Commission may need to apply for a warrant or equivalent measure in order to have the legal means to overcome any opposition by the undertaking.[823] Therefore, as mentioned above, national courts have a role to play in providing the Member State authorities with the means to overcome opposition encountered during the inspection. Article 20(8) of Regulation 1/2003 provides that in deciding on the need to allow the possible use of coercive measure (through service of warrants or other means), the national court may consider the arbitrariness and proportionality of the envisaged measure, but it may not call into question the necessity for the inspection. Normally, such a warrant is applied for as a precautionary measure. Should a judicial authorisation not be available, inspections on business premises can of course still proceed based only on a Commission decision, even though in such cases it may be impossible to overcome opposition other than by using the force of persuasion.[824]

2. Determining the addressee of an inspection decision—the notion of 'undertaking' **8.340** **for the purpose of inspections** Inspections, whether announced or unannounced, can be directed at 'undertakings and associations of undertakings'. As also explained in paras 8.553 and 8.591, the term 'undertaking' in EC law is an economic concept and refers to any entity engaged in an economic activity, regardless of the legal status of the entity and the way in which it is financed.[825] Governments or government institutions cannot be the subject of an inspection under Article 20 of Regulation 1/2003, but undertakings that are state owned or operated can be investigated.[826]

---

[822] *Hoechst*, n 813 above, para 35. Prior review by a national court is not required to validate the inspection itself. Indeed, one of the main issues dealt with in *Roquette Frères* was whether the validity of coercive measures in the framework of the assistance of the national authorities to a Commission inspection, depended on substantive judicial review by the national court of the Commission decision. The ECJ's clarification about limits of the authority of the national courts in this respect was reflected quite literally in Art 20(8) of Regulation 1/2003: the national court may review whether the coercive measures which it is asked to authorise (that may be applied under national law) are not disproportionate ('arbitrary or excessive'), but it has no power to call into question the necessity for the inspection, ie replace with its own judgment that of the Commission.

[823] Arts 20(6) and 20(7) of Regulation 1/2003. Whether or not a judicial authority is required depends on the provisions of national law. In the Netherlands, for instance, police assistance can be provided in cases of opposition without a judicial warrant.

[824] Indirect, but nevertheless severe consequences may follow, however: should the Commission face opposition, it may issue procedural penalties on that basis, as provided in Arts 23 and 24 of Regulation 1/2003 or it may take the obstructive behaviour of the undertaking into account as an aggravating circumstance in determining the fine in the final decision. Although these measures would not help to overcome opposition at the time it occurs, the ultimate financial consequences can be severe. (See para 8.384. in this respect).

[825] Case C-41/90 *Höfner and Elsner* [1991] ECR I-1979, para 21.

[826] See CS Kerse and N Khan, *EC Antitrust Procedure* (5th edn, 2005), at para 3.037.

8.341 Although the Commission may identify 'an undertaking' (using the concept in the economic sense) as the intended focus of the inspection, in its authorisation or decision the Commission will identify the relevant legal person (or persons) within the undertaking that will be the specific subject(s) of the inspection. Still, in order to make clear that 'the undertaking' is the target of the inspection, the Commission normally uses a 'top down' approach: it names in the authorisation or decision the highest entity within the undertaking and refers generically to all entities directly or indirectly controlled by it. The Commission will then consider itself legally covered for inspecting any of the subsidiaries in the group. Then, and in order to pre-empt any possible discussion on the spot, it specifically names the entity(ies) thought to have been involved in the infringement.[827] (As regards the question as to which one of these entities the Commission can validly *notify* the decision to, see below, para 8.343). The physical location(s) at which the Commission may carry out its inspections is a separate matter, but generally all locations from which the undertaking referred to in the decision carries out its activities are covered, even if they are not the formal property of any legal person covered by the inspection decision.[828]

8.342 *Inclusion of the address of the undertaking is not a requirement*   The inclusion of the address of an undertaking/legal entity(ies) is not required for an inspection, authorisation or decision, as long as the addressee has been described correctly with its legal designation. What matters is that the addressee is appropriately identified. The mention of an address is merely an additional aspect in this regard. If an address *is* included it would not limit the physical scope of the inspection either: the Commission is entitled to inspect other premises of the same undertaking.[829]

8.343 **3. Notification of the inspection decision**   It is through notification that the inspection decision takes effect and the Commission cannot commence any investigative action based on the Commission decision without having formally delivered the decision. Regarding announced inspections, a formal 'notification' does not need to take place, given that there is no *decision* that requires such a formal step. Nevertheless, for all practical purposes, an authorisation must also be submitted to the undertaking so that it can verify the basis for the inspection and consider whether or not to cooperate. As stated, the Commission will usually name the entities it intends to visit in the decision or authorisation (apart from its

---

[827] The Commission usually uses terminology such as: 'This decision is addressed to Company X, as well as to its wholly or partially owned subsidiaries, and in particular subsidiaries A, B, C.'

[828] See *Greek Ferries* (Order of 17 November 2005 in Case C-121/04 P *Minoan Lines v Commission*, not yet published, at paras 37–39 and Order of 30 March 2006 in Case C-110/04 P *Strintzis Lines Shipping v Commission*, (not yet published), paras 39–41), where the Commission inspected an agent of the addressee of the decision.

[829] See Commission Decision in *Akzo Chemicals BV* [1994] OJ L294/31, at para 17. Indeed, many of the Commission's investigations might be frustrated if relevant information were to be kept by the same undertaking but at an address other than that identified in the authorisation or decision. The fact that the address is not a limiting factor in the scope of the Commission's powers also flows, though somewhat implicitly, from the Court's judgment in *Hoechst*, where it is acknowledged that the Commission must be able to 'search' for items that have not been previously identified. The Court stated that: 'The right of access would serve no useful purpose if the Commission officials could do no more than ask for documents or files which they could identify in advance. On the contrary, such a right implies the power to search for various items of information which are not already known or fully identified. Without such power it would be impossible for the Commission to obtain the information necessary to carry out the investigation if the undertakings refused to co-operate or adopted an obstructive mode.' (See Joined Cases 46/87 and 227/88 *Hoechst AG v Commission* [1989] ECR 2859, para 27.)

usual catch all provision). Notification must be made to a legal entity that is part of the undertaking to whom the decision is addressed, but, as stated, it is not a *per se* requirement that that legal entity is itself named: if the 'undertaking' has been referred to in the decision (or authorisation), the Commission considers itself entitled to notify the decision (or authorisation) to any other entity that belongs to the undertaking, so that the inspection may be carried out.[830]

Notification is deemed to have taken place when the undertaking has been put in a position to 'take cognisance' of the decision.[831] It is usually made to an individual who is formally authorised to represent the undertaking, but this is not a requirement. An undertaking cannot refuse notification—there is no need for any 'acceptance' by the recipient before it is deemed validly notified—and the Commission can choose to notify the decision to any member of staff.[832] Notification may even be valid if—ultimately—the decision is delivered to the reception desk or the letterbox if no one can (or wishes to) receive the document.[833] If the inspection is ordered by decision, the undertaking has a duty, as from notification, to allow the inspection to take place. Should an undertaking still refuse entry when the Commission has notified it of an inspection decision, it can ask the relevant Member State authority to intervene and to ensure that any opposition is overcome. In the case of an outright refusal of an inspection by authorisation, the inspection team must return with an inspection decision. (On the procedure in case of opposition see furthermore para 8.384).

8.344

4. The Commission's on-the-spot powers   The powers of the Commission investigators when carrying out on-the-spot investigations are the same for both announced and unannounced inspections, and are set out in Article 20(2) of Regulation 1/2003,[834] as follows:

8.345

> The officials and other accompanying persons authorised by the Commission to conduct an inspection are empowered:
>
> (a) to enter any premises, land and means of transport of undertakings and associations of undertakings;

---

[830] According to the Court of Justice in *Orkem*, a decision that has been notified to a subsidiary may be considered to have been validly notified to the parent company. (Case 374/87 *Orkem v Commission* [1989] ECR 3283, para 6.)

[831] *Orkem*, ibid, para 6; also Case 6/72 *Europemballage Corp and Continental Can v Commission* [1973] ECR 215, para 10. The Commission will consider that notification of the decision is once and for all, ie that it does not have to re-notify each time the premises of a different legal entity of the same undertaking are inspected.

[832] The advantage of submitting the inspection authorisation to a member of the company's management is that that person has the authority to decide whether or not the company will submit and can also instruct other members of staff on what their obligations are during the inspection.

[833] If this were not the case, an undertaking could avoid an inspection by its own refusal to receive the inspection decision. Equally, a refusal to receive the authorisation in the case of an inspection under Art 20(3) would not, it is submitted, affect the validity of the 'notification', but the opposition will in practice mean that the Commission has to return with a decision under Art 20(4) in order to be able to carry out the inspection.

[834] It is noted that the powers which already existed under Regulation 17/62 have been put into a more 'chronological' order in Regulation 1/2003. The power to enter premises is now mentioned first, as this usually constitutes the first step in on the spot investigations, before any examination of the books and business records, and before the taking of copies and sealing any premises. Under Regulation 17/62, in Art 14(1), the power to enter premises was listed last.

(b) to examine the books and other records related to the business, irrespective of the medium on which they are stored;

(c) to take or obtain in any form copies of or extracts from such books or records;

(d) to seal any business premises and books or records for the period and to the extent necessary for the inspection;

(e) to ask any representative or member of staff of the undertaking or association of undertakings for explanations on facts or documents relating to the subject-matter and purpose of the inspection and to record the answers.

8.346 Before discussing the above five investigative powers,[835] it is important to note in relation to the persons who may take part in an inspection, that any person who has been 'authorised by the Commission' can participate. This means that the Commission can, for instance, appoint outside forensic computer experts to assist during inspections, or can engage personnel to provide the necessary language skills for the undertaking to be inspected (for instance where subsidiaries in the EU of non-EU-based companies are being investigated).[836]

8.347 The different elements of each of the powers of Article 20(2) are discussed below.

A. 'To enter any premises, land and means of transport of undertakings and associations of undertakings'

8.348 *Entry*[837] The right of entry serves merely to allow the other investigative powers to become operational. A refusal to let the Commission enter is regarded as obstruction and may lead to the considerable fines under Articles 23 and/or 24 of Regulation 1/2003.[838] Where a company refuses entry, the Commission can call upon Member States' officials to overcome the opposition with the assistance of the police or of an equivalent enforcement authority, in accordance with Article 20(6) of Regulation 1/2003.

8.349 *To enter any premises of the undertaking* 'Any premises' refers to all places used by the company under inspection for the conduct of its business. The term includes production sites, warehouses, offices, archive rooms or buildings, data rooms, etc, and also furniture, including filing cabinets, desk drawers, safes, etc. The ownership of the premises is not relevant and premises that are rented are also covered; what matters is whether the premises can be recognised as being used for business purposes by the undertaking that is the subject of the inspections. In *Greek Ferries*, the Commission investigated the offices of a commercial agent of the addressee of an inspection decision and the Commissions's authority in that

---

[835] For a discussion of the Commission's powers, both the current position and the powers granted under Regulation 17, see for instance, CS Kerse and N Khan, *EC Antitrust Procedure* (5th edn, 2005), chapter 3; JL Joshua, 'The Element of Surprise: EEC Competition investigations under Article 14(3) of Regulation 17', (1983) 8 EL Rev 3; Kreis, 'EEC Commission Investigation Procedures in Competition Cases', (1983) 17 Int Lawyer 19. JS Venit, 'Search and Seizure Powers in EU Antitrust Investigations' [1996] *Antitrust*, Vol 10 No 2; L Garzaniti, J Gudofsky, J Moffatt, 'Dawn of a New Era? Powers of Investigation and Enforcement under Regulation 1/2003' [2004] *Antitrust L J*, Vol 72, No 1, p 159. See also the Commission's own publication, *Dealing with the Commission* (1997), which, although referring to Regulation 17, is still largely applicable.

[836] Under Art 14 of Regulation 17, only 'officials' of the Commission could take part and persons outside the Commission were excluded from acting as 'inspectors' for the Commission. ('Officials' included not only statutory officials, but also temporary personnel and so-called 'national experts on secondment' to the Commission.)

[837] See para 8.380 for more details about the practicalities of the on-the-spot process for gaining entry.

[838] Alternatively, the Commission may take a refusal by the undertaking into account when establishing the final amount of the fine for the infringement. (For the alternative use of procedural fines and increase in fines see the discussion in relation to requests for information in para 8.314.)

regard was upheld by both the CFI and ECJ.[839] The term 'premises' is interpreted widely so as to render accessible information that can be obtained from the physical office location, and also documents stored electronically on servers located off-site.[840]

Although the Commission inspectors may enter any area of business of the undertaking[841] and are entitled to inspect the documents in the places where they can be found, the Commission has no power to *search*, ie to use force in executing an inspection.[842] Therefore, the Commission officials may not *obtain* access to premises or furniture (eg desks, cabinets, etc): access is to be *allowed* by the undertaking when so requested and indeed, an undertaking has an obligation to allow it, under its duty of co-operation. If admission is refused a search could only take place by relying on procedures of national law to overcome the opposition.[843] **8.350**

'Means of transport of undertakings' The Commission can inspect any means of transport used for professional purposes, which includes not only cars or lorries used for the transport of goods, but also 'company cars' used by executives and members of staff.[844] It is submitted that it is irrelevant whether such cars are owned by the company or leased: as with business premises, ownership is not the determining factor: what matters is that the vehicles are used in some way by the company for the conduct of its business. **8.351**

B. 'To examine the books and other records related to the business, irrespective of the medium on which they are stored'

To examine the books and other records . . . but no fishing expeditions The Commission's powers, and the obligation of the undertaking to co-operate, are circumscribed by the subject matter of the inspection authorisation or decision. The Commission is not permitted to go on a 'fishing expedition' for evidence of other infringements. Nevertheless, as the purpose of the inspection is to look for information that can be linked to the investigation, it has been confirmed by case law that *all* business information[845] in the undertaking can at least be verified as to its relevance.[846] In other words, an undertaking cannot refuse to provide access **8.352**

---

[839] Case C-121/04 P *Minoan Lines v Commission*, Order of 17 November 2005, not yet published; Case C-110/04 P *Strintzis Lines Shipping v Commission*, Order of 30 March 2006, not yet published. See also: De Bronett, *Kommentar zum Europaischen Kartellverfahrensrecht* (Luchterhand Kommentar, 2005), p 121.

[840] L Ortiz Blanco, *EC Competition Procedure* (2nd edn, 2006), at para 8.35.

[841] See Joined Cases 46/87 and 227/88, *Hoechst AG v Commission* [1989] ECR 2859, at para 26 and para 31, where the Court in para 31 refers to the fact that officials '[. . .] have the power [. . .] to enter such premises as they choose [. . .]'.

[842] *Hoechst*, ibid, para 31, where the Court stated: '. . . the Commission officials have, inter alia, the power to have shown to them the documents they request, to enter such premises as they choose, and to have shown to them the contents of any piece of furniture which they indicate. On the other hand, they may not obtain access to premises or furniture by force or oblige the staff of the undertaking to give them such access, or carry out searches without the permission of the management of the undertaking.'

[843] For the procedure for obtaining access in case of a refusal of the company to co-operate, see para 8.384.

[844] If applicable, other conceivable means of transport, such as company helicopters, airplanes or other means of transport are also covered.

[845] Business records have been defined as 'documents concerning the market activities of the undertaking'. (See *A.M.&S.*, n 674 above para 16, Case C-94/00 *Roquette Frères SA*, ECR I-9011, para 45). See also para 8.297 on the issue of the information that the Commission may request.

[846] Case 31/59R *Acciaieriae Tubificio di Brescia v High Authority* [1960] ECR 98. See also case Case 155/79 *Australian Mining and Smelting Europe v Commission (A.M.&S.)* [1982] ECR 1575, para 17; *Hoechst*, n 813 above at para 31, *Orkem*, n 830 above at para 15. See also the Commission Decision in *FNICF* [1982] OJ L319/12. In the words of Ortiz Blanco: 'The fact that the Commission must observe certain limits in collecting information from undertakings does not mean that those limits apply to what the inspectors may *see* or *examine*.' (L Ortiz Blanco, *EC Competition Procedure* (2nd edn, 2006) at para 8.36).

to documents claiming that they are irrelevant to the case.[847] There is special treatment for documents to which legal professional privilege applies, the content of which does not have to be surrendered to the Commission. But even in respect of privileged documents the Commission must be satisfied that the privilege does indeed apply.[848]

8.353 Even though the Commission is entitled to see any business record accessible at the premises of the undertaking, the Commission has at the same time acknowledged that the inspectors should not examine business records, or should cease examining them, if they are obviously not related to the subject matter of the investigation.[849] Whilst the Commission thus recognises that no fishing expedition should take place, this does not mean that the Commission may not use the information as a basis for starting another investigation: the Commission cannot be considered to suffer from 'acute amnesia'.[850] It is noted that whilst the Commission inspectors may have access to all records of the undertaking, they will only take copies or extracts of those that fall within the subject matter of the investigation. Should the Commission have copied documents which the undertaking continues to consider to be outside the subject matter of the investigation, it should request the return of those documents from the Commission.[851] A refusal by Commission decision to return them can be appealed before the Court of First Instance under Article 230 EC.

8.354 *Duty of active co-operation to indicate the location of information*   As described above, an undertaking must allow an inspection to take place and the Commission is free to look for business records anywhere within the undertaking.[852] Beyond merely consenting to the inspection, the undertaking has a positive duty of co-operation.[853] That obligation places a

---

[847] See Commission Decision in *CSM NV* [1992] OJ L305/16. It is also possible that the Commission itself, after reviewing the inspection materials in its offices, may return documents which it considers not to be relevant to the case. The Commission's Notice on Access to the File allows for this possibility. In excluding documents from its investigation file, the Commission must take account of its obligation expressed by the Court of First Instance in Case T-7/89 *Hercules Chemicals v Commission* [1991] ECR II-1711, to allow the defendants to examine all documents that are in the Commission's file, so that their probative value for the defence can be established. In other words, the Commission should only exclude from its files information that is manifestly unconnected to the infringement. In this regard see point 9 of the *Commission Notice on the rules for access to the Commission file in cases pursuant to Article 81 and 82 of the EC Treaty, Articles 53, 54 and 57 of the EEA Agreement and Council Regulation (EC) No 139/2004* [OJ] C325/7, hereinafter also referred to as the Access to File Notice.

[848] Legal privilege and the procedure for any claims based on legal privilege are discussed in paras 8.260ff.

[849] Commission Decision in *CSM NV* [1992] OJ L305/16. In relation to the guarantees for undertakings the ECJ stated '. . . the rights of the undertakings concerned . . . would be seriously compromised if the Commission could rely on evidence against undertakings which was obtained during an investigation but was not related to the subject matter thereof . . .' (Case C-94/00 *Roquette Frères* [2002] ECR I-9011, para 48 and the case law cited there.)

[850] *Spanish Banks*: Case C-67/91 *Dirección General de Defensa de la Competencia v Asociación Española de Banca Privada* [1992] ECR I-4785, para 39.

[851] Commission Decision in *CSM NV* [1992] OJ L305/16. The Commission may also itself decide to return documents where upon further examination they appear to be unrelated to the investigation: *Commission Notice on the rules for access to the Commission file in cases pursuant to Article 81 and 82 of the EC Treaty, Articles 53, 54 and 57 of the EEA Agreement and Council Regulation (EC) No 139/2004, 2005* [OJ] C325/7. The Commission should do so with care, to avoid attracting the suspicion that it has excluded exculpatory materials from its files, and possible legal claims relating to access to the file (below, paras 8.547ff).

[852] Though the Commission may not carry out a 'search' (see para 8.350).

[853] The obligation of co-operation is discussed more generally in paras 8.308ff.

requirement on the undertaking, for instance, to indicate the location of business records and to submit specific documents upon request.[854] It must also provide reasonable means for access and permit the use of any medium needed (a computer or other means) to inspect the business records.[855] An undertaking's representative cannot refuse the production of documents on the grounds that they may not be disclosed without the approval of a higher ranked officer (or another legal entity) within the undertaking.[856] Failure on the part of the undertaking in relation to any of these obligations can result in fines being imposed under Article 23 and/or Article 24, or in an increase in the final amount of the cartel fine as an 'aggravating circumstance'.

Document retention   In relation to EC competition procedures, there are no particular **8.355** rules as regards the retention of documents, as there may be for, for instance, tax purposes under the national laws of the Member States. Therefore, the suppression or destruction of documents in the absence of any Commission investigation (or if there is no known likelihood that one would be forthcoming) is not sanctionable through any of the provisions of EC competition law. However, destruction or concealment of documents before an investigation could be taken into account by the Commission in setting its ultimate fine, when such destruction is a deliberate attempt to cover up evidence.[857] If destruction or concealment takes place during or after an on-the-spot investigation the undertaking may be liable to sanctions under Articles 23 and/or 24 of Regulation 1/2003, or to an increase in the ultimate fine for obstruction.[858]

Production of business records located outside the premises   It should be noted that each of the **8.356** subparagraphs of Article 20(2) establishes separate powers. In other words, the provision of subsection (b)—the power to examine business records—must not be interpreted on the basis of subsection (a)—the power to enter premises. This means that the Commission is not confined to inspecting documents that are to be found in or are (electronically) accessible from the premises that are inspected: the Commission can also require the undertaking to produce records that may be located outside, or would be accessible from, the premises that are visited.[859]

Books and other records relating to the business   Regulation 1/2003 contains no definition **8.357** of what constitute 'books and other records relating to the business'. In *A.M.&S.*, the Court of Justice defined business records as 'documents concerning the market activities of the

---

[854] See Commission Decision in *Fabbrica Pisana* [1980] OJ L75/30, para 33; See also *Hoechst*, n 841 above, para 31.

[855] Similarly, CS Kerse and N Khan, *EC Antitrust Procedure* (5th edn, 2005), at para 3-053.

[856] See *FNICF*, n 846 above.

[857] In *Cartonboard*, the fact that minutes were missing, although these would have existed, was taken as an aggravating factor as it demonstrated the parties' intent to hide the infringement. (Case T-347/94 [1998] ECR II-1751, para 212.)

[858] Note *Industrial Bags* (Case COMP/F-3/38.354, decision of 30 November 2005 (press release IP/05/1508), in which the Commission imposed a 10% increase in fines for document destruction during inspection.

[859] See CS Kerse and N Khan, *EC Antitrust Procedure* (5th edn), at para 3-053. L Ortiz Blanco, *EC Competition Procedure* (2nd edn, 2006), at para 8.35.

undertaking'.[860] The term therefore encompasses a wide range of business information,[861] including handwritten notes and electronically stored documents. The information contained in it may include any kind of information as long as it is related to the business activities of the undertaking, eg financial information, production and sales records, travel records, diaries, minutes and notes of meetings, copies of correspondence with third parties, phone records, etc. It excludes only information of a private nature and other information that has no relation to the business. (However, the Commission will still need to verify whether the documents concerned do fall within or beyond the scope the investigation.)[862]

8.358　*Stored on Any Medium*　Regulation 1/2003 has clarified that business records stored electronically (or stored otherwise), ie documents stored on magnetic tape, diskette, CD ROM, memory stick, etc are equally subject to inspection. This was in fact already the interpretation under Regulation 17,[863] but it was not spelled out in the text of that Regulation. Information stored on hard drives may also be scrutinised, although at the time of writing the Commission itself has not been known to use forensic technology to uncover deleted (but nevertheless traceable) information stored on hard drives.[864] As mentioned above, as regards access to electronic data that are stored on servers located outside the premises, the Commission considers that there is an obligation to provide admission to these as well, in so far they are accessible from the premises that are inspected.

C. 'To take or obtain in any form copies of or extracts from such books or records'

8.359　*To take or obtain*　One difference from Regulation 17 is that that Regulation only referred to the 'taking' of copies and not to 'obtaining' them. This subtle change suggests that the Commission, if were not in a position to 'take' copies that have been prepared for it, should be empowered to obtain them from the undertakings and that undertakings have a duty to provide them.

8.360　*In any form*　The Commission will take copies of records in their original format. In respect of electronic documents, the Commission considers that it need not first make a printout, as has often been argued by undertakings. Instead it can take a digital copy of the document, so that all information electronically stored within the document is in the possession of the Commission. To ensure that the copies are authentic, it is advisable, both for the Commission

---

860 Case 155/79 *Australian Mining and Smelting Europe (A.M.&S.) v Commission* [1982] ECR 1575, at para 16. See also Case C-94/00 *Roquette Frères SA*, ECR I-9011, para 45. Reference is made to para 8.297 which deals more generally with the issue of the information that the Commission may request.

861 See also Dealing with the Commission, section 5.6.

862 See also para 8.297 regarding the type of business information that the Commission may request and the principle established by the ECJ in *A.M.&S.*, that it is for the Commission to decide whether or not a document must be produced to it. Should an undertaking consider that documents are not covered by the inspection decision it should ask for their return, so that the Commission will have to take a reasoned decision on that request, which is challengeable under Art 230 EC. Also, where the documents have been unlawfully obtained, the Commisson cannot use these documents in evidence. (See Order of the Court in Case 46/87 R *Hoechst v Commission* [1987] ECR 1549, para 34 and the Order of the Court in Case 87/87 R *Dow Chemical Nederland v Commission* [1987] ECR 4367, para 17.)

863 See *Dealing with the Commission* (European Commission, 1997).

864 Reportedly, the Commission has in the past relied on the support of national officials of certain of the Member States, assisting the Commission under Art 20(5) of Regulation 1/2003, to provide a forensic technology capability.

and the undertaking, that the exact digital content and the copying procedure is put on the record in a protocol and that the undertaking obtain a second, identical copy of the electronic copy to avoid any argument that the records have been manipulated.

The question may arise whether the Commission may copy entire (aggregated) electronic files **8.361** or *folders* (as opposed to individual selected documents), without having reviewed the different documents they contain for their relevance to the investigation. To review each document within such files or folders individually would probably prolong the Commission's presence at the premises significantly. It is submitted that where the Commission has been able to identify, with a reasonable measure of certainty, that the information is within the subject-matter of the investigation[865], it may indeed proceed on this basis (ie copy the information and take it away for further examination), and that there is no obligation to review each document separately *in situ*.[866]

Copies of or extracts   The Commission does not seize original material during an inspec- **8.362** tion, but will only take copies. The Commission can also take extracts of documents, for instance by taking handwritten notes of (part of) the contents of a document, or copying only certain pages of larger records. The significance of being able to take extracts is primarily of a practical nature.[867] It is common practice for the Commission to provide the opportunity for the undertakings to make a set of identical copies of the materials the Commission has taken.[868] A copy of the inventory listing the documents the Commission has copied is always made available to the undertaking.

D. 'To seal any business premises and books or records for the period and to the extent necessary for the inspection'

The power to seal was first introduced under Regulation 1/2003. The reason for asking for **8.363** this power from the Council was to enhance the efficiency of inspections by making sure that the risk of information disappearing would be reduced.[869] This risk existed primarily where the inspection team was not large enough to be able to cover all relevant places at once or not able to finish its business within one working day, so that material remaining to be inspected could possibly be destroyed or concealed overnight. Until the entry into force of Regulation 1/2003 the Commission often relied on the assistance of the Member States to seal offices, at least in those countries where domestic law permitted the national competition authority to assist the Commission in this manner. It is surprising that there are no other legal provisions in Regulation 1/2003 or Commission Regulation 773/2004

---

[865] For example, if the Commission were copying information stored on an electronic device used by a member of staff working for the business concerned, based on a key-word search that includes the product under investigation, the information is sufficiently likely to fall within the scope of the investigation.

[866] By proceeding in this way, however, there may be a risk that the Commission will obtain records that are protected by legal privilege. That problem could be overcome by permitting the undertaking to be present when the Commission verifies the contents of the records in its offices.

[867] Extracts may be taken where photocopying does not produce satisfactory results of, for instance, documents containing handwritten (pencil) notes.

[868] The Commission offers to reimburse the companies for the costs of such copies (see the Commission's *Explanatory Note* that is submitted to undertakings at the start of inspections).

[869] See point 4 of the Explanatory Memorandum which accompanied the Proposal for a Council Regulation on the Implementation of the Rules on Competition (COM (2000) 582 final, OJ [2000] C365E/284).

governing the attaching and lifting of the seals other than the provision regarding fines where the seals have been broken.[870] Indeed, the procedure surrounding the affixing of seals, their removal and the obligations (and rights) of undertakings is important, as a hefty fine may be incurred (a maximum of 1 per cent of annual turnover) if the Commission finds that the seals have been broken, even where this has occurred 'negligently'.[871] There has so far been one known case of a breaking of seals. This occurred where the Commission was carrying out an inspection at the premises of the German energy company, *E.ON Energie AG* in May 2006. The seal had been fixed on an office door by Commission officials in order to secure documents found in the course of an unannounced inspection. It was found that the seals affixed had been broken, intentionally or negligently, and a Statement of Objections, expressing the intention to issue a procedural fine, was issued.[872] An oral hearing before the Commission took place at the end of 2006 and at the time of writing the formal decision is not yet known, E.ON having contested the preliminary conclusions by the Commission. If it does come to a formal decision (which presumably will be made public), it will be important to assess the Commission's considerations in (provisionally) holding E.ON liable for having tampered with the seals.

8.364 *Geographical/physical scope: which places can be sealed?* The Commission's power to seal is widely defined in terms of the places or items that can be sealed ('. . . any business premises or books . . .'). Although the power to seal refers to 'premises', it is considered unlikely that the Commission would use the power, for example, to seal an entire office building. Apart from the practical considerations, such a step would be likely to render the exercise of the power disproportionate.[873] It is more likely that the Commission will use it for sealing particular offices, filing cabinets, desk drawers, etc, or for sealing portable computers or specific file holders. Indeed, the power is to be applied with reference to the principle of proportionality[874] ('. . . to the extent necessary . . .'). This is taken to mean that, for example, if it suffices to seal a filing cabinet instead of an entire office, the Commission should seal the cabinet. In order to ensure that there can be no misunderstanding between the undertaking and the Commission about the places which have been sealed, the Commission may draw up a list of the exact places and items that have been sealed, for countersignature by a representative of the undertaking.

8.365 *Temporal scope: the duration of the application of seals* Regulation 1/2003 states that seals may be affixed 'for the period . . . necessary for the inspection'. As stated, Regulation 773/2004 provides no further rules as regards the use of the power to seal. It seems therefore that it is

---

[870] A maximum of 1% of the total turnover of the undertaking in the preceding business year (Art 23(1)(e) of Regulation 1/2003).

[871] No further provisions are included in Commission Regulation 773/2004, unlike, for instance, the procedure for asking oral questions during inspections.

[872] See Commission Press Release of 22 November 2006, 'Commission confirms sending Statement of Objections to E.ON Energie AG concerning the breach of a seal' (Memo/06/443, available at: <http://europa.eu/rapid/pressReleasesAction.do?reference=MEMO/06/443&format=HTML&aged=0&language=EN&guiLanguage=en>

[873] See point 2(C)(1)(c) of the Explanatory Memorandum to the Proposal for a Council Regulation (n 869 above), which speaks of an empowerment 'to seal cupboards or offices', indicating the intention of the Commission in terms of the scope of the power.

[874] For a discussion of the principle of proportionality, see para 8.294ff.

once more a question of proportionality as to how long seals can be kept in place. The only guidance can be found in recital 35 of the preamble of Regulation 1/2003. It states that seals should 'normally' not be affixed for more than 72 hours. It is not made clear, however, whether this period of 72 hours relates to the time the inspection team is on the spot (inspections rarely lasting for more than three days) or whether the seals can even be left in place as a precautionary measure (for a maximum of 72 hours) after the inspection team considers it has finished its work and has left the premises. It is submitted in this regard that that the power to seal may extend beyond the presence of Commission inspectors at the undertaking, particularly since there is no formal end to the inspection when the investigators leave the undertaking.[875] (In practice Commission officials cannot always be certain whether or not there is a need to continue the investigation the next day or even thereafter. This may depend, for instance, on information gathered by other inspection teams, which would need to be (re-)checked at the premises of the undertaking where the seals have been placed. If that is the case, it would appear logical that the case team could decide that seals be affixed even when at first instance they did not intend to return to the premises. If in the end the inspectors do not need to return to inspect the sealed premises or books, it is submitted the Commission may be expected to inform the undertaking (in writing, so that a record exists) that the seals can be removed by the undertaking without sanction.)

Consequences of breaking the seals   A breach of the seals may have significant consequences   **8.366**
for the undertaking. Following Article 23(1)(e) of Regulation 1/2003, the undertaking would be liable to a financial penalty of up to 1 per cent of group turnover, even if the seals have been broken through negligence. Alternatively, the Commission may take the violation into account, as a form of obstruction to the investigation, in determining the amount of the fine to be fixed in the final decision. Commission Regulation 773/2004 provides no clarification as regards the procedure for the affixing or the removal of the seals, or for the determination as to whether the seals are considered to have been 'broken'.[876] It must be assumed, therefore, that the undertaking at the premises of which the seals are affixed is at risk of incurring a sanction regardless of how the seals have been broken and of the circumstances under which it has occured.[877] The Regulation therefore places a considerable burden upon undertakings to ensure that the seals remain untouched, and they are well advised to take appropriate precautionary measures.[878]

---

[875]   This also follows from the text of Art 20(1)(d), which reads '. . .to the extent necessary for the inspection'.

[876]   It is submitted that the notion of 'broken' may cover a wide range of situations where the seals are no longer in their original condition, as affixed. The term broken would therefore also cover seals which have been damaged, partially broken (though not fully ruptured), lifted and glued back, etc. (The Commission has been using seals that do not rupture when they are removed, but partially unstick and hence leave a trace on the seal as well as the surface that they were glued on to. Strictly speaking, these seals are difficult to 'break'.)

[877]   At least, it is submitted, the burden of proof as regards the liability on the undertaking for the breaking of the seals would be reversed.

[878]   It would thus be advisable for undertakings to indicate clearly, for instance to the proverbial cleaning lady, that a particular room or office has been sealed and that it should remain untouched. Also, filing cabinets and drawers should preferably be locked whilst they are sealed to minimise the risk of damage to the seals if someone were to try to open them inadvertently.

***E. 'To ask any representative or member of staff of the undertaking or association of
undertakings for explanations of facts or documents relating to the subject-matter and
purpose of the inspection and to record the answer'***

8.367 *Explanations of facts or documents* The fundamental purpose of on-the-spot investigations is to gather (documentary) evidence on the spot, rather than to seek information which the Commission could obtain using formal information requests. The power to ask questions on the spot as it existed under Regulation 17/62 was regarded merely as an auxiliary power,[879] but the new drafting suggests that this power will enjoy a more prominent role in inspections.[880] The limits on the Commission's power to ask for explanations during inspections as they existed under Regulation 17—and the corresponding duty of the undertaking to comply—had never been clarified fully, notably as regards the question of whether the Commission could ask questions relating to anything other than the documents being inspected.[881] It has now been unequivocally stated in the legislation that questions can be posed not only about *documents*, but also more generally about *facts*, as long as they relate to the subject matter of the investigation. Another important clarification, which was specifically highlighted by the Commission when it put forward its proposal for Regulation 1/2003, is that the Commission can put questions to *any* member of staff, as is further explained below.

8.368 *Specific procedural provisions contained in Regulation 773/2004* An important legislative addition to the power under Article 20(2)(e) is formed by the rules governing the process for asking questions during inspections set out in Article 23(1)(d) of Regulation 1/2003 and notably Article 4 of Commission Regulation 773/2004. Article 4 deals with how a record can be made, the provision of a copy of the recording to the undertaking and the procedure for submitting rectifications, amendments or supplements to any clarifications given on the spot. These provisions will be referred to in the relevant sections below.

8.369 *To ask any representative or member of staff of the undertaking* The fact that the Commission can put questions to 'any' member of staff is an important feature. As mentioned, Regulation 17, although including the option to request oral information, did not make clear to *whom* the Commission could put questions. The practice was often that the undertaking would designate a (senior) representative who was considered by the undertaking to be 'best placed' to answer questions on behalf of the company, even if that individual

---

[879] See *Dealing with the Commission* (European Commission, 1997), at section 5.6.

[880] Under Regulation 17/62 it was codified in much shorter terms, as the power 'to ask for oral explanations on the spot' (Art 14(1)(c) of Council Regulation 17/62). Note that under Art 19 of Regulation 1/2003 interviews may take place relating to the subject-matter of 'the investigation', whereas Art 20((2)(e) refers to the subject matter and purpose 'of the inspection'. This may indicate a more restrictive scope of the latter power. (In this regard see CS Kerse and N Khan, *EC Antitrust Procedure* (5th edn, 2005), at para 3-059.)

[881] As explained by Kerse and Khan, it was generally considered that the power of the Commission was restricted to specific concrete questions arising out of documents, and that for other questions the Commission had another power available, ie requests for information (CS Kerse and N Khan, *EC Antitrust Procedure* (5th edn, 2005), at para 3-058). In this respect see also point 4 (of the article-by-article explanation) of the Explanatory Memorandum that accompanied the Proposal for a Council Regulation on the Implementation of the Rules on Competition COM (2000) 582 final, OJ [2000] C365E/284. There the Commission states that the previous Regulation only allowed the Commission to ask questions about *documents*. It is not clear why the Commission held this restrictive view, as Art 14(1)(c) of Regulation 17/62 reads 'to ask for oral explanations on the spot', which hence appears to include no such limitation.

was possibly not the most knowledgeable about the clarifications sought.[882] That said, it is arguable that based on the duty of co-operation even under the former Regulation, the answer to a question ought to be supplied, on behalf of the undertaking, by the member of staff considered most knowledgeable about the facts or circumstances in question.[883] In any case, the text of Regulation 1/2003 now makes clear that questions can be put to a member of staff designated by the Commission.[884]

Although the Commission is entitled to ask questions of any member of staff, it is not likely **8.370** that it will use this power to pressure personnel of the targeted undertaking into admitting the undertaking's participation in the cartel. In this regard the Commission has stated (referring to the power that existed under Regulation 17) that the purpose of the provision was to ensure that a person best placed to answer would be put forward to provide a response, rather than that it would not be used to pressure the officials of a company into making submissions which they would not make if they had the time for reflection afforded them by a written request under Article 11 (now Article 18).[885]

An obligation on staff members to remain present during an inspection for providing explanations? **8.371** The fact that the Commission can ask questions to designated members of staff raises the question of whether such members of staff can be required by the Commission to stay on the premises during inspections. Regulation 1/2003 confers no such power on the Commission. However, it is submitted that the undertaking, based on its duty of co-operation, can be required to use its best efforts to ensure that such individuals are available to the Commission. The management of the undertaking could reasonably be expected to use its authority over members of staff in order to ensure their availability, at the request of the Commission.

Another question is whether the individuals who are asked questions may refuse to answer **8.372** them, for instance because they fear disciplinary action from the undertaking or even criminal prosecution under national law. It is clear that Community law cannot impose on the individual an obligation to respond. However, here again the undertaking can be required to use its best efforts to make sure that the individual does answer. In this respect it is noted that the *undertaking* can be held liable where members of staff refuse to answer entirely,

---

[882] In *Fabbrica Pisana*, a decision imposing a procedural fine on the undertaking for having wrongly informed the Commission during an announced inspection, the Commission expressed this in the following terms: '[. . .] it is not for the Commission inspectors to assess or dispute the competence or extent of the knowledge of the representatives of the undertakings that they are investigating. The undertakings named in investigating authorisations are alone responsible for their representatives.' (However, in this case it was the undertaking itself making a claim that it could not be held liable for answers given by its representatives, to which the Commission responded by stating that is the undertaking's own responsibility to designate competent representatives.) (Commission Decision in *Fabbrica Pisana* [1980] L75/30, recitals 10 and 12.)

[883] See for example CS Kerse, *EC Antitrust Procedure* (4th edn, 1998), at para 3.63.

[884] This addition was not uncontested, the argument having been expressed on behalf of businesses that since it is 'the undertaking' which will be liable for the sanctions provided for by the Community competition rules, and not the individual concerned, that the undertaking should therefore be able to determine who should provide a reply. That concern was remedied, at least in part, by allowing a mechanism for providing additional information on behalf of the undertaking (see Art 4 of Regulation 773/2004).

[885] *Dealing with the Commission*, European Commission, 1997, section 5.6. See also speech by Philip Lowe, Director-General for Competition at the 2003 Conference 'Understanding Global Cartel Enforcement', British Chamber of Commerce, 11 February 2003.

where the answer is otherwise incomplete, incorrect or misleading, unless the undertaking provides a corrected answer within a time-limit set by the Commission, following the procedure provided for in Article 4 of Regulation 773/04 (as further explained below). As regards the reason for not responding being the possible personal exposure of the individual giving the response eg the risk of (criminal) prosecution under national law, it is submitted that the safeguards that have been built into the (ECN) system will prevent such a scenario.[886] First, the information gathered may not be used for a purpose other than the relevant request or investigation, pursuant to Article 28(1) of Regulation 1/2003. Secondly, as provided in Article 12(3) of Regulation 1/2003, information acquired by the Commission cannot be exchanged with the national authorities for use in evidence in national (criminal) proceedings against natural persons.[887] Nevertheless, it remains the case that an individual cannot be forced to speak and that, as an individual, the Commission could impose no penalty upon him/her for a lack of co-operation.[888]

8.373 *Procedure regarding oral explanations*   Article 4(1) of Regulation 1/2003 states that the explanations provided may be recorded 'in any form'. This means in practice that the explanations can be registered in written form, on tape, or as a digital recording. The Commission will have to consider whether the authenticity and accuracy of the chosen method of registration is appropriately safeguarded, to avoid disputes at a later stage in the proceeding. According to Article 4(2), a copy of the recording is to be made available to the undertaking (or association of undertakings), after the inspection. It does not state clearly whether this would be the moment the inspection team has concluded its investigation on the spot or a later point in time, though it is submitted that both are possible depending on the method of recording chosen.[889]

8.374 There is no obligation to record questions and answers that are exchanged between the undertaking and the Commission inspectors. Indeed, where, for instance, the Commission asks a rather trivial question that is merely intended to help progress the investigation on the spot (eg a clarification about the physical location of particular documents) and the undertaking replies to such a question, there is no reason to make a record. For other questions, however, it may be appropriate to make a record of the answer, if it provides information that is of wider relevance to the Commission's investigation. As stated above, whether or not an answer is recorded is at the discretion of the Commission. An undertaking is free, however, to submit to the inspection team any information that it may wish to bring to the attention

---

[886]   Similarly, see L Ortiz Blanco ed, *EC Competition Procedure* (2nd edn, 2006), at para 9.27.

[887]   See Art 12(3), first indent. A question may remain as regards the use of such information as intelligence by the national authorities, in view of the case law in *Spanish Banks* (n 850 above). See for instance JM Joshua, 'The UK's new cartel offence and its implications for EC competition law: a tangled web', European Law Review, Vol 28, No 5, October 2003, at p 633. Ortiz Blanco, however, considers that the inbuilt safeguards even mean a departure from the Spanish Banks scenario which allowed for the use of such information as leads for a (separate) national investitagtion. (L Ortiz Blanco, *EC Competition Procedure* (2nd edn, 2006), at para 9.27).

[888]   For example, see B Vesterdorf, 'Legal Professional Privilege and the Privilege against Self-incrimination in EC Law: Recent Developments and Current Issues' [2005] Fordham International Law Journal, 1197–1215, at p 1214.

[889]   It may for instance not be possible to duplicate a tape recording at the premises of the undertaking during the inspection, whereas a record made in written form may easily be copied on the spot.

of the Commission (or it can do so at a later stage in writing), which may include answers that the Commission was not intending to record.

Misleading, incorrect, or incomplete answers, and applicable penalties Article 23(1) of **8.375** Regulation 1/2003 provides for sanctions for procedural breaches, including the provision of misleading, incorrect or incomplete answers to questions posed during inspections. In determining the circumstances in which sanctions are imposed, a distinction has been made between answers provided by 'the undertaking' (ie by an individual authorised by the undertaking to answer on its behalf) and answers provided by a member of staff (ie someone designated by the Commission to answer).[890] Any fine, which can be a maximum of 1 per cent of annual turnover, is of course always imposed on the undertaking, and not the individual.

Where an answer has been given by the *undertaking*, it may be penalised for having pro- **8.376** vided an 'incorrect' or 'misleading' answer, whether during an inspection by authorisation or an inspection by decision.[891] In addition, but only in case of an inspection ordered by decision, an 'incomplete' answer can attract a fine.[892]

Where an untruthful answer has been provided by a *member of staff* designated by the **8.377** Commission, no sanction applies to that individual. The undertaking may, however, be punished where it fails to rectify an answer of a member of staff that is incorrect, incomplete or misleading. This is regardless of whether the question was asked during an inspection one by authorisation or one by decision.

Procedure for rectifications, amendments, supplements Article 4(3) of Regulation 773/2004 **8.378** complements Regulation 1/2003 as to the procedure to follow for complementing oral explanations given by a member of staff who was not authorised by the undertaking to answer on its behalf but was designated by the Commission.[893] First, the Commission is to set a time limit for any additional declaration by the undertaking.[894] Secondly, the undertaking or association of undertakings must, within the time limit, communicate to the Commission 'any rectification, amendment or supplement to the explanations given by the member of staff'.[895] It is made clear in Article 4(3), however, that such additions made by the undertaking to the recorded statement will not replace the answer originally given, but will be appended to it and remain on the file. This, it seems, will allow the Commission to have regard to the explanations originally provided should these appear (more) credible in the light of the investigation.[896]

---

[890] The difference would appear to be based on the notion that an answer provided by 'the undertaking' is held to a higher standard of truthfulness and completeness than that provided by an individual employee.

[891] Art 23(1)(d), first indent, of Regulation 1/2003.

[892] Art 23(1)(d), third indent, of Regulation 1/2003.

[893] Depending on the case, without any indication of bad faith it would appear equitable that the undertaking can also provide rectifications, amendments, or supplements where the answer had been given by member of staff authorised by the undertaking. The same would then apply, it is presumed, to the original answer provided, ie that it would remain on the file.

[894] Art 23(1)(d), second indent, refers to this time limit, but does not state that such a time limit is binding upon the Commission. Art 4(3) of Regulation 773/2004 closes this loophole.

[895] The provision of Art 4(3) mirrors that of Art 23(1)(d), second indent, on the basis of which the undertaking can be fined for not having rectified an incorrect, incomplete or misleading answer.

[896] See L Ortiz Blanco, *EC Competition Procedure* (2nd edn, 2006) at para 8.52 and CS Kerse and N Khan, *EC Antitrust Procedure* (5th edn, 2005), at para 3-060.

8.379   *Explanations that may be self-incriminating for the undertaking*   Questions during inspections should remain factual in nature, as they are intended to provide explanations with regard to 'facts' or 'documents'. The likelihood of queries arising that are out of bounds in terms of their self-incriminating nature is thus restricted.[897] Nevertheless, questions may arise that go beyond factual limits, or the intended answer of the undertaking may go beyond its duty to respond. If confronted with a self-incriminating question and the undertaking does not wish to answer, it is in the interest of the undertaking to submit to the Commission the reasons for its position in order to prevent the Commission regarding its refusal to answer as an outright refusal to co-operate. This may provoke procedural penalties,[898] or even be taken into account by the Commission as an aggravating factor when the fine for the substantive infringement is established. Where it does choose to answer (or provide self-incriminating explanations to an otherwise *Orkem*-legitimate question) the undertaking is well-advised to make clear that the information has been submitted on a voluntary basis and to claim a benefit under the Leniency Notice explicitly.[899]

(iii)   Other Practical Aspects Relating to Inspections

8.380   *Procedure upon arrival of the Commission inspectors*   As stated above, the decision to inspect does not take effect until notification.[900] In the case of an inspection by authorisation, formal 'notification' is not a prerequisite, but the authorisation will be put to the undertaking in much the same way. On arrival, the Commission inspectors will normally ask to be received by a senior member of staff (typically an officer of the undertaking who is listed in the commercial registry and has the power to bind the undertaking). The Commission inspectors will identify themselves when so requested. The inspectors will wish to notify the decision quickly and will not allow possible delaying tactics by the undertaking. Upon notification, the inspectors will want to take initial measures, for example settling themselves in the offices of particular members of staff, in order to limit the opportunities for the destruction or concealment of documents. The members of staff of the undertaking with whom contact is made will be requested not to communicate, until further notice, with any outside party about the inspection (apart from legal counsel). Together with the notification,

---

[897]   As described in para 8.276, if the information requested is factual or concerns the supply of pre-existing documents, an answer must be supplied, even if that has incriminating effects on the undertaking.

[898]   Undertakings may then be subject to fines for obstruction under Art 23 of Regulation 1/2003, periodic penalties or (alternatively) an increased ultimate fine under Art 24.

[899]   In fact, the Commission should take into account voluntary co-operation where the undertaking assists the Commission in establishing the infringement, regardless of whether it has made a formal application. The issues will be whether (a) the information provided went (far) beyond what the undertaking was required to supply, (b) whether the information facilitated the task of the Commission in finding the infringement, and (c) whether the undertaking acted in a 'spirit of cooperation'. (Case T-48/02 *Brouwerij Haacht v Commission*, judgment of 6 December 2005, not yet reported, para 106 and the case law cited therein: Case T-279/02 *Degussa AG v Commission*, judgment of 5 April 2006, not yet reported, para 380, and the case law cited therein; and Case C-301/04 *Commission v SGL Carbon*, judgment of 29 June 2006, not yet reported, para 68, and the case law cited therein). (See also para 8.224 on Leniency in this regard). It is noted that under the 2006 Leniency Notice, the Commission insists that any application, even for reduction of fines, be made explicitly. (See point 27 of the 2006 Leniency Notice.)

[900]   *Dealing with the Commission*, Publication of the European Commission, 1997, available at <http://europa.eu.int/comm/competition/publications/dealen1_en.pdf>, p 36. Although this document dates from 1997, the procedure it describes therein is still of application today.

the inspectors will produce their individual inspection mandates[901] and prove their identity by showing their staff cards. The Commission inspectors are usually assisted by officials from the competition authority of the Member State in which the inspection is taking place, who will also identify themselves and inform the undertaking of the mandate under which they act.[902] These Member State officials actively assist the Commission and are vested with the same on-the-spot powers as the Commission inspectors.[903] The representatives of the Commission will furthermore provide the undertaking with a copy of an 'Explanatory Note', which outlines the undertaking's rights and obligations (eg the right to legal assistance). The Commission team will indicate which member of the team will act as contact for the undertaking and the undertaking should address all queries to that person. In order to ensure that the inspection is conducted as smoothly as possible, the undertaking may also wish to indicate which of its officers will act as the contact point for the Commission team. The undertaking is free to designate who will perform that function but it is preferable that an officer in a sufficiently senior position is appointed in order that he or she is able to give instructions to other members of staff. The inspection team can be requested by the undertaking, within limits, to provide explanations on the subject matter of the proposed inspection and must clarify procedural matters.

8.381 Upon submission of the decision and after the undertaking has taken cognisance of it, it will be asked to sign a 'minute of notification'. This merely records that the decision has been *submitted* to the undertaking. It does not confirm the submission of the undertaking to the inspection; that obligation flows from the inspection decision itself and whether or not the undertaking behaves in accordance with that obligation is subject to a factual assessment. The inspection is deemed accepted until such time as the Commission team leader decides that a refusal has occurred and, where warranted, requests the authority of the Member State to take measures to overcome the opposition.

8.382 *Activity of inspectors during the inspection*   When the inspection is ongoing, the inspectors will sift through documents that can be found in offices, secretariats, archive rooms, computers, etc. Staff must be available to answer questions, at least about the whereabouts of materials. Usually one or more IT (information technology) specialists are present within the team to search for data electronically stored. The inspectors may ask for documents to be produced and may also select documents themselves. The undertaking cannot first review materials that are subsequently handed to the Commission if this leads to any delays. Selected documents will be coded and listed by the inspectors. Copies of those documents may be made immediately or by the end of the day. The Commission team is normally unwilling to discuss any matter relating to the substance of the investigation. The purpose of an inspection is mere fact-finding and more often than not, the members of the inspection team are not those responsible for the investigation as a whole.[904]

---

[901] Separate inspection mandates are only required in case of an inspection by decision.

[902] The mandate under which officials of the national authorities act is governed by national law.

[903] Art 20(5) of Regulation 1/2003.

[904] The undertaking will normally receive a data sheet listing the hierarchy responsible for the overall investigation.

8.383 *Right to legal assistance*   As described above in para 8.292, the undertaking is entitled to consult and/or have a legal advisor(s) present during the inspection.[905] Such presence is not, however, a precondition for the validity of the inspection.[906] The Commission's interpretation is that if the undertaking has in-house legal counsel present, the right of the undertaking is in any case respected.[907] If there is no in-house lawyer, the Commission is normally prepared to wait a short period for legal advisors to arrive, which is normally about 20–30 minutes, or such time as can be agreed with the leader of the inspection team. Waiting for legal assistance may not unduly delay the inspection and is subject to the condition that the Commission is satisfied that business records will not be interfered with in the meantime. (As mentioned above, a condition that the inspection team normally insists on is that during the waiting period the Commission team can take precautionary measures, for instance by spreading the inspectors over the offices of certain members of staff or blocking the e-mail accounts of particular individuals.) The role of an (external) legal counsel would be to defend the client in view of the the rights of defence of the undertaking that apply during the investigation. For instance, legal counsel can assist the undertaking in any discussions about the (alleged) legally privileged nature of certain materials. It would appear that the need for any legal assistance of individual members of personnel does not arise because, for the reasons discussed in paras 8.296 and following, Commission investigations target the behaviour of undertakings and safeguards in relation to the use of any information for other purposes, eg national (criminal) procedures are in place.[908]

8.384 *Penalties in case of a refusal to submit to (or obstruct) an inspection by decision*   An undertaking has a duty to submit to an inspection ordered by decision, and indeed to co-operate actively with it.[909] Failure to submit, which can consist of a general refusal (denial of entry) or a more specific one (eg refusal to allow access to certain filing cabinets or documents) can lead to the imposition of a fixed penalty of a maximum of 1 per cent of total (group) turnover as provided in Article 23(1)(c) of Regulation 1/2003. A periodic penalty can be imposed for each day that admission is refused (a maximum of 5 per cent of daily (group) turnover, as provided in Article 24(1)(e)).[910] If an inspection decision includes any such penalties it would need to be adopted in accordance with the general rules applicable to such penalties.[911] As described in para 8.339, the Commission may not gain entry or access to documents by force. In case of opposition, it must rely on assistance from the Member State, under Article 20(6) of Regulation 1/2003. The duty to submit is a continuing one, and at any stage during the inspection the Commission can note an instance of refusal.

---

905   The right to legal representation is referred to in Case C-94/00 *Roquette Frères SA v Directeur-Général de la Concurrence, de la Consommation et de la Répression des Fraudes* [2002] ECR I-9011, para 46 and the case law cited there.

906   Consultation may also take place by phone. Following the judgment of the ECtHR in *Camenzind* (judgment of 16 December 1997, (1999) 28 EHRR 458) the presence of a lawyer is not indispensable as long as there is no risk of irreparable damage to the undertaking's rights of defence.

907   This is without prejudice to the right to obtain assistance from outside counsel.

908   For a similar opinion see L Ortiz Blanco, *EC Competition Procedure* (2nd edn, 2006), para 8.28.

909   On the duty of co-operation, see para 8.308.

910   An example of a procedural fine imposed, then under Art 15(1)(c) of Regulation 17/62, is the *MEWAC* case, OJ 1993 L20/6.

911   L Ortiz Blanco ed, *EC Competition Procedure* (2nd edn, 2006), para 8.17 and ch 9.

Each such instance can give rise to the payment of procedural penalties. It is noted that a refusal to submit, depending on the circumstances, may also be categorised as obstructing the investigation, and may be taken into account as an aggravating circumstance when determining the cartel fine in the final decision.

Commission present during normal business hours   The Commission will endeavour to be **8.385** present at the undertaking only during 'normal business hours'.[912] This is a self-imposed rule rather than a constraint following from any particular legal provision.[913] It depends on the situation within the undertaking as to what normal business hours are, but an undertaking could hardly claim that the Commission could not continue the inspection whilst officers of the company continue to be present in the building. Still, the inspection would not suddenly become illegal if it continued beyond the normal closing of business. In practice, little dispute has arisen over this. In any case, given that since 1 May 2004 the Commission has had the power to seal premises, the need for the Commission to prolong its stay after normal business hours, in order to avoid business records being removed or destroyed, has been reduced considerably.

Protocols made up during an inspection and the possibilities for submitting exculpatory **8.386** *information*   Where the Commission wishes to record specific occurrences that take place during an inspection, including oral explanations relating to facts or documents, it will usually set these out in a protocol. The Commission will ask the undertaking to sign the protocol, but there is no obligation to do so. An undertaking may wish to comment on the protocol, and is free to draw the Commission's attention to any information that it considers to be in its favour and provide any declaration in this respect. The Commission inspectors will normally sign a receipt for that information. Of course, the undertaking may also submit any information post-inspection to the competent case team.

Taking of copies and creating a document inventory   As indicated above, the Commission **8.387** may take copies of inspected documents and does not take originals of any materials. In order to make copies, the Commission usually relies on the equipment available on the premises of the undertaking. Although there is no specific obligation on the undertaking to put such facilities or personnel at the disposal of the Commission, it is considered to be within its duty of co-operation to do so. The Commission offers, in its Explanatory Note, to reimburse the company for the copies made. Co-operating by providing administrative assistance may also be in the undertaking's interest: to enhance the efficacy with which the inspection is being carried out will avoid unduly extending the disruption to the normal course of business. A set of the copied documents is made available to the undertaking.

Treatment of business secrets and confidential information   The confidentiality of docu- **8.388** ments is no reason to keep them from being scrutinised and copied by the Commission.

---

[912] This follows from the Commission's Explanatory Note.

[913] The Commission will endeavour to intervene in the least disruptive way, so that the undertaking can carry on its business in as normal a manner as possible. To oblige an undertaking to continue to permit access after business hours may be considered disproportionate, particularly in view of the Commission's power to affix seals overnight.

All inspected documents benefit from confidential treatment, in line with the Commission's obligation of professional secrecy. All documents are treated confidentially as a matter of course after the inspection and during the investigative phase. Should the Commission issue a Statement of Objections, the undertaking, in preparation for the access to the file that will be granted to all addressees, will have an opportunity to make its claims as regards business secrets and other confidential information. Identifying documents by virtue of their confidentiality during an inspection therefore is of no particular benefit to the undertaking.

8.389 *End of the inspection* The inspection decision refers only to a starting date, but does not indicate when it must finish. This is quite logical, as the Commission cannot predict before the inspection how much information it will find and how speedily it can conclude its work. In practice, inspections usually take between two and three days, but they can be shorter, and can sometimes even be concluded within a matter of hours.

8.390 Although the inspection decision does not refer to the end of the inspection, and the inspection team does not formally announce the end of the inspection when leaving,[914] undertakings do have an interest in knowing when they are freed from the obligations ensuing from the application of Article 20. Also, undertakings that may wish to file an application for immunity or reduction in fines need to know when the inspection has finished. This is because the Commission is likely to consider that undertakings cannot, while an inspection is still continuing, make use of information that should be available to the Commission as part of the inspection for the purpose of applying, for benefit under the Leniency Notice.[915] So the question arises, when can 'the inspection' be presumed to have finished? That issue has never been clarified by the Commission and has not been dealt with by the European Courts. After the inspection the Commission normally sends a so-called 'post-inspection' letter, in which it is stated for purposes of formality that the inspection has been concluded. However, such a letter may follow weeks after the inspection. It is submitted that the Commission could resume the inspection, on the basis of the same inspection decision, if it is probing the same behaviour as that referred to in the inspection decision, and the continuation takes place within a reasonable time from the original action. But this would depend on a case-by-case evaluation.[916]

8.391 *Post-inspection procedure* Following the inspection, the undertaking that has been visited will normally receive a letter requesting it to provide the Commission with a non-confidential version of the inspection documents. In that letter the case officers responsible for following up the investigation are also named. Any subsequent correspondence can be

---

[914] There may be an overnight decision to return to the premises, based on further analysis of the information taken, or instructions received from the Commission's 'headquarters'.

[915] In that case the Commission may well consider that information had been withheld from the inspection and view such behaviour as an act of obstruction. However, the Commission has adopted a practice of handing out a copy of the Leniency Notice when the case team considers that its on the spot work has been concluded. The submission of the Leniency Notice would in any case, it is submitted, imply that the undertaking could make an admissible request under the Leniency Notice as from that moment.

[916] By contrast, if the Commission wishes to return to the premises, for instance only several weeks after the original inspection and on the basis of new information and in order to investigate additional facts, it is submitted that there no longer exists a sufficient link between the original inspection decision and the new action to consider this a continuation of the inspection. Accordingly, a new decision is required (adopted in accordance with all procedural requirements) that will allow for a second intrusion into the private sphere of the undertaking.

conducted with that case team. Should the undertaking wish to file an application under the Commission's Leniency Notice, it can do so using the Commission's dedicated fax number[917] and/or request a meeting with DG Competition in order to deliver an application and accompanying statement.[918]

(iv) The adoption of inspection decisions under Article 20(4)

1. Requirements relating to the substance of the inspection decision

Reference in the decision to the subject matter and purpose   The decision must state, in accordance with Article 20(4), the 'subject matter' and the 'purpose' of the inspection.[919] Although it is perhaps difficult to distinguish between those two notions, the inclusion of the *subject matter* is considered to require a description of the product(s) or service(s) concerned in the investigation and a (short) description of the allegedly infringing behaviour for which the Commission's intervention is taking place. That description does not need to be very detailed, however, as the Commission cannot be expected to know in advance what information relating to the infringement is available or the documents it will find.[920] The *purpose* of an inspection can be described as the need to check, on the premises, facts which might constitute evidence of the suspected infringement as well as other information that may help to clarify the factual and economic circumstances in which the alleged agreements or concerted practices occurred. An example of how the subject matter and purpose have been described can be found in the Commission inspection decision in its *Sodium Gluconate* investigation that eventually led to the *Roquette Frères*[921] judgment. In the ECJ's judgment,[922] on the request for a preliminary ruling by the French *Cour de Cassation*, part of the Commission's inspection decision (then based on Article 14(3) of Regulation 17/62, the equivalent of Article 20(4) of Regulation 1/2003), was reproduced. In the Commission's inspection decision, the *subject matter* of the investigation was described as follows:

> [. . .] The Commission has information to the effect that officers of the above mentioned undertaking held regular meetings with competitors, during which shares of the sodium

8.392

---

917 The dedicated fax no. is: +32 2 299 45 85. The documents regarding the Commission's leniency policy can be accessed at <http://ec.europa.eu/comm/competition/cartels/leniency/leniency.html>. The procedure for making an application and delivering an oral statement to the Commission is discussed in the section on Leniency, especially paras 8.154ff.

918 Referred to in para 8.160.

919 Case T-10/89 *Hoechst v Commission* [1992] ECR II-629, para 29. Case C-94/00 *Roquette Frères SA v Directeur-Général de la Concurrence, de la Consommation et de la Répression des Fraudes* [2002] ECR I-9011, para 47; Case C-110/04 P *Strintzis Lines Shipping v Commission*, Order of 30 March 2006, not yet published, para 31, referring to *Hoechst* and *Roquette*.

920 See Case 31/59 *Acciaieria e Tubificio di Brescia v High Authority of the European Coal and Steel Community* [1960] ECR 71, pp 80–81, point 4. By contrast, in *Minoan Lines* the CFI repeated that the Commisssion is under a requirement to state '. . . as precisely as possible what it is looking for and the matters to which the investigation must relate . . .'. (Case T-66/99 *Minoan Lines SA v Commission* [2003] ECR II-5515, para 55 and the case law cited there.)

921 The litigation concerned a challenge by the undertaking Roquette Frères against the authorisation granted by the *Tribunal de grande instance de Lille* for the entry and seizure of documents.

922 The question referred to the Court of Justice in essence related to the scope of review which may be carried out by a court of a Member State where that court is called upon to act on a request by the Commission for assistance pursuant to Art 14(6) of Regulation 17/62 (the principle which is now contained in Art 20(6) of Regulation 1/2003).

gluconate market were allocated and minimum prices agreed for the users in the various areas of the market. The sales levels - both global and relating to the various areas—were also fixed. At each meeting the degree to which the agreements had been observed was assessed, and it appears that any undertaking exceeding the sales allocated to it had to try to reduce its sales during the following period.

The addressee of this decision is also a producer of glucono-delta-lactone. Glucono-delta-lactone is used in the production of cheese, meat-based products and tofu.

The Commission has information indicating that the above mentioned contacts with competitors also extended to glucono-delta-lactone. In particular, bi- or multilateral talks were held, often on the fringe of the meetings relating to sodium gluconate (before or after them, or during breaks). On those occasions, the participants exchanged information relating to the market, market prices and levels of demand. They also held talks on manufacturing capacity and sales volumes. The contacts were aimed at controlling prices and, it appears, were such as to result in co-ordination of the participants' behaviour on the market.

If their existence were established, the above mentioned agreements and/or concerted practices might constitute a serious infringement of Article 85 of the Treaty establishing the European Community. The very nature of such agreements and/or concerted practices suggests that they are implemented by secret means and that, in this connection, an investigation is the most appropriate means of gathering evidence of their existence.

As regards the *purpose* of the inspection, the Commission decision stated:

8.393   In order to enable the Commission to discover all the facts concerning the possible agreements and/or concerted practices and the context in which they fit, it is therefore necessary to carry out an investigation pursuant to Article 14 of Regulation No 17.

The addressee of this decision may hold information which the Commission needs in order to pursue its inquiries into the matter described above.

[. . .]

8.394   The statement of reasons in the inspection decision is important not only to show that the entry into the premises of the undertakings is justified, but also to enable the undertakings to assess the scope of their duty to co-operate.[923] Furthermore, it serves as a safeguard for undertakings against so-called 'fishing expeditions'.[924]

8.395   ***Requirement to mention the starting date***   The decision must indicate the date on which the inspection is to begin.[925] However, decisions often state that the inspection can begin 'on or after' a particular date, so as to ensure that it does not become void eg in circumstances where there is a last-minute delay as a result of which the Commission cannot start on the planned day. An undertaking cannot claim that, if the inspection starts after the indicated date, its rights of defence have been violated, as it is only through notification that the decision takes effect.[926] Inspection decisions do not need to indicate a particular

---

[923]   Case T-10/89 *Hoechst v Commission* [1992] ECR II-629 para 29; Case C-94/00 *Roquette Frères SA v Directeur-Général de la Concurrence, de la Consommation et de la Répression des Fraudes* [2002] ECR I-9011 para 47.

[924]   '. . .the rights of the undertakings concerned . . . would be seriously compromised if the Commission could rely on evidence against undertakings which was obtained during an investigation but was not related to the subject matter thereof. . .' (Case C-94/00 *Roquette Frères* [2002] ECR I-9011, para 48 and the case law cited there.)

[925]   Art 20(4) of Regulation 1/2003.

[926]   Similarly, G Miersch in D Dalheimer, C Feddersen, G Miersch, n 817 above, at p 164, para 50.

hour of commencement. Equally, they do not state an end or expiration date (though commonly inspections last between one and three days).[927]

Reference to procedural penalties for non-compliance   Inspection decisions must state the   **8.396**
penalties for non-compliance provided for in Articles 23 and 24 of Regulation 1/2003. In case an undertaking does not submit to an inspection, Article 23(1) provides for a fine of up to 1 per cent of annual turnover. Furthermore, periodic penalties can be imposed, for the duration of the refusal, of up to 5 per cent of daily turnover. (On procedural penalties for the different violations that can occur during an inspection see para 8.384.)

Reference to the possibility of Court review   A final element that a decision must contain   **8.397**
is the fact that the addressee can appeal the inspection decision before the European Courts.[928] However, it is unlikely, as explained below, that an appeal (even if combined with a request for interim measures) will have the effect of stopping the investigation. An appeal itself in any case has no suspensory effect.[929]

2. Procedural formalities relating to the adoption of inspection decisions

Inspection decisions can be signed by the Director-General for Competition   In terms of pro-   **8.398**
cedural requirements, an inspection decision is an act of the Commission and must there-fore be adopted by the College of Commissioners. The power to adopt decisions to carry out inspections has been delegated to the Commissioner responsible for competition. The power to sign inspection decisions has, in turn, been conferred on the Director-General of DG Competition.[930] The individual mandates for the inspectors are normally signed by the Director-General or a Deputy Director-General.

Consultation of the Member State concerned   According to Article 20(4), the Commission   **8.399**
must consult the Member State in whose territory the inspection is to be conducted. It is notable that such consultation must take place *before* the inspection decision is adopted, although it is not entirely clear in relation to the substance of the decision what useful pur-pose the advance consultation serves. The purpose seems to be rather that the Member State receives an early warning so that it can organise any assistance that it is required to provide, including applying for warrants as a precautionary measure. In order to avoid the consultation being a delaying factor, consultation can take place in writing or informally, eg by telephone, and no minutes need to be taken.[931]

---

[927] On the issue of the end of an inspection, see paras 8.389 and 8.390.

[928] Art 20(4) of Regulation 1/2003.

[929] Art 242 EC.

[930] In accordance with Art 13(1) and (3) of Commission Rules of Procedure (amended), Commission Decision of 15 November 2005, [2005] OJ L347/83. On 28 April 2004 the Commission adopted a decision with a comprehensive set of empowerments (PV(2004) 1655, SEC(2004) 520/2) for the Competition Commissioner for the application of the Modernisation Regulation No 1/2003 and implementing Commission Regulation No 773/2004. The decision to order inspections under Art 20(4) is amongst those that can be taken by the Director-General, following the decision of 27 May 2004 of the Commissioner for Competition (PH/2004/769). Inspection decisions that include procedural fines (periodic penalties) under Art 24(1)(e) have not been subdelegated to the Director-General. Signature can be further delegated in cases where the Director-General is prevented from exercising his functions, and in accordance with Art 27 of the Commission Rules of Procedure, to a Deputy Director-General.

[931] Case 5/85 *Akzo Chemie BV v Commission* [1986] ECR 2585, para 24. ('It is of little importance that the consultation was carried out informally and, as in the case of the British authorities, by telephone and without a

(v) Additional Substantive and Procedural Aspects of Inspections by Written Authorisation (announced inspections)

8.400 The procedural requirements relating to inspections by authorisation are discussed below with a focus on how they differ from the requirements for inspections by decision. It is repeated here that the authorisation to carry out an unannounced inspection can be signed by the Director-General for Competition or, in his/her absence, a Deputy-Director General.

8.401 **Substantive elements of the authorisation** The authorisation must mention the name of the undertaking or association to be visited. No address is required.[932] Naming the Commission officials or other individuals ('accompanying persons') mandated to carry out the investigation in the authorisation is not formally required, but it is customary to do so. The document shall also mention the subject matter and purpose of the inspection. Article 20(3) stipulates furthermore that the penalties provided for in Article 23 of Regulation 1/2003 must be specified in the authorisation.[933] The potential grounds for applying the penalties in Article 23 in the case of inspections under authorisation only relate to the incomplete production of business records and incorrect or misleading answers to questions.[934] The penalties serve rather as a means of ensuring that the (voluntary) co-operation which the company has chosen to provide is comprehensive. There is no requirement to refer to the periodic penalties provided for in Article 24, because an undertaking is not obliged to allow an inspection under authorisation to take place.[935] (The Commission must first order the inspection by decision under Article 20(4) before it is possible to impose a periodic penalty, in case of (continued) opposition.)

8.402 **Prior notice to—not consultation of—the Members State concerned** In terms of formal steps to be taken, the Commission must, 'in good time before the inspection', give notice to the competition authority of the Member State concerned that an inspection is going to be carried out on its territory.[936] This procedure is less demanding than that for inspections by decision in that no formal *consultation* is necessary.[937]

---

minute of it being drawn up. Since the purpose of Article 14(2) of Regulation no 17 is to enable the Commission to carry out investigations without prior warning on the premises of undertakings suspected of infringements of Articles 85 and 86 [now 81 and 82] of the Treaty, the Commission must be able to adopt its decision without being made subject to conditions of a formal nature which would have the effect of delaying such adoption.')

[932] See paras 8.340 and 8.341 on the requirements for identifying the undertaking.

[933] See Art 20(3) and (4) of Regulation 1 and Case 136/79 *National Panasonic (UK) v Commission* [1980] ECR 2033 at para 11, and Joined Cases 46/87 and 227/88 *Hoechst AG v Commission* [1989] ECR 2859, at para 22 and para 29.

[934] That is logical since a breach of Art 20(2)(a) (entry), and (c) (taking of copies), must require the Commission to obtain an inspection decision first. As regards the use of seals it is presumed that the Commission considered that no separate sanction was necessary as the company would in any event take the necessary measures to ensure the (overnight) protection of sensitive materials. Also, where there is a risk that relevant materials may disappear, the Commission would surely resort to an inspection by decision, with the stronger procedural powers attached to it.

[935] Answer to Written Question No 667/79 [1979] OJ C31/30.

[936] Art 20(3) of Regulation 1/2003.

[937] It will be sufficient to simply give notice because for announced inspections the Member States would not need to take preparatory action such as obtaining national warrants. Hence, no 'consulation' is necessary. Nevertheless, Member States still have to provide assistance to the Commission under Art 20(5) of Regulation 1/2003.

(vi) Opportunities to Challenge the Inspection Decision and/or the Use of the Evidence Collected in Inspections

Little scope in practice for preventing the inspection from going forward   In order to   **8.403**
protect itself from the consequences of what it considers to be an undue intervention by
the Commission, an undertaking may consider challenging an inspection decision before
the CFI.[938] It can do so under the 'standard' provision of Article 230 EC. However, such an
appeal does not have any suspensory effect. Also, it may be difficult to demonstrate a convincing case on the merits, as the substantive and formal requirements for the Commission
to issue a valid decision can be satisfied relatively easily.[939] Even if an undertaking were to
succeed with an appeal, a judgment would never be made soon enough to prevent the
inspection from taking place. A further option is to combine the appeal with a request for
suspension of the investigative measure (stay of execution), based on an application under
Article 242 EC. The CFI will balance[940] the need for the inspection and the risk of the loss
of evidence, against any serious and irreparable harm that may be done to the undertaking.
Such direct harm is rather difficult to imagine, however, in the case of a purely investigative
measure,[941] whereas the likelihood of concealment or disappearance of important information, seriously impacting the investigation, is much greater. Also, even if an undertaking
could convince the CFI of the existence of detrimental circumstances, it is optimistic to
expect that an order would be forthcoming within a sufficiently tight timeframe.[942] By the
time an order was issued the inspection would probably have already been well under way
or completed. Consequently, preventing an inspection from taking place by invoking judicial protection cannot be considered a realistic option for the undertaking.[943] The maximum benefit an undertaking would achieve if it succeeded in having the inspection
decision declared illegal would be to obtain the return of the documents seized during the
inspection or at least that the Commission would be rendered powerless to use these documents in support of any final decision[944] (although for that it would not need to have

---

[938] One cannot challenge an inspection under authorisation because the inspection takes place with
the agreement of the undertaking. An undertaking can oppose an inspection under authorisation as a whole.
For an explanation see Miersch, in D Dalheimer, C Feddersen, G Miersch, *EU Kartellverfahrensverordnung*
(Verlag C.H. Beck, 2005), at p 162, para 41.

[939] A succinct description of the subject matter (the suspected infringement) and the purpose of the
inspection will suffice. See para 8.392.

[940] The CFI may grant interim relief, based on its Rules of Procedure, Art 105(2).

[941] Unless one accepts the view that if the inspection is indeed taking place on illegal grounds, the fact that
the Commission inspectors have had access to incriminating information, combined with the fact that they
cannot be held to suffer from 'acute amnesia', leads to irreparable harm to the undertaking. The argument is
that the further investigation by the Commission will have been because it had access to the information, even
if the information would have to be returned following a successful appeal. (For a further explanation of the
'acute amnesia' argument, see para 8.278 in relation to access to materials to which legal privilege attaches.)

[942] In this respect, Kerse and Khan refer to 'at best within days'. (CS Kerse and N Khan, *EC Antitrust
Procedure* (5th edn, 2005), at para 3-062.)

[943] Furthermore, a challenge to the inspection decision combined with refusing the inspection, should be
weighed against the possibility that the Commission will sanction the undertaking for its refusal, with potentially heavy pecuniary sanctions (discussed in para 8.384). Should a refusal lead to the use of coercive measures
under national law, the undertaking may seek recourse under national law against the use of such coercive
mesasures. However, in the light of the decision in *Roquette*, and the limited scope of review that a national
court can exercise when deciding on the issuing of a national warrant (arbitrary or excessive nature of coercive
measures—Art 20(8) of Regulation 1/2003), the chances of success under national law appear equally slim.

[944] Case C-94/00 *Roquette Frères* [2002] ECR I-9011, para 49 and the case law cited therein.

recourse to interim measures). If this is what the undertaking seeks to achieve, it only needs to ensure that it lodges such an appeal within two months of the inspection having taken place. Otherwise the collection and use of documents is probably not challengeable at a later stage, at least not on the basis of the invalidity of the inspection decision.[945]

8.404   **Challenging the admissibility and use of evidence collected**   In challenging the collection of evidence (and hence attempting to have information collected struck from the Commission's file), a claim about the illegality of the inspection decision itself should be clearly separated from the possible illegality of the investigative actions during the inspection, such as the collection of material covered by legal privilege. Hence, if an undertaking were not in a position to successfully appeal the inspection decision itself, it can still attempt to challenge the admissibility and use in evidence of documents or information taken. The success of such a claim may depend on its substance (whether the Commission's action was illegal), but may also hinge on its (procedural) timing. The question in that regard, discussed below, is whether the undertaking wishing to make such a claim should (first) seek redress before the Commission during the administrative phase, and/or whether it should (and could) raise any arguments in this respect at the stage of an appeal against the final decision. (Reference is also made to other sections in this chapter dealing with the admissibility of evidence and arguments raised by undertakings in this regard, notably paras 8.156 and 8.157.)

8.405   If an undertaking wishes to have the information struck from the file at a prior stage in the administrative process, one possible option consists of provoking an earlier (procedural) Commission decision concerning the documents at stake. This may be done by requesting the return of the documents, so that the Commission will either comply with the request, or adopt a formal decision of refusal to return the document. A separate appeal against that decision may then be possible. This is essentially the course of action used by Akzo in the *Akzo/Ackross* case discussed in para 8.280 above, where it asked for the return of documents

---

945   An undertaking that does not challenge the inspection decision within the set time period cannot later claim the illegality of the inspection and on that basis challenge the use by the Commission of the inspection results. Once the time period for lodging an appeal has expired, the decision is deemed to be definitive and the evidence presumed to have been collected legally in so far as the legality depends on the validity of the inspection itself. That was the view of the CFI in the *PVC* cases. (See Case 46/87 R *Hoechst v Commission* [1987] ECR 1549, para 34, and Case 85/87 *Dow Chemical Nederland BV v Commission* [1987] ECR 4367, para 17. Kerse and Khan question whether that interpretation still stands, ie whether a later claim would still be possible in view of the jurisprudence after *PVC*, (CS Kerse and N Khan, *EC Antitrust Procedure* (5th edn, 2005), at para 3-063, n 48 and n 50, notably referring to the case law in *Greek Ferries* (Case T-66/99 *Minoan Lines SA v Commission* [2003] ECR II-5515 at para 93, where the CFI suggested that an applicant could still make such a claim when appealing the final decision. On appeal, Case C 121/04 P *Minoan Lines SA v Commission*, Order of 17 November 2005, not yet published.) It is noted that, insofar as an undertaking wants to base a claim to the CFI about the admissibility of inspection documents obtained at *another* undertaking on the illegality of an inspection at that other undertaking, it can still make that claim in an appeal to the CFI against the final decision (and possibly subject to the condition that such claim had also been made during the administrative procedure, see Case T-330/01 *Akzo Nobel NV v Commission*, judgment of 17 September 2006, not yet reported, at paras 87–89. This applies *mutatis mutandis* to simple requests for information and requests for information by decision. See Joined Cases C-238/99 P, C-244/99 P, C-245/99 P, C-247/99 P, C-250/99 P to C-252/99 P and C-254/99 P *Limburgse Vinyl Maatschappij (LVM) and others v Commission* [2002] ECR I-08375, para 267, confirming on this point the judgment of the CFI in the same matter in Joined Cases T-305/94 to T-307/94, T-313/94 to T-316/94, T-318/94, T-325/94, T-328/94, T-329/94 and T-335/94 *Limburgse Vinyl Maatschappij (LVM) and others v Commission* [1999] ECR II-931, paras 410–412 and 441–442.

that it claimed were legally privileged.[946] However, the Courts may be expected to be less than enthusiastic about dealing with preliminary matters arising during the course of the investigation itself, when such issues can be properly raised in appeal against the final decision.[947] In order to do so, however, an undertaking is well advised to make at least a procedural claim as regards the documents at stake, in order to safeguard its rights. If the undertaking has not made such a claim at least in reply to a Statement of Objections, it is submitted that it may lose the possibility of a claim when appealing the decision.[948]

Subject to the above, a challenge to the collection and use of evidence is also possible in an appeal to the CFI against the final Commission decision after the administrative phase.[949] A drawback for undertakings of not endeavouring to have documents returned or taken out of the file at an earlier stage and to contest the use of the evidence only in the administrative procedure and after the final decision, is the possibility that an impression of guilt based on the evidence may have been established and more generally the investigation may have been influenced by having had access to the information for the duration of the investigation. Therefore, even though case law clearly shows that the Decision cannot rely on the evidence obtained in contravention of procedural rules and that no conclusions can result from it[950]—though they may still result from other evidence—(partial) damage may have been done as the Commission may have used the information to orientate its investigation.

8.406

(vii) The Role of the Member States in Commission Inspections under Article 20

General duty to provide assistance   Within the framework of assisting the Commission in carrying out inspections, the Member States must ensure that the Commission's actions

8.407

---

[946] Case T-125/03 *Akzo Nobel Chemicals Ltd and Ackros Chemicals Ltd v Commission*. In that case, the undertaking requested the return of particular documents seized during an inspection, based on a claim of legal privilege. The Commission refused, by separate Commission decision, to return the documents. This was subsequently challenged by Akzo and its subsidiary Ackros Chemicals. Certain documents were sealed in an envelope to allow for a subsequent discussion about their legal privilege status. The undertaking wanted to prevent the Commission from even seeing the documents, and attempted to prevent this by making an application for interim measures before the CFI, after the Commission had informed the undertaking of its decision to open the envelope and add the documents to the file.

[947] However, in *Akzo/Ackros* the president of the CFI showed a willingness to deal with a procedural issue in an interim procedure and granted (partial) relief to the undertaking. (Order of the president of the CFI in *Akzo/Ackros*, Case T-125/03 R and T-253/03 R *Akzo Nobel Chemicals Ltd and Ackros Chemicals Ltd v Commission* [2004] ECR II-4771.) At the time of writing, the case in the main proceeding is still before the CFI and awaiting judgment. (Case T-125/03 *Akzo Nobel Chemicals Ltd and Ackros Chemicals Ltd v Commission*). On the issue of the (un)willingness of the courts to deal with such matters see also CS Kerse and N Khan, *EC Antitrust Procedure* (5th edn, 2005), at para 3-033, n 43.)

[948] That opinion is derived from Case T-330/01 *Akzo Nobel NV v Commission*, judgment of 17 September 2006, not yet reported, at paras 87–89, where the CFI refers to the principles and rules governing the administrative procedure and states that the Statement of Objections must have 'practical effect'. An argument that an undertaking failed to raise in the administrative procedure could not be invoked later before the CFI. The CFI stated that 'Accordingly, on the basis of the information contained in the statement of objections, Akzo could not have been unaware that it was likely to be the addressee of a final decision of the Commission. In such a situation, the onus was on it to react during the administrative procedure, or be faced with the prospect of no longer being able to do so. . .' (para 87).

[949] Likewise, see Miersch, in D Dalheimer, C Feddersen, G Miersch, *EU Kartellverfahrensverordnung* (Verlag CH Beck, 2005), at p 134, para 49 and CS Kerse and N Khan, *EC Antitrust Procedure* (5th edn, 2005) at para 3-063.

[950] Case C-94/00 *Roquette Frères* [2002] ECR I-9011, para 49, and the case law cited therein.

are 'effective'.[951] Article 20(5) places a duty on the Member States to 'actively assist' the Commission, which includes being present on the spot during inspections.[952] In practice, the Commission's inspection team is accompanied by one or more officials from the Member State concerned. In accordance with Article 20(5), these officials can execute the same tasks in searching for information as the members of the Commission's inspection team.

8.408 **Role in case of opposition** The Member States have a particular role to play where the undertaking, at any stage, opposes the inspection. Opposition may arise upon entry into the undertaking (an outright refusal), but the opposition may also occur in the course of the inspection, for instance when the undertaking refuses access to a particular office or file, or even to a single document. In these instances, the Commission may call upon the national authorities to overcome the opposition. Article 20(6) of Regulation 1/2003 prescribes that the Member State concerned '[. . .] shall afford the necessary assistance, requesting where appropriate the assistance of the police or of an equivalent enforcement authority [. . .]'. The manner in which the Member State provides such assistance is a matter of national law.[953] Measures typically include obtaining a court warrant (often acquired as a precautionary measure) that will oblige the undertaking to allow entry, possibly with the help of the police. Not all Member States seek recourse to national judicial authorities before forceable measures are taken.[954] It is important to note that the obligation to assist in Article 20(6) rests on 'the Member State concerned' and thus also on the judicial authorities,[955] which means that when confronted with a request for a warrant they have to act promptly. Note that it is only the overcoming of the opposition that is governed by national law: the inspection otherwise continues under Commmunity law.[956]

8.409 **Review by national courts is limited to the arbitrariness and proportionality of the coercive measures** National courts that make decisions about permitting the use of coercive measures as referred to in Article 20(7) may not question the lawfulness of the Commission decision. In other words, they may not call into question the Commission decision and substitute their own assessment for that of the Commission about the need for the inspection. In *Roquette Frères*,[957] the Court of Justice clearly confirmed that an opinion on the *necessity* for an on-the-spot investigation and the adequacy of the reasons submitted by the Commission is reserved to the European Courts.[958] The Court stated that what the

---

[951] Based also on the general obligation of cooperation in good faith as enshrined in Art 10 EC. (Case C-94/00 *Roquette Frères* [2002] ECR I-9011 at paras 30–35; See also *Hoechst*, n 945 above, para 33.)

[952] See also preamble 24 of Regulation 1/2003, which reads: '[. . .] The competent authorities of the Member States should actively assist in the exercise of these powers.'

[953] See C-94/00 *Roquette Frères* [2002] ECR I-9011, para 34 and *Hoechst*, n 945 above, paras 33 and 34.

[954] To give two examples: in the Netherlands no prior judicial approval is necessary, whereas in the UK it is. It is possible that undertakings that have been faced with coercive measures without a judicial warrant will challenge such measures as failing to comply with the *Colas Est* case law, from which it may be concluded that, depending on the situation arising under national law, coercive measures require a prior judicial warrant. (*Société Colas Est and Others v France* (2004) 39 EHRR 17, para 49). On this point see also L Ortiz Blanco, *EC Competition Procedure* (2nd edn, 2006), para 8.63.

[955] That obligation of good co-operation applies reciprocally to the Community institutions. See *Roquette Frères*, n 953 above, at para 31 and the case law to which it refers.

[956] National law regulates only: (a) the body in charge of the force (police or national competition authority), (b) the procedural requirements for the use of force, and (c) the procedural guarantees for the undertaking regarding the overcoming of the opposition.

[957] *Roquette Frères*, n 953 above, paras 39 and 96.

[958] See also *Hoechst*, n 945 above para 35.

national court *can* do—but what its power of review is limited to - is to verify the authenticity of the Commission decision and judge on the possible arbitrariness and excessive nature of the coercive measures applied for.[959] In making its assessment, the national court can ask to be provided with detailed explanations about the grounds that the Commission has for the suspected infringement (including the nature of the infringement and the nature of the involvement of the undertaking concerned), but it cannot demand that it obtain (part of) the Commission's file.[960]

Coercive measures can lead to sanctions under national law—even against private persons Since the use of coercive measures in case of a refusal is a matter of national law, undertakings and their officers are possibly subject to sanctions available under domestic legislation.[961] In the UK, for example, if a court order has been obtained to enforce, in the case of opposition, a Commission inspection by decision, it can be served on (an employee of) the company by the OFT.[962] Non-compliance with the national warrant would be regarded as contempt of court, which under national law may lead to an unlimited fine and/or imprisonment of maximum two years for those involved.[963] Once the opposition has been surmounted with the help of national law, the question may arise whether the inspection is presumed to be conducted for the remaining period under the national law, or whether the inspection continues to be carried out under Regulation 1/2003 regime. As mentioned in para 8.408, the intention of the legislator appears to be the latter.[964]

8.410

(viii) Inspections Carried Out by the Competition Authorities of the Member States on Behalf of the Commission—Article 22(2)

Article 22 of Regulation 1/2003 empowers Member States to carry out inspections on each other's behalf [965] and on behalf of the Commission.[966] This section only discusses inspections carried out on behalf of the Commission under Article 22(2).

8.411

---

[959] Hence, it seems that only where recourse to coercive measures would be manifestly disproportionate, for example in the framework of cartels, perhaps where the potential involvement of the undertaking concerned cannot be assessed, a national judicial authority can refuse to grant an authorisation. See also L Ortiz Blanco, *EC Competition Procedure* (2nd edn, 2006), para 8.63. As regards the element of the seriousness of the infringement, mentioned in Art 20(8) of Regulation 1/2003, in cartel cases the infringement will normally be qualified as 'very serious', so that this is unlikely to be a valid ground for refusing a warrant.

[960] See Art 20(8) of Regulation 1/2003. It may also check the authenticity of the decision. The national court may, however, make its own assessment as to whether any *national measures* may be arbitrary or disproportionate. In light of that assessment the Commission may be required to provide the court with detailed explanations (though it does not have to grant access to its files) showing that there are reasonable grounds for suspecting an infringement. (*Roquette Frères*, paras 59–61.)

[961] See, eg, Commission Decision in *UKWAL* [1992] OJ L121/45.

[962] Competition Act 1998, s 63.

[963] Competition Act 1998, s 65. In practice, the mere threat of such sanctions usually means that any opposition is abandoned, but the refusal that has occurred may still lead to a procedural sanction under Art 23(1)(c) or may lead to an increase in the ultimate cartel fine that the Commission imposes.

[964] It is submitted that the wording of Art 20(6) suggests that only the surmounting of opposition takes place under national law because the purpose of the assistance of the Member State concerned is intended '*to enable* them *to conduct* the inspection' (emphasis added). ('Them' refers to officials and other accompanying persons authorised by the Commission). The 'conduct' of 'the inspection' and the powers that the inspectors avail themselves of, remain those under Community law.

[965] Art 22(1) of Regulation 1/2003.

[966] Under Art 22(2) the Commission can also request a national competition authority to carry out inspections on behalf of another authority, as envisaged in Art 22(1). That possibility is not discussed further in this section.

8.412   The Commission may, on the one hand, be expected to use the Article 22(2) option with increasing frequency in the ECN setting, as more and more Member States have efficient competition agencies with sufficient resources and experience of carrying out inspections. Inspections through the use of Article 22(2) will save the Commission from using its own resources.[967] On the other hand, the use of Article 22(2) may have some procedural side effects, since the inspections carried out by the Member State are conducted via application of national law. For instance, if subsidiaries of the same undertaking located in different Member States are being inspected, reliance on Article 22 may mean that they become subject to different procedural regimes during the same inspection. For the Commission, the use of Article 22(2) may mean that it has to allow national procedures to be followed in full, including possible appeals by the undertakings before national courts (for instance about the legality under national law of the seizure of documents), before it can have access to the evidence. This could lead to considerable delays in the investigation.

8.413   **Member States are obliged to execute Article 22(2) inspections when requested**   An inspection under Article 22(2) may take place where the Commission simply considers it 'necessary' or through a decision pursuant to Article 20(4). Member States have a duty ('shall undertake') to conduct inspections under Article 22(2) when the Commission requests them to do so on either of the above bases. This obligation in relation to the Commission can be contrasted with the regime for assistance that is applicable between the Member States under Article 22(1) in which the provision of assistance is optional.

8.414   **Inspections under Article 22 are executed under national law**   As mentioned above, in Article 22(2) inspections, the inspection procedures and evidence gathering takes place under national law.[968] It is noted that the national regime may be stricter than the Commission's, for instance as regards the taking of copies or of originals of documents. Even if this were the case, the Commission would not be prevented from using materials collected under the national regime, even if the Commission itself would not have had the ability to obtain the documents itself.

8.415   **Commission officials may participate in the inspection carried out by the Member State**   Under Article 22(2) and at the request of the Commission or the NCA concerned, it is possible that inspectors authorised by the Commission can assist the NCA in carrying out its inspection. That appears to be a useful means of ensuring that the inspection team is properly informed about the intricacies of the investigation. It will also help them to make an informed decision about the documents that may be relevant to the investigation when they are at the premises of the undertaking. A question that arises is what powers the

---

[967] Reportedly, the Commission has used Art 22(2) in coordination with inspections by the Commission itself in cases where the Commission was already inspecting a considerable number of sites itself (ie with the assistance of the Member State officials, but not based on Art 22(2)), and requested the Member State(s) to inspect additional sites.

[968] De Bronett considers the wording in Art 22(2) which refers to national official carrying out 'their powers' in accordance with national law, and queries whether the powers themselves are those referred to in Art 20(2), or whether that expression also relates to the provisions under national law. See G De Bronett, *Kommentar zum Europaischen Kartellverfahrensrecht* (Luchterhand, 2005), at p 137.

Commission officials are deemed to have when they are participating in such inspection under national law.[969]

(f) Inspections on Other Premises (Private Homes)—Article 21

(i) Rationale and Use

Article 21 of Council Regulation 1/2003 provides the Commission with the power to order **8.416** by decision '. . . an inspection to be conducted in other premises, land and means of transport, including the homes of directors, managers and other members of staff of the undertaking and associations of undertakings concerned'. The rationale for including this investigative tool in the Commission's list of powers is found in the preamble to Regulation 1/2003 which states that 'there are cases where business records are kept in the homes of directors or other people working for an undertaking.'[970] The background to this is that the Commission's experience in cartel investigations has involved instances where communications between cartel participants had taken place by way of communications from or to private homes (fax machines or computers), or where cartel evidence had been stored away from the office premises, in order to prevent detection.[971] A flaw under Regulation 17/62 was that although the undertaking had an obligation to make such business records available during an inspection[972] or through a request for information, the Commission was not permitted to capture such data directly from the premises where they were located. Despite the new power receiving a lot of publicity when it was created,[973] at the time of writing there were no reported instances of inspections having been carried out at domestic premises. Therefore, many of the questions that Article 21 raises, for example who the addressee of an Article 21 decision is to be, have so far remained unanswered in practice.

Meaning of 'other premises', land and means of transport   Article 21 of Regulation 1/2003, **8.417** is headed '*Inspections in other premises*'. It allows for the inspection of 'other premises, land

---

[969]   Art 20(5) of Regulation 1/2003 makes clear that national officials enjoy the powers of Art 20(2) when they accompany the Commission in an inspection under Art 20. Whether the same is true for Commission officials 'assisting' the competition authority in that Member State would appear to depend on the national laws of the relevant Member State. Regulation 1/2003 is silent on this point. It is submitted that, by analogy to the provision of Art 20(5), and by reference to the wording of Art 22(2) and the notion of the '*efffet utile*' of Community law, the Commission officials would indeed enjoy the same powers as national officials. But the extent to which the Commission officials could in fact carry out the same functions and have the same powers as national officials would still depend on the relevant provisions of national law.

[970]   See recital 26 to the Preamble of Regulation 1/2003. Reportedly, the main case on which the Commission relied was *SAS/Maersk* where important cartel evidence was kept at the private homes of employees, in respect of which the Commission could not have obtained in an inspection. (Commission Decision in *SAS/Maersk* [2001] OJ L265/15, para 7). Another case in point is that of *Fine Art Auction Houses*, where the director of Christie's had kept information at his private residence, which was later used in Christie's application for immunity. (Commission Decision of 31.10.2002, available at: <http://europa.eu.int/comm/competition/antitrust/cases/decisions/37784/en.pdf>, summary published in [2005] OJ L200/92). For a narrative history of the cartel, see C Mason, *The Art of the Steal—Inside the Sotheby's-Christie's Auction House Scandal*, GP Putnam's Sons, 2004.

[971]   See also section B(2)(b) on the organisational aspects of cartels.

[972]   The Commission can, during an inspection, request the production of any business records, even if these are located outside the premises of the undertaking (see para 8.356). The problem for the Commission is, however, that it would first have to identify which particular documents it would want to have produced to it, rather than going to the site and checking all available information at the other premises for itself.

[973]   See for instance: P Shishkin, 'European Regulators Spark Controversy with Dawn Raids', *The Wall Street Journal,* 1 March 2002, p A-1.

and means of transport'. As explained, its main envisaged target concerns the homes of executives or other employees, but premises that are not used for business purposes of the undertakings subject to the investigation may also be covered.[974]

8.418 **Applicability of principles of law and fundamental rights** Although the Commission's investigation is ultimately aimed at undertakings and not individuals, fundamental rights apply equally in the case of inspections under Article 21.[975] Some commentators have argued that although a national judicial warrant is needed, it is questionable whether such authorisation is actually compliant with the ECtHR case law.[976] That is because, in spite of the fact that the scrutiny of the national judge is wider than in the case of deciding coercive measures under Article 20, it still does not permit the national judicial authority to make its own assessment of the evidence and can thus only conduct a marginal test of the Commission's inspection decision.

8.419 **'Reasonable suspicion' about information being stored at the premises** The Commission can use this power only in situations where there is a 'reasonable suspicion' that books or other records related to the subject matter of the inspection are being kept on other premises.[977] A general belief that documents may be stored at private premises will not suffice. It is submitted that the principles of proportionality and protection against arbitrary intervention would furthermore require that the information sought has particular relevance to the Commission's ability to prove an infringement.[978] The concrete information that may provide grounds for the 'reasonable suspicion' may come, for example, from an informant or an immunity applicant who has informed the Commission of the likelihood of documents being kept at private premises. The reasonable suspicion may equally arise during an inspection at the undertaking under Article 20, either from information acquired on the premises of the undertaking (for example, documents found in an executive's office which appear to have been sent or received through a private fax), or from oral explanations given by the undertaking, which indicate that documents are located in 'other premises'. In brief, the Commission may consider carrying out inspections on private premises in two circumstances, either: (a) before the Commission has launched any

---

[974] It is not entirely clear what the notion of other premises could mean other than directors' homes. It is believed, for instance, also to refer to other private premises, such as the homes of previous employees. As regards means of transport, it is possible that what the Commission wanted to cover by this provision, for example, was that during an inspection at a private residence to which a decision under Art 21 applies, the car on the driveway might be inspected too. (See CS Kerse and N Khan, *EC Antitrust Procedure* (5th edn, 2005) at para 3-065.)

[975] See paras 8.266ff above as regards the applicability of general principles and fundamental rights to Commission competition investigations, the relevance of Arts 6 and 8 ECHR, and the case law of the ECtHR. Particularly in *PVC II* it was recognised that there is a general principle of Community law that ensures protection against intervention by the public authorities in the private sphere of any person, whether natural or legal. (See Joined Cases C-238/99P, C-244/99P, C-245/99P, C-247/99P, C-250/99P, C-252/99P and C-254/99P *Limburgse Vinyl Maatschappij and others v Commission* (*PVC II*) [2002] ECR I-8357, para 252.)

[976] That view is expressed by Kerse and Khan (CS Kerse and N Khan, *EC Antitrust Procedure* (5th edn, 2005), at para 3-067).

[977] This would also follow from the Charter of Fundamental Rights and Art 8 of the ECHR. (see also G Miersch, in D Dalheimer, C Feddersen, G Miersch, *EU Kartelsverfahrensverordnung* (Verlag CH Beck, 2005), at p 172.)

[978] The principle of proportionality also implies that the Commission could only resort to inspections at private homes when the evidence sought is unlikely to be available at business premises of the undertaking. (Compare Miersch, ibid, at p 172.)

inspections under Article 20, or (b) during an inspection pursuant to Article 20. In both cases the Commission must have obtained a decision and warrant under national law before conducting the inspection.

Only to be used in case of 'serious violations'   Article 21 refers to the books or business   **8.420** records that may be relevant to proving a 'serious violation' of Article 81 or Article 82. What this term is intended to mean is not exactly clear, but the terminology is similar to that in the 1998 Guidelines on Fines[979] which distinguish between 'minor', 'serious' and 'very serious' infringements. As cartel infringements are almost without exception classified as very serious, inspections into private homes for such types of violation are possible, provided the other conditions are met.[980]

Expected frequency of use   The publicity that this new power attracted at the time of its   **8.421** inception is unlikely to be matched by the frequency of its use. Indeed, it is not certain that before having started an investigation the Commission would have obtained the requisite evidence to allow it to resort to Article 21. Information indicating that incriminating evidence is to be found in other premises is more likely to surface during inspections, for example when it becomes clear that particular individuals have used home offices for sending and receiving information. If a judicial authorisation needs to be obtained while inspections at the business premises are taking place, it is not certain that the Commission and national authorities, including the judicial authorities, could complete all the procedural steps to allow a timely, useful intervention at private premises.[981] Nevertheless, the Commission, together with the NCA, may be expected to have carried out the necessary preparatory work to ensure that they can obtain a speedy authorisation if it is expected that an intervention at private premises will become necessary. Alternatively, information detected in an on-the-spot investigation may be treated with the necessary circumspection and as a basis for an (unexpected) intervention at private premises at a later date, in which case the ability to obtain a speedy Commission decision and warrant is less of an issue.

(ii) Legal Framework

A two-part basis required for executing an inspection under Article 21   The legal basis   **8.422** for executing an inspection decision under Article 21 is in two parts. First, a Commission decision of the type required under Article 249 EC is needed.[982] Secondly, before the decision

---

[979] Guidelines on the method of setting fines imposed pursuant to Art 15(2) of Regulation No 17 and Art 65(5) of the ECSC Treaty, [1998] OJ C9/3.

[980] Although the primary use of these inspections will be in hardcore cartel cases, the Commission may have wanted to retain the option to conduct private home searches in cases concerning, for example, abuse of dominance cases under Art 82 EC.

[981] Obtaining a Commission decision and the subsequent necessary authorisation from a judicial authority is likely to take several hours, at the very least. The longer the time that passes between the indications that documents are being kept in other premises and obtaining the necessary authorisation, the greater the likelihood that such documents may be destroyed or concealed in another location.

[982] In accordance with Art 13(1) and (3) of the Commission Rules of Procedure (amended), Commission Decision of 15 November 2005, [2005] OJ L347/83. On 28 April 2004 the Commission adopted a decision with a comprehensive set of empowerments (PV(2004) 1655, SEC(2004) 520/2) for the Competition Commissioner for the application of the Modernisation Regulation No 1/2003 and implementing Commission Regulation No 773/2004. The decision to order inspections under Art 21 is amongst those that can be taken by the Director-General, following the decision of 27 May 2004 of the Commissioner for Competition (PH/2004/769).

can be executed, an authorisation granted by the national judicial authority (usually a court) of the Member State concerned is required.[983]

8.423 Neither Regulation 1/2003 nor Regulation 773/2004 provides a specific procedural framework in relation to inspections in other premises, apart from elaborating on the degree of involvement of the relevant national judicial authorities. Certain of the provisions regarding inspections under Article 20 are declared applicable under Article 21 (see below).[984]

(iii) Procedural Aspects

8.424 **The Commission decision** According to Article 21(1), the Commission decision should state the reasons that have led the Commission to conclude that a reasonable suspicion exists that books or other records related to the business and to the subject matter of the inspection, which may be relevant to prove a serious violation of Article 81 (or Article 82), are being kept on other premises. Taking into account the specific features of Article 21, as well as the standard content of a decision under Article 20(4), a decision to inspect other premises should probably contain the following elements: the subject matter and purpose of the inspection; the involvement of the undertaking concerned in the alleged infringement; an explanation as to the serious nature of the violation; the relationship between the addressee of the decision and the undertaking concerned; the grounds for the suspicion that books or records are kept in the premises; and how those books or records would be relevant to proving a (serious) violation of Article 81 (or Article 82). Also, the decision will need to indicate the possibility of court review.[985]

8.425 **The authorisation by a national judicial authority** According to Article 21(3), in deciding on the judicial authorisation the national court shall verify that the coercive measures envisaged are neither arbitrary nor excessive. The national court shall make its assessment '[. . .]having regard in particular to the seriousness of the suspected infringement, to the importance of the evidence sought, to the involvement of the undertaking concerned and to the reasonable likelihood that business books and records relating to the subject-matter of the inspection [and that may constitute evidence of the infringement][986] are kept in the premises for which the authorisation is requested'.[987] So, the proportionality test to be applied by the national judicial authorities is more extensive than when deciding on coercive measures for business premises inspections. One explanation lies in the fact that the Commission would be invading the privacy of natural persons rather than legal persons.

---

[983] Art 21(3) of Regulation 1/2003.

[984] Furthermore, as explained above, the general principles of law and fundamental rights, including the relevant rights of defence of the undertaking, as well as the other general aspects considered in paras 8.266ff regarding inspections under Art 20, apply equally, *mutatis mutandis*, to inspections under Art 21.

[985] Furthermore, the decision must probably indicate the date on which the inspection is to start (although this would seem difficult to reconcile with the need for flexibility for the Commission in this regard).

[986] Although not specified in Art 20(8), in *Roquette Frères*, the importance of the evidence sought was relevant to determining the proportionality of the investigative action. (Case C-94/00 *Roquette Frères*, n 953 above at para 79 *et seq.*)

[987] The last requirement, about the likelihood of finding evidence on the spot, is not included in Art 20(8) in relation to inspections at business premises. It is submitted that this information would be equally relevant to a decision by a national court under Art 20(8), so that the difference in the proportionality test in the case of business premises or private home inspections may actually be perceived rather than real.

In order to make an assessment as regards the proportionality of the proposed action, the national judicial authority may ask the Commission for detailed explanations.[988] However, as in the case of business premises, it may not call into question the need for the inspection and the Commission is not required to provide it with information from the Commission's files.[989]

Addressee of the decision   Although Article 21 suggests that a decision to inspect is aimed   **8.426** at 'premises' (and not persons), it must refer to an addressee to whom notification can be made.[990] Given the lack of practical examples, it is as yet uncertain who the addressee of a decision under Article 21 will be: is it the owner of the premises, or its occupants, or one identified occupant (eg the employee concerned)? Whichever it is, it appears clear that the decision will need to be addressed to a natural person, and not the legal person/undertaking the target of the Commission's investigation. The most likely standard addressee of an Article 21 decision would be the 'occupant of the premises'.

Notification of the decision and the judicial authorisation   The decision will only take   **8.427** effect upon its notification to the addressee.[991] The national judicial warrant is to be provided at the same time. In order for the decision to be considered as notified, the addressee must be put in a position which enables him/her to take cognisance of it.[992] Difficulties may arise if the addressee is absent and when for example only a spouse, child or another person (such as a cleaner) is at home. In such instances it is not certain when the addressee can be considered to have been put in a position to take cognisance of the decision. It is submitted that the solution (ultimately) available in the case of an inspection at business premises, of dropping the decision into the letterbox, may possibly not be a sufficient means of notification as regards the Commission decision if the addressee is not present.[993] There is also the question of what the national law prescribes in terms of the notification of the judicial authorisation pursuant to which possible coercive measures can be taken.

On-the-spot powers   The officials and other accompanying persons authorised by the   **8.428** Commission to conduct an inspection of other premises have three of the five powers that are available for the inspection of business premises. These are the powers to enter, to examine books or business records, and to take copies of such information.[994] The other two powers

---

[988] That said, there is no requirement, contrary to the provisions for inspections in business premises (see Art 20(8) of Regulation 1/2003), that the national judicial authorities provide information as to the likelihood that an infringement has been committed. Nevertheless, such information may be relevant to the decision of the national judicial authority and it is presumed that upon request such information is to be provided.

[989] Art 21(3) of Regulation 1/2003.

[990] The decision should of course also identify the premises concerned (eg in the case of a private home, the exact address). Note that in this respect the Commission decision may be quite different from a national warrant (which may be used for any coercive measures), which will relate first and foremost to the premises that are to be inspected, rather than to a particular individual.

[991] In conformity with Art 254(3) EC.

[992] See Case 6/72 *Continental Can*, n 831 above. See further para 8.343.

[993] For undertakings, during business hours personnel will normally be available to receive a decision, so that the possibility of the undertaking being aware of the decision is much more certain. Problems relating to notification due to the absence of the addressee are certainly not theoretical (executives may frequently be away on business trips). In this regard, the Commission will need to provide appropriate solutions in applying its new power.

[994] For a description of these on-the-spot powers in relation to business premises see section C(3)(e)(ii)(4).

that are provided in the case of business premises inspections (ie the power to seal premises or records and the power to ask for oral explanations), are not included in Article 21.[995]

8.429 **Assistance by officials from the national authorities**   As mentioned above, pursuant to Article 21(3), the provisions regarding assistance during inspections by the Member States under Article 20(5) (ie active assistance carrying out the same tasks as the inspectors authorised by the Commission) and Article 20(6) (ie assistance in case of opposition) apply equally to inspections of other premises. It is noted, however, that Article 22, which permits the Commission to ask Member States to carry out inspections on its behalf, cannot be used for inspections in other premises.

8.430 **Sanctions for non-compliance, pursuant to national law**   In the event of a refusal to comply with a decision under Article 21, the Commission does not have the power to apply (procedural) sanctions.[996] However, given that inspections under Article 21 are also based on a national warrant, it would appear that coercive measures and other sanctions could be applied by the national authorities under domestic law based on the underlying judicial authorisation.[997]

(iv) Other Aspects

8.431 **Right to legal assistance**   As mentioned above, the individuals concerned, as addressees of an Article 21 decision, enjoy certain fundamental rights that are at least analogous to the rights attributed to undertakings.[998] The right to legal assistance is one such right. Inspectors can be expected to allow a reasonable time for the addressee to obtain such legal assistance, equivalent to what would occur at business premises.[999]

---

[995] The power to seal may have been omitted since inspections in private homes only need to cover a smaller space and the Commission may be presumed to be able to finish inspecting a private residence within a day. The absence of the power to ask for clarifications on facts or documents is perhaps surprising. During an inspection at a private residence it would appear that there may possibly be a greater need for the inspectors to receive clarifications, for instance in order to distinguish business records from private materials. An explanation of the absence of that power may lie in the fact that the individual concerned may not be present when the inspection is carried out and it was considered inappropriate to include a general obligation on anyone present at the premises to answer questions. An alternative explanation may be that inspections at other premises will only take place when the Commission knows with a relatively high degree of certainty what it is looking for (Article 21(3) refers to a pre-established 'reasonable likelihood' of relevant material being present) so there should be less of a need to ask for any clarifications another (obvious) explanation is referred to in para 8.432, ie that none of the Commission's powers apply directly to individuals. Nevertheless, there is an apparent inconsistency between inspections at business premises and those in private premises. For example, when the office of an executive is being inspected as part of an inspection of business premises under the framework of Art 20, the executive could be asked to provide clarifications about facts or documents related to the subject matter of the investigation, whereas if identical questions arise during an inspection of his/her 'home office' under Art 21, the same executive could not be asked for clarifications on the spot. (Of course, in such an instance the Commission can follow up using its formal powers to request information under Art 18 of Regulation 1/2003.)

[996] The penalties under Arts 23 and 24, which apply in the case of an inspection ordered by Art 20(4), do not apply in the case of an inspection ordered by Art 21.

[997] Art 21(4) declares that Art 20(5) and (6) also applies to inspections at other premises.

[998] Note that the Commission has no power to ask for clarifications on the spot.

[999] This right may also depend on provisions of national law given the 'double basis' under which the inspection takes place. As regards the right not to incriminate oneself, that privilege could not be invoked, since first and foremost, under Art 21 an individual may refuse to answer altogether, without sanction. Should the individual nevertheless answer a question, it is submitted that the answer could not incriminate the individual, because under Commission investigations no personal incrimination can follow and the evidence collected in this manner cannot be used by a national authority for the purposes of prosecuting the individual. (On the issue of the protection for individuals under Art 12 of Regulation 1/2003 see C Gauer,

A duty of active co-operation for the addressee?   Is the addressee required actually to   **8.432**
assist the Commission in the search or can he/she assume a completely passive role? It is
submitted that an addressee would not have an obligation of (active) co-operation similar
to that imposed upon an undertaking.[1000] In this respect it is noteworthy that a duty to
respond to questions has not been included amongst the powers the Commission has in the
case of inspections under Article 21 (which would in any case be problematic given that the
Commission procedures in general do not address private individuals.) Indeed, Community
law provides no sanctions for non-cooperation on the individual, and the degree to which
obstructive behaviour can be sanctioned would thus depend entirely on the provisions of
national law that govern the judicial warrant.[1001]

(g) *European and International Co-operation in Cartel Investigations*

In view of the increasingly global nature of trade and transborder effects of international car-   **8.433**
tels, co-operation between jurisdictions in anti-cartel enforcement has become an important
topic. Indeed, trans-jurisdictional infringements in such cases as *Vitamins*[1002] and *Lysine*[1003]
and *Graphite Electrodes*[1004] have aptly demonstrated that cartels frequently operate on a global
basis. Competition authorities have taken a number of steps to increase the level of co-operation
between themselves.[1005] Co-operation can take place on a bi-lateral level based on formal
agreements, or informally, or on a multilateral basis under the umbrella of an international
structure. The most notable forms of co-operation in the field of cartels from the EC's perspective are discussed below and are divided into two sections, dealing first with co-operation
in the European context, and second with co-operation in the wider international arena.

(i) *European Co-operation*

The European Competition Network (ECN)   The EC antitrust modernisation pro-   **8.434**
gramme that culminated in the adoption of Regulation 1/2003 has provided for greater

---

'Due Process in the Face of Divergent National Procedures and Sanctions', paper prepared for the
International Bar Association/EC Commission Conference *Anti-trust reform in Europe: a year in practice*,
Brussels, March 2005. See also B Vesterdorf, 'Legal Professional Privilege and the Privilege against Self-
incrimination in EC Law: Recent Developments and Current Issues' [2005] Fordham International Law
Journal, 1197–1215. Should the Commission discover documents at the private premises that are legally
privileged as regards the undertaking, the Commission would have to treat them in the same way as it would
have done if the documents been found at the premises of undertaking.

[1000]   For a description of that obligation in relation to undertakings, see para 8.308.

[1001]   An interesting question might arise if, for instance, the private residence of the Chief Executive
Officer of an undertaking is inspected and the person obstructs the investigation. Would that allow the
Commission, by analogy with the consequences of obstruction by the same individual when inspecting
his/her business offices, to take that behaviour into account as an aggravating circumstance for the cartel fine
ultimately imposed on the undertaking?

[1002]   Commission Decision [2003] OJ L6/1.

[1003]   Commission Decision [2001] OJ L152/24.

[1004]   Commission Decision [2002] OJ L100/1.

[1005]   See speech by Scott Hammond, US Department of Justice, Antitrust Division: 'Beating cartels at
their own game—Sharing information in the fight against cartels' (November 2003), available on the DOJ
website at <http://www.usdoj.gov.atr/public/speeches/201614.htm>. See also OECD papers: 'Fighting
Hardcore Cartels: Harm, Effective Sanctions and Leniency Programmes' (2002), 'Hardcore Cartels—Recent
Progress and Challenges Ahead' (2003), 'Best Practices for the formal exchange of information between competition authorities in hard core cartel investigations' (2005) and 'Hard Core Cartels—Third Report on the
Implementation of the 1998 Recommendation' (2006).

decentralisation the application of (EC) competition law. As Articles 81 and 82 EC were meant to be applied more intensively by the Member States,[1006] there was a consequent need to provide for increased possibilities for co-operation. Regulation 1/2003 provides certain ground rules for co-operation and the exchange of information between the Commission and the NCAs (National Competition Authorities of the Member States), and amongst the NCAs themselves.[1007] In order to provide for a structure to manage the exchange and use of information, the European Competition Network (ECN) was established, within which the members can assist each other in gathering and exchanging information for use in evidence. More detailed practical rules for the functioning of the Network were laid down in a Notice.[1008] Chapter 2 deals in greater detail with the functioning of the ECN, and section C(2)(e) of this Chapter deals more specifically with the some of the leniency related aspects of co-operation within the ECN. Some (other) relevant aspects regarding cartel investigations are mentioned in this section.

8.435   The ECN is designed to allow consultation, co-operation and, significantly, the exchange of information, in a system of parallel competences between members, with the overall aim of creating and maintaining common competition culture in Europe.[1009] In terms of assistance in investigations, under the various mechanisms of Articles 20–22 of Regulation 1/2003, the Commission can rely on the NCAs, and the NCAs can support each other, in information gathering. The power to exchange and use information in evidence provided for in Article 12 of Regulation 1/2003 is a strong mechanism in enforcement. However, as explained below, the exchange of information is not without procedural safeguards, and these are provided for in the Regulation and in the Network Notice.[1010] These safeguards notably deal with the conflict arising from the possible use of information exchanged for the application of criminal and/or custodial sanctions, as well as serving to protect the position of applicants under the leniency programmes of the Commission and of the Member States.

8.436   Article 12 of Regulation 1/2003 hence establishes far-reaching, but well-defined possibilities for exchanging information. It provides for the NCAs and the Commission to exchange information on any matter of fact or law, even if confidential in nature, but only in so far as it is used for the purpose of the application of Articles 81 or Article 82 of the Treaty and in respect of the subject matter for which it was collected by the transmitting authority. The use of information exchanged is even allowed in (parallel) proceedings under national law, as long as such proceedings do not lead to a 'different outcome'. Article 12(3) provides that the information exchanged may not be used for sanctions on natural persons,

---

[1006]   Art 3(1) of Regulation 1/2003 prescribes that where trade between Member States may be affected, Member States must apply Arts 81 and 82 EC, either separately or in parallel to national law.

[1007]   See notably Chapter IV, Arts 11–16 of Regulation 1/2003.

[1008]   The Commission Notice on co-operation within the Network of Competition Authorities, OJ [2004] C101/03, also referred to as the 'Network Notice'. The Member States and their respective competition authorites have signed a declaration signalling their adherence to the Network Notice. (Available at < http:// ec.europa.eu/comm/competition/antitrust/legislation/network.html >.)

[1009]   For more on the interplay of the various provisions governing the exchange of information and use in evidence see C Gauer, 'Due Process in the Face of Divergent National Procedures and Sanctions', paper prepared for the International Bar Association/EC Commission conference *Anti-trust reform in Europe: a year in practice*, Brussels, March 2005.

[1010]   See n 1008 above.

unless the law of the transmitting authority provides sanctions of a similar kind (eg where at both ends similar sanctions can be imposed, even if these are criminal/custodial), or unless a similar level of protection of the rights of defence has been respected as that provided under the rules of the receiving authority. But even in these last instances, the information may only be exchanged if the the information exchanged will not be used to impose custodial sanctions.[1011]

Special consideration has been given to the position of applicants under the leniency pro-   **8.437**
grammes of the Commission and the NCAs. Within the ECN, it may happen that one NCA commences an investigation on the basis of (confidential) information provided by another NCA. In order to ensure, within the ECN system, adequate protection for appli-cants under leniency programmes, section 2.2.3 of the Network Notice includes a require-ment that applicants must give consent to the transmission of information that they have provided. In the absence of consent, information can only be exchanged if the applicant has already applied for leniency with the requesting authority or if the requesting authority has agreed not to use the information to impose sanctions.[1012]

Co-operation with the EFTA Surveillance Authority (ESA)   Since this co-operation   **8.438**
takes place within the framework of the *sui generis* relationship between the Community and the European Free Trade Association (EFTA), the particularly close collaboration with ESA under the EEA Agreement is not classified here as 'international co-operation', in con-trast to the relationships with other jurisdictions described in the following sections.[1013] Co-operation between the EU and the EFTA States (through the EFTA Surveillance Authority—ESA) is closer than with other (non-EU) jurisdictions in terms of the possibil-ities that exist, for instance, for co-operation on enforcement and the exchange of informa-tion. In general, in cases which the Commission is investigating, the EEA Agreement allows information to be collected by the ESA and transferred to the Commission for use in its investigations.[1014] This is comparable to what the Commission can request an EU Member State to do under Article 22 of Regulation 1/2003.

(ii) International Co-operation, Multilateral and Bilateral[1015]

Co-operation on cartel issues takes place in a number of multilateral international fora.   **8.439**
It is to be noted that none of these fora discuss particular legislative proposals, but they do provide an arena for discussion of issues of joint interest with the aim of achieving a common understanding and a soft form of harmonisation of laws and practices. Bilaterally, the Commission has treaties with the USA, Canada and Japan.[1016] These agreements do include

---

[1011]   This is relevant to regimes such as that of the UK, where criminal (custodial) sanctions can be imposed on individuals for entering into cartel arrangements (UK Enterprise Act 2002, s 188).

[1012]   Commission Notice on Co-operation within the Network of Competition Authorities [2004] OJ C101/03, recitals 40 and 41. For more detail about the safeguards for leniency applicants, see section C(2)(e) above.

[1013]   See section C(1) of this chapter, as regards the possibilities for co-operation pre-investigation and in evidence gathering.

[1014]   See Protocol 23 to the Agreement on the European Economic Area (concerning the co-operation between the surveillance authorities).

[1015]   For a general discussion on international co-operation in cartel cases see C Canenbley and M Rosenthal, 'Co-operation Between Anti-trust Authorities In- and Outside the EU: What Does it Mean for Corporations?', Part 1 [2005] ECLR, Vol 26, Issue 2; Part 2 [2005] ECLR, Vol. 26, Issue 3.

[1016]   For reference to the agreements see n 1022 below.

provisions for closer co-operation, although, as will be explained, they are of lesser significance in cartel cases as a result of the fact that there is no provision for assistance in (simultaneous) investigations and because of the limits to the exchange of case-related information. In general, international co-operation in cartel investigations is seen as being 'sub-optimal' and there is a recognised need amongst competition agencies that they need to 'strengthen their hand faced with cartellists whose ability to exchange information is unhindered'.[1017]

1. Multilateral co-operation

8.440 *OECD* The Organisation for Economic Co-operation and Development (OECD) is a group of some 30 countries which are committed to democratic government and the market economy. Its Competition Committee has been particularly active in this field since the introduction of its anti-cartel programme initiated by the 1998 *Recommendation Concerning Effective Action against Hard-core Cartels*. The reports issued about cartels are particularly instructive.[1018]

8.441 *International Competition Network (ICN)* The International Competition Network (ICN) is an informal group of a significant number of competition agencies, including those from developing nations. It was established in 2001 and has quickly become a leading forum for co-operation on competition matters.

8.442 The majority of the ICN's work is performed by working groups which specialise in defined issues. A cartels working group was set up in 2004 and is divided into two subgroups: the first deals with matters of principle relating to cartels and the second deals with cartel enforcement issues. Both subgroups produce reports on relevant cartel issues although publication, particularly in the case of subgroup 2, is dependent on the sensitivity of the information collected. As at mid 2006, several publications had been issued, including publications on the definition of hardcore cartel conduct, effective institutions and effective penalties, as well as on international co-operation in cartel investigations and digital evidence gathering.[1019]

8.443 One key component is the International Cartel Workshop, which annually brings together cartel enforcers from around the globe to discuss cartel issues and exchange views. The Cartel Workshop was brought under the umbrella of the ICN in 2004 (workshop in Sydney), prior to which it was organised on a more informal basis.[1020]

[1017] ICN Report (International Competition Network), *Co-operation between Competition Agencies in Cartel Investigations*, Report to the ICN Annual Conference, Cape Town, 2006, available at <http://www.internationalcompetitionnetwork.org>. The report divides the means for international co-operation in cartel cases into six parts: (1) informal co-operation, (2) Co-operation based on waivers, (3) Co-operation based on national law provisions, (4) Co-operation based on non-competition related agreements and instruments, (5) Co-operation base on competition-specific agreements and (6) Regional co-operation instruments (such as the ECN).

[1018] Recent papers include 'Fighting Hardcore Cartels: Harm, Effective Sanctions and Leniency Programmes' (2002), 'Hardcore Cartels—Recent Progress and Challenges Ahead' (2003), 'Best Practices for the formal exchange of information between competition authorities in hard core cartel investigations' (2005) and 'Hard Core Cartels—Third Report on the Implementation of the 1998 Recommendation' (2006). OECD Reports can be accessed at <http://www.oecd.org>.

[1019] The reports can be accessed at <http://www.internationalcompetitionnetwork.org>.

[1020] In 2005, the ICN Cartel Workshop took place in Seoul. The ICN Cartel Workshop for 2006 was hosted by the Dutch Competition Authority (The Hague).

WTO   Discussions on competition were introduced into the World Trade Organisation   **8.444**
(WTO) in 1996. In the Doha Round of trade negotiations that started in November 2001,
conclusions were reached about the adoption of a WTO competition agreement, covering
at least a ban on hardcore cartels and the respect of core principles (non-discrimination,
transparency and procedural fairness). The subject proved controversial, notably for the
USA. In July 2004, it was decided to suspend any talks within the Doha Round on a
possible competition agreement.

UNCTAD   Within the framework of the United Nations Conference on Trade and   **8.445**
Development (UNCTAD), a set of competition principles was agreed upon in 1980 (the
'UNCTAD set'). A model law has been created and is periodically updated, the purpose of
which is to provide guidance for countries wishing to introduce competition laws.
UNCTAD is also actively involved in technical assistance.[1021]

2. Bilateral co-operation

In addition to the above multilateral arrangements, practical international co-operation is   **8.446**
undertaken in the form of bilateral arrangements. The EU has notably concluded co-operation
agreements with the US, Canada and Japan. The most intensive co-operation is between
the EU and the US, and is based on the 1991 EC-US Agreement.[1022]

These bilateral arrangements cover such matters as notification of activities relevant to the other   **8.447**
agency, exchange of information (subject to confidentiality requirements), co-ordination of
enforcement activities, and mutual assistance. Even though the agreements provide for
such mechanisms, in cartel cases the most significant co-operation takes place in the planning and co-ordination of enforcement actions, particularly in respect of the timing of
inspections and other investigative steps.[1023] Indeed, the co-ordination of investigations
has become a matter of routine. Ensuring that investigative actions take place simultaneously will help to create optimal chances for each agency of obtaining evidence in a given
case. Indeed, an independently planned action by one authority may lead to the concealment of evidence in another jurisdiction.

So far the actual co-operation at international level that the European Commission is   **8.448**
involved in does not extend beyond the co-ordination of investigations and into the actual

---

[1021]   See the Competition & Consumer policies section of the UNCTAD web site (<http://r0.unctad.org/
en/subsites/cpolicy/>) for materials, including the UN Set of Multilaterally Agreed Equitable Principles and
Rules for the Control of Restrictive Business Practices (the 'UNCTAD set') and the Model Law on Competition
(UNCTAD Series on Issues in Competition Law and Policy) 2004.

[1022]   The agreement with the US is the 1991 'Agreement between the Government of the United States of
America and the Commission of the European Communities regarding the application of their competition
laws' (Endorsed by the Council in 1995, see [1995] OJ L95/47 and 50). This was supplemented by the 1998
'Agreement between the European Communities and the Government of the United States of America on the
Application of Positive Comity Principles in the enforcement of their competition laws' ([1998] OJ L173/21).
Cooperation with Canada and Japan is based on the 'Agreement between the European Communities and
the Government of Canada regarding the application of their competition laws' ([1999] OJ L175/50), and the
Council Decision of 16 June 2003 concluding the Agreement between the European Community and
the Government of Japan concerning co-operation on anti-competitive activities ([2003] OJ L183/12).

[1023]   Examples of such co-ordinated rates are: *Heat Stabilisers and Impact Modifiers* (press release of
14 February 2003, MEMO/03/33), *Copper Concentrate* (press release of 14 May 2003, MEMO/03/107, and
Deep Sea Chemical Shipping (press release of 19 March 2003, MEMO/03/38).

exchange of evidence, contrary to the common belief.[1024] This is because in accordance with the Commission's rules on professional secrecy (contained in Article 287 EC,[1025] the Commission's Staff Regulations,[1026] and Article 28 of Regulation 1/2003) information that has been gathered in the framework of (competition) investigations cannot be exchanged by the Commission[1027] with other authorities (even with those with whom the EU has a bilateral agreement). As a result, fuller co-operation during and after investigations is restricted.[1028] Stringent rules also exist, for instance, in the US, where Rule 6(e) of the Federal Rules of Criminal Procedure prevents staff of the Department of Justice from disclosing information that has come before the Grand Jury, such as witness testimony. The exchange of actual cartel evidence between the Commission and the US, as well as other agencies, however desirable for furthering their respective investigations, will require new 'second generation' agreements.[1029] If new rules permitting exchange of evidence are adopted in future, they are likely to contribute significantly to tightening the net around cartel participants and hence to increasing deterrence against international cartels.

[1024] This section does not consider the use of instruments that go outside agreements covering the application of competition rules. It is noted, however, that national jurisdictions including EU Member States have Mutual Legal Assistance Treaties (MLATs) with other countries, or may avail themselves of the system of 'letters rogatory' between judicial authorities, that may allow for the collection and exchange of information. A description of these two instruments can be found in the ICN Report (International Competition Network), *Co-operation between Competition Agencies in Cartel Investigations*, at pp 15-17. (The report can be accessed at <http://www.internationalcompetitionnetwork.org>.) Reportedly, the US has resorted to the use of MLATs in order to obtain evidence located in EU Member States and elsewhere. See JM Joshua, PD Camesasca—'An antitrust NATO—the DOJ's "foreign policy" in the war against international cartels', Global Competition Review (can be found at <http://www.globalcompetitionreview.com>). For MLATS and their use by the US DoJ in antitrust cases see also Scott D Hammond, Deputy Assistant Attorney General for Criminal Enforcement, Antitrust Division US Department Of Justice, 'Charting New Waters In International Cartel Prosecutions', presented at the *Ninth Annual Transnational Crime Conference*, International Bar Association, Madrid, 16 June 2006.

[1025] Art 287 EC: The members of the institutions of the Community, the members of committees, and the officials and other servants of the Community shall be required, even after their duties have ceased, *not to disclose information* of the kind covered by the obligation of *professional secrecy, in particular information about undertakings, their business relations* or their cost components [emphasis added].

[1026] Staff Regulations, Art 17:

1. An official shall exercise the *greatest discretion* with regard to *all facts and information* coming to his knowledge in the course of or in connection with the performance of his duties; he shall *not in any manner whatsoever disclose to any unauthorised person any document or information not already made public*. He shall continue to be bound by this obligation after leaving the service.

2. An official shall not, whether alone or together with others, publish or cause to be published without the permission of the appointing authority, any matter dealing with the work of the Communities. Permission shall be refused only where the proposed publication is liable to prejudice the interests of the Communities. [emphasis added.]

For the notion of professional secrecy and its application in competition procedures see Case T-198/03 *Bank Austria Creditanstalt AG v Commission*, judgment of 30 May 2006, not yet reported.

[1027] The exchange of interpretative letters with the Government of the United States of America contained in the Corrigendum to Decision 95/145/EC, ECSC of the Council and the Commission of 10 April 1995 concerning the conclusion of the Agreement between the European Communities and the Government of the United States of America regarding the application of their competition laws ([1995] OJ L95) makes clear that information gathered by the Commission in exercising its investigation powers can not be the subject of an exchange of information. ([1995] OJ L 132).

[1028] See Rule 6(e) of the US Federal Rules of Criminal Procedure (Title 18A USC).

[1029] Neelie Kroes, *The First Hundred Days*, Speech at the 40th Anniversary of the Studienvereinigung Kartellrecht 1965–2005, International Forum on European Competition Law, Brussels, 7 April 2005.

D. The Finding of Infringement

(1) The Procedure Leading to a Final Decision

This section describes the procedure that the Commission follows between the end of the **8.449** fact-finding stage and the making of the final decision, in which the cartel behaviour is prohibited and a fine is (usually) imposed. The description below is a summary of the procedures aimed at highlighting their most important aspects, in particular for cartel cases.[1] It is crucial that the Commission follows all the relevant procedures, especially in relation to the respect of the rights of defence, because a procedural failure may affect the validity of the final decision and thus lead to a reduction or annulment of the fine by the Courts, even if the Commission has produced convincing evidence of an infringement.[2]

General outline of the procedure followed between the fact-finding stage and the final **8.450** **decision**   In coming to a final decision, the Commission's respect of the rights of defence is of central procedural importance. Before the Commission can come to a final decision in a cartel case it must apply the *audi alteram partem* rule (the right to be heard) to enable the parties concerned to express their views on the evidence against them and the conclusions that the Commission seeks to draw from it.[3] The Commission issues a Statement of Objections (SO) in which it sets out the relevant evidence and formulates in legal terms its objections concerning the practices that it has identified as being contrary to Article 81 EC. The parties can defend themselves by obtaining access to the Commission's file and by submitting a written answer to the Commission. They can also request an oral hearing. When drafting the final decision, the Commission must then take into account the arguments presented by the parties, whether in writing or orally, although it is not obliged to reply to each and every argument put forward by the defendant(s) in reply to the SO or at the oral hearing. The Commission may halt the investigation at any stage. Formal proceedings are normally only opened at an advanced stage of investigation, ie when the Commission has completed the fact-finding stage and has drafted its objections. Where proceedings have been formally opened, they will be closed by a decision and the parties informed accordingly.[4] It should

---

[1] For a more detailed overview of the competition procedures before the European Commission see, amongst other literature, CS Kerse and N Khan, *EC Antitrust Procedure* (5th edn, 2005); L Ortiz Blanco, *EC Competition Procedure* (2nd edn, 2006); R Whish, *Competition Law* (5th edn, 2003); Mestmäcker/Schweitzer, *Europäisches Wettbewerbsrecht* (2nd edn, 2004) Van Bael and Bellis, *Competition Law of the European Community* (4th edn, 2005). See also K Lenaerts and J Maselis, 'Procedural Rights and Issues in the Enforcement of Arts 81 and 82 of the EC Treaty' [2001] Fordham International Law Journal 1615–1654.

[2] Reference to 'The European Courts' or 'the Courts' indicates both the Court of First Instance (CFI) and the Court of Justice (ECJ).

[3] See Art 27(1) of Regulation 1/2003 and Art 11(2) of Regulation 773/2004. Joined Cases C-238/99 P etc *Limburgse Vinyl Maatschappij NV (LVM) and others v Commission* [2002] ECR I-8375, paras 316 and 321.

[4] In exceptional cases the Commission may reach an outcome other than a formal decision with fines. For example, in proceedings relating to Euro currency conversion the Commission concluded that measures taken by the undertakings concerned were sufficient for it to halt the proceedings against those undertakings (IP 01/1159—'Commission action results in reduced conversion charges for Euro-zone conversion'). That solution did not apply to all the parties that had received an SO, and the proceedings against certain German banks were continued (Commission Decision of 11 December 2001 in Case 37.919 (ex 37.391)—*Bank charges for currency exchange within the Euro zone* [2003] OJ L15/1).

be noted that, although the final decision takes the form of a single document, in legal terms that document contains individual decisions against each addressee.[5]

8.451 The various steps involved in coming to a final decision, including aspects such as access to the file and the involvement of the Hearing Officer, are discussed in greater detail below. It must be underlined that the procedures are only described in abridged form, highlighting aspects relevant to cartels.

(a) The Statement of Objections

8.452 In cases where the Commission comes to the preliminary conclusion that an infringement has occurred, following the fact-finding phase described in section C of this chapter, it will formulate its objections. The Statement of Objections (SO) is the document in which the Commission sets out in detail those provisional conclusions concerning the existence of an infringement. In cartel cases, an SO usually consists of between 100 and 200 pages, depending on the number of undertakings that are involved in a case, but it may be shorter or longer than that. The sending of an SO is a pre-condition of the Commission adopting a final decision.[6] It provides the undertakings involved with an opportunity to exercise their rights of defence, notably the right to be heard. The Commission usually issues a single document to the various addressees, although separate versions may be prepared if business secrets or other confidential information relating to one or more parties are included in the SO.[7] As mentioned, although the issue of the SO usually marks the formal opening of proceedings, under Regulation 1/2003 the Commission may open proceedings independently of and prior to (but no later than) the sending of the SO.[8] The issuing of the SO and the opening of proceedings are not challengeable acts under Article 230 EC.[9] The language in which the SO is issued is the language of the country where the relevant addressee is formally based (if it is within the European Union), although the right to receive the SO in its 'native' language can be waived by the addressee.[10] Undertakings located outside the European Union will normally receive the SO in the English language.

---

[5] Joined Cases C-238/99 P etc *Limburgse Vinyl Maatschappij NV (LVM) and others v Commission* [2002] ECR I-8375, para 100.

[6] Joined Cases T-45/98 and 47/98 *Krupp Thyssen Stainless GmbH and Acciai Speciali Terni SpA v Commission* [2001] ECR II-3757, para 67, and Joined Cases C-204/00 etc *Aalborg Portland and others v Commission* [2004] ECR I-123, para 60 and the case law cited therein.

[7] Under certain circumstances third parties may also receive a (non-confidential) version of the complaint. See, amongst others, Art 13 of Regulation 773/2004, which deals with the hearing of 'other persons'. See also generally the Commission Notice on the Handling of Complaints by the Commission under Arts 81 and 82 EC ([2002] OJ C101/65) and specifically point 65 of that Notice. For a further discussion of the rights of third parties in competition proceedings, see L Ortiz Blanco, *EC Competition Procedure* (2nd edn, 2006), sections 10.03 and 10.72 *et seq*. The rights of third parties and the opportunity to receive a copy of the SO (as applicable under the regime of Regulation 17) were also dealt with in Joined Cases T-213/01 and T-214/01 *Österreichische Postsparkasse AG and Bank für Arbeit und Wirtschaft AG v Commission*, judgment of 7 June 2006, not yet reported.

[8] See Art 11(6) of Regulation 1/2003 and Art 2(1) of Regulation 773/2004. The opening of proceedings has the effect of relieving the Member States of their competence to apply Art 81 EC or 82 EC to the case.

[9] Like the closing of proceedings, the opening of proceedings is an internal act of the Commission.

[10] Council Regulation 1 of 25 April 1958 [1952–58] OJ Spec edn 59. In practice, undertakings often request or agree to receive the SO in the English language, for example because the *lingua franca* of the group is English.

Objections must be clearly formulated   The conduct to which objection is taken must be **8.453** sufficiently identifiable to allow a proper defence.[11] The Commission may include various infringements in a single SO (and in its final decision) as long as the above requirement has been met.[12] It must disclose the information on which it relies in respect of each addressee.[13] It must also explain the way in which it interprets the information.[14] The format of SOs issued by the Commission may vary but they are usually divided into four main parts: (a) an introduction describing the structure of the industry and its players, (b) an account of the facts as understood by the Commission (ie a description of what has occurred), (c) the legal implications of those facts (ie how Article 81 EC applies) and (d) the reasoning showing which undertakings and legal entities the Commission intends to hold liable.

The Commission will also state its intention to impose fines[15] in the SO, as this is a pre- **8.454** condition for the actual levying of fines in the final decision.[16] However, the Commission is not required to specify in detail the criteria it intends to take into account when determining

---

[11] The SO '[m]ust be couched in terms that, albeit succinct, are sufficiently clear to enable the parties concerned properly to identify the conduct complained of by the Commission' (Case T-15/02 *BASF AG v Commission* [2006] ECR II-497, para 45). See also Joined Cases C-89/85 etc *Ahlström Osakeyhtiö and others v Commission* [1993] ECR I-1307, at para 42, and Case T-352/94 *Mo och Domsjö v Commission* [1998] ECR II-1989, at para 63, upheld on appeal, Case C-283/98 P *Mo och Domsjö v Commission* [2000] ECR I-9855.

[12] Joined Cases C-204/00 etc *Aalborg Portland and others v Commission* [2004] ECR I-123, paras 60 and 67.

[13] On the requirements of an SO in terms of reasoning, see Case T-330/01 *Akzo Nobel NV v Commission*, judgment of 17 September 2006, not yet reported, at para 87 and the case law cited therein. (The SO must '. . . . contain the essential findings against that undertaking, such as the acts complained of, their classification and the eveidence on which the Commission relies, in order to enable that undertaking to put forward its arguments effectively during the administrative procedure. . .'.)

[14] Case C-62/86 Akzo *Chemie BV v Commission* [1991] ECR I-3359, at para 29: '[t]he statement of objections must specify clearly the facts upon which the Commission relies and its classification of those facts.'

[15] This involves specifying how the undertaking has allegedly infringed the competition rules, the gravity and the duration of the offence, the fines the Commission intends to impose and the (general) grounds on which those fines will be based. See also Case T-15/02 *BASF AG v Commission* [2006] ECR II-497, at para 48: 'With regard to exercise of the rights of the defence in respect of the imposition of fines, it is settled case-law that, provided the Commission indicates expressly in the statement of objections that it will consider whether it is appropriate to impose fines on the undertakings concerned and sets out the principal elements of fact and of law that may give rise to a fine, such as the gravity and the duration of the alleged infringement and the fact that it has been committed "intentionally or negligently", it fulfils its obligation to respect the undertakings' right to be heard. In doing so, it provides them with the necessary elements to defend themselves not only against a finding of infringement but also against the fact of being fined (Joined Cases 100/80 to 103/80 *Musique Diffusion Française and others v Commission* [1983] ECR 1825, para 21, and judgment of the Court of First Instance in Case T-16/99 *Lögstör Rör v Commission* [2002] ECR II-1633, para 193, upheld on appeal by judgment of the Court of Justice in Joined Cases C-189/02 P, etc *Dansk Rørindustri and others v Commission* [2005] ECR I-5425, in particular para 428)'.

[16] See Joined Cases T-25/95 etc *Cimenteries CBR SA and others v Commission* [2000] ECR II-491, para 480: 'The Commission is not entitled to impose a fine on an undertaking or an association of undertakings without its having previously informed the party concerned, during the administrative procedure, that it intended to do so. The SO must make it possible for the undertaking or association of undertakings to defend itself not only against a finding of an infringement but also against the imposition of a fine.', and para 484: 'An SO must provide the person to whom it is addressed with details of the deliberate or negligent nature of the infringement he is alleged to have committed and of the gravity and duration of that infringement relevant to determining the amount of the fine, so that he can foresee that a fine may be imposed on him.' See also Case T-15/02 *BASF AG v Commission* [2006] ECR II-497, para 48 and the case law cited therein.

the fines (although it is not barred from doing so),[17] nor is the Commission required to indicate the level of the fine that may be imposed.[18]

8.455 **The Statement of Objections represents the provisional position of the Commission**
The SO cannot be challenged before the Court as it is only an intermediate procedural step towards a final decision.[19] Indeed, the Commission may withdraw objections or change the SO. The Commission should issue a supplementary SO if it wishes to add objections.[20] If it seeks merely to rely on new facts in support of existing objections an opportunity must be provided to comment on these.[21] No matter what form the Commission chooses to use to inform the undertakings of additional objections or (new) facts which it intends to rely on, the undertakings should be given an opportunity to comment on the allegations and the main factual elements that underlie them.[22]

8.456 **Time limit for replies to the SO**   The cover letter that accompanies the SO will set a time limit within which an undertaking may reply.[23] The minimum period for responding to the SO is four weeks,[24] but in cartel cases, which are normally complex multi-party investigations with lengthy SOs, it is normally extended to two months.[25] Any (further) extension of a time limit for the replies is the responsibility of the Hearing Officer.[26]

---

17 For instance, the Commission does not have to mention in the SO that it intends to hold recidivism against an undertaking as an aggravating circumstance (Case T-38/02 *Danone v Commission* [2005] ECR II-497, para 56).

18 Case T-31/99 *ABB Asea Brown Boveri Ltd v Commission* [2002] ECR-II 1881, para 85; Case T-23/99 *LR AF 1998 A/S v Commission* [2002] ECR II-1705, para 206; Joined Cases C-189/02 P, etc *Dansk Rørindustri A/S and others v Commission (Pre-Insulated Pipes)* [2005] ECR I-5425 para 428 and the case law cited therein.

19 Case 60/81 *International Business Machines Corporation (IBM) v Commission* [1981] ECR 2639, paras 19–21.

20 Art 27(1) of Regulation 1/2003 and Art 11(2) of Regulation 773/2004.

21 Joined Cases T-236/01 etc *Tokai Carbon and others v Commission* [2004] ECR II-1181, para 47 and the case law cited therein. ('According to settled case-law, the statement of objections must allow those concerned to have effective knowledge of the conduct in respect of which they are accused by the Commission. That requirement is met when the final decision does not find that the undertakings have committed infringements different from those referred to in the Statement of Objections and establishes only facts on which the persons concerned have had the opportunity to explain themselves'). See furthermore Case T-15/02 *BASF AG v Commission* [2006] ECR II-497, para 47. When merely wishing to rely on certain new facts in support of existing objections, the Commission has issued a so-called 'statement of facts' with a reasonable deadline within which to reply.

22 Case T-23/99 *LR AF 1998 A/S v Commission* [2002] ECR II-1705, at para 190: 'However, there is no provision which prevents the Commission from sending to the parties after the statement of objections fresh documents which it considers support its argument, subject to giving the undertakings the necessary time to submit their views on the subject (Case 107/82 *AEG v Commission* [1983] ECR 3151, para 29)'. See also Case T-15/02 *BASF AG v Commission* [2006] ECR II-497, paras 46–48 and the case law cited therein.

23 Art 10(2) of Regulation 773/2004.

24 Art 17(2) of Regulation 773/2004.

25 According to Art 17(1) of Regulation 773/2004, when the Commission sets the time limit it should take into account the time required to respond and the urgency of the case. In more complex cases, the time limit can be two weeks longer, with additional time being added in the event that the relevant period includes Christmas, Easter or the month of August (see XXIIIrd Report on Competition Policy (1993), point 207). An extension of the deadline for the reply is decided by the Hearing Officer (Art 10 of the Terms of Reference of the Hearing Officers, Commission Decision 2001/462/EC (OJ L162, 19.6.2001, p 21), hereinafter referred to as the 'Terms of Reference of the Hearing Officers').

26 Art 10 of the Terms of Reference of the Hearing Officers.

The undertaking can make written representations on the basis of the SO and access to the Commission's file, although there is no obligation on parties to respond. In their response, the parties may provide relevant documents which support their arguments.[27] The cover letter will also offer the parties the opportunity to request an oral hearing, which will take place under the supervision of the Hearing Officer.[28] The parties will not have access to each other's replies to the SO,[29] although (through their presence at the oral hearing) they may be exposed to the main arguments that other addressees put forward and thus have an opportunity to comment on them.

(b) Access to the File

When an SO has been issued, the Commission gives the parties access to the information **8.457** gathered during the fact-finding phase, in order to allow them to exercise their rights of defence. This is known as 'access to the file'. Access to the file is provided in respect of the principle of 'equality of arms', expressed by the Court in *Soda Ash*.[30] The Commission must reveal to the parties not only the material which it is using to establish the infringement, but also all other (accessible) information that is in the Commission file.[31] Indeed, the

---

27 Art 10(3) of Regulation 773/2004.

28 See Arts 12 and 14 of Regulation 773/2004 and Art 4 of the Terms of Reference of the Hearing Officers.

29 On the issue of the right to access to (parts of) the answers of other parties to the SO, see Case T-43/02 *Jungbunzlauer AG v Commission*, judgment of 27 September 2006, not yet reported, at paras 342 *et seq* and the case law mentioned there. This issue was also under appeal, at the time of writing, in the appeal lodged by the undertaking *Knauf* (T-52/03) against the prohibition decision in *Plasterboard* [2005] OJ L1166/8. As regards access to any information not contained in the investigative file, including materials submitted in reply to the SO, a clear distinction is made in this regard between incriminating information that is used by the Commission in an incriminating fashion, which must be submitted to the undertaking for comment in any event, and exculpatory material, which only has to be provided if its availability to the undertaking could affect the course and the outcome of the proceedings against that undertaking (and in any appeal it is for the undertaking to demonstrate this). But the validity of the Commission's decision—supposing the above principles have been violated—will only be affected if the Commission's conclusions could not be justified in the absence of the (incriminating) evidence or if the arguments that the undertaking might have presented on the basis of any (exculpatory) materials would have affected the decision. In *Jungbunzlauer*, the CFI concluded that—after finding that information was indeed withheld from the applicant—even if the incriminating and exculpatory information had been supplied to the undertaking, it would not have affected the conclusions reached by the Commission.

30 See Case T-30/91 *Solvay SA v Commission* [1995] ECR II-1775 (especially at para 83). See also Case T-36/91 *ICI v Commission* [1995] ECR-II 1847 (especially at paras 93, 111 and 116); Case T-37/91 *ICI v Commission* [1995] ECR II-1847, para 64. Case T-7/89 SA *Hercules Chemicals NNV v Commission* [1991] ECR II-1711, para 54. Joined Cases C-204/00 etc *Aalborg Portland and others v Commission* [2004] ECR I-123, para 68. See also paras 1 and 7 of the Commission Notice of 13 December 2005 on the rules for access to the Commission file in cases pursuant to Arts 81 and 82 of the EC Treaty, Arts 53, 54 and 57 of the EEA Agreement and Council Regulation (EC) No 139/2004 ([2005] OJ C235/7, hereinafter referred to as the 'Notice on Access to the File' or the 'Access to File Notice'). The right of access to the file is also enshrined in Art 41(2)(b) of the EU Charter of Fundamental Rights ([2002] OJ C364/1).

31 Art 27(1) of Regulation 1/2003 and Art 11(2) of Regulation 773/2004. See notably Joined Cases C-204/00 etc *Aalborg Portland and others v Commission* [2004] ECR I-123, at para 66: 'Equally, respect for the rights of the defence requires that the undertaking concerned must have been afforded the opportunity, during the administrative procedure, to make known its views on the truth and relevance of the facts and circumstances alleged and on the documents used by the Commission to support its claim that there has been an infringement of the Treaty (see Joined Cases 100/80 to 103/80 *Musique Diffusion française and others v Commission* [1983] ECR 1825, para 10, and Case C-310/93 P *BPB Industries and British Gypsum v Commission* [1995] ECR I-865, para 21)'. See also Case T-38/02 *Danone v Commission* [2005] ECR II-4407, paras 34 and 65, citing in para 34 Joined Cases T-191/98 etc *Atlantic Container Line AB and others v Commission* [2003] ECR II-3275.

parties must be able to examine all the documents and assess whether or not they are relevant to their defence, and may use exculpatory information included in those files.[32] The preparation for access to the file may be a formidable task for the Commission since case files in cartel cases normally contain thousands of documents.[33]

8.458 The right of access to the file and the procedure that surrounds it have been set out in a Commission notice (the 'Access to File Notice').[34] This notice describes what constitutes the 'Commission file'[35] and then distinguishes between 'accessible' and 'non-accessible' documents.[36] All information obtained, produced and assembled in the investigation[37] is in principle accessible, save for internal documents, business secrets and other confidential information.[38] Internal documents and correspondence with public authorities are not made accessible[39] as they cannot serve either as incriminating evidence or as exculpatory material for the defence. Access to the Commission's file is given after the Statement of Objections has been sent and is normally available only once.[40] It is now common for the entire accessible file to be put on CD ROM, DVD or comparable electronic medium, and to be sent to the undertakings at the same time as the SO, although it is for the Commission to choose the basis on which it provides access.[41] Regarding corporate statements made to the Commission under its Leniency Notice, the Commission has adopted a procedure whereby access to the information is given on the Commission premises, but no mechanical copies of the information (written statements, transcripts and/or recordings) are allowed to be made.[42] The Notice on Access to the File also establishes a principle that the information that is made accessible can only be used within the framework of the application of

---

[32] The principle that has followed from *Soda Ash* is that it is not for the Commission to decide which elements in the file are relevant to the rights of the defence. Case T-30/91 *Solvay SA v Commission* [1995] ECR II-1775, at para 81.

[33] The administrative burden cannot be used by the Commission to limit the right of access. See Case T-36/91 *ICI Chemicals Industry v Commission* [1995] ECR II-1847, at para 112, where the Court stated that: '... respect of the rights of defence should not be allowed to conflict with technical and legal difficulties which an effective administration must overcome'. It is true, however, that the Commission's task is made more burdensome because it has to ensure the protection of business secrets and other confidential information even in respect of the (large) part of its files which have no incriminating or exculpatory value.

[34] Notice on Access to the File, n 30 above. Arts 15 and 16 of Regulation 773/2004 also include certain ground rules on the access to the file.

[35] Point 8 of the Notice on Access to the File.

[36] 'Documents' is defined in n 12 of the Notice on Access to the File as including 'all forms of information support, irrespective of the storage medium'.

[37] Information that has been gathered and that has no 'objective link' with the investigation may be excluded from the file and may be sent back (see point 9 of the Notice on Access to the File).

[38] Point 10 of the Notice on Access to the File.

[39] Points 12 and 13 of the Notice on Access to the File.

[40] Point 27 of the Notice on Access to the File. However, for the Commission to rely on new information as incriminating evidence it must provide access to that information and allow the party(ies) concerned time to comment.

[41] Access to information may be provided at the Commission premises, cf point 44 of the Notice on Access to the File.

[42] The procedure has been set out in detail in section IV of the 2006 Commission Notice on Immunity from Fines and Reductions of Fines in Cartel Cases ([2006] OJ C298/17) and is applicable to all corporate statements, even if made for cases that fall under the 2002 Leniency Notice. (See for a description of that procedure, paras 8.160–8.162).

Community competition rules (ie Articles 81 and 82 EC). This is intended to prevent the disclosure in other (civil) proceedings, notably in the US, of information contained in applications in cartel cases under the Leniency Notice.[43] If undertakings consider that they need further access to particular documents which have not been made accessible or have only been made partially accessible, they can make a request to the competent directorate or unit of DG Competition[44] and if necessary turn to the Hearing Officer.[45] One should note that undertakings which have not raised a procedural claim in relation to access to the file during the administrative procedure may be estopped from doing so before the Courts.[46] If a request for further access is denied by the case team, an undertaking can petition the Hearing Officer.[47]

Protection of business secrets and other confidential information[48] Information **8.459**
gathered by the Commission in its investigations is afforded protection under the EC Treaty,[49] Regulation 1/2003[50] and Regulation 773/204.[51] These strict and wide rules of professional secrecy are 'mitigated' by the requirements concerning access to the file.[52] Regulation 773/2004[53] and the Access to File Notice contain procedural provisions on how claims for confidential treatment are handled.[54] Although in principle the Commission

---

[43] See Arts 15(4) and 8(2) of Regulation 773/2004 and point 48 of the Notice on Access to File. No sanction is applicable although point 48 of the Notice on Access to the File mentions that any violation by outside counsel may lead to a complaint to the bar. As regards statements submitted under the 2002 Leniency Notice and the 2006 Leniency Notice (respectively [2002] OJ C45/3 and [2006] OJ C298/17), points 33 and 34 of those Notices emphasise that such statements may not be disclosed for purposes other than the application of Art 81 EC and within the administrative proceedings. For an explanation see also B Van Barlingen and M Barennes, 'The European Commission's Leniency Notice in Practice', Competition Policy Newsletter, issue No 3, Autumn 2005, p 8.

[44] The request must be well-defined, identify the documents as clearly as possible and explain how the content of the Commission decision would be influenced by not having access to the documents (Case T-175/95 *BASF Coatings AG v Commission* [1999] ECR II-1581, at paras 47–51, and case C-204/00 etc *Aalborg Portland and others v Commission* [2004] ECR I-123, at paras 74–75.

[45] In respect of the obligation on the Commission to make such information available, see n 30 above.

[46] Case T-38/02 *Danone v Commission* [2005] ECR II-4407, para 79 and the case law cited therein. In this regard see also Case T-330/01 *Akzo Nobel NV v Commission*, judgment of 17 September 2006, not yet reported, at para 89, where the CFI refers to the principles and rules governing the administrative procedure and states that the Statement of Objections must have 'practical effect'. Here too, an argument that an undertaking failed to raise in the administrative procedure could no longer be invoked before the CFI.

[47] Point 47 of the Notice on Access to the File. The Hearing Officer will not grant any frivolous claims in this regard. Art 3 of the Terms of Reference of the Hearing Officers applies also.

[48] For a more elaborate overview of the applicable rules and practices, see L Ortiz Blanco, *EC Competition Procedure* (2nd edn, 2006) sections 9.24–9.33.

[49] Art 287 EC. A discussion of the principles of professional secrecy can be found in Case T-279/02 *Degussa AG v Commission* [2006] ECR II-897, para 409 and the case law cited therein, and in Case T-198/03 *Bank Austria Creditanstalt AG v Commission*, judgment of 30 May 2006, not yet reported, at paras 29 and 69 *et seq*. (Note that the latter case deals not with an issue regarding the disclosure of information in the context of access to the file, but with the disclosure of information in a public version of a final decision).

[50] Art 28 of Regulation 1/2003, and as regards the publication of decisions, Art 30(2) of Regulation 1/2003.

[51] Art 16(1) of Regulation 773/2004.

[52] Case 53/85 *Akzo v Commission* [1986] ECR 1985, paras 26–27.

[53] Arts 15 and 16 of Regulation 773/2004.

[54] Section IV(B) of the Notice on Access to the File.

will not provide access to business secrets or other confidential information,[55] depending on the circumstances, such disclosure may be needed because the information constitutes evidence of the infringement or is necessary to give effect to the rights of the defence.[56] Indeed, the Commission cannot undermine the rights of the defence by restricting access with a general argument that the information in question contains business secrets or other confidential information. However, access to information for which confidential treatment has been requested can only be provided after the proprietor of the information has been given the opportunity to express its views and ultimately to appeal any decision in this regard before the European Courts.[57] Reconciling the two rights—the protection of confidential information and the right to defend oneself—may be a difficult balancing exercise for the services of DG Competition and/or the Hearing Officer (and ultimately the Courts). In practice, undertakings are requested to provide a justification for the confidential treatment of information, together with a non-confidential version or summary of the materials (expurgated of business secrets or other confidential data), so that other undertakings can use the information in its non-confidential form or request further access if deemed necessary for their defence.[58]

8.460 **Business secrets** Although the relevant provisions do not contain any precise definition of business secrets, they are generally described as information about an undertaking's business activity the disclosure of which could result in serious harm to that undertaking.[59] The concept covers at least the following categories of information: technical and/or financial information relating to a company's know-how, methods of assessing costs, production secrets and processes, supply sources, quantities produced and sold, market shares, customer and distributor lists, marketing plans, cost and price structure and sales strategy.[60] Business information that is more than five years old is presumed to have lost its commercial value, unless proved otherwise by the undertaking concerned.[61] (The opposite conclusion, that any business information less than five years old can safely be claimed as confidential cannot be drawn, however. An undertaking must always provide a justification for its claim.)

8.461 **Other confidential information** The Access to File Notice makes a distinction between business secrets and 'other confidential information'.[62] Other confidential information

---

[55] Art 15(2) of Regulation 773/2004. In the words of Ortiz Blanco and Jörgens, the concept of professional secrecy is an obligation attaching to the Community administration, whereas the protection of business secrets is a right enjoyed by undertakings (L Ortiz Blanco, *EC Competition Procedure* (2nd edn, 2006) section 10.37, n 135).

[56] Art 15(3) of Regulation 773/2004 and point 24 of the Notice on Access to the File.

[57] The procedure is contained in Art 9 of the Terms of Reference of the Hearing Officers and point 25 of the Notice on Access to the File. It incorporates the so-called 'Akzo procedure' of allowing a party the opportunity to express itself on the intended disclosure, including the possibility of court review based on a decision of the Commission, prior to any disclosure.

[58] Case T-198/03 *Bank Austria Creditanstalt AG v Commission*, judgment of 30 May 2006, not yet reported, at para 29.

[59] See point 18 of the Notice on Access to the File, which refers to Case T-353/94 *Postbank NV v Commission* [1996] ECR II-921, para 87.

[60] See point 18 of the Notice on Access to the File.

[61] Point 23 of the Notice on Access to the File.

[62] Point 19 of the Notice on Access to the File. The CFI makes no particular distinction between business secrets and other confidential information, but applies an overall test relating to whether (a) the information is known to a limited number of persons, (b) it is liable to cause serious harm, and (c) the harm would affect

includes information which does not fall within the definition of business secrets, but which may be considered confidential insofar as its disclosure would *significantly* harm a person or undertaking (compared with 'serious' harm to the undertaking in the case of business secrets).[63] Therefore, information that is not categorised as business secrets can still be protected, and the scope of such protection seems to be somewhat wider.[64]

Procedure for requesting confidential treatment   The procedure is that the undertaking   **8.462** must request and justify its claim of business secrets or confidentiality, and supply a non-confidential version or summary,[65] as stated above. The non-confidential version or summary should allow the recipient of the information to identify whether or not the information is relevant to its defence, so that it can request further access.[66] The Hearing Officer will endeavour to resolve disagreements between the Commission services and an undertaking claiming that certain information constitutes business secrets or other confidential information.[67] If it is found that the information does not merit protection or should be disclosed in view of the rights of defence,[68] and the undertaking still disagrees, the Hearing Officer can take a formal decision under his mandate, which can then be appealed before the CFI.[69]

Irregularities concerning access to the file and potential effects on the Commission   8.463 Decision   A finding that the Commission did not give a party appropriate access to the file cannot *in itself*, with automaticity lead to the entire annulment of a decision. Such a possible violation '[m]ust . . . be examined in relation to the specific circumstances of each particular case'.[70] It is necessary to assess whether the applicant's defence was capable of

---

an interest that is worthy of protection. Case T-198/03 *Bank Austria Creditanstalt AG v Commission*, judgment of 30 May 2006, not yet reported, at para 71. As mentioned above (n 49), note that this case deals not with an issue regarding the disclosure of information in the context of access to the file, but with the disclosure of information in a public version of a final decision.

    [63] For example, 'other confidential information' might be information of a private nature, or information about the identity of a complainant.

    [64] An example of such information may be a diary, a copy of which has been put in the case file for the purpose of confirming presence at certain meetings, but that contains entries of a purely private nature. According to Kerse and Khan, the threshold for obtaining protection appears to be lower in the case of 'other confidential information' than in the case of 'business secrets'. Therefore, information that does not qualify as a 'business secret' may instead qualify as being 'other confidential information'. CS Kerse and N Khan, *EC Antitrust Procedure* (5th edn, 2005), section 4-046.

    [65] Art 16 of Regulation 773/2004 and point 39 of the Notice on Access to the File. If a party fails to comply with the above requirements, the Commission may assume that the documents do not contain confidential information and are therefore 'accessible'.

    [66] See point 47 of the Notice on Access to the File in conjunction with Art 8 of the Terms of Reference of the Hearing Officers.

    [67] Point 42 of the Notice on Access to the File.

    [68] Disclosure would also take place in cases where the information is used as evidence by the Commission; this would depend upon the public interest in enforcing the competition rules and the rights of defence of the other undertakings being deemed to outweigh the private interests of the party whose information is at issue (see point 24 of the Notice on Access to the File).

    [69] See Art 9 of the Terms of Reference of the Hearing Officers. See also Case 53/85 Akzo *v Commission* [1986] ECR 1965, which is at the origin of the so-called 'Akzo procedure' that is now set out in Art 9. For an appeal based on Art 9 of the Hearing Officer's mandate, in relation to the publication of allegedly confidential information in a public version of a Commission Decision, see Case T-198/03 *Bank Austria Creditanstalt AG v Commission,* judgment of 30 May 2006, not yet reported.

    [70] Case 36/91 *Imperial Chemical Industries plc v Commission* [1995] ECR II-1175, at para 70.

being affected by the infringement of its procedural rights.[71] The CFI has taken the view that the rights of the defence will have been infringed if there was 'even a small chance' that the outcome of the administrative procedure might have been different as regards the gravity and duration of the conduct, had the applicant been able to rely on a document.[72] If the Commission relied on other evidence to prove the facts in question, the claim will not affect the Commission's finding.[73] When an undertaking does succeed in making such a claim, the *whole* decision will only be annulled where there is no other remedy for the procedural infringement.[74] The Commission services will normally endeavour to allow parties access to file widely, in order to prevent a decision being affected by a procedural irregularity in this regard or at least to prevent having to deal with procedural contestations in this regard, while trying to reconcile access to the file with the need for efficient administration of the investigation.

(c) The Oral Hearing

8.464 The right to an oral hearing has been enshrined in Article 12 of Regulation 773/2004. An oral hearing will normally be held after the written reply has been received. The hearing is presided over by the Hearing Officer[75] and usually takes place within four to six weeks of the undertakings' reply to the SO. Although the SO is addressed separately to different undertakings and may ascribe different roles to each undertaking, the hearing is normally joined (ie with all the addressees of the SO that have requested a hearing present at the same time), primarily for reasons of administrative convenience. The Commission does not grant access to the written replies of the other undertakings to the SO, unless there are elements in those replies which are clearly exculpatory to other undertakings or that are of an incriminating nature and the Commission intends to rely on them. *In camera* hearings are also possible[76] to enable, for example, confidential elements pertaining to only one

---

[71] Cases T-25/95 etc *Cimenteries CBR SA and others v Commission* [2000] ECR II-491, paras 156 and 157. See also Case T-43/02 *Jungbunzlauer AG v Commission*, judgment of 27 September 2006, not yet reported, at para 342 *et seq* and the case law mentioned there, discussed above in n 29. Furthermore see Case T-44/02 etc *Dresdner Bank and others v Commission*, judgment of 27 September 2006, not yet reported, paras 157–160 and the case law cited therein.

[72] Cases T-25/95 etc *Cimenteries CBR SA and others v Commission* [2000] ECR II-491, para 241, confirmed in appeal and in Joined Cases C-204/00 etc *Aalborg Portland and others v Commission* [2004] ECR I-123, para 131.

[73] If the Commission relied on other evidence to prove the facts in question, the claim will not affect the Commission's finding. Case C-308/04 P *SGL Carbon AG v Commission* [2006] ECR I-5977, para 97: 'It follows from settled case-law that the mere failure to communicate a document constitutes a breach of the rights of the defence only if the undertaking concerned is able to show, first, that the Commission relied on that document to support its objection concerning the existence of an infringement and, second, that the objection could be proved only by reference to that document (see, *inter alia*, Case 107/82 *AEG v Commission* [1983] ECR 3151, paras 24 to 30, and Case 322/81 *Michelin v Commissions* [1983] ECR 3461, paras 7 to 9)'. (See also Case T-311/94 *BPB de Eendracht NV v Commission* [1989] ECR II-1129, at para 256, and Joined Cases C-204/00 etc *Aalborg Portland and others v Commission* [2004] ECR I-123, para 75). See also Case T-43/02 *Jungbunzlauer AG v Commission*, judgment of 27 September 2006, not yet reported, at paras 342 *et seq* and the case law mentioned there, discussed in n 71 above.

[74] cf Schermers/Waelbroeck, *Judicial Protection in the European Union*, Kluwer Law International, (6th edn, 2001), at para 116.

[75] Art 14(1) of Regulation 773/2004. The Hearing Officer decides which parties are allowed to participate, the speaking time that they will have, etc. Hearings in cartel cases usually last between one and two days.

[76] Art 14(6) of Regulation 773/2004.

undertaking to be discussed. Apart from allowing the parties to express their views, the hearing provides an opportunity for clarification of certain facts.[77] That said, the hearing is not an extension of the investigation. At the hearing the parties may ask the Commission to hear persons on their own behalf who may corroborate the facts set out in their submissions,[78] but it should perhaps be considered a general flaw in terms of evidentiary standards that those who speak at the oral hearing are not subject to any sanctions if they provide incorrect or misleading information (in contrast to information supplied in response to requests for information or request for clarification during inspections).[79] The system of oral hearings has also been criticised for not allowing the summoning of particular individuals to the hearing. That criticism has sometimes followed from the fact that the Commission may have had access during the investigation to persons, such as employees of other incriminated undertakings, who may have particular knowledge about the facts and whom another incriminated undertaking would like to question (as a form of cross-examination). However, this is not possible: undertakings can neither be forced to be present at oral hearings, nor can they be compelled to produce certain individuals.

The procedure at the Oral Hearing[80] is not fixed and depends on the circumstances (eg how many parties will be present), but usually follows the procedure outlined below. The person in charge of the case in DG Competition briefly presents the facts and arguments on behalf of the Commission. The parties each then present their own case on an individual basis. Members of the national competition authorities can question the parties, followed by the Hearing Officer and DG Competition staff. The parties are given a chance to respond, although they are not obliged to do so.[81] The parties are also given a chance to put questions to the other parties present and even to the Commission,[82] as well as to comment generally on any arguments that have been put forward.[83] An audio recording is made of the oral hearing and is made available to the participants.[84] In this procedure, the role of third parties, who are not addressees of the Statement of Objections, is limited, particularly in cartel cases. Nevertheless, under special circumstances third parties, notably complainants, may be allowed to participate in hearings.[85]

8.465

---

[77] ibid. See also Art 11(1) of Regulation 773/2004.

[78] Art 13(2) of Regulation 773/2004.

[79] The same holds true for the replies to the SO: undertakings are not compelled through any procedural sanctions to provide complete and truthful information (Art 23 of Regulation 1/2003 restricts which procedural violations can attract fines). The intention is that, in the exercise of their rights of defence, undertakings must be free to submit any information and arguments they consider helpful to their defence (if the Commission wants to obtain or verify certain information presented, it can use its means of inquiry, notably requests for information, to ensure that truthful and complete replies to its questions are being given). However, if an undertaking were to make representations in the reply to the SO and/or the Oral hearing intended to mislead the Commission and thereby obstruct its enquiry, this may be taken into account as an aggravating circumstance in the calculation of the ultimate cartel fine.

[80] On the conduct of Oral Hearings, see Art 14 of Regulation 773/2004.

[81] CS Kerse and N Khan, *EC Antitrust Procedure* (5th edn, 2005), para 4-064.

[82] However, it is submitted that the purpose of questioning the Commission is unclear. Oral argument by the Commission cannot determine the outcome of the investigation. The Commission must make its case in writing, in a final decision. Also, there is no obligation on the Commission officials to answer.

[83] Art 14(7) of Regulation 773/2004.

[84] Art 14(8) of Regulation 773/2004.

[85] Art 13 of Regulation 773/2004 deals with the hearing of 'other persons'. It is accordingly up to the Commission to determine whether or not a complainant may intervene, provided that the complainant made

(d) The Role of the Hearing Officer

8.466 The primary function of the Hearing Officer—a role created in 1982 to provide more checks and balances—is to ensure that the rights of the defence are respected during the administrative procedure, and that both the proceedings and Commission decisions adhere to the proper standards of impartiality and quality.[86] The mandate of the Hearing Officer is set out in a Commission Decision (the Terms of Reference of Hearing Officers).[87] An important task of the Hearing Officer is to organise and conduct oral hearings,[88] but the role is not limited to this. In cartel proceedings the Hearing Officer may frequently intervene, for instance, to adjudicate between requests for confidential treatment of business information on the one hand and opposing requests for access to such information in full exercise of the rights of defence on the other.[89]

8.467 The Hearing Officer[90] produces an interim report on the progress of the proceedings and then a final report when the decision is adopted.[91] These reports deal principally with how the rights of the defence have been upheld. However, according to Article 3(3) of the Terms of Reference of the Hearing Officers, they may present observations on 'any matter' arising out of case. Only the final report will be made public, while the interim report (which is more of a progress report) is supplied to the competent member of the Commission.[92] As stated above, the Hearing Officer may also be called upon to deal with any issue between the Commission services and the parties as to whether documents may be classified as 'accessible' or not. Furthermore, in cartel cases, where the investigative files to which access must be given are voluminous and many parties may be implicated, the Hearing Officer is

---

a request to be heard in the first place. See also generally on this point the Commission Notice on the Handling of Complaints by the Commission under Arts 81 and 82 EC ([2002] OJ C101/65) and specifically point 65 of that Notice. For a further discussion of the rights of third parties in competition proceedings, see L Ortiz Blanco, *EC Competition Procedure* (2nd edn, 2006), sections 10.03 and 10.72 *et seq*. See also the judgment of the CFI in Joined Cases T-213/01 and T-214/01 *Österreichische Postsparkasse AG and Bank für Arbeit und Wirtschaft AG v Commission*, judgment of 7 June 2006, not yet reported.

[86] The Hearing Officers are not formally staff of DG Competition. In order to emphasise their internal independence from the services that deal with the investigation, they are formally attached to the staff (cabinet) of the Commissioner responsible for competition.

[87] Terms of Reference of Hearing Officers, n 25 above.

[88] See Arts 4–6 and 11–12 of the Terms of Reference of the Hearing Officers.

[89] In cases of conflict, the Hearing Officer can, after following the procedure of Art 9 of the Terms of Reference, release information for which confidentiality has been claimed. Alternatively, the Hearing Officers may grant continued protection to information for which confidentiality has been requested, if the rights of defence are not considered to outweigh the reasons for further confidential treatment (under Art 8 of the Terms of Reference of the Hearing Officers). Commission Decisions on the basis of Art 9 can be challenged under Art 230 of the Treaty, as their effect can be immediate (potential prejudice to the undertaking following from the divulging of business secrets or other confidential information) (see Case T-198/03 *Bank Austria Creditanstalt AG v Commission* judgment of 30 May 2006, not yet reported, at paras 26–36). Decisions under Art 8 are not challengeable, as they only have effect when the Commission takes a final adverse decision at the end of the administrative procedure.

[90] At the time of writing, the two Hearing Officers were Mrs K Williams and Mr S Durande.

[91] The final report is communicated to the addressees as an attachment to the final decision of the Commission in which reference is made to the final report (Art 16(3) of the Terms of Reference).

[92] And to the Director-General of DG Competition and the responsible Director (Arts 13, 15 and 16 of the Terms of Reference of Hearing Officers, Decision 2001/462/EC).

usually called upon repeatedly, especially in the period between the sending of the Statement of Objections and the settling of any issues arising from the Oral Hearing.[93]

(e) The Final Commission Decision

After the Oral Hearing has taken place, the Commission can take a formal prohibition decision[94] finding the infringement and ordering the undertakings concerned to end the behaviour in question and refrain from it in future. In 2005, Commissioner Kroes alluded to the possibility that the Commission would consider settling cases—rather than adopting the traditional decisions—with a form of 'plea bargaining'. At the time of writing there were no known instances of any direct settlements having been concluded.[95] (The possibility of 'direct settlements' and certain issues surrounding their possible introduction are discussed below in paras 8.480–8.486) In most cartel cases, the final decision will also entail the imposition of fines. As mentioned above, although the Commission issues a single document as its decision, in legal terms it contains individual decisions against each addressee.[96]   **8.468**

Decisions must have a coherent structure and include adequate reasoning   This princi-   **8.469**
ple follows first from Article 253 of the EC Treaty, but also from the case law of the Courts.[97] The ECJ has held that where fines are imposed a decision must 'set out, in a concise but clear and relevant manner, the principal issues of law and of fact upon which it is based and which are necessary in order that the reasoning which has led the Commission to its decision may be understood'.[98] The final decision may not allege that the persons concerned have committed infringements other than those referred to in the SO and should take into consideration only facts on which they have had the opportunity to make known their views.[99] In its decisions the Commission does not have to respond to every argument or point raised by each party in reply to the SO. The extent to which the Commission must provide reasoning also depends on the type of decision and its novelty.[100] Each addressee should be able to obtain a clear picture of the findings against it in the decision. The name of the addressee must also be mentioned in the 'operative part' of

---

[93] For instance, certain parties present at an Oral Hearing may apply to the Hearing Officer with a request to be given further access to (new) information presented by other parties, with additional time to comment.

[94] In exceptional cases the Commission may reach an outcome that is different from a formal decision with fines, as was the case in the Commission investigation relating to bank charges for currency exchanges within the Euro zone referred to in note 4 above.

[95] Neelie Kroes, *The First Hundred Days*, speech at the occasion of the 40th anniversary of the Studienverein Kartellrecht, Brussels 7 April 2005, accessible at: <http://europa.eu/rapid/pressReleasesAction.do?reference=SPEECH/05/205&format=HTML&aged=0&language=EN&guiLanguage=en>.

[96] See for instance *PVC II*, Joined Cases C-238/99 P etc *Limburgse Vinyl Maatschappij NV (LVM) and others v Commission* [2002] ECR I-8375, para 100.

[97] Art 253 EC states that: '... decisions ... [of] the Commission ... shall state the reasons on which they are based ...'.

[98] Case 24/62 *Federal Republic of Germany v Commission* [1963] ECR 63. For a more recent reflection of that principle, see Joined Cases C-189/02 etc *Dansk Rørindustri and others v Commission* [2005] ECR I-5425, at para 462.

[99] Art 27(1) of Regulation 1/2003 and Art 11(2) of Regulation 773/2004. See also Case T-15/02 *BASF AG v Commission* [2006] ECR II-497, para 47 and the case law cited therein.

[100] Case C-350/88 *Delacre v Commission* [1990] ECR I-395, at para 15.

the decision, for the decision to apply against that legal entity.[101] In the case of undertakings that take the form of a group of companies, the Commission may choose to issue the decision to the various legal entities that it considers to be liable for the infringement. Another general point is that any entity receiving a decision must have had the opportunity to defend itself, ie it must have received an SO that was addressed to it.[102]

8.470 In view of the rights of defence, a Commission decision must relate only to the objection(s) that was (were) referred to in the SO,[103] but the decision does not need to be a replica of the SO.[104] The Commission is allowed to revise its factual and legal assessment in the light of the replies of the parties and–of course–to drop certain objections. Should there be a discrepancy between the SO and the final decision, the objections can be maintained if they were drafted 'in a manner sufficient to enable the addressee to defend their interests'.[105] The Commission need not include all the available evidence in its decision,[106] nor does it as mentioned, need to respond to all the points of fact and law that the addressees have raised in the administrative procedure.[107] If during the administrative proceedings it is found that an undertaking has committed no infringement (or that there are insufficient reasons to continue the inquiry against it), then the Commission will close the investigation against that undertaking. Where formal proceedings had been instigated, these will be closed by internal Commission action, of which the undertaking will be informed by letter.

8.471 **The 'cease and desist order'** In a cartel decision, in addition to levying a fine, the Commission formally requires undertakings to bring the infringement to an end[108] with a

---

[101] Cases 40/73 etc *Coöperatieve Vereniging 'Suiker Unie' UA and others v Commission* [1975] ECR 1663, para 315. As regards determining the appropriate addressees, see section D(3), on the establishing of liability.

[102] Joined Cases T-45/98 and 47/98 *Krupp Thyssen Stainless GmbH and Acciai Speciali Terni SpA v Commission* [2001] ECR II-3757, para 67, and Joined Cases C-204/00 etc *Aalborg Portland and others v Commission* [2004] ECR I-123, para 60 and the case law cited therein.

[103] See also Art 11(2) of Regulation 773/2004.

[104] Case T-15/02 *BASF AG v Commission* [2006] ECR II-497, at para 93. See also Joined Cases T-4/93 etc *Compagnie Maritime Belge Transports SA v Commission* [1996] ECR II-1201, para 113.

[105] Case T-15/02 *BASF AG v Commission* [2006] ECR II-497, para 95. In the decision the Commission may well supplement or redraft its arguments both in fact and in law in support of an existing objection which it maintains. In the view of the CFI, the assessment of the facts is a part of the decision-making act itself and the right to be heard extends to all matters of fact and law which form the basis for the decision but not the final position which the administration intends to adopt (Case T-15/02 *BASF AG v Commission* [2006] ECR II-497, para 94 and the case law cited therein). The Court seems to be giving the Commission considerable leeway in this respect, given that in the same judgment it found that even in the case of 'confusion and inconsistency' the outcome is not necessarily affected (Case T-15/02 *BASF AG v Commission* [2006] ECR II-497, para 96). See also para 8.455 above and n 21 on the possibility of adding fresh objections and/or relying on new facts.

[106] Case T-2/89 *Petrofina v Commission* [1991] ECR II-1087, para 39.

[107] See, for instance, Case C-338/00 P *Volkswagen AG v Commission* [2003] ECR I-9189, at para 127: 'With regard to the second limb of the seventh ground of appeal, although the Commission is required under Art 190 of the Treaty to set out all the circumstances of fact and law justifying the adoption of a decision and the legal considerations which led the Commission to adopt it, that Article does not require the Commission to discuss all the matters of fact and law which may have been dealt with during the administrative procedure (Joined Cases 43/82 and 63/82 *VBVB and VBBB v Commission* [1984] ECR 19, para 22, and Case 246/86 *Belasco and others v Commission* [1989] ECR 2117, para 55).'

[108] Art 7 of Regulation 1/2003.

'cease and desist order'. An *order to cease* the cartel may be considered necessary where the Commission suspects that the behaviour could be ongoing. In a typical cartel investigation companies will normally have stopped the illicit behaviour from the moment the Commission intervened with inspections or other investigative steps, so that the order to cease may actually be redundant. Nevertheless, the Commission usually includes it 'for the avoidance of doubt'. The *order to desist* has a prospective value: it is aimed at ensuring that undertakings abstain from the same behaviour in future. It also serves to indicate that any repeated infringement will be punished more severely.[109]

Other procedural aspects   Before a final decision is taken, the Advisory Committee,[110] **8.472** consisting of representatives of the Member States, must be consulted, both as to the substance of the case and with regard to the fines.[111] The taking of the ultimate decision is a collegiate act of the Commission for which no sub-delegation exists. Once the decision has been adopted by the Commission, only administrative (grammatical and spelling) corrections can be made to the text of the decision.[112] Addressees are notified of the decision on an individual basis.[113]

Legitimate interest in adopting a decision against an undertaking even if no fine is **8.473** **imposed**   The Commission may issue a cartel decision against undertakings against whom the imposition of a fine is no longer possible due to the provisions on limitation periods.[114] This may occur where an undertaking has been a member of a cartel, but by virtue of the rules on limitation periods avoids being fined because it had left the cartel more than five years before the Commission started the investigation. One reason why the Commission may nevertheless want to adopt a decision is to promote exemplary behaviour by undertakings in general. Also, a prohibition decision can be used later as a basis for imposing or increasing the fine in case of recidivism, so as to discourage any repeat infringement on the part of the undertaking. Another possible reason is that the Commission may want to enhance the potential for claims for damages in civil litigation before national courts[115] and to place all of the undertakings that contributed to the cartel, irrespective of

---

[109] Under the 1998 Guidelines on Fines, section 2, the Commission can apply an increase in the fine for aggravation due to recidivism. The application of the increase, however, is not dependent on the inclusion of a 'desist' order in prior decisions (Guidelines on the method of setting fines imposed pursuant to Art 15(2) of Regulation No 17 and Art 65(5) of the ECSC, OJ C9, 14.01.98). Recidivism will be sanctioned more severely under the 2006 Guidelines on Fines (para 28, first indent). The 2006 Guidelines are discussed in paras 8.808–8.834.

[110] The Advisory Committee on Restrictive Practices and Dominant Positions.

[111] Art 14 of Regulation 1/2003.

[112] Case C-137/92 P *Commission v BASF* [1994] ECR I-2555, para 68. The decision that is notified to the addressees must correspond to the text of the decision as agreed by the College of Commissioners. (See also Case T-141/94 *Thyssen Stahl v Commission* [1999] ECR II-347, para 150.)

[113] Art 254 EC. A legal person cannot escape service upon it by, for instance, refusing to receive the document on its doorstep. This was further clarified by the ECJ when it held that: 'a decision is properly notified within the meaning of the [EC] Treaty, if it reaches the addressee and puts the latter in a position to take cognizance of it' (Case 6/72 *Europemballage Corporation and Continental Can Company Inc v Commission* [1973] ECR 215, para 10).

[114] Art 26 of Regulation 1/2003.

[115] Art 16 of Regulation 1/2003 provided a basis for doing so. See also Case C-453/99 *Courage Ltd v Bernard Crehan*, [2001] ECR I-06297. For more on the possibility of obtaining damages for competition law infringements see paras 8.859–8.867.

when they exited the cartel, on an equal footing in that regard. Where the Commission considers that there are reasons for issuing a decision without fines, it should be careful to provide a particular justification related to the case at hand, as the CFI made clear in *Sumitomo*.[116]

8.474 **Public version of the decision and press release**   On the day of the final decision the Commission usually issues a press release, indicating the type of behaviour identified, the duration of the infringement, the participants and the fines imposed.[117] It also states that the addressees can appeal to the CFI. Interestingly, the Commission has also started to include, in its press releases, a reference to the possibility of obtaining civil damages based on the Commission Decision.[118] The decision is published in accordance with Article 30 of Regulation 1/2003. In practice a redacted version of the decision is made available on DG Competition's web site, and a summary is published in the Official Journal. Publication on the Commission's web site (most often initially in one language version, usually English)[119] normally precedes publication of the summary of the decision in the Official Journal.

8.475 In publishing (a summary of) the decision, the Commission must have regard to the legitimate interest of undertakings in the protection of their business secrets, in accordance with Article 30 of Regulation 1/2003.[120] It should be noted that the considerations underlying the treatment of confidential data for the purposes of the SO and the decision sent to the parties are different from those relating to the publication of the decision. For the SO and the (unpublished) decision, the protection of business secrets must be balanced with the rights of defence (the protection of which is a fundamental right of EC law), whereas for publication it is rather the public interest which is at stake. Hence, there is a somewhat broader scope for the protection of data in the case of public versions of the decisions.[121] Where (additional) secrecy claims are made, it can take several months before a solution can be found, leading to considerable delays in the publication of versions that are accessible to the public. The Hearing Officers may be called upon to resolve any problems in this regard,

---

[116] Joined Cases T-22/02 and T-23/02 *Sumitomo Chemical and Sumika Fine Chemicals v Commission* [2005] ECR II-4065, at para 136 *et seq.*

[117] See for instance Commission Press Release IP/05/1508 of 30 November 2005, 'Competition: Commission fines 16 firms €290 million for industrial bags cartel', available at <http://ec.europa.eu/comm/competition/antitrust/cases/index.html >.

[118] ibid.

[119] Publication is normally in the languages of the authentic decision, and in any case in English and/or French. If there is more than one authentic language, an English language version is usually published first, the other (authentic) languages following later.

[120] Art 30(2) of Regulation 1/2003, in combination with Art 28 of Regulation 1/2003, which refers to the obligation of professional secrecy. It is somewhat awkward, by comparison with Art 16 of Regulation 773/2004 and the Notice on Access to the File, that Art 30 only refers to 'business secrets' and not to 'other confidential information'. It is considered, however, that what applies with regard to the treatment of business secrets applies *ipso facto* to confidential information. In practice, the Commission will also allow information other than pure business secrets to be removed, such as the names of employees.

[121] However, there should be no material difference between the decision as sent to the parties and its published version. In public versions, the main additional aspects that undertakings will want to seek protection for are certain (recent) financial data concerning the undertaking (such as its turnover in the product concerned) and the names of employees. On both points the Commission will usually agree to adapt the final version.

based on Article 9(3) of their Terms of Reference. Ultimately, a dispute between a party and the Commission about the public version may be adjudicated by the Court.[122]

(f) Appealing the Decision

The CFI is the initial competent court to hear challenges to Commission cartel decisions.[123] **8.476** As stated in the EC Treaty, the addressee of a decision has two months from the date of the notification within which to challenge the decision.[124] Judgments of the CFI may be appealed to the ECJ on points of law, within two months of the CFI's verdict. Should the ECJ decide that the judgment of the CFI was incorrect, it may refer the case back to the CFI for final judgment.

The nature of appeals   Article 231 of the EC Treaty states that 'if the action [under **8.477** Article 230] is well founded, the [Courts] shall declare the act concerned to be void'. In respect of cartel cases, the Courts will assess whether the alleged infringement has been proved to the required standard. As stated above, parties rarely succeed in completely disproving the evidence that an infringement has actually occurred,[125] and it is unusual for a case to be dismissed as a whole for lack of proof.[126] In cartel cases particularly, a correction of the fines by the Court is often due to the Court taking a different view from the Commission on issues such as the weight to be given to aggravating or mitigating factors (which can (considerably) affect the level of the fine), rather than the (partial) annulment being based on a flaw in the establishment of the facts.[127]

---

[122] See for instance Case T-474/04 *Pergan GmbH v Commission* (pending) in which Pergan has petitioned the CFI to annul the Commission Decision of 1 October 2004 in so far as it failed to accede to the applicant's request for removal of all references to the applicant in the definitively published version of the Commission's decision of 10 December 2003 imposing fines in Case 37.857 *Organic Peroxides* (in the contested decision, the Commission refused in part the applicant's request for removal of all references to the conduct of the applicant in the published version of the Commission's decision). In support of its action, the applicant claims, first, that, under Art 21 of Regulation No 17/62, the published version of a decision imposing fines for an infringement may name only the participating undertakings. Since the applicant was not the addressee of the decision imposing fines, the Commission is prohibited, Pergan claims, from publishing its findings in respect of it. Moreover, it argues that it was not permissible for the Commission to assume that a decision finding an infringement on the part of the applicant would be adopted. In the applicant's view, the Commission has no competence under Regulation No 17/92 to adopt such a decision and is unable to establish a legitimate interest in doing so. Finally, the applicant alleges infringement of its right to an effective legal remedy laid down in the first paragraph of Art 47 of the Charter of Fundamental Rights of the European Union. In that connection, the applicant argues that, although the Commission alleges that it is guilty of comprehensive breaches of cartel law, it omitted to address the decision imposing fines to it and thus restricted its ability to avail itself of a legal remedy.

[123] Art 225(1) EC.

[124] Arts 230 EC and 225 EC, and Art 120 of the Rules of Procedure of the Court of First Instance.

[125] In the past, this was more often the case. See for instance Cases T-68/89 etc *Società Italiana Vetro and others v Commission* ('*Italian Flat Glass*') [1992] ECR II-1403, para 172 *et seq*, where the CFI decided that various aspects of the Commission's decisions had not been proved 'to the requisite legal standard', and therefore (partially) annulled the decision.

[126] For one such case see Case T-44/02 etc *Dresdner Bank and others v Commission* judgment of 27 September 2006, not yet reported.

[127] See, eg, the reduction of the fines for the companies BASF and Daichi, following the judgments of the CFI relating to the Commission Decision in *Vitamins*. In *BASF*, the CFI decided to cancel the increase in the fine that the Commission had imposed for ringleadership in relation to four infringements, thereby reducing the Commission's uplift of 35% for those infringements. The company, Daichi benefited from the fact that the CFI re-evaluated the importance of their voluntary information and increased Daichi's reduction under the [2006] ECR II-497 (1996) Leniency Notice. (Cases T-15/02 *BASF AG v Commission* [2006] ECR II-497and T-26/02 *Daichi Pharmaceutical Co Ltd.*)

8.478 **Grounds for appeal** When a Commission decision is appealed, the Courts can annul the decision, or part of it, on the basis of any of four different grounds that follow from Article 230 of the EC Treaty.[128] They are: (1) lack of competence, (2) infringement of an essential procedural requirement, (3) infringement of the Treaty or any rule of law relating to its application, or (4) misuse of powers. In practice, the CFI, based on the arguments of the parties, will consider whether the conclusions as presented by the Commission are supported by the facts and/or whether any procedural errors have occurred that could affect the validity of the decision.[129] It will not readily substitute its own opinion for that of the Commission in the case of complex assessments, but in cartel cases the CFI has shown itself to be willing to make a very detailed analysis of the arguments of the parties in order to see whether the facts and legal assessment of the Commission decision can be upheld. Procedurally, undertakings should take care to exercise their rights of defence and present any relevant arguments of which they are aware during the administrative procedure. Depending on the circumstances, undertakings may be estopped from presenting arguments before the CFI if they could have been presented during the administrative procedure,[130] although as regards the fines the Commission's Statement of Objections will normally contain few conclusions, so arguments necessarily have to be brought before the CFI. The Courts have 'full jurisdiction' for determining the fines to be imposed, based on Article 229 of the Treaty.[131] Penalties can be cancelled, reduced or even increased.[132]

---

[128] Art 230 EC.

[129] Note that arguments made about facts that have been expressly admitted during the course of the administrative procedure cannot succeed before the Courts (see Joined Cases T-236/01 etc *Tokai Carbon and others v Commission* [2004] ECR II-1181, para 108: 'As to whether Nippon can go back on that cooperation and claim before the Court that it had not participated in the infringement between May 1992 and March 1993, it has consistently been held that where the undertaking involved does not expressly acknowledge the facts, the Commission must prove the facts and the undertaking is free to put forward, in the procedure before the Court, any plea in its defence which it deems appropriate (Case C-297/98 P *SCA Holding v Commission* [2000] ECR I-10101, para 37). It may be concluded, *a contrario*, that that is not the case where the undertaking expressly, clearly and specifically acknowledges the facts: *where it explicitly admits during the administrative procedure the substantive truth of the facts which the Commission alleges against it in the statement of objections, those facts must thereafter be regarded as established and the undertaking estopped in principle from disputing them during the procedure before the Court.*' (emphasis added).

[130] In this regard see Case T-330/01 *Akzo Nobel NV v Commission* judgment of 17 September 2006, not yet reported, at paras 87–89, where the CFI refers to the principles and rules governing the administrative procedure and states that the SO must have 'practical effect'. In that case, an argument that an undertaking failed to raise in the administrative procedure could not be invoked later before the CFI. The CFI stated that, 'Accordingly, on the basis of the information contained in the statement of objections, Akzo could not have been unaware that it was likely to be the addressee of a final decision of the Commission. In such a situation, the onus was on it to react during the administrative procedure, or be faced with the prospect of no longer being able to do so . . .' (para 87).

[131] See also Art 31 of Regulation No1/2003, which states: 'The Courts shall have unlimited jurisdiction to review decisions whereby the Commission has fixed a fine or periodic penalty payment; it may cancel, reduce, or increase the fine or periodic penalty payment imposed'.

[132] See paras 8.580–8.834 as regards the determination of the fines and the role of the Court. An increase in the fine will rarely be imposed. An exception occurred in *Graphite Electrodes*, where the court re-established a portion of the fine imposed on Nippon Carbon for which the Commission had granted a reduction because of the co-operation of the undertaking in the form of a recognition of the facts (which the undertaking then contested before the CFI) (Joined Cases T-236/01 etc *Tokai Carbon and others v Commission* [2004] ECR II-1181, para 112). For a further discussion and explanation of the Courts' role and their reluctance to increase the fines, see CS Kerse and N Khan, *EC Antitrust Procedure* (5th edn, 2005), sections 8.025–8.027.

Differences between review by the CFI and the ECJ   Judgments of the CFI may be   **8.479**
appealed before the ECJ within two months of notification of the judgment, but only on
points of law.[133] The grounds for appeal to the ECJ include specifically: lack of competence of
the CFI, a breach of procedure by the CFI that adversely affects the interests of the appellant,
and the incorrect application of EC law by the CFI.[134] The subject matter of the appeal to
the ECJ is limited to the grounds raised before the CFI.[135] A fundamental difference
between the two Courts is, therefore, that the CFI will consider both the Commission's
appraisal of the facts and its legal reasoning, but the ECJ will not question findings of fact
by the CFI, unless it can be shown that the clear sense of the evidence has been distorted.[136]
If the ECJ finds that an appeal is well-founded then it will annul the decision of the CFI,
partially or completely. The ECJ can then give final judgment itself[137] or refer the case
back to the CFI for final determination.[138] The CFI will be bound on matters of law by the
judgment of the ECJ.

(g) *'Direct Settlements' for Cartel Cases?*

As mentioned above, in 2005, Competition Commissioner Kroes alluded to the introduction   **8.480**
of a form of 'plea bargaining' in cartel cases,[139] or more appropriately in the European
context, 'direct settlements'. The aim was to speed up decision-making, thereby ensuring a
more efficient use of Commission resources,[140] whilst not compromising the deterrent
effect of enforcement. In the present decision-making system, apart from the investigative
phase, Commission resources are devoted to the (adversarial) administrative stage of
progressing from an SO, through written representations and oral hearing, to a final, fully
reasoned decision (in as many languages as are required, depending on the location of the
administrative base of the addressees). Furthermore, as appeals are brought against most
cartel decisions, case-handlers at DG Competition and in the Commission's Legal Service
spend a considerable amount of time defending decisions before the CFI and the ECJ,
where arguments often concentrate on the appropriateness of the fines rather than on the sufficiency of the evidence. The result is that a full cartel procedure, including court review(s),

---

[133] Art 225 EC and Art 58 of the Statute of the Court of Justice.

[134] Art 58 of the Statute of the Court of Justice.

[135] Art 113(2) of the Rules of Procedure of the Court of Justice.

[136] See Joined Cases C-189/02 etc *Dansk Rørindustri and others v Commission* [2005] ECR I-5425, para 122
and the case law cited therein: '. . . considerations . . . based on series of findings of fact . . . are not amenable to
discussion on appeal, unless the relevant facts or evidence have been distorted or the material inaccuracy of
the findings of the Court of First Instance is apparent from the documents placed on the case file'. See also
Case C-121/04 P *Minoikes Grammes ANE (Minoan Lines SA) v Commission* judgment of 17 November 2005,
not yet reported, paras 58 and 59.

[137] Based on Art 61 of the Statute of the Court. For an example see Case C-301/04 P *Commission v SGL
Carbon AG* [2006] ECR I-5915, para 61 *et seq*, where the ECJ reinstated part of the fine for which the CFI
had given a reduction.

[138] Art 61 of the Statute of the Court.

[139] Neelie Kroes, *The First Hundred Days*, speech at the occasion of the 40th anniversary of the
Studienverein Kartellrecht, Brussels 7 April 2005, accessible at: <http://europa.eu/rapid/pressReleasesAction.
do?reference=SPEECH/05/205&format=HTML&aged=0&language=EN&guiLanguage=en>.

[140] This would have an impact not only on DG Competition staff but also on other departments, such as
the Legal Service and the Directorate-General for Translations.

may last for many years. For example, in the case of *Graphite Electrodes*, some nine years elapsed between the start of the Commission investigation and the final judgment of the Court of Justice.[141] Hence, the attractions of a system of direct settlements are clear from the Commission's perspective and also from the point of view of the European taxpayer. Such a system should also have considerable appeal for the undertakings involved: it is a chance to avoid[142] lengthy proceedings that consume resources, are financially burdensome, and which may lead to adverse publicity at various stages of the case. Direct settlements would permit an early halt to the administrative process with an outcome that provides earlier certainty for undertakings (as opposed to waiting for the determination of the fines in the Commission's final decision and in any subsequent judgments by the European Courts).[143] Nevertheless, it is thought likely that the formal result of a settlement process would be that the Commission would still make a formal finding of infringement against the undertaking, as discussed below, though in a different format from that which is currently known.

8.481 At the time of writing, the Commission has not issued any (consultation) document or guidance in relation to how it would seek to introduce this option for concluding its cartel investigations. Hence this section will only discuss the main questions that arise in contemplating a form of European-style plea bargaining. A level of speculation is unavoidable, as it is not presently known what result, if any, will emerge from the Commission's deliberations, despite the fact that Commissioner Kroes seemed keen to bring about a settlement system. Nevertheless, it is useful for readers to be aware of the debate and the issues at stake.[144]

8.482 **Possible legal basis** Regulation 1/2003 does not provide a particular framework for direct settlements, but nor does it preclude them. Of the provisions in the Regulation, Article 9—dealing with 'commitments'—may seem to be a possible legal basis, but upon consideration it is apparent that it was actually designed to deal with 'remedies' that are aimed at curing an identified competition problem. Such an instrument would not be appropriate in cartel cases for which the only remedy is an immediate halt to the illegal behaviour, which would normally have occurred at the start of an investigation in any event. Also, fines cannot be considered to be a 'remedy' in the sense of Article 9: they merely serve as a punishment for what has occurred and are intended to deter (individually and in general) future conduct. Moreover, the recitals to Regulation 1/2003 would appear to exclude the use of commitment decisions in cartel cases, stating that Article 9 procedures are 'not appropriate in cases where the Commission intends to impose a fine'.[145]

---

[141] See one of the appeals: Case C-289/04 P *Showa Denko KK v Commission* [2006] ECR I-5859. The Commission investigation started in June 1997.

[142] The Commission could not, however, take away any fundamental rights of undertakings, which include a right to court review, as discussed further below.

[143] That said, the undertaking might still need to be involved in the proceedings that may continue against other undertakings, as explained below, notably where it has made contributions under the Leniency Notice.

[144] For a discussion on the workings of a possible system of plea bargaining, see J Burrichter and D Zimmer, 'Reflections on the Implementation of a "Plea Bargaining/Direct Settlement" System in EC Competition Law', paper presented at the 11th EUI Competition Law and Policy Workshop, 2006, *Enforcement of Prohibition of Cartels*. See also J Ratliff, 'Plea Bargaining in EC Anti-Cartel Enforcement—A System Change?' (2006), paper presented at the same conference.

[145] See recital 13 of the preamble to Regulation 1/2003.

What the Commission may be able to achieve, however, is a system that is constructed **8.483** around Article 7 of Regulation 1/2003, which is the traditional basis, in combination with Article 23 of Regulation 1/2003, for issuing prohibition decisions with fines. Indeed, it is conceivable that a direct settlement might take the form of a (short-form) decision with fines, and that such a decision would be adopted with the procedural safeguards contained in Regulation 1/2003, using where possible the established administrative processes. Additional features of direct settlements may require further legislation, however, possibly in a separate Commission Regulation, and perhaps in combination with a Notice.[146]

Certain general preconditions   It is suggested that any system of settlements would need **8.484** to take into account the following considerations. One (evident) requirement seems to be that undertakings would obtain a (financial) benefit from settling early. Such a benefit should not only be linked to considerations of quickly halting the procedure and the avoidance of prolonged (negative) publicity, but also from reduced pecuniary sanctions. From the Commission's point of view, applying a *quid pro quo* reasoning, the undertaking would have to accept an obligation to co-operate. Thus, not only could undertakings that apply under the Leniency Notice be candidates for a settlement, but any undertaking, even one with nothing or very little to offer as evidence of significant added value, could also be regarded as a potential settlement candidate and would be obliged to show a co-operative attitude from the time of the settlement. Such undertakings would not contest the Commission's arguments at a later stage without the risk of losing the benefit of the settlement.[147] Another requirement, linked to the respect of fundamental rights, is that the Commission would have to respect the rights of defence, whichever procedure is chosen. The principle against self-incrimination is particularly relevant in this respect. Of course, if an undertaking agrees to a settlement, any admissions that the decision may contain would be self-incriminating, but the decision would not be illegal because the admission would have been given voluntarily. That said, an undertaking must not be put in a position where the pressure that follows from the offer of a direct settlement would be so compelling, when viewed against the alternative of a full procedure with a higher, as yet undetermined fine, that the undertaking could somehow have felt bound to admit to an infringement.[148] Furthermore, if a procedure under Article 7 of Regulation 1/2003 is chosen, parties must have a right to be heard.[149] (In this respect, the role of the Hearing Officer in the settlement procedure would also have to be defined.) Equally, the right to judicial

---

[146] The appropriate functioning of a system of direct settlements, and the decisions taken within it, will in all likelihood not impose obligations on the Commission, but also on the undertakings. For example, undertakings will probably be required to keep confidential any settlement discussions with the Commission. If such obligations on undertakings are indeed intended, then a Commission Notice would appear insufficient as an instrument to underpin the direct settlement procedure, as a Notice binds the Commission but not third parties. Hence, a Commission Regulation, it is argued, would provide the appropriate legal framework, possibly in conjunction with a Commission Notice.

[147] However, the Commission might need to find a way of combining a system of direct settlements with the functioning of the Leniency Notice. Indeed, it is arguable that the combination of reductions under the Leniency Notice and settlements could lead to over-compensation for co-operation.

[148] US plea bargains contain a standard provision in this regard, which underscores that the undertaking has not felt compelled in any way to adhere to the plea bargain.

[149] Art 27 of Regulation 1/2003.

review of a Commission decision could not be withheld.[150] A way of discouraging undertakings that are subject of a settlement decision from going to court could lie in the drafting of that decision. If the Commission were to design the settlement decision in such a way as to contain reference to an admission by the undertaking of the infringement described, and confirmation that the undertaking 'agrees' to the fine, the basis for the undertaking to contest the decision later before the CFI would be significantly reduced.[151] A further key consideration is that the Commission would need to have some discretion in applying the instrument. There is unlikely to be a 'right' to settle and the Commission would want to retain the possibility of reverting to a traditional decision-making process in appropriate cases. That may be so for example where certain parties wanted to settle but other parties in the same case did not. In such circumstances, the Commission would surely wish to be able to simplify the handling of the case by following a single (full) procedure for all the undertakings concerned rather than allowing a more tailored approach.

8.485 **Institutional framework** The institutional framework will determine a number of the boundaries within which a direct settlement system might operate. Assuming that any direct settlement would take the form of a Commission decision (rather than, for example, the combination of a unilateral act by the undertaking—to pay a fine—and one by the Commission—to close the investigation)[152] it can be expected that the Commission, as a College of Commissioners, in the same way as it makes prohibition decisions with fines following a proposal by the Commissioner for Competition, would also arrive at a settlement decision in the same manner. However, the question is on what basis and with whom discussions about a settlement would take place. It appears highly unlikely that such talks would be held with the entire College of Commissioners, but equally it cannot be expected that the College would delegate that power in an unqualified form to the Commissioner for competition. One solution could be, for instance, first to adopt an (internal) act that empowers DG Competition to open discussions within certain limits that have been decided by the College of Commissioners. The possibility of the Commission services participating in such discussions, with the backing of the College of Commissioners, appears a necessary condition for a system of direct settlements to function: undertakings would want to be able to discuss seriously any settlement to be arrived at and would want the outcome to be binding, in principle at least, on the Commission. Another important element in the institutional design that would need to be taken into account is the Advisory Committee on Restrictive Practices and Dominant Positions. Under the existing system, this committee's opinion is required at the stage of the draft decision, in respect of both substance and

---

[150] Also enshrined in Art 31 of Regulation 1/2003.

[151] The Commission would still need to consider what solution to adopt if an undertaking were to appeal (or if it were to violate one of the conditions of the settlement decision). Conceivably, the Commission could withdraw its decision and replace it with a fully reasoned decision with (different) fines or it could ask the Court to impose a fine that would withdraw the benefit accorded by the Commission, in a similar way to what occurred in Joined Cases T-236/01 etc *Tokai Carbon and others v Commission* [2004] ECR II-1181, para 112.

[152] The closing of an investigation is purely administrative and no formal action is required. However, if formal proceedings have been opened (normally at the stage when a Statement of Objections is issued) the closing of proceedings is an act of the Commission that has been delegated to the Director-General for Competition.

fines. In a new procedure for settlements, the Commission might have to ensure that a form of consultation could take place at an appropriate time.[153] As mentioned above, as regards the opportunity for court review, a solution might be to ensure that the settlement decision contains an explicit acknowledgement of both the facts and the legal basis of the infringement, as well as agreement to the resulting level of the fine, so that on those aspects the possibility of obtaining an annulment by the court would be significantly reduced.

Other aspects   If a system of direct settlements is introduced, it is likely to lead to a number **8.486** of other administrative changes. Indeed, one question is when and on what evidentiary basis the Commission would start discussions. In all likelihood, the Commission would want to have performed the necessary investigatory work so that it could have a firm view of its preliminary conclusions. Also, undertakings would want to have at least some access to the evidence upon which the Commission relies (although full access to the file is a procedure that the Commission would probably want to avoid).[154] It is therefore not unlikely that the Commission would first issue an SO, or submit to the parties a document akin to an SO which would outline the factual basis for the Commission's arguments and preliminary conclusions. However, it is possible that the Commission might convey its preliminary conclusions orally to the undertaking in a meeting. Another question is how to determine which legal entity(ies) that form part of 'the undertaking' that is found liable would (have to) consent to the settlement. It remains to be seen, in relation to direct settlements, whether the Commission would want to deviate from its standard practice of imputing liability to the highest ranked entity of the corporate group.[155] Similarly, an important question is what the actual level of the 'proposed' fine would be. To assess whether a fine is 'reasonable' for an undertaking is always difficult to answer, but at least the 2006 Guidelines on Fines[156] provide some certainty as to the maximum amount of a potential fine.[157] If the Commission cannot settle with all undertakings simultaneously, another consideration is whether the settlement decision would also mean that an undertaking that did settle would thereby be excluded from any further procedure. It is submitted that it is

---

[153] On the one hand, the Commission is unlikely to wish to consult the Advisory Committee at too early a stage, but, on the other hand, it would not be useful to present the Member States with what may be considered to be a *fait accompli* after the Commission Services have concluded their settlement discussions with the undertaking(s) concerned.

[154] As regards access to the file, it may be expected that the Commission would also seek administrative efficiencies in that regard and therefore only prepare a 'core file' for review.

[155] Further complications in this regard may follow from the 'joint and several' liability that the Commission imposes on entities that have (consecutively) been involved in an infringement. For example, the imposition of a fine that was established on the basis of the conduct of a subsidiary but for which two parent companies were consecutively responsible, would probably mean that the allocation of that liability between them would need to have been settled before the Commission could accept a final settlement. Another aspect of the attribution of liability for the infringement would be the potential for the Commission to consider recidivism in any future decisions.

[156] Guidelines on the method of setting fines imposed pursuant to Art 23(2)(a) of Regulation No 1/2003, [2006] OJ C210/0.

[157] See also the views of Ratliff about the need for predictability of the fine for companies to want to enter into settlement discussions. He states that the maximum level of the fine is considered to be the most important aspect in this regard, and not necessarily the knowledge of the exact level or the minimum/maximum range. (See J Ratliff, 'Plea Bargaining in EC Anti-Cartel Enforcement–A System Change?' (2006), paper presented at the 11th EUI Competition Law and Policy Workshop, 2006, *Enforcement of Prohibition of Cartels*.)

likely that a condition of the settlement would be the continued co-operation of the under-taking in the investigation/procedure against other undertakings so that the settlement would not be a guarantee against any further involvement in the overall procedure (such as a request for information or the requirement of its presence at a hearing). A further question is the extent to which publicity would be given to a settlement. It is unrealistic for undertakings to hope that the Commission would not want to make the conclusion of an investigation by settlement decision public. As regards information to be made available to third parties, further thought would also need to be given to the position of complainants in a shortened procedure and the (non-)accessibility of the information in the Commission files—information that might otherwise have appeared in a full (public) decision—to third parties that may wish to start actions for private damages.[158]

(2) Evidence in Cartel Cases[159]

8.487 The climax of the typically long and complex Commission investigation is a formal Commission decision in which the existence of an infringement of Article 81 is established and which is addressed to each legal entity found liable. In fact, a Commission decision comprises a group of individual decisions against each of the addressees.[160] In such deci-sions, the illicit behaviour of each undertaking is described and classified as a violation of the Treaty. That conduct is then formally prohibited, a 'cease and desist' order is addressed to the undertakings and (usually) a fine is imposed on them.

8.488 The ever more complex nature of cartels and the increasingly assiduous efforts of partici-pant undertakings to prevent detection render it more and more difficult for the Commission to gather evidence proving the existence of a cartel. In establishing an infringement, the Commission seeks to rely, where possible, on contemporaneous written evidence gathered during the investigation, but such evidence may not be available to prove the necessary elements of the infringement over its full duration. The question of what cat-egories of information the Commission can actually use as proof of the infringement, and the evidentiary value to be attributed to each category, is therefore a vital one.[161] It is sur-prising that only limited legislative guidance exists in this regard. Regulation 1/2003 merely sets out one basic principle regarding to the application of Article 81, namely that the Commission (or the national authority alleging the infringement) bears the burden

---

[158] See for instance Art 6 of Regulation 773/2004 which refers to the right of complainants to a non-confidential version of an SO. It may be that in settlement procedures no such Statement of Objections is issued.

[159] The authors are especially grateful for the assistance of Mr Elliot Milton, Mr Lars Albath, and Mr Jindrich Klouh, whose contributions have been crucial to the preparation of this section on evidence.

[160] See para 8.419 above.

[161] The production of evidence is central to the finding of the existence of cartels, yet it is remarkable how comparatively little studied this subject has been. One study of cartel evidence is that of JM Joshua, 'Proof in Contested EEC Competition Cases', Eur L Rev, Vol 12, 1987. See also M Guerrin and G Kyriazis, 'Cartels: Proof and Procedural Issues', Fordham International Law Journal Vol 16:266, 1992–1993; JM Joshua and C Harding, *Regulating Cartels in Europe, A Study of Legal Control of Corporate Delinquency* (Oxford: Oxford University Press, 2003) in particular chapter VI; L Ortiz Blanco, *EC Competition Procedure* (2nd edn, 2006), paras 4.20–4.23 and 10.22 *et seq*; Ruiz Calzado and A Castro, chapter 7a, 'Cartels and Horizontal Collusive Conduct', in V Korah, *Competition Law of the European Community* (Matthew Bender, 2003).

of proof.[162] Indeed, in EC competition law, *rules* of evidence have not been codified in any collected form,[163] but some guidance and principles for determining what constitutes valid evidence can be gleaned from past practice of the Commission and the European Courts. A synopsis of those principles, focusing on cartel investigations, is provided below.

What does the Commission need to prove?   The Commission's task of proving an   **8.489** infringement can be divided into four steps. The Commission must first substantiate the facts of the case. Second, it must demonstrate that those facts constitute a violation of the competition. Third, it must determine which undertakings can be held responsible for the infringement (and for what duration). Fourth, the Commission must decide—and justify—which legal entity(ies) it will hold liable in respect of each of the undertakings that has taken part in the infringement. This last step is one to which the Commission must pay great attention, as undertakings may have changed identity during and after the lifespan of the cartel. Internal restructuring may have taken place, and changes may have affected the (identities of the) legal entities within each undertaking. Also, part of the undertaking, together with the corresponding legal entities or merely the assets that form that part of the business, may have changed ownership.

In each of the above steps evidential issues are crucial. Evidence is normally put to the test in   **8.490** any appeal before the European Courts as appellants claim that the proof the Commission seeks to rely on to make its case is inadmissible or insufficient or has been misinterpreted. This section deals with the main issues concerning evidence of cartels. It first examines the issue of the *burden of proof* and the instances in which that burden is reversed. Next it discusses the *standard of proof* to which the Commission must adhere in adducing evidence. The discussion then turns to the *admissibility and evidentiary value of information* used by the Commission, and categorises the types of evidence that the Commission has actually relied on in its cartel decisions. The last section deals in greater depth with the issue of how the Commission determines the *addressees of the decision*, on whom fines will be imposed.

---

162 Art 2 of Regulation 1/2003, which states that any party claiming the benefit of the application of Art 81(3) bears the burden of proof as regards the conditions to be fulfilled. Some further legislative guidance on the use of evidence is provided by Art 12 of Regulation 1/2003, which governs certain aspects of the admissibility of evidence within the framework of the exchange of information within the European Competition Network. See also Arts 3 and 4 of Regulation 773/2004, in relation to the taking of evidence through interviews and during inspections. Another source is section Nr. II 4 of Form C (Complaint Form pursuant to Art 7 of Regulation 1/2003, Annex to the Commission Notice on the handling of complaints by the Commission under Arts 81 and 82 of the EC Treaty [2004] OJ 101/65), which envisages a number of different types of evidence. Furthermore, some rules governing issues relevant to (cartel) evidence are provided by the 2002 and 2006 Commission Notice on Immunity from Fines and Reduction of Fines in Cartel Cases ([2002] OJ C45/03, [2006] OJ C298/17; the Leniency Notice is discussed in paras 8.104–8.257), with regard to the evidential value of information relevant to granting a reduction in fines (see notably point 22 and 23 of the 2002 Leniency Notice and point 25 of the 2006 Leniency Notice). The Commission Notice on Access to the File [2005] OJ C325/07 (discussed in paras 8.457–8.463), includes certain rules relating to the exclusion of the use of 'internal documents' as evidence, and to the use of minutes of meetings, which the Notice states may only be used in evidence after the source has agreed to such use (section 3.1.1. of the Notice on Access to the File).

163 By contrast, such codification may exist at the level of national law. The preamble of Regulation 1/2003 specifically recognises this, stating that '[T]his Regulations affects neither national rules on the standard of proof nor obligations of competition authorities and courts of the Member States to ascertain the relevant facts of a case, provided that such rules and obligations are compatible with general principles of Community law'.

(a) The Burden of Proof

8.491   **The burden of proof on the Commission**   Article 2 of EC Regulation 1/2003 provides that 'the burden of proving an infringement of Articles 81 and 82 of the Treaty shall rest on the party or authority alleging the infringement'.[164] In a cartel decision, therefore, the burden of proof is clearly on the Commission to establish the participation of the relevant undertakings in the infringement.[165] In the words of the ECJ, '[…] it is incumbent on the Commission to prove the infringements which it has found and to adduce evidence capable of demonstrating to the requisite legal standard the existence of circumstances constituting the infringement. […] In doing this, the Commission must establish in particular all the facts enabling the conclusion to be drawn that an undertaking participated in such an infringement and that it was responsible for the various aspects of it.'[166] The Courts have confirmed on a number of occasions that until the Commission discharges that burden of proof, the defendant undertaking benefits from a presumption of innocence.[167]

8.492   **An alleviated burden of proof?**   The Commission's task of proving the existence of a cartel is a considerable one: cartels are often complex and of long duration, the behaviour often dates back many years, and firms are increasingly adept at covering their tracks. This means that evidence will inevitably be scarce and/or difficult to uncover. In light of the inherent difficulties in detecting and investigating cartels, the European Courts have eased the Commission's burden of proof to a certain degree with regard to the issues discussed below.[168]

---

[164] Art 2 of Regulation 1/2003. See also the fifth recital to Regulation 1/2003 where the Council states that it should be for the party or the authority alleging an infringement of the competition rules to prove the existence of the infringement and it should be for the undertaking or association of undertakings invoking the benefit of a defence against a finding of an infringement to demonstrate that the conditions for applying the defence are satisfied, so that the authority will then have to resort to other evidence. See also Case C-204/00 *Aalborg Portland A/S and others v Commission* [2004] ECR I-123, para 79, where the Court states that although the 'legal burden of proof is borne either by the Commission or by the undertaking or association concerned, the factual evidence on which a party relies may be of such a kind as to require the other party to provide an explanation or justification, failing which it is permissible to conclude that the burden of proof has been discharged.'

[165] Joshua believes it is misleading to speak of a burden of proof being placed on the Commission in an inquisitorial, administrative procedure like that followed by the Commission, where the latter is a decision-making authority, rather than a party to the proceedings: see JM Joshua, 'Attitudes to Antitrust Enforcement in the EU and the United States: Dodging the Traffic Warden or Respecting the Law?', Annual Proceedings of the Fordham Corporate Law Institute, International Antitrust Law & Policy, 1996 (New York: Sweet & Maxwell, 1996) pp 115–116. See as examples Case T-337/94 *Enso-Gutzeit Oy v Commission* [1998] ECR II-1571, paras 91, 108, 128, 131, 143, Joined Cases T-25/95 etc *Cimenteries CBR SA and others v Commission* [2000] ECR II-491 paras 1852 and 4270, and Joined Cases C-204/00 P etc *Aalborg Portland A/S and others v Commission* [2004] ECR I-123, para 78. K Lenaerts and I Maselis, 'Procedural Rights and Issues in the Enforcement of Articles 81 and 82 of the EC Treaty', Annual Proceedings of the Fordham Corporate Law Institute [2000], v. 27, at p 281.

[166] Case C-49/92 P *Commission v Anic* [1999] ECR I-4125, para 86, and the case law cited therein.

[167] See for instance Case T-44/02 etc *Dresdner Bank and others v Commission*, judgment of 27 September 2006, not yet reported, at para 61. See also joined Cases T-67/00 etc *JFE Engineering Corp and others v Commission* [2004] ECR II-2501 para 178, Case C-199/92 P *Hüls AG v Commission* [1999] ECR I-4287, paras 149 and 150, and Case C-235/92 P *Montecatini v Commission* [1999] ECR I-4539, paras 175 and 176. The principle of the presumption of innocence is also enshrined in Art 6(2) of the European Convention for the Protection of Human Rights (ECHR) and is protected in Community law through the case law of the Court of Justice, as reaffirmed in the preamble to the Single European Act and by Art 47 of the Charter of Fundamental Rights of the European Union. As regards the question on when the burden of proof may switch to the other party, see Case T-120/04 *Organic Peroxides v Commission*, judgment of 16 November 2006, not yet reported, at para 53 and the case law cited there.

[168] See Joined Cases T-67/00 etc *JFE Engineering Corp and others v Commission* [2004] ECR II-2501, para 203.

The 'cartel offence': a concept that embraces both 'agreements' and 'concerted practices'[169] **8.493**
Article 81 EC refers to, on the one hand, 'agreements' and on the other hand to 'concerted practices' that restrict competition. Supported by the Court, the Commission treats agreements and concerted practices as two aspects of a single 'cartel offence',[170] contrary to Article 81. It is recognised, particularly in the case of complex cartels of long duration, that collusive behaviour between undertakings may simultaneously display the characteristics of an agreement and a concerted practice or an inextricable combination of both.[171] In this context, the European Courts have endorsed the view of the Commission that it would be artificial and overly legalistic to consider these elements separately. In most, if not all, cartel cases there is an actual agreement, whether written or oral, explicit or tacit, accompanied by ancillary concerted practices, such as the exchange of sales data, which are intended to monitor adherence to an agreement. Where concerted practices are part of the overall cartel offence that includes (an) agreement(s), or it can be established that the concerted practices have as their object the restriction of competition, the Commission does not need to consider what impact the agreement(s) or concerted practices have had: the violation is punishable in itself.[172] The Commission, with the support of the Courts, therefore regards cartels as 'complex infringements'[173] or 'multiform infringements',[174] capturing anti-competitive cartel behaviour irrespective of its precise legal classification.

Reliance on the concept of a 'single and continuous infringement' As is clear from the **8.494** earlier examination of their typology,[175] cartels are rarely, if ever, characterised by a single meeting at which the entire game-plan of the cartel is drawn up in one neat and

---

[169] See paras 8.14–8.93 for a further description of the meaning of 'agreement' and 'concerted practice'.

[170] Certain legal commentators have described this as the creation of a 'cartel offence' by the European Courts. See JM Joshua and C Harding, *Regulating Cartels in Europe, A Study of Legal Control of Corporate Delinquency* (Oxford: Oxford University Press, 2003), pp 154–155.

[171] Case T-7/89 *SA Hercules Chemicals NV v Commission* [1991] ECR II-1711, para 264: 'The Commission was also entitled to characterize that single infringement as "an agreement and a concerted practice" since the infringement involved at one and the same time factual elements to be characterized as "agreements" and factual elements to be characterized as "concerted practices". Given such a complex infringement, the dual characterization by the Commission in Article 1 of the Decision must be understood not as requiring, simultaneously and cumulatively, proof that each of those factual elements presents the constituent elements both of an agreement and of a concerted practice, but rather as referring to a complex whole comprising a number of factual elements some of which were characterized as agreements and others as concerted practices for the purposes of Article 85(1) of the EEC Treaty, which lays down no specific category for a complex infringement of this type.'

[172] It is only where it appears that the cartel does not operate by way of an agreement, but just by way of a concerted practice, and for which the anti-competitive *object* is not established, that the Commission would have to identify the conduct that follows from the collusion in order to conclude that a violation of Art 81 has taken place. Although the very concept of concerted practice presupposes conduct by the participating undertakings on the market, it does not necessarily imply that that conduct should produce the specific effects of restricting, preventing or distorting competition. Case C-49/92 *Commission v Anic Partezipacioni SpA* [1999] ECR I-4125, paras 122–124 and Case C-199/92 P *Hüls AG* [1999] ECR I-4287, paras 164–165. See also Case T-4/89 *BASF AG v Commission* [1991] ECR II-1523, para 242. However, even in those instances the Commission's burden is reduced: according to the ECJ in *Hüls*, a presumption exists, subject to proof to the contrary, that undertakings taking part in such collusion will take account of the information exchanged with competitors in order to determine their own conduct on the market (See Case C-199/92 P *Hüls AG v Commission* [1999] ECR I-4287, para 162.)

[173] Joined Cases T-305/94 *Limburgse Vinyl Maatschappij NV and other v Commission* [1999] ECR II-931, para 696.

[174] Case COMP/E-1/38.069 [2006] OJ L192/21—*Copper Plumbing Tubes*, recital 16.

[175] See paras 8.14–8.93.

simple document. Rather, cartels usually consist of a complex arrangement of collusive contacts over an extended period of time, each of which on its own may be an infringement of Article 81. The Commission, with the support of the European Courts, has recognised that it would be artificial and contrary to the spirit of Article 81—which prohibits all forms of anti-competitive behaviour—to split this web of collusive conduct into a series of separate infringements when the reality is that they are merely constituent elements linked by a single ongoing economic objective.[176] The Commission has also recognised that it would be prohibitively difficult, from an evidential point of view, to attempt to link every participant in the cartel to each of these contacts.[177]

8.495 In order to capture the different aspects of, and participants in, a single collusive scheme, the concept of a *single and continuous infringement* was developed.[178] Participation in a single and continuous infringement does not mean that the role of each undertaking in that infringement cannot differ (an issue of which the Commission must take account).[179] Also, undertakings can only be held liable for an infringement of which they were aware, as the CFI confirmed in its *Sigma* judgment in *Pre-Insulated Pipes*.[180] However, parties that are aware of the existence of a collusive scheme are considered to be part of the infringement as a whole.

8.496 As is clear from its description, a 'single and continuous infringement' is both a 'single' infringement in that the facts and circumstances involved are interwoven, and a 'continuous' one, in that the behaviour can be seen as belonging to an (uninterrupted, or at least inter-related) string of occurrences.[181] (It should be noted that where the Commission concludes that separate infringements exist for different products, it may nevertheless deal with such infringements in a single administrative decision.)[182]

---

[176] An undertaking might seek to challenge the idea of the cartel as a single complex by arguing that the meetings which form the central basis of the Commission's evidence concerned different products. This was the case, for instance, in *Electrical and Mechanical Carbon and Graphite Products*. The Commission responded in its decision by stating that the substitutability of products is just one factor that it will consider when determining the existence of a single continuous infringement. Other factors play an important role, especially the functioning of the cartel itself. (Case COMP/E-2/38.359—*Electrical and Mechanical Carbon and Graphite Products* recital 230 ([2004] OJ L125/45).)

[177] Case T-1/89 *Rhône-Poulenc v Commission* [1991] ECR II-867, para 127, Case C-49/92 P *Commission v Anic Partezipacioni SpA* [1999] ECR I-4125, para 203; Case T-25/95 etc *Cimenteries etc v Commission* appeal, n 164 above, paras 258–263, Case T-310/94 *Grüber + Weber v Commission* [1998] ECR II-1043, para 37. For another example, see also Case COMP/E-1/38.069—*Copper Plumbing Tubes* [2006] OJ L192/21 recital 444–449.

[178] Reference is made to para 8.175, as regards the granting of immunity per infringement.

[179] See Joined Cases C-189/02 P etc *Dansk Rørindustri A/S and others v Commission* [2005] ECR I-5425, para 145.

[180] Case T-28/99 *Sigma Tecnologie v Commission* [2002] ECR II-1845, para 40. See also Joined cases C-189/02 P *Dansk Rørindustri A/S and others v Commission* [2005] ECR I-5425, para 143.

[181] This does not mean, however, that the evidence cannot have any gaps relating to contacts between cartel members. Even where a cartel has gone through 'quiet periods' it may still be seen as 'continuous'. See for instance Case COMP/E-1/38.069—*Copper Plumbing Tubes* [2006] OJ L192/21, recital 28, and Case T-279/02 *Degussa AG v Commission* [2006] ECR II-897, paras 129 and 135.

[182] For example, see the Commission Decision in *Vitamins* ([2003] OJ L6/1), where the Commission dealt with 12 separate infringements in a single decision. For the appeal against this decision see Case T-15/02 *BASF AG v Commission* [2006] ECR II-497, paras 88–91. For another decision that dealt with more than one infringement, see the Commission Decision in Case COMP/37.667—*Specialty Graphite*.

The notion of a single and continuous infringement first appeared in the Commission's **8.497** *Polypropylene* decision where a cartel involving 15 firms in the petrochemicals sector was uncovered.[183] The Commission considered that the various arrangements by which the cartel operated during the period of its existence[184] were all part of a 'single overall agreement', which infringed Article 81. In the view of the Commission, each of the 15 firms was guilty of the infringement despite not having participated in every meeting nor having materially contributed to the key decisions of the cartel.

Determination of a single and continuous infringement: possible consequences for the **8.498** **fines**   The decision as to whether behaviour can be classified as one infringement or as separate infringements can have important ramifications. If, on the one hand, the Commission were to regard the behaviour as separate infringements, it would impose separate fines, which may (each) go as high as the 10 per cent of annual turnover threshold, contained in Article 23(2) of Regulation 1/2003. On the other hand, if certain unlawful acts are viewed as one and the same infringement, the maximum fine threshold of 10 per cent of the undertaking's annual turnover may kick in more quickly for that single fine. Hence, conceivably, a determination of separate infringements could lead to a higher overall fine amount, though that remains speculative.[185] Another potential consequence may be that behaviour which may be time-barred if viewed as separate infringements (for instance a cartel which has seen a significant period of interruption), might still be punishable when considered as part of a continuous scheme of unlawful behaviour.[186] Also, whether a decision finds one or more infringements may be relevant when rewarding co-operation under the Leniency Notice, since such rewards are assessed on a 'per infringement' basis.[187] Lastly, as the CFI

---

[183] [1986] OJ L230/1.

[184] It appears that gaps in time between the meetings of participants may be relevant to the consideration of whether a single continuous infringement exists, although in the *Cimenteries,* judgment, the Court of Justice dismissed as 'immaterial' a gap of several months between meetings. Joined Cases C-204/00 P etc *Aalborg Portland A/S and others v Commission* [2004] ECR I-123, para 260. On the issue of the continuous nature of the infringement, see also Case T-279/02 *Degussa AG v Commission* [2006] ECR II-897, para 153, where the CFI, referring to its judgment in Case T-62/98 *Volkswagen AG v Commission* [2000] ECR II-2707, para 188, confirms that the 'Commission should adduce at least evidence of facts sufficiently proximate in time for it to be reasonable to accept that infringement continued uninterruptedly between two specific dates'.

[185] For a discussion see the judgment of the CFI in Case T-15/02 *BASF AG v Commission* [2006] ECR II-497 para 69. In para 73 the CFI, referring to the fact that separate infringements had been found instead of a single one, stated that: '(. . .) if the Commission had found in the present case that there had been a single infringement covering all the vitamin products referred to in the Decision, it could probably also have taken into account, for the purposes of calculating the fine to be imposed on the applicant, the latter's collusion in respect of Vitamins B1 and H, which the Commission did not punish in the Decision, as it regarded them as separate infringements relating to which its power to impose penalties was time-barred under Regulation No 2988/74.'

[186] See also Case T-15/02 *BASF AG v Commission* [2006] ECR II-497, para 72.

[187] A hypothetical example may help to explain this. Suppose a violation has occurred between undertakings X, Y and Z covering products A, B and C. Company X applies for immunity in respect of the three products. It will get immunity for all three, regardless of the classification as a single infringement or multiple infringements. Suppose the cartel is seen as a single infringement. If company Y then applies for a reduction of fines with information on only product B, it will be the first in line for a reduction in fines and could therefore benefit from a maximum reduction of 50%, for the infringement ABC as a whole. If company Z subsequently applies with information on product C, it will be the third company in the door for the ABC cartel, and second in line for a reduction of fines, and get a maximum reduction of 30%. If, on the other hand,

showed in *Vitamins*, the application of attenuating and aggravating factors may produce different results, depending on whether the conduct is seen as part of a single scheme or not.[188]

8.499 **Single infringement** How then does the Commission decide whether behaviour will constitute a 'single' infringement or not? The Commission can have regard to 'objective elements', some of which the CFI referred to in *Specialty Graphites* and in *Citric Acid*.[189] Such elements may include: the *common objective* of the collusive behaviour, whether or not different *products or services* were involved, whether the behaviour was (dis)similar in different *geographic areas*, as well as commonalities between the *undertakings that participated*, the *individuals concerned* and *cartel meetings and/or other contacts*. Each of these elements will be discussed in greater detail below, but it must be emphasised that it is usually a combination of the above factors that guides the Commission's approach, rather than dependence on a single element. It is submitted that as long as it considers the relevant objective elements when deciding on the 'single' nature of an infringement, the Commission has a margin of discretion, because a variety of factors, whose weight varies according to the facts of each individual case, have a bearing on the decision. The CFI has made clear that the available elements are to be looked at together in determining whether the Commission's conclusions are well founded.[190]

8.500 One important consideration is whether there was a common overall *objective*, which was subscribed to by all the participants, either consciously, or implicitly as shown by their behaviour. A common objective might be, for instance, that the (agreed) purpose of the collusion was to increase prices for a particular product.[191] The fact that the objective itself may have undergone certain mutations at different points during the lifespan of the cartel, eg a switch from fixing prices to limitation of production capacity, does not preclude it from being considered 'single' in nature.[192] Another possible consideration is whether

---

the behaviour concerning products A, B and C are seen as a separate infringements, company Z would become first in line for a reduction for the infringement covering product C, and could obtain the maximum 50% reduction for that infringement. However, whether that calculation based on separate infringements turns out positively for C or not depends on the circumstances and the (full) fine it may otherwise get for products A and B, for which it did not supply information. In general, the fact that the Commission finds a single infringement, rather than a series of separate infringements does not necessarily mean that the fine imposed will be lower. (See Case T-15/02 *BASF AG v Commission* [2006] ECR II-497, para 69.)

[188] For example, as regards an aggravating circumstance such as being an instigator or having a leadership role. In its *Vitamins decision*, the Commission attributed a leadership role to BASF for a range of separate infringements, and therefore applied an across the board aggravation factor of 35% to the fine. The CFI reduced the fine for vitamins C and D3, beta-carotene and carotinoids because the Commission had failed to establish that BASF had actually acted as instigator or leader in relation to those four products (although it did confirm the increase for vitamins A, E and B5 (and B2)). (See Case T-15/02 *BASF AG v Commission* [2006] ECR II-497, para 273 *et seq.* and, for the conclusion relating to the increase of 35% in the fine for the various infringements, see para 464.)

[189] See Joined Cases T-71/03 etc *Tokai Carbon Co Ltd. and others v Commission* [2005] ECR II-10, paras 118–124; Case T-43/02 *Jungbunzlauer AG v Commission*, judgment of 27 September 2006, not yet reported, para 312.

[190] See Joined Cases T-259/02 etc *Raiffeisen Zentralbank Österreich and others v Commission (Lombard Club)*, judgment of 14 December 2006, not yet reported, para 121.

[191] Case T-43/02 *Jungbunzlauer AG v Commission*, judgment of 27 September 2006, not yet reported, para 312, where the CFI refers to a 'joint project' (own translation) in combination with a single purpose. See also Joined Cases T-259/02 etc *Raiffeisen Zentralbank Österreich and others v Commission (Lombard Club)*, judgment of 14 December 2006, not yet reported, para 111 *et seq.* and the case law cited there.

[192] Case COMP/E-1/38.069—*Copper Plumbing Tubes* [2006] OJ L192/2121, recital 444.

different *products* have been involved in the behaviour. However, cartels are not circumscribed by reference to a product market definition and, unlike for instance, competition proceedings under Article 82 of the Treaty, the Commission is not required to define 'relevant product markets' in order to find an infringement.[193] Nevertheless, the fact that different products are involved may constitute one reason, amongst others, for finding that separate cartels are in operation.[194] In other cases, however, the Commission has found that even though the collusion involves different products or services, the behaviour should nevertheless be classified as a single infringement for other reasons.[195] Another relevant consideration may be that the *undertakings* that are engaged in or are aware of the collusion are (largely) the same. A considerable overlap may point to a single collusive scheme, whereas in the fact that the participants differ would point in the opposite direction.[196] A further pertinent factor to consider in this regard is similarities in the *contacts/meetings between the parties* involved in the cartel. If it can be established that different products were discussed on the same occasions, that would point more strongly in the direction of a single overall scheme. Also, similarity as to the *personnel involved* in the collusion may be relevant, but is not in itself conclusive. Another aspect concerns the *geographic area(s) covered*. If various markets with their own characteristics that, for instance, can each be defined as national, are subject to collusion, this may indicate separate cartel schemes. Nevertheless, the fact that a cartel covers different geographic areas does not necessarily mean that the collusion should be seen as a number of separate infringements.[197] As with the definition of the product market, it is relevant that the Commission does not have to define the market in order to conclude that the infringement has taken place (although the Commission does normally have to consider the geographic scope of the market for determining that an effect on trade between Member States has taken place[198] and for deciding on the appropriate amount of the fines). The Commission may find that, notwithstanding the fact that the undertakings and products involved in the collusion are the same, the behaviour should nevertheless be regarded as constituting separate schemes due to the fact that they occur in

---

[193] See also para 8.502.

[194] See Joined Cases T-71/03 etc *Tokai Carbon Co Ltd. and others v Commission* [2005] ECR II-10, para 124 and Case T-15/02 *BASF AG v Commission* [2006] ECR II-497, para 88. See also Case T-43/02 *Jungbunzlauer AG v Commission*, judgment of 27 September 2006, not yet reported, at para 312.

[195] See Case T-15/02, *BASF AG v Commission* [2006] ECR II-497, paras 76–77. For an example concerning services (banking) see Joined Cases T-259/02 etc *Raiffeissen Zentralbank Österreich and others v Commission (Lombard Club)*, judgment of 14 December 2006, not yet reported, in which various different banking services were subject to a common cartel scheme.

[196] By way of contrast, in *Specialty Graphites* (Case COMP.37.667 [2006] OJ L180/20), the Commission decided to treat as separate infringements the behaviour for extruded and isostatic graphite products, one of the principal reasons being that the cartel in isostatic graphite products involved six undertakings, whereas the collusion on the market for extruded graphites product only concerned two of those six undertakings. See also the judgment of the CFI in *Citric Acid*, (Case T-43/02 *Jungbunzlauer AG v Commission*, judgment of 27 September 2006, not yet reported, para 312), where the fact that only two of five undertakings participated in what the appellant claimed was a single scheme with the Sodium Gluconate cartel, was one reason why the CFI considered that there were two separate cartels.

[197] See Case COMP/38.354—*Industrial Bags* (IP/05/1508) where the Commission found that cartel participants had secretly agreed among themselves, some for over 20 years, to increase sale prices, in Germany, the Benelux countries, France and Spain.

[198] Joined Cases T-259/02 etc *Raiffeissen Zentralbank Österreich and others v Commission (Lombard Club)*, judgment of 14 December 2006, not yet reported, paras 162 *et seq.* and the case law mentioned there.

different national markets or in different levels/segments of the market (eg, at retail level, as opposed to wholesale).

8.501 **The 'continuous' nature of the infringement** The decision of the Commission to consider certain illegal acts as part of the same continuous infringement may have important implications for the fine,[199] not only in relation to the overall duration of the infringement but also because behaviour which occurred more than five years before the Commission started its investigation if it were severable as an infringement from subsequent behaviour, would be time-barred from the imposition of fines and therefore beyond the sanction of fines. The fact that there are certain gaps in the sequence of events established by the Commission does not mean that the infringement cannot be regarded as uninterrupted.[200] Indeed, where cartel contacts diminish temporarily or where they have been interrupted, for instance as a result of an upturn in the market during which market prices are rising, therefore removing the need for collusion, this does not mean that the collusion has actually stopped. As regards the continuous nature of an infringement for individual participants, an undertaking in the cartel cannot avoid responsibility if it is shown that it knew, or must have known, that the collusion in which it participated was part of a common design or overall plan intended to distort competition and that the plan included all the constituent elements of the cartel.[201] For as long as an undertaking has adhered to the cartel arrangements and contributed to the realisation of its overall objective, it will be held to have been a participant and will be equally responsible for the acts of the other participants carried out in accordance with that objective.[202]

---

[199] Under the 1998 Guidelines on Fines, for cartels that last longer than one year an additional increase of 10% is applied to the starting amount for each additional year of infringement (or, normally, 5% for each six month period). (See Commission Guidelines on the method of setting fines imposed pursuant to Art 15(2) of Regulation 17 and Art 65(5) of the ECSC Treaty [1998] OJ C9/03). Under the 2006 Guidelines on Fines the value of sales in the last full year of the infringement will count for each year of the infringement. (See Commission Guidelines on the method of setting fines imposed pursuant to Art 23(2)(a) of Regulation No 1/2003, available on the Commission web site. See also paras 8.624–8.834 on the calculation of fines.)

[200] The CFI has allowed the Commission a degree of flexibility with regard to demonstrating the continued duration of an infringement. If there is no evidence 'directly establishing the duration of an infringement', it is sufficient for the Commission to adduce 'evidence of facts sufficiently proximate in time for it to be reasonable to accept that that infringement continued uninterruptedly between two specific dates': Case T-43/92 *Dunlop Slazenger v Commission* [1994] ECR II-441, para 79; Case T-62/98 *Volkswagen AG v Commission* [2000] ECR II-2707, para 188, and Case T-279/02 *Degussa AG v Commission* [2006] ECR II-897, para 153. Case T-120/04 *Peróxidos Orgánicos SA v Commissions*, judgment of 16 November 2006, not yet reported, para 51. See also Case COMP/E-1/38.069—*Copper Plumbing Tubes* [2006] OJ L192/21 recital 28 and Case No IV/E-1/35.860-B—*Seamless Steel Tubes* [2003] OJ L140/1.

[201] 'According to the case law, an undertaking may be held responsible for an overall cartel even though it is shown that it participated directly only in some of the constituent elements of that cartel, if it is shown that it knew, or must have known, that the collusion in which it participated was part of an overall plan and that the overall plan included all the constituent elements of the cartel.' (Case T-9/99 *HFB Holding für Fernwärmetechnik Beteiligungsgesellschaft mbH & Co. KG and othersv Commission* [2002] ECR II-1487, para 231 and the case law cited therein.). See also Case C-49/92 P *Commission v Anic Partezipacioni SpA* [1999] ECR I-4125, para 83, Joined Cases T-25/95 etc *Cimenteries CBR SA and others v Commission* [2000] ECR II-491, para 83, Joined Cases T-305/94 etc *Limburgse Vinyl Maatschappij NV and others v Commission* ('*PVC II*') [1999] ECR II-931, para 773 and Joined Cases T-67/00 etc *JFE Engineering Corp. and others v Commission* [2004] ECR II-2501, para 370. Conversely, where an undertaking could not have had knowledge of its participation in a wider infringement, it will only be held liable for its own infringement. See also Case T-28/99 *Sigma Tecnologie di rivestimento Srl v Commission* [2002] ECR II-1845, paras 44–52, to which the CFI accorded a reduction of 25% in the starting amount of the fine based on its unawareness of the wider infringement.

[202] The participant undertaking must participate in the cartel in such a way that its conduct forms part of the collusive behaviour constituting the infringement: Case C-49/92 P *Commission v Anic Partezipacioni SpA*

A party claiming that it did not participate in meetings and asserting that it has ceased participation in a collusive scheme will, in the absence of other proof, have to show that it publicly distanced itself from the cartel in an unambiguous manner that leaves its erstwhile co-participant undertakings in no doubt that it has left the cartel.[203]

No market definition required   As mentioned, the Commission is not obliged to define the relevant market in a decision applying Article 81 of the Treaty, except where it would be impossible without such a definition to determine whether the agreement or concerted practice in question was liable to affect trade between Member States and had as its object or effect the prevention, restriction, or distortion of competition within the Common Market.[204] In most cartel cases the effect on trade between Member States or competition within the Common Market will be easily demonstrated without the need to define the relevant market.[205] However, the Commission will place the conduct in its relevant context by describing the sector and the position of the parties on the market. The Commission will also take into account the geographical impact of a cartel when determining the appropriate level of the fine, and thus will consider the geographic dimension of the collusion.

8.502

No need to demonstrate the precise mechanism by which the restrictive object was sought   Related to the acceptance by the European Courts of a more generic concept of what constitutes a cartel offence, is their view that the Commission does not have to produce evidence of the specific mechanism by which a cartel operated.[206] The justification cited by

8.503

[1999] ECR I-4125, para 83. See also Commission Decision in Case COMP/37.533—*Choline chloride* recitals 145–148 ([2005] OJ L190/22. The full text of the decision is available on the DG COMP web site, <http://ec.europa.eu/comm/competition/index_en.htm>).

[203] The undertaking must publicly distance itself from the cartel in such a way that the other participants are aware that it does not subscribe to the conclusions of meetings and will not act in conformity with them, or is participating in the meetings in a spirit which is different from theirs. (Case T-7/89 *SA Hercules Chemicals NV v Commission* [1991] ECR II-1711, para 232; Case T-12/89 *Solvay et Compagnie SA v Commission* [1992] ECR II-907, para 98; Case T-141/89 *Tréfileurope Sales SARL v Commission* [1995] ECR II-791 paras 85 and 86; Case T-15/89 *Chemie Linz AG AG v Commission* [1992] ECR II-1275, para 135; Case T-61/99 *Adriatica di Navigazione SpA v Commission* [2003] ECR II-5349, para 135. See also Joined Cases T-25/95, etc. *Cimenteries CBR SA and others v Commission* [2000] ECR II-491 para 81 and para 3199. See also Case C-199/92 P *Hüls AG v Commission* [1999] ECR I-4287, para 155, and Case C-49/92 P *Commission v Anic Partecipazioni SpA* [1999] ECR I-4125, para 96; Case T-56/99 *Marlines SA v Commission* [2003] ECR II-2003, para 56 confirmed on appeal, Case C-112/04 P *Marlines SA v Commission*; order of 15 September 2005, not yet reported. ('[T]herefore, only by openly and publicly distancing itself from the cartel upon receiving the correspondence in question could the applicant avoid infringing Article 85 [now 81] of the Treaty.') C-204/00 *Aalborg Portland A/S and others v Commission* [2004] ECR I-123, paras 81–86. See further, Joined Cases T-259/02 etc *Raiffeissen Zentralbank Österreich and others v Commission (Lombard Club)*, judgment of 14 December 2006, not yet reported, para 486 and the case law cited therein.

[204] Case T-38/02 *Groupe Danone v Commission* [2005] ECR II-4407, para 99, and the case law mentioned therein.

[205] Another rationale is that in cartel cases, the companies that conclude anti-competitive agreements have, in so doing, themselves determined the boundaries of competition between them. See *Electrical and Mechanical Carbon and Graphite Products* (Case 38.359, [2004] OJ L125/45; the full text of the decision is available on the DG COMP web site, <http://ec.europa.eu/comm/competition/index_en.htm>, recital 13). The position as regards market definition under Art 81 can be contrasted with the position under Art 82 where a market definition is a necessary pre-condition to a finding of abuse of a dominant position: an undertaking could not be judged dominant in a market unless that market is properly defined. also Case 37.784— *Fine Art Auction Houses* ([2005] OJ L200/92, recitals 28 and 29 (the full text of the decision is available on the DG COMP web site, <http://ec.europa.eu/comm/competition/index_en.htm>).

[206] See Case T-310/94 *Grüber + Weber GmbH & Co. KG v Commission* [1998] ECR II-1043, para 214; Joined Cases T-67/00 etc *JFE Engineering Corp. and others v Commission* [2004] ECR II-2501, para 203.

the CFI for this rule is, again, a pragmatic one: due to the furtive nature of cartels and the consequent difficulty the Commission has in obtaining much documentary evidence, the Court must allow the Commission a certain leeway as regards the burden of proof. Therefore, provided the existence and anti-competitive purpose of the agreement(s) has been sufficiently established, the Commission is not required to demonstrate the operation of the cartel in detail. Were it otherwise, the CFI reasoned, '[i]t would be too easy for an undertaking guilty of an infringement to escape any penalty if it was entitled to base its argument on the vagueness of the information produced'.[207]

8.504 **No requirement to prove subjective intent to act illegally**   Similarly helpful to the Commission in its effort to demonstrate the existence of an infringement is the fact that the Court has deemed it unnecessary to prove subjective intent[208] on the part of the cartel participants to break the competition rules.[209] It is also immaterial that the undertakings did not consider themselves bound—in law, in fact, or morally—by the cartel agreement. Rather than having to show wrongful intent or awareness that their behaviour was contrary to Article 81, it is sufficient for the Commission to prove that the participant undertakings shared a common goal of adopting certain conduct in the market, and that the undertakings could not have been unaware that such conduct had as its object or effect the restriction of competition.[210] Article 81 infringements can therefore be characterised as a form of strict liability: the subjective intent or awareness of an undertaking that it has infringed the competition rules is not a necessary element in the establishment of liability.

8.505 **The concept of a *per se* infringement—no requirement to prove impact**   Also of significant assistance to the Commission in its task of proving the existence of an infringement is the fact that is the Court does not require it to prove that the anti-competitive behaviour in question had any impact in the market-place.[211] This applies to the cartel as a whole, as well as to its individual members.[212] The question of 'impact' is one that may be seen as different

---

[207] Joined Cases T-67/00 etc *JFE Engineering Corp. and others v Commission* [2004] ECR II-2501, para 203.

[208] Art 81 refers to the 'object' of anti-competitive practices, but it is submitted that this term refers more to the 'subject-matter' of the collusion than to the subjective intent of the participants. See also R Whish, *Competition Law* (5th edn, 2003), p 110. On the absence of a requirement to prove illegal intent see Joined Cases T-259/02 etc *Raiffeissen Zentralbank Österreich and others v Commission (Lombard Club)*, judgment of 14 December 2006, not yet reported, paras 205 and the case law cited therein.

[209] However, the intentional nature of the infringement may be considered as an aggravating circumstance, see paras 8.713–8.738.

[210] Joined Cases C-238/99 P etc *Limburgse Vinyl Maatschappij NV and others v Commission* [2002] ECR I-8375, para 715. Thus, the level of intent that the Commission is required to prove is that the undertaking concerned 'intended to contribute' by its own conduct to the common objectives pursued by all the participants, and that it was aware of the actual conduct planned or put into effect by other undertakings in pursuit of the same objectives or that it could reasonably have foreseen that such conduct would ensue and was prepared to take the risk of it taking place. Joined Cases C-204/00 P etc *Aalborg Portland and others v Commission* [2004] EC I-123, para 291 and Case C-49/92 *Commission v Anic Partezipacioni SpA* [1999] ECR I-4125, para 87. See also Case T-61/89 *Dansk Pelsdyravlerforening v Commission* [1992] ECR II-1931, para 157; Case T-59/99 *Ventouris Group Enterprises SA v Commission* [2003] ECR II-5257, paras 54 and 92 and the case law cited therein.

[211] For a definition of *per se* infringements see also para 8.03.

[212] Joined Cases T-236/01 etc *Tokai Carbon Co Ltd. and others v Commission* [2004] ECR II-1181, para 81 and Case T-304/94 *Europa Carton AG v Commission* [1998] ECR II-869, para 141. ('For an undertaking to be classified as a perpetrator of an infringement it is not necessary for it to have derived any economic advantage from its participation in the cartel in question.')

from that of the 'implementation' of the cartel, though they are normally associated with each other. The existence of an infringement does not require proof of its implementation either. Indeed, the concept of *per se* infringements[213] is now well established in Community law,[214] all infringements having as their object price-fixing or market sharing, which are amongst the anti-competitive practices, considered to be prohibited 'by definition'.[215] However, the issue of market effects, or presumed effects, although irrelevant to the finding of an infringement as such, may be taken into account in deciding the quantum of fines imposed.[216] That link can be explained as follows: for the Commission to take account of the impact of the cartel, it must be established that such an impact did indeed occur. The Commission is entitled to presume such an impact from the fact that the cartel was implemented. (The Commission cannot be required to quantify that impact, however, and such calculations are in any event regarded as 'hypothetical' by the Courts.)[217] Hence, although the Commission is not required to prove the implementation of an illicit agreement, it normally signals in its decisions factors showing implementation, so that the impact of the cartel can be considered for the determination of the fines.

Concluding comments on the burden of proof   It has been seen that the fundamental rule as **8.506** regards the burden of proof is that the onus is manifestly on the Commission to establish convincingly the participation of the relevant undertakings in the infringement. However, the apparent rigidity of this rule is offset somewhat by two key factors. First, once the Commission has established that the undertaking in question has participated in an anti-competitive practice, the onus shifts to that undertaking to produce evidence which can explain the undertaking's conduct in a way which is consistent with competitive behaviour.[218] So, for example, where the Commission proves the participation by an undertaking in cartel meetings, there is a presumption that the undertaking complied with the overall objective of the cartel. It is then for the undertaking to come up with a different, coherent explanation[219] and in its reply to the Statement of Objections and in any later

---

[213] Case C-49/92 *Commission v Anic Partezipacioni SpA* [1999] ECR I-4125, para 123.

[214] Joined Cases C-204/00 etc *Aalborg Portland and others v Commission* [2004] ECR I-123, para 261. See also Case 277/87 *Sandoz prodotti farmaceutici Spa v Commission* [1990] ECR I-45, para 30, Case T-143/89 *Ferriere Nord SpA v Commission* [1995] ECR II-917, para 30, Case T-141/94 *Thyssen Stahl AG v Commission* [1999] ECR II-1347, para 277; Joined Cases T-204/98 etc *British Sugar plc and others v Commission* [2001] ECR II-2035, paras 72 and 73.

[215] Joined Cases T-374/94 etc *European Night Services Ltd and others v Commission* [1998] ECR II-3141, para 136. See also R Whish, *Competition Law* (5th edn, London: Butterworths, 2003) p 114. Whish lists six different types of agreements which amount to *per se* infringements: (1) to fix prices; (2) to share markets; (3) to limit output; (4) to limit sales; (5) to exchange price information; (6) for collective collusive dealing.

[216] For a discussion see paras 8.634–8.639 on fines.

[217] Joined Cases T-259/02 etc *Raiffeissen Zentralbank Österreich and others v Commission (Lombard Club)*, judgment of 14 December 2006, not yet reported, para 286 and the case law mentioned therein.

[218] Joined Cases C-204/00 P etc *Aalborg Portland and others v Commission* [2004] ECR I-123, para 132.

[219] T-44/02 etc *Dresdner Bank and others v Commission*, judgment of 27 September 2006, not yet reported, at para 65, where, in view of the general indications of cartel behaviour, the Court stated that the undertaking needed to produce a different, coherent explanation of the circumstances and indications that the Commission had relied on. In this regard, the CFI stated that it would make no finding of manifest error of assessment by the Commission if the explanation given by the Commission was more plausible than that of the undertaking (para 58).

challenge before the CFI, the burden of proof will be on the undertaking to produce such an explanation and/or evidence of its (publicly) distancing itself from the cartel.[220]

8.507 Second, it has been shown that the Commission and the European Courts take an expansive, purposive view of what constitutes cartel behaviour.[221] As early as 1972, the Court of Justice indicated in its judgment in *ICI v Commission* that the aim of Article 81 was to prohibit any form of co-ordination between undertakings 'by which, without having reached the stage where an agreement properly so-called may have been concluded, they knowingly substitute practical co-operation between them for the risks of competition'.[222] Article 81 seeks to ensure that each economic operator determines its commercial policy in the market-place independently. It thus prohibits any form of contact, either direct or indirect, between competitors, the aim or effect of which is to distort competition.[223] It is for this reason that the Commission in its role as enforcer of Article 81 will look purposively at what constitutes cartel behaviour and, supported by the European Courts, will not allow legalistic argument by the defendant undertakings to obstruct the Commission in carrying out that task. Undertakings can still defend themselves properly in such circumstances provided that they have an opportunity to comment on all the evidence against them relied upon by the Commission.[224]

(b) The Standard of Proof

8.508 As stated above, the majority of Commission cartel decisions are appealed to the Court of First Instance, and the court does not confine itself to judicial review of the strict legality of the decision. Under its power of unlimited jurisdiction, the CFI examines the evidence to ensure, *inter alia*, that there has not been an error of interpretation. In conducting this review, the question arises as to the standard of proof required of the Commission in decisions which find a cartel infringement.[225] Although the Court has avoided using the term 'standard of proof',[226] it has in recent judgments set out more precisely what it considers

---

[220] For relevant case law see n 203 above. See also Case T-56/99 *Marlines SA v Commission* [2003] ECR II 2003, para 56 where the Court of First Instance held that the mere fact that an undertaking had received from another participant undertaking a certain number of telexes referring to price agreements could suffice to prove that the undertaking had participated in those agreements. (Confirmed on appeal, Case C-112/04 P *Marlines SA v Commission*, order of 15 September 2005, not yet reported).

[221] Whish, n 215 above, p 97.

[222] Case 48/69 *ICI Ltd v Commission* [1972] ECR 619, para 64.

[223] Joined Cases 40/73 etc *Coöperatieve Vereiniging 'Suiker Unie' UA and others v Commission* [1975] ECR 1663, para 174.

[224] Joined Cases T-67/00 etc *JFE Engineering Corp. v Commission* [2004] ECR II-2501, para 203.

[225] For a discussion of this issue, see B Louveaux and P Gilbert, 'The Standard of Proof under the Competition Act', ECLR [2003] Vol. 26, p 173, L Ortiz Blanco, *EC Competition Procedure* (2nd edn, 2006), paras 4.20–4.23 and CS Kerse and N Khan, *EC Antitrust Procedure* (5th edn, 2005), para 5-057. See also JM Joshua and C Harding, *Regulating Cartels in Europe, A Study of Legal Control of Corporate Delinquency* (Oxford: Oxford University Press, 2003), Chapter VI.

[226] The CFI and Court of Justice appear to have used this term notably in certain merger cases. See, for instance, Case C-12/03 P *Commission v Tetra Laval BV* [2005] ECR I-987, para 41 and Case T-464/04, judgment of 13 July 2006 *Independent Music Publishers and Labels Association (Impala) v Commission*, judgment of 13 July 2006, not yet reported, para 328, referred to in Joined Cases T-44/02 etc *Dresdner Bank and others v Commission*, judgment of 27 September 2006, not yet reported, para 57 *et seq.*

the 'requisite legal standard' that the Commission must adhere to in its decisions. The Court has held that the Commission must adduce a 'firm, precise and consistent body of evidence'[227] or, in the words used in *JFE Engineering*, 'the Commission must produce sufficiently precise and consistent evidence to support the firm conviction that the alleged infringement took place'.[228] This notion does not go as far as the standard of proof in criminal law proceedings in common law jurisdictions of 'proof beyond any reasonable doubt'.[229] Nevertheless, the CFI has held that any area of doubt which exists in the Commission's evidence must be construed in favour of the undertakings accused of the infringement[230] and that the CFI cannot be expected to consider lightly the question of whether the Commission has discharged its burden of proof in a decision which involves the imposition of substantial fines.[231] Accordingly, the Court will demand a high standard of proof.[232]

---

[227] See, for example, Joined Cases 29/83 etc *Compagnie Royale Asturienne des Mines SA (CRAM) and others v Commission* [1984] ECR 1679, paras 16–20. See also Case T-68/89 *Società Italiana Vetro SpA (SIV) and others v Commission* [1992] ECR II-1403, paras 193–195, 198–202, 205–210, 220–232, 249, 250 and 322–328; and Case T-62/98 *Volkswagen AG v Commission* [2000] ECR II-2707, paras 43, 72 and 58. See also Case C-235/92 P *Montecatini SpA v Commission* [1999] ECR I-4539, para 179, Case C-185/95 P *Baustahlgewebe GmbH v Commission* [1998] ECR I-8417, para 58, and Case C-49/92 *Commission v Anic Partezipacioni SpA* [1999] ECR I-4125, para 86: '[a]dduce evidence capable of demonstrating to the requisite legal standard the existence of the circumstances constituting an infringement'; Case T-44/02 *Dresdner Bank and others v Commission*, judgment of 27 September 2006, not yet reported, para 62.

[228] Joined Cases T-67/00 etc *JFE Engineering Corp. v Commission* [2004] ECR II-2501, para 179. See also Case T-56/02 *Bayerische Hypo- und Vereinsbank AG v Commission* [2004] ECR II-3495, para 77, where the CFI held that the Commission had not established to the 'requisite legal standard' that there was an agreement between certain German banks on a method of charging for currency exchange services. The Court found that there was a lack of proof of a meeting of wills and so annulled Art 1 of the contested decision which referred to an agreement whose object was 'to fix . . . the way of charging for the exchange of in-currency banknotes (ie a percentage commission)'. This case was decided by default judgment against which the Commission appealed. See also Case T-464/04, judgment of 13 July 2006 *Independent Music Publishers and Labels Association (Impala) v Commission*, not yet reported, para 328, where the CFI cites Case C-12/03 P *Commission v Tetra Laval BV* [2005] ECR I-987, para 232 where the ECJ requires that the Community Courts establish whether the evidence is 'factually accurate, reliable and consistent but also whether that evidence contains all the information which must be taken into account in order to assess a complex analysis and whether it is capable of substantiating the conclusions drawn from it'.

[229] In *JFE Engineering*, the Japanese applicants, JFE-NKK, argued that the Commission must prove the existence 'beyond any reasonable doubt'. However, the Court did not refer to this language in its finding, instead just making reference to the requirement for 'sufficiently precise and consistent evidence'. See Joined Cases T-67/00 etc *JFE Engineering Corp. v Commission* [2004] ECR II-2501, para 341. AG Darmon suggested using this standard in his Opinion in Joined Cases C-89/85 etc *Ahlström Osakeyhtiö and others v Commission* [1993] ECR I-1307, para 195 but the Court of Justice did not follow him in this respect. See also the CFI judgment in *Euro Currency Exchange—Germany* (T-44/02 etc *Dresdner Bank and others v Commission*, judgment of 27 September 2006, not yet reported, at para 58, where the CFI stated that the Commission cannot be held to a standard that obliges on it to bring 'irrefutable evidence' (own translation). Note, however, para 144 of the same judgment where the CFI refers to the fact that any conclusion drawn must be 'beyond a reasonable doubt' (own translation). See also JM Joshua, 'Proof in Contested EEC Competition Cases', ELR, Vol 12, 1987, pp 321–324, where the author characterises the standard as one amounting to proof beyond reasonable doubt.

[230] See, for example, Case 27/76 R *United Brands Company v Commission* [1976] ECR 425, para 265. Joined Cases T-67/00 etc *JFE Engineering Corp. and others v Commission* [2004] ECR II-2501, para 177.

[231] See also Opinion of Advocate-General Sir Gordon Slynn in Joined Cases 100/80 etc *SA Musique Diffusion Française and others v Commission* [1973] ECR 1914, at p 1931: where an applicant is able to show that there is uncertainty as to the merits of the Commission's finding of an infringement, that will suffice to obtain the annulment of the decision containing the finding.

[232] B Vesterdorf, acting as Advocate General, in his influential Opinion in *Rhône-Poulenc* (in *Polypropylene*), considered the fines to be 'of a criminal nature' and hence to require a high standard of proof. He spoke of 'the tension which can clearly be felt . . . between the procedural framework of the cases, consisting of an

8.509 **What matters is the balance of evidence as a whole** Although this exacting standard of proof applies to all the elements of the Commission's decision, including the duration[233] of the infringement,[234] as discussed above, the Court is mindful that evidence of hardcore cartels is often extremely difficult to uncover and that the Commission should not be held to a standard of proof which is unworkable.[235] Therefore, the Court has stated that it is not necessary for every item of evidence produced by the Commission to satisfy those criteria in relation to every aspect of the infringement and it has also allowed reconstruction by deduction.[236] That being said, even a single piece of evidence, including a statement from only one source, can be sufficient to establish an infringement provided that the probative value is such that it attests definitively to the existence of the infraction.[237] Moreover, evidence may take the form not only of documents, but also of oral statements.[238] The European Courts are willing to adopt a holistic approach in their examination of the evidence: the evidence will be looked at as a whole in order to determine whether it constitutes sufficient proof of an infringement.[239] It is sufficient, therefore, if the body of evidence relied on by the Commission, viewed as a whole, meets the standard of proof.[240] The Courts have stated

---

administrative procedure followed by judicial review of legality and the substance of the cases, which all broadly exhibit the characteristics of a criminal case'. See Joined Opinions of Advocate General Vesterdorf delivered on 10 July 1991 in Cases T-1/89 *Rhône-Poulenc SA and others v Commission* [1991] ECR II-867, section I.A.3. Joshua and Harding remark that although the fines are administrative in formal legal terms, they are penal in character (J Joshua and C Harding, note 170, p 240).

[233] Joined Cases T-25/95 etc *Cimenteries CBR SA and others v Commission* [2000] ECR II-491, para 4270.

[234] Joined Cases T-67/00 etc *JFE Engineering Corp. and others v Commission* [2004] ECR II-2501, paras 61 and 177, Case 27/76 *United Brands Company v Commission* [1978] ECR 207, para 265.

[235] Case C-204/00 etc *Aalborg Portland A/S and others* [2004] ECR I-123, paras 55–57. See also the Commission Decision in case COMP/38.443 *Rubber Chemicals* (IP/05/1656), no public version available and Joined Opinions of Advocate General Vesterdorf delivered on 10 July 1991 in Cases T-1/89 etc *Rhône-Poulenc SA and others v Commission* [1991] ECR II-867.

[236] Case C-204/00 etc *Aalborg Portland A/S and others* [2004] ECR I-123, para 56, and Case T-44/02 etc *Dresdner Bank and others v Commission*, judgment of 27 September 2006, not yet reported, at para 58.

[237] Joined Cases T-25/95 etc *Cimenteries CBR SA and others v Commission* [2000] ECR II-491, para 1838; Joined Cases T-67/00 etc *JFE Engineering Corp v Commission* [2004] ECR II-2501, para 148. Similarly, corroboration may not be needed if the undertakings concerned do not expressly deny their participation. In view of the greater probative value of statements where they have been made on behalf of an undertaking, one such statement may be sufficient to establish facts such as the participation of other undertakings in meetings. See also Opinion by AG Geelhoed in Case C-403/04 P and C-405/04, *Sumitomo Metal Industries Ltd and Nippon Steel Corp v Commission*, Opinion of 12 September 2006, not yet reported, para 100.

[238] See for instance the judgment of the CFI in *BASF*, referring to *Tokai*, that not only 'documents' but also 'information' may be 'evidence', adding that the oral disclosure of information has no major disadvantage from the point of view of legal certainty. (Case T-15/02 *BASF AG v Commission* [2006] ECR II-497, paras 496 and 498; and Joined Cases T-236/01 etc *Tokai Carbon Co Ltd and others v Commission* [2004] ECR II-1181, para 431.)

[239] Vesterdorf stated that 'whoever is to judge the evidence must be satisfied, upon an overall assessment of the weight of the evidence, that the case made out by the Commission is sound'. See also Case T-337/94 *Enso-Gutzeit Oy v Commission* [1998] ECR II-1571, paras 152 and 153.

[240] Joined Cases T-25/95 etc *Cimenteries CBR SA and others v Commission* [2000] ECR II-491, para 3708. See to that effect Joined Cases T-305/94 etc *Limburgse Vinyl Maatschappij NV and others v Commission* [1999] ECR II-931, paras 768–778, and in particular para 777, confirmed on the relevant point by the Court of Justice in Joined Cases C-238/99 P etc *Limburgse Vinyl Maatschappij NV and others v Commission* [2002] ECR I-8375, paras 513–523. See also Joined Cases T-67/00 etc *JFE Engineering Corp and others v Commission* [2004] ECR II-2501, para 180. See also the Opinion of Advocate-General Vesterdorf in Joined Cases T-1/89 etc *Rhône-Poulenc SA and others v Commission* [1991] ECR II-87, section I.E.2, 'even where it is possible to give a reasonable alternative explanation of a specific document, which may be isolated from a

that the Commission is not held to a standard of 'irrefutable evidence' and allows a cartel to be proved by deduction, by reference to circumstances and indicia in respect of which the Commission's conclusions are more plausible than the alternative explanation offered by the undertaking concerned.[241]

(c) Admissibility of Evidence

It is important to make a distinction between the *admissibility* of information as evidence, ie the question of whether or not information can be adduced as proof, which is dealt with in this section, and the *evidentiary value* which any given item of information may have, which is dealt with in the next section.[242] **8.510**

Although the European Courts have held on a number of occasions that the 'prevailing principle' in Community law is the 'unfettered evaluation of evidence, the only relevant criterion for such evaluation being the reliability of the evidence',[243] this does not mean that absolutely any information can be admissible as evidence before the European Courts. Certain legal principles and rules apply to the Commission's gathering of evidence.[244] These have largely been elaborated by the ECJ and CFI but are also found, to some degree, in Community legislation.[245] Some of these rules, where they concern the gathering of evidence, have been discussed above in the section on the Commission's investigative powers (see Section C(3)). **8.511**

Evidence collected in contravention of general principles or fundamental rights is not admissible It is a well-established rule of Community law that the Commission, along **8.512**

---

number of documents, the explanation in question might not withstand closer examination in the context of an overall evaluation of a whole body of evidence. It must accordingly be permissible to apply, as the Commission does, conclusions drawn from periods where the evidence is fairly solid to other periods where the gap between the various pieces of evidence is perhaps larger'.

241 T-44/02 etc *Dresdner Bank and others v Commission*, judgment of 27 September 2006, not yet reported, para 58.

242 The Court made this distinction in Case T-44/00 *Mannesmannröhren-Werke AG v Commission* [2004] ECR II-2223, paras 81–95, where it stated that it was not possible to contest the admissibility of the document involved but an argument could be made concerning its reliability.

243 Case T-50/00 *Dalmine SpA v Commission* [2004] ECR II-2395, para 72 and Joined Cases T-67/00 etc *JFE Engineering Corp and others v Commission* [2004] ECR II-2501, para 273. See also the Opinion of AG Vesterdorf, in Joined Cases T-1/89 etc *Rhône-Poulenc SA v Commission* [1991] ECR II-00867. See also, for example, Joined Cases C-406/98 etc *Met-Trans and others* [2000] ECR I-1797, para 29, and Joined Cases T-141/99 etc *Vela and others v Commission* [2002] ECR II-4547, para 223.

244 However, its powers are less fettered than the powers of the prosecution in the criminal law sphere. See the comments of JM Joshua in 'Oral Statements in EC Competition Proceedings: a Due Process Short-Cut?' Competition Law Insight, 7 December 2004.

245 See also Arts 3 and 4 of Regulation 773/2004, in relation to the taking of evidence through interviews and during inspections. Another source is section II 4 of Form C (Complaint Form pursuant to Art 7 of Regulation 1/2003, Annex to the Commission Notice on the handling of complaints by the Commission under Arts 81 and 82 of the EC Treaty, [2004] OJ 101/65) which envisages a number of different types of evidence. Furthermore, some rules governing issues relevant to (cartel) evidence are provided by the Commission's Notice on Immunity from Fines and Reduction of Fines in Cartel Cases, [2002] OJ C45/03 (discussed in paras 8.104–8.257), with regard to the evidential value of information for granting a reduction in fines (see notably point 22 and 23 of the Leniency Notice). The Commission Notice on Access to the File [2005] OJ C325/07 (discussed in paras 8.457–8.465), sets out certain rules relating to the exclusion of the use of 'internal documents' as evidence, and the use of minutes of meetings, which, the Notice states may only be used in evidence after the source has agreed to their contents (section 3.1.1. of the Notice on Access to the File Notice).

with the other institutions, is bound to respect the general principles of law, including fundamental rights, which are recognised as part of the Community legal order.[246] This rule extends to the Commission's competition law enforcement function and means, *inter alia*, that evidence that has been collected or processed in contravention of fundamental rights is inadmissible.[247] Undertakings frequently argue before the European Courts that their fundamental rights, most notably their rights of defence,[248] have been infringed by the Commission. These rights embrace the following issues, relevant to the admissibility of evidence, which will each be dealt with briefly in turn.

8.513 *(i) Information Covered by Legal Privilege* Communications between outside counsel and client, which relate to the subjectmatter of the relevant procedure, are protected.[249] It is debatable whether the Commission can have *access* to such information at all, or whether the privilege only precludes the *use* of the information. What is undisputed, however, is that information to which legal privilege extends cannot be relied upon as evidence. (For further discussion of legal privilege see paras 8.280–8.291.)

8.514 *(ii) Self-incriminating Information* As discussed in paras 8.264–8.274 above, the Commission cannot compel an undertaking to provide it with answers which might involve an admission on its part of the existence of an infringement which it is incumbent upon the Commission to prove.[250] To do so would breach the rights of defence of the undertaking concerned. (Note that in principle this is also the case for evidence obtained by third country authorities.)[251] Such information would be admissible only if submitted

---

[246] Art 6 EU Charter; in Part II of the draft Constitution OJ C310, 16.12.2004. For a short discussion to fundamental rights reference is made to paras 8.266–8.293.

[247] See more generally on this issue, EM Ameye, 'The Interplay Between Human Rights and Competition Law in the EU', [2004] ECLR, Vol. 26, Issue 6; Dieckmann in Wiedemann, *Handbuch des Kartellrechts*, 1999, p 1284; WPJ Wils, *Principles of European Antitrust Enforcement* (Hart Publishing, 2005); WPJ Wils, 'Powers of Investigation and Procedural Rights and Guarantees in EU Antitrust Enforcement', World Competition, Vol 29, No 1, March 2006. See also Case 46/87 R *Hoechst AG v Commission* [1987] ECR 1549, para 34, Case 85/87 R *Dow Chemical Nederland BV v Commission* [1987] ECR 4367, para 17, and Case C-94/00 *Roquette Frères SA* [2002] ECR I-9011, para 49. In Case T-224/00 *Archer Daniels Midland and Archer Daniels Midland Ingredients v Commission* [2003] ECR II-2597, paras 340–341, the Court recalls the general principle of protection against arbitrary public intervention in the private sphere and infers from it the inadmissibility as evidence of clandestine audio and video recordings, which are not covered by Regulation No 17.

[248] Also referred to as the 'right to be heard' or 'right to a fair hearing' or 'right to fair legal process'. See for an example of a reference to that right, see Joined Cases T-236/01 etc *Tokai Carbon Co Ltd. and others v Commission* [2004] ECR II-1181, para 406.

[249] Joined Cases T-125/03 R etc *Akzo Nobel Chemicals Ltd and others v Commission*, Orders of the President of the CFI of 30 October 2003, para 100; Case 46/87 *Hoechst AG v Commission* [1987] ECR 1549, para 16; Case 85/87 *Dow Benelux NV v Commission* [1989] ECR 3137, para 27; Dieckmann in Wiedemann, *Handbuch des Kartellrechts*, 1999, p 1308; However, the Commission must be put in a position enabling it to verify whether documents are covered by legal privilege, Case 155/79 *AM & S Europe Limited v Commission* [1982] ECR 1575, paras 29, 30.

[250] See Case 374/87 *Orkem v Commission* [1989] ECR 3283 para 35; See also the preamble of Regulation 1/2003, para. 23, stating that 'undertakings cannot be forced to admit that they have committed an infringement, but they are in any event obliged to answer factual questions and provide documents, even if this information may be used to establish against them [. . .] the existence of an infringement'.

[251] In relation to evidence obtained from another, third country authority and the application of the right against self-incrimination as regards that evidence, the CFI has ruled that rights equivalent to those established under Community law do indeed need to be respected. (Case T-59/02 *Archer Daniels Midland Co v Commission*, judgment of 27 September 2006, not yet reported, at para 229 *et seq.*)

willingly, or if the undertaking did not object to the Commission's questions in a 'simple' request for information or during an inspection (in which case it is presumed to have been submitted voluntarily).[252] While it is clear that the Commission may not use self-incriminating evidence which it obtains compulsorily in order to impose a fine against the undertaking concerned, it is submitted that it could rely on such evidence in respect of other undertakings, as the information is not being used to 'incriminate' the undertaking from which it was obtained.[253]

(iii) Evidence on which the Undertakings have not been Heard is Inadmissible   Evidence   **8.515** may also be ruled inadmissible if it is used in a manner which infringes the undertaking's right to be heard. It is clear from Regulation 1/2003 that the Commission can only base its decisions on objections upon which the parties have had an opportunity to comment.[254] The question is whether that also means that the Commission is limited to relying in its decisions only upon evidence that has been used or at least referred to in the SO or on which the parties have had an opportunity to be heard. In principle, the answer to that question is positive. According to the Court in *JFE Engineering*, 'undertakings are able properly to defend themselves [...] provided that they have an opportunity to comment on all the evidence relied on against them by the Commission' (emphasis added).[255] Therefore, if the Commission bases its conclusion on material upon which the undertaking could not comment, that evidence will be held inadmissible and any conclusion, in so far as it is not supported by other evidence, dismissed.[256] In other words, a Commission decision imposing fines must not include any material facts or analyses that have not been included in the

---

[252] In such instances, however, the Commission must be prepared to provide a reduction in fines. See Case T-48/02 *Brouwerij Haacht NV v Commission* [2005] ECR II-5259, para 106 and Opinion of AG Geelhoed in Case C-308/04 P *SGL Carbon AG v Commission*, Opinion of 19 January 2006, not yet reported, paras 103–104.

[253] Joined Cases T-25/95, etc. *Cimenteries CBR SA and others v Commission* [2000] ECR II-491, paras 731–733.

[254] Art 27 of Regulation 1/2003 and Art 11(2) of Regulation 773/2004.

[255] Joined Cases T-67/00 etc *JFE Engineering Corp. and others v Commission* [2004] ECR II-2501, para 203. T-44/02 etc *Dresdner Bank and others v Commission*, judgment of 27 September 2006, not yet reported, at para 160.

[256] Or at least the undertaking could not challenge the basis on which the evidence was obtained. On these aspects, see also paras 8.510–8.514 above. This was a key issue in the appeal in *Cement* (Joined Cases C-204/00 P etc *Aalborg Portland A/S and others v Commission* [2004] ECR I-123) where the defendant undertakings claimed that evidence crucial to their defence had not been disclosed to them in the access to file procedure. The Court of Justice rejected this argument stating that it was necessary to determine whether there was an objective link between the documents which were not made accessible during the administrative procedure and an objection adopted against the undertaking concerned in the judgment under appeal. See the CFI judgment in Joined Cases T-25/95 etc *Cimenteries CBR SA and others v Commission* [2000] ECR II-491, para 241 and the ECJ judgment in Joined Cases C-204/00 P etc *Aalborg Portland A/S and others v Commission* [2004] ECR I-123, paras 55–57, 129 and 208. For access to files: Case T-30/91 *Solvay v Commission SA* [1995] ECR II-1775, para 58; for the right to be heard see Mestmäcker/Schweitzer, *Europäisches Wettbewerbsrecht* (2nd edn, 2004) p 481; see furthermore Joined Cases T-67/00 etc *JFE Engineering Corp and others v Commission* [2004] ECR II-2501, para 203, where the Court justified its decision in favour of the Commission by stating that 'undertakings are able properly to defend themselves in such circumstances provided that they have an opportunity to comment on all the evidence relied on against them by the Commission'. See also Joined Cases 204/00 etc *Aalborg Portland A/S and others v Commission* [2004] ECR I-123, para 208. See also Case T-38/02 *Groupe Danone v Commission* [2005] ECR II-4407, paras 34–35, and Joined Cases T-191/98 etc *Atlantic Container Line AB and others v Commission* [2003] ECR II-3275, para 138.

Statement of Objections or on which the undertaking concerned has not otherwise had sufficient opportunity to comment.[257]

8.516 Inspection documents must be covered by the scope of the inspection decision It is clear that evidence found during an inspection which was based on an unlawful decision can be held inadmissible, as explained in paras 8.403–8.406. A separate issue, however, is the admissibility of evidence that is not covered by the scope of an otherwise lawful decision to inspect. The ECJ has confirmed that documents collected during inspections are only admissible as proof if the scope of the inspection decision embraced the information concerned.[258] Evidence of anti-competitive behaviour which has been discovered, accidentally or otherwise, during an investigation and then seized, but which is unrelated to the scope of that investigation, may not be used as direct evidence in another procedure, though it can nevertheless be used as a lead for a new investigation.[259]

8.517 Documents obtained on the premises of an undertaking that is not an addressee of the inspection decision This issue arose in the Commission's investigation in the *Greek Ferries* case where the Commission carried out an inspection at an agent of an undertaking, that agent not being referred to as addressee in the inspection decision. In its judgment the CFI interpreted the scope of the Commission's powers of inspection widely as regards the premises covered by the inspection decision and found that the inspection had actually been lawfully carried out on the premises of the agent of the formal addressee (the principal). The CFI rejected the contention of the principal that the Commission had gathered evidence unlawfully because that evidence had been obtained in the course of an investigation carried out at the offices of a company that was not the addressee of the investigation decision.[260]

---

257 See Joined Cases T-67/00 etc *JFE Engineering Corp. and others v Commission* [2004] ECR II-2501, para 203; Case T-38/02 *Groupe Danone v Commission* [2005] ECR II-4407, paras 34–35, and Joined Cases T-191/98 etc *Atlantic Container Line AB and others v Commission* [2003] ECR II-3275, para 138. See also Mestmäcker/Schweitzer, *Europäisches Wettbewerbsrecht* (2nd edn, 2004), p 481.

258 Case 46/87 R *Hoechst AG v Commission* [1987] ECR 1549, para 34; Case 85/87 R *Dow Chemical Nederland BV* [1987] ECR 4367, para 17; Case T-66/99 *Minoan Lines v Commission* [2003] ECR II-5515, paras 53–56 and the case law cited therein. As regards the opportunities to challenge that use, see paras 8.403–8.406.

259 Case 85/87 *Dow Benelux v Commission NV* [1989] ECR 3155, para 19; Case C-67/91 *Asociación Española de Banca Privada (AEB) and others* [1992] ECR I-4785, paras 39–42.

260 Case T-66/99 *Minoan Lines v Commission* [2003] ECR II-5515. Commission officials had arrived at what they believed were the offices of the Greek ferry company Minoan, to carry out an inspection. In fact, the offices were those of ETA, legally a separate entity from Minoan. However, because the two companies were very closely linked (ETA was Minoan's agent and had full authority to act as, and to refer to itself in commercial matters as Minoan, and also used the latter's logo), and because, through previous correspondence with the Commission, Minoan were aware of the Commission's investigation, the Court held that the Commission had not infringed its powers of inspection. The Court was of the view that ETA, as Minoan's representative, was 'in a position to comprehend the extent of its duty to cooperate with the Commission officials' and that 'its rights of defence remained fully protected, given the detailed statement of reasons provided in [the inspection documents presented by the Commission] and the express mention of its right to bring an action against the investigation decision before the Court of First Instance'. The use of the evidence gathered by the Commission during the inspection at the agent's premises were challenged unsuccessfully by both Ventouris and Strinitz as third parties affected by that evidence, and by the principal, Minoan. See Case T-59/99 *Ventouris Group Enterprises SA v Commission* [2003] ECR II-5257, paras 111–164, Case T-65/99 *Strintzis Lines Shipping v Commission* [2003] ECR II-5433, paras 33–84 and Case T-66/99 *Minoan Lines v Commission* [2003] ECR II-5515, paras 43–97; the latter two judgments of the CFI were appealed without

Confidential information is admissible as evidence   The Commission may seize and use   **8.518**
confidential documents. Confidential information can be protected in respect of third parties during the subsequent procedure under the Commission's Notice governing access to
the file, but there are two exceptions that may apply. Subject to the necessary procedural safeguards for the undertaking as set out in the Notice on Access to File,[261] these exceptions are:
(a) in so far as the documents are used as direct evidence of the infringement, the need to
divulge the information to the addressees of a Statement of Objections and final decision
trumps the interest of keeping the information confidential; and (b) information that includes
material tending to exculpate the party requesting it may be rendered accessible to that party.
(As regards the rules and procedure governing access to the file, see paras 8.457–8.463.)

Evidence provided orally   Nothing precludes the Commission from using evidence pro-   **8.519**
vided orally and such evidence is fully admissible. Indeed, the CFI has stated that the provision and use of oral evidence does not diminish its reliability. In the context of the
Leniency Notice, the Court has stated that information and evidence need not be provided
in documentary form and, furthermore, that the oral disclosure of information has no
major disadvantage from the point of view of legal certainty, since information provided
orally to a public administration is normally likely to be preserved by sound recording
and/or in written minutes.[262]

Use of evidence obtained under the national laws and procedures of a Member State and   **8.520**
evidence obtained in third countries   Article 12 of Regulation 1/2003 provides for the
exchange and use in evidence of any matter of fact or law, including confidential information, between the Commission and the competition authorities of the Member States.[263]
Information collected by the Member States, even where their investigative powers are more
far-reaching than the Commission's, can be freely exchanged and no rule precludes its use

---

success before the ECJ, see Case C-121/04 *Minoan Lines v Commission*, Order of 17 November 2005, not
yet reported and Case C-110/04 *Strintzis Lines Shipping v Commission*, Order of 30 March 2006, not yet
reported. It is interesting to note that the CFI dealt with Ventouris' and Strinitz' challenge against the evidence
even though it was obtained at the premises of Minoan's agent, who was in any case independent from these
two applicants. It is also noteworthy that the CFI was faced with a situation in which the inspected entity had
neither opposed the inspection nor brought legal action against it, while the principal and the other addressees
of the final Commission decision had not been inspected. In deciding on the appeal by those other addresses,
the CFI scrutinised the legality of the inspection and stressed that the relevant applicant '(. . .) now avails itself
of its right to ask for judicial review of the intrinsic lawfulness of the investigation as part of its present action
for annulment of the final decision (. . .)' (see Case T-59/99 *Ventouris Group Enterprises SA v Commission*
[2003] ECR II-5257, para 161; Case T-65/99 *Strintzis Lines Shipping v Commission* [2003] ECR II-5433,
para 81 and Case T-66/99 *Minoan Lines v Commission* [2003] ECR II-5515, para 93). The CFI thus appears
willing to allow any addressee of a final decision, even in this particular case the principal of an inspected
agent, to invoke the illegality of an inspection which was not carried out at its own premises, and to make that
claim only at appeal, rather than requiring that this (also) be done during the administrative proceeding.

261   Those safeguards and the Access to File Notice in general are discussed in paras 8.457–8.463.

262   See Joined Cases T-236/01 etc *Tokai Carbon Co Ltd. and others v Commission* [2004] ECR II-1181, para 431,
and Case T-15/02 *BASF AG v Commission* [2006] ECR II-497, paras 496 and 498.

263   The specific mechanisms of this exchange are provided by the Commission Notice on cooperation
within the Network of Competition Authorities (the 'Network Notice'). Art 40 of the Network Notice provides that no information received by the Commission or an NCA by way of an application under the
Leniency programme may be exchanged without the consent of the applicant. Art 41 of the Network Notice
provides for certain instances when that consent is not required.

in evidence.[264] Only where the subject matter is different as regards the basis on which the information was collected and its intended use by the Commission would the information become inadmissible.[265] The mechanisms for this exchange are operated within the framework of the European Competition Network. (On the functioning of the European Competition Network, see paras 8.434–8.437.) As regards evidence obtained by third country authorities, there is no rule that would *per se* exclude its use by the Commission. The CFI was faced with a question concerning the use of a document produced in the US, in the appeal by ADM against the Commission Decision in *Citric Acid*.[266] The evidence at issue was an FBI report which had been obtained through the Grand Jury process in the US and which had been used as an exhibit in a trial in the US. The Court stated that the Commission would, in its unfettered evaluation of evidence, be entitled to consider this information as reliable, especially since it had been declared before a court (Grand Jury).[267] ADM claimed that the information had been collected without respecting the procedural safeguards of Community law, in this case the right against self-incrimination, and the CFI confirmed that rights equivalent to those established under Community law should indeed be respected. However, in this particular case, the CFI considered that since ADM had itself relied on the document in the administrative procedure in support of its own argument, an argument based on self-incrimination could not succeed.[268]

8.521 **Anonymous evidence can be admissible**   Anonymous information can be used by the Commission. In *Seamless Steel Tubes*, where the use of information from an anonymous source formed part of the evidence used to prove the existence of the seamless steel tubes cartel, the CFI stated that the protection of the anonymity of an informant could not in itself require that the Commission set aside the evidence.[269]

(d) Factors Determining the Value of Evidence

8.522 Having considered the admissibility of evidence, the next issue to examine is how its reliability or credibility is assessed.

8.523 In his much-cited Opinion in *Rhône-Poulenc*, Advocate General Vesterdorf not only considered the issue of the standard of proof, but also the question of the evidentiary value of information. Vesterdorf provided a non-exhaustive checklist for the assessment of the reliability of a 'reporting document' (ie a report from a meeting) but his guidelines could apply equally to any potential piece of evidence. Vesterdorf stated that when assessing a document used by the Commission, account should be taken of the 'credibility of the account

---

[264] For a further discussion on this topic see WPJ Wils, 'Powers of Investigation and Procedural Rights and Guarantees in EU Antitrust Enforcement', World Competition, Vol 29, No 1, March 2006.

[265] See Art 12(2) of Regulation 1/2003.

[266] Case T-59/02 *Archer Daniels Midland Co v Commission*, judgment of 27 September 2006, not yet reported, at para 229 *et seq*.

[267] Also because the information did not contain any 'outward sign' that would put in doubt its evidential value (ibid, para 267).

[268] ibid, para 270.

[269] Case T-50/00 *Dalmine SpA v Commission* [2004] ECR II-2395, paras 72, 73 and the case law cited therein. See also para 8.540.

it contains; of the person from whom the evidence originates; of the circumstances in which it came into being; whether, on its face, the document appears sound and reliable; and the person to whom the evidence is addressed'.[270]

The European Courts have subsequently added to the number of factors to be considered **8.524** when assessing the reliability of evidence, and it is useful to consider each one in turn. For the sake of clarity, this analysis covers both information obtained under the Commission's formal powers of investigation and information submitted voluntarily.

Whether, on its face, the evidence appears sound and reliable   This is clearly an overar-   **8.525** ching, common-sense consideration.[271] The soundness and reliability of a piece of evidence is directly proportional to the extent to which that evidence is in accord with other known facts. The nature of the evidence, its origin, the degree of detail and the purpose for which it was created are all relevant considerations in this respect, and each is discussed in further detail below.

The time when the evidence came into being   The evidence will be considered to have   **8.526** greater probative force if it came into being at the time of the infringement, when the parties to the infringement were not under investigation (*in tempore non suspecto*).[272] Under general evidentiary rules, the fact that the documents were drawn up immediately after the meetings and clearly without any thought for the fact that they might fall into the hands of third parties and/or the authorities must be regarded as having great significance.[273] Finally, evidence of furtiveness or concealment of contemporaneous evidence whose existence is revealed by other evidence might provide useful probative evidence of a cartel.[274]

The level of detail of the evidence   As the Opinion of Advocate General Vesterdorf in   **8.527** *Rhône Poulenc* made clear,[275] the greater the level of detail provided in the evidence, the more its credibility is enhanced. This consideration is particularly relevant to oral statements provided to the Commission, which the Commission may wish to rely on as direct evidence or corroborating material. But it also applies to documents, such as minutes of meetings, or handwritten notes, where the level of precision is a key determinant of their evidentiary value.

---

[270] Opinion by AG Vesterdorf in Joined Cases T-1/89 etc *Rhône-Poulenc SA and others v Commission* [1991] ECR II-867, section I.E.4. See also Case T-3/89 *Atochem v Commission* [1991] ECR II-1177, paras 31–38. See furthermore the discussion on principles of evidence in the Opinion by AG Geelhoed in Cases C-403/04 P and C-405/04 *Sumitomo Metal Industries Ltd and Nippon Steel Corp v Commission*, Opinion of 12 September 2006, not yet reported.

[271] See Case T-1/89 *Rhône-Poulenc SA v Commission* [1991] ECR II-867, para 273.

[272] JM Joshua, 'Proof in Contested EEC Competition Cases', Eur L Rev, Vol 12, 1987.

[273] Opinion by AG Vesterdorf in Joined Cases T-1/89 etc *Rhône-Poulenc SA and others v Commission* [1991] ECR II-867, section I.E.4.

[274] When there is a series of secret meetings it is reasonable to assume that meetings for which a detailed account is available may typify those for which no notes are found. A similar concept exists in US jurisprudence, namely, presumption of continuance—if a state of affairs is proved to exist at a particular moment it is logical to assume that it continued for some time afterwards.

[275] Opinion by AG Vesterdorf in Joined Cases T-1/89 etc *Rhône-Poulenc SA and others v Commission* [1991] ECR II-867, section I.E.4.

8.528   **The source of the information has direct knowledge**   The source of the information is a crucial issue. Evidence is considered more compelling if the source has direct knowledge of the events. [276] If, for example, the evidence consists of an account of a meeting, the evidence would be of a higher probative value if the person giving the account had attended that meeting. Similarly, if the evidence consists of a document which records facts of which a participant in the actual cartel meeting/discussions has knowledge, it is considered more credible. Nevertheless, the CFI in *JFE Engineering* rejected the argument that evidence of which a witness does not have direct knowledge is *necessarily* of lower probative value.[277] Moreover, even hearsay evidence (where a person provides an account of what he has heard) may be relied upon if the surrounding circumstances point to its reliability. However, an assertion of fact based on the belief of a party cannot constitute evidence unless the basis for that belief is indicated.[278] This is particularly the case where that belief implicates a third party.

8.529   **Evidence which goes against the interests of the source providing it has greater probative value**   A higher probative value is normally attributed to evidence which goes against the interests of the person providing it. This has been confirmed by the CFI on a number of occasions, including in *JFE Engineering* where it referred to a 'general principle that, in terms of taking evidence, statements which go against the interests of the person making the statement must be regarded as probative'.[279] This is based upon the assumption that no-one would admit to having broken the law if they believed that they had not done so, given the adverse consequences that might follow from such an admission.

8.530   **Where a witness provides more (self-incriminating) evidence than he is obliged to, in answer to a question from the Commission**   The value of such evidence was made clear by

---

[276] Joined Cases T-67/00 etc *JFE Engineering Corp v Commission* [2004] ECR II-2501, para 207. That is not to say that evidence which has not originated with any of the cartel participants, such as correspondence between third parties, cannot be used as evidence: Joined Cases 40 etc *Coöperatieve Vereniging 'Suiker Unie' UA and others v Commission* [1975] ECR 1663, para 164; Case T-56/99 *Marlines SA v Commission* [2003] ECR II 2003, para 46.

[277] Joined Cases T-67/00 etc *JFE Engineering Corp v Commission* [2004] ECR II-2501, para 299.

[278] Case T-337/94 *Enso-Gutzeit Oy v Commission* [1998] ECR II-1571, para 131.

[279] Joined Cases T-67/00 etc *JFE Engineering Corp and others v Commission* [2004] ECR II-2501, para 211. In *Seamless Steel Tubes* (Commission Decision in Case 35.860-B [2003] OJ L140/1) the statements made by Mr Verluca, an employee of one of the companies involved in the investigation, were admissible against the undertaking to which he belonged. Joshua (In 'Oral Statements in EC Competition Proceedings: a Due Process Short-cut?' Competition Law Insight, 7 December 2004) suggests that this argument should not be applied to statements made as part of a leniency application because such statements are 'inherently self-serving since the object is to secure a reduced or even zero fine'. He suggests, therefore, that evidence obtained by way of a leniency application requires a 'high degree of corroboration as regards both precision and depth by a body of consistent and independent evidence'. It is submitted that, in relation to the opinion that leniency statements are 'inherently self-serving' account should also be taken of the fact that in principle, where such statements are also provide evidence against the supplier of that information, the information is indeed also (potentially) harmful for the source. That may be so for instance where: (a) the undertaking loses its conditional immunity and the information provided will also be used to fine the undertaking; (b) the information does not qualify for a reduction of fines for its 'significant added value' under the Leniency Notice, as other information was already in the Commission's possession (in which case the information could nevertheless be used against the source); and (c) the information becomes known through the (public version of) the Commission's final decision. Moreover, the Commission's decision may be used as evidence in claims for civil damages in national courts. Hence, such statements should not necessarily be seen as 'self-serving', but they should rather be assessed in view of the other criteria relating to the reliability of the information provided.

the Court in *JFE Engineering* where it explained that the statements of a Mr Verluca (an executive of the undertaking Vallourec) which included an admission of participation in the cartel, went beyond merely commenting on a document as requested by Commission officials and thus showed that he had 'resolved to tell the truth'.[280]

Evidence from an undertaking that has resolved to cooperate with the investigation has a high probative value   In *JFE Engineering*, the applicants argued that the undertaking Vallourec, of which Mr Verluca was an executive, was attempting to conceal the existence of a cartel that shared the market between its members. The Court dismissed this claim, saying it would be highly unlikely that an undertaking would admit its participation in one infringement but conceal evidence of its participation in another. By doing so it would risk losing the immunity or reduction in fines that it was hoping to obtain, something it would be unlikely to do.[281] However, where a co-operating undertaking submits evidence which only incriminates third parties, that submission must be assessed with caution (see also under para 8.536 below).   **8.531**

Evidence provided where there is a risk of sanction   The ECJ has stated that evidence given before a public prosecutor is more valuable, as would be evidence given under oath, due to the requirement to answer the questions and the adverse consequences of perjury.[282] The Commission itself is not empowered to take any evidence from witnesses under oath, but does have other compulsory investigative powers (such as sending requests for information with sanctions applicable for misleading, incorrect or incomplete replies, and asking questions during inspections, see section 3.3). Interestingly, in *Fine Art Auction Houses*, amongst other evidence, the Commission relied on sworn witness statements from the trial of Sotheby's former chairman, which had been submitted as evidence before the Federal District Court of the Southern District of New York.[283] In *Citric Acid*, the Commission relied on an FBI report produced in trial in the US.[284]   **8.532**

Evidence provided after mature reflection is more credible   The CFI also stated in *JFE Engineering* that a statement which is made after 'mature reflection' is more credible.[285] This, it is submitted, would suggest that the Commission should exercise a certain amount of restraint when asking for clarifications from employees during inspections, because their answers might not be considered to have been given after mature reflection and therefore in the eyes of the Courts may carry less probative value.   **8.533**

---

280 Joined Cases T-67/00 etc *JFE Engineering Corp v Commission* [2004] ECR II-2501, para 212.
281 ibid, para 214.
282 ibid, para 312.
283 See Case 37.784—*Fine Art Auction Houses*, recitals 57, 74. ([2005] OJ L200/92. The full text of the decision is available on the DG COMP web site, <http://ec.europa.eu/comm/competition/index_en.htm>). This is one of the very few Commission cartel decisions lasting recent years that has not been appealed. In its judgment in the *Aalborg* case the Court stated that there is no obligation on the Commission to afford the undertaking concerned the opportunity to cross-examine a particular witness and to analyse his statements at the investigation stage, as the procedure before the Commission is solely administrative. (Joined Cases C-204/00 P etc *Aalborg Portland A/S etc v Commission* [2004] ECR I-123, para 200). See also Joined Cases C-189/02 P etc *Dansk Rørindustri A/S v Commission* [2005] ECR I-5425, para 64.
284 Case T-59/02 *Archer Daniels Midland Co v Commission*, judgment of 27 September 2006, not yet reported, at para 229 *et seq*.
285 Joined Cases T-67/00 etc *JFE Engineering Corp and others v Commission* [2004] ECR II-2501, para 210.

8.534 **Evidence or statements provided by company executives are of greater probative value**
The function or position of the person within the undertaking is also important. A statement
given by an executive on behalf of an undertaking is considered to have a higher probative
value than that of an employee of the undertaking, acting as a private person, whatever his
individual experience or opinion.[286] This is because a company executive is considered to
be under a professional obligation to act in the interests of that company, and is therefore
unlikely to confess lightly to the existence of an infringement without weighing the consequences of so doing. Where there is nothing in the evidence to support the view that an executive might have failed to fulfil that obligation, the evidence is of particular probative value.[287]
Another closely linked factor is that an executive may be formally authorised to represent
the undertaking, in which case the statements gain credibility for that reason alone.

8.535 **Evidence supplied by one entity may be used against another**   The CFI held in *PVC II*
that 'no provision or any general principle of Community law prohibits the Commission
from relying, as against an undertaking, on statements made by other incriminated undertakings'. This is in line with the principle that documentary evidence seized during inspections of the premises of an undertaking may be used as evidence against another
undertaking, even if the latter undertaking is not expressly mentioned in the relevant document.[288] Were it otherwise, the CFI has stated, 'the burden of proving conduct contrary
to Article 81 and Article 82, which is borne by the Commission, would be unsustainable
and incompatible with the task of supervising the proper application of those provisions
which is entrusted to it by the EC Treaty'.[289]

8.536 **Evidence which tends to exculpate the entity supplying it, while incriminating another
entity, should be treated with caution**   An issue may arise in relation to evidence which
involves recriminations by an undertaking against its fellow cartel members.[290] The
Commission stated in *Pre-Insulated Pipes* that such evidence 'must be treated with some
caution' as it may be intended to be 'self-serving'.[291] Nevertheless, such statements may be

---

[286] Case T-23/99, *LR af 1998 A/S v Commission* [2002] ECR II-1705, para 45; Joined Cases T-67/00 etc
JFE Engineering Corp and others v Commission [2004] ECR II-2501, para 205.

[287] Joined Cases T-67/00 etc *JFE Engineering Corp. and others v Commission* [2004] ECR II-2501,
paras 205–206. Also Joined CasesCase T-25/95 etc *Cimenteries CBR SA and others v Commission* [2000] ECR
II-491, paras 1852, 4270. See also Joined Cases C-204/00 P etc *Aalborg Portland A/S and others v Commission*
[2004] ECR Page I-123, para 207 where the Court of Justice confirmed that in carrying out the task conferred
on it by Art 89 of the Treaty, the Commission is entitled to question the undertaking under investigation
about the conduct of all the other undertakings concerned.

[288] Case T-3/89 *Atochem SA v Commission* [1991] ECR II-1177, paras 31–38; Cases T-59/99 *Ventouris
Group Enterprises SA v Commission* [2003] ECR II-5257, para 91 and the case law cited there.

[289] Joined Cases T-305/94 etc *Limburgse Vinyl Maatschappij NV and others v Commission (PVC II)* [1999]
ECR II-931, para 512, upheld by the ECJ on appeal in Joined Cases C-238/99 P etc *Limburgse Vinyl
Maatschappij NV and others v Commission* [2002] ECR I-8375, para 280; Joined Cases T-67/00 *JFE
Engineering Corp. and others v Commission* [2004] ECR II-2501, para 192.

[290] At the same time, undertakings which do not provide a complete and truthful account to the
Commission in an application for immunity risk losing their immunity or a reduction of fines, pursuant to
point 11(a) of the 2002 Leniency Notice and, as regards applicants for reduction of fines pursuant to the obligation to act in a spirit of co-operation. Under the 2006 Leniency Notice, 2006 OJ C298/17 (point 24 combined with point 12(a)) an obligation of genuine co-operation also exists for applicants for reduction of fines.

[291] Case No IV/35.691/E-4 [1999] OJ L24/1, recital 120.

given some credence, particularly where they are corroborated or are consistent with the overall pattern of behaviour disclosed by the documentary evidence.[292]

Motives of the witness   Apart from relying on submissions by 'undertakings', the **8.537** Commission can also use information derived from other sources, including private individuals. These may be, for example, independent complainants or disgruntled (ex-) employees. A key question, therefore, is whether the witness had a motive to misrepresent the facts. The witness may be seeking to exculpate himself by pinning the blame on another person, may simply have a grudge against that other person or, in the case of an undertaking, may wish to cause it damage. The Commission needs to be particularly aware of this issue when acting on formal or informal complaints and when conducting interviews under Article 19 of Regulation 1/2003. The Commission also needs to take account of this factor, for instance, when obtaining information at an oral hearing. Note that the undertakings potentially affected by such statements cannot ask to hear or cross-examine witnesses,[293] nor is there any obligation on the witnesses' employers to ensure that the relevant individuals are present at the Oral Hearing.

Use of the admission of one party as evidence against others   Parties applying under the **8.538** Leniency Notice, or otherwise co-operating with the Commission, may provide an admission of their participation in a cartel.[294] Although such an admission may facilitate the Commission's task as regards the provider, the question arises whether such an admission could have any probative value in respect of third parties. It is suggested that in assessing what evidentiary value may be attributed to such a statement a distinction should be drawn between admissions as regards the facts of the case and admissions as to the legal interpretation of those facts. It is submitted that it would be more difficult for a third party to rebut a factual admission by an undertaking that was directly involved in those facts (eg an admission about the existence of a meeting and what was discussed at it). Statements as to the legal implications of those facts (ie the question of whether they concerned a violation of EC law, would appear to carry less weight, as any conclusions in this regard must be drawn by the institutions responsible for applying EC law, ie the Commission and/or the European Courts.[295] Factors such as any ulterior motive that the undertaking may have and/or whether the admission could be damaging to the undertaking's own interests may also influence the credibility of the admission, as discussed above.

Information provided by applicants for immunity or for a reduction of fines   It has been **8.539** claimed that because applicants for immunity 'need' to supply the Commission with information that qualifies as evidence of an infringement, they therefore have an interest in making self-serving statements, notably those that incriminate others, so as to maximise their

---

[292] ibid. See also the Court's appreciation in relation to the oral statements made in Joined Cases T-67/00 *JFE Engineering Corp and others v Commission* [2004] ECR II-2501 para 120.

[293] The Court confirmed in *Cement* that as the procedure before the Commission is administrative, the Commission is not required to afford the undertaking concerned the opportunity to cross-examine a particular witness or to analyse his statements at the investigation stage. Joined Cases T-25/95 etc *Cimenteries CBR SA and others v Commission* [2000] ECR II-491, para 1399.

[294] Such an obligation is found in the 2006 Leniency Notice, 2006 OJ C298/17 (point 24 combined with point 12(a)).

[295] Compare Case T-337/94 *Enso-Gutzeit Oy v Commission* [1998] ECR II-1571, para 131.

chances of receiving immunity or receiving a reduction in fines.[296] As indicated in the preceding paragraphs,[297] the Commission must exercise caution when making use of such uncorroborated and potentially self-serving materials, but it is for the Commission to decide whether, in all of the circumstances relating to the evidence, the information is reliable.[298] Part of that assessment will be to consider whether it is against the interests of the applicant to provide the evidence that is being submitted, in which case the credibility of the evidence may be enhanced. In this respect account should be taken of the fact that an applicant for immunity, unless it makes a hypothetical application, will not know if it will be accorded immunity from fines when applying, so puts its own position at risk. Similarly, applicants for reduction in fines have no guarantee that they will receive any benefit in terms of a reduction in fines when they apply. In any case, the Commission should not apply different standards of evaluation to evidence depending on who the provider is. As with any other evidence, the Commission should take into account whether the information is sufficiently detailed and corroborated or consistent with the overall pattern of behaviour disclosed in other evidence.[299]

8.540 **Anonymous or unidentified sources of evidence**   Another issue is the probative value of information that originates from an anonymous source. As stated previously, such evidence is generally permissible. The leading case law on this issue is the series of judgments relating to *Seamless Steel Tubes*[300], in which the CFI stated that a document where 'the context in which it was drafted is largely unknown and the Commission's assertions regarding that context cannot be verified' will have reduced credibility.[301] However, if the document is specific and corroborates other reliable evidence, it can be regarded as 'mutually supporting'. Even when there are discrepancies with other evidence on which the Commission relies, if the evidence corresponds on crucial points, then it is of probative value as it will serve to enhance the credibility of the other evidence.[302]

(e) Types of Evidence

8.541 This section considers the *types of evidence* on which the Commission relies in its cartel decisions. Evidence is usually described as being either direct or indirect and written or oral. However, evidence relating to cartels does not always lend itself to such straightforward

---

296 JM Joshua in 'Oral Statements in EC Competition Proceedings: a Due Process Short-Cut?' Competition Law Insight, 7 December 2004.

297 See also n 290 above for a discussion of why such statements may nevertheless be potentially damaging to the undertaking.

298 In this respect, it should be noted that such statements are normally taken on a voluntary basis under Art 19 of Regulation 1/2003, but that no provisions exist under Art 19, not even for undertakings, that allow the Commission to sanction procedurally the submission of false statements. It is submitted that this is a flaw in the legal provisions, at least as concerns undertakings.

299 See para 8.509 and Joshua n 272 above.

300 Case T-44/00 *Mannesmannröhren-Werke AG and others v Commission* [2004] ECR II-2223, para 86 and Joined Case T-67/00 *JFE Engineering Corp and others v Commission* [2004] ECR II-2501, para 274.

301 In *Belgian Brewers* the physical location was considered relevant context. A document which implicated Danone's subsidiary Brouwerijen Alken-Maes NV was found in the drawer of the office of a director of Heineken. The document was unsigned. The use of such anonymous evidence by the Commission was permitted by the Court which, citing Advocate General Vesterdorf's criteria for evidentiary evaluation, considered that the fact that the document in question was found in the office of a senior director of a different undertaking made it reliable. (Case T-38/02 *Groupe Danone v Commission of the European Communities* [2005] ECR II-4407, para 288.)

302 Case T-44/00 *Mannesmannröhren-Werke v AG Commission* [2004] II-2223, para 84; Joined Cases T-67/00 etc *JFE Engineering Corp and others v Commission* [2004] ECR II-2501, para 273.

classification. For instance, should an oral statement reproduced in writing and giving an account of a cartel meeting be described as direct documentary evidence or indirect oral evidence? Such questions relating to the classification of evidence have not been satisfactorily and definitively resolved by the Community Courts.

If it is possible to speak of a hierarchy of evidence, then the greatest probative value can be **8.542** attributed to documentary evidence produced contemporaneously with the infringement. However, establishing a hierarchy among the other categories of evidence, for instance, ranking non-contemporaneous written evidence against contemporaneous indirect evidence, is more difficult. Evidentiary value is a function of the factors that determine the reliability of the information (discussed in the previous section) and, indeed, it is the credibility of evidence when assessed in its totality that is most important in practice. (Reference is also made to the 2006 Leniency Notice, which refers to the notion of 'compelling evidence', discussed in para 8.201.)

(i) Documentary Evidence

Due both to the elaborate methods by which cartels cover their tracks and also, as Joshua **8.543** has expressed it, to 'their often well-rehearsed ability to destroy the evidence in the first few minutes of a dawn raid'[303] documentary evidence is more difficult to obtain. However, complex cartels will almost inevitably involve some written material, often because participants attempt to keep some form of record of what has been agreed, being suspicious of potential cheating by their fellow cartel members.[304]

Examples of documentary evidence which the Commission has referred to in its decisions **8.544** include:[305] written formal agreements,[306] 'gentlemen's agreements',[307] minutes or notes of meetings or contacts,[308] notes about monitoring systems,[309] as well as a range of other materials.[310] In many cases it is only as a result of piecing together various types of document and information that the facts are reconstructed to a degree sufficient to support the conclusion that the infringement has occured. For example, handwritten notes taken during a meeting of a trade association may prove the illegal content of the discussions, but they may

---

[303] JM Joshua, 'Proof in Contested EEC Competition Cases', Eur L Rev, Vol 12, 1987.

[304] See Joshua, ibid above, p 3. See also J Griffin, 'An Inside Look at a Cartel at Work: *Common Characteristics of International Cartels*', paper presented at the 48th Annual Spring Meeting of the American Bar Association, 6 April 2000.

[305] Only examples are given here, but the more than 80 Commission cartel decisions contain a wealth of references to specific documentary evidence.

[306] A reference to a formal agreement can be found in the Commission Decision in Case 37.857—*Organic Peroxides*, Decision of 10 December 2003, available at <http://ec.europa.eu/comm/competition/antitrust/cases/decisions/37857/en.pdf>. Recitals 83 *et seq* of the decision describe the formal market sharing agreement that was signed in 1971 and that formed the basis for a cartel lasting for 28 years, which was finally denounced to the Commission by the undertaking Akzo.

[307] Case 41/69 *ACF Chemiefarma NV v Commission* [1970] ECR 661, paras 110–114.

[308] Commission Decision in Case 38.069—*Copper Plumbing Tubes* [2006] OJ L192/21, recitals 237 and 278.

[309] Commission Decision in Case 37.027—*Zinc Phosphate*, [2003] OJ L153/1, para 105.

[310] For example, in the Commission Decision in Case 31.149—*Polypropylene* (([2003] OJ L230/1), documents obtained on the premises of the undertaking ATO related to the exchange of information on deliveries by the French producers in the EEC and the operation of quotas on the French market in 1979, as well as details of the European quota plan for 1980; *Graphite Electrodes* (Commission Decision in Case 36.490 [2002] OJ L100/1 eg recitals 63–65): direct evidence of the existence and implementation of the agreement was obtained in the form of the 'budget' documents and extensive meeting notes.

not state who actually attended. The official minutes of the same trade association assembly may list the attendees that day, but these may, in turn, not report on the illegal content of the discussions. As separate items these documents may not amount to conclusive proof against the attendees, but viewed together they constitute decisive evidence.

(ii) Oral Evidence

8.545 Commission decisions were for a long time based predominantly on written evidence,[311] although the Commission was not prevented from relying on oral evidence, and sometimes it did so to a significant degree.[312] In more recent times, oral accounts have of necessity started to play a more significant role in the investigation of cartels, given the measures taken by companies to prevent written material from being created in the first place.[313] Oral evidence may be used as direct evidence of a cartel and, although the usefulness of the oral account depends on the factors discussed in the previous section, there is in principle nothing to prevent the Commission from proving a cartel infringement solely on the basis of oral statements.[314] Indeed, the CFI stated in *BASF*, referring to *Tokai*, that not only 'documents' but als 'information' may be 'evidence', adding that the oral disclosure of information has no major disadvantage from the point of view of legal certainty.[315]

8.546 Oral evidence can be obtained by the Commission[316] in a variety of ways:

— oral explanations given by employees during inspections, under Article 20(2)(e) of Regulation 1/2003;

---

[311] Commission Decision in *Wood Pulp* (Case 29.725 [1985] OJ L85/1, para 25). Traditionally, the greater probative value accorded to documentary evidence can be attributed to the fact that oral evidence cannot be given under oath, although the greater reliance now being placed on oral evidence seems to suggest that this is no longer seen as a weakness in the adjudication of evidence. See *Dealing with the Commission*, European Commission, 1997, p 22.

[312] See for instance the Commission Decision in Case 35.860-B—*Seamless Steel Tubes* [2003] OJ L140/1, referred to in the previous section n 279.

[313] The value of oral evidence and its reliability as evidence was underlined by the CFI in *Vitamins*, Case T-15/02 *BASF AG v Commission* [2006] ECR II-497, para 495–506. See also the Commission Decision in *Seamless Steel Tubes*, which relied to a significant degree on the oral statement of an executive of the undertaking Vallourec. (Commission Decision in Case 35.860-B, [2003 OJ L140/1.) One earlier example of a case where oral evidence was used was *Theal/Watts* (Commission Decision in Case 28.812 [1977] OJ L39/19), where an oral agreement was notified to the Commission and was the subject of a decision under Art 85 of the Treaty.

[314] Case T-15/02 *BASF AG v Commission* [2006] ECR II-497, paras 495–506. However, statements that are contested by several undertakings do need corroboration, as follows from the Court's judgment in Case T-337/94 *Enso-Gutzeit Oy v Commission* [1998] ECR II-1571, para 91. See also, for an example at Member State level, the judgment of the UK Competition Appeal Tribunal (CAT) in *Argos Limited & Littlewoods Limited v Office of Fair Trading*, where witness testimony was relied on to a significant degree. (Procedural documents of this case are available at < http://www.catribunal.org.uk/archive/default.asp?keywords=&Page=12>.)

[315] Case T-15/02 *BASF AG v Commission* [2006] ECR II-497, paras 496 and 498; and Joined Cases T-236/01 etc *Tokai Carbon Co Ltd. and others v Commission* [2004] ECR II-1181, para 431.

[316] One further potential source of oral evidence, although very rare, is that which may be provided in testimony during proceedings before the CFI. (See Art 68(1) of the Rules of Procedure of the Court of First Instance which provides that the CFI may, either of its own motion or on application by a party, and after hearing the parties, order that certain facts be proved by witnesses. Art 44(1)(e) of the Rules of Procedure of the Court of First Instance provides that the application must state, where appropriate, the nature of any evidence offered.) The issue of the hearing of witnesses arose, for instance, in the appeal in Case C-185/95 *Baustahlgewebe GbmH v Commission* [1998] ECR I-8417, para 70, where the ECJ confirmed the CFI's judgment to reject a request to hear witnesses. See also the discussion on this issue by the Court of Justice in *Pre-Insulated Pipes*, see Case C-189/02 P *Dansk Rørindustri A/S* [2005] ECR I-5425, paras 51–76. See as regards

— statements made under Article 19 of Regulation 1/2003, which include (oral) corporate statements submitted as part of an application under the Leniency Notice;[317]

— accounts otherwise provided to the Commission by legal or natural persons, for instance by complainants;

— information given by a natural or legal person at an oral hearing under Article 27 of Regulation 1/2003.

(iii) Direct and Indirect (Circumstantial) Evidence

Direct evidence can be described as 'first-hand' proof of a cartel originating directly from one or more participants in cartel meetings, and normally directly implicating the participants in the cartel. Typical examples of direct evidence would be a written cartel agreement,[318] minutes of a cartel meeting[319] or (handwritten) notes made by a participant to a cartel meeting.[320] Direct evidence can exist either in documentary form, as contemporaneous evidence created at the time when the events to which it relates occurred, or as an oral account of the cartel contacts, provided later.[321] The level of credibility of such information is normally high—it cannot be easily contested—and it therefore requires little or no corroboration. Indirect evidence, on the other hand, tends to be of circumstantial value and usually requires corroboration or is itself used to corroborate other evidence. There is often a thin dividing line between direct evidence and indirect or circumstantial evidence. Evidence may directly implicate one undertaking but only circumstantially implicate another.[322] Circumstantial evidence on its own might suffice to prove an infringement, if, viewed in its totality, an overall pattern of

8.547

---

the obligation by the Commission to hear witnesses Case C-204/00 *Aalborg Portland v Commission* [2004] ECR I-123, paras 236, where the Court explained: 'As the procedure before the Commission is purely an administrative procedure, the Commission is not required to afford the undertaking concerned the opportunity to cross-examine a particular witness and to analyse his statements at the investigation stage. As for the ECHR, it does not lay down the rules on evidence as such (see the *Mantovanelli v France* judgment, § 34).'

[317] Oral statements provided under the Leniency Notice are considered to fall under the regime of Art 19 of Regulation 1/2003. For an example of oral evidence being used in evidence, though prior to the application of Art 19, see Commission Decision in Case 35.860—*Seamless Steel Tubes* [2003] OJ L140/1 as well as the ensuing court case (Joined Cases T-67/00 etc *JFE Engineering Corp. and others v Commission* [2004] ECR II-2501, para 130). See also the recent judgment of the CFI in Case T-15/02 *BASF AG v Commission* [2006] ECR II-497, where the Court stated at para 469 that 'there is nothing in the text of the [1996] Leniency Notice to suggest that evidence must be given in writing. Section B of the 2002 Leniency Notice differentiates between 'information', 'documents' and 'evidence', which suggests that decisive evidence is not necessarily documentary evidence. (See also point 25 of the 2006 Leniency Notice). Likewise, there is no reason connected with legal certainty or administrative efficiency why oral evidence should not be sufficient. The Commission can keep minutes of meetings, and can also, in the interests of certainty, compile a version of such meetings which is agreed with the participants.'

[318] Commission Decision in Case 37.857 *Organic Peroxides*, Decision of 10 December 2003, available in full text at <http://ec.europa.eu/comm/competition/antitrust/cases/decisions/37857/en.pdf>.

[319] See for instance Case T-59/99 *Ventouris Group Enterprises SA v Commission* [2003] ECR II-5257, para 136.

[320] See for instance Commission Decision in Case COMP/37.533 *Choline chloride*, n 120 to recitals 145–148 ([2005] OJ L190/22. The full text of the decision is available on the DG COMP web site, <http://ec.europa.eu/comm/competition/index_en.htm>.) Such information would fall within the category of compelling evidence, referred to in point 25 of the 2006 Leniency Notice.

[321] For an explanation of what constitutes direct documentary evidence, see Joined Cases T-25/95 etc *Cimenteries CBR SA and others v Commission* [2000] ECR II-491, para [903] and on appeal Joined Cases C-204/00 *Aalborg Portland and others v Commission* [2004] ECR I-123, paras 236 *et seq*.

[322] Commission Decision in Case 29.725 *Woodpulp* (Case 29.725 [1985] OJ L85/1, recital 44–59 and 125–131): a document can be both direct documentary evidence with regard to those to whom it refers and circumstantial evidence against others.

guilt emerges.[323] In practice, circumstantial evidence will be used to point to the existence of an agreement or an intention to infringe competition rules. The following types of circumstantial evidence, though not an exhaustive list, have all been adduced by the Commission as evidence: restaurant receipts or expense accounts and travel records confirming attendance at meetings[324], e-mail contacts, telexes, telephone records[325], meeting invitations[326], diary entries concerning meetings[327] and various miscellaneous (internal) documents, including, in one instance, those relating to the constitution of a trade association.[328] Such circumstantial evidence, if it relates to participation in cartel meetings, may in fact be highly relevant in proving participation in an infringement. Importantly, it may also lead to a de facto shifting of the burden of proof from the Commission to the undertaking.[329]

(iv) When is Corroboration Necessary?

8.548 A single piece of evidence, including a statement from only one source, can be sufficient to establish an infringement provided that the probative value is such that it attests definitively to the existence of the infraction.[330] However, it would in practice be highly unusual for a single piece of evidence to confirm definitively that an infringement has taken place. Therefore, corroborating material is usually required so that the overall evidence can reach the appropriate legal standard. Where the evidence from a single source has been presented in the form of a statement, such a statement may in itself be conclusive, depending on the level of detail and other circumstances that determine its reliability, discussed above.

---

[323] Joined Cases 40/73 etc *Coöperatieve Vereniging 'Suiker Unie' UA and others v Commission* [1975] ECR 1663, paras 271–294. The Court spoke of a combination of presumptions provided they are strong, precise and relevant. See also T-44/02 etc *Dresdner Bank and others v Commission*, judgment of 27 September 2006, not yet reported, at para 58, which speaks of indices which considered as a the whole would constitute sufficient proof in the absence of a more probable explanation by the appellants.

[324] Commission Decision in Case 38.069 *Copper Plumbing Tubes* [2006] OJ L192/21 recital 317.

[325] Commission Decision in Case 37.614 *Belgian Brewers* [2003] OJ L200/1 recital 85.

[326] Commission Decision in Case 38.069 *Copper Plumbing Tubes* [2006] OJ L192/21 recitals 304 and 328.

[327] Commission Decision in Case 37.027 *Zinc Phosphate* [2003] OJ L153/1 recitals 169 and 171 and Commission Decision in Case 38.069 *Copper Plumbing Tubes* [2006] OJ L192/21 recital 331.

[328] Commission Decision in Case IV/400 *IFTRA Rules on Glass Containers* OJ [1974] OJ L160/1 recital 35 where the Commission ruled that the constitution of a glass manufacturers' association would lead to reduced price competition as a result of an obligation on its members not to offer discounts and requiring them to charge uniform delivered prices. For a further example of the use of circumstantial evidence, see *Polypropylene* (Commission Decision in Case IV/31.149 [1986] OJ L230/1 recitals 15 and 26), where pricing instructions were sent from the head offices of the various producers to their various national sales offices requiring or requesting them to apply or move towards price levels which corresponded with those shown to have been agreed in the relevant producer meetings. In *PVC*, relevant documents were found to have been internal but this was held to be irrelevant as the documents revealed a plan to organise the cartel. See also Commission Decision in Case 38.069 *Copper Plumbing Tubes* [2006] OJ L192/21 recital 321 and Commission Decision in Case 35.691 *Pre-Insulated Pipes* [1999] OJ L24/1, eg recitals 49 and 52).

[329] T-44/02 etc *Dresdner Bank and others v Commission*, judgment of 27 September 2006, not yet reported, at paras 58 and 65.

[330] Joined Cases T-25/95 etc *Cimenteries CBR SA and others v Commission* [2000] ECR II-491, para 1838; Joined Cases T-67/00 etc *JFE Engineering Corp v Commission* [2004] ECR II-2501, para 148. Similarly, corroboration may not be needed if the undertakings concerned do not expressly deny their participation. In view of the greater probative value of statements where they have been made on behalf of an undertaking, one such statement may be sufficient to establish facts such as the participation of other undertakings in meetings. See also Opinion by AG Geelhoed in Case C-403/04 P and C-405/04, *Sumitomo Metal Industries Ltd and Nippon Steel Corp v Commission*, Opinion of 12 September 2006, not yet reported, para 100.

However, such a statement will normally be contested by the other members of the cartel who are incriminated by the evidence. If so, the statement requires corroboration.[331] Hence, it may be concluded that in practice, oral statements will have to be corroborated by other evidence in order to be accorded sufficient probative value by the European Courts.[332]

In assessing the probative value of a statement taken on its own (ie regardless of the fact that it might be contested, the principle is that the greater the detail of the information, the less corroboration it requires. For instance, if a verbal submission involves a very detailed statement which is particularly reliable, then it needs only slight corroboration. If it is less detailed, it needs more corroboration.[333] However, the Commission's view, as stated in its *Graphite Electrodes* decision, is that minor inconsistencies which are revealed on a close comparison of the statement of one producer with the statement or documents provided by another, for example as to the exact date of or the participation in a particular meeting, do not undermine the essential credibility of the statement.[334] **8.549**

(v) Economic Evidence

The issue of economic evidence has been dealt with more fully earlier in this chapter.[335] In terms of proving the existence of cartels, economic evidence is not usually used to incriminate cartel members and may best be viewed as another category of indirect evidence or (possibly) corroborating material. Economic data alone can hardly ever serve as sufficient proof of a cartel infringement, as, in the absence of other evidence, the economic activity can usually be given a different explanation.[336] Since the *Wood Pulp* and *Dyestuffs* cases,[337] **8.550**

---

[331] Case T-337/94 *Enso-Gutzeit Oy v Commission* [1998] ECR II-1571, para 91. Joined Cases T-67/00 etc *JFE Engineering Corp. and others v Commission* [2004] ECR II-2501, para 291.

[332] For an example of such corroboration, see *Cement* (Joined Cases T-25/95 etc *Cimenteries CBR SA and others v Commission* [2000] ECR II-491, para 1399) where the statement of Mr Kalogeropoulos did not constitute the sole or decisive basis of the finding made against Irish Cement Ltd, since other documents, which Irish Cement Ltd had the opportunity to consult and to comment on, showed that the 'Cembureau agreement' was concluded at the 'Head Delegates meetings' and that Irish Cement had indeed participated in those meetings.

[333] *JFE Engineering Corp. v Commission* [2004] ECR II-2501, para 219. Here the Commission relied on a written statement made by an executive of Vallourec during a dawn raid in response to an oral request for explanations. This was corroborated by various contemporary documents. The different versions of the events in question provided by the different producers, including the principal actors, demonstrated a remarkable coherence and consistency with one another as regards the salient facts. On the question of the level of corroboration needed in particular circumstances, see also Case T-337/94 *Enso-Gutzeit Oy v Commission* [1998] ECR II-1571, para 91, and Joined Cases T-25/95 etc *Cimenteries CBR SA and others v Commission* [2000] ECR II-491, para 1838.

[334] Case COMP/E-1/36.490 [2002] OJ L100/1 *Graphite Electrodes*, recital 504.

[335] See paras 8.52–8.57.

[336] See for example the judgment of the CFI in *Cartonboard*, referring to *Wood Pulp* (Case T-337/94 *Enso-Gutzeit Oy v Commission* [1998] ECR II-1571, para 149. 'The pricing conduct of the applicant and that of Iggesunds Bruk and of Finnboard, as set out in the tables annexed to the Decision (tables B, C, D and G), do not display such a degree of similarity that the possibility that the applicant adapted its conduct to that of its competitors on the market seems less plausible than the possibility that it participated in collusion on prices. It is settled law that, although Article 85 of the Treaty prohibits any form of collusion which distorts competition, it does not deprive economic operators of the right to adapt themselves intelligently to the existing and anticipated conduct of their competitors (see, inter alia, *Ahlström Osakeyhtiö and Others v Commission*, cited above, paragraph 71).'

[337] See Commission Decision in Case *Woodpulp* (Case 29.725 [1985] OJ L85/1) and Commission Decision in Case *Dyestuffs* [1869] OJ L195/11.

where the Commission attempted to prove the existence of a cartel to largely on the basis of economic data, the Commission has not relied on economic evidence to actually prove cartels. Also, given the absence of a requirement to measure the impact of a cartel in proving the infringement, the Commission has not dealt with economic evidence in its decisions to any significant extent.

8.551   As stated above, economic evidence may nevertheless be used to corroborate other material indications of collusion. For example, the Commission might use economic evidence such as simultaneous price movements following contacts between cartel participants to establish that an agreement was *implemented* (but the establishment of the infringement should not depend on those factors). Also, the Commission may look at the economic impact of a cartel as an aggravating circumstance when determining a possible increase in the fine, in accordance with point B(2) of the Guidelines on Fines.[338]

8.552   **The use of economic evidence as an exculpatory factor**   An undertaking that is accused of anti-competitive behaviour might seek to adduce economic evidence in order to demonstrate that the alleged cartel agreement was never implemented and/or that it had no impact on the market. Those issues are considered in paras 8.624–8.834 below, dealing with the calculation of the fines. Suffice it to say here that neither the fact that a cartel has had no economic impact nor that it was not (successfully) implemented can be used as a defence to the charge of infringement itself.[339] Neither the Commission nor the European Courts will entertain a debate about the (non-) impact of a cartel when it is clear that a *per se* and very serious violation of the competition rules has taken place.[340] Also, it has been made clear that for an undertaking to be classified as a perpetrator of an infringement it is not necessary for it to have derived any economic advantage from its participation in the cartel in question.[341] As regards the use of economic data to disprove the existence of a cartel, the Courts have stated that in cases where the Commission itself has endeavoured to prove a cartel by reference to economic data, an *alternative explanation* of the occurrences would suffice to dismiss the Commission's evidence. However, where the Commission has relied on other substantive evidence, which is usually the case in cartel cases, the undertaking must itself provide *a different, coherent explanation* for the events.[342] Economic indicators would be of little avail in this respect.

---

[338]   See paras 8.624–8.834 as regards the application of the Guidelines on Fines.

[339]   The Commission may nevertheless, according to the 1996 Guidelines on Fines, consider the economic impact of the cartel, if such impact is measurable, in assessing the gravity of an infringement for the purposes of calculating the fines. However, such a demonstration will be hypothetical given the absence of a benchmark of price development in normal competitive conditions. In any case, proof of *lack* of impact, supposing it is possible to demonstrate this, would not lead to a lowering of the fine. (See paras 8.734–8.776 for the determination of fines and the application of attenuating circumstances.)

[340]   See paras 8.634–8.639 on the issue of 'impact' as regards the determination of the fine.

[341]   Joined Cases T-236/01 etc *Tokai Carbon Co Ltd. and others v Commission* [2004] ECR II-1181, para 81; Case T-304/94 *Europa Carton v Commission* [1998] ECR II-869, para 141.

[342]   This conclusion can be drawn from Case T-44/02 etc *Dresdner Bank and others v Commission*, judgment of 27 September 2006, not yet reported, at paras 64–67. In *Sodium Gluconate*, the Commission dismissed the economic evidence supplied by ADM, stating that the scenario it had described could indeed occur in the absence of a cartel, but equally was fully consistent with a situation where a cartel did exist. (See Case T-322/01 *Roquette Frères v Commission*, judgment of 27 September 2006, not yet reported, at para 66.)

(3) Establishing Liability

(a) The 'Undertaking' as the Infringing Entity

EC competition law applies to 'undertakings'.[343] As explained elsewhere in this chapter **8.553** and in accordance with Article 23 of Regulation 1/2003, it is the *undertaking* that is held accountable for a violation of Article 81 (see paras 8.591 and 8.340). Although undertakings that participate in cartels will usually be corporate entities, a natural person is not excluded from being considered as an undertaking if that person is engaged in economic activity.[344] The notion of undertaking is an economic concept rather than a formal legal one and an undertaking may be composed of several legal entities. This is clear from the decision of the ECJ in *Hydrotherm* in which the Court stated that the concept as it applies to competition law 'must be understood as designating an economic unit for the purpose of the subject-matter of the agreement in question, even if in law that economic unit consists of several persons, natural or legal'.[345]

Attribution of liability is usually made with regard to entities having legal personality. The **8.554** Commission may find more than one part (legal entity) of an undertaking liable—jointly and severally—for the infringement that was committed by 'the undertaking' as a whole. Such is typically the case for corporate groups where (certain) subsidiaries and their parents are held liable for their participation in their infringement of the undertaking as a whole.

Due to the dynamic nature of the market economy, where legal entities are easily incorporated, **8.555** dissolved, bought and sold, and where corporate restructuring is commonplace, correctly identifying the addressees of the decision often presents a challenge for the Commission. This is especially so when, as is frequently the case, the cartel is of long duration and/or several years have passed between the ending of the illegal practices and the final Commission decision.

The general scheme for attributing liability in Commission decisions can be stated as **8.556** follows: first, the Commission will determine which economic unit (or undertaking) took part in the infringement; second, the Commission will consider which legal entity or entities within that undertaking can be held liable for the infringement;[346] and third, the Commission will consider whether any other legal entities are to be held responsible, wholly or partially, for the infringement, which may be the case where another legal entity is the successor to an entity which was found to have committed the infringement.

---

[343] On the notion of 'undertaking' in EU competition law, see WPJ Wils, 'The undertaking as subject of EC competition law and the imputation of infringements to natural or legal persons' (Apr 2000) EL Rev, 99–116.

[344] *AOIP v Beryrard* OJ [1976] L 6/8, [1976] 1 CMLR D 14; Case 35/83 *BAT v Commission* [1985] ECR 363. See also R Whish (2003), *Competition Law* (5th edn, London: Butterworth), pp 82–83).

[345] Case 170/83 *Hydrotherm v Compact* [1984] ECR 02999, para 11. For a more recent reference to the notion of 'undertaking' see Joined Cases T-71/03, *Tokai Carbon and others v Commission* [2004] ECR II-01181, para 54. See furthermore Case T-11/89 *Shell v Commission* [1992] ECR II-757, para 311 and Case *Mo och Domsjö v Commission* [1999] ECR II-1989, para 87.

[346] The principle of legal personality means that despite the fact that Art 81 only applies to undertakings and the concept of undertaking has an economic scope, only entities with legal personality can be liable for their infringements.

(b) Attribution of Liability to the Undertaking as a Whole: Underlying Reasons

8.557 It is the Commission's prerogative to decide upon the entities to which it addresses its decisions.[347] To ensure the maximum deterrent value of any fines, the Commission will impose—if the circumstances of the case allow it—responsibility at the highest level in a corporate group, by addressing the decision to the parent company within the group. In that way a general (implicit) message is sent, both to the individual undertaking (as specific deterrence), and to the business community at large (as general deterrence), that eliminating cartel behaviour is a matter for the undertaking and within the parent entity to ensure at the highest level. Indeed, the wider objective of cartel fines—apart from punishment—is to create an incentive for undertakings to deploy all necessary means to ensure that cartel behaviour is prevented from occurring within the whole of their corporate group. It needs to be remembered that the imposition of administrative fines is the sole means the Commission has at its disposal for deterrence. What it does not have in its arsenal are (custodial) sanctions on the individual perpetrators (company personnel). Neither can it count to a significant degree on civil claims for damages to serve as deterrence.[348]

8.558 Consistent with this overall objective of deterrence, there are a number of more particular policy reasons why the Commission may wish to attribute liability to more than one legal entity within the same undertaking. First, the maximum fine that can be imposed is 10 per cent of the worldwide turnover of 'the undertaking' to which the decision is addressed. The scope of the undertaking for the purpose of establishing the fine is delineated by the addressees.[349] Hence, attributing liability to a legal entity placed higher within the corporate group makes it possible to take into account a larger (consolidated) turnover, leading to the possibility of imposing a higher maximum fine.[350] Second, attributing liability to a parent company allows the Commission more readily to demonstrate recidivism on the part of the undertaking as a whole,[351] and hence to apply an aggravation factor to the fine.[352] Furthermore,

---

[347] Case T-304/02 *Hoek Loos NV v Commission*, judgment of 4 July 2006, not yet reported, para 129.

[348] For a more detailed analysis see paras 8.580–8.874 on sanctions.

[349] Art 23(2) of Regulation 1/2003. Case T-304/02 *Hoek Loos NV v Commission*, judgment of 4 July 2006, not yet reported, para 71.

[350] In its decision in *Hoek Loos*, the CFI did not discount the possibility of the Commission imposing a fine based on the turnover of the overall group to which a subsidiary addressee of a decision belongs, stating that 'the determination of the amount of the fine is based on a legal assessment by the Commission, subject to review by the Court of First Instance, namely attribution of the infringement to one or several undertakings, which is the only view consistent with the principle of personal responsibility'. (It is to be noted that the Court rather confusingly uses the term 'undertaking', although its actual reference is to legal entities. See Case T-304/02 *Hoek Loos NV v Commission*, judgment of 4 July 2006, not yet reported, para 129.) A parallel exists in *Michelin* where the Court held that the Commission, when considering the issue of the recidivism of a subsidiary, may consider the past behaviour of another entity in the undertaking, as long as the same parent company was able to exercise decisive influence. Thus both subsidiaries can be considered, along with the parent, as one economic entity (Case T-203/01 *Michelin v Commission* [2003] ECR II-4071, para 290.)

[351] See note above, in respect of *Michelin*. Recidivism is dealt with in paras 8.713–8.718. See also Case T-38/02 *Groupe Danone v Commission* [2005] ECR II-4407, para 363, where the Court stated that it is not the previous imposition of a fine that leads to a finding of recidivism, but the fact that a previous finding of infringement has been made against the person concerned.

[352] Including the parent entity may either have the effect that a past infringement of another entity in the undertaking can be taken into account for the purposes of the decision in hand (subject to what has been said about the solution found in *Michelin* and *Danone*, see n 350 and 351 above) and/or help create the basis for a finding of recidivism in the future, as regards any new or ongoing infringement of an entity within the group.

the inclusion of other, more highly placed entities within the group may allow the Commission to decide to increase the fine incrementally for deterrence purposes.[353] Finally, in cases of intra-group restructuring, where the entity held liable is transferred to another legal entity within the same group, but continues to operate under the same control as prior to the transfer, the Commission may want to prevent potential complications that could arise in terms of the imposition and recovery of the fine. By finding the ultimate parent company liable, difficulties in recovering a fine may be avoided. In summary, therefore, it has become the firm policy of the Commission to hold the ultimate parent entity liable when the requisite conditions are met.[354]

(c) Principal Grounds for Liability

The principal grounds for attributing liability to a legal entity—which will now be discussed in greater depth—are the following: **8.559**

(a) The primary basis for liability is what may be called 'direct involvement' in the infringing behaviour. Direct involvement of a legal entity is typically established by proving that personnel of the legal entity have taken part in illegal meetings or in other contacts.[355] However, direct involvement can also be demonstrated where personnel of a different legal entity (which is part of the same undertaking) were aware of the illicit behaviour, but did not intervene to stop it.[356] Direct involvement as a ground for liability is not discussed further here, in view of the relative clarity of the concept, though of course each case must be decided in accordance with the conclusions that can be drawn from the available facts.

(b) Other entities forming part of the same undertaking (parent companies within a corporate group or sister entities) may be held liable for the infringement, without having been directly involved in the infringing behaviour, if the Commission can establish that during the infringement those other entities 'actually exercised decisive influence' over the entity which was directly involved in the cartel. (See paras 8.560–8.568 below on the notion of the exercise of decisive influence.) The issue here is primarily one of business autonomy seen in a broader context.[357] Note that the actual exercise of decisive

---

[353] The larger the financial base of the undertaking, the greater the amount needed in order for the fine to be deterrent, as further explained in paras 8.688–8.697. Thus, the sheer size of the undertaking may itself lead to a deterrence factor being applied.

[354] Exceptionally, there may be reasons why it decides not do so. See Joined Cases 32/78 and 82/78 *BMW Belgium SA and others v Commission*, paras 24 and 25. See also Case T-304/02 *Hoek Loos NV v Commission* judgment of 4 July 2006, not yet reported, where the Commission decided not to attribute a decision to the ultimate parent.

[355] For example, in *Copper Plumbing Tubes* Outokumpu OYj was held liable for the infringement of its subsidiary, OCP, after the Commission found that the CEO of Outokumpu OYj had arranged OCP's participation in the cartel meetings and had sometimes represented OCP at those meetings: COMP/E-1/38.069— *Copper Plumbing Tubes*, recital 578.

[356] Case T-309/94 *Koninklijke KNP BT v Commission* [1998] ECR II-1007, para 48.

[357] See the Commission's Memo, issued upon the adoption of the fines in the Bitumen Netherlands cartel, where that policy was expressed in the following terms: 'The European competition rules apply to undertakings. "Undertaking" is an economic concept. But Commission decisions are necessarily addressed to legal entities. An undertaking consists of all the legal entities within a group of companies that together perform the functions of an economic operator. Therefore, if a parent company within the group is responsible for the most important strategic decisions regarding the commercial behaviour of its subsidiaries then the subsidiary cannot be said to be an autonomous economic actor. Instead it forms part of a larger undertaking, which is managed by the (ultimate) parent company. It is that larger undertaking that committed the infringement. The Commission may therefore address its decision not only to the subsidiary that actually participated in the cartel activity, but also to the parent company or parent companies that exercised decisive influence over

influence ('*l'exercice effectif d'un pouvoir de direction*') need not be linked to the cartel behaviour itself.[358] As regards sister companies, the concept of the exercise of decisive influence does not normally apply. The Commission therefore needs to establish a more direct form of involvement in the cartel or, in the absence of a parent entity that can be held responsible, establish that the sister company formed a component part of the undertaking that is to be held liable.[359]

It should be noted that entities falling under both sections (a) and (b) above may be (jointly) referred to as 'participants' in the infringement. The Commission and the Courts have adopted the approach that participation in the infringement occurs through the economic entity, the undertaking, rather than attempting to distinguish between legal entities within the undertaking that have been 'directly involved' and those that have not but which are held liable on other grounds.[360]

(i) Parent Company Liability: the Concept of the 'Actual Exercise of Decisive Influence'

8.560 As stated above, as far as parent companies are concerned the Commission must establish that the subsidiary did not act autonomously, by demonstrating that the parent *actually exercised decisive influence* over the subsidiary at the time of the infringement. In the words of the Courts, the anti-competitive conduct of an undertaking can be attributed to another undertaking 'where it has not decided independently upon its own conduct on the market, but carried out, in all material respects, the instructions given to it by that other undertaking, having regard in particular to the economic and legal links between them'.[361] The exercise of decisive influence must have deprived the subsidiary of 'autonomy in determining its course of action in the market'.[362] It appears that it is not enough to show that the parent

---

the commercial behaviour of that subsidiary, as together they form a single undertaking. This approach has been endorsed by the case law of the European Court of Justice.' ('Competition: Commission fines companies for road bitumen cartel in The Netherlands–frequently asked questions', MEMO/06/324 of 13 September 2006, available at < http://europa.eu/rapid/pressReleasesAction.do?reference=MEMO/06/324&format= HTML&aged=0&language=EN&guiLanguage=fr>.)

[358] Note that awareness of the cartel at the level of the parent entity provokes liability on account of 'direct involvement' rather than on account of parental liability (even though such awareness can also strengthen the conclusion that the parent exercised influence on the commercial operations of the subsidiary). See also para 8.566 below.

[359] See Case T-9/99 *HFB and others v Commission* [2002] ECR II-1487, para 66. (See also L Ortiz Blanco, *EC Competition Procedure* (2nd edn, 2006), para 11.11.)

[360] See n 358 above, in respect of *Hoek Loos*.

[361] See Joined Cases T-339–342/94 *Metsä-Serla v Commission* [1998] ECR II-1727, para 27. See also Case 48/69 *ICI v Commission* [1972] ECR 619, paragraphs 132 and 133.

[362] However, the Community Courts have also used terms which suggest that a lower level of influence, such as a 'stimulating and coordinating role', is sufficient. (Case T-11/89 *Shell v Commission* [1992] ECR II-757, at para 311–312). As has been argued by Wils, it is submitted that when deciding on the corporate responsibility of parent companies, it would be at least equally justifiable to use the notion of *capacity* to exercise decisive influence, as it would use only the criterion of *actual exercise* of decisive influence. Particularly where a parent company has sole control over another entity, it should not only be active use of that control, but also passive failure to control (or 'negligence by omission') that should render the parent company responsible for cartel behaviour. Indeed, the exercise or non-exercise of decisive influence are two sides of the same coin: the key is the *capacity* to exercise control. See WPJ Wils, 'The undertaking as subject of EC competition law and the imputation of infringements to natural or legal persons' (2000) EL Rev, 99–116. The Community Courts have, however, taken a different approach as described above. Nevertheless, applying the

was *capable* of exercising decisive influence, but that the influence was indeed actually exercised. In this respect a (rebuttable) presumption can apply, as explained below.[363]

A parent entity may have played a greater or lesser part in the management of the **8.561** subsidiary. Although the level of influence necessary to trigger liability has not been defined in Community law, a number of factors have been cited by the European Courts as relevant to indicating a lack of autonomy on the part of the subsidiary undertaking. Indeed, it is clear from Commission decisions that the Commission also holds parent entities liable where they control subsidiaries indirectly (ie through other subsidiaries). The criteria used to define control under the European Merger Control Regulation can assist in determining whether decisive influence has been exercised, although the concept of 'control' under the Merger Regulation applies differently and has a different purpose.[364] A number of determining factors are listed below, though it should not be assumed that the list is exhaustive. The level of shareholding is often the most decisive factor, although other elements are also considered, and these are provided in random order.

The parent company's shareholding in the subsidiary This is often a key factor in estab- **8.562** lishing liability. Where a subsidiary is wholly owned (ie where there is a shareholding of 100 per cent or just under 100 per cent, even if held indirectly), the actual exercise of decisive influence is presumed, though that presumption is rebuttable.[365] Nevertheless, in order to

---

rebuttable presumption of the 'exercise of decisive influence' (see below) mitigates any differences that might result from that different approach, at least in cases of (approaching) 100% shareholding.

[363] *AEG* suggests that the higher placed entity must have *actually* exercised that influence. See Case 107/82 *AEG v Commission* [1983] ECR 3151, para 50. This is where the assessment of 'control', on the basis of which liability may be attributed in cartel cases, may differ from the notion of control in merger cases. In merger assessments, the *potential* to exercise decisive influence on the day-to-day business of another entity is considered sufficient to regard two entities as belonging to the same undertaking. In the case of cartels, where past behaviour is considered, the requirement seems stronger: the decisive influence must actually have been exercised. (On the requirement of the actual exercise of influence see also case Case C-286/98 P *Stora Kopparbergs Bergslags v Commission* [2000] ECR I-9925, para 29.) Wils considers that this difference in approach is unjustified: See WPJ Wils, 'The undertaking as subject of EC competition law and the imputation of infringements to natural or legal persons' (2000) EL Rev, Apr, at 106–107.

[364] For a further discussion of the elements relevant to establishing control under the Merger Regulation see M Broberg, 'The Concept of Control in the Merger Control Regulation' (2004) ECLR 742, and WPJ Wils, 'The undertaking as subject of EC competition law and the imputation of infringements to natural or legal persons' (2000) EL Rev, Apr, 99–116.

[365] See eg Case T-314/01 *Avebe BA v Commission*, judgment of 27 September 2006, not yet reported, at para 136 and the case law mentioned therein. Such a presumption means that the onus rests on the parent company to rebut the presumption by producing sufficient proof of automony. See Case T-325/01 *Daimler Chrysler v Commission* [2005] ECR II-3319, paras 218–220. Note that in *Daimler Chrysler* the Court stated (initially) that the fact that the parent company held 100% of the shareholding of the subsidiary could not on its own demonstrate the existence of control. There must also be 'an actual exercise of a power of direction' (own translation of 'l'exercice effectif d'un pouvoir de direction'). But the Court then went on to say that in the event of a 100% shareholding, the Commission can presume that the parent company exercises decisive influence, in particular where the parent has presented itself to the Commission during the administrative procedure effectively as the sole interlocutor on behalf of the other undertakings in the group. See also Joined Cases T-71/03 *Tokai Carbon and others v Commission* [2004] ECR II-1181, para 60, referring to Case T-354/94 *Stora Kopparbergs Bergslags v Commission* [1998] ECR II-2111, para 80, confirmed by Case C-286/98 P *Stora Kopparbergs Bergslags v Commission* [2000] ECR I-9925, paras 27–29. Account should be taken of the fact that if the same commercial name is used by the subsidiary, this may be a relevant factor. (Case T-66/99 *Minoan Lines SA v Commission* [2003] ECR II-05515, confirmed by the ECJ in Case C-121/04 P *Minoikes Grammes ANE (Minoan Lines SA) v Commission,* Order of the Court of 17 November 2005, not yet reported.

turn the presumption into a more positive demonstration of the exercise of decisive influence, the Commission often presents additional elements of proof in this regard.[366] In order to successfully rebut the presumption, the parent company/shareholder would have to demonstrate true corporate independence on the part of the subsidiary and provide details of the nature of the relationship, or absence of a relationship, between itself and the subsidiary.[367] However, to demonstrate that a wholly-owned (or nearly wholly-owned) subsidiary is truly autonomous is far from straightforward, especially where certain corporate functions (finance, legal) are centralised within a group, creating a degree of interdependence.[368] In any case, an undertaking cannot make general assertions when putting forward arguments to rebut the presumption. Where the shareholding is rather less than 100 per cent, but still a majority shareholding, the case law suggests that, although the size of the shareholding remains important, the Commission must rely on other elements to prove the exercise of decisive influence.[369] Each of the factors discussed below may be relevant in this regard, but, as stated, this list may not be exhaustive.

8.563 **The Articles of Association/Statutes**   Provisions in the company's statutes or articles of association may allow to determine whether a particular level of shareholding translates

---

[366] In *Stora*, a further factor suggestive of control other than a 100% shareholding, was mentioned: if the parent entity presented itself to the Commission as the sole interlocutor, on behalf of the subsidiary as well as itself, this would support other arguments which entitled the Commission to attribute the conduct of its subsidiaries to Stora. It should be noted that Advocate-General Mischo did not suggest that this factor was essential for attribution of the behaviour of a subsidiary to its parent. See Opinion of Advocate-General Mischo in Case C-286/98 P *Stora Kopparbergs Bergslags AB v Commission* [2000] ECR I-9925, para 49 *et seq*.

[367] Case C-286/98 P *Stora Kopparbergs Bergslags AB v Commission* [2000] ECR I-9925, para 29.

[368] For a discussion of a case where an undertaking failed to demonstrate autonomy see Opinion of Advocate-General Mischo in Case C-286/98 P *Stora Kopparbergs Bergslags AB v Commission* [2000] ECR I-9925, notably para 49 where he writes: 'When a parent company owns all the shares in another company, it can be assumed that it is much more probable that it will exercise tight control over the subsidiary in regard to strategic decisions on pricing, salaries and major investments than that the parent company is not interested in such matters and that the subsidiary enjoys complete autonomy.' There is no known case law or Commission decision to show how autonomy can be demonstrated in cases of 100% or nearly 100% ownership. It would appear that a legal entity needs to prove full autonomy, for example by reference to such factors as its financial structure, funding, capacity to enter into loan agreements, credit rating, independence in deciding on investments, freedom to source raw materials and so on. This is an issue that, at the time of writing, is under appeal in Case T-175/05 *Akzo Nobel NV v Commission* against the Commission decision in Case 37.773-MCAA, Decision of 19 January 2005, available on the Commission's web site. (Para 242 is particularly interesting in this respect. The fact that Akzo Nobel NV was not itself involved in the production and sale of MCAA did not determine the question whether it should be considered as constituting a single economic unit with the operational units in the group that were directly involved in the production and sale of MCAA. Division of tasks is normal within a group of companies. An economic unit by definition performs all of the main functions of an economic operator within the legal entities of which it is composed. Group companies and business units that are dependent on a corporate centre for the basic orientation of their commercial strategy and operations, for their investments and finances, for their legal affairs and for their leadership cannot be considered to constitute an economic unit in their own right.) In one case, *BMW*, it was held that a particular type of behaviour could not be attributed to the parent as it had occurred in contravention of its explicit instructions (Joined Cases 32/78 and 82/78: *BMW Belgium SA and others v Commission*, paras 24 and 25.) However, it is submitted, that this does not actually demonstrate autonomy on the part of a subsidiary, but rather its insubordination.

[369] This appears to be a common belief, based on the fact that the presumption of the actual exercise of decisive influence has only been accepted by the Courts in cases of full (or nearly full) ownership. It is submitted however that, subject to proof to the contrary, majority ownership can have the same consequences as a 100% (or near 100%) ownership of shares when it comes to depriving the subsidiary of its autonomy in the market.

into real control. In most situations, ownership of a majority of the shares suggests the existence of control, as the majority shareholder will have the power to influence decisions in shareholders' meetings, or because it will have the power to nominate (the majority of) the directors on the board. However, even a minority shareholding may result in the actual exercise of decisive influence over another company, for example because the shares enjoy specific voting rights or a right of veto over strategic decisions, or simply because the statutes determine that commercial decisions that relate to the day-to-day operation of the business also require the approval of the minority shareholders.[370] Although such characteristics indicate the *power* to exercise decisive influence, other evidence may be available to demonstrate that such decisive influence was actually exercised. A company's statutes may provide, for instance, that any investment of reasonable size which may affect the daily conduct of the company is subject to prior approval by a (qualified) majority of shareholders, of which supplementary documentary proof would be available in board minutes.

The parent entity being active on the same or adjacent markets This is also a factor that **8.564** makes it more likely that the parent is commercially intertwined with the subsidiary and that it will have exercised decisive influence, as the parent will want to control output, investment, costs, prices, etc of the product at stake.[371] Advocate-General Mischo referred to it as follows, in *Cartonboard*, where a relationship existed in terms of supplier/ purchaser between parent and subsidiary: 'Furthermore, where a company producing a particular raw material purchases other companies which transform that material, it does so in particular in order to benefit from the added value which results from the transformation of that material. It will therefore necessarily be interested in the prices at which those transformed products are sold, and that must cause it to become aware of the concerted price increase practices existing in that sector.'[372]

The use of the same commercial name by the parent and subsidiary This may also sig- **8.565** nal that the commercial interests of the undertaking and its subsidiaries are intertwined. The Commission reportedly relied on this factor in its decision in *Hydrogen Peroxide*, in relation to the undertaking Air Liquide, whose subsidiary Chemoxal was referred to by the

---

[370] See point 19 of the Commission Notice on the concept of concentration under Council Regulation (EEC) No 4064/89 on the control of concentrations between undertakings (98/C 66/02). Strategic decisions may include decisions on the appointment of management, on the subsidiary's financial or business plans, investments, choice of technology or product development. It is submitted that if (minority) shareholders are considered to have had (joint) control over an entity, and have manifested their influence by playing an active role in the decision-making of the company, the Commission can also attribute liability for an infringement in which the affiliated company was involved to the minority shareholder. Reference can be made in this regard to the Commission Decision in *Sodium Gluconate* against which both Avebe and Akzo Nobel lodged an appeal befor the CFI. The CFI agreed with the Commission that under the particular circumstances of the case, Akzo and Avebe, both 50% stakeholders in a common subsidiary, could each be held (jointly and severally) liable for the infringement of the subsidiary. In that case, both undertakings had certain statutory rights in terms of their influence over the subsidiary as laid down in a joint-venture agreement. (See Case T-330/01 *Akzo Nobel NV v Commission*, judgment of 17 September 2006, not yet reported, and Case T-314/01 *Avebe BA v Commission*, judgment of 27 September 2006, not yet reported.)

[371] In this regard see Cases T-308/94 *Cascades v Commission* [1998 ECR II-925, para 158; T-347/94 *Mayr-Melnhof v Commission* [1998] ECR II-1751 paras 387, 398; T-354/94 *Stora Kopparbergs Bergslags AB v Commission* [1998] ECR II-2111, para 83.

[372] Opinion of Advocate-General Mischo in Case C-286/98 P *Stora Kopparbergs Bergslags AB v Commission* [2000] ECR I-9925, para 50.

other cartel members as Air Liquide.[373] In *Minoan Lines*, in the context of an inspection, the ECJ concluded, confirming the findings of the CFI, that the use of the same logo by the principal and the agent implied that they could be 'assimilated' commercially.

8.566 **Instructions from a parent company to a subsidiary** Apart from any particular link based on shareholding, evidence that the Commission can adduce of instructions being given by the parent company to its subsidiary may be a key factor in determining the exercise of decisive influence. These instructions need not be directly linked to the cartel participation or to the commercial issues (eg pricing) that were part of the discussions between cartel members in order to be of decisive evidential influence. It suffices that such instructions generally relate to the question of the (lack of) autonomy of the subsidiary[374] and they need not relate to to the illegal behaviour at stake.[375] Board minutes may provide compelling evidence of control by showing the manner in which the shareholder(s) have exercised their power over the subsidiary.[376] Moreover, where the parent company has put in place controlling mechanisms or management systems allowing it to direct the market behaviour of the subsidiary or to monitor its actions, this will amount to strong evidence of decisive influence.

8.567 **Functional links through personnel** If parent company personnel are (statutory) members of the governing body of the subsidiary, this may be relevant since it suggests that the parent company will be informed of, and may be involved in, the commercial strategy of the subsidiary.[377] This may be especially true in the case of undertakings which operate on the basis of a 'business unit' structure, as the economic activities of the undertaking may cut across its formal legal structure so that a manager of one entity can simultaneously perform a management function in the other legal entities.[378] As a result of such personnel links, a parent company, or even a sister company, can be held to have exercised decisive influence over the day-to-day operations of the entity which committed the infringement.

8.568 **The attitude of the parent company during the administrative procedure** The Commission has only exceptionally taken this circumstance into account. In *AEG* and *Stora*, the parent company presented itself to the Commission as the 'sole interlocutor' for itself and its

---

[373] Press release available at: <http://europa.eu/rapid/pressReleasesAction.do?reference=IP/06/560&format=HTML&aged=0&language=EN&guiLanguage=en>. Note that neither Air Liquide or Chemoxal received a fine as their participation was time-barred.

[374] In other words, the instructions may be part of a pattern of previous instructions or particular to the infringement. In case of the former, the Commission will be able to argue that it is probable that the subsidiary's participation in the infringement was directed by the parent company. In *ICI* the Court held that as the Commission had found instructions from the parent company regarding the first of three consecutive price increases, it could be assumed, in the absence of evidence to the contrary, that the subsidiaries had been similarly instructed in relation to the other price increases. (Case T-48/69 *ICI v Commission* [1972] ECR I-619, para 132.)

[375] Case T-11/89 *Shell v Commission* [1992] ECR II-757, para 312.

[376] See, for instance, the Commission Decision in *Sodium Glocunate*, recitals 307 and 308, where reference is made to board minutes establishing the involvement of Avebe in its subsidiary Glucona. (See Case T-314/01 *Avebe BA v Commission*, judgment of 27 September 2006, not yet reported, at para 37.)

[377] For an example, see Case T-354/94 *Stora v Commission* [1998] ECR II-2111, para 80.

[378] See, for instance, the discussion as regards Akzo in Case 37.773-*MCAA*, Commission Decision of 19 January 2005, available at <http://ec.europa.eu/comm/competition/antitrust/cases/index/by_nr_75.html#i37_773>.

subsidiary during the administrative procedure before the Commission.[379] This was viewed as an element demonstrating the parent's exercise of decisive influence over the subsidiary.

(ii) Sister Companies

In certain exceptional circumstances, a company may be held jointly and severally liable for the participation of its sister company in a cartel. According to the CFI in *HFB*, sister companies may be held jointly and severally liable where, notwithstanding the absence of a holding group, several participant companies act in such a coordinated fashion that they can be considered together as forming a single economic unit.[380] In *Aristrain*, two subsidiaries within a group that was family owned participated in various infringements in the steel beams sector and the Commission was unable to distinguish between them as regards the extent of their individual participation in the infringements. As the CFI has stated, where 'owing to the family composition of the group and the dispersal of its shareholders, it may be impossible or exceedingly difficult to identify the legal person at its head to which, as the person responsible for co-ordinating the group's activities, responsibility may be imputed', the Commission is entitled to hold the subsidiaries jointly and severally liable for all the acts of the group.[381] However, according to the ECJ, reversing the judgment of the CFI in this case, the simple fact that the share capital of two separate commercial companies is held by the same person or the same family is insufficient, in itself, to establish with regard to sister companies that one company should be held liable for the actions of another. In spite of that judgment, it is submitted that liability may still be attributed to sister companies, based on the 'economic entity' criterion.[382] The Commission must be careful, however, to adduce further evidence, apart from the shareholding relationship (which exists via the parent), to demonstrate that sister companies are indeed part of a single economic unit.[383] It should be noted that a sister company may be held liable even if its role in the infringement

8.569

---

[379] Case 107/82 *AEG v Commission* [1983] ECR 3151, para 49. Case C-286/98 *Stora v Commission* [2000] ECR I-9925, para 29. It is submitted, however, that in line with the above case law which suggests that the Commission must have regard to the circumstances of control at the time of the infringement, the fact that a parent company acts in defence of a subsidiary *ex post facto* should not be decisive in attributing formal liability for having exercised decisive influence during the infringement. Only where the control structure of the undertaking has remained unchanged since the end of its participation in the infringement might it be appropriate, it is suggested, to serve as one of a number of possible indicators of decisive influence.

[380] Case T-9/99 *HFB v Commission* [2002] ECR II-2429, paras 66 and 75.

[381] Case C-196/99 P *Siderurgica Aristrain Madrid SL v Commission* [2003] ECR I-11005, at para 99, overturning on this point the CFI in Case T-156/94 *Siderurgica Aristrain Madrid SL v Commission*. L Ortiz Blanco, *EC Competition Procedure* (2nd edn), para 11.12.

[382] In *Metsä-Serla*, Finnboard was deemed by the Commission to form a single economic entity with each of the cartonboard-producing member companies, and the Commission held each of them jointly and severally liable with Finnboard for payment of part of the fine imposed. For a discussion, see Joined Cases T-339/94 etc *Metsä-Serla v Commission* [1998] ECR II-1727, para 59.

[383] Although the court did not accept joint liability, this is somewhat surprising in view of the fact that, in *Aristrain*, both sister companies were involved in the same market, which would have been a strong indication that they were component parts of the same economic unit. The ECJ appears simply to have found that the Commission had provided insufficient proof to hold both entities liable on these grounds. See Case C-196/99 P *Siderurgica Aristrain Madrid SL v Commission* [2003] ECR I-11005, para 94. In *Jungbunzlauer*, the CFI endorsed the Commission's approach of holding a sister entity liable, because although not formally the overall parent of the group, the sister company performed the function of the group's parent (Case T-43/02 *Jungbunzlauer AG v Commission*, judgment of 27 September 2006, not yet reported, at para 122 *et seq*). It is noted that a company will not always be held liable for the acts of its related companies within the group where

takes a different form from that of the other entity(ies). In other words, internal task allocation within the group of companies is considered irrelevant to the establishment of liability.

(d) Liability in Cases of Succession [384]

8.570 The long lifespan of many cartels, together with the length of the Commission's investigations, means that a problem often arises of how to deal with situations where undertakings, either during the infringement or subsequently, assume new corporate identities or sell the relevant businesses (either as assets or in the form of entire legal entities). The entity(ies) liable for the infringement may cease to exist altogether following such a transfer. In order to avoid a situation in which liability can be evaded in cases of succession—the aim being that *someone* must answer for the infringement—certain rules have been developed by the Courts, though it must be noted that the existing case law does not cover all possible scenarios. The European Courts have applied the concept of succession in a variety of situations that have been put before them.[385] It is important to note that succession of liability for infringements of EC competition law is determined based on self-standing criteria of EC law, and not by rules of national (corporate) law.[386] Various scenarios of succession that can be discerned from the case law are discussed below. It must be borne in mind that succession in terms of liability for competition law infringements covers the situation where liability is attributed to an entity for the *past* participation of another entity or of assets it acquired. If the acquirer continues the infringement, the rules for the attribution of liability as discussed in the previous sections apply, and it may be held liable on account of its own direct involvement or as a parent entity, depending on the circumstances.

8.571 In dealing with the attribution of liability in cases of succession, the following scenarios can be distinguished: (1) where a legal entity changes its legal denomination, resulting in the dissolution of the previous legal person; (2) where a legal entity that is liable for an infringement remains in existence, but has been sold or transferred to another undertaking; (3) where a legal entity is not transferred, but only sells certain assets to another undertaking, and otherwise remains in existence; (4) where, after a transfer of the assets/activities of a legal entity to another undertaking, the entity is dissolved; (5) situations of intra-company restructuring. These scenarios are discussed below, together with some possible exceptions

---

it is demonstrated that that company acted independently from those related companies. This was the case in the Commission's *Copper Plumbing Tubes* decision where the Commission considered that one company (KME) was a separate undertaking from its sister companies in the same group (EM and TMX) until 1995, in spite of the fact that KME had joined the group in 1990. (See Commission Decision in Case 38.069—*Copper Plumbing Tubes*, recital 564, available on the Commission's web site.)

[384] On this issue generally, see K Dyekjaer-Hansen and K Hoegh, 'Succession of Liability for Competition Law Infringements with Special Reference to Due Diligence and Warranty Claims', ECLR [2003], Issue 5. See also WPJ Wils, 'The undertaking as subject of EC competition law and the imputation of infringements to natural or legal persons' (2000) EL Rev, Apr, 99–116.

[385] For the notion of succession based on 'economic continuity', see notably Case C-49/92 *Commission v Anic Participacione* [1999] ECR I-04125, para 145 and the case law cited therein; Joined Cases T-305/94 etc *Limburgse Vinyl Maatschappij NV and others v Commission* [1999] ECR II-931, para 953; Joined Cases T-259/02 etc *Raiffeisen Zentralbank Österreich and others v Commission (Lombard Club)*, judgment of 14 December 2006, not yet reported, paras 325 *et seq*.

[386] See Case T-134/94 *NMH Stahlwerke v Commission* [1996] ECR II-537.

to the general rules that can be discerned. It must be underlined, however, that in many instances the reasoning of the Courts should be seen as case specific. It should also be stressed that for any entity, even successor companies, that the Commission intends to hold liable, the Commission must respect the rights of defence of those entities and first address a Statement of Objections to them before an adverse decision against these entities can be taken.[387]

Cases of change of legal denomination, resulting in the dissolution of the previous legal person The Courts, which have been instrumental in developing the principle of succession, have wanted to ensure that, as a matter of competition policy, fines could still be levied and collected even where the infringing undertaking no longer legally exists in the same legal form. The theory was first established by the Court of Justice in *Suiker Unie* as early as 1975. Suiker Unie was an addressee which claimed that it could not be held responsible for the past competition law infringements of a (former) sugar co-operative, the assets, rights and obligations of which it had taken over. Suiker Unie argued that the previous co-ordinating body (the co-operative) had no assets or goodwill which it could have transferred to it. Nevertheless, in holding Suiker Unie responsible for the competition law infringements, the ECJ attached importance to the fact that the new entity comprised the same undertaking(s) as its subsidiaries and was to a large extent operated by the same people, had the same office address and behaved in exactly the same manner in the market as the former co-ordinating body. The former co-operative had ceased to exist but the ECJ was anxious to ensure that fines could still be levied and so found an economic continuity between the former infringing undertakings and the new entity, allowing it to attribute liability to the latter.[388] In *CRAM & Rheinzink v Commission*, Rheinzink argued that although it was the legal successor to an entity which had participated in certain agreements and was subsequently dissolved, it could not be held responsible as the violations had ceased before Rheinzink was created. The ECJ made clear that a change in the legal form (the new company was a limited liability company, whereas the former was a limited partnership) and in the name of an undertaking would not free the new company from responsibility when 'from an economic point of view, the two are identical'.[389]

Transfer of a liable entity, which remains in existence, to another undertaking As stated above, succession for the purposes of a competition law infringement occurs when a legal entity (including the business it operates), which can be held liable for its participation in an infringement, changes ownership but otherwise continues to exist. The succession rule applied by the Courts, laid down in *Cascades*, is that liability remains with the entity as long as it remains in existence, irrespective of its legal form or any corporate function it may acquire.[390] (Of course, if a legal entity is sold to a different undertaking, the new parent may

8.572

8.573

---

[387] See Case C 176/99 P *ARBED v Commission* [2003] ECR I-10687, para 23. The position could only be different where a mere renaming of an entity takes place, without any other change to the corporate identity. Issues of succession that may occur after the imposition of a fine, ie dealing with the issue of recovery, are not discussed here.

[388] Joined Cases 40/73 etc *Suiker Unie and others v Commission* [1975] ECR 1663, para 236.

[389] Joined Cases 29/83 and 30/83 *CRAM and Rheinzink v Commission* [1984] ECR-1679, paras 6–9.

[390] Case C-279/98 P *Cascades v Commission* [2000] ECR I-9709, para 79. A purchaser will only be liable for the past infringement of the acquired entity when it expressly assumes such liability, as discussed below.

be liable for any (continued) infringement for the period after the acquisition, based on the previously discussed rules of attribution of liability to parent companies.)

8.574 **Transfer of assets/activities to another undertaking, the entity previously operating the business remaining in existence** In the case of a transfer of the assets/ activities which were involved in a competition law infringement (eg human and capital resources without a legal identity), the main rule is that the legal entity previously responsible for those assets continues to be liable where it remains in existence.[391] This will be the case even where the previous owner has altered its name, moved location or started to conduct an entirely different business activity. However, the fact that a legal entity which was involved in an infringement is still in existence does not necessarily preclude the Commission from attributing liability to a successor entity, notably in cases of restructuring within a group.[392] Those issues relating to intra-group succession are dealt with further below.

8.575 **Transfer of a legal entity or of assets/activities, the entity previously operating the business ceasing to exist** In situations where the legal entity that committed the infringement no longer exists, the undertaking that has acquired the physical and human assets that were responsible for the infringement will attract liability for the infringement. Established by the CFI in its decision in *Anic*,[393] this principle could be described as a rule of 'legal

---

[391] The ECJ reiterated its view in Case C-297/98 P *SCA Holding Ltd v Commission* [2000] ECR I-10101, para 27) stating that 'it falls to the legal or natural person managing the undertaking in question when the infringement was committed to answer for that infringement, even if, at the date of the decision finding the infringement, the operation of the undertaking was no longer its responsibility'.

[392] See C-204/00 *Aalborg Portland v Commission* [2004] ECR I-123, paras 355 and 358.

[393] Case C-49/92 *Commission v Anic* [1999] ECR I-4125, para 145, where the ECJ stated that it is necessary to 'identify the combination of physical and human elements which contributed to the infringement and then to identify the person who has become responsible for their operation'. In its decision in *PVC II*, the Commission stated that the question is whether there is 'functional and economic continuity' between the original infringer and the undertaking into which it is merged. (See Joined Cases T-305/94 etc *Limburgse Vinyl Maatschappij NV and others v Commission* [1999] ECR II-931, para 953; Commission Decision of 27 July 1994 in case IV/31.865 (*PVC*), [1994] OJ L239/14). Also relevant is the case of *HFB*, where the CFI alluded to the fact that applying the succession theory with regard to part or a function of the infringing undertaking may be acceptable. (See also Case T-9/99 *HFB and others v Commission* [2002] ECR II-1487, paras 103 *et seq*. In that case new (holding) entities were held liable by the Commission for the entirety of the infringement, but the CFI dismissed that approach in the particular case). Specifically, when intra-group successions are set up to escape liability, the Commission and Courts will look at all the options to make sure that an infringement does not go unpunished (in application of the principle of the 'useful effect' of the competion rules). It should be noted that proof of circumvention is not relevant in this respect, although the Courts will consider possible strategies in this regard, as signalled in para 106 of *HFB*. (Also compare Case T-33/02 *Brittania Alloys & Chemichals Ltd. v Commission* [2005] ECR II-4973, at para 49, where the CFI refers to evasion by the undertaking that could justify using a different reference year for the 10% turnover limit as regards the fine.) In a scenario where the activities of an entity are fully transferred to another entity, but the first entity remains in existence, the Commission may choose a different solution in order to impose a fine that provides sufficient deterrent effect in respect of the assets involved in the infringement. (If the fine were imposed on the former entity alone, the statutory maximum of 10% may be reached effect in respect of that old entity.) Instead of seeking to solve this problem by holding the new entity liable according to an approach based on the internal restructuring the Commission could take account of a year of normal economic activity of the former subsidiary in order to establish the fine on it, rather than the turnover in the year prior to establishing the fine. That solution would be analogous to that accepted in *Brittania Alloys* where the CFI stated that that the turnover used for establishing (the 10% maximum of) the fine should be calculated not by reference to the last year before the decision but a year of normal economic activity of the entity concerned (at para 38).

succession' when regarded from the point of view of national corporate law. It is, in fact, a logical extension of the rule from *Cascades* (referred to above) that the legal entity which committed the infringement remains responsible for the infringement, but only as long as it remains in existence. The CFI confirmed in *All Weather Sports* and later in *Austrian Banks* (*Lombard Club*) that the Commission could, if properly reasoned, attribute liability for past infringements to the purchasers of the assets that were involved in the infringement.[394] This may particularly be the case where the business concerned has been 'purely and simply absorbed'.[395] One should not go as far as to say that the purchase of a few machines or the hiring of certain sales personnel will invoke a transfer of liability.[396] There may indeed be cases where the previous owner of a business disappears and no new owner of the business (the 'combination of physical and human elements') which contributed to the infringement can be detected. As an exception to the rule that the entity that was involved in an infringement has to have disappeared before the new owner can be held liable, the case of *NMH Stahlwerke* should be mentioned. In that case, the preservation of legal personality by the undertaking previously owning the business was for the sole purpose of its judicial liquidation and it had ceased actual trading. The Court found that the rescue company was formed specifically to guarantee and maintain the continuing operation of certain production units of the liquidated company, and there was hence economic continuity in behaviour between the two companies (the rescue company even continuing the infringement).[397] As explained below, the principle that another undertaking may attract liability for the past infringement of another if that previous owner no longer exists may also apply in situations of intra-group restructuring. Furthermore, it is worth reiterating that if a subsidiary was transferred and dissolved but a parent entity of that subsidiary was (jointly) liable for the infringement of its (previous) subsidiary (ie before the transfer), that parent will of course retain that liability.[398]

---

[394] Case T-38/92 *All Weather Sports Benelux BV v Commission* [1994] ECR II-211, where it is stated, in para 30: 'The Court notes on this point that for a Commission decision, which in its statement of reasons merely identifies as the party committing an infringement the legal entity which existed prior to the date of the purchase of its assets, lawfully to be able to impute liability for that infringement to the purchaser of the undertaking, there must be no dispute as to the identity of the legal entity which is the legal successor of the party committing the infringement, or as to the reality of the continuance by that entity of the activity, carried on by the undertaking in question, which gave rise to the proceedings (see the judgment of the Court of Justice in Joined Cases 29 and 30/83 *CRAM and Rheinzink v Commission* [1984] ECR 1679, paragraph 6 et seq.). That is not the case here, where the party which committed the infringement continues to exist as a legal person, as stated above, even though the economic activity which it carried on before the takeover of its assets is now carried on by a different legal entity.'

[395] Such may be derived, *a contrario*, from the reasoning of the Court in *Cascades*: 'In the present case, it is apparent from the contested Decision that Djupafors and Duffel participated in their own right in the infringement from mid-1986 until their acquisition by the appellant in March 1989 (see paragraph 18 of the contested judgment). Moreover, those companies were not purely and simply absorbed by the appellant but continued their activities as its subsidiaries. They must, therefore, answer themselves for their unlawful activity prior to their acquisition by the appellant, which cannot be held responsible for it.' (Case C-279/98 P *Cascades v Commission* [2000] ECR I-9709, para 79.)

[396] At the same time, in *NMH Stahlwerke*, the CFI indicated that the transfer of business from one undertaking to the other need not be complete: in cases where a part or function is transferred, the new entity may also attract liability. (Case T-134/94 *NHM Stahlwerke v Commission* [1997] ECR II-2293, para 130.)

[397] Case T-134/94 *NHM Stahlwerke v Commission* [1997] ECR II-2293.

[398] As a result of *Anic*, n 385 above, an undertaking cannot evade responsibility by disposing of the assets that were involved in the infringement and dissolving the entity that committed the infringement.

8.576 **Scenarios of intra-group restructuring and succession** As regards cases where a transfer of a legal entity takes place and/or the transfer of activities/assets occurs within a group, reference can be made to the principles explained above that apply *mutatis mutandis*. However, it appears that in cases of intra-group restructuring the Commission has been granted more leeway in holding acquiring entities[399] liable for the past infringement of another entity, even when that previous entity remains in existence. It would seem that the Courts see such a transaction as a form of intra-group restructuring, to which it has special regard in view of the 'structural links' between the transferor and transferee. This conclusion principally follows from what occurred in *Aalborg*, where the ECJ upheld the decision of the CFI in holding that the Commission was entitled to find the entity Aalborg liable for the infringement of the entity Aktieselskabet Aalborg Portland-Cement Fabrik (AAPCF), even though Aalborg had been formed as a subsidiary subsequent to the infringement of AAPCF and despite the fact that AAPCF continued in existence (but in a different role, as a parent entity).[400] Another situation, which may not be confined to intra-group restructurings, is where a new owner may inherit responsibility for a past infringement where the original infringing entity is still in existence but is incapable of paying the fine (because, for instance, it is in liquidation), and, in economic terms the 'undertaking' continues through a different legal entity, ie a similar scenario to that of *NHM Stahlwerke* discussed above. Another case in which purely internal restructuring occurred, and where responsibility of one entity could lawfully be passed on to a new entity within the same group, even for a period before the new entity came into existence, was that of *Sodium Gluconate*. The undertaking *Jungbunzlauer AG*, which had been newly created and had assumed the responsibilities of its (functional) predecessor Jungbunzlauer GmbH, was held liable for the entirety of the infringement including for the period of involvement of Jungbunzlauer GmbH, in spite of the fact that the latter undertaking had remained in existence.[401] By way of contrast to these

---

[399] The acquisition has to be one that can be considered as a transfer of a significant part of the activity/assets. If the (legal) person(s) remain(s) in existence with a commercial activity in the business concerned, and where the new entity only complements the activity of those still existing enitities, it may not be possible to rely on succession. (T-9/99 *HFB and others v Commission* [2002] ECR II-1487, paras 103 *et seq.*)

[400] C-204/00 *Aalborg Portland v Commission* [2004] ECR I-123, paras 344–360. However, a company will not always be held liable for the acts of its related companies within the group where it is demonstrated on the facts that it acted independently from those related companies. This was the case in the Commission's *Copper Plumbing Tubes* decision where the Commission considered that one company (KME) was a separate undertaking from its sister companies in the same group (EM and TMX) until 1995, in spite of the fact that KME had joined the group in 1990. (See Commission Decision in Case 38.069—*Copper Plumbing Tubes*, recital 564.)

[401] When intra-group successions are set up to escape liability, the Commission and Courts will want to make sure that an infringement does not go unpunished (in application of the principle of the 'useful effect' of the competion rules, according to Case *Commission v Anic*, n 385 above, para 146 and Case T-9/99 *HFB and others v Commission* [2002] ECR II-1487, paras 107). It should be noted that in general, ie regardless of the question of whether the restructuring is internal or there is a case of succession to a different undertaking, proof of circumvention is not relevant. (But compare Case T-33/02 *Brittania Alloys & Chemichals Ltd v Commission* [2005] ECR II-4973, at para 49, where the CFI refers to 'evasion' by the undertaking that could justify using a different reference year for the 10% turnover limit as regards the fine.) In a scenario where the activities of an entity are fully transferred to another entity, but the first entity remains in existence, the Commission may choose a different solution in order to impose a fine that provides sufficient deterrent. (If the fine were imposed on the former entity alone, the statutory maximum of 10% may be reached as regards that old entity.) Instead of seeking to solve this problem by holding the new entity liable according to the internal restructuring approach, the Commission could take account of a year of normal

cases where succession was accepted, the case of *HFB* should be mentioned, where the CFI did not agree with the Commission's decision to hold the new parent entity(ies) that had been created within the group liable for the entirety of the infringement. These parent entities had been created after the infringement and had only absorbed part of the functions of the subsidiaries, which had retained their commercial activity.[402]

(e) Voluntary Acceptance of Liability by the Acquiring Undertaking

One notable exception to the foregoing principles is where an acquiring entity expressly accepts liability for the past infringement of another entity. In *Krupp Thyssen and Acciai Speciali Terni SpA v Commission* one company (KTN) agreed formally in writing to accept liability for the infringement of the company it acquired (Thyssen Stahl), notwithstanding the fact that the infringement had ended before it had acquired the business. Although the CFI confirmed that this voluntary acceptance of liability is a permissible exception to the principle that the natural or legal person running the undertaking concerned at the time of the infringement should answer for it, the exception must be interpreted strictly. In this case, the Court found, on procedural grounds, that the acquiring company could not be considered to have waived its rights of defence and ought to have been able to exercise those rights in the same way as the undertaking initially held liable.[403] Therefore, and in spite of KTN's formal written acceptance of liability, the CFI annulled the part of the decision attributing liability to KTN, because the Statement of Objections sent to it in respect of its own participation did not state that it was also being held liable for the past infringement of Thyssen Stahl.[404]

8.577

(f) Determination of Liability and the Application of the Leniency Notice

An issue may arise where a legal entity (eg a subsidiary of a group) applies for immunity or a reduction in fines under the Leniency Notice but its application does not formally cover the other entities of the group, notably the parent company, which may be held (formally) liable for the infringement. It is therefore advisable for the highest placed entity in a group to make the application, so that all entities under its control, which together form part of a single economic unit, are covered by any grant of immunity or reduction of fines which it receives from the Commission.[405]

8.578

---

economic activity of the old subsidiary in order to establish the fine on it, rather than the turnover in the year prior to establishing the fine. That solution would be analogous to that accepted in *Brittania Alloys* (not a case of internal restructuring) where the CFI stated that that the turnover used for establishing (the 10% maximum of) the fine should be calculated not by reference to the last year before the decision but a year of normal economic activity of the entity concerned (at para 38).

[402] Case T-9/99 *HFB and others v Commission* [2002] ECR II-1487, paras 103 *et seq.*

[403] Case T-45/98 *Krupp Thyssen and Acciai Speciali Terni SpA v Commission* [2001] ECR II 3757, paras 62–64.

[404] ibid, para 68. See also Commission Decision of 24 July 2002 in Case COMP/E-3/36.700—*Industrial and Medical Gases*, in which AGA AB accepted liability for AGA Gas and, unlike KTN, did not later challenge the Commission's decision.

[405] Although immunity can only be attributed to a single legal entity according to the Notice, it is possible for that legal entity to request that other entities under its control benefit from the immunity. See also B van Barlingen and M Barrenes, 'The European Commission's 2002 Leniency Notice in practice', Competition Policy Newsletter (Autumn 2005), pp 7–8.) See also para 8.176 in this regard.

8.579   In the absence of an application by the parent company, the Commission may nevertheless deem that other entities that are part of the same economic undertaking are covered by the immunity or reduction in fines. That was the approach adopted by the Commission in its 2005 decision in *MCAA*.[406] There is, however, no obligation on the Commission to extend the benefit of immunity to entities other than the applicant, even if they do belong to the same group. Hence, if it appears that the (parent) entity, which was not the formal applicant for immunity, has not provided full co-operation, it risks being excluded from the grant of immunity that covers the subsidiary. Similarly, in considering whether a *reduction* in fines should cover an entire group (where the parent has not applied), if a member of the group other than the applicant has failed to show the required co-operation during the administrative procedure, it also risks losing a benefit that may be granted to the applying entity.[407]

E. Sanctions Against Cartel Participants

(1) Introduction

8.580   In addition to its power to issue 'cease and desist' orders, the Commission can also punish cartel behaviour through the imposition of fines. Whilst the Commission has been using its power to impose financial penalties ever more rigorously, it is debatable whether the current legal framework gives the EC sufficient power to challenge and eradicate cartels since such sanctions have intrinsic limitations in terms of their deterrent effect.

(a) In Search of the Optimal Regime of Sanctions Against Cartel Behaviour under EC Law

8.581   **The 'retributive' versus 'utilitarian' aspects of sanctions**   First and foremost, cartel behaviour should be minimised through the use of preventive measures, such as efforts by public authorities to develop a genuine culture of competition or corporate initiatives designed to ensure that the rules are observed (compliance programmes). However, where clear-cut and other deliberate infringements such as cartels have been found, adequate sanctions must be imposed. From an economic standpoint, sanctions have two complementary dimensions, one 'retributive', the other 'utilitarian'.[408] The retributive object of the sanction is to confiscate the illicit gain and to stigmatize the offender for its conduct.

---

[406]   See the Commission decision in Case 37.773-*MCAA*, Decision of 19 January 2005, available at <http://ec.europa.eu/comm/competition/antitrust/cases/index/by_nr_75.html#i37_773>.

[407]   Under the 2002 Leniency Notice, co-operation with the Commission is not a condition for obtaining a reduction, although the case law suggests nevertheless that a 'spirit of cooperation' is required from any entity wishing to benefit from leniency. Under the 2006 Leniency Notice, genuine co-operation is a formal requirement. (Both Notices are discussed in section C(2) of this chapter.) Arguably, where a parent company does not co-operate expeditiously and fully, the Commission may also withdraw immunity from the subsidiary, since it may be considered that a breach of that duty will also affect the position of the undertaking as a whole, mirroring the approach taken by the Commission that immunity may benefit the whole undertaking even if only requested by the subsidiary.

[408]   This corresponds to the two traditional purposes of punishment. See eg C Harding and J Joshua, *Regulating Cartels in Europe–A study of Legal Control of Corporate Delinquency* (2002), pp 229–230 and WPJ Wils, 'EC Competition Fines: To Deter or Not to Deter' in WPJ Wils *The Optimal Enforcement of EC Antitrust Law–Essays in Law and Economics* (2002), pp 12–13.

Its utilitarian object is to discourage the offender from repeating the infringement and, by way of the exemplary nature of the punishment, to deter all other potential offenders from engaging in similar violations.[409]

The Commission's focus on deterrence   It is the Commission's responsibility to steer   **8.582** companies towards a culture of compliance by imposing sufficiently deterrent sanctions.[410] When faced with a cartel infringement, the Commission must therefore not only restore effective competition in the market, but also deter any repetition of the cartel behaviour and, most importantly, send a strong signal to other potential offenders. This utilitarian focus has been emphasised by the ECJ since its very first judgment in a cartel case. The Court held in *Quinine* that the object of the fines imposed by the Commission 'is to suppress illegal activities and to prevent any recurrence' and that '[t]his object could not be adequately attained if the imposition of a penalty were to be restricted to current infringements alone'.[411] In its judgment in *Citric Acid* the CFI has held that 'if the fine were set at a level which merely negated the profits of the cartel, it would not be a deterrent. It is reasonable to assume that when making financial calculations and management decisions, undertakings take account rationally not only of the level of fines that they risk incurring in the event of an infringement but also the likelihood of the cartel being detected. In addition, if the purpose of the fine were to be confined merely to negating the expected profit or advantage, insufficient account would be taken of the fact that the conduct in question constitutes an infringement of Article 81(1) EC'.[412]

Optimal features of a policy of sanctions against cartel behaviour   From a 'deterrence'   **8.583** standpoint, cartels raise specific issues. Collusive behaviour may on the one hand be condoned in the highest corporate circles and be supported by the shareholders of the company, or on the other hand may originate in the individual tactics of senior or middle managers pursuing their own goals, for example seeking bonuses or a promotion within the company, possibly against a broader policy defined by the company owners. Any policy aimed at deterring cartel behaviour should take such variations in circumstances into account.

Imposing financial penalties on companies creates an incentive for shareholders or managers   **8.584** to put in place mechanisms aimed at ensuring the compliance of their employees with competition rules. The effectiveness of such penalties, however, will depend critically on the

---

[409]   On the exemplary value of punishment, see Case T-279/02 *Degussa v Commission* [2006] ECR II-897, para 360.

[410]   Joined cases 100 to 103/80 *Musique Diffusion française and others v Commission* [1983] ECR 1825, paras 105 and 106; Case T-150/89 *Martinelli v Commission* [1995] ECR II-1165, para 59; Case T-49/95 *Van Mengen Sports v Commission* [1996] ECR II-1799, para 53; Case T-229/94 *Deutsche Bahn v Commission* [1997] ECR II-1689, para 127; Case T-224/00 *Archer Daniels Midland v Commission* [2003] ECR II-2597, para 56.

[411]   Case 41/69 *Chemiefarma* [1970] ECR 661, paras 173–174.

[412]   Case T-329/01 *Archer Daniels Midland v Commission*, not yet reported, para 141. Interestingly, the CFI also emphasized the retributive dimension of the fine. Thus, it added that '[t]o regard the fine merely as compensating for the damage incurred would be to overlook not only the deterrent effect, which can relate only to future conduct, but also the punitive nature of such a measure in relation to the actual infringement committed. Thus, both the deterrent effect and the punitive effect of the fine are reasons why the Commission should be able to impose a fine which, depending on the circumstances of the case, may even substantially exceed the profit expected by the undertaking in question'.

level of the sanctions actually faced by the company in case of a failure by its staff to adhere to the rules. Indeed, where sanctions are incurred exclusively by undertakings, some employees may still consider that it is in their interest to embark on collusive strategies, depending on their personal cost/benefit analysis. Therefore, sanctions on individuals who take part in cartels, in particular non-monetary sanctions such as disqualification or imprisonment, may have greater deterrent effect.[413] In the absence of a power to impose such sanctions, enforcers are left with the alternative of increasing the level of the fines on companies to such an extent that the pressure on management and the shareholders to control their staff becomes irresistible.

8.585 Enforcement authorities should also take into account the possible effect of private actions for damages on the overall level of deterrence. In a system where customers who have suffered harm can easily and successfully sue cartel members for significant damages, the contribution of private parties to law enforcement may be considerable. The damages paid to plaintiffs will form part of the overall sanction against cartel behaviour and thus greatly contribute to the deterrent effect. Conversely, in a system where civil action is not developed, public authorities alone must carry the burden of enforcement and will therefore need to impose higher sanctions.

8.586 **Constraints upon the Commission's policy of sanctions**   As yet, the Community system has not made any provision for the imposition of sanctions on individuals for collusive behaviour.[414] The Commission can thus only impose fines on 'undertakings'. Moreover, whilst in the US private actions, which by far outnumber public prosecutions, greatly contribute to cartel enforcement, this has not been the case in the EU, where, in spite of the opportunity offered to affected customers to bring actions for damages before national Courts,[415] such initiatives have remained extremely rare, notwithstanding the efforts of the Commission and the ECJ on that front.

8.587 This situation has led the Commission, within the limits of the powers conferred on it, progressively to increase the level of fines imposed on companies taking part in cartels, in the

---

[413] In this regard it should be kept in mind, first, that in view of the procedural requirements associated with the prosecution of individuals, such a policy would imply high enforcement costs. Second, such a policy should necessarily come only as an addition to strong sanctions on corporate entities, in order to avoid undertakings and their shareholders being tempted to put pressure on their staff to engage in collusive behaviour at no cost to the undertaking or shareholders.

[414] Contrary to the Northern American model, and in particular that of the US where cartel behaviour is considered a criminal offence liable to imprisonment.

[415] In Case C-453/99 *Courage v Crehan* [2001] ECR I-6297, paras 25–27, the ECJ recalled that it is settled case law that national courts, whose task it is to apply the provisions of Community law in the areas within their jurisdiction must ensure that those rules have full effect and must protect the rights which they confer on individuals. Thus, '[t]he full effectiveness of Article [81 EC] and, in particular, the practical effect of the prohibition laid down in Article [81(1)] would be put at risk if it were not open to any individual to claim damages for loss caused to him by a contract or by conduct liable to restrict or distort competition. Indeed, the existence of such a right strengthens the working of the Community competition rules and discourages agreements or practices, which are frequently covert, which are liable to restrict or distort competition. From that point of view, actions for damages before the national courts can make a significant contribution to the maintenance of effective competition in the Community'. See also Commission Notice on co-operation between the Commission and the courts of the EU Member States in the application of Arts 81 and 82 EC [2004] OJ C101/54.

pursuit of an appropriate level of deterrence. Whilst fines remained low in the first decades of enforcement, despite a noticeable increase at the turn of the 1980s, the Commission increased the level of its fines considerably from the end of the 1990s onwards, notably in the context of the adoption of its 1998 Guidelines on the method of setting fines.[416] In the years that followed, as the Commission intensified its fight against cartels, the fines imposed on offenders reached unprecedented levels. With the adoption of revised Guidelines on the method of setting fines on 28 June 2006,[417] another increase in the average level of fine is generally expected. The European Courts have so far condoned this evolution, emphasising the wide discretion enjoyed by the Commission in the fulfilment of its duty to deter cartel behaviour.

'Impossibly high' fines? The current dilemma   The increase in the level of the fines, com-   **8.588**
bined with the effects of the increased attractiveness of the Commission's leniency policy,[418] has no doubt contributed to a higher level of deterrence in the EC. However, there is evidence that the level of fines is still insufficiently deterrent by comparison with the benefits that can be extracted from collusion, and some commentators have submitted that effective deterrence cannot be achieved if the imposition of fines remains below the statutory maximum of 10 per cent of total annual turnover.[419] On the other hand, as the level of the fines has increased, a growing number of companies have claimed an inability to pay the anticipated fine, in order to seek a reduction in advance.

The Commission is therefore faced with a dilemma. On the one hand, it may be reluctant   **8.589**
to increase fines to a level that would entail companies being wiped off the market, with the negative consequences this would have on the competitive process, and without necessarily guaranteeing deterrence. On the other hand, it cannot accept that the level of financial penalties be capped at an under-deterrent level, nor undertake to significantly reduce the fines imposed on companies facing financial difficulties, since this would confer on them an unfair advantage over their healthier competitors. In this context, one may wonder whether the Community system of sanctions, based exclusively on financial penalties on companies, is not reaching its limits. This question will be discussed at the end of this section.

(b) The Legal Framework Governing the Commission's Powers to Impose Fines

Sanctions set out in the implementing regulations   Article 81 EC does not specify sanc-   **8.590**
tions for its violation, apart from nullification of restrictive agreements as provided in Article 81(2) EC. However, Article 83 EC empowers the Council[420] to establish 'the appropriate regulations or directives to give effect to the principles set out in Articles 81 and 82'.

---

[416] Guidelines on the method of setting fines imposed pursuant to Art 15(2) of Regulation No 17 and Art 65(5) of ECSC Treaty [1998] OJ C9/3.

[417] Guidelines on the method of setting fines imposed pursuant to Art 23(2)(a) of Regulation No 1/2003.

[418] By increasing the probability of detection and facilitating the investigation of cartels, the leniency policy increases the level of 'expected' fine even if the nominal level of fines remains stable.

[419] See eg JM Connor, *Price-fixing Overcharges: Legal and Economic Evidence*, available at SSRN: <http://ssrn.com/abstract=787924>; WPJ Wils, 'EC Competition Fines: To Deter or Not to Deter' in WPJ Wils *The Optimal Enforcement of EC Antitrust Law–Essays in Law and Economics* (2002), pp 37–44. The notion of 'impossibly high fines' is taken from Wils.

[420] Upon proposal by the Commission and after consulting the European Parliament. Qualified majority voting applies.

Article 83(2) EC provides that such regulations or directives 'shall be designed in particular to: (a) to ensure compliance with the prohibitions laid down in Article 81(1) [...] by making provisions for fines'. From 1962 to 1 May 2004, the rules governing the enforcement of Articles 81 and 82 EC were set out in the first implementing Council Regulation, namely Regulation 17, and the power for the Commission to impose fines was laid down in Article 15(2) of that Regulation. On 1 May 2004, Regulation 1/2003 replaced Regulation 17. Article 23(2) of the former has replaced Article 15(2) of the latter and is today the legal basis of the Commission's power to impose fines.[421]

8.591 **Fines imposed upon 'undertakings'**   The Treaty remains silent as to which entities fines should be imposed on. Article 23(2) of Regulation 1/2003 provides, as did Article 15(2) of Regulation 17, that '[t]he Commission may by decision impose fines on undertakings and associations of undertakings where, either intentionally or negligently: (a) they infringe Article 81 [...]'. Whilst neither the Treaty nor Regulation 1/2003 contains any definition of the term 'undertaking', the ECJ has held that 'in competition law, the term "undertaking" must be understood as designating an economic unit for the purpose of the subject matter of the agreement in question even if in law that economic unit consists of several persons, natural or legal'.[422] A fine may thus be imposed on any 'economic unit'. The latter may be either a legal or a natural person. Indeed, the European Courts held that 'when [...] a violation is found to have been committed, it is necessary to identify the natural or legal person who was responsible for the operation of the undertaking at the time when the violation was committed, so that that person can answer for it'.[423] Although the Commission might theoretically hold a natural person liable for a violation of Article 81 and accordingly impose a fine on that person in respect of his unincorporated business activity, it has in fact never done so. The Commission focuses its efforts on the identification of the legal person(s) who must be held liable for the conduct of the infringing undertaking.[424]

8.592 **'Intention' or 'negligence' is largely irrelevant in cartel cases**   According to Article 23(2), the Commission may only impose fines on undertakings or associations of undertakings which have 'intentionally' or 'negligently' infringed Article 81 EC. These criteria can however be considered largely irrelevant as regards cartels, where intent is generally well established. In its most recent cartel decisions, the Commission has not even bothered to demonstrate the intention to infringe, which is deemed self-evident, especially when cartel participants do not contest the deliberate nature of their conduct as part of their co-operation with the Commission under the Leniency Notice. An argument of 'negligence' or 'lack of awareness' that the restrictive conduct constituted a breach of Article 81 EC will be rejected fairly automatically. Indeed, it is established case law that 'an infringement of the competition rules may be regarded as having been committed intentionally if the

---

[421] The drafting of Art 23(2) of Regulation 1/2003 is largely identical to that of Art 15(2) of Regulation 17. Unless otherwise stated, observations regarding Art 23(2) can therefore be deemed to be relevant, *mutatis mutandis*, to Art 15(2) as regards the period during which the latter was in force.

[422] Case 170/83 *Hydroterm v Compact* [1985] ECR 3016, para 11.

[423] Case T-6/89 *Enichem Anic v Commission* [1991] ECR II-1695, para 236 and Case C-279/98 P *Cascades v Commission* [2000] ECR I-9709, para 78.

[424] See section D(3) of this chapter on liability.

undertaking could not have been unaware that the object of its conduct was the restriction of competition. It is not therefore necessary for an undertaking to have been aware that it was infringing those rules'.[425]

Two criteria relevant to the setting of the fine: 'gravity' and 'duration'   Article 23(3) pro-   **8.593**
vides that '[i]n fixing the amount of the fine, regard shall be had both to the gravity and to the duration of the infringement'. All of the factors taken into account by the Commission when determining fines must relate either to the gravity or to the duration of the infringement. Accordingly, as regards the Commission's duty to state reasons when setting the fine, the European Courts have repeatedly held that such a requirement 'is satisfied where the Commission indicates in its decisions the factors which enabled it to determine the gravity of the infringement and its duration'.[426]

Upper limit of the fine set at 10 per cent of annual turnover   Article 23(2) provides that   **8.594**
'[f]or each undertaking and association of undertakings participating in the infringement, the fine shall not exceed 10% of its total turnover in the preceding business year'. The rule is identical in substance to the one that was spelled out by Article 15(2) of Regulation 17. However, the wording has been simplified. In fact Article 15(2) indeed provided an alternative, as it stated that the Commission could impose on undertakings or associations of undertakings 'fines from 1,000 to 1,000,000 [euros], or a sum in excess thereof but not exceeding 10% of the turnover in the preceding business year of each of the undertakings participating in the infringement'.[427]

---

[425] Case 246/86 *Belasco and others v Commission* [1989] ECR 2191, para 41; Case 96/82 *IAZ v Commission* ECR 3369, para. 45; Case T-143/89 *Ferriere Nord v Commission* [1995] II-917, para. 41; Joined Cases T-45/98 and T-47/98 *Krupp Thyssen v Commission* [2001] ECR II-3757, para 200.

[426] Case C-291/98 P *Sarrió v Commission* [2000] ECR I-9991, para 73. On the Commision's duty to state reasons regarding fines, see paras 8.609–8.610 below.

[427] This simplification is to be welcomed. The wording of Art 15(2) could probably be explained by the fact that when Regulation 17 was drafted, a range of fines from one thousand to one million euros was perceived as likely to encompass most possible fines, and that the 10% ceiling was rather perceived as a 'safeguard' for exceptional cases. However, with the impact of inflation over time and as the level of fines has increased, the maximum amount of one million euros was regularly exceeded and the upper limit of the 10% of total turnover in the preceding business year de facto became the sole reference. On the problems of interpretation raised by the wording of Art 15(2), see fn 486 below.
This wording did still raise problems. Indeed, a literal interpretation of those alternatives meant, on the one hand, that as long as the Commission did not impose a fine exceeding 1 million euros, it was not bound by the 10% upper limit. On the other hand, it meant that in the absence of any significant turnover in the preceding business year, the Commission could not impose a fine exceeding one million euros. In *Greek Ferries* [1999] OJ L109/24, one of the addressees of the decision had ceased its activities and closed all its subsidiaries in Greece a number of years previously, and the Commission lacked information as to the turnover of that company during the year preceding that of the adoption of the decision. Referring to the wording of Art 19(2) of Regulation 4056/86 (the equivalent of Art 15(2) of Regulation 17 for maritime transport), the Commission imposed a fine of 1 million euros on Karageorgis in the absence of any available data on is turnover. In *Zinc Phosphate* however, the Commission took a different approach. Faced with the fact that one company was to be held liable for a given period of the infringement but had ceased all commercial activities a couple of years before, whilst still existing in law, the Commission chose, for the purpose of calculating the upper limit applicable to the fine on Britannia, to take into account its global turnover for the business year ending four years earlier, which was deemed to be the 'last available figure reflecting an entire year of normal economic activity' (see n 196 of the decision).

8.595   **Fines on associations of undertakings**   In contrast to Article 15(2) of Regulation 17, which included no reference to fines imposed on associations of undertakings, Article 23 of Regulation 1/2003 makes detailed provision for such fines. It provides the Commission with a powerful legal tool enabling the Commission to hold a member of an association in effect liable for the whole fine imposed on the association. Article 23(2) reads that '[w]here the infringement of an association relates to the activities of its members, the fine shall not exceed 10 % of the sum of the total turnover of each member active on the market affected by the infringement of the association'. Article 23(4) adds that

> [w]hen a fine is imposed on an association of undertakings taking account of the turnover of its members and the association is not solvent, the association must call for contributions from its members to cover the amount of the fine. Where such contributions have not been made to the association within a time-limit fixed by the Commission, the Commission may require payment of the fine directly by any of the undertakings whose representatives were members of the relevant decision-making bodies of the association. After the Commission has required payment [. . .], where necessary to ensure full payment of the fine, the Commission may require payment of the balance by any of the members of the association which were active in the market in which the infringement occurred. However, the Commission shall not require payment [. . .] from undertakings which show that they have not implemented the infringing decision of the association and either were not aware of its existence or have actively distanced themselves from it before the Commission started investigating the case. The financial liability of each undertaking in respect of the payment of the fine shall not exceed 10% of its total turnover in the preceding business year.

8.596   **Fines not of a criminal nature**   Article 23(5) states, in terms identical to those of former Article 15(4) of Regulation 17, that '[d]ecisions taken pursuant to [Article 23(1) and 23(2)] shall not be of a criminal law nature'. The non-criminal nature of fines has also been confirmed repeatedly by the European Courts.[428] However, such fines should perhaps be regarded as having a 'quasi-criminal' nature. The ECJ has acknowledged that the sanctions imposed under Regulation 17 (now Regulation 1/2003) meet the requirement defined by the European Court of Human Rights[429] and that competition proceedings leading to the imposition of such sanctions may be classified as criminal within the meaning of the Convention.[430]

8.597   **Statute of limitations**   Under Article 25 of Regulation 1/2003, the Commission's power to impose fines upon cartels is subject to a limitation period.[431] The Commission cannot impose a fine more than five years after the infringement was committed, or, in the case of

---

[428] Case C-338/00 P *Volkswagen v Commission* [2003] ECR I-9189, para 96; Case T-83/91 *Tetra Pak International v Commission* [1994] ECR II-755, para 235.

[429] See K Dekeyser and C Gauer, 'The new enforcement system for Articles 81 and 82 and the rights of defence', paper given at the 31st Annual Fordham Corporate Law Institute Conference on International Antitrust Law and policy, New York, 7–8 October 2004. The European Court of Human Rights has developed, within the framework of Art 6 of the European Convention of Human Rights, an autonomous concept of 'criminal matters'. This concept covers administrative proceedings if the following conditions are fulfilled: (i) the offences are defined by a general rule, applicable to all citizens and not only to some of them; (ii) the rule is linked to penalties in the event of non compliance; iii) the sanctions are intended not as pecuniary compensation for damage but essentially as a punishment to deter re-offending; iv) the sanctions are severe. See in particular *Engel and others v The Netherlands*, judgment of 8 June 1976, Series A No 22, para 82; *Özturk v Germany*, judgment of 21 February 1982, Series A No 73, para 50; *Bendenoun v France*, judgment of 24 February 1994, Series A No 284, para 47.

[430] Case C-199/92 P *Hüls v Commission* [1999] ECR 4287, para 150.

[431] Art 25 of Regulation 1/2003 has replaced Art 1 of Regulation 2988/74, [1974] OJ L319/1.

a continuing infringement, more than five years from when the infringement ceased, unless a formal step to investigate or prosecute the infringement has been taken by the Commission or a national competition authority during that period.[432] Each time such a formal step is taken, a new limitation period of five years starts to run. Furthermore, notwithstanding any intervening 'formal steps' the Commission cannot impose a fine more than ten years after the infringement took place or ceased for the addressee in question. The limitation period is suspended for as long as the decision of the Commission is the subject of proceedings pending before the Court of Justice.

For a formal step to interrupt the limitation period it must be necessary to the investiga- **8.598** tion. In *CMA CGM v Commission*, the CFI held that the limitation period could not be extended by a request for information where the figures requested were not necessary, and thus the sole purpose of the request for information seemed to be to prolong the limitation period without proper justification.[433] The findings of the CFI were overturned by the Court on appeal, however, as the ECJ found that the CFI was incorrect in asserting that the request for information did not serve any useful purpose.[434]

(c) Evolution of the Commission's Fining Policy

The Commission's policy regarding the imposition of sanctions against cartels has become **8.599** more rigorous over time. As the average level of fines has increased, the Commission's practice in this field has become subject to more detailed scrutiny by the European Courts and has resulted in abundant case law. A turning point in the Commission's policy on fines and in its judicial review, however, was the publication in 1998 of the first Commission guidelines on the method of setting fines. These guidelines were thoroughly revised in 2006.

(i) Progressive Stepping Up of Enforcement

From 1969 to 1980: sporadic fines The first fines ever imposed by the Commission were **8.600** set in July 1969 in two separate cartel cases, *Quinine* and *Dyestuff*. However, fines remained a relatively rare phenomenon over the first two decades of EC competition law enforcement. The next fines were not imposed until four years later, in *European Sugar Industry*.[435] Four cartels had been prohibited in the meantime (a *Cardboard tubes*[436] cartel and three *Cement*[437] cartels), but they attracted no fine, because the agreements in question had been notified. This was not uncommon at the time, even for what are now considered to be

---

[432] Such formal steps include in particular written requests for information, written authorisations to carry out inspections, the initiation of proceedings or the notification of a Statement of Objections. The limitation period is interrupted with effect from the date on which the action is notified to at least one undertaking or association of undertakings which has participated in the infringement. The interruption applies for all such undertakings.

[433] Case T-213/00 *CMA CGM and others v Commission* [2003] ECR I-913, paras 480–517.

[434] Order of the Court of 28 October 2004 in Case C-236/03 P *Commission v CMA CGM and others* (not published), paras 53–58.

[435] [1973] OJ L140/17.

[436] [1970] OJ L242/18.

[437] *NCH* [1972] OJ L22/16; *Cementregeling voor Nederland* [1972] OJ L303/7; *Cimbel* [1972] OJ L303/24.

hardcore cartels. For the same reasons, although a significant number of cartels were prohibited during the 1970s,[438] the imposition of fines remained sporadic.[439]

8.601 **Systematic fining of cartels since the 1980s** The Commission started to impose fines on cartels regularly in the 1980s. As companies became generally aware of the legal consequences of collusive behaviour, hard core restrictions ceased to be notified, and the Commission focused its attention on secret cartels. In the *SSI* decision in 1982, it imposed fines on tobacco producers for price-fixing practices which they had failed to mention in the notification of their agreements.[440] In the following two years, the Commission imposed fines in a series of cases relating to fully-fledged cartels, such as *Cast Iron and Steel Rolls* (1983), or *Flat Glass (Benelux)*, *Zinc*, and *Peroxygen Products* (1984). Fines were regularly imposed thereafter, and the mid-1990s were marked by unprecedented total fines in *Cartonboard* (ECU 131.7 million)[441] and *Cement* (ECU 248 million)[442]. After an apparent slowdown between 1995 and 1997, the Commission again became more active in cartel enforcement from 1998 onwards, in the wake of the adoption of the first Leniency Notice in 1996. This signalled a considerable stepping up of the Commission's activity in this field, culminating in 2001 in the adoption of 10 cartel decisions in the same year, representing a total amount of fines of over EUR 1,800 million. This effort has been continued, with the adoption of nine cartel decisions in 2002 (EUR 944 million), five in 2003 (EUR 404 million), six in 2004 (EUR 390 million) and five in 2005 (EUR 683 million). In 2006, five more cartel decisions were adopted (*Hydrogen peroxide*,[443] *Methacrylates*,[444] *Road Bitumen Netherlands*,[445] *Copper Fittings*[446] and *Synthetic Rubber*),[447] totalling fines over EUR 1,840 million, a new annual record for the Commission.

8.602 **Progressive increase in the level of fines** As mentioned, over the period 1969–1994, the level of the fines imposed on cartel participants remained quite low.[448] However, the Commission's stance over this period reflects repeated concerns as to its capacity to ensure a sufficiently deterrent effect in its fines. In this respect, the *Pioneer* case,[449] in 1979, marked a clear evolution towards heavier fines. The Commission admitted during the related Court proceedings that it had imposed fines considerably higher than in the past, as the

---

[438] See eg *Dutch Nitrogeneous Fertilizers* (CSV) [1978] OJ L242/15, *Gas Water-Heaters and Bath-Heaters* [1973] OJ L217/34, *Franco-Japanese Ball Bearings* [1974] OJ L343/19, *IFTRA rules for producers of virgin aluminium* [1975] OJ L228/3, *Italian Flat Glass* I [1981] OJ L36/32.

[439] See eg *Belgian Wallpaper* [1974] OJ L237/3, *Tinned Mushrooms* [1975] OJ L29/26, and *Vegetable parchment* [1978] OJ L70/54.

[440] [1982] OJ L232/1.

[441] Fines for some undertakings were subsequently reduced on appeal by the CFI and the ECJ.

[442] idem.

[443] IP/06/560.

[444] IP/06/698.

[445] IP/06/1179.

[446] IP/06/1222.

[447] IP/06/1647

[448] Interestingly, Wils even notes that, in real terms, fines (irrespective of the type of infringement concerned) were on average lower over the period 1974–84 than in the period 1969–1973. WPJ Wils, 'EC Competition Fines: To Deter or Not To Deter', in WPJ Wils, *The Optimal Enforcement of EC Competition Law–Essays in Law an Economics* (2002), pp 10–12.

[449] [1980] OJ L60/21. This was not a cartel case.

fines ranged from 2 to 4 per cent of the companies' total turnover whilst they had never previously been higher than 2 per cent.[450] In its Thirteenth Report on Competition Policy in 1983, the year of the Court's judgment in *Pioneer,* the Commission confirmed that due to insufficient deterrent effect over the preceding period, it had applied a tougher policy since that decision.[451] In its Twenty-first Report on Competition Policy in 1991, the Commission again stated its intention to 'make fuller use of the possibility offered by Regulation 17 to impose fines of up to 10% of the annual turnover of the companies involved, in order to reinforce the deterrent effect of penalties under Community competition law'.[452] It was, however, only after the Commission adopted a new methodology for setting fines in 1998 that fines became decisively heavier.

(ii) Setting the Fine Before the 1998 Guidelines: the Practice of the Commission and Review by the Courts

No explanation of method used   From 1969 to 1998, the Commission did not explain **8.603** in its decisions the methodology that it had used to calculate the fines. It limited itself to listing a variety of elements relevant to the assessment of the gravity and duration of the infringement—the only criteria set out in Regulation 17—without specifying how the starting point of the fine had been determined or the extent to which each criterion had affected this amount. In spite of this opacity, it became apparent, especially during Court proceedings,[453] that the Commission's method consisted of calculating the fine as a percentage of the annual turnover in the product concerned within the EC when the cartel was Community wide, or of the annual product turnover in the geographical market concerned when the scope of the infringement was smaller. The fines would typically work out at between 2 and 4 per cent of the annual product turnover.[454]

Wide discretion enjoyed by the Commission   The ECJ immediately confirmed the wide **8.604** margin of discretion enjoyed by the Commission in setting the amount of the fines. In its first judgments on fines in *Quinine*, the Court made it clear that the fines imposed must be aimed at deterrence, as their 'object is to suppress illegal activities and to prevent any recurrence. This object could not be adequately attained if the imposition of a penalty were

---

[450] *Musique Diffusion Française v Commission*, para 103. The Commission stated before the Court that 'after 20 years of Community competition policy, an appreciable increase in the level of fines [was] necessary, in its view, at least for types of infringement which [had] long been well defined and [were] known to those concerned [. . .]'. The Commission added that 'many undertakings carry on conduct which they know to be contrary to Community law because the profit which they derive from their unlawful conduct exceeds the fines imposed hitherto. Conduct of that kind can only be deterred by fines which are heavier than in the past' (para 104).

[451] 13th Report on Competition Policy (1983), para 65.

[452] 21st Report on Competition Policy (1991), para 139.

[453] See eg Case T-148/89 *Tréfilunion v Commission* [1995] ECR II-1063, para 136: 'The Commission replies [to the applicant] that it took as the basis for calculation of the fine the turnover in welded steel mesh achieved by the undertakings on the relevant geographical market [. . .] and did so because the geographical market as a whole was affected by all the agreements. It explains that, in view of the seriousness of the infringement and the fact that Tréfilunion I participated in agreements on the French market, the Benelux market and the German market, the Commission took as its basis for calculating the fine imposed on Tréfilunion I 3.6% of the relevant turnover [. . .]'.

[454] M Reynolds, 'EC Competition Policy on Fines' (1992), European Business Law Review, 263.

to be restricted to the infringement alone'. Thus, 'the Commission's power to impose penalties is in no way affected by the fact that the conduct constituting the infringement has ceased and that it can no longer have detrimental effects'.[455] The Commission's margin of discretion in assessing the apparent level of the fine is therefore particularly focused upon the need for deterrence. To that end, the Commission is entitled, for the purpose of fixing the amount, to assess the gravity of the infringement by taking into account in particular the nature of the restrictions on competition, the number and size of the undertakings concerned, the respective proportions of the market controlled by them within the Community, and the state of the market when the infringement was committed.[456] In *Musique Diffusion Française*, a landmark case as regards fines, the ECJ largely upheld the Commission's initiative in *Pioneer* of increasing the level of fines considerably, thereby reaffirming the wide discretion enjoyed by the Commission in the exercise of its powers to impose sanctions.[457]

8.605 **Large number of factors to be taken into account** The Court stated in *Musique Diffusion Française* that 'in assessing the gravity of an infringement, regard must be had to [a] large number of factors, the nature and importance of which vary according to the type of infringement in question and the particular circumstances of the case. Those factors may, depending on the circumstances, include the volume and value of the goods in respect of which the infringement was committed and the size and economic power of the undertaking and, consequently, the influence which the undertaking was able to exert on the market'.[458] But the Commission may also take into account other factors, such as the duration of the established infringement and all the factors capable of affecting the assessment of its gravity, such as the conduct of each of the undertakings, the role played by each of them, the profit which they were able to derive from the infringement, their size, the value of the goods concerned and the threat that the infringement in question posed to the objectives of the Community.[459]

8.606 **Power to raise the level of fines without prior notice** The Court also held in *Musique Diffusion Française* that the Commission's power to impose fines on undertakings 'is one of the means conferred on the Commission to enable it to carry out the task of supervision conferred on it by Community law'. It added that whilst this task 'certainly includes the duty to investigate and punish individual infringements, it also encompasses the duty to pursue a general policy designed to apply, in competition matters, the principles laid down by the Treaty and to guide the conduct of undertakings in the light of those principles'.[460] Thus, in

---

[455] Case 41-69 *Chemiefarma* [1970] ECR 661, paras 173–175.

[456] Case 45-69 *Boehringer Mannheim v Commission* [1970] ECR 769, para 53.

[457] Joined cases 100 to 103/80 *Musique Diffusion française and others v Commission* [1983] ECR 1825, paras 105–108.

[458] Para 120. See also Case 322/81 *Michelin v Commission* [1983] ECR 3461, para 111; Joined Cases 96–102, 104, 105, 108 and 110/82 *IAZ v Commission* [1983] ECR 3369, para 52.

[459] Para 129. This has been confirmed in subsequent case law. In particular, the European Courts have held that 'the gravity of infringements must be determined by reference to numerous factors such as, in particular, the particular circumstances of the case, its context and the dissuasive element of fines; moreover, no binding or exhaustive list of the criteria which must be applied has been drawn up' (Case C-137/95 P *SPO v Commission*, para 54; Case C-219/95 P *Ferriere Nord v Commission* [1997] ECR I-2411, para 33; Case T-334/94 *Sarrió* [1998] ECR II-1439, para 328; Case T-23/99 *LR AF 1998* [2002] ECR II-1705, para 236).

[460] Joined Cases 100 to 103/80 *Musique Diffusion française and others v Commission* [1983] ECR 1825, para 105.

assessing the gravity of an infringement for the purpose of fixing the amount of the fine, the Commission must take into consideration 'not only the particular circumstances of the case but also the context in which the infringement occurs and must ensure that its action has the necessary deterrent effect, especially as regards those types of infringement which are particularly harmful to the attainment of the objectives of the Community'.[461]

In this respect, the fact that the Commission imposed fines of a certain level for certain **8.607** types of infringement in the past does not mean that it is estopped from raising that level within the limits indicated in the implementing Regulation if that is necessary to ensure the implementation of Community competition policy. The proper application of the competition rules in fact requires that the Commission may at any time adjust the level of fines to the needs of that policy.[462] This principle has been systematically confirmed by subsequent case law. Thus, the CFI has held on several occasions that 'fines constitute an instrument of the Commission's competition policy. That is why it must be allowed a margin of discretion when fixing their amount, in order that it may channel the conduct of undertakings towards observance of the competition rules'.[463] In light of the above, the CFI has confirmed that that a change from previous practice in the level of the fines imposed does not infringe the principle of equal treatment.[464] Consequently, the mere fact that in one decision the Commission has taken into account a given factor in the assessment of gravity does not mean that it is also obliged to do so in a subsequent decision or that it must attribute the same weight to it.[465] Following the same line of reasoning, the ECJ has also confirmed that the application of a new method of calculation of fines resulting in higher fines in pending cases infringes neither the principle of protection of legitimate expectations nor that of non-retroactivity as long as the fines are still fixed in accordance with the legal framework set out in the implementing Regulation.[466]

---

[461] Joined Cases 100 to 103/80 *Musique Diffusion française and others v Commission* [1983] ECR 1825, para 106.

[462] ibid, para 109; Case T-12/89 *Solvay v Commission* [1992] II-907, para 309.

[463] Case T-150/89 *Martinelli v Commission* [1995] ECR II-1165, para 59; Case T-49/95 *Van Mengen Sports v Commission* [1996] ECR II-1799, para 53; Case T-229/94 *Deutsche Bahn v Commission* [1997] ECR II-1689, para 127; Case T-224/00 *Archer Daniels Midland v Commission* [2003] ECR II-2597, para 56.

[464] Joined Cases T-305/94, T-306/94, T-307/94, T-313/94 to T-316/94, T-318/94, T-325/94, T-328/94, T-329/94 and T-335/94 *Limburgse Vinyl Maatschappij NV an others v Commsion (PVC II)*, para 1232.

[465] Case T-347/94 *Mayr-Melnhof Kartongesellschaft mbH v Commission* [1998] ECR II-1751, para 368; Case T-23/99 *LR AF 1998 v Commission*, para 337.

[466] In Case C-189/02 P *Dansk Rørindustri and others v Commission* [2005] ECR I-5425, paras 228–232, the ECJ found that 'undertakings involved in an administrative procedure in which fines may be imposed cannot acquire a legitimate expectation in the fact that the Commission will not exceed the level of fines previously imposed or in a method of calculating the fines. Consequently, the undertakings in question must take account of the possibility that the Commission may decide at any time to raise the level of the fines by reference to that applied in the past. That is true not only where the Commission raises the level of the amount of fines in imposing fines in individual decisions but also if that increase takes effect by the application, in particular cases, of rules of conduct of general application, such as the Guidelines. It must be concluded that [. . .] the Guidelines and, in particular, the new method of calculating fines contained therein, on the assumption that this new method had the effect of increasing the level of the fines imposed, were reasonably foreseeable by undertakings such as the appellants at the time when the infringements concerned were committed. Accordingly, in applying the Guidelines in the contested decision to infringements committed before they were adopted, the Commission did not breach the principle of non-retroactivity'.

8.608   **Control of proportionality by the Court by virtue of its unlimited jurisdiction**   The fact that the Commission enjoys a wide margin of discretion in setting the fine does not mean that the Court does not exercise strict control over the exercise of this power. Pursuant to Article 31 of Regulation No 1/2003, the Court of Justice has unlimited jurisdiction within the meaning of Article 229 EC to review the fines set by the Commission. The Court may cancel, reduce or increase the fine imposed. In the exercise of its jurisdiction, the Court must consider whether the amount of the fine imposed is proportionate to the gravity and duration of the infringement.[467] It must also balance the seriousness of the infringement against the mitigating circumstances invoked by the applicant.[468]

8.609   **Limited scope of the duty to state reasons**   As far as the duty to state reasons regarding the setting of fines is concerned, the ECJ has found that 'the essential procedural requirement to state reasons is satisfied where the Commission indicates in its decision the factors which enabled it to determine the gravity of the infringement and its duration'.[469] Although the ECJ had found in a 1975 judgment that the Commission must give an account of its reasoning when there was an appreciable change in its approach,[470] the reasoning in the Commission's Decisions as regards fines nevertheless remained very short. This approach attracted much criticism, as the fines imposed tended to become heavier over time. In the judgments in *Welded Steel Mesh*, the CFI, whilst rejecting the appellant's arguments that the Commission had failed to state reasons, sent a signal to the Commission by stating that it was 'desirable for undertakings, in order to be able to define their position in full knowledge of the facts, to be able to determine in detail, in accordance with any system which the Commission might consider appropriate, the method of calculation of the fine imposed upon them, without being obliged to bring Court proceedings against the Commission decision in order to do so, which would be contrary to the principle of good administration'.[471]

8.610   The CFI went further in its judgments in *Cartonboard*. Whilst again rejecting the plea that the Commission had failed in its duty to state reasons, the CFI stated that the Commission was under an obligation, 'if it systematically took into account certain basic factors in order to fix the amount of fines, to set out those factors in the body of the decision'.[472] However, on appeal, the ECJ overturned the CFI on this point. The Court held that the Commission 'cannot, by a mechanical recourse to arithmetical formulas alone, divest itself of its own power of assessment. However, it may in its decision give reasons going beyond [the factors

---

[467] See eg Case T-229/94 *Deutsche Bahn v Commission* [1997] ECR II-1689, para 127; Case T-220/00 *Cheil Jedang v Commission* [2003] ECR II-2473, para 93; Case T-38/02 *Danone v Commission* [2005] ECR II-4407, para 136.

[468] See eg Case C-333/94 P *Tetra Pak v Commission* [1996] ECR I-5961, para 48; Case T-38/02 *Danone v Commission* [2005] ECR II-4407, para 136.

[469] Case C-291/98 P *Sarrió v Commission* [2000] ECR I-9991, para 73; Joined cases T-305/94, T-306/94, T-307/94, T-313/94 to T-316/94, T-318/94, T-325/94, T-328/94, T-329/94 and T-335/94 *Limburgse Vinyl Maatschappij NV and others v Commission (PVC II)* [2002] ECR I-8375, para 463.

[470] Case 73/74 *Groupement des Fabricants de Papiers Peints de Belgique and others v Commission* [1975] ECR 1491, para 31.

[471] Case T-148/89 *Tréfilunion v Commission* [1995] ECR II-1063, para 142.

[472] Case T-334/94 *Sarrió v Commission* [1998] ECR II-1439, para 352.

which enabled it to determine the gravity of the infringement and its duration], inter alia by indicating the figures which, especially in regard to the desired deterrent effect, influenced the exercise of its discretion when setting the fines imposed on a number of undertakings which participated, in different degrees, in the infringement'.[473] The Court added that '[i]t may indeed be desirable for the Commission to make use of that possibility in order to enable undertakings to acquire a detailed knowledge of the method of calculating the fine imposed on them. More generally, such a course of action may serve to render the administrative act more transparent and facilitate the exercise by the Court of First Instance of its unlimited jurisdiction, which enables it to review not only the legality of the contested decision but also the appropriateness of the fine imposed. However, [. . .] the availability of that possibility is not such as to alter the scope of the requirements resulting from the duty to state reasons'.[474]

(iii) A Turning Point in the Commission's Fining Policy: the 1998 Guidelines

On 14 January 1998, the Commission for the first time published Guidelines on the method **8.611** of setting fines[475] (the '1998 Guidelines'). The 1998 Guidelines were revised in 2006, with the adoption of new Commission Guidelines on the method of setting fines imposed pursuant to Article 23(2)(a) of regulation No 1/2003[476] (the '2006 Guidelines'). This chapter will nonetheless provide an extensive analysis of practice under the 1998 Guidelines, as they form an essential backdrop to any discussion of the 2006 Guidelines.[477]

Rationale: increased transparency and stronger deterrence Faced, on the one hand, with **8.612** increased criticism as to lack of transparency of the methodology used to set increasingly higher fines and, on the other hand, with the concern that such fines nevertheless remained insufficiently deterrent, the Commission decided to introduce drastic changes to its policy and in 1998 published Guidelines on the method of setting fines for the first time. It stated in the introductory section that the new methodology should 'ensure the transparency and the impartiality of the Commission's decisions, in the eyes of the undertakings and of the Court of Justice alike, while upholding the discretion which the Commission is granted under the relevant legislation to set fines within the limit of 10% of overall turnover'.

Through the publication of a detailed methodology structured in successive steps, the **8.613** Commission both offered guidance and obliged itself to provide the addressees of fines with a detailed statement of reasons, thereby making it easier for companies to contest the amount of the fine before the European Courts. Transparency was also increased, since the detailed calculation of the fines became available in published decisions. Such transparency

---

[473] Case C-291/98 P *Sarrió v Commision* [2000] ECR I-9991, para 76.

[474] idem, para 77.

[475] Guidelines on the method of setting fines imposed pursuant to Art 15(2) of Regulation No 17 and Art 65(5) of ECSC Treaty [1998] OJ C9/3.

[476] [2006] OJ C210/2.

[477] Three reasons justify such an extensive discussion of the 1998 Guidelines: first, they have been applied in most of the cartel decisions on the basis of which the case law on fines has developed. Second, they continue to be applied in all cartel cases where a Statement of Objections was sent before the publication of the 2006 Guidelines. Third, much of the practice developed by the Commission in application of the 1998 Guidelines can be expected to remain relevant in the context of the application of the 2006 Guidelines.

was made more feasible by the fact that the fines were no longer based on turnover figures, which were usually considered as business secrets. The Commission nevertheless retained a wide discretion, as the Guidelines provide only for 'likely' ranges for the fines. The Commission refused to put in place any 'tariffication' system that might have allowed companies to conduct a cost-benefit analysis of cartel behaviour.

8.614 Although not mentioned in the 1998 Guidelines as a separate objective, the new methodology led to a significant increase in the level of fines, as their starting amount was essentially to be determined by reference to the intrinsic gravity of the infringement, and not on the basis of the turnover relating to the infringement. This was the case particularly in respect of cartels, as the 1998 Guidelines provided for 'likely fines' of over EUR 20 million in the case of 'horizontal restrictions such as price cartels and market sharing quotas'. Although the 1998 Guidelines provided various mechanisms of adjustment, the Commission regularly issued fines greatly exceeding EUR 20 million. On numerous occasions, the Commission ultimately had to reduce the level of the fine because of its obligation not to exceed the upper limit of 10% of the overall turnover of the undertaking concerned.

8.615 **An approach based on the principle of 'fixed penalty'** The method for calculating fines set out in the 1998 Guidelines consisted of four main successive steps. First, a '*basic amount*' was set for each undertaking, in respect of the two relevant criteria laid down by Article 23(2) of Regulation 1/2003 (formerly Article 15(2) of Regulation 17), namely the gravity and the duration of the infringement. This was obtained by increasing the amount based on the gravity by a percentage reflecting the duration of the undertaking's participation in the infringement. Secondly, the basic amount was increased, or decreased, as appropriate, in relation to relevant *aggravating or mitigating circumstances*. Thirdly, the fine was reduced, if appropriate, in application of the *Leniency Notice*. Fourthly, further adjustments could be considered in respect of *exceptional circumstances*.

8.616 The major new development introduced by the 1998 Guidelines was that the starting point used for the calculation of the fine was no longer based on the turnover of the undertaking in the market affected by the infringement, but on a 'fixed penalty', the amount of which was determined by reference to the gravity of the infringement. Infringements were classified within a *category of gravity*, in respect of which the fine was set within an indicative range. Three categories of gravity were set out, as follows:

- Minor infringements (likely fines from EUR 1 000 to EUR 1 million);
- Serious infringements (likely fines from EUR 1 million to EUR 20 million);
- Very serious infringements (likely fines above EUR 20 million).

8.617 The 1998 Guidelines did set out *three criteria* for the purpose of determining the relevant category of gravity,:

- the nature of the infringement;
- the actual impact on the market, when this can be measured; and
- the size of the relevant geographic market.

8.618 **Importance of adjustment mechanisms** In spite of a clear willingness to impose fixed penalties based on the type of infringement committed, the 1998 Guidelines provided for the possibility of applying *differential treatment* to companies and stated that 'the principle of equal punishment for the same conduct may, if the circumstances so warrant, lead to different fines being imposed on the undertakings concerned without this differentiation being governed by arithmetic calculation'. The amount of fine determined on the basis of gravity could be invididualized from case to case and from undertaking to undertaking by applying the following criteria:

- the nature of the infringement committed;
- the effective capacity to cause significant damage to other operators, in particular consumers;
- the need to set the fine at a level ensuring that it has a sufficient deterrent effect;
- the need to take into account the fact that large undertakings have legal and economic knowledge which enables them to recognise more easily that their conduct constitutes an infringement and to be aware of the legal consequences stemming from it under competition law;
- in the case of a collective infringement (cartels), the need to apply weightings in order to take account of the specific weight and, therefore, the real impact of the offending conduct of each undertaking on competition, particularly where there is considerable disparity between their sizes.

In relation to the last criterion mentioned above, the Commission agreed from the outset **8.619** in the case of cartels, which are by nature collective infringements, to depart from the principle of imposing a similar penalty on each participant (based on the gravity of the single infringement committed) and to proceed to sophisticated adjustments of the general starting amount. This resulted in a high degree of sophistication in the method of calculation, so that the way in which each criterion should be taken into account could not readily be deduced from the wording of the Guidelines.[478] Despite the fact that the 1998 Guidelines had created a more defined scope for the setting of fines, the Commission was sometimes accused of giving a false impression of scientific rigour, as it ultimately retains a broad discretion over the general starting point of the fine. Nevertheless, the methodology was unambiguously upheld by the European Courts.

The Court's review of the legality of the 1998 Guidelines   The validity of the 'fixed- **8.620** penalty' (or 'flat rate') approach was soon contested before the CFI. Appellants argued that the 1998 Guidelines were illegal as the Commission was required to calculate the fines by reference to a proportion of the turnover of the undertakings concerned and to ensure equality of treatment in this regard. This argument was rejected by the CFI, which stated that under the 1998 Guidelines the fines continued to be calculated according to the two criteria referred to in the implementing Regulation, namely the gravity of the infringement and its duration,

---

[478] For instance, in cartel cases, the evaluation of the 'effective capacity to cause significant damage to other operators' (second indent) is not clearly distinguished from the 'weightings' (fifth indent). Both criteria seem to be applied indistinguishably, as the 'real impact of the offending conduct of each undertaking in competition' corresponds precisely to its (relative) 'effective capacity to cause damage to other operators'. Similarly, the need to set the fine at a sufficiently deterrent level can hardly be distinguished from that of taking into account the fact that large undertakings are better armed to be aware of the illicit character of their conduct (and therefore need additional deterrence).

and that the upper limit of 10 per cent of the annual turnover as laid down in that provision continued to be observed. The Guidelines therefore could not be regarded as going beyond the legal framework for the fines. The CFI also observed that, pursuant to settled case law, the gravity of the infringements had to be established in accordance with numerous factors,[479] and pointed out that there was no obligation on the Commission to take into account the various turnover figures of the undertakings concerned.[480] Furthermore, a difference in the fines imposed on several undertakings for the same infringement in terms of the percentage of their turnover did not constitute a violation of the principle of equal treatment.

8.621 The CFI also found that the change from the Commission's existing administrative practice did not constitute an alteration of the underlying legal framework for determining the fines, and therefore was not contrary to the principle of non-retroactivity.[481] By resorting to the new methodology set out in the 1998 Guidelines in cases initiated before their publication, the Commission did not violate the principle of legitimate expectations either, as the Commission exercised its powers within the limits of the discretion conferred on it by the Implementing Regulation. Indeed, according to settled case law traders cannot have a legitimate expectation that an existing situation which is capable of being altered by the Community institutions in the exercise of their discretion will remain unchanged.[482] The Commission was therefore entitled to raise the general level of fines, within the limits laid down in the implementing Regulation, if that was necessary to ensure implementation of Community competition policy.[483] These findings have been upheld by the ECJ on appeal.[484]

8.622 Appellants have also argued that the Commission could at no time, in the process of its calculations, exceed the statutory upper limit of 10 per cent of annual turnover as set out in the implementing regulation, as may be the case if the 'fixed-sum principle' is applied.[485] The CFI has responded that Article 15(2) of Regulation No 17 (now Article 23(2) of Regulation 1/2003) only requires that the fine ultimately imposed on an undertaking be reduced if it exceeds 10 per cent of its turnover, and that this 'cap' is independent of the intermediate stages in the calculation intended to take the gravity and duration of the infringement into account. The legislative framework for the imposition of fines therefore does not prohibit the Commission from referring, during its calculation, to an intermediate amount exceeding 10% of the turnover of the undertaking concerned, provided that the

---

[479] See in particular Joined Cases 100 to 103/80 *Musique Diffusion française and others v Commission* [1983] ECR 1825, paras 120 and 121; Case T-77/92 *Parker Pen v Commission* [1994] ECR II-549, para 94; Case T-327/94 *SCA Holding v Commission* [1998] ECR II-1373, para 176.

[480] Case T 23/99 *LR AF 1998 v Commission* [2002] ECR II-1705, paras 277–282.

[481] ibid, para 233.

[482] See Case 245/81 *Edeka* [1982] ECR 2745, para 27, and Case C-350/88 *Delacre and others v Commission* [1990] ECR I-395, para 33.

[483] Case T 23/99 *LR AF 1998 v Commission* [2002] ECR II-1705, paras 241–248.

[484] Joined cases C-189/02 P, C-202/02 P, C-205/02 P to C-208/02 P and C-213/02 P *Dansk Rørindustri and others v Commission* [2005] ECR I-5425.

[485] Appellants argued that if the Commission were at liberty to calculate the fine on basic amounts exceeding the 10% limit, any adjustment which it made to the amount of the fine would be purely illusory and devoid of any impact on the final amount of the fine, which in any event would not exceed 10% of total turnover.

amount of the fine ultimately imposed on the undertaking does not exceed that maximum limit. This was also confirmed by the ECJ on appeal.[486]

The Commission is bound by its Guidelines   The CFI has found, as a matter of settled   **8.623**
case law, that the Commission may not depart from rules which it has imposed on itself[487] and that in particular, whenever the Commission adopts guidelines for the purpose of specifying, in accordance with the Treaty, the criteria which it proposes to apply in the exercise of its discretion, there arises a self-imposed limitation on that discretion in as much as it must then follow those guidelines. It follows that the Commission is required, when setting the fines, to adopt the method set out in its Guidelines and to take into account the relevant factors mentioned therein,[488] and where it departs from those Guidelines in any particular regard, it must expressly set out the reasons justifying such a departure.[489] In appropriate circumstances the Guidelines can therefore be used against the Commission, and the CFI has already corrected fines on the basis of a finding that the Commission had disregarded the Guidelines.[490]

(2) Setting the Fine under the 1998 Guidelines: Practice of the Commission

Overview   In setting fines under the 1998 Guidelines the Commission took a seven-stage   **8.624**
approach. First, it evaluated *the 'objective' gravity of the infringement taken as a whole*, by taking account of all factors relevant to the assessment of the overall impact of that infringement on the economy. Such evaluation allowed the 'general starting amount' to be determined,[491] the level of which reflected the scale of gravity of the cartel. Second, it determined an 'individual starting amount' for each member of the cartel by evaluating the (relative) *'objective' responsibility of each cartel participant* for economic damage caused, having regard to their individual objective characteristics, such as economic weight (both within the cartel and in the market in general) as well as overall size and resources. Third, the Commission applied, when appropriate, an *increase percentage* to those individual starting amounts, which reflected *the additional impact caused by the duration of the infringement* committed by each cartel participant. The resultant amount was then the 'basic amount' of the fine. Fourth, the Commission considered the *'subjective' responsibility of each cartel participant* by taking into account all relevant factors relating to a participant's individual conduct and/or to the

---

[486] Joined Cases C-189/02 P, C-202/02 P, C-205/02 P to C-208/02 P and C-213/02 P *Dansk Rørindustri and others v Commission* [2005] ECR I-5425.

[487] See Case T-7/89 *Hercules Chemicals v Commission* [1991] ECR II-1711, para 53, confirmed on appeal in Case C-51/92 P *Hercules Chemicals v Commission* [1999] ECR I-4235, and the case law cited therein.

[488] Case T-224/00 *Archer Daniels Midland Company and Archer Daniels Midland Ingredients v Commission* [2003] ECR II 2597, para 157.

[489] Case T-213/00 *CMA CGM and others v Commission* [2003] II-913, para 271; Joined Cases T-236/01, T-239/01, T-244/01 to T-246/01, T-251/01 and T-252/01 *Tokai Carbon v Commission* [2004] ECR II-1181, para 353.

[490] See eg Case T-224/00 *Archer Daniels Midland Company and Archer Daniels Midland Ingredients v Commission* [2003] ECR II-2597, paras 181–197. The CFI found that the Commission had disregarded the Guidelines on the method used for applying differential treatment. In the exercise of its unlimited jurisdiction, the CFI finally concluded that the starting amount determined for the applicant was appropriate and that 'the Commission's failure to adhere to the Guidelines ha[d] not [...] led it to breach the principle of proportionality' (para 206).

[491] Sometimes referred to as the 'general starting point'.

context in which such conduct took place, (ie whether there were aggravating or attenuating circumstances). Fifth, it considered whether the *upper limit of 10 per cent* of the annual turnover applicable to the fine had been exceeded. Sixth, where relevant and as appropriate, it reduced the fine, in *application of the Leniency Notice*. Finally, the Commission took account of any *exceptional circumstances* justifying an adjustment to the final amount of the fine.

(a) Evaluating the 'objective' gravity of the cartel 'as a whole': the 'general starting amount'

8.625 The 'general starting amount' was determined in two successive steps. First, the Commission determined into which of the three 'categories' of gravity set out by the 1998 Guidelines the infringement fell. From the range of fines applicable in each category, the Commission then calculated a 'general starting amount', the value of which, at this stage of the procedure, was equal for all cartel participants.

(i) Defining the 'Category' of Gravity of the Infringement

8.626 **Three assessment criteria, three categories of gravity**   Under the 1998 Guidelines, to assess the gravity of an infringement 'as a whole', the Commission applied three objective criteria relating to the *overall* characteristics of that infringement: the *nature* of the infringement, its *actual impact on the market where this can be measured* and the *size of the relevant geographic market*.[492] Following the application of those criteria, infringements were put into one of three categories:[493]

- *Minor infringements*, defined as 'trade restrictions, usually of a vertical nature, but with a limited market impact and affecting only a substantial but relatively limited part of the Community market'. The fines corresponding to such infringements ranged from EUR 1000 to EUR 1 million.
- *Serious infringements* were 'more often than not ... horizontal or vertical restrictions of the same type as [minor infringements], but more rigorously applied, with a wider market impact, and with effects in extensive areas of the common market. There might also be abuse of a dominant position (refusals to supply, discrimination, exclusion, loyalty discounts made by dominant firms in order to shut competitors out of the market, etc.)'. Fines in this category ranged from EUR 1 million to EUR 20 million.
- *Very serious infringements* would 'generally be horizontal restrictions such as price cartels and market-sharing quotas, or other practices which [would] jeopardize the proper functioning of the single market, such as the partitioning of national markets and clear-cut abuse of a dominant position by undertakings holding a virtual monopoly'. Fines in this category were likely to exceed EUR 20 million.

8.627 **Cartels classified as 'very serious' infringements**   According to the 1998 Guidelines, cartels automatically belonged in the category of 'very serious' infringements.[494] In terms of the 'nature of the infringement' (ie the first relevant criterion as mentioned above), it is clear that

---

[492] Point 1 A, para 1 of the 1998 Guidelines states: '[i]n assessing the gravity of the infringement, account must be taken of its *nature*, its *actual impact on the market where this can be measured*, and the *size of the relevant geographic market*'.

[493] Point 1 A, para 2 of the 1998 Guidelines.

[494] In this respect, the Guidelines explicitly refer to the following decisions: 91/297/EEC, 91/298/EEC, 91/299/EEC, 91/300/EEC and 91/301/EEC—*Soda Ash*; 94/815/EC—*Cement*; 94/601/EC—*Cartonboard*; 92/163/EC—*Tetra Pak* and 94/215/ECSC—*Steel Beams*.

cartels are considered the most serious violations of competition law, as consistently con-firmed by case law.[495] However, as account had to be taken of all three criteria together, one could question whether a lack of measurable impact of the cartel or its limited geographical scope could thus be deemed capable of mitigating the 'very serious' character of the infringement by its 'nature'.

However, a more careful reading of the 1998 Guidelines makes it clear that this would not **8.628** have been the case. Whereas the criteria of market impact and geographical scope are explic-itly mentioned with reference to the categories of 'minor' and 'serious' infringements,[496] no mention of those criteria is made with reference to the 'very serious infringement' category (other than the fact that such infringements would include, inter alia, 'practices which jeopardize the proper functioning of the single market'). It can therefore be concluded that, restrictions such as cartels are very serious 'by nature', and that such infringements should (or at least could) thus always be categorised as 'very serious', irrespective of their actual impact when measurable, or of their geographical scope.

The Commission's practice: an initially flexible approach evolving towards stricter **8.629** **application** The practice of the Commission in determining the categories of infringe-ment has, however, been more flexible. In more than 45 cartel decisions taken under the 1998 Guidelines between 1998 and 2006, on only 10 occasions has the Commission con-cluded that the cartel in question constituted a 'serious' infringement' and not a 'very seri-ous infringement'.[497] Analysis shows that the determination of the category of gravity to which a cartel belongs is a result of the complex interplay of the three relevant criteria. It seems that, in the first decisions taken under the 1998 Guidelines, an initial reluctance to consider certain types of cartel behaviour as infringements that were 'very serious' by nature contributed to the overall classification of the corresponding infringements as merely 'seri-ous'. In other decisions, the combination of restrictions deemed very serious 'by nature', together with evidence of either a limited impact and/or a limited size of the geographical market, also led to an overall classification of the infringements in question as 'serious'.

However, that 'lenient' approach tends to be evident mainly in early decisions adopted **8.630** under the 1998 Guidelines, which would indicate that the Commission may have initially been reluctant to apply the criteria for the new method of calculation strictly. Over the years,

---

[495] According to settled case law, to assess the gravity of an infringement account must be taken in partic-ular of the nature of the restrictions on competition (Joined Cases T-213/95 and T-18/96 *SCK and FNK v Commission* [1997] ECR II-1739, para 246, and the case law cited therein). Thus, infringements which directly or indirectly fix prices or other trading conditions, or which limit or control production, markets, technical development, or investment, particularly where they concern horizontal agreements, are classified as 'particularly serious' (Case T-141/94 *Thyssen Stahl* [1999] ECR II-347, para 675) or as 'clear infringements of the Community competition rules' (Case T-148/89 *Tréfilunion v Commission* [1995] ECR II-1063, para 109, and Case T-311/94 *BPB de Eendracht v Commission* [1998] ECR II-1129, paras 303 and 338).

[496] The Guidelines state that *minor infringements* concern restrictions 'with a limited market impact' that affect 'only a substantial but relatively limited part of the Community market'. As for *serious infringements*, they are essentially of the same type as minor infringements but will be 'more rigorously applied, with a wider market impact" and 'with effects in extensive areas of the common market'.

[497] *Alloy Surcharge, British Sugar, Greek Ferries, FEG/TU, FETTCSA, Luxemburg Brewers, Belgian Beer (Private Labels), German Banks, Industrial and Medical Gases, French Beer.*

as the Commission's practice in opposition to cartels developed, it took a stricter stance regarding the categorization of gravity. That evolution appears to have developed in three successive steps. First, the Commission has shown progressively greater determination to consider cartel behaviour as a 'very serious' infringement by nature. Second, the possibility of mitigation of gravity initially included in the criterion of the 'actual impact' has been neutralized by a very restrictive application of this condition. Third, the fact that a cartel may have limited geographical scope has increasingly played a more minor role in the mitigation of gravity.

8.631 **Gravity 'by nature': evolution towards stricter application** In *Alloy Surcharge*, the first cartel decision taken under the 1998 Guidelines, the Commission found that arrangements aimed at a uniform increase of a cost component were, by nature, merely a 'serious' infringement.[498] This seems to have resulted in the overall classification of the cartel as a 'serious' infringement in spite of evidence of its significant impact and wide geographical coverage.[499] In the following cartel decision, *British Sugar*, the Commission found that although the arrangements in question 'pursued the object of restricting competition by coordinating pricing policy on the horizontal level' and consisted of 'a collaborative strategy of higher pricing', there was 'not sufficient evidence to state that minimum prices, or prices to be charged to specific customers, [had] jointly [been] fixed'.[500] The Commission concluded that the infringement at issue constituted a 'serious' infringement overall, since there was no proof of an actual restrictive effect on competition and as the 'geographical scope of the relevant market was confined to Great Britain'.[501] That conclusion could reasonably be interpreted to mean that in the presence of an infringement that was only 'serious' in nature, a lack of evidence of any actual impact and the limited geographical scope of the infringement would prevent it being classified as 'very serious'.

8.632 In its subsequent decision, *FEG/TU*, the Commission was not explicit as to its findings concerning the criterion of gravity 'by nature'. It stated that the infringement in question included arrangements supporting horizontal price agreements, concluded in the FEG framework, which were intended to restrict competition by coordinating pricing policy at a horizontal level, and that the aim of such arrangements was to create or maintain a stable price level with a sufficiently large margin for wholesalers.[502] However, the Commission appeared to mitigate such finding by noting that 'in general, the FEG and its members were

---

[498] [1998] OJ L100/55, para 74.
[499] Paras 48–49. The Commission did not refer explicitly to the criterion of actual impact but noted that the undertakings concerned accounted for almost 90% of stainless steel flat products and that the impact on the market of the concerted increase in prices had thus necessarily been considerable. The Commission added that the alloy surcharge was a major component of the final price and that although the price increase resulting from the alloy surcharge depended partly on the amount of alloy used in the steel and partly on fluctuations in alloy prices, it could account for as much as 25% of the total price. The Commission also pointed out that the change in the reference values for the alloy surcharge was followed by a virtual doubling of stainless steel prices during a certain period. While such a sharp increase could not be explained solely by the implementation of the restrictive arrangements, such arrangements did greatly contribute to it through the mechanical price increase that it caused.
[500] [1999] OJ L76/1, para 193.
[501] Paras 193–194.
[502] [2000] OJ L39/1, paras 137–138.

not so concerned to fix uniform prices for all electro-technical products as to keep the degree of price competition which existed under control and within limits, in order not to jeopardise price stability and wholesalers' margins'.[503] Taking account of the limited geographical scope of the infringement (the Netherlands), and despite evidence of its significant impact,[504] the Commission concluded that, overall, the infringement was of a 'serious' nature.[505] Again, the Commission hesitated to classify the infringement as 'very serious' by nature in spite of the existence of certain practices amounting to price collusion.[506]

However, this seemingly lenient approach towards practices amounting to price-fixing was soon abandoned. In subsequent decisions, cartel arrangements were systematically described as 'very serious' infringements by nature, even in cases where the overall gravity was ultimately considered only as 'serious'. Thus in *Greek Ferries*, the Commission stated that an agreement by which the price of transporting passengers and freight by roll-on roll-off ferries was agreed by some of the most important ferry operators in the relevant market constituted, by its nature, a 'very serious' breach of Community law.[507] Similarly, in *Luxembourg Brewers*, the Commission stated that the infringement was intended to maintain the clientèles, and hence the market shares, of the main brewing undertakings established in Luxembourg and to restrict the penetration of foreign brewers on this market. It concluded that this was a very serious level of gravity 'by nature'.[508] The same line of reasoning was taken in *Belgian (Private Label) Beers*[509] and in *Industrial and Medical Gases*.[510] Thus, the evolution towards increased severity in the categorization of level of gravity was clear. This has been confirmed by case law. The CFI has found that 'horizontal price agreements are particularly injurious under

8.633

---

504 The Commission pointed out that the infringements had occurred in a market where the FEG members had a joint market share of 96%. It stated that the repercussions of the collective exclusive dealing arrangement on the market could not be measured precisely but that it was however certain that the infringement considerably delayed the complainant's entry into the Dutch market and made it appreciably more difficult. Although there were indications that the price level for electro-technical products on the Dutch market was relatively high, the Commission pointed out that it was equally impossible to determine precisely the repercussions of the horizontal price agreements.

505 Para 142.

506 A similar tendency to play down the gravity 'by nature' of the infringement in spite of its clear-cut anti-competitive object also appears evident in *FETTCSA* ([2000] OJ l268/1). As in *British Sugar*, the Commission described the infringement as a horizontal agreement aiming to restrict price competition between undertakings with a high market share. It also pointed out that a restrictive agreement between Conference members and independent lines was particularly serious in the liner shipping sector, where the existence of actual and potential competition from non-Conference lines is one of the principal justifications for the group exemption (liner shipping maritime conferences benefited at the time from a Block Exemption Regulation). However, the Commission stated that an agreement not to discount from published prices was, however, 'a less serious form of horizontal price agreement than an agreement fixing the level of prices' (para 181). The subsequent statement that 'horizontal price agreements will normally be considered very serious infringements' seems to suggest that the Commission tended to view the infringement as 'very serious' by nature although it was, again (whether deliberately or not), not explicitly conclusive on this point. However, the Commission immediately added that in light of its (lack of) actual impact (its geographical scope was not mentioned in the statement of reasons regarding fines) the infringement had to be classified as 'serious' and added that the basic level of fine should be set at the 'very lowest end' of the scale of fines appropriate for a serious infringement (para 181).

507 [1999] OJ L109/24, para 147.

508 [2002] OJ L253/21, para 92.

509 [2003] OJ L200/1, para 335.

510 [2003] OJ L84/1, paras 415–417.

Community competition law and may, by reason of that fact alone, be classified as "very serious"' (Joined Cases T-202/98, T-204/98 and T-207/98 *Tate & Lyle and others v Commission* [2001] ECR II-2035, para 103 and Case T-38/02 *Groupe Danone v Commission* [2005] ECR II-4407, para 147.) In spite of that however, the Commission nevertheless remained pragmatic and its practice still left room for flexibility.[511]

8.634 **'Actual impact when this can be measured': a progressive neutralisation of this potentially mitigating factor** Prior to the application of the 1998 Guidelines, the Commission had often considered evidence of the limited impact of a cartel (or the lack of evidence of its significant impact) as a factor which would mitigate its gravity.[512] In early cartel decisions under the 1998 Guidelines, the Commission continued to consider the lack of evidence of actual impact as a mitigating factor in the assessment of the overall gravity of an infringement. In *British Sugar*, the Commission appeared to consider the gravity of the infringement 'by nature' mitigated by its statement that 'although it [was] by no means out of the question that an actual restrictive effect on competition and an actual effect on trade between Member States resulted from the parties' behaviour, the Commission [did] not rely on the demonstration of such effects'.[513] In *Seamless Steel Tubes*, the Commission stated that the impact of the infringement had been limited with regard to the residual competition resulting from substitutable products.[514] In *FETTCSA*, it noted that it had 'not obtained any evidence as to the effects of the infringement on the price levels' and that 'any harmful effects [were] in any event likely to have been short lived'.[515] In *Greek Ferries*, the Commission noted that the infringement had had a limited actual impact in the market. It accepted in this regard that the parties had 'not applied in full all the specific price agreements' and had 'engaged, during the period of the infringement, in price competition through discounting'.[516]

8.635 However, this tendency to allow the level of the 'impact' to influence the determination of gravity was rapidly replaced by a much stricter approach. In contrast to *Alloy Surcharge*, in which the Commission established an actual impact, in its assessment of the impact of the

---

[511] In *French Beer* ([2005] OJ L184/57, full text of the decision available on DG COMP's web site) the Commission concluded that an 'armistice' agreement which was intended to control the cost of acquiring wholesalers and to establish, in the French 'on-trade' beer market, an equilibrium between the two leading brewers in France was 'a horizontal agreement designed to restrict competition between undertakings holding large market shares'. However, it added that 'an agreement designed to bring wholesalers' acquisition costs under control in the short term by putting an end to an acquisition war cannot be regarded as a clear infringement on a par with a price fixing agreement'. As for the plan to establish longer-term equilibrium between the two brewers' distribution networks, the Commission stated that although it was 'akin to a market-sharing agreement', it was not 'market-sharing in the "conventional sense" since the agreement was intended mainly to prevent one group from dominating the market rather than to eliminate all competition between the groups or impede third parties' (para 83). Interestingly, as in *FETTCSA* ([2000] OJ L268/1), contrary to what had already become a well established practice the Commission seems to have been reluctant to draw explicit conclusions as to the gravity of the agreement 'by nature'. It is clear however that the specific characteristics of the agreement contributed to the mitigation of its assessment of the overall gravity of the infringement. Indeed the infringement was finally classified as 'serious', although the fact that the agreement was never implemented and that it had had a limited geographical scope was also relevant (see paras 84–88).
[512] See eg *Preserved Mushrooms*, paras IV (3); *Zinc Producer Group*, paras 100–103; *Polypropylene*, para 108; *Ferry Operators—Currency surcharges*, para 68.
[513] [1999] OJ L76/1, para 193.
[514] [2003] OJ L140/1, para 160.
[515] [2000] OJ L268/1, para 181.
[516] [1999] OJ L109/24, para 148.

infringement in *Pre-Insulated Pipes* the Commission noted that '[t]he unlawful scheme [had been] aggressively pursued and implemented' without, however, specifying a concrete impact in the market.[517] This decision marked a new approach, whereby the Commission considers whether a cartel has had an actual impact insofar as it has been 'implemented', irrespective of whether that impact can be proved in economic terms. In the following cartel decision, *Amino Acids*, the Commission simply stated that the cartel in question had had an EEA-wide impact.[518] Since then, however, the Commission has almost systematically stated in its decisions that evidence of 'implementation' of the cartel agreements satisfies the criterion of 'actual impact', with the consequence that arguments of a lack of practical effects of a cartel in the market cannot mitigate the degree of gravity of the infringement.[519]

In that regard, one should bear in mind that the criterion set out in the 1998 Guidelines **8.636** was that of actual impact on the market '*when this can be measured*'. This can probably be interpreted as meaning that clear evidence of a complete absence of impact or, alternatively, of a particularly important impact, should be taken into account by the Commission. This is illustrated, for example, in *French Beer*, where, in the presence of a clear absence of actual impact (since the cartel agreement was not implemented), the Commission classified the infringement as 'serious' and not 'very serious', in spite of the severity that the Commission considered the infringement to have by nature. Conversely, in the absence of such evidence, the argument that the cartel did not produce its expected effects in the market cannot be taken as a mitigating factor of the overall gravity of the infringement.[520]

The CFI has confirmed that 'where it appears that [the impact of the infringement] can be **8.637** measured', the Commission is required to take the magnitude of this impact into account in the calculation of the fine.[521] Thus, if the Commission relies on the explicit finding of a concrete impact beyond the mere statement that there must have been an impact in the market as the restrictive action was implemented, (partial) failure to establish that finding to the requisite standard will result in a reduction of the fine imposed, as in *Degussa v Commission*.[522] However, the frequent reluctance of the Commission to rely on a specific impact has so far been condoned by the Court.

Thus, in *Scandinavian Airline System v Commission*, the CFI stated that 'since, according to **8.638** the 1998 Guidelines, the Commission does not, for the purposes of assessing the seriousness of the infringement, have to take its actual market impact into account unless it is measurable, and the overall agreement was designed to restrict potential competition, the actual effect of which is ex hypothesi difficult to measure, [...] the Commission was not

---

[517] [1999] OJ L24/1, para 165.

[518] [2001] OJ L152/24, paras 298–302.

[519] See eg *Specialty Graphite* (paras 443–446), *MCAA* (paras 183–286), *Spanish Raw Tobacco* (paras 412–413) or *Industrial Bags* (paras 757–763). It should however be noted that in *Industrial Tubes* (paras 295–314) and *CopperPlumbing Tubes* (paras 610–673), the Commission went to great effort to rebut the alleged evidence of an absence of impact submitted by certain cartel participants.

[520] This argument, used almost routinely by cartel participants, is now systematically rejected by the Commision. See eg *Electrical and Mechanical Carbon and Graphite Products* (paras 280–286); *Organic Peroxides* (paras 437–446); *Thread* (paras 423–427).

[521] Case T-224/00 *Archer Daniels Midland Company and Archer Daniels Midland Ingredients v Commission*, [2003] ECR II-2597, para 143, and Case T-279/02 *Degussa v Commission* [2006] ECR II-897, para 216.

[522] Case T-279/02 *Degussa v Commission* [2006] ECR II-897, paras 214–254.

required precisely to demonstrate the actual impact of the cartel on the market and to quantify it, but could confine itself to estimates of the probability of such an effect'.[523] In its judgment *Danone v Commission*, in the context *of Belgian Beer*, the CFI found that 'the fact that an agreement having an anti-competitive object is implemented, even if only in part, is sufficient to preclude the possibility that the agreement had no effect in the market'.[524] This does not mean, it is submitted, that the 'impact' criterion has no relevance for the purpose of determining the category of gravity of an infringement, but rather that if restrictive arrangements have been implemented, the fact that their effect on the market cannot be quantified does not mitigate the gravity of the infringement.

8.639 In its judgments in the context of *Sodium Gluconate*, the CFI indicated that it was 'necessary to analyse the exact meaning of the words "where this [ie the actual impact] can be measured" [and to] establish whether those words mean that the Commission can take account of the actual impact of an infringement for the purpose of calculating fines only if, and in so far as, it is able to quantify that impact'. The CFI clarified that 'consideration of the impact of a cartel on the market in question necessarily involves recourse to assumptions. In this respect, the Commission must in particular consider what the price of the relevant product would have been in the absence of a cartel. When examining the causes of actual price developments, it is hazardous to speculate on the part played by each of those causes. Account must be taken of the objective fact that, because of the price cartel, the parties specifically waived their freedom to compete with one another on prices. Thus, the assessment of the influence of factors other than that voluntary decision of the parties to the cartel not to compete with one another is necessarily based on reasonable probability, which is not precisely quantifiable'. It follows that 'the Commission cannot be criticised for referring to the actual impact of a cartel on the relevant market, notwithstanding the fact that it cannot quantify that impact or provide any assessment in figures in this respect'. Consequently, the actual impact of a cartel on the relevant market must be regarded as having been sufficiently demonstrated if the Commission is able to provide specific and credible evidence indicating with reasonable probability that the cartel had an impact on the market.[525]

8.640 **Size of the relevant geographical market: increasingly irrelevant** In its early cartel decisions under the 1998 Guidelines, the Commission tended to take account of the limited size of the geographical scope of the market as a mitigating factor when assessing gravity.[526] However, the Commission very soon adopted a stricter stance. In *Seamless Steel Tubes*, it determined that the overall gravity of the infringement was 'very serious', despite the fact that that infringement had been confined to four Member States.[527] In *SAS/Maersk*, a similar

[523] Case T-241/01 *Scandinavian Airline System v Commission* [2005] ECR II-29117, para 122.
[524] Case T-38/02 *Groupe Danone v Commission* [2005] ECR II-4407, para 148. See also to that effect Joined cases T-259/02 to T-264/02 and T-271/02 *Raiffeisen Zentralbank Österreich and others v Commission*, not yet reported, para 288.
[525] See eg Case T-329/01 *Archer Daniels Midland v Commission*, not yet reported, paras 175–178.
[526] This was the case, for example, in *British Sugar* (cartel limited to Great Britain), *FEG/TU* (the Netherlands), or *Greek Ferries* (all Greece-Italy Adriatic sea routes). However, in these decisions, the 'geographical' criterion seemed to contribute to mitigation only in conjunction with other factors (mere 'serious' gravity by nature or acknowledgement of a limited impact).
[527] [2003] OJ L141/1, paras 161–162.

line was taken. The infringement was classified as 'very serious' because the Commission considered that although the cartel concerned only routes from and to Denmark, the affected geographic market extended throughout the EEA and beyond.[528] The Commission went even further in later decisions, where it classified cartels as 'very serious' infringements in spite of their purely national scope. In the first of such decisions was *Belgian Beer*, where, after stating that the cartel in question concerned the whole territory of Belgium (which was found to constitute 'a substantial part of the common market'),[529] the Commission determined the gravity of the infringement to be 'very serious'. The Commission took the same line of reasoning in *Austrian Banks*[530] and in *Concrete reinforcing bars* (cartel limited to Italy), *Raw Tobacco Spain* (Spain) and *Raw Tobacco Italy* (Italy).

The CFI has confirmed the validity of the Commission's approach. In *Scandinavian Airline* **8.641**
System v Commission, it stated in particular that 'concerning the geographic extent, the fact that, as simple examples of infringements classified as "very serious", the 1998 Guidelines have referred only to infringements concerning most Member States, cannot be interpreted as meaning that only infringements of such a geographic extent are capable of receiving that classification. Moreover, even if most of the decisions of the case law concerning infringements held to be "very serious" did relate to very extensive geographic restrictions, none of the Treaty, the Regulation, the 1998 Guidelines or the case law support the conclusion that only the latter may be considered as such'.[531] The CFI confirmed this in *Danone v Commission*, where it recalled that according to settled case law, 'where a geographic market extends to the whole of a country, that market represents a substantial part of the common market'.[532]

Market value: a 'fourth' criterion?   By adopting a new methodology based on the princi- **8.642**
ple of the 'fixed penalty', the Commission clearly intended to abandon its previous practice, which linked the amount of the fine with turnover in the market affected by collusion. This was explicitly recognised by the European Courts.[533] However, in spite of its intention to break that link, the Commission continued to take account of the economic value of the market concerned when determining the gravity of the infringement. In *Sodium Gluconate*, which concerned a cartel covering the whole of the EEA, the Commission

---

[528] [2001] OJ L265/15, paras 90-91.

[529] [2003] OJ L200/1, para 301.

[530] [2004] OJ L56/1, para 51.

[531] Case T-241/01 *Scandinavian Airline System v Commission* [2005] ECR II-29117, para 87. The CFI, after noting that certain infringements had in any event been classified as 'very serious' even though they were not 'very extensive', added at para 89 that 'moreover, the territory of a single Member State, or even a part of it, may be regarded as constituting a substantial part of the common market within the meaning of Article 82'. It should be understood that by analogy, a cartel covering only a part of a Member State could be considered as covering a substantial part of the common market and therefore be classified as 'very serious'.

[532] Case T-38/02 *Groupe Danone v Commission* [2005] ECR II-4407, para 150. See also Joined cases T-259/02 to T-264/02 and T-271/02 *Raiffeisen Zentralbank Österreich and others v Commission*, not yet reported, paras 308–313.

[533] See Joined Cases C-189/02 P, C-202/02 P, C-205/02 P to C-208/02 P and C-213/02 P *Dansk Rørindustri and others v Commission*, para 225 and Case T-15/02 *BASF v Commission* [2006] ECR II-497, para 134, where the Courts note that the main innovation and essential feature of the Guidelines is that 'fines are determined on a tariff basis, albeit one that is relative and flexible'.

found that the infringement in question was 'very serious', and in response to the parties' claim that the limited value of the product market should be taken into consideration, it pointed out that a distinction had to be made between the question of the size of the market in terms of value and that of the real impact of the infringement in that market. The Commission stated in that regard that the economic importance of the product market had never been taken into account in determining the category of gravity of an infringement and emphasised that that had not been the case in *Alloy Surcharge*, *British Sugar*, or *Greek Ferries*.[534] However, the Commission clearly admitted the relevance of the 'market size' criterion in subsequent cartel decisions. In *Vitamins*, the Commission explicitly stated that 'for the purpose of determining the starting amount of the fines, [it took] into consideration the size of each of the different vitamins market'.[535] Other examples are provided in *Belgian Beer*,[536] *Industrial and Medical Gases*[537] and *Concrete Reinforcing Bars*.[538]

8.643 The Commission's method in this regard has been endorsed by the CFI. In one of its judgments in *Vitamins*, the Court stated that the method set out in the 1998 Guidelines 'does not require—but does not preclude—that the size of the affected market be taken into account for the purposes of determining the general starting amount and still less does it require the Commission to set that amount according to a fixed percentage of the total turnover on the market'.[539] In the context of *Sodium Gluconate*, the CFI stated that in view of the large number of factors that the Commission may take into account when setting the fines, 'the size of the market may constitute a factor to take into consideration when determining the gravity of the infringement', but that 'its significance varies according to the particular circumstances of the case'.[540] In view of the intrinsically very serious nature of infringements such as cartels, 'the small size of the relevant market . . . is of only secondary importance in relation to all the other factors attesting to the gravity of the infringement'.[541] The CFI has also ruled that when considering the size of the affected markets for determining several starting amounts in a decision where distinct infringements are found, the Commission is not obliged to set those starting amounts at a level that represents the same proportion of the value of the respective affected markets considered.[542]

---

[534] Para 376.

[535] [2003] OJ L6/1, para 675.

[536] [2003] OJ L200/1. Two separate infringements where found, namely a bilateral cartel concerning the general beer market in Belgium, and the so-called 'private label' cartel, which concerned only a small segment of the beer market. In the first cartel, the Commission found that the infringement was 'very serious' and imposed heavy fines. However, the 'private label' cartel was only considered a 'serious' infringement, because of the limited economic importance of the segment.

[537] [2003] OJ L84/1. The Commission found that the cartel constituted only a 'serious' infringement as it was confined to the Netherlands '*and to a sector of medium economic importance*' (para 422).

[538] The infringement was considered 'very serious' and the Commission stated that the limitation of the effects of the infringement solely to the Italian market did [not] permit the assessment of the overall gravity of the infringement to be reduced from very serious to serious, '*as the importance of the Italian production had to be taken into account*' para 529. Full text of the decision available on DG COMP's web site.

[539] Case T-15/02 *BASF v Commission* [2006] ECR II-497, para 134.

[540] Case T-329/01 *Archer Daniels Midland v Commission*, not yet reported, paras 102–103.

[541] ibid, para 103.

[542] Case T-15/02 *BASF v Commission* [2006] ECR II-497, paras 134–137.

Conclusion   Initially, in terms of both the qualification of the infringement and the level   **8.643A**
of fines, the Commission appeared reluctant to apply the new method of calculation introduced
by the 1998 Guidelines strictly. However, over time, the Commission took a stricter line.
It then became apparent that all cartels were, by their nature, to be considered 'very serious'
infringements,[543] although the Commission proceeded to a subtle gradation of the overall
level of gravity having regard to the specific circumstances of each case. In addition, it was
established that the 'actual impact' criterion could not lead to any mitigation of gravity unless
solid evidence of a complete absence of impact was adduced. Finally, cartels were to be considered as 'very serious' infringements even if they applied only to a single Member State. This
strict application of the method for calculation of fines was fully upheld by the CFI.[544]

(ii) Determining the Level of the 'General Starting Amount'

Notion of 'general starting amount'   Once the category of gravity had been determined,   **8.644**
the Commission proceeded to calculate a base value for the fine, from which the 'individual
starting amount' for each undertaking would be derived through the application of 'differential treatment', notably by dividing the undertakings into groups and applying a number
of 'multiplying factors'. This base value was known as the 'general starting amount' of the
fines.[545] It took the form of a specific monetary figure corresponding to the level of gravity
of the infringement (ie 'minor', 'serious', 'very serious').

The 'general starting amount' was not provided for in the 1998 Guidelines. Nor did it   **8.645**
appear as such in Commission decisions. Indeed, this was only an intermediate step, taking
place before the application of differential treatment, where applicable. Commission decisions generally directly indicated the individual starting amount determined for each
undertaking, after the application of all factors warranting differential treatment. In any
case, it was the Commission's practice that, even if not identified as such, the 'general starting amount' corresponded to the amount which was set with regard to the 'first group' (ie
the group of companies with the highest market shares) defined under the 'weighting' procedure.[546] The respective starting amounts applicable to the other groups therefore always
represented a proportion of the 'starting amount' set for the 'first' group.[547]

---

[543] In any case, the Commission seems reluctant to classify a 'hard core cartel' practice explicitly as 'serious'
by nature (See *FETTCSA* and *French Beef*).

[544] As is summarised in Case T-241/01 *Scandinavian Airline System v Commission* [2005] ECR II-29117,
para 84, 'even if the size of the geographic market concerned and the impact on the market must also be taken into
account, the nature of the infringement constitutes an essential criterion for assessing the seriousness of an infringement'. In a similar vein, the CFI stated in Case T-38/02 Groupe *Danone v Commission* [2005] ECR II-4407,
para 150, that 'agreements or concerted practices involving in particular [. . .] price-fixing and customer-sharing
may be classified [as a very serious infringement] on the basis of their nature alone, without it being necessary
for such conduct to have a particular impact or cover a particular geographic areacan lead, on the basis of their
sole nature, to their classification as "very serious" without it being necessary to characterize such conduct by
a particular impact or geographical scope'.

[545] Or the 'general starting point', or the 'starting amount of reference'.

[546] See paras 8.665–8.687 below.

[547] This has been clarified in the context of the Court proceedings in *Vitamins*. The Commission indicated
to the CFI that where the Commission had divided the undertakings into categories where differential
treatment was applied, the general starting amount remained linked to the first category for each infringement. See Case T-15/02 *BASF v Commission* [2006] ECR II-497, paras 111 and 123.

8.646   **A 'critical' stage in the calculation of fines in cartel cases**   Under the 1998 Guidelines, the calculation of the 'general starting amount', together with the classification of the infringement within one of the three categories of gravity, was one of the most significant steps in setting a fine in cartel cases. The general starting amount provided a marker within the bands stipulated for each category of gravity. In cartel cases, this was all the more important since the 1998 Guidelines did not stipulate a maximum limit for the starting amount in the case of very serious infringements: stating merely that fines were likely to be *above* EUR 20 million. The methodology used to arrive at the 'general starting amount' was undoubtedly the most controversial aspect of the Commission's practice under the 1998 Guidelines. Some commentators questioned the opacity of that process, which had a decisive impact on the overall level of the fines, claiming that it undermined the objective of transparency pursued by the 1998 Guidelines.[548]

8.647   **The level of the 'general starting amount': a pragmatic approach**   The Commission did not hesitate to set the general starting point at very high levels, particularly in the case of worldwide cartels. At 31 December 2006, the highest starting amount (and therefore the highest general starting amount) in a cartel case was EUR 80 million in the *Plasterboard* case. This was followed by *Carbonless Paper* and *Copper Plumbing Tubes*, in which the general starting amount was set at EUR 70 million, *Methacrylates* (EUR 65 million), *Fittings* (EUR 60 million), *Pre-Insulated Pipes* and *Hydrogen Peroxide* (EUR 50 million), *Belgian Beer* (EUR 45 million) and *Graphite Electrodes* (EUR 40 million).

8.648   Nonetheless, the Commission appears to have taken a very pragmatic approach to determining the level of general starting amounts. It has not hesitated to depart from the notion of a 'fixed penalty' to introduce some flexibility in the methodology used to calculate the starting amount and to tailor the level of the starting amount to each specific case. In *Seamless Steel Tubes*, the Commission found that, overall, the cartel constituted a 'very serious' infringement. However, in its decision in that case the Commission stated that it had taken account of the fact that the relevant sales by the cartel participants in the four Member States concerned amounted 'only to about EUR 73 million a year' and that, consequently, the starting amount of the fine was to be fixed at EUR 10 million.[549] This was the first departure by the Commission from the application of the system of 'fixed penalties'. For the first time, an infringement characterised as 'very serious' incurred a fine below the likely amount of EUR 20 million.[550]

---

[548]   See eg S Mobley and M Arakistain 'How the Commission Sets Cartel Fines', Antitrust (2000); J-F Bellis 'La Détermination des Amendes pour Infraction au Droit de la Concurrence—Bilan de Cinq Années d'application des Lignes Directrices' (2003) 3–4 Cahiers de Droit Européen; I Simic and P Geffriaud 'Evolution of the European Commission's Policy on Fines' (2004) International Business Law Journal; J-F Bellis 'Review of the Commission's Decisions on Fines by the Community Courts', written version of a presentation delivered at the ERA Conference 'Current Developments in Competition Law: Case Law of the Community Courts', Trier, 8–9 December 2005.

[549]   [2003] OJ L140/1, para 162.

[550]   The amounts referred to in the 1998 Guidelines with regard to each of the three categories of gravity are presented as 'likely fines', which suggests that lower levels may be considered as regards their 'starting point'. However, from Commission decisions it is clear that those amounts have always been considered by that institution to be 'starting' amounts of the fines, and not 'final' amounts.

From the beginning it seems to have proved quite difficult for the Commission to keep to **8.649** a 'fixed amount' of a minimum of EUR 20 million for 'very serious' infringements.[551] As the Commission found itself in a position of having to impose fines for European-wide cartels concerning markets of very limited value, a practice emerged under which it was possible to set the 'general starting amount' below the EUR 20 million threshold without the cartel having to have been confined to a small number of Member States.[552]

'General starting amounts' below EUR 20 million for very serious infringements The **8.650** Commission's practice of setting the 'general starting amount' below EUR 20 million for fines in cases concerning cartels classified as 'very serious' became well established.[553] However, the Commission had difficulty reconciling its concern to take account of an array of factors and to avoid imposing unreasonable fines on the one hand, with the principles set out in the 1998 Guidelines on the other hand. That difficulty was particularly highlighted in *Concrete Reinforcing Bars*. The Commission found the infringement in that case to be 'very serious' but stated, without prejudice to that finding, that it had taken account of the specific characteristics of the case, namely that the relevant market was a national one, that it was subject, over the relevant period, to ECSC Treaty rules and that the cartel participants controlled only a limited part of the product market concerned at the beginning of the relevant period.[554] This highlights the fact that notwithstanding the principles set out in the 1998 Guidelines, the Commission continued to take account of a wide array of factors when determining the starting amount for fines in cases concerning cartels. Indeed, the notion of a fixed (minimum) penalty became in effect largely redundant as it appeared that the Commission took account of a large number of factors when determining starting amounts for the calculation of fines. The economic value of the market remained a decisive factor in determining the starting amount, but it remained difficult to predict the starting amount solely on this basis, and significant variations between cases can be observed.

---

[551] *Seamless Steel Tubes* was only the second decision adopted under the Guidelines under the 'very serious category' (following *Pre-Insulated Pipes*). At the time, one may have been tempted to deduce from the Commission's reasoning in the decision that the fact that the scope of the infringement was limited to four Member States had been taken into account as a factor specific to that case, and that it was that factor that justified the low starting amount in spite of the classification of the infringement as 'very serious'. However, subsequent decisions have confirmed that the setting of the general starting amount at a level below EUR 20 million tends to result from the value of the sales concerned rather than from their limited geographical scope.

[552] Thus, in *Sodium Gluconate*, concerning a cartel covering the whole EEA, the Commission categorised the infringement as 'very serious'. After pointing out that it was not its general practice to take account of the value of the product market when determining gravity, it acknowledged it had nevertheless done so in *Seamless Steel Tubes* and decided to do the same in the case before it. Thus, because of the limited size of the sodium gluconate market in the EEA the starting amount was set at EUR 10 million.

[553] With the benefit of hindsight, it seems surprising that in *Seamless Steel Tubes* the Commission considered a market of EUR 73 million to be 'small' in value. In *Vitamin D3*, the starting amount was set at EUR 10 million regarding a sales value in the Community totalling EUR 20 million. In *Raw Tobacco Spain*, a market value of approximately EUR 25 million warranted a general starting amount of EUR 8 million. In *Zinc Phosphate*, the Commission set a low starting amount of EUR 3 million, in respect of an EEA market value of EUR 15–16 million and it set an even lower starting amount in *Methylglucamine*, (EUR 2.5 million in respect of an EEA market value of EUR 3 million).

[554] Para 212 (full text of the decision available on DG COMP's web site). From its statement of reasons, it appears that the precautions taken by the Commission result from the fact that the value of the market affected by the infringement was very high, thereby making it difficult to justify setting a starting amount of less than EUR 20 million on the basis that the market was of limited value, unlike previous cases.

8.651 **Can standard 'rates' be deduced from the Commission's practice?** An analysis of Commission practice leads to the conclusion that a cartel relating to a market value of around EUR 40–80 million would incur fines with a starting amount of EUR 20 million.[555] Below that, markets with a value of approximately EUR 20 million appear to have warranted a general starting amount of around EUR 10 million (*Sodium Gluconate, Vitamin D3, Raw Tobacco Spain*), or possibly less (*Automotive Thread*: EUR 5 million, *Zinc Phosphate*: EUR 3 million). The minimum general starting amounts appear to have been in the region of EUR 2.5 million (*Methylglucamine*). As for fines above the EUR 20 million threshhold, cartels affecting markets of a value of around EUR 150–250 million attracted general starting amounts of approximately EUR 30 million (*Vitamin A, Vitamin C, Vitamin E, Methionine*), rising to EUR 35 million as the market value approached EUR 300 million (*Electrical and Mechanical Carbon and Graphite Products, Industrial Copper Tubes, Industrial Bags*). Markets valued between EUR 400 to 500 million would result in the calculation of a fine from a starting amount of around EUR 40–50 million (*Pre-Insulated Pipes, Graphite Electrodes, Fine Arts Auction Houses, Hydrogen Peroxide*). In *Fittings* and *Methacrylates*, market values of EUR 660 million and EUR 530 million respectively resulted in starting amounts of EUR 60 million and EUR 65 million. At the higher end of the spectrum, cartels affecting market values in the region of EUR 800–1,000 million seemed to incur general starting points in the region of EUR 70–80 million (*Copper Plumbing Tubes, Plasterboard*).

8.652 The above analysis notwithstanding, any attempt to predict the level of the starting amount in a given case remained unreliable, in light of the various factors that could be taken into account of the weight of such factors in the particular case. The Commission's relatively mild approach in *Seamless Steel Tubes*, compared to later decisions regarding markets of the same value, can perhaps be explained by the fact that that case was one of the first decisions in which the Commission set a fine for a very serious infringement under the 1998 Guidelines. In *Zinc Phosphate* or *Concrete Reinforcing Bars*, on the other hand, it is likely that the average size of the firms involved was a factor that favoured the lowering of the starting amount. In *Belgian Beer* and *Austrian Banks*, the confinement of the infringement to a single Member State also clearly played a role, since the starting amounts were kept at EUR 45 and EUR 25 million respectively, in spite of relatively large market values. The effect of the conjunction of those two factors, together with others, was particularly striking in *Concrete Reinforcing Bars*, in which the starting amount was set at EUR 5 million in the context of a market value around EUR 1 billion.

8.653 **Conclusion** The new methodology for calculation of fines set out in the 1998 Guidelines was intended to sever the link between the starting amount and the product turnover, whilst giving the Commission a margin of discretion above EUR 20 million to tailor the level of the 'general starting amount' to the complex circumstances of each case. While the Commission did indeed abandon its previous 'relevant turnover' method,[556] it then had to deal with the difficulty that, under the criteria set by the 1998 Guidelines, it appeared that

---

[555] In *Vitamins*, where separate infringements were found in respect of each product, general starting amounts of EUR 20 million were set with regard to markets worth EUR 34.35 million and 76 million respectively. The same general starting amount was set in *Specialty Graphite* (isostatic product), and in *Sorbates*, in respect of markets worth EUR 45 million In *Needles*, the same general starting amount was set in regard of a market value varying over time from EUR 60 million (needles and pins) to EUR 30 million (needles only).

[556] ie calculation of the fine based on a percentage of the product turnover of each the cartel participants.

cartels were 'automatically' to be classified as 'very serious' infringements which, in turn, would normally oblige the Commission to set the general starting amount of the fine at a minimum of EUR 20 million. It seems that the Commission was not ready to accept what it considered to be excessively high fines in certain cases. The Commission's dilemma resided in the fact that it could not classify a cartel as a 'serious' infringement and then be seen to take a lenient stance towards the 'most egregious infringements' of competition law by applying a lower fine than the likely minimum indicated in the 1998 Guidelines.[557]

(b) Individualising Objective Responsibility: the 'Individual Starting Amount'

Once the overall gravity of the infringement had been established both in terms of the *category of gravity* and the *level of the general starting amount*, the Commission divided the 'general starting amount' into specific 'individual starting amounts'. This step in the procedure for calculation of fines stemmed from the possibility offered by the 1998 Guidelines of applying 'differential treatment' to undertakings.[558] The aim of setting individual starting amounts was to reflect the individual 'objective' gravity of the infringement committed by each participant in the cartel. **8.654**

(i) 'Tuning' the Commission's Practice

Ambiguity of the provisions relating to differential treatment   Paragraphs 3 to 7 of point 1 **8.655** A of the 1998 Guidelines read as follows:

> [3] Within each of [the categories of gravity], and in particular as far as serious and very serious infringements are concerned, the proposed scale of fines will make it possible to apply differential treatment to undertakings according to the nature of the infringement committed.

> [4] It will also be necessary to take account of the effective economic capacity of offenders to cause significant damage to other operators, in particular consumers, and to set the fine at a level which ensures that it has a sufficiently deterrent effect.

> [5] Generally speaking, account may also be taken of the fact that large undertakings usually have legal and economic knowledge and infrastructures which enable them more easily to recognize that their conduct constitutes an infringement and be aware of the consequences stemming from it under competition law.

> [6] Where an infringement involves several undertakings (e.g. cartels), it might be necessary in some cases to apply weightings to the amounts determined within each of the three categories in order to take account of the specific weight and, therefore, the real impact of the offending conduct of each undertaking on competition, particularly where there is considerable disparity between the sizes of the undertakings committing infringements of the same type.

> [7] Thus, the principle of equal punishment for the same conduct may, if the circumstances so warrant, lead to different fines being imposed on the undertakings concerned without this differentiation being governed by arithmetic calculation.

Each of the above provisions allowed for a possible differentiation in the fine set for individual participants within a given case. However, those provisions were not clearly articulated **8.656**

---

[557] The problem, however, seems to be more of a symbolic nature than anything else. In this regard, one may wonder whether the Commission did not make its life excessively difficult by deciding to distinguish as clearly as it did in the Guidelines between 'serious' and 'very serious' infringements.

[558] The 1998 Guidelines state that 'the principle of equal punishment for the same conduct may, if the circumstances so warrant, lead to different fines being imposed on the undertakings concerned without this differentiation being governed by arithmetic calculation' (Point 1. A, para 7 of the 1998 Guidelines).

and certain paragraphs seemed to overlap. Thus paragraph 4 seemed to be an application to collective infringements—in particular cartels—of the general principle set out in the first part of paragraph 2, namely that fines may be differentiated according to the effective economic capacity of offenders to cause damage to the economy. Similarly, paragraph 3, which implies that account may be taken of the fact that large undertakings usually have large resources, seemed to derive in part from the general principle, set out in the last part of paragraph 2, that fines should be set at a level which will ensure sufficient deterrence.[559]

8.657 **Initial variation in the Commission's practice.** In relation to cartels, it became the Commission's established practice that the paragraphs cited above allowed the general starting amount to be customised in each case according to two basic principles, in *two successive steps*. First, the Commission adjusted the starting amounts in order to reflect the '*effective economic capacity*' of each offender to cause damage in the market concerned. To that end, a weighting of the 'general starting amount' was applied on the basis of the sales of each relevant company in the market(s) covered by the cartel. Secondly, the Commission ensured that the fine had a *sufficiently deterrent effect*, by applying, where appropriate, a '*deterrence multiplying factor*' relative to the global means and resources of the undertaking concerned. However, the Commission did not always clearly distinguish between these two steps: indeed, different methods were initially used to calculate the individual starting amounts.

8.658 In *TACA*,[560] where the Commission used its power to differentiate fines for the first time, no distinction was made between the evaluation of the 'effective economic capacity' of each company and the need to ensure sufficient deterrence,[561] but simply divided the parties into four groups according to their *worldwide (liner shipping) turnover*, as opposed to their turnover in the relevant market (transatlantic services).[562] The same approach was adopted two years later, in *FETTCSA*, another case regarding maritime transport,[563] and again in *Amino Acids*[564] and *SAS/Maersk*.[565] In other decisions, however, the Commission

---

[559] It should also be mentioned that to date the first paragraph seems to have been of little practical use, since the Commission has rarely used the grounds of a difference in the nature of infringements committed to differentiate starting amounts to be imposed in a given case (cartel members being necessarily members of the same conspiracy).

[560] This case mainly concerned a collective abuse of dominant position.

[561] [1999] OJ L95/1. The Commission stated at para 596 that '[i]n order to take account of the effective capacity of the undertakings concerned to cause significant damage and the need to ensure that the amount of the fine ha[d] a sufficiently deterrent effect, [it] considered it appropriate that larger fines be imposed on the larger TACA parties than on the smaller ones because of the considerable disparity between their sizes'.

[562] The Commission stated that it was appropriate to take world-wide liner shipping turnover as the basis for the comparison of the relative size of the undertakings because that enabled it to assess the real resources and importance of the undertakings concerned.

[563] [2000] OJ L268/1. Para 183 in this case is almost identical to para 596 of *TACA*.

[564] [2001] OJ L152/24. In this case, which concerned a worldwide cartel, the Commission noted that it was necessary to apply differential treatment in respect of the considerable disparity between the sizes of the undertakings involved. As in *TACA* and *FETTCSA*, the Commission did not distinguish between the assessment of the 'effective economic capacity' and the need to ensure sufficient deterrence. It simply divided the companies into two groups according to their overall size and set a starting amount for each group. The Commission stated that it was 'appropriate to take worldwide turnover as the basis for the comparison of the relative size of the undertakings because it enable[d] the Commission to assess the real resources and importance of the undertakings concerned in the markets affected by their illegal behaviour' (paras 303–304).

[565] [2001] OJ L265/15. The Commission also chose to differentiate the starting amounts on the basis of the overall size of the two companies (paras 104–105).

did not weight the starting amounts relative to the relative overall size of the companies involved, but on the basis of their *relative importance in the relevant market*. Such was the approach in *British Sugar*, the second case in which a differentiation in the starting amount was applied. In that case, no 'deterrence multiplying factor' was applied.[566] The same approach was taken in *Greek Ferries*, where the seven cartel participants concerned were divided into three groups, in accordance with their turnover in the market concerned.[567] Again, no deterrence multiplying factor was applied.

In *Pre-insulated Pipes*, the Commission adopted a two-step weighting method for the **8.659** first time. First, the Commission divided the undertakings into four categories according to their relative importance in the relevant market in the Community, 'subject to adjustment where appropriate to take account of other factors and especially the need to ensure effective deterrence'.[568] Second, the Commission carried out such a subsequent adjustment in relation to ABB. The Commission stated that 'in the case of ABB, the appropriate starting point for a fine resulting from the criterion of the relative importance in the relevant market require[d] further upward adjustment to take account of ABB's position as one of Europe's largest industrial combines'.[569] The Commission confirmed that this adjustment was intended to serve two objectives, namely to ensure that the fine had a sufficiently deterrent effect and to take account of the fact that large undertakings have legal and economic knowledge and infrastructures which enable them more easily to recognise that their conduct constitutes an infringement of competition law and to be aware of the consequences stemming from such infringement.

However, it was only since *Graphite Electrodes* [570] in 2001, that the Commission systemati- **8.660** cally applied the two-step approach. In its decision in that case, the Commission applied the same methodology as it had applied in *Pre-Insulated Pipes*, and in the case of two companies applied a deterrence multiplying factor. Since *Graphite Electrodes*, all of the Commission's cartel decisions under the 1998 Guidelines followed the same line of reasoning. First, the undertakings were grouped in accordance with their shares in the relevant market, and second, if necessary, 'deterrence' multiplying factors were applied to specific companies.

Ambiguity in the CFI's case law on differential treatment The initial variations in **8.661** the Commission's approach as to the method to be used under the 1998 Guidelines to

---

[566] [1999] OJ L76/1. In this case the highest fine (EUR 18 million) was imposed on British Sugar due to the fact that that company had been essential to the operation of the cartel because of its share in the relevant markets and its position as price leader. A starting amount of EUR 10 million was imposed on Tate & Lyle, which was considered the second most important member of the cartel on account of its share in the relevant markets. The merchants Napier Brown and James Budgett were found, among other factors, to have been dependent on supplies from British Sugar and Tate & Lyle for a significant part of the sugar that they sold in their capacities as principal or nominal merchants. Consequently, their influence on the relevant market was considered limited and their respective starting amounts were set at EUR 1.5 million each.

[567] [1999] OJ L109/24. The Commission stated that this was 'the appropriate basis for the comparison of the relative size of the undertakings because it enable[d] the Commission to assess the specific weight and importance of the undertakings in the relevant market and, therefore, to evaluate the real impact of the offending conduct of each undertaking on competition' (para 151).

[568] [1999] OJ L24/1, para 166.

[569] Para 168.

[570] [2002] OJ L100/1.

individualise the 'general starting amount' in respect of each undertaking highlights the fact that it took some time for the Commission to establish a uniform method for calculating fines in the case of collective infringements. [571] However, the case law of the CFI in this regard also evolved over time, and itself appeared not to be entirely free from contradictions.

8.662 In *British Sugar* and *Pre-Insulated Pipes*, the CFI was not called upon to rule on the method and figures used by the Commission to apply differential treatment or, in particular, to divide companies into groups. However, in *CMA CGM v Commission (FETTSCA)*, one of the applicants argued that the Commission had erred in law by taking account, when dividing the companies into groups, of their worldwide liner shipping turnover rather than their size in the geographic market that was subject to collusion. The CFI rejected that argument and found that the Commission, when determining the size of the undertakings concerned, was entitled to refer to their total turnover rather than to their turnover on the relevant markets. The CFI pointed to previous case law in which it had in fact been held that the total turnover of an undertaking constitutes an indication, albeit approximate and imperfect, of its size and economic power.[572] It therefore followed that the Commission was entitled to adjust the starting amount determined in respect of the gravity of the infringement on the basis of the sole criterion of the total turnover of the FETTCSA parties.[573] The same line of reasoning was taken in *Atlantic Container Line v Commission*, relating to *TACA*, where the Commission had followed the same approach. [574]

8.663 At the same time, however, in *Cheil Jedang v Commission* (relating to *Amino Acids*) the CFI took a different approach.[575] Again, one of the applicants in the case argued that the Commission had erred in law by solely referring to the *total turnover* of each undertaking concerned when taking account of their effective capacity to cause significant damage to the lysine market in the EEA (along with the dissuasive effect of the fine and the relative size of each undertaking). The CFI stated in response that, for the purposes of assessing the 'effective capacity of the undertakings concerned to cause significant damage to the lysine market in the EEA', an assessment of the real importance of the undertakings in the market affected by their unlawful conduct (ie their influence on that market,) was necessary, and in that respect total turnover was an imprecise guide.[576] The CFI found in

---

[571] However, it should be borne in mind, and indeed it is clear from settled case law, that the Commission enjoys a wide margin of discretion in the exercise of its power to impose fines. Thus, for the purpose of applying differential treatment, it can rely on the turnover of its choice, ie either the sales of the relevant product or the overall turnover of the undertaking (see Joined Cases 100 to 103/80, *Musique Diffusion Française and others v Commission* [1983] ECR 1825). On the other hand, in light of the Commission's declared intention to adhere to the methodology set out in the Guidelines and to follow a coherent and non-discriminatory policy, it is reasonable to expect the defined methodology to be applied in a consistent manner.

[572] The CFI referred to Joined Cases 100 to 103/80, *Musique Diffusion Française and others v Commission* [1983] ECR 1825, para 121).

[573] Case T-213/00 *CMA CGM and Others v Commission* [2003] ECR II-913, paras 399–400.

[574] Joined Cases T-191/98, T-212/98 to T-214/98 *Atlantic Container Line and others v Commission* [2003] ECR II-3275, paras 1525–1531.

[575] Case T-220/00 *Cheil Jedang v Commission* [2003] ECR II-2473.

[576] It was indeed possible for a powerful undertaking with a multitude of different business activities to have only a very limited presence in certain specific markets, such as the lysine market. Similarly, an undertaking with a strong position in a geographical market outside the Community may have had only a weak position in the Community or EEA market. The CFI pointed out that in such cases, the mere fact that the undertaking in question has a high total turnover does not necessarily mean that it has a decisive influence in

that case that the Commission had made no explicit reference to taking account of the 'specific weight and, therefore, the real impact on competition of the offending conduct of each undertaking', as required under the 1998 Guidelines when it considered, as in *Amino Acids*, that the starting amounts of the fines should be weighted because the infringement in question (a cartel) involved several undertakings, among which there was considerable disparity in size.[577] Thus, by relying on the applicant's worldwide turnover, without taking into consideration its turnover in the market affected by the infringement, the EEA lysine market, the Commission had disregarded the fourth and sixth paragraphs of Section 1.A of the 1998 Guidelines.[578]

In its judgment in *Cheil Jedang v Commission*, the CFI seems not only to have stated that **8.664** the Commission was incorrect to compare the *total* turnover of the companies concerned in order to measure their effective economic capacity to cause damage in the relevant market, but also that the figures that should have been taken into account for such purposes were, even in the case of a cartel extending beyond the limits of EC (or EEA) territory, the sales made in the EC (or EEA). However, in *Tokai Carbon and others v Commission*, relating to *Graphite Electrodes* (another worldwide cartel), the CFI took a slightly different approach. In that case, the Commission had divided the companies into groups on the basis of their worldwide sales of the product concerned, on the grounds that, in the case of a worldwide cartel, the worldwide product turnover of each party gave a relevant indication of its contribution to the effectiveness of the cartel as a whole or, conversely, of the instability to which would the cartel would have been subject had the party concerned not participated. Some applicants in the case contested this reasoning before the CFI, arguing that the Commission should have taken account only of the EEA-wide product turnover, whilst others contended that the overall turnover should have been considered. The CFI stated first (citing *Musique Diffusion Française*) that the sole explicit reference to turnover in Article 15, paragraph 2 of Regulation 17 concerned the upper limit of 10 per cent. It then added that within these limits, the Commission could, in principle, set the fine by reference to the turnover of its choice. Finally, it stated that although the 1998 Guidelines did not provide that fines were to be calculated according to a specific turnover, they did not preclude such a figure from being taken into account, provided that the choice made by the Commission was not vitiated by a manifest error of assessment.[579] The Court's line of reasoning in *Tokai Carbon* seemed therefore to be more in tune with economic reality than that followed in *Cheil Jedang*.[580]

---

the market affected by the infringement. The CFI relied in this respect on the ECJ judgment in *Baustahlgewebe* (Case C-185/95 P *Baustahlgewebe v Commission* [1998] ECR I-8417) and stated that although the market shares of an undertaking cannot be a decisive factor in concluding that such undertaking belongs to a powerful economic entity, they are nevertheless relevant in determining the influence which it may exert on the market. In the case in question, however, the Commission had taken no account of the undertakings' market shares in terms of volume in the market affected by the cartel (the EEA lysine market).

[577] Para 89.
[578] Para 92.
[579] Para 195.
[580] Such an approach is welcome. As the Commission now systematically states in its decisions, in the case of worldwide cartels, the relevant benchmark of an undertaking's power to cause damage to competition in the EC or EEA market is, logically, its weight on the 'board' of the cartel, which is accurately reflected by its worldwide market share, and not by its EC/EEA-wide market share (see paras 8.670–8.671 below).

(ii) Assessing the Effective Economic Capacity to Cause Significant Damage: the 'Weighting'
of the 'General Starting Amount'

8.665 **Rationale**   The negative effect of cartels results from the fact that their members are joining together in an attempt to eliminate competition amongst themselves. While the damage caused to the economy is the result of this collective conduct, each cartel member is
considered to contribute, to a specific extent, to the harm done. The specific degree of
responsibility of each participant, or, as the 1998 Guidelines put it, 'the effective economic
capacity [of each offender] to cause significant damage to other operators, in particular
consumers' is reflected by its weight in those product and geographic markets subject to
collusion.[581] It is therefore logical to take this into account by weighting the general starting amount according to the importance of each cartel participant in the market.[582]

8.666 **Methodology (1)—Division of the companies into groups ('groupings')**   As regards cartels, it was Commission practice to divide the offending companies into a number of
groups and then to apply to the 'general starting amount' a 'weighting' specific to each
group in order to obtain an individual 'starting amount' applicable to each company within
the same group. This division of companies into groups (the so-called 'groupings') has been
contested before the CFI,[583] but the court has upheld the practice. In *LR AF 1998 v
Commission*, relating to *Pre-Insulated Pipes*, the CFI confirmed for the first time that the
Commission was entitled to divide cartel participants into groups.[584] This was set out more
clearly in *CMA CGM v Commission*, where the CFI stated that 'it is true that the effect of
that method is to make the basic amounts[585] for all undertakings in the same group the
same, and therefore has the effect of ignoring the differences in size between undertakings
in the same group. However, the Commission is not required, when determining fines on
the basis of the gravity and duration of the infringement in question, to ensure, where fines
are imposed on a number of undertakings involved in the same infringement, that the final
amounts of the fines resulting from its calculations for the undertakings concerned reflect
any distinction between them in terms of their overall turnover'.[586] This finding, repeatedly
confirmed by the CFI, was upheld by the ECJ on appeal in *Pre-Insulated Pipes*.[587]

8.667 In *BASF v Commission*, concerning *Vitamins*, the CFI clarified that the application of 'differential
treatment' as set out in the 1998 Guidelines was not compulsory and would only be justified, as

---

[581] As the Commission stated in *Industrial Tubes*, 'the market share of any given party to the cartel [. . .]
gives an indication of its contribution to the effectiveness of the cartel as a whole or, conversely, of the instability which would have affected the cartel had it not participated' ([2004] OJ L125/50, para 322 (full text of
the decision available on DG COMP's web site)).

[582] There is a theoretical counter-argument that the 'weight' of a cartel participant in terms of market share
is irrelevant. If smaller players do not support it, the cartel will not be sustainable. Consequently, one might
argue that all participants should be held equally responsible, irrespective of their market share.

[583] Applicants have variously claimed that such groupings are arbitrary and constitute a violation of the
principle of equal treatment.

[584] Case T 23/99 *LR AF 1998 v Commission* [2002] ECR II-01705, para 278.

[585] This should, in fact, read 'starting amounts', since the basic amount relating to companies in the same
group will not necessarily be the same, but will depend on the duration of their respective participation in the
infringement.

[586] Case T-213/00 *CMA CGM and others v Commission* [2003] ECR II-913, para 385.

[587] Joined Cases C-189/02 P, C-202/02 P, C-205/02 P to C-208/02 P and C-213/02 P *Dansk Rørindustri
and others v Commission* [2005] ECR I-5425, paras 312–313.

the 1998 Guidelines themselves suggested, 'where there is considerable disparity between the sizes of the undertakings committing infringements of the same type'. In *Vitamins*, the Commission found that the members of the cartel relating to beta-carotene and carotinoids consisted of 'essentially two main producers' (Roche and BASF) and it was therefore not appropriate to create separate groups of undertakings for the purpose of setting the appropriate starting amounts for the fines.[588] The applicant (BASF) pleaded that as its market share was smaller than that of Roche, it should have been placed in a second group and had its starting amount reduced. Interestingly, the CFI stated that 'since, in a market in which there are only two operators, a cartel can exist only if both operators participate, it is necessary to take the view, as the defendant does, that the participation of the second operator in terms of market shares is as essential for the very existence of the cartel as that of the first operator. Moreover, the operators in question were two large producers. In those circumstances, despite the undeniable differences in the relevant turnovers and in the market shares of those undertakings [...], it was possible for the Commission, without exceeding the limits of its discretion, not to differentiate between its treatment of the applicant and of Roche when it calculated the starting amounts for the fines imposed on them for the infringements committed in those markets.'[589]

Methodology (2)—Sales figures relevant to the 'groupings'   The division of the relevant   **8.668**
undertakings into groups would generally be based on a comparative assessment of their shares of the market subject to the cartel arrangements during the most recent full year of the infringement.[590] When one or more undertakings left the cartel on an earlier date than that on which the overall cartel agreement came to an end, the relevant market share of that undertaking was calculated with reference to the last full year that preceded its exit from the cartel.

As regards the *product(s) (or services) to be taken into consideration* for the calculation of   **8.669**
market shares, some undertakings have submitted, either during administrative proceedings before the Commission, or in an application before the CFI, that the Commission should conduct a complete analysis of the relevant product market before evaluating market shares. However, the Commission has consistently rejected such claims. First, in the case of an infringement by object, it is not necessary to define the relevant market in order to find an infringement of Article 81(1) EC, as long as it is established that the conduct in question affects trade between Member States and appreciably restricts competition (which is usually obvious in international cartel cases).[591] It would thus seem unnecessarily burdensome for the Commission to be obliged to proceed to such a definition for the mere sake of weighting the general starting amount in the context of calculation of fines.[592] Second, the

---

[588] [2003] OJ L6/1, paras 695 and 696.

[589] Paras 181 and 182.

[590] As far as weightings are concerned, the relevant figures are generally those of the most recent full year of the infringement. As regards the figures taken into consideration for calculating the deterrence multiplying factor (see paras 8.688–8.697 below), they are generally that of the year preceding the adoption of the Commission decision.

[591] Case T-38/02 *Groupe Danone v Commission* [2005] ECR II-4407, para 99 and the case law cited therein.

[592] Rather, it would seem that the calculation of fines should be based exclusively on the Commission's findings regarding the characteristics of the infringement. It would be illogical for the Commission to take, for the purpose of evaluating effective economic capacity, the sales of each company in a product other than the one that was the subject of collusion. See Case T-48/02 *Brouwerij Haacht v Commission* [2005] ECR II-5259, para 59.

cartel participants may be deemed to have defined the relevant product market themselves, since it was those participants who determined which product(s) were to be the subject of their collusion. Indeed, it seems inconceivable that companies would attempt to raise the price of a product if, from the beginning, they were aware that this was bound to fail due to the presence of effective substitutes in the market. This line of reasoning was upheld by the CFI in *Specialty Graphite*[593] and other judgments.

8.670 As regards the *geographic scope to be taken into consideration*, undertakings have also claimed that the Commission should only take account of the sales made within the EC (or within the EEA), even in the case of cartels extending beyond the limits of these territories, on the grounds that the Commission's jurisdiction is limited to the damage caused by the cartel in the EC (or the EEA).[594] This argument is consistently rejected by the Commission, which considers that, in the case of a cartel the scope of which extends beyond the European territory, the Europe-wide sales of an undertaking do not adequately reflect its real power in the cartel, in particular because the small market share in the EC (or in the EEA) of a worldwide market player may result precisely from the collusive plan in question. Thus, the sales used for the purpose of the 'weightings' in the case of cartels with a scope wider than the European territory are the total sales covered by the restrictive arrangement. This method of calculation was first used in *Graphite Electrodes*[595] and subsequently applied in all relevant cases.[596]

8.671 In spite of an apparent initial hesitation[597] the CFI has fully endorsed this approach. In *Graphite Electrodes*, the Japanese applicants, who had a relatively small market share within

---

[593] Joined Cases T-71/03, T-74/03, T-87/03 and T-91/03 *Tokai Carbon and others* [2005] ECR II-10, paras 86 and 90. In those cases, non-European producers claimed that the Commission had violated the principle of equal treatment by defining the relevant market as that for isostatic graphite 'in blocks', when non-European producers sold almost exclusively in blocks within Europe whereas European producers sold both machined graphite and graphite in blocks. The CFI stated that the plea was manifestly irrelevant as 'it [was] not the Commission which arbitrarily chose the relevant market but the members of the cartel [. . .] who deliberately concentrated their anti-competitive conduct on unmachined products, that is isostatic graphite in blocks and cut blocks'.

[594] See for instance the claims of the Japanese producers in Joined Cases T-236/01, T-239/01, T-244/01 to T-246/01, T-251/01 and T-252/01 *Tokai Carbon and others v Commission* [2004] ECR II-1181, paras 176–177.

[595] [2002] OJ L100/1, para 149.

[596] See, for instance, *Sodium Gluconate* (para 381), *Vitamins*, *Citric Acid* (para 237), *Methionine* (para 297), *Food Flavour Enhancers* (para 247), *Specialty Graphite* (para 471). The logic behind this approach was clearly explained in *Graphite Electrodes*, where the Commission stated that it was 'supported by the fact that this was a global cartel, the object of which was, inter alia, to allocate markets on a worldwide level, and thus to withhold competitive reserves from the EEA market. Moreover, the worldwide (product) turnover of any given party to the cartel also gives an indication of its contribution to the effectiveness of the cartel as a whole or, conversely, of the instability which would have affected the cartel had it not participated' (para 149).

[597] As discussed in paras 8.666–8.668 above, from the CFI's judgment in Case T-220/00 *Cheil Jedang v Commission* [2003] ECR II-2473, it initially seemed that the correct figures to take into account for the purpose of assessing effective economic capacity to cause damage were, even in the case of a cartel extending beyond the limits of the EC or EEA, the sales made in the EC or EEA. The applicant in that case, which concerned the first worldwide cartel to be fined under the Guidelines, argued that the Commission had erred in law by referring solely to the total turnover of each undertaking for the purpose of determining the effective capacity of the undertakings concerned to cause significant damage to the lysine market in the EEA, the dissuasive effect of the fine and the relative size of each undertaking. The CFI stated that the total turnover of the companies was not the relevant indicator to assess the effective capacity of the undertakings concerned to cause significant damage to the relevant market, and that the relevant sales figures had to be taken into account. The CFI then went further, stating that the relevant sales figures in that case were *those of the sales made in the EEA*, and indicated that it was possible that an undertaking with a strong position in a geographical market outside the Community may have had only a weak position in the Community or EEA market (para 92).

the EEA but a much stronger worldwide market share, claimed that the Commission should have divided the companies into groups on the basis of the product turnover made in the EEA rather than on the worldwide product turnover. The CFI found however, that in respect of the intrinsic nature of the infringement, the Commission was fully justified in referring to the worldwide product turnover for the purpose of assessing effective economic capacity.[598] In its judgment in *Specialty Graphite*, the CFI provided a clear endorsement of the Commission's approach, stating that what the CFI itself termed the 'worldwide approach' was justified even in the absence of any specific market-sharing mechanism.[599] The soundness of the Commission's practice was therefore clearly recognised.[600]

Calculating the respective market shares of cartel participants can nevertheless be a difficult exercise in the absence of precise information regarding the size of the market concerned and the sales of each company.[601] In this context, certain applicants have claimed before the CFI that the Commission had miscalculated their market shares. In *Specialty Graphite* the question was raised as to whether the Commission should define groups on the basis of the

8.672

---

[598] Indeed, the cartel in question in that case included a sharing out of markets based on the principle of the 'domestic producer'. Thus, producers outside the EEA had to withdraw from the EEA market instead of competing in it. The CFI found that '[i]f the Commission had calculated [the] starting amounts [of the producers located outside of the EEA] on the basis of their low turnover in the EEA for the relevant product, it would have rewarded them for having complied with one of the basic principles of the cartel and for having agreed not to compete on the EEA market, while their conduct in accordance with that principle of the cartel enabled the "home" producers in Europe [. . .] to fix prices in the EEA unilaterally' (para 198). The CFI added that 'the worldwide cartel [. . .] harmed consumers in the EEA because [the European producers] had been able to increase their prices in the EEA without being threatened by [the producers located outside of the EEA] which, owing to the principle of reciprocity at global level, were able to do likewise on their home markets, namely Japan and the Far East and [. . .] the United States' (para 199). Finally, and most importantly, the CFI stated that the fact that the Commission's competence for imposing sanctions is limited to the EEA does not prevent it from taking the worldwide product turnover into consideration for the purpose of evaluating cartel participants' effective economic capacity to cause damage to competition within the EEA.

[599] Indeed, the CFI stated that whilst 'a "worldwide approach" is particularly appropriate in the case of the sharing of markets on geographic grounds [. . .], it cannot be concluded a contrario from this that a "worldwide approach" should strictly be excluded in the case of a price-fixing cartel which does not have a market-sharing system'. Joined Cases T-71/03, T-74/03, T-87/03 and T-91/03 *Tokai Carbon and others* [2005] ECR II-10, para 194.

[600] This practice nevertheless continues to cause misunderstandings and the Commission is regularly accused of violating the principle of *non bis in idem* since sales beyond the EC (or EEA) territory are often taken into account by other competition authorities for the purpose of imposing their own fines. However, there should be no cause for confusion in this respect. In the present context, overall cartel sales are only used for the purpose of dividing companies into categories reflecting their 'power' within the cartel. This was explicitly confirmed by the CFI in its judgment in *Specialty Graphite*, where it stated that 'the allegation of an infringement of the principle of *non bis in idem* must also be rejected in so far as [the applicant] claims that the Commission took into account its worldwide turnover and market share [. . .], *all the more since those figures in respect of the worldwide market were only used by the Commission to distinguish the relative impact of the undertakings implicated in the cartel*'. (Joined Cases T-71/03, T-74/03, T-87/03 and T-91/03 *Tokai Carbon and others* [2005] ECR II-10, para 115, emphasis added). As regards the level of the general starting amount, from which individual starting amounts are derived, it takes account only of the impact of the cartel within the Community or within the EEA. Indeed, under the criterion of the scope of the relevant geographic market, EEA-wide coverage may be considered the maximum degree of gravity. Similarly, when specified, the value of the market concerned will always be determined relative to its EEA-wide dimension.

[601] In particular, there may be no industry data available in respect of the specific products in question on which objective findings can be based (since the undertakings' published or internal accounts may not be accessible). In such cases the Commission may have to rely exclusively on figures specially calculated and forwarded by each undertaking in reply to requests for information.

'objective' market share of each cartel participant with reference to the entire market, or whether it could resort, as it did in that case, to a 'relativist' method by defining groups on the basis of the relative importance of each undertaking in relation to the others, evaluated on the sole basis of the cartel participants' sales figures.[602] The CFI found in that case that 'in the particular circumstances of the case, the Commission cannot be criticized on the merits of having chosen the "relativist" method [...]', in particular because none of the applicants had submitted that the Commission could have made its decision on a more solid and objective basis by obtaining official figures relating to the market as a whole.[603]

8.673   It is for the CFI to determine whether or not the Commission has committed a manifest error of judgement in calculating the sales of each undertaking for the sake of defining groups. In *Specialty Graphite*, the CFI found that the Commission had committed a manifest error by significantly overestimating SGL's sales of the relevant product. The Commission had relied upon the sales figures provided by SGL in reply to a request for information, in spite of the fact that it was apparent that the sales figures provided included not only sales for the relevant product, but also those corresponding to other industrial applications. The CFI stated that the Commission could not criticise the company for having supplied an insufficiently precise breakdown of the sales by product, as no such query had been made by the Commission in its request for information. The Commission could not, therefore, rely on the clearly overestimated sales and should have checked the accuracy of the figures further. This was particularly the case as SGL had indicated its willingness to cooperate with the Commission and had pointed out, in its reply to the statement of objection, that the figures in question did not represent solely the sales of the relevant product.[604]

8.674   In its judgment in *Roquette v Commission*, relating to *Sodium Gluconate*, the CFI found that the Commission had overestimated Roquette's share of the sodium gluconate market for the purpose of defining the groups, as it had included in its calculation the sales of an upstream product which was not subject to the cartel agreement. This error had resulted in the Commission's placing Roquette in the first group, thereby violating the principles of proportionality and non-discrimination. Under its unlimited jurisdiction, the CFI placed Roquette in a new intermediary group and reduced its starting amount accordingly. However, the CFI added that the necessity of correcting the objective error made by the Commission did not prevent the Court from taking into account the responsibility for the error committed. In this respect, the CFI noted that Roquette had been negligent in its replies to the Commission's requests for information aimed at quantifying the cartel members'

---

[602] Although in order to be successful a cartel must generally include most of the players in a market and, therefore, will represent a large proportion of the overall sales in the market concerned, it is not unusual for the cartel to represent only 70% or 80% of the overall market.

[603] Joined Cases T-71/03, T-74/03, T-87/03 and T-91/03 *Tokai Carbon and others* [2005] ECR II-10, para 233. Interestingly, the CFI added at para 234: 'In any event, the applicants have no legitimate interest in challenging the principle underlying the method chosen by the Commission. If no distinction were made between the applicants by dividing them into categories, each could, in application of the first and second paragraphs of section 1 A of the Guidelines, be allocated a starting amount of EUR 20 million, which is the lowest "likely" amount for taking part in the cartel in question. None of the applicants would therefore gain any benefit, in terms of a reduction in the starting amount, from the annulment of the method chosen by the Commission [...]'.

[604] Paras 239–258 (full text of the decision available on DG COMP's web site).

sales of the products subject to collusion. Roquette's replies had not made clear that its sales of the upstream product should not be taken into account, and thus the Commission were left legitimately believing that they should indeed be included. Having regard to what it called the 'serious negligence' on the part of Roquette, the CFI in the exercise of its unlimited jurisdiction increased Roquette's fine by EUR 5,000.[605]

Methodology (3)—The number of groups and their thresholds   The determination of **8.675** the appropriate number of groups and of the thresholds between them was a delicate exercise: the classification of a company in one group rather than another could have potentially significant consequences as regards the ultimate level of fine imposed. At 31 December 2006, the Commission's practice ranged from defining two groups (a 'group' could consist of a single company, as in the case of *Vitamins* and *Belgian Beer*) to six groups (in *Industrial Bags, Road Bitumen Netherlands* and *Fittings*). The number of groups most frequently identified was three. The Commission thus generally distinguished between large players, medium sized players, and much smaller, 'fringe' players.

The Commission's practice consisted, first, of evaluating the characteristics of the most **8.676** important cartel participant and establishing a reference point, on the basis of either its size (*FETTCSA, TACA* and *Amino Acids*), or its position in the market concerned (*Pre-Insulated Pipes, Greek Ferries, Graphite Electrodes*, and most subsequent decisions). Secondly, the Commission defined the appropriate number of groups in the cartel and then divided the remainder of the cartel participants into those groups according to their characteristics as compared to the original reference point. It appeared that the Commission's practice was to rank the undertakings concerned on a scale (an 'index') and to distinguish groups according to where the 'gaps' between those undertakings were the greatest. However, that method was contested before the CFI, which subjected the Commission's practice to detailed scrutiny.

In an application before the CFI against the *FETTCSA* decision, a number of applicants **8.677** claimed that the Commission's division of the parties into (four) groups for the purpose of calculating the fines was contrary to the principle of non-discrimination and lacked a sufficiently extensive statement of reasons.[606] They submitted that shipping companies (lines) of very different sizes had been grouped together by the Commission and that as a result companies of a similar size, but in different groups (ie at the 'top' and 'bottom' ends of the scale in adjacent groups) had been treated differently from each other, whereas companies which rather different in size but were in the same group (ie at the top and bottom ends of the scale in that group) were treated similarly to each other.[607] The CFI noted, first, that though the effect of such division into groups was that certain

---

[605] Case T-322/01 *Roquette Frères v Commission*, not yet reported, paras 51–56 and 293–316.
[606] In *FETTCSA* [2000] OJ L268/1, the companies concerned were divided into four groups on the basis of their relative size in 1994 (the year in which the FETTCSA was abandoned) in comparison with Maersk, the largest of the FETTCSA parties. The four groups and the relative size of the FETTCSA parties which make up those groups were defined as follows: the 'large carrier' (Maersk [100]), the 'medium to large carriers' (NYK [58], MOL [55], P&O [52], K Line [49], Nedlloyd [46] and Hanjin [41]), the 'small to medium carriers' (Hapag-Lloyd [34], Evergreen [30], NOL [28], DSR-Senator [23] and Yangming [23]) and the 'small carriers' (Cho Yang [17], MISC [14], OOCL [11] and CGM [6]).
[607] Case T-213/00 *CMA CGM and others v Commission* [2003] ECR II-913, para 359.

applicants were allocated the same basic amount even though they differed in size, that difference in treatment was objectively justified by the importance attached to the nature of the infringement, in comparison with the size of the undertakings, in the assessment of the gravity of the infringement. The CFI went on to state, however, that whilst the Commission does have a margin of discretion when fixing the amount of each fine and is not bound to apply a precise mathematical formula for that purpose, the amount of the fines imposed must at least be proportionate in relation to the factors taken into account in the assessment of the seriousness of the infringement.[608] It concluded that where the Commission divided the undertakings concerned into groups for the purpose of setting the amount of the fines, the thresholds for each of the groups thus identified had to be coherent and objectively justified.[609]

8.678 The CFI found that this had not been the case in *FETTCSA*, since the difference in size between companies from two different groups was sometimes less than that between companies in the same group as each other.[610] It concluded that the Commission had failed in the contested decision to justify the choice of thresholds between the four groups identified, and that the choice had not been based on any objective criterion, lacked consistency and infringed the principle of non-discrimination.[611] The CFI thus modified the fines accordingly.

8.679 In its judgment in *Graphite Electrodes*, the CFI again carried out a detailed examination of the way in which the Commission had divided the companies into groups in that case. The Commission had placed the companies concerned in four different groups, ranked in accordance with their worldwide product turnover. The CFI reiterated what it had held in its judgment in *FETTCSA*: that the thresholds separating each of the groups identified must be coherent and objectively justified, and proceeded to examine whether that was true in the case before it. The CFI found that, although the first and second groups had been adequately defined, the composition of the first group was incorrect, as Tokai Carbon had been grouped together with the companies C/G and SDK even though it was approximately half the size of SDK. The CFI stated that the classification of Tokai in the same group as SDK went beyond the limits of what was acceptable under the principles of proportionality and equality of treatment.[612] This was all the more the case since the difference in size between Tokai and SDK (which were in the same group) was greater than the difference in size between Tokai and Nippon, which the Commission had placed in the third group. The CFI rejected the Commission's argument that it was under no obligation to distinguish companies on the basis of their turnover and that therefore, it could not be obliged, if it did make such a distinction, to apply a strict ratio between the relative turnovers. The CFI pointed out that in this respect the Commission was bound to comply with the methodology set out in the 1998

---

[608] Para 383.

[609] Para 416.

[610] Para 415.

[611] Para 426.

[612] Joined cases T-236/01, T-239/01, T-244/01 to T-246/01, T-251/01 and T-252/01 *Tokai Carbon and others v Commission* [2004] ECR II-1181, para 228.

Guidelines unless it had specific reasons not to do so. In the exercise of its unlimited juris-diction, the CFI then proceeded to create a fifth group, in which it placed both Tokai and C/G, and to which it attributed a specific starting amount. In its judgment in *Specialty Graphite*, the CFI also modified the groups initially created by the Commission, having found that the Commission had erroneously overestimated the market position of the undertaking placed in the first group.[613]

It is clear from the above that the CFI was determined to ensure that the Commission **8.680** acted in accordance with the principles of coherence and objectivity set out in the 1998 Guidelines when dividing cartel participants into groups for the purpose of setting fines. However, a detailed analysis of the above judgments (in particular the *FETTCSA* judg-ment) reveals that the CFI relies exclusively on comparison of undertakings in pairs, on the basis of the ratio of their respective size. In doing so, the CFI seems to lose sight of the fact that the very purpose of the Commission's practice, in line with the objective of eval-uation of the (relative) effective capacity to cause damage to the economy, was to *distrib-ute* a significant number of companies along a *continuous scale* in accordance with their relative size as compared to the *same reference point* (namely the size of the largest under-taking). The method apparently suggested by the CFI in *FETTCSA*, however, does not allow that to be done, since it enables only a comparison of one company with another, which does not take account of those companies' size in relation to the size of all the other cartel participants. If the objective was that the starting amount adopted for each company should reflect its *relative* importance as compared to the largest company in the cartel, then comparison must be made between each of the companies concerned and the largest company respectively, which is what the Commission had endeavoured to do in the *FETTSCA* decision.[614]

However, the CFI's analysis in this area appears to have evolved—as can be seen in its **8.681** judgment in *Vitamins*. In that case, the Commission had found several separate infringe-ments (in respect of separate vitamin markets), and had systematically divided the pro-ducers concerned into only two groups, in spite of the fact that they had greatly differing market shares. While reiterating that the division of the undertakings into groups for the purpose of setting fines in cartel decisions must be coherent and objectively justified, the CFI stated that 'a division of producers into two categories, the major producers and the others, is a not an unreasonable way of taking account of their relative importance on the market in order to adjust the specific starting amount, provided that it does not produce a grossly distorted picture of the markets in question'.[615] That statement appears to be a less demanding standard of examination of the Commission's practice than what was

---

[613] In that case, the CFI moved the undertaking in question from being the sole company in the first group to a new 'group' (in which it was also the sole undertaking) placed between the original second and third groups. The CFI imposed a starting amount of EUR 11.3 million on that company, instead of the initial EUR 20 million that the Commission had imposed.

[614] The Commission contested the CFI's reasoning on appeal before the ECJ, but since the CFI's condem-nation of the Commission's methodology in this respect was not contained in the operative part of that court's judgment, the plea was rejected as inadmissible. See Case C-236/03 P *Commission v CMA GCM and others* (not published).

[615] Case T-15/02 *BASF v Commission* [2006] ECR II-497, para 159.

implied in the judgments in *FETTCSA* and *Graphite Electrodes*. Even more interesting is the reasoning followed by the CFI in its judgment in *Daiichi Pharmaceutical v Commission*. In that case, the applicant objected to the fact that it had been placed in the first group because of its 29 per cent share in the vitamin B5 market, whereas BASF, which had the *same* market share of 29 per cent in the vitamin B2 market, had been placed in the *second* group. The CFI dismissed the submission that the Commission had thereby breached the principle of equal treatment, stating that 'since the Commission was assessing the importance of the undertakings on each market *in relative terms*, the two circumstances raised by the applicant could not be appraised without account being taken of the distribution of market shares. That distribution was not comparable in the two cases considered'. Having explained why the distribution was not comparable,[616] the CFI concluded that 'therefore, even supposing that, when Article 81 EC is being applied, an infringement of the principle of equal treatment could be pleaded otherwise than in the case where the members of one and the same cartel are treated differently, the fact that the applicant, in relation to the vitamin B5 infringement, and BASF, in relation to the vitamin B2 infringement, were subject to different classification does not appear to lack objective justification and therefore does not infringe the principle of equal treatment'.[617] Although the facts considered here are not the same as those of the cases mentioned above, the reference by the CFI to the importance of an assessment *in relative terms* suggests that the Court may be more open in future to the methodology that the Commission has traditionally followed for the purpose of dividing undertakings into groups.

8.682 **Methodology (4)—Determination of the 'weighting key'** Once the groups were defined, the Commission proceeded to individualise the starting amounts for each group on the basis of a 'weighting key'. The starting amount set for the first group was the 'general starting amount'. This starting amount was then weighted according to the key, in order to calculate the starting amounts for each of the other groups. In its first decisions in which it applied such weightings, the Commission did not appear to maintain a strict link between the ratios of the (average) size or market shares within each group and those of the various starting amounts adopted.[618] However, the Commission's practice shows that in spite of its initial hesitation in deciding the most appropriate method to follow, it

---

[616] First, the position of the first operator was clearly stronger in the case of the vitamin B2 infringement than that of the first operator in the vitamin B5 infringement. Second, in the case of the vitamin B2 infringement, BASF's market share (29%—the same as Daiichi's market share in the vitamin B5 market) was closer to that of the third operator (12%) than to that of the first operator (47%), 17 and 18 percentage points separating it from the third and first operator respectively; by contrast, in relation to the vitamin B5 infringement (as has been stated above) Daiichi's market share (29%) was closer to that of the first operator (Roche 36%) than to that of the third operator (BASF, 21%), 7 and 8 percentage points separating Daiichi from the first and third operator respectively.

[617] Case T-26/02 *Daiichi Pharmaceutical v Commission* [2004] ECR II-713, paras 92–93.

[618] In *Pre-Insulated Pipes*, the Commission did not indicate what weighting key it had used or whether the ratios between the different starting amounts corresponded to those of the average relative size of the companies within each group. In *Greek Ferries*, the Commission indicated that the starting amounts of the second and third groups were respectively 65% and 20% of that of the first group. However, this did not correspond to the ratios corresponding to the average difference in size of the companies placed in these three groups. In *FETTCSA*, the Commission set the starting amount of each group by applying a successive reduction of 25% of the starting amount applied to the first group. As for *Amino Acid*, the Commission defined two groups and simply divided the starting amount of the first group by half to obtain the starting amount applicable to the second group.

rapidly adopted an objective, almost arithmetical approach to the weighting key. The starting amount of each group was thus generally set as a result of applying the ratio between the average market shares of the companies placed in the first group and the average market share of the companies in the group concerned to the 'general starting amount'.[619] Particularly clear illustrations of this method can be seen in *Electrical and Mechanical Carbon and Graphite products*,[620] *Industrial Tubes*[621] and *Choline Chloride*.[622]

This evolution in the Commission's method of 'weighting' was probably driven by the Court's tight control over the Commission's practice. In its judgment in *FETTCSA*, the CFI stated that, since the Commission was not required to calculate fines on the basis of a precise arithmetical formula, it had not exceeded its margin of discretion in that case. In fixing the basic amounts of the fines by making successive reductions of 25 per cent from the basic amount imposed on the 'large carriers'.[623] However, the judgment of the CFI in *Graphite Electrodes* suggests that the Commission's margin of discretion is now being construed more narrowly by the CFI. In that case the CFI overruled the Commission with regard to the link between the relative size of the companies placed in different groups and the starting amounts for each group.[624] In its subsequent judgment in *Specialty Graphite*, the CFI, having found that the Commission had greatly overestimated the market position of the undertaking placed in the first group, removed this group altogether and instead placed the undertaking concerned in a *sui generis* group between the original second and third groups. The CFI then proceeded to calculate a new individual starting amount for that undertaking. **8.683**

As regards the mechanism of the 'weighting key', the CFI's decision in *Specialty Graphite* led to an interesting situation insofar as the Commission had erroneously placed a single undertaking (SGL) in the first group because it was 'by far the largest producer' of the relevant product. When the CFI placed the undertaking concerned in a 'new group' between the initial second and third groups, questions arose regarding the consequences of that change for the individual starting amounts calculated by the Commission. Since the original 'second group' had become, in effect, the first group and so on, would the CFI consequently apply a new weighting key based on the new starting amount of EUR 20 million imposed on the undertakings that had initially been placed in the second group but were now in the first group, and so on. In fact, the CFI found that there was **8.684**

---

[619] For example, if the first group consists of two companies with respective market shares of 30% and 26%, a second group consists of two companies with market shares of 14% and 12% respectively, and a third group is made up of two other companies with respective shares of 4% and 2% each. The average market share of each group will be 28%, 13% and 3% respectively. The ratios of the average market share of the second and third group compared to that of the first group are 0.46 (13/28) and 0.10 (3/28) respectively. If the 'general starting amount' set for the first group is EUR 20 million, then the starting amount for the second group will be in the region of EUR 9 million (46% of EUR 20 million), and the starting amount for the third group will be in the region of EUR 2 million (10% of EUR 20 million).

[620] [2004] OJ L125/45 (full text of the decision available on DG COMP's web site), paras 297–298.

[621] [2004] OJ L125/50 (full text of the decision available on DG COMP's web site), paras 326–328.

[622] [2005] OJ L190/22 (full text of the decision available on DG COMP's web site), paras 201–202.

[623] Since the Commission had defined four groups on the basis of the relative size of the companies concerned, the successive reduction for each group in steps of 25% of the basic amount used for the group containing the largest applicant could be regarded as a coherent method which could be objectively justified.

[624] Joined Cases T-236/01, T-239/01, T-244/01 to T-246/01, T-251/01 and T-252/01 *Tokai Carbon and others v Commission* [2004] ECR II-1181, para 227.

'no need to adjust the system of categories as a whole'. It left the starting amounts initially attributed to each group unchanged and determined a new starting amount for the company now placed in a new (third) group. The CFI stated that although the Commission had faithfully converted the turnover figures of the cartel members into starting amounts and set those amounts for the undertakings other than SGL in the form of a percentage of the amount of EUR 20 million allocated to SGL, it was nevertheless the case, in spite of the 'disappearance' of that 'reference amount', that the proportions between the undertakings concerned, other than SGL, remained unchanged in terms of turnover. It followed that the starting amounts attributed to those undertakings correctly reflected their relative sizes.[625]

8.685 **Specific issues in relation to the establishment of 'groupings'** Two specific issues regarding the methodology used by the Commission in the weighting of the 'general starting amount' have been raised and merit discussion.

8.686 *Taking 'in-house' production for the purposes of calculating product turnover* In *Organic Peroxides*, Atochem submitted that its market share throughout the relevant period was 12 per cent rather than the 20–25 per cent estimated by the Commission, as the latter had included the captive consumption within the Atochem group. The Commission rejected that argument and took Atochem's full production into account. It stated that the products that required organic peroxides as an input could be sold more cheaply by Atochem than by its competitors, since those competitors (who did not produce organic peroxides themselves) had to buy the product in a cartelised market.[626] The same approach was followed in *Electrical and Mechanical Carbon and Graphite Products*.[627] In that case the Commission relied upon case law on this point, according to which 'to ignore the value of internal deliveries would inevitably give an unjustified advantage to vertically integrated companies. In such a situation the benefit derived from the cartel may not be taken into account and the undertaking in question would avoid the imposition of a fine proportionate to its importance in the product market to which the infringement relates'.[628]

8.687 *Trade associations and 'groupings'* In *French Beef*, in which the parties concerned were federations of farmers, the Commission stated that the fines had to reflect each party's relative strength and thus degree of responsibility for the infringement, but it was faced with the

---

[625] Joined Cases T-71/03, T-74/03, T-87/03 and T-91/03 *Tokai Carbon and others* [2005] ECR II-10, para 264. Most interestingly, the CFI added that 'it is true that the Court is not prevented—in order to remain within the general logic of the Commission [. . .] which classified the infringement as "very serious"—from imposing a starting amount of EUR 20 million on [the undertaking initially placed in the second group] which has in fact proved to be the largest producer, and from increasing proportionally the starting amounts for the other applicants. However, the difference between EUR 20 million and EUR 14 million, as the "reference amount" is not so great that the adoption of EUR 14 million as the reference amount would deprive the fines of their practical effect. Moreover, the second paragraph of section 1A of the Guidelines, far from imposing a starting amount of EUR 20 million in every case involving a 'very serious' infringement, merely describes such an amount as "likely"' (para 265).
[626] [2005] OJ L110/44 (full text of the decision available on DG COMP's web site), para 457.
[627] [2004] OJ L125/45 (full text of the decision available on DG COMP's web site), paras 292–295.
[628] Case C-248/98 P *KNP BT v Commission* [2000] ECR I-9641, para 62; Case T-304/94 *Europa Carton v Commission* [1998] ECR II-869, para 128; Case T-16/99 *Lögstör Rör v Commission* [2002] ECR II-1633, para 360.

problem that the parties' market shares in that case did not provide an appropriate criterion. First, because the parties were federations, they did not have 'market shares'. Second, in the case of farmers' federations even the market shares of the members of those federations did not provide a basis for comparison between the federations themselves. As an alternative, the Commission used the ratio between the amount of the annual membership fees collected by each of the farmers' federations and that collected by the main farmers' federation, which the Commission considered an objective criterion reflecting the relative sizes of the different farmers' federations, and consequently their individual degree of responsibility in the infringement. The same criterion was applied to the two slaughterers' federations. The Commission rejected the objection that the slaughterers' federations did not operate on the same market as the farmers federations as irrelevant, since the starting amounts of the fines could not, in any event, be determined by reference to market shares.[629]

(iii) The 'Deterrence' Multiplying Factor

The concept   In its early decisions under the 1998 Guidelines, the Commission did not distinguish between the application of the criterion of the effective economic capacity to cause damage and that of the need to ensure sufficient deterrence.[630] The first case in which a multiplying factor for deterrence was applied was *Pre-Insulated Pipes*. After setting the starting amount of the fine for ABB at EUR 20 million, the Commission indicated that '[i]n determining the penalty to be imposed on ABB, the Commission takes account of its economic capacity to cause significant damage to competition and the need to set the fine at a level which ensures by its deterrent effect that there is no repetition'. The Commission pointed out that in the case of ABB, the starting point for the fine resulting from the criterion of relative importance in the relevant market required further upward adjustment to take account of ABB's position as one of Europe's largest industrial combines. This adjustment was held to serve two objectives: first, to ensure that the fine had a sufficiently deterrent effect and, second, to take account of the fact that large undertakings have legal and economic knowledge and infrastructures which enable them more easily to recognise that their conduct constitutes an infringement and to be aware of the consequences stemming from such an infringement under competition law. A multiplying factor of 2.5 ('deterrence multiplying factor') was thus applied to ABB's starting amount. **8.688**

Rationale   The Commission justified the application of deterrence multiplying factors by reference to the fact that the weighting of the 'general starting amount' in respect of the criterion of the effective capacity to cause significant damage tended to lead, in effect, to a significant lowering of the fines of very large companies with a limited share of the market subject to collusion. Yet it is clear from settled case law that the consideration of the need to ensure sufficient deterrence is an essential element of the evaluation of gravity, which in **8.689**

---

[629] [2003] OJ L209/12, paras 169–170.

[630] See paras 8.657–8.660 above. In *FETTSCA* and *Amino Acid*, both criteria were deemed to be fulfilled by a division of the companies into groups according to their overall size. In *Greek Ferries*, cartel participants were, for the first time, divided into groups by reference to their share of the relevant market. However, no mention was made of any need to ensure sufficient deterrence with regard to certain companies.

turn determines the amount of the fine to be imposed.[631] Thus, the Commission considered that in order to prevent a potential repetition of the infringement it was entitled to take the overall resources of an undertaking into consideration and to set the level of the fine accordingly. Indeed, if fines were to remain very low in comparison with the overall resources of the undertaking concerned, they may not have any deterrent effect, since a risk analysis might indicate that it would remain comparatively beneficial for such undertaking to adopt collusive behaviour.

8.690 Commission's practice   The Commission tended to apply a deterrence multiplying factor to a limited number of companies in each case, where such companies were considerably larger than the average cartel participant. The application of multiplying factors therefore seemed to be conditional on the existence of important disparities in the size of the addressees of a cartel decision. However, the final decisions taken under the 1998 Guidelines would seem to indicate that the Commission was simply applying deterrence factors in the case of undertakings with large turnovers, even if there was no considerable disparity between the sizes of the addressees of the decisions. The deterrence multiplying factor to be applied tended to be determined in relation to the overall (worldwide) turnover of the undertaking during the year immediately preceding the *adoption* of the decision in question.[632] The highest deterrence factor to be applied was in *Luxemburg Brewers*, where the Commission multiplied the starting amount applicable to Brasserie de Luxembourg by five. In that case, the Commission took account of the fact that Brasserie de Luxembourg was owned by Interbrew, which was a considerably larger undertaking than the other addressees of the decision.[633] The deterrence multiplying factors most commonly applied in Commission decisions have been 2 or 2.5.

8.691 Legality of the deterrence multiplying factor   The legality of applying a deterrence multiplying factor has been challenged before the CFI. In *ABB v Commission*, the applicant claimed that such a practice constituted a breach of the principle of proportionality.[634] The CFI rejected ABB's arguments, stating that 'the fact that, in fixing [a deterrence factor], the Commission took into account the deterrent effect that fines must have, [was] wholly consistent with the established principle that the gravity of infringements must be determined by reference to several factors, such as the particular circumstances of the case, its context and the dissuasive effect of fines, although no binding or exhaustive list of the criteria which must be applied has been drawn up [...]. In that regard, the Commission's

---

[631] See eg Case 45/69 *Boehringer Mannheim v Commission* [1970] ECR 769, para 53; Joined Cases 100 to 103/80, *Musique Diffusion française and others v Commission* [1983] ECR 1825, para 106, and Case C-289/04 P *Showa Denko v Commission* [2006] ECR I-5859, paras 16–18.

[632] As opposed to the Commission's practice of determining the undertaking's effective economic capacity to cause significant damage', on the basis of the sales in the last year preceding *the end of the infringement* by the undertaking concerned (see para 8.668 above).

[633] The validity of this approach can be questioned, as the decision was only addressed to *Brasseriè de Luxemborg*. See [2002] OJ L253/21.

[634] Case T-31/99 *ABB Asea Brown Boveri v Commission* [2002] ECR II-1881. In particular, ABB argued that the need to ensure that the fine had a sufficiently deterrent effect could not justify increasing the penalty according to the size of the undertaking. Deterrence could not be a separate factor for determining the gravity of an infringement: a fine fully reflecting the gravity of the infringement would automatically have the requisite deterrent effect. If the Commission were able to rely on the argument of sufficient deterrence, it would have 'carte blanche' to set fines as high as it pleased.

power to impose fines [. . .] is one of the means conferred on the Commission in order to enable it to carry out the task of supervision conferred on it by Community law. [. . .] It follows that, in assessing the gravity of an infringement for the purpose of fixing the amount of the fine, the Commission must take into consideration not only the particular circumstances of the case but also the context in which the infringement occurs and must ensure that its action has the necessary deterrent effect, especially as regards those types of infringement which are particularly harmful to the attainment of the objectives of the Community'.[635] The CFI added that 'since the deterrent effect of a fine is one of the factors which case law confirms must be taken into account in determining the gravity of the infringement, the applicant [could not] criticise the Commission for having taken the deterrent effect of the fines into account when fixing the starting point corresponding specifically to the gravity of its infringement. The taking into account of the deterrent effect of the fines forms an integral part of weighting the fines to reflect the gravity of the infringement, since the purpose of so doing is to ensure that the method of calculation does not lead to fines which, in the case of certain undertakings, would not be sufficiently high to ensure that the fine had a sufficiently deterrent effect'.[636]

The CFI also pointed out that 'the Commission ... was entitled to refer to the fact that **8.692** large undertakings have legal and economic knowledge and infrastructures which enable them to recognise more easily that their conduct constitutes an infringement and to be aware of the consequences stemming from it under competition law. It does not matter whether the management of a large undertaking is always aware of all the anti-competitive activities of its subsidiaries, or whether, in a specific case, the infringement is of such gravity that none of the undertakings participating in it could fail to be aware that it is illegal, the CFI has found that the Commission is correct in assuming that large undertakings generally have resources which enable them to have a greater awareness of the requirements and consequences of competition law than smaller undertakings'.[637] This has been clearly reiterated by the CFI in *BASF v Commission*.[638]

Limited scope of the duty to state reasons   The scope of the obligation to state **8.693** reasons remains rather limited as regards the setting of fines (see paras 8.609–8.610 above). The CFI has implied that the obligation to state reasons is also limited in relation to the determination of the deterrence multiplying factor. In *BASF v Commission*, the CFI found that a mere reference by the Commission to the necessity to increase the starting amount set for BASF in order to ensure sufficient deterrence given its size and overall resources did not constitute a failure to fulfil the obligation to state reasons. The CFI noted that the Commission had not specified the facts on which it had based its assessment of the applicant's size and overall resources, but that it was apparent from the decision that the Commission had 'relied in that connection on the total worldwide turnover of the undertaking' which, according to settled case law, 'is an indication, albeit approximate and imperfect, of the size of

---

[635] Paras 165–166. This is largely a quotation of Joined Cases 100 to 103/80 *Musique Diffusion française and others v Commission* [1983] ECR 1825, paras 105–106.
[636] Para 167.
[637] Para 169.
[638] Case T-15/02 *BASF v Commission* [2006] ECR II-497, paras 235–253.

an undertaking and of its economic power'.[639] The CFI concluded in this respect that the statement of reasons had been sufficient, since it is clear from settled case law that 'it is desirable, but not a requirement of the obligation to state reasons, that the Commission indicate the figures which influenced the exercise of its discretion when setting the fines, especially in regard to the desired deterrent effect'.[640]

8.694 **Basis for the assessment and level of the deterrence multiplying factor**   The level of the deterrence multiplying factor was determined by the Commission by reference to the overall (ie worldwide) turnover of the undertaking concerned in the year immediately preceding the adoption of the decision imposing the fine. In *Tokai Carbon v Commission*, the company SDK contested the application of a multiplying factor of 2.5 to its starting amount. The CFI referred to its previous judgment in *ABB v Commission* and confirmed the legality of the principle of the deterrence factor and stated that the Commission was therefore 'entitled to take the view that, owing to its enormous worldwide turnover by comparison with the turnovers of the other members of the cartel, SDK could more readily raise the necessary funds to pay its fine, which, if the fine was to have a sufficiently deterrent effect, justified the application of a multiplier'.[641]

8.695 As at 31 December 2006, the CFI has never reduced the amount of a deterrence factor merely on the ground of a breach of the principle of proportionality. It can be assumed, in the light of such case law, that the Commission enjoys a wide margin of discretion in this respect and that the CFI will intervene only in the case of a manifest error. However, in *Tokai Carbon v Commission*, the CFI examined the deterrence factor that had been applied to SDK in respect of the principle of equal treatment. In its decision in *Graphite Electrodes*, the Commission had applied deterrence factors of 2.5 and 1.25 to SDK and VAW respectively. The CFI noted that SDK's overall turnover was only twice that of VAW, whereas the increase in the starting amount of the fine imposed on SDK was 150 per cent, as compared to the 25 per cent increase applied to the starting amount of the fine imposed on VAW, ie six times higher. The CFI concluded that there was no objective justification for such differential treatment and reduced the deterrence factor applied to SDK to 1.5.

8.696 **Appropriateness of the stage at which the deterrence factor is applied in the calculation of the fine**   In *BASF v Commission*, the applicant argued that the stage at which the deterrence multiplying factor was taken into account in the methodology set out by the 1998 Guidelines was inappropriate, since it was applied before the duration of the infringement and any aggravating or attenuating circumstances were taken into account. The CFI rejected this argument on the grounds that the latter was 'based on a false premise, namely that the increase in question is based on an assessment that a particular amount of a fine is appropriate to the deterrent objective of the fine assessed in the light of the size and overall resources of the undertakings'.[642] The CFI added that 'the decision as to whether there is

---

[639] Case T-15/02 *BASF v Commission* [2006] ECR II-497, paras 208–212.
[640] Para 214. The CFI relied in this regard on Case C-279/98 P *Cascades v Commission* [2000] ECR I-9693, paras 47–48.
[641] Joined Cases T-236/01, T-239/01, T-244/01 to T-246/01, T-251/01 and T-252/01 *Tokai Carbon and others v Commission* [2004] ECR II-1181, para 241.
[642] Case T-15/02 *BASF v Commission* [2006] ECR II-497, para 239.

any need for a deterrent factor is not influenced by the stage in the calculation in which it occurs'. From a more technical standpoint, it also confirmed that because deterrence factors are applied to the starting amount of the fine in the same way as adjustments due to the duration the infringement and/or aggravating and attenuating circumstances are, the final amount of the fine is not affected by the stage at which deterrence factors are applied.[643]

Exact purpose of the deterrence multiplying factor It follows from *BASF v Commission* **8.697** that the notion that the specific increase required in relation to an undertaking on the grounds of deterrence should result from the determination (in respect of its size and resources) of a *particular appropriate amount* is 'based on a false premise'. In other words, the application of a deterrence factor is not justified by the need to reach a scientifically calculated 'optimal level of deterrence', but rather by a broader need to 'apply differential treatment to the members of each individual cartel to take account of the way in which they are actually affected by the fine'.[644] Whilst this distinction is a subtle one, it seems to imply that the Commission is not obliged to determine the exact amount of what should be the 'optimally deterrent' sum, but that it is entitled, in a general way, to increase the amount of the fine to ensure that its overall level will have a deterrent effect.

(c) Taking into Account Duration: From the 'Starting Amount' to the 'Basic Amount'

According to Article 23(2) of Regulation 1/2003, the duration of the infringement is one **8.698** of the two criteria which the Commission must take into account when setting the amount of the fine. The Commission must therefore clearly indicate to the addressees of a decision imposing such a fine the relevant period in respect of which infringements have been found.[645] The application of such a (separate) duration factor to the 'starting amount' resulted in what the 1998 Guidelines referred to as the 'basic amount'.

Previous practice Prior to the adoption of the 1998 Guidelines, the Commission did **8.699** not specify the role played by the duration of the infringement in the calculation of the fine to be imposed, and it was difficult do identify a clear policy in that regard from the Commission's practice. In *Cartonboard* and *Cement*, the Commission found that the infringements, which lasted almost five years and ten years respectively, had been of a 'long duration'. Short duration, on the other hand, was sometimes considered as a mitigating factor. In *Italian Flat Glass I*, the Commission refrained from imposing fines, partly on the grounds that 'the agreements and decisions were applied for a relatively short period'.[646] However, in *Rolled Zinc Products*, the Commission imposed substantial fines with regard to a cartel infringement which lasted for only a few days,[647] in spite of its statement that short duration should be taken into account.[648] Overall, the duration of an infringement appeared to play a minor role in the level of the fine imposed in a given case.

---

[643] Paras 242–243.
[644] Para 241.
[645] See Joined Cases 100 to 103/80, *Musique Diffusion française and others v Commission* [1983] ECR 1825, paras 15–16.
[646] [1981] OJ L326/32, p 41.
[647] [1982] OJ L362/40, p 51.
[648] In *Ferry Operators—Currency surcharges* [1997] OJ L26/23, the Commission also imposed fines in respect of an infringement which lasted only a few weeks (para 67).

However, the validity of such an approach was questionable, since, as a result, the level of the fine imposed was not set in proportion to the actual harm on the economy.

8.700 **Relevant provisions under the 1998 Guidelines** With the adoption of the 1998 Guidelines, the Commission showed its intention to attach greater importance to the duration of the infringement in the calculation of the fine. The 1998 Guidelines provided that a distinction should be made between three categories of infringement. As regards infringements of *short duration* (in general, less than one year), no increase in the amount set with regard to gravity should be applied. As regards infringements of *medium duration* (in general, one to five years) an increase of up to 50 per cent should be applied. As for infringements of *long duration* (in general, more than five years), an increase of up to 10 per cent per year should be applied.[649]

8.701 **No increase in fines for infringements under one year** On several occasions, the Commission found that infringements had been of short duration, and applied no increase in the starting amount with regard to duration. Such was the case in *FETTCSA*, where the infringement in question was found to have lasted only three months, in *Belgian Beer* (*private label*), where the infringement had lasted nine months, in *French Beef*, where the infringement had lasted for only a couple of months, and in *French Beer*, where the Commission found that there had been no duration of infringement since the restrictive arrangements were never implemented.

8.702 **The same method of calculation for infringements over one year** In spite of a slight difference in the description of the method of calculation applicable to infringements of 'medium duration' ('increase of up to 50%') and 'long duration' ('increase of up to 10% per year') the Commission generally used the same method of calculation for all infringements exceeding one year, which was to apply a percentage increase for each full year of infringement. There were initially some variations in approach as to whether to take account of the first year of the infringement in the calculation of the increase.[650] However, it soon became Commission practice to include the first year of the infringement in the calculation. Thus, as became established practice under the 1998 Guidelines, an infringement of two years would have warranted an increase of twice the applicable annual percentage of increase.[651]

8.703 **Normal percentage of increase: 10 per cent per full year/5 per cent per full semester** The 1998 Guidelines indicated that fines could be increased by 'up' to 50 per cent of the starting amount (medium duration) or 'up' to 10 per cent of the starting amount

---

[649] The Commission indicated in the 1998 Guidelines that this new approach would potentially lead to an increase in the size of fines imposed. It stated that the increase in fines for long-term infringements represented 'a considerable strengthening of the previous practice with a view to imposing effective sanctions on restrictions which have had a harmful impact on consumers over a long period'. It also pointed out that this new approach was consistent with the expected effect of the 1996 Leniency Notice, as the risk of having to pay a much larger fine, proportionate to the duration of the infringement, would necessarily increase the incentive for companies to denounce such infringements or to co-operate with the Commission.

[650] Although in *Alloy Surcharge*, *British Sugar* and *Greek Ferries* the Commission took into account the first year of infringement in the calculation, it did not do so in *Pre-Insulated Pipes* and *Amino Acids*.

[651] The 1998 Guidelines indicate that for infringements of medium duration (up to five years) the increase can go up to 50%.

per year (long duration). Accordingly, the Commission was entitled to increase the starting amount of the fine by a smaller percentage per year. In *Volkswagen*,[652] *Opel Nederland*[653] and *Belgian Beer*, the Commission adopted smaller increases for certain years due to the lower 'intensity' of the infringement over the period concerned.[654] However, that approach was only infrequently used and was subsequently abandoned.[655] It became normal Commission practice under the 1998 Guidelines to almost automatically apply the maximum percentage of increase, ie 10 per cent per full year. As regards periods of infringement shorter than a full year, it seemed initially that the Commission had not devised a clear method for calculating the additional increase to be applied. However it finally became established practice to increase the fine by 5 per cent for each full semester (six months) of infringement.[656]

Global increase for average duration of distinct restrictive practices   In cartel cases, the **8.704** percentage increase in the fine with regard to the duration of the infringement is usually fixed by reference to the duration of the participation of each undertaking in the overall, single infringement. In *FEG/TU* however, the Commission did not find one single infringement, but a series of distinct infringements, although it imposed a single fine in respect of all of those infringements. In that case, the Commission applied a single increase of 80 per cent in respect of the duration of the infringement reflecting the average duration for the various incriminatory arrangements.[657] A similar approach was followed in *Yamaha*.[658]

No capping of the increase in the fine with regard to duration   The 1998 Guidelines did **8.705** not set any overall limit on the amount by which fines could be increased with regard to the duration of the infringement, but simply provided that the Commission could increase the starting amount of fines by up to 10 per cent per year in that regard. However, in *AAMS*[659] the Commission found that one of the two infringements had lasted for 13 years, but it increased the fine by only 100 per cent. The same approach was followed in *Luxemburg Brewers*.[660] Those decisions gave the impression that the Commission tended to apply a cap, thereby limiting the increase in fines in respect of the duration of the infringement to a maximum of 100 per cent for any infringement

---

[652] [1998] OJ L124/60. This is not a cartel case. The Decision concerned vertical restrictions.

[653] [2001] OJ L59/1. idem.

[654] It is submitted that this approach is incorrect, since the 'intensity' of the infringement is more to do with its overall gravity than with its duration.

[655] Another example of the confusion between gravity and duration can be found in *Amino Acids*, where the Commission took account of the 'passive role' of an undertaking by reducing the increase retained on account of duration by 20%. The CFI subsequently found that this constituted a breach of the principle of equal treatment and modified the fine imposed on one applicant in the exercise of its unlimited jurisdiction (see Case T-220/00 *Cheil Jedang v Commission* [2003] ECR II-24/73, paras 223–230).

[656] Thus, for example, an infringement of three years and seven months would result in an increase of 35% in the starting amount, whilst an infringement of six years and three months would justify an increase of 60%.

[657] [2000] OJ L39/1, paras 146–147. The Commission found that the incriminatory arrangements had lasted eight, fifteen, nine, four and six years respectively.

[658] This is not a cartel case. Full text of the decision available on DG COMP's web site.

[659] [1998] OJ L252/47. This is not a cartel case.

[660] [2002] OJ L253/21. A 100% increase was applied in relation to an infringement of 14 years.

exceeding 10 years. Subsequently, however, the Commission appeared to abandon that approach. In *Methionine*, an increase of 125 per cent was applied in respect of a cartel that had lasted 12 years and 10 months. Similar examples rapidly followed. In *Concrete Reinforcing Bars*, *Sorbates*, *Electrical and Mechanical Carbon and Graphite Products*, *Industrial Copper Tubes*, *MCAA*, *Industrial Thread* and *Industrial Bags*, the Commission applied multiplying factors in respect of duration that sometimes significantly exceeded 100 per cent. Increases of 175 per cent and 200 per cent were applied in *Sorbates* and *Industrial Bags* respectively.

8.706 **Reduction of the percentage of increase per year over 10 years** In *Organic Peroxides*, the Commission found itself faced with an infringement of extremely long duration, amounting to 29 years for three companies. It decided to apply an increase of only 245 per cent to the fines imposed on those companies, consisting of an increase of 10 per cent per year for the final 20 years of infringement (1980–1999), and of 5 per cent per year for the part of the infringement which had taken place in the previous years (1971–1979). The Commission explained that this was 'justified by the less strict approach of competition policy in the seventies, when companies where less aware that their behaviour infringed competition and fines were lower'.[661] However, the validity of this argument is debatable, since the companies in question might have been expected to stop their infringement as soon as they became aware of the illegal nature of their conduct, or at least when fines became higher.

(d) Individualising 'Subjective' Responsibility: Aggravating and Mitigating Circumstances

8.707 Once the basic amount of the fine was set, the Commission took any potential aggravating or mitigating circumstances into account. At this stage of the process, the fine was individualised to take account of the *subjective* dimension of the responsibility of each cartel participant.[662] The Community Courts have confirmed the Commission's entitlement to take aggravating or attenuating circumstances into account.[663] Indeed, where an infringement has been committed by several undertakings, it is necessary, when calculating the amounts of the fines to be imposed, to examine the relative gravity of each undertaking's participation.[664]

---

[661] [2005] OJ L110/44, para 466 (full text of the decision available on DG COMP's web site).

[662] The Commission follows the same approach under the 2006 Guidelines. In this respect, the subsequent developments regarding aggravating and attenuating circumstances can be deemed to remain largely relevant under the new Guidelines.

[663] See eg Case T-202/98 *Tate & Lyle and others v Commission* [2001] ECR II-2035, para 109. The CFI stated in particular that taking into account such circumstances, '[f]ar from being contrary to the letter and the spirit of Article 15(2) of Regulation No 17, [...] allows the Commission, particularly in the case of infringements involving many undertakings, to take account of the different role played by each undertaking and its attitude towards the Commission during the course of the proceedings in its assessment of the gravity of the infringement'.

[664] Joined Cases 40 to 48, 50, 54 to 56, 111, 113 and 114-73 *Suiker Unie and others v Commission* [1975] ECR 1663, para 623; Case T-224/00 *Archer Daniels Midland Company and Archer Daniels Midland Ingredients v Commission* [2003] ECR II-2597, para 238. The CFI has found that this 'follows logically from the principle that penalties and sanctions must fit the offence, according to which an undertaking may be penalised only for acts imputed to it individually. That principle applies in any administrative procedure that may lead to the imposition of sanctions under Community competition law' (see, as regards fines, Joined Cases T-45/98 and T-47/98 *Krupp Thyssen Stainless* and *Acciai speciali Terni v Commission* [2001] ECR II-3757, para 63; Case T-224/00 *Archer Daniels Midland Company and Archer Daniels Midland Ingredients v Commission* [2003] ECR II-2597, para 260).

That implies, in particular, establishing the respective roles of each undertaking in the infringement during the period of their participation in it.[665] The 1998 Guidelines provided a non-exhaustive list of such circumstances.[666]

Individual conduct vs overall gravity of the infringement   Initially, there was some con-   **8.708**
fusion between the assessment of the gravity of the infringement as a whole and the application of the mitigating circumstance of 'non-implementation in practice of the offending
agreements'.[667] The CFI made it clear in *Amino Acids*, however, that no confusion should
exist between the assessment of the gravity of the *infringement as a whole* (first paragraph of
Section 1.A of the 1998 Guidelines) and that of the *individual conduct of each undertaking*,
which it must carry out in order to assess any aggravating or mitigating circumstances (sections 2 and 3 of the 1998 Guidelines). In the former, the Commission considered the
effects resulting from the infringement as a whole rather than from the individual conduct
of each undertaking. In the latter, in accordance with the principle of individuality of
penalties and sanctions, the Commission examined the relative importance of the individual undertaking's involvement in the infringement.[668]

The Commission is bound by the Guidelines, but not by prior decisions   The fact that   **8.709**
the Commission may have considered that certain factors have constituted mitigating circumstances for the purposes of determining the amount of the fine in previous decisions
does not mean that it is obliged to make the same assessment in a subsequent decision.[669]
However, since it may not depart from rules that it has imposed on itself,[670] the Commission
is bound by the Guidelines when assessing potential aggravating and/or mitigating circumstances. Nevertheless, the Commission still enjoys a certain discretion, first as to whether
an aggravating or attenuating circumstance is applicable in a given case and, second, rea-
garding the appropriate size of the corresponding increase or reduction. In relation in particular to attenuating circumstances, the CFI has held that the Guidelines do not list the
attenuating circumstances which the Commission *must* take into account. The CFI has
also found that 'although the circumstances in the list at point 3 of the Guidelines are certainly among those which may be taken into account by the Commission in a specific case,
[the Commission] is not required to grant a further reduction as a matter of course when

---

[665] Case C-49/92 P *Commission v Anic Partecipazioni* [1999] ECR I-4125, para 150; Case T-224/00
Archer Daniels Midland Company and Archer Daniels Midland Ingredients v Commission [2003] ECR II-2597,
para 238.

[666] In Case T 23/99 *LR AF 1998 v Commission* [2002] ECR II-01705, para 321, the CFI confirmed that
'as regards the list of aggravating circumstances set out in the guidelines, the guidelines clearly state that the
list is given purely by way of example'.

[667] In its assessment of the gravity of the infringement in *Greek Ferries*, the Commission took account of
the limited implementation of the agreement but did not cite that factor as an attenuating circumstance.
Subsequently, in the context of the judicial review of *Amino Acids*, the Commission submitted that the expression 'non-implementation in practice of the offending agreements' referred to situations where a cartel as a
whole remains unimplemented or is inoperative for a given period and that it did not refer to the individual
position of members of an active cartel.

[668] Case T-224/00 *Archer Daniels Midland Company and Archer Daniels Midland Ingredients v Commission*
[2003] ECR II-2597, para 265.

[669] Case T-347/94 *Mayr-Melnhof Kartongesellschaft v Commission* [1998] ECR II-1751, para 368; Case
T-23/99 *LR AF 1998 v Commission* [2002] ECR II-01705, para 337.

[670] See Case T-7/89 *Hercules Chemicals v Commission* [1991] ECR II-1711, para 53, confirmed on appeal
in Case C-51/92 P *Hercules Chemicals v Commission* [1999] ECR I-4235, and the case law cited therein.

an undertaking puts forward evidence of the existence of one of those circumstances. Whether it is appropriate to grant a reduction of the fine on grounds of attenuating circumstances must be determined on the basis of a global assessment which takes account of all the relevant circumstances'.[671]

8.710 **Method of calculation when both aggravating and attenuating circumstances apply** According to the 1998 Guidelines, the correct way to calculate the increases and/or reductions to reflect aggravating and/or mitigating circumstances was to apply a percentage to the basic amount of the fine. In a case where both aggravating and mitigating circumstances were applicable to the same undertaking, or in a case where several attenuating or several aggravating circumstances were applicable to it, each applicable reduction or increase of the fine had to be calculated by applying the corresponding percentage successively to the same basic amount of the fine.[672] However, the Commission did not always employ that method. Its initial practice was first to calculate the amount of the fine resulting from the increase applied to the basic amount with respect to aggravating circumstances, and then to decrease that amount by a percentage relating to the applicable attenuating circumstances. This initial method of calculation was more favourable to the undertakings concerned than the method set out in the 1998 Guidelines.[673]

8.711 In *Amino Acids*, the Commission departed further still from the method set out in the Guidelines. In that case it allowed Sewon the benefit of two mitigating circumstances. The first was in respect of that undertaking's passive role over a given period and led to a reduction of 20 per cent in the increase applied to its fine on account of the duration of the infringement. The second circumstance related to the fact that the infringement had been terminated as soon as a public authority had intervened, and that led to a reduction of 10 per cent in the figure derived following the first reduction. However, the CFI ruled in *Cheil Jedang v Commission*, that this practice was in breach of the principle of equal treatment. Contrary to its treatment of Cheil Jedang, the Commission had not calculated the aggravating and attenuating circumstances applicable to Sewon by reference to the basic amount of its fine. The CFI stated clearly that '[g]iven the wording of the Guidelines, [...] any percentage increases or reductions decided upon to reflect aggravating or mitigating circumstances must be applied to the basic amount of the fine set by reference to the gravity and duration of the infringement, not to the amount of any increase already applied for the duration of the infringement or to the figure resulting from any initial increase or reduction to reflect aggravating or mitigating circumstances'.[674]

8.712 In view of very specific factual circumstances, it was in the applicant's interest in *Cheil Jedang v Commission* that the CFI proceeded to amend the amount of the fine, in line with the method of calculation set out in the Guidelines. A question thus arose as to whether the CFI would also amend the method of calculation of a fine when such an amendment would

---

[671] Case T-50/00 *Dalmine v Commission* [2004] ECR II-2395, para 325. See also Joined Cases T-71/03, T-74/03, T-87/03 and T-91/03 *Tokai Carbon and others*, [2005] ECR II-10, para 289.

[672] For instance, for a basic amount of 100, an aggravating circumstance of 40% and an attenuating circumstance of 10%, the calculation should be the following: 100 + (40% of 100)–(10% of 100) = 130.

[673] For instance, with the same figures: 100 + 40 % = 140–10 % = 126.

[674] Case T 220/00 *Cheil Jedang v Commission* [2003] ECR II 24/73, para 299.

be detrimental to the applicant. In fact, the CFI did just that in *Danone v Commission* (relating to the *Belgian Beer* decision).[675] In that case the CFI, by choosing to correct the mistake made by the Commission in favour of the applicant, reduced the favourable impact of the reduction of the fine for that applicant.[676]

(i) Aggravating Circumstances

1. Repeated infringements of the same type by the same undertaking

Rationale   Repetition by an undertaking of an infringement of the same type as one for   **8.713**
which it has already been found liable will be regarded as an aggravating circumstance. This was the Commission's position even before the introduction of the 1998 Guidelines.[677] The Commission considers that recidivism shows that a previous finding of an infringement and, in most cases, the prior imposition of a fine has not had the expected deterrent effect. Such recidivism justifies an increase in the fine imposed specifically in order to ensure an effective level of deterrence.

Court review   In *Enichem Anic SpA v Commission*, the CFI held that 'the fact that the   **8.714**
Commission has in the past already found an undertaking guilty of infringing the competition rules and penalized it for that infringement may be treated as an aggravating factor as against that undertaking'.[678] This was confirmed in *Michelin v Commission*, where the CFI stated that '[r]ecidivism is a circumstance which justifies a significant increase in the basic amount of the fine. Recidivism constitutes proof that the sanction previously imposed was not sufficiently deterrent' and that the Commission was entitled to increase the basic amount of the fine 'in order to direct [the undertaking's] conduct towards compliance with the Treaty's competition rules'.[679] In *Danone v Commission*, in response to the argument

---

[675]   See Case T-38/02 *Danone v Commission* [2005] ECR II-4407, paras 519–525.

[676]   In this case, the CFI concluded that the Commission had erred in law in its finding of one of the two aggravating circumstances applied in the calculation of the fine imposed on Danone and reduced that fine accordingly. On that occasion, the CFI observed on its own initiative that the Commission had not followed the methodology prescribed by the Guidelines in calculating the cumulative impact of the applicable aggravating and mitigating circumstances and recalculated the fine on the basis of the methodology indicated in the Guidelines. Although this resulted in an overall decrease in the fine imposed on Danone, that decrease was less than what would have resulted from the mere recalculation of the fine on the basis of the revised percentage adopted for aggravating circumstances (from 50% to 40%) based on the Commission's initial method of calculation. The judgment was appealed by Danone on this point. In his Opinion delivered on 16 November 2006 (Case C-3/06 P), Advocate-General Poiares Maduro concluded that the Court should set aside the judgment of the CFI on this point, as the latter failed to hear the applicant on its intention to correct the Commission's error. The Advocate-General nonetheless proposed that the Court also apply the calculation method set out in the 1998 Guidelines and set the amount of the fine at the same amount as the CFI has done in its judgment.

[677]   See for instance *Flat Glass (Benelux)*, para 53; *Polypropylene*, para 107; *Soda Ash (A)*, para 65; *Steel Beams*, para 306; *PVC II*, para 51. In *Steel Beams* (paras 305 and 306) the Commission increased the fine imposed on certain undertakings by one third in respect of their prior involvement in the *Stainless Steel* cartel, but the CFI subsequently annulled that decision on this point on the grounds that it was insufficiently reasoned and that the conditions for finding recidivism had not been met. See Case T-141/94 *Thyssen Stahl v Commission* [1999] ECR II-347, paras 614–618.

[678]   Case T-6/89 *Enichem Anic v Commission* [1991] ECR II-1623, para 295.

[679]   Case *Michelin v Commission* [2003] ECR II-4071, para 293. In Joined Cases C-204/00 P, C-205/00 P, C-211/00 P, C-213/00 P, C-217/00 P and C-219/00 P *Aalborg Portland and others v Commission* [2004] ECR I-123, para 91, the Court confirmed that 'any repeated infringements' must be taken into account, for the purpose of setting the fine, in the assessment of the gravity of the infringement committed'.

that the repetition of an infringement is not relevant to the circumstances that aggravate an infringement (the 'objective assessment of the gravity of facts') but to recognition of a fact specific to the perpetrator of the infringement, namely its tendency to commit such infringements, the CFI replied that 'contrary to the applicant's contention, although repeated infringement relates to a characteristic specific to the perpetrator of the infringement, namely its propensity to commit such infringements, it is precisely, for that very reason, a very significant indication of the gravity of the conduct in question and, accordingly, of the need to increase the level of the penalty in order to achieve effective deterrence'.[680]

8.715   *Three cumulative conditions*   The finding of recidivism is conditional upon three cumulative conditions.[681] First, the Commission must be able to establish a common identity between the undertaking which is found to be recidivist and that undertaking which was subject to the prior finding of an infringement. To that end, the Commission relies on the concept of undertaking in the broad economic sense, as established by the case law.[682] Recidivism may thus be adduced against a subsidiary within one group with reference to a past infringement by a different subsidiary within the same group provided that both subsidiaries received instructions from the same parent company, even if the parent company was not an addressee of the prohibition decisions.[683] Secondly, recidivism may only be adduced if similar behaviour can be identified. Thus, the previous finding of an infringement of Article 82, or of another type of infringement of Article 81 (for example vertical restrictions) would not lead to the finding of recidivism in a cartel Decision.[684] However, the previous infringement need not have been exactly identical and may have concerned a different product or a different geographic market.[685] Nor is it necessary that the earlier infringement related to similar

---

680   Case T-38/02 *Danone v Commission* [2005] ECR II-4407, para 349.

681   See Case T-203/01 *Michelin v Commission* [2003] ECR II-4071, paras 284–293.

682   See section D(3) of this chapter.

683   In Case T-203/01 *Michelin v Commission* [2003] ECR II-4071, para 290, both addressees of the Commission's decision were subsidiaries which were more than 99% owned, directly or indirectly, by the same parent company, namely the Compagnie Générale des Établissements Michelin. The CFI considered that there were therefore reasonable grounds for concluding that those subsidiaries did not independently determine their own conduct on the market and that they formed part of an economic unit and therefore comprised an undertaking within the meaning of Arts 81 EC and 82 EC. Since, in accordance with settled case law, the Commission, had it so wished, could have imposed a fine on the same parent company in both decisions, the Commission was entitled to consider in the contested decision that the same undertaking had already been censured in 1981 for the same type of infringement.

684   In *British Sugar*, the Commission stated that it did not make a finding of recidivism against this company although it had previously been fined in the *Napier Brown* decision for abusing its dominant position in the British retail sugar market, as the finding of recidivism required the repetition of the same kind of infringement. However, the Commission maintained that the fact that the new infringement committed by British Sugar constituted a breach of the compliance programme which was set up in the context of the proceedings that resulted in the *Napier Brown* decision constituted an aggravating circumstance. Indeed, in the latter decision, the establishment of the compliance programme had been taken into account by the Commission as a mitigating factor when setting the fine. In cases of similar types of infringement, the fact that the cartel has operated in distinct product or geographic markets will not be an obstacle to the finding of recidivism.

685   In *Belgian Beer*, the Commission adduced recidivism against Danone as it found that the undertaking had been found to have committed similar infringements twice already, namely in *Flat glass (Benelux)* and *Agreements between Manufacturers of Glass containers*. The Commission noted that the two previous infringements consisted of the exchange of information, restrictions concerning prices and terms and conditions of sale and, in one situation, market-sharing agreements. In *Plasterboard*, the Commission adduced recidivism against both BPB and Lafarge, as BPB's subsidiary BPB De Eendracht had previously been fined in the *Cartonboard* case, whilst Lafarge had already been fined in the *Cement* case.

Treaty provisions.[686] Thirdly, recidivism may be taken into account only from the date on which the first infringement was established by a Commission decision.[687] However, the Commission does not have to establish that the new infringement started after the first finding of infringement in order to make a finding of recidivism.[688] Also, it is not necessary for the Commission to have imposed a fine for the prior infringement in order to make a finding of recidivism: What is relevant is the finding of a previous infringement and the application of an associated 'cease and desist' order under Article 7 of Regulation 1/2003.[689] The fact that the prior finding of an infringement resulted from a notification also does not prevent the Commission from making a finding of recidivism.[690]

The *Organic Peroxides* case provides a good illustration of the implementation of the above **8.716** principles. In this case, the Commission found that three addressees of the decision had, directly or indirectly, already been addressees of prohibition decisions relating to similar infringements and that they had participated or continued to participate actively in the organic peroxides cartel having been notified of those decisions. Although certain companies had not been the formal addressees of those decisions, the Commission stated that the concept of an undertaking allowed the Commission to adduce the aggravating circumstance of repeat offence against those companies.[691]

Commission's practice   The Commission has found recidivism to be an aggravating circum- **8.717** stance in a significant number of cartel cases.[692] This finding indicates the endemic nature of

---

[686] In *Industrial Tubes* and *Copper Plumbing Tubes*, the Commission rejected the argument that a prior infringement of Article 65 of the ECSC Treaty could not be adduced for the purpose of finding recidivism on the grounds of a dissimilarity of the treaty provisions (see paras 349 and 724 respectively).

[687] See Case T-141/94 *Thyssen Stahl v Commission* [1999] ECR II-347, paras 617–618. The Commission therefore cannot adduce it in the case of parallel proceedings concerning cartels which took place over roughly identical periods of time. For instance, whilst German company SGL was subject to three prohibition decisions (*Graphite Electrodes, Specialty Graphites, Electrical and Mechanical Graphite Products*) and fined for four distinct cartel infringements over a period of two years and a half, no aggravating circumstance was found as the infringements concerned had all ceased before the first decision intervened.

[688] In the case of cartels that run in parallel, it is sufficient for the Commission to have previously found an infringement in relation to one of them for it to be able to adduce recidivism in the case of subsequent infringements. This occurred, for example, in *Plasterboard* (paras 559–564). In *Organic Peroxides*, the Commission adduced recidivism against three companies in respect of an infringement which started as early as 1971. As the basis of this finding, the Commission referred to previous findings of infringements relating to cartels that interestingly, took place after the *Organic Peroxides* cartel had begun to operate (paras 470–477).

[689] See *Industrial Tubes* and *Copper Plumbing Tubes*, at paras 349 and 274 respectively. In Case C-38/02 *Danone v Commission* [2005] ECR II-4407, para 363, the CFI found that 'the concept of repeated infringement does not necessarily imply that a fine has been imposed in the past, but merely that a finding of infringement has been made in the past. [...] It is not the previous imposition of a fine that determines that conduct constitutes repeated infringement, which is determinative of recidivism, but the fact that a previous finding of infringement has been made against the person concerned'.

[690] See *Flat Glass (Benelux)*, para 53; *Belgian Beer*, para 314. In Case T-38/02 *Danone v Commission* [2005] ECR II-4407, para 363, the CFI stated that 'the concept of repeated infringement does not necessarily imply that a fine has been imposed in the past, but merely that a finding of infringement has been made in the past. Repeated infringement is taken into account, for a particular infringement, so that a more severe penalty may be imposed on the undertaking responsible for the relevant facts when it transpires that a previous finding of infringement on its part has not been sufficient to prevent the repetition of unlawful conduct. It is not the previous imposition of a fine that determines that conduct constitutes repeated infringement, which is determinative of recidivism, but the fact that a previous finding of infringement has been made against the person concerned'.

[691] Paras 470–477.

[692] See for instance *Belgian Beer* (Danone), *Plasterboards, Concrete Reinforcing Bars, Industrial Tubes* (Outokumpu, paras 348 to 354); *Choline Chloride* (BASF), *MCAA* (Atofina and Hoechst), *Industrial Bags*.

cartel behaviour in certain economic sectors. In a number of decisions, the Commission has found that various addressees had previously been held responsible for several other cartel violations.[693] Some companies have even had repeated findings of recidivism made against them.[694] The Commission has not hesitated to highlight individual personal responsibility in the repetition of infringements.[695]

8.718 Under the 1998 Guidelines, recidivism typically incurred a 50 per cent increase in the basic amount of the fine. In *Choline Chloride*, the Commission stated that '[a] 50% rate is the normal rate employed by the Commission in cases involving recidivism'.[696] The Commission refrained from differentiating the amount of the increase according to the number of times a similar infringement was repeated. Quite surprisingly, in *Organic Peroxides*, the Commission applied the same increase of 50 per cent to the fine imposed on Atochem, which was found responsible for its fifth cartel infringement, as well as to Laporte and PC, which had each only committed one prior infringement.[697] In this respect, it must be noted that no time limit applies in relation to the Commission's entitlement to take into account, for the purpose of finding recidivism, facts which occurred far in the past. The argument that time limits should apply in this respect was dismissed by the CFI in *Danone*.[698]

8.719 **2. Refusal to cooperate with or attempts to obstruct the Commission in carrying out its investigations**   In addition to the specific procedural fines that may be imposed on undertakings as a result of their refusal to cooperate with the Commission or attempts to obstruct the Commission's investigations,[699] such conduct may also be considered an aggravating circumstance for the purpose of calculating fines for the main infringement. Such conduct may consist of attempts to mislead the Commission as to the relevant facts, or to prevent it from properly conducting its investigation.

---

693 In *Organic Peroxides*, the Commission found that Atochem had already been found responsible for no less than four previous cartel infringements, namely in the *Peroxygen*, *Polypropylene*, *LdPE* and *PVC* cases. In *Belgian Beer*, the Commission pointed out that Danone (previously BSN) has already been found responsible twice for a similar infringement of Art 81 EC. Danone was again condemned for cartel behaviour in *Kronenbourg/Heineken*, and recidivism was adduced once more. However, the Commission did not refer to the *Belgian Beer* decision, but only to the *Flat Glass (Benelux)* decision (paras 91–95). In *Soda Ash*, the Commission found that Solvay had previously been condemned for taking part in the *Peroxygen*, *Polypropylene* and *PVC* cartels. As to BASF, it has also been condemned in four cartel decisions so far, namely *Dyestuff*, *PVC*, *Vitamins* and *Choline Chloride*.

694 For instance Danone (*Belgian Beer*, *Kronenbourg/Heineken*).

695 In *Belgian Beer*, it underlined that during the period in which the three infringements were committed by BSN/Danone the same person occupied the post of chairman and chief executive. In addition, at least two of Danone's directors who were involved in the beer cartel had been employed in the company's glass division during the time of the earlier infringements (para 314).

696 [2005] OJ L90/22. Para 208 (full text of the decision available on DG COMP's web site). In *Danone*, the applicant contested what it thought was an unreasonable increase in the fine for repeated infringement (40%). This was dismissed by the CFI, which found that the level of the fine '[did] not arise from a manifestly unreasonable conception of the context of repeated infringement [. . .]'.

697 [2005] OJ L110/44, para 477 (full text of the decision available on DG COMP's web site).

698 See Case T-38/02 *Groupe Danone v Commission* [2005] ECR II-4407, paras 360, 365 and 366.

699 See paras 8.314–8.316 and para 8.384. The question of whether the imposition of procedural fines should exclude the application of an aggravating circumstance relating to the same facts remains open.

Supplying misleading information   In *Greek Ferries*, the Commission found that after the   **8.720**
parties had received requests for information, the undertaking Minoan proposed that
the cartel members should differentiate their price artificially for the purpose of deceiving
the Commission. The Commission considered that, as well as demonstrating Minoan's role
as instigator, such behaviour constituted an attempt to obstruct the Commission's investigation, and justified increasing the basic amount of the fine determined by 10 per cent.[700]
In *Pre-Insulated Pipes* the Commission found that Henss/Isoplus had systematically
attempted to mislead the Commission as to the true relationship between the companies
in the group. This was considered a deliberate obstruction of the Commission's investigation which, had it succeeded, might well have enabled the undertaking to evade the appropriate penalty or rendered its recovery more difficult. This, together with the fact that the
undertaking in question played a leading role in the implementation of the cartel, justified
increasing the basic amount determined by 30 per cent.[701] When reviewing that decision,
the CFI found that inaccurate information had been supplied and upheld the
Commission's finding. This was confirmed on appeal by the ECJ, which also clarified that
the Commission's simultaneous refusal to grant a reduction of fine and finding of an aggravating circumstance with regard to the same conduct was not in breach of the principle *ne bis
in idem*.[702] It rejected the appellant's argument that its conduct was justified on the grounds
of confidentiality, emphasising that the Commission is under an obligation to protect the
confidentiality of information covered by professional secrecy.[703] It also noted that the companies concerned, which were held jointly and severally liable, could have escaped part of the
fines due from them, had the Commission relied on the information initially supplied.[704]
In *Fittings*, the Commission found that the misleading information supplied by one undertaking justified an increase of the basic amount of the fine imposed on it by 50 per cent.[705]

Obstruction of on-the-spot investigations   In *Graphite Electrodes*, SGL was found to have   **8.721**
attempted to obstruct the Commission's investigation by warning other companies of
forthcoming investigations.[706] This was one of the factors contributing to the 85 per cent
increase applied to the basic amount of the fine imposed on SGL. When reviewing the
Commission's decision, the CFI confirmed that warning other cartel members of forthcoming investigations could be properly characterised as an aggravating circumstance since
such conduct added to the gravity of the initial infringement.[707] By warning other members

---

[700] [1999] OJ L109/24, paras 160–161. This was upheld by the CFI in Case T-66/99 *Minoan Lines v Commission* [2003] ECR II-5515, paras 335–339.

[701] [1999] OJ L24/1, para 179.

[702] Joined Cases C-189/02 P, C-202/02 P, C-205/02 P to C-208/02 P and C-213/02 P *Dansk Rørindustri and other v Commission* [2005] ECR I-5425, para 403. The Court stated that 'the fact that an undertaking is not rewarded for cooperation which did not allow the Commission to establish an infringement with less dif-ficulty and, where appropriate, to put an end to it cannot be classified as a sanction additional to the punish-ment consisting in recognition of an aggravating circumstance'.

[703] Case T-9/99 *HFB and others* [2002] ECR II-1487, paras 561–562.

[704] ibid, para 564.

[705] See IP/06/1222.

[706] [2002] OJ L100/1, para 160.

[707] Joined Cases T-236/01, T-239/01, T-244/01 to T-246/01, T-251/01 and T-252/01 *Tokai Carbon and others v Commission* [2004] ECR II-1181, para 312. The CFI cited in that regard Case T-334/94 *Sarrio v Commission* [1998] ECR II-1439, where at at para 320 the CFI held that the Commission had been fully entitled to regard steps taken to conceal collusion as aggravating circumstances.

of the cartel, SGL sought to conceal the existence of the cartel and to ensure its continued operation, an aim which was successfully achieved until March 1998. In *Industrial Bags*, the Commission considered the fact that, in spite of repeated warnings, one of the managing directors of a cartel participant had destroyed a document which had been selected by the inspectors, to be an aggravating circumstance.[708] This behaviour justified increasing the basic amount of the fine of the undertaking concerned by 10 per cent.[709] In *Road Bitumen Netherlands*, one cartel participant was found to have attempted to obstruct the Commission investigation by twice refusing access to its premises by Commission inspectors, thereby forcing the Commission to seek the aid of the Dutch competition authority and police. This resulted in a 10 per cent increase in the basic amount of the fine imposed on that undertaking.[710]

3. Role of leader in, or instigator of, the infringement

8.722   *Rationale*   In many of its decisions adopted under the 1998 Guidelines, the Commission has considered the fact that one or more undertakings were the instigator(s) and/or the leader(s) in an infringement to constitute an aggravating circumstance in relation to such undertaking(s). The rationale behind this approach is that those companies bear a specific responsibility for the damage caused to the economy because of their critical contribution to the establishment or implementation of the collusive scheme.[711] In its decisions the Commission has considered a variety of elements to be evidence of such contributions. Among the most relevant are the fact that the undertakings have taken the initiative in contacting competitors, brought collusive plans to their attention, convened cartel meetings, tried to convince or even force others to engage in collusion, or acted as brokers in case of trouble.

8.723   *The need to distinguish between role of 'instigator' and role of 'leader'*   The 1998 Guidelines state that the 'role of leader in, or instigator of the infringement' can be taken into account as an aggravating circumstance. While in certain decisions the Commission has referred only to the role of 'instigator'[712] or 'leader',[713] in others it has adduced both classifications

---

[708]   The company in question claimed that only the procedural fines provided for in Article 15(1)(c) of Regulation 17 could be applied to such behaviour. However, that argument was rejected by the Commission. It also rejected the argument that the destruction of the document had had no real impact on the investigation as it had been reproduced shortly after the end of the inspection. The Commission stated that it could not be ascertained whether the document subsequently provided was a copy of the same document that had been destroyed.

[709]   Paras 790–795.

[710]   See IP/06/1179.

[711]   Before the implementation of the Guidelines it was already common practice to take the role of leader or instigator played by an undertaking into account when setting a fine. In *Cartonboard*, the Commission stated that six of the major producers of cartonboard and one of the leading producers in the paper industry had acted as the 'ringleaders' and had to bear a special responsibility since they clearly constituted the main decision-makers and were the prime movers of the cartel ([1994] OJ L243/1, para 170). In *PVC II*, on the other hand, the Commission stated that although some indications pointed to two undertakings as prime movers in the cartel, the Commission could not identify with certainty any ringleaders who should bear the major responsibility for the infringement ([1994] OJ L239/14, para 53). In *Cement*, the Commission did not identify 'ringleaders', but stated that it had taken account of the role played by each undertaking in the conclusion of the cartel agreement and in the arrangements and measures agreed to supplement the agreement or principle and/or assist in its implementation. To that end the Commission classified the undertakings in groups according to the importance of their role in the cartel ([1994] L343/1, para 65, point 9).

[712]   See for instance *Greek Ferries*.

[713]   See for instance *Alloy Surcharge*, *Amino Acids*, *Sodium Gluconate*, *Citric Acid*.

against the same undertaking(s).[714] Where it has referred to both, the Commission has not always clearly distinguished between the factors relied upon for the purpose of finding that an undertaking was the 'instigator' and those relied upon for the purpose of finding that the undertaking was the 'leader'. It seems, therefore, that although the Commission may have emphasised either one characteristic or the other, it nevertheless considered that both characteristics were part of the same concept. However, in the context of the *Vitamins* case, the CFI stated that when both characteristics have been adduced against an undertaking, 'it is necessary to distinguish between the concept of leader in and that of instigator of an infringement and to carry out two separate analyses to check whether the applicant was one or the other'.[715] In the case in question, the CFI found that the Commission's conclusion that BASF had been the instigator in certain infringements in *Vitamins* had been insufficiently substantiated.[716] When the Commission finds that an undertaking has been both the instigator *and* the leader of the infringement, there is therefore a clear obligation on the part of the Commission to demonstrate that the undertaking did in fact play both roles.

Role of 'instigator' or 'leader' must be established for each particular infringement   In the **8.724** context of *Vitamins*, the CFI found that the role of 'instigator' or 'leader' must be established for each particular infringement. In *Vitamins*, where the Commission found several closely connected but nonetheless distinct infringements, the Commission relied on general aspects of the market position and conduct of BASF and Roche as a basis for its finding that both undertakings had been instigators and leader of the infringements. This line of reasoning was not accepted by the CFI, which stated that 'since the Commission found in the decision several distinct infringements and imposed separate fines in respect of them, it must [when adducing a role of instigator or leader as an aggravating circumstance] demonstrate in respect of each of those infringements, by referring to and proving facts peculiar to each undertaking, that one or other of the participants in the different cartels was a leader or instigator'.[717] Thus, the CFI concluded that general arguments relating to the overall economic power[718] or the 'common front'[719] formed by BASF and Roche in respect of their presence on all vitamins markets could not be evidence of the aggravating circumstance in question.

---

[714] See for instance *British Sugar, Pre-Insulated Pipes, Graphite Electrodes, Vitamins, Carbonless Paper, Specialty Graphite.*

[715] Case T-15/02 *BASF v Commission* [2006] ECR II-497, para 316.

[716] However, the CFI ultimately found that even if the Commission had not validly found, on the basis of the evidence adduced, BASF to be an instigator of the infringements in question, the increase of 35% in the basic amount of the fines applied to BASF remained fully justified in light of the fact that BASF was, jointly with Roche, a leader in those infringements, albeit to a lesser degree than Roche (see para 354).

[717] Para 294.

[718] The CFI stated in this respect that 'it [could not] be presumed from the fact that Roche and BASF produced a broad range of vitamins, or from the advantages which they derived from it, that those undertakings were in fact leaders in or instigators of the infringements in the present case' (para 298) but that such factors 'could not be ruled out as factors in the assessment of the gravity of the infringement within the meaning of Section 1A of the Guidelines, as being evidence of the effective economic capacity of offenders to cause significant damage to other operators or of 'the specific weight' of the individual offending conduct' (para 297).

[719] The CFI stated in this regard that these were '[. . .] factors which may reveal [the undertaking's] motives in the cartel arrangements but which do not in themselves show that they bore individual and specific liability for the creation and operation of the cartels in question. Furthermore, the objective of eliminating mutual competition is characteristic of the involvement of any undertaking in an illegal cartel and the fact that that objective covers the entire range of BASF's and Roche's vitamins merely reflects the scope of that range and does not, at least in the absence of more detailed explanations, have any particular significance' (para 300).

8.725 *Role of 'instigator' vs role of 'leader'*   In the context of the *Vitamins* case, the CFI gave some interesting indications as to what may characterise the role of 'instigator' of an infringement. The CFI stated that '[w]hereas instigation is concerned with the *establishment* or *enlargement* of a cartel, leadership is concerned with its *operation*' (emphasis added). The CFI went on to state that 'in order to be classified as an instigator of a cartel, an undertaking must have persuaded or encouraged other undertakings to establish the cartel or to join it. [...] That classification should be reserved to the undertaking which has taken the initiative, if such be the case, for example by suggesting to the other an opportunity for collusion or by attempting to persuade it to do so'.[720]

8.726 *Indicia of a role of 'instigator' or 'leader': the Commission's practice and Court review*   As detailed in paras 8.723 and 8.724 above, it was only in its judgment in *BASF v Commission* in the *Vitamins* case that the CFI made clear that it is incumbent on the Commission, when it has found that an undertaking has been both an 'instigator' and a 'leader' to establish both characteristics specifically. An analysis of the Commission's practice prior to that judgment shows that such a distinction had not previously been systematically made. It should therefore be noted that the examples of the Commission's practice given below may relate either to a finding that the undertaking was the 'instigator' or that it was the 'leader'. Where relevant, clarifications given by the Community Courts in respect of one or other characteristic are also mentioned.

8.727 *A. Market power not relevant for the purpose of establishing leadership*   On certain occasions, the Commission has referred to evidence of market power for the purpose of establishing cartel leadership. In *Amino Acids*, the Commission noted that ADM and Ajinomoto were by far the most powerful cartel members, holding the same ambition to be the leader in the world lysine market.[721] In *Carbonless Paper*, the 'economic leadership' of AWA was considered to be an aggravating circumstance.[722] In *Vitamins*, the Commission considered that Roche and BASF had been joint leaders and instigators of the collusive arrangements affecting the common range of vitamin products they produced.[723] It indicated that the anti-competitive agreements in question were most effective for those companies which produced and sold the widest range of vitamin products. As suppliers of a wide range of vitamin products Roche and BASF enjoyed a number of advantages. In particular their position in relation to their customers was stronger than that of companies selling a single or limited number of products. As a result of possessing a broad range of products in separate but closely related product markets, the overall ability of these companies to implement and maintain the anti-competitive agreements into which they had entered increased considerably.[724] This conclusion was rejected by the CFI however. The Court found that the Commission had not explained the relationship between the extent of the range of vitamin products and the actual role played by the companies in question in those infringements.

---

[720] Case T-15/02 *BASF v Commission* [2006] ECR II-497, para 321.
[721] [2001] OJ L152/24, para 355.
[722] [2004] OJ L115/1, paras 418–424.
[723] [2003] OJ L6/1, paras 712–718.
[724] The Commission pointed out that both major European producers had effectively formed a common front in conceiving and implementing the collusive arrangements with the Japanese and other European producers.

The Court's criticism in that case focused mostly on the fact that, whilst it had found several distinct infringements the Commission had relied on general statements regarding market position in the whole range of products without explaining why its reasoning on market power was relevant in *each specific case*. In spite of that, however, it seems to follow from the Court's judgment that evidence of market power is not a relevant element for the purpose of establishing which cartel participant is the ringleader.[725]

B. Critical role in the set-up or management of the cartel   Evidence pointing to a critical role **8.728** in the initiation of the collusive scheme will generally be decisive. In *Alloy Surcharge*, Usinor was found to have been the leader of the cartel as it had made calculations pertaining to the collusive scheme at the initial cartel meeting and had sent its operational conclusions together with the final collusive plan to the other producers.[726] In *British Sugar*, the Commission found that the undertaking had acted as the instigator and remained the driving force behind the cartel.[727] In *Amino Acids*, the Commission considered, among other factors, that ADM had acted as an instigator since it was the prime mover in ensuring that the other Asian producers agreed to cooperate in the framework of the global cartel. As for Ajinomoto, it was also found to have been a leader as, among other things, it had manned and organised the secretariat of the quantity monitoring system. In *Graphite Electrodes*, the Commission used as evidence of leadership the fact that both SGL and UCAR had initiated the earliest contacts, developed the collusive plan and organised the first 'Top Guy' meeting, at which they had adopted a 'common position' in respect of the other producers. In *Citric Acid*, the Commission stated that the efforts deployed by Hoffmann-La Roche to integrate the undertaking Cerestar Bioproducts in the cartel indicated its leadership role.[728] In *Specialty Graphite*, the Commission found that SGL had taken the initiative in launching the cartel and had continuously steered its development. Other interesting examples can also be found in *French Beef* [729] and *Raw Tobacco Spain*.[730]

C. Evidence of prominent decision-making power, such as conduct of price increases.   The **8.729** Commission also relies on evidence that undertakings took the main decisions within the cartel. In *Graphite Electrodes*, the Commission found that SGL and UCAR had taken the main decisions with regard to target prices and market allocation, and had had regular

---

[725] Interestingly, the CFI nonetheless indicated that evidence of market power 'could not be ruled out as factors in the assessment of the gravity of the infringement within the meaning of Section 1A of the Guidelines, as being evidence of the effective economic capacity of offenders to cause significant damage to other operators or of "the specific weight" of the individual offending conduct' (Case T-15/02 *BASF v Commission* [2006] ECR II-497, para 297).

[726] [1998] OJ L100/55, para 53.

[727] [1999] OJ L76/1. This conclusion was borne out in particular by the fact that the key meeting which launched the cartel had been convened at British Sugar's initiative (para 207).

[728] [2002] OJ L239/18. A representative of Hoffmann-La Roche had approached the General Manager of Cerestar Bioproducts and explained to him the basic mechanisms of the cartel (para 129).

[729] [2003] OJ L209/12. FNB, the federation of livestock farmers, was found to have been the leader in the infringement because of its significant role in the preparation and implementation of the infringement. The Commission considered that it was clear from the evidence available that the initiative for the restrictive measures came from the FNB, which was also especially emphatic in support of an oral agreement (para 175).

[730] The Commission considered Deltafina's leadership to be illustrated by the fact that it had persuaded the Spanish processors to coordinate their purchasing strategies and had acted as the repository and arbiter of the processors' anticompetitive agreements (paras 435–436).

contacts with the other cartel members. With regard to the EEA market, UCAR and SGL had agreed on new target prices for each national market, in respect of home markets and the maintenance of 'key account clients'. UCAR had itself admitted that it had generally led the price increases in France and the United Kingdom. For several other EEA markets it was decided on each occasion whether UCAR or SGL would take the lead.[731] In *Vitamins*, the Commission relied on the fact that Roche and BASF had taken the lead in the price increases by being the first to make the price announcement to the market. This finding was subsequently upheld by the CFI. The Court found that 'the fact that the price increases were decided jointly at meetings between the cartel members, including their amount, timing and the mechanism by which they would be implemented, does not remove the special responsibility assumed by a particular undertaking when it decided to be the first in fact to implement the agreed increase. By taking such an initiative, without being under a specific and individual obligation to do so pursuant to the agreement to increase prices entered into at a cartel meeting, the undertaking was voluntarily giving a major boost to the performance of that agreement by ensuring that, instead of remaining unimplemented, it had an effect on the market'.[732]

8.730 *D. Pressure on others to join the cartel*   Putting pressure on other undertakings to join the cartel may also be considered as evidence of leadership or of a role of instigator. In *Pre-Insulated Pipes*, the Commission found that ABB had put pressure on other undertakings to persuade them to enter the cartel. In *Greek Ferries*, the Commission found that Minoan had tried to persuade another company to join the cartel, and had organised and directed meetings with the companies involved in the infringement. The Commission pointed out that Minoan had not only monitored the cartel's operations but had also tried to extend the scope of the companies' collaboration.[733] In *Amino Acids*, the Commission considered the fact that ADM and Ajinomoto had envisaged economic sanctions against a Japanese undertaking and threatened it with an anti-dumping action in Europe to be evidence of their leadership in the cartel in question. Also decisive was the fact that following its entry into the market, ADM repeatedly used the threat of lowering the price of lysine to force other lysine producers to enter into agreements with it for the purpose of restricting competition on the lysine market. ADM was found to have intimidated the other producers with the possibility price wars and to have predicted that Sewon would be severely damaged not only in the overseas markets but also in the Korean market.

8.731 *Percentage increase and number of ringleaders*   In the first decisions taken under the 1998 Guidelines, an increase of 25 per cent in the fine imposed was applied to ringleaders (*Alloy Surcharge*, *Greek Ferries*). It should be noted however that these decisions concerned agreements classified only as 'serious'. In *Pre-Insulated Pipes*, a global increase of 50 per cent was applied to the fine imposed on ABB as a result of several aggravating circumstances. However, in the following decisions, the Commission took a firmer stance and generally applied a 50 per cent increase to the basic amount of the fine imposed on the ground of

---

[731] [2002] OJ L100/1, paras 160–164 and 189–192.
[732] Case T-15/02 *BASF v Commission* [2006] ECR II-497, para 348.
[733] [1999] OJ L109/24, para 159.

leadership alone. In the majority of such cases, the Commission had identified a single company as the leader or the instigator of the cartel. However, there were cases where the Commission identified two joint leaders and/or instigators in the infringement. However, that had not necessarily resulted in more moderate increases in the individual fines imposed. In certain decisions, the Commission distinguished between the roles played by each undertaking.[734] In other decisions, the Commission seems to have concluded that responsibility was shared evenly between two undertakings. This led to similar, smaller increases in their respective fines.[735]

4. Retaliatory measures against other undertakings with a view to enforcing practices **8.732** **which constitute an infringement**   Companies that have induced others to take part in cartels or have enforced illegal arrangements by using retaliation are also considered to bear a particular responsibility for damage caused to the economy, and proof of such conduct will be considered an aggravating circumstance by the Commission.

Forcing undertakings to take part in the infringement   In *French Beef*, the Commission **8.733** found that some of the members of three farmers' federations had used violence in order to compel the slaughterers' federations to accept the unlawful restrictive agreement. The Commission also found that they had used physical force to set up mechanisms to verify that the agreement was being applied, such as illegal 'inspections' to establish the place of origin of meat. The basic amount of the fines imposed on those three farmers' federations was consequently increased by 30 per cent.[736]

Retaliatory measures aimed at expelling a reluctant undertaking from the market   In *Pre-* **8.734** *Insulated Pipes*, the Commission found that ABB had employed a systematic orchestration of retaliatory measures against Powerpipe, aimed at its elimination from the market.[737] This was also found against Løgstør, because of its active role in the retaliatory measures against Powerpipe, although the Commission did not regard Løgstør's role as being on a par with ABB's in this respect.[738] Retaliatory measures included concerted dumping practices in Powerpipe's domestic markets, attempts to buy the company out, a systematic campaign of luring away its key employees and a boycott aimed at cutting off Powerpipe's supplies.[739]

---

[734] In *Pre-Insulated Pipe* [1999] OJ L24/1, ABB was clearly identified as the main instigator and leader of the cartel, but Henss/Isoplus was also considered a leader in view of its active role, although the increase in its fine was smaller. The same approach was followed in *Vitamins*, where Hoffmann-La Roche, the ringleader, had the basic amount of its fine increased by 50% whilst BASF received only a 35% increase in view of its less decisive role in the enforcement of the cartel.

[735] In *Citric Acid* [2003] OJ L239/18, the Commission increased the fines of Hoffmann-La Roche and ADM by 35% and indicated that this mild increase reflected the fact that whilst both these undertakings had had a prominent role in the infringement, other members of the cartel had also carried out activities usually associated with a leadership role, such as the chairing of meetings, or the centralisation of data collection and distribution. In *Belgian Beer (private label)* [2003] OJ L200/1, the Commission also found that both Interbrew and Alken-Maes had taken the initiative in the cartel. This justified an increase of only 30% of the basic amount of their respective fines.

[736] [2003] OJ L209/12, para 173.

[737] [1999] OJ L24/1, para 171.

[738] Para 176.

[739] Paras 90–107.

8.735 *Threats in order to expand the cartel arrangements*   In *Belgian Beer*, the Commission found that Danone had threatened to destroy Interbrew in the French market if a quota of beer of 500,000 hectolitres was not transferred to its subsidiary Alken-Maes. This led to an extension of the co-operation between Interbrew and Alken-Maes. The Commission concluded that Danone had compelled Interbrew to extend the scope of the illicit cooperation to a market sharing agreement by threatening to take measures against Interbrew if the latter did not co-operate. This was found to be an aggravating circumstance and, together with a finding of recidivism, justified the overall 50 per cent increase applied to Danone's basic fine.[740] However this finding was subsequently annulled by the CFI. The CFI did not deny the possibility of relying on the alleged facts as an aggravating circumstance but considered that the Commission had failed to establish a clear causal link between the extension of the scope of the infringement and the threat made by Danone.[741]

8.736   5. **Other aggravating circumstances**   Two other types of aggravating circumstances, not falling into one of the above categories, have also been taken into account by the Commission, as discussed in the following paragraphs.

8.737 *Continued infringement after the initiation of the investigation*   Continuation of an infringement after the initiation of an investigation had already been considered an aggravating circumstance before the implementation of the 1998 Guidelines.[742] In *Pre-Insulated Pipes*, the Commission found that four companies had deliberately continued a manifest infringement after the investigation into that infringement had been carried out by the Commission. This justified increasing the basic amount of their fine by 20 per cent,[743] a finding that was upheld by the CFI in *ABB v Commission*.[744] The same finding was made against five companies in *Graphite Electrodes*,[745] where the basic amounts were increased by 10 per cent. In *French Beef*, the Commission held that the fact that the six parties had continued their agreement in secret, in another form, even though they had received a letter of formal notice from the Commission, and had given an assurance that a written agreement to which the Commission had objected would not be extended was an aggravating circumstance. The basic amount of their respective fines was increased by 20 per cent.[746]

---

[740] [2003] OJ L200/1, paras 315–316.

[741] Case T-38/02 *Groupe Danone v Commission* [2005] ECR II-4407, paras 310–311.

[742] See eg *Belgian Wallpaper* [1974] OJ L237/3, section IV/3 (the situation in this case is, however, slightly different: the infringement had persisted despite the warning of a National court; *PVC II* [1994] OJ L239/14, para 51).

[743] OJ [1999] L24/1, para 179.

[744] Case T-31/99 *ABB Asea Brown Boveri v Commission* [2002] ECR II-1881. The CFI stated at para 213 that '[...] the fact that terminating an infringement after the Commission has first intervened may be regarded as a mitigating circumstance does not mean that continuing an infringement in such a situation cannot be regarded as an aggravating circumstance. An undertaking's reaction to the opening of an investigation into its activities can be assessed only by taking account of the particular context of the case. Since the Commission cannot therefore be required, as a general rule, either to regard a continuation of the infringement as an aggravating circumstance or to regard the termination of an infringement as a mitigating circumstance, the fact that it may classify such termination as a mitigating circumstance in one particular case cannot deprive it of its power to find that such continuation constitutes an aggravating circumstance in another case'.

[745] SGL, UCAR, Tokai, SEC and Nippon. See [2002] OJ L100/1.

[746] [2003] OJ L209/12, para 174.

In *Fittings*, the Commission increased by 60 per cent the basic amount of the fines imposed on several cartel participants because they continued the illegal arrangements after the inspections.[747]

Breach of a compliance programme   In *British Sugar*, the Commission adduced as an **8.738** aggravating circumstance the fact that the infringement by the undertaking in question constituted a breach of a compliance programme that had been introduced in the context of another prohibition decision and the introduction of which had then been considered as a mitigating circumstance.[748] However, the Commission now appears to take a neutral stance as regards compliance programmes. While it systematically refuses to consider their existence to be a mitigating circumstance (see para 8.774 below), it is generally understood that it would not consider their breach to be an aggravating factor.[749]

(ii) Mitigating Circumstances

1. Exclusively passive or 'follow-my-leader' role in the infringement   According to the **8.739** 1998 Guidelines, an 'exclusively passive or "follow my leader" role' in the infringement could constitute an attenuating circumstance. Companies thus frequently claimed that their participation in a cartel was merely passive and attempted to rely on mitigation in this respect. However, the Commission's practice under the 1998 Guidelines shows that, in contrast with its previous practice,[750] it has taken a very restrictive approach in that regard. Such arguments by cartel participants are therefore often rejected.[751]

Commission practice   In *Greek Ferries*, the Commission reduced the basic amount of the **8.740** fines of four undertakings by 15 per cent on the grounds that they had played an exclusively 'follow my leader' role in the infringement.[752] However, the Commission did not state the reasons for this finding and it is difficult from the account of the facts to deduce the criteria that were used. While there are other examples of decisions in which the Commission did not clearly explain the grounds on which this attenuating circumstance was found,[753] it has been more explicit in a number of decisions.

---

[747] See IP/06/1222.

[748] [1999] OJ L76/1, para 208.

[749] In the context of the 'modernisation' of the EC antitrust rules with the adoption of Regulation No 1/2003, and as it became solely the responsibility of the undertakings to evaluate the legality of their conduct under EC competition rules, the Commission gave certain assurances that evidence of warnings by internal company lawyers (who are not covered by the legal professional privilege) as to the illegality of a given conduct would not be considered an aggravating circumstance. According to the same logic, one should not punish an undertaking for its failure to successfully implement a compliance programme.

[750] See eg *Cartonboard* [1994] L243/1, para 171.

[751] See eg *French Beer* [2005] OJ L184/57, para 97.

[752] *Marlines, Adriatica, Anek* and *Ventouris*. See [1999] OJ L109/24, para 164.

[753] In *Industrial and Medical Gases* [2003] OJ L84/1, the Commission found that both BOC and Westfallen had not participated in all the different aspects of the infringement and had played an exclusively passive role in that infringement. The Commission concluded that such attenuating circumstances justified a decrease of 15% in the basic amount of the fine imposed on these two companies (paras 440–442). In *French Bee* [2003] OJ L209/12, the Commission stated that it had no evidence to show that FNPL, the federation representing milk producers, had played any special part in the conclusion or the application of the agreement at issue. It appeared on the contrary that the FNPL had played a passive or 'follow-my-leader' role in the agreement. The amount of the fine imposed on that federation was therefore reduced by 30% (para 178).

8.741   In *Amino Acids*, the Commission rejected most of the arguments made by the Korean company Sewon to the effect that it had been forced to participate in the cartel and had played an exclusively passive role. The Commission nevertheless considered that, at a certain stage, Sewon had changed its behaviour from that of an active to a passive member in the infringement.[754] In the light of these circumstances, the Commission reduced the increase in Sewon's fine on account of duration by 20 per cent.[755] In *Graphite Electrodes*, the Commission found that there were attenuating circumstances in respect of C/G's behaviour, since it had not attended any 'Top Guy' or 'Working Level' meetings and had taken the position of a mere 'price follower'.[756] In *Vitamins*, the Commission rejected most of the cartel participants' claims of passivity but nevertheless accepted that Rhône-Poulenc (now Aventis) had adopted such a position in the vitamin D3 market. This was deemed to justify decreasing by 50 per cent the basic amount of the fines imposed on Aventis for its infringement regarding the vitamin D3 market.[757] In *Specialty Graphite*, the Commission considered that the involvement of Intech in the Isostatic cartel was special insofar as it was to a considerable extent under instruction from Ibiden to implement by its participation in the European and local meetings, as Ibiden's distributor, the decisions of principle taken at a higher level, in which Ibiden, but not Intech, had been involved. The Commission concluded that those specific circumstances justified a reduction of 40 per cent in the basic amount of the fine imposed on Intech.[758]

8.742   *Court review*   On appeal in *Amino Acids*, the CFI stated that a 'passive role' within the meaning of the 1998 Guidelines 'implies that the undertaking will adopt a "low profile", that is to say not actively participate in the creation of any anti-competitive agreements'.[759] It then set out the circumstances that may indicate the adoption by an undertaking of a passive role within a cartel. Among those circumstances are the fact that the undertaking's participation in cartel meetings may be significantly more sporadic than that of the 'ordinary' members of the cartel,[760] the fact that it may have entered the market affected by the infringement late, regardless of the length of its involvement in the infringement,[761] or the fact that a representative of another undertaking which has participated in the infringement

---

[754] [2001] OJ Ll52/24. It did not enter into the agreement on quantities, and although it remained a participant in the agreement on the exchange of information, it ceased to inform the other producers about its sales quantities.

[755] Para 365. This practice, consisting of taking into account the passive role of an undertaking by reducing the percentage of increase retained on account of duration is surprising and has not been used since by the Commission. This approach was criticized by the CFI, which found that it constituted a breach of the principle of equal treatment (see Case T-220/00 *Cheil Jedang v Commission* [2003] ECR II-2473, paras 182–183 and 223–231).

[756] [2002] OJ L100/1, paras 234–235.

[757] [2003] OJ L6/1. The Commission found that Rhône-Poulenc's role had been limited to providing its historic volumes data to Solvay at the latter's request and that it had never attended any of the tripartite cartel meetings. A decisive element was also that Rhône-Poulenc had never been granted an independent market quota, as its allocation had always been included under Solvay's allocation (paras 724–725).

[758] Paras 516–516. Full text of the decision available on DG COMP's web site.

[759] Case T-220/00 *Cheil Jedang v Commission* [2003] ECR II-2473, para 167.

[760] See on this point Case T-311/94 *BPB de Eendracht v Commission* [1998] ECR II-1129, para 343.

[761] See on this point Joined Cases 240, 241, 242, 261, 262, 268 and 269/82 *Stichting Sigarettenindustrie v Commission* [1985] ECR 3831, para 100.

may have made an express declaration to such effect.[762] Those criteria were reiterated by the CFI in its subsequent judgment in *Tokai Carbon v Commission*.[763] However, it can be assumed that these criteria are not restrictive and that whether an undertaking has played merely a passive role can only be assessed on a case by case basis.

Overall, it it is rare for the Commission to consider an undertaking's passive role an **8.743** attenuating circumstance, since those who only (knowingly) followed the more active cartel members also ensured the (smooth) functioning of the cartel. Such passive players, were they to adopt a more independent commercial stance, could in fact cause a cartel to collapse.

2. Non-implementation in practice of the offending agreements or practices Before **8.744** the introduction of the 1998 Guidelines, the Commission reduced the fines imposed on particular undertakings on several occasions, on the grounds that cartel arrangements had not been fully implemented.[764] However, the Commission has since taken a much stricter stance and it is only exceptionally that this may be considered an attenuating circumstance.

Non-implementation not to be confused with lack of effect The inclusion of non- **8.745** implementation of cartel arrangements as an attenuating circumstance in the 1998 Guidelines refers only to the specific attitude of one (or more) undertaking(s) within the cartel, as opposed to the behaviour of the other members, and not to an alleged global lack of effect of the cartel arrangements. However, many undertakings have argued that the lack of effect of a cartel's arrangements in the market should be viewed as an attenuating circumstance. The CFI clarified this issue in *Cheil Jedang v Commission*, where, in response to the submission that such an attenuating circumstance should have been recognised in favour of the applicant, the Commission quite surprisingly submitted that 'non-implementation' referred to situations where a cartel remains unimplemented as a whole or is inoperative for a given period and not to the individual behaviour of members of an active cartel. The CFI made it clear however that under the 1998 Guidelines, attenuating circumstances are'[. . .] all particular to the individual conduct of each undertaking concerned'. The Commission was thus wrong to interpret the notion as referring only to cases where a cartel as a whole was not implemented and not to the individual conduct of each undertaking. The CFI stated that the Commission was in fact 'confusing its appraisal of the actual effect of an infringement on the market, which it must carry out in order to assess the gravity of the infringement [. . .] and in the context of which it must consider the effects arising from the infringement as a whole rather than the actual conduct of each undertaking, with its appraisal of the individual conduct of each undertaking, which it must carry out in order to assess any aggravating or mitigating circumstances [. . .]'.[765]

The need to demonstrate independent competitive behaviour Faced with numerous **8.746** claims by undertakings that they had not implemented the cartel arrangements, or had not

---

[762] See on this point Case T-317/94 *Weig v Commission* [1998] ECR II-1235, para 264.
[763] Joined Cases T-236/01, T-239/01, T-244/01 to T-246/01, T-251/01 and T-252/01 *Tokai Carbon and others v Commission* [2004] ECR II-1181, para 331.
[764] See *Italian Cast Glass* ([1980] OJ L39/51), *Italian Flat Glass I* (OJ 1981, L326/32).
[765] Case T-220/00 *Cheil Jedang v Commission* [2003] ECR II-2473, paras 188–189.

fully done so, the Commission adopted a restrictive interpretation of this attenuating circumstance, and, as a consequence, the argument is almost automatically rejected.[766] In that regard, the Commission relies in particular on *Cascades v Commission*, in which the CFI found that 'the fact that an undertaking which has been proved to have participated in a cartel did not behave on the market in the manner agreed with its competitors is not necessarily a matter which must be taken into account as a mitigating circumstance when determining the amount of the fine to be imposed. An undertaking which, despite colluding with its competitors, follows a more or less independent policy on the market may simply be trying to exploit the cartel for its own benefit'.[767] This principle was expressly confirmed by the CFI in *Specialty Graphite*.[768] Thus, in order to benefit from such mitigating circumstances, an undertaking must be able to show that that, during the period in which it was party to the infringing agreements, it avoided applying those agreements by adopting competitive conduct in the market.[769] In this respect, a mere difference in the degree to which an undertaking implemented the agreements cannot be regarded as a failure to implement them.[770] Also worth noting is the fact that the CFI has upheld the Commission's conclusion that non-implementation can only be adduced as an attenuating circumstance above a certain 'efficiency' threshold.[771]

8.747 *Commission practice* In *Pre-Insulated Pipes*, the Commission took account of the fact that the undertaking KWH did not comply with the boycott organised by the cartel against Powerpipe.[772] In *Graphite Electrodes*, C/G was granted the benefit of a mitigating circumstance as it only partially implemented the offending agreements. Over three years of the cartel duration, C/G actually increased its sales in Europe, thereby disregarding the basic principle of the cartel of restricting sales in 'non-home' markets. This accounted, together with the finding that G/C had played only a passive role, for a 40 per cent reduction of C/G's basic amount. In *Plasterboard*, the Commission granted the benefit of a mitigating circumstance to Gyproc on the grounds, first, that it may not have been in a position to prevent

---

766 See eg *Food Flavour Enhancers* [2004] OJ L75/1, paras 277–278.

767 Case T-308/94 *Cascades v Commission* [1998] ECR II-925. The CFI explicitly confirmed that 'the fact that [the applicant] did not charge the agreed price in full does not mean that there was a non-implementation "in practice" of the collusive agreements. An undertaking which, notwithstanding that it acts in concert with its competitors, follows a more or less independent policy on the market may merely be seeking to use the cartel for its own advantage' (para 230). See also Case T-220/00 *Cheil Jedang v Commission* [2003] ECR II-2473, para 150 and Case T-64/02 *Heubach v Commission* [2005] ECR II-5137, para 101.

768 Joined Cases T-71/03, T-74/03, T-87/03 and T-91/03 *Tokai Carbon and others* [2005] ECR II-10, para 297.

769 See, to that effect, Joined Cases T-25/95, T-26/95, T-30/95 to T-32/95, T-34/95 to T-39/95, T-42/95 to T-46/95, T-48/95, T-50/95 to T-65/95, T-68/95 to T-71/95, T-87/95, T-88/95, T-103/95 and T-104/95 *Cimenteries CBR and others v Commission* [2000] ECR II-491, paras 4872–4874 and Case T-220/00 *Cheil Jedang*, para 192.

770 Case T-220/00 *Cheil Jedang v Commission* [2003] ECR II-2473, para 199.

771 Joined Cases T-236/01, T-239/01, T-244/01 to T-246/01, T-251/01 and T-252/01 *Tokai Carbon and others v Commission* [2004] ECR II-1181, para 339. Tokai claimed that it had penetrated the German market, one of SGL's and UCAR's home markets, and quadrupled its EEA sales between 1992 and 1997. However, the CFI found that the Commission was entitled to conclude, that in spite of Tokai's non-implementation of the offending agreements, non-implementation had remained below a threshold of reasonable effectiveness for the purposes of the mitigating circumstance under consideration. The CFI did not, therefore, consider it appropriate to review that assessment, even in the exercise of its unlimited jurisdiction.

772 [1999] OJ L24/1, para 182. The Commission considered that this mitigating circumstance simply offset the aggravating circumstance that would otherwise have been imposed on KWH and therefore no reduction in the basic amount of the fine was granted.

sensitive information being transmitted to competitors, due to the presence of an active (physical) member of the cartel on the board of the company; and, second, that it had constantly been a destabilising element contributing to the limitation of the effect of the cartel in the German market, and that it was absent from the British market, where the cartel was most active. Those circumstances together objectively placed Gyproc in a different situation from the other members of the cartel and justified a reduction of its basic amount by 25 per cent.[773]

3. Termination of the infringement as soon as the Commission intervenes (in particular when it carries out inspections)

Rationale   The 1998 Guidelines indicated that the termination of the infringement as **8.748** soon as the Commission intervenes, in particular when it carries out inspection visits, could be considered as an attenuating circumstance. That provision aimed at rewarding the fact that an undertaking under investigation, notwithstanding the principle of presumption of innocence, took the initiative in putting an end to the incriminating practice before the Commission had actually found the conduct in question to be illegal.

No longer applicable in cartel cases   However, what seems justified in cases involving verti- **8.749** cal restrictions or under Article 82 EC (where the finding of an infringement is conditional upon the Commission being able to demonstrate, through complex economic evaluations—including a definition of the market concerned—that the conduct actually constitutes an infringement of competition rules) is more controversial in the case of cartels where the infringing nature of the behaviour is self-evident. In the case of the most blatantly illegal conduct the immediate cessation of the infringement is the least a cartel member can do once it has been caught 'red-handed'. This dilemma was highlighted in *Pre-Insulated Pipes*, in which the Commission considered that the continuation of the infringement after the investigation had begun constituted an aggravating circumstance. However, in early cartel decisions taken under the 1998 Guidelines, the Commission took the view that the termination of the agreement did justify a reduction of the fine imposed. In *FETTCSA*, the reduction of the fine could be deemed justified because the parties had ended the infringement upon receipt of a warning letter sent by DG Competition.[774] That was not the situation, however, in the case of blatantly illegal secret cartels such as *Amino Acids*[775] or *Belgian Beer*,[776] where the Commission nonetheless applied a reduction of the fines imposed on the same grounds.

---

[773] [2005] OJ L166/8, paras 570–575 (full text of the decision available on DG COMP's web site). It is worth noting that this is not a pure 'non-compliance' mitigating factor, but that the relevance is that these are factors purely specific to Gyproc.

[774] [2000] OJ L268/1, para 180. This justified a reduction of the basic amount of the fine on each of the parties by 20%.

[775] [2001] OJ Ll52/24, paras 381–384. This was all the more the case since the Commission recognised that it had carried out its first investigation at a time when the undertakings concerned had already ended the infringement. However, the Commission stated that although the termination of the infringement had been brought about by the intervention of another authority, such termination had been immediate and that this justified the application of the attenuating circumstance.

[776] [2003] OJ L200/1, paras 318–320. The Commission took into consideration the fact that Alken-Maes did terminate the exchange of information with Interbrew after the Commission's inspection on 26 and 27 October 1999. This circumstance was deemed to justify a reduction of the basic amount of the fine by 10% in the case of Alken-Maes/Danone.

8.750 Following such apparent contradictions in its decisions, the Commission has adapted its approach and stopped granting reductions in fines for the immediate termination of cartels. This change of practice was accepted by the CFI in *ABB v Commission*, where the court stated that 'the Commission cannot [. . .] be required, as a general rule, either to regard a continuation of the infringement as an aggravating circumstance or to regard the termination of an infringement as a mitigating circumstance [and that] the fact that it may classify such termination as a mitigating circumstance in one particular case cannot deprive it of its power to find that such continuation constitutes an aggravating circumstance in another case'.[777] The Commission has since routinely rejected claims that the immediate termination of a cartel agreement constitutes a mitigating circumstance, stating that the illegal nature of cartel behaviour is self-evident and that the Commission is entitled to expect that such conduct would cease immediately following inspections.[778] In its judgment in *Specialty Graphite*, the CFI supported the Commission's approach by stating that 'the Commission is under no obligation in the exercise of its discretion [. . .] to reduce a fine for the termination of a manifest infringement, whether that termination occurred before or after its investigation'.[779]

> **4. Existence of reasonable doubt on the part of the undertaking as to whether its restrictive conduct does indeed constitute an infringement**

8.751 *Applicable only in exceptional circumstances in cartel cases*   The mitigating circumstance resulting from the existence of doubt as to whether the restrictive conduct of the undertaking constitutes an infringement is not normally applicable in cartel cases for obvious reasons. However, in certain exceptional circumstances, the Commission may take account of the fact that some contextual factors raise doubts as to the illegal nature of the behaviour in question.[780]

8.752 *Doubt due to the attitude of public authorities*   In *Greek Ferries*, the Commission considered that the common practice (not directly imposed by the legal or regulatory framework) of fixing domestic fares in Greece through consultation with all domestic operators (whereby they were expected to submit a common proposal) and the ex-post confirmatory decision of the Ministry for the Merchant Navy could have created some doubt among Greek companies operating on domestic routes, as to whether the price fixing consultation for international routes constituted an infringement of EC competition law. This finding justified a reduction of 15% in the basic amount of the fine imposed on each undertaking.[781]

---

[777]   Case T-31/99 *ABB Asea Brown Boveri v Commission* [2002] ECR II-1881, para 213.

[778]   See eg *Plasterboard* (paras 568–569), *Specialty Graphite* (paras 502–503), *Industrial Tubes* (paras 378–380).

[779]   Joined Cases T-71/03, T-74/03, T-87/03 and T-91/03 *Tokai Carbon and others* [2005] ECR II-10, para 292.

[780]   In *Welded Steel Mesh*, before the implementation of the 1998 Guidelines, the Commission took into consideration the fact that the German Federal cartel office had authorised the formation by German welded mesh producers of a structural crisis cartel over a certain period of time. The Commission found that the existence of this authorised cartel had given parties in other Member States a motive for seeking to protect themselves, and that although that did not justify the illegal measures which were taken, it provided an element of mitigation. The Commission added, a contrario, that the establishment of the cartel to protect the German market against competition from other Member States by measures which are illegal under Community law could not be validated by the existence of a cartel authorization by the Federal cartel office.

[781]   [1999] OJ L109/24, para 163.

Doubt created by the legal context   In *Luxembourg Brewers*, the Commission stated that   **8.753**
the national case law relating to the question of the validity of certain beer ties may have created doubts over a certain period of time (including the time of the conclusion of the cartel agreement), as to whether the restrictions relating to the mutual observance of beer ties
constituted an infringement. The basic amount of the fines imposed was therefore reduced
by 20 per cent.[782] In *Raw Tobacco Spain* the Commission noted that the 'standard contracts'
negotiated between tobacco producers and processors stated that all the producer representatives would negotiate jointly with each individual processor regarding the price schedules
and the additional conditions relating to the sale of tobacco. The Ministry of Agriculture
either approved the price schedules jointly negotiated by the producers and the processor,
or convened meetings of the two parties, some of which were held at the Ministry itself,
with a view to agreeing the price schedules. The Commission concluded that the legal
framework surrounding the infringement engendered a considerable degree of uncertainty
as to the legality of the producers and processors' conduct. This justified the imposition of
a merely symbolic fine on the producers and was considered to be a mitigating circumstance in the case of the processors, justifying a reduction of 40 per cent in the basic amount
of their fines.[783]

Rejected arguments   In *French Beer*, Heineken submitted that there was reasonable doubt   **8.754**
on its part as to whether the agreement on a temporary freeze on acquisition of wholesalers
and the establishment of equilibrium between the respective distribution networks of the
two main players in the market constituted an infringement of EC competition law. This
argument was rejected by the Commission, which stated that the parties could not ignore
the fact that their 'armistice agreement' which was intended to limit investments, constituted an infringement of competition rules.[784] In *Belgian Beer*, Danone submitted that the
system of price control applied in Belgium up until the first few months of the infringement and the long established tradition of price regulation in the sector concerned had cast
doubt on the illegal nature of its conduct. The Commission rejected this argument, stating
that while the price control system obliged parties to request approval for a price increase
either individually or collectively through their trade association, it did not oblige them to
conclude agreements or consult about prices.[785] The Commission's decision in that regard
was upheld by the CFI.[786]

5. Infringements committed as a result of negligence or unintentionally   The fact that   **8.755**
an infringement has been committed either unintentionally or as a result of negligence can
be considered an attenuating factor for the purpose of setting the fine.[787] However, this will

---

[782] [2002] OJ L253/21, para 100.
[783] Paras 426–431 and 437–438 (full text of the decision available on DG COMP's web site).
[784] [2005] OJ L184/57, para 99 (full text of the decision available on DG COMP's web site).
[785] [2003] OJ L200/1, para 320.
[786] Case T-38/02 *Groupe Danone v Commission* [2005] ECR II-4407, paras 404–409.
[787] Intent warrants a higher fine than negligence: See Joined Cases C-89/85, C-104/85, C-114/85, C-116/85,
C-117/85 and C-125/85 to C-129/85 *A Ahlström Osakeyhtiö and others v Commission* (*Woodpulp*) [1993]
ECR I-1307, para 195.

not usually apply to cartels, where a deliberate effort to restrict competition is assumed, or at the very least the parties concerned could not have been unaware of the restrictive nature of their behaviour.

6. Effective co-operation by the undertaking in the proceedings, outside the scope of the Notice of 18 July 1996 on the non-imposition or reduction of fines in cartel cases

8.756 *Not normally applicable in cartel cases* This mitigating circumstance is not normally applicable to cartels since cooperation in such cases would usually take place within the context of the Leniency Notice. In *French Beer*, the Commission rejected the parties' claims that, since they had not filed an application for leniency, their cooperation should have been taken into account as a mitigating factor. The Commission stated that in the case of secret cartels, cooperation could only be assessed within the framework of an application under the Leniency Notice, as proceeding otherwise would undermine the objective of such programmes.[788]

8.757 *Anticipated application of point 23 of the 2002 Leniency Notice* In a number of decisions adopted after the entry into force of the 2002 Leniency Notice, however, the Commission, although bound by the 1996 Leniency Notice, made use of the mitigating circumstance of cooperation to apply by analogy the principle set out in the last section of point 23 of the 2002 Notice. According to point 23, an applicant that provides the Commission with evidence of facts previously unknown to it, which has a direct a bearing on the gravity or the duration of the infringement, should be immune to the corresponding increase in the fine. In *Organic Peroxides*, the Commission found that, without the voluntary submission of Atochem, it would probably have had to reduce the duration of the infringement found by a period of 22 years. Consequently, 'in line with a principle of fairness', the Commission declared that Atochem's cooperation outside of the 1996 Leniency Notice amounted to a specific circumstance which could be taken into account as a mitigating factor. This prevented Atochem from having to pay a higher fine than it would have paid without co-operation.[789] The same approach was subsequently followed in *Industrial Tubes*,[790] *Copper Plumbing Tubes* and *Choline Chloride*.[791]

8.758 *Reward for co-operation under the Guidelines on Fines after the revocation of conditional immunity from fines* In *Raw Tobacco Italy*, the company Deltafina had its conditional immunity from fines revoked on the grounds that it had failed to comply with its duty of full cooperation.[792] The Commission also refused to consider Deltafina's cooperation alternatively under section B of the 2002 Leniency Notice.[793] However, although the Commission

---

[788] [2005] OJ L184/57, para 100. (Full text of the decision available on DG COMP's web site.)

[789] [2005] OJ L110/44, paras 493–496. (Full text of the decision available on DG COMP's web site). This resulted in a considerable reduction of EUR 94.19 million.

[790] [2004] OJ L125/50, paras 384–387. (Full text of the decision available on DG COMP's web site.) Outokumpu benefited from a reduction EUR 22.22 million of its fine on these grounds.

[791] [2005] OJ L190/22, paras 218, 570–575. (Full text of the decision available on DG COMP's web site.) UCB benefited from a reduction of its fine of 25.8% on these grounds.

[792] See paras 8.147 and 8.170.

[793] See para 8.189.

stated that it is only in exceptional circumstances that a claim of co-operation under the Leniency Notice can be considered as an attenuating circumstance under the Guidelines, it nevertheless considered that this should be the case in *Raw Tobacco Italy*. The Commission stated that, in spite of its failure to comply with the conditions for immunity, Deltafina had substantially co-operated by providing information concerning elements which proved decisive in the finding of the infringement and had never substantially contested the facts which were the subject matter of the final decision. Deltafina was therefore granted a reduction of 50 per cent of the basic amount of its fine.[794]

Other circumstances   In *MCAA* the Commission found, on the sole basis of Akzo's volun-   **8.759**
tary submission under the 1996 Leniency notice, that certain of that company's subsidiaries had been independently involved in the cartel before they became part of the Akzo group and that as a consequence of the liability of those subsidiaries, the Akzo group faced a higher fine overall. In light of the specific circumstances of the case, and on the grounds of fairness, the Commission cancelled the additional fines that would have been borne by Akzo. The Commission stated in this regard that Akzo should not ultimately pay a higher fine than it would have done had it not co-operated.[795]

7. Other accepted attenuating circumstances   The following circumstances have also   **8.760**
been accepted by the Commission as mitigating factors when calculating the fine to be imposed.

Crisis in the sector concerned: progressively abandoned   In cartel cases prior to the imple-   **8.761**
mentation of the 1998 Guidelines, the Commission had frequently taken account of a crisis situation in the sector concerned as a mitigating factor when calculating the fine.[796] Although initially it took the same approach after the adoption of the Guidelines,[797] the Commission soon adopted a stricter stance with regard to the 'crisis' argument. That argument was rejected in *Pre-Insulated Pipes*, and even more emphatically in *Graphite Electrodes*, where the Commission refused to allow the undertakings concerned to rely on the alleged structural overcapacity in the sector, stating that in attempting to cope with difficult market conditions or falls in demand, undertakings must only use means that are consistent with the competition rules. The Commission stated that 'price-fixing and

---

[794] Paras 385–398. Full text of the decision available on DG COMP's web site.

[795] Para 318. Full text of the decision available on DG COMP's web site.

[796] See, for instance, *AROW/BNIC* [1982] OJ L379/1, *MELDOC* [1986] OJL 348/50, and *Cement* [1994] OJ L343/1.

[797] In *Alloy surcharge* [1998] OJ L100/55, the Commission recognised that the economic situation in the sector at the end of 1993 was particularly critical. The price of nickel was rising rapidly, whereas the price of stainless steel was very low. The Commission noted that although that particular situation applied only at the very beginning of the concerted action, was nonetheless justified a reduction of 10% in the basic amount for all the undertakings on the grounds of attenuating circumstances (para 84). In *Seamless Steel Tubes* [2003] OJ L140/1, the Commission took account of the fact that the steel pipe and tube industry had been in crisis for a long time and that the situation in the sector had deteriorated at the beginning of the infringement period, which, combined with the growing influx of imports, had resulted in capacity reductions and plant closures. These considerations warranted a reduction of 10% in the basic amounts on the grounds of attenuating circumstances (paras 168 and 169).

market-sharing are certainly not legitimate means of combating difficult market conditions. Nor are undertakings entitled to flout Community competition rules because of alleged overcapacity'.[798] Since then, similar arguments have been rejected in many other cartel decisions.[799] In *Lögstör Rör v Commission*[800] and *Tokai Carbon and others v Commission*,[801] the CFI confirmed that the Commission is not obliged to accept the poor economic state of the sector concerned as an attenuating circumstance.

8.762 *Pressure exerted by the intervention of public authorities* In *French Beef*, the Commission granted the benefit of an attenuating circumstance to each of the slaughterers' federations on the grounds of the forceful intervention of the French Minister for Agriculture in favour of the conclusion of the unlawful agreement, as had been reflected in his speeches in parliament and his press release on the day that the agreement was concluded. The Commission considered that his intervention had put strong pressure on the slaughterers to conclude an agreement—it having been established that, prior to the Minister's intervention, the slaughterers had refused to sign the agreement presented to them by the farmers. The slaughterers' federations consequently received a reduction of 30 per cent in the basic amount of their respective fines.[802]

8.763 *Compensation paid to prejudiced customers* Restitution to undertakings which have suffered as a result of the cartel may be taken into consideration by the Commission as a mitigating factor. In *Pre-Insulated Pipes*, the cartel instigator was granted a EUR 5 million reduction in its fine for the compensation it had already paid to Powerpipe, the company that had reported the infringement and which was subject to boycott by the cartel, and to Powerpipe's previous owner.[803] In *Nintendo* (which was not a cartel case), following its decision to collaborate and at the instigation of the Commission, Nintendo offered substantial financial compensation to third parties identified in the Statement of Objections as having suffered financial harm as a result of the infringement. Those offers were accepted by almost all of the companies concerned. In recognition of this fact, Nintendo was granted a reduction of its fine of EUR 300,000.[804]

8.764 *Undertakings playing a minor role or which are active in only a very limited part of the geographical market affected by the infringement* In *Pre-Insulated Pipes*, the fact that two undertakings had played a minor role and that their participation was confined to Austria

---

[798] [2002] OJ L100/1, paras 197 and 238.

[799] See for instance *Zinc Phosphate* [2003] OJ L153/1, *Belgian Beer* [2003] OJ L200/1, *Industrial Tubes* [2004] OJ L125/50 (full text of the decision available on DG COMP's web site), paras 370–374, *Copper Plumbing Tubes* [2006] OJ L192/21 (full text of the decision available on DG COMP's web site), *Choline Chloride* [2005] OJ L190/22 (full text of the decision available on DG COMP's web site).

[800] T-16/99 [2002] ECR II-1633, paras 319–320.

[801] Joined Cases T-236/01, T-239/01, T-244/01 to T-246/01, T-251/01 and T-252/01 [2004] ECR II-1181, para 345.

[802] [2003] OJ L209/12, para 176. It is worth noting that the Commission refused to grant the benefit of the same circumstance to the farmers' federation, because it considered that the Minister's intervention in that instance was the result of several weeks of demonstrations by farmers who were members of the farmers' federations involved, aimed at securing the slaughterers' signature to an agreement (176).

[803] [1999] OJ L24/1, para 172.

[804] [2003] OJ L255/33, para 440.

and Italy, two relatively small markets for district heating, was taken into consideration as a mitigating factor in favour of those undertakings. Their respective fines were reduced by two thirds on those grounds.[805] A similar approach was followed in *Industrial Thread*, in which the Commission found that certain cartel members had joined the anticompetitive discussions relating to certain geographical areas (the Nordic countries) only in the last two years, justifying a reduction of the basic amount of their fine by 15 per cent.[806] In *Raw Tobacco Italy*, the Commission found that similar arguments justified a reduction of the fines.[807]

8. Rejected arguments The following arguments have been put forward by undertak‑ **8.765** ings as mitigating factors but have been rejected by the Commission.

No benefit from the cartel The argument that an undertaking did not benefit from **8.766** the infringement has been systematically rejected under the 1998 Guidelines. In *Amino Acids*, the Commission rejected an undertaking's claim that it suffered substantial losses for most of the years during which it took part in the cartel.[808] In *Citric Acid*, the Commission stated that it did not consider that 'in general, either failure to benefit from a cartel or any economic disadvantage suffered due to participation in a cartel' constituted an attenu‑ ating circumstance for the purpose of fixing the fine.[809] The same line was taken in *Zinc Phosphate*,[810] *Industrial Tubes*[811] and in many other cases. The validity of this approach is confirmed by settled case law, according to which the fact that an undertaking has derived no profit from the infringement cannot prevent it from being fined, since otherwise the fine would lose its deterrent effect.[812] It follows that, for the purpose of fixing the amount of a fine, the Commission is not required to establish that the infringement in question secured an improper advantage for the undertaking concerned, nor to take into consideration, where applicable, the fact that no profit was derived from the infringement in question.[813]

Positive contribution to the European economy In *Amino Acids*, two undertakings stated **8.767** that they had contributed significantly to the development of the European agricultural industry, creating employment in Europe and generating revenues. In *Vitamins*, one undertaking claimed that the goal of its participation in the cartel was not the realization of profits, since it manufactured the product at a loss, but the maintenance of its industrial infrastructure at its plant at a city in Germany. The Commission rejected the arguments in

---

[805] [1999] OJ L24/1, para 182.
[806] Paras 371–372.
[807] Full text of the decision available on DG COMP's web site.
[808] [2003] OJ L255/1, paras 395–396.
[809] [2002] OJ L239/18, paras 286–287.
[810] [2003] OJ L150/1, para 329.
[811] [2004] OJ L125/50 (full text of the decision available on DG COMP's web site), paras 365–369.
[812] Case C‑219/95 P *Ferriere Nord v Commission* [1997] ECR I‑4411, paras 46–47. Order of the Court of 28 October 2004 in Case C‑236/03 P *Commission v CMA CGM and Others* (not published), para 340; Case T‑229/94 *Deutsche Bahn* [1997] ECR II‑1689, para 217; Case T‑241/01 *Scandinavian Airline System v Commission* [2005] ECR II‑29117, para 146.
[813] *Cement* [1994] OJ L343/1, para 4881.

both cases, stating that neither failure to benefit from a cartel nor any economic disadvantage suffered due to participation in a cartel would constitute an attenuating circumstance in the fixing of the fine, and that the commercial benefits of industrial and commercial activity could not be used to offset the negative effects of the infringement of competition rules.[814]

8.768 *Defensive measures against 'distortions of competition'*   An alleged need to take private defensive measures against economic threats has also been rejected. In *Citric Acid*, an undertaking submitted that the cartel agreements in question were a defensive measure against cheap imports from China which were 'causing serious distortions of competition'.[815] It added that the Chinese producers had received State assistance for their exports and that those products had been offered for sale in Europe below cost price. The Commission dismissed the argument by stating that it is 'certainly not for the main players of a given market segment to take concerted private actions regarding the price they charge to their customers in order to compensate, in any manner whatsoever, for "dumping strategies" employed by undertakings from third countries'.[816]

8.769 *Customers not opposing the illegal practice*   The argument that customers were in favour of the cartel arrangements is also rejected. In *Alloy Surcharge*, some of the undertakings concerned had claimed that a number of customers were in favour of the contested surcharge. The Commission replied that the fact that customers may accept a practice which is contrary to competition rules does not make such practice lawful and that it was precisely owing to complaints from certain other customers that the Commission had undertaken its investigations. It added that it had obtained evidence of the difficulties that the producers had encountered with their customers introducing the surcharge.[817]

8.770 *First time violation of EC competition law*   The fact that an undertaking has violated EC competition rules for the first time cannot be treated as an attenuating circumstance. This was confirmed by the CFI in *Enichem Anic v Commission*.[818] In *Specialty Graphite*, the Commission pointed out that recidivism is an aggravating circumstance and that 'the absence of an aggravating circumstance does not amount to an attenuating circumstance'.[819]

8.771 *Cessation of the infringement before the Commission intervened*   The Commission will reject a claim that cessation of the infringement prior to the Commission's intervention should constitute an attenuating circumstance. The Commission's general argument in

---

[814] *Amino Acids* [2003] OJ L255/1, paras 393–394; *Vitamins* [2003] OJ L6/1, paras 733–734.

[815] [2002] OJ L239/18, para 290.

[816] [2002] OJ L239/18, para 291.

[817] [1998] OJ L100/55, para 57.

[818] Case T-6/89 *Enichem Anic v Commission* [1991] ECR II-867, para 295: 'the fact that the Commission has in the past already found an undertaking guilty of infringing the competition rules and penalized it for that infringement may be treated as an aggravating factor as against that undertaking but that the absence of any previous infringement is a normal circumstance which the Commission does not have to take into account as a mitigating factor, especially since the present case involves a particularly clear infringement of Article 8[1](1) of the EEC Treaty'.

[819] *Specialty Graphite*, decision of 17 December 2002 (full text of the decision available on DG COMP's web site) paras 512–513.

that regard is that cartel members ought to be aware of the illegal nature of their practices and that the fact that a company terminates such illegal behaviour before any intervention by the Commission does not merit any particular reward, other than the resulting shorter period of infringement being taken into account in the calculation of the fine. This line of reasoning has been followed in many cases, such as *Vitamins*,[820] *Specialty Graphite*,[821] *Organic Peroxides*[822] and *Choline Chloride*,[823] and has been upheld by the CFI.[824]

Coercion or pressure exercised by the ringleader   The argument that pressure has been   **8.772** brought to bear on an undertaking by the ringleader or another undertaking has also been systematically rejected by the Commission.[825] The Commission's approach in this regard has been upheld by the CFI, which has stated that an undertaking which participates with others in anti-competitive behaviour cannot rely on the fact that it did so under pressure from the other participants. The undertaking could have complained to the competent authorities about the pressure being brought to bear on it and lodged a complaint with the Commission, rather than participating in the activities in question.[826]

Gradual drift to illegality   Arguments that the cartel evolved from initial discussions of law-   **8.773** ful matters, and that the infringement resulted from a gradual drift in behaviour, have also been rejected. In *Zinc Phosphate*, a cartel member submitted that the hazardous nature of the product in question obliged the producers to comply with numerous laws, which led to frequent legitimate contacts between competitors and that in this context the step towards unlawful contacts was easily made. The Commission dismissed this argument, stating that a duty to comply with the relevant legislation can in no way relieve companies operating in the same market from their obligation to respect competition rules.[827] In *Industrial Tubes*, a cartel member argued that collusion had been initiated and had intensified gradually over the years alongside the lawful activities of the trade association, and that the transition from legal discussions to anti-competitive behaviour was blurred. The Commission rejected this argument, pointing out that the cartel members had been aware of the illegal nature of their activities, as evidenced by the efforts made to conceal their discussions.[828]

Compliance programmes and disciplinary measures   The Commission has maintained a   **8.774** consistently neutral position regarding (the introduction of) compliance programmes, in

---

[820] [2003] OJ L6/1, paras 730–732. The Commission stated that an attenuating circumstance could be adduced if a direct link could be established between the intervention of the Commission and the end of the infringement but not in cases where the infringement had ceased before the intervention. However, that line of reasoning has been abandoned and no finding of an attenuating circumstance should now be expected from a mere cessation of the infringement, before or after the Commission's intervention.

[821] Decision of 17 December 2002 (the full decision available on DG COMP's web site), paras 502–503.

[822] [2005] OJ L110/44 (full text of the decision available on DG COMP's web site), paras 482–485.

[823] [2005] OJ L190/22 (full text of the decision available on DG COMP's web site), para 210.

[824] Joined Cases T-236/01, T-239/01, T-244/01 to T-246/01, T-251/01 and T-252/01 *Tokai Carbon and others v Commission* [2004] ECR II-1181, para 341.

[825] See for instance *Pre-Insulated Pipes* [1999] OJ L24/1, *Copper Plumbing Tubes* [2006] OJ L192/21 (full text of the decision available on DG COMP's web site), para 756.

[826] Cases T-9/89 *Hüls v Commission* [1992] ECR II-499, para 128; Case T-141/89 *Tréfileurope v Commission* [1995] ECR II-791, para 58; Case T-23/99 *LR AF 1998 v Commission* [2002] ECR II-1705, paras 142 and 339.

[827] [2003] OJ L153/1, paras 333–334.

[828] [2004] OJ L125/50 (full text of the decision available on DG COMP's web site), paras 376–377.

spite of the ambiguity of some early decisions. The Commission had originally considered the introduction of a compliance programme as a potential mitigating factor for the purpose of setting fines,[829] but that position was soon abandoned. In *Hercules Chemicals v Commission*, the CFI stated that although it was indeed important that the applicant had taken measures to prevent future infringements of Community competition law by its personnel, that did not alter the fact of the infringement found in the present case.[830] Such arguments have been systematically rejected since the adoption of the 1998 Guidelines. In *Pre-Insulated Pipes*, ABB attempted to rely on the 'strengthening' of its existing compliance programme as a mitigating factor. This was rejected by the Commission, which found that in any case the stated policy had not been applied or had been flouted by the most senior management.[831] In *Graphite Electrodes*, the Commission again rejected such an argument, stating that although it welcomed the fact that following the cartel investigations the undertaking concerned had conducted an internal investigation and had set up a compliance programme, that initiative could not relieve the Commission of its duty to sanction a very serious infringement of competition rules.[832] The argument was also rejected in many other cases,[833] and this approach has been upheld by the CFI. In *LRAF 1998 v Commission*, the Court specified that although the implementation of a compliance programme demonstrates an intention to prevent future infringements and therefore constitutes a factor which better enables the Commission to accomplish its task, the mere fact that the Commission has taken the implementation of a compliance programme into consideration as a mitigating factor in certain of its previous decisions does not mean that it is obliged to act in a similar manner in another case.[834] In addition, arguments to the effect that internal sanctions have been taken against the employees involved in the cartel have consistently been rejected. Such was the case in *Graphite Electrodes*,[835] *Pre-Insulated Pipes*[836] and *Choline Chloride*.[837]

---

829 See eg *National Panasonic* (not a cartel case) [1982] OJ L354/28, paras 67–68, where the Commission substantially reduced the fine because the firm in question had introduced an effective compliance system following the Commission investigation

830 Case T-7/89 *Hercules Chemicals v Commission* [1991] ECR II-1711, para 357.

831 [1999] OJ L24/1, para 172.

832 [2002] OJ L100/1, para 194.

833 See, for instance, *Citric Acid* [2002] OJ L239/18, paras 288–289; *Zinc Phosphate* [2003] OJ L153/1, paras 331–332; *Food Flavour Enhancers* [2004] OJ L75/1, para 279; *Industrial Tubes* [2004] OJ L125/50 (full text of the decision available on DG COMP's web site), paras 381–383, or *Choline Chloride* [2005] OJ L190/22 (full text of the decision available on DG COMP's web site), para 217.

834 This was confirmed in Joined Cases T-236/01, T-239/01, T-244/01 to T-246/01, T-251/01 and T-252/01 *Tokai Carbon and others v Commission* [2004] ECR II-1181 (para 345).

835 [2002] OJ L100/1, para 193.

836 [1999] OJ L24/1, para 172(3). ABB claimed that it should have been given credit for having 'relieved from their duty' the senior managers principally responsible for the infringement. The removal of those company officers was supposedly intended to prevent any recurrence of the infringement and to send a strong message to all personnel. Rejecting the argument, the Commission stated in particular that 'the deterrent effect of such message on ABB personnel must have been diluted by the selective nature of the 'disciplinary measures' taken: the most senior of those involved escaped all sanctions entirely and only one relatively middle-ranking executive left the group. The Commission also took note of the announcement by ABB that the chairman of Adtranz (who played a leading role in the cartel while executive-vice president of ABB) was leaving the group, but the Commission said that this departure, which was decided on the eve of the Commission's decision and had not been presented as a sanction, could not alter its decision.

837 [2005] OJ L190/22 (full text of the decision available on DG COMP's web site), para 217.

Poor financial situation of the company   Claims that the poor financial situation of an   **8.775**
undertaking should be considered a mitigating circumstance have consistently been
rejected by the Commission. The Commission's stance in that regard has been upheld by
the CFI, which has held that the Commission is not required, when determining the
amount of the fine, to take into account the poor financial situation of an undertaking,
since recognition of such an obligation would be tantamount to giving an unjustified competitive advantage to those undertakings least well adapted to market conditions[838] Inability
to pay may nevertheless be taken into consideration by the Commission when applying the
Guidelines (see paras 8.790 to 8.792 below).

Other arguments   The Commission has also refused to consider the following arguments   **8.776**
as attenuating circumstances: the fact that the agreement related to only one element of the
final price;[839] the fact that the applicant is a medium-sized family company;[840] the smaller size
of the market or of the undertaking at the beginning of the infringement;[841] the fact that a cartel member was established in a non-member country over a period of the duration of the
infringement;[842] the oligopolistic structure of the market;[843] legitimate expectations with
regard to the Commission's failure to object to the illegal conduct;[844] market transparency
provoked by a specific regulatory context.[845]

---

[838] Case 96/82 *IAZ and others v Commission* [1983] ECR 3369, paras 54 and 55; Case T-319/94 *Fiskeby Board v Commission* [1998] ECR II-1331, paras 75 and 76, Case T-348/94 *Enso Española v Commission* [1998] ECR II-1875, para 316; Case T-23/99 *LR AF 1998 v Commission* [2002] ECR II-1705, para 338.

[839] Case T-48/98 *Acerinox v Commission* [2001] ECR II-3859, para 114.

[840] *Zinc Phosphate* [2003] OJ L153/1 (paras 342, 343). See also Case T-23/99 *LR AF 1998 v Commission* [2002] ECR II-1705, para 338.

[841] *Organic Peroxides* [2005] OJ L110/44 (full text of the decision available on DG COMP's web site), para 488.

[842] ibid, para 489.

[843] See, for example, *Alloy Surcharge* [1998] OJ L100/55. The CFI upheld such a rejection in Case T-48/98 *Acerinox v Commission* [2001] ECR II-3859, and stated that, on the contrary, the fact that the undertakings participating in the infringement accounted for almost 90% of the sales of the product considerably exacer-bated the restriction of competition on the market resulting from the concerted increase in the price of the product (para 105).

[844] In *Alloy Surcharge* [1998] OJ L100/55, several undertakings attempted to rely upon the principle of legit-imate expectation and claimed that the Commission could have deduced from the price lists sent to it under Art 60 that a single method of calculation had existed. The fact that it did not initiate proceedings under Art 65 created a legitimate expectation on the part of the firms that the use of a common method was lawful (para 60). The Commission dismissed that argument, pointing out that the undertakings had simply notified the Commission of the amounts of the alloy surcharges they were applying, in the different currencies. Neither the calculation method itself nor the data on its implementation had ever been sent to the Commission (para 61).

[845] In *Alloy Surcharge* [1998] OJ L100/55, several undertakings invoked the principle of market trans-parency laid down in Art 60 of the ECSC Treaty. They stated that the price control system known as the 'bas-ing point system' provided specifically for an element of concerted action, that the transparency requirements of Art 60 of the Treaty required the suppliers to provide general information on their intended prices and that the harmonisation of the alloy surcharge resulted from the ECSC system of price controls. The Commission replied that it was true that Art 60 of the Treaty stipulated that 'the price lists and conditions of sale applied by undertakings within the common market must be made public', but that the prices or decisions to add a sur-charge to a price list and the fixing of its amount was a matter for each individual firm and conditions had to be adopted independently by each firm. They could not in any event be communicated to the parties con-cerned before the Commission was informed. The obligation to make the prices public did not justify hold-ing a meeting having the object or effect of either influencing the conduct on the market of an actual or potential competitor or of disclosing to such a competitor the course of conduct which they themselves have decided to adopt or contemplate adopting on the market.

(e) Calculating the Statutory Maximum of 10 Per Cent of Annual Group Turnover

8.777 **Upper limit set by Article 23(2)**   Article 23(2) of Regulation 1/2003 provides that '[f]or each undertaking and association of undertakings participating in the infringement, the fine shall not exceed 10% of the total turnover in the preceding business year'. That provision appears to be a simplified version of Article 15(2) of Regulation 17, which provided that the Commission could impose on undertakings or associations of undertakings 'fines from 1,000 to 1,000,000 [euros], or a sum in excess thereof but not exceeding 10% of the turnover in the preceding business year of each of the undertakings participating in the infringement'.⁸⁴⁶ Point 5(a) of the 1998 Guidelines noted that the final amount calculated under the methodology set out could not in any case exceed that limit.

8.778 **10 per cent of the total turnover**   The total turnover referred to in Article 23(2) is the global (worldwide) annual turnover of the undertaking that is the addressee of the Decision in question. Undertakings have often claimed that the 10 per cent upper limit should be applicable to the turnover of the product covered by the cartel agreement, but the CFI has confirmed that this applies to the entire turnover of the undertaking.⁸⁴⁷ The level within the corporate group at which the Commission attributes liability for the infringement is therefore of great significance. (See section D(3) of this chapter.)

8.779 **Preceding business year**   Article 23(2) establishes that the turnover with reference to which the upper limit must be calculated is that relating to 'the preceding business year'. Point 5(a) of the 1998 Guidelines stated that 'the accounting year on the basis of which the turnover is determined must, as far as possible, be the one preceding the year in which the decision is taken or, if figures are not available for that accounting year, the one immediately

---

⁸⁴⁶ This simplification in wording is welcome. The wording of Art 15(2) could probably be explained by the fact that at the time when Regulation 17 was drafted, a range of fines from one thousand to one million Euros was perceived as likely to encompass most possible fines, and that the 10% ceiling was perceived rather as a 'safeguard' in the exceptional cases where the level of the fine would exceed one million. However, with the passing of time (inflation) and as the level of fines increased, the maximum amount of one million euros was regularly exceeded and the upper limit of 10% of total turnover in the preceding business year became the sole point of reference.

The wording of Art 15(2) did raise problems of interpretation, however. Indeed, a literal reading could lead to the conclusion, on the one hand, that as long as the Commission did not impose a fine exceeding one million euros, it was not bound by the 10% upper limit and, on the other hand, that in the absence of any significant turnover in the preceding business year, the Commission could under no circumstance impose a fine above one million euros. In *Greek Ferries*, one of the addressees of the decision, Karageorgis, had ceased its activities and closed all its subsidiaries in Greece years before its adoption and the Commission lacked information as to the turnover of the company during the 'preceding business year'. Referring to the wording of Art 19(2) of Regulation 4056/86 (the equivalent of Art 15(2) of Regulation 17 for maritime transport), the Commission used the first branch of the alternative and imposed a fine of one million euros on Karageorgis in the absence of any available data on its turnover. In *Zinc Phosphate* however, the Commission took a different approach. Faced with the fact that one undertaking, Britannia Alloys, was to be held liable for a period of the infringement but had ceased all commercial activities some time beforehand (whilst still being legally constituted), the Commission chose, for the purpose of calculating the upper limit applicable to the fine, to take into account Britannia's global turnover for the business year ending *four years earlier*, which was deemed to be the 'last available figure reflecting an entire year of normal economic activity' (see n 196 of the decision). This approach was upheld by the CFI on appeal (see Case T-33/02 *Britannia Alloys & Chemicals v Commission*, [2005] ECR II-4973, currently under appeal).

⁸⁴⁷ Joined cases 100 to 103/80 *Musique Diffusion française and others v Commission* [1983] ECR 1825, para 119; Case T-43/92 *Dunlop Slazenger v Commission* [1994] ECR II-441, para 160, and Case T-220/00 *Cheil Jedang v Commission* [2003] ECR II-2473, para 60.

preceding it'. In order to calculate the applicable upper limit, the Commission has normally taken the turnover of the last available complete accountancy year into account. To that end, it sends requests for information to the undertakings concerned shortly before the adoption of the final decision.

In certain instances, the Commission has not been able to rely on any significant turnover **8.780** in the preceding business year, even though the undertaking concerned continued to exist in law during that time. In such cases, the Commission has taken a number of different approaches. In *Greek Ferries*, one of the addressees of the decision had ceased its activities and had closed all its subsidiaries in Greece a number of years previously, and the Commission lacked information as to the company's turnover during the year preceding that of the adoption of the decision. Referring to the wording of Article 19(2) of Regulation 4056/86 (the equivalent of Article 15(2) of Regulation 17 for maritime transport), the Commission relied on the alternative set out in that Article (ie a fine in the range EUR 1,000 to EUR 1 million) and imposed a fine of EUR 1 million on Karageorgis in the absence of any available data on its turnover. In *Zinc phosphate* however, the Commission took a different line. Since the company, Britannia Alloys & Chemicals ('Britannia'), was to be held liable for a given period of the infringement but had ceased all commercial activities a couple of years earlier (although it still existed in law), the Commission chose, for the purpose of calculating the upper limit applicable to the fine imposed on Britannia, to take account of its global turnover for the business year ending four years earlier, which was deemed to be the 'last available figure reflecting an entire year of normal economic activity'.[848] This line of reasoning was subsequently upheld by the CFI.[849] In *Electrical and Mechanical Carbon and Graphite products* for one of the undertakings, the Commission took into account for the last complete business year before the one in which it fell into bankruptcy.[850]

Joint and several liability within the same undertaking   When several legal entities **8.781** which form part of the same economic group (insofar as they do not behave in an autonomous way in the market) are held jointly and severally liable for an infringement and for the payment of the corresponding fine, the 10 per cent upper limit is calculated with reference to the consolidated turnover of the group that those legal entities form.[851] The underlying rationale is that although they have distinct legal personalities, the companies concerned are one and the same undertaking for the purpose of the application of the EC competition rules.[852]

The 10 per cent cap is calculated before leniency   Any reduction in the fine made to con- **8.782** form with the applicable upper limit is made before the calculation of any reduction under

---

[848] [2003] OJ L153/1. See n 196 of the decision.

[849] Case T-33/02 *Britannia Alloys & Chemicals v Commission* [2005] ECR II-4973. The judgment of the CFI has been appealed by Britannia. See case C-76/06 *Britannia Alloys & Chemicals v Commission* (case pending).

[850] Para 317.

[851] See eg *Electrical and Mechanical Carbon and Graphite Products* [2004] OJ L125/45 (full text of the decision available on DG COMP's web site), para 318 and *MCAA* (full text of the decision available on DG COMP's web site).

[852] On this question, see section D(3) of this chapter.

the Leniency Notice.[853] This is intended to preserve the effectiveness of the leniency programme. If such calculation were to be made at the final stages of the calculation of the total fine, it would be possible that an undertaking might be subject to a fine which was still equal to the maximum admissible amount in spite of it having been substantially reduced. This would remove any incentive for an undertaking to come forward to co-operate, since the undertaking concerned would find itself in no better position than if it had not co-operated.

8.783 **The 10 per cent cap applies only to the final amount (before leniency)** It has been clarified by case law that while the 10 per cent cap applies to the final amount of the fine before the application of the Leniency Notice, that capping does not apply to the intermediary stages of the calculation of the fine, which may well involve an amount exceeding that threshold. The ECJ has confirmed on appeal that the legislative framework (now Article 23(2) of Regulation 1/2003) only requires that *the fine ultimately imposed* be reduced if it exceeds 10 per cent of turnover, independent of the intermediate stages in the calculation intended to take the gravity and the duration of the infringement into account.[854]

(f) Application of the Leniency Notice

8.784 Reductions in fines resulting from the application of the Leniency Notice, as referred to in point 4 of the Guidelines, are dealt with in section C(2) of this chapter.

(g) 'Other factors' to be Taken into Account

8.785 Once the fine was calculated in accordance with the standard methodology set out in the 1998 Guidelines, the Commission could still take into account specific circumstances which in its view justifed a further adjustment in the amount of the fine. Certain circumstances were specifically detailed in point 5(b) of the Guidelines. However, that list was not exhaustive, and, on occasion, the Commission took other circumstances into account.

(i) 'Objective Factors' as set out in point 5(b) of the Guidelines

8.786 The 1998 Guidelines provided in point 5(b) that 'depending on the circumstances, account should be taken [...] of certain objective factors such as a specific economic context, any economic or financial benefit derived by the offenders,[855] the specific characteristics of the undertakings in question and their real ability to pay in a specific social context, and the fines should be adjusted accordingly'. That provision, which was far from being explicit as to the criteria used by the Commission to evaluate the applicability of so-called 'objective factors', was rarely used.

8.787 1. **Specific economic context** A crisis in the economic sector in which the cartel was based was not considered to be a 'specific economic context' which would justify a reduction of the fine under point 5(b). The Commission repeatedly stated that the poor economic

---

[853] See eg *Pre-Insulated Pipes* [1999] OJ L24/1, para 176; *Graphite Electrodes* [2002] OJ L100/1, para 199; *Citric Acid* [2002] OJ L239/18, paras 292–293; *Organic Peroxides* [2005] OJ L110/44 (full text of the decision available on DG COMP's web site), paras 498–500.

[854] Case C-189/02 P *Dansk Rørindustri and others v Commission* [2005] ECR I-5425.

[855] Reference is made to the 21st Report on Competition Policy, point 139.

or financial situation of a given sector could not mitigate the size of the fines to be imposed on cartel participants, and that is also applicable under point 5(b).[856] However, the conjunction of specific, exceptional factors relating to the economic context in which the cartel arose could be considered.

So far, the sole example of application by the Commission of the notion of 'specific context' **8.788** under point 5(b) is *French Beef*. In that case two separate grounds were considered to justify the Commission's approach. First, the Commission stated that this decision was the first 'to penalise an agreement concluded entirely between federations and which relates to a basic agricultural product and involves two links in the production chain'.[857] Secondly, and more importantly, the Commission took note of a conjunction of elements. First, beef consumption had been falling considerably for some ten years, as the result of two successive 'mad cow crises' and, consequently, the infringement in question took place at a time when the sector was already weakened. Second, far-reaching Community measures had already been taken, including authorisation for France to grant aid to the farmers most seriously affected, based on a finding of the existence of 'exceptional occurrences' within the meaning of Article 87(2)(b) of the Treaty.[858] Third, at the time the cartel agreement was concluded, the prices farmers were receiving for cattle had fallen again, despite the Community adjustment measures, reaching levels that were even lower than when the second 'mad cow' crisis was at its worst, although the final consumer prices had remained stable. The Commission concluded that this specific context, created in particular by a loss of consumer confidence linked to the fear of Creutzfeld-Jakob disease, went beyond a straightforward collapse in prices or the presence of a well-known disease. On these grounds, the fines were reduced by 60 per cent.[859] On appeal, and in the exercise of its unlimited jurisdiction, the CFI found that the very exceptional circumstances of the case justified a reduction in the fines of 70 per cent rather than 60 per cent.[860]

2. Economic or financial benefit derived by the offenders   To date, the Commission has **8.789** not used its power to consider the economic or financial benefit derived by the offenders when calculating fines. One may assume that this would have been applicable in cases where evidence of the gain resulting from the infringement was found to be particularly obvious.

3. Ability to pay in a specific social context
'Inability to pay' claims are systematically rejected.   As the financial penalties on cartels **8.790** have risen greatly, it has become common for an undertaking to claim that it is unable to pay the prospective fine because of its financial situation. That situation first arose in

---

[856] See for instance *Amino Acids* [2001] OJ L152/24, paras 436–438.

[857] It is not clear from the wording of the Decision (para 181) whether this was considered as part of the 'specific economic context' or whether this constituted another, distinct specific circumstance taken into account under point 5(b). It is considered here that this was analysed as part of the 'specific economic context'.

[858] The authorising decisions emphasised in particular that the 'crisis' that the beef sector was facing was not merely a short-term fall in prices or the presence of a well-known disease.

[859] [2003] OJ L209/12, paras 180–185.

[860] See Joined cases T-217/03 and T-245/03 *FNCBV and others c Commission*, not yet reported, paras 357–361.

Graphite Electrodes, where three undertakings claimed that they would not be able to pay the fine. Several factors were put forward, including the poor economic situation of the sector, the high level of fines already paid in other jurisdictions and the civil damages paid to injured customers. The Commission asked the undertakings concerned to provide detailed information as to their exact financial situation, but subsequently rejected the argument. Referring to settled case law,[861] the Commission stated that taking account of the mere fact of an undertaking's loss-making financial situation due to general market conditions or changes in the company's corporate structure would be tantamount to conferring an unjustified competitive advantage on these undertakings least well adapted to the conditions of the market. The Commission also added that there was no justification for off-setting fines imposed by other competition authorities or civil damage payments.[862]

8.791 Since then many other undertakings have claimed that they are unable to pay the fine imposed, but the Commission has always rejected such claims on the same grounds.[863] In *Specialty Graphites*, the Commission rejected such an argument in spite of its acknowledgement that the two companies considered were, on the basis of the financial data they had provided, 'undergoing serious financial constraints'.[864] This strict stance, however, is consistent with settled case law, according to which taking account of a loss-making situation would have the effect of conferring an unfair competitive advantage on the undertakings least well adapted to the conditions of the market.[865] Nevertheless, it would seem that in its recent decisions, the Commission has tended to carry out an ever more in-depth analysis of the financial situation of those undertakings claiming inability to pay. In *Industrial Tubes*, the Commission reviewed in great detail the financial figures submitted by the undertakings before rejecting their argument.[866] However, such efforts are not based in recent case law. Indeed the CFI has recently clarified the judicial approach to this issue. In its judgments in *Graphite Electrodes* and *Specialty Graphites*, the CFI recalled that 'the fact that a measure taken by a Community authority leads to the insolvency or liquidation of a given undertaking is not prohibited as such by Community law' and added that 'although the liquidation of an undertaking in its existing legal form may adversely affect the financial

---

861 Joined Cases 96/82 to 102/82, 104/82, 105/82, 108/82 and 110/82 *IAZ and others v Commission* [1983] ECR 3369, paras 54 and 55, Case T-319/94 *Fiskeby Board v Commission* [1998] ECR II-1331, paras 75 and 76, and Case T-348/94 *Enso Española v Commission* [1998] ECR II-1875, para 316.

862 [2002] OJ L100/1, paras 185 and 206–207.

863 See, eg, *Zinc Phosphate* [2003] OJ L153/1 (paras 367–369), *Carbonless Paper* [2004] OJ L115/1 (paras 459–460); *Fine Arts Auction Houses* [2005] OJ L200/92 (Full text of the decision available on DG COMP's web site), paras 234–237; *Specialty Graphites*, decision of 17 December 2002 (full text of the decision available on DG COMP's web site), paras 554–555, *Electrical and Mechanical Carbon and Graphite Products* [2004] OJ L125/45 (full text of the decision available on DG COMP's web site), paras 340–357; *Industrial Tubes* [2004] OJ L125/50 (full text of the decision available on DG COMP's web site), paras 426–431.

864 Decision of 17 December 2002 (full text of the decision available on DG COMP's web site), para 555.

865 Cases *LR AF 1998 v Commission* [2002] ECR II-1705, para 308; Case T-99/09 *HFB and Others v Commission* [2002] ECR II-1487, para 596. See also Joined Cases T-71/03, T-74/03, T-87/03 and T-91/03 *Tokai Carbon v Commission* [2005] ECR II-10 (full text of the judgment available on ECJ's web site).

866 [2004] OJ L125/50 (full text of the decision available on DG COMP's web site). See in particular paras 429–430.

interests of the owners, investors or shareholders, it does not mean that the personal, tangible and intangible elements represented by the undertaking would also lose their value'.[867]

Critical importance of the 'specific social context'? One possible explanation for the systematic rejection of claims of inability to pay the fine is that the Commission took the view that such inability to pay should only be taken into account in the case of a 'specific social context', as laid down by the Guidelines. Although the meaning of that term has not been clarified, it can be presumed to be linked to the potential social consequences of the bankruptcy of an undertaking as a result of fines imposed, such as significant numbers of redundancies in a disadvantaged region. In *Electrical and Mechanical Carbon and Graphite Products* and *Copper Plumbing Tubes*, the Commission stated that the undertakings which had submitted such arguments had not demonstrated that their alleged inability to pay should be considered within a specific social context.[868] The Commission pointed out that the previous redundancies detailed by the undertakings concerned might well have occurred as part of a company's normal efforts at achieving greater efficiencies. The CFI referred to the concept of 'specific social context' as set out in the 1998 Guidelines in *Tokai Carbon and others. v Commission*, and appeared to endorse the principle that such a context could lead to a reduction in the fine to be imposed. The Court proceeded to identify the applicable criteria, stating that the consideration of an undertaking's ability to pay in a specific social context would consist of evaluating the 'consequences which payment of the fine would have, in particular, by leading to an increase in unemployment or deterioration in the economic sectors upstream and downstream of the undertaking concerned'.[869] The CFI found that in the case under consideration the applicants had adduced no evidence capable of determining such a specific social context.

8.792

(ii) Other Factors that may be Taken into Account

In addition to the 'objective' factors considered under point 5(b) of the Guidelines, the Commission has in certain cases accepted other exceptional circumstances as a basis for reducing the amount of the fine. To date such circumstances have been, on the one hand, a combination of the previous imposition of fines and the poor financial situation of the undertaking and, on the other hand, the excessive length of the administrative procedure.

8.793

Poor financial situation and previous payment of fines in other proceedings In *Speciality Graphites*, the Commission rejected the company SGL's claim that it would be unable to pay the fine, whilst acknowledging that that company did have serious financial constraints. The Commission noted, however, that SGL had already been fined EUR 80.2 million one and a half years before, as a result of its involvement in the *Graphite Electrodes* cartel. The Commission stated that it followed that SGL was *both* in a serious adverse situation and

8.794

---

[867] Joined Cases T-236/01, T-239/01, T-244/01 to T-246/01, T-251/01 and T-252/01 *Tokai Carbon and others v Commission* [2004] ECR II-1181, para 372, referring, to that effect, to Cases 52/84 *Commission v Belgium* [1986] ECR 89, para 14, and C-499/99 *Commission v Spain* [2002] ECR I-6031, para 38). This has been reaffirmed in the judgment in Joined Cases T-71/03, T-74/03, T-87/03 and T-91/03 *Tokai Carbon v Commission* [2005] ECR II-10, at para 333.

[868] [2004] OJ L125/45 (full text of the decision available on DG COMP's web site), paras 350 and 357.

[869] Joined Cases T-236/01, T-239/01, T-244/01 to T-246/01, T-251/01 and T-252/01 *Tokai Carbon and others v Commission* [2004] ECR II-1181, para 371.

had relatively recently received a significant fine from the Commission. In these particular circumstances, it did not appear necessary to impose the full amount of the fine in order to ensure sufficient deterrence. The Commission added that that conclusion took account, in particular, of the fact that the aggravating circumstance of recidivism did not apply to SGL, since the infringements in question had been committed concurrently.[870] The fine imposed on SGL was thus reduced by 33 per cent.

8.795 A similar situation arose in *Electrical and Mechanical Carbon and Graphite Products* involving two undertakings including, once again, SGL. Inspired no doubt by the decision in *Speciality Graphites*, SGL suggested that in light of the two fines previously imposed on it, there was no need for further deterrence and that it should receive no fine. That argument was rejected by the Commission, which stated that each separate infringement merits a separate fine. Otherwise, an undertaking involved in one or more cartels would have nothing to lose by entering into further cartels. It could then derive unjustified profits from additional cartels without any risk of a fine for that behaviour. Imposing a fine for each separate infringement serves to deter such behaviour.[871] However, in the case of SGL, the Commission again took account of the combination of the serious financial difficulties faced by the undertaking, and the two fines that had been previously imposed in *Graphite Electrodes* and *Specialty Graphite*. Again, the fine imposed on SGL was reduced by 33 per cent.

8.796 It appears from the wording used that the Commission was determined to confine this rather lenient approach to cases where an undertaking that has previously been fined was placed in a seriously adverse financial situation. Thus, in *Electrical and Mechanical Carbon and Graphite Products*, the Commission refused to reduce the fine imposed on Le Carbone Lorraine ('LCL'), even though that undertaking had claimed inability to pay and had previously been fined in *Specialty Products*. The Commission stated that the fine previously imposed on the undertaking in question represented a much smaller amount of its total turnover than was the case for SGL and that the financial situation of SGL was much worse than that of LCL.[872]

8.797 *Excessive duration of administrative procedure*   Excessive duration of the administrative procedure or other irregularities in the Commission's investigation may justify reductions in fines. In *FETTCSA*,[873] the Commission took account of the time elapsed between the sending of the Statement of Objections, which caused the termination of the infringement, and the adoption of the final decision. Since the Commission was not time barred from imposing fines, it saw no reason not to do so, but that the Commission was also bound by the general principle of Community law that decisions following administrative

---

[870] [2002] OJ L100/1, paras 556–558.

[871] [2004] OJ L125/45 (full text of the decision available on DG COMP's web site), para 359. See also *Industrial Tubes*, [2004] OJ L125/50 (full text of the decision available on DG COMP's web site), paras 343–346. The validity of this approach was confirmed in Joined Cases T-236/01, T-239/01, T-244/01 to T-246/01, T-251/01 and T-252/01 *Tokai Carbon and others v Commission* [2004] ECR II-1181.

[872] See paras 358–363. A similar line was followed in *Copper Plumbing Tubes* [2006] OJ L192/21 (full text of the decision available on DG COMP's web site), where the Commission refused on similar grounds to take into account the fines imposed on KME in the previous *Industrial Tubes* decision. See paras 715–718.

[873] [2000] OJ L268/1.

proceedings relating to competition policy must be adopted within a reasonable time.[874] Whilst stating that it did not believe that the lapse of time had affected the outcome or the rights of the defence of the parties, the Commission nonetheless acknowledged that the duration of the administrative proceedings had been considerable and reduced the basic amount of the fine imposed on each of the parties by EUR 100,000.[875] In *FEG/TU*, the Commission also referred to settled case law according to which the Commission is required to act within a reasonable time when adopting decisions following administrative proceedings relating to competition policy. The Commission acknowledged that the duration of the proceedings in question had been considerable and that the reason for this could partly be attributed to the Commission itself. The Commission therefore acknowledged its responsibility and reduced the amount of the fines imposed.[876]

(iii) Other Factors Rejected

Ne bis in idem *(in an international context)*   In the context of the investigation of world-   **8.798** wide cartels, many undertakings have submitted (possibly as an alleged attenuating circumstance) that the Commission should take into account, and deduct from any fine, the penalties already imposed in third country jurisdictions in respect of the same facts. This would allegedly be justified, on the one hand, by the principle *ne bis in idem* and, on the other hand, by the fact that such previously imposed penalties had had a sufficient deterrent effect. In this regard, certain undertakings argued in particular that they had had to pay considerable civil damages in the context of subsequent class actions and that there was thus no further need for deterrence.[877] The Commission has always strongly rejected such arguments, stating that the exercise by third countries of their jurisdiction in respect of cartels can in no way limit or exclude the Commission's jurisdiction under Community competition law.[878]

In its judgments in *Amino Acids*, *Graphite Electrodes* and *Specialty Graphite*, the CFI con-   **8.799** firmed that, when setting fines, the Commission is under no obligation to take into account penalties imposed by other jurisdictions. In *ADM v Commission*, the CFI confirmed that the principle of *ne bis in idem*, enshrined also in Article 4 of Protocol No 7 to the ECHR, is a general principle of Community law upheld by the European Courts. However, it reiterated that this principle could not be applied to procedures and penalties imposed by different authorities who were clearly pursuing different ends, i.e. the protection of competition

---

[874]   The Commission referred to joined Cases T-213/95 and T-18/96 *SCK* and *FNK v Commission* [1997] ECR II-1739, para 56; Joined Cases T-305/94 etc. *LVM and others v Commission* [1999] ECR II-931, para 121. Concerning the duration of proceedings before the CFI, see Case C-185/95 P *Baustahlgewebe v Commission* [1998] ECR I-8417, paras 47 and 141, in which the ECJ reduced by ECU 50,000 the applicant's fine of ECU 3 million to compensate for the excessive duration of proceedings before the CFI.

[875]   [2000] OJ L268/1, paras 192–196.

[876]   [2000] OJ L39/1, para 145.

[877]   The Commission has repeatedly stated that by virtue of the principle of territoriality, third countries only exercise jurisdiction to the extent that the conduct has a direct and intended effect on their territory. Furthermore, it has held that the possibility that undertakings may have been required to pay damages in civil actions does not have any bearing on the fines to be imposed for infringing Community competition rules. Payment of damages in civil law actions which have the objective of recouping the damage caused by cartels to individual companies or consumers cannot be compared with public law penalties for illegal conduct. See eg *Vitamins* [2003] OJ L6/1, paras 769–774; *Citric Acid* [2002] OJ L239/18, paras 327–335, *Specialty Graphite*, decision of 17 December 2002 (full text of the decision available on DG COMP's web site), paras 545–522.

[878]   See eg *Citric Acid* [2002] OJ L239/18, paras 332–335.

in their respective territories.[879] This was set out particularly clearly in the context of *Speciality Graphite*, where the CFI stated that 'it is settled case law that where the facts on which two offences are based arise out of the same set of arrangements but they nevertheless differ as regards both their object and their geographical scope, the principle of *ne bis in idem* does not apply [...]'.[880] The argument that sufficient deterrence had already been attained through the imposition of the previous penalties was also rejected.[881] That stance had already been confirmed in the context of *Gaphite Electrodes*.[882]

(h) Critical Assessment of the 1998 Guidelines

8.800 Given the wide margin of discretion enjoyed by the Commission in the setting of fines, the publication of the 1998 Guidelines was clearly a forward step in terms of transparency and legal security. However, in spite of the Commission's efforts to make its practice more objective, the methodology set out in the Guidelines and the Commission's ensuing practice was subject to criticism on the part of the business and legal community.[883]

8.801 **Fixing the starting amount: an arbitrariness exercise?** One of the main points of criticism was that while, at first sight, the 1998 Guidelines presented an appearance of increased objectivity, they provided the Commission with excessive discretion as regards the setting of the starting amount, the most critical step in the calculation of the fine. Although the classification into categories of gravity indicating a specific range of 'likely fines' was based on three objective criteria, the Commission in effect possessed a significant margin of discretion when setting the starting amount. The factors taken into account to set reference points at a given level within each range were not indicated. The perceived risk of arbitrariness was particularly strong as regards very serious infringements like cartels, where at that stage of the procedure the Commission did not have to respect any upper limit, the sole limitation being the global upper limit of 10 per cent of the undertaking's total turnover applicable to the final amount of the fine. As a result of the uncertainty characterising the earliest stage of the calculation, all efforts deployed to develop a rigorous and objective approach to differential treatment and to take account of further relevant factors were bound to be considered insufficient.

---

[879] Case T-224/00 *Archer Daniels Midland Company and Archer Daniels Midland Ingredients v Commission* [2003] ECR II 2597, paras 85–104.

[880] Joined Cases T-71/03, T-74/03, T-87/03 and T-91/03 *Tokai Carbon and others* [2005] ECR II-10, para 112. The CFI also clarified that the so-called 'comity agreement' between the EU and the US (regarding the application of positive comity principle in the enforcement of their competition laws) does not entail the application of the principle *ne bis in idem* in relations between them. The CFI stated in particular that 'it is clear from [...] that agreement that the legal interests protected by the Community authorities and the US authorities are not the same and that the purpose of the agreement is not the principle ne bis in idem but solely to enable the authorities of one of the contracting parties to take advantage of the practical effects of a procedure initiated by the authorities of the other' (para 116).

[881] ibid, paras 105–112.

[882] Joined Cases T-236/01, T-239/01, T-244/01 to T-246/01, T-251/01 and T-252/01 *Tokai Carbon and others v Commission* [2004] ECR II-1181, paras 130–148.

[883] See eg articles cited in n 548. Certain weaknesses of the 1998 Guidelines were also discussed by Commission officials. See eg F Arbault 'La politique de la Commission en matière d'amendes: bilan et perspectives', Competition Policy Newsletter, Summer 2003. The article is based on a speech by then Deputy Director General of DG Competition G Rocca before the Institut d'Études Européennes de l'Université Libre de Bruxelles, on 4 February 2003. See also M Debroux 'L' "imprésibilité transparente": La politique de sanction de la Commission en matière de cartels, Concurrences (2006).

A breach of the principle of equal treatment?   Another criticism was that the lack of a   **8.802**
connection between the starting amount and the value of the relevant market resulted, in
the context of an increase in fines, in a breach of the principle of proportionality, as well as
a violation of the principle of non-discrimination. This was because SMEs tended to be
more heavily sanctioned than large companies for similar infringements, in proportion to
their overall turnover. That was all the more true, it was argued, in the case of relatively
undiversified or 'monoproduct' companies whose sales of the product concerned are close
to their overall turnover. It can be observed in this respect that the alleged discrimination
may lie in the insufficient level of the fines imposed on large multinational companies. That
is not, however, a satisfactory response to the objection. Yet it may also be argued that the
application of deterrence multiplying factors to large companies tends to place small and
large companies on a more equal footing. However, deterrence factors have generally
remained relatively low in relation to the overall size of the companies considered. In his
opinion in *Pre-Insulated Pipes*, Advocate General Tizzano pinpointed the risk of discrimination against small companies resulting from the 1998 Guidelines, although that did not
lead him to question the legality of those Guidelines.[884] Competition Commissioner
Neellie Kroes had in the meantime stated that the rigidity of the Guidelines could be questioned and that 'the [. . .] system of fixed minima according to the gravity of the infringement appear[ed] to hit small and medium sized enterprises harder than larger businesses'.
She added that the 1998 Guidelines could be improved in that respect.[885]

The 'deterrence' issue   The use of the concept of 'sufficient deterrence' has also been sub-   **8.803**
ject to debate. First, the recourse to deterrence multiplying factors and the methods used
to determine their level were sometimes criticised as being too arbitrary. Again, the
Commission's approach was perceived as reintroducing an element of considerable uncertainty to a supposedly more objective approach. Multiplying factors could potentially
result in a doubling (or more) of the starting amount, thereby having a considerable impact
on the final amount of the fine and making any prediction of its size highly uncertain.
Second, it was pointed out that the application of a deterrence factor, when appropriate,
came at an early, intermediary step of the calculation of the fine, ahead of various subsequent adjustments. This arguably undermined the relevance of the Commission's
approach, since the concept of 'sufficient deterrence' would seem to be more applicable to

---

[884] Although Advocate General Tizzano proposed that the Court should dismiss the applications, he indicated that certain issues raised (discrimination and proportionality) were not totally devoid of relevance and
that although 'a system of adjusting fines by reference to a lump sum [did] not appear to be entirely alien to
the logic of Regulation No 17' (point 123), the tightening of the policy on fines 'deriving as it does from a calculation method based on flat-rate amounts, [was] liable for the most part to hit small and medium-sized
undertakings' (point 131). Interestingly, the Advocate General mentioned that the Dutch Competition
authority, when it adopted its Guidelines on fines, chose to depart voluntarily from the Commission's
methodology, stating that 'a disadvantage of a system of fixed fines is that small undertakings are affected
relatively more harshly than larger undertakings' and that its policy with regard to fines 'must be applicable
both to (very) large undertakings and to small and medium-sized undertakings, without losing the intended
preventive effect, on the one hand, and generating disproportionate results, on the other' (n 59 of Avocate
General Tizzano's opinion in that case).
[885] Neelie Kroes, 'The First Hundred Days', Speech at the 40th Anniversary of the Studienvereinigung
Kartellrecht 1965–2005, International Forum on Competition Law, Brussels, 7 April 2005.

the final stages of calculation of a fine and the possible need ultimately to increase the fine on such grounds, once all other relevant factors have been taken into consideration. Third, the relevance of deterrence multiplying factors were questioned insofar as such factors had always been used in support of an increase of the fine and never as a reason to reduce it.[886]

8.804 **The refusal to deal with inability to pay** Another important question related to the attitude that the Commission should adopt regarding undertakings that claim that they are unable to pay a fine, a situation that was becoming more frequent as fines continued to increase. In line with the strict approach adopted by the European Courts, the Commission had so far taken a rather inflexible approach and refused to reduce the fine to be imposed on an undertaking on the grounds of its poor financial situation.[887] However, whether such a strict approach was completely satisfactory is debatable. Indeed, in many cases, the liquidation of a competitor may result in a further concentration of the market, with the ensuing risks for competition. On the other hand, as stated in settled case law, reducing the fine on the basis of financial difficulties would clearly confer on a company an unfair competitive advantage, all the more since, in view of the cyclical nature of business, recovery may be very quick, resulting in the possibility of a cartel member returning to high profits just a few years after having had its fine reduced. In that context, one could wonder whether the solution would not lie in an approach combining flexible payment facilities with new monitoring techniques enabling the Commission to maintain the viability of the companies whilst making sure that the appropriate fine is paid once it is made possible by financial recovery.

8.805 **Duration: an appropriate role in the determination of the fine?** Another criticism that could be made of the 1998 Guidelines was that duration, although it played a more significant role in determining the amount of the fine than it had previously, still accounted for only a minor proportion of the final amount of the fine. Whilst the damage caused by a cartel can be deemed to be roughly the same each year, the increase in the starting amount remained limited to 10 per cent each year, thereby seriously underestimating the impact of the duration of a cartel on the overall damage caused to the economy. A significant increase in the role played by duration in calculating the final amount of the fine could therefore be justified from a 'deterrence' standpoint.

8.806 **Conclusion** In light of the criticism of the 1998 Guidelines, and based upon the experience and insights gained from their application in 70 decisions involving fines (45 of which concerned cartel decisions) and from over 35 Court judgments dealing with the 1998 Guidelines,[888] the Commission decided to revise its Guidelines on fines.

---

[886] With regard to the potential risk of discrimination raised by the application of the 'fixed sum' principle to small undertakings, one may wonder whether the solution could not have lied in the application of 'negative' deterrence factors when it appears that a sufficient level of deterrence would be achieved with a level of fine below that resulting from the calculation as set out in the Guidelines.

[887] As stated above in paras 8.790–8.791, the CFI has indeed found that a fine leading to the insolvency or liquidation of a given undertaking is not prohibited as such by Community law, since it does not mean that the personal, tangible and intangible elements represented by the undertaking would also lose their value.

[888] On 1 July 2005.

(3) The 2006 Guidelines

(a) Main Features of the 2006 Guidelines

Two complementary objectives   New Guidelines on the method of setting fines were **8.808** adopted by the Commission on 28 June 2006 and published on 2 September 2006.[889] The objective pursued is twofold. First, the new method of calculating fines intends to reflect more accurately the economic significance of the infringement committed and the specific share of responsibility of the undertaking concerned. Secondly, the 2006 Guidelines seek to ensure greater deterrence than was previously achieved.

Three main changes   The method of calculation set out in the 2006 Guidelines seems at first **8.809** sight quite similar to that of the 1998 Guidelines in that a 'basic amount' is first set, which is increased or decreased in accordance with aggravating or attenuating circumstances as the case may be, and subsequently subject to further adjustment. However, the method of calculation is in fact radically different from that of the previous Guidelines. First, the *basic amount* is now to be set as a *percentage of the sales of the products to which the infringement relates*, in the geographical area concerned, normally during the last full year of participation in the infringement. The 'flat rate' approach is therefore abandoned. Secondly, the *duration* of the infringement is now to be taken into account by *multiplying the figure based on the relevant sales by the number of years* during which the undertaking participated in that infringement. This will give considerably more weight to the impact of the duration of the infringement on the level of the sanction imposed. Thirdly, in order to increase deterrence, the Commission is to systematically apply a so-called '*entry fee*' in cartel cases by virtue of which any participation in a cartel infringement will cost the undertaking 25 per cent of its annual sales in the relevant sector.

Nine successive steps in the calculation   The methodology set out in the 2006 Guidelines **8.810** consists of nine distinct steps. First, the 'value of the sales' relevant to the determination of the fine is to be calculated. Second, a percentage applicable to the value of the relevant sales, of up to 30 per cent, is to be set. Third, the figure thus obtained is to be multiplied by the number of years during which the undertaking participated in the infringement. Fourth, the 'entry-fee' set at between 15 to 25 per cent of the value of sales as described in the first step is to be added. This will result in the 'basic amount'.

Fifth, the Commission will adjust the basic amount in relation to aggravating or attenuat- **8.811** ing circumstances, as applicable. Sixth, it will further increase the fine, if it deems it necessary, to ensure the appropriate deterrent effect. Seventh, the Commission will check whether the statutory limit set out in Article 23(2) of Regulation No 1/2003 is respected. Eighth, where relevant, the Commission will reduce the fine by virtue of the applicable Leniency notice. Finally, the Commission will consider whether there is a need to reduce the fine in regard to the undertaking's inability to pay in a specific social context.

(b) Detailed Overview of the Method of Setting Fines under the 2006 Guidelines

(i) The Basic Amount of the Fine

The basic amount of the fine will be calculated in relation to a proportion of the value of **8.812** the sales, depending on the degree of gravity of the infringement, multiplied by the number

---

[889] Guidelines on the method of setting fines imposed pursuant to Art 23(2)(a) of Regulation No 1/2003 [2006] OJ C210/2.

of years of infringement (point 19 of the 2006 Guidelines). The Commission has indicated that the assessment of gravity will be made on a case-by-case basis for all types of infringements, taking into account all the relevant circumstances of the case (point 20). Cartels, as one of the most serious infringement of EC competition law, can be expected to be placed at the higher end of the scale of gravity.

8.813 **Calculation of the value of the sales**   In determining the basic amount of the fine to be imposed, the Commission will take the value of the undertaking's sales of goods or services to which the infringement *directly* or *indirectly*[890] relates in the relevant geographic area within the EEA (point 13 of the 2006 Guidelines). It will normally take the sales made by the undertaking during the last full business year of its participation in the infringement ('value of sales').[891] Where the infringement by an association of undertakings relates to the activities of its members, the value of sales will generally correspond to the sum of the value of sales by its members (point 14).

8.814 In determining the value of sales by an undertaking, the Commission will take that undertaking's best available figures. Where the figures made available by an undertaking are incomplete or not reliable the Commission will determine the value of its sales on the basis of the partial figures it has obtained and/or any other information which it regards as relevant and appropriate. The value of sales will be determined before VAT and other taxes directly related to the sales (points 15–17).

8.815 Where the geographic scope of the cartel extends beyond the EEA (for example in the case of worldwide cartels), the relevant sales of the undertakings within the EEA may not properly reflect the weight of each undertaking in the infringement, in particular in the case of market-sharing arrangements.[892] In such circumstances, in order to reflect both the aggregate size of the relevant sales within the EEA and the relative weight of each undertaking in the infringement, the Commission 'may assess the total value of the sales of goods or services to which the infringement relates in the relevant geographic area (wider than the EEA), may determine the share of the sales of each undertaking party to the infringement on that market and may apply this share to the aggregate sales within the EEA of the undertakings concerned. The result will be taken as the value of sales for the purpose of setting the basic amount of the fine' (point 18).

8.816 **Gravity: determination of the percentage applicable to the value of the sales**   The determination of the gravity of the infringement remains a key aspect of the 2006 Guidelines, although it is no longer expressed in terms of categories of gravity as was the case in the 1998 Guidelines, but as a 'gravity percentage' applicable to the value of the sales. The Commission has indicated that 'as a general rule, the proportion of the value of sales taken

---

[890]   The Commission indicates that the notion of 'indirect relation' will be used in the case, for instance, of horizontal price-fixing arrangements on a given product, where the price of that product then serves as a basis for the price of lower or higher quality products.

[891]   The Commission has indicated that where the value of sales by undertakings participating in the infringement is similar but not identical, it reserves the right to set an identical basic amount for the undertakings concerned. Moreover, the Commission has indicated that it will use rounded figures in determining the basic amount of the fine.

[892]   On this aspect, see paras 8.670–8.671 above.

into account will be set at a level of up to 30% of the value of sales' (point 21). In order to decide whether the proportion of the value of sales to be considered in a given case should be at the lower end or at the higher end of that scale, 'the Commission will have regard to a number of factors, such as the *nature* of the infringement, the *combined market share of all the undertakings* concerned, the *geographic scope* of the infringement and whether or not the infringement has been *implemented*' (point 22, emphasis added).

The criteria used for the purpose of determining the level of gravity of the infringement are no   **8.817**
longer limitative, as they had been under the 1998 Guidelines where only three criteria were considered (gravity by nature, actual impact if measurable, geographical scope of the infringement). However, the analysis conducted by the Commission in this regard can be expected to remain quite similar. Indeed, two of the criteria set out in the 2006 Guidelines for the purpose of determining gravity remain identical to those of the 1998 Guidelines, namely the *nature* of the infringement and its *geographical scope* (for a detailed discussion of those, see paras 8.631–8.633 and 8.640–8.641 above). The criterion of the *implementation* of the infringement replaces that of the 'actual impact when this can be measured' in the 1998 Guidelines. This appears to be a codification of the Commission's existing practice, which had progressively focussed exclusively on the notion of implementation by presuming an impact on the sole basis of the evidence of the implementation of the infringement and by disregarding arguments as to the alleged lack of effect of the infringement (see paras 8.634–8.639 above). A new method for the measurement of the (presumed) impact of the cartel is also introduced in the 2006 Guidelines through the criterion of the 'combined market share of all the undertakings concerned'. This approach also appears to reflect what was already the Commission's practice in analyzing the actual impact of the infringement under the 1998 Guidelines.

The Commission has stressed that 'horizontal price-fixing, market-sharing and output-   **8.818**
limitation agreements, which are usually secret, are, by their very nature, among the most harmful restrictions of competition. As a matter of policy, they will be heavily fined. Therefore, the proportion of the value of sales taken into account for such infringements will generally be set at the higher end of the scale' (point 23).

Duration: multiplication by the number of years of participation in the infringement   **8.819**
In order to take fully into account the duration of the participation of each undertaking in the infringement, the amount determined on the basis of the value of sales will be multiplied by the number of years of participation in the infringement. Periods of less than six months will be counted as half a year; periods longer than six months but shorter than one year will be counted as a full year (point 24).

This is a radical change in the Commission's approach and seems to reflect a concern that   **8.820**
the amount of the fine imposed should reflect more accurately the extent of the economic damage created to the economy. Under the new method of calculation, the duration of the infringement committed should contribute to a considerable increase in the level of the fine, as its impact on the amount of the fine set for gravity will be 10 times higher than under the 1998 Guidelines.

Payment of the 'entry-fee'   Irrespective of the duration of the undertaking's partici-   **8.821**
pation in the infringement, the Commission will include in the basic amount a sum of

between 15 and 25 per cent of the relevant value of sales 'in order to deter undertakings from even entering into horizontal price-fixing, market-sharing and output-limitation agreements' (point 25).[893] For the purpose of deciding the proportion of the value of sales to be considered in a given case, the Commission will have regard to the same factors as those used to determine the level of gravity of the infringement (point 25).

(ii) Adjustments to the Basic Amount of the Fine

8.822 **Aggravating circumstances** According to the 2006 Guidelines, the basic amount may be increased where the Commission finds that there are aggravating circumstances, such as: (i) where an undertaking continues or repeats the same or a similar infringement after the Commission or a national competition authority has made a finding that the undertaking infringed Article 81 or 82; (ii) refusal to co-operate with or obstruction of the Commission in carrying out its investigations; (iii) role of leader in, or instigator of, the infringement. In this respect, the Commission has indicated that it 'will also pay particular attention to any steps taken to coerce other undertakings to participate in the infringement and/or any retaliatory measures taken against other undertakings with a view to enforcing the practices constituting the infringement' (point 28).

8.823 The most notable aspect of the 2006 Guidelines as regards aggravating circumstances is that the Commission makes clear that it reserves the right to increase the basic amount of the fine by *100 per cent* for any repeat offence found in respect of the prior finding of a similar infringement by the Commission or *a national competition authority* (applying EU antitrust rules). This is another element in a strategy clearly aimed at boosting the deterrent effect of the fines imposed. A further change is that the 'need to increase the penalty in order to exceed the amount of gains improperly made' is (logically) no longer mentioned as an aggravating circumstance, but instead under section C of the 2006 Guidelines allowing for a 'specific increase for deterrence'.[894] The detailed discussion of the Commission's practice as regards aggravating circumstances under the 1998 Guidelines remains largely valid under the 2006 Guidelines. See section E(2)(d) of this chapter.

8.824 **Mitigating circumstances** According to the 2006 Guidelines, the basic amount of the fine may be reduced where the Commission finds that mitigating circumstances exist, such as: (i) where the undertaking concerned provides evidence that it terminated the infringement as soon as the Commission intervened: this will not apply to secret agreements or practices (in particular, cartels); (ii) where the undertaking provides evidence that the infringement has been committed as a result of negligence; (iii) where the undertaking provides evidence that its involvement in the infringement is substantially limited and thus demonstrates that, during the period in which it was party to the offending agreement, it actually avoided applying it by adopting competitive conduct in the market: the mere fact that an undertaking participated in an infringement for a shorter duration than others will not be regarded as a mitigating circumstance since this will already be reflected in the basic

---

[893] The Commission may also apply such an additional amount in the case of other infringements.

[894] Another change is that the previously existing aggravating circumstance of 'retaliatory measures against other undertakings with a view to enforcing practices which constitute an infringement' is no longer singled out (but grouped in a single section together with leadership/instigation/coercion. However, each of those factors may separately be an aggravating circumstance.

amount; (iv) where the undertaking concerned has effectively co-operated with the Commission outside the scope of the Leniency Notice and beyond its legal obligation to do so; (v) where the anti-competitive conduct of the undertaking has been authorised or encouraged by public authorities or by legislation (point 29).

The most notable change introduced in this regard concerns the appraisal of the extent **8.825** to which an undertaking should benefit from an attenuating circumstance in regard to its relatively limited contribution to the infringement. The previously existing attenuating circumstances for 'an exclusively passive of "follow my leader" role in the infringement' and for the 'non-implementation in practice of the offending agreements and practices' have been replaced by the single attenuating circumstance where the involvement of the undertaking in the infringement was 'substantially limited' in that it 'actually avoided applying it by adopting competitive conduct in the market'.[895] Again this appears to be a codification of the Commission's existing practice and of the case law on this aspect (see paras 8.739–8.747 above). Otherwise, the Commission's policy appears to remain unchanged, and reference is made here to the detailed discussion of attenuating circumstances under the 1998 Guidelines in section E(2)(d) of this chapter. It should be noted, however, that the 2006 Guidelines state that it is for the undertaking concerned to provide evidence of the existence of any of the mitigating circumstances mentioned in point 29.

Specific increase for deterrence   The Commission has indicated that it will pay particu- **8.826** lar attention to the need to ensure that fines have a sufficiently deterrent effect; to that end, it may increase the fine to be imposed on undertakings which have a particularly large turnover beyond the sales of goods or services to which the infringement relates (point 30). The Commission will also take into account the need to increase the fine in order to exceed the amount of gains improperly made as a result of the infringement where it is possible to estimate that amount (point 31).

Legal maximum   The 2006 Guidelines reiterate that the final amount of the fine shall **8.827** not, in any event, exceed 10 per cent of the total turnover in the preceding business year of the undertaking or association of undertakings participating in the infringement, as laid down in Article 23(2) of Regulation No 1/2003 (point 32). Where an infringement by an association of undertakings relates to the activities of its members, the fine shall not exceed 10 per cent of the sum of the total turnover of each member active on the market affected by that infringement (point 33).

Leniency Notice   The Commission indicates that it will apply the leniency rules in line **8.828** with the conditions set out in the applicable notice (point 34).

Ability to pay   In spite of the strict stance it adopted in respect of this criterion in its practice **8.829** under the 1998 Guidelines, the Commission has retained the possibility of applying this criterion under the 2006 Guidelines. It has indicated that 'in exceptional cases, [it] may, upon

---

[895] The Commission has indicated, for the avoidance of doubt, that the mere fact that an undertaking participated in an infringement for a shorter duration than others will not be regarded as a mitigating circumstance since this will already be reflected in the basis amount.

request, take account of the undertaking's inability to pay in a specific social and economic context. It will not base any reduction granted for this reason in the fine on the mere finding of an adverse or loss-making financial situation. A reduction could be granted solely on the basis of objective evidence that imposition of the fine as provided for in these Guidelines would irretrievably jeopardise the economic viability of the undertaking concerned and cause its assets to lose all their value' (point 35).

(iii) Final Considerations

8.830 The Commission may, in certain cases, impose a symbolic fine. The justification for imposing such a fine should be given in its decision (point 36). Although the 2006 Guidelines present the general methodology for the setting of fines, the particularities of a given case or the need to achieve deterrence in a particular case may justify departing from such methodology or from the limits specified in point 21 (point 37).

(iv) Conclusion on the 2006 Guidelines

8.831 The adoption of the 2006 Guidelines marks an important change in the Commission's policy on fines. The 'flat rate' approach taken in the 1998 Guidelines has been abandoned in favour of a system under which the starting amount of the fine is more objectively linked with the economic reality of the infringement committed. This change in approach can be interpreted as a response to (1) the concern that the duration of the infringement was not adequately reflected in the 1998 Guidelines and (2) a criticism that the 'flat rate approach' raised questions regarding proportionality and equality of treatment.

8.832 In spite of this significant change, there are nevertheless important similarities between the 1998 and the 2006 Guidelines. The Commission retains a wide margin of discretion in setting the starting amount of the fine on the basis of its gravity (the relevant percentage can vary within a band of 30 per cent). Also, the criteria retained for the evaluation of the gravity of the infringement are similar to those used by the Commission under the 1998 Guidelines. As regards the aggravating and attenuating circumstances listed, they remain broadly in line with the Commission's practice under the 1998 Guidelines.

8.833 The most striking aspect of the 2006 Guidelines is their strong focus on ensuring a sufficient level of deterrence. The Commission's policy in that respect is threefold. First, the new method of calculation gives a considerably greater weight to the duration of the infringement potentially increasing the fine incurred by a much more significant proportion than the 10 per cent per annum increase under the 1998 Guidelines. Second, the Commission has shown more determination to prevent ongoing infringement by sanctioning any repeat offence more severely. Third, the Commission reserves the right to increase the fine where it considers further deterrence is necessary, without being bound by any specific criterion and with no limit other than the statutory one set out in Article 23(2) of Regulation No 1/2003.

8.834 The application of the 2006 Guidelines can nevertheless be expected to result in divergent outcomes. By reason of the Commission's intention to render fines more proportionate to the economic impact of the infringement, it may turn out that fines are reduced for infringements committed by small players in a market of limited economic importance and for a limited duration. However, infringements committed by large, multinational, repeat offenders with large market shares in high value markets can be expected to be much more severely sanctioned.[896]

(4) Enforcing the Fine

Payment of the fine Fines imposed by the Commission must be paid within three months of the date of service of the decision. They are payable to a Commission bank account indicated in the operative part of the Decision. After expiry of the three months, default interest is automatically payable at the rate applied by the European Central Bank ('ECB') to its main refinancing operations on the first day of the month in which the decision was adopted plus 3.5 percentage points. Companies may undertake to negotiate payment facilities with the Commission (DG Budget) if they face difficulties in payment. In the case of payment by instalment, the interest rate applicable to the remainder of the fine will be the ECB rate plus 1.5 per cent. However, negotiation of payment in instalments is conditional upon the provision of a bank guarantee covering the amount of the fine and the corresponding interest. Pursuant to Article 242 EC, appeal before the CFI has no suspensory effect on the payment of the fine. However, when the decision is challenged, the Commission suspends the claim for payment subject to the provision of a bank guarantee covering the fine and the interest. The applicable interest is the ECB rate plus 1.5 per cent.

8.835

Bank guarantee by way of securing payment A precondition for the negotiation of payment facilities or for the suspension of the claim for payment when the decision is challenged is the provision of a bank guarantee covering the full amount of the fine and the related outstanding interest.[897] This condition has been much criticised, since in terms of the financial liabilities of an undertaking, the provision of a bank guarantee does not make much difference in comparison to the effective payment of the fine. However, the Commission is obliged to take all necessary steps to secure the payment of debts in order to comply with its Financial Regulations and to its obligation to protect the Community's financial interests. The obligation to provide a bank guarantee has been held lawful by the CFI.[898] The costs incurred in the provision of a bank guarantee are not 'recoverable costs' in the context of the Court proceedings.[899] Claims for reimbursement of the costs incurred

8.836

---

[896] In support of this view see Case Notes, 'New Penalty Guidelines', Case Associates, July 2006.

[897] The Commission letter notifying the Decision to its addressee encloses a standard financial guarantee. Any undertaking lodging an application for annulment of such decision before the CFI and claiming the benefit of the suspension of the payment of the fine must send to the Commission the required bank guarantee. The Accounting Officer of the Commission will then confirm that the payment of the fine can be deferred until the final outcome of the case is known. The undertaking is free, at any moment in time, to replace the bank guarantee in total or in part by a provisional payment.

[898] See eg Case T-275/94 *Groupement des Cartes Bancaires CB v Commission* [1995] ECR II-216, paras 46–47, Case T-23/99 *LR AF 1998 v Commission* [2002] ECR II-1705, paras 395–396 and Joined Cases T-236/01, T-239/01, T-244/01 to T-246/01, T-251/01 and T-252/01 *Tokai Carbon a.o. v Commission* [2004] ECR II-1181, para 475, where the CFI stated that the power conferred on the Commission to impose fines 'covers the power to determine the date on which the fine is payable and that on which default interest begins to accrue, the power to set the rate of such interest and to determine the detailed arrangements for implementing its decision by requiring, where appropriate, the provision of a bank guarantee covering the principal amount of the fine imposed plus interest'. The President of the CFI has also held that '[t]he possibility of requiring the provision of a financial guarantee [...] is a general and reasonable way for the Commission to act'. See Order in Case T-79/03 R *IRO v Commission* [2003] ECR II-3027, para 25.

[899] See Case 183/83 *Krupp v Commission* [1987] ECR 4611 and Case T-77/92 *Parker Pen v Commission* [1994] ECR II-549, paras 99–101.

in the provision of a bank guarantee have also been turned down thus far.[900] The European Courts have found that the conditionality of the suspension of the Commission decision upon the provision of financial guarantees is in the interest of the proper administration of justice, save in exceptional circumstances.[901]

8.837 **Interim suspension of the obligation to provide a bank guarantee** Interim relief from the requirement to pay the fine or to provide a bank guarantee is granted only in very exceptional cases.[902] The European Courts have thus far almost always rejected such requests. Arguments relating to the adverse effects of the provision of a bank guarantee in terms of financial liabilities have in general been rejected.[903] (Partial) release from the obligation to provide a bank guarantee has only been granted to small undertakings which were able to establish that they would not be able to obtain such guarantee without suffering irreparable damage such as bankruptcy,[904] or that obtaining such a guarantee was objectively unfeasible.[905] When the undertaking belongs to a group, the financial circumstances of that group must be taken into consideration. In assessing the ability of the undertaking to supply the bank guarantee, account must be taken of the group of undertakings to which it directly or indirectly belongs.[906] Suspension of the obligation to provide the guarantee may in theory be granted if there are particularly serious doubts as to the legality of the Decision.[907]

8.838 Compromise solutions are often found, and a release from the obligation to provide the bank guarantee will generally be only partial and subject to the effective payment of part of the fine. In the context of *Cartonboard*, the undertaking Cascades was given the option to initially provide a guarantee covering 30 per cent of the amount of the fine and obtained an extension for the provision of a guarantee for the remainder within six months.[908] However, the CFI imposed on the undertaking an obligation to provide to the Commission, on a monthly basis, information enabling the Commission to monitor its financial situation.[909] In *French Beef*, the president of the CFI released an undertaking from its obligation to give a bank guarantee for the full amount of the fine (EUR 480,000) for two months, and left it with the option, within one month, to either pay EUR 200,000 in full or to pay some of that sum and provide a bank guarantee for the remainder.[910]

---

[900] See Case T-28/03 *Holcim v Commission* [2005] ECR II-1357.

[901] Order in Case 86/82 R *Hasselblad v Commission* [1982] ECR 1555.

[902] Case 107/82 R *AEG v Commission* [1982] ECR 1549, para 6, and Case C-7/01 P(R) *FEG v Commission* [2001] ECR I-2559, para 44.

[903] Order in Case 392/85 R *Finsider v Commission* [1986] ECR 959.

[904] Order in Case 213/86 R *Montedipe SpA v Commission* [1986] ECR 2623, para 23.

[905] See, eg, Order in Case T-245/03 R *FNSEA and others v Commission* [2004] ECR II-271, para 78, and Order in case T-11/06 R *Romana Tabacchi v Commission*, not yet reported.

[906] See, eg, Order in Case T-301/94 R *Laakman v Commission* [1994] ECR II-1279, para 26, and Order in Case 86/82 R *Hasselblad v Commission* [1982] ECR 1555, para 4. Unilateral refusal of assistance by the principal shareholder does not prevent the overall financial situation of the group from being taken into account in order to evaluate its ability to provide a bank guarantee. See Order in Case 364/99 P(R) *DSR Senator Lines v Commission* [1999] ECR I-8733, paras 48–49.

[907] See in particular Order in Case T-301/94 R *Laakman v Commission* [1994] ECR II-1279 and Order in Case T-156/94 R *Siderurgica Aristrain Madrid SL v Commission* [1994] ECR II-715.

[908] Order in Case T-308/94 R *Cascades v Commission* [1995] ECR II-265.

[909] At para 117.

[910] Order of the president of the CFI in Case T-217/03 R *FNCBV v Commission* [2004] ECR II-239.

Default interest   The charging of default interest for an undertaking's failure to pay a fine   **8.839**
is justified by the need to ensure that the Treaty is not rendered ineffective by practices
applied unilaterally by undertakings to delay payment of the fines imposed on them.[911]
If the Commission did not have such power, undertakings which delayed paying their fines
would enjoy an advantage over those which paid their fines within the period laid down.[912]
Addressees of a decision imposing a fine may challenge the interest rate set by the Commission
before the CFI, which has held that the interest rate fixed in the operative part of the decision cannot be regarded as being extraneous to the latter and can therefore also be challenged.[913] In *Pre-Insulated Pipes*, the CFI rejected the plea that a 7.5 per cent default interest
rate was excessive. It confirmed that the rate corresponded to the rate of the ECB plus
3.5 percentage points and found that the Commission had not exceeded its discretion
when fixing the default interest rate.[914] The CFI noted that the default interest rate must
not be so excessively high that the undertakings are effectively obliged to pay the fines even
though they may consider that they have good grounds for challenging the validity of the
Commission decision. The Commission may nonetheless adopt a point of reference higher
than the applicable market rate offered to the average borrower, in order to discourage
dilatory behaviour.[915]

No defence of 'exchange rate fluctuation'   Since European economic and monetary   **8.840**
union, the Commission has set fines in euros.[916] The argument that the amount of the fines
imposed has changed because of the movements in exchange rates between the date of imposition of the fine and the date of payment of the fine has been rejected by the Community
Courts, which have held that the risks of fluctuating exchange rates remain inevitable and
that currency fluctuations are an element of chance which may produce advantages and disadvantages which undertakings realising part of their sales on export markets have to deal
with regularly in the course of their business activities and the very existence of which is not
such as to render inappropriate the amount of a fine lawfully fixed.[917]

No possibility of 'renegotiating' default interest rate   In *Cementir v Commission*,[918] an   **8.841**
undertaking lodged an application for the annulment of a Commission decision turning
down the applicant's request to obtain a reduction of the interest paid on the principal of a
fine in *Cement*. The applicant had obtained a bank guarantee in exchange for the payment of
interest on the principal of the fine at the level of 7.25 per cent per year, ie the market rate plus
1.5 per cent. Market rates having considerably decreased since 1994, the year during which

---

[911] Case T-275/94 *Groupement des Cartes Bancaires CB v Commission* [1995] ECR II-216, para 48.
[912] Idem, para 49.
[913] Joined Cases T-24 to 26 and 28/93 *Compagnie Maritime Belge de Transport and others v Commission*
[1996] ECR II-2101, para 250.
[914] Case T-23/99 *LR AF 1998* [2002] ECR II-1705, paras 397–398.
[915] Idem, para 398. See also, more recently, Joined Cases T-71/03, T-74/03, T-87/03 and T-91/03 *Tokai
Carbon and others v Commission* [2005] ECR II-10, para 411.
[916] Fines were set in 'unit of account' and subsequently in ECUs. They were generally also expressed in the
currency of the Member State where the addressee of the fine was established.
[917] See, for instance, Case C-291/98 P *Sarrió v Commission* [2000] ECR I-9991, para 89 and Joined Cases
C-238/99 P, C-244/99 P, C-245/99 P, C-247/99 P, C-250/99 P to C-252/99 P and C-254/99 P *Limburgse
Vinyl Maatschappij NV a.o. v Commission* [2002] ECR I-8375, para 604.
[918] Case T-138/04 *Cementir v Commission*, not published.

the fine was imposed, the applicant asked the Commission, once the judicial procedure came to an end, to reduce the interest payable, which amounted to 60 per cent of the principal. That request was turned down by the Commission, whose negative decision formed the subject of the application in question. The CFI found that the application was inadmissible on the ground that the Commission decision in question was a purely confirmatory act of the initial decision to apply the interest rate. The CFI nonetheless stated obiter dictum that in a market economy where interest rates are subject to downwards or upwards fluctuations, the inherent risk that a debtor may suffer from a downward movement is equivalent to the risk that it may benefit from an upward movement in the interest rates.[919]

8.842 **Repayment of the annulled fine and the interests**   When a final Court judgment partially or totally annuls the fine, the Commission repays the corresponding amount to the undertaking. Initially, the Commission did not usually repay the interest it had received between the date of payment and the date of repayment. However, in *Corus UK v Commission*, the CFI held that the obligation to repay the fine applies not only to the principal amount of the fine overpaid, but also to default interest on that amount.[920] Not only does this allow the applicant company to be restored to its original position,[921] but it also prevents any unjust enrichment of the Community, which would be contrary to the general principles of Community law.[922]

8.843 **Provisional payments are put on an interest bearing bank account**   Provisional payments are deposited in an interest-bearing Commission bank account offering the minimum refinancing rate (REFI) as applied by the European Central Bank to its main operations in Euro increased by a small percentage amount. The applicable interest rate follows the changes in the REFI-rate and interest is accrued on the account at the end of each trimester. Interest on provisional payments made by undertakings in satisfaction of their fine will be repaid if the fine is successfully appealed.[923]

8.844 **Enforceability of the fines**   Under Article 256 EC: '[d]ecisions of the Council or of the Commission which impose a pecuniary obligation on persons other than States, shall be enforceable. Enforcement is governed by the rules of civil procedure in force in the State in the territory of which it is carried out. The order for its enforcement shall be appended to the decision, without other formality than verification of the authenticity of the decision, by the national authority which the government of each Member State shall designate for this purpose and shall make known to the Commission and to the Court of Justice'. The payment

---

[919] Para 161.

[920] T-171/99 *Corus UK v Commission* [2001] ECR II-2967, para 53.

[921] Since complete reimbursement of a fine that has been wrongly paid cannot omit from the account factors such as the effluxion of time, which may in fact reduce its value (see, by way of analogy, Case C-271/91 *Marshall* [1993] ECR I-4367, para 31, and Joined Cases C-397/98 and C-410/98 *Metallgesellschaft and others* [2001] ECR I-1727, paras 94–95). Proper compliance with such a judgment therefore requires, in order fully to restore the applicant to the position in which it legally should have been, that account be taken that such restoration only occurred after an appreciable lapse of time, during which the applicant did not have the use of the sums it had wrongly paid (see, by way of analogy, Case 266/83 *Samara v Commission* [1985] ECR 189, para 9).

[922] Case 259/87 *Greece v Commission* [1990] I-2845, summary publication, para 26.

[923] Joined Cases T-71/03, T-74/03, T-87/03 and T-91/03 *Tokai Carbon and others v Commission* [2005] ECR II-10, para 410.

of the fine is enforced on the initiative of the Commission, in accordance with national law, by bringing the matter directly before the competent authority. Under Article 256 EC, enforcement may be suspended only by a decision of the CFI. However, national courts have jurisdiction over complaints that enforcement is being carried out in an irregular manner.

(5) Judicial Review of the Fines

The Court's unlimited jurisdiction   According to Article 229 EC, 'Regulations adopted **8.845** jointly by the European Parliament and the Council, and by the Council, pursuant to the provisions of this Treaty, may give the European Court of Justice unlimited jurisdiction with regard to the penalties provided for in such regulations'. Article 31 of Regulation 1/2003[924] has accordingly established that 'the Court of Justice shall have unlimited jurisdiction to review decisions in which the Commission has fixed a fine or periodic penalty payment. It may cancel, reduce or increase the fine or periodic penalty payment imposed'. If the CFI partially annuls the findings of the Commission as regards, for instance, the gravity of the infringement committed, or the extent of the participation of an undertaking in the cartel, it will modify the amount of the fine accordingly. However, such modification does not have to be proportionate to the extent to which the Commission's Decision is annulled. The CFI will normally take all of the relevant facts into consideration and proceed to what it considers a fair assessment of those facts when setting the fine.

No re-examination of the size of the fine by the ECJ   On appeal against a CFI judgment **8.846** before the ECJ, appellants have often sought a re-examination by the ECJ of the amount of fines. However, the ECJ has systematically refused to do this, stating that 'as regards the allegedly disproportionate nature of the fine [. . .] it is not for the Court of Justice, when ruling on questions of law in the context of an appeal, to substitute, on grounds of fairness, its own assessment for that of the Court of First Instance exercising its unlimited jurisdiction to rule on the amount of fines imposed for infringements of Community law'.[925] According to settled case law, the purpose of review by the ECJ in the context of an appeal is, first, to examine to what extent the CFI took into consideration, in a legally correct manner, all the essential factors to assess the gravity of particular conduct under Article 81 EC and the provisions on fines in the implementing regulation and, second, to consider whether the CFI responded to a sufficient legal standard to all the arguments raised by the appellant with a view to having the fine cancelled or reduced.[926]

Article 229 EC applications cannot by made independently from applications for annul- **8.847** **ment**   The CFI has found that an application seeking the reduction of the fine pursuant to Article 229 EC and to the corresponding provision in the implementing regulation

---

[924] This provision is identical to former Art 17 of Regulation 17.

[925] Case C-310/93 P *BPB Industries and British Gypsum v Commission* [1995] ECR I-865, para 34; Case C-219/95 P *Ferriere Nord v Commission* [1997] ECR I-4411, para 31; Case C-185/95 P *Baustahlgewebe v Commion* [1998] ECR I-8417, para 129, Joined Cases C-189/02 P, C-202/02 P, C-205/02 P to C-208/02 P and C-213/02 *Dansk Rørindustri and others v Commission* [2005] ECR I-5425, para 245.

[926] See in particular Case C-185/95 P *Baustahlgewebe v Commission* [1998] ECR I-8417, para 128, Case C-359/01 P *British Sugar v Commission* [2004] ECR I-4933, para 47, and Joined Cases C-189/02 P, C-202/02 P, C-205/02 P to C-208/02 P and C-213/02 *Dansk Rørindustri and others v Commission* [2005] ECR I-5425, para 244.

cannot be lodged independently from an application pursuant to Article 230 EC.⁹²⁷ Therefore, an application seeking the exercise of the European Courts' full jurisdiction as regards a decision imposing a sanction necessarily includes a request seeking the total or partial annulment of this decision. Therefore, the introduction of such an application must respect the time limit set out in Article 230 EC. This may also be construed to imply that an undertaking may not ask for a reduction of fines in respect of a finding of the decision if it does not request the annulment of the corresponding finding. For instance, an undertaking cannot seek the reduction of a fine under Article 229 EC on the grounds that the duration of the infringement has been incorrectly assessed if it does not simultaneously seek the annulment of the finding of the duration.⁹²⁸ This is an important point, as undertakings could be tempted to contest certain facts laid down in the decision whilst pretending, with a view to keeping the reduction granted to them by the Commission on this basis, that they do not substantially contest the facts as set out by the Commission. However, it should be noted that applicants are entitled to ask the CFI to reduce their fine in the absence of any express claim of illegality, but simply on grounds of 'appropriateness'.

8.848 **Does the exercise of unlimited jurisdiction require a prior finding of illegality?** An important question is whether the exercise by the Court of its full jurisdiction is conditional upon a prior finding of illegality on the part of the Commission, or whether it does not require any such prior finding. A second question is whether the exercise of full jurisdiction is conditional upon a request of the applicant, or whether the Court may exercise its full jurisdiction 'ex officio'. Answering these questions is far from easy since, to a certain extent, the relevant case law appears to lack consistency. In certain cases, the CFI has limited the exercise of its full jurisdiction to reviewing whether the fine appears 'proportionate' in relation to the facts adduced by the Commission.⁹²⁹ This would seem to suggest that any exercise of the full jurisdiction is conditional upon the finding of illegality on the part of the Commission, even if it is simply a breach of the principle of proportionality in the exercise of

---

⁹²⁷ Order of the CFI of 9 November 2004 in Case T-252/03 *FNICGV v Commission*. In the context of the *French Beef* case, a trade union of beef slaughterers lodged an application exclusively seeking the annulment or the reduction of its fine pursuant to Art 229 EC. The Commission submitted that the application was manifestly inadmissible, since it had been lodged after the expiry of the time limit of two months set out by Art 230 EC. However, the applicant submitted that an application pursuant to Art 229 EC was not subject to any time limit. The CFI however dismissed the application as inadmissible, stating that the EC Treaty does not provide for any autonomous proceedings pursuant to Art 229 EC, and that the unlimited jurisdiction granted to the Court can only be exercised in the context of the control of the Community acts, and in particular the legality control. The CFI added that the sole effect of Art 229 EC is to extend the powers granted to the European Courts in the context of an application under Art 230 EC.

⁹²⁸ In Case T-38/02 *Danone v Commission*, judgment of 25 October 2005 [2005] ECR II-4407, the CFI noted that the applicant disputed the increase of the fine determined in respect of duration on the grounds that the infringement had stopped earlier than had been found by the Commission, but that Danone did not expressly seek annulment of the operative part of the decision where the Commission had determined the duration of the cartel. The CFI concluded that 'it should therefore be held that by the [. . .] plea relating to the duration of the infringement, the applicant seeks not only a reduction in the fine but also the partial annulment of the contested decision, in particular Article 1 of its operative part, in that the Commission wrongly held that the infringement continued until 28 January 1998' (para 213).

⁹²⁹ See eg Case T-229/94 *Deutsche Bahn v Commission* [1997] ECR II-1689, para 127, Case T-368/00 *General Motors Nederland and Opel Nederland v Commission* [2003] ECR II-44911, para 189, Joined Cases T-236/01, T-239/01, T-244/01 to T-246/01, T-251/01 and T-252/01 *Tokai Carbon and others v Commission* [2004] ECR II-1181, para 165.

the Commission's discretion. However, in other cases, the CFI has determined whether the amount of the fine is 'appropriate', which seems to suggest that the amount of the fine can be modified on considerations of equity, in the absence of any prior finding of illegality.[930] It also appears that the Court does not hesitate to exercise its full jurisdiction in the absence of any such request from the applicant.[931]

In this regard, the line taken by the CFI in *Compagnie Générale Maritime and others v Commission*[932] is interesting. In that case the Commission had imposed a symbolic fine of EUR 10,000 on each of the 14 members of the Far Eastern Freight Conference. Thirteen of the addressees sought the annulment of the decision. The CFI rejected all of the submissions presented by the applicants but nevertheless ultimately annulled the fines. The CFI stated notably that the agreement in question could not be equated with a secret cartel, that it had taken time for the Commission to take a position on the agreement, that the evaluation of the legality of the agreement raised a number of complex legal and economic issues, and that a number of factors had led the applicants to believe that the contested agreement was lawful. On those grounds, the CFI considered, in the exercise of its full jurisdiction, that there was justification not to impose a fine in the case.[933] Thus the CFI annulled the fine without having found any illegality in the Commission's decision. This would seem to suggest that the CFI is entirely free in the exercise of its unlimited jurisdiction. Similar reasoning was followed in the CFI's judgments in the *FEG/TU*[934] and *French Beef*[935] cases. It should also be noted that the CFI has gone even further in the past, where it has annulled a finding of the Commission in the absence of a request of the applicant to that effect.[936]

8.849

---

930 See eg Case 8/83 *Bertoli v Commission* [1984] ECR 1649, para 29; Case 7/73 *Istituto Chimioterapico and Commercial Solvents v Commission* [1974] ECR 223, paras 51 and 52, Case T-13/89 *ICI v Commission* [1992] ECR II-1021, paras 393 and 394 and Case T-220/00 *Cheil Jedang v Commission* [2003] ECR II-2473, para 100.

931 Case T-43/92 *Dunlop Slazenger v Commission* [1994] ECR II-441.

932 Case T-86/95 *Compagnie Générale Maritime v Commission* [2002] ECR II-1011.

933 Idem, para 488.

934 Case T-5/00 *FEG v Commission* [2003] ECR II-5761. After noting that the Commission could be held responsible for the excessive duration of the administrative procedure, the CFI stated that 'although that finding has no consequence regarding the legality of the contested decision, the fact remains that, in the exercise of the unlimited jurisdiction enjoyed by the Court under Article 229 EC and Article 17 of Regulation No 17, the Court may consider whether a reduction of the fine imposed is justified' (para 436).

935 Joined Cases T-217/03 and T-245/03 *FNCBV and others v Commission*, not yet reported. In this case, the CFI noted that the Commission had very significantly reduced the fine on account of exceptional circumstances. However, the CFI stated that despite the Commission's enjoyment of a margin of appreciation when setting the fine, the Court can, in exercise of its full jurisdiction, suppress, reduce or increase the fine imposed. The CFI went on to find that the reduction granted by the Commission did not sufficiently take into account the very exceptional character of the circumstances surrounding the infringement and concluded that the fine had to be reduced by 70% rather than by 60% (see paras 357–361). Thus, whilst the CFI neither expressly identifed any illegality in the Commission decision nor found a violation of the principle of proportionality, it nonetheless set the fine at a level which it considered more appropriate.

936 In Case T-43/92 *Dunlop Slazenger v Commission* [1994] ECR II-441, the applicant had sought, *inter alia*, the annulment of a decision on the ground that the date retained by the Commission for the beginning of the infringement was incorrect and requested a consequent reduction in the fine imposed by that decision. The CFI first concluded that the Commission had indeed erroneously determined the date of the beginning of the infringement. Secondly, the CFI, in the exercise of its full jurisdiction, reduced the fine accordingly. However, on this occasion, the CFI also determined that the Commission had also erroneously determined the date of the end of the infringement. Therefore, the CFI also reduced the fine for that reason, although no views on the end date had been submitted by the applicant.

8.850 **The CFI's practice in the exercise of its full jurisdiction**   In light of the above, it appears that the CFI has so far followed diverging approaches. In certain cases, the CFI has reduced the fine on its own initiative, without any prior finding of illegality. However, in most cases, the CFI has used its full jurisdiction to reduce the amount of a fine as a consequence of the finding that the Commission had erred in law in certain of its conclusions in the contested Decision.

8.851 It took some time for the CFI to make use of its power to increase a fine.[937] In *JFE Engineering a.o. v Commission*, the CFI found that the principle of equality of treatment would have justified imposing an increase in the fine imposed on the European applicants.[938] However, it did not impose such an increase as it noted that, first, the Commission had not come to the same conclusion and, secondly, the applicants had not been given the opportunity to comment on this point.[939] However, the CFI had on several occasions de facto increased the fine imposed on an undertaking by not reducing it in spite of a finding of an error by the Commission detrimental to the applicant.[940] In *Danone v Commission*, the CFI went a step further. In order to correct an error made by the Commission to the detriment of the applicant (when the CFI annulled the finding of an aggravating circumstance), the CFI recalculated the fine. On that occasion and on its own initiative, the CFI found that the method which had been used by the Commission for calculating the cumulative effect of aggravating and attenuating circumstances was not in line with the method indicated in the Guidelines and therefore proceeded to recalculate the fine on the basis of the correct method, with the consequence that it attenuated the favourable impact on the applicant of the partial annulment of the decision on its fine. By so doing, the CFI de facto

---

937 The Commission had invited it to do so where it considered that the applicant contested the facts of a cartel decision for the first time before the Court in spite of the fact that they had been awarded a reduction of fine, under the 1996 Leniency Notice, on the basis that they had not substantially contested the facts. The CFI did not follow the Commission's recommendation in the context of the litigation relating to *Greek Ferries*. See Case T-61/99, *Adriatica di Navigazione v Commission* [2003] ECR II-5349, paras 208–209. However, in the context of the litigation in *Graphite Electrodes*, the CFI did follow the Commission's request and increased the fine imposed on the undertaking Nippon by 2%. See Joined Cases T-236/01, T-239/01, T-244/01 to T 246/01, T 251/01 and T-252/01 *Tokai Carbon and others v Commission* [2004] ECR II-1181, paras 98–112.

938 Case T-67/00 *JFE Engineering v Commission* [2004] ECR II-2501. The CFI found that the Commission had erroneously set the same level of fines for the Japanese and European producers, whereas the latter had taken part in two separate infringements and the Japanese had only taken part in one. The CFI found that, in principle, it could have increased the fine on the European applicants, as they had requested it to make use of its full jurisdiction.

939 Paras 576–579.

940 This was the case on several occasions in the context of the *Cartonboard* case. For instance, in Case T-311/94 *BPB de Eendracht NV v Commission* [1998] ECR II-1129, paras 337–339, the CFI stated that the applicant could not be held responsible for collusion on market shares, but that despite that finding, it considered, in the exercise of its unlimited jurisdiction, that the gravity of the infringement committed, namely participation in the collusion on prices and on downtime, was still such that the amount of the fine should not be reduced. A similar approach was followed in *Volkswagen v Commission*. As a result of its finding that the duration of the infringement to be taken into account in order to fix the fine had to be reduced and that the description of the infringement given by the Commission in order to assess the gravity of the infringement was not wholly correct, the Court said that it had to reduce the amount of the fine imposed on the applicant. However, it added that the reduction of the fine did not necessarily have to be proportionate to the reduction in the duration of the infringement. The CFI added that, in the exercise of its jurisdiction in the matter, it had to carry out its own assessment of the circumstances of the case and that in the present case, the very serious nature of the infringement committed, and the intensity with which the unlawful measures were implemented,

increased the fine as compared to the fine that would have resulted from the recalculation of the fine on the basis of the method used by the Commission in the decision.[941]

Interestingly, it would appear from recent judgments that the CFI now tends to make increasing use of its unlimited jurisdiction 'for the sake of completeness'. This has been illustrated on various occasions when, having dismissed the applicant's plea that the Commission erred in fact or in law, the CFI nevertheless proceeds to an additional assessment of the point at issue under its unlimited jurisdiction. For instance, in the context of *Specialty Graphite*, the CFI stated in several places that the applicant's pleas that the Commission had erred in law had to be dismissed but that 'in any event' [it found] no reason, in the exercise of its unlimited jurisdiction, to alter [the Commission's findings]'.[942] A similar approach can be found in the CFI's judgment in *Sodium Gluconate*.[943]   **8.852**

Exercise of unlimited jurisdiction by the CFI must ensure equal treatment   In the exercise of its unlimited jurisdiction, the CFI must comply with the principle of equal treatment.[944] However, it has long been established that it is necessary to reconcile respect for this principle with the principle of legality, according to which a person may not rely, in support of his claim, on an unlawful act committed in favour of a third party.[945] Nevertheless, in the CFI's judgment in *JFE Engineering a.o. v Commission* the principle of equal treatment seems to have prevailed.[946] In that case, the CFI found that the Commission had committed a breach in the principle of equal treatment by imposing the same starting amount for the fines on both the Japanese and European producers, although the Japanese producers had   **8.853**

---

called for a fine that would act as a real deterrent. In light of those considerations, the reduction of the fine was limited. A similar approach can be found in Case T-360/00 *General Motors Nederland and Opel Nederland v Commission* ECR [2003] II-4491, para 199.

[941] The CFI judgment was appealed (Case C-3/06 P) and the Court of Justice had not issued its judgment at the time of writing. In his Opinion of 16 November 2006, Advocate-General Poiares Maduro concluded that the judgment should be annulled on this point, as the CFI did not give the applicant an opportunity to comment on the point at issue, but that the fine should nonetheless be set by the Court at the same level.

[942] Joined Cases T-71/03, T-74/03, T-87/03 and T-91/03 *Tokai Carbon and others* [2005] ECR II-10, paras 273 and 275–276.

[943] Case T-329/01 *Archer Daniels Midland v Commission*, not yet reported, para 114. The CFI stated, after rejecting the argument that the Commission had erred in law (in particular by violating the principle of non-discrimination in regard of *Zinc Phosphate*) by failing to take into account the limited size of the market when setting the fine, that 'in any event, even if all the circumstances relevant for the purposes of determining the appropriate amount in the *Zinc Phophate* decision could be regarded as comparable to those of this case, the Courts considers, under its unlimited jurisdiction, the the basic amount set . . . is appropriate in the light of all the factors referred to by the Commission in this Decision and in the light of the assessment of some of these factors in this judgement'.

[944] In its judgments regarding *Cartonboard*, the CFI found that the Commission had committed errors in the calculation of the fines in respect of the duration and had accordingly reduced the amount of certain fines. One undertaking noticed however that its fine had not been reduced in the same way as the other fines had been reduced pursuant to the Commission's method of calculation. The ECJ annulled the CFI's judgment on this point, holding that 'the exercise of unlimited jurisdiction must not result in discrimination between undertakings which have participated in an agreement of concerted practice contrary to Article [81(1) EC]' (Case C-280/98 P *Moritz J. Weig GmbH & Co KG v Commission* [2000] ECR I-9757, para 63).

[945] See for example, case 134/84 *Williams v Court of Auditors* [1985] ECR 2225, para 14; Case T-347/94 *Mayr-Melnhof Kartongesellschaft v Commission* [1998] ECR II-1751, para 334; Case T-9/99 *HFB and others v Commission* [2002] ECR II-1847, para 515; Joined Cases T-236/01, T-239/01, T-244/01 to T-246/01, T-251/01 and T-252/01 *Tokai Carbon and others v Commission* [2004] ECR II-1181, para 354.

[946] Cases T-67/00, T-68/00, T-71/00 and T-78/00 [2004] ECR II-2501, paras 566 to 580.

taken part in only one infringement, whereas the European producers had participated in two separate infringements. The CFI found that the fines imposed on the Japanese producers were fully justified and that the fines imposed on the European producers had been set at an excessively low level. After concluding that it was not in a position to increase the level of the fines set for the European producers (although it could, in principle, have done so in the exercise of its unlimited jurisdiction) the CFI proceeded, pursuant to the principle of equal treatment, to reduce the fines imposed on the Japanese producers.[947] However, that approach may be criticised. Since the CFI had previously stated that the fines imposed on the Japanese producers were fully justified, it would indeed seem that the Japanese producers also ended up benefiting from the error initially made by the Commission in favour of the European producers. This means that the CFI reduced a fine that was nonetheless considered fully justified in view of the objective of deterrence pursued by the Commission's competition policy.

8.854 **Potential consequences of the CFI's unlimited jurisdiction on fines** The exercise by the CFI of its full jurisdiction has far ranging implications. According to the 'conservative' approach to the notion of full jurisdiction, its exercise is conditional, on the one hand, upon a request by one of the parties to the litigation and, on the other, on the finding of an error in law by the Commission. From that traditional standpoint, the exercise of full jurisdiction appears to be a judicial tool enabling the Court to correct errors made by the Commission, thereby avoiding the need for a referral of the case back to the Commission and a possible subsequent application before the CFI against the new decision. However, as shown above, there are indications that, as regards fines, the CFI may adopt a broader interpretation of the notion of full jurisdiction whereby, even in the absence of any illegality on the part of the Commission, it may review factual and legal assessments made by the Commission in their entirety, to the extent that it may substitute its own assessment for that of the Commission. Thus, the CFI may not confine itself to reviewing the legality of the decisions taken by the Commission, but in essence would act as a full 'court of appeal' proceeding to its own assessment of the facts gathered by the Commission in the course of its investigation. Although perhaps an attractive prospect at first sight, it is submitted that the consequences of such an evolution should not be underestimated. First, the CFI would thus be granted considerable responsibility for implementing competition policy; and such a development would blur the traditional division between the judiciary and the executive. This would undoubtedly represent an important change in the institutional equilibrium established by the Treaties. Secondly, it is debatable whether the CFI would be any better placed than the Commission to carry out this new function, since one could not expect the CFI to be in a position to carry out its own investigations. Such an evolution might, in effect, lead to the evolution of the Commission's role towards that of a prosecutor pleading its case before the Court in the same way as the defendant. This, in turn, would have wide ranging implications for the way in which the Commission conducts its investigations. The consequences of such an evolution would certainly require careful consideration.

---

[947] ibid, para 579.

(6) Towards a More Optimal Community System of Sanctions?

Over the years, in pursuance of its mission to orientate the conduct of undertakings towards **8.855** compliance with the competition rules, the Commission has stepped up its fight against cartels by considerably increasing the level of fines. Through the application of the 1998 Guidelines, financial penalties for cartels have reached an unprecedented level, with fines of several hundred million euros being imposed on single undertakings. This has been broadly endorsed by the Community Courts. In spite of this, however, cartel conduct does not seem to have disappeared. It is difficult to establish whether the increasing number of cartel decisions results from an increased tendency by firms to adopt collusive behaviour in a more concentrated and globalised economy, or whether it arises from better enforcement of competition law. The truth probably lies somewhere between the two. What is certain is that while the level of fines imposed is often considered high, it can nonetheless reasonably be argued that the penalties remain insufficiently deterrent insofar as collusion seems to remain attractive to certain undertakings. The question therefore arises as to what alternative means, in addition to fines, might be made available to law enforcers. Two suggestions have traditionally been discussed, both inspired by the US experience. The first would be the development of a culture of civil actions for damages in Europe, leading to a greater contribution by private enforcement to the overall level of enforcement of competition law. The other would be the criminalisation of cartel behaviour, aimed at ensuring better deterrence through the stigmatisation and punishment of individuals who, ultimately, do remain the actors in the collusive behaviour.

(a) Is the Community's System of Fines Sufficiently Deterrent?

The main stakeholders under EC antitrust law are undertakings, and the goal pursued by **8.856** those participating in cartels is the maximisation of profit. Colluding parties can therefore be assumed to determine their behaviour in a rational way, and, as opposed to other types of criminality, the behaviour expected of them can be analysed particularly efficiently through the economic theory of crime. In economic terms, offenders will engage in price-fixing only if the benefit they can expect to receive from it exceeds the costs incurred. Fines will therefore have a deterrent effect in an economic sense provided that the result of the cost-benefit analysis conducted by potential offenders is negative, thereby inducing the undertakings to refrain from engaging in illegal conduct. In order to achieve that, fines would have to be set at a level equalling the illicit gained derived from the infringement, plus a 'safety' margin. However, account must also be taken of the probability of detection. In the case of secret infringements like cartels, the probability of detection is never 100 per cent. Thus, the deterrent effect of a pecuniary sanction will correspond to the nominal amount of the expected fine multiplied by the probability that the infringement will be detected and punished.[948] Competition enforcement regimes should therefore take action on both fronts, namely the nominal amount of the fines imposed and the probability of detection.

There is evidence that, in view of the detection rates, fines imposed on undertakings should **8.857** be much higher than has been the case so far in order to be effective. Wils has attempted to

---

[948] For example, if a fine of EUR 1 million is imposed on a given infringement, but the probability that the infringer gets caught is 20%, the 'expected fine' will correspond to 20% of EUR 1 million, that is to say EUR 200,000.

estimate the minimum fine required to attain an effective level of deterrence in a price-fixing cartel.[949] He notes that the gain that cartel members derive from their collusive conduct depends on the turnover of the product concerned, the price increase caused by the cartel, the price elasticity of the demand in the product concerned and the life span of the cartel. Wils notes first that it seems to be widely accepted that the average price increase due to cartels is at least 10 per cent of the selling price.[950] As regards average duration, he notes that it is common for cartels to last at least five years.[951] Assuming a zero price-elasticity, the illicit gain from a price cartel achieving a 10 per cent price increase over five years would therefore amount to 50 per cent of the annual turnover in the product concerned in the violation. Assuming, then, that the price elasticity would result in a division by two of the gain resulting from collusion, a cartel operated over five years would still result in a gain in the order of 25 per cent of the annual turnover in the product. Estimating the probability of detection of a cartel is, of course, virtually impossible, since the number of undetected cartels is unknown. However, relying on a US-wide study carried out between 1961 and 1988, Wils estimates a rate of detection of 16 per cent in the EU (an optimistic average according to him). He concludes that 'assuming a 10% price increase, and a resulting increase in profits of 5% of turnover, a 5-year duration and a 16% probability of detection and punishment, the floor below which fines will generally not deter price-fixing would be in the region of 150% of the annual turnover in the products concerned by the violation'.[952]

8.858 In spite of the dramatic increase in the fines imposed and notwithstanding the higher probability of detection induced by leniency programmes and, within Europe, the activities of the competition agencies of the European Competition Network, fines may thus still be considered insufficiently deterrent. However, several elements indicate that an increase in the fines to such levels as indicated above may not be desirable either. Such an increase might result in such high fines that they may become economically intolerable and would produce side-effects running counter to the objective of restoring and ensuring competitive market conditions. In addition to the fact that such high fines would in most cases exceed the maximum 10 per cent cap of annual turnover contained in Regulation 1/2003, their addressees would probably not be in a position to pay them, as illicit gains are not retained over time, but rather put back into the undertaking's business operations.[953] Bankruptcy of the companies concerned would in effect not suffice to pay the fine, and such liquidation would often result in the removal of a competitor from the market, thus reducing the scope for effective competition, and incurring high social costs. Moreover, should the addressee of the fine survive, the excessive level of the fine might nonetheless induce negative effects by inducing the companies fined, in the context of imperfect competition, to recoup the costs by charging higher

---

[949] WPJ Wils, 'Does Effective Enforcement of Articles 81 and 82 Require Imprisonment?', in *The Optimal Enforcement of EC Antitrust Law*, p 199.

[950] More recent studies (see introduction) hint at the fact that this figure is far greater in reality.

[951] This figure is conservative in respect of recent Decisions. Wils noted that a US study estimated the average life span of price-fixing arrangements to be over six years.

[952] WPJ Wils, 'Does Effective Enforcement of Articles 81 and 82 Require Imprisonment?', in *The Optimal Enforcement of EC Antitrust Law*, p 201.

[953] An empirical study quoted by Wils, based on a sample of 386 firms convicted of price-fixing in the US between 1955 and 1993 estimated that 58% of the firms would not have been able to survive the imposition of an optimal fine.

prices to customers. Consequently, the Commission is faced with a dilemma, as the level of the fines necessarily have limits as to their capacity to deter and they have other effects on undertakings which may be undesirable. It may thus be necessary to explore new possibilities.

(b) Should Private Enforcement be Encouraged?

Private enforcement of EC competition law   Private enforcement of EC competition **8.859** law refers to civil actions brought by private parties before national courts to obtain redress for the injury they have suffered as a result of infringements of EC competition law. Private enforcement is to be contrasted with public enforcement, which refers to the administration of competition law by public authorities in the general interests of society. While the primary goal of public enforcement is to *deter* anti-competitive practices, private enforcement enables victims to be *compensated* for their losses.[954] The direct applicability of Treaty provisions allows private parties in principle to avail themselves of Article 81 EC.[955] As early as 1973,[956] the ECJ recognised that Article 81(2) EC[957] could be used as a *shield*[958] which enabled parties to resile from a contractual obligation that was contrary to EC competition rules. The ECJ also embraced the use of Article 81(2) as a *sword* to enable victims of cartel behaviour to be compensated for the injury they suffered.[959] Finally, by empowering national courts to apply Article 81 EC in its entirety,[960] Regulation 1/2003 further encourages cartel victims to sue for damages before national civil courts.[961]

Private damage actions in Europe—a rare phenomenon   The ECJ has ruled that in the **8.860** absence of Community rules on the matter it is for the Member States to provide detailed rules for bringing actions for damages within national legal systems. Since the European Courts have no jurisdiction in civil cases (outside of the procedure for preliminary rulings), Member State courts provide the fora for such proceedings.

In spite of the fact that private parties have had the option to sue for damages before **8.861** national courts for some time, a study commissioned by DG Competition in 2004 found that, in practice, there was 'total underdevelopment' of actions for damages in national fora. This study found that from 1962 to 2004, no more than 12 actions for damages were

---

[954] Rocca then deputy Director-General of DG Competition, 'La Politique de la Commission en matière d'Amendes Antitrust: Récents Developpements, Perspectives d'Avenir', speech at the Université Libre de Bruxelles, 4 February 2003.

Available at <http://europa.eu.int/comm/competition/speeches/text/sp2003_004_fr.pdf>.

[955] Case C-453/99 *Courage v Crehan* [2001] ECR I-6314.

[956] See for instance Case 127/73 *BRT v SABAM* [1973] ECR 51, para 16.

[957] Pursuant to Art 81(2) EC, 'any agreements [. . .] prohibited pursuant to this Article shall be automatically void'.

[958] WPJ Wils, 'Should Private Antitrust Enforcement Be Encouraged in Europe?', World Competition 26(3): 473–488, 2003.

[959] Case C-453/99 *Courage v Crehan* [2001] ECR I-6314, para 26: '[. . .] Article 81 would be put at risk if it were not open to any individual to claim damages for loss caused to him by a contract or by conduct liable to restrict or distort competition'.

[960] Art 6 of Regulation No 1/2003.

[961] See recital (7) of Regulation No 1/2003, 'when deciding disputes between private individuals, [national courts] protect the subjective rights under Community law, for example by awarding damages to the victims of infringements'. See also the accompanying notices to Regulation 1/2003 that entered into force on 1 May 2004, notably the Commission Notice on the handling of complaints by the Commission under Articles 81 and 82 of the EC Treaty [2004] OJ C101/65.

brought before courts in Member States. This study also noted the 'astonishing diversity' in the approaches taken in the enforcement of EC competition law by the Member States' legislatures and courts. While some commentators have concluded that its absence is a major weakness in the EU competition enforcement system, others consider that private enforcement adds little to the effective protection of competition in Europe. For its part, the Commission considers that private and decentralised enforcement is a tool that is complementary to public enforcement by the Commission and national competition authorities (NCAs). It considers that the threat of private actions may act as an additional deterrent together with the prosecution and fining of undertakings by the Commission and national authorities. Moreover in the Commission's view, private enforcement can contribute to the development of a real 'culture of competition', resulting from an increasing number of infringements that are actually punished.

8.862 **On the road to increased private damages in Europe?**   On the basis of the above-mentioned study, the Commission published a consultative Green Paper on 19 December 2005. The intention behind the Green Paper was to consult all stakeholders and to foster a public debate on all aspects of damages actions for breach of the EC antitrust rules. It disclosed the existing (significant) obstacles to the effective operation of damages actions for infringement of Community antitrust law, both for 'follow-on' actions (that is cases in which the civil action is brought after a prior finding by a competition authority of an infringement) and for 'stand-alone actions' (that is actions which do not follow on from a public enforcement action). The Green Paper lists a series of options which, if implemented, could allow a private enforcement culture to develop, involving European consumers more actively in enforcement of the competition rules. Public comments on the Green Paper were requested by April 2006 and are available at DG COMP's web site. At 31 December 2006, further policy announcements were still awaited.

8.863 **Key issues to tackle**   The hurdles identified in the Green Paper, and the options put forward for developing private damages actions in Europe can be summarised as follows. First, access to courts needs to be improved by, for instance, broadening the provisions on standing, which are considered too restrictive in certain Member States. The option of allowing indirect purchasers—who may or may not have been overcharged—to have standing is also considered. Second, the legal costs involved for private parties in a civil suit are often prohibitive when compared with the potential compensation available. One means of reducing costs for individuals would be allow 'collective actions', so that individuals with smaller claims (and purses) can join others and thereby pool responsibility for their legal costs. Third, the lack of experience of national courts in the field of competition law and particularly the lack of experience in the assessment of damages may act as a significant disincentive to potential litigants. A possible remedy to that could be publication by the Commission of guidelines on the quantification of damages. Fourth, there is the difficulty for claimants in satisfying the burden of proof especially where evidence is not easy to gather since, if it exists, it is held by the party who has committed the anti-competitive behaviour. Access by claimants to such evidence is the key to making damages claims effective, therefore it may be necessary to introduce special rules on the disclosure of documentary evidence ('discovery'). Plaintiffs in (European continental) civil law jurisdictions, for instance, suffer the disadvantage of being unable to benefit from the scope of the broad discovery rules which are available in common law systems.

Relationship between public and private enforcement: interplay between leniency applications and damage actions   The Commission's interest as a public enforcement agency lies in creating maximum deterrence for cartels. That is best achieved when public and private enforcement complement one another. Commission decisions already have evidentiary value in national courts and more generally decisions of competition authorities can have a significant impact on the ability of claimants to prove their case.

8.864

Optimum co-ordination between private and public enforcement cannot be achieved without regard to the interest of applicants under leniency programmes. Both contribute by their effects to the same aim: more effective deterrence against entering into cartels. Indeed, the operation of leniency programmes is generally helpful for private litigants in damages actions, as leniency programmes uncover secret cartels. Nevertheless, claims for damages could affect the incentives for undertakings to use leniency: a more developed culture of private enforcement would increase the exposure of undertakings to private litigation, thus possibly reducing their willingness to confess under leniency programmes.

8.865

Solutions explored in relation to the interplay of private damages actions and leniency   The significance of the interplay of leniency programmes and private damages actions was clearly identified in the Green Paper. One of the alternatives proposed was that whereas cartel members would generally become liable for double damages, successful applicants for immunity would only be liable for single damages. An added benefit for leniency applicants could be that they would not be held jointly and severally liable with the other cartel members for the (double) civil damages of the whole cartel. Their liability would be limited only to the share of the single damages corresponding to the applicant's share in the cartelised market. These measures would offer further incentives for corporations to self-report illegal conduct. Another noteworthy option set out in the Green Paper in relation to leniency is the protection of the confidentiality of submissions made to the competition authority as part of leniency applications, i.e. excluding the discoverability of the leniency submissions. Where any party to proceedings before a competition authority may be obliged to turn over to a litigant in civil proceedings all documents which have been submitted to competition authorities, it is suggested that an exception will apply for submissions made within the framework of leniency applications. In summary, the solutions proposed by the Commission in order to increase the incentives for private parties to sue for damages must not impair the effectiveness of the Leniency programme.

8.866

Conclusion as to the possible future of private damages actions in Europe   Whether there is a real future for private damages actions in Europe will depend on a number of variables. Certain obstacles may prove insurmountable in the short or medium term, such as creating sufficient possibilities for the discovery of evidence through revised national civil procedures. It seems hardly conceivable that Member States will agree to the adoption of new laws of civil procedure for damages claims in antitrust cases that would deviate significantly from current legislation for other claims for damages. In other words, the options proposed will have implications that go far beyond the mere scope of claims for damages in antitrust cases and may therefore be very difficult, to put into practice. Other barriers may prove less obstructive, notably those which the Commission can influence itself, such as ensuring wider access to the information produced by the parties in the course of an investigation.

8.867

However, even in such situations, the Commission must take great care not to create effects that are counterproductive to its public enforcement policy. Whatever the outcome of the debate, and whatever final proposals the Commission puts forward, it is certain that in developing a culture of enforcement, striking the right balance in promotion of competition through the use of public and private enforcement will be a daunting task.

(c) Should Cartel Behaviour be Criminalised?

8.868 As identified above, cartel behaviour is attributed to undertakings, even though the actual behaviour is effected through the actions of individuals. Many consider, therefore, that deterrence should be targeted not only at undertakings, but also at individuals.

8.869 **Do financial penalties on undertakings ensure adequate deterrence for undertakings and their employees?** While developing private enforcement may significantly contribute to the overall level of enforcement, it does not help to solve the European dilemma of 'impossibly high' financial sanctions. As seen above in paras 8.588–8.589, even exceedingly high fines may fail to be sufficiently deterrent, and can even have negative consequences, ie result either in the passing on of the sanction to consumers,[962] or in the disappearance of a competitor, with the consequent risks associated with increased concentration. Hence, the imposition of non-monetary sanctions on undertakings and/or on their employees has been suggested[963] as a possible alternative. In addition to the possibility of giving wide publicity to the condemnation of the undertaking ('naming and shaming') such sanctions could take the form of correction orders ('corporate probation orders'[964] or 'punitive injunctions')[965] in respect of community service, or of 'equity fines', ie restitution to customers who have suffered harm, in the form of the attribution of shares of the undertakings for the same value as the fine that should have been imposed.[966] However, such measures have generally been considered as excessively complex and costly.

8.870 **Personal sanctions, up to imprisonment?** Another potential means of overcoming the limitations associated with monetary fines might be to include the imposition of consequences on individuals as part of the arsenal of sanctions. Such personal sanctions would be intended to induce employees to resist potential pressure from the shareholders or higher management, and to deter them from pursuing personal goals that could ultimately go against the interests of the undertaking that they work for. Individual sanctions would have a stigmatising effect that would probably significantly alter the perception of the risks

---

[962] This risk is limited however, since raising the prices to supra-competitive level is normally not possible in properly functioning markets. However, it is also true that cartels generally occur in markets where competition is already reduced (eg oligopolistic markets).

[963] See eg Brent Fisse, 'Reconstructing Corporate Criminal Law: Deterrence, Retribution, Faults and Sanctions', 1983, 56 S. Cal. L. Rev.

[964] Probation orders involve the sentencing authority suspending the imposition of a sanction, on condition that the offender complies with certain requirements. The primary aim of probation is rehabilitation of the offender to prevent further offending.

[965] Punitive injunctions take the form of an intervention by the sentencing authority in the organisation of the undertaking, by means of an order requiring the convicted corporate offender to introduce specifically ordered internal controls, at the risk of a further punishment for failure to do so.

[966] Equity fines have several advantages: they encourage shareholders to exert greater control over the managers, they induce managers to comply with the law for fear of a decrease in the value of their stock-options, they limit the risk that fines be passed on to consumers and increase the of the undertakings 'ability to pay'.

associated with cartel behaviour by potential offenders, thereby ensuring a deterrent effect at a level equivalent to fines imposed on undertakings.

Imposing financial penalties on individuals may still fail to deter cartel perpetrators sufficiently. **8.871** Certain undertakings may indeed be tempted to 'circumvent' such sanctions by providing compensation to their employees for payment of penalties incurred by them, for instance by paying higher salaries to those exposed to cartel liabilities. However, other personal sanctions can also be considered and may be expected to have a strong stigmatising effect, such as the 'disqualification' of the managers responsible for collusive behaviour. Few countries have adopted this approach, but such a system has been in place in the UK since 1986.[967] Against this background, some commentators consider that such sanctions are still not fully deterrent, and that imprisonment is the most appropriate sanction.[968] Because of their purely personal impact, jail terms could indeed be expected to have a high deterrent effect on cartel behaviour.

Sending cartel participants to jail: the US experience   In the United States, under the **8.872** Sherman Act, cartel behaviour is subject to punishment in the form of prison sentences. However, US judges have long remained reluctant to impose such sanctions.[969] Between 1966 and 1974, prison sentences for price-fixing were on average less than 13 days. However, as public opinion became increasingly aware of the damage caused by cartels, condemnations became more severe. The year 1997 was a turning point for the policy of the US Department of Justice. Fines on individuals and jail sanctions became much higher. In *Fine Art Auction Houses*, a jail term of one year was imposed.[970] In 2002, sentences amounting to more than 10,000 days' imprisonment were imposed, and the average jail term for price-fixing was 18 months. The number of custodial sentences has increased dramatically since 1996 and 20 sentences were imposed in 2002.[971] When determining adequate sanctions,

---

[967] The UK Company Directors Disqualification Act 1986 (CDDA) provided that the person sanctioned could no longer run a company until a judge decided otherwise. Under the Enterprise 2002 Act the OFT can now apply for a Competition Disqualification Order (CDO) against any director or directors (including persons acting as directors) of an undertaking which has participated in a cartel. Such a disqualification makes it a criminal offence for the disqualified person to be a director of a company or be involved in the management of a company, whether directly or indirectly. The maximum period of disqualification is 15 years. The disqualification is recorded on a publicly accessible register. In the Netherlands, similar legislative proposals were made in 2005, that would lead to individual monetary penalties for directors, of a maximum of EUR 450.000 (Global Competition Review News, 18 April 2005).

[968] See eg GJ Werden and MJ Simon, 'Why Price Fixers Should Go to Prison' (1987); WPJ Wils, ''Is Criminalization of EU Competition Law the answer?' (2005); WPJ Wils, 'Does the Effective Enforcement of Articles 81 and 82 EC Require Not Only Fines on Undertakings But Also Individual Penalties, in Particular Imprisonment? In CD Ehlermann (ed) *European Competition Law Annual 2001: Effective Private Enforcement of EC Antitrust Law* (Hart Publishing, 2002); PH Roschowicz, 'The Appropriateness of Criminal Sanctions in the Enforcement of Competition Law' [2004] ECLR 12.

[969] From 1890 to 1940, only 24 custodial sentences were given in 252 criminal cases. All concerned cases where violence or pressure had been exercised. Sanctions were often suspended and it was only in 1959 that a sentence of imprisonment was imposed for price-fixing where no pressure was involved.

[970] On the intensification of the prosecution of individuals, see eg SD Hammond, 'An overview of recent developments in the Antitrust Division's Criminal Enforcement Program', speech before the ABA Midwinter Leadership Meeting, Hawaii, 10 January 2005.

[971] See eg SD Hammond, Deputy Assistant Attorney General for Criminal Enforcement, Antitrust Division US DoJ, 'An Update of the Antitrust Division's Criminal Enforcement Program', speech before the ABA Section of Antitrust Law Cartel Enforcement, Washington, DC, 16 November 2005 and 'Charting New Waters in International Cartel Prosecutions', speech at the 20th Annual National Institute on White Collar Crime, 2 March 2006.

US judges take into account intent, recidivism and the co-operation of the individual, in the context of the leniency policy. Jail terms are perceived as particularly necessary in the case of large, international cartels and are viewed as particularly effective because of the social stigma they impose on the white collar staff who are subject to them.

8.873 **Cultural and practical issues** The criminalisation of cartel behaviour raises both cultural and practical issues. Criminal penalties are generally associated with acts that imply a strong moral condemnation or a direct threat to public order. However, in the context of economic regulation prohibitions are set out in view of their contribution to the pursuance of a collective goal of economic welfare, but do not stem from a condemnation of the conduct as such. In the US, the cultural background is such that price-fixing is perceived directly as a morally unacceptable behaviour. However, this has not been the case for very long in Europe, where it was not until recent decades that cartel behaviour was regarded as dishonest conduct.[972] One may therefore wonder whether the EU is culturally ready to accept that price fixers be sent to jail. Moreover, subjecting individuals to criminal penalties raises complex practical issues. Determining the degree of responsibility of a natural person is far from easy. This could be particularly difficult, for instance, in the case of mid-level managers who may be involved in the cartel without being necessarily aware of the restrictive goals pursued. Companies may also be tempted to blame their executives—possibly after having exercised pressure on them in favour of the infringement—in exchange for a lower fine. Finally, the overall cost-efficiency of criminal penalties may also be put into question. Sanctions such as jail terms are much more onerous on society than monetary fines. Cartel investigations would also be made be more difficult because of the additional efforts that would be deployed by cartel members, and more costly due to the procedural guarantees that would be associated with the adoption of a criminal system.

8.874 **Criminal sanctions for cartel conduct in Europe: already a reality** Criminal sanctions for cartel behaviour already exist in a number of EU Member States (eg France,[973] Germany, Ireland,[974] UK,[975] Estonia), and the EEA (Norway). In certain countries, however, they are rarely resorted to, such as in France, where criminal prosecution is generally limited to cases involving bid rigging, or in Germany, where the procedural constraints associated with criminal sanctions tend to discourage criminal prosecution. Since the adoption of the Enterprise Act in 2002, the UK has been at the forefront of the criminalisation of cartel behaviour, making it a criminal offence with a maximum penalty of five years imprisonment and/or an unlimited fine.[976] This has contributed to the development, in the other Member States, of a debate regarding the legitimacy of a criminalisation of cartel behaviour.

---

[972] See C Harding and J Joshua, *Regulating Cartels in Europe: A Study of Legal Control of Corporate Delinquency* (2003); DJ Gerber, *Law and Competition in Twentieth Century Europe: Protecting Prometheus* (1998).

[973] Under Art L420-6 of the Code of Commerce, an individual responsible for cartel behaviour is liable to a maximum fine of EUR 75,000 and to imprisonment for a maximum term of four years.

[974] Under point 8(b) of the Competition Act 2002, an individual responsible for cartel behaviour is liable to a maximum fine of EUR 4 million or 10% of the individual's turnover and/or to imprisonment for a term of a maximum of five years.

[975] Under the Entreprise Act 2002, an individual responsible for cartel behaviour is liable to an unlimited fine and to imprisonment for a maximum term of five years.

[976] Enterprise Act 2002, s 188.

Interestingly, in Ireland in 2006, a (suspended) sentence was imposed upon a participant in a cartel concerning home heating oil.[977]

Are minimum standards for criminal penalties at EU level possible? The criminalisa- **8.875**
tion of cartel behaviour has so far been left to the discretion of national governments, as it is a general rule that neither criminal law nor the rules of criminal procedure fall within the Community's competence.[978] However, in view of the unanimous condemnation of cartel behaviour in the EU, resulting from an ever greater awareness of its harmful effect on the economy, one may wonder whether the Community would not be entitled to oblige Member States to amend their legislation in accordance with minimum standards defining an EC criminal 'cartel offence'. In an important judgment of 13 September 2005, the ECJ ruled that in view of the fact that protection of the environment constitutes one of the essential objectives of the Community and despite the fact that, as a general rule, neither criminal law nor the rules of criminal procedure fall within the Community's competence, this 'does not prevent the Community legislature when the application of effective, propor-tionate and dissuasive criminal penalties by the competent national authorities is an essen-tial measure for combating serious environmental offences, from taking measures which relate to the criminal law of the Member States which it considers necessary in order to ensure that the rules which it lays down on environmental protection are fully effective".[979] By analogy, and in view of the importance of competition rules in the Treaty, the possibil-ity of the Community legislature taking measures relating to the criminal law of the Member States if such measures were deemed necessary in order to ensure the full effective-ness of Article 81 EC in relation to the most egregious violations of EC competition law cannot be entirely ruled out. As at 31 December 2006, however, no initiatives of any kind in this direction had been announced by the Commission. Indeed, for the Commission itself, linking its investigations to any possible criminal sanctions (at national level) would in all likelihood disturb the existing balance of the Commission's administrative enforce-ment tools on the one hand and defence rights on the other. At the same time, when it comes to the benefits to the Commission of criminal legislation in Member States, the pol-icy initiative of the Office of Fair Trading, linking corporate immunity granted by the Commission to individual immunity at national level, is a useful one. [980]

F. Conclusion

Over the last 50 years, the perception of cartels in Europe has undergone a truly **8.876**
Copernican revolution. Business practices which only half a century ago were often consid-ered a legitimate means of regulating the economy are now depicted as 'cancers' on the economy and energetically prosecuted. This evolution, which results from an ever greater

---

[977] W Prasifka (Chairman of the Irish Competition Authority) speech before the American Chamber of Commerce, Brussels, 20 October 2006.
[978] See, to that effect, Case 203/80 *Casati* [1981] ECR 2595, para 27, and Case C-226/97 *Lemmens* [1998] ECR I-3711, para 19.
[979] Case C-176/03 *Commission v Council* [2005] ECR I-7879, paras 47 and 48.
[980] See brochure by the OFT 'The Cartel offence: Guidance on the issue of no-action letters for individuals', available at the OFT's web site at <http://www.oft.gov.uk/Business/Cartels/default.htm>.

awareness of the considerable damage caused by collusion, owes much to the deepening of the European Union, the foundation of which consisted in constitutionalising certain basic economic principles, including that of free competition.

8.877 Since the mid 1990s the fight against cartels in the EU has gained intensity and resulted in considerable fines, which have often made the headlines. The efforts devoted to strengthening the fight against cartels have certainly paid off. However, one should not forget that, as with any kind of violations, whether white collar or not, better enforcement records may only reveal that the illegal activity is more widespread than believed. Whilst trade liberalisation, both within Europe and beyond, has helped to promote competition, one should not lose sight of the fact that economic globalisation also has the potential to render cartels even more efficient and damaging.

8.878 As the possible benefits of a successful elimination or reduction of competition in the market will always have the potential to make collusion attractive, the only way to prevent cartels is to render more daunting the penalties that might be incurred for engaging in such conduct. Deterrence is key. But as new technological developments make collusion ever more efficient and more difficult to detect, and as financial penalties on companies seem to be reaching their limits in terms of deterrence, one may wonder whether competition agencies should not be looking for other means of deterrence, both for the undertakings involved and for the natural persons by whom they are represented.

8.879 Where criminalising a form of conduct is considered, this implies that taking such a considerable step has broad acceptance in society. Although the much stricter position that has been adopted by the enforcement authorities in Europe in recent years appears to have been largely accepted, insofar as it has resulted in significant fines imposed mostly on large multinational companies, one may nevertheless wonder, in view of the degree of relative tolerance collusive behaviour has long enjoyed in continental Europe,[981] whether public opinion is ready for the criminalisation of cartel behaviour. One should also certainly not underestimate the increase in enforcement costs that would necessarily result from such a radical change. In this context, it would seem that the most important priority is to develop a more widely accepted culture of competition within Europe, using all the other means at the disposal of public authorities and private actors.

---

[981] See C Harding and J Joshua, *Regulating Cartels in Europe: A Study of Legal Control of Corporate Delinquency* (2003).

9

VERTICAL AGREEMENTS

Mario Filipponi, Luc Peeperkorn and Donncadh Woods

A. Introduction

(1) Applicability of Article 81 to Vertical Restraints

The early jurisprudence of the Court of Justice confirmed that Article 81 (former Article 85) **9.01** of the Treaty applies not only to horizontal agreements between traders operating at the same level in the chain of supply but also to vertical agreements between traders at different levels in the chain of supply. The first case submitted to the Court of Justice under Article 234 (former Article 177) of the Treaty concerned vertical restraints whereby a German manufacturer, Bosch, had in 1903 granted its Dutch distributor, van Rijn, an exclusive right of sale of all its products on the Netherlands market.[1] In his Opinion Advocate General Lagrange stated, *inter alia*: 'The first point which seems clear, and does not seem to have been contested in the main action, is that Article 85 [now Article 81] refers as much to "vertical" as to "horizontal" agreements . . .'.[2]

This view was endorsed by the Court in that it did not 'exclude the possibility that the restric- **9.02** tions on export . . . come within the words "agreements . . . which may affect trade between Member States" '.[3] Nevertheless, in *Italy v Council & Commission*,[4] the Government of Italy argued, *inter alia*, that Article 81 'covers dealings between persons trading on the horizontal level, whereas Article 86 [now Article 82] governs the relationships between persons trading at successive stages, vertically'. In its judgment the Court definitively rejected the view that only Article 82 applied to vertical restraints:

> Neither the wording of Article 85 [now Article 81] nor that of Article 86 [now Article 82] justifies interpreting either of these Articles with reference to the level in the economy at which the undertakings carry on business. Neither of these provisions makes a distinction between businesses operating in competition with each other at the same level or between businesses not competing with each other and operating at different levels. It is not possible to make a distinction where the Treaty does not make one.

> It is not possible either to argue that Article 85 can never apply to an exclusive dealing agreement on the ground that the grantor and grantee thereof do not compete with each other. For the competition mentioned in Article 85 (1) means not only any possible competition between the parties to the agreement, but also any possible competition between one of them and third parties.

The Court has also upheld the application of Article 81 to vertical restraints affecting both **9.03** inter-brand and intra-brand competition. In the *Consten and Grundig* case,[5] the Commission had restricted its analysis of the effects of the vertical restraints relating to exclusive distribution and non-compete in terms of their effects on intra-brand competition. Grundig and Consten and the German government argued that Article 81(1) only applied to vertical restraints which have a negative economic effect on inter-brand competition. It was argued

---

[1] Case 13/61 *de Geus v Bosch & van Rijn* [1962] ECR 45.
[2] ibid at 69.
[3] ibid at 53.
[4] Case 32/65 *Italy v Council & Commission* [1966] ECR 389. See the related judgments in Joined Cases 56/64 and 58/64 *Consten and Grundig v Commission* [1966] ECR 299.
[5] Joined Cases 56/64 and 58/64 *Consten and Grundig v Commission* [1966] ECR 299, 342.

that exclusive distribution agreements of the type granted to Consten are not only not harmful to competition but also have the beneficial effect of increasing inter-brand competition.

9.04 The Court rejected the view that Article 81 did not apply to vertical restraints relating to intra-brand competition:

> Although competition between producers is generally more noticeable than that between distributors of products of the same make, it does not thereby follow that an agreement tending to restrict the latter kind of competition should escape the prohibition of Article 85(1) [now Article 81(1)] merely because it might increase the former.

(2) History of the Application of Article 81 to Vertical Restraints

9.05 The unique character of EC competition policy towards vertical restrictions can largely be explained by its twofold aims. The main aim of EC competition policy is to ensure undistorted competition but it also has the aim of market integration. This latter aim has created a two-way pull on policy makers. On the one hand vertical restraints, including territorial exclusivity, were recognised as necessary to enable both producers and distributors to benefit from the opportunities of the common market. The penetration of new markets takes time and investment and is risky. The process is often facilitated by agreements between the producer who wants to break into a new market and a local distributor.

9.06 On the other hand territorial exclusivity in particular was considered as contrary to the fundamental aim of creation of a true internal/single market. Arrangements between producers and distributors can be used to continue the partitioning of markets or exclude new entrants who would intensify competition and bring about downward pressure on prices. Therefore, agreements between producers and distributors can be used pro-competitively to promote market integration and efficient distribution or anti-competitively to block integration and competition.

9.07 In response to the two-way pull in vertical restraints the Commission adopted a wide interpretation of the application of Article 81(1) coupled with a regulatory approach using block exemptions to establish the types of agreements and detailed clauses that would be permitted or not permitted.

9.08 This approach is reflected in the *First Report on Competition Policy 1971*, where it is stated that:

> During the first stage in the application of the rules on competition set out in the EEC Treaty, the problem of exclusive dealing[6] agreements was in the foreground of the Commission's competition policy . . . The attention given to the exclusive dealing agreements was fundamentally due to the fact that such agreements are particularly likely to create obstacles with regard to the integration of national markets into a single market, to the extent that they guarantee to the holder of the concession not only the exclusive right to obtain supplies direct

---

[6] The term 'exclusive dealing' is no longer used by the Commission. It was used primarily to describe what is now more commonly referred to as exclusive distribution; however, it was also used to describe exclusive purchasing and non-compete obligations. See in particular the 8th preamble of Commission Regulation (EEC) 67/67 of 22 March 1967 [1967] OJ 57/849.

from the manufacturer but also to be the only distributor allowed to introduce the relevant products into the territory allocated to him.[7]

(3) Theory of Active/Passive Sales

To counteract absolute territorial protection arising from territorial exclusivity, the Commission developed the theory of active/passive[8] sales and parallel trade. While distributors and producers may be allowed to agree not to sell actively outside their allotted territory, the possibility of passive (ie unsolicited) sales outside the exclusive territory and parallel trade must never be excluded. This mechanism was seen as a safety or pressure valve. It was believed that if price differences between Member States became excessive, then parallel traders would start to exploit the possibilities of arbitrage. The possibility of passive sales was also seen as necessary to protect what was seen as the fundamental right of consumers or their agents to purchase wherever they wanted. This right is a symbol of the internal market. Such was the strength of feeling with respect to the right to make parallel trade and passive sales, that any attempt in a distribution system to frustrate these rights was almost treated as a *per se* infringement of Article 81.

9.09

This approach of the Commission was first given concrete expression in its decision in the *Consten and Grundig* case,[9] which was confirmed in its essential points by the judgment of the Court of Justice.[10] Both the decision and judgment showed that the exclusive distribution agreement concluded between the German manufacturer and his distributor for the sale of the former's products in France fell within the scope of Article 81(1) and did not qualify for exemption under Article 81(3) because the concession of exclusivity was combined with absolute territorial protection.[11]

9.10

---

[7] *First Report on Competition Policy 1971* point 45.

[8] Art 2.2(c) of Commission Regulation (EEC) 1983/83 of 22 June 1983 on the application of Art 81(1) of the Treaty to categories of exclusive distribution agreements [1983] OJ L173/1, exempted, *inter alia*, the imposition on the exclusive distributor of 'the obligation to refrain, outside the contract territory and in relation to the contract goods, from seeking customers, from establishing any branch and from maintaining any distribution depot'. This obligation is commonly referred to as a prohibition on active sales. The imposition of such a prohibition on active sales outside the appointed territory does not restrict the freedom of the exclusive distributor to respond to unsolicited orders received from parties outside his appointed territory, commonly referred to as passive sales.

[9] [1964] OJ 2545/64.

[10] Joined Cases 56/64 and 58/64 *Consten and Grundig v Commission* [1966] ECR 299, 342.

[11] Absolute territorial protection occurs where, as a result of agreed restraints, a dealer faces no intra-brand competition within his territory. Such competition could arise from passive sales by other network dealers, or imports by parallel traders/consumers. The concept of absolute territorial protection as used by the Court appears to be somewhat wider than the use of the word 'absolute' might suggest. In *Consten and Grundig* the Court used this term to refer to the 'wish to eliminate any possibility of competition at the wholesale level in Grundig products in the territory specified' (343). Therefore, it would appear that the absence of arbitrage at the wholesale level is sufficient to establish absolute territorial protection despite the possibility of arbitrage by consumers. An example of the narrow definition of absolute territorial protection, where even arbitrage by consumers was impossible, is to be found in the *BMW Leasing* case (see n 133 below). In any event the dividing line between absolute territorial protection and an intra-Community export ban is less important given that under current case law they both constitute restrictions by object. In April 1998 the Court of Justice reaffirmed in para 14 of the *Javico* case (see n 154 below) that 'an agreement which requires a reseller not to resell contractual products outside the contractual territory has as its object the exclusion of parallel imports within the Community and consequently restriction of competition in the common market . . . Such provisions, in contracts for the distribution of products within the Community, therefore constitute by their very nature a restriction of competition.'

9.11   The most recent description of active and passive sales is found in point 50 of the Guidelines on Vertical Restraints.[12] Here it is stated that in the context of Block Exemption Regulation 2790/1999 'the Commission interprets "active" and "passive" sales as follows:

— "Active" sales mean actively approaching individual customers inside another distributor's exclusive territory or exclusive customer group by for instance direct mail or visits; or actively approaching a specific customer group or customers in a specific territory allocated exclusively to another distributor through advertisement in media or other promotions specifically targeted at that customer group or targeted at customers in that territory; or establishing a warehouse or distribution outlet in another distributor's exclusive territory.

— "Passive" sales mean responding to unsolicited requests from individual customers including delivery of goods or services to such customers. General advertising or promotion in media or on the Internet that reaches customers in other distributors' exclusive territories or customer groups but which is a reasonable way to reach customers outside those territories or customer groups, for instance to reach customers in non-exclusive territories or in one's own territory, are passive sales.'

In the remainder of this chapter the above definitions are used when active or passive sales are mentioned.

(4) System of Block Exemption Regulations

9.12   The Commission's approach to vertical restraints together with the notification system that was provided for in Council Regulation 17/62[13] gave rise to a 'mass' problem with almost 30,000 notifications concerning vertical agreements.[14]

9.13   Under the complex procedures laid down in Regulation 17 the Commission was unable to adopt many formal decisions. The possibility of closing cases informally was also limited. Therefore an approach of 'block exemptions' was adopted.

9.14   Under Council Regulation 19/65,[15] the Commission is empowered to adopt block exemption regulations which define certain categories of agreements which generally fulfil the conditions of exemption under Article 81(3). Under this Regulation the Commission adopted in the 1980s and early 1990s block exemption Regulations in the field of distribution, in particular relating to exclusive distribution,[16] exclusive purchasing,[17] and franchising.[18]

---

[12] OJ C291, 13.10.2000, pp 1–44.

[13] This Regulation not only gave the Commission its exclusive competence to grant exemptions under Art 81(3) but also set up a system of notification to the Commission for agreements for which an exemption or negative clearance was sought. This Regulation has been replaced by Council Regulation 1/2003, see Chapter 2.

[14] *First Report on Competition Policy 1971* point 48.

[15] Council Regulation (EEC) 19/65 of March 1965 [1965] OJ 36/533.

[16] Commission Regulation (EEC) 1983/83 of 22 June 1983 on the application of Art 85(3) [now Art 81(3)] of the Treaty to categories of exclusive distribution agreements [1983] OJ L173/1.

[17] Commission Regulation (EEC) 1984/83 of 22 June 1983 on the application of Art 85(3) [now Art 81(3)] of the Treaty to categories of exclusive purchasing agreements [1983] OJ L173/5.

[18] Commission Regulation (EEC) 4087/88 of 30 November 1988 on the application of Art 85(3) [now Art 81(3)] of the Treaty to categories of franchise agreements [1988] OJ L359/46.

As these three block exemption Regulations are no longer in force the reader is referred to the previous edition of this book, chapter 7, for an analysis of their details.

(5) Green Paper on Vertical Restraints

After the adoption of these first Block Exemption Regulations distribution changed and it was against the background of changed business practices between suppliers and buyers such as just-in-time production and a growing feeling of unease with the effectiveness of its own competition policy towards vertical restraints that the Commission started a thorough review of its policy in this field. The Commission commenced this review by adopting in 1997 a Green Paper on Vertical Restraints in EU Competition Policy.[19] **9.15**

A number of points became clear during the consultation process that followed publication of the Green Paper: **9.16**

(1) that the Block Exemption Regulations on exclusive distribution/exclusive purchasing/franchising were too legalistic and form based and created an unnecessary compliance burden, especially for companies without significant market power;
(2) that changes in the methods/formats of distribution made these Block Exemption Regulations work more and more as a straitjacket;
(3) that these Block Exemption Regulations exempted clear cases of market power where vertical restraints can have serious negative effects;
(4) that a new policy would require a more economic approach, analysing vertical restraints in their market context and making the assessment dependent upon the (likely) effects on the market;
(5) that a new policy should, as far as possible, take account of the wish for legal certainty and limitation of compliance costs.

The Commission subsequently sketched the new policy approach it favoured in a Communication on the Application of the EC Competition Rules to Vertical Restraints,[20] the follow-up to the Green Paper. It proposed to create a safe harbour with a broad umbrella block exemption regulation covering all vertical restraints for the distribution of goods and services.[21] The regulation would use the concept of a market share threshold to distinguish between agreements that are block exempted and agreements that are not block exempted. In addition the regulation would not any more contain a long 'white' list of clauses that may or must be contained in vertical agreements but would be based primarily on a 'black'-clause approach, ie a hardcore list which defines what is not block exempted even when the relevant market share threshold is not exceeded. In the Communication the Commission also proposed that vertical agreements not containing restraints from the hardcore list but which fall outside the regulation, for example because of a too high market share, would not be presumed illegal.[22] **9.17**

---

[19] COM (96) 721 final.
[20] COM (98) 544 final.
[21] Motor vehicle distribution was the only sector not covered by the policy review, see the Green Paper on Vertical Restraints, 2, n 2.
[22] Communication, 23–4.

(6) Two New Council Regulations

9.18 When the Commission adopted the Communication it also submitted to the Council two draft Council amending regulations in order to enable it to adopt the new policy approach described above. The Council adopted the two new Council Regulations which both entered into force on 18 June 1999.[23] Council Regulation (EC) 1215/99 amends Regulation (EEC) 19/65 and Council Regulation (EC) 1216/99 amended Regulation 17/62. The latter Regulation, which introduced the possibility of retroactive exemption for vertical agreements in general, has been cancelled with the replacement of Council Regulation 17/62 by Council Regulation 1/2003 (see Chapter 2). The practical effect of Council Regulation 1216/1999 was that companies no longer had to notify vertical agreements which they believed did not cause competition concerns, simply to ensure legal security. Instead, companies could place greater weight on their own analysis of the economic effects of the vertical restraints at issue, knowing that in the event of subsequent litigation it would not be too late to apply for an exemption under Article 81(3).[24] This was a first step towards the abolition of the exemption system realised by Council Regulation 1/2003.

(a) Extension of the Power to Block Exempt

9.19 Council Regulation 1215/99 relates to an amendment of Council Regulation (EEC) 19/65. Amendment was required to extend the power of the Commission to block exempt categories of vertical agreements. Such extension was considered necessary:

> because the current enabling regulation is restricted to a limited number of vertical restraints, namely, exclusive distribution of goods for resale, exclusive purchase of goods for resale, obligations in respect of exclusive supply and exclusive purchase for resale, and restrictions imposed in relation to the assignment or use of industrial property rights. It is also limited to agreements entered into between two parties . . .

> The current Commission block exemption regulations in the field of distribution . . . cannot be satisfactorily amended to provide for the change in policy proposed in this Communication. Therefore, subject to the adoption of the two Council Regulations outlined above, a new Commission Regulation will be proposed. This regulation will extend to all vertical restraints in all sectors of distribution other than motor vehicles, covering, inter-alia, selective distribution, services, intermediate goods and agreements between more than two parties each operating at different levels in the distribution chain.[25]

(b) Definition of a Vertical Agreement

9.20 In Article 1 of Council Regulation (EC) 1215/99 a new definition of vertical agreements is introduced. Agreements are vertical when they are 'entered into by two or more undertakings, each operating, for the purposes of the agreement, at a different level of the production or distribution chain, and relate to the conditions under which the parties may purchase, sell or resell certain goods or services'. This is a rather wide definition of what is a vertical agreement. It covers agreements between more than two undertakings as long as each of the undertakings operates at a different level of the production or distribution chain, for

---

[23] Council Regulation (EC) 1215/99 of 10 June 1999 amending Regulation (EEC) 19/65 and Council Regulation (EC) 1216/99 of 10 June 1999 amending Regulation 17 [1999] OJ L148 1 and 5, respectively.
[24] Communication, 35.
[25] Communication, 35 and 36.

example between a manufacturer, a wholesaler, and a retailer. It also covers agreements between competitors, as long as for the purposes of the agreement they are operating at different levels, for example when one manufacturer becomes the exclusive distributor for another manufacturer's products. Lastly, it covers such agreements when these relate to the conditions under which the parties may purchase, sell, or resell certain goods or services. These general terms mean that all forms of distribution agreements like exclusive distribution, selective distribution, exclusive purchasing, customer allocation, non-compete obligations, resale price maintenance, etc, are covered, for both final and intermediate goods and services. This new definition made it possible for the Commission to adopt a broad umbrella block exemption covering all distribution agreements.

The new Council Regulation in Article 1 further amends Council Regulation 19/65 in such **9.21** a way that the Commission is no longer obliged to specify a so-called white list of clauses which must be present, or other conditions which must be satisfied, in the agreements. This created the possibility of having a block exemption regulation with only a black list.

In addition to these two important amendments, Council Regulation (EC) 1215/99 con- **9.22** tains two further amendments of Council Regulation 19/65. The first concerns general disapplication of a block exemption regulation, the second concerns individual withdrawal of a block exemption regulation by Member States.

(c) Disapplication of a Block Exemption Regulation

Article 1(2), by inserting a new Article 1a into Council Regulation 19/65, allows the **9.23** Commission to include the power to disapply a block exemption regulation for parallel networks of similar agreements or concerted practices on a particular antitrust market. Any block exemption regulation providing for this possibility must stipulate the conditions which may lead to the exclusion of its application. Such conditions may be based on criteria such as the market coverage rate of the relevant networks of agreements.

This power to disapply is a new instrument, which the Commission may use for a particular **9.24** market instead of withdrawing the block exemption for individual companies. The difference in an individual withdrawal is that the Commission, in the case of disapplication, does not need to prove Article 81(1) is violated and/or that Article 81(3) cannot be applied. It only needs to establish that in a particular market the specified condition, like the coverage ratio, is fulfilled for a particular type of agreement. Whereas an individual withdrawal decision normally contains the prohibition of certain restraints applied by a particular company, general disapplication merely brings certain restraints applied by a group of companies in a particular market back under the direct applicability of Article 81. The Commission may subsequently take individual decisions to prohibit the agreements of individual companies. Or it may, for example, try to solve a perceived competition problem through a settlement with the companies involved.

Procedural safeguards are provided in the Council Regulation in Article 1(2) and 1(3) of **9.25** this new instrument. The Commission must establish the fulfilment of the specified condition by means of a regulation. It needs therefore to respect all the requirements for adopting a block exemption regulation, including consultation of the Advisory Committee on Restrictive Practices and Monopolies and all persons concerned by publishing a draft text for comment. The only difference from the procedure for a block exemption regulation is that the consultation of the Advisory Committee on Restrictive Practices and Monopolies is not required before publication of a draft regulation if no Member State requests such a consultation. The Commission must fix a period in such a disapplication regulation at the expiry of which the block exemption regulation would no longer be applicable in respect of the relevant agreements. This period may not be shorter than six months.

(d) Withdrawal of a Block Exemption Regulation by Member States

9.26 Article 1(4) of Council Regulation 1215/99, by inserting a new paragraph into Article 7 of Regulation 19/65, allows the competent authority of a Member State to withdraw, by way of an individual decision, the benefit of any new, or already existing, block exemption regulation adopted under Council Regulation 19/65. Unlike a disapplication, such a decision must establish, in respect of the relevant agreements, that Article 81.1 is infringed and the conditions for exemption are or are no longer fulfilled. This power is granted to the Member States where agreements or concerted practices covered by the block exemption regulation have certain effects which are incompatible with Article 81(3) in the territory of that Member State, or in a part thereof, which has all the characteristics of a distinct geographic market.

(7) A New Block Exemption Regulation and Guidelines

9.27 The new definition of vertical agreements and other changes to Council Regulation 19/65 enabled the Commission to adopt Commission Block Exemption Regulation (EC) 2790/1999 (the 'BER'), which forms a package with the Guidelines on Vertical Restraints (the 'Guidelines').[26]

B. When is a Vertical Restraint Likely to Fall within the Scope of Article 81(1)?

(1) General

9.28 Article 81(1) prohibits 'all agreements between undertakings, decisions by associations of undertakings and concerted practices which may affect trade between Member States and which have as their object or effect the prevention, restriction, or distortion of competition within the common market'. A vertical restraint will only fall within the scope of Article 81(1) where all of these criteria are fulfilled. Although in Article 81(1) the criterion of effect on trade between Member States appears before that of restriction of competition, it is common practice both in the decisions of the Commission and judgments of the Community Courts to examine the issue of restriction of competition prior to that of effect on trade.

(2) Agreement between Undertakings

9.29 This concept is dealt with in greater detail in paragraphs 3.47 to 3.99 of this book. In summary, Article 81 does not apply to unilateral acts or to agreements between traders who do not constitute separate undertakings.

---

[26] Commission Regulation (EC) 2790/1999 of 22 December 1999 on the application of Art 81(3) of the Treaty to categories of vertical agreements and concerted practices, OJ L336, 29.12.1999, pp 21–5, and Commission notice—Guidelines on Vertical Restraints, OJ C291, 13.10.2000, pp 1–44.

(a) Unilateral Acts versus Agreements

In vertical cases the distinction between the concept of agreement and unilateral act is not **9.30** always so clear-cut. The Commission may well find that what appear at first glance to constitute unilateral actions if looked at in isolation are in fact agreements or concerted practices because they form part of wider business relations. For example, in Joined Cases 25/84 and 26/84 *Ford v Commission*,[27] the Court held that the refusal by a motor vehicle manufacturer to supply its authorised dealers in Germany with right hand drive vehicles did not constitute a unilateral act which fell outside the scope of Article 81(1) but was an agreement within the meaning of that provision if it formed part of a set of continuous business relations governed by a general agreement drawn up in advance. The January 2004 judgment of the ECJ concerning the January 1996 *Adalat* decision of the Commission[28] has clarified that the mere fact that a measure adopted by an undertaking falls within the context of ongoing business relations is not sufficient in itself to establish the existence of an agreement.[29] The ECJ upheld the judgment of the CFI[30] annulling the decision of the Commission and requiring acquiescence of the wholesalers in the measures imposed by the manufacturer Bayer.[31] However the Court also confirmed that tacit acquiescence is sufficient, as occurred in the *Sandoz* case where '[t]he existence of a prohibited agreement . . . rested not on the simple fact that the wholesalers continued to obtain supplies from a manufacturer which had shown its intention to prevent exports, but on the fact that an export ban had been imposed by the manufacturer and tacitly accepted by the wholesalers'.[32] It should also be noted that the Court drew a distinction between the business relations at issue between manufacturers and wholesalers, as in the *Adalat* case, and those between manufacturers and the members of their selective distribution system as in the *AEG*,[33] *Ford*,[34] and *BMW Belgium*[35] cases.[36] Thus, it would appear that it is much easier to establish acquiescence in selective distribution cases. However, this does not absolve the Commission from having to establish a '*concurrence of wills*'[37] on the part of at least two parties in selective distribution cases.

In his opinion of 22 May 2003 in the *Adalat* case, Advocate General Tizzano not only gives a **9.31** helpful summary of the case law in this area but also draws attention to the need for an offer/request by one party and its acceptance by the other. He states at paragraphs 60–61 of his opinion:

> 60. That seems to me to be the crucial point for our purposes. I am of the opinion that it was only the request (or requirement) by Sandoz not to export that enabled the Court to find

---

[27] [1985] ECR 2725, para 21.

[28] OJ 1996 L201, p 1.

[29] See in this respect judgment of 6 Jan. 2004 in Joined Cases C-2/01 P and C-3/01 P, *Bundesverband der Arzneimittel-Importeure e V* and *Commission of the European Communities v Bayer AG* [2004] ECR I-23, para 141.

[30] Judgment of the Court of First Instance of 26 October 2000 in Case T-41/96 *Bayer v Commission* [2000] ECR II-3383 by which the Court annulled Commission Decision 96/478/EC of 10 Jan. 1996 relating to a proceeding under Art 85 of the EC Treaty (Case IV/34.279/F3—ADALAT) (OJ 1996 L201, p 1).

[31] See in particular para 142 of the judgment of the ECJ.

[32] Para 142 of the judgment of the ECJ.

[33] Case 107/82 *AEG v Commission* [1983] ECR 3151.

[34] Joined Cases 25/84 and 26/84 *Ford v Commission* [1985] ECR 2725.

[35] Joined Cases 32/78 and 36/78 to 82/78 *BMW Belgium and Others v Commission* [1979] ECR 2435.

[36] Para 143 of the judgment of the ECJ.

[37] See judgment of the Court of Justice of 13 July 2006 in Case C-74/04 P in *Commission v Volkswagen AG*, at para 36.

a form of 'tacit acceptance' in the fact that the wholesalers continued to order supplies from the manufacturer as usual and without demur, because an offer or a requirement—however expressed, even implicitly—is to my mind always necessary in order for an agreement to be regarded as having been made by way of tacit acceptance.

61 While the Sandoz judgment interpreted the concept of agreement very broadly, I do not think that one can go still further, to the point of regarding an agreement on an export ban as having been made by virtue of the mere fact that wholesalers continue to obtain supplies from a manufacturer who is attempting to prevent the possibility of their exporting but without requiring anything of them. In any event, doing so would lead to the absurd result that such an agreement could be formed even by the tacit acceptance of an offer that was never (even implicitly) made!

9.32 At paragraph 68 of his opinion he draws attention to an important issue when stating his view that in those cases where the Court found that measures of manufacturers constituted agreements because they formed part of ongoing commercial relations with resellers 'the Court did not consider whether the measures adopted constituted agreements in themselves but rather whether they were separate and distinct with respect to the agreements by which the selective distribution systems were established and governed, and hence unilateral, or whether on the contrary they were in fact governed by those agreements, of which they effectively came to form an integral part'.

9.33 In its October 2003 judgment in the *Opel Nederland* case, the Court of First Instance recalled, in citing the case law of the European Court of Justice, that 'in the absence of agreements between undertakings, a unilateral act by one undertaking without the express or tacit participation of another does not fall within Article 81(1)'.[38] The Court went on to uphold the Commission's finding that there was an agreement in this case, not on the basis of the adoption by Opel Nederland of a general policy aimed at restricting all exports from the Netherlands, but on the basis of three individual measures[39] taken in the context of this strategy, and which according to the Commission became an integral part of Opel's distribution agreements with its dealers.

9.34 This contrasts with the December 2003 judgment of the Court of First Instance in the *Volkswagen Passat* case.[40] In this case Volkswagen had sent circulars to dealers in its selective distribution network concerning the pricing of the Passat motor vehicle. Volkswagen argued, successfully before the Court, that these circulars were an attempt to influence the behaviour of dealers, which in the absence of consent, express or tacit, fell short of an agreement.[41] The Commission argued, unsuccessfully, that the calls at issue had become integral parts of the dealership agreement and therefore constituted agreements within the meaning of Article 81(1) EC.[42] The principal argument of the Commission is set out in paragraph 25 of the judgment:

25. As its principal argument, the Commission claims, first of all, that, according to the AEG, Ford, BMW, and Volkswagen judgments, it is not necessary, at least in the case of selective distribution systems such as that in this case, to look for acquiescence to a call by the manufacturer in the behaviour which the dealer adopts in the context of that call (for example after its receipt).

---

[38] Case T-368/00 *General Motors Nederland BV* and *Opel Nederland BV v The Commission* [2003] ECR II-04491, para 58.

[39] The three individual measures related to a restrictive supply policy, a restrictive bonus policy, and a direct export ban. See paras 25 and 60 of the judgment.

[40] Case T-208/01 *Volkswagen AG v Commission* [2003] ECR II-05141.

[41] Para 19 of the judgment.

[42] Para 24 of the judgment.

Such acquiescence must be regarded as established as a matter of principle, from the mere fact that the dealer has entered the distribution network. It is therefore deemed to have been given by the dealer. According to the Commission, that case-law, which serves as the basis of the contested decision, is not put in doubt by the judgments cited by the applicant, indeed on the contrary.

This argumentation of the Commission is dismissed in paragraph 47 of the judgment: **9.35**

47 The Court considers that the Commission is proceeding from a mistaken interpretation of the case-law which it cites in support of its case, when it argues that, according to the AEG, Ford, BMW and Volkswagen judgments, it is not necessary, at least in the case of selective distribution systems such as the one in this case, to look for acquiescence to a manufacturer's call in the conduct adopted by the dealer in the context of that call (for example after its receipt), and that such acquiescence ought to be regarded as having been established as a matter of principle by the mere fact that the dealer has entered the distribution network.

The Court then proceeds to analyse each of the *AEG, Ford, BMW,* and *Volkswagen* judgments and finds acquiescence in each case, with the exception of the *BMW* case, which it distinguishes.[43] Acquiescence was found in the *Ford* case on the basis that the dealers, despite some protests, had complied with the relevant circular.[44] **9.36**

In its appeal to the Court of Justice[45] the Commission argued that, according to settled case law,[46] a call by a motor vehicle manufacturer to its authorised dealers does not constitute a unilateral act which falls outside the scope of Article 81(1) EC but is an agreement within the meaning of that provision if it forms part of a set of continuous business relations governed by a general agreement drawn up in advance. In dismissing the appeal of the Commission, the Courts stated, inter alia, that 'the case-law to which the Commission refers does not imply that any call by a motor vehicle manufacturer to dealers constitutes an agreement within the meaning of Article 81(1) EC and does not relieve the Commission of its obligation to prove that there was a concurrence of wills on the part of the parties to the dealership agreement in each specific case'.[47] **9.37**

(b) Agreements between Separate Undertakings

The issue of separate undertakings arose in the *Viho* case.[48] This case concerned the dismissal by the Commission of a complaint lodged with it concerning the distribution by Parker Pen and its subsidiaries of its products throughout the European Union. The Court stated as follows at paragraphs 16–18 of its judgment: **9.38**

16 Parker and its subsidiaries thus form a single economic unit within which the subsidiaries do not enjoy real autonomy in determining their course of action in the market, but carry out the instructions issued to them by the parent company controlling them . . .

---

[43] Paras 50–4 of the judgment.
[44] Para 51 of the judgment.
[45] Case C-74/04 P in *Commission v Volkswagen AG*; judgment of the Court of Justice of 13 July 2006.
[46] The Commission referred to the following judgments; *Ford v Commission*, para 21; *Bayerische Motorenwerke*, paras 15 and 16; and Case C-338/00 P *Volkswagen v Commission* [2003] ECR I-9189, para 60. Para 60 of the latter judgment reads as follows: 'It is settled case-law that a call by a motor vehicle manufacturer to its authorised dealers is not a unilateral act which falls outside the scope of Art 85(1) of the Treaty but is an agreement within the meaning of that provision if it forms part of a set of continuous business relations governed by a general agreement drawn up in advance (*Ford v Commission*, paragraph 21, and *Bayerische Motorenwerke*, paragraphs 15 and 16)'.
[47] Para 36 of the judgment.
[48] Case C-73/95 [1996] ECR I-5457.

17 In those circumstances, the fact that Parker's policy of referral, which consists essentially in dividing various national markets between its subsidiaries, might produce effects outside the ambit of the Parker group which are capable of affecting the competitive position of third parties cannot make Article 85(1)[now Article 81(1)] applicable, even when it is read in conjunction with Article 2 and Article 3(c) and (g) of the Treaty. On the other hand, such unilateral conduct could fall under Article 86 [now Article 82] of the Treaty if the conditions for its application, as laid down in that article, were fulfilled.

18 The Court of First Instance was therefore fully entitled to base its decision solely on the existence of a single economic unit in order to rule out the application of Article 85(1) to the Parker group.

9.39   The issue of separate undertakings also arose in the September 2005 judgment of the Court of First Instance in the *DaimlerChrysler* case.[49] This case is summarised in section D.3, paragraph 9.172 on agency agreements. Finally, while 'intra-group' distribution agreements normally fall outside the scope of Article 81 because of the absence of an agreement between undertakings, they may, as stated by the Court in *Viho*, fall within the scope of Article 82 where the undertaking concerned is in a dominant position.[50] The question as to whether and in what circumstances a dominant pharmaceutical company could, by way of unilateral act, refuse under Article 82 to meet orders placed with it by wholesalers so as to restrict parallel trade in its products arose in an Article 234 reference by the Greek Competition Commission. The Court declined to answer the question, finding instead that the Greek Competition Commission was not a 'court or tribunal' able to refer a case to the European Court for a preliminary ruling.[51] Nevertheless, in his opinion, Advocate General Jacobs had suggested that, in defined circumstances, such a refusal might not be an abuse.[52] This case is discussed in greater detail in Chapter 4 on abuse of dominance.

(3) Object or Effect of Restricting Competition and Appreciability

9.40   For an agreement or concerted practice to be caught by Article 81(1) it must have either the object or effect of restricting competition. These are alternative and not cumulative requirements.[53] In assessing the compatibility of a distribution system with Article 81 it is essential first to identify whether there are any restrictions by object. This is because restrictions by object can be held to infringe Article 81(1) without the requirement for a detailed economic analysis required to establish a restriction by effect.[54] Therefore, even undertakings

---

[49] Case T-325/01 *DaimlerChrysler AG v Commission*, judgment of 15 Sept. 2005.

[50] In the settlement in the *Interbrew* case reported in the *Report on Competition Policy 1996* (Vol xxvi), the Commission states, *inter alia*, 'DG IV's intervention in this case confirms its policy of prohibiting any barrier to parallel trade resulting either from an agreement between undertakings or from an abuse of a dominant position'. See also judgment of the Court of First Instance in Case T-198/98 *Micro Business Leader v Commission* [1997] ECR II-03989, discussed below in paras 9.117 to 9.120.

[51] Judgment of the Court of Justice of 31 May 2005 in case C-53/03 *Syfait and Others v GlaxoSmithKline*.

[52] Opinion of Advocate General Jacobs of 28 Octber 2004.

[53] Case 56/65 *Société Technique Minière v Maschinenbau Ulm GmbH* [1966] ECR 235, 249.

[54] 'It is settled case law that for the purpose of the application of Art 85(1) there is no need to take account of the actual effects of an agreement when it has as its object the prevention, restriction or distortion of competition within the common market. Consequently, it is not necessary to show actual anti-competitive effects where the anti-competitive object of the conduct in question is proved (see Joined Cases 56/64 and 58/64 *Consten and Grundig v Commission* [1966] ECR 299, 342, and Case C-219/95 P *Ferrière Nord v Commission* [1997] ECR I-4411, paras 12 to 14). As the Court has just held, the Commission has proved that the applicant adopted measures whose object was to partition the Italian market (see in particular paras 88 and 89 above). The Commission was not therefore required to investigate the actual effects which those measures had on competition within the common market.' (Judgment of the Court of First Instance of the European Communities in Case T-62/98 *Volkswagen v Commission* [2000] ECR II 02707, para 178.)

with relatively small market shares have been found to infringe Article 81, when restrictions by object are involved.[55]

Vertical restraints with the object of resale price maintenance, absolute territorial protection, or exclusion of parallel imports/exports constitute, by their very nature, restrictions of competition and will normally fall within the prohibition of Article 81(1). The concepts of restriction by object and restriction by nature are synonymous.[56] Restrictions that are black-listed in block exemptions or identified as hardcore restrictions in guidelines and notices are generally considered by the Commission to constitute restrictions by object.[57]   **9.41**

The jurisprudence does not support the assertion that all impediments to parallel trade constitute restrictions by object. For example, a purely qualitative selective distribution system will normally not fall within the scope of Article 81(1) even though the inherent nature of a selective distribution system is that parallel trade by non-network dealers is excluded. Common distribution formats such as exclusive distribution, exclusive purchasing, and selective distribution have never been held by the Community Courts to constitute restrictions by object unless implemented with the direct or indirect objective of achieving absolute territorial protection, exclusion of parallel trade, or resale price maintenance. While there is no definitive list of those vertical restraints which constitute restrictions by object, provided these three latter elements are absent from the distribution system, other vertical restraints will, in all likelihood, be assessed as restrictions by effect and not restrictions by object. Non-exhaustive guidance on what constitute restrictions by object in vertical agreements can be found in Article 4 of the BER, paragraphs 46 to 56 of the Guidelines and other notices.[58] The Commission's 2004 Guidelines on the application of Article 81(3) of the Treaty[59] state, in paragraph 23, that '[a]s regards vertical agreements the category of restrictions by object includes, in particular, fixed and minimum resale price maintenance and restrictions providing absolute territorial protection, including restrictions on passive sales'. Further guidance can be gained from Commission instruments and the case law of the European Courts discussed below.   **9.42**

While Article 81(1) does not contain the word 'appreciable', it is clear from the jurisprudence of the Court and administrative practice of the Commission that a restriction of competition, and in particular a restriction by effect, will not fall within the scope of Article 81(1) unless it has an appreciable impact on competition in the relevant market. The concepts of 'object', 'effect', and 'appreciability' are further discussed below.   **9.43**

---

[55] Case 19/77 *Miller International Schallplatten GmbH v Commission* [1978] ECR 131. This case is summarized in para 9.70 to 9.74 of this chapter.

[56] See paras 14, 20, 21 of the judgment of the Court of Justice in Case C-306/96 *Javico International and Javico AG v Yves Saint Laurent Parfums SA* [1998] ECR I-1983.

[57] Guidelines on the application of Art 81(3) of the Treaty, [2004] OJ C101/08, para 23.

[58] Of particular relevance is the 2001 De Minimis Notice [Commission Notice on agreements of minor importance which do not appreciably restrict competition under Art 81(1) of the Treaty, OJ C368, 22.12.2001, p 13] and the accompanying press release (IP/02/13), the latter stating, *inter alia*, that '[t]he new Notice defines in a clearer and more consistent way the hardcore restrictions, ie those restrictions, such as price fixing and market sharing, which are normally always prohibited irrespective of the market shares of the companies concerned. Hardcore restrictions cannot benefit from the de minimis Notice. For agreements between non-competitors the new Notice has taken over the hardcore restrictions set out in Block Exemption Regulation 2790/1999 for vertical agreements.'

[59] [2004] OJ C101/08.

(a) Restriction by Object and Appreciability

9.44   The concept of restriction by object is also dealt with in paragraphs 3.145 to 3.164 of this book. This section concentrates on the vertical aspects of these restrictions. According to the Commission, no effect on the market is required for Article 81(1) to apply if the agreement has the object of restricting competition.[60] This statement requires clarification in three respects, relating first to subjective intent, secondly to the concept of restriction by nature, and thirdly agreements of minor importance.

9.45   **(i) Subjective Intent not Determinative**   The first clarification is that the existence of a restriction by object is not dependent on the subjective intent of the parties to the restriction. While subjective intent is relevant, the determination as to whether an agreement has as its purpose a restriction of competition is dependent on 'its terms, the legal and economic context in which it was concluded and the conduct of the parties'.[61] Thus, the Court of First Instance has stated that 'when examination of the clauses of an agreement, carried out in their legal and economic context, reveals in itself the existence of an alteration of competition, it may be presumed that that agreement has as its object the prevention, restriction or distortion of competition'.[62] The way in which an agreement is actually implemented may reveal a restriction by object even where the formal agreement does not contain an express provision to that effect.[63] Of the wide range of vertical restraints available to distributors very few have been held by the European Courts to constitute restrictions by object. For example, in *Delimitis* the Court was of the opinion that a beer supply agreement involving both an exclusive purchase and non-compete obligation did not constitute a restriction by object and that it was necessary to analyse its effects.[64] In *Javico*,[65] the Court stated that 'an agreement in which the reseller gives to the producer an undertaking that he will sell the contractual products on a market outside of the Community cannot be regarded as having the object of appreciably restricting competition within the common market'.

9.46   **(ii) Restriction by Nature**   Secondly, restrictions by object are restrictions which by their very nature constitute a restriction of competition. In the absence of horizontal elements,[66] vertical restraints have only been held to constitute restrictions by object where they are used to impede parallel trade within the Community or enforce resale price maintenance.[67]

---

[60] *Report on Competition Policy 1994* (Vol xxiv) point 145. This statement finds support in the case law of the Court. In *Consten and Grundig* cited above the Court of Justice states at p 342 of its judgment that 'for the purposes of applying Art 85(1) [now Art 81(1)], there is no need to take account of the concrete effects of an agreement once it appears that it has as its object the prevention, restriction or distortion of competition'. See also judgment of the Court of First Instance of the European Communities in Case T-62/98 *Volkswagen v Commission* [2000] ECR II 02707, para 178.

[61] Joined Cases 96/102, 104, 105, 108, 110/82 *NV IAZ International Belgium and others v The Commission* [1983] ECR 3369, paras 23–5.

[62] Case T-168/01 *GlaxoSmithKline Services Unlimited v Commission of the European Communities* [2006] ECR 0000, para 111. Judgment of the Court of First Instance of 27 September 2006.

[63] Guidelines on the application of Art 81(3) of the Treaty, [2004] OJ C101/08, para 22.

[64] Case C-234/89 *Stergios Delimitis v Henniger Brau AG* [1989] ECR 935, 984, para 13.

[65] Case C-306/96 *Javico International and Javico AG v Yves Saint Laurent Parfums SA* [1998] ECR I-01983.

[66] It is important to recognise that vertical distribution arrangements may also have horizontal aspects which contain restrictions by object, particularly where there is territorial or customer allocation as between the parties to the vertical restraint—see *BP Kemi—DDSF* [1979] OJ L286/32.

[67] Although normally only concluded in horizontal agreements, it is likely that a vertical agreement limiting output would also constitute a hardcore restriction.

(iii) Agreements of Minor Importance   The third clarification relates to *agreements of*   **9.47**
minor importance. The *Volk v Vervaeke* case,[68] which concerned absolute territorial protection, established the principle that even in relation to restrictions by object it remains necessary to analyse the actual or potential effect of the vertical restraint involved so as to rule out the possibility that it may only have an insignificant effect on the market. The 'insignificant effect' doctrine of *Volk v Vervaeke* applies to both the restriction of competition and effect on trade criteria. However, as will become apparent from the case law analysed below, the real litmus test for restrictions by object appears not to be one of appreciability of the restriction but rather whether it is capable of having an appreciable effect on trade between Member States.

It is not possible to give a precise quantitative definition of 'insignificant effect'. While the   **9.48**
Court did not say that distribution arrangements for Volk's products in Belgium had an insignificant effect on the market, because the case arose from an Article 234 reference, this is the clear inference of the judgment. In its submission to the Court the Commission stated that the production of washing machines by Mr Volk's company represented 0.08 per cent of the total production of the common market and 0.2 per cent of production in the Federal Republic of Germany. Its market share of sales in Belgium and Luxembourg, the territory of its exclusive distributor Vervaeke, was approximately 0.6 per cent. On the basis of these small market shares the Commission 'admitted that even when an agreement guaranteeing strict "territorial protection" is concluded, the manufacturer does not appreciably restrict competition'. Neither did the Commission believe that the criteria 'may affect trade between Member States' was fulfilled.

In the *Miller* case,[69] which concerned a territorial restriction by object, the Court found   **9.49**
that the company concerned, which had a market share of the German market in sound recordings which varied between 5 and 6 per cent could not be compared with the undertakings in the *Volk* case and that the prohibition of Article 81(1) was infringed. While market share is not the only criterion for assessing the impact of a vertical restraint, it can be stated as a general rule for restrictions by object that below 1 per cent market share the effect on the market is likely to be insignificant and Article 81(1) is unlikely to apply, while above 5 per cent the effect is likely to be appreciable and Article 81(1) is likely to apply. Between 1 per cent and 5 per cent is best described as a grey area. It is important to note that for restrictions by object the Commission no longer gives any comfort under

---

[68] Case 5/69 *Volk v Vervaeke* [1969] ECR 295, 302, paras 5–7, where the Court stated: 'If an agreement is to be capable of affecting trade between Member States it must be possible to foresee with a sufficient degree of probability on the basis of a set of objective factors of law or of fact that the agreement in question may have an influence, direct or indirect, actual or potential, on the pattern of trade between Member States. Moreover, the prohibition in Art 85(1) [now Art 81(1)] is applicable only if the agreement in question also has as its object or effect the prevention, restriction or distortion of competition within the Common Market. These conditions must be understood by reference to the actual circumstances of the agreement. Consequently, an agreement falls outside the prohibition of Art 85 when it has only an insignificant effect on the markets, taking into account the weak position which the persons concerned have on the market of the product in question. Thus an exclusive dealing agreement, even with absolute territorial protection, may, having regard to the weak position of the persons concerned on the market in the products in question in the area covered by the absolute protection, escape the prohibition laid down in Art 85(1).'

[69] Case 19/77 *Miller International Schallplatten GmbH v Commission* [1978] ECR 131.

its de minimis notice. Unlike the 1986 De Minimis Notice, the 1997,[70] and current 2001[71] Notice of the Commission offer no comfort to undertakings in this grey area. The 1986 Notice applied to both restrictions by object and effect. Both the 1997 and current 2001 Notice exclude defined vertical hardcore restraints from the benefit of the notice. Therefore, even companies with little market power who enter into restrictions by object run the risk of infringing Article 81(1).

9.50 While restrictions by object are subject to the appreciability doctrine, it will be seen from the analysis of the leading cases summarised in paragraphs 9.69 to 9.100 below that the doctrine does not appear to have been consistently applied to both the restriction of competition and effect on trade criteria. In many cases the appreciability of the restriction appears to be assumed (ie restriction by nature), with the analysis of appreciability concentrating upon effect on trade between Member States. This contrasts with the Commission's 2001 Notice which confines its de minimis threshold to the restriction of competition criteria. Guidance on the de minimis threshold for the effect on trade criteria is to be found in the Commission's 2003 Notice on effect on trade.[72] The earlier 1997 De Minimis Notice did not distinguish between the effect on trade and restriction of competition criteria and applied the de minimis threshold to the general application of Article 85(1), now 81(1). Greater attention is now being be paid to the effect on trade criteria as it determines the scope of application of Article 3 of Regulation 1/2003 on the implementation of the rules on competition laid down in Articles 81 and 82 of the Treaty.[73] Both the De Minimis Notice and the Notice on effect on trade are considered below under the heading of De Minimis Notices of the Commission.

(b) Restriction by Effect and Appreciability

9.51 In *Technique Minière*,[74] the Court states that where the analysis of the clauses of an agreement, in the economic context in which it is to be applied, does not reveal the effect on competition to be sufficiently deleterious as to constitute a restriction by object

> the consequences of the agreement should then be considered and for it to be caught by the prohibition it is then necessary to find that those factors are present which show that competition has in fact been prevented or restricted or distorted to an appreciable extent.

> The competition in question must be understood within the actual context in which it would occur in the absence of the agreement in dispute. In particular it may be doubted whether there is an interference with competition if the said agreement seems really necessary for the penetration of a new area by an undertaking.

9.52 In the 1971 *Béguelin case*, concerning the legality of an exclusive distribution agreement, the Court ruled that the effect on competition must be appreciable: 'in order to come

---

[70] [1997] OJ C372/13. The 1997 Notice states that the applicability of Art 81(1) cannot be ruled out below the de minimis threshold, defined solely in terms of market share, 'for vertical agreements which have as their object—to fix resale prices, or—to confer territorial protection on the participating undertakings or third parties'.

[71] Commission Notice on agreements of minor importance which do not appreciably restrict competition under Art 81(1) of the Treaty, OJ C368, 22.12.2001, p 13.

[72] OJ C101, 27.04.2004, pp 81–96.

[73] OJ L1, 4.1.2003, p 1.

[74] See n 53 above.

within the prohibition imposed by Article 85 [now Article 81], the agreement must affect trade between Member States and the free play of competition to an appreciable extent'.[75] The Court also gave some guidance on the elements to be examined when applying the criteria of appreciability:

> 17. In order to examine whether this is the case, these factors must be considered in the light of the situation which would have existed but for the agreement in question.

> 18. It follows that, in order to determine whether a contract which contains a clause conferring an exclusive right of sale is caught by that Article, account must be taken in particular of the nature and quantity, restricted or otherwise, of the products covered by the agreement; the standing of the grantor and of the grantee of the concession on the market in the products concerned; whether the agreement stands alone or is one of a series of agreements; the stringency of the clauses designed to protect the exclusive right or on the other hand, the extent to which any openings are left for other dealings in the products concerned in the form of re-exports or parallel imports.[76]

(i) Ancillary Restraints Doctrine   The Court of Justice has further narrowed the scope   **9.53** of application of Article 81(1) to vertical restraints which are not restrictions by object, by applying the concept of necessity (the 'ancillary restraints doctrine'). This approach of the Court is partly reflected in its judgment in *Pronuptia*,[77] where it ruled, *inter alia*, that 'provisions which are strictly necessary in order to ensure that the know-how and assistance provided by the franchisor do not benefit competitors do not constitute restrictions of competition for the purposes of Article 85(1) [now Article 81(1)]'.[78] The Court stated that this would cover 'a clause prohibiting the franchisee, during the period of validity of the contract and for a reasonable period after its expiry, from opening a shop of the same or a similar nature in an area where he may compete with a member of the network'.[79]

Nevertheless, extreme caution must be taken in applying an entirely effects-based approach   **9.54** where the distribution system affords territorial protection. In the *Pronuptia* case the Court, basing itself on its judgment in *Consten and Grundig*, was of the opinion that franchise agreements typically result

> in a sharing of markets between the franchisor and the franchisees or between franchisees and thus restricts competition within the network . . . a restriction of that kind constitutes a limitation of competition for the purposes of Article 85(1) [now Article 81(1)] if it concerns a business name or symbol which is already well-known. It is of course possible that a prospective franchisee would not take the risk of becoming part of the chain, investing his own money, paying a relatively high entry fee and undertaking to pay a substantial annual royalty, unless he could hope, thanks to a degree of protection against competition on the part of the franchisor and other franchisees, that his business would be profitable. That consideration, however, is relevant only to an examination of the agreement in the light of the conditions laid down in Article 85(3).[80]

(ii) No Balancing of Positive and Negative Effects under Article 81(1)   In the first edi-   **9.55** tion of this book, it was suggested that in its judgment in Case T-374/94 *European Night*

---

[75] See the judgment of the Court of Justice of 25 November 1971 in Case 22/71 *Béguelin* [1971] ECR 960, para 16.

[76] Case 22/71 at paras 17 and 18.

[77] Case 161/84 *Pronuptia de Paris v Pronuptia de Paris Irmgard Schillgalis* [1996] ECR 374.

[78] Case 161/84, 388.

[79] Case 161/84, para 16.

[80] Case 161/84, para 24.

Services [ENS] & Others v The Commission,[81] the Court of First Instance had potentially further reduced the scope of application of Article 81(1), leaving the door open for a balancing of positive and negative effects under Article 81(1). The court appears to have closed this door stating clearly that the balancing of anti-competitive and pro-competitive effects is to be conducted exclusively within the framework laid down by Article 81(3).[82] Nevertheless, the *European Night Services* judgment remains essential reading for those wishing to understand the scope of Article 81, and is discussed in some detail in paragraphs 3.218 to 3.220 of this book.

9.56 **(iii) Adoption of more Economic Approach by the Commission**   Until the late 1990s, the Commission resisted this more economic approach of the Court which effectively narrowed the scope of application of Article 81(1) and continued to apply Article 81(1) relatively widely to vertical restraints and exempt them from Article 81(1). It was not until the adoption of the Guidelines in 1999 that the Commission first set out a framework for analysis that was clearly based on the economic impact on the market. This was followed in 2000 with Guidelines on horizontal co-operation agreements[83] and in 2004 by Guidelines on technology licensing agreements.[84] The new effects-based approach of the Commission is confirmed and summarised in paragraph 24[85] of the Commission's 2004 Guidelines on the application of Article 81(3) of the Treaty:

> For an agreement to be restrictive by effect it must affect actual or potential competition to such an extent that on the relevant market negative effects on prices, output, innovation or the variety or quality of goods and services can be expected with a reasonable degree of probability (31). Such negative effects must be appreciable. The prohibition rule of Article 81(1) does not apply when the identified anti-competitive effects are insignificant (32). This test reflects the economic approach which the Commission is applying. The prohibition of Article 81(1) only applies where on the basis of proper market analysis it can be concluded that the agreement has likely anti-competitive effects on the market (33). It is insufficient for such a finding that the market shares of the parties exceed the thresholds set out in the Commission's *de minimis* notice (34). Agreements falling within safe harbours of block exemption regulations may be caught by Article 81(1) but this is not necessarily so. Moreover, the fact that due to the market shares of the parties an agreement falls outside the safe harbour of a block exemption is in itself an insufficient basis for finding that the agreement is caught by Article 81(1) or that it does not fulfil the conditions of Article 81(3). Individual assessment of the likely effects produced by the agreement is required.

> (31) It is not sufficient in itself that the agreement restricts the freedom of action of one or more of the parties, see paragraphs 76 and 77 of the judgment in *Métropole television (M6)* cited in note 10 [of the 2004 Guidelines on the application of Article 81(3)] . This is in line with the fact that the object of Article 81 is to protect competition on the market for the benefit of consumers.

> (32) See eg Case 5/69, *Völk*, [1969] ECR 295, paragraph 7. Guidance on the issue of appreciability can be found in the Commission Notice on agreements of minor importance

---

81 [1998] ECR II 3141.

82 See Case T-65/98, *Van den Bergh Foods*, [2003] ECR II-4653, para 107 and Case T-112/99, *Métropole télévision (M6)* and others, [2001] ECR II-2459, para 74, where the Court of First Instance held that it is only within the precise framework of Art 81(3) that the pro- and anti-competitive aspects of a restriction may be weighed.

83 Commission Notice on Guidelines on the application of Art 81 of the Treaty to horizontal co-operation agreements, OJ C3, 6.1.2001, p 2.

84 Commission Notice on Guidelines on the application of Art 81 of the Treaty to technology transfer agreements, OJ C101, 27.4.2004, p 2.

85 [2004] OJ C101/08, para 24.

which do not appreciably restrict competition under Article 81(1) of the Treaty (OJ C368, 22.12.2001, p 13). The notice defines appreciability in a negative way. Agreements, which fall outside the scope of the de minimis notice, do not necessarily have appreciable restrictive effects. An individual assessment is required.

(33) See in this respect Joined Cases T-374/94 and others, *European Night Services*, [1998] ECR II-3141.

(34) See note 32 [of the 2004 Guidelines on the application of Article 81(3)].

It should also be noted that paragraph 18 of these Guidelines set out two counterfactuals **9.57** or questions which provide a framework for assessing whether an agreement or its individual parts may restrict competition. These two counterfactuals, which are discussed in greater detail in Chapter 3 above (see paragraphs 3.295 to 3.303), reflect the wording of paragraphs 17 and 18 of the *Béguelin* judgment quoted above:

Does the agreement restrict actual or potential competition that would have existed without the agreement? If so, the agreement may be caught by Article 81(1).

Does the agreement restrict actual or potential competition that would have existed in the absence of the contractual restraint(s)?

The Guidelines on vertical restraints provide criteria for the assessment of the most common vertical restraints. These criteria are examined in detail later on in this chapter.

(4) May Affect Trade between Member States and Appreciability

The concept of 'capable of appreciably affecting trade between Member States' is addressed **9.58** in the 2004 Commission Guidelines on the effect on trade concept contained in Articles 81 and 82 of the Treaty.[86] This concept is dealt with in general in Chapter 3, paragraphs 3.365 to 3.378 of this book. The vertical aspects of the negative rebuttable presumption of appreciability of effects on trade set out in paragraph 51 of the 2004 Effect on Trade Notice, however, are summarised in the following section on de minimis requirements.

(5) De Minimis Notices of the Commission

The concept of de minimis is also dealt with in paragraphs 3.238 to 3.242 of this book. **9.59** This section concentrates on the vertical aspects of this concept. It is important to stress that the de minimis notices are only binding on the Commission,[87] however they can be of persuasive influence before national courts.[88] The Court of Justice has also recognised that they can create legitimate expectations.[89]

Subject to the exceptions described below, the 2001 De Minimis Notice[90] provides a safe **9.60** harbour for agreements between non-competitors (the Notice does not use the term vertical agreements but distinguishes 'agreements between competitors' and 'agreements

---

[86] OJ C101, 27.04.2004, pp 81–96.

[87] Para 4 of 2001 Notice.

[88] See judgment of the UK Court of Appeal of 22 July 1998 in *Gibbs Mew plc v Graham Gemmell*, where the national court gave considerable weight to the Commission's definition of de minimis in the beer sector (as set out in the Commission's Notice concerning Regulations (EEC) 1983/83 and 1984/83 [1984] OJ C101/2) in rejecting the application of Art 81(1) to certain beer tie (ie exclusive purchase and non-compete) agreements.

[89] Judgment of the Court of Justice of 28 June 2005, in case C-189/02, para 211.

[90] OJ C368, 22.12.2001, p 13.

between non-competitors'[91]) which affect trade between Member States provided that the market share on the relevant market of each party does not exceed 15 per cent. Such agreements are presumed not to appreciably restrict competition within the meaning of Article 81(1). The 1997 Notice[92] had a threshold of 10 per cent for vertical agreements while the 1986 Notice had a threshold of 5 per cent for 'agreements between undertakings engaged in the production or distribution of goods or in the provision of services' (ie a common threshold for both vertical and horizontal agreements). The current 15 per cent threshold for agreements between non-competitors reflects the Commission's economic approach to assessing vertical restraints and the recognition that competition concerns cannot generally be expected when companies do not have a minimum degree of market power. It also reflects, with a lower 10 per cent threshold for agreements between competitors, that such agreements can lead more readily to anti-competitive effects than agreements between non-competitors. It should be noted that the 15 per cent threshold is a negative definition of appreciability. Exceeding this threshold does not imply that agreements appreciably restrict competition.[93]

9.61 The 1997 De Minimis Notice excluded from its benefit agreements operated on a market where 'competition is restricted by the cumulative effects of parallel networks of similar agreements established by several manufacturers or dealers'.[94] This meant in practice that firms operating in sectors like the beer and petrol sector could usually not benefit from the De Minimis Notice. The 2001 Notice introduces a 'de minimis' market share threshold of 5 per cent for markets where there exist such parallel networks of similar agreements. Therefore, individual suppliers or distributors with a market share not exceeding 5 per cent are in general not considered to contribute significantly to a cumulative foreclosure effect. For those cases where the 5 per cent threshold is exceeded the Notice helpfully states that '[a] cumulative foreclosure effect is unlikely to exist if less than 30 per cent of the relevant market is covered by parallel (networks of) agreements having similar effects'.[95]

9.62 The 2001 Notice, like its 1997 predecessor, clearly confirms the application of the condition of 'appreciability' to both restrictions of competition and effect on trade between Member States, irrespective of whether a restriction by object or effect is involved.[96] However, unlike its predecessors, the thresholds in the current 2001 Notice create a negative presumption only in relation to the concept of 'appreciably restrict competition' and not in relation to the concept of 'capable of appreciably affecting trade between Member States'.[97] It is therefore possible that an agreement which constitutes an appreciable restriction of competition may fall outside the scope of Article 81 because it is not capable of appreciably affecting trade between Member States. This probably explains the difference in title between the 1997 and 2001 texts with the former entitled 'Notice on agreements of minor importance which do not fall within the meaning of Article 85(1) of the Treaty', and the latter entitled 'Commission Notice on agreements of minor importance which do not appreciably restrict competition under Article 81(1) of the Treaty'.

---

[91] Most but not all vertical agreements will be agreements between non-competitors.
[92] [1997] OJ C372/13.
[93] See para 2 of the 2001 Guidelines.
[94] On cumulative effect see section C below.
[95] See para 8 of the 2001 Guidelines.
[96] See para 1 of the Notice.
[97] See para 3 of the 2001 Guidelines.

It is interesting to note that despite the statement set out in paragraph 3 of the 2001 Notice **9.63** that '[i]t does not quantify what does not constitute an appreciable effect on trade' it goes on to state that agreements between small and medium-sized undertakings (SMEs) as defined in the Annex to Commission Recommendation 96/280/EC[98] are normally not capable of affecting trade between Member States. Therefore the Commission considers that agreements between SMEs generally fall outside the scope of Article 81(1). The reason for this presumption is the fact that the activities of SMEs are normally local or at most regional in nature.

In cases covered by the new Notice, the Commission will not institute proceedings either **9.64** upon application or on its own initiative. Where companies assume in good faith that an agreement is covered by the Notice, the Commission will not impose fines.[99] Although not binding on them, the Notice also intends to give guidance to the courts and authorities of the Member States in their application of Article 81.

(a) De Minimis and the Commission Guidelines on the Effect on Trade Concept

The concept of 'capable of appreciably affecting trade between Member States' is addressed **9.65** in the 2004 Commission Guidelines on the effect on trade concept contained in Articles 81 and 82 of the Treaty,[100] which for vertical agreements (including restrictions that have been identified as hardcore restrictions in Commission block exemption regulations and guidelines) sets out the following negative[101] rebuttable presumption based on a double threshold of market share and turnover:

> 52 The Commission holds the view that in principle agreements are not capable of appreciably affecting trade between Member States when the following cumulative conditions are met:
>
> (a) The aggregate market share of the parties on any relevant market within the Community affected by the agreement does not exceed 5 per cent , and
> (b) In the case of vertical agreements, the aggregate annual Community turnover of the supplier in the products covered by the agreement does not exceed 40 million euro. In the case of licence agreements the relevant turnover shall be the aggregate turnover of the licensees in the products incorporating the licensed technology and the licensor's own turnover in such products. In cases involving agreements concluded between a buyer and several suppliers the relevant turnover shall be the buyer's combined purchases of the products covered by the agreements.

(b) Application of De Minimis to Hardcore Restrictions

It is interesting to note that though the legal assessments of the Commission in the 1992 **9.66** *Parker Pen* case[102] and 1994 *Tretorn* case,[103] both involving an export ban, a restriction by

---

[98] OJ L107, 30.4.1996, p 4. With effect from 1 Jan. 2005 this Recommendation has been replaced by Commission Recommendation 2003/361/EC concerning the definition of micro, small, and medium-sized enterprises (OJ L124, 20.5.2003, p 36).

[99] Art 4 of the Notice.

[100] OJ C101, 27.04.2004, pp 81–96.

[101] This negative definition of appreciability does not imply that agreements which do not fall within the criteria are automatically capable of appreciably affecting trade between Member States. A case-by-case analysis is necessary (ref para 51 of the Notice).

[102] *Viho/Parker Pen* [1992] OJ L233/27.

[103] *Tretorn and others* [1994] OJ L378/45.

object, contain no analysis of the condition of appreciability in relation to restriction of competition they do however consider it in relation to the effect on trade. On the other hand, the Commission's later 1998 decision in the *VW-Audi* case,[104] which found both restrictions by object and effect, analysed both the restriction of competition and effect on trade in terms of their appreciability.[105] Nor has it been clear from the jurisprudence of the Community Courts that the concept of 'appreciability' applied to both of these conditions.[106] Nevertheless, in the 1997 De Minimis Notice the Commission has interpreted the jurisprudence of the Court of Justice as having 'clarified that this provision [ie Article 81(1)] is not applicable where the impact of the agreement on intra-community trade or on competition is not appreciable'.[107] This statement is repeated in paragraph 1 of the 2001 Notice. While the interpretation of the Commission is helpful, it should, as regards restrictions by object, be treated with some caution.

9.67   Paragraph 11(2) of the 2001 Notice defines certain vertical restraints which cannot benefit from the Notice. These are vertical restraints having as their direct or indirect object the fixing of resale prices or the conferring of territorial protection. In an improvement over its predecessor, the 2001 Notice defines in a clearer and more consistent way the excluded hardcore restrictions. This is because the excluded hardcore restrictions are the same as those set out in Article 4 of the BER. Article 4 is discussed below in paras 9.206–9.231.

(6) Analysis of Leading Cases on Vertical Restraints

9.68   The following section presents an overview of what Community Courts have considered to amount to restriction by object or restriction by effect.

(a) *Restrictions by Object*

9.69   (i) *Consten and Grundig*[108]—**Exclusive Distribution**[109] **combined with Absolute Territorial Protection (1966)**   This case arose from proceedings in France taken by Consten, the exclusive distributor in France of Grundig electrical appliances, against a French parallel importer UNEF who had been sourcing Grundig appliances from German wholesalers and reselling them in France to retailers at prices below those of Consten. The national proceedings were stayed following UNEF's March 1962 application to the Commission for a declaration that the distribution arrangements between Consten and Grundig infringed Article 81 of the Treaty. In January 1963, Grundig notified, *inter alia*, its agreements with Consten. The decision of the Commission in the *Grundig and Consten* case,[110] which was confirmed in its essential points by the judgment of the Court of Justice,[111] showed that the exclusive distribution agreement fell within the scope of Article 81(1) and did not

---

104   *VW-Audi* [1998] OJ L124/60.

105   *VW-Audi* [1998] OJ L124/60, paras 149 and 150.

106   See paras 37–41 of the Opinion of Advocate General Mischo in Case 27/87 *SPRL Louis Erauw-Jacquery v La Hesbignonne SC* [1988] ECR 1919.

107   Para 2 of the 1997 De Minimis Notice [1997] OJ C372/13.

108   Joined Cases 56/64 and 58/64 *Consten and Grundig v Commission* [1966] ECR 299.

109   The BER recognises the rationale for allocating exclusive territories or customer groups and the need to protect an exclusive distributor against, for instance, free riding by other distributors on its promotional investments; see paras 9.213–9.222.

110   [1964] OJ 161.

111   Joined Cases 56/64 and 58/64 *Consten and Grundig v Commission* [1966] ECR 299.

qualify for exemption under Article 81(3) because absolute territorial protection was combined with the concession of exclusivity. The Court clearly assessed the distribution arrangements as a restriction by object because of the absolute territorial protection granted to Consten.[112] Absolute territorial protection arose from Consten's agreement not to deliver directly or indirectly to the markets of other countries, the imposition by Grundig on its German wholesalers and distributors in other countries of the obligation to refrain from making deliveries from their contract territories to other contractual territories, and the exclusive assignment to Consten of certain trademark rights for the duration of the distribution agreement.[113]

(ii) *Miller*[114]**—Prohibition on Exports (1978)**   This case was an appeal against a   **9.70** Commission decision in which it was found that the prohibitions on the exports of records, tapes, and cassettes inserted by Miller, a German producer of sound recordings, in an exclusive dealing agreement with a French distributor infringed Article 81(1) of the Treaty. Under EC competition law, being an exclusive distributor can normally only protect you from active, but not passive, sales by exclusive distributors[115] in other territories within the Community. The situation can be different where the exclusive distributor is outside the Community.[116] What is interesting about this case is that Miller did not dispute the facts but maintained 'that they cannot have appreciably affected trade between Member States in view of the insignificance of the undertaking on the market in sound recordings, the nature of its products, which are chiefly intended for the German-speaking public, and the nature of its customers'. Between 1970 and 1975 the market share of Miller on the total German market in sound recordings varied between 5 and 6 per cent in terms of volume.

While Miller did not challenge the appreciability of the export ban as a restriction of com-   **9.71** petition (it did claim that 'it did not correspond to a blameworthy objective') the Court of Justice held at paragraph 7 that:

> by its very nature, a clause prohibiting exports constitutes a restriction on competition, whether it is adopted at the instigation of the supplier or of the customer since the agreed purpose of the contracting parties is the endeavour to isolate a part of the market.

Miller supports the thesis that export prohibitions are restrictions by object which consti-   **9.72** tute *per se* restrictions of competition within the meaning of Article 81(1) with no evidence being required as to the appreciability of the restriction.[117] This supports the policy of the Commission in the current 2001 De Minimis Notice discussed above, where hardcore restrictions are excluded from protection by the negative de minimis thresholds.

With regard to effect on trade the Court concluded at paragraphs 10 to 15 that: **9.73**

> Miller, far from being comparable to the undertakings concerned in the judgments of 30 June 1966 (*Technique Minière v Maschinenbau Ulm*, case 56/65 (1965) ECR 235), of

---

[112] Joined Cases 56/64 and 58/64 *Consten and Grundig v Commission* [1966] ECR 299, 342.

[113] Joined Cases 56/64 and 58/64 *Consten and Grundig v Commission* [1966] ECR 299, 343.

[114] Case 19/77 *Miller International Schallplatten GmbH v Commission* [1978] ECR 131.

[115] On analysis of exclusive distribution under the BER see paras 9.213–9.222. Outside of the BER see paras 9.318–9.325.

[116] See the *Javico* case at n 154.

[117] For an example of a case where an export prohibition was held not to fall within Art 81(1) on the grounds of objective necessity see the case of *Louis Erauw-Jacquery v La Hesbignonne SC*, summarised below.

9 July 1969 (*Volk v Vervaeke*, Case 5/69 (1969) ECR 295) and of 6 May 1971 (*Cadillon v Hoss*, Case 1/71 (1971) ECR 351), is an undertaking of sufficient importance for its behaviour to be, in principle, capable of affecting trade.

… In prohibiting agreements which may affect trade between Member States and which have as their object or effect the restriction of competition Article 85(1) [now Article 81(1)] of the Treaty does not require proof that such agreements have in fact appreciably affected such trade, which would moreover be difficult in the majority of cases to establish for legal purposes, but merely requires that it be established that such agreements are capable of having that effect.

The Commission, basing its assessment on Miller's position on the market, its scale of production, ascertainable exports and price policy, has provided appropriate proof that in fact there was a danger that trade between Member States would be appreciably affected.

9.74 Therefore, where a restriction by object is involved, *Miller* is authority for the applicability of the appreciability test to potential effects on trade between Member States. However, as demonstrated by this case, the actual or potential effects do not have to be economically significant before the appreciability criteria are satisfied. It is likely that the Court was particularly influenced by the fact that Miller was trying to protect its home market 'against the re-importation of products exported at low prices'. It is noteworthy that the Commission has retained a 5 per cent market share threshold as one of the two cumulative conditions for the establishment of a negative rebuttable presumption for capacity to affect trade (see para 9.65 above).

9.75 **(iii)** *Binon*[118]—**Resale Price Maintenance (1985)**   This case, an Article 234 reference to the Court of Justice, concerned the distribution of newspapers in Belgium by way of a selective distribution system. SA Binon & Cie, an undertaking which carried on a business in Charleroi selling books, stationery, and educational toys, had brought a case before the national court against SA Agence et Messageries de la Presse (hereinafter referred to as 'AMP'). The purpose of the action was to obtain an order directing AMP to cease refusing to sell or deliver to Binon the newspapers and periodicals, both Belgian and foreign, which it distributed in Belgium. AMP was responsible for the distribution to retailers of close to 70 per cent of Belgian newspapers and periodicals and virtually all newspapers and periodicals published abroad.

9.76 On resale price maintenance the Court stated as follows :

44 It should be observed in the first place that provisions which fix the prices to be observed in contracts with third parties constitute, of themselves, a restriction on competition within the meaning of article 85(1) [now Article 81(1)] which refers to agreements which fix selling prices as an example of an agreement prohibited by the Treaty.

9.77 Therefore, it can be concluded that restrictions on resale prices are restrictions by object and constitute a *per se* restriction of competition within the meaning of Article 81(1). However, they do not fall within the scope of Article 81(1) unless they may appreciably affect trade between Member States.

9.78 While the Court did not expressly apply the criteria of appreciability to the restrictions by object in this case, the criteria were probably fulfilled given the high market shares involved. Paragraph 46 of the judgment is important in that it provides for the possibility

---

[118] Case 243/83 *SA Binon & Cie v SA Agence et Messageries de la Presse* [1985] ECR 201.

for exemption, albeit under very limited conditions:

> 46 If, in so far as the distribution of newspapers and periodicals is concerned, the fixing of the retail price by publishers constitutes the sole means of supporting the financial burden result-ing from the taking back of unsold copies and if the latter practice constitutes the sole method by which a wide selection of newspapers and periodicals can be made available to readers, the Commission must take account of those factors when examining an agreement for the purposes of Article 85(3) [now Article 81(3)].

It is noteworthy that the court opined that the objective necessity test in this case, ie assum- **9.79**
ing that RPM was the sole method of assuring a wide selection of newspapers, fell to be cleared under Article 85(3) (now Article 81(3)). This contrasts with the later 1988 judgment in the case of *Louis Erauw-Jacquery v La Hesbignonne SC* (see below), where the objective necessity test is confined to Article 81(1). Nevertheless, it can be argued from this judgment that the Commission's statement at paragraph 276 of the Green Paper on Vertical Restraints that resale price maintenance and impediments to parallel trade are 'unlikely to benefit from an exemption under Article 85(3) [now Article 81(3)]', appears to be going slightly further than the case law of the Community Courts. As the Court of First Instance has stated 'in prin-ciple, no anti-competitive practice can exist which, whatever the extent of its effects on a given market, cannot be exempted, provided that all the conditions laid down in Article 85(3) [now Article 81(3)] of the Treaty are satisfied and the practice in question has been properly notified to the Commission'.[119] In other words, there is always the possibility of exemption even for so called *per se* infringements. The Commission now appears to recognise this possi-bility in paragraph 20 of its 2004 Guidelines on the application of Article 81(3) of the Treaty:

> for the purpose of applying Article 81(1) no actual anti-competitive effects need to be demonstrated where the agreement has a restriction of competition as its object. Article 81(3), on the other hand, does not distinguish between agreements that restrict competition by object and agreements that restrict competition by effect. Article 81(3) applies to all agree-ments that fulfil the four conditions contained therein.[120]

However, when the latter principle is repeated later in paragraph 46 of the Guidelines it is **9.80**
followed by a more negative statement on the possibility of a restriction by object meeting the criteria for exemption:

> Article 81(3) does not exclude *a priori* certain types of agreements from its scope. As a mat-ter of principle all restrictive agreements that fulfil the four conditions of Article 81(3) are covered by the exception rule (61). However, severe restrictions of competition are unlikely to fulfil the conditions of Article 81(3). Such restrictions are usually black-listed in block exemp-tion regulations or identified as hardcore restrictions in Commission guidelines and notices. Agreements of this nature generally fail (at least) the two first conditions of Article 81(3). They neither create objective economic benefits (62) nor do they benefit consumers (63).
>
> (61) See paragraph 85 of the *Matra* judgment cited in note 52.
>
> (62) As to this requirement see paragraph 49 below.
>
> (63) See eg Case T-29/92, *Vereniging van Samenwerkende Prijsregelende Organisaties in de Bouwnijverheid (SPO)*, [1995] ECR II-289.

---

[119] Case T-17/93 *Matra Hachette SA v Commission* [1994] ECR II-595, para 85.
[120] [2004] OJ C101/08, para 20.

9.81 Therefore, while both the Commission and the Court recognise the possibility of exemption for hardcore restrictions, the Commission has clearly expressed the view that such restrictions are unlikely to satisfy the criteria for exemption. It is also worth noting that in the Binon case the Court considered that the resale price provision could only be saved under Article 81(3). The Commission, on the other hand, appears, in certain limited circumstances, to be prepared to hold that Article 81(1) does not apply to a hardcore restriction which gives rise to intra-brand and not inter-brand restrictions. Paragraph 18 of the 2004 Guidelines on the application of Article 81(3) of the Treaty sets out two questions which must be asked in order to establish whether there is a restriction of Competition. The first question relates to the impact of the agreement on inter-brand competition while the second question relates to the impact of the agreement on intra-brand competition. The question on intra-brand restrictions foresees the possibility of an objective justification under Article 81(1):

> (2) Does the agreement restrict actual or potential competition that would have existed in the absence of the contractual restraint(s)? If so, the agreement may be caught by Article 81(1). For instance, where a supplier restricts its distributors from competing with each other, (potential) competition that could have existed between the distributors absent the restraints is restricted. Such restrictions include resale price maintenance and territorial or customer sales restrictions between distributors. *However, certain restraints may in certain cases not be caught by Article 81(1) when the restraint is objectively necessary for the existence of an agreement of that type or that nature* (23). Such exclusion of the application of Article 81(1) can only be made on the basis of objective factors external to the parties themselves and not the subjective views and characteristics of the parties. The question is not whether the parties in their particular situation would not have accepted to conclude a less restrictive agreement, but whether, given the nature of the agreement and the characteristics of the market, a less restrictive agreement would not have been concluded by undertakings in a similar setting. For instance, territorial restraints in an agreement between a supplier and a distributor may for a certain period of time fall outside Article 81(1), if the restraints are objectively necessary in order for the distributor to penetrate a new market (24). Similarly, a prohibition imposed on all distributors not to sell to certain categories of end users may not be restrictive of competition if such [a] restraint is objectively necessary for reasons of safety or health related to the dangerous nature of the product in question. Claims that in the absence of a restraint the supplier would have resorted to vertical integration are not sufficient. Decisions on whether or not to vertically integrate depend on a broad range of complex economic factors, a number of which are internal to the undertaking concerned. [emphasis added]

> (23) See in this respect the judgment in *Société Technique Minière* cited in note 20 and Case 258/78, *Nungesser*, [1982] ECR 2015.

> (24) See rule 10 in paragraph 119 of the Guidelines on vertical restraints cited in note above, according to which inter alia passive sales restrictions—a hardcore restraint—are held to fall outside Article 81(1) for a period of 2 years when the restraint is linked to opening up new product or geographic markets.

9.82 The objective justification reasoning is also reflected in the 2000 Vertical Guidelines, where the Commission recognises that in the case of the genuine testing of a new product in a particular territory or with a particular customer group, the distributors appointed to sell the new product on the test market can be restricted in their active selling outside the test market for a maximum period of one year without infringing Article 81(1).[121]

---

121 Rule 10 in para 119 of the Vertical Guidelines.

(iv) *Erauw-Jacquery*[122]**—Export Prohibition and Minimum Resale Prices (1988)**   Like   **9.83**
Nungesser (see below) this case concerns plant breeders' rights; however, unlike *Nungesser*
it does not concern the exclusive assignment of those rights for a particular territory but rather
the use of those rights by its holder to control the propagation and sale of seed by a third party
grower. This case arose from proceedings before the Belgian courts between SPRL Louis
Erauw-Jacquery (the breeder), the holder of plant breeders' rights, and La Hesbignonne
SC (the grower), a co-operative authorised by it to propagate basic seed and to sell seed of the
first or second generation produced from that basic seed and intended for cereal production.
The licence agreement contained a provision prohibiting the sale and export of basic seed and
a minimum resale price obligation. The grower did not abide by the minimum resale price
communicated to it by the breeder. In the national proceedings the breeder claimed that this
had in turn obliged other growers to lower their prices, causing them to incur losses for which
they claimed compensation. Therefore, the breeder was seeking to pass on those claims in
the national proceedings. In response to an Article 234 reference the Court of Justice ruled:

> (1) A provision of an agreement concerning the propagation and sale of seed, in respect of
> which one of the parties is the holder of certain plant breeders' rights, which prohibits the
> grower from selling and exporting the basic seed, is compatible with Article 85(1) [now
> Article 81(1)] of the Treaty in so far as it is necessary in order to enable the breeder to select
> the growers who are to be licensees.

> (2) A provision in an agreement such as that described in paragraph 1, which obliges the
> grower to comply with minimum prices fixed by the other party falls within the prohibition
> set out in Article 85(1) only if it is found, having regard to the economic and legal context of
> the agreement containing the provision in question, that the agreement is capable of affect-
> ing trade between Member States to an appreciable degree.

In relation to the first ruling the Court refers at paragraph 10 of the judgment to its earlier   **9.84**
judgment in the *Nungesser* case and describes the circumstances in which a sale and export
prohibition may fall outside of the scope of Article 81(1):

> the development of the basic lines may involve considerable financial commitment.
> Consequently, a person who has made considerable efforts to develop varieties of basic seed
> which may be the subject-matter of plant breeders' rights must be allowed to protect himself
> against any improper handling of those varieties of seed. To that end, the breeder must be
> entitled to restrict propagation to the growers which he has selected as licensees. To that
> extent, the provision prohibiting the licensee from selling and exporting basic seed falls out-
> side the prohibition contained in Article 85 (1) [now Article 81(1)].

Advocate General Mischo gives a much clearer insight as to why the sale and export prohi-   **9.85**
bition for basic seed does not fall within Article 81(1):

> 11 Basic seed is to a certain extent comparable to a manufacturing process protected by a
> patent, since certified seed of the first and second generation intended for sale to farmers for
> use in cereal production is produced from it. The breeder (or his agent) must therefore
> remain in a position to control the destination and the use of the basic seed; otherwise he
> would risk the de facto loss of the exclusive rights granted to him in respect of the new vari-
> eties which he has developed. The Commission is right to point out that the propagation
> agreement is an agreement where the identity of the other party is essential.

---

[122] Case 27/87 *SPRL Louis Erauw-Jacquery v La Hesbignonne SC* [1988] ECR 1919.

12 The situation of a breeder or his agent therefore resembles in certain respects the situation of a franchisor, in respect of whom the Court has stated that he 'must be able to communicate his know-how to the franchisees and provide them with the necessary assistance in order to enable them to apply his methods, without running the risk that know-how and assistance might benefit competitors, even indirectly. It follows that provisions which are essential in order to avoid that risk do not constitute restrictions on competition for the purposes of Article 85(1) [now Article 81(1)]' (judgment of 28 January 1986 in Case 161/84 *Pronuptia* (1986) ECR 353, paragraph 16).

9.86   In relation to the second ruling the Court states at paragraph 12 of the judgment that the minimum resale price provision constitutes both a restriction by object and effect. The Court then proceeded to find that the agreement may affect trade between Member States but recalled that 'an agreement is subject to the prohibition contained in Article 85 [now Article 81] only if it appreciably affects trade between Member States'.[123] This case also supports the thesis that where a restriction by object is concerned the test of appreciability applies to the 'effect on trade' but not to the restriction of competition. The Court gave the following guidance on assessing appreciability in this case:

18 In this respect it must be stressed that the impact of the contested agreement on intra-community trade depends, in particular, on whether it forms part of a cluster of similar agreements concluded between the breeder and other licensees, on the breeder's market share in respect of the seed concerned and on the ability of the producers bound by those agreements to export that seed.

19 It is for the national court to decide, on the basis of the relevant information at its disposal and taking into account the economic and legal context of the agreement of 26 February 1982, whether that agreement is capable of affecting trade between member states to an appreciable degree.

9.87   Advocate General Mischo, while of the opinion that the test of appreciability should be applied to both the restriction of competition and effect on trade in this case, points out that in two earlier judgments involving resale price maintenance[124] the Court appears not to have applied the appreciability test, and 'after having found that an agreement of the type in question in the main proceedings entailed a restriction on competition and was capable of affecting trade between Member States, immediately concluded that such an agreement was incompatible with Article 85(1) [now Article 81(1)] of the Treaty and prohibited by that article'. It is interesting to note that despite the observations of Advocate General Mischo on appreciability, the Court, in its judgment, appears only to have applied the criterion to effect on trade.

9.88   (v) *Parker Pen*[125]—**Export Prohibition(1994)**   This case arose from an appeal by Parker Pen Ltd. against a decision of the Commission[126] fining Parker Pen 700,000 ECU for

---

[123]   See para 17 of the judgment.

[124]   Case 311/85 *ASBL Vereniging van Vlaamse Reisbureaus v ASBL Sociale Dienst van de Plaatselijke and Gewestelijke Overheidsdiensten* [1987] ECR 3801 and Case 123/83 *BNIC v Clair* [1985] ECR 391, at 425. The latter case concerned an agreement which, *inter alia*, fixed the price of spirits used in the manufacture of cognac, that is to say an intermediate product which is not normally sent outside the Cognac region. The Court declared in that context that: 'any agreement whose object or effect is to restrict competition by fixing minimum prices for an intermediate product is capable of affecting intra-Community trade, even if there is no trade in that intermediate product between the Member States, where the product constitutes the raw material for another product marketed elsewhere in the Community'.

[125]   Case T-77/92 *Parker Pen Ltd v Commission* [1994] ECR II-549.

[126]   *Viho/Parker Pen* [1992] OJ L233/27.

including an export ban in an agreement with a German distributor, Herlitz. Parker did not deny the existence of the clause prohibiting exports, but claimed that it was not capable of affecting trade between Member States to an appreciable extent and also that the clause was not implemented. Relying on *Volk v Vervaeke*, and *Miller*, Parker Pen argued that an agreement which by its nature restricts competition falls outside the prohibition of Article 81(1) if it has only an insignificant effect on the markets. It further argued that the relevant geographic market was Community-wide and that the relevant market share was that of Herlitz in the Community. While the market shares have been deleted from the public version of the judgment it would appear that Herlitz's market share on the Community market was below 5 per cent, a level which in the *Miller* case was considered as being of sufficient importance for Miller's conduct to be, in principle, capable of affecting trade to an appreciable extent. Parker Pen also relied on the argument that the agreement's 'potential effect on intra-Community trade was practically nil because the wholesale prices charged by Parker were similar in the various Member States'.

In its appraisal, the Court of First Instance confirmed that a clause prohibiting exports constitutes a *per se* restriction of competition without any need to assess the appreciability of its actual or potential impact on competition: **9.89**

> The Court of Justice has consistently held that 'by its very nature, a clause prohibiting exports constitutes a restriction on competition, whether it is adopted at the instigation of the supplier or of the customer, since the agreed purpose of the contracting parties is to endeavour to isolate a part of the market' (see the judgments of the Court of Justice in *Miller v Commission*, cited above, paragraph 7, and, most recently, in Cases C-89/85, C-104/85, C-114/85, C-116/85, C-117/85 and C-125/85 to C-129/85 *Ahlstroem Osakeyhtioe and Others v Commission* [1993] ECR I-1307, paragraph 176 ('Woodpulp')).[127]

The Court of First Instance also confirmed the application of the test of appreciability to effect on trade but clarified that the test of 'appreciability' is not any greater than that of 'insignificant effect' used in the *Volk* case: **9.90**

> To be capable of affecting trade between Member States, a decision, an agreement or a concerted practice must make it possible to foresee with a sufficient degree of probability, on the basis of a set of objective elements of law or fact, that it may have an influence, direct or indirect, actual or potential, on the pattern of trade between Member States capable of hindering the attainment of the objectives of a single market between States. That influence must also be appreciable (Volk, cited above, paragraph 5, and, most recently, the judgment of the Court of First Instance in Case T-66/89 *Publishers' Association v Commission* [1992] ECR II-1995, paragraph 55). Accordingly, even an agreement according absolute territorial protection escapes the prohibition laid down in Article 85 [now Article 81] of the Treaty where it affects the market only insignificantly, regard being had to the weak position of those concerned on the market for the products in question (judgment of the Court of Justice in Joined Cases 100/80 to 103/80 *Musique diffusion française and Others v Commission* [1983] ECR 1825, paragraph 85).[128]

[127] Case T-77/92, see n 125 above, para 37.
[128] ibid, para 39.

9.91 The Court of First Instance also rejected the claim that the relevant market share for assessing the appreciability of the effect on trade was solely that of Herlitz, since it is sufficient that the sales of one of the parties are not inconsiderable:

> The influence which an agreement may have on trade between Member States is to be determined by taking into account in particular the position and importance of the parties on the market for the products concerned (judgment of the Court of Justice in Case 99/79 *Lancôme v ETOS* [1980] ECR 2511, paragraph 24).[129]
>
> The Court of Justice has held that when it is evident that the sales of at least one of the parties to an anti-competitive agreement constitute a not inconsiderable proportion of the relevant market, Article 85(1) [now Article 81(1)] of the Treaty should be applied (see the judgment in Miller, cited above, paragraph 10).

9.92 Unfortunately the market shares of Parker Pen and Herlitz on the German and Community markets are deleted from the public version of the judgment. Nevertheless, the Court of First Instance states that the 'figures show that Parker and Herlitz are undertakings of sufficient importance for their conduct to be, in principle, capable of affecting intra-Community trade. Moreover, it is not disputed that Herlitz is a major client of Parker on the German market.'[130] 'Having regard to the importance of the position which Parker holds, the size of its production, its sales in the Member States and the proportion of sales of Parker products made by Herlitz', the Court found that the export prohibition was 'capable of affecting appreciably patterns of trade between Member States in such a way as to jeopardize the attainment of the objectives of the common market'.[131]

9.93 Interestingly, the Court of First Instance did not go into detail as regards Parker Pen's argument relating to similarity in wholesale prices charged by Parker in the various Member States, simply noting at paragraph 42 that the Commission had observed 'price differences between the Member States which might give rise to a parallel trade'. However, it did reduce the level of the fine from 700,000 to 400,000 ECU, 'having regard in particular to the low turnover to which the infringement relates'.[132]

9.94 (vi) *BMW Leasing Case*[133]—**Absolute Territorial Protection (1995)** This case, an Article 234 reference to the Court, arose from national proceedings between Bayerische Motorenwerke AG (BMW) and ALD Auto-Leasing D GmbH (ALD) concerning a circular letter sent by BMW, a motor vehicle manufacturer, to its authorised dealers in Germany, in which it called upon them not to supply leasing companies that made vehicles available to customers residing or having their seat outside the contract territory of the dealer in question. The Court found that the letter constituted an agreement granting absolute territorial protection to the BMW dealer on whose territory the customer of ALD is established. Interestingly, while the Court stated that for the agreement to fall within the scope of Article 81(1), 'it must be considered whether the ban on supplies resulting from the

---

129 ibid, para 40.
130 ibid, para 45.
131 ibid, para 46.
132 ibid, para 95.
133 Case C-70/93 *Bayerische Motorenwerke AG v ALD Auto-Leasing D GmbH* [1995] ECR I-3439.

agreement has as its object or effect the restriction to an appreciable extent of competition within the common market and whether it may affect trade between Member States',[134] the judgment contains no reference to the position of BMW on the German or other markets. In fact there is no economic assessment of the word 'appreciable'. With regard to effect on trade, the Court states that 'the agreement in question, since it relates to vehicles of the BMW mark, which are the subject of significant international trade, may affect trade between Member States'.[135]

In this case the Court applied the criterion of appreciability to both the 'object' and 'effect' of the restriction. It is not clear that the Court applied this criterion to effect on trade, though reference is made to 'significant international trade'. **9.95**

(vii) *GlaxoSmithKline*[136]**—Restriction on parallel imports within the EC (2006)** This **9.96** case arose from an appeal by GlaxoSmithKline (GSK), against a decision of the Commission of May 2001[137] which found an infringement of Article 81 as a result of GSK's general sales conditions to wholesalers in Spain. GSK (then Glaxo Wellcome) had notified these conditions to the Commission in 1998 seeking negative clearance or an exemption under the then applicable Council Regulation No. 17 of 6 February 1962.[138] The notified conditions included two different prices for Glaxo products, a so-called 'clause 4A' price for products resold in Spain and a more expensive 'clause 4B' price for products sold outside Spain. Glaxo's distributors were requested to sign these terms and conditions as a condition for obtaining supplies from Glaxo. The Commission found that Clause 4 of the General Sales Conditions had both the object and the effect of restricting competition.[139]

The Court annulled the Commission's finding as to the establishment of a restriction by **9.97** object but upheld that there was a restriction by effect.

The Court, having noted that GSK does not dispute that Clause 4 was inserted with the **9.98** intention of limiting parallel trade between Spain and other Member States and that agreements that are clearly intended to treat parallel trade unfavourably must in principle be regarded as having as their object the restriction of competition,[140] goes on to state at paragraph 121 of the judgment:

> While it has been accepted since then that parallel trade must be given a certain protection, it is therefore not as such but, as the Court of Justice held, in so far as it favours the development of trade, on the one hand, and the strengthening of competition, on the other hand (Case C-373/90 X [1992] ECR I-131, paragraph 12), that is to say, in this second respect, in

---

[134] ibid, para 18.

[135] ibid, para 20.

[136] Case T-168/01 *GlaxoSmithKline Services Unlimited v Commission of the European Communities* [2006] ECR 0000. Judgment of the Court of First Instance of 27 September 2006.

[137] Decision 2001/791/EC relating to a proceeding pursuant to Art 81 of the EC Treaty (Cases: IV/36.957/F3 Glaxo Wellcome (notification), IV/36.997/F3 Aseprofar and Fedifar (complaint), IV/37.121/F3 Spain Pharma (complaint), IV/37.138/F3 BAI (complaint), IV/37.380/F3 EAEPC (complaint)) (OJ 2001 L302, p 1).

[138] First Regulation implementing Arts [81] and [82] of the Treaty (OJ, English Special Edition 1959-62, p 87).

[139] Recitals 116 to 143 and 189 of the Decision.

[140] Paras 114 to 116.

so far as it gives final consumers the advantages of effective competition in terms of supply or price (Tepea v Commission, paragraph 118 above, paragraphs 43 and 56). Consequently, while it is accepted that an agreement intended to limit parallel trade must in principle be considered to have as its object the restriction of competition, that applies in so far as the agreement may be presumed to deprive final consumers of those advantages.

9.99 The Court appears to be stating here that a restriction by object can only be presumed in those cases where final consumers are denied the advantages of effective (inter- and intra-brand) competition in terms of supply or price. The Court then proceeds to an analysis of the specific and essential characteristics of the pharmaceutical sector and lists seven distinguishing factors, including the fact that the price of medicines reimbursed by the national health insurance schemes is not determined as a result of a competitive process throughout the Community but is directly fixed following an administrative procedure in most Member States and indirectly controlled by the other Member States. These distinguishing factors enable the Court to conclude that 'it cannot be presumed that parallel trade has an impact on the prices charged to the final consumers of medicines reimbursed by the national sickness insurance scheme and thus confers on them an appreciable advantage analogous to that which it would confer if those prices were determined by the play of supply and demand'. In other words, it is only because the pharmaceutical markets are heavily regulated, that it cannot be presumed that the restrictions of parallel trade will harm consumers. Accordingly, it cannot be considered that Clause 4 'reveals in itself' that competition is prevented, restricted, or distorted.[141]

9.100 The Court did not find a restriction by object in this case due to the specificities of the pharmaceutical market, a market 'which is characterised by the fact that the price of the products in issue, which is finally set by the Member States, falls structurally outside the play of supply and demand and is established at structurally different levels throughout the Community, notwithstanding a residual competition which may be revealed by parallel trade'.[142] Therefore, the reasoning of the Court on the limitation of the concept of a restriction by object is not readily transferable to a market where the restrictions arise primarily from the actions of the market players.

(b) *Restrictions by Effect*

9.101 (i) *Béguelin*[143]—**Exclusive Distribution (1971)**   This case arose from proceedings in France taken by Béguelin, the exclusive distributor in France for cigarette lighters of the mark 'WIN' against a parallel importer which had imported a consignment of the lighters from Germany and the exclusive distributor for the mark in Germany from whom it had sourced the lighters. Based on the exclusivity granted by the distribution agreement Béguelin sought an injunction preventing sale of the imported lighters and damages. The defendants pleaded before the national court that the exclusive agreement infringed Article 81. In response to an Article 234 reference the Court of Justice ruled:

> An exclusive dealing agreement . . . comes within the prohibition imposed under Article 85 [now Article 81] of the Treaty in cases when, *de jure* or *de facto* it prevents the distributor from

---

[141] Para 136.
[142] Para 141.
[143] Case 22/71 *Béguelin Import Co. v SAGL Import Export* [1971] ECR 949.

re-exporting the products in question to other Member States or prevents the products from being imported from other Member States into the protected area and from being distributed therein by persons other than the exclusive dealer or his customers.

It is not clear from the case that the distribution contract granted Béguelin absolute **9.102** territorial protection,[144] which probably explains why the Court assessed this case in terms of its 'effect' and not 'object'. This is evident from paragraphs 13 and 14 of the judgment:

13 In order to determine whether this is the position [ie prevention of imports or exports], account must be taken not only of the rights and obligations arising from the clauses of the agreement but also of the economic and legal conditions under which it operates and particularly of the existence of any similar agreements entered into by the same producer with exclusive dealers established in other Member States.

14 More especially, an exclusive dealing agreement is liable to affect trade between Member States and may have the effect of impeding competition if, owing to the combined effects of the agreement and of national legislation on unfair competition, the dealer is able to prevent parallel imports from other Member States into [a] territory covered by the agreement.

The Court also confirmed that 'in order to come within the prohibition imposed by **9.103** Article 85 [now Article 81], the agreement must affect trade between Member States and the free play of competition to an appreciable extent'.

(ii) *Nungesser*[145]**—Territorial Protection in the Form of 'Open Exclusivity' (1982) 9.104** This case arose from an appeal by Nungesser and others against a decision of the Commission which found an infringement of Article 81(1) as a result of the content and application of two contracts relating to the assignment of plant breeders' rights for certain maize seeds in the Federal Republic of Germany. The decision also rejected an application for the exemption of the agreements under Article 81(3).

While the judgment of the Court is limited to the licensing of plant breeders' rights, it is **9.105** submitted that the reasoning of the judgment is also relevant to the consideration of territorial protection relating to the distribution of goods and services where substantial levels of investments are involved and distributors may be deterred from making such investments unless they have assurances that they will not face active competition from the grantor of the distribution rights. First, the Court rejected the submission that the Commission had failed to take into account the particular nature of plant breeders' rights, the exercise of which demands strict observance of territorial protection:

It is therefore not correct to consider that breeders' rights are a species of commercial or industrial property right with characteristics of so special a nature as to require, in relation to the competition rules, a different treatment from other commercial or industrial property rights. That conclusion does not affect the need to take into consideration, for the purposes of the rules on competition, the specific nature of the products which form the subject-matter of breeders' rights.[146]

---

[144] See Opinion of Advocate General Dutheillet de Lamothe, [1971] ECR 949, 965.
[145] Case 258/78 *LC Nungesser KG and Kurt Eisele v Commission* [1982] ECR 2015.
[146] ibid, para 43.

9.106   Secondly, the Court accepted the argument that the Commission was wrong to consider that every exclusive licence of breeders' rights by its nature falls within the terms of Article 81(1). The Court drew a distinction between two types of territorial protection, namely *open exclusivity* and *closed exclusivity*:

> the first case concerns a so-called open exclusive licence or assignment and the exclusivity of the licence relates solely to the contractual relationship between the owner of the right and the licensee, whereby the owner merely undertakes not to grant other licences in respect of the same territory and not to compete himself with the licensee on that territory. On the other hand, the second case involves an exclusive licence or assignment with absolute territorial protection, under which the parties to the contract propose, as regards the products and the territory in question, to eliminate all competition from third parties, such as parallel importers or licensees for other territories.[147]

9.107   Having drawn this distinction, the Court proceeded to analyse the former in terms of its effects on competition, rather than treating it as a restriction by object.

> 57 In fact, in the case of a licence of breeders' rights over hybrid maize seeds newly developed in one Member State, an undertaking established in another Member State which was not certain that it would not encounter competition from other licensees for the territory granted to it, or from the owner of the right himself, might be deterred from accepting the risk of cultivating and marketing that product; such a result would be damaging to the dissemination of a new technology and would prejudice competition in the community between the new product and similar existing products.

> 58 Having regard to the specific nature of the products in question, the court concludes that, in a case such as the present, the grant of an open exclusive licence, that is to say a licence which does not affect the position of third parties such as parallel importers and licensees for other territories, is not in itself incompatible with Article 85(1) [now Article 81(1)] of the Treaty.

9.108   Much the same arguments could be used in relation to the distribution of goods and services which require considerable levels of investment. In the first edition of this book, it was suggested that if the Commission were to permit all forms of distribution to avail of this reasoning the two parties to a distribution agreement could agree territorial sales restrictions as between themselves without falling within the scope of Article 81(1). Article 81(1) would then only apply where distributors were granted territorial protection from other distributors or parallel traders. The Commission has not followed this approach, and instead continues to exempt protection of the distributor or licensee against sales by the supplier or licensor. Restrictions on active and passive sales by the supplier are exempted up to the 30 per cent threshold of the BER and above subject to individual analysis under Article 81(3).[148] A similar approach has been adopted in the 2004 Technology Transfer Block Exemption Regulation[149] as regards sales restrictions on the licensor for licensing between non-competitors.[150]

---

[147] ibid, para 53.
[148] See para 9.216 below.
[149] Commission Regulation (EC) 772/2004 of 27 April 2004 on the application of Art 81(3) of the Treaty to categories of technology transfer agreements, OJ L123, 27.4.2004, p 11.
[150] See Art 4.2 (b) of the Technology Transfer Block Exemption Regulation.

(iii) *Binon*[151]—**Qualitative Selective Distribution (1985)** The facts of this newspaper **9.109**
distribution case are summarised above under the heading of restriction by object. In relation to qualitative selective distribution the Court stated as follows in paragraphs 31 and 32
of the judgment:

> 31 It must be noted that according to the Court's decisions and in particular its judgment of
> 25 October 1977 in case 26/76 (*Metro SB-Grossmarkte GmbH and Co Kg v Commission*,
> (1977) ECR 1875) selective distribution systems constitute an aspect of competition which
> accords with Article 85(1) [now Article 81(1)], provided that re-sellers are chosen on the
> basis of objective criteria of a qualitative nature relating to the technical qualifications of
> the re-seller and his staff and the suitability of his trading premises in connection with the
> requirements for the distribution of the product and that such criteria are laid down
> uniformly for all potential re-sellers and are not applied in a discriminatory fashion.

> 32 Such a system may be established for the distribution of newspapers and periodicals, with-
> out infringing the prohibition contained in Article 85(1), given the special nature of those
> products as regards their distribution . . .

Therefore, qualitative selective distribution, where justified by the nature of the product,[152] **9.110**
is in general considered to fall outside Article 81(1), both for lack of object and effect.[153]
This contrasts with the position of quantitative selective distribution in respect of which
the Court, at paragraph 35, appears, at first sight, to find a restriction by object:

> a selective distribution system for newspapers and periodicals which affects trade between
> Member States is prohibited by Article 85(1) [now Article 81(1)] of the Treaty if re-sellers are
> chosen on the basis of quantitative criteria. However, the Commission may, within the
> framework of an application for exemption under Article 85(3), examine whether, in a
> particular case, criteria of that kind may be justified.

In a selective distribution system the right of resale of members of the network is normally **9.111**
restricted to final users or other network members. Intermediaries are excluded from the
distribution of the particular branded product or service which is distributed by way of
selective distribution. Therefore, it can be used to isolate national markets and impede
parallel trade. Where search costs are high, arbitrage by network dealers is the only feasible
mechanism to ensure parallel trade in a selective distribution network. However, the
tighter the control which a supplier has over its distribution network the greater the potential to block parallel trade between network members. While a qualitative system could
be used for the same purpose, the higher number of (potential) network dealers should
limit the control exercised over individual network dealers and the potential for isolation
of national markets. It is submitted that these factors, together with the high market share
of AMP (close to 70 per cent) explains the Court's finding on quantitative selective distribution in this case. It is further submitted that in the absence of a significant level of
market power a quantitative selective distribution system should only be assessed as a
restriction by effect.

---

[151] Case 243/83 *SA Binon & Cie v SA Agence et Messageries de la Presse* [1985] ECR 201.
[152] The nature of the product requirement is not applied within the BER but it can be important for
individual assessment outside the BER. See para 9.287 below on nature of the product.
[153] See also Case 75/84 *Metro v Commission* [1986] ECR 3021, para 40.

9.112 **(iv)** *Javico*[154]—**Export Prohibition from a Third Country (1998)**   Vertical restraints can be used to prevent the re-importation of products into the Community. This is evidenced by the judgment of the Court of Justice in the *Javico* case. This case arose from national proceedings brought by Yves Saint Laurent Parfums SA (YSLP) against Javico International and Javico AG (Javico) for breach of the terms of two contracts for the distribution of its products, one covering the territory of Russia and Ukraine and the other the territory of Slovenia,[155] in which Javico had agreed to confine its sales activities to the relevant territories. The contract for Russia and Ukraine stated, *inter alia*, 'our products are intended for sale solely in the territory of the Republics of Russia and Ukraine. In no circumstances may they leave the territory of the Republics of Russia and Ukraine'.[156] The distribution contract for Slovenia stated, *inter alia*, 'in order to protect the high quality of the distribution of the products in other countries of the world, the distributor agrees not to sell the products outside the territory or to unauthorised dealers in the territory'.[157] Shortly after the conclusion of those contracts, YSLP discovered in the United Kingdom, Belgium, and the Netherlands products sold to Javico which should have been distributed in Russia, Ukraine, and Slovenia.

9.113 The Court confirmed that an export prohibition of the type at issue would, if contained in a contract relating to the distribution of goods within the Community, constitute by its very nature a restriction of competition and fall within the scope of the prohibition of Article 81(1) if it was capable of affecting trade between Member States. In other words, an export prohibition in an agreement relating to the supply of goods within the Community is a restriction by object.

9.114 However, the Court did not treat the export prohibition in this case as a restriction by object because it was not 'intended to exclude parallel imports and marketing of the contractual product within the Community but as being designed to enable the producer to penetrate a market outside the Community by supplying a sufficient quantity of contractual products to that market . . . it follows that an agreement in which the reseller gives to the producer an undertaking that he will sell the contractual products on a market outside the Community cannot be regarded as having the object of appreciably restricting competition within the common market or as being capable of affecting, as such, trade between Member States'.[158]

9.115 The Court stated that to constitute a restriction by effect the agreement must be examined in its economic and legal context and in particular the fact that YSLP had a selective distribution system in the Community which had been exempted by the Commission. In paragraphs 23–26 it gave some guidance as to the other economic and legal factors which should be taken into account:

> 23 In that regard, it is first necessary to determine whether the structure of the Community market in the relevant products is oligopolistic, allowing only limited competition within the Community network for the distribution of those products.

---

[154] Case C-306/96 *Javico International and Javico AG v Yves Saint Laurent Parfums SA (YSLP)* [1998] ECR I-1983.

[155] This case arose prior to Slovenia's entry into the European Community on 1 May 2004.

[156] Case C-306/96, see n 154 above, para 5.

[157] ibid, para 6.

[158] ibid, paras 19–20.

24 It must then be established whether there is an appreciable difference between the prices of the contractual products charged in the Community and those charged outside the Community. Such a difference is not, however, liable to affect competition if it is eroded by the level of customs duties and transport costs resulting from the export of the product to a non-member country followed by its re-import into the Community.

25 If that examination were to disclose that the contested provisions of the agreements concerned had the effect of undermining competition within the meaning of Article 85(1) [now Article 81(1)] of the Treaty, it would also be necessary to determine whether, having regard to YSLP's position on the Community market and the extent of its production and its sales in the Member States, the contested provisions designed to prevent direct sales of the contractual products in the Community and re-exports of them to the Community entail any risk of an appreciable effect on the pattern of trade between the Member States such as to undermine attainment of the objectives of the common market.

26 In that regard, intra-Community trade cannot be appreciably affected if the products intended for markets outside the Community account for only a very small percentage of the total market for those products in the territory of the common market.[159]

9.116 The application of the effects principle to this type of vertical restraint is likely to make it difficult for parallel importers to source goods outside the EEA. However, the situation of parallel importers will be even more difficult in respect of branded goods where the brand owner is able to rely on the principle of EEA exhaustion of trademark rights. EEA exhaustion, when incorporated into national trademark legislation, enables trademark owners to block the importation of products which they have put on the market outside the EEA. The judgment in the *Silhouette* case[160] emphasizes the obligation upon Member States to provide for EEA exhaustion in their national legislation implementing the Trademarks Directive.[161] This case arose from proceedings brought in Austria by Silhouette against Hartlauer, to block the sale by Hartlauer on the Austrian market of 21,000 out-of-fashion spectacle frames which Silhouette had placed on the market in Bulgaria and the former USSR.

9.117 **(v) *Micro Leader Business*—Export Prohibition from a Third Country (1999)** This case concerns the assessment of a unilateral exportation prohibition by a dominant company under Articles 81 and 82. It contains, *inter alia*, elements found both in the *Viho* case, where the agreement, if any, was intra-group, and did not fall within the scope of Article 81 and in the *Javico* case where the prohibition on exports was from a third country.

9.118 This case arose from the putting in place of a prohibition against exporting copies of certain software marketed in Canada. Micro Leader Business (MLB) sold, in France in

---

[159] The judgment is unclear as to whether the economic factors of oligopolistic Community market (para 23) and appreciable price difference (para 24) are alternative or cumulative conditions. In para 24 the words 'it must then' indicate that the factors are cumulative while in the dispositive of the judgment in para 28 the word 'or' indicates that they are alternative.

[160] Case C-355/96 *Silhouette International Schmied GmbH & Co KG v Hartlauer Handelsgesellschaft GmbH* [1998] ECR I-4799. In response to questions from the Austrian court pursuant to Art 234 of the Treaty, the Court responded, *inter alia*: 'National rules providing for exhaustion of trade-mark rights in respect of products put on the market outside the EEA under that mark by the proprietor or with his consent are contrary to Art 7(1) of First Council Directive (EEC) 89/104 of 21 December 1988 to approximate the laws of the Member States relating to trade marks, as amended by the Agreement on the European Economic Area of 2 May 1992.'

[161] First Council Directive (EEC) 89/104 of 21 December 1988 to approximate the laws of the Member States relating to trademarks [1989] OJ L40/1, as amended by the EEA Agreement.

particular, French-language products marketed by Microsoft Corporation (MC) in Canada, identical or similar to products marketed in France by Microsoft France (MF). In an information bulletin of 27 September 1995 entitled 'Flash Microsoft News', MF informed its dealers in France that a number of measures had been taken to reinforce the ban on the marketing of Canadian products outside Canada. One of the passages in that information bulletin, headed 'The importation of French-language Canadian products will in future be illegal' reads:

> For 18 months certain distributors had been bringing Canadian French-language Microsoft products on to the French market through importers. Those products were distorting our market because they were marketed at markedly lower prices than those generally found and adversely affected distributors who used the usual Microsoft sales network. In the face of this unfair competition and to stem such illegal imports, Microsoft has introduced a number of measures intended to reinforce the ban on the sale of Canadian products outside Canada . . .

9.119 MLB subsequently lodged a complaint with the Commission, initially under Article 81 and later extended to Article 82. On 15 October 1998, the Commission rejected the complaint by way of a formal decision, expressing the view that there had been no breach of Articles 81 and 82 of the Treaty. MLB appealed the decision to the CFI, who squashed the Commission's decision on the grounds of manifest error of assessment, under Article 82.[162]

9.120 With regard to the alleged infringement of Article 81 the Commission contended, first, that MC and MF cannot be accused of collusion in breach of Article 81 of the Treaty since they form a single economic unit (Case C-73/95 *Viho v Commission* P [1996] ECR I-5457). Secondly, that all the information supplied by MLB indicates that measures were taken by the Microsoft group, only without any intervention by the Canadian distributors, and finally, that, under Article 4(c) of Directive 91/250, the first sale of a copy of a computer program by MC to Canada did not exhaust the distribution right within the Community of that copy. The measures taken by Microsoft were, therefore, merely a lawful means of protecting its rights. The Court agreed with the Commissions assessment under Article 81. There is an important statement in paragraph 34 of the judgment to the effect that 'even if MC did in fact restrict in that way the opportunities for Canadian distributors to sell their products outside Canada, MC would merely have been enforcing the copyright it holds over its products under Community law. Under Article 4(c) of Directive 91/250, the marketing in Canada of copies of MC software does not exhaust MC's copyright over its products since that right is exhausted only when the products have been put on the market in the Community by the owner of that right or with his consent.'

9.121 With regard to the alleged infringement of Article 82 the Commission argued, *inter alia*, that the prohibition by Microsoft on illegally importing copies of its software from Canada is not an abuse within the meaning of Article 82 of the Treaty, since that prohibition constitutes a lawful enforcement of its copyright under Article 4(c) of Directive 91/250. Whilst the Court recognised that the marketing by MC of copies of software in Canada does not, in itself, exhaust MC's copyright over its products in the Community, it noted in paragraph 54 that the factual evidence put forward by MLB constituted, at the very least, an indication that, for equivalent transactions, Microsoft applied lower prices on the

---

[162] Case T-198/98 *Micro Leader Business v Commission of the European Communities* [1999] ECR II-3989.

Canadian market than on the Community market and that the Community prices were excessive. It also noted that the resale price in France of the parallel traded products was significantly lower than the products marketed by Microsoft in France. The court, referring to the 1995 *Magill* judgment went on to state that '[i]t is clear from the case-law that whilst, as a rule, the enforcement of copyright by its holder, as in the case of the prohibition on importing certain products from outside the Community in to a Member State of the Community, is not in itself a breach of Article 86 [now 82] of the Treaty, such enforcement may, in exceptional circumstances, involve abusive conduct'. It is interesting that the court uses the word 'involve' rather than constitute, implying that blocking parallel trade constitutes only one element of the potential abuse. Although it is not clear what the exceptional circumstances mentioned by the court are it would appear that this refers to the possibility of excessive pricing, a subject addressed in Chapter 4.

(vi) *GlaxoSmithKline*[163]—Restriction on parallel imports within the EC (2006) The **9.122** facts of this parallel trade case are summarised above under the heading of restriction by object. This is a case where the Court of First Instance annulled the Commission's finding as to the establishment of a restriction by object but upheld that there was a restriction by effect. As regards the determination of a restriction by effect it is necessary, in the words of the Court, 'to examine the effect of the agreement and to prove to the requisite legal standard that it actually or potentially prevents, restricts or distorts competition'.[164] The Court, quoting earlier case law, confirms that the examination 'entails a comparison of the competitive situation resulting from the agreement and the situation that would exist in its absence'.[165] This required the Commission to demonstrate how Clause 4 of the General Sales Conditions had the actual or potential effect of restricting competition to the detriment of the final consumer.

In this regard, the Court noted that the Commission had found that some national sick- **9.123** ness insurance schemes took advantage, to various degrees and according to different procedures, of parallel trade in order to reduce the cost of the medicines which they reimburse. The Court also noted that GSK does not deny that parallel trade may have such an effect and that some Member States have adopted measures in order to recover a proportion of the savings which pharmacists have made by means of parallel trade.[166]

The Court therefore concluded that the Commission was entitled to find that Clause 4 had **9.124** the effect of reducing the welfare of final consumers by preventing them from taking advantage, in the form of a reduction in prices and costs, of the participation of the Spanish wholesalers in intra-brand competition on the national markets of destination of the parallel trade originating in Spain.[167]

Finally, it should be noted that the Court annulled that part of the Commission's Decision **9.125** rejecting GSK's request for an exemption under Article 81(3). The Commission's analysis had focused on the first condition of Article 81(3), which is 'contribution to technical

---

[163] Case T-168/01 *GlaxoSmithKline Services Unlimited v Commission of the European Communities* [2006] ECR 0000. Judgment of the Court of First Instance of 27 September 2006.
[164] ibid, para 112.
[165] ibid, para 162.
[166] ibid, para 188.
[167] ibid, para 190.

progress or improvement of distribution'. The Court found that the Commission Decision had failed to take into account all the factual arguments and the relevant economic evidence brought by GSK to show that its sales conditions generated a contribution to innovation outweighing the possible anti-competitive effects. The Article 81(3) aspects of this case are addressed in Chapter 3, paragraphs 3.137 to 3.138.

(7) Conclusion

9.126   As a general rule, resale price maintenance, absolute territorial protection, exclusion of parallel imports/exports, and restrictions of cross-supplies within a selective distribution system have been held to constitute restrictions by object and will fall within the prohibition of Article 81(1) unless they fail to satisfy the doctrine of appreciability established in the *Volk v Vervaeke* case. However, the jurisprudence does not support the assertion that all impediments to parallel trade constitute restrictions by object. For example, a purely qualitative selective distribution system will normally not fall within the scope of Article 81(1) even though the inherent nature of a selective distribution system is that parallel trade by non-network dealers is excluded.

9.127   Guidance on what constitute restrictions by object in vertical agreements can be found in Article 4 of the BER, paragraphs 46 to 56 of the Guidelines and notices.[168] The Commission's 2004 Guidelines on the application of Article 81(3) of the Treaty[169] states, in paragraph 23, that '[a]s regards vertical agreements the category of restrictions by object includes, in particular, fixed and minimum resale price maintenance and restrictions providing absolute territorial protection, including restrictions on passive sales'.

9.128   The Community Courts have never quantified appreciability, but have confirmed the application of Article 81(1) in cases involving relatively low market shares. The greater the anti-competitive nature of the restriction of competition, the greater the likelihood that the criteria of appreciability will be satisfied. Therefore it is not surprising to find the Community Courts upholding the application of Article 81(1) in a case involving absolute territorial protection even though the parties to the vertical restraint had market shares not exceeding 6 per cent.[170]

9.129   As highlighted in the Opinion of Advocate General Mischo, in the *Erauw-Jacquery* case, the Court's application of the appreciability doctrine has not been consistent. Of the cases analysed above, the Court appears to have (1) not applied the criterion in the *Binon* judgment, (2) applied the criterion to both the restriction of competition and effect on trade in the *Béguelin* judgment, (3) applied the criterion to only the restriction of competition in

---

[168]   Of particular relevance is the 2001 De Minimis Notice [Commission Notice on agreements of minor importance which do not appreciably restrict competition under Art 81(1) of the Treaty, OJ C368, 22.12.2001, p 13] and the accompanying press release [IP/02/13], the latter stating, *inter alia*, that '[t]he new Notice defines in a clearer and more consistent way the hardcore restrictions, ie those restrictions, such as price fixing and market sharing, which are normally always prohibited irrespective of the market shares of the companies concerned. Hardcore restrictions can not benefit from the de minimis Notice. For agreements between non-competitors the new Notice has taken over the hardcore restrictions set out in Block Exemption Regulation 2790/1999 for vertical agreements.'

[169]   [2004] OJ C101/08.

[170]   Case 19/77 *Miller International Schallplatten GmbH v Commission* [1978] ECR 131.

the *BMW* judgment (it is unclear whether the Court also applied this criterion to effect on trade, though reference is made to 'significant international trade'), and (4) applied the criterion only to the effect on trade in the *Miller*, *Erauw-Jacquery*, and *Parker Pen* judgments. Therefore, it would appear that in many cases involving restrictions by object, the appreciability of the restriction is assumed (ie restriction by nature), with the analysis of appreciability concentrating upon effect on trade between Member States.

C. Cumulative Effect

An individual agreement which when looked at in isolation has neither an appreciable **9.130** effect on competition or trade between Member States may nevertheless fall within the scope of the prohibition of Article 81(1) where the overall impact of that agreement and similar agreements have such an appreciable effect. In other words agreements must be assessed in their economic and legal context. Where the anti-competitive effects on a market arise not from the agreements of one undertaking but from the cumulative effects of similar agreements of a number of undertakings, the Community Courts have ruled that the prohibition of Article 81(1) applies to the agreements of those companies which make a significant contribution to the cumulative effect.

(1) Foreclosure

The anti-competitive effect most likely to arise from a parallel series of vertical agreements is **9.131** foreclosure. While neither the Community Courts nor the Commission have defined the concept of foreclosure, paragraph 21 of the judgment of the Court of Justice in the *Delimitis* case offers some guidance in that it refers to the 'necessity to examine whether there are real concrete possibilities for a new competitor to penetrate the bundle of contracts' and enter the market. Therefore, foreclosure can only be said to occur when the cumulative effect of a parallel series of agreements makes it difficult to enter the market and there are no concrete ways of bypassing those agreements such as by acquisition or use of other distribution formats.[171] While the concept of foreclosure is normally used to describe a market where a potential entrant is unable to gain entry, it is clear from relevant case law discussed below that it also applies to a situation where an existing player is unable to expand.[172]

(2) Assessment Required to Find a Cumulative Effect which Falls within the Scope of Article 81(1)

In practice, this assessment is carried out under three headings, namely the effect of the network, **9.132** other factors, and significant contribution.[173] Each of these three headings is considered below.

(a) *Effect of the Network*

In the case *Brasserie De Haecht v Wilkin*,[174] the Court of Justice held that the effects of an **9.133** exclusive purchase agreement for beer had to be assessed in the economic and legal context

---

[171] Case C-234/89 *Delimitis v Henninger Brau* [1991] ECR I-935, paras 21–2.
[172] Case T-65/98, see n 177 para 113.
[173] Case C-234/89, see n 171 above, paras 21–2.
[174] Case 23/67 [1967] ECR 407.

in which they occur and where they might combine with others to have a cumulative effect on competition:

> by basing its application to agreements, decisions or practices not only on their subject-matter but also on their effects in relation to competition, Article 85(1) [now Article 81(1)] implies that regard must be had to such effects in the context in which they occur, that is to say, in the economic and legal context of such agreements, decisions or practices and where they might combine with others to have a cumulative effect on competition. In fact, it would be pointless to consider an agreement, decision or practice by reason of its effects if those effects were to be taken distinct from the market in which they are seen to operate and could only be examined apart from the body of effects, whether convergent or not, surrounding their implementation. Thus in order to examine whether it is caught by Article 85(1) an agreement cannot be examined in isolation from the above context, that is, from the factual or legal circumstances causing it to prevent, restrict or distort competition. The existence of similar contracts may be taken into consideration for this objective to the extent to which the general body of contracts of this type is capable of restricting the freedom of trade.[175]

(b) Other Factors

9.134   The Court of Justice has also held that the effect of the network of exclusive purchasing agreements is only one factor, among others, pertaining to the economic and legal context in which an agreement must be appraised.[176] The other factors to be taken into account are, in the first instance, those also relating to the opportunities for access and, secondly, the conditions under which competitive forces operate on the relevant market.

9.135   (i) **Opportunities for Access**   Paragraph 21 of the *Delimitis* judgment referred to the:

> real concrete possibilities for a new competitor to penetrate the bundle of contracts by acquiring a brewery already established on the market together with its network of sales outlets, or to circumvent the bundle of contracts by opening new public houses. For that purpose it is necessary to have regard to the legal rules and agreements on the acquisition of companies and the establishment of outlets, and to the minimum number of outlets necessary for the economic operation of a distribution system. The presence of beer wholesalers not tied to producers who are active on that market is also a factor capable of facilitating a new producer's access to that market since he can make use of those wholesalers' sales networks to distribute his own beer.

9.136   Therefore, assuming that the untied independent outlets on a particular market are insufficient to facilitate entry, this is not sufficient in itself to support a finding that the relevant market is foreclosed. It is also necessary to examine whether there are real concrete possibilities for a new competitor to enter the market such as by purchasing or opening new retail outlets. This also raises the issues as to whether new entrants are confined to existing distribution formats. Other forms of entry must be taken into account in the assessment of foreclosure.

9.137   In paragraph 112 of the *Van den Bergh Foods* judgment,[177] the Court of First Instance uses similar language:

> However, the extent of tying-in brought about by networks of agreements, although of some importance in assessing the partitioning of the market, is only one factor amongst others

---

[175] ibid, at 415.

[176] Case C-234/89 see n 171 above, para 20.

[177] Case T-65/98 *Van den Bergh Foods v Commission and others* [2003] ECR II-4653. This judgment of the Court of First Instance was upheld on appeal to the Court of Justice in Case C-552/03P *Unilever Bestfoods (Ireland) Ltd v Commission* [2006] ECR of 28 September 2006.

pertaining to the economic and legal context in which the network of agreements must be assessed (see Delimitis, paragraphs 19 and 20, and Langnese-Iglo v Commission, paragraph 101). It is also necessary to analyse the market conditions and in particular the real and specific opportunities for new competitors to penetrate that market notwithstanding the existence of those networks.

(ii) Competitive Forces on the Market   Account must be taken of competitive forces on **9.138** the market, including number and size of producers, degree of market saturation, consumer fidelity, and dynamics of the market.[178]

In *Van den Bergh Foods* the Court of First Instance, having analysed the market conditions **9.139** found that:

> the Commission rightly held in the contested decision that the provision to retailers of freezer cabinets subject to a condition of exclusivity and the running maintenance costs of those freezers represent a financial barrier to the entry of new suppliers on the relevant market and to the expansion of existing suppliers. The Court finds that there is no objective link between the supply of freezer cabinets subject to a condition of exclusivity and the sale of ice creams. It is apparent from the contested decision that retailers are not inclined to accept freezer cabinets from suppliers who do not offer terms that are at least as advantageous as those offered by the suppliers of the cabinets already in place in the outlets concerned, or those offered by suppliers to that market in general. In the context of the relevant market, that means that the supplier must be ready to offer a freezer cabinet 'without charge' and to service it. It follows that, in accordance with the Commission's findings in the contested decision (see in particular recital 189), the expense involved in acquiring a stock of freezer cabinets for installation in outlets which will ensure that the supplier's products can achieve viable distribution levels, renders it very difficult to enter the relevant market, particularly for small companies and the suppliers of impulse ice-creams which occupy quite specific niches, because it is difficult to justify the investment in freezer cabinets from suppliers who offer a smaller range of products. Moreover, HB's [Van den Bergh Foods Ltd was formely known as HB Ice Cream Ltd] argument, set out in paragraph 59 above, that it is viable for 47 per cent of outlets to have a freezer owned by the retailer, must be rejected because, given the practice not only of HB but also of other suppliers of making freezers available 'without charge' to retailers, the latter have no reason to buy their own freezer.[179] The European Courts are indicating that it is necessary to look beyond the legal provisions which act as a barrier to entry to establish what is economically feasible in the market place. It would appear that in complex foreclosure cases, where the conditions on the ground may reduce the opportunities for access beyond those set out in contractual provisions, that it is necessary to carry out detailed market research.[180]

(c) Significant Contribution

Where it has been established that competition has been restricted because of a cumulative **9.140** effect the prohibition of Article 81(1) can only be applied to those undertakings whose

---

[178] Case C-234/89 see n 171 above, para 22.
[179] Case T-65/98, see n 177 above, para 113.
[180] In its Decision 98/531 of 11 March 1998 in the *Irish Ice-cream* case [1998] OJ L246/1, the Commission refers extensively to research from three market research surveys, one of which was carried out on its own behalf. This is noted by Advocate General Cosmas in his opinion in Case C-344/98 *Masterfoods Ltd v HB Icecream Ltd* of 16 May 2000, when he states, *inter alia*, 'that the Commission's decision is based, principally on market research carried out in 1996 . . . .' [2000] ECR I-13369, para 19.

network of tied or other agreements make a significant contribution to the restriction. As the Court clarified in paragraph 24 of the *Delimitis* judgment:

> Under the Community rules of competition, responsibility for such an effect of closing off the market must be attributed to the breweries which make an appreciable contribution thereto. Beer supply agreements entered into by breweries whose contribution to the cumulative effect is insignificant do not therefore fall under the prohibition under Article 85(1) [now Article 81(1)].

9.141   This principle was applied by the Commission in the *Van den Bergh* decision[181] (hereinafter referred to as the Irish ice cream decision), where the Commission applied Article 81(1) to the network of a dominant supplier with a market share exceeding 75 per cent of the relevant market for single-wrapped items of impulse ice cream in Ireland, and not to similar networks of other suppliers because they did not make a significant contribution to the foreclosure of the relevant market.[182] This case is also interesting because unlike the *Langnese-Iglo*[183] and *Scholler*[184] cases (hereinafter referred to as the German ice cream cases), the foreclosure arose not from *de jure* exclusive purchase contracts but from freezer cabinet agreements[185] which were said to result in de facto exclusivity.[186]

9.142   The principle of significant contribution was also applied in the *Greene King* decision,[187] where, while considering the UK on-trade beer market to be foreclosed, the Commission was of the opinion that Greene King, a regional brewer with a tied market share of 1.3 per cent, was too small to contribute significantly to the foreclosure. The Commission's *Greene King* decision was upheld, on appeal to the Court of First Instance in a judgment of 5 July 2001.[188] In this case the applicants' arguments were aimed at attributing, for the purposes of the

---

[181]   *Van den Bergh Foods Limited* [1998] OJ L246/1. This decision, which prohibits the practice of freezer exclusivity by Van den Bergh Foods Limited, was suspended by the President of the Court of First Instance on 7 July 1998 pending the hearing of an appeal in the matter. The decision was subsequently upheld by the Court of First Instance in its judgment of 23 October 2003 in Case T-65/98 and the Court of Justice in Case C-552/03P, see n 177.

[182]   See para 204 of the decision.

[183]   Case T-7/93 *Langnese-Iglo GmbH v Commission* [1995] ECR II-1533.

[184]   Case T-9/93 *Scholler Lebensmittel GmbH & Co KG v Commission* [1995] ECR II-1610.

[185]   The freezer cabinet agreements contain provisions requiring the cabinets to be used exclusively for the storing of products for sale which are supplied by Van den Bergh Foods (ref. para 142 of the decision).

[186]   See para 184 of the decision. The economic implications of freezer exclusivity are examined by Aidan Robertson and Mark Williams, 'An ice cream war: the law economic of freezer exclusivity I' [1995] 1 ECLR 7. See also Valentine Korah, 'Exclusive purchasing obligations: Mars v Langnese and Scholler' [1994] 3 ECLR 171; Julian Maitland-Walker, 'Ice cream wars: an honourable peace or the beginning of a greater conflict?' [1995] 8 ECLR 451, and Michael Rowe 'Ice cream: the saga continues' [1998] ECLR 479.

[187]   Rejection of complaint by Commission Decision of 6 November 1998 in Case IV/36511, not published. At time of writing available on DG COMP's Internet site at http://ec.europa.eu/comm/competition/antitrust/closed/en/1998.html#563.

The Commission's press release IP/98/967 of 6 November 1998 states that '[t]he Commission continues to consider the UK on-trade beer market as foreclosed. However, the Commission concludes that Greene King is too small to contribute significantly to this foreclosure. Indeed, Greene King's sales in its managed, tenanted and loan-tied estate account for only 1.3% of the UK on-trade market. This is considerably less than 5% (or more) that each of the big UK brewers (Scottish&Newcastle, Bass, Whitbread and Carlsberg-Tetley) realises in their tied network (including the restrictive agreements with non-brewing pub companies).'

[188]   Case T-25/99, *Roberts v Commission* [2001] ECR II-01881.

analysis of the applicability of Article 85(1) of the Treaty, the Greene King network of agreements, which, according to the Commission's findings, did not in itself contribute significantly to foreclosure of the market, to the national breweries' networks of agreements, which did contribute significantly to foreclosure.

In its judgment, the Court noted that a brewery holding a relatively small share of the market which ties its sales outlets for many years may contribute to foreclosure of the market as significantly as a brewery with a comparatively strong position in the market which regularly frees its outlets at frequent intervals.[189]   **9.143**

For a brewery's network of agreements, which does not in itself contribute significantly to foreclosure of the market, to be attributed, for the purposes of the analysis of the applicability of Article 81(1), to the national breweries' networks of agreements, which do contribute significantly to foreclosure, the court stated, in paragraphs 106 and 107, that two conditions must be satisfied.   **9.144**

> First, the beer supply agreements concluded between the wholesaling brewery, in this case Greene King, and the supplying breweries, namely the national breweries—the upstream agreements—may be regarded as forming part of the supplying breweries' networks of agreements if they contain terms which may be analysed as a purchasing obligation (commitments to purchase minimum quantities, stocking obligations or non-competition obligations). It follows that a supply contract which does not contain a purchasing obligation, in whatever form, does not form part of the network of agreements of a supplying brewery, even if it relates to a substantial proportion of the beer sold by the establishments tied to the wholesaling brewery.

> Next, for not only the upstream agreements but also the agreements concluded between the wholesaling brewery and the establishments tied to it—the downstream agreements—to be attributed to the supplying breweries' networks of agreements, it is also necessary for the agreements between the supplying breweries and the wholesaling brewery to be so restrictive that access to the wholesaling brewery's network of downstream agreements is no longer possible, or at least very difficult, for other breweries in the United Kingdom or elsewhere.

(d) The 2001 De Minimis Notice

The 2001 De Minimis Notice introduces a 'de minimis' market share threshold of 5 per cent for markets where there exist such parallel networks of similar agreements. Therefore, individual suppliers or distributors with a market share not exceeding 5 per cent are in general not considered to contribute significantly to a cumulative foreclosure effect. For those cases where the 5 per cent threshold is exceeded the Notice helpfully states that '[a] cumulative foreclosure effect is unlikely to exist if less than 30 per cent of the relevant market is covered by parallel (networks of) agreements having similar effects'.[190]   **9.145**

(3) Does a Finding of a Restrictive Effect for a Network of an Undertaking Apply to each of its Constituents?

On the basis of the 1998 judgment of the Court of First Instance in *Langnese-Iglo*, the first edition of this book stated that the finding of a restrictive effect for a network of an undertaking   **9.146**

---

[189] ibid, para 76.
[190] See para 8 of the 2001 Guidelines.

would apply equally to each of its constituents.[191] This statement requires qualification following the December 2000 judgment of the Court of Justice in the *Neste Markkinointi Oy* case.[192] This judgment arose from an Article 234 reference by a Finnish national court which was trying to draw a distinction between the contribution of fixed-term contracts concluded for a number of years and those which may be terminated at any time on one year's notice, with the objective of excluding the latter from the scope of Article 81.[193]

9.147 In this case the Court reasoned in paragraph 37 that:

> subdividing, exceptionally, a supplier's network is not arbitrary nor does it undermine the principle of legal certainty. Subdividing the network in that way results from a factual assessment of the position held by the operator concerned on the relevant market, the aim of the assessment being, on the basis of an objective criterion of particular relevance in that it takes into account the market's distinctive features, to limit the number of cases in which a supplier's contracts are declared void to those which, together, contribute significantly to the cumulative effect of sealing off the market.[194]

9.148 The Court then went on to rule as follows:

> The prohibition laid down by Article 85(1) of the EC Treaty (now Article 81(1) EC) does not apply to an exclusive purchasing agreement entered into by a motor-fuels supplier which the retailer may terminate upon one year's notice at any time where all that supplier's exclusive purchasing agreements, whether considered separately or as a whole, taken together with the network of similar agreements made by the totality of suppliers, have an appreciable effect on the closing-off of the market but where the agreements of the same kind as the agreement at issue in the main proceedings by reason of their duration represent only a very small part of the totality of one supplier's exclusive purchasing agreements, of which the majority are fixed term contracts entered into for more than one year.

9.149 From this judgment it may be concluded that where the network of a particular supplier falls within the scope of Article 81 because of its significant contribution to foreclosure, it may be possible to carve out and exclude from the scope of Article 81 a category of agreements whose foreclosure effects are significantly less than the main category of agreements. Although the Court did follow the thrust of the recommendation of its Advocate General, it is noteworthy that in its ruling it did not expressly state that the category of agreements excluded from the scope of Article 81 should have an insignificant effect on access to the relevant market.[195] This could, however, be inferred from paragraph 37 of the judgment quoted above.

---

[191] The Court of First Instance pointed out in Cases T-7 & 9/93 *Langnese-Iglo & Scholler* [1995] ECR I-1539 & 1611, para 129/95 that 'where there is a network of similar agreements concluded by the same producer, the assessment of the effects of that network on competition applies to all the individual agreements making up the network'. The judgment of the Court of First Instance was upheld on appeal by the Court of Justice in its judgment of 1 October 1998 in case C-279/95P.

[192] Case C-214/99, *Neste Markkinointi Oy, Yötuuli Ky and Others* [2000] ECR I-11121.

[193] Para 19 of the judgment.

[194] Para 37 of the judgment.

[195] [2000] ECR I-11121. In his Opinion of 6 July 2000, Advocate General Fennelly had recommended that the Court answer the question as follows: 'Art 85(1) of the EC Treaty (now Art 81(1) EC) does not apply to an exclusive purchasing agreement concluded by a particular supplier which, because it is terminable on giving a short period of notice, is economically distinguishable, as regards its effects on competition, from the majority of the other exclusive purchasing agreements of the same supplier, provided the agreement in question has

(4) Quantification of Contribution

Quantification of the contribution primarily takes account of overall market share, tied **9.150** market share, and duration. The Court has ruled in the *Delimitis* judgment[196] that 'the extent of the contribution made by the individual agreement depends on the position of the contracting parties in the relevant market and on the duration of the agreement'. In paragraphs 25 and 26 of the judgment, the Court has clarified that 'that position is not determined solely by the market share held by the brewery and any group to which it may belong, but also by the number of outlets tied to it or to its group, in relation to the total number of premises for the sale and consumption of drinks found in the relevant market'.

As to the duration, the Court states at paragraph 26 of the judgment that 'if the duration is **9.151** manifestly excessive in relation to the average duration of beer supply agreements generally entered into on the relevant market, the individual contract falls under the prohibition under Article 85(1) [now Article 81(1)]. A brewery with a relatively small market share which ties its sales outlets for many years may make as significant a contribution to a sealing-off of the market as a brewery in a relatively strong market position which regularly releases sales outlets at shorter intervals.'

In the German ice cream cases, the Court of First Instance, in assessing the significant con- **9.152** tribution of the companies in question to 'the closing-off of the market', referred to 'the strong position occupied by the [company concerned] in the relevant market, and, in particular, its market share'.[197] Therefore, it would appear that in this case the Court of First Instance, when taking into account all the factors referred to in *Delimitis*, placed greater emphasis on the overall market share as opposed to the tied market share. This was probably because of the highly concentrated nature of the market.[198]

The general rule is that the longer the duration of the exclusive purchase arrangement the **9.153** greater the foreclosure effect. In the Irish ice cream decision Van den Bergh Foods argued that freezer exclusivity agreements which can be terminated on two months' notice are evidence of a temporary relationship and cannot lead to a de facto tie which foreclosed other suppliers from the market. The Commission did not agree, pointing out that the cabinet agreements were of indefinite duration and that market research showed that the relationship was not temporary.[199] The argument of temporary relationship also appears in the *Whitbread* decision,[200] where it was argued that since it was possible to terminate a loan tie upon three months' notice, such ties should no longer be considered as hindering any opportunities for

---

insignificant effects on access to the market. This is so even if all the exclusive purchasing agreements concluded by that supplier, considered as a whole or together with the parallel networks of similar agreements concluded by the other suppliers active on the market, have a significant influence on foreclosure of the market.'

[196] Last sentence of point 1 of the operative part of the judgment.

[197] See para 87 of *Scholler* case and para 112 of *Langnese-Iglo* case.

[198] The two leading companies had between them a tied market share exceeding 30 per cent (ref. para 105 of the *Langnese-Iglo* case) and a total market share exceeding 70% (ref. para 96 of *Langnese-Iglo* and para 73 of *Scholler*).

[199] See para 208 of the decision.

[200] *Whitbread plc* [1999] OJ L88/26. See also press release IP/99/104 of 11 Feb. 1999. This decision was upheld on appeal to the Court of First Instance in Case T-131/99, *Shaw and Falla v Commission* [2002] ECR II-02023.

access to the market. The Commission considered that the average duration of four years for such loan ties indicated that the contractual relationship was not a temporary one.[201]

9.154   It should be noted that in assessing the contribution to foreclosure made by a supplier the Commission takes into account any retail/buyer outlets owned by the supplier. Therefore, in the beer sector, while the managed estate of the brewer does not of itself fall under Article 81(1) as it does not concern an agreement between independent operators, the brewer's market share acquired via its managed estate is assessed as a part of its tied market share and taken into account in the Commission's assessment of foreclosure.[202]

(5) The New Block Exemption Regulation (BER)

(a) *Withdrawal of the benefit of the BER*

9.155   The presumption of legality conferred by the BER may, under Article 6 of the BER, be withdrawn if a vertical agreement, either on its own or together with similar agreements enforced by competing suppliers or buyers, comes within the scope of Article 81(1) and does not fulfil all the conditions of Article 81(3). The Guidelines explain[203] that withdrawal may in particular be required where access to the relevant market or competition therein is significantly restricted by the cumulative effect of parallel networks of similar vertical agreements enforced by competing suppliers or buyers. The Guidelines recognise that this may occur more readily in the case of distribution of products to final consumers, who are often in a much weaker position than professional buyers of intermediate products. Agreements entered into by undertakings whose contribution to the cumulative effect is insignificant do not fall under the prohibition provided for in Article 81(1)[204] and are therefore not subject to the withdrawal mechanism.

(b) *Disapplication of the BER*

9.156   Article 8 of the BER enables the Commission to exclude from the scope of the BER, by means of regulation, parallel networks of similar vertical restraints where these cover more than 50 per cent of a relevant market. Unlike in the case of withdrawal, such a measure is not addressed to individual undertakings but concerns all undertakings whose agreements are defined in the regulation disapplying the BER (see also paras 9.23–9.25 and paras 9.264–9.265). Whereas the withdrawal of the benefit of the BER under Article 6 implies the adoption of a decision establishing an infringement of Article 81 by an individual company, the effect of a regulation under Article 8 is merely to remove, in respect of the restraints and the markets concerned, the benefit of the application of the BER and to restore the full application of Article 81(1) and (3).[205]

(c) *Analysis of Different Categories of Vertical Restraints*

9.157   The possible negative effects arising from cumulative effects differ as between the different categories of vertical restraints. These are analysed in paras 9.298–9.359 below.

---

[201] Para 115 of the decision.
[202] Para 134 of the decision.
[203] Guidelines points 71–4.
[204] Judgment in the *Delimitis* case. See also the De Minimis Notice (OJ C368, 22.12.2001), which contains in para 8 a specific 5 per cent market share threshold in the case of cumulative effects.
[205] Guidelines points 80–1.

(6) Exemption under Article 81(3)

(a) Non-exemptable Foreclosure

In the Irish ice cream case the Commission refused to exempt the freezer exclusivity agree- **9.158** ments because (1) any improvements in distribution arising from the freezer exclusivity agreements did not outweigh the restrictive effects of those agreements and in particular the limitation they place on access by competing ice cream suppliers; (2) there was no guarantee that benefits will be passed on to consumers; (3) the exclusivity condition was not indispensable for the attainment of the alleged benefits; and (4) they constitute an important barrier to entry which in combination with the strength of the supplier's position on the relevant market contributes substantially to an elimination of competition on the relevant market.[206] In the German ice cream cases the Court of First Instance rejected a plea that the exclusive purchase agreements satisfied the conditions of Article 81(3) on the grounds that it had not been shown that the Commission had committed a manifest error of assessment in considering that the contested agreements did not fulfil the first condition laid down by Article 81(3). Commenting on this first condition the Court of First Instance stated that 'it is settled law that the improvement cannot be identified with all the advantages which the parties obtain from the agreement in their production or distribution activities. The improvement must in particular display appreciable objective advantages of such a character as to compensate for the disadvantages which they cause in the field of competition.'[207] The Court considered that the applicant had 'failed to produce any factual evidence such as seriously to challenge the Commission's analysis regarding the barriers to entry to the market raised by the supply agreements and, consequently, the resulting weakening of competition'.[208]

(b) Exemptable Foreclosure

This contrasts with the *Whitbread* decision[209] where the Commission exempted the exclu- **9.159** sive purchase contracts with pubs in the United Kingdom despite the fact that they were considered to result in foreclosure effects. It should be noted that the exclusive purchase contracts in this case relate to premises which are owned by the brewer and which are rented to tenants by way of leasehold/tenancy agreements. In respect of the first condition of Article 81(3) the Commission concluded that the notified leasehold agreements, including the tying restrictions, contributed to an improvement of distribution on the UK on-trade beer market. This conclusion was justified by a complex analysis of a number of factors[210] including recognition of the fact that:

> Beer supply agreements generally lead to an improvement in distribution as they make it significantly easier to establish, modernise, maintain and operate premises used for the sale and consumption of drinks;
>
> The letting of premises at an agreed rent, particularly in view of the restrictive UK licensing system, is a method of providing the means for a lessee to operate premises and, as such, allows a low cost entry of a newcomer on the on-trade market for the distribution of beer;

---

[206] See paras 221–54 of the decision.
[207] Case T-7/93 at para 180.
[208] ibid, at para 182.
[209] See n 200 above.
[210] See paras 150–70 of the decision.

The incentive on the reseller, following from the exclusive purchasing and the non-competition obligation, to devote all the resources at his disposal to the sale of the contract goods will generally lead to an improvement in the distribution of the contract goods;

They allow long-term planning of sales and consequently a cost-effective organisation of production and distribution and the pressure of competition between products of different makes obliges the undertaking involved to determine the number and character of premises used for the sale and consumption of drinks in accordance with the wishes of customers; and

The higher prices for beer payable by tied tenants vis-à-vis untied or free tenants do not negate the improvements in distribution because they are compensated for by countervailing benefits arising from the overall business relationship with the tying brewer.

9.160 It is submitted that analysis of the fourth and final criterion of Article 81(3) (ie possibility of eliminating competition in respect of a substantial part of the market in question) is why the exclusive agreements were looked at more favourably in this case than in the ice cream cases discussed above. In this case there was sufficient inter-brand competition[211] so that the benefit of efficiencies was likely to be passed on to consumers. In paragraph 177 of the decision the Commission states:

It is evident that Whitbread cannot eliminate competition from a substantial part of the market, as they account for only 13 per cent of the UK on-trade beer market in 1997. Moreover, even taking into account the fact that in 1997 at most 58 per cent of the UK on-trade market for beer was foreclosed through the parallel networks of brewers' agreements, Whitbread's notified agreements do not lead to the elimination of competition in respect of a substantial part of the UK on-trade beer market.

9.161 It should be noted that the Commission applied a narrow test of foreclosure in the *Whitbread* case. This related to the possibility for independent access to the market. The Commission recognised that other forms of access were possible:

It is not disputed that the tied volume might still offer indirect access for other brewers in so far as the (property on loan) tying brewer/wholesaler is prepared to supply to its tied outlets beer from other brewers. However, the assessment on foreclosure focuses on opportunities for independent access for other brewers which clearly does not result from 'horizontal' co-operation between actual competitors. Such co-operation may limit the level of inter-brand competition between the brewers in question and the tying brewer will only allow another brewer's beer in his outlets when this is in the tying brewer's interest.[212]

9.162 The narrow test of foreclosure applied in the *Whitbread* case focuses primarily on the pure vertical aspects of entry, ie the ability of a foreign brewer to get its beers directly into retail outlets rather than indirectly through the network of an incumbent brewer. Access via the network of an incumbent brewer will normally have horizontal aspects. It would appear that the Commission takes these horizontal aspects of entry into account when deciding whether to grant an exemption to the vertical aspects of foreclosure.

---

[211] The Herfindahl-Hirschmann Index (hereinafter HHI), used to help describe market concentration, for the UK beer market increased, on the basis of the market shares of the national brewers, from 1350 in 1991 to 1678 in 1996. With an HHI of between 1000 and 1800, the market is described as 'moderately concentrated' (ref. para 19 of the decision).

[212] Para 116 of the decision.

D. The New Block Exemption Regulation and Guidelines

(1) Background

The new definition of vertical agreements and other changes to Council Regulation 19/65   **9.163**
enabled the Commission to adopt Commission Block Exemption Regulation (EC) 2790/
1999 (the 'BER'), which forms a package with the Guidelines on Vertical Restraints (the
'Guidelines').[213] The BER creates a safe harbour for most vertical agreements whereas the
Guidelines provide guidance on the application of the BER as well as on the application of
Article 81 outside the scope of the block exemption. The Guidelines aim to help companies to
make their own assessment of vertical agreements. Vertical agreements that prevent, restrict, or
distort competition are referred to in the Guidelines and the BER as 'vertical restraints'.[214]

The BER is composed of three main elements. First, the BER creates a safe harbour for ver-   **9.164**
tical restraints below a 30 per cent market share threshold. The approach of limiting the
scope of the safe harbour by a market share threshold was later followed in other block
exemption regulations in the fields of horizontal co-operation agreements and technology
transfer agreements.[215] Secondly, the BER contains a list of hardcore restrictions. The hardcore list is arguably the most important part of the BER. These restrictions of competition
by object have such a high potential for negative effects on competition that it is not considered necessary for the purposes of applying Article 81(1) to demonstrate any actual
effects on the market. Moreover, the conditions of Article 81(3) are considered unlikely to
be fulfilled in the case of hardcore restrictions. When an agreement contains such a restriction, it follows from Article 4 of the BER that the agreement as a whole falls outside the
scope of the block exemption. For the purposes of the BER hardcore restrictions cannot be
severed from the rest of the agreement. In the context of an individual assessment the
Commission considers that hardcore restrictions will only in exceptional circumstances
fulfil the four conditions of Article 81(3). Thirdly, the BER contains a limited list of
excluded restrictions, called conditions in the Guidelines. These conditions are not block
exempted but, unlike hardcore restrictions, the inclusion in an agreement of any of these
excluded restrictions does not prevent the application of the block exemption to the rest of
the agreement. It is only the individual restriction that is not block exempted and that
requires individual assessment. Unlike the hardcore restrictions, there is also no negative
presumption against these restrictions when individually assessed.

The Guidelines, as indicated above, provide interpretative guidance on the application of the   **9.165**
BER and on the application of Article 81 outside the safe harbour of the BER. This is an important aspect given the need for undertakings to self-assess their agreements that fall outside the
safe harbour of the block exemption. As stated in the Guidelines, there is no presumption that
agreements falling outside the block exemption are caught by Article 81(1) or fail to satisfy the
conditions of Article 81(3). In particular, the mere fact that the market share threshold is

---

[213] See n 26 above.
[214] See Guidelines point 5 and BER Art 2(1).
[215] See Commission Regulation (EC) 2658/2000, Commission Regulation (EC) 2659/2000 and
Commission Regulation (EC) 772/2004.

exceeded is not a sufficient basis for finding that the agreement is caught by Article 81(1) or does not fulfil the conditions of Article 81(3).[216] Individual assessment of the likely effects of the agreement is required. It is only when an agreement contains one or more hardcore restrictions that it can normally be presumed that the agreement is prohibited by Article 81.

9.166 Self-assessment is made easier by following the steps in the flow chart in Figure 1.[217] The first step is usually to assess whether the agreement falls within the scope of application of Article 81(1). This concerns in the first place whether or not the agreement is a genuine agency agreement or can benefit from the De Minimis Notice and may therefore be considered to fall outside the scope of Article 81(1). This is first dealt with below. After that the BER and Guidelines are dealt with in detail.

(2) The De Minimis Notice

9.167 The Guidelines in points 8–11 deal with the issue of appreciability of vertical restraints. This concerns in the first place agreements of minor importance as defined in the current

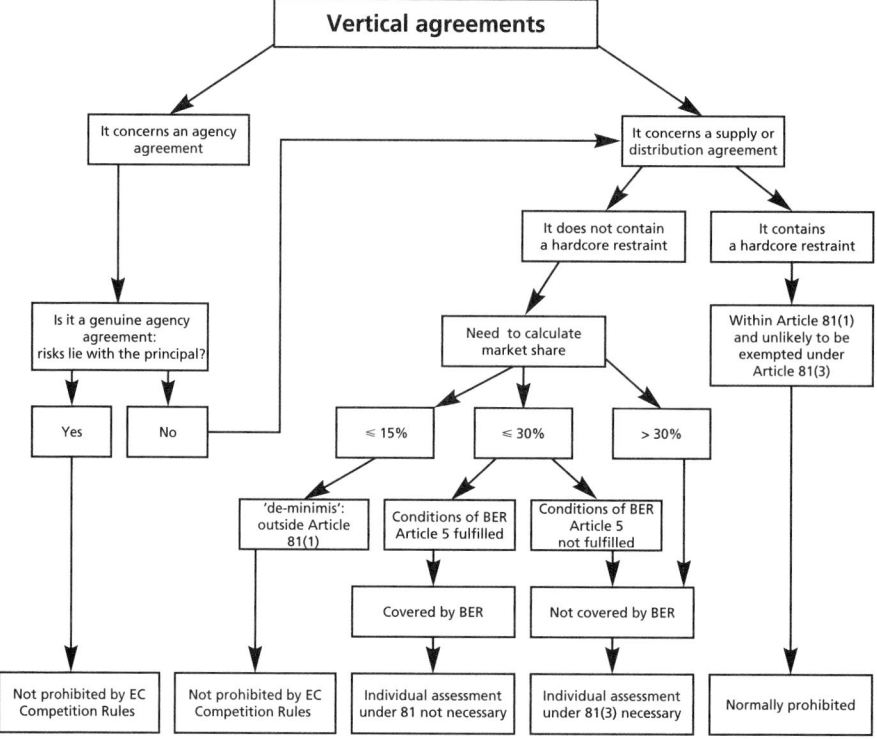

Figure 1 Flow chart for assessing vertical agreements

---

[216] Guidelines, in particular point 62.
[217] The flow chart is derived from *Competition Policy in Europe: The Competition Rules for Supply and Distribution Agreements* (European Commission, Office for Official Publications of the European Communities, 2002).

or any future 'de minimis' notice. The Guidelines refer to the 1997 De Minimis Notice, which has been replaced by the 2001 De Minimis Notice.[218] The text of the Guidelines needs to be read in the light of this new notice and the Notice on effect on trade (see para 9.58).

(3) Agency Agreements

(a) Introduction

Agency contracts are commonly used for the distribution of goods and services. An agent **9.168** is a natural or legal person who negotiates contracts with third parties on behalf of its principal. Once the contract is concluded the agent drops out, with performance of the contract being left to the principal or third party. The Commission has looked favourably upon such contracts where the principal appoints the agent as his sole agent for a given territory and the agent agrees to work exclusively for the principal for a certain period of time. The Commission has considered such exclusivity provisions as the natural result of the special relationship between a commercial agent and its principal which required them to protect each other's interests and therefore as not restricting competition. In such circumstances the exclusive agent has been treated as an auxiliary of its principal.

The Commission took the view that Article 81(1) did not apply to such agreements where **9.169** two conditions were fulfilled, namely integration of the agent in the business of the principle and the absence of financial risk on the part of the agent who did not take title on the goods being traded. This thinking was expressed in Part II of the Commission's 1962 Notice on Exclusive Dealing Contracts with Commercial Agents.[219] This Notice has become outdated for a number of reasons, including the adoption of an EC Council Directive on self-employed commercial agents,[220] developments in the administrative practice of the Commission and case law of the Community Courts, and adoption of the Guidelines.

However, perhaps the most fundamental change relates to changes in the systems of distri- **9.170** bution. In 1962, goods were, in general, manufactured, stored, and pushed down the supply chain by way of arm's length transactions between independent manufacturers, wholesalers, and retailers. The whole nature of distribution has been changed by the information technology revolution and the adoption of just-in-time (JIT) principles.[221] The absence of risk relating to individual transactions, which was the main criterion used for differentiating an agent from an independent trader, is no longer the preserve of the commercial agent. Combined with modern technology, JIT has facilitated a shift from 'push' (ie where products

---

[218] See paras 9.60–9.67 above.

[219] [1962] OJ 139 2921/62. The Notice, now outdated, is described in some detail in the first edition of this book.

[220] Council Directive (EEC) 86/653 of 18 December 1986 on the coordination of the laws of the Member States relating to self-employed commercial agents [1986] OJ L382/17. For the purposes of the Directive a 'commercial agent' is defined as a 'self-employed intermediary who has continuing authority to negotiate the sale or the purchase of goods on behalf of another person hereinafter called the "principal", or to negotiate and conclude such transactions on behalf of and in the name of that principal' (it should be noted that services are excluded from this definition).

[221] JIT is based on the principle that no products should be made, and no components ordered, until there is downstream demand. For a useful summary of changes in distribution see paras 40–5 of the Green Paper on Vertical Restraints.

are manufactured and stored in anticipation of demand) to 'pull' (ie where consumer demand pulls products towards the market and behind those products the flow of components is also determined by that same demand) in the supply chain.

9.171 One of the implications of the shift from push to pull is that manufacturers/suppliers have fewer incentives to organise their distribution chains in a manner which requires their distributors to maintain stocks over which they hold legal title and act as resellers. With the reduction in risks relating to the holding of stocks, distributors will have greater scope to switch their legal status from that of resellers to agents. This is demonstrated by the 1996 *Ford Service Outlet* case[222] which related to Ford's reorganisation of its European dealer network. As part of this reorganisation, smaller dealers who mainly offered servicing and sold a small number of cars ceased to be Ford Dealers and instead became service outlets. The service outlets, while having no legal obligation to sell cars, could continue to 'do so in the name and on behalf of their affiliated main dealer with remuneration by way of commission on each sale'.[223] Therefore, in relation to the sale of new cars these service outlets bore no financial risk and were acting as commercial agents. What is interesting about this case is that the 1997 Report on Competition Policy lists this case as having been closed by the Commission by way of an exemption type comfort letter and not negative clearance.[224] This tends to suggest that the Commission examined the financial risks associated with the service obligations of the outlet together with the sales of new cars by way of agency and applied Article 81(1).[225] This contrasts with the recent 2005 jurisprudence in the *DaimlerChrysler* case,[226] discussed in paras 9.172–9.181 below, where the Court of First Instance focuses more on the assessment of the agent's independence in terms of the financial risk of the transaction on the market concerned (ie the sale of new cars) and less on broader considerations as to the financial risks of the agent's business on related markets (ie after-sales servicing and repair).

(b) The Role of Financial Risk: 2005 Judgment of the Court of First Instance in the DaimlerChrysler case

9.172 In its judgment of 15 September 2005,[227] the CFI annulled a number of the Commission's findings in its 2001 decision[228] and reduced the fine from EUR71.8 million to EUR9.8

---

[222] The notification in this case is summarised in a notice published in [1996] OJ C227/11. The *Report on Competition Policy 1997* (Vol xxvii) 124 reports that the case was closed by way of comfort letter.

[223] See ibid, para 2.

[224] ibid 137 lists the case as having been closed by way of an 'individual exemption 85(3)' type comfort letter.

[225] The case Notice states that '(t)he agreement provides that service and parts sales targets have to be mutually agreed'. See ibid, para 2.

[226] Case T-325/01 *DaimlerChrysler AG v Commission*, judgment of 15 September 2005. See also judgment of the Court of Justice of 14 December 2006 in Case C-217/05 *Confederación Española de Empresarios de Estaciones de Servicio v Compañia Española de Petróleos SA*. This judgment arises from a reference for a preliminary ruling from the Spanish Supreme Court and concerns, *inter alia*, 'agency contracts' between service-station operators and oil companies. Paragraph 46 of the judgment is important as the Court stresses that 'the decisive factors for the purposes of determining whether a service-station operator is an independent economic operator is to be found in the agreement concluded with the prinicipal and, in particular, in the clauses of that agreement, implied or express, relating to the assumption of the financial and commercial risks linked to sales of goods to third paries. As the Commission rightly submitted in its observations, the question of risk must be analysed on a case-by-case basis, taking account of the real economic situation rather than the legal classification of the contractual relationship in national law.'

[227] ibid.

[228] Commission Decision 2002/758/EC of 10 October 2001 relating to a proceeding under Art 81 of the EC Treaty (Case COMP/36.264—*Mercedes-Benz*) (OJ 2002 L257, p 1).

million. At the time of writing, the English version of this judgment was not available, which explains the lack of English-language quotations in the following summary of such an important case. In its 2001 decision the Commission had found that DaimlerChrysler had infringed Article 81 of the Treaty by:

(1) giving its German agents instructions to sell new cars as far as possible only to customers in their own contract territory; to support this DaimlerChrysler also required its agents to insist on the payment of a deposit of 15 per cent of the price of the vehicle for orders for new cars from customers from outside the territory;

(2) prohibiting German agents and Spanish dealers from supplying cars to leasing companies where no customer was identified, thus preventing them from establishing a stock; and

(3) participating in agreements to restrict the granting of discounts in Belgium.

With respect to the alleged anti-competitive conduct of DaimlerChrysler in Germany, the **9.173** Court found that DaimlerChrysler had acted unilaterally. The German agents were to be assimilated to employees of DaimlerChrysler and regarded as integrated into that undertaking and forming an economic unit with it. Neither their activity of soliciting orders for cars with a view to transmitting them to DaimlerChrysler nor the other services supplied by them for DaimlerChrysler, such as repairs and after-sales service, carried a commercial risk which could allow them to be classified as independent operators.

With respect to the conduct of DaimlerChrysler in Spain, the Court found that under **9.174** Spanish law every leasing company already had to have an identified customer for the leasing contract at the time of acquiring the vehicle. The restrictions of which DaimlerChrysler was accused thus derived from the applicable legislation, so that they were not contrary to the prohibition of such restrictions in agreements under Article 81 of the EC Treaty.

However, the Court upheld the Commission's finding that DaimlerChrysler had partici- **9.175** pated, through its Belgian subsidiary, in an agreement intended to restrict price competition in Belgium by introducing detection and deterrent measures against discounts of more than 3 per cent for the E-class motor vehicle.

As regards the analysis of agency agreements under Article 81, the most important part of **9.176** the judgment is the assessment of the German aspects of the case and annulment of the Commission's finding of an agreement between economic operators in Germany. The CFI found that the Commission had both incorrectly assessed certain of the financial risks borne by German agents and provided insufficient evidence of the appreciable nature of others. Unlike dealers in Belgium and Spain, German agents do not buy new cars from Mercedes-Benz for resale.[229] The German agent has no power of sale, because its function is confined to seeking orders and passing these on to Mercedes-Benz, at sales prices fixed by the manufacturer.[230] It was Mercedes-Benz and not the agent who transferred title to the customer. Also, the agent had no authority to grant a rebate on the sale price of the manufacturer and any rebate given by the agent came out of his own commission.[231] In Spain and Belgium the dealer

---

[229] Case T-325/01, see n 226 above, paras 96 and 117.
[230] ibid, para 93.
[231] ibid, para 94.

is required to maintain a stock of cars. The Court noted that the dealers in Spain and Belgium took on a significant financial risk as regards the sale of cars, a risk which in Germany fell on the manufacturer.[232] In light of this, the Court concluded that the Commission was wrong to assimilate German agents with Belgian and Spanish dealers and to find that these dealers were as strongly integrated into Mercedes-Benz's distribution system as German agents.[233]

9.177 The CFI also found that the Commission had overstated the risk of transportation of the cars (approximately 35 per cent were picked up by purchasers at the factory) and the risks related to the obligation of agents to purchase demonstration cars (these were supplied at preferential rates and could be sold 3 to 6 months later having clocked up 3,000 km). It was also not established that obligations on agents to provide after-sales guarantee services were a real financial risk, since it had not been shown that reimbursement from the manufacturer was inadequate. The Court addressed the financial risks borne by the agent in providing after-sales services (retention of workshop, repair facilities, trained staff, and spare parts) by stating that these activities had not been shown by the Commission to involve appreciable risks.[234]

9.178 Crucially, the Court followed its analysis of the financial risks borne by the German agent with the following statement in paragraph 113:

> Il s'ensuit que la qualification du statut de l'agent allemand Mercedes-Benz en application de l'article 81, paragraphe 1, CE exposée au point 102 ci-dessus n'est pas infirmée par le fait que les agents allemands Mercedes-Benz sont tenus d'assumer un certain nombre d'activités et d'obligations financières en application du contrat d'agence. Il convient de souligner également qu'il s'agit d'activités exercées sur d'autres marchés que le marché en cause en l'espèce. En effet, même s'il devait être admis que ces obligations impliquent certains risques limités pour les agents, il y a lieu de considérer qu'elles ne seraient pas susceptibles à elles seules de modifier la qualification de la relation entre la requérante et ses agents en application du droit de la concurrence quant au marché en cause en l'espèce.

9.179 This is an important paragraph, where the Court states that its finding in paragraph 102 that Mercedes-Benz and not its agents bears the principle risks on the relevant market for the sale of new cars, is not called into question by the fact that German agents are, under their agency contract, responsible for a certain number of activities and financial obligations. The court emphasises that these activities are undertaken on markets separate from the relevant market for the sale of new cars. It then states that even if one were to admit that these obligations involve certain limited risks for the agent, they are not, on their own, sufficient to alter the qualification of the relationship between Mercedes-Benz and its agents as regards the relevant market for the sale of new cars.

---

[232] ibid, para 98.

[233] Commission decision at n 232 above, para 226 and Case T-325/01, see n 230 above, para 116.

[234] Case T-325/01, see n 226 above, para 111, where the Court stated 'Le Tribunal considère que la Commission n'a pas établi que l'indemnité de garantie est commercialement inadéquate et qu'il existe, par conséquent, pour l'agent, un risque financier réel associé à l'obligation d'effectuer des réparations sous garantie. Il y a lieu de considérer qu'il ne ressort pas de la décision litigieuse que cette activité associée à la vente de voitures Mercedes-Benz comporte en fait des risques exceptionnels même s'il est vrai que, si elle n'est pas gérée correctement et effectivement, elle peut être déficitaire et réduire, voire éliminer, les bénéfices de l'agent associés à la vente de voitures. De même, il y a lieu de considérer que la Commission n'a pas prouvé que les obligations imposées à l'agent d'installer un atelier de réparation, de proposer un service après-vente et d'acquérir et de stocker des pièces de rechange comportent des risques économiques sensibles.'

What the Court is saying in paragraph 113 is that on the facts of this case certain limited **9.180** risks related to activities on markets other than that for the resale of new cars (the Commission failed to prove that these activities had involved appreciable risks[235]) do not modify the characterisation of the relationship between Mercedes-Benz and its agents on the (new car supply) market concerned here.

This is an important ruling where the Court of First Instance focuses more on the assess- **9.181** ment of the agent's independence in terms of the financial risk of the transaction on the market concerned (ie the sale of new cars) and less on broader considerations as to the financial risks of the agent's business on related markets (ie after-sales servicing and repair). However, it is submitted that it would be going too far to interpret this judgment as meaning that appreciable financial risks on related markets are no longer relevant.

(c) Agency and the 2000 Guidelines on Vertical Restraints

Paragraphs 12 to 20 of the Guidelines replace the 1962 Notice on exclusive dealing con- **9.182** tracts with commercial agents. For the purposes of the Guidelines agency agreements cover the situation in which a legal or physical person (the agent) is vested with the power to negotiate and/or conclude contracts on behalf of another person (the principal), either in the agent's own name or in the name of the principal, for the:

— purchase of goods or services by the principal, or
— sale of goods or services supplied by the principal.

The determining factor in assessing whether Article 81(1) is applicable is the financial or **9.183** commercial risk borne by the agent in relation to the activities for which he has been appointed as an agent by the principal.[236] Unlike the 1962 Notice, it is not material for the assessment whether the agent acts for one or several principals.

Paragraph 14 of the Guidelines identifies the two types of financial risk that are material to **9.184** the assessment of the genuine nature of an agency agreement under Article 81(1). First there are the risks which are directly related to the contracts concluded and/or negotiated by the agent on behalf of the principal, such as financing of stocks (in the *Mercedes-Benz* case discussed above there were no such risks). Secondly, there are the risks related to market specific investments. These are investments specifically required for the type of activity for which the agent has been appointed by the principal, ie which are required to enable the agent to conclude and/or negotiate this type of contract. Such investments are usually sunk, if upon leaving that particular field of activity the investment cannot be used for other activities or sold other than at a significant loss. (In the *Mercedes-Benz* case discussed above the Commission failed to prove that these were appreciable risks.)

In paragraph 15 of the Guidelines the Commission states that '[t]he agency agreement is **9.185** considered a genuine agency agreement and consequently falls outside Article 81(1) if the agent does not bear any, or bears only insignificant, risks in relation to the contracts concluded and/or negotiated on behalf of the principal and in relation to market specific investments for that field of activity. In such a situation, the selling or purchasing function

---

[235] See n 234 above.
[236] Guidelines para 13.

forms part of the principal's activities, despite the fact that the agent is a separate undertaking.' It is noteworthy that the Commission guidelines refer to financial risks in the overall 'field of activity' of the agent whereas in the *DaimlerChrysler* case discussed above the court focuses more on the financial risks in the relevant market. It is likely, following the *DaimlerChrysler* judgment, that only appreciable risks on related markets risk to bring the agency agreement within the scope of Article 82.

9.186   The question of risk must be assessed on a case-by-case basis having regard to the economic reality of the situation rather than the legal form.[237] Nonetheless, the Guidelines state the opinion of the Commission that Article 81(1) will generally not be applicable to the obligations imposed on the agent as to the contracts negotiated and/or concluded on behalf of the principal 'where property in the contract goods bought or sold does not vest in the agent, or the agent does not himself supply the contract services and where the agent:

— does not contribute to the costs relating to the supply/purchase of the contract goods or services, including the costs of transporting the goods. This does not preclude the agent from carrying out the transport service, provided that the costs are covered by the principal;

— is not, directly or indirectly, obliged to invest in sales promotion, such as contributions to the advertising budgets of the principal;

— does not maintain at his own cost or risk stocks of the contract goods, including the costs of financing the stocks and the costs of loss of stocks and can return unsold goods to the principal without charge, unless the agent is liable for fault (for example, by failing to comply with reasonable security measures to avoid loss of stocks);

— does not create and/or operate an after-sales service, repair service, or a warranty service unless it is fully reimbursed by the principal;

— does not make market-specific investments in equipment, premises or training of personnel, such as for example the petrol storage tank in the case of petrol retailing or specific software to sell insurance policies in case of insurance agents;

— does not undertake responsibility towards third parties for damage caused by the product sold (product liability), unless, as agent, he is liable for fault in this respect;

— does not take responsibility for customers' non-performance of the contract, with the exception of the loss of the agent's commission, unless the agent is liable for fault (for example, by failing to comply with reasonable security or anti-theft measures or failing to comply with reasonable measures to report theft to the principal or police or to communicate to the principal all necessary information available to him on the customer's financial reliability).'

(4) The Underlying Philosophy of the BER and the Guidelines

9.187   The overall philosophy is expressed in point 6 of the Guidelines: 'For most vertical restraints, competition concerns can only arise if there is insufficient inter-brand competition, ie if there is some degree of market power at the level of the supplier or the buyer or at both levels. If there is insufficient inter-brand competition, the protection of inter- and intra-brand competition becomes important.' And in point 102: 'In the assessment of

---

[237]   Guidelines para 16 and Case T-325/01, see n 226 above.

individual cases, the Commission will adopt an economic approach in the application of Article 81 to vertical restraints. This will limit the scope of application of Article 81 to undertakings holding a certain degree of market power where inter-brand competition may be insufficient. In those cases, the protection of inter-brand and intra-brand competition is important to ensure efficiencies and benefits for consumers.'

It is recognised that vertical restraints are generally less harmful than horizontal restraints. **9.188** The main reason for treating a vertical restraint more leniently than a horizontal restraint lies in the fact that the latter may concern an agreement between competitors producing identical or substitutable goods or services. In such horizontal relationships the exercise of market power by one company (higher price of its product) may benefit its competitors. This may provide an incentive to competitors to induce each other to behave anti-competitively. Also efficiencies may be less obvious in the case of horizontal agreements where the combination of assets are not always complementary. In vertical relationships the product of the one is the input for the other. This means that the exercise of market power by either the upstream or downstream company would normally hurt the demand for the product of the other. The companies involved in the agreement therefore usually have an incentive to prevent the exercise of market power by the other.[238] This made it possible to apply a market share threshold of 30 per cent instead of the lower threshold of 20 per cent applied in other horizontal block exemption regulations.

The market share threshold is applied in a simplified way in the BER. While it could be **9.189** argued that the 30 per cent threshold should apply to both sellers and buyers, it was felt that having to define and calculate market shares for both sellers and buyers would make it more difficult for market players to determine whether they fall within the scope of application of the BER. This is why, as a general rule, it is the market share of the supplier that is used, for the purposes of the BER, as the proxy of market power. However this proxy is only measuring selling power and not buying power. The presence of strong buyers can generate some concerns, as it can cause a further reduction in intra-brand competition.[239] Therefore, where a vertical agreement contains restraints linked to buying power, namely exclusive supply obligations in favour of the buyer, the market share of the purchaser and not the seller is used as the proxy of market power. Both market shares are however relevant in the case of an individual analysis outside the BER.

In short, applicability of the block exemption depends either on the market share of the **9.190** supplier, and if so on the market where it sells the contract products, or on the market share of the buyer, and if so on the market where it purchases the contract products, but not on both. It is in general the market share of the supplier which determines the applicability of the block exemption. Only where the agreement contains an exclusive supply obligation, as defined in Article 1(c) of the BER, is it the buyer's market share which may not exceed the threshold of 30 per cent in order for the block exemption to apply. Of course the Commission recognises that from an economic point of view, a vertical agreement may have effects not only on the market between supplier and buyer but also on markets downstream of the buyer. The simplified approach of the Block Exemption Regulation, which

---

[238] Guidelines point 100.
[239] The negative effects of buying power are considered in paras 9.343–9.349 below.

only takes into account the market share of the supplier or the buyer (as the case may be)[240] on the market between these two parties, is justified by the fact that below the threshold of 30 per cent the effects on downstream markets will in general be limited. In addition, only having to consider the market between supplier and buyer makes the application of the Block Exemption Regulation easier and enhances the level of legal certainty.[241]

(5) The Scope of the BER and Guidelines

(a) *Definition of Vertical Agreements*

9.191 The BER applies to vertical agreements, that is 'agreements or concerted practices entered into between two or more undertakings each of which operates, for the purposes of the agreement, at a different level of the production or distribution chain, and relating to the conditions under which the parties may purchase, sell or resell certain goods or services' (Article 2(1) BER). This definition, as explained above, is derived from Council Regulation (EC) 1215/99.

9.192 This definition contains three main elements. First, it covers agreements between two or more undertakings. Secondly, each of these undertakings must operate, for the purposes of the agreement, at a different level of the production or distribution chain, for instance manufacturer-wholesaler-retailer. Thirdly, the agreement must be a purchase or distribution agreement, ie must relate to the conditions under which the parties to the agreement purchase, sell, or resell the products supplied by the supplier and/or sell the products into which the buyer has incorporated the products of the supplier. The last element implies that the BER applies to goods sold for renting to third parties but not to rent and lease agreements as such agreements do not involve a transfer of ownership.[242]

(b) *Vertical Agreements between Competitors*

9.193 Articles 2(2) to 2(5) directly or indirectly exclude certain vertical agreements from the application of the BER. Of major importance is Article 2(4), which excludes 'vertical agreements entered into between competing undertakings'. The definition of a vertical agreement as an agreement where the undertakings must operate, *for the purposes of the agreement*, at a different level of the production or distribution chain, includes in principle vertical agreements between competitors. However, for the reasons explained above on the difference between agreements between competitors and non-competitors, the Commission did not want to cover most vertical agreements between competitors. The first and most important competition concern that may arise with such agreements is possible collusive effects between the competitors. Only after these anti-competitive risks have been assessed under the rules for horizontal agreements (see Chapter 7), is there a need to assess the vertical aspects of these agreements under the Guidelines (point 26 Guidelines).

9.194 Article 1(a) of the Block Exemption Regulation defines competing undertakings as 'actual or potential suppliers in the same product market', irrespective of whether or not they are competitors on the same geographic market. The Guidelines (point 26) define a potential supplier

---

[240] The use and calculation of market shares for the purposes of the BER is explained in paras 9.266–9.279 below.
[241] Guidelines point 22.
[242] Guidelines point 25.

as 'an undertaking that does not actually produce a competing product but could and would be likely to do so in the absence of the agreement in response to a small and permanent increase in relative prices. This means that the undertaking would be able and likely to undertake the necessary additional investments and supply the market within 1 year. This assessment has to be based on realistic grounds; the mere theoretical possibility of entering a market is not sufficient.'

There are three exceptions to the general exclusion of vertical agreements between competi- **9.195**
tors, all relating to non-reciprocal agreements. 'Non-reciprocal agreements between competitors are covered by the Block Exemption Regulation where (1) the buyer has a turnover not exceeding EUR 100 million, or (2) the supplier is a manufacturer and distributor of goods, while the buyer is only a distributor and not also a manufacturer of competing goods, or (3) the supplier is a provider of services operating at several levels of trade, while the buyer does not provide competing services at the level of trade where it purchases the contract services.'[243] The second exception covers situations of dual distribution, where for instance a brewer which also operates a number of pubs also has supply agreements with independent competing pubs to sell its beer. On the other hand, an agreement between two brewers in which one of the two becomes the distributor of the other brewer's beer does not fall within the scope of the BER, unless the distributing brewer's total turnover does not exceed EUR100 million. The third exception covers similar situations of dual distribution, but in this case for services.

The Guidelines[244] indicate that a distributor who provides specifications to a manufacturer **9.196**
to produce particular goods under the distributor's brand name is not to be considered a manufacturer of such own-brand goods. A supply agreement between a manufacturer and a distributor in such a situation therefore does fall within the scope of the BER.

(c) Vertical Agreements Concluded by Associations of Retailers

An association of competing undertakings is based on horizontal agreements between **9.197**
competitors, for instance the agreement to set up the association. These agreements and also the decisions of the association, such as a decision to require the members to purchase all their requirements from the association, have to be assessed under the rules for horizontal agreements (see Chapter 7). Only after this assessment has led to the conclusion that cooperation between these undertakings in the area of purchasing or selling is acceptable, will they need to be assessed under the vertical rules.

As a general rule, the BER does not cover vertical agreements concluded by an association. **9.198**
However, there is an exception:[245]

> Vertical agreements entered into between an association and its members, or between an association and its suppliers, are covered by the Block Exemption Regulation only if all the members are retailers of goods (not services) and if each individual member of the association has a turnover not exceeding EUR 50 million. Retailers are distributors reselling goods to final consumers . . .[246]

---

[243] Guidelines point 27.
[244] Guidelines point 27.
[245] BER Art 2(2).
[246] Guidelines point 28.

9.199 In addition the Guidelines make it clear that if only a limited number of the members of the association have a turnover not significantly exceeding the EUR50 million threshold, this will normally not change the assessment under Article 81.[247]

(d) Vertical Agreements Containing IPR Provisions

9.200 Article 2(3) of the BER sets out to what extent vertical agreements, that do not only concern the purchase, sale, or resale of goods or services but that also involve the assignment or licensing of IPRs (intellectual property rights), are covered by the BER. The BER 'applies to vertical agreements containing IPR provisions when five conditions are fulfilled:

— The IPR provisions must be part of a vertical agreement, ie an agreement with conditions under which the parties may purchase, sell or resell certain goods or services;
— The IPRs must be assigned to, or for use by, the buyer;
— The IPR provisions must not constitute the primary object of the agreement;
— The IPR provisions must be directly related to the use, sale or resale of goods or services by the buyer or his customers . . .;
— The IPR provisions, in relation to the contract goods or services, must not contain restrictions of competition having the same object or effect as vertical restraints which are not exempted under the Block Exemption Regulation.'[248]

9.201 These conditions ensure that the BER applies to vertical agreements where the use, sale, or resale of goods or services can be performed more effectively because IPRs are assigned to or transferred for use by the buyer. In other words, restrictions concerning the assignment or use of IPRs can be covered when the main object or centre of gravity of the agreement is the purchase or distribution of goods or services.[249] This means that pure licensing agreements or more general agreements where the emphasis lies on the transfer of technology are not covered by the BER (see Chapter 10 for the assessment of technology transfer agreements). Also subcontracting involving the transfer of know-how to a subcontractor does not fall within the scope of application of the BER, as the IPR is transferred to the supplier instead of the buyer of the products. Subcontracting is still assessed under the Notice on subcontracting.[250] However, vertical agreements under which the buyer provides only specifications to the supplier which describe the goods or services to be supplied are covered by the BER. The last condition in the previous paragraph signifies in particular that the IPR provisions should not have the same object or effect as any of the hardcore restrictions listed in Article 4 of the BER or any of the restrictions excluded from the coverage of the BER by Article 5 (see below).

9.202 Points 39–41 of the Guidelines state that obligations not to infringe copyrights that go together with the sale of products are, to the extent that they fall at all within Article 81(1), covered by the BER. This essentially covers two types of situations. The first type is the sale of goods covered by copyright, such as books and software, where the copyright holder usually obliges the reseller and/or the final user not to infringe the copyright. This may take the form of so-called 'shrink wrap' licences, where the end user is deemed to accept the conditions

---

[247] Guidelines point 28.
[248] Guidelines point 30.
[249] Guidelines point 31.
[250] OJ C1, 3.1.1979, p 2.

included in the package of the hard copy by opening it. The second type concerns the sale of hardware that incorporates copyright protected software and where the right holder wants to prevent the buyer of the hardware from infringing its copyright, for instance by preventing the buyer from making copies.

The Guidelines also make it clear that the Commission intended to cover most non-industrial **9.203** franchising agreements by the BER. Franchise agreements are mentioned as the most obvious example where know-how is communicated to the buyer for marketing purposes and where the licence of a trademark or sign helps the distribution of goods or the provision of services. In addition to the licensing of IPR, the Guidelines also mention that 'the franchisor usually provides the franchisee during the life of the agreement with commercial or technical assistance, such as procurement services, training, advice on real estate, financial planning etc'.[251]

To fall within the scope of the BER it is of course a condition that the IPR provisions do not **9.204** constitute the primary object of the agreement. This may easily be fulfilled where the franchisor is also the producer of the products distributed through the franchise system. Where such is not the case because the agreement only or mainly concerns the licensing of IPRs, the Guidelines state that 'such an agreement is not covered by the Block Exemption Regulation, but it will be treated in a way similar to those franchise agreements which are covered by the Block Exemption Regulation'.[252]

(e) The Interface between the BER and other Block Exemption Regulations

Article 2(5) states that the BER does 'not apply to vertical agreements the subject matter of **9.205** which falls within the scope of any other block exemption regulation'. This means for instance that the BER does not apply to vertical agreements that concern a transfer of technology and that are covered by Commission Regulation (EC) 772/2004[253] or car distribution agreements covered by Commission Regulation (EC) 1400/2002.[254]

(6) Hardcore Restrictions under Article 4 BER

A central feature of the BER is its so-called blacklist approach: restrictions that are not **9.206** explicitly excluded are covered by the block exemption. This contrasts with the previous block exemption regulations which also contained a white list, specifying the restrictions that could or even should have been included in a distribution agreement to be block exempted. The blacklist approach creates more contractual freedom for the parties to design a vertical agreement to their commercial needs. Below the market share threshold the parties only need to take account of what is excluded from coverage, the hardcore restrictions listed in Article 4, and the excluded restrictions in Article 5.

Of these two articles Article 4 is clearly the more important. It contains restrictions which **9.207** the Commission normally considers to be severely anti-competitive. These restrictions of competition by object have such a high potential for negative effects on competition that it is not considered necessary for the purposes of applying Article 81(1) to demonstrate any

---

[251] Guidelines para 42.
[252] Guidelines para 43.
[253] OJ L123, 27.04.2004, p 11.
[254] OJ L203, 01.08.2002, p 30.

actual or likely effects on the market. Moreover, the conditions of Article 81(3) are considered unlikely to be fulfilled in the case of hardcore restrictions. When a vertical agreement contains such a restriction, it follows from Article 4 of the BER that the agreement as a whole falls outside the scope of the block exemption. For the purposes of coverage by the BER, hardcore restrictions cannot be severed from the rest of the agreement.[255] In the context of an individual assessment the Commission considers that hardcore restrictions will only in exceptional circumstances fulfil the four conditions of Article 81(3).[256]

9.208 The hardcore list applies only to vertical agreements concerning trade within the Community. Insofar as vertical agreements concern exports outside the Community or imports/re-imports from outside the Community, an effects-based approach is normally applied.[257]

9.209 The text of Article 4 reads as follows:

> The exemption provided for in Article 2 shall not apply to vertical agreements which, directly or indirectly, in isolation or in combination with other factors under the control of the parties, have as their object:
>
> (a) the restriction of the buyer's ability to determine its sale price, without prejudice to the possibility of the supplier's imposing a maximum sale price or recommending a sale price, provided that they do not amount to a fixed or minimum sale price as a result of pressure from, or incentives offered by, any of the parties;
>
> (b) the restriction of the territory into which, or of the customers to whom, the buyer may sell the contract goods or services, except:
>
> — the restriction of active sales into the exclusive territory or to an exclusive customer group reserved to the supplier or allocated by the supplier to another buyer, where such a restriction does not limit sales by the customers of the buyer,
>
> — the restriction of sales to end users by a buyer operating at the wholesale level of trade,
>
> — the restriction of sales to unauthorised distributors by the members of a selective distribution system, and
>
> — the restriction of the buyer's ability to sell components, supplied for the purposes of incorporation, to customers who would use them to manufacture the same type of goods as those produced by the supplier;
>
> (c) the restriction of active or passive sales to end users by members of a selective distribution system operating at the retail level of trade, without prejudice to the possibility of prohibiting a member of the system from operating out of an unauthorised place of establishment;
>
> (d) the restriction of cross-supplies between distributors within a selective distribution system, including between distributors operating at different levels of trade;
>
> (e) the restriction agreed between a supplier of components and a buyer who incorporates those components, which limits the supplier to selling the components as spare parts to end-users or to repairers or other service providers not entrusted by the buyer with the repair or servicing of its goods.

(a) Vertical Price Fixing under Article 4(a) BER

9.210 The hardcore restriction set out in Article 4(a) concerns vertical price fixing, that is agreements having as their direct or indirect object the establishment of a fixed or minimum sale

---

[255] The rule of nonseverability is described in paras 66 and 67 of the Guidelines. It means that it is not possible to separate a hardcore provision from the rest of the agreement, so that what is left is covered by the BER. The presence of a hardcore provision results in the loss of the benefit of the BER for the entire agreement.

[256] Guidelines point 46.

[257] See the judgment in *Javico v Yves Saint Laurent* referred to in para 9.45.

or resale price to be observed by the buyer. The exception is the imposition of a maximum (re)sale price or recommended (re)sale price. Such a maximum or recommended price is not a hardcore restriction, provided that it does not amount to a fixed or minimum (re)sale price as a result of pressure from, or incentives offered by, any of the parties. In the case of contractual provisions that directly establish the fixed or minimum (re)sale price, the restriction is clear cut. However, vertical price fixing can also be achieved through indirect means. The Guidelines provide a non-exhaustive list of examples such as fixing the distribution margin, fixing the maximum level of discount the distributor can grant from a prescribed price level, making the grant of rebates or reimbursement of promotional costs by the supplier subject to the observance of a given price level, linking the prescribed resale price to the resale prices of competitors, threats and delay or suspension of deliveries or contract terminations in relation to observance of a given price level.[258]

The Guidelines recognise that price fixing can be made more effective when combined **9.211** with measures to identify price-cutting distributors, such as the implementation of a price monitoring system or the obligation on retailers to report other members of the distribution network who deviate from the standard price level. Similarly, price fixing can be made more effective when combined with measures which reduce the buyer's incentive to lower the resale price, such as the supplier printing a recommended resale price on the product or the supplier obliging the buyer to apply a most-favoured-customer clause. While, in isolation, these supportive measures are normally not sufficient to establish price fixing, the Commission appears to regard them in a critical manner as it states that they 'can be used to make maximum or recommended prices work as resale price maintenance'.[259] Therefore, great care should be taken and legal advice sought when seeking to monitor or limit the pricing behaviour of buyers.

In the case of an agency agreement it is normally the principal who establishes the sales price **9.212** as the agent does not become the owner of the goods. The Guidelines advise that the agent be left free to lower the effective price paid by the customer by sharing his commission with the buyer, without reducing the income for the principal.[260] The Guidelines point out that were the agency agreement to fall within the scope of Article 81(1) (see paras 9.168–9.186 above) an obligation preventing or restricting the agent from sharing his commission, fixed or variable, with the customer would be a hardcore restriction under Article 4(a).

(b) Territorial and Customer Sales Restrictions under Article 4(b) BER

The hardcore restriction set out in Article 4(b) concerns agreements that have as their direct **9.213** or indirect object the restriction of sales by the buyer where those restrictions relate to the territory into which or the customers to whom the buyer may sell the contract goods or services. This hardcore restriction relates to market partitioning by territory or by customer. Here too the Guidelines give examples of direct obligations, such as the obligation not to sell to certain customers or to customers in certain territories or the obligation to refer orders from these customers to other distributors, and examples of indirect measures aimed

---

[258] Guidelines point 47.
[259] Guidelines point 47.
[260] Guidelines point 48.

at inducing the distributor not to sell to such customers, such as refusal or reduction of bonuses or discounts or profit pass-over obligations.[261]

9.214 Paragraph 49 of the Guidelines makes specific reference to after-sales guarantees. It describes as an indirect measure which may fall under the hardcore provision in Article 4(b) the situation where the supplier does not provide a Community-wide guarantee service. A Community-wide guarantee service is described as requiring all distributors to provide the guarantee service, even in relation to products sold into their territory by other distributors. Distributors are entitled to be reimbursed for this service by the supplier.

9.215 However, a prohibition imposed on all distributors to sell to certain end users is not classified as a hardcore restriction if there is an objective justification related to the product, such as a general ban on selling dangerous substances to certain customers for reasons of safety or health. It implies also that the supplier himself does not sell to these customers. Nor are obligations on the reseller relating to the display of the supplier's brand name classified as hardcore.[262]

9.216 The fact that only restrictions of the buyer's sales are declared hardcore implies that all sales restrictions on the supplier are block exempted, except for what is said on this below in the context of aftermarkets and Article 4(e). This means that in general the buyer can be protected against active and passive sales from the supplier. In this way the BER recognises that without protection from active and passive sales from his supplier a distributor may not be willing to invest (sufficiently) to distribute the products optimally. It also recognises that the main competition concern is market partitioning between parties operating at the same level of the production or distribution chain.

9.217 In addition to this implied limitation to the hardcore restriction in Article 4(b), there are also four explicit exceptions provided in the indents. The first indent allows a supplier to restrict active sales by his direct buyers into a territory or to a customer group which the supplier has allocated exclusively to another buyer or which he has reserved to itself. The BER thereby recognises the rationale for allocating exclusive territories or customer groups and the need to protect an exclusive distributor against, for instance, free riding by other distributors on its promotional investments. This protection of exclusively allocated territories or customer groups must, however, permit passive sales by the (other) buyers to such territories or customer groups.

9.218 The Guidelines explain that a 'territory or customer group is exclusively allocated when the supplier agrees to sell his product only to one distributor for distribution in a particular territory or to a particular customer group and the exclusive distributor is protected against active selling into his territory or to his customer group by the supplier and all the other buyers of the supplier inside the Community'.[263] This means that if the supplier wants to limit active

---

[261] The Guidelines were adopted before the *Adalat* judgment (see paras 9.30–9.32 above) and also mention reduction of supplied volumes or limitation of supplied volumes to the demand within the allocated territory or customer group as an indirect means to obtain a hardcore restriction. The Court has made it clear in *Adalat* that such a measure on its own however is not sufficient to establish the existence of an agreement and it is thus necessary to first establish the existence of an agreement on other grounds before such a restriction can be assessed under Art 81.

[262] Guidelines point 49.

[263] Guidelines point 50.

sales by the other distributors into a particular distributor's exclusive territory or customer group, the supplier himself should also be restricted from selling actively into that territory or customer group. If the supplier nonetheless wants to continue selling actively to a certain group of customers inside the distributor's exclusive territory, this can be arranged under the block exemption by carving out that particular group of customers from the territory and, for instance, reserving it exclusively to the supplier. More generally, the BER covers the combination of an exclusive territory and an exclusive customer group, for instance when an exclusive distributor is appointed for a particular customer group in a certain territory or for a particular territory except for a certain customer group inside that territory. Neither the BER nor the Guidelines specify how an exclusive territory or customer group must be defined and it can thus be concluded that this is left to the discretion of the parties. A territory can for instance be defined as a particular street or a customer group as a specific list of customers. The way in which such a territory or customer group is defined is not relevant for coverage by the block exemption, but may be of relevance outside the block exemption in case of individual assessment of the agreement, as it may influence the likelihood of possible negative effects and efficiencies.

Under the exception of the first indent the supplier can also reserve a territory or customer group exclusively for itself by disallowing all its direct buyers to sell actively into that territory or to that customer group. This allows the supplier to protect its own sales or to reserve the territory or customer group for future exploitation by itself or another distributor. **9.219**

The second indent of Article 4(b) brings under the block exemption the obligation imposed on a buyer who acts as a wholesaler not to sell to end users and thus to limit its sales activities to the wholesale level. In this case both active and passive sales restrictions are block exempted. **9.220**

The third indent of Article 4(b) block exempts the restriction of sales to unauthorised distributors by the members of a selective distribution system. Here too both active and passive sales restrictions are covered and this brings selective distribution systems under the block exemption. As defined in Article 1(c) a selective distribution system is a distribution system where the supplier undertakes to sell the contract goods or services, either directly or indirectly, only to distributors selected on the basis of specified criteria and where these distributors undertake not to sell such goods or services to unauthorised distributors. **9.221**

The fourth indent of Article 4(b) brings under the block exemption agreements that restrict a buyer of components supplied for incorporation from reselling them to competitors of the supplier. The term 'component' includes any intermediate goods and the term 'incorporation' refers to the use of any input to produce goods. This should allow a supplier with spare capacity which it does not need for its own internal needs, to produce for certain buyers, without the risk that this extra output is sold by its buyers directly to its competitors downstream. Both active and passive sales restrictions are block exempted in this case. **9.222**

(c) Internet Sales and Selling by Catalogue—Territorial and Customer Sales Restrictions under Article 4

The Guidelines clarify how to apply the distinction of active and passive sales to sales and promotion over the internet. The Guidelines state that every distributor must be free to use the Internet to advertise or to sell products. A restriction on the use of the Internet by **9.223** distributors could only be compatible with the Block Exemption Regulation to the extent that promotion on the Internet or sales over the Internet would lead to active selling into other distributors' exclusive territories or customer groups. In general, the use of the Internet is not considered a form of active sales into such territories or customer groups, since it is a reasonable way to reach every customer. The fact that it may have effects outside one's own territory or customer group results from the technology, ie the easy access from everywhere. If a customer visits the web site of a distributor and contacts the distributor and if such contact leads to a sale, including delivery, then that is considered passive selling.[264] In other words having access to the internet is seen as having a telephone, it extends the potential reach of a distributor, but having a telephone or having an internet address or web site is not a form of active selling.

9.224   In line with this general reasoning a number of more detailed questions can be answered. For instance, it is made clear that the language used on the web site or in the communication has no bearing on the assessment as passive sales.[265] This can be compared to having a telephone and helping customers in several languages, which is also not considered a form of active selling. Similarly, it can be expected that general domain name endings such as '.com' or '.int' do not imply active selling into other territories. It becomes different if the web site is specifically targeted at customers primarily inside the territory or customer group exclusively allocated to another distributor, for instance with the use of banners or links in pages of providers specifically available to these exclusively allocated customers or with the use of a domain name ending specific to that exclusive territory. Also the use of meta-tags, the hidden codes that help search engines to find a web site and which one could compare to entries in a telephone directory, can be specific, for instance by their language, to another distributor's exclusive territory and be a form of active selling. The most clear-cut form of active selling is of course the sending of unsolicited e-mails to individual customers or specific customer groups. The Guidelines make it clear that the same considerations apply to selling by catalogue.

9.225   The Guidelines make it clear that the hardcore restrictions do not prevent the supplier from requiring quality standards for the use of the web site to resell its goods, just as the supplier may require quality standards for a shop or for advertising and promotion in general. The latter may be relevant in particular for selective distribution. However, an outright ban on internet or catalogue selling is only possible if there is an objective justification, which normally cannot be based on considerations of image or presentation of the products involved but which may be based on reasons of safety or health. In any case, the supplier cannot reserve to itself sales and/or advertising over the internet. The requirements that the supplier can impose on or agree with the distributor on the latter's use of and promotion on the internet are not circumscribed in the Guidelines and can for instance relate to the presentation of the products, the general appearance of the web site, more technical features such as the stability of the web site or average response time in case of questions, the use of hyperlinks to other web sites including web sites of the supplier or other distributors inside the

---

[264] Guidelines point 51.
[265] ibid.

distribution system, the web site domain name and the ownership of this domain name. The parties should only be careful not to use these requirements directly or indirectly to agree a hardcore restriction such as the restriction of passive sales by the distributor. For instance, the requirement to have a hyperlink on the distributor's web site to the web sites of the supplier or other distributors inside the distribution system should not be used as a tool to (automatically) reroute customers to these other web sites. Similarly, requirements agreed for internet sales or promotion should not be more onerous or burdensome than the (equivalent) requirements agreed for sales in the brick and mortar shop or other forms of advertising and thereby prejudice internet sales and promotion. Lastly, while the use of a location clause, which limits the distributor to perform its distribution function from a particular location, cannot be used to limit the distributor's use of the internet, it can be used effectively to limit selling by catalogue. If a distributor is required to operate from particular premises, this may effectively limit the size of its storage and distribution activities, including selling by catalogue.

(d) Selective Distribution Systems—Territorial and Customer Sales Restrictions under Article 4

9.226 As explained above, the third indent of Article 4(b) block exempts the restriction of sales to unauthorised distributors by the members of a selective distribution system. As can be deduced from the definition of a selective distribution system in Article 1(c), the restriction not to sell to unauthorised distributors is the essential element for a distribution system to be called a selective distribution system.

9.227 The hardcore restrictions in Article 4(c) and 4(d) relate to active and passive sales by the authorised members of a selective distribution system. In order to be block exempted Article 4(c) requires that the members of a selective distribution network operating at the retail level are not restricted in their active or passive sales to end users, whether professional end users or final consumers. The words 'operating at the retail level' indicate that, in accordance with Article 4(b) second indent, a wholesale member of the system can be restricted in its sales to end users. The only limit that can be imposed on the authorised retailer in this respect is a location clause, ie the obligation to run its business from particular premises and not to open a new outlet in a different location. If the dealer's outlet is mobile ('shop on wheels'), an area may be defined outside which the mobile outlet cannot be operated.[266]

9.228 The hardcore restriction set out in Article 4(d) concerns the restriction of cross-supplies between the authorised distributors. A selective distribution agreement may not restrict the active or passive selling of the contract products between the selected distributors. Selected distributors must remain free to purchase the contract products from other appointed distributors within the network, operating either at the same or at a different level of trade. This implies that selective distribution cannot be combined with, for instance, exclusive purchasing which forces distributors to purchase the contract products directly from the supplier or a specified wholesaler. The authorised retailers and wholesalers within the selective distribution system must remain free to sell to and purchase from each other. In practice the Commission is unlikely to take action against an obligation on the retailer to purchase

---

[266] Guidelines points 53–4.

a certain amount directly from the supplier or a specified wholesaler as long as this amount does not exceed 40 per cent of the requirements of the average authorised retailer.[267]

(e) The Combination of Exclusive and Selective Distribution

9.229 From the description and analysis above of Article 4(b) and 4(c) it is clear that the combination of exclusive and selective distribution, if applied by the same supplier for the same contract products and within the same territory, is only block exempted as long as the exclusive distribution is limited to what is sometimes also called 'sole distribution'. The supplier can agree with the distributor only to supply this particular authorised distributor in a specific area inside the wider territory and thereby provide a certain territorial exclusivity, but the appointed distributors must remain free to sell actively and passively to all end users where the selective distribution system is applied.

9.230 The supplier may also wish to combine exclusive and selective distribution for the same contract products but apply them within different territories, for instance operating selective distribution in one Member State and exclusive distribution in another Member State. This raises a number of issues, in particular in relation to the selective distribution system. The third indent of Article 4(b) block exempts the restriction of sales to unauthorised distributors by the members of a selective distribution system. The Guidelines add that such a restriction can be applied only in the market(s) where the selective distribution is operated, thus making it clear that selective distribution can be operated in for instance one Member State while other distribution forms are applied elsewhere in the EU.[268] The authorised dealers in the Member State with a selective distribution system can be obliged not to sell actively to buyers in the exclusive territories of distributors in the Member State where exclusive distribution is operated, but must be free to sell passively to any buyers in the latter Member State. The exclusive distributors in this Member State can be obliged not to sell actively into each others' exclusive territories. But they must remain free to sell actively and passively to any buyer, including unauthorised distributors, in the Member State where selective distribution is applied, because that Member State is not, and according to Article 4(c), cannot be exclusively allocated. This means that if the products are sold at an appreciably higher price in the Member State with selective distribution, such a combination of systems will make it difficult to apply a selective distribution system that is 'watertight', as an important grey market may develop from sales from the other Member State. If the higher price is found in the Member State with exclusive distribution, this may provoke passive sales and parallel trade from the Member State where selective distribution is applied.

(f) Aftermarkets

9.231 The last hardcore restriction, set out in Article 4(e), concerns agreements that restrict end users, independent repairers, and independent service providers from obtaining spare parts

---

[267] Guidelines point 55. As to the 40%, see Case IV/33.242 *Yves Saint Laurent Parfums*, OJ L12, 18.01.1992, p 24 and Case IV/33.542 *Parfums Givenchy* system of selective distribution, OJ L236, 19.08.1992, p 11. Also in a number of cases exclusive purchasing obligations in selective distribution agreements were assessed as a hardcore restriction and prohibited; see Case COMP.F.1/35.918 *JCB*, OJ L69, 12.03.2002, p 1, and the judgment of the CFI in this case upholding this finding (Case T-67/01 of 13.01.2004), and Case COMP/37.975 *PO/Yamaha* http://europa.eu.int/comm/competition/antitrust/cases/decisions/37975/en.pdf.

[268] Guidelines point 52.

directly from the manufacturer of those spare parts. An agreement between a manufacturer of spare parts and an original equipment manufacturer may not, either directly or indirectly, restrict sales by the manufacturer of these spare parts to end users, independent repairers, or independent service providers. It would, for instance, be an indirect restriction if the supplier of the spare parts was restricted from supplying technical information or special equipment to the users, independent repairers, or independent service providers which they need in order to make use of the spare parts. However, the agreement may place restrictions on the supply of the spare parts to the repairers or service providers entrusted by the original equipment manufacturer with the repair or servicing of its own goods. In other words, the original equipment manufacturer may control sales of the spare parts to its own repair and service network and require its own repair and service network to buy the spare parts from it.[269]

(7) Excluded Restrictions

As stated above, a central feature of the BER is its so-called blacklist approach which means **9.232** that below the market share threshold the parties only need to take account of what is excluded from coverage: namely the hardcore restrictions listed in Article 4 and the excluded restrictions in Article 5. Article 5 lists three obligations that are not block exempted. However, unlike hardcore restrictions, the inclusion in an agreement of any of these obligations does not prevent the application of the block exemption to the rest of the agreement. It is only the individual restriction that is not block exempted and which requires individual assessment.[270] Unlike hardcore restrictions, there is also no presumption of illegality for these restrictions when individually assessed. The principle is one of neutrality, ie there is neither a negative nor a positive presumption.

Article 5 contains the following three excluded restrictions: **9.233**

(a) any direct or indirect non-compete obligation, the duration of which is indefinite or exceeds 5 years. A non-compete obligation which is tacitly renewable beyond a period of 5 years is to be deemed to have been concluded for an indefinite duration. However, the time limitation of 5 years shall not apply where the contract goods or services are sold by the buyer from premises and land owned by the supplier or leased by the supplier from third parties not connected with the buyer, provided that the duration of the non-compete obligation does not exceed the period of occupancy of the premises and land by the buyer;

(b) any direct or indirect obligation causing the buyer, after termination of the agreement, not to manufacture, purchase, sell or resell goods or services, unless such obligation

— relates to goods or services which compete with the contract goods or services, and
— is limited to the premises and land from which the buyer has operated during the contract period, and
— is indispensable to protect know-how transferred by the supplier to the buyer, and provided that the duration of such non-compete obligation is limited to a period of one year after termination of the agreement; this obligation is without prejudice to the possibility of imposing a restriction which is unlimited in time on the use and disclosure of know-how which has not entered the public domain;

(c) any direct or indirect obligation causing the members of a selective distribution system not to sell the brands of particular competing suppliers.

---

[269] Guidelines point 56.
[270] Guidelines points 57 and 67.

(a) Non-compete Obligations Exceeding Five Years

9.234 The first excluded restriction in Article 5(a) concerns non-compete obligations. Non-compete obligations are defined in Article 1(b) of the BER as obligations that require the buyer to purchase from the supplier or from another undertaking designated by the supplier more than 80 per cent of the buyer's total purchases during the previous year of the contract goods and services and their substitutes.[271] Such an obligation prevents the buyer from purchasing competing goods or services or limits such purchases to less than 20 per cent of total purchases and may thus have the effect of foreclosing competitors of the supplier from the market. Because of its potential to foreclose, also in situations of cumulative use by several suppliers each having a market share below 30 per cent, and because it was considered that efficiency arguments do usually justify these obligations only for a limited period, such non-compete obligations are not covered by the BER when their duration is indefinite or exceeds five years.

9.235 This five-year duration limit does not apply when the products are resold by the buyer 'from premises and land owned by the supplier or leased by the supplier from third parties not connected with the buyer'. In such cases the non-compete obligation may be of the same duration as the period of occupancy of the point of sale by the buyer. The Guidelines explain that the reason for this exception is that it is normally unreasonable to expect a supplier to allow competing products to be sold from premises and land owned by the supplier without his permission. But it also gives the warning that artificial ownership constructions intended to avoid the five-year limit cannot benefit from this exception.[272]

9.236 The Guidelines are quite detailed on this excluded restriction, probably because of the Commission's experience under the previous block exemption regulations with long-term non-compete obligations in particular sectors such as for beer and petrol distribution. For instance, it is explained that non-compete obligations that are tacitly renewable beyond a period of five years are not covered by the BER but they are covered when renewal beyond five years requires explicit consent of both parties and no obstacles exist that hinder the buyer from effectively terminating the non-compete obligation at the end of the five-year period. The Guidelines explain that the structure of repayment of a loan, provided by the supplier to the buyer, could form such an obstacle and that the repayment of such a loan should not hinder the buyer from effectively terminating the non-compete obligation at the end of the five-year period. For this purpose it is stated that the repayment needs to be structured in equal or decreasing instalments and that the buyer must have the option to repay the remaining debt where there is still an outstanding debt at the end of the non-compete obligation. At the same time the Guidelines acknowledge that in the case of a new distribution outlet, it may be necessary to delay repayment for the first one or two years until sales have reached a certain level. In a similar vein it is explained that in order to be covered by the BER, where the supplier provides the buyer with equipment, the buyer should have the

---

[271] The Guidelines, point 58, explain that where for the year preceding the conclusion of the contract no relevant purchasing data for the buyer are available, the buyer's best estimate of his annual total requirements may be used.

[272] Guidelines point 59.

opportunity to take over the equipment at its market asset value at the end of the non-compete obligation.[273]

While these explanations go into quite some detail, it should not be forgotten that they are **9.237** provided in the Guidelines with the aim of clarifying what is covered by the BER and what is not. As stated earlier, for these excluded restrictions there is no negative presumption. These clarifications, and coverage by the BER, generally are only important in cases where an appreciable foreclosure effect can be established. If the agreements of a supplier do not have such a foreclosing effect and do not contribute significantly to a cumulative foreclosure effect, the duration and other aspects of the non-compete obligations are irrelevant under Article 81.

(b) Post-term Non-compete Obligations

The second excluded restriction in Article 5(b) concerns post-term non-compete obliga- **9.238** tions. Such obligations are only covered by the BER if the obligation is indispensable to the protection of know-how transferred by the supplier to the buyer, is limited to the point of sale from which the buyer has operated during the contract period, is limited to products which compete with the contract products, and is limited to a maximum period of one year. According to the definition in Article 1(f) of the Block Exemption Regulation the know-how must be 'substantial', meaning 'that the know-how includes information which is indispensable to the buyer for the use, sale or resale of the contract goods or services'.

These conditions for coverage are very strict. For instance, if a retailer has resold the contract **9.239** products from a certain shop, the post-term non-compete obligation can only prohibit sales by the same retailer from that particular shop and not from any other shop in the same street. These conditions are so strict because of the serious potential negative effects of post-term non-compete obligations in general. These obligations can effectively eliminate distributors from the market after the agreement has ended, with possible serious foreclosure effects for competing suppliers. However, as stated above, for these excluded restrictions there is no negative presumption. The limitations are only important in cases where an appreciable foreclosure effect can be established. If the agreements of a supplier do not have such a foreclosure effect and do not contribute significantly to a cumulative foreclosure effect, the duration and other aspects of the post-term non-compete obligations are irrelevant under Article 81, as the aim is not to protect individual distributors but to protect competition.

(c) Boycott under Selective Distribution

The third excluded restriction in Article 5(c) concerns the sale of competing goods in a **9.240** selective distribution system. The BER covers the combination of selective distribution with a non-compete obligation, obliging the dealers not to resell competing brands in general. However, if the supplier prevents his appointed dealers, either directly or indirectly, from buying products for resale from specific competing suppliers, such an obligation is not covered. The objective of this exclusion is to avoid a situation whereby a number of suppliers possibly using the same selective distribution outlets, prevent one specific competitor

---

[273] Guidelines point 58.

or certain specific competitors from using these outlets to distribute their products which would effectively lead to a form of collective boycott.[274]

(d) Recent Commission Decisions on the Hardcore Provisions under Article 4 BER

9.241 (i) *Yamaha* (**Article 4(a) and (b)**) In July 2003 the Commission adopted a decision concluding that Yamaha violated EU competition rules by entering into agreements or concerted practices aimed at partitioning the market and fixing resale prices in the markets for the provision of traditional and electronic musical instruments and equipment in Europe.[275] Such practices had the object of restricting competition, within the meaning of Article 81(1) of the EU treaty, in Germany, Italy, France, Austria, Belgium, the Netherlands, Denmark, and Iceland.

9.242 The restrictions implemented by Yamaha were aimed at preventing parallel imports and to insulate national markets. In order to achieve these objectives, Yamaha used the following restrictions:

- Obligations on official dealers to sell only to final customers;
- Obligations on official dealers to purchase exclusively from the Yamaha subsidiaries;
- Obligations on official dealers to contact Yamaha before exporting via the Internet.

9.243 Furthermore, in certain Member States, Yamaha also engaged in minimum resale price maintenance. Although the infringement was qualified as serious, some of the contractual provisions were applied to only a limited number of dealers and products were not systematically included in all Yamaha agreements throughout the EEA and were not simultaneously implemented.

9.244 The fact that Yamaha terminated a majority of the restrictions as soon as the Commission intervened was also considered a mitigating circumstance. The Commission imposed a EUR2.56 million fine on Yamaha.

9.245 (ii) *JCB* (**Article 4(b)**) On 21 December 2000, the Commission adopted a decision finding that the company JCB Service, the parent company of the UK-based JC Bamford Group, had infringed Article 81 of the EC Treaty.[276] The distribution agreements for construction and earth-moving equipment concluded between the JCB Group and its network of exclusive distributors were aimed at walling off the French, UK, Irish, and Italian markets within the Community.

9.246 The restrictive agreements or practices between JCB and its distributors consisted of:

- Restrictions on sales outside allotted territories;
- Restrictions on purchases of machines between authorised distributors in different EU states;
- Bonuses and fees systems which disadvantaged out of territory sales.

9.247 The Commission concentrated its analysis on the latter point and, in particular, on the discount scheme and the so-called 'service fee'. Under the discount scheme, JBC had the right

---

[274] An example of indirect measures having such exclusionary effects can be found in Commission Decision 92/428/EEC in Case No. IV/33.542 *Parfum Givenchy* (OJ L236, 19.8.1992, p 11).

[275] Not yet published in OJ, a non-confidential version of the decision may be found on the Commission's web site at http://ec.europa.eu/comm/competition/antitrust/cases/decisions/37975/en.pdf.

[276] Case COMP.F.1/35.918 *JCB*, OJ L069,12/03/2002 pp 1–49.

to withdraw discounts granted to its dealers in case of sales to customers based outside the dealer's Member State. Under the 'service fee' provision, distributors selling outside their Member State were obliged to pay back a set percentage of the retail price in order to compensate the cost incurred in servicing the product by distributors located in other Member States. The Commission found that both provisions had the effect of preventing distributors from selling outside their Member State.

The Commission found that each of these measures and, a fortiori, their combination, ran **9.248** contrary to the ban on restrictive agreements in Article 81(1) of the EC Treaty. The Commission came to the conclusion that the BER did not apply because JCB's market share was well in excess of 30 per cent. The text of the decision points out, though, that even if JCB's market share had been below 30 per cent, the block exemption would still not have applied because the above described restrictions amounted to hardcore restraints within the meaning of Article 4(b) of the BER.

The Commission ordered JCB to lift the measures and to bring its agreements and practices **9.249** in line with EC competition rules applicable to distribution. Given the seriousness of the infringement and their long duration the Commission also imposed a EUR39.6 million fine.

JCB appealed the Commission decision before the Court of First Instance.[277] In its ruling **9.250** dated 13 January 2004 the CFI upheld the Commission decision but found that the mere imposition of a 'service fee' for out of territory sales did not amount, in itself, to a ban on cross-border trading. The Court argued that before reaching such a conclusion, the Commission should have proved that the 'service fee' imposed by JCB was disproportionate and did not actually reflect the cost incurred by the 'receiving distributor' to service the imported product. As a consequence, the CFI reduced the fine imposed by the Commission to EUR30 million. JCB has lodged an appeal against the judgment of the CFI.[278]

(iii) *Nintendo* (**Article 4(b)**)   In October 2002 the Commission adopted a decision against **9.251** Nintendo and seven distributors of Nintendo products.[279] During the investigation, the Commission collected evidence showing that Nintendo and its distributors colluded to maintain artificially high price differences in the EU between January 1991 and 1998.

The investigation showed that during the seven-year period price differences in the **9.252** European Economic Area (EEA) were frequent and significant. The UK usually had the lowest prices by far, which understandably tempted traders into re-exporting cheap goods to high-price countries.

According to the arrangements, each distributor was under the obligation to prevent par- **9.253** allel trade from its territory. Under the leadership of Nintendo, the companies intensively collaborated to find the source of any parallel trade. Traders that allowed parallel exports to occur were punished by being given smaller shipments or by being boycotted altogether.

---

[277] Case T-67/01, *JCB v Commission* [2004] ECR II-00049.

[278] Pending before the Court of Justice. Case C-167/04 P OJ C156, 12.06.2004, p 3; Opinion of AG Jacobs on 15.12.2005 opines that appeal be dismissed.

[279] Cases COMP/35.587 PO *Video Games*, COMP/35.706 PO *Nintendo Distribution* COMP/36.321 *Omega-Nintendo*, OJ L255 of 08/10/2003 pp 33–100.

9.254 The Commission imposed a EUR163.8 million fine on Nintendo and its seven distributors. An action brought by Nintendo against this decision is pending before the CFI.[280]

9.255 **(iv)** *B&W* (**Article 4(a) and 4(c)**)   In January 2000, B&W Loudspeakers notified a selective distribution system for its products requesting clearance under the EU competition rules. In December 2002, the Commission came to the preliminary conclusion that the agreement was in breach of Article 81(1), would fall outside the scope of the BER, and did not qualify for an individual exemption. The Commission, therefore, opened formal proceedings and issued a statement of objections.[281]

9.256 In particular, the Commission found that B&W's distribution agreement contained several 'hardcore' restrictions of competition, namely minimum retail prices (even though disguised as a prohibition on 'bait pricing'[282]), restrictions on cross-supplies between authorised dealers, and a prohibition on distant sales including through the Internet.

9.257 Following the opening of formal proceedings, B&W Loudspeakers undertook to delete the restrictions on pricing, cross-supplies, and distance selling from its agreements. The revised agreements also provide that retailers can request to engage in distant selling. B&W can only refuse such requests in writing and based on criteria that concern the need to maintain the brand image and reputation of the products. The criteria must be applied indiscriminately and must be comparable to those for sales from a traditional retail outlet. Based on the above described modifications the European Commission issued a comfort letter.[283]

9.258 **(v)** *Topps* (**Article 4 (b)**)   On 26 May 2004, the Commission adopted a decision imposing a fine of EUR1.59 million on the Topps Company Inc. and its European subsidiaries, Topps Europe Ltd., Topps International Ltd., Topps UK Ltd., and Topps Italia SRL (Topps) for infringing Article 81(1) of the Treaty.[284] The Topps group produces collectible products such as stickers or trading cards featuring soccer players or cartoon characters.

9.259 The Commission found that Topps had entered into a series of agreements and concerted practices with several of its intermediaries in the United Kingdom, Italy, Finland, Germany, France, and Spain with the object of restricting parallel imports of Pokémon collectibles. In particular, the Commission found evidence that Topps had, in 2000, developed a strategy to prevent imports from low-price into high-price countries. The price it invoiced to its distributors was up to 243 per cent more expensive in Finland compared with Portugal where it was the cheapest. According to that evidence, Topps repeatedly asked its distributors to trace back parallel imports and to monitor the final destination of the products. Those who did not comply were threatened with supply cuts.

9.260 The decision was addressed to all four European Topps subsidiaries which participated in the anti-competitive agreements and concerted practices and to the ultimate US parent

---

[280] Case T-13/03 *Nintendo v Commission* OJ C70, 22.03.2003, p 27.

[281] On 6 December 2000 the Commission issued a Press Release announcing the opening of proceedings in case COMP/37.709 *B&W Loudspeakers*, IP/00/1418.

[282] 'Bait pricing' relates to the practice of offering a certain product at a very attractive price with the aim of attracting customers to the sales outlet.

[283] On 24 June 2002, the Commission issued a Press Release announcing closure of the case, IP/02/916.

[284] COMP/37.980 *Souris Bleue/TOPPS +*. Commission Press release IP/04/682.

company in view of its decisive influence on the conduct of its wholly owned subsidiaries. The decision was not addressed to Topps's intermediaries because their responsibility for the infringement was less significant.

(8) Transitional Period and Expiry Date of the BER

The BER, adopted on 22 December 1999, entered into force on 1 January 2000. Article 12 **9.261** of the BER exempted for a transitional period until 31 December 2001 vertical agreements already in force prior to 1 June 2000 which, while not satisfying the conditions for exemption provided in the BER, did satisfy the conditions for exemption under the Block Exemption Regulations which expired on 31 May 2000 (Commission Regulations (EEC) 1983/83, (EEC) 1984/83 and (EEC) 4087/88). In addition, the Guidelines clarify that the Commission Notice concerning Regulations (EEC) 1983/83 and 1984/83 also ceased to apply on 31 May 2000. Furthermore, the Guidelines explain that, for suppliers with a market share not exceeding 30 per cent, non-compete agreements with a duration exceeding five years are covered by the BER if on 1 January 2002 the non-compete agreements have no more than five years to run.[285] The BER will expire on 31 May 2010 (Article 13).

(9) Withdrawal of the benefit of the BER

The presumption of legality conferred by the BER may be withdrawn if a vertical agree- **9.262** ment, either on its own or together with similar agreements enforced by competing suppliers or buyers, comes within the scope of Article 81(1) and does not fulfil all the conditions of Article 81(3). The Commission may withdraw the benefit of the BER under Article 6 and establish an infringement of Article 81(1). Under Article 7 of the BER, the competent authority of a Member State may withdraw the benefit of the BER in respect of vertical agreements whose anti-competitive effects are felt in the territory of the Member State concerned or a part thereof, which has all the characteristics of a distinct geographic market (see also section A.6.d above). The Commission has the exclusive power to withdraw the benefit of the BER in respect of vertical agreements restricting competition on a relevant geographic market which is wider than the territory of a single Member State. Where the withdrawal procedure is applied, the Commission or national authority bears the burden of proof that the agreement falls within the scope of Article 81(1) and that the agreement does not fulfil all four conditions of Article 81(3). A withdrawal decision can only have an *ex nunc* effect, which means that the exempted status of the agreements concerned will not be affected for the period before the date on which the withdrawal becomes effective.

The Guidelines explain[286] that withdrawal may in particular be required where access to the rel- **9.263** evant market or competition therein is significantly restricted by the cumulative effect of parallel networks of similar vertical agreements enforced by competing suppliers or buyers. The Guidelines recognise that this may occur more readily in the case of distribution of products to final consumers, who are often in a much weaker position than professional buyers of intermediate products. Responsibility for an anti-competitive cumulative effect can only be attributed to those undertakings which make an appreciable contribution to it. Agreements entered

---

[285] Guidelines point 70.
[286] Guidelines points 71–4.

into by undertakings whose contribution to the cumulative effect is insignificant do not fall under the prohibition provided for in Article 81(1)[287] and are therefore not subject to the withdrawal mechanism. Lastly, it should be stressed that enforcement by withdrawal is rarely used.

(10) Disapplication of the BER

9.264 Article 8 of the BER enables the Commission to exclude from the scope of the BER, by means of regulation, parallel networks of similar vertical restraints where these cover more than 50 per cent of a relevant market. Unlike in the case of withdrawal, such a measure is not addressed to individual undertakings but concerns all undertakings whose agreements are defined in the regulation disapplying the BER (see also paras 9.23–9.25 above). Whereas the withdrawal of the benefit of the BER under Article 6 implies the adoption of a decision establishing an infringement of Article 81 by an individual company, the effect of a regulation under Article 8 is merely to remove, in respect of the restraints and the markets concerned, the benefit of the application of the BER and to restore the full application of Article 81(1) and (3).[288]

9.265 The Guidelines explain that disapplication is appropriate when it is likely that access to the relevant market or competition therein is appreciably restricted. This may occur in particular when parallel networks of selective distribution covering more than 50 per cent of a market make use of selection criteria which are not required by the nature of the relevant goods or discriminate against certain forms of distribution capable of selling such goods. In assessing the need to apply Article 8, the Commission will consider whether individual withdrawal would be a more appropriate remedy. Like withdrawal, disapplication is a rarely used enforcement action which in fact, at the time of writing, has never been applied.

(11) Market Definition and Market Share Calculation

9.266 As stated above, the BER creates a safe harbour for vertical restraints below a 30 per cent market share threshold. The text of Article 3 reads as follows:

1. Subject to paragraph 2 of this Article, the exemption provided for in Article 2 shall apply on condition that the market share held by the supplier does not exceed 30 per cent of the relevant market on which it sells the contract goods or services.
2. In the case of vertical agreements containing exclusive supply obligations, the exemption provided for in Article 2 shall apply on condition that the market share held by the buyer does not exceed 30 per cent of the relevant market on which it purchases the contract goods or services.

9.267 The market share threshold is applied in a simplified way in the BER. The applicability of the block exemption depends either on the market share of the supplier where it sells the contract products or the market share of the buyer where it purchases the contract products, but not on both. It is in general the market share of the supplier which determines the applicability of the block exemption. Only where the agreement contains an exclusive supply obligation, as defined in Article 1(c) of the BER, is it the buyer's market share which may

---

[287] Judgment in the *Delimitis* case. See also the De Minimis Notice (OJ C368, 22.12.2001), which contains in para 8 a specific 5 per cent market share threshold in the case of cumulative effects. See also para 9.145.
[288] Guidelines points 80–1.

not exceed the threshold of 30 per cent in order for the block exemption to apply. It is recognised that:

> From an economic point of view, a vertical agreement may have effects not only on the market between supplier and buyer but also on markets downstream of the buyer. The simplified approach of the Block Exemption Regulation, which only takes into account the market share of the supplier or the buyer (as the case may be) on the market between these two parties, is justified by the fact that below the threshold of 30 per cent the effects on downstream markets will in general be limited. In addition, only having to consider the market between supplier and buyer makes the application of the Block Exemption Regulation easier and enhances the level of legal certainty . . .[289]

Article 1(c) of the BER defines an exclusive supply obligation as 'any direct or indirect obligation causing the supplier to sell the goods or services specified in the agreement only to one buyer inside the Community for the purposes of a specific use or for resale'. As the definition specifies that there must be only one buyer inside the whole of the EU, this will only concern a limited number of agreements, certainly where goods for resale are concerned. That is why for most exclusive distribution agreements it is the supplier's market share on the market where it sells its product to the distributors which is decisive for coverage by the BER. **9.268**

Article 9 deals with some specifics of how to calculate a market share under the BER. Article 9(1) requires that the calculation of the market share is based on value figures. Only where value figures are not available can substantiated estimates be made based on other reliable market information such as volume figures. Article 9(2)(a) requires that the market share is calculated on the basis of data relating to the preceding calendar year. Article 9(2)(b) requires that, in the case of dual distribution of final goods, ie where a producer of final goods also acts as a distributor on the market, the market share of the producer not only includes the goods sold by him to independent distributors but also includes the goods sold by him through daughter companies operating as distributors (so-called 'integrated distributors'). **9.269**

In order to calculate the market share, it is necessary to determine the relevant market. The Guidelines refer to the Commission Notice on definition of the relevant market for the purposes of Community competition law [290] to provide guidance on the rules, criteria, and evidence which the Commission uses when considering market definition issues. In line with that Notice it is noted that to determine the relevant market the relevant product market and the relevant geographic market must be defined. 'The relevant product market comprises any goods or services which are regarded by the buyer as interchangeable, by reason of their characteristics, prices and intended use. The relevant geographic market comprises the area in which the undertakings concerned are involved in the supply and demand of relevant goods or services, in which the conditions of competition are sufficiently homogeneous, and which can be distinguished from neighbouring geographic areas because, in particular, **9.270**

---

[289] Guidelines point 22. In block exemption regulations and notices adopted at a later date the Commission has not pursued such a simplified approach but instead has consistently chosen to make the safe harbour dependent on the parties to the agreement respecting the market share threshold on all the relevant markets affected by the agreement, see for instance Commission Regulation (EC) 772/2004 dealt with in Chapter 10 of this book and the De Minimis Notice dealt with earlier in this chapter.

[290] OJ C372, 9.12.1997, p 5. See Chapter 1 of this book.

conditions of competition are appreciably different in those areas.'[291] In addition to referring to the market definition Notice the Guidelines provide a number of useful comments in relation to market definition and applying the threshold.

9.271 It is recognised that the definition of a product market depends in the first place on substitutability from the buyers' perspective. When the agreement concerns an intermediate product which is used as an input to produce other products and is not recognisable in the final product, the product market is normally defined by the direct buyers' preferences. The customers of the buyers will not normally have a strong preference concerning the inputs used by the buyers. In the case of distribution of final goods, what are substitutes for the distributors will normally be influenced or determined by the preferences of the final consumers.[292]

9.272 It is also recognised that, because the purchasers concluding supply and distribution agreements are professional buyers, the geographic market relevant for coverage by the safe harbour is usually wider than the market where the product is resold to final consumers. This will often lead to the definition of national markets or wider geographic markets.[293]

9.273 It is noted that where suppliers sell a portfolio of products, the entire portfolio may determine the product market when the portfolios and not the individual products are regarded as substitutes by the buyers. Where this is not the case, coverage by the safe harbour will depend on the market share for each individual product. This may lead to the result that certain products are covered by the BER and others not. In respect of the products not covered by the BER, if there is an infringement of Article 81(1) where the conditions of exception under Article 81(3) are not fulfilled, the Commission will endeavour to find appropriate remedies to solve the competition problem within the existing distribution system.[294]

9.274 Where a vertical agreement involves three parties, for instance an agreement between a manufacturer, a wholesaler, and a retailer, then the market share of both the manufacturer and the wholesaler must not exceed 30 per cent in order to benefit from the block exemption.[295]

9.275 Where a supplier produces both original equipment and the repair or replacement parts for that equipment, the supplier will often be the major or sole supplier on the aftermarket for the repair and replacement parts. The relevant market for application of the BER may be the original equipment market including the spare parts or a separate original equipment market and aftermarket depending on the circumstances of the case, such as the effects of the restrictions involved, the lifetime of the equipment, and importance of the repair or replacement costs.[296] In the case of individual assessment outside the BER, the situation on a separate aftermarket

---

[291] Guidelines point 90.

[292] Guidelines point 91.

[293] Guidelines point 91.

[294] Guidelines points 69 and 91.

[295] Guidelines point 93.

[296] See for example *Pelikan/Kyocera* in xxv Report on Competition Policy, point 87, and Commission Decision 91/595/EEC in Case No. IV/M.12 *Varta/Bosch*, OJ L320, 22.11.1991, p 26, Commission Decision in Case No IV/M.1094 *Caterpillar/Perkins Engines*, OJ C94, 28.3.1998, p 23, and Commission Decision in Case No IV/M.768 *Lucas/Varity*, OJ C266, 13.9.1996, p 6. See also *Eastman Kodak Co. v Image Technical Services, Inc. et al.*, Supreme Court of the United States, No. 90 1029. See also point 56 of the Commission Notice on the definition of relevant market for the purposes of Community competition law.

will be evaluated by reference to the situation on the original equipment market. It is recognised that a less significant position on the original equipment market will normally reduce possible anti-competitive effects on the aftermarket.[297]

Where the vertical agreement, in addition to the supply of products, also contains IPR provisions (see paras 9.200–9.204 above), the supplier's market share concerning the products is decisive for the application of the BER. There is no need to define a technology market and determine a possible market share on the latter market.[298] **9.276**

The Guidelines also clarify a particular point of market share calculation in relation to franchising agreements: **9.277**

> Where a franchisor does not supply goods to be resold but provides a bundle of services combined with IPR provisions which together form the business method being franchised, the franchisor needs to take account of his market share as a provider of a business method. For that purpose, the franchisor needs to calculate his market share on the market where the business method is exploited, which is the market where the franchisees exploit the business method to provide goods or services to end users. The franchisor must base his market share on the value of the goods or services supplied by his franchisees on this market. On such a market the competitors may be providers of other franchised business methods but also suppliers of substitutable goods or services not applying franchising. For instance, without prejudice to the definition of such market, if there was a market for fast-food services, a franchisor operating on such a market would need to calculate his market share on the basis of the relevant sales figures of his franchisees on this market. If the franchisor, in addition to the business method, also supplies certain inputs, such as meat and spices, then the franchisor also needs to calculate his market share on the market where these goods are sold.[299]

Outside the safe harbour all relevant markets affected by the agreement and the position of both parties on these markets are relevant for an individual assessment. In the case of intermediate products often only the market between supplier and buyer will be concerned, but in the case of final products more often the effects on downstream resale markets will also have to be evaluated.[300] **9.278**

Lastly, the Guidelines clarify that for the purpose of market definition and the calculation of market share, in-house production, that is production of an intermediate product for own use, will not be taken into account. However, in-house production may be very important in a competition analysis as one of the competitive constraints or to highlight the market position of a company and may thus play a role in the individual assessment of an agreement.[301] **9.279**

(12) The Framework of Analysis for Individual Assessment

The underlying philosophy of the BER and the Guidelines has already been discussed above (see paras 9.187–9.190). For most vertical restraints, competition concerns can only arise if there is insufficient inter-brand competition, in which case the protection of inter- and intra-brand competition becomes important. In the assessment of individual cases, the **9.280**

---

[297] Guidelines points 94 and 96.
[298] Guidelines point 95.
[299] Guidelines point 95.
[300] Guidelines point 96.
[301] Guidelines point 98.

Commission will adopt an economic approach, which will limit the scope of application of Article 81.

9.281 The first thing the Guidelines do in this respect is describe the possible negative effects from vertical restraints that EC competition law should prevent:

(i) foreclosure of other suppliers or other buyers by raising barriers to entry;

(ii) reduction of inter-brand competition between the companies operating on a market, including facilitation of collusion amongst suppliers or buyers; by collusion is meant both explicit collusion and tacit collusion (conscious parallel behaviour);

(iii) reduction of intra-brand competition between distributors of the same brand;

(iv) the creation of obstacles to market integration, including, above all, limitations on the freedom of consumers to purchase goods or services in any Member State they may choose.[302]

9.282 It is possible to analyse which type of restraint may bring about a particular negative effect. Vertical restraints are divided into four groups, with restraints within each group having largely similar negative effects.

9.283 First, the 'single branding group' contains those restraints which have as prime effect to induce the buyer to place all or most of his orders for a particular type of product with one supplier. This is the case, for example, where there are non-compete and quantity requirements on the buyer and in tying. There are four main negative effects on competition that restraints within this group may have: (1) other suppliers in that market cannot sell to these particular buyers, which may lead to foreclosure of the market, or, in the case of tying, to foreclosure of the market for the tied product; (2) it makes market shares more rigid and this may encourage collusion when applied by several suppliers; (3) as far as the distribution of final goods is concerned, the retailers concerned will only sell one brand and there will therefore be no inter-brand competition in their shops (no in-store competition); and (4) in the case of tying, the buyer may pay a higher price for the tied product than he would otherwise do. These effects may lead to a reduction in inter-brand competition. This reduction in inter-brand competition may however be mitigated by strong competition between suppliers to obtain the single branding contracts, but the longer the duration of the contract, the less likely it is that the reduction in inter-brand competition is counterbalanced.[303]

9.284 Secondly, the 'limited distribution group' contains those restraints whose main feature is that the manufacturer sells to only one or to a limited number of buyers. This is the case, for example, in exclusive and selective distribution agreements and exclusive supply agreements. There are three main negative effects on competition that restraints within this group may have: (1) certain buyers within that market can no longer buy from that particular supplier, which may lead to foreclosure of the purchase market, (2) when most or all of the competing suppliers limit the number of retailers, this may facilitate collusion, either at the distributor's level or at the supplier's level, and (3) since fewer distributors will offer the product, it will also lead to a reduction of intra-brand competition. This reduction of intra-brand competition can in turn lead to a weakening of inter-brand competition.[304]

---

[302] Guidelines point 103.
[303] Guidelines points 106–8.
[304] Guidelines points 109–10.

Thirdly, the 'resale price maintenance group' contains those restraints whose main feature is **9.285** that the buyer is obliged or induced to resell at a certain price or not to resell above or below a certain price. This group comprises minimum, fixed, maximum, and recommended resale prices. It is noted that maximum and recommended resale prices, which are not hardcore restrictions, may still lead to a restriction of competition by effect. There are two main negative effects of resale price maintenance on competition: (1) a reduction in intra-brand price competition, and (2) increased transparency on prices. In the case of fixed or minimum RPM, distributors can no longer compete on price for that brand, leading to a total elimination of intra-brand price competition. A maximum or recommended price may work as a focal point for resellers, leading to a more or less uniform application of that price level. Increased transparency on price and responsibility for price changes makes horizontal collusion between manufacturers or distributors easier, at least in concentrated markets. It is also noted that the reduction in intra-brand competition, as it leads to less downward pressure on the price for the particular goods, may have the indirect effect of reducing inter-brand competition.[305]

Fourthly, the 'market partitioning group' contains those restraints whose main feature is **9.286** that the buyer is restricted in his choice of where to source or resell a particular product. This group comprises exclusive purchasing obligations, territorial resale restrictions, the allocation of an area of primary responsibility, restrictions on the location of a distributor, and customer resale restrictions. The main negative effect on competition is a reduction of intra-brand competition that may help the supplier to partition the market and thus hinder market integration. This may facilitate price discrimination. When most or all of the competing suppliers limit the sourcing or resale possibilities of their buyers this may facilitate collusion, either at the distributors' level or at the suppliers' level.[306]

The Guidelines recognise that many vertical agreements may contain restraints from more **9.287** than one of the above mentioned groups, combining certain negative effects. For instance, in an exclusive distribution arrangement the supplier may not only promise to supply only one distributor in a particular territory (limited distribution group), but may also impose on the distributor certain territorial resale restrictions (market partitioning group) and a non-compete obligation (single branding group). It is nonetheless considered useful to analyse the different effects for a correct evaluation.

In order to assess the likelihood that appreciable negative effects result from an agreement **9.288** and thus fall within Article 81(1), the Guidelines indicate that the Commission will have to make a full competition analysis. The following factors are listed as relevant for assessing whether a particular vertical agreement is more or less likely to bring about an appreciable restriction of competition under Article 81(1):

— market position of the supplier;
— market position of competitors;
— market position of the buyer;
— entry barriers;
— maturity of the market;

---

[305] Guidelines points 111–12.
[306] Guidelines points 113–14.

— level of trade;
— nature of the product;
— other factors.[307]

9.289   The importance of these individual factors may vary from case to case and will depend on the total picture that emerges when all factors are taken into account. For instance, a high market share may usually indicate that the supplier has market power, but it is recognised that this is not the case in the absence of entry barriers. Most of these factors are standard in an analysis of the possibilities and likelihood of unilateral and collective use of market power and are already described in Chapter 1, of this book. A particular point to note about the list is that buying power, under market position of the buyer, is not described as a factor mitigating the use of market power by the supplier, but it is stressed that its effect on the likelihood of anti-competitive effects is not the same for the different vertical restraints and that buying power may increase the negative effects in case of restraints from the limited distribution and market partitioning groups. Another particular point to note, in relation to the nature of the product, is that it is stated that when the product is more heterogeneous, less expensive, and resembles more closely a one-off purchase, vertical restraints are more likely to have negative effects. Issues such as a possible cumulative effect, the regulatory environment, and the (collusive) history of the sector are mentioned under 'other factors'.

9.290   It is only after an appreciable negative effect on competition has been established, that an assessment under Article 81(3) becomes important. For the principles and general factors relevant to such an assessment the reader is referred to Chapter 3 where the Guidelines on the application of Article 81(3) of the Treaty are dealt with. In the Guidelines on Vertical Restraints it is only briefly indicated that 'there are four cumulative conditions for the application of Article 81(3):

— the vertical agreement must contribute to improving production or distribution or to promoting technical or economic progress;
— the vertical agreement must allow consumers a fair share of these benefits;
— the vertical agreement must not impose on the undertakings concerned vertical restraints which are not indispensable to the attainment of these benefits;
— the vertical agreement must not afford such undertakings the possibility of eliminating competition in respect of a substantial part of the products in question.'[308]

9.291   The last criterion of elimination of competition for a substantial part of the products in question is related to the question of dominance. The Guidelines state that 'where an undertaking is dominant or becoming dominant as a consequence of the vertical agreement, a vertical restraint that has appreciable anti-competitive effects can in principle not be exempted. The vertical agreement may however fall outside Article 81(1) if there is an objective justification, for instance if it is necessary for the protection of relationship-specific investments or for the transfer of substantial know-how without which the supply or purchase of certain goods or services would not take place.'[309] The Commission has provided some

---

[307] Guidelines points 121–33.
[308] Guidelines point 134.
[309] Guidelines point 135.

further clarification on the relationship between Articles 81 and 82 in the Guidelines on the application of Article 81(3) of the Treaty:

> The concept in Article 81(3) of elimination of competition in respect of a substantial part of the products concerned is an autonomous Community law concept specific to Article 81(3).[310] However, in the application of this concept it is necessary to take account of the relationship between Article 81 and Article 82. According to settled case law the application of Article 81(3) cannot prevent the application of Article 82 of the Treaty.[311] Moreover, since Articles 81 and 82 both pursue the aim of maintaining effective competition on the market, consistency requires that Article 81(3) be interpreted as precluding any application of this provision to restrictive agreements that constitute an abuse of a dominant position.[312,313] However, not all restrictive agreements concluded by a dominant undertaking constitute an abuse of a dominant position.[314]

A recent discussion paper on the application of Article 82[315] indicates a willingness to consider an Article 81(3) type efficiency defence under Article 82. If this were to lead to Commission guidelines on Article 82 the above mentioned parts of the Guidelines on Article 81(3) would have to be re-evaluated. **9.292**

Where the supplier and the buyer are not dominant, the other three criteria of Article 81(3) become important. The first, concerning the improvement of production or distribution and the promotion of technical or economic progress, refers to efficiencies that can be realised with the help of vertical restraints. The Guidelines provide a list of the type of efficiencies or positive effects that vertical restraints may have.[316] It is recognised that the usual arm's length dealings between a supplier and buyer, determining only price and quantity of a certain transaction, can lead to a suboptimal level of investments and sales and that vertical restraints may be helpful to overcome such a suboptimal situation. It is noted that certain vertical restraints may help to overcome various types of free riding problems. Free riding between distributors on each others' promotional efforts or efforts to develop new markets may be overcome by market partitioning and limited distribution-related restraints. Free riding between suppliers may be overcome by single branding type. It is recognised that if there are client-specific investments to be made, either by the supplier or the buyer, this may lead to a so-called 'hold-up problem'. This can be solved by applying an appropriate vertical restraint for the period needed to depreciate the investment. The appropriate vertical restraint will be of the single branding type when the investment **9.293**

---

[310] See Joined Cases T-191/98, T-212/98, and T-214/98, *Atlantic Container Line (TACA)* [2003] ECR II-3275, para 939, and Case T-395/94, *Atlantic Container Line* [2002] ECR II-875, para 330.

[311] See Joined Cases C-395/96 P and C-396/96 P, *Compagnie Maritime Belge* [2000] ECR I-1365, para 130. Similarly, the application of Art 81(3) does not prevent the application of the Treaty rules on the free movement of goods, services, persons, and capital. These provisions are in certain circumstances applicable to agreements, decisions, and concerted practices within the meaning of Art 81(1); see to that effect Case C-309/99, *Wouters* [2002] ECR I-1577, para 120.

[312] See in this respect Case T-51/89, *Tetra Pak (I)* [1990] ECR II-309, and Joined Cases T-191/98, T-212/98, and T-214/98, *Atlantic Container Line (TACA)* [2003] ECR II-3275, para 1456.

[313] This is how para 135 of the Guidelines on vertical restraints and paras 36, 71, 105, 134, and 155 of the Guidelines on horizontal co-operation agreements should be understood when they state that in principle restrictive agreements concluded by dominant undertakings cannot be exempted.

[314] Guidelines on the application of Art 81(3) of the Treaty, OJ C101, 27.04.2004, pp 97–118.

[315] DG Competition discussion paper on the application of Art 82 of the Treaty to exclusionary abuses, December 2005, in particular points 8 and 77–92.

[316] Guidelines points 115–18.

is made by the supplier and of the limited distribution type when the investment is made by the buyer. It is also recognised that if the supplier wants to transfer know-how to the buyer this may create a specific hold-up problem, as the know-how, once provided, cannot be taken back. In order to prevent the know-how from being used to the benefit of its competitors the supplier may require a non-compete type of restraint. Economies of scale in transport may be a reason for a manufacturer to limit the number of distributors or to increase the minimum required amount to be purchased. Capital market imperfections may mean that the supplier of a particular product is better able to judge the risks and opportunities of its distributors and provide loans to these distributors, for which it may require a single branding type of restriction. Lastly, it is recognised that selective distribution restraints in particular can help to achieve uniformity and standardisation in distribution and thereby may help to create and support a brand image.

9.294 The Guidelines make it clear that these efficiencies have to be substantiated and must produce a net positive effect. Speculative claims on avoidance of free riding or general statements on cost savings will not be accepted. For instance, where concerns about free riding between distributors on each others' promotional efforts is concerned it is noted that such free riding:

> can only occur on pre-sales services and not on after-sales services. The product will usually need to be relatively new or technically complex as the customer may otherwise very well know what he or she wants, based on past purchases. And the product must be of a reasonably high value as it is otherwise not attractive for a customer to go to one shop for information and to another to buy. Lastly, it must not be practical for the supplier to impose on all buyers, by contract, effective service requirements concerning pre-sales services.[317]

9.295 Similarly, concerning possible hold-up problems it is noted that:

> there are a number of conditions that have to be met before the risk of under-investment is real or significant. Firstly, the investment must be relationship-specific. An investment made by the supplier is considered to be relationship-specific when, after termination of the contract, it cannot be used by the supplier to supply other customers and can only be sold at a significant loss. An investment made by the buyer is considered to be relationship-specific when, after termination of the contract, it cannot be used by the buyer to purchase and/or use products supplied by other suppliers and can only be sold at a significant loss . . . Secondly, it must be a long-term investment that is not recouped in the short run. And thirdly, the investment must be asymmetric; ie one party to the contract invests more than the other party.[318]

9.296 Cost savings that arise from the mere exercise of market power or from anti-competitive conduct are also not accepted.

9.297 To conclude its general framework for the assessment of individual agreements, the Commission formulates in the Guidelines ten general rules which can be summarised as follows:[319]

(1) For most vertical restraints competition concerns can only arise if there is insufficient inter-brand competition, ie if the supplier or the buyer or both have a certain degree of market power. Where there are many firms competing in an un-concentrated market,

---

[317] Guidelines point 116.
[318] Guidelines point 116.
[319] Guidelines point 119.

it can be assumed that non-hardcore vertical restraints will not have appreciable negative effects on competition.

(2) Vertical restraints which reduce inter-brand competition are generally more harmful than vertical restraints that reduce intra-brand competition. Hence, non-compete obligations are likely to have more negative effects on competition than exclusive distribution agreements which are not combined with non-compete obligations.

(3) However, in the absence of sufficient inter-brand competition, restrictions on intra-brand competition may significantly restrict the choice available to consumers. They are particularly harmful when more efficient distributors or distributors with a different distribution format are foreclosed.

(4) Exclusive dealing arrangements are generally worse for competition than non-exclusive arrangements. For instance, under a non-compete obligation the buyer may only purchase and sell one brand, whereas a minimum quantity requirement leaves the buyer some scope to purchase competing goods.

(5) Vertical restraints are in general more harmful in relation to branded products than in relation to non-branded products. The distinction between branded and non-branded products will often coincide with the distinction between intermediate products and final products.

(6) In general, a combination of vertical restraints aggravates their negative effects. However, certain combinations may actually be better for competition than the use in isolation of each restraint.

(7) Negative anti-competitive effects of vertical restraints can be reinforced when several suppliers organise their distribution on the same market in a similar way (parallel networks of similar agreements).

(8) The more the vertical agreement involves transfer of know-how to the buyer, the more reason there is to expect efficiencies to arise and the more a vertical restraint may be necessary to protect the know-how transferred or the investment costs incurred.

(9) The more the vertical agreement involves relationship-specific investments, the more justification there is for certain vertical restraints for the period necessary to depreciate the investments.

(10) Vertical restraints required to open up new product or geographic markets generally do not restrict competition. This applies for two years after the product is first placed on the market. This rule only applies to non-hardcore vertical restraints, except in the case of a new geographic market where it also applies to restrictions on active and passive selling to intermediaries in the new market when such restrictions are imposed on the direct buyers of the supplier located in other markets. In the case of genuine testing of a new product in a particular territory or with a particular customer group, the distributors appointed to sell the new product on the test market can be restricted in their active selling outside the test market for a maximum period of one year without infringing Article 81(1).

E. Analysis of Different Categories of Vertical Restraints

(1) Single Branding

The first set of restraints analysed in section IV 2 of the Guidelines are those belonging to **9.298** the so-called single branding group. In this group we find all those restrictions that have the object or the effect of forcing distributors to sell mainly or exclusively products of a given brand. This effect can be achieved through different contractual tools, the most common of which is the so-called non-compete obligation, ie a contractual provision obliging the buyer not to sell competing products. An explicit ban on selling competing products, however, is not the only way to implement a single branding strategy and similar effects can be achieved by financial incentives. This is the case, for example, when suppliers are offered non-linear pricing schemes such as quantity rebates, fidelity rebates, or two-part tariffs.[320]

9.299 Another way to implement a single branding strategy is through quantity forcing, where distributors remain (in principle) free to sell competing products, but they are obliged to buy a certain minimum amount of their requirements from only one supplier, thus making it de facto impossible for them to distribute meaningful quantities of competing goods.[321]

9.300 Finally, single branding can also be achieved through the so-called 'English clause'. This clause provides that the distributor is free to sell competing products but is obliged to report to the existing supplier any more advantageous offer from competing suppliers. If the incumbent supplier matches the new offer, the distributor is not entitled to purchase the competing products.[322]

9.301 The Guidelines identify three anti-competitive effects of single branding.[323] The first and most obvious is foreclosure. By forcing distributors to sell only or mainly one brand, these restrictions limit the number of distributors available, thus raising the cost of getting access to the market. The second potential anti-competitive effect of single branding is facilitation of collusion. The difficulty in getting access to or switching distributors can cause a certain degree of market rigidity, which in the medium and long run can facilitate tacit or explicit collusion among suppliers. This effect, however, is only likely to occur when single branding is implemented by most of the suppliers active in the market and where the buyers are distributors acting at the retail level.[324] Finally, single branding can lead to a reduction of in-store competition, as a result of the lack of competing products within the same distribution outlet.

9.302 Single branding restrictions are block-exempted by the BER when implemented by a supplier holding a market share for the contract product below 30 per cent. As far as non-compete obligations are concerned (ie those obligations forcing the distributor to buy more than 80 per cent of its annual requirement from one supplier),[325] Article 5 of the BER makes the

---

[320] See para 152 of the Guidelines.

[321] It should be noted that, for the purpose of the application of both the Block Exemption and the Guidelines, non-compete and quantity forcing are two different forms of restraints. According to Art 1(b) of the Block Exemption, non-compete occurs when the distributor is obliged to purchase at least 80 per cent of its annual requirement exclusively from one supplier, while there is quantity forcing when the distributor is obliged to purchase from a single supplier a certain quantity that amounts to less than 80 per cent of its annual requirement. This differentiation is relevant particularly in the context of the application of Art 5 of the BER, which establishes that the benefit of the block exemption shall not apply to non-compete obligations established for a period in excess of five years. This provision does not apply to quantity forcing obligations, which are covered irrespective of their duration.

[322] The single branding effect of the English Clause has been recently restated by the Italian Competition Authority in its decision against Telecom Italia for abuse of dominant position (Case A351 *Telecom Italia*).

[323] See para 138 of the Guidelines.

[324] See para 107 of the Guidelines.

[325] See n 321 above.

applicability of the block exemption subject to the fact that the duration of the obligation does not exceed five years. Single branding restrictions falling outside the scope of the block exemption are not automatically prohibited but need to be analysed on a case-by-case basis.

The Guidelines identify seven relevant criteria for assessing whether single branding **9.303** restrictions give rise to appreciable anti-competitive effects. These criteria are: market position of the supplier, incidence of the obligation, duration of the obligation, market position of the supplier's competitors, presence of entry barriers, existence of countervailing power, and relevant level of trade. These seven criteria are analysed in turn.

(a) Market Position of the Supplier

The Guidelines identify the supplier's market position as the primary factor for the assess- **9.304** ment of possible anti-competitive effects of single branding. The Guidelines seem to suggest that the higher the market share of the supplier imposing single branding, the more likely it is that the obligations will raise anti-competitive effects. This is based on the assumption that the supplier will implement single branding throughout its entire distribution network, thus foreclosing a percentage of distributors comparable to its market share in the supply market.[326]

The Guidelines specifically provide that individual exemption will not be possible for sin- **9.305** gle branding obligations imposed by dominant suppliers, unless the restriction amounts to an objectively justified practice as defined by the jurisprudence on the application of Article 82 of the Treaty.[327]

(b) Incidence of the Single Branding Obligation

A very important factor in the assessment of single branding is the incidence of the non- **9.306** compete obligation. This is normally measured by the percentage of distributors that are exclusively tied to the supplier (so called 'tied market share'). The higher this percentage, the more likely it is that the agreements will produce foreclosure effects. It is worth noting that this percentage does not necessarily equate to the supplier's overall market share in the relevant market.[328] The supplier, in fact, may well decide (and often does) to distribute through tied distributors only a part of its production, while distributing the rest in a 'multi-brand' environment. Unfortunately, the Guidelines do not provide any indication of the level of 'tied market share' at which anti-competitive effects are likely to arise. It seems relatively safe to assume, however, that—given that single branding is block-exempted up to 30 per cent market share on the relevant market—a 'tied market share' of roughly the same level should not pose great concerns unless there are specific reasons to presume that the tied distributors are particularly important for rivals to access the market or to expand their position therein.

(c) Duration of the Single Branding Obligation

One other important factor in assessing the potential anti-competitive effects of single **9.307** branding is the duration of the obligation. Time, in fact, is the second factor (together with

---

[326] See para 140 of the Guidelines.
[327] See para 141 of the Guidelines.
[328] See above section on the supplier's market position.

the incidence) that contributes to the foreclosure effect of single branding. In this respect, the longer the duration the more significant foreclosure is likely to be. On this point paragraph 141 states:

> Non-compete obligations shorter than one year entered into by non-dominant companies are in general not considered to give rise to appreciable anti-competitive effects or net negative effects. Non-compete obligations between one and five years entered into by non-dominant companies usually require a proper balancing of pro- and anti-competitive effects, while non-compete obligations exceeding five years are for most types of investments not considered necessary to achieve the claimed efficiencies or the efficiencies are not sufficient to outweigh their foreclosure effect.

(d) Market Position of Competitors

9.308   Competitors' market position is also an important factor in the assessment. Single branding is likely to produce foreclosure only insofar as competing suppliers have no appreciable market power. In this respect the Guidelines point out that the presence of suppliers with market shares comparable to that of the supplier imposing the single branding obligation makes foreclosure less likely. On the other hand, equivalent market shares can become an aggravating factor if all suppliers implement a single branding strategy. There are two reasons for this. First, there can be a cumulative effect leading to an even greater degree of foreclosure. Second, the widespread use of single branding can introduce a considerable degree of market rigidity, which might facilitate collusion.[329] The Guidelines link the occurrence of cumulative effect problems essentially to two factors: the market share of the largest supplier and the degree of market concentration. In this respect, paragraph 143 states:

> In cases where the market share of the largest supplier is below 30 per cent and the market share of the five largest suppliers (concentration rate (CR) 5) is below 50 per cent, there is unlikely to be a single or a cumulative anti-competitive effect situation.

9.309   The Guidelines point out that, in the event that the cumulative effect is produced by companies individually exempted by the BER, the benefit of the block exemption might be withdrawn for those companies with a tied market share above 5 per cent.[330]

(e) Barriers to Entry

9.310   Barriers to entry are important for assessing the risk of foreclosure. It should be noted that the relevant market for assessing the presence of barriers to entry is the distribution market, rather than the supply market. The relevant question, therefore, is how easily suppliers can establish their own distribution network or find alternative distributors. Needless to say, in the case of high barriers to entry foreclosure will be more likely.

(f) Countervailing Power

9.311   Countervailing power is relevant because powerful buyers are unlikely to accept single branding obligations. This means that in markets where there are big distributors, even if a

---

329 This is due to the combined effect of high market concentration, lack of potential competition, and difficulty in gaining market share due to the fact that the vast majority of available distributors are already tied to one of the existing suppliers.

330 A tied market share below 5% is assumed not to produce any significant contribution to the cumulative effect. See also the De Minimis Notice, para 9.59 ff above.

certain share of the demand is tied exclusively to certain suppliers, foreclosure is unlikely to occur. It should be noted, however, that if single branding were imposed on strong buyers the foreclosure effect would be magnified.

(g) Level of Trade

The likelihood of foreclosure depends to a considerable extent on the level of trade at which single branding is implemented. As a general rule it can be said that the 'higher' the level of trade, the less likely foreclosure is. The Guidelines distinguish between intermediate products (ie products that are used as an input for the production of other goods or services) and final products. Within the latter category, the Guidelines further distinguish between distribution at the wholesale level and distribution at the retail level. **9.312**

As regards intermediate products, the Commission believes that single branding is unlikely to produce foreclosure unless implemented by a dominant supplier. The Guidelines however warn that foreclosure of actual or potential competitors may also occur below the level of dominance when single branding is widely used in the relevant market and when this leads to a cumulative tied market share of at least 50 per cent. **9.313**

With regard to the distribution of final products at the wholesale level, the Guidelines link the likelihood of foreclosure to the presence of barriers to entry at the wholesale level and to the characteristics of the wholesaling activity in the specific market. Single branding is, in fact, unlikely to lead to foreclosure if competing suppliers are able to establish their own wholesalers. This largely depends on whether, in light of the specific market characteristics, it is efficient to carry out wholesaling for only one product or whether the presence of economies of scope and scale requires the distribution of a whole range of products. **9.314**

For the same reasons, foreclosure is considered more likely to occur at the retail level. Here, in fact, it is generally less efficient for suppliers to establish their own distribution network. In addition, the Guidelines point out that single branding at the retail level can be conducive to lowering in-store competition.[331] In light of this, the Guidelines state that at the retail level anti-competitive effects may already arise when a non-dominant supplier ties more than 30 per cent of the available distributors, while 'for a dominant company, even a modest tied market share may already lead to significant anti-competitive effects'. **9.315**

As far as cumulative effects are concerned, paragraph 149 of the Guidelines states: **9.316**

> When all companies have market shares below 30 per cent a cumulative foreclosure effect is unlikely if the total tied market share is less than 40 per cent and withdrawal of the block exemption is therefore unlikely. This figure may be higher when other factors like the number of competitors, entry barriers etc are taken into account. When not all companies have market shares below the threshold of the Block Exemption Regulation but none is dominant, a cumulative foreclosure effect is unlikely if the total tied market share is below 30 per cent.

Having analysed the factors that might give rise to anti-competitive effects, the Guidelines move on to describe the possible efficiencies that could be assessed for the purpose of the application of Article 81(3). In this context, paragraph 153 identifies three different **9.317**

---

[331] Para 148 of the Guidelines.

possible efficiencies linked to the use of single branding: (1) elimination of free-riding among suppliers, (2) resolution of 'hold-up' problems, and (3) remedy to capital market imperfections.[332] In relation to a possible hold-up problem, the Guidelines clarify that relationship-specific investments and a transfer of substantial know-how could justify a single branding in excess of five years. The Guidelines also specify that there are very limited circumstances under which capital market imperfection problems can justify single branding. In particular, paragraph 156 states:

> Even if the supplier of the product were to be the more efficient provider of capital, a loan could only justify a non-compete obligation if the buyer is not prevented from terminating the non-compete obligation and repaying the outstanding part of the loan at any point in time and without payment of any penalty.

(2) Exclusive Distribution

9.318 The Guidelines define exclusive distribution agreements as agreements whereby the supplier agrees to sell his products only to one distributor for resale in a particular territory and whereby the distributor agrees not to sell actively into other exclusively allocated territories.[333] As for single branding, the Commission identifies three possible anti-competitive effects. First, because of the limitation in the number of distributors and the prohibition on active sales, exclusive distribution can lead to less intense intra-brand competition. Second, due to the reduction in intra-brand competition, exclusive distribution can facilitate market partitioning and price discrimination. Finally, when applied extensively throughout a market, exclusive distribution can lead to collusion both at the supply and distribution level.

9.319 Exclusive distribution is block exempted insofar as the supplier's market share does not exceed 30 per cent. This is the case also when exclusive distribution is associated with other non-hardcore restraints. As regards the joint use of exclusive distribution and selective distribution, the Guidelines point out that such combination is only possible insofar as distributors are allowed to sell actively into other exclusive territories.[334]

9.320 The Guidelines identify five main factors to assess whether exclusive distribution might give rise to anti-competitive effects. These are: market position of the supplier, market position of the supplier's competitors, buying power, level of trade, and maturity of the product.

(a) Supplier's Market Position

9.321 The supplier's market position is of major importance in assessing whether exclusive distribution is likely to produce anti-competitive effects. As noted above, the main competitive concern related to exclusive distribution is the reduction in intra-brand competition. Low intra-brand competition, however, is unlikely to become a problem insofar as there is sufficient inter-brand competition. If the supplier implementing exclusive distribution has

---

[332] For details on each efficiency see para 116 of the Guidelines. See also above paras 9.291–9.297.

[333] Para 161 of the Guidelines.

[334] A restriction on active sales would be contrary to the provision of Art 4(c) of the BER. This provision is a departure from past policy of the Commission on vertical restraints included in franchising agreements. A combination of selective distribution and exclusive distribution (including the restrictions on active sales) was one of the main features of Regulation 4087/88 on Franchising.

a strong position in the market, it is more likely that inter-brand competition will not be sufficient to remedy a loss in intra-brand competition. In this respect, the Guidelines state that above the market shares threshold of 30 per cent exclusive distribution may lead to significant restrictions in intra-brand competition.

(b) Competitors' Market Position

Generally speaking, the presence of strong competitors is a positive factor, as fierce inter-brand competition mitigates the loss in intra-brand competition. If, however, the number of competitors is too small and their market shares are similar, collusion might become an issue. The Commission points out that this may happen in particular when different suppliers appoint the same exclusive distributor (so-called 'multiple exclusive dealerships'). In this regard, paragraph 164 of the Guidelines states:

> If a dealer is granted the exclusive right to distribute two or more important competing products in the same territory, inter-brand competition is likely to be substantially restricted for those brands. The higher the cumulative market share of the brands distributed by the multiple dealer, the higher the risk of collusion and the more inter-brand competition will be reduced. Such cumulative effect situations may be a reason to withdraw the benefit of the Block Exemption Regulation when the market shares of the suppliers are below the threshold of the Block Exemption Regulation.

(c) Buying Power

The presence of strong distributors normally generates some concerns, as it can cause a further reduction in intra-brand competition. Strong distributors, in fact, may have the power to obtain very large exclusive territories, thus substantially limiting the number of distributors for the contract product. This problem can be exacerbated if those distributors also enjoy a significant degree of market power in the downstream market.[335] Furthermore, buying power can also increase the risk of collusion among distributors.[336]

(d) Level of Trade

The Guidelines make clear that exclusive distribution is more likely to have anti-competitive effects at the retail level than at the wholesale level. The reduction in intra-brand competition inherent to exclusive distribution systems tends to affect final consumers more than professional buyers. On this point, paragraph 170 states:

> A manufacturer which chooses a wholesaler to be his exclusive distributor will normally do so for a larger territory, such as a whole Member State. As long as the wholesaler can sell the products without limitation to downstream retailers there are not likely to be appreciable anti-competitive effects if the manufacturer is not dominant. A possible loss of intra-brand competition at the wholesale level may be easily outweighed by efficiencies obtained in logistics, promotion etc, especially when the manufacturer is based in a different country. Foreclosure of other wholesalers within that territory is not likely as a supplier with a market share above 30 per cent usually has enough bargaining power not to choose a less efficient wholesaler. The possible risks for inter-brand competition of multiple exclusive dealerships are however higher at the wholesale than at the retail level.

9.322

9.323

9.324

---

[335] Anti-competitive effect can be even more severe in the case of multiple exclusive dealerships.
[336] See para 167 of the Guidelines.

(e) Maturity of the Market

9.325 Exclusive distribution is more likely to be problematic if implemented in mature markets. Market partitioning—one of the possible anti-competitive effects of this restraint—may be a serious problem in markets characterised by stagnant demand, mature technologies, and stable market positions.

9.326 The Guidelines point out that the negative effects of exclusive distribution can be amplified when implemented together with other vertical restraints.

9.327 First, the combination with single branding restrictions may increase the anti-competitive effects of exclusive distribution by adding the reduction in inter-brand competition to the reduction in intra-brand competition.[337] Second, the Guidelines warn about the combination of exclusive distribution and exclusive purchasing,[338] which would normally magnify the restriction of intra-brand competition.[339] This combination is unlikely to be individually exempted, unless the parties are able to demonstrate substantial efficiencies. With regard to agreements covered by the block exemption, the Commission points out that the lack of demonstrable efficiencies could be the basis for the withdrawal of the exemption.

9.328 As far as the assessment of efficiencies is concerned, the Guidelines identify the nature of the product as the most relevant factor. Paragraph 174 says:

> Exclusive distribution may lead to efficiencies, especially where investments by the distributors are required to protect or build up the brand image. In general, the case for efficiencies is strongest for new products, for complex products, for products whose qualities are difficult to judge before consumption (so-called experience products) or of which the qualities are difficult to judge even after consumption (so-called credence products). In addition, exclusive distribution may lead to savings in logistic costs due to economies of scale in transport and distribution.

(3) Exclusive Customer Allocation

9.329 Exclusive customer allocation is a restriction based on the same type of obligation as exclusive distribution. The only difference is that in exclusive customer allocation the limitation on the distributor's freedom to resell is based on the identification of a customer group rather than on the definition of a geographic area.[340] This means that the framework of analysis laid down in the previous section for exclusive distribution is also applicable to exclusive customer allocation. It should be noted, however, that the Commission seems to have a more cautious approach to exclusive customer allocation than to exclusive distribution.

---

[337] Para 171 of the Guidelines, however, says that such a combination is problematic only when the supplier has a considerable tied market share. If this is not the case, the combination of exclusive distribution and single branding may be pro-competitive, because it can increase the distributor's incentives to focus on a given brand. In this respect para 171 states that: 'in the absence of such a foreclosure effect, the combination of exclusive distribution with non-compete is exemptable for the whole duration of the agreement, particularly at the wholesale level'.

[338] Para 172 of the Guidelines.

[339] Exclusive purchasing obliges the buyer to source the contract good only from the designated supplier, therefore eliminating the possibility of arbitrage by the buyer.

[340] The exclusive customer groups can be defined in several ways. Typically, customers are identified on the basis of criteria such as turnover (above and below a certain turnover threshold), quantities ordered (above and below a certain quantity), nature of the activity (resellers vs final users) etc.

This is because exclusive customer allocation could reduce the possibility of arbitrage by the customers. On this issue the Guidelines point out that exclusive customer allocation is unlikely to be individually exempted unless clear and substantial efficiency effects can be demonstrated.[341]

As far as the identification of the relevant efficiencies is concerned, Paragraph 182 states: **9.330**

> Exclusive customer allocation may lead to efficiencies, especially when the distributors are required to make investments in for instance specific equipment, skills or know-how to adapt to the requirements of their class of customers. The depreciation period of these investments indicates the justified duration of an exclusive customer allocation system. In general the case is strongest for new or complex products and for products requiring adaptation to the needs of the individual customer. Identifiable differentiated needs are more likely for intermediate products, that is products sold to different types of professional buyers. Allocation of final consumers is unlikely to lead to any efficiencies and is therefore unlikely to be exempted.

(4) Selective Distribution

Selective distribution has two distinctive features: distributors are selected on the basis of **9.331** quantitative or qualitative selection criteria,[342] and the selected distributors are obliged not to sell—either actively or passively—to other distributors not belonging to the authorised distribution network.[343] The combination of these two features brings selective distribution within the scope of the 'limited distribution' group, ie those vertical restraints that have the effect of limiting the number of distributors. This means that the main competition risk associated with the implementation of selective distribution is the reduction in intra-brand competition. As a result of foreclosure of certain types of distributors, selective distribution may facilitate collusion among supplier or buyers. These risks are particularly high when selective distribution is applied extensively in the market.

It should be noted from the outset, however, that the Guidelines point out that not all **9.332** forms of selective distribution are likely to raise competition concerns. In particular, purely qualitative selective distribution may fall outside the scope of Article 81 (1) provided that:

(1) The nature of the product distributed is such that selective distribution is necessary to preserve its quality and ensure its proper use,[344]

---

[341] See para 180 of the Guidelines.

[342] This is a major shift in policy. Under the old Commission policy on vertical restraints, in fact, quantitative selective distribution was considered as a *per se* restriction of competition and, therefore, not exemptable. See J. Faull and A. Nikpay, *The EC Law of Competition* (1st edn, Oxford: Oxford University Press, 1999), para 7.198.

[343] The ban on sales to distributors outside the authorised distribution network is the first feature that potentially brings selective distribution within the scope of Art 81(1). The selection process is a second possible restriction of competition, in particular when it forecloses more competitive distribution formats.

[344] This is the so-called 'nature of the good' requirement that can be tracked back both in Commission practice and in Court jurisprudence. In Givenchey [1992] OJ L236/11, for example, the Commission said 'Certain products which are not ordinary products or services have properties such that they cannot properly be supplied to the public without the intervention of specialized distributors'. Generally speaking, products for which selective distribution can be deemed necessary are products characterised by technological complexity, luxury and sophisticated image, high quality, or strong safety implications.

(2) The selection criteria are objective, qualitative in nature, and are applied in a non-discriminatory manner,[345] and

(3) The selection criteria do not go beyond what is necessary to preserve the quality of the product and to ensure its proper use.[346]

9.333   For those agreements that do fall within the scope of Article 81(1), the Commission identifies six relevant factors to assess anti-competitive effects, which are analysed below.

(a) Nature of the Product

9.334   The block exemption regulation exempts selective distribution regardless of the nature of the product. However, the nature of the product can become relevant for assessing selective distribution applied by a producer with a market share exceeding the 30 per cent threshold of the BER and to assess the likelihood of withdrawal of the block exemption. On this last point, paragraph 186 of the Guidelines says:

> However, where the nature of the product does not require selective distribution, such a distribution system does not generally bring about sufficient efficiency enhancing effects to counterbalance a significant reduction in intra-brand competition. If appreciable anti-competitive effects occur, the benefit of the Block Exemption Regulation is likely to be withdrawn.

(b) Supplier's Market Position

9.335   As for the other restrictions belonging to the limited distribution family, the supplier's market share is of central importance: the higher the supplier's market share the more problematic the anti-competitive effects will be. It should be noted, however, that—unlike exclusive customer allocation—the Guidelines do not state that agreements entered into by suppliers holding a market share in excess of 30 per cent are unlikely to be exempted. This seems to suggest that the Commission considers selective distribution to be less harmful for inter-brand competition. In this respect, paragraph 187 states that:

> Where selective distribution is applied by only one supplier in the market which is not a dominant undertaking, quantitative selective distribution does not normally create net negative effects provided that the contract goods, having regard to their nature, require the use of a selective distribution system and on condition that the selection criteria applied are necessary to ensure efficient distribution of the goods in question.

(c) Competitors' Market Position

9.336   The existence of strong competitors is normally considered a mitigating factor, in the case of restraints affecting intra-brand competition. This also applies to selective distribution. Having said that, the presence of strong competitors can become problematic if selective distribution is widespread throughout the relevant market.[347] In this case the loss in

---

[345] Discriminatory application normally occurs when the supplier refuses to appoint a dealer that would otherwise fit the selection criteria (see *Report on Competition Policy 1983* (Vol xiii), para 11) or when the selection criteria are not applied in a uniform manner to different categories of dealers (see *Binon* [1985] ECR 20105).

[346] On the notion of necessity see: Case T-19/91 *Vichy v Commission* [1992] ECR II-415, para 65, Case 107/82 *AEG* [1983] ECR 3151, para 35; Case 26/76 *Metro* [1977] ECR 1875 paras 20 and 21; Case 31/80 *L'Oréal v PVBA* [1980] ECR3775, paras 15 and 16.

[347] This is often the case, since the use of selective distribution is normally related to the nature of the product distributed.

intra-brand competition is less likely to be compensated by strong inter-brand competition and collusion might become more likely.

The Guidelines point out that net negative cumulative effects are unlikely to arise when: **9.337**

(a) The share of the market covered by selective distribution is below 50 per cent, or
(b) The cumulative market share of the five largest suppliers is below 50 per cent:

> Where the Block Exemption Regulation applies to individual networks of selective distribution, withdrawal of the block exemption or disapplication of the Block Exemption Regulation may be considered in case of cumulative effects. However, a cumulative effect problem is unlikely to arise when the share of the market covered by selective distribution is below 50 per cent. Also, no problem is likely to arise where the market coverage ratio exceeds 50 per cent, but the aggregate market share of the five largest suppliers (CR5) is below 50 per cent. Where both the CR5 and the share of the market covered by selective distribution exceed 50 per cent, the assessment may vary depending on whether or not all five largest suppliers apply selective distribution. The stronger the position of the competitors not applying selective distribution, the less likely the foreclosure of other distributors. If all five largest suppliers apply selective distribution, competition concerns may in particular arise with respect to those agreements that apply quantitative selection criteria by directly limiting the number of authorised dealers. The conditions of Article 81(3) are in general unlikely to be fulfilled if the selective distribution systems at issue prevent access to the market by new distributors capable of adequately selling the products in question, especially price discounters, thereby limiting distribution to the advantage of certain existing channels and to the detriment of final consumers.[348]

(d) Barriers to Entry

Barriers to entry are relevant for assessing the risk of distributors' foreclosure. In this **9.338** respect, the higher the barriers at the supply level the more likely it is that distributors will be foreclosed. As selective distribution is usually implemented by producers of branded products, barriers to entry are generally considerable.[349]

(e) Buying Power

The Guidelines consider the presence of strong distributors as a factor that could exacer- **9.339** bate the anti-competitive effects of selective distribution. The reason is twofold. First, the presence of buying power—associated with low intra-brand competition—could facilitate downstream collusion. Second, strong distributors could require suppliers to adopt very stringent selective criteria, and thus foreclose competing distributors from the retail market.[350]

(f) Maturity of the Market

The maturity of the market is relevant for assessing possible anti-competitive effects of selec- **9.340** tive distribution, as the loss of intra-brand competition in a market characterised by stagnant demand, mature technologies, and stable market shares can be conducive to collusion.

As far as efficiencies are concerned, the Guidelines point out that selective distribution can **9.341** be particularly effective in the development of new brands. This efficiency, however, is

---

[348] Para 189 of the Guidelines.
[349] Para 190 of the Guidelines.
[350] This scenario is particularly likely in case of strong retail organisations. See para 191.

likely to occur only when the products distributed through the selective network are either new or complex or are products the qualities of which cannot be judged before the purchase (so-called experience and credence products).[351]

(5) Franchising

9.342   The Guidelines portray franchising as a combination of elements of selective distribution, exclusive distribution, and single branding, associated with the transfer of intellectual property rights. For its analysis, therefore, the Commission relies on the guidance provided in relation to the individual restraints forming the franchising scheme. The only two additional elements of guidance are set out in paragraph 200, which states:

(1)   In line with general rule 8 (see paragraph 119), the more important the transfer of know-how, the more easily the vertical restraints fulfil the conditions for exemption.

(2)   A non-compete obligation on the goods or services purchased by the franchisee falls outside Article 81(1) when the obligation is necessary to maintain the common identity and reputation of the franchised network. In such cases, the duration of the non-compete obligation is also irrelevant under Article 81(1), as long as it does not exceed the duration of the franchise agreement itself.

(6) Exclusive Supply

9.343   The Guidelines define exclusive supply as an agreement whereby the supplier undertakes to supply its products only to one buyer within the Community for the purpose of a specific use or for resale.[352] The main competition risk associated with exclusive supply is the foreclosure of other buyers and the elimination of intra-brand competition. The Commission identifies the following factors of analysis.

(a) Buyer's Market Share

9.344   The most important factor for assessing potential anti-competitive effects of exclusive supply is the buyer's market share on both the upstream purchase market and on the downstream supply market. The first is relevant to measuring the extent to which other buyers will be foreclosed.[353] The second provides an indication of whether foreclosure on the buying market is likely to result in a competition problem in the downstream market. Even in the presence of high upstream market shares, no significant anti-competitive effect should be expected if the buyer has no downstream market power. In this regard, paragraph 204 of the Guidelines says: 'Negative effects can however be expected when the market share of the buyer on the downstream supply market as well as the upstream purchase market exceeds 30 per cent'. The same paragraph states that where the upstream market share is below 30 per cent but the buyer's market share on the downstream market is greater than 30 per cent, the Commission may withdraw the benefit of the block exemption.[354]

---

[351] See para 195 of the Guidelines.

[352] See para 202 of the Guidelines.

[353] It should be noted that, for the purpose of measuring foreclosure, the tied upstream market share of the buyer (ie the share of purchase realised through exclusive supply agreements) is definitely more important than the overall upstream market share (see para 205 of the Guidelines).

[354] Art 3(2) of the BER provides that for exclusive supply the buyer's market share on the upstream market is the relevant market share for the purpose of the block exemption (see above paragraph 9.190).

(b) Duration of the Agreement

Another important factor in assessing the likelihood of anti-competitive effects is the duration of the supply agreement. The longer the agreement the more likely it is that exclusive supply will cause foreclosure of other buyers. The Guidelines indicate that for most investments agreements longer than five years are not considered exemptable, because they will not be necessary to achieve the claimed efficiencies or because those efficiencies are not sufficient to outweigh foreclosure. On the other hand, agreements shorter than five years entered into by non-dominant buyers will usually require a case-by-case balancing of pro- and anti-competitive effects.[355] **9.345**

(c) Competitors' Market Position

The market position of competing buyers is important because it helps in assessing the likelihood of foreclosure. Foreclosure is only likely to occur when competing buyers are significantly smaller than the buyer implementing exclusive supply. In this regard, the presence of strong competitors on the downstream market is regarded as a positive factor. As always, however, the presence of strong competitors has the drawback of increasing the likelihood of foreclosure in case of parallel implementation of exclusive supply agreements. In such circumstances, the Commission may withdraw the benefit of the block exemption.[356] **9.346**

(d) Countervailing Power

Suppliers' countervailing power normally mitigates the possible anti-competitive effects of exclusive supply agreements. Strong suppliers are unlikely to agree to be foreclosed from other distribution channels unless this generates substantial efficiencies. Strong suppliers may tend to combine exclusive supply with single branding obligations. This combination is normally exemptable (always below the level of dominance) in the presence of strong relation-specific investments for both parties to the agreement.[357] **9.347**

(e) Level of Trade and Nature of the Product

The Guidelines state that buyers' foreclosure is less likely to happen for intermediate products than for final products. Buyers of intermediate products are generally more flexible in adapting to changing supply conditions so, even if foreclosed, they may create or find alternative sources of supply. This is particularly the case for homogeneous intermediate products, for which exemption is normally possible up to the level of dominance. The opposite is true for differentiated final products, where the loss of a supplier more easily results in foreclosure. **9.348**

As far as efficiencies are concerned, the Guidelines indicate that exclusive supply can be helpful in resolving 'hold-up' problems, particularly in the case of intermediate products. **9.349**

---

[355] It is interesting to note that the Commission does not provide any 'de minimis' rule for the length of the Exclusive Supply obligations. This seems to suggest that even short-term agreements could be considered restrictive.

[356] See para 206 of the Guidelines.

[357] See para 208 of the Guidelines.

(7) Tying

9.350   The Guidelines define tying as an agreement whereby the supplier makes the sale of a certain product (tying product) conditional on the purchase of another distinct[358] product (tied product). Tying is considered a vertical restraint insofar as it can result in single branding for the tied product.

9.351   The main competitive risk of tying is foreclosure of other suppliers in the tied product market. Tying may also lead to higher prices and it might increase entry barriers in both the tying and tied markets. The Guidelines identify three main criteria for the assessment of tying, all of which try to evaluate whether the supplier has some degree of market power in the tying market.

(a) Supplier's Market Position on the Tying Market

9.352   The supplier's market position on the tying product market is of main importance. The stronger its position, the more likely it is that the supplier will be able to impose the purchase of a second product.

(b) Competitor's Market Position on the Tying Market

9.353   The presence of strong competitors on the tying market makes anti-competitive effects less likely. A sufficient number of strong competitors, in fact, makes it possible for buyers to purchase the tying product without having to accept the obligation to buy the tied product.

(c) Buying Power

9.354   Similar considerations apply to buying power. Paragraph 202 of the Guidelines state that strong buyers are unlikely to accept tying obligations unless these generate considerable efficiencies from which the buyers would also benefit.

9.355   The analysis of foreclosure in the tied market uses the concept of tied market share (similar to what happens in the analysis of single branding). In this regard, it should be noted that the combination with non-compete obligations in the tied market is considered to increase the possibility of foreclosure effects.

9.356   As far as individual exemptions are concerned, the Guidelines point out that Article 81(3) can only apply below the level of dominance. However, as described in paragraph 9.292 above there is increased discussion on allowing an efficiency defence also under Article 82. Tying can generate efficiencies related to joint production or joint distribution of products or arising from the purchase of large quantities of the tied products or from obtaining uniform distribution conditions. Paragraph 222, however, warns that cost efficiencies cannot be claimed when the buyer is able to obtain a constant supply of the tied product at conditions comparable to or more advantageous than those offered by the supplier of the tying

---

[358] One problem that arises from this definition is the identification of what constitutes a 'distinct' product. In this regard, the Commission suggests that the starting point for identifying what constitutes a distinct product should be the analysis of demand. In particular, the crucial question should be whether, in the absence of a tying obligation, buyers would buy the two products separately.

product. As for the possible efficiencies linked to increased uniformity, it must be borne in mind that the indispensability requirement provided by Article 81(3) requires that:

> the positive effects cannot be realised equally efficiently by requiring the buyer to use or resell products satisfying minimum quality standards, without requiring the buyer to purchase these from the supplier or someone designated by the latter. The requirements concerning minimum quality standards would not normally fall within Article 81(1). Where the supplier of the tying product imposes on the buyer the suppliers from which the buyer must purchase the tied product, for instance because the formulation of minimum quality standards is not possible, this may also fall outside Article 81(1), especially where the supplier of the tying product does not derive a direct (financial) benefit from designating the suppliers of the tied product.[359]

(8) Recommended and Maximum Resale Price

The Guidelines indicate that recommended and maximum resale prices often may not restrict competition but that under certain circumstances, however, these provisions can raise anti-competitive effects. In particular they can lead to the creation of a 'price floor' at the retail level and to facilitation of collusion at the supply level. The main factors to be taken into account in assessing the likelihood of these anti-competitive effects are the market position of the supplier and the market position of the competitors. **9.357**

(a) Market Position of the Supplier

As a general rule, the stronger the market position of the supplier implementing recommended prices and maximum resale prices, the more likely it is that these restrictions can have anti-competitive effects, because retailers may find it difficult to diverge from the price level that seems to be preferred by the main supplier. **9.358**

(b) Market Position of Competitors

Recommended and maximum resale prices when applied in a tied oligopoly could facilitate collusion. This could be particularly true when recommended and maximum resale prices are made public through marketing or advertising campaigns and operate as a means of information exchange. **9.359**

---

[359] Para 222 of the Guidelines.

10

INTELLECTUAL PROPERTY

Kevin Coates, Lars Kjølbye and Luc Peeperkorn

A. Introduction

(1) Overview

10.01 The application of the competition rules to the field of intellectual property (IP) protection is complex. This is due in part to the varied scope and nature of that which can benefit from intellectual property right protection, and in part to the development over time of the jurisprudence on the relationship between intellectual property rights, often granted nationally, and Community law. This chapter sets out the application of EC competition law to licensing of, and refusals to license, intellectual property, and draws out the underlying principles governing the area as a whole.

10.02 A complete treatment of intellectual property licensing under Community law would require an analysis both under the Community competition rules, and the rules on free movement. As this book is concerned solely with the competition rules, the latter laws are beyond the scope of this chapter, save where there is a direct impact on the application of the competition rules. This is most notably the case in the discussion of the existence/exercise distinction and the consequent definition of the specific subject matter of an intellectual property right.

IP rights may be relevant to an appraisal under the competition rules in the absence of **10.03** licensing issues or allegations of abusive behaviour, such as an analysis of barriers to entry on a particular market.[1] These issues are similarly beyond the scope of the present chapter.

(2) Purpose of Intellectual Property Rights

Intellectual property law confers certain exclusive rights in relation to the exploitation of **10.04** intellectual endeavour—invention, design, or expression—which would otherwise not be protected by traditional property laws. Intellectual property may be costly to develop: attempts to develop new intellectual property often fail and successful projects sometimes take a long time to complete. The end result of a successful development of intellectual property may often be easily reproduced at a fraction of the original development cost. This makes free riding on others' development commercially attractive, and protection of that development important if further development is to be encouraged.

The intellectual property right gives the developer certain rights over the exploitation of the **10.05** work, discussed in more detail below. However it is important to distinguish exclusive intellectual property rights from a position of market power: unfortunately, intellectual property lawyers frequently refer to the former rights in the same terms as antitrust lawyers refer to the latter position—as a monopoly. The term is not being used in the same way.

The position is further confused when one considers that the profits resulting from the **10.06** exploitation of intellectual rights appear monopolistic compared to the costs of exploiting the work, even taking into account development costs. The relationship between legitimate exploitation of an intellectual property right, and abusive exploitation contrary to Article 82 is far from clear.

For example, once a new drug has been developed and tested, manufacturing the drug is a **10.07** relatively simple and low cost exercise. The researchers can only enjoy the reward for their successful work if they can prevent 'free riders' reproducing it at low cost. The profits earned by the manufacturer of a successful drug may seem high, even compared to the cost in time and resources of developing the drug. However, this is to examine the situation *ex post*. Given the high proportion of development projects that do not come to fruition, no development would take place were there not a right to recoup the development costs of both the failed and the successful drugs.

The literature on the economic benefits of providing this legal protection for intellectual **10.08** property is extensive, although the optimum level and form of intellectual property protection for the various types of intellectual property remains controversial.

---

[1] Commission Regulation (EC) 447/98 of 1 March 1998 on the notifications, time limits and hearings provided for in Council Regulation (EEC) 4064/89 on the control of concentrations between undertakings (text with EEA relevance) [1998] OJ L61/1, Art 8(9).

(3) The Relationship between Intellectual Property Protection and EC Law

10.09 Intellectual property rights interact with Community law mainly in the areas of free movement and competition law. The position is complicated by intellectual property law remaining primarily the responsibility of the Member States. Article 295 EC requires the Community to respect national systems of property ownership. Neither the single market rules nor Community competition law can be interpreted so as to negate nationally granted intellectual property rights.

(a) Intellectual Property Protection and the Free Movement Provisions

10.10 The (still largely) national granting of intellectual property rights sits uneasily with the single market objective of the European Community as most notably expressed in Article 28 EC. This single market conflict, largely played out before the ECJ, is relevant to the application of the competition rules in that the scope and extent of intellectual property rights under Community law have largely been defined by the ECJ in the context of these cases. The ECJ developed the conceptual distinction between the existence of an intellectual property right and its exercise: this necessitated an elaboration of the concept of the specific subject matter of the intellectual property right—that package of rights which together make up the intellectual property right itself. A separate means of addressing parts of this problem is through the harmonisation of certain aspects of intellectual property rights at the Community level.[2]

(b) Intellectual Property Protection and the Competition Rules

10.11 The second area where intellectual property rights and Community law interact relates to the application of the EC competition rules to the licensing of intellectual property rights, or the refusal to do so. An intellectual property right gives its holder the ability to impose conditions on licensors, who may be actual or potential competitors of the right holder. Competition law limits the restraints to which actual or potential competitors can be subject, and imposes further obligations where the licensor has a position of dominance on a relevant market. This latter point is complicated by the fact that it may be the IP right itself which leads to the dominant position on the market. Articles 81 and 82 are therefore both relevant to a determination of the permissible restrictions which can be imposed on licencees. The existence/exercise distinction referred to above is also relevant here, the competition rules limiting the latter, and not the former.

10.12 **(i) General Approach** The application of Article 81(1) to an intellectual property licence is therefore complicated by the need to determine whether the licence provisions are

---

[2] See, for example: Council Directive (EEC) 89/104 of 21 December 1988 to approximate the laws of the Member States relating to trademarks [1989] OJ L40/1; Council Directive (EEC) 92/100 of 19 November 1992 on rental right and lending right and on certain rights related to copyright in the field of intellectual property, [1992] OJ L346/61; Council Directive (EEC) 93/98 of 29 October 1993 harmonising the term of protection of copyright and certain related rights, [1993] OJ L290/9; Council Directive (EEC) 93/83 of 27 September 1993 on the coordination of certain rules concerning copyright and rights related to copyright applicable to satellite broadcasting and cable retransmission [1993] OJ L248/15; Directive 98/71/EC of the European Parliament and of the Council of 13 October 1998 on the legal protection of designs [1999] OJ L289/28; Council Regulation (EC) No 6/2002 of 12 December 2001 on Community designs [2002] OJ L3/1; and Directive 2001/29/EC on copyright and related rights in the information society [2001] OJ L167/10.

necessary to secure the specific subject matter of the intellectual property right. Use of an intellectual property right in a manner which ensures for the right holder the benefit of the specific subject matter of that right is regarded as preserving the existence of the right. Use of an intellectual property right in a manner which goes beyond the specific subject matter of the right is regarded as being an exercise of that right which must be analysed in light of the competition provisions of the Treaty. Therefore, only those provisions of a licence which go beyond the specific subject matter are potentially caught by Article 81(1).

The Commission has in the past taken the view that the permissible content of a licence has **10.13** varied depending on the form of intellectual property right covered by the licence. This has required the Commission to determine what is the preponderant element of a licence (is it, for example, mostly a patent licence, with ancillary trademark elements, or vice versa?), and then apply certain rules relevant to that intellectual property right.[3] This practice has been accused of artificiality given the complex package of rights often included in a single licence.

(ii) Block Exemptions This was also largely the approach taken in the earlier block **10.14** exemption regulations. However, the technology transfer block exemption, discussed in detail below, takes a slightly different line, encompassing both patent and know-how rights, together with other ancillary intellectual property rights within a single approach.

(4) Form of the Following Analysis

The sections of this chapter are as follows: **10.15**

Section B outlines the distinction in Community law between the existence of an intellectual property right and its exercise. It then outlines the various types of intellectual property right and their specific subject matter. It describes the common features of all types of intellectual property, and describes how the distinction between the existence of the intellectual property right (its specific subject matter) and its exercise is used to determine how competition law is applied to an intellectual property licence.

Section C analyses technology transfer and the block exemption.

Section D looks at trademark licences.

Section E looks at copyright.

Section F discusses the special considerations in applying Article 82 to the actions of owners of intellectual property.

B. Intellectual Property Rights and EC Law

(1) Introduction

Within the Community, the granting of intellectual property rights has historically fallen **10.16** within the competence of the Member States. More recently EC legislation has given rise

---

[3] See, for example, *Moosehead/Whitbread* [1990] OJ L100/32, at para 16 (only the English text is authentic).

to new or harmonised intellectual property rights throughout the EU, for example in relation to trademarks,[4] rental and lending rights,[5] the harmonisation of the term of protection of copyright,[6] satellite broadcasting and cable retransmission rights,[7] and the legal protection of databases.[8]

10.17   The relationship between EC law and Member State laws granting intellectual property rights has been most extensively explored in cases involving the free movement of goods. The EC Treaty provisions on the free movement of goods do not override national laws on intellectual property rights. First, Article 30 EC provides a specific exception from the free movement provisions where they conflict with national intellectual property rights.[9] Secondly, Article 295 EC[10] contains a general protection against the provisions of the Treaty undermining national systems of property ownership. The *Grundig Consten* case[11] established that Member State intellectual property rights were a form of property that enjoyed the protection of Article 295. This protection is limited, however. First, the Court is prepared to examine the extent of the rights granted at the national level to ensure that they do not conflict with the overall objectives of the Treaty. Secondly, the extent of Article 295 is unclear in that the use of the term 'system' of property ownership may imply that Article 295 is aimed more at the distinction between public and private ownership.

10.18   This section looks at the relationship between intellectual property rights and EC law under the following headings:

— Existence v Exercise and the Specific Subject Matter of an Intellectual Property Right;
— The Specific Subject Matter of Intellectual Property Rights;
— Exhaustion of Intellectual Property Rights;
— Exhaustion Concept in EC Intellectual Property Legislation.

---

   [4] Council Directive (EEC) 89/104 of 21 December 1988 to approximate the laws of the Member States relating to trademarks [1989] OJ L40/1.
   [5] Council Directive (EEC) 92/100 of 19 November 1992 on rental rights and lending rights and on certain rights related to copyright in the field of intellectual property [1992] OJ L346/61.
   [6] Council Directive (EEC) 93/98 of 29 October 1993 harmonising the term of protection of copyright and certain related rights, [1993] OJ L290/9.
   [7] Council Directive (EEC) 93/83 of 27 September 1993 on the coordination of certain rules concerning copyright and rights related to copyright applicable to satellite broadcasting and cable retransmission [1993] OJ L24 Directive (EEC) 96/9 of the European Parliament and of the Council of 11 March 1996 on the legal protection of databases [1996] OJ L77/20.
   [8] Directive (EEC) 96/9 of the European Parliament and of the Council of 11 March 1996 on the legal protection of databases [1996] OJ L77/20.
   [9] Art 30: 'The provisions of Articles 28–32 shall not preclude prohibitions or restrictions on imports, exports or goods in transit justified on grounds of public morality, public policy or public security; the protection of health and life of humans, animals or plants, the protection of national treasures possessing artistic, historic or archaeological value; *or the protection of industrial and commercial property.* Such prohibitions shall not, however, constitute a means of arbitrary discrimination or a disguised restriction on trade between Member States.' Emphasis added.
   [10] Art 295: 'This Treaty shall in no way prejudice the rules of Member States governing the system of property ownership.'
   [11] Joined Cases 56/64 and 58/64 *Consten and Grundig v Commission* [1966] ECR 299.

(2) Existence v Exercise and the Specific Subject Matter of an Intellectual Property Right

(a) Existence and Exercise

This distinction between existence and exercise of an intellectual property right was initially drawn in the *Grundig Consten* case.[12] The existence of an intellectual property right is protected by Articles 30 and 295; its exercise falls to be examined under the Treaty.

10.19

This distinction has been attacked as being artificial, giving the EC institutions an arbitrary ability to limit the scope of Member State law on intellectual property rights.[13] The converse, however, would appear equally arbitrary: were the existence of an intellectual property right to prevent any analysis of how that right were used in practice, then intellectual property rights would be effectively exempt from the free movement and competition law provisions of the Treaty.

10.20

(b) Specific Subject Matter

The distinction between the existence and exercise of an intellectual property right is based on the 'specific subject matter' of the intellectual property right. Use of an intellectual property right in a manner which ensures for the right holder the benefit of the specific subject matter of that right is regarded as preserving the existence of the right and cannot be overruled by the free movement or competition provisions of the Treaty. Use of an intellectual property right in a manner which goes beyond the specific subject matter of the right is regarded as being an exercise of that right which must be analysed in light of the free movement and/or competition provisions of the Treaty. Once the intellectual property owner has received the benefit of the specific subject matter of the intellectual property right, the right is said to be 'exhausted'.

10.21

(3) The Specific Subject Matter of Intellectual Property Rights

The above distinction between the existence and exercise of intellectual property rights, and the doctrine of exhaustion, makes the definition of the specific subject matter of the right fundamental to any appraisal under the competition rules.

10.22

(a) Patents

For the purposes of Community law, the specific subject matter of a patent has been defined as follows:

10.23

> the specific object of industrial property is inter alia to ensure to the holder, so as to recompense the creative effort of the inventor, the exclusive right to utilise an invention with a view to manufacture and first putting into circulation of industrial products either directly or by the grant of licences to third parties, as well as the right to oppose any infringement.[14]

(b) Know-how

The technology transfer block exemption defines know-how as a body of technical information that is secret, substantial and identified in any appropriate form.[15] Know-how is

10.24

---

[12] Joined Cases 56/64 and 58/64 *Consten and Grundig v Commission* [1966] ECR 299.
[13] For example, V Korah, *Technology Transfer Agreements and the EC Competition Rules* (1st edn, Oxford: Clarendon Press, 1996) 2.1.1.
[14] Case 15/74 *Centrafarm BV v Sterling Drug Inc* [1974] ECR 1147, at para 9.
[15] TTBER, at Art 1.

not a form of intellectual property right, but is closely analogous to patents. A firm which has certain knowledge or technology which is potentially patentable has a choice as to whether or not to seek patent protection. The firm may prefer not to disclose the information (required if a patent is sought), but instead to protect its investment in developing the technology by maintaining the confidentiality of the information. Such a decision would be appropriate, for example, where enforcement of the patent would be more difficult than maintaining the confidentiality.

10.25 Although such 'know-how' does not therefore enjoy a specific legal protection, owners of know-how can protect it through the general law on confidentiality. Conceptually, therefore, it may be appropriate to regard know-how as being protected not by virtue of it being an intellectual property right in itself, but by virtue of its being an aspect of the general law on confidentiality.

10.26 Presumably as a consequence of this, there is no clear definition of the specific subject matter of know-how in the case law of the Court.

10.27 One commentator suggests that in early Commission competition decisions, only the maintenance of confidentiality was regarded as being part of the specific subject matter of know-how, which led to know-how licences being treated more strictly than patent licences. This position changed over time, and the know-how Regulation accepted that the weaker legal protection afforded to know-how under the general law was a reason for more contractual protection not less.[16]

10.28 It is likely that the specific subject matter of know-how would now be regarded as essentially the same as that for patents. The common treatment of patents and know-how in the technology transfer block exemption suggests that this is at least the case for the purposes of the competition rules.

(c) Copyright

10.29 Copyright takes the form not of giving the author an exclusive right to the ideas in the work, as is the case with patents, but in giving the author rights over the specific expression of these ideas. The precise scope of the rights varies, however, and the specific subject matter of copyright cannot be stated with precision.

10.30 The specific subject matter of copyright comprises several different elements, reflecting the different ways in which a copyrighted work can be exploited. There is no single definition of the specific subject matter of copyright, but the following elements emerge from the case law:

— a right to decide on the first placing of a work on the market;[17]
— a right to require fees for public performance;[18] and
— a right to rent out a work.[19]

---

[16] V Korah, *Technology Transfer Agreements and the EC Competition Rules* (1st edn, Oxford: Clarendon Press, 1996) at 4.1.3.

[17] Joined Cases 55 and 57/80 *Musik-Vertried Membran GmbH v GEMA* [1981] ECR 147.

[18] Case 62/79 *SA Compagnie Générale pour la Diffusion de la Télévision, Coditel v SA Ciné Vog Films* [1980] ECR 881.

[19] Case 158/86 *Warner Brothers and Metronome Video ApS v Christiansen* [1988] ECR 2605.

A complicating factor is the variation between Member States as to what can be **10.31** copyrighted. One of the more controversial intellectual property cases, the *Magill* decision discussed below, related to TV listings—copyrightable in the UK and Ireland, but not in other Member States. One commentator has identified this as the reason for the Court's controversial judgment.[20]

(d) Trademarks

For the purposes of Community law, the specific subject matter of a trademark has been **10.32** defined as the right:

> inter alia to ensure to the holder the exclusive right to utilise the mark for the first putting into circulation of a product, and to protect him thus against competitors who would take advantage of the position and reputation of the mark by selling goods improperly bearing that mark.[21]

The EC has also issued a Directive harmonising national trademark protection[22] and estab- **10.33** lished a Community trademark system.[23]

(e) Plant Breeders' Rights

Plant breeders who develop a new strain of plant are entitled to a monopoly in production **10.34** and sale of seeds for this new variety of plant under a variety of Member State laws. In addition there is a separate Community-wide right established by EU law.[24]

There is no clear single definition of the specific subject matter of a plant breeder's rights, **10.35** but the Court has held that the constant need to care for and monitor seed means the right extends beyond mere marketing.[25]

(4) Exhaustion of Intellectual Property Rights

(a) Exhaustion Requires Consent

A holder (H) of intellectual property rights in Member State A cannot oppose the import **10.36** of a product protected by those intellectual property rights into that Member State, where that product was put on the market of Member State B by H or with H's consent.

(i) *Centrafarm v Sterling Drug*[26] This principle was set out in the context of pharmaceu- **10.37** ticals protected by patent and trademark law. Sterling Drug and its subsidiaries had registered the patent for a drug marketed as 'Negram' in several Member States including the UK and the Netherlands. The company had also registered the trademark in a number of Member States including the UK and the Netherlands. The UK National Health Service purchases the majority of the human pharmaceuticals used in the UK, and has the power

---

[20] W R Cornish, *Intellectual Property: patents, copyright, trademarks and allied rights* (3rd edn, London: Sweet & Maxwell, 1996).

[21] Case 16/74 *Centrafarm BV v Winthrop BV* [1974] ECR 1183.

[22] Council Directive (EC) 89/104 to approximate the laws of the Member States relating to trademarks [1989] OJ L40/1.

[23] Council Regulation (EC) 40/94 on the Community trademark [1994] OJ L11/1.

[24] Council Regulation (EC) 2100/94 of 27 July 1994 on Community plant variety rights [1994] OJ L227/1.

[25] *Breeders' rights—maize seed* [1978] OJ L286/23 at I.E(4) (only the German and French texts are authentic).

[26] Case 15/74 *Centrafarm BV v Sterling Drug* [1974] ECR 1147.

to obtain compulsory licences to pharmaceutical compounds. As a result it enjoys a position of considerable market power with respect to pharmaceutical companies operating in the UK. Perhaps as a result of this, Sterling Drug sold the Negram product in the UK for approximately half of the price that it obtained for the product in the Netherlands.

10.38 Centrafarm obtained supplies of Negram from UK wholesalers and resold these in the Netherlands, undercutting the prices in the Dutch market. Sterling Drug alleged that these sales were in breach of the Dutch patent and trademark held by Sterling Drug and its subsidiaries. However, the ECJ held that the specific subject matter of Sterling Drug's intellectual property protection was to obtain a financial reward by ensuring that Sterling Drug had an exclusive right to be the first to market a product protected by the intellectual property rights. Sterling Drug had obtained this benefit by selling the product in question on the UK market. Sterling Drug had received the benefit of the specific subject matter of its intellectual property rights in the products in question by selling them in the UK, and had therefore exhausted its rights in the products. Its attempt further to limit transactions in these goods by relying on its Dutch intellectual property rights contravened Article 30 of the Treaty.

10.39 (ii) **Consent does not have to be explicit**   Consent may be given implicitly or may be inferred from the behaviour of the IP owner,[27] however that behaviour must be unequivocal and cannot be implied by silence. Once marketing has occurred, however, further consent is not necessary, and any further restrictions on marketing within the EEA are a matter for contract between the parties.[28]

(b) *For a Sale to Exhaust Intellectual Property Rights it is not Necessary for that Sale to be Made in a Jurisdiction where it Enjoys Intellectual Property Right Protection*

10.40 A holder (H) of intellectual property rights in Member State A cannot oppose the import of a product protected by those intellectual property rights into that Member State, where that product was put on the market of Member State B by H or with H's consent, even where that product did not enjoy intellectual property protection in Member State B.

10.41 (i) *Merck v Stephar*[29]   A sale in a Member State where the good in question is not protected by intellectual property rights can exhaust protection of the goods in other Member States where it would otherwise be so protected. Italian law did not allow pharmaceutical products to be patented. Despite this, a pharmaceutical called Monuretic, which was protected by patents owned by the Merck group in other Member States, including the Netherlands, was being sold in Italy by a subsidiary of Merck. Stephar purchased Monuretic in Italy and imported it into the Netherlands. The Court held that Merck had exhausted its rights in the Monuretic product in question by selling it in Italy, and that it could not invoke its Dutch patents to prevent the import of goods which had been produced and sold by it in Italy.

---

[27] Joined Cases C-414/99 to C-416/99 *Zino Davidoff and Levi Strauss*.
[28] C-16/03, *Peak Holding AB v Axolin-Elinor AB, formerly Handelskompaniet Factory Outlet i Löddeköpinge AB*, judgment of 30 November 2004.
[29] Case 187/80 *Merck & Co Inc v Stephar BV* [1981] ECR 2063.

(c) Exhaustion Requires the Consent of the Right Holder even if the Goods were Lawfully Put on the Market in Another Member State without that Consent

A holder (H) of intellectual property rights in Member State A can oppose the import of a **10.42** product protected by those intellectual property rights into that Member State, where that product was put on the market of Member State B without H's consent, even if the placing of the product on the market of Member State B was itself lawful (for example, because there was no intellectual property protection of the product in Member State B).

(i) EMI/Patricia[30]

EMI UK and its German subsidiary owned the UK and German **10.43** copyrights to certain recordings. A German company, Patricia, produced copies of these recordings in Germany without the consent of EMI. These were exported to Denmark and sold there. The Danish copyright on the recordings had expired so Danish law could not be used to prevent this sale. Some of the recordings were reimported into Germany. The Court held that EMI could invoke its German copyright to prevent the sale of these imported recordings despite the fact that they had first been sold on a market where EMI did not benefit from copyright, as EMI had not consented to this first sale.

(ii) Keurkoop/Nancy Kean Gifts[31]

Nancy Kean imported handbags of a particular design **10.44** from Taiwan. As the first importer of goods of this design it was able to register the design in the Netherlands, despite not having been the original designer. Keurkoop imported handbags of the same design from Taiwan and sold them in the Netherlands. Some of the bags imported by Keurkoop were first imported from Taiwan into Germany and then re-exported to the Netherlands. Nancy Kean did not own design rights to the handbags in Germany, and could not own such rights as the German law only allowed the original designer of a product to register the design. Keurkoop argued that as the initial sale in Germany did not infringe any intellectual property rights, Nancy Kean could not invoke its rights under Dutch law to prevent the import of the bags to the Netherlands. The Court ruled that since Nancy Kean had not consented to the sale in Germany of the handbags, its intellectual property rights were not exhausted, despite the fact that the sale in Germany was legal.

(d) Exhaustion Depends on the Specific Subject Matter of the Right in Question

A holder (H) of intellectual property rights in Member State A can oppose the import of **10.45** a product protected by those intellectual property rights into that Member State, even if that product was put on the market of Member State B by H or with H's consent, provided that the putting on the market did not exhaust the specific subject matter of the right in question.

Exhaustion in any particular case can, by definition, only be analysed in light of the specific **10.46** subject matter of the intellectual property right. This is most clearly apparent in the area of copyright, where sale, public performance, and rental have all been identified as distinct elements of the subject matter of the right.

---

[30] Case 341/87 *EMI/Patricia* [1989] ECR 79.
[31] Case 144/81 *Keurkoop BV v Nancy Kean Gifts BV* [1982] ECR 2853.

10.47   *Warner v Christiansen*[32]   In *Warner v Christiansen* the Court of Justice recognised that the specific subject matter of copyright extended not only to the right to sell copies for home use, but also to the right to rent copies of the film. A sale for home use did not therefore exhaust the right to obtain revenue by renting the copy to several users.

10.48   Warner owned the copyright to certain films in both the UK and Denmark. UK law gave Warner the exclusive right to make the first sale of a video cassette recording, but once the sale had been made they could not prevent the recording from being rented out. The Danish law recognised a rental right, ie it had recognised that there was a market for short term rentals of video cassette recordings as well as one for the purchase of copies for personal use. In Denmark, Warner could sell a recording for home use and prohibit the purchaser from renting it out. Alternatively it could sell copies at a higher price to firms that wished to rent out the recording to third parties. Christiansen, a Danish operator of a video rental business, purchased video cassettes in the UK and imported them into Denmark where they rented them out. The Court held that the rental right created by the Danish law was a separate right, which was not exhausted by the purchase of a copy of the video cassette in the UK for home use.

10.49   The Court later clarified the nature of the rental right further: 'it is not contrary to Articles 30 and 36 [now Articles 28 and 30] of the Treaty . . . for the holder of an exclusive rental right to prohibit copies of a film from being offered for rental in a Member State even where the offering of those copies for rental has been authorised in the territory of another Member State'.[33]

(e) Exhaustion for the Purposes of EC Law Requires Use in the EEA

10.50   A holder (H) of intellectual property rights in Member State A can oppose the import of a product protected by those intellectual property rights into that Member State, where that product was put on the market outside the EEA, even if the placing of the product on the market outside the EEA was done by H or with H's consent.

10.51   A sale outside the EEA does not exhaust intellectual property rights for the purposes of Community law. In *EMI v CBS*,[34] the Court found that even if an owner of intellectual property rights in a Member State of the EC had consented to the sale outside the EC of goods covered by these rights they could invoke their rights to prevent the import of these goods into the EC.

10.52   As a result of agreements and transactions pre-dating the formation of the EC the 'Columbia' trademark was owned by EMI and it subsidiaries in the EC, and by CBS in the United States. CBS had a UK subsidiary which imported goods bearing the Columbia

---

[32] Case 158/86 *Warner Bros and Metronome v Christiansen* [1988] ECR 2605.

[33] Case C-61/97, *Foreningen af Dansk Videogramdistributører, acting for Egmont Film A/S, Buena Vista Home Entertainment A/S, Scanbox Danmark A/S*, judgment delivered on 22 September 1988, not yet reported. See also, in relation to the right of public performance, Case 395/87 *Ministère Public v Tournier* [1989] ECR 2521.

[34] Joined Cases 51, 86 & 96/75 *EMI Records Ltd v CBS United Kingdom Ltd, CBS Grammofon A/S and CBS Schallplatten GmbH* [1976] ECR 811, 871 & 913.

trademark from the United States and placed them on the market in several Member States. Despite the fact that these goods had been legitimately produced and sold in the US by CBS, and that CBS's ownership of the trademark in the United States was as the result of an agreement between EMI and CBS, EMI could invoke its trademark rights in the Member States of the EC to prevent the import of these goods from the United States.

In the more recent *Silhouette* case,[35] the Court's interpretation of the 1988 Trademark **10.53** Directive maintained this position. Hartlauer is an Austrian discount retailer of spectacles. Silhouette is an Austrian producer of high-quality and high-price spectacles, which it sells throughout the EEA under its own registered trademark. Silhouette had in the past refused to supply Hartlauer with its spectacles on the grounds that to do so would damage Silhouette's brand image. In 1995 it had sold a single consignment of old model Silhouette spectacles in Bulgaria at a price considerably lower than that which its spectacles would command in the EC market. Hartlauer had bought these in Bulgaria and had reimported them into Austria. Silhouette sought to use its trademark rights to prevent the sale of these goods.

Hartlauer argued in the Austrian courts that Silhouette's trademark rights should be con- **10.54** sidered as exhausted by Silhouette's sale of the goods, even outside the EC, in line with the Austrian legislation. In answer to a question put to it by the Austrian courts the ECJ stated that the Trademark Directive[36] provides that the protection of a trademark is only exhausted by a sale of a good bearing the trademark inside the EEA, and that national law could not go beyond this to deem the protection exhausted by a sale outside the EEA.

(f) Exhaustion and Licensing under the Competition Rules

Although the majority of cases have been examined under the free movement provisions of **10.55** the Treaty, the same principles apply to the relationship between intellectual property rights and the competition rules. For example in *EMI v CBS*, the court held that 'a trademark right as a legal entity does not possess those elements of contract or concerted practice referred to in Article 81(1). Nevertheless, the exercise of that right might fall within the ambit of the prohibitions contained in the Treaty.'[37]

Once the specific subject matter of an intellectual property right has been secured, any further **10.56** use of the rights conferred by the intellectual property law is subject to scrutiny under the EC competition rules.

(5) Exhaustion Concept in EC Intellectual Property Legislation

The concept of exhaustion of intellectual property right protection throughout the EEA **10.57** after a sale anywhere in the EEA has been explicitly provided for in the EC legislation

---

[35] Case C-355/96 *Silhouette International v Hartlauer* [1998], judgment delivered on 16 July 1998, not yet reported.
[36] Council Directive (EEC) 89/104 of 21 December 1988 to approximate the laws of the Member States relating to trademarks [1989] OJ L40/1.
[37] Cases 51, 86 & 96/75 *EMI Records Ltd v CBS United Kingdom Ltd, CBS Grammofon A/S and CBS Schallplatten GmbH* [1976] ECR 811, at paras 26 and 27.

on trademarks.[38] Similar provisions on exhaustion exist in other EC legislation conferring or harmonising intellectual property rights. For examples, see Article 1(4)(c) of the software Directive,[39] or Article 9(2) of the copyright and related rights Directive.[40]

C. Technology Transfer Agreements

(1) Introduction

10.58   Intellectual property laws confer exclusive rights on holders of patents, copyright, design rights, trademarks, and other legally protected rights. The owner of intellectual property is entitled under intellectual property laws to prevent unauthorised use of his intellectual property and to exploit it, *inter alia*, by licensing it to third parties. Indeed, as previously explained these rights constitute the core of the specific subject matter of intellectual property. Moreover, licensing of technology is a common feature of an open market economy. It is therefore of considerable importance for market participants to be aware of the interface between intellectual property law and competition law. While the distinction between existence and exercise and the concept of specific subject matter provide some degree of conceptual guidance, they are often of limited use in the assessment of individual cases. It is often more useful, at least in addition, to consider the economic role played by each type of intellectual property and the benefits stemming from licensing.

10.59   It is very important to keep in mind that the fact that intellectual property laws grant exclusive rights to owners of intellectual property does not imply that there is an inherent conflict between intellectual property rights and the Community competition rules. Indeed, as stated in the Commission's Guidelines on the application of Article 81 to technology transfer agreements[41] (the Guidelines) both bodies of law share the same basic objective of promoting consumer welfare and an efficient allocation of resources. Innovation constitutes an essential and dynamic component of an open and competitive market economy. Intellectual property rights promote dynamic competition by encouraging undertakings to invest in developing new or improved products and processes. So does competition by putting pressure on undertakings to innovate. Therefore, both intellectual property rights and competition are necessary to promote innovation and ensure a competitive exploitation thereof. It is submitted that an analytical approach based on the economics of intellectual property and licensing is more fruitful than an approach based on legal concepts such as existence and exercise. Such legal concepts have been useful in terms of allowing the Community Courts to strike the necessary balance between the requirements of Article 295 EC and the free movement and competition rules. However, in the field of competition law, where legal rules should be based on sound economic principles, it is necessary to have due regard to likely economic effects in devising the applicable rules.

---

[38] Council Directive (EEC) 89/104 of 21 December 1988 to approximate the laws of the Member States relating to trademarks [1989] OJ L40/1, at Art 7.

[39] Council Directive (EC) 91/250 on the legal protection of computer programs [1991] OJ L122/42.

[40] Council Directive (EEC) 93/98 of 29 October 1993 harmonising the term of protection of copyright and certain related rights [1993] OJ L290/9.

[41] [2004] OJ C101/2, para 7.

Technology transfer agreements are subject to a Commission Block Exemption Regulation[42] **10.60** (the TTBER) and the Guidelines and the present section focuses on these texts. There is little (recent) case law and Commission practice in the field of technology licensing. The TTBER and the Guidelines therefore constitute the most recent and most comprehensive source of guidance in this area. The TTBER creates a safe harbour for certain categories of technology transfer agreements whereas the Guidelines provide guidance on the application of the TTBER as well as on the application of Article 81 outside the scope of the block exemption. This is an important aspect given the need for undertakings to engage in self-assessment of the compatibility of their agreements with the Community competition rules.[43]

(2) The Basic Framework and Underlying Philosophy of the TTBER and the Guidelines

The TTBER is composed of three main elements. First, the TTBER creates a safe harbour **10.61** for technology transfer agreements concluded by two undertakings, covering all restraints that are not expressly excluded from its scope of application. In other words, if a restraint is not expressly excluded from the scope of the block exemption, it is exempted. The safe harbour is circumscribed by market share thresholds of 20 per cent in the case of agreements between competitors and 30 per cent in the case of agreements between noncompetitors. In limiting the scope of the safe harbour by market share thresholds the TTBER follows the approach of the block exemption regulations in the fields of vertical restraints and horizontal co-operation agreements.[44] Secondly, the TTBER contains a list of hardcore restrictions. There are separate lists for agreements between competitors and agreements between non-competitors. Agreements containing hardcore restrictions fall outside the scope of the block exemption in their entirety. Thirdly, the TTBER contains a limited list of excluded restrictions that are not block exempted. Such restrictions are subject to individual assessment. However, their inclusion in the agreement does not exclude the application of the block exemption to the rest of the agreement.

Agreements that fall outside the scope of the safe harbour are subject to individual assess- **10.62** ment. As repeatedly stated in the Guidelines[45] there is no presumption that technology transfer agreements falling outside the block exemption are caught by Article 81(1) or fail to satisfy the conditions of Article 81(3). In particular, the mere fact that the market shares of the parties exceed the market share thresholds set out in the TTBER is not a sufficient basis for finding that the agreement is caught by Article 81(1). Individual assessment of the likely effects of the agreement is required. It is only when agreements contain hardcore

---

[42] Commission Regulation (EC) No 772/2004 on the application of Art 81(3) of the Treaty to categories of technology transfer agreements [2004] OJ L123/11.

[43] See Chapter 2, paras 2.12–2.27.

[44] See Commission Regulation (EC) No 2790/1999 on the application of Art 81(3) of the Treaty to categories of vertical agreements and concerted practices [1999] OJ L336/21, Commission Regulation (EC) No 2658/2000 on the application of Art 81(3) of the Treaty to categories of specialisation agreements [2000] OJ L304/3 and Commission Regulation (EC) No 2659/2000 on the application of Art 81(3) of the Treaty to research and development agreements [2000] OJ L304/7.

[45] See paras 37, 65 and 130.

restrictions of competition that it can normally be presumed that they are prohibited by Article 81.[46]

10.63 The overall philosophy expressed in the Guidelines is that most licence agreements do not restrict competition and create pro-competitive efficiencies.[47] Licensing leads to dissemination of technology and promotes innovation. By stating that the great majority of licence agreements are compatible with Article 81[48] the Guidelines adopt a positive attitude towards technology transfer agreements. This positive attitude is reflected in a number of places in the TTBER and the Guidelines. For instance, Article 4(2)(b) block exempts restrictions on active and passive sales into exclusive territories and customer groups reserved for the other party and active sales restrictions between licensees irrespective of whether they have been granted an exclusive territory or customer group. This is quite far-reaching when compared to the treatment of, in particular, passive sales restrictions in the context of vertical distribution agreements.[49] In the TTBER the Commission has made a deliberate choice to treat more favourably certain restrictions with a view to promoting licensing and dynamic competition even where it might result in a short run loss of static competition. *Ex ante* factors are taken duly into account. Indeed, the Commission expressly recognises[50] that the creation and exploitation of intellectual property rights often entails substantial investment and that it is often a risky endeavour. In view thereof the Guidelines provide[51] that:

> in order not to reduce dynamic competition and to maintain the incentive to innovate, the innovator must not be unduly restricted in the exploitation of intellectual property rights that turn out to be valuable. For these reasons the innovator should normally be free to seek compensation for successful projects that is sufficient to maintain investment incentives, taking failed projects into account. Technology licensing may also require the licensee to make significant sunk investments in the licensed technology and production assets necessary to exploit it. Article 81 cannot be applied without considering such *ex ante* investments made by the parties and the risks relating thereto. The risk facing the parties and the sunk investment that must be committed may thus lead to the agreement falling outside Article 81(1) or fulfilling the conditions of Article 81(3), as the case may be, for the period of time required to recoup the investment.

10.64 Certain restraints may be necessary in order to induce the licensor to license his technology and the licensee to take a licence. For instance, as regards field of use restrictions the Guidelines provide[52] that if the licensor could not prevent licensees from operating in fields where he exploits the technology himself or in fields where the value of the technology is not yet well established, it would be likely to create a disincentive for the licensor to license

---

[46] It should also be noted that the fact that an agreement is covered by the block exemption does not give rise to any presumption that it is caught by Art 81(1) in the first place. Block exemption merely signifies that if the agreement is caught by Art 81(1), it is block exempted.
[47] See para 9.
[48] See paras 9 and 17.
[49] See Art 4(b) of Regulation 2790/1999.
[50] See Guidelines para 8.
[51] ibid.
[52] See para 182.

or would lead him to charge a higher royalty. Similarly, as regards output restrictions the Guidelines provide[53] that in the application of Article 81(3) it must be taken into account that such restrictions may be necessary in order to induce the licensor to disseminate his technology as widely as possible and that a licensor may, for instance, be reluctant to license his competitors if he could not limit the licence to a particular production site with a specific capacity.

The fact that the licensee may need to commit significant and risky investments is *inter alia* **10.65** reflected in the treatment of passive sales restrictions between licensees in agreements between non-competitors. The Guidelines state[54] that:

> licensees often have to commit substantial investments in production assets and promotional activities in order to start up and develop a new territory. The risks facing the new licensee are therefore likely to be substantial, in particular since promotional expenses and investment in assets required to produce on the basis of a particular technology are often sunk, ie they cannot be recovered if the licensee exits the market. In such circumstances, it is often the case that licensees would not enter into the licence agreement without protection for a certain period of time against (active and) passive sales into their territory by other licensees. Restrictions on passive sales into the exclusive territory of a licensee by other licensees therefore often fall outside Article 81(1) for a period of up to two years from the date on which the product incorporating the licensed technology was first put on the market in the exclusive territory by the licensee in question.

In arriving at this conclusion the Commission applies the test set out in paragraph 12(b) of the Guidelines. Paragraph 12 of the Guidelines contains two counterfactual tests providing a framework for assessing the impact of agreements on inter-technology competition and intra-technology competition respectively. These tests are in substantive terms the same as those contained in paragraph 18 of the Guidelines on the application of Article 81(3).[55]

(3) The Scope of the TTBER and the Guidelines

The TTBER applies to technology transfer agreements entered into between two under- **10.66** takings.[56] Under Council Regulation 19/65[57] the Commission is only empowered to block exempt 'categories of agreements to which only two undertakings are party and which include restrictions imposed in relation to the acquisition or use of industrial property rights'. However, the Guidelines acknowledge[58] that licence agreements concluded between more than two undertakings often give rise to the same issues. The Commission therefore undertakes to apply by analogy the principles of the TTBER to such agreements provided that they are of the same nature as those covered by the block exemption.

---

[53] See para 175.
[54] See para 101.
[55] These tests are dealt with in Chapter 3, paras 3.295 to 3.303 above.
[56] See Art 2(1).
[57] Council Regulation No 19/65 7EEC on the application of Art 81(3) of the Treaty to certain categories of agreements and concerted practices [1965] OJ P36/533 as amended by Council Regulation (EC) No 1215/1999 [1999] OJ L148/1.
[58] See para 40.

(a) Agreements for the Production of Contract Products

10.67 It is a condition for the application of the TTBER that the agreement must concern 'the production of contract products'.[59] The agreement must identify a contract product to which the licensed technology relates. Contract products are goods and services produced with the licensed technology. This condition is satisfied where the technology is used in a production process or where the technology is incorporated into the product itself. There is no contract product for the purposes of the TTBER where the licence is granted in order to allow the licensee to license on the technology to third parties. Agreements authorising sublicensing are not covered by the TTBER except where the primary object of the agreement is not sublicensing.[60] However, the Commission undertakes to apply by analogy the principles of the TTBER and the Guidelines to agreements that have as their main purpose to allow the licensee to sublicense.[61] Agreements establishing technology pools are also not covered by the TTBER, but are dealt with in a separate section of the Guidelines.[62]

10.68 It is not a condition that the transferred technology must be ready for commercial exploitation. The TTBER and the Guidelines also apply where the licensee must carry out development work before obtaining a product or a process that is ready for commercial exploitation.[63] However, the TTBER and the Guidelines do not apply where the technology is licensed for the purpose of enabling the licensee to carry out further research and development in various fields.[64] The framework of the TTBER and the Guidelines is based on the premise that there is a direct link between the licensed technology and an identified contract product. The greater the R&D content of the agreement the more likely it is that the framework of the Guidelines would be unduly restrictive, *inter alia*, taking insufficiently into account the additional risk facing the licensee and the uncertainty as to the commercial success of the arrangement. Certain issues may also be particular to such arrangements. For instance, it is likely that royalty payments have to be linked to the results of future R&D work and thus take the form of reach through royalties, ie royalties on the revenues generated by such future developments. The Guidelines should not be interpreted as creating obstacles to such particular arrangements.

10.69 The TTBER also covers subcontracting. Subcontracting occurs when the licensor licenses technology to the licensee who undertakes to produce certain products on the basis thereof exclusively for the licensor. Subcontracting may also involve the supply of equipment by the licensor to be used in the production of the goods and services covered by the agreement. However, in this case the TTBER only applies if the licensed technology and not the supplied equipment constitutes the primary object of the agreement. It is also important to note that subcontracting is covered by the Commission's Notice concerning the assessment

---

[59] See Art 2(1).
[60] Licence agreements concluded between the sub-licensor or a technology pool and third parties are covered by the TTBER.
[61] See Guidelines para 42.
[62] See section IV.4.
[63] See Guidelines para 45.
[64] ibid.

of certain subcontracting agreements in relation to Article 81(1) of the Treaty.[65] According to this Notice, which remains applicable, subcontracting agreements whereby the subcontractor undertakes to produce certain products exclusively for the contractor generally fall outside Article 81(1). However, other restrictions imposed on the subcontractor such as the obligation not to conduct or exploit his own research and development may be caught by Article 81.[66]

(b) Technology Transfer Agreements

The application of the TTBER and the Guidelines do not require that there is an 'active' flow of technology from the licensor to the licensee. For a transfer of technology to occur it is sufficient that the licensor undertakes not to exercise his intellectual property rights against the licensee.[67] The essence of a pure patent licence is the right to operate inside the scope of the exclusive right of the patent. It follows that the TTBER also covers so-called non-assertion agreements and settlement agreements whereby the licensor permits the licensee to produce within the scope of the patent. **10.70**

The TTBER does not cover all intellectual property rights. Due to the limitations imposed by Regulation 19/65 only 'industrial property rights' are covered. The Council Regulation mentions as examples patents, utility models, designs, trademarks and know-how and the TTBER covers such property rights except trademarks which do not constitute technology for the purposes of the TTBER. In addition to the industrial property rights specifically mentioned in the Council Regulation the TTBER covers plant breeders' rights, topographies of semiconductor products, supplementary protection certificates for medicinal products or other products for which such supplementary protection certificates may be obtained, and software copyright. Other types of copyright are not covered. Software copyright is thus considered to constitute industrial property whereas that is not the case with other types of copyright. **10.71**

The Guidelines provide that as a general rule the Commission will apply the principles set out in the TTBER and the Guidelines when assessing the licensing of copyright for the purpose of reproduction and distribution of the protected work, ie the production of copies for resale. Such agreements are considered to be of a similar nature as technology transfer agreements and to raise comparable issues. The TTBER and the Guidelines on the other hand do not apply to the licensing of rights in performances and other rights related to copyright. In the case of performance rights value is created not by the reproduction and sale of copies of a product but by each individual performance of the protected work. The licensing of such rights raises particular issues that may warrant distinct analysis.[68] **10.72**

The Guidelines also do not apply to trademark licensing. It could be argued that it would have been useful to apply the framework of the Guidelines to at least certain types of trademark licensing, in particular merchandising. The Guidelines cover copyright licensing for **10.73**

---

[65] See OJ 1979 C 1, p 2.
[66] See para 3 of the subcontracting notice.
[67] See Guidelines para 43.
[68] See Guidelines para 52.

the purpose of reproduction and sale of a product. An agreement authorising a licensee to produce for instance T-shirts with a copyright protected picture of say a Coca-Cola bottle is thus covered. On the other hand the Guidelines do not cover an agreement to produce T-shirts with the Coca-Cola trademark in spite of the fact that the two transactions are equivalent. Given these similarities one would expect that in practice the Commission will treat such transactions in a similar way.

10.74 The only exception to the exclusion of trademarks and certain types of copyright is the rule in Article 1(1)(b) of the TTBER according to which such intellectual property rights are covered by the block exemption when they are directly related to the exploitation of the licensed technology and do not constitute the primary object of the agreement. This condition ensures that an agreement covering for instance a trademark is only block exempted to the extent that this trademark serves to enable the licensee better to exploit the licensed technology.[69]

10.75 Similarly, agreements containing provisions relating to the purchase and sale of products are only covered by the TTBER to the extent that those provisions do not constitute the primary object of the agreement and are directly related to the application of the licensed technology. According to the Guidelines this is likely to be the case where the tied products take the form of equipment or process input which is specifically tailored to exploit efficiently the licensed technology.[70] If, on the other hand, the product is simply another input into the final product, it must be carefully examined whether the licensed technology constitutes the primary object of the agreement. For instance, in cases where the licensee is already manufacturing a final product on the basis of another technology, the licence must lead to a significant improvement of the licensee's production process, exceeding the value of the product purchased from the licensor. The requirement that the tied products must be related to the licensing of technology implies that the TTBER does not cover the purchase of products that have no relation with the products incorporating the licensed technology.

(c) The Interface between the TTBER and other Block Exemptions

10.76 The main interface to be established is that between the TTBER and Regulation 2790/1999 on vertical restraints.[71] These two Regulations are in an upstream/downstream relationship given that the licensee is a supplier of goods and services on the market. The agreement between licensor and licensee is subject to the TTBER whereas agreements concluded between a licensee and its buyers are subject to Regulation 2790/1999 and the Guidelines on Vertical Restraints.[72] Technology transfer agreements may contain

---

[69] In Commission Decision in *Moosehead/Whitbread* [1990] OJ L100/32 this condition was found not to be satisfied. The value of the licensed technology to the licensee was limited because he already employed an identical or very similar technology. The trademark was therefore considered to constitute the main object of the agreement.

[70] See para 49.

[71] Commission Regulation (EC) No 2790/1999 on the application of Art 81(3) of the Treaty to categories of vertical agreements and concerted practices [1999] OJ L336/21.

[72] [2000] OJ C291/1.

obligations as to the way in which the licensee must sell the contract products. Such obligations are covered by the TTBER. However, the distribution agreements concluded for the purposes of implementing such obligations must, in order to be block exempted, comply with Regulation 2790/1999.[73]

For the purposes of Regulation 2790/1999 each licensee is considered a separate supplier. **10.77** Distributors appointed by one licensee must in principle be free to sell both actively and passively into territories covered by the distribution systems of other licensees. However, the Guidelines[74] explain that when the products incorporating the licensed technology carry a common brand identity, there may be the same efficiency reasons for applying the same types of restraints between licensees' distribution systems as within a single vertical distribution system. In such cases the Commission is unlikely to challenge restraints where by analogy the requirements of Regulation 2790/1999 are fulfilled. For a common brand identity to exist the Guidelines require that the products are sold and marketed under a common brand, which is predominant in terms of conveying quality and other relevant information to the consumer. It is not sufficient that in addition to the licensees' brands the product carries the licensor's brand, which identifies him as the source of the licensed technology. It is submitted that for instance the 'Intel inside' logo which is affixed to computers containing an Intel processor does not convey a common brand identity for the purposes of the Guidelines.

Regulation 2658/2000 on certain specialisation agreements[75] covers *inter alia* agreements **10.78** whereby undertakings establish a production joint venture and license technology to the joint venture to produce goods or services. Such agreements are not covered by the TTBER. However, where the joint venture engages in licensing of the technology to third parties, the activity is not linked to production by the joint venture and therefore not covered by Regulation 2658/2000. Such licensing arrangements, which license the technologies of the joint venture to third parties, are covered by the TTBER and the Guidelines.

Regulation 2659/2000[76] covers licensing between the parties and by the parties to a joint **10.79** entity in the context of a research and development agreement. In the context of such agreements the parties can also determine the conditions for licensing the fruits of the research and development agreement to third parties. However, since third party licensees are not party to the research and development agreement, the individual licence agreement concluded with third parties is not covered by Regulation 2659/2000. Such licence agreements are subject to the TTBER.

(4) Competitors versus Non-competitors

An important element of the economic approach of the TTBER and Guidelines is the differ- **10.80** ent treatment of licensing between competitors versus licensing between non-competitors.

---

[73] See recital 19 of the TTBER.
[74] See para 64.
[75] Commission Regulation (EC) No 2658/2000 on the application of Art 81(3) of the Treaty to categories of specialisation agreements [2000] OJ L304/3.
[76] Commission Regulation (EC) No 2659/2000 on the application of Art 81(3) of the Treaty to research and development agreements [2000] OJ L304/7.

Agreements between competitors pose in general a greater risk to competition than agreements between non-competitors.[77] This general conclusion has led to substantial differences in terms of the market share thresholds, the hardcore list and also the assessment outside the safe harbour of the block exemption.

10.81　The fact that agreements between competitors may pose greater risks to competition does not imply that licensing between non-competitors is without competition risks. Such licensing may have a negative effect on both inter-technology and intra-technology competition. As to the latter, the Guidelines point out that intra-technology competition is an important complement to inter-technology competition. Competition between licensees using the same technology is worth protecting because such competition may lead to lower prices, better quality and improved product differentiation of the products incorporating the licensed technology.[78]

10.82　To test the competitive relationship between the parties the TTBER and Guidelines start with the question 'whether the parties would have been actual or potential competitors in the absence of the agreement. If without the agreement the parties would not have been actual or potential competitors in any relevant market affected by the agreement they are deemed to be non-competitors.'[79] In other words, it is the situation but for the agreement that is relevant to judge whether the parties are competitors. Becoming a competitor as a result of the licence is not relevant for this assessment.

10.83　The TTBER contains a number of modifications to this general distinction between competitors and non-competitors. These modifications limit the situations in which parties are treated as competitors. The first modification concerns the markets on which the parties may compete. The TTBER in Article 1(1)(j) limits the definition of competing undertakings to undertakings which compete on the relevant technology and/or the relevant product market. So-called innovation markets are not taken into account under the TTBER. In the Guidelines[80] it is explained that, also outside the safe harbour of the TTBER, the Commission will normally confine itself to examining the impact on product and/or technology markets.

10.84　The second modification concerns potential competition on the technology market. For the application of the TTBER potential competition on the technology market is not taken into account. If the licensee owns a competing technology that he would be likely to license out in case of a small but permanent increase in royalties, such potential competition on the technology market is only taken into account outside the safe harbour. For the application of the market share threshold and the hardcore list licensee and licensor will be considered non-competitors, provided of course that they are in addition neither actual nor potential competitors on the product market.[81] The Commission apparently considered the assessment

[77] See Guidelines para 26. See also for instance paras 100 and 101 of the Guidelines on Vertical Restraints.
[78] See Guidelines para 26.
[79] See Guidelines para 27.
[80] See para 25.
[81] See Guidelines paras 30 and 66.

of potential competition on the technology market too difficult or uncertain for a proper application of the TTBER. The TTBER is already quite complex due to the need to cover agreements between competitors and non-competitors operating on both technology and product markets.

Undertakings are considered actual competitors on the technology market if, but for the **10.85** agreement, both licensor and licensee license out competing technologies. Licensor and licensee are also considered actual competitors on the technology market if the licensee was already licensing out a competing technology and the licensor enters the technology market by granting a licence for a competing technology to the licensee.[82] The second situation deviates from the general principle according to which the competitive relationship is assessed 'in the absence of the licence agreement'. In this way, while in general not taking potential competition on the technology market into account for the application of the TTBER, the Commission does take into account the situation of (potential) competition on the technology market where the licensee is already licensing out its own technology and the licensor enters the technology market by licensing to the licensee. In this particular situation the assessment is not too difficult or uncertain for a proper application of the TTBER.

As far as the product market, ie the relevant market for goods or services, is concerned, the **10.86** application of the TTBER requires assessment of whether the parties would have been actual or potential competitors absent agreement, see Article 1 (1)(j)(ii). The parties are actual competitors when they both sell on the same relevant product market. A company is considered a potential competitor on the product market if in the absence of agreement it is likely that it would have undertaken the necessary additional investment to enter the relevant market in response to a small but permanent increase in product prices. In order to constitute a realistic competitive constraint and be assessed as potential competition, such entry should be 'timely', ie has to be likely to occur within a relatively short period. According to the Guidelines a period of one to two years is normally considered appropriate. However, in individual cases longer periods can be taken into account if, for instance, capacity adjustments in the industry in general take longer also for incumbent companies.[83]

The third modification to the general distinction between competitors and non-competitors **10.87** concerns infringement of the licensor's or licensee's intellectual property rights. Undertakings are not considered actual or potential competitors if, in the absence of the licence agreement, their activity on the relevant product and/or technology market would infringe the intellectual property rights of the other party. Both in case of a one-way blocking position—ie where the intellectual property rights of only one of the parties would be infringed—and in case of a two-way blocking position—where the intellectual property rights of both parties would be infringed—the parties are considered to be non-competitors.[84] In assessing

---

[82] See Art 1(1)(j)(i) of the TTBER and para 28 of the Guidelines.
[83] See Guidelines paras 28 and 29.
[84] See TTBER Art 1(1)(j).

whether a blocking position exists the Guidelines provide that the Commission will rely on objective factors such as court decisions and opinions of independent experts. Expert evidence from the parties may also be taken into account. The parties have an incentive to claim that a blocking position exists so as to avoid being identified as competitors. The Commission is therefore likely to treat information coming from the parties with some scepticism. The Commission will want to exclude in particular sham licensing of competing technologies between competitors on the product market.[85]

10.88 The fourth modification concerns drastic innovations and their effect on the competitive relationship between licensor and licensee. A drastic innovation by the licensor may have as a result that while the licensor and licensee were competitors on the product market before the innovation, they have become non-competitors since. For this to happen, the new technology should represent such a drastic innovation that the licensee's technology has become obsolete or uncompetitive. The licensor's innovation has created a new market or has excluded the licensee's technology from the market. In case the drastic nature of the innovation only becomes apparent sometime after the licence agreement has been concluded, it is only from that time onward that the parties can be considered non-competitors. Article 81 must be applied in the light of the actual context in which the agreement is operated and the assessment is therefore sensitive to material changes in the facts. The classification of the relationship between the parties may therefore change over time into a relationship between non-competitors.[86]

10.89 The fifth and last modification is not concerned with competitors becoming non-competitors as described in the previous paragraph, but with non-competitors becoming competitors. This is the situation where licensor and licensee are non-competitors at the time of concluding the licence agreement but become competitors afterwards for reasons other than the licence itself, for instance because the licensee develops its own competing technology which it starts to exploit or because the licensor, who was not active on the product market before concluding the licence agreement, enters the product market at a later point in time. The Commission could have chosen to apply here too the general policy explained in the previous paragraph, ie that Article 81 has to be applied in the actual context in which the agreement occurs. However the Commission decided to deviate from this policy in the case of non-competitors becoming competitors. It seems that the Commission considers that agreements which at the material time were negotiated by non-competitors are less suspect and that as a consequence it would have been disproportionate at a later point in time to subject the commercial arrangement to the full force of a stricter hardcore list. For such agreement the hardcore list for non-competitors remains the applicable hardcore list, unless the agreement is subsequently amended in any material respect, see Article 4(3) of the TTBER. In other words, whereas the lower market share threshold of 20 per cent starts to apply from the moment that the parties to the agreement have become competitors, the hardcore list of competitors only becomes applicable after the agreement, in any of its parts,

---

[85] See Guidelines para 32.
[86] See Guidelines para 33.

has been materially changed. More generally, the Commission will focus its assessment on the impact of the licence agreement on the newly developed source of competition.[87] The Commission has so far not given any indications as to how it interprets the concept of 'material change'.

(5) The Hardcore Restrictions

A central feature of the TTBER is its so-called black-list approach: restrictions that are not explicitly excluded are covered by the block exemption. This contrasts with the old Regulation 240/96 which contained also a white list, specifying the restrictions that could or even should be included in a licensing agreement for it to be block exempted. The black-list approach creates more contractual freedom for the parties to design a licence to their commercial needs. Below the market share thresholds the parties only need to take account of what is excluded from coverage, ie the hardcore restrictions listed in Article 4 and the excluded restrictions in Article 5.

10.90

Of these two articles Article 4 is clearly the more important one. Indeed, the hardcore list is the most important part of the TTBER. It contains restrictions which the Commission considers normally to be severely anti-competitive. These restrictions of competition by object have such a high potential for negative effects on competition that it is unnecessary for the purposes of applying Article 81(1) to demonstrate any effects on the market.[88] Moreover, the conditions of Article 81(3) are considered unlikely to be fulfilled in the case of hardcore restrictions. When a licence agreement contains such a restriction, it follows from Article 4(1) and 4(2) of the TTBER that the agreement as a whole falls outside the scope of the block exemption. For the purposes of the TTBER hardcore restrictions cannot be severed from the rest of the agreement. In the context of an individual assessment the Commission considers that hardcore restrictions will only in exceptional circumstances fulfil the four conditions of Article 81(3).[89]

10.91

As remarked before, the hardcore list in Article 4 makes a distinction between licensing between competitors (Article 4(1)) and non-competitors (Article 4(2)). The hardcore list of Article 4(1) is inspired by the hardcore list in other 'horizontal' block exemption regulations.[90] The hardcore list in Article 4(2) is inspired by the hardcore list in the vertical distribution block exemption Regulation.[91] However, while there are similarities with the other block exemption regulations, Article 4(1) and (2) also have licensing specific features which differentiate this hardcore list from these other regulations.

10.92

The text of Article 4 reads as follows:

10.93

    (1) Where the undertakings party to the agreement are competing undertakings, the exemption provided for in Article 2 shall not apply to agreements which, directly or indirectly,

---

[87] See Guidelines para 31.
[88] See eg Case C-49/92 P *Anic Partecipazioni* [1999] ECR I-4125, para 123.
[89] See Guidelines paras 14, 18 and 75.
[90] See for instance Regulation 2658/2000 on specialisation agreements and Regulation 2659/2000 on research and development agreements.
[91] Commission Regulation 2790/1999 on vertical agreements.

in isolation or in combination with other factors under the control of the parties, have as
their object:

(a) the restriction of a party's ability to determine its prices when selling products to
third parties;

(b) the limitation of output, except limitations on the output of contract products
imposed on the licensee in a non-reciprocal agreement or imposed on only one of
the licensees in a reciprocal agreement;

(c) the allocation of markets or customers except:

(i) the obligation on the licensee(s) to produce with the licensed technology only
within one or more technical fields of use or one or more product markets,

(ii) the obligation on the licensor and/or the licensee, in a non-reciprocal agreement,
not to produce with the licensed technology within one or more technical fields
of use or one or more product markets or one or more exclusive territories
reserved for the other party,

(iii) the obligation on the licensor not to license the technology to another licensee in
a particular territory,

(iv) the restriction, in a non-reciprocal agreement, of active and/or passive sales
by the licensee and/or the licensor into the exclusive territory or to the exclusive
customer group reserved for the other party,

(v) the restriction, in a non-reciprocal agreement, of active sales by the licensee into
the exclusive territory or to the exclusive customer group allocated by the licensor to another licensee provided the latter was not a competing undertaking of
the licensor at the time of the conclusion of its own licence,

(vi) the obligation on the licensee to produce the contract products only for its own
use provided that the licensee is not restricted in selling the contract products
actively and passively as spare parts for its own products,

(vii) the obligation on the licensee, in a non-reciprocal agreement, to produce the
contract products only for a particular customer, where the licence was granted
in order to create an alternative source of supply for that customer;

(d) the restriction of the licensee's ability to exploit its own technology or the restriction
of the ability of any of the parties to the agreement to carry out research and development, unless such latter restriction is indispensable to prevent the disclosure of
the licensed know-how to third parties.

(2) Where the undertakings party to the agreement are not competing undertakings, the
exemption provided for in Article 2 shall not apply to agreements which, directly or indirectly, in isolation or in combination with other factors under the control of the parties,
have as their object:

(a) the restriction of a party's ability to determine its prices when selling products to
third parties, without prejudice to the possibility of imposing a maximum sale price
or recommending a sale price, provided that it does not amount to a fixed or minimum sale price as a result of pressure from, or incentives offered by, any of the parties;

(b) the restriction of the territory into which, or of the customers to whom, the licensee
may passively sell the contract products, except:

(i) the restriction of passive sales into an exclusive territory or to an exclusive customer group reserved for the licensor,

(ii) the restriction of passive sales into an exclusive territory or to an exclusive customer group allocated by the licensor to another licensee during the first two
years that this other licensee is selling the contract products in that territory or to
that customer group,

(iii) the obligation to produce the contract products only for its own use provided
that the licensee is not restricted in selling the contract products actively and passively as spare parts for its own products,

   (iv) the obligation to produce the contract products only for a particular customer, where the licence was granted in order to create an alternative source of supply for that customer,

   (v) the restriction of sales to end-users by a licensee operating at the wholesale level of trade,

   (vi) the restriction of sales to unauthorised distributors by the members of a selective distribution system;

  (c) the restriction of active or passive sales to end-users by a licensee which is a member of a selective distribution system and which operates at the retail level, without prejudice to the possibility of prohibiting a member of the system from operating out of an unauthorised place of establishment.

(3) Where the undertakings party to the agreement are not competing undertakings at the time of the conclusion of the agreement but become competing undertakings afterwards, paragraph 2 and not paragraph 1 shall apply for the full life of the agreement unless the agreement is subsequently amended in any material respect.

For a number of hardcore restrictions in licensing agreements between competitors the **10.94** TTBER makes a distinction between reciprocal and non-reciprocal agreements. A reciprocal agreement is a cross-licensing agreement where the licensed technologies are competing technologies or can be used for the production of competing products. A non-reciprocal agreement is an agreement where only one of the parties is licensing its technology to the other party or where in case of cross-licensing the licensed technologies are not competing technologies and cannot be used for the production of competing products.[92] The hardcore list is stricter for reciprocal than for non-reciprocal agreements. Reciprocal agreements are considered to have more easily an anti-competitive object (and effect). There is more alignment of incentives and restraints in case of reciprocity whereas non-reciprocity creates an asymmetry in terms of technology flows and restraints. In addition, it is also considered that in a reciprocal situation there is usually less need for restrictions: both parties have a technology the other wants to license-in and there is thus less risk that the licence agreement would not be concluded without the possibility for the parties to restrain each other. A non-reciprocal agreement may more often not be concluded unless the licensor and licensee are allowed to agree certain restrictions.[93]

(a) Price Fixing

The first hardcore restriction concerns price fixing. Both in case of licensing between com- **10.95** petitors and non-competitors it is a hardcore restriction to fix the price of products sold to third parties, see Article 4(1)(a) and 4(2)(a). Licensor and licensee must be free to set the price of their own products, whether produced with the licensed technology or another technology. The only exception is the imposition of a maximum sale price or recommending a sale price in a licence agreement between non-competitors. Such a maximum or recommended price in an agreement between non-competitors is not a hardcore restriction,

---

[92] See Guidelines para 78.

[93] In the case of agreements that restrict competition that would have existed but for the agreement such a finding does not imply that the agreement falls outside Art 81(1). When the agreement (appreciably) affects inter-technology competition it is caught by Art 81(1). Any benefits resulting from the agreement fall to be considered in the context of Art 81(3).

provided that it does not amount to a fixed or minimum sale price as a result of pressure from, or incentives offered by, any of the parties.

10.96   The Guidelines provide further clarification on what is considered hardcore price fixing.[94] It is explained that indirect price fixing can be achieved in several ways, such as fixing the margin, fixing the maximum level of discounts, linking the sale price to the sales prices of competitors or providing that the royalty rate will increase if product prices are reduced. Again in the context of licensing between competitors, it is made clear that running royalties to be paid on the basis of all product sales irrespective of whether the licensed technology is being used, is a hardcore restriction under Article 4(1)(a) and also under Article 4(1)(d).[95] Such requirement raises the cost for the licensee of using his own technology and this is considered seriously to restrict competition, whether it concerns a reciprocal or non-reciprocal agreement between competitors. It is however indicated that exceptionally the conditions of Article 81(3) may be fulfilled in an individual case if in the absence of the restraint it would be impossible or unduly difficult to calculate and monitor the royalty payable by the licensee, for instance because the licensor's technology leaves no visible trace on the final product and the licensee at the same time uses his own technology to produce the same final product. The Guidelines further explain that in the context of cross-licensing between competitors running royalties on the licensed products can be used to coordinate prices on a product market through their impact on the marginal costs of the products of both parties. However, the Guidelines provide that the Commission will only treat cross-licensing with reciprocal running royalties as price fixing within the meaning of Article 4(1)(a) where the agreement is devoid of any pro-competitive purpose and therefore does not constitute a bona fide licensing arrangement ('sham licensing').

(b) Output Limitations

10.97   The second hardcore restriction concerns output limitations. Limitation of output is not a hardcore restriction where the licensing is between non-competitors. Limitation of output only features in the hardcore list of licensing between competitors, in Article 4(1)(b). Article 4(1)(b) provides that a limitation of output is considered a hardcore restriction in general, except where the limitation is imposed on the licensee in a non-reciprocal agreement or imposed on only one of the licensees in a reciprocal agreement. It follows that an output limitation is hardcore if it concerns a reciprocal restriction on both parties or if it concerns a restriction on any of the parties' output produced with its own technology. An output limitation is not hardcore if it is limited to a non-reciprocal restriction, on the licensee in case of non-reciprocal licensing or on only one of the licensees in reciprocal licensing. It is considered that when the restraint is asymmetrical there is a lower risk of reducing output on the market. In case of such a one-way restriction it is also considered more likely that the agreement leads to a real integration of complementary technologies or an efficiency enhancing integration of the licensor's superior technology and that the

---

[94] See Guidelines paras 79–81 and 97.
[95] See below.

restriction may be necessary to induce the licensor to license-out.[96] It would therefore not be appropriate to treat it as a hardcore restriction.

(c) Territorial and Customer Sales Restrictions

10.98 The third hardcore restriction concerns territorial and customer sales restrictions. This provision consists of a general hardcore restriction with an important number of exceptions in both Article 4(1) and 4(2) and as those Articles are materially different, licensing between competitors and non-competitors are dealt with separately below.

10.99 **(i) Territorial and Customer Sales Restrictions between Competitors** In case of licensing between competitors it is hardcore to allocate markets or customers. However, given the various exceptions, the hardcore restriction is effectively narrowed down to (1) exclusivity and territorial and customer sales restrictions between the parties in a reciprocal agreement and (2) most active and passive sales restrictions between licensees in case the licensor is licensing to more than one licensee.

10.100 The first part concerning exclusivity and sales restrictions signifies that competitors in a reciprocal agreement should not (and need not) restrict each other as to where to produce or where or to whom to sell. This applies irrespective of whether the licensee remains free to use his own technology. In the words of the Guidelines, once the licensee has tooled up to use the licensor's technology to produce a given product, both his possibilities and incentive to produce under his own technology may have been reduced significantly.[97]

10.101 At the same time it is important to note that exclusivity agreed in a non-reciprocal agreement is covered by the block exemption.[98] To be more precise, in a non-reciprocal agreement the licensor and licensee can agree not to produce in the exclusive territory reserved for the other party. This means that both licensor and licensee may have an exclusive territory where the other is not allowed to produce. It is also possible for only one of them to have such an exclusive territory. The restriction need not be symmetrical. This restriction also entails that the licensor abstains from entering or remaining on the market if the licensee's exclusive territory is world-wide. However, it is a condition for the application of the block exemption that the protected territory of the licensee and/or licensor is exclusively reserved for the other party, ie that the latter is the only one authorised to produce with the licensed technology in that territory. Active and passive sales restrictions between licensor and licensee to protect the exclusive territory or territories or customer group(s) reserved for one or both of them, are also block exempted if contained in a non-reciprocal agreement.[99] The block exemption thus covers absolute territorial production between licensor and licensee in such a situation.

10.102 It is further made clear that field of use restrictions are covered by the block exemption, whether in a reciprocal or non-reciprocal agreement.[100] The licence can thus be limited to

---

[96] See Guidelines paras 82 and 83.
[97] See Guidelines para 85.
[98] See Art 4(1)(c)(ii).
[99] See Art 4(1)(c)(iv).
[100] See Art 4(1)(c)(i).

one or more product markets or technical fields of use. It is important to note that the licensee can only be limited in the use of the licensed-in technology and not in the use of its own technology, as this would constitute a hardcore restriction under Article 4(1)(d).[101] This implies that in a reciprocal agreement, where each party is both licensor and licensee at the same time, none of the parties can be restricted in the use of its own technology. However, in the case of a non-reciprocal agreement, Article 4(1)(c)(ii) explicitly block exempts field of use restrictions limiting the licensor's use of its own technology. The TTBER thus block exempts in general field of use restrictions imposed on the licensee concerning the licensed technology and block exempts in addition field of use restrictions imposed on the licensor in case of non-reciprocal licensing. The risk of market sharing is considered less in the case of field of use restrictions than in the case of territorial or customer restrictions. The Commission considers that a licensee will be less inclined to withdraw from a product market as long as he is still able to use his own, possibly inferior, technology. Withdrawal from a product market will often be costly as it may for instance involve plant closures and re-entry at a later point in time may be difficult. Field of use restrictions may also be necessary to promote pro-competitive licensing, in particular to ensure design freedom to the licensee within the scope of the licence and to avoid having to license for fields of use for which the value is not yet well established.[102]

10.103   In Article 4(1)(c)(iii) it is clarified that sole licensing is not a hardcore restriction. In other words a licensor can appoint a licensee as his only licensee in a territory and agree not to license to third parties in the same territory. As the licensor is not restricted in the use of its own technology under sole licensing, it is anyhow difficult to see how such licensing could lead to allocation of markets or customers. Article 4(1)(c)(iii) seems therefore somewhat superfluous, making an exception to the hardcore restriction for clarification purposes only. Article 4(1)(c)(iii) does not make a distinction based on whether or not the agreement is reciprocal. As explained in the Guidelines the block exemption of sole licensing 'applies irrespective of whether the agreement is reciprocal or not given that the agreement does not affect the ability of the parties to fully exploit their own technology in the respective territories'.[103] This could be said to conflict with Article 4(1)(d) where it concerns reciprocal agreements. Under Article 4(1)(d) a licensee should be free to exploit its own technology, including according to the Guidelines[104] licensing his own technology to third parties. In a reciprocal agreement both parties are by definition both licensor and licensee and sole licensing would in such a case restrict one or both licensees to license to third parties and could thus be said to contravene Article 4(1)(d). In view of the explicit exception from the hardcore list made for both reciprocal and non-reciprocal sole licensing and the Commission's statement that sole licensing in general does not affect the ability of the parties to exploit their own technology, it can be expected that the exception defined in Article 4(1)(c)(iii) would prevail over Article 4(1)(d) if a possible case of conflict were to be argued.

---

[101] See below.
[102] See Guidelines paras 90 and 91.
[103] See Guidelines para 88.
[104] See para 95.

The above-mentioned exceptions to the hardcore restriction of Article 4(1)(c) all relate to **10.104** exclusivity and sales restrictions between the parties. In Article 4(1)(c)(v) there is an exception to the general hardcore on active and passive sales restrictions between licensees that all use the technology of the same licensor.[105] Active sales restrictions imposed on the licensee to protect the exclusive territory or customer group allocated by the licensor to another licensee are block exempted on condition that the sales restrictions are part of a non-reciprocal agreement and the protected licensee was not a competitor of the licensor at the time it concluded its own licence agreement. With this somewhat complex construction it is achieved that in general in the case of licensing between competitors sales restrictions between licensees are hardcore, but in cases where the licensor is licensing to competitors and non-competitors at the same time, the latter can be protected against active selling by other licensees as would be possible if the licensor was only licensing to non-competitors. This allows the licensor to address the asymmetry that arises when some licensees are already operating on the market whereas others are not.

Lastly there are two specific exceptions to the hardcore restriction of market sharing, one **10.105** for captive use restrictions (Article 4(1)(c)(vi)) and another to create an alternative source of supply for a particular customer (Article 4(1)(c)(vii)). The captive use exception allows the licensor to prohibit the licensee to sell the products, usually a component produced with the licensed technology, except where this would restrict the supply of these products as spare parts for the licensee's own product. The possibility to create an alternative source of supply for a particular customer enables the licensor to conclude a licence agreement under which the licensee is only allowed to produce the contract product for and sell the contract product to a specific customer. These exceptional situations are not considered to lead easily to market sharing.

(ii) Territorial and Customer Sales Restrictions between Non-competitors The hardcore **10.106** territorial and customer sales restrictions in licensing agreements between non-competitors are dealt with in Article 4(2)(b) and 4(2)(c). The hardcore restrictions found here are similar to but more lenient than the corresponding hardcore restrictions in Commission Regulation 2790/1999 for distribution agreements.

In Article 4(2)(b) it is declared hardcore to restrict the licensee's passive sales of the contract **10.107** products. The Guidelines[106] explain that passive sales restrictions may result from direct obligations on the licensee, such as the obligation not to sell to certain customers or refer orders from these customers to other licensees. Passive sales are also restricted if provision, delivery, or installation of the product at the customer's premises is hindered. Passive sales restrictions may also result from indirect measures aimed at limiting such sales. While an output limit imposed on the licensee will not as such be considered an indirect means to restrict passive sales, this will be the case if the output limit is, for instance, combined with an obligation to sell a minimum amount in the licensee's 'own' territory. Another indirect way to obtain passive sales restrictions is differentiated royalties depending on the destination of the products.

---

[105] See para 10.93. above.
[106] See para 98.

10.108 The fact that only restrictions of the licensee's passive sales are declared hardcore implies that all sales restrictions on the licensor are block exempted. It also implies that all active sales restrictions on the licensee are block exempted, except for what is said on this below in the context of selective distribution and Article 4(2)(c).[107] The block exemption of passive sales restrictions imposed on the licensor and active sales restrictions imposed on the licensee is considered appropriate to promote the licensee's investment in view of potential free riding problems and hold-up problems.[108]

10.109 In addition to the implied limitations to the hardcore restriction in Article 4(2)(b), there are also a number of exceptions provided in this Article. First, in Article 4(2)(b)(i), it is made clear that passive sales restrictions on the licensee to protect the exclusive territory or customer group of the licensor, are block exempted. This allows licensor and licensee to have absolute territorial protection between them. The Guidelines indicate that a licensor can in this way also reserve a territory for future exploitation.[109] Secondly, Article 4(2)(b)(ii) block exempts restrictions of the licensee's passive sales into another licensee's exclusive territory or to the latter's exclusive customer group during the first two years that this other licensee is selling the contract products. This thereby allows protection of start-up costs and other, often sunk, investments made by the new licensee.[110] Thirdly, Articles 4(2)(b)(iii) and 4(2)(b)(iv) block exempt passive sales restrictions that are necessary to impose a captive use restriction or to create an alternative source of supply for a particular customer.[111] Fourthly, Article 4(2)(b)(v) brings under the block exemption the obligation imposed on the licensee not to sell to end users and thus to limit its sales activities to the wholesale level. Finally, Article 4(2)(b)(vi) allows the licensor to set up a selective distribution system by prohibiting the member-licensee to sell to unauthorised distributors. In that case, however, a licensee active at the retail level of trade must, according to Article 4(2)(c), be permitted to sell both actively and passively to end-users. In such a case of selective distribution the licensee-retailer can only be restricted in its place of establishment.

(d) Restrictions on the Use of Own Technology or to do R&D

10.110 The last hardcore restriction concerns (a) restriction of the licensee to exploit its own technology and (b) restriction of any of the parties to carry out research and development, unless this second restriction is indispensable to prevent disclosure of licensed know-how, see Article 4(1)(d). This hardcore only applies to licensing between competitors. Where the licence is concluded between non-competitors the same restriction is excluded from the block exemption under Article 5.[112] Paragraph 94 of the Guidelines makes clear that the mere fact that the parties agree to share future improvements of their licensed technologies will not be assessed as a restriction of the parties to carry out independent research and development. It is also made clear that Article 4(1)(d) does not apply when the restriction

---

[107] For the distinction between active and passive sales, reference is made to para 50 of the Guidelines on Vertical Restraints (see also Chapter 9, paras 9.09 to 9.11 of this book)

[108] See Guidelines para 99.

[109] See Guidelines para 100.

[110] See Guidelines para 101.

[111] See also para 10.105 above.

[112] See below.

is indispensable to prevent the foreclosure of the licensed know-how to third parties. In order not to be caught by Article 4(1)(d) the restrictions imposed to prevent disclosure of licensed know-how must be necessary and proportionate to ensure such protection and must, where possible, not impose a total ban on the licensee to do R&D with third parties.

This last hardcore restriction reflects the aim of the TTBER to promote innovation and not **10.111** to let the competitive significance of technologies and innovation be reduced. The licensing should not lead to a reduced effectiveness of existing technologies or a reduced incentive to improve or replace these technologies. The licensee should be free to produce with his own technology and sell the resulting products without restriction, including not having to pay royalties on these products. The licensee should also be free to license out his own technology.[113] Both parties should be free to carry out R&D to improve their position.

(6) Excluded Restrictions

Article 5 lists four types of excluded restrictions. These restrictions are not block exempted **10.112** but, unlike in the case of hardcore restrictions, the inclusion in an agreement of any of these excluded restrictions does not prevent the application of the block exemption to the rest of the agreement. It is only the individual restriction that is not block exempted and that requires individual assessment. There is, also unlike in the case of hardcore restrictions, no presumption of illegality of these restrictions when individually assessed.

Article 5(1) contains the following three excluded restrictions: **10.113**

(a) any direct or indirect obligation on the licensee to grant an exclusive licence to the licensor or to a third party designated by the licensor in respect of its own severable improvements to or its own new applications of the licensed technology;

(b) any direct or indirect obligation on the licensee to assign, in whole or in part, to the licensor or to a third party designated by the licensor, rights to its own severable improvements to or its own new applications of the licensed technology;

(c) any direct or indirect obligation on the licensee not to challenge the validity of intellectual property rights which the licensor holds in the common market, without prejudice to the possibility to provide for termination of the technology transfer agreement in the event that the licensee challenges the validity of one or more of the licensed intellectual property rights.

Article 5(1)(a) and 5(1)(b) concern exclusive grant backs and assignments to the licensor of **10.114** severable improvements of the licensed technology. An improvement is severable if it can be exploited without infringing the licensed technology. An obligation to grant the licensor an exclusive licence to severable improvements of the licensed technology or to assign such improvements to the licensor is considered likely to reduce the licensee's incentive to innovate since it hinders the licensee in exploiting his improvements, including by way of licensing to third parties. The exclusion of exclusive grant backs and assignments of severable improvements does not depend on whether or not the licensor pays a price for acquiring the improvement or for obtaining an exclusive licence. However, if a price is paid this will be

---

[113] See also para 10.103. above.

a relevant factor in the context of an individual assessment under Article 81. Depending on the level of the price it may be less likely that the obligation creates a disincentive for the licensee to innovate. The block exemption does cover non-exclusive grant back obligations in respect of severable improvements. This is so even where the grant back obligation is non-reciprocal, ie only imposed on the licensee, and where under the agreement the licensor is entitled to feed-on the severable improvements to other licensees. It is mentioned in the Guidelines that a feed on clause may promote the dissemination of technology because each licensee knows at the time of contracting that he will be on an equal footing with other licensees in terms of the technology on the basis of which he is producing. Also, an obligation not to license severable improvements to third parties, ie what could be termed a sole grant back obligation where only the licensee and licensor can use the former's improvements, is covered by the block exemption as it does not concern an exclusive grant back obligation. Finally, exclusive grant backs and obligations to assign non-severable improvements are considered not restrictive of competition within the meaning of Article 81(1) since non-severable improvements can anyhow not be exploited by the licensee without the licensor's permission.[114]

10.115 The excluded restriction set out in Article 5(1)(c) concerns non-challenge clauses. The Guidelines mention, as reason for excluding non-challenge clauses from the scope of the block exemption, that licensees are normally in the best position to determine whether or not an intellectual property right is invalid and that in the interest of undistorted competition and in conformity with the principles underlying the protection of intellectual property, invalid intellectual property rights should be eliminated. Invalid intellectual property stifles innovation rather than promoting it. However, the Guidelines also indicate that the Commission takes a favourable view of non-challenge clauses relating to know-how where once disclosed it is likely to be impossible or very difficult to recover the licensed know-how. In such cases, an obligation on the licensee not to challenge the licensed know-how promotes dissemination of new technology, in particular by allowing weaker licensors to license stronger licensees without fear of a challenge once the know-how has been absorbed by the licensee. Similarly, the Commission takes a favourable view of non-challenge clauses in the context of settlements.[115] Moreover, the exclusion of Article 5(1)(c) does not extend to the possibility for the licensor to terminate the licence agreement in the event of a challenge of the licensed technology. Accordingly, the licensor is not forced to continue dealing with a licensee that challenges the very subject matter of the licence agreement, implying that upon termination any further use by the licensee of the challenged technology is at the challenger's own risk. The provision thereby ensures that the licensee is in the same position as third parties.[116]

10.116 Article 5(2) excludes from the scope of the block exemption, in the case of agreements between non-competitors, any direct or indirect obligation limiting the licensee's ability to exploit his own technology or limiting the ability of the parties to the agreement to carry

---

[114] See Guidelines paras 109 and 110.
[115] See section 9(i) below.
[116] See Guidelines paras 112 and 113.

out research and development, unless such latter restriction is indispensable to prevent the disclosure of licensed know-how to third parties. The content of this condition is the same as that of Article 4(1)(d) of the hardcore list concerning agreements between competitors.[117] However, in the case of agreements between non-competitors there is no presumption that such restrictions generally have negative effects on competition or that the conditions of Article 81(3) are generally not satisfied. Individual assessment is required. For such individual assessment it is considered important whether or not the licensee owns a competing technology. The Guidelines stress that in case the licensee already owns a competing technology it is important to ensure that the licensee is not restricted in his ability to exploit his own technology and further develop it. This technology constitutes a competitive constraint in the market, which should be preserved. In such a situation restrictions on the licensee's use of his own technology or on research and development are normally considered to be restrictive of competition and not to satisfy the conditions of Article 81(3). In cases where the licensee does not own a competing technology or is not already developing such a technology, a restriction on the ability of the parties to carry out independent research and development may be restrictive of competition where only a few technologies are available. In that case the licensee may be an important (potential) source of innovation in the market. This is particularly so where the licensee possesses the necessary assets and skills to carry out research and development. In that case the Guidelines indicate the conditions of Article 81(3) are unlikely to be fulfilled. In other cases where several technologies are available and where the licensee does not possess special assets or skills, the restriction on research and development is likely either to fall outside Article 81(1) for lack of an appreciable restrictive effect or satisfy the conditions of Article 81(3). The restraint may promote the dissemination of new technology by assuring the licensor that the licence does not create a new competitor and by inducing the licensee to focus on the exploitation and development of the licensed technology.[118]

(7) The Safe Harbours

10.117 Article 3 of the TTBER establishes a safe harbour based on market share thresholds. The market share thresholds are 20 per cent for agreements between competitors and 30 per cent for agreements between non-competitors. Outside the safe harbour individual assessment is required. The fact that market shares exceed the thresholds does not give rise to any presumption either that the agreement is caught by Article 81(1) or that the agreement does not fulfil the conditions of Article 81(3).

10.118 In the case of technology markets, it follows from Article 3(3) of the TTBER that the licensor's market share is to be calculated on the basis of the sales of the licensor and all his licensees of products incorporating the licensed technology and this for each relevant market separately. The relevant market share is thus the licensed technology's footprint on downstream product markets on which the products incorporating the licensed technology are sold. Where the parties are competitors on the technology market, sales of products

---

[117] See paras 10.103 and 10.110 above.
[118] See Guidelines paras 114–116.

incorporating the licensee's own technology must be combined with the sales of the products incorporating the licensed technology.

10.119 With regard to product markets, the licensee's market share is calculated on the basis of the licensee's sales of products incorporating the licensor's technology and competing products, ie the total sales of the licensee on the product market in question. Where the licensor is also a supplier of products on the relevant market, the licensor's sales on the product market in question must also be taken into account. In the calculation of a product market share, sales of other licensees are not taken into account.

10.120 The market share threshold, whether the 20 per cent or 30 per cent threshold, is applied relevant market by relevant market. If the agreement covers several relevant markets and the market share threshold is exceeded only on one or some markets, the block exemption continues to apply to the remaining markets where the threshold is not exceeded.[119] This rule clearly applies in cases involving distinct product and geographic markets. However, it is not entirely clear whether it also applies where the threshold is exceeded on an upstream technology market but not on a downstream product market.[120] It is submitted that the better view is that it does not. Given that technology markets are analysed on the basis of a technology's position on the downstream product market, it would be artificial to make a distinction between the upstream and the downstream market for the purpose of applying the block exemption. Once the threshold is exceeded on either market, an arrangement covering these two markets should be subject to individual assessment in order to ascertain the overall impact of the agreement on competition. This interpretation corresponds to the general principle according to which block exemptions, being derogations, must be interpreted restrictively.[121]

10.121 The Guidelines contain in paragraph 131 an additional safe harbour. The Commission takes the view that except in the case of hardcore restrictions, Article 81 is unlikely to be infringed where there are four or more independently controlled technologies, in addition to the technologies controlled by the parties to the agreement that may be substitutable for the licensed technology at a comparable cost to the user.[122] It is not required that the technologies are already being used. It is sufficient that they are likely to come to market within a reasonable period of time.[123] The technologies must be of competitive significance. Their commercial strength must therefore be taken into account. The competitive constraint imposed by a technology is limited if it does not constitute a commercially viable alternative to the licensed technology. The Guidelines give the example where due to network

---

[119] See Guidelines para 69.

[120] The example given in para 69 of the Guidelines refers to the situation involving distinct geographic markets or distinct product markets. Moreover, in example 3 in para 73 it is stated that 'As the agreement is between competitors, their combined market share, both on the technology and on the product market, has to be below the 20% market share threshold in order to benefit from the safe harbour.'

[121] See eg Case C-70/93 *Bayerische Motorenwerke* [1995] ECR I-3439, para 28, and Case 234/89 *Delimitis* [1991] ECR I-935, para 46.

[122] This safe harbour is identical to the safe harbour contained in section 4.3. of the 1995 US Guidelines for the Licensing of Intellectual Property.

[123] See Guidelines para 131.

effects in the market consumers have a strong preference for products incorporating the licensed technology.[124] In such circumstances other technologies may not constitute a real alternative and may therefore impose only a limited competitive constraint.

(8) Withdrawal and Disapplication

According to Article 6 of the TTBER, the Commission and the competition authorities of the Member States may withdraw the benefit of the block exemption in respect of individual agreements that do not fulfil the conditions of Article 81(3). The power of the competition authorities of the Member States to withdraw the benefit of the block exemption is limited to cases where the relevant geographic market is no wider than the territory of the Member State in question. Withdrawal implies that the agreement in question restricts competition within the meaning of Article 81(1) and does not fulfil the conditions of Article 81(3). Withdrawal is therefore necessarily accompanied by a negative decision under Regulation 1/2003. **10.122**

According to Article 6(1), withdrawal may in particular be warranted in the following circumstances: **10.123**

(a) access of third parties' technologies to the market is restricted, for instance by the cumulative effect of parallel networks of similar restrictive agreements prohibiting licensees from using third party technology;

(b) access of potential licensees to the market is restricted, for instance by the cumulative effect of parallel networks of similar restrictive agreements preventing licensors from licensing to other licensees;

(c) without any objectively valid reason the parties refrain from exploiting the licensed technology.

The reference to market access for potential licensees must be read in light of paragraphs 164 and 165 of the Guidelines dealing with exclusive licensing. Contrary to the draft published for public consultation, the final version of the Guidelines does not highlight foreclosure of potential licensees as an area of particular concern. Indeed, in the case of agreements between non-competitors it is stated that the Commission will only exceptionally intervene against exclusive licensing, irrespective of the territorial scope of the licence. The example of a dominant licensee obtaining an exclusive licence to one or more competing technologies is described as a situation where exceptionally intervention may be required. However, in the case of dominance it is highly unlikely that the block exemption applies in the first place given the market share thresholds. It would therefore appear that Article 6(1)(b) is a 'left over' from the more restrictive approach of the published draft. **10.124**

Article 7 of the TTBER enables the Commission to exclude from the scope of the TTBER, by means of regulation, parallel networks of similar agreements where such agreements cover more than 50 per cent of a relevant market. Such a measure is not addressed to individual undertakings but concerns all undertakings whose agreements are defined in the regulation disapplying the TTBER. The instrument of disapplication was first introduced **10.125**

---

[124] ibid.

in Commission Regulation 2790/1999 on the application of Article 81(3) of the Treaty to categories of vertical agreements and concerted practices.[125] The main purpose was to allow the Commission to deal with cumulative effects of networks of, in particular, selective distribution agreements and non-compete agreements. In the field of licensing it is more difficult to identify obvious candidates for disapplication. It is submitted that in so far as networks of agreements give rise to foreclosure of competing technologies the appropriate action is withdrawal and prohibition. Disapplication is not sufficient given the fact that it merely restores the full application of Article 81. It does not in itself render the identified agreements null and void.

(9) Application Outside the Scope of the Block Exemption

(a) Introduction

10.126 Outside the scope of the block exemption, agreements are subject to individual assessment. There is no presumption of illegality of agreements that fall outside the scope of the block exemption provided that they do not contain hardcore restrictions of competition. The Guidelines provide guidance on the application of Article 81 to various types of licensing restraints and practices.

10.127 The analysis of licence agreements under Article 81 follows the same basic approach as that applied to other types of agreements. Licence agreements are assessed in the economic and legal context in which they occur with a view to determining their impact on competition on the market. In the application of Article 81(1) and 81(3) the dynamic aspect of licensing must be taken into account.[126] For licence agreements to be restrictive of competition they must affect actual or potential competition to such an extent that on the relevant market negative effects on prices, output, innovation or the variety or quality of goods and services can be expected with a reasonable degree of probability.

10.128 Such effects on competition may arise where the agreement restricts competition between the parties or between the parties and third parties. In certain circumstances licence agreements may facilitate collusion on the market or create barriers to entry or expansion of rivals. Licence agreements may also, by imposing contractual restraints on licensees, restrict competition that would otherwise have occurred between licensees. The Guidelines distinguish two sources of competition, namely inter-technology competition and intra-technology competition.[127] The same agreement may be capable of affecting both inter-technology competition and intra-technology competition, in which case the impact of the agreement on both needs to be assessed.

10.129 Appreciable anti-competitive effects are likely to occur when at least one of the parties has or obtains some degree of market power and the agreement contributes to the creation, maintenance, or strengthening of that market power or allows the parties to exploit such market power. The Guidelines use the term 'significant degree of market power' to indicate

---

[125] [1999] OJ L336/21.
[126] See Guidelines para 9.
[127] See paras 11 and 12.

the threshold where competition concerns will normally arise whereas the term 'substantial market power' appears to be used to indicate dominance. However, no attempt is made to quantify these terms. Market power is a question of degree and the two terms indicate two points on a continuum.

Licence agreements also have substantial potential for generating pro-competitive efficiencies. **10.130** Licensing may often promote innovation by enabling licensors to obtain a return on their investment and by creating design freedom for licensees that would otherwise face the risk of infringement action by the licensor. Through the dissemination of technology the licensing also creates scope for synergies at the level of the licensee. When combining the licensed technology with his own technology and production assets the licensee may be able to achieve a cost/output configuration that would otherwise not be possible or to produce a new or improved product.

(b) Royalty Obligations

The parties to a licence agreement are normally free to determine the royalty payable by the **10.131** licensee and its mode of payment without being caught by Article 81(1). This principle applies both to agreements between competitors and agreements between non-competitors.[128]

In agreements between competitors it is a hardcore restriction when royalties are charged **10.132** on products produced with the licensee's own technology. Such an obligation may also give rise to competition concerns when applied to third party technologies. When royalties extend also to products produced with third party technology, that technology is rendered less attractive. Irrespective of whether it is concluded between competitors or not such an agreement may therefore give rise to foreclosure and should be analysed in the same way as other foreclosure restraints such as non-compete obligations, to ensure that the royalty obligation does not create an obstacle to the use of competing technologies.

Reciprocal running royalties in agreements between competitors increase marginal costs **10.133** and feed directly into product prices. They can therefore be used to elevate prices. When the licensing arrangement is a sham in that it serves no pro-competitive purpose, reciprocal running royalties are caught by the hardcore list given the fact that the object of the agreement is to raise prices. In other cases Article 81(1) may also apply to reciprocal running royalties provided that the royalties are clearly disproportionate compared to the market value of the licence and where such royalties have a significant impact on market prices.[129] Given the difficulties in determining the market value of a technology and the fact that royalties must be disproportionate it is likely that the Commission will only rarely intervene against reciprocal running royalties outside the scope of the hardcore list.[130]

---

[128] See Guidelines para 156. The Guidelines specifically mention that in the case of software licensing royalties based on the number of users and royalties calculated on a per machine basis are generally compatible with Art 81(1).

[129] See Guidelines para 158.

[130] It is recalled that under Art 2 of Regulation 1/2003 it is for the Commission to prove an infringement of Art 81(1).

(c) Exclusive Licences and Sales Restrictions

10.134   The TTBER makes a distinction between exclusivity relating to production on the basis of the licensed technology and restrictions on the sale of products incorporating the licensed technology. The two types of restrictions may be combined. If a single worldwide exclusive licence is granted, sales restrictions are irrelevant given the fact that for the duration of the agreement only the licensee can legally produce on the basis of the licensed technology. The block exemption covers non-reciprocal exclusive licensing between competitors and exclusive licensing between non-competitors, whereas reciprocal exclusive licensing between competitors is identified as a hardcore restriction.

10.135   The assessment of exclusivity outside the scope of the block exemption depends on the competitive relationship between the parties. Greater concerns arise in the case of agreements between competitors due to the possible impact on the ability and incentive for the licensor to compete on the market. If the licensor has limited capacity to compete in the licensed territory because he lacks the necessary production or distribution capacity, the agreement is unlikely to be caught by Article 81(1).[131] The same is true where the location of production capacity is of little competitive significance and where as a consequence the granting of an exclusive production right does not significantly affect the ability of the licensor to compete on the market. Conversely, competition concerns arise if the parties have a significant degree of market power and the agreement reduces competition between the parties that would have occurred in the absence of the agreement.

10.136   In agreements between non-competitors exclusivity is unlikely to be caught by Article 81(1) irrespective of the market position of the parties and the scope of the licence. To intervene against the exclusivity once the licensee has made a commercial success of the licensed technology would deprive the licensee of the fruits of his success and would be detrimental to competition.[132] The main situation where intervention may be warranted is where an undertaking has already become dominant or near dominant on the basis of one technology it has licensed-in and subsequently obtains an exclusive licence for one or more other competing technologies thereby foreclosing the market.[133]

10.137   The treatment of sales restrictions also depends on the competitive relationship between the parties and whether the restriction applies between the parties or restricts sales between one or both parties and other licensees. The TTBER block exempts, in non-reciprocal agreements between competitors, the restriction of active and passive sales into an exclusive territory or customer group of the other party and the restriction of active sales into the exclusive territory or customer group of another licensee who was not a competitor of the licensor at the time of contracting. Outside the block exemption the application of Article 81(1) as always depends on the degree of market power held by the parties. It also needs to be carefully analysed what is the likely impact of the agreement on the licensee's

---

[131] See Guidelines para 164.
[132] See Guidelines para 165.
[133] See Guidelines para 166. This situation resembles that pertaining in Case T-51/89 *Tetra Pak (I)* [1990] ECR II-309, except for the fact that the dominant technology was not licensed.

use of his own technology and the incentive for the parties to compete. If the royalty earned by the licensor is expressed as a percentage of the licensee's selling price, the licensor's royalty income will be affected by price reductions resulting from competition. The licensor will necessarily take this effect into account when determining his commercial strategy on the market, which may affect his incentive to compete. Under Article 81(3) it must, according to the Guidelines,[134] be taken into account whether the restrictions are necessary for licensing to occur. If the licensor and the licensee have a relatively weak market position in their protected areas restrictions may be indispensable in order to induce the licensor to grant the licence and the licensee to take the licence. In such circumstances the conditions of Article 81(3) are likely to be satisfied provided that the licensed technology generates real efficiencies.

In the case of agreements between non-competitors the block exemption covers all active **10.138** sales restrictions and restrictions on passive sales into an exclusive territory or customer group reserved for the other party. The block exemption also covers passive sales restrictions between exclusive territories and customer groups allocated to different licensees the first two years the licensee is selling the contract product. Beyond this period the latter restrictions are covered by the hardcore list. In the case of individual assessment outside the block exemption it is important to note that sales restrictions fall outside Article 81(1) altogether when on the basis of objective factors it can be concluded in the individual case that in the absence of the restrictions licensing would not occur.[135] This is particularly likely to be the case with regard to restrictions in favour of the licensor. A technology owner cannot normally be expected to create direct competition with himself on the basis of his own technology. It may also be the case that a licensee would not be willing to take a licence if he had to face direct competition from the licensor. Sales restrictions between the parties are therefore likely often either to fall outside Article 81(1) or satisfy the conditions of Article 81(3). Sales restrictions between licensees are likely to be caught by Article 81(1) when the individual licensee has a significant degree of market power.[136] Active sales restrictions may fulfil the conditions of Article 81(3) when they are necessary in order to prevent free riding or induce the licensee to invest optimally in the licensed technology. Passive sales restrictions are unlikely to satisfy the conditions of Article 81(3) beyond the two-year period covered by the block exemption.[137] In other words, when passive sales restrictions between licensees in agreements between non-competitors fail the test of paragraph 12(b) of the Guidelines they are likely to be caught by Article 81(1) and unlikely to satisfy the conditions of Article 81(3).

(d) Output Restrictions

Most output restrictions are block exempted and subject to individual assessment outside **10.139** the scope of the block exemption. Only reciprocal output restrictions in licence agreements between competitors constitute a hardcore restriction covered by Article 4(1)(b) of the TTBER.

---

[134] See para 170.
[135] See Guidelines para 172, which applies the rule laid down in para 12(b) of the Guidelines.
[136] See Guidelines para 174.
[137] See in this respect Case 258/78 *Nungesser* [1982] ECR 2015.

In the case of non-reciprocal output restrictions in agreements between competitors competition concerns start to arise when the parties have a significant degree of market power.[138] The Commission appears to assume that when the parties have a significant degree of market power a limitation of the output produced by the licensee with the licensed technology will restrict competition that would have occurred in the absence of the agreement. However, whether that is true depends on the specific circumstances facing the licensee. If the agreement is not likely to lead the licensee to reduce output produced with his own technology compared to the output that he would have produced but for the agreement, there is no restriction of inter-technology competition.

10.140 In cases where Article 81(1) applies, output restrictions may satisfy the conditions of Article 81(3). According to the Guidelines[139] Article 81(3) is likely to apply in cases where the licensor's technology is substantially better than the licensee's technology and the output limitation substantially exceeds the output of the licensee prior to the conclusion of the agreement. In that case the effect of the output limitation is limited even in markets where demand is growing. The Guidelines also express a favourable opinion of site licenses whereby the agreement limits the licence to a particular production site with a specific capacity.[140] The Guidelines opine that, where such agreement leads to a real integration of complementary assets, it is unlikely to fall foul of Article 81 below the level of dominance.

10.141 Output restrictions in agreements between non-competitors may in particular restrict intra-technology competition between licensees. This impact is exacerbated when such restrictions are combined with territorial and customer restrictions. However, there is no presumption that output restrictions serve to restrict active and passive sales by licensees.[141] Moreover, it can be argued that output restrictions imposed on licensees often are not caught by Article 81(1). The licensor should normally be entitled to determine the scope of the transfer of his property by imposing limitations on the output of the licensee.[142] As stated in the Guidelines,[143] if the licensor were not free to do so, a number of licence agreements might not come into existence in the first place, which would have a negative impact on the dissemination of new technology. It is likely that the licensor would be particularly reluctant to license where he is also a producer, since in that case the output of the licensees may find their way back into the licensor's main area of operation and thus have a direct impact on these activities.

(e) Field of Use Restrictions

10.142 Under a field of use restriction the licence is either limited to one or more technical fields of application or one or more product markets.[144] Fields of use must be defined objectively by reference to identified and meaningful technical characteristics of the licensed product.

---

[138] See Guidelines para 175.

[139] ibid.

[140] ibid.

[141] See Guidelines para 98.

[142] Arguably, this right belongs to the specific subject matter of the intellectual property right.

[143] See para 178.

[144] When assessing field of use restrictions from the perspective of product markets it is essential that such markets be defined at the appropriate level, namely the level at which the licensed technology is used as an input. This can be illustrated by an example based on Case 234/89 *Delimitis* [1991] ECR I-935, which concerned

This is necessary in order to distinguish field of use restrictions from customer restrictions, which under the TTBER are subject to stricter treatment. The Guidelines[145] give the following examples of field of use restrictions: an engine technology that may be employed in four cylinder engines and six cylinder engines and a technology may be used to make chipsets with up to four CPUs and more than four CPUs. Licences limiting the use of the licensed technology to produce four cylinder engines and chipsets with up to four CPUs constitute technical field of use restrictions. It follows that field of use restrictions are based on the characteristics of the products and not on the characteristics of the buyer.

Field of use restrictions are treated favourably irrespective of whether the agreement involves competitors or non-competitors. The Guidelines[146] recognise that if the licensor could not prevent licensees from operating in fields where he exploits the technology himself or in fields where the value of the technology is not yet well established, it would likely create a disincentive for the licensor to license or would lead him to charge a higher royalty. It is also recognised that in certain sectors licensing often occurs to ensure design freedom by preventing infringement claims. Within the scope of the licence the licensee is able to develop his own technology without fearing infringement claims by the licensor. This is particularly important in high tech and other industries where a multitude of intellectual property rights create thickets hampering innovation. Cross-licensing between competitors may be an effective way to resolve such problems and create necessary design freedom. Allowing the parties to impose field of use restrictions promotes the conclusion of such generally pro-competitive agreements. **10.143**

In the case of agreements between competitors the main competitive concern is the risk that the licensee ceases to be a competitive force outside the licensed field of use. According to the Guidelines[147] this risk is greater in the case of cross licensing between competitors where the agreement provides for asymmetrical field of use restrictions, ie an arrangement where one licensee is licensed one field of use and the other licensee is licensed another field of use. Symmetrical licenses on the other hand are less likely to give rise to competition concerns. Clearly, it cannot be excluded that such agreements may facilitate collusion by creating a high degree of commonality of costs. Undertakings that have similar costs are more likely to have similar views on the terms of coordination.[148] However, even where production on the basis of the same technologies makes up a substantial part of the cost structures of the undertakings concerned, individual undertakings may differ in efficiency **10.144**

---

the issue of foreclosure at the distribution level. In its judgment the Court of Justice held that there are two relevant beer distribution markets, namely a market for off-premise consumption and a market for on-premise consumption. However, in the case of a licence of beer technology it would not be appropriate to apply the same market definition. There would likely be one market for beer technology, and the grant of a distinct licence for production for off-premise consumption should be qualified as a customer restriction and not a field of use restriction.

145 See para 179.
146 See para 182.
147 See para 183.
148 See Commission Notice on Guidelines on the application of Art 81 of the Treaty to horizontal cooperation agreements [2001] OJ C3/2, para 23. As is clear for Case T-342/99 *Airtours* [2002] ECR II-2585, para 62, for a finding of tacit collusion it is not sufficient that the undertakings in question are able tacitly to agree on the desired outcome, which may be facilitated by a commonality of costs. They must also be able to monitor each other's market conduct and retaliate in the case of deviation.

in exploiting the technology and may also use different inputs, leading to different costs. It is therefore submitted that in the case of licensing cost commonalities should only rarely lead to licence agreements being caught by Article 81(1).

10.145 According to the Guidelines[149] it must also be taken into account whether the licensee's production facility, which is tooled up to use the licensed technology, is also used by the licensee to produce with his own technology outside the licensed field of use. If the agreement is likely to lead the licensee to reduce output outside the licensed field of use, the agreement is likely to be caught by Article 81(1).

10.146 Field of use restrictions in agreements between non-competitors whereby the licensor reserves one or more product markets or technical fields of use for himself are according to the Guidelines generally either non-restrictive of competition or efficiency enhancing.[150] They promote dissemination of new technology by giving the licensor an incentive to license for exploitation in fields in which he does not want to exploit the technology himself.

(f) Captive Use Restrictions

10.147 A captive use restriction is an obligation on the licensee to limit production of the licensed product to the quantities required for the production of his own products and for the maintenance and repair of his own products.[151] In the case of agreements between competitors the main issue to be assessed is how the agreement affects the ability and incentive for the licensee to supply components based on his own technology. Competition concerns are likely to arise where, prior to the agreement, the licensee was an actual or likely supplier of components on the market and the agreement is likely to impact negatively on this activity. This may particularly be the case where, by tooling up to use the licensor's technology, the licensee ceases to use his own technology on a stand alone basis.[152]

10.148 When the parties to the agreement are non-competitors captive use restrictions may limit intra-technology competition on the market for inputs. However, according to the Guidelines,[153] if the licensor is a supplier of components, the restraint may be necessary in order for the dissemination of technology between non-competitors to occur. In the absence of the restraint the licensor may not grant the licence or may do so only against higher royalties, because otherwise he would create direct competition to himself on the component market. In such circumstances the restraint will normally escape Article 81. Where the licensor is not a component supplier and the licensees have a significant degree of market power, the restraint is likely to be caught by Article 81 as it restricts intra-technology competition that would otherwise have occurred between the licensees.

(g) Tying and Bundling

10.149 In the context of technology licensing, tying occurs when the licensor makes the licensing of one technology (the tying product) conditional upon the licensee taking a licence for

---

[149] See para 183.
[150] See para 184.
[151] See Guidelines para 186.
[152] See Guidelines para 187.
[153] See para 189.

another technology or purchasing a product from the licensor or someone designated by him (the tied product). Bundling occurs where two technologies or a technology and a product are only sold together as a bundle. In both cases it is a condition that the products and technologies involved are distinct. It is sufficient in this respect that due to product differentiation there is distinct demand for each of the products and technologies forming part of the tie or the bundle. It is not required that in addition they belong to separate product markets.

The main restrictive effects of tying are: (a) foreclosure on a downstream market as a means of maintaining market power in the upstream tying market. Tying may raise barriers to entry when it obliges an undertaking, contemplating entry in the market for the tying product, to also enter the market for the tied product. (b) Foreclosure of competing suppliers on the market for the tied product, producing negative effects such as reduced product variety and product innovation. (c) Tying may also allow the licensor to increase royalties, in particular when the tying product and the tied product are partly substitutable and the two products are not used in fixed proportion. Tying prevents the licensee from switching to substitute inputs in the face of increased royalties for the tying product. These competition concerns are independent of whether the parties to the agreement are competitors or not. **10.150**

For tying to produce likely anti-competitive effects the licensor must have a significant degree of market power in the tying product so as to restrict competition in the tied product. In the absence of market power in the tying product the licensor cannot use his technology for the anti-competitive purpose of foreclosing suppliers of the tied product.[154] The tie must also cover a sufficient portion of demand on the tied market so as to produce likely foreclosure effects. **10.151**

Tying can also produce pro-competitive efficiencies. The Guidelines give two examples of such efficiencies.[155] First, the tied product is necessary for a technically satisfactory exploitation of the licensed technology or for ensuring that production under the licence conforms to quality standards respected by the licensor and other licensees. Second, tying is likely to be pro-competitive where the tied product allows the licensee to exploit the licensed technology significantly more efficiently. **10.152**

(h) *Exclusive Dealing*

Under a non-compete obligation the licensee is obliged not to use third party technologies which compete with the licensed technology. The main competitive risk presented by non-compete obligations is foreclosure of third party technologies.[156] Foreclosure effects may result from agreements concluded by a single licensor or by a cumulative effect of agreements concluded by several licensors, even where each individual agreement or network of agreements is covered by the TTBER.[157] **10.153**

---

[154] See Guidelines para 193. If the licensor has market power in the tied product the restraint should be analysed as exclusive dealing on the tied market or in the case of bundling as bundling based on market power in the tied market.

[155] See paras 194 and 195.

[156] Non-compete obligations may also facilitate collusion between licensors in the case of cumulative use.

[157] In the latter case the application of Art 81 requires withdrawal of the block exemption.

10.154   Foreclosure may arise where a substantial part of all possible licensees are tied to one or, in the case of cumulative effects, more sources of technology and are prevented from exploiting competing technologies. According to the Guidelines a serious cumulative foreclosure effect is unlikely to arise as long as less than 50 per cent of the market is tied.[158] In the case of a single undertaking foreclosure effects may arise where the undertaking in question has a significant degree of market power and there are significant barriers to entry.[159] The stronger the market position of the licensor the higher the risk of foreclosing competing technologies. The risk of foreclosure is particularly high where there is only a limited number of potential licensees and the licence agreement concerns a technology which is used by the licensees to make an input for their own use. In such cases the entry barriers for a new licensor are likely to be high.[160] The reason is the fact that in such circumstances the licensees represent demand in the market. If this demand is tied, new entry requires not only that the licensee produce the input but also the final product that incorporates the input. Entry is therefore required at two levels. However, also in the case where a single undertaking holds a strong position on the market, foreclosure is generally only likely where a substantial part of the market is foreclosed.[161]

10.155   Non-compete obligations may also produce pro-competitive effects. First, such obligations may promote dissemination of technology by reducing the risk of misappropriation of the licensed technology, in particular know-how. If a licensee is entitled to license competing technologies from third parties, there is a risk that particularly licensed know-how would be used in the exploitation of competing technologies and thus benefit competitors.[162] Secondly, non-compete obligations, possibly in combination with an exclusive territory, may be necessary to ensure that the licensee has an incentive to invest in and exploit the licensed technology effectively.[163]

(i) Settlements

10.156   Licensing may serve as a means of settling disputes or avoiding a situation in which one party exercises his intellectual property rights to prevent the other party from exploiting his own technology. Such agreements are treated like any other licence agreement.[164] Licensing including cross-licensing in the context of settlement agreements and non-assertion agreements is not as such restrictive of competition since it allows the parties to exploit their technologies post agreement. However, the individual terms and conditions of such agreements may be caught by Article 81(1).[165] Agreements whereby the parties cross-license each other and impose restrictions on the use of their technologies, including restrictions on

---

[158]   See para 199. The threshold is the same as that applied in the Guidelines on Vertical Restraints (2000 OJ C291/1, para 146) in the case of intermediate products.

[159]   See Guidelines para 200.

[160]   ibid.

[161]   If it is not, it needs to be substantiated that the tied licensee(s) are the most likely to deal with new entrants for instance because they have the most flexible production assets that can most readily be adapted to use alternative technologies.

[162]   See Guidelines para 201.

[163]   See Guidelines para 202.

[164]   See Guidelines para 204.

[165]   ibid.

licensing to third parties, may be caught by Article 81(1).[166] Where the parties have a significant degree of market power and the agreement imposes restrictions that clearly go beyond what is required in order to unblock the technologies concerned, the agreement is likely to be caught by Article 81(1) even if it is likely that a mutual blocking position exists. Article 81(1) is particularly likely to apply where the parties share markets or fix reciprocal running royalties that have a significant impact on market prices.[167]

The Commission takes the view in the Guidelines[168] that non-challenge clauses in the context of settlement agreements generally are not caught by Article 81(1). According to the Commission it is inherent in such agreements that the parties agree not to challenge *ex post* the intellectual property rights covered by the agreement. The Commission expressed the same view in *Bayer v Sülhöfer*.[169] However, the Court of Justice rejected the argument, referring to the fact that Article 81(1) makes no distinction between agreements whose purpose is to put an end to litigation and those concluded with other aims in mind and that a non-challenge clause included in a patent licensing agreement may, in the light of the legal and economic context, restrict competition within the meaning of Article 81(1). It is submitted that the Commission's approach is correct and in line with other judgments where the Court of Justice has held certain restraints to fall outside Article 81(1) because they formed an inherent part of a particular type of agreement.[170]

10.157

(j) Licensing of Future Developments

Agreements whereby the parties cross-licence competing technologies and agree to share future improvements and developments may negatively affect the parties' incentives to innovate. Such agreements are likely to be caught by Article 81(1) where they prevent the parties from gaining a competitive lead over each other.[171] This approach is based on standard patent race theory.[172] Innovation can be seen as a race to develop future successful products. Uncertainty as to the innovative efforts made by rivals and the risk of being left behind creates incentives to invest in innovation. If the parties commit to exchanging future innovations they know that they will remain on an equal technological footing, eliminating the gain from competing on innovation. However, for this concern to materialise the parties must have a strong position on the market. If there are several other competitors investing in innovation, the competitive pressure from such third parties will suffice to maintain the incentive of the parties to innovate. Moreover, the agreement to exchange future innovations must have a significant impact on overall competition between the parties. As stated in the Guidelines, 'the agreement must prevent the parties from gaining a competitive lead over each other'. This is not the case where the agreement

10.158

---

[166] See para 207.
[167] See in this respect the decision of the US Federal Trade Commission of 23.2.1999 in *Summit Technology and VISX*.
[168] See para 209.
[169] Case 65/86 *Bayer v Süllhöfer* [1988] ECR 5249.
[170] See eg Case C-519/04 P *Meca-Medina* [2006] ECR I-0000, Case C-399/93 *Luttikhuis* [1995] ECR I-4515, Case C-250/92 *Gøttrup-Klim* [1994] ECR I-5641, and Case 161/84 *Pronuptia* [1986] ECR 353.
[171] See Guidelines para 208.
[172] See eg Tirole, *The Theory of Industrial Organisation* (MIT Press, 1988) p 394 *et seq*.

only covers a limited aspect of the competing products sold by the parties. For instance, the fact that two car manufacturers agree to licence future improvements of their brake technology is unlikely to have a significant impact on future competition between them. The parties are also unlikely to be prevented from gaining a competitive lead over each other where the purpose of the licence is to allow the parties to develop their respective technologies and where the licence does not lead them to use the same technological solutions.[173] Such agreements merely create design freedom by preventing future infringement claims by the other party.

(10) Technology Pools

10.159   The notion of technology pools covers agreements whereby two or more parties agree to pool their respective technologies and license them as a package. It also covers arrangements whereby two or more undertakings agree to license a third party and authorise him to license on the assembled package of technologies.[174] Agreements establishing technology pools and setting out the terms and conditions for their operation are not covered by the block exemption. They are only covered by the Guidelines. However, the individual licences granted by the pool to third party licensees are treated like other licence agreements and may therefore be covered by the block exemption.[175]

10.160   Technology pools may give rise to mainly two types of efficiencies. Pooling reduces transaction costs where licensees need the various technologies in the pool in order to produce the product to which the pool relates. Only one agreement needs to be concluded. Pooling also ensures that a single overall royalty can be fixed, thereby avoiding a stacking of royalties with resulting double marginalisation. As is clear from these efficiencies, the benefits relating to technology pools stem from the complementary nature of the pooled technologies. Conversely, the anti-competitive potential of pools relates largely to the technologies in the pool being substitutable with other technologies in the pool or technologies outside the pool.

(a) *The Nature of the Pooled Technologies*

10.161   Two basic distinctions must be made, namely between (a) technological complements and technological substitutes and (b) essential and non-essential technologies. Two technologies are *complements* as opposed to *substitutes* when they are both required to produce the product or carry out the process to which the technologies relate.[176] Conversely, two technologies are substitutes when either technology allows the holder to produce (part of) the product or carry out (part of) the process to which the technologies relate. A technology is *essential* as opposed to *non-essential* if there are no substitutes for that technology inside or outside the pool and the technology in question constitutes a necessary part of the package of technologies for the purposes of producing the product(s) or carrying out the process(es) to which the pool relates.

---

[173] See Guidelines para 208.
[174] See Guidelines paras 41 and 210.
[175] See Guidelines para 212.
[176] See para 216.

The reference in the Guidelines to 'technologies' might seem contradictory given the fact   **10.162**
that technology pools generally purport to create a technology or part of a technology that
can be used to produce a certain product. For instance, the technology required to produce
DVD discs and players is controlled by a number of undertakings that have formed distinct
pools each licensing part of the overall technology. However, the term 'technologies' is useful
in the sense that it also encompasses the situation where the pool covers competing
technologies or competing technological solutions for at least part of the technology as well
as the situation where there are competing technological solutions for at least part of the
overall technology outside the pool. A pool can be compared to a jigsaw puzzle. The pool
consists of a number of pieces that make up the overall technology that is licensed by the
pool. Each piece is a technology for the purposes of the Guidelines. If all the pieces are
needed to make the puzzle the technologies are complements. If there are also no substitutes outside the pool, the pieces are also essential. If there are substitute pieces inside the
pool, these technologies are substitutes and the technologies in question are no longer
essential. The same is true where there are substitute pieces outside the pool.[177]

The Guidelines use a narrower notion of substitutability in relation to pools than that used   **10.163**
in other parts of the Guidelines. It is acknowledged that technologies may be substitutes in
part and complements in part. When due to efficiencies stemming from the integration of
two technologies licensees are likely to demand both technologies the technologies are
treated as complements even if they are partly substitutable. This test may be difficult to
apply given that demand is a function of value and price. However, it is positive that the
Commission recognises that the distinction between substitutes and complements is not
necessarily clear cut.

(b) Competition Concerns relating to the Creation of the Pool

When a pool is composed only of technologies which are essential and which are therefore   **10.164**
by necessity also complements, the creation of the pool as such generally falls outside
Article 81(1) irrespective of the market position of the parties.[178] Conversely, the
Commission considers that the inclusion of substitute technologies in the pool constitutes
a violation of Article 81(1). The Commission also considers that it is unlikely that the conditions of Article 81(3) will be fulfilled in the case of a pool comprising to a significant
extent substitute technologies.[179] When substitute technologies are included, the pool does
not generate efficiencies and allows competitors to coordinate their prices. When the pool
is to a substantial extent composed of substitute technologies the pool amounts to a price
fixing cartel. The Guidelines are rather categorical when they state that inclusion of substitute technologies in the pool constitutes a violation of Article 81(1). However, given the
practical difficulty in determining the competitive relationship between two technologies

---

[177] This example illustrates a possible difficulty in applying the requirement under the Guidelines according to which a technology is only essential when it forms a necessary part of the overall technology to which
the pool relates. This may be question of design. If the puzzle makes up a castle with a blue sky and one white
cloud, the piece with the white cloud forms a necessary part of the puzzle as designed. However, in itself the
chosen design says very little about the importance of the cloud and its colour.
[178] See Guidelines para 220.
[179] See Guidelines para 219.

and the fact that a pool which is composed mainly of essential technologies can hardly be qualified as a restriction by object, it is likely that in practice the Commission will have regard to whether or not the inclusion of substitute technologies is likely to have an appreciable effect on royalties. For instance, the inclusion of substitute technologies of minor importance is unlikely to create competition concerns. As long as the main parts of the puzzle that make up the relevant technology are essential, the inclusion of substitutes is unlikely to have an appreciable impact on price as long as the essential pieces are owned by non-competitors. In this context it must be taken into account that royalties may be negotiated *ex ante*.[180] It is likely that in such negotiations the key parts of the technology will obtain a lion's share of the royalties. If the pool is mainly composed of complementary pieces the owners of these technologies are unlikely to let the owners of substitute elements use the pool as a vehicle for price fixing. It is likely that these latter contributors will compete to be included in the pool and therefore collectively attract little more than the royalty which they would be able to obtain individually.

10.165   Competition concerns may also arise when there are substitute technologies outside the pool. Once a technology is included in the pool and is licensed as part of the package, licensees are likely to have little incentive to take a licence for a competing technology when the royalty paid for the package already covers a substitute technology.[181] However, foreclosure is only an issue if the pool has a strong position on the market. According to the Guidelines[182] a pool is likely to be caught by Article 81(1) where it has a significant position on any relevant market. Given the benefit to licensees of one-stop licensing it is submitted that the conditions of Article 81(3) are likely to be satisfied unless the pool holds a dominant position. In individual cases, the significance of the technology for which substitutes exist outside the pool should also be taken into account. The aim of Article 81 is to protect competition on the market. It is not sufficient for the application of Article 81(1) that any third party technology is being excluded. The exclusion must have an appreciable impact on dynamic competition which presupposes that the excluded technology is of some significance.

10.166   Given that substitute and complementary technologies may be developed after the creation of the pool the assessment of essentiality is an ongoing process. One way to deal with this reality is to exclude from the pool technologies that have become non-essential. However, the Guidelines[183] also outline a number of factors that may provide a basis for keeping the technology in question inside the pool. The listed factors are the following: (a) any pro-competitive reasons for including the non-essential technologies in the pool; (b) the possibility for licensors to license independently;[184] (c) where the pooled technologies have different applications the possibility for licensees to obtain a licence for separate packages for distinct applications; and (d) the possibility for licensees to obtain a licence for only part

---

[180] See Guidelines para 225.
[181] See Guidelines para 221.
[182] ibid.
[183] See para 222.
[184] If licensors are free to license independently licensees may be able to assemble their own package. However, the benefits of pools, namely reduction of transaction costs and double marginalisation, will in many cases render this option a rather theoretical one.

of the package with a corresponding reduction of royalties. Factor (c) seeks to address the situation where technologies that are non-essential in relation to one or more applications are bundled with essential ones. However, such a situation is only caught by Article 81(1) in the first place if bundling is likely to lead to higher prices. It is therefore necessary to consider the importance of the technology in question to the overall package. Factor (d) seeks to address the situation where there are substitutes outside the pool that risk being foreclosed and where it may be a relevant option for the pool to offer a licence that excludes the substitute technology. The main difficulty is setting the royalty for such an alternative licence. To avoid foreclosure of competing technologies the royalty must be reduced by an amount reflecting the relative value of the technology in question. However, in practice it may be very difficult to assign a true value to the technology. In cases where real foreclosure concerns arise it may therefore be simpler to eject the technology in question from the pool.

(c) Assessment of Individual Restraints

The individual licence agreements concluded by the pool are subject to the TTBER including the hardcore list contained in Article 4. The Guidelines further provide that where the pool has a dominant position on the market, royalties and other licensing terms should be fair and non-discriminatory and licences should be non-exclusive.[185] It is further provided that when the pool has a strong position on the market, licensors and licensees must be free to develop competing products and standards and must also be free to grant and obtain licences outside the pool.[186] These requirements are said to be necessary in order to limit the risk of foreclosure of third party technologies and to ensure that the pool does not limit innovation and preclude the creation of competing technological solutions. Where a pool supports a (de facto) industry standard and where the parties are subject to non-compete obligations, the pool is said to create a particular risk of preventing the development of new and improved technologies and standards.

10.167

The Guidelines also address the fixing of pool royalties and the sharing of these royalties amongst the participants.[187] Undertakings setting up a technology pool are generally[188] free to negotiate and fix royalties for the technology package and to determine each technology's share of the royalties either before or after the standard is set. It is very important that royalties can be negotiated before the selection of the technologies that eventually form part of the pool. The value of a technology which is being proposed for a pool is a function of price and performance. *Ex ante* negotiations are likely to lead to the selection of the technologies with the best price/performance ratio. Where the pool creates a standard, *ex post* negotiations may confer a significant degree of market power on one or more essential technologies.[189]

10.168

---

[185] See Guidelines para 226.

[186] See Guidelines para 227.

[187] See Guidelines para 225.

[188] This statement presupposes that the pool does not give rise to price fixing concerns between substitute technologies.

[189] *Ex ante* negotiations may in some circumstances lead to buyer power concerns. If the pool supports an industry standard, negotiations involving suppliers of substitute technology could drive prices down to marginal costs, which in the case of licensing are close to zero. In sectors where standards are commonplace this could have a chilling effect on the incentive to innovate.

10.169 The value of a technology package does not depend on the number of essential technologies contained in the pool. An essential patent or other intellectual property right can be equated with a key that unlocks the whole or part of an overall technology. The value of such an overall technology is the same irrespective of the number of keys required to gain access to it. In cases where there is more than one holder of essential technologies and where a pool may therefore be relevant, there is no mechanical relationship between the number of intellectual property rights and royalties. In other words, there is no reason why royalties should be higher when there are four essential technologies in the package compared to when there are only two. The Guidelines do not deal with this issue explicitly, which is particularly relevant in cases where patents are registered asymmetrically in the sense that not all essential technologies are patent protected in all territories covered by the pool. In such cases there would appear to be no reason to expect that the undertakings will fix distinct royalties depending on the number of patents registered in each territory and it is submitted that Community competition law does not oblige them to do so.

D. Trademark Licences

10.170 The commercial risks of, and consumer benefits accruing from, investment in innovation and manufacturing are clearly recognised under Community competition law, in particular by the technology transfer block exemption. Distribution arrangements are generally regarded under Community law as less in need of protection, and the permitted restrictions in agreements are consequently more limited. It is unclear whether this is because of a perception of lower commercial risk, fewer third party benefits, or the increased risks to the single market of market partitioning through territorial distribution.

(1) Licences and Assignments

(a) *Territorial Protection*

10.171 The Court established early that absolute territorial protection using trademarks was liable to infringe Article 81 in that it led to a partitioning of markets. The Court even went so far as to suggest that trademark rights were less important than other forms of intellectual property.[190] The Court's relatively strict jurisprudence on trademark restrictions seems to have placed an undue reliance on the importance of intra-brand competition without necessarily taking into account the existence and extent of inter-brand competition.[191]

10.172 In *Consten/Grundig*[192] Grundig had appointed Consten as its exclusive distributor in France and had assigned the GINT (Grundig International) mark to Consten. Grundig had agreed not to appoint any other distributors in France or to sell the goods itself in France. In addition it restrained its distributors outside France from selling to French customers. In return Consten agreed not to deal in goods competing with Grundig's products. Consten was able to obtain significantly higher prices for Grundig products on the French market than those prevailing

---

190 Case 40/70 *Sirena Srl v Eda Srl and others* [1971] ECR 69, at para 7.
191 See, for example, Case 28/77 *Tepea BV v Commission* [1978] ECR 139, at para 43.
192 Joined Cases 56 & 58/64 *Consten and Grundig v Commission* [1966] ECR 299.

in Germany. Consten used the agreements to obtain injunctions from the French courts blocking the parallel imports of Grundig products. The Court held:

> Consten's right under the contract to the exclusive use in France of the GINT trademark, . . . is intended to make it possible to keep under surveillance and to place an obstacle in the way of parallel imports. Thus, the agreement by which Grundig, as the holder of the trade-mark by virtue of an inter-national registration, authorized Consten to register it in France in its own name tends to restrict competition.
>
> . . .
>
> That agreement therefore is one which may be caught by the prohibition in Article 85(1) [now Article 81(1)]. The prohibition would be ineffective if Consten could continue to use the trade-mark to achieve the same object as that pursued by the agreement which has been held to be unlawful.[193]

The Court's belief in the risks to the single market inherent in trademark rights appears to have reduced over the years. In relation to the free movement of goods, for example, the position of the Court in respect of Article 28 in the first *Hag* case[194]—that trademarks could not be used to oppose the import of products into a Member State where the trademarks had a common origin—was abandoned in the *Hag II*[195] litigation. The current position is that under Article 7(1) of the First Trademarks Directive,[196] the trademark cannot be employed to oppose its use ('use' here includes import) in relation to goods where the goods have been put on the market in the Community by the trademark proprietor, or with its consent.[197] **10.173**

In the *Moosehead* case,[198] the Commission regarded territorial restrictions on Whitbread's activities as falling within Article 81(1). Whitbread entered into a licensing agreement to manufacture Moosehead Canadian lager in the UK. Whitbread was prevented from making active sales outside the territory. These restrictions fell within Article 81(1) as Whitbread, given its size, would otherwise have been in a position to supply other markets. However, the Commission accepted that the restrictions were exemptable in view of the benefits of the agreement. It seems safe to assume that the position on open and closed exclusive licences is essentially the same in respect of trademarks as it is in respect of other forms of intellectual property.[199] **10.174**

The Court has recently adopted a less restrictive approach in respect of assignments of trademarks to different entities in different Member States. While recognising that this may be used as a market partitioning mechanism, the Court went on: **10.175**

> that rule and the accompanying sanction cannot be applied mechanically to every assignment. Before a trade-mark assignment can be treated as giving effect to an agreement prohibited under

---

[193] Joined Cases 56 & 58/64 *Consten and Grundig v Commission* [1966] ECR 299.

[194] Case 193/73 *Van Zuylen Frères v Hag AG* [1974] ECR 731 (Hag I).

[195] Case C10/89 *CNL Sucal v Hag GF AG* [1990] ECR I–3711 (Hag II). See also Case C-9/93 *IHT Internationale Heiztechnik v Ideal-Standard* [1994] ECR I-2789.

[196] Directive 89/104/EEC (OJ 1989 L40/1).

[197] It should be noted however that Art 7(2) of the same Directive disapplies Art 7(1) where legitimate reasons exist for the proprietor to oppose further commercialisation of the goods, especially where the conditions of the goods is changed or impaired after they have been put on the market.

[198] *Moosehead/Whitbread* [1990] OJ L100/32 (only the English text is authentic).

[199] See, *inter alia*, the discussion of *Maize Seeds: Breeders' rights—maize seed* [1978] OJ L286/23; Case 258/78 *LC Nungesser KG and Kurt Eisele v Commission* [1982] ECR 2015.

Article 85 [now Article 81], it is necessary to analyse the context, the commitments underlying the assignment, the intention of the parties and the consideration for the assignment.[200]

10.176 As such, it appears more likely that such clauses would fall outside Article 81(1), provided that, for example, inter-brand competition was sufficiently strong.

(b) Prohibition on Competing Products

10.177 In *Campari*, the Commission was prepared to exempt a ban on trade in competing goods given the consequent benefits to the distribution system, and contrasted non-competition clauses in respect of trademarks with those in respect of patents:

> Although a non-competition clause in a licensing agreement concerning industrial property rights based on the result of a creative activity, such as a patent, would constitute a barrier to technical and economic progress by preventing the licensees from taking an interest in other techniques and products, this is not the case with the licensing agreements under consideration here. The aim pursued by the parties, as is clear from the agreements taken as a whole, is to decentralize manufacture within the EEC and to rationalize the distribution system linked to it . . .

> The prohibition on dealing in competing products, therefore, makes for improved distribution of the relevant product in the same way as do exclusive dealing agreements containing a similar clause, which are automatically exempted by regulation no 67/67/EEC.[201]

10.178 A similar clause was exempted in the *Moosehead* case in light of the availability of competing brands.[202]

(c) No-challenge Clauses (Ownership)

10.179 The Commission has found that such a clause falls outside Article 81(1) as: 'Whether or not the licensor or licensee has the ownership of the trademark, the use of it by any other party is prevented in any event, and competition would thus not be affected.'[203]

(d) No-challenge Clauses (Validity)

10.180 In the *Moosehead* case, the Commission decided that this could potentially fall within Article 81(1) as it could contribute to the maintenance of a trademark that could be an unjustified barrier to entry on a given market. Whether or not a particular trademark could constitute a barrier to entry would depend on the status of the trademark on the particular market. In this case, as Moosehead was comparatively new to the relevant market, the Commission found that the clause did not fall within Article 81(1).

10.181 As indicated above, the Commission is likely to take a stricter approach where there appears to be a risk of market partitioning,[204] or the obligation appears to have been imposed on one of the parties without justification. The Commission condemned a no-challenge

---

200 Case C-9/93 *IHT Internationale Heiztechnik GmbH and Uwe Danzinger v Ideal-Standard GmbH and Wabco Standard GmbH* [1994] ECR I-278, at para 59.
201 *Campari* [1978] OJ L70/69 (only the German, Danish, French, Italian, and Dutch texts are authentic).
202 *Moosehead/Whitbread* [1990] OJ L100/32, at para 16(2) (only the English text is authentic).
203 *Moosehead/Whitbread* [1990] OJ L100/32, at para 15(4)(only the English text is authentic).
204 *Toltecs-Dorcet* [1982] OJ L379/19 (only the German and Dutch texts are authentic).

clause in the *Windsurfing* case without having examined the impact of the clause on the particular market: the Commission may have been influenced in that case by the no-challenge clause being 'imposed on the licensees in the agreements relating to the exploitation of the patent even though the subject-matter of the clause was quite different'.[205]

(e) *Prohibition on Sub-licensing or Assignment*

In the *Campari* case,[206] the Commission cleared a clause prohibiting assignment of the trademark as this was essential to ensure that the licensor could continue to select its preferred licensees.

10.182

(f) *Quality Control Measures*

Given the importance of maintaining the brand, the Commission has regarded quality control measures as falling outside Article 81(1).[207]

10.183

(2) Trademark Delimitation Agreements

The single market increases the risks of confusion of nationally granted trademark rights. Parties owning marks capable of being confused may wish to avoid consumer confusion by agreeing some form of territorial restrictions on the scope of use of certain trademarks.

10.184

(a) *Market Partitioning*

The Commission has taken a strict line in respect of Article 81(1) where it believed that the agreements in question were being used simply to partition the market.[208] The principals can agree what trademarks they will use in various jurisdictions but they cannot agree not to compete with each other in those jurisdictions. BAT owned the German rights to the 'Dorcet' trademark. A smaller Dutch firm, Segers, sought to export its cut tobacco to Germany under its 'Toltecs' brand name. BAT began proceedings under German law based on the fact that the two trademarks were confusingly similar. To avoid the costs of a lengthy legal battle with a larger rival, and because of the breadth of protection sometimes given to German trademarks Segers entered into a settlement with BAT. Under the terms of this settlement Segers could only export a limited number of types of tobacco to Germany under the Toltecs brand name, and could only make these exports through distributors approved by BAT. Subsequently when Segers's initial distributor ceased trading, Segers found it difficult to gain BAT's approval for a new distributor and ceased exporting their products to Germany and complained to the Commission.

10.185

The Commission, and later the Court, held that the agreement between BAT and Segers went beyond what was necessary to avoid confusion of trademarks. The agreement served to limit severely competition to BAT from Segers. Accordingly it infringed Article 81(1) and did not meet the conditions for the grant of an exemption under Article 81(3).

10.186

---

[205] Case 193/83 *Windsurfing International Inc v Commission* [1986] ECR 61, at para 80.
[206] *Campari* [1978] OJ L70/69 (only the German, Danish, French, Italian, and Dutch texts are authentic).
[207] *Moosehead/Whitbread* [1990] OJ L100/32, at para 15(2) (only the English text is authentic) and *Campari* [1978] OJ L70/69 (only the German, Danish, French, Italian, and Dutch texts are authentic).
[208] *Toltecs-Dorcet* [1982] OJ L379/19 (only the German and Dutch texts are authentic). Upheld on the substance in Case 35/83 *BAT Cigaretten-Fabriken GmbH v Commission* [1985] ECR 36.

(b) Confusion of Marks

10.187 However, where restrictions only go so far as is necessary to avoid confusion, the Commission will take a more positive view. In the *Penneys* case,[209] the Commission gave a negative clearance to an agreement to settle a range of trademark disputes in a number of jurisdictions. The Penneys trademark was owned both by a US clothing retailer and an Irish clothing retailer. This had given rise to a number of trademark disputes. Under the terms of the settlement the US firm agreed not to trade as Penneys in Ireland and the Irish firm agreed to use the Penneys business name only in Ireland, and not to register it outside Ireland.

E. Copyright

(1) Community Directives Relating to Copyright

10.188 The following EC Directives have been adopted which add to or modify Member States' copyright systems.

10.189 First, there is a Directive on semiconductor topographies[210] which introduced a form of protection for the design of products made by etching electronic circuits onto semiconducting surfaces ('chips').

10.190 Secondly, there is a Directive on computer software[211] which extended copyright protection to computer software by providing that software should be considered as literary works.

10.191 Thirdly, there is a Directive on rental lending, and neighbouring rights.[212] The emergence of a market for the sale and rental of recordings of copyright works such as films coupled with the technological possibility of making high-quality copies of these works at home, led to a need to clarify and extend copyright. This Directive clearly established a right to rent out a copy of a copyrighted work, and so to control the use of this rented copy and to prohibit the owner of a copy of a work from renting it out.

10.192 Fourthly, there is a Directive on satellite broadcasting and cable retransmission[213] establishing that a copyright owner has the right to control the broadcast or transmission of their work via satellite or cable network.

10.193 Fifthly, there is a Directive on copyright duration[214] which aims to facilitate a single market in products protected by copyright by harmonising the term of copyright protection throughout the EEA. Since the terms were harmonised upwards to the longest term

---

209 *Penneys* [1978] OJ L60/19.

210 Council Directive (EC) 54/87 on the legal protection of semiconductor topographies [1987] OJ L24/36.

211 Council Directive (EC) 91/250 on the legal protection of computer programs [1991] OJ L122/42.

212 Council Directive (EC) 92/100 on rental right and lending right and on certain rights related to copyright in the field of intellectual property [1992] OJ L346/61.

213 Council Directive (EC) 93/83 on the co-ordination of certain rules concerning copyright and rights related to copyright applicable to satellite broadcasting and cable retransmission [1993] OJ L248/15.

214 Council Directive (EC) 93/98 harmonising the term of protection of copyright and certain related rights [1993] OJ L290/9.

granted in any Member State this had the effect of renewing the copyright protection on certain classic works. The work of an individual author is protected until 70 years after his or her death. Where the right owner is a corporate body copyright extends for 50 years.

Sixthly, there is a Directive on the legal protection of databases.[215] Computer and commu-   **10.194**
nication technology allows the creation of ordered collections of information. This information may be the copyright of the person assembling the database or one or more third
parties, non-copyrighted material in the public domain, or a mixture of the two. The creator
of the database adds value by assembling the material, maintaining it, and providing facilities for searching the database. Certain Member States' copyright law would protect such
an assembly of material, but in others it could not meet the requirement for originality.[216]
This Directive creates a specific, *sui generis*, protection for the database.

Finally, there is a Directive harmonising certain aspects of copyright and related rights in the   **10.195**
information society [217] which clarifies the copyright protection of data in an online environment, covering all original works including computer programs and databases. The
Directive recognises the importance of the technical measures that a right holder may use to
prevent illicit copying or reuse of their work, and the importance of the visible and hidden
'rights management' information that a right holder may include in a copy of their work.

(2) Territorial Protection through Exclusive Licences

Exclusive territory does not necessarily infringe Article 81(1)   A licence granting the   **10.196**
licensee exclusive rights in a particular jurisdiction is not necessarily restrictive of competition. In the *Coditel II* case,[218] the Court noted that assigning part of an exclusive right did
not amount to a restrictive agreement or practice[219] and ruled that such an exclusive licence
did not *in itself* breach Article 81.[220] However, there might be factual circumstances where
the effect of such a licence would be to restrict competition.[221] Since the reference had not
described the commercial and economic background to the case the court found that:

> it is for national courts . . . to establish whether or not the exercise of the exclusive right to
> exhibit a cinematographic film creates barriers which are artificial and unjustifiable in terms
> of the needs of the cinematographic industry, or the possibility of charging fees which exceed
> a fair return on investment, or an exclusivity the duration of which is disproportionate to
> these requirements, and whether or not, from a general point of view, such exercise within

---

[215]   Council Directive (EC) 96/9 on the legal protection of databases [1996] OJ L77/20.
[216]   One of the issues raised in the *Magill* case was that the television listings in question were only protected
by copyright due to the nature of UK and Irish copyright law. The Court of First Instance noted that the Irish
courts had determined that the listings in question were in fact protected by the relevant Irish copyright law
and did not need to consider the issue further. (Case T-69/89 *RTE v Commission* [1991] II–ECR 485, in particular paras 10 and 75.)
[217]   [2001] OJL167, pp 10–19.
[218]   Case 262/81 *Coditel v Cine-Vog* [1982] ECR 3381.
[219]   Case 262/81 *Coditel v Cine-Vog* [1982] ECR 3381, at para 15.
[220]   Case 262/81 *Coditel v Cine-Vog* [1982] ECR 3381, at para 20: 'a contract whereby the owner of the
copyright in a film grants an exclusive right to exhibit that film for a specific period in the territory of a member state is not, as such, subject to the prohibitions contained in Article 85 [now Article 81] of the Treaty'.
[221]   Case 262/81 *Coditel v Cine-Vog* [1982] ECR 3381, at paras 16 and 17.

a given geographic area is such as to prevent restrict or distort competition within the common market.[222]

10.197   The test set out by the Court can be criticised as it appears to focus on whether the restriction is necessary to safeguard the continuation of the cinematographic industry, whereas arguably the test should be more focused on whether the rights owner can continue to be appropriately remunerated for the supply of its content. Focusing on the circumstances of the industry rather than the incentive effects of the rights owner risks protecting the industry against new products or services that could better satisfy consumer demand.

(a) Collective Refusals to License

10.198   Refusals to licence only fall within Article 81(1) where it can be shown that the refusals are themselves part of an agreement or concerted practice.[223] Horse racing in France is organised by a number of regional bodies (*sociétés de course*), each of which has the sole authorisation to organise horse races in their area, and owns the copyright to any recordings or broadcasts of these races. Each of them had granted a firm jointly owned and controlled by them (the PMU) an exclusive licence, for France and Germany only, to broadcast the races that they organised. The PMU broadcast these races itself in France for the purpose of taking off-course bets, and licensed the German rights to a German firm, Deutscher Sportverlag Stoof GmbH & Co (DSV).

10.199   Ladbrokes operated a chain of betting shops in Belgium, and wished to show these French races in their Belgian shops in order to take bets on the races. Ladbrokes applied for a licence for these races to DSV, who informed them that they only held a licence for Germany and so could not grant licences for Belgium. Ladbrokes applied to PMU and to each of the individual *sociétés de course*. PMU informed Ladbrokes that it only held a licence to the races for France and so could not grant the licence that Ladbrokes sought. It also informed Ladbrokes that each of the individual *sociétés de course* had asked it to inform Ladbrokes that they had individually decided not to license the Belgian rights to their races to Ladbrokes.

10.200   The combination of the exclusive, limited licence from the *sociétés de course* to PMU, the exclusive licence from PMU to DSV, and the independent refusal of each *société de course* to grant a licence to Ladbrokes meant that it was not possible for Ladbrokes to broadcast French horse races and take off-course bets on them as was done in France and Germany by PMU and DSV respectively. The Court held, *inter alia*, that each of these refusals to licence did not individually or collectively infringe Article 81(1). Only if it could be shown that there was an agreement or concerted practice between the *sociétés de course* not to licence certain third parties would any question of a breach of Article 81(1) arise:

> a horizontal agreement between sociétés de courses which prevented each of them from granting a licence to transmit the sound and pictures of the races which it organized to a third party such as the applicant would be liable to impede the entry of each of them on to the Belgian market in sound and pictures in general and thereby restrict such potential competition as

---

222   Case 262/81 *Coditel v Cine-Vog* [1982] ECR 3381, at para 19.
223   Case T-504/93 *Tiercé Ladbroke SA v Commission* [1997] ECR II-923.

might exist on that market, to the detriment of the interests of bookmakers and ultimate consumers. Moreover, the effect of such an agreement might be to 'limit or control . . . markets' and/or to 'share markets' within the meaning of Article 85(1)(b) and (c) [now Article 81(1)(b) and (c)] of the Treaty.[224]

(b) Specific Subject Matter of Copyright and Article 81(1)

In *Ladbroke*, the Court allowed a system of exclusive licences with prohibitions on sub-licensing. Although prohibitions on sub-licensing are also allowed in other areas, the effect in relation to copyrighted works is more severe. Whereas a patent licence would normally lead to a saleable product, the distribution of which cannot be subject to absolute territorial protection,[225] the broadcast element of copyright does not lead to such a product. The only product is in effect the broadcast transmission itself. In these circumstances, allowing the possibility of making a passive sale would largely undermine any exclusive licensing system. Copyright licensing, because of its specific subject matter, therefore allows a greater degree of territorial protection than other intellectual property rights. The Court has taken a similar approach under Article 59.[226]   **10.201**

Given the Court's recognition that rental rights are a distinct element of the specific subject matter of copyright, licensing sale and rental separately is not in itself a breach of Article 81.[227]   **10.202**

(3) Collecting Societies

(a) Artists' Licences to a Collecting Society

An exclusive licence of copyright to a collecting society is not necessarily restrictive of competition.[228] The exclusivity merely describes the extent to which the owner of intellectual property rights has licensed those rights to another. However, as with the other types of licensing contract described above, a contract which goes beyond describing to what extent an owner of intellectual property is licensing those rights is subject to Article 81. In the *GEMA I* case, a contract between an artist and a collecting society where the artist granted the society an exclusive licence not only to his existing body of work but also to any future work infringed Article 81. The Commission has issued a Statement of Objections to the International Confederation of Societies of Authors and Composers (CISAC) concerning certain aspects of the CISAC model contract and its implementation at a bilateral level between some of its members. The press release confirming the Statement of Objections indicates that the Commission believes that 'the membership restrictions which oblige authors to transfer their rights only to their own national collecting society (whatever the subsequent exploitations of the rights)' may infringe Article 81.[229]   **10.203**

---

[224] Case T 504/93 *Tiercé Ladbroke SA v Commission* [1997] ECR II-92, at para 159.

[225] Save, under the technology transfer block exemption, for a limited start-up period.

[226] Case 62/79 *SA Compagnie générale pour la diffusion de la télévision, Coditel, and others v Ciné Vog Films and others* [1980] ECR 88.

[227] Case 158/86 *Warner Bros. and Metronome v Christiansen* [1988] ECR 2605.

[228] Case 125/78 *GEMA v Commission* [1979] ECR 3173.

[229] Competition: Commission sends Statement of Objections to the International Confederation of Societies of Authors and Composers (CISAC) and its EEA members, MEMO/06/63 of 7 February 2006.

(b) Licensing Agreements between Collecting Societies

10.204 Collecting societies tend to be organised nationally, but will often want to exploit their rights internationally. There is an obvious efficiency benefit if collecting societies grant each other licences in the work of their 'home' artists since any potential licensee can then go to their own 'home' collecting society and obtain a single licence to all of the rights they might need. The Court has therefore held that reciprocal contracts do not in themselves fall within Article 81(1), although the position might be different if the reciprocal contracts contained exclusivity clauses. In addition a concerted practice between collecting societies so as to restrict direct access to their repertoires from foreign users would fall within Article 81(1).[230]

10.205 Technological developments have highlighted the difficult area of where territorial exclusivity falls foul of Article 81. The first indicator of this trend came with the Commission's 2002 decision in the *Simulcasting* case.[231] Simulcasting is the simultaneous broadcasting of material through both traditional broadcast channels and the Internet. The International Federation of Phonographic Industries (IFPI) applied for an exemption for a system whereby its collecting society members instituted a one stop shop allowing individual collecting societies to grant multi-territory multi-repertoire licences. The original notification provided that customers wishing to purchase one of these licences must do so from the collecting society in their home Member State. The Commission required amendments to the notified agreements and granted an exemption only on condition that broadcasters could seek a licence from any collecting society in the EEA, and also provided that the collecting societies began reforming their accounting system making it more transparent.

10.206 Another group of collecting societies notified an agreement—the Santiago agreement—with a similar multi-territorial / multi-repertoire purpose and containing similar territorial restrictions to the original Simulcasting agreement. The Commission expressed the same concerns as to the territorial restrictions and sent a Statement of Objections. Some parties to the agreement agreed not to enforce the territorial restrictions, and the Commission issued an Article 27(4) Notice[232] with a view to adopting a commitments decision under Article 9 of Regulation 1/2003. However, the parties did not agree to institute an agreement absent those territorial restrictions.

(c) Licences from Collecting Societies to Manufacturers

10.207 Collecting societies also enter into licensing arrangements with manufacturers of recordings. Once the recordings have been manufactured and placed on to the market, the performing right society's intellectual property rights are exhausted and any term in the licensing

---

[230] Joined Cases 110/88, 241/88 and 242/88 *François Lucazeau and others v Société des Auteurs, Compositeurs et Editeurs de Musique (SACEM) and others* [1989] ECR 281, at para 17.

[231] Commission Decision of 8 October 2002 relating to a proceeding under Art 81 of the EC Treaty and Art 53 of the EEA Agreement (Case No COMP/C2/38.014—*IFPI 'Simulcasting'*) (notified under document number C(2002) 3639) (only the English text is authentic) (text with EEA relevance) (2003/300/EC), OJ L107/58, 30/04/2003.

[232] Notice published pursuant to Article 27(4) of Council Regulation (EC) No 1/2003 in Cases COMP/C2/39152—BUMA and COMP/C2/39151 SABAM (Santiago Agreement—COMP/C2/38126), OJ C200/11, 17.8.2005.

agreement or action by the society that seeks to control the further sales of the recordings is potentially a restriction of competition subject to Article 81 of the EC Treaty.

The collecting society cannot, for example, seek to influence the retail selling price of the product. In *BIEM/IFPI*,[233] a collecting society had granted a licence to a record manufacturer where the royalty payable by the manufacturer was expressed as a percentage of the average retail selling price of records on the market on which the manufacturer operated. This would have the effect of penalising the manufacturer if it sold the record at a price below the average price prevailing in the market, and would consequently give the manufacturer an incentive to charge as high a price as possible. This was found to infringe Article 81 and the collecting society was required to charge a royalty calculated as a percentage of the actual prices charged by the licensee. **10.208**

F. Article 82

(1) Introduction

The application of Article 82 to intellectual property issues is controversial, and the existing precedents under Community law are neither comprehensive nor models of clarity. It is useful to distinguish between two main categories of case, the first of which—as with other forms of property—has proved extremely controversial: **10.209**

— those of refusals to grant licences to any third party; and
— the granting or refusal of licences on discriminatory or otherwise abusive terms.

This section looks in turn at issues of market definition, dominance, and abuse. **10.210**

(2) Intellectual Property and Market Definition

It is useful to distinguish between upstream and downstream markets. **10.211**

First, there may be a market for the supply to producers of the particular technology needed to produce the good in question, which may or may not be covered by intellectual property rights. Where a good could be produced using different substitutable technologies, some or all of which are protected by intellectual property, the intellectual property rights holders would compete in the supply of that intellectual property to producers. This is essentially the same position as a component manufacturer whose components are used in the manufacture of a downstream product. **10.212**

Secondly, there may be the downstream market for the sale of the good produced using the intellectual property right(s). **10.213**

This distinction between upstream and downstream markets has been recognised explicitly by the Commission in the related area of standardisation, where the Commission identified: 'the market for telecommunications standards and the downstream markets which use those standards'.[234] **10.214**

---

[233] *BIEM/IFPI, Report on CompetitionPolicy (1983)* (Vol XIII), points 147–150.
[234] *ETSI interim IPR policy* (Notice pursuant to Art 19(3) of Regulation 17) [1995] OJ C76/5.

10.215 In standardisation cases, intellectual property rights holders seeking to have their intellectual property included in a standard will be doing so either implicitly or explicitly on the basis that these intellectual property rights will be licensed to third parties who wish to manufacture goods compliant with the standard. In these cases, the distinction between the upstream and downstream markets will be relatively clear.

10.216 However, the distinction between the upstream and downstream markets will not always be so apparent. Where the intellectual property holder is vertically integrated and no third party licence has been granted, whether or not the upstream market exists will depend on whether a market is defined as actual commerce, or the existence of a demand together with the potential to supply.

10.217 The Commission's decision in the *Magill* case implicitly uses this dual market analysis. In the original decision, the Commission identified two distinct products: 'the advance weekly listings of ITP and BBC regional programme services and those of RTE and also the TV guides in which these listings are published (or broadcast)'.[235] The Commission did not make it clear whether it considered the products of weekly listings and TV guides to constitute separate product markets. However, such a distinction does appear to be implicit in the decision, where the Commission referred to the parties as being: 'dominant on the market for their own listings, [and seeking to] retain for themselves also the derivative market for weekly TV guides'.[236]

10.218 The existence of upstream and downstream markets was raised in the *IMS Health* case discussed below, where IMS maintained that there was no upstream market for the intellectual property needed to produce the 1860 brick structure and that NDS intended to produce an essentially identical product on the downstream market. The Court held, at paragraph 45, that:

> it is determinative that two different stages of production may be identified and that they are interconnected, inasmuch as the upstream product is indispensable for the supply of the downstream product.

10.219 In other words, it was not necessary for there to have been prior supply of the intellectual property in question on an open market; potential supply and potential demand are sufficient. It is important to note, however, that even once this separate upstream market is shown, it is still necessary to demonstrate that a new product will be provided on the downstream market. Therefore a simple repackaging of the upstream product onto the downstream market will not be sufficient to make a refusal to supply abusive.

(3) Intellectual Property and Dominance

10.220 Although intellectual property rights give the owner the exclusive right to use the intellectual property this does not necessarily equate to a position of dominance.

10.221 An intellectual property right generally gives an exclusive right in relation to the incorporation of that right into downstream products. However, whether or not that right holder

---

235 *Magill TV Guide/ITP, BBC and RTE* [1989] OJ L78/43, at para 20 (only the English text is authentic).
236 *Magill TV Guide/ITP, BBC and RTE* [1989] OJ L78/43, at para 23(14) (only the English text is authentic).

would have market power in respect of the intellectual property depends not on that exclusive right *per se*, but on the relationship between that intellectual property right and its proprietary and/or non-proprietary substitutes. Whether or not dominance arises in respect of the intellectual property depends on the extent to which substitutes for that intellectual property right which could be used to manufacture the good (or the relevant part of the good) exist. A company may own a patent in a particular technology, used to create a downstream product, but if alternative technologies could also be used to create that product, then the company may not be dominant. In looking at substitutability it is necessary to look at both supply and demand side issues: the downstream market may, for example, be locked into a particular technology even though competing technologies exist.

The technology transfer block exemption differentiates between licences where the parties **10.222** enjoy market power and those where they do not. The Regulation states that the benefit of the block exemption may be withdrawn where the licensee is placed in a situation where it does not face competition for the goods produced under the licence. The Regulation states that this may in particular be the case where the licensee has a market share of 40 per cent or over on the market for the licensed goods and other goods considered interchangeable by consumers. Market power is being assessed by reference to the market for goods produced using the licensed intellectual property.

(4) Abuse

The distinction between the specific subject matter of an intellectual property right, which **10.223** relates to its existence and which cannot be called into question by Community law, and its exercise, which can be constrained by Community law, is set out above.

Generally, therefore, decisions on whether or not to license relate to the specific subject **10.224** matter of the right and cannot be called into question by Community competition law. The extent to which such decisions can be examined under the competition rules is a contentious area. However, the manner in which licensing is carried out (including, for example, choice of which third parties licences should be granted to) is clearly subject to competition law scrutiny.

(a) *Refusals to License Intellectual Property Rights*

(i) **The IBM Undertaking**   In 1984 the Commission obtained an undertaking from **10.225** IBM[237] closing a case relating to IBM's practices in the market for 'mainframe' computers, particularly those compatible with IBM's 'System 370' range of mainframe computers. At the time of this case IBM's System 370 was the single most popular type of large 'mainframe' computer. Users of these computers such as banks and large commercial firms would typically have a large computer installation comprising several processor units, disk drives, and other storage devices all working together and sharing information because they were compatible with the IBM System 370 system. IBM's practice in the past had been to make public significant amounts of information about how the various parts of an IBM System 370 system fitted together. As a result a number of competing manufacturers such

---

[237] *IBM Undertaking, Bull EC* 7/8-1984 Point 1.1.1 and *Bull EC* 10-1984 Point 3.4.1.

as Siemens, Hitachi, Fujitsu, and Amdahl designed and manufactured mainframe computer equipment that was compatible with System 370 and could be added to an installation built on IBM components, or could run software written for an IBM mainframe system. These manufacturers designed their own technology and merely used interface type information to design their products in such a way that they interfaced with users, information, and other computer equipment in the same way as the equivalent IBM machines. IBM then changed its commercial policy and started to withhold or delay certain of the 'interface information' required by its competitors.

10.226   Following a Statement of Objections, IBM undertook to provide its competitors with interface information about its current and future mainframe products in accordance with a fixed timetable and format. IBM also undertook to supply on request processor products with only the memory needed for proper testing of the product. The undertaking remained in force for eleven years and during its life numerous requests were made for interface information, and a significant number of competing firms continued to offer competing products to IBM's 370 range computers and their successor products.

10.227   IBM reserved its position that the information disclosed was protected by intellectual property rights and reserved the right to charge royalties for any information it disclosed under the undertaking. The undertaking appears analogous to a know-how licence in that it provided competitors with information necessary to design competing machines in such a way that they would be compatible with IBM machines, in circumstances where this information would otherwise have been, at least, confidential to IBM and, possibly, covered by intellectual property rights. As outlined above, a similar situation is created for computer software by the software Directive, where the subject matter of the right created by the Directive does not extend to protecting information about the interfaces in a piece of Software.

10.228   (ii) *Volvo/Veng* [238]   Veng was an importer into the UK of spare parts for Volvo cars which had been manufactured without Volvo's consent, and in respect of which Volvo held intellectual property rights. Volvo instituted proceedings against Veng for infringement of those rights. The UK High Court referred three questions to the ECJ, the latter answering only the second. The ECJ therefore avoided the difficult first question of the extent to which intellectual property rights can confer a dominant position:

(1) If a substantial car manufacturer holds registered designs which, under the law of a Member State, confer on it the sole and exclusive right to make and import replacement body panels required to effect repair of the body of a car of its manufacture (if such body panels are not replaceable by body panels of any other design), is such a manufacturer, by reason of such sole and exclusive rights, in a dominant position within the meaning of Article 86 [now Article 82] of the EEC Treaty with respect to such replacement parts?

(2) Is it prima facie an abuse of such dominant position for such a manufacturer to refuse to licence others to supply such body panels, even where they are willing to pay a reasonable royalty for all articles sold under the licence (such royalty to represent an award which

---

[238] Case 238/87 *AB Volvo v Erik Veng (UK) Ltd* [1988] ECR 6211.

is just and equitable having regard to the merits of the design and all the surrounding circumstances, and to be determined by arbitration or in such other manner as the national court shall direct)?

(3) Is such an abuse likely to affect trade between Member States within the meaning of Article 86 by reason of the fact that the intending licensee is thereby prevented from importing the body panels from a second Member State?[239]

The Court held that since the right to be the only manufacturer of the protected product **10.229** was part of the specific subject matter[240] of the intellectual property rights concerned, a refusal to license could not in itself be considered prima facie abusive. Other circumstances could, however, render the refusal abusive, and the Court went on to list potentially abusive conduct going beyond a simple refusal to license, provided that such conduct is liable to affect trade between Member States, such as:

— the arbitrary refusal to supply spare parts to independent repairers;
— the fixing of prices for spare parts at an unfair level; or
— a decision no longer to produce spare parts for a particular model even though many cars of that model are still in circulation.[241]

In all of these cases the intellectual property owner is limiting the use of the technology **10.230** concerned (designs for car parts), to limit competition in other markets for repairs or the manufacture of new cars where the technology is not necessarily used. However, only in the third case is it the use of, or rather the refusal to use, the intellectual property right itself which is being regarded as potentially abusive.

(iii) *Magill* The Magill case arose from a refusal to license copyrighted information. **10.231** Magill published a weekly magazine in Ireland containing details of television programmes to be broadcast by the three broadcasters whose programmes were widely available in Ireland at the time: BBC, the UK public broadcaster; ITV, the UK commercial broadcasting network; and RTE, the Irish national broadcaster. These listings infringed a copyright owned by the three broadcasters, each of which published a weekly magazine containing detail of their own broadcasts for the coming week. The broadcasters exercised their copyright to prevent Magill from producing its listings magazine. The Commission found by decision that this was a breach of Article 82 and required the broadcasters to grant licences.[242] The Commission's decision was upheld by the Court of First Instance and the Court of Justice.

The ECJ's judgment reiterated the position from *Volvo/Veng* cited above that a 'refusal to **10.232** grant a licence, even if it is the act of an undertaking holding a dominant position, cannot in itself constitute abuse of a dominant position'.[243] However, the Court held that the exercise of an intellectual property right could, in exceptional circumstances, involve abusive conduct, and that these circumstances were present in this case. The Court therefore

---

[239] Case 238/87 *AB Volvo v Erik Veng (UK) Ltd* [1988] ECR 621, at para 4.
[240] Case 238/87 *AB Volvo v Erik Veng (UK) Ltd* [1988] ECR 621, at para 8.
[241] Case 238/87 *AB Volvo v Erik Veng (UK) Ltd* [1988] ECR 621, at para 9.
[242] *Magill TV Guide/ITP, BBC & RTE* [1989] OJ L78/43.
[243] Joined Cases C-241/91P and C-242/91P *Radio Telefis Eireann (RTE) and Independent Television Publications Ltd (ITP) v Commission* [1995] ECR I-74, at para 49, citing Case 238/87 *Volvo*, paras 7 and 8.

affirmed the decision of the Commission and the ruling of the Court of First Instance, and set out three arguments on which the CFI had based its finding, and on the basis of which the ruling of the CFI should be upheld.[244]

10.233 First, there was no actual or potential substitute for the intellectual property requested from each broadcaster.[245] As such, the refusals to license had prevented the emergence of a new product for which there was a potential consumer demand.[246] Daily or weekend guides were not an adequate substitute, and consumers would otherwise have no choice but to buy each individual weekly guide. The ECJ does not explicitly state whether this new product should be such as to fulfil demand on a new market, or whether it was sufficent for the new product to fulfil an identified but unfulfilled demand on an existing market. As a composite weekly guide would clearly compete with all of the individual weekly guides, the latter possibility appears to be the more likely.

10.234 In this, the Court deviated from the recommendation of the Advocate General, who had argued that a refusal to supply could be abusive if the purpose of the supply was to create a new product which did not compete with the existing products and which therefore must be fulfilling a consumer demand not currently fulfilled. Where, however, the purpose of the demand was in order to be able to supply a product which did compete with existing products on the market, a refusal would not be abusive:

> Where the product is one that largely meets the same needs of consumers as the protected product, the interests of the copyright owner carry great weight. Even if the market is limited to the prejudice of consumers, the right to refuse licences in that situation must be regarded as necessary in order to guarantee the copyright owner the reward for his creative effort.[247]

10.235 Secondly, there was no objective justification based on the activities carried out by the right owner for the refusal to license.[248]

10.236 Thirdly, the broadcasters had exercised their copyright over expressions of listings information to reserve for themselves the secondary market for guides containing that information.[249]

10.237 The *Magill* case seems to create a limited obligation on an owner of intellectual property to grant licences to that intellectual property, where the licensee needs the intellectual property to create a new product for which there is potential demand.

10.238 The rationale for the judgment is not entirely clear. The Advocate General argued that an undertaking's refusal to license intellectual property rights to ensure that its own down-

---

[244] Joined Cases C-241/91P and C-242/91P *Radio Telefis Eireann (RTE) and Independent Television Publications Ltd (ITP) v Commission* [1995] ECR I-74, at paras 48–58.
[245] Joined Cases C-241/91P and C-242/91P *Radio Telefis Eireann (RTE) and Independent Television Publications Ltd (ITP) v Commission* [1995] ECR I-74, at para 52.
[246] Joined Cases C-241/91P and C-242/91P *Radio Telefis Eireann (RTE) and Independent Television Publications Ltd (ITP) v Commission* [1995] ECR I-74, at para 55.
[247] Joined Cases C-241/91P and C-242/91P *Radio Telefis Eireann (RTE) and Independent Television Publications Ltd (ITP) v Commission* [1995] ECR I-74, Opinion of Advocate General Gulmann at para 97.
[248] Joined Cases C-241/91P and C-242/91P *Radio Telefis Eireann (RTE) and Independent Television Publications Ltd (ITP) v Commission* [1995] ECR I-74, at para 55.
[249] Joined Cases C-241/91P and C-242/91P *Radio Telefis Eireann (RTE) and Independent Television Publications Ltd (ITP) v Commission* [1995] ECR I-74, at para 56.

stream operations did not face competition from the licensed party is of the essence of intellectual property right protection. The Court appears to have agreed in part, in that the Court requires that the request for a licence be made in the context of an intention to produce a new product for which there is untapped consumer demand. It may be that the Court regarded the refusal to license as an infringement of Article 82(b) in that it limited products, markets, or technical development. This interpretation would be consistent with the position of the Advocate General in *Macrotron*:

> where national law confers an exclusive right on someone—whether in the form of a patent, a registered design or a monopoly in the provision of certain services—and he fails to produce the goods or services covered by the exclusive right, that failure may amount to abuse of a dominant position, in which case the prohibition laid down in Article 86 [now Article 82] will apply.[250]

This interpretation appears consistent with the approach taken by the CFI in *Tiercé Ladbroke*.[251] In this case, Ladbroke was not only present on the Belgian market in respect of which it had requested the right, but was the leading operator. In these circumstances: **10.239**

> The refusal to supply the applicant could not fall within the prohibition laid down by Article 86 [now Article 82] unless it concerned a product or service which was either essential for the exercise of the activity in question, in that there was no real or potential substitute, or was a new product whose introduction might be prevented, despite specific, constant and regular potential demand on the part of consumers.

Whatever the underlying rationale for the rule, as regards refusal to supply intellectual property rights, the case law now appears clear as to the need for a 'new product' analysis. **10.240**

(iv) *IMS Health* In the IMS case, IMS maintained that it held the copyright in a database structure ('the brick structure') used to collate reports from pharmacies in Germany. A competitor, NDC, wished to compete with IMS on the downstream market. IMS brought national proceedings against NDC alleging that, operating without a licence which IMS did not wish to supply, NDC was violating IMS's copyright. NDC brought a complaint before the Commission maintaining that the refusal to supply the licence was abusive. Remarkably for such a contentious area of law, the Commission granted interim measures, but this was suspended by Order of the President of the Court of First Instance. The President's order indicated that the applicant intended not to offer a new product, but to compete with IMS on the same market and with the same product/services.[252] **10.241**

The national copyright infringement proceedings led to an Article 234 reference being made to the ECJ. The President's analysis of the law in his Order was supported by the ECJ judgment on the reference,[253] which confirmed the *Magill* criteria: **10.242**

> The undertaking which requested the license intends to offer, on the market for the supply of the data in question, new products or services not offered by the owner of the intellectual property right and for which there is a potential consumer demand;

---

[250] Case C-41/90 *Klaus Höfner and Fritz Elser v Macrotron GmbH* [1991] ECR I-197, Opinion of Advocate General Jacobs at para 46.

[251] Case T-504/93 *Tiercé Landbroke v Commission* [1997] ECR II-923, discussed at para 10.198 above.

[252] Case T-184/01, *IMS Health Inc v Commission* [2001] ECR II-3193 at para 106

[253] Case C-418/01, *IMS Health v NDC*, judgment of 29 April 2004.

The refusal is not justified by objective considerations;

The refusal is such as to reserve to the owner of the intellectual property right the market for the supply of data on sales of pharmaceutical products in the Member State concerned by eliminating all competition on that market.

10.243 This strongly suggests that a new product analysis is required for this category of cases, though it is unclear how burdensome this requirement would be: competition tends to drive innovation, so opening a monopolised market to competition will tend to produce new products and services. Nevertheless this requirement would seem to protect, for example, pharmaceutical companies from having to license their drugs to manufacturers: the latter would typically produce the same pharmaceutical on the same downstream market as the licensor company. Although it is possible to envisage a new product scenario, where a licensee had developed separate technology improving the delivery of the drug, such cases seem likely to be extremely rare events in the already exceptionally rare circumstances of essential facilities cases.

10.244 (v) *Microsoft*   The Commission's Decision in *Microsoft* provides a useful perspective on the new product analysis. Microsoft is a provider of computer software with a quasi-monopolistic position on the market for desktop PC operating systems. It has attracted extensive antitrust scrutiny in various jurisdictions around the world, mostly focusing on two general types of conduct: first that Microsoft stifled competitive threats to its desktop operating systems; second that Microsoft sought to use its quasi-monopoly over desktop operating systems to move into new markets and garner new sources of revenue.

10.245 In July 1994 the European Commission obtained an undertaking from Microsoft which led to the closure of a case arising from a complaint made by Novell in June 1993 which touched on the first of these issues.

10.246 Then, as now, Microsoft had an extremely large share in the market for operating systems for microcomputers. Most microcomputers were sold with an operating system already installed, as a result of an original equipment manufacturer (OEM) licence contract between the microcomputer manufacturer and a developer of operating system software. The Commission had been investigating these OEM licences between Microsoft and microcomputer manufacturers and was concerned that certain aspects of these licences had the effect of excluding Microsoft's competitors from the market. The main practices causing concern were:

— the use of 'per processor' and 'per system' licences; (under these licences the manufactures paid a royalty to Microsoft for all or practically all of their production even if they installed non-Microsoft operating systems on some of the machines concerned);
— the inclusion of large 'minimum commitments' to pay royalties in licence contracts regardless of the number of copies used; and
— the long duration of the licence contracts.

10.247 The Commission was concerned that the cumulative effect of these would be to foreclose Microsoft's competitors from licensing operating systems to computer manufacturers.

10.248 Under the terms of the undertaking Microsoft agreed:

— to limit the term of its licences to one year;
— not to enter into per processor licences;

— to enter into per system licences only where it was clear that the manufacturer could simply name a new model of computer, and not have to pay a royalty on these machines; and

— not to impose minimum commitments on licensees.

In 1998, Sun Microsystems complained to the Commission about the second aspect of Microsoft's conduct mentioned above, leveraging into related markets. Sun alleged that Microsoft was behaving illegally in the supply of, or refusal to supply, information which would allow operating systems on computers dedicated to server functions—such as file and print servers—to communicate with computers running Microsoft's desktop operating system software, performing typical office desktop functions. Essentially the complaint was that Microsoft had initially provided extensive information allowing third party server software to interoperate with the desktop. However once Microsoft began developing its own competing server operating system software, its behaviour changed—it reduced the information available, and refused to supply it to certain competitors. In its 2004 decision against Microsoft, the Commission cited a number of different factors, why this conduct was abusive, including creating artificial barriers to entry,[254] discriminatory supply,[255] ending of previous supply (bringing the case closer to the *Commercial Solvents* line of reasoning),[256] and leveraging of dominance into related markets.[257] Even assuming the *Magill/IMS* new product reasoning is essential to the case—which, given that it relates to distortion/withdrawal of pre-existing levels of supply is at least doubtful—then the fact that there were pre-existing distinct products on the market would appear to be sufficient. **10.249**

(b) Licensing of Intellectual Property Rights and Article 82

The main focus of attention in recent years has been on the issue of refusal to license intellectual property rights to third parties. **10.250**

Less controversial—in principle at least—are the cases where the question is not whether or not there is an obligation to license third parties, but on what terms and conditions a licence can be granted to ensure that the licensing complies with Article 82. **10.251**

Here, the interrelationship between the competition rules and the specific subject matter of an intellectual property right is clearer. Once an undertaking has chosen how it intends to exploit its intellectual property—for example by licensing it to a third party—then the intellectual property right has been exhausted and the competition rules apply in the normal way. **10.252**

If the undertaking is dominant, therefore, a traditional Article 82 analysis can be used. Thus, for example, the following are potentially abusive exercises of intellectual property rights: **10.253**

— charging or attempting to charge excessive royalties;[258]

— discriminating in the granting of licences or in the terms under which licences are granted, where such discrimination affects competition. This may be what the Court

---

[254] Para 524.
[255] Para 574.
[256] Para 587.
[257] Para 697.
[258] Case 402/85 *Basset v SACEM* [1987]ECR 174,7 at para 19, and Case 395/87 *Ministère Public v Tournier* [1989] ECR 2521, at para 38.

had in mind when it referred to an 'arbitrary' refusal to license in the *Volvo* case, and discrimination of supply was one of the elements of the abusive conduct found by the Commission in the Microsoft case.[259]

(c) Misuse of Regulatory Process

10.254 The Commission's decision in *AstraZeneca* established for the first time in the EU that a dominant company's use or misuse of regulatory procedures might constitute an abuse of a dominant position. In that case AstraZeneca had invented and marketed a successful ulcer drug, Losec which by the time its patent on the drug was close to expiration, had given the company a dominant position on the market. Wishing to frustrate market entry by generic manufacturers following the expiry of the patent, AstraZeneca first misled patent authorities as to when the drug was first manufactured in several Member States and second withdrew the capsule form of the drug from the market, replacing it with—medically identical—tablets. The first conduct led to the grant of supplementary protection certificates, extending the life of the patent beyond that to which AstraZeneca was properly entitled. The second conduct prevented generic competitors from using the market authorisation granted to the capsules in order to market their own products. The Commission, finding that both of these sets of conduct were aimed at delaying generic entry, condemned the conduct as abusive. The case is now on appeal.

(d) Conclusions on Abuses

10.255 Neither the Court nor the Commission has purported to produce a definitive list of abuses of intellectual property rights, or a definitive list of exceptional circumstances where refusals to licence may be abusive. The following provides broad indications of the type of situations which may arise, and summarises the likely current state of the law as regards dominant holders of IP rights:

— *No actual or potential substitutes exist, refusal to license a competitor to produce the same products as currently exist.* This does not appear to be abusive (ECJ and the Attorney General in *Magill*, ECJ in *IMS Health*), unless, perhaps, there is evidence of a failure to fulfil demand on the downstream market, possibly through lack of innovation or inefficiency leading to higher prices (*Port of Genoa, Macrotron, Ladbroke*).

— *No actual or potential substitutes exist, refusal to license a competitor to produce a new, but competing product, or to produce a product in a different market.* This may be abusive if there is evidence of potential consumer demand (ECJ in *Magill, Ladbroke, IMS*, Commission in *Microsoft*).

— Licensing of at least one third party, whether or not *actual or potential substitutes exist.* The ordinary Article 82 rules apply on discrimination, withdrawal of supply, excessive pricing, etc (*Basset v SACEM, Tournier,* Commission in *Microsoft*).

— *Refusal to license any third party, where some actual or potential substitutes exist.* This is unlikely to be regarded as abusive (implicitly, ECJ and Attorney General in *Magill*).

---

[259] Para 574.

PART III

SPECIAL SECTORS

11

FINANCIAL SERVICES

Stephen Ryan, Eduardo Martinez Rivero and Albert Nijenhuis

A. Introduction

The financial services sector is traditionally defined as consisting of three elements: banking, **11.01** insurance, and securities, although the boundaries between those activities are increasingly blurred. This chapter respects that definition, with the addition of social security, an activity akin to insurance in some respects, traditionally a State prerogative, but where reforms in several Member States, introducing private sector involvement and an element of competition, have raised issues as to the application of the competition rules. However, this chapter is not a financial services handbook, and cannot explain in any detail the functioning or specific regulation of the sector, except where this is pertinent or necessary for an understanding of the Community competition rules and case law. In particular, it leaves many important aspects of the financial services sector unmentioned, since they have not so far seen any application of the EU competition rules, and the chapter does not enter into speculation as to how the rules might possibly be applied in those areas in the future.

11.02 One of the features of the financial services sector is that many market participants can be retailers and wholesalers, customers and suppliers, in different respects, and that competition on wholesale markets can affect retail customers in indirect ways of which they are not aware. For example, insurance companies, pension funds, and banks are all customers of stock exchanges and other securities markets, and high trading or other costs on such markets can increase their costs and thus contribute to higher prices for end consumers of the products they offer. Banks provide payment systems of which they themselves, and also other financial institutions, are large-scale users. Banks need insurance and insurers need banking services. With the increasing development of financial conglomerates, different departments of the same undertaking can provide services to each other. Wholesale financial services markets often differ significantly from retail markets ('retail' being understood as involving both personal and small business customers)—wholesale markets are often worldwide in scope, with many sophisticated participants, and based on advanced technology with real-time information, while retail markets are often geographically limited, with fewer participants, and with information for customers less readily available. The complex interrelationships in the financial sector, as often with network-based industries, are such that many financial institutions are reluctant to bring formal complaints against other such institutions with which they have to deal every day in order to carry out their normal business.

11.03 The importance of the financial services sector to the economy, which hardly needs emphasising, would seem clearly to necessitate a vigorous application of the competition rules. However, representatives of the sector long argued that the uniqueness of the sector precluded a full application of Articles 81 and 82, despite the absence of any such exclusion in the Treaty. In the 1980s the Court had the opportunity to reject this hypothesis, both for banking and for insurance. In the *Züchner* case,[1] the Court rejected arguments that banks are not fully subject to Articles 81 and 82. In 1984 the Commission took its first decisions in the insurance sector. On appeal from one of those decisions the applicant association of insurers argued, in a variation on the 'destructive competition' argument, that unlimited competition in the insurance industry would increase the risk of insolvency to the detriment of consumers, that co-operation between insurers was required to avoid that risk, and that special rules should therefore be adopted under Article 83 (former Article 87) to limit

---

[1] Case 172/80 *Züchner v Bayerische Vereinsbank AG* [1981] ECR 2021, 2030. The judgment, a preliminary ruling on a reference from a German court, concerned a concerted practice between banks on customer fees.

the applicability of Articles 81 and 82. The Court rejected those arguments: Articles 81 and 82 are fully applicable in the absence of any special rules adopted under Article 83.[2]

A further point of general relevance to the financial services sector is the importance, for **11.04** competition within the sector, of Community-level legislation aiming to establish a fully effective single market in financial services. The various banking, insurance, and investment services Directives all aim, by establishing the principle of home country regulation, and a single 'passport', to facilitate cross-border activities and increase competition in the sector. This legislation has been accompanied by Community regulation on matters such as capital adequacy for banks, prudential requirements for insurance companies, and settlement finality. Cross-border electronic payments have also been the subject of a specific legislative framework. This huge and ongoing activity of single market regulation, which in itself falls outside the scope of this chapter, interacts with the application of the competition rules. Examples where this interaction is particularly close, cross-border electronic payments and clearing and settlement, are dealt with later in this chapter.

The Commission's efforts to establish a complete and fully-functioning single market for all **11.05** financial services is ongoing. However, many financial services are still produced and consumed domestically, and cross-border competition is limited, at least in retail financial markets. The Commission's Financial Integration Monitor[3] has found that as a rule, the closer to the end consumer, the less integration and intra-EU competition there is, which poses challenges for passing on the benefits of financial integration to the consumer. At the same time cross-border merger and acquisition activity in financial services is increasing, and there has been consolidation at wholesale level (such as in the area of clearing and settlement of securities transactions), which only benefits end consumers indirectly. Consumers are however not benefiting from consolidation in the area of retail banking, which is one of the reasons why the Commission has launched a sector enquiry in this area, as will be seen below.

Against this background, the case law on the existence of an appreciable effect on trade **11.06** between Member States is relevant. The Court's 1999 judgment in the Bagnasco case[4] cast some light on this question. The case concerned agreed uniform banking conditions decided by the Italian Banking Association ABI in relation to the opening of current account credit facilities and guarantees. These agreements had been notified to the Commission, and benefited from a comfort letter in 1993, on the grounds of lack of effect on trade between Member States. In a national case brought against the same agreement, the Court was asked to make a preliminary ruling. In its judgment (§51), the Court refers to three arguments advanced by the Commission in concluding the absence of effect on trade between Member States, first that the banking service in question involved economic activities which have a very limited impact on trade between Member States, secondly that the participation of the subsidiaries or branches of non-Italian financial establishments was limited, and thirdly that the standard conditions in question were not a factor of decisive

---

[2] Case 45/85 *Verband der Sachversicherer* [1987] ECR 405, 454–455.
[3] See Commission press release IP/04/601.
[4] Court judgment of 21 January 1999, Joined Cases C-215/96 and C-216-96 *Bagnasco v Banca Popolare di Novara* [1999] ECR I-00135.

importance in the choice made by foreign banks as to whether or not to establish themselves in Italy (that is, not a potential barrier to entry on the market).

11.07   Shortly after the *Bagnasco* judgment, the Commission gave a clear signal of following the principles laid down in that judgment by adopting a formal negative clearance decision, on the grounds of lack of effect on trade between Member States, in a financial services case which had been under consideration for some time. The *Dutch Banks (Acceptgiro)* decision,[5] concerned a fixed interbank fee for automated domestic interbank payments in the Netherlands.[6] The Commission had previously sent a statement of objections in June 1993, but several months after the *Bagnasco* judgment concluded that the agreement, even though it covered the totality of the territory of a Member State, did not appreciably affect trade between Member States in that it did not meet any of the three 'Bagnasco' criteria.

11.08   It is arguable that the Commission's *Acceptgiro* decision, by taking a strict approach to the question of effect on trade between Member States in the financial services sector, is perhaps overinterpreting the *Bagnasco* judgment. For example, the decision states (§61), that the coverage of the totality of the territory of a Member State is no longer sufficient alone to justify an effect on trade between Member States, whereas the subsequent *Arduino* and *Austrian Banks* judgments of the Court reaffirm that an act covering the entire territory of a Member State is susceptible of affecting trade.[7] The issue of an effect on trade between Member States should therefore not pose a barrier to effective antitrust enforcement in the financial services area, especially given the increased level of co-operation between the Commission and national competition authorities in the wake of the modernisation of the competition rules.[8] Indeed, since the entry into force of Regulation 1/2003, national competition authorities have started to use Article 81 of the Treaty as a base for decisions concerning financial services agreements on a national level.[9]

B. Banking

(1) Introductory/Preliminary Remarks

11.09   The banking sector has certain specific characteristics which distinguish it from most other sectors of the economy. These include:

- the important role which it plays in monetary creation, by triggering a 'multiplier effect' in its lending activities;

---

[5] Commission Decision of 8 September 1999, [1999] OJ L271/28.

[6] For a discussion of the competition issues relating to interbank fees, see paras 11.33–11.51 below.

[7] Case C-35/99 (Reference for a preliminary ruling from the Pretore di Pinerolo): *Manuele Arduino* [2002] ECR I-01529, para 33 and the CFI decision of 14 December 2006 in joined Cases T-259/02 to T-264/02 and T-271/02 (*Raffeisen Zentralbank Österreich AG and others v Commission of the European Communities*, not yet published in ECR, see press release 104/06). See the Commission Notice Guidelines on the effect on trade concept contained in Articles 81 and 82 of the Treaty, [2004] OJ C101/81-96. *Bagnasco* is in fact the only case where the Court has considered that an agreement affecting the totality of the territory of a Member State had no effect on trade between Member States.

[8] See Chapter 2, section E.

[9] As Regulation 1/2003 obliges them to do when there is an effect on trade between Member States. One example of this is the MasterCard decision of 6 September 2005 by the UK OFT, referred to below (para 51).

- its intermediation role between those with surplus money to invest and those needing to borrow, thus facilitating economic activity;
- the fact that some key determinants of pricing of banking services, namely interest rates, are led by decisions taken by public authorities (central banks);
- the need for a specific regulatory framework for banking activities, including capital adequacy requirements and settlement finality rules, due to the systemic risk which can arise from the failure of a bank to meet its commitments;
- the important role of payment systems, which requires a greater level of systematic coordination between competing banks than would be the case in other sectors.

However, no specific competition law framework for the banking sector has ever existed in community law (unlike in transport, for instance), and thus the competition rules applying to the banking sector are no different from those applying to other sectors. Indeed, it can be argued that the key importance of banking to individual consumers and the economy as a whole makes it especially essential to detect and prevent anti-competitive practices in that sector. **11.10**

The Commission's enforcement policy in the banking sector has so far focused on two areas: hardcore price-fixing agreements, and payment systems (particularly retail means of payment, especially cards). This focus is not hard to understand, as price-fixing is the most serious type of antitrust offence, with direct and indirect costs for business customers and consumers, and payment systems play an increasingly important role in everyday economic activity, involving very substantial flows of money, and often significant revenue for banks. As they also involve agreements between banks on their rules and management, many precautionary notifications have been received over the years, not to mention complaints. In what follows, it should be borne in mind that only wholesale payment systems, such as inter-bank clearing systems, are payment systems *stricto sensu*, while retail means of payment (such as payment cards), are normally not independent payment systems but merely ways of facilitating payments between retail customers using the wholesale systems.[10] **11.11**

(2) Banking other than Payment Systems

(a) Price Agreements

There have been three prohibition decisions with fines imposed on banks for cartelistic pricing agreements, of which the most recent was the Austrian banks ('Lombard Club') decision of 11 June 2002, which fined eight Austrian banks a total of over EUR124 million for a long-established, far-reaching and highly institutionalised cartel covering every area of banking activity.[11] The extensive structure of committees and sub-committees reaching 'down to the smallest village' according to one cartel participant, prompted the then Competition Commissioner Mario Monti to distinguish the cartel with the term 'shocking' in his press release.[12] The fine only covered the period from Austrian EU membership in 1995, but the cartel had existed long before. Committees included the 'Lending Rates **11.12**

---

[10] The term 'card payment systems', used *passim* in this chapter, is merely convenient shorthand.
[11] *Austrian banks* decision of 11 June 2002, [2004] OJ L56/1.
[12] IP/02/844 of 11/6/2004.

Committees', the 'Deposit Rates Committees' and a pan-Austrian committee called Federal Lending and Deposit Rates Committee in which bank representatives from Vienna met with their opposite numbers from the provinces. Between January 1994 and the end of June 1998, in Vienna alone at least 300 meetings took place. A large part of the 75-page decision consists of quotations from cartel committee meetings, culled from documents seized in the Commission's inspections of June 1998. A typical example from a meeting of 1995 suffices to convey the spirit of the cartel: 'The exchange of experience between banks in relation to interest rates has repeatedly proved to be a useful means of avoiding uncontrolled price competition.'

11.13 The Austrian banks case is illustrative of the shock of transition to a competition-based free market system consequent on EU membership for a hitherto corporatist economy. The cartel had existed for decades before Austrian EU membership, and during most of the period of the existence of the cartel, including a period after Austrian EU accession, Austria did not have a national competition law in force prohibiting cartels. In their submissions during the procedure, the Austrian banks emphasised the cartel's roots in Austrian political and economic traditions, even mentioning 'social' pressures to take part, and evoking 'fear of the negative consequences of a too rapid, and in particular, a poorly prepared transition to free competition'.[13] On the other hand, the cartel took measures to maintain secrecy concerning its meetings, indicating an awareness of its illicit nature. On 14 December 2006 the Court of First Instance rejected the appeal of the parties, the main argument of which was that the cartel did not affect trade between Member States. However, the Court reduced the fine of one of the cartelists, on the basis of an unjustified calculation of market share (see n 7).

11.14 Prior to the Austrian banks decision, in August 2001, the Commission had imposed fines totalling over EUR100 million on five German banks, for fixing commissions charged on certain currency-exchange operations during the three-year transitional phase of the introduction of the euro.[14] On 1 January 1999 the bilateral exchange rates for euro-zone currencies set to be replaced by the euro were irrevocably locked, and those currencies became in fact internal denominations of the euro. This eliminated exchange rate risk between those currencies, and put an end to the justification for the lucrative selling and buying 'spread' charged by banks and bureaux de change for exchanging those euro-zone currencies. According to the Commission's decision, in order to compensate for loss of revenue from the 'spread', in late 1997 several German and Dutch banks concluded an agreement on a commission of about 3 per cent for the buying and selling of euro-zone banknotes during the three-year period which preceded the final arrival of euro notes and coins in 1 January 2002.

11.15 The Commission's investigation into such agreements had extended much more widely than Germany. Following inspections, statements of objections had been sent to banks in seven Member States for similar agreements on the charges for exchange between the 'euro-in' currencies.[15] However, in the other cases the banks in question agreed to reduce the

---

[13] *Austrian banks* decision, §367–9.
[14] *German banks* decision of 11 December 2001, [2003] OJ L15/1-34.
[15] Belgium, Portugal, Ireland, Finland, Germany, the Netherlands, and Austria (see press releases IP/00/704, IP/00/784, IP/00/908, and IP/00/1358).

commissions charged, following the receipt of a statement of objections, and in return the Commission agreed to drop proceedings.[16] The German banks had been the only recipients of a Statement of Objection to reject any kind of 'deal' with the Commission. This highly unusual arrangement is explained in the Commission's press release on adoption of the *German banks* decision:[17]

> The Commission agreed to end proceedings against the banks [other than German banks] as it took the view that it would be in the consumer interest for it to secure an immediate and substantial reduction in the charges. The Commission's unusual attitude was justified by the exceptional circumstances of the present case. Euro notes and coins will be introduced next January replacing the national currencies of the participating euro-zone countries and, therefore, putting an automatic end to the cartel behaviour.

However, the *German Banks* decision was annulled by the Court of First Instance in a judgment **11.16** of 14 October 2004, and the fines cancelled. The Court found, without being able to take the Commission's defence into account, that the evidence adduced by the Commission was insufficient to demonstrate an agreement on the level of fees or on the manner of setting fees. The Commission subsequently opposed the default judgments. However on 27 September 2006, the CFI confirmed its finding that there was insufficient evidence.[18]

The Commission's first decision with fines in the banking sector, the French banks (*Helsinki* **11.17** *agreement*) case, occurred much earlier, in 1992.[19] Apparently, in order to promote the use of payment cards in France, a number of French banks, members of an organisation called Groupement des Cartes Bancaires, and Eurocheque International, adopted the 'Helsinki Agreement', under which, in respect of purchases paid for by eurocheques, the banks participating in the agreement would charge their affiliated merchants a commission not exceeding the commission applicable to payments by Carte Bleue and Eurocard payments. The Commission considered this to be both an agreement to charge a commission and an agreement on the amount of the commission. It imposed a fine of ECU 5 million on the Groupement des Cartes Bancaires 'CB' and ECU 1 million on Eurocheque International. The Groupement's fine was reduced on appeal, the Court of First Instance holding that there had been an agreement to charge a commission but no agreement as to the amount of the commission.[20]

(b) Other Issues

There are very few Commission decisions on the banking sector outside the area of payment **11.18** systems, other than the price-fixing and cartel cases described above. One exception is the

---

[16] For Austria, these proceedings were merged into the proceedings of the *Lombard* case described above, but no mention is made of the fixing of currency exchange commissions in the Austrian banks decision of 11 June 2002.

[17] Press release IP/01/1796.

[18] Cases T44/02, T54/02, T56/02, T60/02, T61/02. The judgment of 27 September 2006 is as yet unreported in ECR. Due to an administrative error, the Commission had failed to submit a reply to the application for annulment of its decision, and the first judgment of the CFI was made by default. The judgment of 27 September 2006 concerned the Commission's opposition against CFI judgments by default.

[19] *Helsinki agreement*: [1992] OJ L95/50.

[20] Joined Cases T-39/92 and 40/92 *Groupement des Cartes Bancaires 'CB' and Europay International v Commission* [1994] ECR II-49.

agreement between Banque Nationale de Paris and Dresdner Bank to which the Commission granted a ten-year exemption in 1996.[21] The very wide-ranging agreement affected in practice all the banking and financial services markets (except insurance) on which the parties operated. The Commission found that the agreement restricted competition between the two banks in France and Germany, but exempted it on the grounds that consumers would benefit from the improved services that would result from the exchange of know-how between the parties and their distribution of each other's products. The agreement originally contained a wide-ranging reciprocal exclusivity clause (under which either bank could veto the other's proposed co-operation with a home country competitor of the former bank) which the Commission did not consider indispensable. At the Commission's request, the parties agreed to limit the scope of this clause to cases where such co-operation would involve the third party gaining access to know-how or business secrets which originate from the vetoing bank or arise out of the co-operation. The agreement has since been discontinued.

(3) Payment Systems

(a) Introduction on Payment Systems

11.19 The great majority of the Commission's interventions in application of the competition rules in the banking sector have involved payment systems. There are a number of reasons for this, beyond the banal one that a number of notifications and complaints were received. Payment systems are of fundamental importance in banking, to such an extent that modern banking could not exist without them; huge volumes of funds pass through payment systems every day, and participation in banking markets is simply not possible without access to at least some payment systems. The terms and fees applicable to the use of payment systems are also of great interest to consumers, merchants, and other undertakings which use them. Moreover, many payment systems are cross-border, and thus their effect on trade between Member States in not in question.

11.20 As concerns the euro zone, the Commission's interventions must be seen in the context of the goal of establishing a 'Single Euro Payments Area' not only for cash payments (which is ensured by the euro notes and coins) but also cashless ones. The European Central Bank (ECB) and the European System of Central Banks (ECSB) are increasingly important actors in this field, thanks to the role conferred on them by the Treaty in promoting the smooth operation of payment systems, including an oversight function and regulatory powers.[22] The ECB and ECSB are also the operator of a cross-border euro payment system, TARGET, which was looked at by the Commission in the 1990s.[23]

---

[21] *BNP/Dresdner*. Commission Decision of 24 June1996, [1996] OJ L188/37.

[22] Art 105(2) of the Treaty establishing the European Community and Art 3 of the Statute of the European System of Central Banks and of the European Central Bank. See 'Towards a Single Euro Payments Area—progress report June 2003', ECB.

[23] TARGET stands for 'Trans-European Automated Real-Time Gross settlement Express Transfer'. See the Report on competition policy for 1997, §95. The Commission reached the provisional conclusion that as concerns TARGET payments effected for banks' customers, unrelated to monetary policy, agreements between the Central Banks in the ECSB concerning TARGET could fall under the scope of Art 81(1), particularly as regards pricing to end users. However, the investigation was closed without opening a formal procedure.

At consumer level, two main means of cross-border payment exist in Europe: credit and **11.21** debit cards, and interbank transfer systems ;[24] in fact, these means of payment merely provide consumers with indirect access to interbank clearing systems, to allow payments between end users to take place, using wholesale banking infrastructure. While the operation of these systems from a consumer's point of view is familiar to most people, it is less well-known that the functioning of such payment systems is underpinned both by a complex technical infrastructure (which falls outside the scope of this book) and extensive rules governing the relations between the parties, which, when they constitute agreements between undertakings, come within the scope of competition rules.

Regardless of the infrastructure used, such retail payment systems can be divided into two **11.22** categories: three-party systems and four-party systems. In a three-party system, the debitor and creditor[25] are always customers of the same bank or payment organisation, making three participants in a payment operation, while in a four-party system, the debitor and creditor are normally customers of different banks, making four participants in a operation.[26] A three-party system does not require any interbank clearing, and therefore no agreements between banks, and therefore its internal rules are unlikely to raise Article 81 issues (although there may be Article 82 issues if it enjoys a dominant position). A four-party system requires agreements between competitor banks concerning its rules, criteria for access, technical arrangements (particularly regarding clearing and settlement), and any fees, and thus can raise both Article 81 and Article 82 issues. For this reason, and because the most important payment systems in Europe are four-party systems (including the card systems Visa and MasterCard), the Commission's attention has focused on four-party systems, as opposed to three-party systems such as American Express or Diners Club, which in any case have lower market shares.

Payment systems raise various kinds of competition issues, including those relating to **11.23** pricing matters, and a range of other issues. The pricing issues include not only prices paid by end users of the systems, but also fees paid at the 'wholesale' level between system participants, in particular interbank fees. Non-pricing issues include a huge range of rules governing, for example, access to payment systems and the obligations on participants in those systems. Often different, apparently unrelated rules, can have a cumulative effect and thus need to be considered in conjunction.

On both the pricing and non-pricing issues, the most comprehensive statement of the **11.24** Commission's position to date has come in two separate decisions in the same case, the

---

[24] Since the eurocheque system became unguaranteed in 2000, eurocheques have become marginal for cross-border payments, and cheques have become essentially a domestic payment instrument in certain Member States.

[25] In a card payment system, the debitor (or payer) is the cardholder, and the creditor (or payee) is normally a merchant. The cardholder's bank is known as the 'issuing bank', and the merchant's bank is known as the 'acquiring bank'. The issuing and acquiring markets are important in the Commission's analysis of pricing restrictions in card systems, see below.

[26] Of course, even in a four-party system, the creditor and debitor may fortuitously be customers of the same bank, in which case the transaction is known as an 'on-us' transaction. See Figure 1 for the functioning of a four-party system.

notification by the card payment system Visa International of its rules. The first decision, of 2001,[27] cleared a number of non-pricing rules in the Visa system, and one pricing rule (the so-called 'no discrimination rule', see below). The second decision, of 2002,[28] conditionally exempted one pricing rule, concerning so-called 'multilateral interchange fees', which are interbank fees in the Visa system. The discussion below will focus essentially on those two decisions. First, however, there will be an explanation of the Commission's approach to competition issues in the field of cross-border transfers, which is somewhat different.

(b) Cross-border Transfers: Competition and Regulation

11.25 The close link between competition law and regulation, and the possibility of using competition or regulatory approaches to tackle the same problem, is illustrated by cross-border interbank transfer systems. In 1995, the Commission adopted a notice on the application of the competition rules to cross-border credit transfers,[29] issued in conjunction with a Commission proposal for a Directive on cross-border transfers,[30] with which it formed a 'package'. The Directive laid down minimal quality standards for cross-border credit transfers, but did not concern the fees charged, except in so far as it stipulated that, in the absence of an explicit request from the sender of the transfer, the beneficiary's bank cannot deduct fees from the amount of the transfer credited to the beneficiary,[31] thus preventing 'double charging' (the unauthorised charging of fees to both the sender and the beneficiary of the transfer). The 1995 notice was consequently much concerned with clarifying what kinds of price restrictions in the rules of cross-border credit transfer systems might be justifiable in order to avoid the risk of double-charging for certain types of transfers.[32] In particular, an agreed fixed interbank fee paid by the remitting bank to the beneficiary's bank along with the transfer itself, could remove any justification for the beneficiary's bank to deduct fees from the beneficiary, thus helping to avoid 'double charging'. Consequently, an agreement between banks on such a fee could, in certain circumstances, benefit from an exemption.

11.26 However, in 2001 the Parliament and the Council adopted a Regulation concerning cross-border payments in euros,[33] which lays down, *inter alia*, that 'charges levied by an institution in respect of cross-border electronic payment transactions in euro up to EUR12,500 shall

---

[27] Decision of 7 August 2001, [2001] OJ L293/24. Hereafter referred to as '*Visa I*'.

[28] Decision of 24 July 2002, [2002] OJ L318/17. Hereafter referred to as '*Visa II*'. According to the Commission, the separation of the Visa notification into two distinct decisions was for practical and not substantive reasons.

[29] [1995] OJ C251/3.

[30] The Directive was adopted on 27 January 1997 as Directive 97/5 (EC), [1997] OJ L043/25.

[31] In doing this, it established the 'OUR' type of transfer (with all fees to be paid by the sender) as the default fee structure.

[32] Specifically, the Notice considers in what circumstances a 'multilateral interbank fee' might be justifiable, concluding that this could only be the case for so-called OUR payments (see previous footnote) and only on certain conditions, namely that the fee be linked to applicable costs and that the fee should be a default fee, leaving banks free to agree a different fee bilaterally (1995 Notice, §56).

[33] Regulation (EC) 2560/2001 of 19 December 2001 on cross-border payments in euro [2001] OJ L344/13.

be the same as the charges levied by the same institution in respect of corresponding payments in euro transacted within the Member State'.[34] That Regulation, by laying down relative limits on the price charged to a consumer, adopted a regulatory solution to some of the pricing issues dealt with from a competition law angle in the 1995 Communication, thus rendering it partially outdated. Specifically, the justification for an exemption for interbank pricing agreements given in the Notice had disappeared, as the double-pricing problem which the agreement aimed at solving had been removed by Regulation, at least for transfers up to EUR12,500 in the euro zone.[35]

The Commission has never formally withdrawn the 1995 Notice, but nor has it referred to it subsequently, and nor have there been any Commission decisions on cross-border transfers. It would seem from this that the importance of the 1995 Notice has been significantly diminished by the 2001 Regulation, at least as concerns the issues covered in the Regulation. **11.27**

An initiative to create a 'Single European Payments Area' (SEPA) is linked to these regulatory developments, since the adoption of Regulation 2560/2001 has led to interest on the part of banks in building European standards and infrastructure. The European Payment Council (EPC), a body of commercial banks, is working on reaching SEPA by 2010 at the latest, so that payments within the Euro area look to the consumer like national payments.[36] Another driving force behind the SEPA project is the European Central Bank, which is concerned to ensure that consumers obtain the full benefit of the euro. Together with regulatory proposals[37] and standards setting by industry,[38] competition law can be an important instrument to make cross-border payments more efficient: payment systems and providers should compete with one another effectively, and innovation must be protected. Rather than enforcement (launching infringement procedures), the activity of DG Competition in relation with SEPA has focused on so-called 'competition advocacy', which includes working together with representative industry bodies such as the EPC to ensure that new frameworks and standards promote competition. **11.28**

On 1 December 2005 the Commission adopted a proposal for a Directive on payment services in the internal market.[39] The proposal would establish a legal framework that **11.29**

---

[34] Art 3.

[35] However, it presumably remains relevant to cross-border transfers made within the EU in currencies other than euro, and indeed Directive 97/5 (EC) was not repealed by Regulation 2560/2001.

[36] See the European Payment Council's webpage <www.europeanpaymentscouncil.org>.

[37] A draft Payment Services Directive (formerly called New Legal Framework) was adopted by the Commission in November 2005. The goal of the draft is to provide a legal framework for SEPA, by establishing rules for cross-border payments, including payments where at least one leg is in the EU, whatever the currency of the operation. Cheques, cash and so-called e-money are outside its scope. The right to operate payment services should, under the proposal, not require a banking license. The type of issue harmonised by the proposal includes who pays for payment transactions, transparency in pricing, execution times, liability in case of default, consumer information and rules on revocability of payment orders.

[38] The EPC is at present developing standards for cross-border credit transfers, direct debit, and credit and debit cards. The possible introduction of a 'multilateral interchange fee' (see below, paras 11.33–11.51) for European direct debit is an issue; in respect of cards, EPC is not creating a new scheme but a framework for which all SEPA card schemes should qualify.

[39] COM (2005) 603 final.

would facilitate the achievement of SEPA. The proposed Directive covers relationships between providers and users of payment services but does not deal with interbank relationships.[40] It is expected that the Directive, once adopted, will enter into force at the beginning of 2008.

(c) Pricing Issues (Wholesale and Retail)

11.30 (i) **Pricing to End Users** Agreements on the level of prices to be charged to end users are of course cartelistic agreements, as is illustrated in the payment systems field by the *Helsinki agreement* case described above. An agreement in card payment systems, of which the competition analysis is more complicated, is the so-called 'no-discrimination rule' (NDR). This rule, widely—but not universally—applied in many card payment systems, takes the form of an obligatory clause in contracts between merchants and their banks prohibiting merchants who accept the card in question from charging a 'surcharge' to consumers for paying with that card rather than other means of payment such as cash. The Visa and MasterCard notifications of their rulebooks included such a rule. In some cases the rule may also prohibit the offering of discounts for payment in cash.

11.31 One way of analysing such a rule is as an example of retail price maintenance with a zero price level. On this approach, since merchants pay a fee to their bank for 'acquiring' card payments, such a rule prevents merchants from passing on that cost to consumers who choose to pay by card, thus limiting the pricing freedom of merchants, imposing cross-subsidisation of card-using consumers by non-card-using consumers, and distorting economic choices, at the expense of efficiency. This line was taken by three national competition authorities in the EU in prohibiting NDRs on their national territory.[41] The Commission also sent statements of objections addressed to both Visa and MasterCard in May 1999 concerning their NDRs.

11.32 However, in the *Visa I* decision of August 2001, the Commission granted a negative clearance to the Visa NDR on the grounds of lack of appreciable effect.[42] This was not however a reversal of its former position: the *Visa I* decision clearly stated that the NDR restricts competition; the only reason for the negative clearance was that the restriction of competition lacked an appreciable effect. This conclusion was based on studies commissioned by the Commission on the effects of the abolition of the NDR in Sweden and the Netherlands,[43] which found that very limited numbers of merchants used their

---

[40] The proposal (Title II) establishes a regulatory regime for payment institutions. It lays down the principle that any payment service provider has to benefit from a licence to be able to provide payment services. This licence can be a banking licence, an electronic money licence, or a payment institution licence. In Title III it harmonises the information requirements for all payment services provided in the European Union. Title IV of the proposal defines the rights and obligations of payment service users and payment service providers, such as execution time or liability rules.

[41] The UK in 1989, the Netherlands in 1994, Sweden in 1995.

[42] *Visa I*, 11–12 and 54–58.

[43] In the UK the abolition of the NDR was combined with other structural interventions on the market (the abolition of a monopoly in card acquiring), making it impossible to determine the exact cause of subsequent market changes. *A priori*, any subsequent falls in merchant fees would probably be more due to the end of the acquiring monopoly.

new freedom to surcharge, and that merchant acquiring fees had not significantly fallen (thus showing that the abolition of the NDR did not increase the bargaining power of merchants vis-à-vis their acquiring banks). The clearance of the NDR was challenged in the Court of First Instance by a complainant in the case (EuroCommerce, a retailing confederation), *inter alia* on the grounds that the Commission's own studies showed an appreciable effect (for example, 10 per cent of merchants in the Netherlands had surcharged at some time since the abolition of the NDR in the Netherlands). However, the appeal was subsequently withdrawn.

As to the pricing of card acquiring services to merchants, the other end user of a card payment system, acquiring banks are free to set their prices, but these are deeply influenced by interbank fee arrangements in four-party card systems, which can effectively set a floor on merchant acquiring fees. Interbank pricing arrangements must therefore now be dealt with. **11.33**

(ii) Wholesale or Interbank Pricing   A significant part of the Commission's attention concerning the application of competition law to payment systems during the 1990s was taken up with the thorny issue of wholesale pricing in four-party systems, that is, the fees which are paid between the two banks involved in the completion of a payment transaction. The *Visa II* decision of July 2002, on the 'multilateral interchange fee' (hereafter MIF) in the Visa system, can without exaggeration be described as the result of over a decade of internal reflection.[44] Those reflections were characterised by a number of developments in the Commission's position over the years, and by a progressively greater element of economic thinking. **11.34**

First, the nature of MIFs will require a word of explanation. Interchange (or interbank) fees are transaction fees paid between the creditor's bank and the debitor's bank as part of the completion of a payment. The fee can be bilaterally agreed between the two banks, or it can be laid down in the rules of the payment system, in which case it is known as a multilaterally-agreed interchange fee, a MIF. The fee can be paid in either direction, or it can be zero. In practice it is almost always paid by the creditor's (merchant's) bank to the debitor's (cardholder's) bank.[45] **11.35**

---

[44] In fact, the Visa notification, made in 1977, was over 25 years old when the *Visa II* decision was adopted. In 1985 a comfort letter was issued, but this was withdrawn and the case re-opened in 1990 following the receipt of a complaint from a UK federation of retailers (in 1997 a complaint from the European retailing confederation EuroCommerce was also received). For the first half of the 1990s, the *Visa* case was not actively dealt with, as the *Eurocheque* and then the *Dutch banks (Acceptgiro)* cases were advanced as the 'leading' MIF cases. See paras 11.43 and 11.07 of this chapter respectively for those cases.

[45] Normally the MIF is netted into the payment transaction itself by the debitor's bank. So if the fee is payable by the creditor's bank to the debitor's bank (as in the Visa and MasterCard systems), the debitor's bank will deduct it from the amount transferred to the creditor's bank, thus transferring less than the nominal amount of the transfer.

11.36   The functioning of a MIF in a Visa card payment is illustrated in the graphical example below, using hypothetical values:[46]

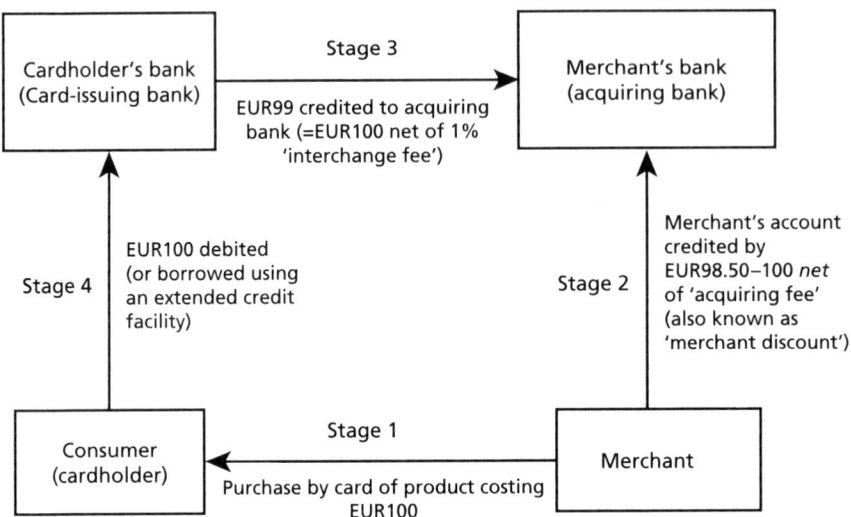

Figure 1   A card payment transaction involving an 'interchange fee'

11.37   In this example it can be seen that for a card payment for a nominal value of EUR100, if the MIF is defined as 1 per cent of the value of the operation, then the cardholder's bank will deduct EUR1 from the amount it reimburses to the merchant's bank, thus in this example only paying EUR99 to the retailer's bank. The retailer's bank then deducts a further amount to cover its own costs and profit margin; in this hypothetical example, that amount is EUR0.50, giving an amount of EUR98.50 actually received by the retailer for a purchase with a face value of EUR100.[47]

11.38   It can thus be seen that a MIF is effectively a device for shifting the burden of the costs of a card payment system between the two banks in the system, and consequently between the two users of the system, namely merchants and cardholders. These two users, both of whom are essential to enable a card payment to take place, have somewhat conflicting interests, in as much as each would prefer the costs of the system to be borne by the other. The MIF in the Visa system, as in the majority of card systems, shifts a significant proportion of the costs of the system onto merchants (who in turn pass it on to all consumers through their prices).[48]

---

[46] Exact MIF levels are considered by card organisations as business secrets, and vary according to the type of card used.

[47] Acquiring banks are free to determine merchant acquiring fees, in negotiation with merchants, but if the merchant fee is below the level of the MIF the acquiring bank will make a loss on the operation. Except if an acquiring bank is willing to accept losses on acquiring in the context of a global relationship with a merchant, price competition between acquiring banks concerns only the 'MIF plus' element of the merchant acquiring fee.

[48] NDR rules, where they exist, prevent merchants from passing on the MIF to those who pay with the card in question via a targeted fee.

There is a significant, and growing, legal and economic literature on the effect on competition of interchange fees, which must be mentioned here (even if it is impossible to do justice to it).[49] Two opposing 'camps' exist, and no consensus has so far been forthcoming. The opponents of interchange fees, on the one hand, characterise them as a price, and describe the multilateral setting of MIF levels by the banks in a payment system as collective price-fixing, which determines the most important input cost for acquiring banks.[50] The huge amount of revenue which accrues to issuing banks from interchange fees,[51] and the secret nature of the levels of the fees, reinforce those concerns. Moreover, the essentially duopolistic structure of the market for international card payment systems can cause upward pressure on MIF levels, as the Commission explains in §80 of its *Visa II* decision:

> The Commission found [in its statement of objections of October 2000] that there were upward pressures on the level of the previous MIF, in particular, the fact that most banks were members of both Visa and the competing Eurocard/MasterCard system, and therefore were likely to issue whichever of the two brands of card had the higher interchange level and brought them the most revenue. The possibility of merchants ceasing to accept Visa cards if the Visa MIF was too high was not sufficiently strong to constrain this upward pressure, as long as the MIF did not reach exceedingly high levels. This was due to the fact that once a merchant already accepts Visa cards, when faced with an increase in the MIF, and consequently an increase in merchant fees, recovering this cost increase through a very small price increase for all goods sold will normally lead to a smaller fall in turnover than ceasing to accept Visa cards.

11.39

An opposing point of view holds that an interchange fee is not a 'price', but rather an essential demand-balancing mechanism with a view to optimising the use of a product (a payment mechanism) characterised by network effects and by joint demand (also by joint supply, in cases where the payment system is a four-party one, according to this point of view).[52] Proponents of this view point out that 'hidden' costs borne by the consumer are a feature of

11.40

---

[49] In recent years (including after the Commission's 2002 *Visa* decision), a number of economists have begun to devote considerable attention to the analysis of 'two-sided markets', that is, markets where the total price is divided between two users with differing demand elasticities, and the volume of transactions is dependent on the price paid by each. Prominent among these are Jean-Charles Rochet and Jean Tirole. See for example their papers, 'Cooperation Among Competitors: Some Economics of Payment Card Associations' [2002] 33(4) Rand Journal of Economics 549-70; and 'Defining two-sided markets' (paper presented at the conference 'The Economics of Two-Sided Markets', Toulouse, 23–24 January 2004).

[50] The 'anti-MIF' position is primarily expressed by DW Carlton and AS Frankel. See their article 'The antitrust economics of credit card networks' in the Antitrust Law Journal, Winter 1995; and AS Frankel's article 'Monopoly and competition in the supply and exchange of money' [1998] 66 Antitrust Law Journal 313–61. D A Balto also criticises interchange fees, in his article 'The Problem of Interchange fees: costs without benefits?' (2000) 4 ECLR 215.

[51] The exact amount of revenue generated from cross-border Visa card transactions in the EU was deleted from the published version of the *Visa II* decision, at Visa's insistence, as a business secret. However, the levels of MIF fees in the USA are publicly known, since the acquiring fees paid by merchants are calculated on a 'MIF plus' basis. Balto (op. cit.) estimates the interchange revenue from domestic credit card transactions in the USA to exceed US$10 billion per year, and a report published in the UK in 2000 estimated the domestic value of interchange revenue in the UK as UK£758 million per year (D Cruickshank, *Competition in UK Banking*, March 2000 (Annex D3,. ISBN 0 11 560075 2). One of the conditions for exemption of the Visa MIF in the *Visa II* decision was an increase in transparency about MIF levels (see below).

[52] This view of MIFs draws on the seminal work of William Baxter 'Bank Interchange of transactional paper: legal and economic Perspectives' [1983] J L E 541, which lays down an economic basis for the existence of MIFs without however reaching conclusions about how their level can practically be determined nor by which bank they should be paid.

most transactions involving an intermediary, and that a card payment transaction cannot take place without both a cardholder and a merchant, who are using a payment mechanism in order to carry out a payment between them. They then argue that it is normal in the case of goods jointly consumed by two different parties that the overall price be divided between the two users in a way that reflects the average marginal utility of a card payment to the two categories of users, otherwise there will be an imbalance of demand between them resulting in less than optimal consumption. A unitary (three-party) payment system, such as American Express, is free to do this by setting prices to cardholders and merchants as it thinks fit, regardless of the costs incurred for servicing each of them; a four-party payment system, in which cardholder and merchant are served by different banks, will be handicapped if it cannot exercise the same pricing flexibility, and an 'interchange' payment between banks is the only practical way to do this. In any case, the argument goes on, without some kind of default rule on the terms of exchange between the banks, there will be a risk of 'hold-up' by the cardholder's bank, which might unilaterally deduct an exorbitant amount for itself from the nominal amount which it transfers to the merchant's bank. An interchange fee is such a default rule, and once it has been accepted as inherent in a payment system it should be irrelevant, for the purposes of analysis under Article 81, whether the fee is set at zero or a positive amount, and which bank must pay it (Article 81 is not concerned with the specific levels of prices, and if the MIF is not a price at all, then even the Article 82 prohibition on excessive prices cannot be applied to it). In legal terms, this amounts to considering MIFs as an ancillary restraint.[53]

11.41   Further background to the Commission's approach to MIFs is provided by interventions by national competition and regulatory authorities under national law, both inside and outside the EU. In 1984 a US District Court rejected a private challenge to MIFs in the USA under the Sherman Act.[54] In the late 1980s, in the first ever intervention of any competition authority against a MIF, the French Conseil de la Concurrence, using national French competition law, ruled against a MIF in the French 'CB' card payment system. The Conseil de la Concurrence had ruled a flat-rate MIF to be unexemptable, but finally exempted a revised MIF, based on a formula involving various parameters, including the level of fraud on cards issued by a bank.[55] Prior to the Commission's *Visa* decisions, several competition and regulatory authorities intervened with regard to different MIFs.[56]

---

[53] Examples of the 'pro-MIF' point of view are: R Schmalensee, 'Payment systems and interchange fees', [2002] 50 Journal of Industrial Economics 103–122; R Schmalensee and D S Evans 'Economic aspects of payment card systems and antitrust policy towards joint ventures', [1995] 63(2) Antitrust Law Journal 861–901; Ahlborn Chang and Evans, 'The problem of interchange fee analysis, case without a cause?' (2001) 8 ECLR 304 (a reply to the Balto article cited in n 50).

[54] The *NaBanco* judgment, upheld on appeal, which has discouraged further attempts to use the Sherman Act against interchange fees in the USA. But the judgment was mainly based on a market definition which placed all means of payment, including cash and cheques, on one market, and thus concluded that credit card organisations exercise no market power.

[55] For a summary of this case in English see the 'Cruickshank report' mentioned in n 51 above (Annex D3, paras 110ff).

[56] On 27 November 2001 the Bank of Italy, in its capacity as competition authority for the banking sector, adopted a decision exempting the MIF in a domestic Italian debit card payment scheme, PagoBancomat, after the level of the MIF was reduced to reflect relevant costs; on 27 August 2002 the Reserve Bank of Australia, using regulatory powers, adopted reforms to credit card schemes in Australia. As concerns MIFs, the RBA, like the Commission in its Visa II decision, imposed the use of an objective, transparent and cost-based benchmark for determining interchange fees.

The Commission has always held MIFs to be, in most circumstances, restrictive of compe- **11.42**
tition in the meaning of Article 81(1), and has never at any time adhered to the conception
of MIFs as ancillary restraints. The most detailed explanation of why the Commission
considers a MIF to restrict competition in the meaning of Article 81(1) is the *Visa II*
decision. A close reading of the Article 81(1) reasoning in that decision[57] gives the impression that the Commission is carefully paving the way for an exemption by, on the one hand,
rejecting the argument that a MIF would be essential for the very existence of the Visa card
system (which would have led to a negative clearance), and on the other hand, avoiding
qualifying the MIF as a hardcore restriction of competition (which would have ruled out
an exemption). First of all, the Commission characterised the MIF as 'an agreement
between competitors, which restricts the freedom of banks individually to decide their
own pricing policies, and distorts the conditions of competition on the Visa issuing and
acquiring markets' (*Visa II*, §66). Even a price agreement can, exceptionally, benefit from a
negative clearance if it is necessary for the supply of a product, for example in a production
jointventure, but the Commission rejects Visa's argument that a card payment system
is aproduction joint venture, on the grounds that each bank provides a distinct service
to adistinct customer. So it would seem that the Commission considers the MIF as an
agreement which affects or impacts prices, but one which falls short of being a price cartel,
and which is not necessary for the existence of the Visa system, although it may have bene-
fitsworthy of consideration under Article 81(3)—indeed the Commission explicitly
accepts that the object of the MIF agreement is to procure efficiencies and not to restrict
competition.

On the analysis of MIFs under Article 81(3), the Commission's position has fluctuated, in **11.43**
four main phases. First of all, in three formal decisions in the 1980s, the Commission
exempted agreements between banks setting MIF levels, with no, or very few, conditions.[58]
The exemption was justified in particular on indispensability grounds, as the alternative to
a default MIF would be thousands of bilateral agreements between banks, which would be
inefficient. The second phase consisted in the sending of a statement of objections in 1990
concerning a MIF in the eurocheque system, and a supplementary statement of objections
in 1992.[59] The third phase, embodied in the statement of objections sent to Visa and
MasterCard in May 1999 concerning *inter alia* their NDR rules,[60] linked the MIF and
NDR, proposing to exempt MIFs in four-party card systems on a number of conditions,

---

[57] *Visa II* decision, §64–69.

[58] *Uniform eurocheques* [1985] OJ L35/43; *Belgian banks* [1987] OJ L7/27; *Italian banks* [1987] OJ L 43/51.
The 'uniform eurocheques' exemption in fact contained a condition for exemption, that the full nominal value
of a eurocheque always be respected by an encashing bank, with no deductions.

[59] This was after the expiry of the exemption granted in 1985 (see previous footnote). No formal decision
was ever taken following those statements of objections, and the eurocheque file was closed on the demise of
the eurocheque system in 2000.

[60] See para 11.31 above. This approach was also exemplified in the publishing of a Article 19(3)
noticeconcerning a MIF in the domestic Dutch inter-bank transfer system *Acceptgiro* ([1997] OJ C273/12).
That case was eventually closed by the negative clearance decision discussed at para 11.07 above, on
the grounds of lack of effect on trade between Member States. See also the first edition of this book, Ch 9,
paras 9.25–9.40.

the most important of which would be that the system must not contain an NDR. The reasoning behind this approach, in a nutshell, was that the effects of any shifting of costs onto merchants via a MIF could be undone, in the absence of an NDR rule and if market forces between merchants and cardholders permitted it, by merchants surcharging cardholders for payment with a card. Thus, on this view, in the absence of an NDR rule, the existence or level of a MIF payment between banks should become irrelevant. This position however became untenable once the studies on the effect of abolition of the NDR in Sweden and the Netherlands (above, paragraph 11.32) showed, on the Commission's interpretation, that the NDR had no appreciable effect.[61] The fourth phase of the Commission's evolution is that embodied in the statement of objections of October 2000 concerning the Visa MIF,[62] followed by the *Visa II* decision of 2002, namely to exempt the MIF on conditions, of which the main one is not the abolition of the NDR but rather that the MIF be linked to, and capped at, the level of applicable costs.

11.44 The exemption granted in the *Visa II* decision was based on an offer of reforms to its systems of MIFs which Visa made following the sending of a statement of objections in October 2000, and which was presumably intended to make the MIF conform to criteria laid down in that statement of objections. The reforms involved three main elements:

- First, Visa was to progressively reduce the level of its MIFs for various different types of consumer cards (that is credit, deferred debit, and direct debit cards).
- Secondly, the MIFs were to be capped at the level of costs for three specific services provided by issuing banks, which the Commission accepted correspond to services provided to those retailers who ultimately pay the cross-border MIF. These services are: transaction processing, payment guarantee,[63] and free funding period.[64] The costs of these services were to be determined by an independently audited cost study, and the 'cost cap' would apply cumulatively with reductions in the level of the MIF offered by Visa.[65]

---

[61] The studies undermined this approach on legal grounds only, since it is not legally possible to prohibit an agreement which has no appreciable effect. In economic terms, if market forces do not permit merchants to surcharge cardholders for using a credit card, even in the absence of a NDR rule, this would seem to suggest that the division of the costs of the system between cardholders and merchants affected by a MIF does correspond closely to the relative price elasticity of cardholders and merchants. The 'safety valve' role played by the merchant's right to surcharge does not necessarily imply that surcharging must take place.

[62] See press release IP/00/1164 of 16 October 2000.

[63] The term 'payment guarantee' is used to describe the promise of the issuing bank to honour payments to the acquiring bank, even those which turn out to be *inter alia* fraudulent or for which the cardholder ultimately defaults, on condition that the retailer undertakes all the security checks necessary to enable the issuing bank to promise payment. This promise is then extended by acquiring banks on to retailers, and effectively constitutes a kind of payment insurance for retailers.

[64] The 'free funding period' corresponds to the cost of any time difference between payment by the cardholders' bank to the acquirer and the time when either payment must be made by the cardholder, or the balance of the credit card bill rolled over into the extended credit facility, to which a rate of interest is applied (that is, it does not include any costs arising from the granting of extended credit to cardholders). This 'free funding period' to cardholders is considered by the Commission to benefit retailers in a cross-border context by stimulating sales and increasing turnover.

[65] That is, if the cost study suggested a MIF level below that offered by Visa as the first part of its reform, the effective 'cap' of the MIF would be the level suggested by the cost study.

- Furthermore, Visa was to allow member banks to reveal information about the MIF levels and the relative percentage of the three cost categories (previously considered business secrets) to retailers at their request.[66]

In its Article 81(3) reasoning used in granting an exemption to this revised MIF, the Commission follows the argumentation of Visa, and of defenders of MIFs, for quite some way: **11.45**

> The Visa network—like any network characterised by network externalities—will provide greater utility to each type of user the greater the number of users of the other type: the more merchants in the system, the greater the utility to cardholders and vice-versa. The maximum number of users in the system will be achieved if the cost to each category of user is as closely as possible equivalent to the average marginal utility of the system to that category of user. The Commission accepts that this is not necessarily achieved with each bank simply charging its own customer . . .[67]

However, the Commission departs from the traditional defence of MIFs in remarking that 'some kind of default arrangement is necessary, but the question of whether it qualifies for exemption or not will depend on the details of the arrangement' (§79), and 'only a MIF which is the least restrictive of competition out of all the possible types of MIF could be considered as indispensable' (§99). The Commission goes on to note: 'Given the difficulties of measuring the average marginal utility of a Visa card payment to each category of user, some acceptable proxy for this must be found, which meets the concerns of the Commission'. This gives the impression that if the MIF had been based on an econometric calculation of the average marginal utility of a Visa card payment to each category of user (presumably via the relative price elasticity of each category of user) the Commission would have been inclined to exempt that MIF unconditionally. Visa's method of setting its MIF before proposing its reforms (a method which was the subject of the statement of objections of September 1999) remains a secret, but clearly it was not based on a calculation of marginal utility. **11.46**

The Commission then goes on to accept that the revised MIF, linked to three categories of costs and rendered transparent, constitutes such an 'acceptable proxy', in particular as it balances sufficiently the conflicting interests of the two users of a card payment system (cardholders and retailers), thus meeting the second condition of Article 81(3), and constitutes the least restrictive feasible method of calculating the MIF, thus meeting the indispensability condition of Article 81(3). In all of its analysis under Article 81(3), the Commission does not mention the first part of Visa's reforms to the MIF—a reduction in the absolute level of the MIF. It is hard to see how a reduction in the level of a price alone could be of relevance for the granting of an exemption, thus presumably this element of Visa's reform was of little **11.47**

---

[66] In May 2004 Visa and MasterCard decided to publish their cross-border MIF rates on their web sites. See Commission press release IP/04/616 of 7 May 2004, and an article in the summer 2005 edition of the Commission's 'Competition policy newsletter' by Lukas Repa ('MasterCard and Visa modify network rules, and increase transparency of cross-border interchange fees', p 57).

[67] *Visa II*, para 83. This reasoning is based on the work of Baxter, (op. cit., n 52 above). But it should be noted that this reasoning does not tell us anything about how a MIF should be calculated nor even in which direction it should be paid, only that it should exist.

importance as far as the legal analysis is concerned. On the other hand, the emphasis on the link to costs suggests that the Commission feared that the MIF was being set at an excessively high level; but if this were the concern, then Article 82 would have been a more appropriate legal instrument.

11.48   Finally, the Commission's definitions of the relevant product market in the *Visa I* and *Visa II* decisions needs to be considered.[68] The definitions in the two decisions are near-identical, but with certain nuances. At the outset, the Commission dismisses any substitutability between payment cards and other means of payment, such as cash, cheques, and interbank transfers, on the grounds principally that those other means of payment lack the convenience or security of card payments. The fact that for some medium-value payments either cards or cheques may be used (functional substitutability) is considered insufficient to constitute economic substitutability (that is, a small but sustained price increase for cards will not lead to consumers switching to cash or cheques). Within payment cards, the Commission explicitly leaves open the question of whether different types of cards (credit and debit cards, for example) constitute separate markets, as even on a wide market definition, of all types of cards, Visa would still hold market power. Finally, a distinction between two levels of competition is introduced, between system-level (or upstream) competition, and intra-system (or downstream) competition. System-level competition is between different card systems, such as Visa and MasterCard, while intra-system competition is between individual banks to issue cards and acquire merchants within a particular card payment system. Different agreements may affect various of these markets; MIFs were considered to affect all of them, to various degrees.

11.49   (iii) **Comment on the *Visa II* Decision**   The *Visa II* decision was a success in pragmatic terms: by it the Commission managed to close a case which had been under investigation, on and off, for twenty-five years, for long periods of which time it seemed paralysed by diverging legal and economic interpretations and the effects of conflicting lobbies. It was also the first time that the Commission had set out in detail its reasoning on this complex issue. Certain key concessions from Visa as to the calculation and transparency of its MIF were obtained, in the overall interest of users of the Visa system. But this success came at the risk of creating a perception that the Commission was making itself into a price regulator, and of a significant resource burden for the Commission itself with ongoing monitoring of Visa's costs. The decision was not appealed.[69]

11.50   The *Visa II* decision does not cover MIFs for certain types of Visa card (notably for so-called 'commercial cards') and explicitly limits itself to MIFs as applied to cross-border payment transactions. Nor does the decision provide a great deal of clarification on precisely what other payment systems similar to Visa would have to do in order to benefit from an exemption. For example, would the Commission insist on a reduction in the absolute level of the MIF (the first element of Visa's reform 'package') as an essential precondition for an

---

[68]   *Visa I*, §34–43; *Visa II*, §43–52.

[69]   This is surprising, since the innovative (and thus vulnerable) reasoning under both Arts 81(1) and 81(3) would seem to invite challenge (Visa might have challenged the reasoning under Art 81(1), arguing that a negative clearance should have been given, and the complainant EuroCommerce might have challenged the justification for the exemption under Art 81(3)).

exemption, and what are the precise cost components which can and cannot be included within the three broad cost categories? The main other four-party card payment system is MasterCard, which received a statement of objections concerning its MIF from the Commission in 2003.[70] That case is still ongoing, and it is not known whether MasterCard will offer reforms to its MIF sufficient to receive an exemption, and if so, what those reforms will be.

One final question which presents itself with regard to the *Visa II* decision is why an inter-   **11.51** vention under the competition rules was considered necessary, in the light of the effects of the Regulation of 2001 on cross-border payments in euros (above, paragraph 11.26), which, in imposing the principle of equal pricing between domestic and cross-border euro payments, applies to cardholder fees and to merchant acquiring fees. This would prevent acquiring banks from passing on the MIF for cross-border payments to merchants via a specific distinct fee rate for such payments, and thus, the effect of any fall in MIF rates for cross-border Visa payments resulting from the revision of the Visa MIF will be largely hidden from merchants. The answer would seem to lie, not so much in the fact that some parts of the EU fall outside the euro zone, and thus escape the effects of that Regulation, but rather that the great majority of card payments in the EU, and consequently the majority of MIF payments, are domestic, not cross-border. Although only MIFs for cross-border payments are covered by the *Visa II* decision, the Commission may have wanted to set a precedent which it would desire national competition authorities to follow when examining MIFs (either under national competition law, or if appropriate, under Article 81, given their new power to grant exemptions under Community competition law).

One recent such decision by a national authority is the September 2005 decision by the UK   **11.52** Office of Fair Trading regarding the MIF applied by MasterCard in the UK,[71] applying Article 81 as well as national law. The OFT found the MIF applied by MasterCard in the UK between 2000 and 2004 to be anticompetitive, in particular as its calculation incorporated 'extraneous costs' which the OFT considered as not inherent in the provision of a card payment service. One of those 'extraneous costs', which accounts for a significant proportion of the total MIF and which the Commission had accepted in the *Visa II* decision, is the 'free funding period' (that is the free credit provided to the cardholder until the card bill must be paid). In the course of the judicial review that followed, the OFT decision was nevertheless set aside, with the OFT's agreement.[72]

In June 2006 the Commission sent a supplementary statement of objections to MasterCard.   **11.53** In the objections, the Commission takes the view that the MasterCard cross-border interchange

---

[70] Report on competition policy for 2003, pt I, paras 182ff.

[71] OFT decision of 6 September 2005, Case CP/0090/00/S, OFT press release 168/05. The decision imposed no fine, and thus has only declarative value. The MasterCard MIF, as applied since 2004, is the subject of an ongoing OFT investigation.

[72] See press release 97/06 of 20 June 2006 from the OFT. Another recent example of a national competition authority taking a cost-based approach, but with a harder line than the Commission's *Visa II* decision, albeit using national competition law only this time, is the decisions adopted in April 2005 by the Spanish Tribunal de Defensa de la Competencia regarding MIFs in three domestic Spanish card payment networks. For debit cards, only transaction processing/authorisation costs were accepted by the TDC; for credit and deferred debit cards, the TDC also accepted costs related to covering fraud, which is a percentage of the transaction value. However, costs relating to the free-funding period were not accepted for either debit or credit cards.

fee agreements restrict competition between member banks by pre-determining a minimum price merchants must pay for accepting credit and debit cards.[73] The *MasterCard* case will be the leading case defining the Commission's position on interchange fees, notably because the Commission's *Visa II* exemption decision described above expires at the end of 2007.

(d) Non-price Issues

11.54   (i) **Issues Relating to Access**   Payment systems are of such fundamental importance in the banking sector, both for interbank payments and for payments on behalf of customers, that lack of access to them can constitute a significant barrier to entry on banking markets, and thus they may even constitute essential facilities. Restrictions of access to payment systems have therefore logically played an important part in the Commission's application of the competition rules in the banking sector. Access to payment systems can be affected not only by specific rules and access criteria but also by fees and pricing, thus overlapping somewhat with pricing issues. The Commission's intervention in the *SWIFT/La Poste* case illustrates these issues.

11.55   SWIFT is a co-operative owned by over 2,000 banks. It operates a specific international telecommunication network which offers reliable and secure data communication and processing to financial institutions located all over the world. SWIFT's network is used by virtually all international payment systems in the world. The French post office, La Poste, which offers retail banking services, applied for membership of SWIFT but was refused on the grounds that membership of SWIFT was limited to banks, and the legal status of La Poste, a part of the French state administration, was different from that of a bank. Following a complaint to the Commission from La Poste, the Commission issued a statement of objections to SWIFT.

11.56   The Commission argued that SWIFT is an essential facility holding the control of a gateway to the international transfer market, for two reasons. First of all, it holds a monopolistic position in the market for international payment message transfer networks. In addition, SWIFT is the only network providing connections to banks located anywhere in the world. The Commission considered that SWIFT had abused its dominant position by excluding La Poste and other entities interested and engaging in cross-border transfers from SWIFT membership on the basis of their legal form rather than objective non-discriminatory criteria.

11.57   Following the opening of proceedings by the Commission, although SWIFT denied both the existence of a dominant position and an abuse, it offered the Commission an undertaking which led the Commission to suspend its investigation. SWIFT undertook to create a new category of participants (as opposed to broadening its category of members who are also shareholders). This new category, called Non-Shareholding Financial Institution (NSFI), would be granted full access to the SWIFT network, products, and services. NSFIs are those institutions that satisfy the criteria laid down by the European Central Bank, for access to any European payment system. To qualify as an NSFI, the entity must be authorised to hold accounts for customers; its direct participation in one or more EU fund transfer systems processing third party payments must have the approval of the central

---

[73] See European Commission MEMO/06/260 of 30 June 2006.

bank; and (a) its public nature must ensure little risk of failure; or (b) its financial service activities must be supervised by a recognised competent authority.[74]

The intervention in the SWIFT case came before the Court judgment in the *Oscar Bronner* **11.58** case, which clarified the circumstances in which an essential facility can be found to exist.[75] Interestingly, in an intervention subsequent to that judgment, again concerning access to a payment system, the Commission found against the existence of an essential facility. The Groupement des Cartes Bancaires (GCB), a French grouping of banks which operates a domestic card payment system in France, known as 'CB', had notified a number of rules and decisions over the years, all of which benefited from a comfort letter in October 2000. Among these was a GCB decision of 1995 on the conditions under which Visa cards and MasterCards issued by banks outside France could be authorised and processed on the GCB's French network. Although the 'CB' system is a domestic system in France, agreements between the GCB, on the one hand, and the Visa and MasterCard systems, on the other, allow Visa cards and MasterCards issued outside France but used for payments in France (for example by visitors to France), to use the GCB's proprietary network for the French leg of their authorising and processing. The creation of a single market for banking in the EU raised the possibility that banks in other EU Member States might issue Visa cards or MasterCards in a cross-border manner to French residents, in which case the Visa and MasterCard systems would become de facto competitors of the 'CB' system for domestic card payments in France. Given this possibility, the notified decision required that any bank which issues cards which are mostly used on the GCB's network (which would normally be the case with such a card held by a French resident rather than an occasional visitor to France) should join the GCB and consequently conform to its internal rules[76] and pay the applicable fees. Failing this, the GCB reserved the right to deny access to its network to cards issued by the bank in question. The Commission's comfort letter for this particular decision was based on the conclusion that the CB network was not an essential facility, as other (albeit less efficient and more expensive) networks for card authorisation and processing exist in France.[77] This conclusion was apparently based primarily on the existence of the American Express and Diners Club card systems in France, as competitors to the 'CB' system, with no access to the GCB's network.

However, a completely separate case involving the same French organisation Groupement des **11.59** Cartes Bancaires,[78] and involving the creation of barriers to entry on a card-related market, led to the sending of a statement of objections in July 2004. A new, and exceedingly complex, system of fees payable by member banks to the GCB for certain activities, in particular card issuing, was notified to the Commission by the GCB at the end of 2002.[79] This fee

---

[74] IP/97/870; Report on competition policy 1997 (Vol XXVII), point 68; [1997] OJ C335/3 (publication of the commitment).

[75] Judgment of the court of 26 November 1998 in Case C-7/97.

[76] Including eg, the obligation for the card to contain a microprocessor.

[77] See Commission annual competition policy report, 2000, paras 205–208. Para 207 notes that in the absence of an essential facility, the GCB 'can decide whether or not to grant access to its competitors (provided that it does not discriminate between them)'.

[78] There have thus been three main cases involving this organisation: the *Helsinki agreement* case referred to in para 11.17 above, the case closed by comfort letter in 2000 referred to in the previous paragraph, and this case.

structure had been adopted by the founder members of the GCB—the major French banks represented on the GCB's steering committee, which effectively control the organisation—without any advance information or consultation of the GCB's over 140 other member banks. Suspecting that the true goal of the notified new fee structure was to bar new entrants to the French card payment market—in particular banks owned by major retailing chains and foreign banks—through deliberately discriminatory measures, the Commission carried out surprise inspections in May 2003, which according to the press release accompanying the statement of objections,[80] corroborated those suspicions. The fees (whose introduction has been suspended by the GCB) would have increased the costs of new entrants, who would no longer have been able to reduce card prices. This reduction of competitive pressure on prices would allow the incumbents not to lose market share to new entrants, maintain card prices at a supra-competitive level, and preserve their revenues. In addition, revenue from the fees collected would be redistributed among members of the GCB not liable to the fees (including all those on the steering committee). The case concerns in effect access to the French retail banking market, as few consumers will consider a bank current account which does not provide a competitively-priced payment card, and the 'CB' card payment brand is by far the most widely accepted by retailers in France, and the best known and most valued by consumers.

11.60   Another interesting case which is still outstanding, concerning access to a payment system, is an Article 81 complaint from Morgan Stanley Dean Witter (MSDW) against Visa for having refused MSDW membership of Visa in Europe, the grounds for the refusal being that MSDW was a competitor of Visa, as it operates in the USA a card payment system called 'Discover' in competition with the Visa system. MSDW introduced a claim for damages in the UK courts, but proceedings were stayed pending a Commission decision. A statement of objections was sent on 3 August 2004,[81] focusing on the effect of Visa's decision on competition in acquiring markets. Since merchants almost always seek an acquiring bank capable of acquiring both Visa and MasterCard payment transactions, exclusion of a bank from Visa effectively prevents it from competing as a merchant acquirer. The discriminatory aspect of Visa's decision was also highlighted in the statement of objections, as Visa had admitted to membership several banks which could be considered as competitors to Visa, notably Citigroup, the owner of the Diner's Club card network. Moreover, MasterCard, Visa's main competitor, had admitted MSDW to membership in Europe.

11.61   **(ii) Honour All Cards Rule**   The honour all cards rule is a rule in many card payment systems obliging merchants who accept a particular brand of card to accept all cards bearing that brand, and not refuse to accept some cards, for example on the basis of which bank issued the card, which country it was issued in, or other characteristics of the card. The honour all cards rule in the Visa system was cleared by the Commission in the *Visa I* decision.[82] The Commission found that the honour all cards rule did not tie unrelated products, even

---

[79]   These fees would in particular penalise banks which issue cards but do not carry out acquiring of merchants (allegedly in order to stimulate competition on the French acquiring market), and banks which rapidly increase their issuing activity of 'CB' cards relative to other banks in the GCB.

[80]   IP 04/876 of 8 July 2004.

[81]   See Commission press release IP/04/1016 of 3 August 2004.

[82]   2001 *Visa* decision, paras 66–69.

though different categories of Visa-branded cards covered by the rule (such as credit cards, debit cards, or corporate cards) might have different characteristics and involve different MIF levels and merchant acquiring fees. In the Commission's view as expressed in *Visa I*, without a guarantee of universal acceptance of all Visa-branded cards wherever the Visa logo is displayed, the Visa brand would lose much of its meaning and value, nor could the Visa system properly function if merchants could pick and choose among Visa cards presented to them for payment.

Certainly, if the Commission had found the honour all cards rule to involve tying in the **11.62** meaning of Article 81(1)(e) of the Treaty, an acceptable remedy would have been hard to find. Obliging Visa to ensure that acquiring banks charge the same fees for all categories of Visa cards would have involved cross-subsidisation and limited the freedom of pricing of acquiring banks; while obliging Visa to launch a new card brand every time a card with different characteristics is launched could have led to a confusing multiplicity of card brands.

(iii) Cross-border Restrictions The Visa rules on cross-border card issuing and acquiring **11.63** of merchants had been one of the subjects of the statement of objections of May 1999, but, following modifications to those rules, they were covered by the negative clearance of the *Visa I* decision. As concerns issuing, the Commission's objection had been to an obligation (with very limited exceptions) on a Visa member bank wanting to issue cards into a country other than its country of domicile to have a branch or subsidiary in the country into which cards are issued, thus effectively eliminating the cross-border nature of the activity. This obligation was removed with effect from April 2001.[83] As regards cross-border acquiring of merchants, the Visa rules in force in 1999 had allowed cross-border acquiring only of international merchants, that is, merchants with outlets in more than one country. From October 2000, this restriction was removed.[84] However, both cross-border issuing and acquiring require a bank to obtain a special licence and are conditional on the respect of certain domestic Visa rules applied in the country where the issuing or acquiring takes place.[85]

(iv) No Acquiring Without Issuing Rule The 'no acquiring without issuing' rule was a **11.64** rule which hitherto applied in the Visa and MasterCard systems in Europe, obliging member banks to issue a substantial number of cards before undertaking the activity of acquiring merchants. Visa's European 'no acquiring without issuing' rule was cleared in the 2001 *Visa* decision, with one brief paragraph of reasoning, which noted that no evidence had been found that the rule created any barriers to entry on the acquiring market.[86] Shortly after the adoption of that decision, an appeal against the negative clearance of the 'no acquiring without issuing' rule was lodged with the CFI by First Data, a specialist acquirer from the USA which claimed that it had failed to gain membership of the Visa system in Europe because of this rule (however First Data had failed to bring its situation to the Commission's attention during the administrative procedure leading to the decision).[87]

---

[83] *Visa I* decision, §14–15.
[84] *Visa I* decision, §16–17.
[85] For cross-border acquiring, this can include the application of the domestically applicable MIF. As the MIF is the most important cost component for acquirers, this can hinder the ability of cross-border acquirers to offer lower merchant fees to domestic acquirers.
[86] 2001 *Visa* decision, para 65.
[87] Case T28/02 [2002] OJ C109/54.

Before any Court hearing on the appeal cound take place, first MasterCard and subsequently Visa repealed their 'no acquiring without issuing' rules.[88]

C. Capital Markets

(1) The Consolidation of European Capital Markets and the Role of Competition Law

11.65   The application of EU competition law to capital markets and in particular to the trading, clearing and settlement [89] of securities (equities, bonds, and derivatives) is recent and cannot be understood in isolation from the creation of the single market in this area.

11.66   Advancing from national markets towards a single capital market is a political objective of the Community.[90] It is also a fact that capital markets within the EU are becoming increasingly integrated. This is already the case with money markets, largely due to the introduction of the euro. Integration is less of a reality as regards securities markets, although there is a continuous increase in cross-border transactions (intra-EU equity trades have increased by 20–25 per cent annually since 1996) and service providers are undergoing consolidation:

— At the trading level, Euronext, the securities exchange, now integrates the formerly independent exchanges of Paris, Brussels, Amsterdam, and Lisbon. Just three companies (the London Stock Exchange, Deutsche Börse and Euronext) represent some 70 per cent of all exchange trades in the EU.

— The London Stock Exchange has been the target of takeover attempts by both Euronext and Deutsche Börse. These transactions were examined by the Competition Commission in the UK, because the envisaged mergers were not of Community dimension. The Competition Commission cleared the transaction subject to remedies, the details of which were being decided at the time of writing.

— Providers of clearing and settlement are also in a consolidation phase. LCH-Clearnet is a large clearinghouse that clears trades for Euronext and the London Stock Exchange. Euroclear is the owner of several central securities depositories (see concept in paras 11.73–11.87 below) in Belgium, France, Ireland and the UK, the Netherlands, and Portugal.

11.67   For securities traded on exchanges, there is as a rule no choice of clearing and settlement providers, as most exchanges have rules—or agreements with clearing and settlement

---

[88]   See the article referred to in n 66 above.

[89]   Securities are traded either in exchanges or off exchange ('over the counter'). Securities clearing and settlement are necessary steps for a securities trade to be completed. Clearing is the process that ensures that the buyer and the seller have agreed on an identical transaction and that the seller is selling securities which it is entitled to sell. Settlement is the final transfer of securities from the seller to the buyer and the transfer of funds from the buyer to the seller, as well as the relevant annotations in securities accounts.

[90]   The Financial Services Action Plan (FSAP) included full review of existing legislative measures and many new directives, such as the Markets in Financial Instruments Directive (MiFID, Directive (EC) 2004/39 [2004] OJ L145/1), which replaced the 1993 Investment Services Directive. In the clearing and settlement area, the Commission has adopted two communications, one on 28 May 2002 and the other on 28 April 2004. Both communications underline the role of competition law. The 2004 Communication announced a new Directive that would include among other provisions the granting of access rights between service providers.

providers—pursuant to which securities trades in the exchange must be cleared and settled in a predetermined company.[91]

Within the wider area of capital markets, the Commission's action in the competition area has **11.68** so far focused on securities markets, and more specifically in the application of antitrust law to securities markets. Despite the increasing consolidation in the sector, even important transactions such as the creation of Euronext exchange or of the LCH/Clearnet clearinghouse did not need to be notified to the Commission under the Merger Regulation. This is because the turnover thresholds in the area of securities markets infrastructure were not met. While the amount of money that transits through the infrastructures is huge, the fees charged, which determine the turnover, did not reach the levels necessary for the merger to be considered of Community dimension.[92]

The existence of links and agreements between service providers at different levels is a pre- **11.69** condition for exchanges to compete effectively. For example, when the London Stock Exchange launched its trading service for Dutch securities in May 2004, in direct competition with Euronext, the new service used LCH/Clearnet as a clearinghouse, the same as that used by Euronext.

Since 2001, high level groups and expert groups such as the Lamfalussy group of wise men **11.70** and the Giovannini group[93] identified cross-border clearing and settlement, and in particular issues related to access and pricing, as one of the main sources of inefficiencies for the proper functioning of European capital markets. Calls for competition enforcement in the clearing and settlement area have also been made on various occasions in speeches by members of the governing council of the European Central Bank.[94]

In such a context, it can be expected that competition law will play an increasing role. Article 81 **11.71** issues will arise for example in the case of exclusive agreements, which have the potential to foreclose markets, and Article 82 may be of application as regards access and pricing.

(2) Commission Practice in the Sector of Financial Markets Infrastructure

(a) The First Cases

The first cases the Commission dealt with in the sector of financial markets infrastructure **11.72** resulted from notifications. No formal decisions were adopted until 2004, in the

---

[91] See 'An overview of current arrangements in securities trading, clearing and settlement in EU 25', compiled by London Economics for DG Competition, February 2004.

[92] To remedy the situation where important mergers in the sector of stock exchanges and other financial infrastructure providers escape review by the Commission, the Commission agreed with the Member States in June 2000 that a 'special co-operation procedure' would apply. The special co-operation procedure consists in the provision of information (merger notifications, requests for information, etc) by the authority which reviews the transaction to all Member States and the Commission, in the same manner as is done by the Commission in those cases where it has exclusive competence. The Commission and Member States may then comment to the competent national authority (see speech of 5 December 2002 by Commissioner Monti to the Association of Private Client Investment Managers and Stockbrokers, APCIMS). The effectiveness of this procedure still has to be demonstrated.

[93] The Giovannini group produced two reports, the first of November 2001 (identifying 15 barriers in the way of efficient clearing and settlement in the EU) and the second of April 2003 (suggesting the types of action needed to remove the barriers).

[94] See for example speech of Mr Padoa-Schioppa, executive board member of the European Central Bank, of 23 June 2004, 'Challenges of financial integration in the post—Financial Services Action Plan period'.

Clearstream case. Some cases were closed because the co-operation was terminated. In other cases, comfort letters were issued:

— *Volbroker* concerned a joint venture between various investment banks,[95] the purpose of which was the development and marketing of an electronic brokerage service for trading among banks in foreign currency options. As the parents were active in the market for foreign currency options, the Commission considered that the fact that they agreed to channel a certain part of their business through Volbroker constituted a restriction of competition caught by Article 81(1). The co-operation was however deemed to meet the conditions for exemption, in particular because Volbroker undertook to allow a certain type of brokers called 'voice' brokers to participate in the system where they act as principals, and took steps to ensure that sensitive business information would not be divulged by the joint venture to the parents. These commitments, often cited as an example of 'Chinese walls', were: (i) none of Volbroker's staff would have any contractual or other obligation towards any of the parents or vice versa; (ii) Volbroker's staff would be in a geographically distinct location from that of the parents; (iii) the representatives of the parents in Volbroker's board of directors would not have access to commercially sensitive information relating to each other or to third parties; (iv) the parents would not have access to the IT and communication systems of Volbroker; and (v) the parents would ensure that all personnel understand the importance of maintaining the confidentiality of sensitive commercial information and that sanctions for breach are established.

— In April 2001, the Commission issued a 'negative clearance' type comfort letter to *Coredeal*,[96] an electronic trading platform that provided an order entry and matching system for corporate bonds. The Commission took the view that Coredeal would face competition from other trading systems for corporate bonds such as those provided by the Swiss Exchange and by Eurex.

— *Eurex* is an exchange for derivatives trading and a joint venture of Deutsche Börse AG and the Swiss Exchange. The joint venture was notified in 1999, and as part of its analysis under Article 81, the Commission examined if there was a risk of coordination of the behaviour of the parents.[97] The Article 19(3) notice outlined a series of possible markets where Eurex is active (such as markets for derivatives trading[98] and derivatives clearing in relation to the securities traded on Eurex), as well as neighbouring markets in which the parents are active (such as listing and trading services for securities, listing and trading services for warrants, the provision of electronic exchange systems, and the sale of

---

[95] DB UK Holdings Limited, UBS AG, Goldman Sachs Vol-Holdings LLC, Citibank Investments Limited, J.P. Morgan and NatWest. See press release IP/00/896 of 31 July 2000.

[96] See 2001 Report on competition policy and speech of Commissioner Monti to APCIMS, cited above.

[97] The joint venture was deemed full-function and therefore a merger, but not of Community dimension. The Commission examined under Art 81(1) the risk of coordination due to the merger of part of the parents' activity. See 2001 Report on competition policy, and Notice pursuant to Article 19(3) of Council Regulation No 17 [2000] OJ C231/2.

[98] Markets for derivatives based on (i) equities listed on Deutsche Börse, the Swiss Exchange, or the Helsinki Stock Exchange; (ii) equity indexes based exclusively on Deutsche Börse, the Swiss Exchange, or the Helsinki Stock Exchange listed shares; (iii) equity indexes not based exclusively on Deutsche Börse or the Swiss Exchange listed shares ands specific interest rates (such as the Bund future).

market information). The case was cleared by comfort letter (of the 'negative clearance' type) as the Commission's examination found no appreciable risk of coordination of parents in neighbouring markets.

— *Centradia*, an electronic trading platform created by four banks to offer foreign exchange and a limited range of money market products to corporate customers, also received a comfort letter. The Commission took the view that the transaction did not create any restriction of competition within the meaning of Article 81(1), because the parents had put in place safeguards to ensure that there would be no exchange through the platform of sensitive commercial information, and because parents remained free to trade on other platforms. The Commission also took into account that most of the foreign exchange transactions were concluded off-line, and not online as in the case of Centradia.[99]

(b) Clearstream[100]

The *Clearstream* case was initiated ex-officio. As mentioned above, this is the first Commission decision in the area of securities markets. The Commission started investigating clearing and settlement from a competition viewpoint in 2001, and progressively narrowed the scope of the investigation to abusive behaviour by Clearstream. In the decision, the Commission found that Clearstream Banking AG, the German Central Securities Depository (CSD), and its parent company Clearstream International SA violated Article 82 by refusing to supply certain clearing and settlement services to one of its customers (Euroclear Bank SA (EB)), and by applying discriminatory prices to that same customer. **11.73**

Market definition is a central element in this decision. As is often the case in financial services, the relevant market is defined in a narrow manner as the provision by the issuer CSD (Clearstream Banking AG) to CSDs in other Member States and to ICSDs of 'primary' clearing and settlement services for securities issued according to German law. This requires some explanations: **11.74**

— Providers of clearing and settlement services may be Central Securities Depositories (CSDs), International Central Securities Depositories (ICSDs) or other intermediaries such as banks.
— A CSD is an entity which holds and administers securities and enables securities transactions to be processed through book entry. In its home country, it provides processing services for trades of those securities that have been deposited with it (which it holds in final custody), and in this function the CSD is referred to as the 'issuer CSD' and is not an intermediary. A CSD can also offer processing services as an intermediary in cross-border clearing and settlement, where the primary deposit of securities is in another country. Clearstream Banking AG is Germany's only Wertpapiersammelbank (CSD).
— An ICSD is an organisation whose core business is clearing and settling securities— traditionally Eurobonds—in an international (non-domestic) environment. There are at present two ICSDs in the EU: Euroclear Bank, based in Belgium, and Clearstream Banking Luxembourg (CBL), a subsidiary of Clearstream International SA and a sister company to Clearstream Banking AG. An ICSD can also provide other services such as intermediary services for equities.

---

[99] See 2002 Report on competition policy and press release IP/02/943 of 27 June 2002.
[100] Decision of 2 June 2004. See press release IP/04/705 of the same day.

— Intermediaries such as banks may also provide clearing and settlement services to their clients.

11.75 To define the relevant market, the Commission considered that, while clearing and settlement may generally be carried out by CSDs, ICSDs or other intermediaries such as banks, only final custodians may perform 'primary' clearing and settlement for the securities actually deposited in final custody. In this case, all securities issued under German law and kept in collective safe custody—the only significant form of custody in Germany for traded securities—were deposited with Clearstream Banking AG, and only this company could conduct the primary clearing and settlement related to these securities. Primary clearing and settlement was therefore occurring when the position of a securities account held with the issuer CSD (Clearstream Banking AG for securities issued according to German law) changed.

11.76 In contrast, secondary clearing and settlement is performed 'downstream' by intermediaries in their own books. Secondary clearing and settlement encompasses both mirror operations through which intermediaries reflect the result of primary clearing and settlement in the accounts of their customers and annotations in account following internalised transactions. Internalisation takes place where the intermediary is able to settle the transaction in its own books because both the buyer and seller happen to hold accounts with that intermediary.

11.77 In the *Clearstream* case, it became apparent that the particular services that Clearstream provided to CSDs and ICSDs could be compared to the standard services provided to what Clearstream called 'non-CSD customers' (banks), who were supplied on the basis of Clearstream Banking AG's General Terms and Conditions.

11.78 An issue that the Commission examined in detail is whether clearing and settlement by intermediaries could be a substitute to the primary clearing and settlement performed by Clearstream Banking AG.

11.79 In the decision, the Commission underlined that, for market definition purposes, it does not need to examine the needs of the intermediaries' clients, but rather the specific needs of the category of clients who require the product or service, that is, in the present case, the needs of financial intermediaries like Euroclear Bank, who desire to provide economically significant, efficient, and competitive secondary clearing and settlement services to their own clients. For this category of customers, the Commission took the view that:

— Indirect access to the issuer CSD—Clearstream Banking AG—through an intermediary is not a substitutable alternative for direct access (given that the use of an intermediary results in slower service, greater risk and complexity, additional costs, and potential conflict of interests[101]).

— No intermediary is able to internalise all transactions with all potential counterparties for all securities safekept in the issuer CSD and therefore access to the issuer CSD is a requirement. The Clearstream case precisely relates to a situation where an intermediary

---

[101] The use of a local agent bank as an intermediary may create conflicts of interest, as the intermediary may be an actual or potential competitor in the downstream market and is informed of the operations of the customer against which it is competing or might start competing in the downstream market.

(Euroclear Bank) required primary clearing and settlement services from the issuer CSD and could not obtain substitutable services either in-house or from another intermediary.

— The issuer CSD is not constrained by the prices applied by intermediaries when primary clearing and settlement is needed. During the time that Euroclear Bank sought unsuccessfully to obtain price reductions for primary clearing and settlement services directly from Clearstream Banking AG and cease using a local agent as an intermediary, the prices applied by that local agent did not constrain Clearstream in its discussions with Euroclear Bank.

Clearstream Banking AG is dominant in the relevant market since it is the only CSD where **11.80** securities issued under German law and kept in collective safe custody are deposited. It is thus the only entity able to perform primary clearing and settlement for these securities. The Commission considered that the position of Clearstream Banking AG was not constrained by any actual or potential competition in the market.

The decision identifies two types of abuse, the first refusing to supply primary clearing and **11.81** settlement services for registered shares (and discriminating against EB in relation to the provision of those services) and the second, the application of discriminatory prices for primary clearing and settlement services.[102]

The qualification of Clearstream's behaviour as refusal to supply follows from the combination **11.82** of a number of factors: Clearstream Banking AG is an unavoidable trading partner, Euroclear Bank could not duplicate the services that it was requesting, and the refusal to supply had the effect of impairing Euroclear Bank's ability to provide a comprehensive and innovative pan-European service in the downstream market for cross-border clearing and settlement of EU securities. In addition, the Commission considered (i) that the growing importance of registered shares in Germany[103] resulted in a reduction of the scope of the services provided to Euroclear Bank, an existing customer of Clearstream, because newly issued shares were mostly registered, and many existing bearer shares were converted into registered shares; and (ii) that Clearstream breached Euroclear Bank's legitimate expectations that it would be supplied by Clearstream with primary clearing and settlement services within a reasonable time.

The Commission also found discrimination as regards the refusal to supply, because the dila- **11.83** tory behaviour vis-à-vis Euroclear Bank contrasted with the reasonable delay within which other comparable customers were supplied: Euroclear Bank asked for access on 3 August 1999 and only obtained access on 19 November 2001, while CSDs that requested access were granted access either almost immediately or in a maximum of one month, and the other ICSD (Clearstream Banking Luxembourg) received access within four months. The Commission considered that the infringement ran between 3 December 1999[104] and 19 November 2001.

---

[102] It should be noted that this concerns the pricing for all transactions processed for Euroclear Bank and is not restricted to registered shares, unlike in the case of the previous abuse.

[103] Registered shares are the most widely internationally traded German shares and therefore likely to be included in transactions of an ICSD's clientele.

[104] The initial four-month period between 3 August and 3 December 1999 can be considered as a reasonable period within which Clearstream would not be refusing to supply. To ascertain what a reasonable maximum period for Clearstream Banking AG to provide direct access to its clearing and settlement services for registered shares would be, the Commission took into account internal companies' plans in the present case and comparative data originating from various customers.

11.84   As regards discriminatory pricing, the Commission found that between 1 January 1997 and 1 January 2002, Clearstream had charged a higher per transaction price to Euroclear Bank than to CSDs outside Germany. In addition, Euroclear Bank, unlike CSDs, also paid an annual fee partly covering settlement services. The Commission examined in detail the information regarding services and costs and concluded that the content of the primary clearing and settlement services for cross-border transactions provided by Clearstream to CSDs and to ICSDs was equivalent, and that there was no objective justification for the difference in prices.

11.85   The *Clearstream* decision was adopted when the infringements had already ceased. The Commission found it necessary to adopt a decision for a number of reasons, including the need to clarify the legal situation and provide guidance, both to Clearstream and to other undertakings active in clearing and settlement, at a moment when the industry is consolidating within the EU.

11.86   The Commission however decided not to impose fines. Among other factors, the Commission took into account that:

— There were no decisions or case law relating to the complex area of clearing and settlement services; the decision analysed for the first time the clearing and settlement processes in the context of market definition, as well as other sector-specific issues such as internalisation, and this analysis had a direct bearing on the legal analysis of the case.

— Clearing and settlement services in the EU are evolving, in particular as regards cross-border transactions. Different institutions and fora have been for some time discussing issues connected with the functions of the various actors in the industry. The scope for internalisation, the role of CSDs and ICSDs and their relationship with large custodian banks are matters being actively debated and connected to the subject matter of the *Clearstream* decision.

11.87   The *Clearstream* decision is currently under appeal.

(c) Euronext

11.88   A more recent investigation concerned possible abusive behaviour by the incumbent exchange Euronext in connection with new competition by the London Stock Exchange (LSE). Although the case was closed without any formal infringement procedure being launched, the main reasoning behind the closure of the case was made public by the DG Competition services.[105]

11.89   In May 2004, LSE launched an alternative service for trading Dutch equities, called the Dutch Trading Service (DTS). In reply, and prior to the launch of the LSE's DTS, Euronext applied two rounds of price reductions in the form of temporary rebates, limited to operations on Dutch securities. The rebates did not cover other markets where Euronext operated, such as France or Belgium. The Commission's reaction was quick and surprise

---

[105] See 'Competition between stock exchanges—findings from DG Competition's investigation into trading in Dutch equities', by Sean Greenaway, Competition Policy Newsletter, 2005, number 3, Autumn.

inspections were carried out in July 2004. However, in September 2005, the Commission decided to close the case without further action.

The services of DG Competition considered Euronext dominant on a market for on-exchange trading services in Dutch equities, but could not demonstrate any abuse, particularly with regard to possible predatory pricing. Given marginal costs close to zero, Euronext continued to make significant—albeit reduced—profits at the new prices. Also, Euronext apparently had genuine reasons to fear migration of the entire market, and there was no evidence of individual targeting in the rebates, or of 'retroactivity' (ie the rebates applied to marginal prices but not to total sales). The case raises interesting issues about how to define predatory pricing, and abuse more generally, in a sector where sunk costs are important and marginal costs minimal. **11.90**

(3) Latest Priorities—Towards a Pro-Active Enforcement of Competition Law in Capital Markets

In the absence of notifications, the Commission needs market monitoring to help it define priorities in an effective manner. Examples of this new approach are: **11.91**

— a study on exclusive agreements commissioned by DG Competitition a few months before the end of the notification system came to an end on 1 May 2004. The study, with the title 'An overview of current arrangements in securities trading, clearing and settlement in EU 25',[106] confirmed that exclusive arrangements—whereby trades in a given exchange must be cleared and settled in pre-determined companies—are widespread throughout the EU, which has the potential to foreclose markets.
— the 'Issues paper on competition in EU securities trading and post-trading' of 24 May 2006.[107] The issues paper states that vertical integration may result in foreclosure at all levels of the trading and post-trading value chain and lead to welfare losses, and that the Commission has seen no convincing evidence to substantiate efficiencies produced by vertically integrated models.

It is clear from these policy documents that vertical agreements and vertically integrated infrastructures are likely to represent a priority area for the future.

D. Insurance

(1) Introductory/Preliminary Remarks

(a) Some Characteristics of Insurance

Although classified as a financial service, it should be borne in mind that insurance is primarily one instrument of risk management, among others; in return for a fee (a premium) an **11.92**

---

[106] The study is published on the DG Competition website, at <http://www.eu.int/comm/competition/general_info/securities/report_june_2005_en.pdf>. An update, with the title 'Securities trading, clearing, central counterparties and settlement in EU 25—an overview of current arrangements' was published on 30 June 2005, and is available at the same web page.
[107] The issues paper is published in the DG Competition website, at: <http://ec.europa.eu/comm/competition/antitrust/others/rep_securities.html>.

insurer undertakes to indemnify the insured party against the consequences of a contingent (that is, uncertain) event. Three levels of insurance exist: direct insurance, for which the purchaser is the end user or insured party; reinsurance, by which insurers themselves obtain insurance cover from other insurers or specialised reinsurers; and finally retrocession, in which providers of reinsurance themselves obtain cover for their risk. A further important distinction in insurance is that between life insurance and non-life insurance. Non-life insurance (for example property damage insurance or liability insurance) corresponds to the traditional idea of insurance, while life insurance increasingly resembles, and overlaps with, investment products, with the insurance element in a life insurance policy sometimes secondary to the investment element.

11.93   The fact that the precise obligations of the insurer are contingent on the happening of future events which may not arise at all, while the premium is paid at the outset of the insurance contract, places the insurer in a unique position as regards cash-flow. Income from premiums can be invested, and the proceeds from investment can be used to subsidise premiums charged to customers, thus enabling an insurer to run an underwriting loss[108] on a long-term basis, if investment income permits.

11.94   This fact, together with the relative ease of entry to certain insurance markets, contributes to what is known as the 'insurance cycle'. During periods when underwriting profits are to be made, and the number of market participants is relatively small, this attracts market entry, and price competition subsequently leads to a period of underwriting losses, or even overall losses, which precipitates some withdrawal of participants from the market. This insurance cycle is characteristic of, for example, maritime and aviation insurance.

11.95   Two further general points about insurance are worth making. First, the very specific regulatory and prudential framework which applies to the insurance sector has had the effect that insurance undertakings tend to be separate entities rather than part of more varied conglomerates (even the trend towards 'bancassurance' has normally involved separate banking and insurance companies, cross-selling each other's products, under a holding company). Secondly, at least as far as mass insurance is concerned, cross-border provision of insurance in the EU is virtually non-existent, despite internal market insurance Directives. Differing legal frameworks and practical issues such as the need for a sales and claims settlement network, make it usually most worthwhile for insurers to enter retail insurance markets in other Member States via the acquisition of local insurers; thus, though many large insurance groups are present in many or most EU markets, they are not fully integrated EU-wide.[109] For large-scale industrial and commercial insurance (which is where most interventions using EU competition law in the insurance sector have occurred), the situation is of course different, with often Europe-wide or even global integration.

11.96   The insurance sector is characterised also by a higher degree of contact between competitors than many other sectors. Exchange of statistical information on claims is near-universal

---

[108] An underwriting profit or loss is the difference between the payments made as a result of claims and the income from premiums.

[109] The Commission's Financial Services Action plan aims to remove such barriers. See: <http://europa.eu.int/comm/internal_market/en/finances/actionplan/index_en.htm>.

(and covered by the insurance block exemption Regulation, see below), while insurers must collaborate for the settlement of claims where there are two parties involved who are clients of different insurance companies (a car accident for example). For particularly large risks, co-insurance is frequent, either on an ad hoc basis or via institutionalised pools. The challenge for a competition authority is to lay down clearly where is the dividing line between legitimate co-operation and anti-competitive collusion.

(b) The Commission's Antitrust Policy in the Insurance Sector

The first Commission antitrust decision in the insurance sector dates from 1984,[110] and **11.97** the first Court judgment from 1987. This judgment, in the *German Fire Insurance (Verband der Sachversicherer)* case, in addition to dealing with the substance at issue (commercial premiums, see paragraph 11.106 below), conclusively rejected the arguments put forward by the parties (German insurance companies) claiming that some special structural role of insurance in the economy precluded the applicability of Articles 81 and 82 of the Treaty.[111]

The Commission's application of the antitrust rules to the insurance sector to date has been **11.98** in large part concerned with the clarification of the status of practices which are widespread or even universal in the insurance sector. A central part of this policy has been a sector-specific block exemption Regulation.[112] The first insurance block exemption Regulation, of 1992,[113] was valid for a period of ten years, until 31 March 2003. On expiry, it was replaced by another block exemption Regulation,[114] valid for seven years, expiring on 31 March 2010.[115] The Council enabling Regulation of 1991,[116] which constitutes the legal basis of the Commission exemption Regulations, authorised the Commission to block exempt six categories of insurance agreements, of which only the first four have been included in the two block exemption Regulations so far adopted (see paras 11.127–11.128 below):

---

[110] *Nuovo Cegam* [1984] OJ L99/29.

[111] The Court judgment (Case 45/68 [1987] ECR 405, 454-5), was on appeal of a Commission decision in the same case ([1985] OJ L35/20).

[112] Insurance is one of the few sectors of the economy to benefit from a sector-specific block exemption Regulation. Outside the area of transport, the only other sectoral block exemption Regulation is that for car distribution. The original reason for the adoption of an insurance block exemption Regulation in 1992 was the large volume of notifications—over three hundred—made following the Court's 1987 judgment in the *German Fire Insurance (Verband der Sachversicherer)* case.

[113] Commission Regulation (EEC) 3932/92 of 21 December 1992 on the application of Art 81(3) of the Treaty to certain categories of agreements decisions and concerted practices in the insurance sector [1992] OJ L398/7. In accordance with the requirements of that Regulation, a report on its application was adopted by the Commission six years after its entry into force (COM (1999) 192 final, 12 May 1999).

[114] The procedure for the adoption of a new Regulation began in July 2002 with the publication of a draft for third party observations ([2002] OJ C163/7, and accompanying press release IP/02/1028). The second Insurance block exemption Regulation was adopted on 27 February 2003 (Regulation (EC) 358/2003 [2003] OJ L53/8).

[115] The period of validity is shortened compared with the previous block exemption Regulation, presumably to allow a review of the Commission's policy on block exemptions in 2010, as a number of other block exemption Regulations expire in that year. Given the future absence, under the modernised antitrust procedural regime of Council Regulation 1/2003, of the factor which led to the adoption of the first insurance block exemption in 1992 (volume of notifications), it will be interesting to see the outcome of any such review, especially for sectoral block exemption Regulations such as this one.

[116] Council Regulation (EEC) 1534/91 of 31 May 1991 [1991] OJ L143/1.

(a) the establishment of common risk premium tariffs based on collectively ascertained statistics or the number of claims;

(b) the establishment of common standard policy conditions;

(c) the common coverage of certain types of risks;

(d) the testing and acceptance of security devices;

(e) the settlement of claims;

(f) registers of, and information on, aggravated risks.

The 2003 block exemption Regulation thus covers the same four categories of agreements as that of 1992; broadly speaking it left the scope of the block exemption largely unchanged for categories (a) and (b) above, while widening the exemption for category (c) (pools) and narrowing it for (d) (security devices).

11.99   The Commission's case-based activity in the insurance sector has been mainly concentrated on the wholesale and corporate insurance sectors (insurance for which the purchasers are companies, and re-insurance). Retail insurance for individuals has been relatively little dealt with by the Commission. This is because retail insurance is provided almost exclusively domestically, which could raise issues concerning the effect on trade between Member States, and national authorities have shown themselves to be vigilant in this area using national competition law.[117]

11.100   The number of formal Commission antitrust decisions in the insurance sector is limited to eight, of which only one was a prohibition decision,[118] and so far no fines have been imposed. However, some of the positive Article 81 decisions were only adopted following modifications to the agreements in question made after a statement of objections was issued,[119] and in some cases policy issues have been clarified by comfort letters publicised either by press releases or in the Annual Report on competition policy.

11.101   In 2003 the European Commission took the initiative to create an expert group dedicated to insurance matters within the European Competition Network (ECN).[120] The group, which brings together representatives of DG Competition of the Commission and insurance experts from national competition authorities, first met on 26 June 2003, and decided to orient its future activities around three axes:

- the structural characteristics of insurance markets;
- the sharing of methodologies for market monitoring;
- specific sector-related issues.

---

[117] The following are examples of this activity. In July 2000 the Italian Autorità Garante imposed fines totalling 700 billion lire on a number of Italian insurance companies for anti-competitive collusion including the exchange of commercially sensitive information. On 24 July 2002 the German Bundeskartellamt conducted a search operation on the suspicion that companies in the insurance sector had agreed on premium increases in the industrial property and liability insurance business. The Irish competition authority has carried out a detailed study into competition in certain sectors of insurance in Ireland.

[118] The *German Fire insurance* case. See para 11.97 above and para 11.106 below.

[119] The *Lloyds of London* and *P&I clubs* cases. See paras 11.107 and 11.120–11.121 respectively below.

[120] See E Caprioli, 'Insurance network: the ECN sectoral group on insurance' (2003) 3 Competition Policy Newsletter 60. For the European Competition Network see Chapter 2, section E.

While the exact significance of this initiative remains to be seen, and information available about it is limited, it would seem to signal an intention on the Commission's part to take a more proactive approach as concerns competition on insurance markets, and to monitor market practices more closely than hitherto, in conjunction with national competition authorities.

(c) Market Definition Issues in the Insurance Sector

Insurance is an exception to the usual principle of market definition methodology laid **11.102** down in the Commission's notice on market definition,[121] that demand substitution is always the starting-point for market definition analysis, and supply substitution secondary. The reason is obvious: since each risk insured is unique, for an insured party, an insurance policy for a different risk is totally unsubstitutable (and even invalid). For example, for the owner of a car of brand A, an insurance policy for a car of brand B is not an alternative, even if it is cheaper. Market definition analysis must therefore start from supply substitutability.[122] As a result, product markets in the insurance sector do not necessarily correspond exactly to the categorisation of insurance products typically used in insurance regulation, although they may well do so in many cases.

Barriers to supply substitutability (that is, barriers to undertakings offering one type of **11.103** insurance switching to offering another type of insurance in the short term), and barriers to market entry, are thus a key element in market definition for insurance. These differ between mass insurance and specialised insurance (including reinsurance). For mass insurance, the most important barriers are the necessary financial resources, access to a distribution network, and claims settlement facilities. For specialised insurance, it is rather the required underwriting skills which may be in short supply and restrict access to the market.

As examples of insurance product market definition in antitrust cases, one can note the **11.104** definition in the nuclear insurance cases (see below, paragraph 11.124), in which the Commission distinguished three markets: for nuclear damage insurance, nuclear liability insurance, and nuclear reinsurance, or the *P&I Clubs* cases (see below, paragraphs 11.120–11.121), where the relevant product market was third-party liability insurance for maritime shipping. In aviation insurance, the Commission has considered that insurance for commercial and non-commercial aviation constitutes distinct product markets (see below, paragraph 11.123). In many merger cases in the insurance sector, the Commission has limited itself to dividing insurance into three broad markets: life, non-life, and reinsurance.[123] In the *Generali/INA* case,[124] however, the Commission was

---

[121] Commission Notice on the definition of the relevant market for the purposes of Community competition law [1997] OJ C372.

[122] Supply substitutability is different from market entry. The Commission Notice on market definition defines supply substitutability as requiring that suppliers be able to switch production to the relevant products and market them in the short term without incurring significant additional costs or risks in response to small and permanent changes in relative prices.

[123] For example Case IV/M.1193 *AXA-UAP/Royale Belge*, Decision of 19 June 1998, [1998] OJ C239/17. Available only in French.

[124] Case COMP/M/1712 *Generali/INA*, Decision of 12 January 2000, [2002] OJ C58/6. Available only in Italian. See press release IP/00/29.

obliged to enter into more detail, rejecting the argument of the parties that life insurance products are substitutable with pure investment products, and concluding that the insurance element in a life insurance product, linked to the uncertainty of the duration of a human life, is sufficiently distinctive to rule out such substitutability (this conclusion was reinforced by a specificity of Italy, namely the application of a distinct fiscal regime to insurance and financial products). As concerns geographical markets, these are almost exclusively national for retail insurance, but often worldwide for commercial insurance, such as aviation or maritime insurance, owing to the use of global insurance broking services.

(2) Agreements on Prices

11.105 In any discussion of insurance prices, it is necessary to clarify at the outset the various uses of the word 'premium' in insurance. The 'commercial premium' is the price charged by an insurer to a client for the coverage of a specific risk. The 'pure premium' is a historic statistic on the average frequency and size of claims for a risk in a given category, based on past information. When the 'pure premium' is corrected to allow for estimated future changes in claims (based for example on new legislation or improved preventive measures), the result is called the 'risk premium'. The pure and risk premiums are not prices, while the commercial premium is a price.[125] The commercial premium may be higher or lower than the risk premium (higher if the insurer chooses to add its administrative costs and a profit margin to the risk premium, lower if it chooses to use revenue from its investments in order to offer lower prices to consumers). Since commercial premiums are prices, it follows that agreements that set or recommend uniform commercial premiums are straightforward price-fixing agreements falling within Article 81(1)(a) and not normally capable of being exempted[126]; as for pure and risk premiums, as they are kinds of statistical indicators, agreements concerning those premiums can be exempted.[127]

11.106 In *German Fire Insurance*,[128] the German Association of Property Insurers (Verband der Sachversicherer), recommended increases in commercial premiums for industrial fire and consequential loss insurance of 10, 20, or 30 per cent in specified circumstances. Although

---

[125] Relevant also in this discussion of insurance prices is the judgment of the Court of Justice of 7 September 2004 concerning the obligatory 'bonus-malus' systems of France and Luxembourg. The Commission had held those systems to infringe the freedom to set prices established in the insurance Directive (EC) 92/49. However, the Court found against the Commission, on the grounds that insurers remain free to set the basic amount of the premium. Cases C-346/02 and C347/02; Court press release 60/04.

[126] Report on competition policy 1972 (Vol II) points 55 and 56; *Nuovo CEGAM* [1984] OJ L99/29, para 21; *Fire Insurance* [1985] OJ L35/20; Case 45/85 *Verband der Sachversicherer* [1987] ECR 405, 454–5; *Lloyd's Underwriters' Association and The Institute of London Underwriters* [1993] OJ L4/26. It is true that co-insurance pools also involve the joint determining of commercial premiums, and that co-insurance pools are exempted by Title IV of the Block Exemption Regulation. However, co-insurance pools are a kind of production joint venture (in the wide sense of the term) and their block exemption should be seen in this context (see paras 11.117–11.119 below).

[127] The Council enabling Regulation 1534/91 explicitly refers to 'the establishment of common risk premium tariffs', but the term 'risk premium' should be understood as comprising pure premiums. In the 2003 insurance block exemption Regulation the terms pure premium and risk premium are not used, at the request of one Member State (Spain) where the definitions of 'pure premium' and 'risk premium' in national legislation are different from those given here.

[128] *Fire Insurance* [1985] OJ L35/20; Case 45/85 *Verband der Sachversicherer* [1987] ECR 405, 454–5.

the recommendation was stated to be non-binding, the Court held that it constituted 'the faithful reflection of the [Association's] resolve to coordinate the conduct of its members'. The recommendation was stated in mandatory terms, and German reinsurers decided to treat premiums not following the recommendation as under-insurance in the event of a claim.

In the *Lloyd's of London* case,[129] two agreements relating to marine hull insurance were found to infringe Article 81(1) in the following ways. The Joint Hull Understandings agreement recommended minimum increases in premiums, fixed the rate of increase in deductibles, and fixed the rebate paid for prompt cash payment and for deferred payment. The Respect of Lead Agreement restricted price competition by prohibiting members from participating in a co-insurance contract unless there were two lead underwriters from each association, and required that the same leading underwriters were to be used upon renewal of co-insured policies. The infringing provisions were abandoned by the associations and the Commission adopted a negative clearance decision.   **11.107**

(3) Jointly Produced Statistics and Studies

Most national associations of insurers produce statistics on pure premiums, based on information annually supplied by insurers on claims, and carry out studies on likely future trends, calculating an indicative risk premium on that basis. The rationale for the joint calculation of pure premiums is that only the biggest insurers are likely to have an adequate sample of risks from their own insurance portfolio (for example cars of a particular brand in a particular city with a particular age and gender of driver) to produce reliable statistics on past claims, and a new market entrant will, at the time of its market entry, have no such information. Joint production of statistical information on pure premiums thus improves the reliability of such statistics, helps smaller insurers, and facilitates market entry.[130] The same reasoning applies to mortality tables used in life insurance. As to studies on the likely future evolution of claims, for the purpose of calculating risk premiums, their joint production engenders cost savings.   **11.108**

The 2003 insurance block exemption, like its predecessor, exempts such statistical collaboration (Title II) with no market share threshold for exemption. The conditions for exemption are also largely unchanged in the 2003 version of the Regulation. For example, in order to benefit from exemption, the statistics and studies must not identify the insurance undertakings concerned or any insured party, and when compiled and distributed, must include a statement that they are non-binding (Article 3.2.a and b[131]). Statistics also must not include any costs or revenues not deriving from claims (Article 3.1.c). Nor does the exemption apply where insurers agree among themselves not to use any other statistics or studies than   **11.109**

---

[129] *Lloyd's Underwriters' Association and The Institute of London Underwriters* [1993] OJ L4/26.

[130] However, the exchange of statistics on claims can easily spill over into the exchange of commercially sensitive information, and joint statistical bodies can act as a front for this, as happened in the domestic Italian insurance case mentioned in n 117.

[131] All references to articles in the block exemption Regulation hereafter are to the 2003 block exemption Regulation.

those jointly produced (Article 4). However, one condition for exemption of joint calculation of indicative risk premiums implicit in the 1992 Regulation was made explicit in its successor: as concerns pure premiums, statistics must be broken down into as much detail as is possible, while leaving a statistically useful sample (Article 3.1.b). The reason for this condition is that the more statistics are broken down, the more freedom insurers have to differentiate their prices to end consumers.[132] A further new condition for exemption is that the statistics on risk premiums be made available on reasonable and non-discriminatory terms, to any insurance undertaking which requests access to them (Article 3.2.c). This condition aims particularly at insurance companies considering entering the market in question, but which need access to the statistics before taking their decision.

11.110 In two individual decisions prior to the 1992 block exemption Regulation, the Commission exempted the joint fixing of pure premiums. In *Nuovo CEGAM*, an Italian association of insurers agreed to apply jointly fixed pure premiums for industrial engineering insurance.[133] This appears a more restrictive arrangement than would be allowed under the block exemption (where companies may not agree to apply the jointly agreed pure premiums). However, the members of the Nuovo CEGAM collectively had a 26 per cent market share while their largest competitor had a 25 per cent market share. The Commission found that the agreement brought new competition onto the market. The facilitation of new entry was also considered a benefit justifying the exemption in the Commission's *Concordato Incendio* decision of 1990, even though the members of the Concordato collectively had over 50 per cent market share and its largest four members had a 28 per cent market share as against the largest four non-members' 23 per cent share.[134]

(4) Standard Policy Clauses

11.111 Standard insurance policy conditions for many types of insurance policy are produced by national associations of insurance undertakings, or by other groupings of insurers. If an insurer wishes, it can use these 'model insurance policies' 'as such', or it may take them as a basis and make its own modifications to them, or it may totally ignore the model clauses and draft its own policies. Such clauses are widely used in some insurance markets, and are claimed to have benefits including the facilitation of market entry (by avoiding inexperienced insurers having to draft their own policies), although if too slavishly followed, they risk leading to standardisation of insurance policy characteristics.

11.112 The block exemption Regulation does not authorise any compulsory clauses comprising standard conditions; all standard conditions must be optional (so insurers must be free to use them or not, as they wish). Article 5(1) limits the block exemption to model policy conditions which: are established and distributed with an explicit statement that they are non-binding and that their use is not in any way recommended; expressly mention that participating undertakings

---

[132] For example, if the jointly produced statistics on vehicle claims are broken down only by geographical region, insurers will be unable to differentiate their commercial premiums according to the town of residence within that region, as they will lack the necessary information, whereas if the statistics are broken down by town, insurers can differentiate their premiums by town if they wish.

[133] *Nuovo CEGAM* [1984] OJ L99/29.

[134] *Concordato Incendio* [1990] OJ L15/25.

are free to offer different policy conditions to their customers; and are accessible to any interested person and provided simply upon request. Also, neither Regulation exempts such standard policy conditions for reinsurance, only for direct insurance.[135] A long list of 'black clauses', which do not benefit from the block exemption even in a non-binding model policy, is contained in Article 6 of the Regulation. The presence of some clauses on the 'black' list seems inspired by consumer protection considerations, as agreements on such clauses would not meet the second condition of Article 81(3),consumer benefit. The black clauses are clauses which:

(a) contain any indication of the level of commercial premiums;

(b) indicate the amount of the cover or the part which the policyholder must pay himself (the 'excess');

(c) impose comprehensive cover including risks to which a significant number of policy-holders are not simultaneously exposed;

(d) allow the insurer to maintain the policy in the event that he cancels part of the cover, increases the premium without the risk or the scope of the cover being changed (without prejudice to indexation clauses), or otherwise alters the policy conditions without the express consent of the policyholder;

(e) allow the insurer to modify the term of the policy without the express consent of the policyholder;

(f) impose on the policyholder in the non-life assurance sector a contract period of more than three years;

(g) impose a renewal period of more than one year where the policy is automatically renewed unless notice is given upon the expiry of a given period;

(h) require the policyholder to agree to the reinstatement of a policy which has been suspended on account of the disappearance of the insured risk, if he is once again exposed to a risk of the same nature;

(i) require the policyholder to obtain cover from the same insurer for different risks;

(j) require the policyholder, in the event of disposal of the object of insurance, to make the acquirer take over the insurance policy;

(k) exclude or limit the cover of a risk if the policyholder uses security devices, or installing or maintenance undertakings, which are not approved in accordance with the relevant specifications agreed by an association or associations of insurers in one or several other Member States or at the European level.

The exemption does not apply to agreements between insurers preventing them from using model policy conditions other than the ones jointly prepared (Article 6.2—this would effectively make the conditions compulsory). Nor does it apply to agreements which exclude the coverage of certain risk categories because of the characteristics associated with the policyholder (Article 6.3). **11.113**

The 2003 block exemption Regulation is little changed from that of 1992 as concerns standard clauses, with the exception that the list of black clauses in Article 6 is slightly length- **11.114**

---

[135] This limitation, not imposed by the Council enabling Regulation, is unexplained in the recitals of either block exemption Regulation but would seem reasonable in so far as the purchasers of reinsurance, namely direct insurers, do not need the same level of protection as end consumers.

ened. Interestingly, however, in the draft new block exemption Regulation published for consultation in July 2002, the Commission had drastically narrowed the scope of the block exemption Regulation for standard policy conditions, but the final version adopted in February 2003 reverts more or less to the coverage of the 1992 Regulation. The press release accompanying the draft of July 2002 explained that the draft would exempt such clauses:

> only if they are agreed in conjunction with the joint calculation of pure premiums and joint studies related to risk premiums, and only in so far they are both necessary and exclusively used for such calculations or studies. This is because, in the Commission's view, the insurance sector has not so far conclusively demonstrated that such standard policy conditions serve consumer interest, except insofar as they are necessary to calculate risk premiums.

In the intervening period the Commission received from the insurance sector strong representations in favour of the benefits of standard policy conditions, while consumer organisations were apparently divided on the issue.[136]

11.115 The *Concordato Incendio* decision of 1990 referred to in paragraph 11.110 above also involved standard policy conditions.[137] In the decision, the Commission exempted not only standard policy conditions, which members were free to derogate from, but also a requirement that members notify the Concordato of any such derogation that might affect the statistics used to calculate the pure premium. The requirement to notify would seem likely to encourage the members to follow the standard conditions, but was held to be necessary to guarantee the reliability of the statistics. The Commission might now be less likely to accept a requirement to notify derogations, given that the block exemption clearly requires standard policy conditions to be non-binding.

(5) Co-insurance and Co-reinsurance Pools

11.116 Permanent institutionalised insurance pooling arrangements involving a number of insurers are frequent for the coverage of large or exceptional risks, such as nuclear and environmental risks, for which individual insurance companies are reluctant to insure the entire risk alone. Insurance pools can usefully be thought of as a kind of production joint venture (although they do not necessarily involve joint control and do not normally fall under the Merger Regulation). A co-insurance pool provides insurance directly to insured parties, and, in its most developed form, involves the member insurers jointly deciding the price (commercial premium) and product characteristics (policy conditions). A co-reinsurance pool, whose customers are first-level insurers, leaves those first-level insurers free to decide the price of the insurance they offer their customers, but inevitably leads to considerable harmonisation of the product characteristics. Pools have been a common thread running through the Commission's consideration of the insurance sector. Not only do they play a prominent role in the block exemption Regulation, but there have been a large number of individual notifications which have led either to Commission decisions or to comfort letters.

---

[136] For more detail see the article in the Competition Policy Newsletter, No 2 2003, p 51, on the new insurance block exemption Regulation.
[137] *Concordato Incendio* [1990] OJ L15/25.

(a) Pools in the Block Exemption

The 2003 block exemption Regulation divides insurance and reinsurance pools into two **11.117** categories, for the purposes of granting a block exemption: pools created after the date of entry into force of the Regulation in order exclusively to cover new risks, and pools which do not fall under that description.[138] Pools falling into the first category benefit from a block exemption for a period of three years from their creation, with no applicable market share threshold (Article 7.1). The rationale, explained in recital 19 of the block exemption Regulation and seemingly inspired by the block exemption Regulation on R&D, is that co-operation resulting in the creation of entirely new commercial products can be exempted without a market share threshold for a limited start-up period, and in the case of a new insurance product it is not possible to determine in advance what capacity is necessary to cover the risk. For this reason, the definition of 'new risks' in Article 2.7[139] is such as to ensure that only risks genuinely requiring the creation of a new insurance product are covered.

Pools falling into the second category (including pools which formerly fell into the first **11.118** category but which have reached the end of the three-year exemption period), can benefit from the block exemption (Article 7.2) with the application of market share thresholds (20 per cent in the case of co-insurance pools, and 25 per cent in the case of co-reinsurance pools).

For both categories of pools, the benefit of the block exemption, is subject to a list of con- **11.119** ditions for exemption in Article 8:

(a) each participating undertaking has the right to withdraw from the group, subject to a period of notice of not more than one year, without incurring any sanctions;

(b) the rules of the group do not oblige any member of the group to insure or re-insure through the group, in whole or in part, any risk of the type covered by the group;

(c) the rules of the group do not restrict the activity of the group or its members to the insurance or reinsurance of risks located in any particular geographical part of the European Union;

(d) the agreement does not limit output or sales;

(e) the agreement does not allocate markets or customers;

(f) the members of a co-reinsurance group do not agree on the commercial premiums which they charge in direct insurance; and

(g) no member of the group, or undertaking which exercises a determining influence on the commercial policy of the group, is also a member of, or exercises a determining

---

[138] The 1992 block exemption Regulation did not make this distinction, and granted a block exemption only on the basis of market share thresholds and of conditions for exemption. The 2003 block exemption Regulation innovated with regard to the 1992 block exemption Regulation, not only in creating a new category of pools exempted with no market share threshold, but in increasing the applicable thresholds for other pools, and adding certain new conditions for exemption.

[139] The definition reads: '"New risks" means risks which did not exist before, and for which insurance cover requires the development of an entirely new insurance product, not involving an extension, improvement or replacement of an existing insurance product'. The most recent example of new pools falling under this narrow definition would be the creation of nuclear pools in the 1950s. Although some recently created war and terrorism pools may claim to cover 'new risks', war and terrorism can hardly be described as new.

influence on the commercial policy of, a different group active on the same relevant market.[140]

(b) Commission Decisions and other Cases on Pools

11.120   In 1985 and then again in 1999 the Commission adopted decisions on a rather unique pooling arrangement, that of the International Group Agreement (IGA) of protection & indemnity (P&I) Clubs active in the field of marine liability insurance. P&I clubs are mutual non-profit associations of shipowners, charterers, and operators which provide their members with insurance for their contractual third party liability (for example injury or death of crew members or third parties, damage to cargo, collision damage, and pollution); the clubs within the IG represent about 90 per cent of the worldwide market for such insurance. The issues at stake in the P&I Clubs case were not the mutualisation of insurance within the Clubs, but the procedures for competition between Clubs, and an agreed obligatory upper level of cover. In 1985, following some easing of restrictions of members changing Clubs, the Commission issued a ten-year exemption.[141] When this expired, a complaint was received from a shipowners' organisation about the compulsory upper limit of cover of US$18 billion, and about remaining restrictions on shipowners changing Clubs: a Club wishing to offer a lower premium rate to a shipowner insured by a different Club had to prove to a committee that the old club's rate was unreasonably high. In the course of the procedure, the compulsory upper level of cover was reduced to US$4.25 billion, and the rate quotation procedures were changed so that a Club's administrative costs fell outside the procedure and could be subject to free competition (the Clubs also agreed to publish information allowing shipowners to compare the administrative costs of different Clubs). Following those changes, the Commission granted an exemption,[142] and determined that there was no violation of Article 82.

11.121   On the issue of the existence of the P&I pooling arrangement, the 1999 decision concluded that the level of cover offered by the IGA required the member pools collectively to have a market share of over 50 per cent, thus effectively constituting a natural monopoly for that level of cover. However, the decision stated that the Commission would revoke the exemption if the members of the IGA collectively were ever to hold a market share larger than twice the minimum scale economically required to provide the level of cover. This has not however been done.

11.122   In two earlier individual exemption decisions for co-insurance pools, the *TEKO* decision of 1990,[143] and the *Assurpol* decision of 1992,[144] the Commission had decided that the pools under examination restricted competition within Article 81(1)—basically because they were permanent and institutionalised co-operation for which there were less restrictive alternatives—but could be exempted without conditions. It is doubtful whether the

---

[140] This last condition is particularly interesting, being new, as compared with the 1992 block exemption Regulation, and not explained in a recital. Presumably it is aimed at preventing the circumvention of the market share thresholds and the hiding of an oligopolistic market behind a multiplicity of pools with similar membership.

[141] *P&I Clubs* [1985] OJ L376/2.

[142] *P&I Clubs* [1999] OJ L125/12.

[143] *TEKO* [1990] OJ L13/34. TEKO is a German space insurance pool.

[144] *Assurpol* [1992] OJ L37/16. Assurpol is a French environmental insurance pool.

Commission would follow this reasoning if the same cases arose today, either on Article 81(1) or on Article 81(3).

The Commission has also closed two groups of pool cases by comfort letter. In 1998, it **11.123** closed an investigation into several notifications of aviation pool cases. It found that for the insurance of large aviation risks (international commercial aviation), the market share of each pool was sufficiently small as to benefit from negative clearance under the Commission's de minimis notice (which at that time laid down a market share of 5 per cent, subsequently raised to 10 per cent). For small aviation risks (private and pleasure aviation), for which markets seemed to be national and where certain pools would enjoy a dominant position on their national markets, the pools did not seem to be necessary in order to allow their members to be present on those markets. The Commission found there to be insufficient Community interest to bring proceedings but warned the pools of the possibility of action by national competition authorities.[145]

In January 2001 the Commission closed its investigation into three nuclear insurance pool **11.124** cases.[146] The Commission considered that three different relevant markets were involved, for nuclear property insurance, nuclear reinsurance, and nuclear liability insurance. The first two of these markets were considered worldwide in extent, and on those markets the share of each of the pools in question again qualified as de minimis. Markets for nuclear liability insurance, however, were considered still national, because of greatly differing national legislative requirements in this field, and the need for locally based claims-settlement facilities. Each of the pools in question had a monopoly on its national market for nuclear liability insurance. Nevertheless, the Commission concluded that without the pooling agreements there would be no supply of nuclear liability insurance with adequate coverage for the risks involved, and therefore the pooling agreements did not restrict competition in that respect. A fourth nuclear insurance pool case was closed in 2002, following the deletion of a clause of the type referred to in Article 8(b) of the block exemption Regulation, obliging members to insure nuclear risks only through the pool.

(c) Conclusions on Pools

It would seem, looking at the Commission's record of tackling insurance pools over twenty **11.125** years, that the Commission's approach combines a basic relatively tolerant attitude to the existence of pools, with a strict approach to restrictive clauses or other restrictive practices linked to a pool. The Commission has never shown any appetite to try to break up an insurance pool, despite its affirmation in a report of 1999 that it would theoretically be prepared to do so.[147] Indeed, given the burden of proof on the Commission in such cases, this would be a hazardous venture. Since insurance pools by their nature insure large risks (airlines, nuclear power stations, terrorist risks), the danger of causing disruption to such sensitive insurance markets seems to have engendered a prudent approach from the Commission as concerns pools.

---

[145] Report on competition policy 1998 (Vol XXVIII), §114–115.
[146] Report on competition policy 2001 (Vol XXXI), §203.
[147] Report referred to in n 113 above, para 33: 'if the size of the pool is so large that it could be replaced by two or more pools in competition with each other, the Commission will insist that it reorganise itself in such a way'.

(6) Security Devices

11.126   In most EU Member States, there are agreements between insurers on technical specifications for safety equipment (for example, alarms, anti-theft, and anti-fire devices); on this basis, devices are tested, and lists of 'approved' devices drawn up. The specifications in question vary from Member State to Member State, and thus a security device which is 'approved' by insurers in one Member State may not be 'approved' in another, which might create difficulties in insuring a property in which it is installed. The scope of the 1992 block exemption Regulation covered all such agreements. However, the 2003 block exemption Regulation narrows the scope of the block exemption so as to exempt such agreements only in areas where no Community-level harmonisation of standards has taken place. This effectively rules out any block exemption for agreements concerning security devices themselves, virtually all of which are covered by such Community-level harmonisation, and restricts it to the installation and maintenance of such devices. The motivation for this narrowing of the scope, according to the press release which accompanied the final adoption of the 2003 block exemption Regulation[148] is that:

> Where there is Community harmonisation legislation in force, agreements between insurers which effectively impose on security devices higher requirements than those imposed by legislation have a major impact on the market for such devices, as a device which insurers are reluctant to insure will have great difficulty gaining access to the market. Given this, the view has been taken that agreements between insurers going beyond harmonising legislation cannot be exempted by Regulation.

It remains to be seen whether the effective withdrawal of the block exemption from agreements concerning security devices will have any concrete effect, given that there are no ongoing cases which could lead to a precedent being set through individual analysis of such an agreement. Certainly it does not seem to have triggered any new complaints about such agreements.

(7) Agreements on Settlement of Claims and on Registers of Aggravated Risks

11.127   Agreements on settlement of claims are increasingly frequent among insurers. The simplest type is known as a 'knock for knock' agreement, in which insurers agree to split between themselves 50–50 the costs for insurance claims where there is no consensus on responsibility between the insured parties, without investigating further. However, more sophisticated types of claims settlement agreements exist. Registers of 'aggravated risks', often compiled by national associations of insurers, inform insurers *inter alia* of insured parties who have been the origin of frequent claims. Despite the benefits in terms of costs savings to insurers, in both cases the risk exists that the agreements in question could work to the detriment of insured parties who have produced, through no fault of their own, numerous claims.

11.128   Although they were included in the 1991 Council enabling Regulation, neither of these types of agreement was included in the 1992 or the 2003 insurance block exemption Regulation. The main explanation for this seems to have been relative lack of experience of such cases on the Commission's part (recital 3), although the Commission was possibly also

---

148 IP/03/291 of 27 February 2003.

influenced by the uncertain benefits to consumers of such agreements. It goes without saying that their exclusion from the two block exemption Regulations does not imply that such agreements should necessarily be prohibited, simply that an individual analysis under Article 81(3) would be necessary.

(8) Other Recent Insurance Cases

In May 2002 the Commission approved, by administrative comfort letter, an agreement forming a business-to-business (B2B) online reinsurance trading platform called *inreon*.[149] Such online B2B platforms have sprung up in recent years, and the competition issues facing such platforms in the insurance sector do not differ radically from those in other sectors.[150] In the *inreon* case specifically, the Commission found that the rules and procedures of the *inreon* exchange did not allow participants to obtain sensitive information on their competitors, allowed access on fair and non-discriminatory terms, and did not facilitate joint selling, by denying participants access to the bids of their competitors.

11.129

The only Commission investigation to date into vertical agreements in the insurance sector, based on a complaint from a federation of insurance intermediaries,[151] was closed in October 2003. The complainant had alleged that a network of agreements between German insurance companies and tied agents, involving exclusivity provisions and non-compete clauses, created a cumulative foreclosure effect, and moreover were not genuine agency agreements. Not only was this the first case in which the Commission applied the guidelines on vertical restraints[152] to the insurance sector, but also the only important insurance case in recent years involving mass or retail insurance. Following a detailed enquiry into the German insurance market, the Commission found that although a high proportion of insurance products in Germany was sold through tied agents, this distribution channel was diminishing in importance and subject to competition from other channels, including electronic commerce; moreover, market entry from abroad was taking place, and few foreign insurers considered the network of tied insurance agents to constitute a significant barrier to entry. Based on this information, the Commission wrote to the complainant on 29 July 2003 explaining its conclusions that the practices complained of did not have a foreclosure effect,[153] following which, the complaint was withdrawn on 6 October 2003.[154]

11.130

Most recently, a Commission investigation into the behaviour of providers of aviation war and terrorism insurance and brokerage in the wake of the terrorist attacks of 11 September 2001 was concluded in March 2005 with a settlement involving far-reaching structural reforms in the aviation insurance sector. The origin of the case was press reports indicating

11.131

---

[149] See press release IP/02/761 of 24 May 2002.
[150] See the paper 'Competition issues in e-commerce' (Competition Policy Roundtable, October 2000), issued by the Committee on Competition Law and Policy of the OECD, published in January 2001.
[151] BIPAR (Bureau International des Producteurs d'Assurances et de Réassurances).
[152] Commission Notice—Guidelines on Vertical Restraints [2000] OJ C291/1-44.
[153] Given this conclusion, it was not necessary to consider whether the agency contracts were genuine or not (see Art 19 of the Vertical Guidelines).
[154] For more details, see the article by J Patrick (2004) 1 Competition Policy Newsletter 32.

that such insurers and brokers (almost universally pools) met within days of the attacks, and subsequently all airlines received notice of termination of their insurance for third party liability as a result of war or terrorism. After this, insurance contracts were re-negotiated with new higher war and terrorism insurance surcharges, which were allegedly identical among all insurers. On the basis of the reports, the Commission started to investigate whether the apparent reaction of aviation insurers following the events of 11 September 2001 could amount to an infringement of Article 81, with the main focus being to establish whether after those attacks, insurers met on a regular basis to agree on a range of terms for providing third party war and terrorism liability insurance cover, including setting the level of premiums.

11.132 The settlement of March 2005 involved undertakings by the International Underwriting Association of London and the Lloyd's Market Association.[155] The undertakings consisted in reforms including *inter alia* greater transparency and customer involvement in key industry committees based in London, including one that establishes standard wordings for aviation insurance policies and clauses. In this respect, a new Aviation Insurance Clauses Group will grant customers—hitherto not involved in the preparation of standard clauses—far reaching rights and opportunities to participate by being consulted on proposed clauses as well as by making proposals themselves.[156]

11.133 In addition, the undertakings provide that if an unforeseeable crisis resulting from war or terrorism arises, insurers will limit any coordinated action to that which is indispensable to ensure that capacity continues to be available and customers can continue to buy insurance, and that the effects on competition from the coordinated action will be kept to a strict minimum. A new Crisis Response Protocol aims at ensuring that competition is maintained even in crisis situations, and that the minimum of disruption is caused to the normal operations of aviation insurance policyholders due to the actual or potential unavailability of adequate aviation insurance.

E. Social Security

(1) Introductory/Preliminary Remarks

11.134 Social security is in some respects clearly related to insurance, as social security schemes usually provide products which are also offered in the commercial insurance markets such as old-age pensions and health care cover. In contrast to commercial insurance, the social security sector is however traditionally characterised by a very high degree of State involvement. Social security schemes have generally been set up and are directly or indirectly operated by the State.[157] The main reason is that many Member States consider it essential that the

---

155 See Commission press release IP/05/361 of 23 March 2005.

156 Such standard clauses, although non-binding (in keeping with Arts 5 and 6 of the insurance block exemption Regulation (see above paras 11.111–11.115), are very widely, indeed almost universally, used in the aviation insurance sector.

157 Certain schemes are set up by the social partners (employers and employees) or by commercial insurers. In the rest of this section essentially schemes set up by the state and social partners are discussed.

population be provided with a minimum income and health cover. As a result the scope for competition in this area has hitherto been extremely limited. However, certain Member States have over time introduced some form of competition in this sector, usually to improve the quality of the services, or simply to reduce expenditure, or both.

The 'three pillars' A broad distinction can be made between three categories of social security **11.135**
schemes. These categories are often referred to as the 'three pillars', in particular as regards the pension sector:

   (i) Basic or first pillar schemes, set up by the State, covering large parts of the population with compulsory affiliation and demonstrating a very high degree of solidarity (eg no link between contributions and benefits, no risk selection).
  (ii) Supplementary or second pillar schemes, set up by the social partners, often for certain categories of the population (eg certain sectors or professions), either with compulsory or optional affiliation, supplementing the basic schemes and containing a high degree of solidarity, although also evidencing elements of commercial schemes.
 (iii) Complementary or third pillar schemes, often set up by commercial insurers, for individuals or certain categories of the population, supplementing basic schemes and with no particular solidarity features other than those that are akin to any commercial insurance.

No general exception for social security There is no doubt that the third pillar schemes **11.136**
(and their operators) are fully subject to Articles 81 and 82 of the EC Treaty. As to the application of these rules to the first and second pillar schemes the situation is less obvious, as will be shown below. Moreover, certain schemes may well have elements of both first pillar and second pillar schemes. What is clear, however, is that there is no general exception for social security in EC competition law. The Court has considered that Member States, when organising their social security systems, must comply with Community law.[158] This obviously includes the EC competition rules.

It seems therefore remarkable that there are hardly any Commission decisions regarding **11.137**
social security in the competition field.[159] This may possibly be due to the highly sensitive political nature of this sector which is often regarded as a State prerogative.[160] In the 1990s

---

[158] The Court held that 'Community law does not detract from the powers of Member States to organise their social security systems and adopt provisions (. . .) to promote the financial stability of their health-care insurance systems (Case C-238/82 *Duphar* [1984] ECR 523)'. It also clearly stated that Member States 'must nevertheless comply with Community law when exercising those powers' (Cases C-120/95 *Decker* [1998] ECR I-1831; and C-158/96 *Kohll* [1998] ECR I-1931).

[159] The Commission has however submitted its observations to the Court in preliminary ruling cases regarding social security. These observations are often briefly summarised in the judgments of the Court and in the opinions of the Advocate-General and provide some guidance on the Commission's thinking on the application of the EC competition rules in the social security sector.

[160] It should also be noted that Arts 81 and 82 are applicable to agreements and practices on the part of undertakings that may affect trade between Member States. This means that certain agreements and/or practices in the social security sector on the part of entities that are undertakings, in particular those covering only local areas of a Member State, may nevertheless not be subject to Art 81 and/or 82 as they may not affect trade between Member States.

however, the Court started to consider the possible application of the EC competition rules to social security schemes and the organisations that are involved in the operation of such schemes, predominantly as a result of requests for preliminary rulings from national courts. Cases have arisen where individuals or companies have attacked schemes (whether compulsory or optional) whose operation is essentially entrusted to a single (or limited number of) generally not-for-profit organisation(s).

11.138 The main questions arising from such cases are: (1) whether the social security scheme in question is an economic activity whose operator is an 'undertaking' within the meaning of Articles 81 and 82; (2) whether the Member State, by entrusting the operation of the scheme to a single organisation, has acted contrary to Articles 86 and 82.

(2) Social Security Organisations as 'Undertakings'

11.139 An undertaking within the meaning of EC competition law is 'every entity engaged in an economic activity, regardless of the legal status of the entity and the way in which it has been financed'.[161] In order to determine whether an activity is economic, the Court usually examines whether the activity may be exercised by private companies.[162] In the context of social security, it appears that the test is essentially whether the activities of the managing organisation of the social security scheme at issue can be compared to those of commercial insurers or pension funds.

11.140 According to the case law of the Court, the main factors that are relevant in determining whether or not the managing organisations of social security schemes are engaged in an economic activity, and thus to be qualified as undertakings, are:

- the exclusive social function and the degree of solidarity of the scheme (if the scheme demonstrates a very high degree of solidarity, the organisation is less likely to be an undertaking);
- the non-profit-making nature of the managing organisation (if the organisation is non-profit making, it is less likely to be an undertaking);
- the organisation's influence over the amount of the contributions and the level of benefits (if the organisation has no or little influence over these parameters, it is less likely to be an undertaking).

11.141 Elements such as the financing method of a scheme and the type of affiliation are important for determining the degree of solidarity. State funding or, in case of pensions, funding on the basis of 'pay as you go' point at a higher degree of solidarity of the scheme than when its funding is based on the principle of capitalisation.[163] Compulsory affiliation is usually evidence of a higher degree of solidarity of the scheme than optional affiliation.

---

[161] Case C-41/90 *Höfner/Macrotron* [1991] ECR I-1979.

[162] Case C-41/90 *Höfner/Macrotron* [1991] ECR I-1979, para 22.

[163] Under the capitalisation principle pension funds are investing the contributions they receive and paying pensions from (the return on) such investments. This is different from the so-called 'pay as you go' method, under which pensions are financed by way of contributions from the working population.

(a) Organisations not Qualified as Undertakings

The Court in *Poucet and Pistre, Cisal* and *AOK* and the CFI in *Fenin* concluded that the **11.142** social security organisations at issue in these cases were not engaged in an economic activity and therefore not undertakings.[164]

In *Poucet and Pistre*, the Court examined two French organisations entrusted by law with the **11.143** management of a first pillar compulsory sickness and maternity and an old-age pension scheme respectively. It concluded that those organisations are not undertakings because they fulfilled an exclusively social function and performed an activity based on the principle of national solidarity and which was entirely non-profit-making. In addition, both the level of contributions and benefits were ultimately fixed by the State, ie not by the managing organisations. One of the solidarity features of the *sickness and maternity* scheme at stake to which the Court specifically referred, was that the statutory benefits were the same for all beneficiaries although contributions were proportional to income. As to the solidarity features of the *pension* scheme at issue, the Court mentioned *inter alia* the fact that the pensions were funded by those in employment and that the pension entitlements were not proportional to the contributions paid. The Court found the compulsory affiliation to the schemes to be indispensable for application of the principle of solidarity and the financial equilibrium of the schemes.

In *Cisal* the Court found basically for the same reasons as in *Poucet and Pistre* that an Italian **11.144** organisation entrusted by law with the management of a compulsory scheme providing insurance against accidents at work and occupational diseases is not an undertaking. The solidarity of the scheme manifested itself *inter alia* in the absence of any direct link between the contributions paid and the benefits granted.

In *AOK* the Court held that sickness funds involved in the management of the German **11.145** statutory health insurance system are not undertakings. The Court considered the funds to be similar to those in *Poucet and Pistre*, given their exclusively social function, the fact that they are based on the principle of solidarity and their entirely non-profit-making character. The Court noted in particular that the funds cannot influence the benefits as they are compelled by law to offer their members essentially identical obligatory benefits (treatment and medicines) which do not depend on the amount of the contributions. The Court held that the sickness funds were not in competition with each other or with private insurers as regards the provision of these statutory benefits.

It should be noted that unlike the organisations in *Poucet and Pistre* and *Cisal*, the German **11.146** sickness funds had some freedom in setting the contribution rates to their members. The Court considered however that this freedom does not lead to the conclusion that the funds were undertakings, by referring to the fact that this freedom was introduced by the legislator to encourage the funds to operate in accordance with principles of sound management. Apparently, this leaves open the possibility that the Court would have considered the funds to be undertakings if the legislator had introduced the freedom to set the contribution rates

---

[164] Joined Cases C-159/91 and C-160/91 *Poucet and Pistre* [1993] ECR I-637; Case C-218/00 *Cisal* [2002] ECR I-00691; Joined cases C-264/01, C-306/01, C-354/01 and C-355/01 *AOK Bundesverband et al.*, [2004] ECR-I-02493; and Case T-319/99 *Fenin* [2003] ECR II-0357.

in order to promote competition as such. It also follows from the judgment that if the funds had had the influence to determine the benefits, they would have been more likely to be qualified as undertakings.

11.147 In addition, in *AOK* the Court kept open the possibility that besides their functions of an exclusively social nature, the sickness funds may engage in activities which have a purpose that is not social in nature and could be economic. The Court considered that the decisions of the funds in respect of such activities could perhaps be regarded as decisions of undertakings or associations of undertakings, as the case may be. Similarly, in *AOK* the Court had to decide whether the determination by the fund associations of fixed maximum amounts payable by sickness funds towards the costs of medicines and treatment materials was a social or an economic activity. The Court concluded that this activity was linked to the funds' functions of an exclusively social nature. The fund associations did not act as undertakings engaged in economic activity as they merely performed a task for management of the German social security system which was imposed upon them by law.

11.148 In *Fenin* the CFI motivated its decision that the managing entities of the Spanish statutory health system were not undertakings by referring to the system operating according to the principle of solidarity, in that it was funded from social security contributions and other state funding and in that it provided services free of charge to its members on the basis of universal cover.

11.149 The importance of *Fenin* is however more related to a different issue decided by the CFI in its judgment. The CFI ruled that it is the activity consisting in offering goods and services on a given market that is the characteristic feature of an economic activity and not the business of purchasing, as such.[165] As, in the CFI's view, the managing entities were not to be regarded as providing an economic activity when offering their services, they could not be qualified as undertakings when purchasing goods or services either. On appeal, the Court of Justice confirmed this view.[166] It considered that the CFI rightly deduced that there is no need to dissociate the activity of purchasing goods from the subsequent use to which they are put in order to determine the nature of that purchasing activity, and that the nature of the purchasing activity must be determined according to whether or not the subsequent use of the purchased goods amounts to an economic activity.

(b) Organisations Qualified as Undertakings

11.150 In contrast to the above-mentioned cases, in *FFSA, Brentjens, Albany, Drijvende Bokken* and *Pavlov*, the Court concluded that the organisations managing the second pillar social security schemes at issue were engaged in an economic activity and thus undertakings.[167]

11.151 In *FFSA* the Court held that a French non-profit-making body which managed an old-age pension scheme intended to supplement a basic compulsory scheme, established by law as an

---

165 The CFI referred in particular to Case C-118/85 *Commission v Italy* [1987] ECR 2599.
166 Case C-205/03 P, *Fenin*, not yet reported in ECR.
167 Case C-244/94 *FFSA v Ministry of Agriculture and Fishery* [1995] ECR I-4013; Case C-67/96 *Albany* [1999] ECR I-5751; Joined Cases C-115/97, C-116/97 and C-117/97 *Brentjens* [1999] ECR I-6025; Case C-219/97 *Drijvende Bokken* [1999] ECR I-6121; and Joined Cases C-180/98 to C-184/98 *Pavlov* [2000] ECR I-645.

optional scheme and operating according to the principle of capitalisation, was an undertaking. The Court stated that the body carried out an economic activity in competition with life insurance companies in view of its optional membership, the application of the principle of capitalisation and benefits depending solely on the amount of contributions paid and on the performance of the investments made by the managing body. The main difference with the pension scheme in *Poucet and Pistre* is that, as a consequence of the optional nature of the *FFSA* scheme, its degree of solidarity is lower than that of the scheme in *Poucet and Pistre*. It should also be noted that the application of the capitalisation principle pointed to a lower degree of solidarity than that of the scheme in *Poucet and Pistre* where the pensions were funded by those in work.

In *Brentjens, Albany* and *Drijvende Bokken*, the Court held that a pension fund entrusted **11.152** with the management of a supplementary pension scheme set up by a collective agreement between labour and management in a given sector in the Netherlands, of which membership had been made compulsory by the public authorities for all workers in that sector, was an undertaking. The Court based its conclusion on three factors. First, the respective funds determined the amount of contributions and benefits. This is clearly different from the organisations at stake in *Poucet and Pistre* and *Cisal* where both contributions and benefits were ultimately determined by the State. It also contrasts with *AOK* where the sickness funds were able to influence the contributions but not the benefits. Secondly, as in *FFSA*, the respective funds operated in accordance with the principle of capitalisation. The Court added that the funds were, like insurance companies, supervised by the insurance supervisor. Thirdly, the respective funds were in certain circumstances required or empowered to exempt undertakings from membership, meaning that they were carrying on an economic activity in competition with insurance companies. The Court stated that in these circumstances, the fact that the funds are non-profit-making and the degree of solidarity of the schemes were not sufficient to deprive the sectoral pension fund of its status as an undertaking.[168]

In *Pavlov*, on the basis of the same criteria as in *Brentjens, Albany* and *Drijvende Bokken*, the **11.153** Court came to the conclusion that the Dutch occupational pension fund at issue was an undertaking.

(3) Exclusive Rights

In *Brentjens, Albany, Drijvende Bokken* and *Pavlov*, the Court examined the compatibility with **11.154** Articles 86 and 82 of exclusive rights granted to the pension funds to manage the supplementary pension scheme concerned.[169] There were a number of issues that the Court had to decide.

---

[168] For a further discussion of the role of solidarity in these judgments, see paras 11.160ff below.

[169] The Court also decided in *Brentjens, Albany* and *Drijvende Bokken* that agreements concluded in the framework of collective negotiations between labour and management in order to improve conditions of work (*in casu* the agreements to set up the pension schemes and to request the public authorities to make affiliation compulsory for all workers in the relevant sectors) do not, by virtue of their nature and purpose, fall within the scope of Article 81. In the same line, Case C-222/98 *Hendrik van der Woude v Stichting Beatrixoord* [2000] ECR I-07111, where the Court held that a collective labour agreement relating to sickness insurance for employees covered by the agreement and under which employers' contributions are paid only in respect of insurance taken out with the insurer(s) selected for the purposes of implementing that agreement, does not, by reason of its nature and purpose, fall within the scope of Article 81.

11.155 First, the Court ruled that where public authorities make affiliation compulsory, as in these cases, this necessarily implies granting to the funds an exclusive right. The exclusive right at issue concerned the right to collect and administer the contributions paid with a view to accruing pension rights. It followed that such funds must be regarded as undertakings to which exclusive rights have been granted in the meaning of Article 86 (1).

11.156 Secondly, the Court held that funds having a legal monopoly in a substantial part of the common market may be regarded as having a dominant position in the meaning of Article 82. Apparently, the Court does not consider it necessary to examine whether or not the supplementary pensions form part of a larger relevant product market. It follows that an undertaking which has a legal monopoly is also in a dominant position.

11.157 Thirdly, the Court considered that merely creating a dominant position by granting exclusive rights within the meaning of Article 86 is not in itself incompatible with Article 82 of the Treaty. A Member State only breaches those provisions if the undertaking merely by exercising the exclusive rights granted to it, is led to abuse its dominant position or when such rights are liable to create a situation in which that undertaking is led to commit such abuses. The Court stated in *Brentjens*, *Albany* and *Drijvende Bokken* that some undertakings in the relevant sectors may wish to provide their workers with a pension scheme superior to the one offered by the fund. It then held that the fact that such undertakings are unable to entrust the management of such a pension scheme to a single insurer, and the resulting restriction of competition, derive directly from the exclusive right conferred on the sectoral pension fund.[170] The Court did however not expressly conclude that the state measures granting these exclusive rights violate Articles 86(1) and 82, but nevertheless assessed them under Article 86(2).

11.158 Fourthly, the Court concluded in *Brentjens*, *Albany* and *Drijvende Bokken* that the exclusive rights of the sectoral pension funds to manage supplementary pensions in a given sector and the resulting restriction of competition were justified under Article 86(2) as a measure necessary for the performance of a particular social task of general interest with which those funds had been charged. The Court was of the view that the supplementary pension scheme fulfilled an essential social function in the Dutch pension system by reason of the limited amount of the statutory pension. In addition, the Court considered the exclusive rights to be necessary as their removal might make it impossible for the funds to perform their task of general economic interest, entrusted to them under economically acceptable conditions, and threaten their financial equilibrium.

11.159 The removal of the rights would lead to the progressive departure of 'good risks' (young employees in good health engaged in non-dangerous activities) to private insurers that offer more advantageous conditions, leaving the sectoral pension fund with the 'bad risks'. As a result the funds could no longer offer pensions at an acceptable cost. The Court added that this would in particular arise in a case, where the supplementary pension scheme, like the ones at issue in the judgments, demonstrates a high level of solidarity (manifested by *inter alia* the contributions not reflecting risk and the existence of an obligation to accept workers without prior medical examination). Such constraints resulting from solidarity render

---

170 In *Pavlov* the Court decided that the case file did not contain evidence of abuse of a dominant position.

the service provided by the funds less competitive than a comparable service provided by insurance companies and go towards justifying the exclusive rights of the fund to manage the supplementary pension scheme.

It is clear from *Brentjens, Albany* and *Drijvende Bokken* that the degree of solidarity of a **11.160** social security scheme does not only play a role in determining whether or not a managing body of such a scheme is engaged in an economic activity and therefore an undertaking, but also as to the question whether or not an exclusive right granted to such a body is necessary to perform a specific social task of general economic interest.[171] As Articles 86(1) and 86(2) only applies to undertakings, the Court will however only come to the latter assessment if a managing organisation of the scheme is considered to be an undertaking.

It follows from the case law that if a managing organisation of a social security scheme is **11.161** found to be an undertaking, the degree of solidarity of the scheme it operates is lower than when the managing organisation is not found to be an undertaking. The degree of solidarity may however still be sufficient to justify the existence of any exclusive right of the organisation to manage the social security scheme at issue. It appears from *Brentjens, Albany* and *Drijvende Bokken* that the Court is easily convinced by the 'good risks/bad risks' argument to conclude that an exclusive right is necessary. In his opinion Advocate General Jacobs pointed out that there are still 15 supplementary pension schemes in the Netherlands that operate without compulsory affiliation. This casts some doubts on the necessity of the exclusive rights. Apparently, this did not prevent the Court from deciding that these rights were necessary. In any event, even though the exclusive rights are justified, the pension funds are subject to Articles 81 and 82 in the exercise of their exclusive rights.

(4) Future Prospects

Given the lack of action by the Commission in the social security sector as far as the **11.162** application of the EC competition rules is concerned, it would seem that the Commission has decided to leave the initiative to national courts (with recourse to the Court under Article 234) and, possibly, national competition authorities. There are currently no signs that this will change in the near future.

In the judgments discussed in this section the Court clarified a number of issues. A very **11.163** important issue concerns the question whether a managing organisation of a social security scheme can be involved in an economic activity as a purchaser of goods and services, even if it is not in its capacity as a provider of services. The CFI in *Fenin* answered the question negatively and this was, on appeal, confirmed by the Court of Justice. The question is of great relevance since social security bodies are often important purchasers of, for example, health care services and pharmaceuticals. Their actions may therefore have a substantial impact on these markets. As the Court ruled that a managing organisation of a social security scheme that is not performing an economic activity in relation to its 'customers', is also not to be regarded as an undertaking in its capacity as a purchaser of goods or services, it follows

---

[171] For a detailed discussion of the role of solidarity, see Winterstein, 'Nailing the jellyfish: social security and competition law' [1999] ECLR 324-33. See also Gyselen, [2000] CMLR 425-48; and Nijenhuis, (2000) 3 EUREDIA 336-51.

that the purchasing activities of such bodies are generally also not subject to the EC competition rules. This could well mean that a significant part of the social security sector falls outside the reach of the EC competition authorities.

F. Current Initiatives—Sector Enquiries

11.164 On 13 June 2005 the Commission decided to open 'sector enquiries' in the financial services sector in the areas of retail banking and business insurance.[172] The retail banking enquiry is focusing on payment cards and current accounts and other services. One reason underlying the Commission's investigation into retail banking is probably that retail banking markets in the EU are not yet integrated and prices for comparable retail banking products vary substantially across the EU. Also, switching costs and product bundling may lead to customer captivity. In the business insurance area, the Commission seems likely to investigate matters such as horizontal co-operation, insurance distribution and broker remuneration, and reinsurance.

11.165 The preliminary results of the retail banking sector enquiry—the only results available at the time of writing[173]—suggest that payment systems, highly fragmented in the EU, are likely to be a priority area for the future:

— In the area of payment cards, the preliminary conclusions of the Commission point to the high profitability of the payment cards business and the high variation of fees (cardholder fees, fees paid by retailers, and fees paid between banks) across the EU. The Commission also identifies potential barriers to competition, which it classifies into (i) structural, such as joint ventures between banks at national level for providing merchants with card acceptance services, which result in the absence of competing offers to merchants and in the foreclosure of foreign competitors from the market where the joint venture operates; (ii) technical (divergent technical standards) and (iii) behavioural, such as agreements on interchange fees paid between banks and membership and governance rules, which in certain payment card systems even require smaller banks to pass sensitive information on payments to the principal members of the system.

— In the area of current accounts and related services, the Commission examined market structures—which differ considerably across the EU—and concentration, the financial performance of retail banks and low customer mobility. In addition to (non-card) payment systems, the interim report examined credit databases: while credit databases are a useful tool for banks to operate in a given market, they can also create barriers to entry when access to them is restricted, in particular when they are owned and managed by joint ventures of local banks.

---

[172] The inquiries were initiated through two Commission decisions of 13 June 2005. See IP/05 of 13 June 2005 and MEMO/05 of the same date. Sector enquiries under Art 17 of Regulation 1/2003 allow the Commission to improve its knowledge about the obstacles to competition in a particular sector where it has concerns that competition may not be working as it should. The knowledge gained about the market can form the basis of specific enforcement initiatives at a later stage.

[173] The interim report I, on payment cards, was published on 12 April 2006, and the interim report II, on current accounts and related services, was published on 17 July 2006. The interim report on insurance has not been published at the time of writing.

12

ENERGY

Harold Nyssens and Dominik Schnichels

A. General Introduction

12.01 This chapter provides an overview of the legal and economic context in which EC competition policy is being applied in the energy sector. Other chapters in this book explain the law with reference to the economic and policy context. Although all types of energy source will be discussed from time to time, the focus of this chapter is on the gas and electricity sectors. One reason for this emphasis is that the latter two sectors are 'network industries' which underwent a recent liberalisation process contrary to the other areas of the energy sector (such as oil,[1] coal, and nuclear energy).

12.02 The network aspect of gas and electricity creates a certain number of challenges for antitrust enforcement, similar to those which arise, for instance, in the railway and air transport or telecommunications sectors. Moreover, energy liberalisation only began in the mid 1990s and is thus at an early stage of development. Competition enforcement in these sectors is therefore even more necessary.

12.03 The competition rules cannot be applied in a policy vacuum. In relation to the electricity sector, and increasingly also the gas sector, application of competition rules is complicated

---

[1] See 'EC competition policy and the motor fuel sector', Commission press release MEMO/00/55.

by the need to accommodate a wider range of public interest factors. Moreover, this is an area where the traditional 'antitrust dilemma' appears with particular force: the right balance should be struck between, on the one hand, maximum short term competition—implying, for instance, an extensive third party access regime to energy networks—and, on the other hand, increased competition in the long run, implying a possible limitation on third party access to incentivise the much needed infrastructure investments.[2]

Finding the right balance is crucial, as this sector is vital for the smooth running of the over-all economy. Its importance goes well beyond its still rather limited contribution to GDP. Any change in the overall business environment can have direct or indirect effects on secu-rity of supply, on the technical integrity of the networks and on the way in which public services are performed in the sector. Antitrust enforcement may also directly affect the revenues generated by the sector—through tax revenue, concession, or participation in public companies—in favour of State bodies. Last but not least, energy policy and antitrust enforcement in the sector is likely to have an impact on the prices paid by the end-user, including low-income households. This policy is thus likely to have a direct impact on the proportion of overall household income spend on energy.[3] **12.04**

In view of the fact that these issues have, in the last five to ten years, been rendered increas-ingly transparent by means of EC legislation, this chapter starts with a brief overview of the legislative framework in which antitrust and merger rules are applied to the gas and electricity sector. **12.05**

(1) Constitutional Framework

(a) Current EC Treaty and Draft Constitution

(i) **Current EC Treaty Rules**   The current EC Treaty does not include a special chapter on the energy sector, although it does contain a few references to it. Therefore, in spite of occa-sional claims by certain operators, the EC antitrust and merger rules apply in full to the energy sector. Moreover, it would be paradoxical if those rules did not apply to the energy sector, as the first antitrust rules developed in history (the US Sherman Act), were developed in order to alleviate problems caused by the monopolisation of the petrol sector by Standard Oil. **12.06**

As a consequence, there is no limitation on the application of competition rules to the energy sector such as exists for agriculture, nor have specific competition rules, such as sector-specific block exemptions, been adopted for this sector (unlike the transport sector, for instance). Even before explicit references to energy were included in the founding treaties, the Court of Justice had ruled that the energy sector was within the scope of competition rules.[4] The only formal Treaty exception has been granted, as outlined in the next section, for nuclear energy, which is subject to a specific Treaty. As a consequence, EC antitrust laws apply to a more limited extent. **12.07**

---

[2] See, amongst others, K B Moen, 'The Gas Directive and third party transport rights—What pipeline volumes are available ?' (hereafter 'Moen') (2003) Journal of Energy & Natural Resources Law 64.

[3] See M Harker and C Waddams Price, 'Consumers and antitrust in British energy markets', in *The pros and cons of antitrust in deregulated markets* (Swedish Competition authority, 2004), pp 30ff.

[4] See Case 6/64 *Costa v ENEL* [1964] ECR 1251; Case C-393/92 *Almelo* [1994] ECR I-1477; and, more recently, Cases C-157/94 *et seq*, *Commission v Netherlands and others* [1997] ECR I-5699ff.

12.08   The absence of a sector-wide derogation does not mean, however—as this chapter demonstrates—that a number of specific features of this sector, for example public service obligations or concerns relating to security of supply, have put their stamp on merger and antitrust enforcement. As a consequence, general block exemptions, like the horizontal and vertical block exemptions and their accompanying guidelines also apply to this sector, although the special characteristics of the energy sector must be taken into account when applying them.[5]

12.09   The EC Treaty, including its provisions on antitrust and energy, applies to the entire energy sector including petrol, electricity, gas, renewable energy, and coal. It is noteworthy that, until 23 July 2002, coal was covered by the Coal and Steel Treaty (ECSC) which included a certain number of specific provisions on antitrust, quite distinct from the EC Treaty.[6] The key transitional issues arising from the expiry of the ECSC Treaty in the antitrust, mergers, and State aid areas have been addressed in a Communication from the Commission.[7]

12.10   **(ii) The draft European Constitution**   For a number of reasons relating to the need to ensure a coherent legal basis for EC energy policy, and to the increasingly cross-border nature of energy challenges (climate change, liberalisation, and import dependency) a new energy title was added in the now defunct draft Treaty establishing a Constitution for Europe.[8] Article 13 of this draft Treaty indicates that energy is a matter of shared competence between the Member States and the European Union. Article III-130 indicates that unanimity is required in the Council for approving rules affecting Member State's choices between different energy sources and the general structure of its energy supply.[9] Article III-157 of the draft constitution, for the first time in Community history, provides that in establishing an internal market and with regard for the need to preserve and improve the environment, Union policy on energy shall aim to: (a) ensure the functioning of the energy market; (b) ensure security of energy supply in the Union; and (c) promote energy efficiency and saving and the development of new and renewable forms of energy. This trilogy largely overlaps what has been called the 'Johannesburg equation', ie the challenge faced by the human species to reconcile the use of energy resources with respect for the environment, whilst at the same time maintaining economic development.[10]

12.11   Although the draft Constitution will probably never see the light of day at least in its current form, this chapter on energy, granting the European Union explicit competencies in this area, highlights the increased attention given to energy policy at European level. Its content also underlines the fact that security of energy supplies and the related concern of management of natural resources have recently gained political prominence.[11]

---

5 See in this sense, generally Case 45/85 *Verband der Sachversicherer/Commission* [1987] ECR 405; and Cases T-374/94, T-375/94, T-384/94 and T-388/94, *ENS/Commission* [1998] ECR II-141, points 136–137.

6 See for an overview of the latest developments in this area, Case C-172/01 P *Naloo* [2003] ECR I-11421.

7 Communication from the Commission concerning certain aspects of the treatment of competition cases resulting from the expiry of the ECSC Treaty [2002] OJ C152/5.

8 See generally, G Rashbrooke, 'Clarification or complication? The new energy title in the draft Constitution for Europe' (2004) Journal of Energy and Natural Resources Law 373–387.

9 See already in this sense, Art 175 of the current EC Treaty.

10 See Jean-Marie Chevalier, *Les grandes batailles de l'énergie* (hereafter 'Chevalier') (2004) Gallimard, Folio Actuel, 363ff.

11 Strategic Energy Review adopted by the Commission on 10 January 2007.

Nevertheless, the principle that market rules in general and antitrust rules in particular also apply to the energy sector remain unaffected.

(b) The Euratom Treaty

The nuclear sector, however, is largely dealt with in the context of the Euratom Treaty **12.12** signed in 1957 together with the EC Treaty. The general objective of the Euratom Treaty is to contribute to the technical development of nuclear energy, thereby enhancing the security of energy supply for the Community. In order to ensure that all users receive regular supplies of nuclear fuels, a 'common supply policy', based on the principle of equal access, has been established. This role is assigned to the Euratom Supply Agency (ESA).

The ESA has an option on ores, source materials, and special fissile materials produced in **12.13** the territories of Member States. The ESA was also granted an exclusive right to conclude contracts relating to the supply of ores, source materials, and special fissile materials coming from inside the Community or from outside.

Apart from these institutional differences, nuclear energy is characterised by specific **12.14** features, which have been acknowledged in a number of antitrust cases.[12] Indeed nuclear reactors are generally considered to operate most efficiently if used continuously and at relatively steady capacity. This technical feature provides a basis for nuclear electricity generators to try to ensure a constant and steady production. The most straightforward scenario for doing so is to enter into long-term supply contracts covering an optimised production level for the plant in question. As in the *Scottish Nuclear* case, and assuming that the company concerned has some price setting power, such long-term supply agreements will only be acceptable if the entire production is not sold on an exclusive basis to a dominant downstream supplier, but rather to a series of downstream competitors.

The Euratom Treaty clearly provides that, where it contains rules that are opposed to those **12.15** of the EC Treaty, the Euratom rules prevail: the *lex specialis* overrides the *lex generalis*. In practice, EC merger rules[13] apply in full to the nuclear sector. Application of antitrust rules is the rule, except were they are overridden by special Euratom provisions, in particular Articles 67 to 76 on prices and supply of nuclear materials.[14]

The application of State aid rules to the nuclear sector is a matter of controversy:[15] only **12.16** Article 40 of the Euratom Treaty refers explicitly to this topic. In our view, this provision does not, however, constitute a sufficient basis for excluding the application of EC State aid rules altogether. This approach has the advantage of maintaining a unified approach to the monitoring of competition in the internal market across different sources of primary energy (gas, nuclear, coal, etc). This is also the way in which the Commission has been dealing with nuclear issues: it tends to apply State aid rules *mutatis mutandis* without fully acknowledging that it is actually applying these rules.

---

[12] See, for instance, the Scottish Nuclear decision of 6 July 1991, [1991] OJ L178/31.
[13] See eg Case M.3099 *Areva/Urenco* (2004).
[14] See L Ritter and WD Braun, *European competition law. A practitioner's guide* (3rd edn, Kluwer, 2004), p 914.
[15] See L Hancher in *Competition Law & Energy markets* (Claeys & Casteels, 2005), pp 467ff.

(2) Economic and Political Background of Liberalisation

(a) *Expected Benefits from Liberalisation*

12.17 The energy sector has become central to the achievement of the goals of the European Community. Indeed, the energy policies currently in place at Community level are intended, first, to integrate numerous national markets into wider European markets and, secondly, to enable these markets to become more efficient, thereby improving the competitiveness of the European industry and, by implication, general consumer welfare. These policies aim to contribute to the road map of economic, social, and environmental reform known as the 'Lisbon strategy'.[16]

12.18 Energy liberalisation is expected primarily to lead to a reduction of suppliers' surplus, which it is assumed will benefit consumers. Thus, if all other factors, such as oil prices and tax, remain constant, the liberalisation process should lead to lower market prices and higher levels of efficiency.

12.19 Liberalisation measures, in two main waves, have challenged what were perceived, from a competition point of view, as inefficiencies, excessive prices, over-investment and inertia in the largely monopolised energy markets in place at the time. It is acknowledged, however, that exclusive rights or similar measures may be helpful in 'infant industries'.[17] In other words, the drive for liberalisation of the EC energy industry was motivated by the conviction that the former legal regime was inferior to a regime based on competition and that the new process would transform dormant industries into competitive ones.[18] Free cross-border trade in energy can indeed offer significant economic benefits both in terms of security, flexibility, and quality of energy and greater competition. Cross-border trade in electricity may, for instance, facilitate the use of the generation plant with the lowest marginal costs at any given moment within an interconnected system.

12.20 Energy transport networks, however, constitute a crucial bottleneck through which incumbents can hamper or delay liberalisation. The legislative framework that has been created thus focuses primarily on third party access to networks, in addition to formally abolishing the legal monopolies. Nevertheless, the ultimate objective of the entire liberalisation exercise was, and still is, to ensure the fundamental principle of freedom of—eligible—customers to choose, from a variety of players, the supplier which responds to their specific needs with the best offer.[19]

---

[16] See Presidency Conclusions of the Lisbon European Council, 23–24 March 2000.

[17] Chevalier, see n 10 above, p 303; and W Wälde and AJ Gunst, 'International energy trade and access to energy networks' (hereafter 'Wälde and Gunst') (2002) Journal of World Trade 197. For a concrete example of such understanding, see Arts 4.4 and 28 of Gas Directive (EC) 2003/55 for delaying liberalisation in 'emergent countries'. For the consequences of the latter provisions on competition policy, see Case T-87/05 *EDP v Commission* [2005], not yet published.

[18] 'Use and Abuse of market power in the Nordic power market', Main report—market power in the Nordic power market—sub project 3 of Copenhagen Economics (hereafter 'Copenhagen Economics study'), 21 October 2002, p 8, available, amongst others on the web site of the Swedish competition authority.

[19] Speech by Commissioner Monti of 21 September 2004, available on DG Competition's web site.

Whether the advantages of this liberalisation exercise outweigh the disadvantages, or vice versa, has for some time been the subject of intense debate.[20] Market liberalisation undoubtedly complicates long-term planning by individual utilities, as they can no longer rely on a secure and captive range of customers within a geographically delimited area. In other words, energy companies must now take into account the risk of losing market share. The effects of these changes must be balanced against the advantages to customers of satisfying their requirements on more competitive or more tailored conditions. **12.21**

Linked to this objective of increased economic efficiency, a second, more political goal, is to realise a further integration of national markets into wider, supranational regional markets and, in the long run, to a united European energy market.[21] **12.22**

(b) The Need for a Combination of Regulatory and Antitrust Instruments

Like a number of other network industries such as telecommunications, transport, or postal services, it was felt that antitrust law alone would not be sufficient to guarantee effective competition in the gas and electricity markets. The protection long enjoyed by legal monopolists, in many Member States, has allowed those companies to obtain broad command of the sectors concerned: they clearly have the best insight into the technical and economic functioning of a market they have largely created themselves. They own, directly or indirectly, the network infrastructure and most of the best locations for constructing upstream production capacity (generation sites, hydrocarbon concessions, or gas storage facilities).[22] The historic structural links between transmission and supply activities have long allowed them privileged access to crucial information earlier than potential competitors.[23] **12.23**

Usually, these companies have also set up networks of long-term supply contracts guaranteeing both upstream input security and captive downstream markets.[24] Existing interconnection capacity with neighbouring countries will, most often, be largely reserved for implementing the long-term contracts of the historic players.[25] The high investment costs required to access this market constitute a further barrier for new entrants. Finally, historic actors have both the means and the knowledge that allows them to behave in the subtlest anti-competitive ways. All these issues will be addressed in the following sections. **12.24**

The combined implementation of the liberalisation legislation, described in the next section, as well as the antitrust and merger enforcement in the area, dealt with thereafter, constitute the two-headed cornerstone of market opening. **12.25**

The importance of structural measures, voluntarily adopted by certain Member States in the context of the liberalisation process should, however, also be emphasised. **12.26**

---

[20] IEA, *Security of supply in open markets: LNG and power at a turning point* (OECD, IEA, 2004).

[21] As regards the link between those two objectives, see Commission guidelines on the application of Art 81(3) EC, point 13.

[22] See in this respect, Preliminary Report of the Sector inquiry under Art 17 Regulation 1/2003 on the gas and electricity markets (hereafter 'Commission's energy sector Inquiry') 16/2/2006, available at <http://ec.europa.eu/comm/competition/antitrust/others/sector_inquiries/energy/>, points 138ff.

[23] ibid, points 229ff.

[24] ibid, points 112ff.

[25] As to the legality of such reservations, see further para 12.272, as well as 12.416ff.

Structural measures like full ownership unbundling of formerly vertically integrated entities, the splitting up of former supply monopolies or divestiture of parts of those monopolies, even if temporary in nature, like gas release programmes, have a decisive impact on the efficiency of the liberalisation process in the area in question, by diminishing market power and increasing liquidity in supply markets.[26]

(3) Legislative Context

(a) *The Choice between Harmonisation Directives and Article 86 Directives*

12.27   Whereas the process of integrating European energy markets began in 1990 with directives concerning the transparency of gas and electricity prices and the transit of electricity and gas, in effect the energy sector only began to be 'liberalised' with the introduction of market opening measures in 1996 in the case of electricity and 1998 in the case of gas.

12.28   Although competition rules could have been used as an alternative instrument[27] to open up markets, the only instruments effectively used, so far, for the purpose of liberalising the energy sector have been Parliament and Council Directives and Regulations based on Article 95 of the Treaty, to the exclusion of Directives based on Article 95 of the Treaty. Unlike the telecommunications sector, where liberalisation was originally initiated using Article 86 EC measures, the Commission's Article 86 powers were first used, in practice, as late as 2003 and then only in individual cases.[28]

(b) *Liberalisation: A Progressive Process*

12.29   It is also crucial to remember that the liberalisation process has been very gradual, as will be outlined in the following sections. The progressive nature of the exercise is best exemplified by the concept of 'eligible customer'. Indeed, even after the adoption of the last set of liberalisation directives, not all energy consumers have yet been able to benefit from the freedom of choosing their supplier: until 11 July 2007, the date at which all individuals will be able to do so, only non-household customers are 'eligible' to benefit from market opening.[29] The gradual nature of the liberalisation process has meant that antitrust enforcement has not yet addressed any retail issues relating to household customers.

12.30   The legislation which will be summarised hereafter is crucial not only for understanding the framework in which antitrust is to be applied. It can also impose explicit boundaries on antitrust enforcement, for instance when temporarily limiting market opening to a limited number of eligible customers. The CFI judgment in the *EDP* case, cited above, also demonstrates that there are limits on applying merger rules to energy sectors not yet fully opened up to competition.

---

[26] See an acknowledgment of this in recital 11 of Directive (EC) 2004/67 described hereafter. See also 'Discussion document on long term contracts, gas release programmes and the availability of multiple gas suppliers' presented by the Commission for discussion at the 5th Madrid Forum. This document is available on the Commission's web site.

[27] Copenhagen Economics study p 53. See also Commission press release IP/01/872.

[28] See initiation of the *Greek lignite* case in Commission press release (IP/04/436).

[29] See, for instance, Art 1, point 28 of Gas Directive (EC) 2003/55. See also points 109 and following in the CFI judgment in Case T-87/05. Member States were free to liberalise faster.

There is no doubt that, in view of the fundamental principle of hierarchy of norms, **12.31** the energy directives cannot be considered to limit the inherent scope of application of the rules of primary EC antitrust law. In practice, however, the burden of proof on the Commission or any party to national litigation to demonstrate that commercial practice explicitly tolerated by Community legislation infringes Articles 81 or 82 EC will be a difficult to meet.

(c) Evolution of the Legal Framework

(i) Pre-liberalisation: Price Transparency and Transit Legislation As indicated above, **12.32** the opening of European energy markets has taken place in several waves.[30] The first measure adopted by the Community in view of creating an integrated European energy market was Directive (EEC) 90/377 laying out a procedure to improve the transparency of gas and electricity prices charged to industrial end-users.[31] This Directive was intended to ensure that gas and electricity undertakings notify their prices to the Statistical Office of the Commission. The Commission still publishes this information regularly in an aggregate form. The purpose of this exercise was, at the time, to determine the level of price differences between Member States in order to determine the level of integration. These aggregates do not generally constitute a completely sound basis of end-users prices for the purposes of an antitrust assessment in a particular case.

This first Directive was soon followed by the electricity and gas transit Directives,[32] which **12.33** essentially created a pre-liberalisation framework for the exchange of electricity and gas respectively between incumbent operators. The purpose of these Directives was to allow for collaboration between existing national operators, which would enhance security of supply and allow for cost reductions. These Directives merely obliged Member States to 'facilitate' transit without creating any market opening within the transited countries. The existing legal monopolies were in fact left unaffected by the Transit Directives.[33]

Although both Directives have now been abolished,[34] some effects are likely to persist long **12.34** beyond market opening, especially in the gas sector.[35] Indeed, both the 'Gas Directive'[36] and the Cross-border electricity Regulation contain transitory provisions relating to the continuity of the transport contracts entered into under the auspices of the transit Directives.[37] The compatibility of such contracts with antitrust rules will be touched upon

---

[30] For an overview of the current rules, see C Jones, *EU Energy Law* (2004).
[31] Council Directive (EEC) 90/377 of 29 June 1990 concerning a Community procedure to improve the transparency of gas and electricity prices charged to industrial end-users [1990] OJ L185/16.
[32] Directive (EEC) 90/547 of 29 October 1990 on the transmission of electricity through transmission grids [1990] OJ L313/30; and Directive 91/296 of 31 May 1991 on the transmission of natural gas through grids [1991] OJ L147/37.
[33] It is noteworthy that 'transit' is widely defined and includes both exports from one country to another as 'transits' in the more traditional understanding, ie exports from one country to another via a third country.
[34] See Art 32 and recital 31 of the Gas Directive, and Art 29 of the Electricity Directive.
[35] See in this respect, Preliminary Report of the Commission's energy sector Inquiry, points 194ff.
[36] The terms 'Gas Directive' refer to the second Gas Directive (EC) 2003/55, whereas the first Gas Directive (EC) 98/30 will be referred to as 'first Gas Directive'.
[37] See Art 32 of the Gas Directive and the chapter 'Position of long term contracts of the guidelines' annexed to the Regulation no 1228/2003 on cross-border electricity exchanges [2003] OJ L176/1.

below when addressing the legality of long-term reservations contracts on gas or electricity interconnectors.

12.35 (ii) **Utilities Procurement Directive**   The Utilities Procurement Directive (EEC) 93/38[38] should also be mentioned in this context. It purports to coordinate the national procurement procedures of publicly controlled entities operating in the energy sector *inter alia* in order to ensure genuine Community-wide competition between operators in these sectors. The Directive applies not only to public authorities and public undertakings, but also to private entities which enjoy special or exclusive rights granted by a Member State. Contracts for fuels intended for power generation are, however, excluded from the scope of the Directive.

12.36 The provisions of this Directive—their structure and the conditions they impose—are relevant for antitrust enforcement to the extent that they have an impact on the assessment of energy infrastructure projects under competition rules. Indeed, as will be outlined in more detail in paragraph 12.344 and following, infrastructure projects for which an open and transparent tender procedure has been followed, will, in practice, benefit from a presumption of compatibility with antitrust rules, at least as far as the project itself is concerned. In such a case, indeed, it can be argued that 'competition *in* the market' can be restricted to the extent there has been a fair 'competition *for* the market'.

12.37 (iii) **The Hydrocarbons Directive**   In order to ensure non-discriminatory access for all enterprises, regardless of their nationality, their ownership (public or private) to the activities of prospecting, exploring for, and producing hydrocarbons in the EC, the Hydrocarbons Directive was adopted in 1994.[39] The Directive allows the Member States the right to determine the areas within their territory to be made available or not for exploration and production. However, it ensures equal treatment of all EC companies as regards access to and exercise of these activities by describing detailed procedures for granting authorisations. This legislation constitutes an important pre-condition for the development of more competition in the upstream gas market, to the extent that it has allowed, in countries like the Netherlands, a greater number of operators to appear in the field of upstream gas exploration and production.[40] To the extent indigenous sources of oil and gas production are clearly declining, this Directive will, in the years to come, gradually lose its practical effect. In order to stimulate upstream gas competition it is therefore crucial that the Commission ensures that measures similar to the Hydrocarbons Directive are no longer taken at EU level, but at wider level, for instance at WTO level. This could, for instance, increase the number of upstream players established in (future) WTO member countries, like Russia, which are important sources of supply to the EU.[41]

---

[38] Directive (EEC) 93/38 of 14 June 1993 coordinating the procurement procedures of entities operating in the water, energy, transport and telecommunications sectors [1993] OJ L199/1, as amended several times subsequently. For an overview, see S Arrowsmith, 'An assessment of the new legislative package on public procurement' (2004) CMLR 1277.

[39] European Parliament and Council Directive (EC) 94/22 of 30 May 1994 on the conditions for granting and using authorizations for the prospection, exploration and production of hydrocarbons [1994] OJ L164/3.

[40] For an overview, see Roggenkamp, Roenne, Redgwell and Del Guayo, *Energy law in Europe National, EU and International Law and Institutions* (Oxford University Press, 2001) 295.

[41] See also para 12.60 relating to the Energy Charter.

As for the existing Directive, its recitals indicate that licensing is limited in time and geography to prevent 'the reservation to a single entity of an exclusive right over an area which can be prospected, explored and brought into production more efficiently by several entities'. Such an approach is warranted to prevent Member States from reserving large exploration blocks for national champions. This second step towards market opening of the upstream gas sector has since been complemented by the Gas Directive, which provides that Member States must ensure that natural gas undertakings and eligible customers are able to obtain access to upstream pipeline networks in order to obtain direct access to upstream gas producers.[42] This has lead, for instance, to improvements in the upstream pipeline regime of the Norwegian Gassco/Gasled system.

12.38

The existence of this EC legislation underlines the importance of a pro-competitive upstream licensing regime and upstream TPA regime in order for competition to develop in gas wholesale markets. Although some timid first steps have been taken in this direction, the absence, for the time being, of effective pro-competitive regimes in third countries which constitute big exporters to the EC is a significant obstacle to the creation of additional competition in Europe, as it tends to support the existing oligopolistic upstream market structure.

12.39

(iv) The First Wave of Liberalisation   In June 1994, the Commission lodged applications pursuant to Article 226 EC before the Court to challenge the exclusive import and/or export rights for electricity and gas which existed in a number of Member States (Spain, France, Italy, the Netherlands).[43] In its judgment, the Court held, in essence, that the exclusive rights in question did indeed infringe Article 31 EC. It decided, however, that the Commission had not sufficiently demonstrated that the justifications under Article 86(2) EC, advanced by the Member States concerned, were invalid. The infringements procedures were dismissed on this basis. This prompted the Commission to take the politically more consensual route of opening up the market by means of harmonisation directives.

12.40

The first real step towards market opening and liberalisation was the Electricity Directive (EC) 96/92 adopted on 19 December 1996.[44] The Directive had to be implemented in the Member States by February 1999. The first Gas Directive (EC) 98/30[45] established common rules on the organisation and functioning of the natural gas sector, including both the transmission and supply of 'natural gas'.[46] Its structure and content was broadly in line with the Electricity Directive. The first Gas Directive had to be implemented in the Member States by August 2000.

12.41

Although these Directives left the Member States considerable freedom of choice to select the types of qualitative measures necessary to ensure liberalisation, they constituted a 'Copernican revolution' for a large number of national energy markets: the world of vertically integrated companies enjoying legal monopolies, which had successfully allowed for

12.42

---

[42] Art 20 of the Gas Directive.
[43] Cases C-157/94 *et seq, Commission/Netherlands, Italy, France and Spain* [1997] ECR I-5699ff.
[44] [1997] OJ L27/20.
[45] [1998] OJ L204/1.
[46] This term includes liquefied natural gas (LNG), biogas, and gas from biomass.

the creation of the electricity and gas markets in Europe, was abandoned: State monopolies were gradually abolished, and 'account unbundling' of network activities from generation and supply activities was introduced. Moreover, the fundamental objectives of transparency and non-discrimination became, for the first time, mandatory under specific legislation, especially as regards access to transmission lines.

12.43 These Directives, as well as all subsequent liberalisation measures adopted by the Community contained two main types of measures: first, those purporting to directly facilitate competition in the supply markets by abolishing, step by step, legal supply monopolies and, secondly, those concerning access to the network, which is a necessary condition to create competition in supply markets. Whereas the former tend to be rather self-explanatory, provisions related to third party access (TPA) to the network tend to be more complex.

12.44 The concept underlying this TPA architecture is that energy networks are considered to constitute a 'natural monopoly'.[47] Creating competition in the provision of network transportation services would therefore not make sense from an economic point of view. Although the Directives impose quasi-tender procedures for the construction of new pieces of infrastructure,[48] the natural monopoly characteristic of these industries leads to a scenario where specialised network companies (transmission system operators or TSOs) are legally entrusted with the task of providing access services, whilst largely operating under exclusive rights to provide the service within their area.

12.45 Under the liberalised system, transmission system operators (TSOs) are responsible for providing access to their networks under equal terms to affiliated companies and third parties. Such third parties will necessarily ask for access in order to compete with the TSOs' affiliated supply companies. The unbundling provisions constitute the cornerstone intended to guarantee the equal treatment of all applicants and to avoid cross-subsidisation. The effectiveness of these rules has been questioned by some operators in the market. At the end of 2005, the Commission was in the process of monitoring the implementation of these rules and their effects both in the context of the 'Progress report' to be established by DG TREN as in the context of the energy sector inquiry launched by DG Competition.

12.46 Although Member States were not formally obliged to introduce a sectoral regulator in charge of overseeing access regimes under the first set of Directives, the vast majority of them had already opted to do so when adopting implementation measures for these liberalisation Directives.

12.47 The main task of these national regulatory authorities (NRAs) is to ensure the effectiveness of access conditions.[49] Implementation of the provisions of these Directives has not been left to national ministries and sectoral regulators alone: the Commission has been

---

[47] It has been argued that this is less true for the natural gas sector, as highlighted by the fact that in certain Member States new entrants have set up entirely new gas networks competing with the incumbent systems. The construction of the Wingas system in Germany in the 1990s constitutes the prime example in this respect. LNG chains also constitute a sub-segment of the gas industry which some argue cannot be characterised as a natural monopoly.

[48] See, for instance, Arts 4 and 24 of the Gas Directive.

[49] About the role of NRAs see further paras 12.72–12.76.

monitoring the developments in the relevant markets closely, attempting to identify obstacles and shortcomings. The benchmarking reports published yearly by the Commission constitute one of the main tools in this perspective.[50] These reports also contain a wealth of factual information which can be useful as a first introduction into the structure and the dynamics of particular products or geographic markets.

The Commission is also trying to ensure harmonised or at least compatible, pro-competitive, implementing measures at national level, in order to avoid national measures—irrespective of their positive effects at the national level—impeding the effective creation of an integrated and competitive energy market. This has been done in the context of the so-called 'Florence Forum' for electricity and 'Madrid Forum' for gas.[51] In these fora, the Commission meets with sectoral regulators, competent ministries, and industry representatives. **12.48**

(v) **The Second Wave of Liberalisation** The huge number of practical obstacles to liberalisation remaining after the adoption and implementation of the first set of Directives, as well as the widely varying levels of market opening chosen by Member States, led the European Council, in Lisbon, to call for an increase in the pace of energy liberalisation. Moreover, the transition phase from monopolised to open markets was considered to involve huge risks for the credibility of the process. Therefore, the second Electricity Directive (Directive (EC) 2003/53,[52] hereafter the 'Electricity Directive') provided for market opening for all non-household customers by July 2004, and for all customers, including households, by July 2007. The second Gas Directive (Directive (EC) 2003/55,[53] hereafter the 'Gas Directive') now includes timing identical to that of the Electricity Directive for market opening. **12.49**

Such synchronicity is crucial, first, because gas constitutes a key (primary energy) input for generating electricity (a so-called 'secondary energy source') by means of combined cycle gas turbines (CCGT) and, secondly, because electricity companies are considered the most likely new entrants into the gas business and vice versa. In view of this, it was necessary to create a level playing field across the two sectors. **12.50**

This second set of Directives also require publication of network tariffs approved by regulators (RTPA), thereby forcing the few Member States[54] which had, until then, opted for negotiated TPA (NTPA) to fundamentally restructure their national framework. **12.51**

These 'second generation' Directives, moreover, contain measures providing for stricter unbundling rules: legal and management unbundling of vertically integrated companies must be implemented, beyond the mere accounting obligations existing before.[55] These unbundling obligations have also been extended from TSOs to the distribution **12.52**

---

[50] These reports are available on the web site of the Commission's Transport and Energy Directorate (hereafter 'DG TREN').

[51] Discussion papers and conclusions can be found on the web site of DG TREN.

[52] Directive (EC) 2003/54 of the European Parliament and of the Council of 26 June 2003 concerning common rules for the internal market in electricity and repealing Directive 96/92/EC [2003] OJ L176/37.

[53] Directive (EC) 2003/55 of the European Parliament and of the Council of 26 June 2003 concerning common rules for the internal market in natural gas and repealing Directive 98/30/EC [2003] OJ L176/57.

[54] Including mainly Germany for both electricity and gas and the Netherlands for gas.

[55] See Hancher and De Vlam, 'Mergers in the electricity sector-relevant markets and related issues' (2004) European Energy Law Report I-34.

system operators (DSOs). Issues of TPA and unbundling relating to these distribution systems are vital in order to ensure that competition will, in the end of the liberalisation process, also benefit small undertakings and households connected to the distribution grids. In 2005, unbundling problems and difficulties linked to obtaining access to networks were much more frequent at DSO than at TSO level, however significant obstacles also prevailed at the TSO level (eg lack of investment).

12.53   Although opening of competition at the distribution level may have ripple effects on national wholesale markets, it should be acknowledged that market distortions affecting transport networks are more likely to have a (potential) effect on trade between Member States,[56] as compared to those affecting distribution systems. Distribution-related restrictive practices are thus more likely to be dealt with by national authorities. In this respect it is less likely that the Commission would consider distribution-related matters as a priority, unless these practices cover, for instance, a large part of a national territory or clearly constitute barriers to importing competition from neighbouring Member States.

12.54   It is noteworthy that DG TREN has published non-binding interpretative notices relating to a number of crucial concepts or provisions of the second generation Directives.[57]

12.55   The Electricity and Gas Directives have been complemented by the adoption of a Regulation 1228/2003 on cross-border electricity trade.[58] This Regulation basically lays down common rules with regard to tarification and capacity allocation, including inter-TSO compensation mechanisms for cross-border flows. It particularly deals with the issue of so-called 'pancaking', ie the charging of tariffs for cross-border flows based on contractual flows,[59] rather than on physical flows. A similarly structured Regulation applying to the gas sector has also been adopted.

12.56   The lack of decisive progress and the bleak outlook for development of efficient competition in energy markets just after the adoption of this 'second liberalisation package' have led to a wide debate on the need for further measures or more forceful implementation of the existing rules. The Commission's first analysis of the state of play of liberalisation was summarised in a 'Progress Report' presented by the Commission to the Council and the Parliament by the end of 2005. Similar observations have also led to the launch of the ongoing sector inquiry into the gas and electricity markets by the Commission's antitrust services.[60] This inquiry, launched in June 2005, constitutes the widest ranging empirical fact finding launched by the Commission in the antitrust field to date. The Commission identified significant shortcomings for the sectors in this inquiry and called for urgent action to complete the liberalisation process. The inquiry has also inspired the Commission to carry out a series of inspections

---

[56] See in this respect Guidelines of the Commission on the effect on trade concept contained in Arts 81 and 82 of the Treaty.

[57] These interpretative notices are available on the Commission's web site and address the following issues: Unbundling; Role of regulators; Public service obligations; Distribution; Exemptions from certain provisions of the Third Party Access regime; Security of electricity supply; Labelling; Security of gas supply; and Gas Storage.

[58] Regulation 1228/2003 of the European Parliament and of the Council of 26 June 2003 on conditions for access to the network for cross-border exchanges in electricity [2003] OJ L176/1.

[59] For an (old) example of an antitrust analysis on the basis of contractual electricity flows, see Reorganisation of the electricity industry in Scotland (Notice pursuant to Art 19(3) of Regulation 17) [1990] OJ C245/9.

[60] See cases 39.172 and 39.173 on the web site of DG COMP. See press release IP/05/716.

both in the gas and the electricity sector in the course of 2006. The final findings of this inquiry are due at the beginning of 2007 and will be presented together with the strategic energy review undertaken by the Commission's services responsible for the implementation of the liberalisation legislation (DG TREN). In this manner, the Commission intends to combine the different available Community instruments—liberalisation directives and antitrust tools—in order to achieve an effective market opening, which will require further legislative measures and effective enforcement of EC competition law.

(vi) The Security of Supply Directives   As the Community is expected, in the longer **12.57** term, to become increasingly dependent on gas imported from non-EU sources, whilst, at the same time, gas markets are being liberalised, a certain number of legislative measures have been adopted in order to ensure the security of gas supplies in this new market environment. Directive (EC) 2004/67[61] thus foresees a relatively flexible, minimal common approach for guaranteeing security of supply, amongst others in case of 'major supply disruptions'. The Directive addresses the roles and responsibilities of the different market players in the new environment in which incumbent monopolies no longer explicitly or implicitly ensure security of supply within the territory of a given Member State.[62]

This Directive especially emphasises the historical role of long-term supply contracts **12.58** between foreign producers and Community importers and indicates 'that such contracts will continue to make a significant contribution to overall gas supplies as companies continue to include such contracts in their overall supply portfolio'.[63] These contracts nevertheless need to remain compatible with antitrust rules, as will be shown below. Whilst promoting the adoption of measures such as long-term gas contracts, minimum stocks in gas storage and sufficiently diversified pipeline and liquefied natural gas (LNG) infrastructure, the Directive explicitly acknowledges the need to avoid placing disproportionate burdens relating to security of supply measures on new entrants.

The most constraining obligation imposed on Member States requires them to ensure, in **12.59** a public service perspective, that supplies for household customers are protected in the event of partial disruption of national gas supplies, like extremely cold temperatures. National measures adopted within the framework of this Directive, continue to underlie the general conditions laid out in Article 86 EC.

(vii) The Energy Charter   The Energy Charter process was initiated in order to stimu- **12.60** late economic recovery in Eastern Europe and the then Soviet Union and to ensure security of supply to the Community. This charter, reaching far beyond Europe's borders, was subsequently complemented by a legally binding agreement called the 'Energy Charter Treaty'.[64] This Treaty is designed to promote East–West industrial co-operation in the

---

[61] Council Directive (EC) 2004/67 of 26 April 2004 concerning measures to safeguard security of natural gas supply [2004] OJ L127/92–96.

[62] A Security of Supply directive was also adapted for the electricity sector: Directive (EC) 2005/89, [2006] OJ L33/22–27.

[63] 11th recital of the Directive.

[64] The Charter was signed in 1994 and entered into force in April 1998: Council and Commission Decision (EC, ECSC, Euratom) of 23 September 1997 on the conclusion, by the European Communities, of the Energy Charter Treaty and the Energy Charter Protocol on energy efficiency and related environmental aspects [1998] OJ L69/1.

energy sector by providing legal safeguards in areas such as investment, transit, and trade. The Treaty has been signed or acceded to by fifty-one states plus the European Communities, but not, for the time being, by Russia, the EC's main interlocutor in this respect.

12.61   The impact of this Charter on competition would be biggest in the area of transit.[65] Indeed, each contracting state must take the necessary measures to facilitate the transit of energy products in line with the principle of freedom of transit and without discrimination on the basis of the origin, destination, or ownership. The Community is to be considered as one entity for the purposes of the Charter Treaty, which means that gas transport between Member States, for instance, is not to be considered as 'transit' and continues to be governed exclusively by EC legislation. The Charter Treaty however is relevant for a number of important existing or future gas import routes from a number of Caspian States, through Russia to the Community.[66]

(4) Interaction between Sectoral Directives and Antitrust Enforcement

(a) Introduction

12.62   The enforcement of competition rules ensures, in general terms, that State barriers which are being removed by the liberalisation Directives, are not replaced by anticompetitive behaviour by commercial operators having the same effect of maintaining national barriers or hampering effective competition.

12.63   From this perspective, it is logical that both the Directives and the antitrust enforcement in the gas and electricity sectors have a common objective: to ensure effective freedom of choice of energy customers, which should lead to competition developing in the market and possibly to competitive pricing, all other parameters remaining constant. The Commission, more particularly, takes the view that competition can only be introduced if three conditions[67] are met: (1) suppliers are free to compete for customers; (2) customers are free to change suppliers;[68] and (3) an effective TPA regime is introduced and kept in place.[69]

12.64   In the case of the gas and electricity sectors, the competence for ensuring competitive markets has not been left solely in the hands of the European and national competition authorities: antitrust law has been supplemented, as set out above, by sector-specific legislation. This legislation has essentially entrusted sectoral regulators with the task of looking after the functioning and the access rules applying to the transport and distribution networks. The basic premise is that sector-specific regulation is required to secure open access to the network, whereas competition law is a more adequate tool to guarantee competition on supply markets. As this chapter on energy demonstrates, antitrust authorities have however intervened on network access issues. Regulators, especially in more mature regulatory systems, also have a number of competencies relating to the monitoring of supply markets.

---

[65] See Wälde and Gunst, above, p 213.

[66] For more information, see <http://www.encharter.org>.

[67] See also L Hancher and R De Vlam, 'Mergers in the electricity sector—relevant markets and related issues'[2004] European Energy Law Report I-29ff.

[68] Recital 20 of the Electricity Directive and recital 18 of the Gas Directive.

[69] Commission Competition Report 2001, p 41, point 96 and the speech of Commissioner Monti of 21 September 2004.

In view of the significant overlap of competencies and the interrelationship between the **12.65**
different elements of the energy chains, competition authorities and NRAs in charge of
implementing the liberalisation legislation, must co-operate closely. Consultation is advisable when fixing enforcement priorities, in order to avoid duplication of work or gaps in
enforcement practice. Consistency becomes mandatory, however, when applying national
energy legislation and competition rules to individual cases.[70]

Both competition authorities and energy regulators have set up networks for co-operation **12.66**
between peers. Whereas the Commission's competition services and the national competition authorities (NCAs) meet within the context of the European Competition Network
(ECN),[71] regulators meet, *inter alia*, in the context of the Florence and Madrid regulatory
fora, mentioned above. Collaboration between authorities in the energy sector has, in practice, become very close. This co-operation is such that meetings and negotiations with the
parties are regularly held jointly in antitrust cases.[72] Co-operation between competition
and regulatory authorities is also important in merger cases.[73]

This co-operation has its limits, however, most obviously in the area of information **12.67**
exchange. This type of collaboration between competition authorities is covered explicitly
in Article 12 of Regulation 1/2003. To the extent that a sectoral regulator has been granted
explicit antitrust competencies, such as the United Kingdom's Ofgem, information
exchange can take place in this formalised environment.[74] Formal information exchange
between the Commission on the one hand, and, pure regulators on the other, currently
remains a 'black box'. Information exchange can obviously take place with the consent of
the companies concerned. Even without such consent, it could be argued that information
which both authorities could have obtained individually through their respective investigatory powers from the company concerned,[75] could possibly be exchanged, if the confidentiality requirements of both authorities are sufficiently similar and the rights of defence
of the companies concerned are adequately protected under the relevant legal regimes. In
the absence of any explicit framework, the solution for this type of exchange should probably be found in the general rules regarding the obligation of loyal co-operation between
the Commission and national administrations, as expressed, amongst others, in the
Zwartveld[76] case law of the ECJ, whilst requesting the obligations of Regulation 1/2003 and
in particular Article 28 thereof.

---

[70] See Klotz and Nyssens, 'Energy day: first sectorial high level meeting within the ECN' (2004) 3 CPL 33.

[71] See Commission notice on co-operation within the network of competition authorities (2004).

[72] eg Commission, Competition Report 2000, p 48, point 136. See more generally the *Synergen*, *Eni-Gazprom* and *Marathon* cases mentioned further in sections E, F and G.

[73] See, for instance, cases M.2947 *Verbund/Energie Allianz (2002)*; and M.3440 *ENI/EDP/GDP (2004)*.

[74] Art 12(1) of Regulation 1/2003 clearly provides, however, that the information exchange takes place 'for the purpose of applying Articles 81 and 82 EC'. This excludes, on the basis of this regulation, the passing of information from competition authorities to regulators for the purpose of applying their (purely) regulatory competencies.

[75] Such an approach would typically cover the exchange of information which both types of authorities could have obtained by means of requests for information. Information obtained by competition authorities in the context of on-the-spot investigations would however typically not qualify for such type of exchange.

[76] Case C-2/88 *Imm., Zwartveld* [1990] ECR I-3365; and C-275/00 *Franex* [2000] ECR I-10943.

12.68   The reservations against full information exchange between competition and regulatory authorities stems from the fact that the former have the single and clear-cut competence of tackling barriers to competition, whereas the latter generally have a role that can go well beyond that of ensuring competitive energy markets. Their role indeed often includes responsibilities relating to planning or ensuring security of supply. Their objectives may also be social and/or environmental in nature.[77] Some authors also point to the risks of so-called 'regulatory capture'.[78] It would indeed be unacceptable for information obtained through antitrust instruments to be used for the purpose of implementing regulatory policy in an unrelated area, for example planning or environmental protection, without violating the companies' rights of defence. It is for this reason that NRAs cannot participate in ECN meetings, in which individual cases are discussed.

(b) Reciprocal Limitations by Sectoral Legislation and Antitrust Law

12.69   It must be emphasised, at this stage, that the existence of sectoral legislation, one of the main purposes of which is to foster competition, does not exclude the application of more general antitrust provisions. In other words, compliance with sectoral legislation, both at national and European level, neither exempts companies from observing antitrust law nor removes them from the scrutiny of the authorities entrusted with their enforcement.[79]

12.70   In view of the fundamental principle of hierarchy of norms, secondary legislation such as the liberalisation Directives, cannot diverge from or even limit the inherent scope of application of the rules of primary EC antitrust law. This means, for instance, that NRAs must exercise their powers in conformity with Community law, ie not only following the relevant sectoral directives, but also in line with the competition provisions of the Treaty.[80] The Commission will not refrain from intervening in cases where the intervention of a sectoral regulator does not, in its opinion, warrant a sufficient degree of competition. In the telecommunications sector, for instance, the Commission has intervened against the tariff structures of Deutsche Telekom, which had been agreed by the competent German regulator.[81]

12.71   Whatever the formal hierarchical legal rule, it must nevertheless be acknowledged that any industry practice explicitly or implicitly approved by Community liberalisation legislation or Commission decisions[82] will somehow benefit from a favourable presumption, under the antitrust rules.[83] Such a presumption is itself based on the assumption that the secondary

---

[77] See Art 25 of the Gas Directive and Art 23 of the Electricity Directive. See, more generally, M Harker and C Waddams Price, 'Consumers and antitrust in British energy markets', above, pp 30ff. See also the study of the Belgian regulator CREG about its co-operation with the Belgian NCA, (F) 020711-CREG-91 of 11 July 2002.

[78] See Ritter and Braun, above, p 924.

[79] Case 66/86 *Ahmed Saeed* [1989] ECR I-838. In certain countries, for example Germany, the situation has historically been different. Indeed, German legislation has long excluded the application of national antitrust law to the electricity and gas sectors.

[80] See as regards the necessity for the enforcement action of regulators to be in line with antitrust law, Case C-198/01 *Consorzio Industrie Fiammiferi* (CIF) [2003] ECR I-8055.

[81] (EC) 2003/77: Commission decision of 21 May 2003, *Deutsche Telekom AG* [2003] OJ L263/9. Such approach is in line with other legal systems like in the US. See, amongst others, CM Naeve and JL Pfeffer, 'Emerging antitrust issues in the transition to deregulated electricity markets', 28th Fordham conference, point IV, B, 1.

[82] For instance, decisions applying Art 22 of the Gas Directive or Art 7 of Regulation 1228/2003.

[83] See, as regards the relationship between the energy Directives and the antitrust rules, for instance, the opinion of Stix-Hackl AG in Case C-17/03, *VEMW*, not yet reported.

legislation is compatible with Treaty rules. This, however, also implies that sector-specific rules should be interpreted in line with the applicable antitrust provisions.[84]

(c) Respective Strengths of Competition and Regulatory Measures

One of the traditional difficulties for antitrust enforcement when it comes to liberalising **12.72** industries is that there are, at best, only limited possibilities for establishing new pro-competitive structures in the market.[85] Antitrust tools were originally conceived to tackle existing barriers to competition, as a 'negative' instrument, whereas kick-starting effective competition may often require more far-reaching pro-competitive measures of a positive nature, especially in the first years of a liberalisation process. Structural measures, like the splitting up of dominant supply companies, and the organisation of gas release programmes, such as those established in the initial phases of liberalisation in the UK, Spain, and Italy, are generally considered measures of legislative or regulatory, rather than antitrust, nature.[86] Some commentators have also claimed that merger enforcement has been used as a means to liberalise markets and as such constitutes a misuse of powers. The CFI, however, clearly rejected such arguments in its *EDP/GDP* judgment, emphasising that liberalisation directives have the effect, if not the object, of introducing competition to a sector. 'It is no surprise therefore that the competition objective of the merger regulation should also be assumed by one of the objectives of the second electricity and gas directives. Consequently, the fact that the Commission pursued the practical realisation of the Second Gas Directive cannot indicate a misuse of powers when that objective is also the objective for which that regulation conferred its powers on the Commission.'[87]

This judgment will most probably encourage the Commission to continue including far- **12.73** reaching, quasi-regulatory measures in a number of antitrust cases, as well as in merger decisions.[88] The virtual power plants (VPP) remedy accepted by the Commission in the *EDF/ENBW* case provides a typical example of such intervention. The *Marathon* cases, dealt with further in section G.3.d, provide clear examples of similar intervention by means of traditional antitrust instruments, as the Commission has largely helped to re-shape access conditions to the gas networks concerned.[89]

Use of such instruments is typical in the transitory phases of the liberalisation process and **12.74** constitutes a succedaneum for incomplete European and/or national regulation. It can therefore be presumed that as the process develops and as differences between national regulatory regimes decrease, fewer quasi-regulatory antitrust interventions will be necessary.

Article 7(1) of Regulation 1/2003, which codifies the competence of the Commission for **12.75** adopting structural measures on the market, will nevertheless reinforce the legal standing of such Commission interventions. Whatever the merits of such involvement, it should be

---

[84] Case T-184/97 *BP Chemicals/Commission* [2000] ECR II-03145, point 64.
[85] See speech of M. Monti of 21 September 2004.
[86] An identical trend can be identified in the US: see Naeve and Pfeffer, point G.
[87] Case T-87/05 *EDP/Commission*, not yet reported, point 96.
[88] See, for instance, Hancher and De Vlam, above, p 69.
[89] For a similar approach at national level, see for instance, the *Elsam* case dealt with by the Danish NCA, mentioned further in paras 12.400 ff.

acknowledged that a purely legislative or regulatory approach for market design problems is preferable to 'regulation by antitrust'. Indeed, the latter type of *ex post* intervention does not offer the same guarantees of predictability and often involves complex monitoring exercises for which competition authorities lack sufficient time and resources.

12.76 Finally, the sheer number of particularly time-critical and technical problems arising during implementation of the liberalisation of a network industry will generally argue in favour of regulators with particular technical expertise taking responsibility for monitoring such issues. The judicial obstacles experienced by the Bundeskartellamt in its attempts to streamline the German access conditions by means of antitrust enforcement[90]—in the absence of a national energy regulator—constitute a clear reminder of the limits of the quasi-regulatory antitrust approach.

(5) Special Characteristics of Energy Markets

(a) Structure of Energy Markets

12.77 In recent years, the Commission has placed greater emphasis on economic criteria in its antitrust assessment. Such assessment is all the more crucial in gas and electricity cases since market power in these sectors is clearly linked to the possibility of supplying energy at times of peak demand, both on a daily and seasonal basis. Market power, in other words, depends not merely on generation capacity or gas volumes available to a market player, but more obviously on its capability to offer 'peak supplies', as opposed to so-called 'base-load'.[91] To analyse market power in such a context it is necessary to look beyond market shares in broadly defined electricity or gas wholesale markets.

12.78 In electricity markets, analysis of market power entails examining the generation mix of electricity companies and the ranking of the power plants in order of merit[92] within the relevant market on the basis of their marginal costs. For gas, the extent to which different market operators have access to 'flexibility instruments' (eg storage, flexible upstream contracts, or linepack) will play an equally crucial role. A detailed economic analysis of the fundamentals of the market is warranted, particularly in view of the oligopolistic nature of these industries.[93]

12.79 In a number of recent merger cases detailed energy-specific econometric models have been used in order to determine the likely price increase which might result from the merger at stake. Although such modelling has, so far, not been used to the same extent in Commission antitrust cases, it could become a more standard practice, especially in the context of assessing large horizontal joint ventures relating, for instance, to infrastructure projects and the effect they might have on the relevant national markets.

---

[90] See paras 12.380–12.385.

[91] See in this regard, Case M.3268 *Sydkraft/Graninge* (2003), points 46ff; and the decision of the Dutch NCA in Case *Nuon/Reliant* (2003) points 14ff, available at <http://www.nmanet.nl>. See, more generally, P Moelgaard and C Kastberg Nielsen, 'The competition law and economics of electricity market regulation' (2004) ECLR 37ff.

[92] See in this respect Arts 2.16 and 11 of Directive (EC) 2003/54 and points 302 and following and point 532 of the M.3440 *ENI/EDP/GDP* decision (2004).

[93] In this sense, amongst others, Case M.1673 *VEBA/VIAG* (2000) point 226; and Case M.3268 *Sydkraft/Graninge* (2003), points 59ff.

One of the key factors that led to the success of telecommunications liberalisation is that this **12.80** sector was experiencing a number of crucial technological changes at the same time as deregulation policies were introduced. An equally radical shift comparable to the introduction of mobile telecommunications or Internet is certainly lacking currently in the gas and electricity sectors.[94] Both sectors are clearly mature industries in the vast majority of Member States.

This should not however, hide the fact that both sectors are currently experiencing a number **12.81** of crucial technological developments. The scale of economies in electricity generation is, for instance, clearly diminishing.[95] Indeed, a key technological driver in the current industry transition is the emergence of smaller, shorter lead-time power plants, using combined cycle gas turbines (CCGT) technology as compared with the more traditional fossil steam plants.

The environmental constraints imposed by the Kyoto Protocol and its implementation **12.82** measures at EU and national level contribute to the technological changes in the industry: they lead to shifts in the type of primary energy sources used to generate electricity, with, for instance, a move away from coal to gas. The CO_2 emissions trading schemes reinforce this tendency by internalising the costs of pollution more clearly than before. The way in which the trading of emissions trading certificates affects electricity wholesale prices is also a current source of debate.[96] Certain aspects of the schemes are reviewed under State aid rules (see further paras 12.97–12.101). There have also been complaints about gaming of the emission trading exchanges. Nevertheless, it is fair to say that, until very recently, environmental issues have had relatively limited direct impact on the assessment of antitrust cases, contrary to State aid cases.

The economics of upstream gas has also been characterised by the rapid development of **12.83** substantially improved exploration and production technology.[97] This trend is most noticeable in the upstream LNG chain, which has seen costs decrease dramatically in recent years. Unlike the telecommunications sector, these developments essentially concern costs efficiencies in the production of a commodity, the nature of which has not intrinsically changed. It nevertheless remains a fact that if a trend develops in Europe for non-incumbents to develop so-called 'merchant' CCGT facilities, as happened in the course of the liberalisation process in the UK, antitrust concerns relating to market power in wholesale supply markets may be allayed. Indeed, the market entry of such new suppliers, at the right point in the merit curve,[98] could inhibit generators from exercising market power. This in turn means that the exercise of market power needs to be surveyed strongly until new plants are commissioned. With the same token, it needs to be maintained that incumbents do not create and maintain entry barriers for new power plants.

The structure of electricity and gas markets is also important for an understanding of how **12.84** competition works in these markets. This structure may take the form of a so-called 'pool'

---

[94] As regards the technological evolution in the electricity sector, see Chevalier, pp 192ff.

[95] Naeve and Pfeffer, point I and V, A. See generally Chevalier, pp 234ff.

[96] See Launch of the antitrust proceedings by the Bundeskartellamt in December 2006 for pricing in costs for CO_2 certificates into electricity prices despite the fact that the certificates were allocated for free. The generators claim that they are entitled to price in costs for CO_2 certificates, as so-called 'opportunity costs'.

[97] See Energy Information Administration (EIA), 'Natural Gas 1996: issues and Trends', ch 4, pp 81ff.

[98] See, as regards this concept, Preliminary Report of the Commission's energy sector inquiry, point 343.

or be contracts based.[99] In certain cases both systems may coexist in the same geographic area with only a limited share of energy being traded via the pool and the remaining share being delivered in accordance with bilateral contracts.

12.85 A 'pool' system is a mandatory, organised market for the trading of electricity or gas where a system operator invites bids from offering parties and instructs those with the lowest bids—following the 'merit order'—to input gas or electricity into the network depending on the demand.[100] In the more common, contracts-based market, each supplier must conclude contracts with customers before delivering electricity or gas on the network in accordance with the estimated off-take of these customers. The network operator has to balance the system and may instruct some suppliers to reduce or increase their deliveries to the system. In any event, it is likely that the quantities input by a supplier will not match the total of the quantities off taken by its customers (or vice versa). The difference between the contractual quantity and the actual quantity delivered to or taken from the system (so-called 'imbalance') must be settled between the suppliers and the network operator. When investigating such pool systems, close attention should be paid to ensure that companies are not able to bend the rules by setting artificially high prices. To date, the only example of a pool to have attracted general praise is the Scandinavian Nordpool system. This pool has the particular advantage of covering different Member States, thereby offering a prime example of regional integration of previously national markets leading to the reduction of market power of each of the incumbent national operators in their traditional supply area.

(b) Impact of Infrastructure and Investment Needs

12.86 Competition cases often depend on a perception of risk. A historical characteristic of the energy sector is the use of large capital investment, significant sunk costs and relatively long lead times. In the pre-liberalisation system, characterised by legal monopolies, economies of scale led to large-scale investments, which were based on security of consumption. This has led, in the gas sector for instance, to a rigid (gas) chain, in which the long-term upstream supply contracts are replicated in the gas transport contracts, and down into the down-stream gas sales contracts.[101] This has given rise to below-market risks, often limited to political and regulatory risks.[102]

12.87 In the new environment, risk in the energy sector, however, should be assessed as in other sectors where large capital investments are made. In other words, in liberalised markets, players should not be allowed to argue that contractual relations be used to maintain risk at lower than market level as an end in itself. Otherwise, investment distortions will arise between the energy sectors and other sectors and within the energy sector between different energy sources, such as, for instance, oil exploration and wind technology.

---

99 For an overview of different types of organised markets, see Chevalier, pp 199ff.
100 Electricity pool systems exist in Portugal, Spain, and Scandinavia, amongst others.
101 See P Roberts, 'Structuring effective gas sales and gas transportation arrangements' (2004) IELTR 190.
102 For further discussion see M Klein, 'The risk premium for evaluating public projects'; and Brealey, Cooper and Habib, 'Investment appraisal in the public sector', both in *Oxford Review of Economic Policy* (1997) 13(4), and the accompanying essays.

In view of these characteristics, amongst others, for the time being, there is little pressure for **12.88** market entry by completely new players in most European countries: 'import competition'[103] from established operators from neighbouring Member States, as well as entry by gas operators in the electricity sector and vice versa, can thus still be considered the main sources of likely rivalry, if at all. [104] Truly new players tend to be more niche players, for instance in co-generation or renewable energy, rather than fully-fledged operators like the existing ones.

One of the key questions that arises in such a context is to what extent the large sunk costs **12.89** and long lead construction times encountered in these industries, justify the conclusion, on the one hand, of long-term purchase contracts for the input of gas or coal and, on the other hand, of downstream sales contracts for the supply of customers. These issues will be dealt with in more detail below.

(6) Impact of State Involvement

In view of the importance of electricity and gas supplies for their national industry, many **12.90** Member States have either retained full ownership of the major suppliers (or have maintained golden shares), or have historically set up mechanisms to regulate, harness, and protect this industry. The latter type of State intervention has taken numerous forms, including shielding demarcation contracts from antitrust law in Germany, imposing co-operation in the production and the supply of electricity between independent generators in the Netherlands or the encouragement of joint gas sales in Norway.

Such State intervention has a direct bearing on the application of the antitrust rules **12.91** provided for in Articles 81 and 82 of the Treaty. Indeed, under the State compulsion doctrine,[105] companies whose behaviour in the market has been specifically imposed on them by compulsory legislation can, for that reason, escape the application of those provisions. This does not, however, mean that the legislation concerned escapes the scrutiny of Articles 86 EC, or the case law prohibiting restrictive legislation in violation of the combined Articles 3, 10, and 81 EC.

(7) Stranded Costs

In order to facilitate the transition from a monopolised (regulated) market to a liberalised **12.92** one, adjustments are necessary. Existing players may have made, in view of a captive consumer basis, investments which are no longer profitable or long-term agreements which are no longer acceptable once the market opens up and the customers become free to switch suppliers. The argument most often heard—probably in view of the historic developments in the UK—is that a drop in prices, after liberalisation, would lead to losses for the suppliers who invested in a pre-liberalisation environment.

---

[103] See also in this respect, Preliminary Report of the Commission's energy sector inquiry, points 174–175ff.
[104] See, as regards the former M.1853 *EDF/EnBW* (2000), point 30 and as regards the latter Case (M.3440) *ENI/EDP/GDP* (2004).
[105] See amongst others, Joint cases C-359/95 P and C-379/95 P *Commission/Ladbroke racing* [1997] ECR I-6265, point 33; Cases 40/73 to 48/73, 50/73, 54/73 to 56/73, 111/73, 113/73 and 114/73 *Suiker Unie/Commission* [1975] ECR 1663, points 12 to 24; and Case C-198/01 *Consorzio Industrie Fiammiferi*, not yet reported, points 45ff.

12.93   Recent experience tends to demonstrate that until now incumbents have not suffered any severe losses as the result of liberalisation. There are provisions in both the Electricity and the Gas Directives[106] that would allow Member States to take transitional measures. The stranded costs issue which has arisen also in the US,[107] has mainly been dealt with under State aid rules and is described in the next section. Indeed, Member States, when confronted with such stranded costs problems, have often opted to offer financial compensation for expected losses.

12.94   However, the issue may also arise, although in less apparent form, in an antitrust context, for instance, when priority access is granted to historic contracts on interconnectors or when the compatibility with antitrust rules of new infrastructure projects dating from before liberalisation is being assessed.[108] In the latter case, one key condition for such (quasi) exclusive use of infrastructure is that it will only be acceptable if the operator effectively also continues to support the costs of construction of the infrastructure.

12.95   The issue of stranded costs was dealt with in the Non Fossil Fuel Obligation (NFFO) and Non Fossil Fuel Purchasing Authority (NFPA) cases, in the beginning of the 1990s.[109] These cases concerned the arrangements made in the context of the privatisation of the UK electricity industry for the continued functioning of the nuclear power stations. An obligation to purchase from nuclear installations was placed on regional distribution companies with a concomitant obligation to buy from renewable sources. In parallel, a Fossil Fuel Levy was raised from sources of electricity derived from fossil fuels. A sum equivalent to the amount raised by these levies was passed on to the distribution companies to compensate them for having to buy the expensive nuclear and renewable electricity.

12.96   The Commission, at the time, accepted these arrangements on the basis that these arrangements ensured security of supply through fuel diversity. The UK measures, however, could have been justified by referring to the temporary pro-competitive effects of the overall scheme of liberalisation and privatisation and, indeed, the threat of a short-term supply disruption occasioned by financial difficulties in the nuclear industry.[110] In any event, it is likely that these long-term supply agreements between distribution companies and Nuclear Electric have contributed to an 'orderly transition' to a more competitive market.

(8) State Aid Enforcement in the Energy Sector

12.97   Although antitrust and merger enforcement constitutes the main topic of the present chapter, it is worth mentioning briefly the areas in which State aid enforcement complements the wider regulatory and antitrust measures. State aid cases in the energy sector can be broadly subdivided into three main clusters.

---

[106] See Art 26 of Electricity Directive 96/62 and Art 27 of the Gas Directive concerning take-or-pay contracts.

[107] See, as regards the US, Naeve and Pfeffer, p 24.

[108] See judgment of the ECJ in Case C-17/03, *VEMW*, described further and *Viking Cable* case: Commission Competition Report 1995, p 125 and Notice pursuant to Art 19(3) of Reg 17 *Viking Cable* [2001] OJ C247/11.

[109] Reorganisation of the electricity industry in England and Wales (Notice pursuant to Art 19(3) of Regulation no 17) [1990] OJ C191/9.

[110] See L Hancher in *Competition Law & Energy markets* (Claeys & Casteels, 2005) pp 467ff.

First, there are the cases which involve individual aid to the incumbents, best illustrated by **12.98**
the aid granted to EDF in the form of unlimited State guarantees which enabled EDF to
obtain better credit ratings and in the form of special tax concessions.[111] Such State support
may aggravate the behaviour of incumbents aggressively protecting their core businesses in
home markets and at the same time expanding into new markets.[112] This type of case therefore complements antitrust enforcement relating to the wholesale supply markets.

Secondly, there are a number of cases concerning aid schemes granted to environmentally **12.99**
friendly ways of generating electricity from such sources as wind, biogas, biomass, or CHP.[113]
Such types of electricity may, for instance, be granted preferential dispatching on the network or benefit from State-imposed wholesale prices. The judgment of the Court in
Preussenelektra/EZH[114] results from one such case. The main issues in this type of case are,
first, whether it really involves State aid and, second, whether the State aid at issue can be
regarded as necessary to ensure environmental protection and sustainable development
without having disproportionate effects on competition and economic growth.[115]

Thirdly, there are the cases related to the so-called 'stranded costs', referred to in the previ- **12.100**
ous section.[116] Stranded costs refer to commitments, such as long-term purchase contracts
or guarantees of operation entered into by historical incumbent energy suppliers before
liberalisation. Public compensation for stranded costs arises generally when old power
plants, built before liberalisation, are no longer sufficiently efficient to be able to participate
in a competitive market. The Commission, in a nutshell, requires that it is proven that
the inefficiency of these investments causes real losses after liberalisation.[117] Although these
cases generally only concern the electricity sector, one case also incidentally concerns the
gas sector.[118]

Finally, the Commission's energy services have investigated how companies generating **12.101**
electricity using nuclear power are making use of the decommissioning funds they have to
set aside for future dismantling of the nuclear plants.[119]

---

[111] See Commission press release IP/03/1737, as well as S Catalan, Paroche and C Goguel, 'Le contrôle des
aides d'Etat dans la mise en place du marché intérieur de l'électricité: le cas EDF' (2004) 1 CPN 4.

[112] EDF has acquired in recent years a number of companies in the UK, Germany, and Spain amongst others.

[113] See, amongst others, M Könings, 'Wind Energy and the context of EU State Aid law'(2004) European
Energy Law Report I-73ff; and B Renner-Loquenz, 'State aid in energy taxation measures: first experiences
from applying the environmental aid guidelines 2001'(2003) European State Aid Law Quarterly 21. See, in
the latter respect also the special tax regimes for energy intensive users, amongst others in Germany
(IP/04/406).

[114] Case C-379/98 *Preussenelektra* [2001] ECR I-2099.

[115] See Community guidelines on state aid for environmental protection [2001] OJ C37/3.

[116] See in this respect, amongst others, B Allibert, 'Compensations of stranded costs in the European
Union electricity sector' (2003) European State Aid Law Quarterly 3.

[117] See Commission Communication relating to the methodology for analysing State aid linked to
stranded costs in the electricity sector of 26/7/2001(Letter to the Member States SG(2001) D/290869 of
6/8/2001) available on the Commission's web site. See the latest decisions relating to Portugal (Commission
press release IP/04/112) and Slovenia (Commission press release IP/05/126).

[118] See 'Italy–Stranded costs of the electricity sector, State Aid no N 490/2000', available on the Commission
web site. The gas aspects related to allegedly irrecoverable costs linked to the take-or-pay contract signed by
Italian electricity generator ENEL with Nigerian gas producer NLNG.

[119] Commission press release IP/04/130.

B. Security of Supply and Public Service Obligations

(1) Introduction to the Security of Supply Issue

12.102 'Security of supply' is a concept which covers a very wide range of issues, including technical elements (the physical availability of an energy source for a certain customer or customer group), economic issues (investments to ensure energy availability over a longer term period) and political issues (import dependency upon sometimes unstable third energy-producing countries and the ensuing risk of large scale interruptions).[120] At times, the concept of security of supply has also been considered to encompass price-related topics, for instance the consideration that energy must always be available at a 'reasonable cost'.[121]

12.103 At the Community level, a number of legislative texts have been adopted to guarantee security of supply.[122] The challenge, for antitrust and regulatory assessment alike, is to balance these values correctly. This involves an exercise, described in more detail in chapter 1 of this book, of balancing short-term maximisation of competition and longer term competition incentives.[123]

12.104 The importance of security of supply, as a matter of fact, should not be underestimated since it is undoubtedly more crucial in the energy industry as compared to other liberalising network industries like telecommunications or transport.

12.105 Pre-liberalisation, decisions of the Commission explicitly limited the application of antitrust rules because of security of supply concerns.[124] Those decisions were made purely within the framework of Articles 81 and 82 EC (to the exclusion of Article 86 EC). It can be doubted whether such approach is still valid in light of the case law of the CFI[125] and the guidelines of the Commission on Article 81(3) EC, primarily as regards so-called 'efficiencies'.[126]

(2) Security of Supply in the Context of Article 86 EC

(a) Pre-liberalisation Precedents

12.106 Security of supply constitutes a public interest ground which can be invoked within the conditions laid down in Article 86 EC. This concept could, for instance, be invoked to

---

[120] See generally as regards security of supply: G Luciani, 'Security of supply for natural gas markets. What is it and what is it not ?', INDES working paper (2004), available at <www.ceps.be>; and J Stern, 'Security of European natural gas supplies. The impact of import dependence and liberalisation' (2002) Journal of the Royal Institute of International Affairs 12ff. For electricity see, amongst others, LJ de Vries and RA Hakvoort, 'The question of generation adequacy in liberalised electricity markets', INDES working paper (2004), available at <www.ceps.be>.

[121] See for instance, Art 3.3 of the Electricity Directive.

[122] See para 12.57.

[123] Speech of M. Monti of 21 September 2004, cited above. It has been argued that the Commission, in its antitrust analysis, often takes a very favourable view of agreements that expand or ensure generation and transmission capacity in the long-term, even if this may be harmful to customers in the short term (Copenhagen Economics study p 5.)

[124] Commission Decision (EEC) 93/126 of 22 December 1992, *Jahrhundertvertrag*, [1992] OJ L50/14; and Commission decision (EEC) 94/153 of 21 February 1994, *International Energy Agency*, [1994] OJ L68/35.

[125] Case T-528/93 *Metropole Television/Commission* [1996] ECR 649.

[126] See Commission guidelines on the application of Art 81(3) EC, points 42, 60.

justify measures relating to the exploitation of natural resources in order to maintain a certain minimum level of domestic energy production.[127] This principle was first recognised by the Court in its *Campus Oil* and *Greek Oil Monopoly*[128] judgments. In the first case, the Court accepted an obligation, imposed by the Irish authorities, on all oil importers, to purchase 35 per cent of their requirements from the only local—state-owned—refinery, *inter alia*, because of the seriousness of the consequences that an interruption in oil supplies may have for the country's security. In the second, the Court condemned a monopoly for importing refined oil products.

This line of case law was further developed in the *Almelo*[129] case and the cases brought **12.107** by the Commission against electricity and gas import and export monopolies,[130] which explicitly raised the issue of the compatibility of the exclusivity practices with Article 86 EC. The latter cases are crucial to the extent that the Court reversed the burden of proof as regards the conditions of Article 86(2) EC in favour of the Member States. Indeed, the Court found that, in view of the allegations of the Member States concerned, the Commission did not sufficiently substantiate why the application of the competition rules in these cases would *not* have obstructed the performance of the public service tasks assigned to the companies concerned which enjoyed exclusive or special rights.

Several Directives adopted since then provide guidance on the type of energy-specific **12.108** justifications which can be invoked in the context of Article 86(2) EC, without however providing much detail about the perilous assessment of the proportionality of the measures concerned.[131]

(b) Formalising Public Service Obligations in Energy Legislation

The Energy Directives do not merely contain provisions concerning market opening. Both **12.109** Directives indeed state that public service requirements are a fundamental prerequisite of the liberalisation process.[132]

(i) **Electricity Sector** In the electricity sector, Member States *may* impose, on undertak- **12.110** ings operating in the electricity sector, public service obligations relating to security, including security of supply,[133] regularity, quality and price of supplies, and environmental protection, including energy efficiency and climate protection. Member States *must* however ensure a universal electricity service: all household customers, at least, must enjoy the right to be supplied with electricity of a specified quality within their territory at

---

[127] Ritter and Braun, above, p 916.

[128] Cases 72/83 *Campus Oil* [1984] ECR 2727; *Greek Oil monopoly* [1990] ECR I-4747.

[129] Case C-393/92 *Almelo* [1994] ECR I-1477.

[130] Cases C-157/94 *et seq, Commission/Netherlands, Italy, France and Spain* [1997] ECR I-5699ff.

[131] More guidance is provided in the interpretative notices published by DG TREN in 1999 (Directive 98/30; 2nd meeting of Follow-Up Group; 29 April 1999; Public Service Obligations) and in 2004 (Note of DG Transport and Energy on Directives 2003/54/EC and 2003/55/EC on the internal market in electricity and natural gas: Public Service Obligations of 16/1/2004), both available on the Commission web site.

[132] See Recitals 24–26 of the Electricity Directive and Recital 27 of the Gas Directive.

[133] The issue of security of supply as a public service obligation in the electricity sector has been addressed explicitly in an Irish State aid case (Commission press release IP/04/913).

reasonable, easily and clearly comparable, and transparent prices.[134] This can be done, for instance, by appointing a so-called 'supplier of last resort'.[135]

12.111 The Directive (EC) 2005/89 concerning measures to safeguard security of electricity supply, and infrastructure investment, moreover indicates that Member States must ensure a 'high level of security of electricity supply'.[136] This Directive is however clear in that it considers appropriate interconnection levels between Member States—ie the development of an effective internal electricity market—and the establishment of liquid wholesale markets as crucial tools for achieving security of supply.[137]

12.112 This underlines the fact that diversity of market players—a necessary condition for liquid wholesale markets—and competitive access to cross-border electricity links are crucial to the security of electricity supplies in general.

12.113 (ii) **Gas Sector** The Gas Directive contains similar provisions to the Electricity Directive.[138] The main difference lies in the absence, in the Gas Directive, of any obligation of universal service towards household customers. This is due to the fact that natural gas is a source of primary energy which, unlike electricity, can be substituted to a certain extent.[139]

12.114 The Directive on security of gas supplies[140] generally obliges Member States to monitor security of supply issues like the national supply/demand balance and ensure measures that cover peak demand and deal with shortfalls of one or more suppliers.

12.115 In practice, once the Energy Directives have been implemented, there should be no doubt as to the existence of such obligations, which will tend to be formally enacted in law. Any problems will thus centre on the issue of proportionality. This—by nature delicate— exercise should be facilitated by the legislative transparency created by the liberalisation process: indeed, it should become increasingly simpler to compare and benchmark national systems against each other and thus determine to which extent some of them are unnecessarily intrusive in guaranteeing the public well-being.

C. Commission Enforcement Policy in the Energy Sector

(1) From Formal Decisions to Settlements and Back Again

12.116 It has been argued that the Commission, in recent years, has taken a rather lenient approach as regards the application of competition law in the gas and electricity sectors, compared to its policy in other sectors.[141] Two explanations for this are traditionally advanced: the first refers to the concern to ensure security of supply following liberalisation.

---

[134] Art 3 of the Electricity Directive
[135] See as regards this concept M.3318 *ECS/Sibelgaz* (2003).
[136] Art 3.1 of the Directive.
[137] Arts 1 and 3.2 of the Directive.
[138] See, for details para 12.109.
[139] This difference has led DG TREN to consider that public service obligations in the gas sector may generally be applied in a more restrictive manner. Note of DG TREN of 1999, cited above, p 4.
[140] See above para 12.57.
[141] See, for instance, Copenhagen Economics study, p 9.

A second, more credible, explanation is that the Commission has been giving priority, in a sector characterised by important lead times and long-term projects, to promoting competition in the long run, rather than just in the short run.

It is also a fact that in between its decision in the *Ijsselcentrale* case in 1991[142] and the *GDF/ENI/ENEL* decisions in 2004,[143] the Commission settled all of its antitrust cases through commitments and contractual amendments rather than taking infringement decisions. Some ongoing antitrust investigations have also been closed in the context of simultaneous merger cases.[144] This settlement approach was probably linked to the fact that, in the first stage of liberalisation, the Commission considered that the companies concerned should be allowed some time to adopt their functioning to the new competitive environment.   **12.117**

This period appears to have come to an end in 2004–2005. Indeed, in 2003, the Commission announced its intention to adopt more formal decisions in the future.[145] This energy-specific tendency corroborates a more general trend which was formalised in Regulation 1/2003. This Regulation is indeed supposed to allow the Commission, and by ripple effect, also the NCA, to concentrate their enforcement activities on the most serious antitrust violations. Even if settlements are to be achieved after May 2004, they are more likely to take the form of Article 9 decisions, rather than of informal settlements.   **12.118**

The Commission has also announced that it would extend its efforts from upstream production activities to downstream wholesale and retail activities, including issues such as long-term exclusive downstream supply contracts. This enforcement practice is likely to be centred on wholesale markets, but to the extent necessary to establish precedents will also include national or even regional retail markets. Equally, it can be expected to centre on cross-border transport networks, rather than on local distribution network issues. Such priority questions will be extensively discussed between European antitrust authorities within the framework of the energy subgroup of the ECN.[146]   **12.119**

Another new phenomenon in the energy sectors is the sector inquiries. The Commission launched a sector inquiry on 13 June 2005,[147] whilst several NCAs or NRAs also possessing antitrust powers have also conducted such inquiries, both for the purpose of better identifying the most damaging antitrust violations and for more general competition advocacy purposes.[148]   **12.120**

---

[142] See *Almelo* case described above in para 12.107.

[143] See below n 298.

[144] See for instance the way in which the Verbändevereinbarungen electricity have been addressed in Case M.1673 *Veba/Viag* (2000). Another example concerns the contracts between Compagnie Nationale du Rhône (CNR) and EDF which have been addressed in Case M.1853 *EDF/EnBW* (2001).

[145] See XXXIIIth Competition report (2003), points 72ff; and speech of M. Monti of 21 September 2004, cited above.

[146] See Klotz and Nyssens, 'Energy day: first sectorial high level meeting within the ECN' (2004) 3 CPL 33.

[147] See 'Energy Sector Inquiry Issues Paper' of 15 November 2005, available at <http://www.europa.eu.int>, as well as Commission press release IP/05/716.

[148] See, for instance, the joint study of the Italian NCA and NRA: Provvedimento of 9/2/2005, available at <http://www.agcm.it>, as well as the joint investigation of the Austrian NCA and NRA, dated 2005, available on <http://www.e-control.at>.

(2) When will the Effects of Liberalisation be felt by Consumers?

12.121 The crucial question is when the consumers can be expected finally to reap the benefits of the liberalisation process. Experience derived from deregulation in the US and the UK suggests that the potential efficiency gains from competitive energy markets may take a decade or longer to be fully realised.[149] It should be emphasised in this respect that the task of liberalising Europe's gas and electricity markets appears more daunting than the deregulation of these sectors in a number of American States. Indeed, apart from the different federal structures of the EC and the US, both gas and electricity sectors in the US were traditionally characterised by a more fragmented structure, whereas the European model traditionally reflected a higher level of centralisation and State control over energy entities.[150] The same observation applies when comparing gas liberalisation in the UK and in the EU: whereas the UK has a relatively diverse gas production structure, the EU as a whole relies heavily on a more limited number of core suppliers.

12.122 The fact that the transformation of the energy markets may, in reality, only constitute a medium-term goal, implies a number of complications for the regulatory and antitrust authorities active in these markets. Those authorities must remain attuned to market developments, and during the transition period must ensure, on the one hand, that the market is not trusted blindly in the initial period while, on the other hand, avoiding over-regulation and micro-management once energy markets have actually become active.[151] During the transition period, both regulators and antitrust authorities are still confronted with high concentration levels and practices or arrangements, such as long-term capacity reservation contracts or tacit collusion, that survived from the previous market structure.[152] Residues of the past which incumbents use strategically should be challenged, whilst one could take a more lenient approach for a while at least, with respect to the legitimate expectations of companies who might claim that certain commercial practices were perfectly acceptable in pre-liberalisation times and have not been addressed explicitly by the liberalisation legislation. A particular difficulty arises from the fact that Articles 81 and 82 EC have been conceived largely to operate as guarantees that competitive markets will not become less competitive, rather than to function as instruments to force monopolised industries into a more competitive structure.[153]

D. Market Definitions in the Energy Sector

12.123 As is true for all other sectors, the definition of the relevant market plays an essential role when applying European competition law to the energy sector. The market definition has great significance for the assessment of the market power by the undertakings concerned

---

[149] Naeve and Pfeffer, point I.

[150] See amongst others, Naeve and Pfeffer, point I and Energy Information Administration (EIA), *Natural Gas 1996: issues and Trends* ch 4, p 81ff.

[151] See in this respect the evolution of the regulatory framework and antitrust enforcement in the telecommunications area.

[152] See in this respect, Preliminary Report of the Commission's energy sector inquiry, section 'Main findings', pp 4–6.

[153] Speech of M. Monti of 21 September 2004, cited above. See also in this respect *EDP/Commission* judgment of the CFI quoted in para 12.72.

(mergers and Article 82 EC). Market share thresholds are also decisive when applying the *de minimis* notice[154] and certain block exemption regulations in Article 81 cases.[155]

The definition of the relevant market requires a definition of the product and geographic **12.124** market concerned. A characteristic peculiar to the energy sector is that it has changed significantly over time and continues to do so. This calls for a careful assessment of temporal issues, particularly in merger cases which require a forward looking approach. Another factor that needs to be taken into account is the scope of national legislation implementing the directives (date of full market opening, possibility to switch from the regulated to the non-regulated segment). The following comments relate to the situation pertaining at the end of the year 2006.

When defining energy markets, the Commission relies on the notice on the definition of the **12.125** relevant markets[156] and case law which, taking into account that there have only been a limited number of antitrust decisions in the energy sector, is mostly found in merger decisions.[157]

Whilst the original structure of the gas and electricity sectors was quite similar (network **12.126** industries) and whilst both sectors underwent the same liberalisation process, it nonetheless appears appropriate to distinguish between the sectors for the purpose of this chapter. In this respect it should also be noted that the situation varies significantly between Member States. Accordingly, the following description can only give an overview of the most important considerations when assessing markets, and does not claim to be complete. In particular, there is no detailed assessment of the situation in the ten Member States that joined the European Union on 1 May 2004, where changes in market structure at times appear particularly dramatic.

(1) The Gas Sector

(a) The Product Concerned

Natural gas is a primary source of energy. Whilst these primary sources of energy can com- **12.127** pete against each other or with electricity in certain applications (eg when taking investment decisions for a new production facility), the Commission has consistently taken the view that natural gas does not form part of the same product market as the other primary energy sources and/or electricity.[158] Only in Germany does the issue of competition between primary sources of energy still appear to constitute a (political) issue, with a section of the gas industry still claiming, for instance, that gas does not constitute a separate

---

[154] [2001] OJ C368/13.

[155] For details on horizontal and vertical restraints in the energy sector see below section E and section F. The market share thresholds do not play a role for core restrictions such as price fixing or territorial sales restrictions.

[156] [1997] OJ C372/5.

[157] As in other sectors, the Commission only defines a market if necessary for the case in question. If all possible market definitions lead to the same result, the definition of the market is generally left open, for example Case M.2443 *E.ON/Powergen* (2001), para 9.

[158] cf Case M.493 *Tractebel/Distrigaz (II)* (1994), para 23. Since then established Commission practice, eg Case M.1383 *Exxon/Mobil* (1999), para 49ff; Case M.2822 *EnBW/ENI/GVS* (2002), paras 10ff; Case M.3440 *EDP/ENI/GDP* (2004), para 14.

market, but is part of a more general 'warmth market' (in German 'Wärmemarkt'). Substitutability with other primary energy sources and/or electricity is however at most partial and once the investment decisions are taken switching costs are generally significant. In any event, the use of natural gas is characterised by different rigidities in consumption, transport, and capacity to store the product, which also result in different cost structures.

12.128 Natural gas is a homogenous product, at least once it is processed following production (ie once it is cleaned of substances such as sulphur, which compromise proper use, be it for technical or commercial reasons) to meet agreed standards. Whilst natural gas can be produced in different countries (eg the UK and the Netherlands in the EU and Russia, Algeria, and Norway outside the EU[159]) or transported in different ways (pipeline gas or so called LNG—liquefied natural gas) or produced from different types of gas fields (associated gas or 'pure' gas fields), the subsequent use of the gas is not determined by these factors. Accordingly, natural gas that comes from different origins or is produced/transported in different ways can form part of the same product market.[160]

12.129 Although it cannot be denied that further quality differences emerge here and there on a geographic basis, nevertheless, there is a traditional distinction between two gas qualities, so called H-gas (high calorific value, which is produced everywhere) and so called L-gas (low calorific value, which is produced mainly in the large Groningen field in the Netherlands and marketed in the surrounding Member States). Whether H-gas and L-gas form part of the same product market is not yet clear under existing Commission practice.[161]

12.130 There are good reasons, however, to assume different product markets taking into account pricing trends and the existence of non-interchangeable pipeline systems rendering switching costs very high. Nevertheless, it should be noted that H-gas can be turned into L-gas by adding nitrogen.[162]

(b) The Product and Geographic Markets

12.131 When defining geographic and product markets, it is necessary to distinguish between upstream and downstream activities. Upstream means all activities until natural gas is sold to wholesalers for subsequent sale/distribution in the EU. Downstream means all activities thereafter.

---

[159] There are some minor quality differences between gas from various origins. However these differences do not determine the use of the gas. For the distinction between H-gas and L-gas see below.

[160] Left open in Case M.1383 *Exxon/Mobil*, (1999)para 18; and Case M.1532 *BP Amoco/Arco* (1998), para 17, as it was claimed that certain customers might have a preference for deliveries from certain (stable) regions for security of supply considerations.

[161] In the merger Case M.1383 *Exxon/Mobil* (1999) the Commission originally took the view that H-gas and L-gas belong to different product markets, but later dropped the distinction (cf paras 112ff of the decision). It is debatable, however, whether the Commission would adopt the same approach today, with the possible exception of the upstream markets. See also E Cabauin *Competition Law & Energy markets* (Claeys & Casteels, 2005), p 84ff.

[162] See, on the technical and commercial possibilities to transform one type of gas into the other (so-called 'quality conversion'), the studies realised by the Dutch regulator DTE (<http://www.dte.nl>) and the Belgian regulator CREG (<http://www.creg.be>).

(i) **Upstream Markets** For the upstream sector the Commission has so far distinguished **12.132** between the following product markets: (1) exploration;[163] (2) development of gas fields, production, and sale of gas[164] generally to wholesalers and to a limited extent also to very large industrial customers or electricity producers;[165] (3) transport through upstream gas pipelines[166] or via LNG ships; and (4) processing of gas, which can take place at the production facility or at the entry point into the downstream systems.[167]

According to established Commission practice the geographic scope of these markets is as **12.133** follows: (1) exploration—world wide;[168] (2) development, production, and sale—EEA and possibly Russia and Algeria;[169] (3) upstream transport—taking into account the fact that transport from A to B cannot be replaced by transport from A to C, the transport markets are generally defined narrowly[170] (demand side perspective), however it might be possible to group certain pipelines or LNG routes together into one market (eg British Northern North Sea and British Southern North Sea);[171] and (4) processing—taking into account that gas is processed to meet the specifications of the transport facilities subsequently used (upstream or downstream), the processing market generally follows the geographic dimension of the transport markets.[172]

Whilst there is established Commission practice for these main markets, a number of ques- **12.134** tions remain open and the ongoing liberalisation process will lead to new questions possibly calling for an adjustment/fine-tuning of the market definitions. These questions relate in particular to the production and sales market, but can also be of relevance to the transport and processing markets. The following issues are particularly noteworthy:

Certain customers have met their entire demand in gas supplies or a large proportion **12.135** thereof on a long-term basis. Accordingly they are no longer an available outlet for suppliers. It has therefore been argued that customers who are not bound by long-term contracts and who are still looking for supplies form a separate product market (so-called forward markets).[173]

---

[163] Case M.1383 *Exxon/Mobil* (1999), paras 15ff. In Case M.3052 *ENI/Fortum Gas* (2002), para 13 the Commission clarified that exploration for oil and gas is part of the same market.

[164] Case M.1383 *Exxon/Mobil* (1999), paras 15ff. Gas production as such cannot be considered to be a market as this requires that supply and demand meet.

[165] For example, sale of natural gas by the Norwegian gas producer Statoil to the Dutch consortium of electricity producers SEP later leading to a court case ((1994) ECR 1911).

[166] Case M.2745 *Shell/Enterprise Oil* (2002), paras 10ff.

[167] Case M.2745 *Shell/Enterprise Oil* (2002), paras 10ff.

[168] Case M.1383 *Exxon/Mobil* (1999), para 15ff.

[169] Case M.3052 *ENI/Fortum Gas* (2002), para 14. However countries which are not connected with other Member States via an interconnector do not form part of the same market (eg Finland). The recent increase of gas sales via LNG ships might lead to a further expansion of the geographic scope of the market concerned.

[170] For further details on the definition of transport markets see below under downstream markets.

[171] Case M.1532 BP *Amoco/ARCO* (1998), paras 38ff. For the upstream transport of Norwegian gas cf Case M.3052 *ENI/Fortum Gas* (2002), para 15.

[172] cf Case M.2745 *Shell/Enterprise Oil* (2002), para 13.

[173] Case M.672 *BP/Sonatrach* (1996), para 12; cf also Commission notice pursuant to Art 19(3) of Regulation 17 in Case IV/E-3/35.354 *Britannia Gas Condensate Field* [1996] OJ C291/10.

12.136 The distinction between the market of committed customers and the market of uncommitted customers is however difficult to draw. It was adopted in only a limited number of decisions and presupposes the validity of long-term contracts.[174] It also renders the assessment of market power in the market of uncommitted customers next to impossible. It furthermore introduces considerations relating to foreclosure effects into the market definition. It is therefore submitted that the distinction between uncommitted and committed customers is not a valid one, possibly with the exception of markets in which capacity restraints are established, eg transport and/or processing infrastructure.[175]

12.137 Another open question relates to the distinction between long-term and short-term supply contracts and whether they are part of the same product market. Long-term contracts in the upstream sector are mainly found on the European continent and can be for up to thirty years. Short-term contracts are often concluded at so called gas hubs (eg Zeebrugge or Emden/Bunde). An important argument in favour of separate markets is the price formula applied. In long-term contracts concluded by continental European wholesalers the gas price is directly linked to oil derivatives.[176] In short-term contracts the price is negotiated freely and generally fixed for the duration of the contract.[177] However, the market players and subsequent use of the gas are identical.

12.138 Yet another open question is whether the sale of LNG (liquefied natural gas) forms part of the same market as the sale of pipeline gas.[178] From a demand perspective—pipeline gas and LNG (following re-gasification) are fully interchangeable as far as their use is concerned. Also the prices for pipeline gas and LNG follow the same trends, even if LNG has been traditionally more expensive than pipeline gas. The main difference relates to the supply rigidities of LNG. LNG cargos do not allow for continuous supply on a daily basis and require additional infrastructure to balance these rigidities, eg short-term storage and re-gasification capacity. On the other hand, LNG can be used to store higher quantities of gas in a reduced volume. As a consequence, LNG is often used, once it has arrived onshore, to meet peak demand, for instance on days of extreme cold weather. Also LNG facilitates spot sales. On balance however, it is assumed that the sale of pipeline gas and LNG form part of the same market.[179]

12.139 The liberalisation process has also led to the creation of new markets, namely access to liquefaction and re-gasification infrastructure. In the past, the infrastructure was exclusively used by the owners. However, the creation of a Third Party Access regime (TPA)

---

[174] See in this respect paras 12.416–12.427.

[175] Case M.1532 *BP Amoco/Arco* (1998), para 56; Case M.2745 *Shell Enterprise Oil* (2002), para 20.

[176] See for a description of this so-called gas-oil link, the Issues Paper published by DG Competition in the context of the gas sector inquiry (Case 39173), as well as DG TREN's inquiry (Case 39173), as well as DG TREN's benchmarking report 2005, both available on the Commission's web site.

[177] For an overview of the different price indices see Final Report of the Sector Inquiry (2007), Chapter B.a.II.5 Price Issues (gas).

[178] In favour of one market Case M.672 *BP/Sonatrach* (1996) para 17. For a full description of the LNG market, see *Security of gas supply in open markets. LNG and power at a turning point*, OECD/IEA, 2004.

[179] For further detail on the relevance of LNG for the gas sector see Final Report of the Energy Sector Inquiry (2007), Chapter C.b.III (gas study).

opens the infrastructure for third parties. No major precedents exist in respect of these facilities, but it would appear possible that complaints are lodged relating to new major infrastructure projects in particular those benefiting from exemptions under Article 22 of the second Gas Directive and for which no more appropriate use it or lose it system and/or short term access possibilities exist.[180]

Last but not least the question arises as to whether upstream gas transports via pipelines are part of the same product market as upstream gas transports via LNG ships, provided they serve similar transport routes. Both methods of transport appear interchangeable from the demand perspective. So far the question has not required an answer as there are only a limited number of potential cases where alternative means of transport exist (eg gas transports from Algeria to Spain and to Italy). **12.140**

(ii) Downstream Markets   For the downstream sector, the Commission has so far distinguished between the following activities: (1) sales; (2) transport; (3) storage/flexibility instruments; and (4) blending. Within these activities the Commission has identified a number of product markets. It should, however, be noted that these categorisations do not necessarily apply to all Member States. **12.141**

A common feature in almost all Member States is however that, in the past, sales and transports were carried out—within a well defined territory—by a single vertically integrated company. The effects of horizontal demarcation (agreement not to enter the supply area of the neighbouring supplier) combined with this vertical integration (transport and supply, and possibly other activities such as storage or retail) can still be found today. They continue to have a significant impact on the definition of the geographic scope of the markets concerned. **12.142**

Sales   As regards sales the Commission today distinguishes between four main customer groups:[181] regional distributors, local distributors, industrial and commercial users, and private households. On the basis of this distinction the Commission has identified the following supply markets:[182] (i) sales (by wholesalers) to power plants; (ii) sales (by wholesalers) to regional distributors; (iii) sales (by regional distributors) to local distributors; (iv) sales (by local distributors) to final users (ie households = retail); and (v) sales to industrial and commercial users. The markets can be distinguished on the basis of the quantities purchased, the respective off-take patterns (most prominently: differences in the consumption during summer and winter and possibility of interrupting the contract), the duration of the contracts, the price formula used, the expertise of the buyers in negotiating gas supply contracts, the connection to the transmission/distribution network, and the margins of profitability when selling to the various customer groups.[183] **12.143**

---

[180] See, for a summary description, of the LNG chain and an antitrust analysis of some of its features, Nyssens and Osborne, 'Profit splitting mechanisms in a liberalised gas market: the devil lies in the detail' (2005) 1 CPN 25.

[181] The distinction between eligible and non-eligible customers, which was a consequence of the 1998 Gas Directive, will increasingly lose its relevance because—according to the 2003 Gas Directive—all non-household customers should be eligible as of July 2004, whilst households must follow at the latest in July 2007.

[182] cf Case M.2822 *EnBW/ENI/GVS* (2002), paras 13ff for the German market and Case M.3440 *EDP/ENI/GDP* (2004), paras 190ff for the Portuguese market. Case M.4810—*Gaz de France/Suez* (2006), not yet published for the French and Belgian markets.

[183] See, for instance, Case M.3440 *EDP/ENI/GDP* (2004), paras 215ff.

12.144 As indicated above, these market definitions are not necessarily relevant in all Member States. In certain smaller Member States or in Member States where liberalisation had an early start, the intermediate levels (regional or local suppliers) might not exist (eg Luxembourg or the UK).[184] In others it might be possible/necessary to distinguish further between industrial customers and commercial customers[185] (at least in some countries small commercial customers could be part of the same product market as households if they buy similar quantities and have a similar off-take pattern). Also the degree of market opening by national legislation might play a part, albeit decreasingly, as full market opening is foreseen by July 2007 (if one disregards certain countries that may have asked for a derogation benefit from exemption).[186]

12.145 As regards the geographic scope of these markets it should be noted that a Europe-wide market cannot yet be assumed to exist. In some (large) Member States such as Germany[187] it might even be necessary to distinguish between separate regional and local supply markets. This assessment is essentially based on the consideration that the existing TPA regimes are not yet sufficient to allow the conclusion that a European or national market exists.[188] The scope of the supply markets to (regional or local) distributors is thus as large as the traditional supply area of the incumbent supplier, whilst for industrial users it is assumed that the markets are local in scope unless the industrial users are or can be connected easily to the pipeline of the supplier on the upper level of trade.

12.146 *Transport*   As regards the transport markets in the downstream sector it is necessary to make the same distinctions as for the supply markets. It is therefore necessary to distinguish between supra-regional, regional, and local transports, but the situation in the individual Member States varies significantly. The relevant market is to be defined on the basis of the underlying request of the shipper taking into account the fact that transport from A to B cannot be replaced by transport from A to C.[189] The shipper inserts the gas at point A and withdraws it at point B, a withdrawal at point C is of no interest to the shipper. In this respect it is irrelevant what is done with the gas following the withdrawal (consumption, sale, or transport).

---

[184] In certain countries, vertical integration of the wholesale and retail supply levels also occurred after the commencement of liberalisation. See for instance the acquisition by Electrabel of the 'intercommunales' traditionally responsible for the retail supply activities in Belgium (Cases M.3318 *ECS/Sibelgaz* (2003) and following).

[185] For very large industrial customers such as large power plants that buy directly from producers see above.

[186] See however Case M.3440 *EDP/ENI/GDP* (2004), paras 210ff for the Portuguese gas market, which qualifies for a derogation as an emerging market, however the Commission also took into account the foreseeable future effects. The argument was rejected by the CFI upon appeal.

[187] Merger E.ON/Ruhrgas, which was dealt with by the German competition authority in cases: B8—109/01 (*E.ON/Gelsenberg*) and B8—149/01 (*E.ON/ Bergmann*), published on the web site of the Bundeskartellamt under <http://www.bundeskartellamt.de/wDeutsch/archiv/EntschFusArchiv/2002/EntschFus02.shtml>. The refusal to authorise the merger by the Bundeskartellamt was later overturned by the German Ministry of Economic Affairs, but the market definition was not challenged. cf also the consultation document of the Bundeskartellamt of 28 January 2005 published as an annex to the press release under <http://www.bundeskartellamt.de/wDeutsch/aktuelles>.

[188] Case M.2822 *EnBW/ENI/GVS* (2002).

[189] cf for the air transport sector, where similar considerations apply, Commission Decision (EEC) 92/213 *British Midland v Aer Lingus* [1992] OJ L96/34, recitals 14ff.

In contrast to other transport markets (air transport, rail) the precise transport route is **12.147** generally irrelevant for customers as long as all other conditions are equal (eg transport tariff, balancing regime). Direct transport from A to B can thus be replaced by transport from A to B via D. For the shipper it is also irrelevant whether the gas molecules inserted into and withdrawn from the pipe are identical. Gas is—within the limits outlined above—a *commodity*. Also there is no need for the physical gas flow to correspond to the contractual gas flow (for example, a shipper may insert gas of Norwegian origin into a downstream pipeline in northern Germany and withdraw gas of Russian origin in southern Germany, since southern Germany is an area primarily served by Russian gas).

Whilst the Commission has not yet taken an explicit position on so called 'back-to-back' **12.148** or 'swap' arrangements (a company sells gas to another company at point A and the latter resells the same volumes back to the first at point B), it would seem plausible that this type of arrangement can also be regarded as forming part of the transport market. From the perspective of the shipper, back-to-back arrangements—although consisting of two supply contracts—have to a large degree the same effects as a transport contract: gas of a certain quantity and quality is inserted at point A of a gas network and withdrawn at point B of the gas network.[190]

It cannot be denied, however, that there are also certain differences between transport and **12.149** back-to-back arrangements, eg as regards the contractual partners who are in charge of the transport[191] and the risk allocation (eg in times of a failure of the gas pipeline). Moreover, such arrangements have a number of implications on the opportunities for the shipper/swapping company to enter the territory of the supply company traditionally active in the supply area concerned: whereas a transport contract could allow a shipper to divert gas along a pipeline (or to choose a different exit point), a back-to-back arrangement will often require the renegotiation of its supply components with the same supply company whose territory is targeted. It could thus also be argued that swaps are part of the supply markets.

Storage   Access to storage is a separate product market.[192] Only access to storage provides **12.150** a shipper with the opportunity to balance the fluctuation in demand from its customers (*swing*), eg during summer and winter. From the demand perspective it does not matter whether the shipper is granted access to physical storage or virtual storage as long as the commercial conditions are comparable. Also other instruments providing shippers with flexibility such as access to flexible supply contracts[193] or to linepack (storage capacity of gas pipelines) can be part of the same product market.[194] Whether it is necessary to make

---

[190]   See for a description of such swap arrangements, the Issues Paper published by DG Competition in the context of the inquiry (Case 39173), available on the Commission's web site.

[191]   In times of legal unbundling, a pure transport contract is concluded with the transport unit of a vertically integrated company, whilst the back-to-back arrangement would be concluded with the supply unit.

[192]   cf Case M.1383 *Exxon/Mobil* (1999), para 261.

[193]   See Case M.3868—*DONG/Elsam/Energi E2* (2006), paras 58ff, in which it is argued that 'flexible trading' is not an alternative (too unpredictable), whilst flexible purchase contracts and interruptible supply contracts (eg with CHP plants) can be a source providing comparable flexibility.

[194]   Different however Case M.3868—*DONG/Elsam/Energi E2* (2006), para 56, in which it is argued that for the Danish market line pack is not part of the same market due to the high costs associated with the use of line pack.

a distinction between pore and cavern storages—given their minimum and maximum input and output capacity as well as their delivery circle—is not yet clear.[195] In two cases, the Commission has, however, provided a number of indications as to the existence of differences between seasonal and daily storage markets.[196]

12.151   The geographic scope of storage markets has been defined narrowly by the Commission in its past practice (eg in *Exxon/Mobil* the Commission considered the area around Munich to be a separate geographic market[197]). In favour of such a narrow market definition it can be argued that flexibility is required in the vicinity of the fluctuation in demand. On the other hand it should be considered that flexibility is needed in a certain supply area (eg balancing zones), which speaks in favour of a congruence of the geographic scope of supply balancing and storage markets.

12.152   *Blending*   The transformation of H-gas into L-gas (the reverse process is not possible) is a separate product market. Gas suppliers that have a portfolio of H-gas, but want to market L-gas to customers, need to transform their H-gas into L-gas. There is no established Commission practice yet as regards the geographic scope of blending markets, but it would seem likely that blending markets correspond to the supply markets.

12.153   *Special issues*   It is still debatable whether interruptible services (whether in supply, transport, or storage) are part of the same product market as firm services or whether they should be considered a separate market. The argument in favour of regarding them as being part of the same market is that the price for interruptible services are generally aligned to the price of firm services and merely reflect the risk of interruption. In favour of separate markets speaks the argument that—from the demand perspective—the products are only interchangeable if the customer does not care about an interruption, eg because he has back-up or because he can reduce the consumption.

12.154   Another open question is whether services at peak demand and stable services offering no flexibilities (eg band deliveries) are part of the same product market. In the past this issue did not arise as customers traditionally met their entire demand with one and the same supplier, ie this supplier was a stable and a flexible supplier at the same time. But following liberalisation an increasing number of customers at least consider multiple supplier models, one offering stable supply and the other offering flexibility or both offering parts of both. From an economic perspective there are good arguments for assuming different markets for peak and stable services (eg price and flexibility), but in practice it will be very difficult to know where to draw the line as many contracts offer some flexibility combined with a certain stable supply.

12.155   It is expected that in future new product markets will evolve, eg as regards financing or transport services.[198] It is also expected that the liberalisation process will lead to wider geographic markets in particular if the obstacles to effective transport are removed.

---

[195] Case M.1383 *Exxon/Mobil* (1999), para 262. See also Case M.3868—*Dong/Elsam/Energi E2* (2006), para 127 (200 km for pore storage and 50 km for cavern storage).

[196] See Cases M.3410 *Total/Gaz de France* (2004); and M.3086 *Gaz de France/Preussag* (2003).

[197] cf Case M.1383 *Exxon/Mobil* (1999), para 262ff. Case M.3868—*Dong/Elsam/Energi E2* (2006), para 127 *et seq*.

[198] cf Case M.2744 *RWE Gas/Lattice International* (2002).

(2) The Electricity Sector

(a) The Product Concerned

Electricity is a homogenous product and accordingly electricity markets have similarities to   **12.156**
other commodity markets.[199] Competition in the supply markets, at least as far as large customers are concerned, essentially takes place on the basis of the price and to some degree on
flexibility which can also be considered to be a price element. Whilst one needs to distinguish between alternating and direct current (also referred to as AC and DC), both types
can be transformed into each other without difficulties. They are thus part of the same
market. A distinction might however be necessary for different time periods—eg hours—
when electricity is supplied (peak supply or off-peak supplies), as a supply during one hour
cannot be replaced by supplies at a later hour (inelasticity of demand).

In continental Europe all transmission system operators have formed the so-called UCTE-   **12.157**
zone,[200] where the frequency of alternating current amounts to 50 Hz and is synchronised.
Scandinavia and the UK/Ireland are not part of the UCTE-system, but are linked to it by
DC interconnectors. There is significant cross-border trade without however allowing the
conclusion that—at this stage—a common (ie European-wide) market exists.[201]

Electricity is produced on the basis of primary energy sources (most prominently nuclear,   **12.158**
coal, and gas) and renewables (most prominently water and wind). The production costs
vary substantially between different plants, which leads to a rather unusual merit order
curve. Also the fuel mix varies significantly from one country to the other, but the bulk is
still produced on the basis of fossil fuels such as coal, lignite, oil, and gas.[202] From the perspective of industrial consumers it generally does not matter how the electricity was generated
or in which country it was generated. The key issues are the commercial conditions (ie price
and flexibility) and possibly the reliability of the supplier. In certain retail markets however
a customer preference for renewable energy can be observed, without suggesting that these
are at this stage separate product markets.

Whilst in certain applications electricity can be replaced by the use of primary energy   **12.159**
sources (eg gas), it has been established that electricity forms a separate product market.[203]
The underlying reason is that once an investment decision for electricity is taken, switching costs to other sources of energy are high. There are also other factors such as price and
flexibility in supply (impossibility to store), which distinguish electricity from other energy
sources.

Over recent years a variety of different legislative frameworks for the electricity sector has   **12.160**
developed in the EU Member States taking into account the possibilities offered by the

---

[199] cf Case M.2801 *RWE/Innogy*, (2002) para 10. For a detailed description of the value chain and in
particular the wholesale markets cf Final Report of the Sector Inquiry (2007), Chapter B.b.I. Introduction
(electricity).

[200] For details see <http://www.ucte.org>.

[201] Final Report of the Sector Inquiry (2007), Chapter B.b.II.1 Concentration and market power
(electricity) and the corresponding annex.

[202] For details see <http://public.eurelectric.org>.

[203] cf Case M.493 *Tractebel/Distrigaz (II)* (1994), para 23. Since then established Commission practice,
eg Case M.3440 *EDP/ENI/GDP* (2004), para 14.

Electricity Directive (pool system, single buyer system, system of bilateral contracts) and the political preferences in the countries concerned. Also the speed of market opening has varied significantly from Member State to Member State. It is thus only logical that the definition of product markets and their geographic scope also varies.[204] Nonetheless the basic features of all markets seem to be comparable and are described below.

(b) The Product and Geographic Markets

12.161 The Commission essentially distinguishes the following activities in the electricity sector:[205] (1) supply; (2) transmission; and (3) other services (eg balancing).[206]

12.162 **(i) Supply Markets** Within the supply activities the Commission identified a number of different product markets. So far the Commission has distinguished between the following markets: (1) generation, imports, and wholesale; (2) sales to small/local distributors; (3) sales to industrial customers; and (4) sales to commercial and final customers/households (retail). In some cases the Commission did not distinguish between the product markets (2) to (4), but established a distinction between price-oriented customers and service-oriented customers.[207]

12.163 In a number of cases the Commission has also considered whether—within the wholesale sector—separate trading markets exist consisting of (1) OTC—over the counter/bilateral contracts; (2) trade with physical products at stock exchanges (eg spot deliveries on an hourly basis); and (3) trade with non-physical financial derivatives, but so far has left open the question whether these are separate markets or part of one and the same wholesale market.[208]

12.164 *Wholesale* Whilst a number of questions—as indicated above—remain unanswered (possibly also because there are differences between national markets rendering it very difficult to reach a uniform answer) the existence of wholesale markets as separate product markets is now generally accepted. These wholesale markets comprise sales of electricity by generators and traders as well as sales of electricity physically imported through interconnectors.[209] On the demand side they generally comprise other wholesalers (including financial traders), regional resellers, and possibly also some large industrial customers, which might decide to buy directly on the wholesale market (eg railway companies). Market places are often power exchanges, brokers platforms (OTC) or bilateral deals. A number of different

---

204 Cf. Case M.2801 *RWE/Innogy* (2002), para 8.

205 The most important merger cases were: Case M.1346 *EdF/London Electricity* (1998), paras 12ff (UK); Case M.1673 *VEBA/VIAG* (1999), paras 11ff (Germany); Case M.1853 *EdF/EnBW* (2000), paras 13ff (France); Case M.2684 *EnBW/EDP/Cajastur/Hidrocantabrico* (2002), paras 16ff (Spain); Case M.2801 *RWE/Innogy* (2002), paras 8ff (UK); Case M.2947 *Verbund/Energie Allianz* (2002), paras 24ff (Austria); Case M.3268 *Sydkraft/Graninge* (2003), paras 8ff (Scandinavia); Case M.3440 *EDP/ENI/GDP* (2004), paras 31ff (Portugal); Case M.3857 *EdF/AEM/Edison* (2005)—(Italy); M.4180—*Gaz de France/Suez* (2006) not yet published (Belgium).

206 See generally E Cabau in *Competition Law & Energy markets* (Claeys & Casteels, 2005), p 9ff. See also Final Report of the Sector Inquiry (2007), Chapter C.c.II. Balancing Market (Electricity).

207 Case M.2947 *Verbund/Energie Allianz* (2002), para 29.

208 Case M.3268 *Sydkraft/Graninge* (2003), para 14; Case M.3440 *EDP/ENI/GDP* (2004), paras 37ff.

209 Case M.1557 *EdF/Louis Dreyfus* (1999), paras 16ff; Case M.1673 *VEBA/VIAG* (2000), para 18, Case M.2947—*Verbund/Energie Allianz* (2002), paras 43ff, and in particular 47; Case M.3268 *Sydkraft/Graninge* (2003), paras 14ff.

products are traded at these markets places, eg spot (day ahead) versus forward/futures (eg year ahead) or peak demand (normally weekdays between 8 am and 8 pm) versus base load.

The geographic scope of these wholesale markets is in most cases national.[210] Factors which **12.165** were considered when analysing the geographic scope of the markets were:[211] (1) the degree of interconnection between the national markets leading to congestion at significant time periods, which in turn leads to significant price differences during these time periods; (2) differences in the market regulation/design; (3) different fuel mixes for the production of electricity leading to different cost/price structures; (4) different policies as regards stranded costs; and (5) different national policies as regards CO_2 emission plans. The general assumption that national markets exist should not be taken (erroneously) to mean that in certain Member States the geographic scope of the markets is even smaller[212] or that certain Member States are part of the same geographic market.[213]

Sales to distributors   Sales to small/local distributors can constitute a separate product **12.166** market. In this respect it is considered that distributors have a specific off-take pattern and conclude a specific type of contract (contracts with a long duration covering the entire demand of the distributor).[214] Also, the distributors often do not appoint personnel specifically for electricity purchases. A difficulty in this market definition is that there is no precise cut-off point (What is the difference between a large distributor that purchases electricity on the wholesale market and a small distributor belonging to a separate market?). If, however, the existence of a separate product market regarding sales to small distributors is assumed, the geographic scope of that market is generally considered to be national.

Sales to industrial clients   Sales to industrial clients can often be distinguished from sales **12.167** to distributors (for reasons given above) and thus form a separate product market. These sales can also be distinguished from sales to commercial customers and households. The latter have a different off-take pattern and are invoiced on the basis of standard consumption profiles (no metering of the consumption on an hourly basis). Also commercial customers and private households do not have trained personnel to negotiate individual supply contracts (which is generally not the case for large industrial customers); in addition costs for electricity are not a significant factor in their spending, which reduces the incentive to switch.[215] Another distinction used is the connection to the transmission or the distribution grid.[216] The geographic scope of most of these markets is national or regional.

(ii) Transmission   With respect to transmission of electricity, the Commission has so far **12.168** distinguished between the high voltage transmission grids (220 kV upwards), medium voltage transmission grids (not lower than 20 kV), and the low voltage distribution grids.

---

[210] Final Report of the Sector Inquiry (2007), Chapter B.b.II.1 Concentration (electricity) and the corresponding annex.

[211] cf Case M.3440 *EDP/ENI/GDP* (2004), paras 76ff.

[212] For the UK cf Case M.2801 *RWE/Innogy* (2002), para 16; for Germany prior to liberalisation Case M.1673 *VEBA/VIAG* (2000), para 32.

[213] Considered for the Scandinavian market in Case M.3268 *Sydkraft/Graninge* (2003), para 27.

[214] Case M.2947 *Verbund/Energie Allianz* (2002), paras 40 and 41, even if ultimately left open in this decision.

[215] Case M.3440 *EDP/ENI/GDP* (2004), paras 68ff.

[216] M.4180—*Gaz de France/Suez* (2006), not yet published.

As long as the respective grids do not overlap, each grid is deemed to constitute a geographic market of its own.[217] The market can be narrower because transmission from A to B cannot be replaced by transmission from A to C. For further explanation, see paras 12.146–12.149 above.

12.169   As regards interconnectors linking two Member States, it is necessary to consider whether there are competing transmission systems (alternative routes) to bring electricity contractually from one Member State to another. Otherwise it would seem that each interconnector (or set of interconnectors) linking two Member States amounts to a separate product and geographic market. Another possibility would be to argue that interconnectors are lines forming part of the respective high voltage transmission grids of the respective transmission system operators.

12.170   **(iii) Other Services—Balancing Power**   Balancing mechanisms are required in all electricity networks to make up for any shortfall in consumption or generation of electricity (deviation from forecasted demand/supply).[218] If the balance is not maintained within a very narrow band, the tension in the grid would either fall causing stability problems or rise beyond acceptable tolerance levels. There is thus a technical necessity for the transmission system operator to keep the system in balance.

12.171   Since electricity cannot be stored, the balancing system can only function properly if the transmission system operator can add/lower generation capacity or add/lower consumption (eg interruptible customers). Needless to say, that the transmission system operator has to book capacity rights in advance in order to be in a position to call upon these reserve capacities when actually needed. The service is paid for by the users of the network. The payments of the transmission system operator for the capacity reservations are, in many Member States, included in the general transmission tariff, whilst the actual deviation will be charged to the user of the network that has causes the deviation (penalty payments).[219]

12.172   One factor that needs to be taken into account, however, is that deviations within a certain geographic area might level each other out without obliging the transmission system operator to take action with a view to maintaining the balance. The transmission system operators therefore create so called 'balancing zones' in which all deviations are summed up, which allows the users of the transmission system—in particular those with a large supply portfolio—to avoid penalty payments or reduce them to a minimum.

12.173   The Commission has not yet taken a position on whether balancing power is a separate product market or whether it could form part of the wholesale market.[220] The argument in favour of a separate product market is that balancing power needs to be available on short notice and that there is only one customer, the TSO, which has such a demand and there are generally only a very few suppliers who can offer the service.

---

[217] Case M.3440 *EDP/ENI/GDP* (2004), para 34.
[218] Final Report of the Sector Inquiry (2007), Chapter C.c.II. Balancing (electricity) for a description of the existing balancing markets.
[219] Case M.2947 *Verbund/Energie Allianz* (2002), paras 51ff.
[220] cf however Case M.3440 *EDP/ENI/GDP* (2004), paras 51ff.

E. Assessment of Vertical Agreements in the Light of Article 81 EC

(1) Introduction

The Commission's policy with respect to vertical restraints has changed significantly over the last few years.[221] The block exemption Regulation for vertical restraints (Commission Regulation (EC) 2790/1999 of 22 December 1999 on the application of Article 81(3) of the Treaty to categories of vertical agreements and concerted practices[222]—hereafter 'Vertical BER') and the respective guidelines (Commission Notice–Guidelines on Vertical Restraints—hereafter 'Vertical Guidelines')[223] have the effect that fewer vertical agreements fall foul of European competition law. **12.174**

The underlying rationale of the reform on vertical restraints was the Commission's intention to concentrate on those anti-competitive agreements and practices that have a real impact—from an economic perspective—in the market. Vertical agreements of companies with limited market power (as long as they did not contain hard-core restrictions) were deemed to have no such impact. **12.175**

The Vertical BER and the Vertical Guidelines apply to all economic activities including the energy sector.[224] There are currently no special rules applying to the energy sector. In practice, many incumbent energy companies, however, are unlikely to benefit from the Vertical BER. This is due to the fact that the market shares of these companies usually exceed the 30 per cent threshold set out in Article 3 of the Vertical BER. In many cases the market share even exceeds the threshold of dominance, which can lead to a parallel application of Articles 81 and 82 EC. Their contracts thus require individual assessment on the basis of other—general—guidelines in force (eg Commission Notice–Guidelines on the application of Article 81(3) of the Treaty[225]) or past practice. **12.176**

Furthermore, it should be noted that the Vertical BER does not apply to vertical agreements entered into between competing companies[226] and that today many energy companies—previously operating at different levels of trade—can be seen to be at least potential competitors,[227] whether in the purchasing markets or in the markets for selling the products concerned at the subsequent level of trade. For these competing companies the Vertical BER only applies if one of the exceptions provided for in Article 2(4) of the Vertical **12.177**

---

[221] For details see the description of the vertical restraints policy contained in this book.
[222] [1999] OJ L336/21ff.
[223] [2000] OJ C291/1ff.
[224] See *Schnichels/Valli*, Competition Policy Newsletter No 2/2003, p 60ff.
[225] [2004] OJ C101/97ff.
[226] cf Art 2(4) of the Vertical BER.
[227] For the definition of 'competing undertaking' cf Art 1(a) of the Vertical BER and para 26 of the Vertical Guidelines. The decisive criteria for establishing whether undertakings are potential competitors is that the undertaking, which is not yet active on the market concerned, 'would be able and likely to undertake the necessary additional investments and supply the market within one year', if there were a small and permanent increase in relative prices and in the absence of the agreement between the parties.

BER applies.[228] However, if the exception does not apply (which is likely to be the case in most cases) the agreement should be assessed under the Vertical and the Horizontal Guidelines.[229]

12.178 Whilst in general one can observe the tendency to place less focus on vertical restraints, the energy sector can be seen as an exception to the rule. There are a number of reasons for this. First, many incumbent operators have—as indicated above—high market shares, which do not allow for the application of the Vertical BER. This calls for an individual assessment under Article 81 (3) EC and the parallel application of Article 82 EC. Secondly, the sector only became subject to the strict enforcement of EC competition law following the liberalisation exercise.[230] It is therefore not surprising that the Commission identified a significant number of hard-core restrictions in existing vertical supply agreements.

12.179 Vertical restraints can be found in all types of contracts. For the purpose of this chapter it was deemed appropriate to distinguish between restraints contained in supply relationships (see below paragraphs 12.181ff), transport relationships (see below paragraphs 12.262ff) and other relationships eg storage (see below paragraphs 12.283ff).

12.180 The provisions contained in these contracts are assessed on a provision-by-provision basis. This follows the Commission approach of first analysing each individual provision found in a vertical contract on its own merits and once it has 'eliminated' all anti-competitive clauses, assessing the potentially restrictive effects of the remaining provisions in their entirety. Obviously there is also a need for market participants to assess whether the incompatibility of one provision leads to nullity of the complete contract.

(2) Vertical Restraints in Supply Relationships

12.181 Vertical restraints in supply contracts are found in the upstream markets (ie contracts between producers/generators and large wholesalers) and in the downstream markets (ie contracts between the wholesalers and regional/local distributors, industrial/commercial clients and/or private households). In the years following the adoption of the first liberalisation Directives for gas and electricity, the Commission focused its activities on the upstream markets, particularly in the gas sector. There were many reasons for these enforcement priorities, the most prominent being (a) that in well established vertical supply chains contractual restraints are often passed on to the next level in the chain (it is therefore essential that the restraints are first removed at its origin); and (b) that national competition authorities are generally well placed to deal with competition concerns in the downstream markets.[231]

---

[228] The exceptions are: Art 2(4)(a) the buyer has an annual turnover not exceeding EUR100 million (ie exemption for small distributors); Art 2(4)(b) the seller is a manufacturer and distributor of the products concerned, whilst the buyer is only a distributor of the products (ie exemption for electricity and gas producers selling to undertakings not active in production) and (3) Art 2(4)(c) the supplier is a provider of the services at several levels of trade, while the buyer does not provide competing services at the level of trade where it purchases the contract services. For details see para 27 of the Vertical Guidelines.

[229] cf para 26 of the Vertical Guidelines.

[230] For France see exclusive rights for EdF and GdF to import electricity and gas into France. The Commission's efforts to remove the monopoly rights prior to liberalisation failed in Court—Case C-159/94 *Commission v France* [1997] ECR I-5815; cf annotation of *Dohms/Levasseur* (1998) 1 Journal of World Trade 18ff. For Germany see §103 of the German competition law (GWB) which explicitly exempted certain agreements and practices in the energy sector from the scope of German competition law until 1998.

[231] This is also in line with the modernisation exercise, cf paras 8 and 9 of the Commission Notice on co-operation within the Network of Competition Authorities [2004] OJ C101/43ff.

This enforcement priority (ie 'supply relationship in upstream markets') also had the posi- **12.182** tive side effect that producers located outside the European Union (in particular the gas producers) were confronted directly with the liberalisation process taking place in the European Union. This liberalisation process offers significant business opportunities to such companies, but at the same time requires them to respect European legislation when doing business in the EU—including European competition law. The fact that these companies are located outside the EU does not protect them against the application of European competition law as their behaviour has an effect on the European markets (eg prevention of cross-border trade through territorial restriction clauses).

For the purpose of this chapter it was deemed appropriate to distinguish between restraints **12.183** imposed on the buyer (see below a), restraints imposed on the supplier (see below b) and other contractual provisions (see below c).

(a) Restraints Imposed on the Buyer

With respect to the buyer the Vertical BER identifies the following hard-core restrictions, **12.184** which are incompatible with EC competition law (Article 4 of the Vertical BER): (a) certain types of resale price maintenance;[232] (b) territorial restrictions and use restrictions; (c) restriction of active and passive sales to end users in a selective distribution system; (d) restriction of cross supplies in a selective distribution system; and (e) restrictions on buyers of components.

The Commission has so far focused on territorial restrictions and use restrictions in the **12.185** energy sector. Whilst it is still possible that resale price maintenance will become an issue at some point in time, it appears unlikely that the other hard-core restrictions mentioned above will play a significant role in the energy sector since energy is—at least for the time being—a commodity product and therefore not susceptible to a selective distribution system[233] and/or sales of components. Accordingly, the Commission's enforcement activities with respect to restraint in vertical supply relationships are likely to remain territorial restrictions, use restrictions, and contractual provisions having similar effects—in particular profit splitting mechanism, all described in more detail below.

Whilst not being a hard-core restriction in the narrow sense of the Vertical BER, long-term **12.186** exclusive purchase obligations, which prevent the buyer from buying significant volumes of the contract goods from a competing supplier, may also fall foul of European competition law. In the terminology of the Vertical BER such clauses are called non-compete obligations.[234] The anticompetitive effects of such clauses stem from the foreclosure of competition which will also be described below.

(i) **Territorial Restrictions**   One of the most flagrant violations of European competi- **12.187** tion law that can still be observed in certain supply agreements—most prominently in the

---

[232] The imposition of a maximum resale price and price recommendations are allowed provided they do not amount to a fixed or minimum resale price as a result from pressure or incentives (cf Art 4(a) Vertical BER and paras 225ff of the Vertical Guidelines).
[233] For details paras 184ff of the Vertical Guidelines.
[234] Arts 1(b) and 5(a) of the Vertical BER.

upstream gas sector—are so called 'territorial restrictions' or 'destination clauses'.[235] These clauses prevent the buyer from reselling the product concerned outside an allocated territory, normally a Member State. The clauses can take different forms, for example 'the product must not be re-exported', 'the product is destined for consumption in country x' or 'the buyer commits to resell the product only in country x'.

12.188   The main reason why the Commission objects to these clauses is that they lead to/maintain market segregation, which undermines the creation of the common market. It allows the seller to maintain different price levels in different territories by preventing each buyer from selling outside its 'allocated' territory. For the subsequent market level the clause means that customers from other Member States can only buy the products from those buyers/resellers that are located in the same territory as the customer, typically a Member State.

12.189   Territorial restrictions or destination clauses are hard-core violations of EC competition law. Article 4(b) of the Vertical BER states that vertical agreements must not contain provisions, which 'directly or indirectly . . . have as their object . . . the restriction of the territory into which . . . the buyer may sell the contract goods or services'.[236]

12.190   In the context of the investigations carried out by the Commission over recent years[237] parties seeking to justify such clauses argued that the possibilities of cross-border sales were rather limited prior to liberalisation (taking into account existing legal monopolies or existing special regimes such as the possibility of concluding demarcation contracts[238]). 'Contractual' territorial restrictions thus merely confirmed an existing legal and economic reality. According to this line of reasoning the clauses did not restrict competition at the time when the respective supply contracts were concluded and should therefore not be contested during the lifetime of these contracts. The Commission rejected these arguments relying on the primacy of Community law over national law and taking into account the fact that certain possibilities for cross-border sales did exist prior to liberalisation. In any event the argument could not be maintained following liberalisation, which explicitly allows/encourages cross-border sales. If the argument had been accepted by the Commission—particularly in the upstream gas sector—it would have meant that in

---

[235]   cf press release for cases *Nigeria LNG* (IP/02/1869) and *Gazprom/ENI* (IP/03/1345), for further information on these cases, cf *Nyssens/Cultrera/Schnichels*, Competition Policy Newsletter No 1/2004, p 48ff; *Nyssens/Osborne*, Competition Policy Newsletter No 1/2005, p 25ff; *Cultrera*, Competition Policy Newsletter No 1/2005, p 45ff.

[236]   Territorial restrictions also identified as hard-core restrictions for the purpose of determining whether agreements *appreciably* restrict competition under Art 81(1) EC: see para11 of the Commission Notice on agreements of minor importance which do not appreciably restrict competition under Art 81(1) of the Treaty establishing the European Community (*de minimis*) [2001] OJ C368/13ff.

[237]   A general overview of the investigations is contained in the article of *Nyssens/Cultrera/Schnichels*, Competition Policy Newsletter No 1/2004, p 48ff. See also the more recent press releases in the cases concerning OMV (IP/05/195) and Ruhrgas (IP/05/710).

[238]   Similar arguments are made for certain national markets, eg in Germany. Here it is maintained that national legislation prevents local distributors owned by the local council to become active outside the area, for which the local council is responsible in order to limit the risk of liabilities for the local council. The legislation does however not prevent local companies from entering into co-operation with other local companies. Thus, the argument cannot be accepted.

the light of the great number of existing long-term contracts the possibility of cross-border sales would not become an economic reality for many years.

Territorial restrictions are highly unlikely to fall within the terms of Article 81(3) EC.[239] In particular it cannot be argued that in the light of existing price differences between Member States the supplier should be entitled to ensure maximum profits in each Member State by making use of territorial restrictions. If the argument had been accepted by the Commission, it would have meant that market segregation could be perpetuated for the lifetime of the contracts, which would not have been compatible with the aim of creating a common market. In this respect it should also be noted that it is not for the supplier to decide when and where its customers resell the product concerned. Once the title and the risk in the products are transferred to the customer, it is for the customer itself—not the supplier—to make such decisions.

12.191

There are four exceptions to the hard-core restriction contained in Article 4(b) of the Vertical BER. The first of these permits—under certain conditions—the restriction of so called 'active' sales into the exclusive territory reserved to the supplier or allocated by the supplier to another buyer. These are to be distinguished from 'passive' sales restrictions, which are allowed under the Vertical BER. So, for example, a buyer could be limited to making sales which respond to unsolicited requests from customers outside the buyer's allocated territory, but could not actively look for sales outside the allocated territory.[240] It is unlikely, however, that the European gas companies, for which classic territorial restrictions were established in the course of the Commission's investigations, could make use of the first exception in Article 4(b) of the Vertical BER, because the suppliers often have market power, while the buyers are often the dominant operators in their domestic markets. Furthermore, the suppliers may have parallel contracts with the buyers in neighbouring countries, which would lead to the unwarranted protection of the dominant suppliers in all countries concerned.

12.192

In reaction to the Commission's approach, gas companies advanced two solutions to protect their interests whilst allegedly being compatible with European competition law. The first was a so-called 'profit splitting mechanism', ie an obligation to pass over a certain part of the profit to the supplier if the buyer resells the product concerned outside its traditional supply area. It was argued that such a clause would be compatible with European competition law because—are title and risk in transformed—it would allow the buyer to resell the product cross-border. The Commission rejected this reasoning because once title and risk is transferred profit splitting mechanisms reduce the incentive for cross-border sales (for further details see below).

12.193

The second solution proposed in the context of the Commission's investigation consisted of a change of the delivery point for the products concerned. In this respect it should be noted that in some cases the contracting parties had agreed upon delivery points, which would require further transport to the market in which the buyer was located and in which the buyer intended—at least originally—to resell the products concerned. However these delivery points rendered it relatively easy for the buyer to resell the products concerned in the transit

12.194

---

[239] cf para 46 of the Vertical Guidelines.
[240] For further details on the definition of active and passive sales, cf para 50 of the Vertical Guidelines.

country/countries as well, ie outside the traditional supply area. The parties therefore suggested to the Commission that they should be able to agree on new delivery points, which would bring the delivery of the products concerned closer to the market in which they would be resold/consumed. The Commission accepted this approach, as long as the buyer was free to re-export the products concerned (including swaps) once the title and the risk in the products had changed. The Commission also insisted that the buyer not be put under an obligation to agree on the change of the delivery point and that the parties should also be free to agree on more than one delivery point facilitating sales outside the traditional supply area in future.[241]

12.195 **(ii) Use Restrictions**   Another hard-core restriction that can still be found in energy supply contracts is 'use restrictions'.[242] Such clauses prevent the buyer from using the product for purposes other than those specified in the contract. The clauses can take different forms such as 'the product can only be used for own consumption' or 'the product cannot be resold' or 'the product can only be resold to customers using the product for the same purpose'. In certain cases a buyer that uses the product for different purposes (eg gas as a source for heating and as a raw material) might even be obliged to sign two or more contracts depending on the use of the product. The contracts provide for different prices and prohibit the buyer from changing the use of the product concerned under each contract.

12.196 The Commission has objected to these provisions as they allow the seller to maintain different price levels for different uses by preventing the buyer from using the product for other purposes or reselling it. Since use restrictions often prevent the buyer from reselling the product altogether, it is fair to state that use restrictions limit the buyer even further than classic territorial restrictions, under which the buyer is at least free to resell the product to other customers located in the same territory. In this respect it has to be said, however, that use restrictions are typically applied in contracts with final users (which are not primarily in the business of reselling the product), whilst territorial restrictions are typically applied in contracts with wholesalers or distributors.

12.197 Use restrictions are incompatible with EC competition law. In this respect Article 4(b) of the Vertical BER provides that vertical agreements must not contain provisions, which 'directly or indirectly, in isolation or in combination with other factors under the control of the parties, have as their object (. . .) the restriction (. . .) of the customers to whom the buyer may sell the contract goods'.[243]

12.198 Similar to territorial restrictions, use restrictions are highly unlikely to fall within the terms of Article 81(3) EC.[244] In this respect it is interesting to note that in the context of the

---

[241] For further explanation see *Nyssens/Cultrera/Schnichels*, Competition Policy Newsletter No 1/2004, p 48ff.

[242] cf most prominently IP/00/297 (*Endesa/GasNatural*) and IP/03/566 (*DONG/DUC*); for further details on use restrictions see *Fernandez-Salas*, Competition Policy Newsletter No 2/2000, p 55ff and *Schnichels/Valli*, Competition Policy Newsletter No 2/2003, p 60ff.

[243] Use restrictions also identified as hard-core restrictions for the purpose of determining whether agreements *appreciably* restrict competition under Art 81(1) EC: see para 11 of the Commission Notice on agreements of minor importance which do not appreciably restrict competition under Art 81(1) of the Treaty establishing the European Community (*de minimis*), [2001] OJ C368/13ff.

[244] cf para 46 of the Vertical Guidelines.

ongoing investigations into territorial and use restrictions in the gas sector it has been argued that gas has no protected market and therefore is in constant competition with other energy sources (eg households can choose between oil and gas for their heating; electricity producers can choose between coal, nuclear and gas to run their power plants; certain industries such as the paper producers can choose between electricity and gas for their production). According to those who put forward this argument, the price for gas varies depending on the competitive conditions in the respective markets. The suppliers argued that they cannot offer the gas at low prices to certain users unless they are entitled to protect themselves against the risk of deviation by those customers. The Commission has not accepted this argument because it leads to market segregation. In this respect the Commission noted in particular that certain large users such as electricity companies intended also to become active in gas supply and that the prohibition to use the gas for purposes other than those specified in the contract would limit their opportunity to do so.[245] Again the underlying assumption was that once the title and the risk in the products concerned are transferred to the buyer, it is for the customer—not the supplier—to establish the subsequent use of the product concerned.

The first exception under Article 4(b) of the Vertical BER, however, allows—under certain conditions—the restriction of so called 'active' sales to exclusive customer groups reserved to the supplier or allocated by the supplier to another buyer. In other words, whilst the supply contract must not contain a straight-forward use restriction, the buyer can be limited to so-called 'passive' sales for certain customer groups, ie from a contractual point of view the buyer would be allowed to respond to unsolicited requests from those customers, but could not actively look for sales in these customer groups.[246] For reasons similar to those outlined for territorial restrictions it is, however, unlikely that many contracts could benefit from the first exception under Article 4(b) of the Vertical BER.[247] **12.199**

In reaction to the Commission's approach, energy companies have proposed two solutions which they felt protected their interests whilst being compatible with competition law. As for territorial restrictions, the main ideas were profit splitting mechanisms (further discussed below) and a change of the delivery point (ie delivery at the factory gate of the user, the compatibility of this approach is further discussed in the chapter on territorial restrictions). **12.200**

A particular type of use restriction to which the Commission objected arose in the *DONG/DUC* case.[248] In the contracts concluded between Danish gas producers and the Danish gas company DONG, the price formula applied to the delivery of certain gas **12.201**

---

[245] cf IP 00/297 (*Endesa/GasNatural*); for further details on this case see *Fernandez-Salas*, Competition Policy Newsletter No 2/2000, p 55.

[246] For further details on the definition of active and passive sales, cf para 50 of the Vertical Guidelines.

[247] Another exception to the prohibition of use restrictions is contained in the second exception under Art 4(b), which allows restrictions of sales to end users by a buyer operating at the wholesale level of trade. So far this exception has not been used in the energy sector.

[248] IP/03/566 (*DONG/DUC*); for further details see *Schnichels/Valli*, Competition Policy Newsletter No 2/2003, p 60ff.

volumes depended on evidence to be provided by DONG that the gas was subsequently sold and delivered to electricity producers. The Commission considered this price provision to be a use restriction, the underlying rationale once again being that as soon as the title and the risk for the gas is transferred from the supplier to the buyer the latter must be free to use or resell the gas as deemed appropriate. This would not have been the case if DONG could only benefit from the special price formula if it declared the customer(s) to whom the gas was subsequently sold.

12.202 (iii) **Profit-splitting Mechanisms**   In the light of the Commission's position in respect of territorial restrictions and use restrictions, the energy industry—in particular the gas producers selling gas in liquid form (LNG)—considered how to replace the contested clauses with new provisions compatible with European competition law.

12.203 They suggested replacing territorial restrictions with so called profit-splitting mechanisms.[249] Profit-splitting mechanisms are clauses that oblige the buyer to pass a certain part of the profit—typically 50 per cent—to the supplier if the products concerned are sold outside the area agreed upon or used for a different purpose than agreed upon. Profit-splitting mechanisms can take different forms, but the essential elements are identical in almost all cases, ie 'when selling or using the products for a different purpose than agreed upon the buyer is obliged to pass over x per cent of the profit to the original supplier'.

12.204 The clauses differ, however, when it comes to the definition of the term 'profit'. In some cases the definition is left open leaving the buyer at a considerable risk in case of a subsequent disagreement (perhaps suggesting that the clause is not really meant for application in practice). In others, profits are taken to mean the difference between the purchase price of the buyer and its resale price (which means that the costs incurred by the buyer in reselling the product are always borne by the buyer rendering the deviation of the product unattractive, if not uneconomic). In yet other cases the term 'profits' is calculated after deducting all costs that the buyer incurs when reselling the product (which means that only 'net profits'—possibly even limited to profits exceeding the profits generated in its traditional market—need to be split, keeping at least a certain incentive for the buyer for cross-border sales).

12.205 Since the supplier has a keen interest in knowing how much of the profits should be split, profit-splitting mechanisms require monitoring to establish how much of the product was diverted into other territories or other uses. In most if not all cases profit-splitting mechanisms would therefore also be combined with reporting obligations imposed on the buyer. This leads to an additional administrative burden for the buyer and creates the risk that the buyer is obliged to provide the supplier with sensitive information/business secrets including resale prices. In order to avoid sensitive information/business secrets being passed from the buyer to the supplier, contracts may provide for reports to go to an independent expert.

---

[249] For an overall overview of the issue of profit splitting mechanisms, see *Nyssens/Osborne*, Competition Policy Newsletter No 1/2005, p 25ff.

In the Commission's investigations relating to international gas supplies, which are still **12.206** ongoing, 'profit-splitting mechanisms' were found in contracts making use of different INCO terms.[250] The most commonly used contract types were (1) 'FOB contracts'; (2) 'CIF contracts'; and (3) 'DES contracts'. The main differences between the clauses are at which point title and risk are transferred from the seller to the buyer and who bears the transport costs etc.[251] In this respect the main feature of DES contracts is that the port of destination is specified in the contracts, where title and risk are transferred. As a consequence deviations of a ship would need prior agreement of both the buyer and the seller. FOB and CIF contracts—on the other hand—foresee that title and risk are legally or de facto with the buyer already prior to the arrival of the LNG tanker in the harbour of destination calling for a different approach.

When analysing profit-splitting mechanisms the Commission started its assessment with **12.207** provisions contained in FOB and CIF contracts, which were the first in which profit-splitting mechanisms were found. The Commission acknowledged that profit-splitting mechanisms— contrary to territorial restrictions which impose a complete prohibition of cross-border sales—do not rule out cross-border sales *de jure*. The Commission also acknowledged that the deviation of ships can, in certain instances, create additional costs when it affects the agreed delivery schedule. The Commission, however, came to the conclusion that profit-splitting mechanisms in FOB and CIF contracts pursue a similar—if not the same—purpose as territorial restrictions. They lead to market segregation and render cross-border sales more burdensome than domestic sales, even if the buyer is entitled to keep a certain portion of the profit. They also prevent the buyer from marketing the product in the manner deemed appropriate following the transfer of title and risk in the product concerned.

The Commission was also of the view that profit-splitting mechanisms presuppose **12.208** reporting obligations which are incompatible with EC competition law. The Commission therefore reached the conclusion that the clauses are incompatible with EC competition law.[252] In this respect it is also important to note that the Vertical Guidelines consider profit-splitting mechanisms as restriction by 'object' (as opposed to restrictions by effect), which would mean that the Commission is not obliged to demonstrate any economic effects of the alleged restriction, but can assume their existence.[253]

The assessment of the profit-splitting mechanisms contained in supply contracts making **12.209** use of other INCO terms than FOB and CIF (ie essentially DES) is still ongoing. However,

---

[250]   The definition of INCO terms 2000 are found under <http://www.iccwbo.org/incoterms/preambles.asp>.

[251]   In a simplified form FOB means that title and risk are transferred to the buyer when the goods pass the ship's rail at the port of *shipment*. DES means that title and risk are transferred to the buyer when the goods pass the ship's rail at the port of *destination*. CIF means that—whilst title and risk are in principle transferred to the buyer when the goods pass the ship's rail at the port of shipment—the seller has to pay the costs of transport to the port of destination and the insurance costs against the buyer's risk of loss and damage.

[252]   cf *Nyssens/Cultrera/Schnichels*, Competition Policy Newsletter No 1/2004, p 48ff and para 49 of the Vertical Guidelines. Differently, however not fully convincing *Nyssens/Osborne*, Competition Policy Newsletter No 1/2005, p 25ff.

[253]   cf however the judgment of the CFI in case T-168/01 *GlaxoSmithKline*, not yet published, for a similar issue relating to the pharmaceutical sector, which is however characterised by State interferences with price setting.

it would appear that, as the buyer and the seller have agreed on a port of destination in their contract and the supplier is not obliged—from a contractual point of view—to give its consent to a change in the destination of the ship, certain forms of profit sharing might be compatible with EC competition law.[254] On the other hand, one must take into account the fact that such clauses might be used to prevent the creation of a common market and have similar if not identical effects as clauses in FOB contracts. A pragmatic solution could therefore be an agreement that the buyer is entitled to divert a certain number of LNG ships per year to a destination of its choice, provided that the delivery schedule of the ships is respected and/or the extra costs for deviating the ship are borne by the buyer.

12.210 **(iv) Long-term Exclusive Purchase Obligations** Another important restriction of competition in the energy sector that can still be observed in the European Union is what can be called the 'long-term exclusive purchase obligation'.[255] Under this, the buyer is obliged to meet its entire demand for the product concerned—or at least a significant part thereof—from the incumbent supplier during an excessive period of time. In the language of the Vertical BER, exclusive purchase obligations are called 'non-compete obligations'.[256]

12.211 Long-term exclusive purchase obligations can take different forms such as 'the buyer is obliged to meet its entire demand for the products concerned with the supplier during each contract year' (legal exclusivity) or 'the buyer is obliged to buy x kWh from the supplier during each contract year', where x corresponds to the average annual demand of the buyer or a large part thereof—so called annual minimum quantity (*de facto* exclusivity). The latter does not provide the buyer with adequate incentives to buy quantities exceeding the annual minimum quantity from an alternative supplier.

12.212 Whilst long-term contracts can be found at all levels of trade (including the upstream level—see in particular contracts between gas producers and wholesalers, which can be for as long as thirty years), it is generally at the downstream level in certain Member States where long-term contracts are combined with an obligation imposed on the customer to

---

[254] See *Nyssens/Osborne*, Competition Policy Newsletter No 1/2005, p 25ff, which might however no longer fully reflect the current views of the Commission services.

[255] Currently a case is pending before the Commission relating to the Belgian gas market (see Memo/06/197 of 16 May 2006—at the time of the writing this case was not yet concluded); cf also Court of Appeal in Düsseldorf, Recht der Energiewirtschaft 2002, p 44ff; and Court of Appeal in Stuttgart, Recht der Energiewirtschaft 2002, p 182ff. Both cases also went to Germany's highest civil court, the Bundesgerichtshof. However before it could render its judgments the appeals were withdrawn, cf press release of the German Federal Competition Authority (Bundeskartellamt) of 7 November 2003; subsequently the Bundeskartellamt launched an investigation into the compatibility of long-term gas supply contracts in the German gas market with EC competition law. In this context the Bundeskartellamt published a consultation document on 25 January 2005 setting out its views on the compatibility of long-term exclusive supply contracts with EC competition law and with a view to reaching a settlement with the gas companies concerned. The settlement efforts failed in September 2005, cf press release of 27 September 2005. In January 2006 the Bundeskartellamt adopted a prohibition decision relating to E.ON Ruhrgas (B8-113/03), which was challenged by the company. At the time of the writing the main proceedings were still pending. However in an interim measures case the Court of Appeal in Düsseldorf confirmed the decision of the Bundeskartellamt; cf on the compatibility of long-term exclusive gas supply agreements with EC competition law see also *Albers*, [2002] Fordham International Law Journal 909ff (915); *Schnichels*, (2003) Europäische Zeitschrift für Wirtschaftsrecht 171ff with further references.

[256] cf Art 1(b) of the Vertical BER.

meet their entire demand from the incumbent supplier (eg sales from gas wholesalers to regional or local distributors where contracts have a duration of ten to fifteen years[257] and sales to certain industrial clients that consume large gas quantities for electricity production or for the manufacture of fertilisers where contracts can have a duration of ten to twenty years. Similar provisions are found in electricity supply contracts).

Long-term exclusive purchase obligations/non-compete obligations raise competition concerns as they can result in significant foreclosure effects.[258] During the lifetime of the contract the buyer is prevented from switching to another supplier. Alternative suppliers lose a possible outlet for their products because the buyer cannot switch supplier. Long-term exclusive purchasing obligations can thus prevent market entry by actual or potential competitors. The anti-competitive effects of this strategy are reinforced if key customers, who would justify a market entry in their own right, are obliged to procure their entire demand from a supplier or if there is a network of parallel contracts sealing off a large part of the consumption in the market concerned. Long-term exclusive purchase obligations can therefore fall foul of Article 81 EC, in particular if they take the form of legal exclusivity. Depending on the market power of the supplier they might also be incompatible with Article 82 EC. **12.213**

So far the Commission has not provided conclusive guidance in individual cases on how it will apply EC competition to long-term exclusive purchase obligations in the energy sector.[259] The *Electrabel* case [260] can no longer be considered to be a valid precedent because it was settled long before Electrabel's customers (in the case at stake local distribution companies in Belgium) became 'eligible' in the sense of first Electricity Directive, ie could choose their supplier. Similarly, the *Endesa/GasNatural* and *Synergen* cases cannot provide conclusive guidance as they are characterised by special circumstances (erection of new gas fired power plants).[261] In addition the market share of the gas supplier in the *Synergen* case was close to the *de minimis* threshold. **12.214**

Guidance can however be found in certain court cases[262] as well as in the Vertical BER and the Vertical Guidelines. Paragraph 141 of the Vertical Guidelines provides that contracts with a duration of a year or less rarely contribute to foreclosure, whilst contracts with a duration exceeding five years rarely lead to efficiencies outweighing foreclosure effects. The latter statement is indirectly confirmed by Article 5(a) of the Vertical BER, which provides that 'any direct or indirect non-compete obligation, the duration of which is indefinite or exceeds five years' is not exempted by the Vertical BER. The concept of 'non-compete obligations' is defined in Article 1(b) of the Vertical BER as 'any direct or indirect obligation causing the buyer not to manufacture, purchase, sell or resell goods or services which **12.215**

---

[257] Case M.2822 *ENI/EnBW/GVS* (2002).
[258] cf also Final Report of the Sector Inquiry (2007), Chapter C.c.I Downstream Markets (electricity).
[259] An investigation relating *inter alia* to industrial customers in Belgium is ongoing, however. It is expected that the case will be decided in 2006. In addition the Bundeskartellamt is expected to conclude its investigation into the German gas markets (sales to local and regional distributors).
[260] IP/97/351.
[261] cf IP 00/297 (*Endesa/GasNatural*); for further details on this case see *Fernandez-Salas*, Competition Policy Newsletter No 2/2000, p 55; IP 02/792 (*Synergen*).
[262] In *Hoffmann-La Roche* ([1979] ECR 461, rec. 109, 114/115) the ECJ considered that even an exclusive purchase obligation of two years can be considered to be an abuse of a dominant position.

compete with the contract goods or services, or any direct or indirect obligation on the buyer to purchase from the supplier (. . .) more than 80 per cent of the buyer's total purchases of the contract goods or services (. . .), calculated on the basis of the value of the purchases in the preceding calendar year'.

12.216   From the above it follows that it is a combination of factors that renders a long-term exclusive purchase obligations incompatible with European competition law. At least two conditions must be fulfilled at the same time in order to reach the conclusion that a long-term exclusive supply obligation amounts to an appreciable restriction of competition in the sense of Article 81(1) EC: (1) the purchase obligation must be of a long duration; and (2) the obligation must cover the entire demand of the customer or at least a significant part thereof. A third element—whilst not explicitly mentioned in the Vertical BER—that will be taken into account by the Commission is the overall economic effect of the contractual practice. In particular, the Commission will look into the question of whether there is a network of parallel contracts containing identical or similar obligations or whether key customers capable of justifying a market entry in their own right are bound by long-term exclusive purchase obligations (for further details see below as well as in the explanations relating to Article 82EC).

12.217   Long-term exclusive purchase obligations falling outside the scope of the Vertical BER can nonetheless be compatible with EC competition law if they fulfil the conditions of Article 81(3) EC (this issue is also discussed in more detail below).

12.218   Whilst no sector specific case law exists at this stage to show how energy suppliers with market power can ensure that their contracts do not fall foul of EC competition law, two models appear possible: suppliers can either aim to address the overall foreclosure effects of their contracts by ensuring that an adequate proportion of their portfolio comes up for renegotiation every year or they can conclude contracts with short durations combined with some exceptions for longer-term contracts meeting the conditions Article 81(3) EC. Both models are explained below in more detail. It should be emphasised from the outset that these models should not only be applied to future contracts, but can also be applied to contracts concluded prior to liberalisation.

12.219   Finally, the civil law consequences of contracts that are incompatible with Article 81(1) EC and do not meet the conditions of Article 81(3) EC must be assessed. It is arguable that the contract is void either in part or in its entirety (see below).

12.220   *Long-term*   The duration of a contract is calculated from the day of the envisaged first delivery to the day of the envisaged last delivery (the analysis will thus not be limited to the remaining contract duration). Contracts which do not provide for a day of last delivery will be deemed to be concluded for an indefinite period.[263] The same applies to contracts which are tacitly renewable.[264]

12.221   It is not yet clear how the Commission will assess contracts which provide the buyers with a unilateral option to terminate a long-term exclusive supply contract. The remedy accepted

---

[263]   cf Art 5(a) of the Vertical BER.
[264]   cf Art 5(a) of the Vertical BER.

by the Commission in the merger case *ENI/EnBW/GVS*[265] (namely the offer by the supplier to introduce certain termination rights for the buyers) seems to suggest that termination rights in long-term contracts with customers that are deemed to make use of it remove the competition concerns. On the other hand, there are often additional incentives for a buyer not to make use of the termination rights or there may be certain limitations to making use of the termination rights. Some customers, for which energy supplies amount only to a small proportion of their total costs, might also suffer from a certain inertia to change suppliers. It is therefore suggested that termination rights as such have no effect on the Commission's assessment concerning the duration of a contract. At the very least, all other factors which limit the incentives to switch suppliers must be taken into account.

In this respect particular attention will also be paid to the existence of so-called 'English clauses'. These clauses allow the buyer to terminate the contracts and switch suppliers at certain times, but they also allow the incumbent supplier to match the offer of the potential new supplier. These contracts cannot be considered to be of a short term nature, as it is the incumbent supplier who may choose to opt for a prolongation of the contract with the buyer. **12.222**

As indicated above, the Commission is not likely to consider contracts with a duration of less than one year as long-term contracts having foreclosure effects, whilst contracts with a duration exceeding five years rarely lead to efficiencies outweighing foreclosure effects, and are thus considered as long term. For contracts lasting for between one and five years, an assessment must be made on the merits of the case taking into account the degree to which customers are bound to procure their demand, the market power of the supplier and possibly other factors (overall foreclosure, type of customer, Article 81(3) considerations). **12.223**

Exclusive purchasing   As indicated above, exclusive purchasing exists in different forms: legal exclusivity where the buyer must meet its entire demand from a particular supplier and *de facto* exclusivity where the parties fix a supply volume that corresponds to the average annual demand of the buyer. The economic effect of both forms of exclusivity is the same—namely foreclosure of alternative suppliers—and this is why they need to be treated in the same manner under European competition law. **12.224**

In addition, the term 'exclusive purchasing' comprises situations in which the buyer is obliged to purchase a 'major part' of its annual demand from the supplier, eg by fixing an annual minimum quantity that must be taken and paid for. In such scenarios alternative suppliers are essentially limited to supplying the flexible demand above the minimum quantity supplied by the incumbent. This type of clause is therefore also assumed to have foreclosure effects if combined with long-term purchase obligations. Alternative suppliers lose a potential outlet because the demand of the buyer is met to a large degree by the incumbent supplier. In this respect it is also considered that it is often uneconomical for the buyer to enter into negotiations for the remaining demand with a new supplier (high transaction costs). **12.225**

The Commission has not yet defined what is meant by 'major part' of the demand in the energy sector. However, if one accepts that the Vertical BER provides for a certain minimum **12.226**

---

[265] cf Case M.2822 *ENI/EnBW/GVS* (2002).

standard, it seems fair to conclude that the Commission will always regard buyers that meet more than 80 per cent of their demand with a supplier as a buyer purchasing a 'major part' from that supplier, cf Article 1(b) of the Vertical BER. The Commission, however, may also regard contracts under which the buyer purchases less than 80 per cent from one and the same supplier as a contract relating to a major part of the consumption depending on the market power of the supplier. But it seems unlikely that contracts with a purchase obligation of less than 50 per cent of the total demand will be regarded as an obligation relating to the 'major part' of the purchases. Here a different assessment might only be warranted if there is a network of parallel contracts (including other contracts where more than 50 per cent of the demand is met by the supplier) leading to an overall foreclosure effect.

12.227 When assessing whether a buyer of electricity or gas is buying a 'major part' from a supplier, it would seem appropriate to calculate the degree of foreclosure on the basis of total purchases of the buyer and not on the basis of its total demand, which might be higher when one considers that the customer might produce electricity for its own consumption eg in a combined heat and power plant or might have some special gas (coke gas) from a production process. The buyer does not take part in the market with respect to these self-generated volumes. Only the demand with respect to the volumes that are not self-generated can be met by third parties. This assessment is also confirmed by Article 1(b) of the Vertical BER, which refers to '80 per cent of the buyer's total purchases' and not of its demand.

12.228 In conclusion, it must be emphasised that the Commission services will look at economic reality (did the customer *de facto* procure its entire demand from the supplier?) rather than the contractual arrangements between supplier and buyer. Thus, a combination of supply contracts, by means of which a supplier meets the demand of a customer (eg a ten year contract for 50 per cent of the demand, a four year contract for 30 per cent of the demand, and a two year contract for the remaining 20 per cent) should be assessed overall and not as separate contracts. In this context, one should not forget that incumbent suppliers may offer certain discounts for those parts of the demand that are sold short term ('remaining volumes'), thus providing the buyer with an additional incentive to fulfil its entire demand requirement with the incumbent supplier (so called fidelity rebates). This might amount to an additional infringement of EC competition law.

12.229 *Individual contracts or overall foreclosure*   Competition authorities have at their disposal the investigative tools to gather all relevant information allowing them to assess whether a given market is foreclosed by long-term exclusive purchase obligations. They will not generally focus on contracts with one single customer unless that customer is regarded as capable of market entry in its own right (key customer concept). They will rather assess whether all the contracts of a given supplier (possibly in conjunction with identical/similar contracts of other suppliers) lead to an overall foreclosure of the market concerned. This is in line with the Commission's 'economic approach', which does not assess the (legal) compatibility of certain contractual provisions with EC competition law, but considers the actual effects on the markets.[266]

---

[266] cf para 5 of the Commission Notice—Guidelines on the application of Art 81(3) of the Treaty (hereafter 'Guidelines on Art 81(3) EC'), [2004] OJ C101/97ff.

For national courts the situation is more complex when a customer initiates civil proceedings with a view to challenging the contract with its supplier containing long-term exclusive purchase obligations. Normally the courts will not have at their disposal adequate information on the overall foreclosure effects in the market concerned. If the parties are unable or unwilling to submit the relevant information and all possible efforts to obtain the information from national competition authorities or the Commission fail (cf Article 15 of Regulation 1/2003), national courts will only have the option to either dismiss the claim as unfounded if they are not convinced that the contract forecloses the market concerned or decide on the basis of the contested contract only, possibly combined with a shift of the burden of proof to the supplier obliging it to demonstrate that the contract does not significantly contribute to foreclosure (see however Article 2 of Regulation 1/2003). **12.230**

Article 81(3) EC Contracts which are incompatible with Article 81(1) EC can be compatible with EC competition law either because they meet the conditions of a block exemption regulation[267] or because they meet the conditions of Article 81(3) EC. Since the conditions of the Vertical BER have already been explained above,[268] the following section concentrates on the conditions of Article 81(3) EC. The undertaking relying on Article 81(3) EC must demonstrate that the four conditions of Article 81(3) EC are fulfilled, broadly (1) efficiency gains; (2) fair share for consumers; (3) indispensability; and (4) no elimination of competition.[269] The burden of proof is on the undertakings concerned (Article 2 of Council Regulation 1/2003). **12.231**

In the past it has been argued that long-term exclusive purchase obligations between gas wholesalers and their customers (downstream market) are always compatible with Article 81(3) EC because these contracts enhance 'security of supply'. The gas wholesalers argued that they themselves are bound by long-term commitments (take or pay contracts[270]) in the upstream markets and that they should be entitled to pass on these long-term obligations, at least partly, to the next level of trade, so that they are put into a position to honour their long-term upstream contracts and ensure security of supply in the downstream market, in which they are active. In this context, reference is also made to Article 27 of the Gas Directive, which provides a certain protection for take-or-pay contracts. **12.232**

The Commission has however not accepted these arguments in any of its recent decisions. The underlying reason for this is that it is normal for wholesalers to bundle the demands of their customers and then negotiate with the suppliers for what is needed to meet the demand of the (actual or expected) customer base. Allowing the wholesalers to pass on **12.233**

---

[267] Block exemption Regulation contains typical constellations, for which the Commission assumes that the conditions of Art 81(3) EC are met.

[268] See above the references to Arts 5(a) and 1(b) of the Vertical BER.

[269] For an analytical framework of these conditions see the Commission 'Guidelines on the application of Art 81(3) of the Treaty', [2004] OJ C101/97.

[270] Take or pay means that the buyer is obliged to pay for a certain part of the gas even if it is not taken in a given year. Take or pay obligations are thus minimum off-take obligations. There are however provisions in almost all take or pay contracts alleviating the adverse effects for the buyers such as carry-forward mechanisms and/or make-up mechanisms, which allow compensation for gas not taken during a certain year with higher gas volumes taken in subsequent or previous years.

the risks associated with their normal business activity to the next level of trade would thus seem an insufficient justification for the adverse effects associated with long-term exclusive purchase obligations (foreclosure of alternative suppliers). The foreclosure effects are not only detrimental to the alternative suppliers, but also to the medium and long-term competitive structure of the markets concerned, which will suffer if alternative suppliers withdraw from the market or decide not to enter it. In this context, it should also be noted that the wholesalers themselves, whilst bound by long-term contracts, are not normally bound by exclusive purchase obligations, ie they would obtain a higher protection from their customers than they are willing to give to their suppliers.

12.234 By the same token it cannot be argued that long-term exclusive purchase contracts between wholesalers and distributors/industrial users are necessary to protect the wholesalers' investments in the 'transmission infrastructure'.[271] In this respect it must be taken into account that energy companies (wholesalers and distributors alike) are obliged to unbundle supply and transmission activities.[272] This means, *inter alia*, that the costs of the transmission activities must be borne by those using the infrastructure (third parties or the supply branch of the vertically integrated energy company). The investments in the infrastructure therefore must not be used to defend the supply interests of a vertically integrated energy company.[273]

12.235 A valid economic reason for long-term exclusive purchase obligations, however, might be found in legitimate amortisation interests, primarily where the buyer makes 'relationship-specific' investments, which cannot be recouped in a short period and which are asymmetric compared to the investment of the supplier.[274] Thus it was considered compatible with EC competition law when a gas supplier concluded a fifteen year exclusive supply contract for gas for a newly erected gas-fired power plant in which it held a minority shareholding.[275] However in that case the Commission stressed that, in addition to the above considerations,[276] the long-term exclusive supply contract was necessary for the gas supplier to enter the market dominated until then by the incumbent operator and that the gas supplier would not have offered the specific price formula for the gas without the fifteen year exclusivity.

12.236 The assessment of how long it takes to achieve the intended efficiency gains (including the amortisation of the investment costs) is to be made on an *ex ante* basis,[277] ie based on when the investments are incurred. However it might turn out in the subsequent course of action that the efficiency gains cannot or can no longer be achieved. If the restrictive agreement in

---

[271] The same applies to distribution companies when selling to the next level of trade.

[272] cf Arts 9 and 13 of the Gas Directive and Arts 10 and 15 of the Electricity Directive.

[273] In line with this reasoning it would seem fair to conclude that the settlement of the Commission case *Electrabel/Intercommunales mixtes* (IP/97/351) is no longer a valid precedent. In any event, one would need to take into account the specificities of this case, such as that the Intercommunales mixtes were not eligible customers under EC law at the time of the settlement, ie they were in any case not free to switch supplier.

[274] cf para 116, point 4 of the Vertical Guidelines.

[275] cf IP/02/792—*Synergen*.

[276] It appears arguable that newly erected power plants are not a relationship specific investment as the power plant can still be used as power plant following the termination of the existing gas supply contract.

[277] cf para 119, point 9 of the Vertical Guidelines.

question (long-term exclusive supply contract) is not an irreversible event, the agreement, which originally was compatible with EC competition law, might subsequently fall foul of European competition law. With the same token amortisation might take place faster than foreseen, no longer justifying any restrictions of competition to ensure that the efficiency gains can be achieved. It is thus submitted that companies should regularly reassess the compatibility of their agreements with EC competition law.[278]

Models to avoid conflicts with EC competition law   Setting aside possible exceptions under   **12.237**
Article 81(3) EC for certain long-term contracts containing exclusive purchase obligations, suppliers with market power essentially seem to have two options for avoiding conflict with EC competition law. They can either conclude contracts in such a manner that every year a sufficient proportion of their portfolio can effectively switch suppliers (overall foreclosure model) or they can conclude contracts with a short duration only (the duration needs to be one to two years depending on the market, if the buyer has no second supplier of significance; if on the other hand a second supplier of significance exists, the duration can be longer, but must not exceed four to five years) (contractual model). Both models have similar effects, namely that a significant number of customers can switch supplier every year allowing new entrants to conclude supply contracts with the customers previously committed long-term to the incumbent supplier.

The challenge of the overall foreclosure model is that so far no clear benchmark has been   **12.238**
established by Commission precedent to show what is meant by 'sufficient proportion of the portfolio'. Taking into account the economic approach favoured by the Commission it would appear that the 'proportion' needs to be calculated in relation to volumes rather than number of customers (which might buy only very limited volumes), eg 70 per cent of the volumes supplied by the supplier. Another difficulty might lie in implementation of the model in practice. It requires the supplier to constantly monitor its portfolio and adapt instructions to its sales personnel on a regular basis. In addition, it would not protect the supplier against challenges to the contracts by certain customers that initially agreed to enter into long-term contracts. On the other hand, the obvious benefit of this model is that it gives the supplier a large degree of flexibility on how to conclude its contracts.

The challenge of the contractual model is also that no clear benchmark has been developed,   **12.239**
so that it is not yet clear what is meant with contract of a 'short duration'.[279] It also appears that many customer might not want a second supplier, *de facto* reducing the current supplier to the conclusion of short-term contracts. Another important issue that would need to be addressed is how suppliers for the same customer share the risk of imbalances. New entrants should not bear a higher risk than the incumbent. Finally, there might be a need to limit the exceptions under Article 81(3) EC by a market share cap.

Civil law consequences   According to Article 81(2) EC contractual provisions that are not   **12.240**
compatible with Article 81(1) and (3) EC, are void. This applies in the same way to provisions contained in contracts concluded prior to liberalisation as well as to provisions

---

[278] Paras 44ff of the Guidelines on Art 81(3) EC.

[279] See however the consultation document published by the Bundeskartellamt on 25 January 2005 as well as the press release of 27 September 2005 setting out how the investigation into the German gas supply market to local and regional distributors could have been concluded by means of a settlement. See also the decision of the Bundeskartellamt against Ruhrgas mentioned above.

contained in contracts concluded thereafter,[280] ie contracts concluded prior to liberalisation are not protected against the application of EC competition law (supremacy of EC law, here of the EC Treaty). Accordingly, exclusive purchase obligations which are contained in supply contracts with an excessive duration are void.

12.241 In line with the jurisprudence of the ECJ in the *Kerpen & Kerpen* judgment,[281] the incompatibility of a contractual provision with EC competition law does not, however, render the entire agreement automatically void. The court also ruled in this judgment that it is not a matter of Community law to decide whether the remaining parts of the agreement are affected by the invalidity of the anti-competitive provision. It is therefore a question of national law whether the remaining parts of the contracts are valid. In practice this means that contractual disputes are likely to come before national courts or arbitration tribunals, unless the parties find a mutually acceptable solution.[282]

12.242 Relying on the *Kerpen & Kerpen* judgment, it has been argued that long-term exclusive purchase obligations are not void altogether, but must just be amended to what would have been legally acceptable, ie either the duration of the contract is shortened to an acceptable level or the off-take obligation is reduced to an acceptable level. This approach, however, does not appear compatible with the *effet-utile* of Article 81(2) EC, if anti-competitive clauses are simply replaced by the acceptable provision. On the contrary, suppliers would be encouraged to take the risk of entering into anti-competitive contracts and then awaiting potential challenges by the buyers in court leading to an amendment of the contract to the legally acceptable level. From a contractual point of view the maximum penalty they would have to fear is the reduction of the contract to the acceptable level. It would thus seem preferable to reassess the situation in the light of '*effet utile*' considerations and come to the conclusion that the incompatibility of the long-term exclusive purchase obligation renders the entire contract void.

12.243 This solution would also be compatible with the liberalisation efforts of the Commission. Whilst of course nothing would prevent the parties concerned from reaching a new supply agreement with a shorter duration or a lower level of the purchase obligation, it would give new suppliers an opportunity to make a competitive offer at the same time, facilitating their market entry.

(b) Restraints on the Supplier

12.244 Whilst the Vertical BER clarifies that a number of provisions limiting the *buyers'* commercial activities are incompatible with EC competition law (see above), it is largely silent on restraints restricting the suppliers' commercial activities. The only exception is contained in Article 3(2) and relates to so-called 'exclusive supply obligations'. Article 1(c) defines exclusive supply obligations as an 'obligation causing the supplier to sell the goods (. . .)

---

[280] With respect to the assessment pursuant to Art 82 EC it has been argued that the decisive question is whether long term exclusivity was already incompatible with Art 82 EC at the time the contract was concluded (eg prior to liberalisation) and if not whether it is an abuse to insist on the fulfilment of the contract legally concluded following liberalisation.

[281] [1983] ECR 4173—recital 11.

[282] cf Säcker/Jaecks (§ 1 GWB, recitals 81ff) in Berliner Kommentar zum Wettbewerbsrecht on significant case law relating to the German market.

only to one buyer in the Community (. . .)'. In the European energy sector, which is characterised by national markets and national champions, such exclusive supply obligations do not exist. As a consequence Article 3(2) of the Vertical BER is of limited relevance for the energy markets.

Nonetheless, vertical restraints applicable to suppliers have played an important role in the **12.245** Commission's recent practice. The main focus was on 'exclusivity clauses'[283] preventing the gas supplier from selling into the territory of their customers (see below) and on so-called 'reduction clauses',[284] ie provisions having effects similar to exclusivity clauses (see below). In the electricity sector the Commission dealt with obligations on certain electricity generators to sell the entire output via so-called power purchase agreements (PPAs) to the incumbent operator [285] (see below).

The underlying competition concern of the Commission in all these cases was that com- **12.246** petitors of the exclusive buyer were deprived of important supply sources. The Commission therefore took into account the fact that the number of alternative suppliers was limited and that the buyer was the incumbent operator in its home market where it often enjoyed a dominant position on the downstream markets concerned. The clauses thus had the effect of rendering market entry more difficult for new operators and protecting the dominant position of the incumbent supplier.

(i) **Exclusive Supply**[286]   In the course of its investigations into upstream gas markets, the **12.247** Commission noted that gas producers had committed to deliver gas only to the incumbent importer in the territory concerned, normally a Member State. Contractually, the supplier was thus prevented from selling gas to other operators in the agreed territory, whether wholesalers (ie competitors of the incumbent importers), distributors or end users (ie customers of the incumbent importers). The underlying contractual provision could take different forms such as: 'The supplier sells the product only to company x in the territory concerned' or 'The supplier is only allowed to sell the product to companies other than company x in the territory concerned upon explicit consent of company x'.

Irrespective of their form, such provisions have a number of adverse effects for competition **12.248** in the European gas markets, primarily that competing wholesalers could no longer buy gas from those gas producers which were contractually committed. As a consequence these alternative wholesalers encountered further difficulties when entering into competition in the downstream supply markets with the incumbent wholesaler (entry barrier). This was detrimental because the number of gas producers was in any case limited, a number of them were bound by similar clauses (network effect) and the incumbent importer often enjoyed a dominant position on the downstream markets concerned. These clauses thus protected the dominant position of the wholesaler benefiting from the exclusivity clause. In addition they had the effect that the gas producer itself could no longer enter the

---

[283] IP/03/1345 (*Gazprom/ENI*), for further details see *Nyssens/Cultrera/Schnichels*, Competition Policy Newsletter No 1/2004, p 48ff.

[284] IP/03/566 (*DONG/DUC*), for further details see *Schnichels/Valli*, Competition Policy Newsletter No 2/2003, p 60ff; IP/02/1293 (*EdF Trading/Wingas*).

[285] Case M.1853 *EDF/EnBW*, remedy relating to CNR.

[286] It should be noted that this provision might also be assessed as a horizontal restriction of competition.

downstream markets by selling directly to large industrial users. Thus the dominant position of the incumbent wholesaler was further protected.

12.249   The Commission did not need to address the issue of exclusivity in a formal decision: the companies concerned were ready to delete the clause from the existing contracts.[287] They also undertook not to introduce such provisions in any future contracts. As a consequence, the Commission closed the investigation.

12.250   **(ii) Reduction Clause**[288]   A contractual provision with economic effects similar to exclusivity clauses is the so-called 'reduction clause'.[289] This provision allows the buyer—normally a wholesaler—to reduce the annual volumes to be purchased from the supplier if the supplier starts selling gas into the territory 'allocated' to the buyer. The clause can take different forms, the main differences being that in some instances the off-take obligations are automatically reduced, whereas in others the buyer merely has an option to reduce the off-take volume.

12.251   In the Commission's view reduction clauses reduce the supplier's economic incentive to sell to customers other than the incumbent buyer, whether they are competitors of the incumbent buyer or its customers (eg end-users). For the supplier, sales to other customers—apart from the need to cover additional transaction costs—are only of interest if the new customer pays a purchase price that is higher than the price paid by the incumbent buyer; otherwise the supplier is better off continuing to sell all volumes to the incumbent buyer, if the overall volumes cannot be increased (the incumbent buyer can reduce the off-take if the supplier sells into the territory allocated to the incumbent buyer). On the other hand the new customer is not likely to buy from the supplier unless it obtains a low purchase price. In this respect, one should note that gas is a commodity product and competition essentially takes place on price.[290] Thus from an economic perspective it seems that reduction clauses have effects similar to exclusivity clauses, namely prevention of sales to alternative buyers. They are not acceptable, for the same reasons as outlined for the exclusivity clause, in particular when the incumbent buyer is a dominant operator and could rely on the provision in order to prevent market entry in its home market or price competition on the subsequent level of trade.

12.252   The incumbent buyers have tried to justify the reduction clause by arguing that these clauses are the appropriate counter-balance to take-or-pay provisions.[291] The buyers maintained that the reduction clause is necessary to prevent the supplier from selling the gas 'twice', once to the incumbent buyer who would be obliged to continue paying for the gas

---

[287]   IP/03/1345 (*Gazprom/ENI*), cf also settlements with *OMV* (IP/05/195) and *Ruhrgas* (IP/05/710); for further details see *Nyssens/Cultrera/Schnichels*, Competition Policy Newsletter No 1/2004, p 48ff.

[288]   It should be noted that this provision might also be assessed as a horizontal restriction of competition because the players are often at least potential competitors.

[289]   IP/03/566 (*DONG/DUC*), for further details see *Schnichels/Valli*, Competition Policy Newsletter No 2/2003, p 60ff; IP/02/1293 (*EdF Trading/Wingas*). See also in this respect, Preliminary Report of the Commission's energy sector inquiry, point 135.

[290]   Sales from the supplier to a new buyer could take place, primarily if the incumbent buyer resells the product in its territory with a very significant margin.

[291]   For the definition see above.

even if it could no longer take it (because its outlets are now directly or indirectly supplied by the supplier), and once to the new customers to which the supplier would deliver the gas directly or via a new wholesaler. The incumbent buyers considered that removal of the reduction clause in existing supply contracts would thus undermine the commercial equilibrium of the supply contracts.

In essence, those who made these points were arguing that each buyer deserved a fully pro-   **12.253**
tected home market—even following liberalisation. However, in the Commission's view, this was not the case because the essential aim of liberalisation is not the protection of home markets and existing supply relationships, but the creation of a common market, ie the facilitation of cross-border sales. The alleged need for a protected home market is thus not a valid justification for the reduction clause other than in exceptional cases, in which the incumbent buyer is prevented from carrying out cross-border sales for other reasons, for example because there is no pipeline link allowing for cross-border sales.

Whilst the assessment described above primarily addresses incumbent buyers with signifi-   **12.254**
cant market power (dominance) or cases in which there is a network of comparable reduction clauses in many contracts relating to the same market (cumulative effect), the Commission dealt with another, although related issue in *EdF Trading/Wingas*.[292] In that case the Commission established that the reduction clause would have allowed the supplier to sell gas—without the application of the reduction clause—to certain companies (primarily those with market power) whilst sales to other companies would have entitled the buyer to reduce the off-take volumes. The Commission considered this to be an inappropriate discrimination in favour of the dominant operators. It could however close the case after the parties had removed the discrimination.

(iii) Power Purchase Agreements with Independent Power Producers   Whilst the exis-   **12.255**
tence of exclusivity and reduction clauses was primarily an issue in the upstream gas sector, where incumbent wholesalers/importers were trying to prevent their suppliers from entering the downstream markets, the electricity sector also suffered from a similar, but slightly different practice, namely the exclusive power purchase agreements (PPAs) between the incumbent producer/wholesaler and independent power producers (IPPs).[293] The IPPs are contractually obliged to sell their entire output to this incumbent producer/wholesaler. These supply contracts are either not limited in time at all or of a long duration.

The economic effect of these agreements is that IPPs are prevented from selling the electric-   **12.256**
ity to competing wholesalers or to operators active at subsequent levels of trade (eg regional distributors or industrial users). At the same time, competing wholesalers and operators active at the next market level are prevented from approaching the IPPs as an alternative supplier. These contracts are a competition concern for the Commission in particular if the incumbent buyer is the dominant operator in the wholesale electricity market concerned

---

[292] IP/02/1293 (*EdF Trading/Wingas*).
[293] The most prominent example was addressed in the merger Case M.1853 *EdF/EnBW* (2000), where the French electricity producer CNR—accounting for approximately 4% of French electricity production—was freed from its obligation to sell the entire output to EdF. It should be noted that power purchase agreements might also be classified as a horizontal restriction of competition.

and/or access to alternative supply sources is limited. The obligation to sell the entire output or a significant part of it to the incumbent operator in the relevant market removes a competitor from the market, which is an even greater concern if the IPP is capable of producing low cost electricity (eg new power plants with low production costs or fully amortised power plants with low variable costs such as power plants running on water).

12.257 On the other hand, it is acknowledged that IPPs may have a legitimate interest in having a secure outlet for their output for a certain period of time in order to secure financing for new plants. To determine this, it is necessary to assess whether the agreements fulfil the conditions of Article 81(3) EC. Disregarding the less problematic scenario that IPPs sell to non-incumbents one of the decisive questions is whether the obligation to sell the entire output or a large part of it to the incumbent is indispensable. It might, for example, be sufficient that the IPP is entitled, but not obliged, to place the entire output with the incumbent operator, ie the IPP could sell to alternative customers upon reasonable notice given to the incumbent buyer. Another option would be that the obligation to sell the entire output of the plant to the incumbent operator is limited to the start-up phase or that the IPP is only obliged to sell a certain percentage of its output on a long-term basis to the incumbent operator (which would be sufficient to secure a part of the financing). It also appears plausible that an obligation to sell the entire output to the incumbent operator could be looked at more favourably, if electricity is just a by-product of an overall production process and therefore the producer cannot guarantee sales on a regular basis (ie the buyer needs a supply portfolio in order to ensure that in times of low sales volumes by the IPP supplies can be made up from other sources).

12.258 The Commission has been able to settle all cases so far, in particular because the incumbent buyers allowed the IPPs to place their output with alternative buyers. The most notable case was settled in the context of the EdF/EnBW merger (M.1853), in which EdF committed to releasing the French electricity producer CNR, which produces low cost electricity on the river Rhone, from its obligation to sell its entire output to EdF. CNR accounts for 4 per cent of French electricity production and could thus—at least in combination with a strong strategic partner—develop into a competitor of EdF in the French electricity markets concerned (at the time sales to eligible customers).

(c) Other Possible Vertical Restraints

12.259 In recent years, two other provisions in gas supply contracts have often been criticised as being incompatible with EC competition law, namely the price formulae under which the price for gas is linked to the price of oil and its derivatives and the so-called take-or-pay obligations.[294] The Commission has not yet pronounced on these two types of clause.[295]

12.260 The oil price link was 'invented' in the 1970s, when gas was introduced as a new primary energy source into the European energy markets. At that time it was argued that gas competed directly with oil and its derivatives in practically all subsequent applications, mainly power production, industrial use and domestic heating. As a consequence, wholesalers deemed it appropriate to link the gas price in the upstream gas supply contracts to the

---

[294] For the definition see above.
[295] The provisions might also be assessed as a horizontal restraint or an abuse of a dominant position in the sense of Art 82 EC.

international oil price so that gas could be offered in competition with the oil derivatives on the downstream markets. Whilst the oil price link made some sense in the 1970s (and even today certain users might choose between oil and gas when taking an initial investment decision eg for domestic heating), more mature gas markets such as the UK have moved away from the gas-oil price link. The mature markets recognise that gas and oil are not part of the same product market and that the costs for producing/supplying gas are not linked to the international oil prices. In continental Europe, which is characterised by long-term gas supply contracts also with non-EU gas producers, this development is yet to come.[296]

Similarly, the Commission has not yet taken a final position on the compatibility with EC competition law of take-or-pay obligations in gas supply contracts. As explained above, take-or-pay provisions merely oblige the buyer to pay for certain gas volumes during the contract year even if the gas is not taken in that year. They are thus nothing but a minimum off-take guarantee for the supplier.[297] On the other hand, it is recognised that in certain markets a large proportion of the demand can be covered on a long-term basis by such provisions. Contracts containing such clauses might then be considered to have foreclosure effects for other suppliers, either on their own or as a network of parallel contracts. The buyers in the market concerned are no longer available outlets for alternative suppliers. **12.261**

(3) Vertical Restraints in Transport Relationships

Whilst the Commission has dealt with a number of cases concerning vertical restraints in supply relationships, it has carried out only a small number of investigations[298] with respect to (vertical) transport contracts.[299] This is due, amongst other things, to the fact that internal market rules facilitate third party access and thus set out the fundamental conditions under which access has to be granted. This does not mean, however, that the Commission (DG Competition) has remained completely passive with respect to the transport markets. **12.262**

Typical restraints in transport contracts, which can be addressed by means of Article 81 EC are territorial restrictions, use restrictions and long-term capacity reservations. Other obstacles to an effective Third Party Access regime require an assessment pursuant to Article 82 (eg the need to introduce a use-it or lose-it principle) and are not addressed in this chapter. **12.263**

(a) Territorial Restrictions

Territorial restrictions in transport contracts prevent the shipper from selling the product concerned in a certain area, normally a Member State.[300] They are typically found in **12.264**

---

[296] For more factual information on the gas-oil price link cf Final Report of the Sector Inquiry (2007), Chapter B.a.II.5 Price Issues (gas).

[297] The take-or-pay provisions do not guarantee the supplier a minimum revenue per year as the price for the gas is linked to the oil price, which varies significantly over time.

[298] See in particular decisions in case COMP/38.662—*GDF (ENEL and ENI)* of 26 October 2004 published at <http://europa.eu.int/comm/competition/antitrust/cases/index/by_nr_77.html#i38_662>; for further details on this case *Cultrera*, Competition Policy Newsletter No 1/2005, p 45ff.

[299] For the purpose of this chapter the term transport includes (long distance) transmission and short distance distribution (excluding the supply activity) in the electricity and the gas sector.

[300] See Commission decisions in Case COMP/38.662 *GDF (ENEL and ENI)* of 26 October 2004 published under <http://europa.eu.int/comm/competition/antitrust/cases/index/by_nr_77.html#i38_662>; for further details on this case *Cultrera*, Competition Policy Newsletter No 1/2005, p 45ff.

transit contracts (ie transports from one border point of a Member State to another). The clauses can take different forms such as 'the product must not be resold in country x' or 'the product transported through the transmission line is destined for consumption in country x'. They thus prevent the shipper from selling the electricity/gas during the transport from the entry point to the exit point.

12.265 The underlying purpose of these clauses is market segregation. It is important to emphasise in this regard that the undertaking offering the transport service traditionally is a vertically integrated company (often a national champion) that is not only active in the transport markets, but also in the supply markets. That company, whilst having an interest in maximising its profits in the transport sector, has a conflicting interest in preventing the shipper from selling the product in the area, which is traditionally supplied by its own supply branch (typically a Member State). Territorial restrictions thus assist the vertically integrated company in maintaining a higher price level in its supply area and prevent customers in this area from buying directly from the shipper.

12.266 In light of the above, territorial restrictions in transport contracts almost always have a horizontal dimension (avoiding competition in the supply market by a potential competitor). They lead to demarcation. Taking into account the fact that a number of such contracts seem to exist in Europe, it seems fair to conclude that territorial restrictions in transport contracts were and possibly still are an important element in particular in the continental European gas industry to ensure that traditional supply areas of the incumbent operators are protected.

12.267 Territorial restrictions in transport contracts constitute a hard-core violation of EC competition law. In this respect it can be left open whether this can be derived from Article 4(b) of the Vertical BER providing that vertical agreements must not contain provisions, which 'directly or indirectly, in isolation or in combination with other factors under the control of the parties, have as their object (. . .) the restriction of the territory into which (. . .) the buyer may sell the contract goods'[301] or from the respective provisions in the regulations/notices dealing with horizontal restraints. Territorial restrictions in transport contracts are incompatible with European competition law because they undermine the creation of a common market, one of the essential aims of European integration.

12.268 In anticipation of potential investigations by the Commission it seems that certain transport contracts were drafted in order to achieve the same economic effect (ie prevent the shipper from entering the supply markets in the area transited), without explicitly making use of territorial restrictions. A typical example would be contracts in which the shipper is limited to one specific entry point and to one specific exit point in the respective transmission system and is not entitled to ask for other exit points along the transmission line: it would seem plausible to argue that these provisions are comparable to territorial restrictions. Another possibility would be to argue that such provisions are use restrictions preventing the shipper from selling the product along the (pipe)line or at least rendering it more difficult.

---

[301] See paras 116ff of the decision relating to ENI in Case COMP/38.662 *GDF*, cf also para 11 of the *de minimis* notice.

(b) Use Restrictions

Transport contracts can also contain use restrictions. The most prominent examples are **12.269** restraints on shippers that want to resell the transport rights acquired in the primary market. These restraints can take different forms, such as a complete prohibition on reselling capacity rights or the obligation on the shipper to request the explicit approval of the owner prior to the transfer of transport rights. All these restraints pursue the same object, namely preventing or limiting the creation of a secondary market in which the capacity rights are traded.

Whilst the owner of the transport infrastructure has a legitimate interest in ensuring that **12.270** certain technical specifications are respected by all shippers, including those acquiring rights in the secondary market, and can thus impose certain conditions on the resale/ sublease of transport rights (eg the obligation that the product respects certain quality standards), shippers must not be prevented altogether from making available transport rights in the market place.

The Commission has not yet carried out investigations directly addressing the issue, but in a **12.271** number of settlements negotiated with infrastructure owners in recent years, those companies committed themselves to introducing and facilitating the creation of secondary markets.[302] This also included accompanying measures such as anti-hoarding obligations (use-it or lose-it principle) and score boards, on which shippers could bundle their access requests.

(c) Long-term capacity reservations

Another important restriction of competition can stem from long-term capacity reserva- **12.272** tions in transport contracts. It must be emphasised that access to the transmission infrastructure is an essential prerequisite for suppliers to reach customers. If the capacity in the transmission infrastructure is booked and used on a long-term basis, new suppliers cannot enter the market, until either the capacity reservation comes to an end or new capacity is built. The same restraints also occur if capacity is booked but not used, and the unused capacity is not made available to the market or is only made available in a manner that does not permit the intended use of the infrastructure (for example, where a shipper needs capacity for a year, but capacity is only offered during the summer months, or a shipper needs firm capacity, but capacity is only available on an interruptible basis).

In addition to the assessment of long-term capacity reservations pursuant to the Electricity **12.273** and Gas Directives[303] as well as pursuant to Article 82 EC (which also leads to the introduction

---

[302] cf the settlements in the *Marathon* case: IP/04/573 (*Ruhrgas and GdF*); IP/03/1129 (*BEB*); IP/03/547 (*Gasunie*); IP/01/1641 (*Thyssengas*); for further details on these settlements see *Fernandez-Salas/Klotz/Moonen/Schnichels*, Competition Policy Newsletter No 2/2004, pp 41ff.

[303] ECJ, C-17/03, judgment of 7 June 2005, *VEMW*, (not yet published) on the incompatibility with the Electricity Directive (EC) 96/92, if pre-liberalisation capacity reservations are granted priority status over new bookings although the Member State did not request an exemption to do so under Art 24 of the Directive. For transit contracts in the gas sector the situation is more complex taking into account the protection of transit contracts pursuant to Art 32 of the Gas Directive. For certain new infrastructure projects an assessment pursuant to Art 22 of the Gas Directive and Art 7 of the Electricity Regulation 1228/2003 is necessary. A list of projects that have been exempted from the existing TPA regimes is published by the Commission on its web site: a) gas: <http://europa.eu.int/comm/energy/gas/infrastructure/exemptions_en.htm>; b) electricity: <http://europa.eu.int/ comm/energy/electricity/infrastructure/exemptions_en.htm>.

of anti-hoarding obligations, whether short term or long term, eg by means of the use-it or lose-it principle), long-term capacity reservations cllllan also amount to an appreciable restriction of competition pursuant to Article 81 EC if they have foreclosure effects. These foreclosure effects can derive from capacity reservations by a single undertaking or from a bundle of parallel long-term capacity reservations by various undertakings.

12.274　Long-term capacity reservations exist in the electricity and gas sectors alike. In the electricity sector, which is characterised by a wide spread of production facilities throughout Europe, long-term capacity reservations are primarily found in contracts relating to so-called inter-connectors, ie transmission lines linking the electricity networks of two Member States.[304] In the gas sector, long-term capacity reservations are found in the upstream and down-stream markets. In the upstream markets capacity reservations allow the producers to bring the gas from the well head to the entry points into the downstream markets (often border points). In the downstream markets they are found in transit contracts (ie transports through Member States) and in contracts allowing the supplier to transport the gas to the customers (either final consumers or distributors). There are also long-term capacity reser-vations relating to the gas interconnector between the continent and the UK[305] and it is expected that similar conditions will apply to new, currently planned interconnectors, the main argument always being that long-term capacity reservations are needed to ensure the financing of the infrastructure and are used in order to fulfil long-term supply contracts.

12.275　Given the high degree of vertical integration in the energy industry, where companies are often active in transport and supply activities within the same territory, it is not surprising that in many instances it is the vertically integrated companies that benefit from long-term capacity reservations.[306] Sometimes these reservations are combined with grandfather rights allowing the capacity holder to renew the reservation. Such capacity reservations not only have the adverse effect that new suppliers cannot enter the market (foreclosure to be assessed under Article 81 EC), but also keep potential competitors out of the supply markets dominated by the incumbent operators (exclusionary conduct to be assessed under Article 82 EC).

12.276　The Commission has not yet defined the duration of contracts that it would consider to be excessive, but in line with the explanations given above for supply contracts, it would seem that transport contracts with a duration of less than a year do not amount to an appreciable restric-tion of competition, whilst contracts with a duration of more than five years would require spe-cial justification. They are likely to be looked at favourably in particular for contracts relating to

---

[304] The Commission dealt with these agreements mostly in the context of merger investigations such as Case M.1673 *VEBA/VIAG* (1999). The Commission also dealt with long-term capacity reservations in cases relating to the Dutch interconnectors and to the Spanish/French interconnectors (Competition Report 2003, 203). At that time, the Commission closed the case on the basis that there are 'insufficient grounds for acting on the basis of antitrust rules' because the capacity reservation contracts were signed pre-liberalisation. In the light of the ECJ judgment in Case C-17/03 (*VEMW*) this argument does seem no longer to be valid.

[305] See most prominently *Bacton-Zeebrugge-Interconnector*, IP/95/550.

[306] It is recalled that vertically integrated companies cannot rely on the fact that the agreement between the supply branch and the transport branch is intra group. The unbundling provisions contained in the liberali-sation directives allow the Commission to treat the supply and transport branches as two separate companies and thus apply Arts 81 and 82 EC to them.

'new' infrastructure.[307] Contracts which were concluded for an indefinite period of time (even if the contract contains termination rights) or which are implicitly renewable following expiry of the original contract period must also be considered to be of a long-term nature.

Of course, the fact that a transmission contract is of a long-term nature does not auto-matically mean that it is not compatible with EC competition law. In the first place it is nec-essary to assess the extent to which the contract contributes to the possible foreclosure effects on its own and in combination with parallel contracts. If adequate capacity remains available, the Commission is unlikely to give priority to cases addressing these long-term capacity reservations. **12.277**

Furthermore it is necessary to assess whether there is legitimate justification pursuant to Article 81(3) EC for the duration and the degree of capacity reservation. The main argu-ments[308] made in this context are: (a) fulfilment of an actual or future supply contract; (b) underpinning of a major new investment; and (c) security of supply. In addition it might be necessary to assess whether the preferential treatment for certain contracts is imposed by a State measure calling for an assessment under Article 86 EC. **12.278**

It should be noted that no consolidated Commission practice exists with respect to these or any other possible arguments.[309] It should be borne in mind that regulated third party access regimes became compulsory under the new liberalisation Directives calling for the introduction of regulatory congestion management regimes. In order to avoid a duplica-tion of efforts it appears likely that the application of competition law will be focused on new infrastructure projects, interconnectors and transit lines, which are of strategic impor-tance or fall outside the scope of the Directives.[310] **12.279**

As regards the first argument (ie that the shipper requires a long-term capacity reservation in order to fulfil a supply obligation), it would appear that a shipper cannot invoke the obligation to fulfil a supply contract if the supply contract in itself is not compatible with EC competition law (eg because it contains a long-term exclusive purchase obligation **12.280**

---

[307] *UK-Belgium Gas Interconnector* [1995] OJ C73/18; Viking electricity cable between Norway and Germany (Notice pursuant to Art 19(3) of Council Regulation 17) [2001] OJ C247/11. See also the provi-sions in Art 22 of the Gas Directive and Art 7 of the Electricity Regulation 1228/2003 applicable to new infra-structure projects. The underlying reason for this approach is that new infrastructure is in most cases seen as pro-competitive allowing for additional imports.

[308] Another argument sometimes made is that the contract was concluded prior to liberalisation. At least for electricity this is no longer a valid argument, cf. ECJ, C-17/03, judgment of 7 June 2005 *VEMW*, (not yet published). In this judgment the Court clarified that a Member State that intended to maintain priority rights for pre-liberalisation contracts should have applied for an exemption under Art 24 of the Electricity Directive (EC) 96/92, which did not happen in the case in question. For gas the situation is more complex taking into account the special provisions for transit contracts in the Gas Directive (for the relationship between sector spe-cific legislation and competition law see above. In this respect it should also be noted that Arts 81 and 82 EC were applicable before liberalisation of the energy markets).

[309] Whilst the ECJ did not address the application of EC competition law in its judgment in Case C-17/03 (see n 83 above), see Stix-Hackl AG in the same matter.

[310] There is however some past practice: Reorganisation of the electricity industry in England and Wales (Notice pursuant to Art 19(3) of Regulation 17) [1990] OJ C191/9; Reorganisation of the electricity sector in Scotland (Notice pursuant to Art 19(3) of Regulation 17) [1990] OJ C245/9; *UK-Belgium Gas Interconnector* [1995] OJ C73/18; Viking electricity cable between Norway and Germany (Notice pursuant to Art 19(3) of Council Regulation 17) [2001] OJ C247/11.

for the customer which is incompatible with EC competition law). If, on the other hand, the supply contract is valid, the Commission will assess the other conditions of Article 81(3) EC, most prominently whether the capacity reservation leads to an elimination of competition.

12.281 As regards the second argument (underpinning significant investments), it would seem possible to take into account investments by the shipper (eg development of a new gas field requiring transport to the downstream markets) and investments by the transmission company (eg construction of a new interconnector). Quite apart from the assessment for new infrastructure projects under sector specific legislation,[311] it is submitted that the conditions of Article 81(3) EC are no longer fulfilled once the investment costs are recouped. From that moment onwards the anti-competitive foreclosure effects stemming from long-term capacity reservations are no longer compensated by the legitimate need to underpin the risks associated with the investment.[312]

12.282 As regards the third argument (security of supply), it would seem that this argument is sometimes used in order to justify the business interests of the operators concerned (for example, it is argued that customers request supply security and in order to meet this request long-term capacity reservations are required). However in most cases these arguments do not go beyond the argument made above concerning the fulfilment of supply contracts.

(d) Restraints in Storage Contracts and LNG Terminals

12.283 Vertical restraints, in particular use restrictions and long-term capacity reservations, can also be found in contracts relating to access to storage and LNG terminals. However, the Commission has not yet actively dealt with these issues. It is however fair to assume that the consideration described above apply *mutatis mutandis* to storage and LNG terminals.

F. Assessment of Horizontal Agreements in the Light of Article 81 EC

(1) Introduction

12.284 The starting point for analysing horizontal agreements in the energy sector is the Horizontal Guidelines.[313] In the energy sector, the following would, *inter alia*, qualify as being horizontal: an agreement between generators to produce electricity jointly; an agreement between oil companies to construct and exploit an upstream exploration and production platform jointly; agreements between energy traders/suppliers to market their products jointly; and agreements by large consumers to buy their energy jointly.

12.285 In most instances, agreements entered into by undertakings in the context of 'associations of undertakings', such as the agreements entered into between the German transmission companies in the context of the so-called 'Association Agreements' or 'Verbändevereinbarungen',

---

[311] See in this respect also Art 22 of the Gas Directive (EC) 2003/55 and Art 7 of the Cross-border electricity Regulation 1228/2003.

[312] para 44ff of the Guidelines on Art 81(3) EC.

[313] Commission guidelines on the applicability of Art 81 of the EC Treaty to horizontal co-operation agreements [2001] OJ C3/2. For an in-depth overview of the issues arising from horizontal agreements in the energy sector, see M Albers, in *Competition Law & Energy markets* (Claeys & Casteels, 2005), pp 113ff.

will tend to include an important number of horizontal features. Agreements between companies which are not competitors, and which are operating at a different stage of the energy supply chain are to be classified as 'vertical' agreements. This type of agreement was dealt with above in section E.

It should be emphasised that the focus for determining whether a contract should be considered as 'horizontal' or 'vertical' lies in the competitive relationship between the contracting parties, rather than in the nature of the contract itself.[314] A contract for the transport of gas or electricity over a particular network tends to have an intrinsic vertical nature. However, when the contract is entered into between a supplier requesting access to the network and a transmission system operator (TSO), which is also active—within the same legal entity or through related undertakings—as a supplier competing with the customer of the transmission services, the contract will have to be assessed under horizontal rules. Indeed, as the contracting parties are competitors on the supply market, the contract could be used to restrain competition in that market, for instance, by disallowing sales to customers in the regions transited. The same principles apply to supply contracts between competing undertakings which might primarily be active in different regions/markets or at a different level of the supply chain, but nevertheless remain at least potential competitors.[315]

12.286

(2) Competition Problems and Benefits arising from Horizontal Agreements

Horizontal co-operation between competitors may lead to a number of competition problems in the energy sector.[316] Price competition, which is generally considered to be the main source of rivalry in most industries, is even more critical in commodity markets such as electricity and gas. In such commodity markets, the scope for competing on the quality of the product is indeed severely reduced.[317] Restrictions likely to affect price, which is the key remaining competition factor, should thus be examined with particular attention.

12.287

As in other sectors, the *first*, most obvious restriction stems from the lessening of competition between the companies entering into the agreement.[318] However, spillover effects are especially likely in the energy sector, because a large number of energy players are vertically integrated. They are, in other words, active on upstream production/generation markets and, at the same time, owners of national, regional, or local transmission grids, as well as directly supplying a certain number of ancillary services (like storage or metering services). Such spillover effects also exist between the gas and electricity sector.[319]

12.288

---

[314] See vertical block exemption, Arts 2.2 and 2.4 and horizontal guidelines, point 1, as explained in the introduction of section E.

[315] See for instance Commission press release IP/02/1293 relating to a gas supply contract between EDF Trading and Wingas.

[316] See horizontal guidelines, point 2.

[317] See amongst others Case M.1673 *Veba/Viag* (2000), point 71 and decision of the Dutch competition authority *Nuon/Reliant*, point 46, mentioned in n 90.

[318] See, for an individual application of this principle in the energy sector, the *Synergen* case mentioned further in para 12.334.

[319] See, amongst others, Merger decisions between electricity and gas companies like Case M.493 *Tractebel/Distrigaz II* (2000); Case M.931 *Neste/Ivo* (1998); and Case M.3440 *ENI/EDP/GDP* (2004).

12.289 The *second* type of restrictive effect that a joint venture can generate, relates to foreclosure of third parties, for instance by substantially increasing the barriers to entry in the market concerned.[320] In addition, where one of the parents of a joint venture is also the operator of a network infrastructure to which competing suppliers should require access, there will be an additional risk of foreclosure by discrimination or refusal to supply.

12.290 On the other hand, horizontal co-operation can lead to *substantial economic benefits*. Indeed, in liberalising energy markets, horizontal agreements can constitute a means to share risks, save costs, pool know-how, penetrate new geographic or customer markets jointly, or to launch new (environmentally friendly) energy products more speedily or tailored more to special industry needs.

(3) Main Types of Horizontal Agreements in the Energy Sector

12.291 The variety of horizontal agreements encountered in the energy sector, the anti- and pro-competitive effects of which must be analysed in detail, are broadly classified in the subsequent sections, starting with agreements unlikely to create efficiencies within the meaning of Article 81(3) EC (demarcation contracts, non-compete clauses, and information exchange). Agreements of a more industrial nature, which are more likely to create efficiencies are dealt with thereafter and are broadly classified starting from the 'upstream' gas production and electricity generation activities down to the 'downstream' retail activities.

12.292 Pure cartels, the most blatant violation of competition rules, will not be addressed in detail in this energy chapter. The reader is generally referred to Chapter 8 which focuses on hardcore cartels. Although the petroleum sector has often been accused of cartel practices, such allegations are more rarely made with respect to the electricity and gas sector. This can probably be traced back to the different market structures of these industries: petroleum markets tend to be more oligopolistic in nature, the gas and electricity sectors still tend to be rather (quasi) monopolies. One of the issues which will deserve attention in the coming years, however, is whether an upstream organisation similar to the OPEC[321] will emerge in the gas sector to form an effective 'OPEG'. The impact of such an organisation, which is currently still in its infancy, could indeed have a serious impact on Europe, primarily with regard to LNG supplies.[322]

(a) Demarcation Contracts

12.293 Historically, the structure of the energy industry has been characterised by a large number of geographic demarcation agreements.[323] Such practices imply that companies active on

---

[320] For an example of an analysis of barriers to entry in the electricity sector, see for instance Case M.3318 *ECS/Sibelgaz* (2003), points 58ff. See also, more generally, the Commission guidelines on the appraisal of horizontal mergers under Council Regulation on the control of concentrations between undertakings [2004] OJ C31/5, especially points 71ff.

[321] See M Albers, in *Competition Law & Energy markets*, p 121ff.

[322] See, amongst others, R Soligo and M Jaffe, 'Market structure in the new gas economy: is cartelization possible?', paper produced in the context of the Program on Energy and Sustainable Development of Stanford University, May 2004, available at <http://www.pesd.stanford.edu>.

[323] See Case M.958 *Watt AG II* (1997), point 14; and Schaub and Alexander, 'Liberalisation of the European Energy markets: the perspective of competition policy' in 'European integration and international coordination', *Studies in Transnational Economic law in Honour of Claus-Dieter Ehlermann* (Kluwer, 2002) pp 403–418.

the same product market, although in neighbouring geographic regions, agree to refrain from entering into each other's territories. Such demarcation leads to a significant rigidity in the markets concerned, as the operators are protected from their most likely effective or potential competitors (completely new operators are rare exceptions in the energy sector). These types of agreement have exactly the same effects as the legal monopolies which are gradually being abolished by the liberalisation Directives.

By the 1990s, the Commission had begun to challenge such arrangements, mainly in the electricity sector.[324] This is evidenced by its investigation into the arrangements between Dutch electricity suppliers, which reserved imports into the Netherlands to a joint whole-sale company (SEP). This system was reinforced by a network of vertical exclusive supply contracts between those incumbents and the eligible clients. The object and effect of the agreements was to prevent the customers from importing electricity, even where their geographic proximity to the border allowed them to purchase directly from foreign suppliers without the need to access the Dutch electricity grid controlled by SEP. The Commission considered that these agreements violated Article 81(1) EC, could not be exempted under Article 81(3) EC, and were not covered by Article 86(2) EC.[325] The Commission decision was followed by a long series of proceedings before the CFI and ECJ, which lasted until 1996.[326]   **12.294**

Equally, in *SHG/EDF-ENEL*,[327] the Commission challenged a horizontal agreement between the French and Italian incumbents, who jointly prevented a smaller French generator established in the Alps from exporting its production directly into Italy. Together, they obliged SHG first to sell its production to EDF, who would subsequently resell it to ENEL. The Commission regarded this as a horizontal market partitioning practice.   **12.295**

Particular attention should also be given to so-called 'crisis supply arrangements', traditionally agreed upon between electricity wholesalers. Although irreproachable in their overall objective, these arrangements must not contain any direct or indirect prohibitions to enter into each other's traditional geographic markets for 'regular supplies'. Some such arrangements have, in recent years, been voluntarily amended without apparent intervention from antitrust authorities.   **12.296**

Finally, it should be pointed out that a number of practices related to vertical agreements, such as territorial restrictions,[328] can have effects very similar to horizontal demarcation contracts. The web of territorial restrictions which the Commission has been challenging can be compared to classical demarcation cartels, although their structure is not purely horizontal, but rather takes place in a triangular relationship with foreign suppliers. The effects of parallel sets of gas supply contracts containing such territorial restrictions, however, are similar to demarcation contracts: competition between geographically close competitors is impeded.   **12.297**

---

[324] See also *Ruhrgas/Thyssengas* decision of the Bundeskartellamt from 1994, cited in Ritter and Braun, above, p 929.

[325] Commission Decision (EEC) 91/50 of 16 January 1991, *Ijsselcentrale* [1991] OJ L28/32.

[326] Last episode was Case T-16/91 *RV Rendo/Commission* [1996] ECR II-1827.

[327] XXIInd Commission Competition Report [1992] points 142–145.

[328] See above paras 12.264–12.268.

(b) Non-compete Clauses under the Guise of 'Use Restrictions'

12.298 Although the Commission has not dealt with cases concerning explicit horizontal non-compete clauses in the electricity or gas sectors recently, it has frequently encountered and challenged clauses having the same effect, most prominently in the form of so-called 'use restrictions'. Under such clauses, gas will typically be sold to an electricity generation company indicating that the gas is 'for generation purposes only'. Such clauses, when found in contracts with clients who cannot be considered to be effective or potential competitors of the gas supplier concerned (for example, a fertilising plant using the gas as an input in its industrial process), should generally[329] be considered to be vertical in nature and are therefore dealt with in section E above.

12.299 However, use restrictions found in contracts between gas wholesalers and electricity wholesalers should, by contrast, be looked at *also* from a horizontal perspective. This is because they can have the effect of enabling gas suppliers to curtail the electricity wholesalers who have gas portfolios from entering the gas market. In *Gas Natural- Endesa*,[330] as well as in a series of subsequent cases,[331] the Commission managed to have this type of restriction removed from the gas supply contracts at issue. The stated intention in the former case was to ensure that the gas supply contract would not allow the dominant gas supplier to impede the entry of new suppliers into the Spanish gas market, on the eve of liberalisation of the European gas market.

(c) Exchange of Confidential Business Information

12.300 The Commission also seeks to avoid anti-competitive exchanges of information between competitors. Indeed, such exchanges may constitute a threat to competition even in the absence of other collusive behaviour.[332] Controlling this type of behaviour is becoming increasingly important in a period where electricity and/or gas exchanges are being set up in an ever-increasing number of Member States.[333] The competition authorities' competencies overlap, in practice, with those of energy regulators and financial watchdogs entrusted with the task of overseeing the functioning of these exchanges.[334]

---

[329] The evaluation of who should be considered as a potential competitor must however be assessed on a case-by-case basis. In the electricity sector, for instance, it is not uncommon for large industrial customers to resell some of the electricity they buy from established suppliers or even some of the electricity they may generate themselves through co-generation facilities, on electricity exchanges in periods where peak prices make such transactions lucrative. This is evidenced by the fact that some of these industrial customers have enrolled as licensed traders on electricity exchanges like Powernext or EEX.

[330] See Commission press release IP/00/297 and 'Long-term supply agreements in the context of gas market liberalisation: Commission closes investigation of Gas Natural', by Mariano Fernandez Salas [2002] CPN 2.

[331] See *NLNG* case (IP/02/1869), *GFU* case (IP/02/1084) and *DUC DONG* cases (IP/03/566). The latter case is described in more detail in Schnichels and Valli, 'Vertical and horizontal restraints in the European gas sector—lessons from the DONG- DUC case', [2003] CPN 2.

[332] See also Case T-34/92 *Fiatagri & New Holland/Commission* [1994] ECR II-905.

[333] The UK-Belgium interconnector investigation (Commission press release IP/02/401) gives an idea of the importance of transparency in the functioning of interconnectors.

[334] See for instance the joint inquiry conducted in parallel in 2004 by the UK energy regulator Ofgem and the watchdog of the financial exchange FSA into the rising gas wholesale prices, available at <www.ofgem.gov.uk>.

However, not all information exchange between competitors need necessarily fall within the scope of Article 81(1). An example of such unobjectionable practice would be an information exchange on issues which do not directly affect key factors of competition such as, for example, information merely designed to reduce the cyber-threats in the energy industry presented by the increasing interconnection, interdependence, and computerisation.[335]   **12.301**

Another example of legitimate information exchange in the energy sector is when several companies jointly create a commodity exchange or new infrastructure, such as the construction of the UK—Belgium gas interconnector. Information exchange between TSOs in order to allow congestion management systems for cross-border links between the respective territories of those (potentially competing) TSOs also appear unobjectionable as long as no information is passed on to related supply companies in a way which prevents anti-competitive use being made of it.[336]   **12.302**

In order to identify appropriate ways for this to happen, a useful parallel can be drawn with cases involving the business-to-business (B2B) electronic market places, such as the one organised by the electricity sector in a joint venture called Eutilia.[337] The solution most often applied in practice is the creation of an independent company in charge of aggregating data flows and administrating the electronic market.   **12.303**

Confidentiality issues might also arise in the context of standardised transport agreements agreed upon by TSOs and their shippers, requiring the latter to provide extremely detailed information about their commercial transactions. Indeed, in this context, the transparency created by the TSO about all shippers' activities might lead to easy identification, by the shippers, of each others' behaviour in the market.[338] These issues, amongst others, were addressed in the context of a case relating to the British Gas Network code.[339] Finally, it is noteworthy that, in certain circumstances, exchanges of information restricting competition have been exempted on the basis that they enable structural measures to be set up in case of supply disruptions.[340]   **12.304**

(d) Joint Production

(i) **Introduction**   The first source of competition problems that may arise from joint production agreements relates to the coordination of the parties' competitive behaviour as suppliers of the jointly produced good. However, the fact that the parties to a joint venture are competitors does not automatically cause the coordination of their entire behaviour in the affected markets. In order for such restrictive coordination to take place, the parties   **12.305**

---

[335] Compare with business review letter of the DOJ addressed to EPRI (2000) available on <www.usdoj.gov>.

[336] See Art 5.1 of Regulation (EC) 1228/2003 which encourages electricity TSOs to put in place such information exchange systems.

[337] See Clerc and Clark, 'Commission clears the creation of three B2B e-marketplaces: Covisint, Eutilia and Endorsia' (2002) 1 CPN 53.

[338] See in this regard the Madrid Forum guidelines for good TPA practice of September 2003 (GGP II), point 5.2, available on the Commission web site.

[339] *British Gas Plc—Network Code* (Notice pursuant to Art 19(3) of Council Regulation 17 [1996] OJ C93/5; and Commission press release IP/96/462.

[340] Commission decision (EEC) 94/153 of 21 February 1994, *International Energy Agency* [1994] OJ L68/35.

normally need to co-operate with regard to a significant part of their activities, or create, in other words a high commonality of costs.

12.306 Another element to take into consideration when analysing the market structure in joint production cases concerns the so-called '*network effects*', ie structural links existing between the competitors on a market. Indeed, in concentrated gas and electricity markets, the creation of an additional link between companies who are already connected through cross-shareholdings and/or joint venture activities may tip the balance and make collusion in this market more likely, even if the parties directly involved in the transaction have a moderate, combined market share of between 10 and 30 per cent.[341]

12.307 Even co-operation between *potential competitors*, like energy suppliers in geographically neighbouring markets which have not yet entered into each other's respective traditional markets, may raise competition concerns. Indeed, the reduction of potential competition is particularly sensitive in the gas and electricity sectors, as many national markets still remain largely dominated by historical incumbents. This may explain the importance the Commission attaches to safeguarding the threat of entry from neighbouring geographical markets as the major source of future competition.[342]

12.308 A second source of competition problems relates to the fact that production agreements may also create *foreclosure problems* for third parties. These problems are not due to a competitive relationship between the parties, but to a strong market position of at least one of the parties in an upstream or downstream market. This may occur for instance, if a powerful generator teams up with a regionally prevailing supplier, which might lead to supply difficulties for competing suppliers.[343] Such foreclosure issues may also arise if a number of energy suppliers, jointly controlling a substantial share of the downstream supply market, decide to create new infrastructure jointly, without previously having organised an 'open season' inviting interested third parties to participate and without allowing for effective TPA on the infrastructure.

12.309 (ii) **Upstream Hydrocarbons Exploration and Production Activities** Upstream exploration and production of oil and gas in a given field is usually undertaken by more than one company. The Commission has accepted the necessity of such co-operation in upstream development because of the need to spread risks during the exploration phase. The Hydrocarbons Directive is also based on this presumption.[344] Indeed, a certain number of restrictions relating to field-specific infrastructure and arrangements relating to timing and implementation of an upstream project are to be considered as 'ancillary' to the realisation of hydrocarbons exploration as such.

12.310 Caution should however be observed in the light of the possible market power of the companies involved in a project, certainly on a regional basis, and the commonality of costs that

---

[341] Horizontal guidelines, point 97.
[342] Horizontal guidelines, point 98 and M Albers, 'Energy liberalisation and EC competition law', Annual proceedings of the Fordham Corporate Law Institute 2001 (2002, pp 519–532 point III 1).
[343] See, for a similar merger issue, the Dutch merger case *Nuon/Reliant* (see <www.nmanet.nl>).
[344] See paras 12.37ff.

multiple joint operations might create. Sharing of confidential commercial information between the—often numerous—members of upstream exploration and production consortia should also be examined carefully.

Provisions that restrict any of the parties from pursuing their individual interests in **12.311** competing projects and which are not intrinsically linked with the main project in question are likely to violate Article 81 EC, as are joint operation agreements creating veto powers in respect of selling or commercialisation opportunities for co-producers. Other exploration-related activities, such as the joint operation of upstream pipelines linking the production facilities with the mainland transmission grid might give rise to foreclosure problems.[345] In such cases, the conditions under which a pipeline can be linked to other pipelines or access can be granted to third parties will, more particularly, have to stand the test of Article 81 EC.

Finally, it should be mentioned that a certain number of the types of co-operation referred **12.312** to above might be imposed by the Member States in whose territories the hydrocarbons are explored. If they can demonstrate that their specific behaviour is not 'autonomous' in any way, the companies concerned could invoke the 'state compulsion' doctrine to avoid the prohibition of Article 81(1) EC.[346]

(iii) Pure Production Joint Ventures   The Commission has not had the opportunity to **12.313** deal with a large number of joint production ventures. The only position taken by the Commission in this area concerned the creation of a structural joint venture named EHP between Germany's integrated energy company E.ON and the Austrian electricity generator Verbund.[347] The venture was limited to joint production of hydropower. There was no intention for EHP to be active directly on the market, but EHP was to deliver all its pooled hydropower production to its parent companies in proportion to their shareholdings. The investigation carried out by the Commission established that the creation of EHP would not restrict effective competition in the Austrian and German power markets, as the market position of the parent companies would not be altered appreciably.

This conclusion was presumably reached on the basis, first, of the low commonality of **12.314** costs that the EHP joint venture was going to create between the parent companies, secondly, that no joint commercialisation activities were being undertaken by the parties and, thirdly, that credible competitors were active on both geographic markets affected by the transaction. In view of the above, the Commission granted the companies a comfort letter.[348]

(e) Combined Production and Commercialisation Ventures and Pure Joint Sales Practices

(i) Introduction   Production joint ventures sometimes reach out beyond the stage of **12.315** pure joint production, extending into joint selling on downstream supply markets.

---

[345] Compare with analysis in Case M.745 *Commission Shell/Enterprise Oil* (2002).
[346] See in this respect, more generally, Case C-198/01 *Consorzio Industrie Fiammiferi* [2003], not yet reported.
[347] See also the Portuguese Pego joint production project. The Commission focused however on the long-term supply agreement entered into by the joint venture with EDP, the Portuguese incumbent (*Electricidade de Portugal/Pego project* [1993] OJ C265/3).
[348] Commission press release IP/02/62.

12.316   The first question that arises in such a case is whether the agreement falls within Article 3 of the Specialisation BER.[349] On the basis of this provision, companies with a combined market share of less than 20 per cent, jointly generating electricity or producing gas, can include in their joint production agreement provisions providing either for the 'ancillary' setting up of a joint distribution venture or for the appointment of a third party for the distribution of their products.[350]

12.317   In order for such combined agreements to qualify for the block exemption, two aspects should be emphasised. First, the 'centre of gravity' of the co-operation must lie with production, commercialisation remaining an activity ancillary to the main production purpose.[351] Secondly, 'joint distribution' as defined in Article 3(b) of the BER should be understood as including the effective integration of the commercialisation activities, as opposed to the mere coordination of sales by the companies concerned without common joint structure providing for distribution efficiencies that can be passed on to customers.[352] The mere coordination of sales without full integration of activities would instead be assessed as a joint sales cartel having the object of restricting competition, rather than as an attempt to jointly rationalise commercialisation activities through integrated cost-savings.

12.318   Whereas in many instances, in the gas sector at least, joint commercialisation ventures will somehow be linked to joint production by the parties concerned, the practices challenged by the Commission so far have tended to concern joint commercialisation without true integration of the sales function. Some of the practices described hereunder as 'pure' joint sales practices did indeed have some links with joint production of gas and could therefore, on a factual basis, be considered as 'joint production *and* sales' practices. However, in view of the fact either that the co-operation realised at the production level—for instance by means of the appointment of a single 'operator' of a field—was not duplicated at the sales level, or that the type of co-operation at the sales level was wider in scope than the technical co-operation at the production level, such practices, for purposes of simplification, are referred to as 'pure' joint sales practices in the following paragraphs.

12.319   It should be noted that a large number of production joint ventures, which also carry out 'joint distribution' in the meaning of the BER, are likely to be considered so-called 'full-function' joint ventures and thus fall under the scope of the Merger Regulation.

12.320   Commercialisation agreements in the energy sector can generally be categorised at the extreme end of the spectrum, leading to a joint determination of all commercial aspects related to the sale of energy, including volume, delivery point, and supply price. Less extreme

---

[349]   Commission Regulation (EC) 2658/2000 of 29 November 2000 on the application of Article 81(3) of the Treaty to categories of specialisation agreements [2000] OJ L304/3.

[350]   This analysis is made on the assumption that the term 'specialisation agreements', provided for in Art 3(b) of the Specialisation BER, also covers joint production agreements in the energy sector, in line with the definition provided in Art 1 of that block exemption. See, in this sense, Schnichels and Valli, 'Vertical and horizontal restraints in the European gas sector- lessons from the DONG- DUC case', (2003) 2 CPN 61.

[351]   See Horizontal guidelines, point 12 as regards the 'centre of gravity' analysis. See also recital 11 of the Specialisation block exemption.

[352]   See point 153 of the Horizontal guidelines; Schnichels and Valli, above, p 61.

forms of integration, addressing only one of these elements, appear to have been rare, although they could develop as liberalisation progresses.

In the context of joint selling, the Commission has essentially dealt with the issue of joint **12.321** selling in the gas industry, as evidenced by the *Britannia, Corrib, GFU,* and *DUC DONG* cases. In the past, it has been alleged that such joint sales arrangements are necessary in order to counter-balance both the power of the State-controlled or State-sponsored competitors (from countries such as Russia, Algeria, or Norway) and the buying power of the national distribution and supply monopolies.

Since liberalisation, however, it has become the Commission's consistent policy not to **12.322** tolerate joint selling practices falling outside the scope of the BER, unless particularly compelling reasons are provided as a justification. Indeed, technical and commercial constraints, *prima facie*, do not seem to require joint selling by gas producers. Moreover, the existence of import monopolies within the EC can no longer be invoked by producers, if they have ever been a valid justification under Article 81 EC.[353]

Agreements exclusively limited to joint selling are considered by the Commission to have **12.323** both the object and effect of coordinating the pricing policy of the competing energy suppliers.[354] As they are commodity products, joint sales of electricity or gas are considered to equate to a restriction on price and volume.[355] Such arrangements therefore fall within the scope of Article 81(1) EC with no realistic chance of qualifying for exemption under Article 81(3) EC.[356] The strict policy of the Commission in this respect, in all likelihood, is driven by its intention to support the liberalisation process in downstream markets, rather than exclusively by concerns relating to the—often widely defined—upstream gas market. Indeed, the overall intention is not only to reduce (artificial) concentration at the upstream level, but also to increase liquidity in wholesale markets and to allow smaller downstream buyers access to a new series of more independent upstream gas suppliers.

When analysing this type of agreement, a distinction should, first, be made between joint **12.324** selling relating to single fields and joint selling relating to multiple fields. A second relevant distinction could be made between large and small consortium members in joint production and commercialisation ventures (although no explicit Commission position has been adopted in this respect in the energy markets). Really small and isolated participants—for instance, those active in only one field, or in only one field linked to a given upstream pipeline system—could indeed claim to face large obstacles when accessing downstream markets, especially if the overall volumes they can sell in downstream markets is small, or because the own gas with an irregular production profile, or quality. Such a line of reasoning finds some support in the policy line under which agreements through which

---

[353] M Albers, above, point III.2. See also Commission press release in the *Synergen* case referred to below.
[354] See Horizontal guidelines, point 144.
[355] For this reason, the presumption in favour of joint commercialisation agreements when the parties' joint market share is below 15 % (see point 149 of the Horizontal guidelines) is unlikely to apply to a commodity market like the energy markets.
[356] Horizontal guidelines, point 144; Specialisation block exemption, Art 5.1.

competitors decide jointly to supply a single identified customer, which they could not reasonably have supplied individually, do not violate Article 81(1) EC.

12.325 **(ii) Joint Sales from Single-field Gas**   Primary evidence of the Commission's policy in
respect of joint exploitation and sales of gas originating from a single field can be found in
the *Corrib* case dating from 2001.[357] Under the regime pre-dating Regulation 1/2003, the
Enterprise, Statoil, and Marathon companies had applied for an exemption from the
Commission jointly to market gas commonly produced at the Irish Corrib gas field during
the first five years of production. This field is one of the two only indigenous gas sources
in Ireland.

12.326 The concession holders argued that joint marketing would be necessary to balance the
countervailing purchasing power of the incumbent Irish gas and electricity companies
BGE and ESB. The Commission, whilst recognising the strong market position of BGE
and ESB, still raised competition concerns. It questioned in particular whether the joint
marketing would bring about any efficiency as required under Article 81(3) EC. There
were also indications in this case that independent marketing was commercially feasible.
The Commission took into account the fact that the ongoing liberalisation process
would increase the number of eligible gas consumers, such as power generators and energy-
intensive industrial consumers.[358] The Commission closed its investigation after the three
Corrib partners had withdrawn their application for an exemption and had accepted the
principle of individual sales.[359]

12.327 This case should be considered as the current policy line and must be distinguished from
the earlier *Britannia* case dating from 1996, ie before the adoption of the first Gas
Directive. In the latter case, the Commission cleared an agreement notified by the companies participating in the development of the Britannia gas field in the United Kingdom.
The notified agreement concerned the decision by the participating companies to appoint
one of their members as the single sales negotiator on behalf of all the participants. The
Commission concluded that this agreement, running from 1992 to 1994, did not affect
trade between Member States and was therefore outside the scope of the European
Community's competition rules. This position was, in all likelihood, taken on the basis
that the agreement, at the time, was only likely to affect the UK[360] (the UK-Belgium gas
interconnector only entered into operation in 1998). The position adopted by the
Commission in this case would certainly no longer apply, unless the case concerned a

---

[357] See before this Britannia gas condensate field (Notice pursuant to Article 19(3) of Regulation 17
[1996] OJ C291/10).
[358] For a similar type of approach linked to the degree of market opening and the realistic possibilities of the competing venture partners finding clients in the downstream market, see the policy of the
Australian competition authority, as outlined in its brochure 'Infrastructure industries. Energy' (2000)
pp 14ff. The industry's traditional vision, opposed to this approach, can be found in a study from Lateral
Economics: 'Accomplishing precisely nothing: requiring joint venture producers to market gas separately'.
A Supplementary submission to the Energy Market Review on behalf of ExxonMobil, September 2002. Both
documents are available at <http://www.accc.gov.au>.
[359] Commission press release IP/01/578.
[360] Commission press release IP/96/1241.

Member State without any realistic direct or indirect gas interconnection with any other Member State.[361]

Whereas these two cases clearly indicate that joint sales from a single field are caught by Article 81 EC, the *DUC DONG* and *GFU* cases, discussed below, concern joint sales of gas originating from different fields, which are clearly considered as restricting, by object, Article 81 EC. It is noteworthy in this respect, that the preliminary results of the sector inquiry point to a persistence of almost identical sales conditions offered by multiple producers of single gas fields.[362]

12.328

(iii) **Joint Sales from Multiple Gas Fields**   In *DUC DONG*,[363] the Commission, in close co-operation with the Danish Competition authority, investigated joint gas sales activities of Denmark's main gas producers Shell, Møller, and ChevronTexaco, acting together as the Danish Underground Consortium (DUC). DUC accounted for 90 per cent of Danish gas production. The case was settled without the adoption of a formal decision after the members of DUC committed to marketing their production individually in the future. In order to facilitate the establishment of new supply relationships, the DUC members also committed to offering in total seven billion cubic metres of gas for sale to new customers over a period of five years starting in 2005.

12.329

The *GFU* case concerned the joint sales of Norwegian natural gas through a single sales entity called 'GFU'.[364] GFU negotiated natural gas sales contracts with buyers on behalf of all the other natural gas producers in Norway and thus fixed the selling price, volumes, and all other trading conditions. The Commission sent a statement of objections to the members of GFU in 2001, warning them that the joint sales of Norwegian gas through GFU infringed Article 81(1) EC.[365] The companies claimed, in particular, that their behaviour was justified by the 'state compulsion doctrine'. The Commission disagreed and required them, in essence, to put an end to the joint selling of gas and eliminate the restrictive effects of the contracts already concluded: these long-term supply contracts perpetuated the adverse effects of the joint selling scheme and led to significant rigidity in the national gas markets affected.

12.330

The Norwegian Government announced, in 2001, that it was going to take measures to dismantle GFU for the future. A year later, the Commission came to a settlement with the GFU members with regard to the implementation of the dismantlement of the existing joint sales scheme.[366] The settlement consisted of two main elements: first the discontinuation of all joint marketing and sales activities. For existing supply relationships, the settlement required individual negotiations when contracts come up for review. Secondly, the main companies concerned, ie Statoil and Norsk Hydro, offered to reserve certain gas

12.331

---

[361] See Art 28 of the Gas Directive relating to emergent and isolated markets.
[362] See in this respect, Preliminary Report of the Commission's energy sector inquiry, points 276ff.
[363] Commission press release IP/03/566.
[364] For an overall description of the case, see Lindroos, Schnichels and Svane, 'Liberalisation of European gas markets—Commission settles GFU case with Norwegian gas producers' (2002) 3 CPN 50–52.
[365] Commission press release IP/01/830.
[366] Commission press release IP/02/1084.

volumes to new customers which, in the past, had not been in a position to buy from the gas producers concerned.[367] In its press release, the Commission also stressed the need to ensure that gas sold by Norwegian gas producers on an individual basis can indeed be transported along national transmission networks and thus reach consumers. The Commission handled a number of cases thereafter, known as the *Marathon* cases, related to access of Norwegian gas to these transmission networks.[368]

12.332 **(iv) Joint Sales in the Electricity Sector**   The Commission has dealt with few cases in the electricity sector of similar importance to the gas cases discussed above. The electricity sector, however, has long been characterised by the fact that smaller generators tended to sell their entire output to the incumbent.[369] As long as legal supply monopoly persisted, such practices were unobjectionable.

12.333 An example of such a contractual arrangement is provided by the case of French hydropower producer Compagnie Nationale du Rhône (CNR), which sold all its electricity to competitor EDF, instead of marketing it on the French market itself. The Commission initiated an investigation into this practice under Articles 81 and 82 EC. EDF eventually agreed to cut its links with CNR in the context of the *EDF/EnBW* merger case, thus allowing CNR to become an independent competitor on the French supply market.[370]

12.334 A more complex example is provided by the *Irish Synergen* case,[371] which related to the joint construction of a generation plant and the subsequent joint sales of the electricity produced. Joint venture agreements had been agreed upon between Ireland's dominant electricity supplier ESB and the Norwegian gas company Statoil for construction of a 400 MW gas-fired power plant in Dublin called 'Synergen'. The supply agreement signed by the parties provided that a subsidiary of ESB would exclusively market all power generated for fifteen years.

12.335 The Commission, in close co-operation with the Irish energy regulator, analysed in particular whether, in the light of Article 81 EC, the creation of the joint venture removed Statoil as a potential competitor from the highly concentrated Irish power wholesale market. The market investigation showed that Statoil was one of a few, if not the most likely, potential new entrant on the electricity market. The conclusion from the joint investigation was that the market structure would be improved on a lasting basis only if a third power producer, independent of ESB and its Northern Irish competitor Viridian, entered the Irish electricity market. The joint venture agreement, however, prevented Statoil from participating in competing power projects or from entering the market independently.

12.336 In the course of the investigation, the companies proposed to address the key competition concerns. The two main elements of the commitments submitted were the following: first, ESB and Synergen would make available 600 MW of electricity per year under an auction

---

367 See Case M.1383 *ExxonMobil* (1999), point 94.
368 Press releases IP/02/1084 and IP/01/1170. See also further paras 12.400–12.415.
369 See Schaub, n 323 above, p 406. See also Case M.568 *EDF/Edison-ISE* (1995).
370 See Case M.1853 *EDF/EnBW* (2001). See also M Albers, 'Energy liberalisation and EC competition law', Annual proceedings of the Fordham Corporate Law Institute 2001 (2002), pp 519–532, point III.1.
371 Commission press release IP/02/792 and XXXIInd Report on Competition Policy (2002), point 86.

system until additional sources of electricity of 400 MW became available on the Irish market. Secondly, the restriction imposed on Statoil not to participate in competing power projects was deleted. These commitments compensated appropriately for the elimination of an important potential horizontal competitor, in the view of the Commission.

(f) Joint Purchasing

Several electricity or gas buyers may have an interest in coming together in order to bundle their energy needs with a view to achieving better commercial conditions from suppliers. Such arrangements, which appear to be more frequent in the gas sector than in the electricity sector, can appear at different stages of the energy chain, from wholesale level down to the retail level. For instance, joint purchasing by EC wholesalers/importers has traditionally been advanced as one of the ways to ensure security of supply.[372] Dismantling restrictive forms of such co-operation, however, constitutes the mirror action to abolishing restrictive forms of joint upstream commercialisation agreements such as those described in the previous section.

12.337

There is no BER applying to joint purchasing agreements. Moreover, the Commission has never yet formally dealt with this type of case in the energy sector. Guidance should therefore be sought on the general lines of reasoning developed in the horizontal guidelines, as well as in cases dealt with in other sectors of industry. Some interesting cases of this nature, however, have been dealt with by national competition authorities.[373]

12.338

Joint purchasing agreements generally involve both horizontal aspects (between the competing purchasers) and vertical aspects (concerning the relationship between the latter and their common supplier). In other words, a two-step analysis is necessary.[374] As far as the horizontal aspects are concerned, there are basically *two markets* which may be affected by joint buying: first, the relevant purchasing market, where the partners could exercise their 'buyer power' and secondly, the selling markets, ie the downstream markets where the participants of the joint purchasing arrangement may be active as competing sellers.[375]

12.339

One considers generally that market power is unlikely to exist if the jointly purchasing parties have a combined market share below 15 per cent on the upstream purchasing market, as well as a combined market share of below 15 per cent on the downstream selling markets.[376] If both conditions are fulfilled, an appreciable restriction of competition is unlikely.

12.340

In this context, it should be noted that, in practice, joint purchasing agreements are often concluded by small and medium-sized energy customers, including local distributors such as the city works in Italy or Germany (Stadtwerke), to achieve volumes and discounts

12.341

---

[372] See Naeve and Pfeffer, point I, 1.

[373] See *inter alia*, the decision of the Italian competition authority of 19 September 2002, Associazioni di categoria/Gas Intensive, available on web site <http://www.agcm.it>.

[374] Horizontal guidelines, points 115 to 118.

[375] Horizontal guidelines, point 119 to 122. Compare with Commission Decision (EC) 2000/400 of 10 May 2000, Eurovision [2000] OJ L151/18, points 72ff. See also joint cases T-185/00 a.o *Métropole/ Commission* [2002] ECR II-3805, particularly points 52ff.

[376] Horizontal guidelines, point 130.

similar to their bigger competitors. Such agreements between small and medium-sized enterprises (SMEs) often have pro-competitive features and are unobjectionable under Article 81(1) EC.[377] The proviso, of course, is that these SMEs are not controlled by one of the large incumbent players at the national or regional wholesale level.

12.342　Given the dominant position which incumbent wholesalers still exercise in many geographic markets at the current stage of liberalisation, the focus of the analysis with regard to joint purchasing practices by wholesalers will generally focus less on the buying power of the partners on the upstream market, and more on the coordination effects of the purchasing agreement on downstream markets. It is true that, in the *Jahrhundertvertrag* case, dating from 1992, the Commission exempted a joint sales scheme of the German coal industry to a joint purchasing consortium of the German electricity generation industry.[378] It is doubtful, however, that an exemption reasoning, similar to the one based on Article 65(2) of the ECSC Treaty in this old case, would still be applicable to joint purchases of important electricity companies since market opening.

12.343　Finally, it should be noted that gas and electricity companies have set up joint purchasing consortia in order to buy technical equipment construction services or other inputs.[379] Such consortia should be assessed under the general rules set out in the Horizontal Guidelines (ie they will be treated like a joint venture relating to the sale and purchase of industrial goods).

(g) *Joint Construction and Management of Energy Infrastructure*

12.344　(i) **Introduction**　The joint construction of energy infrastructure by competitors raises a series of particular antitrust issues. As a general rule, additional infrastructure, like new LNG terminals, or a novel interconnection between Member States will be considered as pro-competitive,[380] as long as the infrastructure does not mainly or exclusively benefit a company that is dominant in a related (downstream or upstream) supply market. Such market power, typically at the downstream level, could cause foreclosure problems in respect of third parties.[381] The absence of such foreclosure risks will be most obvious when a project is financed and operated by fully unbundled transmission system operators who are not active on upstream or downstream supply markets and where capacity is not made available (exclusively) on a long-term basis to such downstream players.

12.345　An alternative hypothesis is that given the size and the considerable investment that the largest of such projects entails, it can be assumed that co-operation between competitors who could not independently carry out a particular project, does not violate Article 81(1) EC.

377　For examples from the US, see Naeve and Pfeffer, point I, 1.

378　Commission Decision (EC) 2000/400 of 22 December 1992, *Jahrhundertvertrag* [1993] OJ L50/14, points 41ff. See also Commission Decision (EEC) 91/329 of 30 April 1991, *Scottish Nuclear*, [1991] OJ L178/31, point 29.

379　See, for instance, C4 gas joint venture set up by Fluxys, Gaz de France International and Transco, [2002] OJ C166/8.

380　M Albers, 'Energy liberalisation and EC competition law', Annual proceedings of the Fordham Corporate Law Institute 2001 (2002), pp 519–532, point IV.2.

381　See Horizontal Guidelines, points 24, 87 and 143. Compare with Commission Decision (EEC) 88/568 of 24 October 1988, *Eurotunnel*, [1998] OJ L311/36.

An example of the way in which the Commission analyses such infrastructure cases and **12.346**
especially possible foreclosure effects, is provided by the *Eurotunnel* case, in which British
Rail and the French SNCF, which participated indirectly in the financing of the channel
tunnel, had obtained 100 per cent of the railway capacity in that tunnel. Thus, third party
railway companies were prevented from obtaining capacity to run trains through the
channel tunnel. The Commission considered that the exclusivity violated Article 81(1) EC.
However, it exempted the agreements on condition that one quarter of the capacity would
be made available to third parties.[382] In the context of such interpretation of Article 81(3)
EC, the extent and duration of the exclusive use of the infrastructure by those financing its
construction, as opposed to the access rights of third parties, will play a crucial role.[383]

(ii) Construction and Management of Access to New Infrastructure

Antitrust aspects   The current gas and electricity Directives provide for mandatory regu- **12.347**
lated TPA to national transmission networks. However, some infrastructure projects,
depending on the rules developed under national regulatory regimes[384] or the historic
reservation contracts still in place, might fall, *de jure* or *de facto*, outside this regime; for
example, some gas transit pipelines or merchant interconnectors, the agreements for which
date from before the entry into force of the current provisions.

In the absence of a TPA regime set up by or with the explicit approval of regulators, **12.348**
antitrust assessment of access conditions appears warranted, especially since such commercial interconnectors or gas transit pipelines play a crucial role for the liberalisation and
market integration process.[385] In the electricity sector, antitrust involvement might be less
necessary to the extent that the Electricity Directive and the Electricity Regulation[386] do
not appear to provide for a protection of historic contracts as extensive as that provided for
by the Gas Directive.[387]

Moreover, as far as the necessity of antitrust scrutiny is concerned, another relevant dis- **12.349**
tinction should be made between (1) standard interconnectors built before liberalisation
(generally by the former vertically integrated incumbents[388]); and (2) 'merchant interconnectors' constructed jointly by several suppliers, often after a private tender procedure.

---

[382] Commission Decision (EC) 94/894 of 13 December 1994, *Eurotunnel*, [1994] OJ L 354/66, especially point 83. This decision was annulled by the CFI on the basis of error of appreciation of the facts, which
does not however necessarily invalidate the core of the Commission's reasoning (Cases T-79/95 and T-80/95
SNCF a.o./ Commission [1996] ECR, II-1491).
[383] It should be considered, in this respect, that the CFI has held, in *ENS*, that the duration of an exemption must take account of the length of time necessary to enable the infrastructure partners to achieve a satisfactory return on their investment, especially where the project concerned is new and involves substantial
financial risks or the pooling of know-how: Cases T-374/94 and following, *ENS/Commission* [1998] ECR
II-3141, point 230. See also point 81 of the Commission Guidelines on the application of Art 81(3) EC.
[384] See next section.
[385] M Albers, 'Energy liberalisation and EC competition law', Annual proceedings of the Fordham
Corporate Law Institute 2001 (2002), pp 519–532, point III.1. See, as regards the electricity supply market,
Case M.3318 *ECS/Sibelga* (2003), point 43; and Dutch merger decision *Nuon/Reliant*, point 47.
[386] See annex to Regulation (EC) 1228/03, title 'Position of long term contracts'.
[387] Art 32 of Gas Directive.
[388] See the agreements relating to the construction and operation of the Viking electricity cable between
Norway and Germany: Notice pursuant to Art 19(3) of Council Regulation 17 [2001] OJ C247/11.

The former type of interconnectors currently tends to be managed jointly by both national TSOs concerned, under close scrutiny by the competent energy regulators.[389]

12.350 The latter type of interconnector has emerged more recently. Since liberalisation, commercial operators, not necessarily linked with TSOs, have developed projects for building additional interconnectors. The historic example of such projects is the gas interconnector linking the United Kingdom and Belgium: nine European gas companies jointly constructed and agreed on operational rules for the first sub-sea gas interconnection between the United Kingdom and Belgium. A joint venture company was set up which both coordinated the construction and provided for the technical operation of the interconnector.

12.351 The Commission has dealt with this interconnector on two occasions, once in 1995 after the parties notified the Commission about their project[390] under Regulation 17/62 and, a second time in 2001, after several operators and authorities had complained to the Commission about the functioning of the interconnector.[391]

12.352 The agreements notified in 1995 raised certain horizontal issues. No foreclosure effects arose from the construction of the project, as the process leading up to construction appeared open and transparent. In fact, all interested companies had been invited to participate in the project through an open season procedure.

12.353 Another issue examined by the Commission related to the fact that, although the marketing and use of the capacity of the pipeline remained with the individual companies, the joint operation agreements made transfer of capacity to third parties contingent upon standardised conditions. These agreements also provided for the possibility, in certain circumstances, of joint sales of spare capacity by the interconnector company operating the pipeline. The Commission did not challenge either practice. Instead it stated explicitly, in its Competition Report 1995, that it considered the entire project to be pro-competitive, as it created opportunities for competition between previously separated markets and because of the realistic possibilities for third parties to acquire capacity on the interconnector. The twenty-year duration of the rights acquired by those initially funding the project was also considered ancillary to the project as a whole.

12.354 In 2001 however, the UK Department of Trade and Industry (DTI) raised concerns about the functioning of the interconnector. In January of that year, the flows on the interconnector changed from reverse flow (ie imports into the UK) to forward flow (ie exports to the Continent) and did not reverse back before the end of that month, although UK prices were higher than those on the Continent. This led the Commission to consider whether any restrictive practice could help in explaining the steep gas price increases in the UK during that period.

12.355 The Commission investigated, more particularly, the following two horizontal issues. First, it analysed whether companies owning shipping rights, some of whom were also major UK

---

[389] See for example, the rules applying to the French–Belgian electricity interconnectors, as approved by both regulators concerned, available at <http://www.creg.be> and <http://www.cre.fr>.

[390] Commission press release IP/95/550 and Commission competition report (1995) p 125–126.

[391] Commission press release IP/02/401.

gas producers and wholesalers, could have colluded in order to influence the flow direction of the interconnector. Indeed, by screening off the UK market, some of them could have benefited from higher gas prices. Secondly, the Commission investigated whether the technicalities, which were allegedly necessary for the proper functioning of the interconnector, justified the rigidities in the procedures determining the flow direction of the interconnector.

In respect of the first issue, the Commission found no evidence that the gas producers **12.356** owning interconnector capacity collectively had an influence on the flow reversal. On the second issue, the Commission identified a series of rigidities within the Standard Transportation Agreement governing the interconnector which restricted shippers in their capacity to transfer capacity to third parties. This was to be seen as a horizontal issue as the companies owning and controlling the interconnector jointly decided, in a uniform manner, to make spare capacity available to interested third parties. These rigidities included the long minimal duration of assignment and sublease contracts and the high minimal amounts due to be delivered through such contracts.

The Commission, however, closed its investigation as the companies jointly controlling **12.357** IUK had agreed upon more flexible operating rules in November 2001. The most salient modifications included swifter flow transition rules and less stringent conditions for sublease to interested third parties. Moreover, IUK had increased the transparency of its operations by announcing flow reversals in advance: this diminished the information gap between the suppliers owning interconnector capacity and their competitors on the neighbouring supply markets, who did not have access to that information.

Regulatory provisions on new infrastructure As far as the construction of energy infrastruc- **12.358** ture is concerned, traditional antitrust analysis must be combined, in a certain number of cases, with an analysis of the regulatory provisions implementing the Electricity Regulation and the Gas Directive.[392] In essence, these new provisions create the possibility for NRAs to derogate, on a case-by-base basis and on request from the companies concerned, from general, regulated TPA rules in favour of new major energy infrastructure, such as gas or electricity interconnectors, LNG terminals, or gas storage facilities. In this case, the antitrust dilemma described in the introduction appears to have been solved by favouring competition in the long run by means of additional investments, rather than the maximum short-term competition through unconditional TPA.

In order to obtain such derogation, however, five cumulative conditions must be ful- **12.359** filled:[393] (1) the investment must both enhance competition and security of supply; (2) the level of risk attached to the investment is such that the investment would not be made unless an exemption were granted; (3) the infrastructure must be owned by a company other than the relevant TSOs; (4) charges are levied on users of that infrastructure; and (5) the exemption is not detrimental to competition or the effective functioning of the

---

[392] Art 22 of Gas Directive and Art 7 of Regulation 1228/2003.
[393] Art 7.1(e) of Regulation (EC) 1228/2003 also requires, in addition, that since the market opening realised by Directive (EC) 96/62, no part of the costs of the electricity interconnector concerned has been recovered through the charges levied for the use of the transmission systems linked to the interconnector.

internal energy market or the transmission system to which the infrastructure is connected. The applicable provisions further indicate that consideration must be given by the national authorities to the duration of the exemption and non-discriminatory access to the interconnector.

12.360   The type of analysis to be made in the context of these provisions should be close to the one generally realised in the context of Article 81 EC. The first condition can be seen as a reference to the inherently pro-competitive nature of new infrastructure, as long as it is not used almost exclusively in favour of a dominant downstream operator, as already indicated above. The second condition relates to the necessity, for the construction partners, to be guaranteed a sufficient rate of return on their investment. This condition can also be compared with the condition imposed by Article 81(3) EC that a competition restriction is indispensable in order to achieve the overall aim of the agreement containing it.[394] The third and fourth conditions essentially guarantee that the construction of the new infrastructure would not be cross-subsidised by charges levied on the users of neighbouring transmission grids, but directly by the users of the infrastructure concerned. Finally, the fifth condition can be interpreted as reflecting the last condition imposed by Article 81(3), namely that an agreement should not allow competition in the (downstream) market to be eliminated.

12.361   The cases in which these TPA exemptions have been applied by NRAs[395] highlight a series of economically complex issues. A first challenge, for all authorities involved, is to determine whether the duration of the exemption is appropriate in view of the necessary return on investment which the project is intended to yield. The second issue is whether the pro-competitive effects of such infrastructure projects can be secured not only in the relevant transport market which the infrastructure itself affects or creates, but also in the downstream wholesale supply markets linked to the infrastructure.

12.362   The first aspect is generally difficult for an authority to assess from a technical point of view. The main problem is that relevant concepts (such as pay-back period or break-even point) are business concepts which rest on a number of economic assumptions. The veracity and reasonableness of the assumptions are not always easy for authorities to gauge. The parties will nevertheless have to provide a detailed quantitative analysis of the risk assessment they have made.[396] Against this particular background, the competition analysis will tend to focus on the downstream effects of the infrastructure projects. Finally, it should be noted that as those legislative provisions constitute derogations to the general principle of regulated TPA, the conditions for its fulfilment are to be interpreted restrictively.[397]

---

[394]   See Guidelines on the application of Art 81(3) of the Treaty, points 44 and 81.

[395]   The first cases concern the British LNG terminals of South Hook and Isle of Grain, an LNG terminal in Brindisi (Italy), a new gas pipeline between the Netherlands and the UK (BBL) and an electricity interconnector between Scandinavia and the Baltic countries.

[396]   See Note of DG TREN on Directives 2003/54 and 2003/55 and Regulation 1228/03 in the electricity and gas market, 'Exemptions from certain provisions of the third party access regime', p 6.

[397]   See Note of DG TREN, p 1. Compare this line of reasoning with the judgments concerning Arts 86(2) and 81(3) EC of the courts: Case C-157/94 *Commission/Netherlands* [1997] ECR I-5699; and Case T-395/94 *Atlantic Container/Commission* [2002] ECR II-875, point 165.

Procedurally, such decisions are adopted by NRAs and notified to the Commission for **12.363** approval. The Commission may request that the NRA concerned amends or withdraws the decision to grant an exemption.[398] If the NRA does not comply with the request within a period of four weeks, the Commission shall take a final decision.

It is noteworthy that even after having obtained such an exemption, the companies **12.364** concerned will remain subject to antitrust rules. As DG Competition is closely involved in the assessment of the exemption decisions, the companies can however presume that, in the absence of substantial changes of circumstances, DG Competition will not, on its own initiative, commence an investigation as regards the aspects being explicitly addressed in the exemption decision.

(iii) Agreements for Standardising Access Conditions on Existing Infrastructure **12.365** Before the acceleration package provided for mandatory regulated TPA (RTPA) to gas and electricity transmission systems, a number of Member States, including Germany, chose to introduce a system of negotiated TPA (NTPA). Following this decision, the German government, acknowledging the difficulties that would result from each of the several hundred German network operators setting up their own access systems, encouraged the bodies representing the main interested parties to conclude a framework agreement formalising common access conditions. As a consequence, shippers and transmission system operators entered into an agreement on common principles for the calculation of network tariffs.

This resulted in the historic Association Agreements or 'Verbändevereinbarungen'.[399] **12.366** These agreements—first adopted in the electricity and subsequently in the gas sector— essentially contained common criteria for calculating transmission fees. They also provided for the exact level of distance-related fees. These Association Agreements contain both horizontal and vertical features. The horizontal aspects stem from the fact that, by reason of their membership of the industry associations directly involved in the negotiations, different sets of actors involved at the same stage of the energy supply chain jointly agreed on common access rules for their network. A preliminary issue is determination of the extent to which different transmission operators are effective or, at least, potential competitors. This requires a careful factual examination of alternative transmission routes between a significant number of network entry and exit points.

In respect of the horizontal aspects of these agreements, one can first observe that they **12.367** included a degree of joint price-setting. These price effects however, in the particular circumstances of the case, also included the beneficial effect of reducing transaction costs for those parties seeking access to several regional parts of the transmission grids.[400]

---

[398] In practice, pre-notification discussions take place between the undertakings concerned, the NRAs and the different Commission services concerned well before the notification to the Commission by the NRAs.

[399] See for a general description, Cameron Peter, *Competition in energy markets: law and regulation in the European Union* (Oxford University Press, 2002), points 7.73ff. See also M Albers, in *Competition Law & Energy markets*, pp 123–124.

[400] Levasseur Christian, 'Liberalisation & State Intervention. Dévelopements les plus récents' (1998) CPN 43ff.

Secondly, these agreements included the risk of allowing the vertically-integrated companies artificially to partition markets on a geographic basis. Various distance-related tarification elements of the Verbändevereinbarungen have been especially criticised in this regard.

12.368   The acceptance by the Commission of the Verbändevereinbarungen for electricity in 1998, even only after a series of amendments,[401] indicated its willingness, at the time, to tolerate imperfect solutions in the first stages of the energy liberalisation process.

G. Abusive Practices in the Energy Sector

(1) Introduction

12.369   This section provides a general description of the abuse cases which the Commission and some NCAs have considered in the energy sector.

12.370   From a policy perspective, one of the main issues to be addressed in the first decade of this century is whether the traditional abuse provisions, as applied until now by the Commission and NCAs, are sufficient to tackle individual profit maximising behaviour which directly hampers market opening and thus leads to a misallocation of resources in the energy sector. In other words, the policy question is whether the existing antitrust arsenal should somehow be superseded or complemented by a regulatory regime addressing certain types of exercise of dominance or substantial market power on supply markets, as has been done, for a time, in the telecommunications area. The following paragraphs will not provide the answer to this question. Only the enforcement of Article 82 EC in the years to come will indicate whether that antitrust rule is sufficient or not.

12.371   Finally, it should be emphasised that the present section addressing Article 82 is substantially shorter than the chapters devoted to Article 81. This is simply due to the fact that the Commission enforcement of this provision has been significantly less. If the market power of the historic incumbents in the energy sector does not decrease, for instance by means of market integration leading to wider relevant markets, this provision can be expected to be used increasingly both at European and national level, albeit within the limits of the ongoing modernisation of that provision by means of the adoption of 'Article 82 guidelines'.

(2) Dominance and Market Power below that Level

12.372   The analysis applied in order to determine whether or not an energy company has a 'dominant position' is, in general terms, the same as for any other sector of industry. It is debatable, however, whether the 40 per cent market share threshold traditionally used as a starting point for dominance constitutes an appropriate first benchmark in the energy markets and especially in the electricity sector. Traditional yardsticks such as market shares and concentration levels (HHI), which provide useful first indications of market structure and the competitive position of an undertaking, can sometimes be misleading in electricity and gas markets.

---

[401] See *Veba/Viag* (M.1673) (2000). See, more generally M Albers, 'Competition law issues arising from the liberalisation process' (2000) Journal of Network Industries, pp 272–273.

The key problem is that, in electricity markets, which are characterised by inelasticity of demand,[402] an undertaking can achieve a decisive impact on price setting with 'market power' below the traditional 'dominance' level of Article 82 EC. Alternatively, one could describe the problem in terms of 'dominance' exercised only in very specific time segments and market circumstances. In such a market, market shares or HHI levels may lead to false conclusions. **12.373**

A clear example of the issues in question is provided by the Danish electricity markets (east and west Denmark respectively) and the two main operators active in each of those two markets: during periods where the geographic market is wider than that half of Denmark, because the interconnectors are not congested, the local operators have only a relatively small market share as compared to their bigger competitors in neighbouring Member States. However, when, due to congestion, the relevant markets shrink to cover only eastern Denmark or western Denmark respectively, the companies concerned have a very significant market share.[403] **12.374**

With respect to an even shorter time period, the Spanish NCA decided, in 2004, that each of three Spanish generators had abused their respective dominant position, by charging excessively high tariffs, when there were exceptional congestion problems on the Spanish electricity transmission network for a period of three days.[404] **12.375**

After encountering similar problems in the US, the Federal Energy Regulatory Commission (FERC) developed a framework to analyse market power in the electricity generation segment called the Supply Margin Assessment (SMA).[405] This SMA assesses market power by reference to a threshold based on whether an undertaking is 'pivotal' in the market: the framework tries to determine whether at least part of a company's generation capacity is necessary to meet the market's peak demand. Where an undertaking is indeed in such a 'pivotal' situation, it is in a position to demand a high price, presumably above competitive levels. **12.376**

In antitrust policy, the relevant authorities have addressed these issues, first, by defining electricity and gas *peak* markets,[406] secondly, by making a detailed analysis of the electricity 'merit order'[407] and, thirdly, by means of the doctrine of unilateral effects in merger cases.[408] All of these techniques purport to allow antitrust authorities to prevent situations arising **12.377**

---

[402] While gas can be stored at least within the limits of existing gas storage facilities, electricity cannot be stored.

[403] See P Moelgaard and C Kastberg Nielsen, above, p 39.

[404] Decision 'Empresas electricas', Case 552/02 *Tribunal de Defensa de la Competencia*, 7 July 2004, as described by M van der Woude in *Competition Law & Energy markets*, p 255.

[405] Copenhagen Economics study, p 14.

[406] First considered in Case M.3268 *Sydkraft/Graninge* (2003), as well as in the *Nuon/Reliant* merger case dealt with by the Dutch NCA (see n 90).

[407] The 'merit order' is the order in which generation plants are called to produce in order to respond to demand, starting with the cheapest base-load production and ending with the most expensive peak production (eg old oil-fired plants). See, for a detailed analysis of such merit order at national level, Case M.3440 *ENI/EDP/GDP* (M.3440) (2004), especially points 163ff and 302ff.

[408] Guidelines on the assessment of horizontal mergers under the Council Regulation on the control of concentrations between undertakings [2004] OJ C31/5.

where electricity generators, with a relatively small generation capacity, are, collectively or individually, in a position to impose supra-competitive prices due to their position in the merit order, or their ability to withhold production strategically in peak times.

12.378 In view of the oligopolistic nature of the industry and the links between competing suppliers in a number of Member States (ie cross-shareholdings, joint operation of networks or production facilities), the doctrine of 'collective dominant positions' may also apply. The Commission has indeed applied this doctrine, in the electricity sector, in the *Almelo* case.[409]

(3) Abuse

(a) Introduction

12.379 As is the case with many other industries, Article 82 abuse cases in the energy sector have tended to deal with exclusionary, rather than with exploitative abuses. Investigations into exploitative abuses (for example, challenging excessive prices) have been rare, and principally undertaken by NCAs like the German Bundeskartellamt or the Spanish Tribunal de Defensa de la Competencia. Whatever the abuse concerned, the following sections show that it is not always easy to draw the line between competition by a powerful incumbent relying on its (natural) advantages and 'abuse' of the dominant position by the incumbent against its competitors.[410]

(b) Excessive Pricing

12.380 The difficulty for antitrust authorities and judges alike in establishing the existence of exploitative abuses is not peculiar to the gas or electricity sectors. It is notoriously challenging to prove this type of abuse, which generally requires the authority to indicate, at least implicitly, what a 'correct' or 'competitive' price would be. The basic issue in all such cases is to try to determine whether price levels can be explained by costs structures and/or habitual fluctuations in a competitive market or whether the price levels are to be considered as the pure consequence of the exercise of unrestrained market power. These issues have been thoroughly examined, as regards the electricity sector, in the context of the energy sector inquiry.[411]

12.381 (i) **The 'Cost Plus' Approach**   Several antitrust authorities have endeavoured to tackle this type of case, with varied success.[412] Two methods have been tried: the first is the 'cost plus' approach, which attempts to calculate, for example on the basis of the Lerner index, how the profit margin compares to the marginal costs. This approach was used, *inter alia*, by the Danish NCA in an investigation into the pricing behaviour of electricity supplier

---

[409] Commission Decision (EEC) 91/50 of 16 January 1991, *Ijsselcentrale*, [1991] OJ L28/32, described in greater detail in para 12.107.

[410] Wälde and Gunst, above n 16, p 206.

[411] See in this respect, Preliminary Report of the Commission's energy sector inquiry, points 399ff.

[412] See for example, a Finnish case, quashed on appeal, as described in Copenhagen Economics study, p 19. See also decision of the French Conseil de la Concurrence (decision no 05-D-15) of 13 April 2005, rejecting the complaint of Regal Pat against Electricité de Strasbourg, available at <http://www.conseil-concurrence.fr>.

Elsam in western Denmark.[413] The Danish authority settled this case on the basis of commitments which boil down, in reality, to (regulatory) market design rules. The electricity companies concerned committed, first, to following a particular policy for the submission of supply fundamentals to the structured electricity exchange Nordpool and, secondly, to operating as so-called 'market makers'. The latter commitment implies that they will always give notice of the prices at which they will buy and sell, which should render the market more liquid.

A similar 'costs plus' approach has been tried by the Bundeskartellamt (BKA) in the **12.382** *Thüringer Energie AG (TEAG)* case.[414] The BKA, acting at the time in the absence of any energy sector regulator in Germany, considered that excessive fees for network use constituted the main obstacle for effective TPA in the German electricity sector. TEAG, a subsidiary of incumbent wholesaler E.ON, had calculated its fees for distribution network use on the basis of the Association Agreements.[415] The calculations made by the BKA focused primarily on the evaluation of the network and management costs. The BKA considered, *inter alia*, that TEAG had erroneously attributed advertisement costs to the network branch, which in reality constituted a cross-subsidisation in favour of TEAG's supply activities. The Bundeskartellamt therefore ordered TEAG to reduce its abusively excessive fees for network use.

On appeal, however, a German court repealed the decision, arguing that the **12.383** Bundeskartellamt had exceeded its competencies by setting an upper limit for TEAG's revenues and hence for taking up a 'price regulation' competence. Another issue raised by the court was whether some inappropriate costs highlighted by the Bundeskartellamt could not be neutralised by other allowable costs which had not been taken into account. Finally, the court did not consider the difference of 10 per cent, as compared to the minimum fee, as being of such importance as to be considered abusive under German cartel legislation.

(ii) **The 'Benchmarking' Approach**   The second method consists of benchmarking **12.384** prices in one geographic area by reference to prices in other similar areas, as the Bundeskartellamt did in the *Stadtwerke Mainz* case.[416] In this case, the BKA compared the fees levied by the Stadtwerke Mainz with those of RWE. As the fees of the companies were not directly comparable because they served different customer groups (the former operated essentially a local distribution network, the other a transmission network), the revenues for a kilometre of network line were, in essence, chosen as the basis for comparison. The Bundeskartellamt considered that the comparison showed there to be a potential for important cost savings mainly related to Mainz's network operation management. The BKA thus ordered a 20 per cent reduction of the network fees. As in the TEAG case, this decision was successfully challenged in court by the addressee of the BKA decision. As well

---

[413]   See P Moelgaard and C Kastberg Nielsen, 'The competition law and economics of electricity market regulation', (2004) ECLR 42 and the web site of the Danish competition authority: <http://www.ks.dk>.
[414]   Decision of 15/1/2003, available at <www.Bundeskartellamt.de>.
[415]   These Associations Agreements, also called 'Verbändevereinbarungen' are described above in paras 12.365ff.
[416]   Decision of 17/4/2003, available at <http://www.Bundeskartellamt.de>.

as the (same) ground of incompetence, the court highlighted in particular the fact that RWE was not to be considered an appropriate comparator with Mainz because of differences in size and structure. This 'comparable market concept' approach is generally comparable to that adopted by the Commission in a series of pending cases relating to international roaming rates in the telecommunication sector.[417]

12.385 These German cases demonstrate the inherent challenges in attempts to determine the reasonableness of network tariffs. However, it might be easier to prove the existence of an abuse in cases where a payment is required for a service that is, in fact, not offered. In a case regarding Dutch electricity transmission charges,[418] the Dutch energy regulator asked the Commission whether the tariff system of the dominant national network operator, which it had been asked to approve at national level, was compatible with Article 82 EC. This system provided that the cost for transmitting electricity through the grid was to be shared, on a 75 per cent/25 per cent basis, between customers and suppliers. The national TSO intended to charge suppliers the same charge, on the one hand, for imports into the Netherlands and transit of electricity through the country, and on the other hand, for local supplies, ie 25 per cent.

12.386 The Commission considered, first, that transmission costs normally arise only from physical and not from merely contractual flows of electricity. The TSO could therefore only charge for import and transit to the extent that those operations gave rise to extra costs on the Dutch high voltage grid. Secondly, the Commission noted that within the framework of an integrated European energy market, it was possible for electricity to be traded financially several times across national borders without physical flows necessarily taking place for the same amount. Therefore, in order to avoid double payments in favour of the TSO—the TSO was, at the time, still vertically linked with a number of local suppliers grouped within SEP[419]—it was necessary to ensure that foreign traders were only charged for electricity which was physically imported and/or exported.

12.387 A similar case is unlikely to arise under the present legislative regime for cross-border electricity lines, as Regulation (EC) 1228/2003 explicitly addresses such issues.[420] In the gas sector, on the other hand, there is a great lack of transparency as regards the difference between physical and contractual flows. This is due, *inter alia*, to the practice of the so-called locational 'swap' arrangements between established wholesalers, who exchange gas volumes at different geographic points within Europe in order to reduce transport costs.[421]

12.388 With increasing scrutiny by energy regulators over transmission activities and the growing harmonisation of TPA rules at European level, one might expect a diminishing need for antitrust intervention with regard to network activities. Experience from the telecommunications

---

[417] The Commission issued press releases (IP/04/994 and IP/05/161) when initiating these cases.

[418] XXIXth Report on Competition Policy (1999) p 165.

[419] See, for a description of SEP, the *Almelo* case described above in para 12.107.

[420] The Regulation underlines, for instance, the necessity of taking into account physical rather than contractual flows (Arts 3.5 and 6.5), as well as a general principle of equal treatment between national transport and cross-border transport (Art 5).

[421] See with respect to the swaps, the Issues Paper published in November 2005 by DG Competition in the context of the energy sector inquiry (Cases 39.172 and 39.173), available at <http://www.europa.eu.int>.

sector, and most prominently the *Deutsche Telekom* case,[422] however, highlights the continuous need for residual antitrust scrutiny.

(c) Discrimination

(i) **Introduction** The duty of TSOs not to discriminate between network users, as laid   **12.389**
down in the liberalisation legislation, should be seen as a parallel to the prohibition against
discrimination[423] found in Article 82(2)(c) EC. The principle of non-discrimination is in
fact one of the cornerstones of the liberalisation process. As the liberalisation Directives
indicate, 'In order to complete the internal [. . .] market, non-discriminatory access to the
network of the transmission and distribution network operators is of paramount importance.'[424] The key non-discrimination provision, however, concerns third party access
rules: TSOs are prohibited from discriminating between system users or between classes of
system users, particularly in favour of related undertakings.[425]

Cross-subsidisation is inherently also a form of discrimination. All directives relating to   **12.390**
market opening processes, including those in the energy sector, address this type of
behaviour by requiring, at least, the unbundling of accounts: vertically-integrated electricity and gas undertakings must keep separate internal accounts for their own network
activities, on the one hand, and their supply activities on the other.

The energy Directives recognise this explicitly.[426] Cross-subsidies can occur either between   **12.391**
network and supply activities or between different supply activities. It is noteworthy in this
respect that the liberalisation process is also likely to unravel explicit or implicit cross-
subsidies which existed. Indeed, consumers with higher than average costs (households) were
often subsidised by those with lower average costs (large industrial customers).[427] Social intervention by authorities in the energy markets, for instance by means of cross-subsidies, is
not incompatible with the liberalisation process and antitrust rules: it should, however,
take place in a transparent manner.

No such cases have yet been dealt with by the Commission in the energy sector. The   **12.392**
Deutsche Post case,[427A] however provides a framework for managing this type of case for
network industries.

(ii) **Discrimination as Regards Access** The extent of the principle of non-discrimination   **12.393**
is very wide: it covers not only allocation of available capacity and tariff setting, but also all

---

[422]   Commission Decision of 21 May 2003, *Deutsche Telekom*, [2003] OJ L263/9.
[423]   Non-discrimination is a general principle of EC law, enshrined most prominently in Art 12 EC. In its
case law, the Court has repeatedly held that this principle requires that comparable situations are not to be
treated differently and that different situations are not to be treated alike, unless such treatment is
justified objectively. See Cases 117/76 and 16/77 *Ruckdeschel* [1977] ECR 1753. On the principle of non-
discrimination, see generally Lenaerts and Van Nuffel, *Constitutional Law of the European Union* (Sweet &
Maxwell, 2004).
[424]   Recital 6 of the Electricity Directive and Recital 8 of the Gas Directive.
[425]   Arts 14(2) and 20 of the Electricity Directive and Arts 12 (2) and 18 of the Gas Directive.
[426]   Art 19(3) of the Electricity Directive.
[427]   See Cave and Crowther, 'Co-ordinating regulation and competition law—ex ante and ex post' in *The
pros and cons of antitrust in deregulated markets* (Swedish Competition Authority, 2004), p 31.
[427A]   COMP/37.821, mentioned in IP/00/919 of 8 August 2000.

access conditions, including ancillary network services, such as portfolio effects.[428] Moreover, the duty of equal treatment applies not only between two (unrelated) third party shippers: it also extends to the treatment granted by the network operators to related supply branches or companies, as compared to third party shippers.[429] These principles have been incorporated, often in great detail, into national legislation implementing the electricity and gas Directives.

12.394 Two issues, however, remain largely contested, even after implementation of the Directives at national level. The first concerns the question as to whether priority access to the grid can be given to pre-liberalisation users, on the basis of (alleged) legitimate expectations raised by existing long-term reservation contracts.

12.395 The second issue is whether discrimination can somehow be proved between, on the one hand, a branch of a completely integrated energy company—where network and supply activities have not (yet) been unbundled into separate entities—and, on the other, a third party shipper. In other words, can a company discriminate between itself and a third party?[430] These issues can arise both in a purely regulatory context and in an antitrust case. This is highlighted by the crucial *VEMW* case.[431] There, addressing the issue of the legality of priority access granted to historic electricity transmission contractors, the Court ruled that such priority treatment amounted to discrimination under the Electricity Directive. The Advocate General had examined the same issue under Articles 81 and 82 EC. This again underlines the overlap which exists between the scope of application of both sets of rules.

12.396 (iii) **Discrimination as regard Supply Issues** Before liberalisation took off at a general EC level, both the Commission and certain national authorities had dealt with a number of price discrimination practices by dominant energy suppliers, although not necessarily under the competition rules.[432] Since 1998, the Commission has not dealt explicitly with cases addressing discriminatory supply practices. Certain decisions relating mainly to foreclosure effects, such as the *Gas Natural—Endesa* case,[433] can however also be analysed in the light of the principle of non-discrimination.

12.397 In this case, the contract at issue in that case provided that Endesa was under an obligation to buy gas from Gas Natural for electricity generation purposes only. The contract included a provision indicating that natural gas for resale purposes would be supplied separately at a higher price. The Commission considered, in this context, that lowering prices to new customers while maintaining a higher price level in other segments of the market (market segmentation), certainly helped to reinforce artificially the market position of the incumbent gas supplier Gas Natural.[434]

---

[428] See with regard to portfolio effects the decision of the French regulator CRE of 2 May 2002 concerning litigation between the French TSO RTE and the Paris metro (RATP), French [2002] OJ128/10002.

[429] For an overview of the discrimination issues in a regulatory context, see Moen, above, p 65.

[430] This issue is often linked to the question whether legally unbundled companies should still be considered to be a single 'undertaking' under Art 82 EC. See in this respect, *inter alia*, Case M.2684 *ENBW/EDP/Cajastur/Hidrocantabrico* (2002).

[431] Case C-17/03 *VEMW* [2005], not yet reported.

[432] See Ritter and Braun, above, pp 928–929.

[433] See paras 12.181ff.

[434] XXIIth Report on Competition Policy (2000) p 154.

The only formal decision from an NCA regarding alleged discriminatory energy supply **12.398** prices was adopted by the British regulator Ofgem under its antitrust powers.[435] Ofgem had received a complaint against London Electricity. That company, the historic operator in the city of London, offered a 'win back offer' to customers who had switched away from it. Special vouchers were offered over a period running for a little over a year. While the company was clearly engaging in price discrimination between, on the one hand, its existing customers and, on the other hand, those customers who had switched away, Ofgem, surprisingly, decided that the discrimination did not have any 'material effect', due to the very limited take-up of the offer.

Ofgem rejected the complaint, on that substantive basis, by a decision similar in nature to **12.399** a decision under Article 7 of Regulation 773/2004. It is regrettable that this is the only precedent available for what is arguably a frequent practice. This is especially so because it sets a very high burden of proof as regards the effects of the practice on the market. This approach might well lead dominant companies to think that practices which are abusive in nature can be exempted as long as, for whatever reason, they are unsuccessful.

(d) Denial of Access to the Network

The case law on refusal to supply starts from the premise that all companies, including **12.400** dominant companies, are, in principle, free to enter into commercial relations with those clients whom they find appropriate: this line of reasoning also applies to the issue of access or the refusal to provide access to energy networks. The controversies relating to access issues are linked to the wider debate on the doctrine of 'essential facilities', which provides, under certain conditions, for a principle of access in favour of competitors to key infrastructure. The Commission has published a notice on the application of the competition rules to access agreements in the telecommunications sector,[436] setting out a framework for the analysis of access agreements or refusals to provide access. There is, for the time being, no similar notice in respect of the energy sector, so the principles contained in the telecommunications notice can be applied by analogy, as many of the conceptual access issues that are raised are similar.

(i) **Advantages of Access Provided by Sectoral Regulation**   Antitrust tools, in most **12.401** instances, do not constitute, for an individual company, the most efficient way to obtain access to gas or electricity infrastructure, because of the long time periods generally needed to litigate such cases. Therefore, legislation has been adopted which contains detailed provisions on access to networks. Not only does legislation provide for general and more predictable rules than antitrust enforcement, it can also go beyond what is required of the owner of an 'essential infrastructure' under Article 82 EC. A regulation can, for instance, indicate that the owner of an energy infrastructure is under an obligation to reduce the flexibility of its own supply business in favour of third parties, for instance through the

---

[435] See Harker and Waddams, pp 38–39.
[436] See also Notice on the application of the competition rules to access agreements in the telecommunications sector—Framework, relevant markets and principles? [1998] OJ C265/2; and more particularly point 6 as regards is application beyond telecommunications.

application of a 'use-it or lose-it' principle. Such a remedy would not appear to be readily available under the antitrust rules.

12.402 Generally, Regulation should thus take over the role of competition enforcement as regards access issues. Moreover, such regulatory intervention leads, in practice, to shifting the *burden of proof* in favour of those requesting access.[437] The main feature of TPA is indeed an obligation on the network owners to provide a transport service for third party shippers. This 'duty to contract', which lies at the heart of the controversies surrounding the 'essential facilities doctrine', was further reinforced, in the process of liberalisation, when the latest directives imposed on Member States a duty to introduce Regulated TPA regimes to the general networks, to the exclusion of Negotiated TPA regimes.

12.403 Another reason for favouring regulation over competition enforcement in the area of access is the level of the tariffs to be imposed on the company requesting access.[438] The *Bundeskartellamt* cases mentioned above in paragraphs 12.380ff, as well as certain Commission decisions regarding intellectual property, (such as *Microsoft* and *IMS*[439]), highlight the difficulties of litigating such issues on a case-by-case basis. In the gas and electricity sectors, the principles for setting access tariffs or, at least, access tariff methodologies, are also outlined in the legislation, and further elaborated in the context of the regulatory fora of Florence and Madrid.[440]

12.404 (ii) **Reasons for Refusing Access**   The EC Energy Directives and Regulations do not provide for an unconditional principle of access for interested shippers-customers to energy networks. These Directives lay down a certain number of conditions under which TSOs may legitimately refuse access. Article 21 of the Gas Directive,[441] for instance, provides in this respect that 'Natural gas undertakings may refuse access to the system on the basis of lack of capacity or where the access to the system would prevent them from carrying out [. . .] public service obligations [. . .]. Duly substantiated reasons shall be given for such a refusal'.[442] It appears undeniable that, in the absence of physical capacity, access to a network can be denied as long as it is not done in a discriminatory manner.[443] This means however that network operators must make the maximum technically available

---

[437] Compare with Art 2 of Regulation 1/2003.

[438] See Ridyard, 'Compulsory access under EC competition law—A new doctrine of 'convenient facilities' and the case for price regulation'(2004) ECLR 669ff.

[439] (Reluctant) licensors will often claim that licensing rates should be set at a level which will compensate them for the loss of profits they suffer from allowing the licensee into the downstream market.

[440] See above para 12.48.

[441] See also Art 20(2) of the Electricity Directive.

[442] The Gas Directive also contains a provision relating to so-called 'take-or -pay commitments'. Art 27 of this Directive provides that if a gas company encounters serious economic or financial difficulties because of its take-or-pay commitments in a gas- purchase contract, it can apply to the regulator concerned for a temporary derogation from TPA rules. This provision now appears largely outdated, first because gas companies have received sufficient time to renegotiate their supply contracts (taking into account the liberalisation process) and secondly because this provision is still based on a confusion of interests between transport and supply branches within vertically integrated companies.

[443] See the debate surrounding this issue in the early stages of the legislative process: 'Report of the Consultative Committees on Third party access to Electricity Networks, Commission', May 1991, document CCEME 91/1 final.

capacity accessible.[444] It is questionable that Commission would accept other justifications during the assessment of a refusal under Article 82 EC.

A crucial question which arises in this context is whether access rights extend to capacity **12.405** contracted by the so-called primary owners, but subsequently unused by them. This issue is addressed, in practice, by applying a form of the 'use-it or lose-it' principle, which allows for rights that are contracted but not used (so-called 'unused capacity') to be made available to third parties, at least on an 'interruptible' basis.[445]

(iii) Antitrust Enforcement as the Stopgap of Access Regulation   Whatever the level of **12.406** detail of the last set of EC Energy Directives and Regulations, as well as the level of detail of the rules implementing these into national law, many access-related issues cannot be addressed at all, or can be addressed to a limited extent only in the current regulatory system. These unregulated access issues will therefore be addressed by TSOs, on a day-by-day basis, leaving some scope for application of Article 82 EC.

The Commission's *Marathon* case[446] offers clear examples of the role of competition law as **12.407** regards setting TPA conditions in a liberalising environment. The case dates from the 1990s, when the Norwegian subsidiary of the American oil and gas producer Marathon had requested access to the gas pipelines of five gas companies in continental Europe on several occasions. It encountered systematic refusals to provide access. The incumbent companies concerned essentially argued that they themselves wanted to buy Marathon's uncommitted gas. The refusals were flagged by the Commission as potential abuses of dominant position and restrictive concerted practices. The complaint was later withdrawn following an out of court settlement, but the Commission continued its investigation because the settlement did not remove the suspected infringements.

The main commitments obtained by the Commission relate to issues such as a gradual **12.408** reduction in the number of tariff and balancing zones, conversion of High calorific gas into Low calorific gas, gas release programmes, the introduction of entry/exit regimes, online balancing services, transparency, booking procedures, and congestion management. In view of the type of commitments offered, the cases were dealt with in close co-operation with the sectoral regulators concerned, such as the French CRE and the Dutch DTE.

In Germany, the Bundeskartellamt has also dealt with an interesting complaint from RWE **12.409** against Bewag, a regional electricity company in Berlin. The latter refused an access request from RWE who sought to supply a customer in West Berlin, on the basis of capacity restrictions

---

[444] See Art 6 of Electricity Regulation and Art 5 of the Gas Regulation.

[445] 'Interruptible' rights are rights obtained by a 'secondary' user, but which might have to be given back (interrupted) if the primary owner claims back its original right of use. Such 'interruptible' rights therefore create additional risks for those using them. Interruptible rights are most useful for those network users, such as certain generation plants, which can switch between heavy fuel oil and gas. Such plants can therefore use the interruptible transport rights in order to benefit from possible inter-fuel competition without being obliged to stop their core activity in case of an interruption. See, for instance, Art 6(4) of the Electricity Regulation.

[446] See Commission press releases IP/04/573 (*Ruhrgas* and *Gaz de France*), IP/03/1129 (*BEB*), IP/03/547 (*Gasunie*), IP/01/1641 (*Thyssengas*). See for a general explanation, Fernandez Salas, Klotz, Moonen and Schnichels, 'Access to gas pipelines: lessons learnt from the Marathon case' (2004) CPN 41.

in the West Berlin area. Bewag referred both to technical security reasons (waiting for further reinforcement of the grid) and to the fact that it needed the existing capacity for its own (unbundled) supply activities. The Bundeskartellamt considered that Bewag, as a network operator, was not entitled to give itself priority use of the network in order to cover its affiliate's supply needs. The Bundeskartellamt decided that it had found no circumstances that could lead to any solution other than equal allocation of the existing capacity and ordered Bewag to allow use of the network by scaling of existing capacity.[447]

12.410 **(iv) Can the Refusal to Expand Network Capacity Constitute an Abuse?** Another relevant question is whether Article 82 EC can be used to 'force' network owners to enhance the capacity of a pipeline or electricity line which is physically fully used, when the company is faced with continuous longer term demand?[448] The existence of Article 21(2) of the Gas Directive shows that the issue of enhancement is a crucial one in practice.[449] It appears doubtful that a company could refuse to expand energy infrastructure, completely or partially, in order to protect its supply interests, when it has organised an open season and received firm commitments from potential shippers which are ready to co-finance the new infrastructure. This type of problematic refusal to enhance capacity tends to arise essentially where the company managing the infrastructure is still somehow vertically integrated with a supplier. Indeed, whereas an infrastructure company confronted with excessive demand for capacity should, in a well-designed regulatory system, have a commercial interest in expanding the network, the implementation of these interests might be hampered by conflicting supply interests within a vertically integrated group of companies.

12.411 The delicate question of the extent to which such 'mandatory enhancement of capacity' could be obtained by means of Article 82 EC, should be examined in conjunction with the extent to which 'legacy contracts' (ie transport contracts signed before liberalisation) continue to benefit, after the entry into force of the liberalisation Directives, from a priority status.[450] The current (over) lenient approach of the Gas Directive, for instance, should be combined with a strict approach with regard to enhancements. A stricter approach concerning legacy contracts could be combined with a more lenient approach concerning capacity enhancements.

12.412 So far, the issue has only arisen indirectly in a pending Italian case. The Italian Autorità Garante della Concorrenza e del Mercato has initiated a case against the Italian oil and gas company, ENI, because together with its affiliate, Trans Tunisian Pipeline Company (TTPC), ENI has blocked the agreed expansion of the TTPC pipeline linking Italy with Algeria.[451]

---

447 Decision of 30/8/1999, available at <www.Bundeskartellamt.de>.

448 See Moen, above, p 53 and pp 79ff.

449 This Art provides that 'Member States *may* take the measures necessary to ensure that the natural gas undertaking refusing access to the system on the basis of lack of capacity or a lack of connection makes the necessary enhancements as far as it is economic to do so or when a potential customer is willing to pay for them [. . .]'. See also Art 20(3) of the Electricity Directive.

450 See in this respect, paras 12.272ff.

451 See Decision of 15 February 2006, (Case A358 *ENI Trans Tunisian Pipeline*) available at <http://www.agcm.it>.

The indictment specifies that ENI controls all of the gas entry points to Italy and is still the leading wholesaler in the relevant Italian wholesale market. In 2002, TTPC had allocated the expanded capacity to seven competitors of ENI. These companies entered into so-called 'ship-or-pay' contracts,[452] thereby guaranteeing the financial viability of the project.

The charge made by the Autorità is essentially that the issue of whether the conditions precedent of these ship-or-pay contracts were met was entirely a matter for ENI: by invoking the risk that ENI's supply interests could be damaged by the overall increased gas imports into Italy in order to block the (already) agreed expansion, ENI has failed to meet the special responsibility laid upon it by Article 82 EC. More particularly, the alleged obstructionist practices would constitute an abuse with the effect of foreclosing competitors from the market for the import of gas into Italy. **12.413**

(v) Neutrality Regarding Capacity Allocation Mechanisms It should be emphasised that, as a matter of principle, it is not for antitrust authorities to choose from among the different capacity allocation mechanisms available, which should be applied in any particular case. The Commission made clear allusions to this in the *Irish interconnector* case in 1999.[453] **12.414**

In that case, the competent Irish ministry asked the Commission for its advice on how to allocate the limited capacity of the UK–Ireland gas interconnector. The Commission confirmed that the equality principle would not be violated if, in the particular context of proven need for imported gas to generate the required amount of electricity by means of gas-fired power stations, priority was given to the allocation of gas to be consumed by power generators when allocating the limited capacity of the gas interconnector. No additional capacity, however, was to be granted to the dominant power supplier, ESB. As far as the allocation methodology was concerned, the Commission emphasised that the choice had to be made by the Ministry, which was only required to respect the principles of transparency and non-discrimination. Since this case, the European liberalisation legislation has, to a large extent, clarified the framework that applies to capacity allocation mechanisms.[454] **12.415**

(e) Long-term Contracts

(i) Long-term Supply Contracts The restrictive effects of both horizontal and vertical energy supply contracts, as analysed under Article 81 EC, have been outlined above.[455] As far as the analysis of such contracts under Article 82 EC is concerned, there has been no guidance from the Commission since the implementation of the first liberalisation Directives, with the exception of the *Gas Natural-Endesa* case mentioned above. **12.416**

---

[452] For an explanation of 'ship-or-pay contracts', see P Roberts, 'Structuring effective gas sales and gas transportation arrangements' (2004) IELTR 190.

[453] *Irish interconnector* case, XXIXth Report on Competition Policy (1999) p 165.

[454] See, for instance, Art 6 of the Electricity Regulation and Art 5 of the Gas Regulation.

[455] See sections E and F. See also the Bundeskartellamt paper 'Kartellrechtliche Beurteilungsgrundsätze zu langfristigen Gasverträgen', 25 January 2005, available at <http://www.Bundeskartellamt.de>.

12.417   An interesting example, however, is provided by a decision of November 2003[456] adopted by the Italian Autorità Garante della Concorrenza e del Mercato. The Autorità found that the incumbent electricity generator and wholesale supplier ENEL had abused its dominant position in the market for the sale of power to eligible customers. In particular, ENEL was found to have violated Article 82 EC by including clauses in its standard supply contracts which prevented customers from switching to competing suppliers. As a result, ENEL had created a 'captive market' foreclosing competitors.

12.418   Beyond these explicit non-compete provisions, clauses providing for exclusivity in the supply of electricity of foreign origin and a prohibition against participating in bids for the allocation of renewable energy or co-generation were found to be abusive. Moreover, ENEL applied price increases when its customers also bought electricity from competing sources. Such a 'customer retention strategy', covering a considerable proportion of the total eligible customers, provides a prime example of why antitrust enforcement is needed to prevent historic players from pre-empting liberalisation.[457]

12.419   Turning to the issue of duration, although the vertical block exemption provides some guidance, it should be acknowledged that the definition of an appropriate duration for an energy supply contract is a recurrent problem both for antitrust authorities and national judges. It is hoped that the ongoing work of the Bundeskartellamt[458] and the Commission will have provided clarity in this respect in the course of 2006.

12.420   **(ii) Long-term Capacity Reservations of Infrastructure**   Long-term capacity reservation of electricity interconnectors or gas pipelines can have severe foreclosure effects,[459] especially when the infrastructure concerned constitutes one of the only energy routes between neighbouring markets. In such circumstances, long-term reservations often allow the capacity holder to bar new entrants from its markets and to benefit exclusively from price differentials between neighbouring geographic markets.

12.421   It must be noted that the length of time permitted by the Commission for exclusive or quasi-exclusive use of such parts of infrastructure in the past[460] for the construction of new infrastructure largely exceeded the duration it has accepted for supply contracts. These positions taken by the Commission, which are reflected in its 'regulatory' policy in respect of new infrastructure projects,[461] can probably be traced back to the need for long-term investments in the sector. Moreover, additional cross-border network infrastructure will generally be considered to have positive effects on competition, on

---

[456]   See AGCM bulletin No 47 of 15 December 2003.

[457]   Compare with the *Electrabel-intercommunales* case as mentioned in Commission press release (IP/97/ 351) (1997). See also, as regards liberalisation pre-emption strategies, Harker and Waddams, cited above.

[458]   See 'Kartellrechtliche Beurteilungsgrundsätze zu langfristigen Gasverträgen', 25 January 2005, available at <http://www.Bundeskartellamt.de>.

[459]   For a factual description of the effects of such reservations contracts see, amongst others, Case M.3075 *ECS/Iveka* (2003), point 31. See also the Issues Paper published by the Commission in the context of the energy sector inquiry in November 2005, available at <http://www.europa.eu.int>.

[460]   20 years in the case of the UK/Belgium interconnector and 25 years in the case of the *Viking Cable* case.

[461]   See paras 12.358ff.

market integration and on security of supply, provided the capacity does not end up in the hands of companies that are already dominant.

Even in the case of new infrastructure, the foreclosure effects must be balanced against the **12.422** need to conclude such contracts in view of the sunk costs and construction lead times which are encountered in the sector.[462] More particularly, these effects must be weighed against the likelihood that the project in question would not proceed if ancillary restrictions (such as capacity reservations and, possibly collateral upstream and/or downstream supply contracts) were not secured for the long term.

A key issue in this context is knowing whether the energy industry, as compared to other **12.423** investment-intensive industries (eg the railway industry), is characterised by higher sunk costs, stricter financial requirements or, more generally, by a higher degree of market risk in order to justify the reservation of capacity for a longer period of time. Such differences would need to be documented in order to justify the application of less stringent antitrust enforcement in gas and electricity sector infrastructure projects as compared to other sectors of industry.

An alternative benchmark would be a comparison with the financing of similar energy **12.424** projects in other market economies in the world. Investments in LNG facilities might, for instance, be compared with equivalent projects in the US or in south-east Asia, arguably the most buoyant LNG market in the world today.[463] In this context the length of long-term contracts will also depend on technical progress in the sector. The costs of both LNG production and transportation chains, pipelines and CCGT electricity generation plants have, for instance, dramatically reduced in recent years.[464] This means that cases dealt with by the Commission a number of years ago may no longer provide accurate guidance as to the acceptability of similar projects under current circumstances.

This antitrust tolerance towards risky energy infrastructure investment, however, is impos- **12.425** sible to justify for existing amortised infrastructure. Foreclosure effects[465] of new long-term reservations on existing capacity, which will hardly ever be directly linked with investment in that infrastructure, cannot be counter-balanced by arguments relating to the need for investment. The same applies to current prolongations of historic contracts, beyond their originally foreseen end date, even if this possibility was foreseen in the historic transport contracts.

---

[462] This line of reasoning is supported by the CFI judgment in European Night Services (ENS), Joint Cases T-374/94 and T-388/94 *ENS/Commission* [1998] ECR II-3141. See also Commission guidelines on the application of Art 81(3) EC, point 44.

[463] See in this regard the trend developing in these markets for the capacity of LNG terminals which are not fully booked in advance, which leaves sufficient margin for spot supplies outside traditional long-term contracts (See LNG terminals in Italy). Some upstream gas production projects have also been initiated without 100% of their full (so-called 'plateau') production being fully allocated in advance. See also the recent US policy as regards TPA to LNG terminals after the Hackberry terminal approval. See, with regard to the US LNG terminal expansion policy, JE Vallee, 'FERC Hackberry decision will spur more US LNG terminal development', (2003) Oil and Gas Journal p 1ff.

[464] See Chevalier, pp 234ff.

[465] See Commission memorandum 'Role of interconnectors in the electricity market. A competition perspective', MEMO/01/76 (2001).

12.426 A substantial number of these issues have arisen in a preliminary ruling[466] of the ECJ. In this case, a Dutch administrative Court enquired, *inter alia*, whether the priority rights granted under national legislation to the four incumbent electricity suppliers for accessing the Dutch electricity interconnectors, was compatible with Article 86 EC and with the Electricity Directive. More particularly, the national Court enquired whether a national regulatory measure, which provides for the preferential allocation of a proportion of the cross-border transport capacity for electricity to these four incumbent players over a period of ten years, is invalid under EC law because it is not proportionate. In a very pro-competitive judgment, emphasising the need for the Electricity Directive to be interpreted in the light of its market opening objective, the Court considered that the preferential allocation was to be considered as discriminatory. In doing so, the Court based its decision, first on the fact that transitional measures and procedures had been put in place by the EC legislator, which the State of the Netherlands had not made use of. Secondly, the Court emphasised that such preferential treatment was likely to lead to severe foreclosure effects, which risked thwarting the very purpose of the liberalisation process.

12.427 It is to be hoped that Community institutions, national regulatory authorities, and interested parties will invoke this judgment in order to force open the door into countries where regulation or commercial behaviour of the TSO have allowed such long lasting preferential treatment to continue.

H. Merger Policy in the Energy Area

(1) Introduction

12.428 The ongoing liberalisation of the energy sector has lead to significant merger activities in recent years.[467] It is expected that this trend will continue. The main drivers for mergers in the energy sector are, as for most other mergers, economies of scale and economies of scope, ie in the newly liberalised world the energy companies pursue the aim of growing by acquiring companies in new geographic markets (often neighbouring markets) or by entering into new product markets (mostly neighbouring markets allowing them to form multi-utilities offering gas and electricity and possibly other products such as water).

12.429 Another reason for increased merger activity is barriers to new entry. Energy companies therefore prefer to acquire existing players to establish a position in the market. Some of the

---

[466] See judgment of the ECJ in Case C-17/03, *VEMW*, not yet reported.

[467] Examples: Case M.3440 *ENI/EdP/GdP* (2004), the Commission's prohibition decision for this Portuguese merger of the gas and electricity incumbents was confirmed by the judgment of the CFI in Case T-87/05 of 21 September 2005 (not yet reported); Case M.2947 *Verbund/Energieallianz* (2002); Case M.2822 *ENI/EnBW/GVS* (2002); Case M.1853 *EdF/EnBW* (2002); Case M.1673 *VEBA/VIAG* (1999); Case M.1532 *BP Amoco/ARCO* (1998); Case M.1383 *Exxon/Mobil* (1999); Case M.3696 *E.ON/MOL* (2005); Case M.3868 *DONG/Elsam/Energi E2* and Case M.3180 *Gaz de France/Suez* (not yet published; national: *RWE/VEW* (available on the web site of the <http://www.bundeskartellamt.de> in the archives for the year 2000); *E.ON/Ruhrgas* (available on the web site of the <http://www.bundeskartellamt.de> in the archives for the year 2002, despite the prohibition decision of the Bundeskartellamt the merger was subsequently cleared by ministerial approval, cf web site of the German ministry for economics and labour (<http://www.bmwa.bund.de>) under press releases).

most significant entry barriers are: (1) third party access regimes, which do not adequately remove existing obstacles for efficient transmission (possibly because of vertical integration); (2) customers who are bound to buy gas or electricity on a long-term exclusive basis from the incumbent supplier; (3) a high degree of loyalty from customers who could potentially change suppliers and very high costs to gain new customers; (4) the existence of dominant operators who defend their traditional supply area against new entrants; and (5) a high degree of state interference.

Another factor contributing to the merger wave is the fact that there were and still are **12.430** significant opportunities for acquisitions. A great number of energy companies are still fully or partially State-owned.[468] A large proportion of energy companies were privatised in recent years because of the financial situation of the public sector in many Member States. It appears likely that this trend will continue. Whilst some Member States allow private operators to take control over the previously State-controlled undertaking, others will only sell minority shareholdings. These minority shareholdings do not give control over the undertakings concerned and thus fall outside the scope of the merger regulation. They are therefore not dealt with in this chapter.

The trend towards mergers has produced and continues to produce many positive effects **12.431** for certain energy markets, with new, often financially stronger, companies entering markets previously dominated by the incumbent operators. The newly formed companies have a long-term interest in staying in the market and can therefore develop into viable competitors for incumbent operators.

On the other hand, certain energy markets are already highly concentrated and further **12.432** mergers therefore entail significant risks for a competitive market structure, particularly in the downstream supply markets.[469] The acquisition of companies which are active in the same product market and the same or neighbouring geographic market, might lead to the removal of an actual or potential competitor in the market where the acquiring company is already dominant.[470] Furthermore, the merger of a dominant gas company with a dominant electricity supplier, if both are active in the same geographic market (creation of a multi-utility), might undermine the competitive strength of competing electricity producers/suppliers, which would have to rely on gas supplies from their competitor for the generation of electricity (raising competitors' costs).[471]

---

[468] Examples of such acquisitions: Case M.2822 *ENI/EnBW/GVS* (2002); Case M.1853 *EdF/EnBW* (2000); Case M.2947 *Verbund/Energieallianz* (2002).

[469] Certain cases also give rise to concerns in the transport markets, cf Case M.1383 *Exxon/Mobil* (1999) for the British North Sea. So far, mergers in the upstream gas markets have not given rise to major concerns, cf the merger between the two Norwegian producers Norsk Hydro and Saga (M.1573) or the transaction relating to the Algerian In Salah JV by Statoil, BP and Sonatrach (M.3230).

[470] Case M.1853 *EdF/EnBW* (2000); Case M.3440 *ENI/EdP/GdP* (2004). It was essentially for this reason that the CFI rejected the appeal of the parties against the Commission's prohibition decision in Case T-87/05 of 21 September 2005, not yet reported.

[471] Case M.493 *Tractebel/Distrigaz II* (1994); Case M.931 *Neste/IVO* (1998); Case M.3440 *ENI/EdP/ GDP* (2005). This line of reasoning was not addressed in the judgment of the CFI (Case T-87/05 of 21 September 2005, not yet reported) assessing the decision of the Commission.

12.433 In relation to both types of merger which raise competition concerns, the Commission aims to ensure that the merger does not significantly impede effective competition in the common market or in a substantial part of it, in particular as a result of the creation or strengthening of a dominant position, compared with Article 2 of Regulation 139/2004.[472]

12.434 Often the Commission uses merger cases to support its liberalisation efforts. In order to remove the competition concerns that are identified, the parties may offer remedies that allow the Commission to clear the merger. The remedies offered support the creation of a common market, eg by facilitating market entry (*VEBA/Viag*—release of import capacity,[473] *EdF/EnBW*—electricity auctions in France,[474] *EnBW/ENI/GVS*[475]—option for customers to terminate long-term contracts).

12.435 Whilst not being an issue that occurs exclusively in the energy sector, it should be noted that energy mergers in smaller Member States are likely to give rise to the issue of a small market fallacy (first raised in the *Volvo/Scania* merger[476]). This is due to the fact that the energy markets are often no greater than national in scope. Mergers in these countries, whilst not being problematic on the Community-wide scale, can give rise to serious concerns for the national market concerned.

12.436 The sections below address the following three issues: energy mergers giving rise to concerns under the merger regulation, remedies developed by the Commission in problematic energy mergers, and the small market fallacy in energy mergers.

(2) Significant Impediment of Effective Competition

12.437 Mergers in the energy sector, as in any other sector, are most problematic in those markets where barriers to entry are significant and high levels of market concentration already exist prior to the merger. For the purpose of present discussions, it is useful to distinguish between the upstream and the downstream markets for supply and transmission. Other markets, such as the storage market and access to LNG terminals, are not dealt with here as they have played only a minor role in the development of precedents.[477]

(a) Transmission Markets

12.438 As indicated above, a high level of market concentration can be found primarily in the downstream transmission markets (for both electricity and gas). This can be explained by the historic development of the sector: there was previously a single vertically integrated company that was responsible for the creation of the transmission network in a given territory and the supply of energy to customers located in that territory. A duplication of the existing network was and still is considered to be uneconomical in most cases.[478]

---

472 [2004] OJ L24/1.
473 Case M.1673 *VEBA/VIAG* (1999).
474 Case M.1853 *EdF/EnBW* (2000).
475 Case M.2822 *ENI/EnBW/GVS* (2002).
476 Case M.1672 *Volvo/Scania* (1999).
477 See however Case M.1383 *Exxon/Mobil* (1999) in respect of the German storage market.
478 One of the few exceptions is the creation of a competing transmission network by Wingas in certain parts of Germany.

The liberalisation of the energy sector has not altered the underlying economic reality that **12.439** continues to exist in the sector. Nonetheless, most mergers between downstream transmission companies, even if they are active in neighbouring territories, would not give rise to significant competition concerns, if one takes into account the fact that the transmission companies are normally not actual or potential competitors: transport from A to B cannot be replaced by transport from A to C.

An important exception, however, does apply if competing transmission lines exist in the **12.440** same geographic area. Disregarding the very limited number of parallel networks, the most common type of competition can be found where a downstream transmission line is owned by at least two companies and each owner can market its capacity separately (in the gas sector this is called 'pipe-in-pipe' competition as opposed to 'pipe-to-pipe' competition). Competition concerns would occur if the owners of the transmission line were to merge. This would reduce customers' choice between competing suppliers of transmission services.

Mergers relating to transmission activities can also give rise to concerns in the upstream **12.441** markets, eg in respect of off-shore pipelines, transit pipelines, or interconnectors linking two Member States. Here, competing infrastructures might exist with the consequence that a merger between the owners of the infrastructure might lead to a significant reduction of choice for actual or potential users of these lines.[479] One would need to assess in particular whether the merger has adverse effects for the downstream supply markets, particularly if a dominant supplier of energy in the downstream market acquires control over infrastructure allowing third parties to serve the same supply markets.[480] In this scenario there is a risk that the new owner of the infrastructure could use its control over the transmission line to raise its competitors' costs, which could lead to a reinforcement of the dominant position in the downstream supply market.

(b) Upstream Supply Markets

Mergers in the electricity sector normally cover not only the generation and wholesale of **12.442** electricity, but also the retail level. This is because many European electricity companies are traditionally vertically integrated in the sense that they combine under the roof of one company generation and retail activities. They are therefore dealt with below in the section on downstream markets. An interesting case relating to the upstream electricity sector, however, was the creation of a new trading house by EdF and Louis Dreyfus[481] called EdF Trading. The case was only cleared after the companies had undertaken not to act as a wholesaler on the French market (structured sales to eligible customers) for as long as the Commission had not certified that the liberalisation of the eligible customer market in France was legally implemented and effective. In this context, the Commission considered

---

[479] Case M.1383 *Exxon/Mobil* (1999) for the pipelines in the UK North Sea.
[480] cf Case M.2791 *GdF/Ruhrgas/SPP* (2002). The case involved the acquisition of the Slovak gas (supply and transmission) company SPP by GdF and Ruhrgas. It was cleared on the basis that competing pipelines for the import of Russian gas into Europe existed and/or were expected to become available within a foreseeable time period.
[481] Case M.1557 *EDF/Louis Dreyfuss* (1999).

that EdF was dominant on the market for eligible customers. Thus its position should not be reinforced by removing a potential market entrant (Louis Dreyfus had significant expertise in trading with energy products).

12.443 In the upstream gas markets the ongoing concentration process is, *inter alia*, linked to the ongoing concentration process in relation to crude oil[482] and the aim to create larger entities in the gas sector (economies of scale).[483] However the level of concentration reached in the upstream gas markets has not yet reached a level that could be considered to raise competition concerns under the merger regulation, because the geographic scope of these markets includes the EEA and possibly Algeria and Russia.[484] Thus the Commission has cleared a number of mergers between gas producers without conditions.[485] It is unlikely that this will change in the near future, in view of the number of players active in this market and the expected new entries (eg LNG producers).

(c) Downstream Supply Markets

12.444 Serious competition concerns occur most frequently in mergers of energy companies in the downstream supply markets, which are historically highly concentrated. As indicated above, geographic markets are, at most, national in scope, and can sometimes be smaller (ie regional or local scope).[486] The situation varies from Member State to Member State, calling for a case-by-case approach that also takes into account the degree of market opening achieved in the countries concerned. Whilst, for example in the UK, markets are (still) said to be relatively competitive, markets in other Member States can be dominated by one incumbent operator in each relevant market.

12.445 Mergers that give rise to competition concerns are likely to be, in particular, those between companies that are active in the same product and the same or neighbouring geographic markets, or mergers between companies that are active on the same geographic market, but in different product markets (ie multi-utilities). A good example was the recent merger between Gaz de France and Suez (Case M.4180).

12.446 (i) **Merging Parties are Active in the Same Product Market** Typical examples[487] of the first category of problematic mergers (ie those between parties who are active in the same product market) include the acquisition of Mobil by Exxon,[488] the acquisition of EnBW by EdF,[489] the merger between VEBA and VIAG leading to E.ON,[490] the merger between

---

[482] Case M.1383 *Exxon/Mobil* (1999); Case M.1532 *BP Amoco/ARCO* (1999); Case M.2745 *Shell/Enterprise* (2002).

[483] Case M.1573 *Norske Hydro/Saga* (1999); Case M.3052 *ENI/Fortum Gas* (2002); Case M.3230 In Shalah JV/Statoil/BP/Sonatrach (2003).

[484] Case M.1383 *Exxon/Mobil* (1999).

[485] cf the merger between the two Norwegian producers Norske Hydro and Saga (M.1573) or the transaction relating to the Algerian In Salah JV by Statoil, BP and Sonatrach (M.3230).

[486] cf for the German gas supply markets the Commission decision in Case M.1383 *Exxon/Mobil* (1999); and the decision of the Bundeskartellamt in *E.ON/Ruhrgas* (available on the web site of the <http://www.bundeskartellamt.de> in the archives for the year 2002).

[487] Other examples are: Case M.2684 *EnBW/EDP/Cajastur/Hidrocantrabico* (2002); Case M.2947 *Verbund/Energie-Allianz* (2002); Case M.3410 *Total/Gaz de France* (2004).

[488] Case M.1383 *Exxon/Mobil* (1999).

[489] Case M.1853 *EdF/EnBW* (2000).

[490] Case M.1673 *VEBA/VIAG* (1999).

EnBW/ENI and GVS⁴⁹¹, the merger between EdP, GdP and ENI⁴⁹² and most recently the merger between Gaz de France and Suez.⁴⁹³

In *Exxon/Mobil* the Commission analysed in particular the effects of the merger on the **12.447** downstream gas supply markets in the Netherlands and Germany, where Exxon, in combination with other operators (Gasunie in the Netherlands and BEB in northern Germany), held a dominant position and Mobil was one of the few active competitors. The merger was only cleared after the parties had offered remedies (see below).

In *EdF/EnBW* the Commission concluded that EdF held a dominant position on the elec- **12.448** tricity supply markets in France and that EnBW, which was active in south west Germany, was one of the few potential entrants in the French electricity supply markets. Again, the merger was only cleared after EdF offered certain remedies facilitating market entry into France.

In *VEBA/VIAG* the Commission came to the conclusion that the geographic scope of the **12.449** German electricity supply markets would soon be national and that VEBA/VIAG would have a combined market share of below 40 per cent on these markets. However, taking into account the fact that the largest competitor, RWE, had a market share of more than 30 per cent, that all other competitors were significantly smaller in size and that market entry was rendered difficult because of a number of factors, the Commission concluded that the merger would lead to joint dominance on the part of VEBA/VIAG and RWE. It only cleared the merger after the companies had offered remedies removing the competition concerns (see below).

In *EnBW/ENI/GVS* the Commission took the view that the geographic dimension of the **12.450** German gas supply markets was regional and that both EnBW and GVS were active in the same geographic area (south west Germany). The merger would thus lead to a reinforcement of GVS' dominant position. Again, the Commission only cleared the transaction after the companies had offered appropriate remedies (see below).

In *EdP/GdP/ENI* the Commission established that GdP was one of the few prominent **12.451** entrants in the Portuguese electricity markets, which had invested and planned to invest further in electricity generation. The merger would thus have led to the reinforcement of a dominant position/impediment of competition in the Portuguese electricity markets. The Commission therefore prohibited this merger,⁴⁹⁴ a decision recently confirmed by the CFI.⁴⁹⁵

---

⁴⁹¹ Case M.2822 *ENI/EnBW/GVS* (2002).
⁴⁹² Case M.3440 *EdP/ENI/GdP* (2004); confirmed by the CFI in Case T-87/05 of 21 September 2005, not yet reported.
⁴⁹³ Case M.4180 *Gaz de France/Suez* (2006)—not yet published.
⁴⁹⁴ In the Commission decision a similar reasoning was developed for the gas market, which was rejected by the CFI in Case T-87/05, not yet reported. The Court argued that the Portuguese gas market benefits from a derogation to introduce competition until 2007. Under these circumstances the CFI took the view that it could not be argued that GdP's dominant position was reinforced by the merger (it benefits from a legal monopoly). This argument is not convincing, as the Court did not adequately consider the effects of the merger for the period after 2007.
⁴⁹⁵ Case T-87/05 of 21 September 2005, not yet reported.

12.452 In *Gaz de France/Suez* the Commission established that GdF was one of the few prominent entrants in the Belgian gas and electricity markets dominated by Suez (and its subsidiaries Electrabel and Distrigaz), whilst Distrigaz was one of the few prominent entrants in the French gas market. The merger would thus have led to the reinforcement of a dominant position/impediment of competition in these markets. The Commission therefore could only accept the merger following the adequate remedies by the parties.

12.453 (ii) **Merging Parties are Active in Different Product Markets** The other type of merger which typically raises competition concerns in the downstream supply markets is that between incumbent electricity and gas suppliers, which creates a multi-utility. Prominent examples[496] of such mergers at the Community level include *Distrigaz/Tractebel*,[497] *Neste/IVO*[498] and *ENI/GDP/EDP*.[499] At the national level, the most significant example is the German merger case *E.ON/Ruhrgas*.[500] The national decision relating to the takeover of the largest Spanish electricity company, Endesa, by the largest gas company, GasNatural, is currently not likely to be of much relevance.

12.454 In mergers dealt with at the European level, the main competition concern relates to the fact that gas is currently regarded as one of the fuels most likely to be used in new power generation plants. The gas consumed in these generators accounts for well over 50 per cent of the total generation costs. Under these circumstances, it is clear that a merger between the dominant gas and electricity suppliers will have adverse effects for all actual or potential electricity producers operating in the same geographic market: for their gas supply, the electricity producers are likely to rely on the dominant gas supplier which is, at the same time, their main competitor in the electricity markets. There is at least a significant potential for the merged entity to abuse its dominant position by raising competitors' costs, which will also create a significant disincentive for potential competitors to enter the electricity markets or for actual competitors to expand their existing activities. As a consequence, this type of merger is unlikely to be cleared or may only be cleared after appropriate remedies have been agreed (see below).

(3) **Remedies**

12.455 Merging companies wishing to obtain clearance from the Commission may offer commitments to overcome the competition concerns that are identified (either at phase I or phase II). Clearance of the merger may be subject to the fulfilment of the commitments by the parties. The Commission will attach to its decision conditions and obligations that are intended to ensure that the companies comply with the commitments, Articles 6(2) and 8(2) of Council Regulation 139/2004.

---

[496] See also Case M.3696 *EON/MOL* (2005); and Case M.3868 *Dong/Elsam/Energi E2*.

[497] Case M.418 and 493 *Tractebel/Distrigaz I and II* (1994 and 2000).

[498] Case M.931 *Neste/IVO* (1998).

[499] Case M.3440 *ENI/GDP/EDP*. In the judgment of the CFI (Case T-87/05) this issue was not discussed.

[500] Available on the web site of the <http://www.bundeskartellamt.de> in the archives for the year 2002; despite the prohibition decision of the Bundeskartellamt the merger was subsequently cleared by ministerial approval, cf web site of the German ministry for economics and labour (<http://www.bmwa.bund.de>) under press releases).

The Commission has made extensive use of these provisions in merger proceedings relat- **12.456**
ing to the energy markets. It has done so also with the view to supporting the ongoing
liberalisation process. However, in contrast to a regulatory approach (where the legislator
decides on appropriate rules for the entire industry), the remedies accepted in the context
of merger proceedings are intended to overcome those particular competition concerns
that have been identified and are directed only to the addressees of the merger decision. The
alternative would be a prohibition of the notified merger.

The commitments offered by companies can be diverse, from structural remedies (eg **12.457**
divestiture) to behavioural remedies (eg auctions of electricity/gas or transmission rights,
termination of long-term contracts etc). They can also relate to the improvement of the
Third Party Access regime. The following are of particular interest for the energy sector:

(a) Divestiture

One of the most frequently used remedies in merger proceedings relating to the energy **12.458**
markets is divestiture.[501] The companies may either divest themselves of interests in market participants in the markets concerned (including cross shareholdings with competitors
that would facilitate the creation of a joint dominance) or sell subsidiaries altogether. The
determining factor is that, following the divestiture, the parties should no longer hold a
controlling stake in the divested companies.

A good example for such a commitment is *Neste/IVO*,[502] which relates to the merger **12.459**
between the Finnish companies Neste (active in oil, gas, petroleum, heat, and chemical
products) and IVO (active in electricity and heat production, transmission, and distribution). In order to obtain clearance from the Commission, the companies and the Finnish
Government, which held controlling stakes in both companies, offered to sell the controlling stake in Neste's subsidiary, Gasum (Gasum was Finland's dominant operator on the gas
supply markets). The divestiture was deemed necessary in order to ensure that IVO's
dominant position on the electricity market was not reinforced by acquiring control over
Gasum. It should be noted that gas-fired power plants were seen as one of the most attractive options for entering the Finnish electricity market or expanding existing activities.

Another very good example for such a commitment is *Gaz de France/Suez*,[503] which relates **12.460**
to the merger between the French incumbent gas supplier Gaz de France and the Belgian
incumbent gas and electricity supplier Suez (through its subsidiaries Electrabel and
Distrigaz). The merged entity is under the obligation to divest parts of its gas sales business
in Belgium and at least loosen control over the transmission grid (Fluxys).

Whilst not falling directly within the category of divestiture, one of the remedies accepted **12.461**
in *EdF/EnBW* [504] had very similar effects. In this case, EdF promised to release the French

---

[501] Case M.1673 *VEBA/VIAG*, IP/00/613; Case M.1853 *EdF/EnBW*, IP/00/1099; Case M.2947
Verbund/Energie- Allianz, (2002), Case 3868 *Dong/Elsam/E2* (2006) and Case M.4180 *Gaz de France/Suez*;
E.ON/Ruhrgas cf ministerial approval published on the web site of the German ministry for economics and
labour (<http://www.bmwa.bund.de>).
[502] Case M.931 *Neste/IVO* (1998).
[503] Case M.4180 *Gaz de France/Suez* (2006).
[504] Case M.1853 *EdF/EnBW*.

electricity producer Compagnie Nationale du Rhone (CNR) from its obligation to sell its entire production output on a long-term basis to EdF. The long-term contract had the effect that CNR could not even develop into a potential competitor of EdF. The discontinuation of its supply obligation would allow CNR to develop into a viable competitor, possibly in combination with a strategic partner.

(b) Auctions

12.462 Another type of remedy used in merger proceedings in the energy sector is the auction/sale of energy and/or transmission capacity with the aim to facilitate market entry.[505]

12.463 The energy sold in the auctions can be bought by traders, *inter alia*, for subsequent resale in the market. Auctions therefore allow traders to build up a customer base in a market without having to make significant investments at the outset (eg investment into a new power plant or a long-term gas supply contract). A drawback to auctions is that the energy may be exported to other markets where price levels are higher, thus reducing the liquidity in the market for which they are destined. On the other hand, the Commission cannot determine the destination. Another risk with auctions relates to the price-finding mechanism: the company offering the energy in the auction will want to achieve a minimum price if demand is low. If demand is very high, however, the price will reach a level which eliminates the auction as a cheap source of energy allowing/facilitating market entry.

12.464 Nonetheless, auctions have proved to be a useful remedy in a number of merger proceedings in the energy sector. A good example is the auction introduced in the context of the merger between EdF and EnBW.[506] In order to counter-balance the elimination of EnBW as a potential new entrant in the highly concentrated French electricity market, not only did EdF have to commit to release CNR from its long-term supply obligations as described above, it also had to agree to conduct an electricity auction for France. The auction period was initially limited to five years, but thereafter the Commission is only obliged to release EdF of its obligations when the French market has developed sufficient alternative supply sources. This has not yet occurred, so the auction continues.

12.465 The sale of the transmission capacity of interconnectors is a remedy intended to produce similar effects. It aims at attracting new market entry by facilitating imports into the markets affected by the merger.[507] Prior to the introduction of the remedy, these import capacities are often reserved on a long-term basis to the incumbent operators, thus preventing operators from other countries from entering the highly concentrated markets. The discontinuation of the long-term reservation of capacity and the opportunity for alternative users to acquire transport rights can therefore facilitate the market entry.

---

[505] Case M.931 *Neste/IVO* (1998); Case M.1383 *Exxon/Mobil* (1999); Case M.1673 *VEBA/VIAG*; Case M.1853 *EdF/EnBW*; Case M.2947 *Verbund/Energieallianz* (2002); Case M.3696 *E.ON/MOL* (2005); Case *E.ON/Ruhrgas* cf ministerial approval published on the web site of the German ministry for economics and labour (<http://www.bmwa.bund.de>).
[506] Case M.1853 *EdF/EnBW*.
[507] Case M.1673 *VEBA/VIAG*.

(c) Termination Rights for Long-term Contracts

Finally, a remedy used in some merger cases is the introduction of termination rights for **12.466** long-term supply contracts. Thus in the joint acquisition of the gas wholesaler GVS[508] (which is active in south west Germany) by EnBW (active mainly in the electricity market in south west Germany) and ENI (the Italian incumbent oil and gas company) which led to the reinforcement of GVS's dominant position in the market for the supply of gas to distribution companies in south west Germany, the Commission accepted as a remedy the introduction of termination rights for GVS's customers. GVS's customers can therefore discontinue their long-term exclusive supply relationship with the dominant supplier, thus facilitating market entry for new operators.[509]

(4) Small Market Fallacy

As explained above, the markets that are most likely to give rise to competition concerns in **12.467** merger proceedings relating to the energy sector are downstream supply markets. The geographic dimension of these markets (at the current stage of liberalisation) is at most national in scope, and sometimes only regional or local. As a consequence, mergers in which the merging companies hold strong positions in the same geographic market are more likely to give rise to competition concerns (whether mergers of gas and electricity businesses forming a multi-utility or mergers relating to the same product market).

Whilst this assessment applies in small and large Member States alike, it is arguable that merg- **12.468** ers in smaller Member States are more likely to be prohibited or to result in stricter remedies (there are often fewer players to start with and they are more likely to have begun to engage in activities outside their traditional markets).[510] Thus smaller Member States may be prevented from creating national champions that could later play an active role in what will be a Europe-wide market or at least regional markets covering several Member States. Even if such national champions were created, they would, in any event, be small in size compared to the energy 'giants' in some of the large Member States (EdF, GdF, RWE, E.ON).

From an industrial policy perspective, this line of reasoning appears plausible. However, it **12.469** overlooks the fact that European merger policy does not have such a perspective: instead it analyses the effects of the merger on competition in the markets concerned. Whilst European merger policy takes into account ongoing liberalisation and future developments of the markets, these developments must, in the assessment of the Commission, be likely to materialise within the foreseeable future. At this stage of liberalisation, it does not seem plausible that downstream supply markets in Europe will have a Europe-wide dimension in the near future. Accordingly, mergers must be assessed on the basis of national markets and on these markets the mergers are considered to have adverse effects.

---

[508] Case M.2822 *ENI/EnBW/GVS* (2002).

[509] It is, of course, a separate question whether these long-term exclusive supply contracts are themselves compatible with EC competition; on this see chapters on horizontal and vertical restraints.

[510] cf Case M.931 *Neste/IVO* (1998); Case M.2947 *Verbund/Energieallianz* (2002), IP/03/825; Case M.3440 *ENI/GDP/EDP* (2004). Case M.1673 *VEBA/VIAG* (1999), IP/00/613; *E.ON/Ruhrgas* cf ministerial approval published on the web site of the German ministry for economics (<http://www.bmwi.bund.de>).

13

COMMUNICATIONS
(TELECOMS, MEDIA AND INTERNET)

Kevin Coates and Wolf Sauter

A. Introduction

(1) Scope of the Chapter

13.01 This chapter sets out the most important issues relating to the application of Article 81 and Article 82 to the telecommunications and media sectors.[1]

13.02 The integrated approach of this chapter in part reflects the convergence of technology between the two sectors: this relates most clearly to issues related to the transmission of telecommunications or media services, but is also relevant to, for example, interface devices such as set top boxes and to retail services. With the development of the Internet, the overlap between content and electronic communications services is likely to become increasingly evident. Nonetheless, these similarities should not be overstated: significant differences between the sectors persist.

13.03 The second reason for writing an integrated chapter is the increasing overlap in legal issues relevant to both areas. Issues of control of bottleneck facilities and therefore requests for access have been most clearly addressed in the telecommunications sector but are increasingly relevant to the media sector, for example in relation to set top boxes. By contrast, the leveraging of market power has been an important issue in a number of formal decisions in the media sector.

13.04 Another feature shared by the two sectors is the relative paucity of formal Commission decisions, although these have been supplemented in part by policy statements from the European Commission, and in the case of electronic communications sector-specific legislation. On many of the most important issues, there is still little in the way of Commission precedent, and even less in terms of jurisprudence.

---

[1] This is not, however, a complete analysis of either sector: telecommunications equipment has been excluded, as have media issues related to books and films.

(2) Structure of the Chapter

Section B provides a basic background to the regulatory framework of the two sectors, including an overview of telecommunications liberalisation. **13.05**

Section C sets out certain procedural issues that are relevant to the sectors given the existence of these overlapping regulatory environments. **13.06**

Sections D to G set out the main competition issues relevant to the various levels of the value chain in the broadcast and telecommunications sectors: content, transmission, enduser interface equipment, and retail services. **13.07**

Section D looks at issues related to content creation, packaging, and distribution. This is most relevant to media, but will increasingly be relevant to Internet based services. **13.08**

Section E examines competition issues related to data and voice transmission, with the emphasis being mostly on the telecommunications sector. This section covers both basic infrastructure problems such as the right to build, and infrastructure related services, such as interconnection. **13.09**

Section F draws together various problems related to set top boxes. **13.10**

Section G looks at issues that are of particular relevance to retail services. **13.11**

Inevitably, a number of legal issues such as access, discrimination, and bundling, will be relevant to more than one of the above sections. Detailed analysis of the principles is set out in the section where most relevant: for example, exclusivity is examined in Section D on content, and many of the basic Article 82 issues are set out in Section E on transmission. **13.12**

B. Regulatory Framework

The sector specific regulatory frameworks of the telecommunications and broadcast industries are quite different. There were proposals to integrate the regulatory framework at the EU level,[2] which eventually occurred at the level of transmission infrastructure, but not of content. **13.13**

The traditional view of the telecommunications sector was that in order to achieve certain public policy objectives—most notably universal service—a single, often state-owned, telecommunications operator must be established in the particular state. Technical developments and changes in economic thinking now mean that this monopolist approach is regarded as unnecessary. The provision of telecommunications infrastructure and services has therefore been subject to a progressive liberalisation, pursuant to Article 86 **13.14**

---

[2] Green Paper on the convergence of the telecommunications, media and information technology sectors and the implications for regulation, COM (97) 623 final, 3 December 1997, Communication to the European Parliament, the Council, the Economic and Social Committee and the Committee of the Regions, Results of the Public Consultation on the Green Paper COM(1999) 108 final.

(formerly Article 90) EC,[3] beginning in 1990.[4] The liberalisation of the sector at the EU level was accompanied by the introduction of a detailed sector specific regulatory regime, Open Network Provision (ONP), enacted under Article 95 (formerly 100A) EC.[5] This regime was supplemented by a Regulation on unbundled local loop access at the end of 2000.[6] Following a policy review that started in 1999, the ONP regime was replaced by a new

---

[3] See Chapter 5 above.

[4] The telecommunications sector was liberalized by Commission Directives adopted pursuant to Art 86 EC. See: Commission Directive (EEC) 90/388 of 28 June 1990 on competition in the markets for telecommunications services [1990] OJ L192/10 (the Services Directive); Commission Directive (EEC) 94/46 of 13 October 1994 amending Directive (EEC) 88/301 and Directive (EEC) 90/388 in particular with regard to satellite communications [1994] OJ L268/15 (the Satellite Directive); Commission Directive (EC) 95/51 of 18 October 1995 amending Directive (EEC) 90/388 with regard to the abolition of the restrictions on the use of cable television networks for the provision of already liberalized telecommunications services [1995] OJ L256/49 (the Cable TV Directive); Commission Directive (EC) 96/2 of 16 January 1996 amending Directive (EEC) 90/388 with regard to mobile and personal communications [1996] OJ L20/59 (the Mobile Directive); Commission Directive (EC) 96/19 of 13 March 1996 amending Directive (EEC) 90/388 with regard to the implementation of full competition in the telecommunications markets [1996] OJ L74/13 (the Full Competition Directive). Certain Member States were granted limited derogations from full competition in telecommunications: Commission Decision (EC) 97/114 of 27 November 1996 concerning the additional implementation periods requested by Ireland for the implementation of Commission Directives (EEC) 90/388 and (EC) 96/2 as regards full competition in the telecommunications markets [1997] OJ L41/8; Commission Decision (EC) 97/310 of 12 February 1997 concerning the granting of additional implementation periods to the Portuguese Republic for the implementation of Commission Directives (EEC) 90/388 and (EC) 96/2 as regards full competition in the telecommunications markets [1997] OJ L133/19; Commission Decision (EC) 97/568 of 14 May 1997 on the granting of additional implementation periods to Luxembourg for the implementation of Directive (EEC) 90/388 as regards full competition in the telecommunications markets [1997] OJ L234/7; Commission Decision (EC) 97/603 of 10 June 1997 concerning the granting of additional implementation periods to Spain for the implementation of Commission Directive (EEC) 90/388 as regards full competition in the telecommunications markets [1997] OJ L243/48; Commission Decision (EC) 97/607 of 18 June 1997 concerning the granting of additional implementation periods to Greece for the implementation of Directive (EEC) 90/388 as regards full competition in the telecommunications markets [1997] OJ L245/6.

[5] See the ONP framework: Directive (EC) 97/13 of the European Parliament and of the Council of 10 April 1997 on a common framework for authorisations and individual licences in the field of telecommunications services [1997] OJ L117/15; Directive (EC) 97/33 of the European Parliament and of the Council of 30 June 1997 on interconnection in Telecommunications with regard to ensuring universal service and interoperability through application of the principles of Open Network Provision (ONP) [1997] OJ L199/32; Council Directive (EEC) 90/387 of 28 June 1990 on the establishment of the internal market for telecommunications services through the implementation of open network provision [1990] OJ L192/1, as amended by Directive (EC) 97/51 of the European Parliament and of the Council of 6 October 1997 amending Council Directives (EC) 90/387 and (EEC) 92/44 for the purpose of adaptation to a competitive environment in telecommunications [1997] OJ L295/23; Council Directive (EEC) 92/44 on the application of open network provision to leased lines [1992] OJ L165 as amended by Directive (EC) 97/51 of the European Parliament and of the Council of 6 October 1997 amending Council Directives (EC) 90/387 and (EEC) 92/44 for the purpose of adaptation to a competitive environment in telecommunications [1997] OJ L295/23; Directive (EEC) 95/62 of the European Parliament and of the Council of 13 December 1995, on the application of open network provision to voice telephony [1995] OJ L321/6, replaced by Directive (EC) 98/10 of the European Parliament and of the Council of 26 February 1998 on the application of open network provision (ONP) to voice telephony and on universal service for telecommunications in a competitive environment [1998] OJ L101/24; Directive (EC) 97/66 of the European Parliament and of the Council of 15 December 1997 concerning the processing of personal data and the protection of privacy in the telecommunications sector [1998] OJ L24/1.

[6] Regulation 2887/2000/EC of the European Parliament and of the Council of 18 December 2000 on unbundled access to the local loop [2000] OJ L336/4.

regulatory framework in 2002 (the 2002 regulatory framework) likewise based on Article 95 EC in April 2002.[7] The 2002 regulatory framework is currently again under review by the Commission.[8] The European Union is also party to the WTO Agreement on Basic Telecommunications Services.[9] Any consideration of the competition rules applying to companies operating in the telecommunications and interactive services sector also requires consideration of these other bodies of law.

The regulation of the Internet is very different. Although originating in a US government research programme, it has developed without significant government support into a world-wide data network capable of connecting anyone with a suitable device and access to a suitable communications system. Some elements of the telecommunications and broadcast regulation could affect the provision of Internet services, and the e-Commerce Directive[10] and the proposed successor to the TV Without Frontiers Directive—the Directive on Audiovisual Media Services—all have an impact on Internet services. More importantly, the competition rules apply automatically to the Internet.   **13.15**

(1) Telecommunications

(a) Liberalisation

(i) **Services Liberalisation**   The position on key competition issues has developed over time across successive regulatory frameworks. The 1990 Services Directive provided for the liberalisation of all telecommunications services except for voice telephony,[11] though the Directive did not apply to mobile or radio telephony, satellite, paging, or telex.[12] That definition of voice telephony was not linked to a market definition, but to a   **13.16**

---

[7] Directive 2002/19/EC of the European Parliament and of the Council of 7 March 2002 on access to, and interconnection of, electronic communications networks and associated facilities (Access Directive) [2002] OJ L108/7; Directive 2002/20/EC of the European Parliament and of the Council of 7 March 2002 on the authorization of electronic communications networks and services (Authorisation Directive) [2002] OJ L108/21; Directive 2002/21/EC of the European Parliament and of the Council of 7 March 2002 on a common regulatory framework for electronic communications networks and services (Framework Directive) [2002] OJ L108/33; Directive 2002/22/EC of the European Parliament and of the Parliament of 7 March 2002 on universal service and users' rights relating to electronic communications networks and services (Universal Service Directive) [2002] OJ L108/51. cf C Koenig, A Bartosch and J-D Braun (eds), *EC Competition and Telecommunications Law: A Practitioner's Guide* (Aspen, 2002); P Nihoul and P Rodford, *EU Electronic Communications Law—Competition and Regulation in the European Telecommunications Market* (OUP, 2004).

[8] cf COM(2006) 334 final, Communication from the Commission to the Couincl, the European Parliament, the Economic and Social Committee and the Committee of the Regions on the Review of the EU Regulatory Framework for electronic communications networks and services; and SEC(2006) 816, Commission staff working document on the same topic.

[9] See, as regards the Community, Council Decision (EC) 97/838, concerning the conclusion on behalf of the European Community, as regards matters within its competence, of the results of the WTO negotiations on basic telecommunications services [1997] OJ L347/45.

[10] Directive 2000/31/EC of the European Parliament and of the Council of 8 June 2000 on certain legal aspects of information society services, in particular electronic commerce, in the Internal Market, OJ L178/1, 17 July 2000.

[11] Commission Directive (EEC) 90/388 of 28 June 1990 on competition in the markets for telecommunications services [1990] OJ L192/10, Art 2.

[12] Commission Directive (EEC) 90/388 of 28 June 1990 on competition in the markets for telecommunications services [1990] OJ L192/10, Art 1(2).

technical configuration.[13] Following *full liberalisation* in 1998 this distinction has become less relevant as it is no longer used to demarcate services that are liberalised from those that are not. Accordingly, under the 2002 regulatory framework for electronic communications, voice telephony is no longer a defined term, although access to the publicly available telephone service at a fixed location remains at the core of universal service obligations.[14]

13.17   (ii) **Full Liberalisation**   All other telecommunications services were liberalised gradually with satellite,[15] mobile,[16] and other services being liberalised over the years following the 1990 Services Directive,[17] culminating in full liberalisation, including the liberalisation of voice telephony, in principle on 1 January 1998.[18]

13.18   The Full Competition Directive envisaged that those Member States with less well-developed or small telecommunications networks could request a temporary derogation from the liberalisation timetable of the Directive. Five derogation decisions were passed[19]—for Greece, Ireland, Luxembourg, Portugal, and Spain. Derogations could be justified, for example, by the need to rebalance tariffs, to invest in infrastructure and/or the digitisation of exchanges, to allow time for the telecoms operator to become market driven, or to allow time to improve the debt and cost structures of the telecoms operator. These derogations have now expired.

13.19   (iii) **Infrastructure Liberalisation**   The 1995 Cable TV Directive[20] abolished all restrictions on the supply of transmission capacity by cable TV networks and allowed the use of cable networks for the provision of telecommunications services, other than voice telephony. The 1998 Full Competition Directive then required the liberalisation of all alternative

---

[13] Commission Directive (EEC) 90/388 of 28 June 1990 on competition in the markets for telecommunications services [1990] OJ L192/10, Art 1(1): 'the commercial provision for the public of the direct transport and switching of speech in real-time between public switched network termination points, enabling any user to use equipment connected to such a network termination point in order to communicate with another termination point'.

[14] Directive 2002/22/EC of the European Parliament and of the Parliament of 7 March 2002 on universal service and users' rights relating to electronic communications networks and services (Universal Service Directive) [2002] OJ L108/51.

[15] Commission Directive (EEC) 94/46 of 13 October 1994 amending Directive (EEC) 88/301 and Directive (EEC) 90/388 in particular with regard to satellite communications [1994] OJ L268/15, Art 2. See also: Satellite Green Paper, COM (90) 490 final of 20 November 1990; Council Resolution of 19 December 1991 on the development of the common market for satellite communications services and equipment [1992] OJ C8/1.

[16] Commission Directive (EC) 96/2 of 16 January 1996 amending Directive (EEC) 90/388 with regard to mobile and personal communications [1996] OJ L20/59.

[17] See European Commission, 1992 Review of the situation in the telecommunications services sector, SEC (92) 1048, 21 October 1992. Communication to the Council and to the European Parliament on the consultation on the review of the situation in the telecommunications sector, COM (92) 159 final, 28 April 1993. Council Resolution of 22 July 1993 on the review of the situation in the telecommunication sector and the need for further development in that market, [1993] OJ C213/1.

[18] Commission Directive (EC) 96/19 of 13 March 1996 amending Directive (EEC) 90/388 with regard to the implementation of full competition in the telecommunications markets [1996] OJ L74/13.

[19] See n 4 above.

[20] Commission Directive (EC) 95/51 of 18 October 1995, amending Directive (EEC) 90/388 with regard to the abolition of the restrictions on the use of cable television networks for the provision of already liberalised telecommunications services [1995] OJ L256/49.

infrastructure. These Directives also contained requirements relating to the interconnection of networks which duplicated certain provisions found in the 1998 Interconnection Directive. This overlap issue was resolved in the 2002 package when the Article 86 Directives were 'consolidated' —in effect, for the main part revoked—in the Consolidated Competition Directive.[21] The scope of the latter was largely pared down to the prohibition of special and exclusive rights without reference to specific provisions on interconnection, which instead are now only covered by the Article 95 Access Directive.

The Commission has also examined the issue of joint ownership of telecommunications **13.20** and cable networks, as the latter are important (potential) local infrastructure competitors for the provision of communications services. The Cable TV Directive announced that the Commission would review this situation by 1 January 1998, an examination which resulted in the 1999 Legal Separation Directive (an amendment of the Service Directive), which required a telecoms operator that also owned a cable network to hold the two operations in legally distinct entities in those cases where the undertaking is (a) controlled by a Member State or benefits from special rights, (b) is dominant, and (c) operates a cable TV network which has been established under special or exclusive right in the same geographic area.[22] This position has been retained in Article 8 of the Consolidated Competition Directive. The Commission has also obtained commitments for the divestiture of cable TV assets in a number of individual cases such as *Telia/Telenor*[23] and *Telia/Sonera*.[24]

More recently the Commission issued a reasoned opinion in an Article 226 procedure **13.21** against Hungary in relation to territorial restrictions on broadcasting transmission services provided by cable TV operators in alleged infringement of the Consolidated Competition Directive.[25]

(iv) Ensuring Effective Liberalisation   In addition to setting out the timetable within **13.22** which the telecommunications sector should be opened to competition, the Liberalisation Directives also set out certain requirements designed to ensure the effectiveness of the liberalisation. These included requirements:

— to publish technical interfaces;
— to make interconnection available and publish a standard interconnection offer; and
— to establish accounting separation between their interconnect and other activities.

These issues are now addressed by the 2002 regulatory framework in the Access Directive, **13.23** and no longer by the Consolidated Competition Directive. A parallel can be drawn between these issues and the consideration of the joint ownership of telecommunications and cable networks referred to above. The issue of how far the Commission can proceed under Article 86 to ensure effective liberalisation of the telecommunications sector was left unresolved.

---

[21] Commission Directive 2002/77/EC of 16 September 2002 on competition in the markets for electronic communications networks and services (Consolidated Competition Directive) [2002] OJ L249/21.
[22] Commission Directive 1999/64/EC of 23 June 1999 amending Directive 90/388/EEC in order to ensure that telecommunications networks and cable TV networks owned by a single operator are separate legal entities (Legal Separation Directive) [1999] OJ L175/39.
[23] *Telia/Telenor* (Case IV/M.1439) (1999) [2001] OJ L40/1.
[24] *Telia/Sonera* (Case COMP/M.2803) [2002] OJ C 201/19.
[25] Commission press release IP/06/487 of 11 April 2006.

The Consolidated Competition Directive adopted in 2002 introduced no significant new obligations. Given the objections against Article 86 Directives raised by the European Parliament and the fact that all special and exclusive rights in this sector are in any event abolished no further such Directives may be expected concerning electronic communications.

(b) Sector Specific Regulation

13.24 The telecommunications sector is also subject to extensive sector specific single market regulation (the 2002 regulatory framework, formerly the ONP rules) enacted under Article 95 EC.[26] These Directives establish national regulatory authorities (NRAs) in each Member State with responsibility in the telecommunications sector (although it is not necessary to establish a sector specific regulator). The Directives cover the availability of and pricing for access and interconnection, authorisation, data protection, and universal service. Whereas under the original ONP Directives regulatory intervention was triggered by 'significant market power' (SMP) established purely on the basis of 25 per cent or above market share in predefined markets, under the 2002 regulatory framework SMP is equivalent to dominance under competition law. Establishing SMP therefore requires a market analysis based on market definition and assessment of the possible existence of SMP based on standard competition law principles. For this purpose, the Commission has provided the NRAs with guidance by means of Guidelines and Recommendations.[27] One important aspect of this is that the starting point in market analysis should be the market that is most upstream in the vertical supply chain, (as if) in the absence of regulation. Downstream markets are then analysed taking into account the expected effects of remedies imposed at wholesale level.[28]

13.25 In addition to providing guidance, the Commission also plays a coordinating role in a notification procedure based on Article 7 of the Framework Directive, which provides for the Commission vetting and commenting on all market analyses (market definition and SMP designation and proportionality of remedies) carried out by the NRAs, and gives it a veto power regarding market definition or SMP designation—but not concerning remedies— in case it considers the measure concerned would create a barrier to the single market or

---

[26] See n 5 above.

[27] Commission guidelines on market analysis and the assessment of significant market power under the Community regulatory framework for electronic communications networks and services [2002] OJ C165/6; Commission Recommendation of 11 February 2003 on relevant product and service markets within the electronic communications sector susceptible to *ex ante* regulation in accordance with Directive 2002/21/EC of the European Parliament and of the Council on a common regulatory framework for electronic communication networks and services [2003] OJ L114/45, and the Commission's Explanatory Memorandum to the latter document. (<http://ec.europa.eu/information_society/topics/telecoms/regulatory/maindocs/documents/explanmemoen.pdf>). Now under review: see SEC(2006) 837 Commission staff working document, consultation on a draft Commission Recommendation on relevant product and service markets susceptible to *ex ante* regulation in accordance with Directive 2002/21/EC of the European Parliament and of the Council on a common regulatory framework for electronic communication networks and services (Second edition).

[28] Commission Recommendation on relevant product and service markets susceptible to *ex ante* regulation in accordance with Directive 2002/21/EC of the European Parliament and of the Council on a common regulatory framework for electronic communication networks and services (Second edition), pp 13–14.

where it has serious doubts about the compatibility with European law.[29] In practice this role is carried out by the Article 7 Committee, consisting of representatives of the Commission's competition and information society DGs acting jointly.[30] The Article 7 procedure is now subject to review (streamlining and simplified procedures in non-complex cases) as part of the general review of the 2002 regulatory framework. In addition, the Commission would like to extend its competence over regulatory remedies, which is presently limited to comments, to a veto power.[31] As the number of vetoes—or indeed decisions not to veto[32]—increases, new case law will develop on the powers of the Article 7 Committee.[33]

From a competition law perspective, the key obligations under the 2002 regulatory framework are related to access. Based on Article 12 of the Access Directive, NRAs can impose obligations on operators with SMP to meet reasonable requests for access to, and use of, specific network elements and associated facilities in the event that a denial of access or unreasonable terms and conditions with a similar effect would hinder the emergence of sustainable competition or harm the interest of end-users. They can also regulate the relevant access prices. Wherever possible, regulatory solutions must be limited to intervention at wholesale level, with intervention at retail level as a measure of last resort. Based on Article 5 of the Access Directive, even in cases where SMP is not at issue, NRAs may impose access obligations (i) on operators who control access to end-users, where necessary to allow end-to-end connectivity (also know as 'interoperability'), and (ii) to application programme interfaces and electronic programme guides, where necessary to ensure accessibility for end-users to digital radio and television broadcasting services. Finally, Article 6 of the Access Directive requires the Member States to impose specific requirements on conditional access systems—including must-carry obligations on fair reasonable and non-discriminatory terms for all broadcasters, which may (but need not) be lifted following an SMP analysis and in accordance with the Article 7 procedure.

13.26

(2) Media

In contrast to the telecommunications sector, there is relatively little regulation of the media sector at the European level. For the purposes of this chapter, brief reference is made only to EC legislation which is directly relevant to the application of the competition rules.

13.27

---

[29] COM(2006) 28, Communication from the Commission on market reviews under the EU Regulatory Framework: Consolidating the internal market for electronic communications. Public versions of decisions and related documents can be found at <http://ec.europa.eu/information_society/policy/ecomm/article_7/index_en.htm> and <http://forum.europa.eu.int/Public/irc/infso/ecctf/library>.

[30] cf Commission Recommendation 2003/561/EC of 23 July 2003 on notifications, time limits and consultations provided for in Art 7 of the Framework Directive, [2003] OJ L190/13.

[31] cf COM(2006) 334 final, Communication from the Commission on the Review of the EU Regulatory Framework for electronic communications networks and services; and SEC(2006) 816, Commission staff working document on the same topic.

[32] cf Case T-109/06: Action brought on 12 April 2006—*Vodafone España and Vodafone Group v Commission* [2006] OJ C131/46.

[33] The Commission in June 2006 reported that by the end of May 2006, a total of 405 notifications had been received including 16 withdrawals by NRAs and 5 cases closed by veto decisions. (A schematic overview is found at <http://ec.europa.eu/information_society/policy/ecomm/doc/article_7/competition-regulation%20first%20round%2001-08-2006_nonewmarkets.pdf>).

Thus, the Television Without Frontiers Directive[34] is examined in the section on exclusive rights contracts,[35] while the section on set top boxes contains references to the 2002 regulatory framework for communications.

(3) Competition Rules and Sector Specific Regulation

13.28   Depending on the facts of the case, sector specific regulation such as the 2002 regulatory framework may provide more far-reaching, more detailed, or more rapid remedies for potential complainants than the competition rules. However, the mere existence of sector specific legislation does not prevent the application of the competition rules to the same area.[36] There are two areas where the relationship between sector specific regulation and competition law is not clear:

— first, to what extent do the competition rules limit the powers of national regulators; and
— secondly, to what extent should sector specific regulation be taken into account in analysing a case under the competition rules?

(a) Competition Law as a Limit on the Role of Sector Specific Regulation

13.29   An open issue is the extent to which the competition rules can be invoked against state action in regulating a sector.[37] Where that regulation has the objective of favouring, or has the clear effect of favouring, a particular operator or class of operators, the Commission can take action under Article 86.[38] A more difficult case arises where the state action is at least overtly intended to serve another objective, such as the development or maintenance of competition. It appears possible that some such measures nevertheless risk infringing Article 86. For example, policies to encourage infrastructure investment, which can include differential interconnection pricing (cheaper interconnection for infrastructure operators), or imposing line of business restrictions on dominant telecommunications companies, could potentially raise competition concerns. The impact on third party investment is also one of the arguments made in relation to a competition authority ordering access to an essential facility, although following the essential facilities analysis embraced by the Court of Justice in the *Bronner* case this should not arise as if investment

---

[34] Council Directive (EEC) 89/552 on the coordination of certain provisions laid down by law, regulation or administrative action in Member States concerning the pursuit of television broadcasting activities [1989] OJ L298/23 as amended by Directive (EC) 97/36 of the European Parliament and of the Council [1997] OJ L202/60.

[35] See para 13.99 below.

[36] Commission Guidelines on market analysis and the assessment of significant market power under the Community regulatory framework for electronic communications networks and services [2002] OJ C165/6, paras 24–31; Notice on the Application of the Competition Rules to Access Agreements in the Telecommunications Sector [1998] OJ C265/2 at para 58; Commission Guidelines on the application of EEC competition rules in the telecommunications sector [1991] OJ C233/2, paras 15 and 16. See also *Bertelsmann/Kirch/Premiere* (Case IV/M.993) [1999] OJ L53/1 and *Deutsche Telekom/BetaResearch* (Case IV/M.1027) [1999] OJ L53/31.

[37] The extent to which regulatory justifications can be used to prohibit what the competition rules would allow is examined below in the section on procedure

[38] Commission Decision of 4 October 1995 concerning the conditions imposed on the second operator of GSM radiotelephony services in Italy [1995] OJ L280/49 (only the Italian text is authentic).

in own infrastructure was a viable proposition then the facility cannot be deemed to be essential.[39]

It is an open question whether NRAs must meet the same standard of proof before requiring access based on the 2002 regulatory framework—the Commission in its Guidelines on market analysis and SMP clearly suggests that establishing SMP is sufficient.[40] As regards local loop unbundling, this issue was preempted by legislative means in the ULL Regulation.[41] More broadly, the NRAs have adopted a 'ladder of competition' approach to remedies, which, while emphasising the importance of facilities-based competition in the long run, recognises that—apart from benefiting consumer choice—promoting compulsory access-based services competition may be necessary in the short run, in order to allow market testing of services, building up a client base, and the necessary track record to enable the outside sourcing of financing generally required to enable infrastructure investment. The argument is that in an attempt to capture a greater share of the value chain, successful services based competitors naturally tend to expand into developing proprietary facilities.[42] **13.30**

(i) **Different Interconnection Prices Risk Being Discriminatory** NRAs may wish to differentiate between (lower) interconnection prices for companies owning their own infrastructure and (higher) prices for service providers who use third parties' infrastructure, for example using cost-plus a reasonable rate of return methodologies for the former, and a retail-minus methodology for the latter. **13.31**

Although under the 2002 regulatory framework the Commission has no veto over remedies, the competition rules set limits to such policies. NRAs' actions must always be subject to the provisions of Articles 10 (former Article 5), 81 and 82, and 86.[43] This is even the case where national law requires outcomes that are incompatible with Community law.[44] In looking at interconnection pricing, for example, it is important to note that the Access Directive itself allows differences only to the extent that there is no distortion of **13.32**

---

[39] Case C-7/97 *Oscar Bronner GmbH & Co. KG v Mediaprint Zeitungs- und Zeitschriftenverlag GmbH & Co* [1998] ECR I-7791. The AG suggested, at para 66 of his Opinion, that the test might be less strict for facilities created under non-competitive conditions—notably with public funding. Moreover, the Court's case law on essential facilities does not appear to have settled. In Case C-418/01 *IMS Health GmbH & Co. OHG v NDC Health GmbH & Co. KG* [2004] ECR I-5039 in relation to compulsory licensing however the Court suggested the application of a less stringent 'indispensability' test similar to that used in the earlier *Magill TV Guide* case law. cf Cases T-69, 70 and 76/89, *RTE, BBC and ITP v Commission* [1991] ECR 485ff.

[40] Commission guidelines on market analysis and the assessment of significant market power under the Community regulatory framework for electronic communications networks and services [2002] OJ C165/6, paras 81–82.

[41] Regulation 2887/2000/EC of the European Parliament and of the Council of 18 December 2000 on unbundled access to the local loop [2000] OJ L336/4. This Regulation will be repealed because once all NRAs have completed their market analysis of the ULL market the Regulation becomes unnecessary.

[42] ERG (06) 33 Revised ERG Common Position on the approach to appropriate remedies in the ECNS regulatory framework ('Remedies' document): <http://www.erg.eu.int/documents/docs/index_en.htm>.

[43] Case 66/86 *Ahmed Saeed* [1989] ECR 838.

[44] Case C-198/01, *Consorzio Industrie Fiammiferi (CIF) v Autorità Garante della Concorrenza e del Mercato* [2003] ECR I-8055, paras 48–49. cf Case FI/2003/0031 Access and call origination on public mobile telephone networks in Finland, Commission Decision of 5 October 2004 (<http://ec.europa.eu/comm/competition/liberalization/decisions/>).

competition (a reiteration of the position under Article 82). It even goes beyond the settled Article 82 case law on discrimination by providing that the operator with SMP which is made subject to a non-discrimination obligation must provide services and information to others under the same conditions and of the same quality as it provides for its own services, or those of its subsidiaries or partners.[45] In practice a distortion of competition would appear to be likely on the basis of even a small differential in price if the service being provided to two companies was equivalent, and those two companies competed on the same downstream market (or at least two closely related markets).[46]

13.33 **(ii) Different Treatment Risks Becoming a Special Right within the Meaning of Article 86**
The policies described above may lead to preferential treatment that could constitute a special right within the meaning of Article 86, or would constitute a breach on the part of a Member State of Article 10 read in conjunction with Article 82. The following analysis looks at the possible implications of Article 86 in the context of public policy objectives.

13.34 In relation to electronic communications networks and publicly available electronic communications services the pursuit of public policy objectives by means of special and exclusive rights is barred by the Consolidated Competition Directive.[47] Individual licensing has been abolished under the 2002 regulatory framework, although the Authorisation Directive provides that specific obligations (not rights) may be attached to general authorisations for those parties designated to provide universal service.[48] Rights of use for radio frequencies, where unavoidable in view of scarcity and the need to ensure efficient use of frequencies, and numbers must be granted based on open, transparent and non-discriminatory procedures.[49] Apart from constituting possible infringements of the Authorisation Directive, deviations from these rules risk running foul of the Consolidated Competition Directive.

13.35 Because under the 2002 regulatory framework the objectives to be pursued by NRAs are defined as promoting competition, consumers' interests, and the internal market, regulatory action in compliance with the framework is likely to be consistent with competition policy and is in any event to Commission scrutiny—and a possible veto—under the Article 7 Framework Directive procedure.[50] The Commission has also taken a clear

---

[45] Art 10, para 2 of Directive 2002/19/EC of the European Parliament and of the Council of 7 March 2002 on access to, and interconnection of, electronic communications networks and associated facilities (Access Directive) [2002] OJ L108/7. See also: Art 3 Commission Directive 2002/77/EC of 16 September 2002 on competition in the markets for electronic communications networks and services [2002] OJ L249/21. There is some support for this proposition under Art 82 EC: Case T-224/94 *Deutsche Bahn v Commission* [1997] ECR II-1689, paras 85–93.

[46] See the discussion on discriminatory pricing, below at paras 13.262 *et seq.*

[47] Art 2, Commission Directive 2002/77/EC of 16 September 2002 on competition in the markets for electronic communications networks and services (Consolidated Competition Directive) [2002] OJ L249/21.

[48] Art 6, para 2 Directive 2002/20/EC of the European Parliament and of the Council of 7 March 2002 on the authorisation of electronic communications networks and services (Authorisation Directive) [2002] OJ L108/21.

[49] Art 5, and Annex, sub B and C Directive 2002/20/EC of the European Parliament and of the Council of 7 March 2002 on the authorisation of electronic communications networks and services (Authorisation Directive) [2002] OJ L108/21.

[50] Art 8, Directive 2002/21/EC of the European Parliament and of the Council of 7 March 2002 on a common regulatory framework for electronic communications networks and services (Framework Directive) [2002] OJ L108/33.

position in the Access Notice that if a regulator infringes the competition rules it is at risk of an action for damages by a third party.[51] Regulatory intervention may also be insufficient to prevent an undertaking from itself being held liable for infringement of the competition rules at least to the extent that it autonomously foreclosed (ie absent regulatory requirements to do so) even the remaining scope for competition.[52] This also answers the question whether there is scope for findings of anticompetitive behaviour on account of undertakings in the context of regulatory actions sanctioned (explicitly or by non-exercise of its veto-powers) by the Commission in the Article 7 Framework Directive procedure.

(b) Relevance of Sector Specific Regulation to an Appraisal under the Competition Rules

(i) Regulation as a Mitigator of Competition Concerns   Commission decisional practice   **13.36**
on this issue appears to vary. Commission decisions in the telecommunications sector have generally either included conditions which mirror or build on pre-existing regulation[53] or have failed to mention the regulatory framework at all.[54]

In *BT/MCI I* however, the Commission did not impose non-discrimination and   **13.37**
transparency conditions on BT given the pre-existing regulatory framework,[55] although the Commission explicitly reserved the right to apply the competition rules should the regulatory regime prove ineffective. The approach seems to have altered slightly in the *Atlas* decision, where the Commission imposed certain obligations even where the parties maintained that at least some of the conditions reflected pre-existing national law.[56] In *Telia/Sonera* the Commission accepted a commitment on non-discrimination in relation to regulated wholesale fixed and network products, including in relation to products that would be regulated in the future.[57] Given increasing criticism of behavioural undertakings it is not clear whether this pattern will persist.

This should be contrasted with the Commission's position on the *Kirch/ Bertlesmann*[58] joint   **13.38**
venture. Here, no reference is made to the TV Standards Directive then in force which at

---

[51] Joined Cases C-6/90 and C-9/90 *Francovich and Others* [1991] ECR I-5357, and Joined Cases C-46/93 and C-48/93 *Brasserie du Pêcheur SA v Bundesrepublik Deutschland* and *The Queen v Secretary of State for Transport, ex parte: Factortame Ltd and others* [1996] ECR I-1029, Notice on the Application of the Competition Rules to Access Agreements in the Telecommunications Sector [1998] OJ C265/2 at para 19.

[52] Joined cases C-359/95 P and C-379/95 P *Commission and French Republic v Ladbroke Racing Ltd.* [1997] ECR I-6265.

[53] *Atlas* [1996] OJ L239/23 (*Atlas*).

[54] *Bertelsmann/Kirch/Premiere* (Case IV/M.993) (1998) [1999] OJ L53/1.

[55] *BT-MCI* [1994] OJ L223/ 36, at para 57: (*BT/MCI I*). 'The abovementioned regulatory constraints, together with the additional explanations provided by the parties, have permitted the Commission to conclude that it is not necessary for it to take any further action as of now, including requesting the parties to make appropriate undertakings to the effect that they will neither discriminate nor cross-subsidise. However, should this conclusion prove to be wrong in the future, the Commission will immediately apply the competition rules of the EC Treaty (and if applicable those of the EEA Agreement) as required.'

[56] *Atlas* [1996] OJ L239/23, at para 30: 'In so far as related to existing obligations under national or Community law, the obligations described below are intended to ensure the Parties' firm commitment to comply with the applicable legal framework.'

[57] *Telia/Sonera* (Case COMP/M.2803) [2002] OJ C201/19.

[58] *Bertelsmann/Kirch/Premiere* (Case IV/M.993) (1998) [1999] OJ L53/1. On appeal to the Court of First Instance.

least in principle regulated the provision of digital conditional access services in Germany, one of the Commission's concerns in the case.

13.39   **(ii) Regulation is Irrelevant if Competition is Decreased**   Where sector specific regulation is intended at least in part to deal with the effects of an absence of competition, that regulation cannot be used as a justification to allow a further decrease in competition. For example, the Access Directive is intended to regulate customer (or: customer-competitor) access in circumstances where there is an operator with SMP, and enables an NRA to impose on such an operator an obligation to interconnect at cost-oriented prices. The TV Standards Directive imposed behavioural obligations on parties, and does not prevent significantly impeding effective competition in particular as a result of the creation or strengthening of dominance, the relevant test under the Merger Regulation. Regulation is often behavioural, taking as its starting point the existence of market power, and seeking to regulate the exercise of that power. If the regulation were to take as its starting point a prohibition on the creation or strengthening of market power, it is likely that it could be taken into account under the Merger Regulation.

C. Procedural Issues

13.40   The relationship between the European Commission and national regulatory authorities is particularly important in these sectors given the overlap between the sector specific regulation and the competition rules. The overlap is greatest in the telecommunications sector, and for that reason, the Commission has issued guidance on the relationship as part of the Access Notice.[59] In addition, the Commission has set out co-operation procedures between NRAs and national competition authorities, between the Commission and NRAs, and between NRAs in its market definition and SMP Guidelines.[60] Certain principles, however, were developed in media cases, and the principles set out below are broadly applicable to both sectors.

(1) Merger Control

Regulatory Jurisdiction of National Authorities

13.41   Regulatory intervention to prohibit agreements or practices that are permitted under Community competition law is possible in certain circumstances.

---

[59] Notice on the Application of the Competition Rules to Access Agreements in the Telecommunications Sector [1998] OJ C265/2, Part I—Framework.
[60] Commission guidelines on market analysis and the assessment of significant market power under the Community regulatory framework for electronic communications networks and services [2002] OJ C165/6, paras 135–143. Moreover Art 7 of Directive 2002/21/EC of the European Parliament and of the Council of 7 March 2002 on a common regulatory framework for electronic communications networks and services (Framework Directive) [2002] OJ L108/33 provides for a notification procedure of all draft decisions taken in respect of market definition and SMP designation that affect trade between the Member States, and for a Commission veto in those instances where a draft measure may create a barrier to the single market or is incompatible with Community law, in particular with the objectives of Article 8 Framework Directive. cf Commission Recommendation 2003/561/EC of 23 July 2003 on notifications, time limits and consultations provided for in Art 7 of Directive 2002/21/EC (Procedural Recommendation) [2002] OJ L190/13.

Article 21 of the Merger Regulation envisages regulatory scrutiny by the Member States on **13.42** the basis of public interest (non-competition) objectives. Public interest objectives could include, for example, plurality of the media.

(2) Complaints

(a) Community Interest

Where other fora have potential jurisdiction over a dispute, complainants should consider **13.43** carefully what elements of their complaint are of Community interest, and should if possible pursue national remedies, where such Community interest is limited.

(b) Other Options Available to Complainants

The Access Notice notes that, as regards complaints to the Commission, other options are **13.44** often available to complainants, such as actions before national competition or regulatory authorities, or national courts. The Notice notes the directly applicable nature of Articles 81 and 82,[61] and reiterates the benefits of national court proceedings first set out in the Commission's Notice on Co-operation with National Courts.

— national courts can deal with and award a claim for damages resulting from an infringement of the competition rules;
— national courts can usually adopt interim measures and order the termination of an infringement more quickly than the Commission is able to do;
— before national courts, it is possible to combine a claim under Community law with a claim under national law;
— legal costs can be awarded to the successful applicant before a national court.[62]

(c) Procedures under the 2002 Regulatory Framework

The Notice notes that the ONP Directives—the precursors to the Directives on the 2002 **13.45** regulatory framework—provide that national regulatory authorities have power to intervene and order changes in relation to both the existence and content of access agreements. The 2002 regulatory framework likewise provides for a full range of access remedies in cases where the existence of SMP is demonstrated, as well as access remedies to ensure interoperability even in the absence of SMP. Among the key objectives listed in the Framework Directive is 'ensuring that there is no distortion or restriction of competition'. SMP measures are based on competition-law based market and dominance analysis carried out in consultation with the national competition authorities and coordinated by the Commission under the procedure provided in Article 7 of the Framework Directive.

(d) Commission's Position

Given the benefits of avoiding a multiplicity of proceedings, the Commission indicates **13.46** that:

Where complaints are lodged with the Commission under Article 3 of Regulation 17 while there are related actions before a relevant national or European authority or court, the

---

[61] Access Notice, para 27, citing Case 127/73, *BRT v SABAM* [1974] ECR 51.
[62] Access Notice, para 25; Notice on co-operation between national courts and the Commission in applying Articles 85 and 86 [now Arts 81 and 82] of the EC Treaty [1993] OJ C39/6, at para 16.

Directorate-General for Competition will generally not initially pursue any investigation as to the existence of an infringement under Article 85 [now Article 81] or 86 [now 82] of the EC Treaty.[63]

13.47 It is likely that, following modernisation, the Commission based on Regulation 1/2003 would take the same approach under the 2002 regulatory framework, in particular given the heavy reliance of the new framework on competition law principles. Moreover the dispute resolution procedures in Article 20 of the Framework Directive are much wider than the old provisions and cross-refer to the regulatory principles in Article 8, which include the promotion of competition. The Article 20 dispute resolution mechanism is used on a regular basis in many jurisdictions and is of greater practical significance than private litigation.

(e) Safeguarding Complainants' Rights

13.48 The Commission cannot abrogate its responsibilities under the competition rules towards those who feel that their rights under the competition rules are being infringed. Undertakings are entitled to effective protection of their Community law rights.[64] These rights would be undermined if the Commission were to refer matters to national authorities without ensuring that those national authorities respected the Community law rights of the applicants. Although the Access Notice refers to national regulatory authorities in the telecommunications sector, it may be that similar principles will be applied in the media sector also.

13.49 The Access Notice sets out certain criteria by which this effective protection should be judged. As the Access Notice is an interpretative text these criteria are unlikely to be interpreted strictly by the Commission and each case will have to be analysed and reasoned on its merits.

(f) Relevance of Timing to Community Interest

13.50 First, the Commission indicates that if a matter is not resolved within six months of it first being brought to the attention of the national regulatory authority, the Commission will then consider intervening.[65] This period was the same as that recommended in the ONP Directives then in force for the resolution of disputes although this is not explicitly referred to in the Notice. Under the 2002 regulatory regime, Article 20 of the Framework Directive provides for a statutory limit of four months triggering a binding decision by the NRA to resolve the dispute concerned within a further four months, thus potentially exceeding the six-month time frame set out in the Notice. The Notice provides no indication of when the six-month time period will start: this is consistent with the six-month provision being more of a guideline than a strict rule. Potential complainants to the Commission would therefore be well advised to inform national regulatory authorities of their problems at the earliest possible stage.

13.51 The Notice goes on to say that timely resolution of disputes is particularly important in this sector given the short innovation cycles. This parallels the importance which the

---

[63] Access Notice, para 28.
[64] Case 14/83 *Von Colson* [1984] ECR 1891.
[65] Access Notice, para 30.

Commission also places on the timely provision of access by dominant operators—delay in providing access could potentially be abusive on the part of a dominant operator.[66] Resolution by the national regulatory authority could take the form of either a final determination of the action or another form of relief which would safeguard the rights of the complainant.

(g) Cross-border/Pan-European Dimension

A caveat likely to remain extremely significant is set out very briefly at paragraph 31 of the **13.52** Access Notice:

> In addition, the Commission must always look at each case on its merits: it will take action if it feels that in a particular case, there is a substantial Community interest affecting, or likely to affect, competition in a number of Member States.[67]

Where there is a substantial cross-border element to a particular case it is likely that no one **13.53** national regulatory authority would have jurisdiction to act. In these circumstances it would be inappropriate for the Commission to refer matters to the national level. However, this paragraph is drafted more widely than that case would require. The paragraph also appears to envisage Commission intervention in a case where the issues are likely to recur in other Member States, even though the particular case is centred in one Member State and where that State's national regulatory authority would therefore have jurisdiction. In addition, the 2002 regulatory framework provides for joint analysis by the NRAs of the Member States concerned in the event transnational markets are concerned.[68]

(h) Interim Measures

(i) Availability of Interim Measures at the National Level   The Commission also notes **13.54** the importance of the availability in principle and in practice of interim measures at the national level. To be relevant, obtaining interim measures at the national level should be no more difficult than before the Commission.

(ii) Substantially the Same Outcome   A principle developed in the media sector, but **13.55** only implicit in the Access Notice, is that matters can only be appropriately referred to a national authority in circumstances where that national authority is applying rules which should lead to substantially the same outcome as an application of the competition rules. Following modernization, this is obviously the case as regards the application of Articles 81 and 82 by national competition authorities (and courts), which is now mandated by Community law, including powers to end infringements, to provide for interim relief, accepting commitments and imposing fines and periodic penalty payments.[69]

---

[66] Access Notice, paras 95 and 125.
[67] This is likely to be influenced by Commission Notice—Guidelines on the effect on trade concept contained in Articles 81 and 82 of the Treaty [2004] OJ C101/81.
[68] Art 15 para 4 and Art 16 para 5 of Directive 2002/21/EC of the European Parliament and of the Council of 7 March 2002 on a common regulatory framework for electronic communications networks and services (Framework Directive) [2002] OJ L108/33.
[69] Council Regulation (EC) No 1/2003 of 16 December 2003 on the implementation of the rules on competition laid down in Articles 81 and 82 of the Treaty [2003] OJ L1/1, Arts 5 and 6.

13.56   National regulatory authorities will often be applying the 2002 regulatory framework in circumstances where there is an overlap with the competition rules, for example in the field of interconnection and access pricing. In such cases, this criterion will usually be satisfied. Because the concept of SMP is equivalent to dominance in the sense of the general competition rules, and given that designations of SMP are subject to notification to, and comments by, the Commission, there is likely to be limited divergence between the two regimes. Nevertheless, the designation of an undertaking as having SMP in a market defined for the purpose of *ex ante* regulation does not automatically imply that this undertaking is also dominant for the purposes of Article 82. Nor does the SMP designation have any bearing on whether that undertaking has committed an abuse within the meaning of Article 82. Consequently, in the same or related relevant markets parallel procedures may arise under *ex ante* regulation and under competition law, competition authorities may carry out their own market analysis and impose appropriate remedies alongside any sector specific measures applied by the NRA.[70]

13.57   Recital 27 of the Framework Directive clearly indicates that *ex ante* regulatory obligations should only be introduced where national and Community competition law remedies are not sufficient to address the problem. The Commission's guidance under the new regulatory framework provides three cumulative criteria that should be applied to identify such markets, which should (i) be subject to high and non-transitory entry barriers; not over time tend towards effective competition; and (iii) *ex ante* regulation should be more efficient in addressing the persistent market failures concerned than competition law by itself. Criteria for the relative efficiency of competition law and complementary *ex ante* regulation are provided in the explanatory memorandum that accompanies the Commission's Recommendation on relevant product and service markets as including cases where the compliance requirements of an intervention to redress a market failure are extensive; where frequent or timely intervention is indispensable; or where legal certainty is of paramount concern. Finally, the Commission recommends that NRAs should consult with their national competition authority in making decisions on this issue.[71]

13.58   Where a national competition or regulatory authority applies national rules that should lead to substantially the same outcome, but the complainant is dissatisfied with the result, the appropriate course of action would be to challenge in national proceedings the finding of the national authority. Article 4 of the Framework Directive provides for a right of appeal against NRA decisions. The Commission is unlikely to prove receptive to being treated as

---

[70] Commission guidelines on market analysis and the assessment of significant market power under the Community regulatory framework for electronic communications networks and services [2002] OJ C165/6, paras 24–32. In the US the Supreme Court is wary of antitrust intervention where adequate sector-specific remedies are available. cf *Verizon Communications inc. v Law Offices of Curtis V. Trinko LLP*, United States Supreme Court 13 January 2004, 540 US (2004).

[71] Commission Recommendation of 11 February 2003 on relevant product and service markets within the electronic communications sector susceptible to *ex ante* regulation in accordance with Directive 2002/21/EC of the European Parliament and of the Council on a common regulatory framework for electronic communication networks and services [2003] OJ L114/45, para 9, and pp 9–12 of the Commission's Explanatory Memorandum to the latter document at <http://ec.europa.eu/information_society/topics/telecoms/regulatory/maindocs/documents/explanmemoen.pdf>.

a court of appeal against decisions of national authorities, particularly in view of the Article 234 jurisdiction of the Court of Justice.

D. Content

Scope of section   This section will deal with the competition issues which arise in respect   **13.59**
of the creation, packaging, and distribution of content. These categories reflect distinct
economic activities but are often carried out by a single integrated company. For example,
most television broadcasters are active in programme production, acquisition of the rights
to further programming, packaging of channels, and their distribution or broadcasting to
end-users.

Creation of content is used here to refer to the production of—usually television—   **13.60**
programmes. Packaging of content refers to the acquisition with a view to distribution of
programming rights by media operators, for example broadcasters wishing to create television channels. Distribution refers to the wholesale distribution of television channels to
pay TV operators. This section thus deals only with the wholesale aspects of content distribution. Issues relating to retail end-user services (advertising-funded and pay television) are
dealt with in section G on retail services.

General issue: effect on downstream markets   Television rights are often sold exclusively   **13.61**
in respect of individual territories, and may be bought or sold collectively. Competition issues
involving exclusive rights agreements, collective purchasing, and collective selling of rights
are therefore common and are likely to raise issues under Article 81 EC. Analysis of the
effects of such agreements, however, is primarily focused on downstream television markets
as lack of access to content may constitute a barrier to entry.[72] In this respect, three issues in
particular have attracted ever growing scrutiny by competition authorities at both the
Community and national levels: the effects of vertical integration; the conclusion by pay
television operators of series of exclusive agreements for sports and film rights; and
collective selling of exclusive sports rights by sports federations or leagues.

General issue: effect on trade between Member States   The Commission has tended to   **13.62**
define content product markets with regard to national, or at broadest linguistic, territories. This has not prevented it from finding agreements confined to the territory of a single
Member State to have an effect on trade between Member States.[73] This seems largely to be
on the basis that appreciable restrictions of competition in a national market can affect
market structure, raise barriers to entry for undertakings from other countries, and thereby
contribute to foreclosure of national markets.

---

[72] *Report on Competition Policy 1996* (Vol XXVI) at para 81: 'Steps must therefore be taken to ensure that the market is not foreclosed and that competition is not distorted . . . by difficulty in gaining access to programmes.'

[73] See, for example, *BBC/BSkyB/Premier League* (Notice pursuant to Art 19(3) of Regulation 17) [1993] OJ C94/6. Press release, IP(93)614 of 20 July 1993 and the *BDB* case referred to in the speech of JF Pons, Deputy Director-General of DGIV, 'The Future of Broadcasting' at the Institute of Economic Affairs on 29 June 1998, <http://europa.eu.int/en:comm/dg04/speech/eight/en/ sp98034>.

(1) Content Creation

(a) Market Definition

13.63 **(i) Content Production** The Commission has discussed product markets for content production in a number of cases,[74] often without having to decide definitively on the precise scope of the market. For example in the *Seagram/Polygram* decision[75] the Commission identified a film production market and discussed—without concluding—whether there might be different markets for, for example, mainstream and arthouse films. In the earlier *RTL/Veronica/Endemol* prohibition decision,[76] the Commission did reach clear conclusions on market definition by defining, *inter alia*, a product market for independently produced Dutch television programmes, ie excluding captive in-house production by Dutch broadcasters.[77] The Commission rejected the parties' arguments that the market should include in-house production on the following grounds. First, such programmes were very rarely sold to other broadcasters. Secondly, their production involved high fixed costs which made a significant increase in the purchase of independently produced programmes a commercially unfeasible strategy. Lastly, independently produced programmes tended to be 'large-scale entertainment programmes'. Broadcasters could not easily produce such programmes in-house. This market definition has since been upheld by the Court of First Instance[78] and the Commission's reasoning confirmed.

13.64 **(ii) Geographic Markets** Geographic markets for content production tend to be national or regional, reflecting linguistic differences. In the *RTL/Veronica/Endemol* case, the Commission concluded that the geographic market for independent television production was the Netherlands as there was very little trade in Dutch language television programmes even with broadcasters in the Belgian Flanders region. This was due to cultural differences between the two areas and to the fact that programmes produced to attract Dutch audiences with well-known Dutch actors were unlikely to be attractive to Belgian audiences and vice versa. This conclusion has been confirmed by the Court of First Instance. It therefore seems likely that the Commission will continue to define national geographic markets, or depending on the facts, broader markets in respect of a homegenous cultural or linguistic area which can surpass national boundaries.[79]

(b) Competition Issues

13.65 The only competition issues to have been examined by the Commission to date have arisen under the Merger Regulation and concerned television programme markets. No significant competition concern has been identified in the majority of these cases. The exception is the *RTL/Veronica/Endemol*[80] prohibition decision. The main interest of this case is for its

---

[74] *ABC/Générale des Eaux/Canal+/WH Smith TV* (Case IV/M.110) (1991), *VOX (II)* (Case IV/M.525) (1995), *Channel Five* (Case IV/M.673) (1996).

[75] Commission Decision M.1219, *Seagram/Polygram*, 21 September 1998.

[76] *RTL/Veronica/Endemol* (Case IV/M.553) [1996] OJ L294/14.

[77] ibid, see in particular paras 24, 89, and 90.

[78] Case T-221/95 *Endemol Entertainment Holding v Commission*, judgment of 28 April 1999, not yet published.

[79] In *ABC/Générale des Eaux/Canal+/WH Smith TV* (Case IV/M.110) (1991) the Commission referred to the possibility of the geographic market in question surpassing national boundaries.

[80] *RTL/Veronica/Endemol* (Case IV/M.553) [1996] OJ L294/14.

analysis of the factors relevant to dominance and to the strengthening of that dominance through vertical integration. The decision has been upheld on appeal by the Court of First Instance.[81]

(i) Strengthening of Dominance through Vertical Integration—*RTL/Veronica Endemol* **13.66**
The case concerned the creation of a joint venture company, HMG, by RTL, the broadcaster of two Dutch-language advertising-funded television channels directed at the Netherlands, Veronica, the broadcaster of a third such television channel, and Endemol, an independent producer of Dutch-language television programmes. In addition to the structural link between Endemol and HMG, a production agreement was concluded under the terms of which HMG agreed to purchase a large percentage of its Dutch-language programme requirements from Endemol. The purpose of HMG was to package and supply television and radio programmes broadcast by itself, CLT, Veronica, or others to viewers in the Netherlands and Luxembourg.

The Commission concluded that Endemol held a dominant position in the market **13.67**
for independently produced Dutch language TV programmes and that this position would be strengthened by its participation in the newly created joint venture, HMG. Furthermore, the Commission concluded that HMG would acquire a dominant position on the Dutch television advertising market. The operation was prohibited. Following this decision Endemol withdrew from HMG.[82] On this basis, and following modifications to the programme supply agreement between Endemol and HMG and to HMG itself, the operation was cleared.[83] The programme supply agreement itself was then notified to the Commission under Regulation 17 but no formal decision was issued.[84]

(ii) Factors Relevant to Dominance in Television Programme Production In calculating **13.68**
Endemol's pre-existing market share, the Commission concluded that the value of programmes sold and not the volume was the most appropriate method. On this basis, Endemol had a market share which was 'clearly more than 50 per cent'. The Court of First Instance has since confirmed the Commission's methodology. The strength of Endemol's market position was confirmed by the fact that it owned a large number of the most popular entertainment programmes, had preferential access to foreign formats which it then adapted to the Dutch audience, and had a high number of the most popular Dutch TV personalities under contract, often on an exclusive basis. Finally, Endemol's single largest competitor had a market share of less than 10 per cent, while the remainder had market shares of less than 5 per cent. The Court of First Instance has since confirmed that these factors were sufficient to establish dominance.

---

[81] Case T-221/95 *Endemol Entertainment Holding v Commission*, judgment of 28 April 1999, not yet published.
[82] The operation had been implemented prior its prohibition by the Commission. This was possible as it was referred by the Dutch authorities to the Commission under Art 22 of Council Regulation (EEC) 4064/89 on the control of concentrations between undertakings [1989] OJ L395/1 which does not provide for a suspensive effect on the operation's implementation.
[83] *RTL/Veronica/Endemol* (Case IV/M.553) [1996] OJ L294/14.
[84] Notice inviting third party comment, OJ C147/5.

13.69 (iii) **Effect of Downstream Vertical Integration**   The Commission concluded that Endemol's dominant position would be strengthened by its participation in HMG (which as stated above, was also found to hold a dominant position) as it would have 'a structural link to the future leading broadcaster in the Netherlands' and would thus secure 'a large sales basis for its product which is safe and cannot be attacked by competitors'.[85] The programme production agreement between Endemol and HMG was used as an illustration of this. De facto joint control of HMG would allow Endemol to 'use its influence in HMG to obtain even more orders from HMG. No other producer in the Netherlands had a similar possibility to have a safe sales basis for its production and to influence the programme acquisition of a broadcaster'.[86] Endemol's structural link with HMG would thus allow it to strengthen its position on the programme production market by foreclosing the access of its competitors to HMG. The Court of First Instance has upheld this reasoning.[87]

13.70 Importantly, even in the absence of joint control, the Commission stated that Endemol's dominant position would be strengthened. Endemol's indirect participation in HMG amounted to 23 per cent. This gave it the right to be represented in the shareholders' meeting in which the major strategic decisions relating to the commercial behaviour of HMG were taken:

> A participation of 23% in a company which is active in a downstream market has to be seen as a strategic participation, rather than a financial one. This is even more the case where this participation is combined with a substantial representation of the shareholder in the decision-making body of this company. The shareholder will be able to obtain all information on the strategic decisions and will be involved in the discussions and decision-making procedure, where it can, in particular, influence decisions related to the upstream market where it is itself active.[88]

13.71 The Commission therefore concluded that 'through its structural link to HMG, Endemol was in a position to influence the general programming and programme acquisition policy of HMG in a manner which strengthens Endemol's current position on the market for independent production'.[89] The Court of First Instance made no reference to this argument as it concluded that HMG was jointly controlled by its shareholders.

(2) Content Packaging

(a) Market Definition

13.72 Defining product markets in respect of the acquisition of television rights by broadcasters is a complicated exercise.[90] Measuring demand substitutability is difficult. Broadcasters' demand for individual forms of programming is a reflection of viewers' preferences.

---

[85] *RTL/Veronica/Endemol* (Case IV/M.553) [1996] OJ L294/14, at para 98.
[86] ibid, at para 99.
[87] Case T-221/95 *Endemol Entertainment Holding v Commission*, judgment of 28 April 1999, not yet published, at paras 167–169.
[88] ibid, at para 100.
[89] ibid, at para 100.
[90] For a general economic analysis of market definition in the media sector see study by Europe Economics available at <http://europa.eu.int/comm/competition/publications/studies/european_economics.pdf>.

However, it is only in respect of pay television services that those preferences are directly expressed by viewers. In respect of advertising-funded television, viewer preferences are expressed by viewing shares which then determine the prices of advertising slots (as does the relationship between the profile of a particular audience and the demands of advertisers). Supply side substitutability between different forms of programming is limited as the producer of one form of programming cannot easily switch to produce another. The existence of both free to air and pay television broadcasters poses a further question, namely whether these different forms of broadcaster compete against each other in the acquisition of programming.

13.73 The lack of simple consistency and clarity in the Commission's decisions on market definition appears to reflect these difficulties and may also explain the Commission's tendency to concentrate on differences in programme characteristics rather than on use of the hypothetical monopolist test as set out in its Notice on market definition.

13.74 In many cases, it has not been necessary to specify market definitions particularly precisely, but there are now some indications that relatively narrow market definitions might be appropriate in particular cases, reflecting viewers' comparatively narrow preferences. The long term evolution of this trend might lead to a move away from the now well established distinction between advertising funded and pay television and towards a set of market definitions defined more closely on consumer preferences. In practice such a move might help to define more accurately some of the competition problems in this area, though it is unlikely to lead to a major change in the approach to particular cases. If, for example, consumers have a demand for first window premium movies sufficiently distinct from other windows or other forms of content, then basing a market definition on that demand would lead to effectively the same market definition as that for pay TV movie channels used in current Commission decisions.

13.75 (i) **Television Rights to Films, TV Films and Series**   There is no explicit market definition in the *ARD* decision.[91] It does appear to imply, however, that the Commission considered the relevant product market to be that for the acquisition of the television rights to feature films.[92] The Commission has now indicated that, at least as regards pay TV services, films and sports constitute separate markets.[93] Given the ability of pay TV services to provide viewers with very narrowly targeted types of content, there may be a range of narrowly definable content markets. The Commission has, for example, also distinguished between films made for cinema release, and those made for television[94] and movies produced by Hollywood studios and other studios.[95]

---

[91] *Film Purchases by German Television Stations* [1989] OJ L284/36.

[92] ibid, at para 22: 'Feature films are a particularly important component of programming. Compared with television product (ie televisions films and television series), they are in many cases on a higher artistic level and are produced with greater financial expense, are therefore often more popular and mostly achieve high ratings.'

[93] *Vivendi Universal*—Commission Decision Case IV/M.2050, 13 October 2000, *Vivendi/Canal+/Seagram*. See also *Newscorp/Telepiù*, Commission Decision in Case COMP M.2876, 2 April 2003 at paras 56 *et seq*.

[94] *Vivendi/Canal+/Seagram* at para 17.

[95] ibid, at para 18.

13.76   **(ii) Narrower Markets**   Rights to films are sold in respect of geographic territories and in respect of exploitation windows: these are time periods during which the film may be exploited for one purpose only.[96] For example, the first exploitation window is generally theatrical release in cinemas, which is then followed by DVD/video release, pay-per-view, pay television, and then free to air television.[97] The rights in respect of each window and territory are also generally sold exclusively within each window. Where the television rights in respect of all exploitation windows are sold to a single intermediary (whether a broadcaster as in the *ARD* decision or a rights agency), there is no need to determine whether a narrower market distinguishing exploitation windows is appropriate. However, broadcasters may also buy rights directly from film studios in respect of only one exploitation window, in which case separate markets are likely to be found to exist, as there is no substitutability between rights for individual windows. This would also appear to be the view of the Commission.[98]

13.77   **(iii) Television Rights to Sports Events**   In the *EBU*,[99] *Eurosport*,[100] *UEFA Champions League*,[101] and *DFB*[102] decisions, the Commission defined product markets for the acquisition of television rights to sports events. The *EBU* decision was annulled by the Court of First Instance but on grounds not related to the definition of the market.[103] In the *Bertelsmann/CLT* decision[104] the Commission justified the existence of a separate market for sports rights largely on the grounds of their 'specific features', namely their popularity with audiences, appeal to advertisers and the fact that they were often acquired before the teams which were to participate in the event, and thus their attractiveness, could be determined.

---

[96] The length of the windows varies between Member States. Indeed, in some countries, such as France, they are determined by statute. In others, they are determined by contract.

[97] There are often sub-windows within each of these categories: for example, first and second pay television exploitation.

[98] In the press release issued by the Commission announcing the dissolution of UIP pay TV, a joint venture between Paramount Pictures International, MGM International, and MCA International for the distribution of film rights to pay TV broadcasters, reference was made to 'the market for the supply of programmes for pay-television transmission in the EU'. IP/97/227 of 17 March 1997—'The Commission imposes the dissolution of UIP Pay TV's distribution joint venture'. The following decisions also suggest that separate markets for the various windows exist: *Seagram/Polygram* (Case IV/M.1219) (1998) (question left open as the operation did not raise a problem of compatibility with the Common Market); *TPS* [1999] OJ L90/6 (also left open). See also *BiB*, *Vivendi/Seagram* and *Newscorp/Telepiù*.

[99] *EBU/Eurovision* [1993] OJ L179/23. See also *ABC/Générale des Eaux/Canal+/WH Smith TV* (Case IV/M110) (1991): the possibility of a separate product market in respect of sports events was raised, but not decided as even on the narrowest market definition the case raised no problems of compatibility with the Common Market.

[100] *Screensport/EBU Members* [1991] OJ L63/32.

[101] Commission Decision of 23 July 2003 relating to a proceeding pursuant to Art 81 of the EC Treaty and Art 53 of the EEA Agreement (COMP/C.2-37.398 —Joint selling of the commercial rights of the UEFA Champions League) OJ L 291, 08.11.2003, pp 25–55.

[102] Commission Decision of 19 January 2005 relating to a proceeding pursuant to Art 81 of the EC Treaty and Art 53(1) of the EEA Agreement (Case COMP/C.2/37.214—Joint selling of the media rights to the German Bundesliga).

[103] Joined Cases T-528/93, T-542/93, T-543/93 and T-546/93 *Metropole television SA and Reti Televisive Italiane SpA and Gestevision Telecinco SA and Antena 3 de Television v Commission* [1996] ECR II-649.

[104] *Bertelsmann/CLT* (Case IV/M.779) (1996), at para 18. However, the Commission did not take a definitive view on whether sports rights constituted a separate market as even on the narrowest market definition the case raised no problems of compatibility with the Common Market.

(iv) Narrower Markets   There are no precedent decisions defining narrower markets, **13.78** either in respect of rights to particular sports events or in respect of the rights to live and deferred transmission and to highlights of sports events. It appears to be the position of the Commission that narrower product markets in relation to the television rights to particular sports may need to be defined in appropriate cases.[105] The Commission also appears willing to consider distinctions in market definition between the rights to live broadcasts and to highlights or deferred transmissions.[106]

In contrast to film rights, it is more difficult to sell sports rights in accordance with exploita- **13.79** tion windows given the great difference in value between live and deferred coverage of a sports event. The UEFA Champions League case suggests that live rights are on a separate market to delayed/deferred rights, leaving open the question of whether other—for example non-sporting rights—might be substitutes for non-live rights. It seems most likely that non-live sports rights are no more substitutable for other forms of content than their live equivalents, but simply the value of the rights is relatively limited. Live coverage to sports events are generally sold exclusively to a single television broadcasters (subject to the distinction between live and deferred transmission and highlights), whether for exploitation on pay or advertising- funded television. This would tend to suggest that, where this is the case, there is no justification for distinguishing between these different forms of television in defining wholesale markets. With the convergence of transmission mechanisms and the ability to deliver TV-quality services over the Internet, it appears increasingly difficult to distinguish separate markets for Internet and television transmission of live sports rights.

(v) Geographic Markets   The Commission's approach to geographic market definition **13.80** seems to be more straightforward. Television rights are protected by intellectual property and generally sold in respect of national territories or sometimes linguistic zones. The Commission has tended to conclude that the geographic market definition follows from this. In *ARD*, for example, the geographic market was said to be coterminous with the territory covered by the agreement, namely the German language territories within Europe.[107]

(b) Competition Issues

(i) Exclusive Rights Contracts

Exclusivity not itself a restriction of competition   The producer of a film owns the copy- **13.81** right in it and is free to exercise that copyright without contravening Community competition law (within certain limits). Thus, exclusivity is inherent in copyright or is part of its 'specific subject matter' and exclusive rights contracts do not necessarily constitute a restriction of competition within the meaning of Article 81(1) EC.

---

[105] In particular, section II of 'Broadcasting of Sports Events and Competition Law' in DGIV's *Competition Policy Newsletter,* No 2 of 1998, which suggests that product markets in respect of certain sports and in respect of important events in a particular sport may need to be defined. See also John Temple Lang, 'Media, Multimedia and European Anti-Trust Law' which also suggests that narrower markets than that defined in the *EBU* decision will now be considered.

[106] See articles quoted in n 105 above.

[107] See also *Seagram/Polygram* (Case IV/M.1219) (1998); *TPS* [1999] OJ L90/6 (also left open); and *BiB* (Notice pursuant to Art 19(3) of Regulation 17) [1998] OJ C322/5.

13.82   The leading case on this issue is *Coditel II*.[108] The Court of Justice was asked for a preliminary ruling on the question of whether a contract whereby the owner of the copyright in a film grants the exclusive right to exhibit that film in cinemas within the territory of a Member State and for a given period falls within Article 81(1). The Court referred to its previous judgment in *Coditel I*,[109] in which it held that the right of the owner of the copyright in a film and his assigns to require fees for any showing of that film is part of the essential function of copyright, and then continued as follows:

> Although copyright in a film and the right deriving from it, namely that of exhibiting the film, are not, therefore, as such subject to the prohibitions contained in Article 85 [now Article 81], the exercise of those rights may, nonetheless, come within the said prohibitions where there are economic or legal circumstances the effect of which is to restrict film distribution to an appreciable degree or to distort competition on the cinematographic market, regard being had to the specific characteristics of that market.

> It is therefore for the national courts, where appropriate, to make such inquiries and in particular to establish whether or not the exercise of the exclusive right to exhibit a cinematographic film creates barriers which are artificial and unjustifiable in terms of the needs of the cinematographic industry, or the possibility of charging fees which exceed a fair return on investment, or an exclusivity the duration of which is disproportionate to those requirements, and whether or not, from a general point of view, such exercise within a given geographic area is such as to prevent, restrict or distort competition within the Common Market.[110]

13.83   The fact that rights owners are able by virtue of copyright to grant exclusive licences is thus not in and of itself a restriction of competition, despite the fact that there is absolute territorial protection.

13.84   ***Duration and/or scope of exclusivity may constitute a restriction of competition***   In accordance with the *Coditel II* judgment, three issues are relevant to consideration of whether an exclusive rights contract may fall within the ambit of Article 81(1) EC:

- the duration and scope of the exclusivity;
- the appreciability of its impact on competition between broadcasters in the acquisition of rights and on downstream television markets; and
- its effect on trade between Member States.

13.85   While it is often unclear whether the owner of the television rights to sports events holds a copyright in the strictest sense,[111] the Commission has nonetheless applied the principles set out in the *Coditel II* judgment by analogy.

13.86   ***Commission's policy objective in respect of exclusive rights contracts***   The Commission's policy objective in seeking to limit the duration and scope of exclusive rights contracts is to

---

[108]   Case 262/81 *Coditel SA, Compagnie générale pour la diffusion de la télévision, and others v Ciné-Vog Films SA and others* [1982] ECR 3381.

[109]   1980] ECR 881.

[110]   ibid, at paras 17 and 19.

[111]   The answer to this question may vary between Member States in view of the differences in national copyright systems. This is in contrast to the situation in the United States where federal copyright protection of live sports broadcasts is assured by the Copyright Act 1976, 17 USC paras 101–801.

maintain a fluid rights market, thereby preserving competition in downstream television markets. The use of exclusive rights agreements to erect barriers to entry to downstream markets has proved to be of particular relevance to pay television. Despite the markets being largely national in scope, the criterion of effect on trade between Member States is often fulfilled whether or not the parties to an exclusive agreement are situated in the same Member State.[112] However, the principles governing the Commission's application of this policy objective to individual cases are less certain. This applies, in particular, to the test for determining whether the duration and scope of a particular agreement are likely to have an appreciable effect on competition such as to fall within Article 81(1) EC. In the *ARD* decision, which is discussed below, the focus was on the proportionality of the exclusivity to the needs of the broadcaster which has acquired the rights. There is little in the way of analysis of the effect of the contract in appreciably restricting competition between ARD and its competitors on the advertising-funded television market. This fact, taken in combination with the lack of clear market definition, and the peremptory treatment of appreciability in the decision, may cast a doubt over its use as an indicator of the Commission's likely future position in relation to exclusive agreements. This section sets out the Commission's past practice with respect to exclusive rights agreements, before considering whether a development is likely in the future.

Past approach to applicability of Article 81(1) to vertical exclusive rights agreements The **13.87** Commission's *ARD decision*,[113] which dates from 1989 (its focus in recent years having been more on horizontal issues of joint selling and joint buying) and its precedent value must therefore be treated with some caution. The Commission finally exempted the agreement, but only after having required major changes. The contract at issue was concluded between ARD (an association of German public broadcasters) and the American film studio MGM. ARD was granted 15 years' exclusivity in respect of each programme covered by the contract beginning with ARD's first exploitation. The contract covered both MGM's library of feature films, TV films, series, and cartoons and its future output of feature films. ARD was granted the right to choose the product it required from MGM's library and future output. MGM could grant no other licences in respect of any programme, regardless of whether ARD had chosen it. The rights granted were in respect of German-language versions of the films and covered all means of transmission: terrestrial, cable, and satellite. The rights also covered both advertising-financed and pay television.[114] In terms of geographic scope, the contract covered German-speaking Europe. With one exception, ARD was free to sub-license broadcasters outside Germany. Inside Germany, ARD could only sub-license related companies. The Commission issued a statement of objections, as a result of which ARD was required to release the product which it had not chosen so that licences could be granted to third parties. To this end, windows of varying duration were

---

[112] For example, *TPS* [1999] OJ L90/6, the exclusive rights contracts concluded in *BBC/BSkyB/Premier League* (Notice pursuant to Art 19(3) of Regulation 17) [1993] OJ C94/6. Press release, IP(93)614 of 20 July 1993.

[113] *Film Purchases by German Television Stations* [1989] OJ L284/36.

[114] In respect of pay television, however, MGM was able to license up to 25% of the films to third parties for pay TV in two pay TV windows of up to a year's duration.

created during which third parties, but not ARD, could have access to the programmes. ARD was also obliged to contribute to the costs of dubbing the product into German and to allow third parties to broadcast the product in a foreign-language version (ie not in German) throughout the contract area or to broadcast into the contract area from elsewhere (both of which were originally prohibited). Despite these changes, the Commission considered both the duration and scope of the agreement to fall within the ambit of Article 81(1) EC (although meeting the criteria of Article 81(3) EC).

13.88 *ARD: duration of agreement*   The Commission found the 15-year duration of the agreement beginning in respect of each programme with ARD's first exploitation to be 'disproportionate' and to result in 'an artificial barrier to trade'.[115] Two further restrictions of competition relating to the duration of the agreement were identified: first, the three-year period after conclusion of the contract during which ARD could choose the programmes it required from MGM's library and during which third parties had no access to the programmes; secondly, ARD's right to match the terms offered by any third party in the event that MGM wished to negotiate a similar contract with another broadcaster.

13.89 *ARD: scope of agreement*   The scope of rights covered by the agreement also constituted a restriction of competition, on the grounds that:

> The stock of suitable feature films cannot be increased at will and therefore large quantities of films must not be withdrawn from the market as a result of long-term exclusive ties. The number of films involved in this case goes well beyond the normal quantity necessitated by the needs of programme acquisition and programming and also well beyond the previous acquisition practice of the ARD broadcasting organisations themselves.[116]

13.90 These restrictions were appreciable, notwithstanding the fact that the contract concerned only 4.5 per cent of the 'total stock [of films] available worldwide' as the popularity of the films covered meant that their importance went beyond 'numeric quantity'.[117]

13.91 *Sports rights*   In 1993, the Commission issued an administrative letter exempting the five-year exclusive agreement to football rights between the BBC, BSkyB, and the English Football Association.[118] It said at the time that, in general, exclusive football rights contracts of a duration of more than a single season would fall within Article 81(1). In this particular case, the Commission was willing to exempt the agreements for the full five years in view of the fact that BSkyB was then a new entrant. Although little can be gleaned from the formal record, it appears that the Commission's focus was primarily on the vertical aspects of the agreement, rather than on the horizontal joint selling, an issue it came back to several years later.

13.92 *Development in Commission approach*   In 1995, the Commission summarised its approach to exclusive rights contracts as follows: 'while acknowledging the importance of exclusivity as

---

[115] *Film Purchases by German Television Stations* [1989] OJ L284/36, at para 44: 'This long duration of the agreements and the extension of the exclusivity beyond the actual licence period are disproportionate within the meaning of the *Coditel II* judgment of the Court of Justice and result in an artificial barrier to trade.'

[116] ibid, at para 43.

[117] ibid.

[118] Notice pursuant to Art 19(3) of Regulation 17 [1993] OJ C94/ 6. Press release, IP(93)614 of 20 July 1993.

a means of safeguarding the value of a programme, [the Commission] takes particular care to ensure that neither the duration nor the scope of such agreements restricts third-party access to rights for too long a period or risks foreclosing the market'.[119] This new emphasis on foreclosure of third party access to substitutable rights is certainly more in line with the Commission's most recent statements on its general approach to vertical restraints[120] than the *ARD* analysis. On this basis, an exclusive agreement would constitute an appreciable restriction of competition only if either its duration or scope result in foreclosure of third party access to substitutable rights. Given the 2004 Notice on Article 81(3), it is likely that this conclusion would also have to be qualified or at least clarified, in that foreclosure would have to be reasonably likely to affect 'prices, output, innovation or the variety or quality of goods and services'. [121]

The importance of proper market definition to such an analysis is crucial. Had this test **13.93** been applied in *ARD*, the agreement seems unlikely to have fallen within Article 81(1) EC given that some 95 per cent of substitutable rights were unaffected by the exclusive agreement and were available for purchase by other German broadcasters.

Recent years have seen an increased focus on exclusive rights contracts, and the Commission **13.94** merger decision in *Telepiù/Stream*[122] provides a strong indication that an accumulation of exclusive rights may be problematic. In that case—which was essentially a merger to monopoly on the Italian pay TV market, the Commission insisted on remedies which limited the exclusive film and sports rights that the merged entity could purchase in the future. The merged entity could only buy exclusive film and sports rights for distribution on its own platform (digital satellite) and for three and two years respectively. If the merged entity bought rights for other distribution platforms such rights could only be non-exclusive.

The various cases into the exclusive and joint sale of football rights by leagues on behalf of **13.95** the individual clubs also suggest that the scope of exclusive rights in the hands of single purchasers is causing concern. In the Article 9 Decision on the FA Premier League's joint selling arrangements, the FAPL undertook to ensure that there will be at least two purchasers of live Premier League football in the future suggesting that the Commission saw the sale of exclusive rights to a single operator as foreclosing the market.

Applicability of Article 81(3)   Again, the only formal decision is *ARD*, the pertinence of **13.96** which for future practice has already been questioned above.[123] However, the 1993 comfort

---

[119] *Report on Competition Policy 1995* (Vol XXV) at para 83.

[120] Communication of 30 September 1999. Indeed, it appears likely that the expected block exemption Regulation on vertical restraints will block exempt vertical agreements provided that the supplier does not have a market share above 30%. It remains to be seen whether rights contracts will fall within the scope of this block exemption.

[121] Commission Notice Guidelines on the application of Art 81(3) of the Treaty [2004] OJ C101/8, para 24.

[122] 2004/311/EC: Commission Decision of 2 April 2003 declaring a concentration to be compatible with the Common Market and the EEA Agreement (Case COMP/M.2876—*Newscorp/Telepiù*).

[123] In *Film Purchases by German Television Stations* [1989] OJ L284/36, the following benefits were said to justify exemption. First a new product was introduced to German consumers which they would not otherwise have had an opportunity to watch. Secondly, the windows system means that other broadcasters also had access to the product, sometimes even before ARD. Thirdly, buying the rights to a large number of films

letter in respect of the *BBC/BSkyB/English Football Association* also provides some pointers. Two points in particular seem relevant to the likelihood of exemption. The first concerns the existence of 'windows' or sub-licensing schemes to attenuate concerns surrounding exclusivity, as in *ARD*. This has also been a feature of subsequent exemption and merger decisions[124] and has been relied upon in place of a reduction in the duration of agreements. The second important point is the market position of the broadcaster acquiring the rights. In the English Football Association case, much was made of the fact that BSkyB was not only a new entrant in the pay television market but would also use a then novel means of transmission, satellite direct-to-home. However, a number of statements have since been made that, in retrospect, a five-year exemption was excessive.[125] It may therefore be that the Commission will take a stricter line in the future on the duration of exclusive sports rights contracts which meet the criteria for exemption. The Commission's approach in merger cases, where issue of rights contracts has sometimes been addressed as part of the remedies, also provides guidance as to what is likely to prove acceptable under Article 81. In the *Telepiù/Stream* case, the pay TV operator created through the merger was prevented from concluding sports contracts of greater than two years in duration (and film contracts of greater than three years in duration—the justification for this difference in duration is unclear).

13.97 The scope of the exclusivity has also been attacked in the *Telepiù/Stream* decision where the merged entity was prevented from buying exclusive rights to distributon platforms other than its own (satellite). Such a condition prevents an operator from foreclosing the market to its competitors. As in this case the merged entity only operated on one platform, it is not clear whether there was an implicit condition in the decision that operating on only one platform would be permissible (thereby keeping other platforms open for new entrants).

13.98 *Cumulation of exclusive pay television film and sports rights contracts* The Commission has made various statements to the effect that the conclusion of a series of exclusive rights contracts can act as a barrier to entry and foreclose competition in television markets.[126] The *FA Premier League* case, and the CFI annulment of the Commission's exemption decision in EBU both suggest that the scope of exclusive rights needs to be examined very carefully to ensure that the remaining rights on the market allow for the possibility of market entry.

---

resulted in a lower cost per film than would have been possible with a series of smaller agreements. Fourthly, only restrictions indispensable to these objectives were maintained. Finally, competition was not likely to be eliminated as a result of the introduction of the windows system and of the fact that sufficient other films suitable for exploitation on German TV remained available.

[124] *Report on Competition Policy 1996* (Vol XXVI) at para 83.

[125] See, for example, Commissioner van Miert's speech on 'Sport et Concurrence: Développements récents et action de la Commission' at the Forum Européen du Sport in Luxembourg on 27 November 1997: 'Avec le recul, la durée acceptée par la Commission était probablement trop longue parce que cette technologie de transmission [ie satellite direct-to-home] s'est implantée plus rapidement que prévu.' <http:/europa.eu.int/en:comm/dg04/speech/seven/fr/ sp97069>.

[126] *Report on Competition Policy 1996* (Vol XXVI) at para 83.

Exclusive rights to 'events of major importance for society' Article 3(a)[127] of the Television **13.99**
Without Frontiers Directive[128]—currently under review—allows Member States to pre-
vent pay television operators from acquiring the exclusive rights to certain events. The
object is to ensure that 'events of major importance for society' are available to most of the
population on 'free' television. The definition of such events, whether national or international, and whether the rights concerned are for live or deferred transmission are a matter
for each Member State. However, those Member States which take advantage of this possibility remain subject to Community law. In terms of competition law, Article 82 EC is the
most relevant provision. The scope of Member State action is therefore constrained.

(ii) Collective Purchasing of Television Rights

In general As stated above, broadcasters will generally acquire rights exclusively. Thus, **13.100**
regardless of whether the rights are purchased individually or collectively, the impact of
exclusive acquisition will often be the first issue to consider. In this section collective purchasing agreements are presumed to be exclusive.

Where rights are acquired collectively, two further broad sets of issue arise. First, does col- **13.101**
lective purchasing of rights affect the vertical relationship between the seller and the buyers, that is, do the buyers have market power which would allow them to buy the rights at
a price which is lower than the competitive level? In terms of rights acquisition, the scarcity
of attractive content seems to make the likelihood of buyer power remote. However, the

---

127 '1. Each Member State may take measures in accordance with Community law to ensure that broadcasters under its jurisdiction do not broadcast on an exclusive basis events which are regarded by that
Member State as being of major importance for society in such a way as to deprive a substantial proportion of the public in that Member State of the possibility of following such events via live coverage or deferred coverage on free television. If it does so, the Member State concerned shall draw up
a list of designated events, national or non-national, which it considers to be of major importance
for society. It shall do so in a clear and transparent manner in due and effective time. In so doing the
Member State concerned shall also determine whether these events should be available via whole or
partial live coverage, or where necessary or appropriate for objective reasons in the public interest,
whole or partial deferred coverage.
2. Member States shall immediately notify to the Commission any measures taken or to be taken pursuant to paragraph 1. Within a period of three months from the notification, the Commission shall
verify that such measures are compatible with Community law and communicate them to the other
Member States. It shall seek the opinion of the Committee established pursuant to Article 23a. It
shall forthwith publish the measures taken in the Official Journal of the European Communities and
at least once a year the consolidated list of the measures taken by Member States.
3. Member States shall ensure, by appropriate means, within the framework of their legislation that
broadcasters under their jurisdiction do not exercise the exclusive rights purchased by those broadcasters following the date of publication of this Directive in such a way that a substantial proportion
of the public in another Member State is deprived of the possibility of following events which are
designated by that other Member State in accordance with the preceding paragraphs via whole or
partial live coverage or, where necessary or appropriate for objective reasons in the public interest,
whole or partial deferred coverage on free television as determined by that other Member State in
accordance with paragraph 1.'
128 Council Directive (EEC) 89/552 on the coordination of certain provisions laid down by law, regulation or administrative action in Member States concerning the pursuit of television broadcasting activities
[1989] OJ L298/23 as amended by Directive (EC) 97/36 of the European Parliament and of the Council
[1997] OJ L202/60.

Commission has made passing reference to its existence in the sector in the past.[129] Secondly, does collective purchasing of rights appreciably affect horizontal competition between the acquiring broadcasters? This appears to be the more relevant question.

13.102 *Applicability of Article 81(1) EC*   Horizontal competition can only be restricted if the purchasers are actual or potential competitors. If this is not the case, then there can be no negative effect on competition. However, competition in two levels of markets could be affected by collective purchasing and both require consideration: competition in upstream markets for the acquisition of television rights and competition in downstream television markets.

13.103 Market definition will thus be crucial to an assessment of the effects of collective purchasing agreements. In this respect, therefore, the Commission's practice in distinguishing between separate downstream television product markets is relevant. It has consistently defined separate downstream markets in respect of advertising-funded television (television advertising market) and pay television (see section G below). As described above in the section on market definition, it is unclear whether the same distinction will be adopted in respect of upstream rights markets. National markets have generally been defined in respect of both downstream and upstream markets.

13.104 In theory, therefore, a collective purchasing agreement between broadcasters operating in different geographic markets seems unlikely to be found to have an appreciable effect on competition as the parties are neither competitors in the acquisition of rights nor in television markets. However, the *EBU* case casts some doubt on this conclusion. Whether a collective purchasing agreement between a free to air broadcaster (advertising-funded or public-funded) and a pay television broadcaster which operate in the same geographic market will be found to have an appreciable effect on competition will depend on the market definition adopted in respect of upstream rights markets.[130]

13.105 *Commission statement that 'in principle' Article 81(1) is applicable*   In circumstances in which the parties are clearly actual or potential competitors in respect either of the acquisition of rights or on a television market, the Commission has stated that: 'the joint acquisition or distribution of television rights, which in principle are covered by Article 85(1) [now Article 81(1)] of the EEC Treaty, could be exempted if they allow rationalisation, provided that they do not prevent market access for competitors'.[131] This statement leaves a number of questions unanswered. In the first place, it is unclear why such agreements are 'in principle' covered by Article 81(1) EC. This may be a reference to the fact that collective agreements inevitably involve agreement on the price to be paid for the rights in question. Article 81(1)(a) explicitly refers to agreements which directly fix purchase prices. Secondly,

---

[129] *Screensport* [1991] OJ L63/32, at para 65: 'the joint purchasing policy operated by the EBU through the Eurovision scheme already confers upon EBU members a certain degree of market power'. *EBU/ Eurovision* [1993] OJ L179/23, collective purchasing of sports rights 'strengthened the negotiating power of the EBU and its members vis-à-vis sports organisers'.

[130] The issue was not raised in *BBC/BSkyB/Premier League* (Notice pursuant to Art 19(3) of Regulation 17) [1993] OJ C94/6. Press release, IP(93)614 of 20 July 1993.

[131] *Report on Competition Policy 1990* (Vol XX) at para 82.

it is unclear whether the Commission's concern over competitors' access to markets concerns access to rights acquisition markets or to television markets. In the first *EBU* decision[132] only restrictions of competition on the sports rights acquisition market were identified. Arguably, however, the more important possible negative effect of collective purchasing agreements would be to restrict competition on the downstream television market. Analysis of the restrictive effect of collective purchasing would therefore focus on the market positions of the purchasers on either the television advertising or pay television market. If those positions were substantial, then coordination of their behaviour should give rise to concern. To date, the Commission does not appear to have considered downstream market positions to be relevant.

EBU The Commission has issued two exemption decisions[133] in respect of the **13.106** collective purchasing of sports rights by the members of the EBU, each then being annulled by the CFI. The first annulment by the Court of First Instance[134] was based on the Commission's failure to assess properly whether the restrictions of competition in the collective purchasing system were indispensable within the meaning of Article 81(3)(c) as it had not examined the conditions for membership of the EBU. The Commission further erred in law by using arguments relevant to Article 86(2) EC to justify exemption under Article 81(3) EC. The Commission re-examined the EBU scheme, and granted a second exemption decision addressing the points raised by the CFI. This was again challenged by third party broadcasters, who put forward seven grounds of annulment. During the oral hearing on the case, all sides expressed a wish for the CFI to rule on all of the grounds of the appeal, in order to provide as much clarity as possible in a difficult area. However, the CFI, in annulling the second Commission decision, did so on the basis of only one ground of appeal—that the Commission had not correctly applied the fourth criterion of Article 81(3)—and remained silent on the others. This might suggest that the Court found difficulty in reaching consensus on these other points. Although Regulation 1/2003 removed the need for the Commission to issue a further exemption, the complaint is pending with the Commission yet to give an indication as to whether it intends to issue a Statement of Objections.

The EBU is an international association of television broadcasters. In general terms, only **13.107** one broadcaster per country meets the criteria for membership. However, there is more than one member in five Member States. The EBU's rules provided that rights to international sports events[135] might be acquired jointly by all interested EBU members, who then share the rights and related fee between them. Analysis of the EBU is complex, as the arrangements touch on a variety of upstream (rights) and downstream (television) markets. While the collective purchasing of a minority sport might have limited impact on competition

---

132 *EBU/Eurovision* [1993] OJ L179/23.
133 *EBU/Eurovision* [1993] OJ L179/23 and [2000] OJ L151/18.
134 Joined Cases T-528/93, T-542/93, T-543/93 and T-546/93 *Metropole television SA and Reti Televisive Italiane SpA and Gestevision Telecinco SA and Antena 3 de Television v Commission* [1996] ECR II-649.
135 The extent to which the rights to national events may also be acquired jointly is somewhat unclear in the decision. Para 30 of the annulled decision states that the rights to national events are not 'normally' the subject of joint acquisition.

where an EBU member faces strong competition on the relevant domestic television market, a different conclusion might be reached if the sport was significant, and the position of the EBU member(s) is comparatively strong domestically. Drawing general conclusions as to the EBU system itself is therefore difficult.

13.108 *Applicability of Article 81(1) to single collective purchasing agreements*   There are no Commission decisions concerning single collective purchasing agreements. The most pertinent question in respect of such agreements appears likely to be whether any restriction has an appreciable effect on competition. In terms of rights acquisition, this will depend largely on the relative importance of the rights in question within the defined market. Whether there is an appreciable effect on downstream markets will depend on the purchasers' market position.

13.109 *Applicability of Article 81(3)*   Before exempting the agreement in *EBU*, the Commission required substantial modifications on the rules governing access of non-members to sports programmes for which the exclusive rights had been acquired collectively. As amended, the Commission considered the agreement to meet the first test of Article 81(3) as the transaction costs of acquiring the rights to international sports events were reduced and cross-border broadcasting was facilitated. Consumers benefited from an increase in the broadcasting of high-quality sports programmes and from the fact that cost savings would allow money to be invested in other forms of attractive programming. The ban on individual negotiations while collective negotiations were ongoing was indispensable as without it the success of collective negotiations would be jeopardized. Likewise, the fact that members agree on the financial conditions and the sharing of rights in respect of each sports event was inevitable as each event was distinct. Competition was not eliminated as only a part of the market for acquisition of sports rights was affected, namely the acquisition of the rights to international events.

13.110 **(iii) Collective Selling of Television Rights to Sports Events**   In general terms, collective selling agreements will normally constitute a restriction of competition within the scope of Article 81(1) EC, provided that the restriction is appreciable. Such arrangements have few redeeming features from a competition point of view as they may well inflate selling prices. They will also often restrict output. As such, at first sight, they seem unlikely to meet the criteria for exemption set out in Article 81(3).

13.111 The television rights to sports events are generally sold either in respect of a particular event (for example, the rights to individual boxing matches) or in respect of all events played within the context of a competition (for example, the rights to domestic football matches in a particular league competition or to the races within the Formula One motor car series). In the case of the latter, the organiser of the competition in question often concludes a single rights contract in respect of all individual matches played in the competition.

13.112 This practice was not questioned under competition rules for many years.[136] However, the question of whether such collective selling arrangements constitute restrictions of

---

[136] For example, the issue of collective selling was neither raised nor investigated by the Commission in the context of the rights contracts concluded between BBC and BSkyB and the English Football Association, Notice pursuant to Art 19(3) of Regulation 17 [1993] OJ C94/6. Press release, IP(93)614 of 20 July 1993.

competition and whether they should be permitted has now arisen at both the national[137] and Community levels.

There are two issues which are particularly relevant to competition analysis of collective **13.113** selling arrangements in respect of television sports rights.

Applicability of Article 81(1) EC: ownership of sports rights   The first question to resolve is who **13.114** is the owner of the television rights in question. By definition, collective selling arrangements can only be at issue if ownership of the television rights vests, at least partly, in the individual clubs or players which participate in the competition rather than in the league or association which has taken on responsibility for the selling of the rights.[138] Determination of ownership of rights to sports events is not a question of competition law. It must rather be determined by national civil law or statute. This issue has already arisen in a number of Member States in the context of the collective selling of football rights. Although, the approach taken has differed, there is a clear tendency towards recognising that ownership vests in individual football clubs.[139] Where national law does not give clear guidance— often the case where the issue has never been litigated—it appears that Article 81 will be applicable. If nothing else, the joint sellers are agreeing to avoid litigation.

Effect on trade between Member States can be presumed where the association is itself an **13.115** international one. However, even national collective selling agreements might well be found to affect trade between Member States given the increasing tendency for such rights to be sold in other European countries and—at least in the case of football—because of the increasingly global nature of marketing and player transfers.

Membership of some sports associations is conditional upon accepting collective selling **13.116** of television rights by the association. In such circumstances, it is evident that the members of the association are the proper owners of the rights. The statute which embodies the

---

[137] In Germany, the Cartel Office prohibited the German Football Association from collectively selling the television rights to home matches of German clubs playing in the UEFA Cup and the European Cup Winners' Cup. This decision was upheld by the Bundesgerichtshof, which is the highest civil court, in its judgment of 11 December 1997. In the Netherlands, the Ministry of Economic Affairs decided on 6 November 1996 that the collective selling by KNVB (Dutch Football Association) of the television rights to football matches was a cartel.

[138] However, for an alternative viewpoint, see John Temple Lang's article, 'Media, Multimedia and European Anti-Trust Law' in which he suggests that the ownership of rights is irrelevant to the question of whether joint selling by football clubs constitutes a restriction of competition within Art 81(1) EC.

[139] In Germany, the Bundesgerichtshof held, in its judgment of 11 December 1997, that the home club is the original owner of the television rights to its matches. 'Even if the DFB [German Football Association] and UEFA set the organisational framework for competitive football, the clubs playing the football matches are the ones that render essential economic services for the marketing of the TV broadcasting rights . . . Moreover, the home club concerned performs the necessary organisational work on site: . . . the home club is the natural market participant that is entitled to market the service produced by acting in combination with the opponent's club on a reciprocal basis agreed upon. As far as the sale of tickets . . . or the leasing of advertising space and similar commercial activities are concerned, there is no room for doubt about the home clubs' rights. The same applies in principle to the granting of film or TV rights in the stadium.' In Spain, in contrast, it has been determined by statute that ownership vests with individual football clubs. Law 10/1990 of 15 October 1990, known as the 'Sports Law', provided that the Spanish Professional Football League (LNPF) was charged with the management of all television rights to matches which it organised until the 1997/98 season. Thereafter, each club was able to manage its rights independently.

members' agreement to form the association seems likely to constitute a decision of an association of undertakings within the meaning of Article 81(1) EC.

13.117 Some sports associations may go further and require members to cede ownership of television rights as a condition of membership. Depending on the circumstances, this may be actionable under Article 82 EC where the sports association holds a dominant position. This would arguably be the case, for example, where the association has regulatory powers over the sport in question which allow it to veto the participation of a particular team in a competition, and where this approval is made conditional on the transfer of television rights.[140] On the basis of *Télémarketing*,[141] this could be said to constitute abusive behaviour.

13.118 **'Special characteristics' of sport** The 'special characteristics' of sport must always be recognised, but the Commission has taken a relatively strict line in analysing whether the restrictions it is examining are indispensable. For example, 'solidarity' between weaker and stronger participants or the training of young players requires redistribution of revenues. However the redistribution could be based on revenues other than those which are jointly sold. There is no necessary link between redistribution and joint selling.

13.119 In the *UEFA Champions League* exemption decision, the Commission exempted UEFA's general rules for the sale of media rights to Champions League matches in the EEA,[142] following certain modifications. Essentially the decision requires that rights be sold in separate packages (several packages of live TV rights, separate packages for mobile, Internet, etc). The decision is silent as to the accumulation of several exclusive packages in the hands of a single purchaser. However any concern as to accumulation of UCL rights is mitigated by UEFA's comparatively low market share—in the order of 20 per cent—and UEFA's policy for live TV whereby separate complementary packages are sold to free and pay TV broadcasters. It is not clear whether UEFA's decision to ensure some live matches are shown on free to air television is driven by political—'good of the sport'—or commercial grounds. One interesting condition which was expanded in the later cases was the non-sale/non-use clause. If any live TV rights remained unused or unexploited, the rights reverted from the joint sales organisation to the clubs. Essentially this ensures that the joint sales arrangements cannot be used to limit output, one of the prime concerns about joint selling.

13.120 This exemption decision was followed shortly afterwards by the Article 9 decision (the first under Regulation 1/2003) in the German *DFB* case. Again here, the Commission insisted on separate packages of rights. Despite the DFB's larger market share on the German national market, the Commission did not insist on an anti-accumulation clause. In light of the *FAPL* case discussed below, this might appear surprising. There are various possible reasons why the *DFB* case was treated differently. First, the situation of pay TV broadcasters on the UK and German markets is rather different. German pay TV has never been as

---

[140] See, for example, COMP/36.776—*GTR/FIA et autres*+5, Press Release IP/01/1523 of 30 October 2001.

[141] Case 311/84 *Centre belge d'études de marché—Télémarketing (CBEM) v SA Compagnie luxembourgeoise de télédiffusion (CLT) and Information publicité Benelux (IPB)* ECR 3261.

[142] The Commission explicitly left open the possibility that the implementation of this policy in particular Member States might, depending on the circumstances of the national market, give rise to additional competition concerns not covered by the exemption decision.

successful as UK pay TV, and shortly before the *DFB* decision, Kirch, the parent company of German pay TV broadcaster Premiere went bankrupt. Second, the value of the free to air TV highlights package in Germany was much higher in relation to the live rights than was the case in the UK, suggesting that German consumers regard highlights as a closer substitute for live TV than do UK consumers. Consequently it would be appropriate to look at both live and highlights rights when deciding whether there was an accumulation problem.

The third joint selling case was into the *English FA Premier League*. An Article 9 Decision **13.121** was issued in March 2006, which built on the commitments in the UEFA and DFB case. The innovation introduced by the *FAPL* case was in the introduction of a no single buyer rule for exclusive live TV rights. As commitments decisions are not reasoned, the decision does not provide guidance as to why such a provision was deemed necessary, though the Commission—supported by the national competition authorities—clearly had concerns as to the foreclosure of the downstream pay TV market.

(3) Content Distribution

(a) Market Definition

(i) Wholesale Supply of Television Channels In the *Télévision par Satéllite*[143] (*TPS*) **13.122** decision, the Commission referred to a market for 'the distribution and operation of special-interest channels' which it said were essential for the composition of a pay television service (although it also said that such channels were not confined to pay television).[144] In the *BiB* case,[145] the Commission indicated that a wholesale market exists for the supply of film and sports channels for pay-television.[146] The Commission justified this on the grounds that such channels are significantly more expensive than others which in turn reflects the fact that the underlying pay TV rights are the most expensive. The price of the rights reflects the fact that viewers' willingness to pay for film and sports channels is higher than willingness to pay for other channels. For a pay TV operator, therefore, these channels are crucial. The Commission did not distinguish between a wholesale market for film channels and a wholesale market for sports channels for pay TV in that case, but a strong suggestion that such a distinction is appropriate can be found in the *Vivendi/Canal Plus* merger decision. Although that is a first phase clearance decision, the merger was cleared subject to remedies and as such the market analysis is more extensive than is usually the case. The existence of separate markets is likely in view of the fact that the characteristics of sport and film programming are different, as are the profiles of their respective audiences. The issues were

---

[143] *TPS* [1999] OJ L90/6.

[144] ibid, at paras 37–39.

[145] *BiB*, Commission Decision 1999/781/EC, *British Interactive Broadcasting / Open* (Case IV/36.539), [1999] OJ L312/1. In this regard, see the undertakings sought by the Commission in *Bertelsmann/ Kirch/ Premiere* (Case IV/M.993) [1999] OJ L53/1 and *Deutsche Telekom/BetaResearch* (Case IV/M1027) [1999] OJ L53/31 to the effect that the pay television channel, Premiere, could be marketed by independent cable operators.

[146] See also Commission Decision COMP M.2876 *Newscorp Telepiù*, Commission Decision in JV.30, 3 Feb 2000, *BVI Television (Europe) Inc/SPE Euromovies Investments Inc/Europe Moveico Partners*, para 15; Commission Decision IV/M.1327, 3 December 1998, *NC/Canal+/CDPQ/Bank America*, para 15.

also considered in the *Telenor/Canal Digital* case[147] where again the reasoning suggests separate markets, although the precise market definition was again ultimately left open.

13.123 (ii) **Geographic Markets**   In *TPS*, the Commission concluded that the geographic market was a national one, and this approach has been followed in subsequent cases[148]

(b) Competition Issues

13.124 A distinction has developed in the pay TV market in the EU between retail pay TV operators, also sometimes referred to as pay TV platform operators, and suppliers of individual channels for pay TV. Pay TV operators package together a number of channels for which they charge subscribers a fee: all individual channels are not available to subscribers separately. The channels may be the property of the pay TV operator, but often also include third party channels. In the case of third party channels, therefore, wholesale supply agreements are concluded between the channel operator and the pay TV operator. The commercialisation of packages of channels in non-subscription-funded television is emerging in some Member States and the Commission pointed out in the TPS decision, that it expected this position to develop over time, in particular with the introduction of digital technologies. While this section concentrates on pay television, the issues raised may increase in importance in advertising-funded television.

13.125 The tendency in pay television to commercialise packages of channels became more pronounced with the digitisation of broadcasting technologies. Digital broadcasting, and digital compression, result in a more efficient use of transmission bandwidth. A greater number of channels can therefore be provided to consumers as part of a single television service. However, to do so, the pay television operator must have access to sufficient content. This need is generally met by the conclusion of wholesale channel supply agreements, which may be exclusive.

13.126 The practice of acquisition of exclusive pay television rights to programmes (which are then packaged to form a channel) further contributes to this development in market structure. This applies above all to pay television film and sports channels. Where one pay television operator has acquired the majority of such rights exclusively, then it may wholesale the channels it creates to its competitors on the retail pay television market.[149]

13.127 The competition law assessment of pay TV services has proven to be a particularly different challenge: historically, television has been based on selected packages of exclusive content. Essentially free to air broadcasters were heavily capacity constrained and competed on the basis of varying offerings of exclusive content. Pay TV—and in particular digital pay TV services—have little or no capacity constraints, leading to an increasing range of content being provided to consumers. However often such content continues to be based

---

[147] Commission Decision of 29/12/2003 relating to a proceeding under to Art 81 of the Treaty and Art 53 of the EEA Agreement (COMP/C.2-38.287 *Telenor / Canal+ / Canal Digital*).

[148] See *BiB, Vivendi/Canal Plus*.

[149] In this regard, see the undertakings sought by the Commission in *Bertelsmann/Kirch/Premiere* (Case IV/M.993) [1999] OJ L53/1 and *Deutsche Telekom/BetaResearch* (Case IV/M1027) [1999] OJ L53/31 to the effect that the pay television channel, Permiere, could be marketed by independent cable operators.

on exclusive rights agreements. This combination of an extensive range of content, licensed exclusively, can quickly lead to price escalation and the foreclosure of new entrants on these markets. Whereas operators on other markets are generally allowed to compete either on range or on exclusivity, many pay TV operators have successfully managed to combine the two with limited competition law intervention. Cases such as the football joint selling cases and the *Telepiù/Stream* merger referred to above suggests that this issue is beginning to receive greater scrutiny.

(i) Article 81 EC   This issue has been examined by the Commission in two separate **13.128** Article 81 cases. Both would tend to suggest that exclusive supply agreements are likely to be found to fall within the scope of Article 81(1). The first concerns Télévision par Satellite,[150] a company established for a period of 10 years to operate a digital pay television platform via satellite direct-to-home transmission in France. TPS's parent companies include three French advertising-funded terrestrial television broadcasters, namely TF1, the public broadcaster France Télévision (which broadcasts two channels, France 2 and France 3) and M6. As part of the agreement constituting TPS, these companies granted TPS the exclusive right to distribute their four channels as part of a pay television service. The poor quality of terrestrial reception in much of France makes this an attractive proposition for viewers. In addition, the parties agreed to give TPS a right of first refusal for the carriage of their special interest channels, and a right of final refusal over any programmes or services offered to third parties. TPS could choose in respect of both whether the contracts with its parents would be exclusive.

The Commission concluded that while the creation of TPS did not constitute an apprecia- **13.129** ble restriction of competition, the exclusive distribution agreement for its parents' general interest channels was caught by Article 81(1) EC and that an exemption of three years to correspond with TPS's start-up period was appropriate. It is noteworthy that the Commission justified this conclusion solely on the basis that the exclusivity 'denied TPS's competitors access to attractive programmes' and without defining the relevant market. Moreover, there is no discussion of the appreciability of the restriction of competition. In similar terms the Commission concluded that TPS's right of first refusal over its parents' special interest channels fell within the scope of Article 81(1) as it resulted in 'a limitation of the supply of special-interest channels and television services'. Again, an exemption of three years was considered appropriate.

The issue of the wholesale supply of channels for pay television was also raised in *British* **13.130** *Digital Broadcasting (BDB)*,[151] which concerned the creation of a digital terrestrial pay television operator in the United Kingdom by two advertising-funded television broad-casters, Granada and Carlton. The creation of the joint venture together with a seven-year channel supply agreement between BDB's parents and BSkyB in respect of three 'premium' channels (ie film and sport channels) and one 'basic' channel (Sky One) was notified to the

---

[150] *TPS* [1999] OJ L90/6.

[151] See the speech of JF Pons, Deputy Director-General of DGIV 'The Future of Broadcasting' at the Institute of Economic Affairs on 29 June 1998, <http:/europa.eu.int/en:comm/dg04/speech/eight/en/sp98034>.

Commission under Regulation 17. In contrast to the situation in *TPS*, the supply agreement between BDB and BSkyB was not exclusive: BSkyB also supplied cable operators with the same channels. Before granting an administrative letter, the Commission insisted that the duration of the programming supply agreement was reduced to a period of five years and that clauses in the agreement were deleted which could have acted as a disincentive on BDB competing with BSkyB for the acquisition of sports and film rights after the expiry of the contract. The precise nature of the Commission's concerns and the legal reasoning underlying its position is unclear. It does seem to be the case, however, that it was principally concerned by the agreement only in so far as it related to the supply of film and sports channels and its duration and terms affected BDB's future possibility to acquire the necessary rights to create such channels itself. The policy objective would be more understandable, however, if the duration of the channel supply agreement had been aligned with the duration of BSkyB's most important rights contracts. In this respect, it is noticeable that the five-year period which was exempted extended two years beyond the end of BSkyB's existing exclusive football rights contracts. At least as regards these rights, the Commission appears to have failed to meet its own declared objective.

13.131 (ii) **Article 82 EC**   The question of dominance in the markets for the wholesale supply of film and sports channels for pay television has not yet been considered by the Commission in the context of Article 82. There is thus little in the way of useful precedent. However, given the apparent importance of these forms of channels to the success of pay television operators, disputes over failure to supply or the terms of supply seem likely to arise under Article 82 EC in the future.[152] Given that the Commission now appears to define a single pay television market, without distinguishing between means of transmission, abusive behaviour in the wholesale supply of film and sports channels would affect competition in pay television.

13.132 (iii) **Factors Relevant to Dominance**   In the abstract, demonstration of dominance would require an undertaking to have a persistently high share in the supply of film and sports channels and for it be improbable that this share would be significantly eroded by its competitors within a reasonable timescale. It seems likely from other precedents[153] that the Commission would adopt the value of channels, rather than their number, as the most appropriate method of calculating wholesale market shares. If this is correct, then the percentage of total expenditure by purchasers on film and/or sports channels which is paid to the channel operator will need to be assessed. If other film and sports channels exist, then the relative numbers of subscribers might also be considered. Indeed, where the channel operator does not wholesale the film and/or sport channel in question, subscriber numbers appear to be the only available indicator of market share. In terms both of the likelihood of the market share being eroded and the endurance of dominance, consideration of the position of the channel operator in relation to the necessary programming rights will be crucial.

Examination of vertical relations with content producers and owners, such as film studios or football clubs, will be relevant, as will the number, scope, and duration of exclusive rights contracts.

(iv) Obligation to Supply There are a number of different scenarios in which the ques- **13.133** tion of obligation to supply by a dominant operator of film and/or sports channels might arise. Legally, the issues are comparable to those analysed under refusals to supply in the section on transmission networks (see section E below) though to the extent that intellectual property rights are involved, as will often be the case, it is likely that the *Magill/IMS* line of case law would be more relevant than the Bronner line (see Chapter 8, paras 225 *et seq*). Where the channel operator already supplies the channel to one third party, then a refusal to supply to others would risk being discriminatory and might objective justification. The most appropriate ground of attack would be the unjustified discrimination between the third parties. Requiring the wholesale supply of a channel in circumstances where it has never been supplied in this way to a third party is more problematic. It would be necessary to demonstrate that the channel constituted an 'essential facility' and that failure to supply would eliminate all competition from the party requesting supply in the pay television market,[154] not merely make competition more difficult. This is an extremely high burden of proof which it would seem difficult to meet.

An obligation to supply was, however, imposed as a remedy in the *Telepiù/Stream* merger. **13.134** In that case, the Commission put in place a range of remedies to ensure the possibility of future market entrance. The limitations on exclusive acquisition of content were referred to above. In addition, the Commission mandated wholesale channel supply on non-discriminatory terms. This seems sensible given that new entrants may face a range of difficulties other than access to content—for example competing with a well established brand, generating sufficient customers to be able to conclude direct agreements with rights owners (who often require minimum payments in addition to per customer payments). Wholesale access to existing channels would appear to overcome these difficulties and provide a means for new entrants to address the market in phases.

(v) Terms and Conditions of Supply: Bundling Bundling can occur in a variety of ways, **13.135** such as buy through requirements, structuring, and tiering of basic and premium packages. Bundling by a dominant company might be prohibited by Article 82(d) EC. Thus, any attempt by a dominant operator of a film and/or sports channel to make supply of the channel conditional upon purchase of other channels could be illegal.

(vi) Terms and Conditions of Supply: Price Discrimination In terms of the price of **13.136** supply, on the other hand, clear guidance is more difficult. It is clear that charging different prices to third parties for the supply of the same channel must be objectively justified to avoid the prohibition of Article 82(c) EC, at least where those parties are actual or potential competitors. Differential pricing on the part of a dominant company might also result in allegations that its price is excessive.

---

[154] Case C-7/97 *Oscar Bronner GMbH & Co KG*, judgment of 26 November 1998.

13.137 **(vii) Terms and Conditions of Supply: Excessive Pricing**   Disputes over the absolute level of the price would be more complicated to resolve. Given that the channel operator is likely to be a competitor on the pay television market of the purchaser, then complaints of excessive, rather than predatory, pricing seem to be more probable. However, there are two difficulties to be overcome if such an action were to succeed. The first is that the Commission appears to have a general reluctance to intervene in questions of pricing for fear of becoming a 'price regulator'. The second is that the economics of television channel production make it difficult to assess the 'economic value of the product supplied' as against which charges of excessive pricing must be evaluated.[155] Indeed, the fixed costs in creating a television channel may be significant, but the marginal cost of its provision are negligible, if not non-existent. In these circumstances, it is far from clear how the appropriate price for wholesale supply of the channel can be determined.

13.138 **(viii) Terms and Conditions of Supply: Margin Squeeze**   Where the dominant channel supplier is also active on the retail pay television market, then allegations of margin squeeze may be made. In *Napier Brown*, the Commission decided that a firm, which is dominant in the markets for both a raw material and a derived product, commits an abuse of a dominant position if the margin between the prices it charges for the two products is insufficient to cover the dominant company's own costs with the result that competition in the supply of the derived product is restricted.[156] This principle has recently been restated in the Access Notice.[157]

13.139 The theory underlying margin squeeze may be clear: in circumstances in which the dominant company as a whole is not making a loss, a margin squeeze means, in effect, that the dominant company is using profit from its wholesale operation to subsidize its retail operation. This affects competition as those downstream competitors of the dominant company which are at least as efficient as the dominant company would nevertheless be prevented from entering the market or forced from the market.

13.140 However, proving in practice that margin squeeze exists will be difficult. In the Access Notice, the Commission envisages two possible ways. The first involves examining whether the dominant company's own retail pay television arm would be profitable if it paid the same wholesale price for channels charged to competitors. Given that in most circumstances, the accounts of the dominant firm will integrate its wholesale and retail arms, an accounting separation exercise must be conducted of the proportion of common operating costs which should be attributed to each. It is only after this cost accounting has been

---

[155] Case 26/75 *General Motors v Commission* [1975] ECR 1367.

[156] *Napier Brown/British Sugar* [1988] OJ L284/41, at para 66. 'The maintaining, by a dominant company, which is dominant in the markets for both a raw material and a corresponding derived product, of a margin between the price which it charges for a raw material to the companies which compete with the dominant company in the production of the derived product and the price which it charges for the derived product, which is insufficient to reflect that dominant company's own costs of transformation (in this case the margin maintained by BS between its industrial and retail sugar prices compared to its own repackaging costs) with the result that competition in the derived product is restricted, is an abuse of a dominant position.'

[157] Notice on the Application of the Competition Rules to Access Agreements in the Telecommunications Sector [1998] OJ C265/2, at para 92.

completed, that an evaluation can be made of whether the retail arm is able to recover both its operating costs and the transfer charges for supply of channels from the wholesale arm. (In the telecommunications sector in contrast, the general regulatory framework simplifies the task as separated accounts must in any event be produced.)[158]

The second option to prove margin squeeze is to demonstrate that a 'reasonably efficient' **13.141** downstream competitor is unable to make a profit on the basis of the wholesale prices charged by the dominant firm. This possibility is raised in the Access Notice at paragraph 92. However, it poses two difficulties. The first is the general difficulty of defining reasonable efficiency: the appropriate marker would seem to be the efficiency of the dominant company itself. The second is that where the dominant company and its competitors use different means of transmission to provide pay television, there may be significant differences in cost structure. In other words, the means of transmission used by competitors may be less efficient, in the sense of more expensive, than that used by the dominant company. In such circumstances, it is suggested that the only appropriate way to demonstrate margin squeeze is to rely on the costs of the dominant company itself.

Generally, addressing abuses at the wholesale level is a difficult task as both the Commission **13.142** and national competition authorities have shown. Where dominance at the wholesale level results from exclusive rights contracts upstream it may be more effective to address those contracts—as the cause of the downstream problems—rather than the behaviour at the wholesale level which is in effect a symptom.

E. Transmission

Issues related to the transmission of information—be it voice or data, communications **13.143** based or content based—are increasingly common to the telecommunications and media sectors. Unfortunately, there are few precedents on the most difficult issues, in particular access and pricing.

This section does not distinguish between the provision of access to infrastructure and the **13.144** provision of a service including access to infrastructure. The distinction underlies some discussions of telecommunications regulation, but has not so far proved useful under the competition rules.

The first subsection below provides a basic introduction to transmission networks, with an **13.145** explanation of the types and elements of telecommunications networks. This is followed by a more direct discussion of infrastructure issues.

Competition problems relating to the creation or strengthening of dominance in transmis- **13.146** sion networks are best examined separately in relation to the separate markets of backbone transmission networks, customer access transmission networks, and networks relevant to the Internet and interactive services. Each of these markets therefore has its own subsection.

---

[158] cf Commission Recommendation 2005/698/EC of 19 September 2005 on accounting separation and cost accounting systems under the regulatory framework for electronic communications [2005] OJ L266/64.

Each subsection looks first at market definition issues, then issues related to the creation or strengthening of dominance on those markets.

13.147 Finally, the extent to which third parties may have rights to access and use transmission networks of dominant companies raises substantially similar issues whichever particular transmission market is being considered. As such, there is a single subsection on this topic.

(1) Introduction to Transmission Networks

13.148 Broadcast infrastructure is designed to convey the same signal simultaneously to a large number of destinations. The network does not need to be capable of directing a signal to a particular destination, although as is discussed below, when the signal is for pay TV, a system for recognising authorised recipients of the signal (conditional access) may need to be included.

13.149 Communications infrastructure is designed to convey a number of different signals to and from a number of different destinations. The network therefore needs to be capable of directing a signal to a particular destination. There are two main ways in which this can be achieved.

(a) Circuit Switched Networks

13.150 First, the network could dedicate part of itself to carrying the signal between two defined points (the houses of two customers who are having a telephone conversation). This is known as circuit switching—switches in the network are used to join together a dedicated line (circuit) between the two end points. For a conversation between Ireland and Greece, this would entail a dedicated line being created between the two countries for the duration of the conversation. This system is not an efficient use of the capacity of the network as the circuit between source and destination is dedicated to the conversation even if no one is speaking (no signals are being sent along the network). Telephone networks are traditionally circuit switched networks. In the past voice telephony under Community law was based on this circuit switching technology and defined in part as being between two fixed points of the public switched telecommunications network. The 2002 regulatory framework no longer refers to a specific technology in relation to telephone networks or services, or to voice telephony.[159] Instead electronic communications networks and services are defined in terms of their functionality.

(b) Packet Switched Networks

13.151 Alternatively, the network can divide the data being transmitted (the telephone conversation) into smaller units (packets of data) and attach address information which describes where the data should be sent. The network then reads the address information on each packet individually and sends each packet to the destination address using whatever route is most convenient at the time. The packets of data are then reassembled into a single unit

---

[159] cf Art 2 Directive 2002/21/EC of the European Parliament and of the Council of 7 March 2002 on a common regulatory framework for electronic communications networks and services (Framework Directive) [2002] OJ L108/33; and Art 2 Directive 2002/22/EC of the European Parliament and of the Parliament of 7 March 2002 on universal service and users' rights relating to electronic communications networks and services (Universal Service Directive) [2002] OJ L108/51.

at the destination address. No two packets of data need follow the same route from source to destination. This system is known as packet switching—switches in the network (routers) are used to send packets of data to their destination. In terms of network usage, this solution is more efficient as if no one is speaking in the conversation no data is transmitted and no network capacity is used. The solution does require the data being transmitted to be in digital format. This makes packet switching well suited to the transmission of data where the source is already digital—as in the case of computer communications. Where the source is analogue—as in the case of human conversations—the data must be digitised, transmitted, and then converted back to an analogue signal. This adds to the expense, makes real-time conversations more difficult, and has affected the quality of using packet switched networks for straightforward telephone conversations. These difficulties are now being overcome.[160]

(c) Network Elements

Both circuit switched networks and packet switched networks are therefore comprised **13.152** of transmission and switching (and/or routing) elements. Transmission elements move the data from one place to another, and switching elements send the data to the right destination.

Transmission elements are often further broken down into local and backbone elements. **13.153** Local elements can broadly be defined as the transmission element necessary to reach an end-user (the end-user could be either the originator or the destination of a particular network transmission). Often this is taken to mean the transmission network connecting the end-user to the first switch in the network. Backbone elements can similarly broadly be defined as the transmission element necessary to connect local elements.

For example: in a standard fixed telephone call, the calling party picks up the phone, and **13.154** dials a number. The signal from the phone is sent across the local network element to the first switch in the network (together these elements are often referred to as the local loop). The switch starts the process which establishes a circuit across the backbone network to connect to the nearest switch in the network to the called party. The signal is sent along the local network connecting the called party to the last switch.

For cellular mobile networks, a distinction can be made between the radio access network **13.155** and the core network. The radio access network includes mast and antenna sites and technical facilities as well as the base stations that control a particular network cell, and the radio network controllers that control a number of cells. The core network is the intelligent part of the network that includes mobile switching centres, services platforms, client home location registers, and centres for operations and maintenance and is linked to the fixed backbone network.

---

[160] cf Communication from the Commission—Status of voice on the Internet under Community law, and in particular, under Directive 90/388/EEC—Supplement to the Communication by the Commission to the European Parliament and the Council on the status and implementation of Directive 90/388/EEC on competition in the markets for telecommunications services [2000] OJ C369/3. A review of this communication is now subject to consultation.

(d) Local Networks and Customer Access Networks

13.156 Telecommunications access issues are often expressed in terms of local network problems—competing operators wish to use the incumbent operator's local network either to originate or to terminate traffic. The use of the term 'local' in this context is, however, potentially misleading. To take the example of the termination of international calls, the termination service being requested of the incumbent operator may often be far from local. To avoid confusion, it may generally be preferable to refer to customer access networks. In the specific context of unbundling however, the term local loop is commonly used to denominate the twisted metallic pair circuit connecting the network termination point at subscriber premises to the main distribution frame or equivalent facility in the fixed public telephone network.[161]

(e) Networks and Market Definition

13.157 An important element to consider in respect of market definition for any network is the service which is to be delivered over it. Different services place different demands on the network infrastructure: different infrastructure markets are likely to exist given these different demands.

13.158 Some of the main categories of networks are set out below, but these should not be regarded as the only relevant market definitions. Market definition in a particular case could require identification of particular technical—such as configurations or interfaces—or geographic—such as country-pairs or localised networks—aspects.[162]

(2) Right to Build Transmission Networks

13.159 Having the right to build infrastructure is a necessary prerequisite for the establishment of competing infrastructure networks. Following full liberalisation, in particular now individual licensing has been abolished under the 2002 regulatory framework, such a general right exists. To the extent that the right to build is denied by state action, Article 86 could apply. Restrictions on the right to install facilities may be justified only for the reasons set out in Article 46(1) of the EC Treaty, ie non-economic justifications related to public policy, public security, and health. This may include in particular the need to protect the environment and town and country planning.[163] A limitative list of the conditions that may be attached to general authorisations is found in Annex A of the Authorisation Directive. Such conditions must be objectively justified, non-discriminatory, proportionate, and transparent.[164] In particular where undertakings are deprived of viable alternatives

---

[161] Art 2 Regulation 2887/2000/EC of the European Parliament and of the Council of 18 December 2000 on unbundled access to the local loop [2000] OJ L336/4 (soon to be revoked); and Art 2(e) Directive 2002/19/EC of the European Parliament and of the Council of 7 March 2002 on access to, and interconnection of, electronic communications networks and associated facilities (Access Directive) [2002] OJ L108/7.

[162] cf *British Telecom/MCI (II)* (Case IV/M.856) [1997] OJ L336/1, para 19; *France Telecom/Equant* (Case COMP/M.2257) [2001] OJ C187/8, para 32.

[163] On the issue of rights of way see Case C-97/01, *Commission of the European Communities v Grand Duchy of Luxemburg* [2003] ECR I-5797; concerning territorial restrictions on the provision of broadcasting transmission services see Commission press release IP/06/487 of 11 April 2006.

[164] Art 6 and Annex A of Directive 2002/20/EC of the European Parliament and of the Council of 7 March 2002 on the authorisation of electronic communications networks and services (Authorisation Directive) [2002] OJ L108/21.

as the result of such conditions Member States may impose the sharing of facilities or property, or otherwise facilitate the coordination of public works.[165] In an Article 86 EC setting it is likely that a State would be obliged to ensure an equitable outcome by, for example, mandating facility sharing (ducts, masts) and/or co-location of equipment.[166]

(3) Backbone Transmission Markets

(a) Market Definition

(i) Backbone Transmission Networks Distinguished from Customer Access Networks   **13.160**
Backbone transmission is required to move voice or data traffic from one place to another. Customer access networks are required to originate calls from or terminate calls to particular customers. The distinction can begin to break down with a sufficiently large business user where the demand for telecommunications capacity is considerable. However in most cases, given the fundamentally different demand characteristics of backbone as opposed to local loop networks, and given the substantial cost differences between building, for example, a national backbone network as compared to a national local loop network, separate markets are likely to exist. Evidence suggests that in a relatively short period after liberalization, competing backbone networks have been established,[167] whereas competing local loop networks remain difficult to establish.

International Backbone Transmission Markets—BT/MCI II [168]   When telecommunications   **13.161**
markets were first opened to competition, and given the consequent quasi-monopolistic market shares enjoyed by most former monopolists in many national markets, dominance was sometimes assumed rather than explicitly analysed in the early Commission decisions in the sector.[169] However, when British Telecommunications sought to merge with the US operator MCI, the case raised issues of dominance over transmission capacity between the UK and the US. Market definition and dominance were therefore examined explicitly.

Although BT's merger proposal proved less attractive than a rival offer from Worldcom and   **13.162**
the merger never in fact took place, this decision provides some useful guidance on the analysis of backbone issues.

As indicated above the decision does not explicitly distinguish between backbone and cus-   **13.163**
tomer access networks, and the precise products and services being analysed in the market definition are sometimes difficult to relate to the competition concern expressed. However, the Commission's concern related to a concentration of capacity on a particular backbone transmission market (transatlantic) in the hands of the merged entity.

---

[165] Art 12 Directive 2002/21/EC of the European Parliament and of the Council of 7 March 2002 on a common regulatory framework for electronic communications networks and services (Framework Directive) [2002] OJ L108/33.

[166] See, for example, Commission Decision (EC) 95/489 of 4 October 1995 concerning the conditions imposed on the second operator of GSM radio-telephony services in Italy [1995] L280/49, Art 1 where the Commission was prepared to accept remedies to counterbalance the anti-competitive effect of the licence fee.

[167] Although evidence from some Member States suggests that competition outside major cities can remain weak several years after liberalisation.

[168] *BT/MCI (II)* [1997] OJ L336/1.

[169] *Atlas* [1996] OJ L239/23 (only the English, French, and German texts are authentic).

13.164 BT/MCI II—*product market*   The Commission identified a market for international voice telephony services, and appeared to narrow that market down into country-pair services.[170] The Commission then analysed in more detail the transatlantic transmission market, and considered that satellite and cable transmission capacity are not adequately substitutable for them to be considered as part of the same market. On the basis of demand, the relevant geographic market for international voice telephony services was defined:

> with reference to call traffic routes between any country pair, since different international routes cannot be considered as viable demand substitutes. From the supply side . . . the possibility of hubbing, ie re-routing US–UK traffic through third countries, does not appear to be a viable commercial possibility at present, since under the existing system of accounting rates and proportionate return it would be more expensive than using direct routes. Furthermore, two distinct geographic markets can be identified within any international route, each comprised of the originating bilateral traffic from the countries concerned.[171]

13.165 BT/MCI II—*vertical integration complicated the market definition*   Market definition was complicated by the vertical integration of the companies, and BT in particular. BT operated local and backbone networks in the UK, provides local, national, and long-distance voice and data services to residential and corporate users, and had extensive international capacity. The Commission's emphasis on call services in analysing the market, although understandable at the time given the vertically integrated nature of the market, would no longer be appropriate.

13.166 With the emergence of carrier companies[172] there appears likely to be a number of separate markets for the provision of telecommunications capacity between States, at least in circumstances where undersea cables are used, given the substantial cost of such cable. This analysis is in fact supported by the remedies imposed by the Commission in this case: BT did not have to reduce its share of call services in the UK—the parties did, however, have to reduce their owership of transatlantic capacity.[173]

13.167 BT/MCI II—*geographic market*   Geographic market definition of transmission networks can be problematic. *BT/MCI II* suggests that country-pair markets (such as UK–US) are appropriate, given that relaying traffic through third countries is commercially unfeasible. Such an analysis would clearly be very fact-specific.

13.168 *Competition issues—dominance in backbone transmission markets*   As indicated above, the Commission did not explicitly identify a market for transatlantic transmission capacity in *BT/MCI II*. However, the idea of such a market appears to underpin a large amount of the Commission's analysis and, in particular, the remedy imposed.

13.169 It appears that the determination of dominance or its strengthening in respect of these markets will be heavily dependent on the current and soon-to-be available capacity on the

---

[170] *BT/MCI (II)* [1997] OJ L336/1, at para 13.
[171] *BT/MCI (II)* [1997] OJ L336/1, at para 19.
[172] An emerging related market for so-called carrier services (provision of services from one telecoms operator to another) was first identified formally in *Unisource/Telefonica* (Case IV/M.544) [1996] OJ C13/3.
[173] This can be contrasted with the *WorldCom/MCI* (Case IV/M.1069) (1999) [1999] OJ L116/1 discussed below, where the Commission refused to accept the parties' offer to divest solely the backbone network of MCI. The Commission required that all of MCI's Internet business (backbone and customers) was divested.

particular route. The Commission will be reluctant to accept future availability of capacity as sufficient to counter current market shares, at least in circumstances where demand is growing rapidly.

Relevance of vertical integration The Commission did not simply look at the available capacity on the transatlantic route, but went further and examined the impact of BT's vertical integration.   **13.170**

The Commission concluded that the possibility of self-corresponding (internal termina-   **13.171**
tion of traffic on a network, rather than passing the traffic to a third party network for termination) provided by the parties' share of transatlantic capacity, and denied to their
competitors by the absence of spare capacity, would lead to a strengthening of BT's dominant position in the market for international voice telephony services on the UK–US
route.

Divestiture of capacity The parties provided an undertaking to the Commission to make   **13.172**
transatlantic cable capacity available to third parties. Moreover, capacity would be made
available on an indefeasible right of use (IRU) basis. An IRU is in effect comparable to an
asset divestiture, a common remedy in merger cases. This allowed competitors cost-based
access to transatlantic capacity. The Commission considered that because the capacity
would be made available at prices corresponding to BT's true cost of purchase, this would
be likely to ease the entry of competitors. On this basis the merger was approved.[174]

The Recommendation on relevant markets for the 2002 regulatory framework includes tran-   **13.173**
sit services in the fixed public telephone network as a market that requires SMP analysis.[175]
The Commission proposes to retain this market in its review.[176] Other markets identified
in the Recommendation that are relevant in relation to backbone capacity are the wholesale terminating segments, respectively the wholesale trunk segments of leased lines.[177]

(4) Customer Access Infrastructure

The importance of customer access infrastructure in voice telephony is clearly recognised,   **13.174**
to the extent that a substantial part of the 2002 regulatory framework is dedicated to ensuring non-discriminatory and cost-oriented access to it. It may be as a result of this extensive
regulation that relatively little recourse to the competition rules has been necessary, and, as
such, market definition under the competition rules remains largely unresolved.

---

[174] There was another issue in relation to audio-conferencing on which undertakings were also provided,
but this is of relatively minor significance.
[175] Commission Recommendation of 11 February 2003 on relevant product and service markets within
the electronic communications sector susceptible to *ex ante* regulation in accordance with Directive 2002/21/
EC of the European Parliament and of the Council on a common regulatory framework for electronic communication networks and services [2003] OJ L114/45. cf *Transit services in the public fixed telephone network
in Austria* (case AT/2004/0090) Commission Decision of 20 October 2004, COM/2004/4070.
[176] SEC(2006) 837 Commission staff working document, consultation on a draft Commission
Recommendation on relevant product and service markets susceptible to *ex ante* regulation in accordance
with Directive 2002/21/EC of the European Parliament and of the Council on a common regulatory framework for electronic communication networks and services (second edition).
[177] The Commission proposes to remove the retail market for the minimum set of leased lines from the
Recommendation as wholesale level regulation is considered sufficient. SEC(2006) 837.

(a) Product Market Definition

13.175 In the *BiB* decision[178] the Commission first expressed its view that a general customer access infrastructure market exists and describes what is known as the last mile or local loop of the telecommunications network—the network from the last switch into the home. Since then, the Commission formally defined local access markets in the context of both mergers and Article 82 cases.[179] The local loop market is generally considered to be a key bottleneck in the context of competitive roll-out. This is the reason why the Commission has required unbundled access to the local loop as a merger remedy,[180] and, following an EU-wide sector inquiry on the conditions for local loop access under the competition rules, has pushed for a regulation on unbundled access to the local loop, which was adopted in December 2000.[181] Apart from the market for local access, where entrants need to purchase access in order to provide their own origination and termination services, separate markets for origination and termination by the operator that owns the relevant infrastructure can be distinguished.

13.176 **(i) Origination and Termination Markets** In essence, the difference between origination and termination services is the difference between making and receiving calls. Origination services are sold either to end-users (as retail telecommunications services) or to intermediate companies competing with the incumbent and wishing to use the network to sell those same services to end-users, either on a full service or, more commonly, on a market segment basis (such as international, long-distance, or Internet access). Termination services are sold to a variety of customers, including competitors originating calls on the same network or on other networks, and companies who are not competitors, for example, because they operate in different geographic markets (international termination).

13.177 The first Commission precedent in favour of separate origination and termination markets resulted from the Internet. The market defined in *Worldcom/MCI* [182] appears to be essentially a global one for Internet termination services. The clearance of certain Internet joint ventures would appear to have been based on a market for retail Internet access for end-users (essentially an origination market) which was national. Since then the practice of defining separate termination and origination markets has been codified in the Commission's Recommendation on relevant product and services markets, which is based on this distinction.[183] Moreover,

---

[178] *British Interactive Broadcasting/Open* (Case IV/36.539) [1999] OJ L312/1.

[179] eg *Telia/Telenor* (Case IV/M.1439) (1999) [2001] OJ L40/1; *Deutsche Telekom AG* (Case COMP/37.451, 37.578, 37.579) [2003] OJ L263/9.

[180] *Telia/Telenor* (Case IV/M.1439) (1999) [2001] OJ L40/1.

[181] Regulation 2887/2000/EC of the European Parliament and of the Council of 18 December 2000 on unbundled access to the local loop [2000] OJ L336/4.

[182] *Worldcom/MCI* (Case IV/M.1069) (1998) [1999] OJ L116/1.

[183] Commission Recommendation of 11 February 2003 on relevant product and service markets within the electronic communications sector susceptible to *ex ante* regulation in accordance with Directive 2002/21/EC of the European Parliament and of the Council on a common regulatory framework for electronic communication networks and services [2003] OJ L114/45, and the Explanatory Memorandum to this document. cf Commission guidelines on market analysis and the assessment of significant market power under the Community regulatory framework for electronic communications networks and services [2002] OJ C165/6.

as regards termination on both fixed and mobile networks, the Commission now clearly regards individual networks as separate markets.[184]

(ii) Fixed and Mobile Customer Access Infrastructure   Given the advantages of mobility, and the premium paid for it, mobile services are in general not substitutable by fixed services. Hence, from the Commission's decision in *GSM Italy*[185] onward it has considered these markets separate.[186]   **13.178**

Residential voice telephony infrastructure   As originating networks, fixed and mobile networks may ultimately prove sufficiently substitutable on the basis of price for the provision of residential voice telephony services. However, given the premium of mobility, substitution is generally one-sided. At wholesale level, separate markets for national roaming, international roaming, wholesale airtime access, and call origination services on mobile networks appear to exist.[187]   **13.179**

Mobile telephony infrastructure   The Commission has indicated that the operation of GSM infrastructure and the provision of GSM services constitute two separate markets.[188]   **13.180**

The extent to which distinct mobile network markets exist (for example 2G/3G,) would appear to depend on the downstream markets. If a distinct wholesale or retail product market can be identified which could only be served by a particular form of mobile infrastructure, then it is likely that that infrastructure could be regarded as constituting a separate market. One example are pan-European corporate mobile services which, it could be argued, would need use of mobile networks in each Member State.[189] Where the use of infrastructure is not specific to a particular mobile technology, no separate market exists.[190]   **13.181**

---

[184] Statement of objections in *MCI/Mobile termination rates* (Case COMP/37.704) IP/02/484; *Telia/Sonera* (Case COMP/M.2803) [2002] OJ C 201/19; *Telefónica/O2* (Case COMP/M.4035) EUR-lex 32006M.4035; cf Explanatory Memorandum to Recommendation on product and service markets and Commission guidelines on market analysis and the assessment of significant market power under the Community regulatory framework for electronic communications networks and services [2002] OJ C165/6, para 65. cf L Garzaniti and F Liberatore, 'Recent Developments in the European Commission's practice in the Communications Sector, Part I', [2004] ECLR 25(3) 169–176.

[185] Commission Decision (EC) 95/489 of 4 October 1995 concerning the conditions imposed on the second operator of GSM radiotelephony services in Italy [1995] OJ L280/49.

[186] *Telia/Telenor* (COMP/M.1439) [2001] OJ L40/1; *Vodafone Airtouch/Mannesmann* (COMP/M.1795) [2000] OJ C141/19; *Pirelli/Edizioni/Olivetti/Telecom Italia* (case COMP/M.2574) [2001] OJ C325/12; *Telia/Sonera* (case COMP/M.2803) [2002] OJ C201/19; *Network sharing Germany* (Case COMP/38.369) [2004] OJ L 75/ 32; *Network sharing UK* (Case COMP/38.370) [2003] OJ L200/59. cf Commission guidelines on market analysis and the assessment of significant market power under the Community regulatory framework for electronic communications networks and services [2002] OJ C165/6, para 66.

[187] *Network sharing Germany* (Case COMP/38.369) [2004] OJ L 75/ 32, at para 61; *Network sharing UK* (Case COMP/38.370) [2003] OJ L200/59, at para 57.

[188] Commission Decision (EC) 95/489 of 4 October 1995 concerning the conditions imposed on the second operator of GSM radiotelephony services in Italy [1995] OJ L280/49.

[189] An emerging market for such services based on intra-group roaming was identified in *Vodafone Airtouch/Mannesmann* (Case COMP/M.1795) [2000] OJ C141/19, at paras 11ff. cf *Telefónica/O2* (Case COMP/M.4035) EUR-lex 32006M.4035; *FT/Amena* (Case COMP/M.3920) EUR-lex 3205M.3920; *Telefónica/Cesky Telecom* (Case COMP/M.3806) EUR-lex 32005M.3806.

[190] For example, the market for sites and site infrastructure for digital mobile radiocommunications equipment identified in *Network sharing Germany* (Case COMP/38.369) [2004] OJ L75/32, at paras 49ff; *Network sharing UK* (Case COMP/38.370) [2003] OJ L200/59, at paras 45ff. The Commission exempted

(b) Geographic Market Definition

13.182   Geographic markets in the telecommunications sector are determined by: the extent and coverage of the network and the customers that can economically be reached and whose demands may be met; the legal and regulatory system and the right to provide a service;[191] and the geographic scope of pricing constraints.

13.183   Residential markets will tend to be national, corporate markets may be national, regional, or global. One potential issue in the future could be the identification of a geographic market which, though identifiable and distinct, is not contiguous. In the telecommunications sector, it could be argued that the conditions of competition are sufficiently different in cities compared to rural areas that separate markets should be identified. It may, for example, be commercially feasible to roll out cable or other competing networks only in areas of sufficiently high population density. If it were possible to discriminate between these areas, separate geographic markets could be identifiable.

13.184   **Competitition issues**   There is only a limited number of decisions on the creation or strengthening of dominance on these markets although the procedure under article 7 of the Framework Directive is giving rise to Commission decisions on such issues by the NRAs.[192] Issues arise most commonly in relation to the abuse of market power on these markets, for which see the subsection on Article 82 below. This section looks first at assessment of dominance and joint dominance on these markets, and then examines some of the issues raised by the *Telia/Telenor* case.

(i) Dominance

13.185   *Different assessment of dominance for origination and termination markets*   It may be the case that the question of dominance would be assessed differently if these markets were distinct.

13.186   For full service origination markets, substitutability of alternative networks is more important than it is for termination markets, where customers are less sensitive to price differentials. A company can therefore be regarded as non-dominant in origination markets if there

---

agreements in the UK and Germany to share networks at the initial rollout stage of 3G mobile. The CFI annulled the Commission's decision on the ground that it had insufficiently demonstrated the existence of a restriction of competition, as it had not fully analysed the competitive situation in the absence of the agreement. Network sharing between network operators would appear to have intrinsic risks of coordination of competitive behaviour on cost, quality, and coverage (and therefore price), on a market with absolute barriers to entry (the availability of licences). However the ruling faulted the Commission for failing to carry out an explicit counterfactual analysis, raising the question of how far the Commission need go in complex hypothetical analysis about future trends. See Case T-328/03, *O2 (Germany) GmbH & Co. OHG v Commission*, judgment of 2 May 2006, not yet reported.

191   *Mannesmann/Olivetti/Infostrada* (Case IV/M.1025) (1998), at para 17 (only the English text is authentic).
192   *Access and call origination on public mobile telephone networks in Finland* (case FI/2004/0082) Commission Decision of 5 October 2004 COM/2004/3682; *Transit services in the public fixed telephone network in Austria* (case AT/2004/0090) Commission Decision of 20 October 2004, COM/2004/4070 (<http://forum.europa.eu.int/Public/irc/infso/ecctf/home>). cf Art 7, Directive 2002/21/EC of the European Parliament and of the Council of 7 March 2002 on a common regulatory framework for electronic communications networks and services (Framework Directive) [2002] OJ L108/33; Commission Recommendation 2003/561/EC of 23 July 2003 on notifications, time limits and consultations provided for in Art 7 of Directive 2002/21/EC (Procedural Recommendation) [2002] OJ L190/13.

are adequate alternative networks available to act as a supply side constraint. The number of connected customers and the reluctance of customers to switch would not appear relevant. For call-by-call origination services, where a particular retail demand is being addressed, market power would, by contrast, appear to be based more on the number of connected customers.

Where the calling party pays principle applies users of electronic communications services **13.187** are unlikely to be sensitive to the price of termination, leading to the definition of a separate market for each network. In assessing dominance on termination markets, where market shares are therefore by definition 100 per cent, the existence of countervailing market power appears to be the most accurate measure of competitive constraints.

Termination markets, and potentially some origination markets, can be regarded as after- **13.188** markets of the relevant downstream service market. The complicating factor is that access to this after market is necessary for companies to enter the downstream service market, making dominance on the downstream service market self-reinforcing.

(ii) **Joint Dominance** With the ending of the legal monopolies on the provision of **13.189** telecommunications services and infrastructure, and the increasing usage of mobile networks, it is likely that the former paradigm of single network dominance in the sector will become increasingly irrelevant. However, there remain significant commercial and/or technical limits to the number of competing networks likely to be present on any geographic market. The telecommunications sector is unlikely to be characterised by a large number of competing networks. As such, it may be the case that the number of networks is insufficient to ensure a competitive market, and competition problems may remain. In these circumstances it may not be possible to demonstrate that any one network operator is dominant. The continued utility of the competition rules to resolve remaining competition problems will therefore depend on the extent to which the doctrine of joint, or collective, dominance can be used.

Commission position There are relatively few precedents in the area of joint dominance.[193] **13.190** The Access Notice stated that two or more undertakings would be considered to be in a collective dominant position where they had substantially the same position in respect of their customers and competitors as a single company has if it is in a dominant position, provided no effective competition existed between them. This lack of competition could be due to the existence of structural links between those companies.[194] However, the existence of such links was not regarded as a prerequisite for a finding of joint dominance.[195]

European Courts The position of the Commission on the role of economic links has sub- **13.191** sequently received support by a Court of First Instance judgment in a Merger Regulation

---

[193] In the electronic communications sector: *Vodafone/Airtouch* (Case IV/M.1430) [1999] C295/2; *MCI WorldCom/Sprint* (Case COMP/M.1741) (2000) [2003] OJ L300/1; *BT/ESAT* (Case COMP/M.1838) [2000] OJ C341/3; *France Télécom/Orange* (Case COMP/M.2016) [2000] C261/6.

[194] In addition there are always close legal links, eg agreements on interoperability, interconnection, roaming, and other forms of access.

[195] Notice on the application of the competition rules to access agreements in the telecommunications sector (Access Notice), [1998] OJ C265/2, para 79.

case (unrelated to telecommunications). The Commission prohibited the proposed merger between Gencor and Lonrho on the basis that it risked creating an oligopoly on the relevant market. The parties contested the Commission's decision, *inter alia*, because the Commission had not proved the existence of the economic links which the Court's earlier judgment *inter alia* in *Italian Flat Glass*[196] had indicated as necessary. The *CFI*,[197] however, upheld the Commission's decision in *Gencor/ Lonrho*,[198] concluding that a demonstration of economic links was not necessary.

13.192 Furthermore, there is no reason whatsoever in legal or economic terms to exclude from the notion of economic links the relationship of interdependence existing between the parties to a tight oligopoly within which, in a market with the appropriate characteristics, in particular in terms of market concentration, transparency and product homogeneity, those parties are in a position to anticipate one another's behaviour and are therefore strongly encouraged to align their conduct in the market, in particular in such a way as to maximise their joint profits by restricting production with a view to increasing prices. In such a context, each trader is aware that highly competitive action on its part designed to increase its market share (for example a price cut) would provoke identical action by the others, so that it would derive no benefit from its initiative. All the traders would thus be affected by the reduction in price levels.[199]

13.193 This ruling was endorsed by the European Court of Justice in *Compagnie Maritime Belge*.[200] In the same case it also stated that in order to show that two or more undertakings are in a collectively dominant position, it is first necessary to consider whether the undertakings concerned together constitute a collective entity vis-à-vis their competitors, their trading partners, and their consumers on a particular market. In this case is it is appropriate to consider whether due to the existence of economic links the collective entity holds a dominant position which enables them to act independently of their competitors, customers, and consumers.[201]

13.194 As regards the criteria to be applied, the Court of First Instance has in *Airtours* set out more clearly which conditions are necessary to prove a finding of collective dominance:

(1) there must be sufficient 'market transparency' so that each member of the dominant oligopoly has 'the ability to know how the other members are behaving in order to monitor whether or not they are adopting the common policy';

---

[196] Joined Cases T-68/89, T-77/89 and T-78/89 *SIV and Others v Commision* [1992] ECR II-1403, para 358. cf Case C-393/92 *Almelo* [1994] ECR I-1477, para 43; Case C-96/94 *Centro Servizi Spediporto* [1995] ECR I-2883, para 33; Joined Cases C-140/94, C-141/94 and C-142/94 *DIP* [195] ECR I-3257, para 62; Case C-70/95, *Sodemare* [1997] ECR I-3395, para 46, and Joined Cases C-68/94 and C-30/95 *France and Others v Commission* [1998] ECR I-1375, para 221.

[197] Case T-102/96 *Gencor v Commission* [1999] ECR II-753.

[198] *Gencor/Lonrho* (Case IV/M.619) (1996) [1997] OJ L11/30.

[199] Case T-102/96 *Gencor v Commission* [1999] ECR II-753, at para 276.

[200] Joined cases C-39596/P and C-396/96P *Compagnie Maritime Belge and others v Commission* [2000] ECR I-1365, paras 41–44.

[201] ibid, at para 39.

(2) there must be a means for other oligopoly members to 'retaliate' against any departures from the common policy, so that members have an 'incentive not to depart from the common policy'; and

(3) the Commission must show that the 'foreseeable reaction of current and future competitors, as well as consumers, would not jeopardize the results expected from the common policy'.[202]

As concerns the 2002 regulatory framework, the criteria the Commission considers relevant for assessing collective dominance are summarised in Annex II to the Framework Directive and repeated in the Guidelines on market definition and SMP.[203] Apart from market concentration and transparency, the relevant characteristics are:

— mature market
— stagnant or moderate growth on the demand side
— low elasticity of demand
— homogeneous product
— similar cost structures
— similar market shares
— lack of technical innovation, mature technology
— absence of excess capacity
— high barriers to entry
— lack of countervailing buying power
— lack of potential competition
— various kinds of informal or other links between the undertakings concerned
— retaliatory mechanisms
— lack or reduced scope for price competition.[204]

13.195 As stated in Annex II and in the Guidelines, this list is not exhaustive, nor are the criteria cumulative. The list is intended to be illustrative of the type of evidence that can be used to support assertions concerning the existence of collective dominance. It is not yet clear to what extent this approach is consistent with the identification of three minimum conditions for a finding of collective dominance by the Court of Justice in *Airtours*.[205]

13.196 *Limited number of network operators* The economic and technical issues relating to the building of infrastructure are fundamentally different to those relating to the provision of services using that infrastructure. Even assuming widespread successful construction (roll-out) of alternative infrastructure networks, it is likely that there will be a relatively limited number of networks available. Local network construction is expensive, currently available services provided over these networks are still limited, and all alternative provision

---

[202] Case T-342/99 *Airtours v Commission* [2002] ECR II-258, para 62.

[203] Commission guidelines on market analysis and the assessment of significant market power under the Community regulatory framework for electronic communications networks and services [2002] OJ C165/6, paras 86–106.

[204] Directive 2002/21/EC of the European Parliament and of the Council of 7 March 2002 on a common regulatory framework for electronic communications networks and services (Framework Directive) [2002] OJ L108/33, Annex II.

[205] The first Community case law on this may arise in the context of Case T-109/06, *Vodafone España and Vodafone Group v Commission* [2006] OJ C131/46. Cf. Case IE/2004/0121 Access and call origination on public mobile networks in Ireland (<http://forum.europa.eu.int/Public/irc/infso/ecctf/library>).

is faced with competition from an incumbent operator with substantial sunk costs in a local network often constructed in a monopoly (non-commercial) environment. The incumbent operator may also remain subject to universal service obligations and benefit from universal service contributions. In addition to commercial problems of network roll-out, there may also be technical limits such as frequency limitations. When looking at the provision of particular services—such as high speed Internet access and video on demand—the number of usable networks is likely to be particularly limited.[206]

13.197 Such a limited number of providers may well be insufficient to provide a fully competitive market: intervention on the basis of the competition rules is likely in these markets. There are strong policy arguments against allowing the network providers (whose numbers are commercially or technically limited) from extending this limit into the service markets. If the only service providers were the downstream arms of the network operators then:

— there would be similar risks that the number of service providers would be insufficient to form a competitive market; and
— there would be no necessary link between ability to trade efficiently as a service provider and presence on the service provision market.

13.198 In the Article 7 context the Commission regards the markets for unbundled local loops and wholesale broadband access to constitute distinct markets. The local loop market is considered to be situated upstream from the wholesale broadband access market as they are only substitutable from a demand perspective if self-provision of an equivalent service to wholesale broadband access is feasible. As regards the wholesale broadband access market, it depends on the scope of geographical coverage of cable TV networks whether they are part of the same product market as the incumbent DSL operator (even when they are not included in the market definition however they may be capable of exercising an indirect pricing constraint to be taken into account in an SMP assessment).[207]

(c) Strengthening of Dominance on Customer Access Infrastructure Markets

13.199 This could arise either through acquisitions on the relevant market, a reduction in potential competition, or through strengthening in upstream or downstream markets which could weaken the structure of the infrastructure market. These issues are discussed in the section on retail services below.

13.200 **(i) Vertical Integration**   Vertical integration combined with control over bottleneck customer access infrastructure markets increases the risk of foreclosure by means of discrimination, bundling, and leveraging *inter alia* in the shape of price abuses. In the *Telia/Telenor* case the Commission found the proposed merger between two vertically integrated incumbents in adjacent geographical markets, would entail a risk of raising rivals' cost by increasing (or not decreasing) the price and/or degrading the quality of interconnection, an increased ability to bundle products and an ability to leverage dominance on access to the

---

[206] *BiB* (Notice pursuant to Art 19(3) of Regulation 17) [1998] OJ C322/6.

[207] Commission Recommendation on relevant product and service markets susceptible to *ex ante* regulation in accordance with Directive 2002/21/EC of the European Parliament and of the Council on a common regulatory framework for electronic communication networks and services (second edition to be adopted in 2007) see SEC (2006) 837.

fixed public telephone network (local loop).[208] It imposed *inter alia* local loop unbundling as a remedy. In *Telia/Sonera*, the Commission found a risk of foreclosure regarding the provision of corporate communications services and mobile communications services based on Telia's dominant position in fixed call termination, and imposed *inter alia* the divestiture of Telia's cable TV network, which the Commission considered the main alternative for the public switched telephone network.[209] In *Deutsche Telekom*, the Commission found a margin squeeze operated by the vertically integrated incumbent between the pricing to its competitors for unbundled local loop access and the prices it charged end-users for access to its fixed network infringed Article 82 of the Treaty.[210] In *Wanadoo*, a similar price squeeze existed between wholesale and retail level prices for broadband Internet access, but was addressed by the Commission on the basis of predatory pricing.[211]

(5) Internet and Interactive Services

(a) Market Definition

(i) Internet Termination—Top Level Networks   The Internet is a network of intercon-   **13.201**
nected networks. In order to provide a full Internet service any company providing customers with access to the Internet (an Internet Service Provider, ISP) will need access to all, or at least the vast majority, of the networks connected to the Internet.

Market definition in this area is difficult. The distinction between competitors to whom an   **13.202**
operator will provide reciprocal access to its customers (peering), and customers to whom an operator will provide access to all other Internet users (transit) appears more fluid than is the case in traditional telecommunications, such as voice telephony. However, *inter alia* due to developments in broadband access, and the provision of voice over DSL and voice over IP it is possible that the traditional vertically integrated nature of voice telecommunications is breaking down, and a market structure more closely aligned to that of the Internet may be emerging. It should also be noted that some commentators predict that voice services will become a subset of the data carried on Internet networks in the medium term. It is conceivable, therefore, that public telephone networks may disappear in the long term as an independent market definition.

The first formal Commission precedent in this area is the decision approving the proposed   **13.203**
merger between Worldcom and MCI.[212] The case arose shortly after the bid for MCI by BT (discussed in the *BT/MCI II* case, above). Worldcom, a relative new entrant in the telecommunications sector, had pursued an aggressive acquisition strategy over the previous years. This had provided Worldcom with operations in a number of countries, and in particular had given Worldcom a substantial presence on Internet markets. Worldcom launched a bid for MCI to counter BT's proposed bid. The main issue which emerged in the case was the position of the merged entity on the so-called 'top level networks' market for the Internet.

---

[208] *Telia/Telenor* (Case IV/M.1439) (1999) [2001] OJ L40/1.
[209] *Telia/Sonera* (Case COMP/M.2803) [2002] OJ C 201/19.
[210] *Deutsche Telekom AG* (Case COMP/37.451, 37.578, 37.579) [2003] OJ L263/9.
[211] *Wanadoo* (Case COMP/38.233), see <http://ec.europa.eu/comm/competition/antitrust/cases/decisions/38233/en.pdf>. Cf L Garzaniti and F Liberatore, 'Recent Developments in the European Commission's practice in the Communications Sector, Part II', [2004] ECLR 25(4) 234–240.
[212] *Worldcom/MCI* (Case IV/M1069) (1998) [1999] OJ L116/1.

13.204   In order to ensure universal connectivity on the Internet, every Internet service provider network has to be connected to every other network. Direct connections from every network to every other network are clearly not technically or commercially feasible, and therefore a system of indirect connection has developed. The Commission distinguished between the two distinct services of peering and transit.

> 32 . . . the usual form of peering arrangement is one under which Network Operator A (or ISP A) agrees to accept from Network Operator B (or ISP B) all traffic originating from B's customers which is to be terminated on A's network. In return, B accepts a reciprocal obligation to terminate all traffic originating from A's customers and destined for B's network . . .
>
> 39 . . . The purchase of a transit service could therefore be . . . described as a right on the part of an ISP to have his traffic treated as the traffic of the transit provider's network for the purpose of exchange across a peering interface.

13.205   This distinction between peering and transit led the Commission to conclude that there was an important distinction between two types of ISPs—essentially dividing-out top level networks.

> 41. Although ISPs may turn successively to yet larger ISPs for the provision of transit services, there is a logical limitation to the process. Traffic which is progressively defaulted to higher level networks will finally end up in the hands of an ISP who has no one else to whom to turn, and must either assume responsibility on its own account for delivering the traffic across peering interfaces, or return it undelivered. These networks (or the ISPs concerned) are referred to hereon as 'top level networks' or 'top level ISPs'.

13.206   This distinction was supported by the activities of the players on the market who appeared to be gradually increasing the criteria which had to be fulfilled before peering were granted.[213] The Commission concluded that alternatives to the top-level networks—resellers or providers of secondary peering[214]—were not adequate substitutes.

13.207   Resellers were by definition dependent on the top-level networks for their services and as such subject to price rises imposed by the top-level networks.[215] Secondary peering ISPs may offer some limited substitutability in terms of allowing them to access some sites without having to transit the networks of the top-level ISPs, but there will be gaps in their coverage. In no case, however, can the second tier connectivity offered by a secondary peering ISP provide a service which is a sufficient substitute for the first tier connectivity provided by the top-level network. Secondary peering ISPs who wanted to offer complete connectivity could not avoid continuing to buy some transit from the top-level networks, and their cost base is therefore captive to the extent that they continue to have to do so.

13.208   **(ii) Residential Internet/Interactive Services Origination Infrastructure**   The majority of Internet users access the Internet via a dial-up connection using a domestic voice telephony line. However, the relevant product market for the infrastructure is not necessarily the same as that for voice telephony. As indicated above for voice services, fixed and mobile

---

213 *Worldcom/MCI* (Case IV/M.1069) (1998) [1999] OJ L116/1, at para 45.
214 Secondary peering ISPs have a collection of peering agreements, either with other similarly placed ISPs or with some, but not all, of the top-level networks.
215 *Worldcom/MCI* (Case IV/M.1069) (1998) [1999] OJ L116/1, at para 67.

networks are likely to converge—however until the data carrying capacity of mobile networks substantially increases,[216] mobile network infrastructure will probably not be an adequate substitute for fixed line Internet access. Cable TV networks capable of carrying two-way communications are certainly substitutable for domestic telephone lines for the purpose of accessing the Internet. In at least two Article 82 Decisions the Commission has defined a separate market for broadband/ high speed Internet access services to the general public.[217]

(b) Competition Issues

(i) Strengthening of Dominance on Internet Markets   The Commission considered   **13.209**
how to assess a strengthening of dominance in the *Worldcom/MCI* case. The Commission determined that traffic was the most appropriate means of measuring market share in the sector. Notably, the Commission rejected a simple revenue test (which the parties suggested) for determining market share on the basis that, given the vertically integrated nature of the parties' Internet operations, this would tend to understate the market share. In a coordinated information gathering exercise with the US authorities, the Commission conducted an extensive investigation of Internet traffic and concluded that a percentage sufficient to give rise to a presumption of dominance was carried on the networks of the merging parties.

The Commission concluded that the merger would result in the creation of a dominant   **13.210**
position on the market for top level networks. In addition to a market share calculation, the Commission based this conclusion on:

— the importance of network effects:

126. Because of the specific features of network competition and the existence of network externalities which make it valuable for customers to have access to the largest network, MCI WorldCom's position can hardly be challenged once it has obtained a dominant position. The more its network grows, the less need it has to interconnect with competitors and the more need they have to interconnect with the merged entity. Furthermore, the larger its network becomes, the greater is its ability to control a significant element of the costs of any new entrant. It can achieve this by denying such entrants the opportunity to peer and insisting that they remain as customers and pay a margin accordingly for all the services they want to offer. The merger could thus have the effect of raising entry barriers still higher. Indeed, it could be argued that, as a result of the merger, the MCI WorldCom network would constitute, either immediately or in a relatively short time thereafter, an essential facility, to which all other ISPs would have no choice but to interconnect (directly or indirectly) in order to offer a credible Internet access service.[218]

— the risk of a snowball effect (market tipping):

131. The merger might well create a 'snowball effect', in that MCI WorldCom would be better placed than any of its competitors to capture future growth through new customers,

---

[216] Such as with the third generation mobile.
[217] *Deutsche Telekom AG* (Case COMP/37.451, 37.578, 37.579) [2003] OJ L263/9; *Wanadoo* (Case COMP/38.233) IP/03/1025.
[218] *Worldcom/MCI* (Case IV/M1069) (1998) [1999] OJ L116/1, at para 126.

> because of the attractions for any new customer of direct connection with the largest network, and the relative unattractiveness of competitors' offerings owing to the threat of disconnection or degradation of peering which MCI WorldCom's competitors must constantly live under. As a result, the merger might provide MCI WorldCom with the opportunity to enlarge its market share still further.[219]

— and the opportunity for incumbent operators to capture market growth:

> At the oral hearing, an intervener stressed the need to avoid the error of assuming that growth could counter market dominance. Indeed, the incumbents rather than newcomers could well be the best placed to capture future growth. For example, the parties pointed to the emergence of new competitors who were engaged in laying substantial fibre networks and could therefore offer a competitive counter-force. However, entry as a top level ISP requires not only physical facilities, but also a customer base and hence traffic flow and thus access to peering interconnection. A dominant network which refused to provide peering could effectively prevent a new entrant from operating as a top level network . . .[220]

13.211 These concerns led the Commission to the conclusion that the proposed merger would have created a dominant position on the market for top-level networks. The Commission therefore determined that MCI should divest its entire Internet activities, removing all overlap between its Internet activities and those of Worldcom. A similar case arose in MCI WorldCom/Sprint, where the Commission found this merger would lead to a dominant position or the reinforcement of a dominant position in the market for the provision of top-level or universal connectivity.[221] In this case the remedies offered by the parties were considered insufficient to re-establish immediate and effective competition, and the merger was blocked.

13.212 Similar concerns in relation to the power of particular networks appear to arise as with traditional telephony and interconnection. These concerns include the risks that a dominant network operator: imposes a price squeeze by means at wholesale or retail level or both; seeks to reinforce its position, for example by concluding lengthy exclusive arrangements with its customers or by delaying interconnection upgrades, or otherwise favours its own operations at the expense of third parties.

(6) Access to Transmission Networks

13.213 Aside from avoiding the creation or strengthening of dominant positions—as in *BT/MCI II* above—a number of competition issues revolve around access to transmission facilities. This problem appears both in relation to those joint ventures or mergers where one or more parents is dominant on a relevant market and in pure Article 82 cases.

(a) Third Party Access to Transmission Networks

13.214 Most access issues in the telecommunications sector are likely to be resolved by NRAs applying the provisions of the Access Directive which sets out the 2002 regulatory framework for interconnection issues. However, Articles 81 and 82 continue to apply and to the extent

---

219 *Worldcom/MCI* (Case IV/M.1069) (1998) [1999] OJ L116/1, at para 131.
220 *Worldcom/MCI* (Case IV/M.1069) (1998) [1999] OJ L116/1, at para 134.
221 *MCI WorldCom/Sprint* (Case COMP/M.1741)(2000) [2003] OJ L300/1.

that problems emerge that do not fit fully within the pre-existing framework, competition law intervention may be necessary.

The Access Notice sets out general competition law principles relating to access to telecom- **13.215** munications facilities by third parties wishing to provide services to end-users.[222] Access is not defined explicitly, but the Commission's intentions can be derived from Part II of the Notice, dealing with market definition. The Notice envisages markets for the provision of services to end-users, and markets in the facilities needed to provide those services to end-users.[223] Facilities are not, however, defined: any definition would risk being interpreted as limitative, whereas legally the concept cannot be limited but is relevant to any type of facility where the underlying principles are applicable. The Notice sets out various possible abuses in the context of access to networks, examined below. Issues of third party access under Article 82 can be examined under several different legal grounds, for example essential facilities, discrimination, and bundling. The relationship between these grounds can be complex, and, given the very different evidential burdens each puts on complainants, an understanding of the circumstances in which each applies is particularly important.

(i) Essential Facilities   The concept of essential facilities is a contentious one under **13.216** Community law, although it now seems clear that it is a principle of general application. The Commission devoted substantial space in the Access Notice to the concept,[224] and indicated that it will apply in circumstances where the company from whom access is being sought has not yet provided any third party with access to the facility in question. This could come under the heading refusal to deal and/or discrimination. Since the publication of the Access Notice, the ECJ has delivered its judgment in *Bronner*,[225] a case involving newspaper distribution in Austria. The reasoning of *Bronner* is far from clear,[226] however, although the basic definition of what constitutes 'essential' appears consistent with the Commission's position.

The Access Notice identified five criteria which must be fulfilled before a refusal to grant **13.217** access could be characterised as abusive.

Essential   First, access to the facility in question must be essential, defined as: **13.218**

> 91 . . . It will not be sufficient that the position of the company requesting access would be more advantageous if access were granted—but refusal of access must lead to the proposed activities being made either impossible or seriously and unavoidably uneconomic . . .

---

[222] The continuing relevance of the Access Notice is illustrated by the statement to this effect in para 216 of the DG Competition discussion paper on the application of Art 82 of the Treaty to exclusionary abuses. (See <http://ec.europa.eu/comm/competition/antitrust/others/discpaper2005.pdf>).

[223] Notice on the Application of the Competition Rules to Access Agreements in the Telecommunications Sector [1998] OJ C265/2, paras 49 *et seq*.

[224] Notice on the Application of the Competition Rules to Access Agreements in the Telecommunications Sector [1998] OJ C265/2, paras 87–98.

[225] Case C-7/97 *Oscar Bronner GmbH & Co KG and Mediaprint Zeitungs- und Zeitschriftenverlag GmbH & Co KG, Mediaprint Zeitungsvertriebsgesellschaft mbH & Co KG, Mediaprint Anzeigengesellschaft mbH & Co KG* [1998] I-7791.

[226] Compare, eg, paras 35 and 43.

13.219 This is an extremely high burden of proof, reaffirmed by Advocate General Jacobs[227] in *Bronner*:

> 67 . . . intervention of that kind [the ordering of access], whether understood as an application of the essential facilities doctrine or, more traditionally, as a response to a refusal to supply goods or services, can be justified in terms of competition policy only in cases in which the dominant undertaking has a genuine stranglehold on the related market. That might be the case for example where duplication of the facility is impossible or extremely difficult owing to physical, geographical or legal constraints or is highly undesirable for reasons of public policy. It is not sufficient that the undertaking's control over a facility should give it a competitive advantage.

13.220 The Court provided no criteria for determining directly whether or not a facility is essential. The Court did, however, indicate that the refusal to provide access must be likely to eliminate all competition on the part of the party requesting access.[228]

13.221 AG Jacobs went on to suggest:

> 68 . . . the possibility that the cost of duplicating a facility might alone constitute an insuperable barrier to entry. That might be so particularly in cases in which the creation of the facility took place under non-competitive conditions, for example, partly through public funding.

13.222 This could clearly be relevant to the telecommunications sector where the demands of universal service required telecoms operators to connect all end-users regardless of the individual cost involved. Universal service is explicitly recognised under the applicable sector specific regulation as a continuing issue in the sector.[229]

13.223 Although the concept of an essential facility is raised in Commission practice under the analysis of abuse, it could also be regarded as essentially a market definition issue. The essential nature derives from the absence of demand or supply side substitutability. Where this essential facility is controlled by a single entity, or, in cases of joint dominance, by two or more jointly dominant entities, competition issues may arise.

13.224 *Available capacity* Secondly, the Notice indicates that there must be '91(b) . . . sufficient capacity available to provide access'.

13.225 There is a certain overlap between this criterion and the fifth, the absence of an objective justification, and it is not clear why in principle a capacity limit should be more important than, or considered separately from, a technical incompatibility in determining whether a refusal to provide access is abusive.

13.226 The Notice is silent as to the legal conclusion to be drawn where capacity is limited. If capacity cannot be increased, the competition rules would argue for an allocation of

---

227 Case C-7/97 *Oscar Bronner GmbH v Mediaprint* [1998] I-7791.

228 cf Case C-418/01, *IMS Health*, Judgment of 29 April 2004, not yet reported; Case C-481/01 P (R) *Commission v IMS Health* [2002] ECR I-3401.

229 cf Directive 98/10/EC of the European Parliament and of the Council of 26 February 1998 on the application of open network provision (ONP) to voice telephony and on universal service for telecommunications in a competitive environment [1998] OJ L101/24; Directive 2002/22/EC of the European Parliament and of the Parliament of 7 March 2002 on universal service and users' rights relating to electronic communications networks and services (Universal Service Directive) [2002] OJ L108/51.

capacity on an objectively justifiable basis. Allocation on other than objective criteria, for example reserving capacity to the dominant operator's own downstream operations, would appear to risk charges of discrimination. However, favouring existing customers over new customers may be permissible, as may rationing between customers or simply selling to the highest bidder.

In certain circumstances there may be an obligation on the dominant operator to expand the available capacity. This would appear to be a legitimate result where only the dominant operator is in a position to expand capacity, indeed where such operator may be the only company in a position to do so, and has a guaranteed return on its investment through third parties wishing to purchase access.[230] A legitimate justification for refusing to expand capacity in those circumstances is difficult to envisage.   **13.227**

Effect on competition or on market development   Thirdly, the refusal to provide access to the facility must have an effect on the market: '91(c) the facility owner fails to satisfy demand on an existing service or product market, blocks the emergence of a potential new service or product, or impedes competition on an existing or potential service or product market'. This criterion is relatively wide-ranging, envisaging not only direct effects on competition but the impeding of technical development by preventing the development of a new product or service. The Notice makes it clear that preventing the emergence of a completely new market would fulfil this test, but is not necessary, thus clarifying the Commission's interpretation of *Magill*.[231]   **13.228**

As the Notice envisages that a refusal which prevents the emergence of a new product market could be abusive, refusals to provide access could be abusive even where the essential facility operator is not present on the market for which access is being requested.   **13.229**

Non-discrimination   Fourthly: '91(d) the company seeking access is prepared to pay the reasonable and non-discriminatory price and will otherwise in all respects accept non-discriminatory access terms and conditions'.   **13.230**

The party requesting access must be prepared to accept non-discriminatory terms and conditions of access. This criterion is unlikely to prove problematic.   **13.231**

Objective justification   Finally: '91(e) there is no objective justification for refusing to provide access'.   **13.232**

There must be no other objective justification for the refusal. As indicated above, there is a certain overlap between this element and the question of limited capacity. This can be a relatively wide concept encompassing a variety of justifications such as technical incompatibilities. However, it is likely that the Commission will treat purported technical problems with a certain scepticism.   **13.233**

(ii) **Discrimination**   Discriminating between equivalent transactions where the discrimination has an effect on competition is specifically mentioned as an abuse under Article 82.   **13.234**

---

[230] *FAG—Flughafen Frankfurt/Main AG* [1998] OJ L72/30.
[231] Joined Cases C-241/91P and C-242/91P *Radio Telefís Eireann (RTE) and Independent Television Publications Ltd (ITP) v Commission* [1995] ECR I-743.

Provision of access to a particular facility to one party while refusing that access to a third party (or providing access but at different prices, see below) could therefore constitute discrimination under Article 82 provided a number of conditions are fulfilled.

13.235 *Notion of an equivalent transaction*   For there to be a case of discrimination, there must be different treatment of equivalent transactions. In terms of transmission networks, the starting point of the analysis is to determine exactly which network elements are required in each case. It is important to note that it is the demand of the company requesting access, not the supply by the network operator that is important.

13.236 *Self-supply*   Under Article 82 there are only a few precedents concerning the relevance of self-supply.[232] Under the 2002 regulatory framework, self-supply is clearly included in the context of discrimination.[233] In a number of merger cases non-discrimination remedies have been imposed on similar grounds.[234] However in at least one decision based on the Framework Directive the Commission has reasoned that self-supply does not constitute part of the relevant market, which would bar a finding of discrimination in relation to the conditions for self-supplied services.[235]

13.237 *Effect on competition*   Discrimination can have effects on competition either on the market for the product being sold (referred to in US law as primary-line discrimination) or on the downstream market on which the product is being used (referred to in US law as secondary-line discrimination). The clearest case of an effect on competition is if the operators between whom there is discriminatory treatment compete on the same downstream market, such as that for voice telephony. Refusing to provide one with access, or supplying access at different prices will clearly affect competition. A more complex case is where the operators between whom there is discriminatory treatment operate on different downstream markets. In these circumstances, there is clearly no direct effect on actual competition. However, the Access Notice indicates that where the markets are closely related there may nevertheless be an effect on competition sufficient for the purposes of the discrimination test:

> 121 . . . Where two distinct downstream product markets exist, but one product would be regarded as substitutable for another save for the fact that there was a price difference between the two products, discriminating in the price charged to the providers of these two products could decrease existing or potential competition. For example, although fixed and mobile

---

232 See however Case T-224/94 *Deutsche Bahn v Commission* [1997] ECR II-1689, paras 85–93.

233 Art 10, para 2 of Directive 2002/19/EC of the European Parliament and of the Council of 7 March 2002 on access to, and interconnection of, electronic communications networks and associated facilities (Access Directive) [2002] OJ L108/7. See also: Art 3 Commission Directive 2002/77/EC of 16 September 2002 on competition in the markets for electronic communications networks and services [2002] OJ L249/21.

234 *Vodafone Airtouch/Mannesmann* (COMP/M.1795) [2000] OJ C141/19; *Telia/Sonera* (Case COMP/M.2803) [2002] OJ C 201/19; *Vodafone/Vivendi/Canal Plus* (Case COMP/JV.48) (2000) [2003] OJ C118/12.

235 *Transit services in the public fixed telephone network in Austria* (case AT/2004/0090) Commission Decision of 20 October 2004, COM/2004/4070. Phase two decision based on Art 7 of Directive 2002/21/EC of the European Parliament and of the Council of 7 March 2002 on a common regulatory framework for electronic communications networks and services (Framework Directive) [2002] OJ L108/33.

voice telephony services at present probably constitute separate product markets, the markets are likely to converge. Charging higher interconnection prices to mobile operators as compared to fixed operators would tend to hamper this convergence, and would therefore have an effect on competition. Similar effects on competition are likely in other telecommunications markets.

On this basis, if an operator were to discriminate in its call-termination charges depending **13.238** on whether the call originates on a fixed or a mobile network this would be very likely to affect competition. A more difficult issue is where the discrimination is between different geographic markets. Clearly there is no direct effect on competition, and indirect effects on competition such as those envisaged in relation to fixed/mobile networks appear more difficult to justify. They cannot be entirely ruled out, however, as discrimination in these circumstances could be said to increase national partitioning of markets, thereby reducing potential competition between the operators on those national markets. Even if a discrimination argument cannot be used, there may be strong arguments in relation to excessive pricing, see below.

(iii) Bundling Although bundling or tying is an issue traditionally related to goods **13.239** rather than services, there appears to be no argument of principle that would prevent its application to services.[236] The Court in *Tetra Pak*[237] held that:

> even where tied sales of two products are in accordance with commercial usage or there is a natural link between the two products in question, such sales may still constitute abuse within the meaning of Article 86 [now Article 82] unless they are objectively justified . . .

Given that key markets in the electronic communications sector are dominated by former **13.240** monopolist operators that have not previously distinguished between their different services, this judgment may prove to be important in relation at least to network access in telecommunications. The Court's interpretation of the concept of bundling appears to dispense with the possible defence that the particular unbundling requested has never been requested. The Commission appears prepared to apply the concept of bundling to the provision of telecommunications services.

An argument that a dominant operator is unjustifiably refusing to unbundle its services **13.241** carries with it a significantly lower burden of proof than an argument that an operator is refusing to provide access to an essential facility.

In order to demonstrate bundling, it would be necessary to demonstrate: **13.242**

— dominance (note: it is not necessary to prove the existence of an essential facility);
— two or more discrete elements that are being sold together;
— an effect on competition resulting from the refusal to unbundle;
— there is, at least prima facie, no objective justification for the refusal to unbundle (technical issues could be relevant here).

---

[236] Notice on the Application of the Competition Rules to Access Agreements in the Telecommunications Sector [1998] OJ C265/2, para 103.
[237] Case C-333/94P *Tetra Pak International SA v Commission* [1996] ECR I-5951.

13.243 Following *Tetra Pak*, there appears to be no requirement to demonstrate that the elements are normally sold separately, or are sold separately elsewhere, although such indications would clearly be beneficial to a complainant's case.

13.244 In relation to network infrastructure, a refusal to provide unbundled access to the network would appear difficult to justify in many cases. Clearly, though, a dominant operator cannot be required to unbundle all elements of its network at the request of every third party, and there must be some element of reasonableness both in relation to the timing and content of the request for unbundling, and in relation to all requests which it has received.

13.245 This relatively broad interpretation of the concept of bundling is consistent with the approach of the competition rules in other areas. The refusal to sell, for example, unbundled wholesale services (interconnection) without the added value of the retail services (voice telephony) could also have been characterised as monopoly leveraging using the Court's definition in *Telemarketing*[238] and *GB-Inno-BM*:[239]

> an abuse within the meaning of Article 86 [now Article 82] is committed where, without any objective necessity, an undertaking holding a dominant position on a particular market reserves to itself an ancillary activity which might be carried out by another undertaking as part of its activities on a neighbouring but separate market, with the possibility of eliminating all competition from such undertaking[240]

13.246 *Unbundled local loop* Unbundling in this sense means the provision of direct access to the telecommunications wire separately from that of the switch.[241]

13.247 The provision of unbundled access to the local loop allows the requesting company to offer both origination and termination services in respect of that line. A competitor that has the benefit of unbundled access to the local loop effectively takes over the customer from the incumbent operator and provides both origination services from and termination services to that customer.

13.248 If a dominant telecoms operator allows its competitors to use its infrastructure to provide origination services to end-users, then it is in effect allowing that competitor access to the switch and to the wire together. In effect the telecoms operator would be ensuring a return on its investment in switching infrastructure in which its competitors have no interest and with which its competitors would rather compete. Similarly, given that the provision of call origination would not normally also entail the competitor being in a position to provide call termination services for that customer, refusing to provide unbundled access can also be seen as an attempt by the dominant operator to reserve the termination market to itself. Unbundling and divestiture of cable TV assets as the main alternative to the public telephone network was first imposed as a competition remedy in the *Telia/Telenor* merger case,[242] cable

---

[238] Case 311/84 *CBEM v CLT and IPB* [1985] ECR 3261.
[239] Case 13/77 *GB-Inno-BM/ATAB* [1977] ECR 2115.
[240] Case 13/77 *GB-Inno-BM/ATAB* [1977] ECR 2115, at para 18.
[241] Unbundled local loops are known by a variety of names, including Direct Access to the Copper Loop (DACL), line-side unbundling, and, occasionally, dark copper access.
[242] *Telia/Telenor* (Case IV/M.1439) (1999) [2001] OJ L40/1.

TV divestiture (following the failure of the Telia/Telenor merger) in *Telia/ Sonera*.[243] Given the key importance of local loop access to the promotion of competition in all Member States, unbundling was imposed by means of a Regulation late in 2000.[244]

(iv) Self-Supply, Supply to Third Parties, and Leveraging: The Relationship between **13.249** **Essential Facilities, Discrimination, and Unbundling** An important element in telecommunications cases is likely to be whether self-supply—the supply by a dominant operator to its own downstream operations—is sufficient to found a case of discrimination. The Access Notice is ambiguous on this point. At paragraph 84, the Notice distinguishes between three scenarios:

(a) a refusal to grant access for the purposes of a service where another operator has been given access by the access provider to operate on that services market;

(b) a refusal to grant access for the purposes of a service where no other operator has been given access by the access provider to operate on that services market;

(c) a withdrawal of access from an existing customer.

The distinction between (a) and (b) depends on whether an operator has been given access, **13.250** but the Notice does not make it clear whether this other operator could also be the downstream operation of the dominant operator.

There are difficulties with either interpretation. For example, if self-supply is insufficient **13.251** to mount a discrimination case, then the incentive placed on a dominant company is to adopt the most restrictive approach possible and to supply its own operations but no one else. As soon as it supplies to a third party, it is obliged to supply subject to the obligations of Article 82.[245]

If, on the other hand, self-supply is sufficient to mount a discrimination case, then there are **13.252** risks that discrimination arguments could be used to unpick the network of the incumbent at any or all levels. Although Article 10 of the Access Directive opts for self-supply as the standard when imposing non-discrimination obligations on undertakings with SMP, it is difficult to conclude on this basis what the rule is in general competition law.

Given the ambivalence in the Access Notice and the lack of conclusive case law on this **13.253** point,[246] it is difficult to predict the outcome of any particular case. The *Bronner* case mentioned above would tend to argue for the former interpretation. However, the impact of other Article 82 analysis, such as bundling, may avoid the issue in practice.

Where a dominant operator refuses to sell a component requested by a third party, but is **13.254** prepared to sell that component combined with other components which the third party

---

[243] *Telia/Sonera* (Case COMP/M.2803) [2002] OJ C 201/19.
[244] Regulation 2887/2000/EC of the European Parliament and of the Council of 18 December 2000 on unbundled access to the local loop [2000] OJ L336/4. Under the 2002 regulatory framework, NRAs will now have to impose bundling, if proportional, based on Directive 2002/19/EC of the European Parliament and of the Council of 7 March 2002 on access to, and interconnection of, electronic communications networks and associated facilities (Access Directive) [2002] OJ L108/7. Consequently under the review of the 2002 regulatory framework the ULL Regulation is likely to be revoked.
[245] Subject to issues of non-discrimination, proportionality, reasonableness, etc.
[246] cf Case T-224/94 *Deutsche Bahn v Commission* [1997] ECR II-1689, paras 85–93.

does not want, it may, as discussed above, be committing an abuse. Thus where an operator seeks to combine various network elements in a single package, access to one of those network elements may be required as a consequence of the jurisprudence on bundling. This would avoid discussions of third party supply and the notion of essential facilities, and would impose a much lower evidential burden on the complainant.

13.255 Given this, the concept of essential facilities appears to be relevant only where no form of access has been given—ie where there are no pre-existing relations between the companies. It is in these circumstances that concerns over the use of the essential facilities doctrine— most notably that it is contrary to the principle of freedom of contract[247]—are most pronounced. Where there are some contractual relations between the companies, recourse to essential facilities may well not prove to be necessary as bundling or discrimination arguments may be more easily proved.

13.256 Thus, for example, if access to local loop infrastructure is already granted to a third party, then any upgrades to the local loop infrastructure—such as higher capacity switches— should be made available on a non-discriminatory basis.

13.257 **(v) Withdrawal of Supply** The Access Notice also refers to the situation where access has been granted in the past but has now been withdrawn. On the basis of *Commercial Solvents*,[248] and in the absence of a clear objective justification, this would appear to be a relatively straightforward case of abuse in particular if, as a result, effective competition on the downstream market is threatened.

13.258 **(vi) Access as a Remedy to a Separate Abuse** Access issues will normally arise in the context of third parties actively seeking access to a network. Where a refusal to provide access falls within one of the categories identified above, access may be ordered under the competition rules. A slightly different access issue arose under Article 81(3) in relation to the *BiB* case.[249] This case is discussed in more detail below (see section F), but is also of interest here given the conditions imposed in relation to BT's cable interests, and its discussion of future possible action in relation to BT's customer access infrastructure.

13.259 BiB was to provide an interactive service using broadband (and one-way) satellite delivery, together with a standard domestic telephone line to provide interactive information. From the perspective of BT, this would allow the delivery of an interactive service with the appearance of a greater broadband communications capacity than was actually the case, thus avoiding the capacity constraints of its using its own PSTN (public switched telecommunications network).

13.260 The Commission's concern was that in diversifying its service provision interests away from its traditional network where it was dominant, BT was reducing its incentive to invest in upgrading its own network to broadband technology. This would have effects both on

---

[247] But see Case C-7/97 *Oscar Bronner GmbH v Mediaprint*, Opinion of 28 May 1998, not yet reported. At para 53, which sets out the laws of a number of Member States holding that an unjustified refusal to contract may constitute an abuse of a dominant position.
[248] Joined Cases 6 and 7/73 *Commercial Solvents* [1974] ECR 223.
[249] *British Interactive Broadcasting/Open* (Case IV/36.539) [1999] OJ L312/1.

competition—in that the transmission mechanisms available to competitors of the BiB service were controlled largely by BT (either in respect of the PSTN or of the broadband cable interests held by BT)—and on technical and economic progress—in that only BT is currently in a position to manage investment in the PSTN. The Commission addressed this concern in two ways: first, by requiring BT to divest its broadband cable interests; secondly, by stating that it would re-examine the development of broadband PSTN in the UK in the short to medium term. The Commission explicitly envisaged unbundling BT's local loop (see below) if investment in BT's broadband infrastructure could be seen to have suffered as a result of BT's investment in BiB. Given that unbundling was subsequently imposed by Regulation a review will in any event be unnecessary.[250]

(b) Access Pricing[251]

The competition rules are generally ill-suited to establishing appropriate prices for goods or services. Although the competition rules do establish parameters within which pricing issues can be analysed, detailed pricing issues are more efficiently dealt with under sector specific regulation, where available. However, large scale fact-finding operations based on the Commission's powers under Article 82 were launched in the form of sector inquiries, followed up by formal and informal investigations into pricing issues.[252] Moreover, the Commission has demonstrated in several cases a willingness to intervene in the pricing of, for example, call-termination services,[253] international mobile roaming,[254] and wholesale and retail broadband Internet access services.[255] In the case of mobile roaming the market failure concerned is considered to be sufficiently widespread and difficult to address by means of the competition rules alone that the Commission has proposed introducing both wholesale and retail price caps by means of an EU Regulation.[256]
13.261

(i) Discriminatory Pricing   If the Commission orders access to be given to a facility, it will order access on non-discriminatory terms, including as compared to the downstream operating arm of the dominant company.[257]
13.262

The issue of non-discrimination has been referred to above. It will be important to determine which services should benefit from non-discriminatory tariffs. For example, should
13.263

---

[250] Regulation 2887/2000/EC of the European Parliament and of the Council of 18 December 2000 on unbundled access to the local loop [2000] OJ L336/4.

[251] Competition aspects of access by service providers to the resources of telecommunications operators, study by Cave *et al*, European Commission, December 1995.

[252] *Sector Inquiries Leased Lines* (Case COMP/37.638); *Roaming* (Case COMP/37.639); and *Local Loop* (Case/37.640). (For further references to these inquiries see <http://europa.eu.int/comm/competition/antitrust/others/>).

[253] Statement of objections in *MCI/Mobile termination rates* (Case COMP/37.704) IP/02/484.

[254] Statements of objections against Vodafone and O2 concerning mobile roaming in *UK Roaming* (Case COMP/38.097) IP/04/994; Statements of objections against T-Mobile and Vodafone concerning mobile roaming in *Germany Roaming* (Case COMP/38.098) IP/05/161.

[255] *Deutsche Telekom AG* (Case COMP/37.451, 37.578, 37.579) [2003] OJ L263/9; *Wanadoo* (Case COMP/38.233) IP/03/1025.

[256] cf COM(2006)382, Proposal for Regulation of the European Parliament and of the Council on roaming on public mobile networks within the Community and amending Directive 2002/21/EC on a common regulatory framework for electronic communications networks and services.

[257] Notice on the Application of the Competition Rules to Access Agreements in the Telecommunications Sector [1998] OJ C265/2, para 86.

mobile network operators be entitled to the same interconnection rates as fixed network operators? As indicated above, even where fixed and mobile voice services are determined to occupy different downstream markets, discriminating between them is likely to affect competition. Secondly, application of the non-discrimination principle may be problematic either because an effect on competition is difficult to demonstrate, or because of the absence of an appropriate cost-accounting system which would demonstrate a non-discriminatory price.

13.264 (ii) **Excessive Pricing** In these circumstances, the concept of excessive pricing may prove useful. To the extent that the service performed in, for example, terminating internationally originated calls, rather than nationally originated calls, is essentially the same in each case, a dominant operator would risk allegations of excessive pricing were it to charge substantially different prices for the provision of comparable services.

13.265 *European competition law on excessive pricing remains sparse*[258] The text of the Access Notice on this point also shows the importance of the relationship between the competition rules and sector specific regulation.

13.266 Excessive prices can be found based on a comparison with costs, including costs based on sector-specific regulation of such costs, with prices for comparable services, or with the prices for the same services in other geographic areas and/or Member States.

13.267 The starting point for an excessive pricing analysis is the actual costs incurred in providing a good or service. This is problematic in the telecommunications sector for a number of reasons. First, telecoms operators have traditionally been heavily vertically integrated and have not identified the costs associated with various operations: although they are now obliged to provide separate accounts for the purposes of interconnection, such accounts would in many cases not yet be established and by definition would be limited to one particular type of service. Secondly, many investments in telecommunications networks would have been made in a non-commercial environment, and the extent to which these should be regarded as having been recovered is difficult to quantify. This is related to the question as to the most appropriate accounting basis on which to calculate the costs. Under the 2002 regulatory framework, at least, different costing methodologies are in principle acceptable when imposing cost-oriented pricing (eg long range average incremental costs, but also benchmarking or 'retail minus' approaches). Thirdly, identifying costs of, for example, interconnection would entail detailed allocation of common costs. All of these would tend to make a cost based analysis difficult in the telecommunications sector.

13.268 In *Ahmed Saeed*, the Court indicated that in order to determine an excessive price, it is possible to have reference to pricing principles contained in sector specific legislation. Given that pricing principles constitute an important part of the 2002 regulatory framework, this type of analysis could be extremely useful in determining an excessive price in the telecommunications sector. This leads to the conclusion in the Access Notice that in determining

---

[258] See, eg, Case 26/75 *General Motors Continental v Commission* [1975] ECR 1367.

an excessive price under the competition rules, regard should be had to relevant sector specific legislation and to recommendations issued by the European Commission which interpret that legislation. When looking at the question of interconnection however, NRAs are generally better placed to impose price regulation, given the potential need to develop complex cost models and ongoing monitoring requirements.[259] Second, it is possible to approach costs by comparing against prices for similar services. Thus in the international roaming cases, the Commission compared the prices at which O2 and Vodafone provided wholesale airtime access to independent service providers to the prices charged to other European mobile network operators for their international roaming services at wholesale level.[260]

A third possible line of argument results from the Court's judgment in *Bodson*. The Court **13.269** held that in determining whether a price charged is excessive, regard can be had to prices charged in other geographic areas. This appears vulnerable to the criticism that prices can differ sharply between Member States and may, for example, be influenced by the degree of competition in the particular market—the absence of competition would tend to lead to inefficient operation, higher costs, and higher prices. Although this is logical, *Bodson* itself dealt with an activity carried out under special and exclusive rights, which could therefore be expected to suffer from these inefficiencies. If the Court nevertheless concluded that comparison with other markets was possible in that case, there appears to be reason to believe that the Court would uphold the practice in the telecommunications sector as well, particularly when full liberalisation has taken place.

F. Set Top Boxes

This section addresses competition issues concerning access to set top boxes. It is therefore **13.270** focused on the media sector. However, the issues which arise may also be pertinent to other sectors. For example, control of intermediate technical standards and/or equipment may be a source of problems in both the telecommunications and information technology sectors.[261]

This section begins with an overview of the purpose and relevance of set top boxes, with a **13.271** particular focus on digital television, before considering the applicable regulatory framework. Thereafter, it discusses the principal decisions in which the Commission has considered issues surrounding set top boxes. Both the facts and the legal reasoning in these

---

[259] cf Commission Recommendation of 11 February 2003 on relevant product and service markets within the electronic communications sector susceptible to *ex ante* regulation in accordance with Directive 2002/21/EC of the European Parliament and of the Council on a common regulatory framework for electronic communication networks and services [2003] OJ L114/45, and the Explanatory Memorandum, pp 11–12.

[260] Statements of objections regarding Vodafone and O2 concerning mobile roaming (IP/04/994).

[261] See, eg, the Symbian joint venture which was dealt with under the Merger Regulation and concerned the development of an operating system for wireless information devices combining the functions of handheld computers and mobile telephones: IP/98/762; IP/98/1181; and IP/99/65. The decisions have not yet been made public.

decisions are complicated. Moreover, given the rapid developments in the technical services market, it may be that their use as precedents should be treated with caution.

(1) Overview

13.272 Analogue set top boxes have been of relevance only for television broadcasters which are funded wholly or mainly by viewers' subscriptions. Television broadcasters which are funded by advertising revenue, public subsidy, or both provide a service to all viewers who possess a television set.[262] Subscription-funded broadcasters, in contrast, must ensure that only those viewers who have paid a subscription are able to watch the television service. This is achieved by broadcasting the signal of the television service in an encrypted form. Subscribers then rent or purchase a set top box which decrypts the television signal and allows them to view the service. The collection of subscriptions is achieved by a subscriber management system.

13.273 Thus, subscription-funded television companies require a special technical infrastructure. It is comprised of a number of basic elements, namely:

— a set top box;
— an encryption system (conditional access system) which is compatible with the set top box; and
— a subscriber management system.

We refer to the combination of these services hereafter as 'technical services'.

(a) Implications of Introduction of Digital Television

13.274 In contrast to analogue set top boxes, both subscription-funded and advertising or state-funded television companies will require access to digital set top boxes, at least in the initial phase of digital broadcasting. This is because the current generation of television sets is analogue. Digital broadcast signals must be converted into an analogue form which can be displayed by current television sets. This process is known as 'demodulation'. All digital broadcasters will require demodulation of the television signal to allow viewers to watch their channels, until all viewers have bought digital television sets. Digital set top boxes will therefore typically include demodulation capabilities, in addition to the conditional access capabilities found in analogue set top boxes. The demodulation function will be included in digital set top boxes. It is likely to take a number of years before the transition to digitial television sets is complete,[263] and in the meantime, digital set top boxes will remain important.

(b) Proprietary Set Top Boxes[264] and Technical Services

13.275 Conditional access systems are generally proprietary and embedded in the set top box. This means that the set top box can descramble only those signals which are encrypted with that

---

[262] Subject only to any legal requirement to pay a fee for ownership of a television.
[263] The target date for ending analogue transmission of terrestrial channels is being discussed in a number of Member States. The UK has been discussing a target date of 2008.
[264] Set top boxes (STBs) are sometimes referred to as decoders.

particular conditional access system. There are a number of different proprietary conditional access systems operating in the EU.

The set top box may contain further proprietary elements, such as: **13.276**

• an electronic programme guide (EPG—the navigational device which basically allows viewers to tune between different channels); and
• an application programming interface (API—the software which allows the features of the box to be controlled and used by broadcasters or interactive services providers; this allows, for example, interactivity in the form of broadcast icons directing viewers to 'side-channels' or interactive services).

These features can be used only by operators which have access to the underlying technology. **13.277**

Access to the proprietary elements in set top boxes is controlled by the company which sup- **13.278**
plies the underlying proprietary technical services.[265] This applies equally to analogue and digital set top boxes.

(c) Structure of Technical Services Market

There are two general points to note about the structure of the technical services **13.279**
market. First, in the EU, suppliers of technical services tend also to be pay TV operators. When pay TV operators entered the market, the technical services necessary for pay TV did not exist. It was therefore logical that they developed the technical services themselves. As stated above, the technology for the technical services they use is generally proprietary. Secondly, there is a considerable first-mover advantage associated with technical services. The pay TV operator which is first to market will install a base of subscribers with set top boxes. As the set top boxes are generally proprietary, they will be compatible only with that pay TV operator's conditional access system and its other technical services. A new entrant in pay TV is unlikely to find launching a second set top box to be an economic proposition. The investment required to do so is substantial and consumers who have already bought a set top box would be reluctant to buy a second (at least until the retail price of set top boxes has significantly decreased).

The combination of these two facts means that a new entrant in subscription-funded tele- **13.280**
vision is often dependent on his incumbent competitor for supply of the technical services necessary to access consumers through existing set top boxes. All pay TV companies which wish to begin a digital service must launch digital set top boxes. In a number of European countries competing digital pay TV services have been launched contemporaneously using different conditional access systems and set top boxes.[266] However, the problem remains in that the 'dominant' digital pay TV supplier will also control the largest number of digital set top boxes in the market and, to the extent that they are proprietary, the access of competitors to those boxes.

---

[265] See reference to common interface in section on Directive 95/47.
[266] This was the case in France with Canal Satéllite and Télévision par Satéllite (TPS) and will be the case in the United Kingdom with BSkyB, BDB, and individual cable operators.

It follows from the above that the controller of a proprietary set top box (whether analogue or digital) is in a powerful gatekeeper position. This raises competition problems in terms of foreclosure of competition in downstream markets. Just as in the telecommunications sector, access issues are therefore central.

13.281 The importance of regulating digital conditional access services has been recognised by the Community legislature, and in practice most issues are likely to be addressed under Community law, as implemented nationally.

(2) Market Definition

13.282 Technical and administrative services for pay TV. *MSG Media Services*[267] was the first formal Commission decision to consider issues relating to set top boxes and conditional access services. One of the markets found to be affected by the operation was that for 'administrative and technical services for pay-TV'. This market primarily concerned:

— the making available of decoders (to pay TV subscribers);
— the handling of conditional access;
— subscriber management in respect of pay TV customers; and
— settlement of accounts with programme suppliers.[268]

13.283 This market definition was followed in the *Kirch/Bertelsmann/Deutsche Telekom* cases,[269] which concerned the successor operation to MSG. In contrast to *MSG* which was focused on digital television, but also concerned analogue, these cases were concerned with technical services for digital television only. The market was described as including the development of conditional access technology and its supply, and the marketing of set top boxes and smart cards. The Commission did not distinguish between markets for technical services for analogue and digital pay TV.

13.284 In the *BiB* case, the Commission indicated that one of the markets affected by the creation of the joint venture is that for 'technical and administrative services for digital interactive TV services and retail pay TV'. In concluding that the market for technical services included those necessary for both pay TV and digital interactive TV services, the Commission noted that:

> There is a very large area of overlap between the technical and administrative services necessary for retail pay TV and the services necessary for digital interactive TV services. These services include the provision of conditional access, access to the Electronic Programme Guide (EPG) and access to the Application Programming Interface (API).

13.285 It went on to conclude that 'access control services', defined as conditional access services for on-line as opposed to broadcast services, and the technical infrastructure necessary to allow transactions to be carried out were also part of the market. Although this market definition is a provisional conclusion, it appears likely to be maintained given that it reflects

---

[267] *MSG* (Case IV/M.469) [1994] OJ L364/1.
[268] ibid, para 26.
[269] *Bertelsmann/Kirch/Premiere* (Case IV/M.993)(1998) [1999] OJ L53/1 and *Deutsche Telekom/ BetaResearch* (Case IV/M.1027) (1998) [1999] OJ L53/31.

the statement made in *MSG* that 'it must be assumed that there will be a single market for services relating to digital pay TV and other digital interactive television communications services'.[270]

The same market definition was used in the *Kirch/BSkyB* case,[271] a first phase merger clear- **13.286** ance, subsequently upheld by the CFI.[272]

(a) Narrower markets

There is no formal decision in which a market has been defined in respect of one or more **13.287** of the individual services comprising the technical services necessary for pay TV and inter-active services. As the services are not substitutable, it appears likely that the Commission would identify narrower markets should it prove necessary in a particular case. The deci-sions cited above do indicate that the Commission would be willing to consider doing so.

The *MSG* decision states that in the future separate markets for subscriber management **13.288** and conditional access services may emerge.[273] The *Kirch/Bertelsmann/Deutsche Telekom* decisions raise the possibility of separate markets in respect of technical services for cable and satellite pay TV.[274] Finally, in the *BiB* case, the Commission refers to the possibility of separate markets existing in respect of the services constituting conditional access, access to the electronic programme guide, and access to the application programming interface.

(b) Geographic markets

The geographic market for the supply of technical services has been defined in light of the **13.289** geographic market definition of the pay TV market for which the technical services are supplied.

(3) Competition Issues

To date, the Commission has been called upon to examine issues relating to technical ser- **13.290** vices only in the context of mergers or joint ventures. The absence of other antitrust action suggests that disputes are settled through the Community regulatory environment, enforced at national level. In the *MSG Media Services*,[275] *Bertelsmann/ Kirch/Premiere*,[276] *Deutsche Telekom/BetaResearch*[277] and *Newscorp/Telepiù*[278] decisions, adopted under the Merger Regulation, the Commission concluded that the operations would create a domi-nant position in the technical services market which would, in turn, create or strengthen the parents' dominant positions in the downstream pay TV and cable networks markets. Inherently, therefore, the operations foreclosed competition from third parties in both the

---

[270] *MSG* (Case IV/M.469) [1994] OJ L364/1, at para 31(f).
[271] Commission Decision, Case COMP/JV.37, 21 March 2000, *BSkyB/Kirch Pay TV* at para 30.
[272] T-158/00, *ARD v Commission*, [2003] ECR II-3825.
[273] *MSG* (Case IV/M.469) [1994] OJ L364/1, at paras 31(f) and 70.
[274] *Bertelsmann/Kirch/Premiere* (Case IV/M.993) (1998) [1999] OJ L53/1, at paras 19–21 and *Deutsche Telekom/BetaResearch* (Case IV/M.1027) (1998) [1999] OJ L53/31, at paras 16–18.
[275] *MSG* (Case IV/M.469) [1994] OJ L364/1.
[276] *Bertelsmann/Kirch/Premiere* (Case IV/M.993) (1998) [1999] OJ L53/1.
[277] *Deutsche Telekom/BetaResearch* (Case IV/M.1027) (1998) [1999] OJ L53/31.
[278] *Newscorp/Telepiù* (see n 93 above).

technical services and downstream markets.[279] (A further prohibition decision, *NSD*,[280] was also adopted under the Merger Regulation, but the issue of technical services arose more marginally.) In the case of the *BiB* joint venture, the Commission exempted the joint venture under Regulation 17,[281] concluding that the creation of BiB would neither create a dominant position in the technical services market, nor strengthen the position of its parents, in particular BSkyB and BT, in downstream markets. The focus of the conditions was to ensure that BiB and its parent BSkyB do not use their position in the technical services market to foreclose competition in downstream markets. Non-discriminatory access to BiB-subsidised set top boxes has thus been crucial.

13.291 The effect of vertical integration has been the central concern. Two basic issues have thus been addressed by the Commission to date: dominance on the market for technical services; and the consequent strengthening of the parents' positions on downstream markets. The parties' positions on downstream markets have been key to a finding of dominance on the technical services market; in turn the Commission has emphasised that dominance on the technical services market can be leveraged into downstream markets. Given the risk that dominance can be leveraged either up- or downstream, there is thus a certain circularity to the analysis set out in the Commission's decisions. This section will consider the questions of dominance on the technical services market and its use to create or strengthen dominance on other markets before considering issues relating to access to set top boxes which may arise in the future under Article 82. Although there are no formal decisions dealing with the abuse of a pre-existing dominant position on the technical services market, the cases dealing with joint ventures give some indication of the Commission's likely position.

13.292 The Commission's thesis appears to be that competition on the technical services market is shaped by the competitive situation on the pay TV market. In this context, it is important to distinguish between retail operators of pay TV, that is those companies which package a selection of channels for which a subscription fee is charged, and providers of individual channels. Pay TV operators may retail both their own and third party channels. This retail activity is often referred to as operation of a pay TV platform. Regardless of the ownership of the channels, it is the pay TV platform operator which will determine the technical services used. This would suggest that where a single company holds a dominant position in the pay TV market (ie as a pay TV platform operator) and is also active on the technical services market, it will also hold a dominant position there.

13.293 The only prospect of competition in the technical services market would be if pay TV competitors emerge, yet even that would not necessarily mean that there would be competition in the technical services market, as a new operator might in commercial practice be forced to use the services of the existing operator.[282]

---

[279] The Commission reached the same conclusion in the *Cablevision* case. A prohibition decision was avoided as the parties withdrew the notification. See *Report on Competition Policy 1996* (Vol XXVI) at points 150 and 151.

[280] *Nordic Satellite Distribution* (Case IV/M.490) (1995) [1996] OJ L53/20.

[281] Notice pursuant to Art 19(3) of Regulation 17 [1998] OJ C322/5.

[282] *Bertelsmann/Kirch/Premiere* (Case IV/M.993) (1998) [1999] OJ L53/1, at para 56.

The Commission is therefore unlikely to focus on the technical services market for its own **13.294** sake, but focus on competition on the related television market.

Dominance in the technical services market may be used to control the supply of their **13.295** technical services to actual or potential competitors on these related television markets. This issue has arisen in the context of undertakings offered by parties with significant downstream positions which were designed to ensure that third parties could supply technical services independently. However, it would also be relevant in the absence of vertical integration as part of an analysis of barriers to entry: a company which did not control the supply of a particular form of technical services would be unable to prevent entry by competitors using the same technology.

Owners and/or exclusive licensees of proprietary technical services control their supply **13.296** to third parties. In such circumstances, and in the presence of vertical integration, the Commission has concluded that the suppliers would be unlikely to license their competitors on fair, reasonable, and non-discriminatory terms as to do so would not be in their economic interest as it would create competition to themselves.[283]

The Commission has not yet been confronted with a situation in which the technical ser- **13.297** vices which are the object of an operation are not proprietary and has not therefore had to consider the factors relevant to dominance in the supply of non-proprietary technical services. This is not surprising given that proprietary technical services are the norm in the EU. The reasoning set out above from the *MSG* decision in relation to the insufficiency of a common interface would certainly suggest that where the parties to a technical services operation hold a dominant position on the pay television market, then they will de facto control the technical services which are the industry standard regardless of whether the technical services are proprietary.

However, this conclusion should be treated with caution. Open standardisation agree- **13.298** ments are generally looked upon favourably under the competition rules. Where the technical services are based on an open, non-proprietary standard then there would appear to be no barriers to entry for other suppliers of those technical services.

(a) Creation or Strengthening of Dominance on Other Markets

The creation of a joint venture to supply technical services by a company which has an **13.299** interest in downstream markets for which the services are relevant (at the moment, pay TV and cable networks, although other services are likely to be relevant in the future) may well create a structural problem. Vertical integration of this sort provides the means to distort competition in downstream markets by refusing to supply technical services to downstream competitors or supplying them on less favourable terms. This is the underlying rationale of the regulation of digital conditional access services.

---

[283] See *Deutsche Telekom/BetaResearch* (Case IV/M.1027) (1998) [1999] OJ L53/31, at para 39: 'BetaResearch might therefore use its licensing policy to hamper other service providers' access to the market.' This was all the more likely given that BetaResearch was jointly controlled by a pay-TV operator, which had no interest to promote competition to itself on the pay TV market: see *Deutsche Telekom/BetaResearch* (Case IV/M.1027) (1998) [1999] OJ L53/31, at para 38. *Bertelsmann/ Kirch/Premiere* (Case IV/M.993) (1998) [1999] OJ L53/1, at para 111.

13.300 **(i) Use of Technical Services to Strengthen Dominance in Pay TV** In several cases the Commission has found that the dominant positions of the parties on the pay TV market would be strengthened by the creation of dominant technical services joint ventures. The Commission has referred to the following ways in which dominance in technical services could be used to distort competition in pay TV:

- Ensuring that the terms and conditions of supply of technical services, and in particular the price, were favourable to the parent's own service and unfavourable to others;[284]
- Charging artificially high prices for technical services. This would not affect the parents' pay TV operations, as they would share in the technical services supplier's profits;[285]
- Delaying market access of competitors through spurious technical problems;[286]
- Placing competitors' services on unattractive positions on the electronic programme guide[287] and preventing differentiation of competitors' services through development of the EPG;[288]
- Manipulating the number of slots on smart cards to ensure that competitors require a second smart card;[289]
- Obtaining information about competitors' programme plans, viewer profile, and viewer preferences facilitates the development of programmes targeted at specific groups;[290]
- Control over the development of the application programming interface and its licensing to third parties gives information about competitors' plans and can be used to delay them/make them more difficult.[291]

13.301 **(ii) Behavioural Undertakings** Where a structural problem of this nature is created, the Commission has generally refused to accept undertakings from the parties that limit the conduct of the dominant technical services joint venture so that it will not be used to strengthen downstream dominance. In the *MSG* decision, behavioural undertakings of this type[292] were characterised by the Commission as a 'commitment not to abuse in certain respects a dominant position held by MSG on the market for technical and administrative services to the detriment of competitors in the market for pay-TV'.[293] 'They are as

---

[284] *MSG* (Case IV/M.469) [1994] OJ L364/1, at para 84. *Bertelsmann/Kirch/Premiere* (Case IV/M.993) (1998) [1999] OJ L53/1, at para 58.

[285] *MSG* (Case IV/M.469) [1994] OJ L364/1, at para 84. *Bertelsmann/Kirch/Premiere* (Case IV/M.993) (1998) [1999] OJ L53/1, at para 58.

[286] *MSG* (Case IV/M.469) [1994] OJ L364/1, at para 85.

[287] *MSG* (Case IV/M.469) [1994] OJ L364/1, at para 87.

[288] *Bertelsmann/Kirch/Premiere* (Case IV/M.993) (1998) [1999] OJ L53/1, at paras 59, 60.

[289] *MSG* (Case IV/M.469) [1994] OJ L364/1, at para 88.

[290] *MSG* (Case IV/M.469) [1994] OJ L364/1, at para 89. *Bertelsmann/Kirch/Premiere* (Case IV/M993) (1998) [1999] OJ L53/1, at para 61.

[291] *Bertelsmann/Kirch/Premiere* (Case IV/M.993) (1998) [1999] OJ L53/1, at paras 113–117.

[292] *MSG* (Case IV/M.469) [1994] OJ L364/1, at para 94—promoting the sale rather than rental of decoders and not preventing the use of rented decoders for programmes not handled by MSG; 'chinese walls' preventing information on other pay TV suppliers' programmes or subscriber data from being passed to its parents; installing a neutral and non-discriminatory electronic programme guide in the decoders with an advisory committee composed of other broadcasters to ensure that this was indeed the case; charging reasonable prices and operating a transparent price policy without discrimination; and, finally, Deutsche Telekom would ensure that further digital capacity was available on its cable networks so as to avoid any shortage of channel capacity.

[293] *MSG* (Case IV/M.469) [1994] OJ L364/1, at para 95.

a matter of principle inappropriate to solving the structural problem, namely that the creation of MSG creates or strengthens dominant positions on the markets for administrative and technical services, pay-TV and cable networks.'²⁹⁴

The fact that the creation of a dominant technical services joint venture affords the parties **13.302** the possibility to distort downstream competition is sufficient. It is not necessary to demonstrate in such a structural analysis that competition will be distorted, but only that distortion is made possible.

Acceptance of behavioural undertakings   Behavioural undertakings may, however, be **13.303** accepted in certain circumstances. In the *BiB* case the Commission accepted undertakings offered by the parties to provide fair, reasonable, and non-discriminatory access to the digital set top boxes to be subsidised by BiB as one of the conditions of exemption under Regulation 17.²⁹⁵ More controversially the Commission accepted behavioural undertakings in the *Newscorp/Telepiù* case,²⁹⁶ where the risks to competition were clear.

(iii) **Structural Solutions**   Where a supplier of technical services has significant down- **13.304** stream interests, the clearest remedy would be a structural one: removing the downstream operators' controlling interest in the technical services joint venture. However, to be acceptable such a solution must remove the controlling interest as a matter of fact, and not only in principle.²⁹⁷

Non-proprietary technical services   The Commission has not yet had to address whether **13.305** dominance in the technical services market can be used to strengthen downstream dominance where the technology underlying the technical services is not proprietary. This will remain a theoretical question for as long as proprietary set top boxes and related set top boxes remain the norm. However, it does appear questionable that downstream dominance could be strengthened if the technical services company has no technical control over access to the set top box.

(iv) **Relevance of Regulation of Digital Conditional Access Services**   As stated above, **13.306** no reference is made to the Advanced Television Standards Directive in the *Bertelsmann/ Kirch/Deutsche Telekom* decisions. Given the limitation of the scope of the Directive (only digital conditional access services), control of further proprietary elements, such as the electronic programme guide or application programming interface, could still be used to strengthen downstream dominance. The *Newscorp/ Telepiù* decision did make reference to the regulatory regime, but concluded that although the regulation mitigated the competition concern, they were not enough to remove it,²⁹⁸ suggesting that the Commission is ready to accept the relevance of regulation, at least in so far as that regulation effectively prevents behaviour which would otherwise constitute or exacerbate a competition concern.

Pre-existing regulation was therefore insufficient to address all of the means by which **13.307** dominance in technical services could be leveraged into downstream markets. It was therefore

---

²⁹⁴ *MSG* (Case IV/M.469) [1994] OJ L364/1, at para 99.
²⁹⁵ Notice pursuant to Art 19(3) of Regulation 17 [1998] OJ C322/5.
²⁹⁶ See section 11 of the commitments.
²⁹⁷ *Bertelsmann/Kirch/Premiere* (Case IV/M.993) (1998) [1999] OJ L53/1, at paras 38, 79.
²⁹⁸ *Newscorp /Telepiù* at 140.

not necessary to address the more difficult question of whether the creation of a structural competition problem can be accepted if it is subject to pre-existing regulation. Given the Commission's strict approach to behavioural undertakings, it may well be that it would not. However, the Commission's *BiB* decision suggests that regulation will be relevant in respect of pre-existing problems where it is sufficient to prevent exacerbation of competition problems.

(4) Access to Set Top Boxes under Article 82

13.308 There are no decisions on this point, perhaps given the detailed regulation of the issue. The following points therefore provide only general indications of the type of issue that may arise. The factors relevant to dominance in the technical services market are set out in paragraphs 11.311 *et seq* above.

(a) Bundling

13.309 Technical services comprise a group of disparate services: for instance conditional access, subscriber management, and access to the application programming interface. It seems likely that the Commission would consider a refusal to supply any one of these services individually as bundling[299] unless it could be objectively justified. The most appropriate justification would seem to be that the security function of the set top box would be affected. A further issue may arise where a company which is dominant in the wholesale supply of channels makes provision of certain technical services conditional on purchase of programming. It is difficult to imagine any acceptable justification for such behaviour.

(b) Excessive Pricing

13.310 There would clearly be an effect on competition if a vertically integrated company were to charge its downstream competitors an excessive price for technical services.[300] However, the Commission has been reluctant to deal with pricing issues in the past.

(c) Price Discrimination

13.311 At the most rudimentary level, a company which is dominant in the supply of technical services which has agreed to supply any of those services individually to a downstream competitor or on more advantageous terms, must offer those terms to all as discrimination would be contrary to Article 82.

(d) 'Simulcrypt'

13.312 In a number of Member States, competing digital pay TV platforms have been, or will be, launched together. These platforms use different proprietary conditional access systems and set top boxes. The question may therefore arise of whether the dominant technical services and pay TV operator can be obliged to enter simulcrypt agreements.[301] Refusal to

---

[299] See, eg, the UK regime—the separate provision of each type of service is a regulatory requirement.

[300] See *MSG* (Case IV/M.469) [1994] OJ L364/1, at para 84. *Bertelsmann/Kirch/Premiere* (Case IV/M.993) (1998) [1999] OJ L53/1, at para 58.

[301] See *BiB* (Notice pursuant to Art 19(3) of Regulation 17) [1998] OJ C322/5: the Notice indicates that one of the proposed conditions of exemption is that BSkyB enter simulcrypt agreements.

do so would prevent pay TV competitors from reaching consumers who have bought or leased an incompatible set top box. Without objective justification, refusal might well be considered to constitute exclusionary and abusive behaviour. In this context, it is interesting to note that BSkyB has been required to enter such agreements as a condition of exemption of *BiB*.

G. Retail

Effects on competition in retail markets can arise either as a result of operations on upstream **13.313** markets or on the retail markets themselves. The importance of upstream markets has been considered in previous sections: access issues related to content, transmission networks, and interface devices, such as set top boxes, can all result in the restriction, distortion, or elimination of downstream competition. As can be seen from these sections, a number of the major competition concerns which manifest themselves in a reduction of competition at the retail level are attributable to competition problems higher up the value chain. Each of these represents a potential barrier to entry into retail markets. The existence of a bottle-neck at any one level is sufficient to affect such entry.

This section focuses on activities on retail markets. In this respect, one of the most important **13.314** points to note about the Commission's decisional practice is its tendency to identify narrow product and geographic markets. In the television sector, for example, advertising-funded and pay television have been considered to be separate product markets.[302] The geographic scope of both has tended to be national, or, at the broadest, linguistic in dimension.

(1) Market Definition

(a) Product Markets in Telecommunications

The clearest general guidance on the Commission's views on market definition in the elec- **13.315** tronic communications sector is provided by its Recommendation on relevant markets and the Explanatory Memorandum thereto.[303] The Commission distinguishes between retail and wholesale services. Retail services are distinguished between access and fixed services (and, by implication, access and mobile services), and between services to residential and to non-residential users. Wholesale services are distinguished between call origination and termination (on fixed and mobile networks separately), transit, wholesale unbundled ser-vices, wholesale broadband access, roaming, and broadcasting transmission services. Separate markets are distinguished for leased lines at retail and wholesale level, and at wholesale level for terminating and trunk segments.

---

[302] The same distinctions in product markets have been made in respect of radio services. Thus, the Commission distinguishes between a market for radio advertising and a market for subscription-funded radio: *Bertelsmann/CLT* (Case IV/M.779) (1996) (national market for radio advertising defined).

[303] Commission Recommendation of 11 February 2003 on relevant product and service markets within the electronic communications sector susceptible to *ex ante* regulation in accordance with Directive 2002/21/EC of the European Parliament and of the Council on a common regulatory framework for elec-tronic communication networks and services [2003] OJ L114/45, and the Explanatory Memorandum.

13.316 These market definitions are not comprehensive as they are proposed for purposes of sector-specific regulation, based on the existence of high and non-transitory entry barriers, with a structure that does not tend towards effective competition within a two- or three-year time frame, and where the application of competition law alone would not adequately address the market failures concerned. This means that in any competition case, relevant markets would have to be defined based on an analysis of demand and supply-side characteristics. However, they form a useful starting point. Markets not listed in the Recommendation that may nevertheless be relevant in particular cases are eg universal Internet connectivity,[304] business data communications services,[305] and broadband Internet access[306] at retail level.

13.317 (i) **Telephone Services** For the purposes of Directive (EEC) 90/388 speech, or voice telephony, was defined as:

> the commercial provision for the public of the direct transport and switching of speech in real-time between public switched network termination points, enabling any user to use equipment connected to such a network termination point in order to communicate with another termination point.[307]

13.318 This definition was necessary in the context of partial liberalisation to draw the dividing line between liberalised and non-liberalised services, and, after 1998, to draw the dividing line between individual licensing and general authorisation requirements. However, the distinction between voice telephony and other voice services which do not fall within the formal definition of voice telephony was technical, rather than economic. Services formally defined as voice telephony sometimes competed with services which fall outside of the definition. The definitions of electronic communication services that apply under the 2002 regulatory framework have no comparable regulatory implications—although 'publicly available telephone services' are more heavily regulated than public eletronic communications services, as in this case in particular universal service obligations persist.[308]

13.319 *Fixed and mobile* The Commission has distinguished between fixed and mobile infrastructure and services in numerous decisions.[309] Where the prices of such services are markedly different, and given the added functionality of mobility for mobile services, it is

---

[304] *WorldCom/MCI* (Case IV/M.1069) (1999) [1999] OJ L116/1; *MCI WorldCom/Sprint* (Case COMP/M.1741) (2000) [2003] OJ L300/1.

[305] *Telia/Telenor* (Case IV/M.1439) (1999) [2001] OJ L40/1, paras 101–104; *France Telecom/Equant*(Case COMP/M.2257) [2001] OJ C187/8, paras 22–27.

[306] cf the Commission's decision in *Deutsche Telekom AG* (Case COMP/37.451, 37.578, 37.579) [2003] OJ L263/9, at para 78ff.

[307] Commission Directive (EEC) 90/388 of 28 June 1990 on competition in the markets for telecommunications services [1990] OJ L192/10, at Art 1.1.

[308] cf Directive 2002/22/EC of the European Parliament and of the Parliament of 7 March 2002 on universal service and users' rights relating to electronic communications networks and services (Universal Service Directive) [2002] OJ L108/51.

[309] (EC) 95/489: Commission Decision of 4 October 1995 concerning the conditions imposed on the second operator of GSM radiotelephony services in Italy (only the Italian text is authentic) [1995] OJ L280/49, at paras 7 *et seq*; (EC) 97/181: Commission Decision of 18 December 1996 concerning the conditions imposed on the second operator of GSM radiotelephony services in Spain (only the Spanish text is authentic) [1997] OJ L76/19.

likely that these should be regarded as constituting separate downstream markets. However, where, as is already the case in some Scandinavian countries, the price of fixed and mobile voice services has almost fully converged, the maintenance of separate retail markets will be more difficult to sustain. There may also be scope for the definition of markets for integrated fixed-mobile services, as in the case of corporate products of this nature.

Internet telephony   Originally the Commission in its Notice on the Status of Voice on the   **13.320**
Internet[310] concluded that for the time being in particular differences in quality meant that Internet telephony could not be considered to fall within the definition of voice telephony and its provision did therefore require a licence to that effect.

In a subsequent review of the Notice, the Commission concluded that Member States   **13.321**
could continue to allow Internet access/service providers to offer voice on the Internet under data transmission general authorisations.[311] Under the 2002 regulatory framework the distinction between voice telephone and other electronic communications services is no longer legally significant from a licensing perspective. Now providers of electronic communications services including incumbent PSTN operators are increasingly bundling their offers of digital telephone services including speech communications with broadband Internet access, for instance as voice over digital subscriber lines (DSL), it is likely that new market definitions will emerge.

(ii) Value Added Services   Prior to full liberalisation of the sector, value added services   **13.322**
were broadly regarded as those not constituting voice telephony. Value added services are no longer a category that is relevant from a regulatory perspective and are therefore not likely to come up under market definition. However, in particular cases, more detailed market definitions emerged that may still be relevant. *Atlas*, for example, identifies customised packages of corporate communications services[312] and packet-switched data services.[313] *Unisource/Telefonica*[314] identifies traveller services.

(iii) Corporate Communications Services   This market is defined in the Commission's   **13.323**
decisions on international alliances, discussed below. Generally large corporate customers

---

[310] Notice on the Status of Voice on the Internet under Directive (EC) 90/388 [1998] OJ C6/4.

[311] Communication from the Commission—Status of voice on the Internet under Community law, and in particular, under Directive 90/388/EEC—Supplement to the Communication by the Commission to the European Parliament and the Council on the status and implementation of Directive 90/388/EEC on competition in the markets for telecommunications services [2000] OJ C369/3. A review of this communication is now subject to consultation.

[312] *Atlas* [1996] OJ L239/23, at para 5 (only the English, French, and German texts are authentic).

[313] *Atlas* [1996] OJ L239/23, at para 8 (only the English, French, and German texts are authentic).

[314] *BT/MCI* [1994] OJ L223/36, at para 5: 'the emerging market for value-added and enhanced services to large multinational corporations, extended enterprises and other intensive users of telecommunictions services provided over international intelligent networks. This market will cover a wide range of existing global trans-border services, including virtual network services, high-speed data services and outsourced global telecommunications solutions specially designed for individual customers requirements . . .'; *Atlas* [1996] OJ L239/23, at para 5 (only the English, French, and German texts are authentic): 'The market comprises mostly customized combinations of a range of existing telecommunications sevices, mainly liberalised voice services including voice communication between members of a closed group of users . . . high-speed data services and outsourced telecommunications solutions specially designed for individual customer requirements . . .'.

have a demand for a range of telecommunications services, often bought from a single supplier. The Commission's decisions indicate that this can be further divided into national, cross-border, regional, and international markets.

(b) Product Markets in the Internet Sector

13.324   The Commission has issued a number of decisions which provide guidance as to market definition in respect of Internet services.

13.325   **(i) Corporate markets**   Internet access would typically be one element of the overall corporate communications services market referred to above, and the Commission decision in *Worldcom/MCI* indicates that, in some circumstances, it may be appropriate to identify a corporate Internet access market separate from that for packaged corporate services.[315] However, if predictions as to the ubiquity of Internet based services prove realistic, then the distinction may cease to have meaning as many if not all corporate services will become Internet protocol based. Market definitions in the future, at least in the corporate sector, will therefore probably not be based on the issue of whether or not a service is Internet based, but on a definition of the type of service being provided.

13.326   **(ii) Residential services**   Looking at residential services, the Commission's decisions[316] indicate that the following markets can be identified:

— Internet access;[317]
— Internet advertising;
— paid for Internet content.

13.327   This suggests, *inter alia*, that the Commission is maintaining the advertising funded versus subscription funded distinction that it uses in the broadcasting sector. In addition the Commission has defined portals as separate markets.[318]

13.328   An area that is likely to be of increasing importance in the future is the availability of Internet services or Internet-like interactive services on domestic television sets. The Commission's decision in *BiB*[319] suggests that the Commission would regard the availability of a service on a TV set, rather than on a PC, as being likely to constitute a separate product market. This conclusion appears to be based on the different price, characteristics, and use, and the consequent household penetration rates, of TVs as opposed to PCs.

---

315 *Worldcom/MCI* (Case IV/M.1069) (1998) [1999] OJ L116/1.

316 /*Telenor/Schibsted* (Case IV/JV.1) (1998) [1999] OJ C220/28; (Case IV/JV1) (1998); *Cegetel/Canal+/AOL/Bertelsmann* (Case IV/JV5) (1998) [2000] OJ C24/4; *Vodafone/Vivendi/Canal Plus* (Case COMP/JV.48) (2000) [2003] OJ C118/12.

317 Possibly divided between dial-up and dedicated access *Telia/Telenor* (Case IV/M.1439) (1999) [2001] OJ L40/1, para 105; on the division between business and residential dial-up access see *BT/ESAT* (Case COMP/M.1838) [2000] OJ C341/3, para 7. A distinction between high speed (broadband) and low speed (narrowband) access is also possible. cf *Deutsche Telekom AG* (Case COMP/37.451, 37.578, 37.579) [2003] OJ L263/9; *Wanadoo* (Case COMP/38.233) IP/03/1025.

318 *Vodafone/Vivendi/Canal Plus* (Case COMP/JV.48) (2000) [2003] OJ C118/12, paras 47–53; *Telia/Oracle/Drutt* (Case IV/M.1982) [2000] OJ C374/10, paras 17–18; *BT/ESAT Digifone* (Case IV/M.2282) [2002] OJ C66/13, paras 7–8. cf L Garzaniti and F Liberatore, 'Recent Developments in the European Commission's practice in the Communications Sector, Part III', [2004] ECLR 25(5) 286–298.

319 *British Interactive Broadcasting/Open* (Case IV/36.539) [1999] OJ L312/1.

The Commission's preliminary view is that the interactive service to be provided by BiB is distinct from traditional broadcast television services, although it is likely that there will be an increased blurring of the boundaries between these services in the future.

(iii) Mobile services   Data services are increasingly made available over mobile telecom-   **13.329** munications networks. Given the bandwidth constraints of the present GSM/ DCS1800 systems, and the price premium likely to be afforded to the UMTS (Universal Mobile Telecommunications System) networks, it appears likely that data services over UMTS will occupy a separate market to GSM based data services. The Commission has so far considered that mobile and fixed data services are in separate markets.[320] However because the highest bandwidth mobile data services are likely to be deliverable only under conditions of optimal coverage and low to no mobility, and because wireless local are network services (WLAN) are emerging that allow limited mobility within a circumscribed area, a similar limited measure of mobility may become the norm for high bandwidth services. In this case, a market for broadband wireless data communications may emerge.[321]

(c) Product Markets in the Television Sector

In defining product markets, the Commission has distinguished between television ser-   **13.330** vices which are funded by advertising and those which are funded by viewers' subscriptions. This has been a controversial and contested approach.

(i) Pay Television   In the *MSG* decision,[322] the Commission concluded that pay televi-   **13.331** sion constituted a separate product market from advertising-funded television and from public television financed through fees and partly through advertising, as in the case of pay TV there is a trade relationship between the viewer as subscriber and the programme supplier, while in the case of advertising-funded television there is a trade relationship only between the programme supplier and the advertising industry. This meant that the conditions of competition were different for the two types of television. The main parameters for competition in advertising-funded television are audience share which determines advertising rates. In the case of pay television, the key factors were the shaping of programmes to meet the interests of the target groups and the level of subscription prices. In addition, the content of pay television and advertising-funded channels differed, in that the former tended to be of a more specialised nature.

This distinction between pay television and advertising-funded television has since been   **13.332** maintained in a series of decisions.[323] The existence of separate markets does not mean that there is no relationship between the two types of television, indeed pay TV operators that also carry advertising will be present on both markets (but usually with a relatively small

---

[320] *Vodafone/Vivendi/Canal Plus* (Case COMP/JV.48) (2000) [2003] OJ C118/12.
[321] *Network sharing Germany* (Case COMP/38.369) [2004] OJ L 75/ 32, at paras 69–71; *Network sharing UK* (Case COMP/38.370) [2003] OJ L200/59, at paras 64–66.
[322] *MSG* (Case IV/M.469) [1994] OJ L364/1. A separate market for pay TV was first referred to in *Kirch/Richemont/Telepiù* (Case IV/M.410) (1994).
[323] See *Kirch/Richemont/Multichoice/Telepiù* (Case IV/M584) (1995); *Nordic Satellite Distribution* (Case IV/M.490) (1995) [1996] OJ L53/20; *BiB* (above); *TPS* (above).

market share of the advertising market). The Commission has accepted that the existence of varied and numerous free television channels in a market has an impact on the ease with which pay television can be introduced, without, however, altering its conclusion that separate product markets exist.[324]

13.333   Analogue and digital pay television have been found to form part of single pay television market.[325] However, the Commission has referred to the fact that digitisation may at some point in the future lead to sufficient convergence between free access and pay television for the definition of a single product market.[326] This has also been said to be the case in respect of pay TV channels which are funded partly by advertising.[327]

13.334   *Cable, satellite, and digital terrestrial pay television*   In the *MSG* and *NSD* decisions, the Commission appeared to define pay television markets in respect of cable and satellite pay television respectively. More recent decisions, however, define a single product market, regardless of the means of transmission used for delivery.[328] This approach was followed following a detailed market analysis in the *Telenor/C+/Canal Digital* case, and is more consistent with the regulatory environment—which explicitly adopts a technology neutral approach—and more consistent with the general market definition concepts of price, characteristics, and intended use.

13.335   *Pay per view*   In the *Premiere* decision, the Commission said that pay-per-channel and pay-per-view were part of the pay TV market.[329] However, this issue was not of central

---

[324] Most recently *Bertelsmann/Kirch/Premiere* (Case IV/M.993) (1998) [1999] OJ L53/1, at paras 18, 44, and 45.

[325] *Bertelsmann/Kirch/Premiere* (Case IV/M.993) (1998) [1999] OJ L53/1, at para 18: 'Digital pay TV is only a further development of analog pay TV and therefore does not constitute a separate relevant product market. Moreover, account should be taken of the fact that in the next few years analog broadcast pay TV will be completely superseded by digital broadcast pay TV.' See also Commission Decision 2001/98/EC, *Telia/Telenor* (Case IV/36.237), [1999] OJ L 90/6 at para 26; Commission Decision, Case COMP/JV.37, 21 March 2000, *BSkyB/Kirch Pay TV* at para 25.

[326] *Bertelsmann/Kirch/Premiere* (Case IV/M993) (1998) [1999] OJ L53/1, at para 18: 'As digitalisation continues to spread, there could admittedly, with the passage of time, be a certain convergence between pay-TV and free-TV, particularly if, at some future stage, freeTV channels too should largely be supplied in digital bouquets by pay-TV operators. However, this possible future development is not enough now to justify the acceptance of a common market for pay and free TV.'

[327] *MSG* (Case IV/M.469) [1994] OJ L364/1, at para 32: '. . . could become blurred in the case of pay-TV programmes that are financed from a mixture of sources'. However, in *BiB* (Notice pursuant to Art 19(3) of Regulation 17) [1998] OJ C322/5, the Commission defined a single pay TV market despite the fact that BSkyB is funded partly by advertising and partly by subscription (albeit that advertising revenue is minor).

[328] *Bertelsmann/Kirch/Premiere* (Case IV/M.993) (1998) [1999] OJ L53/1; *TPS* [1999] OJ L90/6; *BiB* (Notice pursuant to Art 19(3) of Regulation 17) [1998] OJ C322/5.

[329] *Bertelsmann/Kirch/Premiere* (Case IV/M.993) (1998) [1999] OJ L53/1, at para 18. To be contrasted with *MSG* (Case IV/M.469) [1994] OJ L364/1, at para 38: '. . . according to what is known at present, pay-TV in the form of pay-per-channel, pay-per-view and near-video-on-demand constitutes a single market, since in such forms of viewing, the broadcaster alone determines the programme sequence and timing and the viewer has only limited choice available (in the case of near-video-on-demand, for example, a specific number of feature films is available for selection, with each being repeated at specific times of the day). Things might be different in the case of video-on-demand proper, with the customer selecting a programme of his choice from an electronic programme library. However, since this form of broadcasting will, according to the information provided by various potential market participants, probably not be achievable for technical reasons over the next few years, it need not be assigned to any particular market.'

importance to the case. In a later decision, the Commission indicated that there could be separate markets for the provision of pay per view films and/or channels at the retail level,[330] with the former potentially being closer to the video rental market than to traditional television markets.

(ii) Television Advertising Market The Commission has distinguished between a   **13.336**
'television broadcasting' or 'viewers' market' on the one hand and a market for television advertising on the other. It has left open the question of whether the former markets in fact exist. 'In view of the fact that there is no direct trade relationship between broadcasters of "free" TV channels on the "supply side" and viewers on the "demand side", it might be argued that TV broadcasting does not constitute a market in the strict economic sense of the notion.'[331] The only economic relationship has been found to be that between advertising-funded broadcasters and advertisers or advertising agencies. However, the Commission has also said that audience shares are a determinative factor for success on the market for television advertising.[332]

The market for television advertising has been found to be separate from those for adver-   **13.337**
tising in other media, and in particular print media, on the basis that the consumers targeted through different types of advertising may vary considerably, and the techniques employed and production costs are different as is the price.[333]

There are no formal decisions in which narrower markets have been defined. However, the   **13.338**
Commission has referred to the possibility of defining narrower television advertising markets by reference to the target audience of the channel and advertiser.[334]

(d) Geographic Markets

This will vary depending on the service being provided. In the electronic communications   **13.339**
sector, the geographic market is determined by:

(a) the extent and coverage of the network and the customers that can economically be reached and whose demands may be met; and
(b) the legal and regulatory system and the right to provide a service.[335]

On this basis, the Commission has identified national markets for residential telecommu-   **13.340**
nications services, and a range of markets—national, cross-border, regional, pan-European, and global—for corporate communications services.[336] Because mobile licensing and the

---

[330] Commission Decision, Case IV/M.2211, *Universal / NTL / Studio Channel*, at para 17.
[331] *RTL/Veronica/Endemol* (Case IV/M.553) [1996] OJ L294/14; *Canal+/UFA/MDO* (Case IV/M.655) (1995).
[332] *RTL/Veronica/Endemol* (Case IV/M.553) [1996] OJ L294/14, para 20.
[333] *RTL/Veronica/Endemol* (Case IV/M.553) [1996] OJ L294/14, para 23. See also *Sunrise* (Case IV/M.176) (1992).
[334] In *CLT/Disney/Super RTL* (Case IV/M.566) (1995), the question of a television advertising market confined to children's channels was raised. However, as such a narrower market definition would not affect the competitive assessment, it was left open.
[335] Commission guidelines on market analysis and the assessment of significant market power under the Community regulatory framework for electronic communications networks and services [2002] OJ C165/6, at paras 55–60.
[336] *Atlas* [1996] OJ L239/23 (only the English, French, and German texts are authentic).

pricing of mobile services is national, mobile markets are generally considered national in scope. The additional connection and communication costs that customers incur when roaming abroad supports this definition.[337] An exception is pan-European services to corporate customers, that may be provided based on networks within the same group of operators.

13.341   In respect of television services, the Commission has often identified linguistic[338] or national markets. The Commission has generally defined national markets in respect of both pay and advertising-funded television. Differences in culture, language, regulatory regime, and competitive conditions have been relied upon in justification. However, the Commission has indicated a willingness to define markets with respect to areas within which the language and culture are relatively homogenous. In the *Premiere* case, it referred to the possibility of the relevant geographic market for pay TV extending beyond Germany to include all German-speaking areas within Europe. This is to be contrasted with the position in *RTL/Veronica/Endemol*,[339] in which the Commission found that the relevant geographic market for television advertising was the Netherlands and excluded Flemish-speaking Belgium.

(2) Competition Issues

13.342   As indicated above, competition problems at higher levels of the value chain often have a significant impact at the retail level. The Commission has dealt with a number of alliances in the telecoms and media sectors that were entered into by operators that were dominant on markets other than those on which the alliance was to operate.

13.343   In addition to abuses of dominance, genuine retail issues fall into three broad categories:

— assessment of actual competition on retail markets;
— assessment of potential competition on retail markets;
— leveraging from related markets.

(a) Telecommunications

13.344   (i) Assessment of Actual Competition on Retail Markets   As indicated above (see section E), many of the important issues in telecommunications cases relate to the dominant positions of the parent companies on related, often transmission, markets. However, where significant established positions on retail markets exist—as in packet-switched data communication on the French and German markets in *Atlas*—the Commission will inevitably look at the overlap and determine whether divestiture (as in *Atlas*)[340] or prohibition might be necessary. Similarly, when looking at incumbent operator mergers such as *Telia/Telenor*[341]

---

[337] *Vodafone/Airtouch* (Case IV/M.1430) [1999] C295/2; *Telia/Telenor* (Case IV/M.1439) (1999) [2001] OJ L40/1, para 124.
[338] *Bertelsmann/Kirch/Premiere* (Case IV/M.993) (1998) [1999] OJ L53/1.
[339] *RTL/Veronica/Endemol* (Case IV/M.553) [1996] OJ L294/14.
[340] *Atlas* [1996] OJ L239/23, at para 68 and Article 4(a) (only the English, French, and German texts are authentic).
[341] *Telia/Telenor* (Case IV/M.1439) (1999) [2001] OJ L40/1.

and *Telia/Sonera*,[342] divestiture of actual overlapping operations on their domestic markets has been imposed. In other cases the Commission has emphasised market dynamics, the absence of capacity constraints, and the lack of evidence of high switching costs to find insufficient proof of dominance in spite of very high market shares.[343]

Actual competition and joint dominance It is possible that the Commission would also **13.345** regard the divestiture of shareholdings in some operations as necessary even in the absence of single operator dominance. For example, in *France Télécom/Orange* the Commission found that given the role of Orange as third operator in breaking duopolistic pricing patterns in Belgian markets for mobile telephony, overlapping shareholdings between FT and Orange in Belgium could raise serious doubts, in response to which FT divested its stake.[344] In such cases, the Commission could object to the overlap of even relatively small minority shareholdings.

(ii) Assessment of Potential Competition on Retail Markets

Alliances addressing domestic markets With the liberalisation of the telecommunications **13.346** sector in 1998, there has been a substantial number of joint venture cases concerning entrants in electronic communications markets that were notified under the Merger Regulation, in particular (but not exclusively) in mobile communications. These involve both companies active in other industrial areas, and telecommunications operators active in other geographic markets. The existence of a dominant player on the market meant that none of these cases raised the risk of creating or strengthening a dominant position. To the extent that these alliances strengthened the viability of the new entrants, there would have been no reduction in potential competition resulting from the alliance as compared to the possibility of the members of the alliance entering independently. Given that these new entrant cases raised no competition concerns, market definition issues tended to be left completely open, and the cases are therefore of little use in predicting market definition and/or competition concerns in more problematic cases in the future.

Incumbent operator mergers The mixed success of international alliances to date has **13.347** been accompanied by only limited consolidation between the incumbent operators.

Mergers between incumbent operators could raise significant concerns, in particular if they **13.348** are located within the same geographical area. New entrant domestic alliances seek to attack the market position of the former monopolist operator and are therefore pro-competitive. Incumbent operator mergers, by contrast, can in part be seen as a defensive response to the loss of market share on domestic markets. One aspect of such mergers relates to a possible strengthening of existing positions through a reduction of potential competition. Assessing the potential competition would be difficult, but, as indicated below in the discussion of leveraging, the Commission in cases such as *Telia/Telenor* and *Telia/Sonera* has regarded national incumbent operators as being potential competitors to each other on certain markets.

---

[342] *Telia/Sonera* (Case COMP/M.2803) [2002] OJ C 201/19.

[343] *Access and call origination on public mobile telephone networks in Finland* (case FI/2004/0082) Commission Decision of 5 October 2004 COM/2004/3682.

[344] *France Télécom/Orange* (Case COMP/M.2016) [2000] C261/6.

The reasons cited below would appear equally applicable as criteria for determining the extent of the reduction in potential competition:

— any overlap in their existing operations whose business scope could be extended into related markets;
— the size and domestic market share of the operators concerned;
— the geographic proximity of their respective markets;
— linguistic or other cultural issues that make their market entry in each other's markets more or less likely.

13.349 When looking at infrastructure issues, the ability to roll-out competing networks, through incremental extension of existing and geographically proximate networks, is considered important. In this context cable TV network divestiture and unbundling remedies have been imposed.

13.350 *International alliances*   Operators that are well established on domestic markets appear highly likely to be considered to be at least potential competitors at the global level.[345] However, given the shifting sands of international alliances, competition issues in this context have revolved around an examination of the domestic positions of the parents to ensure that there is no strengthening or possibility of leveraging. The Commission's decisions in *BT/MCI I*, *Atlas/Phoenix*, and *Unisource/Uniworld* are therefore examined below.

13.351 By contrast, the Commission gave a negative clearance to *International Private Satellite Partners*,[346] given the need to obtain authorisations and licences, and to arrange the financing, construction, launch, and operation of two satellites in circumstances where none of the partners was in a position to do this alone.[347] The Commission also concluded that the joint venture could be expected to increase the level of competition in a fast-growing segment of the overall telecommunications market.[348]

13.352 The Commission is further investigating the *Freemove* and *Starmap* alliances aimed at competing with the Vodafone group in offering seamless transnational services, notably including roaming services, to MNCs.[349]

(iii) Leveraging and Related Markets

13.353 *Incumbent operator mergers*   The final issue which may have to be considered is whether the parties will derive additional benefits from the consolidation of their operations and from the vertical integration of their activities. The clearest consolidation benefit is likely to be the ability to self-correspond in place of national or international interconnection arrangements. While arguably a legitimate economy of scale, such benefits may prove problematic where the existing market positions of the parties are very large and lead to a strengthening of the parties' position in downstream retail services markets.

---

345 *BT/MCI* [1994] OJ L223/36, at para 34.
346 *International Private Satellite Partners* [1994] OJ L354/75 (IPSP).
347 *International Private Satellite Partners* [1994] OJ L354/75, at para 53.
348 *International Private Satellite Partners* [1994] OJ L354/75, at para 56.
349 cf *Telefónica/O2* (Case COMP/M.4035) EUR-lex 32006M.4035; *FT/Amena* (Case COMP/M.3920) EUR-lex 3205M.3920; and IP/05/1217.

International alliances   Although the purpose of strategic alliances is usually to deliver **13.354** value added retail services to corporate users, many of the most important competition issues relate to the position of the parent companies (often dominant, former monopolist telecommunications operators) on national markets. The participating companies would tend not to have substantial market presence on the relevant retail markets at the global level—but the existence of dominance on national markets would raise risks of those dominant positions being used to favour the retail joint ventures.

The Commission has regarded the cases as falling within Article 81(1) as such operators **13.355** would normally be regarded as actual or potential competitors on each other's markets, and their alliance would tend to reduce actual or potential competition between them on those markets.

BT/MCI I   BT and MCI entered into a joint venture to provide telecommunications ser- **13.356** vices to large corporate customers whose demands could not be satisfied by national telecommunications providers.

The competition concern was relatively limited given the limited extent to which MCI **13.357** could be regarded as a significant competitor to BT on its domestic markets. In addition, the Commission recognised the existence of a strong national regulatory framework relevant to third party access to transmission facilities, and chose not to impose further conditions as part of the decision. The Commission therefore exempted the creation of the joint venture and the appointment of BT as an exclusive distributor for the joint venture's services in the EEA.

The parties later decided to merge their entire activities, leading to the Commission's deci- **13.358** sion in *BT/MCI II*. As the main issue in this case related to the availability of transatlantic capacity, this case is discussed above.

Atlas/GlobalOne   The Commission's decision in *BT/MCI I* contrasts markedly with its **13.359** decision in *Atlas*. BT/MCI I was an alliance between a European and an American operator some time after the home market of the European operator had been largely liberalised (albeit with limited practical success in some areas). *Atlas* involved an alliance between Deutsche Telekom and France Telecom at a time when both operators benefited from legal monopolies. The purpose of the alliance was essentially the same as that in *BT/MCI I*—the creation of a joint venture which could provide international telecommunications services to large corporate customers whose demands could not be met by national telecommunications operators. The parties in this case, however, included two European monopolists in addition to the US company Sprint. The alliance between Deutsche Telekom and France Telecom (Atlas) and the alliance between Atlas and Sprint (Phoenix) were the subject of separate notifications and therefore separate decisions. For all practical purposes, they should be regarded as a single decision.[350]

---

[350] Similar issues arose in the *Unisource/Uniworld* decisions. See *Unisource* [1997] OJ L318/1; and *Uniworld* [1997] OJ L318/24.

13.360   The Commission imposed significantly more extensive conditions on DT/FT than it had on BT/MCI. These conditions sought to prevent any strengthening of DT and FT's existing market positions or favouring of the joint venture. Conditions included:

— early liberalisation of the German and French markets before the joint venture was allowed to operate. The effectiveness of this liberalisation was to be demonstrated by the availability and granting of licences;

— divestiture of Info AG to prevent the creation of a dominant position on the packet-switched data services market;

— non-discrimination obligations in respect of leased lines, access to PSTN/ISDN services and other reserved services;

— prohibitions on cross-subsidisation of the Atlas joint venture;

— obligations to keep separate accounts identifying transfers between France Telecom and Deutsche Telekom on the one hand, and the Atlas entities on the other;

— prohibitions on bundling of France Telecom and Deutsche Telekom services with those of the Atlas entities.

(b) Television

13.361   **(i) Assessment of Potential Competition in Television Markets**   Whether analysed under the Merger Regulation or Articles 81 and 82, agreements between companies with largely complementary geographic activities or limited activities in neighbouring markets are unlikely to give rise to any serious competition problems in television markets.[351] While such agreements are most unlikely to raise serious concerns, there is no clear line as to when they will be found to fall outside of Article 81(1) EC or whether they will be exempted under Article 81(3) EC. Relatively few cases have been examined thus making firm conclusions impossible.

13.362   *Geographic activities*   It seems to be the case that companies with activities in one geographic market will not be considered potential competitors in respect of another geographic market.[352] Given the linguistic and cultural differences between the television services offered in various countries, it appears unlikely that an operator established in one country could, or would, establish itself elsewhere without local expertise. As indicated above, the Commission appears to believe that there are fewer such constraints in the telecommunications sector.

---

[351] See the following clearance decisions under the Merger Regulation: *Kirch/Richemont/Telepiù* (Case IV/M.410) (1994); *Kirch/Richemont/Multichoice/Telepiù* (Case IV/M.584) (1995); *CLT/Disney/Super RTL* (Case IV/M.566) (1995); *Canol+/UFA/MDO* (Case IV/M.655) (1996); *RTL 7* (Case IV/M.878) (1997) (creation of advertising-funded channel in Poland would not affect structure of EEA markets); *Bertelsmann/CLT* (Case IV/M.779) (1996). Under Regulation 17: *TPS* [1999] OJ L90/6 (negative clearance); BDB joint venture referred to in the speech of JF Pons, Deputy Director-General of DGIV, 'The Future of Broadcasting' at the Institute of Economic Affairs on 29 June 1998, <http://europa.eu.int/en/comm/dg04/speech/eight/en/sp98034> (exemption comfort letter); Channel 5 joint venture (negative clearance comfort letter) referred to in *Report on Competition Policy 1996* (Vol XXVI) 153.

[352] See, for example, the statements in *Bertelsmann/CLT* (Case IV/M.779) (1996) to the effect that CLT which was mainly active in other geographic markets could not realistically be considered a potential competitor to Bertelsmann in the German pay TV market.

Activities in Separate Television Markets It is less clear whether companies with activities **13.363**
in one of the television product markets (ie advertising-funded or pay television) in a single
Member State would be considered potential competitors in respect of the other. The *TPS*
decision[353] would suggest that even the most established of advertising-funded television
operators would not be considered potential competitors in respect of pay television in the
same country.[354] 'Télévision par Satellite' (TPS) was a company established for a period of
ten years to operate a digital pay television platform via satellite direct-to-home transmission in France. Its parent companies were three French advertising-funded terrestrial
television broadcasters, namely TF1, the public broadcaster France Télévision (which
broadcasts two channels, France 2 and France 3), and M6, the telecoms operator, France
Télécom, and Suez Lyonnaise des Eaux. The Commission concluded that the creation of
the company itself did not fall within Article 81(1) EC as the parents did not jointly control TPS. Any risk of spill-over effects was excluded as none of the parents were otherwise
active on the French pay television market. On this basis, the Commission granted a
negative clearance.[355]

There are two caveats to this apparently restrictive interpretation of potential competition. **13.364**
First, in the *Eurosport* decision,[356] the Commission prohibited under Regulation 17 the
creation of a joint venture between EBU members and News International's then subsidiary, Sky Television, to operate a pan-European advertising-funded sports TV channel,
Eurosport. However, the reasoning in the decision appears open to question, notably on the
question of the appreciability of the restriction of competition and elimination of competition which was essentially judged by the parties' intent rather than the likely effect of the
agreement. Secondly, the Commission has referred to the possibility that a network of separate agreements between companies with very strong positions in individual geographic
markets could ultimately give rise to concern.[357] However, this situation has not yet arisen.

---

[353] *TPS* [1999] OJ L90/6.

[354] However, it would seem that the BDB joint venture was found to fall within Art 81(1) EC, although
meeting the conditions of Art 81(3) EC. BDB was a joint venture between Carlton and Granada. It was
awarded the franchise to operate digital terrestrial pay TV in the United Kingdom. Both of the parents had
significant interests in the markets for advertising-funded television and programme production in the
United Kingdom. Their interests in pay TV channels were relatively minor. The creation of BDB was notified
to the Commission under Regulation 17, together with a programming supply agreement between Carlton
and Granada on the one hand and BSkyB on the other. The Commission closed the file by means of an administrative letter exempting the BDB agreements. As such, the Commission's legal reasoning was not explained
and it is unclear whether the Commission considered the creation of the joint venture itself to fall within the
ambit of Art 81(1) EC or only certain of the provisions in the notified programme supply agreement. See references in the speech of JF Pons, Deputy Director-General of DGIV, 'The Future of Broadcasting' at the
Institute of Economic Affairs on 29 June 1998, <http://europa.eu.int/en:comm/dg04/speech/eight/en/
sp98034>.

[355] As discussed above, certain clauses in the TPS agreement were found to restrict competition, although
they fulfilled the conditions for exemption under Art 81(3).

[356] *Screensport/EBU Members* [1991] OJ L63/32.

[357] *Report on Competition Policy 1996* (Vol XXVI) at para 82: 'At present, more and more cross-border
alliances are being planned or forged, typified by a pan-European outlook. If all these projects come to
fruition, most major television distributors in Europe may well be linked through networks of alliances. The
Commission will accordingly have to examine these transactions carefully. In particular, it will have to evaluate the alliances' overall impact at European level, going beyond the direct consequences for the specific
national markets.' See also *Bertelsmann/CLT* (Case IV/M.779) (1996), at paras 40–41.

13.365 (ii) **Assessment of Actual Competition in Television Markets** Operations between actual competitors with significant market positions are likely to attract close scrutiny under both Article 81/82 and the Merger Regulation. A number of prohibition decisions under the Merger Regulation in respect of such agreements in television markets have been adopted by the Commission, concerning both advertising-funded and pay television. More recently, however, the Commission has allowed the Sky Italia pay TV merger that would appear to strengthen pre-existing dominance on the Italian pay TV market. The following describes the factors considered by the Commission to be relevant to dominance in the television advertising and pay television markets. The common theme is the importance attached to the effects of vertical integration. The *Premiere* decision is particularly interesting in this respect: the barriers to entry created by the parties' positions at all levels of the value chain—content, transmission networks, and technical services for pay television (set top box)—were relevant to the Commission's finding of dominance in pay television. The Sky Italia decision reiterates the importance of content, imposing significant restrictions on exclusive content acquisition in return for allowing what would otherwise appear to be a highly problematic retail pay TV merger.

(iii) Dominance in Television Advertising Market

13.366 *RTL/Veronica/Endemol*[358] The case concerned the creation of a company, HMG, by RTL, Veronica, and Endemol. The Commission concluded that, de facto, if not *de jure*, HMG would be jointly controlled.[359] The purpose of HMG was to package and supply advertising-funded television and radio programmes broadcast by itself, CLT, Veronica, or others to viewers in the Netherlands and Luxembourg. All of the parent companies were already active in television markets in the Netherlands. RTL operated two Dutch-language advertising-funded television channels, RTL4 and RTL5, directed at the Netherlands. Veronica operated the third such channel in the Netherlands, having recently changed status from a public broadcasting organisation to become a commercial broadcaster. Endemol was an independent producer of Dutch language television programmes. [360]

13.367 The Commission prohibited the operation on the grounds that HMG would have a dominant position on the Dutch market for television advertising and that Endemol's existing dominant position on the market for the independently produced Dutch language television programmes would be strengthened.[361] The case is currently under appeal, *inter alia* on the grounds that the Commission wrongly assessed the competitive constraint to HMG which was posed by the public channels and by the then recent commercial new entrant, SBS.

---

[358] *RTL/Veronica/Endemol* (Case IV/M.553) [1996] OJ L294/14.

[359] This conclusion has since been upheld by the Court of First Instance: Case T-221/95 *Endemol Entertainment Holding v Commission*, judgment of 28 April 1999, not yet published. In other respects, the Court of First Instance did not examine the Commission's conclusions in respect of the television advertising market as Endemol challenged the findings only in respect of the independent television programme production market which is discussed above.

[360] See section D above.

[361] See section D above.

RTL/Veronica/Endemol: measurement of market share   In analysing the effect of the opera- **13.368**
tion on the television advertising market, the Commission stressed that viewing shares were
crucial. The parties' television channels attracted the highest viewing figures. HMG would
thus become the strongest broadcaster in the Netherlands, in particular in view of its link
to Endemol. An econometric study was relied upon which correlated viewing share figures
with advertising market shares. On this basis, the Commission concluded that HMG
would have a market share of more than 60 per cent in the television advertising market.
This was found to be sufficient to establish dominance.

RTL/Veronica/Endemol: barriers to entry   Various strengths of HMG were found to pre- **13.369**
vent public broadcasters or new entrant advertising-funded broadcasters from acting as
competitive constraints. First, the target audiences of two of the HMG channels were complementary, RTL4 and Veronica, and together covered the main target groups for advertisers.
While HMG could coordinate programming to maximise advertising revenues, the regulatory regime prevented public broadcasters from doing the same. HMG would also be
able to negotiate package deals with advertisers as a result of the breadth of its channels' target audiences. Secondly, prior to the operation the third HMG channel, RTL5, had had
the same target audience as Veronica. As a result of the joint venture, HMG would be able
to use RTL5 'as a fighting channel which can directly counteract the programming of competing channels and in particular the programmes of new entrants on the market'.[362] SBS
which was a recent entrant was said to be particularly vulnerable to the use of RTL5 in this
way. Thirdly, the structural link to Endemol further strengthened the position of HMG's
channels. Endemol produced the most popular programmes and HMG was guaranteed
preferential access to the most successful productions made by Endemol. HMG's viewing
shares would therefore remain high.

This combination of factors meant that buyers of television advertising time would not be **13.370**
able to prevent an increase in prices by switching easily between advertising on HMG's and
other broadcasters' channels. Moreover, the combined strength of the parents meant that
'the existence of HMG is in itself dissuasive for the market entry of any potential new-
comer'.[363] The Commission further concluded that even if there was high growth in the
advertising sales markets, the largest part of any growth would be captured by HMG.

RTL/Veronica/Endemol: remedy   The case was considered by the Commission following **13.371**
an Article 22 reference by the Netherlands. The operation was thus implemented prior to
the Commission prohibition decision. Subsequently, Endemol withdrew from HMG and
RTL and Veronica undertook to cease operating RTL5 as a general interest channel and
instead to operate it as a news channel. This operation was re-notified,[364] and, combined
with recent developments in the market, the Commission considered the changes to be
sufficient to restore effective competition in the Dutch television advertising market.
It should be noted that the Commission rejected the parties' undertaking during the first

---

[362] *RTL/Veronica/Endemol* (Case IV/M.553) [1996] OJ L294/14, at para 44.
[363] *RTL/Veronica/Endemol* (Case IV/M.553) [1996] OJ L294/14, at para 86.
[364] Case M.553 [1996] OJ L294/17.

procedure to reduce their influence in RTL5 on the basis that there was too great a risk both that the parties would run down RTL5 prior to divestiture and that no potential buyer would be found.

13.372 **(iv) Dominance in the Pay Television Market**   The Commission has prohibited horizontal agreements between pay television competitors in two cases, *Nordic Satellite Distribution (NSD)*[365] and *Bertelsmann/ Kirch/Premiere* [366] and authorised a merger in *Newscorp/ Telepiù*.[367] In all cases, the horizontal agreements formed part of broader operations involving upstream markets and this was an important element in the Commission's analysis of dominance in pay television.

13.373 *Bertelsmann/Kirch/Premiere*   The facts were as follows. The *Premiere* case involved the concentration of Bertelsmann and Kirch's pay TV interests in Germany and Kirch's pay TV and pay-per-view programme rights contracts in the pay TV channel, Premiere. The parties intended to develop Premiere into a digital pay TV platform which would sell its own and third party channels in packages to viewers either via satellite direct-to-home transmission or via cable networks. As part of the operation, Bertelsmann was to acquire joint control of BetaResearch (together with Deutsche Telekom) and BetaDigital, both of which had until then been subsidiaries of Kirch. BetaResearch and BetaDigital were to supply the technical services necessary for digital pay television.

13.374 The Commission concluded that Premiere would obtain a near monopoly on the pay TV market in Germany/the German-speaking area of Europe. The operation would also result in both BetaDigital and BetaResearch holding dominant positions in respect of the supply of technical services for pay TV. Finally, Deutsche Telekom's existing dominant position in respect of cable networks would be strengthened. The operation was prohibited.

13.375 *Bertelsmann/Kirch/Premiere: measurement of market share*   Market share in pay television is measured by subscriber numbers. On this basis, prior to the operation the Commission found that Premiere already held a dominant position. Kirch's digital pay television service, DF1, was the only other service in Germany.

13.376 *Bertelsmann/Kirch/Premiere: barriers to entry*   The Commission identified barriers to entry on all relevant markets upstream of pay television. In terms of content, the extent of Bertelsmann and Kirch's exclusive pay TV and pay-per-view rights, especially to films and sports events, was found to prevent the emergence of competition to Premiere. The involvement of Deutsche Telekom further secured Premiere's market position: its future entry into pay television could be excluded. Entry by private cable operators was excluded by their lack of access to film and sports rights. Moreover, private cable operators had only local networks and were dependent on Deutsche Telekom for backbone transmission. The Commission considered the possibility of their investing in a second backbone cable network to be economically unfeasible. By virtue of their participation in BetaDigital and BetaResearch, Bertelsmann and Kirch (together with Deutsche Telekom) controlled the set

---

[365] *Nordic Satellite Distribution* (Case IV/M.490) (1995) [1996] OJ L53/20.
[366] *Bertelsmann/Kirch/Premiere* (Case IV/M.993) (1998) [1999] OJ L53/1.
[367] *Sky Italia*.

top box infrastructure which any new entrant in pay television would require as it would be economically impossible for a new entrant to replicate this infrastructure. Moreover, control of technical services would allow the parties to steer competition in pay television to their advantage.

Bertelsmann/Kirch/Premiere: relevance of television advertising market Together, **13.377** Bertelsmann and Kirch had a market share of almost 90 per cent of the television advertising market in Germany. This position could be used to strengthen Premiere's dominance in pay television. While advertising-funded and pay television constituted separate markets, the Commission stated that the more attractive the programming on advertising-funded television, the less interest viewers had in subscribing to pay TV. As Bertelsmann and Kirch had a leading position in both advertising-funded and pay TV and owned the most important programming rights in respect of both, then after the operation they would be in a position to direct the relationship between the two forms of TV. First, they would be able to buy packages of free and pay TV rights. Secondly, Bertelsmann and Kirch were in a position to co-ordinate the programming available on free TV in order to attract subscribers to Premiere. This strategy would be profitable as there was only a very limited possibility for advertisers to switch to public advertising- funded channels as these channels had restrictions on the amount of advertising they could broadcast, and, in particular, could not do so in 'prime-time'. Thus, Bertelsmann and Kirch would lose revenue if they followed such a strategy only if advertisers substituted advertising on television with other media which seemed unlikely.

It is striking that the Commission did not argue, as would have been logical, that the **13.378** parties' interest in Premiere allowed them to secure their position on the television advertising market (nor did it define television advertising as an affected market). Had the Commission done so, it would have amounted to an admission that the operation did not fall under the then Merger Regulation as it led to coordination of Kirch and Bertelsmann's interests in a related market. This seems to be the only convincing explanation for the omission.

Bertelsmann/Kirch/Premiere: remedies rejected The parties offered various undertakings. **13.379** First, making available 25 per cent of Kirch's pay TV film rights to third parties. Secondly, opening the share capital of BetaResearch to third parties and allowing them the same voting rights as the parties. Thirdly, allowing private cable operators to market Premiere's pay TV service (but not its pay-per-view services) in competition with Premiere. However, they would be obliged to package Premiere as the parties determined and would be obliged to give Premiere all relevant subscriber information. Finally, Deutsche Telekom making two digital cable channels available for third party pay television channels until the end of 1999. These were all rejected as insufficient.

Newscorp/Telepiù The decision in the *Bertelsmann* case might appear difficult to recon- **13.380** cile with the conditional approval given to the merger of the Stream and Telepiù pay TV platforms to form Sky Italia. The facts, market structure and competition concerns were relatively similar to the earlier German case, and the Commission maintained its market definitions and competition assessment including an emphasis on vertical integration and content agreements. However, the transaction was cleared subject to a range of remedies focused at restricting the merged entity's activities to digital satellite distribution.

13.381 These remedies[368] included divesting non-digital satellite businesses, granting contract termination rights to content providers, waiving exclusivity over non-satellite platforms for existing contracts, limiting the scope and duration of future film and sports rights contracts including ensuring that exclusivity would in future be limited to satellite transmission only. In addition the merged entity would be obliged to make a wholesale offer of its channels to competing pay TV operators. These remedies were designed to ensure the possibility of market entry, at least by companies wishing to provide pay TV services other than via digital satellite.

> The main thrust and the underlying ultimate objective of any remedy package should be to create the conditions for actual competition to subsist and/or potential competition to emerge. In a case like the one at stake, this aim must be achieved by lowering barriers to entry in the affected markets and through the creation of competitive constraints which effectively operate as a disciplining and restraining factor vis-à-vis the dominant player. The package of remedies proposed by Newscorp has been conceived and constructed with this ultimate objective in mind.[369]

13.382 The decision provides relatively little analysis, however, as to why a merger to quasi-monopoly was permitted subject only to largely behavioural remedies focused on future market entry. After explicitly rejecting the failing firm defence, raised by the parties, the Commission nevertheless accepts that:

> the risk of Stream exiting the market, if it were to materialise, would be a factor to take into account when assessing the present merger. The Commission further considers that an authorisation of the merger subject to appropriate conditions will be more beneficial to consumers than a disruption caused by a potential closure of Stream.[370]

13.383 **(v) Leveraging and Related Markets** The positions of the parties to an operation on a retail television market may be relevant in two respects. First, as has been stated in the introduction their positions on upstream markets can be leveraged to prevent entry to downstream markets. Secondly, as is clear from the *Bertelsmann/Kirch/Premiere* decision, the positions of the parties to an operation on one of the retail television markets on the other such market will be examined. There are two potential points of concern: first, the use of an operation on one market as a vehicle for the coordination of their activities on the other; secondly, the leveraging of market power from one market to another in order to foreclose competition in the latter.

---

[368] Set out at para 225 onwards of the decision.
[369] Decision at para 228.
[370] Decision at para 221.

14

TRANSPORT

Monique Negenman, Maria Jaspers, Rita Wezenbeek and Joos Stragier

A. Introduction

(1) Economic Significance of the Transport Sector

14.01 The transport sector represents a major part of the European economy. In 2000, within the EU the sector as a whole, it generated a turnover of more than EUR650 billion, which corresponded to about 10 per cent of the Community GDP.

14.02 In 2001 about 7 million people were employed in the transport services sector throughout the EU, of whom 57 per cent worked in land transport (road, rail, inland waterways), 3 per cent in sea transport, 6 per cent in air transport, and 34 per cent in supporting and auxiliary transport activities (such as cargo handling, storage and warehousing, travel and transport agencies, tour operators).[1]

14.03 In goods transport, transport by road accounts for 45 per cent of the kilometres travelled, rail for 7.8 per cent, inland waterways for 4 per cent, sea transport for 40.4 per cent, and pipelines for 2.8 per cent. In passenger transport, cars account for 78 per cent of the kilometres travelled, bus and coach transport for 8.6 per cent, rail transport for 6.6 per cent, tram and metro for 1 per cent, and air transport for 5.9 per cent.[2]

14.04 Since 1970, there has been over 75 per cent growth in the transport of goods in the EU and over 110 per cent, growth in passenger transport. There is every reason to believe this growth will continue. It is therefore essential that transport markets are competitive and that, where necessary, the Community's competition rules are enforced effectively.

(2) Regulatory Framework

14.05 For a long time the European Community was not able to implement the common transport policy provided for by the EEC Treaty. It was only in 1985, when the Court of Justice

---

[1] Source: Eurostat, EU energy and transport in figures 2003.
[2] Source: as above.

ruled that the Council had failed to act,[3] that the Member States had to accept that the Community should legislate in this area.

The Treaty of Maastricht later reinforced the institutional and budgetary foundations of transport policy. Unanimity was replaced by qualified majority voting and the European Parliament was allowed to co-legislate through the co-decision procedure. The Treaty also introduced the concept of the trans-European network, which made it possible to develop a plan for transport infrastructure at European level with the help of Community funding. (see below at para 14.257). **14.06**

Transport policy was placed in a separate title of the EEC Treaty (now Articles 70–80 of the EC Treaty, previously Articles 74–84 of the EEC Treaty).[4] The question therefore arose whether the rules for transport contained an exception to the common market rules similar to the exemption for agricultural products. In the *French Seamens'* case[5] the Court ruled that, far from involving a departure from the fundamental rules of the Treaty, the object of the rules relating to the common transport policy was to implement and complement the other treaty rules by means of common action: 'Whilst under Article 84 (2) (now 80 (2)), therefore, sea and air transport as long as the Council has not decided otherwise, is excluded from the rules of Title IV of Part II of the Treaty relating to the common transport policy, it remains, on the same basis as other modes of transport, subject to the general rules of the Treaty'. In the *Nouvelles Frontières* case,[6] the Court held that the competition rules form part of the general rules of the Treaty and that they apply fully in the transport sector. **14.07**

However, the transport sector had been excluded from Regulation 17, which contained general procedural rules in relation to the competition provisions of the Treaty. Regulation 141[7] removed from the scope of Regulation 17: **14.08**

> agreements, decisions and concerted practices in the transport sector which have as their object or effect the fixing of transport rates and conditions, the limitation or control of the supply of transport or the sharing of transport markets nor shall it apply to the abuse of a dominant position, within the meaning Article 86 [now Article 82] of the Treaty, within the transport market.

A separate regulation, Regulation 1002/67,[8] determined that in relation to rail, road, and inland waterways, Regulation 141 only applied until 30 June 1968. The reason for this was that, in 1962, it was possible, as regards transport by rail, road, and inland waterway, 'to envisage the introduction within a foreseeable period of rules on competition'. On 18 July 1968, the Council adopted Regulation 1017/68, applying rules of competition to transport by rail, road, and inland waterways.[9] On 22 December 1986, Regulation 4056/86, laying down rules for the application of Articles 85 and 86 of the Treaty to maritime transport,

---

[3] Case 13/83 *European Parliament v Council of the European Communities* [1985] ECR 1600.
[4] Arts 70–80 EC Treaty were incorporated almost without change in the text of Arts III-236-245 of the Treaty establishing a Convention for Europe that was available on 1 August 2004.
[5] Case 167-73 [1974] ECR 359 (ECJ 4 April 1974).
[6] Joined Cases 209 to 213/84 *Ministère Public v Asjes et al.* [1986] ECR 1425.
[7] Council Regulation 141/62 exempting transport from the application of Council Regulation 17 [1962] OJ L124/2751.
[8] [1967] OJ L306/1.
[9] [1968] OJ L175/1.

was adopted.[10] Finally, on 14 December 1987, Regulation 3975/87, laying down the procedure for the application of the rules on competition to undertakings in the air transport sector, was adopted.[11]

14.09 Consequently, until 1 May 2004, air, maritime, and rail transport services were subject to special procedural rules contained in three sector-specific implementing regulations. Regulation 1/2003 repealed the procedural provisions of these Regulations and brought transport services under the same enforcement rules as all other areas of activity.

14.10 Regulation 1/2003 did, however, maintain the exclusions previously contained in the air and maritime implementing Regulations for air services between the Community and third countries, maritime cabotage, and tramp vessel services.[12] It became clear that the transfer of the existing exclusions to the new Regulation was not to be seen as an acknowledgement that the justifications for the exclusions were still valid when the Council, in February 2004, decided to repeal the exclusion in the air sector.[13]

14.11 In the following paragraphs, the substantive and procedural rules and the development of the application of the competition rules in each sector will be addressed separately.

B. Air Transport

(1) Introduction

14.12 The aim of competition policy in the air transport sector is to ensure that liberalisation of the EU aviation market[14] is not hampered by private or public action, intended to have or having the effect of defending established positions, without generating additional efficiencies to the benefit of consumers. Competition enforcement in aviation as in other network industries, is often complex. The competition assessment has to be made against the background of the specific characteristics of the air transport sector, such as:

— Growing globalisation (ie an extension in scope of global aviation alliances such as *Star, OneWorld, Skyteam*) and a trend towards consolidation of the internal EU aviation market (alliances and mergers).
— Increasing importance of low-cost carriers, putting pressure on traditional network carriers to cut costs, in particular in the field of distribution (ie growing importance of direct internet booking), Computer Reservation Systems (CRSs), airport charges, etc.

---

[10] [1986] OJ L378/4.

[11] [1987] OJ L374/1.

[12] White Paper on modernisation of the rules implementing Arts 85 and 86 of the EC Treaty, [1999] OJ C132/1 and Proposal for a Council Regulation on the implementation of the rules on competition laid down in Arts 81 and 82 of the EC Treaty and amending Regulations (EEC) 1017/68, (EEC) 2988/74, (EEC) 4056/86 and (EEC) 3975/87, [2000] OJ C365/284–96.

[13] See paras 14.84–14.85 below.

[14] The liberalisation of intra-Community air transport was achieved in 1997, following the adoption of three successive packages of Council Regulations. The third package, which is currently being reviewed by the Commission, introduced in particular the Community carrier's licence, freedom of access to the Common market, and freedom for carriers to set their fares and rates. The liberalisation process of international air transport (ie air transport services between the EU and third countries), on the other hand, is still ongoing (see paras 14.84–14.91 below).

— Growing airport congestion problems and environmental challenges (ie impact on allocation of slots, airport charges, etc).

— Vulnerability of the industry (eg security problems).

This chapter discusses competition issues in the aviation sector, which are a policy priority for the Commission.[15] It will address, in particular, the Commission's assessment of co-operation arrangements between airlines, hardcore restrictions and abusive practices, block exemptions, and international aviation issues. Before looking at these issues in further detail, it is useful, however, to give an overview of the relevant competition regulations applicable in the aviation sector and address the important preliminary question of defining the relevant market in aviation cases.

(2) Legal Framework

Since the preliminary ruling of the European Court of Justice in the *Nouvelles Frontiéres* **14.13** case in 1986,[16] there is no doubt that air transport, like any other economic sector, is fully subject to the EC competition rules laid down in Articles 81 and 82 of the Treaty. However, for many years the air transport sector was to remain subject to specific competition implementing rules.[17]

This specific procedural regime for air transport came to an end when Council Regulation **14.14** (EC) 1/2003[18] became applicable on 1 May 2004. Regulation (EC) 1/2003 provides the Commission with efficient tools for fact finding and effective enforcement of the EC competition rules, for example by giving the Commission the direct power to bring infringements to an end and to make commitments legally binding on the undertakings concerned. The Regulation applies to the whole of the air transport sector, including air transport on routes between the EU and third countries. The latter was achieved through the adoption

---

[15] See also J Stragier, 'Outlook of European Commission's competition policy and enforcement priorities in transport' [2002] European Air Law Association Conference Stockholm, published on the Commission's website at <http://europa.eu.int/comm/competition/speeches/text/sp2002_038_en.pdf>. See, on the application of EC competition law in the transport sector, also J Goh, *European Transport Law and Competition* (New York; Chichester/ Wiley, 1997); B van Houtte, 'Community Competition Law in the Air Transport Sector (I)' [1993] Air and Space Law 61–70; B van Houtte, 'Community Competition Law in the Air Transport Sector (II)' [1993] Air and Space Law 275–7; L Ortiz Blanco, B van Houtte, *EC Competition Law in the Transport Sector* (Oxford; New York/ Clarendon Press, 1996); C Pietro, 'Les restrictions de concurrence des companies aériennes' [2004] Receuil Dalloz 2134–8.

[16] Joined Cases 209-213/84 *Nouvelles Frontières* [1986] ECR 1425. Previously, in Case 167/73 *French Seamen* [1974] ECR 359, the European Court of Justice had held that economic sectors could only be excluded from the Treaty by an express provision thereof and had concluded that sea and air transport were, although not part of a common transport policy, nevertheless on the same basis as other modes of transport, subject to the general provisions of the Treaty. It remained, however, disputed by some Member States whether the EC competition rules would qualify as such general provisions. This question was finally answered in the affirmative by the Court in the *Nouvelles Frontières* judgment.

[17] Council Regulation (EEC) 3975/87 of 14 December 1987 laying down the procedure for the application of the rules on competition to undertakings in the air transport sector [1987] OJ L374/1, as last amended by Council Regulation (EC) 411/2004 of 26 February 2004, repealing Regulation (EEC) 3975/87 and amending Regulation (EEC) 3976/87 and Regulation (EC) 1/2003, in connection with air transport between the Community and third countries [2004] OJ L68/1.

[18] Council Regulation (EC) 1/2003 of 16 December 2002 on the implementation of the rules on competition laid down in Arts 81 and 82 of the Treaty [2004] OJ L1/1.

of Council Regulation (EC) 411/2004 on 26 February 2004,[19] which finally empowered the Commission to apply the competition enforcement rules to all air transport, irrespective of the routes affected.[20]

14.15 The last remaining specific competition Regulation in the air transport sector is Council Regulation (EEC) 3976/87,[21] enabling the Commission to adopt block exemptions under Article 81(3) of the Treaty for certain listed activities.[22] On the basis of this Regulation the Commission adopted, in 1993, Regulation (EEC) 1617/93.[23] This Regulation was amended several times and its scope has over the years been reduced to only two activities, passenger tariff consultations for interlining purposes and consultations on slot allocations at airports. Both block exemptions expired on 30 June 2005 and the Commission launched a consultation to examine whether there are reasons to prolong the exemptions, which resulted in the adoption of a new block exemption in 2006. [24]

(3) Market Definition

(a) Air Transport of Passengers

14.16 (i) **Starting Point: O&D Approach**   The starting point of market definition in air transport for the purpose of EC competition law is a so-called 'point-of-origin/point-of-destination' (O&D) or 'city-pair' approach.[25] According to this approach, every combination of point-of-origin and point-of-destination should be considered as a separate market from the customer's point of view. This demand-based approach has been applied by the Commission consistently in aviation cases[26] and has been supported by the European Court of Justice.[27]

---

[19] [2004] OJ L68/1.

[20] Council Regulation (EC) 411/2004 effectively repealed all remaining (substantive) provisions of Council Regulation (EEC) 3975/87, with the exception of Art 6(3), which shall continue to apply to individual exemption decisions adopted pursuant to Art 81(3) of the Treaty until their date of expiry.

[21] Regulation (EEC) 3976/87 of 14 December 1987 on the application of Art 85(3) of the Treaty to certain categories of agreements and concerted practices in the air transport sector [1987] OJ L374/9, as last amended by Council Regulation (EC) 411/2004 of 26 February 2004 [2004] OJ L68/1. The last amendment also empowered the Commission to grant block exemptions in air transport to and from third countries.

[22] Council Regulation (EC) 1/2003 does not modify the existing powers of the Commission to declare Art 81(1) of the Treaty inapplicable to certain categories of agreements.

[23] Commission Regulation (EEC) 1617/93 of 25 June 1993 on the application of Art 85 (3) of the Treaty to certain categories of agreements and concerted practices concerning joint planning and coordination of schedules, joint operations, consultations on passenger and cargo tariffs on scheduled air services and slot allocation at airports [1993] OJ L155/18, as last amended by Commission Regulation (EEC) 1105/2002 [2002] OJ L167/6.

[24] See paras 14.72–14.83 below.

[25] See also B van Houtte, 'Relevant Markets in Air Transport' [1990] CMLR 521–46; P Larouche, 'Relevant Market Definition in Network Industries: Air Transport and Telecommunications' [2001] Journal of Network Industries 407.

[26] See eg Commission decision of 7 April 2004, *Air France/Alitalia*, paras 39–41 (published on the Commission's website at <http://europa.eu.int/comm/competition/antitrust/cases/decisions/38284/en.pdf> (confirmed by the CFI (Case T-300/04—*easyJet Airline Company Ltd/Commission*—not yet reported and Commission decision of 11 February 2004, case M.3280, *Air France/KLM* para 9 (published on the Commission's website at <http://europa.eu.int/comm/competition/mergers/cases/decisions/m3280_en.pdf>). The demand-side approach is also reflected in the Commission Notice on the definition of the relevant market for the purposes of Community competition law [1997] OJ C372/5.

[27] Case 66/86 *Ahmed Saeed Flugreisen* [1989] ECR 803. *Idem* the Court of First Instance in Case 2/93 *Air France/Commission* [1994] ECR 323.

(ii) Type of Passenger Furthermore, in determining the relevant market, the Commission **14.17** usually makes a distinction between different groups of passengers, that is between *time-sensitive passengers* on the one hand and *non-time-sensitive* passengers on the other hand. Generally time-sensitive passengers focus primarily on flexibility. The main criteria on the basis of which they select a carrier are: the number of daily flights offered or the convenience of departure/arrival times; the location of the airport; and the possibility of changing their reservation at short notice. The ticket price is not usually of paramount importance for time-sensitive passengers, although there is evidence that it is becoming more important for these passengers. Non-time-sensitive passengers are generally more price-sensitive; they accept longer journey times and need less flexibility. The distinction between time-sensitive and non-time-sensitive passengers largely coincides with the distinction between business and leisure travellers, but there is no complete overlap. For example, leisure travellers going on a short trip will prefer to keep their travel time as short as possible.[28]

(iii) Possible Alternatives (Substitutability) After having identified the relevant O&D **14.18** routes, the Commission looks at the different transport possibilities which could possibly be considered as substitutable for the services provided by the parties. Naturally this needs to be assessed for each individual case on a route-by-route basis. Usually the Commission carries out a market test with interested third parties, such as the parties' main competitors and customers. Whether the potential alternatives are viable substitutes depends on a multiplicity of factors, such as travel time, frequency of service, service features, price, etc. The Commission has considered the following alternatives:

— Direct services from adjacent airports (*airport substitution*). Passengers beginning or ending their journey in the catchment area of two or more airports have a choice from or to which airport they wish to fly. Whether an adjacent airport would provide a suitable alternative will depend on a number of factors, such as the number of potential passengers living in the overlapping catchment areas, frequency of service, duration of the journey, ticket prices, and the type of passenger (whether time-sensitive or not). For flights within Europe, the radius of an individual airport's catchment area will normally be rather small, given the short travel time, while for long-distance flights the situation might be different.[29]

---

[28] See eg Commission decision of 11 August 1999, case JV.19 *KLM/Alitalia* para 21 (published on the Commission's website at <http://europa.eu.int/comm/competition/mergers/cases/decisions/jv19_en.pdf>); Commission decision of 18 July 2001, *SAS Maersk* para 30 ([2001] OJ L265/15); *Air France/Alitalia* (see n 26 above) paras 41 and 44–46. However, as regards long-haul routes, the distinction between time-sensitive passengers and non-time-sensitive passengers may be less clear, compare eg Commission decision of 12 January 2001 and case M.2041, *United Airlines/US Airways*, para 18 (published on the Commission's website at <http://europa.eu.int/comm/competition/mergers/cases/decisions/m2041_en.pdf>).

[29] For example, in *Air France/Alitalia* (see n 26 above) (paras 48–49) the Commission concluded that the two main airports in Paris (Charles de Gaulle and Orly) were located in the same catchment area as regards the affected routes between France and Italy. The Commission also concluded that all five London airports are sufficiently substitutable for non-time-sensitive passengers on certain routes between the UK and Spain. However, for time-sensitive passengers this was not accepted *prima facie* (Commission decision of 10 March 2003, *British Airways/Iberia* paras 21–24, published on the Commission's website at <http://europa.eu.int/comm/ competition/ antitrust/cases/decisions/38477/en.pdf>). As regards traffic between Austria and Germany, the Commission concluded in its decision of 5 July 2002 in *Austrian Airlines/Lufthansa* (paras 54–55) ([2002] OJ L242/25) that overlapping catchment areas do not play an important role. In *United Airlines/US Airways* para 20 (see n 28 above) the Commission did not accept that, for certain long-haul routes, the Frankfurt catchment area would overlap with other European hubs within a radius as large as 250 km, such as Brussels, Amsterdam, and Munich.

— Services by *low cost carriers*. Traditional full-service carriers face increasing competition from low cost carriers.[30] Typical characteristics of low cost carriers are that they provide (point-to-point) 'no frills' services (eg no in-flight meals service, no premium cabins, limited amount of luggage, etc.) and usually operate from secondary airports (with lower airport charges, but often less accessible). Whether they are considered as viable alternatives to scheduled service providers depends on their specific product. For example, notably for business passengers it will be of importance whether they provide a similar service in terms of flexibility (in terms of number of daily operated flights, convenience of schedules, choice of tickets, etc.) and accessibility (eg whether they also fly from main airports).[31]

— Services by *charter operators*, typically providing services from Northern Europe to leisure destinations, are still generally not considered to be sufficiently substitutable for scheduled flights, in any event not for time-sensitive and flexibility focused travellers. Charter services primarily fly leisure passengers on 'package holidays'; only a minority of seats are normally sold without a package tour. Furthermore, although charter services appear in computer reservation systems (CRSs), the frequency of flights is often insufficient to exercise competitive constraints on traditional scheduled airlines.[32] However, in the *British Airways/Iberia* case, given the apparent year-round availability of charter flights on certain routes between the UK and Spain and the substantial percentage of seat-only charters on those routes, the Commission could not rule out substitutability between scheduled services and charter flights for non-time-sensitive passengers on some of those routes. The issue was however left open.[33]

— *Indirect flights* (in particular one stop services) could in certain circumstances provide a convenient alternative to direct service on an O&D route. This would depend in particular on the duration of the flight, the connection time, flight schedules, and price. In general indirect services are more likely to be substitutable for direct services on long-haul and medium-haul flights.[34] On relatively short routes, where only a relatively small percentage of passengers use indirect flights, these will not provide a suitable alternative.[35]

— *Alternative modes of transport* (eg high speed trains, transport by road). In order to assess whether other means of transport could be suitable alternatives to the air transport services provided by the parties, instead of distance the total travelling time should be taken

---

[30] Initially low cost carriers established themselves in the UK, but they have expanded rapidly into other parts of Europe.

[31] The Commission has not yet concluded that services by low cost carriers are a viable alternative for business passengers. However, in a number of cases the Commission came to the conclusion that services offered by low cost carriers were an alternative for non-time-sensitive passengers. See eg *Air France/Alitalia* (see n 26 above) paras 54–55; *British Airways/Iberia* (see n 29 above) para 28.

[32] See eg *KLM/Alitalia* (see n 28 above) paras 55–56; *British Airways/Iberia* (see n 29 above) paras 29–32; and *Air France/Alitalia* (see n 26 above) para 56.

[33] *British Airways/Iberia* (see n 29 above) paras 29–32.

[34] For example, in *United Airlines/US Airways* (see n 28 above) (paras 13–19) the Commission accepted that certain indirect services effectively competed with the direct services operated by the parties on the transatlantic routes in question. The Commission came to similar conclusions in the *KLM/NorthWest* (Commission Decision of 28 October 2002, see notice in [2002] OJ C264/11); and *Lufthansa/SAS/United Airlines* (Commission Decision of 28 October 2002, see notice in [2002] OJ C264/5) cases.

[35] For example, in *Austrian Airlines/Lufthansa* (see n 29 above) (para 53) the Commission concluded that, on the short-haul routes concerned between Austria and Germany, indirect services did not represent a suitable alternative. The Commission came to the same conclusion with regard to routes between France and Italy in *Air France/Alitalia* (see n 26 above) (para 57).

into account. Generally, for time-sensitive passengers, alternative means of transport may be a viable substitute only where the travel time is not significantly longer than by air. In this regard it is generally considered that, for total travel time by air, one hour should be added to the flight duration at each end of the route for check- in and out, plus the travel time to and from the respective airports.[36] However, for price-sensitive passengers travel time might be less important, so for them the price of the journey should also be taken into account. Where there is no correlation between the price of air transport and other means of transport, it will generally be difficult to conclude that the other means of transport impose competitive constraints on the parties.[37]

(iv) Network Effects   In various aviation cases the Commission has been confronted with **14.19** the question whether the traditional demand-side approach to defining the relevant market is still appropriate. Network carriers, operating a hub-and-spoke system, have argued that network effects (eg competition between airline hubs and between alliances) should be taken into account (more) in defining the relevant market. The Commission acknowledges that, in the business model for network carriers, network competition is relevant from a supply-side perspective.[38] However, in the *United Airlines/US Airways* case,[39] the Commission concluded that network competition was still not sufficient to modify its traditional demand-based approach. First, from the demand side, consumers continue to ask for a transport service between two points. Arguably, if confronted with high prices due to a monopoly on a particular O&D route, a passenger may find little comfort in the fact that air carriers compete worldwide in the development of their respective networks. Furthermore, in *United Airlines/US Airways*, the Commission found that there were no indications that airlines could start services between all city pairs concerned in the short term without incurring significant costs and risks.

The demand-side approach is basically still the approach of the Commission today. This **14.20** approach does not mean that the Commission ignores the existence of networks; in fact, the Commission has in various cases, implicitly considered network competition, for instance accepting, under certain conditions, substitutability of indirect services or direct services on long-haul routes.[40] Network effects also play a role in identifying barriers and remedies.

---

[36] In its decision of 10 December 2003, *British Airways/SN Brussels Airlines* (paras 18–21) (published on the Commission's website at <http://europa.eu.int/comm/competition/antitrust/cases/decisions/38479/en.pdf>), the Commission concluded that the Eurostar provided a sufficient alternative to the direct flights of the parties on the Brussels–London route, for both non-time-sensitive and time-sensitive passengers. In *Air France/Alitalia* (see n 26 above) (paras 58–60) the Commission concluded that road transport was an alternative to the direct flights on some of the affected routes between Italy and France. However, rail transport, due to the total travelling time involved, was not considered a viable alternative.

[37] For example, in *Austrian Airlines/Lufthansa* (see n 29 above) (paras 57–61) the Commission rejected the argument of the parties that transport by road and rail provided competitive constraints on the direct air services provided by the parties on the affected routes between Austria and Germany, given the significantly longer travelling time and the fact that the air travel was twice as expensive as travelling by train or car.

[38] Carriers operating with a different business model, such as low cost operators (providing point-to-point services) and regional carriers, however, generally tend to agree with the O&D approach.

[39] See paras 11–12.

[40] See eg *United Airlines/US Airways* (see n 28 above); *KLM/NorthWest* (see n 34 above); *Lufthansa/SAS/United Airlines* (see n 34 above). Compare also Commission decision of 16 January 1996, *Lufthansa/SAS* para 35 ([1996] OJ L54/28); and *KLM/Alitalia* (see n 28 above) paras 45–46.

In *Air France/KLM*, the Commission, while applying an O&D approach, explicitly recognised that for corporate customers demand is in some cases driven by both network effects and O&D considerations.[41]

(b) Air Transport of Cargo

14.21   In the case of air cargo transport the relevant market is in principle wider than the direct services on the point of origin/point of destination (O&D) route, since, unlike passengers, cargo may be transported with a higher number of stopovers, provided the total travel time and cost remain reasonable. Moreover, from the freight forwarder's point of view, not only is there wider substitution between direct and indirect services, but also wider overlapping catchment areas between airports.

14.22   For intra-European cargo transport the relevant market would be, in principle, Europe-wide, including road transport and, to a limited extent, transport by rail.[42] For intercontinental routes, where at least one of the points of origin or destination is located outside Europe, the catchment area would generally cover continents, at least for those routes where local infrastructure is adequate to allow for onward connections, such as North Atlantic routes.[43] Generally, the nature of the product transported makes no difference, with some exceptions such as perishable goods which require greater frequency of service and a better inter-connectivity and are therefore normally best transported by air.

(c) Distribution of Air Transport

14.23   Air transport services cover not only the provision of air transport services (passenger and cargo services) but also the *distribution* of air transport services, either direct by the carrier itself (eg via Internet sales or via the carrier's web site, as is increasingly the case) or indirect (eg via travel agents and tour operators).

14.24   In the *Virgin/British Airways* case,[44] concerning a complaint by Virgin against British Airways' incentive schemes for UK travel agents, the Commission defined the relevant product market as the market for air travel agency services, which are purchased from travel agents by airlines for the purpose of marketing and distributing their airline tickets. In geographic terms the market was considered to be national, as customers were normally found to book their tickets in their country of residence and relations between travel agents and airlines are established on a country-by-country basis. These conclusions were upheld by the Court of First Instance, which found that the services of air travel agencies represented an economic activity for which (at the time of the decision) airlines could not substitute another form of distribution of their tickets and therefore constituted a market for services distinct from the air transport market.[45]

---

[41] *Air France/KLM* (see n 26 above) paras 10–16 and 130–135.
[42] Eg *Lufthansa/SAS* (see n 40 above) para 33.
[43] *KLM/Alitalia* (see n 28 above) paras 23–25; *Air France/KLM* (see n 26 above) paras 36–37.
[44] Commission decision of 14 July 1999, *Virgin/British Airways* [2000] OJ L30/1.
[45] Case T-219/99 *British Airways/Commission* [2003] ECR-II-05917, paras 89–117. The judgment has been appealed by British Airways (Case C-95/04 *British Airways/Commission*, pending).

(4) Airline Alliances and Mergers

(a) Introduction

One of the main priority areas for the Commission in the transport sector so far has been **14.25** the assessment under the EC competition rules of aviation alliances and mergers.[46] It has dealt with a number of aviation alliances, both intra-Community alliances and alliances between EU carriers and non-EU carriers.[47] In addition, a number of mergers in the aviation sector have been assessed under the EC Merger Regulation.[48] The Commission is expected to remain very active in this area; a number of important alliance cases are pending[49] and new cases are expected in the near future.[50]

The difference between an alliance and a merger depends on the economic and legal speci- **14.26** ficities of the transaction. In short, if the transaction amounts to a concentration within the meaning of the EC Merger Regulation, it should be assessed under that Regulation.[51] If the parties coordinate their competitive conduct but remain independent, their co-operation agreement will be assessed under Regulation (EC) 1/2003. Although the legal framework is therefore different, the assessment of alliances and mergers in the aviation sector is broadly similar in substance. Hereinafter the focus will be on the assessment of alliances (antitrust aspects); however, where useful, for example for market definition issues, reference is also made to merger cases.

Generally the Commission takes a positive approach to alliances in the air transport sector, **14.27** since in most cases they generate benefits for consumers. Competition policy should not

---

[46] See, for the assessment of aviation alliances under competition law, also: European Competition Authorities, 'Report of the ECA Traffic Working Group, Mergers and Alliances in civil aviation' [2004] available at the Commission's website at <http://europa.eu.int/comm/competition/publications/eca/report_air_traffic.pdf>; R Miller, 'International Airline Alliances' [1998] Air and Space Law 125–32; T Soames and G Goeteyn, 'Airline Mergers and Alliances: EU Regulatory Issues' [2001] European Air Law Association Conference, Athens; J Stragier, 'Airline Alliances and mergers—the emerging Commission policy' [2001] European Air Law Association, published on the Commission's website at <http://europa.eu.int/comm/competition/ speeches/text/sp2001_040_en.pdf>; O Stehmann and J Raya Aguado, 'The Air France–KLM Merger: A First Step Towards the Consolidation of the European Aviation Industry' [2005] ECLR 258–71.
[47] The assessment under EC competition law of intra-Community alliances on the one hand and international alliances (in so far as these alliances affect trade between Member States) on the other hand is practically the same, though there are some differences in nuance (eg on the definition of the relevant market). International aviation alliances that have been assessed so far by the Commission are mainly alliances between EU and US carriers (see eg *KLM/NorthWest, Lufthansa/SAS/United Airlines* (see n 34 above)).
[48] Eg *KLM/Alitalia* (see n 28 above); *United Airlines/US Airways* (see n 28 above); and, more recently, *Air France/KLM* (see n 26 above).
[49] For example, in 2003 Austrian Airlines and SAS notified a bilateral co-operation agreement to the Commission which is currently being examined. The Commission is also examining the international aspects of *Skyteam* alliance (that is, affected routes between the EU and third countries—the intra-Community aspects of the Sky team agreements, in particular the France–Italy bundle of routes, have been dealt with in the *Air France/Alitalia* case, resulting in a formal exemption decision with conditions, adopted on 7 April 2004 (see n 26 above)).
[50] Eg the *Open Skies* judgments of the European Court of Justice (see paras 14.89–14.90 below) are likely to trigger increased merger activity between EU carriers, notably between network carriers and smaller feeder carriers.
[51] In the case of a joint venture this will be the case if it performs, on a lasting basis, all the functions of an autonomous entity.

stand in the way of pro-competitive restructuring and co-operation between carriers that lead to more efficient output. Furthermore, competition policy should not give preference to any specific institutional design or airline size, but should ensure that consolidation is not at the expense of competition and consumer welfare. The core aim is to identify the remaining competitive constraints on the alliance partners. Naturally, this is a case-by-case assessment, but some general principles have emerged from the Commission's practice so far.[52]

(b) Assessment under Article 81(1) of the Treaty

14.28 Alliances between air carriers are generally caught by the prohibition of Article 81(1) of the Treaty, because of their close co-operation and integration on key competition parameters.[53] Although the provisions of alliance agreements vary, the alliance partners usually agree to coordinate prices, frequency, schedules, and sales strategies. Furthermore, they often share capacity, revenues, and sensitive information and pool frequent flyer programmes. Sometimes even profits are shared.

14.29 Generally there are two types of affected market:

— *Overlap routes:* O&D routes on which two or more parties to the alliance operated competitive services, either direct-direct services and/or (on long-haul routes) direct-indirect or indirect-indirect services. The alliance will restrict actual competition between the alliance partners on these routes, since they will stop competing with each other;[54] and

— *Non-overlap routes:* O&D routes on which at least one of the alliance parties operated a service and the other(s) could be considered as a potential entrant. In order to determine whether a carrier would be a potential entrant on a particular route, the Commission applies an economic-based approach, based on a set of objective criteria that make it possible to determine whether entry on this route would be commercially realistic for the non-operating party.[55] This is generally considered to be the case if the route in question is linked to one of its hubs or if the route is sufficiently large and frequented by local traffic to allow market entry on a point-by-point basis, while taking into account the operational requirements and benchmarks of the respective business strategy.[56]

---

[52] Compare also the report of the ECA (see n 46 above).

[53] Air transport services have a geographical dimension in themselves and an agreement between carriers on such services covering a substantial part of the Community is liable to affect trade between the Member States. Compare Commission Notice Guidelines on the effect of trade concept contained in Arts 81 and 82 of the Treaty [2004] OJ C101/81.

[54] In most cases it will be relatively easy to determine whether the parties, prior to the alliance, competed with each other on a particular route. However, where prior to the alliance the parties were already involved in some sort of co-operation agreements, for example a code-sharing agreement, it will depend on the specific provisions in that agreement and their behaviour in practice whether the parties could be said to be actual competitors before the alliance.

[55] Compare Joined Cases T-374, 375, 384, 388/94 *European Night Services/Commission* [1998] ECR II-3141, para 137.

[56] Relevant elements in this regard could be, for example, whether the carrier in question operates routes of similar size/characteristics, whether it has already a local market presence, and whether it operates appropriate aircraft. See eg *Air France/Alitalia* (see n 26 above) para 111.

(c) Assessment under Article 81(3) of the Treaty

(i) General   Article 81(3) of the Treaty provides that Article 81(1) may be declared inap- **14.30**
plicable if four cumulative conditions are fulfilled.[57] The provision provides for a balancing
of anti-competitive and pro-competitive effects, in principle market by market. However,
where affected consumers are substantially the same, balancing across markets may be
undertaken.[58] Particularly in the case of network industries, there could be spillover effects
of benefits from one market to another. For example, the creation of new or enhanced connections is also likely to have an effect on the overall economy of hub-to-hub operations.

(ii) Efficiencies   The first condition requires that the alliance should achieve economic **14.31**
benefits, such as cost efficiencies and/or qualitative efficiencies. In order to enable the
Commission to assess whether this condition is fulfilled, carriers should substantiate and
quantify in concrete terms, as far as is reasonably possible, the benefits achieved by their
alliance agreement, and how and when these benefits will be achieved.

In the aviation alliance cases that the Commission has dealt with so far, this condition was gen- **14.32**
erally considered to be fulfilled. Fully fledged alliances are likely to contribute to improving the
production and distribution of air transport services and to promote technical and economic
progress. Possible efficiencies could, for example, include a more extensive network in terms of
increased numbers of flights on routes served, improved connectivity, new online connections,
and better support and coverage on thin routes (network efficiencies). One could also think of
possible cost savings, due to a higher load factor, better planning of frequencies, more efficient
use of resources, etc. The alliance could also result in efficiencies in terms of improved organisation of sales systems and better organisation of ground-handling services.

Efficiencies are likely to occur, in particular, where the parties have largely complementary **14.33**
networks (and the effects of synergies are thus likely), where the number of connecting passengers is relatively high (with a high potential for improved connectivity), and where there
is concrete proof of new or improved airline services (eg new services have been and/or will
be created by the parties in the near future).[59]

(iii) Consumer Benefits   Pursuant to the second condition of Article 81(3) of the Treaty, **14.34**
consumers must receive a fair share of the identified efficiencies. For example, consumers
could benefit from increased frequencies and/or additional seats, more convenient scheduling, better spread of flights during the day, resulting in a wider choice of destinations and
connections, shorter waiting times, seamless travel, improved service in terms of quality,
reciprocal lounge products, benefits derived from pooling of frequent flyer programmes,
and possibly reduced fares as a result of cost efficiencies.

---

[57] The agreements or concerted practices concerned must contribute to improving the production or distribution of goods or to promoting technical or economic progress, while allowing consumers a fair share of
the resulting benefit. The restrictions of competition imposed by these agreements, however, should be indispensable to the attainment of these objectives and they should not lead to the elimination of competition in
respect of a substantial part of the products in question.

[58] Compare Commission Notice Guidelines on the application of Art 81(3) of the Treaty [2004] OJ
C101/97 para 43.

[59] See eg *British Airways/SN Brussels Airlines* (see n 36 above) paras 55–56; *British Airways/Iberia* (see n 29 above)
para 45; *Austrian Airlines/Lufthansa* (see n 29 above) para 86; and *Air France/Alitalia* (see n 26 above) para 132.

14.35 It cannot just be assumed that, if efficiencies have been established, these will also be passed on to consumers. The alliance partners must provide concrete evidence that this has occurred. Furthermore, the efficiencies must at least compensate consumers for the likely negative effects of the restrictions on competition. While connecting passengers are generally likely to receive a fair share of the benefits (notably in terms of improved connectivity), this might be less obvious for point-to-point (local) passengers.[60] The latter may benefit from increased and better-scheduled frequencies. However, in some alliance cases, the Commission has considered that the parties have no incentive to pass on cost savings and synergies to point-to-point passengers, in instances where the alliance threatens to eliminate competition.[61]

14.36 (iv) **Indispensability**   The restrictions of competition in the alliance agreement must be reasonably necessary to produce the identified efficiencies. In short, the test is whether the envisaged cost savings and qualitative benefits could only materialise if the parties enter into a close co-operation regarding their respective business strategies. Furthermore, the Commission must assess whether each individual restriction is indispensable, in other words whether the alliance is more efficient with the restriction concerned than without.

14.37 In previous cases, the Commission usually considered this condition had been fulfilled. Once efficiencies have been established in terms of an improved range of services as a result of joint route planning and network planning, it is usually accepted that these can only be achieved by a fully fledged co-operation between the carriers concerned in respect of, for instance, pricing, scheduling, and capacity. This is true in particular for routes linking hubs used by the parties. It is generally believed that the growing demand for networks can only be met through the implementation of multi-hub systems.

14.38 However, the restrictions of competition in the alliance agreement must not go beyond what is necessary. In previous cases the Commission has accepted that joint pricing by the alliance partners is necessary in order to offer seamless unified services to customers and that profit sharing is needed to achieve cost savings and synergies. The Commission also accepts in principle that cost sharing between the carriers concerned is necessary, to ensure that the parties will equally share the burdens of the alliance. Limitations on the parties' freedom to operate additional routes and frequencies are also generally held to be indispensable for the good functioning of an aviation alliance agreement.[62]

14.39 (v) **No Elimination of Competition**   In order to assess whether the alliance threatens to eliminate competition, each O&D route where appreciable restrictions of competition have been identified must be examined. By entering into the alliance the parties have ensured that there is no longer any (actual or potential) competition between them on the routes covered by the alliance. The degree of competition between the parties and third parties must therefore be examined, also taking into account possible commitments that have been offered by the parties. This examination covers essentially two elements.

14.40 First, the level of *actual competition* remaining on each of the affected routes. To that end the combined market position of the parties after the alliance as well as the number and

---

[60] See eg *Air France/Alitalia* (see n 26 above) paras 133–137.
[61] See eg *Air France/Alitalia* (see n 26 above) para 137.
[62] See eg *Air France/Alitalia* (see n 26 above) paras 138–141.

strength of their competitors should be assessed. Generally, market shares in aviation are measured in terms of (point-to-point) O&D passenger numbers (where appropriate distinguishing between time-sensitive and non-time-sensitive passengers). In addition, operated frequencies (eg number of flights per week) might also give an indication of the parties' market position. Airline alliances, in particular on the overlap routes, often lead to relatively high combined market shares. That in itself would not, however, be sufficient to conclude that competition is eliminated.

Therefore, a second element to be taken into account is the likelihood of competitive con- **14.41**
straints on the alliance partners resulting from *potential competition*. To that end the
Commission examines the existence of possible entry barriers that could prevent existing
competitors from increasing their services or impede new entrants from starting services on
the routes concerned. Entry barriers could have different forms. They could include structural factors, such as the lack of availability of commercially usable slots at congested airports,[63] existing 'grandfather rights',[64] and ground-handling infrastructure. Entry barriers
may also result from the reinforcement of the parties' position and market power in the relevant market as a result of the alliance, for example in terms of increased frequencies, network effects resulting from pooling of the parties' frequent flyer programmes, joint travel
agency incentives, corporate discount schemes, improved connectivity, hub and spoke system, etc. One could also think of 'behavioural' barriers, such as (potentially) exclusionary
practices like predatory pricing and frequency increases aimed purely at keeping competitors out. Furthermore, although liberalisation has removed regulatory barriers to entry into
the EU aviation market, regulatory barriers could still exist in respect of routes to and from
the EU (international aviation) where the liberalisation process is still ongoing.[65]

In general, entry barriers are high on markets where parties operate a hub airport at both ends of **14.42**
the route. On such routes the ability of new entrants to attract connecting traffic is essential.[66]

(d) Commitments

(i) **General** Commitments essentially aim at removing or substantially reducing exist- **14.43**
ing entry barriers for competitors, to ensure that affected consumers obtain a fair share of
the benefits resulting from the co-operation. Commitments must be unambiguous and
self-executing, that is, their implementation must not be dependent on any action by third
parties who are not bound by corresponding commitments. Commitments must respect
the principle of proportionality, ie they should not go beyond what is necessary to solve the
competition concerns. This also implies that there should be a causal link between the competition concerns identified and the commitments offered. Furthermore, commitments
must be effective, and must take into account the significance of the competition concerns.[67]

---

[63] A new entrant would need to operate a sufficient number of frequencies at commercially viable slots in order to also attract time-sensitive passengers.

[64] Grandfather rights entitle a carrier to claim the same slot in the next scheduling period which it had been operating in the previous equivalent period. See para 14.80 below.

[65] An example of such a regulatory barrier is price control on indirect services (so-called 6th freedom services); see para 14.56 below.

[66] See eg *Air France/KLM* (see n 26 above), para 69.

[67] Prior to 1 May 2004 the Commission could exempt the alliance under Art 81(3) of the Treaty subject to certain conditions and obligations. Under Art 9 of Regulation (EC) 1/2003, the Commission can conclude cases by means of a so-called commitment decision, in which the commitments offered by the undertaking are rendered binding on it. Such a decision also concludes that there are no longer grounds for action by the Commission.

Commitments also raise monitoring issues. In merger cases, a Monitoring Trustee is usually nominated to ensure effective implementation of the undertakings given.[68]

14.44 There are various types of commitments. Whether they are appropriate to solve the identified competition problems can only be assessed on a case-by-case basis. Usually the parties propose a package of commitments, which may be further refined following discussions with the Commission and comments from third parties following a market test. Examples from previous Commission cases include the following types of commitments.

14.45 **(ii) Slots** In order to remedy the slot shortage at congested airports, where potential entrants would not have been able to obtain take-off and landing slots through the normal slot allocation procedure, the parties are required to make available to competitors slots aimed at supporting new or additional services. The number of slots to be surrendered is normally set on the basis of a certain number of new daily/weekly round trips. The number must be sufficient to impose effective competitive constraints on the parties. Slot remedies normally include specifications on timing, turn-around times, and slots at peak times. Slots should be made available without charge.

14.46 In past decisions the Commission in principle accepted selection by the parties of the carriers to whom the slots were to be allocated. However, in more recent decisions, in order to ensure that slots are given to carriers that offer the most effective competitive constraints, the Commission has imposed further requirements relating to the selection of eligible recipients of slots. For example, in *Air France/Alitalia* the Commission stipulated that the slots should be made available on a preferential basis to the competitor operating the most frequencies on the route, on the basis that it is more effective to add frequencies to an existing service than to start a new service.[69] In *Air France/KLM* the Commission required that slots be allocated, preferably in block, to a single new entrant. For the important city pair Paris–Amsterdam it also stipulated that, if no third party applied for any slots within a certain time period, a new entrant should be granted so-called grandfather rights, once it had operated a service on a particular route for a certain period of time.[70] The purpose of this remedy was to offer an additional incentive for potential entrants; obtaining grandfather rights with permission to use such slots freely after a certain length of time reduces the commercial risk of entering a new route.

14.47 The principle of proportionality implies that the parties are free to choose at which airport to surrender slots, provided that this is sufficient to solve the identified competition problems. However, the commitments must also be effective and, in certain circumstances the choice of the parties as to the airport at which they wish to offer slots to new entrants may be restricted, for example if potential entrants can demonstrate that, due to cost differences in their existing operations, they can only operate from a specific airport.[71] Furthermore, from a user-perspective, the principle of proportionality implies that slots could normally only be used for the purpose of operating on the routes in respect of which they were made available.

---

[68] Such a trustee is not normally nominated in alliance cases assessed under Art 81 of the Treaty.
[69] *Air France/Alitalia* (see n 26 above) paras 164–169.
[70] *Air France/KLM* (see n 26 above) para 158.
[71] See, for example, *Air France/Alitalia* (see n 26 above) paras 168–169.

In Commission decisions under Article 81(3) of the Treaty, the maximum length of time **14.48** for which slots were made available was the same as the length of the exemption. Since a merger is not limited in time, in *Air France/KLM* slot undertakings are, in principle, unlimited as well. In addition, with a view to addressing the problem of hub dominance, a structural element was introduced. Eventually slots will not be returned to the merged entity but to the slot coordinator.

(iii) Frequencies A commitment from the parties to freeze or even to reduce their fre- **14.49** quencies aims at preventing the parties from increasing frequencies with the sole purpose of making new entry difficult. From the point of view of competition policy, the imposition of such commitments on carriers, in particular an imposed frequency reduction, should be considered with some caution. The positive effects on competition in terms of facilitating new entry should be weighed against possible negative effects on competition in terms of limiting the commercial freedom of the parties and notably impeding their response to market changes. It should also be borne in mind that the Commission could, in appropriate cases, open a proceeding under Article 82 of the Treaty, if carriers were to decide on increasing their frequencies with the sole purpose of eliminating competition. In any event, in light of the proportionality principle, the duration of any freeze or reduction in frequency should not be longer than necessary to solve the competition problems.[72]

(iv) Interlining Agreements An interline agreement with the alliance partners would **14.50** allow the new entrant to combine its services with those of the incumbents. Interlining is a widespread industry practice that provides carriers with access to routes which they do not serve, beyond the scope of individual alliances. It enables passengers to purchase a single ticket to travel on two or more airlines involving multiple sectors across each carrier's network. Interlining is considered very important for small and medium-size carriers, in particular to attract time-sensitive passengers who require flexible and seamless travel. In more recent cases (eg *Austrian Airlines/Lufthansa*) the Commission has imposed on the parties an obligation to interline, not just on the affected routes but also for travel within and/or beyond the two countries concerned. Furthermore, rather than requiring interlining 'on industry standard' terms, the commitments specified the conditions under which the interlining should occur, in particular in respect of pricing.[73]

(v) Block-space Agreements The parties could also be required to commit themselves to **14.51** conclude so-called block-space agreements with new entrants. Under a block-space agreement the new entrant (the marketing carrier) could sell a certain number or percentage of

---

[72] This should be assessed on a case-by-case basis. Eg in *Air France/KLM* (see n 26 above) (para 157) a frequency freeze was imposed for a period of 6 IATA seasons. In *Air France/Alitalia* (see n 26 above) (para 173) a frequency freeze was imposed for at least two full consecutive IATA seasons from the moment a new entrant received slots from the parties. However, in *Austrian Airlines/Lufthansa* (see n 29 above) (para 105) the Commission considered it necessary, in view of the economic weight of the parties and their market position on the routes concerned, that they should freeze their frequencies for a period of two years. So far, only in *KLM/Alitalia* (see n 26 above) (para 69) has the Commission imposed an obligation to reduce frequencies.

[73] *Austrian Airlines/Lufthansa* (see n 29 above) para 112. Notably, the parties committed themselves to enter into a special pro rata agreement (dividing the revenues generated by interline tickets) with a potential new entrant, on the same conditions as those that applied to the parties' alliance partners. A similar undertaking was offered by the parties in *Air France/KLM* (see n 26 above) (para 157).

reserved seats on flights of the incumbent (the operating carrier). Such an agreement would allow the new entrant to offer customers, notably time-sensitive passengers, greater flexibility as regards outward and return flights. Under a block-space agreement, the commercial risk lies with the marketing carrier. This remedy was applied for the first time in the *KLM/Alitalia* case. Further conditions were imposed in more recent cases, such as *Austrian Airlines/Lufthansa*. [74]

14.52 **(vi) Inter-modal Agreements** Furthermore, in some cases an obligation on the parties to enter into inter-modal agreements, for instance with railway companies, has been imposed in order to ensure greater choice and better multi-modal transport services for consumers. By combining air and rail travel, travellers could benefit from greater frequency and flexibility. Rail companies could start competing for certain time-sensitive passengers who may wish to benefit from attractive conditions in the inter-modal agreement. For example, by waiving restrictions normally attached to promotional air tickets, such as a minimum stay before the return trip can be undertaken, travellers could benefit from the promotional air fare on one leg of the journey while choosing the rail company for the second leg.[75]

14.53 **(vii) Frequent Flyer Programmes** A Frequent Flyer Programme (FFP) is a marketing tool that can be used by a carrier to attract business traffic and to develop customer loyalty. This is especially true for a hub carrier; because of its large network at the hub, the FFP allows business travellers in particular to collect more points and to redeem those points for a wider number of destinations. Since, in addition, the business traveller is usually not paying for the ticket, but is benefiting from the FFP free flight, it will be difficult for a new entrant without a competitive FFP or without a developed network at the hub in question to attract business customers to its flights. Pooling of FFPs by different carriers will make this even more difficult. Access to the FFP of the co-operating parties will therefore be important, in particular, for small and medium carriers that have networks that are too small to make such schemes attractive. In a number of aviation alliance and merger cases the Commission therefore imposed on the parties an obligation to offer to new entrants who do not already participate in a FFP the possibility of participating in their FFP.[76]

14.54 **(viii) Price Commitments** An innovative type of remedy was imposed in the *Austrian Airlines/Lufthansa* case, where the Commission introduced a so-called price reduction mechanism, according to which the parties, if they reduce prices on a route where they face competition, must apply an equivalent price reduction on routes where they still enjoy a monopoly, allowing consumers to enjoy the benefit of lower fares on these other routes as well. Furthermore, such a mechanism would make predatory pricing more costly. A similar

---

[74] See eg *Austrian Airlines/Lufthansa* (see n 29 above) para 105; and *Air France/KLM* (see n 26 above) para 157. A block-space agreement should be distinguished from a so-called free-flow code sharing agreement, where there is no pre-determined capacity attributed to the marketing carrier. Under a free-flow agreement the operating carrier controls the inventory and the inventory risk remains with him. It is generally recognised that competition is fiercer under block-space agreements than under free-flow code sharing.

[75] See eg *Austrian Airlines/Lufthansa* (see n 29 above) para 113; *Air France/Alitalia* (see n 26 above) para 172; *Air France/KLM* (see n 26 above) para 165.

[76] See eg *Lufthansa/SAS* (see n 40 above) para 105; *KLM/Alitalia* (see n 28 above) paras 66–67; *Lufthansa/SAS/United Airlines* (see n 34 above); *Air France/KLM* (see n 26 above) para 157.

remedy was imposed in *Air France/KLM*.[77] However, in view of the risk that the competition authority may be perceived as a price regulator, some caution may be required in imposing such conditions on fares.

(ix) Behavioural Commitments   In some cases the Commission has obliged the parties **14.55** to refrain from abusive behaviour, such as applying loyalty remuneration schemes to travel agents or to corporate customers.[78] The value of such remedies is arguable. Apart from the fact that behavioural remedies are difficult to monitor and that therefore structural remedies should be preferred, where possible,[79] it goes without saying that such remedies must be without prejudice to the application of Article 81 and Article 82 of the Treaty to the use of such loyalty schemes.

(x) 'Regulatory' Commitments   Although EU air transport has been liberalised, inter- **14.56** national aviation is still regulated by a web of bilateral air service agreements,[80] from which specific regulatory barriers may flow, making it difficult for new entrants to compete with the parties on routes between the EU and third countries. For example, in the course of some of its investigations the Commission discovered that some Member States require published fares for indirect services on long-haul routes to be filed with them and they may prohibit these so-called indirect service providers from undercutting fares for direct services offered on the same route by national designated carriers (so-called 6th freedom price-leadership restrictions).[81] Naturally, such regulatory barriers remove effective competition from indirect services on the routes concerned.

The lack of availability of traffic rights (5th freedom rights)[82] may also amount to a regula- **14.57** tory barrier. Some Member States impose restrictions on traffic rights, which may make it difficult for carriers from third countries to enter the routes concerned.

In a number of cases dealt with by the Commission to date, the Member States concerned **14.58** have agreed, where appropriate, to grant traffic rights and not to impose other restrictions on price and capacity, thus facilitating new entry on the routes in question.[83] The Commission has taken these agreements into account when deciding on the compatibility of the alliances and mergers concerned under EC competition law.

(xi) Effectiveness of Commitments   Commitments should aim at fully removing all com- **14.59** petition concerns. The effectiveness of remedies which have been imposed is best assessed

---

[77] See *Air France/KLM* (see n 26 above) (para 158 sub g), para 166. Compare *Austrian Airlines/Lufthansa* (see n 29 above) para 105.

[78] See eg *KLM/Alitalia* (see n 28 above).

[79] Compare Commission Notice on remedies acceptable under Council Regulation (EEC) 4064/89 and under Commission Regulation (EC) 447/98 [2001] OJ C68/3.

[80] See paras 14.86–14.91 below.

[81] For example, the competent German authorities could prohibit KLM from offering an indirect flight from Bonn to New York via Amsterdam at a lower price than the direct flight offered by Lufthansa from Bonn to New York. In the Netherlands and France the national authorities may impose similar restrictions on 6th freedom price leadership.

[82] 5th freedom is carriage between two foreign countries on a route with origin/destination in its home country, eg Singapore Airlines operating Amsterdam–New York with origin in Singapore.

[83] See eg *Lufthansa/SAS/United Airlines* (see n 34 above); *Air France/KLM* (see n 26 above) paras 103–104, 155, and 163.

by the extent to which the remedies have indeed resulted in new entrants entering the market. In the early aviation alliance cases examined by the Commission the imposed remedies did not always lead to real market entrance and the effects have been more indirect. In more recent cases the Commission has adjusted its remedy approach towards making actual entry more likely. For example, the exemption decision in the *Austrian Airlines/Lufthansa* case was granted, because market entry by a new competitor on certain key routes did actually transpire. In cases like *Air France/Alitalia* and *Air France/KLM*, the Commission imposed specific conditions, for instance on the slot commitments, to make the remedies as effective as possible by introducing certain priority rules. As a result, in these cases commitments have been actually taken up by existing competitors and/or new entrants. Travellers have benefited from this additional choice and in many cases from lower prices.

(5) Hardcore Restrictions and Abuses

(a) Market Sharing

14.60 In the *SAS/Maersk* case, the Commission fined Scandinavian airlines SAS and Maersk Air for having concluded a secret market sharing agreement.[84] Documents found during on-site inspections showed that both carriers had agreed to an overall non-compete clause, according to which Maersk Air would not launch new international routes from Copenhagen without approval from SAS. Conversely, the parties had agreed that SAS would not operate on Maersk Air's routes out of Jutland, where Denmark's second airport is located. In addition to the overall non-compete clause, SAS and Maersk Air had agreed on entry into and withdrawal from a number of specific routes, providing the other party essentially with a monopoly.

14.61 Clearly, such market sharing arrangements are to be considered as hardcore restrictions of competition, detrimental to passengers. By their very nature, market sharing agreements have the object of restricting competition and are therefore caught by Article 81(1) of the Treaty. Furthermore, the arrangements had the effect of significantly restricting actual and potential competition on the routes concerned, to the detriment of passengers.

(b) Exclusionary Practices

14.62 **(i) Travel Agency Incentive Schemes**   Travel agency incentive schemes may amount to market foreclosure. Case law shows that a fidelity rebate, ie a rebate based not on economically justified considerations (eg cost savings) but on loyalty, if granted by a dominant undertaking, constitutes an exclusionary abuse under Article 82 of the Treaty. In the *Virgin/ British Airways* decision,[85] the Commission made clear that travel agency incentive schemes that are loyalty discount driven and used by a dominant carrier create market entry barriers. In the case concerned, British Airways paid extra commissions to travel agents dependent upon the travel agents meeting or exceeding their previous year's sales of British Airways' tickets. In order to qualify for the payment of an extra commission, travel agents had to increase their sales of British Airways' tickets year after year. The Court of First Instance[86]

---

[84] Commission Decision of 18 July 2001, *SAS/Maersk*, [2001] OJ L265/15. The appeal by SAS was dismissed by the Court of First Instance (Case T-241/01 *SAS/Commission* [2005] not yet reported).

[85] See n 44 above.

[86] Case T-219/99 *British Airways/Commission* [2003] II- 05917. The CFI judgment has been appealed by British Airways (Case C-95/04 *British Airways/Commission*, pending).

confirmed the Commission's finding that such a performance scheme had a fidelity-building effect and discouraged travel agents from selling air transport services to other airlines and consequently restricted access of competitors of British Airways to the UK market for travel agency services.[87] Following the Commission's decision, British Airways adopted a new scheme consisting essentially of a flat rate booking fee and, in addition, sales and marketing agreements that reward travel agents for meeting certain quality targets.

In order to provide guidance for other airlines in a similar situation, the Commission set out, in a press release, certain principles concerning travel agents' commissions.[88] The travel agency incentive schemes of a number of other carriers have been scrutinised by the Commission on the basis of these principles. In several cases the Commission's investigation led to a substantial revision or even complete replacement of existing incentive schemes, with a view to bringing them into conformity with EU competition rules.[89]   **14.63**

(ii) **Corporate Discount Schemes**   Anti-competitive effects can also result from discount schemes granted to large business customers, which are a widespread practice in the aviation industry. Corporate discount schemes, under certain circumstances, may constitute a barrier to entry on certain routes. For example, the presence of a network carrier, which has the potential to grant corporate discounts across its whole network, could make it difficult for point-to-point carriers or for carriers with less complete networks to enter or stay in the market. The existence of corporate deals is therefore an element to take into account when assessing a carrier's or an alliance's position in the relevant market.   **14.64**

Corporate deals might also amount to an infringement of Article 82 of the Treaty. For example, by tying corporate discounts on one route, where it is dominant, to market share targets on other routes where it faces competition, a dominant carrier could abuse its dominant position. Corporate deals could also, under certain circumstances, amount to fidelity or loyalty rebates, notably when no evidence of cost savings in the provision of large volumes of service to business customers could be provided.   **14.65**

The Commission has not taken any formal decision on corporate deals in the aviation sector under Article 82 of the Treaty so far,[90] although it has stated in the context of some alliance cases, as a principle, that corporate deals may not be designed to reward loyalty directly or indirectly.[91]   **14.66**

---

[87] It also upheld the Commission's decision that British Airways had abused its dominant position by discriminating between travel agents since, under British Airways' incentive schemes, two travel agents handling the same number of British Airways tickets and providing the same level of service to British Airways received a different commission rate if their sales of British Airways tickets had been different in the previous year.

[88] Annex to the Commission's press release IP/99/504 of 14 July 1999.

[89] See, for further details, Report on Competition Policy 2003 (Vol XXXIII) at para 132 and Competition Policy Newsletter Number 2 of 2003, pp 65–7.

[90] In *Virgin/British Airways* (see n 44 above), the complainant, Virgin, requested that the Commission also take action against British Airways' discount schemes for corporate customers, arguing that they could be assimilated as fidelity/loyalty rebates. The Commission's decision, however, does not cover British Airways' arrangements with corporate customers. Apparently, the possibility that there were some cost savings for British Airways (*inter alia* in the marketing and distribution of tickets) in the provision of large volumes of service to corporate customers could not be excluded, so the discounts could not be considered merely as payments for loyalty.

[91] eg in *KLM/Alitalia* (see n 28 above) (para 69) the parties undertook to place limits on the type of commission schemes that KLM and Alitalia are able to operate for travel agents and large corporate customers.

14.67   (iii) **Frequent Flyer Programmes**   Under certain circumstances Frequent Flyer Programmes (FFPs) applied by carriers could amount to an exclusionary practice.[92] A FFP is a marketing tool that can be used by a carrier to attract business traffic and to develop customer loyalty. So far the Commission has assessed the competitive impact of FFPs mainly under Article 81 of the Treaty, in the context of airline alliances.[93] The Commission has not yet taken a formal decision on FFPs under Article 82 of the Treaty.[94] EC competition law does not prohibit *a priori* large airlines from taking advantage of their networks and thus exploiting certain size-related advantages when marketing their services. As long as the marketing strategies employed by an airline do not amount to an abuse in the sense of Article 82 of the Treaty, difficulties that may arise for smaller competitors from such legitimate exploitation of size-related advantages must be accepted. Generally speaking, FFPs can to a certain extent be considered as competition on prices, constituting legitimate behaviour under the EC competition rules.

14.68   However, according to precedent, unless there is an objective justification, a dominant supplier cannot give loyalty incentives to its customers with the object or effect of restricting their freedom to choose their sources of supply freely, thus impeding market access of competitors.[95] Therefore, to the extent that the effects of a particular FFP operated by a dominant airline are equivalent to a 'loyalty' discount scheme or represent a comparable exclusionary practice, the FFP may be caught by Article 82 of the Treaty. Whether a particular FFP must be considered an abuse of a dominant position can only be assessed on a case-by-case basis.

14.69   (iv) **Predatory Pricing**   Lowering prices below cost combined with increasing capacity and matching timetables could be indicators of a predatory pricing strategy, which has the object or effect of excluding competitors from the market, in breach of Article 82 of the Treaty.[96] Predatory pricing in the air transport sector could occur, for example, as a strategic response by a network carrier to the entry of low cost carriers on a particular route. A predatory strategy would in principle only be rational if the incumbent carrier succeeds in monopolising the market and if there are high entry barriers which prevent competing carriers from re-entering the market.[97]

---

[92] Compare, on frequent flyer programmes, also S Storm, *Air Transport Policies and Frequent Flyer Programmes in the European Community* (Nexo: Bornholms Forsknincenter, 1999).

[93] See paras 14.25–14.59 above.

[94] As regards the National Competition Authorities, following a complaint by certain associations of travel agents the Swedish Competition Authority, in a decision of November 1999, fined Scandinavian Airline Systems (SAS) for abusing its dominant position, in breach of national competition law, by applying its Eurobonus FFP on domestic flights. The decision was upheld by the Swedish Market Court in February 2001. A similar decision was taken by the Norwegian Competition Authority, on 18 March 2002, prohibiting SAS from awarding FFPs on domestic Norwegian routes. According to both Competition Authorities, SAS's FFP scheme functioned as an important barrier to entry into domestic Scandinavian air transport markets. The FFP scheme concerned was viewed as a loyalty programme designed to restrict competition among airlines.

[95] For the distinction between rebates which merely constitute non-abusive competition on their merits and rebates which fall within the scope of Art 82 of the Treaty, see the European Court of Justice in eg Case 85/76 *Hoffmann-La Roche* [1979] ECR 461; and Case 322/81 *Michelin* [1983] ECR 3461.

[96] The European Court of Justice established two equivalent tests to identify predation; either it is proved that prices are below average variable costs, or there is evidence that prices are below average total costs (variable costs plus fixed costs) and the incumbent plans to eliminate the competitor. See in particular Case C-62/86 *AKZO* [1991] ECR I-3359; and Case C-333/94 *Tetra Pak II* [1996] ECR I-5951.

[97] The traditional approach to predation is that the incumbent, as the dominant carrier, tries to drive the competitor out of the market by reducing prices below cost. As it has a large market share, it thereby runs significant losses. After having monopolised the market it then can recoup the earlier losses by raising its fares.

The Commission has not yet taken a formal decision on predatory pricing in the airline **14.70** sector.[98] However, the Commission was confronted with the issue in a number of cases.[99] In its preliminary assessment of these cases the Commission did not focus on marginal costs, ie the costs for producing an extra unit, since in the context of air transport this would have led to a series of assumptions and uncertainties.[100] Instead, the Commission looked at the total costs and revenues and at evidence of an intention to eliminate a competitor.

Predation cases in the air transport sector are complex.[101] Running an air service at a loss **14.71** can be a strong indicator of a predatory pricing strategy. However, the losses suffered must be substantial over a certain period of time, mounting to a level which would not permit the maintenance of the service under the present circumstances without substantial cross-subsidies. Otherwise they could be explained by a temporary recession or simply incorrect business expectation. A realistic approach would assume that the incumbent aims to establish the reputation of being a predator, thus deterring other carriers from entering routes on which the incumbent is already operating. In that case, from the incumbent's point of view, the main benefit does not arise on the route where it actually has attacked a competitor, but on all other routes where it can maintain its dominant position because it has scared away potential competitors. While the cost of predation would arise only on a specific route, benefits could be obtained from a multiplicity of routes on which the dominant carrier could maintain high prices.

(6) Block Exemptions in the Aviation Sector

(a) General Remarks

Regulation (EEC) 3976/87[102] empowers the Commission to adopt block exemption **14.72** Regulations in the air transport sector for a specific period of time with regard to a certain number of listed activities. Initially such block exemptions could only be granted in respect of air transport between Community airports. However, in 2004 the Council broadened the scope of Regulation (EEC) 3976/87 by empowering the Commission, in addition, to grant block exemptions in respect of air transport between the Community and third countries.[103]

---

[98] As regards the National Competition Authorities, it is worth mentioning that the German Bundeskartellamt (BKA), on 18 February 2002, took a decision against Lufthansa for predatory pricing against the low-cost carrier Germania on the route Frankfurt-Berlin. In the past, Lufthansa had had a monopoly on this route. When Germania entered this route, charging tariffs of about one fifth of the tariffs charged by Lufthansa, the latter reacted by reducing its own fares to the level charged by Germania. In its decision, the Bundeskartellamt considered the behaviour by Lufthansa to be a predatory pricing strategy with the aim of eliminating the competitor from the market and requested Lufthansa to raise its tariffs. The decision was upheld by a provisional decision of the Higher Regional Court.

[99] All these cases concerned complaints by low cost carriers against alleged predatory behaviour of flag carriers. The cases were closed, either because a settlement was reached or because the alleged behaviour did not continue over time.

[100] Taking marginal costs as a yardstick may be useful in the manufacturing business, where those costs can easily be calculated. However, in the airline business, the costs for an extra unit produced, ie the costs of an extra seat, are very difficult to calculate. Those costs are either rather low (eg in the case of costs for extra meals, travel agent commission) or it is difficult to allocate them to a single seat (as in the case of extra fuel required to carry extra weight; extra expenditure on ticketing and passenger handling).

[101] Compare also A Ryan and T Soames, 'Predatory pricing in air transport' [1994] ECLR 151–64.

[102] See n 21 above.

[103] Council Regulation (EC) 411/2004 (see n 17 above).

14.73 On the basis of Regulation (EEC) 3976/87, the Commission adopted, in 1993, Regulation (EEC) 1617/93[104] which permitted carriers, under certain conditions, to agree on passenger tariffs. Furthermore, the Regulation provided, subject to certain conditions and obligations, for a block exemption for agreements on slot allocation and airport scheduling.[105] Both block exemptions expired on 30 June 2005 but the Commission launched a review as to whether the exemptions should be prolonged

(b) IATA Tariff Conferences

14.74 Commission Regulation (EEC) 1617/93 permitted carriers, under certain conditions, to hold consultations on passenger tariffs in respect of routes within the Community.[106] The consultations must aim at facilitating interlining, that is to say they must allow passengers to travel with one single ticket on more than one airline, where available, to reach their final destination.[107] Furthermore, participation in the consultations should be voluntary, open to any carrier operating a service on the route concerned, and the tariffs concerned should be non-binding and applied without discrimination.[108]

14.75 By way of background, it was considered important in particular that the tariff conference block exemption should ensure that passengers had the option to interline. The Regulation was initially applicable for a period of five years and was renewed several times thereafter. In 2002 the Commission expressed doubts as to the continued justification for the block exemption and imposed on participating carriers the obligation to collect and report certain data, with the primary aim of making it easier for the Commission to assess the effects and concrete consumer benefits of the conferences at the time of the next revision.

14.76 In practice, the exemption for passenger tariff consultations applied to the activities of just one organisation, the International Air Transport Association (IATA). The 25 EEA members of IATA (all the EEA flag carriers plus nine regional airlines) meet several times a year to agree on non-binding prices for international journeys involving interlining. Both business and full economy fares are agreed for all EEA city pairs for one year at a time. For some city pairs discounted fares are also agreed. Furthermore, carriers in the passenger tariff conferences agree on conditions for different types of interlining ticket.

14.77 IATA interlinable tickets are comparable to carrier-specific tickets, in so far as both types of ticket entitle a consumer to travel by air from a point of origin to a point of destination.

---

[104] See n 23 above.

[105] Originally Regulation (EEC) 1617/93 also block exempted consultations on cargo tariffs, joint planning and coordination of schedules, and agreements on joint operations. These block exemptions were not renewed, however, when the Regulation was amended in 1996 (cargo tariffs) and 1999 (the other activities) respectively.

[106] The block exemption initially adopted covered services between Community airports. By extension through the EEA agreement and the EC–Switzerland Air Transport Agreement the exemption also covers routes within the area of the EEA and Switzerland, respectively.

[107] Compare Art 4(1)(b) of Regulation (EEC) 1617/93. For example, passengers may start a journey with a given carrier, who will issue the ticket for the entire journey, although the passengers continue their journey onwards to destinations not served by the carrier who has issued the ticket. Alternatively, a passenger may, on a single segment round-trip journey, leave on the issuing carrier and return on another airline. Moreover, to the extent that the conditions governing the initial reservation allow it, interlining extends to reservation changes onto other airlines' flights.

[108] Art 4 of Regulation (EEC) 1617/93.

It follows that the joint setting of passenger tariffs by carriers in the context of the IATA passenger tariff conferences is liable to restrict competition within the meaning of Article 81(1) of the Treaty. It is indeed one of the rare instances in EC competition law where the Commission has exempted a (retail) price agreement, which is normally regarded as a hardcore restriction.[109] Although the agreed IATA tariffs are not binding, in practice airlines seem to be reluctant to grant any up-front rebates on IATA interlinable tickets and the bulk of these tickets appear to be issued at the actual rates agreed in the IATA passenger tariff conferences. In practice, on the main computerised reservation systems, the IATA interlinable fares offered by airlines participating in the tariff conferences are all the same. Furthermore, the IATA Tariff Conferences can provide a forum in which carriers exchange sensitive information, which is likely to reinforce restrictive effects.

On routes within the EU in particular, it is arguable whether the tariff conferences, in the **14.78** present market circumstances, could still be said to fulfil the four cumulative conditions of Article 81(3) of the Treaty. Passenger tariff conferences are one of the main pillars of the IATA multilateral interlining system.[110] It is not disputed that interlining as such benefits consumers, by providing them with a 'through fare' for their journey and a 'through check' of their baggage. Furthermore, interlining provides consumers with flexibility in respect of changing airlines and itineraries. However, it seems that most of these consumer benefits could also be generated now through means other than multilateral price fixing in the IATA conferences. In particular, due to the development and increasing importance of code share agreements and airline alliances in the EU since the mid-nineties, as well as recent mergers such as *Air France/KLM*, passengers now have a choice of interlining facilities. In light of this, one might ask whether the restrictive consultation system set up by IATA is still indispensable within the meaning of Article 81(3) of the Treaty.[111]

(c) IATA Slot Allocation and Airport Scheduling Conferences

Regulation (EEC) 1617/93 also provided for a block exemption for arrangements **14.79** between carriers on slot allocation and airport scheduling, subject to certain conditions and obligations. As airports become increasingly congested, there is a practical need for carriers and authorities competent in the area of slot allocation at airports to combine efforts to ensure a more efficient use of airport capacity. The block exemption accepted this, subject to certain conditions, notably that all carriers should be afforded equal opportunities to access congested airports and that the criteria for slot allocation should be transparent and non-discriminatory.[112]

---

[109] Another example being the block exemption for price-fixing, market, and supply regulation by liner shipping conferences in Council Regulation (EEC) 4056/86 of 22 December 1986 laying down detailed rules for the application of Arts 85 and 86 of the Treaty to maritime transport [1986] OJ L378/24. This block exemption is currently under review.

[110] The other pillars include the Multilateral Interline Traffic Agreement (requiring the participating airlines to issue and accept each other's tickets on a reciprocal basis in accordance with the fares and conditions set by the carrying airline), the IATA Clearing House (through which interline billings are settled), and the IATA pro rata system (according to which the revenues generated by interline ticket are divided).

[111] It should be noted that, in 1997, the Commission did not renew a similar block exemption for cargo tariff consultations, in essence because the tariffs fixed by cargo tariff conferences appeared to be much higher than the market rates and the system no longer seemed essential for interlining.

[112] Art 5 of Regulation (EEC) 1617/93.

14.80   The block exemption should be viewed in the context of Council Regulation (EC) 95/93 on common rules for the allocation of slots at Community airports,[113] which forms the legal basis of the present slot allocation process. The aim of Regulation (EC) 95/93 is to ensure optimum use of capacity at congested airports by means of a non-discriminatory and transparent system. To that end Regulation (EC) 95/93 entitles an air carrier to claim the same slot in the next scheduling period that it had been operating in the previous equivalent period (so-called 'grandfather rights').[114]

14.81   It should be noted that the present slot allocation system based on grandfather rights has shortcomings from a competition point of view. Given the significant excess demand for slots at a number of EU airports, the current system of grandfather rights inhibits new competitors from entering the market, as there are often very few suitable slots in the pool. The Commission has announced, following a market study,[115] that a fundamental review of the current Regulation on allocation of slots in airports will be carried out, with the primary aim of introducing a more market oriented approach.[116] From a competition standpoint it is indeed essential to guarantee as much market flexibility as possible for both incumbents and new entrants (slots at congested airports should primarily be allocated by the market), while at the same time providing a framework for stable air services.

(d) Review

14.82   In June 2004 the Commission launched a review of the block exemptions in the air transport sector with the publication of a DG Competition consultation paper, setting out the main issues and inviting interested parties to comment.[117] The Commission's preliminary position in this paper was that there does not appear to be a strong case for an extension of the block exemption for passenger tariff conferences within the Community but that such a block exemption for air transport between the Community and third countries might be appropriate for a certain period of time. As regards the slot consultation, the Commission did not initially consider major amendments to the block exemption because of the pending review of Regulation (EC) 95/93.

14.83   On the basis of the submissions received on its consultation paper, the Commission published a discussion paper in March 2005, confirming its preliminary view on tariff conferences.[118] The discussion paper was followed, in February 2006, by a Commission proposal for a revised

---

[113] As last amended by Regulation (EC) 793/2004 ([2004] OJ L138/50). The amendment amounts basically to a technical update seeking to clarify the application of the existing regime on a number of issues.

[114] Furthermore, Regulation (EC) 95/93 establishes the 'use-it-or-lose-it rule': an operator who has utilised a slot less than 80 per cent of the time for which it had been allocated in that period must hand it back to the slot pool. Any slots not covered by grandfather rights are allocated according to administrative criteria. This includes a requirement that 50 per cent of this 'pool' should be made available to new entrants.

[115] See <http://europa.eu.int/comm/transport/air/rules/doc/2004_01_24_nera_slot_study.pdf>.

[116] See Commission Staff Working Document of 17 September 2004, published on the Commission's website. at <http://www.europa.eu.int/comm/transport/air/rules/competition2/doc/2004_09_17_consultation_paper_en.pdf>.

[117] The consultation paper was published at the Commission's website at <http://europa.eu.int/comm/competition/antitrust/others/consultation_paper_en.pdf>.

[118] The discussion paper has been published on the Commission's website at <http://europa.eu.int/comm/competition/antitrust/others/discussion_paper_en.pdf>.

block exemption Regulation.[119] On 28 September 2006 the Commission adopted the new block exemption Regulation.[120] The new Regulation ends the exemption for passenger tariff conferences for routes within the EU as of 1 January 2007 but continues to exempt tariff conferences on routes between the EU and the US or Australia until 30 June 2007 and routes between the EU and other EU countries until 31 October 2007, subject to certain conditions. Since the consultation revealed that in their present form slots allocation and scheduling conferences are compatible with the competition rules there was felt to be no longer a need for legal certainty provided by a block exemption in this regard and the Commission did not prolong the block exemption for slots and scheduling.[121]

(7) International Aspects

(a) *Effective Enforcement Tools*

Before 1 May 2004 the Commission did not have effective enforcement rules for applying **14.84** the EC competition rules to air transport between the EU and third countries. Instead the Commission had to rely on the cumbersome proceeding of Article 85 of the Treaty.[122] Over the years the Commission submitted several proposals to the Council in order to end this anomaly, most recently in 2003. This last proposal, which was presented against the background of the growing importance of global alliances, led to the adoption by the Council of Regulation (EC) 411/2004,[123] effectively amending Regulation (EC) 1/2003 so that it also applies to air transport between the Community and third countries.

In terms of competition policy these new enforcement powers are particularly important for **14.85** the Commission's assessment of cases relating to pending and future global alliances. They will allow the Commission to examine the impact of such alliances, such as *Star*, *Wings*, and *Skyteam*, on all routes that may affect trade between the Member States, without having to separate procedurally the intra-Community routes from the third country routes.[124]

(b) *Bilateral Air Service Agreements*

As stated above, while intra-Community transport has been liberalised, air transport services **14.86** between the EU and third countries ('international aviation') are still regulated by a web of bilateral air service agreements between States. There exist some 1,500 bilateral air service agreements concluded by EU Member States and third countries. The terms of these agreements vary, but generally speaking they determine all aspects of the scope and degree of freedom that carriers have to provide air services between specific city pairs. For example, the agreements usually determine which routes may be served by which carrier(s) and regulate

---

[119] [2006] OJ C42/15.

[120] [2006] OJ L272/3.

[121] Commission press release IP/06/1294 of 2 October 2006.

[122] Art 85 of the Treaty allows the Commission, if it finds an infringement of the EC competition rules, to propose appropriate measures to bring that infringement to an end and, if needed, record the infringement in a reasoned decision and authorise the Member States concerned to take the appropriate action needed to remedy the situation. Examples of proceedings under Art 85 of the Treaty in the aviation sector are the *KLM/NorthWest* and *Lufthansa/SAS/United Airlines* cases (see n 34 above).

[123] See n 17 above.

[124] This is also in line with the assessment of aviation mergers under the Merger Regulation, which does not make a distinction between intra-Community air traffic and air traffic between the EU and third countries.

seat capacity, flight frequency, size of aircraft, etc on the agreed route. The agreements may in addition contain provisions on prices, ranging from agreements where the parties' competent authorities agree on the prices to be charged and impose them on airlines, to agreements where pricing is entirely unfettered and not subject to any filing requirement with a competent authority. Some agreements also refer to the tariffs decided in the IATA tariff conferences.

14.87   Some bilateral air service agreements concluded by Member States and third countries appear to contain provisions requiring or favouring the adoption of agreements, decisions, or concerted practices between air carriers that are contrary to Articles 10 and 81 of the Treaty.[125] This is the case, for example, in respect of agreements containing provisions that require or encourage designated carriers to agree or coordinate tariffs between themselves.[126] The same is true of provisions requiring, encouraging, or allowing airlines to agree capacity restrictions among themselves.

14.88   The Commission has not initiated formal proceedings against Member States on this point.[127] Arguably, formal proceedings would have made little sense in the absence of specific enforcement powers on routes between the EU and third countries. However, now that such enforcement powers are in place, such proceedings would not be excluded.[128] A priority of the Commission in this regard is to promote a pro-competitive reform of the regulatory framework applicable to international aviation. In this context the Commission has shown determination in applying Regulation (EC) 847/2004, which entered into force on 30 May 2004 and which requires Member States to notify the Commission of their intended negotiations and bring their existing air service agreements into conformity with Community law.[129]

---

[125] As confirmed by case law, Arts 81 and 82, read in conjunction with Art 10 of the Treaty, require Member States not to introduce or maintain in force measures, even of a legislative or regulatory nature, which may render ineffective the competition rules applicable to undertakings. Such would be the case if a Member State were to require or favour the adoption of agreements, decisions, or concerted practices contrary to Art 81 or reinforce their effects (judgment of the Court of 21 September 1988 in Case 267/86 *Pascal Van Eyke v ASPA NV* [1988] ECR 4769, para 16).

[126] See, for example, the bilateral agreement between Austria and Australia. In its decision of 15 July 2005 on the application of Regulation (EC) 847/2004 (C(2005)2667 final), the Commission ordered Austria to bring the agreement into conformity with Community law within 12 months.

[127] Following a complaint by *bmi British Midland Airways*, the Commission examined in 2001, on a preliminary basis, the Bermuda II Air Service Agreement, concluded between the UK and the US under Art 86 combined with Arts 81 and 82 of the Treaty. However, the case was closed when the complaint was withdrawn, without the Commission taking a final position.

[128] In principle, terms in air service agreements that are restrictive of competition could give rise to an infringement procedure, under Art 226 of the Treaty, against the Member States for breach of the combined application of Art 81 with Art 10(2) and Art 3(1)(g) of the Treaty. In the case of undertakings entrusted with exclusive or special rights such terms could also give rise to proceedings under Art 86(1) of the Treaty against the Member States. In both cases, this could amount to procedures against the carriers concerned for breach of Art 81(1) of the Treaty.

[129] Regulation (EC) 847/2004 of the European Parliament and the Council [2004] OJ L157/7 governs the negotiation and implementation of air service agreements between Member States and third countries. Pursuant to the Regulation, Member States may negotiate air service agreements with third countries subject to, *inter alia*, a notification procedure laid down in the Regulation. Member States must notify the Commission of their planned negotiations. In these negotiations, Member States must seek the agreement of the third countries to insert 'standard clauses' in their existing air service agreements with a view to bringing the latter into conformity with Community law. Member States must then notify the Commission of the results of their negotiation. Where it is possible to incorporate all the relevant standard clauses in an agreement, Member States are allowed to conclude the agreement. In other instances it is for the Commission, subject to the advisory procedure, to authorise Member states to conclude the agreements that they have negotiated.

(c) *Towards an EU–US Open Aviation Area Agreement*

As a consequence of the Court's *Open Skies* judgments of 5 November 2002,[130] in which **14.89**
the Court ruled that the so-called nationality clause[131] in air service agreements is contrary
to Community law, Member States are obliged to introduce the so-called 'Community
carrier' principle in such agreements between Member States and third countries.[132]

Following this judgment, the Commission received a mandate from the Council to start **14.90**
negotiations with the US with a view to reaching a comprehensive EU–US air service
agreement replacing the existing bilateral agreements concluded between the United States
and each individual Member State. As far as competition policy is concerned, the main
objective is to set up an institutional framework for co-operation between the Commission
and the US Department of Transportation for the assessment of transatlantic aviation
alliances, similar to the type of co-operation provided for in the 1991 EC/US competition
co-operation agreement with the US.[133]

The Commission wishes to negotiate similar comprehensive air services agreements with **14.91**
third countries other than the United States. For this purpose it will have to obtain the necessary mandates from the Council. This process is most likely to start with countries neighbouring the EU.[134] It can be expected that these agreements should include a section on
competition co-operation between the enforcement agencies.

C. Maritime Transport

(1) General Remarks

Maritime transport services cover a huge spectrum of different services, ranging from non- **14.92**
regular bulk operations to regular ferry and liner shipping services. The Commission's
enforcement activities have to date focused on liner shipping and ferry services.

Due to the uncertainty concerning the application of the competition rules to the transport **14.93**
sector, secondary legislation empowering the Commission to use its traditional enforcement powers with reference to maritime transport was only provided by the adoption of
Council Regulation (EEC) 4056/86. This Regulation was adopted as part of a legislative
package, including in particular Council Regulation (EEC) 4055/86, applying the principle

---

130 Joined Cases C-466, 467, 468, 469, 471, 472, 475 and 476/98 *Open Skies* [2002] ECR I-09427.
131 According to a nationality clause, the contracting party has the right to refuse traffic rights to an airline
if that airline is not effectively owned and controlled by nationals of the other contracting party.
132 This means, for example, that Lufthansa should have the potential to operate on an international route
departing from Paris under the auspices of the bilateral agreements concluded between France and other third
countries.
133 Agreement between the Government of the United States of America and the European Communities
regarding the application of their competition laws ([1995] OJ L95/45–50 as corrected by [1995] OJ L131\38),
providing for co-operation between the European Commission, on the one hand, and the US Department of
Justice and the Federal Trade Commission, on the other. Such envisaged co-operation with the US Department
of Transportation could comprise, for example, mutual notification of relevant cases; exchange of information
both on general and case-related issues; and regular meetings to discuss developments in the market as well as
issues of common interest.
134 See Communication from the Commission of 9 February 2004 (COM(2004) 74 final), available at
<http://europa.eu.int/comm/transport/air/international/doc/com_2004_0074_en.pdf>.

of freedom to provide services to international maritime transport.[135] This liberalisation Regulation was accompanied by two other regulations, which provided for corrective measures to counter unfair pricing practices by third countries in the Community and coordinated safeguard measures in response to third country measures restricting access to their own market.[136] Regulation 4056/86 followed an earlier Community maritime policy instrument known as the 'Brussels Package',[137] which itself had been the result of discussions between the Commission and the Member States on the incompatibility of the UNCTAD Code of Conduct for Liner Conferences with the provisions of the EC Treaty. In the 'Brussels Package', the Community had accepted that international liner shipping services should be provided on the basis of the traditional conference system. Consequently, the central feature of Regulation 4056/86—apart from laying down detailed rules on the application of the competition rules—was to authorise the way in which the industry has traditionally organised itself, through a block exemption for liner shipping conferences.[138] Following a three-year review of Regulation 4056/86, the Regulation was in September 2006 repealed by Council Regulation 1419/2006. The repealing Regulation however foresees a two-year transition period for the provisions relating to liner conferences.[139]

14.94 The second maritime sector-specific legislation is Commission Regulation 823/2000, which contains a block exemption for consortia arrangements.[140] Following the entry into force of Regulation 1/2003, maritime services, with two exceptions, became subject to the same enforcement regime as all other services. The exceptions concerned cabotage and tramp vessel services, for which the Commission continued to lack specific enforcement powers and where its actions had to be based directly on Article 85 of the Treaty.[141] With the entry into force of Regulation 1419/2006 in October 2006, these services have also been brought under the scope of the common competition implementing rules.[142]

(2) Market Definition

14.95 In the *liner shipping sector*, the Commission has applied a trade lane analysis where the geographic scope of the relevant service market is defined by the points of origin and destination

---

[135] Council Regulation (EEC) 4055/86 of 22 December 1986 applying the principle of freedom to provide services to maritime transport between Member States and between Member States and third countries [1986] OJ L378/1.

[136] Council Regulation 4057/86 [1986] OJ L378/14; and Council Regulation 4058/86 [1986] OJ L378/21.

[137] Council Regulation (EEC) No 954/79 concerning the ratification by Member States of, or their accession to, the United Nations Convention on a Code of Conduct for Liner Conferences [1979] OJ L121/1.

[138] For more information on the legislative background of Regulation 4056/86 and the Brussels packages, see Luis Ortiz Blanco, *Shipping Conferences under EC Antitrust Law* (Hart Publishing, not yet published); Luis Ortiz Blanco and Ben van Houtte, *EC Competition Law in the Transport Sector* (Clarendon Press, Oxford, 1996); and Felix Dinger, *The Future of Liner Conferences in Europe* (Peter Lang, 2004).

[139] See Council Regulation (EC) No 1419/2006 of 25 September 2006 repealing Regulation (EEC) No 4056/86 laying down detailed rules for the application of Arts 85 and 86 to maritime transport, and amending Regulation (EC) No 1/2003 as regards the extension of its scope to include cabotage and international tramp vessel services, [2006] OJ L269/1. See also press release IP/06/1249 and MEMO/06/344 and the Commision Proposal COM (2005) 651 of 14 December 2005, available on the Commission's website at <http://europa.eu.int/comm/competition/antitrust/others/#review>.

[140] See section 5 below.

[141] See section 4 below.

[142] See n 139 above.

of the relevant services. The Commission has been reluctant to include other modes of transport (air) or other forms of maritime transport (conventional liner transport (bulk or reefer)) in the relevant service market for containerised cargo. It has made clear that the essential question for determining demand substitutability is not whether the same goods can be transported in both containers and bulk, but whether the choice of mode of transport is made on the basis of the characteristics of the mode.[143] Finding that, for the vast majority of categories of goods and users of containerised liner shipping, other forms of maritime transport do not normally offer a reasonable alternative to containerised liner shipping services, the Commission has held that the latter forms a separate market. The Court has endorsed the Commission's use of the concept of one-way substitutability for this analysis.[144] Supply-side substitutability can also play a role if there are clear indications that, for example, operators of conventional vessels can easily convert their vessels to carry large numbers of containers or, taking into account the mobility of the Community fleet, containerised vessels active in other trades could exercise a sufficient competitive constraint on the services concerned.[145] The Commission has also found that a distinction between the two directions of a trade is justified where trade imbalances or different characteristics of the products shipped would result in different market conditions depending on the direction.[146] The geographic market (as opposed to the geographic element of the relevant service market)[147] has been defined as the area in which the services are marketed, which would normally consist of the catchment area of the ports within the defined port range.

The Commission has had relatively little experience of defining the market for *non-containerised* **14.96** *cargoes*. The above principles concerning the substitutability between different modes of maritime transport are, however, likely to be of equal importance for such assessments. The Commission has in one case refuted the argument that general roll-on/roll off (ro-ro) and

---

[143] See Commission Decision of 16 September 1998 in Case No IV/35.134 Trans-Atlantic Conference Agreement [1999] OJ L95/1 (the '*TACA* decision'), para 71. The Commission has, however, in one consortia case (the Europe to Caribbean Consortium) accepted that in respect of the transport of one specific category of goods, traditional reefer ships would still be included in the same market as container ships carrying reefer containers. This was due to highly exceptional circumstances specific to the market in question and should not be seen as a change in the Commission's policy.

[144] The Commission has found that, as the degree of containerisation increases, shippers of non-containerised cargoes turn towards containerised services. Once those shippers have become accustomed to shipping in containers, they do not revert to non-containerised shipping. In a mature market, the substitution of containerised transport for break-bulk transport once put into effect, is therefore conclusive. Judgment of the Court of First Instance in Joined Cases T-191/98, 212/98 and 214/98 *Atlantic Container Line AB and Others v Commission* [2003] ECR II-3275 (hereinafter the *TACA* judgment) paras 790 to 795; and the *TACA* decision (see n 143) paras 62 to 75. The Commission came to a similar conclusion in the *Maersk/PONL* merger with regard to substitution between reefer containers and bulk reefer vessels, Commission decision of 29 July 2005 in case COMP/M.3829 (published on the Commission's website at <http://europa.eu.int/comm/competition/merger/cases/decisions/m3829_en.pdf>).

[145] Although potential competition and supply-side substitution are conceptually different issues, these factors will also normally be considered when assessing the existence of effective competition under the liner conference and consortia block exemption.

[146] See, for example, the *Maersk/PONL* merger case referred to in n 144.

[147] The definition of the relevant service would generally include a geographic element in its own right, since the place where the service is provided must be taken into account in determining whether the service is substitutable for another service.

container/ro-ro operators compete in the same market as specialised car carriers, despite the fact that the latter can and sometimes do transport the same types of cargo.[148]

14.97 As regards *ferry services*, freight and passenger traffic would normally represent different demands, which would impact on the question of substitutability between alternative modes of transport and routes, provided that the operators can distinguish and target the different categories of customer. The Commission has accepted that other modes of transport can constitute a substitute for ro-ro freight ferry services.[149] Following the evolution of passenger services provided by low cost carriers, it may be that the Commission will consider further the competitive constraint exercised by such services.

14.98 The Commission has made a distinction between *stevedoring services* provided to deep-sea container ships and similar services provided to short-sea container vessels or vessels carrying non-containerised cargo. Moreover, it has found that the provision of stevedoring services in respect of hinterland traffic and transhipment traffic constitute two discrete relevant product markets.[150]

(3) Council Regulation 4056/86

(a) Introduction

14.99 Regulation 4056/86 was adopted after the Court had explicitly confirmed that Community competition rules were fully applicable in the transport sector.[151] This Regulation, like Regulation 1017/68, is nevertheless based on two Treaty provisions—Articles 80(2) and 83 EC. This is explained by the fact that Article 9 of Regulation 4056/86 deals with the question of conflicts of law with third countries.[152] The purpose and use of Article 9 and its relevance for the dual legal base of Regulation 4056/86 is, however, far from obvious.[153]

---

[148] Commission decision of 29 November 2002 in Case M.2879 *Wallenius Lines AB/Wilhelmsen ASA/Hyundai Merchant Marine*, paras 20–27 (published on the Commission's website at <http://europa.eu.int/comm/competition/merger/cases/decisions>).

[149] In its *P&O Stena Line I* decision, the Commission concluded that ro-ro ferry services of unitised freight provided by the parties faced competition from lift-on/lift-off ferry operators. Furthermore, door-to-door intermodal services and freight services via the Channel Tunnel (freight trains and Eurotunnel's Le Shuttle service) were found to be substitutes for unitised freight ferry services. Commission Decision of 26 January 1999 in Case IV/36.253 *P&O Stena Line* [1999] OJ L163/61.

[150] Commission Decision of 3 July 2001 in Case COMP/JV.55 *Hutchison/RCPM/ECT* [2003] OJ L223/1, paras 23–36; Commission decision of 29 November 2001 in Case COMP/JV.56 *Hutchison/ECT* [2002] OJ C113/7, paras 12–16; and Commission Decision of 22 December 2004 in Case M.3576 *ECT/PONL/Euromax* [2005] OJ C61/4.

[151] Judgment of the Court in Joined Cases 209 & 213/84 *Nouvelles Frontières* [1986] ECR 1425.

[152] The Commission's original proposal for Regulation 4056/86 was based solely on Art 83 EC. The Council, however, accepted the line argued in the opinions of the Economic and Social Committee as well as the European Parliament, which appear to have been driven by a desire to ensure that the Community's maritime transport policy would not be trumped by Community competition policy. See Opinion on the Proposal for a Council Regulation Laying Down Detailed Rules for the Application of Arts 85 and 86 of the Treaty to Maritime Transport [1983] OJ C77/13 (European Economic and Social Committee (1983)).

[153] A conflict of law would only occur if one jurisdiction required something that another jurisdiction prohibits. The Commission, in its review of Regulation 4056/86, questioned the justification for maintaining Art 9 while noting that such a situation has never arisen and is unlikely to arise in the future; see the Commission's White Paper and its attachment of 13 October 2004. In its Proposal for a Council Regulation repealing Regulation 4056/86, the Commission takes the position that the legal basis of the original measure can be considered incorrect and therefore only proposes to base the repealing regulation on Art 83 of the Treaty. Both the White Paper and the Proposal for a Council Regulation are published on the Commission's website at <http://europa.eu.int/comm/competition/antitrust/others/#review>.

The sections in Regulation 4056/86 dealing with the implementation of the competition rules in **14.100** the maritime sector have been repealed with the entry into force of Council Regulation 1/2003. In September 2006, the Commission adopted Regulation 1419/2006, repealing all the remaining provisions but allowing for a two-year transitional period for the exemption for liner shipping conferences. This Chapter will consequently focus on those articles of Regulation 4056/86 that are subject to these transitional rules.

(b) Block Exemption for Liner Shipping Conferences—Article 3 of Regulation 4056/86 [154]

Regulation 4056/86 defines a liner conference as being: **14.101**

> a group of two or more vessel-operating carriers which provide international liner services for the carriage of cargo on a particular route or routes within specified geographical limits and which has an agreement or arrangement, whatever its nature, within the framework of which they operate under uniform or common freight rates and any other agreed conditions with respect to the provision of liner services. [155]

A liner conference is not a joint service. The objective is to agree to offer, through a regularly scheduled service, the same freight rates for the transport of the same category of goods, no matter which conference carrier the transport user addresses himself to.

The definition of a liner conference makes it clear that the agreements between the carriers **14.102** in a conference must have as their objective the fixing of rates and conditions of carriage for maritime transport services. A liner conference therefore, by definition, restricts competition between its members.[156] In addition to horizontal price-fixing, the block exemption also authorises a number of other co-operative measures, if carried out by the members in addition to fixing prices and conditions of carriage. These additional activities are:

(a) the coordination of shipping timetables, sailing dates, or dates of calls;
(b) the determination of the frequency of sailings or calls;
(c) the coordination or allocation of sailings or calls among members of the conference;
(d) the regulation of the carrying capacity offered by each member;
(e) the allocation of cargo or revenue among members.

The block exemption is both highly generous and unique. It is generous because it permits liner conferences to engage in activities that would normally constitute hardcore restrictions of competition (collective price-fixing and capacity regulation) which are unlikely to fulfil the conditions of Article 81(3) of the Treaty.[157] It is unique because it is contained in a

---

[154] For a general overview of liner shipping services and the block exemptions, see Louis Ortiz Blanco in *Shipping Conferences under EC Antitrust Law* (Hart Publishing, not yet published); Luis Ortiz Blanco and Ben van Houtte, *EC Competition law in the transport sector* (Clarendon Press, Oxford, 1999); and Mary R Brooks, *Sea Change in Liner Shipping* (Pergamon, 2000).

[155] Art 1(3)(b).

[156] Confirmed by the Court of First Instance in its judgment of 28 February 2002 in Case T-395/94 *Atlantic Container Line AB and Others v Commission* [2002] ECR II-875, para 324 (hereinafter the *TAA* judgment). The block exemption, in other words, requires a certain level of restriction of competition between the members in order to permit the restrictions.

[157] See the Commission notice on Guidelines on the application of Art 81(3) of the Treaty, [2004] OJ C101/97, para 46.

Council Regulation which was adopted even though the Commission had not gained any experience in granting individual exemptions in the sector. Furthermore, it contains no market share thresholds and it is unlimited in time. The justification given in the Regulation for this generous exemption is, in essence, that price-fixing by liner conferences is assumed to lead to price stability, assuring reliable scheduled transport services.[158] The adoption of this exceptional block exemption can only be explained by its historical and political context.

14.103　The application of the block exemption has been marked by a series of Commission interventions against the industry's perception that the block exemption would cover all activities the carriers deemed useful or necessary in order to adapt to changing market conditions. The Court has made clear that the block exemption—despite its exceptional nature—cannot derogate from the Treaty competition provisions and—because of its exceptional nature—must be given a strict interpretation.[159]

(c) The Scope of the Block Exemption

14.104　The scope of the block exemption is determined by the scope of the Regulation itself, the definition of a liner shipping conference, as well as the aim and objective of the exemption. The dual legal base of Regulation 4056/86 does not change the nature and scope of the block exemption. The Court has clarified that the Council did not derogate, and indeed could not have derogated, from Article 81(3) when adopting the Regulation.[160]

14.105　The Commission has in the past relied on the wording of Article 1(2) of the Regulation to refute the industry's conception that the block exemption would also cover the fixing of inland transport rates in the context of intermodal transport services. In the *FEFC* case, the Court endorsed the Commission's position that the scope of the block exemption could not be wider than the scope of the Regulation itself, which is applicable to 'international maritime transport services from or to one or more Community ports'.[161] The Court applied a similar reasoning when it found that the TACA conference's collective fixing of freight brokerage and freight forwarder remuneration was not covered by the block exemption.[162] The same considerations explain the Commission's findings in the *Revised TACA* case—that the common imposition of certain charges relating to cargo-handling services in ports might not fall within the scope of the Regulation and consequently would not benefit from the block exemption.[163]

14.106　The definition of a liner shipping conference would exclude certain categories of co-operations. The reference to 'international liner shipping services' means that agreements in non-liner shipping services, such as bulk pools or specialised neo-bulk transport co-operations, are not

---

[158] See recital 8 of Regulation 4056/86.

[159] See the Court of First Instance in its judgments of 28 February 2002 in case T-86/95 *Compagnie General Maritime v Commission* [2002] ECR II-1011, para 254 (hereinafter the *FEFC* judgment); the *TACA* judgment (see n 144) para 118; and the *TAA* judgment (see n 156) para 146.

[160] *TAA* judgment (n 156) para 162.

[161] *FEFC* judgment (n 159) para 241, which also makes references to an earlier judgment of the European Court of Justice in Case C-96/94 *Centro Servizi Spediporto* [1995] ECR I-2883.

[162] The Court held in its *TACA* judgment (n 144) para 568, that the exemption could not be extended to services which, even if they could be considered to be ancillary to or even necessary for maritime transport to and from ports, were not maritime transport services as such.

[163] Commission Decision of 14 November 2002 in Case COMP/37.396 *Revised TACA* [2003] OJ L26/53.

covered by the block exemption.[164] Similarly, the reference 'for the carriage of cargo' would exclude restrictive agreements between passenger shipping companies, such as ferry operators offering passenger transport, from the block exemption.[165] The situation is less clear with regard to freight-only ferry services or ferries carrying both passengers and freight. The organisation of traditional ferry co-operation as well as the rationale for the block exemption argue against extending the exemption to cover such ferry co-operations. Apart from the fact that co-operation between ferry operators would normally cover activities that go beyond those exempted under the conference block exemption, it is unlikely that joint ferry services will operate freight services under a fixed tariff or fulfil the conditions and obligations associated with the exemption. Moreover, the justification for authorising the very serious restrictions of competition is that those restrictions are necessary in order to guarantee reliable scheduled services in an environment supposedly characterised by unstable demand from shippers.[166] That justification is valid only where the service is predicated wholly, or at least overwhelmingly, on demand from shippers. It follows that a service that is predicated partly on demand from passengers and partly on demand from shippers cannot be regarded as a liner conference service covered by the block exemption provisions. Indeed, the Commission has not considered the application of the block exemption in its examination of co-operations between ferry operators.

The relevance of the definition of a liner shipping conference as well as the objective of the block exemption is illustrated by the *TAA* case. In this case, the Court confirmed the Commission's position that the words 'uniform or common freight rates' in the definition must be read conjunctively, so that the conference tariff must be identical for all conference members for the same category of goods.[167] In order to determine the meaning of this notion, the Court had regard to the terms used, as well as the mechanism of the block exemption, the context of the Regulation, and the objectives it pursues.[168] Since the TAA members had structured the tariff in a way that enabled a group of its members to charge different prices (so called two-tier pricing or differentiated rate agreements), the Court found that the TAA did not constitute a liner conference within the meaning of the Regulation and could therefore not benefit from the exemption. The block exemption, for the same reasons, would not cover so-called 'discussion agreements'.[169] **14.107**

A controversial issue has been whether the block exemption would also cover service contracts. In the *TACA* case, the Court upheld the Commission's position that the block exemption concerns tariff arrangements only and cannot be applied to the totally different concept of contract carriage.[170] **14.108**

---

164 See, in this respect, the Commission's findings in the *Wallenius* case (see n 148) that car carrier services did not constitute liner shipping services, but, rather, specialised transport.

165 It should be mentioned that the 1981 draft Regulation included an explicit reference to 'carriage of cargo and passengers', which was later removed and replaced with a definition that was consistent with the UNCTAD Code.

166 See recital 8 of Regulation 4056/86.

167 The shipowners had argued that the words should be read disjunctively and that the condition was fulfilled if prices were agreed in common and published in a uniform tariff.

168 *TAA* judgment, (n 156) para 145.

169 Discussion agreements, which are common on the US and Australian trades, are explained in the Commission White Paper and its attachment of 13 October 2004 (see n 195).

170 See paras 14.113 *et seq* below.

(d) Exempted Activities

14.109 (i) **Capacity Regulation**   Article 3(d) provides that conferences may engage in 'the regulation of the carrying capacity offered by each member'. To date, the Court has not ruled on which type of capacity regulation schemes would fall within the scope of this provision.[171] The Commission, in two prohibition decisions, has concluded that this provision does not cover capacity non-utilisation agreements, where the operators agree to 'freeze' capacity without undertaking any actual vessel withdrawals.[172] The Commission argued that the aim of Article 3(d) is to improve the scheduled transport services provided by the conference members. Therefore, the provision cannot be used as a means of maintaining excess capacity on the market and/or artificially increasing freight rates. Capacity withdrawals would only be permitted if they are carried out in such a way as to bring about definable benefits, for example if there was a true withdrawal of inefficient or outdated capacity that would result in a reduction of costs, leading to price reductions for transport users. A temporary capacity withdrawal would be covered by the block exemption if it is a proportionate response to a short-term fluctuation of demand from transport users.

14.110 The *Revised TACA* case[173] provides useful guidance as to the limits within which conference members may engage in the collective regulation of vessel capacity. Following discussions with the Commission, the TACA members decided to include new provisions in the conference agreements, which established safeguards against abuses and enabled the Commission to conclude that the provisions concerned would be covered by the block exemption. First, the conference has undertaken not to increase any tariff rates in conjunction with a capacity regulation programme on any trade covered by such programme or to create an artificial peak season. Secondly, detailed reporting obligations were included in order to allow the Commission to monitor any capacity regulation programme decided by the conference.[174] The conference has carried out several seasonal capacity withdrawal schemes of about five weeks each in the off-peak Christmas and New Year periods, which the Commission has so far not found any reason to intervene against. The Commission has, however, taken a strong position against a planned capacity regulation programme on a different and much larger scale by the members of the FEFC conference. The initiative was announced in October 2001, when the FEFC parties decided to implement a six-month coordinated vessel withdrawal scheme intended to respond to the combined effects of a drastic fall in demand for the concerned trades and the introduction of significant new capacity.

---

[171] The Court considered this issue in the appeal against the *TAA* decision. Since the Court concluded that the TAA did not constitute a conference, there was in this case no need for it to examine further whether the capacity management programme would be covered by the block exemption provision. The Court did find, however, that the capacity management aspects of the TAA would lead to the elimination of competition on the market and for that reason could not qualify for individual exemption.

[172] The *TAA* case (Commission Decision of 19 October 1994 in Case IV/34.446 *Trans-Atlantic Agreement* [1994] OJ L376/1) concerned a capacity management programme on the westbound transatlantic trade and the *EATA* case (Commission Decision of 30 April 1999 in Case IV/34.250 *Europe Asia Trade Agreement* [1999] OJ L193/23) concerned similar programmes on the Europe/Far East trades. The Commission also concluded that the assessed capacity management programmes could not qualify for individual exemptions.

[173] See n 163 and press release IP/02/1677 of 14 November 2002.

[174] See the *Revised TACA* decision (n 163), paras 81-83, which further explains the reporting obligations in particular.

The Commission queried whether such a programme would be consistent with the interpretation given in the *TAA* and *EATA* decisions (ie that it should have the objective of addressing a short-term fluctuation in demand). The Commission also doubted whether the possible benefits to transport users would outweigh the negative impact the programme would have on the transport users' costs. In response to the Commission's concerns, the programme was immediately terminated.

(ii) Inland Price-fixing The Court has upheld the Commission's position that the block **14.111** exemption does not cover the fixing of a joint tariff for the inland leg of a multimodal transport operation (such as from a factory to a port) or the joint fixing of door-to-door prices.[175] Moreover, the Court has stated that the bare fixing of the price for the inland leg of a multimodal shipping service that is unaccompanied by any co-operation that might provide benefits to transport users, would not satisfy the Article 81(3) EC criteria.[176] These findings would not exclude the possibility that carriers can engage in some form of inland co-operation.

The Commission has recognised the possibility that inland prices set below cost level might **14.112** jeopardise the stabilising effect which the setting of a common freight rate for the maritime leg is deemed to have under the block exemption. Although maintaining its view that such rules are not covered by the block exemption, the Commission has therefore accepted that the members of a liner conference can agree that no member would charge a price for inland transport services which is less than the direct out-of-pocket costs incurred by it in buying the inland transport service.[177] This rule is referred to as the 'not-below cost' rule. It was challenged by transport users in the *Revised TACA* case. In June 2003, the Court held that there was no longer any need to adjudicate in the case, since the original exemption had expired and the members had applied for a renewal.[178] Even though the Court has not yet ruled on the conformity of the 'not-below cost' rule with Community law, it can be argued that the Commission's policy in this respect has already been endorsed implicitly by the Court in the *FEFC* case.[179]

(iii) Service Contracts A service contract is a contract between a shipper (customer) and **14.113** carrier(s) in which the shipper undertakes to provide a minimum quantity of cargo over a fixed period of time and the carrier commits to a certain rate or rate schedule as well as a defined service level (including, for example, assured space, transit time, or port rotation). A shipper can enter into a service contract either bilaterally with one carrier (individual service contracts (ISCs)) or with some or all members of a conference (joint service contracts).[180]

In the past there have been several attempts by conferences to prohibit or restrict the avail- **14.114** ability or content of individual and confidential service contracts. The Commission has

---

175 *FEFC* judgment (n 159) para 241.

176 *TAA* judgment (n 156) paras 369 and 372.

177 Such out-of-pocket costs would not include repositioning costs or overhead/administrative costs.

178 Order of the Court of First Instance of 4 June 2003, in Case T-224/99 *The European Council of Transport Users ASBL a.o. v Commission* [2003] OJ C-213/34. The *Revised TACA* parties' application for renewal expired with the entry into force of Regulation 1/2003.

179 See *FEFC* judgment (n 159) paras 398 to 400.

180 Joint service contracts could either be entered into with one conference (conference service contracts, sometime referred to as 'agreement service contracts') or with several, but not all members of a conference (so called multi-carrier service contracts).

strongly defended the view that the free availability of such contracts is a crucial element in ensuring that the conference members are subject to effective internal competition. The Commission took issue with the practice of conferences in the *TACA* decision,[181] where it found that the TACA parties had infringed Article 81 EC by agreeing the terms and conditions under which they could enter into service contracts with shippers and that the same parties had also abused their joint dominant position by placing restrictions on the availability and content of service contracts. In reaching that conclusion, the Commission considered that the block exemption covered tariff arrangements only and could not be extended to price-fixing activities for contract carriage, which was a completely different concept.

14.115 The Court confirmed the Commission's position that service contracts were not covered by the block exemption. It also held that the practices applied by the TACA parties, with one exception, constituted an abuse of a dominant position.[182]

14.116 The Commission does not prohibit conference members from entering into conference service contracts or from determining the content of such contracts, so long as such agreements do not prevent the conference members from entering into individual service contracts, from departing from the terms of conference service contracts by way of independent action, or restrict the terms which may be included in individual service contracts. This is confirmed by its decision in the *Revised TACA* case. The Commission found that the joint service contract types applied by the Revised TACA conference did satisfy the Article 81(3) criteria, to the extent that they may be restrictive of competition, since they provided benefits to shippers and did not lead to the elimination of competition due to the market environment prevailing in the transatlantic trade. In the same case the Commission addressed concerns raised by transport users that, although no longer contractually regulated, restrictions in the content and availability of individual service contracts still existed in practice. The Commission concluded that this was not the case, notably because of the safeguards introduced concerning the restrictions on the exchange of commercially sensitive information relating to service contracting.

14.117 **(iv) Information Exchanges** The extent to which information exchanges between competitors can constitute an appreciable restriction of competition must be assessed on a case-by-case basis taking into account the structure of the market, and the nature and type of information exchanged, as well as the frequency and organisation of the system. In light of the fact that the block exemption allows the members of the conference to set a common freight rate for spot cargo, the Commission appears to accept that members should also be able to exchange the information necessary to give them a rough idea of the average current market price for the types of service in respect of which the common freight rate is intended to apply. On some trades, that price would depend on the spot rate as well as the service contract rates.

14.118 In the *Revised TACA* case, the Commission considered how information on service contract rates could be exchanged between conference lines without allowing an insight into the

---

[181] See n 143.
[182] *TACA* judgment (n 144). The exception concerned mutual disclosure of the availability and content of individual service contracts.

commercially sensitive terms of individual contracts. Following discussions with the Commission, the parties in the *Revised TACA* case introduced amendments to the conference agreement which were designed to limit the nature and the amount of commercially sensitive information that could be exchanged between the members. In essence, the revisions ensure that neither the conference secretariat, nor any of its members would have access to non-aggregated carrier-specific information relating to cargoes travelling under individual or multi-carrier service contracts.[183] The parties also undertook to provide the Commission with periodic reports on their contract activity, in order to allow the Commission to assure itself that the information exchanges would not lead to a decrease in the number of individual service contracts. The Commission's position in this case is understandable in view of the fact that conference members are allowed to fix a common freight rate that should reflect the prevailing market price. The possibility that the Commission may take a different position in an environment where such joint price-fixing is not exempted from the competition rules should not be excluded.[184]

(e) Conditions and Obligations

Regulation 4056/86 attaches one condition and several obligations to the block exemption. The condition is a non-discrimination provision set out in Article 4, according to which the co-operation must not cause detriment to ports, transport users, or carriers by applying rates and conditions of carriage which vary without justification according to the country of origin or destination or port of loading or discharge. Non-conformity with this condition means that the agreement or parts of it are automatically void pursuant to Article 81(2) of the Treaty. **14.119**

A failure to observe the obligations stipulated in Article 5 of the Regulation does not automatically result in the non-application of the block exemption. However, it may cause the Commission to withdraw the benefits of the block exemption and impose fines. The obligations in Article 5 require the lines to consult with transport users.[185] For that purpose, Article 6 contains a parallel exemption for arrangements that may be necessary between transport users on the one hand and the conferences on the other hand as well as agreements between transport users relating to the rates, conditions, and quality of the services. **14.120**

(f) Monitoring (Articles 7 and 8)

Under Article 7, the Commission may withdraw the benefit of the block exemption where there is a breach of an obligation and shall do so where the acts of a conference or a change in market conditions in a given trade result in the absence or elimination of actual or potential competition. **14.121**

---

[183] The Revised TACA members have adopted, *inter alia*, a resolution setting out the categories of information that may and may not be exchanged between the members and have appointed an independent third party to be responsible for collecting, aggregating, and disseminating commercially sensitive data.

[184] See the preliminary position of the Commission expressed in its White Paper, paras 124–126 (see n 195). The Commission has announced that it will issue appropriate guidelines on competition in the maritime sector so as to help smooth the transition to a fully competitive regime. As an interim step in the preparation of such guidance, DG Competition issued a staff paper on 29 September 2006, focusing on information exchanges (available on the Commission's web site).

[185] Art 5 stipulates furthermore that loyalty arrangements must contain safeguards for transport users and that transport users must be free to make their own arrangements concerning inland transport and quayside services. Lastly, tariffs and other conditions applied by the conference must be made available to transport users on request, or must be otherwise available for examination.

At the same time the Commission shall decide whether to accept commitments offered by the undertakings.[186] The Commission has never used this provision, but in two cases has announced its intention to do so. The Commission may also withdraw the benefit of the block exemption where it finds that it results in effects incompatible with Article 82 of the Treaty (Article 8(2)).

(g) Article 82

14.122 The Court has found that a liner conference, by its very nature and because of its objectives, could be seen as a collective entity presenting itself as such in the market and therefore capable of holding a dominant position within the meaning of Article 82 of the Treaty.[187] The Court has also confirmed that the same practice of a liner conference may simultaneously give rise to an infringement under both Articles 81 and 82 of the Treaty.[188]

(h) Revised TACA Principles and Outstanding Issues

14.123 The Commission has made clear that, although the exceptional circumstances of the *Revised TACA* case limit the possibility of using the Commission's findings in this case as a 'blue-print' for conferences trading in less competitive trades,[189] there are certain pro-competitive provisions of the *Revised TACA* decisions that should be respected by all EU-related conferences. The principles identified by the Commission are:

(a) conferences should refrain from inland price-fixing;
(b) no restrictions should be placed on the right of conference members to enter into confidential individual service contracts with transport users; and
(c) the collective regulation of capacity by members of a conference is only permissible where it is necessary in order to adapt to a short-term fluctuation of demand. Furthermore, it must not be combined with a price increase.[190]

There are still, however, some important outstanding issues on which neither the Commission nor the Community Courts have so far taken a clear position. One unresolved legal issue concerns the common fixing and imposition of charges for services carried out in the ports which may be economically and physically closely related to maritime services. The cargo-handler (terminal operator or stevedoring company) would generally invoice the carrier directly for these services. The latter would then pass on these costs in the form of charges and surcharges to the shipper. In certain conference agreements, not only the rate charged for the sea transport service as such, but also prices for cargo-handling in the ports of departure and destination, would be set in the conference tariff, which could in practice be higher or lower than the costs actually incurred by the carrier. To date, neither

---

[186] Art 7 of Regulation 4056/86, as amended by Art 38 of Regulation 1/2003.

[187] Judgment of the European Court of Justice of 16 March 2000 in Joined Cases C-395/96 P and 396/96 P *Compagnie Maritime Belge Transport and Others v Commission* [2002] ECR I-1365 (hereinafter referred to as the *Cewal* judgment). In the *TACA* judgment (n 144), the Court also rejected the parties' position that the extent and intensity of internal competition at that time would preclude a collective assessment of the TACA parties' position on the market: paras 694 to 736.

[188] *Cewal* judgment (n 187).

[189] The special circumstances in the *Revised TACA* case were the exceptional competitive market conditions prevailing on the transatlantic trade, in terms of both external and internal competition.

[190] See Commission press release IP/00/486.

the Court nor the Commission has taken a clear position on the precise dividing line between cargo handling services and maritime transport services, which would be decisive for assessing whether the joint fixing and imposition of such charges are permitted under Community law. In the *FETTCSA* case,[191] the members of the FEFC conference and their main independent competitor had agreed not to grant any discounts to customers on certain charges additional to the basic ocean freight rate, including so-called terminal handling charges (THCs). The Commission found that THCs did not fall within the scope of Regulation 4056/86. The Court did not find it necessary to rule on that question in the appeal.[192]

The closest guidance can be found in the *Revised TACA* decision. Guided by the Court's **14.124** findings in the *FEFC* case concerning the scope of the Regulation itself, the Commission found that the Revised TACA tariff charges for such activities would only fall within the scope of the block exemption to the extent that such activities are inseparable from the sea voyage. If they are not, the charges could only be permitted if the Article 81(3) criteria are fulfilled. In the case in question, the Commission found that the very special circumstances of the case allowed it to conclude that those aspects of the conference tariff that would fall outside the scope of Regulation 4056/86 but within that of Regulation 17 could be considered exemptible. It was consequently not necessary to identify, in that case, exactly which activities fell into which category. In reaching the conclusion that the tariff arrangements in the case would satisfy the conditions of Article 81(3) of the Treaty, the Commission recognised that the shippers, as end-users, could benefit from the interposition of carriers, since the latter will generally have greater bargaining power in relation to the cargo-handler.[193] The Commission, however, has emphasised that the finding was due to the exceptional circumstances of the *Revised TACA* case, where only a very small proportion of the cargoes is carried under the conference tariff and where the conference members have a collective market share of no more than 50 per cent. This should be a clear indication that a similar assessment cannot be taken for granted in relation to other conference agreements and in other markets.

(i) Review

The Commission launched a review of Regulation 4056/86 in March 2003 with the pub- **14.125** lication of a consultation paper, concluding that there was a need to re-examine in particular the justification for the liner conference block exemption. Special attention would be given to the alleged causal relationship between the exempted activities and the supposed benefits for transport users (stability of prices and the provision of reliable, adequate, and efficient scheduled liner shipping services). The review has also examined whether there are still

---

191 Commission decision of 16 May 2000 in Case IV/34.018 *Far East Trade Tariff Charges and Surcharges Agreement (FETTCSA)* [2001] OJ L268/1. The Commission found that a restrictive agreement relating to such charges could fall at least partly within the scope of Regulation 17 and, to the extent that the object or effect of an agreement relating to a THC is the fixing of rates and conditions for inland transport, within the scope of Regulation 1017/68 (see particularly para 128).

192 Judgment of the Court of First Instance of 19 March 2003 in Case T-213/00 *CMA CGM a.o v Commission* [2003] ECR II-913, para 85. The Court found that the Commission had failed to state reasons justifying the non-application of Regulation 4056/86. The alleged error concerning the choice of legal basis for the decision, however, did not have any adverse consequences for the applicants, and it was therefore not necessary for the Court to rule on the merits of those findings. By order dated 28 October 2004, the European Court of Justice dismissed the Commission's appeal (Case C-236/03, *Commission v CMA CGM a.o.,* [2005] OJ C106, p. 10)).

193 See *Revised TACA* decision (n 163) para 96.

valid reasons to maintain the exclusion of cabotage and tramp vessel services from the competition implementing rules, as well as maintaining the specific exclusion for purely technical agreements (Article 2) and the provision on conflict of laws (Article 9). The review was triggered by the fact that, despite authorising exceptionally serious restrictions of competition, no review had been carried out during the 16 years the block exemption had been in force, which was not consistent with the regular scrutiny the Commission undertakes of its policy in other areas.[194] Following an extensive consultation with the industry and the Member States, including a public hearing, the Commission formulated its position in a White Paper issued on 13 October 2004.[195] Having assessed numerous submissions and opinions from stakeholders and other Community institutions, the Commission submitted its proposal to repeal Regulation 4056/86 to the Council on 14 December 2005.[196] The Council, finding that liner shipping conferences no longer fulfil Article 81(3) conditions and that the block exemption should consequently be abolished adopted on 25 September 2006 the Regulation 1419/2006 repealing the remaining provisions of Regulation 4056/86. Conferences satisfying the requirement of Regulation 4056/86 on the date of entry of the Regulation can however continue to benefit from the provisions relating to the block exemption until October 2008. The Regulation also extends the scope of Regulation 1/2003 to include also maritime cabotage and tramp vessel services.

(4) Maritime Cabotage and Tramp Vessel Services

14.126   Article 81 and 82 of the Treaty apply fully and without exception to all maritime transport services that may affect trade between Member States. Maritime cabotage and tramp vessel services have, however, until October 2006, been excluded from the scope of Community implementing Regulations.[197] These exclusions have had important practical consequences in terms of how the Commission as well as national competition authorities and national courts have enforced Community competition rules in these sectors. Despite the fact that these sectors are now subject to the normal enforcement rules, general principles of temporal application of Community acts may prevent the application of such rules to situations existing before October 2006. The question what constitutes maritime cabotage and tramp vessel services will therefore continue to be of relevance for enforcers and practitioners in the years to come.

14.127   Maritime cabotage services are services between ports within the same Member States. Despite the geographical limits of the services, it is clear that cabotage services may nevertheless, in certain cases, affect trade between Member States to an appreciable extent. Maritime cabotage services *per se* do not therefore fall outside the scope of Community competition law although the justification for having excluded these services from the scope of Regulation 4056/86 appears purely to be the assumption that such services are unlikely to have an appreciable effect on trade between Member States, given the limitations in the service and

---

[194]   The review must also be seen in the context of the conclusions of the OECD secretariat in its 'Liner Shipping Competition Policy Report', where it recommended the removal of antitrust exemptions for common pricing and rate discussions and encouraged the OECD members to review their existing regulations to ensure that these took changed market circumstances into account.

[195]   COM(2004) 675 final. See also press release IP/04/1213 of 13 October 2004.

[196]   See n 139 above. All documents concerning the review can be found on DG Competition's web site at <http://europa.eu.int/comm/competition/antitrust/others/#review>.

[197]   See Art 32 of Regulation 1/2003 and para 14.94 above.

the volumes provided. While the justification for having excluded such services from effective enforcement rules may be disputed,[198] the scope of the exclusion is clearly defined and easy to apply. The same cannot be said for the exclusion for tramp vessel services.

Tramp vessel services are non-regular maritime transport services of goods in bulk or break-bulk. **14.128** Bulk and break-bulk transport cover a wide range of highly diversified services of significant economic importance, and co-operation arrangements such as pool agreements are common. Regulation 4056/86 defines the tramp vessel services that are to be covered by the exclusion from Regulation 1/2003.[199] The definition contains four main elements that describe the categories of goods transported, the nature of the service, including its operational characteristics (transport on demand, type of contract, and non-regularly scheduled sailings), as well as the commercial terms under which they are performed (freely negotiated freight rates). The definition leaves room for significant doubt as to which services would fall under the exclusion and the Commission has not yet taken a formal position on the exact meaning of tramp vessel services for the purpose of applying Regulation 4056/86.[200] Although it is clear that the exclusion, like any other exclusion from the normal rules, must be interpreted restrictively, it remains open to question whether the terms in the definition should be viewed as a mere description of the characteristics of tramping or as legal conditions which must be fulfilled at any point in time.[201] The Court appears to have taken the position that the definitions contained in Article 1(3) of the Regulation are intended to have legal consequences. In the *TAA* case, it found that, because the TAA did not meet the definition in Article 1(3)(b) of a liner conference (it did not operate under 'uniform or common freight rates'), it could not benefit from the block exemption contained in Article 3. The notion of uniform and common freight rates is not mentioned as a condition for the block exemption in Article 3, but only as one of the elements in the definition of a liner conference in Article 1(3)(b). The Court findings can therefore only be explained if the elements in the definition constitute legal conditions. It would consequently be fair to assume that the Court will adopt the same position concerning the definition of tramp vessel services.

The elements that are likely to cause most concern in terms of applying the exclusion are **14.129** the qualification of 'goods in bulk or in break-bulk' and 'non-regularly scheduled sailings', as well as the question as to when freight rates can be said to be 'freely negotiated case by case in accordance with the conditions of supply and demand'. The service should concern

---

[198] See recital 13 of Regulation 1419/2006. The Commission has indicated that the facts and arguments put forward to date in the context of the review have not convinced it of the need to maintain the exclusion for such services. See White Paper, paras 24–25 (n 195) and the Commission Proposal to the Council to repeal Regulation 4056/86 (see n 139 above).

[199] Art 1(3)(a) of Regulation 4056/86 reads: 'tramp vessel services means the transport of goods in bulk or in break-bulk in a vessel charter wholly or partly to one or more shippers on the basis of a voyage or a time charter or any other form of contract for non-regularly scheduled or non-advertised sailings where the freight rates are freely negotiated case by case in accordance with the conditions of supply and demand.'

[200] In the *TAA* decision, the Commission made a distinction between tramp services, liner services, and specialised transport (para 33). The distinction was made in the context of defining the relevant market and therefore does not provide clarification as to which services constitute tramp vessel services within the meaning of the Regulation.

[201] See, in this respect, also Niels Christian Ersbøll, 'The European Commission's Enforcement Powers: An Analysis of the Exclusion of Tramp Vessel Services from Regulation 4056/86 and Regulation 1/2003' [2003] ECLR 375.

the transport of goods in bulk or break-bulk, which seems to exclude not only container-ised services, but also possibly so-called specialised cargo.[202] The irregularly scheduled or non-advertised element can be difficult to assess in cases where a certain regularity is inherent in the service for operational or commercial reasons.[203] The existence of specific geographic trade patterns might not in itself be sufficient to constitute a regularly scheduled service. Rather, emphasis would be put on the regularity of the service and particularly on the exis-tence of some type of schedule or announcements to the market of planned sailing. It is clear that the element concerning the freely negotiated freight rates relates to the relation-ship between the vessel operator and the shipper and can only be fulfilled where the price is not fixed in advance by a tariff rate or other general rate arrangements, but negotiated on the basis of the service offered. The definition not only stipulates that freight rates should be freely negotiated, but also that this should be done on a 'case-by-case' basis 'in accor-dance with the conditions of supply and demand'. This could imply that a rate agreement between an operator and a shipper cannot qualify as a freely negotiated freight rate in a market where the supply and demand functions have been set aside *de facto* by horizontal price agreements between the operator and his competitors.

14.130   The result of the previous exclusion of cabotage and tramp vessel services is that for these services the Commission could not use its traditional fact-finding tools, such as the power to conduct on the spot investigations or enforce legal deadlines for replies to requests for information. Nor could the Commission itself bring infringements to an end, accept legally binding remedies and commitments, or impose fines, but instead had to rely on the transi-tional provisions in Article 85 of the Treaty.[204]

14.131   The exclusion has also restricted the role of national competition authorities and courts. The aim of Regulation 1/2003 was to create a new enforcement regime where national competition authorities and courts could apply Article 81 of the Treaty in full. While Article 82 of the Treaty is directly applicable by national courts, precedents show that in the absence of an applicable implementing Regulation such courts can only rule on Article 81 when the Commission or a national competition authority has held that a given practice infringes Article 81.[205]

14.132   The Commission, in its White Paper, has questioned the justification for maintaining the exclusion of maritime cabotage and tramp vessel services from the normal enforcement regime, laid down in Regulation 1/2003.[206] Regulation 1419/2006 deleted Article 32 of Regulation 1/2003, thereby bringing cabotage and tramp vessel services under the scope of the

---

[202]   As, for example, so-called neo-bulkers or cargo that is heavy and outsized.

[203]   This would, for instance, be the case when the vessel operator provides specialised services or focuses mainly on a particular type of good for which the number of loading and discharge areas is limited. The same considerations would apply when the services need to be organised in such a way that the operators fulfil their contractual obligations further to long-term contracts with large customers.

[204]   Art 85 of the Treaty empowers the Commission to propose appropriate measures to bring an identified infringement to an end; these include the right to record such infringement in a reasoned decision and to authorise Member States to take the measures necessary to remedy the situation. The Commission may deter-mine the conditions and details of the measures to be undertaken by the Member States.

[205]   Judgment of the Court in Case 66/86 *Ahmed Saeed* [1989] ECR 803; and judgment of the Court of 30 April 1986 in Joined Cases 209 to 213/84 *Ministére Public v Asjes et al* [1986] ECR 1425. It may well be, however, that this case law will evolve following the abolition of the notification system.

[206]   See n 195 above.

common competition implementing rules. Contrary to the provisions concerning the liner conference block exemption, this change was not subject to a transitional period, but entered into effect 20 days after the publication of the Regulation in the Official Journal. General principles of the temporal application of Community acts may however prevent the Commission from applying all its normal enforcement powers to situations existing before the entry into force of such regulation.[207] The above described uncertainty concerning the notion of tramp vessel services may therefore continue to play a role in the enforcement of Community competition rules in this sector. The Commission has commissioned a study on the economic and legal assessment of tramp shipping markets and intends to issue guidelines.

(5) Consortia (Regulation 823/2000)

(a) Background

The second sector-specific Regulation is Commission Regulation 823/2000 (as amended by **14.133** Regulation 611/2005) containing a block exemption for consortia agreements. A consortium is a grouping of shipping lines that co-operate to provide a joint liner shipping service. Consortia emerged as a common means of organising the industry in the 1960s with the growth of container vessels, which necessitated major capital investment in new vessels and containers. Most consortia comprise highly integrated joint ventures where the members co-operate on technical, operational, and commercial matters. By contrast with traditional mergers, the members, however, remain free to join other consortia or indeed to act independently on other routes. The Commission has therefore stated that the Merger Regulation does not apply to consortia in the liner trades sector.[208]

(b) Legislation

The first consortia block exemption (Commission Regulation 870/95)[209] was adopted by **14.134** the Commission in April 1995, on the basis of the Council enabling Regulation 479/92.[210] The five-year period of validity of the Regulation expired on 22 April 2000, when the block exemption was renewed until 25 April 2005 by Commission Regulation 823/2000.[211]

---

[207] Whereas procedural rules are generally held to apply to all proceedings pending at the time when they enter into force, substantive rules are usually interpreted as not applying to situations existing before they enter into force (see Joined Cases 212-217/80, *Salumi and Others v Amministrazione delle Finanze dello Stato*, [1981] ECR 2735). Arts 7 to 10, 14 and 17 to 22 of Regulation 1/2003 would appear to be procedural in nature and therefore applicable as from the entry into force of any repeal of Art 32 of Regulation 1/2003. Art 23 (imposition of fines) could on the other hand arguably qualify as a substantive rule.

[208] See Commission statement for the Council Minutes 9296/97 ADD 1, 20 June 1997, reproduced in Merger Control law in the European Union, Situation in March 1998, at p 66.

[209] Commission Regulation (EC) 870/95 of 20 April 1995 on the application of Art 85(3) [now Art 81(3)] of the Treaty to certain categories of agreements, decisions and concerted practices between liner shipping companies (consortia) pursuant to Council Regulation (EEC) 479/92 [1995] OJ L89 ([1995] OJ L89/7).

[210] [1992] OJ L55/3. The Council at the time of the adoption of Regulation 4056/86 had already invited the Commission to study the situation regarding liner shipping consortia. The result was a communication submitted to the Council in June 1990, in which the Commission pronounced itself in favour of adopting a block exemption for this type of agreement (COM 90 (260) final of 18 June 1990).

[211] Commission Regulation (EC) 823/2000 of 19 April 2000 on the application of Art 81(3) of the Treaty to certain categories of agreements, decisions, and concerted practices between liner shipping companies (consortia) [2000] OJ L100/24. See also Working paper of DGIV 'Report on Commission Regulation No 870/95' of 28 January 1999.

On 12 March 2004, Regulation 823/2000 was amended to align its procedural rules with Regulation 1/2003. The changes included in particular the repeal of the opposition procedure and the notification requirement for consortia exceeding the block exemption ceiling.[212] The changes did not, however, affect the substantive provisions of the block exemption itself. These were the subject of a second revision, resulting in Commission Regulation 611/2005 which extended the application of Regulation 823/2000 for a further five years.[213] Regulation 611/2005 also introduced some minor modifications in the substantive provisions of the block exemption, in order to provide greater clarity as to the application of the Regulation.[214] Taking account of the possible consequences that the at that time ongoing review of the liner shipping regime might entail for the consortia block exemption, the Commission nevertheless considered that it was neither necessary nor appropriate to introduce substantial modifications to the consortia block exemption before the end of the review.[215] It is to be anticipated that the Commission will thoroughly review the scope and conditions of the consortia block exemption once it has been able to observe the result of the repealing of Council Regulation 4056/86.

(c) Consortia and Conferences

14.135 The objective of a consortium agreement is to bring about co-operation in the joint operation of a maritime transport service, so as to improve the productivity and quality of liner shipping services and to encourage greater utilisation of the containers and the more efficient use of vessel capacity. It may restrict competition between its members by provisions concerning capacity, sailing schedules, port rotations, and marketing. The Commission has, however, recognised that such a form of co-operation usually leads to substantial economies of scale, which would in turn lead to lower prices for consumers, provided that there is sufficient competition on the market.

14.136 Even if most consortia operate within a conference, the two forms of co-operation are fundamentally different, which is reflected in the scope and aim of the two block exemption Regulations. The most obvious difference is that a consortium offers a joint shipping service whereas a conference offers no such service. The consortia block exemption Regulation is intended to reduce the costs and risks of launching a containerised liner

---

[212] Commission Regulation (EC) 463/2004 of 12 March amending Regulation (EC) 823/2000 [2004] OJ L77/23. Like its predecessor, Regulation 823/2000 originally contained a simplified opposition procedure under which consortium agreements with market shares between the block exemption ceiling and 50 per cent could still benefit from the block exemption if the Commission did not oppose exemption within six months of notification. A consortium with a market share above 50 per cent on any market could also qualify for an individual exemption.

[213] Commission Regulation (EC) 611/2005 amending Regulation (EC) 823/2000 [2005] OJ L101/10. A corrigendum was published in [2005] OJ L103/41. See also press release IP/05/477 issued on 25 April 2005 and the publication of the draft Regulation published in [2004] OJ C319/2.

[214] The amendments extended the initial period within which members cannot withdraw from the agreement without a financial penalty and clarified that such an initial period could also be agreed when the members have made a substantial new investment in the service offered by the consortium. Lastly, it clarified that the existence of individual service contracts may also be taken into consideration when demonstrating the existence of effective price competition.

[215] DG Competition, in its Consultation document published on 25 April 2004, had already outlined a renewal of the Regulation without any modifications as the most likely of three policy options available to the Commission when Regulation 382/2000 expired.

shipping service, by allowing the operators to engage in various types of co-operation to provide such services. The conference block exemption, on the other hand, focuses on the revenue side and is based on the assumption that allowing the conference members to agree on common freight rates will contribute to price stability, which will in turn ensure that there is a constantly reliable supply of liner shipping services, to the ultimate benefit of the customers.

(d) Scope and Exempted Activities

Regulation 823/2000 recognises the wide variety of consortia arrangements that exists and covers all agreements whose objective is the joint operation of liner shipping services, provided that they fulfil the conditions and obligations set out in the Regulation.[216] The block exemption covers both consortia operating within a liner conference and consortia operating outside such conferences, in so far as they provide international liner shipping services to or from one or more Community ports. The scope of the application therefore excludes cabotage services operating solely within a single Member State. The exemption is further limited to services exclusively for the carriage of cargo, chiefly by container, and consequently does not cover agreements in respect of passenger transport or traditional bulk pool arrangements. Taking into account the fact that consortia are rarely active in only one trade nowadays, Regulation 823/2000 makes it clear that the exemption also covers multi-trade and global consortia. Each trade which the consortium operates, however, will be assessed separately. The Regulation does not cover restrictive agreements between different consortia.[217]   **14.137**

The exempted activities are listed in Article 3 of the Regulation and cover a range of technical, operational, and commercial activities, such as the joint operation of the transport service and port terminals, temporary capacity adjustments, and joint marketing.[218] The possibility of making temporary capacity adjustments (which is more justified in this context than in the liner conference block exemption) should be read in conjunction with Article 4, which makes clear that any agreement seeking to freeze the use of a fixed percentage of capacity leads to the non-applicability of the block exemption.   **14.138**

Price-fixing agreements are expressly excluded from the scope of the consortia block exemption. This does not, however, prevent consortium members from also being members   **14.139**

---

[216] Despite the broad definition, normal (non-reciprocal) slot charter arrangements would not qualify as a consortium, unless they are combined with other forms of co-operation between the parties or reciprocal undertakings (see Working paper of DGIV 'Report on Commission Regulation No 870/95' of 28 January 1999, para 81).

[217] See recital 21 of Regulation 823/2000.

[218] Art 3(2) reads in full: 'The declaration of non-applicability shall apply only to the following activities: (a) the joint operation of liner shipping transport services which comprise solely the following activities: (i) the coordination and/or joint fixing of sailing time-tables and the determination of ports of call; (ii) the exchange, sale or cross-chartering of space or slots on vessels; (iii) the pooling of vessels and/or port installations; (iv) the use of one or more joint operations offices; (v) the provision of containers, chassis and other equipment and/or the rental, leasing or purchase contracts for such equipment; (vi) the use of a computerised data exchange system and/or joint documentation system; (b) temporary capacity adjustments: (c) the joint operation or use of port terminals and related services (such as lighterage or stevedoring services); (d) the participation in one or more of the following pools: cargo, revenue or net revenue; (e) the exercise of voting rights held by the consortium in the conference within which its members operate, in so far as the vote being jointly exercised concerns the consortium's activities as such; (f) a joint marketing structure and/or the issue of a joint bill of lading; (g) any other activity ancillary to those referred to above in points (a) to (f) which is necessary for their implementation.'

of liner conferences, which is in fact mostly the case.[219] The fact that Regulations 823/2000 (as amended by Regulation 611/2005) and 4056/86 do not exclude a parallel application *per se* does not mean that the concurrent membership of a consortium and of a conference may not have implications with regard to the conditions that are attached to the respective regulations. This could be an issue particularly in cases where the membership of the consortium coincides exactly with the membership of the conference (ie the same carriers have formed both a conference and a consortium). It is unlikely that in such cases there would be sufficient effective internal competition on price and on service, which is a condition which must be fulfilled in order to benefit from the consortia block exemption.[220]

14.140   Article 3(2)(g) provides that any other activity ancillary to the one listed and necessary for its implementation is exempted. This 'additional' exemption should be interpreted restrictively. This provision allows the members, *inter alia*, to exchange information relating to the co-operation. Article 3(3) explicitly states that so called exclusivity and third party clauses, which are very common in consortia agreements, albeit in a variety of different forms, shall be considered ancillary activities.[221] The Commission has also accepted that the provision could cover common feeder services if these are offered as an integral part of the consortium service. Notwithstanding the fact that the Commission also appears to have accepted the joint purchase of port terminal services as a related service exempted under Article 3(2)(c), it has indicated that the joint purchase of feeder services would not generally seem to be necessary for the implementation of the exempted activities and could not therefore be subsumed under the exempted ancillary activities.[222]

(e) Conditions

14.141   The Regulation contains four sets of conditions and obligations for exemption.

14.142   First, Article 5 stipulates that the consortium must operate in an environment where at least one of the following situations prevails: (a) there is effective price competition between the members of the conference within which the consortium operates; (b) there exists within the conference within which the consortium operates a sufficient degree of effective competition in terms of services provided between consortium members and other conference members; and (c) consortium members are subject to effective competition from non-consortium lines (whether or not a conference operates in the relevant trade).

14.143   This condition can give cause for concern if the consortium is operating within a conference that has a strong position in the market, especially when a very large proportion of the conference cargoes is carried under the tariff rather than under contract rates (which

---

219   See recital 8 of Regulation 823/2000.

220   See Art 5 of Regulation 823/2000 (as amended by Art 2 of Regulation 611/2005), further explained below.

221   Exclusivity clauses are obligations on the consortium members to use only those vessels that are allocated to the consortium service on the relevant trade route and to refrain from chartering slots on vessels belonging to third parties. Such provisions guarantee that the members bring all available cargo to the joint shipping service and have therefore been treated as an ancillary service. Third party clauses restrict the ability of the consortium members to assign space charter or sub-space charter to other vessel-operating carriers except with the prior consent of the other members. The term vessel-operating carrier is used to avoid a situation whereby the third party clause can be applied towards freight forwarders and other non-vessel-operating intermediaries.

222   See working paper of DG IV, 'Report on Commission Regulation No 870/95', 28 January 1999, para 110.

provide some internal competition between the conference lines). This was the situation in the *Grand Alliance* case. Following careful examination, the Commission concluded that the fact that shippers appeared to switch frequently between different carriers (both members and non-members of the consortium), as well as evidence of considerable fluctuation in the market shares of the individual consortium members, indicated that the members were subject at least to effective competition on service.[223]

Secondly, Article 6 contains the relevant market share thresholds. In order to benefit from the block exemption, the market share of a consortium must, in each market in which it operates, not exceed 30 per cent (if it operates within a conference) or 35 per cent (when it operates outside a conference). Market shares are calculated by reference to the volume of goods carried.[224] The distinction between consortia within and outside a conference is due to the fact that the former are agreements superimposed onto an already existing restrictive conference agreement operating within the trade. The Regulation also contains a 'margin of tolerance' for temporal and marginal excess of the thresholds. It should be remembered in this context that the definition of the relevant service market, upon which the market shares are to be calculated, would not normally include conventional maritime operators.

14.144

Until March 2004, the block exemption was also applicable to consortia with a market share not exceeding 50 per cent in any market provided that such arrangements were notified to the Commission and that the Commission did not oppose such exemption within a six-month period (the 'opposition' procedure).[225] It is clear, however, that consortia agreements that exceed the market share thresholds of the block exemption may also still be legal in the new enforcement regime, provided that they satisfy the Article 81(3) EC criteria.

14.145

Thirdly, Article 8 aims at ensuring that the trade in which the consortium operates is kept flexible and competitive. It provides that a consortium must preserve the right of each individual line to offer individual service arrangements. Furthermore, each individual line must be allowed to withdraw from the agreement following a six-month notice period. The Regulation, however, provides for possible agreement to an initial lock-in period of 18 months or, in the case of a highly integrated consortium, 30 months, under which no notice can be given.[226] Notice and lock-in periods that extend beyond these periods are not covered by the block exemption.[227] The initial period starts to run from the 'entry into force of the agreement'. Unless there is a specific provision in the agreement regulating its entry into force, the assumption must be that it enters into force when it has been signed, which will usually be before the commencement of the actual service. Regulation 611/2005 has, in this respect, introduced two welcome amendments. In cases where the date of entry into force of the agreement is earlier

14.146

---

[223] See Eric FitzGerald, 'The Grand Alliance' [2000] Competition Policy Newsletter 26.

[224] The volume of goods carried is calculated in freight tonnes or twenty-foot equivalent unit (TEU), the standard term for containerised cargo.

[225] The opposition procedure, contained in Art 7 of Regulation 823/2000, was repealed in the procedural revisions undertaken in Regulation 463/2004.

[226] Art 8(b) of Regulation 823/2000. The types of highly integrated consortia that can benefit from the exceptional 30-month lock in period comprise such consortia as have a net revenue pool and/or high level of investment due to the purchase or charter by its members of vessels specifically for the purpose of setting up the consortium.

[227] The Commission has on one occasion opposed a consortium under the previously applicable non-opposition procedure partly because the agreement contained a lock-in period of 31 months.

than the date of the commencement of the service, the members can agree on an initial lock-in period of a maximum of 24 months (or 36 months in the case of a highly integrated consortium). Furthermore, it is now clear that changes and upgrades in the services offered after the establishment of the service can justify a new lock-in period of similar duration, provided that such upgrades can be regarded as a substantial new investment in the joint maritime service.[228]

14.147   Lastly, Article 9 provides for various obligations attaching to the exemption, which have been partly revised with the procedural amendments introduced in May 2004. The most important of the remaining conditions is the initiation of real and effective consultations between the consortium and the shippers on issues that are related directly to the consortium service. As in Regulation 4056/86, the consortia Regulation also provides an exemption for agreements between transport users on the one hand and the consortium on the other concerning the use of scheduled maritime services in so far as they arise out of the consultations required under Article 9 (Article 10).

(f) Commission Practice

14.148   The Commission has so far looked favourably on consortia, due to the improvement they usually bring about not only in the productivity but also in the quality of liner shipping services by rationalisation and economies of scale. This position is illustrated by the fact that since the entry into force of Regulation 823/2000 the Commission has in only one case opposed a notification under the now repealed opposition procedure. The issues that appear to have given rise to most uncertainty during the application of Regulation 823/2000 concern the assessment of effective competition, the maximum notice period (including the lock-in period), and the question when an agreement would constitute a new agreement. The Commission has taken the position that the initial period starts on the day the agreement becomes legally binding on the consortia members, irrespective of when the service commenced. It has also been reluctant to accept that upgrades in the service or changes of consortia members will necessarily trigger the establishment of a new agreement under which the consortia members would benefit from a new initial lock-in period. The amendments introduced by Regulation 611/2005 have hopefully solved the issues deemed most problematic by the industry. The amendments also clearly show that the Commission is prepared to ensure that the block exemption provisions are attuned to industry practice, as long as such practice can be subsumed under the four conditions of Article 81(3) EC.

D. Inland Transport

(1) Introduction

14.149   Inland transport comprises transport by road, rail, and inland waterway. These are the sectors covered by Regulation 1017/68,[229] which is still applicable and is one of the oldest regulations in the competition area.

---

[228] Art 3 of Regulation 611/2005, amending Art 8 point (b) of Regulation 823/2000. The Regulation specifies in clear terms what constitutes a 'substantial new investment' as well as the 'commencement of the service' within the meaning of the Regulation.

[229] Regulation 1017/68 of 19 July 1968 applying rules of competition to transport by rail, road, and inland waterway [1968] OJ L175/1.

(a) Transport of Goods by Road

The European road haulage market is fully liberalised. Since 1 January 1993, any road **14.150** transport operator wishing to provide haulage between Member States must hold a Community licence issued by the Member State of establishment. This document entitles the operator to access the single market.[230] On 1 July 1998 road cabotage in the movement of freight was liberalised. This means that from that date an EU haulier, meeting the conditions for admission to the occupation of road haulage operator and holding a Community licence, can transport goods between destinations anywhere in the European Union, including within a Member State which is not his own: thus a Belgian operator can load a consignment in Rome and unload it in Milan.[231]

Road haulage has seen spectacular growth during the last decades: the volume of road **14.151** freight haulage grew by 34 per cent between 1991 and 2000. Furthermore, road haulage accounted for about 75 per cent of freight traffic within the European Union in 2000 compared to 50 per cent in 1970.

(b) Transport of Passengers by Road

The carriage of passengers by coach and bus is the subject of a Community Regulation[232] **14.152** that lays down common rules, defines the conditions for applying the principle of free movement, and simplifies administrative procedures.

The Community licence in principle allows bus operators to provide international passen- **14.153** ger services on European Union territory, regardless of nationality or place of establishment. However, national authorisations are still required for scheduled services. For charter services, special regular services, and own-account transport, special rules apply. Cabotage operations (national passenger transport operations carried out on a temporary basis by non-resident operators), generally speaking, are limited to specialised regular services and occasional services.[233] Cabotage is permitted for regular services, on a temporary basis, provided that it forms part of an international service (for example, an Italian transport operator can only take passengers between Lyon and Paris on a Turin-Lyon-Paris-Brussels line) and that the laws, regulations, and administrative provisions in force in the Member State where the cabotage operation is performed (the host country) are observed (relating to *inter alia* authorisations, the routes to be operated, and frequency).

(c) Inland Waterways

The current inland waterway markets are largely liberalised. Regulations (EEC) 3921/91 **14.154** and (EC) 1356/96 give EU vessels the right to carry out cabotage and international transport operations within the European Union. Operators of such vessels must prove a 'genuine link' with a Member State. Council Regulation (EEC) 3921/91 of 16 December 1991[234]

---

[230] See Council Regulation (EEC) 881/92 of 26 March 1992 [1992] OJ L095/1–7.

[231] It was also permitted from 1990 to 1998, though subject to annual licensed quotas for each Member State. A 1998 Commission report on the application of this scheme (COM/98/0047) showed that by and large these quotas were underused.

[232] Regulation 684/92 of 16 March 1992, as amended by Regulation 11/98 of 11 December 1997.

[233] Council Regulation 12/98 of 11 December 1997.

[234] [1991 OJ L373/1–3.

deals with cabotage, while Regulation (EC) 1356/96 of 6 July 1996[235] specifies the conditions for inland waterway traffic between EU countries and in transit through them. All carriers of goods or passengers by inland waterway have the right to carry out transport operations between Member States and in transit through them without discrimination on grounds of nationality and place of business if they are registered in a Member State in accordance with the laws of that State and comply with a number of other conditions.

14.155 These provisions do not affect the rights of third country carriers under the revised Rhine Navigation Convention (Mannheim Convention), the Danube Navigation Convention (Belgrade Convention), or the Community's international obligations.

14.156 Inland waterways carry 12 per cent of the freight in the EU. The industry has grown by 17 per cent in the last 10 years.

(d) Transport of Goods by Rail

14.157 In the railway sector, market opening is less advanced than in the other transport sectors. Although the markets for rail freight transport have been opened in three stages since 15 March 2003 (international transport via the so-called Trans-European Rail Freight Network), 1 January 2006 (international transport via the whole network), and 1 January 2007 (domestic freight transport), the markets for international and national transport of passengers have until now not been opened at a European level.

14.158 Nevertheless, the European rail transport market is in a critical condition. It has experienced a worrying decline over almost thirty years now. In 1970 the railways carried 21 per cent of all freight in the fifteen countries that were members of the EU in 2000. By 2000 the figure was down to 8.1 per cent. In the US, rail's share of the freight market in 1999 was 40 per cent. The modal share of railway passenger traffic has also declined during the last thirty years, though less dramatically: passenger transport, which accounted for 10.2 per cent of total rail transport in 1970, fell to 6.3 per cent in 2000.

14.159 The downward trend in respect of rail transport is also reflected in the fact that the average speed by which goods are transported by rail is only 18 km per hour. Further, rail transport of goods is less reliable than road haulage as regards delivery times, which are far less predictable in the case of rail. On some international routes, delivery times have even doubled or trebled in recent years. This is due mainly to very long stopping times en route, because other trains (passenger services especially) have priority, and because procedures at borders are complicated (train crews and locomotives have to be changed because of differences in signalling systems from one country to another, etc).

14.160 At the same time, Member States and the European Union continue to provide considerable funding to the sector. About EUR50 billion of public resources are spent annually in the railway sector (on railway infrastructure and services)[236] in order to subsidise an industry that generates a turnover of EUR100 billion.

---

[235] [1996] OJ L175/7–8.

[236] Including EUR2 billion from the European structural funds and EUR3–4 billion in loans granted by the EIB, but exclusive of the railway projects that are part of the EUR600 billion recently earmarked for the trans-European transport network (which also concerns projects for modes of transport other than rail).

Nevertheless, it is widely recognised that railways play a key role in contributing to the **14.161** overall Community objectives of greater competitiveness and sustainable development. They provide services at distances, times, frequencies, and fares attractive enough to persuade people to switch from road to rail, and thereby help to relieve road traffic congestion and pollution. They are a safe and clean mode of transport and one train can contain up to 50 or 60 truckloads of goods. Also, the high-speed train network spreading across the European Union, with its excellent environmental performance and energy efficiency, proves that the railways are a mode of transport with a future, and not of the past.

Therefore, one of the particular priorities identified in the White Paper on European Transport **14.162** Policy adopted by the Commission in October 2001 was the revitalisation of the railways. The need to act had been given added urgency by the Lisbon European Council of June 2000 which concluded that liberalisation of sectors such as transport should be accelerated.

(2) EU Liberalisation in the Railway Sector   **14.163**

The Railway Packages

Liberalisation of the railway sector started with Directive (EEC) 91/440.[237] This Directive **14.164** introduced financial accounting changes as the first step towards separating train services from track management. The Directive opened the door, for the first time, to the provision by third parties of cross-border combined transport freight services. The Directive also introduced the concept of the 'international grouping', an association of at least two train operators based in different Member States operating cross-border passenger or freight services. This requirement to form a grouping for all types of cross-border services except combined transport has given significant power to the incumbent national railway undertakings.[238]

(i) **First Railway Package**   With regard to freight services, this dependence on the incum- **14.165** bent undertaking was abolished under Directive 2001/12.[239] As part of the first railway package of Directives, it has freed individual operators to provide all types of cross-border freight services (ie not just in respect of combined transport). For a transitional period, these new opportunities are limited to the so-called Trans-European Rail Freight Network (TERFN). However, from 2007 onwards,[240] access rights will be the same as for combined transport and will extend across the whole of the EU rail network. In addition, the Directive takes separation in the sector a stage further by requiring separate balance sheet accounting for train operations and infrastructure management and clearer accounting separation between passenger and freight services. The Directive also states that certain essential functions,[241] concerning track charging, train path allocation, operator licensing,

---

[237] Directive of 29 July 1991 on the development of the Community's railways [1991] OJ L237/25.

[238] An interesting study commissioned by DG TREN finished in June 2005 highlights the regulatory and competition issues raised by the fact that much of the cross-border traffic in rail still takes place on the basis of the 'old' structure of multilateral and bilateral agreements based, *inter alia*, on the requirement of an international grouping. See Colin Buchanan and Partners, a study on compliance of rail border traffic agreements with EU rail and competition ligislation, <http://ec.europa.eu/transport/rail/research/doc/buchanan-report.pdf>.

[239] Directive 2001/12 of the European Parliament and of the Council of 26 February 2001 amending Council Directive (EEC) 91/440 on the development of the Community's railways [2001] OJ L75/1.

[240] The initial date of 2008 was brought forward by the second package.

[241] With some derogations for Ireland, Northern Ireland, and Greece.

monitoring compliance with public service obligations and setting standards of safety, can only be carried out by entities who do not themselves provide rail transport services.

14.166   (ii) **Second Railway Package**   The second package of reforms, adopted on 23 April 2004, included market opening for *national* rail freight markets with effect from 1 January 2007.

14.167   The second package also provided for the establishment of a European Railway Agency, to be located in Lille/Valenciennes (France).[242] Its main task is to develop common safety standards, monitor safety performances, and manage systems for establishing, registering, and monitoring technical specifications for interoperability.

14.168   (iii) **Controlled Competition for Public Transport**   As regards *railways*, a recurrent concern is the need to guarantee socially necessary universal services that cannot be operated on a commercial basis. It was for this reason that, in the 2004 DG TREN proposal to open up the market for international transport of passengers (the 'free access proposal'), access to stations served by universal service providers was ring-fenced to a certain extent.[243] It is now proposed that Member States retain the option of limiting such access should it put at risk the economic equilibrium of the universal service.

14.169   In 2000 the Commission had already presented a proposal with respect to public services in passenger transport by rail, road, and inland waterway. The effect of the Commission proposal[244] would be to extend the system of so-called controlled competition right across the EU rail, road, and inland waterway passenger markets. Controlled competition involves open, competitive bidding for fixed term contracts where the contracting authority wants to procure a service with exclusive rights and/or subsidy. Such a system has already been instituted on a voluntary basis for public services in passenger transport by rail and road in a number of EU Member States.

14.170   The 2000 proposal on controlled competition was held up for a long time in Council, and in July 2005 the Commission presented a new proposal.[245] The July 2005 proposal concerning public services in rail and road transport requires Member States to award public service contracts in these sectors by public tender. However, the proposal contains major exceptions that severely reduce its potential market opening effects, for instance in relation to Member States whose public bus and railway companies are not active in other Member States' territory and with respect to regional and long distance rail transport. The Transport Council reached a common position on this proposal during its meeting of 8 and 9 June 2006.

14.171   (iv) **Third Railway Package**   In the third package, presented on 3 March 2004, the Commission, keeping its promise to the European Parliament, issued a specific proposal on

---

[242] The tasks of the Agency, its organisation, and its methods of working with the representatives of the railway sector are regulated in Regulation 881/2004.

[243] See Art 7 of the proposal, inserting a new para 3 (b) in Art 10 of Directive 91/440.

[244] *Amended proposal for a Regulation of the European Parliament and of the Council on action by Member States concerning public service requirements and the award of public service contracts in passenger transport by rail, road and inland waterway* COM(2002) 107 final of 21 February 2002.

[245] COM (2005) 319 final.

the opening up of the market for international rail passenger services.[246] On 24 July 2006, the Transport Council reached a common position on this proposal which will now be discussed in Parliament. The proposal to liberalise the market for the international transport of passengers was accompanied by proposed measures concerning protection of passenger rights, the certification of locomotive drivers, and minimum quality clauses in contracts between railway undertakings and their customers.[247]

It is proposed that, as from 1 January 2010, railway undertakings that have a licence and **14.172** the required safety certificates should be able to operate international services in the Community. For example, existing services such as Thalys and Eurostar could see the arrival of competitors. In order to create realistic economic conditions for developing the services, it is proposed that operators be permitted to pick up and set down passengers at any station on an international route, including stations located in the same Member State. It is intended that the general principle should be one of opening the market on the basis of free competition, while allowing Member States the option of limiting such access if it could put at risk the economic equilibrium of a public service contract for a specific service, subject to strict compliance with (the regulation replacing) Regulation 1191/69. The solution proposed is balanced, since it allows national or local authorities, if they so wish, to award public service contracts jointly, while leaving the way open for the development of new initiatives and retaining the cabotage option to enable international services to develop under realistic economic conditions. According to the Commission, the expansion of the high-speed network (from 2600km to 6000km in 2010) and its interconnection by 2010, together with progress on interoperability, should open up important new markets for rail transport and provide an opportunity for new commercial initiatives.

(v) Railway Interoperability The technical fragmentation of rail networks is a major **14.173** handicap to the development of this mode of transport. Community legislation is gradually establishing mandatory Technical Specifications for Interoperability (Directives (EC) 96/48, (EC) 2001/16, and (EC) 2004/50 on the interoperability of the trans-European rail system).

The first set of Technical Specifications for Interoperability was adopted in 2002 for high **14.174** speed systems. Specifications now need to be developed for conventional systems, with priority given to freight. Work is being done by the European Association for Railway Interoperability (AEIF), which groups together the various players in the sector. The newly founded Railway Agency will be responsible for drawing up and revising the Technical Specifications for Interoperability, on the basis of work completed or being done by the AEIF.

(3) Legal Framework for Competition in Inland Transport

(a) Regulation 1017/68

(i) Scope of Regulation 1017/68 Regulation 1017/68 was adopted in 1968. The Regulation **14.175** contained both substantive and procedural rules on competition including an exception

---

[246] Proposal for a Directive of the European parliament and of the Council amending Council Directive 91/440/EEC on the development of the Community's railways (presented by the Commission), COM (2004) 0139 final.

[247] Press release IP/04/291, Memo <http://www.europa.eu.int/comm/transport/rail/package2003/doc/memo-fr.pdf>, COM(2004)139–144 final of 3 March 2004.

for 'technical agreements' and a block exemption for certain groups of small and medium-sized undertakings.[248] The Regulation applies, in the field of transport by rail, road, and inland waterway, to:

- all agreements, decisions, and concerted practices which have as their object or effect:
— the fixing of transport rates and conditions;
— the limitation or control of the supply of transport;
— the sharing of transport markets;
— the application of technical improvements or technical co-operation; or
— the joint financing or acquisition of transport equipment or supplies where such operations are directly related to the provision of transport services and are necessary for the joint operation of services by a grouping, within the meaning of Article 4, of road or inland waterway transport undertakings; and
- the abuse of a dominant position on the transport market.

These provisions also apply to operations by providers of services ancillary to transport, which have any of the objects or effects listed above.

14.176 **(ii) Modernisation**   Apart from the acts of accession and one corrigendum in 1973,[249] Regulation 1017/68 was never substantially changed. However, Regulation 1/2003[250] considerably reduced the scope and effect of Regulation 1017/68 by introducing direct references to Article 81 of the EC Treaty and repealing the procedural rules of the Regulation.

14.177 As a consequence, Article 2, which essentially re-formulates the prohibition of Article 81 (1) of the EC Treaty in relation to the transport sectors referred to, is repealed and, wherever applicable, references to this provision are replaced by references to Article 81 (1). In addition, Article 5, containing a specific 'Article 81 (3)-like' exemption for the relevant transport sectors, and Article 7, containing the equivalent of Article 81 (2) of the EC Treaty, are repealed. References to the first Article are replaced by references to Article 81 (3) of the EC Treaty.

14.178 Furthermore, the possibility that the prohibition contained in the former Article 2 may be declared inapplicable in the event of a crisis in part of a transport market has been removed.

14.179 The same applies with respect to the provisions on abuse of dominant position in the relevant transport sectors (Article 8) and to undertakings with special or exclusive rights (Article 9).

14.180 Finally all the procedural rules regarding complaints, applications for exemptions, requests to declare the prohibition of Article 2 inapplicable, and the enforcement powers of the Commission (Articles 9–29) have been repealed.

14.181 As a result, the only substantial provisions remaining in Regulation 1017/68 concern:

- the scope of the Regulation (Article 1);
- the exception for technical agreements (Article 3); and
- the exemption for groups of small and medium-sized undertakings (SMEs) (Article 4).

---

[248] For an extensive comment on Regulation 1017/68, see also Oliver Stehmann, 'Chapter 2 (Verordnung 1017/68)' in Frohnmeyer and Mückenhausen, *Kommentar EG Verkehrsrecht* (Beck, 2004, EL 4).
[249] [1999] OJ L999/28.
[250] Regulation 1/2003 of 16 December 2002 [2003] OJ L1/1.

(b) Dividing Line between Regulation 1017/68 and other Regulations

Before the introduction of a common regime for the application of the EU rules through **14.182** Regulation 1/2003, the question was often raised as to where the dividing lines lay between Regulation 17 and specific transport Regulations and between the transport Regulations themselves. In future, since Regulation 1/2003 is now the only Regulation determining the procedural framework of competition law enforcement, the relevance of the dividing line will be limited to situations in which the parties wish to rely on the exception for technical agreements or the exemption for groups of small and medium-sized undertakings.

In the *Fenex* case,[251] concerning recommended forwarding charges by a Dutch trade organi- **14.183** sation of forwarders regarding, *inter alia*, customs declarations and formalities, handling costs and pallet tariffs, the Commission based its decision on Regulation 17. Although the Commission did not dispute that, in certain circumstances, forwarders may perform a direct role as providers of transport services, it held that the recommended prices circulated by Fenex related to services that did not fall within the scope of Regulation 1017/68.

In *UIC*,[252] the Commission fined the International Rail   Union (UIC) for breach of **14.184** Article 81(1) for issuing a leaflet recommending the way in   hich member railways should appoint travel agents and setting a standard rate of com   sion for travel agents. The Commission applied Regulation 17 arguing, in particular, th   ravel agency services are nei- ther transport services nor services 'directly relating' to the p   ision of transport services.

On appeal,[253] the Court of First Instance annulled the decision upholding the UIC's argu- **14.185** ment that the procedure in Regulation 1017/68, and not that i. Regulation 17, should have been used. The Commission's appeal to the Court of Justice was rejected.[254] The Court upheld the Court of First Instance's reasoning that Article 1 of R   lation 1017/68 does not mention agreements, etc 'directly' related to transport, but agree   nts, etc 'in the transport sector which have as their object or effect the fixing of transport   ates and conditions . . .'.

According to the Court, it follows from the wording of Article 1 of Regulation 1017/68 **14.186** that its application depends upon the nature of the relevant agreements, which have the object or effect, *inter alia*, of fixing transport rates or limiting or controlling the supply of transport, and not, as the Commission had maintained, upon the prior identification of the market on which those agreements produce their effects.

Interestingly, however, in (later) judgments concerning Regulation 3975/87 on compe   ion **14.187** in air transport, the Court seems to have taken a slightly different approach. In *Aérop* *Paris*,[255] the Court relied on the express wording of Regulation 141 to establish that the th... recital of the preamble to that Regulation explains that the distinctive features of transport justify exempting from the application of Regulation 17 only agreements, decisions, and con- certed practices '*directly* relating to the provision of transport services'. Therefore, it could

---

[251] Commission Decision of 5 June 1996.
[252] Decision 92/568/EEC relating to a proceeding under Art 85 of the EEC Treaty (IV/33.585—Distribution of railway tickets by travel agents) OJ 1992 L366, p 47.
[253] Case T-14/93 *UIC v Commission* [1995] ECR II-1503.
[254] Case C-264/95P *Commission v UIC* [1997] ECR I-1287.
[255] Case C-82/01 P *Aéroports de Paris* [2002] ECR I-09297.

not be inferred from the judgment in *UIC* that the activity of an airport manager such as that carried out by ADP necessarily fell within the transport sector and the Court agreed that Regulation 3975/87 only applied to activities directly relating to the supply of air transport services, which was not the case as regards the activities carried out by ADP.

14.188 In *British Airways/Commission*,[256] which concerned BA's agreements with IATA travel agents established in the United Kingdom, the Court of First Instance again examined the differences between, on the one hand, Regulation 17 and Regulation 1017/68, and, on the other hand, Regulation 17 and Regulation 3975/87. Referring again to the use of the word 'directly' ('*directly* relating to the provision of transport services') in Regulation 141, the Court pointed out that the wording of Regulation 3975/87 (ie 'lays down the procedure for the application of the rules on competition to undertakings in the air transport sector') was different from that of Regulation 1017/68 (ie 'applies the rules of competition to transport by rail, road and inland waterways'). According to the Court, that difference in wording confirms that an activity falls within the scope of Regulation 3975/87 only if it is *directly* linked to the provision of air transport services.

(4) Market Definition

14.189 As in all sectors undergoing liberalisation, defining the market in inland transport has turned out to be an evolving process. A distinction must be made between passenger transport and transport of goods.

(a) Freight

14.190 In both rail freight and rail passenger transport, a distinction is generally made between the market for rail *services* and that for rail *transport*. In *Deutsche Bahn*,[257] the Court of First Instance found that the rail services market constituted a sub-market distinct from the rail transport market in general. According to the Court, the rail services market offered a specific range of services, in particular the provision of locomotives, traction, and access to the railway infrastructure, which, while admittedly provided according to the demands of the railway transport operators, was in no way interchangeable or in competition with their services. The distinct character of railway services also derived from the demand and supply factors that were specific to those services. On the one hand, it was not possible for transport operators to provide their services if they did not have railway services available to them. On the other hand, the railway undertakings, at the material time, enjoyed a statutory monopoly as regards the provision of railway services within their respective countries.

14.191 Citing precedents, the Court held that a sub-market which has specific characteristics from the point of view of demand and supply and which offers products which occupy an essential and non-interchangeable place in the more general market of which it forms part must be considered to be a distinct product market.[258] The Court held that, in the light of precedent, the Commission was justified in not taking into consideration the services provided by the rail transport operators and especially those provided by road hauliers and inland waterway transport operators.

---

[256] Case T-219/99, [2003] ECR II-05917.
[257] Case T-229/94 *Deutsche Bahn AG/ Commission* [1997] ECR II-01689.
[258] Case T-69/89 *RTE v Commission* [1991] ECR II-485, paras 61 and 62.

As in other sectors, the general principles of market definition as defined in the Commission's **14.192** Notice of 1997 apply.[259] The concept of relevant market is closely related to the objectives pursued under Community competition policy. For instance, in Article 82 cases, market definition is usually linked to the alleged abuse. In rail freight transport, this would mean that, if the alleged abuse affects a consignor or shipper, an investigation should take place to determine whether he has an alternative to the railway. Could he use road, inland waterway, sea, or possibly even air transport? This would depend partly on the particular type of freight commodity to be moved. For example, road is the preferred mode for low volume, high value goods, whereas rail is used far more for transporting large quantities of bulk freight—coal, iron ore and petroleum, for example—for which road haulage is not practicable. Thus, road transport may be substitutable in the case of some goods, but not necessarily for all types of freight.

However, if the alleged abuse affects a new entrant railway undertaking and that undertak- **14.193** ing complains about the exclusionary behaviour of the incumbent, the relevant market is the provision of railway infrastructure capacity or the provision of traction services, depending on the type of abuse alleged.

On the basis of the Commission's (merger) decisions in *Deutsche Bahn/Stinnes*[260] and **14.194** *SNCF/Trenitalia/AFA*,[261] the following more detailed principles can be formulated:

- A distinction can be made between the general market for rail transport and the distinct sub-market for rail services, consisting of, *inter alia*, the provision of locomotives, traction, and access to railway infrastructure.
- Bearing in mind the different locations of customers and different characteristics of the products being transported, one cannot assume that all modes of transport (car, inland waterways, and rail) are interchangeable.
- In general, pure carriers—transporters—on the one hand and forwarders and logistics providers on the other hand belong to different markets.
- Environmental legislation (aimed at greatly reducing road transport in favour of rail transport) could play a role in reducing interchangeability of road and rail.
- Geographically, a Member State may in itself constitute a substantial part of the common market (see also the Court in *Deutsche Bahn/Commission* in the context of rail services).
- The 'origin-destination' principle generally used for market definition in the transport sector is also appropriate for defining geographic markets in rail transport.

In *ERS*,[262] the Commission granted and renewed an exemption for a joint venture between **14.195** Maersk Intermodal BV and P&O Nedlloyd BV which provided scheduled rail transport services for the containers of both parent companies between deep sea ports and inland terminals in the Netherlands, Italy, Germany, Poland, Hungary, the Czech Republic, and Slovakia. Because of the substitutability of the principal ports of Germany, Belgium, the Netherlands, and Italy, the Commission took the view that the geographic market to be taken into consideration included all those territories.

---

[259] See the Commission's Guidelines on definition of the relevant market, <http://europa.eu.int/comm/competition/antitrust/relevma_en.html>.

[260] Case IV/M.2905.

[261] Case IV/M.3150.

[262] COMP/38.086—European Rail Shuttle + Maersk Intermodel Europe + P&O Nedlloyd, final version of Art 19(3) notice [2002] OJ C13/5-6.

(b) Passenger Transport

14.196 In passenger transport, as with air transport, a distinction is generally made between 'business' and 'leisure' passengers,[263] sometimes also referred to as 'time- sensitive' and 'non-time-sensitive' passengers. The basis for the distinction is that 'time- sensitive' travellers—mainly but not exclusively those travelling on business—are prepared to pay a premium for increased flexibility regarding when they start and finish their journey, as well as for higher standards of comfort and other facilities. By contrast, non-time-sensitive—mainly but not exclusively leisure passengers—are prepared to give up some of this flexibility, and accept lower standards of comfort, etc in return for a lower price. Thus, in *Eurostar*[264] the Commission held that, whereas sea crossings and the car 'Shuttle' service through the Channel Tunnel would not constitute a valid alternative for time-sensitive passengers, air transport would. Conversely, for non-time-sensitive passengers, various other modes of travel, from coach to the car shuttle, were considered as viable alternatives.

14.197 In *GVG/FS*,[265] which concerned a complaint by a German rail passenger transport operator about the refusal by the Italian incumbent rail operator, FS, to provide access to infrastructure and traction or to enter into a so-called international grouping, the Commission distinguished three relevant markets:

— the market for access to infrastructure;
— the traction market; and
— the international rail passenger transport market.

Since GVG intended to provide a service between several German cities and Milan, the relevant geographic market for access to infrastructure was that of access to the Italian network between Domodossola, a place at the Italian border where the railway entered Italian territory, and Milan.

14.198 In relation to the market for the provision of traction (the provision of a locomotive and a driver), the Commission demonstrated that the renting or purchasing of a locomotive was not a substitute for traction since it involved only the provision of rolling stock. Traction, however, also included the provision of a driver, maintenance and repair services, and the back-up. These additional elements were necessary to ensure the continuity of a scheduled passenger transport service.[266]

14.199 The Commission also referred to the general 'point of origin/ point of destination (O&D) pairs' approach for passenger transport services.[267] Comparing air transport and transport by own car from a perspective of pricing, travelling time, and other elements such as opportunity to work while travelling, the Commission came to the conclusion that air transport and own car transport would not be a realistic alternative.

---

[263] See, for instance, Case IV/M.1305 *Eurostar*, decision of 9 December 1998.
[264] See n 263.
[265] COMP/37.685—*Georg Verkhrsorganisation / Ferrovie dello Stato*, decision of 25 August 2003.
[266] See para 54 of the Decision.
[267] See, for example, Commission Decision (EC) 2002/746 of 5 July 2002 *Austrian Airlines/ Lufthansa* [2002] OJ L242/25.

(5) Prohibited Agreements and Behaviour

Article 2 of Regulation 1017/68 restated Article 81(1) of the Treaty with some minor and **14.200** immaterial differences. The Commission used to interpret Article 2 of Regulation 1017/68 no differently from Article 81. In the *FEFC* decision,[268] the Commission stated that:

> Regulation (EEC) No 1017/68 applying rules of competition to transport by rail, road and inland waterway was the first Regulation implementing competition rules in the transport sector. Having been adopted before the Court of Justice's express confirmation that the competition rules contained in the Treaty apply to the transport sector [in the *French Seamen's* case], Regulation (EEC) No 1017/68 reproduces with little variation the text of Articles 85 and 86 [now Articles 81 and 82] of the Treaty.

> As part of the Community's secondary legislation, Regulation (EEC) No 1017/68 cannot derogate from the provisions of the Treaty. Consequently, Regulation (EEC) No 1017/68 must be interpreted in the light of the case law of the Court, as providing the Commission with the necessary means to enforce Articles 81 and 82 of the Treaty in inland transport, without deviating from the basic competition rules contained in the Treaty.[269]

Consequently, the Commission's practice in applying the prohibition in Article 2 of Regulation 1017/68 can be used to indicate how it will apply Article 81(1) EC directly to the rail sector in the future.

For instance, in its decision concerning tariff structures in the combined transport of **14.201** goods, the Commission applied the prohibition in Article 2 of Regulation 1017/68 to an agreement concerning a common tariff structure for the sale of rail haulage in the international combined transport of goods. The agreement on the one hand comprised provisions on the structure of sales prices and methods for determining such prices, and on the other hand a common decision on the incidental costs set at a flat rate of 1 per cent of the total rail haulage price. The Commission held that the agreement on the tariff structure would have at least an indirect effect on tariff levels. It therefore restricted competition on combined transport routes between the existing operators and potential competition between them and any newcomers who would be able to take advantage of the provisions of Directive (EC) 91/440.

Similarly, in *CIA*,[270] the Commission expressed serious doubts concerning a co-operation **14.202** agreement between nearly all the EC railway companies relating to the international carriage by rail of new motor vehicles. The agreement established, *inter alia*, tariffs for 'sets of links' (links between two economic areas, usually two Member States). The Commission held that, where a set of links comprised alternative routes enabling railway undertakings or international groupings to compete, the application of a single tariff for each set of links prevented those companies or groupings from competing on price.

In *HOV SVZ/MCN*,[271] the Article 2 prohibition was applied to the so-called 'Maritime **14.203** Container Network Agreement', concluded between Deutsche Bahn, SNCB, Nederlandse

---

[268] *FEFC* (n 159 above): Commission Decision IV/33.218 of 21 December 1994 *Far Eastern Freight Conference* [1994] OJ L378/17 at paras 60–61.
[269] See also Commission Decision of 24 February 1993 concerning tariff structures in the combined transport of goods [1993] OJ L73/38–45.
[270] Case IV/D/36.535 *Communauté d'inérêts automobiles (CIA)*, XXIX Competition report 1999, para 153.

Spoorwegen and Intercontainer and Transfracht, so-called combined transport operators (transport undertakings that have specific equipment and organise and handle the transport, *inter alia*, by purchasing railway traction services and access to infrastructure from the railway undertaking). The Commission held that competition between the railway undertakings (DB, NS, and SNCB), which could sell their services directly to shippers and shipping companies, was restricted because the parties would be making joint offers instead of competing with each other. Also, potential competition between them and the combined operators Intercontainer and Transfracht, who also offered their services to shippers and shipping companies, was restricted. Lastly, competition between the operators Intercontainer and Transfracht, which technically could operate in the market from either the northern ports or the western ports, was restricted. In addition, the MCN agreement had the effect of restricting competition on the relevant market by making access more difficult for new competitors, who would not enjoy the same advantages as Intercontainer and Transfracht. In its judgment in *Deutsche Bahn*,[272] the Court of First Instance confirmed this assessment, on the basis *inter alia* that one of the purposes of the agreement was to set up a common administration for the fixing of prices and tariffs.[273]

14.204 In *Eurotunnel*,[274] the application of Article 2 of Regulation 1017/68 was highly dependent upon the interpretation of the notified agreement. The case concerned a conditional individual exemption granted by the Commission on 13 December 1994 to Eurotunnel, SNCF, and BR in respect of their agreement on the use of the Channel Tunnel. This usage contract gave BR and SNCF 50 per cent of the capacity of the fixed link, per hour in each direction, with the remaining 50 per cent left to Eurotunnel. The usage contract was exempted for a period of thirty years beginning on 16 November 1991.

14.205 The Commission considered that the arrangements restricted competition in two ways. First, they restricted competition between Eurotunnel and BR/SNCF in the rail transport markets since the contract provided for a division of the markets between Eurotunnel for the operation of shuttles, and BR/SNCF for the operation of international trains carrying passengers and freight.

14.206 Secondly, BR and SNCF were effectively given a monopoly of the hourly paths for rail transport in the Eurotunnel available for international passenger and freight trains. Therefore, other railway undertakings could not obtain from Eurotunnel the hourly paths necessary to operate international passenger or freight trains in competition with SNCF and BR. Consequently the Commission made the exemption subject to the condition that BR and SNCF should not withhold their agreement to the sale to other railway undertakings of at least 25 per cent of the hourly capacity of the tunnel in each direction allocated to run international passenger and freight trains.

14.207 On appeal, the Court of First Instance found, however, that the Commission's statements in the decision to the effect that half of the tunnel capacity was reserved for shuttle services

---

271 Commission Decision of 29 March 1994 *HOV SVZ/MCN* [1994] OJ L104/34.
272 Case T-229/94 *Deutsche Bahn* [1997] ECR II-1689.
273 See paras 35 and 36.
274 Commission Decision of 13 December 1994 [1994] OJ L354/66.

and the other half for international trains and that BR/SNCF were entitled to all the capacity reserved for international trains were wrong.[275] The assessment in the decision on the restrictive effects of the contract on competition was based on that error. Thus, in its evaluation of those effects as regards other railway undertakings, the Commission had failed to have regard to the possibility that Eurotunnel might still transfer some of its own capacity to other undertakings wishing to run international trains through the tunnel.

In 1999 the Commission examined the agreement again, taking into account new Directives **14.208** that had by then entered into force. The Commission established that the agreement did not divide the market and did not aim at restricting competition, either, while the railway undertakings and Eurotunnel were active on different markets.[276]

In *ENS* the Commission found that the agreement between British Rail (BR), Deutsche Bahn **14.209** (DB), Nederlandse Spoorwegen (NS), the Société Nationale des Chemins de Fer Français (SNCF), and the Société Nationale des Chemins de Fer Belges (SNCB) concerning the running of night passenger trains between the United Kingdom and the Continent was likely to restrict competition between the parties and between them and other operators. In view of the advantages for consumers the Commission decided to authorise the agreement for eight years. However, in order not to prevent other operators from offering similar services, the Commission required the railway undertakings to sell to them the rail services they had agreed to sell to their subsidiary, on the same terms.

The *ENS* decision was annulled by the Court of First Instance in October 1998,[277] on the **14.210** basis that the Commission's finding that the arrangements brought about a material restriction of competition was not supported by the evidence put forward in the decision. Also, the Court held that the Commission had not shown to the required standard that the infrastructure products and services that the parties had to provide to third parties, on the basis of the conditions imposed by the decision, were effectively necessary or essential for entry into the market.

The *Deutsche Bahn*, *Eurotunnel*, and *ENS* cases illustrate how difficult it is to analyse the **14.211** effects of agreements in the context of the liberalisation of the railway sector. Whereas in *Deutsche Bahn* the Court of First Instance was willing to accept that the railway undertakings were potential competitors on the northern and western routes, in *ENS* it was not willing to regard the railway undertakings as potential competitors. However, although in international passenger transport by rail, access rights to the rail infrastructure of another Member State are limited to railway undertakings that have entered into an 'international grouping' with a railway undertaking of that Member State, this does not prejudice the possibility of railway undertakings entering into agreements with new entrants or with their own subsidiaries established in the Member State of destination. Nevertheless, the

---

[275] Joined Cases T-79/95 and T-80/95 *Société nationale des chemins de fer français and British Railways Board v Commission* [1996] ECR II-1491.
[276] Commission Decision of 21 May 1999, IV/32.490, *Eurotunnel II*, XXIX report on competition policy, 184.
[277] Joined Cases T-374/94, T-375/94, T-384/94 and T-388/94 *European Night Services Ltd (ENS), Eurostar (UK) Ltd, formerly European Passenger Services Ltd (EPS), Union internationale des chemins de fer (UIC), NV Nederlandse Spoorwegen (NS) and Société Nationale des chemins de fer français (SNCF) v Commission*, Judgment of the Court of First Instance of 15 September 1998, [1998] ECR II-3141.

Court considered this to be 'a hypothesis unsupported by any evidence or analysis of the structures of the market from which it might be concluded that it represented a real, concrete possibility'.[278] The Court therefore did not conceal that it did not have much faith in the effects of Directive 91/440 in terms of liberalisation. In *Eurotunnel*, although the contract did not actually prevent Eurotunnel from granting hourly paths to competitors of SNCF and British Railways Board, the fact remains that 17 years after the signing of the contract no such paths have been granted and 50 per cent of the Eurotunnel capacity still remains reserved for the (successors of the) British and French incumbents. These cases leave the observer with the impression that, in a market where competition has difficulty gaining a foothold, the existence of (only) theoretical possibilities of entering the market will work in favour of incumbents rather than to the advantage of newcomers.

(6) Article 3 of Regulation 1017/68—Technical Agreements

14.212 In accordance with its view that Regulation 1017/68 did not modify Articles 81 and 82, the Commission has interpreted Article 3 of Regulation 1017/68, the provision relating to 'technical agreements', as follows:

> Article 3 of Regulation No 1017/68 is merely declaratory and lists a number of different kinds of agreement which do not fall within the scope of Article 85(1) [now Article 81(1)] of the Treaty when their sole object and sole effect is to achieve technical improvements or technical co-operation.[279]

14.213 The technical agreements listed in Article 3 are the following:

- the standardisation of equipment, transport supplies, vehicles, or fixed installations;
- the exchange or pooling, for the purpose of operating transport services, of staff, equipment, vehicles, or fixed installations;
- the organisation and execution of successive, complementary, substitute or combined transport operations, and the fixing and application of inclusive rates and conditions for such operations, including special competitive rates;
- the use, for journeys by a single mode of transport, of the routes which are most rational from the operational point of view;
- the coordination of transport timetables for connecting routes;
- the grouping of single consignments;
- the establishment of uniform rules on the structure of tariffs and their conditions of application, provided such rules do not lay down transport rates and conditions.

The Court of First Instance has held that the introduction of a legal exception for agreements of a purely technical nature cannot amount to an authorisation, on the part of the Community legislature, which allows agreements to be concluded if their purpose is the joint fixing of prices.[280]

---

[278] See para 142 of the CFI's judgment in *ENS*, 15 September 1998, Joined Cases T-374/94, 375/94, T-384/94 and T-388/94 [1998] ECR II-3141.

[279] ibid, at para 66. This also follows from *HOV SVZ/MCN* (n 271 above) at para 91. The English language version of Art 3 of Regulation 1017/68 has omitted the word 'sole', which is included in the original language version of Regulation 1017/68 as well as in Regulations 4056/86 (Art 2) and 3975/87 (Art 2).

[280] *Deutsche Bahn* (n 272 above).

In a number of cases the Commission has held that the exception for technical improve- **14.214** ments and technical co-operation must be applied strictly.

In 'Tariff structures in the combined transport of goods',[281] the Commission established **14.215** that the notified agreement aimed at preventing a reduction in the revenue of railways (freight operators had built new types of wagons in order to obtain a reduction in price). Also, it was based on the railways' jointly developed strategy for their combined transport activities. Furthermore, the agreement would affect prices for certain routes and for individual consignments. Therefore, the Commission concluded that the notified agreement did not have the sole object of applying technical improvements or achieving technical co-operation.

Similarly, in *ACI*,[282] the Commission established that the co-operation between British **14.216** Rail, SNCF, and Intercontainer in order to sell terminal-to-terminal combined rail transport services of goods loaded in road vehicles, containers, swap-bodies, semi-trailers, or other loading units suitable for intermodal transport between the United Kingdom and continental Europe had a number of commercial motives. The Commission accordingly took the view that the ACI agreement was not an agreement the sole object of which was to apply technical improvements or to achieve technical improvements.

(7) Article 4 of Regulation 1017/68—Exemption for Groups of Small and Medium-Sized Companies

Article 4 of Regulation 1017/68 provides a group exemption for agreements, decisions, **14.217** and concerted practices whose purpose is:

- the constitution and operation of groupings of road or inland waterway transport undertakings with a view to carrying on transport activities;
- the joint financing or acquisition of transport equipment or supplies, where these operations are directly related to the provision of transport services and are necessary for the joint operations of the aforesaid groupings.

The scope of the group exemption is limited to cases where the total carrying capacity of any grouping does not exceed 10,000 metric tons in the case of road transport or 500,000 metric tons in the case of transport by inland waterway. The individual capacity of each undertaking belonging to a grouping shall not exceed 1,000 metric tons in the case of road transport or 50,000 metric tons in the case of transport by inland waterway.

The block exemption is unlimited in time. Where there are effects that are incompatible with **14.218** the requirements of Article 5 and that constitute an abuse of the exemption from the provisions of Article 2, the Council is given the power to order undertakings or associations of undertakings to make such effects cease.

(8) Conditions for Exemption

So far as individual exemptions are concerned, the Commission has taken the position **14.219** that the four conditions set out in Article 5 of Regulation 1017/68 set out a test identical

---

281 Commission Decision of 24 February 1993, Case IV/34.494, [1993] OJ L73/38–45.
282 Decision of 27 July 1994, [1994] OJ L224/28–54.

to the conditions for exemption set out in Article 81(3) of the Treaty. Therefore the way in which Article 5 of Regulation 1017/68 has been applied in the past should provide a useful indication of how Article 81(3) EC is likely to be directly applied in this sector in the future.

(a) Cases in which an Exemption was Granted

14.220 In 'Tariff structures in the combined transport of goods',[283] the Commission granted an exemption for five years, subject to a number of conditions. The Commission concluded that a common tariff structure increased the efficiency of combined transport compared with other modes of transport since it made it easier for operators to compare routes. It also provided combined transport operators with the stability they needed to invest in rolling stock. Perhaps surprisingly, the Commission held that the common rate for incidental costs (1 per cent) was 'absolutely secondary to the total price'. Also, the Commission thought that the common rate might, 'in view of the special features of the sector', facilitate transactions between haulage suppliers and operators by eliminating unnecessary procedures and invoices involving quite small sums. The Commission recognised that after the implementation of Directive (EEC) 91/440 railway undertakings would be able to operate international combined transport on their own. However, it noted that technical difficulties and the absence of technical harmonisation would still make some forms of co-operation necessary for a transitional period. By way of a condition the Commission required the common rate to be optional. Also, railway companies applying the common tariff were required to apply the same structure to all enterprises seeking to acquire rail haulage services.

14.221 In *ACI*,[284] the Commission also granted a five-year exemption in respect of co-operation between British Rail, SNCF, and Intercontainer in order to sell terminal-to-terminal combined rail transport services of goods loaded in road vehicles, containers, swap-bodies, semi-trailers, or other loading units suitable for intermodal transport between the United Kingdom and continental Europe. The Commission held that the formation of ACI took advantage of the new opportunities created for railway undertakings and combined transport operators by the opening of the Channel Tunnel. Although British Rail and SNCF were entitled to provide the services themselves, account was taken of the fact that the service was completely new and had to be laid on immediately, which would involve considerable financial risks which a single undertaking would be unable to bear alone. Therefore, an exemption was granted, imposing, however, *inter alia*, the condition that the railway undertakings had to supply to any consignor or combined transport operator on a non-discriminatory basis the same rail services as they supplied to their own subsidiary ACI.

14.222 In *European Rail Shuttle (ERS)*,[285] the Commission granted an exemption with respect to a joint venture between P&O Nedlloyd and Maersk, engaged in the movement of deep-sea containers by scheduled rail shuttle services between Rotterdam and points in Germany

---

[283] Commission Decision of 24 February 1993, Case IV/34.494, [1993] OJ L73/38–45.
[284] Decision of 27 July 1994, [1994] OJ L224/28–54.
[285] Commission notice pursuant to Art 12 (2) of Council Regulation (EEC) 1017/68 concerning Case No IV/35.592, [1997] OJ C328/2 and Commission Notice pursuant to Art 12 (2) of Council Regulation (EEC) 1017/68 concerning Case COMP-D2-38.096, [2002] OJ C13/5, Press release IP/02/575.

and Italy. ERS also offered spare train capacity to third parties. In 2002, when the exemption was extended by a further three years, the Commission took the view that, while ERS continued to have the potential to distort competition, there were countervailing benefits, notably that the expansion of the ERS network would further enhance competition in a market which, until recently, had been almost the sole preserve of the state owned railways.

(b) Cases in which an Exemption was Withheld

In *HOV SVZ/MCN*,[286] the Commission refused to grant an exemption because it had not **14.223** been demonstrated that the joint selling agreement between DB, SNCB, NS, Intercontainer, and Transfracht improved the quality of the services. Moreover, the reductions of competition were significant and could not be deemed to be essential to the attainment of an improvement in the quality of the services. For all other European international combined traffic, several operators were able to compete with one another without impairing the functioning of the market.

In *Compagnie générale maritime*,[287] the Court accepted the Commission's refusal to grant **14.224** an exemption on the basis of Article 5 of Regulation 1017/68, holding that it had not been established that the charging of a collectively agreed price for inland transport services by a liner conference contributed to improving the quality of those services. In that respect, the fact that the direct costs of inland transport represent only a small proportion of the total costs of inland transport services was deemed irrelevant; it had not been shown that the collective fixing of rates rendered intermodal transport services, and in particular the management of empty containers, more efficient. It had not been shown, either, that the collective fixing of prices would contribute to the continuity and stability of the relevant market or would stimulate the introduction of new technology. On the contrary, the collective price fixing was likely to discourage new investment.

(9) Abuse of Dominant Position

After the repeal of Article 8 of Regulation 1017/68, there is no longer any specific provision **14.225** defining the prohibition on abuse of dominant position for transport via rail, road, and inland waterways. Article 82 therefore also directly applies in this sector.

This would not seem to be an important change. In *HOV SVZ/MCN* (the decision leading to **14.226** the *Deutsche Bahn* judgment),[288] the Commission referred only to Article 82 and not to Article 8 of the Regulation. The Court of First Instance[289] accepted that the aim of Article 8 of the Regulation was no different from that of Article 82. It was therefore already the Commission's practice to refer both to Article 82 of the EC Treaty and to Article 8 of the Regulation.[290]

In this initial phase of rail transport liberalisation, most national railway undertakings still **14.227** enjoy monopoly powers in a number of areas. Consequently, new entrants face many issues

---

[286] Commission Decision of 29 March 1994 *HOV SVZ/MCN* [1994] OJ L104/34.

[287] Case T-86/95 *Compagnie générale maritime* [2002] ECR II-1011.

[288] *HOV SVZ/MCN* [1994] OJ L104/4.

[289] Case T-229/94 *Deutsche Bahn v Commission* [1997] ECR II-1689 at para 77.

[290] See Oliver Stehmann and Georg Zellhofer, 'Dominant Rail Undertakings under European Competition Policy' (2004) 10 European Law Journal 327–53.

generally connected with abuse of dominant position, for instance regarding conflicts of interest of incumbent railway undertakings involved in both infrastructure management and the provision of services, including access to a whole variety of facilities (electricity, stations, maintenance facilities, and marshalling yards), and excessive track charges. A number of these issues have been addressed in the directives currently in force regarding rail transport liberalisation. In principle, the Regulatory Bodies, to be instituted by Member States on the basis of Article 30 of Directive 2001/14,[291] are competent to deal with those issues. Although with considerable delays, all Member States have now implemented this Directive.[292] However, in the current situation, competition law enforcement still has an important role to play by underpinning the liberalisation process and addressing issues that for the time being cannot be solved on the basis of the sectoral regulatory regime.

14.228 For instance, there are several provisions dealing with the *separation of essential functions* (separation between infrastructure and services). The general provision is Article 6(3) of Directive 91/440 (as amended by Directive 2001/12[293]), which reads as follows:

> Member States shall take the measures necessary to ensure that the functions determining equitable and non-discriminatory access to infrastructure, listed in Annex II, are entrusted to bodies or firms that do not themselves provide any rail transport services. Regardless of the organisational structures, this objective must be shown to have been achieved.

The essential functions listed in Annex II of the Directive are operator licensing, train path allocation and charging, and monitoring public service obligations.

14.229 Articles 4(2) and 14(2) of Directive 2001/14 specify the extent of separation required as regards the levying of infrastructure charges and the allocation of capacity respectively. Where the infrastructure manager, in its legal form, organisation, or decision-making functions, is not independent of any railway undertaking, those tasks must be performed by a body that is 'independent in its legal form, organisation and decision-making from any railway undertaking'.

14.230 Having regard to the general application of the concept of 'control' in European competition law as laid out in the *De Minimis* Notice,[294] the case law on 'intra group behaviour',[295] and the Merger Regulation,[296] it would seem these provisions must be interpreted in such a way that the functions mentioned in these provisions must be carried out by a legal entity outside the holding structure of the railway undertaking. This would also seem to follow

---

[291] Directive 2001/14 of the European Parliament and of the Council of 26 February 2001 on the allocation of railway infrastructure capacity and the levying of charges for the use of railway infrastructure and safety certification [2001] OJ L75/29.

[292] See the report from the Commision on the implementation of the first railyway package SEC(2006) 530, <http://ec.europa.eu/transport/rail/overview/doc/report-final_en.pdf>.

[293] Note, however, that in certain cases the EC competition rules (in particular Arts 86 jo. 82 EC) have also been interpreted as imposing independence between the provider of infrastructure and the providers of services on that infrastructure (see, for instance the Commission's Decision 2002/344 on the relationships between La Poste and mail preparation companies, and the Court's judgments in *ERT* (Cases C-241 and 242/91 P) and *RTT v INNO* (Case C-18/88)).

[294] Commission Notice on agreements of minor importance which do not appreciably restrict competition under Art 81 (1) of the Treaty establishing the European Community[2001] OJ C368/13.

[295] See, *inter alia*, Case C-73/95 *Viho Europe BV/ Commission* [1996] ECR I-5457.

[296] Council Regulation (EC) 139/2004 of 20 January 2004 on the control of concentrations between undertakings [2004] OJ L24/1–22.

from the case law regarding the application of Articles 86 and 82 EC with respect to potential conflicts of interest of undertakings with special and exclusive rights,[297] on the basis of which a situation in which the mere exercise of a monopoly enables an undertaking to distort in its favour the equal conditions of competition between the various competitors on a services market on which it is also active constitutes, in itself, a violation of Articles 82 and 86 of the EC Treaty.[298]

Problems related to *safety certification procedures* also primarily concern the correct imple- **14.231** mentation of the Directives. Article 1.8 of Directive 2001/12 provides that 'Member States shall ensure that safety standards and rules are laid down, rolling stock and railway undertakings are certified accordingly and accidents investigated. These tasks shall be accomplished by bodies or undertakings that do not provide rail transport services themselves and are independent of bodies or undertakings that do so, in such a way as to guarantee equitable and non-discriminatory access to infrastructure.'[299]

As to track *access charges*, Directive 2001/14 provides, in Article 7, a framework based on **14.232** short run marginal cost pricing but also, in Article 8, permits market pricing in certain circumstances. Article 9 allows for discounts 'without prejudice to Articles 81, 82, 86 and 87 of the Treaty . . .'.

As to access to *sidings, maintenance facilities, ports, refuelling points, energy supply, informa-* **14.233** *tion, driver education, etc*, it is important to note that a number of these items appear on the list of items in Annex I.A to Commission Regulation (EEC) 2598/70 of 18 December 1970. Consequently, they fall under the concept of 'infrastructure' as defined in Directive 91/440. Railway undertakings that have a right of access to infrastructure also have a right of access to these facilities. New Article 10 of Directive 91/440, as amended by Article 1.11 of Directive 2001/12, provides that 'track access to, and supply of, services in the terminals and ports linked to rail activities referred to in paragraphs 1, 2 and 3, serving or potentially serving more than one final customer, shall be provided to all railway undertakings in a non-discriminatory manner, and requests by railway undertakings may be subject to restrictions only if viable alternatives under market conditions exist.'[300]

Article 5 of Directive 2001/14 confers entitlement on all railway undertakings to access to elec- **14.234** trical supply equipment for traction current; refuelling facilities; passenger stations; freight terminals; marshalling yards; train formation facilities; storage sidings; and maintenance and other technical facilities. Requests to access such facilities may be refused only if there are viable alternatives. If the national network provider is not the manager of the facility in question,

---

[297] See Case C-202/88 *France/ Commission, competition in the markets in telecommunications terminals equipment* [1991] ECRI-01223, para 51; Case C-18/88 *RTT/ INNO* [1991] ECR I-05941; Case C-260/89 *ERT* [1991] ECR I-2925; and Case C-163/96 *Raso* [1998] ECR I-0533. See also Oliver Stehmann and Georg Zellhofer, 'Dominant rail undertakings under European competition policy' (2004) 10 European Law Journal 327–53 at 344–52.

[298] See in particular ECJ in *Raso*, para 29.

[299] The Article also provides that Member States may require railway undertakings to be involved in ensuring the enforcement and monitoring of the safety standards while at the same time guaranteeing the neutral and non-discriminatory execution of those functions.

[300] Paras 1, 2, and 3 of the above Article concern, respectively, international passenger services provided by international groupings, combined transport services, and other freight services.

he must use all reasonable endeavours to facilitate access to it. In applying these provisions, it is therefore not necessary to demonstrate either an impact on inter-state trade or dominance.

14.235 Finally, *access to training facilities* has been regulated by the recently adopted Railway Safety Directive 2004/49[301] (part of the 2nd railway package). Article 13 of the Directive states that applicants for a safety certificate must have fair and non-discriminatory access to training facilities for train drivers and staff accompanying the train. The services offered must include training on necessary route knowledge, operating rules and procedures, the signalling and control command system, and emergency procedures applied on the route operated.

14.236 An example of the application of Article 82 in the railway sector is the *Deutsche Bahn* case.[302] As mentioned above, the Commission established that the MCN agreement concluded between DB, SNCB, NS, Intercontainer, and Transfracht had the effect of restricting competition in the relevant market. However, no fine was imposed on the parties since the agreement was considered by SNCB, NS, and Intercontainer as an attempt to remedy the tariff discriminations practised by Deutsche Bahn of which they had been victims for many years in respect of traffic from the western ports. Further, SNCB and NS had no other option but to conclude an agreement with DB in order to operate international rail services. The Commission therefore held that it was apparent that the conclusion of the MCN agreement was a result of the tariff practices imposed by DB, which were subsequently examined under Article 82 of the EC Treaty.

14.237 The Commission found that, in view of its statutory monopoly, DB held a dominant position on the market for the supply of rail transport services in Germany. DB had abused that dominant position by acting in such a way that tariffs for carriage between a Belgian or Dutch port and Germany were appreciably and unjustifiably higher than for carriage between points within Germany and the German ports. The Commission imposed a fine on DB of ECU 11,000,000.[303] The Commission's decision was upheld by the Court of First Instance in October 1997.[304]

14.238 In the case *GVG/FS*, Georg Verkehrsorganisation (GVG), a small German railway operator, had been trying to get access to the Italian railway market since 1995 to provide a twice-daily passenger service from various points in Germany via Basle to Milan. The service would have reduced journey times by about an hour, mainly because it would be non-stop and timed to interconnect at Basle with Intercity trains from and to Germany. To be able to provide the service, GVG needed access to the Swiss and Italian railway networks. It obtained the necessary train path in Switzerland in 1996. However, the company also had to form an international grouping with an Italian railway undertaking, pursuant to Directive 91/440. Ferrovie dello Stato (FS), the Italian state-owned railway company, was the only Italian train operator equipped to enter into such a grouping. Furthermore, GVG needed traction services (ie locomotives and train crew), which, at the relevant stage in the European railway liberalisation process, it needed to rent and only FS was capable of providing.

---

[301] The Directive must be implemented by 30 April 2006.
[302] Case T-229/94 *Deutsche Bahn AG/ Commission* [1997] ECR II-01689.
[303] *HOV SVZ/MCN* (n 271 above).
[304] *Deutsche Bahn* (n 272 above).

Following discussions with the Commission and in order to come to a settlement, FS **14.239** entered into an international grouping agreement with GVG and agreed on the terms of a traction contract with the company. FS and its subsidiary RFI, which manages the Italian railway infrastructure, had promised to use their best endeavours to provide GVG with train paths. FS had also undertaken to enter into international grouping agreements with any duly licensed train operator, which had concrete proposals to start an international rail service into Italy. Furthermore, FS had undertaken that, for a period of five years, it would provide traction to other railway companies for such services.

The Commission adopted a decision requiring FS to allow new train operators to provide **14.240** cross-border passenger services into Italy. The decision found that FS had prevented GVG from providing passenger services from Germany to Milan, by refusing to enter into an international grouping,[305] by refusing to discuss terms for access to the track and by refusing to provide traction services. This had deprived rail passengers of the benefits of price competition and customer choice.

However, taking account of the concessions made by FS, the Commission came to the con- **14.241** clusion that the infringement had been terminated and, in view of the novelty of the case and the substantial commitments offered by FS, decided not to impose a fine.[306]

E. Transport Infrastructure

(1) Airport Infrastructure

(a) Introduction

Access on a non-discriminatory basis to airports and to services related to the airport infrastruc- **14.242** ture, such as for example ground-handling services, is of vital importance for airlines. As there is often only one commercial airport in a given geographic market, airports usually have a dominant position as regards a very high proportion of their traffic. This implies that they have a special responsibility not to distort competition and particularly to treat their customers (ie airlines) and other potential airport service providers equally in comparable situations.

The Commission's competition policy on airport infrastructure has been shaped in a num- **14.243** ber of decisions, which can broadly be divided into two categories. First, the Commission has examined the landing fees systems applied at various European airports and concluded that some systems, by discriminating in favour of national airlines, infringed the EC competition rules.[307] Secondly, the Commission has ensured that access to airport services is open to competitors on a non-discriminatory basis.

---

[305] <http://europa.eu.int/rapid/pressReleasesAction.do?reference=IP/03/1182&format=HTML&aged=1&language=EN&guiLanguage=en#file.tmp_Foot_1#file.tmp_Foot_1>.

[306] See also Oliver Stehmann, 'Applying essential facility reasoning to passenger rail services in the EU—the Commission decision in the case GVG' [2004] ECLR 390–4.

[307] Discriminatory landing fees might also constitute a restriction on the freedom to provide air transport services, in breach of Art 49 of the Treaty combined with Art 3(1) of Council Regulation 2408/92 on access for Community air carriers to intra-Community air routes (compare Case C-70/99 *Commission v Portugal* [2001] ECR I-04845).

(b) Discriminatory Landing Fees

14.244 In return for services in connection with the landing and take-off of planes, airlines must pay a fee to the airport authority. These landing fees as well as the methods for calculating them are usually set by law or royal decree and administered by a public authority that has been granted an exclusive right by the State.[308]

14.245 The Commission first dealt with the issue of discriminatory landing fees under the EC competition rules in 1995, in its decision in the *Zaventem* case.[309] This case concerned a complaint by British Midland about a system of discounts on landing fees applied at Brussels National Airport. In its decision the Commission concluded that this system of discounts, which increased in line with the airline's volume of traffic, favoured carriers with a high number of landing frequencies and placed small carriers at a disadvantage. In fact, the threshold to be attained in order to qualify for the higher discounts was so high that in practice only the national flag carrier could benefit from it, to the detriment of other Community carriers.

14.246 The Commission concluded that the airport authority, which held a dominant position in the market for aircraft landing and take-off services at Brussels airport, had not provided an objective justification for this difference in treatment. In particular, since the handling of the landing or take-off of an aircraft requires the same service, irrespective of the individual airline, economies of scale were found not to exist.[310] The discount system, although it applied to all airlines, therefore had the effect of applying dissimilar conditions to airlines for equivalent transactions and constituted an abuse within the meaning of Article 82(c) of the Treaty.

14.247 Following this decision the Commission sent a letter to all airport authorities within the EU at which similar discounts or differentiated charges were applied, setting out its approach towards landing fees and calling on them to alter their landing fees systems. Most authorities agreed to carry out the necessary changes. Nevertheless three further decisions of the Commission on landing fees systems proved necessary. On 10 February 1999 the Commission adopted two decisions, one against Portugal[311] and one against the Finnish airport authority,[312] in which it explained that a system of landing charges differentiating according to the type of the flight (domestic or international—where charges were higher for international flights) amounted to discrimination within the meaning of Article 82(c) of the Treaty. On 26 July 2000 the Commission adopted a further decision with regard to landing fees, explaining that discounts based on landing frequencies and a differentiation of landing charges according to the origin of the flight, as prescribed by the Spanish Government, discriminated in favour of national airlines and thereby infringed Article 82(c) of the Treaty.[313]

---

[308] Depending on the modalities of the landing fees system in question, competition decisions in this field are addressed either to the Member States concerned (on the basis of Art 86(1) of the Treaty, read in conjunction with Art 82 thereof) or to the airport authority (on the basis of Art 82 of the Treaty).

[309] [1995] OJ L216/8.

[310] The services provided do not depend on the individual owner of the aircraft or whether they are, for example, rendered for the first or the 10th aircraft of the same airline.

[311] *Portuguese airports* [1999] OJ L69/31, upheld by the ECJ in Case C-163/99 *Portuguese Republic v Commission* [2001] ECR I-02613.

[312] *Finish airports* [1999] OJ L69/24.

[313] *Spanish airports* [2000] OJ L208/36.

(c) Access to Airport Services (Ground-handling)

Council Directive (EC) 96/67 of 15 October 1996 on access to the ground-handling **14.248** market at Community airports[314] aims at liberalising the ground-handling market. The Commission has, however, also used the EC competition rules to guarantee access on a non-discriminatory basis to this market.

In a decision adopted on 14 January 1998, the Commission ended a ground-handling **14.249** monopoly at Frankfurt airport.[315] The decision related to a complaint by Air France, KLM, and British Airways, according to which the operator of Frankfurt/Main airport (FAG) abused its position as exclusive provider of airport facilities for the landing and take-off of aircraft by not granting to airlines the right to provide ground-handling services[316] themselves (self-handling) nor giving access to other companies to provide such services (third party handling). The Commission upheld the complaint and concluded that FAG had not put forward any objective justification for reserving to itself the market for the provision of ground-handling services and thereby had infringed Article 82 of the Treaty. The Commission in particular rejected FAG's arguments that constraints on space and capacity justified the monopoly.

In another decision, adopted on 11 June 1998,[317] the Commission prohibited a discrimi- **14.250** natory system of commercial fees for the provision of ground-handling services under Article 82 of the Treaty. The case concerned a complaint by Alpha Flight Services (AFS), a firm that provided aircraft catering services at certain Paris airports, in competition with, among others, airlines that provided their own ground-handling services. The operator of the Paris airport, Aéroports de Paris (ADP), charged different fees to suppliers of certain ground-handling services, including catering services, without objective justification for this differentiation. The Commission concluded that ADP infringed Article 82 of the Treaty by using its dominant position as manager of the Paris airports to impose discriminatory commercial fees. The system was found to distort competition in the ground-handling services market and, also, indirectly, in the air transport market.

On 12 December 2000, the Court of First Instance[318] dismissed ADP's appeal on all grounds. **14.251** In substance, the judgment, which was confirmed by the European Court of Justice,[319] is important in at least two aspects. First, it categorises the management and operation of an airport in return for a commercial fee as an economic activity and the airport operator as an undertaking. Secondly, it confirms, further to a judgment in *Corsica Ferries*,[320] that the undertaking in question need not be operating in the markets where the effects of the abuse were felt in order to be caught by Article 82 of the Treaty.

---

[314] [1996] OJ L272/36.

[315] *Flughafen Frankfurt Main (FAG)* [1998] OJ L72/30.

[316] Ground-handling services comprise all the activities performed on the occasion of a stopover of an aircraft at an airport: ground-handling services that take place on the ramp (or apron) of the airport, such as provision and operation of equipment for the embarkation and disembarkation of passengers, cabin cleaning, fuelling of aircraft, etc.

[317] *Alpha Flight Services/Aéroports de Paris* [1998] OJ L230/10.

[318] Case T-128/98 *Aéroports de Paris v Commission* [2000] ECR II-03929.

[319] Case C-82/01P *Aéroports de Paris v Commission* [2002] ECR I-09297.

[320] Case C-18/93 *Corsica Ferries* [2004] ECR I-1783.

(2) Maritime Infrastructure

14.252 The relationship between the infrastructure providers and the transport service providers also plays a role in the maritime sector. The issue has arisen particularly in cases where ferry operators also own and operate the port facilities. This allows them the possibility of giving favourable treatment to their own ferry operations by either refusing competing ferry operators access to the port facilities or granting access on less favourable terms than those offered to its own ferry services. The first situation was at issue in the *Port of Roscoff* case,[321] where the Commission, acting under (what is now) Article 85 of the Treaty, ordered CCI Morlaix, who both managed the port and was a shareholder in the principal user of the port, to grant access to the ferry operator Irish Continental Group for a temporary period.

14.253 The question of discriminatory harbour duties has been addressed by the European Court of Justice in the *GT-Link* case. This preliminary ruling concerned harbour duties, which the Danish national rail company (DSB) had charged the ferry operator GT-Link for the use of the port of Gedser, owned by DSB. The ECJ held, *inter alia*, that it was contrary to (what is now) Article 86(1) in conjunction with (what is now) Article 82 for a dominant public undertaking which owned and operated a commercial port to exempt its own ferry services (and those of its trading partners) from payment of harbour duties in so far as such exemptions entailed the application of dissimilar conditions to equivalent services.[322]

14.254 Port duties are, however, not the only means by which the port operator can give favourable treatment to its own ferry operations. In the *B&I* case, the port authority had given its own ferry operator (Sealink) sailing times that seriously disrupted the loading and discharge possibilities for the competing ferry operator (B&I). Sealink was permitted to sail past a B&I vessel while the latter was in its berth; however, due to the physical conditions of the port, as the water in the harbour rose, this permission on occasion necessitated the disconnection of the loading ramp from the B&I vessel. The Commission adopted interim measures in the case, ordering Sealink temporarily to change some of the sailing times.[323]

14.255 It is possible that the increasing trend of dedicated or controlled terminals in the liner shipping sector will also, in the future, raise vertical problems of a similar nature.

(3) Railway Infrastructure

(a) General

14.256 Competition issues related to railway infrastructure generally concern the application of Article 82 EC and/or the application of sector-specific rules. As indicated above, given the

---

[321] Commission decision of 16 May 1995 (not published). Similarly, in the *Port of Rødby* case, the Commission found that the refusal of the Danish government to (a) allow a ferry operator, competing with the state-owned ferry operator, to build a port in the immediate vicinity of the port of Rødby; or (b) to operate from the existing port facilities at Rødby was incompatible with (what is now) Art 86(1) in combination with (what is now) Art 82 of the Treaty. Commission Decision of 21 December 1993 in Case 119/94[1994] OJ L55/52–57.

[322] Judgment of the Court of 17 July 1997 in Case C-242/95 *GT-Link A/S v De Danske Statsbaner* [1997] ECR I-449.

[323] Commission decision of 11 June 1992 in Case IV/34.174 relating to proceedings under (now) Art 85 of the Treaty (not published).

transitional character of the railway sector and the continued existence of many—vertically integrated—dominant players, there is a wide range of problems concerning infrastructure access in the European railway market, problems which are often closely related to the extent to which the Member State concerned has instituted separation between infrastructure management and the provision of railway services.[324] Because of their interrelatedness with issues concerning safety certification, access to sidings, maintenance facilities, ports, refuelling points, energy supply, information, driver education, and track access charges, infrastructure issues have been dealt with under abuse of dominant position in the railway sector (see para 14.225ff above).

(b) Trans-European Network

Mooted as early as the 1980s, trans-European networks (TENs) for transport and energy were incorporated into the Maastricht Treaty as a major policy objective. The aim was to create truly trans-European routes for all modes of transport (road, rail, air, sea, inland waterway, etc), concentrating essentially on big-ticket cross-border projects to link up separate national systems. A list of fourteen priority projects was drawn up for completion by 2010.   **14.257**

The programme got off to a slow start. By 2003, only three of the fourteen projects identified as priorities had been completed. These included the Oeresund bridge and tunnel linking Denmark and Sweden and the Malpensa airport in Italy. Part of the reason was the huge cost of the first phase of TENs projects, estimated at EUR400 billion.   **14.258**

More recently, the Van Miert High Level Group on the trans-European transport network has proposed that the priority status given to a large number of railway projects, including projects on the high-speed passenger services network, should be maintained.[325] Following up on the recommendations, the Council and Parliament adopted new Guidelines for the trans-European network including a list of thirty priority projects (with a total cost of EUR220 billion), some 70 per cent of which concern railway infrastructure.   **14.259**

The Trans-European Rail Freight Freeways will be a series of railway corridors on which railway operators will be granted open access on a non-discriminatory basis. These corridors will connect the main European economic centres having high density of freight traffic. Competition issues arise since rail infrastructure managers will have to co-operate in the organisation of these freeways.   **14.260**

In essence, in assessing the TENs transport projects under EC competition rules, the Commission has said that it will apply the following basic principles:[326]   **14.261**

• Where the infrastructure manager wishes to allow transport undertakings to reserve capacity as from the launch of the project, all EC undertakings that might be interested should be given the chance of doing so.

---

[324] A full separation has, for instance, been carried out in Denmark, Finland, France, the Netherlands, Spain, Sweden, and the United Kingdom.
[325] <http://europa.eu.int/comm/ten/transport/revision/hlg_en.htm>.
[326] Clarification of the Commission recommendations on the application of the competition rules to new infrastructure projects, 30 September 1997, [1997] OJ C298/5.

- The capacity reserved to an undertaking should be in proportion to the direct or indirect financial commitments entered into by it and should be in line with planned operational requirements over a reasonable period.
- As new infrastructure is not generally congested right from the start of operation, an operator should not be able to reserve all of the capacity available. Some of the capacity should remain available so as to allow competing services to be operated by other undertakings.
- The period covered by capacity reservation agreements must not exceed a reasonable period, to be determined on a case-by-case basis.

According to the Commission, these principles are intended to reconcile the need to maximise the financial viability of rail infrastructure projects with the provision of free and non-discriminatory access to infrastructure. By clarifying the application of the competition rules, the Commission's intention has been to provide legal guidance and thus facilitate the creation of TENs.

15

MOTOR VEHICLES

Konrad Schumm and Hubert Gambs

A. Introduction

Motor vehicles, spare parts and after sales services are traditionally distributed by distributor **15.01** and repairer networks set up by vehicle manufacturers or their national importers. There are eight large passenger car manufacturer groups and five large commercial vehicle manufacturers operating in Europe, and the relevant vertical distribution agreements of these groups contain similar vertical restraints. Furthermore, motor vehicles are expensive and long-lasting products which need repair and maintenance throughout their lifetime.

15.02 Since there were so many agreements with similar content, and because distribution and the necessary after sales service activities involved large investments in showrooms, repair shops and tools, stocks of spare parts and staff training, the European Commission decided as early as 1985 to clarify the application of Article 81(3) to such agreements by adopting the block exemption Regulation 123/85, to facilitate the purchase and servicing of vehicles by consumers throughout Europe. In 1995 a slightly modified Regulation 1475/95 was adopted, which applied for the next seven years. In 2002 a major overhaul of the existing rules led to the third block exemption, Regulation 1400/2002.

15.03 This chapter starts with an explanation of the characteristics of the relevant products and services. It then provides an overview of the two earlier Regulations and the process leading to the adoption of the new Regulation 1400/2002.[1] Thereafter, the chapter discusses the content of the new Regulation, following its structure and explaining the various topics addressed within it. The rules for the distribution of new vehicles and the distribution of repair services by authorised repairers operating within a vehicle manufacturer's network are explained in separate sections, followed by a section on the distribution of spare parts and on independent repairers. The chapter ends by reviewing some procedural issues.

(1) The Characteristics of the Motor Vehicle Sector

15.04 Motor vehicles are technically complex products, which are used on public roads and need proper repair and maintenance throughout their lifetime to ensure their safe and reliable use. They are generally the second most expensive purchase for most consumers, after the purchase of a house or apartment. Servicing and repair over the lifetime of a car are more or less as costly as the price of the new vehicle itself. This differentiates motor vehicles from any other consumer goods. Prices for motor vehicles,[2] spare parts,[3] and repair and maintenance services differ considerably between Member States. Motor vehicles are traditionally distributed by a network of distributors established by the vehicle manufacturer or the importer in a given country. In the past, these distributors were selected by the manufacturer and were allocated a defined sales territory.

(2) The Situation Pre-1985

15.05 In the years after 1970, the Commission had hoped that it could set the guiding principles for the application of the EC competition rules by adopting a number of individual decisions.[4] However, this hope proved to be in vain because the automobile industry did not fully adapt its distribution systems to the principles set out in the leading *BMW* decision of 1974. In view of the large number of notifications received by the Commission for individual exemption pursuant to Article 3 of Regulation 17/62, the Commission decided to clarify

---

[1] Commission Regulation (EC) 1400/2002 of 31 July 2002 on the application of Art 81(3) of the Treaty to categories of vertical agreements and concerted practices in the motor vehicle sector [2002] OJ L203/30.

[2] As regards cars, see the Commission's bi-annual car price reports, published on the Commission's website at: <http://ec.europa.eu/comm/competition/car_sector/>; for trucks see Commission decision of 14 March 2000 case COMP/M.1672 *Volvo/Scania* [2001] OJ L143/74, para 39.

[3] See study of the Danish competition authority, *The car repair market*, 2001, in particular table 11.1 with price indexes for spare parts in 15 Member States showing that spare parts were on average 55% more expensive in Denmark than in Germany.

[4] *Bayerische Motoren Werke* [1975] OJ L29/1; *Peugeot* [1986] OJ L295/19, in particular para 8.

the conditions under which such agreements were permissible pursuant to Article 81(3) by adopting a block exemption regulation.

(3) Regulation 123/85 and Regulation 1475/95

Commission Regulation (EEC) 123/85 of 12 December 1984 on the application of Article 85(3)   **15.06**
of the Treaty to certain categories of motor vehicle distribution and servicing agreements[5] was the first motor vehicle block exemption and remained in force until 30 June 1995. It was replaced by Commission Regulation (EC) 1475/95 of 28 June 1995 on the application of Article 85(3) of the Treaty to certain categories of motor vehicle distribution and servicing agreements.[6] Both regulations allowed manufacturers to use a combination of selective and exclusive distribution agreements: manufacturers[7] were allowed to prohibit sales of new vehicles to independent resellers (selective distribution), and also to allocate an exclusive sales territory to each distributor (exclusive distribution).

The Commission considered, however, that Regulation 123/85 only partly achieved its   **15.07**
aims, for example of contributing to the functioning of the internal market and the development of efficient and flexible distribution structures encouraging relationships based on partnership.[8] Furthermore the Commission had to deal with a large number of complaints. To resolve these problems, a considerable number of amendments were introduced in 1995 by Regulation 1475/95, such as the right of distributors to sell more than one brand (multibranding), the setting of sales targets by agreement,[9] the right of distributors to obtain and use spare parts of matching quality, the prohibition of differences in the remuneration of distributors depending on the destination of a vehicle, and the right to refer disputes to an arbitrator or independent expert. Distributors had to be allowed to advertise outside their sales territory albeit in a manner that was not targeted at specific individual customers. In order better to protect the distributors' investments, the minimum duration of fixed term contracts was extended from four to five years and the notice periods in agreements concluded for an unlimited duration were extended from one to two years. Furthermore, manufacturers had to give independent repairers access to technical information if they wanted to benefit from the new Regulation. In order better to explain consumers' rights and the content of the Regulation, an explanatory brochure[10] was published by the Commission's

---

[5] [1985] OJ L15/16.

[6] [1995] OJ L145/25.

[7] The term manufacturer is used throughout this chapter. However in some cases manufacturers have transferred their rights and obligations to set up a distributor and repairer network to other suppliers such as importers, wholesalers, or even large distributors. These operators will then enjoy the rights and have the obligations of the vehicle manufacturer through delegation. The vertical agreements they conclude must also comply with the applicable regulations.

[8] See IP/95/420 of 26 April 1995.

[9] In case of disagreement on sales targets, each party had to be in a position to refer to an arbitrator or independent third expert pursuant to Art 4(1)(3) and Art 5(3); see also the explanatory brochure on Regulation 1475/95, reply to question 13. Regulation 1400/2002 is based on the same approach: see Art 3(6) of Regulation 1400/2002.

[10] Explanatory brochure on the Commission Regulation (EC) 1475/95 of 28 June 1995 on the application of Art 85(3) of the Treaty to certain categories of motor vehicle distribution and servicing agreements; available at: <http://ec.europa.eu/comm/competition/car_sector/>.

Directorate-General for Competition giving additional clarification on many issues which had not been addressed in two previous Commission notices.[11]

(4) The Evaluation Report on Regulation 1475/95 and Decisions Enforcing Regulation 1475/95

15.08   Article 11 of Regulation 1475/95 required the Commission to draw up an evaluation report on the operation of the Regulation[12] before 31 December 2000, because the Regulation was due to expire on 30 September 2002. This evaluation report concluded that Regulation 1475/95 had not achieved all the aims stated by the Commission in 1995 when it renewed the block exemption.[13] In the Commission's view, competition between distributors was not strong enough and distributors remained too dependent on car manufacturers. Consumers had in practice found it difficult to exercise their right in the Internal Market to take advantage of price differentials between Member States to buy their vehicle wherever the price was the lowest. Consumers did not derive a fair share of benefit from the system, even though this is a requirement for any exemption pursuant to Article 81(3).

15.09   Between 1998 and 2001, the Commission adopted four decisions imposing fines on vehicle manufacturers and importers. The infringements of Article 81 related to impediments of parallel trade,[14] resale price maintenance,[15] the restriction of the supply of new cars to leasing companies and a price cartel.[16] These decisions covered practices which existed when

---

[11] Commission Notice concerning Regulation (EEC) 123/85 of 12 December 1984 on the application of Art 85(3) of the Treaty to certain categories of motor vehicle distribution and servicing agreements [1985] OJ C17/4. Information from the Commission—Clarification of the activities of motor vehicle intermediaries [1991] OJ C329/20. These notices remained in force until 30 September 2002: see Commission press release IP(95) 648, 21 June 1995, p 3 which points out that after the entry into force of Regulation 1475/95 the clarifications in these notices only concerned those provisions which in substance had been left unchanged by this Regulation.

[12] Commission Report on the evaluation of Regulation (EC) 1475/95 on the application of Art 85(3) [now 81(3)] of the Treaty to certain categories of motor vehicle distribution and servicing agreements, 15 November 2000, COM(2000)743 final; available at: <http://ec.europa.eu/comm/competition/ car_sector/>.

[13] See also the speech of Commissioner Mario Monti, 'Who will be in the driver's seat?' at the Forum Europe Conference, Brussels, 11 May 2000.

[14] *Volkswagen I* Decision of 28 January 1998, imposing a fine of EUR102 million; [1998] OJ L124/60; press release IP/98/94. This Decision was largely confirmed by the CFI, Case T-62/98, which reduced the fine to EUR90 million, [2000] ECR II-02707; Commission press release IP/00/725; CFI press release 50/00. This judgment was confirmed by the Court of Justice on 18 September 2003, Case C-338/00 P, [2003] ECR I-09189. See also Opinion of Ruiz-Jarabo Colomer AG delivered on 17 October 2002, [2003] ECR I-09189.

Opel Nederland BV / General Motors Nederland BV Decision of 20 September 2000, imposing a fine of EUR43 million; [2001] OJ L59/1; press release IP/00/1028. The judgment of the Court of First Instance of 21 October 2003, Case T-368/00, reduced this fine to EUR35.475 million, ECR II-4491; see CFI Press release 91/03. The appeal (Case C-551/03 P) lodged by GM and Opel Nederland at the Court of Justice was dismissed by a judgment of 6 April 2006, [2006] ECR I-3173.

Mercedes-Benz Decision of 10 October 2001, imposing a fine of nearly EUR72 million; [2002] OJ L257/1; press release IP/01/1394. DaimlerChrysler launched an appeal to the CFI (Case T-325/01). In its judgment of 15 September 2005, [2005] ECR II-3319, the CFI annulled 2 of the 3 infringements identified by the Commission and reduced the fine to EUR9.8 million.

[15] *Volkswagen II* Decision of 29 June 2001, imposing a fine of EUR30.96 million; [2001] OJ L262/14; press release IP/01/760; annulled by CFI judgment of 3 December 2003, Case T-208/01; ECR II-5141; see also opinion of Tizzano AG of 17 November 2005 and the judgment of the Court of Justice of 13 July 2006 which upheld the CFI judgment although the CFI's reasoning was considered to be partly erroneous, Case C-74/04 P, not yet published in the ECR.

[16] See above *Mercedes-Benz* decision.

Regulation 123/85 and Regulation 1475/95 applied. They showed that neither Regulation was fully respected. A further decision concerning restrictions of parallel trade was adopted in 2005.[17]

Following the evaluation report, the decisions that were adopted and the many informal **15.10** complaints received from consumers, intermediaries and distributors, and taking account of the findings of four studies[18] commissioned by the Commission, a new block exemption Regulation was prepared.

(5) Effects of a Possible Application of Regulation 2790/1999 to the Car Sector

Without a sector specific block exemption regulation, motor vehicle distribution, servicing **15.11** and spare parts distribution would have come under the general block exemption for vertical restraints, Regulation 2790/1999. However, such an approach would not have solved the problems identified in the evaluation report on Regulation 1475/95 and would have constituted a big step backwards.

The evaluation report came to the conclusion that inter-brand competition amongst **15.12** motor vehicle distributors was weak due to the limited number of multi-brand distributorships that would sell competing brands. If Regulation 2790/1999 had applied, it would have allowed a total ban of multi-branding on the condition that non-compete clauses would be renegotiated after five years. This would have been a significant step backwards and inappropriate in this sector also because in 1995 restrictions banning multi-branding by distributors had been excluded from the scope of Regulation 1475/95. Furthermore, tying sales and servicing activities covered by Regulation 1475/95 was not considered justified. However, Regulation 2790/1999 would have covered such ties.

Finally, Regulation 2790/1999 would have covered restrictions of competition in the area **15.13** of spare part distribution such as a ban on authorised repairers to sell spare parts to independent repairers or a ban for spare part manufacturers to supply spare parts directly to authorised repairers, which had not been covered by the previous Regulation and which would have placed independent repairers, who provide about 50 per cent of all repair and maintenance services, in a very difficult position. To avoid such effects, the new set of rules carried over and strengthened the existing rules on distribution of spare parts. Another very important issue concerned the access to technical information which vehicle manufacturers had to give to independent repairers under Regulation 1475/95. Such access is vital for preserving competition in a market relating to long-lasting, ever more complex technical products which need repair and maintenance throughout their lifetime. Applying Regulation 2790/1999 would have allowed manufacturers under Article 81 to operate

---

[17] *Peugeot* Decision of 5 October 2005, imposing a fine of EUR49.5 million for having obstructed parallel trade; summary at [2006] OJ L173/20, the full text can be found at: <http://ec.europa.eu/ comm/competition/index_en.html>. The strategy consisted of two measures. First, a portion of the remuneration of Peugeot's Dutch dealers was made dependent on the final destination of the vehicle, discriminating against sales to foreign consumers. In particular, performance bonuses were refused if dealers sold cars to non-Dutch citizens. Secondly, Automobiles Peugeot SA exercised, through Peugeot Nederland N.V. direct pressure on those dealers who were identified as having developed a significant export activity, for example by threatening to reduce the number of cars supplied to them. See also press release IP/05/1227.

[18] <http://ec.europa.eu/comm/competition/car_sector/>.

their distribution and servicing networks without granting such access. The new regime broadened the obligation of vehicle manufacturers to grant such access to all independent operators directly or indirectly involved in the repair and maintenance of motor vehicles.

15.14   Moreover, in certain areas such as making corresponding vehicles available to distributors, the right of distributors to sell spare parts to independent repairers, the right of distributors to source spare parts from other suppliers or access to technical information for independent repairers, all of which were well established and competition-enhancing elements of Regulation 1475/95, would not have been preserved, had the Commission decided to apply Regulation 2790/1999 to the motor vehicle sector.

B.   Overview of Regulation 1400/2002

(1)   The Essential Features of the New Regulation

15.15   The new regime is based on the principles governing the new generation of block exemption regulations: it exempts vertical agreements only up to certain market share thresholds and it only lists restrictions and measures which are not covered by the block exemption, thus covering all restrictions of competition which are not explicitly mentioned in the lists of hardcore restrictions of competition (Article 4) or general (Article 3) or specific conditions (Article 5). As regards substance, the main aim of the new regime is to allow manufacturers to choose between selective and exclusive distribution, to allow distributors to choose whether they wish also to run a repair shop or to subcontract repair and maintenance services, to operate from one or several locations (this option exists for authorised repairers and spare part distributors from 1 October 2002 and for distributors of passenger cars and light commercial vehicles from 1 October 2005), to make it easier for distributors to become multi-brand distributorships, to strengthen the distributors' independence from manufacturers by allowing them to acquire other distributorships within the same network and by obliging manufacturers to give reasons if they end a distributor agreement concluded for an unlimited time. Furthermore, Regulation 1400/2002 aims to make the Single Market a reality for the European consumer and to promote competition, quality, and choice in the repair sector: to this end a manufacturer will normally only be able to select authorised repairers on the basis of quality criteria, ie it will have to allow every qualified repairer who fulfils the quality standards to join its network of authorised repairers. As regards spare parts distribution, all authorised repairers will be allowed to use spare parts from the relevant manufacturer, but will also be permitted to use spare parts of good quality made by competitors. A novelty of the new regime in the area of spare parts distribution relates to the fact that manufacturers will also have to use qualitative selective distribution for the distribution of their spare parts if their market share is above 30 per cent. Since this is the case for many spare parts, motor vehicle manufacturers must appoint all wholesalers and distributors who want to sell only the vehicle manufacturer's spare parts. Finally, independent repairers and other independent operators directly or indirectly involved in the repair of motor vehicles must be given access to all technical information and to all spare parts. The aims and content of the

Regulation have been further clarified through an explanatory brochure and replies to frequently asked questions.[19]

(2) Legal Basis and Procedure for Adoption

Council Regulation 19/65 of 2 March 1965 on the application of Article 85(3) of the Treaty to certain categories of agreements and concerted practices[20] empowers the Commission to adopt block exemption regulations for categories of agreements of undertakings, decisions of associations of undertakings, and concerted practices that are presumed normally to satisfy the conditions for exemption laid down in Article 81(3). **15.16**

The adoption of Regulation 1400/2002 resulted in Regulation 2790/1999, the general block exemption Regulation on vertical restraints, not being applicable to vertical agreements in the motor vehicle sector. Pursuant to Article 2(5) of Regulation 2790/1999, it 'shall not apply to vertical agreements the subject matter of which falls within the scope of any other block exemption regulation'. This means that if Regulation 1400/2002 is not applicable, for instance, because the distribution agreement does not provide an arbitration mechanism in case of contractual disputes, it is neither necessary nor possible any more to examine whether the conditions for exemption in Regulation 2790/1999 would be applicable. If an agreement which comes under Article 81(1) is not covered by a block exemption, it must be assessed directly on the basis of Article 81(3). In the context of such an individual assessment one must bear in mind that the Regulation is a sector specific regulation in which the Commission has addressed certain aspects of vertical restraints in the automobile sector in a very detailed way after careful consideration of the specific context. This makes it much harder for an undertaking to show that a vertical restraint which is not covered by the Regulation nevertheless complies with Article 81(3).[21] **15.17**

As is stated in Recital 2 of the Regulation, the reason for the non-application of Regulation 2790/1999 is that the experience acquired by the Commission in the application of Article 81 in the motor vehicle sector, ie the distribution of new motor vehicles, spare parts, and after sales services, led the Commission to the conclusion that stricter rules than those provided in Regulation 2790/1999 were necessary in this sector. **15.18**

The procedure for adoption of the block exemption Regulations is laid down in Articles 5 and 6 of the empowering Regulation 19/65: in the case of Regulation 1400/2002, the Commission **15.19**

---

[19] Explanatory brochure on Commission Regulation (EC) No 1400/2002 of 31 July 2002 on the application of Art 81(3) of the Treaty to categories of vertical agreements and concerted practices in the motor vehicle sector, published on 1 October 2002 (hereafter 'explanatory brochure') and Frequently asked questions on the new motor vehicle block exemption, published in October 2003. In this respect, Geelhoed AG underlined in his opinion in case C-125/05 *VW-Audi Forhandlerforeningen acting on behalf of Vulcan Silkeborg A/S v Skandinavisk Motor A/S*, paras 33–39, that such guidelines are a tool by which the Commission creates legal certainty for undertakings and which have a self-binding effect on the Commission; judgment of the Court of Justice of 7 September 2006, not yet published in the ECR.

[20] [1965] OJ L36/533.

[21] Based on Regulation 1/2003 and the direct application of Art 81(3), judges are now in a position to assess whether vertical restraints which are not covered by a block exemption regulation and which are not within the 'save harbour' created by such a regulation, nevertheless fulfil the conditions of Art 81(3); see Geelhoed AG, joint cases C-376/05 and C-377/05 *A Brünsteiner GmbH* and *Autohaus Hilgert GmbH v Bayerische Motorenwerke AG (BMW)*, para 37, judgment of the Court of Justice of 30 November 2006, not yet published in the ECR.

adopted on 5 February 2002 a first draft block exemption Regulation.[22] Then the Commission presented the draft Regulation to the Member States in the framework of the Advisory Committee on Restrictive Practices and Dominant Positions in March 2002. The draft Regulation was published in the Official Journal of the European Communities on 16 March 2002[23] for comment from interested third parties. A second consultation of the Member States took place in June 2002.[24] On 31 July 2002 the Commission adopted Commission Regulation (EC) 1400/2002 of 31 July 2002 on the application of Article 81(3) of the Treaty to categories of vertical agreements and concerted practices in the motor vehicle sector (hereafter 'the Regulation').[25]

(3) Structure of the Regulation

15.20 Article 1 of the Regulation contains in paragraph 1 a set of definitions for the purpose of this Regulation. Paragraph 2 extends those definitions that concern market operators to include connected undertakings. The definition of 'connected undertakings' follows that contained in Regulation 2790/1999. An undertaking which is linked directly or indirectly to another undertaking which has, or within which it has, the power to exercise more than half the voting rights or to appoint more than half the members of bodies legally representing the undertaking, such as the supervisory board or the board of management, or which has the right to manage the undertaking's affairs, must be considered as a connected undertaking. This is relevant for the calculation of market shares and of turnover figures.

15.21 Article 2 describes the scope of the Regulation. The Regulation covers vertical agreements that relate to the conditions under which the parties may purchase, sell or resell new motor vehicles, spare parts, or repair and maintenance services for such vehicles. The distribution of accessories does not fall under the Regulation.[26] As regards the distribution of financial services, such as credit or insurance contracts, the situation is less clear. The principle that specific rules must be interpreted narrowly suggests that the distribution of these products comes under Regulation 2790/1999. However, for many of these products, distributors merely act as intermediaries and do not bear any risk associated with the relevant financial service. If the distributor acts as a commercial agent,[27] this activity does not come under Article 81(1) and there is no scope for the application of a block exemption regulation or an assessment of such agreements under Article 81(3).

15.22 Article 3 of the Regulation lists the general conditions necessary for agreements to be covered by the Regulation. The most important general condition relates to the market shares of the supplier (or the buyer, in the case of exclusive supply obligations). The non-fulfilment of a general condition leads to a situation where the block exemption Regulation is not applicable to the vertical agreement as such and any restriction of competition contained in the agreement must be examined directly in the light of the conditions laid down in Article 81(3).

---

[22] See IP/02/196 of 5 February 2002.
[23] [2002] OJ C67/2.
[24] See MEMO/02/174 of 17 July 2002.
[25] [2002] OJ L203/30.
[26] See explanatory brochure, reply to question 95. Available at: <http://ec.europa.eu/comm/ competition/ car_sector/>.
[27] See Guidelines on vertical restraints, paras 12ff.

Article 4 of the Regulation contains a list of hardcore restrictions of competition. If any of **15.23** these restraints is included in the agreement, this excludes the application of the Regulation to the whole agreement. It is also unlikely that such a restriction would fulfil the conditions of Article 81(3).[28]

The specific conditions required to apply the block exemption to an agreement are laid **15.24** down in Article 5 of the Regulation. This provides a list of restrictions of competition which are not covered by the Regulation. However, the inclusion of such a restriction in the agreement, if it is severable, does not affect the applicability of the Regulation to the remainder of the agreement: the non-exemption is limited only to the relevant restrictive clause.[29]

Articles 6 to 9 of the Regulation are to a large extent aligned to the corresponding provisions **15.25** of Regulation 2790/1999: Article 6 describes the power of the Commission and national competition authorities to withdraw the benefit of the Regulation if agreements covered by the exemption nevertheless have effects that are incompatible with Article 81(3). Pursuant to Article 7, the Commission may declare the Regulation to be inapplicable to vertical agreements containing specific restraints where parallel networks of similar vertical restraints cover more than 50 per cent of a relevant market. Articles 8 and 9 specify the rules for the calculation of market shares and turnover, respectively.

Article 10 of the Regulation provides for a transitional period of one year for agreements **15.26** that were covered by Regulation 1475/95. Manufacturers and distributors have the possibility to end existing distribution agreements covered by Regulation 1475/95 with one year's notice if the entry into force of the new Regulation makes it necessary to reorganise the whole or a substantial part of the network.[30]

Article 11 of the Regulation establishes the duty of the Commission to monitor the opera- **15.27** tion of the Regulation and to draw up an evaluation report at the latest two years before its expiry in 2010.[31]

Finally, Article 12 contains the rules on the entry into force and the expiry of the Regulation. **15.28**

(4) Scope of Application

The substantive scope of the Regulation is defined in Article 2. Paragraph 1 constitutes the **15.29** exemption provision, stating that Article 81(1) shall not apply to vertical agreements concerning the purchase, sale, or resale of new motor vehicles,[32] spare, parts for motor vehicles or repair and maintenance services for motor vehicles. The exemption is subject to the fulfilment of the conditions in Articles 3 and 5 and the non-inclusion of hardcore restraints enumerated in Article 4. Agreements that do not contain any vertical restraints, ie restrictions

---

[28] See Guidelines on vertical restraints, para 46.
[29] See Guidelines on vertical restraints, para 57.
[30] Art 5(3), first indent, Regulation 1475/95; see also para 15.83 below.
[31] Based on its obligation to monitor the operation of the Regulation pursuant to its Art 11(1), the Commission has commissioned a study on 'Developments in car retailing and after-sales markets under Regulation 1400/2002, June 2006', published at: <http://ec.europa.eu/comm/competition/car_sector/>.
[32] According to Art 5(2)(a) and Recital 30 the distributor can also sell leasing services or run his own leasing company; see also section 5.3.1.2 of the explanatory brochure.

of competition contained in a vertical agreement and falling within the scope of Article 81(1),[33] do not need an exemption.

15.30   The scope of Regulation 1475/95 was narrower. It only covered agreements that concerned both the sales of new vehicles and spare parts, on the one hand, and the provision of repair and maintenance services, on the other: Article 1 established the exclusive nature of the network of distributors for new vehicles and spare parts and Article 5(1) made the application of the block exemption dependent on there being an obligation on the part of distributors to honour guarantees, to perform free servicing and vehicle-recall work, and to carry out repair and maintenance. These provisions established an obligatory link between the, in principle, separate economic activities of selling new vehicles, selling spare parts, and repairing and maintaining vehicles.

15.31   The wider scope of Regulation 1400/2002 offers a distributor of new vehicles the opportunity to provide after sales service himself or to subcontract it to authorised repairers of that brand of vehicles.[34] It is therefore logical that it also covers agreements that are limited to the sale of new vehicles or the sale of spare parts or the provision of repair and maintenance services.

15.32   As is the case with Regulation 2790/1999, the Regulation also applies to agreements between an association of undertakings, on the one hand, and its members or suppliers on the other hand, as long as all members are distributors of new motor vehicles or spare parts for motor vehicles, or repairers, and no individual member has a total annual turnover of more than EUR50 million. The Regulation equally covers provisions on the assignment of intellectual property rights.[35]

15.33   Vertical agreements between competitors are in principle excluded from its scope.[36] There are three permissible exceptions, and in all three scenarios the agreements must be non-reciprocal. The first exception is an agreement with a buyer who has a total annual turnover not exceeding EUR100 million. This might be relevant, for instance, for an agreement between a manufacturer that also distributes its vehicles and a distributor of limited size. This type of dual distribution is also covered—in particular in the case of distributors with a higher turnover—by the second exception, according to which the supplier is a manufacturer and also a distributor of goods, while the buyer is a distributor who does not manufacture goods which compete with the contract goods. The Regulation does not prevent manufacturers of vehicles from also acting as distributors of their vehicles. These 'direct sales' have been criticised in the past in particular by the associations of distributors. In view of their competition-enhancing effect, however, it would not have been justified to deny manufacturers the opportunity to establish or purchase distributorships. The third exception concerns a clause akin to dual distribution, but in this case concerning the provision of services. It allows the manufacturer to establish its own repair shops and therefore also to be active as an authorised (or independent) repairer and set up on the same market a network of authorised repairers.

---

[33] Art 1(1)(d).
[34] Art 4(1)(g).
[35] Art 2(2)(b).
[36] Art 2(3).

(5) Application to the Ten New Member States and within the EEA

The geographic scope of the Regulation was extended from the EU to include the territo- **15.34**
ries of the countries participating in the European Economic Area (EEA).[37] Consequently,
the Regulation became fully applicable in the EEA with effect from 1 October 2002.

With regard to the accession of the ten new Member States on 1 May 2004, the Regulation **15.35**
was modified by the Act of Accession. An additional transition period of six months was
granted during which Article 81(1) would 'not apply to agreements existing at the date of
accession for the Czech Republic, Estonia, Cyprus, Latvia, Lithuania, Hungary, Malta,
Poland, Slovenia and Slovakia and which, by reason of accession, fall within the scope of
Article 81(1) if, within six months from the date of accession, they are amended and
thereby comply with the conditions laid down in this Regulation'.[38]

C. Sales of New Vehicles

(1) Definition of Motor Vehicles and of Vertical Agreements

A motor vehicle is defined in Article 1(1)(n) as having the following characteristics: (1) it is **15.36**
self propelled; (2) it is intended for use on public roads; and (3) it has three or more road
wheels. Consequently, the Regulation covers agreements on passenger cars, light commercial
vehicles, trucks, buses, and coaches while, for instance, motorcycles (only two road wheels) or
quads (which have four wheels but no body[39]), tractors and earth-moving machines (in general not intended for use on public roads) are excluded from the scope of the Regulation.

**(2) Choice between Selective Distribution and Exclusive Distribution of
New Motor Vehicles**

For the sale of new motor vehicles, the supplier can choose whether to opt for selective **15.37**
distribution or to establish a network of exclusive distributors. He may also mix the two
systems by establishing selective distribution in some markets and exclusive distribution in
others.[40] The large majority of manufacturers of motor vehicles[41] have chosen selective networks for distributing their goods because in a selective distribution system they have more
control over who is selling their goods and in what way the sale takes place because they can
establish criteria for distributors.

---

[37] Decision of the EEA Joint Committee No 136/2002 of 27 September 2002 amending Annex XIV
(Competition) to the EEA Agreement, [2002] OJ L336/38.

[38] See List referred to in Art 20 of the Act of Accession, Ch 5, point 11 published at: <http://ec.europa.eu/
comm/enlargement/negotiations/treaty_of_accession_2003/pdf/3_act_of_accession/aa00011_re03_en03.pdf>.

[39] The definition of 'a motor vehicle which corresponds to a model within the contract range' in Art 1(1)(r)
makes a reference to the 'body style' of the relevant vehicles, which indicates that the Regulation was designed
to cover vehicles which have a body.

[40] For further details on mixed distribution systems see para 15.43.

[41] The only exception is Suzuki, which distributes its new cars via dealers who have been allocated an
exclusive sales territory. One should bear in mind that unlike dealers operating within a selective distribution
system, the exclusive dealers are allowed to sell new cars to unauthorised resellers as such sales may not be
banned pursuant to Art 4(b)(iii).

15.38   (i) **Selective distribution**   A selective distribution system for new motor vehicles is characterised by two features[42]: first, the manufacturer of the vehicles, or the company which the manufacturer has designated to supply its vehicles in a given territory, undertakes only to sell the vehicles that are the subject matter of the agreement to distributors that are selected on the basis of specified criteria. Secondly, this obligation on the part of the manufacturer is mirrored by an obligation on the distributors or repairers not to sell the vehicles to unauthorised distributors, ie independent resellers that are not members of the distribution network.

15.39   If the selection criteria directly limit the number of distributors, for instance if the manufacturer fixes the total number of members of its distribution system in a given market, this is a 'quantitative selective distribution system'.[43]

15.40   The selective distribution is of a qualitative nature if the criteria:

- are only of a qualitative nature;
- are required by the nature of the goods or services;
- are laid down uniformly for all distributors or repairers applying to join the distribution system;
- are not applied in a discriminatory manner; and
- do not directly limit the number of distributors.[44]

In a system of selective distribution, the distributor is free to sell new vehicles actively and passively to end-users in any markets where selective distribution is used,[45] and the supplier must not limit these sales.

15.41   'Active sales' means actively approaching individual customers by, for instance, direct mail or visits, through advertising in the media, or by other promotions not normally available or in circulation at the authorised place of establishment of a distributor or repairer; or by establishing a warehouse or sales or delivery outlet at another place of establishment [46] to facilitate dealings with customers or their intermediaries. 'Passive sales' means responding to unsolicited requests from customers or their duly authorised intermediaries including delivery of motor vehicles or spare parts to such customers or intermediaries. General advertising or promotions in the media which are normally available or in circulation at the authorised place of establishment of the distributor or repairer or on the Internet are passive sales methods.[47] Therefore, any distributor, be it in selective (or exclusive) distribution, can sell new motor vehicles or indeed spare parts for motor vehicles by using the Internet or Internet referral sites.[48]

15.42   (ii) **Exclusive distribution**   In a system of exclusive distribution, either a territory or a customer group is exclusively attributed to one or more distributors. It is also possible for

---

[42] Art 1(1)(f).

[43] Art 1(1)(g).

[44] Art 1(1)(h).

[45] Art 4(1)(d) and (e).

[46] As regards the right of dealers to open additional sales or delivery outlets located elsewhere than his 'main' dealership from 1 October 2005 on, please refer to the section below on location clauses.

[47] See Guidelines on Vertical Restraints [1999] OJ C336/21, para 50, and reply to question 12 of the explanatory brochure.

[48] Recital 15.

the supplier to reserve a territory or a customer group to itself. Other distributors are not allowed actively to approach the end-users in this territory or the members of this group.[49] However, the exclusive distributor cannot be prohibited from selling new vehicles to independent resellers.[50] He can do so actively in respect of independent resellers that are located in his territory, but only passively when they are located in the exclusive territory of another distributor. The exclusive distributor may sell actively to end-users in his territory, and may also engage in passive sales to end-users located in the territories of other exclusive distributors, ie the end-users that approach him.

(iii) Mixing distribution systems   If a supplier of new vehicles intended to mix the distribution systems by establishing selective distribution in some markets and exclusive distribution in others, he would have to take into account the fact that he cannot prevent the exclusive distributors from selling to independent resellers who would then be free to resell the vehicles wherever they wished. Furthermore, a selective distributor of new vehicles cannot be prohibited from also selling the vehicles to independent resellers located in territories where exclusive distribution is used and which approach the selective distributor. This is therefore an exception to the obligation of authorised distributors and repairers in a selective distribution system not to sell goods to distributors that are not members of the distribution network. It would, however, be feasible for a supplier to reserve a certain area, for instance a metropolitan area, for itself and establish its subsidiaries as exclusive distributors in this area. In the surrounding territories, the supplier could establish a selective distribution network. He could decide not to carry out sales from such exclusive distributors to independent resellers in order not to undermine the selective distribution system. Sales from the selective distributors to independent resellers would most likely only take place if the price differentials between the metropolitan area and its surroundings were substantial. **15.43**

(iv) The role of sales agents and intermediaries
Sales agents   In selective and exclusive distribution, the manufacturer decides whether or not to prevent its distributors from appointing sales agents, whether or not they are 'genuine' sales agents, who do not bear any financial or commercial risk in relation to the activities for which they have been appointed by the principal.[51] A sales agent sells vehicles on behalf of a manufacturer or distributor. Although, strictly speaking, the number of distributors would not rise if distributors were allowed to appoint sales agents, the manufacturer has the right to organise its distribution network, and to decide whether or not to have sales agents in his distribution system. If a manufacturer can prohibit the use of sales agents, it is logical and less restrictive that, if he accepts the appointment of sales agents by the authorised distributor, he can set criteria that such agents must fulfil in order to be appointed. Such criteria could, for instance, relate to the size of the showroom, the signage, or the training of the agent's sales personnel. **15.44**

When sales agents are used, one must first consider whether the agency agreement falls within the scope of application of Article 81(1) and assess in particular the obligations imposed **15.45**

---

[49] Art 4(1)(b)(i).
[50] Art 4(1)(b)(ii).
[51] Guidelines on vertical restraints, paras 13ff.

on the agent in the contracts negotiated and/or concluded on behalf of the distributor as principal. In principle, in the case of genuine agency agreements, Article 81(1) is not applicable to restrictions agreed between an undertaking and its agents.[52] Although agents conduct an economic activity and therefore must be considered as undertakings within the meaning of this provision, they operate as auxiliary organs forming an integral part of the principal's undertaking due to the fact that they act on behalf of another undertaking. The restrictions contained in agreements between the principal and its agents, therefore, are not in general considered to be restrictions of competition within the meaning of Article 81(1).

15.46 For motor vehicle distribution, the Commission examined this question in the *Mercedes-Benz* decision.[53] DaimlerChrysler, which sells a large proportion of its new vehicles in Germany via a network of 'agents', claimed that these agents should not be equated with distributors as they would not bear any of the contractual risks associated with selling new vehicles. However, in the Commission's view the application of Article 81 to the restrictions agreed between DaimlerChrysler and its German agents resulted from the fact that these agents had to bear considerable financial and commercial risks linked to their activity: a share of the price risk associated with the vehicles whose sale they negotiated because the agent had to make a financial contribution if rebates on new vehicles were granted to individual customers or to specific customer groups by accepting a lower commission; transport and transport cost risk; use of own resources for sales promotion (the agent had to buy and resell demonstration vehicles and the vehicles displayed in the showroom); and there were contractual risks linked to the manufacturer's guarantee. From the point of view of EC competition law, the Commission, therefore, did not regard these agents as genuine commercial agents but as distributors, and applied Article 81 to the agreements between them and DaimlerChrysler.

15.47 The Commission's reasoning was based on the case law of the Court of Justice.[54] It is also in line with the Commission Guidelines on vertical restraints[55] according to which the determining factor in assessing whether Article 81(1) applies to the activity of a sales agent is whether or not the agent has to bear financial or commercial risks in relation to the activities for which he has been appointed as an agent by the principal, unless these risks are insignificant.

15.48 In its judgment of 15 September 2005[56] the CFI quashed the reasoning of the Commission decision relating to the assessment of the DaimlerChrysler agency agreements. The CFI found that the DaimlerChrysler agents do not buy, stock, and resell new cars and do not bear the price risk. As regards the risk linked to the purchase and resale of demonstration

---

[52] Guidelines on vertical restraints, para 13.

[53] [2002] OJ L257/1, paras 153–168. See also CFI Case T 325/01, judgment of 15 September 2005, not yet published in the ECR.

[54] See Case C-266/93 *Bundeskartellamt v Volkswagen AG and VAG Leasing GmbH* [1995] ECR I-3477, para 19.

[55] [2000] OJ C291/1. It is noted that these Guidelines were not applicable in that case as the infringement predated them. Paras 12 to 20 of the Guidelines replace the Notice on exclusive dealing contracts with commercial agents of 1962 ([1962] OJ 139/2921).

[56] Case T 325/01 [2005] ECR II-3319.

vehicles and the risks resulting from the obligation to honour the manufacturer's warranties, it took the view that the Commission had not shown the exact magnitude of the risks. The Commission had also not demonstrated that the *compensation* paid to the agent for an activity which must normally be carried out by the principal was *commercially inadequate*, in which case *the agent can also lose its status as a genuine agent.*[57] As to the risks linked to the provision of normal repair and maintenance and the sale of spare parts, it also emphasised that the Commission had not shown that appreciable risks were associated with these activities. The CFI added that these latter activities of the agent were in any event conducted in a market other than the new car market and on their own could not in any event lead to the conclusion that the DaimlerChrysler agents are not genuine commercial agents and that Article 81 can be applied to the agency agreement.

Intermediaries   Intermediaries must be distinguished from sales agents. An intermediary **15.49** is a person or undertaking which purchases a new vehicle on behalf of an end-user while not being a member of the supplier's distribution network. Intermediaries therefore are not independent resellers as they do not acquire a vehicle and resell it afterwards to a customer, but operate on behalf of a named end-user.

In 1985, the Commission issued a notice concerning Regulation 123/85[58] which addressed **15.50** the issue of intermediaries. It obliged the intermediary or the consumer to give the distributor documentary evidence that the intermediary was acting on behalf of and for the account of the consumer. This notice was supplemented in 1991 by a Clarification of the activities of motor vehicle intermediaries.[59] This second notice included limitations on the activities of intermediaries. For instance, the outlet of the intermediaries could not be within the same premises as those where the principal activities of a supermarket were carried out. An intermediary could also not establish a 'privileged' relationship with one or more authorised distributors. Such a relationship would have been created if an authorised distributor had sold more than 10 per cent of his annual sales of new vehicles through a given intermediary. In such a situation, the distributor would have infringed his contractual obligations stemming from the distribution agreement.

The Regulation makes clear that a selective distributor has the right to sell vehicles to end- **15.51** users via intermediaries. It abolishes all criteria for acting as an intermediary that would be additional to having a valid mandate from an end-user. A valid mandate must be in writing, give the end-user's name and address and must be signed and dated. The authorisation given in the mandate may concern all or one or some of the following actions: purchasing, taking delivery of, transporting or storing a new motor vehicle on behalf of the end-user. Normally the intermediary will not become the owner of the vehicle which he has purchased for an end-user. However, even if the intermediary becomes for a short and transitional period of time the owner of a vehicle which he has purchased for a specific customer, the distributor is allowed to sell the vehicle to that intermediary. In order to implement such a sale of a new vehicle, which has been clearly identified in the mandate given to the

---

[57] See in particular paras 106, 109 and 111 of the judgment.
[58] [1985] OJ C17/4.
[59] [1991] OJ C329/20.

intermediary, the distributor selling the vehicle can also 'pro forma' bill it to the intermediary and pass the ownership to the intermediary on condition that the vehicle is transferred in due course to the buyer who has given the authorisation to the intermediary.[60] Such sales do not undermine a selective distribution system and are therefore not contrary to the rights of manufacturers to protect their selective distribution systems[61] and to prohibit sales of new vehicles to unauthorised resellers, who buy, stock, promote and resell new vehicles on their own initiative to any buyer in the market without being subject to any of the obligations of the distributors belonging to the manufacturer's network regarding investments into showrooms, training of sales persons, etc and who take advantage of investment (by others) in the distributor network of the manufacturer.

15.52   The intermediary acts on behalf of the customer who has given the mandate. The mandate may also allow or oblige the intermediary to pick up the new car at the premises of the selling distributor and to ship it to the buyer. Normally and unless otherwise agreed the manufacturer's warranty period starts when the car leaves the distributor network at the time when it is handed over to the intermediary.

15.53   **(v) Cross-supplies between distributors**   An important means of increasing competition within a system of selective distribution is provided by cross-supplies between distributors of new vehicles who are members of such a distribution system.[62] The manufacturer must not indirectly or directly restrict the opportunities for a distributor to sell vehicles to or purchase from another authorised distributor. Such transactions can take place between distributors operating at different levels of trade and can also be cross-border in nature, for instance, a retailer in Member State A purchasing vehicles from a wholesaler in Member State B. This measure fosters market integration between Member States. If a manufacturer imposed on its distributors the requirement to source vehicles only from him or from a specified importer/wholesaler or distributor, this would restrict the distributor's ability to source vehicles from other undertakings within the distribution system and, consequently, constitute a hardcore restriction under Article 4(1)(c). Thus, an obligation for the distributor to purchase up to 30 per cent of his total purchases of the vehicles or their substitutes from the manufacturer, which is one of the non-compete obligations permitted pursuant to Article 1(1)(b) in combination with Article 5(1), cannot be used to impose an obligation to source certain or all new vehicles from the manufacturer or a certain other importer/wholesaler or distributor. On the contrary, cross-supplies from other authorised distributors must, eg, be included in the calculation of this percentage.

15.54   **(vi) Bonus schemes and cross supplies**   Bonus schemes must be designed in such a way that bonuses are also paid for cars which have been cross-supplied between distributors. For instance, if a bonus were only paid for cars which have been sourced from the manufacturer or importer and which are sold to end consumers, the scheme would restrict cross-supplies: the bonus would neither be paid for cars sourced from another importer or another distributor

---

[60]   See <http://www.kfzbetrieb.de/einfo/einfo_1608401.html> where the text of the relevant letter of DG Competition is published.

[61]   See Art 4(1)(b)(iii).

[62]   Art 4(1)(c); see also para 55 of the Guidelines on vertical restraints.

of the same brand nor for cars sold by a distributor to another distributor in the network. In fact, many bonus schemes are used as a means of boosting the sale of certain car models, eg in order to reduce the stock of new unsold cars of a certain model. In practice, such bonuses provide a flexible means of reducing the wholesale price of certain vehicles in one or several Member States. The bonuses should thus be available for all sales of such vehicles carried out by a distributor, whether they are sold directly to end-users coming from the Member State in which the distributor is located or from another Member State, or whether they are sold to an end-user who has given a mandate to an intermediary. However, such bonuses must also be available if a vehicle is cross-supplied by one distributor to another distributor in or outside the relevant Member State: otherwise the bonus scheme could make cross-supplies economically unattractive or impossible. Furthermore, if, for example, a bonus paid for a certain car in Member State A could be withheld if this car is cross-supplied to a distributor located in Member State B, where no bonuses are paid, the distributor in Member State B could not make an attractive offer to a customer living in Member State B. This would put him at a disadvantage because this customer has the opportunity to buy that specific car model directly or via an intermediary from a distributor in Member State A and thus indirectly benefit from the bonus (ie the lower wholesale price for that car).[63] This approach contributes to the creation of a level playing field between distributors in the Single Market which operate within the distribution system of a manufacturer.

15.55 Most vehicle manufacturers own banks and leasing companies, which offer favourable loan or leasing conditions for new vehicles. The relevant loan or leasing contract is concluded by the car manufacturers' bank or leasing company with the buyer or lessee of the new vehicle. Such contracts, if limited to the loan for or leasing of the vehicle, do not come under Article 81 and the Regulation does not apply. The favourable loan or leasing conditions must therefore not be made available for cars which have been cross-supplied between distributors and can thus be limited to cars sourced by the distributors from the factory or the national importer or wholesaler.

15.56 **(vii) The use of location clauses** In selective distribution systems, the restriction of active or passive sales to end-users constitutes a hardcore restriction that results in the non-application of the Regulation to the agreements that include such a restriction. It is, however, permissible to include a clause in the agreement with a selected distributor by which the manufacturer determines the location of the distributor's business premises (location clause).[64] Such a clause prevents the distributor from operating out of an unauthorised place of establishment, ie from moving its primary outlet or opening additional outlets without the consent of the supplier. In accordance with this principle, the use of location clauses is not limited to the sale of new vehicles other than passenger cars or light commercial vehicles.[65] However, the prohibition is not exempted if it limits the expansion of the

---

[63] Manufacturer W in Member State A pays a 'conquest' premium of EUR2,000 to its dealers to allow them to make better offers for used cars from brand X, which are traded in by the customers. If a dealer located in Member State A cross-supplies such a car to a dealer in Member State B who sells the car to a customer who trades in a car of brand X, then the premium has to be paid either to the dealer in Member State A (who passes it on to the dealer in Member State B) or directly to the dealer in Member State B.

[64] See Guidelines on vertical restraints, para 54.

[65] Art 4(1)(e).

distributor's business at the authorised place of establishment.[66] If there is a contractual dispute about whether a provision in an agreement limits such an expansion, the issue could be the subject of arbitration.[67] Vehicles such as medium and heavy trucks, buses and coaches are normally used in a commercial context. It is assumed that most of their buyers are therefore in a better position to purchase this kind of vehicle from distributors located in other areas and can obtain more favourable sales conditions more easily than can private consumers.

15.57 For passenger cars or light commercial vehicles, the Regulation limits the ability of the manufacturer using a selective distribution system to include location clauses in its agreements by making this subject to a specific condition.[68] After a transition period lasting until 30 September 2005,[69] this provision protects the ability of the distributor to establish additional sales or delivery outlets in areas where selective distribution is applied. The distributor is not allowed to close or move its initial outlet from the location that has been agreed between him and the supplier, unless the supplier agrees.[70] He can however open additional outlets in markets where selective distribution is used and where he sees business opportunities. These additional outlets serve either the purpose of selling new vehicles, for instance a showroom, or of delivering them to the end-users. In order to prevent these additional outlets free-riding on the investment of incumbent distributors, they must comply with the same qualitative criteria and standards that are applicable to similar outlets in the same geographic area.[71] However, such criteria may only be related to the design and quality of the premises, the quality of sales persons and other elements which are necessary to protect the brand image. As regards, for instance, the size of the showroom or the number of cars which must be displayed, the additional showroom must comply with the standards applicable to the smallest distributor operating in that area due to the fact that quantitative requirements for secondary outlets are not covered by Regulation 1400/2002.[72] Requirements regarding back-office equipment, such as having an additional IT system or accounting system for the secondary outlet, in addition to the one the distributor has already at his primary location, are not covered by Regulation 1400/2002 because they are already present at the primary location of the distributor. It is not necessary for the distributor to ask for permission or to enter into additional agreements for these outlets. Such obligations would give the supplier an opportunity to limit, or at least delay, the opening of such additional outlets.[73]

15.58 There has been some debate on the question whether the opening of delivery outlets would inevitably lead to a situation where the relevant distributor free-rides on the investment in showrooms, demonstration vehicles, and sales staff of distributors located in the neighbourhood of the delivery outlet. This is clearly not the case if the delivery outlet is only used to

---

[66] Recital 18.

[67] Art 3(6)(f).

[68] Art 5(2)(b).

[69] See Art 12(2).

[70] This follows from the wording of Art 5(2)(b) which excludes from the cover of the Regulation restrictions to open *additional* sales or delivery outlets. See also reply to question 55 in the explanatory brochure.

[71] Recital 29.

[72] See Recital 29, last sentence.

[73] See also the Commission press release IP/05/1208 of 30 September 2005 on the abolition of the location clauses with effect from 1 October 2005.

deliver new vehicles. If a manufacturer finds that a distributor uses a delivery outlet to sell new cars, it can impose sanctions on that distributor, but no more. A general ban on delivery outlets for all distributors would not be covered by the Regulation and could also not be justified under Article 81(3).

(viii) Availability clause   Pursuant to Article 4(1)(f), a supplier must not restrict the distributor's ability to sell any new motor vehicle which corresponds to a model within its contract range. The contract range means all the different models of motor vehicle available for purchase by the distributor from the supplier.[74] A motor vehicle corresponds to a model within the contract range if it is the subject of a distribution agreement with another authorised distributor of the manufacturer and if it is manufactured or assembled in volume by the manufacturer, and identical as to body style, drive-line, chassis and type of motor to a vehicle within the contract range.[75] The purpose of this 'availability clause' is to enable a distributor in one country also to sell vehicles with specifications offered in any other Member State, under the condition that he sells the corresponding model. The most obvious example is the sale of right-hand drive vehicles on the continent to British or Irish end-users. The availability clause covers all motor vehicles which are sold anywhere in the EU, not only passenger cars as in the previous Regulations 123/85 and 1475/95. If a manufacturer does not honour the orders of a distributor in one Member State for vehicles with specifications of another Member State, or if he has applied discriminatory or objectively unjustified supply conditions, such as longer delivery times or higher prices which cannot be justified, for instance by higher transport costs, this would infringe the availability clause which is a hardcore restriction,[76] and the distribution system of that manufacturer would no longer benefit from the Regulation. In some Member States, vehicles that fulfil higher requirements in respect of environmental standards, for example with regard to emissions, benefit from tax advantages. A consumer must be able to order such a vehicle in another Member State with the specifications from his own Member State, as long as the vehicles that the manufacturer puts on sale in the home country of the customer fulfil these requirements. If the manufacturer sells identical vehicles, but distinguishes in the certification of the emission standards fulfilled, this would also run counter to the right to sell actively and passively to end-users.

15.59

(ix) Sales of new vehicles to leasing companies   Leasing companies must be treated as end-users unless the leasing contracts used provide for a transfer of ownership of the motor vehicle or an option to purchase it prior to the expiry of the contract.[77] This means that leasing companies must be treated in the same way as end customers as long as the leasing contract does not allow the lessee to purchase the vehicle before the leasing contract expires, and distributors are free to sell new cars to independent leasing companies. A corresponding provision was already included in a provision of Regulation 1475/95 according to which 'the term resale shall include all leasing contracts which provide for a transfer of ownership or an option to purchase prior to the expiry of the contract'.[78]

15.60

---

[74] Art 1(1)(q).
[75] Art 1(1)(r).
[76] Art 4 (1)(f).
[77] Art 1(1)(w).
[78] Art 10(12), last sentence.

15.61 In the *Mercedes-Benz* decision,[79] the Commission examined clauses in distribution agreements by which DaimlerChrysler limited the sale of new vehicles by Mercedes agents in Germany and Mercedes distributors in Spain to independent leasing companies. The agents and distributors were only allowed to supply them if the leasing companies had already found customers for the vehicles concerned. Consequently, the undertaking restricted the competition between its own leasing companies and independent leasing companies because the latter were not able to put cars on stock or benefit from rebates which are granted to fleet owners. The independent leasing companies were therefore not able to pass on favourable conditions, in particular concerning the price and availability of cars, to their clients. The Commission concluded that the behaviour of DaimlerChrysler aimed at avoiding a situation where independent leasing companies could offer leasing rates that undercut those which the leasing companies belonging to DaimlerChrysler were prepared to offer.

15.62 DaimlerChrysler argued that the prohibition of selling vehicles to leasing companies for stock would be justified by the obligation of the selective distributor not to sell the vehicles to independent resellers. This is in contradiction to Regulations 1475/95 and 1400/2002 since a leasing company is not a reseller as long as, under its leasing contracts, it is not possible to transfer the ownership of the vehicle to the lessee prior to the expiry of the leasing contract and the lessee cannot exercise an option to purchase the vehicle before the end of the contract. Nearly all leasing contracts used in Europe fulfil these conditions. If a leasing contract provides for the transfer of ownership or the option to purchase the vehicle after the end of the contract, the 'sale' does not concern a new vehicle and the leasing company is therefore not an independent reseller of new vehicles to which a selective distributor would not be allowed to sell.

15.63 Without addressing the above issues concerning the interpretation of the Regulation in its judgment of 15 September 2005, the CFI took the view that the German DaimlerChrysler sales agents are genuine agents. Consequently, Article 81 and the Regulation do not apply. DaimlerChrysler was therefore in a position to instruct the sales agents not to sell new cars to leasing companies who wish to put them into their stock for future use as leasing vehicles. As regards the agreement between the Spanish DaimlerChrysler importer and its distributors prohibiting sales of new cars to leasing departments of financial institutions that wanted to use them for financial leasing contracts, the CFI referred to the Spanish law 26/1988.[80] This law states that the goods which are the subject matter of a financial leasing contract must be purchased by the leasing company based on the specifications determined by the lessee. A financial leasing company therefore cannot buy a stock of cars to be used for future financial leasing contracts. The CFI stated that the prohibition of selling cars to such companies does not restrict any competition which would be possible under Spanish law. As regards sales to other leasing companies, these were not prohibited in the distributor contracts by DaimlerChrysler España.

---

[79] [2002] OJ L 257/1. See also case T 325/01, judgment of the CFI of 15 September 2005 (not yet published).

[80] See additional provision no 7 of the law 'Discipline and intervention of credit institutions', Law 26/1988, of 29 July 1988. An English translation of this law can be found at: <http://www.bde.es/normativa/be/l2688.pdf>, at p 27.

The judgment does not put into question the Commission's reasoning pursuant to which **15.64** distributors must be allowed to sell new cars to leasing companies which will use them for upcoming leasing contracts even if the lessee is not yet known.

(3) Market Share Thresholds

In comparison with the earlier motor vehicle block exemptions, the Regulation follows a **15.65** more economics-based approach. Vertical agreements can have efficiency-enhancing effects on the distribution of goods. But it is likely that the positive effects outweigh any anti-competitive effects of the restrictions of competition included in vertical restraints only if the market power of the undertakings concerned does not exceed certain limits reflected in market share thresholds.

As a first step for calculating the market share, the relevant product and geographic markets **15.66** must be defined. Here, the Commission's traditional instruments are applicable.[81] Pursuant to the Commission Notice on the definition of the relevant market for the purposes of Community competition law,[82] the most important point of reference is demand substitution. The Regulation states that, for the distribution of new motor vehicles, the market share shall be calculated 'on the basis of the volume of the contract goods and corresponding goods sold by the supplier, together with any other goods sold by the supplier which are regarded as interchangeable or substitutable by the buyer, by reason of the products' characteristics, prices and intended use'.[83] The view of the authorised distributors of new vehicles as buyers will be determined by the preferences of the end-users. The Regulation takes account of the fact that market shares in the markets for new motor vehicles are traditionally based on the volumes of new vehicles sold—due to the availability of detailed national registration statistics, the reference to the volume facilitates the calculation of market shares, whereas the market shares in the markets for the provision of repair and maintenance services and for the sale of spare parts are based on the value of the services or products sold.

The Commission has so far only defined relevant markets in formal decisions which con- **15.67** cern heavy vehicles. The truck market is commonly subdivided into three sub-markets: a segment of vehicles below 5 tons, the segment between 5 and 16 tons and the segment of above 16 tons.[84] The bus market is composed of three segments: city buses, intercity buses and touring coaches, each representing a relevant market.[85]

In the *Mercedes-Benz* decision, the Commission stated that the market for passenger cars **15.68** could be divided into a number of segments based on factors such as purchase price and

---

[81] See Ch 6 of the explanatory brochure which deals with market definition; see also: Verboven, *Quantitative Study to Define the Relevant Market in the Passenger Car Sector*, 17 September 2002, who takes the view that either one or in certain cases two of the traditional car segments are to be considered as a relevant market.
[82] [1997] OJ C372/5.
[83] Art 8(1)(a).
[84] See eg Case IV/M.004—*Renault/ Volvo*, decision of 7 November 1990. In case Comp/M.1672 *Volvo/Scania*, decision of 25 October 1999, it was decided that a relevant market is the market for heavy trucks above 16 tonnes.
[85] See Case IV/M.477—*Mercedes-Benz/Kässbohrer*, decision of 14 February 1995; confirmed in Case IV/M.1202—*Renault/IVECO*.

vehicle length,[86] while factors such as engine capacity, quality and brand image would play a smaller role in determining the segment to which a vehicle belongs. A distinction widely used in the industry divides the passenger car market into the following segments: A: very small cars; B: small cars; C: medium cars; D: upper-medium cars; E: executive cars; F: luxury cars; and G: multi-purpose vehicles and sports cars. From the perspective of the end-user, it is unlikely that all passenger cars together fall within one relevant product market, nor is it likely that each of the above-mentioned categories of passenger car constitutes a separate market as there exist chains of substitution which are not limited to vehicles from one of the segments.

15.69 For passenger cars, a preliminary analysis was carried out in the assessment of the new Porsche distribution agreements.[87] Based on the information available, the assessment of the agreements was carried out for both relevant product markets concerned, ie the relevant market for high end sports cars which includes the traditional sports coupes and cabriolets and high end passenger cars fitted with strong engines and sports chassis and the relevant market for sport utility vehicles.

15.70 The market threshold for the application of the block exemption lies generally at 30 per cent of the market share of the supplier.[88] If the market share of a given supplier exceeds this limit, the block exemption does not cover the agreements in question. The exceptions to this rule are threefold and depend on the type of distribution system:

- In a system of exclusive supply obligations, it is obviously the market share of the buyer that must not exceed 30 per cent if the application of the Regulation is not to be excluded.[89]
- A quantitative selective distribution system for the sale of new motor vehicles is block-exempted up to a supplier's market share not greater than 40 per cent.[90]
- No thresholds are applicable if a supplier chooses to distribute his goods by means of a qualitative selective distribution system.[91]

Manufacturers of motor vehicles often supply vehicles of different brands as connected undertakings. If the vehicles belong to the same product market, the market shares of the different brands must be added in order to calculate the 'group' market share.[92]

15.71 As far as the geographic market is concerned, the Commission practice in merger and antitrust cases so far is to consider that these markets are normally still national.

(4) Protection of Distributors' Independence

15.72 One of the main objectives of the Regulation is to offer distributors more options for developing new channels of distribution and acting pro-competitively. In order to avoid pressure from manufacturers to limit such behaviour, the position of the distributors in relation to

---

[86] [2001] OJ L257/1, para 23.
[87] IP/04/585 of 3 May 2004.
[88] Art 3(1), first subparagraph.
[89] Art 3(2).
[90] Art 3(1), second subparagraph.
[91] Art 3(1), third subparagraph.
[92] See Art 3(7).

the manufacturers and their respective national importers is strengthened. The various measures are: promoting multi-branding; facilitating the transfer of distributorships within the network; and extending the contractual protection against the termination of agreements (minimal requirements for termination of a distributor agreement; minimum duration of agreements; obligatory arbitration clause).

(i) Multi-branding　Multi-branding describes a situation where one distributor sells **15.73** more than one brand of vehicles that do not belong to the same manufacturer or group of connected undertakings of manufacturers. This measure has the main objective of promoting inter-brand competition. Since they have contractual relationships with more than one manufacturer, the independence of the distributors is strengthened. Any direct or indirect non-compete obligation included in an agreement would not be covered by the exemption.[93] The term 'non-compete obligation' describes two situations: the first comprises any obligation on the buyer not to manufacture, purchase, sell, or resell vehicles which compete with the contract goods. In the second scenario, a non-compete obligation can also take the form of an obligation on the buyer to purchase from the supplier or from another undertaking designated by the supplier—including for example other members of the distribution system, ie importers and distributors, in the same country or in other countries—more than 30 per cent of the buyer's (ie the distributor's) total purchases of the contract goods, corresponding goods and their substitutes on the relevant market. The percentage must be calculated on the basis of the value of the buyer's purchases in the preceding calendar year.[94] Furthermore, a requirement not to sell vehicles of other manufacturers could be more targeted and only concern specified brands. The Regulation explicitly bans such non-compete restrictions against certain brands.[95]

The distributor was already permitted to sell different brands of vehicles under Regulation **15.74** 1475/95. The conditions were, however, very cumbersome and made multi-branding costly: the sale had to take place on separate sales premises, by means of a distinct legal entity with separate management, and in a manner avoiding confusion between brands.

The Regulation now allows the distributor to sell motor vehicles of other suppliers as long **15.75** as the sale takes place in separate, brand-specific areas of one showroom, so that there is no confusion between brands. The manufacturer must not impose conditions on these brand-specific areas that would render multi-branding impossible or unreasonably difficult. While the manufacturer can impose qualitative criteria on the sales personnel, for instance in terms of training, the supplier cannot oblige the distributor to have sales personnel who only sell its brand. Such a clause would hinder multi-branding because the distributor could end up having to employ brand-specific sales personnel for each different brand. If, however, it was the decision of the distributor to have brand-specific sales personnel and if the supplier paid all the additional costs involved in having such brand-specific sales personnel, an obligation to employ brand-specific sales personnel would not constitute a non-compete obligation for the purposes of the Regulation.

---

[93] Art 5(1)(a).
[94] Art 1(1)(b).
[95] Art 5(1)(c).

15.76 An important issue in this context concerns contractual requirements pursuant to which the distributor must have a showroom of a certain size and/or must display a certain number of vehicles.[96] Sometimes these requirements depend on additional factors, such as the number of cars the distributor sells. In order to allow the distributor to sell another brand in his existing showroom, better to use his investment and other resources, such criteria are not covered by the Regulation if they make it impossible for the distributor to allocate appropriate space for the display of vehicles of another brand in his existing showroom. Many distribution agreements do not address this issue. However the criteria in a selective distribution system must be specified.[97] If the relevant contract clauses provide for the exclusive use of the showroom for one brand, they would not be block exempted. A straightforward way to address this issue would be the justification of display obligations insofar as they are indispensable to the proper promotion of the relevant products. This obligation applies in the same manner to small and large distributors alike. The distributor can use the space which he does not need for his primary brand to display one or several other brands. However, this approach seems to be unfairly strict for the existing brand and could be very advantageous for the second and further brands which the distributor takes on as the distributor could use a very large and disproportionate part of his showroom for the second brand. This would not be in line with the loyalty obligations of the distributor towards all the brands he sells. It therefore seems more appropriate to use a proportionality rule based on, for example, the existing or planned sales or on the number of models each brand offers. If the obligations of distributors to display a certain number of car models in their showroom are such that nearly all distributors are able to take on a second brand, the distribution system may not appreciably restrict inter-brand competition and the conditions of Article 81(1) may not be fulfilled. In case of a dispute concerning the practical implementation of these principles the distributor or manufacturer must refer the dispute to the arbitrator or independent expert based on the relevant procedure which must be included in each distributor agreement.[98]

15.77 Distributors must be in a position to sell at least three [99] different brands without asking the existing supplier for permission. They must be in a position to use a single generic distributor management system which complies with the quality and functionality standards of the manufacturers involved. Furthermore, they may not be required to reveal commercially sensitive information to a manufacturer regarding sales of competing vehicles.[100]

15.78 If a manufacturer were to grant higher margins or pay a bonus to distributors for not selling brands of vehicles of other suppliers, this would constitute an indirect non-compete obligation. The manufacturer must not treat multi-brand distributors differently from

---

[96] For further details see press releases IP/06/302 'Competition: Commissions welcomes changes to BMW's distribution and servicing agreements' and IP/06/303 'Competition: Commissions welcomes changes to General Motors' distribution and servicing agreements' and XXXVIth Report on Competition Policy 2006 on the *BMW* and *General Motors* cases.

[97] Art 1(1)(f).

[98] Art 3(6).

[99] This follows from the fact that the Regulation allows each manufacturer to impose an obligation on its dealers to sell at least 30 per cent of cars of the manufacturer's brand (Arts 5(1)8(a) and 1(1)(b)).

[100] IP/06/302 on the *BMW* case and IP/06/303 on the *General Motors* case.

mono-brand distributors. Obligations linked to corporate identity, such as the use of brand-specific furniture in the sales area, would have to be waived if they hindered the sales of other brands. Similarly, it would not be possible for a manufacturer to impose separate entrances to the showroom for the different brands.

Targets, whether concerning sales, orders or based on accurate sales forecasts or other objec-   **15.79**
tives which create a direct or indirect obstacle to the distributor becoming a multi-brand distributor, are not covered by the Regulation: they are not enforceable. In order to benefit from the block exemption, the only way to continue to have such targets is to seek the distributors' approval on reviewed targets which remove this obstacle and which reflect in a realistic way the distribution opportunities of the new multi-brand distributor.[101] However, there is one requirement as regards the setting of targets which would in any event be covered by the Regulation: Article 5(1)(a) in combination with Article 1(1)(b) allows the manufacturer to require that the distributor achieves at least 30 per cent of his turnover with motor vehicles sourced from the manufacturer.

(ii) Transfer of distributorships   In order to enable distributors to grow through acqui-   **15.80**
sition of other distributors and in this way gain greater independence from the manufacturer, the Regulation abolishes any right of veto of the manufacturer in the case of a sale of a distributorship between members of the distribution system. The distribution agreement must include the supplier's agreement to the transfer of the rights and obligations resulting from the vertical agreement to another authorised distributor of the same brand chosen by the former distributor.[102] The permission granted in advance by the supplier concerns only the transfer of a distributorship between undertakings of the same type. It does not enable a distributor to sell his business to an authorised repairer of the same brand without the manufacturer being able to retain a veto right against such a deal.

(iii) Termination of agreements   The Regulation strengthens the rights of the distribu-   **15.81**
tor in the case of termination of the distribution agreement in order to introduce a certain degree of legal stability into the contractual relationship between a manufacturer and its distributors. The measures are twofold.

Termination notice   If a supplier wants to terminate a distribution agreement, the notice   **15.82**
of termination must be given in writing. It must also set out the reasons for the termination. These reasons must be detailed, objective and transparent. This provision is particularly relevant in the case of agreements which have been concluded for an indefinite period, but applies also in the case of agreements concluded for a definite period if such agreements are terminated before the end of the agreed period, a possibility that can be foreseen under national contract law. Its purpose is to ensure that it is clear to the distributor why the distribution agreement is being terminated and to render it easier for him to challenge the notice before national courts. Furthermore, if it turns out that a supplier can end a distribution agreement because the distributor entered into pro-competitive practices which must not be restricted under the Regulation,[103] the distribution agreement will not come under the Regulation.

---

[101] See IP/06/303 on the *General Motors* case.
[102] Art 3(3).
[103] Art 3(4).

15.83 *Termination period*   The Regulation provides for specific rules on the periods of notice in case of non-renewal or termination of a distribution agreement.[104] Such clauses are not new in Regulation 1400/2002, but have been carried over from Regulation 1475/95. They take account of the sometimes very high investments which distributors or repairers have to make. If distributors had no assurance that this investment would be recouped over a certain period of time and feared that their agreement could end at any moment, they would be reluctant to invest. This could not only be detrimental for their business, it would also have a negative effect on competition. In order to allay these concerns, it is important that any vertical agreement coming under the Regulation contains the essential[105] rights and obligations of both parties and that these elements remain unaltered during the notice periods and may not be changed unilaterally by the manufacturer. If an agreement is concluded for a definite period, its duration must be at least five years. In such a case, the supplier or the distributor must announce its intention not to prolong the agreement at least six months before the scheduled end of the agreement. In this case, no reasons need to be given. For normal termination of agreements of indefinite duration, the supplier or the distributor must be given a period of notice of at least two years before the termination takes effect. The Regulation does not exclude the possibility that national law might impose a longer period of notice. In two scenarios, this period is reduced to one year: (1) the supplier has agreed with the distributor—or is obliged by law—to pay appropriate compensation when terminating the agreement; or (2) the supplier reorganises its network and therefore ends the agreement. The reorganisation might concern the whole network or be limited to a substantial part of it. It must be a significant change, both substantially and geographically, to the distribution structures of the manufacturer concerned. As the Court pointed out, this change must be convincingly justified on grounds of economic effectiveness based on objective circumstances internal or external to the manufacturers' network which, in the absence of a swift reorganisation, would be liable to prejudice the effectiveness of the manufacturer's distribution network. The entry into force of the Regulation does not in itself require such a reorganisation of a manufacturer's network. However, depending on the structure of an existing network, such a reorganisation may be justifiable. It is not necessary that the manufacturer presents reasons or has drawn up a reorganisation plan when it gives one year's notice to its distributors. However, in case of dispute, it is for the manufacturer to prove that the conditions to terminate the agreement with one year's notice are satisfied.[106]

---

104 Art 3(5).

105 Such essential rights and obligations of a distributor agreement are the right to distribute vehicles of a certain brand at a certain location and the obligation for the manufacturer to supply the distributor with new vehicles. As regards the distributor's remuneration, there has been some debate if the fixed margin paid to the distributor or even the variable margin (bonuses, sales subsidy systems, etc) are essential elements of a distribution agreement. In answering this question account could have been taken of the notice periods or periods of minimum duration for a distribution agreements imposed by the Regulation: their aim is to create a stable basis for the distributors allowing them to recoup during the relevant period the investments required by the manufacturer. In view of this aim of the Regulation, the overall level of the remuneration offered by the manufacturer to the dealer when signing the distribution agreement could have been considered an essential element of the distribution agreement. However, complaints relating to perceived lack of contractual fairness have been considered by the Commission to be unfounded in terms of competition rules; see IP/06/302 on the *BMW* case and IP/06/303 on the *General Motors* case.

106 Case C-125/05, judgment of 7 September 2006, *VW-Audi Forhandlerforeningen acting on behalf of Vulcan Silkeborg A/S v Skandinavisk Motor A/S*, not yet published in the ECR.

Ending the agreements of a single distributor or a very limited number of distributors cannot be considered a reorganisation.

It is for the national judge or arbitrators to decide whether the manufacturer has a legitimate **15.84** reason to reorganise the network.[107] Giving notice can only be used as a last resort. Manufacturers may only issue such notices if other solutions are not available, such as adapting the contract to a new legal framework.[108] Otherwise, the notices are not covered by the Regulation and may be void.

(iv) Dispute settlement   Distribution agreements and agreements on the provision of **15.85** repair and maintenance services are long lasting and any dispute on a contractual matter between the parties can negatively affect their competitive behaviour. It is therefore appropriate to make sure that the parties can have recourse to a procedure which helps them to resolve such disputes quickly. As already provided under Regulation 1475/95 for specific subject matters, Regulation 1400/2002 makes it a condition for the exemption that all contractual disputes can be referred to an arbitrator or expert third party.[109] This procedure, however, may not exclude the right of the parties to make an application to a national court. If a party has recourse to an arbitrator who adopts a decision to settle the dispute, national law may provide that such a recourse is not possible as to the substance of the decision taken by the arbitrator but may be possible as regards the procedure followed by the arbitrator. In such a case the conditions of the Regulation are fulfilled, even if the national court cannot review the substance of the decision of the arbitrator and can only check whether certain essential rules of the national law and certain procedural rules have been observed.

(5) Reorganisation of the Link between Sales and After Sales Servicing   **15.86**

Pursuant to Articles 1 of Regulation 123/85 and Regulation 1475/95, motor vehicle manufacturers could only benefit from the block exemption if their distributor agreements covered the distribution of motor vehicles together with the distribution of spare parts in addition to the provision of repair and maintenance.[110] These regulations obliged manufacturers to conclude distribution agreements which covered all three activities. Agreements which only concerned the latter activity were not covered.[111] Based on the findings in the evaluation report on Regulation 1475/95[112] and a study,[113] both showing that the sale of new motor vehicles and the provision of repair and maintenance services including the distribution of spare parts are distinct activities, the Regulation no longer covers such ties. The existence of many stand alone repairers or distributors who only sell spare parts indicates that tying these activities is not indispensable.

---

[107] Case C-125/05; explanatory brochure, reply to question 68.

[108] The explanatory brochure states that the entry into force of Regulation 1400/2002 is not in itself a valid reason to reorganise the network and to give a single year's notice.

[109] Art 3(6).

[110] See Art 5(1)(a) of Regulation 123/85 and Regulation 1475/95.

[111] See IP IP/97/740 of 4 August 1997 on the *Ford Service outlet* case; see also IP/03/80 of 20 January 2003 concerning the obligation of Volkswagen and Audi to conclude agreements with repair shops for the provision of after sales services.

[112] See Ch 6.1 and the conclusion on p 81 of the evaluation report on Regulation 1475/95.

[113] Autopolis, *The Natural Link between Sales and Service*, 2000, published at: <http://ec.europa.eu/ comm/ competition/car_sector/>.

15.87   However, there is one limited exception: distributors selling new vehicles normally have an obligation to honour warranties, which are offered by the vehicle manufacturer on a voluntary basis, and the guarantees which are based on the sales contract. Furthermore, they are also involved in recall operations and in some cases they offer free servicing (eg the first inspection). In order to take account of these obligations, Article 4(1)(g) does not totally de-link the distribution of new vehicles from the provision of repair and maintenance services. In order to maintain a very limited responsibility in this area, the Regulation 'reorganises' the sales/after sales service link. A distributor can either offer repair and maintenance services himself or, if he wants to specialise in selling new vehicles, subcontract these activities to one or more official authorised repairers of the same brand. In such a case he can refer customers who need repair and maintenance services or who want to make a claim under their warranties to the subcontractor.

15.88   The distributor's interest in having an efficient subcontractor is clear: if the subcontractor is not able to fix the problem, the consumer can rescind the sales contract and return the car to the distributor or ask for a reduction of the sales price.[114] Despite the fact that a distributor should not have a permanent obligation to supervise the subcontractor,[115] it was held that a manufacturer is allowed to pay a bonus to the distributor which rewards the performance of the distributor's own repair shop or, in the case of subcontracting, that of the subcontractor. Such a scheme would give an incentive to distributors to select their subcontractors properly and would not restrict competition.

15.89   In a situation where a distributor has subcontracted after sales servicing and the subcontractor's workshop is not in the vicinity of the showroom, the distributor can be obliged by the manufacturer to inform his customers before the conclusion of the sales contract of the location of the subcontractor and of the distance between the sales outlet and the repair shop;[116] however, such an obligation is subject to the condition that a similar obligation is also imposed on distributors whose own repair shop is not in the vicinity of the showroom.

15.90   For the sake of clarity, the Regulation also states that authorised repairers cannot be obliged to sell new motor vehicles.[117]

(6) The Link between the Distribution of New Motor Vehicles and the Distribution of Spare Parts

15.91   As regards the link between the distribution of new motor vehicles and the distribution of spare parts, the Regulation contains no explicit ban or condition. However, for most spare parts the market share of the vehicle manufacturers is considerably higher than the 30 per cent market share threshold, above which the Regulation only covers qualitative selective distribution. In such a system it is not possible to link the distribution of spare parts to the provision of repair

---

[114] See recital 17 and explanatory brochure, questions 35 and 36.
[115] The subcontractor has to be an authorised repairer of the relevant manufacturer, who is supervised by the latter as regards the fulfilment of the qualitative standards for authorised repairers.
[116] See Art 4(1)(g).
[117] Art 4(1)(h).

and maintenance services. The reason is simple: the proper performance of one activity does not require performance of the other.[118] This means that as regards authorised repairers, the manufacturer may only request that the repairer has a stock or easy access to the spare parts needed for his own business. The authorised repairer cannot be forced also to stock and sell spare parts to third parties, although he normally carries out such sales, because of their high profitability.[119] Furthermore, manufacturers whose market shares in the market for spare parts are above 30 per cent and who wish to benefit from the Regulation as regards their spare part distribution agreements will have to allow all qualified operators to distribute such parts without being obliged to sell new vehicles or to offer repair and maintenance services.[120]

D. After Sales Servicing

(1) Authorised Repairers

(i) General remarks and comparison with the previous regulations Until Regulation **15.92** 1400/2002 came into force, the setting up of networks of authorised repairers was not covered by block exemption regulations.[121] The earlier Regulations 123/85 and 1475/95 only covered distributor agreements which obliged the distributors to sell spare parts and run repair shops in which they had to provide warranty repairs and normal repair and maintenance services. Under Regulation 1400/2002 such tying practices are no longer covered and contract clauses which oblige a distributor of new vehicles also to sell spare parts and run a workshop are not exempted by the new Regulation.[122]

In line with the latest generation of block exemption regulations, the new Regulation is also **15.93** based on a more economic approach and covers certain restrictive agreements up to a given market share threshold. Above this threshold the relevant restrictive agreement must be assessed under Article 81(3).[123]

A further principle of the Regulation is that the higher the market shares the less generous **15.94** is the block exemption. In light of this principle the Regulation covers quantitative selective or exclusive distribution systems for the provision of after sales services and the distribution of spare parts up to a market share threshold of 30 per cent.[124] Above this threshold it only covers qualitative selective distribution.[125]

---

[118] See also reply to question 16 in the explanatory brochure.

[119] Art 4(1)(i) protects the right of the authorised repairer to sell spare parts to independent repairers who use them for the repair and maintenance of motor vehicles. This is a specific hardcorehardcore restraint not included in Regulation 2790/1999 and which is necessary to ensure that independent repairers can compete with authorised repairers.

[120] Peugeot Deutschland accepted this interpretation and announced that it would appoint any qualified company as a Peugeot spare parts distributor (see Autohaus online, 2 October 2003, at: <http://www.autohaus.de/sixcms/detail.php?id=63927&nachrichten>).

[121] See Press release IP/03/80, 20 January 2003, Volkswagen and Audi to conclude agreements with repair shops for the provision of after sales services; see also Press release IP/97/740, 4 August 1997, on the 'Ford service outlet agreement' and XXVIIth Report on Competition Policy, 1997, First Part, Section I, B 3.

[122] Art 4(1)(g).

[123] Guidelines on vertical restraints, para 62.

[124] Art 3 (1), first subparagraph.

[125] Art 3 (1), third subparagraph.

15.95 Before considering which rules apply in practice to this type of business, one must look at the markets for the provision of after sales servicing, which includes both the business of repairing a defective vehicle and the provision of maintenance services. As has been clarified in the Notice on the definition of the relevant market,[126] supply substitution from the user's point of view is crucial for determining the relevant markets.

15.96 **(ii) The relevant markets for after sales servicing**   In view of the ever increasing electronic content of modern motor vehicles, any market analysis must take account of the different types of after sales services: some require brand-specific tools, training of staff and garage equipment, whereas others are simpler and require less or no brand-specific knowledge and can easily be carried out by any repair shop. As regards the more complex repair and maintenance services which the members of a manufacturer's[127] network of authorised repairers have to offer, it is likely that they are not, or are only to a limited extent, substitutable by such services offered by others, namely independent repairers or authorised repairers of other brands. There are also no signs that real competitive constraints exist between a given network of authorised repairers of one brand, as regards price or quality of after sales servicing of the vehicles of that brand, and the authorised repairers of other brands and most of the independent repairers. This indicates that the relevant product market for after sales servicing relating to complex repairs is limited to the authorised repairers of the relevant car or truck brand and may include a small number of independent brand specialists. As for more simple repair and maintenance services, such as changing the oil, battery or tyres or simple body repairs, authorised repairers of other brands and independent repairers may be real alternatives to the authorised repairers. This type of repair and maintenance constitutes another relevant product market.

15.97 Once the different relevant after sales service market(s) have been identified, the market shares must be calculated. Especially in view of the high market shares of the authorised repairer networks of each manufacturer on the market for complex repairs, which throughout the industry is higher than 30 per cent, it is generally accepted that manufacturers can only apply qualitative selective distribution when they set up a network of authorised repairers.

15.98 However, as has already been mentioned, the market analysis also reveals that certain more simple maintenance services offered by authorised repairers working within a motor vehicle manufacturer's network strongly compete with the same type of services offered by other authorised and independent repairers. If a vehicle supplier wants to set up a network of authorised repairers who only offer such simpler maintenance services, then in most cases it will be able to use quantitative selective distribution.

15.99 **(iii) The 'reorganisation' of the sales—after sales service link**   It has already been explained (in paragraph 15.86 above) that a key element of Regulation 1400/2002, as

---

[126] Commission Notice on the definition of the relevant market for the purposes of Community competition law, [1997] OJ C372/5.

[127] Normally the supplier is the manufacturer or an undertaking connected to the manufacturer, such as a wholesaler or an importer. The supplier can also be a company which is independent and which is the authorised importer of the relevant vehicles. This company is normally also entrusted by the vehicle manufacturer with the task of setting up and supervising the network of new vehicle and spare part distributors and of authorised repairers.

compared to the previous regulations,[128] is that the distribution of new vehicles and the provision of after sales servicing by distributors has been 'de-linked' or 're-organised'. The opposite obligation is also not covered by the Regulation: therefore, authorised repairers cannot be forced to sell new vehicles and any such obligation is a hardcore restriction.[129]

A distributor who decides not to run a repair shop can subcontract this activity.[130] The **15.100** Regulation does not further specify what 'subcontracting' means. However, one should bear in mind that distributors have a legal obligation under national law to honour guarantees. To fulfil this obligation properly, any distributor must have at least one preferred authorised repairer. The distributor has a clear interest in having an efficient subcontractor: if the subcontractor is not able to fix the problem covered by the guarantee, the consumer can rescind the sales contract and return the car to the distributor or ask for a reduction in the sales price.[131] Any subcontract concluded by the distributor and an authorised repairer would at least cover these issues. Furthermore, it was felt that before signing the sales contract customers should be made aware that the distributor does not run a repair shop. The manufacturer can therefore impose an obligation on its distributors to give the name and address of their possible authorised repairer(s) and subcontractor(s) to the customers before they sign the sales contract. Furthermore, the manufacturer can impose an obligation on distributors whose subcontractor is not in the vicinity of the showroom to inform customers about the location of the repair shop and its distance from the showroom, on condition that such an obligation is also imposed on distributors whose own repair shop is not in the vicinity of their showroom.

The aim of allowing the distributor to subcontract after sales servicing was also to enable him **15.101** to specialise in the sale of new vehicles. Despite the fact that a distributor may not have a permanent obligation to supervise the subcontractor, a manufacturer is allowed to pay a bonus to the distributor to reward the performance of the distributor's own repair shop, but also, in the case of subcontracting, that of the subcontractor. Such a scheme would give an incentive to distributors to select their subcontractors properly and does not restrict competition.

(iv) Requirements within a qualitative selective distribution system for the provision **15.102** **of repair and maintenance services** Based on the definition of qualitative selective distribution,[132] the criteria must be:

- qualitative in nature;
- required by the nature of the contract goods or services;
- laid down uniformly for all repairers;
- may not be applied in a discriminatory manner; and
- may not directly limit the number of repairers.

---

[128] See Arts 1 and 5(1)(1)(a) of Regulation 123/85 and Regulation 1475/95; see Press release IP/03/80, 20 January 2003, on the obligation on Volkswagen and Audi to conclude agreements with repair shops for the provision of after sales services; see also Press release IP/97/740, 4 August 1997, on the *Ford service outlet agreement* and XXVIIth Report on Competition Policy, 1997, First Part, Section I, B 3.

[129] Art 4(1)(h).

[130] Art 4(1)(g).

[131] See recital 17 and explanatory brochure, questions 35 and 36.

[132] Arts 1(1)(f) and (h).

Consequently motor vehicle manufacturers and any other supplier of new motor vehicles[133] had to draw up for the first time[134] clear criteria for their authorised repairers. In applying the above criteria, some issues may arise which are discussed in the following paragraphs.

15.103 *Qualitative nature of the criteria*   As regards criteria which are related to the core business of a repair shop, ie the provision of repair and maintenance services for the motor vehicles of the relevant brand, an objective justification generally exists if the relevant criteria aim at ensuring the quality of the services sold by the repairer. Qualitative justification also means that the criteria must describe a result and not prescribe the means of achieving the result.[135]

15.104 A requirement that equipment or staff can only be used to carry out after sales servicing on the vehicles of one brand would not be a qualitative criterion.[136]

15.105 *Requirements as to the equipment of the repair shop, the type of services which must be provided and the size of the repair shop*   The requirements which may be imposed on authorised repairers must be dependent on the nature of the services, ie they must be necessary for the provision of certain repair and maintenance services. This is clearly a technical question which can easily be answered by experts.

15.106 Objective customer expectations can also be taken into account when the manufacturer asks the authorised repairer to provide certain types of services.[137]

15.107 Manufacturers may also try to fix the minimum number of work places for mechanics or the number of work bays which the authorised repairer must install. In a qualitative selective system, this number must be defined on the basis of technical needs relating to the vehicles of the relevant brand. Enquiries have lead to the conclusion that for most car brands, two to

---

[133] In particular the authorised, official vehicle importers in a given territory or country.

[134] Under Regulations 123/85 and 1475/95 a combination of quantitative selective and exclusive distribution was covered as regards dealer networks within which the dealers were selling new vehicles and providing after sales services. A number of manufacturers used to operate parallel networks of authorised repairers, which were not covered by these regulations (see IP/97/740 of 4 August 1997 on the *Ford Service outlet* case; IP/03/80 of 20 January 2003 concerning Volkswagen and Audi repair shops).

[135] For instance, the authorised repairer must have access to tools of a certain quality; it is however not possible to force the repairer to purchase these tools from the supplier or a third party undertaking or to force him to own the tools instead of leasing or merely having access to them in a way which is compatible with the relevant task, such as borrowing a rarely needed tool from a tool pool which has been set up by several authorised repairers; equally, a repairer cannot be required to operate his own car wash. The supplier can only request that the repairer cleans a car if the consumer requests such a service; the choice of whether the job is done by hand, or at a public car wash in the neighbourhood or a car wash run jointly by several garages must be left to the authorised repairer. This also relates to training requirements: if a mechanic already has the necessary technical skills and knowledge or if he prefers to follow training courses provided by an independent body, the manufacturer cannot require that the mechanic must follow a training course offered by the manufacturer.

[136] See also IP/06/303 on the *General Motors* case.

[137] This played a role eg in the following context: the manufacturers rightly claimed that customers might nowadays expect to be able to call a hotline of the vehicle manufacturer in case of a break down of the vehicle and the manufacturer may wish to ask the nearest authorised repairer to arrange local assistance. To provide 24-hour breakdown assistance every day of the year would however place an excessive burden on each authorised repairer. The relevant manufacturer allowed its authorised repairers to co-operate and to provide this service on the basis of a rota at night and on weekends. All repair shops located in an area of a diameter of around 50km were allowed to co-operate in this way to fulfil the obligation to participate in a brand-specific emergency service. An alternative solution would be to allow the repairer to subcontract these services to a qualified on-road assistance organisation, such as an automobile club.

three work bays and a staff of three will suffice to repair all vehicles of the relevant brand. If the manufacturer were to require from repairers who wish to join its network of authorised repairers more equipment or personnel than is necessary to run a small workshop, the system would become quantitative.[138]

If a certain authorised repairer has acquired over time a larger customer base and if the **15.108** capacity of his repair shop is insufficient to deal with this demand within reasonable time limits, the manufacturer can require that this authorised repairer invest in additional staff and workshop equipment.[139] Today's customers expect that authorised repairers will be able to repair or service a vehicle within a reasonable time. Many customers even take account of this factor when buying a new vehicle. Waiting times therefore constitute a qualitative criterion and manufacturers can request that an authorised repairer, who has increased his customer base over time, is able to offer his services to his customers within reasonable time limits.

Differentiation between different authorised repairers The manufacturer can take account **15.109** of the local market conditions and/or customer expectations when setting the criteria for authorised repairers. It is therefore permissible for the manufacturer to apply less demanding criteria in rural areas than in urban areas.[140] Because of existing objective differences in the relevant customer base and their habits, such differentiations are justifiable. An adaptation of the criteria to the local market conditions is indeed pro-competitive because it avoids the application of inadequate criteria and over- or under-investment. The definition of qualitative selective distribution in Article 1(1)(h) however sets certain limits for such adaptations: the relevant criteria must always be laid down uniformly for all authorised repairers operating in the relevant area or market conditions and the criteria may not be applied in a discriminatory manner.

If a manufacturer who has set up a qualitative selective distribution system for the provision **15.110** of after sales services and decides to conclude vertical agreements with some of its authorised repairers, the principle of non-discrimination requires that it offers a contract to all its authorised repairers.

Obligations on authorised repairers to provide replacement vehicles An obligation on the **15.111** authorised repairer to provide replacement vehicles to customers while the vehicle is being repaired is also a qualitative requirement. However, the manufacturer cannot require that such vehicles be provided to customers free of charge. This would amount to resale price maintenance for this service, which is a hardcore restriction pursuant to Article (4)(a). Also, the manufacturer cannot force an authorised repairer to buy such cars as long as the repairer has access to them. A repairer could thus fulfil such an obligation by asking a rental company to supply a car to the customer.[141] The rental charge of such a car would have to be paid by the customer. If the authorised repairer decides to have a fleet of replacement cars, the brand of the cars cannot be prescribed, for two reasons: the imposition of an obligation to provide replacement vehicles is intended to ensure adequate mobility; in this respect the brand of the replacement vehicle is irrelevant. Furthermore insisting that the

---

[138] See IP/06/302 on the *BMW* case and IP/06/303 on the *General Motors* case.
[139] See IP/06/303 on the *General Motors* case.
[140] See reply to frequently asked question 14.
[141] See reply to frequently asked question 12, last bullet point.

replacement vehicles must be of a particular brand would increase the financial burden on multi-brand authorised repairers dramatically.

15.112 *IT systems* It is essential that authorised repairers can communicate with their vehicle manufacturer in an efficient way, for example when they order spare parts or send bills for warranty claims. To this end the manufacturer may require that the authorised repairer uses software which is compatible with the IT equipment used by the manufacturer. By contrast, the manufacturer may not impose an obligation to buy IT hardware or software from certain undertakings, provided the software used by the repairer can communicate with the manufacturer's IT system. In order to allow companies to develop the relevant software, vehicle manufacturers are obliged to publish information on the interface that they use. The vehicle manufacturer may require that the relevant software has to be certified before it is used by its authorised repairers.[142]

15.113 *Tools, including scan tools* In order to be able to provide high quality repair and maintenance services, the manufacturer may require that the authorised repairer has access to the necessary tools, including diagnostic tools, and workshop equipment. The prospect of immediate access is a frequently used qualitative criterion in relation to tools or equipment. Having access does not mean that the authorised repairer is obliged to buy and own the relevant tools and equipment: he may also lease them or use available facilities. As regards tools which are rarely used, the manufacturer must accept, for instance, that they can be shared by several authorised repairers.[143]

15.114 Based on these principles, the manufacturer cannot request that the authorised repairer uses brand-specific diagnostic tools if the job can be done with generic diagnostic tools. The same goes for repair shop IT management systems.[144] Furthermore, authorised repairers may not be forced to disclose commercially sensitive information regarding the repair of vehicles from other brands.

15.115 As regards the purchase of the necessary tools and workshop equipment, the principle that within a qualitative selective distribution system the manufacturer may only lay down performance-related requirements means that the manufacturer cannot impose an obligation on its authorised repairers to purchase such goods from specified suppliers.

15.116 *Corporate identity standards* Manufacturers must observe the principles for qualitative selective distribution when they lay down corporate identity standards which concern, for example, the signage, the exterior and interior decoration of the premises, or the clothing of the staff of their authorised repairers.

---

[142] This was the result of proceedings before the German Bundeskartellamt regarding complaints from several software companies against Opel. The plaintiffs had supplied software to Opel dealers and repairers which was used to order spare parts and to clear warranty claims. After the entry into force of the new Regulation, Opel rejected the software and imposed the use of the software of a single supplier which it had selected. Following intervention by the Bundeskartellamt, Opel modified its policy as indicated above. See *Bericht des Bundeskartellamtes über seine Tätigkeit in den Jahren 2003/2004 sowie über die Lage und Entwicklung auf seinem Aufgabengebiet*, Bundestagsdrucksache 15/5790, p 140, available at: <http://www.bundeskartellamt.de>; see also IP/06/303 on the *General Motors* case.

[143] See answer to frequently asked question 12, in particular the 2nd and 3rd bullet point.

[144] See also above para 15.77.

Authorised repairers claimed that the manufacturer must allow them to use the same exterior **15.117** design and logos as those used by distributors.[145] Based on the criteria for qualitative selective distribution systems, such a claim is not justifiable. Under the Regulation, a manufacturer may allow its distributors to use a certain logo or indicate the brand name of the vehicle in a certain size outside the showroom. The manufacturer can also allow these distributors and all authorised repairers to use other means to inform customers about the location of an authorised repair shop, for example by allowing the repairers to display the brand name in smaller letters or to use only a specific logo created for all authorised repair businesses of that brand, whether they are operated by a distributor or stand alone authorised repairers.[146]

Whatever policy the manufacturer adopts, the signage and logos which authorised repairers are **15.118** allowed or have to use must enable a customer, who passes by on the public road or who looks at advertisements or visits the manufacturer's website, to identify a repairer clearly and easily as an authorised repairer for vehicles of a certain brand belonging to that manufacturer's network.[147]

(v) Multi-branding by authorised repairers and manufacturers' obligations to adapt or relax certain qualitative criteria which impede multi-brand authorised repairers

The basic principles   The Regulation does not cover clauses which directly or indirectly **15.119** prevent the repair of motor vehicles from competing manufacturers.[148] This approach is very strict: it does not matter whether there is competition between the repair of the vehicles of one brand and the repair of vehicles of another brand: according to the Regulation, the supplier cannot prevent an authorised repairer from also being an authorised repairer of another brand or from operating at the same time as an independent repairer[149] who repairs motor vehicles of any brand. Because multi-branding may not be prohibited under the Regulation, authorised repairers can decide to take on further brands at any time and without prior authorisation from their existing supplier(s). Since quantitative or qualitative selective distribution is only covered if the criteria used for the selection of authorised repairers have been defined in advance,[150] suppliers must clearly indicate which criteria are relaxed or waived in the case of multi-brand repair shops.[151] A system where a supplier has

---

[145] BMW does not allow authorised repairers to use the brand logo, the so-called white and blue propeller, which can only be used by authorised BMW distributors for the new car sales activity. Mini has adopted a similar approach. Some other vehicle manufacturers allow authorised repairers to use the normal brand logo, but in a smaller format.

[146] According to the definition in Art 1(1)(h), a supplier is not allowed to discriminate against one category of authorised repairers in relation to another.

[147] If a car manufacturer has an address list of repairers (for example, a printed list or one that is available on the Internet) all repairers must be listed, not only those who are also dealers.

[148] Art 5(1)(a) and (b).

[149] It should be noted that in a qualitative selective distribution system for repair and maintenance services a clause which would not allow an authorised repairer to also repair vehicles from other brands would not be qualitative.

[150] See definition of selective distribution in Art 1(1)(f).

[151] Qualitative criteria for authorised repairers may therefore not require that the reception area, office equipment, tools, personnel, or even the warehouse for spare parts must be dedicated to one brand. As already mentioned, the criteria may also not require that the temporary replacement vehicles are from a certain brand. In order to make sure that these principles are properly applied, the Commission clarified this issue in its replies to frequently asked questions, see questions 17 and 5. The frequently asked questions are available at: <http://ec.europa.eu/comm/competition/car_sector/ distribution/#car_faq>.

one set of criteria for mono-brand repairers and another for multi-brand repairers does not comply with the Regulation since the qualitative criteria must be applicable uniformly to both mono- and multi-brand authorised repairs.

15.120 *An exception: non-compete obligations in authorised repairer agreements if the relevant supplier is de minimis on the market for new cars—the Porsche case* Although non-compete obligations for authorised repairers are not covered by the Regulation, the Commission has not felt a need to intervene against a limited non-compete obligation imposed by Porsche on its authorised repairers.[152] In fact, Porsche does not allow its authorised repairers also to be at the same time distributors of cars which directly compete with Porsche cars. The reasoning which led to the conclusion that this limited non-compete obligation does not appreciably restrict competition is based on the fact that it only excludes about 8 per cent of all potential operators[153] active in the car sector from becoming an authorised Porsche repairer, which does not appreciably restrict competition. However, an alternative reasoning would have led to the same conclusion: Porsche has a market share of less than 5 per cent in the market of luxury sports cars and limousines and in the market for sports utility vehicles in the various national markets in the EU. In such a case Porsche is de minimis in the market for new sports cars and limousines and the market for sport utility vehicles and can thus impose a non-compete obligation[154] on its distributors and ask them not to sell competing vehicles,[155] thereby keeping competing brands 'away' from its customers. The question is whether this lenient approach can be 'extended' to authorised Porsche repairers. In fact, if an authorised Porsche repairer were at the same time a distributor of a competing car brand, that distributor would have direct access to the Porsche customers (who turn to him to have their Porsches serviced). In view of his obligations to promote sales of the competing car brand he would probably try to (and have to) use this direct access to Porsche customers to sell them a car of the other brand. This would seriously undermine and pre-empt the right of Porsche as a car manufacturer which is 'de minimis' to impose a non-compete obligation on its new car distributors and to 'keep competing car brands at distance' from its clients.

(vi) The obligations of authorised repairers—in particular in the context of manufacturers' warranties and guarantees

15.121 *Obligations to honour warranties, carry out free servicing and recalls* Motor vehicles are long lasting goods which need repair and maintenance throughout their lifetime. In order to allow end-users to buy their vehicle anywhere in the Single Market, it is important that manufacturers do not use their after sales service network to undermine consumers' choice. Therefore the two previous Regulations for the automobile sector made it a condition of

---

[152] See Press release IP/04/585 of 3 May 2004.

[153] It should be borne in mind that the following undertakings can become a Porsche repairer: (1) Porsche dealers, whether they only sell new Porsche cars or also cars of other (including competing) brands; (2) independent or authorised repairers of any other brand who are not dealers of that brand; (3) dealers of car brands, who do not sell competing sports cars or sport utility vehicles.

[154] A non-compete obligation is a specific condition of the Regulation pursuant to Art 5(1)(a). The specific conditions listed in Art 5 and the general conditions listed in Art 3 of the Regulation do not apply to companies which are *de minimis* on the relevant market; see explanatory brochure, reply to question 7.

[155] It should be noted that Porsche does not impose a non-compete obligation on its distributors, as it could: it merely asks them to sell other car brands in different showrooms. Furthermore Porsche sales persons must be brand specific (ie they may only sell new Porsche cars).

exemption that all network members of the relevant brand offering after sales services[156] must honour warranties and carry out free servicing and recalls without regard as to where a vehicle has been purchased. The same also applies for normal repair and maintenance. Under Regulation 1400/2002 the refusal to offer these services is a hardcore restriction.[157]

Obligations to honour the manufacturer's guarantees The question arises whether the principles set out in the Regulation for warranties also apply to guarantees given by a manufacturer on a voluntary basis.[158] The relevant case law suggests that it does not matter whether a manufacturer's contractual obligation towards an end-user is called a warranty or a guarantee.[159] In both instances a manufacturer must require its whole network of authorised repairers to honour its commitments.[160]   **15.122**

Warranties or guarantees may not lapse if the car has been repaired or serviced by an independent repairer The Regulation does not prescribe a certain content and duration as regards the substance of the manufacturers' warranties or guarantees. However, warranties and guarantees may not be designed in a way which hinders consumers from having their vehicles serviced or repaired by independent repairers.[161] If warranties or guarantees, which are a valuable asset for end-users, were to become invalid once a vehicle has been repaired or serviced outside the network, they would usually refrain from turning to an independent repairer for normal servicing or repair. Such a scheme forecloses the repair market for independent repairers for vehicles which are still under warranty for the duration of the manufacturer's warranty or guarantee, ie for a considerable period of time, of two or possibly more years.[162] In the case where a consumer turns to an independent repairer during the warranty or guarantee period, the manufacturer may not subsequently refuse to honour the warranty or guarantee unless the defect is due to an incorrect intervention by an independent repairer.[163]   **15.123**

Extended warranties or guarantees The above obligations exist if a manufacturer offers a warranty on the new vehicle free of charge to the end-user. If, in contrast, the manufacturer offers such a scheme through its distributors who offer it free of charge to the buyer of any vehicle, the same principles apply if the manufacturer has set up the scheme and subsidises it   **15.124**

---

[156] Under Regulations 123/85 and 1475/95 the dealers.

[157] Art 4(1)(b) and recital 17.

[158] Guarantees find their legal basis in the sales contract; see Directive (EC) 1999/44 of the European Parliament and of the Council of 25 May 1999 on certain aspects of the sale of consumer goods and associated guarantees, [1999] OJ L171/12.

[159] Case 31/85 *ETA Fabriques d'ébauches v SA DK Investment and others* [1985] ECR-3933. See also Case C-376/92 *Metro SB-Großmärkte GmbH & Co. KG v Cartier SA* [1994] ECR I-15.

[160] See the reply of the Commission to the written question E-2110/04 (published on the European Parliament's website).

[161] See answer to question 37 in the explanatory brochure.

[162] It should be borne in mind that in some Member States, such as the United Kingdom, manufacturers' warranties and guarantees are traditionally longer than in Continental Europe, and may cover a period of up to 5 years. Furthermore, many manufacturers offer extended warranties which protect against rust or problems with paint for periods of up to 10 years.

[163] See explanatory brochure, reply to question 37. The Bundeskartellamt has asked several car manufacturers to modify their warranty and guarantee conditions in order to avoid the lapsing of a warranty when a car has been repaired using spare parts obtained from sources other than the vehicle manufacturer. See *Bericht des Bundeskartellamtes über seine Tätigkeit in den Jahren 2003/2004 sowie über die Lage und Entwicklung auf seinem Aufgabengebiet*, Bundestagsdrucksache 15/5790, p 141, published at: <http://www.bundeskartellamt.de>.

completely or partially. If the extended warranty or guarantee, whether provided by the manufacturer, an insurance company or the distributor, is sold by distributors or authorised repairers to customers, who can freely decide whether they wish to purchase it, the Regulation does not apply and the scheme can provide that spare parts supplied by the vehicle manufacturer must be used for the repair services.

15.125 *Compulsory guarantees under national law and the authorised repairer's obligations to honour these guarantees* Warranties or guarantees supplied by the vehicle manufacturer with the new vehicle are voluntary[164] and should be distinguished from the guarantees which are mandatory consumer rights pursuant to national contract law. If the purchased good is not in conformity with the contract of sale, the seller is liable for a period of at least two years, during which the consumer has the right to have the good brought into conformity free of charge either by repair or replacement. It is the distributor as the final seller who is liable to fulfil these obligations, but the distributor has a right of redress against the previous seller in the same contractual chain. In certain cases the consumer may require an appropriate reduction of the price or that the contract be rescinded.[165] If a vehicle is defective and if the authorised repairers of the relevant brand are not in a position to repair the vehicle, the end-user has the opportunity of taking action against the distributor who sold the relevant vehicle and to request that the contract be rescinded or the purchase price reduced.[166]

(2) Spare Parts Distribution

15.126 (i) **Definition and relevant markets**
The definition of spare parts Spare parts are goods which are installed in or upon a motor vehicle in replacement of components of that vehicle, including goods such as lubricants which are necessary for the use of a motor vehicle, with the exception of fuel.[167] Components, ie parts which are used to manufacture a new vehicle and which are necessary for its operation are not considered as spare parts.[168] The same applies for accessories.[169]

15.127 Four categories of spare part can be distinguished:

- Original spare parts[170] distributed by the vehicle manufacturer: on average about 20 per cent of these spare parts are produced by the vehicle manufacturer and 80 per cent are produced by spare part and/or component suppliers according to the specifications and production standards of the relevant vehicle manufacturer. On most of these spare parts, the trademark

---

[164] See the reply of the Commission to the written question E-2110/04 (published on the website of the European Parliament; not yet published in the OJ).

[165] See in particular Art 3(2) and (5) of Directive (EC) 1999/44.

[166] See also explanatory brochure on Regulation 1400/2002, reply to question 35.

[167] See definition in Art 1(1)(s).

[168] This follows from the definition of spare parts in Art 1(1)(s).

[169] For further details see explanatory brochure, reply to question 95; the sale of accessories does not fall under Regulation 1400/2002 and is therefore governed by Regulation 2790/1999. It is important to note that authorised repairers selected on the basis of qualitative criteria may not be forced to sell accessories as well. It goes without saying that normally the sale of accessories generates additional income and any authorised repairer may be interested in selling accessories.

[170] See definition in Art 1(1)(t).

or logo of the vehicle manufacturer and, if relevant, of the manufacturer of the part can be found. In order to allow the consumers and repairers to identify the manufacturer of a car part which needs to be replaced, the part manufacturer cannot be prevented from placing its trademark or logo on the component used to manufacture the new vehicle.[171]

• Original spare parts not distributed by the vehicle manufacturer: these are spare parts which are of the same quality as the components used to build the new vehicle and which are produced on the same production line as those components or manufactured according to the specifications and production standards of the vehicle manufacturer. It is presumed that parts constitute original spare parts if in addition the part manufacturer certifies that these parts match the quality of components used for the assembly of the vehicle in question and have been manufactured according to the specifications and production standards of the vehicle manufacturer. The spare part manufacturer has the right to place its trademark or logo on them[172] and must be able to sell these parts directly to any authorised or independent repairer or spare part distributor.[173]

• Spare parts of matching quality[174] are parts which are made by any undertaking which can certify at any moment that the parts in question match the quality of the components which are or were used for the assembly of the motor vehicle in question.

• Other spare parts, which may be of lesser quality, that do not fall within the above definitions.

In order to ensure competition for spare parts of good quality, the Regulation deals with issues relating to the first three of the above categories of spare parts.

The relevant product market for spare parts   Most spare parts are brand-specific and/or **15.128** even specific to a certain motor vehicle. For example, a headlamp or a brake disc for a given car, in most cases, can only be used for a particular vehicle model. This suggests that there are many rather narrowly defined markets for specific types of spare part and that motor vehicle manufacturers' market shares in the relevant spare part markets, which normally include the first three of the above categories of spare parts, are in most cases far greater than 30 per cent.

(ii) Spare part distribution through authorised repairers   **15.129**
Spare part stocking requirements   In order to offer a good quality service to consumers, authorised repairers must have a stock of certain readily available spare parts to enable them to carry out routine repairs and maintenance. An obligation to hold such a stock is therefore permissible in a system of qualitative selective distribution for authorised repairers. However, the requirement to have a stock of spare parts is only justified as far as such stocks are 'required by the nature of the . . . services'.[175] It should also be borne in mind that manufacturers operate efficient spare part delivery systems which normally allow an authorised repairer to order and obtain spare parts within a few hours. Requiring the repairer to keep a large stock of spare parts which are normally not needed (such as body panels or engines or gearboxes) or which can be obtained at very short notice from a central warehouse of the

---

[171] See Art 4(1)(l).
[172] See Art 1(1)(l).
[173] Art 1(1)(j) and (k).
[174] Art 1(1)(u).
[175] See definition of qualitative selective distribution in Art 1(1)(h).

manufacturer or a spare part warehouse jointly owned by several authorised repairers, would be excessive and not covered by the Regulation.[176]

15.130 *Right for authorised repairers to resell spare parts to independent repairers* Pursuant to Article 4(1)(i), authorised repairers, even when operating within a selective distribution system, must be allowed to sell spare parts on to independent repairers to use for the repair and maintenance of motor vehicles, ie not for resale. However, such activity is voluntary on the part of an authorised repairer[177] and therefore it is not permissible to impose on each authorised repairer a stocking requirement for spare parts without regard as to whether or not he sells spare parts to independent repairers. Only if the authorised repairer regularly sells spare parts to independent repairers is the manufacturer allowed to impose an obligation on the authorised repairer to have a sufficient stock of spare parts to cover both the spare part consumption by his own repair shop and his over-the-counter business.

15.131 *Two-tier spare part distribution system* Some manufacturers operate a two-tier qualitative selective distribution system of authorised repairers for the purchase of spare parts: the first tier generally consists of larger authorised repairers who have agreed to supply spare parts, which they also use for their own repair shop, to a number of smaller authorised repairers (the authorised repairers of the second tier) located in the same geographic area. The latter do not obtain their spare parts from the factory or the importer. While such a two-tier system may entail certain efficiencies as compared to a one-tier system, especially as regards logistics, it must be designed in such a way that it avoids any discrimination in terms of price and availability of spare parts for all authorised repairers operating within the same network. This follows from the fact that all such authorised repairers, whether they are tier one or tier two, operate within the same qualitative selective distribution system for the provision of after sales services. Pursuant to the definition of qualitative selective distribution in Article 1(1)(h), such a system may not be applied in a discriminatory manner towards its members. However, a manufacturer which pays a bonus or agrees on a higher margin with tier one authorised repairers, who also act as spare part wholesalers for a sub network of tier two authorised repairers in order to compensate for their additional costs as spare part wholesalers, would not apply a discriminatory margin system.

15.132 *The use of competing spare parts by authorised repairers* The Regulation strengthens the approach introduced in 1995 by Regulation 1475/95: it aims to ensure that authorised repairers can offer, and consumers can choose between, different types of spare parts.

15.133 Therefore, a motor vehicle manufacturer may not impose a non-compete obligation on its authorised repairers: pursuant to Article 5(1)(a), in combination with Article 1(1)(b), this means that the motor vehicle manufacturer can only impose an obligation on its authorised repairers to purchase 30 per cent of the required spare parts from it or any other member of its network authorised to distribute such spare parts. All such spare parts are parts belonging

---

[176] See also IP/06/303 on the *General Motors* case.

[177] It is not a qualitative criterion for the selection of authorised repairers that they must distribute spare parts to third parties on a large scale, as this business is not necessary for the core task of the authorised repairer, ie to offer repair and maintenance services for the vehicle of the brand for which he is an authorised repairer.

to the first category mentioned above.[178] The 30 per cent figure must be applied to each of the many different markets for spare parts,[179] or, as the Regulation puts it, contract goods,[180] corresponding goods[181] and their substitutes.[182] This approach ensures that the authorised repairer will be able to repair a vehicle only by using original spare parts of the first category. However, the fact that 70 per cent of the spare parts stocked and used by the authorised repairer can be either original (the second category of spare parts mentioned above) or matching quality spare parts sourced from other suppliers (the third category of spare parts mentioned above), allows the authorised repairer and the consumer ample opportunities to use alternative high quality parts as well.

The Regulation adequately protects the right of an authorised repairer to source up to 70 per cent of the spare parts from suppliers who sell such original or spare parts of matching quality. Article 4(1)(k) blacklists clauses which limit the authorised repairer's ability to source such spare parts from third parties and Article 4(1)(j) blacklists restrictions which a vehicle manufacturer may impose on the manufacturer of such spare parts. **15.134**

The authorised repairer has the freedom to use the first three categories of spare parts for the repair of the relevant motor vehicles. There is one exemption from this freedom: as regards repairs under warranty, free servicing, and in the context of a recall operation, the authorised repairer can be obliged by the vehicle manufacturer to use only spare parts supplied by the manufacturer.[183] This obligation is justified because the motor vehicle manufacturer has to reimburse the authorised repairer in these three cases of repairs: the vehicle manufacturer should therefore also be in a position to decide which parts are used for such repairs. **15.135**

Free servicing and spare part use Although this exception addresses specific situations, there have been attempts by vehicle manufacturers to extend the scope of this specific rule by offering longer warranty periods or by including packages of 'free servicing' in the car price. Whereas longer warranty periods extend the end-user's protection against defaults, free servicing was initially and is still designed to cover the first and rather limited maintenance service which is carried out shortly after a vehicle had been put into use, ie typically, previously 1,000 km or 2,000 km, now often the service is after one year or 10,000 km or more after delivery of the car to the user. If, however, a manufacturer were to offer, for example, **15.136**

---

[178] The parts can be bought from the manufacturer or any other undertaking within its network, ie wholesalers or authorised repairer or authorised spare part distributors. All these undertakings must be considered as having been 'designated' in the sense of Art 1(1)(b) by the manufacturer to distribute spare parts.

[179] If 5 different types of oil filters are fitted on the engines of the different car models of the car brand for which the repairer is authorised and if he must stock 10 of each, then the authorised repairer has to have 3 filters (=30% of 10 filters) of filter type A, 3 of filter type B, etc in his warehouse. He can buy the other 7 filters of filter type A, etc from other suppliers.

[180] These are the spare parts which are sold by the manufacturer or importer to the authorised repairer. Normally these are the spare parts sold under the brand name of the vehicle manufacturer.

[181] Based on the definition in Art 1(1)(r) this relates mainly to new motor vehicles. However, an authorised repairer in Continental Europe may also need the specific spare parts for the right hand drive versions of the cars which he repairs. The Regulation forces manufacturers to also make such spare parts available to its authorised repairers.

[182] These are the original spare parts, see definition in Art 1(1)(t), and spare parts of matching quality, see definition in Art 1(1)(u).

[183] Art 4(1)(k).

a five year 'free' servicing package (because it is purchased at a single inclusive price with the car) and were to require the use of spare parts provided by it (the manufacturer), this would not come within the above exception: this is, because the provision of maintenance services over a period of several years is costly and manufacturers would have to include a lump sum for the 'free' servicing package in the price of the new vehicle, which is paid by the customer. Such servicing packages are therefore in reality not 'free servicing' in the sense of Article 4(1)(k) of the Regulation. By contrast, if the consumer freely decides to buy a servicing package from the manufacturer or authorised repairer and if the manufacturer does not subsidise it, the package may provide that the repairer must use spare parts of a certain brand.

15.137 (iii) **Spare part distribution by authorised spare part distributors**
The basic principles The Regulation also covers[184] vertical agreements for the distribution of spare parts which manufacturers or wholesalers of spare parts may conclude with their distributors. In general, such vertical agreements do not appear to pose any problem under the Regulation.

15.138 However, the Regulation contributes to the emergence of authorised spare part distributors who sell original spare parts of a motor vehicle manufacturer for the following reasons: many spare parts are not only brand-specific, but are even vehicle model-specific. Taking all spare parts which can be used for a certain type of repair into account, it becomes clear that the market shares for the relevant spare parts[185] of the motor vehicle manufacturer who is able to supply them is much higher than 30 per cent. The Regulation therefore only covers qualitative selective distribution systems in respect of the distribution of spare parts by motor vehicle manufacturers.

15.139 In a qualitative selective distribution system, the question is whether a proper distribution of spare parts is only possible if the spare part distributor also has a repair shop. Reality shows that this is not the case: there are many spare part distributors who only sell spare parts and who do not have workshops.[186] Under the Regulation, such a link is no longer covered, in particular in cases where the relevant goods can only be sold through qualitative selective distribution systems, as is the case for the distribution of spare parts by motor vehicle manufacturers.[187] Motor vehicle manufacturers must therefore appoint authorised spare part distributors if an operator wishes only to sell spare parts. In the field of distribution of

---

[184] See Art 2(1), first subparagraph.

[185] These spare parts are original spare parts of the first category mentioned previously.

[186] Under Regulations 123/85 and 1475/95, manufacturers were forced to tie together the sale of spare parts, the sale of new motor vehicles and the provision of after sales services. Indeed, both previous block exemption regulations explicitly stated that in order to make the full range of spare parts readily available, and in relation to spare parts with a low turnover, manufacturers should be allowed to prevent the emergence of wholesalers not belonging to their distribution system; see recital 6 of Regulations 123/85 and 1475/95; see also IP/94/159 of 24 February 1994 regarding the Fiat spare part distribution system. Fiat operated, alongside its official Italian network of car and truck dealers, a parallel network of 315 exclusive distributors of its spare parts. By creating two selective distribution systems for spare parts, Fiat had acted in breach of the block exemption under Regulation (EEC) 123/85. The Commission informed Fiat that it intended to initiate proceedings. This prompted Fiat to undertake to abandon over a period of not more than five years the parallel network of Fiat spare part distributors. Furthermore, Fiat undertook to relinquish a threshold above which car and truck dealers would obtain a discount, which forced them to source Fiat spare parts exclusively.

[187] See reply to frequently asked question 16.

spare parts by vehicle manufacturers, the Regulation does indeed contribute to the emergence of a new distribution channel, ie spare part wholesalers and distributors working within a vehicle manufacturer's network who only sell spare parts to authorised and independent repairers and end-users.

Since the Regulation covers vertical agreements with spare part wholesalers and retailers, all general conditions, hardcore restrictions, and specific conditions apply to these agreements. As a consequence, the relevant distribution agreements must include notice periods of two years in the case of agreements concluded for an unlimited duration; in the case of fixed term agreements, the agreements must last for at least five years. Location clauses are not covered for spare part distributors.[188] Furthermore, multi-branding (ie the fact that they sell spare parts for cars of different brands) by authorised spare part distributors cannot be restricted.[189] As regards the sourcing of spare parts for cars of a particular brand, it must be borne in mind that the relevant market for spare parts consists only of the spare parts for a vehicle model of a given brand, and the non-compete obligation of Article 5 (1)(a) and Article 1(1)(b) must be applied to that market: consequently the spare part wholesaler or distributor must purchase at least 30 per cent of the spare parts for a given model from the relevant vehicle manufacturer or any other authorised repairer or spare part distributor within that vehicle manufacturer's network. Thus the Regulation could well lead to the emergence of large multi-brand authorised spare part distributors, which should make the market more competitive and efficient by concentrating the spare part supply and by avoiding duplication in the area of delivery systems and other overheads. **15.140**

The distribution of 'spare part' lubricants and non-compete obligations imposed by the **15.141** *lubricant supplier* Lubricants are also considered to be spare parts.[190] Therefore, a vertical agreement concluded between a lubricant supplier and an authorised or independent repairer which contains restrictive clauses falls under the Regulation.

The Regulation covers an obligation on authorised repairers to purchase up to 30 per cent of the spare parts from the relevant supplier.[191] However, in many cases lubricant supply agreements which oil firms conclude with authorised and independent repair shops combine trade loans, garage equipment loans, or other incentives with a minimum purchase obligation which de facto covers most if not all of the repairer's requirements over a five-year period, thereby amounting to an indirect non-compete obligation. These agreements are of widespread use in the sector. In the *BP* case,[192] the Commission restated and applied its policy on vertical restraints which are not covered by the Regulation, although indirect 'non-compete obligations' of the kind notified by BP would be block-exempted under Article 5(a) of Regulation 2790/1999. **15.142**

---

[188] Art 5(3).

[189] The Regulation does not contain an explicit clause excluding non-compete clauses for spare part dealers from its coverage. However, as under the Regulation spare part dealers operate within a qualitative selective system, a ban on selling spare parts of another brand would not be a qualitative criterion and would not be covered by the Regulation.

[190] See Art 1(1)(b).

[191] See Arts 5 (1)(a) and 1(1)(b).

[192] Notified in accordance with Arts 2 and 4 of Regulation 17. See Notice on the notification of the relevant standard supply agreements published in [2003] OJ C126/5.

15.143 The assessment of BP's agreements showed that, in many Member States, the agreements were unlikely to restrict competition appreciably. Where Article 81(1) could apply, it appeared that, although the agreements did not meet the conditions of the Regulation, Article 81(3) applied on an individual basis to the restraints as they stood in almost all the other Member States. The reasons included the fact that BP was not dominant, that it supplied only a minor fraction of all the products needed to provide repair and maintenance services, and it did not apply other restraints which would have aggravated the negative effects of the non-compete obligation. Moreover, BP also modified the notification in order to bring the notified agreements into line with the Commission's policy on vertical restraints[193] in Member States where one of the following conditions is met:

- BP's market share exceeds 30 per cent; or
- provided that where parallel networks of restraints producing effects on competition similar to those notified by BP cover no less than 30 per cent of a relevant market, BP's 'tied market share' exceeds 15 per cent.

15.144 In those Member States, BP undertook to inform and give those buyers tied by the notified agreements a right to give six months' notice to terminate the agreements at the earliest two years after their entry into force. Such a right would also be exercisable at six-monthly intervals thereafter. The exercise of that right would be subject to the buyer repaying any outstanding monies without any penalty whatsoever. A penalty was to be understood as any sum which would be paid by the buyer in excess of costs incurred by BP and thereafter at the end of each period of six months. Following these modifications, the Commission closed the case without adopting a formal decision and informed lubricant industry associations that it intended to apply the above principles to similar agreements.[194]

(3) Independent Operators, in Particular Independent Repairers

15.145 **(i) The basic principles**   In order to protect competition in the market for repair and maintenance of motor vehicles, the Regulation aims to ensure that consumers have a wide choice between different service providers, ie not only can they turn to any of the authorised repairers who belong to the network of the relevant vehicle manufacturer, but also to other types of repairers, who are independent from the relevant vehicle manufacturer and who may be stand-alone businesses, members of a franchise system[195] or a group[196] or who might also be specialists in certain types of repair[197] or maintenance. In fact, in the EU prior to the 2004 round of enlargement, about 50 per cent of all maintenance and repair was carried out by independent repairers, who clearly are an important driver of competition and innovation in this market.

15.146 In order to promote competition in the after sales servicing market, the Regulation ensures that independent repairers, including roadside assistance operators, must have full access to

---

193 Guidelines on Vertical Restraints: as to single branding or non-compete arrangements see paras 138–158 and, especially, para 156. See also explanatory brochure, reply to question 17.
194 See Annual Report 2003, pt 158.
195 For example, Quick fit or Speedy.
196 For example, ATU.
197 For example, body shops, tyre specialists.

spare parts and technical repair information. In this respect the Regulation is based on the same principles as those which were introduced in 1995 by Regulation 1475/95.

Since 1995, Regulation 1475/95 has required all motor vehicle manufacturers wishing to **15.147** benefit from the block exemption to give independent repairers access to technical information. However, evaluation of the relevant blacklisted clause revealed that the extent of the access provided under Article 6(1)(12) of Regulation 1475/95 was generally insufficient.[198] In view of the ever increasing mechanical and electronic complexity of motor vehicles, the Regulation extends the right of access to technical repair information to all other operators[199] directly or indirectly involved in the repair and maintenance of motor vehicles, such as manufacturers of repair equipment or tools, independent distributors of spare parts, publishers of technical information, automobile clubs, operators offering inspection and testing services, and operators offering training to repairers.

(ii) Independent repairers' access to all types of spare parts Independent repairers **15.148** (including roadside assistance operators) must have access to all types of spare parts.[200] To facilitate this, authorised repairers and distributors of spare parts for a vehicle manufacturer must be allowed to sell original spare parts to independent repairers[201] so that the latter can repair vehicles properly. It is noteworthy that the relevant clauses of Regulation 1400/2002 differ from those in Regulation 2790/1999, where a manufacturer using selective distribution can prohibit the sale of spare parts to independent repairers. Moreover, under Regulation 1400/2002 vehicle manufacturers cannot prevent the original equipment manufacturers, or any other manufacturers who produce spare parts, from selling spare parts to any independent repairer.[202] The protection of the independent repairer's access to all categories of spare parts by defining certain restrictive clauses as hardcore restrictions also emphasises the fact that the Regulation is intended to allow independent repairers to compete fully with authorised repairers.

(iii) Independent operators' access to technical information **15.149**
The legal instrument used to protect independent operators' full access to all technical information and background for this approach Independent operators, who should be given access to technical repair information, are not normally linked by vertical agreements to motor vehicle manufacturers. The vertical agreements which come under Article 81(1) and which are block exempted pursuant to Article 81(3) are those vertical agreements which a motor vehicle manufacturer concludes with its distributors and authorised repairers.

According to Article 1(2)(b) of Regulation 19/65, a block exemption regulation may set **15.150** out not only those restrictions which must not be included in a vertical agreement, it may also clarify that certain conditions must be met if a vertical agreement is to benefit from the

---

198 See evaluation report on Regulation 1475/95, section 6.2.3.2, paras 291–298.
199 Art 4(2), last sub-paragraph.
200 ie original spare parts manufactured or distributed by the motor vehicle manufacturer; original spare parts from the manufacturer of the corresponding parts used for the assembly of the new car; matching quality spare parts; any other spare part.
201 Art 4(1)(i).
202 Art 4(1)(j).

block exemption. Article 4(2) of the Regulation is contained within the hardcore restrictions, while being a condition in its legal construction.

15.151   The importance of ensuring full access to technical information by independent repairers is underlined by the fact that, as early as in 1995, Regulation 1475/95 was adopted, containing a similar hardcore clause.[203] When preparing the new Regulation the Commission carefully analysed the extent to which independent repairers and other independent operators needed to have access to technical repair information. The Commission came to the conclusion that such access is necessary not only in order to ensure the safe and reliable functioning of motor vehicles, but also to ensure that competition in the after sales service markets remains possible. Indeed, modern motor vehicles are equipped with even more electronic and other complex devices, which cannot be properly maintained and repaired without the necessary repair information. The Commission's investigation also revealed that the access should be given not only to those undertakings which provide repair and maintenance services, ie the independent repairers, but also to other undertakings whose involvement is less direct, such as roadside assistance operators, providers of training, publishers of technical information, or manufacturers of scan tools, all of whom need such information. Furthermore it is a matter of fact that throughout Europe, a large share of all repair and maintenance is carried out by independent repairers. Without the necessary repair information, such operators could no longer compete effectively with authorised repairers. Even if there is competition among authorised repairers of the relevant vehicle brand, it is a fact that authorised repairers of a given brand operate on the basis of the same requirements set by the relevant vehicle manufacturer. Such intra-brand competition was considered to be insufficient and it was decided that inter-brand competition between authorised and independent repairers needed to be protected.

15.152   In view of these considerations, the Commission decided that a vehicle manufacturer who refused to give full access to technical information to independent operators could not benefit from the exemption provided by the Regulation and that such a refusal should be considered a hardcore restriction. A consequence of this strict approach is that a manufacturer who refuses[204] to give such access also cannot claim that its distribution system meets the requirements of Article 81(3).[205]

15.153   *The manner in which access must be given*   The provision concerning access to technical information is very detailed. Access must be given to any repair information as well as to all diagnostic and other equipment and tools, including the relevant software.[206]

---

[203] Art 6(1)(12) Regulation 1475/95.

[204] See: Institut für Kraftfahrwesen Aachen (IKA), Study 'Do motor vehicle suppliers give independent operators effective access to all technical information as required under the EC competition rules applicable to the motor vehicle sector?', October 2004. The study revealed that most manufacturers do not provide access to technical repair information as required by the Regulation. For the time being, the Commission is discussing solutions with the manufacturers concerned; see also Neelie Kroes, 'Market developments and future perspectives in the automotive sector', conference organised by the European Council for Motor Trades and Repairs (CECRA), Brussels, 25 September 2006, available at: <http://ec.europa.eu/rapid/pressReleasesAction.do?reference=SPEECH/06/527&format=HTML&aged=0&language=EN&guiLanguage=en>.

[205] See Guidelines on vertical restraints, para 46 at the end.

[206] Art 4(2), first sub-paragraph.

The Regulation emphasises that the access must be given in a non-discriminatory, prompt, and proportionate manner and that the information must be provided in a usable form. The obligation to give non-discriminatory access means that the content and extent of the information which must be made available may not differ between authorised and independent repairers. Furthermore, the access must be given to both authorised and independent repairers at the same time,[207] and upon request without undue delay, ie promptly. The information must be provided in a usable form.[208] These examples given in the Regulation clarify the notion of non-discriminatory access, ie independent repairers cannot be treated less favourably than authorised repairers. However, the Regulation goes even further: it stipulates that an independent repairer must not be obliged to buy more information than necessary to do a specific repair job.[209] In this respect the Regulation forces manufacturers to provide more favourable and tailored access conditions to independent repairers than for members of their own network.

In respect of technical information that is covered by an intellectual property right within **15.154** the meaning of Article 1(1)(i) or which constitutes know-how within the meaning of Article 1(1)(k), the Regulation states that access may not be withheld in an abusive manner. This wording takes account of the fact that a manufacturer normally holds a dominant position[210] as regards the technical information for the motor vehicles that it produces, including the information which is covered by the above mentioned rights. Article 4(2), however, does not require that the vehicle manufacturer must be shown to hold a dominant position[211] in the market for technical information per Article 82. It is nevertheless legitimate to interpret the notion of abuse in the same way as in the context of the application of Article 82. In Article 82(2)(b) 'limiting production, markets or technical development to the prejudice of consumers' is considered to be an abuse. The Court of Justice has clarified that the refusal by the proprietor of a registered design right for spare parts to sell those parts to independent repairers or to fix the prices for such parts at an unfair level constitutes an abuse.[212] By analogy, the same principles must also be applied in relation to access to technical repair information.

---

207 See recital 26.

208 See Art 4(2), third sub-paragraph, and Recital 26.

209 This is important in view of the specialisation of independent repairers. For instance, tyre specialists, specialists in suspensions, body repair shops, climate control specialists, fast fitters focusing on more simple repairs, roadside assistance operators who carry out certain simple repairs at the roadside after a vehicle breakdown, fitters of alarm systems and radio and other entertainment devices, only require very specific information for a particular vehicle.

210 Case 238/87 *AB Volvo v Erik Veng (UK) Ltd.* [1988] ECR-6211 concerning design rights for body panels.

211 Case 226/94 *British Leyland PLC v Commission* [1986] ECR-3263, para 9, concerning the monopoly conferred by law on a vehicle manufacturer regarding the issuance of certificates of conformity; Case 26-75 *General Motors Continental NV v Commission* [1975] ECR-425.

212 Case 238/87 *AB Volvo v Erik Veng (UK) Ltd.* [1988] ECR-6211, para 9; Case 53/87 *Consortio Italiano della componentistica di ricambio per autoveicoli and Maxicar v Renault* [1988] ECR-6039: see also XIII Report on Competition Policy, 1985, point 49, regarding Ford which in the context of an application requesting interim measures granted a licence to independent body panel producers for the production of body panels for all cars save the latest models. See also judgment of the Rechtbank Utrecht, 3 November 2005, Case 201038 / KG ZA 05-911, point 4.14, where the court held that the refusal by Peugeot Netherlands to give independent repairers access to the technical repair information, which was also used by its authorised repairers and which is necessary to carry out all types of repairs, was considered to be abusive in the sense of Art 4(2) of the Regulation. The Rechtbank ordered Peugeot to remedy the situation by granting access to all independent Peugeot repairers.

15.155 *Publishers' and scan tool manufacturers' access to technical information* Publishers of technical information and scan tool manufacturers are also considered to be independent operators. Publishers of technical information compile the information in a database covering all or many motor vehicles from different brands to which independent repairers can have access for a fee.[213] Scan tool manufacturers use the information to develop and produce scan and other tools which can be used on vehicles of different brands and which are not offered by any of the motor vehicle manufacturers, who instead sell scan and other tools for the repair of the vehicles of the relevant brand only. Publishers compile the information from different car manufacturers and also create data which form the basis for specific types of activities, such as body shops, tyre traders, brake repair services, or climate control repairers. In such scenarios there are precedents[214] to show that it would be abusive to withhold information which is necessary to generate new products or services and for which demand exists, where there is no objective justification for withholding it.[215] The argument that an independent repairer could also search for the information on the website of the car manufacturer and download it and either read it or upload it onto a suitable scan tool, or buy brand-specific scan tools for each make of vehicle that he repairs, is not valid. The lack of harmonisation in respect of methods of access, structure of the data, and data formats makes it very difficult and time-consuming for independent repairers to obtain the necessary data.[216] As regards scan tool manufacturers, these produce multi-brand testers which no car manufacturer is willing to produce and which are the only viable solution for independent repairers who repair vehicles of many brands and who cannot afford to buy brand-specific scan tools for each.

E. Procedural Issues

(1) Entry into Force, Transitional Period and Expiry

15.156 **(i) Entry into force and expiry** The Regulation was adopted on 31 July 2002 and entered into force on 1 October 2002. It will remain in force until 31 May 2010. This date is the same as the expiry date of Regulation 2790/1999. Some factors which explain why the Commission adopted a new sector-specific regulation, and which are linked to the fact that long-lasting technical products such as motor vehicles also need repair and maintenance for longer periods after their sale, might be valid in other product areas, such as motor bicycles, scooters, or watches. Should both Regulations be merged in 2010, it is

---

[213] See also frequently asked questions, reply to question 92, where it has been clarified that publishers of technical information must be allowed to redistribute the information received from a vehicle manufacturer.

[214] Joined Cases C-241/91 P and C-242/91 *Radio Telefis Eireann (RTE) and Independent Television Publications Ltd (ITP) v Commission of the European Communities* [1995] ECR I-743, §§ 52ff.

[215] The only objective justifications are mentioned in recital 26 of the Regulation: it states that it is legitimate and proper for a vehicle manufacturer to withhold access to technical information which might allow a third party to bypass or disarm onboard anti-theft devices, to recalibrate electronic devices, or to tamper with devices, which, for instance, limit the speed of a motor vehicle, unless protection against theft, re-calibration, or tampering can be attained by other less restrictive means than withholding the information. The explanatory brochure in the reply to question 94 mentions as examples of such less restrictive means: access codes and encryption by imposing so called pass-through-programming techniques by which the vehicle is directly connected to the vehicle manufacturer.

[216] Study by Institut für Kraftfahrwesen Aachen (IKA) on access to technical information, p 256, available at: <http://ec.europa.eu/comm/competition/car_sector/ika/ika.html>.

possible that the rules for after sales servicing might be extended to vertical agreements concerning after sales servicing of other long-lasting technical goods. However, at this stage one cannot make any forecast if there will be a successor to the Regulation.

As regards location clauses for distributors of passenger cars and light commercial vehicles **15.157** operating within a selective distribution system, the Regulation provided for a transitional period of three years after the entry into force of the Regulation, so that as since 1 October 2005 location clauses have been excluded from the cover of the Regulation.[217]

(ii) **Transitional period**   Article 10 of the Regulation provided for a one-year transitional **15.158** period until 30 September 2003 in order to give all interested parties time to adapt their distribution agreements to the new legal framework. The transitional period only applied to agreements meeting two conditions: the vertical agreements had to be in force on 30 September 2002 and had to be compatible with Regulation 1475/95. If these conditions were not fulfilled, the vehicle manufacturer had to amend its agreements as from 1 October 2002.

The Audi case   The first case involving the application of Regulation 1400/2002 presented **15.159** the Commission with the opportunity to clarify two important issues: the authorisation of repairers in the networks of vehicle manufacturers and the application of the Regulation during the transitional period.

In Autumn 2002, a large number of former Audi distributors and repairers complained to **15.160** the Commission about Audi's refusal to conclude authorised repairer agreements with undertakings that fulfilled the qualitative criteria for being authorised Audi repairers before the end of the transitional period on 30 September 2003. Before the Regulation came into force, Audi and some other vehicle manufacturers had concluded agreements with authorised repairers who only provided after sales services. This network of authorised repairers existed alongside the network of authorised distributors of the Audi brand, who were selling new cars and at the same time providing after sales services. Because vertical agreements concerning the provision of after sales services did not fall under Regulation 1475/95,[218] Audi could not benefit from the transitional period in respect of its network of authorised repairers. In addition, the market share of the Audi network on the market for after sales service for Audi cars was above the 30 per cent threshold specified in Article 3(1). Consequently, Audi had to establish a qualitative selective distribution system in order to be covered by the Regulation. If this type of distribution system is applied in a non-discriminatory manner, it follows that undertakings which fulfil the qualitative criteria must be free to enter the network of the manufacturer. Audi and Volkswagen therefore agreed to conclude servicing agreements with repairers that satisfied the criteria already set by Audi and the other brands of the Volkswagen group even before the end of the transitional period on 30 September 2003.

The Commission clarified that for vertical agreements concerning products such as lubri- **15.161** cants, or agreements such as wholesale agreements for spare parts, which were not covered

---

[217] Art 5(2)(b).

[218] Under Regulations 123/85 and 1475/95, a combination of quantitative selective and exclusive distribution was covered as regards dealer networks within which the dealers were selling new vehicles and providing after sales services. A number of manufacturers used to operate in parallel networks of authorised repairers, which were not covered by these regulations (see IP/97/740 of 4 August 1997 on the *Ford Service outlet* case).

by Regulation 1475/95, the Commission did not consider enforcement of Regulation 1400/2002 within the above transition period to be a priority.[219]

(2) Withdrawal of the Benefit of the Regulation

15.162 Article 6 of the Regulation provides for the withdrawal[220] of the benefit of the Regulation from particular vertical agreements which formally comply with the Regulation but which are nevertheless incompatible with the conditions laid down in Article 81(3) of the Treaty. Furthermore, it is not only the Commission that can apply this procedure. In line with the decentralised application of the Community competition rules, Article 6(2) also allows national competition authorities to withdraw the benefit of the Regulation if the vertical agreement produces effects which are incompatible with the conditions laid down in Article 81(3) in the territory of the relevant Member State or a part thereof, if the relevant territory has all the characteristics of a distinct geographic market.

15.163 Article 6 lists four examples, in particular, where the Commission takes the view that the conditions for withdrawal may be met. The first example relates to cumulative effects of parallel networks of similar vertical restraints which impede market access or competition in that market. For example, the conditions for such a withdrawal would be met in the case of warranties if, after a repair or maintenance job has been undertaken by an independent repairer, a vehicle manufacturer could refuse to honour the warranty because a car had been repaired or maintained during the warranty period by an independent repairer.[221] Were manufacturers able to decide otherwise (and there are many indications that they would do so in order to ensure that consumers exclusively used authorised repairers during the warranty period) consumers' access to independent repairers would be excluded to a large extent for the duration of the warranty period, as consumers would not want to risk undermining the validity of their warranties. In view of the sometimes very long warranty periods of up to ten or more years, such a policy could exclude consumers' choice for nearly the whole lifetime of the vehicle. The second example given in Article 6 where a withdrawal may be envisaged relates to a situation where the supplier is not exposed to effective competition from other suppliers. The third example concerns prices and conditions for the supply of contract goods and whether they differ substantially from one Member State to the other. This example was carried over from Regulations 123/83 and 1475/95. The Commission gave a detailed interpretation of this clause in its Notice on Regulation 123/85[222] which remained valid[223] under Regulation 1475/95. The Commission stated in that Notice that it would not intervene regarding pre-tax price differentials between Member States if they were less than 12 per cent in the long run and below 18 per cent within a period of one year. This notice was however withdrawn by the Commission when it adopted

---

[219] See explanatory brochure, reply to question 24.

[220] See also Vertical Guidelines, paras 71–79.

[221] See explanatory brochure, reply to question 37; see also *Bericht des Bundeskartellamtes über seine Tätigkeit in den Jahren 2003/2004 sowie über die Lage und Entwicklung auf seinem Aufgabengebiet*, Bundestagsdrucksache 15/5790, p 140, published at: <http://www.bundeskartellamt.de>.

[222] The Commission Notice concerning Regulation (EEC) 123/85 of 12 December 1984 on the application of Art 85(3) of the Treaty to certain categories of motor vehicle distribution and servicing agreements, [1985] OJ C17/4.

[223] See Commission press release IP(95) 648, 21 June 1995, p 3.

Regulation 1400/2002.[224] The fourth example concerns discriminatory services on sales conditions within a geographic market.

(3) Non-application of the Regulation

Article 7(1) provides for possible modification of the Regulation or certain parts of it **15.164** through a new Commission regulation in cases where parallel networks of similar vertical restraints cover more than 50 per cent of a relevant market.[225] It follows from the text of this provision that the modification would consist of a declaration that the Regulation does not apply to certain specific restraints relating to that particular market. In practice this would mean that, in all likelihood, the list of hardcore restrictions or specific conditions would be extended. In the case of an extension of the hardcore list, the Regulation would no longer apply to the whole agreement if it contained the relevant hardcore restriction. In the case of an extension of the list of specific conditions, the relevant vertical restraint would no longer be covered by the Regulation.

Article 7 does not entail an obligation on the part of the Commission to act where the **15.165** 50 per cent market coverage ratio is exceeded, which is probably the case today in the motor vehicle sector both in respect of the sale of new vehicles and also as regards after sales servicing. According to the Vertical guidelines,[226] disapplication of a regulation could be appropriate where access to the relevant market is appreciably restricted. A disapplication could also be envisaged if more than 50 per cent of a market were covered by networks of selective distribution systems and if the selection criteria were not required by the nature of the relevant goods or services or would discriminate against certain forms of distribution capable of selling such goods.[227] Such a regulation disapplying Regulation 1400/2002 would only enter into force after a transition period of one year[228] in order to give the operators in the market sufficient time to adapt their agreements to the new regime.

(4) Monitoring and Evaluation Report

The Commission has committed itself to regular monitoring of the operation of the **15.166** Regulation.[229] In this context it should in particular monitor its effects on competition in motor vehicle retailing and after sales servicing within the Common Market and in relevant parts of it, ie also within certain geographic markets which are smaller than the EU. Furthermore, it should also monitor the effects of the Regulation on the level of concentration in the area of motor vehicle distribution and any consequent effects on competition. To this end a study has been commissioned by DG Competition.[230] In addition to this constant monitoring obligation, the Commission must draw up an evaluation report on the Regulation not later than 31 May 2008.

---

[224] See explanatory brochure, fn 101.

[225] See also Guidelines on vertical restraints, paras 80–87.

[226] See Guidelines on vertical restraints, para 83.

[227] See Guidelines on vertical restraints, para 83.

[228] This transition period is longer than the 6 months period provided for in Art 8(2) of Regulation 2790/1999.

[229] Art 11.

[230] Study, 'Developments in car retailing and after-sales markets under Regulation 1400/2002, June 2006' published at <http://ec.europa.eu/comm/competition/car_sector/>.

15.167 One regular monitoring activity concerns the publication of bi-annual car price reports.[231] These reports list the prices of approximately 90 passenger car models and show prices both including and excluding taxes.[232] Furthermore the reports list the prices for some major additional specifications and for the so-called right-hand drive supplement (which is a mark up of the price when a consumer wants to buy a car with the steering wheel on the right-hand side). The index included in the reports is based on both pre-tax prices and prices including taxes, in order to make it easier for customers to compare the recommended retail prices quoted in different Member States.

---

[231] See <http://ec.europa.eu/comm/competition/car_sector/>.
[232] See study on H Degryse and F Verboven, *Car Price Differentials in the European Union*, November 2000, published at: <http://ec.europa.eu/comm/competition/car_sector/>.

PART IV

STATE AID

16

STATE AID

Andreas Knaul and Francisco Pérez Flores

16.01 The EC Treaty distinguishes between distortions of competition due to the actions of undertakings and those due to the intervention of the State. Other chapters of this book deal with distortions caused by undertakings. This chapter focuses on distortions caused by the State. Since State aid is prohibited in principle by the EC Treaty, we will first analyse the concept of State aid and will then turn to the exceptions to the prohibition principle with a particular focus on Services of General Economic Interest. Since prior notification to the Commission is a requirement for State aid in most cases (unless the aid is exempted under Block Exemption Regulations), the notification procedure will be examined in a separate section of this chapter. The final section of this chapter will cover remedies in situations where aid has been granted unlawfully. At the time of writing, the Commission has adopted a State aid Action Plan outlining the guiding principles for a comprehensive reform of state aid rules and procedures over the next five years.[1]

A. Definition of State Aid

Public intervention in the economy is a common feature in modern States and may take **16.02** several forms, pursue different objectives and have different effects. Some measures adopted by the State aim generally at favouring its business sector and may make demands on the public purse. Such measures may serve general economic purposes of the State in which case the Community has no competence to deal with them. However, where a measure fulfils the conditions of Article 87(1), the State intervention amounts to State aid which, by virtue of Article 88(3), must be notified to the Commission prior to its implementation. The direct effect of Article 88(3) recognised by the Court of Justice means that national courts are empowered to verify whether a measure is State aid and, if it has been put into effect unlawfully, may also adopt the necessary measures to restore the status quo. If a national court is asked to order the recovery of the unlawful aid, it must normally grant that application.[2] Hence the importance of properly understanding the definition of State aid.

According to Article 87(1), save as otherwise provided in the Treaty, any aid granted by a **16.03** Member State or through State resources in any form whatsoever which distorts or threatens to distort competition by favouring certain undertakings or the production of certain goods in so far as it affects trade between Member States is incompatible with the common market and hence prohibited.

In order for a measure to fall within the scope of Article 87(1) of the Treaty and constitute **16.04** State aid, four cumulative criteria must be met:

— the measure must involve the use of State resources;
— the measure must confer an advantage on the beneficiary;
— the advantage must be selective, in that it is limited to certain undertakings or the production of certain goods;
— the measure must distort competition and affect trade between Member States.

It should be noted as a preliminary point, that according to settled case law, State aid measures are defined by reference to their effects and not to their causes or aims.[3] Therefore, the social character of State assistance, for instance, is not sufficient to exclude it from being categorised as State aid from the outset.[4] The Commission will consider the aim of a measure when examining its compatibility with the common market (ie whether it should be authorised).

---

[1] <http://www.europa.eu.int/comm/competition/state_aid/others/action_plan/saap_en.pdf>.
[2] Case C-39/94 *SFEI v La Poste* [1996] ECR I-3547.
[3] Case C-173/73 *Italy v Commission* [1974] ECR 709, para 27; Case C-241/94 *France v Commission* ('*Kimberley-Clark*') [1996] ECR I-4551, para 20; Case C-480/98 *Spain v Commission* [2000] ECR I-8717, para 16; and Case C-5/01 *Belgium v Commission* ('*Cockerill*') [2002] ECR I-11991, para 45.
[4] Case C-75/97 *Belgium v Commission* [1999] ECR I-3671, para 25; Case C-251/97 *France v Commission* [1999] ECR I-6639, para 37; Case C-5/01 *Belgium v Commission* ('*Cockerill*') [2002] ECR I-11991, para 46.

(1) Aid Granted by the State or through State Resources

16.05 First of all, it should be pointed out that the definition of State is very broad, covering both regional or local authorities[5] and public authorities and public bodies, including publicly owned companies.

(a) Origin of the Resources

16.06 For the Court of Justice only advantages granted directly or indirectly through State resources are to be considered aid within the meaning of Article 87(1). The distinction made in the provision between 'aid granted by a Member State' and aid granted 'through State resources' does not mean that all advantages granted by a State, whether financed through State resources or not, constitute aid but is intended merely to bring within that definition both advantages which are granted directly by the State and those granted by a public or private body designated or established by the State.[6] The measure in question must necessarily mean that the State will incur a cost of some kind. Therefore, in *PreussenElektra*[7] the Court concluded that the obligation imposed on private undertakings to purchase electricity at fixed minimum prices did not involve any direct or indirect transfer of State resources. The Court reached that conclusion after acknowledging the fact that the purchase obligation is imposed by statute and it confers an undeniable advantage on certain undertakings.

16.07 In the following cases the Court found that no State resources were involved:

(a) In *Sloman Neptun*,[8] a measure enabling certain shipping undertakings flying the German flag to subject seafarers who were nationals of non-member countries to working conditions and rates of pay less favourable than those applicable to German nationals was not considered to involve State resources.

(b) In *Kirsammer-Hack v Sidal*,[9] the exclusion of SMEs from the national system of protection against unfair dismissal was not considered to entail any direct or indirect transfer of State resources.

(c) In *Viscido*,[10] a national provision relieving one undertaking of the obligation to comply with the generally applicable legislation concerning fixed term contracts was found not to entail any transfer of State resources.

In the following two cases, by contrast, the Court found that State resources could be involved:

(a) In *Ecotrade v AFS*[11] and *Piaggio*,[12] the Court was asked to give guidance to the national court under Article 234 on the Italian special administration procedure for large

---

[5] Case C-248/84 *Germany v Commission* [1987] ECR 4013, para 17.

[6] Case 82/77 *Van Tiggele* [1978] ECR 25, paras 24 and 25; Joined Cases C-72/91 and C-73/91 *Sloman Neptun v Bodo Ziesemer*, [1993] ECR I-887 para 19; Case C-189/91 *Kirsammer-Hack* [1993] ECR I-6185, para 16; Joined Cases C-52/97, C-53/97 and C-54/97 *Viscido* [1998] ECR I-2629, para 13; Case C-200/97 *Ecotrade* [1998] ECR I-7907, para 35; Case C-295/97 *Piaggio* [1999] ECR I-3735, para 35.

[7] Case C-379/98 *PreussenElektra AG* [2001] ECR I-02099.

[8] Joined Cases C-72/91 and C-73/91 *Sloman Neptun v Bodo Ziesemer* [1993] ECR I-887.

[9] Case C-189/91 *Kirsammer-Hack v Sidal* [1993] ECR I-6185.

[10] Joined Cases C-52/97, C-53/97 and C-54/97 *Viscido and Others v Ente Poste Italiane* [1998] ECR I-2629.

[11] Case C-200/97 *Ecotrade v AFS* [1998] ECR I-7907.

[12] Case C-295/97 *Piaggio v IFITALIA and Others* [1999] ECR I-373.

companies in difficulties. The Court considered that in view of the priority accorded to debts connected with the pursuit of economic activity, authorisation to continue trading might involve an additional burden for the public authorities; as might involve an additional burden for the State other features of the system such as the State guarantee, a reduced rate of tax, exemption from the obligation to pay fines and other pecuniary penalties or waiver in practice of public debts wholly or in part. The Court, however, did not rule out the possibility for the national court to establish that this procedure did not in fact entail or should not entail an additional burden for the State, taking into account the situation that would have arisen had the ordinary insolvency provisions been applied.

(b) In *Ladbroke*,[13] the Court considered that the fact that certain sums were continuously subject to the State's control, and therefore at the disposal of the competent national authorities, was sufficient for them to be categorised as State resources.

Special levies imposed by the State in order to finance measures in favour of certain sectors, so-called sectoral funds, may be considered State resources since the State imposes the levy and it therefore becomes a State resource. The Court has established three cumulative criteria for assessing the involvement of State resources where money is transferred by a fund: the fund must be established by the State, it must be financed by contributions imposed or managed by the State, and it must be used to favour specific undertakings.[14] In *Kinderkanal and Phoenix*,[15] the Commission found that the licence fees collected in Germany from each individual owner of a television set were State funds since they were compulsory and had to be paid irrespective of whether the owner actually watched the programmes of public broadcasters and were collected and distributed pursuant to State regulations.   **16.08**

(b) Imputability to the State

Nonetheless, the requirement that the State should be the ultimate source of the funds is not sufficient for the aid to be categorised as State resources; it is also necessary that the State be involved in some way in the adoption of the measure. This is the so-called 'imputability test' which arises when the measure itself is taken by an entity other than a public authority, usually a public undertaking. The Court examined this issue in detail in *Stardust Marine*.[16] In its judgment, the Court rejected the interpretation that the imputability of a measure to the State can be inferred from the mere fact that it was taken by a public undertaking. According to the Court, 'even if the State is in a position to control a public undertaking and to exercise a dominant influence over its operations, actual exercise of that control in a particular case cannot be automatically presumed. A public undertaking may act with more or less independence, according to the degree of autonomy left to it by the State' (paragraph 52). Consequently, it is necessary to determine whether the public authorities were involved in any way in the adoption of those measures. The Court, however, did   **16.09**

---

[13] Case C-83/98 P *France v Ladbroke Racing and Commission*, judgment of 16 May 2000, confirming the judgment of the Court of First Instance in Case T-67/94 *Ladbroke Racing v Commission* [1998] ECR II-1.

[14] Case C-173/73 *Italy v Commission* [1974] ECR 709; Case C-78/76 *Steinike und Weinlig v Commission* [1977] ECR 595.

[15] State aid NN-70/98 ([1999] OJ C238/3).

[16] Case C-482/99 *France v Commission* [2002] ECR I-4397.

not go so far as to require proof that the public authorities specifically encouraged the public undertaking to take the aid measures in question in that particular case. It considered that the imputability to the State of a measure could be inferred from a set of indicators amongst which the Court listed the following: the integration of the public undertaking into the administrative structures of the State; the nature of its activities and how they are carried out on the market in normal conditions of competition with private operators; the legal status of the undertaking; the intensity of the supervision exercised by the public authorities over the management of the undertaking or any other indicator showing an involvement of the public authorities in the adoption of the measure.

16.10   In *Pearle*,[17] the Court was asked by the national court under Article 234 whether the funding of advertising campaigns by the Board (a trade association governed by public law) for the benefit of opticians' businesses could be regarded as State aid. The advertising campaigns were organised at the request of a private opticians' association, the Nederlandse Unie van Opticiîns ('the NUVO') and funded through a compulsory earmarked levy. The Court concluded that the necessary conditions, namely that the advantages be granted directly or indirectly through State resources and be imputable to the State, were not met. The Court considered first that 'Since the costs incurred by the public body for the purposes of that campaign were offset in full by the levies imposed on the undertakings benefiting therefrom, the Board's action did not tend to create an advantage which would constitute an additional burden for the State' (paragraph 36). Then, after having ascertained that 'the initiative for the organisation and operation of that advertising campaign was that of the NUVO, a private association of opticians, and not that of the Board' it considered that 'the Board served merely as a vehicle for the levying and allocating of resources collected for a purely commercial purpose previously determined by the trade and which had nothing to do with a policy determined by the Netherlands authorities' (paragraph 37).

(2) Advantage to a Firm or Firms

16.11   It is settled case law that the concept of aid is much wider than that of subsidy because it embraces not only direct financial benefits to the undertaking but also, and more generally, any advantages granted by public authorities which, in various forms, alleviate the charges which are normally included in the budget of an undertaking.[18]

16.12   Thus, public financing of a bonus paid to workers in the coal sector was found by the Court to give an advantage to the undertakings concerned since it led to an increase in workers' pay which artificially reduced the production costs of the undertakings.[19]

16.13   A reduction in social security charges as compensation for additional costs which undertakings incurred as a result of collective agreements with unions was also found by the Court

---

[17] Case C-345/02 *Pearle BV, Hans Prijs Optiek Franchise BV, Rinck Opticiëns BV v Hoofdbedrijfschap Ambachten*, judgment of the Court of 15 July 2004, not yet reported.

[18] Case 30/59 *Steenkolenmijnen Limburg* [1961] ECR 19; Case C-387/92 *Banco Exterior de España* [1994] ECR I-877, para 13; Case C-241/94 *France v Commission* [1996] ECR I-4551, para 34; Case C-256/97 *DM Transport* [1999] ECR I-3913, para 19; Case C-143/99 *Adria-Wien Pipeline* [2001] ECR I-8365, para 38; Case C-5/01 *Belgium v Commission* ('*Cockerill*') [2002] ECR I-11991, para 32.

[19] Case 30/59 *Steenkolenmijnen Limburg* [1961] ECR 19.

to confer an advantage. The Court noted that the agreements had been voluntarily concluded by the companies concerned on the basis of the parties' economic evaluation.[20]

Similarly, the public financing of a transitional supplement paid to the employees of an **16.14** undertaking and intended to maintain their level of pay despite a reduction in their working hours was considered by the Commission and, on appeal, confirmed by the Court, to constitute an advantage to the undertaking since it alleviated the undertaking's normal budgetary burdens. This conclusion was reached despite the fact the undertaking was under no legal obligation to provide financial compensation for the reduction in pay of its salaried employees as a result of a reduction in their working week, and that no such obligation was included in the collective agreement.[21]

(a) The Private Investor Principle

It is easier to find an advantage when the aid is granted in the form of a subsidy, but for other **16.15** forms of State intervention in the economy it has been necessary to develop specific approaches in order to guarantee some legal certainty. This is the case for State shareholdings where the Commission started using the so-called Market Economy Investor Principle (MEIP), subsequently designated as the private investor principle. Although it was already used in some form to assess certain individual aid cases, it was not until 1981 (with the first Steel Aid Code[22] and the first shipbuilding directive[23]) that the Commission adopted a general formulation in this respect: 'aid elements in the financing measures taken by Member States in respect of the companies that they control and which do not count as the provision of equity capital according to standard company practice in a market economy'. This principle has been endorsed by the Court of Justice in a large number of judgments. It allows the Commission to consider the specific circumstances of each case, for example taking into account certain strategies of a holding company or group of companies or distinguishing between short- and long-term investors.

In essence, this principle establishes that no State aid is involved where an investment is **16.16** made by the State in an undertaking on terms and conditions that would be acceptable to a private investor of a size comparable to that of bodies managing the public sector operating under normal market conditions.[24] If that is the case, the company obtains no particular benefit since it could have obtained the same financing on the market. The question that arises, however, is how to determine the benchmark in order to measure the 'acceptability' of the behaviour of the public authorities.

The most obvious benchmark is the *actual behaviour of a private investor*.[25] If a private **16.17** and a public investor take part in the same transaction, then there is no State aid if both do

---

[20] Case C-251/97 *France v Commission* [1999] ECR I-06639.

[21] Case C-5/01 *Belgium v Commission* ('*Cockerill*') [2002] ECR I-11991.

[22] Commission Decision (ECSC) 2320/81 [1981] OJ L228/14.

[23] Council Directive (EEC) 81/363 [1981] OJ L137/39.

[24] Case C-142/87 *Belgium v Commission* [1990] ECR I-959, para 29; Case C-305/89 *Italy v Commission (Alfa Romeo)* [1991] ECR I-1603, paras 18 and 19; Case T-16/96 *Cityflyer Express v Commission* [1998] ECR II-757, para 51.

[25] Commission communication on the application of Articles 92 and 93 of the EC Treaty to public authorities holdings. Bulletin EC 9 1984. Point 3.2 (iii).

so on the same terms and conditions. Three elements must be ascertained in this instance. First, the genuine private nature of the investor must be demonstrated. For instance, in *Crédit Lyonnais*[26] the Commission considered that the public control exercised by the State over the three main shareholders of Crédit Lyonnais meant that the behaviour of those shareholders could not be adduced as *per se* evidence of private investor behaviour. Secondly, it is necessary to prove that the terms and conditions which apply to the private and public investor are the same, ie if they take part in the transaction *pari passu*. This means, for instance, that where the public holding in a company is to be increased, the capital injected by the private and the public shareholder must be proportionate to the number of shares, that the timing of the participation and the price paid are identical, etc. Thirdly, the private investor holding must have real economic significance. In *Air France*,[27] the Commission considered that the private parties' shareholdings in Air France represented only 0.132 per cent of its capital and the share of the securities to which they had subscribed was negligible. The Court upheld this decision.[28]

16.18 Where there are *no other private investors* taking part in the transaction, other parameters must be found to provide a comparator for the public authorities' behaviour. First, if the company is listed on the stock market, the quotation will determine the market price. This works in both ways: if the State is the seller, the price paid by the private buyer should not be lower than the quoted price; if the State is the buyer, the price should not be higher than the quoted price (nevertheless, a higher price would be justified if the State intended to acquire minority control). If the company is not listed on the stock market, the parameter will be the expected profitability of the investment. Public authorities must obviously use methods of analysis similar to those used by private investors in adopting their investment decisions.[29]

16.19 In its aforementioned Communication of 1984 on the application of the State aid rules to public authorities' holdings, the Commission outlined certain circumstances where a private investor operating under normal market economy conditions would refuse to provide fresh capital to a company. These are as follows:

  (i) where the financial position of the company, and particularly the structure and volume of its debt, is such that a normal return (in dividends or capital gains) cannot be expected within a reasonable time after the capital is invested;
 (ii) where, because of its inadequate cash flow (and for this reason alone), the company would be unable to raise the funds needed for an investment programme on the capital market;
(iii) where the holding is short term, with duration and selling price fixed in advance, so that the return to the provider of capital is considerably less than could be expected from a capital market investment for a similar period;
 (iv) where the public authorities' holding involves the taking over or the continuation of all or part of the non-viable operations of an ailing company through the formation of

---

[26] Commission Decision (EC) 95/547 [1996] OJ L308/92.
[27] Commission Decision (EC) 94/662 of 27 July 1994 [1994] OJ L258/26.
[28] Case T-358/94 *Air France v Commission* ECR [1996] II-2109.
[29] [1993] OJ C307/3 point 31.

a new legal entity (excluding, however, the straightforward takeover of the assets of a company which has become insolvent or gone into liquidation);

(v) where the injection of capital into companies whose capital is divided between private and public shareholders makes the public holding reach a significantly higher level than before and the relative disengagement of private shareholders is largely due to the companies' poor profit outlook;

(vi) where the amount of the holding exceeds the real value (net assets plus value of any goodwill or know-how) of the company, except in the case of SMEs with excellent prospects which because of their size are unable to provide adequate security on the private financial market.

In fact, with the exception of (v) which refers to a concomitant shareholding by a private **16.20** investor, all the above circumstances can be summarised as follows: would the likely return on investment be accepted by a private investor? In *WestLB*,[30] the Commission developed in some detail the reasoning underlying the private investor principle which was subsequently endorsed by the Court. The case concerned the transfer of the assets of a publicly owned institution (WfA) to a publicly owned bank (WestLB) in order to strengthen the latter's equity capital. The key question was whether a market economy investor would have supplied WestLB with capital which presented the specific characteristics of WfA's assets and under the same conditions, particularly in view of the probable return on investment. As to the appropriate remuneration for the equity capital provided, in respect of some of the assets transferred, the Commission assumed an expected minimum remuneration of 12 per cent after tax at the time of their transfer (which was essentially based on historical average returns). It then modified that rate by taking into account three features of the transaction which it considered crucial for fixing the appropriate remuneration: the size of the investment and its decisive effect on WestLB; the absence of new shares and associated voting rights; and the fact it was a permanent investment in unquoted stock. These three elements led the Commission to consider that a premium of 1.5 per cent should be added on top of the 12 per cent. The Commission then took into account the financing costs arising from the lack of liquidity of the assets transferred and reduced by 4.2 percentage points the resulting 13.5 per cent, therefore reaching the rate of 9.3 per cent as an appropriate remuneration of the capital. In its judgment,[31] the Court considered at paragraph 314 that 'normally, a private investor is not content merely with the fact that an investment does not cause him a loss or that it produces only limited profits. He will seek to achieve the maximum reasonable return on his investment, according to the particular circumstances and the satisfaction of his short-, medium- and long-term interests, even when he is investing in an undertaking of which he is already a shareholder'. The Court also endorsed the use of the average return as a tool for the purpose of applying the private investor principle. The Court, however, annulled the decision in view of the lack of reasoning underlying the Commission's choice of both the basic rate of return of 12 per cent and the 1.5 per cent rate of increase.

---

[30] Commission Decision (EC) 2000/392 [2000] OJ L150/1.
[31] Joined Cases T-228/99 and T-233/99 *Westdeutsche Landesbank Girozentrale et Altri v Commission*, judgment of 6 March 2003 (not yet reported).

16.21   In *Neue Maxhütte Stahlwerke*,[32] the Court acknowledged that even in the private sector a parent company may, for a limited period, take over the losses of its subsidiary companies. Such action could be motivated by a desire to protect the image of the group or to redirect its activities. However, the Court found that there had to be a prospect of the subsidiary's finding its way back to profitability. A private investor could not afford to inject private capital after years of continuous losses if this were more costly than winding up the company.

(b) Extensions of the Private Investor Principle

16.22   The Court has developed what may be called two extensions of the private investor principle: the private creditor principle and the private buyer principle. In *Tubacex*,[33] the Court held that when deciding whether or not to waive or reschedule debts, the public creditor should act as a private one would do since otherwise the company gains an advantage. In *Grupo de Empresas Alvarez*,[34] the Commission considered that failure by Spain to take measures available under Spanish law (bankruptcy proceedings, separate forced collection procedures) against a company that had not paid its social security contributions persistently and systematically was not consistent with private creditor behaviour. In *P&O Ferries*,[35] the Commission concluded that the agreement between public authorities and a shipping company for passenger transport did not conform to the public authorities' genuine social needs and did not constitute a normal commercial transaction. It inferred this both from the fact that the total number of travel vouchers purchased by the public authorities was not fixed on the basis of their actual needs and that the agreement contained several provisions which a normal commercial agreement concerning the purchase of travel vouchers would not include. The Court upheld the Commission's decision and considered that the public authorities had not adduced sufficient evidence to prove that the purchase of the travel vouchers met a real need and that they had acted in a similar way to a private investor operating under normal market conditions. The Court considered the mere fact that a Member State should purchase goods and services on the basis of prevailing market conditions is not sufficient for that transaction to constitute a commercial transaction concluded under conditions which a private investor would have accepted or, in other words, a normal commercial transaction, if it turns out that the State did not actually need those goods and services.[36]

16.23   (i) **State Guarantees**   The benefit of a State guarantee means that the risk associated with the guarantee is incurred by the State. This incurring of a risk by the State should normally be remunerated by an appropriate premium. The Commission considers that the fulfilment of certain conditions prevents any benefit arising from a State guarantee:[37]

(a) the borrower is not in financial difficulty;

(b) the borrower would in principle be able to obtain a loan on market conditions from the financial markets without any intervention by the State;

---

[32] Case T-129/95, T-2/96, and T-97/96 *Neue Maxhütte Stahlwerke v Commission* [1999] ECR II-17.
[33] Case C-342/96 *Tubacex* [1999] ECR I-02459.
[34] Commission Decision (EC) 2002/935 [2002] OJ L329/1.
[35] Commission Decision (EC) 2001/247 [2001] OJ L89/28.
[36] Joined Cases T-116/01 and T-118/01, not yet reported.
[37] Commission Notice on the application of Arts 87 and 88 of the EC Treaty to State aid in the form of guarantees, point 4.2 ([2000] OJ C71/14).

(c) the guarantee is linked to a specific financial transaction, is for a fixed maximum amount, does not cover more than 80 per cent of the outstanding loan or other financial obligation (except for bonds and similar instruments) and is not open-ended;

(d) the price paid for the guarantee is the market price (which reflects, amongst others, the amount and duration of the guarantee, the security given by the borrower, the borrower's financial position, the sector of activity and the prospects, the rates of default, and other economic conditions).

(ii) Guidelines on Sales of Land and Buildings by Public Authorities Having gained **16.24** experience in a number of cases where the main issue was the possible use of State aid in the sale of publicly owned land and buildings, the Commission set out specific guidance in this area in a Communication published in 1997.[38] Depending on whether or not the sale takes place through an unconditional bidding procedure, the guiding principles for establishing the absence of State aid are as follows:

In the case of a sale through an unconditional bidding procedure, four conditions must be met:

(a) the bidding procedure must be sufficiently well-publicised, ie repeatedly advertised over a period of at least two months;

(b) the bidding procedure must be open, ie not exclude any potential buyer;

(c) the sale must be unconditional, ie the buyer is free to acquire the land and buildings and use it for his own purposes;

(d) the best or only bid is accepted.

When the sale is made without an unconditional bidding procedure, an independent evaluation should be carried out by one or more independent asset valuer prior to the sale negotiations in order to establish the market value, ie the price at which the land and buildings could be sold under private contract between a willing seller and an arm's length buyer on the date of valuation, assuming that the property is on the market, that market conditions permit an orderly disposal, and that a normal period is available for the negotiation of the sale. If, after a reasonable effort, the market value cannot be obtained, a reduction of 5 per cent can be accepted. If, after a reasonable period, no buyer is found, a new valuation may be carried out to take account of the experience gained and the offers received. Where special obligations are attached to the sale in the public interest, ie when the sale is not unconditional, every potential buyer should be able to fulfil them and the economic disadvantage entailed should be evaluated separately by independent assessors.

In any case, when the sale is to be carried out in the first three years after acquisition by the **16.25** public authorities, the market value should not be less than the acquisition cost unless the independent valuers specifically identified a general decline in market prices for land and buildings in the relevant market.

---

[38] [1997] OJ C209/3.

16.26 **(iii) Privatisation of Publicly Owned Companies** In order to determine whether a given privatisation includes State aid elements, the Commission assesses whether:[39]

— the company is sold through a competitive tender or an equivalent procedure that is open, transparent, and unconditional;
— the company is sold to the highest bidder; and
— bidders have enough time and information to carry out a proper valuation of the assets on which to base their bids.

16.27 **(iv) Infrastructure Projects** State support granted to an infrastructure manager, private or public but separate from the State for the maintenance, management, or provision of infrastructure, is presumed to be compatible with the common market if that manager was chosen by an open and non-discriminatory tender, thereby ensuring that the amount of State support represents the market price necessary to achieve the desired result.[40]

(3) Selectivity

16.28 For a measure to constitute State aid within the meaning of Article 87(1), it must favour 'certain undertakings or the production of certain goods'. This is the so-called 'selectivity' or 'specificity' test. Generally speaking, the State intervenes in the economy in various ways and through a series of different measures, a number of which do not favour only certain undertakings but may apply to all the undertakings of a Member State. These are general measures which do not meet the selectivity test. The fact that some undertakings may benefit more than others from a particular measure does not necessarily mean that the measure is selective. For instance, measures which aim to reduce the taxation of labour are of more benefit to undertakings in labour intensive sectors than in capital intensive sectors. This does not make them 'State aid'.

16.29 Selectivity can result from limiting the benefit of the measure to one or several sectors of activity where this is not justified by the nature or general scheme of the system. This occurs when neither the large number of eligible undertakings nor the diversity and size of the sectors to which those undertakings belong provide any grounds for concluding that a State initiative constitutes a general measure of economic policy.[41] Measures applying to the manufacturing sector to the exclusion of the service sector are therefore selective in principle.[42]

16.30 Selectivity of a measure can also result from the fact that it is reserved to certain undertakings irrespective of their sector of activity by virtue of certain criteria. For instance, the Court has acknowledged that measures in favour of large undertakings can meet the selectivity test,[43] as can measures in favour of SMEs.[44]

---

[39] 23rd Competition Report (1993) point 403ff. See for instance decision on Case N-353/2004 on the Privatisation of the Czech State involvement in the Unipetrol Group.
[40] See for instance decision in State aid N 264/2002—UK London Underground Public Private Partnership; Decision in Case N 355/2004 Belgium Krijgsbaan Tunnel Public Private Partnership.
[41] Case C-75/97 *Belgium v Commission* [1999] ECR I-3671, para 32.
[42] Case C-143/99 *Adria-Wien Pipeline* [2001] ECR I-08365.
[43] Case C-200/97 *Ecotrade v AFS* [1998] ECR I-7907.
[44] Case T-55/99 *CETM v Commission* [2000] ECR II-03207.

A measure may appear to be open to all undertakings, but be de facto reserved to some of them. For example, the Commission found that a tax deduction open in principle to all undertakings, only applied to those which had export activities and made certain investments.[45]   **16.31**

Another source of selectivity can lie in the fact that the measure applies only to undertakings located in a particular area within a Member State. This is so-called regional selectivity which presents certain problems in the taxation field, particularly when the tax measures are adopted by authorities who are able to raise taxes which by their very nature only apply in their jurisdiction (see 16.38ff below).   **16.32**

Finally, selectivity can result from the discretionary power of the public authorities in the application of the measure. In *FNE*,[46] the Court concluded the measure was selective because the public authority enjoyed a degree of latitude which enabled it to adjust its financial assistance in the light of a number of considerations, namely the choice of beneficiaries, the amount provided and the conditions under which it was granted. In *Ecotrade*,[47] the Court held that as a result of the discretion enjoyed by the public authorities in determining which companies would benefit from the measure, the selectivity test was met.   **16.33**

Taxation and State Aid

The field of taxation is without doubt an area where the difference between a general measure and State aid, ie the selectivity criterion, is of vital importance. In order to increase transparency, predictability, consistency, and equality of treatment between Member States, the Commission has issued a notice on the application of the State aid rules to measures relating to direct business taxation.[48] In 2004, having drawn lessons from experience, the Commission published a report on the application of the notice.[49]   **16.34**

The first issue to be examined is whether a tax measure is available to all economic agents operating within a Member State. If it is effectively available to all firms on an equal basis and is not de facto reduced in scope, for example, through the discretionary power of the public authorities, it is a general measure. The fact that a tax measure is intended to bring charges in a given sector more in line with those of its competitors in another Member State does not alter the fact that it constitutes aid. Such divergences between tax systems, which are covered by Articles 100–102 of the Treaty, cannot be corrected by unilateral measures targeting the undertakings which are most affected by the disparities between tax systems.   **16.35**

(i) Material Selectivity   Tax measures restricted to certain economic sectors or types of company meet the selectivity test. For instance, tax credits in favour of large undertakings,[50]   **16.36**

---

[45] Joined Cases 6 and 11-69 *Commission v France* [1969] ECR 52; Commission Decision (ECSC) 168/2001 (Spain's corporation tax laws) [2001] OJ L60/57.
[46] Case C-241/94 *France v Commission* [1996] ECR I-04551.
[47] Case C-200/97 *Ecotrade v AFS* [1998] ECR I-7907.
[48] [1998] OJ C384/3.
[49] Report of 9 February 2004 on the implementation of the Commission notice on the application of the State aid rules to measures relating to direct business taxation (C(2004)434).
[50] Joined Cases T-269/99, T-271/99 and T-272/99 *Territorio Histórico de Guipúzcoa–Diputaciún Foral de Guipúzcoa, Territorio Histórico de Álava–Diputación Foral de Álava and Territorio Histórico de Vizcaya–Diputación Foral de Vizcaya v Commission* [2002] ECR II-04217.

tax credits in favour of newly created undertakings,[51] tax rebates in favour of the manufacturing sector,[52] and tax credits in favour of undertakings carrying out export activities or investment[53] have been held by the Court not to be general measures.

16.37 The Commission has considered that certain tax measures meet the selectivity test, namely, measures restricted to foreign companies,[54] measures limited to intra-group transactions,[55] measures limited to companies meeting certain turnover thresholds,[56] and measures restricted to firms set up after the entry into force of the legislation concerned.[57]

16.38 **(ii) Geographic Selectivity**   The Commission expressed its view on the issue of regional selectivity in its decision on the tax system in the Azores Islands.[58] In this case the Commission had to assess the selectivity of a tax measure involving a reduction in corporation tax granted by the Regional authorities in the Azores under the fiscal autonomy granted to them by the Portuguese constitution. The Commission found that the selectivity of the measure was based on a comparison between the advantageous tax treatment granted to certain firms and the treatment applied to other firms within the same frame of reference, which it defined as the territory of a Member State.

16.39 Similarly, the Commission decided that the planned reform of Gibraltar's company taxation was not in line with EU rules.[59] The reform sought to replace the current 35 per cent corporate tax rate by a payroll tax and a business property occupation tax, both capped at 15 per cent of corporate profit. The Commission considered that undertakings in Gibraltar would have an advantage over undertakings operating in the UK, where the normal rate of corporate tax is 30 per cent of profit.

16.40 **(iii) Justification of a Derogation by 'the Nature or General Scheme of the System'**   The differential nature of some measures does not necessarily mean they must be considered State aid. This is the case of measures whose economic rationale makes them necessary to the functioning and effectiveness of the tax system. According to the Commission, a distinction must be made between, on the one hand, the external objectives assigned to a particular tax scheme (in particular, social or regional objectives) and, on the other, the objectives inherent in the tax system itself. For instance, the Commission has found that exemptions from land tax in the agricultural field were justified by the specific role of land in agricultural production.[60] It also accepted that an exemption from transfer taxes on the

---

[51] Joined Cases T-92/00 and T-103/00 *Ramondín* [2002] ECR II-01385.

[52] Case C-143/99 *Adria-Wien Pipeline* [2001] ECR I-08365.

[53] Case C-501/00 *Kingdom of Spain v Commission*, judgment of 15 July 2004 (not yet reported).

[54] Commission Decision (EC) 2003/512 on Control and coordination centres of foreign companies in Germany [2003] OJ L177/17; Decision of 27 November 2002 in State aid E-7/2002 Gibraltar Exempt Offshore Companies.

[55] Commission Decision (EC) 2003/81 on Coordination Centres in Biskaia [2003] OJ L31/26; Commission Decision (EC) 2003/501 on Coordination Centres Luxembourg [2003] OJ L170/20; Commission Decision (EC) 2003/755 on Coordination Centres Belgium [2003] OJ L282/25.

[56] Commission Decision (EC) 2003/755 on Coordination Centres Belgium [2003] OJ L282/25.

[57] Commission Decision (EC) 2002/540 [2002] OJ L174/31; Commission Decision (EC) 2003/86 [2001] OJ L40/11.

[58] Commission Decision (EC) 2003/442 [2003] OJ L150/52.

[59] Commission Decision (EC) 2005/261 [2005] OJ L85/1.

[60] State aid N 20/2000 (Netherlands) and N 53/99 (Denmark).

conversion of certain public undertakings into joint stock companies was justified by the principle of tax neutrality.[61] Likewise, it considered that a Danish measure allowing credit institutions to make provision for losses inherent in credit risks was justified by the specific features of banking or financial transactions.[62]

The Commission considers it is difficult to justify, by invoking a logic inherent in the tax system, a more favourable treatment of non-resident companies or grant of tax benefits to head offices or to firms providing certain services (for example, financial services) within a group. The need to restructure the banking sector was not considered by the Commission as sufficient justification for the tax breaks for mergers in the banking sector carried out within a certain period.[63] Likewise, the Commission did not accept a measure allowing international companies to establish a tax-exempt risk reserve provided they carried out financing activities for parts of a group in at least four countries or on at least two continents.[64] It acknowledged that international transactions entailed specific and real risks that could justify a derogation but the specific requirements as to the number of countries or continents in which the activities had to be carried out was not justified by the rationale of the system. **16.41**

(iv) Indirect Taxation Notwithstanding the fact that, in principle, the Commission notice referred to above covers only direct taxation, the Commission has referred to it in a number of cases relating to indirect taxation measures, particularly as regards the principle that a measure is justified by the nature and general scheme of the system. However, indirect taxation measures present specific features. Thus, while VAT reductions are subject to strict Community rules and conform to the principle of equality of taxation for similar products, the same is not true of excise duties, a reduction in which favours certain undertakings and may therefore constitute State aid. **16.42**

(4) Distortion of Competition and Effect on Trade

When the State confers even a limited advantage on an undertaking which is active in a sector where competition prevails, there is a distortion or risk of distortion of competition. The condition is therefore easily fulfilled. Actual distortion of competition is not necessary since the State aid rules apply to planned aid. The Court always examines this together with the effect on trade.[65] **16.43**

The concept of effect on trade used in Article 87(1) of the EC Treaty is extremely broad in scope. In *CETM*,[66] the Court recalled that when: **16.44**

> aid from State resources strengthens the position of an undertaking compared with other undertakings competing in intra-Community trade, the latter must be regarded as affected

---

[61] Commission Decision (EC) 2003/193 [2002] OJ L77/21.

[62] State aid N-482/2001 (Denmark), Decision 27 May 2003.

[63] Commission Decision (EC) 2002/581 [2002] OJ L184/27.

[64] Commission Decision (EC) 2003/515 [2003] OJ L180/52.

[65] See for instance Joined Cases T-298/97, T-312/97, T-313/97, T-315/97, T-600/97 to T-607/97, T-1/98, T-3/98 to T-6/98 and T-23/98 *Alzetta v Commission* [2000] ECR II-2319, paras 91–97; and Case T-288/97 *Friuli Venezia Giulia v Commission* [2001] ECR II-01169, para 54.

[66] Case T-55/99 *Confederación Española de Transporte de Mercancías v Commission* [2000] ECR II-03207, para 86.

by that aid . . . Furthermore, an aid may be of such a kind as to affect trade between Member States and distort competition even if the recipient undertaking, which is in competition with undertakings from other Member States, does not itself participate in crossborder activities. Where a Member State grants aid to an undertaking, internal supply may be maintained or increased, with the consequence that the opportunities for undertakings established in other Member States to offer their services to the market of that Member State are reduced.

16.45   In *Altmark*,[67] the Court established that 'it is not impossible that a public subsidy granted to an undertaking which provides only local or regional transport services and does not provide any transport services outside its State of origin may none the less have an effect on trade between Member States'. It also found that:

> Where a Member State grants a public subsidy to an undertaking, the supply of transport services by that undertaking may for that reason be maintained or increased with the result that undertakings established in other Member States have less chance of providing their transport services in the market in that Member State.

16.46   Furthermore, according to the Court, 'the relatively small amount of aid or the relatively small size of the undertaking which receives it does not as such exclude the possibility that intra-Community trade might be affected'.[68]

16.47   In order to establish the impact of this distortion on trade between Member States, it is therefore sufficient to conclude that the beneficiary conducts, even on a partial basis, activities involving trade between Member States.

16.48   The Commission thus concluded in *Marina di Stabia*[69] that a marina on the southern Italian Tyrrhenian coastline might also attract limited demand from as far away as the southern French coast and thereby affect trade between Member States.

16.49   On the other hand, in *Dorsten swimming pool*,[70] the Commission considered that the annual grant made to the private operator of the swimming pool in Dorsten would not affect trade since it would be used essentially by the inhabitants of the town and its surrounding area.

16.50   In *Capital allowances for Irish hospitals*,[71] the Commission considered that the tax benefit granted to individuals investing in the construction, extension, and refurbishment of hospitals in Ireland would not affect trade since, given the prevailing undercapacity, it would not result in the construction of hospital complexes likely to attract patients from other Member States.

16.51   In *Brighton West Pier*,[72] the Commission considered that the aid granted to the owner of the West Pier in Brighton would not affect trade since the pier's international reputation was insufficient to attract tourists from other Member States.

---

[67] Case C-280/00 *Altmark Trans GmbH* [2003] ECR I-07747, paras 77 and 78.
[68] Case C-142/87 *Belgium v Commission* [1990] ECR I-959, para 43.
[69] State aid N-582/99, [2000] OJ C40/2.
[70] State aid N-258/2000 Germany; Commission press release IP/00/1509 of 21 December 2000.
[71] State aid N-543/2001 Ireland [2002] OJ C154/4.
[72] State aid N-560/01 and NN 17/02 [2002] OJ C239/3.

(a) The De Minimis Regulation[73]

This Regulation provides that aid not exceeding EUR 100 000 over any period of three **16.52** years does not affect trade between Member States and/or does not distort or threaten to distort competition. However, in view of the risk that even small amounts of aid may distort competition and/or affect trade, the sectors of transport, agriculture, fisheries, and aquaculture are excluded from the scope of this de minimis Regulation. Similarly, as a result of the WTO Agreement on Subsidies and Countervailing Measures, aid to export-related activities and aid contingent upon the use of domestic over imported products are not exempted by the Regulation and must therefore be notified to the Commission.

(b) The 2004 Commission's Proposals to Deal with Small Amounts of Aid and with Aid with Limited Effects on Intra-community Trade

In 2004, with a view to introducing a greater degree of flexibility in the assessment of lower **16.53** amounts of State aid or of State aid with limited effects on intra-community trade, the Commission examined the possibility of proposing two new frameworks.[74] The idea was to introduce two new categories of State aid: LASA (lower amounts of State aid) and LET (limited effect on trade).

LASA is State aid that, while exceeding the de minimis ceiling could still, subject to certain **16.54** safeguards, be regarded as too modest in size to present a significant threat to competition at Community level and to trade between Member States provided the aid is granted in a manner which favours the achievement of general Community objectives of common interest. LASA would still have to be notified, but Member States would have greater flexibility to conceive and implement measures adapted to local conditions. The Commission would therefore be able to focus resources on cases where a major impact on competition appears likely.

Under the LET approach, there would be a simplified assessment procedure. First, there **16.55** would be a list of activities that, by their very nature, do not produce significant cross-border effects or do not appear to be characterised by a high level of concentration or barriers to entry. Once it has been established that an activity is on the list, additional conditions, intended to ensure that the negative effects of the aid measure are kept to a minimum, would apply to the aid intensity, the total amount of aid, and the form it takes.

B. Compatibility of State Aid with the Common Market

(1) Introduction

Once it has been determined that a measure constitutes State aid, it is the Commission's **16.56** task (and, in exceptional circumstances, within the Council's competence) to verify its compatibility with the common market. The EC Treaty has established an *ex ante* system of control of State aid whereby Member States must notify the Commission of any plans to

---

[73] Commission Regulation (EC) 69/2001 [2001] OJ L10/30. This regulation will be replaced as of 1 January 2007 by Commission Regulation (EC) 1998/2006 [2006] OJ L379/5.

[74] <http://europa.eu.int/comm/competition/state_aid/others/limited/en.pdf> and <http://europa.eu.int/comm/competition/state_aid/others/lesser/en.pdf>.

grant aid (unless exempted from the requirement of prior notification) and refrain from implementing such aid without the prior authorisation of the Commission.

16.57   The conclusion that a State aid measure is compatible with the common market can be reached in different ways:

(a) there is compatibility *ex lege* where the aid fulfils the conditions established in a Commission block exemption Regulation. Regulations can be directly applied by national courts;

(b) the Commission, having followed the appropriate procedure (see below), adopts a decision of compatibility in respect of an individual project or the aid is granted under a scheme already approved by the Commission;

(c) compatibility is declared by the Council.

(2) Compatibility *Ex Lege:* Block Exemption Regulations

16.58   Council Regulation (EC) 994/98,[75] adopted on the basis of Article 89 of the Treaty, empowered the Commission to declare by means of regulations that certain categories of aid do not fulfil the criteria of Article 87(1) or that they are compatible with the common market and exempted from the notification obligation contained in Article 88(3). Regulations adopted on this basis can be directly applied by national courts. According to its preamble, the aim is to simplify administration in areas where the Commission has sufficient experience to define general compatibility criteria, thus following law and established practice under Article 81(3).

16.59   The Commission has made use of these powers in four Regulations to date: one establishing that certain kinds of aid do not fulfil the conditions of Article 87(1), namely the de minimis Regulation, and three other Regulations defining the general compatibility criteria for aid to SMEs, aid for employment and aid for training. The Commission has not yet adopted block exemption Regulations in the fields of research and development (except as far as SMEs are concerned), environmental protection, or regional aid.

(a) Aid for SMEs

16.60   Under Commission Regulation (EC) 70/2001,[76] as amended by Commission Regulation (EC) 364/2004,[77] aid to SMEs fulfilling certain conditions is compatible with the common market and not subject to the notification requirement of Article 88(3) of the Treaty. In order for a scheme or an individual grant of aid outside a scheme to benefit from the exemption, they must contain an express reference to the Regulation.

16.61   (i) **Definition of SMEs (as from 1 January 2005)**[78]   A medium size enterprise is an enterprise employing between 50 and 250 persons and which has an annual turnover of between EUR 10 million and EUR 50 million and/or an annual balance sheet total of between EUR 10 million and EUR 43 million. A small enterprise is an enterprise employing fewer than 50 persons and whose annual turnover and/or annual balance sheet total does not exceed

---

[75] [1998] OJ L142/1.
[76] [2001] OJ L10/33.
[77] [2004] OJ L63/22.
[78] Annex I to Commission Regulation (EC) 364/2004 [2004] OJ L63/22.

EUR 10 million. If an enterprise has structural links with other undertakings, the data of all related undertakings will also be taken into account.

The main provisions of this Regulation are as follows: **16.62**

(ii) Costs Eligible for Aid

- Investment in tangible assets (land, buildings, plant/machinery) and intangible assets   **16.63**
  (acquisition of technology).
- Costs entailed by R&D activities on the basis of the same conditions as those included in
  the R&D Guidelines (cf 16.139ff below), including the costs of technical feasibility
  studies and patenting costs.
- Costs of consultancy services by outside consultants, provided that the services concerned
  are not a continuous or periodic activity nor refer to the enterprise's usual operating costs,
  such as routine consultancy, regular legal services, or advertising.
- Costs of renting, setting up, and running a stand incurred the first time an enterprise
  participates in a particular fair or exhibition.

(iii) Aid Intensity[79]

- The maximum aid intensity for investment is 30 per cent of eligible costs in the case of   **16.64**
  Article 87(3)(c) regions and 75 per cent in the case of Article 87(3)(a) regions. In non-
  assisted regions, the maximum aid is 15 per cent for small enterprises and 7.5 per cent for
  medium enterprises.
- The maximum aid intensity for consultancy services is 50 per cent.
- The maximum aid for R&D activities is 100 per cent for fundamental research, 50 per cent
  for pre-competitive research, and 75 per cent for industrial research.

(iv) Aid Subject to Individual Notification   In the case of investment aid, any individ-   **16.65**
ual grant of aid meeting one of the following thresholds must be notified individually to the
Commission:

(a) The total eligible costs of the whole project are at least EUR 25 million; and
   — in non-assisted areas or in sectors not eligible for regional aid, the gross aid intensity
     is at least 7.5 per cent for small enterprises or 3.75 per cent for medium enterprises;
   — in assisted areas[80] and in sectors eligible for regional aid, the aid intensity is at least
     50 per cent of the aid ceiling determined by the regional map.
(b) The total gross aid amount is at least EUR 15 million.

In the case of R&D aid, the conditions for individual notifications contained in the R&D
Framework apply (see 16.139ff below).

---

[79] Aid intensity is the correlation, expressed as a percentage, between the amount of aid granted to a project and the amount of the costs that the Commission considers as eligible for aid. The aid intensity is expressed
in terms of Net Grant Equivalent (NGE) or Gross Grant Equivalent (GGE), the former taking into account
taxation and discounting contrary to the latter. The detailed method of calculation for this purpose is
explained in the Community guidelines for National Regional aid.
[80] Assisted regions or regions eligible for regional aid are the areas of a Member State that have been
approved by the Commission acting on a proposal made by the Member State and applying the criteria contained in the Community guidelines for National Regional aid.

(b) Aid for Employment

16.66 Under Commission Regulation (EC) 2204/2002,[81] aid schemes for the creation of employment, for the recruitment of disadvantaged or disabled workers or to cover the additional costs of employing disabled workers that fulfil certain conditions are compatible with the common market and not subject to the notification requirement of Article 88(3) of the Treaty. Any individual award of aid made under such schemes and fulfilling those conditions is also exempted from the notification requirement. In order for the scheme to benefit from the exemption it must contain an express reference to the Regulation in question.

16.67 The main provisions of this Regulation are as follows:

(i) Aid for the Creation of Employment
Conditions

16.68 • The employment created must represent a net increase in the number of employees, both in the establishment and in the enterprise concerned, compared with the average of the previous twelve months. Where the creation of employment is linked to the carrying-out of an investment project, the application for aid must have been submitted before the work on the project is started.
• The employment created must be maintained for a minimum period of three years (two in the case of SMEs).
• The new workers employed as a result of the creation of employment must never have been employed before or they have lost or will lose their previous job.

Eligible costs

16.69 • Wage costs of the employment created over a period of two years.

Aid intensity

16.70 • In regions or in sectors eligible for regional aid the maximum aid must not exceed 15 per cent (small enterprises) of the eligible costs.
• In regions and in sectors eligible for regional aid, the maximum aid must not exceed 75 per cent of the eligible costs (SMEs in Article 87(3)(a) regions).

16.71 **(ii) Aid for the Recruitment of Disadvantaged and Disabled Workers** The conditions for compatibility with the common market of aid for the recruitment of disabled and disadvantaged workers as defined in the Regulation are as follows:

(a) When there is no net increase in the number of workers the posts must have fallen vacant by reasons attributable to the workers (and not as a result of redundancy) and the disadvantaged or disabled worker must be entitled to continuous employment for a minimum of twelve months.
(b) The maximum aid intensity must not exceed 50 per cent (disadvantaged workers) or 60 per cent (disabled workers) of the wage costs of the workers concerned over a period of one year following recruitment.

---

[81] [2002] OJ L337/3.

Additional costs of employment of disabled workers These are the costs of adapting prem- **16.72**
ises, of employing staff for time spent on the assistance of the disabled workers, and of
adapting or acquiring equipment for their use.

(iii) Aid Subject to Prior Notification to the Commission The Regulation does not **16.73**
exempt:

— aid targeted at particular sectors;
— aid to a single enterprise or establishment exceeding EUR 15 million over any three-year
  period.

(c) Aid for Training

Under Commission Regulation (EC) 68/2001,[82] aid schemes and individual aid for train- **16.74**
ing that fulfil certain conditions are compatible with the common market and not subject
to the notification requirement of Article 88(3) of the Treaty.

The main provisions of this Regulation are as follows: **16.75**

(i) Eligible Costs
• trainers' personnel costs; **16.76**
• trainers' and trainees' travel expenses;
• materials and supplies;
• depreciation of tools and equipment;
• costs of guidance and counselling services with regard to the training project;
• trainees' personnel costs corresponding to the hours actually spent in the training and up
  to the amount of the total of the other eligible costs mentioned above.

(ii) Aid Intensities The aid intensities vary according to the nature of the training, the **16.77**
size, the location of the beneficiary and the qualification of the trainee as disadvantaged:

• For general training, ie training which provides qualifications that are largely transferable
  to other firms or fields of work, the aid intensities can go from 50 per cent (large undertaking in a non-assisted region) to 90 per cent of the eligible costs (training for disadvantaged workers in SMEs located in an Article 87(3)(a) region).
• For specific training, ie training involving tuition directly and principally applicable to
  the employee's present or future position in the assisted firm, the aid intensities can rise
  from 25 per cent (large undertaking in a non-assisted region) to 55 per cent of the eligible costs (training for disadvantaged workers in SMEs located in an Article 87(3)(a)
  region).

(iii) Aid Subject to Prior Notification to the Commission The Regulation does not **16.78**
exempt aid exceeding EUR 1 million granted to one enterprise for a single training project.

(3) Compatibility Declared by the Commission on the Basis of Article 87(2)EC

The Commission's State aid control is based on the principle of compulsory prior notification **16.79**
of all new aid measures (schemes as well as individual grants of aid) to the Commission.

---

[82] [2001] OJ L10/20.

Under the standstill clause of Article 88(3) the aid measure may not be put into effect until the Commission has reached a decision. State aid that meets the criteria of Article 87(2) is automatically compatible with the common market although the Commission has some margin of discretion when assessing whether the conditions are met as can be seen in the following paragraphs.

(a) Aid having a Social Character granted to Individual Consumers

16.80 This provision has been used mainly in the field of air transport. In its Communication on the application of the State aid rules in the aviation sector[83] the Commission established three conditions in this context:

(a) the aid must effectively be for the benefit of final consumers;

(b) the aid must have a social character, ie it must, in principle, cover only specific categories of passengers travelling on a route (eg children, handicapped, or low income persons). However, if the route concerned links an underprivileged region, mainly islands, the aid could cover the entire population of that region;

(c) the aid must be granted without discrimination as to the origin of the services, that is to say no matter which EEA air carriers operate the services. This also implies the absence of any barrier to entry on the route concerned for all Community air carriers.

In *Corsica passengers*,[84] the Commission ascertained that those conditions were fulfilled. In *PO Ferries*,[85] the Commission considered that the condition concerning the absence of discrimination was not met. The Court upheld the Commission decision.[86]

(b) Aid to make good Damage caused by Natural Disasters or Exceptional Occurrences

16.81 Although it must be notified to the Commission prior to its being put into effect, this type of aid is compatible with the common market. The Commission must verify however that: (a) it is a true natural disaster or exceptional occurrence; (b) that there is a direct relationship between the natural disaster or exceptional occurrence and the damage; and (c) that there will not be overcompensation.

16.82 The Commission's policy on the use of this provision is summarised in the Community Guidelines for State aid in the agriculture sector:[87]

> 11.2.1. Because they constitute exceptions from the general principle of the incompatibility of State aid with the common market laid down by Article 87(1) of the Treaty, the Commission has consistently held that the notions of "natural disaster" and "exceptional occurrence" contained in Article 87(2)(b) must be interpreted restrictively. Hitherto the Commission has accepted that earthquakes, avalanches, landslides and floods may constitute natural disasters. Exceptional occurrences which have hitherto been accepted by the Commission include war, internal disturbances or strikes, and with certain reservations and depending on their extent, major nuclear or industrial accidents and fires which result in

---

[83] [1994] OJ C350/07.

[84] State aid N 24/2000—France [2004] OJ C67/9.

[85] Commission Decision (EC) 2001/247 [2001] OJ L89/28.

[86] Joined Cases T-116/01 *P&O European Ferries (Vizcaya) SA* and T-118/01 *Diputación de Vizcaya v Commission* [2003] ECR II-2957.

[87] [2000] OJ C28/2.

widespread loss. On the other hand the Commission did not accept that a fire at a single processing plant which was covered by normal commercial insurance could be considered as an exceptional occurrence. As a general rule, the Commission does not accept that outbreaks of animal or plant diseases can be considered to constitute natural disasters or exceptional occurrences. However, in one case the Commission did recognise the very widespread outbreak of a completely new animal disease as an exceptional occurrence. Because of the inherent difficulties in foreseeing such events, the Commission will continue to evaluate proposals to grant aid in accordance with Article 87(2)(b) on a case-by-case basis, having regard to its previous practice in this field.

11.2.2. Once the existence of a natural disaster or an exceptional occurrence has been demonstrated, the Commission will permit aid of up to 100 per cent to compensate for material damage. Compensation should normally be calculated at the level of the individual beneficiary, and in order to avoid over-compensation, any payments due, for example under insurance policies, should be deducted from the amount of aid. The Commission will also accept aid to compensate farmers for loss of income resulting from the destruction of the means of agricultural production, provided that there is no over-compensation.

The Commission considered that the sinking of the oil tanker Erika in 2000[88] constituted an exceptional occurrence that caused damage. It therefore approved an aid scheme proposed by the French government to assist SMEs which suffered in the course of the dispersion of the oil slick. Under the scheme, the costs arising from the replacement of damaged facilities, the destruction of stocks and exceptional financial losses were eligible for aid. The aid covered costs not otherwise covered by insurance. **16.83**

The Commission considered the terrorist attacks of 11 September 2001 as exceptional occurrences because of their unforeseeable nature, the number of victims and the impact on the world economy. It considered that the costs arising directly from the closure of US airspace between 11 and 14 September 2001 and the extra costs of insurance could give rise to compensation under Article 87(2)(b) on certain conditions, mainly concerned with avoiding overcompensation.[89] **16.84**

Under this provision, the Commission also approved five aid schemes aimed at compensating victims in the agricultural sector for the damage caused by the floods which occurred in Germany in the summer of 2002.[90] **16.85**

In its decision of 11 December 2002,[91] the Commission refused the application of Article 87(2)(b) to aid granted by Spain in the agricultural sector following an increase in fuel prices because Spain had not demonstrated any link between the aid granted and the damage sustained by beneficiaries as a result of the rise in fuel prices. Furthermore, according to the Commission, Spain had not demonstrated either that all the beneficiaries of these aid measures had suffered damage from the rise in prices or that the amount of the aid related to and did not exceed the damage sustained by the farmers. **16.86**

---

[88] Commission Decision of 4 October 2000 [2000] OJ C380/9.

[89] Communication from the Commission to the European Parliament and the Council, *The repercussions of the terrorist attacks in the United States on the air transport industry* COM (2001) 574 final of 10 October 2001.

[90] State aid N 567/2002, 581/2002, 595/2002, 647/2002 and 682/2002.

[91] Commission Decision (EC) 2003/293 [2003] OJ L111/24.

16.87 Similarly, in April 2003[92] the Commission expressed its doubts that the strike carried out by road hauliers in Sicily constituted an exceptional occurrence that could justify the application of Article 87(2)(b).

(c) Aid to compensate for the Economic Disadvantages caused by the Division of Germany

16.88 Although this provision has lost virtually all its usefulness, it was not repealed after German reunification by successive Treaty amendments and is even retained in the draft Constitution of the European Union.

16.89 As the Court has held in three judgments:

> the expression 'division of Germany' refers historically to the establishment of the dividing line between the two occupied zones in 1948, and the 'economic disadvantages caused by that division' can therefore only mean the economic disadvantages caused in certain areas of Germany by the isolation which the establishment of that physical frontier entailed, such as the breaking of communication links or the loss of markets as a result of the breaking-off of commercial relations between the two parts of German territory.[93]

> The Court has rejected Germany's interpretation that Article 87(2)(c) permits full compensation for the undeniable economic backwardness of the new Länder. It is only the economic disadvantages directly caused by the geographical division of Germany which may be compensated for within the meaning of that provision; the differences in development between the original and the new Länder are explained by causes other than the geographical split caused by the division of Germany, in particular by the different politico-economic systems set up in each part of Germany.[94]

(4) Compatibility Declared by the Commission on the Basis of Article 87(3)EC—Commission Guidelines

16.90 The Court had the opportunity to rule as early as 1980, that Article 87(3), unlike Article 87(2), 'gives the Commission a discretion by providing that the aid which it specifies "may" be considered to be compatible with the common market'.[95] Also, according to case law:

> the Commission, in the application of Article 87(3)(c), has a wide discretion, the exercise of which involves complex economic and social assessments which must be made in a Community context. Judicial review of the manner in which that discretion is exercised is confined to establishing that the rules of procedure and the rules relating to the duty to give reasons have been complied with and to verifying the accuracy of the facts relied on and that there has been no error of law, manifest error of assessment in regard to the facts or misuse of powers.[96]

---

[92] [2003] OJ C127/3.

[93] Case C-156/98 *Germany v Commission* [2000] ECR I-6857, para 52; Case C-334/99 *Germany v Commission* [2003] ECR I-1139, para 120; Case C-301/96 *Germany v Commission* [2003] ECR I-9199, para 67.

[94] Case C-301/96 *Germany v Commission* [2003] ECR I-9199 paras 68–76.

[95] Case C-730/79 *Philip Morris Holland BV v Commission* [1980] ECR 2671, para 17.

[96] Case 310/85 *Deufil v Commission* [1987] ECR 901, para 18; Case C-351/98 *Spain v Commission* [2002] ECR I-8031, para 74; Case C-409/00 *Spain v Commission* [2003] ECR I-1487, para 93; and Case C-91/01 *Italy v Commission* [2004] ECR I-4355, para 43.

(a) Aid to Promote the Economic Development of Areas where the Standard of Living is Abnormally Low or where there is Serious Underemployment (Article 87(3)(a))

The methods for determining the areas covered by this provision and the types and amount **16.91** of permissible aid are defined in the Community guidelines on National Regional aid (see paragraphs 16.101ff below).

(b) Aid to Promote the Execution of an Important Project of Common European Interest (Article 87(3)(b))

Under Article 87(3)(b) aid to promote the execution of an important project of common **16.92** European interest may be considered compatible with the common market. The Commission has the competence to define a project as being of common European interest and to gauge its importance. Thus, in *Glaverbel*[97] the Commission considered that a project could not be considered as being of common European interest for this purpose unless it formed part of a transnational European programme supported jointly by a number of Member States or arose from concerted action undertaken by them to combat a common threat such as environmental pollution. The Court upheld the Commission's view.[98]

The Commission has found that some R&D projects could fall under this provision and **16.93** attract maximum aid intensities. However, the common European interest of an R&D project must be demonstrated in practical terms: for example, it must be proved that the project represents a major advance over specific Community R&D programmes or that it enables significant progress to be made towards achieving specific Community objectives. For the Commission, this may apply particularly to transnational projects of major qualitative and, in principle, quantitative significance (eg projects related to the formulation of industrial standards that could enable the Community's industries to secure the full benefit of the single market).[99] In *Medea+*,[100] the Commission found that the quantitative and qualitative importance of the co-operation between public or university laboratories and industrial research centres in different Member States envisaged by the project justified its categorisation as an important project of common European interest.

(c) Aid to Remedy a Serious Disturbance in the Economy of a Member State (Article 87(3)(b))

Although Article 87(3)(b) makes it possible to declare compatibility with the common **16.94** market aid to remedy a serious disturbance in the economy of a Member State, this provision has rarely been used.

Apart from three decisions adopted in the period 1974–1975 on aid in Denmark, France, **16.95** and Italy, the last decision where the Commission based its assessment of compatibility on this provision dates from 1988. In the *Greek austerity programme*,[101] the Commission approved an aid scheme for the financial recovery of 23 companies accounting for 20 per cent of

---

[97] Commission Decision (EEC) 87/195 [1987] OJ L77/47.
[98] Joined Cases 62 & 72/87 *Executif Régional Wallon v Commission* [1988] ECR 1573, paras 22–23.
[99] Community Framework for State aid for R&D, point 3.4.
[100] State aid N 702/B/2001—France [2002] OJ C292/6.
[101] Commission Decision (EEC) 88/167 [1988] OJ L76/18.

industrial employment in Greece and a considerably larger percentage of its industrial output and international trade. In its assessment, the Commission took into account the fact that, due to the critical economic situation, the government had been forced to introduce a drastic austerity programme and that the success of the programme could be compromised if the beneficiaries of the aid were allowed to go into liquidation. The Commission, however, required prior notification of individual aid grants to companies of a certain size in order to ascertain that the aid did not promote expansion of production capacity and that it did, in fact, provide a genuine solution for the companies concerned.

16.96 The Court has ruled that the disturbance mentioned in this provision must affect the economy of a Member State, not merely one of its regions or areas.[102]

16.97 In *Crédit Lyonnais*,[103] the Commission conceded that circumstances outside the control of the banks could cause a crisis of confidence in the system and that Article 87(3)(b) could therefore be invoked. However, for aid to be compatible with the common market it must be granted in a neutral fashion from the viewpoint of competition in the State concerned; moreover, it must cover the whole of the banking system and must be confined to what is strictly necessary. In the case in question, the Commission considered that the aid was not designed to remedy a serious disturbance in the economy but to remedy the difficulties of a single aid recipient. Moreover, in the Commission's view, Crédit Lyonnais' problems were specific to this bank and appeared to be related to its aggressive commercial policy which lacked a sufficiently strict monitoring of risks and a proper evaluation of assets acquired.

(d) Aid to Promote Culture and Heritage Conservation (Article 87(3)(d))

16.98 Although the Commission had previously authorised State aid with cultural aims, it was the Maastricht Treaty that included in Article 87(3)(d) a new specific possibility of derogation from the prohibition of State aid embodied in Article 87(1). However, as with other exceptions, it must be applied strictly. The main area where the Commission has developed a policy concerning aid to culture relates to cinema and TV production. In its decision of 3 June 1998 on a French scheme,[104] the Commission set out four specific compatibility criteria to authorise aid to cinema and TV production in accordance with the derogation contained in Article 87(3)(d). Those criteria were subsequently included in its Communication of 16 February 2002[105] and are as follows:

(a) The aid is directed to a cultural product. It is up to each Member State to establish verifiable national criteria as to what constitutes cultural content.

(b) The Commission admits that a certain degree of territorialisation of the expenditure may be necessary to ensure the continued presence of human skills and technical expertise required for cultural creation. However, the producer must be free to spend

---

[102] Case C-301/96 *Germany v Commission*, judgment of 30 September 2003 (not yet reported) para 106.

[103] Commission Decision (EC) 95/547 [1996] OJ L308/92.

[104] State aid N 3/98, [1998] OJ C279/4. Decision of 3 June 1998.

[105] Communication from the Commission to the Council, the European Parliament, the Economic and Social Committee and the Committee of the Regions on certain legal aspects relating to cinematographic and other audiovisual works [2002] OJ C43/6.

at least 20 per cent of the film budget in other Member States without suffering any reduction in the aid provided for under the scheme.

(c) With a view to stimulating normal commercial initiatives inherent in a market economy and avoiding a bidding contest between Member States, the aid intensity must be limited to 50 per cent of the production budget. However, 'difficult' and low budget films are excluded from this limit. It is up to each Member State to establish a definition of difficult and low budget film according to national parameters.

(d) Aid supplements for specific film-making activities (eg post-production) are not allowed.

(e) Aid to Facilitate the Development of Certain Economic Activities or of Certain Economic Areas (Article 87(3)(c))

Under Article 87(3)(c) aid can be authorised to facilitate the development of certain eco- **16.99** nomic activities or of certain economic areas, where such aid does not adversely affect trading conditions to an extent contrary to the common interest. It is on the basis of this provision that the Commission adopts the vast majority of its decisions of compatibility with the common market. Furthermore the aid pursues in most cases one of the objectives that the Commission considers in need of incentives and for which it has developed Community guidelines with a view to increasing transparency and legal certainty. There are two main types of guidelines: those applying to all sectors of the economy (horizontal guidelines) and those applying to certain sectors (sectoral guidelines). The Commission is bound by the guidelines and the notices that it issues in the area of supervision of State aid where they do not depart from the rules in the Treaty and are accepted by the Member States.[106] The parties concerned are therefore entitled to rely on those guidelines and the Court will ascertain whether the Commission complied with the rules it has itself laid down when it adopted the contested decision.[107]

Aid that does not fit into any of the guidelines or frameworks, however, may still be approved **16.100** by the Commission on the basis of the conditions established in Article 87(3)(c), namely:

(a) that the aid facilitates the development of certain economic activities or areas;

(b) that the aid does not adversely affect trading conditions to an extent contrary to the common interest.

(i) **Guidelines on National Regional Aid**[108]   According to the Treaty, aid to promote the **16.101** economic development of areas where the standard of living is abnormally low or where there is serious underemployment (Article 87(3)(a)) and aid to facilitate the development of certain economic areas where such aid does not adversely affect trading conditions to an extent contrary to the common interest (Article 87(3)(c)) may be considered compatible with the common market. This is the so-called national regional aid which is designed to develop the less-favoured regions of the Community.

---

[106] Case C-351/98 *Spain v Commission* [2002] ECR I-8031, para 53.
[107] Case T-35/99 *Keller and Keller Meccanica v Commission* [2002] ECR II-261, paras 74 and 77.
[108] [2006] OJ C54/08.

16.102 It should be pointed out that, unless shown otherwise, the advantages to be gained in terms of development of a less-favoured region from individual ad hoc payments made to a single firm or aid confined to one sector are likely to be rather limited. This is why the Commission considers that compatibility of aid can normally be granted only when multisectoral aid schemes are open, in a given region, to all firms in the sectors concerned.

16.103 For a regional aid scheme to benefit from one of the derogations established in Article 87(3)(a) or (c), the region must be included in the regional map approved by the Commission for the Member State in question. The detailed criteria to be used for establishing the regional maps are set out in Chapter 3 of the guidelines. Regions can be eligible for aid under Article 87(3)(a) or (c). This affects the intensity of the permissible aid: higher aid intensities are authorised for Article 87(3)(a) regions.

16.104 *Aid for initial investment*   Initial investment means investment in material and immaterial assets relating to the setting-up of a new establishment, the extension of an existing establishment, diversification of the output of an establishment into new, additional products or a fundamental change in the overall production process of an existing establishment. Replacement investment is thus excluded.

16.105 Aid for initial investment is calculated as a percentage of the value of the investment which may include land, buildings, plant/machinery, and intangible assets (patents and know-how). In the case of Article 87(3)(a) regions, the maximum aid intensity is 70 per cent (in the outermost regions).[109] For Article 87(3)(c) regions, the maximum aid intensity is 15 per cent. SMEs may also be entitled to a bonus.

16.106 *Aid for newly created small enterprises*   This aid can be granted in addition to regional investment aid, in order to provide incentives to support business start-ups and the early development of small enterprises in the assisted areas. The maximum amount of the aid is up to EUR 2 million in Article 87(3)(a) regions and the aid intensity may not exceed 40 per cent of eligible expenses in certain Article 87(3)(a) regions.

16.107 Eligible expenses include legal, advisory, consultancy, and administrative costs related to the creation of the enterprise.

16.108 *Operating aid*   Operating aid is aid aimed at reducing a firm's current expenses and is normally prohibited. Exceptionally, however, Article 87(3)(a) regions are eligible for such aid provided that three conditions are met:

(a) the aid is justified in terms of its contribution to regional development and its nature and level are proportional to the handicaps it seeks to alleviate. It is for the Member State to demonstrate the existence of any handicaps and gauge their importance;

(b) the aid is limited in time;

(c) the aid is progressively reduced.

The guidelines also contain special provisions for aid intended to offset additional transport costs in outermost regions or to prevent depopulation in regions of low density population.

---

[109] The French overseas departments, the Azores, Madeira, and the Canary Islands.

Regional aid for large investment projects   In its Communication on the Multisectoral **16.109** Framework for large investment projects[110] the Commission considered that a restriction of the level of incentive for large projects was needed in order to avoid unnecessary distortions of competition. Therefore, an automatic limitation of aid intensities will be applied as described below.

For projects whose eligible expenditure exceeds EUR 50 million the maximum aid inten- **16.110** sity will be reduced according to the following formula: maximum aid amount $= R \times (50 + 0.50B + 0.34C)$ where R is the regional ceiling approved by the Commission in the regional map, B is the eligible expenditure between EUR 50 million and EUR 100 million and C is the eligible expenditure above EUR 100 million, if any.

Member States that wish to grant a higher amount of aid than the maximum allowable aid **16.111** that an investment of EUR 100 million may obtain under the above formula, must notify the project to the Commission. In this case, the Commission will approve the aid only after opening the procedure provided for in Article 88(2) if the company has a high market share (more than 25 per cent) or where the project increases existing sectoral production capacity by more than 5 per cent without a corresponding increase in demand for the products concerned.

It is for the Member State concerned to prove the aid beneficiary's market share is lower **16.112** than 25 per cent or that the increase in production capacity is less than 5 per cent.

(ii) State Aid for Environmental Protection   According to Article 2 EC the Community **16.113** must promote a high level of protection and improvement of the quality of the environment. Under Article 6 EC environmental protection requirements must be integrated into the definition and implementation of all Community policies and activities. Therefore, the requirements of environmental protection must be integrated into the definition and implementation of State aid policy, in order to promote, in particular, sustainable development.

The Commission's current guidelines on State aid for environmental protection[111] were **16.114** adopted in 2001 and are valid until the end of 2007. For the purposes of the guidelines, 'environmental protection' means any action designed to remedy or prevent damage to our physical surroundings or natural resources, or to encourage the efficient use of these resources. The design and manufacture of machines or means of transport which can be operated using fewer natural resources are excluded from the scope of the guidelines, as is any action taken within production units with a view to improving safety or hygiene.

The Commission considers that if environmental requirements are to be taken into account **16.115** in the long term, the prices of goods or services should incorporate the external costs associated with the negative impact on the environment of their production and marketing. Moreover, the polluter who causes the pollution should bear the costs of measures to deal with this pollution (the 'polluter pays' principle).

---

[110] [2002] OJ C70/8. These rules have been integrated into the Regional Aid guidelines for the period 2007–2013: [2006] OJ C54/08, point 4.3.
[111] [2001] OJ C37/3.

16.116 Ensuring that prices reflect costs at all stages of the economic process is, in the Commission's view, the best way of making all parties aware of the cost of protecting the environment. If these costs were to be diminished by State aid, firms would not pass on their costs of environmental protection to consumers. Therefore, in the long term, some forms of State aid run counter to the objective of sustainable development.

16.117 *Investment aid* In general, the 'polluter pays' principle and the need for firms to incorporate in their prices the costs associated with the negative impact on the environment of their activities would appear to rule out the granting of State aid for investment. However, the Commission considers that such aid is justified in certain circumstances and within certain limits. Investments that may be eligible for aid in this context are investments in land which are strictly necessary in order to meet environmental objectives, investments in buildings, plant and equipment intended to reduce or eliminate pollution and nuisance, and investments to adapt production methods with a view to protecting the environment. The acquisition of operating licences or of know-how may also qualify provided that: (a) it is regarded as a depreciable asset; (b) it is purchased on market terms from a firm independent from the buyer; and (c) it remains in the firm for at least five years.

16.118 In *Ferriere Nord*,[112] the Commission considered that there was not enough evidence that a productive investment carried out by a firm was for the purpose of environmental protection. The Court upheld the Commission decision.[113]

16.119 In *Waste and Resources Action Programme-WRAP*,[114] the Commission concluded that the environmental guidelines did not apply to the scheme. It considered that the guidelines applied to investments that aim at reducing pollution caused by the aid beneficiary but not to situations where the whole economic activity of the beneficiary (waste recycling in the case at hand) is environmentally beneficial. Nevertheless, the Commission approved the scheme directly under Article 87(3)(c) of the Treaty. In reaching this conclusion, the Commission took into account the fact that waste recycling is a priority environmental objective of the Community; that the aid was necessary because certain waste products are hardly reprocessed at all; that the amounts of aid were relatively small and an open tender procedure was used to select the beneficiaries and to determine the amount of aid. In these circumstances, the Commission could conclude that the aid was proportionate to the objectives pursued and did not cause an undue restriction of competition.

16.120 In *UPM-Kymmene Shotton*,[115] an individual aid project notified under the WRAP scheme, the Commission concluded that the investment as a whole was not eligible for environmental aid since only part of it (the building of a sludge combustor) was meant to reduce Shotton's own pollution. The rest of the investment, although intended to help the UK to fulfil its obligations under the EU landfill and packaging Directive, was not considered eligible for investment aid for environmental protection purposes.

---

[112] Commission Decision (EC, ECSC) 2001/829[2001] JO L310/22.
[113] Case T-176/01 *Ferriere Nord* judgment of the CFI of 18 November 2004 (not yet reported).
[114] Commission Decision (EC) 2004/317 [2004] JO L102/59.
[115] Commission Decision (EC) 2003/814 [2003] OJ L314/26.

Different types of investment

Investment aid to help SMEs adapt to new Community standards   In order to address the **16.121**
special difficulties encountered by SMEs, the Commission considers that they can receive
aid for adapting to new compulsory Community standards for a period of three years from
their adoption.

Investment aid to firms improving on Community standards   The Commission considers that **16.122**
aid might be useful where it serves as an incentive to achieve levels of environmental protection that are higher than those required by Community standards.[116] Therefore, investment aid enabling firms to improve on the Community standards applicable may be
authorised within certain limits.

Investments in energy saving   These are investments enabling firms to reduce the amount of **16.123**
energy used in their production cycle.

Investments in the combined production of electric power and heat   This type of investment **16.124**
might be eligible for aid if it can be shown that: (a) the conversion efficiency is particularly
high; or (b) the investment will allow energy consumption to be reduced; or (c) the production process will be less damaging for the environment.

Investments to promote renewable sources of energy   Renewable energy sources include **16.125**
renewable non-fossil sources, like wind, solar ray energy, geothermal, wave, sea currents, tidal
and hydroelectric installations with a capacity below 10 MW, biomass,[117] and landfill gas.

Investments to relocate firms   The relocation of a firm to a more suitable area can receive **16.126**
investment aid provided that:

— the firm carries on an activity which creates major pollution in an urban area or in a
  Natura 2000 designated area;[118]
— the change of location is ordered by administrative or judicial decision on environmental protection grounds;
— the firm must comply with the strictest environmental standards applicable in the new
  region.

Eligible costs   Eligible costs must be confined strictly to the extra investment costs neces- **16.127**
sary to meet the environmental objectives.

Thus, where the cost of investment in environmental protection cannot be easily identified **16.128**
in the total cost, the Commission will apply objective and transparent methods of calculation, for example, taking into account the cost of a technically comparable investment that
does not however provide the same degree of environmental protection. This is a way of

---

[116] Mandatory Community standards setting the levels to be attained in environmental terms and the obligation under Community law to use the best available techniques (BAT) which do not entail excessive costs.
[117] Products from agriculture and forestry, vegetable waste from agriculture, forestry and the food production industry, and untreated wood waste and cork waste.
[118] This is a network of protected areas comprising sites designated under the Community Birds and
Habitats Directives (Council Directive (EEC) 92/43 of 21 May 1992 on the conservation of natural habitats
and of wild fauna and flora).

ensuring, as far as possible, that mere replacement investments are not aided under cover of environmental investments.

16.129 Eligible costs must in any case be calculated net of the benefits accruing from any increase in capacity, cost savings arising during the first five years of the life of the investment and additional ancillary production during that five-year period.

16.130 The additional investment costs are those needed to:

— attain the level of environmental protection required by new standards (where SMEs are adapting to standards that have entered into force);
— achieve a level of protection higher than the level required by Community standards, or, in the absence of Community standards, a higher level of protection than that which the firm would achieve in the absence of aid. The cost of investments needed to reach the level of protection required by the Community standards is not eligible for aid.

16.131 In *Nerefco*,[119] the Commission approved only part of an environmental investment aid measure proposed by the Dutch government to support investment in the construction of a process-integrated gas turbine.

16.132 In *UPM-Kymmene Shotton*,[120] the economic benefits over a five-year period of the construction of a sludge combustor, ie the value of electricity and steam produced by the combustor and the cost savings of spreading the sludge, were deducted from the eligible investment costs. The Commission then determined whether the eligible cost was confined to the extra investment costs necessary to meet the environmental objectives by comparing the planned investment with a smaller gas-fuelled sludge combustor.

16.133 For renewable energy, eligible investment costs are normally the extra costs borne by the firm compared with a conventional power plant with the same capacity in terms of effective production of energy. In 2002, the Commission approved a planned German scheme for aiding the construction of a solar power station.[121] The Commission accepted the method used by the German authorities to ensure that the eligible costs were limited to the additional costs incurred by a firm that had decided not to install a traditional energy production plant.

16.134 *Aid intensity*   The following thresholds apply to aid granted to investment for environmental purposes:

• Investments by SMEs to adapt to new Community standards: up to 15 per cent of eligible costs.
• Investments to improve on Community standards: the maximum aid intensity can rise from 30 per cent (large undertaking in a non-assisted region) to 50 per cent or the regional ceiling plus 10 percentage points (SME located in an Article 87(1)(a) region).
• Investments in energy savings and investments in the combined production of electric power and heat: the maximum aid intensity can rise from 40 per cent (large undertaking

---

[119] Commission Decision (EC) 2000/17 [2000] OJ L6/46.
[120] Commission Decision (EC) 2003/814 [2003] OJ L314/26.
[121] State aid N 345/2002, Commission Decision of 13 November 2002.

in a non-assisted region) to 60 per cent or the regional ceiling plus 10 percentage points (SME located in an Article 87(1)(a) region).

- Investments to promote renewable sources of energy: the maximum aid intensity can rise from 40 per cent (large undertaking in a non-assisted region) to 70 per cent or the regional ceiling plus 10 percentage points (SME located in an Article 87(1)(a) region) or exceptionally 100 per cent where it can be shown to be necessary. For instance, in 2003 the Commission considered that the need of an aid intensity of 75 per cent was proved for a scheme which included, *inter alia*, support for investment in photovoltaic plants.[122]

Rehabilitation of polluted industrial sites   A firm is eligible for State aid towards the costs **16.135** of rehabilitation of polluted industrial sites provided that:

— the person responsible for the pollution is not identified or cannot be made to bear the cost;
— the aid does not exceed the actual expenditure incurred by the firm;
— the intensity of the aid does not exceed 115 per cent of the cost of the work less the increase in the value of the land.

On 11 June 2003, the Commission adopted a decision on a British aid measure aimed at **16.136** recovering contaminated land, brownfield land, and derelict land.[123] The British measure intends to bring this land back into productive use by addressing detrimental effects of previous usage and making it reusable, thereby reducing pressure on greenfield land and limiting urban sprawl. The Commission approved the scheme after assessing: (a) under the environmental guidelines, the measures aimed at the rehabilitation of contaminated polluted industrial sites; and (b) directly under Article 87(3)(c), the measures aimed at recovering land on which there are derelict buildings, structures, or works.

Operating aid   The guidelines contain a detailed set of criteria used by the Commission **16.137** when assessing the following types of operating aid:

— To promote waste management and energy saving: where firms temporarily lose competitiveness at international level because national standards are introduced which are more stringent than the applicable Community rules or in the absence of Community rules, they can receive operating aid provided that the aid is limited to five years.
— Reductions or exemptions from taxes levied for reasons of environmental protection: temporary exemptions are justified by the absence of harmonisation at European level or by the temporary risks of a loss of international competitiveness. Different criteria apply depending on whether the tax is a Community one or a national one.
— Production of renewable energy and combined production of electric power and heat: aid is justified in order to cover the difference between the cost of producing energy from renewable energy sources and the market price of that energy. The form of the aid may vary depending on the kind of energy involved and the support mechanism worked out by the Member State. In 2002, the Commission adopted three decisions concerning

---

[122] State aid C 60/2002 (ex N 747/2001) Tuscany (Italy).
[123] State aid N 385/2002 UK, [2003] OJ C195/16.

excise duty rates on biofuels in the UK,[124] in Italy,[125] and in France.[126] The Commission concluded in all three cases that overcompensation was ruled out and aid was restricted to covering the difference in production cost from a renewable energy source in relation to the market price of energy.

16.138 *Large individual aid grants*   Even if they are covered by a scheme approved by the Commission, investment projects where the costs eligible for environmental protection exceed EUR 25 million and where the aid exceeds EUR 5 million, are subject to prior individual notification to the Commission.

16.139 **(iii) Aid for Research and Development**   According to Article 163(1) of the EC Treaty, the Community shall pursue the objective of strengthening the scientific and technological bases of Community industry, encouraging it to become more competitive at international level. Competition policy can contribute to the pursuit of this objective.

16.140   The criteria currently used by the Commission for the assessment of State aid for R&D are those in force since 1996.[127]

16.141 *Stage of R&D*   In the Commission's view, the closer the R&D is to the market, the more significant the distorting effect of the State aid may be. In order to determine the proximity to the market of the R&D receiving the aid, the Commission has established a distinction in Annex 1 of the Framework between:

— fundamental research;[128]
— industrial research;[129] and
— pre-competitive development activity.[130]

The differentiation between the different stages above is essential in order to determine the maximum aid intensity of any given project.

16.142   Innovation does not qualify as a separate category of R&D and, therefore, is not eligible as such for R&D aid.

---

[124] State aid N 804/2001, [2002] OJ C238/13.

[125] State aid N 461/2001, [2002] OJ C146/7.

[126] State aid C 64/2000, [2003] OJ L94/1.

[127] Community Framework for State aid for Research and Development [1996] OJ C45/5 as amended in [1998] OJ C48/2 and extended in [2001] OJ C78/24 and in [2002] OJ C111/3. This framework will be replaced as of 1 January 2007 by a new framework adopted on 22 November 2006 [2006] OJ C323/1.

[128] An activity designed to broaden scientific and technical knowledge not linked to industrial or commercial objectives.

[129] Planned research or critical investigation aimed at the acquisition of new knowledge, the objective being that such knowledge may be useful in developing new products, processes or services or in bringing about a significant improvement in existing products, processes, or services.

[130] The shaping of the results of industrial research into a plan, arrangement, or design for new, altered, or improved products, processes, or services whether they are intended to be sold or used, including the creation of an initial prototype which could not be used commercially. This may also include the conceptual formulation and design of other products, processes, or services and initial demonstration projects or pilot projects, provided that such projects cannot be converted or used for industrial applications or commercial exploitation. It does not include the routine or periodic changes made to products, production lines, manufacturing processes, existing services, and other operations in progress, even if such changes may represent improvements.

Incentive effect of R&D aid   State aid for R&D should serve as an incentive for firms to **16.143** undertake R&D activities in addition to their normal day-to-day operations or to encourage firms not carrying out R&D to undertake such activities. Except in the case of SMEs, where the incentive effect is presumed, Member States must demonstrate that the aid is necessary as an incentive, and that it is on no account operational aid. Some elements the Commission will consider when assessing the incentive effect of the aid are:

— quantifiable factors: changes in R&D spending, changes in the number of people
    assigned to R&D activities, changes in R&D spending as a proportion of total turnover;
— market failures;
— additional costs connected with cross-border co-operation;
— contribution of the aid towards expanding the scope of research or speeding it up.

The Commission will scrutinise closely the incentive effect in the case of large companies carrying out individual close-to-the-market projects and all cases in which a significant proportion of the R&D expenditure has already been made prior to the aid application. In *BMW Steyr*,[131] the Commission considered that the incentive effect of the aid had not been proved as far as certain R&D projects were concerned. The Commission concluded they would have been undertaken anyway by the company in the absence of aid in order to retain its competitiveness. Aid for those projects was therefore considered incompatible with the common market.

Eligible costs   According to Annex II of the Framework eligible costs for the purpose of **16.144** calculating the aid intensity include the following:

— personnel costs (researchers, technicians, and other supporting staff used solely on the
    research activity);
— costs of instruments, equipment, and land and premises used solely and on a continu-
    ous basis (except where transferred commercially) for the research activity;
— cost of consultancy and equivalent services used exclusively for the research activity,
    including research, technical knowledge, and patents, etc bought from outside sources;
— additional overheads incurred directly as a result of the research activity;
— other operating expenses (eg costs of materials, supplies, and similar products) incurred
    directly as a result of the research activity.

Aid intensities   The basic aid intensities are 50 per cent for industrial research and **16.145** 25 per cent for pre-competitive development activities. In addition to these basic rates, the following bonuses are possible, but the aid intensity must not in any case exceed 75 per cent for industrial research and 50 per cent for pre-competitive development:

(a) 10 percentage points if the beneficiary is an SME;
(b) 5–10 percentage points if the project is carried out in an assisted region;
(c) 15–25 percentage points if the project is in accordance with the objectives of a specific
    programme undertaken as part of the Community's framework programme;

---

131 State aid C 63/2002, [2003] OJ L229/24.

(d) 10 percentage points if it is not in accordance with the objectives of a specific programme undertaken as part of the Community's framework programme but either the project involves effective intra-Community cross-border co-operation between two independent partners or effective co-operation between firms and public research bodies or the project's results are widely disseminated and published.

Technical feasibility studies may qualify for aid amounting to 75 per cent of study costs if they are preparatory to industrial research or to 50 per cent if they are preparatory to pre-competitive development.

16.146 Whatever the size of the firm or the location, R&D projects of common European interest within the meaning of Article 87(3)(d) can benefit from the maximum aid permitted for industrial research (75 per cent) or for pre-competitive development (75 per cent) (see below).

16.147 *Large individual aid grants* Any individual research project costing more than EUR 25 million and for which the proposed aid exceeds EUR 5 million is subject to prior notification even if it falls within the scope of authorised R&D schemes.

(iv) Aid for Rescuing and Restructuring Firms in Difficulty

16.148 *Introduction* Aid for rescue and restructuring operations has given rise to some of the most controversial State aid cases. This type of aid interferes with the normal functioning of the competition process by allowing inefficient firms to remain active in the market. These firms are normally very large companies which have many thousand employees.

16.149 The distortion through rescue and restructuring aid has a particularly negative impact on competition because it tends to cover the operating expenses of companies and sometimes allows excess capacity to remain in the market. Consumers may benefit in the short term from a better supply of goods and services. However, in the long term it harms the most efficient producers and, thus the consumer, who will have to pay for the inefficiencies.

16.150 Moreover, rescue and restructuring aid to companies in one Member State (or region) frequently harms companies in other Member States. It thus represents an 'export' of the structural economic problem to another country. It can lead to the closure of mainly healthy businesses in other regions because they can no longer compete with the subsidised products or services. The ultimate consequence is the survival of the incompetent—but aided—firm. That runs contrary to any European competitiveness initiative and the selection process of market forces.

16.151 In light of this, the Commission's policy has been to allow rescue and restructuring aid only in exceptional circumstances as a sort of *ultima ratio*.

16.152 Legitimate purposes for granting rescue and restructuring aid can be found in economic, social, or regional policy considerations, and above all, in the economically beneficial role of small and medium-sized enterprises (SMEs). These are a natural counterweight to the market power of large companies. They are often more flexible and provide jobs in disadvantaged regions and under difficult economic and trading conditions.

16.153 Keeping large companies alive through rescue and restructuring aid may, nevertheless, be justified on competition grounds. If a large competitor disappears from the market, the other players will take over its market share and increase their market power, potentially resulting in a monopoly or tight oligopoly. Thus the granting of rescue and restructuring aid to a large company can sometimes help to avoid the concentration of market power with all its negative effects on competition.

Keeping a large market player afloat may also help to avoid a so-called domino effect. In **16.154** some regions the downfall of the dominant regional industrial player or bank might entail the bankruptcy of many smaller—in principle healthy—companies which depended on it. If the large company falls, all the other connected companies would also collapse in a domino effect. The breakdown of a large regional player can lead to an economic crisis in that region ('desertification').[132]

The need to guarantee economically important services on a countrywide basis might also **16.155** justify rescue and restructuring aid. Utilities, such as energy, telecom, rail and air transport, are of great importance for the whole national economy. In the absence of credible competitors, ready to take over their business, the State often has no choice but to support the ailing (former) monopolist.[133]

The First Report on Competition Policy of 1971 emphasised the exceptional character **16.156** of aid given for company reorganisation. This has since been the Commission's guiding principle.

As the European courts have acknowledged, the Commission may provide guidance for the **16.157** exercise of its powers of assessment by adopting acts such as the guidelines on undertakings in difficulty in so far as they contain indications as to the direction to be followed by the Commission and do not depart from Treaty rules.[134] The Commission issued its first Guidelines in 1994.[135] In 1997, amendments included specific rules for restructuring aid in the agriculture sector.[136] The 1999 revision of the Guidelines[137] underlined the principles of rescue and restructuring aid having exceptional character and of limited aid to companies in difficulty. Moreover, the rescue and the restructuring phase of an aid operation were strictly separated. New Guidelines came into force in October 2004 (hereinafter 'the 2004 Guidelines'). These will remain in place in principle until 2009. The 2004 Guidelines have been built on previous experience and have clarified some important issues.

Common provisions for rescue and restructuring aid alike   The 2004 Guidelines contain **16.158** certain common provisions for rescue and restructuring aid which concern the eligibility of the beneficiary, the scope of the Guidelines, the 'one time—last time principle' and the strengthening of state aid enforcement (recovery) policy.

Eligible firms   Only a 'firm in difficulty' can be eligible for rescue and/or restructuring aid **16.159** (points 9–11). A company generally speaking is in difficulties if it is unable to stem losses

---

132 Commission press release IP/05/447 of 19 April 2005, *MG Rover: Danuta Hübner offers support for the West Midlands region.*

133 cf State Aid Scoreboard, 9th edition of Spring 2005, published 20 April 2005, COM (2005) 147 final, pp 13, 17, 19.

134 Case T-35/99 *Keller v Commission* [2002] ECR II-261, para 77.

135 [1994] OJ C368/12.

136 [1997] OJ C283/2.

137 [1999] OJ C288/2.

or to continue business without state intervention.[138] The Guidelines give specific examples of this situation.

16.160   A limited liability company is in 'difficulty' when it has lost half of its capital and more than 25 per cent of it over the last twelve months (point 10 a/b). A firm is in difficulty in any case if it meets the conditions for bankruptcy under national law (point 10 c). Since bankruptcy law is national law which is not harmonised substantively, it means at least theoretically that a company may be in difficulty under the insolvency law of one Member State but not another. However, this situation will only rarely arise in practice. If a company fulfils the conditions for bankruptcy in one Member State it will most certainly also be in difficulty under the European part of the definition.

16.161   Other criteria showing 'difficulty' for a firm include combinations of signs of economic distress, eg increasing losses, diminishing turnover, excess capacity, declining cash flow, mounting debt, etc (point 11).

16.162   Newly created firms are not eligible for these types of aid. Such firms are firms that were set up after the liquidation of a previous firm or have merely taken over the previous company's assets. A firm is 'new' for three years 'from start of operations in the relevant field of activity' (point 12).

16.163   Firms that form part of a larger group are not eligible either, unless they can show that the difficulties are their own and not the result of an arbitrary allocation of costs within the group. The difficulties must be too serious to be solved by the group itself (point 13).

16.164   *Scope*   The Guidelines apply to all sectors of the economy. However, in the coal and steel sector rescue and restructuring aid is strictly prohibited.[139] Specific rules exist for the aviation sector, agriculture, and fisheries (point 18).

16.165   *The 'one time, last time' principle*   Rescue and restructuring aid should be given to a specific undertaking only once every ten years. Unless certain special circumstances are met (cf point 73), the Commission will not approve additional aid. This principle applies to the beneficiary firm understood as the continuing entity doing business on a specific market. It is not affected by changes in ownership of the company. This is true for a group of companies and for any company belonging to it. The one time, last time requirement does not apply in the case of the purchase of assets of the beneficiary firm at market prices.

16.166   *Recovery against recipients of previous unlawful aid*   The guidelines restrict new rescue or restructuring aid for firms that have not repaid previous unlawful aid as ordered by the Commission. The Guidelines thus underline the so-called *Deggendorf* rule[140] and subsequent practice of the Commission (point 23). However, the wording leaves some flexibility short of an outright prohibition, in so far as 'the assessment of any rescue and restructuring aid to be granted to the same undertaking shall take into account, first, the cumulative

---

[138]   A recent case in point is MG Rover. 'The ghost of industry past'; *The Times*, 19 April 2005, 'Commission must approve Rover loan' 11 April 2005, *EU Observer*.
[139]   [2004] OJ C244/4.
[140]   Case C-355/95 P *Textilwerke Deggendorf v Commission* [1997] ECR I-2549.

effect of the old aid and of the new aid and, secondly, the fact that the old aid has not been repaid'. In any case, the refusal of new aid can ultimately lead to the bankruptcy of the firm concerned.[141]

Rescue aid　This is temporary and reversible assistance to keep an ailing firm afloat for the time needed to work out a restructuring plan (point 15). It can be granted in case of serious social difficulties and must have no adverse spill-over effects (point 25 b).　**16.167**

Urgent structural measures, eg closure of company branches or loss-making business activities can be taken during the rescue phase.　**16.168**

The aid must be reversible. That means that it is limited to short-term liquidity support, in the form of loans or guarantees (point 25 a). Rescue aid can still be granted only in the form of reimbursable loans, for example as a six-month repayable loan guarantee at normal interest rates until the restructuring plan is in force (following notification and authorisation by the Commission). Irreversible capital injections by public authorities or the participation of the State into the equity capital of the beneficiary remain prohibited (point 15).　**16.169**

The rescue measure must be temporary, ie the loan must be repaid and the guarantee must come to an end within a period of not more than six months after the disbursement of the first instalment to the beneficiary. This six-month period is considered to be the time needed to devise the restructuring plan (point 25 c). At the end of this rescue period, the aid must be reimbursed. The restructuring plan must follow within the six months (point 25 c). Extension is possible only until the approval of a restructuring plan which was delivered within the initial six-month period (point 26).[142]　**16.170**

The rescue aid must be the minimum amount needed to keep the business going (point 25 d). This minimum is defined by the liquidity needs of the company and must be proved by the Member State concerned.　**16.171**

The 2004 Guidelines introduced a simplified—faster—procedure for the approval of some form of rescue aid (point 30). The Commission will render its decision under the simplified procedure within one month, if the 'strict eligibility criteria' of point 10 are fulfilled and the amount of the aid does not exceed the result of a standard formula (calculated on the basis of operating cash flow, Annex 1 of the New Guidelines) and, in any event, EUR 10 million.　**16.172**

Due to the urgency of injecting fresh cash into a company in difficulty, rescue aid is often granted in breach of the standstill obligation of Article 88(3) EC. In this case, the competitors can ask a national court for remedies. However, if the rescue aid was duly notified with the Commission, the court will most certainly await the decision of the Commission in order to avoid possible contradictions.　**16.173**

Restructuring aid　The provisions on restructuring aid constitute the core and the largest part of the Guidelines (points 31–71). The provisions on rescue aid must be interpreted in the light of the rules on restructuring aid.　**16.174**

---

[141] Case C-10/2004, Commission Decision of 1 December 2004 favouring restructuring aid to BULL.
[142] NN-101/2002, Commission Decision of 27 November 2002 favouring aid to British Energy plc.

16.175 *Form of aid* Restructuring aid can adopt any form, eg loans, capital injection, tax relief, or equity participation by the State. There is a basic distinction (point 17) between, on the one hand, financial restructuring, including capital injections, debt reduction and, on the other hand, physical restructuring, such as cost reductions, abandonment of certain production lines, taking up new business lines and structures, improvement of management, and cost control.

16.176 After the establishment of the restructuring plan and after the plan is put into effect ('is being implemented') all further aid is considered to be restructuring aid (point 16).

16.177 *Restoration of long-term viability* The restoration of long-term viability of the firm in difficulty is the final goal of the restructuring aid. The Commission will approve the aid only if there is a high probability that it will succeed in bringing the company back into profit.

16.178 To evaluate the likelihood of achieving this goal, it is crucial to have a feasible, coherent, and far-reaching restructuring plan (point 17). The plan is compiled by the Member State authorities and their financial and legal advisers with the assistance of the ailing company. In practice, it is generally the company and its advisers who draft the plan for acceptance by the State authorities.

16.179 The plan must include a market survey (point 35) and show that after completion of the restructuring phase the beneficiary can compete in the market-place on its own merits (point 37). The plan will normally include significant financial information about the ailing firm, accounts, and forecasts.

16.180 The plan must show how the company will regain its viability within a reasonable time-frame. It must describe the reasons for the difficulties and the means of achieving future business success. The plan must detail the beneficiary's ability to cover all costs, charges, and depreciation on return on capital, to cease the loss-making activities, and to achieve the turnaround of the business.

16.181 The Commission will evaluate the plan from several angles. In social terms, the Commission will look at the number of jobs maintained or newly created. From a commercial point of view the chances of success and profitability must be evaluated. Last but not least, competition considerations in the sense of antitrust provisions are taken into consideration. The main question is whether the plan will require the minimum amount of aid needed to ensure return to viability and cause the smallest possible distortion of competition (point 31).

16.182 Under the 2004 Guidelines, the Commission will no longer assess the viability of restructuring plans for SMEs. This allows the Commission to concentrate resources on cases that pose a genuine threat to competition, ie large companies with significant market shares.

16.183 *Avoidance of undue distortions of competition* The positive effects of the restructuring must outweigh the negative effects (point 38). The avoidance of undue distortions of competition must be secured by means of compensatory measures.

16.184 Compensatory measures can take many different forms, for example, the divestiture of assets or a reduction in capacity or market presence which can rise to 100 per cent in markets with long-term structural overcapacity (points 39 and 42). The finding of structural overcapacity in a given market can prove problematic.

Antitrust considerations, such as avoiding increasing the market power of monopolists or the tightening of oligopolies, also play an important role in the Commission's assessment (point 39). Reductions in market presence are not necessarily in the interest of the consumers but rather of competitors. A consumer-oriented approach may favour the opening of markets over capacity reductions. Thus compensatory measures could also be reductions of entry barriers to the market. **16.185**

The compensatory measures must be proportionate to the distortive effects of the intended aid. They must be assessed on a case-by-case basis taking into account the size and influence of the beneficiary on its markets. Measures which would have been taken anyway are not deemed compensatory (point 40). The question of what was already foreseen and which measure is an additional compensation is debated in most cases. **16.186**

This requirement does not apply to small enterprises (points 41 and 57) since their market share is considered to be negligible and they present no danger to competition or of increased market power. **16.187**

Aid must be limited to the minimum needed The amount and intensity of aid must be limited to the strict minimum of the restructuring costs necessary to enable restructuring to be undertaken (point 43). The 2004 Guidelines further clarify that the beneficiary should make a real contribution towards the cost of its restructuring. Future expected profits such as cash flow are not considered to be real contribution.[143] The contribution must itself be free of aid. **16.188**

A significant proportion of the restructuring costs must be borne by private investors or the beneficiary. This shows that the market believes in the long-term viability of the enterprise. The private contribution minimises the level of aid and hence the distortion of competition. It demonstrates the feasibility of achieving viability within a reasonable time because otherwise no reasonable private investor would fund the restructuring. **16.189**

The Guidelines for the first time set thresholds for the contribution as a percentage of the overall restructuring costs, taking into account the size of the beneficiary. For large undertakings the threshold of the contribution should be around 50 per cent of the overall restructuring cost. For medium-sized undertakings whose activities do not distort competition within the Union in the same way, the threshold is fixed at 40 per cent. Small companies need only bear around 25 per cent of their restructuring cost. However (point 44), 'In exceptional circumstances and in cases of particular hardship which must be demonstrated by the Member State, the Commission may accept a lower real own contribution'. **16.190**

Under no circumstances should the beneficiary receive by way of restructuring aid surplus cash it could use for aggressive marketing. The beneficiary should obtain just enough money **16.191**

---

[143] Joined Cases C–328/99 and 399/00 *Italian Republic and SIM 2 Multimedia SpA v Commission (Seleco)* [2003] ECR I–4035.

to be able to survive and to continue to function on the market. It is not the goal of the aid to push competitors out of the market.

16.192   *Other conditions and special provisions on restructuring aid*   The Commission may add any conditions it considers necessary to achieve the success of the restructuring. This can include, for example, an obligation upon Member States to open up certain markets or to refrain from giving any other type of aid during the restructuring period (point 46). The Commission can request the payment of the aid in instalments and subject it to the successful completion of specifically identified phases of the restructuring plan (point 48).

16.193   The full implementation of the restructuring plan and observance of all conditions must be guaranteed by the Member State (point 47). The failure to implement the plan and all its conditions constitutes misuse of aid and entitles the Commission to take judicial action against the Member State under Article 88(2) EC.

16.194   Regular reporting (points 49–51) enables the Commission to monitor the progress of the restructuring effort and the implementation of the conditions. The first report is usually due after six months. The later reports are due annually. They must contain all information necessary for the Commission to evaluate the state of the restructuring. The simplified reporting requirements for SMEs comprise only the balance sheet and the profit and loss account.

16.195   Amendments to the restructuring plan and in the amount of aid can be approved by the Commission under certain conditions (points 52–54). Restructuring aid in assisted areas (points 55–56) must follow the same criteria as those listed in points 32–54. However, the conditions applied to compensatory measures and the beneficiary's own contribution may be less stringent.

16.196   The conditions for granting restructuring aid for SMEs (points 57–59) are less strict as far as compensatory measures and reporting are concerned. The restructuring plan need not be approved by the Commission. Only the Member State assesses the restructuring plan of the SME.

16.197   Social measures (points 60–67) which the Member State takes to soften the impact of reductions in the workforce are not State aid if they are applied generally without sectoral limitations. Aid is involved if the measures favour particular industries or cover the normal costs of business. Where they constitute State aid within the meaning of Article 87, the Commission adopts a favourable view towards aid provided in connection with a particular restructuring case for training, counselling, assistance with relocation and professional training, and assistance for employees wishing to start new businesses.

16.198   Information requirements guarantee that large and medium-sized companies cannot accumulate aid and thus circumvent the control provisions under these Guidelines (points 68–71).

16.199   *Special provisions for rescue and restructuring aid schemes*   Rescue and restructuring aid schemes are possible only for SMEs (points 78–86). Basically the same conditions apply as for the approval of individual rescue or restructuring aid. However, approved aid schemes for rescue and restructuring of SMEs do not apply in markets with structural over capacity.

The schemes must specify the maximum amount of aid which can be awarded to any single firm. This cannot be more than EUR 10 million for any one firm. The annual reports on the restructuring must include a list of all beneficiaries and detailed information about each of them.

The rules for rescue and restructuring aid in agricultural markets (points 87–98) have been **16.200** considerably simplified. For the processing and marketing of agricultural (Annex I) products, the normal rules will apply. A modification is the application of the one time, last time principle, which will only apply for a period of five years instead of ten (point 97). The rules are stricter for compensatory measures. Specific targets for production capacity reduction are given (point 91). Structural excess capacity will be defined by the Commission on a case-by-case basis (point 88).

The Commission will propose appropriate measures with regard to existing aid schemes. **16.201** Member States must bring their existing aid schemes into line with these Guidelines within six months (points 99–101).

Conclusions   One of the main problems in analysing rescue and restructuring aid is the **16.202** difficulty of assessing the restructuring plan. The most difficult part is not the analysis of the mistakes of the past which led to the financial difficulty but the prognosis for the future. The evaluation of often voluminous plans takes a lot of time and economic knowledge. It requires market expertise and management experience which the Commission cannot always provide from its own ranks. If it seeks outside expertise, this can be costly and time-consuming.

An ideal solution has not yet been found. As acknowledged by the European courts, the **16.203** Commission enjoys a wide margin of discretion to allow aid by way of derogation from the general prohibition, since the problems raised make it necessary to examine and appraise complex economic facts and conditions. Judicial review is therefore limited to checking that the rules on procedure and the reasons have been complied with, that the facts are materially accurate, and that there has been no manifest error of assessment and no misuse of powers. It is not for the Court, therefore, to substitute its economic assessment for that of the Commission.[144]

(5) Compatibility Declared by the Council: Article 88(2)

Article 88(2) provides that: 'On application by a Member State, the Council may, acting **16.204** unanimously, decide that aid which that State is granting or intends to grant shall be considered to be compatible with the common market, in derogation from the provisions of Article 87 or from the regulations provided for in Article 89, if such a decision is justified by exceptional circumstances.'

From a procedural point of view, this provision requires an application by a Member **16.205** State in order to prevent the Commission from initiating proceedings against the aid or

---

[144] Case T-149/95 *Ducros v Commission* [1997] ECR II-2031, paras 61–63; Case T-35/99 *Keller v Commission* [2002] ECR II-261, para 77.

suspending a procedure that it might already have initiated. If after three months from the date of application the Council has not made its position known, the Commission is free to initiate or to close proceedings.

16.206 As to the question of the substance, the Council is required only to justify the existence of exceptional circumstances. The Court has acknowledged that the Council has a wide margin of discretion on this point.[145]

16.207 Nevertheless, the Council cannot declare the compatibility of an aid measure already declared incompatible by the Commission or bypass the effects of such a decision adopted by the Commission. As the Court has ruled:

> where a decision finding an aid incompatible with the common market has been adopted by the Commission, the Council cannot paralyse the effectiveness of that decision by itself declaring the aid compatible with the common market on the basis of the third subparagraph of Article 88(2). Nor, therefore, can the Council thwart the effectiveness of such a decision by declaring compatible with the common market, in accordance with that provision, an aid designed to compensate the beneficiaries of the unlawful aid declared incompatible with the common market for the repayments they are required to make pursuant to that decision.[146]

This case concerned aid intended specifically for the beneficiaries of an award of aid previously declared incompatible by the Commission and the amount provided aimed at allowing them to meet the repayments which they were required to make pursuant to two Commission decisions.

16.208 It should be noted that four months after the adoption of the above decision, the Council adopted under the same provision three decisions on aid by the Netherlands, Italy, and France in favour of road transport undertakings. In this instance, however, the three Member States in question had sought from the Council an acknowledgement that exceptional circumstances prevailed before the Commission adopted a decision of incompatibility. The Commission did not institute proceedings against those decisions before the Court.

(6) Sectoral Aid

16.209 Owing to the specific nature of competition conditions prevailing in certain sectors, the Commission has adopted guidelines for the assessment of the compatibility with the common market of aid granted to undertakings in those sectors.

16.210 The sectors currently covered by these specific rules are as follows:

(a) *Shipbuilding*: Framework on State aid to shipbuilding;[147]
(b) *Steel*: Point 27 of the Multisectoral Framework on regional aid for large investment projects;[148] Communication from the Commission on rescue and restructuring aid and closure aid to the steel sector;[149]

---

[145] Case C-122/94 *Commission v Council* [1996] ECR I-881.
[146] Case C-110/02 *Commission v Council*, judgment of the Court of 29 June 2004 (not yet reported), paras 44 and 45.
[147] [2003] OJ C317/11.
[148] [2002] OJ C70/8.
[149] [2002] OJ C70/21.

(c) *Coal*: Council Regulation (EC) 1407/2002;[150]

(d) *Air transport*: Council Regulation (EC) 659/1999 of 22 March 1999;[151]

(e) *Sea transport*: Community guidelines on State aid to maritime transport;[152]

(f) *Transport by rail, road, and inland waterway*: Council Regulation (EEC) 1107/70[153] as completed by Council Regulation (EEC) 1658/82;[154]

(g) *Agriculture*: Community guidelines for state aid in the agriculture sector,[155] Commission Regulation (EC) 1/2004;[156]

(h) *Fisheries*: Guidelines for the examination of State aid to fisheries and aquaculture;[157]

(i) *Electricity*: Stranded costs.[158]

(7) Services of General Economic Interest

(a) Introduction: Definition and Legal Basis

Services of general economic interest (SGEI) are general interest services subject to specific public service obligations imposed by Member States.[159] Examples of SGEI are to be found in public utility networks (eg energy, transport, telecommunications), social services (eg services for elderly people, nursing homes, hospitals, social housing), certain bank services (eg basic current bank account), radio and television broadcasting, health services, cultural services, water, sewage, removal and treatment of waste, and other, mainly locally produced services. **16.211**

A related and partly overlapping term is 'universal services'. This term is used mostly in the context of liberalisation of network services. Universal services should ensure the continued accessibility and quality of established services for all users and consumers during the passage from State monopoly to market competition. For example, in the area of telecommunications it means that a minimum set of services must be maintained at a defined level of quality, accessible to all users at an affordable price. The same is true for postal services and energy markets. The public service must be provided efficiently at a reasonable price, and be sustainable and socially just. **16.212**

SGEI are traditionally and still often provided through 'Public Service'. This term is ambiguous, since it can mean the public body which provides the services or the service as such. Liberalisation can be understood as the opening of the provision of SGEI to competition. **16.213**

According to economic theory, SGEI exist to correct market failures. The under-provision by the market of certain services regarded as essential for the functioning of the Community, makes state intervention necessary. These market failures can be found especially in 'social' **16.214**

---

[150] [2002] OJ L205/1.
[151] [1999] OJ L083/1.
[152] [1997] OJ C205/5.
[153] [1970] OJ L130/1.
[154] [1982] OJ L184/1.
[155] [2006] OJ C319/1.
[156] [2004] OJ L1/1.
[157] [2004] OJ C229/3.
[158] <http://europa.eu.int/comm/competition/state_aid/legislation/stranded_costs/en.pdf>.
[159] <http://europa.eu.int/comm/competition/state_aid/others/1759_sieg_en.pdf>.

services areas, where the market does not provide sufficient (profit) incentive for entrepreneurs to open and conduct profitable business. The reason is sometimes to be found in legislation which renders business in such sectors unprofitable from the outset. Through the use of SGEI the Member States correct the results of failed or insufficient market action. SGEI are considered to be one of the pillars of the European model of a market economy with strong social dimension as opposed to an unrestrained free market system.

16.215 SGEI cover both market and non-market services. State aid control deals in principle only with services of general interest where an economic activity is involved. Indeed, when there is no economic activity, the competition rules are not applicable. Clear criteria are needed to make this distinction.

16.216 An activity is 'economic' if it involves the offer of goods or services in a given market. Examples of non-economic activities are basic school teaching, the functioning of compulsory basic social security schemes which implement the principle of pure solidarity in the sense that there is no equivalence between contributions and benefits, or specific activities involving the exercise of power by the public authority, such as the justice system or internal and external security.

16.217 Article 16 EC provides a legal basis to the concept of SGEI. It stresses the important role of these services by referring to 'the place occupied by services of general economic interest in the shared values of the union as well as their role in promoting social and territorial cohesion'.

16.218 The article goes on to state that 'the Community and the Member States, each within their respective powers and within the scope of application of this Treaty, shall take care that such services operate on the basis of principles and conditions which enable them to fulfil their missions'.

16.219 In Article II 36 of the Draft Constitution, the necessity of access to SGEI is further emphasised: 'The Union recognises and respects access to services of general economic interest as provided for in national laws and practices, in accordance with the Constitution, in order to promote the social and territorial cohesion of the Union.'

16.220 In the absence of specific Community legislation, all Member States have considerable freedom to define the nature and the extent of 'their SGEI' or 'public services', ie the services that they wish to provide according to their own domestic political choices.

16.221 Due to the relationship between SGEI and market-oriented services, a delicate balance may need to be struck between play of market forces and state intervention. The key terms in this context are 'Common Market', 'Subsidiarity', and 'Distortion of Competition'. The principle of subsidiarity places the definition of SGEI within the ambit of the Member State. The common market obligation requires the control and avoidance of 'Distortions of Competition'.

16.222 The control of State aid has an important role to play in reconciling apparently diverging interests in this respect, since a number of these economic services cannot be provided without the continued financial support of the Member State. Permanent financial support of the state intended to deal with all or some of the specific costs resulting from the public service obligations can interfere with the common market obligation.

Article 86(2) EC therefore provides that 'Undertakings entrusted with the operation of **16.223**
services of general economic interest . . . shall be subject to the rules contained in this Treaty,
in particular to the rules on competition, in so far as the application of such rules does not
obstruct the performance, in law or in fact, of the particular tasks assigned to them'. An
important provision is added: 'The development of trade must not be affected to such an
extent as would be contrary to the interests of the Community.'

(b) Role of the Commission: Safeguard against Distortions of Competition

The Member States and the Commission have different roles in the definition and control **16.224**
of SGEI. The Member States define the character of the services within their national legal
framework. The EU State aid rules control unjustified distortions of competition which
can come about as a result of over-compensation for or cross-subsidisation of the provision
of SGEIs.

Competition problems in this area can take various forms: **16.225**

(a) First, activities that in practice do not fall within the definition of an SGEI are classified
as SGEI. This can be either because companies performing within a competitive framework already provide the services in a satisfactory way, or because the activities concerned
are not really in the general interest. Such practices, in particular in recently liberalised
sectors of the economy (eg electricity), can have negative effects on companies that do not
provide the supposed public service and can amount to cross-subsidisation.[160] These
practices are therefore not justified by the need to ensure the effectiveness of the SGEI.

(b) Secondly, considerable difficulties also arise if the advantages granted to companies
providing the public services go beyond what is necessary for the operation of the
service in question, ie are over-compensated. The clear risk is that the advantages conferred on the companies are used to foster economic activities over and above the provision of the public service obligation and therefore distort competition in that specific
market. If the company providing the public service is also involved in commercial
activity, over-compensation may also give rise to undesirable and even illicit cross-
subsidisation.

(c) Before 'Altmark': Compensation and State Aid Approach

Before the *Altmark* judgment there were two main approaches to the general approach to **16.226**
the control of SGEI:[161] the 'compensation or non-aid approach' and the 'State aid approach'.
Even though it may seem that in the end all approaches come to the same final result the
dichotomy has important legal consequences. The approach chosen depends on the existence or non-existence of State aid which must be notified under Article 88(3) EC. The
application of the standstill clause and thus the possibility for courts in the Member States
to intervene (and even to order suspension injunctions) will determine which approach is
taken.

---

[160] From an antitrust point of view they create new barriers to entry into the market.
[161] Case C-280/00 *Altmark* [2003] ECR I-7747.

16.227   The starting point for the *State aid approach* is that State funding for the financing of undertakings providing SGEI under a public service obligation falls under Article 87(1) EC and thus constitutes State aid. This is true, even if there is no over-compensation. However, such aid can be compatible with the common market under Article 86(2) EC. This interpretation gives rise to the notification and standstill obligation of Article 88(3) EC and gives the Commission the power to control that aid. Violations of these provisions fall within the jurisdiction of the national judges in the Member States.

16.228   Under the *non-aid approach or compensation approach* the compensation of costs for the provision of an SGEI (discharge of a public service obligation) does not give an advantage to the entity concerned. It constitutes a payment for the value of the services rendered, provided that there is no over-compensation going beyond costs. Since the compensation does not constitute State aid, there is no obligation to notify under Article 88 (3)—and no standstill obligation.

16.229   The Commission held for a long time that financial support granted by the Member States to companies charged with the provision of SGEI did not constitute State aid within the meaning of Article 87(1) EC, when this support only compensated the SGEI providers for the additional costs incurred for providing the public service. This line was, for example, taken in the *FFSA* case.[162] The French Post Office had received a tax exemption and the Commission concluded that the derogation of Article 86(2) EC applied. The financial advantage did not exceed the amount necessary to guarantee the discharge of the public service in question. Consequently, the Commission concluded that there was no aid (State aid approach).

16.230   The Court of First Instance (CFI) did not agree with this approach and held that the benefit was State aid because it was not obtained under market conditions. However, in the second step of the analysis, the Court found that the aid could be considered compatible with the common market under Article 86(2) EC.

16.231   In a case concerning a different type of public service—broadcasting—the CFI confirmed its approach. In the *SIC* case, the CFI once again considered money paid to the public service provider—this time in the form of grants—to be a financial advantage and consequently aid.[163] The fact that the money was paid as compensation for the specific public service charge was not to be taken into account. It came under consideration only when assessing its compatibility, the second step of the State aid assessment.

16.232   In the *CELF* case the Court of Justice considered the applicability of the standstill clause of Article 88(3) EC to this type of aid, which qualified for a derogation under Article 86(2) EC.[164] France had argued that it was a special type of aid in compensation for the discharge of public service obligations and did not fall under the standstill obligation. This was rejected by the Court, confirming that there is no special exemption for aid which is intended as compensation for public service charges.

---

[162] Case T-106/95 *FFSA v Commission* [1997] ECR II-229.
[163] Joined Cases T-297/01 and T-298/01 *SIC v Commission*, judgment of 19 February 2004.
[164] Case C-322/98 *Kachelmann/Lampe* [2000] ECR I-7505.

The ECJ reversed this line of precedent on 22 November 2001 in the judgment delivered **16.233**
in the *Ferring* case.[165] This came as a surprise to the 'State aid community'. *Ferring* related
to the wholesale distribution of medicines in France. In this judgment, the ECJ sets out the
conditions under which a tax exemption granted to companies charged with the provision
of public service obligations is to be considered State aid. If the tax advantage only compensates for the excess cost of the public service, the companies that benefit do not receive any
advantage within the meaning of Article 87(1) EC. Therefore, the measure in question
does not constitute State aid, and does not require notification.

Altmark introduced a third approach which might be called the 'compensation plus' **16.234**
approach, which effectively endorses the 'compensation approach'.

(d) The Altmark Judgment

This case concerned the public transport sector in Germany. In 1990, Altmark Trans **16.235**
obtained licences and subsidies for the transport of people by bus in the area of Stendal (in
Sachsen-Anhalt). In 1994, the German authorities renewed the licences and refused a
licence application from a competing company. The competitor brought an action before
a German court arguing that the subsidies paid to Altmark Trans were aid incompatible
with the common market. The German Court asked the ECJ whether such subsidies
should be regarded as State aid.

In response to this question, the ECJ set out four main criteria under which such compen- **16.236**
sation does not constitute State aid, under Article 87 (1) EC:

First, the beneficiary must actually have public service obligations to discharge. These obli- **16.237**
gations must be clearly defined under the relevant national legislation, for example, giving
quality parameters, from tenders or comparison criteria, or definitions for the protection of
the environment or handicapped people. The addressees of the public service obligation
must be defined.

Secondly, the parameters on the basis of which the compensation is calculated must be **16.238**
established in advance of the award of any aid in an objective and transparent manner. This
is to avoid conferring an economic advantage that would favour the aid recipient over competing companies.

Payment by a Member State of compensation for the loss incurred by an undertaking with- **16.239**
out the parameters for such compensation having been established beforehand constitutes
a financial measure which must be assessed under the State aid rules. The rationale for this
is based upon the fact that it may become clear that the operation of certain services in connection with the discharge of public service obligations was not economically viable.

Thirdly, the compensation cannot exceed what is necessary to cover the costs incurred in **16.240**
the discharge of public service obligations. The calculation of the compensation must take
into account a 'reasonable profit' margin for the company. Compliance with such limits for
compensation ensures that the SGEI provider will not receive an advantage that could distort competition by strengthening its commercial position.

---

[165] Case C-53/00 *Ferring* [2001] ECR I-9067.

16.241   The *fourth* criterion provides two options to the Member State for avoiding over-compensation. The first option allows the Member State to choose to select the company providing the public service following a public procurement procedure which permits selection of the bidder offering the lowest or the economically most advantageous price.

Alternatively, the Member State must be satisfied that the proposed level of compensation is determined on the basis of an analysis of the costs which a 'typical undertaking' would have incurred in providing such services. This 'typical' company must be well run and adequately provided with the necessary means (means of transport—in this case) to be able to provide the specific service at the required level of quality. Thus, only if these conditions are satisfied, State financing for discharging public service obligations constitutes mere compensation not conferring an advantage and therefore, does not fall not under Article 87(1) EC.

16.242   In conclusion, *Altmark* confirms *Ferring*, and its compensation approach is explained in great detail.

(e) Analysis of Altmark: *Positive Effects and Open Questions*

16.243   The ECJ has confirmed the Commission's general approach to SGEI. *Altmark* has clarified to some extent what is meant by compensation for SGEI, but it has also created a need for further clarification on the interpretation of the rules. Increased transparency and legal certainty will be introduced by the Transparency Directive. The Directive supports the Commission's regulatory approach by referring to the use of public procurement and objective accounting practices. It confirms the Member States' prerogative to define 'their' SGEI and grants a greater role to national courts. Competitors can still sue in national courts if they believe that a company has received unlawful State aid. The national court will be required to apply the four *Altmark* criteria.

16.244   The ECJ has introduced a new element in the second condition. It requires that the criteria for the calculation of the compensation, must not only be objective and transparent, but also have been established before the award of SGEI or the public service obligation. This implies a change of behaviour on the part of the public authorities, because it used to be normal practice to establish or to adapt these criteria *a posteriori*. One example of that is the financing of public broadcasting in certain Member States. In future, national authorities will define these parameters in advance, and will no longer be able to ignore them without exposing themselves to examination of the compatibility of their State aid.

16.245   The reference to the element of a 'reasonable profit' under the third criterion is also new. Profit must be added to the costs of the public service, in order to determine the permitted level of compensation. Although *Altmark* emphasises this element explicitly for the first time—*Ferring* being silent on profit—there is no further explanation of the calculation of the allowed profit margin. When is a profit reasonable? Is it the average return of investment in the national economy? Is the benchmark the industry average in the Member State concerned or in the EU as a whole? Future decisions by the Commission and the case law of the courts in Luxembourg must provide answers to these questions.

16.246   Probably the most important innovation of the *Altmark* judgment lies in the two options of the fourth criterion, which states—in its first option—that the compensation escapes qualification as State aid only if it results from a public procurement procedure that allows for selection of the company which offers the public service in question at the least cost for the community. Choosing the cheapest, and therefore—it is assumed—most efficient operator would *a priori* exclude a distortion of competition. However, this is not entirely new, since in State financing of infrastructure the application of public procurement rules eliminates the aid.

The Commission has always considered that there is a close relationship between State aid and **16.247** public procurement law. The implementation of transparent, open, and non-discriminatory public tenders gives rise at least to a presumption that over-compensation is excluded. Under the conditions of an unbiased bidding process, market forces and not a public administration determine the price of the (public) service concerned. Problems remain, however, both from a theoretical and a more practical point of view.

The tender procedure might either eliminate the State aid element as such or render it com- **16.248** patible, depending whether or not there is State aid: in other words, whether the previous three conditions of *Altmark* are fulfilled or not. Linked to the specifics of public procure- ment law, other questions arise: how should one deal with the so-called external bidding factors, such as environmental or social conditions added to the tender conditions? Does the introduction of those bidding factors 'pollute' the tender procedure? The application of procurement law therefore, may not always lead to the cheapest provider. Other factors can be included in the evaluation and determine the final choice of a public service provider. However, it is the Member State that pre-determines the specifications of the bidding for the public service obligations.

The Court sets out in the fourth criterion a second option for excluding over-compensation. **16.249** The compensation can be compared with the costs of an average well-managed and well- equipped undertaking. The introduction of the benchmark criterion of an averagely effi- cient company goes far beyond the traditional approach of taking into account only the observed net additional costs in discharging the public service. This new situation entails a number of difficulties.

In practical terms, a comparable company may simply not exist. What are the comparative **16.250** factors for the determination of such an 'equivalent' company? Must it be active in the same industry, in the same market? Can large companies be compared with small and medium- sized companies? Assuming that the Member States produce lists of hypothetical compa- nies, how can the Commission check the data? Who has the burden of proof? Can the Commission prove whether State aid was given if the Member States present contradicting data on 'equivalent' companies?

The issue of the 'comparable company' had already arisen in '*Chronopost*'.[166] This judg- **16.251** ment was handed down just three weeks before *Altmark*. Here, the Court held that in the absence of any possibility of comparing the situation of 'La Poste' (the French state-owned postal service) with that of a private group of undertakings not operating in a reserved

---

[166] Joined Cases C-83/01 P, C-93/01 and C-94/01 P *Chronopost* [2003] ECR I-6993.

sector, normal market conditions (which are necessarily hypothetical) must be assessed by reference to the objective and verifiable elements which are available. The Court is called upon to clarify this in future decisions.

16.252 When the comparison of costs proves that the public service provider, often a traditional incumbent, has higher costs than the reference company, these higher costs would have to be classified as State aid. Then, the second step is to ask if this aid is compatible with the Common Market. Normally, over-compensation would be incompatible. However, this would lead to an implicit assessment of the efficiency of market operators by the Commission. Not only has the Commission never made such an assessment, but also, in *FFSA*, the CFI stated: '. . . the Commission is not entitled to rule on the basis of public service tasks assigned to the public operator, such as the level of costs linked to that service, . . . or La Poste's economic efficiency in the sector reserved to it . . .'

16.253 There are more open questions. In the case of locally provided services, sometimes there is no effect on trade between Member States. This can be because the service and those using it are all based in the same locality. It may also be the case that the service cannot be provided by outsiders but only locally.

16.254 Another difficult case, already mentioned, is public service broadcasting. The character of State aid might be excluded because the finance comes not from the state but from the TV set owners. This question is similar to the questions raised in the *PreussenElektra* case.[167]

16.255 If not all of the four *Altmark* criteria are fulfilled, ie there is State aid, is it possible that there is no over-compensation? Cases fall into three groups: (1) the subsidiarity principle[168] is applicable; (2) the *ex-post* payment of deficit is State aid; (3) there is no tender and no comparison but, for example, an assessment. What then is the role of Article 86(2) EC? Can it still apply?

16.256 Two judgments handed down after *Altmark* (*GEMO*[169] and *Enirisorse*[170]) did not add any further clarification to the outstanding issues.

(f) Legislative Consequences of Altmark

16.257 (i) **Outline for Legislative Measures** The upshot of *Altmark* is to increase legal certainty. The effect of the conditions set out in *Altmark*, and in particular the fourth condition, is such that the public services currently provided within the EU must be considered, for the most part, as involving State aid. The majority of the operators of public service obligations in the Member States were designated in a discretionary way and not on the basis of public procurement procedures. Furthermore, the level of compensation was not calculated on the basis of comparable companies but was determined more loosely and largely at the Member States' discretion. The relationship between the fourth *Altmark* criterion, ie the

---

[167] Case C-392/00 *PreussenElektra* [2002] ECR I-7397.

[168] According to Art 5, para 2 of the EC Treaty, the Community shall take action in areas which do not fall within its exclusive competence only if and in so far as the objectives of the proposed action cannot be sufficiently achieved by the Member States but better by the Community.

[169] Case C-126/01 *GEMO* [2003] ECR I-13769.

[170] Case C-34/01 *Enirisorse* [2003] ECR I-14243.

State aid rules and the procurement rules, concerning the possible use of the negotiation procedure in particular, must be explored further.

Consequently, if the compensation for the discharge of current public service obligations **16.258** is State aid, it should have been notified. If is not notified, it is unlawful and should be treated as such. This situation is critical for Member States as it means that any competitor can apply to a national court to suspend the compensation payment or even request recovery pursuant to Article 88 EC. Generally, the Commission encourages the use of this provision as an effective means to force the Member States to comply with their notification obligation.

The Commission has enacted three legal instruments to give effect to *Altmark*.[171] They take **16.259** the form of a Decision, a Community Framework for State aid in the form of public service compensation, and a modification of the Commission Directive ((EC) 80/723) on financial transparency. These legal measures initiate implementation of the Commission's new State aid Action Plan.[172]

(ii) Decision on 'Small Public Services'[173]   The first measure is a Commission decision **16.260** on relatively small-scale public funding of certain enterprises entrusted with the provision of a service in the public interest. This funding, provided it does not exceed a yearly threshold of EUR 30 million of public funding and as long as its beneficiaries do not achieve an annual turnover greater than EUR 100 million, is exempt from the obligation of prior notification. The compensation for public services provided by hospitals and social housing is also exempt from notification, irrespective of the amounts involved. Furthermore, the exemption covers compensation payments for maritime transport to islands, granted in accordance with sectoral regulation, where annual traffic does not exceed 100,000 passengers.[174]

The underlying justification is that the relatively small scale of this funding does not distort **16.261** competition and trade to a degree that would be contrary to the EU goal of creating an internal market for goods and services. Therefore, the decision on small-scale funding seeks to exempt States that compensate such—mostly local—undertakings from the obligation of prior notification.

The Decision is in effect a block exemption Regulation for State aid based on Article 86(3) **16.262** EC. The instrument gives Member States legal certainty for measures granted in the past to offset the cost of public service obligations that have not been notified to the Commission but do not give rise to over-compensation. It (automatically) exempts small-scale public funding from the obligation of prior notification because there is no relevant distortion of competition (or trade). There is State aid but it does not need to be notified. The de minimis Regulation[175] is not affected.

---

[171] Commission press release IP/05/937.
[172] Commission press release IP/05/680.
[173] <http://europa.eu.int/comm/competition/state_aid/others/interest/en.pdf>.
[174] Commission communication (2003) on the experience of the Cabotage Regulation, COM(1999) 182; Commission Decision (EC) 2005/842 of 28 November 2005 on the application of Art 86(2) of the EC Treaty to State aid in the form of public service compensation granted to certain undertakings entrusted with the operation of services of general economic interest (notified under document no C(2005) 2673) [2005] OJ L312, 29 November 2005, pp 67–73.
[175] Regulation 69/2001 [2001] OJ L10/30.

16.263 (iii) **Framework on Large Public Services**[176] The 'Legal Framework for Large Scale Funding Subject to Prior Notification' gives guidance on public funding of other undertakings providing SGEIs that are not exempt from the obligation of prior notification by the Commission decision. Due to the higher risk of distortion of competition, such compensation does need to be notified to the Commission. It concerns mainly the larger public service companies.

16.264 The framework clarifies, on the one hand, the conditions under which compensation will not be considered State aid. On the other hand, it describes in detail the criteria for compatibility when the four conditions of *Altmark* are not satisfied. The framework sets out the criteria for the assessment of compensation which, due to the amount of the compensation and the size of the beneficiary, remains subject to the obligation of prior notification.

16.265 For example, compatibility criteria include the existence of special tasks for companies defined by the Member States. There might be a transfer of tasks by a legal act including the consideration of the *Altmark* criteria. The geographic extension of the services and rules for clawing back any over-compensation will also be taken into account. In principle, compensation which exceeds the costs of the service of general economic interest, or which is used by enterprises on other markets open to competition, is incompatible with the EC Treaty's State aid rules.

16.266 (iv) **Modification of the Transparency Directive**[177] The primary goal of the Transparency Directive was to enable the Commission and competitors to control cross-subsidisation in large SGEI providers in the public sector. It obliges companies to account separately for all SGEI for which they receive financial support from the State and market services.[178] Through its accounting a company which provides SGEI must differentiate between the costs and revenues for its public and commercial operations. There must be an accurate allocation of costs to each of the undertakings concerned. This is important for creating a basis for making a comparison between these costs and the equivalent costs of its competitors, otherwise it would be impossible to assess whether there has been any over-compensation or not.

16.267 It remains to be determined whether actual separate accounts or just analytical accounting is needed for application of the *Altmark* criteria.

(g) Conclusions

16.268 The Commission had hoped that the Court of Justice would clarify how public service compensation is to be assessed in State aid terms. The *Altmark* judgment—and to a lesser extent *GEMO* and *Enirisorse*—provide some helpful guidance but by no means answer all possible questions. However, these judgments have raised many important additional issues.

16.269 The Commission's legislative measures follow the general practice of the Commission which is to approve all compensation necessary for the provision of services of public interest.

---

[176] <http://europa.eu.int/comm/competition/state_aid/others/public_service_comp/en.pdf>. Community framework (adopted on 13 July 2005) for State aid in the form of public service compensation [2005] OJ C297, 29 November 2005, pp 4–7.

[177] Directive 80/723 [2000] OJ L193/75. Commision Directive 2005/81/EC, Amending Directive (EEC) 80/723 on the transparency of financial relations between Member States and public undertakings as well as on financial transparency within certain undertakings, [2005] OJ L312, 29 Novermber 2005, pp 47–48.

[178] <http://europa.eu.int/comm/competition/state_aid/others/interest/directive_en.pdf>.

The Commission limits itself to preventing abuses, such as the payment of excess compensation payments that are used to cross-subsidise activities in competitive markets. The role of the Commission is thus to safeguard the proper functioning of competition in relation to public services by preventing unfair competitive practices, such as predatory pricing in activities open to competition.

16.270 For all public service providers, it may be wise to recommend that they study the relationship between State aid and public procurement, since the organisation of public tenders seems to be the safest way to ensure legal certainty in respect of the State aid character of a measure and its compatibility with the common market.

C. Notification and Assessment of State Aid

(1) Objective of the Notification and Assessment Procedure

16.271 The notification and assessment procedure is intended to enable the Commission to understand the nature of a measure proposed by a Member State and thus decide whether it constitutes State aid and, if so, assess its compatibility with the Internal Market in the shortest possible time. The decision of the Commission provides the requisite legal certainty for all parties involved.

16.272 Some factual background: in 2004,[179] 570 measures were notified to the Commission as State aid. About 12 per cent of all State aid cases registered were non-notified measures. Italy registered the most, with 23 per cent, and Germany followed with 22 per cent of these 87 non-notified measures. 93 per cent of the notifications were found compatible. Only 7 per cent were found incompatible after formal investigation.

16.273 Experience shows that good co-operation between all parties involved—on the basis of the largest possible transparency of the procedure—can help to process the notification as quickly and smoothly as possible. This co-operation should begin at a very early stage in the process. The following paragraphs explain the purposes and the different stages of the notification procedure and offer recommendations of what to do and what to avoid.

(2) Legal Basis and the Principle of Notification Requirement

16.274 Article 88(3) of the EC Treaty (EC) provides the legal basis of the notification and authorisation procedure:

> The Commission shall be informed, in sufficient time to enable it to submit its comments, of any plans to grant or alter aid. If it considers that any such plan is not compatible with the common market having regard to Article 87, it shall without delay initiate the procedure provided for in paragraph 2. The Member State concerned shall not put its proposed measures into effect until this procedure has resulted in a final decision.

Council Regulation (EC) 659/1999[180] sets out the general procedural rules to be followed for the notification and approval of State aid (the Procedural Regulation). Commission

---

179 COM (2005) 147 final of 20 April 2005.
180 Council Regulation (EC) 659/1999 of 22 March 1999 establishing detailed rules for the application of Art 93 of the Treaty [1999] OJ L83/1.

Regulation 794/04 (the Implementing Regulation)[181] sets out the details of the procedure to be followed, including notification forms, annual reports, calculation of time limits, and of interest.

16.275 The Commission's internal Manual of Procedure (currently in the course of revision) also covers the handling of State aid cases (both notified and unnotified) and in particular the procedure leading to the adoption of the final Commission decision. In order to speed up the notification and authorisation procedure the Directorate General of Competition (DG COMP) has established a standard notification form set out in Part I of Annex I to the Implementing Regulation. This standard form is based on Article 27 of the Procedural Regulation. In addition, there are fifteen standard letters the Commission uses in its communications with the Member States. The Commission utilises these letters, for example, to request further information or to remind a Member State about an outstanding answer.

16.276 Community supervision of State aid is based on a system of *ex-ante* authorisation. Under this system, Member States are required to inform the Commission beforehand (*ex ante*) of any plan to grant or alter State aid. They are not allowed to grant, put such aid into effect,[182] or alter an award of aid before receiving authorisation from the Commission (Article 3 of the Procedural Regulation, the standstill principle).

16.277 The Commission is the ultimate authority (subject to control by the European Courts) for determining whether or not the notified state measure constitutes State aid within the meaning of Article 87(1) EC, and if it does, whether or not it qualifies for exemption under Article 87(2) or (3) EC.[183]

(3) Consequences of Violation of Notification Requirement

16.278 Any aid, granted in the absence of Commission approval, thus violating the standstill obligation, is automatically classified as unlawful aid (Article 1(f) of the Procedural Regulation), as Article 88(3) EC prohibits the Member State from executing the intended measure. If the Member State does actually grant the aid or even takes preliminary steps towards granting it, the Commission has the power to order suspension of the measure (including suspension of the State guarantee) or even the provisional recovery of the aid.

16.279 The Commission must, however, assess the compatibility of the measure with the common market.[184] Under Community law, there is no other sanction or penalty against a Member

---

[181] Commission Regulation (EC) 794/2004 of 21 April 2004 implementing Council Regulation (EC) 659/1999 of 22 March 1999 setting out detailed rules for the application of Art 93 (now 88) of the Treaty [2004] OJ L140/1.

[182] Definition of 'putting info effect' pursuant Quigley/Collins, *EC State Aid Law and Policy* (Hart Publishing, Oxford, 2002), p 265: 'not the granting of the aid, but rather by the prior action of instituting or implementing the aid at a legislative level.' This means that as soon as the legislative machinery enabling it to be granted without further formality has been set up (ref. Commission letter to the Member States dated 27 April 1989, SG (89) D/5521).

[183] Luebbig/Martín-Ehlers, *Beihilfenrecht der EU* (Munich, 2003), p 3, para 7; Ehlermann, State aid control: failure or success? speech of 18 January 1995, <http://europa.eu.int/comm/competition/speeches/text/sp1995_001_en.html>. Last reviewed 20 December 2005.

[184] Case C-301/87 *France v Commission* [1990] ECR I-307.

State for the act of granting unlawful aid as such and thus breaching the standstill obligation under Article 88(3) EC.[185] However, nobody has yet taken action against a Member State for breach of its Treaty obligation under Article 227 EC.

In the absence of notification, the Commission is not bound to complete its investigation within the prescribed eighteen-month period.[186] The Commission, however, cannot order the recovery of unlawful aid if it has taken no action in respect of that aid in the ten years following the grant of the aid. Article 15 of Regulation 659/99 provides that, in the absence of any such interrupting action, the unlawful aid becomes existing aid which can only be reviewed for the future but cannot be recovered. **16.280**

A second negative consequence of unlawful aid is that any competitor of the beneficiary can choose to complain against the aid in a national court.[187] In this case the national court may order the recovery of the aid if it finds that aid was given unlawfully. It cannot, however, adjudicate on the compatibility of the aid. It must decide solely on the basis of the existence or absence of notification.[188] This can lead not only to recovery claims but also to claims for damages. The national Court is expected to co-operate with the Commission or refer questions to the European Court of Justice. **16.281**

(4) Exemptions from the Notification Requirement

There is no notification requirement for individual aid grants under an approved aid scheme[189] or for aid for rescue and restructuring of small companies (but not for large companies, which must always be notified individually).[190] In addition, investments under the Multisectoral Framework,[191] for research and development[192] and environmental aid[193] below a certain threshold are also exempted. **16.282**

---

[185] This has given rise to a demand for the introduction of such penalties in order to reduce the number of cases of unlawful aid.

[186] The investor will normally obtain certainty in respect of the State aid character of his investment within about 18 months. This certainty will not be granted in the case of unlawful aid, ie aid which has not been notified. This is a major disadvantage of granting unlawful aid. The deadlines in the notification procedure which are in the interest of the Member State, and ultimately the beneficiary, do not apply.

[187] Whether the competitor has standing depends to some extent on national law.

[188] *French Ryan Air* case, French Cour administrative d'appel de Nancy, 18 December 2003, n° 03NC00859. Also: Case C-39/94 *SFEI and others*, [1996] ECR I-3547; and Case C-354/90 *FNCE* [1991] ECR I-5505. Recent jurisprudence of the German Bundesgerichtshof (BGH), judgments of 4 April 2003 and 20 January 2004 (Deufil) on Art 88(3) EC as a 'prohibition law' under para 134 of the German Civil Code (BGB). As a result of this French and German jurisprudence, unlawful aid measures are null and void. This is the concept of 'formal' illegality.

[189] Quigley/Collins, *EC State Aid Law and Policy* (n 182 above), 77.

[190] Community Guidelines on State Aid for Rescuing and Restructuring Firms in Difficulty [2004] OJ C244/89.

[191] Commission communication—Multisectoral framework on regional aid for large investment projects [2002] OJ C70/8.

[192] Commission communication—Community framework for state aid for research and development [1996] OJ C45/5.

[193] '. . . any individual case of investment aid must be notified in advance to the Commission where the eligible costs exceed EUR 25 million and where the aid exceeds the gross grant equivalent of EUR 5 million.' Commission communication: Community guidelines on state aid for environmental protection [2001] OJ C37/3.

16.283   However, under a number of block exemption Regulations for State aid,[194] the Commission can declare certain categories of State aid compatible with the Treaty if they meet the required conditions, thus exempting them from the requirement of prior notification and approval. Aid schemes that satisfy all the conditions laid down in one of the block exemption Regulations adopted by the Commission do not need to be notified to the Commission.

16.284   The Commission has adopted three block exemption Regulations so far. They create exemptions for aid to small and medium-sized enterprises,[195] employment aid,[196] and training aid.[197] As a result, Member States are able to grant aid that meets the conditions laid down in these three Regulations without the prior approval of the Commission.

16.285   A fourth Regulation codifies the application of the de minimis rule.[198] It establishes that aid to an enterprise that does not exceed EUR 100,000 over a period of three years and that respects certain conditions, does not constitute State aid in the sense of Article 87(1) of the EC Treaty, since it is deemed not to affect trade or distort competition. Such aid therefore does not need to be notified. The de minimis Regulation does not apply to the transport sector or to the agricultural and fisheries sectors.[199]

16.286   In the case of an aid measure that satisfies all the conditions of the SME, training, or employment aid Regulation, the Member State is, nevertheless, required to submit to the Commission a summary description of the aid measure within twenty working days following the implementation of the measure.[200] Where the aid measure satisfies all the conditions laid down in the de minimis Regulation, there is no such requirement.

(5) Steps in the Notification and Assessment Procedure

16.287   The notification and assessment process can be divided into different stages:[201]

(a) *Preparation and Filing of Notification*

16.288   It is for the Member State to decide which authority will handle the notification and co-operation with the Commission. Generally, the central authorities of the Member State concerned (in the case of federal states) notify planned aid measures. In order to speed up the process, the Commission has drawn up standard notification forms for most types

---

194   Council Regulation (EC) 994/98 of 7 May 1998 on the application of Articles 92 and 93 of the Treaty establishing the European Community to certain categories of horizontal State aid [1998] OJ L142/1 constitutes the basis for adopting any such block exemptions.

195   Commission Regulation (EC) 70/2001 of 12 January 2001 on the application of Articles 87 and 88 of the EC Treaty to state aid to small and medium-sized enterprises [2001] OJ L10/33.

196   Commission Regulation (EC) 2204/2002 of 12 December 2002 on the application of Articles 87 and 88 of the EC Treaty to State aid for employment [2002] OJ L337/3.

197   Commission Regulation (EC) 68/2001 of 12 January 2001 on the application of Articles 87 and 88 of the EC Treaty to training aid [2001] OJ L10/20.

198   Commission Regulation (EC) 69/2001 of 12 January 2001 on the application of Articles 87 and 88 of the EC Treaty to de minimis aid [2001] OJ L10/30.

199   ibid, Art 1 and consider para 3.

200   Aid to SMEs: Commission Regulation (EC) 70/2001, Art 9 (1); Training Aid: Commission Regulation (EC) 68/2001, Art 7(1); Employment Aid: Commission Regulation (EC) 2204/2002, Art 10(1).

201   The description follows the procedures applied by DG COMP. In other DGs there may be variations, but the principles are the same.

of aid.[202] Notifications must be sent to the Secretariat General (SG) of the Commission through the Permanent Representation of the Member State concerned (Article 3(1) of the Implementing Regulation). All formal correspondence involves the Permanent Representation, but apart from the notification most other correspondence directly involves the relevant DG within the Commission. For DG COMP all correspondence should be sent to the State Aid Registry.

The notification must be sent to the SG which is *inter alia* the registrar of the Commission **16.289** for incoming documents. It distributes incoming mail, notifications, and complaints to one of the four Directorates General (DG)—Competition, Energy & Transport, Agriculture & Rural Development and Fisheries & Maritime Affairs—that deal with State aid. These DGs can also initiate inquiries themselves.

The notification is registered as a case with the relevant DG which allocates the handling of **16.290** the case internally to a directorate and further to a unit and a specific case handler. In large cases, eg *British Energy*,[203] *Alstom*,[204] or the *German Landesbanken*,[205] a case team is formed. Such case teams can include case handlers from different units or even directorates, including the DG Competition Chief Economist's team.

(b) Preliminary Investigation (Phase A)

First, the Commission has two months to examine the proposed aid (Article 4(5) of the **16.291** Procedural Regulation). This two-month period runs from the date on which the Commission receives all the information it needs to assess the case. If the notification is incomplete, the Commission will request further information. The Member State concerned is usually given 20 days to supply this information.

This preliminary investigation will normally be concluded either by a decision not to raise **16.292** objections or by a decision to initiate formal Article 88(2) EC proceedings (phase B).[206] If the Commission decides not to raise any objection, the aid measure concerned can be implemented.

The Commission addresses its correspondence principally to the Member State and only **16.293** exceptionally to a complainant or even to the beneficiary of the aid.[207]

The Commission can use all available sources of information to verify the facts of the case. **16.294** In case of information from sources other than the Member State, the Commission will normally submit the comments received from any interested parties to the Member State to ensure that the right to be heard is given effect[208] and will ask the Member State to comment on or clarify points raised. Although there is no obligation on the Commission at this stage other than to submit the third party comments, the CFI has held that in accordance

---

[202] Commission webpage, DG Competition, State Aid, Other documents.
[203] Commission press release of 22 September 2004, IP/04/1125.
[204] Commission press release of 7 July 2004, IP/04/859.
[205] Commission press release of 21 September 2004, IP/04/1119.
[206] Quigley/Collins, *EC State Aid Law and Policy* (n 182 above), pp 272ff.
[207] According to Art 5 of Council Regulation (EC) 659/1999 the Commission requests all necessary information from the Member State. The complainant and the beneficiary of the aid play a tangential role.
[208] Quigley/Collins, *EC State Aid Law and Policy* (n 182 above), p 287.

with the Commission's duty of good administration, it may enter into correspondence with the notifying State or with third parties to overcome difficulties already encountered during the preliminary procedure.[209]

(c) Formal Investigation Proceedings (Phase B)

16.295 The Commission initiates Article 88(2) EC proceedings if it has doubts about the compatibility of the notified aid measure with the common market (Article 6 of the Procedural Regulation). In such cases, the Commission opens a formal investigation.[210] It publishes its decision in the language of the case, and a meaningful summary of the measure in any other official language, in the Official Journal. The Commission thereby invites the Member State concerned and any interested parties[211] to comment.[212]

16.296 In its final decision, the Commission can only use information it has introduced into the procedure through the opening decision of the formal investigation procedure.

16.297 The formal investigation normally ends with the Commission's final decision. This may be either positive (aid can be implemented), negative (aid cannot be implemented), or positive but subject to conditions.[213] The indicative maximum time limit set out for such an enquiry is eighteen months (Article 7(6) of the Procedural Regulation). However, where there is agreement with the Member State, an extension of time is permissible to ensure that the Commission has sufficient time to examine extensive aid plans (Article 7(6) sentence 3 of the Procedural Regulation).[214] During the investigation period the Commission officials hold meetings with the Member State authorities, including the beneficiaries and other third parties.

16.298 Once the investigating DG believes that it has sufficient information, it will inform the competent Commissioner about the intended further procedure by means of a short memorandum or 'Note to the Commissioner' (usually about five pages long). The note will be more comprehensive if the case raises policy or (significant) legal problems.

16.299 The case will be discussed in one of the regular meetings between the DG and the Commissioner. These meetings are attended by a representative of the Commission's Legal Service who will already have been informed about the note. The Commissioner then determines the further procedure. These meetings are minuted.

16.300 The DG drafts a decision based on the guidance given by the Commissioner at the meeting. At any stage the Legal Service or other services may be consulted if the case raises difficult

---

[209] Case T-73/98 *Société Chimique Prayon-Ruppel SA v Commission* [2001] ECR II-867, para 45.

[210] Quigley/Collins, *EC State Aid Law and Policy* (n 182 above), p 284 give five examples of cases in which the formal investigation procedure must be initiated.

[211] Council Regulation (EC) 659/1999, Art 1(h); Case 323/82 *Intermills v Commission* [1984] ECR 3809, para. 17 and *per* Advocate General Verloren van Themaat, at 3837 provided a definition of the 'interested parties': Member States, any person, undertaking or association of undertakings whose interests might be affected by the granting of the aid (eg beneficiary of the aid, competing undertakings, and trade associations) as well as customers, suppliers, and employees, also including representatives of employees of the recipient.

[212] Lübbig/Martíns-Ehlers, *Beihilfenrecht der EU* (Munich, 2003), p 194, para 514; ibid, Art 20(1).

[213] Quigley/Collins, *EC State Aid Law and Policy* (n 182 above), p 290.

[214] *Sinnaeve*, EuZW 1998, 268, 270.

legal or other questions. The Legal Service will be consulted together with other services of the Commission during the Inter-Service Consultation (ISC).

The ISC is a formal consultation procedure among relevant or affected DGs of the **16.301** Commission. Some DGs are always consulted, ie Legal Service, Secretariat General, DG ECFIN, and DG ENTR, along with others as the case requires. For example, DG REGIO will be consulted on regional aid, DG Environment on environmental aid, DG Employment and Social Affairs on employment aid, and DG RTD on research and development aid. The ISC normally lasts for three weeks and is coordinated by the SG.

The ISC is normally completed on a Thursday. The case is then transferred to the 'preparatory **16.302** Monday meeting'. The 'Chefs de Cabinets' special meeting takes place on the following Thursday. It is only after that meeting that the case is put on the agenda of the Commission meeting, usually held on a Wednesday, otherwise on a Tuesday. In case of agreement a case will be a so-called A-point (all agree) and it passes on to the next meeting without discussion. In case of disagreement, it will be a B-point (needs to be discussed).

If the ISC does not lead to full agreement between the various sections of the Commission **16.303** involved, the case will be discussed in a regular bi-weekly meeting held by the SG. The SG has a coordinating role throughout the whole procedure. The DGs which were not consulted in the ISC do not normally participate in this round of discussions.

(d) Review of Decisions by European Courts

All Commission decisions are subject to review by the European Court of Justice under **16.304** Article 230 of the EC Treaty. The period for bringing an action in the European Courts will be usually be two months and ten days: Article 230(5) stipulates a period of two months to bring an action in court, from the date of publication of the measure or its notification to the plaintiff, or the date on which it came to the knowledge of the plaintiff. Competitors do not participate in any stage of the proceedings, whether preliminary or formal and therefore, the decision will not be formally notified to them. Thus, the period for commencing proceedings will normally run from publication of the decision in the Official Journal, which takes place ten days after the decision is made. Unless the decision was neither published nor formally notified, press reports about a decision will not be relevant to this commencement date.[215]

Normally after between one and three years or so, the Court will either uphold the **16.305** Commission decision or annul it.

An important factor for the notifying Member State and the beneficiaries throughout the **16.306** whole procedure is early and close contact with the Commission and its Services. So-called pre-notification meetings between the Member State (beneficiaries) and the Commission services are common in difficult cases. On the basis of a pre-notification document DG COMP usually agrees to meet the Member State and sometimes company representatives for an early and informal analysis of the intended aid project. Even though this goes against the principle that the State aid procedure is between the Commission and the Member

---

[215] Case T-110/97 *Kneissl Dachstein v Commission* [1999] ECR II-2881, paras 40ff.

States, it is nevertheless current practice. The justification for this lies in the valuable input provided by the beneficiary. The direct—but informal—inclusion of the beneficiary in the procedure saves time. Thereafter, the Member State may provide a (more) complete notification, modify the project, or sometimes even decide to abandon the aid project completely.

(6) Use of the Prescribed Forms

16.307 In order to facilitate the preparation of State aid notifications by Member States and their assessment by the Commission, the Commission has established a new and compulsory notification form.[216]

16.308 This form is intended to be as comprehensive as possible. The Implementing Regulation sets out detailed provisions concerning the form, its content and details of other notifications and annual reports referred to in the Procedural Regulation. It also sets out provisions for the calculation of time limits in all procedures concerning State aid and of the interest rate applicable in the recovery of unlawful aid.

16.309 The standard form must be used for all State aid notifications. The form is divided into three parts. The first or 'General Information' part must be completed in all cases. The initial classification of the notification under Article 88(3) EC, as possible unlawful aid or non-aid measure for the purposes of obtaining legal certainty provides an important starting point. The form requires the provision of a number of details which may speed up the processing of the notification. The information requested relates to the granting authority, the aid itself, the legal basis in the Member State, the beneficiaries, the amount, form and financing of the aid, its duration, accumulation of different types of aid, professional confidentiality, compatibility, and outstanding recovery orders (*Deggendorf* principle[217]).

16.310 The second part of the form requests a summary of the information for publication in the Official Journal. The third part contains Supplementary Information Sheets depending on the type of aid, eg SME aid, training aid, employment aid, etc.

16.311 Failure to complete the form may result in the notification being considered incomplete. A different problem may arise out of point 14 in the first part of the form, which requires the notifying authority, ie a named officer thereof, to'certify that to the best of my knowledge the information provided on this form, its annexes and its attachments is accurate and complete'. The officials in the national ministries drafting and signing the notification will not normally be able to give this declaration. Since most of the information in the form concerns the beneficiary, they have only limited means of checking its reliability and accuracy. It would be difficult to find the officials (personally) liable in the case of incompleteness or inaccuracy.

16.312 On the other hand, one might argue that national authorities should know what they are doing when they grant aid. Beneficiaries should provide reliable information to the

---

[216] Annex I of Implementing Regulation 794/2004.
[217] Case C-355/95 P *Textilwerke Deggendorf v Commission* [1997] ECR I-2549. In short, the Commission will approve new aid only if previous unlawful aid has been paid back in the meantime.

authorities. Overall, this requirement increases the likelihood that the Commission will receive more reliable information.

Article 4 of the Implementing Regulation provides a simplified procedure for certain alter- **16.313** ations to existing aid. It applies when the budget increase of an authorised aid scheme exceeds 20 per cent, when the scheme is prolonged for up to six years or when the criteria are tightened, the aid intensity or the eligible expenses are reduced. Annex II of the Implementing Regulation provides the simplified notification form.

(7) Delays and Mistakes in the Notification Procedure and How to Avoid Them

One important reason for delaying a State aid investigation is that the notifying Member **16.314** States do not describe the measure in clear and unambiguous terms. Lack of clarity and insufficient information trigger questions and misunderstandings between the notifying Member States and the Commission. It can take considerable time to put a project which started on the wrong track onto the right one. The Commission tries to be flexible. Often the problem is that the Member State does not really understand the procedural requirements or know how best to describe its project clearly on paper. Especially in cases where time is of the essence, as in rescue and restructuring cases in particular, the utmost care should be taken to give a clear and cogent description of the measure.

Some of the common and repeated mistakes in the notification procedure can be avoided. **16.315** First, the aid programme in the Member State must be developed not only with one eye on the beneficiary but with the other eye on the Community State aid law. If the Member State notifies an incompatible measure, a negative decision will follow. If the aid programme does not take into account the realities of Community State aid control, the notification is likely to founder.

The description of the aid project should be precise in legal and economic terms. The stan- **16.316** dard format is obligatory, but it may be useful to add a general introduction which gives a clear overview of the nature of the project and the rationale behind the aid.

Notification and investment documents must be consistent. There should be no contradic- **16.317** tions between the national support request and the European notification request, unless a clear explanation is given (and of course, a Member State may grant less aid than it was initially asked for). The national aid terminology may be different from the terminology of the Community State aid control law. If this is the case, a sufficient explanation should be provided. Special provisions apply in certain sectors.

The aid intensity must be shown clearly and transparently. That is particularly important **16.318** for aid in the form of loans and guarantees. There are specific formulae for calculating aid involved in State guarantees.[218] The interest rate, the net and gross grant equivalent, and the risks covered should be clearly indicated.

---

[218] cf para 5.4 of the Commission Standard notification form for regional aid schemes, DG Competition web site.

16.319 Provisions that lead to accumulation of aid should not be forgotten. One company may receive aid from different programmes or from different sources. This must be made clear. Individual notification thresholds must be applied in any case.

16.320 There are also problems as regards indirect beneficiaries (since it is not always clear who benefits from the aid) and the role of competitors. Member States should also consider their aid project from the perspective of a competitor and take its concerns into account, in order to verify the justification for the proposed aid. Furthermore, the errors in notifications of schemes may be different from those in individual aid cases. The latter require far more detail, but it is not always helpful to 'swamp' the Commission with all kinds of background documents which add nothing to the substance of the case.

16.321 These few examples show that, by preparing a notification thoroughly and providing all necessary information at the start, delays and misunderstandings in the notification process can be largely avoided. This results in smoother and faster procedures and greater legal certainty in a shorter time. Finally, it should not be forgotten that if the Commission is given wrong information, it has the right to revoke its decision.

D. State Aid Enforcement—Recovery of Unlawful State Aid

(1) Introduction[219]

16.322 Under Article 88(1) EC the Commission keeps all existing aid 'under constant review'. The enforcement of State aid law involves several different but connected areas. The recovery of unlawful State aid is the best known and currently of foremost importance. Enforcement includes the monitoring of and possible corrective intervention relating to conditional State aid decisions,[220] the monitoring of decisions under the Multisectoral Framework, the application of the various block exemption Regulations, and decisions approving aid schemes.

16.323 The compliance of the Member States with all State aid decisions must be monitored constantly. The recovery of unlawful State aid has been even more of a priority of the Commission in recent years. The Commission has the power and the duty to require that (unlawful) aid granted by Member States which is incompatible with the common market be repaid by the beneficiaries to the State (or the institution) which granted it. However, not only the Commission, but also national courts can order recovery.

16.324 Case law of the European Courts shows that the logical legal consequence of the grant of unlawful aid is recovery.[221] All aid granted prior to authorisation by the Commission is unlawful (unless exempt from notification). This includes aid provided or committed without notification and aid that has already been put into effect when it is notified or is put into effect after being notified but before the Commission reached a decision.

---

[219] For comprehensive discussion, see Heidenhain, *Handbuch des Europäischen Beihilfenrechts* (Munich, 2003), Ch 10. Alexander Schaub in a speech of 18 July 1996 stressed the importance of recovery, '4 Enforcement of the State aid discipline in the EU'.

[220] cf Commission Decision (EC) 2005/345 of 18 February 2004 on restructuring aid implemented by Germany for Bankgesellschaft Berlin AG (notified under document number C(2004) 327), [2005] OJ L116/1.

[221] See eg ECJ Case C-142/87 *Belgium/Commission (Tubemeuse)* [1990] ECR I-959 (1020).

Once the Commission orders recovery, the Member State must recover the aid immediately **16.325** in accordance with its domestic legal procedures provided that such procedures allow for an effective and immediate recovery.

The goal of the recovery action is to remove the advantage that has been provided by the aid **16.326** to a specific undertaking (selectivity) and rectify the distortion of competition through restoration of the *status quo ante*.[222] This is impossible in a strictly logical sense since time cannot be reversed. However, the recipient of unlawful aid must give back the benefit received. Recovery is the nullification of any advantage which favoured one undertaking in a given market over those of its competitors who did not receive a similar benefit from the State.

In the first half of 2005, there were about ninety outstanding recovery cases pending before **16.327** DG COMP. About one third concerned aid schemes. About forty of the pending cases concerned Germany and twenty related to Spain. Together with Italy and France, these Member States 'account[ed] for more than 90% of the pending recovery cases'.[223] About 120 recovery cases came before the Commission in total, including cases before DG Energy and Transport (DG TREN), DG Fisheries and Maritime Affairs (DG FISH),[224] and DG Agriculture and Rural Development (DG AGRI).[225] This number covers all recovery cases with decisions taken from 1995 onwards.

The amount of aid involved in these cases is estimated to be at least EUR 9.3 billion, being **16.328** the capital amount excluding interest. This figure is, however, an underestimate in any event, because it is impossible to identify the exact amount of incompatible aid in cases where aid is awarded to a large number of beneficiaries through a scheme or when a certain type of instrument is used for which it is difficult to quantify the effect of the aid, for example guarantees. Two major awards of aid were recovered[226] from Deutsche Post in January 2003 (about EUR 1 billion) and Eléctricité de France (EdF) in February 2004 (EUR 1.2 billion).[227] A total of EUR 4.25 billion has been recovered from the German Landesbanken. So far there is no decision on the recapitalisation, but it is expected to be made soon.

(2) Legal Basis and General Principles of Recovery

(a) Legal Basis of Recovery

The legal basis for the recovery of unlawful State aid is to be found in the Procedural **16.329** Regulation which is the equivalent of Antitrust Regulation 1/2003 but applies to State aid procedures. The Procedural Regulation establishes the main legal basis for the recovery of unlawful aid. Article 11(2) of the Regulation provides for an injunction to recover aid on a provisional basis.[228]

---

[222] Schaub in speech of 18 July 1996. See also Schaub on AEA congress 20/21 November 2000. Case C-75/97 *Belgium v Commission* [1999] ECR I-3671, para 66. Case C-24/95 *Alcan* [1997] ECR I-1591, para 23.
[223] Commission press release, 20 April 2005, IP/05/457.
[224] DG FISH now has one recovery case.
[225] Overall number of recovery cases. Cases from DG TREN and DG AGRI are included.
[226] These were paid into a frozen account pending litigation as to the justification for the recovery order.
[227] Commission press release, 20 April 2005, IP/05/457, seems to indicate that the outstanding amount is somewhat lower.
[228] See also 'whereas 12'.

16.330 The main recovery provision is Article 14, the first paragraph of which requires the Commission to request the concerned Member State to recover immediately any incompatible aid which was granted unlawfully. This aid must be recovered with interest according to paragraph 3 of Article 14. This Article further states that the aid will be recovered according to national rules. These rules must provide for an immediate and effective recovery procedure. Article 15 establishes a limitation period of ten years for the recovery of aid.

16.331 It is a fundamental principle of recovery that the aid must be repaid with interest. The Commission's Communication of 8 May 2003[229] and Articles 9–11 of the Implementing Regulation explain the legal basis and the details of interest calculation. The Commission recently published a study and a consultation on the use of interest rates.[230]

(b) Immediate and Effective Recovery According to National Laws

16.332 The leading questions for recovery are how much and from whom. Recovery is effected in accordance with national law by the authorities of the Member State that granted the aid. This includes interim measures:

> One weak point in our current [state aid law] system lies in the difficulty of ensuring the effective recovery of aid. Community law places an obligation on Member States to ensure effective recovery in accordance with national legal procedures. However, those national procedures do not in general give a high priority to the recovery of illegal aid, particularly when, as is frequently the case, the beneficiary is in financial difficulties.[231]

16.333 On the other hand, it is the Commission and not the Member State that makes a binding decision on how the unlawful aid is to be recovered and on the date when the aid was granted. The aid is granted from the moment that the beneficiary can make use of it. It may even have economic effects preceding this date, if the knowledge of the fact that the aid will definitely be granted influences economic decisions. It is possible, for example, that the beneficiary, knowing that aid will be granted in the (near) future, will receive favourable borrowing terms it would not otherwise have received. In such a case, the benefit derived from the aid precedes the point in time when the beneficiary actually received the aid. Determining the time when the aid was granted is crucial for pin-pointing the start of the interest-bearing period. In practice, the amount of interest can reach or even exceed the capital to be recovered.

16.334 The courts of the Member State which are faced with difficulties of recovering the unlawful aid need to co-operate with the Commission to find ways of overcoming these difficulties. The duty of co-operation with the Commission under Article 10 EC applies in full.[232] The Member State must make specific proposals to the Commission. General proposals: tentative suggestions are not enough.[233]

---

229 [2003] OJ C110/21.

230 Reference and recovery rates for the new Member States are published in [2005] OJ C48/2.

231 Commissioner Monti in his speech of 1 December 2003 in Brussels. See also his speeches of 19 June 2003 in Brussels and 17 October 2003 in Berlin.

232 Case C-303/88 *Italy/Commission ('ENI-I')*[1991] ECR I-1433 (1485). Recovery from the company which actually enjoyed the benefit of the aid.

233 Case C-209/00 *WestLB* [2002] ECR I-11695.

The principle of immediate and effective execution means that national law cannot be **16.335**
invoked to frustrate the recovery or to make it impossible in practice. As was held in *Alcan I*,[234]
procedural obstacles, just like administrative deadlines, cannot be used to prevent recovery.

The reimbursement must normally be in cash, although as an exception to this rule, it is **16.336**
sometimes possible to convert debt into equity. Here, the State receives shares in the beneficiary company in exchange for the recovery debt. This occurs in several areas, particularly
in respect of publicly owned enterprises. The two operations, reimbursement and reinvest-
ment, are clearly separated or the reimbursed amount is reinvested in the beneficiary by the
State. In the latter case, the reimbursement falls practically *uno actu* together with the rein-
vestment of the original amount of aid.

A recurring problem in this type of case is how to evaluate the equity share in market terms. **16.337**
If the equity is overvalued, then the difference from the market price would constitute new
State aid. There is also a general rule excluding reimbursement by instalments, even if the
instalments are paid with market rate interest.

The calculation of tax on the amounts to be recovered is a matter of national law.[235] The **16.338**
Commission only monitors the recovery of the aid and will not prescribe how any applica-
ble domestic tax is applied, as long as the distortion of competition is effectively abolished.
If, however, the recovery amount is expressed as a post-tax figure, as in most of the
Landesbanken cases, then the issue arises as to whether the repayment based on the post-
corporate tax figure can be deducted as an expense. DG COMP rejected this suggestion.

(c) Imposition of Compound Interest

Article 14(2) of the Procedural Regulation and Articles 9–11 of the Implementing **16.339**
Regulation require the imposition of compound interest[236] on the sum to be reimbursed.
Since the purpose of recovery is to recreate the situation that existed before the aid was
unlawfully granted, interest must also be paid. The recovery decision will normally require
interest to be charged from the date when the unlawful aid was awarded until it is fully
recovered.[237]

The interest rate for recovery is fixed as an annual percentage and varies between Member **16.340**
States (within and outside the Eurozone). The starting point for the calculation is the
reference rate of the year in which the aid was given. A State aid grant may be deemed to
reduce a beneficiary undertaking's medium term financing requirements. For these purposes, and in line with general financial practice, the medium term is defined as five years.
The recovery interest rate should therefore be calculated on the basis of an annual percentage
rate fixed for five years.

The Commission established a single recovery interest rate for each Member State on the **16.341**
basis of inter-bank swap rates. The volume and frequency of transactions between banks

---

[234] Case C–94/87 *Alcan I* [1989] ECR 175.
[235] Case T-459/93 *Siemens v Commission* [1995] ECR II-1675.
[236] 'Zinseszins' or 'intéret composé'.
[237] <http://europa.eu.int/comm/competition/state_aid/legislation/unno_en.html>.

result in an interest rate that is consistently measurable and statistically significant, and therefore forms the basis of the recovery interest rate. The inter-bank swap rate, however, is adjusted in order to reflect general levels of increased commercial risk outside the banking sector. The Commission publishes the recovery interest rate applicable at any given moment, as well as relevant previously applicable rates.

16.342 In accordance with general financial practice, the recovery interest rate is compounded annually. The Commission Communication of May 2003 clearly states that this rule applies to all pending recovery cases. it should be noted in practice that DG COMP accepts exceptions to this rule if certain conditions are satisfied which are considered to constitute legitimate expectations. A case is pending, as long as the aid has not been fully reimbursed. The specific rules on fixing the interest rate, publication and the method for applying interest in Articles 9–11 of the Implementing Regulation apply to recovery decisions notified after the date of entry into force of this Regulation (Article 13 of the Implementing Regulation).

16.343 No interest rate is applied from the moment the amount is placed into a frozen account after the recovery decision.[238]

(d) Defences against Recovery

16.344 There is little material defence against a recovery order, ie the recovery part of a negative decision. The legal defence against the recovery order must be separated from the defence against the negative decision as such. Legal action brought against a recovery order in the European courts has no suspensory effect (Article 242 EC). Thus, the recovery must still be made, in spite of any ongoing litigation in European courts against the negative decision.[239] One might call this principle 'pay first—argue later'.[240] There are two main material defences against recovery: absolute impossibility and breach of legitimate expectations.

16.345 No recovery takes place if the implementation of the recovery decision is absolutely impossible.[241] This rule has never been fully applied as such by the European Courts. There may be only one (partially) successful case.[242] The ECJ's interpretation of this exemption has been always very narrow.[243] In another case, mere perception of (technical) difficulties was judged insufficient to establish absolute impossibility.[244]

16.346 Recovery is not possible if it is contrary to a general principle of Community law, ie the protection of legitimate expectations.[245] This exemption has been interpreted strictly by

---

[238] Cases T-231/94, T-232/94 and T-234/94 *Transacciones Maritimes* [1994] ECR II-247.

[239] Art 7(5) of the Procedural Regulation: 'Where the Commission finds that the notified aid is not compatible with the common market, it shall decide that the aid shall not be put into effect (hereinafter referred to as a "negative decision").'

[240] National courts would normally suspend the recovery pending the ECJ or CFI decision.

[241] Case C-499/99 *Commission v Spain (Magefesa II)* [2002] ECR I-6031, paras 36ff; Case C-480/98 *(Magefesa I)* [2000] ECR I-8717.

[242] Case C-47/91 *Italy v Commission (Italgrani)* [1994] ECR I-4635.

[243] Case C-52/84 *Commission v Belgium* [1986] ECR 89, para 14; Case C-295/97 *Piaggio v Ifitalia & others* [1999] ECR I-3735.

[244] Case C-75/97 *Belgium v Commission ('Maribel')* [1999] ECR I-3671, para 90.

[245] 'Vertrauensschutz' in German, 'confiance legitime' in French legal terminology. Case C-24/95 *(Alcan II)* [1997] ECR I-1591.

the Commission and the ECJ. A legitimate expectation can be inferred only from the Commission's behaviour. The Member State cannot refuse to recover the aid on the grounds of the supposed legitimate expectations of the aid recipients.

Normally, because of the notification requirement for new aid under Article 88(1) EC, a beneficiary should know whether the aid was notified or not (and approved as compatible). Recipients cannot usually invoke legitimate expectations, because they have a duty of care to ensure before receiving aid that it is granted lawfully. The required degree of care is the 'diligent entrepreneur' who would check the legal terms and conditions carefully before making an investment. Recent case law in the Member States has strengthened this approach explicitly.[246]   **16.347**

The ECJ confirmed its jurisprudence on legitimate expectations in the recent case *Fleuren*   **16.348**
Compost.[247] The Court first emphasises the general principle of the legitimate expectation defence:

> Admittedly, the case-law does not preclude the possibility that, in order to challenge its repayment, the recipients of unlawful aid may, in the procedure for the recovery of the aid, plead exceptional circumstances which could legitimately have given rise to a legitimate expectation that the aid was lawful . . .[248]

The Court then continues with the restrictive conditions for its application, ie what a diligent entrepreneur must check before he can rely on legitimate expectations:

> However, it is implicit in the case-law of the Court of Justice . . . that those recipients can rely on such exceptional circumstances, on the basis of the relevant provisions of national law, only in the framework of the recovery procedure before the national courts, and it is for them alone to assess the circumstances of the case, if necessary after obtaining a preliminary ruling on interpretation from the Court of Justice.[249]

A different situation is to be found in the *Salzgitter* case.[250] The Court of First Instance   **16.349**
annulled the Commission's recovery order on the grounds of violation of the principal of legal certainty. *Salzgitter* did not plead legitimate expectations, but rather that the Commission had acted in a manner contrary to the principle of legal certainty.[251] The Court found in favour of the applicant on the basis of the way in which the Commission had dealt with aid

---

[246] German Supreme Court (BGH) 20 January 2004, XI ZR 53/03 referring to ECJ judgment of 20 March 1997—Case C-24/95 *(Alcan II)* [1997] ECR I-1591 (1617), para 25—'Das Vertrauen der Beklagten in den Bestand der rechtswidrigen Beihilfe ist schon deshalb nicht schutzwürdig, weil es einem sorgfältigen Kaufmann regelmäßig möglich und zuzumuten ist, sich der Einhaltung der Beihilfevorschriften (Notifizierungspflicht) zu vergewissern . . .'. The trust of the defendant in the continuation of the unlawful aid does not constitute a legitimate expectation because a diligent merchant would have at least checked whether the State aid had been duly notified.

[247] Judgment of the Court of First Instance of 14 January 2004, in Case T-109/01.

[248] *Fleuren*, point 136, referring to Case C-5/89 *Commission v Germany* [1990] ECR I-3437, para 16; Case C-183/91 *Commission v Greece* [1993] ECR I-3131, para 18.

[249] Fleuren, point 137; See also Case C-24/95 *(Alcan)* [1997] ECR I-1591, paras 24 and 25; Case T-459/93 *Siemens v Commission* [1995] ECR II-1675, paras 104 and 105; and Case T-67/94 *Ladbroke Racing v Commission* [1998] ECR II-1, para 83.

[250] Case T-308/00 *Salzgitter v Commission* 'Seventh plea: breach of the principle of legal certainty', paras 148ff (not yet reported).

[251] *Salzgitter*, paras 166, 167.

to the steel sector. *Salzgitter* was a rather exceptional case and it remains to be seen whether the court has begun a new line of case law or whether this case remains unusual.

(3) Specific Problems and Situations of Recovery

(a) Domestic Motivation for Recovery

16.350 The Member State authority which awarded the State aid normally has no particular interest in its recovery. However, it may be different for other authorities in the Member State, especially the budgetary authority, usually the Ministry of Finance. This is perhaps a starting point for creating incentives in the Member States to recover aid, in particular in times of lower State revenues. For example, the French budget received EUR 1.2 billion from Eléctricité de France (EdF) in February 2004. At times of budgetary shortfall, this may be an attractive prospect for the State.

16.351 A general obstacle to supervision by the Commission of recovery is related to the fact that recovery is subject to a variety of different national laws. Unlawful aid must be recovered according to twenty-five different national enforcement laws and twenty-five bankruptcy laws. There is no unified or even harmonised European recovery procedure or law, because the Member States themselves are in charge of their own recovery procedures.[252]

16.352 The Member States are obliged to give effect to European law. Therefore, if the national law is inadequate, they have a duty to make it effective. An award of damages can be made against Member States that do not implement or apply European law correctly. Some Member States have started to consider drafting specific State aid recovery laws to improve the national recovery procedures and produce more efficient and faster results. Germany is the most advanced in this respect, having presented a first draft text to the Commission. The Netherlands have undertaken a study to see if such a law would be helpful.

16.353 Recovery in bankruptcy proceedings is very important since in about one third of all recovery cases, the beneficiary is involved in bankruptcy proceedings. In the case of Germany, since reunification and the ensuing economic problems, the relevant numbers are even higher. In such cases, recovery takes place under national insolvency procedures since there is no harmonised European insolvency law.

16.354 A number of Member States, including some of those which joined the EU in 2004, have recently adopted new insolvency laws. These are often modelled to a greater or lesser extent on the US Chapter 11 insolvency statute. In line with the US model, these new laws include an option under which the insolvent company could continue its business. In that event, the insolvency law would shield the economic activities of the insolvent company against its creditors. This includes the State aid recovery claims and therefore harbours a potential conflict.

16.355 The ECJ has supported the Commission's policy of continuing recovery proceedings vigorously, even if that leads to the liquidation of the recipient company.[253] That clearly means

---

[252] Schaub in speech of 20/21 November 2000.
[253] Case 40/85 *Belgium v Commission* [1986] ECR 2321; Case 234/84 *Belgium v Commission* [1986] ECR 2263.

that insolvency and liquidation can be the result of the recovery procedure. The Member State must also register its claim in bankruptcy proceedings.[254] A recurring problem is that bankruptcy proceedings are often closed before the issue of the Commission's recovery decision or because the Member State did not act swiftly enough. The Member State must use any means available to have the recovery claim registered even after official closure of the registration period (and accept late registration penalties, etc).

It must be noted that the Member State in the recovery procedure is not a normal market **16.356** economy creditor. The Market Economy Investor Principle finds no application in the context of recovery. In this situation, the State is expected not to act as a market player but as the guarantor of the recovery order. Since the purpose of the recovery procedure is to remedy the distortion of competition, the Member State cannot be in the same position as a private party to the insolvency procedure. The private creditor wishes to maximise his outcome or to minimise his losses. The State must restore competition. The State's main interest, unlike that of private parties, is not to receive as much money as possible. Its primary interest is to correct the distortion of competition. All the steps taken by the Member State under its bankruptcy laws must be governed by the recovery imperative.

If a company which received unlawful aid goes out of business, competitors can fill the gap **16.357** by buying that company or its assets under market conditions (ideally by auction).

Only in rare cases has the European Court accepted that full recovery could not be achieved **16.358** because of the application of national bankruptcy laws. In one such case no interest was payable on the recoverable State aid, because in the Member State concerned (Spain) obligations under bankruptcy administration cannot bear interest.[255]

(b) The Correct Addressee for the Recovery Claim

In some cases, there have been difficulties identifying the true recipient of the aid, in par- **16.359** ticular, in cases where the recipient of the aid has been acquired. When the beneficiary company or its assets are sold the first question is who is the correct addressee for the recovery claim. Two different situations can be distinguished. Either the legal ownership of the beneficiary company changes (a share sale) or the production facilities, ie the assets, are sold to a competitor or investor (an asset sale). The sale of assets does not involve a change in the ownership of the beneficiary company as such.

There is a group of aid recovery cases under insolvency procedure which pose difficult ques- **16.360** tions under the competition rules. These are the cases in which the business activity continues in successor companies ('Auffanggesellschaften').[256] In order to approve their activity, strict criteria must be applied. The costs of the continuation of business must be calculated in relation to expected sales result. There should be no additional aid to the successor company. The *Deggendorf* principle can also apply in the context of successor companies, in case of circumvention of recovery.

---

[254] Commission Decision (EC) 2000/567 of 11 April 2000—*SMI* [2000] OJ L238/50. See also Commission Decision (EC) 2000/536 of 2 June 1999—*Seleco* [2000] OJ L227/24; and Commission Decision (EC) 2000/796 of 21 June 2000—*CDA* [2000] OJ L318/62.

[255] Case C-480/98 *Spain v Commission (Magefesa I)* [2000] ECR I-8717.

[256] Case T-181/02R *(Erba Lautex and Neue Erba Lautex)* [2002] ECR II-5081.

16.361   The Commission and the Member State must prevent circumvention of the recovery order. A typical circumvention case is one where all the valuable assets have been sold, leaving only the company's debts.

16.362   In a share sale, the situation is, however, relatively simple. If it is just the ownership of the beneficiary that has changed, the recovery obligation is not affected. Under a share sale[257] the recovery order stays with the company, since it is not attached to the owner. This is clearly the case when the beneficiary is a publicly held joint stock company with hundreds or even thousands of owners (shareholders). The change of ownership is irrelevant for recovery purposes. A comparison with the Rescue and Restructuring Guidelines[258] in point 22 shows the same principle applied in a different area of State aid law. The assessment of rescue or restructuring aid should not be affected by changes in the ownership of the business in receipt of the aid.

16.363   The situation is different in case of an asset deal. In the recent cases *Seleco*[259] and *SMI*[260] the ECJ clarified its position on asset sales and the potential follow up on recovery from parties other than the original beneficiaries. The Court refers to the criterion of the market price for the sale of assets, either as single assets or bundled together. If the acquirer pays (at least) the market price for the assets, the money received for that sale replaces the outgoing asset.

16.364   There is no pursuit of recovery from the new owner, if market prices were paid for the assets. Market prices result typically from an open, transparent and unconditional bidding process. They can also be proved otherwise.[261] It is interesting to note in this context the fourth criterion in the *Altmark* judgment. According to *Altmark*, a tender as described above rules out overcompensation in the granting of services of general economic interest.

16.365   Although in *SMI* the Court did not formally abolish the original circumvention concept, it was considerably weakened by the emphasis put on the market price for the assets. Only where the acquirer pays less than market value to the beneficiary, can he be considered an additional target for recovery. Whether he faces recovery claims up to the market value of the acquired assets or to the value of the difference from the market rate (pro rata or fully), remains to be decided. Many questions remain to be answered.

16.366   In any case, the European Courts made it clear that they expect a high level of proof from the Commission, showing whether or not a market price has been paid. It is up to the Commission to prove that the asset transfer took place at less than market value.

16.367   Since this will be difficult to prove, the Commission may in future seek a reversal of the burden of proof, because the acquirer is best placed to know whether he has paid a market price or not. However, for the time being, the burden of proof rests with the Commission.

---

[257]   Case C-390/98 *(Banks)* [2001] ECR I-6117; Case C-350/93 *(ENI-Lanerossi I and II)* [1995] ECR I-699.
[258]   Communication from the Commission, *Community Guidelines on State Aid for Rescuing and Restructuring Firms in Difficulty* [2004] OJ C244/2.
[259]   Joined Cases C-328/99 and C-399/00 *(Seleco)* [2003] ECR I-4035.
[260]   Case C-277, *Germany v Commission (SMI)* ECR I-3925, (29 April 2004) with annotation by Andreas Knaul, (2004) 3 European State Aid Law Quarterly 427.
[261]   See Advocate General Tizzano in his opinion on *SMI*, 19 June 2003, point 101. *Altmark* criterion no 4.

(c) Separation of Competences between Commission and Domestic Courts

According to *Van Calster*[262] a final Commission decision declaring an award of aid compatible does not extinguish the prior illegality. The Commission cannot order a recovery of unlawful aid if it considers the aid to be compatible. The authorisation of the aid by the Commission operates without retroactive effect. The *ex post* Commission approval of unlawful aid cannot 'cure' the effects of illegality. Therefore, a competitor of the beneficiary may claim in a national court the annulment of any act authorising unlawful aid under Article 88(3). He may also claim damages.[263]   **16.368**

This judgment reinforces the standstill obligation.[264] If a national court suspended its judgment until the Commission made a decision on compatibility, the standstill obligation would be largely meaningless.   **16.369**

Van Calster reflects the established 'division of labour' between the Commission and domestic courts in recovery cases. The national court adjudicates only on the illegality of aid under Article 88. The Commission has exclusive competence in respect of the compatibility test. This derives from the *Boussac* judgment,[265] according to which the roles of Commission and national courts are different and complimentary.   **16.370**

(4) Conclusions

Since summer 2003, the Commission has significantly accelerated its recovery activity. A new enforcement unit has collected and disseminated models of best practice in this area. With close co-operation and integration of enforcement work into the investigative units the enforcement activity has become more efficient. Further action can be expected on three levels: (1) legislation (European or national); (2) better quality of factual information; and (3) legal analysis.   **16.371**

The Commission is determined to make the rules of recovery of unlawful aid clearer and more effective. There are several possibilities, including perhaps the creation of a European Recovery Regulation. European law might give competitors increased rights to sue the beneficiary in national courts. This would be in line with the growth of private enforcement of competition law.   **16.372**

Legislative action is also, at least theoretically, possible in the field of harmonisation or unification of insolvency laws. Unification or harmonisation of this very intricate field of law is, however, not on the Commission's agenda at present.   **16.373**

Some Member States are endeavouring to clarify and improve their national recovery legislation. Germany has already produced a draft by the Ministry of Finance. This is in part due to the increased pressure for enforcement coming from the Commission. Member States   **16.374**

---

[262] Joined Cases C-261/01 and C-262/01 *Van Calster and others* [2003] ECR I-12249.

[263] See also the opinion of AG Jacobs in Case C-39/94 *SFEI* [1996] ECR I-3547, para 32, ruling out the possibility of damages action against a recipient of unlawful aid by a competitor.

[264] It might even be argued that the Commission should charge interest on the illegal aid between the date when it was put at the disposal of the beneficiary and the date of the approval by the Commission.

[265] Case C 301/87 *Boussac* [1990] ECR I-307.

may try to comply with the recovery pressure by more effective application of their internal recovery relevant legislation.

E. Judicial Review in State Aid Matters and the Role of the Courts

(1) Introduction: Forms of Legal Protection

16.375 This chapter does not deal with infringement cases against the Member States under Articles 88(2) or 228(2) EC. In such cases, the Commission starts legal procedures at the European Court of Justice against Member States which have violated State aid law, in particular through the breach of the standstill obligation (Article 88(2)).

16.376 An exceptional case is the recourse to the Council by Member States. The ECJ annulled in 2004 a Council Decision[266] authorising the government of Portugal to grant aid to Portuguese pig farmers who were beneficiaries of measures granted in 1994 and 1998. The Court held that the Council did not have the right to adopt a decision reversing a prior negative Commission decision on the same aid measure. The principle of pre-emption applies. Once the Commission has made a decision, any other Community institution is pre-empted from deciding the same issue.[267]

16.377 The focus of this chapter is on legal protection for Member States, beneficiaries, and third parties, in particular competitors (of the beneficiary) against decisions of or failure to act by the Commission.

16.378 Legal protection should be secured in the administrative procedure by the European Commission and by the Courts. These Courts can be the European Courts, ie the Court of First Instance (CFI) and the European Court of Justice (ECJ) in Luxembourg. At the national level it can be the administrative or the civil courts, acting at the instigation of competitors of the aid recipients.

16.379 It is a basic procedural principle of State aid law that the parties to the State aid procedure can only be the Commission and the Member State concerned. Interested third parties can be the beneficiary, other Member States and any person or company which might be affected by the granting of the aid. These are normally the competitors of the aid recipient.[268]

16.380 Typical situations involving legal protection arise when the Commission refuses to approve a notified aid measure ('negative decision'). In such circumstances, the Member State or the envisaged beneficiary can bring an action against the negative Commission decision before the ECJ or the CFI. If the notification is accepted, the competitors of the aid recipient may bring an action against the positive Commission decision before the CFI.

16.381 In the case of unlawful, ie non-notified, aid the competitor has two main options: one at European level, and the other at the level of the Member State. It can complain to the Commission against the (alleged) unlawful aid and ask the Commission to intervene

---

[266] Decision (EC) 2002/114 of 21 January 2002.
[267] Case C-110/02 *Commission v Council (Portuguese Pigs)*, judgment of 29 June 2004.
[268] Case 323/82 *Intermills* [1984] ECR 3809. See definition in Art 1(h) of the Procedural Regulation.

(using the complaint form). It can also—and in parallel—ask a competent national Court to give judgment under Article 88(3) EC.

The following review of legal protection analyses the different levels of protection in the administrative procedure of the Commission and judicial protection provided by the European and domestic Courts. There is a distinction between legal protection provided to the Member State and 'its' beneficiary and that enjoyed by the competitors of the beneficiary. **16.382**

(2) Legal Protection within the Commission's Administrative Procedure

State aid control proceedings are, by nature, bilateral: the Commission and the Member State concerned are the only parties. However, in practice the (present or future) beneficiary often plays a role in the administrative proceedings before the Commission. In many cases the undertaking concerned participates in the notification and assessment procedure as a kind of expert witness, and may be involved in meetings with the Commission. **16.383**

This makes sense, as the beneficiary usually has the greatest knowledge of the economic facts which can determine the granting of aid. He has first hand knowledge of the market and his specific economic situation. In order to shorten the chain of information the Commission thus regularly admits the beneficiaries into the assessment process. This helps the Commission to clarify the quality and possible effects of the intended aid. **16.384**

Third parties, including the beneficiary, but in particular competitors or trade associations, do not enjoy a strong position in the administrative procedure. As regards various procedural rights, one must distinguish between the preliminary examination procedure and the formal investigation procedure. **16.385**

In the preliminary examination procedure, neither the EC Treaty nor the Procedural Regulation[269] gives any procedural rights to third parties. This suggests that interested parties are in principle excluded from this phase of the proceedings. There is no formal mechanism provided to supply them with information. If third parties do not know about the notification, they have no chance to intervene. **16.386**

In the formal investigation procedure, however, Articles 6 and 20(1) of the Procedural Regulation allow third parties to submit comments to the Commission. This is the most significant opportunity for influencing the Commission's assessment of the State aid measure. The competitor or a trade association (acting in the interest of fair competition) can submit any information it believes relevant for the Commission's decision. **16.387**

In order to protect interveners from the potentially damaging repercussions of their intervention, they can request that their identity be withheld from the Member State concerned (Article 6 of the Procedural Regulation). After taking a decision, the Commission must send a copy of the non-confidential version of the final decision to the third parties who submitted comments (Article 20(1) of the Procedural Regulation). **16.388**

If the Commission decides not to open or to close a formal investigation, a third party can bring an action before the CFI against that decision. A competitor must fulfil all conditions **16.389**

---

[269] Procedural Regulation 659/99 of 22 March 1999 [1999] OJ L83/1–9.

under Article 230(4) EC. In particular, the decision must be of direct and individual concern to the plaintiff. The CFI can then declare the act concerned to be void or it can judge that the Commission has failed to act, in breach of the EC Treaty.

16.390   Independent of the administrative procedure, any interested party may inform the Commission about State measures which could be State aid (Article 20(2) of the Procedural Regulation). The Commission must open an investigation if it has doubts about the compatibility of an aid measure with the common market.

16.391   Access to documents and the role of business secrets in State aid procedures follow in principle the general rules for competition cases. Article 24 of the Procedural Regulation on 'Professional Secrecy' obliges the Commission and the Member States to safeguard professional secrets.

(3) Legal Protection through the European Courts

16.392   The most important means of legal protection in State aid cases is through the European Courts in Luxembourg. While the ECJ is the first and last instance Court for actions by Member States against the Commission, in overall State aid practice the jurisprudence of the CFI has gained importance, due to beneficiaries or other third parties complaining to the CFI.

(a) General Information about Pending Cases

16.393   Some figures show the growing importance of European State aid litigation. At the end of 2003 there were about 300 pending State aid cases. Forty-seven cases were closed in 2003 and 58 new cases opened in the same period. The languages used in these Court cases were as follows: Italian in 99 cases (58 cases from Venice and other joined cases), Dutch in 85 cases (66 concerning petrol stations), Spanish in 45 cases (including a number of Basque cases), German in 33 cases, English and French each in 14 cases, and Portuguese and Greek each in five cases.

16.394   The Court of First Instance is the European Court of first instance for all direct actions brought by private plaintiffs. Up to 2004, the Member States directed their litigation exclusively to the ECJ which decided their complaints as first and last instance. Article 51 of the ECJ Statute states that for actions by the Member States against Commission decisions, the CFI now has jurisdiction.[270]

16.395   Court procedures are regulated in a number of different documents and by jurisprudence.[271]

16.396   In a direct action, the application will be notified to the defendant by the registry of the Court. A notice of action is published in the Official Journal of the European Union (C Series).

---

[270] Council Decision of 26 April 2004 amending Articles 51 and 54 of the Protocol on the Statute of the Court of Justice [2004] OJ L132/5–6; and Corrigendum to Council Decision (EC) 2004/407 Euratom of 26 April 2004 amending Arts 51 and 54 of the Protocol on the Statute of the Court of Justice [2004] OJ L194/3.

[271] See: Court of Justice, Court of First Instance, Practice Directions [2002] OJ L87/48–51. Practice directions relating to direct actions and appeals [2003] OJ L98/9–13. Notes for the guidance of Counsel in written and oral proceedings before the Court of Justice of the European Communities, February 2003, <http://www.curia.eu.int/en/instit/txtdocfr/autrestxts/txt9.pdf>.

As a next step interim measures may be discussed, although this is unusual. The defence can raise objections on the grounds of admissibility. After the reply and rejoinder, normally the end of the written procedure is reached. Exceptionally, the procedure may be completed by other pleadings or the intervention of third parties, or response to questions raised by the Court in writing or in meetings with the parties.

The Judge-Rapporteur (and the Advocate General—at the ECJ) is designated, usually during the written procedure. The Judge-Rapporteur draws up his preliminary report which is discussed in the general meeting of Judges (and Advocates General). This may lead to the referral of the case, where appropriate, to a Chamber and measures of inquiry. If the oral procedure is not waived the hearing takes place, on the basis of a report for the Hearing prepared by the Judge-Rapporteur. The opinion of the Advocate General proposes a course of action to the Court. After deliberation by the Judges on the basis of a draft judgment, their judgment closes the procedure.   **16.397**

The Commission is represented in all legal actions by the Legal Service. The Legal Service has a State aid team comprised of nine lawyers who are in charge of all judicial State aid cases involving the Commission. The Legal Service is the sole litigator before all Courts and judicial bodies. It works in close contact with the State aid Directorates General. It also regularly delegates to external lawyers some of the heavy work load (more than 300 pending cases).   **16.398**

(b) Action for Annulment

Different Court procedures apply to the various types of action that can be brought by the plaintiff. The action for annulment of the Commission decision under Article 230 EC comprises applications lodged by Member States before the ECJ or before the CFI—for cases brought after April 2004. About 20 cases are currently pending before the ECJ. These also include applications lodged by private parties with the CFI against either positive or negative decisions.   **16.399**

The actions for annulment constitute the vast majority of State aid cases, comprising overall around 260 pending cases. The deadline for this type of action according to Article 230(5) EC is two months from the time that the plaintiff obtained knowledge of the relevant action, plus ten days.   **16.400**

The action for annulment is assessed by reference to the factual and legal matters existing at the time when the decision was adopted.   **16.401**

(c) Other Court Actions

An undertaking can complain to the Commission about alleged unlawful aid awarded to a competitor. The Commission must respond to a complaint (Article 10(1) of the Procedural Regulation), and will need to investigate whether there is sufficient information and merit to take the complaint further. It must take a decision according to Articles 13(1) and 4 of the Procedural Regulation.   **16.402**

If the competitor believes that the Commission has not acted properly on its complaint, it can file an action under Article 232 EC after giving the Commission time to do its duty. No minimum period for this is explicitly stated. Two months are certainly not sufficient.   **16.403**

The CFI ruled that forty-seven months delay after the first complaint and twenty-seven months delay in acting after the second complaint were too long and criticised the Commission for failure to act properly. [272]

16.404 The actions for failure to act are very limited in number. There were only six pending cases at the end of 2003. In May 2004, the German private hospital company Asklepios sued the Commission for failure to act.[273] It felt that its complaint against subsidies for State owned hospitals was not being dealt with properly.[274]

16.405 The availability of injunctive relief under Articles 242 and 243 of the EC Treaty has had little significance in practice. The same is true for actions for damages. However, some recent attempts show that such action may gain importance in the future, in particular in national Courts against beneficiaries. Requests for preliminary rulings under Article 234 of the EC Treaty concern two possible situations: either a competitor attacks (allegedly) unlawful aid in a national Court[275] or the modalities of a recovery action are in dispute and the beneficiary goes to Court.

16.406 This type of action is often very important for the development of State aid case law.[276]

16.407 In a recent case a party made a claim against the Commission for damages allegedly caused by a (negative) State aid decision. This claim relates to the *Stardust* decision and judgment. The case is at an early stage of proceedings.[277]

16.408 It is possible that beneficiaries of unlawful aid may turn against their own Member State for breach of Article 88(3) EC and seek damages under domestic rules for failure of the Member State to act lawfully, ie failure to notify the State aid measure to the Commission.

(d) Locus Standi

16.409 In State aid cases the general rules on *locus standi* or entitlement to bring an action apply. Under Article 230(4) EC private parties must prove that they are directly and individually concerned by the Commission decision.[278] Parties that have responded to the Article 88(2) EC notice will normally be admitted. The same applies *mutatis mutandis* in the case of an action for failure to act. The third party must show that it had taken part in the administrative proceedings, ie the formal investigation phase, by making comments or lodging a complaint, and that the decision would cause it considerable competitive harm.[279]

---

[272] *Gestevision Telecinco* [1998] ECR II-3407, para 76.
[273] Case T-167/04 *Asklepios Kliniken GmbH v Commission of the European Communities* [2004] OJ C201/16.
[274] <http://www.asklepios.com/pressezentrum/Pressemitteilungen/PM_EUKlageneu.pdf>.
[275] *Altmark*, ECJ of 24 July 2003.
[276] The *PreussenElektra* case was based on a preliminary ruling.
[277] Case T-344/04 *Me Denis Bouychou (Stardust Marine) v Commission*, registered by the CFI on 27 August 2004.
[278] Case T-358/02 *Deutsche Post AG and DHL International Srl v Commission*, 27 May 2004, paras 31ff.
[279] Case T-157/01 *Danske Busvognmaend v Commission*, 16 March 2004, para 41; Case T-158/99 *Thermenhotel Stoiser Franz and others v Commission*, 13 January 2004, paras 69–73; Case T-358/2002 *Deutsche Post AG and DHL International Srl v Commission*, 27 May 2004, para 21; Case T-41/01 *Perez Escolar v Commission* [2003] ECR II-2157, paras 35–45.

(e) Challengeable Acts

Not every action by the Commission is a challengeable act. In addition to a final decision, a **16.410** decision opening the formal investigation procedure (Article 6 of the Procedural Regulation) can be challenged. Opening decisions can be challenged if they produce legal effects of their own which are not only of a preliminary nature.

The CFI has held that the definitive nature of the classification of the aid determined in the **16.411** opening decision may produce independent legal effects. However, the opening decision is normally only a preparatory step for the final decision. Only the final decision determines the Commission's position.[280]

The Commission's initial determination of a measure as new aid can be revised on the basis **16.412** of a later finding that it is existing aid.[281] An initiation decision which recognises that the measure is existing aid cannot be challenged separately. Injunctions and administrative letters cannot be challenged since they are not final and definitive acts by the Commission.

(f) The Scope of Judicial Control

The scope of judicial control is defined by the objective definition of State aid.[282] The **16.413** Court will verify the interpretation of this term by the Commission.[283] As regards compatibility, however, the Commission has a wide margin of discretion. The CFI has confirmed recently that decisions which involve economic and social assessments in a European Community context are the prerogative of the Commission. The Court is restricted to examining whether the Commission committed a manifest error of judgment or misused its powers.[284]

The Commission's discretion is restricted by the law (ie the Procedural Regulation), the **16.414** Commission's own guidelines, notices or equivalent measures and case law. The Courts guarantee that the Commission applies its own guidelines in a non-discriminatory way. Once the Commission has established guidelines, which are usually based on earlier written Commission or Court practice, it must follow them through in an objective and transparent manner.

The Court also monitors whether the Commission respects the procedural rights of all par- **16.415** ties concerned. This includes the duty of diligence, the rights of defence (ie to a fair hearing) for Member States and the right to be heard for interested parties, beneficiaries, and competitors depending on the phase of the administrative procedure.

The Commission is more than just a party to the procedures. The Commission is in the **16.416** first instance a European institution, ie a political body with the overriding political goal of fostering integration. The main goal of every Commission action is to strengthen its

---

[280] Case T-190/00 *Regione Siciliana v Commission*, 27 November 2003.
[281] Case T-276/02 *Forum 187 v Commission (Centres de coordination, initiation decision)* [2003] ECR II-2075, paras 43–46.
[282] Case T-109/01 *Fleuren Compost v Commission*, paras 52ff.
[283] An exception is the market economy operator test.
[284] Case T-109/01 *Fleuren Compost v Commission*, point 90; Case C-456/00 *France v Commission* [2002] ECR I-11949, para 41.

position and credibility as a European institution. The Commission's intention in a case before the European Courts is, of course, to win the case, but it also seeks to clarify the law and the principles of the policy underlying the law.

16.417 Consistency of decision making is a major source of legitimacy. Equal treatment of all parties, transparency, and thus predictability, must underlie the administrative procedure before the Commission. The right to be heard is tantamount in this respect:

> . . . having regard to the Member State's central role in that procedure, it must be held that the Member State's right to be heard in the same procedure constitutes an essential procedural requirement and that failure to comply with that requirement entails the nullity of a Commission decision ordering that aid be abolished or altered . . . (point 141) Consequently, the beneficiary of the aid, and the local government body which has granted it, have a legitimate interest in pleading such a defect in the Commission's decision where a failure to comply with the Member State's right to be heard may have a bearing on the legality of the contested measure . . . (point 142)[285]

The Commission must give reasons for its decisions (Article 253 EC). The degree of reasoning must be appropriate to the measure at issue and disclose in a clear and unequivocal manner the rationale behind the decision. It is on the basis of such reasoning that the Courts determine whether or not the Commission has correctly applied State aid law, both substantially and procedurally.[286]

16.418 Rights of defence of the beneficiaries in the European Courts are the same as for any party in Court. During the administrative procedure, the beneficiary or other third parties have only minor rights,[287] but they are fully entitled to all legal rights in the judicial procedure.

(4) Protection of Third Parties (Competitors) in National Courts

16.419 In addition to the protection of Member States and beneficiaries, legal protection of competitors is receiving increasing attention.[288] Looking at the division of responsibilities between the Commission and the domestic Courts, one can distinguish between actions for suspending the aid, recovery, and claims for damages.

(a) General: Legal Basis and Division of Tasks between Commission and National Courts

16.420 Under the State aid rules in the Treaty the competitor's position in the administrative proceedings before the Commission is rather weak. The European Courts, however, have been trying to apply general Community law principles to provide some legal protection when competitors make complaints. However, in such proceedings, the position of a competitor will never be equivalent to that of a competitor complaining to the Commission under the Antitrust Regulation, unless new legislation is introduced or the Treaty itself is amended.

---

285 Cases T-228/99 *Westdeutsche Landesbank Girozentrale v Commission*; and T-233/99 *Land Nordrhein-Westfalen v Commission* [2003] ECR II-435.

286 Case T-109/01 *Fleuren Compost v Commission*, point 119.

287 Case T-109/01 *Fleuren Compost v Commission*, paras 42–44.

288 Report on the application of EC State aid law by the Member State courts, 1999, Jestaedt, Ottervanger, van Cutsem,<http://europa.Eu.Int/comm/competition/state_aid/legislation/app_by_member_states/>, reviewed on 17 December 2005.

The action for annulment at the CFI takes a long time and is uncertain in its outcome. The **16.421** competitor has a strong interest in fast and effective legal protection against alleged unlawful assistance given to its competitor.

The weak position of the competitor in the Commission and the time-consuming **16.422** procedure at the CFI is somehow balanced by the competitor's right to enforce the standstill obligation for non-notified aid through an action in a competent national Court. The legal basis for this action is the standstill obligation of Article 88(3) EC. Its implementation by domestic Courts results from the direct effect and primacy of Community law over national laws of the Member States.

The violation of the standstill obligation by a Member State may trigger different actions **16.423** by a competitor of the aid recipient. In these proceedings the competitor is a party to the proceedings.

The national Court's action under Article 88(3) EC is based on a division of tasks[289] between **16.424** the Commission and the Courts in the Member States. The Commission exercises preventive control for which it enjoys a large discretion under Article 87(3) EC. Its role is safeguarded through the notification obligation and the standstill obligation under Article 88(3) EC. The violation of this obligation creates direct effects, ie individual rights, which must be enforced by national Courts.

The domestic Courts in the Member States enforce the standstill obligation and conse- **16.425** quently can order recovery. The national Court determines whether the measure constitutes unnotified, ie unlawful, State aid. The national Court has no right to adjudicate on the compatibility of the aid with the Common Market. That is the prerogative of the Commission. The national Court can decide only the formal illegality (ie absence of notification) of the aid measure.

National Courts are increasingly active in this respect. A series of cases in Germany and a **16.426** legal action against Ryanair in France in 2003 are indicative of this trend.

The German Supreme Court in Civil Matters (Bundesgerichtshof, BGH) ruled in three **16.427** cases in 2003 and 2004 that civil law contracts concluded in violation of Article 88(3) EC are null and void under §134 of the Civil Code (Bürgerliches Gesetzbuch, BGB).[290] As a consequence, the German Federal Ministry of Finance has prepared a draft recovery law which provides *inter alia* for the possibility of saving the parts of a contract which are not linked to the effects of the unlawful aid.

The French regional administrative Court of Nancy confirmed the outcome of an earlier **16.428** judgment of the administrative Court of Strasbourg depriving the Irish low-cost airline Ryanair of aid received for operating at an airport in Alsace. The Court ruled that the Chamber of Commerce and Industry of Strasbourg had not acted as a private market

---

[289] C-354/90 *FNCE* [1991] ECR I-5505; C-39/94 *SFEI* [1996] ECR I-3547, paras 41ff.
[290] Judgment of 4 April 2003, V ZR 314/02, EuZW 2003, 444; BGH 20 January 2004, XI ZR 53/03.

investor when it gave support to Ryanair. This support thus constituted State aid and was unlawful for lack of notification to the Commission.[291]

16.429　There is a constant risk of divergence between judgments of national Courts and the Commission over the definition of State aid in case of parallel procedures, for example in the case of equity investment by the Member State. A reference to the ECJ for a preliminary ruling is not always efficient or helpful. This procedure does not protect competitors sufficiently[292] because it takes too long. The same is true of a suspension of the judgment until the Commission reaches a decision. There seems to be no perfect solution. Flexible solutions on a case-by-case basis are needed to avoid divergent decisions.

(b)　Court Proceedings to Stop the Granting of the Aid and Recovery

16.430　Action by a competitor against the State for granting aid must be distinguished from actions against the beneficiary for accepting or using the aid. A competitor may take action in national courts to prevent the State from granting the aid or in order to instigate its recovery. The type of action depends on how the aid was granted, whether by public administrative act or public contract. This distinction determines which Court is competent to hear the competitor's complaint. A civil Court is competent only if the aid is in the form of a purely civil law grant.

16.431　Usually the competitor will bring his action for annulment or suspension or recovery of aid against the State in an administrative Court, but in exceptional circumstances, actions for information and injunctive relief may be possible.

16.432　Action by the competitor against the aid recipient has no basis in Community law. There may be actions under national law, but the evidential requirements will be high. It will be difficult to prove that the aid recipient used the aid to engage in price competition (akin to 'dumping'). The internal price structure of the aid recipient is not usually known to the competitor.[293] Moreover, discovery is very expensive, takes a long time and is uncertain in its outcome. Any litigation against the aid recipient to stop using the grant faces the same evidential problems.

(c)　Claim for Damages

16.433　The competitor can bring a claim for damages against either the Member State or the aid recipient. The main problems in this procedure also lie in respect of evidence. A claim can be justified under the case law which established state liability for failure to implement or follow European law (*Francovich* jurisprudence). State aid rules protect the individual since the State aid articles of the EC Treaty confer subjective rights.

---

[291] Cour administrative d'appel de Nancy, 18 December 2003, n° 03NC00859, *Ryan Air*, <http://www.rajf.org/article.php3?id_article=2108>.

[292] Notice on co-operation between national Courts and the Commission in the State aid field [1995] OJ C312/8–13.

[293] Procedures for obtaining evidence, such as the discovery procedures in the US are not generally applicable in the Community except to some extent in the UK Civil Procedure Rules, where disclosure issues (akin to discovery in the US) are covered by Part 31.

Member States are liable for damages caused by wrongful judgments in breach of **16.434** European law. Under Community law, the conditions governing State liability for breach of Community law:

> are threefold: the rule of law infringed must be intended to confer rights on individuals; the breach must be sufficiently serious; and there must be a direct causal link between the breach of the obligation incumbent on the State and the loss or damage sustained by the injured parties . . . State liability for loss or damage caused by a decision of a national Court adjudicating at last instance which infringes a rule of Community law is governed by the same conditions.[294]

Claims under national unfair competition legislation may also be possible. The common **16.435** problem is the difficulty of proving the existence of a causal link. The competitor must prove that the aid was responsible for the beneficiary's price reduction and that the harm suffered by the competitor was due to the lower prices.

An additional problem arises if the national Court of Last Instance orders recovery, but the **16.436** Commission later finds that the measure is not State aid. A solution to this might be a finding of damage on the basis that the aid was paid too early, ie before approval by the Commission.

(5) Conclusions

Legal protection of the Member State and the beneficiary can be considered sufficient. The **16.437** European Courts have increased the level of proof required from the Commission, obliging the Commission to conduct better and more intensive fact gathering and analysis.

The competitor of the aid recipient can obtain legal protection in a number of ways. **16.438** Though his formal position is rather weak in the Commission's administrative procedure, the competitor can take action in the European and national Courts. However, because he does not have access to the internal documents of the beneficiary, he may have evidential problems, such as difficulty in proving the State aid character of a measure.

One of the most effective means for a competitor to enforce his rights is still to complain to **16.439** the Commission.

---

[294] Case C-224/01 *Köbler v Austria* [2003] ECR I-10239, paras 51, 52.

INDEX